Financial Management

SECOND EDITION

RAJIV SRIVASTAVA
Professor
Indian Institute of Foreign Trade
New Delhi

ANIL MISRA
Associate Professor – Accounting & Finance
Management Development Institute
Gurgaon

OXFORD
UNIVERSITY PRESS

OXFORD
UNIVERSITY PRESS

Oxford University Press is a department of the University of Oxford. It furthers the University's objective of excellence in research, scholarship, and education by publishing worldwide. Oxford is a registered trademark of Oxford University Press in the UK and in certain other countries

Published in India by
Oxford University Press
YMCA Library Building, 1 Jai Singh Road, New Delhi 110001, India

First published in 2011
Third impression 2012

ISBN-13: 978-0-19-807207-2
ISBN-10: 0-19-807207-4

Typeset in Times New Roman
by Anvi Composers, New Delhi 110063
Printed in India by Tara Art Printers (P) Ltd., Noida

Dedicated to

With great love and affection, for sacrifice of their invaluable
personal time they
are entitled to, providing all encouragement and support and
bearing with me, my dear wife
Mrs Anita Srivastava
and
two lovely daughters
Juhi and Shruti

Rajiv Srivastava

With respect to the medium of my worldly manifestation and the
foundations of my value system,
my father
Prof. D. P. Mishra
and mother
Mrs Renu Mishra

Anil Misra

Features of

CHAPTER

8 Portfolio Theory

LEARNING OBJECTIVES

After going through this chapter, you will be able to:

- understand the concept of a portfolio, and its return and risk
- learn about feasible portfolios, and the difference between efficient and inefficient portfolios
- measure the relationship of returns of two securities
- understand covariance and coefficient of correlation, and their relationship
- understand the concept of an efficient frontier
- learn how to compute portfolio variance and standard deviation
- examine how the utility of money is related to returns and risks
- understand the concept of capital allocation line (CAL)
- learn to find an efficient frontier using Markowitz Model of portfolio design
- analyse the implications of portfolio theory for portfolio managers
- design an optimum portfolio using Sharpe's Single Index Model
- understand the concept of diversification and the issues to be considered while diversifying
- learn how risk can be segregated into unique risk and market risk
- examine superfluous diversification
- determine an optimum portfolio

Each chapter begins with learning objectives that focus learning and the knowledge you should acquire by the end of the chapter.

TENNIS STOCK AND CRICKET PORTFOLIO

In the hot summer afternoon of June, Ek and Anek, both bosom friends and enthusiastic knowledgeable wagers, sat watching news on the television and sipping beer in a local bar. Announcing the Indian cricket team, the BCCI spokesperson informed, 'We have an extremely balanced side with some very adventurous and some not so adventurous players. We expect to win the next series with this team.' The next news item was on Wimbledon. The seeding is declared. Federer is expected to lift the title and is the top-seeded player in the tournament.

Ek, as his name would imply, always believed in betting on individual performances, told Anek, 'Federer would certainly win the championship. He is unbeatable and his track record is too good. I will put my money on him.'

Anek, differing with the philosophy of Ek reacted, 'But the odds would be too low. I suspect you get only ₹1.20 for a bet on him. I would rather bet on the Indian team winning the test series in England. I think I will get ₹1.60 if India wins.'

Ek suggested, 'Well if you want more return, why don't you bet on Sania Mirza winning the women's Wimbledon title.'

Anek, refusing to accept the suggestion, explained his thinking 'Agreed that the return will be very good if I bet on Sania Mirza, but it is highly risky because chances of her winning are extremely remote. I would rather bet on the performance of the Indian cricket team. Not that I love cricket more than tennis, but putting money on cricket is not as risky as betting on individual performance. It is better to bet on the team performance rather than individual performance.'

Anek further explained, 'Whether or not Tendulkar would hit a century is a poorer bet than a bet on the Indian team's win. It is a risky bet because your fortunes depend upon the performance of single individual. If he fails, you are doomed.'

With a strange look on his face, Ek asked, 'How is the bet on Indian team different? A bet is a bet.'

Each chapter starts with an opening case to introduce you with the theme of the chapter.

Box 20-2 Tata Steel Issues Perpetual Bonds

Tata Steel, the world's seventh-largest steel maker has made the debt market and probably the equity investors sit up with a very interesting perpetual bond product. Tata Steel has boasted about raising ₹1,500 crore through these high-yield perpetual bonds.

Perpetual bonds means the issue has no maturity period, and only the company has the option to buy-back the bonds at any time it chooses. Tata Steel has listed this bond in the wholesale debt market and expects it to fetch an interest of 11.8% per annum.

In an interview with CNBC-TV18's Latha Venkatesh, Koushik Chatterjee, Group CFO of Tata Steel, said that the company wanted to come up with a product which captures the essence of equity at a lower cost than equity cost and gives a higher yield to the investors. 'We started working on a product which meets the legal requirement, the regulatory framework and the accounting disclosure issues and this is what we have arrived at,' he said.

According to him, this product will fetch benefits to investors from the insurance companies and pension funds, who have long-term asset liability requirements to match. He also said that perpetual bond issue helps funding sources and this bond is lesser expensive compared to equity.

'Appetite for this bond should be high. It is an important product for companies with value-accretive investments,' added Chatterjee.

Talking about the tenure of the product, he said that technically it has a tenure of 10 years but it doesn't create obligation on the issuer to repay the distribution cost.

JP Morgan Securities India and ICICI Bank were the arrangers for the issue.

Source: www.moneycontrol.com accessed on 25 March 2011

Boxes reflect industry and business trends that are relevant to financial decision-making.

Example 4-3 Implied Interest Rate

A finance firm has announced a scheme called 'Lakhpati in 10 years'. It has promised to pay ₹1,00,000 after 10 years for every ₹20,000 deposited today. The advertisement states that the firm pays ₹80,000 as interest at ₹8,000 every year and therefore offers a 40% annual return. Do you agree with the claim made in the scheme? Explain. What would be the maturity value if the finance firm really had to offer 40% return annually?

Solution

The claim made by the finance company is simply erroneous as it ignores the time value of money. The real rate of return offered by the finance company can be calculated using Equation 4-1:

$20{,}000 \times (1 + r)^{10} = 1{,}00{,}000$

or, $(1 + r)^{10} = 5$

Using the Table given in Appendix A-1 for a period of 10 years and looking for value of 5, we find the future value factors of 4.807 and 5.234 at 17% and 18% respectively. By linear extrapolation we may arrive at the approximate rate of return of 17.45% $\left(17\% + \frac{5.000 - 4.807}{5.234 - 4.807}\right)$.

For a more exact answer, we may solve Equation 4-1 for r

$r = 5^{1/10} - 1 = 17.46\%$

If the firm really had to offer the 40% return for every ₹20,000 deposited today, it would be required to pay ₹5,78,500 (Using table in Appendix A-1).

$20{,}000 \times 1.4^{10} = 20{,}000 \times 28.925 = ₹5{,}78{,}500$

DISCOUNTING AND PRESENT VALUE

The inverse of the compounding process is termed as *discounting*. Here we find the value of future cash flow as on today. We know that the future value (F) is given by Equation 4-1. By restating Equation 4-1 we may find the present value as given by Equation 4-2.

Effect of discounting is more pronounced as the time extends or as the discount rate increases.

$$P = \frac{F}{(1 + r)^n} \qquad (4\text{-}2)$$

Factor of $1/(1 + r)^n$ is known as present value discount factor at interest rate of r for n period, and is denoted as PVDIDF(r,n). A

Numerous solved examples interspersed throughout the text will help you to further understand the concepts discussed in the text.

Important concepts appear as sidebars throughout the text for quick recapitulation. This will come handy for revision before exams.

Table 3-3 Classification of cost of SG Footwear

Profitability	*₹ lakh*	*Nature of Cost*	*Variable Cost ₹ lakh*	*Fixed Cost ₹ lakh*
Revenue	5,040.00			
Raw Materials	2,646.00	Variable	2,646.00	—
Packing Material	151.20	Variable	151.20	—
Consumables	75.60	Variable	75.60	—
Electricity	115.20	Variable	115.20	—
Wages	240.00	Fixed	—	240.00
Repairs & Maintenance	50.00	Fixed	—	50.00
Salaries	300.00	Fixed	—	300.00
Travelling & Conveyance	100.00	Fixed	—	100.00
Business Promotion	500.00	Fixed	—	500.00
Freight	25.20	Variable	25.20	—
Selling Commission	504.00	Variable	504.00	—
Administrative Overheads	100.00	Fixed	—	100.00
Total Cost	**4,807.20**		**3,517.20**	**1,290.00**

The breakeven (sales quantity) can also be computed using the model:

$$= \frac{\text{Fixed Costs}}{\text{Contribution per unit}}$$

Contribution = Sales − Variable cost.

Using the above formulae the breakeven point for SG Footwear is computed at sales of ₹4269.50 lakh equivalent to 21.35 lakh pairs of shoes and capacity utilization of about 51% as shown below.

Breakeven Sales (in terms of sales revenue)

$$= \frac{\text{Fixed Cost}}{\text{Sales} - \text{Variable Cost}} \times \text{Sales}$$

$$= \frac{1290.00}{5040.00 - 3517.20} \times 5040.00 = ₹4{,}269.50 \text{ lakh}$$

Breakeven Sales (in terms of sales quantity)

$$= \frac{\text{Breakeven Sales}}{\text{Selling Price}} = \frac{4269.50}{200} = 21.35 \text{ lakh pairs}$$

Breakeven Sales (in terms of % capacity utilization)

$$= \frac{\text{Breakeven Sales}}{\text{Capacity Sales}} = \frac{4269.50}{8400.00} = 50.83\%$$

Since marketing and production functions normally monitor their performance and progress in terms of revenues and physical quantities respectively knowing the breakeven point in terms of revenue and quantity helps them to easily figure out whether the level of activity is above breakeven point.

Various representations of breakeven point are condensed in Table 3-4.

Table 3-4 Breakeven point for SG Footwear

(a) In terms of revenue (₹ Lakh)	4,269.50
(b) In terms of number of pairs of shoes sold (Lakh)	21.35
(c) In terms of capacity utilization (%)	50.83

A graphical view of breakeven point is presented in Figure 3-5. Observe that as the level of sales rise the variable costs also rise linearly and the fixed costs remain constant. Variable cost and fixed cost together account for a firm's total cost.

Total cost line would be parallel to the variable cost line. Sales rise linearly and the breakeven point is the intersection of total cost and sales, where sales equals total cost. Selling price being higher than the variable cost, the revenue line would rise faster than the cost line. To the right of the breakeven point is the profit area and to its left is the loss area. This means that until the firm reaches the point of breakeven it incurs losses. These losses are due to the fact that the firm has not been able to cover its fixed costs. Although every unit sold covers up the variable costs and also leaves some surplus (known as contribution), it requires a certain minimum number of units to be sold in order to recover the total fixed costs incurred. The higher the amount of fixed costs incurred by the firm, higher is the number of units that it needs to sell in order to reach the breakeven point and start earning profits. The businesses should make sure that the amount of fixed costs that they commit to are not too high as it would shift the breakeven point further. However there are certain businesses such as power generation, telecom, etc. that have a long gestation period. take a long time to breakeven and start earning profits. Such businesses should try and stick to the production and delivery schedule so as to ensure that the breakeven point does not get delayed.

Until a firm reaches the point of breakeven, it incurs losses. Beyond this point, it is the profit zone.

A firm should try to reach BEP as quickly as possible. For this, the fixed costs should be contained within manageable limits.

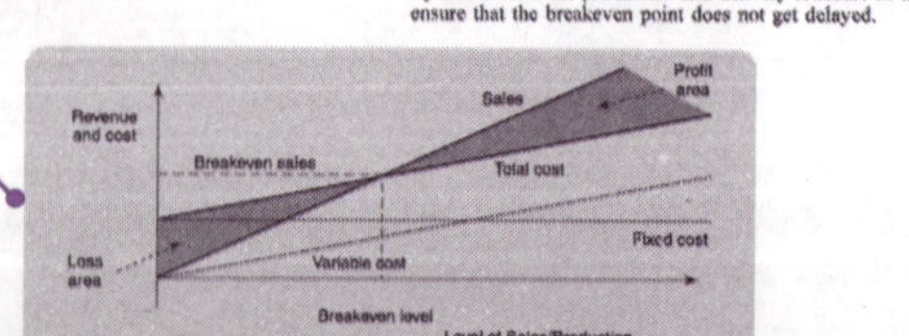

Figure 3-5 Breakeven point

All chapters contain figures and tables to illustrate the topics discussed in the chapter.

the Book

Each chapter contains a series of concept review, critical thinking, and project assignments that highlight the major topics covered in the chapter. The questions enhance learning and can be used for review and

EXERCISES

Concept Review Questions

1. Why do firms invest in inventory? What are the benefits from the investment in inventory? What are the costs of investing in inventory?
2. Distinguish between the economic order quantity and the just-in-time inventory models of inventory management.
3. What are carrying costs and ordering costs and how are they important in inventory management?
4. What is the reorder point and how is it relevant to inventory management? What is the role of safety stock in the determination of reorder point?

Critical Thinking Questions

1. Where inventory occupies a prominent position in business operations, it will usually play a key role in deciding the success of the venture. Comment.
2. Compare and contrast the motives for holding cash and inventory. What are the similarities and differences in these motives?
3. 'Inventory provides cushion against demand side and supply side uncertainties.' Comment.
4. 'The inventory policy of a firm is intricately linked with the overall corporate strategy.' Discuss.
5. 'Although the proportion of the different components of inventories is industry-specific, its importance is universal.' Elaborate.
6. 'Alteration in the level of inventory is justified only if the expected rate of return on incremental investments in inventory exceeds the cost of funds blocked in them.' Examine.

Practical Assignments

1. Select a manufacturing company of your choice and study the inventory holding pattern of the company, using the inventory turnover ratio (or the inventory holding period). Based on these measures, compare the inventory management trend with other companies in the industry.

   If the inventory turnover of the firm has improved, find out the measures taken by the firm that have facilitated the improvement in the inventory management. Are these measures similar to those adopted by MUL in the case study?
2. Select a manufacturing sector of your choice. Based on the sample of the prominent firms falling in the sector do the value chain mapping of the sector so as to find out whether the sector has moved up the value chain during the past 5–7 years or not.

   (Hint: one of the possible ways could be studying the inventory level and composition over the period and also vis-à-vis the competitors). If there has been upscaling, find out the ways the firm has been able to move downstream.

Numerical Problems

1. Determining the EOQ

A unit manufacturing bangle containers consumes 17,500 units of plastic fibres every month. The material is consumed uniformly throughout the month. Based on the data available, the current per unit cost of acquisition is ₹55 and the carrying cost for the firm is 35% on an average, and the

Each chapter ends with a case study that is designed to consolidate your understanding of the chapter subject and broaden your financial decision-making skills.

CASE STUDY

Maruti Udyog Limited (MUL)-II*

Inventory Management at MUL

With raw material consumption cost (including the cost of raw material stores and spares) as a percentage of net sales ranging from 75–83%, the management of inventory for the firm has always assumed importance from the viewpoint of operational efficiency, and also the bottom line of the firm. Around 70% of the firm's components are outsourced. Inventory management, therefore, plays a key role in the company's operations. The average inventory turnover ratio of the company has increased from 11.9 in 2005–06 to 13.9 in 2006–07. In the light of the significant importance of inventory, the firm has been paying special attention to its inventory management. The inventory management performance at MUL for six consecutive financial years is given in Table A.

Table A Inventory management performance at MUL

	2001-02	2002-03	2003-04	2004-05	2005-06	2006-07
Net Sales (₹ crore)	70677.00	71265.00	93456.00	109108.00	120034.00	145922.00
Average Stock of raw materials (₹ crore)	477.00	317.85	246.15	269.00	296.30	315.35
Average Stock of stores and spares (₹ crore)	123.10	69.70	47.70	51.05	50.10	23.70
Average Stock of semi-finished goods (₹ crore)	28.80	22.70	19.15	33.85	37.35	27.85
Average Stock of finished goods (₹ crore)	144.40	173.80	150.40	199.30	390.15	430.30
Average days of raw materials stock	38.52	25.45	16.10	14.04	14.14	12.00
Average days of finished goods stock	7.38	8.76	6.38	7.37	13.34	12.29
Average days of semi-finished goods stock	1.56	1.28	0.85	1.29	1.29	0.85

Source: Prowess database of Centre for Monitoring of Indian Economy, India.

Solved examples which will help you understand the concepts well and give you adequate practice before you start solving the various exercises given at the end of the chapters.

PRACTICE PROBLEMS

1. Determining the Economic Order Quantity

A unit manufacturing electronic meters consumes 20,000 units of moulded steel boxes every month. The material is consumed at an uniform rate during the month. The cost of acquiring the inputs is ₹100 per month for the firm and the carrying cost for the firm is 27.5% on an average. The acquisition cost is likely to remain constant in the near future. The cost of placing an order is ₹50,000 per order. Compute the optimal inventory for the year ahead using EOQ model.

Solution

Annual demand $D = 20{,}000 \times 12 = 2{,}40{,}000$

Ordering cost $O = ₹50{,}000$

Carrying cost $C = ₹27.5$ (27.5% of acquisition cost of ₹100)

$$\text{EOQ}(Q) = \sqrt{\frac{2 \times D \times O}{C}}$$

$$= \sqrt{\frac{2 \times 2{,}40{,}000 \times 50{,}000}{27.5}} = 29{,}542 \text{ units}$$

2. Incorporating Quantity Discount in the Basic EOQ Model

Spring Enterprises require 30,000 units of inputs annually to sustain its production at the current level. The carrying cost is ₹32 per unit while the ordering cost is ₹5,000 per order. The cost per unit of input is also ₹32.

Determine the EOQ for Spring Enterprises. What would be the firm's policy of inventory acquisition if the firm's suppliers offer quantity discount as follows:

Order Size (Units)	Discount (%)
1000–3999	0.00
4000–7999	1.00
8000–11999	1.25
12000–15999	2.00
16000 and above	3.00

Solution

Demand $D = 30{,}000$ units

Ordering cost $O = ₹5{,}000$

Carrying cost $C = ₹32$

Exhibits analyse the financial tools/concepts discussed in the text.

Exhibit 19-1 Important dates for dividend

Declaration date: Dividends are declared in a meeting of the Board of Directors that needs to be notified to stock exchanges at least seven days in advance. The date on which the directors of the company declare dividend is called the *dividend declaration date*.

Record date: The *record date* is the date on which all those shareholders whose names are on the books of the firm are paid dividend. It is announced on the date of declaration of dividend. This date needs to follow notice of duration of a minimum of 15 days to stock exchanges. The company closes its stock transfer book on this date.

Ex-dividend date: The *ex-dividend date* is the date on which prices on stock exchanges are adjusted for the amount of dividend. All buyers prior to this date get the dividend. This is normally a day before the record date, to enable the company to update its stock transfer book.

Payment date: The *payment date* is the date of actual payment of the dividend. The payment date has to be within 30 days of the declaration date.

The summary at the end of each chapter draws together the main concepts discussed within the chapter. This will help you to reflect and evaluate important concepts

SUMMARY

The total costs incurred do not vary proportionately with the level of activity as some part of total costs is fixed in nature. Such fixed costs refer to such components of costs that remain constant with the changing activity level. They are alternatively referred to as period costs as they change with time and not with volume. Rent, salaries, etc., are examples of fixed costs. These costs remain fixed only within a relevant range of production/sales. The moment the volume increases and crosses this relevant range, there is a sudden increase in such costs.

The costs that vary in direct proportion to the change in the volume are termed as variable costs. Due to the feature of variability with the activity level (level of volume or production) such costs are also referred to as product costs. Cost of raw materials, power, and fuel are some of the prominent examples of variable costs.

There is a third category of costs termed as semi-variable costs. These are the combination of variable and fixed costs. These costs are also referred to as mixed costs. The examples of semi-variable costs include repairs and maintenance, salaries paid to the supervisors, etc. This understanding of costs concept and its behaviour is important from the viewpoint of profit planning and cost management and control.

CVP analysis determines the relationship between cost, volume, and profit. Such an analysis aids in certain key financial decisions. Breakeven point is the most significant techniques in CVP analysis. Breakeven point refers to a point of no profit, no loss. It is that level of sales where firm's revenues are equal to its total costs. Until a firm reaches the point of breakeven, it incurs losses. If the sales of a firm are rightwards of the breakeven point the firm is said to be operating in the profit zone. A firm should try to reach breakeven point as quickly as possible. To achieve this, fixed costs should be contained within manageable limits.

The difference between the actual sales and the sales at breakeven point is termed as the margin of safety. It measures the cushion available to firms against the decline in volume (sales). The higher the margin of safety, the better it is for the business. In order to have a high safety margin, the firm should cut down its fixed costs, volumes remaining the same.

Breakeven analysis, though very useful in decision-making, is sometimes criticized for its unrealistic assumptions that may not hold well in the real life. The analysis is based on the assumption of constant selling price, fixed costs, per unit variable costs, and product mix. These assumptions of constancy are the limitations of the model.

All technical terms have been explained at the end of each chapter as key terms. This will help you to retain all the new terms that you have learnt in the chapter.

KEY TERMS

Fixed costs Fixed costs are the costs that remain constant with the level of production sales. They are also known as period costs.

Variable costs Costs that change directly with the level of operations are called variable costs. They are also known as product cost.

Operating risk Operating risk refers to the chances that a firm's revenues are not sufficient to cover the operating costs. It is the fixed costs that cause operating risk due to their invariance to sales. Higher the fixed costs higher is the operating risk.

Degree of operating leverage (DOL) DOL measures the variability of operating profit with a given change in sales.

Financial risk The degree of financial risk depends upon the usage of fixed cost bearing sources of financing (i.e., debt) and is measured by the degree of financial leverage.

These have been identified by equation numbers throughout the text and will help you to retain the important formulae discussed in a chapter.

KEY FORMULAE

$$\text{Total Cost} = \text{TFC} + (\text{UVC} \times \text{N})$$

$$\text{Breakeven Sale} = \frac{\text{Fixed Cost}}{\text{Sales} - \text{Variable Cost}} \times \text{Sales}$$

$$\text{Breakeven Quality} = \frac{\text{Breakeven Sales}}{\text{Selling Price}}$$

$$\text{Breakeven Capacity} = \frac{\text{Breakeven Sales}}{\text{Capacity Sales}}$$

$$\text{Margin of Safety} = \frac{\text{Actual Sales} - \text{Breakeven Sales}}{\text{Actual Sales}} \times 100$$

$$\text{Target Sales for Profit of } x = \frac{\text{Fixed Cost} + \left(\frac{x}{1-T}\right)}{\text{Sales} - \text{Variable Cost}} \times \text{Sales}$$

Preface to the Second Edition

Sensible financial management practices create organizational value by allocating scarce resources among various business opportunities. It helps in the execution and supervision of an organization's business policies. The importance of sound financial management practices cannot be stressed more in an ever-changing global economy. The book is targeted at students taking the post-graduate management course. We have continued to provide a balanced attention to both conventional and non-conventional areas of financial decision making.

We are very happy to learn about the enthusiastic response that this book has received. The second edition of this well-accepted textbook continues to provide an exhaustive yet lucid coverage of the subject. We sincerely hope that the revised edition of the book will further aid students in understanding the basic concepts and principles of this subject.

Since the publication of the first edition three years back, we have received feedback from faculty members regarding the inclusion of certain topics. We have included their suggestions while revising the text.

Extended Chapter Material

The second edition improves upon the coverage of the original edition, making the text much more comprehensive and lucid.

Chapter 6 Valuation and Management A new section on ratings has been included in this chapter. Rating symbols facilitate decision making by investors. The section includes in-depth discussions on how ratings ascertain the adequacy of cash flows to service debt and the risks associated with them. It also discusses rating exercises by agencies and the ratings assigned by them.

Chapter 10 Valuation and Corporate Governance This chapter, which was titled Valuation in the first edition, has been revised and expanded to include extended coverage on economic value added (EVA) and corporate governance.

The section on EVA, one of the most popular value-based measurements, has been expanded in order to provide in-depth coverage of the factors that influence wealth maximization.

In the light of new industry developments, the section on corporate governance has been revised and updated. The section discusses how the corporate governance framework should ensure the accountability of the company to its stakeholders and board, and management of the company to its shareholders.

Chapter 17 Designing Capital Structure A new section on corporate debt restructuring has been introduced in this chapter. This section discusses the need for debt restructuring, which essentially involves the revival of units with potential.

Chapter 20 Financing Options This chapter has been revised extensively to focus on the long-term as well as short-term sources of funds. The chapter discusses long-term sources of funds such as equity, American depository receipts (ADR), global depository receipts (GDR), debentures and bonds, and project finance. India continues to be an attractive investment destination. The importance of venture capital (VC) funding and private equity (PE) in an emerging economy cannot be understated. These two topics have been expanded keeping in mind the latest industry trends. The section on short-term sources of finance discusses lines of credit, commercial papers, factoring, and forfaiting at length.

Chapter 21 Working Capital Management A new section on regulation of working capital finance has been included in this chapter. It discusses working capital financing by the banks in response to the working capital loan application by firms. The chapter discusses the implications of the Tandon study group. Banks follow the norms proposed by the committee regarding the assessment of working capital gap and the determination of maximum permissible bank finance.

About the CD

The book is accompanied with a CD. The enclosed CD contains Excel templates related to a few illustrations and unsolved problems from the book. It also includes additional reading material related to portfolio theory.

Additional Resources

Instructor's manual and *PowerPoint presentations* are available to lecturers on the password-protected website to the book—www.oupinheonline.com.

Acknowledgements

We are grateful to Dr Arya Kumar, BITS Pilani; Prof. Ashok Malhotra, BIMT, Greater Noida; Prof. Suman Kumar, NDIM, New Delhi; Kousik Guhathakurta, Army Institute of Management, Kolkata; Ashok Kumar Mishra IMIS, Bhubaneswar; and Dr Udayan Kumar Basu, Kolkata for their valuable feedback.

Your feedback will help us improve the book. All feedback can be sent to: rajiv1234 @ hotmail.com and anil.a.misra @ gmail.com.

Praise f.or the First Edition

'This book deals with every aspect of financial management.'

Prof. Suman Kumar
NDIM, New Delhi

'The presentation is interesting and lucid. The excel illustrations are a welcome addition.'

Kousik Guhathakurta
Army Institute of Management, Kolkata

Preface to the First Edition

Financial management as a discipline pertains to the management of financial resources. Broadly speaking, every decision/action having financial implications comes under the domain of finance. Specifically, there are three key areas of financial decision-making: *investment decisions, financing decisions, and dividend decisions*. Investment decisions are concerned with selecting the most optimal avenues of physical and financial investments. Financing decisions pertain to the choice of suitable sources to meet the firms' financing needs. The nature, composition, and above all, timing of financing are the main considerations in financing decisions. How much to retain for future financing needs of the firm and how much to distribute to the shareholders in the form of dividends is the key issue in dividend decisions.

The business environment, particularly in India, has undergone a major transformation with liberalization and growth of firms in Indian industry. The number of stakeholders has multiplied over the years on account of:

(a) quantum increase in the scale of business operations,
(b) proactive role being played by the stock market regulators,
(c) increased participation of institutional investors,
(d) pervasiveness of media that has put businesses to a closer scrutiny, and
(e) the threat of hostile takeovers.

In this changed business milieu, the focus of business decision-making is on the expectations and perceptions of these external stakeholders, though the considerations of shareholders remain dominant.

Financial management as a subject has gone through a 360-degree makeover—from insiders-looking-out approach to outsiders-looking-in approach—the nucleus of this metamorphosis being the requirement to put more emphasis on managerial decision-making skills. Sustainable growth in today's dynamic business environment demands a clear perception of market trends with the ability to take prudent managerial decisions. With the emergence of computing tools like spreadsheets, the emphasis of financial management is more on understanding and application of decision-making models and less on number crunching. Today, the thrust of the course is on resource optimization through quick and quality decisions related to both sides of the balance sheet.

Although the established areas of financial decision-making are still relevant, the changing business milieu has widened their framework to include certain non-conventional options of investment and financing. On one hand, the scale and the complexity of business has grown manifold; while on the other, the investors' expectations for the returns on investment are growing amidst the shrinking volumes and margins caused by increased competition. This has widened the purview of investment decisions to include avenues such as options, futures, forward, and other derivative instruments. From financing viewpoint, newer and creative sources of financing such as leasing, external commercial borrowings, securitization, ADRs, etc., have evolved to give wider choice and flexibility in financing. Also, the increased rate of internationalization of business has given prominence to issues pertaining to international finance such as currency risk and exposure, hedging, etc.

About the Book

This textbook on Financial Management is primarily designed keeping in view the requirements of MBA students undergoing the course in Business Schools in India. The book aims at explaining the concepts in the simplest possible manner without burdening the readers with unwarranted text.

The book devotes an equal attention to both conventional and non-conventional areas of finance decision-making.

Owing to its liberal resort to managerial and decision-making applications, the book will prove to be a useful ready reckoner for the readers for referring to important concepts in finance, first as aspiring managers and later as working professionals.

Pedagogical Features

The book adopts a simplified approach while presenting the basic concepts and policy issues in finance. To ensure that the readers do not get bogged down by the mathematical trivia and are able to assimilate and appreciate the broader issues of financial policy making, complex financial/mathematical models have been simplified, without in any way compromising with the inherent technical nature of the subject. Each chapter starts with a caselet to sensitize the readers with the theme of the chapter. To facilitate understanding of complex concepts in finance, the text in each chapter is interspersed with suitable examples/exhibits.

Besides the Learning Objectives and the Introduction that unfold the chapter, the end-chapter summary provides a bird's eye view of the topics discussed. All the technical terms that warrant explanation and recapitulation have been defined at the end of each chapter as Key Terms. A compendium of formulae too has been provided at the end of each chapter to facilitate revision and to put the readers at ease before attempting the numerical problems. End-chapter Practice Problems aid the readers in mapping the concepts with the real-world situations. Most of the chapters end with a case study that focuses upon the policy issue(s) discussed in the chapter. Most of these case studies have been developed from the real-world situations to expose the readers to virtual business environment of financial decision making.

To assist the readers traverse through the chapters without missing crucial details, the chapters are provided with a number of side-boxes that collect the essence of important sections.

Coverage and Structure

The course on financial management covers three broad areas: investment decisions, financing decisions, and dividend decisions, besides the basic tools and techniques such as time value of money, valuation, risk management, etc., that facilitate decision-making in these areas.

The book follows the style of moving from simple and fundamental issues to complex issues and models in financial decision-making. The fundamental concepts like ratio analysis, CVP analysis, and valuation techniques that find their application in subsequent chapters have been discussed in Part I and Part II of the book. Important corporate finance decisions of *Investment, Financing,* and *Dividends* are covered in later chapters for which the foundations are already created in earlier sections.

Part I of the book (Chapters 1–3) discusses the tools for financial analysis and managerial decision-making. Chapter 1 lays down the conceptual framework for financial decision-making in a "for-profit" business setting. The goals of "for-profit" business organization, the decision areas in financial management, the issue of multiplicity of stakeholders and related conflicts of interests in a typical corporate set up, etc., are the issues discussed in the chapter. Chapters 2 and 3 deal with the arithmetic tools of ratio and CVP analysis, respectively that are frequently used in managerial analysis and decision-making.

Part II that comprises seven chapters (Chapters 4–10), focuses upon the concepts and models that are fundamental to the understanding of financial decision-making. Vital concept of Time Value of Money presented in Chapter 4 finds application in investment and financing decisions in Part III and Part IV of the book. The concepts of Risk and Return (Chapter 5) find their application in almost all the subsequent chapters as the decisions whether related to the asset side or the liabilities side involve risk-return analysis. Determining the investment yield and the intrinsic value of securities is the key to making worthwhile investment in securities. Chapter 6 and 7 discuss at length the various models for determining the value and yield from securities, primarily bonds and shares. Such models facilitate the selection of right kind of securities for investment/disinvestment. The CAPM and Arbitrage Pricing Models that form the basis of Portfolio Theory have been taken up in Chapter 8. Chapter 9 on Portfolio Theory takes the discussion in Chapter 8 further. How to reduce the risk by diversifying the portfolio and how to design an optimal portfolio have been discussed therein. Chapter 10 explores the corporate valuation models that are used for the valuation of firms for different purposes such as mergers, acquisitions, takeovers, restructuring, etc.

Part III (Chapters 11–15) deals with the theoretical framework and the practical techniques used in investment decisions. This part deals with the asset side of the balance sheet with a focus on long-term investment. Short-term investment decisions and financial investment decisions have been dealt with separately in Part V (Working Capital Management) and Chapter 8 (Portfolio Theory) respectively. Chapters 11 and 12 take up the conceptual framework and the decision criteria for the long-term investment decisions. While the former discusses the basic issues in capital budgeting decisions like cash flow estimation and appraisal techniques for investment decisions, the latter takes up the advanced issues in investment decisions like decisions under the conditions of uncertainty and capital rationing. The techniques to incorporate risk in investment decisions have also been taken up in the chapter. The cost of capital is one area that finds its application in almost every financial decision, be it investment decision, financing decisions, or performance appraisal, to name a few. Since cost of capital acts as a hurdle rate for evaluating the investment options, it has been taken up under the investment decisions in the scheme of the book. Chapter 13 (Cost of Capital) focuses upon determining the cost of different sources of financing and eventually the overall cost of capital (or the weighted average cost of capital) that acts as the hurdle rate or the discount rate in the investment appraisal models. Real options that have lately emerged as the tools for incorporating uncertainty in investment decisions have been taken up in Chapter 14. The options to expand, delay, and abandon, and the valuation of these options have been discussed therein. Chapter 15 deals with the decision involving big ticket investment, i.e., mergers and acquisitions (M&A). Besides the theoretical aspects of M&A, the chapter also discusses the crucial aspect of valuing an M&A deal.

Part IV (Chapters 16–20) deals with long-term financing and dividend decisions. Chapter 16 lays down the theoretical foundations of the capital structure (or financing decisions) that find their application in the designing of capital structure in Chapter 17, where the crucial issue of determining the optimal capital structure has also been addressed. The propositions of Miller and Modigliani being common to both capital structure and dividend decisions, the two issues have been clubbed together and dealt with in the capital structure decisions. The focus is on application of principle of arbitrage. Leasing, an important source of indirect financing (long-term), is discussed in Chapter 18. The rationale and the structure of a lease transaction have been dealt with, *inter alia* in the chapter. Dividend decision, though an independent financial decision, affects the availability of the internal finances of the firm. The impact of the dividend policy on the internal financing (retained earnings) and hence the financing decisions, has convinced us to deal with the dividend decision along with the financing decisions. Chapter 19 discusses the theoretical framework of dividend decisions, designing of a dividend policy, and the methods of dividend payments. Chapter 20 on Financing Options discusses financial markets, financial products available, and the services offered by financial markets. In addition, this chapter throws light into domestic capital markets and their constituents, venture capital funding, and investment banking. It also discusses the sources of short-term and long-term financing.

Part V (Chapters 21–24) discusses working capital decisions that are concerned with the management of day-to-day operations. The focus of this part is on managing the level and financing of investment in the working capital. Chapter 21 lays down the framework for working capital decisions. The chapter is introductory in nature and discusses the generic issues that have been taken up subsequently in Chapters 22–24 that deal with the specific components of working capital management. Chapter 22 deals with one of the most important component of working capital, the inventory. Optimizing the investment in inventory is the basic thrust of this chapter. Receivables Management (Chapter 23) deals with the credit policy variables and their impact on the firms' value. The vexed issue of 'how to maximize the cash availability to support business operations, yet minimize idle cash' has been covered in Chapter 24 (Cash Management).

Part VI (Chapters 25–27) deals with the issues of international finance. Globalization has significantly widened the horizons of the domestic firms. Trade is no more confined to geography of a nation and has instead expanded its reach across borders. Now, many domestic firms are engaged in transactions with international suppliers and clients. A complete understanding of various currencies and their values is indispensable to pull off these transactions successfully. Moreover, such transactions have exposed the firms to the additional risks of appreciation/depreciation of currencies. Foreign exchange markets, transactions, determination of exchange rates, etc. have been taken up in Chapters 25 and 26. Chapter 27 discusses transaction exposure, economic exposure, translation exposure, and their management using the techniques such as hedging, risk sharing, forward, etc.

Part VII (Chapters 28–30) deals with the different types of risks and their management using the tools of derivatives such as forwards, futures, options, and swaps. With increased globalization and recent financial innovations, the choice available to managers has not only expanded but has become complex too. The elements of risks are getting added, so are the tools and techniques of managing them. A host of new financial instruments have emerged as an outcome of financial innovations. Such instruments have complexities in description as well as usage. A separate chapter has been devoted to each of the instrument focussing on the description, features, valuation, and applications of each. Understanding of these concepts has become inevitable in today's environment in the areas of corporate finance, risk management, and security analysis.

About the CD

The enclosed CD provides some additional readings on a few important concepts related to portfolio theory. Students having an inclination towards mathematical modelling and those who are interested in deeper understanding of portfolio theory would find the additional material useful. Besides additional reading material, the CD also contains a number of Excel applications that are aimed at providing practice to students with respect to a few useful mathematical concepts in finance. Related Excel applications for the Chapter are listed at the end of each chapter. These applications include (i) finding standard deviation and expected return as per CAPM; (ii) finding value, duration, and yield of bonds; (iii) valuing equity shares; (iv) finding IRR and NPV of the cash flows; (v) finding cost of capital; (vi) calculating lease rentals; (vii) finding the fair value of a futures contract; (viii) valuing options using Black Scholes Model; etc. These applications are central to understanding of finance and pricing of various instruments, and therefore need to be understood and practised by all users.

ACKNOWLEDGEMENTS

This book would not have seen the day of fruition without the direct and indirect support and cooperation of many individuals whom we would like to briefly acknowledge here.

We are grateful to Mr K.T. Chacko, Director, IIFT, Delhi, for providing an environment conducive for learning and creative thinking without which this work would not have been possible. We also express our sincere gratitude to Prof. J.N. Shukla, former Professor, University of Lucknow; Prof. D.K. Bandyopadhyay, Vice Chancellor, GGS Indraprastha University; Prof. S. Chakraborty, Director, JIM, Lucknow; and Prof. Deepak Chawla, Professor, IMI, Delhi; for all their encouragement, guidance, and support.

We are immensely indebted to Dr Dheeraj Mishra, Professor (Finance), JIM, Lucknow, for the entire academic and research stimulus that he has provided over the years. Dr Naval Bajpai, Associate Professor, IITM, Gwalior, a former colleague and friend of Dr Misra, deserves special mention for all the motivation that he has provided over the years.

We also express our sincere acknowledgements to all our employers, State Bank of India, CMC Limited, Uflex Limited, Jaipuria Institute of Management, and Lucknow University for providing invaluable opportunities for practical learning, which has immensely helped in expressing the financial concepts with a number of applications.

Our special thanks are also due for our faculty colleagues in the area of finance at IIFT, Prof. Satinder Bhatia, Prof. Harkirat Singh, Prof. V. Raveendra Saradhi, Prof. T.P. Ghosh, and Prof. Jacqueline Symss for their support and encouragement from time to time. A special thanks to the staff of the computer center at IIFT, particularly Mr S. Balasubramanian, Assistant Systems Manager, for extending help towards the development of the CD.

We would also like to acknowledge the contribution of all our present and former students. It is their inquisitiveness shown in the form of their incisive and intriguing questions that enabled us to identify the areas that needed a special emphasis and guided us to present the contents of the book in a simplified manner.

We are specially grateful to Dr Pinaki Dasgupta, Associate Professor, IIFT, for introducing us to each other and being such a good friend. Dr Dasgupta was instrumental in sowing the seeds for the fruitful collaboration of this book.

We would like to thank the production and the editorial team of Oxford University Press for all their support and dedication to the project.

Last but not the least, we are indebted to our better halves, Mrs Anita Srivastava (wife of Mr Rajiv Srivastava) and Dr Kanwal Anil (wife of Dr Anil Misra) Assistant Professor, Jaypee Business School, for their beliefs, confidence, patience, and support that made our efforts see the light of day.

Rajiv Srivastava
Anil Misra

Contents

Contents of CD

Appendices

Excel Applications

PART ONE

INTRODUCTION

CHAPTER 1

Financial Management—An Overview

LEARNING OBJECTIVES

The chapter is aimed at

- discussing the nature and scope of financial management
- explaining the role of finance function in an organization
- elaborating the key decision areas in financial management – investment, financing, dividend, and working capital management
- discussing the principles underlying the four broad areas of financial decision-making
- enunciating the objective function of financial management
- discussing the issue of multiplicity of stakeholders in business and the associated agency problems and costs
- highlighting the relationship between financial accounting, management accounting, and financial management
- expressing the relationship between financial objective and organizational strategy

SHAPE UP OR SHIP OUT

Electro Korea, a Korean electronic giant, was forced into bankruptcy post-South East Asian currency crisis in 1997. Mr Gupta, the President of Electronica India Limited, an Indian MNC, with an eye on expanding his company to global level visited Seoul to explore the possibility of taking over Electro Korea. Mr Gupta called upon Mr Chin-Hwa, erstwhile CFO of the Korean company, now working as a consultant, to figure out the problems that caused the firm's closure.

The following conversations took place between Mr Gupta and Mr Chin-Hwa:

Mr Gupta: Tell me Mr Chin what financial problems did Electro Korea encounter that caused the demise of the firm?

Mr Chin: Sir! The problem was not one or two, but three-dimensional. The company faltered on three basic financial management tenets, i.e., investment selection, finance sourcing, and fund utilization.

Mr Gupta: Please go ahead.

Mr Chin: The problem started with a strong urge to meet the demand and capitalize on the booming market conditions. In view of the overwhelming demand for electronic products not only locally but in the global markets too in post 1990s, the company added a wide range of products to its existing product line. We became over-enthusiastic and to tap the growing market, expanded production capacity by 500%. Between 1990 and 1992, five new manufacturing units were set up.

Mr: Gupta: Oh! that is a phenomenal growth in a short period of time.

Mr Chin: Yeah, true but most of this expansion was debt financed using either short-term loans from Korean banks or long-term foreign currency loans. With the ongoing phase of expansion the banks were very open-hearted in lending to the firm. By 1995, the debt–equity ratio reached a catastrophic level of 5:1. To make hay while the sun shines was the common phrase that was used by all from top, middle, and lower rungs of people. A wide array of products and brands emerged by 1995, causing a glut.

Mr Gupta: I can visualize some of the problems now.

Mr Chin: Recessionary conditions started setting in early 1996 and the company began to witness idle capacity that started dragging down its ROI. Theorists say that investment decisions are irreversible, we witnessed precisely that. Due to recessionary conditions there were no buyers for the three idle manufacturing units that we wanted to sell off. There was a huge pile up of raw material, semi-finished and finished goods inventory, which could be disposed off with a great difficulty at a value that was significantly below the book value.

Mr Gupta: That would have caused lenders to panic.

Mr Chin: Exactly. The banks that were hitherto pumping in money on demand were unwilling to roll over short-term loans. To complicate matters further due to devaluation, the local value of foreign currency loan of the company skyrocketed.

Another major problem was that in the first half of 1990 when the company's growth rate was in double digits, the company followed a very liberal dividend policy, which became unsustainable by 1995 with nose-diving revenues, profits, and cash flows. A sharp cut in dividends conveyed an adverse signal and the stock price of the company crashed in 1997.

Mr Gupta: We also witnessed a similar situation in 1990s but could avert the crisis as we stuck to fundamental principles of finance. Our expansion was need based, market driven and came in a phased manner. We tried to finance the additional investments as much as possible through internal sources, i.e., our past retentions. We maintained a stable dividend payout of 40% even amidst the very high growth period of 1990s and never allowed the debt–equity ratio to go beyond 2.5:1. Through better supply chain management and successful implementation of Just-In-Time inventory management, we ensured that even during this high-growth phase we were carrying close to zero level of inventories.

Mr Chin: I appreciate what you did. I presume that only because of sound financial management policies you are here on a buying spree.

INTRODUCTION

Businesses, whether new or existing, may vary from one another in terms of the industry they operate in, the environment they function in, the products/services they render, or the operations that they undertake. However, the finance issues that businesses grapple with, notwithstanding their industry characteristics, geographical location, product profile etc. are largely universal. These are:

- From where to raise the most cost-effective financial resources needed to carry out the operations and how to manage the risks associated with such financing?
- Where to invest the scarce business resources so as to maximize the returns on the investments, i.e., selecting the right nature and optimal scale of businesses, projects, etc. and at most suitable locations?
- How to manage the routine production–distribution functions in the most optimal and cost-effective manner so as to maximize the wealth of the stakeholders?
- How much of the profits to retain for future investment needs and how much to distribute as dividends to shareholders?

The scope of financial management extends to the decisions pertaining to optimal utilization of financial resources. The role of a finance manager is to resolve the aforesaid issues that are commonly categorized into—financing decisions, investment decisions, working capital decisions, and dividend decisions. All these issues are resolved in the light of their probable impact on the wealth of the shareholders, which is commonly accepted goal for all 'for-profit' organizations.

NATURE AND SCOPE OF FINANCIAL MANAGEMENT

The term financial management has emerged from the generic discipline of management. In order to understand financial management, it is better to start with an understanding of the term *management*. Management, simply put, is all about securing the optimal use of the resources at the disposal of a firm towards the attainment of some predetermined goals. These resources are of many kinds such as human capital, production machines, distribution channels, etc. Resources are put under the charge of their respective departments that are responsible for their management and control. Each department contributes towards the organizational objectives by effectively managing the resources they are in charge of. As can be seen in Figure 1-1, financial management is concerned with the management of financial resources of the organization. Many terms such as capital, funds, cash flow, money, etc. are used synonymously and interchangeably to describe financial resources. The finance department of the organization is responsible for the financial management of the firm, which it does through the means of financial decision-making.

Financial management is concerned with managing financial resources in the most optimal manner.

Financial management performs facilitation, reconciliation, and control functions in an organization. The sourcing of finances needed by various departments and its rational allocation for various activities is done by the finance department. This facilitates the attainment of the various departmental goals along with the

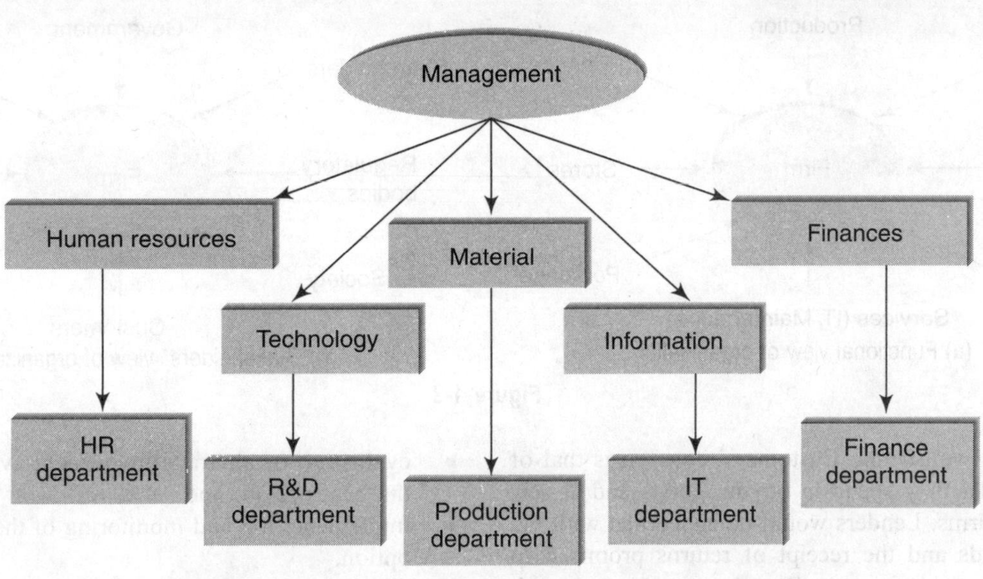

Figure 1-1 Financial management as a sub-discipline of management

realization of the overall organizational goal. The rational and balanced allocation of resources done by the finance department reconciles the interests of the various departments and pre-empts any kind of probable conflict for resources between the various departments of an organization. Also, the finance department maintains a constant control over the various activities of the organization and makes different departments accountable for the resources that they consume.

Through the process of financial decision-making the finance department performs facilitation, reconciliation, and control functions.

All decisions that have monetary implications come under the purview of financial management. Decision related to other functions such as the decision to launch a major advertising campaign or to go ahead with a comprehensive training programme for middle-level managers are although under the control of marketing and HR functions respectively, their financial implications require ratification by the finance department. This widens the scope of financial decision-making practically to all the decisions. It is due to this fact that it is said that 'the finance manager is on the top and not on the tap'.

ROLE OF FINANCE FUNCTION

Finance is central to all business activities—for survival and growth alike. All business performance, targets, and goals though set in absolute terms have a common measurement in financial terms. Similarly all comparisons either with the past or with competitors are measured or analysed with financial data.

An organization can be viewed from two different perspectives—functional and stakeholders'. From the functional viewpoint, each organization can be divided into various functional areas such as marketing, production, personnel, etc., which discharge different duties and perform different roles to achieve organizational goals. The functional division of organizational structure helps to translate wider goal into smaller and perceivable sub-unit or functional goals. It also helps establish the relationship of each individual with the organizational goals. Sales revenue and the effectiveness of the marketing strategy are some of the issues that the sales and marketing function evaluates. The results of a new machine installation, the cost of production of various items, etc., are some of the issues that fall in the domain of the production function. Similarly, personnel function needs to decide upon the executive compensation, establish training needs, and measure individual performance in quantitative and/or qualitative terms.

An organization can be viewed from two different perspectives—functional and stakeholders'.

Like different functions of an enterprise, there are different stakeholders associated with business. There exist shareholders who contribute capital and expect to earn a return on equity contributed. There are debt-holders who also provide capital but feel satisfied with the returns at a fixed rate. Employees work to earn their emoluments, suppliers provide material and services, and customers derive satisfaction by consuming the products and services offered by the firm. Besides there are various government and regulatory bodies who monitor performance in compliance with the rules and regulations aimed at general welfare of the society and nation as a whole.

Different stakeholders of a firm have varied concerns, which can only be addressed by finance function. Shareholders need to know how their wealth would increase and how safe are they in their investment with the firm. Creditors want to know whether or not to supply materials on credit to the firm, and if yes, for what period and to what extent. Employees of the firm are also concerned about the timely receipt of salary and their personal

Finance function is significant for all organizations from both functional and stakeholders' perspectives.

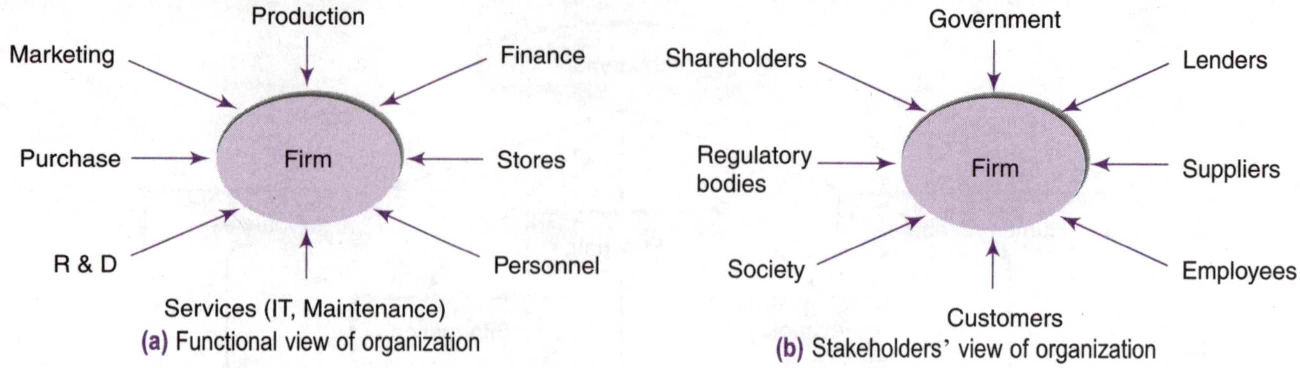

Figure 1-2

growth and general well-being. Customers' concern is that of value for money that they spend in buying goods and/or services rendered by firms. Lenders would be concerned with the security of the funds and the receipt of returns promised to them. Government would want to collect the taxes as projected.

Finance function reconciles the potential conflicts between functional goals on one hand and between stakeholders' interests on the other.

Two separate views of the firm are depicted in Figure 1-2(a) and (b). Irrespective of the perspective of different functions and stakeholders, finance function serves as a common denominator by taking decisions that are in consonance with the interests of different stakeholders; by facilitating the decisions and by providing the information that the stakeholders need for evaluation and analysis of the firm's performance.

FINANCE DECISIONS BY THE FIRMS

The thrust of financial decision-making is on procurement of funds and their optimal utilization through investment, financing, dividends and working capital decisions.

There are a host of decisions that the finance managers have to take throughout the life of the firm. Some of these decisions are routine operating decisions that are repetitive in nature and affect the business on a day-to-day basis. While other decisions such as the decision to set-up a new business unit, decision to merge with another company, etc., are of strategic nature as they have long-term implications for the business. Financial management is concerned with the procurement and utilization of funds in an optimal way so as to achieve the desired goals of an organization. The scope of financial management extends to four key decision areas—*investment, financing, dividend, and working capital.*

Investment Decisions

Investment decisions involve putting the resources in avenues that give a return that is in excess of the cost incurred on procuring such resources. This maximizes the wealth of the shareholders. These decisions are alternatively referred to as capital budgeting decisions. Basic issues involved in investment decisions are:

- evaluation of alternate investment avenues so as to select the best option; and
- implementation and monitoring of the selected investment option.

Investment decisions pertain to selection of the most productive avenues with a view to maximize the returns on investment.

For a new business such decisions usually relate to setting up of production–distribution facilities, while for an existing business they are mainly in form of replacement, modernization, and research and development (R&D) expenditure decisions. These decisions depend upon the nature of industry that the firm operates in, the kind of products/services offered, scale of its operations, etc. They have long-term implications, involve large capital outlay, and are normally irreversible. Drawing an analogy from our day-to-day life, we can say that the decision to buy a car or a house property is an investment decision that not only involves relatively large capital outflows but also has long-term implications as we do not take such decisions frequently unlike the decision to buy a pair of shoes.

Investment decisions are concerned with the expansion, modernization, and replacement of long-term assets (fixed assets).

These decisions are significantly important for the business not only for huge capital outlay that they entail and the element of irreversibility in them but also from the risk–return perspective. A wrong nature or scale of investment may not only bring down the return on investment but may also enhance the operating risk of the business.

In finance, we distinguish investment decisions based on the nature of assets. The assets deployed in business are broadly of two kinds—fixed asset and current asset. Fixed assets are those assets that serve the business for a long time, at least beyond one year period, while current assets have a short life and are held for sale, either in the same form or after transforming them, within a year's time. Examples of fixed assets include land, building, machinery, etc. Inventories, account receivable, and cash are the typical current assets of the firm.

Investment decisions which are alternatively referred to as capital budgeting decisions are crucial for survival and growth of any firm.

The decision to invest in the long-term assets (fixed assets) by the firm is referred as investment decision (or capital budgeting decisions). Right investment

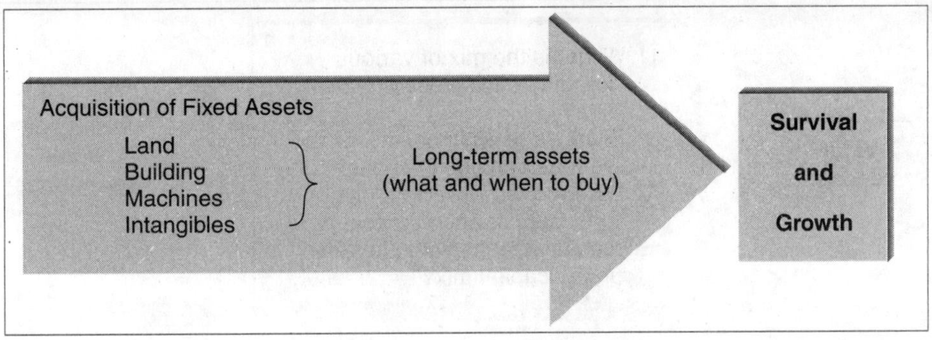

Figure 1-3 Investment decision

decisions, as indicated in Figure 1-3, are critical for long-term survival and growth of the firm. The decision to invest or not is taken in the light of the probable impact of such investments on the wealth of the shareholders. If the investment option is likely to create/enhance the wealth, it is acceptable, otherwise it is not. In case of multiple investment options, the option that is likely to maximize the wealth is acceptable.

Managers devote considerable time and energy in the selection of various businesses and in identifying, choosing, and acquiring the assets required to remain in the selected business. It requires conceptually a different framework and set of skills different from those needed to examine routine business issues.

Long-term assets are bought to perform production–distribution functions and earn a net rate of return that should satisfy the various contributors of capital. The basic issue in investment decisions is whether the cash generated from operations carried out by using or consuming such assets is sufficient enough, in real value terms, to meet the expectations of investors. If yes, the investment is acceptable, else managers reject the proposed investment. Investment decisions are benchmarked against the expectations of investors.

Productive capacity of a business depends upon the quality and the scale of its investments.

The issues in investment decisions and their implications are depicted in Figure 1-3.

Financing Decisions

The second question that finance managers face is how to fund the investments. Financing decisions relate to the procurement of required amount of funds, as and when needed, at lowest possible cost and on most convenient terms. These decisions are mainly concerned with the identification of potential sources of funds and tapping of these sources as per the funding requirements of the firm. Often these decisions are loosely referred to as *capital structure decisions*. Although capital structure or debt–equity structure is of prime importance, there are other issues as well that are covered under the rubric of financing decisions in addition to the capital structure. The main issues involved in such decisions are:

Financing decisions are concerned with the procurement of the required amount of funds on most convenient terms as and when needed.

Financing decisions are commonly referred to as capital structure decisions.

- Where from to procure the requisite capital?
- What should be the optimal mix of various sources of capital?
- How much should be the proportion of short-term and long-term capital?
- How do the expectations of providers of each source of capital change with alteration in the capital mix?

Financing decisions are as important as the investment decisions in the valuation of a firm. They determine the financial risk profile of the business.

While investment decisions deal with the creation of assets by the firm, financing decisions are concerned with the sources of financing such assets. Firms have two options of financing their long-term investments— debt and equity. While equity holders do not seek a fixed return (it does not mean that they have no expectation of return), the debt holders do expect a fixed return at periodic intervals as well as redemption of the original capital contributed. Debt, due to the associated tax advantage, is a cheaper source of finance than equity. Due to the lower cost of debt, increased usage of debt financing brings down the overall cost of financing for the firm. However, since debt carries the obligation for fixed interest payment and principal repayment, increased dosage of debt financing increases the risk of financial bankruptcy for the firm. A right blend of debt-equity assumes significance as it affects the risk return profile of the business. Decisions regarding the sources and mix of financing are taken in the light of their likely impact on the wealth of the stockholders. Such decisions may enhance or erode the value of the firm as shown in Figure 1-4. The other issue associated with the debt is the desire of the lenders for control over the business. With the increase in the debt component in the firm's financing the lenders start perceiving the firm to be risky and want, as a precautionary measure, a participation in its decision-making and control. Sometimes they may also put some restrictions on the firm as a pre-condition to their lending to the firm. Such interference in the decision-making of the firm may circumscribe the managerial decisions and may, at times, interfere with the goal of the shareholders' wealth maximization.

Another related issue in financing decisions is to determine the mix of short-term and long-term financing. This assumes significance as long-term financing enhances the liquidity position of the firm. But at the same time there is a risk that the funds may be lying idle for some part of the year and the

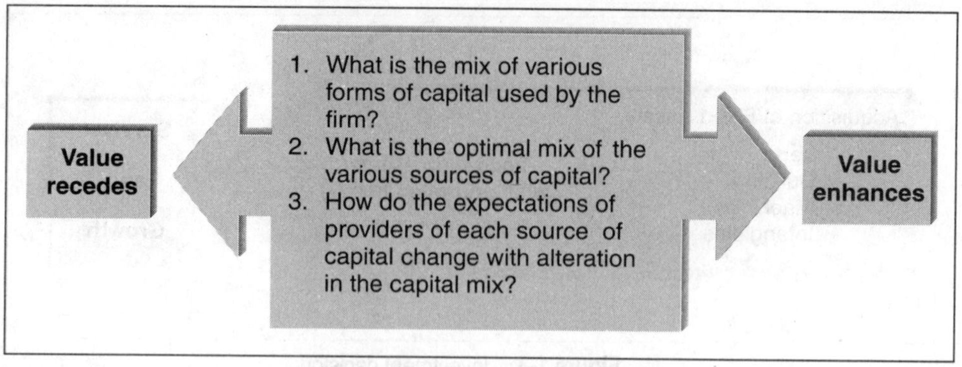

Figure 1-4 Financing decision

business may have to bear the cost of funds even for the period it does not need them. Short-term funds provide the flexibility to the business as they could be tied up with the needs of the business. For the periods additional financing is needed funds can be raised on a short-term basis and could be repaid at the time the need for funds comes down. However, there is a risk with short-term funds as well; they may not be available when needed. Even if they are available they may be available on terms that are inconvenient for the borrowers.

The thrust of financing decisions is on bringing down the cost of financing keeping the risk constant.

The thrust of financing decisions is to bring down the cost of financing the firm's investments and operations for a given level of risk.

Dividend Decision

Coupled with capital structure decisions is the dividend decision. The *dividend decision* focuses upon identifying what portion of residual profits to distribute to shareholders as dividends and how much to peough back for future financing needs of the business. Having generated cash, the firm must decide whether to retain or distribute the cash to the providers of capital. The providers of equity capital, who opted to link their fortunes with that of the firm and did not explicitly demand their investment back or return thereon, have to make a choice of retention or distribution of cash once it becomes available. Such a decision depends on trade off between future financing needs of the firm and current consumption requirements of the shareholders. Generally firms in sectors with a high-growth rate follow a policy of high retention and low payout. This is to plan for the future financing requirements in view of the high rate of projected growth and expansion for such firms. Firms that are in the sectors, which have matured and where the growth has been stabilized, normally follow a policy of high payout. In the absence of strong financing requirements, such firms, by having a high payout ratio, pass on the earnings to the shareholders in the form of dividends and enable them to make a choice to consume the income or invest in the firms/sectors that give them a better growth and a higher return on investment.

Rate of dividends and the method of its payment are the two key issues that the dividend policy is concerned with.

Payout ratio depends on the future financing requirements and the expectations of the shareholders for current income.

The payout ratio is decided in the light of its likely impact on shareholders' wealth. Normally firms follow a policy of stable dividends and do not make any significant change in their rate of dividend payout on an annual basis. Dividends are normally increased in a gradual manner to a level that is sustainable in foreseeable future. Since investment in assets is desired on a continuous basis and cash is also generated simultaneously, the question of retention of cash or its distribution assumes significance. Another related issue addressed by the dividend policy is the method of dividend payment. Should the dividend be paid in form of cash or should it be paid in form of stocks (stock dividends/ bonus shares)?

One may argue that given an investment policy and the financing mix, the dividend is automatic. Dividend policy is considered as a residue of investment and financing policy. High investment and financing requirements mean low payout and high retention policy and vice versa. However, another view is that dividend decision by itself can impact the value of the firm. It can be used as a tool of conveying some meaningful information about the firm, which is valuable for stakeholders. Therefore, dividend decision need not be residual of investment policy and financing decision. All the three decisions that the finance function has to take are intricately linked as depicted in Figure 1-5, and cannot be viewed in a simplistic manner. Any decision in isolation cannot be guaranteed as optimal.

There are two views on dividend decisions—dividend decisions as a residue of investment and financing decisions and dividend as an independent policy decision.

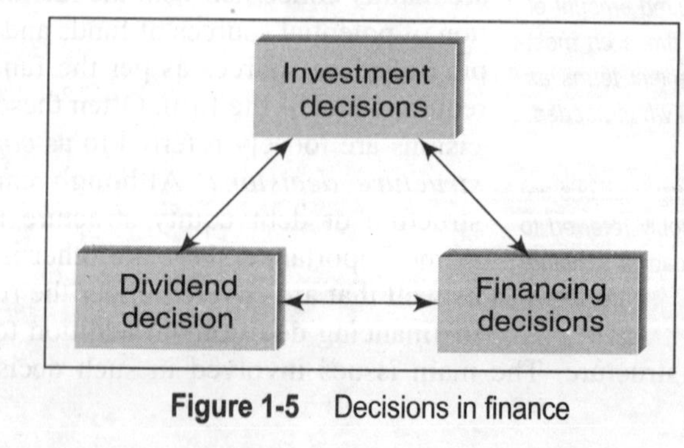

Figure 1-5 Decisions in finance

Working Capital Decisions

Besides long-term assets, the firm also requires short-term assets known as current assets. These assets comprise cash and bank balances, account receivable and stocks of finished goods, work-in-process, and raw material. These assets are required for day-to-day functioning of the firm. Basic issues in working capital decisions are: determing the optimal level of current assets and deciding the most suitable sources of their financing. Questions such as what level of inventory should be maintained and for how long the credit should be given to the customers are of significant importance for any business as they affect the profitability–liquidity position of the business.

Working capital decisions are related to the management of current assets.

The two key decision points are the level of investment in current assets and mode of their financing.

Working capital decisions are classified as a separate group because short-term assets need a different approach than what is required for long-term assets. Constraints and decision-making criteria for working capital are substantially different from long-term assets.

The key decision issues in each of the aforesaid decisions areas of financial management are enumerated in Table 1-1.

An Integrated View of Finance Decision-making

All the four key areas of finance decision-making are very much interlinked and form part of the integrated framework of financial decision-making. As can be seen in Figure 1-6, the firm carries out its operations to achieve its goal. These operations, depending on the nature of the business, may be manufacturing, trading, or service and require certain economic resources (assets) that are both long-term and short-term in nature. Acquisition of these assets requires financial resources (liabilities). The figure can be read bottom upwards indicating the sequence of activities undertaken by the firm. This is shown by dotted lines in the figure. There are three key issues with regards to financing—the duration of financing, the sources of finance, and the financing mix. Normally short-term funds are tapped for working capital financing, while the long-term sources of funds are relied upon for long-term investments.

The four key decision areas in finance are the part of an integrated decision-making framework. They are directly linked to and reinforce each other.

Table 1-1 Key issues in financial decision making

Investment Decisions	• What business to be in? • What growth rate is appropriate? • What assets to acquire?
Financing Decisions	• What mix of debt and equity to be used? • Can we change the value of the firm by changing the capital mix? • Is there an optimal debt–equity mix?
Dividend Decision	• How much of the profit should be distributed as dividends and how much should be ploughed back? • Can we change the value of the firm by changing the amount of dividend? • What should be the mode of dividend payment?
Working Capital Decisions	• What level of inventory of goods is ideal? • What level of credit should be given to the customers? • What level of cash should be maintained? • How can the blockage of funds in the current assets be minimized without compromising profits?

Financing decisions also assume significance due to their impact on the business risk. Excessive usage of debt, which is a cheaper source of financing, though brings down the overall cost of financing, increases the bankruptcy risk for the firm. Another key decision that is intricately linked to the financing decision is the dividend decision. It is concerned with the allocation of the surplus (residual profits) between the dividends and the retained earnings, which are ploughed back to meet the future financing requirements of firms. Since retained earnings, which are an outcome of firm's dividend policy, represent the internal component of financing, the dividend policy is sometimes considered as a part of financing policy. Also, by altering its dividend policy, the firm can alter the mix of internal and external sources of financing.

The four decision areas of financial decision-making mentioned above are largely universal. However, the relevance and the importance of these decision areas vary from firm to firm depending upon industry characteristics and the nature of operations. For example, for firms in the Information Technology (IT) sector such as Microsoft Corporation or Infosys Technologies Ltd, investment decisions are of less significance as these firms are knowledge intensive firms and operate with low levels of fixed asset investments. The nature of their business demands huge investments in intellectual capital as opposed to physical capital. Similarly, since most of the IT firms are, at least till date, cash-rich firms the dividend decisions assume importance for them. As there is no production taking place in these firms and also because these firms mostly have project-based operations, the issue of working capital management does not hold much relevance for them.

Although the key financial decisions are universal, their importance varies.

Unlike this, the firms that are capital intensive such as those manufacturing consumer durables and capital goods require a large outlay for investment, particularly for creating and maintaining production, storage, and distribution facilities. Since manufacturing firms have long assembly lines, the management of working capital also assumes special significance for them.

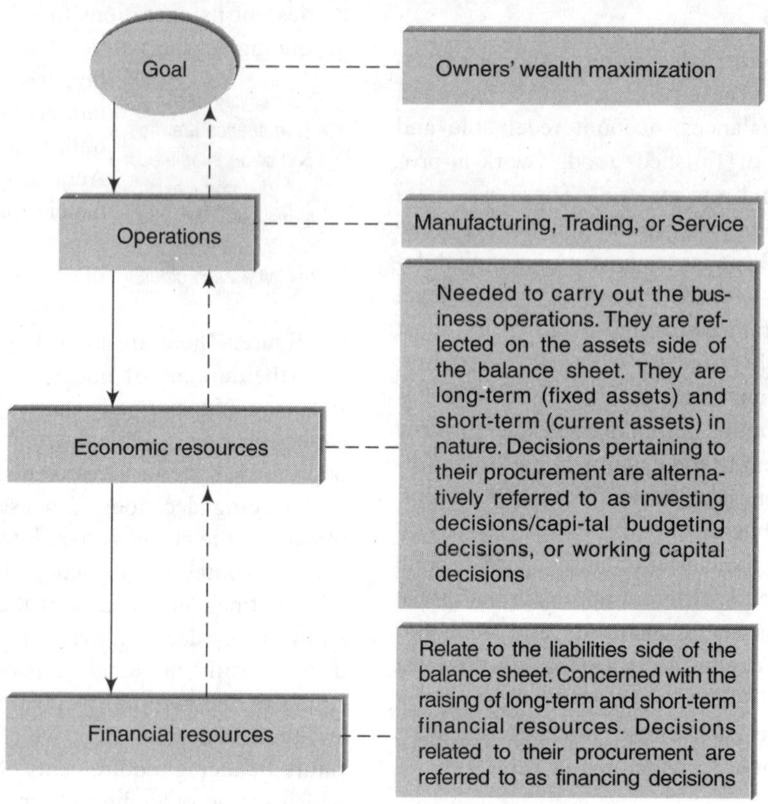

Figure 1-6 Financial decision-making framework

OBJECTIVE FUNCTION IN FINANCE

Different functions and different stakeholders of a firm view its existence and objectives differently. At times these different set of objectives of various functions and stakeholders can be conflicting. Conflict may arise among different suppliers of capital—debt and equity. Debt holders may want the firm to play safe to ensure the safety of their stake in it. For this they may put some restrictive covenants in the loan agreement restricting the freedom of the shareholders to pursue some risky ventures. On the other hand, the shareholders in their endeavour to maximise their wealth may be interested in exploring some new and more profitable, though somewhat riskier business opportunities.

The stakes of the different stakeholders in the firm vary and so do their expectations from the firm.

Similarly different functions see an organization differently. The marketing function of a firm may want to reduce the price and improve the quality of the product with the objective of beating the competition though this may adversely affect the profits. They may also want to have inordinately high levels of inventory of finished products to ensure timely supply of products and to convert any unanticipated demand into sales. However, such a high level of investment in the inventory carries the risk of obsolescence and may result in pile up of non-moving inventory. Similarly, the production function would want adequate time to produce goods and plan procurement activities, much to the discomfort of marketing function.

The focus of different functional areas in organizations are at variance with one another.

There are several objectives that are associated with the for-profit firms. Some of the common ones are:

- Maximization of market share
- Maximization of profit/earnings
- Maximization of return on investment
- Achieving a specified service level
- Satisfying all stakeholders

Though all the stated objectives are valid and appealing, they do not provide an unfailing framework for financial decision-making. The aforesaid objectives suffer from the following limitations:

Objective function of the business should be in consonance with the interests of the multiple stakeholders.

1. they ignore view points of other stakeholders;
2. they are too vague and are non-quantifiable;
3. they do not take into account the changing value of money with time.

Due to these limitations the aforesaid objectives are not acceptable as the overarching goal of the firms that have multiple stakeholders with varied stakes. Various decisions of finance, i.e., investment, financing, dividend, and working capital need a guiding principle that serves the objectives of all stakeholders and functions of an enterprise.

The only objective that seems to stand the rigorous test that each decision is subjected to is the maximization of shareholders' wealth. Finance scholars, managers, and the society in general are unanimous in the opinion that the sole objective of the firm is to maximize the shareholders' wealth. Let us view this objective in some detail.

As stated earlier and depicted in Figure 1-2(b), there are many stakeholders in the firm. A firm sells its products and/or services, pays the suppliers of raw material, pays wages and salaries to employees, and then meets other expenses. Thereafter, it services the obligations towards lenders by paying interest on borrowed capital before generating profit. As a good corporate citizen, it must also pay taxes to the government. If any profit is left, it goes to the shareholders. In a nutshell, although shareholders are the owners, they are entitled to the residual profit only. After meeting the commitments to all other stakeholders they get the remaining. Shareholders' claim cannot precede that of any other stakeholders. The flow of benefits is depicted in Figure 1-7. With maximization of residual as the objective of the firm, it can safely be stated that all preceding commitments have been satisfied adequately.

The goal of wealth maximization is widely accepted as it reconciles the varied, often conflicting, interest of the stakeholders.

Despite the overwhelming evidence and the unfailing nature of the objective, there are many critics of the goal of maximization of shareholders' wealth. It may be argued by some that shareholders being owners, managers, and controllers of the firm serve their own interests by maximizing their wealth. The objectives of other stakeholders are ignored. Instead, they may argue that a balanced approach with respect to all stakeholders would be better. However, it poses some practical problems of defining the right balance because of inherent conflicts of interests among the various stakeholders. Maximization of shareholders' wealth ensures that conflict, if any, must be resolved in favour of real owner of the firm. Firms focusing on the goal of wealth maximization ensure that they, in the process, take care of the interest of all the stakeholders as the individual goals of the varied stakeholders are in congruence with the goal of wealth maximization.

AGENCY COSTS AND CORPORATE GOVERNANCE

The company form of business organization has emerged due to the limitations of its preceding forms of businesses—sole proprietorship and partnership—in terms of their capacity to raise capital, hire professionals to manage their operations, scale of operations, and their legal status. Joint stock company is a form of business organization, which is commonly referred to as a body where the public is substantially interested. The stakeholders in a company are multiple and their stakes are varied. This multiplicity of stakeholders is on account of the following features of such firms:

The stakeholders in the company form of business organization are multiple, their stakes are varied and their objectives are often conflicting.

- The ownership lies with the shareholders who are widely scattered.
- Due to scattered interest, split between ownership and management makes management a key stakeholder.
- The large size and the wide impact makes the community at large interested in the firms.
- Capital comprises borrowed funds too. Hence, lenders are also stakeholders.
- These firms operate in a regulated environment. This makes the government a stakeholder.

Figure 1-7 shows clearly the various stakeholders in publicly-held firms. As it is evident from the figure, there are multiple stakeholders with varied stakes (interests) in a typical firm. The multiplicity of stakeholders with varied stakes and expectations leads to the pursuit of varied objectives by different stakeholders in the firm. These objectives are more often than not conflicting. To reconcile these conflicting objectives, the overall goal of 'for-profit' firms is stated as maximizing the wealth of the owners (maximizing the market value of equity shares in case of firms that are listed on stock exchanges). Pursuit of this all-encompassing goal by the firm ensures that the interest of all the different stakeholders is taken care of in the process as this wealth maximization as the goal of weath maximization is in congruence with the objectives of the varied stakeholders. No firm can bring about a sustained increase in the wealth of its owners without taking care of the interest of its other stakeholders. For example, deteriorating liquidity position of a firm makes the lenders, current and prospective, apprehensive about its creditworthiness, which eventually gets reflected in its share prices and consequently the wealth of the shareholders. Similarly, a firm that cannot retain its existing customers will witness a decline in its sales and consequently the market price of its shares.

Agency Issues

Theoretically the goal of wealth maximization provides a comprehensive framework to resolve the conflict of interest between the different stakeholders as it is consistent with the individual interests and objectives of the varied stakeholders. However, reality may be quite contrary to the theory. As per the theory, there exists a principal–agent relationship between the shareholders and the management, whereby the management is ex-

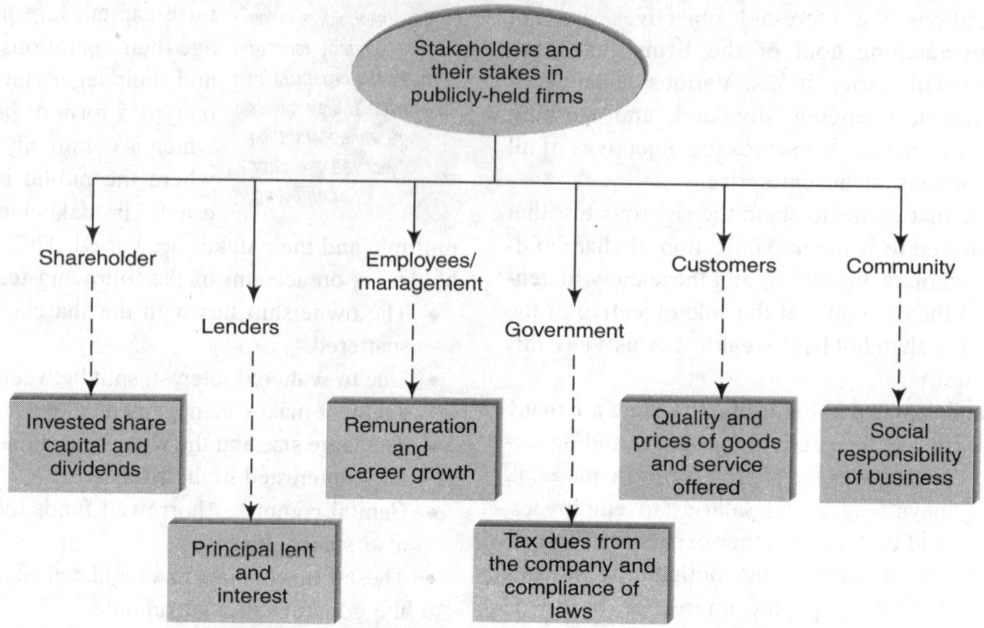

Figure 1-7 Multiple stakeholders and their respective stakes

Conflicting interest between the varied stakeholders particularly the stockholders and the management causes agency problems.

pected to manage the resources of the firm in the best interest of shareholders. However, contrary to the theory, as has been witnessed in several real life cases, the management instead of acting as an arbitrator of the stakeholders and the agent of the stockholders has been found to be acting in their own interest and trying to maximize their own wealth. This brings forth the issue of agency problem and the associated costs.

Agency problems occur on account of conflicts of interest between shareholders and management. Shareholders who are the principal stakeholders, delegate decision rights to the manager to act in their best interests. This implies a loss of effective control by shareholders over managerial decisions. The cases of insider trading, i.e., acquisition of shares by the management in view of an impending merger for which no information is available with the shareholders suggest agency problems. Similarly the cases of companies such as Enron and Worldcom, where the management in collusion with the auditors have been responsible for destruction of shareholders' wealth suggest the tendency of management to create an illusion of wealth creation so that they are not dislodged from their positions. Under the guise of shareholders' wealth maximization, management have been pursuing the agenda of self-aggrandizement, that too at the cost of erosion in the shareholders' wealth. In such a scenario, which emerges on account of conflicting stakes and interests of the multiple stakeholders, particularly the management and the stockholders, some kind of control on management becomes imperative. All such control mechanisms entail costs that are termed as agency cost.

To resolve the agency problems, monitoring and control mechanisms become imperative. Such mechanisms entail costs that are termed as agency costs.

Agency cost is a type of internal cost that arises from, or must be paid to, an agent acting on behalf of a principal. They arise on account of agency problems such as conflict of interest between various stakeholders such as management and shareholders, lenders and shareholders, etc. Such costs are inevitable within an organization whenever the principals are not completely in command such as the company form of business organization where the principal (the shareholders) put in their resources in the business but the resources are in control of the agent (the management). Such costs can either take the form of incentives to the management such as bonuses, profit sharing, stock options, etc., which align the interests of the agent with the principal or they can be incurred on monitoring and control such as audit fees, credit rating fees, etc. Such costs have their major financial implications from the perspective of shareholders' wealth. Irrespective of who pays such costs, they are eventually borne by the stockholders as the other stakeholders would always build these costs in the returns they expect from the firm. Thus, such costs eat into the wealth of the shareholders.

Agency costs take the form of either incentives to management like bonuses, stock options or monitoring and control costs like audit fees, credit rating fees, etc.

Corporate Governance

Another mechanism to ensure that the affairs of the firm are being managed in the best interests of the shareholders is the system of effective corporate governance. Corporate governance refers to the set of rules, processes, and customs that affect the manner in which an organization is administered. As discussed, the need of corporate governance emerges on account of divergence of interest, particularly between the owners (principal) and the management (agent). The essence of corporate

Set of rules, processes, and customs that enable effective management of the firms in the best interests of the shareholders are termed as corporate governance.

governance is on improving the trust between the principal and the agent through increased transparency and better management conduct. This is brought about by introducing certain procedures, mechanisms, and guidelines that reinforce the accountability of management towards the shareholders.

Corporate governance rests upon the four pillars of transparency, full disclosure, independent monitoring, and fairness to all the stakeholders, especially to minority shareholders. The mechanisms of corporate governance controls are:

1. Disclosure of certain crucial information that is considered important from the viewpoint of transparent governance of the company. Such information is disclosed not only for listing purpose, it is also disclosed on a quarterly basis to Securities Exchange Board of India (SEBI), a regulatory body safeguarding the interests of shareholders in listed companies in India. Also, it is included in the annual report for the purpose of reporting. The information includes—composition of board in terms of executive and non-executive members; details of meetings attended by each of the board member; disclosure of board level committees such as audit committee, remuneration committee, etc.; remuneration paid to the members of the board; details of related party transactions etc.
2. Monitoring by the board of directors
3. Restrictive covenants in the debt contracts
4. Regulations by Government, regulatory authorities such as SEBI (clause 49 of listing agreement issued by SEBI.)
5. Threat of takeover
6. Media's pressure

The issue of corporate governance has been discussed in detail in Chapter 10 of the book.

FINANCIAL MANAGEMENT AND ACCOUNTING

Financial management is a decision function that is related to both financial accounting and management accounting. Financial management shares a symbiotic relationship with financial accounting and management accounting as it affects and gets affected by the financial and management accounting statements.

Financial management is intricately related to financial and management accounting.

On one hand, financial management becomes an input function for the purpose of financial reporting that is done by financial and management accounting. What gets reflected in the different accounting statements is an outcome of firm's financial management. For example, the firm's performance in terms of its finance and investment functions is reflected in the firm's profit and loss account and the analysis of various statements.

The accounting information provides inputs for financial decision making. Financial decisions in turn get reflected in the accounting statements.

On the other hand, financial management depends on the inputs provided by the financial statements such as profit and loss account and balance sheet and the different management accounting statements such as budgets, cost statements, etc. The information provided by different financial and management accounting statements facilitates the process of financial decision making and thereby leads to better financial management and control. The relationship that exists is that of mutual interdependence as reflected in Figure 1-8.

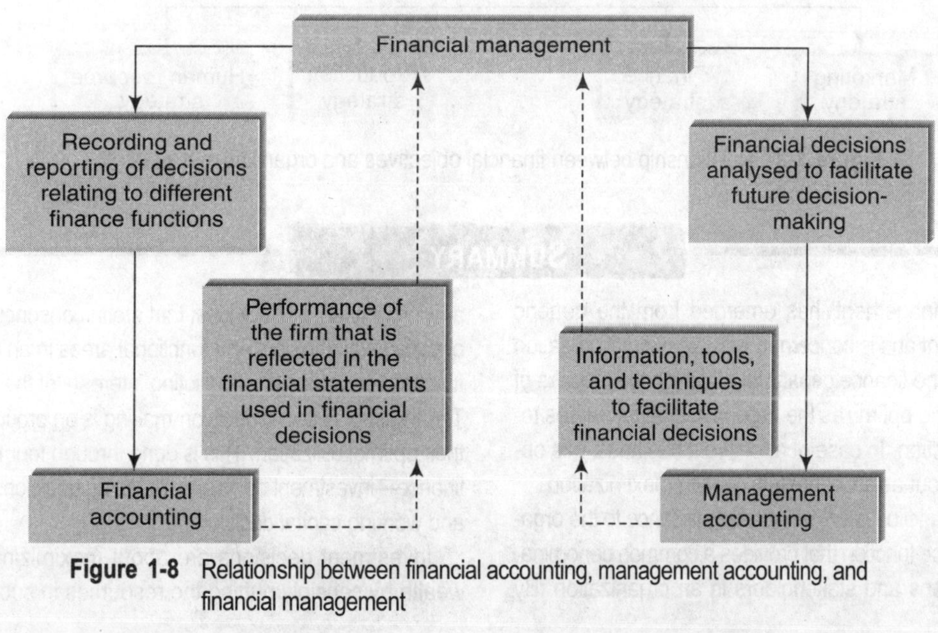

Figure 1-8 Relationship between financial accounting, management accounting, and financial management

FINANCIAL OBJECTIVES AND ORGANIZATIONAL STRATEGY

Organizational strategy refers to a course of action designed to achieve a specific organizational goal. Given the organizational goal to be achieved, the strategy indicates how to reach there and where to get the resources from. Thus, it includes a detailed planning of structure, processes, and resources. It is in the light of this organizational or corporate strategy that the objectives of the other functional areas are decided. All the functional strategies such as marketing, finance, and human resources are formulated to reinforce the organizational strategy. Figure 1-9 explains this relationship.

Financial objectives of firms depend on their overall organizational strategy.

A firm's financial objectives and its financial strategy are guided by its corporate strategy. An expansionary corporate strategy will find its reflection in different finance functions too. The focus of investment function, in such a case, would be on expanding the physical capacity to handle the increased level of activity. Financing decisions in such a situation would focus on raising the required financial resources to support such expansion plans. Even the dividend policy of the firm with expansion strategy would normally be of a low payout. Similarly, if the organizational strategy is that of cost cutting, the finance function through the means of financial decision-making would reinforce this focus. On such occasions, the firm is likely to follow the techniques such as capital rationing and capital restructuring to cut down the costs. The working capital decisions of the firm would also reflect the overall corporate strategy. An expansionary strategy is normally accompanied with the tying up of additional resources in the different components of working capital such as inventory, receivables, etc. On the other hand the emphasis, during the contraction phase, is on unlocking the additional funds that may be blocked in the working capital.

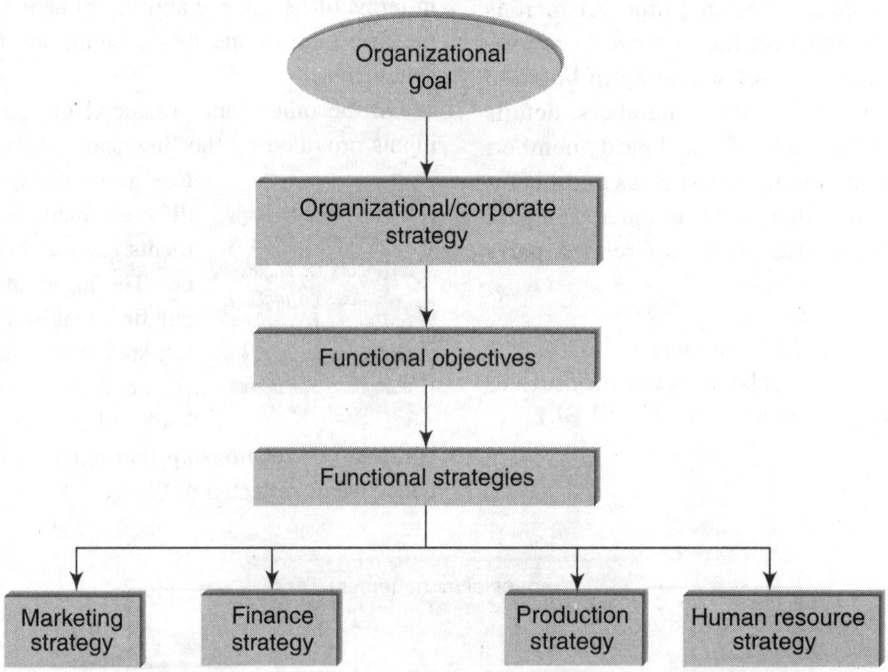

Figure 1-9 Relationship between financial objectives and organizational strategy

SUMMARY

The term 'financial management' has emerged from the generic discipline of management and is concerned with the optimal utilization of financial resources. The finance department through the process of financial decision-making optimizes the organizational resources towards an objective function. In case of a for-profit business, this objective function is spelt out as shareholders' wealth maximization.

The role of finance function is of immense significance to the organization as it is the finance function that provides a common denominator to the varied functions and stakeholders in an organization. By arriving at financial decisions, that are in consonance with the interests of varied stakeholders and functional areas in an organization, finance function reconciles the conflicting interests of the varied stakeholders. The thrust of financial decision-making is on procurement of funds and their optimal utilization. This is done through four key decision areas in finance—investment decisions, financing decisions, dividend decisions, and working capital decisions.

Investment decisions are about maximizing the shareholders' wealth by sensibly putting the resources in such avenues that give a return in excess of the cost incurred on operating and financing such resources. Such decisions are alternatively referred to as capital budgeting decisions.

Financing decisions are concerned with the procurement of the required amount of funds at the right time on most convenient terms. By tapping the funds most economically and by maintaining the right blend of the debt and equity and short- and long-term sources, the returns are enhanced while the risk is minimized.

The decision as to what portion of profits to distribute to equity shareholders and how much to plough back for future financing needs of business is known as dividend decision. Dividend policy is concerned with rate of dividends and the method of dividend payment. The payout ratio is decided in light of its likely impact on shareholders' wealth.

Working capital decisions are related to the management of current assets. The two key decision points in working capital management are—level of investment in current assets and financing of such assets.

The four key decision areas in finance are the part of an integrated decision-making framework in finance. They are directly linked to each other and reinforce each other. Also, each one has a common objective function—shareholders' wealth maximization.

The goal of wealth maximization is the widely accepted goal of the business as it reconciles the varied, often conflicting, interests of the stakeholders. Also, it is free from the limitations that other objectives are faced with.

The company form of business organization has multiple stakeholders who have varied stakes and divergent expectations. This leads to pursuit of varied objectives by different stakeholders in the firm. These objectives are more often than not conflicting. This causes agency problems. To resolve the conflicting interests of diverse stakeholders, firms have to incur certain costs that are termed as agency costs. Corporate governance system is another mechanism used to resolve the problem of conflicting interests of the stakeholders. The corporate governance framework should ensure the accountability of the company to its stakeholders and board, and management of the company to its shareholders.

KEY TERMS

Firm Any business entity, large or small, privately run or publicly traded. It could be engaged in any kind of operation—manufacturing, retailing, or service. In the context of corporate finance, it normally connotes company form of business organization.

Restrictive covenants Restrictive conditions imposed by the lenders on certain corporate decisions to safeguard their stakes in the firm. Examples include restriction on declaration of dividends or restriction on further issue of debt, etc.

Shareholder Any individual, company, or institution that has fractional ownership in a company. They have a potential to profits if the company does well, but to loss if the company does poorly.

Stakeholders All parties that have an interest, financial or otherwise, in a firm. The various stakeholders in a typical firm are—shareholders, creditors, bondholders, employees, customers, management, community, and the government.

EXERCISES

Concept Review Questions

1. Discuss the nature and the scope of financial management.
2. What is the role of finance function in an organization?
3. What are the key decision areas in finance? Discuss the key decision points of each area.
4. What is the objective function in financial management?
5. The multiplicity of stakeholders in a firm causes the conflict of interests. Comment.
6. How is financial management related to financial accounting and management accounting?
7. Discuss the relationship that exists between financial objectives and organizational strategy.

Critical Thinking Questions

1. Finance function performs facilitatory, reconciliatory, and control functions in an organization. Discuss.
2. Key decisions in financial management are a part of an integrated decision framework. Discuss.
3. The pursuit of wealth maximization as the overall goal of the business reconciles the conflicting interests of the varied stakeholders. Elaborate.
4. Agency conflicts are the direct outcome of the multiplicity of stakeholders in a firm and their resolution lies in the convergence of the interests of varied stakeholders. Analyse.

Practical Assignments

1. Go through the annual report of a firm of your choice and find out what does it state with respect to the four decision areas of financial management discussed in the chapter. Note down the critical points that emerge in this context as they will form the basis of further discussion in the course. (Management discussion and analysis and the Directors' report sections of the report may be of special relevance in this regard.)

2. Go back again to the annual report that you have selected and see what reporting has the company made under the heading corporate governance. Now find out what clause 49 issued by SEBI says with respect to corporate governance. See whether the issues mentioned therein have been covered in the corporate governance disclosure. Note down the issues that emerge with respect to corporate governance and relate to the discussion on multiplicity of stakeholders, particularly the conflict of interest between owners and managers.

CASE STUDY

Financial Management at Hero Honda Motors Ltd*

Background

Hero Honda Motors Limited came into existence on 19 January 1984. The company was formed by creating a joint venture between Hero Group and the Honda Motor Company of Japan. Owned by Hero (Munjal) Group, the company's current Chairman is Mr Brij Mohan Lal Munjal and Mr Pawan Kant Munjal is its Managing Director. The promoters of the company hold approximately 29% of the equity shares and the Indian public holds 9% of the total shares, while the institutional investors hold about 35%.

The company produces motorcycles and scooters. Some of the brand names of its products are Achiever, Karizma, CBZ, Splendor, Super Splendor, Splendor Plus, Glamour, Passion, Passion Plus, CD Deluxe, CD 100 SS, Sleek, and CD Dawn. The company also manufactures the spare parts of these two wheelers. Besides, the company provides mobile after-sales service to its existing customers. The company has two plants located in Haryana, one at Dharuhera and the other at Gurgaon. In a little over two decades, it has emerged as the world's largest manufacturer of bicycles and a global leader in motorcycles. The company has sold over 15 million motorcycles and has consistently grown at double digits since its inception and today, every second motorcycle sold in the country is a Hero Honda. Hero Honda is a world leader because of its excellent manpower, proven management, extensive dealer network, efficient supply chain, and world-class products with cutting edge technology from Honda Motor Company, Japan.

Progressively through the 1980s, the 1990s, and now in the 2000s, Hero Honda has relied on 3 R's—*reach*, *research*, and *reliability* as its basic building blocks. Using feedback from the market, a fully-equipped R&D centre has consistently created best practices in designing, testing, and harmonization, besides placing strong emphasis on road safety and ride quality. This emphasis has helped Hero Honda build products that are ahead of their time. Hero Honda became the first company in India to prove that it was possible to drive a vehicle without polluting the roads. The company introduced new generation motorcycles that set industry benchmarks for fuel thrift and low emission.

Financing Policy

The company has been a debt-free company for the last five years. The unsecured loan of ₹186 crore from the state government of Haryana on account of sales tax deferment is interest-free and has no holding costs. The company has been meeting its expansion and growth needs from its internal sources of financing. The financing mix of the company for the past six years has been as follows (Table A):

Table A Financing mix of Hero Honda

Time	*Debt–equity ratio*
March 2001	0.11
March 2002	0.17
March 2003	0.16
March 2004	0.15
March 2005	0.15
March 2006	0.09

The financing mix of the closest competitor, Bajaj Auto Ltd, stood as follows (Table B):

Table B Financing mix of Bajaj Auto Ltd

Time	*Debt–equity ratio*
March 2003	0.25
March 2004	0.27
March 2005	0.29
March 2006	0.30

*The case study has been developed based on the information collected from the annual reports, managerial discussions and analyses, and other information available at the company's official website, besides the various secondary sources of information including reports, new items, etc. Some of the views expressed in the case study may not be in conformity with the official viewpoint. The purpose of the case study is to enable the reader to see the application of specific concepts discussed in the chapter and not to illustrate either effective or ineffective handling of an administrative situation.

Performance

The executive summary of Hero Honda Ltd is as follows (Table C):

Table C Executive Summary of Hero Honda (*₹ in crores*)

	March 2001	*March 2002*	*March 2003*	*March 2004*	*March 2005*	*March 2006*
Net sales	3171.22	4466.48	5097.95	5833.01	7419.86	8708.13
Other income	10.63	47.21	23.25	53.60	44.05	75.81
Cost of production	2581.28	3463.47	3922.35	4502.45	5842.09	6878.70
PBDIT	459.55	750.01	903.65	1054.60	1227.21	1438.05
PBDT	424.45	717.09	878.83	1031.65	1209.45	1422.47
PBT	380.18	666.08	815.44	958.32	1120.07	1307.85
PAT	250.10	434.63	511.64	614.18	713.29	866.95
Gross fixed assets	614.66	704.52	780.88	901.45	1074.73	1421.54
Current assets	663.83	536.46	1666.57	2068.80	2577.72	2850.92
Net worth	608.99	675.54	860.33	1138.81	1493.38	2009.33
Equity capital	39.94	39.94	39.94	39.94	39.94	39.94
Long term borrowings	66.48	116.44	134.28	174.70	201.76	185.78
Capital employed	675.47	791.98	994.61	1313.51	1695.14	2195.11
Current liabilities & provisions	460.12	880.21	1116.21	1260.05	1500.47	1562.80
Total assets/liabilities	1125.47	1733.34	2176.67	2652.08	3294.68	3875.07
Growth (%)						
Gross sales	40.97	40.75	14.22	32.24	27.42	17.32
Cost of production	41.61	34.18	13.25	14.79	29.75	17.74
PBDIT	34.19	63.21	20.49	16.70	16.37	17.18
PAT	35.66	73.78	17.72	20.04	16.14	21.54
GFA	22.45	14.62	9.30	13.95	19.09	29.27
Total assets	33.26	54.01	25.58	21.84	24.23	17.62
Profitability Ratios (%)						
PAT/sales	7.87	9.72	10.02	9.09	8.29	8.59
PAT/net worth	47.52	67.67	66.63	61.44	54.20	49.50
PAT/total assets	25.39	30.41	26.17	25.44	23.99	24.18
PAT/capital employed	42.75	59.24	57.28	53.22	47.42	44.57

Investment Policy

The company keeps on increasing the production capacity from time to time to cope up with the rising demand. During the year 2005-06, the company added ₹399 crore in fixed assets to expand the manufacturing capacity. The production capacity of Gurgaon plant was increased from 5,000 to 6,500 units a day in the previous year. To tap the increasing demand for the motorbikes, the company decided to carry the process of expansion further and increase the capacity at the Dharuhera plant to 6,500 units by the fall of 2006. This would take the installed capacity to roll out 13,000 units a day. This capacity expansion will take care of the growing demand in the short run. The company is in the process of setting up a third plant to take care of the demand in the medium-term as it would also enable the company to realize its mandate of becoming a global scale and world-class manufacturer. A state-of-the-art manufacturing plant with an investment of ₹400 crore to be operational by mid-2007 at Haridwar with an initial production capacity of 5,00,000 is proposed. Besides, the company, in order to improve its efficiency and to cut down the cost, has made investment in augmenting its welding capacity. The company has also invested in technology that will help in localizing the production of gear boxes. By 2010, Hero Honda and its ancillaries will invest ₹1,900 crore in the new plant, achieving a capacity expansion to 15 lakh units, thereby enabling the company to cater to future market demand and consolidate its market leadership.

Working Capital

The company has already endeavoured to set benchmarks in its working capital management and has continued to operate on negative working capital for the past several years. The continued focus on working capital has helped the company to enhance cash flows through better management of inventory, receivables, and payables. As a part of cost rationalization drive, the company has aggressively availed cash discount from its vendors by making the payments before due date. This has not only helped to improve its operating margins but has also allowed it to deploy the surplus funds in its core business operations. The tight monitoring and control of the working capital components has been the main source of satisfactory working capital management, which is reflected in the following figures:

Table D Working capital management and liquidity ratios

	2004-05	*2005-06*
Inventory period (days)	11.30	10.50
Operating cycle (days)	14.00	14.90
Cash cycle (days)	–33.00	–23.90
Current ratio	0.53	0.74
Acid-test ratio	0.34	0.54

The company has made sustained efforts to prune manufacturing variable costs over the years through the process of localization and process improvement. To a large extent, these costs have been controlled and the cost per vehicle came down from ₹837 to ₹353 in March 2005. However, due to sharp increase in the cost of electricity and its erratic supply, the declining trend in the variable manufacturing costs was reversed in 2005-06. To address this problem, the company has commissioned HFO-based generator sets at each of its facilities. In the coming months and years, these measures will help Hero Honda to prune its material and manufacturing costs substantially.

As 60–70% of the revenue of the company is made up of material costs, vendor management is a critical factor. To improve plant efficiency and inventory turns, the company has extended Just-In-Time (JIT) beyond the shop floor. An online vendor connectivity programme has been implemented and extended to 94 vendors from 46 in the previous year. As a result, the company has been able to access 70% of the materials (in value terms) by maintaining zero inventory. For the balance, the average inventory period is about 34 days. The cost of raw materials as a percentage of total sales decreased from 70.1% in 2004-05 to 69.5% in 2005-06 primarily due to favourable changes in sales mix and continued focus on cost rationalization. To rationalize the supply chain further, the company is now switching to system purchases and also looking at the possibilities for global procurements. The working capital performance of Hero Honda Motors Ltd. is given in Table E.

Compared to the company, the working capital cycle of the other firms in the automobile sector was as follows:

Dividend

The company has been continuing with a liberal dividend policy during the past few years. The company believes that the shareholders should benefit appropriately from the company's continued success consistently. The company is extremely conscious about the efficient use of capital employed and has always endeavoured to earn a return higher than the cost. Further, after giving due consideration to the cash generating capacity, expected capital needs of the business and strategic considerations, the board has recommended a dividend of 1000% for the third year in succession.

Table E Working capital performance of Hero Honda Motors Ltd

	March 2001	March 2002	March 2003	March 2004	March 2005	March 2006
Working Capital (₹ in crore)	203.71	–343.75	550.36	808.75	1077.25	1284.57
Average current assets (₹ in crore)	488.89	600.14	1101.51	1867.68	2323.26	2714.32
Avg. days of debtors	4	5	8	5	2	4
Avg. days of creditors	31	32	35	42	40	32
Gross working capital cycle (days)	33	27	28	22	16	17
Net working capital cycle (days)	2	–5	–7	–20	–24	–15
Liquidity ratios (times)						
Current ratio	1.44	0.61	1.49	1.64	1.72	1.82
Quick ratio	0.18	0.25	1.21	1.30	1.42	1.52
Interest cover	11.83	21.23	33.85	42.76	64.07	84.94

Table F Working capital cycle of automobile companies

Company Name	2004		2005		2006	
	Gross working capital cycle	Net working capital cycle	Gross working capital cycle	Net working capital cycle	Gross working capital cycle	Net working capital cycle
	(in days)					
Bajaj Auto	30.38	–15.43	24.18	–18.76	14.24	–10.56
Maharashtra Scooters	69.49	–74.21	78.40	–72.33	108.66	–63.08
TVS Motors	39.31	–11.93	38.71	–14.23	42.30	–11.01
Yamaha	113.16	50.38	85.01	44.85	94.29	54.45

Table G Dividend payout by Hero Honda

Year	*Dividends (₹ in crore)*	*Retained earnings (₹ in crore)*	*Total Dividend Rate (in percentage)*	*Dividend per share (in ₹)*
March 2001	66.01	180.86	150	NA
March 2002	349.67	113.26	850	17
March 2003	405.49	175.27	900	18
March 2004	450.54	277.78	1000	20
March 2005	455.90	354.57	1000	20
March 2006	455.39	515.95	1000	20

The dividend payout by Bajaj Auto Ltd during past four years was as follows:

Year	*Dividends per share (in ₹)*	*Payout ratio (%)*
March 2003	14.00	29.68
March 2004	25.00	38.64
March 2005	25.00	39.55
March 2006	40.00	41.89

The adjusted closing prices of shares of Hero Honda Motors Ltd were as follows:

Year	*Share Price (in ₹)*
March 2001	140.35
March 2002	333.70
March 2003	188.40
March 2004	490.45
March 2005	548.15
March 2006	888.30

Discuss

1. Is the financing policy of Hero Honda Motors satisfactory? How is the unlevered capital structure of the firm justified?
2. What are the factors that are favouring a zero debt capital for the company? Is it always beneficial to have a low debt in the capital structure?
3. Is investment policy driving the growth of the firm? What are the key issues that the investment policy of the company is trying to address?
4. Are you satisfied with the working capital management of the company? Give reasons.
5. Is the dividend policy of the firm appropriate? What factors determine the existing dividend policy of the firm?

CHAPTER

2 Comparative and Historical Analysis

LEARNING OBJECTIVES

The chapter is aimed at

- discussing the relevance of financial statements for different stakeholders
- developing a clarity on the conceptual framework of financial statements and the items contained therein
- creating a conceptual framework for the analysis of financial performance using the tool of ratio analysis
- dealing elaborately with the four categories of ratios namely liquidity, profitability, capital structure, and valuation
- analysing the inter-linkages between the ratios through the DuPont analysis to develop a comprehensive view on financial performance
- demonstrating how the problems of scales in inter-firm and intra-firm comparisons can be taken care of by using the standardized financial statements
- discussing the purpose served by the tool of ratio analysis and highlighting its limitations that should be borne in mind while using it

INVESTIGATING THE FINANCIAL HEALTH

'Just 30 years ago, the rules governing corporate accounting filled only two volumes and could fit in a briefcase. Since then, the standards have multiplied so rapidly that it takes a bookcase shelf—and a long one—to hold all the volumes.'

'...............the collapse of Enron, WorldCom, and the likes is ample testimony to the fact that the simple accounting concepts like earnings, revenues, etc., have today become impenetrable for investors and perplexing for the analysts. Creative accounting is fast emerging as one of the most lucrative innovations of our times. Notwithstanding their adherence to the norms of adequate disclosure, the corporate financial statements are more often than not so obscure that their darkness survives the light of day.' With these words of caution, Louis Balmer, the leading trainer in the area of advanced financial statements analysis started his talk on analysis of financial statements with the fresh batch of trainee financial analysts at the Chartered Financial Analysts' Institute.

'Whether you watch analysts on CNBC or read articles in business periodicals', he added further 'you'll hear experts insisting on the importance of doing proper homework before investing in a company. In other words, investors should dig deep into the company's financial statements and analyse everything from the auditor's report to the footnotes. Expecting an average investor to bypass the labyrinth of complicated accounting details and unearth the hidden information is really a tough ask.'

'The role of a financial analyst is immense and his responsibilities are onerous in facilitating informed decision-making by the investors. As an analyst, you are expected to be well-versed with the anatomy of financial statements so that you are able to read in between the lines and decipher the red flags in the financial reporting.'

The trainer in his usual allegorical style added further, 'always remember that financial analysis is like a medical examination where the measures for the different medical tests should be seen in the light of some commonly accepted benchmarks. The pulse rate, for instance, of a patient under investigation does not hold any meaning until it is compared to the pulse rate of 60 to 100 beats per minute, which is the normal pulse rate for a healthy adult, while resting. Also, the investigator should bear in mind that these benchmarks too vary from season to season. Due to contraction of arteries, for instance, in the winter months the blood pressure has a general tendency to surge. The phase of natural cycle should always be kept at the back of mind while analysing a case.'

'Last but not the least; a patient's history is of immense importance in the entire process of investigation and diagnosis. A blood pressure of 160/90 may be alarming for one patient while it may not be so for the next one. It all depends on the family history and past readings of the patients under investigation.'

Balmer ended his monologue with a deep pause and urged the participants to be very meticulous and watchful in their careers as financial analysts.

INTRODUCTION

Understanding the historical background of the situation is the basic prerequisite for creating a framework for financial decision-making. For a firm, no decision can be taken without the consideration of the past activities as the future is, normally, inexorably linked to the past. Hence, there has to be a consistency between past performance and future projections. Future projections that are devoid of consideration of past situations lack credibility and conviction. This problem of lack of credibility can be very conveniently overcome if supported by past performance.

In financial terms, all the activities of the firm are translated and recorded in the form of three documents known as the *profit and loss account*, *balance sheet*, and *cash flow statement*. These documents are prepared at periodical intervals, mostly annually and at a specified date, which is by convention 31 March in India. The information contained in these statements is available publicly and can be used by different stakeholders for taking decisions relating to their stake in the firm. This financial information is put in the decision compatible framework applying the analytical tools like ratio analysis, common size statements, etc. Notwithstanding their limitations, these analytical tools facilitate inter-firm and intra-firm analysis.

Before moving on to the analysis framework, let us look at the structure of these financial statements and the meaning attached with items contained therein.

BALANCE SHEET

The balance sheet of a firm reflects its financial condition as on a particular date. It is like an X-ray report of a firm that reveals its state of health on a specific date and thus, holds tremendous significance for the purpose of analysis. To facilitate comparison of performance, the balance sheet normally provides figures of preceding period too. A typical structure of balance sheet is shown in Table 2-1.

Table 2-1 Structure of balance sheet

Liabilities	Assets
• Share capital • Reserves and surplus • Secured loans • Unsecured loans • Current liabilities and provisions	• Fixed assets • Investments • Current assets, loans, and advances • Miscellaneous expenditure

The balance sheet of any firm has two sides and three components. The two sides are known as *assets* and *liabilities*. These also form the two components. The third component known as the *owners' equity*, also referred to as shareholders' fund or net worth, is shown on the liability side of the firm's balance sheet. Any business creates assets and the assets need to be acquired through some funds. These funds can be generated from many sources and must necessarily be equal to the value of the assets. The funds mobilized from various sources need to be recognized as liability of the firm. Therefore, the value of assets created and liabilities generated must match at all points of time. This can be represented as:

The balance sheet of a firm reflects its financial position on a given date. Assets, liabilities, and owners' equity are the constituents of a balance sheet.

Assets = Liabilities

Assets represent uses of funds, and liabilities are sources of funds. Although assets and liabilities are further classified into various groups and sub-groups, the liability of the firm towards its shareholders is of special importance. In the real sense, liability towards shareholders is substantially different from other liabilites, because shareholders are owners of the firm. The liability arises due to the fact that the shareholders and the firm are treated as two separate legal entities.

Assets represent uses of funds, and liabilities are sources of funds. They must be equal at all points of time.

Liabilities

Starting a business needs some assets such as land, building, machinery, etc. Cash is required to buy assets. The initial cash needed to acquire assets, is normally contributed by individuals or a group of individuals known as *promoters* or *shareholders*. After the start-up, the firm (company registered as the one in which the public is substantially interested) may go for further capitalization by inviting public at large to participate in its ownership. Those who accept this offer and invest in the firm are issued shares and are called shareholders. Promoters too are shareholders. The sum contributed by them, known as *share capital* or *equity*, has to be recognized as liability of the business entity. Equity is contributed without any commitment to pay a fixed return; instead, it is a claim on the residual profits.

Preference capital is also classified under share capital. The obligation to pay is fixed in the case of preference capital. Equity holders cannot get any return before the firm discharges obligations towards preference capital holders.

Reserves and Surplus

Running an enterprise is expected to result in some profit for the owners/shareholders. In fact, this is the precise reason it has come into existence. After induction of the initial capital, the business generates cash, which is first used to pay off the claims of stakeholders other than the shareholders. The residual belongs to the shareholders, who face a choice of either consuming it or ploughing it back into the business. The distributed profit is referred to as *dividend* and the remaining amount that is kept in business is termed as *reserves and surplus.*

Undistributed profit is termed as reserves and surplus.

Share capital together with reserves and surplus is known as *shareholders' fund* or *net worth* of the firm. It represents the amount of funds contributed by the owners. It becomes an important parameter for other stakeholders, such as lenders and creditors, to judge the financial soundness of the firm.

Secured and Unsecured Loans

Most firms need to raise loans to finance the acquisition of assets. Loans are repayable with interest as per the terms of agreement between the firm and its lenders.

Secured loans are secured by assets to reduce the risk of lending, while an unsecured loan is supported only by the borrower's creditworthiness.

The providers of loans are classified into two categories—secured and unsecured. *Secured loans* are given against specific assets with protective covenants of superior claim of the lender on the assets so procured (known as primary security) or other assets (known as collateral security). This claim of the lender lasts till the obligations of loans are discharged.

The loans taken without any security are classified as *unsecured loans*. These include fixed deposits by the public, inter-corporate loans, issuance of commercial paper, etc. Lenders of such funds do not have any claim against the specific assets of the firm. Their credit risk is higher than that of lenders of secured loans and consequently they charge higher rates of interest.

Unsecured loans are costlier than secured loans.

The division of loans into secured and unsecured helps other stakeholders assess the assets that are free from encumbrances and those that are charged to specific lenders.

Current Liabilities and Provisions

The liabilities are normally classified as short-term or long-term. *Short-term* liabilities are those which are payable in near future, conventionally defined as payable within next 12 months. The liabilities that mature beyond 12 months are classified as *long-term* liabilities.

Current liabilities are obligations payable in the next 12 months.

Current liabilities arise as the firm procures material or services from suppliers on credit. The liability towards suppliers is classified under the head 'sundry creditors'. Similarly, a firm may receive advance from customers against future supplies. This too is recognized as current liability. To have a fair view of the current liabilities of the firm, the amount of instalments falling due within next 12 months, included otherwise in loans, must also be included in the current liabilities.

Provisions refer to the liability for which amount and/or timing is uncertain. Such amounts are provided on the basis of estimate, but these are deemed to be payable in next 12 months. The examples would include provision for dividend (timing of cash flow is uncertain), provision for tax (amount of tax is estimated), provision for leave encashment (payable when employee claims or leaves), etc. Such provisions are made to reflect the present obligations of the firm that may arise any time and to present a fair view of the earnings, profit, or cash flows.

Contingent liabilities

Provisions are made for the expenses and income for which only estimates are available. They are recognized in the balance sheet to provide a true and fair view of the financial position of the firm. Apart from provisions, there are certain liabilities that may arise contingent upon actions totally beyond the control of the firm. For example, some demands made by regulating agencies, such as sales tax authorities or the pollution control board, may be disputed or subjudice. The outcome of the dispute, decided by a court or tribunal, may or may not be favourable to the firm. Such kinds of claims by outsiders on the firm too are potential liabilities. Liabilities that are not crystallized are known as *contingent liabilities*. They are not disclosed in the financial statement, but instead information is provided by way of *notes to accounts*.

Liabilities that arise on occurrence of an event beyond firm's control are called contingent liabilities.

Assets

Assets side of the balance sheet represents the uses of funds. Assets so created provide economic benefits to the firm in future. Assets are classified broadly into four categories—*fixed assets, investments, current assets, loans and advances, and miscellaneous assets and losses.*

Fixed assets

They are expected to last for a long time and provide economic benefits to the firm for more than one year. Items such as land, building, and plant and machinery are included in fixed assets. These can further be divided into *tangible assets* and *intangible assets*. Items mentioned earlier are examples of tangible assets. Intangibles assets include copyrights, patents, goodwill, software, etc.

Fixed assets provide benefit over an extended future period.

Recognizing that fixed assets have a definite life and would require replacement if the firm has to continue, the firm is allowed to set apart a fixed sum every year during the economic life of the asset. The sum set aside every year for the purpose of replacement is referred to as *depreciation*, which is recognized as an expense. The value of the asset reduces every year by the amount of depreciation charged on it. Similarly in case of an intangible asset, the sum set aside every year is referred to as *amortization*. The original purchase value of the asset is referred to as *gross block* and the value net of depreciation or amortization is referred to as *net block*. The balance sheet depicts the fixed assets as below:

Gross block
Less: Accumulated depreciation/amortization
Net block

Investments

The cash generated by the business is normally invested to earn an income. The firm may invest the surplus money in various financial securities such as shares, bonds, etc. This is represented in the balance sheet under the head 'investments'. Investments can be classified as *marketable investments*, and *long-term* and *short-term investments*. Marketable investments have high liquidity and a low risk of value erosion. Due to their high liquidity they can be marketed (or converted into cash) early. Long-term and short-term investments are classified according to the contemplated period of holding. Investments intended to be held beyond 12 months are classified as long-term, else they are short-term.

Surplus funds over and above the immediate requirements are invested in financial securities. These are called investments.

Current Assets, Loans, and Advances

By definition, current assets are those assets that get converted into cash within a short period of time conventionally in the next 12 months. Broadly they are further broken into three major heads in terms of their proximity to cash—*cash and bank balances, sundry debtors or account receivable, and inventory.*

Most firms are required to maintain some cash and bank balances to meet their day-to-day needs. Cash and bank balances as on the date of balance sheet are stated under this head.

Normally products or services are supplied by a firm to its customers on credit. *Sundry debtors* represent the amount recoverable from the customers for the supplies made or services rendered. Not only the amount outstanding on a particular date is important for analytical purposes, it is equally important to know— (1) for how long the amount is outstanding; and (2) whcther the amount is considered good or doubtful for recovery. For proper analysis, age-wise schedule of debtors, which provides information about the time for which the dues are pending, is required. As per the requirement of law, debtors for more than 6 months old are to be stated separately. Further provision is to be made in case the amounts are considered doubtful of recovery.

Like liabilities, assets too are classified based on the life and ease of convertibility into cash. Current assets are quickly convertible into cash.

Inventory is classified into three categories—raw materials, work-in-process, and finished goods. Such a classification is aimed at knowing how soon or late these stocks can be converted into cash. Finished goods can be sold rather readily and cash is realized immediately. Raw material would need to be converted to finished products before they can be sold and hence, would take longer to get converted into cash. Raw material is, therefore, shown separately. Work-in-process stocks are those materials which have progressed from raw material stage but yet are not converted into finished product. Stocks of consumable stores and packing materials are also shown separately.

Loans and advances, another item of current nature, are the sums of money advanced in the usual course of business, which are recoverable in cash or kind. Loans given to employees and associates, security deposits given to landlords and utilities companies, money deposited with the Government, etc., are mentioned under this head.

Miscellaneous Expenses not written off, and Losses

These assets represent certain expenses, the benefit of which is supposed to accrue over a long period. These are expensed over the period of benefit. The amount to the extent not written off as on the date of balance sheet is shown under the miscellaneous expenses head. Examples include preliminary expenses and developmental expenditure.

Losses are shown in the balance sheet on the asset side and not adjusted against reserves and surplus because loss is use of funds and not a source like profit. Profit would be reflected as liability towards the shareholder. Presentation of losses on the asset side also facilitates immediate recognition that the firm is incurring a loss.

Net Working Capital

As stated earlier, based on their maturities, assets can broadly be classified as current and non-current. Assets convertible into cash in 12 months are referred to as current assets, while all the other assets are non-current. Similarly liabilities are also grouped into—current and non-current or long-term liabilities. The liabilities to be paid within 12 months are classified as current while rest are long-term. Current assets and current liabilities normally arise due to regular and normal operations of the firm. Normally cash realizable in 12 months through liquidation of current assets must be adequate to cover the liabilities arising in the same period.

The excess of current assets over current liabilities is defined as *net working capital*. A positive net working capital implies the amount coming from long-term sources of the funds, and is viewed favourably. Financial statements normally show directly the surplus/deficit of the current assets over current liabilities as *net current assets*.

PROFIT AND LOSS ACCOUNT

Profit and loss account (P&L account), also referred to as the income statement, presents operations of the firm for a given period, which is usually 12 months. It reflects earning capacity and profitability of the firm. It summarizes the activities of the firm for a given period under various heads of income and expenses. The presentation of information in the P&L account (or income statement) has no prescribed format.

Operational vs Non-operational Income/expenditure

The P&L account of the firm is supposed to reflect operational capabilities to generate funds, which must flow through its routine and normal activities. However, firms do have incomes and/or expenditures that arise from activities other than their core business operations. All such incomes and expenditures that are non-operational, non-recurring, or exceptional in nature should be indicated separately. For example, a firm engaged in manufacturing and selling products, may decide to sell some property it owns. It may result in phenomenal and comparable profit as generated from the manufacturing and selling activities. Such profit/income, if not shown separately, may cause misleading inferences about potential of profitability of the firm through its regular operations. Analysts must be careful about such items while analysing past performance or projecting future performance.

> *Profit and loss account or income statement reflects income earned and expenses incurred during a given period.*

CASH FLOW STATEMENT

The third statement that is reported by firms on a periodic basis is known as the *cash flow statement*, which is derived from the earlier two statements—the balance sheet and the P&L account—and contains no fresh items. This is also known as the statement of changes in the financial position. In fact, it does not contain any information that is not available in the balance sheet and/ or profit and loss account. Yet, the cash flow statement provides very important information for financial decision-making and analysis. It forms the core of framework of decision-making for capital budgeting, capital structure, and dividend discussed in subsequent chapters.

> *Cash flow statement is vital for financial decisions of capital budgeting, capital structure and dividend.*

Cash Flow

A cash flow statement summarizes the sources of cash and its uses. Besides profit of the firm, there are many ways additional cash can be generated. Similarly, the uses of funds can be diverse. Besides ploughing back in the business, the funds may be used for other activities. All these sources and uses would be reflected in the balance sheet. As the balance sheet is cast on a specific date, it provides a static position of funds as on a date. It does not describe the flow of funds. The origin and utilization of funds during the period is not known directly from balance sheet and profit and loss account. A cash flow statement provides this information, even though derived. It reveals how the funds have been generated and how they have been used. To prepare a cash flow statement, we need a company's balance sheet as at the start and at the end of the period and its profit and loss account for the period. The changes in financial position then can be obtained and classified as per the needs.

Rules of Cash Flow

The method to find out the changes in the cash position of the firm is to record all transactions involving inflows and outflows of cash. This is known as the *direct method.* However, we can use a rather convenient *indirect method* of arriving at cash flows from balance sheets and P&L account. The initial cash flow statement can be prepared from the balance sheet by recording the changes in liabilities and assets. Any increase in liability is equivalent to inflow of cash. For example, owners bringing in fresh funds would increase the liability of the firm towards its shareholders, which shall be visible from the balance sheet of two dates. Similarly, any loans taken/repaid by the firm would show an increase/decrease in the secured loans.

Cash may be generated from the asset side too. For example, if a fixed asset such as a machine is sold, it would generate cash and reduce the fixed assets in the balance sheet.

Cash is used to procure assets that would increase the value of assets in the balance sheet. Similarly repayment of loans would be a use of cash reducing the liabilities of the firm.

From our discussion, certain conclusions can be made:

Sources of cash	Any increase in liability Any decrease in asset
Uses of cash	Any decrease in liability Any increase in asset (Excluding cash)

Based on this principle, the sources and uses of cash from the balance sheet of the firm using figures from preceding period may be calculated.

Structure of Cash Flow

A cash flow statement prepared from the balance sheet provides useful information. For the purpose of a cash flow statement, all inflows and outflows of cash are included under one of the three categories of activities that a firm engages in. These are cash flows from—*operating activities, investing activities, and financing activities*. Although the cash balance gets reflected in the balance sheet, it is the details of the sources and applications of cash that makes the cash flow a mandatory constituent of reported financial statements. The interrelationship between the three aforesaid heads is important from the analyst's perspective.

Cash flow from operating activities This includes cash generated from and utilized for the activities conducted in the normal course of business. If it is a manufacturing or services organization, the management as well as other stakeholders would like to know what amount of cash has been generated from the core activities of supply of goods and services by the firm.

The source of preparing the cash flow from operations is the profit and loss account of the firm. Is the profit/loss of the firm as presented in the income statement real cash flow? Certainly not, because besides operational activities of sale/purchase of goods, incurring various expenses, etc., there are many items in the profit and loss account that impact the bottom line but do not entail a cash flow. Examples of such items would include depreciation, provisions for bad debts, bad debt written off, etc., which are mere accounting entries and decrease profit but not cash. If profit and loss account is the starting point, all such items become sources of cash.

Under normal circumstances, increase in reserves and surplus would indicate funds generated from operations. However, it would not indicate what dividend has been paid or if any cash has been generated from non-conventional activities. This is essentially a financing activity. Similarly, any interest or dividend received from the investment made by the firm included in its profit cannot be referred to as cash from operations. It would be better to classify such receipts as part of the investment activity.

Cash flow from operations is calculated by (a) adjusting profit for non cash flow items of expenses and income and (b) excluding cash flow due to investing and financing activities.

Any profit generated from sale of fixed assets is not equivalent to cash generation from expected and routine activities of the firm. Generation or uses of cash from activities other than normal operation must be indicated separately.

While considering the funds available from operations of the firm, another aspect that deserves special mention is working capital. A firm needs to invest funds not only in the long-term assets but also in the working capital. Growing a business would require increased credit to customers and higher levels of inventory and cash. Some of the increased requirements can be met by getting larger credit from suppliers of raw materials. All these activities are certainly investing and financing, but they are specifically meant for sustaining operational activities. Such investing and financing activities are short-term in nature. Therefore, any change in the working capital should more appropriately form part of operational cash flow.

While projecting cash flow, the following aspects should be taken care of:

1. Exclude items of accounting nature that impact the profit but not cash.
2. Exclude items that are related to investing or financing activities.
3. Separately classify the changes in working capital but include it in the operational cash flows.

Cash flow from investing and financing activities Besides normal business activities, the firm also generates cash from other sources such as mobilizing additional funds from shareholders, from financial institutions, etc., which augment the resources of the firm. Similarly, profits of the firm may be used in repaying loans and interest. Profits are also used in distributing the dividend to shareholders. Such activities are financing activities and are distinct from operational activities, and need to be grouped separately.

Cash flows from investing activities include purchase and sale of fixed assets, investing temporary surplus in marketable financial securities and income earned from such financial investments. The cash flows related to fixed assets and other investments are grouped under a separate head, as distinct from normal operations of the firm.

A cash flow statement facilitates a better understanding and analysis of a firm by classifying cash flows under three heads.

ANALYSING FINANCIAL STATEMENTS—RATIO ANALYSIS

After basic understanding of the financial statements, we now turn our attention as to how the information contained therein can be used beneficially for decision-making by different stakeholders. Balance sheet, profit and loss account, and cash flow statement contain a lot of numbers that can be used to draw some meaningful inferences. These inferences can further be used as inputs for planning/decision making. The numbers contained in the financial statements carry a host of information that can be put to use in making judgements regarding financial strengths and weaknesses of the firm, efficacy of past policies, and remedial measures or corrective actions to be taken.

Information contained in financial statements can be analysed by different stakeholders to draw inferences regarding the firm's performance vis-á-vis their expectations.

Different stakeholders view the firm differently in their own ways. Although the common area of focus of all stakeholders remains the level of profit and profitability of the firm, there are specific areas that are of greater interest than others for a particular stakeholder. While profits serve the common objective for all stakeholders, the other issues involve aspects such as security, safety, and growth potential. Each stakeholder has to make a decision with respect to his/her desirability to continue as stakeholder in future depending upon whether the specific objectives are met or not.

Various stakeholders seek answers to issues pertinent to them. Some of the questions that each group seeks answers to are:

Shareholders:

- Is the profit adequate?
- How much dividend can be expected from the firm?
- Will dividend continue to flow?
- What appreciation in the value of shares can take place?

Suppliers:

- How much credit period can be allowed to the firm?
- What quantum/level of credit the supplier may assume?

- Will the firm be able to pay on time and as promised?
- How creditworthy is the firm vis-à-vis its competitors?

Customers, Dealers, and Distributors:
- How much credit period can be availed?
- What is the quality of products?
- Does the firm spend enough on advertising, sales promotion, etc.?

Competitors:
- Where does the firm stand in competition?
- Is the firm spending enough on modernizing, capacity enhancement?

Lenders:
- Does the firm have adequate capability to service the debt burden?
- Does the firm have adequate assets to protect the amount lent in case of default?

Employees:
- Does the firm pay adequate wages and salaries and on time?
- Is the firm growing fast enough to meet their career aspirations?

Government regulatory bodies and Society
- Does the firm pay all taxes?
- Does the firm follow all regulatory guidelines and rules?
- Is it contributing to the welfare of the society?

Review and analysis of financial statements reported by the firms at regular intervals can provide an answer to the most of these questions. The technique of ratio analysis is one of the potent tools for the purpose of such a review and analysis.

DEFINITION AND USES OF RATIOS

A ratio can be defined as one number divided by another. By division of one number by another, we eliminate the problem of size and the bias that creeps in because of it. Two numbers when viewed as ratio provide a relationship of one with respect to another.

A ratio can be used either as an absolute figure, a series over time, or compared with respect to a benchmark.

Financial ratios can be used in any one or more of the following three ways—as *an absolute number; as a historic sequence or time series; or as a comparison with the industry or a benchmark.*

As an absolute number: Ratio provides a direct relationship of one number with another. For example, a ratio of current assets with current liabilities would indicate whether the current assets are adequate to meet the current liabilities.

As a historic sequence or time series: When the same ratio is seen over financial statements of successive intervals, it provides an insight not only on the comparison, but the progression of the ratio over time. A qualitative judgement can be made on the rate at which the improvement or deterioration is taking place with respect to the parameter being studied.

As a comparison with the industry or a benchmark: A comparison of a given ratio of a firm with that of the competitors, industry, or a benchmark gives an understanding of relative strength or weakness of the firm with respect to its competitors and industry.

TYPES OF RATIOS

Financial statements contain a vast set of numbers and, therefore, numerous combinations of two numbers can be chosen for analysis. The caveat is that such a combination should reflect some rational and meaningful relationship. Selection of two numbers has to be made depending upon the parameter to be examined. For convenience and ease of understanding, ratios are divided in various groups aimed at analysing performance in specific domain. These are—*liquidity ratios, capital structure or leverage ratios, working capital ratios, profitability ratios, and valuation ratios.*

To explain each of the term and the ratios associated with it, we take an example. Tables 2-2 and 2-3 contain the balance sheet and P&L account of CMC Limited for five consecutive years. These financial statements will illustrate the computation of various ratios. We will analyse each category of ratios one by one.

LIQUIDITY RATIOS

Liquidity of a firm refers to its ability to pay short-term liabilities from the short-term assets. Current assets of the firm are defined as those assets that are convertible into cash within a short period of time. Normally a firm raises funds by way of credit for its purchases. Payment to suppliers for credit purchases is normally due within 12 months. Similarly, there could be other sources of funds that may mature for payment in 12 months' time. All such obligations that need to be fulfilled in short-term are classified as current liabilities.

Liquidity denotes the firm's capacity to pay its short-term obligations on time. There are three prominent measures of liquidity: current ratio, acid test ratio, and cash ratio.

It is expected that the liabilities of a firm towards the suppliers would be met from the collections made from its customers. If the receivable amount is less than what is payable, it is a sign of poor ability to discharge obligations. Extending the logic further, the firm must have adequate assets that are readily convertible into cash in the normal course of business so as to meet the liabilities that are also created during normal operations. The liquidity of a firm is measured by calculating whether the current assets are adequate to meet current liabilities.

There are three prominent measures of firms' liquidity performance—current ratio, acid test ratio, and cash ratio. The following section deals elaborately with these three measures of liquidity position.

Table 2-2 Balance sheet of CMC Limited

(₹ in thousands)

Year	*1998*	*1999*	*2000*	*2001*	*2002*
Sources of Funds					
Share Capital	151,500	151,500	151,500	151,500	151,500
Reserves & Surplus	251,423	305,069	395,769	595,257	776,326
Net Worth	**402,923**	**456,569**	**547,269**	**746,757**	**927,826**
Secured Loans					
a) Short-term Loans	138,357	104,393	145,989	65,000	98,060
b) Long-term Loans	43,602	29,066	95,000	111,970	25,000
	181,959	**133,459**	**240,989**	**176,970**	**123,060**
Unsecured Loans					
a) Short-term Loans	32,000	32,000	32,000	81,835	13,038
b) Long-term Loans	213,297	176,437	132,554	132,397	132,397
	245,297	**208,437**	**164,554**	**214,232**	**145,435**
Deferred Tax	—	—	—	—	88,147
Total Liabilities	**830,179**	**798,465**	**952,812**	**1,137,959**	**1,284,468**
Application of Funds					
Gross Block	972,338	1,014,245	1,101,763	1,226,555	1,215,271
Less: Accumulated Depreciation	474,005	494,674	530,266	589,841	605,094
Net Block	**498,333**	**519,571**	**571,497**	**636,714**	**610,177**
Investment	**18,366**	**81,801**	**81,801**	**81,801**	**81,801**
Current Assets, Loans & Advances					
Inventories	251,354	288,959	242,850	220,708	116,573
Sundry Debtors	849,038	871,307	1,282,882	1,565,630	1,500,584
Accrued Revenue	35,281	68,846	150,853	329,480	409,993
Loans & Advances	192,275	284,940	380,877	522,967	761,530
Cash and Bank Balances	166,488	186,656	216,839	224,117	191,850
	1,494,436	**1,700,708**	**2,274,301**	**2,862,902**	**2,980,530**
Current Liabilities & Provisions					
Sundry Creditors	458,203	500,546	637,491	1,210,517	973,298
Other Current Liabilities	534,905	735,466	971,480	694,143	675,130
Provisions	187,848	267,603	365,816	538,798	739,612
	1,180,956	**1,503,615**	**1,974,787**	**2,443,458**	**2,388,040**
Net Current Assets	313,480	197,093	299,514	419,444	592,490
Total Assets	**830,179**	**798,465**	**952,812**	**1,137,959**	**1,284,468**
Loans Repayable within 12 months					
In Secured Loans	14,536	14,536	20,000	80,000	25,000
In Unsecured Loans	124,575	146,575	119,575	119,525	87,525
	139,111	**161,111**	**139,575**	**199,525**	**112,525**

Table 2-3 Profit & Loss Account of CMC Limited

(₹ in thousands)

Year	*1998*	*1999*	*2000*	*2001*	*2002*
Net Sales	2,881,650	3,388,867	4,570,656	5,376,763	5,466,980
Income from services	77,391	72,817	116,788	149,336	186,336
Total Revenue	**2,959,041**	**3,461,684**	**4,687,444**	**5,526,099**	**5,653,316**
Purchases	1,300,601	1,371,887	2,007,399	2,212,552	2,113,445
Operating & Other Expenses	1,433,213	1,864,595	2,380,999	2,800,947	2,928,870
Profit Before Interest, Tax and Depreciation	**225,227**	**225,202**	**299,046**	**512,600**	**611,001**
Depreciation	69,233	69,071	60,639	90,984	80,425
Interest (Net of interest earned)	40,499	30,537	31,405	24,496	19,524
Net Profit Before Tax	**115,495**	**125,594**	**207,002**	**397,120**	**511,052**
Provision for Current Tax	46,000	52,500	80,000	146200	181,579
Deferred Tax	–	–	–	–	–6,916
Net Profit After Tax	**69,495**	**73,094**	**127,002**	**250,920**	**336,389**
Appropriations					
Dividend	15,150	15,150	30,300	53,025	60,600
Dividend Tax	1,515	1,515	6,666	5,409	
Transfer to Reserves and Surplus	**52,830**	**56,429**	**90,036**	**192,486**	**275,789**

Current Ratio

Liquidity of the firm is gauged from the level of current assets and current liabilities.

Current ratio is defined as ratio of current assets to current liabilities.

$$\text{Current ratio} = \frac{\text{Current assets}}{\text{Current liabilities}}$$

Current ratio is the simplest measure of liquidity. It is the ratio of current assets to current liabilities.

Current assets would include debtors, inventories, and cash, while current liabilities would include payment due to suppliers of materials and services, provisions, and instalments of loans falling due in next 12 months (the balance sheet normally does not provide this information). Depending upon the need, some analysts especially bankers are inclined to include bank borrowings, normally forming part of secured loans, for working capital in the current liabilities.

For the year 2002, CMC has a current ratio of

$$\text{Current ratio} = \frac{\text{Current assets}}{\text{Current liabilities}} = \frac{2980530}{2388040} = 1.25$$

With instalments of loans falling due in next 12 months included in current liabilities, the current ratio falls to:

Current ratio (with loan amount payable in next 12 months)

$$= \frac{2980530}{2388040 + 112525} = 1.19$$

A current ratio of more than 1 indicates the excess of current assets over current liabilities and the firm is said to be *liquid*. Excess of current assets over current liabilities signifies that part of current assets are created by long-term liabilities. Although there is no specific value considered as optimum current ratio, a value between 1.33 and 2.00 is deemed adequate by most analysts and financial institutions. Generally speaking,

A current ratio of more than 1 indicates liquidity. Higher the current ratio better is the liquidity. But a very high current ratio affects profitability adversely.

larger the current ratio better is the firm's liquidity position. However, over-liquidity exhibited by very high current ratio is viewed as extra precautionary tendency on part of the management and is likely to have an adverse impact on the firm's profitability. This is on account of cost (explicit or implicit) that the firm has to bear on this excess level of assets that the firm carries.

Current ratios with and without loan instalments payable in next 12 months, for the last 5 years for CMC are given below:

CMC Ltd - Trend Current Ratio	1998	1999	2000	2001	2002
Current Ratio	1.27	1.13	1.15	1.17	1.25
Current Ratio with loan instalments payable in next 12 months	1.13	1.02	1.08	1.08	1.19

The trend of current ratio can be examined to know if the liquidity of the firm is deteriorating or improving, and whether or not the change is keeping pace with the target set. The figures of current ratio for CMC Ltd show a healthy trend of improved liquidity for the last four years.

Further qualitative insight is obtained by comparison of the current ratio with the prevalent norms of the industry. The major determinants of the current ratio are—(1) inventory holding period; (2) amount and days of credit provided to the customers; and (3) amount and days of credit availed from suppliers, all of which are characteristics of a particular industry. A firm keeping inventory and availing/providing credit as per the requirements of the industry must exhibit the current ratio consistent with what is prevalent in the industry. The judgement whether or not current ratio of 1.25 in the year 2002 for CMC Ltd is adequate depends upon the normal acceptable level in the industry.

Acid Test Ratio

Acid test ratio, also referred to as quick ratio, provides a deeper look at the liquidity of the firm. Of the three major components of the current assets—debtors, inventory, and cash—inventory takes maximum time to get converted into cash as the goods first have to be produced, sold, and finally realized as cash to be available for liquidation of liabilities. Therefore, true test of liquidity of a firm is measured by exclusion of inventory from current assets.

Acid test ratio is a more stringent measure of liquidity than the current ratio. It is the ratio of all the current assets excluding inventory to the current liabilities.

Acid test ratio is calculated as

$$\text{Acid Test or Quick Ratio} = \frac{\text{Current Assets} - \text{Inventory}}{\text{Current Liabilities}}$$

It is a more stringent measure of liquidity than the current ratio as it is based on assets that are cash or near cash and excludes those, which are likely to take a longer time to convert into cash.

For the year 2002, the acid test ratio for CMC works out to 1.20 and the trend for the ratio during the five-year period (1998–2002) is given below:

CMC Ltd - Trend Acid Test Ratio	1998	1999	2000	2001	2002
Acid Test Ratio	1.05	0.94	1.03	1.08	1.20

Analytically, current ratio and acid test ratio communicate the same message and lead to similar conclusions. A simultaneous study of current ratio and acid test ratio isolates the impact of inventory over liquidity of the firm. Quick ratio indicates the extent to which a firm would be able to meet its current liabilities if they become too pressing with time. Inventory is excluded from the list of current assets in the numerator, as it is the slowest moving item of current assets. Conversion of inventory into cash takes the longest time. If inventories constitute unduly large proportion of current assets then the firm though may have acceptable current ratio but would exhibit a poor quick ratio. Generally, a quick ratio in excess of 1.00 is regarded as satisfactory.

Quick ratio indicates the extent to which a firm will be able to meet its current liabilities at a very short notice as inventory is excluded in computing the quick ratio.

Cash Ratio

The severest measure of liquidity of the firm is the cash ratio. It is calculated as:

$$\text{Cash Ratio} = \frac{\text{Cash} + \text{Marketable Securities}}{\text{Current Liabilities}}$$

The cash available to a firm includes current investments, more particularly marketable financial securities. Measure of liquidity through cash ratio seems to be more of academic interest rather than of practical significance as firms flush with cash only invest in financial securities to earn some income, and the liquidity as measured from current ratio or quick ratio is expected to be good in such cases. Large values of cash ratio, therefore, may be an indicator more of the profitability of the firm rather than its liquidity. The availability of large amount of cash in a firm also implies that by economic prudence the firm has paid of creditors before investing surplus in the marketable securities. Firms with large cash or marketable securities may not have current liabilities of significant proportions.

Cash ratio is the most stringent measure of firm's liquidity. It denotes the extent to which cash and near cash marketable securities are sufficient to meet the current liabilities.

With no marketable investments, CMC keeps roughly 8% of liabilities in cash or cash equivalent. A large cash ratio here would indicate poor utilization of funds as idle cash translates into high opportunity cost. The trend of the past five years reflects a declining cash ratio, suggesting a better use of cash.

CMC Ltd—Trend Cash Ratio	1998	1999	2000	2001	2002
Cash Ratio	0.14	0.12	0.11	0.09	0.08

CAPITAL STRUCTURE RATIOS

Arguably the most important set of ratios are capital structure ratios. Also known as leverage ratios, they indicate how the assets of a firm are funded. In other words, these ratios indicate the type of liabilities used to finance assets.

Capital structure ratios measure the relationship between owners' funds and borrowed funds. A high usage of borrowed funds brings down the cost of financing but makes the firm more risky.

From the perspective of capital structure, liabilities can be divided into two broad categories—the one created towards owners of the firm and those towards non-owners. The liability of the firm towards the owners, who contribute equity and are prepared to accept the residual, is different from the liabilities towards others, i.e., the debt providers who have prior claims on cash flows and profit. The use of debt commits fixed and legally binding obligation of payments to the lenders on scheduled dates, irrespective of level of earnings of the firm.

Debt providers have two crucial questions—(1) how much of funds owners have put in and how much has been borrowed by the firm to acquire assets; and (2) whether the firm has adequate earning capacity to service the contractual obligations undertaken while raising debt. Since debt is provided on a long-term basis, the earning capacity is useful not only in deciding the quantum of borrowing but also in setting the repayment schedule of the loan.

Debt–Equity Ratio

The capital structure of the firm refers to the proportion of debt in relation to equity or assets. There are many ratios that can throw light on the capital structure. The most prominent of them are—(1) the debt–equity ratio defined as amount of long-term debt divided by amount of shareholders' funds; (2) debt to asset ratio; (3) total outside liabilities (TOL) to net worth; and (4) TOL to net assets ratio.

Debt–equity ratio, debt to asset ratio, total outside liabilities to net worth, and total outside liabilities to assets, are the most prominent measures of capital structure.

The computation of debt ratios of CMC Ltd for the year 2002 and the trend of all the ratios is given below:

$$\text{Debt Equity Ratio} = \frac{\text{Long-term Debt}}{\text{Net Worth}}$$

$$= \frac{25000 + 132397}{927826}$$

$$= 0.17$$

Debt to Assets Ratio

$$= \frac{\text{Long-term Debt}}{\text{Net Assets}}$$

$$= \frac{25000 + 132397}{1284468}$$

$$= 0.12$$

TOL to Net Worth Ratio

$$= \frac{\text{Total Outside Liabilities}}{\text{Net Worth}}$$

$$= \frac{123060 + 145435 + 88147 + 2388040}{927826}$$

$$= 2.96$$

TOL to Assets Ratio

$$= \frac{\text{Total Outside Liabilities}}{\text{Net Assets}}$$

$$= \frac{123060 + 145435 + 88147 + 2388040}{1284468}$$

$$= 2.14$$

While current ratio is more meaningful for short-term creditors of the firm, who are concerned about cash generation in immediate future, the long-term creditors prepared to look farther into the future are more concerned about debt–equity ratio. They may even overlook some weaknesses apparent in the short-run if they believe in the potential and the abilities of the firm to overcome such shortcomings in the long run.

As current ratio assumes significance for the short-term lenders, capital structure ratios are important for the long-term lenders.

Unlike current ratio where higher values are favoured, debt ratios are considered better if they have low values. Lenders feel more secured with an increasing stake of the owners. With increasing debt, as reflected in higher debt ratios, the firm is considered more vulnerable to external shocks and its operations are deemed risky. However, low values of debt ratios imply foregoing the advantages of debt. Since debt is a cheaper source of funds than equity, its use enhances shareholders' earnings.

The trend of debt–equity ratios for the five years for CMC is presented below. The trend of debt ratios indicates reduction in the proportion of debt over the years suggesting that growth is coming more and more from shareholders' funds rather than debt.

CMC Ltd - Capital Structure Ratios	1998	1999	2000	2001	2002
Debt to Equity (Only Long-term Debt)	0.64	0.45	0.42	0.33	0.17
Debt to Equity	1.06	0.75	0.74	0.52	0.38
Debt to Asset (Only Long-term Debt)	0.31	0.26	0.24	0.21	0.12
Debt to Asset	0.51	0.43	0.43	0.34	0.28
Total Outside Liabilities to Net Worth	3.99	4.04	4.35	3.80	2.96
Total Outside Liabilities to Assets	1.94	2.31	2.50	2.49	2.14

Generally a large value of debt ratio is disliked by one and all as the increased debt makes the firm more vulnerable to economic or business cycles. Debt always carries with it a fixed interest burden that remains insensitive to the declining revenues and/or profitability under unfavourable economic conditions.

Depending upon the risk profile and other factors, each industry develops an acceptable norm for the proportion of debt. Most interested in development of such norms are financial institutions and banks, which provide debt to the firm. For instance, acceptable debt proportion for capital-intensive industries such as cement, steel, and infrastructure would be higher than that for industries such as software development, consumer goods, etc. A firm having debt ratio in excess of the acceptable level or prescribed norm is considered more risky in its operations.

A substitute to reduction in the risk of operations of the firm is the security aspect of the loan. Industries in the infrastructure sector are capital intensive and have large fixed assets and hence, lenders relax the capital structure norms in such cases by providing larger debt as compared to firms in industries such as software development. A lower value than the established norm helps determine the amount of further debt that can be afforded by the firm.

Treatment of preference share capital and that of lease payments are the two issues that deserve special attention in the computation of debt–equity ratios. As regard to preference share capital, one opinion is to include it in debt as it bears a fixed rate of dividend and has a claim prior to that of equity shareholders. Another opinion is to include it in equity as the payment is not binding but only preludes the dividend payments to equity shareholders. The treatment, however, depends upon the objective. If debt ratio is calculated to assess financial risk, preference capital must form the part of equity since inability of the firm to meet the promised dividend cannot lead to financial bankruptcy. If debt ratio is considered to analyse the capital structure, it must be included in the debt because of the fixed obligations that preference capital carries.

Preference share capital and lease payments must be added to the debt while computing debt–equity ratios.

In case assets are acquired on lease, the value of lease must be added to the debt of the firm while computing debt ratios.

Example 2-1 Applying Ratios

A condensed balance sheet of ABC Ltd is presented below:

Net Worth	350	Net Fixed Assets	450
Debt	250	Current Assets	400
		Less: Current Liabilities	250
Total	**600**	**Total**	**600**

You are a banker providing funds for fixed assets and working capital. The norms of the bank prescribe a minimum current ratio of 1.3 and maximum debt–equity ratio of 1.00. Find out how much funds you can sanction for—(1) acquisition of fixed assets and (2) for working capital, assuming no further equity contribution by the firm. Also project the balance sheet of the firm assuming deployment of newly-sanctioned funds.

Solution

Amount of new long-term funds sanctioned = x

The new debt–equity ratio of the firm = $(250 + x)/350$ should not exceed 1.00. Hence,

$$\frac{250+x}{350} \le 1.00 \text{ gives } x \le 100$$

With the sanction amount of y towards working capital, the current assets too will increase at least by the same amount. The new current ratio should not be more than 1.3. Hence,

$$\frac{400+y}{250+y} \le 1.30 \text{ gives } y \le 250$$

The projected balance sheet of the firm after awailing the maximum loans would be as below:

Net Worth	350	Net Fixed Assets	550
Debt	350	Current Assets	650
		Less: Current Liabilities	500
Total	**700**	**Total**	**700**

Debt Coverage Ratios

While debt ratios are only concerned with the maximum debt the firm can avail, an equally important issue of recovery and safety of the loan is not addressed by these ratios. It is presumptive that debt, if given within the prescribed limit, is safe and its repayment is rather certain. This at best is a generalization that leaves many questions unattended. While granting debt, the question of how soon the recovery can be made must also be answered. Also, the repayment schedule of the loan cannot be determined by the debt–equity ratio. Debt ratios do not provide any quantitative measure for the ability to service debt obligations and the level of comfort the lender can enjoy. Therefore, we turn our attention to another set of ratios known as debt coverage ratios.

Debt coverage ratios are the measure of the firm's capacity to service its debt obligations. Higher the coverage, safer is the firm from the lenders' perspective.

Interest Cover The most prominent among debt coverage ratios is the interest cover ratio. The ability to service debt obligation is dependent on the earning capacity of the firm and is calculated by dividing earnings by the interest obligations. Interest coverage ratio is defined as:

$$\text{Interest Cover} = \frac{\text{Profit Before Interest and Taxes (PBIT)}}{\text{Interest Obligation}}$$

Interest coverage ratio measures quantitatively how many times the earnings are to the interest obligations. Larger the ratio, larger is the earning capacity and better is the assurance of recovery of interest. Firms are subject to the risks associated with a constantly changing business environment. This leads to fluctuations in their cash flows. High earnings as multiple of interest denote that the firm is safe for the lender.

Interest coverage ratio indicates the extent to which profits (PBIT) are sufficient to pay the existing interest obligations. Higher the ratio more is the cushion available to lenders.

In the formula for calculating interest cover, the numerator, profit before interest and taxes (PBIT) measures the earning potential of the firm. From the perspective of shareholders, the earning potential is profit after taxes (PAT). The consistency of figures in the numerator and denominator demands use of matching figures. Since interest is tax deductible, PBIT is the more appropriate figure to represent funds available for payment of interest.

Since PBIT as stated in the profit and loss account includes many items such as depreciation, amortization, write offs, etc., which do not reflect cash flows, interest cover can be calculated on the basis of cash available for payment of interest. It can be computed as follows:

Interest Cover (on cash basis)

$$= \frac{\text{PBIT} + \text{Depreciation} \pm \text{Non Cash Expense/Income}}{\text{Interest Obligation}}$$

Debt Service Coverage Ratio Besides recovery of interest on the loan, the firm also must pay back the principal amount borrowed from the earnings made. Normally loans are payable in equal instalments spread over tenure of the loan. To assess the ability of the firm to meet the debt service obligations (interest and the principal amount), debt service coverage ratio (also known as fixed charge coverage ratio) is computed as below:

Debt service coverage ratio measures the ability of the firm to meet its total debt obligations (both interest and principal).

Debt Service Coverage Ratio

$$= \frac{\text{PBIT} + \text{Depreciation} \pm \text{Non Cash Expense/Income}}{\text{Interest Obligation} + \dfrac{\text{Loan Instalment}}{1 - \text{Tax Rate}}}$$

The numerator represents the cash available to the firm before taxes. The denominator includes interest obligation and instalment for the loan repayable. Since taxes have to be paid before loan instalment and the numerator is pre-tax earning, the loan instalment must be modified to pre-tax basis by dividing the amount by the factor of (1 – tax rate). For example, if a loan instalment of ₹100 is payable and the firm pays 40% tax on funds available on pre-tax basis, the loan amount is 100/0.6 = ₹166.67

The three ratios for CMC for the year 2002 are calculated below:

$$\text{Interest Cover} = \frac{\text{Profit Before Interest and Taxes (PBIT)}}{\text{Interest Obligation}}$$

$$= \frac{530576}{19524} = 27.18$$

Interest Cover (on cash basis)

$$= \frac{\text{PBIT} + \text{Depreciation} \pm \text{Non Cash Expense/Income}}{\text{Interest Obligation}}$$

$$= \frac{611001}{19524} = 31.29$$

Debt Service Coverage Ratio

$$= \frac{\text{PBIT} + \text{Depreciation} \pm \text{Non Cash Expense/Income}}{\text{Interest Obligation} + \dfrac{\text{Loan Instalment}}{1 - \text{Tax Rate}}}$$

$$= \frac{611001}{19524 + \dfrac{112525}{1 - 0.36}} = 3.15$$

The trend for three ratios for last five years is as below:

CMC Ltd - Debt Coverage	*1998*	*1999*	*2000*	*2001*	*2002*
Interest Cover	3.85	5.11	7.59	17.21	27.18
Interest Cover - Cash Basis	5.56	7.37	9.52	20.93	31.29
Debt Service Cover	0.83	0.73	1.16	1.51	3.15

Trend analysis over the period of last five years indicates an improvement in debt paying capacity because of increased earnings and reduced debt obligations.

WORKING CAPITAL RATIOS

Effective utilization of funds blocked in working capital is an issue of predominant concern to the management as investment in working capital occupies a significant percentage. At the same time, it is variable and controllable to some extent, particularly for manufacturing and trading businesses. Various components of working capital such as funds blocked in inventory, debtors and creditors are utilized as much as possible by turning them over and over.

Working capital ratios denote the efficiency of firms in handling its operations. More quickly a firm turns over the different current assets eventually into cash, more efficient is the firm.

An organization procures raw material by incurring cash expenses or creating a liability, processing materials to convert into finished goods, selling the finished product on credit to customers, and ultimately realizing cash from them at the end of the credit period. Cash gets blocked at the time of procurement of inputs if inputs are paid for in cash. If the firm enjoys credit facility from its suppliers the cash blockage starts from the point the suppliers are paid for their supplies at the end of the credit period extended by them. The cash thus blocked is realized from customers at the end of the credit period extended to them. The duration of the time gap between the blockage of funds for the prounsement of inputs and their realization from customers is known as the *cash cycle*. The efficiency of a firm in utilization of resources is reflected in the cash cycle. The shorter the cash cycle, the more efficient is the firm in the utilization of cash resource. This section elaborately handles the various working capital ratios that reflect the efficiency of firm's operations.

Current Asset Turnover

Generally utilization of working capital is gauged from the turnover of each component of working capital. A high turnover of current assets implies better utilization and quicker conversion into cash. Current assets turnover ratio is calculated as:

Current assets turnover ratio indicates how many times the current assets are turned over into sales in a given period (usually a year). An increasing ratio is a sign of improving efficiency.

Current Assets Turnover Ratio

$$= \frac{\text{Sales}}{\text{Average Current Assets}}$$

Current assets turnover computes how many times current assets are turned over in a year. This can easily be converted into number of days current assets take to get converted into cash (i.e. the current assets holding period).

Current Assets Holding Period

$$= \frac{\text{Average Current Assets}}{\text{Sales}} \times 365 \text{ days}$$

Expressing current assets as holding period in number of days provides an estimate about the length of the firm's working cycle. A higher turnover ratio or shorter current assets holding period denotes better utilization of funds deployed in current assets. With smaller holding period—lower level of funds in current assets—it is implied that the firm can achieve larger sales with smaller capital, and exhibits better profitability to the extent of savings made in the cost of funds.

A related measure is the current assets holding period. There is an inverse relationship between current assets turnover and the holding period.

Net Current Assets Turnover

An alternative measure of efficiency in the working capital is to calculate the turnover on the basis of net current assets instead of gross current assets. Since the firm builds current assets partly from the current liabilities and partly from long-term sources (equity or borrowed funds), the efficiency of owned or borrowed long-term funds used for working capital financing is assessed on the basis of net assets turnover.

Net current assets turnover ratio expresses the relationship between the sales and long-term financed component of current assets. A very high ratio indicates poor liquidity.

Net Current Assets Turnover Ratio

$$= \frac{\text{Sales}}{\text{Average Net Current Assets}}$$

This can also be expressed in days as follows:

Net Current Assets Holding Period

$$= \frac{\text{Average Net Current Assets}}{\text{Sales}} \times 365 \text{days}$$

The current asset turnover and net current turnover for CMC for the year 2002 are calculated at as below:

Current Assets Turnover Ratio

$$= \frac{\text{Sales}}{\text{Average Current Assets}}$$

$$= \frac{5653316}{2980530} = 1.90$$

Net Current Assets Turnover Ratio

$$= \frac{\text{Sales}}{\text{Average Net Current Assets}} = \frac{5653316}{592490} = 9.54$$

The trend for the current asset turnover for CMC for the five years is as follows:

CMC Ltd Working Capital Turnover	1998	1999	2000	2001	2002
Current Assets Turnover	1.98	2.04	2.06	1.93	1.90
Net Current Assets Turnover	9.44	17.56	15.65	13.17	9.54

From the description of the current asset turnover ratios, it is logical to associate larger values with greater efficiency. Can we say the same for net current asset turnover ratio? In general yes, but it does have a relationship with current asset turnover ratio and must be interpreted cautiously. Net asset turnover would always be higher than the current asset turnover, but how much higher can it be? As minimum value could be equal to current asset turnover where the firms avail no credit. However, at the other extreme, a firm may avail extraordinarily high credit from suppliers suggesting large proportions of current assets being financed by them. Net current assets close to zero would give inordinately high returns for the net working capital, but it also implies rather lower net working capital than desired. Although net current asset turnover that is more than four times the current asset turnover indicates high returns on net working capital, it is undesirable. High proportion of financing of current assets by current liabilities means lower proportions being financed from the firm's own capital. A very high net current asset turnover ratio as compared to current assets turnover ratio signals poor liquidity and/or unsatisfactory capital structure.

As can be seen from the data for CMC, the net current asset turnover is more than four times the current asset turnover.

Current assets turnover, either on gross basis or on net basis, is an aggregate measure of efficiency of working capital. It does not tell us which part of the working capital the efficiency or inefficiency comes from. To examine this, we turn our attention to the utilization of funds blocked in each component of current asset and working capital.

Inventory Turnover Ratios

Each area of working capital can be analysed separately to gain further insight into the functioning of the firm. Inventory as a part of current assets deserves attention as it takes the longest to convert inventory into cash. Inventory turnover ratio is expressed as ratio of inventory to cost of goods sold (COGS)[1]. This can also be expressed as number of days inventory is held, a number that is more convenient and simple to understand. It presents the same information as the inventory turnover ratio. These are expressed as:

Inventory turnover ratio expresses the relationship between cost of goods sold and inventory. It denotes the efficiency in inventory management. An increasing ratio signifies better inventory management.

[1]Cost of Goods Sold (COGS) is calculated as All direct cost (material, labour, manufacturing expenses, etc., including depreciation ± decrease/increase value of work-in-process and finished goods stocks during the period.

$$\text{Inventory Turnover Ratio} = \frac{\text{Cost of Goods Sold (COGS)}}{\text{Average Inventory}}$$

$$\text{Inventory Holding Period} = \frac{\text{Average Inventory}}{\text{COGS}} \times 365 \text{ days}$$

Inventory is generally held in three forms—raw material, work-in-process, and finished goods. For deeper insight and analysis, the turnover ratios for each of the component of inventories can be analysed separately. The three components of inventory in terms of turnover or number of days held are defined in terms of cost of production and cost of sales as follows:

Inventory holding period denotes the shelf life of inventory. It shares an inverse relationship with inventory turnover ratio.

Raw Material Turnover Ratio

$$= \frac{\text{Raw Material Consumption}}{\text{Average Raw Material Inventory}}$$

Raw Material Holding Period

$$= \frac{\text{Average Raw Material Inventory}}{\text{Raw Material Consumption}} \times 365$$

Work-in-Process (WIP) Turnover Ratio

$$= \frac{\text{Cost of Production}}{\text{Average WIP Inventory}}$$

WIP Inventory Holding Period

$$= \frac{\text{Average WIP Inventory}}{\text{Cost of Production}} \times 365$$

Finished Goods (FG) Turnover Ratio

$$= \frac{\text{Cost of Sales}}{\text{Average FG Inventory}}$$

FG Inventory Holding Period

$$= \frac{\text{Average FG Inventory}}{\text{Cost of Sales}} \times 365$$

Consistency of numerator and denominator is required for appropriate interpretation. Note that the numerator in each of the ratios of inventories turnover is different. The numerator is chosen depending upon the linkage of the type of inventory with the appropriate stage of production and equivalent financial data. Raw materials holding period or turnover are better indicated when measured with respect to raw material consumption. Similarly work-in-process turnover and holding period is expressed in relation to cost of production[2] while the finished goods turnover ratio and finished goods holding period are computed in relation to cost of sales.

Although an appropriate combination of numerator and denominator is desired, there is no harm in using a common numerator for all turnover ratios. On the contrary, using figure of sales as a common numerator for all ratios may be preferred for reasons of—(1) uniformity of interpretation; (2) non-availability of relevant figures of raw material consumption, cost of production, and cost of sales in publicly available financial statements; and (3) as a matter of convenience. Inventory-holding periods, which are expressed in terms of days of sales, for all kinds of inventories facilitate comparison and comprehension. The use of single figure really does not affect the analysis as long as the same parameter is used for different periods of time.

Inventory-holding period can be curtailed by ordering more frequently (for raw materials), by reducing the idle time between different stages of production (for work-in-process), and by faster despatches of orders (for finished goods). To a large extent, inventory-holding period is governed by industry characteristics. For example, seasoning of wood, maturing of wines, etc., takes a long time and production is determined by natural processes. The time of processing cannot be curtailed in such industries. Subject to the constraints of the industry and technical parameters, all efforts must be made to keep inventory-holding periods as low as possible.

Inventory turnover ratios or holding periods can be used as:

- *measurement tools* for determining the efficiency of inventory management, and the trend over successive periods;
- *diagnostic tools* to find weak areas such as accumulation of non-moving or slow-moving stocks;
- *norm-setting tools* for developing guidelines for financing; and
- *comparative tools* for assessing relative performance of a firm with respect to its competitors, industry, and against a benchmark.

Debtors's Turnover Ratio

Debtors' turnover ratio helps determine how fast the receivable are realized by the firm. Firms extend credit to its customers to boost sales, increase market share, beat the competition, overcome shortcomings in the product, etc. Most of the reasons are needs of the marketing function. However, it adversely affects the firm's financial performance.

Debtors' turnover ratio reflects the efficiency with which debts are turned into cash. Improvement in the ratio indicates better receivables management.

Like inventory ratios, debtors' performance can also be measured in terms of turnover as well as in number of days.

$$\text{Debtors' Turnover Ratio} = \frac{\text{Sales}}{\text{Average Debtors}}$$

$$\text{Average Collection Period} = \frac{\text{Average Debtors}}{\text{Sales}} \times 365 \text{ days}$$

Debtors' turnover refers to how fast the collection from customers is made while the average collection period reflects the average number of days it takes for a form to realize money

[2]Cost of Production is calculated as All direct cost (material, labour, manufacturing expenses etc including depreciation ± decrease/increase value of work-in-process stocks during the period. The difference in cost of production and cost of goods sold (COGS) is that COGS provides for adjustment of change in the finished goods stocks.

from its debtors. Debtors' turnover is alternatively referred to as receivables turnover ratio. It is a function of the credit policy of a firm and its collection efforts.

Credit sales figures should ideally be used for computing the debtor turnover ratio. However, if the credit sales figures are not available, net sales figures should be used for computing the debtors' turnover ratio. The uses of this ratio are similar to those of inventory turnover ratios.

Debtors' turnover ratio can be used as a:

- *measurement tool* to know the speed of collection and efficiency of collection department;
- *comparative tool* to assess the collection policy with respect to competitors and industry;
- *policy determinant* for deciding the cash discount incorporating the cost of capital of the firm;
- *norm-setting tool* to formulate guidelines for financing by the banks and financial institutions;
- *predictive tool* for understanding the level of competition and likely changes in the profitability. Normally increasing credit implies hotter competition and declining profitability; and
- *analytical tool* for cost volume profit planning by ascertaining the impact of changes in the collection and credit policy on sales, volume, and profit.

Ageing of Debtors

Besides measurement of collection period, another related tool is the ageing schedule of debtors. The ageing schedule categorizes outstanding receivables on the basis of duration for which they have been outstanding.

> *Debtors' ageing schedule categorizes the debtors as per the period outstanding. It is the device for monitoring of receivables and identifying potential defaulters.*

While the average collection period provides information about the quality of debtors at an aggregate level, the debtors ageing schedule concentrates on specific customers. It is used to identify the potential defaulters, and determine the intensity of efforts required for collection from each customer. It establishes the need for monitoring specific customers for whom dues are outstanding beyond the terms of sale. Ageing schedule also helps in estimating the risk of non-realization and making provision for bad debts.

Average Credit Availed

As the firm extends credit, it also avails credit from the raw material and services suppliers. Efficiency of working capital in terms of net assets is also dependent upon how much credit the firm is able to obtain from its suppliers. Larger the credit availed from suppliers, lesser is the amount of funds needed to replenish the gap between the current assets and current liabilities.

> *Creditors' turnover ratio reflects the number of times average dues to the suppliers is settled.*

Average credit availed can be ascertained from creditors' turnover or directly from average credit period availed.

$$\text{Creditors Turnover Ratio} = \frac{\text{Purchases}}{\text{Average Creditors}}$$

$$\text{Average Credit Availed} = \frac{\text{Average Creditors}}{\text{Purchases}} \times 365 \text{ days}$$

Reverse of what was stated for debtors and inventory applies to creditors. It is better for the firm if it has low creditors' turnover or larger credit period availed from the creditors. Since higher credit from suppliers means deferment of cash, it provides more leeway to the firm in managing the cash resource.

The inefficiency in the management of current assets, in certain cases, can be partly compensated by efficiency in the management of current liabilities. However, this should not be construed as a welcome situation. Both current assets and current liabilities are managed independently of each other. The firm must continue to strive for better management of current assets irrespective of what can be achieved through management of current liabilities.

> *For effective working capital management, both current assets and current liabilities should be managed independently.*

Working capital turnover ratios for CMC for the year 2002 are computed below:

$$\text{Inventory Turnover Ratio} = \frac{\text{Sales}}{\text{Inventory}} = \frac{5466980}{116573} = 46.9$$

$$\text{Inventory Holding Period} = \frac{\text{Inventory}}{\text{Sales}} \times 365 \text{ days}$$

$$= \frac{116573}{5466980} \times 365$$

$$= 7.78 \text{ days of sales}$$

$$\text{Debtors Turnover Ratio} = \frac{\text{Sales}}{\text{Debtors}} = \frac{5653316}{1500584} = 3.77$$

$$\text{Average Collection Period} = \frac{\text{Debtors}}{\text{Sales}} \times 365 \text{ days}$$

$$= \frac{1500584}{5653316} \times 365$$

$$= 96.88 \text{ days of sales}$$

$$\text{Creditors Turnover Ratio} = \frac{\text{Purchases}}{\text{Creditors}} = \frac{2113445}{973298} = 2.17$$

$$\text{Average Credit Availed} = \frac{\text{Creditors}}{\text{Purchases}} \times 365 \text{ days}$$

$$= \frac{973298}{2113445} \times 365$$

$$= 168 \text{ days of purchase}$$

The trend of working capital turnover ratios for five successive years as presented below indicates improvement in the inventory turnover over the period from 11.46 (holding period of about 32 days) in 1998 to 24.36 (holding period of about 15 days) in 2001. Substantial improvement in the year 2002 needs a further and deeper study of circumstances before any conclusion is made.

Debtors' collection period remains almost constant at about 100 days, which appears to be the industry norm.

CMC Ltd (Turnover Ratios)	1998	1999	2000	2001	2002
Inventory Turnover Ratio	11.46	11.73	18.82	24.36	46.90
Debtors' Turnover Ratio	3.49	3.97	3.65	3.53	3.77
Creditors' Turnover Ratio	2.84	2.74	3.15	1.83	2.17
Average Collection Period (Days)	104.73	91.87	99.89	103.41	96.88
Average Credit Availed (Days)	128.59	133.17	115.91	199.70	168.09

Use of Average Figures

Note that in each of the ratios of working capital, average of the opening and closing values of stock, debtors, and creditors is used because the corresponding figure relates to the period rather than at one point of time. As sales are made over a period, the accretion or depletion of inventory/stocks/debtors/creditors also takes place over the same period of time. As sales increase so will the stocks, debtors, and creditors. Therefore, the average of the opening and closing figures is more appropriate. Another reason for the use of average is to smoothen out the changes over the period of time. However, use of the end-of-the-period values of stocks, debtors, creditors or assets is not detrimental as long as changes in the activity levels are moderate. In case of high-growth firms, use of average figures rather than end-of-the-period values would lead to more sound conclusions.

PROFITABILITY RATIOS

Profits are essential for any firm to survive and service all stakeholders. Although profit is said to be belonging to shareholders, its absence is detrimental to all stakeholders. Examining the profitability of the firm is of interest to all and it is not the exclusive domain of shareholders.

Profitability ratios refer to a business's ability to generate earnings.

Profit can be defined in many ways. In general, it is excess of revenue over cost. Various definitions of profit would depend upon the definition of revenue and cost for the purpose of profit. Different stakeholders are interested in different kinds of surplus an enterprise would generate. For example, share-holders are concerned about profit after taxes but the Government (tax authorities) would be keen to know profit before taxes. Similarly the management would want to know the value addition done by the firm, while lenders will focus on earnings before interest and taxes. The following section discusses the different metrics of firms' profitability.

Value Addition

At the broadest level a firm is interested in value addition it makes to the product it sells. For example, a transformer producer would normally procure various inputs such as copper, plates, oil, etc., to convert them into the finished product of ready-to-use transformers. The excess of the selling price of the finished product sold by the firm over the price paid to procure the inputs is known as *value addition*.

Value addition is the enhancement made to the value to customers. Higher the value added, better is the bottom-line for the firm.

Value addition

= Sales – Purchases

Value addition in %

= (Sales – Purchases)/Sales

Value addition percentage for CMC for the year 2002 is about 61%.

Value Addition

$$= \frac{\text{Sales} - \text{Purchases}}{\text{Sales}} \times 100$$

$$= \frac{5466980 - 2113445}{5466980} \times 100 = 61.34\%$$

For good firms, value addition would show an increasing trend. The increase in value addition in absolute terms can come from better procurement at competitive prices and/or ability of the firm to market its products at better prices. The ratio of value addition to sales would show an increase if the firm has added features to create product differentiation that fetches more value than the increase in procurement prices. If the value addition as absolute number remains constant but value addition percentage increases, it would imply creativity, product innovation, etc., on part of the firm. Increasing value addition in absolute terms without the increase in the value addition ratio implies increasing volumes and market share but stagnation in the area of product development.

Contribution Margin

The value addition by the firm is done through processing of inputs procured. The firm has to incur expenses on the processing of basic inputs for transforming them into output (finished goods). These expenses can be categorized as variable and fixed. Variable expenses vary with the level of activity while fixed expenses do not. Examples of variable expenses include wages to workers, electricity charges, etc. Examples of fixed expenses are rent, salaries, etc.

The margin available once the variable costs have been covered up is known as contribution margin. This margin goes to meet the fixed costs.

The firm is concerned with how much it can have to itself when it sells its products. How much the firm is left with after it has met variable costs is referred to as contribution margin that goes to meet the fixed expenses and profit. Contribution margin is defined as:

Contribution = Sales – Variable cost

Contribution in % = (Sales – Variable cost)/Sales

It is desirable to have as large contribution as possible both in absolute and percentage terms. The conclusions from the analysis of value addition and contribution are almost similar, except that the contribution may be analysed with respect to proportions of variable cost.

Contribution margin percentage for CMC for the year 2002 is about 37% assuming that 50% of the operating expenses as variable and sales revenue includes other income, also known as non-operational income, such as interest earned, rent received, etc.

$$\text{Contribution Margin \%} = \frac{\text{Sales} - \text{Variable cost}}{\text{Sales}} \times 100$$

$$= \frac{5653316 - 3577880}{5653316} \times 100$$

$$= 36.71\%$$

The trend of value addition and contribution margin for five years for CMC Ltd is shown below:

CMC Ltd Value Addition & Contribution (%)	1998	1999	2000	2001	2002
Value Addition	55	60	56	59	61
Contribution Margin	32	33	32	35	37
(50% of operating expenses taken as variable)					

Gross Profit Margin

Gross profit margin, also referred to as gross margin, is defined as excess of sales over cost of goods sold. While computing gross profit margin, the following must be kept in mind:

Gross profit margin is the excess of total sales revenue over its cost of goods sold. It reflects production efficiency.

- depreciation is to be included in the cost of production;
- selling, general, and administrative overheads must be excluded from the cost; and
- non-operational income must be excluded from the revenue.

Gross profit margin is measured to assess production or operational efficiency. Therefore, all expenses up to the stage of production must be included and all expenses post manufacturing must be excluded. Similarly, any non-operational income such as dividends and interest earned, that are generated from investing or other activities of the firm, should be excluded from the sales/revenue.

The desired figures for calculating gross profit margin are generally not available easily. Instead the figures of earnings before interest and taxes (EBIT) are easily available and hence, can be used as a substitute to establish profitability and operational efficiency of the firm as a matter of convenience. Besides, EBIT being readily available for all firms the gross margin measure based on EBIT facilitates comparison among competing firms as well as with the industry. Using EBIT as measure of profit also eliminates the problem of choosing which items of expenditure to exclude or include in the definition of gross profit.

Gross Profit Margin

$$= \frac{\text{Sales} - \text{Cost of Goods Sold (COGS)}}{\text{Sales}} \times 100\%$$

$$\text{Or, } \frac{\text{EBIT}}{\text{Sales}} \times 100\%$$

A high gross margin reflects the ability of the firm to meet production expenses while EBIT-based profitability reflects ability to recover all expenses of procurement, production, and sales. Financial expenses, which depend upon the capital structure, are excluded. The comparison of EBIT-based profit of various firms excludes the leverage employed in financing by the enterprise. A low gross profit margin could be on account of one or more of the following reasons:

- inability of the firm to procure inputs at competitive prices;
- selling finished product at lower prices;
- excessive production overheads;
- high capital investment resulting in higher depreciation; or
- poor utilization of production capacity.

Adequate value added ratio and contribution margin but inadequate EBIT to sales ratio indicates excessive selling and general overheads.

EBIT-based profit margin of CMC for the year 2002 is around 9.39% as calculated below:

$$\text{Gross Profit Margin} = \frac{\text{EBIT}}{\text{Sales}} \times 100\%$$

$$= \frac{530576}{5653316} \times 100\% = 9.39\%$$

Net Profit Margin

Net profit margin, also known as net margin, is the final level of profit. Net profit is the residue available for the shareholders after the coverage of all direct and indirect costs, and interest and taxes. The net profit margin reflects the overall profitability of the business.

Net profit margin is calculated by dividing profit after taxes by sales. Net profit margin measures the efficiency of the firm in managing production, procurement, sales, financing, and tax planning.

Net profit margin for CMC Ltd for 2002 works out to 5.96% as calculated below:

$$\text{Net Profit Margin} = \frac{\text{PAT}}{\text{Sales}} \times 100\%$$

$$= \frac{336389}{5653316} \times 100\% = 5.96\%$$

The trend of profitability for CMC indicates growth over the years.

CMC Ltd (Profitability)	1998	1999	2000	2001	2002
Gross Profit Margin using EBIT	5.27%	4.51%	5.09%	7.63%	9.39%
Net Profit Margin	2.35%	2.11%	2.71%	4.54%	5.95%

Return on Capital Employed

Return on capital employed (ROCE) provides a measure of efficiency of capital. It is also known as *return on investment* (ROI) and is calculated as:

The efficiency of a firm in using the capital at its disposal is reflected by its ROCE.

Return on Capital Employed (ROCE)

$$= \frac{\text{EBIT}(1 - \text{T})}{\text{Net Assets}} \times 100\%$$

It can be observed that the numerator has the term EBIT (1 – T) as a measure of return where T is the corporate tax rate. To assess the efficiency of capital, one needs to isolate the impact of capital structure since the earning power of the assets depends upon the capital and not on its source. The true measure of the earnings of the assets is the earning before interest and taxes (EBIT). Since interest

Since the total capital employed includes both debt and equity, the return is taken as EBIT (1 – T) and not PAT.

payable on the debt capital is tax deductible, we examine the return as if the entire capital were in the form of equity. If entire capital were equity, the net earning that will flow to the capital suppliers would be net of taxes. EBIT (1 – T) can be alteranately expresed as (PAT + Interest) with PAT belonging to equity shareholders while interest is for lenders.

The denominator is equal to net assets since investment must equal assets. Net assets would represent capital from all sources—equity and both long-term and short-term debt. Since earnings are made over a period, it is desirable to smoothen the end-of-the-period values by taking the average of the opening and closing net assets. This would be particularly required if there are substantial changes in the net assets/capital during the period under review.

Most analysts prefer to measure earning power of the firm by earnings before interest, taxes and depreciation and amortization (EBITDA) and replace the numerator accordingly to arrive at ROCE.

ROCE reflects the post-tax earning power of the firm. It facilitates comparison with the cost of capital of the firm. If ROCE is greater than the weighted average cost of capital, the firm can be classified as efficient. ROCE of the firm can also be compared with the competing firms in the industry to establish classification of relatively efficient and inefficient firms.

ROCE for CMC Ltd for the year 2002 is determined below:

Return on Capital Employed (ROCE)

$$= \frac{EBIT(1-T)}{\text{Net Assets}} \times 100\%$$

$$= \frac{530576(1-0.36)}{1284468} \times 100\% = 26.63\%$$

Return on Equity

Although overall efficiency of capital or investment is assessed from ROCE, the main concern for the equity shareholders is the return they get on the part of the capital supplied by them, i.e., net worth. Return on equity (ROE) measures the efficiency of a firm in managing its shareholders' funds. Since profit after tax (PAT) goes to the equity shareholders, ROE is defined as

$$\text{Return on Equity (ROE)} = \frac{\text{Profit After Tax (PAT)}}{\text{Net Worth}} \times 100\%$$

If change in net worth during the period is large, it is advisable to use average of beginning and end of the period values of net worth in the denominator. Net worth would include the capital contributed directly by shareholders and the accumulated undistributed profit of the firm. ROE is not only important for owners of the firm but also to the managers as they have the responsibility towards the shareholders on whose behalf they manage the firm. ROE is affected by several factors such as capital structure, tax rates, efficiency of assets, cost of debt, etc.

ROE is the return that the firm generates on the funds provided by equity holders. Increasing ROE denotes improving efficiency of the firm in handling its shareholders' funds.

Return on equity for CMC Ltd for the year works out to 36.25%.

$$\text{Return on Equity (ROE)} = \frac{\text{Profit After Tax (PAT)}}{\text{Net Worth}} \times 100\%$$

$$= \frac{336389}{927826} \times 100\% = 36.25\%$$

The trend of ROCE and ROE for five years presented below indicates consistent improvement over the years, with ROCE rising from 11.3% to 26.6% and ROE improving from 17.2% to 36.2%.

CMC Ltd – Return on Capital %	*1998*	*1999*	*2000*	*2001*	*2002*
Return on Capital Employed	11.31	11.38	15.35	23.41	26.63
Return on Equity	17.25	16.01	23.21	33.60	36.25

Earning per Share and Dividend per Share Earning per share (EPS) is an alternative representation of ROE. It is not a ratio but an absolute figure stating the amount of profit earned on per share basis. It is calculated as:

EPS is the return (profit) earned on per share basis.

Earnings Per Share (EPS) (*₹/Share*)

$$= \frac{\text{PAT}}{\text{Number of shares outstanding}}$$

While ROE measures the earnings for the shareholders on the funds provided by them, EPS measures the profit that accrues on each share. Further, ROE signifies current return on original capital subscribed as well as the accumulated undistributed profits in the past. EPS is not concerned with the past profit retained on behalf of and belonging to the shareholders, but instead considers only the original amount of capital contributed as reflected in the number of shares for the period under consideration. Since net worth is the fund contributed by shareholders as a group, the individual investor is required to work around on ROE to determine how much belongs to him/her. EPS provides that answer directly.

The part of EPS that the firm proposes to distribute to the shareholders is known as dividend per share (DPS).

Of the earnings made by the firm, the management, in the interest of the shareholders, may decide to distribute only a part of it while retaining some to be deployed in the business to provide growth in future earnings. Dividend per share (DPS) provides the amount of money that the shareholders receive out of his/her entitled earnings. It is calculated as

Dividend Per Share (DPS) (*₹/Share*)

$$= \frac{\text{Dividend}}{\text{Number of shares outstanding}}$$

Both EPS and DPS are of interest to the market as they are considered to be most important determinants of the price of the share.

For the year 2002, CMC Ltd had EPS and DPS of ₹22.20 per share and ₹4.00 per share as shown below:

Earning Per Share (EPS) (₹/Share)

$$= \frac{\text{PAT}}{\text{Number of shares}} = \frac{336389}{15150} = ₹22.20$$

Dividend Per Share (DPS) (₹/Share)

$$= \frac{\text{Dividend}}{\text{Number of shares}} = \frac{60600}{15150} = ₹4.00$$

The trend of EPS and DPS for CMC Ltd for five years is shown below:

₹ Per Share	1998	1999	2000	2001	2002
Earning Per Share	4.59	4.82	8.38	16.56	22.20
Dividend Per Share	1.00	1.00	2.00	3.50	4.00

VALUATION RATIOS

Valuation ratios judge the value the stock market places on any given company. The prominent valuation ratios are: earnings. and dividends yield, price earnings, and price to book ratios.

The ratios mentioned so far analyse the performance of the firms on various fronts such as liquidity, leverage, and profitability. The true measure of performance of the firm lies in its market value. In a way it can be said that market evaluates the complex interrelationship of various aspects of business and the price it assigns to the firm is a manifestation of how the firm is rated on an aggregate basis. It not only takes into account the comprehensive view of the existing performance measuring variables such as liquidity, capital structure, and profitability, the market price also discounts the expected future performance.

In view of what is stated above, market-based information is always more important and gets precedence over accounting information available in the financial statements. When market-based information is not available, the accounting information can be used as substitute.

Earnings Yield and Dividend Yield

Due to the difference of scale, absolute earnings and dividends may be of little relevance while comparing different firms. Hence, they are better expressed as a percentage of market price. This is known as yield.

The previous section explained the concepts of EPS and DPS. These earnings are in absolute values. An investor needs to know the rate of return offered by a firm. From the investor's viewpoint two firms having identical amount of earnings of ₹10 per share and paying identical dividend of ₹5 per share but having different market price, are not same in terms of returns. If the market price of one firm is ₹100 and the other trades at ₹200, the returns offered by the first firm is twice as much as that of second firm.

Assuming market price of ₹500, earnings yield and dividend yield are defined and calculated for CMC Ltd for the year 2002 as given below:

$$\text{Earnings Yield} = \frac{\text{Earning Per Share (EPS)}}{\text{Market Price}} \times 100\%$$

$$= \frac{22.20}{500} \times 100\% = 4.44\%$$

$$\text{Dividend Yield} = \frac{\text{Dividend Per Share (DPS)}}{\text{Market Price}} \times 100\%$$

$$= \frac{4.00}{500} \times 100\% = 0.80\%$$

It should be noted that earnings and dividend yields keep changing since the market price changes on a continuous basis.

Price–Earnings Ratio

Price–earnings ratio, commonly referred to as P/E multiple in the financial markets, is inverse of earning yield and is calculated as

$$\text{Price Earnings Ratio} = \frac{\text{Market Price}}{\text{Earnings Per Share (EPS)}}$$

The price earnings ratio shows how much the investors are willing to pay per rupee of reported profits. It reflects the confidence the market reposes in a given firm/scrip.

P/E multiple serves as a measure of faith the investors and financial market pose in the firm and its management. Although calculated on the basis of current market price and current earnings, the P/E multiple reflects the confidence the financial markets have in the continued ability of the management and the firm to perform in future. A higher P/E multiple reflects higher level of confidence in the overall functioning of the firm in terms of growth and stability of earnings. It also encompasses factors such as liquidity, leverage, asset utilization, and future business prospects. It is taken as a summary measure of performance of the firm as market determines the price of the share factoring in the complex relationship of all the variables of performance measure.

Since markets are supposed to be operating on expected future performance rather than current performance, the P/E multiple is often calculated using expected earnings instead of current earnings. It is often taken as a benchmark of corporate image and projects the future market price for the firm.

Using current earnings and assumed market price of ₹500 for the CMC shares the P/E ratio works out to 22.5. It indicates that the market discounts the earnings of CMC about 22 times. If the P/E ratio is assumed to remain constant at existing level of about 22.5 and the next year's earnings are projected at say ₹28, the expected price after one year is 22.5 × 28 = ₹630.

$$\text{Price Earnings Ratio} = \frac{\text{Market Price}}{\text{Earnings Per Share (EPS)}}$$

$$= \frac{500}{22.20} = 22.52$$

$$\text{Expected Market Price} = \text{PE ratio} \times \text{Expected EPS}$$

$$= 22.5 \times 28 = ₹630$$

Market Value to Book Value Ratio

Book value of the share is calculated as:

$$\text{Book Value Per Share (₹/Share)} = \frac{\text{Net Worth}}{\text{Number of Shares}}$$

Book value of the shares would indicate the extent to which the profits have been retained in the business on a per share basis. Let us assume that a shareholder contributes ₹10 in the firm initially and over a period of time the firm follows the policy of distributing some of the earnings while retaining the balance in the business. By doing so the net worth increases and gets reflected in the book value. If the book value of the share is say ₹30, it would imply that for each ₹10 contributed, the firm is able to accumulate ₹20.

The ratio of market price to its book value also reflects the perception of investors towards the stock. Firms with relatively higher returns on equity generally sell at higher multiples of book value as compared to the ones with low returns.

Comparing book value to market value gives an indication of the firm's growth potential as perceived by the market. If the market value is in excess of book value (market value to book value ratio > 1.00), it indicates a positive outlook of the market in the retention of the funds by the firm.

Assuming the market price of ₹500 for CMC, the book value and the price to book value ratio for year 2002 are:

$$\text{Book Value Per Share (₹/Share)} = \frac{\text{Net Worth}}{\text{Number of shares}}$$

$$= \frac{927826}{15150} = ₹\ 61.24$$

$$\text{Price to Book Value Ratio} = \frac{\text{Market Price}}{\text{Book Value}}$$

$$= \frac{₹\ 500}{₹\ 61.24} = 8.16$$

INTERLINKING THE RATIOS: DuPont ANALYSIS

Introduced and used by DuPont Co. of USA, the DuPont analysis establishes relationship of few ratios. Return on assets (ROA) is the product of net profit margin and assets turnover as can be seen from the formula here.

Return on Total Assets

$$= \frac{\text{Profit After Tax}}{\text{Total Assets}}$$

$$= \frac{\text{Profit After Tax}}{\text{Sales}} \times \frac{\text{Sales}}{\text{Total Assets}}$$

= Net Profit Margin × Asset Turnover

The return on capital is a function of margin on sales and the speed of the utilization of the assets. It is a product of profitability and operating efficiency of the firm. Firm 'A' having net profit margin of 10% and sales to asset turnover of 3 would have a return on capital employed of 30%. Firm 'B' too can have same return on capital employed of 30% by having a net profit margin of 7.5% and asset turnover of 4. Two firms can achieve identical return on total assets by different strategies. One may have greater profit margin and lower turnover of assets, while the other may decide to compensate lower profit margin by increased turnover of assets.

Asset turnover can be defined as sales divided by total assets. For CMC Ltd, for the year 2002, the asset turnover works out to 4.40.

$$\text{Total Assets Turnover} = \frac{\text{Sales}}{\text{Total Assets}} = \frac{5653316}{1284468} = 4.40$$

Similarly fixed asset turnover can be stated as sales divided by net fixed assets and its calculation for CMC Ltd for the year 2002 is given as:

$$\text{Fixed Assets Turnover} = \frac{\text{Sales}}{\text{Fixed Assets}} = \frac{5653316}{610177} = 9.26$$

Both the ratios indicate the operational efficiency of assets. Fixed assets turnover indicates the ability of fixed assets to generate sales while total assets turnover indicates the operational efficiency of the capital employed.

The trend of fixed assets turnover and total assets turnover for CMC for five years is presented below:

CMC Ltd: Assets Turnover	*1998*	*1999*	*2000*	*2001*	*2002*
Fixed Assets Turnover	3.47	4.24	4.80	4.72	4.26
Total Assets Turnover	3.56	4.34	4.92	4.86	4.40

For a firm that is 100% equity financed, return on equity (ROE) would be same as return on assets, (ROA). If a part of equity is replaced by debt, and making a fair assumption that the (ROA) exceeds cost of debt, the return on equity would increase. ROE can be studied in greater detail by dividing it into three components as below:

Return on Equity (ROE)

$$= \frac{\text{Profit After Tax}}{\text{Net Worth}} = \frac{\text{Profit After Tax}}{\text{Assets}} \times \frac{\text{Assets}}{\text{Net Worth}}$$

$$= \frac{\text{Profit After Tax}}{\text{Assets}} \times \frac{\text{Loans + Net Worh}}{\text{Net Worth}}$$

= ROA × (1 + Debt/Equity)

= Net Profit Margin × Asset Turnover × (1 + Debt/Equity)

= Operating Margin × Operating Efficiency × Financial Leverage

ROE is said to be product of operating margin, operating efficiency, and the financial leverage. Improved margin, higher efficiency, and increased debt would lead to higher return on equity.

Dividing ROE into its components helps diagnose the problem in case the ratio is found to be inadequate or does not meet expectations of the shareholders. It provides a convenient and systematic way for the management to address the weak areas and formulate strategies to enhance the return to shareholders.

The return on equity of CMC Ltd is 36.13%. Using DuPont analysis, this ROE of 36.13% can be said to be composed of net profit margin of 5.95% on sales, rolling assets over 4.4 times a year, and with 38% of the assets financed by debt.

Return on Equity (ROE)

$$= \text{Net Profit Margin} \times \text{Asset Turnover} \times (1 + \text{Debt/Equity})$$

$$= \frac{\text{Net Profit}}{\text{Sales}} \times \frac{\text{Sales}}{\text{Assets}} \times \frac{\text{Assets}}{\text{Equity}}$$

$$= \text{Operating Margin} \times \text{Operating Efficiency} \times \text{Financial Leverage}$$

$$= 5.95\% \times 4.40 \times (1 + 0.38) = 36.13\%$$

In case ROE of 36.13% does not meet the benchmark of the industry or expectations of the investors, a further inquiry would be required as to what causes it to be low. Many options are available to improve upon the ROE. Broadly speaking, operating margin, operating efficiency, and financial leverage are subjects corresponding to marketing, production, and finance function respectively. Depending upon the feasibility and scope available, the management may adopt a suitable strategy to reward the shareholders.

STANDARDIZED FINANCIAL STATEMENTS

Analysis of financial statements poses a problem of size. Financial statements are normally not seen in isolation but instead are compared either with the past results of the firm or with the results of competing firms. The results are often evaluated against the benchmark. Such a comparison with the past or with a competing firm is made to make qualitative judgement on the performance of the firm being examined. Differing sizes of the two firms make this comparison deceptive. Let us assume that a firm's sales revenue amounts to ₹100 crore, the cost of goods sold is ₹85 crore, and its net profit is ₹15 crore. It cannot be compared directly with another firm having sales of ₹1 crore.

A common size financial statement displays all items as percentages of revenues assets. This allows easy analysis and comparison of the firm with others and is past performance

To make the comparison easier, financial statements are converted into common size. In case of a balance sheet, the total assets or total liabilities serve as the common denominator. For the profit and loss account, total sales serve as a convenient base for representing all figures. Although most firms do not report their financial statements in a common size format, such a format reduces the bias that can occur when analysing companies of differing sizes. It also allows for the analysis of a company over various time periods, revealing, for example, what percentage of sales is cost of goods sold and how that value has changed over time.

Common size balance sheet and profit and loss account of CMC Ltd for two years are presented in Tables 2-4 and 2-5, respectively.

Table 2-4 Balance Sheet of CMC Ltd - Common Size

Year	*2001*		*2002*		
	Amount	***%***	***Amount***	***%***	***Change***
Sources of Funds					
Share Capital	151,500	13.31	151,500	11.79	–1.52
Reserves & Surplus	595,257	52.31	776,326	60.44	8.13
	746,757	**65.62**	**927,826**	**72.23**	**6.61**
Secured Loans					
(a) Short-term Loans	65,000	5.71	98,060	7.63	1.92
(b) Long-term Loans	111,970	9.84	25,000	1.95	–7.89
	176,970	**15.55**	**123,060**	**9.58**	**–5.97**
Unsecured Loans					
(a) Short-term Loans	81,835	7.19	13,038	1.02	–6.18
(b) Long-term Loans	132,397	11.63	132,397	10.31	–1.33
	214,232	**18.83**	**145,435**	**11.32**	**–7.50**
Deferred Tax	—	—	88,147	6.86	6.86
Total Liabilities	**1,137,959**	**100.00**	**1,284,468**	**100.00**	**0.00**
Application of Funds					
Gross Block	1,226,555	107.79	1,215,271	94.61	–13.17
Less: Accumulated Depreciation	589,841	51.83	605,094	47.11	–4.72
Net Block	**636,714**	**55.95**	**610,177**	**47.50**	**–8.45**
Investment	**81,801**	**7.19**	**81,801**	**6.37**	**–0.82**
Current Assets, Loans & Advances					
Inventories	220,708	19.40	116,573	9.08	–10.32
Sundry Debtors	1,565,630	137.58	1,500,584	116.83	–20.76
Accrued Revenue	329,480	28.95	409,993	31.92	2.97
Loans & Advances	522,967	45.96	761,530	59.29	13.33
Cash and Bank Balances	224,117	19.69	191,850	14.94	–4.76
	2,862,902	**251.58**	**2,980,530**	**232.04**	**–19.54**
Current Liabilities & Provisions					
Sundry Creditors	1,210,517	106.38	973,298	75.77	–30.60
Other Current Liabilities	694,143	61.00	675,130	52.56	–8.44
Provisions	538,798	47.35	739,612	57.58	10.23
	2,443,458	**214.72**	**2,388,040**	**185.92**	**–28.81**
Net Current Assets	**419,444**	**36.86**	**592,490**	**46.13**	**9.27**
Total Assets	**1,137,959**	**100.00**	**1,284,468**	**100.00**	**0.00**

This makes the comparison of two years rather easy and more meaningful. We can conclude that the firm improved upon the net worth from 65% to 72% of total liabilities over the period of one year. Similarly net current assets have gone up from 37% in 2001 to 46% in 2002, registering an increase of 9% during the year. Similarly, inventories have declined from 19.4% to about 9% over the same period. Thus, reducing the balance sheet to common size helps identify areas where improvement has taken place. Weak areas too can be marked for monitoring and further study.

Common size profit and loss account of CMC Ltd indicates that income from services increased from 2.70% in 2001 to 3.30% in

2002. The purchases changed from 40% to 37%, which contributed towards improved profit of 5.95% in 2002 from 4.54% in 2001.

Table 2-5 Profit & Loss Account of CMC Ltd–Common Size

Year	*2001*		*2002*	
	Amount	*%*	*Amount*	*%*
Net Sales	5,376,763	97.30	5,466,980	96.70
Income from services	149,336	2.70	186,336	3.30
Total Revenue	**5,526,099**	**100.00**	**5,653,316**	**100.00**
Purchases	2,212,552	40.04	2,113,445	37.38
Operating & Other Expenses	2,800,947	50.69	2,928,870	51.81
Profit Before Interest, Tax and Depreciation	**512,600**	**9.28**	**611,001**	**10.81**
Depreciation	90,984	1.65	80,425	1.42
Interest (Net of interest earned)	24,496	0.44	19,524	0.35
Net Profit Before Tax	**397,120**	**7.19**	**511,052**	**9.04**
Provision for Current Tax	146200	2.65	181,579	3.21
Deferred Tax		—	–6,916	–0.12
Net Profit After Tax	**250,920**	**4.54**	**336,389**	**5.95**
Appropriations				—
Dividend	53,025	0.96	60,600	1.07
Dividend Tax	5,409	—	—	—
Transfer to Reserves and Surplus	**192,486**		**275,789**	

Common size statements, as stated earlier, are also useful for making inter-firm comparison by eliminating the size problem because all elements of balance sheet and profit and loss account are converted to a common base.

USES OF RATIO ANALYSIS

Ratio analysis is the most powerful and widely used tool for financial analysis. It provides an insight into the operations of the firm that otherwise are not apparent from mere scanning of financial statements. Some of the uses of ratio analysis are described in this section.

Analysing performance objectively

The primary use of the ratio analysis is to render meaning to the performance of the firm. People often form opinions on the performance of the firm rather subjectively. Individual biases in the opinions are inevitable. However, by ratio analysis an attempt is made to eliminate subjectivity while analysing a firm's performance. Ratios would provide the number either to contradict or reinforce subjective evaluation. Ratio analysis reduces ambiguity in judgement and provides an objective analysis by supplying data to support the view.

Financial planning

Another use of financial statement analysis is to facilitate planning for immediate future. Financial statements of the past and its analysis serve as basis for projecting future financial performance by making reasonable assumptions. The analysis also throws light on the reasonableness and realism of the assumptions made. Common size statements are specifically useful in financial planning.

Decision-making by creditors

Lenders and other creditors are often interested in the financial soundness of the firm while extending credit to the firm. These decisions are often based on the performance of the firm reflected in the financial statements. Credit rating agencies, banks, financial institutions, and creditors often rely heavily on the financial statements of the firm. These are available in public domain and enable stakeholders to take their own decision with regard to the quantum of exposure and risk associated.

Diagnostic

Analysis of financial statements in terms of ratios has found exploratory use in attempting to forecast failures of firm. Studies focused on ratios are being done to examine whether ratio analysis can predict corporate failure. If the financial condition of a firm deteriorates gradually, it is presumed that a historical analysis of various ratios can help determine the direction the firm is headed for. Comparing the historical trends of the same ratios and analysing them for the healthy and sick firms may provide clues to predict corporate failures.

Establishing a benchmark

Ratios of the same firm over an extended period of time provide an insight into the normal or acceptable value. A firm exhibiting a rising trend of debt–equity ratio demands a further investigation as to the reason behind the rising debt. It raises several questions about raising debt. Many possibilities exist. Were the profits not adequate to pursue growth, or were they raised to fund the losses and solve the liquidity problem, did the growth not result in adequate profits to keep debt level within limits, etc. History of the ratio may be used to establish a benchmark for the firm against which the subsequent performance is measured.

Another way to establish a benchmark is to find ratios of the competing firms that are regarded as better performers and to average out their ratios. This average of the competing firms serves as a benchmark. For example, leading firms in software business may have a current ratio of 2.5. This value can be taken as a benchmark not only by management of the firm but by the lenders too in determining the credit to be extended by them.

LIMITATIONS OF RATIO ANALYSIS AND FINANCIAL STATEMENTS

Analysis of financial statements, though widely used by large number and categories of people for variety of purposes, suffers from some deficiencies. Some of these limitations have been discussed in this section.

Arbitrary Selection

From the standpoint of market value, financial statements do not provide any benchmark or guidance as to which figures in the financial statements and which ratios are useful. The selection of figures and the ratios is left to the discretion of the user. Lack of standardization makes comparisons difficult. Although various regulatory and monitoring agencies issue guidelines for presentation and classification of financial data, they are often conflicting and have failed to achieve the desired standardization and uniformity.

Definitional Issues

Apart from presentation and classification, the definition of various ratios is also not standardized. There is no unanimity over the definition of ratios among various groups and stakeholders. Although the guiding principle is common, the definition of ratios is changed according to the purpose and the user. The differences in business practices of various industries and various companies in the same industry make the comparison of ratios a difficult task. Increased globalization also makes the process of standardization of presentation and classification of financial data difficult due to varying accounting standards and policies of various nations. Different practices in different countries make the task of inter-firm comparison difficult on a global basis.

Differences in Businesses, Location, Accounting

Even the firms in the same industry and same country adopt different accounting policies. Valuation of inventories and policies of depreciation are few examples where accounting statements of different firms make the comparison invalid. Further problems may be encountered due to different fiscal years used by different firms. The financial data does not remain comparable if it is not for the same period or not on the same date.

SUMMARY

The past financial performance of a firm, which is crucial to the basis of decision-making by various stakeholders, gets reflected in its financial statements. The financial statements comprise of balance sheet, profit and loss account, and cash flow statement. The balance sheet of a firm reflects its financial condition as on a particular date. The profit and loss account reflects the earning capacity and profitability of the firm during a given period, and the cash flow statement summarizes the sources of cash and its uses.

The stakeholders in a firm are varied and so are their interests in the firm. Depending upon their individual stake in the firm, these stakeholders look for a particular set of information in the financial statements. Although the common area of focus of all stakeholders remains the level of profit and profitability of the firm, there are specific areas that are of greater interest than others for a particular stakeholder. Review and analysis of financial statements reported by the firms at regular intervals provide an answer to most of the questions regarding the firm's performance sought by the different stakeholders. The technique of ratio analysis is one of the potent tools often taken recourse to for the purpose of such a review and analysis.

A financial ratio expresses the relationship between two financial variables. It facilitates analysis by eliminating the problem of size and the bias that creeps in because of it. There are five prominent categories of ratios that cover the entire gamut of firm's financial performance. These are—liquidity ratios, capital structure or leverage ratios, working capital ratios, profitability ratios, and valuation ratios.

Liquidity denotes the firm's capacity to pay its short-term obligations on time. It depends on the level of current assets owned by the firm. There are three prominent measures of liquidity—current ratio, acid test ratio, and cash ratio. Current ratio is the ratio of current assets to current liabilities. A current ratio of more than 1 indicates that the current assets are in excess of current liabilities. The higher the current ratio, the better is the firm from its lenders' perspective. Acid test ratio is a more stringent measure of liquidity than the current ratio. It is the ratio of all the current assets excluding inventory to the current liabilities. It is also referred to as quick ratio. Cash ratio is the most stringent measure of a firm's liquidity. It denotes the extent to which cash and near-cash marketable securities are sufficient to meet the current liabilities.

Capital structure ratios measure the relationship between owners' funds and borrowed funds deployed by the firm in financing its assets. A high usage of borrowed funds brings down the cost of financing and increases returns to shareholders, but also makes the firm more risky. These ratios can be further subdivided into structural ratios and coverage ratios. Debt–equity ratio, debt to asset ratio, total outside liabilities to net worth, and total outside liabilities to assets are structural ratios providing insight to the capital structure. Interest coverage ratio, and the debt service coverage ratio are the most prominent measures of a firm's ability to service debt and are categorized as coverage ratios.

Debt–equity ratio expresses the relationship between borrowed funds and its own funds. Generally a large value of debt ratio is not favoured as the increased dosage of debt makes the firm more vulnerable to economical and business cycles. Coverage ratios indicate the cushion available for the firm to service its debt obligation. Higher the value of coverage ratios, safer is the firm from the lenders' perspective. Interest coverage ratio indicates the extent to which profits (PBIT) are sufficient to pay existing interest obligations. Higher ratio provides a cushion to lenders. Debt service coverage ratio measures the ability of the firm to meet its total debt obligations (both interest and principal).

Working capital ratios denote the efficiency of firms in handling its operations. The more quickly a firm turns over different current assets eventually into cash, more efficient is the firm. Inventory turnover, debtors' turnover, and creditors' turnover are the key measures of working capital management. Current assets turnover ratio indicates how many times the current assets have been turned over into sales in a given period (usually a year). An increasing ratio is a sign of improving efficiency. Inventory turnover ratio expresses the relationship between cost of goods sold and inventory. It denotes the efficiency in inventory management. An increasing ratio signifies better inventory management. Debtors' turnover ratio expresses the relationship between sales and debtors. It reflects the efficiency with which the firm is able to convert its debtors into cash. Improvement in the ratio indicates better receivables management. The creditors' turnover ratio reflects the number of times average dues to the suppliers is settled. Higher the turnover, lower is the payment period offered by the suppliers.

Profitability ratios refer to those financial metrics that are used to assess a business's ability to generate earnings. Some examples of profitability ratios are profit margin, return on capital employed, return on assets, return on equity, etc. Generally a higher profitability ratio relative to a competitor's ratio or the same ratio from a previous period is indicative of better performance. Contribution refers to the margin available once the variable costs have been covered. As this margin is used to meet the fixed costs, a larger margin is desirable. Gross profit margin is the excess of total sales revenue over its cost of goods sold. It reflects production efficiency. A higher gross margin provides more cushion to meet the overheads. Net margin is arrived by deducting from revenues all direct and indirect expenses. Net margin as a percentage of sale reflects the overall efficiency of the business. Return on capital employed (ROCE), also known as return on investment (ROI), provides a measure of the efficiency of capital, while the return on equity (ROE) is the return that the firm has been able to earn on the equity financed portion of its capital. Increasing ROE denotes improving efficiency of the firm in handling its shareholders' funds. Earnings per share (EPS) is the return (profit) earned on a per share basis. It is one of the prominent measures of financial performance. The part of EPS that the firm proposes to distribute to the shareholders is known as dividend per share (DPS).

Valuation ratios judge the value the stock market places on any given company. The prominent valuation ratios are earnings and dividends yield, price earnings, and price to book ratios. Expressing the earnings and the dividends as a percentage of market price gives earnings and dividends yields respectively. The price earnings ratio shows how much the investors are willing to pay per rupee of reported profits. It reflects the confidence that the market reposes in a given firm/scrip. The ratio of market price of a stock to its book value also reflects the perception of investors towards the stock. Firms with relatively higher returns on equity generally sell at higher multiples of book value as compared to the ones with low returns.

DuPont analysis establishes the relationship of a few important ratios. Such an analysis enables the management to address the weak areas and formulate strategies to create value for shareholders. As per the analysis, return on assets (ROA) is product of net profit margin and assets turnover, i.e., the utilization of assets. Return on equity is a function of operating margin, operating efficiency and financial leverage. Improved margin, high efficiency, and increased debt lead to higher return on equity.

A common size statement is a financial statement that displays all items as percentages of a common base figure. This allows for easy analysis between companies or between time periods of a company. The values on the common size statement are expressed as percentages of a statement component such as revenue or assets.

Ratio analysis helps in an objective analysis of financial performance. It also aids financial planning and decision-making by creditors besides acting as a diagnostic tool and setting a benchmark for performance. However, due to some limitations on account of arbitrariness in the selection and variations in the definitions of the different ratios, they should be used with caution.

KEY TERMS

Balance sheet Balance sheet is financial position of a firm as on a date providing details of sources and uses of fund.

Profit and loss account P&L account contains the summary of operations of a firm in a given period providing details of revenue, cost, and profit.

Reserves and surplus The amount of funds belonging to shareholders/owners of the firm is called reserves and surplus.

Current liabilities Liabilities of the firm that are payable in short-term, usually within next 12 months by convention are current liabilities.

Current assets Assets of the firm that can be converted into cash readily and in short-term, usually within next 12 months by convention are current assets.

Contingent liabilities Liabilities that have not crystallized and may arise upon the happening of an event which is not in the control of the firm are called contingent liabilities.

Net working capital (NWC) NWC is excess of current assets over current liabilities. It also represents the part of working capital financed from long-term sources of funds.

Liquidity Liquidity refers to the ability of the firm to pay short-term liabilities from assets readily convertible into cash.

Leverage Leverage is the extent of debt in relation to owned funds in financing of the firm.

Debt coverage Debt coverage reflects the ability of the firm to service its debts.

Value addition Excess of revenue over raw materials purchased from outside is value addition and reflects the ability of the firm to add value to its finished products.

Contribution margin Contribution margin is the excess of revenue over variable cost and represents firm's ability to recover fixed cost and provide profit.

Return on capital employed (ROCE) ROCE is the percentage of profit over the capital employed and reflects productivity of capital.

Return on equity (ROE) ROE the return on the capital provided by the shareholders after providing for the returns to debt holders.

P/E ratio P/E ratio is the ratio of market price to the earnings per share and reflects market perception of the firm's ability to produce earnings

KEY FORMULAE

Current Ratio $= \dfrac{\text{Current Assets}}{\text{Current Liabilities}}$

Acid Test or Quick Ratio $= \dfrac{\text{Current Assets} - \text{Inventory}}{\text{Current Liabilities}}$

Cash Ratio $= \dfrac{\text{Cash} + \text{Marketable Securities}}{\text{Current Liabilities}}$

Debt Equity Ratio $= \dfrac{\text{Long-term Debt}}{\text{Net Worth}}$

Debt to Assets Ratio $= \dfrac{\text{Long-term Debt}}{\text{Net Assets}}$

TOL to Net Worth Ratio $= \dfrac{\text{Total Outside Liabilities}}{\text{Net Worth}}$

TOL to Assets Ratio $= \dfrac{\text{Total Outside Liabilities}}{\text{Net Assets}}$

Interest Cover $= \dfrac{\text{Profit Before Interest and Taxes}}{\text{Interest Obligation}}$

Debt Service Coverage Ratio

$$= \frac{\text{PBIT} + \text{Depreciation} \pm \text{Non-cash Expense/Income}}{\text{Interest Obligation} + \dfrac{\text{Loan instalment}}{1 - \text{Tax Rate}}}$$

Current Assets Turnover Ratio $= \dfrac{\text{Sales}}{\text{Average Current Assets}}$

Current Assets Holding Period

$$= \frac{\text{Average Current Assets}}{\text{Sales}} \times 365 \text{ days}$$

Net Current Assets Turnover Ratio $= \dfrac{\text{Sales}}{\text{Average Net Current Assets}}$

Inventory Turnover Ratio $= \dfrac{\text{Cost of Goods Sold}}{\text{Average Inventory}}$

Inventory Holding Period $= \dfrac{\text{Average Inventory}}{\text{COGS}} \times 365 \text{ days}$

Raw Material Inventory Turnover Ratio

$$= \frac{\text{Raw Material Consumption}}{\text{Average Raw Material Inventory}}$$

Raw Material Inventory Holding Period days

$$= \frac{\text{Average Raw Material Inventory}}{\text{Raw Material Consumption}} \times 365$$

Work-in-Process (WIP) Turnover Ratio $= \dfrac{\text{Cost of Production}}{\text{Average WIP Inventory}}$

WIP inventory Holding Period days

$$= \frac{\text{Average WIP Inventory}}{\text{Cost of Production}} \times 365$$

Finished Goods (FG) Turnover Ratio $= \dfrac{\text{Cost of Sales}}{\text{Average FG Inventory}}$

FG inventory Holding Period days

$$= \frac{\text{Average FG Inventory}}{\text{Cost of Sales}} \times 365$$

Debtors' Turnover Ratio $= \dfrac{\text{Sales}}{\text{Average Debtors}}$

Average Collection Period $= \dfrac{\text{Average Debtors}}{\text{Sales}} \times 365 \text{ days}$

Earning Yield $= \dfrac{\text{Earning Per Share}}{\text{Market Price}} \times 100\%$

Dividend Yield $= \dfrac{\text{Dividend Per Share}}{\text{Market Price}} \times 100\%$

Price Earnings Ratio $= \dfrac{\text{Market Price}}{\text{Earning Per Share}}$

Price to Book Value Ratio $= \dfrac{\text{Market Price}}{\text{Book Value}}$

Gross Profit Margin

$$= \frac{\text{Sales} - \text{Cost of Goods Sold}}{\text{Sales}} \times 100\% \quad = \frac{\text{EBIT}}{\text{Sales}} \times 100\%$$

Net Profit Margin $= \dfrac{\text{Profit After Tax}}{\text{Sales}} \times 100\%$

Return on Capital employed = $\frac{\text{EBIT}(1-T)}{\text{Net Assets}} \times 100\%$

Return on Equity = $\frac{\text{Profit After Tax}}{\text{Net Worth}} \times 100\%$

Earning Per Share (₹/Share) = $\frac{\text{PAT}}{\text{Number of Shares}}$

Dividend Per Share (₹/Share) = $\frac{\text{Dividend}}{\text{Number of shares}}$

PRACTICE PROBLEMS

1. Cash Flow Statement

Balance sheet for two consecutive years as on 31 March, P&L account for the year ended as on 31 March 2007 and other relevant financial information of Alpaso Ltd are given below. Prepare the cash flow statement for the firm for the year 2006-07 and analyse its cash flow position.

Liabilities & Equity	*Mar-07 (₹ in lakh)*	*Mar-06 (₹ in lakh)*
Equity Share Capital	1100	1000
Reserves & Surplus	400	200
P&L Balance	270	250
L.T borrowings	600	500
Current Liabilities	270	200
Provision for taxation	240	150
Proposed Dividends	110	100
Total	**2990**	**2400**
Assets		
Gross Fixed Assets	1500	1200
Less: Accumulated Dep.	780	600
Net Fixed Assets	720	600
Long-term Investments	500	400
Inventories	380	200
Debtors	240	160
Cash and Bank Balance	100	60
Loans and Advances	1050	980
Total	**2990**	**2400**

P&L Account for the year 2006-07

Income	*(₹ in lakh)*
Sales	2520
Other income	304
Stock Adjustment	36
Total	**2860**
Expenditure	
Raw Material consumed	1430
Manufacturing expenses	280
Administrative expenses	160
Selling & distribution expenses	130
Depreciation	180
Interest	110
Total	**2290**
Profit before tax (PBT)	570
Provision for Taxes	240
Profit after tax (PAT)	330
P&L at the beginning of the year	250
Profit available for appropriation	580
Transfer to reserves	200
Proposed dividends (incl. div. tax)	100
Balance profit carried to B/S	270

The following additional information has been provided regarding the firm:

(i) Current liabilities denote amount that is payable to suppliers.
(ii) Raw materials constitute 80% of the inventory balance of the firm.
(iii) Loans and advance include income tax paid ₹240 lakh (previous year ₹150 lakh).
(iv) During 2006-07 10 lakh of equity shares of ₹10 each were issued at par. Long-term loans raised during the year amounled is ₹160 lakh
(v) The interest shown in the P&L account has actually been paid for in cash and other income is realized in cash.

Solution

Step 1: Computation of cash from operation

Although there are two methods (direct and indirect) for computing cash from operations, we will use here the indirect method. External analysts and other external stakeholders use indirect method to analyse the cash flow position of the firm as they do not have access to cash receipts and payments information. They have to dig out information hidden in the financial statements indirectly. In any case the method that we we use does not make a difference as the result of the two methods is same.

(All figures in ₹ lakh)

PBT		570
Add: Depreciation	180	
Add: Interest	110	
Less: Other income	–304	–14
Operating profit before WC changes		556
Adjustments for WC changes		
Increase in inventories	–180	
Increase in debtors	–80	
Increase in current liabilities	70	–190
Cash generated from operations		366
Less: Income tax paid		–240
Net cash flow from operations		**126**

Step 2: Computation of cash from investing activities

Cash paid to acquire fixed assets	–300	
Cash paid to acquire long term investments	–100	
Cash receipts from repayments of loans and advances made to third parties	20	
Receipts of other incomes	304	
Net cash flow from investing activities		**–76**

Step 3: Computation of cash from financing activities

Proceeds from equity issue	100	
Raising of L.T loans	160	
Repayment of L.T loans	–60	
Interest paid	–110	
Dividend paid (inclusive of div. tax)	–100	
Net cash flow from financing activities		**–10**

Step 4: Reconciliation of cash flows

Cash flow *from operating activities*	126
Cash flow *from investing activities*	–76
Cash flow *from financing activities*	–10
Net Increase in cash & cash equivalents	40
Add: Cash and bank balance at the beginning of 2006-07	60
Cash and bank balance at the end of 2006-07	100

Interpretation of Cash Flow Statement

Although the firm has been able to earn cash surplus from its operations but this surplus is not sufficient enough to service the capital of the firm.

Cash flow from operating activities	(126 lakh)
Interest payments	(110 lakh)
Dividend payments	(100 lakh)
Cash shortfall (126 – 210) =	84 lakh

This shortfall has been compensated by the receipt from other incomes of ₹304 lakh. Although the firm has been, in the year 2006-07, able to pay its dividends and interest from its other income but this may not be sustainable in future. To be in a sound cash position, a firm should be able to not only service its capital from the cash surplus from its operations but should also partly finance its investments. But in this case the firm is expanding rapidly as is evident from the growth in its assets due to which it is facing a cash crunch.

Receipts from other incomes	304 lakh
Less: Cash shortfall	84 lakh
= surplus for investment purposes	220 lakh

Return from investment in shares/ securities of other firms are impressive. The firm has earned an average return of around 70%. This has prompted the firm to make further investments in securities to the tune of 100 lakh during the year. The firm has also acquired fixed assets of ₹300 lakh. This has been financed as follows:

Acquisition of fixed assets	300
Long term investments	100
Total cash required (a)	**400**
Financed by:	
Surplus from other income	220
Proceeds from issue of shares	100
Long-term loan (net)	100
Total finances available (b)	**420**
Surplus cash (b) – (a)	20
Add: Receipts from third parties	20
Net additions to cash and cash equivalents during the year	40

Cash receipts from repayment of loans and advances made to third parties has been calculated as follows:

	Mar-07	Mar-06
Loans and advances	1050	980
Less: Advance tax (as it has already been included in operating activities)	240	150
= Other loans and advances	810	830
Decrease in loans and advances during the year	20	—
	830	830

2. Profitability and Liquidity Ratios

Given below are the financial statements of Safal enterprises. Using the tool of ratio analysis comment on the profitability and liquidity position of the firm for the year 2006-07. Total number of shares outstanding for the firm is 2.69 crores. In view of growth opportunities in the near future the firm has been maintaining a policy of 45% payout.

Summarized P&L A/c of Safal Enterprises
for the year ended 31 March

	2006	2007
	(₹ in crores)	
Sales	132.00	144.00
Other income	12.00	15.00
Cost of Sales	102.96	110.02
Gross Margin	**29.04**	**33.98**
Operating expenses		
Administration	12.44	14.36
Selling and Distribution	4.42	5.36
Profit before interest and tax (PBIT)	**24.18**	**29.26**
Interest	3.00	4.01
Profit before tax (PBT)	**21.18**	**25.26**
Provision for taxes	7.94	9.47
Profit after tax (PAT)	**13.24**	**15.79**

Balance Sheet of Safal Enterprises as on

	31/03/06	31/03/07
	(₹ in crores)	
Assets		
Fixed Assets (Net)	31.25	37.50
Current Assets		
Inventory	14.56	16.64
Accounts receivable	13.20	15.43
Cash	1.50	1.75
Less: Current Liabilities	8.55	11.25
Net Current Assets	20.71	22.57
Total Assets	**51.96**	**60.07**
Liabilities and owners' equity		
Share capital	27.00	27.00
Reserves and surplus	4.96	6.36
Debt (long-term)	20.00	26.71
Total	**51.96**	**60.07**

Solution

Various ratios of profitability and liquidity of Safal Enterprises are as given below:

Profitability ratios	***Years***	
	2005-06	**2006-07**
Gross Margin $=\left(\frac{\text{Gross Margin}}{\text{Sales}}\right)\times 100$	$\left(\frac{29.04}{132}\right)\times 100 = 22.00\%$	$\left(\frac{33.98}{144}\right)\times 100 = 23.60\%$
Net Margin $=\left(\frac{\text{Net Margin}}{\text{Sales}}\right)\times 100$	$\left(\frac{13.24}{132}\right)\times 100 = 10.03\%$	$\left(\frac{15.79}{144}\right)\times 100 = 10.96\%$
Expenses Ratio $=\left(\frac{\text{Expenses}}{\text{Sales}}\right)\times 100$ Expenses = Cost of Sales + operating expenses	$\left(\frac{102.96+16.86}{132}\right)\times 100 = 90.77\%$	$\left(\frac{110.02+19.72}{144}\right)\times 100 = 90.09\%$
Return on Capital Employed (ROCE) % ROCE $=\left(\frac{\text{PBIT} - \text{Provision for tax}}{\text{Total assets}}\right)\times 100$	$\left(\frac{24.18-7.94}{51.96}\right)\times 100 = 31.25\%$	$\left(\frac{29.26-9.47}{60.07}\right)\times 100 = 32.94\%$
Return on Equity (ROE) % ROE $=\left(\frac{\text{PAT}}{\text{Share Capital} + \text{Reserves \& Surplus}}\right)\times 100$	$\left(\frac{13.24}{27+4.96}\right)\times 100 = 41.43\%$	$\left(\frac{15.79}{27+6.36}\right)\times 100 = 47.33\%$
Earnings Per Share (EPS in ₹) EPS $=\frac{\text{PAT}}{\text{No. of shares outstanding}}$	$\frac{13.24}{2.69}$ = ₹4.92	$\frac{15.79}{2.69}$ = ₹5.87
Dividend Per Share (DPS in ₹) DPS = EPS × Pay out ratio	4.92 ×0.45 = ₹2.21	5.87 × 0.45 = ₹2.64
Liquidity ratios		
Current Ratio $=\frac{\text{Current Assets}}{\text{Current Liabilities}}$	$\frac{29.26}{8.55} = 3.42$	$\frac{33.82}{11.25} = 3.01$
Acid Test Ratio $=\frac{\text{Current Assets} - \text{Inventory}}{\text{Current Liabilities}}$	$\frac{29.26-14.56}{8.55} = 1.72$	$\frac{33.82-16.64}{11.25} = 1.53$
Cash Ratio $=\frac{\text{Cash} + \text{Marketable Securities}}{\text{Current Liabilities}}$	$\frac{1.5}{8.55} = 0.18$	$\frac{1.75}{11.25} = 0.16$

Analysis

Profitability performance of the firm as indicated by the profitability ratios has improved in the year 2006-07. Both gross margin and net margin have improved marginally (by 1.6% and 0.93% respectively) during the year. Similarly ROCE, EPS and DPS have improved during the financial year 2006-07.This improvement in the profitability performance of the firm has been mainly on account of better cost management by the firm. The firm has been able to bring down its cost of sales from 78% of the sales in 2005-06 to 76.4% in 2006-07. Another noteworthy aspect of firm's profitability performance has been a significant increase in ROE from 41.42% in 2005-06 to 47.32% in 2006-07. This has been, inter alia, due to the benefit of financial leverage. The increased usage of long-term debt by ₹6.71 crores in the financial year 2006-07 has magnified the return to the equity shareholders.

The profitability performance of Safal Enterprises, though satisfactory, should be analysed on a longer time scale and also compared with that of other comparable firms in the industry to arrive at more meaningful conclusion.

Liquidity position of Safal Enterprises in the year 2006-07 has weakened compared to what it was in 2005-06. This is evident from the fall in current ratio, acid test ratio, and cash ratio for the firm. All the three ratios have declined marginally in 2006-07. Before commenting whether it is good or bad for the financial health of the firm we need to find out the reasons for this decline.

As can be seen from the financial statements of the firm, the decline in liquidity position has to do more with the financing side than the investment side of the balance sheet. During the period 2006-07 aggregate current assets of the firm grew by around 16% as compared to total current liabilities that saw a growth of approximately 32%. This disproportionate change in the current liabilities has brought down the liquidity ratios for the firm during the year 2006-07.

The liquidity ratios of the firm are still on the higher side if compared with the benchmark (current ratio of 1.33 and the acid test ratio of 1). Reduction in liquidity ratio is not always bad and also the increase in the liquidity ratio is not always good. Since liquidity has opportunity cost, too high a liquidity may not be good for firms as it may be on account of unwarranted tying up of funds and may adversely affect the profits.

3. Capital Structure Ratios

The summarized assets and liabilities of G&T Ltd for three consecutive financial years ending 31st March are as follows:

Assets	*Mar 2005*	*Mar 2006*	*Mar 2007*
		₹ crore	
Gross fixed assets	2100.89	2582.13	3340.59
Less: Cumulative depreciation	1014.76	974.44	1112.83
Net fixed assets	1086.13	1607.69	2227.76
Investments	969.97	2027.80	3106.60
Deferred tax assets	123.95	132.51	164.69
Current assets loans and advances			
Cash & bank balance	828.02	583.23	1094.43
Inventories	2261.26	2210.27	3001.14
Receivables	5201.56	6110.82	7220.99
Loans & advances	495.53	522.88	565.94
	8786.37	9427.20	11882.50
Less: Current liabilities	5559.74	6913.68	9340.42
Net current assets	3226.63	2513.52	2542.08
Deferred revenue expenditure	39.89	21.98	9.84
Total assets	**5446.57**	**6303.50**	**8050.97**

Liabilities	*Mar 2005*	*Mar 2006*	*Mar 2007*
		₹ crore	
Net worth			
Paid up equity capital (net of forfeited capital)	25.98	27.48	56.65
Reserves & surplus	3343.15	4612.69	5711.78
Long-term borrowings	1858.96	1453.54	2077.66
Deferred tax liability	218.48	209.79	204.88
Total liabilities	**5446.57**	**6303.50**	**8050.97**

The summary of income statements for three consecutive financial years of G&T stood as follows:

	2004-05	*2005-06*	*2006-07*
Income	13748.26	15198.63	18041.13
Expenditure	12446.81	13886.47	16037.68
Profit before tax (PBT)	1301.45	1312.16	2003.45
Tax	455.51	492.06	751.29
Profit after tax (PAT)	845.94	820.10	1252.16
Depreciation (included in expenditure above)	93.25	115.98	171.45
Interest	139.42	109.02	155.82
Loan repayment	50.05	125.25	112.60

The tax rate applicable to the firm is 37.5%.

Solution

Computation of Capital Structure Ratios

	2004-05	*2005-06*	*2006-07*
Debt Equity Ratio $= \frac{\text{Long Term Debt}}{\text{Net Worth}}$	$\frac{1858.96}{25.98 + 3343.15} = \mathbf{0.55}$	$\frac{1453.54}{27.48 + 4612.69} = \mathbf{0.31}$	$\frac{2077.66}{56.65 + 5711.78} = \mathbf{0.36}$
Debt to Assets Ratio $= \frac{\text{Long Term Debt}}{\text{Net Assets}}$	$\frac{1858.96}{5446.57} = \mathbf{0.34}$	$\frac{1453.54}{6303.50} = \mathbf{0.23}$	$\frac{2077.66}{8050.97} = \mathbf{0.26}$
TOL to Net Worth Ratio $= \frac{\text{Total Outside Liabilities}}{\text{Net Worth}}$	$\frac{1858.96 + 218.48 + 5559.74}{25.98 + 33343.15}$ $= \mathbf{2.26}$	$\frac{1453.54 + 209.79 + 6913.68}{6303.50}$ $= \mathbf{2.27}$	$\frac{2077.66 + 204.88 + 9340.42}{56.65 + 5711.78}$ $= \mathbf{2.01}$
TOL to Assets Ratio $= \frac{\text{Total Outside Liabilities}}{\text{Net Assets}}$	$\frac{1858.96 + 218.48 + 5559.74}{5446.57}$ $= \mathbf{1.40}$	$\frac{1453.54 + 209.79 + 6913.68}{6303.50}$ $= \mathbf{1.36}$	$\frac{2077.66 + 204.88 + 9340.42}{8050.97}$ $= \mathbf{1.44}$
Interest Coverage Ratio (ICR) $= \frac{\text{Profit Before Interest and Taxes (PBIT)}}{\text{Interest Obligation}}$	$\frac{1301.45 + 139.42}{139.42} = \mathbf{10.33\ times}$	$\frac{1312.16 + 109.02}{109.02} = \mathbf{13.04\ times}$	$\frac{2003.45 + 155.82}{155.82} = \mathbf{13.86\ times}$
Debt Service Coverage ratio (DSCR) $= \left(\frac{\text{PBIT} + \text{Depreciation} \pm \text{Non Cash Expense/Income}}{\text{Interest Obligation} + \frac{\text{Loan Instalment}}{1 - \text{Tax Rate}}} \right)$	$\frac{((1301.45 + 139.42) + 93.25)}{139.42 + \left(\frac{50.05}{1 - 0.375}\right)}$ $= \mathbf{6.99}$	$\frac{((1312.16 + 109.02) + 115.98)}{109.02 + \left(\frac{125.25}{1 - 0.375}\right)}$ $= \mathbf{4.97}$	$\frac{((2003.45 + 155.82) + 171.45)}{155.82 + \left(\frac{112.60}{1 - 0.375}\right)}$ $= \mathbf{6.96}$

Analysis

G&T's dependence on debt as a source of financing has come down. Only 26% of the assets of the firm have been debt financed in the 2006-07 compared to 34% in 2004-05. The increased reserves and surplus has reduced the firm's dependence on debt financing. This declining level of debt in the firm's capital structure not only makes the existing lenders safer but it also increases the company's debt raising capacity. Although the total outstanding liabilities to assets ratio has gone up in 2006-07 to 1.44 from 1.36 in the preceding year, this is not a cause of alarm as it has been due to increased long-term borrowings and current liabilities during the year. In fact usage of debt within manageable proportion is good for the financial health of the firm as it gives the shareholders the benefit of leverage. In any case the firm is still having a low debt capital.

The interest coverage ratio of the firm has increased from 10.23 times to 13.86 times. This improves the cushion available for lenders. Although the debt service coverage ratio has declined marginally but this decline is not on account of decline in profits but it is due to increased interest out go on account increased borrowing of the firm in 2006-07. Although solvency position of the firm is satisfactory, it should be also evaluated against the industry performance during the period.

4. Turnover Ratios

Summarized financial statements of Matrix Ltd for two consecutive years are given below. Analyse the firm's performance using the turnover ratios.

Summarized Income Statement of Matrix Ltd as on 31 March

(₹ *in lakh*)

	Previous year	*Current year*
Sales	150	164
Less: Sales returns	4.12	3.26
Net Sales	145.88	160.74
Cost of sales	97.5	106.60
Gross Profit	48.38	54.14
Administrative Overheads	3.46	3.14
Selling and distribution overheads	4.61	4.15
Interest and other non operating expenses	0.168	0.19
Operating income	40.14	46.65
Other incomes	2.34	3.12
Profit Before Tax (PBT)	42.48	49.77
Tax	14.86	17.42
Profit After Tax (PAT)	**27.61**	**32.35**

Summarized Balance Sheet of Matrix Ltd as on 31 March

(₹ *in lakh*)

	Previous Year	*Current Year*
Assets		
Cash and bank balance	1.05	1.10
Marketable securities	4.75	5.25
Sundry Debtors	6.45	7.25
Stock	8.75	10.45
Prepaid expenses	1.25	2.50
Current Assets	22.25	26.55
Fixed Assets (Net)	83.50	98.20
Total Assets	**105.75**	**124.75**
Liabilities and Owners Equity		
Sundry Creditors	8.75	9.25
Notes payable	7.00	10.50
Long term debt	15.00	30.00
Equity	75.00	75.00
Total Liabilities and Shareholders' equity	**105.75**	**124.75**

Solution

Computation of Turnover Ratios*

Ratios	*Previous year*	*Current year*
Assets turnover $\frac{\text{Sales}}{\text{Total Assets}}$	$\frac{145.88}{105.75} = 1.38$	$\frac{160.74}{124.75} = 1.29$
Fixed assets turnover $\frac{\text{Sales}}{\text{Fixed Assets (net)}}$	$\frac{145.88}{83.50} = 1.75$	$\frac{160.74}{98.20} = 1.64$
Current assets turnover* $\frac{\text{Sales}}{\text{Average current assets}}$	$\frac{145.88}{22.25} = 6.56$	$\frac{160.74}{26.55} = 6.05$
Current assets holding period* (days) $\left(\frac{\text{Average current assets}}{\text{Sales}}\right) \times 365$	$\left(\frac{22.25}{145.88}\right) \times 365 = 55.67$	$\left(\frac{26.55}{160.74}\right) \times 365 = 60.29$
Inventory turnover ratio* $\frac{\text{Cost of goods sold}}{\text{Average inventory}}$	$\frac{97.5}{8.75} = 11.14$	$\frac{106.6}{10.45} = 10.20$
Inventory holding period* (days) $\left(\frac{\text{Average inventory}}{\text{Cost of goods sold}}\right) \times 365$	$\left(\frac{8.75}{97.5}\right) \times 365 = 32.76$	$\left(\frac{10.45}{106.6}\right) \times 365 = 35.78$
Debtors turnover ratio* $\frac{\text{Sales}}{\text{Average debtors}}$	$\frac{145.88}{6.45} = 22.62$	$\frac{160.74}{7.25} = 22.17$
Average collection period* (days) $\left(\frac{\text{Average debtors}}{\text{Sales}}\right) \times 365$	$\left(\frac{6.45}{145.88}\right) \times 365 = 16.14$	$\left(\frac{7.25}{160.74}\right) \times 365 = 16.46$

*Since the data given is only for two years getting the average figures for both the years is not possible hence year end values have been taken for the purpose of ratio computation.

Analysis

All the turnover ratios, as can be seen in the table above, indicate a decline in the firm's performance. Does this necessarily mean that the firm's efficiency in the utilisation of its resources has deteriorated? Is the decline in the turnover ratio always bad? No, wherever the decline is on account of expansion in the assets it denotes the growth which may soon transform into better turnover. Whenever a firm infuses more resources into the business the turnover ratios come down, at least initially. As can be seen in case of Matrix Ltd, the growth in its assets during the current year far exceeds the growth in sales (sales growth during the period was about 10% while the growth in current assets was 19% and the growth in fixed assets was around 18% making it an average rate of 17% growth in assets). This is a typical case where the firm anticipating an expansion in sales increases its capacity. This may temporarily have an adverse impact on the efficiency of the business due to pile up of current assets but later when this value gets unlocked it benefits the business by increasing the profitability and also improving efficiency.

5. Common-size Financial Statements

Prepare a common-size income statement and balance sheet of Matrix Ltd from the financials given in Problem 4 above. Analyse the firm's financial performance using the common-size statements.

Solution

Common-Size Income Statement

	Previous Year	Current Year
	(%)	
Net Sales	100	100
Cost of sales $\frac{\text{Cost of Sales}}{\text{Net Sales}}\times 100$	$\frac{97.5}{145.88}\times 100$ = 66.84	$\frac{106.60}{160.74}\times 100$ = 66.32
Gross Profit $\frac{\text{Gross Profit}}{\text{Net Sales}}\times 100$	$\frac{48.38}{145.88}\times 100$ = 33.16	$\frac{54.14}{160.74}\times 100$ = 33.68
Administrative Overheads $\frac{\text{Administrative overheads}}{\text{Net Sales}}\times 100$	$\frac{3.46}{145.88}\times 100$ = 2.37	$\frac{3.14}{160.74}\times 100$ = 1.95
Selling and distribution overheads $\frac{\text{Selling and distribution Overheads}}{\text{Net Sales}}\times 100$	$\frac{4.61}{145.88}\times 100$ = 3.20	$\frac{4.15}{160.74}\times 100$ =2.58
Interest and other non operating expenses $\frac{\text{Interest and other non operating Expenses}}{\text{Net Sales}}\times 100$	$\frac{0.168}{145.88}\times 100$ = 0.115	$\frac{0.19}{160.74}\times 100$ = 0.123
Operating income $\frac{\text{Operating income}}{\text{Net Sales}}\times 100$	$\frac{40.14}{145.88}\times 100$ = 27.52	$\frac{46.65}{160.74}\times 100$ = 29.02
Other incomes $\frac{\text{Other income}}{\text{Net Sales}}\times 100$	$\frac{2.34}{145.88}\times 100$ = 1.60	$\frac{3.12}{160.74}\times 100$ = 1.94
Profit Before Tax (PBT) $\frac{\text{Profit before tax}}{\text{Net Sales}}\times 100$	$\frac{42.48}{145.88}\times 100$ = 29.12	$\frac{49.77}{160.74}\times 100$ = 30.96
Tax $\frac{\text{Tax}}{\text{Net Sales}}\times 100$	$\frac{14.86}{145.88}\times 100$ = 10.19	$\frac{17.42}{160.74}\times 100$ = 10.83
Profit After Tax (PAT) $\frac{\text{Profit after tax}}{\text{Net Sales}}\times 100$	$\frac{27.61}{145.88}\times 100$ =18.93	$\frac{32.35}{160.74}\times 100$ = 20.13

Common-Size Balance Sheet

	Previous Year	Current Year
	(%)	
ASSETS		
Cash and bank balance $\frac{\text{Cash and bank balance}}{\text{Total assets}}\times 100$	$\frac{1.05}{105.75}\times 100$ = 0.99	$\frac{1.10}{124.75}\times 100$ = 0.88
Marketable securities $\frac{\text{Marketable Securities}}{\text{Total assets}}\times 100$	$\frac{4.75}{105.75}\times 100$ = 4.49	$\frac{5.25}{124.75}\times 100$ = 4.21
Sundry Debtors $\frac{\text{Sundry Debtors}}{\text{Total assets}}\times 100$	$\frac{6.45}{105.75}\times 100$ = 6.10	$\frac{7.25}{124.75}\times 100$ = 5.81
Stock $\frac{\text{Stock}}{\text{Total assets}}\times 100$	$\frac{8.75}{105.75}\times 100$ = 8.27%	$\frac{10.45}{124.75}\times 100$ = 8.38%
Prepaid expenses $\frac{\text{Prepaid expenses}}{\text{Total assets}}\times 100$	$\frac{1.25}{105.75}\times 100$ = 1.18	$\frac{2.50}{124.75}\times 100$ = 2.00
Current Assets $\frac{\text{Current assets}}{\text{Total assets}}\times 100$	$\frac{22.25}{105.75}\times 100$ = 21.04	$\frac{26.55}{124.75}\times 100$ = 21.28
Fixed Assets (Net) $\frac{\text{Fixed assets (net)}}{\text{Total assets}}\times 100$	$\frac{83.50}{105.75}\times 100$ = 78.96	$\frac{98.20}{124.75}\times 100$ = 78.72
Total Assets	**100.00**	**100.00**
LIABILITIES AND OWNERS EQUITY		
Sundry Creditors $\frac{\text{Sundry creditors}}{\text{Total liabilities}}\times 100$	$\frac{8.75}{105.75}\times 100$ = 8.27	$\frac{9.25}{124.75}\times 100$ = 7.41
Notes payable $\frac{\text{Notes Payable}}{\text{Total liabilities}}\times 100$	$\frac{7.00}{105.75}\times 100$ = 6.62	$\frac{10.50}{124.75}\times 100$ = 8.42
Long term debt $\frac{\text{Long term debt}}{\text{Total liabilities}}\times 100$	$\frac{15.00}{105.75}\times 100$ = 14.18	$\frac{30.00}{124.75}\times 100$ = 24.05
Equity $\frac{\text{Equity}}{\text{Total liabilities}}\times 100$	$\frac{75.00}{105.75}\times 100$ = 70.92	$\frac{75.00}{124.75}\times 100$ = 60.12
Total Liabilities and Shareholder's equity	**100.00**	**100.00**

Analysis

Profitability performance of the firm has improved during the current year. PAT (as a % of sales) has gone up from 18.93% to 20.13%. This improvement has been on account of increased operating income and non-operating income of the firm indicating better performance from both core and non-core business operations of the firm.

While the sales grew by around 10% and the other income grew by 33% the total expenses came down from 72.52% of sales to 70.97%. This combination of increased growth in revenues and decrease in expenses gave a boost to the firm's Profit after tax from 18.93% of sales to 20.13%. Overall the profitability position for the firm appears to be satisfactory

Looking at the common size balance sheet it can be noticed that all the current assets of the firm, with an exception of prepaid expenses, declined during the current year. Even the fixed assets as a percentage of sales have declined from 78.96% to 78.72% of sales. This when seen in the light of a sales growth of 10% during the year highlights the better capacity utilisation and improved efficiency of the firm.

On the financing side of the common-size balance sheet it can be noticed that the proportion of equity has come down from approximately 71% to 60% of total financing. Debt has gone up from 14% to 24% of the total financing. The firm has replaced equity with debt financing, perhaps to get the benefit of leverage.

EXERCISES

Concept Review Questions

1. What are different kinds of ratios? What purpose do they serve? Who would look into which ratios more keenly?
2. What are the different ways in which ratios can be used?
3. Differentiate between current ratio and acid test ratio.
4. What are valuation ratios?
5. What is the difference between capital structure ratios and debt coverage ratios?
6. As a banker, which two ratios would you look into most and why?
7. What are the benefits of common size statements?
8. What is DuPont analysis?
9. What are the limitations of ratio analysis?

Critical Thinking Questions

1. How does increased leverage enhance return on equity? If returns keep increasing with increasing debt, explain why firms fix their level of debt to some limit.
2. A firm that has a good profitability ratio must have excellent liquidity and low leverage. Do you agree? Justify your answer.
3. Which single set of ratio would you consider to be most important as—(a) shareholder, (b) a raw material supplier, (c) a lender, (d) an employee, and (e) a customer? Why?
4. The first sign of sickness of a firm emerges from deteriorating liquidity as reflected in time series of current ratios and acid test ratios. Comment.

Practical Assignments

1. Select an industrial sector such as cement or steel and its major listed firms at NSE/BSE. Find out their P/E ratio and develop a benchmark for P/E ratio.
2. Select three firms from the same industry based on high, medium, and low P/E ratios. From the financial data of the three chosen firms, develop norms by taking the weighted average for current ratio, debt–equity ratio, profitability ratio, and turnover ratios. Assign reasons for variations in P/E ratios based on financial parameters of liquidity, capital structure, and profitability of the three firms.
3. Choose a firm and obtain financial statements for the preceding three years. This will give you financial data for four years. Evaluate liquidity, capital structure, profitability, and turnover ratios, and comment upon the performance of the firm over the period of four years.

Numerical Problems

1. Profitability and Liquidity ratios

The summarized financial statements for Zoom Ltd are as follows:

Summarized Profit and Loss Account of Zoom Ltd
for the year ended 31 March

	2006 (₹ in lakh)	***2007 (₹ in lakh)***
Sales	64.00	79.00
Cost of Sales	49.25	59.85
Gross Margin	**14.75**	**19.15**
Operating expenses		
Administration	4.46	5.32
Selling and Distribution	2.78	2.99
Profit before interest and tax (PBIT)	**7.51**	**10.84**
Interest	2.43	3.32
Profit before tax (PBT)	**5.07**	**7.51**
Provision for taxes	1.95	2.89
Profit after tax (PAT)	**3.12**	**4.62**

Note:

1. Credit sales have been 89.13% and 90.9% of the total sales in the years 2005-06 and 2006-07, respectively.
2. Total number of shares outstanding for the firm is 1.25 lakh.
3. The company follows a policy of 40% payout as there are tremendous expansion opportunities.

Balance Sheet of Zoom Ltd as on

	March 2006 (₹ in lakh)	March 2007 (₹ in lakh)
Assets		
Fixed Assets (Net)	25.50	36.25
Current Assets		
Inventory	12.60	14.45
Accounts receivable	11.20	13.43
Cash	1.25	1.50
	25.05	29.38
Less: Current Liabilities	6.70	9.60
Net Current Assets	18.35	19.78
Total Assets	**43.85**	**56.03**
Liabilities and owners' equity		
Share capital	25.00	25.00
Reserves and surplus	5.45	8.22
Debt (long-term)	13.4	22.81
Total	**43.85**	**56.03**

Using the tool of ratio analysis, you are required to comment on the profitability and liquidity performance of Zoom Ltd.

2. Capital Structure Ratios

From the summarised financial statements of Zoom Ltd given above, calculate the capital structure ratio and comment on the firm's performance.

Assume that the repayment of debt amounted to ₹4 lakh during the year 2005-06 and 7 lakh during 2006-07. The depreciation provision amounted to ₹2.15 lakh and ₹2.75 lakh respectively during 2005-06 and 2006-07.

3. Working Capital Ratios

Evaluate the working capital performance of Zoom Ltd for the years 2005-06 and 2006-07 using the information given in Problem 1. Apply the tool of ratio analysis for the purpose. The following additional information may be used:

1. Creditors account for 92% of the current liabilities in both the years
2. Purchases constitute 56% of the sales in the year 2005-06 and 58% in 2006-07.
3. The current assets and liabilities position on 1 April 2005 stood as follows:

	(₹ in lakh)
Current Assets	
Inventory	10.50
Accounts Receivable	9.45
Cash	0.89
	20.84
Current Liabilities	5.40
Net Current Assets (NCA)	15.44

4. Valuation Ratios

Using the summarized financial statements of Zoom Ltd given in Problem 1, comment on the firm's performance using the following ratios:

(a) Earnings yield
(b) Dividends yield
(c) Price Earnings (P/E) Ratio
(d) Market Price to Book Value (P/B) Ratio

Assume the current market price of Zoom Ltd's shares is ₹135, while the price in 2005-06 was ₹105.

5. Ratio Analysis—Comprehensive Problem

The financial performance of Trinetra Ltd is as given below:

Profit and Loss Account for Trinetra Ltd for the year ended 31 March

	2006 (₹ in lakh)	2007 (₹ in lakh)
Sales and Other Income	8015.00	9013.50
Cost of goods sold	3767.05	4134.55
Administrative Expenses	2244.20	2312.14
Profit Before Taxes (PBT)	2003.75	2566.81
Taxes	771.45	988.22
Profit After Tax (PAT)	1232.31	1578.59

Balance Sheet of Trinetra Ltd as on

	31 March 2006	31 March 2007
Liabilities and Share Capital	(₹ in lakh)	(₹ in lakh)
Share Capital	237.61	237.61
Reserves and Surplus	1157.15	1267.39
Secured Loans	115.02	78.49
Unsecured Loans	195.23	144.10
Current Liabilities and Provisions	1729.64	2480.74
Total	**3434.66**	**4208.34**
Assets		
Fixed Assets (Net)	861.02	947.38
Investments	392.24	634.17
Inventories	1078.64	1246.60
Sundry debtors	171.24	173.53
Cash and Bank Balances	242.61	685.40
Other Current Assets	12.51	17.34
Loans and Advances	676.41	503.92
Total	**3434.66**	**4208.34**

Based on the given financial information, calculate the following ratios:

(a) Profitability ratios
(b) Liquidity ratios
(c) Turnover ratios
(d) Capital structure ratios
(e) Valuation ratios
(f) DuPont ratios

Comment on the financial performance of Trinetra Ltd based on the above ratios.

6. Common-Size Income Statement

The summary of Income Statement of Zeta Ltd for two consecutive years is given below. Prepare a common-size income statement and interpret the changes.

Income Statements
for the year ended

	2005-06 (₹ in lakh)	2006-07 (₹ in lakh)
Sales	79.5	84.6
Less: Sales returns	2.15	1.76
Net Sales	77.35	82.84
Cost of sales	61.12	63.37
Gross Profit	16.22	19.46
Administrative Overheads	1.85	1.94
Selling and distribution overheads	2.63	2.90
Interest and other non operating expenses	0.17	0.20
Operating income	11.75	14.63
Other incomes	0.19	0.94
Profit before tax (PBT)	11.77	15.37
Tax	4.53	5.92
Profit after tax (PAT)	7.24	9.46

7. Common-Size Balance Sheet

Given here are the balance sheets of the two firms—Gloria Ltd and Victoria Ltd as on 31 March:

(*₹ in lakh*)

	Gloria Ltd	Victoria Ltd
Assets		
Cash and bank balance	12.70	38.60
Marketable securities	10.00	21.00
Sundry Debtors	22.00	23.70
Stock	93.50	162.45
Prepaid expenses	1.12	2.14
Current Assets	139.32	247.90
Fixed Assets (Net)	589.00	642.00
Total Assets	**728.323**	**889.895**
Liabilities and Owners Equity		
Sundry Creditors	6.75	26.45
Notes payable	6.56	6.45
Long term debt	130.01	345
Equity	585.00	512.00
Total	**728.32**	**889.89**

(a) Can the financial position of the two firms be compared assuming that the two firms fall in the same industry?

(b) Prepare a common size balance sheet for the two firms and compare their financial position in terms of the size and mix of their assets and liabilities.

CASE STUDY

Bajaj Auto Limited: The Unprecedented Growth Story*

Bajaj Auto Limited ('Bajaj Auto', 'BAL', or 'the company') is the flagship company of the Bajaj Group. The company manufactures two- and three-wheelers. Mr Rahul Bajaj is the present Chairman of the company. The company was incorporated in the year 1945 as M/s Bachraj Trading Corporation Private Ltd. The promoters hold about 30% equity, whereas Indian public holds about 26% and institutional investors have more than 27% stake in the company.

The products manufactured by Bajaj Auto are scooters, motorcycles, auto spare parts, machine tools, steel and engineering products. The company also produces three-wheelers as goods carriers such as pick-up or delivery vans and passenger carriers such as auto-rickshaws. Bajaj Auto has a network of 498 dealers, 1,500 authorized service centres and 162 exclusive three-wheeler dealers spread across the country.

Bajaj Auto has also diversified into the general as well as life insurance business through its subsidiaries Bajaj Allianz General Insurance Company Ltd, and Bajaj Allianz Life Insurance Company Ltd, respectively. The Bajaj brand has presence in many countries such as Sri Lanka, Mexico, Bangladesh, Columbia, Peru, Egypt, etc. The main competitors of the company in the two-wheelers and three-wheelers segment are—Hero Honda Motors Ltd, Kinetic Motor Co. Ltd, LML Ltd, Maharashtra Scooters Ltd, and TVS Motor Co. Ltd.

The company sold close to 23 lakh vehicles in 2005-06, which is a record performance in its history. The sales of motorcycles manufactured grew by 32% in 2005-06 compared to a market growth of below 19%. For the fifth successive year, the company raised its market share in the motorcycle segment. Today it stands at almost 31%. Sales increased by almost 31% to an all-time high of ₹9,285 crore in 2005-06. The export performance of the company in all its product categories has also been unprecedented during the FY 2005-06 as is reflected in the figures given in Table A:

Table A Product-wise exports of Bajaj Auto Ltd

Product	2005-06	2004-05	Growth
	(in numbers)		(in percentage)
Motorcycles	165,288	123,946	33
Total two-wheelers	174,907	130,945	34
Three-wheelers	75,297	65,765	14
Total vehicles	250,204	196,710	27

*The case study has been developed based on the information collected from the annual reports managerial discussions and analyses and other information available at the company's official website besides the various secondary sources of information including reports, news items etc. Some of the views expressed in the case study may not be in conformity with the official viewpoint. The purpose of the case study is to enable the reader to see the application of specific concepts discussed in the chapter and not to illustrate either effective or ineffective handling of an administrative situation.

Even more impressive has been the growth in company's operating EBITDA, which increased by 47% to touch ₹1805 crore during 2005-06. Consequently the operating EBITDA margin grew by 220 basis points to 17.9% of sales and operating income. Earnings per share have risen from ₹75.60 to ₹111.00 in the current year. Dividend too has grown to ₹40 per share (400%) for the year ended 31 March 2006 as against ₹25 per share in 2005.

Over the past few years, Bajaj Auto has focused on technology development, and product development in anticipation of market needs, scaling up its manufacturing facilities, implementing best-in-class production systems, rationalizing vendors, slashing costs while upgrading quality, restructuring dealerships, and distribution channels. These capabilities enabled the company to create exciting new products, which have set benchmarks in styling, design, and technology. The company's products are creating a customer pull at all price points and the company has now transformed from being a price warrior to a price leader. The results of these strategies are reflected in its financial statements as follows (refer Table B and C):

Notwithstanding its excellent financial performance in the years following its major strategic shift, the management of the firm believes in the philosophy that the *quest for perfection is eternal.*

Table B Profit and Loss Account for Bajaj Auto Ltd for the year ended

	Mar 2003	Mar 2004	Mar 2005	Mar 2006
	₹ in crore			
Sales	4987.05	5721.44	7078.06	9284.84
Other income	297.10	507.04	516.41	602.52
Change in stocks	32.92	10.87	–11.57	50.10
	5317.07	6239.35	7582.90	9937.46
Expenditure	4335.16	5017.92	6286.91	8131.87
PBDIT	981.91	1221.43	1295.99	1805.59
Interest	1.12	0.94	0.67	0.34
Depreciation	171.42	184.32	185.66	191.28
PBT	809.37	1036.17	1109.66	1613.97
Tax provision	274.44	285.41	349.32	509.37
PAT	534.93	750.76	760.34	1104.60
Dividends	159.81	285.37	288.64	461.50

To preclude the complacency from setting in, the management not only sets higher standards it also continuously monitors its performance and benchmarks with the industry performance in general and their closest competitors' results in particular.

Table C Assets and Liabilities of Bajaj Auto Ltd as on 31 March 2006

Liabilities	Mar 2005	Mar 2006	Assets	Mar 2005	Mar 2006
	₹ in crore			₹ in crore	
Net worth	4447.16	5349.79	Gross fixed assets	2870.02	3092.28
Paid-up equity capital	101.18	101.18	Capital WIP	9.14	25.26
Bonus equity capital	114.17	114.17	Less: cumulative depreciation	1660.32	1834.19
Minority interest	89.46	148.79	Net fixed assets	1205.64	1230.77
Reserves & surplus	4256.52	5099.82	Investments	5273.83	6865.43
Free reserves	4233.28	5076.58	Deferred tax assets	9.20	6.43
Share premium reserves	87.07	285.78	Inventories	224.70	274.47
Other free reserves	4146.21	4790.80	Receivables	3116.05	5799.11
Specific reserves	23.24	23.24	Sundry debtors	176.97	302.54
Borrowings	1229.17	1469.44	Debtors exceeding six months	0.20	1.13
Deferred tax liabilities	139.90	87.58	Advances/loans to corporate bodies	62.29	33.66
Current liabilities & provisions	4284.64	7773.20	Group/associate companies	34.44	19.41
Sundry creditors	833.86	1404.40	Other companies	27.85	14.25
Other current liabilities	1169.04	3674.37	Advance payment of tax	1823.60	1869.40
Provisions	2281.74	2694.43	Other receivables	1053.19	3593.51
			Cash & bank balance	266.88	476.48
			Intangible/DRE not written off	4.57	27.32
Total liabilities	10100.87	14680.01	Total assets	10100.87	14680.01

Discuss

1. Is the profitability performance of the firm satisfactory? If not, how can it be improved?
2. How attractive is the firm from the short-term and the long-term lenders' perspective? Does the firm appear to be the favourite destination in the automobile sector (two wheelers' and three-wheelers segment) for the lenders?
3. How efficient has the firm been in utilizing the resources at its disposal? How do you think the company can improve upon its efficiency?

In the CD

Ratio Calculator

CHAPTER 3

CVP and Breakeven Analysis

LEARNING OBJECTIVES

The chapter is aimed at

- explaining the nature of costs and their behaviour
- highlighting relevance of different costs for decision-making
- discussing the cost volume profit (CVP) decision-making framework
- elaborating the meaning of breakeven point (BEP) – its assumptions and its determination
- demonstrating how to determine the BEP for a multi-product firm
- explaining the concept of margin of safety and its relevance in decision-making
- emphasizing the role of breakeven analysis in managerial decisions

LOOK BEFORE YOU LEAP

Nikhil Ramesh, a software engineer, returned home one evening dejected and utterly perplexed! He had lost his job that fetched him a package of ₹75,000 a month. That morning what happened to him was literally a nightmare. As soon as he reached his office in the morning he found, to his dismay, that his ID cards did not work, his PC was disabled, and passwords were disqualified—just about anything, to give the message across that he is being shown the door. Then came the worst—the pink slip.

Ramesh had been working with an information technology (IT) company Infitech, the company he got placed with on day one of his campus placement. Although still a bachelor, Ramesh had taken a home loan from HDFC for tax planning purposes. The equated monthly instalment (EMI) on the loan amounts to ₹12,500 per month. Besides, he had also taken an auto loan to buy his new Hyundai Santro. The EMI for which comes to ₹10,000 a month. With the debt servicing obligation of ₹22,500 a month, Ramesh is broke.

Till last year everything was going fine and smooth. Even middle-sized IT companies such as Infitech were witnessing soaring bottom line. The employees were getting huge bonuses. Last year only the company announced stock options and Ramesh was also one of the beneficiaries. The company had been expanding for the past five years and the growth in manpower was around 35% during this period. The company shifted its Bangalore operations to bigger premises two years back that it had hired in view of its expanding human resource base.

It all started with the slowdown in the US. Cost cutting became the order of the day, with overheads being axed first. Venture capitalists, unsure of returns, began dictating terms. Even IT companies with finances in order and new frontier software to offer found growth rates dipping. All of which meant one thing: lay offs. The less skilled were the first to go. Freshers are not the only ones to be kicked around. Even those with supposedly permanent jobs were also at the receiving end.

Ramesh was really dreading as to how should he share this news with his parents who incidentally were there with him for vacation. But his father had already come to know of this from his pal, Ravi. The father trying to give him solace said, 'Son, it is not your fault. It is pure economics. Every economy witnesses such business cycles and they are only a passing phase. You learn from them and move ahead.' Ramesh's response was prompt 'Actually both I and my company were sailing on the same boat. The company in the wake of growing business became overenthusiastic in expanding its physical and human resources which led to surge in its salary bills and rentals. Till the time expansion phase was on, all was fine but the moment the projects started shrinking all went haywire.' Adding further, Ramesh said, 'The growing salary bills that were being taken as a measure of growth suddenly became burdensome fixed costs. The physical expansion started to be seen as overcapacity causing fixed costs. To reach the breakeven in wake of receding revenues, the finance people started to look at options to cut down the costs. First step was to lay off the extra workforce so as to bring down the salary bill along with the other overheads. Next was to cut down the capacity by shifting to smaller premises as this would bring down the rentals and costs on maintenance.

The mistake I committed was to create a very high fixed interest obligation oblivious of the nature of fixed costs. They do not change with the changing seasons.'

Source: Adapted with changes from 'Of job-cuts in IT: The lost pride', *http://www.cybermediadice.com/*. Accessed on 18 January 2007.

INTRODUCTION

Besides ratio analysis, another analytical tool that is comprehensively used in the decision-making process is cost volume profit (CVP) analysis. Decisions such as change in cost and profit for a given level of change in activity level (volume), the adjustments to be made in costs and/or volume to change the profits by a desired margin, the required change in costs to enhance the volume, etc., depend upon the relationship that exists between cost, volume, and profit. The CVP analysis focuses upon the relationship between these three key parameters of financial decision-making to arrive at such important business decisions.

Breakeven analysis is the most prominent and widely used technique of CVP analysis. The concept of breakeven analysis is built around the breakeven point (BEP), which is a no-profit, no-loss point. Fixed costs are the focus of breakeven analysis as the coverage of such costs is crucial for the firm to breakeven. Breakeven analysis is used in profit planning and cost control besides being useful for several other managerial decisions.

NATURE AND BEHAVIOUR OF COSTS

Increased business activity (volume) requires increased resources to carry out those activities. This increases the costs associated with the procurement of additional resources. However, this increase in cost is not in the same proportion as the increase in the volume. The disproportionate change in cost is due to the fact that all the costs do not vary with the changing activity levels. Before proceeding further to the discussion on CVP and breakeven analysis, let us understand costs, their nature, and behaviour vis-à-vis volume.

The total costs incurred on carrying out activities do not vary proportionately with the level of activity.

The total costs incurred by firms can be divided into two categories—*variable* and *fixed*. The costs that vary in direct proportion to the change in the volume are termed as *variable costs*. On an aggregate basis, variable costs vary proportionately with volume; but on per unit basis, they remain constant as can be seen in Table 3-1.

Costs that vary directly with the change in the level of activity (volume) are termed as variable costs.

Table 3-1 Variable costs

Volume (No. of units)	*Cost per unit (In ₹)*	*Total variable costs (In ₹)*
100	1,000	1,00,000
200	1,000	2,00,000
2500	1,000	25,00,000
5000	1,000	50,00,000
7500	1,000	75,00,000
10000	1,000	1,00,00,000
12500	1,000	1,25,00,000

Raw material costs, power and fuel costs, wages paid on the piece rate basis, target-based incentive/commission to salespersons are some of the examples of variable costs. From the decision-making point of view, variable costs are termed as controllable because the total variable costs can be changed by altering the level of production and these costs are within the control of a cost/responsibility centre.

Since variable costs fluctuate automatically with the activity level, they are controlled during adverse times. For example, if the sales are down due to decline in demand the variable costs will come down automatically and will pose no problems for the management. The behaviour of variable costs vis-à-vis the level of activity is shown in the Figure 3-1. Although the variable costs are positively correlated with sales, the degree of their correlation may not be necessarily one.

Fixed costs refer to such components of costs that remain constant to the changing activity level. Such costs are alternatively referred to as *period costs* as they change with time and not with volume. The examples of fixed costs include rent, salaries, etc. It is not that the fixed costs do not change at all but the change happens only if the level of activity of the firm goes beyond a certain range, which is known as the relevant range. As the activity level of the firm reaches the end point of this relevant range, it becomes necessary to expand the capacity. Capacity expansion causes a sudden spurt in the total fixed costs. Till the time the firm operates within the range, these costs remain fixed. For example, if a firm has a capacity to store 10,000 units of output in its warehouse then till the time the output reaches the level of 10,000 units the rent for the warehouse, which is a fixed cost, remains the same. Although it may go up on account of factors

Costs that remain volume are known as fixed costs. They are also called period costs.

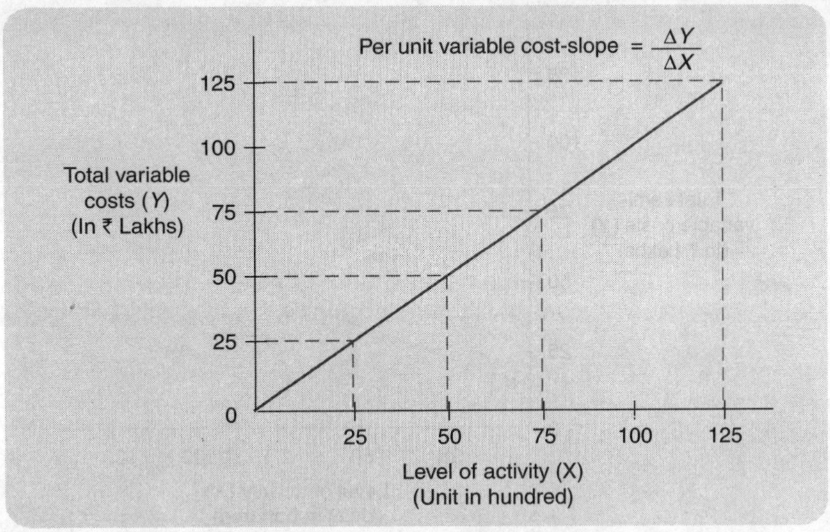

Figure 3-1 Behaviour of variable costs

Fixed costs remain fixed only within a particular range of volume.

such as inflation and annual increment as per the lease agreement, it does not increase with an increase in the production level. The moment the output level of the firm exceeds the level of 10,000 units, the firm will have to hire additional warehousing facility and this would lead to an increase in rent. Thus in such a situation, the relevant range within which the fixed costs remain fixed is 1–10,000 units. This behaviour of fixed costs vis-à-vis the volume is demonstrated in Figure 3-2.

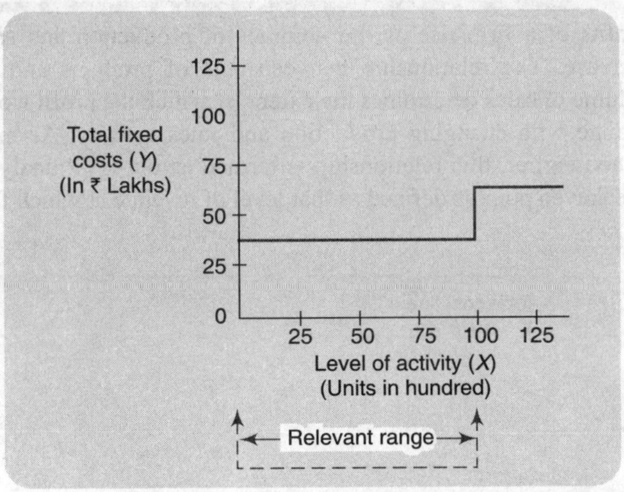

Figure 3-2 Behaviour of fixed costs

Through the total fixed costs remain constant within the relevant range the per unit fixed costs are inversely related to the level of activity. Fixed costs are also termed as uncontrollable costs because once they are incurred they remain fixed at a given level. Changing the level of such fixed costs requires major restructuring decisions, which are not within the control of a responsibility centre or a cost centre. Such decisions due to their strategic implications and under repercussions fall within the domain of authority of top management. For example, to cut down the salary bill, which is a fixed cost, if a decision to lay off employees needs to be taken. It is only the top management that can take such a decision. Similarly, the decision to change the nature of firm's operation—to shift from production as a core activity to distribution as a core business function may bring down the fixed production costs incurred by the business, but this again is a strategic business decision that has to be taken by the top management. Thus by and large, fixed costs are uncontrollable costs. Since fixed costs are constant, they assume significance in financial decision-making. The management has to keep the fixed costs within a manageable limit as they cannot be reversed easily.

Since the fixed costs are not easily reversible, management should be cautions while committing fixed costs.

The total fixed costs can be divided into—fixed operating and fixed financing costs. Fixed operating costs include costs such as rent, salary, and other fixed administrative, and selling and distribution expenses that are incurred to carry out the firm's operations. The fixed costs incurred on financing the firm's operations are termed as fixed financing costs. The two main financing costs are interest and lease rent. To put it simply, it can be said that all business-related fixed costs except for interest and lease rentals are fixed operating costs.

Fixed costs can be categorized into operating and financing costs. While fixed operating costs depend upon the cost structure, the fixed financing costs depend upon its the capital structure.

One may wonder as to how it matters whether a cost falls under the category of fixed operating costs or fixed financing costs! After all both of them remain fixed. We let you ponder over this issue for a while and take up the issue a little later in the chapter under the section on operating and financial leverage.

Besides variable and the fixed costs, there is a third category of costs termed as semi-variable costs. These costs are a combination of variable and fixed costs. As can be seen in Figure 3-3 these costs change but not in the direct proportion to the change in the volume. If the volume increases by 5% the total amount of semi-variable costs will increase by less than 5%. These costs are also referred to as mixed costs, semi-fixed costs, or partly variable costs. Costs incurred on repairs and

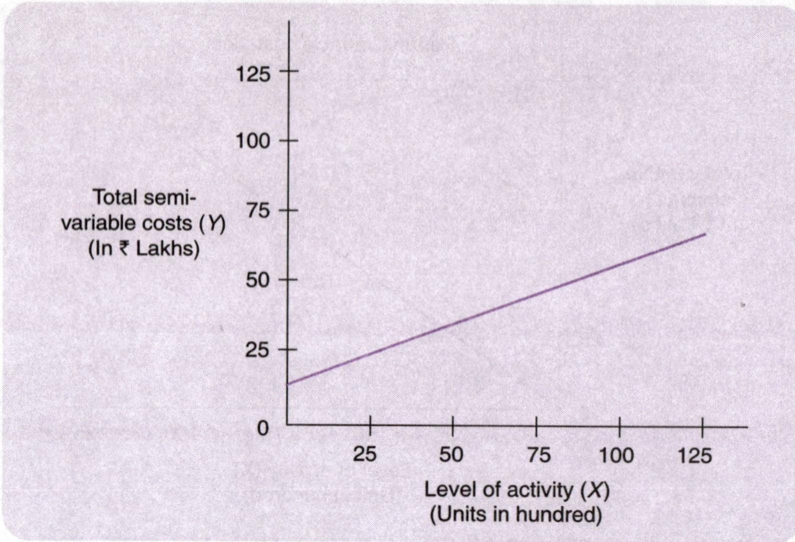

Figure 3-3 Behaviour of semi-variable costs

Semi-variable costs have features of both variable and fixed costs. Such costs need to be segregated into variable and fixed components for decision-making.

maintenance, salaries paid to supervisors, etc., are examples of semi-variable costs. Even the cost of electricity and telephone is put under this category as there is some minimum rental that has to be paid even if the consumption is zero as is analogous to the *y* intercept in Figure 3-3. Semi-variable costs should be segregated into the variable and fixed component for decision-making purposes.

The total costs, as shown in Figure 3-4, comprise of both fixed and variable costs and can be represented using the Equation 3-1.

$$TC = TFC + (UVC \times N) \quad (3\text{-}1)$$

where,

TFC = Total fixed costs

UVC = Unit variable costs (or variable cost per unit)

N = Activity level (Volume)

The understanding of costs and their behaviour is important not only from the viewpoint of cost management and control, but also for taking certain important decisions using CVP analysis. The next section discusses the concept of CVP and breakeven analysis.

CVP AND BREAKEVEN ANALYSIS

Profits of a firm rise as the volumes of production and sales increase. The relationship between cost of products and the volume of sales determines the extent by which the profit would change with changing production and sales activity. As mentioned earlier, this relationship is termed as the CVP analysis. Breakeven point is defined as that level of revenue at which firm

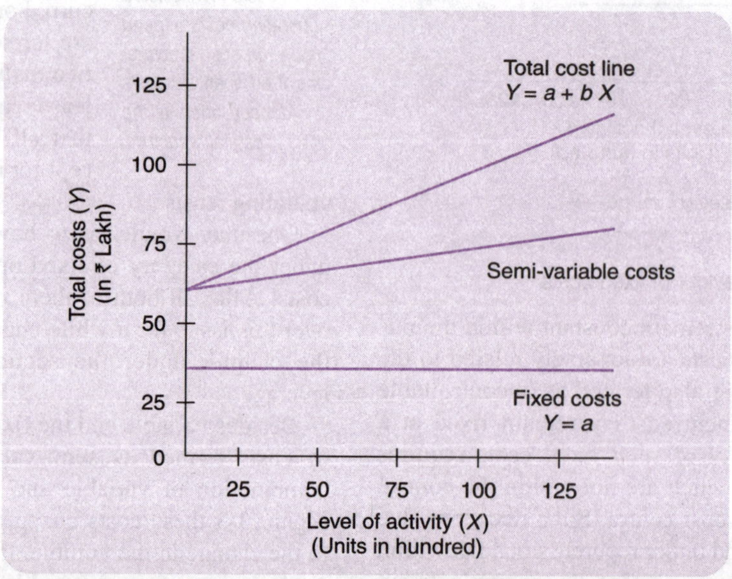

Figure 3-4 Total costs

CVP analysis is the relationship between cost, volume, and profit. It aids in certain key financial decisions.

recovers all its cost. In other words, it is a level of no profit or no loss. Operating beyond breakeven point would result in profit, while operating below it would mean loss for the firm. Breakeven point is of significance to all stakeholders of the firm. Knowing the breakeven point is important as it tells how safe the stakeholders are should the sales decline. Breakeven point is the most significant techniques in CVP analysis. Although there are other techniques like profit volume analysis, marginal cost analysis, key factor analysis etc. in addition to breakeven analysis that aid in CVP analysis but the BEP is normally used as a sine qua non for the CVP analysis.

Breakeven point refers to a point of no profit, no loss. It is that level of sales where firm's revenues are equal to its total costs.

To have a clear understanding of breakeven point (BEP) analysis and CVP analysis, the profit and loss account of a firm is analysed. For easier understanding and illustration, let us take an example of a single product firm, though in the real world it is rare to find such firm. Ideally firms would like to produce single product to keep management of the firm simple. However, market conditions, desire for growth, and prevailing competition force the management to produce more than one product.

Let us assume that a firm named SG Footwear is in the business of producing PVC shoes. It has installed 10 sophisticated direct injection process (DIP) moulding machines by importing them from Taiwan. These extremely sophisticated machines are capable of producing full, single piece PVC cloth and leather shoes. Each machine has 16 stations producing 8 pairs of shoes in one production cycle lasting for 5 minutes. The capacity of the firm can be estimated as about 7,000 pairs per shift equivalent to 42 lakh pairs per annum as shown.

Capacity = No. of pairs per cycle × No. of cycles per shift × No. of machines

No. of pairs of shoes per shift = 8 × (480/5) × 10 = 7,680

Less: Wastage and set up time approx 8–9% = 680

Annual Capacity = Capacity per shift × No. of Shifts per day × No. of Days per annum
= 7,000 × 2 × 300
= 42 lakh pairs of shoes per annum

Assuming that the selling price per pair of shoes is ₹200 the capacity revenue of SG Footwear is ₹8,400 lakh.

Capacity revenue
= No. of pairs per shift × Shifts per days × Days per annum × Selling Price
= 7,000 × 2 × 300 × 200 = ₹8,400 lakh

The management of SG Footwear is hopeful of booking the machine to the extent of 60% of capacity utilization as more than 25 lakh pairs of shoes can be sold. Based on the above target the management has prepared a profitability statement as shown in Table 3-2. The cost of raw materials, packing materials, and consummarles (including wastages) have been estimated as ₹1.5, ₹6, and ₹3 per pair respectively.

Table 3-2 Profitability statement of SG Footwear

Capacity (pair of shoes in lakhs)		42.00
Capacity Utilization		60%
Nos. of pairs of shoes (in lakhs)		25.20
		₹ per pair of shoe
Selling Price		200.00
Raw Material		105.00
Packing Material		6.00
Consumables		3.00
Profitablity	**Basis**	**₹ lakh**
Revenue	**at ₹200 per pair of shoe**	**5,040.00**
Raw Material	at ₹105 per pair of shoe	2,646.00
Packing Material	at ₹6 per pair of shoe	151.20
Consumables	at ₹3 per pair of shoe	75.60
Electricity	₹4/unit, 100 KW/Machine	115.20
Wages	20 lakh per month	240.00
Repairs & Maintenance	Estimated	50.00
Salaries	at ₹25 lakh per month	300.00
Travelling & Conveyance	Estimated	100.00
Business Promotion	Estimated	500.00
Freight	at 0.5% of selling price	25.20
Selling Commission	at 10% of selling price	504.00
Administrative Overheads	Estimated	100.00
Total Cost		**4,807.20**
Earnings Before Intesrest and Taxes		**232.80**

Since all the figures are estimates, the management is keen to know the minimum level at which the firm needs to operate in order to recover the entire cost, i.e., to find the breakeven point. To compute the BEP, we need to segregate various heads of cost into fixed and variable. The reason that we need to segregate costs into fixed and variable is that with each additional unit produced or sold, the firm would earn an amount equivalent to the difference of selling price and variable cost defined as contribution. For example, if the selling price of a product is ₹100 and the variable cost is ₹60, the firm will earn revenue of ₹100 by selling one additional unit. It will incur a cost of ₹60 and generate a contribution of ₹40 that goes to meet the fixed expenses and profit. For SG Footwear the classification of cost into fixed and variable is shown in Table 3-3.

To arrive at breakeven point, we need to work out the level of sales that will yield a contribution equal to the fixed cost. This can be found using following formulae:

Breakeven Sales (in terms of sales revenue)

$$= \frac{\text{Fixed Cost}}{\text{Sales} - \text{Variable Cost}} \times \text{Sales}$$

Breakeven Sales (in terms of sales quantity)

$$= \frac{\text{Breakeven Sales}}{\text{Selling Price}}$$

Breakeven Sales (in terms of % capacity utilization)

$$= \frac{\text{Breakeven Sales}}{\text{Capacity Sales}}$$

Table 3-3 Classification of cost of SG Footwear

Profitability	*₹ lakh*	*Nature of Cost*	*Variable Cost ₹ lakh*	*Fixed Cost ₹ lakh*
Revenue	5,040.00			
Raw Materials	2,646.00	Variable	2,646.00	—
Packing Material	151.20	Variable	151.20	—
Consumables	75.60	Variable	75.60	—
Electricity	115.20	Variable	115.20	—
Wages	240.00	Fixed	—	240.00
Repairs & Maintenance	50.00	Fixed	—	50.00
Salaries	300.00	Fixed	—	300.00
Travelling & Conveyance	100.00	Fixed	—	100.00
Business Promotion	500.00	Fixed	—	500.00
Freight	25.20	Variable	25.20	—
Selling Commission	504.00	Variable	504.00	—
Administrative Overheads	100.00	Fixed	—	100.00
Total Cost	**4,807.20**		**3,517.20**	**1,290.00**

The breakeven (sales quantity) can also be computed using the model:

$$= \frac{\text{Fixed Costs}}{\text{Contribution per unit}}$$

Contribution = Sales – Variable cost.

Using the above formulae the breakeven point for SG Footwear is computed at sales of ₹4269.50 lakh equivalent to 21.35 lakh pairs of shoes and capacity utilization of about 51% as shown below.

Breakeven Sales (in terms of sales revenue)

$$= \frac{\text{Fixed Cost}}{\text{Sales} - \text{Variable Cost}} \times \text{Sales}$$

$$= \frac{1290.00}{5040.00 - 3517.20} \times 5040.00 = ₹4,269.50 \text{ lakh}$$

Breakeven Sales (in terms of sales quantity)

$$= \frac{\text{Breakeven Sales}}{\text{Selling Price}} = \frac{4269.50}{200} = 21.35 \text{ lakh pairs}$$

Breakeven Sales (in terms of % capacity utilization)

$$= \frac{\text{Breakeven Sales}}{\text{Capacity Sales}} = \frac{4269.50}{8400.00} = 50.83\%$$

Since marketing and production functions normally monitor their performance and progress in terms of revenues and physical quantities respectively knowing the breakeven point in terms of revenue and quantity helps them to easily figure out whether the level of activity is above breakeven point.

Various representations of breakeven point are condensed in Table 3-4.

Table 3-4 Breakeven point for SG Footwear

(a) In terms of revenue (₹ Lakh)	4,269.50
(b) In terms of number of pairs of shoes sold (Lakh)	21.35
(c) In terms of capacity utilization (%)	50.83

A graphical view of breakeven point is presented in Figure 3-5. Observe that as the level of sales rise the variable costs also rise linearly and the fixed costs remain constant. Variable cost and fixed cost together account for a firm's total cost.

Until a firm reaches the point of breakeven, it incurs losses. Beyond this point, it is the profit zone.

Total cost line would be parallel to the variable cost line. Sales rise linearly and the breakeven point is the intersection of total cost and sales, where sales equals total cost. Selling price being higher than the variable cost, the revenue line would rise faster than the cost line. To the right of the breakeven point is the profit area and to its left is the loss area. This means that until the firm reaches the point of breakeven it incurs losses. These losses are due to the fact that the firm has not been able to cover its fixed costs. Although every unit sold covers up the variable costs and also leaves some surplus (known as contribution), it requires a certain minimum number of units to be sold in order to recover the total fixed costs incurred. The higher the amount of fixed costs incurred by the firm, higher is the number of units that it needs to sell in order to reach the breakeven point and start earning profits. The businesses should make sure that the amount of fixed costs that they commit to are not too high as it would shift the breakeven point further.

A firm should try to reach BEP as quickly as possible. For this, the fixed costs should be contained within manageable limits.

However there are certain businesses such as power generation, telecom, etc. that have a long gestation period. take a long time to breakeven and start earning profits. Such businesses should try and stick to the production and delivery schedule so as to ensure that the breakeven point does not get delayed.

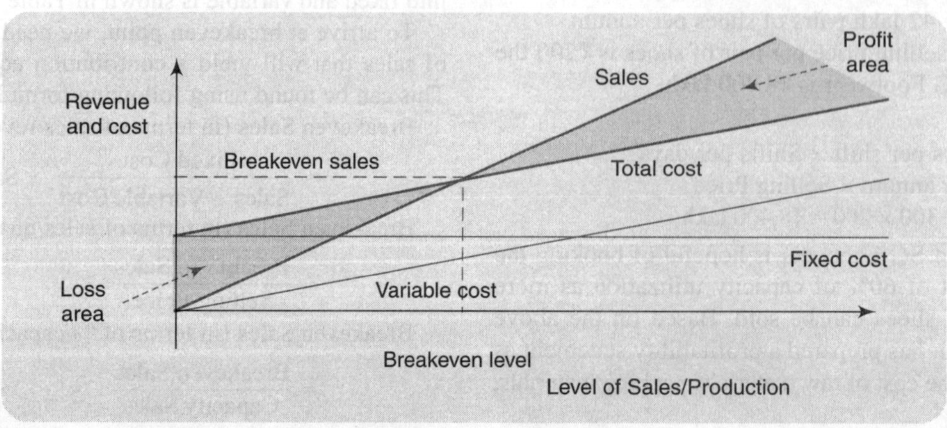

Figure 3-5 Breakeven point

Let us look at another related concept—margin of safety—that is important for decision-making.

Margin of Safety

The difference between the actual sales and the sales at breakeven point is termed as margin of safety. It measures the cushion available to firms against the decline in volume (sales).

Breakeven point also helps in establishing the level of risk the firm is facing depending upon how far are the current sales from the breakeven point. Operating at a sales level close to the breakeven point poses risk for the firm as the margin available to such firm in case of a downward slide in sale will be low.

The margin of safety is the difference between the sales at the breakeven point and the actual sales level. It is calculated as follows:

$$\text{Margin of Safety (\%)} = \frac{\text{Actual Sales} - \text{Breakeven Sales}}{\text{Actual Sales}} \times 100$$

It represents the cushion that is available to the firm in case the sales decline. Given the actual sales fall on the right side of the breakeven point, higher the difference between actual sales and the breakeven point, greater is the margin of safety.

It indicates that the business would be in position to tide over any temporary setback in its revenues. If the margin of safety is thin or shows a declining trend it is the cause of concern for the business as even a slight decline in sales may push the company below the breakeven (in the loss area).

In the SG footwear's case the margin of safety would be:

Margin of Safety (in absolute terms)

$$= \text{Actual Sales} - \text{Sales at BEP}$$
$$= 5040 - 4269.50 = ₹770.50 \text{ lakh}$$

$$\text{Margin of Safety (\%)} = \frac{5040 - 4269.50}{5040} \times 100$$
$$= 15.29\% \text{ approx.}$$

Breakeven analysis is based on certain assumptions that may not hold well in the real life.

This implies that if the sales decline by more that 15.29% then only SG footwear will incur loss in its operations. Till the time the decline in sales is less than 15.29% firm will manage to remain profitable.

Assumptions of Breakeven Analysis

Breakeven analysis, although very useful in decision-making, has been criticized for its unrealistic assumptions. Let us understand these assumptions and their limitations. Margin of safety also assumes importance as a higher margin of safety would cover up for the limitations of the breakeven analysis.

Let us understand these assumptions and their limitations in the case of SG Footwear. These assumptions are:

Constancy of selling price In the analysis, we assumed that the selling price of the shoes will remain constant at ₹200 per pair. In practice, this assumption holds good for a limited range of sales. Normally firms have to decrease the price if they wish to increase their sales significantly. In case of SG footwear the company will have to decrease the price substantially if it wants to increase the sales say from 21 lakh pairs to 30 lakh pairs. However, if the company decides not to change its price its sales may still increase owing to the growing demand for its products. But such an increase in sales will only be marginal. In the graphical presentation, the constancy assumption implies linear relationship of revenue and the quantity sold.

Constancy of fixed costs and proportionate variability of variable costs For the purpose of breakeven analysis, costs are clearly segregated into variable and fixed. Graphically the fixed cost is a horizontal straight line and variable cost is a rising straight line. In real life situations, as discussed earlier, fixed costs remain constant only within the relevant range. Beyond that even the fixed costs go up suddenly. Similarly, the assumption that the variable costs per unit remain constant may also not hold well in a real life. The increase in the prices of inputs and other variable costs on account of the impact of inflation and other external factors may affect the contribution and thus the breakeven point. Are the costs strictly classifiable into fixed and variable? Strictly speaking the answer is no. It may be difficult to segregate some of the costs into fixed and variable components. Although there are techniques to segregate such mixed costs into variable and fixed components, these techniques are not universal.

Production process remains the same Breakeven analysis assumes that the production process, technique, etc. do not undergo any change. However, in view of an increased competitive environment and to maintain/enhance their operating efficiency, firms are forced to bring in the necessary changes in the production processes and technology. Many a times such a change is thrust upon the firm by the changing external environment. For certain businesses, the rate of such a change is very high.

Constant product mix The breakeven analysis assumes that the product mix and the sales mix remain constant for a multi-product firm. However, in reality both production mix and sales mix are neither constant nor are they under the control of the firm. The market forces are equally responsible in deciding the production–sales mix. Firms with a view to increase their profits may keep on altering their production–sales mix.

The assumptions of the breakeven analysis mentioned above may not be compatible with the dynamic environment that the firms are faced with today where there is nothing constant, be it variable costs per unit, total fixed costs, or the selling price per unit. Despite the assumptions and their limitations, we feel that these assumptions are made to highlight the application of the concept and in no way do they dilute the power of this analytical tool. There is nothing that restricts from relaxing these assumptions in the light of the prevailing/emerging scenario. For example, if a hike in the sales price is expected, multiple breakeven points could be computed for the expected levels of selling prices besides the breakeven point at the prevailing selling price.

Having discussed the assumptions of breakeven point and their limitations, we now move on to the computation of breakeven point for a multiproduct firm.

BREAKEVEN POINT: MULTIPLE PRODUCTS

Most firms produce and market multiple products. Breakeven point analysis can be extended to firms dealing in multiple products with some adjustments by converting all the products of the firm into a composite. Data requirement for conducting a breakeven point analysis for a multiple product company is the same as that for a single product firm—selling price, variable cost per unit, and aggregate fixed cost. Besides this, we need to have the sales–product mix.

The breakeven point for a multiproduct firm can be computed using the contribution margin of each product and the product mix of the firm.

Let us understand how to compute the breakeven point for a multi-product firm. Assume that Label Maker, a firm manufacturing labels, produces three different kinds of labels namely large, medium, and small. The relevant cost details and the product mix are given below:

Product	Selling Price (₹/thousand)	Variable Cost (₹/thousand)	Product Mix
Large Labels	1,000	500	20%
Medium Labels	700	400	30%
Small Labels	300	200	50%

Label Maker has a fixed cost of ₹72 lakh per month and wants to find the level at which it must operate in order to breakeven.

The way to calculate the breakeven point in this case is to convert different products into a single composite product. The above products with the given product mix can be treated as a composite product 'grand label' consisting of 20% large label, 30% medium label, and 50% small label with selling price and variable cost as follows:

Selling price of 'grand label'

$= 0.20 \times 1000 + 0.30 \times 700 + 0.50 \times 300 = ₹560$

Variable cost of 'grand label'

$= 0.20 \times 500 + 0.30 \times 400 + 0.50 \times 200 = ₹320$

Contribution of 'grand label' = ₹240

To breakeven, Label Maker must produce 30,000 (72,00,000/240) grand labels each month. The breakeven sales would be = ₹168 lakh (30,000 × 560) per month.

This is equivalent to

Large labels = 20% of 30,000 = 6,000 per month
Medium labels = 30% of 30,000 = 9,000 per month
Small labels = 50% of 30,000 = 15,000 per month

The limitations of the analysis are rather obvious. Besides the assumptions made under single product case of constancy of prices and costs and its nature we additionally assume constancy of product mix. If the product-mix changes, the conclusions drawn above would be fallacious. Nevertheless, breakeven point remains a powerful tool for analysis and profit planning. In the example of label maker we can relax the assumptions and calculate the breakeven point for various prices and with varying product mix and variable casts.

OPERATING LEVERAGE

As discussed earlier, total fixed costs can be categorized into fixed operating costs and fixed financing costs. Now let us understand how these fixed costs affect the risk.

Operating leverage measures the sensitivity of the profits (PBT) to the change in sales.

Operating leverage measures the sensitivity of the firm's profits (PBT) to the change in sales. The degree of operating leverage (DOL) is computed as follows:

$$\text{DOL} = \frac{\text{Contribution}}{\text{Profit Before Tax}}$$

A degree of operating leverage of 2 implies that if the firm's sales (represented by contribution margin) change by 100%, its profits before tax would change by 200%.

A firm with a high proportion of fixed operating costs in its cost structure will have a high degree of operating leverage. Operating leverage is a measure of both risk and opportunity. Other things remaining the same, a higher degree of operating leverage signifies greater opportunity of profits with increasing sales. So in the previous case, with the sales increasing by 100%, the firm's PBT will increase by 200%. This high degree of operating leverage also magnifies the operating risk of the firm.

A Degree of Operating Leverage of 2 indicates that if the sales change by 100%, the profit before tax would change by 200%.

In the situation discussed earlier, the degree of operating leverage of 2 would become a cause of concern for the firm in times of declining sales as it will precipitate the decline in PBT, which would decline by a rate that is twice the decline in the sales. Operating leverage can make or break a firm depending upon the way it is managed. Two firms that are identical in all respects other than their fixed operating costs will have a different risk–return profile.

Assume that Alpha and Beta are two identical firms. The firms are similar in all ways except for their cost structure. The information for both the firms for the month of January stood as follows:

	Alpha Ltd (In ₹)	Beta Ltd (In ₹)
Selling price (per unit)	20	20
Variable costs (per unit)	8	8
Contribution margin (per unit)	12	12
Total contribution margin	1,20,000	1,20,000
Fixed operating costs	40,000	70,000
Profit before tax	80,000	50,000
Degree of operating leverage	1.5	2.4

Thus, the two firms have everything in common except for the fixed costs in their cost structure. This difference has changed the risk–return scenario for the two otherwise identical firms. If the sales of the two firms increase by 20% the PBT of the two firms will increase as follows:

	Alpha Ltd	Beta Ltd
Increase in sales (%)	20	20
Degree of operating leverage	1.5	2.4
Increase in PBT (%) = Increase in sales × Degree of operating leverage	30	48

The high DOL magnifies the risk-return of the firm with the change in the volume (sales).

Thus during the phase of increasing sales, Beta Ltd will be better off as its profits increase by 48%, which is much higher than the rate of increase for Alpha Ltd However, Beta Ltd would become worse off compared to Alpha Ltd if the sales were to decline. Due to high degree of operating leverage, its profits would decline at a much faster rate than that for Alpha Ltd.

These risk–return implications of fixed costs for the firms are important from the viewpoint of decision-making. In case of a probable decline in the sales level, the management should try to cut down the fixed operating costs to ensure that their high proportion does not take the degree of operating leverage to a level that makes the firm very risky. Thus while designing and monitoring the cost structure, the degree of operating leverage and its implications for the risk–return of the firm should be kept in mind.

Financial leverage is the measure of sensitivity of firm's EPS to a change in operating profits. The degree of financial leverage depends on the level of debt financing.

Another concept that is intricately linked to risk-return profile is financial leverage. Financial leverage measures the sensitivity of the firm's earnings per share (EPS) to a change in operating profit (EBIT). The degree of financial leverage depends on firm's capital structure. Higher the usage of debt financing in its capital structure higher the fixed financing costs (the interest) and higher will be its degree of financial leverage. As the degree of operating leverage determines the operating risk of the business, the degree of financial leverage determines its financial risk. Together they go on to determine the overall risk of the business. To contain the risk within manageable limits, a firm should either have a low degree of operating leverage or a low degree of financial leverage. The possibility of bankruptcy increases if both the degree of operating leverage and degree of financial leverage are high. Since financial leverage relates to the capital structure of a firm it has been taken up in detail in the chapter on capital structure.

DECISIONS USING BREAKEVEN ANALYSIS

The CVP analysis is a very handy tool to understand the relationship that exists between the elements of financial decision-making—cost, volume, and profit. Some of these decisions that are facilitated by the CVP analysis are discussed below:

Planning for a Target Level of Profit

Some of the prominent decisions that the CVP analysis helps in arriving at are: determining sales for targeted profits, determining optimum product mix, etc.

All firms work on specific targets of sales, production, and profit. It is desirable to know the level of sales or production that will generate the required or the target level of profit. The profit for the firm at breakeven point is zero by definition. If we treat the desired profit as part of the fixed cost, the breakeven formula can be used to plan for the target profit level.

Since costs are tax deductible and profit is not, the inclusion of profit in the fixed cost must be done on pre-tax basis. With 40% tax (T) a profit before tax (PBT) of ₹100 will yield ₹60 {PBT × (1 – T)} only. The volume required for a target profit of x can be calculated as follows:

$$\text{Target Sales} = \frac{\text{Fixed Cost} + \dfrac{x}{1-T}}{\text{Sales} - \text{Variable Costs}} \times \text{Sales} \qquad (3\text{-}2)$$

$$\text{Target Quantity} = \frac{\text{Target Sales}}{\text{Selling Price}}$$

$$\text{Target \% capacity utilization} = \frac{\text{Target Sales}}{\text{Capacity Sales}}$$

The select data from the breakeven analysis of SG Footwear is reproduced in Table 3-5 below:

Table 3-5 Select breakeven point data: SG Footwear

	(₹ lakh)
Capacity Revenue	8400.00
Current level of Sales	5040.00
Variable cost	3517.20 (69.79%)
Contribution Margin	1522.80 (30.21%)
Fixed Cost	1290.00
Profit Before Tax	232.80

Assuming a tax rate of 40%, the level of sales SG Footwear needs to achieve to generate a post tax profit of ₹500 lakh can be calculated by using Equation 3-2.

$$\text{Target Sales} = \frac{\text{Fixed Cost} + \dfrac{x}{1-T}}{\text{Sales} - \text{Variable Costs}} \times \text{Sales}$$

$$= \frac{1290.00 + \dfrac{500.00}{0.60}}{1522.80} \times 5040.00 = ₹7027.58 \text{ lakh}$$

$$\text{Target Quantity} = \frac{\text{Target Sales}}{\text{Selling Price}} = \frac{7027.58}{200}$$

$$= 35.14 \text{ lakh pairs of shoes}$$

$$\text{Target \% capacity utilization} = \frac{\text{Target Sales}}{\text{Capacity sales}} = \frac{7027.58}{8400.00}$$

$$= 83.66\%$$

Decision to Optimize the Product Mix

In case of a multi-product firm, one of the key decision points is to determine the product mix or sales mix that would yield the maximum profit for the business. CVP analysis facilitates such decision by comparing the different production and sales mix in the manner it was done to compute the BEP for a multi-product firm in the previous section. In this way, the firm is able to select the optimal product mix.

Similarly, there are several other managerial decisions that are taken with the help of breakeven analysis. Some of these decisions are—decision to shut down the business unit/ operation or to continue them, the decisions to alter prices, and decision to outsource or manufacture the product in-house, etc.

SUMMARY

The total costs incurred do not vary proportionately with the level of activity as some part of total costs is fixed in nature. Such fixed costs refer to such components of costs that remain constant with the changing activity level. They are alternatively referred to as period costs as they change with time and not with volume. Rent, salaries, etc., are examples of fixed costs. These costs remain fixed only within a relevant range of production/sales. The moment the volume increases and crosses this relevant range, there is a sudden increase in such costs.

The costs that vary in direct proportion to the change in the volume are termed as variable costs. Due to the feature of variability with the activity level (level of volume or production) such costs are also referred to as product costs. Cost of raw materials, power, and fuel are some of the prominent examples of variable costs.

There is a third category of costs termed as semi-variable costs. These are the combination of variable and fixed costs. These costs are also referred to as mixed costs. The examples of semi-variable costs include repairs and maintenance, salaries paid to the supervisors, etc. This understanding of costs concept and its behaviour is important from the viewpoint of profit planning and cost management and control.

CVP analysis determines the relationship between cost, volume, and profit. Such an analysis aids in certain key financial decisions. Breakeven point is the most significant techniques in CVP analysis. Breakeven point refers to a point of no profit, no loss. It is that level of sales where firm's revenues are equal to its total costs. Until a firm reaches the point of breakeven, it incurs losses. If the sales of a firm are rightwards of the breakeven point the firm is said to be operating in the profit zone. A firm should try to reach breakeven point as quickly as possible. To achieve this, fixed costs should be contained within manageable limits.

The difference between the actual sales and the sales at breakeven point is termed as the margin of safety. It measures the cushion available to firms against the decline in volume (sales). The higher the margin of safety, the better it is for the business. In order to have a high safety margin, the firm should cut down its fixed costs, volumes remaining the same.

Breakeven analysis, though very useful in decision-making, is sometimes criticized for its unrealistic assumptions that may not hold well in the real life. The analysis is based on the assumption of constant selling price, fixed costs, per unit variable costs, and product mix. These assumptions of constancy are the limitations of the model.

KEY TERMS

Fixed costs Fixed costs are the costs that remain constant with the level of production sales. They are also known as period costs.

Variable costs Costs that change directly with the level of operations are called variable costs. They are also known as product cost.

Operating risk Operating risk refers to the chances that a firm's revenues are not sufficient to cover the operating costs. It is the fixed costs that cause operating risk due to their invariance to sales. Higher the fixed costs higher is the operating risk.

Degree of operating leverage (DOL) DOL measures the variability of operating profit with a given change in sales.

Financial risk The degree of financial risk depends upon the usage of fixed cost bearing sources of financing (i.e., debt) and is measured by the degree of financial leverage.

KEY FORMULAE

Total Cost = TFC + (UVC × N)

$$\textbf{Breakeven Sale} = \frac{\text{Fixed Cost}}{\text{Sales} - \text{Variable Cost}} \times \text{Sales}$$

$$\textbf{Breakeven Quality} = \frac{\text{Breakeven Sales}}{\text{Selling Price}}$$

$$\textbf{Breakeven Capacity} = \frac{\text{Breakeven Sales}}{\text{Capacity Sales}}$$

$$\textbf{Margin of Safety} = \frac{\text{Actual Sales} - \text{Breakeven Sales}}{\text{Actual Sales}} \times 100$$

$$\textbf{Target Sales for Profit of } x = \frac{\text{Fixed Cost} + \left(\frac{x}{1-T}\right)}{\text{Sales} - \text{Variable Cost}} \times \text{Sales}$$

PRACTICE PROBLEMS

1. Breakeven Point and Margin of Safety

The sales and profit figures of Midas Inc. for two successive years are as follows:

	Previous year	*Current year*
Number of units sold	15000	20500
Sales (₹ in lakh)	3750.00	5125.00
Profit/ Loss (₹)	825.00	1178.75

Based on the above information on sales and profit/ loss you are required to determine the following:

(a) The amount of fixed costs incurred by the firm
(b) The break even point for the firm (in rupees and in units)
(c) The amount of sales to earn a profit of ₹25 crores
(d) Margin of safety if actual sales of Midas Inc. is 17.5 crores

Solution

	Previous year	*Current year*
Sales	37,50.00 ₹/lakh	51,25.00 ₹/lakh
Profit	8,25.00 ₹/lakh	11,78.75 ₹/lakh

(a) ***Fixed cost computation***

$$\frac{P}{V} = \frac{\Delta \text{Contribution}}{\Delta \text{Sales}} \times 100$$

$$\frac{P}{V} = \frac{₹\ 1178.75 - ₹\ 8{,}25.00}{₹\ 51{,}25.00 - ₹\ 37{,}50.00} \times 100$$

= 0.2573 = 25.73%

$$\text{Contribution} = \text{Sales} \times \frac{P}{V}\ \text{Ratio}$$

Contribution (Previous year) = ₹3750 × 0.2573
= ₹964.875 lakh

Fixed Cost = Contribution ± Loss/Profit
= 964.875 – 825.000 = ₹139.875 lakh

(b) ***Breakeven point***

$$\text{BEP (in ₹)} = \frac{\text{Fixed Cost}}{P/V\ \text{Ratio}}$$

$$= \frac{139.875}{0.2573} = ₹543.626\ \text{lakh}$$

$$\text{BEP (in units)} = \frac{\text{Breakeven Point (in ₹)}}{\text{Selling price}}$$

$$= \frac{543.626\ \text{lakh}}{\frac{37{,}50{,}00{,}000}{15{,}000}} = 21{,}745\ \text{units}$$

(c) Sales to earn a desired profit of ₹25 crore

$$\text{Sales at Desired Profit (in ₹)} = \frac{\text{Fixed Cost} + \text{Desired Profit}}{P/V\ \text{Ratio}}$$

$$= \frac{139.875 + 2500}{0.2573} = \frac{2639.875}{0.2573}$$

= ₹10,260 lakh

$$\text{Sales (in units) at Desired Profit} = \frac{\text{Sales at desired profit (in ₹)}}{\text{Selling Price per unit}}$$

$$= \frac{10{,}260\ \text{lakh}}{2500} = 4{,}10{,}396\ \text{units}$$

(d) Margin of safety if actual sales are 17.5 crores

Margin of Safety = Actual Sales (in ₹) – Breakeven sales (in ₹)
= 1750.00 – 543.626 = ₹1206.374 lakh

2. Breakeven Point for Multi-product Firm

ABS Ltd is the manufacturer of florescent lamps. There are three types of lamps—'Flore Light', 'Flore Medium', and 'Flore High' manufactured and sold by the firm. The sales mix in value comprises 35%, 42%, and 23% of 'Flore Light', 'Flore Medium', and 'Flore High' respectively.

The total budgeted sales for the firm are ₹50 lakh per month. The operating costs as a percentage of sales are 55%, 62% and 76.5% for 'Flore Light', Flore Medium', and 'Flore High' respectively. The firm incurs an average fixed cost of ₹18.25 lakh per month.

What will be the overall break even point for the firm? Also indicate the product-wise contribution margin for the firm.

Solution

Computation of Contribution margin

	Flore Light	*Flore Medium*	*Flore High*	*Total*
Sales Mix (%)	**35.00**	**42.00**	**23.00**	**100.00**
Sales (₹ In lakh)	17.50	21.00	11.50	50.00
Variable cost (₹ In lakh)	9.63	13.02	8.80	31.44
Contribution (₹ In lakh)	7.88	7.98	2.70	18.56
P/V Ratio (%)	45.00	38.00	23.50	37.12
Fixed costs (₹ In lakh)	—	—	—	18.25
Profit (₹ In lakh)	—	—	—	0.31

$$\text{Breakeven point (in ₹ lakh)} = \frac{\text{Fixed Cost}}{P/V\ \text{Ratio}}$$

$$= \frac{18.25\ \text{lakh}}{0.3712} = ₹49.17\ \text{lakh}$$

3. Operating Leverage

Based on the financial information given below for Amada Ltd, answer the following.

(a) What is the Degree of Operating Leverage for the firm? What are its implications for financial decision-making?

(b) How much would the firm's sales have to come down so that its EBT is equal to zero?

Sales (Units)	5,55,665
Selling Price ₹/unit	125
Fixed Cost (₹)	12,50,0000
Variable Cost (₹/unit)	68
Debt (₹)	100,00,000
Interest Rate (%)	12

Solution

Sales (5,55,665 × 125)	₹6,94,58,125
Variable cost (5,55,665 × 68)	₹3,77,85,220
Fixed Cost	₹1,25,00,000
Total Cost (Variable cost + Fixed cost)	₹5,02,85,220
EBIT (Sales – Total cost)	₹1,91,72,905
Interest (10,000,000 × 0.12	₹12,00,000
EBT (EBIT – Interest)	₹1,79,72,905

(a) *Degree of Operating Leverage (DOL)*

$$\text{DOL} = \frac{Q(P-V)}{Q(P-V)-F}$$

where

Q = Sales (Units)

P = Selling Price

V = Variable Cost

F = Fixed Cost

$$\text{DOL} = \frac{5,55,665(125\text{-}68)}{5,55,665(125\text{-}68) - 1,25,00,000}$$

$$= \frac{3,16,72,905}{1,91,72,905} = 1.652$$

This implies that if the sales of the firm change by 100% the EBIT would change by 165.2%. This may be good for the firm in periods when sales are showing an increasing trend but may have an adverse impact on the bottom line in phase of declining sales. So firms should plan their fixed operating costs in a manner that it is able to bring down the DOL in phase of declining sales.

(b) *Margin of reduction in Sales till EBIT becomes zero*

As it is known

$\text{EBIT} = (P - V) \times Q - F$

EBT becoming zero means that the EBIT is equal to Interest. Assuming that it happens at Level Q^* of sales.

$(P - V) \times Q^* - F = \text{Interest}$

$(125 - 68) \times Q^* - 1,25,00,000 = 12,00,000$

$57\, Q^* = 1,37,00,000$

$Q^* = 2,40,351$ units approx.

Thus Sales should come down to 2,40,351 units for EBT to become zero.

4. Profit Planning Decisions

The cost sheet of Transco, manufacturer of Chips used in colour televisions, for the current financial year is as follows:

	Per unit of output (in ₹)
Material	875
Labour	175
Variable overheads	189
Total variable cost	1,239
Selling Price	2,000

In the previous year the company sold 120000 units. The total fixed costs incurred by the firm are ₹62.55 lakh. The company management, in view of growing competition especially from China, is contemplating to bring down its selling price per unit. But the management wants to keep the current profit margin intact.

In this regard you are expected to determine the number of units that the firm is expected to sell if:

(a) Selling price is reduced by 7.5%

(b) Selling price is reduced by 10%

Solution

Calculating the present level of profits

Sales (in units)	1,20,000
Sales (in ₹)	24,00,00,000
Variable Cost (in ₹)	14,86,80,000
Fixed Cost (in ₹)	62,55,000
Total Cost (in ₹)	15,49,35,000
Profit (Sales – Total cost)	**8,50,65,000**

(a) If the Selling Price is reduced by 7.5%:

The new Selling Price for the firm will be	1850
New P/V ratio for the firm will be	0.33
Fixed Cost (₹)	62,55,000
Desired Profit (will be same as the current profits) (₹)	8,50,65,000

$$\text{Sales for Desired Profit} = \frac{\text{Fixed Cost} + \text{Desired Profit}}{P/V\ \text{Ratio}}$$

$$\text{Sales for Desired Profit} = \frac{62,55,000 + 8,50,65,000}{0.33}$$

Level of Sales (in ₹) to earn a profit of ₹8,50,65,000 = 27,65,00,818.3

Level of Sales (in units) to earn a profit of ₹8,50,65,000 = 149460

(b) If the Selling Price is reduced by 10%:

The new Selling Price for the firm will be	1800
New P/V ratio for the firm will be	0.31
Fixed Cost (₹)	62,55,000
Desired Profit (will be same as the current profits) (₹)	8,50,65,000

$$\text{Sales for Desired Profit} = \frac{62,55,000 + 8,50,65,000}{0.31}$$

Level of Sales (in ₹) to earn a profit of ₹8,50,65,000
= ₹29,30,05,347.6

Level of Sales (in units) to earn a profit of ₹8,50,65,000
= 1,62,781 units

5. Optimizing the Product Mix

The following are the figures of the current sales-mix of Adventure Ltd:

	Products				
	A	B	C	D	Total
Sales (₹)	4,55,000	5,25,000	2,25,000	1,35,000	13,40,000
Variable Costs (₹)	3,25,000	3,98,000	1,75,625	49,000	9,47,625
Fixed Costs (₹)					4,15,255

Find out the maximum profitable sales-mix for the company. The maximum production and sales capacity for Adventure Ltd is as follows:

	Products				
	A	B	C	D	Total
Sales (₹)	5,00,000	6,00,000	2,50,000	3,00,000	16,50,000

Solution

The decision to arrive at the optimal product mix is taken in the light of its impact on profits. If any alteration in the product mix increases the profit then such a change is better. Profit as per the current product mix needs to be estimated to compare it with that under the proposed mix.

Calculation of current profits (₹)

	Products				
	Total	A	B	C	D
Sales	13,40,000	4,55,000	5,25,000	2,25,000	1,35,000
Variable Costs	9,47,625	3,25,000	3,98,000	1,75,625	49,000
Contribution	3,92,375	1,30,000	1,27,000	49,375	86,000
Fixed Cost	4,15,255				
Profit	–22,880				
P/V Ratio	0.29	0.29	0.24	0.22	0.64
P/V Ratio (%)	29	29	24	22	64

To decide the optimal mix the different products should be ranked in the descending order of their P/V ratio.

Proposed Sales-Mix (in descending order of P/V ratio)

Products (%)	P/V Ratio (₹)	Max. Capacity (₹)	Proposed Mix
D	64	3,00,000	3,00,000
A	29	5,00,000	5,00,000
B	24	6,00,000	3,90,000
C	22	2,50,000	1,50,000
Total			13,40,000

The total sales (₹13,40,000) will remain constant as the sales are market ordained and do not change by the mere change in the product mix by the firm. The optimization process focuses on giving the maximum weightage in the product mix to the products with higher *P/V* ratio. Product D and Product A that give the highest contribution margin (64% and 29% respectively) should be up-scaled to 100% of their capacity (of course under the assumption that there is a demand for them). The remaining capacity of ₹5,40,000 (13,40,000-(3,00,000+ 5,00,000)) should be shared between products with low *P/V* ratio (i.e. *B* and *C*). Supposing *B* is reduced to 65% of its maximum capacity available while *C* Is reduced to 60%. The profit for the new product mix will be:

Profit for the proposed product-mix (₹)

	Products				
	Total	A	B	C	D
Sales	1340,000	500,000	390,000	150,000	300,000
Variable Costs	878,772	357,143	295,657	117,083	108,889
Contribution	461,228	142,857	94,343	32,917	191,111
Fixed Cost	415,255				
Profit	45,973				

As can be seen from the table above that by maximizing the production of Product D and A that give the highest contribution of 64% and 29% respectively the profits of the firm have increased by ₹68,852.98 (i.e., from a loss of ₹22,880 under the present plan to a profit of ₹45,973 under the proposed mix). This is due to the diversion of production capacity towards products with higher contribution margin. Now let us look at a scenario where Product C that has the lowest *P/V* ratio is discontinued and the capacity created is diverted towards *B*.

Profit in case the least contributing Product C is discontinued (₹)

	Products				
	Total	A	B	C	D
Sales	13,40,000	5,00,000	5,40,000	0	3,00,000
Variable Costs	8,75,403	3,57,142	4,09,371	0	1,08,889
Contribution	4,64,597	1,42,857	1,30,629	0	1,91,111
Fixed Cost	4,15,255				
Profit	49,342				

If Product C, which is the least contributing product, is discontinued the profits of the firm increase by another ₹3369. This is the optimal mix.

EXERCISES

Concept Review Questions

1. The cost-volume-profit relationship assumes importance in several business decisions. Discuss.
2. The problem with fixed costs is that they are insensitive to the changes in the volume. Comment.
3. Breakeven point becomes an important reference point in business decisions. Examine.
4. Margin of safety provides the business with a cushion to tide over a temporary decline in the revenues. Discuss.

Critical Thinking Questions

1. Operating leverage is a double-edged sword, it cuts both ways. What is your opinion?
2. Why are fixed costs important for some crucial financial decisions?
3. A balanced cost structure is necessary for the survival and growth of a firm. Explain.
4. Unrealistic assumptions of CVP analysis limit its utility in unstable business environment. Discuss.

Practical Assignments

1. Make an industry-wise comparison of fixed to variable cost or fixed to total cost ratio to have an understanding of the impact of industry characteristics on cost structure.
2. Select firm(s)/industry of your choice and find out the key initiatives in the different functional areas that have been taken in the recent past to cut down the fixed costs. Study the impact of such initiatives on the operating and financial risks besides studying how they have influenced profits.

Numerical Problems

1. Breakeven Point

The sales of Incubator Ltd during the two years' period have been as follows:

	2005-06	2006-07
Units sold	10,000	15,500
Sales (₹)	2,50,0000	3,87,5000

The profit earned by the firm in the two consecutive years was as follows:

	2005-06	2006-07
Profit/Loss (₹)	50,000	82,000

Based on the above information on sales and profit/loss, you are required to determine the following:

1. The amount of fixed costs incurred by the firm
2. The breakeven point (in rupee and unit terms)
3. The amount of sales to earn a profit of ₹5 lakh

2. Margin of Safety

In the previous problem if the actual sale for Incubator Ltd is 15000 units, calculate the margin of safety (MOS) for Incubator Ltd. Also, indicate the relevance of MOS for the firm.

3. Breakeven Point for Multi-product Firm

ABC Ltd manufactures and sells four types of products under the brand names of *A*, *B*, *C*, and *D*. The sales mix in value comprises $33^1/_3$%, $41^2/_3$%, $16^2/_3$%, $8^1/_3$% of products *A*, *B*, *C*, and *D* respectively. The total budgeted sales are ₹60 lakh per month. The operating costs are:

	Product A	Product B	Product C	Product D
Variable costs (as a % of selling price)	60	68	80	40

The fixed cost incurred by *ABC* Ltd is ₹14.70 lakh per month. Based on the above information calculate the contribution margin for the firm on a product basis and the overall breakeven point.

4. Operating Leverage

Given below is the financial information for Lemofiz, a carbonated soft drink manufacturing company.

Sales (Units)	3,00,000
Selling Price (per unit) in ₹	32
Fixed Cost (₹)	4,50,000
Variable Cost (₹ per unit)	24
Debt (₹)	10,00,000
Interest Rate	12%

Based on the above information, answer the following:

1. What is the degree of operating leverage for the firm? What are its implications for the firm's financial decision-making?
2. How much would the firm's sales have to come down so that its earnings before taxes (EBT) is equal to zero?

5. Profit Planning Decisions

Adarsh Electro, manufacturer of AM/FM radios has prepared the following cost-sheet for the current financial year:

Particulars	Per unit of output (In ₹)
Material	700
Labour	150
Variable overheads	150
Total	1,000
Selling Price	2,000

In the previous year, the company sold 1 lakh units. The total fixed costs incurred by the firm amounted to ₹50 lakh. The company was the pioneer in the production of AM/FM radios when it entered this space in the year 2000-01. Over a period of time, the electronics goods sector has witnessed intense competition. Since the market size has gone up significantly, the company is contemplating a strategic shift by changing its focus from the bottom line to volumes.

The company management is considering revising its selling price so as to keep its margin intact. In this regard you are expected to determine the number of units that the firm is required to sell if:

1. The selling price is reduced by 5%
2. The selling price is reduced by 10%

6. Optimizing the Product Mix

The following are the figures of the current sales-mix of Regalia Enterprises:

Particulars	Products				
	A	B	C	D	Total
Sales (₹)	4,00,000	5,00,000	2,00,000	1,00,000	12,00,000
Variable Costs (₹)	2,40,000	3,40,000	1,60,000	40,000	7,80,000
Fixed Costs (₹)					2,94,000

The maximum production and sales capacity for Regalia Enterprises is as follows:

Particulars	Products				
	A	B	C	D	Total
Sales (in ₹)	5,00,000	6,00,000	2,00,000	3,00,000	16,00,000

Find out the maximum profitable sales-mix for Regalia Enterprises.

CASE STUDY

Salron Electronics: Moving up the Value Chain

Background

Salron Electronics Ltd was incorporated in the year 1968 under the name Electronics Consortium Pvt Ltd. It is engaged in manufacturing, distribution, and service of consumer electronics, IT and telecommunications. More than 60% of the company's equity is held by promoters while around 30% is owned by individuals. It has one subsidiary. At present, Mr Jairaman Hooda is the Chairman of the company.

The company is also involved in direct sales of telecom and IT products of different companies such as Sony Ericsson, Panasonic, Acer, etc. The product range under the consumer electronics category includes colour television of different sizes. The product range under telecom products includes faxes and mobiles while IT products comprise computers, floppy disk drive, keyboards, optical mouse, printers, etc.

The operations of the company can be classified into three main areas of business:

1. Infocom division
2. Component division
3. Consumer electronics division

Scenario

While the infocom and component divisions are doing very well, the consumer electronics division of the company has of late started facing problems. Consumer electronics division is operating in a fiercely competitive market where large MNC players are constantly defining the benchmarks for pricing and quality. The market continues to remain highly competitive with customers becoming increasingly demanding for better price and improved features.

On the price front too, the industry has witnessed continuous erosion of margin over the years. The key factors contributing to this trend are rising input costs, increased competition, and lower technology costs. With multinational companies focusing more on high-end sets, the market is shifting from curved to flat TVs, LCD, and plasma TVs.

Performance

The summary profit and loss account for consumer electronics division of Salron Ltd for the past four years is given in Table A and the key ratios are given in Table B.

Table A Divisional profit & loss account: Summary

	Mar 2004	Mar 2005	Mar 2006	Mar 2007
Income				
Sales	434.72	511.72	556.50	582.30
Other income	0.24	0.46	0.27	0.63
Non-recurring income	0.65	1.62	2.57	5.02
Expenditure				
Raw materials, stores, etc.	326.04	393.00	450.76	494.95
Wages	6.52	7.67	8.35	8.73
Energy (power & fuel)	1.74	2.30	2.61	2.91
Salaries	6.52	7.17	7.89	8.68
Indirect taxes (excise, etc.)	18.52	20.98	22.26	22.13
Advertising & marketing expenses	3.83	4.50	3.57	3.98
Distribution expenses	3.42	5.09	5.96	11.02
Others	12.70	14.47	14.50	16.86
Profits / losses				
PBDIT	56.32	58.61	43.43	18.68
Financial charges (incl. lease rent)	1.14	1.75	1.15	2.75
PBDT	55.18	56.86	42.28	15.93
Depreciation	4.19	4.63	4.42	5.21
PBT	50.99	52.23	37.86	10.72
Tax provision	15.30	15.67	11.30	3.20
PAT	35.69	36.56	26.50	7.50

Table B Key Ratios

	Mar 2004	*Mar 2005*	*Mar 2006*	*Mar 2007*
Ratios				
PAT/Sales (%)	8.21	7.14	4.76	1.29
PAT/Equity Capital (%)	404.69	414.50	300.49	85.10
PAT/Capital employed (%)	36.58	33.73	23.27	5.12
(PAT+Int)/Total Assets (%)	23.51	21.83	15.92	3.60
Debt/Equity	0.98	1.17	1.08	3.46
Current Ratio	2.09	2.10	2.37	1.69
Interest coverage (times)	45.73	30.84	33.92	4.90
Gross working capital cycle (days)	171.00	176.00	196.00	257.00
Net working capital cycle (days)	142.00	144.00	163.00	227.00
Avg. days of debtors	27.00	29.00	29.00	34.00
Avg. days of creditors	29.00	32.00	33.00	30.00

The total number of units sold in 2006-07 was 9,45,600. Product-wise sales and sales price for the 2006-07 was as follows:

	Sales Price *(Per unit)*	Sales *(units)*
20″, 200 w coloured TV	6000	1,13,372
20″, 100 w coloured TV	5600	75,648
21″, 200 w Stereo ZX	6500	4,25,520
21″, 100 w conventional	5900	3,30,960

If the company adheres to the existing production–sales mix, the total sales (projected) for the coming financial year is estimated to be 9,87,205 units. The product-wise sales mix and estimated sales price projections are as follows:

	Estimated Sales Price	*Projected Sales mix (Per unit)*
20″, 200 w coloured TV	5450	0.12
20″, 100 w coloured TV	5115	0.08
21″, 200 w Stereo ZX	6500	0.47
21″,100 w conventional	5900	0.33

A meeting of top management executives was convened to discuss the problems faced by the consumer electronics division of the company and the strategy to confront them. Mr Gupta, the CFO of the company, appraised about the future plans of the company to tide over the crisis. He said 'intensification of competition and the import of components especially from China have put a significant pressure on margins. Growing input costs have put further pressure on margins particularly for low-end products.

Till about 2005, market penetration was high for the conventional products as there was a huge demand for colour TVs from the first time buying households and also from those graduating from B&W television sets to colour television sets. However, in the coming years, the market will be driven primarily by the replacement demand particularly for the high value products like Plasma TV, LCD TV, etc. We have to realize that in its next phase, the consumer electronics segment will be less of a volume game and more of a margin game with high value products driving the revenue.'

Management's Response

Explaining further the CFO said, "In view of the changing dynamics of the sector, we plan to move up the value chain both by altering our production–sales mix and also by shifting our focus from manufacturing to our core strength—distribution network. We have entered into strategic alliance with the Korean consumer electronics manufacturing giant Electro Korea, which has started its production operations in India and wants distribution partners. Starting from the beginning of next year we, as per the agreement with our strategic partners, will outsource our manufacturing to our Korean strategic partner.

Electro Korea's competencies are in engineering, manufacturing, R&D, business process, and supply chain. A strategic partnership with Electro Korea will not only bring down the cost of production/procurement but will also free personnel, manufacturing equipment, and inventory investment for other more useful corporate purposes." Mr Gupta added furth that "Additional space that will be created due to discontinuing of production can be utilized for expanding our telecom division operations that are growing at a rate of 20% annually. The fixed assets base is likely to come down by 45% on account of outsourcing. The proceeds realized from the sale of fixed assets would be utilized towards the repayment of debt. This will bring down the leverage of the firm."

To a query by VP (Human Resources) regarding the status of employees consequent upon restructuring, Mr Gupta said, "We are aware of the implications of large-scale retrenchments and there will be only 10–15% lay offs on account of such a business transformation. After proper training and orientation, we will shift 85–90% of the workforce to our infocom division. In any case, the HR department is planning to expand the workforce for the infocom business by 15% in view of the exponential growth witnessed by the sector. I would like to flag the quality issue. Electro Korea has received OHSAS 18001:1999 certification from the British Standard Institution (BSI). Besides ISO 9001:2000 certification, the products of Electro Korea have been getting quality certification from Bureau Verita."

"Now allow me to come to the financials of the strategy. Since the demand for 20 inches colour televisions has thinned out, we propose to discontinue the production/sales of these models under the new option. The total sales (in units) projected for the coming year as per the new strategy is estimated as 1,73,137 units."

The projected sales (in units) are given in Table C:

Table C Projected Sales

	Sales Price (Per unit)	*Sales Units*	*Price of purchase from Electro Korea (₹)*
21″, 200 w Stereo ZX	6500	51941	4600
21″, 100 w conventional	5900	43284	3900
42″ Plasma TV with revolutionary Claro filter	83000	34627	68000
42″ Plasma TV with revolutionary Claro filter	78000	25971	61000
Time Machine, 42" Plasma TV with 80 GB built in hard disk	102000	17314	86000

Switching over from in-house production to outsourcing of manufacturing function is likely to bring down the breakeven point for the firm besides improving its bottom line and realigning its debt–equity ratio.

With respect to cost the following additional information is available:

1. Raw materials, wages, and energy as variable costs.
2. Salaries as fixed costs. Normally there is around 10% per annum increase in the salary bill on account of yearly increments and dearness allowances.

Indirect taxes comprise mainly of excise duty and sales tax. They vary directly with sales. In the previous year, indirect taxes were around 3.8% of the sales and are likely to go up to 4% due to marginal increase in excise duty.

Discuss

1. What are the reasons for the firm to consider the option of outsourcing the production function?
2. Do you recommend the plan of firm moving up the value chain?
3. Do you subscribe to Mr Gupta's view that the company will be able to breakeven earlier under the outsourcing option as compared to in-house production option?
4. What will be the impact of alternative strategy on the firm's PAT?

In the CD

- BEP and Margin of Safety
- BEP of a Multi Product Firm
- Sales to Earn Desired Profit

PART TWO

VALUATION CONCEPTS

CHAPTER 4

Time Value of Money

LEARNING OBJECTIVES

After going through this chapter, you will be able to:

- understand the concept of time value of money
- compute the time value of money
- calculate the future value as well as the present value of money
- understand the concept of present value and future value of annuities
- compute equated monthly instalments (EMIs)
- segregate the components of interest and principal from the EMIs

DE-CONFOUNDING AJAY WITH COMPOUNDING

Vijay is a professional banker whose son Ajay just passed his seventh standard examination with excellent scores. Ajay is very keen to become an engineer and pursue an MBA thereafter.

Vijay, equally keen and concerned about his son's future, informed Ajay, 'I have started saving ₹2,000 every month in a bank deposit, and I will do so for the next 5 years when you would be ready for admission in an engineering college.'

Ajay who is fond of arithmetic promptly calculated and said, 'At ₹2,000 per month, the annual amount would be ₹24,000. Over 5 years, it would become ₹1,20,000. Do you think this is enough to cover the admission expenses to an engineering college?'

Vijay smilingly said, 'No I would get much more than this, because the bank would pay interest @12% every year.' Ajay again scratched his head for a while and responded, 'That would mean you would get ₹2,880 as interest each year. Your interest would be ₹14,400 for 5 years and that makes a total of ₹1,34,400. Even that is not enough.'

Vijay again smiled, 'Your maths seems alright, but you need to understand something more. Even interest earns interest.' 'Banks pay you interest on a quarterly basis. If you do not withdraw the interest amount, it gets added to the original amount. So, money grows faster than you think,' explained Vijay. 'I do not understand this. What is a quarter?' Ajay asked curiously.

'A quarter means one-fourth and is equal to 3 months. Since it is one-fourth of a year, it is called a quarter. For the first payment of ₹2,000, I get an interest of ₹60 for the first quarter. This is equivalent to 12% per year. So for the next quarter, the principal becomes ₹2,060 on which I get an interest of ₹61.80 for the second quarter. This is more than what I got in the first quarter. This goes on till I do not withdraw the money.'

'You mean—even on interest, we get interest. Is it not too complicated to know the amount you will get after 5 years,' queried Ajay.

Vijay quickly referred to his table and said '₹2,000 with a quarterly interest of 3% each quarter for 5 years would give me about ₹3,312.'

'That means without doing anything, you can get ₹1,312 extra. Why is it so?' asked Ajay.

Vijay further elaborated, 'When I deposit this money with the bank, I cannot use it elsewhere. I forego some alternative. For example, I could have used ₹1,000 for buying a shirt for you.

'What about the second instalment and all the other monies that you would deposit with the bank?' asked Ajay.

'It would also be done the same way as I did for the first ₹2,000. But, it would be less because the bank had this money for a period less than 5 years. If I deposit ₹2,000 every month for 5 years, I would get', Vijay paused for a while to refer a table, 'about ₹1,63,340'.

Ajay got assured of his future and went to play with his friends.

INTRODUCTION

Time value of money is central to the concept of finance. It recognizes that the value of money is different at different points of time. Since money can be put to productive use, its value is different depending upon when it is received or paid. In simpler terms, the value of a certain amount of money today is more than its value in future. It is not because of the uncertainty involved with time but purely on account of timing. The difference in the value of money at present and in future is referred to as time value of money.

The value of money is different at different points of time due to several reasons. These are—(1) presence of inflation; (2) preference of individuals for current consumption over future consumption; and (3) investment opportunities that make the money grow with time possibly without taking risk.

Presence of inflation, preference for current consumption, and investment opportunities available are the three causes that change the value of money with time

Generally speaking, decrease in the value of money with time is due to inflation. Inflation is all pervasive and is a universal phenomenon, the causes of which are a subject matter of economics. For the purpose of our discussion, we will define inflation as the rise in the prices of goods, leading to a reduction in the value of money. The prices of goods and services increase with time. Hence, a lesser quantity of the same goods can be bought in future than at present. This applies to most products in general, though some products such as computers and durables may defy the trend. The presence of inflation makes money more valuable today than tomorrow.

The second reason for the decreasing value of money is the preference of individuals to consume now than later. Each one of us faces a situation of trade-off between present and future consumption. Ideally speaking, each one of us wants to fulfil all our needs today rather than in future. Consumption is postponed in the hope of having more in the future. This sacrifice of present consumption in favour of having more tomorrow must have some value.

Last but not the least; money has time value because capital can be put to productive use, if it is not consumed now. Like any other commodity, money too is scarce. The surplus money with one unit (individual firm) can be utilized by another who requires finance. The latter can put it to some productive use and derive some benefit. For passing the benefit to another party, some reward must accrue to the lending unit. While accepting deposit from individuals, banks are willing to pay some interest on deposit because they would lend to someone who needs money and thus receive a greater reward. Therefore, even the idle money has value because of the lost opportunity to invest and earn an income on it.

The application of time value of money is an invaluable tool in financial analysis. The scope of application of this concept is very vast. Since all financial issues almost invariably deal with the analysis of cash flows that occur at different points of time, it makes them non-comparable. In order to compare the cash flows occuring at different points in time they need to be brought at the common point in time. The concept of time value of money is used for this purpose.

The concept of time value of money is used in valuation of financial securities such as bonds, shares, etc. It is also used in corporate finance in the areas of valuation of firms, capital budgeting, and mergers and acquisition. Time value of money finds its applications in personal finance decisions such as determining instalments of loans in leasing and hire-purchase transactions.

BASIS OF TIME VALUE

Having recognized that the value of money is greater today than it is tomorrow, the next natural question is to determine how much worth can be attached to time factor. As stated in the earlier section, the value of money differs with time. The difference in value can be attributed to two broad factors—(1) the risk involved in getting the returns; and (2) the wait involved in deferring the consumption.

Capital can be put to alternative uses depending upon the host of investment opportunities available. The choice of investment options depends on the preference of users of capital. Different people use capital in different ways. Despite diversity of uses the returns offered by capital are determinable unlike most commodities that have rather undeterminable consumption value. Since the value of money is primarily dependent upon the investment opportunities available, the returns offered can form the basis of time value of money. The returns foregone on the investment is referred as the *opportunity cost of capital*. It is dependent upon the risk associated with the investment avenues. This aspect is discussed in detail in later chapters.

Time value of money does not account for the risks associated with investments.

The second component of basis of value of money comes from the waiting time for the investment to mature. The element of waiting isolates the risk component from the basis of the value of money. Investment opportunities yield uncertain returns. This uncertainty of return is referred to as *risk*. The return obtainable without risk is the reward for waiting. Although it is impossible to obtain a risk-free return, one can come fairly close to identifying an opportunity that makes return fairly certain.

The basis of finding time value of money is normally specified by the rate per period usually denoted in percentage terms. Normally the chosen period is annual more by convention than by rule.

Compounding and Discounting

Financial analysts examine cash flows at different points of time. For meaningful comparison, all these cash flows should have occurred at the same point of time. Either the cash flow occurring today has to be converted into its equivalent at a future date or the cash flow occurring later has to be converted back to its value today.

The future value of money that is available today can be calculated using the concept of compounding. Similarly, the present value of money accruing later is estimated by discounting.

FINDING FUTURE VALUE

Suppose you are given ₹100 today. You decide not to use it now and instead deposit in a bank that pays you an interest of 10% per annum. How much does it grow in one year? This rate of 10% becomes the basis of time value of money. The future sum payable will be equal to the original amount known as principal plus interest thereon. The value after one year becomes:

> Compounding is the process of applying interest over interest. Discounting is the reverse of compounding.

₹100 + 10% of ₹100 = 100 + 10 = ₹110

or $P \times (1 + r) = 100 \times (1 + 0.1) = 100 \times 1.1 =$ ₹110

where P is principal amount invested and r is the interest rate per annum represented in decimal form.

If you invest this money for a further period of one year the amount after two years becomes 110 × 1.1 = ₹121.00, with ₹110 becoming principal amount for the second period. The interest for the first period becomes entitled for interest during the second period. The earning of interest over interest is referred to as *compounding*. Interest earned only on the original principal amount is known as simple interest. If ₹100 were invested for two years with simple interest the payable amount would have been ₹120. The additional Re 1 is the effect of the compounding.

This can be alternatively established by using the formula $P \times (1 + r)^2$. Extending the logic further, for investment of amount P for n periods at interest rate of r per period, we may generalize that the future value of money (F) as given in Equation 4-1.

$$F = P \times (1 + r)^n \tag{4-1}$$

If the original principal amount is taken as Re 1, Equation 4-1 gives the future value after n periods at interest rate of r. It is known as *future value interest factor*, FVIF(r, n).

The future value interest factors are given in Appendix A-1 for 30 years and up to 40%. One can easily compute them using a computer in MS Excel or a calculator using Equation 4-1.

The impact of compounding becomes larger and larger as the period of investment increases. For example, investing Re 1 for one year at 25% yields only ₹1.25 but it increases by over 9 times at ₹9.313 if investment horizon is increased to 10 years. The rate of increase is larger with the increase in the investment

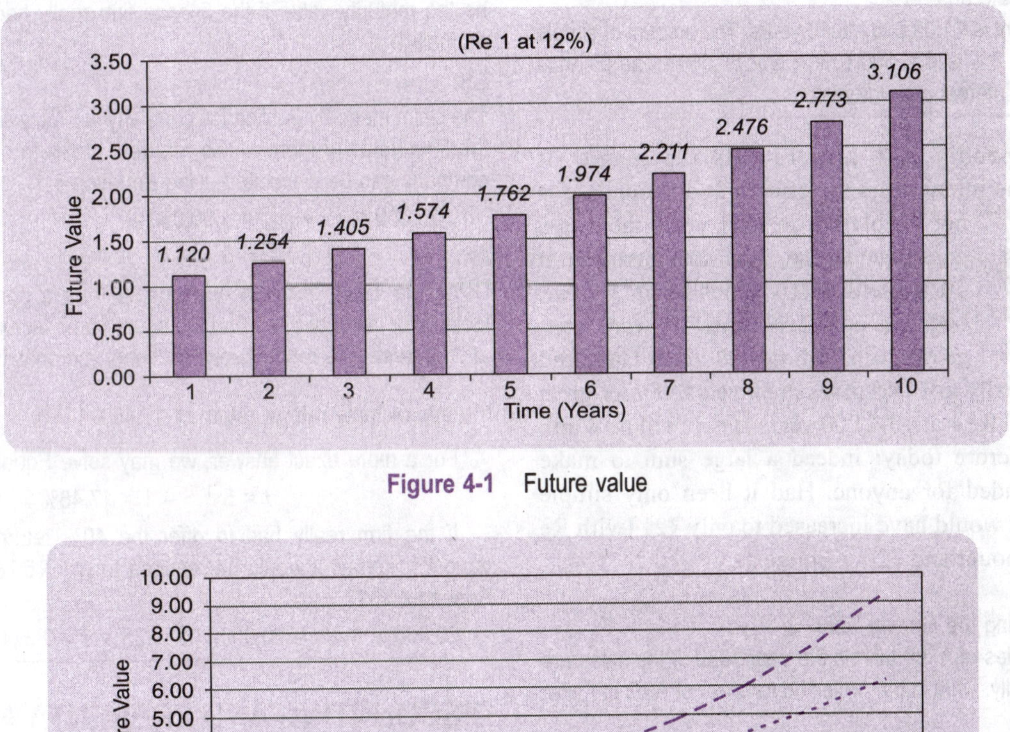

Figure 4-1 Future value

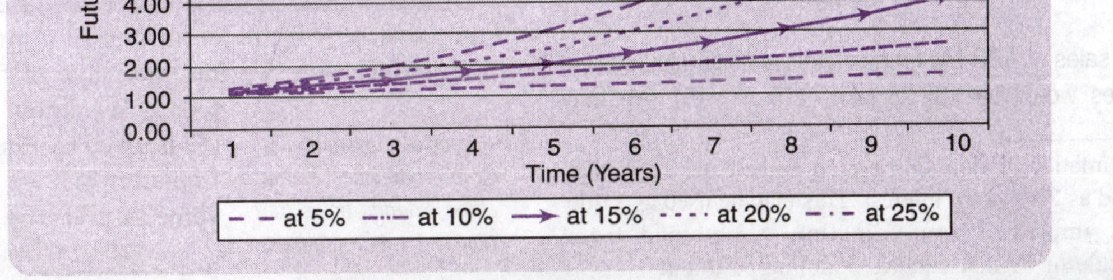

Figure 4-2 Growth of future values

horizon. Figure 4-1 displays the value of Re 1 at 12% at the end of each of the 10 years.

It can be observed in Figure 4-1 that the increase each year is larger than what it was in any of the previous years. The increase in value from 5th to 6th year is 0.212 (1.974 –1.762) while from the 6th to 7th year there has been an increase of 0.237. This is because additional amount of interest becomes available in subsequent periods. Impact of future values with varying interest rates is depicted in Figure 4-2.

Example 4-1 Compounding and Simple Interest

You have ₹50,000 available today for investment. A bank has offered 8% interest payable annually. For how long should you invest with the bank so that the amount is doubled? How much would be the simple interest for this period?

Solution

Scanning Appendix A-1 for a value of 2.000 at 8% reveals that the period of investment must be close to 9 years. We may also find the exact answer using Equation 4-1.

$50{,}000 \times (1 + 0.08)^n = 1{,}00{,}000$

or $(1.08)^n = 2$

This is difficult to solve[1]. The trial and error procedure may be adopted to obtain an approximate answer.

The maturity amount is ₹1,00,000 after 9 years. The amount of simple interest for 9 years at 8% is ₹36,000 (8% × 9 × 50,000). The balance amount of ₹14,000 is interest over interest.

A look at Appendix A-1 also reveals the magic of compounding. In the initial years the effect of compounding is not visible but in later years there is a conspicuous rise. Any sum invested at 10% yields 1.10 times after 1 year, becomes only 2.59 times 10 years later, grows to 6.73 times 20 years later, and increases phenomenally to 17.45 times in 30 years. If your great grandfather invested Re 1 at 10% 200 years ago, it will be worth more than ₹18.99 crore today; indeed a large sum to make happiness compounded for anyone. Had it been only simple interest, the amount would have increased to only ₹21 (with Re 1 as the original amount and ₹20 as interest).

Compounding effect is greater with increasing interest and increasing time.

Example 4-2 Finding the Growth Rate

ABC Ltd registered sales of ₹100 lakh in the year 1990. If the sales are growing at 15% annually, what is the projected turnover of ABC Ltd after 10 years?

Solution

We can find out the sales of ABC Ltd for next year at ₹115 lakh. For the year 1992, the sales would be 132.25 lakh (115 × 1.15). We may continue this exercise for 10 years. Instead we may use the table in Appendix A-1 and use the factor of 4.046 and project the sale of ₹404.60 lakh (100 × 4.046) in the 10th year.

The impact of compounding is more and more pronounced as the rate of interest increases. This can be seen from Figure 4-2 as it displays how fast the future values grow as time elapses and as rate of interest increases. Notice that at 15% the value grows to about 4 times in 10 years while for the same parameters the value becomes about 9.5 times if the rate of interest is increased to 25%.

Averaging out the compounded returns to estimate the annual returns is a mistake often committed by people. This is also misused by a large number of firms to make large claims that have the capacity to mislead many investors. Example 4-3 highlights such practices.

Example 4-3 Implied Interest Rate

A finance firm has announced a scheme called 'Lakhpati in 10 years'. It has promised to pay ₹1,00,000 after 10 years for every ₹20,000 deposited today. The advertisement states that the firm pays ₹80,000 as interest at ₹8,000 every year and therefore offers a 40% annual return. Do you agree with the claim made in the scheme? Explain. What would be the maturity value if the finance firm really had to offer 40% return annually?

Solution

The claim made by the finance company is simply erroneous as it ignores the time value of money. The real rate of return offered by the finance company can be calculated using Equation 4-1:

$20{,}000 \times (1 + r)^{10} = 1{,}00{,}000$

or, $(1 + r)^{10} = 5$

Using the Table given in Appendix A-1 for a period of 10 years and looking for value of 5, we find the future value factors of 4.807 and 5.234 at 17% and 18% respectively. By linear extrapolation we may arrive at the approximate rate of return of 17.45% $\left(17\% + \dfrac{5.000 - 4.807}{5.234 - 4.807}\right)$.

For a more exact answer, we may solve Equation 4-1 for r

$r = 5^{1/10} - 1 = 17.46\%$

If the firm really had to offer the 40% return for every ₹20,000 deposited today, it would be required to pay ₹5,78,500 (Using table in Appendix A-1).

$20{,}000 \times 1.4^{10} = 20{,}000 \times 28.925 = ₹5{,}78{,}500$

DISCOUNTING AND PRESENT VALUE

The inverse of the compounding process is termed as *discounting*. Here we find the value of future cash flow as on today. We know that the future value (F) is given by Equation 4-1. By restating Equation 4-1 we may find the present value as given by Equation 4-2.

Effect of discounting is more pronounced as the time extends or as the discount rate increases.

$$P = \frac{F}{(1+r)^n} \tag{4-2}$$

Factor of $1/(1 + r)^n$ is known as present value discount factor at interest rate of r for n period, and is denoted as PVDIDF(r,n). A

[1]Fairly good approximation of doubling period is the Rule of 72 that gives doubling period as 72/Rate of interest. This may be used as a rule of thumb. Further improved approximation is obtained from what is referred as rule of 69 that equates doubling period at

$$0.35 + \frac{69}{\text{Rate of interest}}.$$

The rules are fairly accurate for interest rates up to 20%.

table containing the present values at different interest rates and for periods up to 30 years is presented in Appendix A-2.

Assuming an interest rate of 10% per annum, the present value of ₹100 expected a year later is ₹90.9090 (₹100/1.1). Alternatively put, the future value of ₹90.9090 after 1 year is ₹100. This may be verified using Equation 4-2. Similarly the present value of ₹100 after two years would decrease to ₹82.6446, which is calculated as:

Value of ₹100 after two years

$$P = \frac{F}{(1+r)^n} = \frac{100}{(1+0.1)^2}$$

$$= \frac{90.9090}{1.1} = ₹82.6446$$

Equations 4-1 and 4-2 form the backbone of financial analysis. These seemingly simple equations are extremely powerful tools for evaluating vast cases of financial applications.

The issue addressed in discounting is opposite to that of compounding. While discussing compounding we addressed the issue of finding the future value of a present sum available if invested at a specific rate for a specified period. Compounding was used to estimate the value of ₹100 invested at 15% for two years. Using the concept of discounting, one can estimate the amount to be invested today at 15% if ₹100 is needed after 2 years. To answer this question, we need to find the PVIF(15%,2) from the table in Appendix A-2 and multiply it by 100. The answer is ₹75.61 (100 × 0.7561) in this case.

Example 4-4 Using Compounding and Discounting Tables

Suppose you have ₹12,000 today and need to preserve it for the next 8 years when you are required to pay fees for your daughter, which is estimated to be ₹40,000.

(a) At what rate should you invest this money so as to have the required sum at the end of 8 years?

(b) If you needed ₹40,000 after 8 years at 12%, what amount should you invest today?

Solution

(a) The problem may be solved using Appendix A-1. The future value required after 8 years is:

$$\frac{40,000}{12,000} = 3.333$$

For a value of 3.333 for 8 years, we find the money grows to 3.059 times the original if invested at 15% per annum and 3.378 times if invested at 16%. Using extrapolation, we can find the approximate rate of investment as:

$$\frac{3.378 - 3.333}{3.378 - 3.059} = \frac{0.045}{0.319} = 0.14,$$

(Gives 16.00% – 0.14%) = 15.86%

(b) The discounting factor at 12% for 8 years from Appendix A-2 is 0.4049

Therefore the principal amount that you must have now

= 40,000 × 0.4049 = ₹16,196.

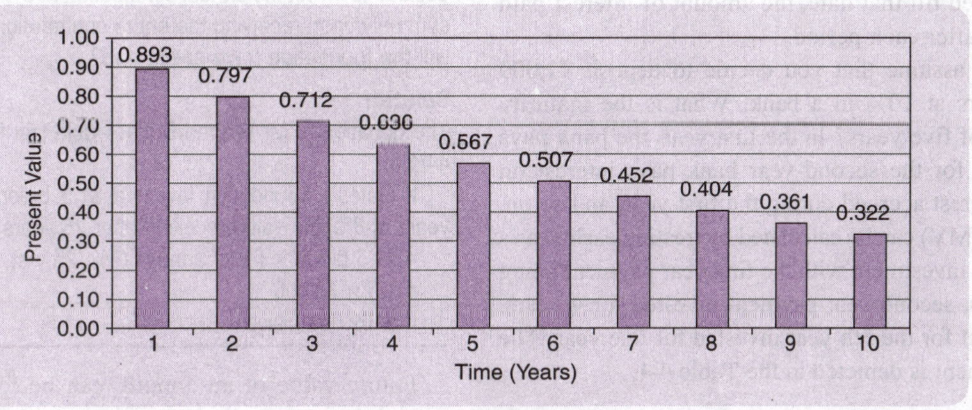

Figure 4-3 Present value

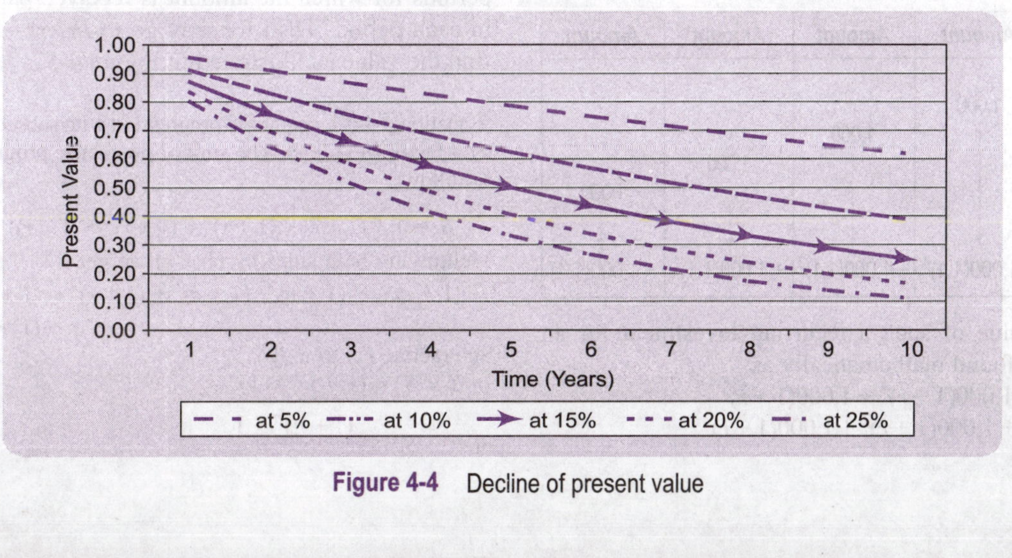

Figure 4-4 Decline of present value

The impact of discounting increases if the time horizons are large and as the discount rate increases. Figure 4-3 depicts the decline in value of Re 1 at 12% for a period from 1 to 10 years. Note that the value of Re 1.00 is Re 0.893 after one year, while it is merely Re 0.322 after 10 years.

A high discount rate signifies a low present value. The impact of change in discount rate in the present value can be seen from Figure 4-4. The decline in value is fairly steep with increase in the discount rate. As the discount rate increases, the change in present value will be more than proportionate.

FUTURE VALUE OF ANNUITY

Some times we make investments on a periodic basis. We either receive or pay a fixed amount in each period for a specified number of periods. A stream of cash flows on a recurring basis at uniform intervals is referred to as *annuity*. Examples of such payments include premium payable when buying an insurance policy and equated monthly instalments (EMIs) when repaying a loan. Although the term annuity refers to annual periods, it can be used for any period that is equally spaced.

A typical example of an annuity is a recurring deposit account in a bank where a customer undertakes to deposit a specified sum at regular intervals (mostly monthly) for specified number of periods on which the bank pays the contracted rate of interest. Since the bank pays interest on specified dates on the amount deposited till that date, the amount of interest paid would accumulate after each period.

As an example, assume that you decide to deposit ₹1,000 annually for 5 years at 10% in a bank. What is the maturity amount at the end of five years? In the first year, the bank pays interest on ₹1,000, for the second year bank pays interest on ₹2,000 plus the interest accrued during the first year, and so on. The maturity value (MV) can be calculated by treating each year's stream as a separate investment with the first year payment being invested for 5 years, second year payment invested for 4 years, and the last payment for the 5th year invested for one year. The time line of investment is depicted in the Table 4-1.

Table 4-1 Time Line of Investment for 5 years

Time	Amount	Amount	Amount	Amount	Amount
1	1,000				
2	↓	1,000			
3	↓	↓	1,000		
4	↓	↓	↓	1,000	
5	↓	↓	↓	↓	1,000
MV	$1{,}000(1.1)^5$	$+\ 1{,}000(1.1)^4$	$+\ 1{,}000(1.1)^3$	$+\ 1{,}000(1.1)^2$	$+\ 1{,}000(1.1)$

The maturity value of such a recurring investment for an interest rate of r is found mathematically as:

$$= 1{,}000(1+r)^5 + 1{,}000(1+r)^4 + 1{,}000(1+r)^3 + 1{,}000(1+r)^2 + 1{,}000(1+r)$$

$$= 1{,}000(1.1)^5 + 1{,}000(1.1)^4 + 1{,}000(1.1)^3 + 1{,}000(1.1)^2 + 1{,}000(1.1)$$

$$= (1{,}000 \times 1.611) + (1{,}000 \times 1.464) + (1{,}000 \times 1.331) + (1{,}000 \times 1.21) + (1{,}000 \times 1.1)$$

$$= ₹7{,}716$$

Mathematically, an amount of Re 1 invested for n years at interest rate of r is represented as Equation 4-3.

Future Value of Annuity of Re 1, FVA (r, n)

$$= \sum_{1}^{n} (1+r)^n \quad (4\text{-}3)$$

The value in Equation 4-3 is referred as *future value annuity factor* at interest rate of r for n periods. A table containing future value annuity factors for 30 years and for interest rates up to 40% is given in Appendix A-3. These values are derived from following formula given as Equation 4-4[2]:

Future Value Annuity Factor at r% for n years, FVA (r, n)

$$= \frac{(1+r)^n - 1}{r} \quad (4\text{-}4)$$

Example 4-5 Finding Annuity Values

Mr Warren Buffet, the second richest man in the world, in June 2006 decided to donate 85% of his $44 billion fortune to Bill & Melinda Gates Foundation in instalments of $ 1.5 billion every year. Mr Buffet stipulated that the annual payments must be distributed to the beneficiaries within a year before the subsequent payment is made. If Mr Buffet did not stipulate the condition and instead, Gates Foundation decided to invest the annual contribution at 8% and spend the aggregate sum only upon receiving the entire contribution promised, what amount will the foundation have at the end?

Solution

The donation of Mr Warren Buffet would last for next 25 years (0.85 × 44/1.5).

If Gates's Foundation invested $1.5 billion every year for next 25 years at 8%, the value received after 25 years would be:

= $1.5 billion × FV of annuity (8%, 25 yrs)
= 1.5 × 73.106
= $109.659 billion

Future value of an annuity can be found using Excel. We need three inputs—the rate of interest per period, the number of periods for which the amount is received/paid, and the amount in each period. Then we may go to *Insert—Function—FV* and find the value as illustrated in Figure 4-5.

[2]Equation 4-4 is a geometric progression with subsequent value increased by a factor of $(1 + r)$. The sum of geometric progression S_n is derived as follows:

$$S_n = 1 + (1+r) + (1+r)^2 + (1+r)^3 + (1+r)^4 \ldots + (1+r)^{n-1} \quad (1)$$

Multiplying both sides by $(1 + r)$ we get

$$(1+r)S_n = (1+r) + (1+r)^2 + (1+r)^3 + (1+r)^4 \ldots + (1+r)^{n-1} + (1+r)^n \quad (2)$$

Subtracting (1) from (2):

$$r \times S_n = (1+r)^n - 1$$

or, $$S_n = \frac{(1+r)^n - 1}{r}$$

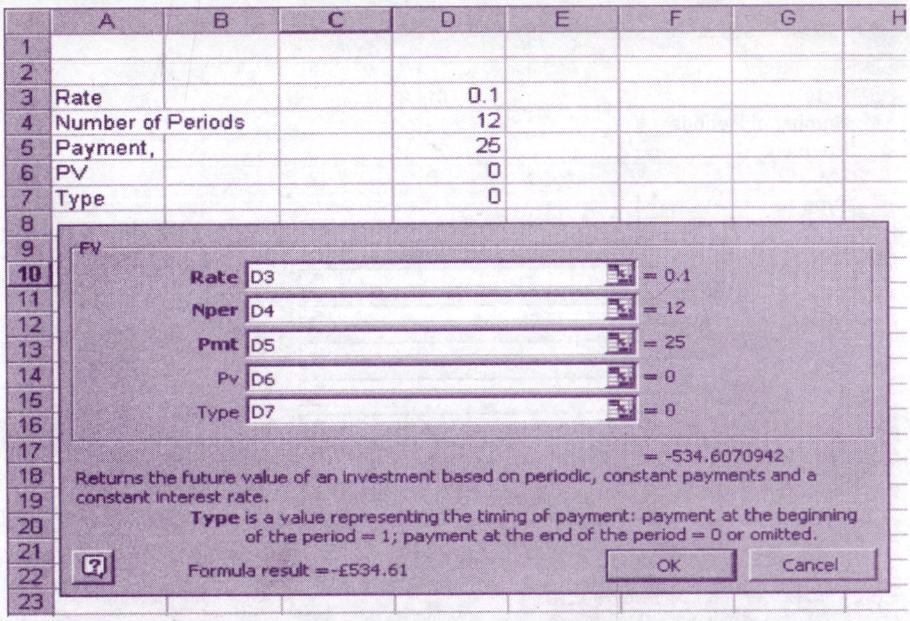

Figure 4-5 Finding future value of an annuity using EXCEL

PRESENT VALUE OF ANNUITY

We considered the issue of making investment on a periodic basis and determined the value of the investment at a future date in Example 4-5. The issue was also considered by making a recurring deposit in the bank for 5 years and analysed from the perspective of the investor. We now address the same issue from the perspective of the bank.

The bank received a stream of cash flows on a recurring basis at uniform intervals. It pays a specified rate of interest on the money deposited with it. Referring to the same example of ₹1,000 invested at 10% for next 5 years, the bank wants to know the present value of the stream of cash flows that it receives for the next five years. Here the contracted rate of interest becomes the cost to the bank.

From common sense we know that the present value of the investment received today is ₹1,000. The present value of second instalment is less than the first instalment. Let us assume that cost of funds for the bank is 10%. If so, the present value of second receipt is ₹1,000/(1+0.1). The present value (PV) of the entire stream of cash flows can be estimated by treating each year's cash flow as a separate independent element with the first year investment received today, second year instalment being received a year later, and with the last payment received at beginning of 5th year. The time line for the purpose of present value is depicted in the Table 4-2.

The present value of such a recurring receipts for an interest rate r is calculated as:

$$= [1{,}000/(1+r)^4] + [1{,}000/(1+r)^3] + [1{,}000/(1+r)^2] + [1{,}000/(1+r)^1] + 1{,}000$$

$$= [1{,}000/(1.1)^4] + [1{,}000/(1.1)^3] + [1{,}000/(1.1)^2] + [1{,}000/(1.1)^1] + 1{,}000$$

$$= [1{,}000 \times 0.6830] + [1{,}000 \times 0.7513] + [1{,}000 \times 0.8264] + [1{,}000 \times 0.9091] + 1{,}000$$

= ₹4,169.80

Table 4-2 Time line of present value for 5 years

Time	*Amount*	*Amount*	*Amount*	*Amount*	*Amount*
1	1,000				
2		1,000			
3			1,000		
4				1,000	
5					1,000
PV	1,000	+ 1,000(1.1)$^{-1}$	1,000(1.1)$^{-2}$	1,000(1.1)$^{-3}$	1,000(1.1)$^{-4}$

Mathematically, the present value of an amount of Re 1 received for n years at interest rate of r is represented as Equation 4-6.

Present Value of Annuity of Re 1,

$$\text{PVA}(r, n) = \sum_{1}^{n} \frac{1}{(1+r)^n} \tag{4-5}$$

The value in Equation 4-6 is referred as to as present value *annuity factor*. A table containing present value annuity factors for 30 years and for interest rates up to 40% are given in Appendix A-4. These values are derived from following formula[3]:

Present Value Annuity Factor at r% for n years,

$$\text{PVA}(r, n) = \frac{(1+r)^n - 1}{r(1+r)^n} \tag{4-6}$$

[3]Equation 4-6 is a geometric progression with subsequent value decreased by a factor of 1/(1+r). The sum of geometric progression S_n is derived as follows:

$$S_n = (1+r)^{-1} + (1+r)^{-2} + (1+r)^{-3} + (1+r)^{-4} \ldots + (1+r)^{-n} \quad (1)$$

Multiplying both sides by $(1 + r)$, we get:

$$(1+r)S_n = (1+r) + (1+r)^{-1} + (1+r)^{-2} + (1+r)^{-3} \ldots + (1+r)^{-(n-1)} \quad (2)$$

Subtracting (1) from (2):

$$r \times S_n = 1 - (1+r)^{-n}$$

or, $$S_n = \frac{(1+r)^n - 1}{r(1+r)^n}$$

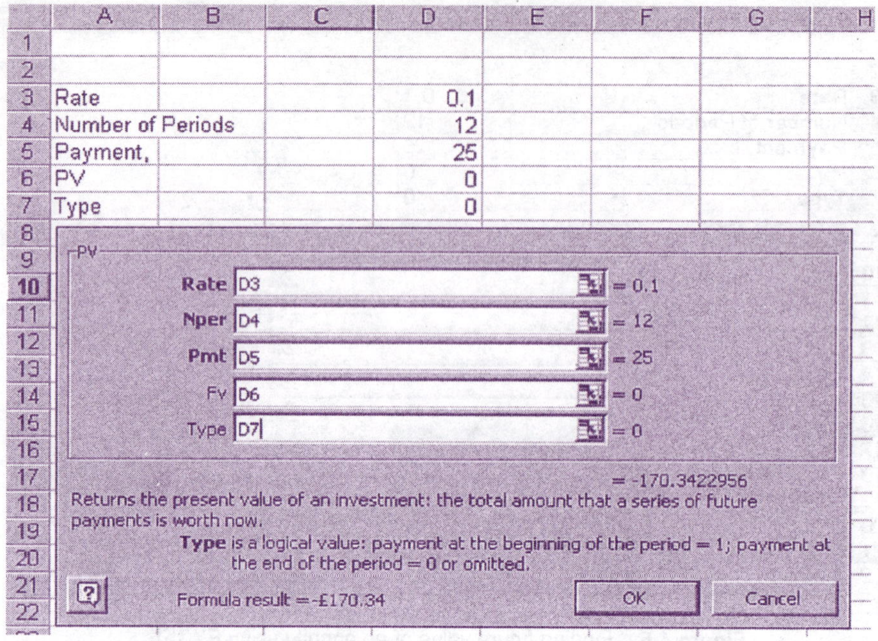

Figure 4-6 Finding present value of an annuity using EXCEL

Example 4-6 Present Value of an Annuity

In Example 4-5, we found that Mr Warren Buffet decided to donate 85% of his $ 44 billion fortune to Bill & Melinda Gates Foundation in instalments of $1.5 billion every year since June 2006. Do you think that Mr Warren Buffet has really donated 85% of the wealth? If not, what is the percentage of wealth that is being really donated by him assuming that he earns 8% on his wealth?

Solution

The donation of Mr Warren Buffet would last for the next 25 years (0.85 × 44/1.5).

If Gates Foundation received $1.5 billion every year for next 25 years, the present value of the amount at 8% would be:

= $1.5 billion × PV of Annuity (8%, 25 yrs) = 1.5 × 10.6748
= $16.0122 billion

$$\text{The fraction of present wealth being donated} = \frac{16.0122}{44} = 36.39\%$$

Like future value of an annuity, we can also find the present value of an annuity using EXCEL. We need three inputs—rate of interest per period, number of periods for which the amount is received/paid, and the amount in each period. Then we may go to *Insert – Function – PV* and find the value as illustrated in Figure 4-6.

PERIODICITY OF COMPOUNDING AND DISCOUNTING

Hitherto we considered rate of interest and periods as annual. Compounding or discounting of cash flows was done for the annual periods. However, if the periodicity of application of interest is changed, the computation also changes. Consider a simple example of a deposit of ₹100 for two years in the bank at 10% annual rate of interest. If the interest compounds annually, the maturity value of the deposit will be ₹121 (₹100 × 1.1^2).

Now let us assume that the interest is compounded quarterly instead of annually. Let us examine if the maturity amount changes. At annual interest of 10%, the bank shall now pay 2.5% interest at the end of first quarter. This would make ₹102.50 as principal for second quarter on which another 2.5% would be paid. Similarly, for the third and fourth quarter, additional amount would be available for earning interest. Since a greater amount of principal is available for earning interest in each quarter, the maturity amount shall be greater in case of quarterly compounding than if it were with annual compounding. We may see that if compounded quarterly, the maturity value of ₹100 at the end of one year is ₹110.38 as against ₹110 with annual compounding.

Time	*Amount*	*Interest %*	*Interest*	*Closing balance*
1st quarter	100.0000	2.5	2.5000	102.5000
2nd quarter	102.5000	2.5	2.5625	105.0625
3rd quarter	106.0625	2.5	2.6265	107.6890
4th quarter	107.6890	2.5	2.6922	110.3812

We may generalize the above in the following Equation 4-7.

$$F = P \times \left(1 + \frac{r}{m}\right)^{m \times n} \qquad (4\text{-}7)$$

where F = future value, r = annual rate of interest, m = total number of periods in a year, and n = number of years.

Using Equation 4-7 we may calculate the maturity value of ₹100 after two years with quarterly compounding as

$$\text{Maturity Value} = 100 \times \left(1 + \frac{0.10}{4}\right)^{4 \times 2} = 100 \times (1.025)^{4 \times 2}$$

= ₹121.84

As the periodicity of compounding increases (or the interest is applied at reduced time intervals) the maturity amount keeps increasing. For example, if the interest is paid monthly, the maturity value shall be ₹122.04 as computed.

$$\text{Maturity Value} = 100 \times (1 + 0.10/12)^{12 \times 2}$$
$$= 100 \times (1.00833)^{24} = ₹122.0391$$

Similarly we may generalize the present value of the future cash flows by Equation 4-8 by re-arranging Equation 4-7.

$$\text{Present value, } P = \frac{F}{\left(1 + \frac{r}{m}\right)^{m \times n}} \quad (4\text{-}8)$$

Continuous compounding and discounting

The maturity value of the deposit keeps increasing as periodicity increases from quarterly to monthly to daily. How far can we reduce the interval of compounding and what ultimate value can be achieved? In the ultimate case the compounding becomes continuous. In case of continuous compounding, the future value and discounted value may be given by Equations 4-9 and 4-10 respectively.

The value rises/falls exponentially if we assume continuous compounding/discounting.

$$\text{Future value, } F = P \times e^{rt} \quad (4\text{-}9)$$

$$\text{Present value, } P = F \times \frac{1}{e^{rt}} = F \times e^{-rt} \quad (4\text{-}10)$$

For a two-year deposit of ₹100 the maximum maturity value (with continuous compounding) at 10% is $100 \times e^{0.10 \times 2}$ = ₹122.14 as against ₹121.00 over a two-year period with annual compounding.

Effective rate of interest

The annual yield on investment increases as compounding interval decreases. The effective rate[4] may be found for a given annual rate of r and m number of compounding in a year by Equation 4-11 as follows:

$$\text{Effective Interest Rate} = \left[\left(1 + \frac{r}{m}\right)^m\right] - 1 \quad (4\text{-}11)$$

In the above example, the effective realization is 10.38%, instead of 10%, with quaterly compounding. This is due to the effect of increased frequency of compounding.

EQUATED MONTHLY INSTALMENTS

Lending institutions while disbursing the loan fix the repayment schedule on the basis of various parameters. Most of these repayments are equally spaced in time. Equal instalments payable at specific intervals (usually monthly) are referred to as equated monthly instalments (EMIs).

[4]For continuous compounding the effective rate of interest may be found from the expression $e^r - 1$.

Loans are repayable normally in equated monthly instalments (EMIs), the computation of which uses the concept of time value of money and annuity factors.

The EMIs are regular periodic payments whose present value, discounted at specified rate of interest, adds to the loan value. Through EMIs the lender recovers the original amount as well as the desired interest on the loan. The determination of EMIs follows the concept of time value of money, specifically the concept of present value of annuity.

As an example, consider a loan of ₹1,000 repayable in 3 yearly instalments with an interest rate of 10%. Referring to Appendix A-4 for 10% for 3 periods, we find PVA(10%,3) as 2.4869. It implies that the present value of Re 1 received each year for 3 years is ₹2.4869 at 10%. Therefore, for a loan of ₹1,000, the annual instalment of ₹402.11 (1,000/2.4869) may be fixed.

Normally the instalments are fixed on a monthly and not an annual basis. To calculate EMIs one requires the use of a calculator or computer. A numerical example will rather easily illustrate the concept and the method to calculate EMIs.

Assume that Mr Mohammad has taken a loan of ₹20,000 against a television from ConsumerBank. The loan amount is repayable in 36 monthly instalments. The bank charges the interest at 10% per annum and the instalments are payable in advance (beginning of the month)[5].

Finding out EMIs

As mentioned earlier, EMIs use the concept of time value of money. The EMIs are fixed in such a manner that the cash flows of the bank yield the desired return of 10%. This can easily be done with the help of EXCEL using *PMT function*, as displayed below:

Principal Amount (₹)	20000	Interest rate (%)	10%
Period (years)	3	EMI (₹per month)	=–PMT (10%/12,3*12,20,000,0,1)

The syntax for PMT function uses five fields—(1) interest rate for the period; (2) number of instalments (periods); (3) value of the loan (the loan amount); (4) residual value at the end of the period of loan (taken as '0' if all loan has to be repaid); and finally (5) a field describing the nature of payment, '1' for payment in advance and '0' for payment in arrears. This is shown in Figure 4-7.

The tables for EMIs for principal amount of ₹1,000 with interest rates up to 40% per annum and periods up to 30 years are given in Appendix A-5 and Appendix A-6 for payment in advance and in arrears respectively. Using the PMT function or the table in Appendix A-5, we find EMI in advance for ₹1,000 at 10% for three years as ₹32.0005 per month, which for the loan of ₹20,000 works out to ₹640.01 (20 × 32.0005) as shown in Figure 4-7.

[5]Where instalments are paid at the end of the period they are referred to as payment in arrears. In terms of time value of money, the payment in arrears and payment in advance will differ by the discount factor of one period.

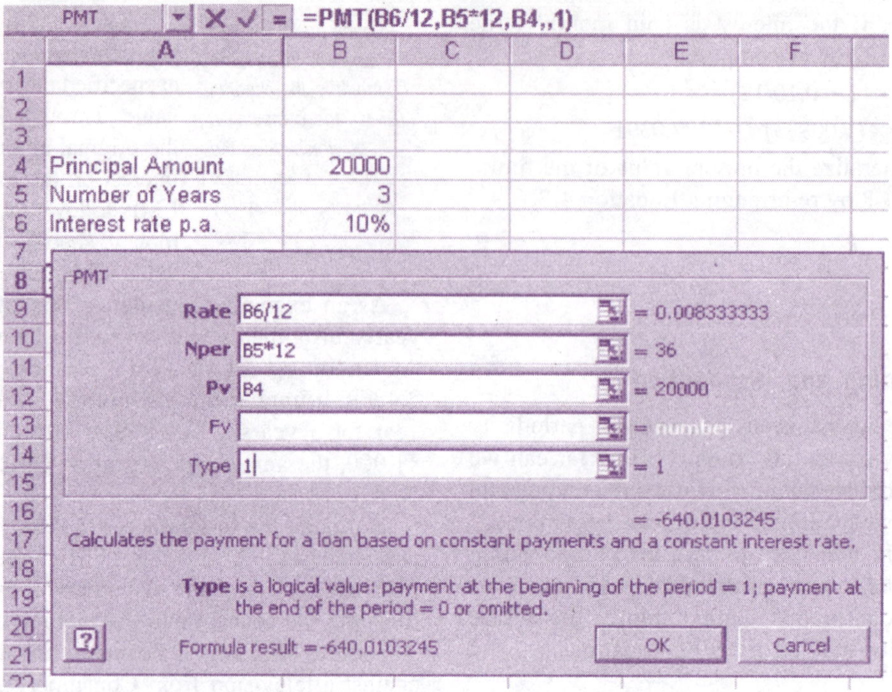

Figure 4-7 Calculating equated monthly instalments (payable in advance)

Segregating the EMIs into Principal and Interest

Each EMI paid consists of two parts—(1) interest on the outstanding loan; and (2) repayment towards the principal amount. For example, an EMI of ₹640.01 for a loan of ₹20,000 for 3 years at 10% would have a part that first goes to liquidate the interest and then the principal amount. With each EMI, the two components vary but in such a manner that total of the two remains same for entire duration of the loan. In the beginning, a major part of EMI is used towards the payment of interest as the outstanding loan is large. As repayment takes place the portion of interest in the EMI falls with each EMI. For the purpose of accounting and taxes both the lender and borrower need to segregate EMI into the interest and principal repayment.

Each EMI consists of interest and principal. The interest declines and the repayment principal increases with successive EMIs in such a manner that the aggregate of the two remains same.

The segregation of EMI for the loan of Mr Mohammad is done in the Table 4-3. Column 2 of Table 4-3 represents the cash flow for each month. Note that since the EMI is payable in advance, the disbursed loan amount is ₹20,000 less EMI of ₹640.01 and the loan lasts for 35 months.

The loan outstanding for the first month is ₹19,359.01 and it carries interest of 10%. The amount of interest for one month works out to ₹161.33. The remainder of the EMI is towards the repayment that reduces the outstanding loan balance by ₹478.61. For the next EMI we proceed in a similar manner. The following may be noted from Table 4-3 in page 85:

1. The discounted present value of the EMI and the loan as in total of Column 4 is zero confirming that the EMI provided a return of 10% to the bank and equals cost of the loan for Mr Mohammad.
2. Mr Mohammad paid an interest of ₹3,040 as total of Column 6.
3. The total of last column in Table 4-3 matches the repayment exactly to the amount of loan that appears in the first line.

A few examples of time value of money are presented in Examples 4-7 to 4-9.

Example 4-7 Finding EMI in Arrears

AB Ltd is borrowing ₹50 lakh for a period of 4 years at interest rate of 15% repayable in equal instalments at the end of each year. Find out the instalment amount, the interest paid each year and the total interest paid for the loan.

Solution

We may find the amount of instalment using EXCEL *function PMT(15%,4,50,00,000,0,0)* = ₹17,51,327. The break up of each instalment into interest and principal is given below:

Year	*Opening Amount of Loan*	*Instalment*	*Interest*	*Repayment of Principal*	*Closing Amount of Loan*
1	50,00,000	17,51,327	7,50,000	10,01,327	39,98,673
2	39,98,673	17,51,327	5,99,801	11,51,526	28,47,147
3	28,47,147	17,51,327	4,27,072	13,24,255	15,22,893
4	15,22,893	17,51,327	2,28,434	15,22,893	—
	Total		**70,05,307**	**20,05,307**	**50,00,000**

The total amount of interest paid is ₹20,05,307.

Table 4-3 Segregating EMI into interest and principal repayment

Principal Amount (₹)		*20,000*	*Interest rate (%)*		*10%*	
Period (Years)		*3*	*EMI (₹ per month)*		*640.01*	
Instalment No. Period (Month)	**Cash Flow for the Period**	**Discount Factor**	**Present Value**	**Principal Outstanding at the Beginning of Period**	**Interest Amount**	**Principal Repaid**
	–19,359.99	1.0000	–19,359.99			
1	640.01	0.9917	634.72	19,359.99	161.33	478.68
2	640.01	0.9835	629.48	18,881.31	157.34	482.67
3	640.01	0.9754	624.27	18,398.65	153.32	486.69
4	640.01	0.9673	619.11	17,911.96	149.27	490.74
5	640.01	0.9594	614.00	17,421.21	145.18	494.83
6	640.01	0.9514	608.92	16,926.38	141.05	498.96
7	640.01	0.9436	603.89	16,427.42	136.90	503.12
8	640.01	0.9358	598.90	15,924.31	132.70	507.31
9	640.01	0.9280	593.95	15,417.00	128.48	511.54
10	640.01	0.9204	589.04	14,905.47	124.21	515.80
11	640.01	0.9128	584.17	14,389.67	119.91	520.10
12	640.01	0.9052	579.35	13,869.57	115.58	524.43
13	640.01	0.8977	574.56	13,345.14	111.21	528.80
14	640.01	0.8903	569.81	12,816.34	106.80	533.21
15	640.01	0.8830	565.10	12,283.13	102.36	537.65
16	640.01	0.8757	560.43	11,745.48	97.88	542.13
17	640.01	0.8684	555.80	11,203.35	93.36	546.65
18	640.01	0.8612	551.20	10,656.70	88.81	551.20
19	640.01	0.8541	546.65	10,105.50	84.21	555.80
20	640.01	0.8471	542.13	9,549.70	79.58	560.43
21	640.01	0.8401	537.65	8,989.27	74.91	565.10
22	640.01	0.8331	533.21	8,424.17	70.20	569.81
23	640.01	0.8262	528.80	7,854.36	65.45	574.56
24	640.01	0.8194	524.43	7,279.80	60.67	579.35
25	640.01	0.8126	520.10	6,700.46	55.84	584.17
26	640.01	0.8059	515.80	6,116.28	50.97	589.04
27	640.01	0.7993	511.54	5,527.24	46.06	593.95
28	640.01	0.7927	507.31	4,933.29	41.11	598.90
29	640.01	0.7861	503.12	4,334.39	36.12	603.89
30	640.01	0.7796	498.96	3,730.50	31.09	608.92
31	640.01	0.7732	494.83	3,121.58	26.01	614.00
32	640.01	0.7668	490.74	2,507.58	20.90	619.11
33	640.01	0.7604	486.69	1,888.47	15.74	624.27
34	640.01	0.7542	482.67	1,264.20	10.53	629.48
35	640.01	0.7479	478.68	634.72	5.29	634.72
Total			**0.00**		**3,040.37**	**19,359.99**

Example 4-8 Fixing the Tenure of Loan

A housing company is willing to lend ₹20 lakh for a house at 10%. You are able to pay no more than ₹20,000 per month at the end of each month.

(a) What tenure of the loan the housing company can fix?

(b) If you need moratorium of two years before you commence repayment of loan and the housing company still wants the loan to be paid back as stipulated in (a), what shall be the new EMI?

Solution

We first convert the amount of instalment per thousand basis to use the tables of EMI. The EMI per thousand rupees is 20,00,000 / 20,000 = ₹10 per 1,000. Scanning EMI table in Appendix A-6 for column at 10%, we find the number of years close to 10 is 18 years at 9.9984. Therefore, the tenure of the loan can be fixed at 18 years.

In case a moratorium of 2 years is granted, the principal amount of loan after two years becomes 1.1 × 1.1 × 20 lakh = ₹24,20,000. This now has to be paid over 16 years at 10%. Again using table in Appendix A-6 for 10%, 16 years the EMI is 10.4590 per thousand. Therefore, the new loan instalment is 10.4590 × 2420 = ₹23,311.

Example 4-9 Understanding Future and Present Values together

A landlord of a flat is willing to rent it for a rent of ₹1,000 per month with annual increase of 10%. Rents are payable in advance for the year. He is also willing to offer the flat for outright purchase if the prospective buyer pays 10 years rent discounted at 12%. What price would you pay for the flat?

Solution

The purchase price of the flat may be found by discounting the rents for 10 years at 12% as follows:

$$\text{Price of the flat} = 12{,}000 + \frac{12{,}000 \times 1.1}{1.12} + \frac{12{,}000 \times 1.1^2}{1.12^2} + \dots + \frac{12{,}000 \times 1.1^9}{1.12^9}$$

Using future value table in Appendix A-1 for the numerator and table in Appendix A-2 for the denominator we get:

Year	*0*	*1*	*2*	*3*	*4*	*5*	*6*	*7*	*8*	*9*
(a) Future Value	1.000	1.100	1.210	1.331	1.464	1.611	1.772	1.949	2.144	2.358
(b) Present value	1.000	0.893	0.797	0.712	0.636	0.567	0.507	0.452	0.404	0.361
c = (a) × (b)	1.000	0.982	0.965	0.947	0.930	0.914	0.898	0.882	0.866	0.850
										Σc = 9.2335

The price of the flat is 12,000 × 9.2335 = ₹1,10,802

SUMMARY

Time value of money is probably one of the most important concepts that form the basis of decision making in almost all areas of finance. Its applications range from personal finance to decisions in corporate finance such as capital budgeting, valuation, derivatives, and risk management. The concept of time value of money states that the timing of the receipt or payment of money is as important as the amount received or paid. It is an important concept as it explains that money has the capacity to increase in value even when it is not put to any use.

The interest rate prevailing in the market forms the basis of finding the time value of money. The value of money increases with time due to the application of interest. It grows at a higher rate when interest is applied on the interest. Application of interest over interest is known as compounding. Similarly the value of the money received or paid later is less than what it is today by the amount of interest for the time. The process of reduction in value eliminating the interest that could have accrued is known as discounting.

Future value of money is simply the amount of principal and the interest earned over it for a specified period of time. Annuities refer to the equal amount of cash flows spaced uniformly over time, normally a year. The value of the equal amount of receivable or payable at evenly spaced intervals of time at a given rate of interest is known as future value of annuity. Similarly the sum receivable or payable at a future date can be equated with the equal amounts evenly spaced over time at a known rate of interest.

Present values and future values of a single cash flows or recurring equal cash flows are normally available in the tables for computational ease because of very frequent applications of these values in finance.

One prominent application of the time value of money that is very widely used in the field of finance is the determination of equated monthly instalments for recovery of loans in specified time period and at a given rate of interest.

KEY TERMS

Future value The value of money at a future date with the given interest rate is called future value.

Present value The worth of the money today that is receivable or payable at a future date is called present value.

Compounding The process of application of interest over interest period after period over a given sum at specified rate for specified time to know the worth of the money at a future date is called compounding.

Discounting The process of removal of interest over interest period after period on the given money at a future date to find out its worth in today's date is discounting.

Annuity A fixed and equal amount of money receivable or payable at periodic intervals evenly spaced over time, usually a year is referred to as annuity.

EMI An equal amount of money payable or receivable at periodic intervals of time usually a month that is equal to the amount of loan principal and the interest thereon at a given rate is called equated monthly instalment (EMI).

KEY FORMULAE

Future Value $F = P \times (1 + r)^n$

Present value $P = \dfrac{F}{(1+r)^n}$

Future Value of Annuity of Re 1,

$$\text{FVA}(r, n) = \sum_{1}^{n}(1+r)^n$$

Future Value Annuity Factor at r% for n years,

$$\text{FVA}(r, n) = \frac{(1+r)^n - 1}{r}$$

Present Value of Annuity of Re 1,

$$\text{PVA}(r, n) = \sum_{1}^{n}\frac{1}{(1+r)^n}$$

Present Value Annuity Factor at r% for n years,

$$\text{PVA}(r, n) = \frac{(1+r)^n - 1}{r(1+r)^n}$$

Future Value with quaterly/monthly compounding

$$F = P \times (1 + r/m)^{m \times n}$$

Present Value

$$P = \frac{F}{(1+r/m)^{m \times n}}$$

Effective Interest Rate $= \left[\left(1+\dfrac{r}{m}\right)^m\right] - 1$

PRACTICE PROBLEMS

1. Relationship between Effective and Nominal Interest

Two financing options are available before a borrower. The first option offers loan at 21% while in case of second option the rate of interest is 22.5%. Compounding is done on a quarterly basis in the first case while it is annual in case of second option. Which of the two options is better for the borrower?

Solution

The interest rate given in the first option is the nominal rate, while in the second option, since it is a case of annual compounding, the interest offered rate is the effective rate.

To compare the two options, the effective interest rate for the first option needs to be computed.

For the first option:

Nominal interest rate (r) = 0.21 or 21%

Number of compounding periods per year (m) = 4

$$\begin{aligned}\text{Effective interest rate } (r) &= [1 + r/m]^m - 1\\ &= [1 + 0.21/4]^4 - 1\\ &= 1.2271 - 1\\ &= 0.2271 \text{ (or } 22.71\%)\end{aligned}$$

Since effective rate in the first option (22.71%) is marginally higher than the second option (22.5%), the second option is better for the borrower.

2. Future Value

Pratyaksh Ltd has generated ₹1.50 crore from the sale of one of its manufacturing units. The company has an option to invest the money for 5 years in an investment avenue that will give an assured compounded return of 11.5%. On the maturity of investment at the end of the 5th year, the firm can invest the money in proposed expansion plans that are projected to cost ₹5 crore. If the firm decides to go ahead with the investments, how much extra financing will be needed at the end of 5th year to finance its expansion plans.

Solution

Future value of investable surplus (₹1.5 crore) at the end of 5th year needs to be estimated for the purpose. This future value should be deducted from the financing required for the expansion plan (₹5 crore) to find out the additional financing required for expansion plan.

$$\text{FV} = \text{PV} \times \text{FVIF}$$
$$\text{FVIF} = (1 + r)^n$$

where

r = rate or return = 11.5%

n = time period of investment = 5 years

PV = ₹1.5 crore

FVIF = $(1 + 0.115)^5$ = 1.7233

Future Value (₹in crore) = 1.50 × 1.7233534 = 2.5850

Additional financing needed for expansion plan

= 5 – 2.5850 = ₹2.4150 crore

3. Future Value of Annuity

How much will a recurring investment of ₹10,000 per annum accumulate to at the end of 30 years where the investment fetches an interest rate of 9.5% per annum if compounding is:

(a) Annual
(b) Quarterly
(c) Monthly

Solution

$$\text{FVIFA}_{r,\,n} = \frac{(1+r)^n - 1}{r}$$

(a) Annual compounding

Interest rate offered by the scheme (r) = 9.5% per annum

Period (n) = 30 years

Amount invested annually (annuity) = ₹ 10,000

$$\begin{aligned}\text{FVIFA}_{9.5\%,\ 30\ \text{years}} &= \frac{(1+0.095)^{30} - 1}{0.095} = \frac{15.22031 - 1}{0.095}\\ &= \frac{14.22031}{0.095} = 149.6875\end{aligned}$$

$$\begin{aligned}\text{FV} &= \text{FVIFA}_{9.5\%,\ 30\ years} \times \text{Annuity}\\ &= 149.6875 \times ₹10000\\ &= ₹14{,}96{,}875\end{aligned}$$

(b) Quarterly compounding

Interest rate per annum (r) = 9.5%

Interest rate per quarter $\frac{r}{m}$ = 2.375%

No. of times compounding is done in each year (m) = 4

Period (n) = 30 years

Amount invested annually (annuity) = ₹10,000

Future Value of annuity increase of quarterly compounding

$$= \frac{(1 \times r/m)^{m \times n} - 1}{r/m}$$

$$\text{FVIFA}_{0.095/4, 30 \times 4 \text{ years}} = \frac{(1 + 0.095/.4)^{30 \times 4} - 1}{0.095/4}$$

$$= \frac{(1.02375)^{120} - 1}{0.02375}$$

$$= 661.9490$$

Future Value of Annuity = $\text{FVIFA}_{0.0975/4, 30 \times 4 \text{ years}}$ × Present Value

= 661.9490 × ₹10,000

= ₹66,19,490

(c) Monthly compounding

Interest rate per annum (r) = 9.5%

Interest rate month = $\frac{r}{m}$ = 0.7917%

No. of times compounding is done in each year (m) = 12

Period (n) = 30 years

Amount invested annually (annuity) = ₹10000

FVA in case of quarterly compounding

$$= \frac{(1 + r/m)^{m \times n} - 1}{r/m}$$

$$\text{FVIFA}_{0.095/12, 30 \times 2 \text{ years}} = \frac{(1 + 0.095/12)^{30 \times 12} - 1}{0.095/12}$$

$$= \frac{(1.007917)^{360} - 1}{0.007917} = 2{,}033.035$$

FVA = $\text{FVIFA}_{0.0975/12, 30 \times 12 \text{ years}}$ × PV

= 2033.035 x ₹10,000

= ₹ 2,03,30,35

4. Determining the Implied Interest Rate

There are two options available to an investor. Scheme (A) promises to pay ₹1,50,000 at the end of 10 years if an investment of ₹10,000 is made annually. Scheme (B) promises to pay ₹1,50,000 at the end of 8 years if ₹15,000 is invested annually. Which of the two schemes is better for the investor?

Solution

	Scheme A	*Scheme B*
Amount to be invested annually (₹)	10,000	15,000
Time period (n)	10	8
Lump sum received at the end (FV)	1,50,000	1,50,000

Implied rates of interest in two schemes for Scheme A and for Scheme B needs to be estimated and compared to take a decision.

The implied interest rates for the two schemes can be computed as follows:

Scheme A

Future Value of Annuity (FVA) = PV × $\text{FVIFA}_{r,n}$

$$\text{FVA} = 10{,}000 \times \frac{(1+r)^{10}}{r}$$

$$1{,}50{,}000 = 10{,}000 \times \frac{(1+r)^{10}}{r}$$

$$15 = \frac{(1+r)^{10}}{r}$$

Now looking at the FVIFA table to locate the FVIFA of 15 against 10 years we can find out the implied rate of return for Scheme A. as per the table lies between 8 and 9%.

Scheme B

$$\text{FVA} = 15{,}000 \times \frac{(1+r)^{8}}{r}$$

$$1{,}50{,}000 = 15{,}000 \times \frac{(1+r)^{8}}{r}$$

$$10 = \frac{(1+r)^{8}}{r}$$

Now looking at the FVIFA table to locate the FVIFA of 10 against 8 years, we can find out the implied rate of return for Scheme B. as per the table lies between 6 and 7%.

Since the implied rate of return in Scheme A is higher than that in Scheme B investing in Scheme A is a better option.

5. Present Value

Select the alternative from the four options given below that gives the highest return

(a) ₹7,50,000 available today

(b) ₹18,00,000 to be received after 8 years

(c) ₹1,00,000 per annum in perpetuity

(d) ₹30,000 per month for a year and ₹ 5,00,000 at the end of the year

Assume that the opportunity cost of capital is 11.5%.

Solution

Since the options have varied maturity they are incomparable. To make them comparable we need to find out the present value of all, the above options.

$$\text{PVIF}_{r,n} = \left(\frac{1}{1+r}\right)^{n}$$

(a) Since it is available today, this is the value given i.e. ₹ 7,50,000 is the present value only.

(b) PV of ₹ 18,00,000 received after 8 years

$$= FV \times PVIF_{11.5\%,\ 8\ years}$$

$$= \left(\frac{1}{1+0.115}\right)^{8} = 0.4186$$

PV = ₹ 18,00,000 × 0.418602 = ₹7,53,48.0

(c) As it is known, PVF of a perpetuity $= \frac{1}{r}$

$$\text{PVF for Perpetuity}_{11.5\%} = \frac{1}{0.115} = 8.6956$$

Present Value of Perpetuity of ₹ 1,00,000

= ₹1,00,000 × PV Factor of Perpetuity $_{11.5\%}$

= ₹ 8,69,56

(d)

$$PVIFA = \frac{1-\frac{1}{(1+i)^n}}{i}$$

$$PVIFA_{11.5\%/12,\ 12\ months} = \left[\frac{1-\frac{1}{(1+0.115/12)^{1\times 12}}}{0.115/12}\right] = 11.2848$$

$$PVIF_{r,\ n\ years} = \left(\frac{1}{1+r}\right)^{n}$$

$$PVIF_{11.5\%,\ 1\ year} = \left(\frac{1}{1+0.115}\right)^{1} = 0.8969$$

Present Value = 30,000 x ($PVIFA_{0.115/12, 12\ months}$) + 5,00,000 × ($PVIF_{0.115, 1year}$)

= (30,000 × 11.2848) + (5,00,000 × 0.8969)

= ₹ 7,86,9994

Option C of a perpetuity of ₹ 1,00,000 per annum has the highest present value and therefore is best suited alternative.

6. Present Value of a Cash Stream

Figurative Ltd is considering the replacement of its existing machinery that is nearing the end of its estimated useful life. The firm is considering two options. First machinery (*Mach One*) entails a cash outflow of ₹2 crore and is likely to have an estimated useful life of 4 years. The second machinery (*Mach Two*) is invoiced at ₹2.25 crore and is likely to serve the business for the next 5 years. Replacement will enable the business to increase its production capacity to tap the growing demand. The incremental cash flows likely to occur to the business are projected as follows:

Year	**Cash Flows (₹)**	
	Mach One	**Mach Two**
0	–2,00,00,000	–2,25,00,000
1	72,00,000	72,00,000
2	75,00,000	75,00,000
3	72,50,000	76,50,000
4	68,00,000	72,50,000
5	—	68,00,000

Assuming the discount rate to be 13.75% find out the present value of the cash outflows. Which of the two options should the firm prefer?

Solution

The problem can be solved in three steps as follows:

Step 1: Finding the PV factor for each of the years. As it is known that

$$PVIF = \left(\frac{1}{1+r}\right)^{n}$$

Year-wise PV factors are given below in Column C. They have been computed using the above model.

Step 2: Finding out the Present Value for both the options.

Present Value = Future Value × PVIF

Step 3: Finding the Net Present Value (NPV) for both the options.

NPV = PV of Cash Inflows — PV of Cash outflows.

Computation of Present Value and NPV for Mach One

Years (n)	***Cash Flows (₹)***	***Present Value Interest Factor (PVIF)***	***Present value (in ₹) (FV × PVIF)***
		$\left(\frac{1}{1+0.1375}\right)^{n}$	***(Col. B × Col. C)***
0	–2,00,00,000	1	–2,00,00,000
1	72,00,000	0.8791	63,29,520
2	75,00,000	0.7729	57,96,750
3	72,50,000	0.6794	49,25,650
4	68,00,000	0.5973	40,61,640
5	—		
NPV			11,13,560

Computation of Present Value and NPV for Mach Two

Years (n)	***Cash Flows (₹)***	***Present Value Interest Factor (PVIF)***	***Present value (in ₹) (FV × PVIF)***
0	–2,25,00,000	1	–2,25,00,000
1	72,00,000	0.8791	63,29,520
2	75,00,000	0.7729	57,96,750
3	76,50,000	0.6794	51,97,410
4	72,50,000	0.5973	43,30,425
5	68,00,000	0.5251	35,70,680
NPV			27,24,785

As purchase of Mach Two gives the higher NPV to the firm it is advised to go for it.

7. Calculation of EMI

The current rate of interest on home loan offered by a commercial bank 'Banko' is 10.5% per annum. Loan is available for a maximum period of 20 years. Rohit is planning to buy a property that will cost him ₹52 lakh. Bank can finance up to a maximum of 85% of the value of property, the remaining 15% has to be paid upfront by the purchaser to the builder before the loan is approved by the bank.

As per the terms of sale, the buyer of property can get a cash discount of 10% of the value of the property. Rohit can manage 15% of the initial deposit to be made to the builder from his past savings. He is not sure about the EMIs that he will have to pay in case he takes the loan repayable in 10 years.

You are expected to advise Rohit. Calculate the EMIs and segregate the EMIs for the first year into interest and principal components for the purpose.

Solution

Rate of Interest (r)	10.5% p.a. (equivalent to 0.875% p.m.)
Value of Property	₹52,00,000
Less: Discount (@ 10%)	₹5,20,000
Net Value of property	₹46,80,000
Up front payment by the purchaser (15%)	₹7,02,000
Loan amount	₹39,78,000
Period of loan	10 years

The EMIs to be paid by Rohit constitutes annuity.

Annuity (EMIs) can be computed as follows:

PVIFA for interest of 0.875% pm and 120 months

$$= \left[\frac{1-\dfrac{1}{(1+r/m)^{n\times m}}}{r/m}\right] = \frac{1-\dfrac{1}{\left(1+\dfrac{0.105}{12}\right)^{10\times 12}}}{(0.105/12)}$$

$$= 74.1098$$

$$\text{EMI} = \frac{\text{Loan Amount}}{\text{PVIFA}_{0.00875,120}}$$

$$= \frac{39,78,000}{74.1098}$$

$$= ₹53,677$$

Segregating EMIs into Principal and Interest components for first year

Time	Beginning Balance	EMI	Principal	Interest	Closing Balance
1	39,78,000	53,677	18,870	34,808	39,59,130
2	39,59,130	53,677	19,035	34,642	39,40,096
3	39,40,096	53,677	19,201	34,476	39,20,894
4	39,20,894	53,677	19,369	34,308	39,01,525
5	39,01,525	53,677	19,539	34,138	38,81,986
6	38,81,986	53,677	19,710	33,967	38,62,276
7	38,62,276	53,677	19,882	33,795	38,42,394
8	38,42,394	53,677	20,056	33,621	38,22,338
9	38,22,338	53,677	20,232	33,445	38,02,106
10	38,02,106	53,677	20,409	33,268	37,81,698
11	37,81,698	53,677	20,587	33,090	37,61,110
12	37,61,110	53,677	20,767	32,910	37,40,343
	Total	**6,44,126**	**2,37,657**	**4,06,469**	

Interest has been computed @ 0.875% on the beginning balance.

EXERCISES

Concept Review Questions

1. What do you understand by time value of money?
2. What are the possible reasons that money must have time value despite not being put to use?
3. What do you understand by (a) future value, and (b) present value of money?
4. What are annuities, and why such values are calculated?
5. How do you determine the equated monthly instalments?

Critical Thinking Questions

1. If a loan carries a fixed rate of interest and it is to be paid over a fixed period the only way to arrive at equated monthly instalment is to add the amount of interest and the principal. Do you agree with the statement?
2. A deposit carries an interest of 10% per annum with quarterly compounding. The effective rate of interest would be 40% because you would receive 10% every quarter, four times a year. What is wrong with the statement? What would be the correct effective rate of interest?

Practical Assignments

1. Visit a car dealer and find out the EMIs for a car loan of ₹2,00,000 repayable over a period of: (a) 3 years, (b) 5 years, and (c) 7 years. Find out the effective rate of interest from the amounts of EMIs.
2. Visit a housing finance company and find out the EMIs for a housing loan of ₹10,00,000 repayable over a period of: (a) 10 years, (b) 15 years, and (c) 20 years. Find out the effective rate of interest from the amounts of EMIs.
3. What difference do you find in the effective rates of interests in Assignments 1 and 2? What is the cause of this difference?

Numerical Problems

1. Relationship between Effective and Nominal Rate of Interest

Financier Ltd 'an NBFC' is offering personal loan within 24 hours of application, without any documentation. The interest rate charged by Financier Ltd is 25% with monthly compounding. The borrower, Anand, has another option, to borrow the required money from Banko 'a national bank' at 27% p.a with annual compounding. The borrower feels that the option of borrowing from NBFC is not only convenient but is also cheaper. Is the first option actually cheaper?

2. Future Value of a Single Sum

Alpha Ltd has a surplus of ₹20 lakh available for the next 5 years. At the end of the period, the firm will need the amount for investing in its business expansion. If the firm decided to invest the surplus in a scheme that offers a 13% per annum, how much would the amount grow to at the end of 5 years.

3. Future Value of Annuity

An investor is thinking of investing in a recurring deposit scheme that offers an interest rate of 12% per annum. The investment that he is planning is for the higher education of his son who is just two years now. In case the investor decides to invest ₹20,000 every year, what will be the total money available to him when his son reaches the age of 20 years?

4. Determining the Implied Rate of Interest

Two investment options are available to Prateek. The first option promises to pay ₹75,000 at the end of 8 years to investors who deposit ₹7,000 annually for 8 years. The second scheme promises a lump sum of ₹50,000 at the end of five years on an annual deposit of ₹7,000 for 5 years. Prateek is confounded as to which of the two schemes give him better returns? Please suggest.

5. Present Value of a Sngle Sum

Assuming a discount rate of 12% find out which one of the following gives the highest returns:

(a) ₹1,60,000 available today
(b) ₹1,75,000 to be received after 8 years
(c) ₹25,000 p.a. in perpetuity
(d) ₹10,000 per month for a year and ₹1,00,000 at the end of the year
(e) ₹25,000 every year for the next 10 years

6. Present Value of a Cash Stream

Shruti Enterprises is considering making investment for expanding its operations to the north zone of the country. Such an expansion is likely to entail a capital expenditure of ₹12 lakh. The incremental inflows from such an investment are likely to be available for the next 10 years. The cash flows on account of such an expansion plan are as follows:

Year	*Cash Flows (₹)*
0	–12,00,000
1	2,10,000
2	3,05,085
3	4,25,060
4	4,05,002
5	3,24,545
6	3,05,689
7	2,45,065
8	1,55,400
9	1,35,600
10	1,25,000

Assuming a discount rate of 14% find the present values of cash inflows from year 1 to year 10.

7. Comparing the Yield

Rahul Sharma is to retire in 15 years' time. He is considering two schemes available for investment. The first scheme pays him an interest rate of 8% per annum while the second scheme will pay him ₹2,000 per annum perpetually beginning from the end of 16 years, if he deposits at the end of every year ₹2,500 till he retires. Which scheme should Mr Sharma opt for?

8. Calculating the Growth Rate

An investor bought a share of a blue chip company 20 years back at a price of ₹50. If the price of the share has gone up to ₹350, what is the compound rate of growth in the price of shares of the firm?

CASE STUDY

Bharat Engineering Works

Bharat Engineering Works (BEW) is promoted by Mr Bharat Singh, a qualified and experienced mechanical engineer. He worked for an automobile major, General Auto Ltd (GAL). Over years of experience, he had developed a sheet metal component that was being procured by GAL through another vendor. GAL was not satisfied with the quality of the sheet metal components. In view of the better product developed by Mr Bharat Singh, his employer encouraged him to set up his own unit and assured him all help. He decided to venture on his own.

Bharat Singh prepared the project report. The project cost was ₹60 lakh—consisting of ₹40 lakh towards plant and machinery and remaining ₹20 lakh as working capital. Mr Bharat Singh with all his resources could accumulate only ₹20 lakh on his own and needed balance ₹40 lakh as loan from a bank.

He approached his banker friend for a loan of ₹40 lakh. After due appraisal of the project and considering the assured orders from GAL, the bank agreed to provide him ₹40 lakh. However, the bank was willing to disburse the fund in a need-based manner according to the requirement of funds as they arise. The bankers asked Bharat Singh to prepare the requirements of funds according to the time when the funds were actually required.

Bharat Singh had negotiated the contracts for machinery on deferred payment basis. On the recommendations of his employer, the machinery supplier had agreed for the deferred terms of payment as follows:

Down payment : ₹10 lakh

After one year : ₹20 lakh plus interest @ 15% on remaining amount

After two years : ₹10 lakh plus interest @ 15% on the remaining amount

Accordingly, the following requirement of fund was presented to the bank to which the bank agreed:

₹(lakh)	*Year 0*	*Year 1*	*Year 2*	*Total*
Funds required	30.00	20.00	10.00	60.00
Equity	20.00	—	—	20.00
Loan	10.00	15.00	15.00	40.00

The bank sanctioned the loan on the following terms:

1. The rate of interest would be 12% per annum.
2. The aggregate period of the loan would be 7 years from now.
3. The loan would have moratorium of two years from date of sanction.
4. The repayment could be done in any of the following methods:
   (a) In equal amount every quarter for 20 quarters along with interest beginning Year 3 onwards on declining basis.
   (b) In equated quarterly instalments (EQIs) for 20 quarters commencing from Year 3 onwards.

Moratorium of two years was given because BEW did not have enough generation in the first two years. However, BEW would pay the interest during the period.

Discuss

If BEW chooses the option of EQI as in 4(b), answer the following:.

1. Work out the EQIs for next 20 quarters for repayment of loan and interest.
2. BEW is required to show interest portion of EQIs in its profit and loss account each year. Find out the amount of interest in each EQI and the sum that would be shown as interest each year.

In the CD

Future Value of a Single Sum

Future Value of Annuity

Present Value of a Single Sum

Present Value of Variable Cash flows

CHAPTER

5 Risk and Return

LEARNING OBJECTIVES

After going through this chapter, you will be able to:

- understand the meaning of return and risk
- know how the return and risk are measured
- understand the various measures of return and situations in which they are used
- learn about the different measures of risk
- understand why standard deviation is most appropriate to measure risk
- know how to find expected return and standard deviation from the historical data of financial assets
- learn about the normal distribution and standard normal distribution
- understand and apply the standard normal distribution to real life data

THE RINGMASTER, CIRCUS, AND SEHWAG

Kinni, a 12-year-old boy, was watching a show of the Royal Circus performing in his town, with his father. He was astonished to see the ringmaster managing 10 fierce lions. 'Why does the ringmaster take such a grave risk?' asked Kinni.

'He gets paid for this,' said his father nonchalantly.

After a while, seeing Kinni's discomfort with the answer, his father added, 'He has mastered the lions. For him there is little risk in this act. Moreover, he gets a reward for this.'

Not happy with the answer Kinni said, 'I guess he gets about ₹20,000 for the whole month in which he must be performing the same act about 30 times. Is this worth the risk he assumes every time? Would you do the same act with this amount of money?'

'Certainly not?' replied his father.

'What if you are paid ₹1,00,000?' queried Kinni.

'I might consider this provided the ringmaster accompanies me,' was the father's reply.

'You mean you would take risk if the reward increased?' Kinni implied.

'Mostly yes, but not every time,' his father replied.

A little later, few girls entered the circus arena on single-wheel cycles. They performed several acrobatic acts.

'They do not fall from the cycles and get hurt. These small delicate girls too are taking the risk. I guess they too are paid the same amount as the ringmaster. But their risk is not as great as the ringmaster's' observed Kinni.

Searching for a suitable answer, the father attempted a justification, 'The risk is not the same for all. The ringmaster had mastered the art of controlling the lions while these girls have perfected maintaining the balance on a single-wheel cycle while performing acrobatics. These two risks seem equivalent and, therefore, deserve an equivalent reward.'

After a pause Kinni's father further added, 'Risk is different for different people. What is risky for one is not as risky for another. Also, different people see the same situation with different perception of risk as you see for ringmaster and girls.'

Now the dialogue became more academic. Kinni asked, 'But, how do we measure risk?'

Again the father somehow explained, 'It is risky when the chances of something untoward happening are lesser than the expectations. The ringmaster facing the lions is expected to control them. The chance that the lions would attack is remote and same as the chances of the girls on the single-wheel cycles losing control.'

Anticipating the next query the father added, 'What if the role of ringmaster and cycle riding girls are changed? They would not agree to do so for the same amount of money. Probably the girls would have to be offered many times more money if they were to face lions.'

The same evening Kinni was watching the news about the Indian cricket team's tour to England and Ireland. He learnt that Virender Sehwag has been dropped from the team. 'Why should selectors do this? Sehwag is such a dynamic batsman, and he can turn the match upside down single-handedly.'

'Yes, I agree. But, probably selectors find him too risky. These days he is failing more often than succeeding' reacted his father.

'What do you mean by this? His average is as good as his captain Rahul Dravid or any other batsman,' asked Kinni.

This time the father was more comfortable answering his son's questions than he was in the afternoon. He said, 'Yes they do consider the average. But the average has little to do with risk. You can get the same average by scoring a triple century in one innings and then get out within the scores of 20s in next 19 as one may get with scoring 40s in each of the innings. Rahul Dravid scores 40s in each innings. That is why Sehwag is more risky than Dravid but both may have similar averages.'

'You mean Dravid is dependable, while Sehwag is risky,' concluded Kinni.

'Exactly and that seems to be the reason why Sehwag has been dropped. Interestingly, we can measure the risk in this case because of the availability of past scores. The deviations from the average are less for David and more for Sehwag, elaborated Kinni's father.

'But as you said unless you take risk you do not get reward,' enquired Kinni.

'You are right,' said Kinni's father agreeing with him.

'We must include Sehwag if we have to win matches. But at the same time we run the risk of losing matches. It depends what you consider important. More risk and more return or safe bet with less return.'

'So now we can quantify risk. Probably it was difficult to do so in the case of the circus, where one had to go by perceptions alone,' explained father.

The dialogue ended and Kinni was beginning to understand the concept of risk.

INTRODUCTION

Investment decisions by individuals and firms alike are done with diverse motives. For firms the decision to invest in business opportunities can be motivated by factors such as desire for control, expansion, status etc. Individuals also make investments with several motives like financial security, wealth maximisation, or speculation. In a nutshell, everybody is looking for some returns, tangible or intangible, from the investment. Irrespective of the motives, the common thread that binds all the investments is the expectation of a return on investment, that is, in most cases, quantifiable.

Although return on investment is a dominant factor, it cannot be the only motive for investments. This is evident from the fact that most businesses are either diversified or intend to diversify. Similarly, seldom do we find investors putting all their eggs in one basket. If returns were the sole criteria we would not find individuals and firms investing in different assets. They simply would invest in single asset that yields the maximum profit. However, this is rarely the case and could happen only with ignorance. All well-informed investors park their funds in multiple assets. They all perceive too much of a risk if all the investment is made in a single asset. Therefore, the return and risks are interdependent with the unfailing rule that higher risk demands higher returns.

The concept of return and risk needs to be understood simultaneously. The understanding is critical from the viewpoint of firms making capital budgeting decisions. The firms need to evaluate the returns that a project can offer and this process of evaluation must necessarily consider the risk associated with the project. The argument applies equally to the individuals investing their savings in different financial securities to earn returns in future.

Return and risk are the two critical factors in investment decisions. They are closely linked and must be studied simultaneously.

This chapter deals with the measurement of return and risk. The measurement can be done with the primary data and the tools that are available, In case when primary date is not available we rely on the data of the company that is a close substitute of the company in question. Fortunately, there is an abundance of data available for return and risk in the traded financial assets. The study of price behaviour of such frequently traded financial assets would serve as an ideal proxy for the expected returns and perceived risk for the firms to assess the returns and risk involved in the projects.

The expected risk and return data thus arrived at using the price data of the proxy financial asset is not only objective but is also an authentic source as millions of investors exchange trades at prices that are rather independently determined among them, and reflect the collective wisdom of millions of investors. There can be no better substitute of the data of the capital markets to understand return and risk associated with investment.

For analysis of return and risk, we depend on data on financial assets, because they are frequently traded and reflect investors' preferences for return and risk.

RETURN

Having appreciated the suitability of data of financial assets as available in the records of the capital markets, we turn our attention to the measurement of returns on financial assets.

Returns on financial assets consist of dividend/interest of holding the security and capital gains, i.e., the difference between the prices at the beginning and at the end of the holding period.

Consider an initial investment in the stock of Reliance, currently selling at a price of ₹500 by an investor, who buys 100 shares making an initial investment of ₹50,000. Assume that this investment is being made for a period of one year after which the investor would make an exit by selling the shares. How do we calculate the returns of the investor? To answer this, the returns on the investment must be broken in two parts:

1. The reward the investor gets by owning this asset over the holding period; one year in this case, referred as *dividend yield*, and
2. The gain the investor makes upon selling the asset after the holding period of one year, referred to as *capital gains*.

Assume that Reliance declares a dividend of ₹10 per share during this period of one year. Further, at the end of one year the share price of Reliance is ₹600 per share. For convenience let us assume that the disinvestment and receipt of dividend are simultaneous and happen exactly after one year. We make this assumption to eliminate the impact of time value of money. The funds received by the investor after one year are:

= Dividend received + Amount realized through sale
= 100 × 10 + 100 × 600 = 1,000 + 60,000
= ₹61,000

The absolute return of the investor would be
= Amount realized – Amount invested
= 61,000 – 50,000
= ₹11,000

We may say that the investor obtained a return of ₹11,000 over a period of one year. As a measure of the return on investment the absolute return has little significance since the return amount would change with the amount of initial investment. Since this change is proportionate to the initial investment the return can be expressed in percentage terms. The % return in the above example will be 22% determined as below:

$$\% \text{ Return} = \frac{\text{Value Realized} - \text{Amount Invested}}{\text{Amount Invested}} \times 100$$

$$= \frac{61{,}000 - 50{,}000}{50{,}000} \times 100 = 22\%$$

This return can be split in two components of dividend yield and capital gains. The total return after a period of one year is ₹11,000 on an investment of ₹50,000. Of this an amount of ₹1,000 is earned as dividend and ₹10,000 is the profit upon selling of the asset. Therefore,

Total Return = Dividend Earned + Capital Gain
= 1,000 + 10,000
= ₹11,000

The % return can be expressed in mathematical terms, assuming P_0 as the initial price, D_1 is the dividend received in the period 1, and P_1 is the price at the end of period 1, as follows:

$$\text{Total \% Return} = \frac{\text{Dividend} + \text{Capital Gain}}{\text{Initial Investment}}$$

$$= \frac{D_1 + (P_1 - P_0)}{P_0}$$

$$= \frac{D_1}{P_0} + \frac{P_1 - P_0}{P_0} \qquad (5\text{-}1)$$

In the above analysis, we have:

(i) ignored the time value of money,
(ii) made no adjustment for inflation and the returns calculated are in nominal terms, and
(iii) not provided for taxes that may be payable on dividend and capital gains taxed at different rates.

It was assumed that the investor sells the share after the holding period of one year. What if the investor holds on to the investment? In such a case the capital gains will be treated as unrealized. Yet the computation of returns remains valid since investor could have sold the stock to realize the return, opportunity for which existed. Whether or not the investor actually sold the stock becomes rather irrelevant for the measurement of return.

Example 5-1 Calculating Dividend Yield and Capital Gains

The current market price of a share is ₹300. An investor buys 100 shares. After one year he sells these shares at a price of ₹360 and also receives the dividend of ₹15 per share. Find out his total return, % return, dividend yield and capital gains.

Solution

Initial Investment = 300 × 100 = ₹30,000
Dividend Earned = 15 × 100 = ₹1,500
Capital Gains = (360 – 300) × 100 = ₹6,000
Total Return = 1,500 + 6,000 = ₹7,500
Total Percent Return = [(1,500 + 6,000)/30,000] × 100 = 25%
Dividend Yield = 15/300 = 0.05 (5%)
Capital Gains = 60/300 = 0.20 (20%)

MEASURING EXPECTED RETURN

In the previous example, the prices at the time of investment as well as at the time of disinvestment were assumed as known. However, in practice only the current price is known. The investor does not know the future price of the financial asset. At best only an estimate can be made about the future price, which generates expectations of the return. In the absence of availability of a future price, the investor acts on the expectations of some return while initiating a position of either buying or selling the financial assets. Here, we are concerned with the expectations of profit rather than its actual realization to make an investment decision. Notice that investor is rewarded positively when (i) he buys first at a lower price and expects to sell later when price increases, or when (ii) he sells first at higher price and expects to buy later when price decreases.

There are several ways one can estimate the expected return. One of the simplest ways of finding the same is to directly address the question to the investor and seek the expected profit percentage. A more complicated approach could be to develop a valuation model and forecast the price a year later or for any other time horizon as considered appropriate by the investor. Yet another way of finding the expected return is to use some standard models such as capital asset pricing model, arbitrage pricing model, etc. Another simple time-tested approach to find the expected return is based on historical returns the financial asset has offered in the past. In this chapter, we will rely on the historical rereturns approach.

Return expected is one of the key determinants of the investment decision. Expected returns are normally calculated from historical data.

Arithmetic Mean (Average)

Let us assume the price data of a share for the last six years in Table 5-1.

Table 5-1 Historical Data of Stock Price

Year	Share Price P_t	Dividend during the year, D_t	Capital Gains $\frac{(P_t - P_{t-1})}{P_{t-1}}$	Dividend Yield $\frac{D_t}{P_{t-1}}$	Rate of Return
1	100	10	—	—	—
2	110	10	10/100	10/100	20.00
3	120	10	10/110	10/110	18.18
4	100	12	–20/120	12/120	–6.66
5	90	12	–10/100	12/100	2.00
6	130	12	40/90	12/90	57.78

From the historical data of the returns on the share, one can estimate the average rate of return the share has offered over a period of time.

The average rate of return is the simple *arithmetic mean* of the return in the last column of Table 5-1 and is defined as sum of the returns divided by number of observations. If n is the number of years and R_n is the rate of return in the nth year the simple arithmetic average R mathematically is represented by Equation 5-2:

Arithmetic mean of the past returns is easiest to find, and it is the best estimate of expected returns.

$$\text{Arithmetic Return; } \bar{R} = \frac{1}{n}(R_1 + R_2 + R_3 + \ldots R_n)$$

$$= \frac{1}{n}\sum_{1}^{n} R_n \qquad (5\text{-}2)$$

For the data in Table 5-1 the arithmetic mean of returns works out to 18.26% as worked out below.

Arithmetic Return;

$$\bar{R} = \frac{1}{5}(20.00 + 18.18 - 6.66 + 2.00 + 57.78)$$

$$= \frac{91.30}{5} = 18.26\%$$

Example 5-2 Calculating Average Return

An investor has bought shares of six companies and invested equally in each of them. The returns offered by the six companies in the last one year have been 21%, 24%, –25%, 18%, 120%, and 16% respectively. Find the average return of the investor in the last year.

Solution

$$\text{The average return} = \bar{R} = \frac{1}{n}(R_1 + R_2 + R_3 + \ldots R_n)$$

$$\bar{R} = \frac{1}{6}(21 + 24 - 25 + 18 + 120 + 16) = 29\%$$

Geometric Mean

Another statistic that is very popular as a measure of return is the *geometric mean.* Let us consider an example to demonstrate how the geometric mean is different from the arithmetic mean and more importantly which one should be used when. Let us assume that Investor A buys a share in 2001 which was trading at ₹100. A year later in 2002 the share price jumps by 100% and becomes ₹200. Two years after the investment in 2003, the share falls by 50% and again quotes at ₹100. Assuming that no dividend was paid in the two year period, we may compute the average return for A by taking the average of the returns over the years 2002 and 2003.

Geometric mean is calculated by prices at the beginning and ending period, and it gives the holding period returns.

Return in first year = (200 – 100)/100 = 100%

Return in the second year = (100 – 200)/200 = –50%

Arithmetic mean, the average return

= (100 – 50)/2 = 25% per annum

The arithmetic mean would indicate that the annual return offered by the share was 25% and therefore Investor A should have earned 50% (25% × 2) over the holding period of two years.

In fact Investor A has earned nothing as whatever was gained in the first year was wiped out in the second year with investment ending at a closing value same as that the initial value. His ending wealth was same as the wealth in the beginning.

Arithmetic mean suggests that he should have had 1.5 times the initial wealth at the end of investment period of two years. Is our interpretation of arithmetic mean wrong? Certainly not. Here is an explanation:

Holding period returns as measured from geometric mean is not an appropriate measure of expected return, because the investment is not held constant, period after period.

While calculating the arithmetic mean we did not take into account the compounding effect of returns. We simply added the returns of each period and divided the sum by number of periods. In the above example of investment over multiple periods, it was assumed that the investor keeps reinvesting the wealth of one period into the next period. This implies that compounding of wealth should have been taken into account, which the arithmetic mean did not.

The geometric mean reflects the holding period return and takes compounding into account. If we take R_g to be the annual rate of return in a holding period of two years in this case (more generally that is different than a year), and first year and second year returns at 100% and –50% respectively, we can write as below:

$$(1 + R_g)^2 = (1 + 1) \times (1 - 0.5) = 2 \times 0.5 = 1$$

Or $\quad R_g = \sqrt{1} - 1 = 0$

More generally, the return over n period investment is given by geometric mean of each period return, $R_1, R_2 \ldots R_n$ being the returns over period 1, 2, …n, respectively can be written as Equation 5-3.

$$(1 + R_g)^n = (1 + R_1)(1 + R_2)(1 + R_3)(1 + R_4)\ldots(1 + R_n)$$

$$R_g = \sqrt[n]{(1 + R_1)(1 + R_2)(1 + R_3)(1 + R_4)\ldots(1 + R_n)} - 1 \qquad (5\text{-}3)$$

The observation that the average rate of return of 25% per annum given by the arithmetic mean is valid when we keep the value of investment constant period after period. Let us compute the return for investor A keeping the investment in each period constant. This will eliminate the compounding effect. After investing ₹100 in 2001, the investor A must sell half the share when price became ₹200 to keep the investment value constant in the next period. Investor A realizes ₹100 and keeps the remaining ₹100 reinvested for the next period. At the end of second year the value of this half share will be ₹50 at which the investor liquidates assuming two-year holding period. After the initial investment of ₹100 the investor A has following income:

Cash realized in Period 1 (Year 2002)	₹100
+ Cash realized in Period 2 (Year 2003)	₹50
– Initial Investment	₹100
Gain over two years	₹50

Rate of return for two years = 50/100 = 50%

Therefore, average annual rate of return = 50/2 = 25%

Arithmetic Mean vs Geometric Mean

The relationship between the geometric mean and arithmetic mean is approximated by Equation 5-4 where R_g is geometric mean and R_a is the arithmetic mean, and σ is the standard deviation of the returns.

$$R_g \approx R_a - \tfrac{1}{2}\sigma^2 \qquad (5\text{-}4)$$

The above relationship of the geometric mean and arithmetic mean is exact when returns follow normal distribution. Also note that the geometric mean is always smaller than the arithmetic mean and the difference depends upon the variability of returns.

The discussion on arithmetic and geometric mean raises the questions as to which one of them is correct and when they are to be used. The answer depends upon what application we are looking at. If the objective is to evaluate the past performance of the return on the financial assets, the geometric mean is the appropriate measure. However, if we have the future in mind and have to evaluate whether or not to invest in a financial asset, the judgment must be based on arithmetic average. Reverting back to the example of share price increasing by 100% in the first year and then decreasing by 50% in the second year, yielding no return it would be appropriate to infer the following:

1. While evaluating the performance of the asset it is correct that the return over two year period is zero, using the geometric mean.
2. While making judgements about the future as to the desirability of investing in the asset, it would be appropriate to state that the average rate of return of the asset is 25%, based on the arithmetic average. Use of geometric average for planning purposes would be erroneous.

Internal Rate of Return (IRR)

Another related issue while measuring returns arises from the changing investment values from period to period. Consider the following simple scenario:

Period	Action
0	Invest ₹100 by purchase of a share
1	Invest ₹110 to buy second share Receive ₹5 as dividend for owning one share
2	Receive ₹12 as dividend for two shares owned, Receive ₹240 as sale proceed of two shares

Here the price of the share has moved from ₹100 to ₹110 and then to ₹120 in two periods and dividend received is ₹5 per share for Period 1 and ₹6 per share in Period 2.

How do we measure the return for the investor in such a case where there is a change in the value of the investment in each period? The best way to find out the return earned is to set up the cash flows for each period and use the discounted cash flow approach. The return r can be found from the following equation:

$$100 + \frac{105}{1 + r} = \frac{252}{(1 + r)^2}$$

By a procedure of hit and trial and after a few iterations, one can find the rate of return r that satisfies the above equation. The solution to the above equation can be easily found using an EXCEL worksheet and the *IRR function* as shown in Table 5-2.

The IRR, which measures the performance of the investment, is 14.70%. In contrast, the average rate of return offered by the share is 14.77% computed on the basis of data available in each period.

Internal rate of return is a cash flow based approach that incorporates changing investments, period after period, and is the best measure of realized returns.

Again the question arises as to which of the two, i.e., IRR and Average Rate of Return, provides the correct answer. The difference between the two again lies in the constancy of amount of the investment in each period. While computing IRR the use of actual cash flows implies that the investment in each period gets moderated with the value.

While computing arithmetic mean, the capital gain, and the dividend yield in each period is computed separately to arrive at the % return in each period implying constancy of investment in each period. Based on the above we can make following observations:

1. While evaluating the past performance one must use the geometric mean taking into account the compounding effect.
2. Use of discounted cash flow technique (using IRR) is appropriate when value of investment is changing from period to period.
3. While making decisions about investing in future use of neither the geometric mean nor the IRR based evaluation is appropriate. It would be appropriate to make investment decisions on the basis of arithmetic mean.

Table 5-2 Finding Return Using Excel and IRR Function

Period	Cash Inflow (₹)	Cash Outflow (₹)	Net Cash Flow (₹)
0	—	100.00	–100.00
1	5.00	110.00	–105.00
2	252.00	—	252.00
Rate of Return (IRR)			**14.70%**

Computation of Average Return of Investment

Period	Price (₹)	Dividend (₹/Share)	Capital Gain (%)	Dividend Yield (%)	Total Return (%)
0	100	—	—	—	—
1	110	5	10.00	5.00	15.00
2	120	6	9.09	5.45	14.55
Average Return					**14.77**

Both the geometric mean and the IRR are subject to change with the amount of investment. For example, the IRR of the investment falls to 14.66% if the investor decides to buy additional two shares instead of one in Period 1, despite the fact that the price as well as the dividend yield of the stock remains the same, as shown in Table 5-3.

While choosing stocks for investment, or including them into the portfolio, or for the purpose of comparison arithmetic mean of returns will provide a judicious basis. The geometric mean will distort the opinion depending upon the timings of investment and disinvestment, and IRR is subject to change if the investment amount is changing in each period.

Table 5-3 Finding Return

Period	Cash In Flow (₹)	Cash Out Flow (₹)	Net Cash Flow (₹)	Remarks
0	—	100.00	–100.00	Bought one share @ ₹100
1	5.00	220.00	–215.00	Bought 25 shares @ ₹110 and earned dividend of ₹ 5/share
2	378.00	—	378.00	Sold 3 shares @ ₹120 and earned dividend of ₹6/share
Rate of Return			**14.66%**	

PROBABILITY DISTRIBUTION

We defined the average return as the sum of observations divided by the number of observations. What meaning do we assign to this value? Does this represent the most likely value? Not really. In fact it was assumed that all observations are equally likely. It implies that if sufficiently large observations were made one would end up with the return equal to the average computed.

For measurement of risk associated with returns, one needs to know the probability distribution of returns.

In fact the returns on the assets are not equally likely. Some values of returns occur more often, while some values occur fewer times when some extraordinary events happen. In such situations the returns are not evenly distributed. There is a greater chance that some values will occur more often than others. A graphical plot of the values of the return on the horizontal axis and the frequency of occurrence on the vertical axis is referred as *frequency distribution*. An example would illustrate the point. Consider the data of returns for 150 observations on a security as given in Table 5-4:

Table 5-4 Returns on Security

Frequency of occurrence	26	34	50	18	12	10
Values of Return in (%)	10	15	20	25	30	35
Probability of occurrence(%)	17	23	33	12	8	7
Probability x Returns (%)	1.73	3.40	6.67	3.00	2.40	2.33
Expected Returns (%)						**19.53**

A total of 150 observations are made. Table 5-4 lists the frequency of observed returns ranging from 10% to 35%. For example, the value of 20% returns occurs 50 times out of the total 150 observations.

In the above example, the likelihood of a 20% return occurring is 33% (50/150). The probability of the occurrence of

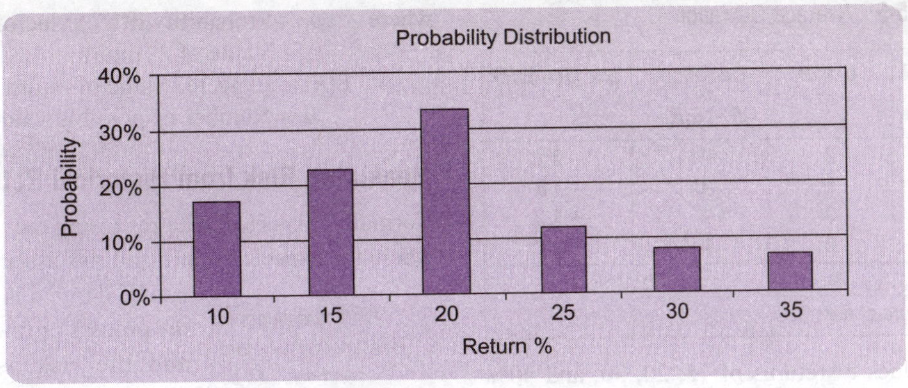

Figure 5-1 Probability distribution of returns

each value is given in row 3 of the Table 5-4 and shown in Figure 5-1.

In a scenario where the frequency of occurrence is not same, the average will not be given by Equation 5-2, which considers all values equally likely. One has to take into account the likelihood of occurrence of each value. The average referred as expected value is the product of probability and the value of the variable. The expected value can be calculated as:

Expected Value = Sum of Product of Probabilities and Values

These values are shown in row 4 of the Table 5-4 and the expected value comes to 19.53%. The expected value can be represented as Equation 5-5.

$$E(R) = \sum_{i=1}^{n} p_i R_i \quad (5\text{-}5)$$

where p_i = Probability of occurrence of ith outcome
R_i = Return for the ith outcome
n = Nos. of possible outcomes

RISK

The second important dimension of any investment decision is the risk associated with it. How do we define risk? In the simplest sense, risk may be viewed as the possibility that the actual outcome will differ from the expected outcome. If one is certain that a particular outcome will occur then there is no risk involved.

We need to develop a yardstick for measuring risk. In the practical world, risk may be expressed in different ways by different investors. Some of the expressions of risk may be:

1. The maximum loss that I can incur is 20%
2. The chances that I will not make a profit are 50%
3. It is a risky investment because the chances that price will exceed the current level are only 20%

Though the above statements may be expressions of risk they fail to quantify it. What is risky for one may be safe for another and what is safe for one is risky for another. Our manner of perceiving risk is more of a subjective matter. We need to eliminate the subjectivity.

Therefore, there is a need to have a measurement of risk that is objective and unambiguously states the fact but leaves the judgement of it being acceptable or otherwise to the individuals.

MEASURES OF RISK

Risk can be measured in many ways. We discuss few of them here.

Range

The difference between the maximum and minimum values of the return is defined as a range. It can also be one indication of the risk. Mathematically it can be stated as:

Range = Maximum Value or Return – Minimum Value or Return (5-6)

For example, consider Share A prevailing at a price of ₹100. Estimates of future price by an analyst reveal that the price can go as high as ₹200 if good conditions prevail and under depressed conditions can fall as low as ₹50. For another Share B, also selling currently at ₹100, the estimated maximum and minimum values can be ₹300 and ₹25 respectively. On the basis of the difference in the extreme values of the stocks, Share B may be regarded as more risky having a larger possible variation of ₹275 (300 – 25) compared to ₹150 (200 – 50) for Share A.

Such a measure of risk as a difference of extreme values, however, ignores the probability of such extreme events happening. If in the above case the likelihood of price of Share A falling to ₹50 is 50%, while for Share B the probability of price falling to ₹25 is only 10% the perception of risk changes. To have a clear view of risk one has to not only consider the range of values that the price/return can take but also the probabilities of the different values. Hence, the range cannot be regarded as an appropriate measure of risk.

Range is one measure of risk that concentrates on the maximum possible loss.

Average Deviation

Another way of measuring risk is to find out the deviation of returns from a reference value such as an expected return. It must also include the probability of such deviations. For an aggregate risk one can add the product of deviations. For example consider the data in Table 5-5.

Table 5-5 Average Deviation

Probability p	Return % R	p × R	Deviation R – E(R)	p × {(R – E(R)}
0.2	15	3	–11	– 2.2
0.3	20	6	–6	– 1.8
0.3	30	9	4	+ 1.2
0.2	40	8	14	+ 2.8
Expected Return, E(R)		26		
Sum of Deviations (As measure of risk)				0

With the possible values of returns of 15, 20, 30, and 40% and probabilities of occurrence of 0.2, 0.3, 0.3, and 0.2 respectively, the expected return works out to 26%. The risk measured as a sum of deviations in the last column of Table 5-5 is nil. This happens because positive and negative deviations cancel out each other. Clearly this too cannot be a dependable and authentic measure of risk.

Average deviation of returns is another measure of risk that attempts to incorporate the probability of each return.

Variance and Standard Deviation

The way of overcoming the deficiency of positive and negative deviations offsetting each other is to square them up before multiplying them with probabilities and adding that up. The sum of squared deviation multiplied by probabilities is known as *variance*. The measurement of risk through variance will have the unit of % squared. In order to be consistent with the unit of measurement of expected return, one can take the square root of the variance, called *standard deviation*, as a measure of risk. By repeating the exercise displayed on Table 5-5 we find that the standard deviation of the returns is 8.89% as shown in Table 5-6.

Table 5-6 Variance and Standard Deviation

Probability p	Return % R	p × R	Deviation R – E(R)	Deviation² {R – E(R)}²	p × {(R – E(R)}²
0.2	15	3	–11	121	24.2
0.3	20	6	– 6	36	10.8
0.3	30	9	4	16	4.8
0.2	40	8	14	196	39.2
Expected Return, E(R)		26			
Variance = Sum of Squared Deviations × Probability (As measure of risk)					79.0
Standard Deviations (As measure of risk)					8.89%

Mathematically, variance, and standard deviation are given by Equations 5-6 and 5-7 respectively, stated below:

$$\text{Variance; } \sigma^2 = \sum_{1}^{n} p_i \times \{(R_i - E(R)\}^2 \quad (5\text{-}6)$$

and Standard deviation,

$$\sigma = \sqrt{\sum_{1}^{n} p_i \times \{(R_i - E(R)\}^2} \quad (5\text{-}7)$$

where p_i = Probability of ith value of return
R_i = Value of ith return
$E(R)$ = Expected value of return
n = Number of possible values of returns

Measuring Risk from Historical Returns

Normally, historical data regarding the prices of securities from where the expected return and risk associated with the securities can be derived is available. We illustrate the process of finding the expected return and the risk associated through an example. Consider the share whose closing price was ₹100 at Week 0. At the end of week one the price became ₹101.50 thereby providing a return of 1.5% in Week 1. The % return for any period may be found by using Equation 5-1.

Both parameters of investment, i.e., return and risk, can be effectively measured from historical data of return on each security.

The return for each week is arrived by dividing the difference of price during the week by the opening price, i.e.,

Table 5-7 Measuring the Average Return and Standard Deviation from Historical Data

Week	Return (%)	Deviation from Mean	Squared Deviation
1	1.50	0.29	0.08
2	1.00	–0.21	0.04
3	1.32	0.11	0.01
4	–1.20	–2.41	5.81
5	1.55	0.34	0.12
6	1.17	–0.04	0.00
7	–2.25	–3.46	11.97
8	3.25	2.04	4.16
9	2.45	1.24	1.54
10	3.26	2.05	4.20
11	–3.10	–4.31	18.58
12	4.20	2.99	8.94
13	0.00	–1.21	1.46
14	0.38	–0.83	0.69
15	1.16	–0.05	0.00
16	1.31	0.10	0.01
17	–1.58	–2.79	7.78
18	3.00	1.79	3.20
19	–0.55	–1.76	3.10
20	1.76	0.55	0.30
21	1.85	0.64	0.41
22	3.72	2.51	6.30
23	2.46	1.25	1.56
24	2.55	1.34	1.80
25	–1.44	–2.65	7.02
26	3.75	2.54	6.45
Sum	31.52		
Mean (%)	1.21		
Sum of squared deviations			95.55
Variance			3.82
Standard deviation (%)			1.96

% return for period *n*;

$$r_n = \frac{P_n - P_{n-1}}{P_{n-1}} \times 100 \text{ with no dividend in the period}$$

$$= \left[\frac{D}{P_{n-1}} + \frac{P_n - P_{n-1}}{P_{n-1}}\right] \times 100 \text{ with dividend during the period.}$$

Proceeding in the same manner, the weekly returns on a share for past 26 weeks is shown in Column 2 of Table 5-7.

The mean value is calculated by dividing the sum of all values by the number of observations, which are 26. The average weekly return works out to 1.21%.

$$\text{Average Return} = \bar{R} = \frac{\sum_{1}^{26} R_i}{n} = \frac{31.52}{26} = 1.21\%$$

Risk as measured by standard deviation is calculated by dividing the sum of squared deviation by $(n - 1)$. Using the formula as given below the standard deviation of the mean is 1.96%.

$$\text{Variance } \sigma^2 = \frac{1}{(n-1)}\sum_{1}^{n}(R_i - \bar{R})^2 = \frac{95.55}{25} = 3.82$$

$$\text{Standard Deviation } \sigma = \sqrt{\text{Variance}} = \sqrt{3.82} = 1.96\%$$

Example 5-3 Using Historical Data to Find Return and Risk

The following price data for a share *A* is available for last 10 years:

Year	Dividend (₹)	Closing Price (₹)
1990	5.00	200.00
1991	6.00	220.00
1992	6.00	240.00
1993	7.00	290.00
1994	7.00	270.00
1995	8.00	325.00
1996	8.00	240.00
1997	9.00	380.00
1998	9.00	380.00
1999	10.00	425.00
2000	10.00	460.00

Find out (1) the expected rate of return for share *A*; (2) its variance and standard deviation; (3) If the return and standard deviation of the market index over the same period are 10% and 15% respectively what meaning do you attach to the answers in (1) and (2).

Solution

1. The data and the calculation of expected return and standard deviation are shown below. The return for each year is found by dividing the capital gain/loss and dividend by the previous price as shown for the year 1997.

$$\text{\% return for period } n;\ r_n = \left[\frac{D}{P_{n-1}} + \frac{P_n - P_{n-1}}{P_{n-1}}\right] \times 100$$

$$\text{\% return for period 1997; } r_n = \left[\frac{9}{240} + \frac{380 - 240}{240}\right] \times 100$$

$$= \frac{149}{240} \times 100 = 62.08\%$$

Year	Dividend (₹)	Closing Price (₹)	Return (%)	Square of Deviation
1990	5.00	200.00		
1991	6.00	220.00	13.00	0.10
1992	6.00	240.00	11.82	2.27
1993	7.00	290.00	23.75	108.70
1994	7.00	270.00	–4.48	317.08
1995	8.00	325.00	23.33	100.19
1996	8.00	240.00	–23.69	1,370.21
1997	9.00	380.00	**62.08**	**2,377.47**
1998	9.00	380.00	2.37	120.02
1999	10.00	425.00	14.47	1.32
2000	10.00	460.00	10.59	7.48
Sum			133.24	4,404.85
Average			13.32	
Variance				489.43
Standard Deviation (%)				22.12

The average of the 10 observations reflects the expected return for share *A* at 13.32%.

2. The variance is found by taking the sum of the squared deviations of the return from the average. The squared deviation for the year 1997 is 2377.47 [$(62.08 - 13.32)^2$]. From the following equation, we find variance of the share as 489.43, leading to the standard deviation of 22.12%.

$$\text{Variance, } \sigma^2 = \frac{1}{n-1}\sum^{n}(R_i - \bar{R})^2 = \frac{4404.85}{9} = 489.43$$

$$\text{Standard Deviation, } \sigma = \sqrt{\text{Variance}} = \sqrt{489.43} = 22.12\%$$

3. As against the market return of 10% the stock offers a better return of 13.32% but at the same time it carries more risk too as reflected in the higher standard deviation of 22.12% as compared to 15% of the market.

One possible objection to variance or standard deviation as measures of risk is that it includes the positive as well as negative deviations from an expected return. Most people believe that a return in excess of expected return (the positive deviation) is in fact not a risk but instead a desirable outcome. Therefore, it will be appropriate to include only the negative deviations (the returns lesser than expected return) while measuring risk. The objection is apparently valid. If one considers only the negative deviations and ignores the positive ones, the measure will be called *semi-variance*. However, if probability distribution of returns is symmetrical around its mean value, which apparently is the case for returns on the individual stocks and portfolios, then semi-variance will be half the variance. Therefore, using variance or semi-variance would make no difference in the analysis when returns are symmetrical around the mean. In case the returns are non-symmetrical; neither variance nor semi-variance will be an appropriate measure of risk. The additional parameter that needs to be considered is the *skewness* of the distribution.

The justification of variance or standard deviation as measures of risk is as follows:

1. Historically, the returns on stocks are observed to have symmetrical distribution. The probability distribution of returns is usually a bell-shaped curve known as *normal*

distribution, which is described completely by its mean and standard deviation.

2. The utility of money for investors is a quadratic function of risk and, therefore, variance as a measure of risk is apt as it reflects the risk aversion tendency of investors.

Coefficient of Variation

Standard deviation or variance is an absolute measure of risk. Sometimes we are keen to find out a relative measure. For example, stock returns for Share A and B may exhibit the standard deviation of 20% each. However, the expected returns of the two may be 15% and 20%. Although in absolute terms both the shares carry the same risk, in relative terms the risk of share B would be lower because its expected returns are higher.

Coefficient of variation given by standard deviation divided by expected return is a relative measure of risk.

The standard deviation when compared with the expected returns is known as the *coefficient of variation*. It is defined as the ratio of standard deviation to the expected value and computed in Equation 5-8.

Coefficient of Variation

$$= \frac{\text{Standard Deviation}}{\text{Expected Value}} = \frac{\sigma}{E(R)} \quad (5\text{-}8)$$

The coefficient of variation must be used cautiously as a measure of risk. For an expected value of zero it would always be infinite, which is a value difficult to interpret. For lower values of mean the coefficient of variation tends to overstate risk, while for a higher expected value, the risk tends to be understated.

Example 5-4 Finding and Understanding the Geometric Mean

Using the data provided in Example 5-3 and assuming that Stock A paid no dividend, what annual return did the stock offer for an investor who bought the share in the end of 1991 and exited in end of 2000, compare it with average return and comment.

Solution

Purchase price of the share in the year 1991 = ₹200

Selling price of the share in the year 2000= ₹460

The return realized by the investor over a 10-year period is given by the geometric mean, R_g is determined as follows:

$$R_g = \sqrt[n]{(1+R_1)(1+R_2)(1+R_3)(1+R_4)\ldots(1+R_n)} - 1$$

$$\text{or, } R_g = \sqrt[n]{R_{10}/R_0} - 1 = \sqrt[10]{460/200} - 1$$

$$= 1.0868 - 1 = 0.0868 \equiv 8.68\%$$

The average return over 10-year period is re-computed and found to be 10.57% as worked out in the table.

Average returns should be used for planning the investment. The geometric mean reflects the return realized over a holding period of 10 years. This would change with a change of the holding period. For example, if the holding period changed to five years the investor would exit at ₹325 which shall yield a return of 10.20% computed below.

$$R_g = \sqrt[n]{R_5/R_{10}} - 1$$

$$= \sqrt[5]{325/200} - 1 = 1.1020 - 1 = 0.1020 \equiv 10.2\%$$

Year	Closing Price (₹)	Return (%)	Square of Deviation
1990	200.00	—	—
1991	220.00	10.00	0.32
1992	240.00	9.09	2.17
1993	290.00	20.83	105.43
1994	270.00	–6.90	304.92
1995	325.00	20.37	96.14
1996	240.00	–26.15	1,348.31
1997	380.00	58.33	2,281.77
1998	380.00	0.00	111.63
1999	425.00	11.84	1.63
2000	460.00	8.24	5.43
Sum		105.65	4,257.75
Average		10.57	
Variance			473.08
Standard Deviation (%)			21.75

Example 5-5 Using Forecast to Estimate Return and Risk

An investor is considering buying a share for which he has made a forecast of returns based on expected economic conditions. The states of economic conditions are described as excellent, good, fair, poor, and bad. The chances of each economic conditions and the forecast of returns are given below:

Scenario	Probability p (%)	Return R (%)
Excellent	15.00	40.00
Good	25.00	20.00
Fair	35.00	10.00
Poor	15.00	–10.00
Bad	10.00	–20.00

Find out the expected return on the share and the standard deviation.

Solution

The expected return and standard deviation are found using Equations 5-3 and 5-4 as shown below:

$$E(R) = \sum_{i=1}^{n} p_i R_i = 0.15 \times 40 + 0.25 \times 20 + 0.35 \times 10 + 0.15 \times (-10) + 0.10 \times (-20) = 11\%$$

$$\text{Variance; } \sigma^2 = \sum_{1}^{n} p_i \times \{(R_1 - E(R)\}^2 = 0.15 \times 29^2 + 0.25 \times 9^2 + 0.35 \times -1^2 + 0.15 \times -21^2 + 0.10 \times -31^2 = 72.78$$

and

$$\text{standard deviation; } \sigma = \sqrt{\sum_{1}^{b} p_i \times \{(R_i - E(R)\}^2} = \sqrt{72.78} = 8.53\%$$

Scenario	Probability p	Return R (%)	p × R (%)	Squared Deviation × p (%)
Excellent	15.00	40.00	6.00	3.75
Good	25.00	20.00	5.00	9.00
Fair	35.00	10.00	3.50	19.69
Poor	15.00	–10.00	–1.50	23.44
Bad	10.00	–20.00	–2.00	16.90
Expected Return %			11.00	
Variance				72.78
Standard Deviation %				8.53

NORMAL DISTRIBUTION

Normal distribution is a probability distribution that is symmetrical around its mean and is a bell-shaped curve as depicted in Figure 5-2(a). It is also referred to as the *Gaussian distribution*. This is the most frequently occurring probability distribution and it is assumed that the returns on the stocks exhibit return characteristics that are similar to that of normal distribution.

Returns on portfolio are found to resemble a bell-shaped curve called normal distribution, which is completely described by its expected value and standard deviation.

The probability of occurrence of any value, x is given by $p(x, \mu, \sigma)$ for a distribution that has mean of μ and standard deviation of σ is given by Equation 5-9.

$$p(x, \mu, \sigma) = \frac{1}{\sqrt{2\pi}\sigma} e^{-\frac{(x-\mu)^2}{2\sigma^2}} \qquad (5\text{-}9)$$

where μ = mean value, σ = standard deviation.

Equation 5-9 is also called the normal density function. Consider a stock having expected returns of 20% and standard deviation of 5% then the probability that the stock return would be 22% can be found using Equation 5-9 by putting x = 22% μ = 20%, and σ = 5%. It is 7.36%.

The other value that is most often required while analysing risk and return is the probability of stock return assuming a value less than or greater than a particular value. For example, we may be more interested in knowing the probability of return less than 22% or more than 22% rather that finding probability of returns being exactly 22%. The area under the normal distribution curve in Figure 5-2(b) gives the probability of value falling below x. It is known as cumulative normal distribution.

Values of probability density function and cumulative density function for any value of return x can be found using EXCEL given the expected value and standard deviation. For value of x = 22% with the expected value of 20% and a standard deviation of 5% the density function and cumulative density function are shown in Figures 5-3(a) and 5-3(b), respectively. The path is *Insert – Function – NORMDIST* where x represent the chosen stock return. For the density function (the probability that the value would exactly equal to x) to choose *false* under cumulative, and for *cumulative* density (the probability that the value would be less than x) to choose *true* under *cumulative*.

The probability that the return would be exactly equal to 22% is 7.36% and the probability that the returns would be less than 22% is 65.54%. It also implies that the probability that the returns would exceed 22% is 34.46% using Equation 5-10.

$$p(x > 0.22) = 1 - p(x \leq 0.22) \qquad (5\text{-}10)$$

Normal distribution is completely defined with two parameters, i.e., mean, μ and standard deviation, σ. The vertical axis gives the probability of occurrence of particular value of return

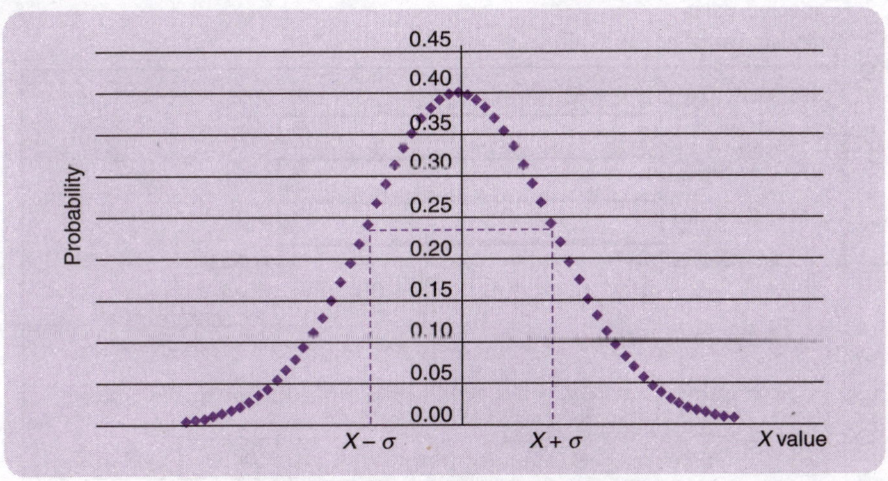

Figure 5-2(a) Normal distribution

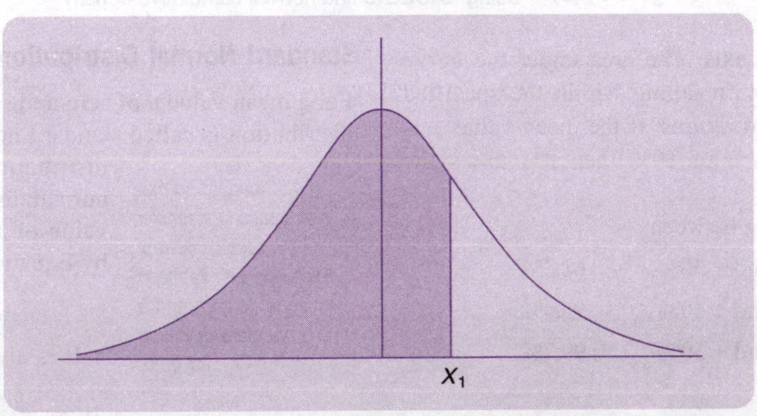

Figure 5-2(b) Cumulative normal distribution

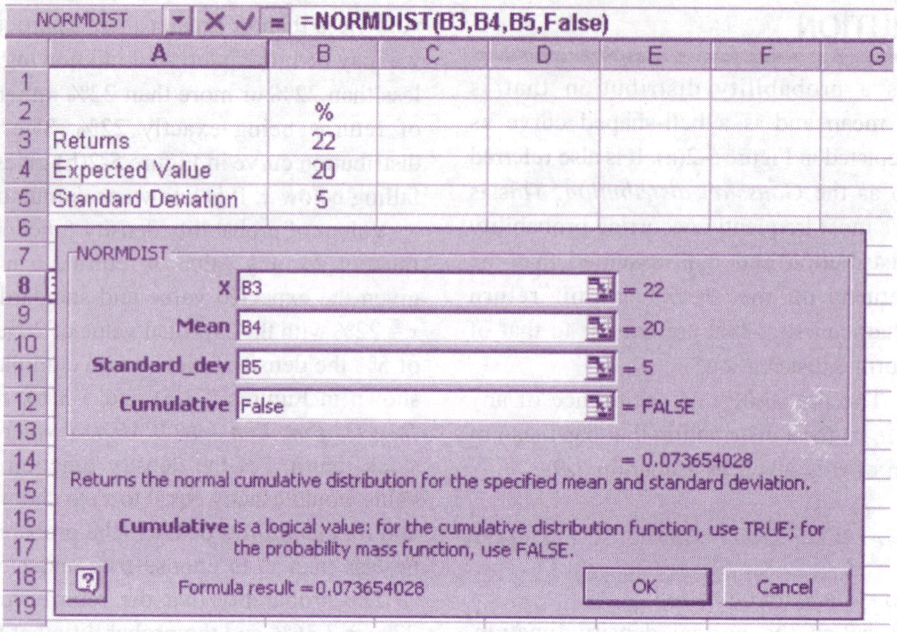

Figure 5-3(a) Using EXCEL to find normal density

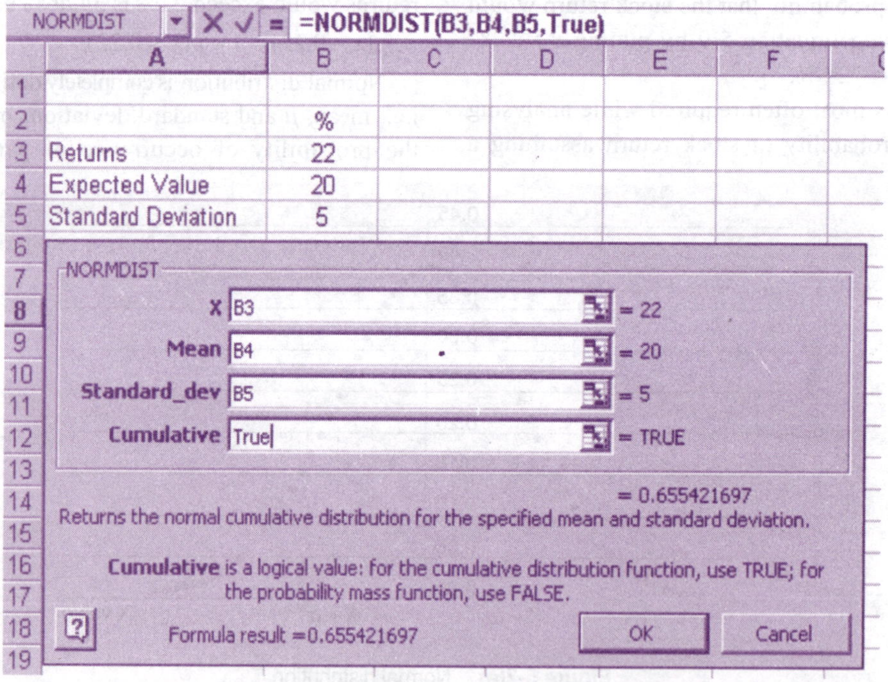

Figure 5-3(b) Using EXCEL to find normal cumulative density

represented on the horizontal axis. The area under the curve provides the probability of return falling within the specified range. For normally distributed returns, if the mean value X is 20% with standard deviation σ of 10% then it implies the following:

Probability of returns falling between

$X \pm 1\sigma = 20 \pm 10 = +10\%$ and $+30\%$	: 68.3%
$X \pm 2\sigma = 20 \pm 20 = 0\%$ and $+40\%$	: 95.4%
$X \pm 1\sigma = 20 \pm 30 = -10\%$ and $+50\%$	: 99.7%

Standard Normal Distribution

For a mean value μ of zero and standard deviation σ of 1.00 the distribution is called standard normal distribution. Any normal distribution is converted into standard normal distribution and the corresponding value of x becomes equal to z as given by Equation 5-11.

Standard normal distribution is a special case of normal distribution with its mean equal to zero and a standard deviation of 1.00.

$$z = \frac{x - \mu}{\sigma} \qquad (5\text{-}11)$$

It is always better to use the standard

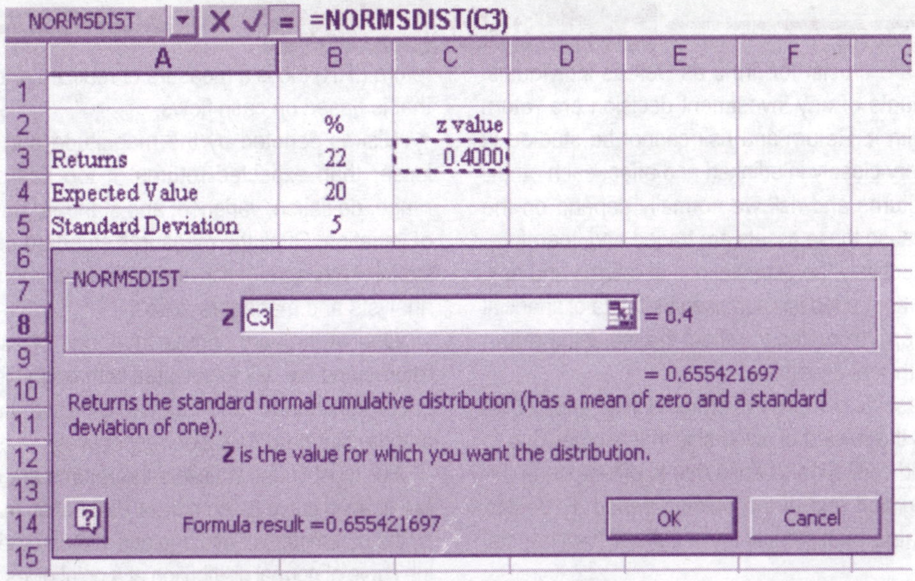

Figure 5-4 Using EXCEL to find cumulative density function with standard normal distribution

normal distribution because we can convert all normal distributions with any value of mean or standard deviation into an equivalent standard normal distribution. The areas under the curve for particular values of z are tabulated in Appendix A-2 at the end of the book. They can also be found using EXCEL exactly in the same manner as described for normal distribution except that one has to choose NORMSDIST function instead of NORMDIST. This is shown in Figure 5-4.

Any normal distribution can be converted into standard normal distribution, values of which are well tabulated for easier application.

With the help of normal or standard normal distribution, we can find probability of returns for a given range using Equation 5-12.

$$p(z_1 \le z \le z_2) = N(z_2) - N(z_1) \qquad (5\text{-}12)$$

where $N(z_1)$, $N(z_2)$ denote the area under the standard normal distribution at values z_1 and z_2 respectively.

For example, if we wish to know what is the probability of returns falling between 18% and 22%, we can convert each value to an equivalent z-value and find cumulative normal distribution using Excel function NORMSDIST. For returns to fall between 18% and 22% the z-values are –0.40 and +0.40 respectively. The probability of returns falling between 18% and 22% is 31.08% as shown below:

$$p(-0.040 \le z \le 0.40) = \text{NORMSDIST}(0.40) - \text{NORMSDIST}(-0.40)$$
$$= 0.6554 - 0.3446$$
$$= 0.3108 \equiv 31.08\%$$

While Excel denotes the standard normal distribution by z, commonly we denote the same figure by d.

Some of the properties of normal distribution that are worth remembering are:

1. The area under the curve between two points on the horizontal axis represents the probability of occurrence of values between those two points.
2. The distribution is symmetrical around its mean with equal area on either side.
3. Three measures of central tendency, i.e., mean, mode and median are at the same point for normal distribution.
4. 50% of the area is covered under $X \pm 0.67\sigma$.
5. Normal distribution with mean as zero and standard deviation as 1.00 is known as *standard normal distribution* and the values of the area under the curve are tabulated.

For small holding periods, the mean and variance of the holding period returns are proportional to those of annually compounded rates and the time interval measured in years. Accordingly, variance and standard deviation are given be Equation 5-13.

Even if security returns are not normally distributed, it is found that portfolio returns are a useful finding that enhances the application of normal distribution.

$$\text{Variance}(r) = \text{Variance}(\tilde{r}, t) = t \times \text{Variance}(\tilde{r})$$

Standard Deviation for holding period t,

$$\sigma_t = \sigma \times \sqrt{t} \qquad (5\text{-}13)$$

If standard deviations of annual, monthly, and daily returns are denoted as σ_a, σ_m, and σ_d respectively, then:

Standard deviation of monthly returns: $\sigma_m = \sigma_d/\sqrt{12}$

Standard deviation of daily returns: $\sigma_d = \sigma_d/\sqrt{250}$

If standard deviation of weekly returns is 2%, then it is equivalent to annual standard deviation of

$$\sigma_t = \sigma \times \sqrt{t} = 2 \times \sqrt{12} = 14.42\%.$$

SUMMARY

Investment decisions are crucial for firms as well as individuals. The two key determinants of any investment decision are return and risk associated with it. Return and risk cannot be studied in isolation as both are very closely interlinked and affect each other.

For estimates of returns and risk we normally depend on the financial securities because these assets are traded and, therefore, assumed to reflect collectively the expectations of returns and risk. Though real assets are not traded it is surmised that data of financial assets can closely be approximated to reflect the expected return and risk associated with real assets.

Return of financial assets comprise of dividend yield and capital gains. Dividend yield is the reward of ownership that accrues due to holding of the asset and capital gains arise due to difference in the prices at the beginning and end of the holding period. Expected returns may be calculated by historical price data of the financial asset.

Arithmetic mean and geometric mean are the two very common measures of expected return. While arithmetic mean is the simple average, geometric mean is computed by the *n*th root of the returns over holding period. The geometric mean tells the holding period's return. For the purpose of decision making for an investment arithmetic mean is an appropriate measure. The internal rate of return (IRR) too is a measure of realized return over holding period that is based on cash flows.

Risk is denoted by the magnitude and likelihood of realizing lesser than expected returns. It too has several measures like range, deviation, variance, and standard deviation, and coefficient of variation. Of all the measures standard deviation is regarded as the best measure of risk and is the unanimous choice of all financial analysts and managers alike.

One of the very popular methods of estimating the expected returns and the risk associated is through historical data. With past price data returns and risk can be estimated by finding average and the standard deviation respectively.

For most financial assets the returns are deemed to resemble a bell-shaped curve called normal distribution that is completely defined by the parameters of average and standard deviation. The area under the curve of normal distribution at a point gives the probability of finding returns lesser than that point. Standard normal distribution is a special case of normal distribution with a mean equal to zero and standard deviation of one. The values of standard normal distribution are tabulated or can be easily found using EXCEL. It is a very handy tool of analysis because any normal distribution with given mean and standard deviation can be converted to standard normal distribution.

KEY TERMS

Dividend yield The amount of dividend as a percentage of the current price is called dividend yield.

Capital gains yield The difference between opening and closing price expressed as a percentage of the opening price.

Arithmetic mean Simple average of data arrived at by dividing the sum of observations by the number of observations.

Geometric mean Geometric mean is the return over holding period and found by *n*th root of the ratio of the prices at beginning and end of holding period less 1, where *n* is the number of periods.

Internal rate of return Internal rate of return is that return which equates the cash flows to the initial investment.

Probability distribution Probability distribution is a tabular or graphic representation that specifies the values of return with the frequency of its occurrence.

Range Range is the difference of maximum price/return and minimum price/return.

Deviation Deviation is the difference between expected value and actual value.

Variance Variance is a measure of risk found by adding the squares of deviation from expected value multiplied by probability of deviation.

Standard deviation Standard deviation is a measure of risk and is the square root of variance.

Coefficient of variation Coefficient of variation is a relative measure of risk and is the ratio of standard deviation and expected value.

Normal distribution It is a bell-shaped probability density function that is supposed to occur most frequently. It is completely described by mean and the standard deviation.

Standard normal distribution Standard normal distribution is a special case of normal distribution with mean equal to zero and standard deviation of 1.

KEY FORMULAE

Return on Security

$$\text{Return on Security} = \frac{D_1 + (P_1 - P_0)}{P_0}$$

Average Return

$$\bar{R} = \frac{1}{n}(R_1 + R_2 + R_3 + \ldots R_n) = \frac{1}{n}\sum_{1}^{n} R_n$$

Geometric Return

$$(1 + R_g)^n = (1 + R_1)(1 + R_2)(1 + R_3)(1 + R_4) \ldots (R + R_n)$$

$$R_g = \sqrt[n]{(1+R_1)(1+R_2)(1+R_3)(1+R_4)\ldots(1+R_n)} - 1$$

Expected Return

$$E(R) = \sum_{i=1}^{n} p_i R_i$$

Range

Maximum Value or Return – Minimum Value of Retrun

Variance, $\sigma^2 = \sum_{1}^{n} p_i \times \{(R_i - E(R)\}^2.$

Standard deviation, $\sigma = \sqrt{\sum_{1}^{n} p_i \times \{(R_i - E(R)\}^2}$

Coefficient of Variation

$$\frac{\text{Standard Deviation}}{\text{Expected Value}} = \frac{\sigma}{E(R)}$$

Normal Probability Density Function

$$p(x, \mu, \sigma) = \frac{1}{\sqrt{2\pi\sigma}} e^{\frac{(x-\mu)^2}{2\sigma^2}}$$

where μ = mean value, σ = standard deviation

Standard Normal Distribution Factor $z = \frac{x-\mu}{\sigma}$

Probability for Return between z_1 and z_2

$$p(z_1 \le z \le z_2) = N(z_2) - N(z_1)$$

Standard Deviation for Time Period *t*

$$\sigma_t = \sigma \times \sqrt{t}$$

PRACTICE PROBLEMS

1. Measuring Returns

The current market price of a share of Maruti Udyog Ltd is ₹746. The company is likely to pay a dividend of ₹4 per share at the end of the year. If an investor buys 250 shares today and holds them for a period of one year before selling them for an expected selling price of ₹1150 what will be his total return on investment? Give the break-up of dividend yield and capital gains on investment.

Solution

Initial Investment = 746 x 250 = ₹1,86,500

Dividend Earned = 4 x 250 = ₹1,000

Capital Gains = (1150 – 746) x 250 = ₹1,01,000

Total Return = 1,000 + 1,01,000 = ₹1,02,500

$$\text{Total \% return for period } n; r_n = \left[\frac{D_n}{P_{n-1}} + \frac{P_n - P_{n-1}}{P_{n-1}}\right] \times 100$$

where

D_n = Dividend during year *n*

P_n = Share price in year *n* (exit price)

P_{n-1} = Share price in the year before year *n*

$$\text{Total \% return for period } n; r_n = \left(\frac{1000 + 101000}{186500}\right) \times 100$$

$$= 54.70\%$$

$$\text{Dividend Yield} = \left[\frac{D_n}{P_{n-1}}\right] \times 100 = \left(\frac{4}{746}\right) \times 100 = 0.54\%$$

$$\text{Capital Gains Yield} = \left[\frac{P_n - P_{n-1}}{P_{n-1}}\right] \times 100$$

$$= \left[\frac{1150 - 746}{746}\right] \times 100 = 54.16\%$$

2. Calculating Dividend and Capital Gains Yield

For the past three years Akhib has been depositing his surplus in a cooperative bank. The average yield earned during the period has been 9.25%. Akhib's boss who is an avid investor in shares is trying to convince him to invest his savings in the stock market as it would give him a much higher yield. His boss shares with him the performance of a stock of Gammon Ltd that he invested in three years back. The share price and dividends data of the same are as follows:

Year	Dividend per Share (₹)	Share Price (₹)
0	—	90
1	4.50	124
2	5.00	146
3	5.25	174

Do you think, based on the figures given by Akhib's boss, that the return from stock market is higher than what Akhib's current yield?

Solution:

$$\text{Capital Gains Yield} = \left[\frac{P_n - P_{n-1}}{P_{n-1}}\right] \times 100$$

$$\text{Dividend Yield} = \left[\frac{D_n}{P_{n-1}}\right] \times 100$$

Computation of Average Return on Investment

Year	Dividend per Share (₹)	Price per Share (₹)	Capital Gains (₹)	Dividend Yield (%)	Capital Gains Yield (%)	Total Returns (%)
0	—	90	—	—		
1	4.50	124	34	5.00	37.78	42.78
2	5.00	146	22	4.03	17.74	21.77
3	5.25	174	28	3.60	19.18	22.77
Average Return (%)				4.21	24.90	29.11

As can be seen from the table above the average return during the past three years from investments made by Akhib's boss in Gammon Ltd was 29.11% with majority of it (24.90%) coming from capital gains yield. The remaining 4.21% was the dividend yield. This is much higher than the average return (9.25%) that Akhib has earned from his deposits made with cooperative bank.

3. Measuring Expected Return and Risk

The expected returns under different business cycles for two firms–Alpha Utility and Alpha Technology that belong to the same group, Alpha Industries are given below:

State of Economy	Probability (p)	Return	
		Alpha Utility (%)	Alpha Tech (%)
Recession	0.25	6.50	–11.50
Normal	0.45	11.75	15.00
Boom	0.30	15.45	35.00

Which of the two firms is likely to give a better average return? Which of the two firms is riskier?

Solution

Alpha Utility

Expected Return ER = Sum of Return under different conditions x Probabilities

$= \Sigma\ (0.25 \times 6.50\%) + (0.45 \times 11.75\%) + (0.30 \times 15.45\%)$

$= 11.55\%.$

Alpha Technology

$= \Sigma\ (0.25 \times -11.5\%) + (0.45 \times 15\%) + (0.30 \times 35\%)$

$= 14.375\%$

Thus expected return is better for Alpha Technology Ltd

Risk is measured by Standard Deviation or Variance

$$\text{Variance}, \sigma^2 = \sum_1^n (\text{Expected return} - \text{Aveage return})^2 \times \text{Probability}$$

$$\sigma = \sqrt{\text{Variance}}$$

Risk Estimation for Alpha Utility Ltd

State of Economy	Expected Return (%)	Average Return (%)	Deviation²	Probability (P)	Dev² × Probability
Recession	6.50	11.55	25.5025	0.25	6.3756
Normal	11.75	11.55	0.0400	0.45	0.0180
Boom	15.45	11.55	15.2100	0.30	4.5630
Variance = 10.9566					
$\sigma = 3.31\%$					

Risk Estimation for Alpha Technology Ltd

State of Economy	Expected Return (%)	Average Return (%)	Deviation²	Probability (P)	Dev² Probability
Recession	–11.5	14.375	669.5156	0.25	167.3789
Normal	15.0	14.375	0.3906	0.45	0.1758
Boom	35.0	14.375	425.3906	0.30	127.6172
Variance = 295.1719					
$\sigma = 17.18\%$					

Thus although Alpha Technology is expected to give marginally higher returns (2.825%) than Alpha Utility, the risk involved in investing in Alpha Technology is significantly higher than Alpha Utility as indicated by the standard deviation of 17.18% for Alpha Technology as compared to 3.31% for Alpha Utility.

4. Using Historical Data to Find Return and Risk

The yearly price data for the scrip of Bikaji Ltd is as follows:

Year	Dividend (D) (₹)	Closing Price (P) (₹)
2000	4.25	150
2001	5.50	256
2002	6.00	296
2003	6.75	354
2004	7.75	450
2005	9.00	375
2006	10.25	315
2007	11.00	395

Find out the following:

(a) The expected rate of return for shares of Bikaji Ltd.

(b) Its variance and standard deviation.

(c) If return and standard deviation of the market index over the same period are 15% and 20% respectively how do you rate Bikaji's risk-return profile?

Solution

Return for each year comprises two components–dividend yield and capital gains yield. The composite yield for a given period is:

$$\%\text{ return for period } n;\ r_n = \left[\frac{D_n}{P_{n-1}} + \frac{P_n - P_{n-1}}{P_{n-1}}\right] \times 100$$

$$\%\text{ return for period 2001};\ r_n = \left[\frac{5.50}{150} + \frac{256 - 150}{150}\right] \times 100$$

$$= \frac{111.50}{150} \times 100 = 74.33\%$$

Year	Dividend (₹)	Closing Price (₹)	Expected Return (%)	Variance
2000	4.25	150		
2001	5.50	256	74.33	2883.58
2002	6.00	296	17.97	7.11
2003	6.75	354	21.88	1.54
2004	7.75	450	29.31	75.23
2005	9.00	375	–14.67	1246.16
2006	10.25	315	–13.27	1149.28
2007	11.00	395	28.89	68.14
Sum			**144.44**	**5431.03**
Average Return →(%)			20.63	

Thus average expected return earned from holding the shares of Bikaji Ltd. for the period (2000-2007) is 20.63%.

Variance is found by taking the sum of the squared deviations of the return from the average. The squared deviation for the year 2001 is $(74.33–20.63)^2 = (53.699)^2 = 2883.69$. From the following equation we find variance of the share as 905.17, leading to the standard deviation of 30.09%

$$\text{Variance}, \sigma^2 = \frac{1}{n-1}\sum^n (R_i - \bar{R})^2 = \frac{5431.03}{6} = 905.17$$

$$\text{Standard Deviation}, \sigma = \sqrt{\text{Variance}} = \sqrt{905.17} = 30.09\%$$

As against the market return of 15% the stock offers a better return of 20.63% but at the same time it carries more risk too as reflected in the higher standard deviation of 30.09% as compared to 20% of the market.

EXERCISES

Concept Review Questions

1. What do you understand by return and risk?
2. What are different measures of return? Compare them.
3. What is understood by risk and what are the different measures of risk?
4. Why do you think standard deviation is an appropriate measure of risk?
5. What do you understand by probability density function and normal distribution?
6. What is the relationship between normal distribution and standard normal distribution?
7. What is the utility of standard normal distribution?

Critical Thinking Questions

1. An investor bought a share at ₹100 and after four years she sold the stock at ₹150. With no dividend paid by the stock her returns were 50% over a period of four years. She, therefore, concluded that her annual returns were 12.5%. Is she right in her conclusion?
2. A financial analyst stated that as compared to markets in developed nations like USA the Indian stock exchanges exhibit extraordinary volatility in the stock prices because daily standard deviation of BSE Sensex was around 1% while the stock exchanges in USA show an annual volatility of 20% only. Do you concur with the views expressed by the analyst?

Practical Assignments

1. Observe the closing prices of the Tata Steel share for every Friday for the last 52 weeks and compute the average return and standard deviation. Compare this figure with the NSE NIFTY and comment about the returns and risk of Tata Steel shares.
2. From the closing prices in the previous assignment segregate the returns into ten different brackets and plot a frequency distribution of returns of Tata Steel for each bracket.

Numerical Problems

1. Measuring Returns

The current market price of a share is ₹525. An investor buys 150 shares. He sells these shares at a price of ₹643 and also receives the dividend of ₹12 per share. Find out his total return, % return, dividend yield and capital gains.

2. Calculating Dividend and Capital Gains Yield

An investor purchased the share of ABC Ltd at a price of ₹150 five years back. During this period the dividends declared by the company and its share prices (closing) have been as follows:

Year	Dividend per Share (In ₹)	Share Prices (In ₹)
0	—	150
1	9.00	176
2	12.00	193
3	13.50	218
4	15.00	299
5	18.00	376

Had the investor invested in a savings bank account scheme he would have earned a return of 5.5%. Was the shareholder compensated for the risk that he undertook by investing in the stocks?

3. Finding Return and Risk from Historical Data

The share price and dividend distribution data for Angel Ltd for the past 10 years is as follows:

Year	Dividend (₹)	Closing Price (₹)
1997	7.00	250
1998	8.00	265
1999	8.00	280
2000	9.00	295
2001	9.00	268
2002	10.00	305
2003	8.00	269
2004	9.00	329
2005	11.00	375
2006	11.00	425
2007	12.00	450

Find out the following:

(a) The expected rate of return for share of Angel Ltd;
(b) Its variance and standard deviation;
(c) If the return and standard deviation of the market index over the same period are 8.5% and 13% respectively, what meaning do you attach to the answers in (a) and (b).

4. Finding and Understanding Geometric Mean

Using the data of Problem 3 and assuming that stock of Angel Ltd paid no dividend. Find out the annual return offered by the stock of Angel Ltd to an investor who bought the share in end of 1997 and exited in end of 2007. Compare it with average return and comment.

5. Projecting Return and Risk

An investor is considering buying a share for which he has made a forecast of returns based on expected economic conditions. The states of economic conditions are described as 'excellent', 'good', 'fair', 'poor', and 'bad'. The chances of each economic conditions and the forecast of returns are given below:

Scenario	Probability, p (%)	Return, R (%)
Excellent	25	50
Good	30	25
Fair	20	15
Poor	15	–10
Bad	10	–20

Find out the expected return on the share and the standard deviation.

CASE STUDY

United Bank's Business

Rahul was working for United Bank, a medium-sized bank in a small town. The bank was increasing its thrust to capture business in the small business segment and was coming out with innovative packages of financing to fulfil the needs of small traders whose requirements were being ignored by large multinational banks. In one of its schemes the bank had decided to finance small traders based on their average weekly sales.

One of the clients of the bank namely, Kwality Stores, was managed by Mr Krishna Talwar. The store sold a variety of merchandize and deposited all its sales on a weekly basis to the United Bank. Mr Talwar enjoyed a good relationship with Rahul. To promote his younger brother, Mr Talwar was planning to open a similar store named as Excellent Store in the adjacent colony. According to his estimates, the new store needed a working capital to the extent of two weeks of sales.

The sales of the new store would be about 75% of the sales of Kwality Stores. Due to frequent festivals the sales of the stores exhibited fair amount of volatility, which was expected to continue for the new store too. As the sales fluctuated wildly the requirement of the working capital would change from period to period. Mr Talwar approached Rahul for help.

Rahul was too pleased to find a walk-in customer to meet his targets in the banking business. He informed Mr Talwar of the requirements of the bank to provide funds. The United Bank was willing to finance 50% of the requirements of funds by way of a loan with balance to be contributed by the promoter. The method of arriving at working capital was as follows:

1. Normal limit would be equal to 50% of the average sales of two weeks, which utilized or not, would carry interest at 13% per annum.
2. In order to meet the enhanced working capital requirements during festivals, United Bank would provide additional funds. This would be met by way of providing a peak limit, which will be computed based on standard deviation of 1.50 of the sales.
3. Any additional amount used for working capital in excess of normal limit would carry an interest at 16%.

To assist Rahul in his computation of working capital for Excellent Traders, Mr Talwar provided him with the following weekly data of sales of Kwality Traders:

Weekly Sales of Kwality Stores for Past One Year (₹ in '000)

Week	*Sales*	*Week*	*Sales*	*Week*	*Sales*	*Week*	*Sales*
1	135	14	225	27	91	40	322
2	400	15	165	28	332	41	398
3	196	16	144	29	229	42	146
4	258	17	98	30	298	43	122
5	354	18	113	31	335	44	189
6	120	19	149	32	146	45	236
7	78	20	256	33	198	46	294
8	96	21	274	34	173	47	336
9	364	22	356	35	228	48	198
10	223	23	389	36	263	49	233
11	198	24	162	37	194	50	155
12	146	25	165	38	225	51	95
13	188	26	123	39	239	52	162

Discuss

1. What are the normal and peak working capital limits computed by Rahul for Excellent Stores based on the weekly sales data of Kwality Stores.
2. What expected income can United Bank have from the interest from Excellent Stores.
3. What would be the standard deviation of such an interest on income?

In the CD

Yield Calculator

CHAPTER

6 Valuation and Management of Bonds

LEARNING OBJECTIVES

After going through this chapter, you will be able to:

- understand the role and features of bonds as instruments of financing
- distinguish between various types of bonds
- identify the cash flow patterns of bonds and their relevance in determining the value of bonds
- understand the term structure of interest rates and various hypotheses
- explore the meaning of implied forward rates
- find out the sensitivity of bond prices with changing interest rates and duration
- understand the concept of ratings of bonds and its significance in debt financing
- implement the various bond management strategies in designing a portfolio

BOND WITH THE SAFEST

The morning after the day he attained superannuation after 35 long years of serving the Indian Airlines in its ground duty operations, Mr Walnut Mattoo, on the advice of his close friend, went to the office of *Secured Investment Consultant* to seek advice on investing.

Mr Mattoo: I have been referred to you by Mr Sridhar. I am looking forward to productively invest my superannuation benefits.

Consultant: To advise you, I need to judge your risk appetite.

Mr Mattoo: I am looking for safer investment avenues that offer fixed and regular returns like the savings bank account but with a higher yield.

Consultant: If safety is your consideration, there is a universe of debt obligations to pick from depending upon the preference and cash flow requirements of the investors. Corporate debentures, government securities, savings certificates, discount bonds, and income schemes of mutual funds are such investment avenues. Recovery of principal is certain along with the interest income on such instruments.

Mr Mattoo: Are bonds truly risk-free as it is commonly believed?

Consultant: Often, investors mistakenly believe that bonds are a 'riskless' investment. This is a big fallacy. While it is true that the risks are lower and the returns more predictable than in the case of investments in shares, investing in bonds is also subject to a variety of risks.

Mr Mattoo: I wonder! It's news to me. But how is that?

Consultant: In an age of inflation, getting back your original principal is less than satisfactory if its purchasing power has seriously shrunk. You can lose money in bonds. Though their life span and interest payments are fixed—thus the term 'fixed-income' investments—their returns are not.

Mr Mattoo: Does it mean that I should not invest all my money in bonds?

Consultant: Inflation erodes the value of bonds' fixed interest payments. Stock returns, by contrast, stand a better chance of outpacing inflation. Despite the drubbing stocks sometimes take, young, and middle-aged people should put a large chunk of their money in stocks. Even retirees should own some stocks, given that people are living longer than they used to.

Mr Mattoo: What advice do you give to bond investors for safe investing?

Consultant: Be aware of the five points and become a happy bond investor.

- Bond prices move in the opposite direction of interest rates.
- Pay attention to total return, not just yield.
- If you want capital gains, stay invested.
- If you want steady income, stick with short- to medium-terms.
- If you fall in a higher tax bracket, consider tax-free bonds.

INTRODUCTION

Bonds have emerged as one of the prominent financial instruments of capital markets the world over. This growing significance of bonds is not only due to the scale at which corporations have started using bonds in the structuring/restructuring of their capital, but also due to the role the yields on such instruments play in the valuation process. The returns offered by bonds act as a benchmark in arriving at the expected returns on other instruments of ownership/borrowing. The bonds, especially those issued by governments, are indicators of the prevailing sentiments in financial markets. A frequent revision of yields on such bonds causes volatility in the interest rates.

Bonds are instruments of borrowing by governments and corporates. Whenever firms and/or governments need to borrow money they can do so by issuing an instrument known as the *bond*. The issue of bonds is similar to loan transactions where the issuer borrows and subscribers lend money for a specified period of time. These bonds promise a fixed rate of return, known as a *coupon rate*, till the date of maturity and the payback of the principal sum in a phased manner or at maturity.

Bonds are the instruments of borrowings. They promise a fixed return until their maturity and the payback of principal upon maturity.

There are two categories of bonds—those issued by government and those issued by firms (also known as *debentures*). From the perspective of risk, the bonds issued by the government are regarded as risk free, while those issued by firms are deemed to bear default risk.

Further, bonds can either be listed or unlisted. Listing of bonds on stock exchanges facilitates their easy transferability from one person to another. Since the ownership of bonds can change over a period of time, the holder of the bond at maturity could be different from the original investor (lender).

The aspects of risk, security, and tradability are important determinants of the return on the bond and affect its valuation.

Over a period of time, with changing needs of the issuers and subscribers of the bonds, many modifications in the features of the bonds have taken place. As a result, different variants of bonds have evolved. Bonds vary from one another in terms of their risk, caslı flow patterns, tradability, etc. Standard features and termino-logy used in the bonds are described in the following section.

FEATURES OF THE BOND

Features of the bond refer to the broad terms and conditions on which bonds are issued. These conditions are pre-decided and are specified by the issuers to the subscribers at the time of the issue. The terms and conditions of the issue of the bonds containing features as well as security provisions are contained in a document commonly known as an *indenture*. The decision of the subscribers to invest or not to invest in a given issue depends on these features. There are five main features of the bonds—face value, coupon rate, periodicity of coupon payment, maturity, and redemption value.

The terms and conditions for the issue of bonds are pre-decided at the time of the issue as a part of bond indenture.

Face Value

Face value, also referred as *par value*, of the bond is the amount of money that is stated on the face of the instrument. The principal sum borrowed is normally repaid at maturity. Usually bonds are issued with the face value of ₹100 or ₹1,000, though there is no such rule that prescribes the face value.

Main features of bond indenture are: face value, coupon rate, periodicity of coupon payments, maturity period and redemption value.

The issue price of the bond— the money that the subscriber pays to the issuer while subscribing—can be different from the face value. More often than not, bonds are issued at face value. When bonds are issued at price higher than the face value the excess amount is referred to as *premium* and when issued at a price lower price than the face value the difference is referred to as *discount*.

Coupon Rate

The rate of interest payable by the issuer to the subscriber of the bond is referred to as the coupon rate. The rate of interest offered is governed by several factors, which predominantly include the current economic conditions, the risk associated with the bond, quality of the issuer, etc.

Periodicity of Coupon Payments

The coupon rate of the bond is specified as annual interest payment. However, the issuer may decide to *pay the interest at regular intervals as opposed to annual payments*. Since timing of the cash flow is important, as elaborated in the concept of time value of money, the periodicity of payment becomes a determinant of the bond value. The returns offered by a bond with coupon payments on a quarterly basis would be higher than the bond with the same coupon but making interest payment on a semi-annual or annual basis. Coupon payments are normally evenly spaced over time.

Maturity

The principal sum borrowed through the issue of bonds is for a finite period of time that is predetermined and specified at the time of issue. The duration from the date of issue until the bonds are redeemed is referred to as the *maturity period* of the bond. It can be as long as 30, 50, or 100 years or as short as 1 to 5 years.

Redemption Value

At the end of maturity, the borrowed sum must be refunded. The amount of money paid at the time of maturity is referred to as the *redemption value*. Normally bonds are redeemed at par value and are represented by the words 'redeemable at par'. Sometimes bonds are redeemed at premium or discount to the par value too.

TYPES OF BONDS

Bonds can be classified on various bases. One classification may be based on the nature of the issuer. Based on this, bonds may be classified as government bonds or corporate bonds. There are not many variants in case of government bonds but corporate bonds keep adding or modifying features of the bonds with time. Some of the bonds are discussed below.

Fixed Rate and Floating Rate Bonds

The first kind of modification takes place on the coupon rate. Normally bonds pay a fixed rate of interest at predetermined intervals of time. However, firms also issue floating rate bonds where the coupon rate is not predetermined, but instead is linked to some benchmark. London Inter Bank Offer Rate (LIBOR) is the most common benchmark used wherein the coupon payment is based on the most recent LIBOR rate. Such floating rate bonds are issued as hedge against the changing interest rates.

Indexed Bonds

Indexed bonds are issued with coupon payments based on inflation rate. As bonds are used for long-term investment with a relatively smaller coupon rate as compared to the returns in an alternative investment, the subscribers are uncertain as to how rich can they get with fixed and small coupon rates if the inflation fluctuates constantly. Issuance of index-linked bonds assures subscribers of some real return over inflation.

Callable/Puttable Bonds

Another innovation relates to the redemption feature of the bond. Although the bonds are issued with fixed maturity, an option for early redemption can be built into the features of the bond by the issuer. The issuer may reserve a right but no obligation to call the bond prior to the prescribed maturity. For example, in case of a bond issued for maturity of 5 years the issuer may, at his/her option, redeem the bond in full say at any time after 3 years. Such bonds granting an option to issuer to redeem earlier than prescribed maturity are referred to as *callable bonds*. While calling the bond, the issuing firms announce the price of repurchase of the bond known as the *call price*. This is done by the issuer to safeguard against a situation of a substantial fall in interest rates subsequent to the issue at a higher coupon. In contrast to callable bonds, we have *puttable bonds* where the option may be given to the subscriber to redeem prior to the maturity. When the interest rates are comparatively higher than the coupon rate of the bond the subscribers may want to reclaim the principal from the issuer to invest in more profitable avenues. Such bonds provide the subscribers with an exit mechanism.

> Bonds that can be redeemed by the issuer prior to the maturity are known as callable Bonds, while those redeemable at the option of subscribers are known as puttable bonds.

Redemption in Lump Sum/Phased Redemption

The third kind of variation emanates from the manner of redemption of bonds. The issuer may like to redeem the principal in instalments or in a lump sum at the maturity, known as *bullet payment*.

Zero Coupon/Deep Discount Bonds

Bonds that pay no coupon are known as *zero coupon bonds*. These bonds have a face value that is redeemed at the end of maturity. In order to provide return to the subscribers these bonds are issued at substantial discount to the face value; hence, they are also referred to as *deep discount bonds*. For example, a 25-year bond with face value of ₹1,00,000 may be issued at say ₹10,000. The subscriber pays ₹10,000 now and after 25 years receives an amount of ₹1,00,000.

> Bonds that do not pay any interest but are issued at discount to the face value and redeemed at face value are called deep discount bonds.

Convertible Bonds

Bonds are difficult instruments to market as they offer paltry returns. To broaden their investor base, firms merge the features of equity with those of bonds in a manner that a part value of the bond becomes convertible into a predetermined number of equity shares after some time from the date of issue. Such bonds are known as *convertible bonds*.

The number of common shares converted per bond at the time of conversion for each convertible bond is termed as *conversion ratio*. Conversion price is a term related to the concept of conversion ratio. It is the price per share at which a convertible bond can be converted into common stock. The relationship between conversion ratio and conversion price can be illustrated with the help of an example. Alpha Surgicals Ltd issued fully convertible bonds at the par value of ₹1,000 per bond in September 2004. At any time prior to maturity on September 20, 2014, a debenture holder can exchange a bond for 20 equity shares. Therefore, the conversion ratio is 20. The bond costs a purchaser ₹1,000, the par value, when it was issued. Dividing the ₹1,000 par value by the 20 shares received gives a conversion price of ₹50 a share. Conversely, by dividing ₹1000 par value by conversion price of ₹50, we get a conversion ratio of 20.

The primary advantage to the issuer of the convertible bonds is that they are issued at less than competitive rate. Since convertibles offer an opportunity to bondholders to convert their bonds into stocks and thereby derive potential benefit from the rise in the price of the underlying stock, companies offer lower yields on convertibles. This expectation of higher return from capital gain works as sweetener and makes these bonds attractive for the investors despite the low rate of return offered by them.

From the investor's perspective, a convertible bond has a value-added component built into it; it is essentially a bond with a stock option hidden inside. Thus, it tends to offer a lower rate of return in exchange for the value of the option to convert the bond into stock. It also renders the bond more attractive as subscribers are assured of a fixed return during the early uncertain period of the project. Later upon conversion into equity, the investors can reap the benefit of good performance as owners once the project succeeds in providing the promised returns.

Another useful feature of these bonds is that they can be used to convey positive financial signals to the market about the firm's expected performance. For example, if an existing public company chooses to issue stock, the market usually interprets this as a sign that the company's share price is somewhat overvalued. To avoid this negative signal, the company may choose to issue convertible bonds, which bondholders will most likely convert to equity anyway should the company continue to do well.

CASH FLOW OF THE BOND

Cash flows of a conventional bond consist of two parts—the periodic coupon payments and the final redemption payment. Consider as an example of a 10% semi-annual bond with face value of ₹100 redeemable at 5% premium at the end of 3 years. The cash flows of the bond from the perspective of the subscriber are as shown below.

Cash flows of bonds are made up of two components: the periodic coupon payments and principal repayment.

Time (months from now)	0	6	12	18	24	30	36
Coupon received	0	5	5	5	5	5	5
Principal paid (–) and redeemed (+)	–100						105
Total cash flow	**–100**	**5**	**5**	**5**	**5**	**5**	**110**

Note that the inflow to the subscriber is an outflow to the issuer. Therefore, the cash flows of the issuer would be same but with opposite signs.

PRICING OF BONDS

The value of the bond is the price one would pay now in exchange of the future cash flows that accrues over the remaining life of the bond to its owner. The value of what is being paid today must be equal to the present value of the future cash flows at a specific discount rate. This discount rate reflects the expectations of the return of the investors, which in turn is dependent upon the quality of cash flows associated with the bond.

The value of bond is calculated by discounting the future cash flows from the bonds at an appropriate discount rate.

Specefically, the discount rate is arrived at after appropriately incorporating the following three factors:

- First, the *risk characteristics* of the cash flow. Higher the risk, higher must be the discount rate. Since bonds offer rather certain cash flows, the discount rate used in finding the value of the bond is normally close to a risk-free rate. We may add the risk premium in the discount rate depending upon the risk profile of the issuer.
- Second, the discount rate *must be in tune with markets and the economy*. If high interest rates prevail in the market, a higher discount rate would be used.
- Third and the last factor affecting the discount rate is the *timing of cash flows*. Cash flows more distant in future must be discounted at a higher rate simply because time adds to the uncertainty.

The discount rate is assumed to take into account risk, economic conditions, and the timing of the cash flow and, therefore, it truly reflects the expectations of the investors. The discount rate thus arrived at is used for discounting the cash flows so as to find out their present values.

Discount rate must appropriately be adjusted for the riskiness of the cash flows, prevalent market conditions and timing of cash flows to truly reflect the expectations of investors.

Let us value a bond paying 10% coupon on a semi-annual basis. The bond has a face value of ₹100 and a remaining life of 3 years at the end of which it would be redeemed at 5% premium. Although the coupon rate of 10% was perhaps appropriate at the time of the issue of the bond, the change in economic conditions and expectations of investors with the passage of time has made it imperative that the value of the remaining cash flows also changes accordingly. Assume that the current discount rate is 12%. The value of the bond would then be given by Equation 6-1.

Value of the bond

$$= \text{Price}, P_0 = \sum_{1}^{n} \frac{C_t}{(1+r)^t} + \frac{R}{(1+r)^n} \qquad (6\text{-}1)$$

Where C_t = Cash flow (coupon payment) at time t
R = Redemption value at maturity after n periods
r = Discount rate and
n = Remaining life in number of periods

Using Equation 6-1, we find the value of the bond[1] at ₹98.62.

Table 6-1 Value of the bond and discount rate

Face Value of the Bond (₹)		***100***							***Redemption Value (₹)***		***100***	
Coupon Rate (%)		***10%***							***Maturity (years)***		***10***	
Periodicity of coupon payment		***Annual***										
Year	**Cash flow**	**Discount Rate**										
	₹	**5%**	**6%**	**7%**	**8%**	**9%**	**10%**	**11%**	**12%**	**13%**	**14%**	**15%**
1	10.00	9.52	9.43	9.35	9.26	9.17	9.09	9.01	8.93	8.85	8.77	8.70
2	10.00	9.07	8.90	8.73	8.57	8.42	8.26	8.12	7.97	7.83	7.69	7.56
3	10.00	8.64	8.40	8.16	7.94	7.72	7.51	7.31	7.12	6.93	6.75	6.58
4	10.00	8.23	7.92	7.63	7.35	7.08	6.83	6.59	6.36	6.13	5.92	5.72
5	10.00	7.84	7.47	7.13	6.81	6.50	6.21	5.93	5.67	5.43	5.19	4.97
6	10.00	7.46	7.05	6.66	6.30	5.96	5.64	5.35	5.07	4.80	4.56	4.32
7	10.00	7.11	6.65	6.23	5.83	5.47	5.13	4.82	4.52	4.25	4.00	3.76
8	10.00	6.77	6.27	5.82	5.40	5.02	4.67	4.34	4.04	3.76	3.51	3.27
9	10.00	6.45	5.92	5.44	5.00	4.60	4.24	3.91	3.61	3.33	3.08	2.84
10	110.00	67.53	61.42	55.92	50.95	46.47	42.41	38.74	35.42	32.40	29.67	27.19
Price (₹)		**138.61**	**129.44**	**121.07**	**113.42**	**106.42**	**100.00**	**94.11**	**88.70**	**83.72**	**79.14**	**74.91**

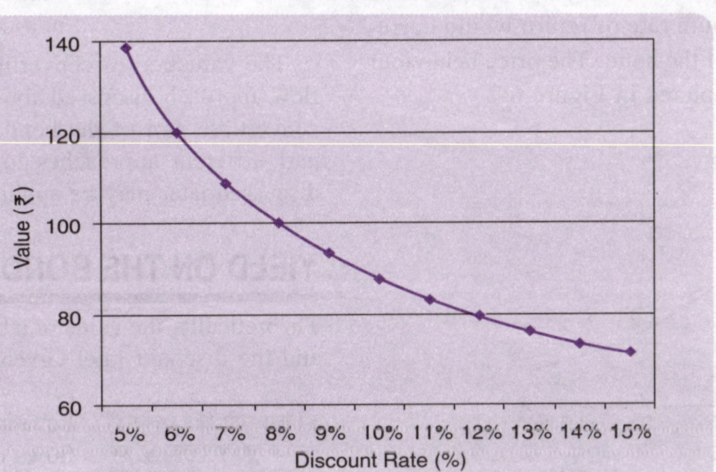

Figure 6-1 Value of the bond and discount rate

Value of the bond P_0

$$= \frac{5}{1.06} + \frac{5}{1.06^2} + \frac{5}{1.06^3}$$

$$+ \frac{5}{1.06^4} + \frac{5}{1.06^5} + \frac{5}{1.06^6} + \frac{105}{1.06^6}$$

$$= 4.72 + 4.45 + 4.20 + 3.96 + 3.74 + 3.52 + 74.03$$

$$= ₹98.62$$

Both discount rate and period have to be consistent. Here the 10% annual rate of interest is assumed equivalent to 5% interest rate for the 6-month period. Similarly the number of period has been taken as 6 to denote six half-yearly coupons in the 3-year period.

There is an inverse relationship between the price of the bond and the discount rate. The value of the bond declines with rise in the discount rate and vice-versa. The value of a 10-year bond with 10% coupon rate payable annually with face value and redemption value of ₹100 with discount range ranging between 5% and 15% is computed in Table 6-1.

There exists an inverse relationship between the price of bond and the discount rate.

At 5% discount rate the value of the bond is ₹138.61, whereas at 15% the price of the bond in the market must be ₹74.91. The price behaviour of the same bond with respect to different discount rates is depicted in Figure 6-1. Note that the price change is not linear but instead is convex to the origin.

As long as coupon rate and the general expectations of return are identical, the value of bond would remain equal to face value. However, as the discount rate increases beyond the coupon rate the value of the bond must fall so as to increase the returns. We state below a general rule that applies to pricing of the bond:

---

[1]The value of the bond can also be found using PV tables. Since coupon payments are equal and occur at regular intervals the value of the bond would be sum of annuity of coupon payments at 6% for 6 periods and present value of redemption amount at 6% after 6 periods. Using tables in Appendix A-4 and A-2 the value of the bond is as below:

Value of the bond = 5 × PVA(6%,6) + 105 × PV(6%,6)
= 5 × 4.9173 + 105 × 0.7050
= 24.59 + 74.03 = ₹ 98.62

When discount rate, $r >$ coupon rate, i : Price < Face Value
When discount rate, $r <$ coupon rate, i : Price > Face Value
When discount rate, $r =$ coupon rate, i : Price = Face Value

Value of the Bond with Risk-free Rate and Time

Discount rate is a function of risk. For increased risk, we use a higher discount rate and vice versa. Therefore, risky bonds trade at lower price as compared to bonds from reputed firms where the discount rate used is lower. Hypothetically if discount rate were to be zero, the value of the bond would be infinite. Is it possible? How low the discount rate could be? Given a risk-free bond the investor would still want some minimum return on investment, and this return must be equal to the risk-free return. The risk-free rate places a limit on how low the discount rate can be. This minimum rate of return would correspond to the maximum price of the bond. The price behaviour of the bond would look as depicted in Figure 6-2.

Discount rate is a function of risk. Higher the risk, higher the discount rate and consequently lower the price of bond.

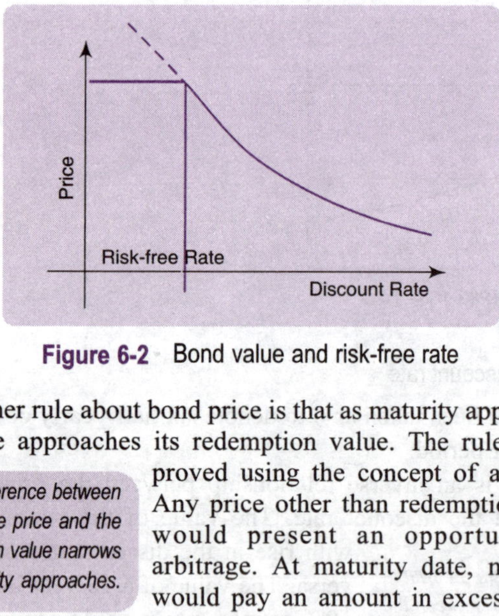

Figure 6-2 Bond value and risk-free rate

Another rule about bond price is that as maturity approaches, the price approaches its redemption value. The rule can be proved using the concept of arbitrage. Any price other than redemption value would present an opportunity of arbitrage. At maturity date, no buyer would pay an amount in excess of the redemption value, which he/she receives upon owning the bond, and nor would the counter-party accept any amount lesser than the redemption value, which he/she receives by continuing to hold. Extending the logic, we may state that the spread between the market price, irrespective of whether it is higher or lower than the redemption value, and the redemption value would decline with time as maturity approaches, assuming that the market interest rates remain constant over time. This is indicated in Figure 6-3.

The difference between the price and the redemption value narrows as maturity approaches.

Value of Convertible Bond

Since the convertible bonds are convertible into shares either fully or partly, their value can be broken into two components. One component is the value of the share and the other component is the value of the conventional bond left after the conversion of the equity share attached.

Value of convertible bond
= Value of equity + Value of the non-convertible portion of the bond

The valuation of convertible bond is complex and the cash flow approach discussed above can only be applied to the non-convertible part of the bond. For the valuation of convertible part different approaches to valuation of shares and options discussed later may be applied.

YIELD ON THE BOND

Theoretically, the value of a bond is a function of its cash flows and the discount rate. Given the cash flows and the discount rate value can be compared using Equation 6-1. In reality however, the cash flows of the bond and its value (market period) are known. The market value of bonds changes just like the prices of stocks change, albeit not by the same magnitude. The question that arises is that with the given cash flows and the price of the bond what return, known as the yield, the instrument offers if one invests at the prevailing price. So what we estimate for a bond is the yield i.e. the rate of return offered by the bond,

There are four types of returns (yields) on bonds: current yield; yield to maturity; realized yield and yield to call (relevant only for callable bonds).

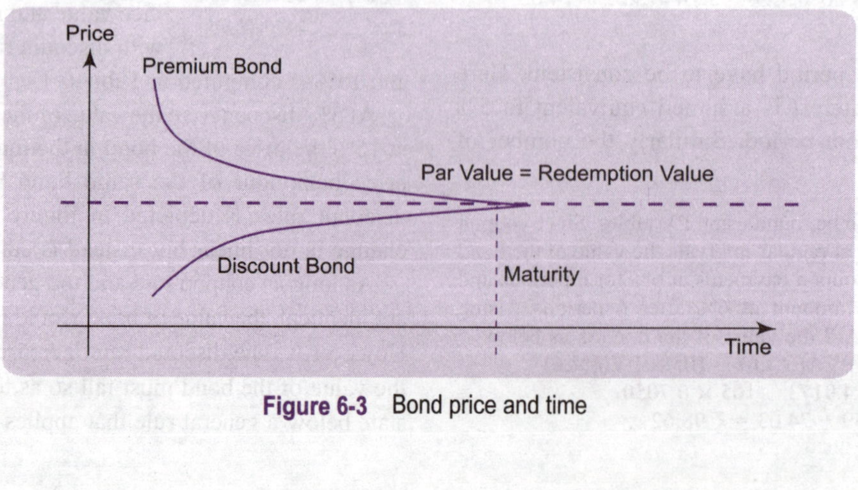

Figure 6-3 Bond price and time

and not the price of the bond. Let us discuss several variants of the yield—current yield, yield to maturity (YTM), and realized yield. For callable bonds another form of yield known as yield to call (YTC) is computed.

Current Yield

Current yield of the bond is the simplest estimate of the return the bond offers. It is calculated by dividing the annual coupon by the current market price of the bond. If a bond pays 10% coupon on face value of ₹100 and is trading at ₹90, the current yield or return is ₹10/90 = 11.11%. Current yield is as given by Equation 6-2.

Current yield is simply the annual coupon payment divided by the current market price of the bond.

$$\text{Current yield} = \frac{\text{Interest}}{\text{Current Price } P_0}$$

$$= \frac{\text{Coupon} \times \text{Face Value}}{\text{Current Price } P_0} \qquad (6\text{-}2)$$

Current yield considers only the regular part of the income that accrues to the bondholder and ignores the return that would be generated as capital gains either on maturity or upon selling prior to maturity. Current yield only serves as an approximate measure of return that does not require much information or computation.

Yield to Maturity (YTM)

YTM reflects the yield that the investor would earn by holding the bond till maturity. The YTM of the bond can be computed by using Equation 6-1 and replacing r in the equation with YTM as shown in Equation 6-3.

$$\text{Value of the bond} = \text{Price}, P_0 = \sum_{1}^{n} \frac{C_t}{(1+\text{YTM})^t} + \frac{R}{(1+\text{YTM})^n} \quad (6\text{-}3)$$

Assuming investment at the current price of the bond P_0, YTM of the bond is the internal rate of return on the investment in the bond. To illustrate the computation of YTM, consider an example of a Bond X with face value of ₹100 redeemable at par after 6 years from now. It carries a coupon of 12% payable annually (assumed for simplicity of computation only) and is currently traded at ₹90. We assume that the investor buys the bond and holds it till maturity. The cash flows of the bond may be inserted in Equation 6-1 and solved for r as follows:

Yield to maturity (YTM) is the return the investor would earn if he holds the bond till maturity.

$$\text{Price}, P_0 = 90.00 = \frac{12}{(1+r)} + \frac{12}{(1+r)^2} + \frac{12}{(1+r)^3} + \frac{12}{(1+r)^4} + \frac{12}{(1+r)^5} + \frac{12}{(1+r)^6} + \frac{100}{(1+r)^6}$$

The solution to determine the YTM of the bond can be attempted through trial and error method by taking an approximate value of r and checking if the right hand side of the equation matches with the price. For approximate initial value of the YTM we may estimate that the return must consist of—(1) the yield which is equal to 13.33% (₹12/90); and (2) the capital appreciation at maturity when ₹100 is received against investment of ₹90 spread over period of holding approximately being equal to 1.67% [(100 – 90)/6]. The total yield therefore must be approximately 15.00% (13.33+1.67). The real yield must be lesser than this if we consider the time value of money. As a starting point we may use 15% as discount rate. If right hand side is greater than P_0 we increase the value of r in the next iteration, else we decrease r. This iterative process continues till satisfactory accuracy is achieved.

Alternatively we resort to Excel and feed the cash flows in the successive columns or rows. The cash flows of the bond are shown in Table 6-2 with the assumption that the investor buys the bond at ₹90 and holds it till maturity. To find out YTM insert the formula IRR for the range containing the cash flow data as shown in Table 6-2.

The solution of YTM at 14.62% implies that with the given cash flows of the bond and the current price of ₹90 the investor would earn a yield of 14.62% per annum. The earlier estimate of yield ignored the time value of money. With time value of money considered, the YTM reduces to 14.62%.

YTM takes into account the capital loss or gain upon maturity as well as the time value of money. *Current yield considers neither*. If the current price of the bond is less than its redemption

Table 6-2 Finding Yield To Maturity (YTM) of the bond

Current Price (₹)	*90.00*		*Time to Maturity*			*6 years*
Coupon Rate	*12%*		*Periodicity of Interest*			*Annual*
Face Value (₹)	*100.00*		*Redemption Amount (₹)*			*100.00*
Cash Flow of the Bond (₹)							

Time (years)	***Now (0)***	***1***	***2***	***3***	***4***	***5***	***6***
Current Price	–90.00						
Interest		12.00	12.00	12.00	12.00	12.00	12.00
Redemption							100.00
TOTAL CASH FLOW	**–90.00**	**12.00**	**12.00**	**12.00**	**12.00**	**12.00**	**112.00**
YTM = *IRR (Range of cash flows)*	→						**14.62%**

YTM considers the time value of money while calculating returns for the investor.

value, YTM shall be greater than the current yield as the investor would have capital gain upon maturity. If the bond trades at a price higher than its redemption value YTM shall be lower than current yield since upon maturity the investor would incur a capital loss.

It is generally assumed that bonds are issued and redeemed at face value. If such a bond trades at face value, its YTM would always be equal to the coupon rate at the time of the issue. For example a bond of face value of ₹1,000 bearing a coupon of 9% and redeemable at ₹1,000 would have YTM of only 9% and the bond would trade at its face value. As long as price stays at ₹1,000 the YTM remains same and equals coupon rate. A change in price would cause YTM to change inversely with the price.

There is an inverse relationship between the price and the YTM of the bond.

Realized Yield

YTM assumes that the bond is held till its maturity. However, if the investor sells the bond before maturity he/she will realize the price prevailing in the market. Although the investor continues to enjoy the same current yield, depending on the selling price, the amount of capital appreciation changes.

Realized yield is the rate of return if the bond is sold before maturity. It has two components: coupons received and the capital appreciation realised on sale.

Realised yield refers to the rate of return earned by the investor if he decides to sell the bond before the maturity. The method to compute the realized yield is identical to that of calculating YTM. Consider the same Bond X but now assuming that the investor rather than holding it till maturity sells at the end of 4 years immediately when the 4th coupon payment is received. We project the cash flows of the bond under this assumption as shown in Table 6-3.

Realized yield is found in the same manner as that of YTM by using IRR formula in EXCEL, which solves the following equation for unknown r representing realized yield at 15.54%:

$$\text{Price, } P_0 = 90.00 = \frac{12}{(1+r)} + \frac{12}{(1+r)^2} + \frac{12}{(1+r)^3} + \frac{12}{(1+r)^4} + \frac{100}{(1+r)^4}$$

The assumption of reinvestment rate

The computation of YTM and the realized yield makes an implicit assumption that the interim coupon payments received till maturity or divestment as the case may be, were re-invested at the YTM itself. While calculating YTM it was implied that all the coupon payments of ₹12 each received prior to the maturity were reinvested at 14.62%. Under computation of realized yield when the investor sold the Bond X at the end of 4th year it was assumed that the three coupon payments of ₹12 each at the end of 1st, 2nd and 3rd year were reinvested at 15.54%, the IRR of the cash flows.

What happens if the reinvestment rate of the interim cash flows is different from the IRR of the entire stream of cash flows? Naturally the realized yield would be at divergence depending upon the rate at which the interim cash flows are reinvested. Reconsider the Bond X that was sold after 4 years at ₹100 after receiving 4 coupon payments. If these interim coupon payments were reinvested at 10% what yield would be realized?

The alternate way of finding the holding period yield is to project the interim cash flows at the given reinvestment rate to the terminal value as at the end of holding period. The 1st coupon payment as at the end of holding period, i.e., 4th year at 10% amounts to ₹15.97. Likewise, the 2nd and 3rd coupon payments would have values of ₹14.52 and ₹13.20 respectively as shown in Table 6-4.

Having transformed the cash flows to the end of holding period, the compounded realized yield can be computed from the following formula:

$$P_0 \times (1 + r_y)^n = \text{TV}_n \tag{6-4}$$

where P_0 = Current price
r_y = Annualized yield over n years
n = Holding period in years

Table 6-3 Finding realized yield of the bond

Current Price (₹)	*90.00*	*Time to Sell at Year*		*4*	
Coupon Rate	*12%*	*Periodicity of Interest*		*Annual*	
Face Value (₹)	*100.00*	*Selling Price (₹)*		*100.00*	
Cash Flow of the Bond (₹)					
Time (years)	Now (0)	1	2	3	4
Buying Price	-90.00				
Interest		12.00	12.00	12.00	12.00
Selling Price					100.00
TOTAL CASH FLOW	**-90.00**	**12.00**	**12.00**	**12.00**	**112.00**
Realized Yield					**15.54%**

Table 6-4 Finding realized yield adjusted for reinvestment rate

Current Price (₹)	*90.00*		*Time to Sell (years)*		*4*
Coupon Rate	*12%*		*Periodicity of Interest*		*Annual*
Face Value (₹)	*100.00*		*Selling Price (₹)*		*100.00*
Cash Flow of the Bond (₹)					
Time (years)	***Now (0)***	***1***	***2***	***3***	***4***
Current Price	−90.00				
Interest		12.00	12.00	12.00	12.00
Redemption					100.00
TOTAL CASH FLOW	**−90.00**	**12.00**	**12.00**	**12.00**	**112.00**
				1.1 × 12 →	13.20
			1.1 × 1.1 × 12 →		14.52
		1.1 × 1.1 × 1.1 × 12 →			15.97
Maturity value at the end of Year 4 with reinvestment at 10%					155.69
Realized yield if reinvestment rate is 10%					14.68%

TV_n = Total of terminal values consisting of all interim cash flows reinvested at given rate and the selling price

Inserting the given values in Equation 6-4, we get realized yield at 14.68%.

$90 \times (1 + r_y)^4 = 155.69$, gives $r_y = 14.68\%$

Note that the YTM of the bond remains constant as long as the price of the bond does not change till maturity. YTM depends upon the current price, coupon payments, and the maturity amount, all of which are observable today. As time progresses, market expectations and interest rates undergo a change leading to a change in bond price. Realized yield is dependent upon the price at the end of holding period.

Yield to Call

Yield to call is the return the investors earn on the callable bonds till the time the bonds are called. It comprises of two components: coupons and the call price.

YTM is the relevant measure of return the investor realizes on a bond if held till maturity. In case the bond is callable the relevance of YTM is diluted because the bond may be redeemed prior to the maturity at the option of the issuer. In such a case it would be more relevant to compute the yield to the point of earliest call. This is known as yield to call (YTC).

For example, if Bond X is callable at ₹105 anytime after 4 years from now, it would be more pertinent to know the yield as if the bond would actually be redeemed after 4 years. The computation of YTC involves Equation 6-1 as indicated below, and solved for YTC:

Value of the bond =

$$\text{Price } P_0 = 90 = \sum_{1}^{n} \frac{C_t}{(1+\text{YTC})^t} + \frac{R}{(1+\text{YTC})^n}$$

$$= \sum_{1}^{4} \frac{12}{(1+\text{YTC})^t} + \frac{105}{(1+\text{YTC})^4}$$

Table 6-5 computes the YTC of the Bond X at 16.59%.

Referring to Figure 6-1, we note that the price of the bond rises if market interest rates fall. Assume the Bond X paying 10% coupon is callable at a price of ₹115. If the market yields fall to 8% subsequent to the issue, the bond price would be ₹113.42 (from Table 6-1). If the interest rates fall further to 7%, the price of the bond shall be ₹121.07. At this point the issuer may decide to call the bond back at ₹115 and reissue the bond with 7% coupon. Hence, in case of callable bond the price would not rise above the call price because the issuer would exercise the option to redeem the bond at pre-announced call price. The rise in price with falling interest rates would limit at call price as shown in Figure 6-4.

Table 6-5 Finding Yield To Call (YTC)

Current Price (₹)	*90.00*		*Earliest Call at year*		*4*
Coupon Rate	*12%*		*Periodicity of Interest*		*Annual*
Face Value (₹)	*100.00*		*Call Price (₹)*		*105.00*
Cash Flow of the Bond (₹)					
Time (years)	***Now (0)***	***1***	***2***	***3***	***4***
Current Price	−90.00				
Interest		12.00	12.00	12.00	12.00
Redemption					105.00
TOTAL CASH FLOW	**−90.00**	**12.00**	**12.00**	**12.00**	**117.00**
YTM = IRR (range of cash flows)	→				**16.59%**

Example 6-1 Valuation of Bond – Redeemable in Instalments

XYZ Ltd has issued a bond with face value of ₹1,000 and coupon rate of 8% payable annually. The bond has exactly 5 years to maturity and sells at ₹900. The redemption of the bond would be done in 4 equal annual instalments in last four years.

(a) What is the YTM of the bond?

(b) What do you think will happen to YTM if the bond pays semi-annual interest?

(c) What would be the price of the bond if the YTM of option (a) applies?

Solution

(a) If the coupon payment is made annually, the cash flows of the bond and the calculation of the YTM work out to 11.70% as shown below.

(Figures in ₹)

Time months from now	*Purchase Price/ Redemption Amount*	*Coupon Payment*	*Total Cash Flow*	*Principal Outstanding*
0	-900.00		-900.00	1000.00
12	0.00	80.00	80.00	1000.00
24	250.00	80.00	330.00	750.00
36	250.00	60.00	310.00	500.00
48	250.00	40.00	290.00	250.00
60	250.00	20.00	270.00	0.00
YTM			**11.70%**	

(b) and (c) When the coupon payments are made on semi-annual basis instead of annual, the value of the bond must rise since part of the coupon would be received earlier. The yield, therefore, would be greater than 11.70% calculated in (a). The price of the bond would rise and is recomputed as ₹906.25 if the yield were to remain constant at 11.70%, as shown below:

(Figures in ₹)

YTM with semi-annual coupon					**New price at 11.70%**	
Time months from now	***Purchase Price/ Redemption Amount***	***Coupon Payment***	***Cash Flow***	***Principal Out-standing***	***PV Factor at 11.70%***	***Present Value***
0	-900.00		-900.00	1000.00	1.0000	
6	0.00	40.00	40.00	1000.00	0.9462	37.85
12	0.00	40.00	40.00	1000.00	0.8953	35.81
18	0.00	40.00	40.00	1000.00	0.8471	33.88
24	250.00	40.00	290.00	750.00	0.8015	232.43
30	0.00	30.00	30.00	750.00	0.7583	22.75
36	250.00	30.00	280.00	500.00	0.7175	200.91
42	0.00	20.00	20.00	500.00	0.6789	13.58
48	250.00	20.00	270.00	250.00	0.6424	173.44
54	0.00	10.00	10.00	250.00	0.6078	6.08
60	250.00	10.00	260.00	0.00	0.5751	149.52
YTM (Semi-annual)		**5.81%**		**Price**		**906.25**
YTM Annualized		**11.96%**				

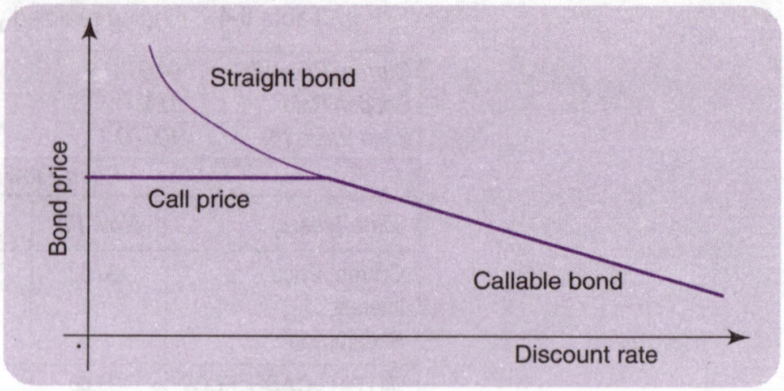

Figure 6-4 Price of callable bond

DEEP DISCOUNT/ZERO COUPON BONDS AND STRIPS

Bonds normally provide returns to investors in two forms—as periodic coupon payments, and as capital gains from the difference between the selling/redemption value and issue/purchase value. In contrast, we may have zero coupon bonds, which do not pay any interest and instead provide all the returns in the form of capital gains by issuing the bond at a price substantially lower than the par value and redeeming them on maturity at par value. The issue price would be dependent upon the interest rates prevailing in the market. Higher the yield expectations lower would be the issue price.

Zero coupon bonds do not pay any interest and instead provide all the returns in the form of capital gains.

Typical examples of zero coupon instruments are the 91-day or 364-day treasury bills (T-bills) issued by government.

These T-bills are auctioned at a price determined by competing investors and redeemed at face value. The investors realize the returns by buying at a discount and redeeming at par value, which is higher than the issue price. T-bills are short-term instruments. However, long-term bonds too can be issued with zero coupon. As time progresses the price of zero coupon instruments gradually rises and approaches the par value, albeit not linearly, assuming constant market conditions for the life of the bond. The price behaviour of 30-year zero-coupon bond is shown in Figure 6-5.

The value of zero coupon bonds is arrived at by discounting the par value (redemption price) at an appropriate discount rate.

Assuming the discount rate of 10% the initial price of 30-year zero coupon bond with face value of ₹1,000 would be ₹57.31 [$1{,}000/(1+0.10)^{30}$], at which it shall be issued. After a year the price would be ₹63.04 [$1{,}000/(1+0.1)^{29}$], provided the market conditions regarding expectations of return remain same as at the time of its issue. The value of the zero coupon bond is easiest to determine with the given expectations of the yield. The value can be found by Equation 6-5.

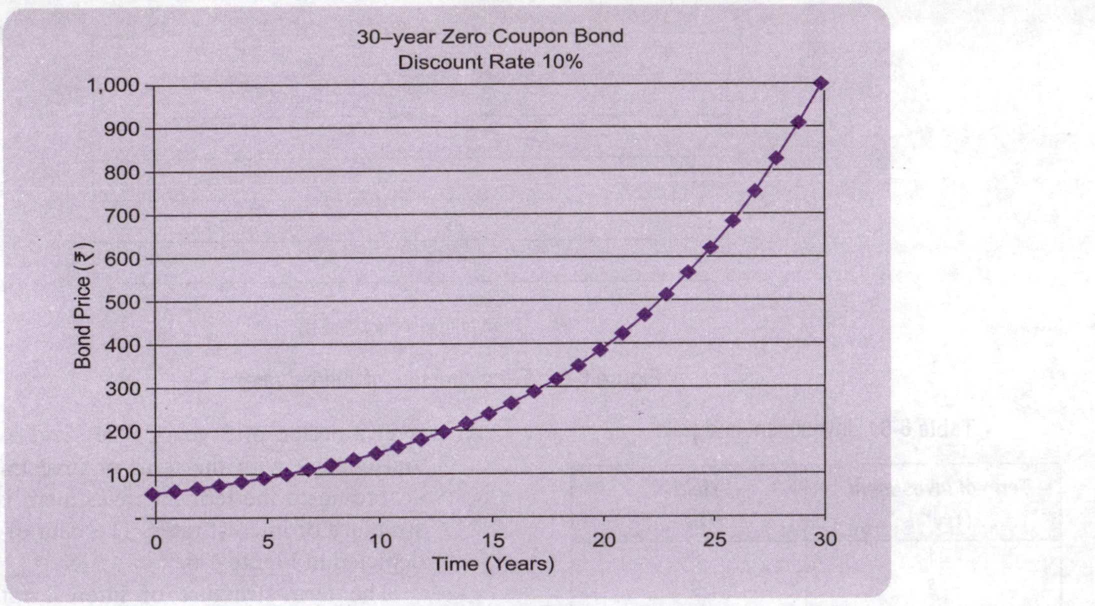

Figure 6-5 Price behaviour of zero coupon bond

$$\text{Value of zero coupon bond} = \frac{\text{Face value}}{(1+r)^T} \qquad (6\text{-}5)$$

where T = Time remaining for maturity and r = Discount rate.

If for next 29 years the market conditions regarding returns remain same at 10%, which is highly unlikely, the price of the bond would be ₹909.09 (1,000/1.1).

Coupon bearing bonds too can be made to look like zero coupon bonds if we treat all the coupon payments as separate instruments. As a simple example consider a 3-year bond of face value of ₹1,000 with annual coupon payment of 10%. This composite instrument provides a set of cash flows to the investor as below:

1st coupon payment	₹100
2nd coupon payment	₹100
3rd coupon payment	₹100
Redemption amount	₹1,000

Here if each of the three coupon payments and the final redemption payment can be seen as separate cash flows, then the composite bond can be said to be constituting of—(1) three separate zero coupon bonds of face value of ₹100 each maturing after 1, 2, and 3 years corresponding to each coupon payment; and (2) one zero coupon bond of face value of ₹1,000 maturing three years later corresponding to the redemption value of the bond. The process of segregating the coupon payments and redemption value and issuing them as separate securities is referred to as *stripping*. Each of the strips then becomes a separate instrument that can be traded independently of the composite instrument. These are known as separate trading of registered interest and principal of securities (STRIPS).

Each coupon payment and the redemption value of the bond can be detached and issued as separate and independent instruments called STRIPS.

The advantages of stripping include—(1) increased liquidity due to increased participation by small investors as coupon stripping results in instruments of smaller denominations; (2) larger number of securities available for trading providing depth to the market; and (3) fair pricing due to increased depth and participation. This also helps in establishing the term structure of interest rates, which is discussed in the next section.

TERM STRUCTURE OF INTEREST RATES

Recall that while computing the price of the bond we used a discount rate to find the present values of the cash flows and later added them up. We also stated the desirable features of the discount rate. The appropriate discount rate must—(1) reflect risk of the cash flows; (2) have consistency with the prevailing interest rate scenario and investor's expectations of return; and (3) consider the timing of the cash flows.

In our analysis of bond pricing, we used a uniform rate of discount for all the cash flows. The same rate of discount was used for the cash flow occurring a year later or 10 years later. It was implied that a single rate is appropriate for all the cash flows irrespective of when they occur. However, this seems far from reality. In general investors are not indifferent to the investment horizon. Investors want a different return for different investment horizons. Therefore, we cannot treat all cash flows with the same yardstick. The timing of the cash flows and the discount rate to be used become inter-dependent.

The timing of cash flows and the discount rates to be used are inter-dependent as the expectations of investors vary with the investment horizon.

Consider a simple example of an investor willing to place a deposit in the bank. The return expectation of the investor depends upon the time for which he/she invests. Assume that expectations of return are 8% for 1-year deposit, 9% for 2-year deposit, and 10% for 3-year deposit, as shown in Figure 6-6 and Table 6-6.

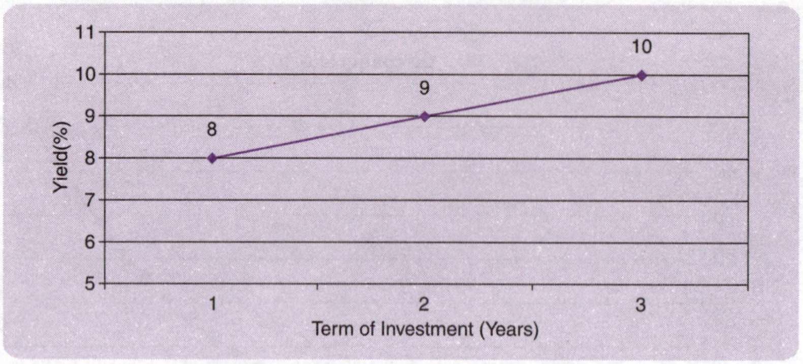

Figure 6-6 Term structure of interest rates

Table 6-6 Investment and yield

Term of investment (Years)	Yield (%)
1	8
2	9
3	10

At the moment we are not concerned about why such return profile is expected. There could be varying reasons for the expectations to change with a change in term of investment. The possible causes are discussed later. Here we merely recognize the fact that the cash flows occurring at different times are not equivalent in terms of returns offered.

If different returns are expected from investment at differing time horizons it is more sensible to discount the cash flows occurring at different points of time with the discount rate appropriate for that time period. Assume a bond that has 3 years remaining for maturity with face value of ₹1,000 and coupon of 12% payable annually and redeemable at par. The value of this bond using current market expectations of 10% as discount rate is ₹1,049.73.

$$\text{Price, } P_0 = \frac{120}{(1+0.10)} + \frac{120}{(1+0.10)^2} + \frac{120}{(1+0.10)^3} + \frac{1000}{(1+0.10)^3}$$
$$= 109.09 + 99.17 + 90.16 + 751.31$$
$$= ₹1{,}049.73$$

Instead of using a uniform discount rate of 10% for all the cash flows, we now calculate the bond price afresh by discounting the cash flows at 8%, 9%, and 10% for the cash flows of first, second, and third year respectively, being appropriate for the timing of the cash flows. The new price works out to ₹1,053.58.

$$\text{Price, } P_0 = \frac{120}{(1+0.08)} + \frac{120}{(1+0.09)^2} + \frac{120}{(1+0.10)^3} + \frac{1000}{(1+0.10)^3}$$
$$= 111.11 + 101.00 + 90.16 + 751.31$$
$$= ₹1{,}053.58$$

The relationship between the yield (interest rate) and the term of investment is called the term structure of interest rates.

If the price of the bond was ₹1,049.73, the YTM of the bond would be 10%. This YTM is the single rate that is applied to equate the cash flows of the bond to the current price. Therefore, YTM can be said to reflect an average rate of yield or return over a period of 3 years. The yield expectations depend upon and change with the term of investment. The yield structure according to the term of investment is referred to as the term structure of interest rates. The data of Table 6-6 is graphically depicted in Figure 6-6.

The term-structure of interest rates can take any shape depending upon market conditions reflecting investors' expectations. There are three prominent types of term-structures of interest rates—rising, flat, and falling as shown in Figures 6-7(a), (b), and (c) respectively.

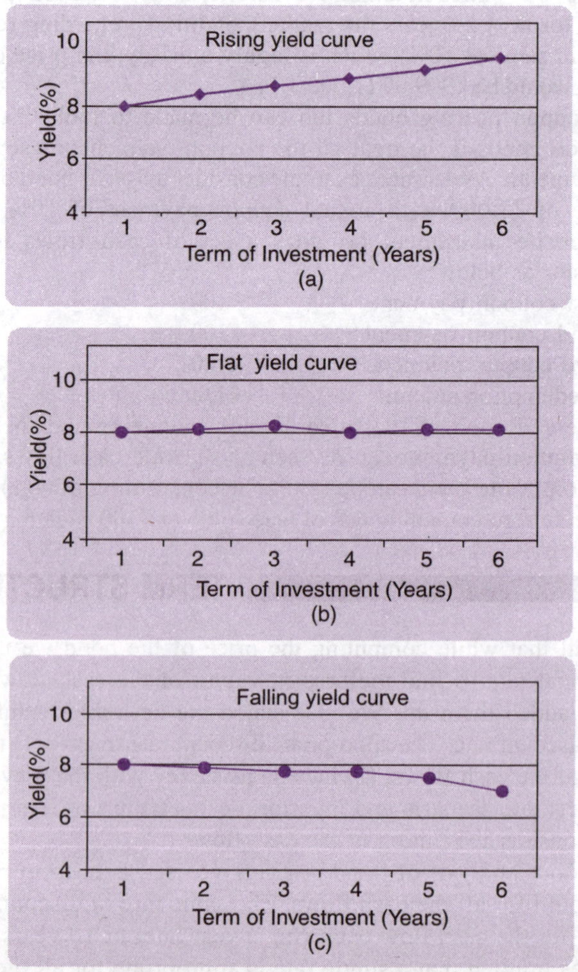

Figure 6-7 (a) Rising yield curve (b) Flat yield curve (c) Falling yield curve

Finding Term Structure

Understanding the term structure of interest rates is easy but calculating it presents many practical difficulties. With the given prices of the bonds the YTM is known which is regarded as average rate of return over the life of the bond. Some may interpret the YTMs of bonds with maturities of 1, 2, 3, etc. years as equivalent to term structure of interest rates. It is erroneous. YTMs of bonds with different maturities cannot be considered as term-structure of interest rates because usually bonds are composite instruments representing cash flows spread over its life occuring at different points of time but treated as one.

Though the YTMs of the bonds are observable, the term structure is not. However, from the observed data of prices of the bonds the term structure can be derived. One way of deriving the term structure of interest rates is to find YTMs of progressively maturing bonds.

Let us illustrate the procedure through an example. Assume that the data shown in Table 6-7 is observed from the capital markets giving prices of three different bonds A, B, and C maturing after 1, 2, and 3 years respectively. For the convenience of computation we further assume that bonds pay their coupon annually.

Though the YTMs are observable, the term structure of interest rates needs to be derived on some rational basis.

From the data in Table 6-7 we may derive the term structure of interest rates for up to three years of investment by analysing the prices of the bonds. Table 6-7 also gives the YTMs of the bonds that correspond to the respective prices. It is note wontaly that these YTMs do not represent the term structure of interest rates though they do impact it.

Using term structure of interest rates we are attempting to find yields denoted by r_1, r_2, and r_3, for investments lasting up to 1, 2, and 3 years respectively and all commencing at $t = 0$. We proceed progressively in steps, i.e., finding r_1 first, then r_2, and finally r_3.

Using the same notations and CF_n as cash flow for period n and the known price of Bond A, P_A we can find the value of r_1 by using the following simple equation:

Table 6-7 Observed prices of the bonds

Bond Features		*Price (₹)*	*YTM*
(A) 1-Year 10% Bond		1018.50	8.00%
(B) 2-Year 12% Bond		1062.50	8.47%
(C) 3-Year 11% Bond		1052.40	8.93%
Cash Flows of the Bonds			**₹**
Time	**Bond A**	**Bond B**	**Bond C**
0	−1018.50	−1062.50	−1052.40
1	1100.00	120.00	110.00
2		1120.00	110.00
3			1110.00
YTM	**8.00%**	**8.47%**	**8.93%**

$$P_A = \frac{CF_1}{(1+r_1)}$$

$$1018.50 = \frac{1100}{(1+r_1)};\ \text{gives } r_1 = 0.08 \text{ or } 8.00\%$$

Since Bond A has only one cash flow, the price truly reflects the investor's expected return for investment horizon of one year. Having obtained r_1 we turn our focus on r_2. The price of Bond B, P_B having maturity of 2 years and only two cash flows is known. P_B is equal to the discounted value of the cash flows of the bond with first year cash flow being discounted at r_1 and second year cash flow with r_2. With P_B and r_1 known, we may solve the following equation for r_2:

Term structure of interest rates is hidden in the YTMs of bonds with progressive maturities.

$$P_B = \frac{CF_1}{(1+r_1)} + \frac{CF_2}{(1+r_2)^2}$$

$$1062.50 = \frac{120}{(1+0.08)} + \frac{1120}{(1+r_2)^2};$$

gives $r_2 = 0.085$ or 8.50%

We repeat the same process for finding r_3 using Bond C. The price of Bond C, P_C again is equal to the discounted value of the cash flows of Bond C with first year, second year, and third year cash flows discounted respectively with r_1, r_2, and r_3. With all values except r_3 known we may solve the following equation to get r_3:

$$P_C = \frac{CF_1}{(1+r_1)} + \frac{CF_2}{(1+r_2)^2} + \frac{CF_3}{(1+r_3)^3}$$

$$1052.40 = \frac{110}{(1+0.08)} + \frac{110}{(1+0.085)^2} + \frac{1110}{(1+r_3)^3};$$

gives $r_3 = 0.09$ or 9.00%

If we have to find the term structure of interest rates beyond three years, we need market data of prices of the bonds for those maturities.

YTMs of bonds with different maturities do not reflect the term structure unless all of them have only single cash flow attached with them.

Through the above example we have obtained the following term structure of interest rates as compared to the YTMs:

	Term Structure	YTM
1 Year	8.00%	8.00%
2 Year	8.50%	8.47%
3 Year	9.00%	8.93%

The limitations of the progressive approach lie in the competitiveness of the market. The term structure is not directly observable except for the bonds with single cash flow. Instead it is derived from the prices of the bonds with progressively increasing maturities.

The validity of the term-structure so derived is obviously dependent upon how truthfully the bond prices reflect the true yields. Although there is great amount of investors' interest in short-term fixed income instruments such as 91-day or 364-day T-bills, the same does not remain valid for long-term instruments. Markets lack depth in terms of the availability of debt instruments and the participants' interest therein.

Using prices of coupon bearing bonds to determine the term-structure of interest rates suffers from the problem of reinvestment rate. Although bonds with same maturities and with different coupon rates are supposed to have same YTMs, due to differential in their interim cash flows (caused by different coupon) and their reinvestment rates they will exhibit different YTMs. To illustrate, let us consider two bonds with the face value or ₹1000 and coupons of 5% and 10%. The maturity period of the bonds is two years and the redemption will be at par value. Assuming the reinvestment rate of 8% today and 10% next year, the prices of the two bonds and their YTMs can be computed.

Bond with 5% coupon:

$$\frac{50}{1.08} + \frac{1050}{(1.08)(1.10)} = ₹930.13, \text{ which corresponds to the YTM of } 8.97\%$$

Bond with 10% coupon:

$$\frac{100}{1.08} + \frac{1100}{(1.08)(1.10)} = ₹1018.52, \text{ which corresponds to the YTM of } 8.95\%$$

The difference in the YTM arises due to differing cash flows of two bonds even though cash the cash flows, have been assumed to be reinvested at the same rate.

Another limitation with term-structure derived from the prices of the coupon bearing bonds is the apprehension that the prices are camouflaged since multiple cash flows are involved. A better measurement could be obtained if there was a single cash flow. The pricing of instruments that have single cash flows would be a fairer representation of the true yield for the period corresponding to the maturity of the financial instrument. Hence, zero coupon bonds must be used as far as possible to determine the term-structure of interest rates. However, such an exercise would have added constraint of the inadequate availability of such instruments, poor liquidity, and increased market imperfection.

The most suitable method to arrive at term structure on interest rates is to get the yields on bonds with increasing maturities but that have single cash flow, as is the case with zero-coupon bonds.

Dealing with prices of zero coupon bonds would straight away give the term structure of interest rates and render computational ease. For example, if we had the prices of the three zero coupon bonds maturing after 1, 2, and 3 years as given in Table 6-8, the YTMs computed using Equation 6-4 would directly provide the term-structure of interest rates up to three years.

Table 6-8 Prices of zero coupon bonds and term structure

Bond	*Maturity*	*Price (₹)*	*Yield (%)*
Zero Coupon Bond	1 Year	925.00	8.11
Zero Coupon Bond	2 Year	845.00	8.79
Zero Coupon Bond	3 Year	770.00	9.10
All bonds are redeemable at par with ₹1,000			
Yields have been worked out using following: $P_0 = \frac{FV}{(1+r_n)^n}$ where n is periods to maturity			

Term Structure and YTMs

Term structure of interest rates provides the correct discount rate for the cash flows depending on when they occur. It will, therefore, be more appropriate to use the discount rate as exhibited in the term-structure of interest rates.

Due to its simplicity, the market is fond of specifying the YTMs of the bond. It must be clarified that it is not the YTM that determines the price of the bond. It is a mathematical equality that makes interpretation of prices easy, comprehendible, and comparable.

Example 6-2 Term Structure and YTM

A 10-year bond with face value of ₹1,000 and redeemable at par was issued with the coupon of 7% payable annually. The coupon rate was consistent with the market interest rates prevalent then. It has got 6 years left for maturity and the market scenario of interest rates has changed since then. The term structure of interest rates prevailing now is as follows:

1-year: 6.00% 2-years: 6.25% 3-years: 6.50%
4-years: 7.00% 5-years: 7.50% 6-years: 8.50%

Find out at what price the bond would sell. Also find the YTM of the bond.

Solution

With the given term structure of the interest rates the cash flows of the bond must be discounted at the rate corresponding to the year of the cash flow to arrive at the price.

Year	*Term Structure*	*Cash Flow (₹)*	*Present Value (₹)*
		–944.01	
1	6.00%	70.00	66.04
2	6.25%	70.00	62.01
3	6.50%	70.00	57.95
4	7.00%	70.00	53.40
5	7.50%	70.00	48.76
6	8.50%	1,070.00	655.85
Price of the bond as per term structure			**944.01**
YTM of the bond			**8.22%**

The price of the bond is ₹944.01.

Using the price so arrived as investment in the Year 0 and the cash flows of the bond, the YTM of the bond works out to 8.22%, which may be deemed as average yield over the period of 6 years.

INTEREST RATES AND IMPLIED FORWARD RATES

Do the prices of the bonds and yields of different maturities tell something about the pattern of future interest rates that are expected? We may attempt to answer this on the basis of argument of equivalency of maturity amounts using two separate strategies that are supposedly equivalent. Consider for example a 2-year investment by following two different strategies known as direct investment and rollover:

Term structure of interest rates not only provides expectations of returns with horizon of investment but also imply forward rates of interest.

Strategy 1: Invest directly for two years at current 2-year yield of r_2. Let us denote this as direct investment strategy.

Strategy 2: Invest for one year at current rate or r_1, and then reinvest the matured amount for another year at 1-year interest rate prevailing then, denoted as ${}_1r_2$. Let this be referred to as rollover strategy.

Under conditions of perfect certainty and knowledgeable investors the direct strategy and rollover strategy must provide an identical outcome. The meaning of r_1, r_2, r_3 etc remain same as before denoting the yields for investment terms of 1, 2, 3 etc years are known today. For strategy of rollover we denote ${}_1r_2$ as interest rate at the end of Year 1 for investment maturing at Year 2. Similarly, ${}_1r_3$ would denote yield at end of Year 2 for investment maturing at Year 3.

Different rollover strategies for periods up to 3 years are shown in Figure 6-8. For investment horizons of more than 3 years, investors may have many rollover strategies.

Assume that the term structure of interest rates is 9% for 1-year investment and 10% for 2-year investment. With direct investment of two years the maturity amount would be:

$(1 + r_2)^2 = 1.10^2 = ₹1.21$

With rollover strategy the first investment is made for a period of 1-year at 9% and then rolled over for another year. The outcome shall be

After one year: $(1 + r_1) = 1.09$

After two years: $(1 + r_1) \times (1 + {}_1r_2) = 1.09 \times (1 + {}_1r_2)$

The direct investment strategy and rollover strategy must result in identical outcome and therefore

$1.09 \times (1 + {}_1r_2) = 1.21$

$(1 + {}_1r_2) = 1.21/1.09$ gives $1 + {}_1r_2 = 1.1101$ or ${}_1r_2 = 11.01\%$

From the value of ${}_1r_2$ of 11.01%, it can be interpreted that the term structure of the interest rates implies that the market expects 1-year yield after one year from today at 11.01%. Of course, future interest rates are uncertain and the interest rate after a year cannot be estimated. The calculation of the future interest rates based on the equivalency argument is the best estimate one can have today about the likely path and the direction the interest rates are expected to follow. The interest rate that actually will prevail after 1 year would in all likelihood be different from the forward rate. It would only be a coincidence that the actual and forward rates turn out to be similar.

Under the conditions of perfect market and well-informed investors, the direct investment strategy and roll over strategy must result in identical returns.

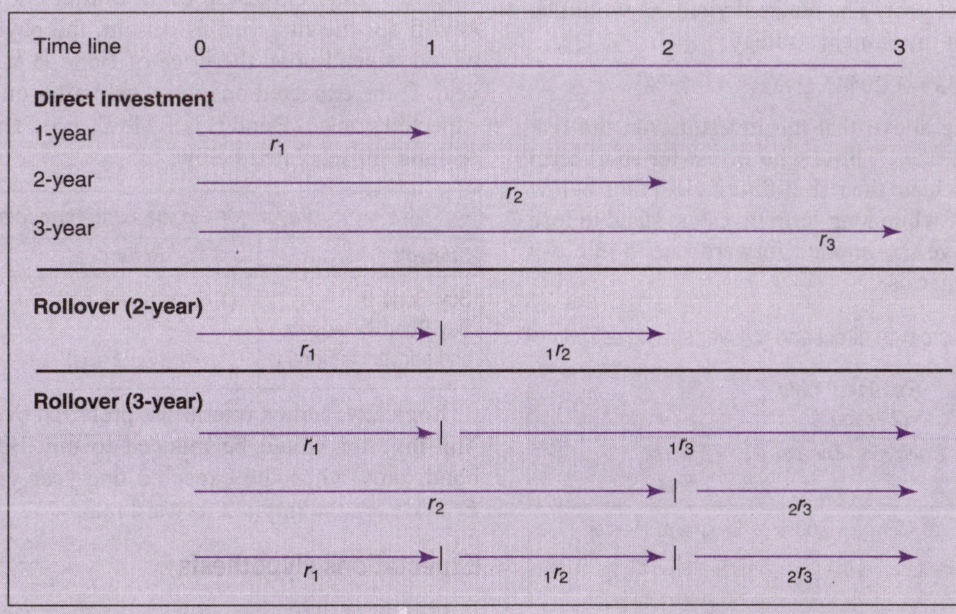

Figure 6-8 Different investment strategies

With uncertainty about the future expected rate the investor faces a choice between the direct investment and rollover strategies. We have seen that with r_1 and r_2 given as 9% and 10% respectively, the implied forward rate for 1–year investment at the end of first year, ${}_1r_2$ is 11.01%. If the actual rate turns out to be equal to the implied forward rate, the investor is indifferent to direct and rollover strategies. Depending upon the actual rate prevailing at the end of first year the investor would be better off in one of the strategies.

Assume two bonds with following information:

Bond A: 1–year zero coupon bond: ₹917.43 Yield 9%
Bond B: 2–year zero coupon bond: ₹826.44 Yield 10%

With direct investment for two years the yield realized would be 10% buying the Bond B at ₹826.44. If an investor adopts a rollover strategy he/she would buy Bond A now, get the par value of ₹1,000 after one year and reinvest in Bond B.

When actual rate is greater than the implied forward rate

If the actual rate turns out to be 12%, Bond B will trade at a lower price of ₹892.86 (1,000/1.12) rather than at the anticipated price of ₹900.82 (1,000/1.1101). The investor will realize a return of 12% in the second year by buying bonds worth ₹1,000 and get ₹1,120 at the end of the second year. The realized yield, r_y, would be 10.49%, higher than direct investment strategy as shown below:

$$(1 + r_y)^2 = 1{,}120/917.43 = 1.2208 \text{ gives } r_y = 10.49\%$$

When actual rate is less than the implied forward rate

If the actual rate turns out to be 10.5%, Bond B will trade at a higher price of ₹904.98 (1,000/1.105) rather than the anticipated price of ₹900.82 (1,000/1.1101). The investor will realize a return of 10.5% in the second year by buying bonds worth ₹1,000 and get ₹1,105 at the end that year. The realized yield, r_y, would be 9.75%, lower than direct investment strategy.

$$(1 + r_y)^2 = 1{,}105/917.43 = 1.20445 \text{ gives } r_y = 9.75\%$$

It is evident from the above that the investors run the risk about the future interest rates. Those who invest for short-term and use rollover strategy have the risk if future yield falls below the implied forward rate, while long-term investors stand to lose if future yield rises above the implied forward rate. Table 6-9 summarizes the two scenarios.

Table 6-9 Risks of investors with direct and rollover strategies

Scenario	Future Rate	Realized Yield (2 years) Rollover	Realized Yield (2 years) Direct	Risk
Future rate > implied forward	12.00%	10.49%	10.00%	Long-term investor better off than short-term investor who bears risk.
Future rate < implied forward	10.50%	9.75%	10.00%	Short-term investor better off than long-term investor who bears risk.

THEORIES OF TERM STRUCTURE

Theories of term structure of interest rates attempt to explain the implied forward rates and expected rates.

Adverting to Bond A and Bond B and the comparison of direct and rollover strategies for investors we take a re-look on the strategies of long-term and short-term investors.

Investors who prefer short-term investment face two choices for investment. A short-term investor can invest in Bond A (one-year zero) and lock-in a return of r_1 at 9%. Alternatively he/she may buy Bond B (two-year zero) but sell after one year. His/her payoff would depend upon the price of Bond B at the end of Year 1. If the expected one year yield after one year is $E({}_1r_2)$, the expected price of Bond B is $1/\{1 + E({}_1r_2)\}$. The returns under the two options are tabulated here:

Payoff for / to the Short-term Investor		
Strategy	**Return**	**Nature of return**
Buy Bond A	$(1 + r_1)$	Certain
Buy Bond B and sell a year later	$\frac{(1+r_2)^2}{\{1+E({}_1r_2)\}} = \frac{(1+r_1)(1+{}_1r_2)}{\{1+E({}_1r_2)\}}$	Uncertain

Since buying of Bond B makes returns uncertain, the strategy would be adopted only when its returns exceed that of buying Bond A. In other words, the short-term investor would be induced to buy the long-term bond, Bond B, only when expected one-year yield after one year is $E({}_1r_2) < {}_1r_2$, the implied forward rate.

Now let us consider long-term investors. They again face two choices for investment. A long-term investor can invest in Bond B (two-year zero) and lock-in a return of r_2 at 10%. Alternatively, he/she may buy Bond A (one-year zero) now, redeem it, and reinvest in Bond B after one year. While his/her Payoff for the first year is certain, the payoff for second year would depend upon the price of Bond B at the end of the first year. If the expected one year yield after one year is $E({}_1r_2)$, the expected price of Bond B is $1/\{1+E({}_1r_2)\}$. The returns under two options are tabulated below:

Payoff for / to the Long-term Investor		
Strategy	**Return**	**Nature of return**
Buy Bond B	$(1 + r_2)^2 = (1 + r_1)(1 + {}_1r_2)$	Certain
Buy Bond A, redeem and reinvest in Bond B	$(1 + r_1)\{(1 + E({}_1r_2)\}$	Uncertain

Logically, certain returns are preferred over uncertain returns. The investor would be induced to buy Bond B, a long-term bond, only when the expected one-year yield after one year, $E({}_1r_2) > {}_1r_2$, the implied forward rate.

Expectations Hypothesis

Expectations hypothesis of term-structure states that expected rates would be equal to implied forward rates. If expected rates are lower than the implied forward rates no investor would be interested in investing in long-term bonds. Similarly, if expected rates are higher than implied forward rates then short-term bonds

The shape of yield curve is dependent upon the expectations of investors about the future interest rates.

would be out of the markets. Since there are investors and markets for both short-term and long-term bonds it necessarily implies that the implied forwards rates are equal to the expected rates. This also means that both the strategies of short-term investing and long-term investing are equally rewarding. The reason that the term-structure would be upward or downward sloping is the expectations of the investors about the future interest rates.

Expectations hypothesis suggests that expected rates of interest would be equal to the implied forward rates. The shape of the yield curve is, therefore, influenced by market participants and their expectations of future interest rates. A rising yield curve would result if market participants expect a rise in interest rates. Likewise, a flat or falling yield curve implies expectations of constant or falling interest rates in the future.

Liquidity Preference Hypothesis

Liquidity preference hypothesis concentrates on investors' preference for liquidity. Investors would be induced to invest for long-term only when they are offered a higher rate than short-term investments. Investors seek greater reward for foregoing the liquidity if they have to remain invested for long. According to liquidity preference theory, long-term bonds ought to offer higher returns to compensate for the additional risk arising out of longer horizons of investment since risk increases with time. More often than not, liquidity preference would assume a rising yield curve.

Liquidity preference theory suggests that the term structure of the interest rates is governed by preferences of investors for liquidity.

Expectations hypothesis ignores the risks associated with future while liquidity preference attaches a liquidity premium to the implied forward rate to reflect the desire for increased reward for assuming additional risk. Therefore, implied forward rates must incorporate the risk premium.

Preferred Habitat Theory/Market Segmentation Theory

Preferred habitat theory recognizes that investors have preferred investment horizons. Short-term investors invest in securities with short maturities and long-term investors prefer securities with long-term maturities. By doing so, investors lock-in the desired rate of return for a certain period and avoid the uncertainty about the reinvestment rate implicit in rollover strategies.

The theory assumes that investors adopt a strategy of maturity matching unless there is a compelling reason to deviate from such practice. According to this theory, if the investors prefer to invest for the period of one year they are unmindful of the yields prevailing for instruments of other maturities. The yields for the specific maturities are determined by forces of demand and supply (the issuers and subscribers of instruments) for those maturities.

DURATION OF THE BOND

Values of bonds change with the change in interest rate. When issued, bonds normally conform to the yields prevalent at the time of the issue by setting the same coupon rate. If a bond is issued at the prevalent rate with coupon of 10%, the subscribers would earn a return of 10%. If subsequent to the issue the yield rises to 11%, the bond prices must fall so that the shortfall of 1% in the return is met by capital gains. Similarly, if interest rates fall to 9% the excess return must be eroded by capital loss by showing an increase in bond price.

With the change in interest rates, all bonds do not change in value by the same amount. It depends upon the duration of the bond.

Do all bonds change by the same amount or in same ratio? The answer apparently is no. We know the value of bond is sum total of present values of all the cash flows attached with the bond. The answer to this question depends upon what proportion each of the cash flows constitutes the price.

Price sensitivity of the bond is measured by the term known as *duration*. Duration is time weighed average of the cash flows as compared to its total value. It is calculated using the following formula:

$$\text{Duration of the bond} = \frac{\sum_{1}^{n} t \times PV \text{ of } CF_t}{P_0}$$

$$= \frac{\left[\frac{1 \times CF_1}{(1+r)^1} + \frac{2 \times CF_2}{(1+r)^2} + \frac{3 \times CF_3}{(1+r)^3} + \cdots\right]}{P_0} \qquad (6\text{-}6)$$

where CF_t represents the cash flow at time t and P_0 is the current price of the bond.

Let us calculate the duration of a bond with following data:

Face value of the bond : ₹1,000 redeemable at par
Coupon rate : 8% payable annually
Time left for maturity : 8 years
Discount rate : 10% p.a.

The duration of the bond is 6.091 years as shown in Table 6-10.

Table 6-10 Duration of the bond

Time (Years)	Cash Flow (₹)	Present Value (₹) @10%	Proportion of Total Value (%)	Time × Proportion of Total Value
1	80.00	72.73	8.14	0.081
2	80.00	66.12	7.40	0.148
3	80.00	60.11	6.73	0.202
4	80.00	54.64	6.12	0.245
5	80.00	49.67	5.56	0.278
6	80.00	45.16	5.06	0.303
7	80.00	41.05	4.60	0.322
8	1,080.00	503.83	56.40	4.512
	Price	893.30	100.00	
	Duration of the Bond (Years)			6.091

The last column of Table 6-10 provides the time-weighted average of the proportionate present value of the cash flows of the bond. The preceding column gives the proportion of each of the cash flows of the bond in present value terms to the total value.

SENSITIVITY OF BOND PRICES

Duration of the bond is a measure of the sensitivity of bond price with the change in the yield. The volatility of the bond is approximately given by the following equation:

$$\text{Volatility of the bond} = -\frac{\text{Duration}}{(1+\text{YTM}/m)} \quad (6\text{-}7)$$

Where duration is measured in years, YTM is expressed as decimal and m is the number of times the coupons payments are made in a year. If the duration is measured in number of periods according to the periodicity of coupon payment then the value of YTM too would be for the periods and value of m would be 1. For semi-annual coupon payments m would be equal to 2. The negative sign in the volatility reflects inverse relationship of the price with YTM.

Table 6-11 Duration of the Bond

Time (Years)	*Cash (₹)*	*Present Flow Value (₹)*	*Present Value (₹)*
Discount Rate		*10.50%*	*9.50%*
1	80.00	72.40	73.06
2	80.00	65.52	66.72
3	80.00	59.29	60.93
4	80.00	53.66	55.65
5	80.00	48.56	50.82
6	80.00	43.95	46.41
7	80.00	39.77	42.38
8	1080.00	485.88	522.53
	New Price	869.02	918.50
% Change in Price		–2.72%	2.82%

Volatility of the bond will give a percentage change in the bond price with 1% change in the YTM. The volatility of the bond in Table 6-11 using Equation 6-7 is –5.54%. It implies that a 1% rise in YTM results in fall in the bond price by 5.54%, and 1% fall in YTM would result in 5.54% rise in bond price.

$$\text{Volatility of the bond} = -\frac{\text{Duration}}{(1+\text{YTM}/m)} = -\frac{6.091}{(1+0.1/1)}$$

$$= -\frac{6.091}{1.1} = -5.54$$

Let us confirm this with an example of the bond whose duration is calculated as 6.091 years in Table 6-10. The bond has a price of ₹893.30 at YTM of 10%. A change in YTM by 50 bp (0.5%) should move the price of the bond by 2.77%. We recalculate the price of the bond at YTM of 9.5% and 10.5% in Table 6-11. The price rises to ₹918.50 when the yield reduces by 0.50% to 9.50% showing a change of 2.82%. The price falls to ₹869.02 when the yield rises by 0.50% to 10.50% showing a change of 2.72%. Note that the change is not exactly equal to 2.77% as is estimated. The sensitivity of price based on duration is presented in Table 6-12.

Table 6-12 Sensitivity of Bond Price

YTM	*9.50%*	*10.50%*
Price (₹)	*918.50*	*689.02*
% Change		
Actual	+2.82%	–2.72%
As per Duration	+2.77%	–2.77%

The reason for deviation of actual change in price from the estimated one is due to convexity of bond price with the discount rate. The change in the price of the bond with respect to discount rate is convex and not linear. This is indicated in Figure 6-9. While estimating the change in price from duration using Equation 6-6, it was assumed that the price change is linear. Due to convexity of price, Equation 6-6 would underestimate the price. The assumption of linearity is reasonable if the change in YTM is small. The advantage of using duration as measure of change in the price is to avoid the complex recalculation of price and directly estimate the interest rate sensitivity of the bond portfolio. It can easily be visualized from

Due to convexity of bond price with interest rate, the change in price of bonds is linear only approximately.

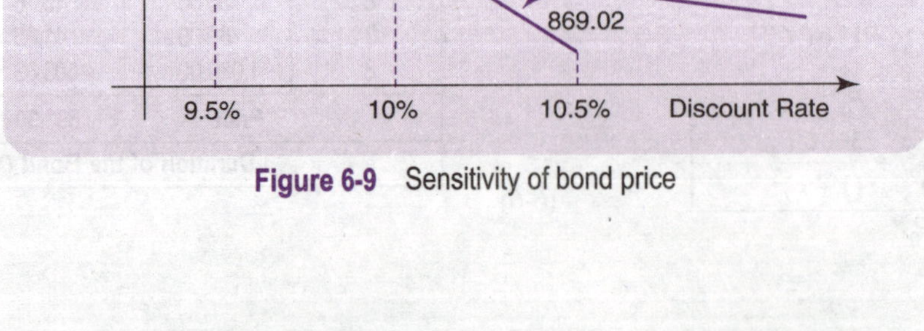

Figure 6-9 Sensitivity of bond price

Figure 6-9 that due to convexity[2] of the price behaviour of the bond the decline in price with the increase in yield will be smaller than the increase in price for the equivalent decrease in yield. This can be noticed from the data in Table 6-11 that when the yield rises by 0.5% from 10% to 10.5% the change in price is ₹24.28 (893.30 – 869.02) and is smaller than the change of ₹25.20 (918.50 – 893.30) in the case when yield declines by same 0.5% from 10% to 9.5%.

Properties of Duration

Few properties of the bond prices that can be rather easily seen from the convexity of the bond prices and the definition of duration are worth noting. They provide useful guidance in design of the portfolios and subsequent planning and management of the changes in portfolios. These are:

Prices of the bonds are more sensitive when the YTM is low. It may be observed from Figure 6-9 that the price behaviour becomes flatter when discount rates are high. At lower YTMs, the changes in the price will be steeper. For example, the price change would be much larger when the yield moves from 15% to 14% than the change when yield moves from say 6% to 5%. Table 6-13 compares the duration and volatility of a bond at YTMs of 5% and 15%.

Duration of low YTM bonds is higher, and hence they are more sensitive as compared to high YTM bonds.

Table 6-13 Volatility at different YTMs

Time (Yrs)	Cash Flow (₹)	Low YTM		High YTM	
		Present Value at 5% (₹)	Time × Proportion of Total Value	Present Value at 15% (₹)	Time × Proportion of Total Value
1	100.00	95.24	0.08	86.96	0.10
2	100.00	90.70	0.16	75.61	0.17
3	1,100.00	950.22	2.51	723.27	2.45
	Price (₹)	1,136.16		885.84	
	Duration (years)		2.75		2.72
	Volatility %		–2.62		–2.36

The volatility of low coupon bonds is higher as compared to bonds with higher coupons. The final payment of the bond, which has the highest value amongst all the cash flows of the bond, contributes a larger proportion of the value of the bond when the coupon is low. This causes duration of the low coupon bond to be higher than when the bonds have high coupon. Table 6-14 presents a comparison of bonds with coupons of 10% and 20% for all other features same.

Duration of low coupon bonds is higher.

Table 6-14 Volatility for different coupons

Time (Yrs)	Low Coupon (10%)			High Coupon (20%)		
	Cash Flow (₹)	Present Value at 5% (₹)	Time × Proportion of Total Value	Cash Flow (₹)	Present Value at 5% (₹)	Time × Proportion of Total Value
1	100.00	95.24	0.08	200.00	190.48	0.14
2	100.00	90.70	0.16	200.00	181.41	0.26
3	1,100.00	950.22	2.51	1,200.00	1,036.61	2.21
	Price (₹) 1,136.16				1,408.49	
	Duration (years)		2.75			2.60
	Volatility %		–2.62			–2.48

The volatility of long-term bonds is higher than that of short-term bonds. This may be seen from the way we compute duration. Since duration is time weighted average of present values of the cash flows of the bond, the weightage of the redemption value will have the highest multiplier causing the duration to be larger than in case of short-term bonds. This multiplier would be larger for long maturity bonds as can be seen from Table 6-15, which compares 10% coupon bonds of 3-year and 5-year maturities at YTM of 5%.

Duration of bonds with longer term to maturity is higher.

Table 6-15 Volatility for different maturities

Time (Yrs)	Short Maturity (3 yrs)			Long Maturity (5 yrs)		
	Cash Flow (₹)	Present Value at 5% (₹)	Time × Proportion of Total Value	Cash Flow (₹)	Present Value at 5% (₹)	Time × Proportion of Total Value
1	100.00	95.24	0.08	100.00	95.24	0.08
2	100.00	90.70	0.16	100.00	90.70	0.15
3	1,100.00	950.22	2.51	100.00	86.38	0.21
4	—	—	—	100.00	82.27	0.27
5	—	—	—	1,100.00	861.88	3.54
	Price (₹) 1,136.16				1,216.47	
	Duration (years)		2.75			4.25
	Volatility %		–2.62			–4.05

Duration is always shorter than the term to maturity and increases as maturity extends. Duration of a zero coupon bond would always be equal to the time remaining for maturity. Since zero coupon bonds have single cash flow at their maturity, they will constitute 100% of the present value of the bond.

---

[2] Convexity $= \dfrac{1}{P_0(1+r)^2}\sum_{1}^{n}\dfrac{CF_t}{(1+r)^t}(t^2+t)$

For elaborate discussion on convexity refer to Bodie, Kane, and Marcus (2002), *Investments*, fifth edition, Tata McGraw-Hill, New Delhi, pp. 493–496.

Table 6-16 364 day T-bill—price and volatility

Time (days)	Cash Flow (₹)	Present Value at 6%	Time × PV of Cash flows	Duration (days)
364	1,000.00	943.55	0.9973	
Price (₹)		**943.55**		
Duration Years/Days		**0.9973**	**364.00**	
Volatility			**0.941%**	
Price and % change with YTM changing to 7%				
Price at 7%		**934.75**		
% Change in Price		**–0.932%**		

For zero coupon bonds, the ratio of percentage value with the value would always be 1.00. The volatility of such bonds would be fairly close to 1 with low YTM. This is demonstrated in Table 6-16 showing the price, duration, and volatility of a 364-day T-bill. We observe that the change in price of the T-bill is approximately equal to the volatility computed using duration.

The duration of the bond has an upper bound governed by YTM and frequency of coupon payments in a year m. The upper bound of duration is given by

$$\text{Upper Bound of Duration} = \frac{(r+m)}{m \times r}$$

where r is YTM expressed as annual and used in decimal form.

Note that the upper bound is independent of the—(1) coupon rate, and (2) remaining time to maturity. Bond that pay coupons annually, the maximum duration would be $(r+1)/r$ and maximum volatility will be $1/r$. For bonds that pay coupon on semi-annual basis the maximum duration would be $(r+2)/2r$.

For a 30-year bond paying semi-annual coupon of 6% and trading at YTM of 10%, the maximum duration is 10.5 years (2.1/0.2), and the maximum volatility is 9.54%.

The additivity property of duration. The duration of a portfolio of bonds that have equal yields can be computed by the weighted average of individual bonds that the portfolio consists of.

Duration of a portfolio of bonds is weighted average of durations of the bonds consisting it.

Duration of bond portfolio

$$= D_p = w_i D_1 + w_2 D_2 + w_3 D_3 \qquad (6\text{-}8)$$

where w_1, w_2, w_3, etc., are the proportions and D_1, D_2, D_3, etc., are the durations of the bonds 1, 2, 3, etc.

Example 6-3 Additive Property of Duration

Assume that Bond 1 and Bond 2 have following features:

	Bond 1	Bond 2
Face value, redeemable at par (₹)	1,000	1,000
Coupon rate, payable annually (%)	8	12
Time to maturity (Years)	5	3

An investor has the portfolio consisting of 75% of Bond 1 and rest in Bond 2. The current YTMs prevailing in the market is 10%.

(i) Find out the price of the Bond 1 and Bond 2
(ii) Find the interest rate sensitivity of each of the bond.
(iii) What would be the interest rate sensitivity of the portfolio?
(iv) Predict the change in the value of the portfolio if yields move from 10% to 10.1%.
(v) What happens to the prices of Bond 1 and Bond 2 if the yields change from 10% to 10.1%?
(vi) What would be the impact on the value of the portfolio if the yield changes from 10% to 10.1%?
(vii) How does it compare with the prediction made in (iv)?

Solution

(i) and (ii): The cash flows, present values at 10%, prices of the bonds and their durations are calculated as below:

Bond 1				
Year	Cash Flow (₹)	Present Value 10%	Proportion	Duration
1	80.00	72.73	7.87%	0.08
2	80.00	66.12	7.15%	0.14
3	80.00	60.11	6.50%	0.20
4	80.00	54.64	5.91%	0.24
5	1,080.00	670.60	72.56%	3.63
Price (₹)		**924.18**	**100%**	
Duration (Years)				**4.28**

Bond 2				
Year	Cash Flow (₹)	Present Value 10%	Proportion	Duration
1	120.00	109.09	10.39%	0.10
2	120.00	99.17	9.45%	0.19
3	1,120.00	841.47	80.16%	2.40
Price (₹)		**1,049.74**	**100%**	
Duration (Years)				**2.70**

The interest rate sensitivity of the bond (with 1% change in YTM) computed from the durations of Bond 1 and Bond 2 are 3.89% and 2.45% respectively.

Bond 1 = –4.28/1.1 = –3.89%; and

Bond 2 = –2.70/1.1 = –2.45%

(iii) The interest rate sensitivity of the portfolio of bonds is dependent upon the duration and the proportions of each bond constituting the portfolio. With proportion of 75% and 25% for Bond 1 and Bond 2 respectively, the duration of the portfolio computed by using Equation 6-8 is 3.89 years and the volatility is 3.53%.

	Bond 1	Bond 2
Proportion	0.75	0.25

Weighted average of duration = 0.75 × 4.28 + 0.25 + 2.70
= 3.210 + 0.675
= 3.885 = 3.89

$$\text{Price sensitivity of the portfolio} = \frac{\text{Duration}}{1+\text{YTM}} = \frac{3.89}{1.1} = 3.53\%$$

(iv) The expected decline in the value of the portfolio with yield changing from 10% to 10.1% is 0.1 × 3.53% = 0.353%.

	Bond 1		Bond 2	
Year	Cash Flow (₹)	Present Value	Cash Flow (₹)	Present Value
	Interest	10.10%		10.10%
1	80.00	72.66	120.00	108.99
2	80.00	66.00	120.00	98.99
3	80.00	59.94	1120.00	839.18
4	80.00	54.44		
5	1,080.00	667.56		
	Price	920.60		1,047.17

(v) The prices for the Bond 1 and Bond 2 at new yield of 10.1% are found to be ₹920.60 and ₹1,047.17 representing a change of 0.387% and 0.2455 consistent with the volatility estimated in (i) and (ii).

(vi) The new value of the portfolio is ₹952.24 showing a decline of 0.349% from the original value of ₹955.57.

Value of the portfolio (₹)	952.24
% Actual Change	–0.349%
Predicted change as per duration	–0.353%

(vii) The actual change of 0.349% is fairly close to the change estimated using duration at 0.353%. The difference is due to non-linearly of price with YTM.

BOND RATING

Seldom do we find that bonds with identical features trade at an identical price. Why do bonds that are same in all respects trade at different prices? One possible reason for the price differential is the ratings of the bonds. Bonds are supposed to make payments of interest and the principal at pre-stated time period(s). Although they are fixed income securities, they cannot be said to be risk-free securities.

Bond rating is an alphanumeric score given to debt issue of a firm by an independent specialized external agency.

Bonds issued by the firms carry some amount of default risk. While lending, such assessment of the ability of the firm to service its borrowings timely is carried out in the due diligence by the lender. However, in case of issue of bonds subscribed by naïve investors the time, effort, and ability on part of subscribers to judge and forecast the cash flows cannot be presumed. They neither have the resources nor the access to privileged information to make an assessment of the firm's ability to generate adequate cash flows and make well-informed investment decisions.

Recognizing the inability of average investors in judging the creditworthiness of borrowing firms, regulatory authorities often make rating of the debt instruments mandatory for the term exceeding a particular period (18 months in India). The objective of such a rating is to subject the borrowing firm to the scrutiny of an independent specialized external agency so as to judge the creditworthiness as regard to its potential for interest payment and principal repayment towards the debt it proposes to raise. Such an independent examination helps investors to make informed judgement about the desirability of the investment.

It broadly signifies the level of risk associated with such an issue of debt.

RATING SYMBOLS

There are many agencies in India that perform the role of rating the issues of debt. CRISIL, ICRA, FITCH, CARE etc are prominent among them. These agencies normally assign an alpha or alphanumeric score to the firm that broadly signifies the level of risk associated with such an issue of debt. Table 6- gives the rating symbol and their interpretation that are assigned by the CRISIL, one of the premier rating agencies of India. These ratings are generally available to the investors.

There are different rating symbols used for different kinds of instruments. Long term instruments mature after 12 months or more. Short term instruments are commercial papers typically having maturity of 90 days. Besides instrument specific rating firms may need general rating because the interest cost is linked to the rating. Higher the rating lower is the interest cost.

It may be understood that rating is only a facilitation mechanism and should not be construed as a guarantee on behalf of the issuer. Rating is not a recommendation to buy or sell a particular financial instrument. It is an independent assessment made by an impartial agency to provide their impression about the timely fulfilment of the obligations. Rating agencies periodically monitor the ratings assigned by them and publicly announce any upgrading or downgrading of the rating symbols.

Rating symbols facilitate decision making by naïve investors

Rating is normally denoted by symbols which are alpha/alphanumerals. A higher rating like AAA denotes safety of interest and principal as to whether the borrowing firm will be able to pay interest regularly and repay the principal on time. This default risk is inter alia, a function of the timely and sufficient availability of cash flows.

The ratings are normally made into three grades, namely *high investment*, *investment*, and *speculative*. They are further assigned a symbol in each grade and are added with a prefix or suffix like '+' or '–' to indicate relative or comparative position within the grade.

Depending upon the rating, the discount rate used for different bonds can be adjusted. Investors assign a higher discount rate for the low rated bonds causing the price of such bonds to be lower.

The advantages of rating debt instruments include making information available at a very nominal cost. Not only the one-time cost of initial rating but also that of constant surveillance is borne by the issuer. On the basis of rating, an investor may decide to invest depending upon his risk appetite.

[1] From www.crisil.com accessed on August 26, 2010

Table 6-17 Rating Symbols and meaning[1]

	LONG TERM INSTRUMENTS AND MEANING
AAA (Triple A) Highest Safety	Instruments rated 'AAA' are judged to offer the highest degree of safety with regard to timely payment of financial obligations. Any adverse changes in circumstances are most unlikely to affect the payments on the instrument
AA (Double A) High Safety	Instruments rated 'AA' are judged to offer a high degree of safety with regard to timely payment of financial obligations. They differ only marginally in safety from `AAA' issues.
A Adequate Safety	Instruments rated 'A' are judged to offer an adequate degree of safety with regard to timely payment of financial obligations. However, changes in circumstances can adversely affect such issues more than those in the higher rating categories.
BBB (Triple B)	Moderate Safety Instruments rated 'BBB' are judged to offer moderate safety with regard to timely payment of financial obligations for the present; however, changing circumstances are more likely to lead to a weakened capacity to pay interest and repay principal than for instruments in higher rating categories.
BB (Double B) Inadequate Safety	Instruments rated 'BB' are judged to carry inadequate safety with regard to timely payment of financial obligations; they are less likely to default in the immediate future than instruments in lower rating categories, but an adverse change in circumstances could lead to inadequate capacity to make payment on financial obligations.
B High Risk	Instruments rated 'B' are judged to have high likelihood of default; while currently financial obligations are met, adverse business or economic conditions would lead to lack of ability or willingness to pay interest or principal.
C Substantial Risk	Instruments rated 'C' are judged to have factors present that make them vulnerable to default; timely payment of financial obligations is possible only if favourable circumstances continue.
D Default	Instruments rated 'D' are in default or are expected to default on scheduled payment dates.
NM Not Meaningful	Instruments rated 'NM' have factors present in them, which render the outstanding rating meaningless. These include reorganisation or liquidation of the issuer, the obligation being under dispute in a court of law or before a statutory authority etc.
	SHORT TERM INSTRUMENTS AND MEANING
P1	This rating indicates that the degree of safety regarding timely payment on the instrument is very strong.
P2	This rating indicates that the degree of safety regarding timely payment on the instrument is strong; however, the relative degree of safety is lower than that for instruments rated 'P1'.
P3	This rating indicates that the degree of safety regarding timely payment on the instrument is adequate; however, the instrument is more vulnerable to the adverse effects of changing circumstances than an instrument rated in the two higher categories.
P4	This rating indicates that the degree of safety regarding timely payment on the instrument is minimal and it is likely to be adversely affected by short-term adversity or less favourable conditions.
P5	This rating indicates that the instrument is expected to be in default on maturity or is in default.
NM Not Meaningful	Instruments rated 'NM' have factors present in them, which render the rating outstanding meaningless. These include reorganisation or liquidation of the issuer, the obligation being under dispute in a court of law or before a statutory authority etc.
	CORPORATE RATING SYMBOLS AND MEANING
CCR AAA ("CCR Triple A")	A **'CCR AAA'** rating indicates **highest** degree of strength with regard to honoring debt obligations.
CCR AA ("CCR Double A")	A **'CCR AA'** rating indicates **high** degree of strength with regard to honoring debt obligations.
CCR A	A **'CCR A'** rating indicates **adequate** degree of strength with regard to honoring debt obligations.
CCR BBB	A **'CCR BBB'** rating indicates **moderate** degree of strength with regard to honoring debt obligations.
CCR BB	A **'CCR BB'** rating indicates **inadequate** degree of strength with regard to honouring debt obligations.
CCR B	A **'CCR B'** rating indicates **high risk** and greater susceptibility with regard to honouring debt obligations
CCR C	A **'CCR C'** rating indicates **substantial risk** with regard to honouring debt obligations.
CCR D	A **'CCR D'** rating indicates that the entity is in **default** of some or all of its debt obligations.
CCR SD	A **'CCR SD'** rating indicates that the entity has **selectively defaulted** on a specific issue or class of debt obligations but will continue to meet its payment obligations on other issues or classes of debt obligations.

[1] Prepared on the basis of content on the respective websites of two agencies accessed on August 25, 2010

PROCESS OF RATING

Rating methodology is an aspect that is left to the rating agency. By and large the methodology is fairly comprehensive and includes assessment of economy, industry, and the firm, competitive position, evaluation of managerial competence, factors effecting the cash flows, cost structure, capital structure, ratio analysis etc. All such quantitative factors are superimposed by a qualitative judgment that is finally transformed in a symbol that are rather easy to understand by normal investor.

Rating is essentially a process of ascertaining the adequacy of cash flows to service the debt and the risk associated with them. As we know that the risk can be classified in two ways – the business risk and financial risk. Business risk is associated with the industry, competition, product, management etc. while financial risk is concerned with the capital structure and levels of debt. Table 6-18 condenses the various parameters considered by CRISIL and ICRA under business and financial risk.

Rating of debt is a complete appraisal exercise as done by financial institutions though the rating agency does no funding.

Table 6-18 Analytical Framework for Rating[2]

Business Risk	
CRISIL	**ICRA**
• Industry risk • Market position • Operating efficiency • Government policies • Technology • Pricc volatility • Access to resources • Level of integration • Human resource	• Industry Risk • Competitive position • Management quality • New project risk
Financial Risk	
CRISIL	**ICRA**
• Accounting quality • Adequacy of cash flows • Financial flexibility • Management risk analysis • Project risk	• Financial position • Profitability • Capital structure • Financial flexibility • Future cash flow adequacy

Assessment of business risk is specific to industry and therefore would require industry specific domain knowledge. Business risk is the variability of the earnings/cash flow from changes in business environment. The environment includes industry status, competitiveness in the industry, technological obsolescence, resourcefulness of the firm in the areas of procurement & distribution and human resources.

The factors of risk would be different for different industries. For example industries subject to regulation and control the factor of "Government policies" assumes significance. For IT sector the "human resource" assessment becomes critical. For relatively new product factors such as "Technology" and "New projects" are important constituents that give rise to business risk. Rating agencies therefore have special group who are equipped with domain knowledge to make right assessment about the ability of the firm to sustain shocks emanating from business environment.

In the financial risk assessment the major emphasis is on the cash flows and ability to service debt. The quantum of cash flow and its stability are the main concerns that are addressed in financial risk analysis.

"Accounting quality" would focus on truthfulness of financial statements, accounting policies for revenue recognition, depreciation, inventory valuation, over or under statement of revenue or expenditure, adherence and consistency with accounting standards and practices etc. This would also include due attention to contingent liabilities that are not provided for. These factors communicate whether the firm is transparent in its presentation and the financial statements can be relied upon. In a way truthfulness of financial statements also reflects upon the integrity of the management of the firm.

"Financial flexibility" concerns with the ability of the firm to generate financial resources through alternative means in case of need. Alternative sources of funding include internal generation, finance from banks/financial institution, recourse to government, access to capital markets, liquidation of marketable securities etc. It can also be measured from the extent of unutilised but sanctioned credit limits from banks and/or the ability to generate deposits from business constituents like dealers, customers, suppliers etc. Improved financial flexibility is better assurance of service of long/short term debt being raised. More diverse the sources of finance better is the rating.

Financial flexibility examines the different avenues the firm has in case it needs to mobilise funds.

The aspects of adequacy of cash flow, favourable capital structure, and sufficient profitability are measured from different kinds of ratios, understanding of trends, comparing with industry or benchmarks, sensitivity of cash flows. Profitability ratios such as operating margin, net margin, return on capital employed are examined in detail. Since issuance of debt affects capital structure the increased leverage may be adverse from the point of view of stability of cash flows. Benchmarking against industry would reveal if the capital structure after issuance of debt remains within the acceptable limits. For capital structure debt equity ratios and coverage ratios are important. Important coverage ratios are cash flow from operations to interest, cash flow from operations to total debt, and retained earnings to total debt are some of the prominent ratios that are looked into. From the perspective of rating for short term instruments the liquidity of the firm is also emphasised upon besides ratios of profitability and capital structure.

Thus rating exercise by the rating agency though not lending is equivalent to complete appraisal of the projects, probably in as much depth as would be for a financial institution for lending.

---

[2] Prepared on the basis of content on the respective websites of two agencies accessed on August 25, 2010

BOND MANAGEMENT STRATEGIES

Fixed income securities are increasingly forming the part of any portfolio as they serve the purpose of providing fixed income to the portfolio. Mutual funds allocate part of their corpus in fixed income securities to maintain liquidity for redemption. There are many ways investors can manage portfolio of bonds depending upon the objectives of the investment and the risk profile. Some of the strategies are discussed in this section.

Buy-and-Hold Strategy

The simplest of the strategy of managing the investment in bonds is to buy-and-hold. The investor makes investment in bonds and holds them for a long time. The focus is on the heavy cash flows that take place on redemption of the bond. The coupon income is used for consumption rather than for returns and, therefore, the aspect of reinvestment is rather ignored. Buy-and-hold strategy does away with the need for prediction of interest rates. The price risk associated with the bond is eliminated as investors hold on till maturity, and reinvestment risk is considered nominal (Discussed under immunization).

Buy-and-hold strategy has the advantage of least transaction cost and suits retired people who need steady stream of income satisfied by coupon payments while preserving the principal with assured gains.

Bond Laddering

Bond laddering strategy is similar to buy-and-hold with the modification that the portfolio of bonds is chosen with staggered maturities. The focus is on creating a portfolio with progressive maturities so as to make available large amounts of cash flow available at periodic intervals. Bond laddering strategy would include bonds with maturities raging from 1 year to 30 years in proportions to be decided by the individual investor.

Since the intention is to hold on to the bond till maturity, the price risk is eliminated. In case the investors need to sell the bonds before maturity they face price risk. As the portfolio includes long-term bonds the risk would be larger as long-term bonds have higher duration and, therefore, are more sensitive to interest rate risk as compared to short-term bonds.

Although transaction costs in bond laddering are nominal, it has the disadvantage of a large initial outlay needed to build a portfolio. It is suitable for investors who have large funds but are conservative and, therefore, do not to take a view on future interest rates.

Maturity Matching vs Duration Matching—Immunization

From the investment in bonds the investor expects to earn the coupons as specified in bond indenture and realize the principal on redemption date. However, the investor has the option of selling the bond prior to its maturity. Investors, who invest in bonds primarily face two kinds of risks that originate from the changes in the interest rate structure subsequent to the investment—*price risk* and *reinvestment risk*.

Price Risk The prices of bonds change constantly, albeit not as much as stock prices, with the changing economic conditions that affect the YTM. The price falls if YTM increases and rises if YTM decreases. In case the investor wants to sell the bond he/she faces uncertainty about the price. This is termed as price risk. Price risk is faced by only those investors who do not hold till maturity.

Reinvestment Risk Reinvestment risk arises due to inability of the investors to reinvest the interim coupon payments at the desired rate. The YTM of the bond implicitly assumes that all the interim coupon payments would be reinvested at the current YTM, which in all probability would not remain constant over the investment horizon.

By matching the maturity of the investment the investors can insulate themselves against the price risk but cannot eliminate the reinvestment risk. If the YTM increases subsequent to the investment, the investor would end up with higher amount than planned. In case YTM falls, the terminal wealth would be lesser than desired because interim coupon payments would get reinvested at a lower rate.

Let us consider an example to illustrate how the maturity amount changes if the investor decides on the strategy of making the holding period equal to the maturity of the bond.

Consider a bond with face value of ₹1,000 redeemable at par after 5 years, paying 10% coupon, and annually currently trading at YTM of 10%. Its price shall be ₹1,000. With no change anticipated in the market conditions and YTM remaining at 10% the investor expects to receive coupon payments and reinvest them at 10% so as to end up with terminal value of ₹1610.51, as shown in Table 6-19. This terminal value comprises:

1. the price of the bond at the end of the holding period, and
2. reinvestment value obtained by reinvesting the first coupon for four periods at 10%, second coupon for next three periods at 10%, and so on.

What may happen to the terminal value if the yield in the market (a) declines to 5% or (b) rises to 20%.

Yield falls to 5% after investment

With fall in the yield to 5%, two things happen.

1. The price of the bond instantly increases to ₹1,216.47 making the investor richer providing an immediate capital gain.
2. Assuming that the investor remains invested, this gain would be accompanied by the loss in the value since now the each of the coupons received would be reinvested at 5% instead of the contemplated 10%. Simultaneously the price too would converge to the redemption value.

The terminal value of the investment would be ₹1,552.56 instead of ₹1,610.51 (Refer Table 6-17, Plate 2)

Yield rises to 20% after investment

With rise in the yield to 20%, again two things happen.

1. The price of the bond instantly decreases to ₹700.94 making the investor poorer. It provides an immediate capital loss.

Table 6-19 Terminal Value with Maturity Matching

Year	*Cash Flow*	*Period (Years)*					
		0	*1*	*2*	*3*	*4*	*5*
YTM 10%		**Reinvestment Rate remains at 10%**					
Price of the bond at end of period		**1,000.00**	**1,000.00**	**1,000.00**	**1,000.00**	**1,000.00**	
0	–1,000.00						
1	100.00		100.00	110.00	121.00	133.10	146.41
2	100.00		—	100.00	110.00	121.00	133.10
3	100.00		—	—	100.00	110.00	121.00
4	100.00		—	—	—	100.00	110.00
5	1,100.00		—	—	—	—	1,100.00
Terminal value at end of period		**1,000.00**	**1,100.00**	**1,210.00**	**1,331.00**	**1,464.10**	**1,610.51**
YTM 5%		**Reinvestment Rate falls to 5%**					
Price of the bond at end of period		**1,216.47**	**1,177.30**	**1,136.16**	**1,092.97**	**1,047.62**	
0	–1,000.00						
1	100.00		100.00	105.00	110.25	115.76	121.55
2	100.00		—	100.00	105.00	110.25	115.76
3	100.00		—	—	100.00	105.00	110.25
4	100.00		—	—	—	100.00	105.00
5	1,100.00		—	—	—	—	1,100.00
Terminal value at end of period		**1,216.47**	**1,277.30**	**1,341.16**	**1,408.22**	**1,478.63**	**1,552.56**
YTM 20%		**Reinvestment Rate rises to 20%**					
Price of the bond at end of period		**700.94**	**741.13**	**789.35**	**847.22**	**916.67**	
0	–1,000.00						
1	100.00		100.00	120.00	144.00	172.80	207.36
2	100.00		—	100.00	120.00	144.00	172.80
3	100.00		—	—	100.00	120.00	144.00
4	100.00		—	—	—	100.00	120.00
5	1,100.00		—	—	—	—	1,100.00
Terminal value at end of period		**700.94**	**841.13**	**1,009.35**	**1,211.22**	**1,453.47**	**1,744.16**

2. This capital loss would be accompanied by gain in the value since now each of the coupons received would be reinvested at higher rate of 20% instead of the contemplated 10%. Simultaneously the price too would converge to the redemption value.

The terminal value of the investment would be ₹1,744.16 instead of ₹1,610.51. (Refer Table 6-19, Plate 3)

The gradual change in the value of investment till maturity is depicted in Figure 6-10. Note that when the yield falls the price rises. The reinvestment of coupons is slower due to reinvestment at lower rate, and when yield increases the price falls but the increase in reinvestment is steeper compensating the capital loss more than adequately. However, in both cases, the terminal value is not same as contemplated.

Another interesting observation from Figure 6-10 is that the three curves at 5%, 10%, and 20% intersect at a point. It implies that at this point the terminal values would be identical irrespective of what happened to the yields. This common point happens to be equal to the duration of the bond computed at 4.17 years. The capital gain or loss happens instantly, whereas compensating reinvestment takes time. There comes a point where the two exactly offset each other. The return at this point shall be equal to the original YTM, which is 10% in this example.

From the above discussion, we can derive an important conclusion for bond management strategy. The investment in bond would have no interest rate risk if the holding period of investment is set equal to the duration of the bond rather than its maturity. The same may be extended to the portfolio of bonds.

By making the holding period equal to the duration of the bond, the portfolio can be immunized from change in value due to change in interest rates.

In this case the investor can lock-in a return of 10% if he/she chooses 4.17 years (the duration of the bond and not maturity) as the holding period of investment. Alternatively, if the holding period is fixed at 5 years, the investor must choose a bond with duration equal to 5 years.

By matching the duration with the holding period, the investor effectively eliminates the interest rate risk associated with maturity matching strategy. Duration matching is also referred as immunization.

The concept of duration strictly applies to flat yield curve as its computation involves discounting of all cash flows at a single rate of YTM. Ideally individual cash flows must be discounted at appropriate discount rate applicable for the term. Immunization based on duration is perfect for flat yield curve and at best may hold good for parallel shift in the yield curve, i.e., at equal change in interest rates for all maturities. In case the shift in the yield curve is not uniform across all maturities, matching investment horizon with duration would not ensure immunization. However, duration matching strategy would still perform better than maturity matching.

Example 6-4 Maturity Matching and Duration Matching

An anxious father needs to send his daughter for an MDA course 7 years from now. He has ₹4 lakh at present. Currently the market interest rates are 8%. In 7 years from now, the amount can grow to ₹6.8553 lakh (4×1.08^7). He has two strategies available—invest in a 7-year, 12% bond (matching maturity) or invest in a 10% bond maturing after 10 years but having a duration of 7 years (matching duration). Find out the amount the father will avail under the two strategies if one year subsequent to his investment the market interest rates— (a) fall to 6% (b) rise to 10%. The price of 7-year 12% bond today is ₹1,208.25 while 10-year 10% bond is trading at ₹1,134.20.

Solution

Under maturity matching, the bond is held till maturity, while under duration strategy the bond is sold after holding period of 7 years at the rate prevailing then.

The two strategies of maturity matching and duration matching when the interest rates fall to 6% after one year are compared on the basis of terminal wealth.

Under maturity matching 7-year 12% bond is bought, while with duration matching 10-year 10% bond is bought.

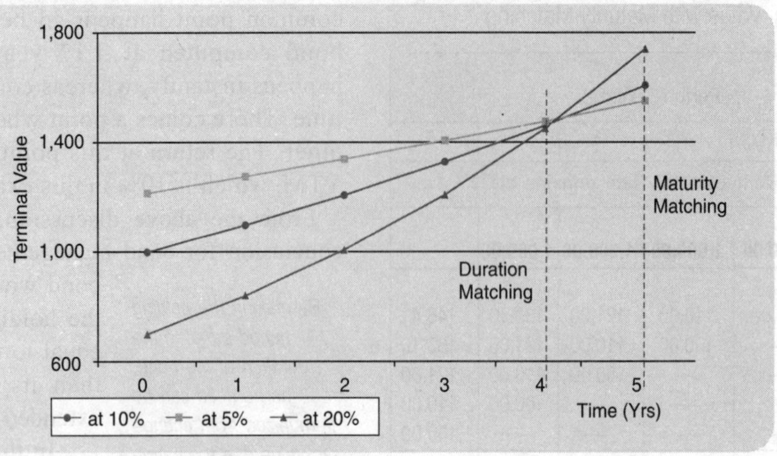

Figure 6-10 Terminal value

We have computed the terminal value of the investment matching first coupon of ₹120 is reinvested at 6% to yield ₹127.20 (1.06 × 120). Added with the second coupon of ₹120 the ending wealth is ₹247.20. This goes on for 7 years as shown below.

Time (Yr)	*Maturity Matching* Cash Flow (₹)	Re-invst Rate	Terminal Value	*Duration Matching* Cash Flow (₹)	Re-invst Rate	Terminal Value
0						
1	120.00	8 %	120.00	100.00	8 %	100.00
2	120.00	6 %	247.20	100.00	6 %	206.00
3	120.00	6 %	382.03	100.00	6 %	318.36
4	120.00	6 %	524.95	100.00	6 %	437.46
5	120.00	6 %	676.45	100.00	6 %	563.71
6	120.00	6 %	837.04	100.00	6 %	697.53
7	1120.00	6 %	*2,007.26*	100.00	6 %	839.38

Under duration matching the bond would be sold after 7 years. The value of bond at that time would be present value of the remaining cash flows discounted at assumed YTM of 6%, as calculated here.

S. No	Cash Flow	PV at 6%
1	100	94.34
2	100	89.00
3	1,100	923.58
Price of bond		1,106.92

Similarly when YTM rises to 10%, the comparison of ending wealth would be as shown below.

Time (Yr)	*Maturity Matching* Cash Flow (₹)	Re-invst Rate (%)	Terminal Value	*Duration Matching* Cash Flow (₹)	Re-invst Rate (%)	Terminal Value
0						
1	120.00	8	120.00	100.00	8	100.00
2	120.00	10	252.00	100.00	10	210.00
3	120.00	10	397.20	100.00	10	331.00
4	120.00	10	556.92	100.00	10	464.10
5	120.00	10	732.61	100.00	10	610.51
6	120.00	10	925.87	100.00	10	771.56
7	1120.00	10	*2,138.46*	100.00	10	948.72

The value of bond, held under duration matching strategy at the end of 7 years would be as shown below.

S. No	Cash Flow	PV at 10%
1	100	90.91
2	100	82.64
3	1100	826.45
Price of bond		₹1,000.00

The comparison of ending wealth under maturity matching a duration matching with YTM following to 6% or rising to 10% is as below:

	Duration Matching 10 year 10% bond		*Maturity Matching 7-year 12% bond*	
New YTM	*6%*	*10%*	*6%*	*10%*
Terminal value of Coupons & Redemption	839.38	948.72	2,007.26	2,138.46
Sale value of the bond	1,106.92	1000.00	—	—
Terminal value (a)	1,946.30	1,948.72	2,007.26	2,138.46
Purchase value (b)	1,134.20	1,134.20	1,208.25	1,208.25
Ratio (a/b)	1.7160	1.7181	1.6613	1.7699
Ending wealth (₹ lakh) (Initial ₹4 lakh)	6.8641	6.8726	6.6452	7.0795

It may be noted that under the strategy of duration matching the end wealth remains the same irrespective of change in the yield subsequent to purchase. By adopting a strategy of duration matching, immunization from interest rate fluctuations can be achieved. Under maturity matching, the end wealth may be higher or lower than the planned terminal value depending upon the direction of change in the interest rates.

Dedication

Dedication refers to immunizing the portfolio by matching the cash flow of assets and liabilities. While duration-based immunization is a single period strategy, dedication is multi-period. When obligations in each period are matched with the maturity amounts of bonds, the interest rate risk is eliminated if the bond portfolio consists only of zero coupon bonds. If coupon bearing bonds are used some element of reinvestment risk would persist. However, it can be reduced by using a conservative reinvestment rate on coupon payments.

Active Bond Management Strategies

Active bond management strategies concentrate on opportunities to exploit the changes in the yield curve by forecasting the direction of change and the spread between the bonds of various kinds. Short-term investors use such strategies. These investors capitalize on the changes in the price by buying and selling the bonds and making a capital gain. The focus is neither on the coupon payments nor on the redemption amount available at maturity.

In contrast, passive strategies such as buy-and-hold focus on coupon income and large cash flows at maturity. These strategies ignore the changes in the yield curve. Passive strategies are concerned with steady cash flows without risk rather than the maximization of returns. Active bond management would constantly change the portfolio by predicting changes in the price based on yield curve movement.

One golden rule is provided by duration in this respect. In times of rising interest rates (when the bond prices are supposed to fall), the portfolio must be constructed with bonds of lower duration to have lesser decline in the portfolio than the market. Similarly when interest rates are expected to decline (bond prices expected to move up) it is advisable to have portfolio dominated by bonds of high duration to register a larger gain in the portfolio than the market. However, in efficient markets the rule of duration is not of much significance, as anticipated changes in the yield curve would already be discounted in the prices.

Another source of earning better returns in the bonds market is to identify the mispricing of bonds of various classes. For example, if the historical yield spread between a government bond and AA rated corporate bond has been 1% while currently it is 2%, the investor is likely to believe that the aberration in the market is temporary and the yield differential will get restored to 1% after some time. The mispricing of bonds also takes place when bonds of same rating trade at different yields whereas in the opinion of the investor they must command the same price. The strategy in this case is to buy the bond with a higher yield (or sell the one with a lower yield) in the hope that the yield differential would shrink in future. For example, two bonds A and B, similar in all respects, trade at ₹1,010 (lower yield) and ₹1,000 (higher yield) respectively. The ideal price for both the bonds in the opinion of investor should be ₹1,005. Under such a scenario of mispricing, the investor would do good to sell Bond A or buy Bond B now and reverse the transaction when mispricing is eliminated.

Mispricing of bonds on the basis of yield differential may exist in bonds with different (i) coupons, (ii) maturities, and (iii) sectors. Depending upon the intelligence of the investors and confidence of forecast about the mispricing getting corrected, investors can employ various kinds of substitution of bonds to benefit.

Riding the Yield Curve

A very popular strategy employed by short-term investors is known as riding the yield curve. This is particularly useful when the yield curve is rising, i.e., bonds with more time to maturity trade at higher yields than the bonds with less time to maturity.

We illustrate this with an example. Assume a zero coupon bond with two years remaining for maturity. The rising yield curve reflects yields of 7% for 1-year term and 8% for 2-year term. The current price of the bond would be ₹857.34 ($100/1.08^2$). If the planned investment horizon is two years, the investor would lock-in the return of 8%. However, if he/she decides to sell the bond after one year, the bond would trade at a price higher than expected. With 8% yield the price should be ₹925.92 (100/1.08). Since after the duration of one year the time left for maturity is only one year, the new price of the bond should be ₹934.58 (1,000/1.07) consistent with the yield curve. The investor would realize a return of 9% if the bond is sold one year after investment, as calculated below:

$$\%\ \text{Gain} = \frac{934.58 - 857.34}{857.43} = 0.0901 = 9.01\%$$

When the yield curve rises and no change is expected in the term structure of interest rates, the longer maturity bonds would provide greater returns than the YTMs, and by trading in these bonds the returns would exceed the YTM. The success of the strategy depends upon the assumption of unchanged yield curve.

SUMMARY

Bonds are the instruments of debt financing available to governments and corporations. They promise a fixed return till the date of maturity and the payback of the principal sum either as a lump sum on maturity or in a phased manner.

The terms and conditions for the issue of bonds are pre-decided and are specified by the issuers to the subscribers at the time of the issue. The key terms on which the subscribers base their decision to invest include—face value, coupon rate, periodicity of coupon payments, maturity period, and redemption value. Each of them has an impact on the value of the bond.

Due to varying needs of issuers and subscribers, bonds have different variants. Based on the nature of rate of return they are classified as fixed or floating rate bonds. Bonds offering coupon payments based on inflation rate are known as indexed bonds. Callable bonds grant an option to issuer while puttable bonds give an option to the subscriber to redeem prior to the maturity. Bonds can also be categorized based on whether the principal is redeemed in lump sum or in instalments. Also there are zero coupon bonds that offer no coupon rates and the convertible bonds that give an option of the holders to convert them into equity.

Zero coupon bonds do not pay any interest and instead provide all the returns in the form of capital gains. They are issued at price substantially lower than the par value and are redeemed at par value on maturity. Due to this feature they are also termed as deep discount bonds. The value of zero-coupon bond is arrived by discounting the par value (redemption price) at an appropriate discount rate.

Cash flows of the conventional bond consist of two parts—periodic coupon payments and final redemption payment. The value of bonds is arrived by discounting the future cash flows from the bonds at an appropriate discount rate. Discount rate is a function of risk and must be appropriately adjusted for cash flow risks, prevalent market conditions, and timing of cash flows to truly reflect the expectations of investors.

There are many ways of expressing returns of the bond. Yield from bonds is the return that investors earn from the bonds and is a function of cash flows, price of the bond (market price or call price), and the required rate of returns from the bonds. There are four variants of yield namely current yield, yield to maturity, realized yield, and yield to call. The most common measure is yield to maturity (YTM), the yield available if bond is held until maturity.

The timing of cash flows and the discount rates to be used are inter-dependent as the expectations of investors vary with the investment horizon. The relationship between the yield (interest rate) and the term of investment is known as the term structure of interest rates. The term structure may be derived from the YTMs of the bonds with varying maturities. Different YTMs of the bonds also reflect expectations of future interest rates termed as implied forward rates. Different theories such as expectation hypothesis, liquidity preference, and preferred habitat attempt to explain the different shapes of yield curve.

Price sensitivity of the bond with changing interest rates is measured by the term called duration, which is the time weighed average of the present values of cash flows in the price of the bond. Duration has additive property, which can be conveniently used to estimate the duration of the portfolio of bonds.

Bond rating is an alphanumeric score given to debt issue of a firm by an independent specialized external agency. The objective of such a rating is to judge the creditworthiness as regard to its interest payment and principal repayment potential towards the debt it proposes to raise. It helps investors to make informed judgement about the desirability of the investment.

There can be various strategies for the investors to manage their bond portfolio. It depends on the objectives of the investment and the risk profile. These strategies may be active or passive. The risks faced by investors of bond are classified as price risk and re-investment risk, both of which act in conflicting manner. By matching duration with the holding period the portfolio of bonds is immunized from the change in interest rates. This dispels a common belief that by matching maturity with the holding period no interest rate risk is faced by the investors.

KEY TERMS

Indenture A contract between an issuer of bonds and the bondholder stating the various terms and conditions of the contract.

Coupon rate The annual interest rate payable on the face value of the bond.

Floating rate bonds The bonds, which pay varying interest according to market conditions prevailing based on a benchmark.

LIBOR LIBOR is an acronym for London Inter-Bank Offer Rate representing the interest rate at which banks can borrow funds, in marketable size, from other banks in the London inter-bank market.

Callable/Puttable bonds The bonds that give an option to the issuer to redeem prior to maturity are callable bonds, while those with option to the subscribers are puttable bonds.

Deep discount bonds The bonds issued with zero coupon, at substantial discount to the face value and redeemed at face value are known as deep discount bonds.

Convertible bond Bonds where part or whole is convertible into equity shares.

Conversion price The price per share at which a convertible security, such as corporate bonds or preferred shares, can be converted into common stock.

Conversion ratio The number of common shares received at the time of conversion for each convertible security.

Current yield A measure of return in percentage given by dividing the coupon payment by the current market price of the bond.

Yield to maturity (YTM) YTM is the percentage return of the bond at current market price assuming investor holds the instrument till maturity.

Realized yield The return obtained by investor when the investment is sold prior to its maturity.

IRR: The internal rate of return. It is the rate of return that equals the present value of cash inflows with the present value of cash outflows

Yield to call The return for the investor assuming that the instrument would be called at the earliest possible time.

STRIPS It is the acronym for Separate Trading of Registered Interest and Principal of Securities. It is used when each coupon payment and the principal of the composite bond are issued as separate and independent securities for trading.

Term structure of interest rates The relationship of investor expectation of return with respect to the investment horizon is referred to as term structure.

Duration Duration is the time weighted average of the present values of each cash flow of the bond with respect to the total value. It is a measure of sensitivity of the price of the bond with respect to changes in the interest rates.

Bond rating An alphanumeric symbol assigned by an independent agency reflecting the quality of the bond to help investors make informed decision regarding investment.

Immunization A strategy aimed at making the value of the portfolio of bonds insensitive to the changes in the interest rates.

KEY FORMULAE

Yield to Maturity of the bond (YTM)

$$P_0 = \sum_{1}^{n} \frac{C_t}{(1+YTM)^t} + \frac{R}{(1+YTM)^n}$$

Realized Yield (r_y)

$$P_0 \times (1 + r_y)^n = TV_n$$

Yield to call (YTC)

$$P_0 = \sum_{1}^{n} \frac{C_t}{(1+\text{YTC})^t} + \frac{R}{(1+\text{YTC})^n}$$

Value of deep discount bond $= \dfrac{\text{Face Value}}{(1+r)^T}$

Duration of the bond $= \dfrac{\sum_{1}^{n} t \times PV \text{ of } CF_t}{P_0}$

Volatility of the bond $= -\dfrac{\text{Duration}}{1+\text{YTM}/m}$

Duration of bond portfolio

$$D_p = w_1D_1 + w_2D_2 + w_3D_3$$

PRACTICE PROBLEMS

1. Valuing a Bond

Powerful Cements Limited had issued 10-year bond with face value of ₹100, coupon of 12% payable semi-annually, and redeemable at par to fund its expansion of capacity from 3 MTPA to 5 MTPA. Five years have already elapsed. Since the time of the issue the interest rates in the market have changed from 12% to 14%. Find out the current market price of the bond.

Solution

The market price of the bond shall be the present value of the remaining cash flows of the bond discounted at current interest rate.

Coupon rate	12.00%
Face value (₹)	100.00
Interest at each semi-annual period (₹)	6.00

The present values of all the cash flows of the bond is:

Current market yield 14.00%		*Figures in ₹*
Periods	*Cash flow (₹)*	*Present Value*
1	6.00	5.61
2	6.00	5.24
3	6.00	4.90
4	6.00	4.58
5	6.00	4.28
6	6.00	4.00
7	6.00	3.74
8	6.00	3.49
9	6.00	3.26
10	106.00	53.89
Price of the bond (₹)		**92.98**

2. Choosing between Bonds

You are an avid investor in fixed income securities. Your portfolio of bond does not have bonds from AAA rated companies. You are considering purchase of an AAA rated bond. Two such bonds from AAA rated companies, Bond A and Bond B are available in the market that have following features:

	Bond A	Bond B
Face value	₹100.00	₹120.00
Coupon rate	15.00%	12.00%
Periodicity of coupon	Semi annual	Semi annual
Time remaining for maturity	3 years	4 years
Current market price	₹110.00	₹130.00

Your expectation of return from the investment in AAA rated bonds is 10%, which is slightly above the yields in the government securities

Which of the bond should you buy and why? Assume that you are indifferent to the investment horizon of 3 or 4 years.

Solution

Fair value of the bond must be compared with the current market price to make a choice of investment.

The bond that sells at lesser than the fair value must be bought and the one that sells at a price higher than the fair value should not be considered since it is overvalued.

Fair values of Bond A and Bond B are computed as cash flows of each bond discounted at current expectation of yield. The current market yield or expectation is 10.00%. The fair value of each of the bond is computed below:

Bond A		*Figures in ₹*	*Bond B*		*Figures in ₹*
Coupon	*Cash flow*	*PV*	*Coupon*	*Cash flow*	*PV*
1	7.50	7.14	1	7.20	6.86
2	7.50	6.80	2	7.20	6.53
3	7.50	6.48	3	7.20	6.22
4	7.50	6.17	4	7.20	5.92
5	7.50	5.88	5	7.20	5.64
6	107.50	80.22	6	7.20	5.37
7	—	—	7	7.20	5.12
8	—	—	8	127.20	86.09
Fair price		**112.69**	**Fair price**		**127.76**
Market price		**110.00**	**Market price**		**130.00**

Clearly Bond A is undervalued by ₹2.69 and therefore must be bought.

Bond B is overvalued by ₹2.24 and must not be considered for inclusion in the portfolio. Buying such a bond would result in decline of returns in the portfolio.

3. Yield on the Bond

Suvidha Enterprises engaged in the business of ship breaking. They have issued a bond whose current market price is ₹120. The bond issued has following features:

Face value	₹100.00
Coupon rate	15.00%
Periodicity of coupon	Annual
Time remaining for maturity	6 years
Redemption value	₹110.00
Current market price	₹124.00

(a) What is the current yield of the bond?

(b) If an investor buys the bond today and holds it till maturity what returns would he realise?

(c) Assuming that the yield in the market has fallen to 9% what impact on price of the bond you see? Work out the price of the bond after two years assuming that yield remains at 9%.

(d) Assume that an investors buys the bond today and sells at the price worked out in (c) above, what returns would he realize?

Solution

(a) Current yield = Coupon interest/Current market price
= 100 × 0.15/124 = **12.10%**

(b) The yield to maturity (YTM) can be found by equating the current market price of the bond with the cash flows of the bond discounted at an appropriate rate. The discount rate that equates the current market price to the cash flows of the bond is YTM and is given by the following equation:

$$P_0 = \sum_{1}^{n} \frac{C_t}{(1+r)^t} + \frac{R}{(1+r)^n}$$

This equation may be solved by hit-and-trial method. Alternatively, we find the IRR of the cash flows of the bond assuming buying at the prevailing market price and reaping the cash flows of the bond till maturity.

This is shown below:

Price of the bond	***₹124.00***
Year	***Cash flows***
1	15.00
2	15.00
3	15.00
4	15.00
5	15.00
6	125.00*
IRR of the bond = YTM	**10.66%**

*Consists of coupon and redemption of ₹110.

(c) If immediately after the purchase the yields have fallen the price of the bond would go up. Yield and price have an inverse relationship. The price of the bond after two years would be the discounted value of the remaining cash flows of the bond discounted at the reduced yield of 9% as worked out below:

		New YTM	9.00%
Price of the bond after 2 years:		Cash flow	PV
Coupon	1	15.00	13.76
	2	15.00	12.63
	3	15.00	11.58
Coupon + Redemption	4	125.00	88.55
Price of the bond after 2 years			**₹126.52**

(d) The returns realised by the investor by buying the bond now and selling after 2 years at reduced yield would consist of two components: 1. capital gain equal to the difference in the price of selling and buying, and 2. re-investment value of the two coupon payments received during the holding period of two years. This re-investment is assumed at prevailing yield of 9%.

The reinvestment value of two coupons at 9% is:

Coupon No	Coupon Amount	Re-investment Value
1	15.00	16.35
2	15.00	15.00
		₹31.35
Sale value		₹126.52
Terminal value of the cash flows		₹157.87

$$S_0(1 + r)^2 = S_2$$

$$124.00 \times (1 + r)^2 = 157.87$$

Solving for r would give the value of 12.83%

4. Zero Coupon Bond—Value & YTM

Government of India is planning to issue a deep discount (zero coupon) bond with the face value of ₹25,000 payable at the end of 10 years. The planned yield for the investors is 12%.

(a) What would be the issue price of the deep discount bond?

(b) If the proposed issue price of the bond is ₹7,500 what yield would it offer to the subscribers of the bond if they hold it till the redemption of the bond?

Solution

(a) Zero coupon bond has only one cash inflow i.e. at the time of maturity equal to the face value.

YTM of the bond, r = 12.00%

Years to maturity, n = 10

Issue price of zero coupon bond = Face Value/$(1+r)^n$
= $25{,}000/1.12^{10}$
= ₹8,049.33

(b) Issue price = ₹7,500.00

$$\text{YTM of zero coupon bond} = \left[\frac{\text{Face Value}}{\text{Issue Price}}\right]^{1/m} - 1$$

$$= \left[\frac{25{,}000}{7{,}500}\right]^{1/10} - 1$$

YTM = 12.79%

5. Term Structure of Interest Rates

There are three bonds with 1, 2, and 3 years to maturity. All these bonds have no coupon payments attached with them and therefore the prices of these bonds would reflect yields with investment horizons of 1, 2, and 3 years.

The prices and par values at which they would be redeemed are as below:

	Price (₹)	Par value (₹)
Zero coupon bond maturing after 1 year	476	500
after 2 years	895	1000
after 3 years	4139	5000

(a) Find out the yield that each bond offers.

(b) What conclusions can you make about the yields for investment for 1, 2, and 3 years?

Solution

(a) The prices and redemption values of the bonds are as below.

Zero coupon bond maturing after	Price (₹)	Par value (₹)
1 year, Bond 1	476	500
2 years, Bond 2	895	1,000
3 years, Bond 3	4,139	5,000

Prices of each of these bonds Bond 1, Bond 2, and Bond 3 would reflect the yields for 1, 2, and 3 years denoted respectively by ${}_0r_1$, ${}_0r_2$, and ${}_0r_3$

Interest rate (yield) for investment horizon of one year

$P_0(1 + {}_0r_1) = R_1$

$(1 + {}_0r_1) = R_1/P_0 = 500/476 = 1.05042$

${}_0r_1 = 5.04\%$

Interest rate (yield) for investment horizon of two years

$P_0(1+{}_0r_2)^2 = R_2$

$(1 + {}_0r_2)^2 = R_2/P_0 = 1000/895 = 1.1173$

${}_0r_2 = 5.70\%$

Interest rate (yield) for investment horizon of three years

$P_0(1 + {}_0r_3)^3 = R_3$

$(1 + {}_0r_3)^3 = R_3/P_0 = 5000/4139 = 1.2080$

${}_0r_3 = 6.50\%$

(b) The term structure of interest rate as reflected in the prices of Bond 1, Bond 2, and Bond 3 is rising (upward sloping) and is as below:

Investment horizon	Yield (%)
One year	5.04%
Two years	5.70%
Three years	6.50%

6. Expectation Hypothesis

Assume that the term structure as arrived in Problem 5 is prevailing. What best estimate based on the term structure can you make for (a) one year interest rate after one year (b) one year interest rate after two years?

Solution

We can make estimate of one year interest rate after one year, i.e., ${}_1r_2$ on the basis of equivalency of two year direct investment with the roll over of one year investment for another year upon the maturity of the first investment.

Mathematically, $(1 + {}_0r_1) \times (1 + {}_1r_2) = (1 + {}_0r_2)^2$

$1.0504 \times (1+ {}_1r_2) = 1.1173$

gives ${}_1r_2 = 6.37\%$

After one year, we expect the interest rate for investment for one year to be 6.37%.

Similarly we can make estimate of one year interest rate after two years i.e., ${}_2r_3$ on the basis of equivalency of three year direct investment with the rollover of two year investment for another year upon the maturity of the first investment.

Mathematically, $(1 + {}_0r_2)^2 \times (1 + {}_2r_3) = (1 + {}_0r_3)^3$

$1.1173 \times (1 + {}_2r_3) = 1.2080$

gives ${}_2r_3 = 8.12\%$

After two years we expect the interest rate for investment for one year to be 8.12%.

7. Term Structure and Value of the Bond

In the fixed income securities market the indicative term structure of interest rates is as follows:

Investment horizon	Yield (%)
One year	8.00%
Two years	8.50%
Three years	9.20%

There exists a bond with the face and redemption value of ₹1,000, coupon of 12% payable annually, and has 3 years remaining to maturity.

(a) Find out the price of the bond based on the term structure of interest rates.

(b) If the actual price of the bond is what you calculated in (a), what YTM does it imply?

Solution

(a) The true value of the bond should be determined by discounting the each year's cash flows of the bond with the appropriate discount rate as reflected in the term structure of interest rate. This means that the cash flow after one year must be discounted with rate applicable for one year investment.

Similarly cash flow occurring after two year must be discounted with the rate applicable for two year investment, and so on. The term structure of interest rate is as follows:

Investment horizon	Yield (%)
One year	8.00%
Two years	8.50%
Three years	9.20%

The value of the bond by discounting the cash flows at a rate applicable for the timings of the cash flow is as below:

Timing of payment, Year	*Cash flow, ₹*	*Discount rate, %*	*Present value, ₹*
1	120.00	8.00%	111.11
2	120.00	8.50%	101.93
3	1,120.00	9.20%	860.10
Price of the bond			**1,073.15**

(b) Assuming that the price as arrived above is the actual market price the YTM of the bond can be found by equating the price of the bond to the sum of present values of the cash flows of the bond discounted at YTM. This is nothing but the IRR of the cash flows of the bond and is found as below:

Time	*Cash flow (₹)*
0	1,073.15
1	120.00
2	120.00
3	1120.00
	IRR = 9.10%

8. Sensitivity of Bond Prices

Augusta Fabricators had issued a convertible bond a few years back. The non-convertible portion had the value of ₹400 and has 5 years remaining for maturity. It promises to pay annual interest rate of 13.50% and would be redeemed at par.

(a) If the current yield for 5-year paper of equivalent quality in the market is 8% what is the price of the bond?
(b) Calculate the Maclaulay's duration of the bond.
(c) What significance you attach to duration computed in (b)?
(d) What would be the price of the bond if YTM changes from current 8% to 9% based on duration?
(e) Compute the price of the bond at revised YTM of 9%.
(f) Do you find the difference in prices computed in (d) and (e) above? What reason do you attribute to the difference in the prices so arrived?

Solution

(a) and (b) Price of the bond at given YTM, r is given by following equation:

$$P_0 = \sum_{1}^{n} \frac{C_t}{(1+r)^t} + \frac{R}{(1+r)^t}$$

Macaulay's duration is the time weighted average of cash flows of the bond relative to its price. It is given by the following equation:

$$\text{Maclaulay's duration, MD} = \frac{\sum_{1}^{n} \frac{C_t \times t}{(1+r)^t}}{P_0}$$

where P_0 = Price of the bond C_t = cash flow of the bond at time t
r = YTM of the bond n = time to maturity

Price and duration of the bond is computed below:

Face value	₹400.00	Redemption value	₹400.00
Coupon	13.50%	Time to maturity	5 years
Interest payments	₹54.00	YTM	8.00%

Price of the bond and its duration are computed as below:

Years	*Cash flow (₹)*	*PV of cash flow (₹)*	*t x PV of C_t*
1	54	50.00	50.00
2	54	46.30	92.59
3	54	42.87	128.60
4	54	39.69	158.77
5	454	308.98	1,544.92
Price of the bond (₹) =		**487.84**	
Time weighted value of cash flows =			**1,974.88**
Maclaulay's duration =			**4.048 years**

(c) The duration of the bond at 4.048 indicates the sensitivity of the price of the bond with respect to changes in the YTM.

It indicates that if YTM increases/decreases by 1% the price of the bond wound decrease/increase approximately by 4.048%

There is inverse relationship between price and YTM. If YTM increases price declines and vice-versa.

Higher the duration of the bond, more sensitive is the price of the bond with respect to changes in the interest rate structure.

(d) We can forecast the change in price of the bond based on modified duration.

Modified duration (MMD) of the bond
= MD/(1 + YTM)
= 4.048/(1 + 0.08) = 3.748

MMD = 4.048/(1 + 0.08) = 3.748

If the YTM increases to 9% from 8% the fall in price of the bond given by modified duration is

Change in price = –MMD × Δ(YTM) × *P*
= –3.748 x 0.01 x 487.84 = ₹18.29

New price of the bond = 487.84 – 18.29 = ₹469.55

(e) The new price of the bond may also be computed as below:

Years	*Cash flow (₹)*	*PV of cash flow (₹)*
1	54	49.54
2	54	45.45
3	54	41.70
4	54	38.25
5	454	295.07
Price of the bond (₹) =		**470.01**
Change in price		**–₹17.83**
% change in price		**-3.65%**

(f) The difference in the price as calculated from the modified duration and cash flow approach is due to the simplified assumption that price of the bond varies linearly with the change in YTM under modified duration approach.

In fact the price change in non-linear. When the change in YTM is small the assumption would be closer to reality.

9. Designing Bond Portfolio

Government of India floats several securities from time to time with varying time to maturities. There are two actively traded bonds in the market: Bond A maturing after 5 years and Bond B maturing after 15 years.

The features of the bonds are as below:

	Bond A	Bond B
Face value	₹1,000.00	₹1,000.00
Coupon	10%	12%
Periodicity of coupon	Annual	Annual
Redemption value	₹1,000.00	₹1,000.00
Time to maturity (years)	5	15

The current yield for 5-year instrument is 8% while for 15-year instrument is 9%.

(a) Find the current price and duration of Bond A
(b) Find the current price and duration of Bond B
(c) An investor has ₹10 lakh to invest. He is looking for average maturity of the 5 years because he cannot assume a risk greater than 5%. Can you devise a portfolio for him to meet his objective of risk?

Solution

(a) Price and duration of Bond A is computed below:

Face value	₹1,000.00	Redemption value	₹1,000.00
Coupon	10.00%	Time to maturity	5 years
Interest payments	₹100.00	YTM	8.00%

Price of the bond and its duration are computed as below:

Years	Cash flow (₹)	PV of cash flow (₹)	$t \times$ PV of C_t
1	100	92.59	92.59
2	100	85.73	171.47
3	100	79.38	238.15
4	100	73.50	294.01
5	1,100	748.64	3,743.21
Price of the bond (₹) =		1,079.85	
Time weighted value of cash flows =			4,539.43
Maclaulay's duration =			4.204 years

Price and duration of the bond is computed below:

Face value	₹1,000.00	Redemption value	₹1,000.00
Coupon	12.00%	Time to maturity	15 years
Interest payments	₹120.00	YTM	9.00%

(b) Price of Bond B and its duration are computed as below:

Years	Cash flow (₹)	PV of cash flow (₹)	$t \times$ PV of C_t
1	120	110.09	110.09
2	120	101.00	202.00
3	120	92.66	277.99
4	120	85.01	340.04
5	120	77.99	389.96
6	120	71.55	429.31
7	120	65.64	459.51
8	120	60.22	481.79
9	120	55.25	497.26
10	120	50.69	506.89
11	120	46.50	511.54
12	120	42.66	511.97
13	120	39.14	508.84
14	120	35.91	502.73
15	1,120	307.48	4,612.24
Price of the bond (₹) =		1,241.82	
Time weighted value of cash flows =			10,342.18
Maclaulay's duration =			8.328 years

(c) Proportion of invested funds in Bond A = X_1

Target duration, $D = 5.00$

The duration of the portfolio consisting of Bond A and Bond B is given by

$$D = X_1D_1 + (1 - X_1)D_2$$

Inserting the value give following:

$$5.000 = X_1 \times 4.204 + (1 - X_1) \times 8.328$$

Solving the above equation would give X_1 = 80.69%

Amount of investment = ₹1,000,000

The portfolio of bond with the duration of 5.00 would therefore be:

	Amount (₹)	Price (₹)	Nos. of bonds
Bond A	806,900	1,079.85	747
Bond B	193,100	1,241.82	155

EXERCISES

Concept Review Questions

1. How do you think the value of the bond would change with (a) increasing face value; (b) increasing coupon rate; (c) increasing the periodicity of coupon; and (d) increasing the term to maturity.
2. With no periodic coupon payment available how do you think the investor gets the desired return in case of deep discount bonds.
3. Differentiate between yield to maturity and yield to call.
4. What do you think are the advantages of convertible bonds?
5. For bonds selling at premium to par value the current yield is less than the coupon rate. What do you think would be the YTM of the bond as compared to current yield and coupon rate? Provide reason/s for you answer.
6. For bonds selling at discount to par value, the current yield is more than the coupon rate. What do you think would be the YTM of the bond as compared to current yield and coupon rate? Provide reason/s for your answer.

7. Term structure of interest rate is flat up to 2 years at 6%. What do you think of the YTMs of the bonds maturing after (a) 6 months; (b) 12 months; and (c) 18 months?
8. What is duration of a bond?

Critical Thinking Questions

1. A firm, Conscious Enterprises (CE) is planning to issue a 10-year bond with a face value of ₹1,000 and a coupon of 10% payable semi-annually and redeemable at par. The coupon rate has been arrived at with the expected yield currently prevailing in the market. What price do you think the bond can be sold as compared to its face value?
2. The Finance Director of Conscious Enterprises feels that the yields would decline in future and, therefore, wants to reserve the right to call the bond at any time after 5 years by issuing a callable bond. Compared to the price of the straight bond what price do you think the callable bond can fetch?
3. A financial wizard opined that bonds with long maturity must always be issued with floating rate rather than fixed coupon. Do you agree with the statement?
4. Term structure of interest rates shows 7%, 7.5%, and 8% returns for investment horizons of 1, 2, and 3 years respectively. A bond of 7.5% coupon payable annually with face value of ₹100, with maturity of 3 years, is selling at par. Do you think the bond is underpriced, correctly priced, or overpriced?

Practical Assignments

1. The bonds issued at around the same point of time must have similar coupon rates to reflect common market expectations. However, it seldom happens because of variations in the terms and conditions of each issue of bonds. Select a block of 3 months and find out the coupon rate of each of the debenture issued during this period. Compare it with the terms of the debenture issue and the features of the bond to arrive at the possible reasons for deviations in the coupon rate.
2. Select 10 different bonds with almost similar maturities and find out their YTMs and the rating assigned by any of the rating agency. Based on the data, what appropriate premium would you assign to the debentures of different ratings of high investment grade, investment grade, and speculative grade.

Numerical Problems

1. Pricing of Bonds

ABC Ltd floated a bond of face value of ₹1,000 on which the interest was payable semi-annually at 16% p.a., which was the yield prevailing in the market then. The bond has 6 years remaining when the principal amount shall be redeemed. If the current interest rate is 12%, at what price would the bond sell in the market? What happens if the market interest rates suddenly change to (a) 14% and (b) 10%?

2. Deciding Initial Price of Bond

ABC Ltd is planning to issue a bond of 5 years maturity with semi-annual payment of coupon of 12%. The face value of the bond is ₹1,000. If market expectation of yield is 14%, at what initial price can ABC Ltd issue the bond?

3. Pricing and YTM of a Zero Coupon Bond

What is the price of a zero coupon bond with the face value of ₹10,000 that provides a yield of 15% over a period of 8 years? What would be the YTM of the bond if it sold for ₹4,000?

4. YTM and Price of Bond

What is the YTM of the bond that pays annual coupon at 8% and has 5 years to maturity if the current price is (a) ₹1,050, (b) ₹1,000, and (c) ₹950.

5. YTM, Price, and Realized Yield of Bond

A bond with face value of ₹1,000 and annual coupon payment of 12% with 6 years remaining for maturity was selling for ₹1,100 immediately after it had paid the coupon. An investor buys the bond. She holds the bond for next 4 years and immediately after receiving the fourth coupon payment sells it for ₹1,075. The investor was able to re-invest the interim coupon payments at 10%. Find the following:

(a) The YTM of the bond when the investor bought the bond
(b) YTM of the bond when the investor sold it
(c) The yield realized by the investor over the holding period.
(d) How does the realized yield compare with the YTM of the bond when the investor purchased it?

6. Finding Duration of Bond

A bond has the face value o ₹ 1,000 and coupon of 12%. The YTM of the bond is 14%. Find out the Maclaulay's duration of the bond if coupon payments are (a) annual, and (b) semi-annual.

7. Sensitivity of Bond Price and Duration

Consider the bond, which pays annual coupon in Problem 6. Assuming that the YTM in the market changes from 14%.

(i) What would be the change in price and new price of the bond if YTM changes to (a) 15%, (b) 13%, (c) 14.1%, and (d) 13.9% as computed from duration of the bond?
(ii) What is the actual price of the bond as computed by discounted cash flow approach?
(iii) What is the reason for the variation?

8. Term Structure and Implied Forward Rates

Following is the term structure of interest rates as reflected from the yields of bond maturing after 1, 2, and 3 years:

Zero-coupon bond maturing after 1 year	10.50%
Zero-coupon bond maturing after 2 years	11.00%
Zero-coupon bond maturing after 3 years	11.50%

Find the following

(i) Expected interest rate after one year for one year investing.
(ii) Expected interest rate after one year for investing for two years.
(iii) Expected interest rate after two years for one year investing.

9. Taking Advantage of Yield Curve

Following are the yields of the zero-coupon Bonds A and B respectively maturing after 1 and 2 years:

Zero-coupon Bond A maturing after 1 year	10.50%
Zero-coupon Bond B maturing after 2 years	11.00%

An investor is happy to note the rising trend of interest rates but he believes that this trend would not last for another year. He would like to cash-in on the opportunity available. What can he do now to assure himself that the improved yields are available to him? How much that yield would be?

10. Immunization with Duration Matching

Two bonds, A and B with identical face value of ₹1,000 and coupon rate of 12% payable annually are trading at YTM of 14%. Bond A has 5 years to maturity while bond B is maturing after 4 years. Both are redeemable at par.

An investor has ₹1 lakh to invest but needs the investment back after 4 years. He faces two alternatives—(1) to invest in Bond A and sell it after 4 years when he needs the money back; and (2) to invest in Bond B that matures after 4 years. He feels that investing in Bond A is riskier because he does not know the price at which he would be able to sell the bond, whereas for Bond B such question does not arise.

Examine the view of the investor by answering the following:

(i) Calculate the price and duration of Bond A
(ii) Calculate the price and duration of Bond B
(iii) Which of the bonds is more sensitive to the changes in the yield?
(iv) Calculate the ending wealth if ₹1,000 is invested in Bond A and Bond B after 4 years.
(v) What happens to the ending wealth if the yield changes to (a) 13% and (b) 15%?
(vi) Between investing in Bond A and Bond B which of the strategy is better from the viewpoint of risk in the terminal wealth?

11. Portfolio Immunization

Consider Bond A and Bond B in Problem 10. What could be an investor's strategy if he now changes his mind and wishes to invest for 3.5 years rather than 4 years and yet maintain immunization?

CASE STUDY

Nature Care India Ltd*

Background

Incorporated in 1974, Nature Care India Ltd is a nature-based solutions company. The products manufactured by Nature Care India Ltd are broadly categorized into health care, personal care, and foods. The company has a far-reaching penetration into urban as well as rural India. Besides this it has global distribution networks spread across Central, North and South America, Australia, Asia, Middle East, North and South Africa, and East and West Europe.

From a strategic perspective, 2005-06 can be considered a positive inflexion point in Nature Care's long-term growth path. Having delivered good results in the last four years, even when the industry was undergoing adverse demand conditions, the company has spelt out its intent of entering a new growth trajectory. The new four-year plan aims at continuing the growth momentum across businesses so as to outperform the sector as a whole. Business strategies have been developed in consonance with the growth objectives, focusing on three key elements—expansion, innovation, and acquisition.

In view of this emerging growth potential across the various segments of its products the Board of Directors of Nature Care have decided to invest 150 crore in its different product segments during in the next two years. The investments will be made primarily to spruce up its R&D, supply chain, and IT infrastructure. The low debt–equity ratio is evident from Table A. The extremely comfortable position in terms of coverage of its interest reflected in the excerpts of its income statement in Table B have been the key factors that have convinced the company management to raise the funds through public issue of non-convertible debentures (NCD).

Table A Own funds to borrowed funds

	Mar 2005 (₹ crore)	*Mar 2006 (₹ crore)*
Net worth	338.07	447.87
Reserves & surplus	309.43	390.54
Total borrowings	48.63	20.57
Secured borrowings	15.70	19.23
Unsecured borrowings	32.93	1.34
Current portion of long-term debt	8.06	

Table B Excerpts of income statement

Profits/losses	*Mar 2005*	*Mar 2006*
PBDIT	186.72	239.85
Financial charges (incl. Lease rent)	4.65	5.73
PBDT	182.07	234.12
Depreciation	17.10	19.05
PBT	164.97	215.07
Tax provision	17.00	25.78
PAT	147.97	189.29
Appropriation of profits		
Dividends	81.37	114.39
Retained earnings	66.6	74.90

On 15 January 2007, the company management announced the public issue of debt to fund their capacity enhancement initiative. The debt offering was given AAA credit rating by CRISIL. The details of the financing plans of the firm are as follows:

Issue 1,50,00,000 non-convertible debentures with fixed interest rates. The issue price of debentures is ₹100, maturity is 9 years, and

*The case study is based on a real Indian company. However, the company's name and the facts stated in the case have been changed and adapted according to the requirements of the chapter.

the rate of interest offered is 10.2%. The debentures have a call option at par after 5 years. During January 2007, the following debt issues were made (Table C):

Table C Debt Issues

Name of the issuer	*Rate*	*Maturity (Years)*	*Rating by the rating agency*	*Amount (₹ crore)*	*Type of instrument*
LIC Housing Finance	9.10	10	AAA	265	Bonds
Punjab State Industrial Development Corpn.	9.32	10	n.a.	30	Bonds
Rural Electrification Corpn. Ltd	8.85	10	AAA	500	Bonds
Sundaram Finance Ltd	9.60	5	AA+	100	NCD
Yes Bank Ltd	9.60	15	A+	75	Bonds
Bank of Rajasthan	9.50	10	A	100	NCD

Key market ratios (%) as on 31 January 2007 were as follows:

Type of Debt Securities	*Rate of Interest*
Government Securities	
10 year	7.62
11 year	7.79
15 year	8.07
PSU Bonds (AAA)—5 years	8.79
Treasury Bill	
91 days	6.98
182 days	7.32
364 days	7.39
Bank Rate	6.00
Commercial Paper (PR+1)—90 days	9.40

A research report titled 'FMCG sector in India: Current Status and Future Outlook' released in the December 2006 read as follows:

Although the growth rate of FMCG sector came down to 11.3% in 2006-07 from 13.5% in 2005-06, India's fast moving consumer goods (FMCG) sector still remains the fourth largest sector in the economy with a total market size in excess of US$13.1 billion. Set to treble from US$11.6 billion in 2003 to US$33.4 billion in 2015, the top 15 FMCG companies clocked sales and profit growth of 23% and 12% respectively for the quarter ended September 2006, compared with the corresponding period for the previous year.

The FMCG sector is set on a rapid growth trajectory with the sector projected to grow by over 60% by 2010. This will translate into an annual growth of 10% over a 5-year period.

Hair care, household care, male grooming, female hygiene, chocolates, and confectioneries are estimated to be the fastest growing segments, says the report. The report estimates that the total size of the FMCG sector will rise from around ₹56,500 crore in 2005 to ₹92,100 crore in 2010.

While the current year is expected to be excellent for rural income growth and increase of rural buying power, urban demand will be the key growth driver over the long-term, says the report. Long-term urban penetration-led growth categories will outperform other categories and urban spend on new category growth will outpace rural spend. This, the report, says will occur due to rising urban incomes, increasing urban population and launch of more affordable products as well as the availability of new categories in urban areas.

Discuss

1. What is the intrinsic value of the bond?
2. What is the yield to maturity that the investor gets from these debentures?
3. If the company calls the debentures at a premium of 10% of the face value at the end of 5th year and the investor decides to put the debentures, how much would be the yield to call for the investors?
4. Comparing the debt offering of Nature Care with the other similar debt issues during the month. Do you think that investing in the debt issue of Nature Care is more rewarding for the investors?

You can assume a 12% discount rate for the purpose of all your computations.

In the CD

Finding Value of the Bond   Finding YTM of the Bond   Finding Duration of the Bond

CHAPTER

7 Shares and Their Valuation

LEARNING OBJECTIVES

The chapter is aimed at

- explaining the features of equity
- determining the value of equity shsres
- providing insights to the Dividend Discount Model (DDM) and its variants
- explaining the impact of growh on the value of equity shares
- establishing the relationship between returns expected by shareholders and growth estimate
- explaining the meaning of P/E multiple and how it can be used in valuation of equity
- presenting the efficient market hypothesis and explaining the various forms of market efficiency
- explaining the implications of efficient market hypothesis on the fundamental valuation, technical analysis, and for portfolio management

MOOL BHOOT, NAKSH LAL, AND GYAN PRAKASH

Mool Bhoot and Naksh Lal are regular wagers on cricket matches. However, both of them hardly ever shared their logic with one another on what and why they bet. They always kept their cards close to their chest like all professional betters. On the evening of 26 May the bets were on a cricket match between India and England.

Watching Sachin Tendulkar batting on 25, Mool Bhoot disclosed to Naksh Lal, 'I have just betted on Tendulkar scoring his 36th century in today's match against England. The odds were 2.2 and I found it too attractive.'

Naksh Lal surprised by the odds offered reacted, 'I feel 2.2 is very attractive. How could bookies offer such high stakes? We have been betting for long. But I have yet to figure out how the bookies work out their odds.'

Mool Bhoot casually stated, 'It is a kind of a rating or valuation of a player's ability to achieve a certain target. If odds are too high it simply means that the likelihood of achieving the landmark is low and vice versa. Bookies feel that the odds of 2.2 are just appropriate for Tendulkar to score a century while he is not out on 25.'

Naksh Lal sounded unconvinced said, 'But there must be some calculation behind the odds being offered. I wonder what all they consider?'

Although not knowing much, Mool Bhoot pretending to be an expert explained, 'They consider many things. It is complex because everything is dependent on the perception. There is hardly any rationale, concrete evidence, or data available for the calculation of odds. All the bookies consider aspects like technique, skill, footwork, ability to adopt, past record, etc.'

Disagreeing with the explanation Naksh Lal countered, 'If that is the case why the odds change with time. How do you relate performance with the odds? When we agree then only we bet.'

Mool Bhoot clarified, 'Wrong, when you disagree with the odds then only you place a bet. For example, I have placed a bet with odds of 2.2 for Tendulkar scoring a century. If for the odds of 2.2, you bet on him it implies that you disagree with the odds. 2.2 is too attractive for me. Probably I would not bet if the odds were say 1.5.'

Naksh Lal asked another question, 'But this was not with one bookie. Other bookies offered much lower stakes. Why all bookies do not offer same stakes?'

Confidently Mool Bhoot responded as if he was preaching, 'It is a tricky business and the collective result of all the bookies. The odds offered by each bookie differ slightly but not substantially. Slowly each bookie modifies the odds and theoretically the odds must converge to a single figure.'

Naksh Lal was quick to ask another question, 'I can understand different bookies having different perceptions about Tendulkar scoring a century. But why do they keep changing with time?'

Mool Bhoot who found an interesting learner in Naksh Lal surmised, 'Again there are many reasons. As time passes and Tendulkar gets closer to the target, the odds would fall. Another reason is demand and supply. If too many people start betting on Tendulkar scoring a century in the match, the bookies realize that most people think this would happen and accordingly they would lower the odds.'

Attempting to understand more and more Naksh Lal seeing an expert in Mool Bhoot asked, 'By the way, when you place a bet what do you consider?'

Hesitantly Mool Bhoot disclosed, 'I bet on fundamental attributes of the player like his ability to play against all bowlers, under varying weather conditions; range of strokes; his footwork; ability to improvise; etc.'

Naksh Lal differing from him disclosed his considerations, 'That is not my way. I rely more on patterns and past record. The law of averages has to catch up with everybody. One cannot remain consistent in a game like cricket forever. Tendulkar is bound to fail now because he has been simply too consistent in the past. I believe that at the top level almost all players have same skills and it is only a matter of time and form. Skills don't count as much as the patterns of past scores. All players play in patches. You can almost predict when one player would go out of form and come in the form.'

Strongly opposing the views Mool Bhoot emphasized, 'I do not believe in such philosophy. If everybody had same or similar set of skills of batting all batsmen would have been equally great players. In such a case the odds offered for Tendulkar and Mohammed Kaif scoring centuries would have been alike.'

Nodding his head Naksh Lal said, 'I can agree with you somewhat that there is a difference in the skill set of different batsmen. Besides skills, bookies necessarily have to consider the statistics of the players and immediate past record and patterns of scoring while deciding the odds. To my mind that plays a major role.'

Mool Bhoot wondered and diverted the focus and stated, 'There is a comparative relationship in the odds. If Mohammed Kaif is half as skilled as Tendulkar his odds would more likely be double that of Tendulkar.'

Gyan Prakash, who was listening to both of them could not resist speaking and came out with the final word, 'Well there is no debate on this. Everything is important—the skills, patterns of scoring, comparison, etc. I wonder if anyone can beat the bookies simply by following only one set of factors. Let Mool Bhoot concentrate on fundamentals, while Naksh Lal can keep his focus on patterns of scoring. Though I do not bet on cricket but I do invest in stocks and use all these techniques.'

By then, Tendulkar had moved from 25 to 76 not out and all three concentrated on the match and more specifically on whether he would score the century.

INTRODUCTION

In the previous chapter, we discussed features of bonds and their valuation. We have another financial instrument known as share. Also referred to as common stock or equity, it is traded in the capital markets. Unlike bonds, shares are instruments that do not assure a fixed return.

Equity is fundamentally different from debt. Debt is commonly issued by security known as bond/debenture. Financial markets deal with the transfer of these securities from one person to another. The price at which such transfer takes place is determined by market forces.

Before we discuss the valuation of equity shares let us devote some attention to the features of equity that will help understand its valuation too.

FEATURES OF EQUITY

The best way to explain equity is to imagine that you want to start the manufacture of special adhesives that needs about ₹1 crore of capital investment. Unfortunately you have no money of your own. You go around convincing many friends to contribute the funding towards the project. Some 100 friends get convinced about the business potential and contribute ₹1 lakh each on your assurance that the income derived from the business would be shared in proportion to the capital contribution made. Each of your friends is now entitled to get 1% share of the profit earned and is called a shareholder.

Equity shares are characterized by (a) ownership and management (b) entitlement to residual cash flows (c) limited liability (d) infinite life and (e) substantially different risk profile.

The above illustration described a share but did not elaborate on all the features that equity shares carry. We discuss them now further in this section.

Ownership and management The most important feature of the equity share is the ownership. This ownership entitles shareholders to manage the business. Usually the ownership is in proportion of the capital contributed. Holding 51% of the entire capital entitles one to the absolute ownership, though the firm can be managed by smaller holding too.

Residual claim The second most important feature of equity is the nature of claim on the cash flows of the firm. While doing business several kinds of cash flows take place. Sales are made and monies realized. The business, therefore, creates claims on others, called assets. Similarly while doing business several others connected with the business enterprise create claims on its cash flows. These are the liabilities created by the business in the usual course. These liabilities include suppliers of materials, salaries for workers, managers, interest to debt holders, dues to government, etc. The owners of the business enterprise first have to satisfy the claims of others and then only share the residual among them.

Limited liability The residual cash flows or the profit that the shareholders derive is extremely uncertain. While having a claim on the residual, it is possible that they are not left with anything at all because liabilities for others may exceed the assets. In fact, if a business has more claims of others than the assets it has, the shareholders may have to make the shortfall good to satisfy the claim of other stakeholders.

To what extent can they lose? The maximum that the owners can lose is to the extent of capital contributed. Hence, the shareholders have limited liability to the extent of their holding in the business. This is not true for all forms of businesses. The extent of liability is dependent upon the constitution of business.

Infinite life The capital contributed by individuals cannot be withdrawn from the business in the normal circumstances. A business is deemed to continue forever while those who promote the business are mortal. Business has its own identity that is separated from the individuals who promote and manage it. Unlike debt that is repayable, the capital contributed as shares in business continues forever unless the whole business is liquidated. For the purpose of valuation we would assume infinite life of the share.

Listing and trading on stock exchanges As stated earlier, the share capital once made cannot be withdrawn. This poses a serious problem if one wants to exit the business. Business is a whole entity that possibly cannot be divided in parts. Therefore, the only alternative that allows continuity of operations and yet provides an exit route to the individual investor is to provide a market for exchange of shares. A stock exchange facilitates the replacement of the exiting investor with the investor wanting an entry into the business. Such markets list these shares for trading amongst those investing and disinvesting. The price for exchange of share is determined between the individuals by their mutual consent.

Risk The entitlement only to the residual claim implies that the earnings on the capital invested are uncertain. There is no promised rate that the business is required to pay to the investor in shares. The uncertainty attached with the return on the share makes the financial asset substantially different from the bonds. The uncertainty of returns on the investment in shares is called risk.

ISSUES IN VALUATION OF EQUITY

While valuation of bonds is rather easy, the valuation of shares on similar lines presents its own difficulties. The cash flows of the bonds are known in its quantum as well as timings. Equity, being owner of the residual, has cash flows that are neither fixed in magnitude nor in its timings. The uncertainty of magnitude and timing of the cash flows attributed to equity makes valuation of equity extremely difficult.

Infinite life, uncertain return and substantially different risk profile makes valuation of equity difficult.

The second critical difference in the valuation of shares emanates from the time frame. The cash flows attached to the equity shares are everlasting rather than for a predetermined time frame as was the case with bonds. Listing and trading on the exchanges provide an exit route to investors. One investor gets replaced by another. The value at which such replacement takes place is the key issue in share valuation.

Lastly, in valuation of equity share one does not know the discount rate that is appropriate. Even if the cash flows are assumed the expectations of the shareholders is anybody's guess. The expectations of reward varies a great deal because of two reasons—(1) the shareholders assume responsibility of managing the business that has its own hazards; and (2) being a claimant of the residual the uncertainty is large as to how much would be left for them.

METHODS OF VALUATION

There are two approaches to equity valuation. One approach is holistic that attempts to estimate the cash flow and value them according to the risk associated with them. Such an approach is called discounted cash flow valuation.

The second approach to valuation rests on the premise that similar assets must sell for similar values. The approach is called comparative or relative valuation. The market prices of similar assets are compared with each other. Then the target asset is valued based on the similarities and dissimilarities of its attributes with the assets whose price is already known. Apparently it is extremely easy to apply but dissimilarities in the assets and the adjustments required to account for these dissimilarities is a challenging area and not free from controversies. It is hard to find two financial assets that are exactly alike. Accounting for dissimilarities lends subjectivity to valuation. Further, such an approach is dependent upon the efficiency of the capital markets, which determines the reliance on relative valuation.

Value of an equity share can be found by estimating its intrinsic worth by discounting its cash flows or in relation to the market price of comparable assets.

The first approach is to find the intrinsic value of the asset while the second approach values any asset relative to another and focuses on market value.

DIVIDEND DISCOUNT MODELS

Dividend discount model for valuation of equity is an extended application of the concept of time value of money. According to time value of money, the cash available today is more valuable than the cash tomorrow. This measurement of difference in the value of cash available at different points of time depends upon many intricate aspects. All the complex factors affecting the value of cash are quite simply captured in a single figure called discount rate denoted as r and is the required rate of return for the investor. Clearly this required rate of return for equity is different from what is used for valuing cash flows of other financial instruments because of the features of equity discussed.

Two important inputs for valuation of equity share are (1) the cash flows attached to the equity and (2) the discount rate that is appropriate for finding present value of the cash flows.

As compared to bonds, equity valuation is difficult because cash flows of equity last for indefinite period of time, unlike bond whose cash flows end with the redemption. Debt has a definite life, but equity lasts forever. The second constraint emanates from the uncertainty of the cash flows attached with the equity. Unlike debt where cash flows are determined in advance and are promised by the issuer, equity does not carry any such undertaking by the issuer though each subscriber to the equity has certain expectations. The cash flows attached with the equity are dividends that are distributed out of the profits the firm earns.

Assuming that the investor holds on to the asset for one period (a year for convenience) we assume that the current price of equity share, P_0 is equal to the dividend expected during the holding period, D_1 and the price of the asset at the end of the holding period P_1. Expressed mathematically the price P_0 is given by Equation 7-1.

$$P_0 = \frac{D_1}{(1+r)} + \frac{P_1}{(1+r)} \tag{7-1}$$

Here the current price is a function of—(1) the dividend expected in next period; (2) the expected price of the share at the end of the period; and (3) the return expected by the investor, all of which must be projected. One would realize that Equation 7-1 is more of a justification for the current price rather than its determination.

Example 7-1 Current Share Price

The equity owners of a firm ABC Ltd need a return of 12%. The current performance of the firm leads to a belief that a dividend of ₹5 would be paid and after a year the price of the share would be ₹20.

(a) If the current price of the share is ₹22, do you think the share is worth buying?

(b) How do you justify that the positive return would be generated despite the price falling to ₹20 after a year?

(c) What maximum price do you think that the investor should pay today for a share of ABC Ltd?

Solution

The current price of the share using Equation 7-1 that would provide a return of 12% is ₹22.32.

$$P_0 = \frac{D_1}{(1+r)} + \frac{P_1}{(1+r)} = \frac{5}{1+0.12} + \frac{20}{1+0.12} = 4.46 + 17.86$$
$$= ₹22.32$$

(a) The current price of the share is ₹22 and buying at this price would provide a return in excess of desired rate of 12%. Hence the share is worth buying.

(b) Despite falling price, the returns are in excess of 12% due to cash flows of dividend of ₹5. This more than compensates the loss in value.

(c) The maximum price that can be paid for the share is ₹22.32. Any price above ₹22.32 would result in lesser than required return of 12%.

Equation 7-1 may be re-arranged to express the return in the form of dividend yield and capital gains. Dividend yield is the return provided by dividend due to ownership of share, while capital gain results with assumed disowning of the asset. Over the investment of P_0 the investor would have the dividend of D_1 and the capital gain of $P_1 - P_0$. Equation 7-2 gives the return r.

$$\text{Return, } r = \frac{D_1}{P_0} + \frac{P_1 - P_0}{P_0}$$
$$= \text{Dividend Yield} + \text{Capital Gain} \tag{7-2}$$

Example 7-2 Required Rate of Return

The share of Reliance Industries Limited is currently trading at ₹700. Financial analysts have projected a price of the share at ₹800 at the end of the year during which a dividend of ₹25 is also expected. What rate of return is implied by the market for Reliance shares?

Solution

Using Equation 7-2 the return is expected to be

$$\text{Return, } r = \frac{D_1}{P_0} + \frac{P_1 - P_0}{P_0} = \frac{25}{700} + \frac{800-700}{700} = 0.0357 + 0.1428$$
$$= 0.1785 = 17.85\%$$

The return consists of 3.57% of dividend yield and 14.28% of capital gains.

Sometimes it is easier to project the growth in the share price rather than its absolute estimate. Given the growth in share price g Equations 7-1 and 7-2 may be modified to incorporate the growth.

$$P_0 = \frac{D_1}{(1+r)} + \frac{P_1}{(1+r)} = \frac{D_1}{(1+r)} + \frac{(1+g)P_0}{(1+r)}$$

By rearranging, we get,

$$P_0 = \frac{D_1}{(r-g)} \tag{7-3}$$

$$\text{and } r = \frac{D_1}{P_0} + g \tag{7-4}$$

Example 7-3 Share Price and Growth

The earnings of Indian Jet Airlines have been growing at 10% for the last 3 years and the same growth is expected to continue in future. The dividends and the share price too have been consistent with the growth in earnings. Last year the firm paid a dividend of ₹10. If investors' expectation from the firm is a return of 20% what do you think is the worth of the share of Indian Jet Airlines?

Solution

The last year's dividend is ₹10. The expected dividend for next year D_1 if assumed to grow at 10% would be ₹11 (10 × 1.10).

The worth of the share today as given by Equation 7-3 is

$$P_0 = \frac{D_1}{(r+g)} = \frac{10 \times 1.10}{(0.20-0.10)} = ₹110.00$$

To calculate the price of the share if the holding period extends beyond one, Equation 7-1 may be reproduced for the price at the end of Period 1. Just as the current price P_0 is given by dividend and price of Period 1, the price at the beginning of Period 1, P_1 depends upon dividend in Period 2 and price at the end of Period 2. Mathematically this can be expressed as:

According to Dividend Discount Model (DDM) the current price of the equity share is equal to the present value of the infinite stream of dividend expected.

$$P_1 = \frac{D_2}{(1+r)} + \frac{P_2}{(1+r)}$$

Substituting the value of P_1 in Equation 7-1 we get,

$$P_0 = \frac{D_1}{(1+r)} + \frac{\frac{D_2}{(1+r)} + \frac{P_2}{(1+r)}}{(1+r)}$$

$$= \frac{D_1}{(1+r)} + \frac{D_2}{(1+r)^2} + \frac{P_2}{(1+r)^2}$$

Similarly the price at the end of Period 2, P_2 can be expressed as:

$$P_2 = \frac{D_3}{(1+r)} + \frac{P_3}{(1+r)}$$

Again substituting the value of P_2 and continuing in this fashion for indefinite period of time, the dividend discount model for equity share price is as given in Equation 7-5

$$P_0 = \frac{D_1}{(1+r)} + \frac{D_2}{(1+r)^2} + \frac{D_3}{(1+r)^3} + \dots + \frac{D_n}{(1+r)^n} \quad (7\text{-}5)$$

Alternatively, for indefinite period of time this may be abbreviated as:

$$P_0 = \sum_{1}^{\infty} \frac{D_n}{(1+r)^n} \quad (7\text{-}6)$$

The dividend discount model is a manifestation of the discounted cash flow approach. It conforms to the idea that the value of any asset is equal to the discounted cash flows attached to it. The owners of equity shares are entitled to the reward of dividend for as long as they want to hold on to the investment, and the price paid by the investor would be equal to the discounted value of the dividends on the share. To value the current price of the equity shares we need to estimate the dividend that would be distributed over infinite period of time; indeed an impossible task. The valuation of equity as given by Equation 7-6 is known as the dividend discount model (DDM).

Throughout the discussion on equations of dividend discount model for valuing equity shares, we had made an implicit assumption that all the earnings of the firm are distributed as dividend to the shareholders. We now discuss few variants of dividend discount models.

DDM with Constant Dividend—No Growth

We stated earlier that the application of dividend discount model (Equation 7-6) to value equity needs projection of dividend for infinite periods—a requirement difficult to fulfil. Normally shareholders would see business grow and, therefore, the dividends grow with time. We make an extremely simplifying assumption of constant amount of dividend in each period, i.e., dividends are constant in each period and do not vary or grow with time. With the given assumption, Equation 7-5 can be rewritten as Equation 7-7.

If dividend for all times to come is assumed constant, then the current price of the share is simply the current dividend divided by the capitalization rate.

$$P_0 = \frac{D}{(1+r)} + \frac{D}{(1+r)^2} + \frac{D}{(1+r)^3} + \dots + \frac{D}{(1+r)^\infty} \quad (7\text{-}7)$$

This is further simplified[1] as:

$$P_0 = \frac{D}{r} \quad (7\text{-}8)$$

The simplest of valuation model as given by Equation 7-8 states that the value of equity is given by the expected dividend divided by the expected discount rate. For example, if the expected dividend on a share is ₹5.00 and the expectation of returns on the investor is 10%, then the expected price would be ₹50 (5/0.10). Stated differently, if one buys the stock for ₹50, he/she would receive a return of ₹5 that is 10% on the investment made.

Notice that the dividend discount model incorporates only dividend in the valuation of equity and leads to a belief that it ignores the capital appreciation on the prices. It is a misconception because the formulation has been done for infinite life and it merely replaces the future price in terms of dividend. The price of the equity at any point of time shall be driven by the dividends subsequent to investment, i.e., the expected dividend. The past dividends are immaterial to the price. For easier visualization, consider an example for an investor who

[1]The simplification is rather easy and as follows:

$$P_0 = \frac{D}{(1+r)} + \frac{D}{(1+r)^2} + \frac{D}{(1+r)^3} + \frac{D}{(1+r)^4} \dots + \frac{D}{(1+r)^\infty} \quad (a)$$

Multiplyiing the above Equation (a) by $(1 + r)$, we get

$$(1+r)P_0 = D + \frac{D}{(1+r)} + \frac{D}{(1+r)^2} + \frac{D}{(1+r)^3} + \frac{D}{(1+r)^4} + \frac{D}{(1+r)^5} \dots + \frac{D}{(1+r)^\infty} \quad (b)$$

Subtractiung (a) from (b) and rearranging, we get

$$P_0 = \frac{D}{r}$$

decides to sell the equity after holding for 4 periods when the price of the share is P_4. The price P_0 then can be stated as:

$$P_0 = \frac{D}{(1+r)} + \frac{D}{(1+r)^2} + \frac{D}{(1+r)^3} + \frac{D}{(1+r)^4} + \frac{P_4}{(1+r)^4} \quad \text{7-8(a)}$$

Here again the price P_4 can be said to be equal to the dividends accruing from period 5 onwards and expressed as:

$$P_4 = \frac{D}{(1+r)} + \frac{D}{(1+r)^2} + \frac{D}{(1+r)^3} + \frac{D}{(1+r)^4} + \frac{D}{(1+r)^5} \cdots \frac{D}{(1+r)^\infty} \quad \text{7-8(b)}$$

Replacing the value of P_4 in Equation 7-8 (a) would lead to what is stated in Equation 7-7.

DDM with Constant Growth

It is difficult to assume that the dividend of the firm would remain constant. If that were the case then equity would be no different than bonds. Investors choose to invest in equity because of the growth anticipated in the earnings and the dividends.

Recognizing the growth and again making a simplifying assumption that dividend grow at a continuous rate of g, Equation 7-5 can be restated as:

$$P_0 = \frac{D}{(1+r)} + \frac{D(1+g)}{(1+r)^2} + \frac{D(1+g)^2}{(1+r)^3} + \frac{D(1+g)^3}{(1+r)^4} + \frac{D(1+g)^4}{(1+r)^5} \cdots \frac{D(1+g)^\infty}{(1+r)^\infty} \quad (7\text{-}9)$$

Here dividend in next period is D. For convenience, we may denote it by D_1, the dividend in Period 1. The dividend in subsequent Period 2 is $D_1 \times (1 + g)$, and in period thereafter is $D_1 \times (1 + g) \times (1 + g) = D_1(1 + g)^2$, and so on. Upon simplification[2] Equation 7-9 reduces to:

$$P_0 = \frac{D_1}{(r - g)} \quad (7\text{-}10)$$

which is same as Equation 7-3, and the expected rate of return would be:

$$r = \frac{D_1}{P_0} + g \quad (7\text{-}11)$$

[2]The simplification is same as for Equation 7-4 and as follows:

$$P_0 = \frac{D}{(1+r)} + \frac{D(1+g)}{(1+r)^2} + \frac{D(1+g)^2}{(1+r)^3} + \frac{D(1+g)^3}{(1+r)^4} + \frac{D(1+g)^4}{(1+r)^5} \cdots + \frac{D(1+g)^\infty}{(1+r)^\infty} \quad \text{(a)}$$

Multiplying the above equation by $(1 + r)/(1 + g)$, we get:

$$[(1 + r)/(1 + g)]P_0 = \frac{D}{(1+g)} + \frac{D}{(1+r)} + \frac{D(1+g)}{(1+r)^2} + \frac{D(1+g)^2}{(1+r)^3} + \cdots + \frac{D(1+g)^\infty}{(1+r)^\infty} \quad \text{(b)}$$

Subtracting (a) from (b) and rearranging, we get:

$$\frac{(1+r)}{(1+g)} P_0 - P_0 = \frac{D}{(1+g)},$$

$$\text{or } P_0 = \frac{D}{(r-g)}$$

The value of equity share is dependent upon the expected dividend, the growth expected in dividend and the shareholders expectations of return.

Valuation model as per Equation 7-11 states that the expected returns are given by the dividend yield and growth expected. For example, if the dividend expected in the next period is ₹2 and is expected to grow at 10% while the stock trades at ₹50 then the expected return is 14% (4% dividend yield + 10% growth).

Implications of DDM

We now discuss some of the implications of Gordon's dividend discount model.

Expectations cannot be less than growth Constant dividend growth model, known as Gordon model, is the same as discounted cash flow approach. This applies only when $g < r$. In other words, the expected return must exceed the growth. This is reasonable since it is difficult to imagine a scenario where expectations of return are 10% while the firm itself offers a growth of 12%. It would be foolish for investors to accept such position. The minimum what the investors expect must be somewhat higher than the potential growth of the firm else the capital markets would be extremely inefficient. The firm must strive to fulfil this extra expectation at all times.

Current price rises with reduced expected return The model implies that the share price would rise with increased dividend, increased growth, and reduced expectation of return by the investor. While the first two factors are comprehendible, the last one may need some explanation. If investors' expectations of return become lower, the only way this can be achieved is by showing an increase in the current price since we assume that the future price is same as before. Only an increase in current price will bring down the returns in line with the expectations.

The price grows as much as dividend The model also implies that the price of the stock grows at the same rate of growth as for dividends. Let us consider an example. Assume that a firm is expected to pay a dividend of ₹20 in the next period. With the expected return of 20% and assumed growth of 15%, the stock price would be ₹400 as shown using Equation 7-10.

The increase in price is same as the growth rate in dividend.

$$P_0 = \frac{D_1}{(r-g)} = \frac{20}{(0.20 - 0.15)} = ₹400$$

The price of ₹400 must grow by 15% to ₹460 at the end of the period. This is confirmed by using Equation 7-3.

$$P_1 = \frac{D_2}{r-g} = \frac{D_1(1+g)}{(r-g)} = \frac{20(1.15)}{(0.20 - 0.15)} = ₹460$$

Different growth estimates cause price volatility To some extent the model provides an explanation for the divergent opinions of financial analysts regarding valuation of the same share. While there could be unanimity over the expected dividend and the expected return, the parameter of growth is an estimate on which substantial differences may arise amongst analysts. For example, an analyst may value a stock at ₹400 based on expected dividend of ₹20, expected return of 20%, and growth of 15%. However, another analyst disagreeing with the first one may estimate the growth at 18% and value the same stock at ₹1,000, i.e., 2.5 times the earlier valuation. Since the sensitivity of the value with respect to estimated growth is very high, any small revision in the growth potential explains the wild movements in the stock price.

Stock that pays no dividend too has value According to dividend discount models the price of non-dividend paying stock must be zero. In fact, all stock, irrespective of whether the dividend is paid or not, have some market value. One plausible explanation for non-zero price of share that does not pay dividend is the assumption that it is the expectation of dividend that drives the price and investors would be correct in assuming that at some point of time the earnings accruing to them would ultimately be distributed to them.

Dividend and Growth

Under the constant dividend growth model of equity valuation, we assumed a constant growth in dividend without bothering about the source of dividend growth. Another convenient assumption was the distribution of all the earnings in the form of dividend. The two assumptions seem to be inconsistent. To propel growth a firm needs funds, which it must get by retaining a part of the earnings and deploying them into assets that provide growth in earnings.

To fund growth, the firm must necessarily curtail dividend. Would a cut in dividend result in decline in the price of the share? A mere look at the dividend discount model would lead to an inference that it would. However, it is not necessarily so. Intuition tells us that the impact on share price would depend on the successful deployment of retained earnings by the firm.

Let us consider an example to illustrate this viewpoint. Assuming a firm called Flat Products presently earns ₹20 per share, which it distributes entirely to its shareholders, implying that the growth rate of dividend is zero. Further assume that the required rate of returns by the shareholders is 20% and, therefore, the price of the share is ₹100, as constant flow of ₹20 as dividend each year provides a 20% return. Also, the dividend discount model provides the value of the share at ₹100 using Equation 7-4 with $g = 0$.

Now let us consider that Flat Products has some business opportunities available for providing growth to the earnings and hence add to the shareholders' wealth. Consider three options called A, B and C. Option A is an opportunity to make product called Square that provides a return of 25%. Option B is an expansion project for the existing Flat product and would give 20% return. Option C is to produce low technology product called Round that would generate a return of 15%. For simplicity of understanding, we assume that all the projects are scaleable, mutually exclusive, and would only be funded through equity. The alternative available to fund any of the projects is to reduce dividend pay out to 50%. This means the dividend would be curtailed from existing ₹20 per share to ₹10 per share.

The retained part of the dividend would be used to fund the selected projects and provide growth in future dividends. That must enhance the price. On the other hand, reduction in dividend would act negatively on the share price. The overall impact on the share price would depend upon whether dividend growth has been able to compensate the fall in price due to cut in the dividend. Under the three different projects, the growth provided depends upon—(1) how much earnings have been retained, denoted by b; and (2) the return on equity offered by the project, ROE. For the three projects the dividend growth provided is:

Value of the share is closely linked to the growth opportunities available with the firm, the re-investment rate, the shareholders expectations and proportions of earnings retained in business.

For Square $g = b \times \text{ROE} = 0.50 \times 25\% = 12.5\%$
For Flat $g = b \times \text{ROE} = 0.50 \times 20\% = 10.0\%$
For Round $g = b \times \text{ROE} = 0.50 \times 15\% = 7.5\%$

Current status is as follows:

Dividend (₹) ₹20
Expected Return 20%
Return on Equity 20%

$$\text{Current Price, } P_0 = \frac{D}{r} = \frac{20}{0.2} = ₹100$$

We may now calculate the price of the share using Equation 7-10. This is presented in Table 7-1.

Table 7-1 Share price and growth opportunities

Options	*Square*	*Flat*	*Round*
Dividend (₹) Expected Return, *r* Return on Equity (ROE)	10 20% 25%	10 20% 20%	10 20% 15%
Growth Rate, *g* = *b* × ROE	0.5 × 25% = 12.5%	0.5 × 20% = 10.0%	0.5 × 15% = 7.5%
New Share Price $P_0 = \frac{D_1}{(r-g)}$			
New Share Price	$\frac{10}{(0.20-0.125)}$ = ₹133.33	$\frac{10}{(0.20-0.10)}$ = ₹100.00	$\frac{10}{(0.20-0.075)}$ = ₹80.00

The value of the share would rise if the firm accepted the Square project, remain same if the Flat project was selected, and fall if Round project was implemented. The increase in price from ₹100 to ₹133.33 when Square project was implemented was due to the fact that Square offered return in excess of required. The price remained the same in case of Flat because the return offered by the project was exactly equal to expected rate of return, while the price declined in case of Round since the return offered by the project was less than the expected return.

Clearly if the retained earnings by the firm are redeployed at a rate higher than expected any announcement of dividend policy in favour of retention would be greeted positively. For example, if the firm decided to retain 75% instead of 50% to implement Square, the share price would further jump to ₹400 (5/(0.20 – 0.1875).

We may simply think that the share price is the sum of the value of the firm already in place, the value with zero growth and the present value of the growth opportunities.

Value of the share = No growth value + PV of growth opportunities

$$P_0 = E_1/r + \text{PVGO} \tag{7-12}$$

In case of Round, the value of the share would decline since the present value of the project is negative (the project offers only 15% against the expected rate of 20%) that brings down the price. For such a project, any increase in the retention ratio would be viewed negatively. If there are no growth opportunities then the value of the share is earnings, E_1 discounted at r.

DDM—Multi-stage Growth Models

Valuation based on the constant growth of dividend is a greatly simplifying assumption that helps explain some of the complex phenomena of valuation. It also explains to a reasonable extent why the prices change as they do.

However, it seems rather unrealistic that the firm would continue to grow at some extraordinary pace forever. A more reasonable and realistic assumption would be to assume high growth during the initial few years, as opportunities for extraordinary growth are available only for a limited time. Slowly these opportunities dry up and firms start registering a rather normal growth consistent with the rest of the economy.

Utilizing the same approach that the price of the share is equal to the present value of the cash flows, we segregate the cash flows of the firm in two distinct phases—high growth phase lasting for n years and normal growth phase continuing thereafter. The cash flows of the firm can be represented as below:

$$P_0 = \left[\frac{D_1}{1+r} + \frac{D_1(1+g_1)}{(1+r)^2} + \frac{D_1(1+g_1)^2}{(1+r)^3} + \ldots + \frac{D_1(1+g_1)^{n-1}}{(1+r)^n}\right] + \left[\frac{P_n}{(1+r)^n}\right] \tag{7-13}$$

High Growth Phase of n years ⟷ Normal growth

where D_1 represents dividend expected in next Period 1, g_1 represents the high-growth rate lasting for n years, and P_n is the price of the share at the end of high-growth period.

Let us consider an example to illustrate the concept further. ABC Ltd, an IT firm, is having a current level of earnings of ₹10 per share. Due to extremely good prospects and opportunities in this field, the firm is experiencing a high growth phase and, therefore, pays only 25% of its earnings as dividend and retains the balance. ABC Ltd is expected to register a high growth of 20% over the next 5 years. Thereafter the growth in earnings is expected to settle down at 6%—the rate at which the economy is growing. Investors of ABC Ltd expect a return of 15%.

To find the current value of its share we apply the dividend discount approach by projecting the dividend separately for each of the next five years at 20% growth and thereafter applying a constant growth of 6%, using a discount rate of 15%. This is done as below:

Current level of dividend, D_0 = ₹2.50

Dividend expected in the next period,

$$D_1 = (1+g) \times D_0 = 1.20 \times 2.50 = ₹3.00$$

Assuming 20% growth for 5 years, the value of the share can be estimated as:

$$P_0 = \frac{3.00}{(1+.15)} + \frac{3.00(1+0.20)}{(1+0.15)^2} + \frac{3.00\,(1+0.20)^2}{(10.15)^3} + \frac{3.00(1+0.20)^3}{(1+0.15)^4} + \frac{3.00\,(1+0.20)^4}{(1+0.15)^5} + \frac{P_n}{(1+0.15)^n}$$

$$= \frac{3.00}{(1.15)} + \frac{3.00(1.20)}{(1.15)^2} + \frac{3.00(1.20)^2}{(1.15)^3} + \frac{3.00(1.20)^3}{(1.15)^4} + \frac{3.00(1.20)^4}{(1.15)^5} + \frac{P_n}{(1.15)^n}$$

$$= \frac{3.00}{(1.15)} + \frac{3.60}{(1.15)^2} + \frac{4.32}{(1.15)^3} + \frac{5.18}{(1.15)^4} + \frac{6.22}{(1.15)^5} + \frac{P_n}{(1.15)^n}$$

$$= 2.61 + 2.72 + 2.84 + 2.96 + 3.09 + \frac{P_n}{(1.15)^n}$$

This value is equal to the present value all dividend streams for next 5 years growing at 20% and discounted at 15% plus the price of the share expected at the end of Period 5. The price at the end of Period 5, P_5 may be obtained from constant growth model with the assumption of normal growth at 6%. With dividend expected in Period 6 at ₹6.22 (1 + 0.06) the price expected is:

$$P_5 = \frac{D_6}{(r-g)} = \frac{6.22(1+0.06)}{0.15-0.06} = \frac{6.59}{0.09} = ₹73.27$$

This price must be discounted back in today's terms at 15% discount rate, which gives the price of ABC as ₹50.65.

$$P_0 = 2.61 + 2.72 + 2.84 + 2.96 + 3.09 + \frac{P_n}{(1.15)^n}$$

$$= 14.22 + \frac{73.27}{1.15^5} = 14.22 + 36.43 = ₹50.65$$

DDM and Actual Price The dividend discount model and its variants are an attempt to find the true worth of a share. In practice shares may have different values, what is suggested by DDM. The difference in the true value and the actual value is an aberration, which is supposed to get rectified with time. The actual price must converge to the theoretical value. Under the assumption that there are millions of investors the market forces would act in a manner that would stabilize price of the share to the true value. When the actual price is greater than the true value there would be more sellers than buyers. This would cause a downward pressure on the price. Similarly when the actual price is below the true value there would be more buyers than sellers. This would cause the price to move up. This process continues till the share achieves its true value.

RELATIVE VALUATION

So far the discussions centred on finding the intrinsic value of shares. The difficulties associated with the valuation of shares were the uncertainty of the amount of dividend, their timing, and the selection of appropriate discount rate. We were not concerned about the actual market value of the share and instead were focused on finding what the market value should have been.

While DDM based valuation focuses on finding the intrinsic value, relative valuation attempts pricing based on the market value of the comparable assets.

We now turn our attention to a different aspect. Here the attempt is to find a comparison with another asset that closely resembles the asset we are attempting to value. This is known as relative valuation. Under the approach of relative valuation the aspect of cash flows and appropriate rate of discounting them is left to the market. We depend upon the value the market assigns to similar assets, and our task is limited to find an equivalent asset in the market that is already valued. Of course, the accuracy of the value would depend upon how efficient the markets are in their valuation of the equivalent asset.

Whether or not the markets are efficient enough in correctly valuing an asset is a question that can be attempted separately. Even if the markets were inefficient in valuing the equivalent asset we presume that as long as similar inefficiencies persist in the valuation, the valuation done on the basis of the relative valuation too would be close to the market value. Remember that we are not trying to assess the intrinsic worth of an asset.

The basic approach to derive the value of an asset is to price the standardized common variable in terms of multiples of market price. The first common variable that is priced is shareholders' earnings.

Price Earning (P/E) Ratio/Multiple

The price earning based approach is extremely popular among the relative valuation techniques. It is hard to imagine any discussion regarding a firm's pricing of shares in the stock market without drawing a reference to a term called P/E ratio. Much of investors' and analysts' attention alike is focussed on the P/E ratio, which as per definition, is the ratio of price of the share divided by the earnings of the firm. P/E ratio or multiple is calculated as given in Equation 7-14.

$$\text{Price Earning Ratio} = \frac{\text{Market Price}}{\text{Earning Per share}} = \frac{P_0}{E_0} \qquad (7\text{-}14)$$

The most common relative valuation is based on the P/E multiple defined as ratio of market price to the earnings.

Some analysts, who believe that the current market price discounts not the present earnings but future earnings too, rely more on another ratio called leading P/E ratio. It is calculated on the basis of expected earnings in the next period, as defined by Equation 7-15.

Leading Price Earning Ratio

$$= \frac{\text{Market Price}}{\text{Expected Earning Per share}} = \frac{P_0}{E_1} \qquad (7\text{-}15)$$

Valuation based on P/E ratio is rather simple. Assume that a firm in the IT sector has an EPS of ₹20 per share. An investor is negotiating with the promoters to offer her 10 lakh shares. The market value of the firm is not known. One basis of negotiations, the price can be the comparison of the prices and the earnings of the competing firms in the same sector of about the same size and engaged in the same activity. Although the exact match may not be possible, some indications can be had from the financial securities of firms in the sector being traded. If an average P/E ratio of such competing firms is 20, the price offered can be ₹400 (EPS of ₹20 × P/E ratio of the comparables).

P/E Multiple and Growth

The P/E ratio of the firm is said to represent its growth prospects. We may see this with the help of the dividend discount model. The value of the share as given by this model can be bifurcated in two components—(1) the value of assets already in place that offer current level of earnings E_1; and (2) value of the potential assets that are yet to be created by the firm by exploiting the growth opportunities available. The first part is the no-growth value of the firm and the second part is the value attached to the growth prospects. The market makes an assessment of both the components to arrive at the price. Equation 7-12 precisely reflects this scenario, which simply adds the two values to arrive at the aggregate value of the share.

P/E multiple reflects the growth prospects of the firm as assessed by the market.

This also explains why two firms are valued differently by the market despite the same level of earnings and dividends. Consider two firms namely 'Slow Growth' and 'Fast Growth' with same earnings at ₹10 per share and same dividend of ₹5 per share. 'Slow Growth' offers a growth of 5% while 'Fast Growth' has opportunities to grow at 15%. The expected return by investors is 20%. The value of 'Slow Growth' as per DDM is ₹33.33 while 'Fast Growth' is valued at ₹100.

If we denote b as the retention ratio and k as the reinvestment rate by the firm for deploying funds for future growth opportunities, then the value of the share is given by Equation 7-16.

$$P_0 = \frac{D_1}{r-g} = \frac{E_1(1-b)}{r-g}$$

$$\text{Or } \frac{P_0}{E_1} = \frac{(1-b)}{r-bk} \qquad (7\text{-}16)$$

Table 7-2 Dividend, growth, and P/E ratio

	Slow Growth	Fast Growth
Earnings (₹ per share)	10	10
Dividend (₹ per share)	5	5
Market Capitalization (%)	20	20
Growth Potential (%)	5	15
Value of the Share (₹)	$P_0 = \frac{5}{(0.20 - 0.05)}$ = ₹33.33	$P_0 = \frac{5}{(0.20 - 0.15)}$ = ₹100.00
Dividend Yield	15% (5/33.33)	5% (5/100)
Capital Gain = growth	5 %	15%
P/E Ratio	3.33	10.00

From Table 7-2, it is evident that the P/E ratio reflects a composite measure of dividend policy, *b*; reinvestment rate, *k*; and market expectations, *r*. The P/E ratio would increase if *k* and *b* increase as long as $k > r$. If the market places a higher value on the firm, it is reflected in its P/E multiple. The firm has the capability to re-invest the funds at a rate higher than what the investors can do by themselves and this value would be higher if the retention ratio is increased. Contrary to this, if the reinvestment rate by the firm is lower than the return expectations the P/E multiple would decline with increased retention ratio. With $r = k$, the P/E ratio is constant and independent of the retention ratio (the dividend policy). It also implies it is not necessary for P/E multiple to increase with growth.

The relationship of the P/E ratio with respect to the market capitalization rate is rather straightforward. A higher value of *r* translates into a lower value of the P/E multiple. Effectively it means that earnings would be more volatile if discounted at higher rate, reflecting the increased risk with cash flows. Firms with more stable cash flows would have higher P/E multiple.

Riskier firms have low P/E multiple while firms with stable cash flows have higher P/E multiple.

The utility of the P/E ratio lies in its simplicity to guide valuation. Without bothering to know the individual constituents of P/E ratio—*r*, *b*, and *k*—one can do valuation in a composite manner. The two parameters needed to arrive at the value are P/E ratio and expected earnings. While P/E ratio is observable, earnings for the next period is not and may have to be projected.

Further, P/E ratio is said to change only gradually. Similarly if the past earnings E_0 is known, analysts can predict E_1 with reasonable accuracy and certainty. With two parameters known, the valuation becomes easy.

One rule of thumb used by investors and analysts is that the growth rate must roughly be equal to the P/E ratio. According to Peter Lynch (1989), the author of *One Up on Wall Street*, the P/E ratio of a firm that is fairly priced will equal its growth rate. If the P/E ratio of a firm is 15, the growth rate must be 15% per annum.

Valuation based on P/E ratio is extremely popular and often provides a basis of comparison of firms within the same industry. The management and the investors' confidence can be measured by the P/E multiple. All other things remaining constant, a higher P/E multiple means greater confidence reposed by the market in the management of the firm.

Some caveats are in order regarding the use of P/E ratio as valuation model. First, the P/E ratios generally available are based on historical data and use past earnings E_0 as the base. Whatever has been stated about the P/E ratio applies to the projected earnings E_1 and one must be careful while making observations and decisions based on the published P/E ratio. Second, the earnings that are used in published P/E ratios are accounting earnings, which are subject to change as accounting policies change from firm to firm, especially those related to depreciation and inventory valuation. The bias generated due to different accounting policies must be eliminated for fair comparison. Third, reported earnings that are computed under one set of laws do not correspond to the economic earnings that form the basis of P/E ratios.

OTHER RELATIVE VALUATIONS

The P/E approach follows these steps in valuing a share:

1. Find out the industry of the firm whose shares are to be valued.
2. Find the P/E multiple of the industry.
3. Project the relative position of the firm in the industry into broad class of good, average, and below average.
4. Project the earnings of the firm.
5. Project the value of the asset by using the appropriate multiples.

The process of using the relative valuation is simple. Suppose we wish to value the share price of an average firm in the cement sector, which has estimated earnings of ₹10 per share. The average P/E multiple of the cement sector as reflected in the data obtained from the stock market is 5.25. Based on the P/E multiple of 5.25 and estimated earnings of ₹10, we may value the share at ₹52.50 (10 × 5.25).

The process of valuation based on multiple can be repeated for any other observable parameter. Besides earnings, there are several other relevant parameters along which relative valuation can be achieved.

Besides PE multiple other popular relative valuations are done on market price multiples of book value, return on net worth and sales.

One common measure is the book value of the assets. Like P/E multiple, this too may be expressed in terms of Gordon's dividend discount model.

$$P_0 = \frac{D_1}{(r-g)} = \frac{E_0(1-b)(1+g)}{(r-g)}$$

Dividing both sides by book value per share, B_0, we get:

$$\frac{P_0}{B_0} = \frac{E_0/B_0(1-b)(1+g)}{(r-g)} = \frac{\text{ROE}(1-b)(1+g)}{(r-g)}$$

Similarly, one can use sales multiple as another indicator of the relative valuation, which too can be expressed in terms of DDM as follows:

$$P_0 = \frac{D_1}{(r-g)} = \frac{E_0(1-b)(1+g)}{(r-g)}$$

Dividing both sides by sale per share, S_0, we get:

$$\frac{P_0}{S_0} = \frac{E_0/S_0(1-b)(1+g)}{(r-g)} = \frac{\text{Net profit \%}\,(1-b)(1+g)}{(r-g)}$$

There are two key issues and assumptions in the relative valuation. The first one relates to if the comparable is appropriate and second relates to the market valuation being appropriate.

The asset being compared must be as close as possible to the asset with the known value. We assume that a comparable asset in terms of size, equity, sales, history, products, etc. already exists in the market. This assumption is difficult to fulfil as no two organizations are exactly same, but nonetheless share some common characteristics. For example, two firms may be in the same line of business, but one is three times the other in terms of sales. Would it be right to value one firm on the basis of second using book value and price per share of the first one? Can we apply the same multiple to the firm being valued as exists for another, or do we need to adjust this multiple?

The success of relative valuation is dependent upon finding a comparable assets and efficiency of capital markets.

The second assumption relates to the fair assessment by the market. We assume that the comparable used as standard to value another has been correctly priced by the market and that the market neither undervalues nor overvalues an asset. If this assumption holds and is true, it ensures that the asset being valued too would be priced correctly.

There is no method to eliminate such errors except to use managerial discretion in a given situation. Such errors can be minimized by using—(1) an average of multiple over industry rather than multiple of one firm; and (2) use combination of many variables rather than one variable to arrive at relative valuation. One must be aware that distortions in the market valuations and multiplicity of variables create opportunities to justify the individual biases people may have in the assessment.

Realizing the limitations of valuation based on the multiple of single parameter such as the P/E ratio, analysts use several multiples for valuation in order to avoid misinterpretation. The industry practice too is the same. For reference, refer to the case in Exhibit 7-1 that highlights the justification offered by the firm for the issue price of its share.

Exhibit 7-1 Offer for Sale to the Public by Binani Cements Ltd*

An offer for sale of 205 lakh shares at ₹75 was made by an investor in Binani Cements Ltd, a leading manufacturer of cement, to off-load their holding to public at an indicative price of ₹75 per share through a book building process in May 2007. It provided the justification of the indicative price on the basis of 3 parameters of P/E ratio, return on net worth (RONW), and net asset value (NAV) per share.

EPS

EPS was calculated based on the performance of last 4 years and then arriving at the weighted average of EPS providing 4 times the weight to the most recent earnings. The weighted average EPS at ₹2.18 was computed as below:

Computation of Weighted Average EPS

Year Ended	*Adjusted PAT (₹ crore)*	*Nos. of Shares (crore)*	*EPS (₹)*	*Weight*
March 31, 2004	3.50	21.70	0.16	1
March 31, 2005	2.10	21.70	0.10	2
March 31, 2006	51.80	20.31	2.55	3
Dec 31, 2006 (9m)	70.10	20.31	3.45	4
Weighted Average			2.18	

P/E Ratio

P/E ratios based on the offer price of ₹75 per share on different values of EPS was:

	Annualized FY 06-07	*Immediate Past FY 05-06*	*Weighted Average*
EPS (₹)	3.45	2.55	2.18
P/E Ratio	21.74	29.41	34.40

Return on Net Worth

The second parameter for relative valuation was return on net worth (RONW). Using the same weights for the past year data, the average RONW was computed at 15.86% as below:

Computation of Weighted Average RONW

Year Ended	*Adj PAT (₹ crore)*	*Adj. Net worth (₹ crore)*	*RONW (%)*	*Weight*
March 31, 2004	3.50	220.9	1.57	1
March 31, 2005	2.10	222.9	0.92	2
March 31, 2006	51.80	240.1	21.57	3
Dec 31, 2006 (9m)	70.10	310.2	22.86	4
Weighted Average			15.96	

Net Asset Value per Share

The third parameter of relative valuation, i.e., NAV per share as on 31 December 2006 was at ₹15.27.

Relative Valuation

Finally the three parameters for the comparables were as under:

Comparative Data of Competition

	EPS (₹)	*P/E Ratio*	*RONW (%)*	*NAV (₹)*
Binani Cement	2.55	29.41	21.57	11.82
Comparables				
Gujarat Ambuja	3.30	23.60	22.30	16.00
Ultratech	4.30	97.60	0.36	85.80
ACC	18.30	23.50	25.70	85.00
Shree Cement	14.70	32.80	10.80	83.10
J K Cement	3.10	50.60	2.50	10.90
Birla Corp	10.20	22.70	31.70	38.50
OCL India	8.80	17.30	17.80	44.60

*All data based on the Prospectus dated 24 May 2007 filed with Registrar of Companies.

EFFICIENT MARKET HYPOTHESIS

We have discussed many models to estimate share prices. If we can forecast the correct price of the share by any method then all that is required to do is to identify and buy undervalued shares, and sell them when the share price increases. Similarly if the stock is overvalued, one could sell it now to buy it back when it is correctly priced.

Many analysts thought that they have the tools and analyses to identify undervalued and overvalued stocks and, therefore, adopted a strategy that would essentially result in profit at all times. Until a study by Maurice Kendall (1953), known as random walk hypothesis, such a belief that the prices of the stock followed a predictable pattern existed. Contrary to general belief, Kendall's study found that there was no predictable pattern in stock prices and instead the prices followed a random walk. Prices were as much likely to go up as go down. The historical price data provided no clue as to in which direction and by how much the prices would move in future.

Random walk theory states that price changes are random and unpredictable.

Subsequent studies by Harry Roberts (1959) revealed that series of random numbers bore resemblance to time series of stock prices. Another physicist, Osborne (1959), observed that stock price behaviour was similar to movement of very small particles suspended in liquid medium. This is referred to as Brownian motion.

Is this randomness in the prices a sign of irrationality or does it reflect the true nature of markets? Initially it was thought that randomness meant irrational markets since randomness follows no logical rules. However, later, it was opined that it is the true behaviour of the market and randomness of the stock prices represented well-functioning markets, and not its irrationality. Price changes are unpredictable. If prices were predictable, all investors would make money in an orderly fashion. Such a market would not need intelligent investing.

The genesis of the randomness of prices lies in the fact that all information is reflected in the current prices. Only new information would cause the price to change and since the inflow of information is random so would the price movement be. The basic premise is that market quickly discounts all information in the prices so as not to permit any extraordinary gains by investors on the basis of differential levels of information. The idea that market price truly reflects all the available information is referred to as the efficient market hypothesis (EMH).

Efficient capital markets imply that the demand and competition among portfolio managers and analysts to outperform one another is so intense that it leads to fair pricing of the securities. Since information flow is continuous and is subject to numerous interpretations by different individuals, there are continuous and minor variations in the prices of the stocks. These variations are not correlated with one another and hover around the intrinsic value of the share.

There are three forms of market efficiency—weak, semi-strong and strong, based on level of information discounted in the current price.

The key to random movements of price is the flow of information. Based on the levels of information, EMH is presented in three different forms. The information pertaining to the stocks is categorized at three levels— the past information, publicly available information, and privately available (privileged) information. These are named respectively as EMH in weak form, semi-strong form, and strong form.

Weak Form of EMH

Weak form of market efficiency states that current prices discount all past information. Such information includes all history of prices, volumes, the past financial performance of the firms, its competitors, etc. All this information already exists and prices have already incorporated such information. If someone learns a new fact today it does not mean that it is new information. In fact, they are new to the information; the information is as such not new.

Weak form of market efficiency states that current price discounts all past information.

If the markets are efficient in the weak form, it implies that investors cannot expect to have extra-ordinary returns on the basis of past information pertaining to the prices of the share. A technical analyst, who dwells on the past data and identifies patterns of prices and volumes in the hope that they shall be repeated and give advance signals for providing extra-ordinary returns, cannot hope to use this technique of charting if markets are efficient in the weak form.

Semi-strong Form of EMH

Semi-strong form of efficient markets assumes that the current prices reflect not only the past information but also publicly available information. In addition to the past data such as prices, volumes, past financial data, etc., the information relating to the firms that has been made public such as capital expenditure plan, preliminary market survey reports, etc., too have already been discounted in the price. Any projections, new projects, and new products that have come in public domain too have been in the price domain. We do not expect the prices to change merely because the information is new to us. In a nutshell, the semi-strong form of efficient markets states that mere knowledge, interpretation or analysis of past, and publicly available information constitutes no ground and must not give rise to any hope to gain extra-ordinary returns from investment.

Semi-strong form of market efficiency assumes that current price discounts all past and publicly available information.

Strong Form of EMH

Strong form of EMH rises above all forms. It states the ultimate—prices of shares not only discount the past information and publicly available information, but also any private information that one may have access to. The proof of strong form of efficiency in the market would be if the people supposed to be possessing privileged information cannot hope to

Strong form of market efficiency says that all information – past, public and private is discounted in price of the shares.

register any extraordinary returns as compared to the investors not privy to such information. The returns of both the groups—the one with privy of information and the other without any such information would be similar if a strong form of market efficiency exists.

Insider trading Regulators of stock markets in most countries believe that people likely to have access to privileged information regarding the performance and plans of the company, such as members of the board, do have an opportunity to exploit the information to their own benefit. Such an advantage is not available to general investors.

To prevent people from exploiting any privileged information, most regulators have made insider trading illegal. Insider trading by and large prohibits specific individuals, supposed to be in possession of privileged information, to trade into the shares where individuals are perceived to have specific information. Imposing such legislation by most countries, including USA, is an evidence of wide recognition that the markets are not efficient in the strong form. Such markets would present an opportunity to group of individuals in possession of privileged information to out-perform the market.

Few tests to measure the efficiency of capital markets are described in the Appendix available in the CD.

Approaches to Valuation

Analysts and investors alike continuously strive for finding methods of identification of suitable financial securities and making handsome returns. Different people use different methods or techniques to achieve this objective. These methods can be broadly classified into—fundamental analysis and technical analysis.

Fundamental analysis begins with the economic fundamentals of understanding the economic environment, followed by analysis of industrial scenario, and then the identification of specific firms in the industry. Fundamentalists believe that the intrinsic value of the firm depends upon economy, industry prospects, and the company's characteristics. It further assumes that prices converge to the intrinsic value. One can make gains by investing in undervalued shares and disinvesting in overvalued shares. All one needs is identification of undervalued and overvalued shares to make decisions of investing and disinvesting to make abnormal returns. Fundamentalists continue to search for firms that are either undervalued or overvalued.

The two distinct basic approaches to valuation are—fundamental analysis and technical analysis.

In contrast to fundamental analysts, technical analysts believe that the price patterns are repetitive and predictable. They are more a function of demand and supply, and as such shares do have 'psychic value', i.e., they are more determined by psychological factors. Technical analysis is study of these patterns. It discerns some meaningful information from them and helps in timing the purchase and sale of the securities to make abnormal gains. Some studies have revealed that technicians have often been able to outperform the markets.

Fundamental analysis is focused on finding the intrinsic worth, while technical analysis emphasizes on detecting discernable patterns in past prices and making future prediction based on these patterns.

Yet another approach could be to combine the two. One may use fundamental analysis for identifying securities and decide the timing of purchase and sale using technical analysis.

EMH and Technical Analysis

Technical analysts believe that prices and volumes of trading from patterns are discernible, recurrent, and predictable. It is up to the skills of an analyst to identify these patterns and predict the next move with respect to timing, direction, and quantum of change in price. These predictions can be exploited by taking suitable investment positions to have better than normal returns.

The philosophy of technical analysis is completely opposite to that of efficient market hypothesis. Even if the markets are deemed efficient in the weak form, the hypothesis does not conform to the belief that any one can make abnormal returns on the basis of past information of price and volume of trading. If technical analysts can outperform the markets, the markets cannot be said to be efficient even in the weakest form.

EMH and Fundamental Analysis

Like technical analysis, the EMH also does not support the views held by fundamental analysts. Fundamental analysis places the value of the share on present and past earnings, dividends, expected returns, interest rates, etc. They opine that based on such factors the intrinsic value of the share may be found. As a profitable trading strategy, it recommends selling securities for which market value is higher than the intrinsic value, and buying those trading at less than their intrinsic values.

Fundamental analysts begin their exercise with the analysis of economy, identifying sectors of industries expected to perform well, and then converging on those firms which are undervalued as compared to the intrinsic worth to recommend a buy strategy. Fundamental analysts possess excellent analytical and computational skills and are proficient in making PowerPoint presentations and preparing complicated Excel work sheets analysing ratios and other financial parameters and projections.

According to EMH, fundamental analysis cannot lead to a portfolio performance better than the market, since all those presentations and complicated mathematical models can only influence investors, not the prices of securities. Fundamental analysis basically relies on the publicly available information that is presented in different formats by different analysts. It does not add any value to the security being analysed.

In an efficient market, there exist too many researchers and analysts who wholeheartedly and on whole-time basis work to find securities that do not conform to intrinsic value. Since there are too many researchers and all of them rely on publicly available information, the findings of one analyst would not be significantly different than others. Efficient market hypothesis suggests that only analysts with unique insight get rewarded. Fundamental analysis unless superimposed with new information does not yield super normal returns.

EMH and Portfolio Management

The two extremes on the spectrum of portfolio management techniques are passive management techniques known as buy-and-hold strategy on one end, and active management techniques with repeated and frequent changes or adjustments on the other end. As the cost of frequent reshuffling of portfolio is large, it discourages small investors to follow active portfolio management strategies. For large investors while active portfolio management may not be an issue, the ability to conduct unique analysis remains a question mark. If they have such ability they may outperform the market, else they would end up with normal returns.

Efficient market hypothesis foresees no role for active portfolio management and the portfolio managers.

Efficient markets imply that passive portfolio management could be as effective as active portfolio management, unless active portfolio management is based on extraordinary insights developed through careful research. The EMH suggests that the key to success in getting normal returns lies in adequate diversification of portfolio and not in the frequent churning. The only constraint a small investor may face in matching returns with that of large investors is the inadequacy of funds to have a well-diversified portfolio. With the route of mutual funds open to investors, the constraint of funds is no more a limiting factor and with index funds, the limitation of adequate diversification too does not exist anymore.

EMH and Portfolio Manager

If the markets are efficient and passive management strategies are likely to be as effective as active portfolio management, the issue of selection of securities for the portfolio is rather trivial. Therefore, the role and functions of security analysts and portfolio managers becomes minimal if EMH holds.

It does not mean that portfolio managers can be dispensed with altogether. The selection of securities in the portfolio cannot be random. The security selection even in efficient markets has to be based on many other attributes of a portfolio that is specific to an investor. The risk appetite of individual investors can vary according to their risk profile. Younger investors may like to increase their return by assuming greater risk and, therefore, may prefer a portfolio of securities of the firm in high technology areas, whereas elderly people may desire to confine the portfolio in favour of firms in conventional industries. Such considerations are not easy to assess for the naïve investor and may require expert guidance from security analysts and portfolio managers.

Limitations of EMH

Efficient market hypothesis tends to suggest that all investors (if not individually but collectively) are intelligent and, therefore, there is hardly any role for security analysts and portfolio managers in the market; a position very difficult to accept by the financial community. The value addition to be made by experts in improving the portfolio returns must be weighed against the cost. If EMH holds, the contribution of portfolio managers to performance becomes difficult to prove due to the following factors:

The inherent volatility of the market We all know that market returns are characterized by normal distribution having an expected value and standard deviation. The standard deviation quantifies the risk and may range around 20% in competitive markets. It implies that the performance of the portfolios would vary due to inherent volatility of the market. The moot question is whether the discriminatory returns on various portfolios result from the contribution of the concerned portfolio managers or are due to the natural volatility of the markets. A portfolio manager's good performance can be buried or over exaggerated in the natural volatility of the market. Statistically, it becomes very difficult to measure the performance of portfolio managers.

Initial selection Besides regular churning of portfolio, the performance of the portfolio depends a great deal on the initial selection of the securities. Many combinations of securities, which are expected to yield the similar results in the portfolio, are possible. The investment plan may be devised based on several considerations and these considerations need not be made public. We all know that some stocks outperform the markets and some do not. The same holds true for portfolio managers too. The method of selection of securities remains confidential till the performance is proven. Failure to outperform the market is disguised in the claim that EMH holds, while those outperforming may prefer to remain quiet as they may not have any interest in proving or disproving EMH. Hence, what gets noticed is the claim that EMH holds. Such a position suits the outperformers too as it bolsters their achievements even further.

Timing of investment Another factor that affects the portfolio performance is the timing of investment. Technical analysts emphasize the issue of timing of the investment, and may outperform the market merely by the timing of investments and disinvestments. The wild fluctuations of the prices without the any fundamental justification for such movements in prices can cause equally wild fluctuations in the performance of the portfolios. The same portfolio constituted at different points of time would have different amount of initial investment and hence varied performance.

Summary

Valuation of equity shares is one of the most challenging exercises a financial analyst faces. The valuation of the equity is similar to that of bonds as it involves the discounting of the cash flows attached with the financial instrument. Equity valuation is an extremely tricky exercise as none of the parameters can be determined accurately and with certainty. The cash flows, their timing and maturity as well as rate of discount are all uncertain.

The difficulties of valuation emanate from the underlying nature of equity. It is a financial instrument characterized by indefinite life with the owner of the instrument bearing total responsibility for managing the business and entitled to only the residual that is unknown. These features of equity make estimation of cash flows uncertain as well as use of definite discount rate a controversial issue.

One way of finding the intrinsic value of equity is to discount the cash flows associated with equity—the dividend. The dividend discount model (DDM) and its many variants attempt to find the intrinsic worth of a share. It states that current price must equal the discounted value of dividends for an indefinite period of time. Under special cases of constant dividend and constant growth, the model is relatively easy to solve. According to DDM, the value of the share is a function of expected dividend, shareholders' expectations, and dividend growth. Shareholders' expectation consists of dividend yield and growth.

Another approach to value equity shares is relative valuation. This is based on the premise that equivalent assets must command the same price. The approach, therefore, concentrates on finding the equivalent asset whose market value is known. The efficacy and accuracy of the approach is dependent upon the existence of a comparable asset and the assumption that the asset is correctly priced.

The most common market-based valuation is P/E multiple. It is calculated by dividing the earnings by the market price. P/E multiple is regarded as a composite single parameter that reflects market perception of how investors view the quality, stability, and growth in the earnings of the firm. It also takes into account the industry average for the P/E multiple and the relative position in that industry. As against the intrinsic worth of the firm, the relative valuation focuses on market valuation. Besides P/E multiple, the other measures used in relative valuation are sales multiple, book value multiple, and return on net worth.

The level of efficiency of capital markets determines how fair the market valuation is. Market efficiency implies that price converges to intrinsic value and changes in the price are random and unpredictable. The price changes as new information flows in. The information that affects the price is categorized into—past, public and private. The efficiency of a market is determined by the level of information built into the current price.

The weakest form of market efficiency implies that all past information is discounted in the current price. The next level called semi-strong form of market efficiency states that price discounts all past and publicly available information. No investor can expect to make abnormal profits merely by better analysis of publicly available information. Finally, the ultimate form of market efficiency, called strong form, rules out abnormal profit even if someone has access to private information.

KEY TERMS

Dividend discount model (DDM) DDM states that current price of the share is equal to the expected dividend discounted at an appropriate rate reflecting the shareholders' expectations.

DDM with constant dividend The current price of the share is given by the expected dividend divided by shareholders' expectation of return. This is DDM with constant dividend.

Intrinsic value The intrinsic value of the share is the present value of the future cash flows attached to it.

P/E multiple Price earning multiple is the ratio of current market price and the earnings of per share.

Random walk theory Random walk theory says that changes in the prices of shares are random and unpredictable.

Weak form of market efficiency The hypothesis that market discounts all past information in its current price is weak form of market efficiency.

Semi-strong form of market efficiency The hypothesis that market discounts all past information as well as all publicly available information in its current price is called semi-strong form of market efficiency.

Strong form of market efficiency The hypothesis that market discounts all past information, publicly available as well as all private/privileged information in its current price is strong form of market efficiency.

Fundamental analysis Fundamental analysis means that the value of the share must converge to its intrinsic value, which depends upon the state of the economy, status of industry, and the competitive position of the firm in the industry.

Technical analysis Technical analysis is an approach that believes that past price patterns are discernable and repeated, and therefore, have predictive powers.

KEY FORMULAE

Current Price of the Share

$$P_0 = \frac{D_1}{(1+r)} + \frac{P_1}{(1+r)}$$

Dividend Discount Model (DDM)

$$P_0 = \sum_{1}^{\infty} \frac{D_n}{(1+r)^n}$$

DDM With No Growth

$$P_0 = \frac{D}{r}$$

DDM With Constant Growth

$$P_0 = \frac{D_1}{(r-g)}$$

Shareholders' Expectations of Return $r = \frac{D_1}{P_0} + g$

P/E Multiple $\frac{\text{Market Price}}{\text{Earning Per Share}} = \frac{P_0}{E_0}$

Leading P/E Multiple $\frac{\text{Market Price}}{\text{Expected Earning Per Share}} = \frac{P_0}{E_1}$

Leading P/E Multiple & DDM $\frac{P_0}{E_1} = \frac{(1-b)}{(r-bk)}$

PRACTICE PROBLEMS

1. Return on Investment

Ramesh bought a share at a price of ₹100. The price of the stock moved to ₹200 a year later. During the period, Ramesh received a dividend of ₹8 per share.

(a) What is the % return Ramesh got on his investment at the end of one year?

(b) If Ramesh paid only 40% of the investment as margin to the broker while the remaining was funded through a loan borrowed at 15%, what is the return for Ramesh?

Solution

(a) Return for Ramesh for a period of 1 year

Purchase price	=	₹100.00
Selling price after one year	=	₹200.00
Profit	=	₹100.00
Dividend during the period	=	₹8.00
% Return	=	108%

% Return may be computed using the following formula:

$$\text{Return (\%)} = \frac{(P_1 - P_0) + D_1}{P_0} \times 100$$

$$= \frac{(200 - 100) + 8}{100} \times 100 = 108\%$$

(b)

Own funds invested (%)	=	40%
Own investment (Equity)	=	₹40.00
Profit and dividend earned	=	₹108.00
less: Interest paid = 15% on ₹60	=	₹9.00
Return on equity	=	99.00
Return on equity %		
=Return/Own investment × 100 = $\frac{99}{40}$ × 100	=	248%

2. Fair Value of a Stock

ABC Corporation had paid a dividend of ₹10 per share in the last year. Now the time for annoucement of next dividend has come. The market expectations are that the new dividend shall be reflecting the growth of the industry and would be ₹12. If the expected return by investors is 25%, what price of the share do you expect?

Solution

Current dividend, D_0	=	₹10.00
Expected dividend, D_1	=	₹12.00
Growth in dividend, g	=	20.00%
Required return, r	=	25.00%

The value of the share is given by:

$$\text{Value of the stock, } P_0 = \frac{D_0(1+g)}{r-g}$$

Value of the common stock = 10 × (1 + 0.20) / (0.25 – 0.20)
= ₹240.00

3. Price and Expected Dividend

Guru Techology Ltd is a listed company whose shares are selling at ₹230 currently. The expectations of the market about the future price of the share is ₹280. If the current dividend is ₹7 per share, what dividend do you expect for the coming year?

Solution

Current price of the share, P_0	=	₹230.00
Expected price of the share, P_1	=	₹280.00
Expected growth rate, g	=	21.74%
Current dividend, D_0	=	₹7.00
Growth in dividend, g	=	21.74%
Expected Dividend, $D_1 = D_0 \times (1 + g)$	=	₹8.52

4. Dividend, Return, and Price

A share of the firm is trading at ₹350 currently. The market estimates that the price next year is going to be ₹420.

(a) What is the growth in price of the share?

(b) If the current dividend is ₹20 per share, what is the dividend expected from the firm in the coming year?

(c) What is the expectation of return by the investors? Would it be same as growth in the price of the share? Why and why not?

(d) If investor decides to sell the share prior to the anticipated dividend at what price would he sell his share?

(e) Would there be any difference in return if investor sells the share before or after the dividend? Why and why not?

Solution

(a)	Current price of the share, P_0	=	₹350.00
	Expected price of the share, P_1	=	₹420.00
	Expected growth rate, g	=	20%
(b)	Current dividend, D_0	=	₹20.00
	Growth in dividend, g	=	20%
	Expected Dividend, $D_1 = D_0 \times (1 + g)$	=	₹24.00

(c) Expected return can be arrived as follows:

$$\text{Value of the stock, } P_0 = \frac{D_0(1+g)}{r-g}$$

or

$$r - g = \frac{D_1}{P_0}$$

Therefore, $r = \frac{D_1}{P_0} + g = \frac{24}{350} + 0.2 = 0.2686 = 26.86\%$

The return of the investor would not be same as growth in price but instead would be higher than that because of the dividend yield earned by holding on to the investment.

The returns comprise two parts – (i) price appreciation and (ii) dividend earned.

Price appreciation would be 20% and dividend earned is 6.86% making total return of 26.86%.

(d) If investor sells prior to the dividend, he would get cum dividend, price.

Ex-dividend price	₹420.00
Dividend	₹24.00
Cum-dividend price	₹444.00

(e) If the investor sells the stock prior to the dividend, his return would be:

$$r = \frac{\text{Cum dividend price} - \text{Current price}}{\text{Current price}}$$

$$= \frac{444 - 350}{350} = 26.86\%$$

Irrespective of when the investor sells, the share (before or after the dividend) his return would stand at 26.86%.

If he sells prior to the dividend, the investor would receive price greater exactly by the amount of dividend. After the dividend, the price would decline by the amount of dividend.

5. Extraordinary Growth and Value

Hira Constructions Ltd has been in the business of constructing residential flats. It has been doing considerably well and constantly growing at 10% annually for the past several years. The last dividend paid by the company was ₹3 per share. Due to its reputation the firm received an overseas contract that would add to the growth and the prospect of the firm. The Managing Director confirmed to some of the investors that for next three years, the company would grow at double the rate at 20% rather than at usual 10%.

(a) What should be the current price of the share?

(b) Assuming that the firm would grow at 20% for next three years before reverting to normal growth of 10% what change in price would be caused due to the annoucement of the contract?

Solution

(a) With current dividend of ₹3 and expected growth of 10% and investors' expectation of return of 25% the stock price of the share is

Current dividend, D_0	=	₹3.00
Growth in dividend, g	=	10.00%
Expected dividend, D_1	=	₹3.30
Required return, r	=	25.00%

The current price of the share (before the annoucement of award of contract) is:

Value of the stock, $P_0 = \frac{D_0(1+g)}{r-g}$

$= 3 \times (1 + 0.10) / (0.25 - 0.10) =$ ₹22.00

(b) With the growth estimate of 20% and investors' expectations remaining unchanged at 25%, the price of the share would be:

= PV of the dividends from Year 1-3 + PV of the dividends from Year 4 onwards.

This is found as follows:

Current dividend	₹3.00
Growth rate for 3 years	20%
Required rate of return	25%

Present value of dividends for next three years:

Year	1	2	3
Dividend	3.60	4.32	5.18
PV at 25%	2.88	2.76	2.65
PV of Dividends from Year 1 – 3			8.30

Present value of the dividends is found using DDM:

Steady state growth rate	=	10%
Dividend in Year 4	=	₹5.70
Value of dividends from Year 4 onwards using DDM, P_3	=	₹38.02

Value of the Stock, $P_3 = \frac{D_3(1+g)}{r-g}$

This value at Year 3 needs to be converted to Year 0 as follows:

PV of Price in Year 3 = $\frac{38.02}{(1.25)^3}$ = ₹19.46

Price today = PV of Dividend (Year 1–3) + PV of P_3

= 8.30 + 19.46 = ₹27.76

6. Realized Return

In the Problem 5, assume that an investor buys the share of the Hira Construction Ltd after the annoucement of the award of contract. His holding period is three years after which he sells the share.

If the investor does so what return would he realise on his investment? Confirm your answer with the data provided.

Solution

Since investors' expectations have remained unchanged during the holding period of three years the return of the investor would be 25%.

His return would comprise of the price appreciation, i.e., the difference of selling price and buying price, and dividend earned in each year with re-investment at 25%.

For this we compare the investment with the terminal value of all the cash flows for the period of holding as shown below:

Initial purchase price, S_0		₹27.76
Selling price after 3 years		₹38.02
Dividend received	**Amount**	**Reinvested value at 25%**
Year 1	₹3.60	₹5.63
Year 2	₹4.32	₹5.40
Year 3	₹5.18	₹5.18
Terminal value of dividend reinvested		= ₹16.21
Sale value plus reinvested value of dividends, S_3		= ₹54.23

The realized return, *r* may be found using following equation

$$S_0(1 + r)^3 = S_3$$

$$27.76 \times (1 + r)^3 = 54.23$$

This gives r = 25%

7. Earnings and P/E Multiple

Multi-Products Ltd has been following a dividend payout of only 20% so that the funds needed for the growth of the firm targeted at 10% is retained. The market expectations of return are 12%.

(a) At what rate the market is discounting the current and future earnings of Multi-Products Ltd?

(b) If the current level of earnings are ₹10 per share at what price the shares of the firm are being traded?

Solution

(a) The dividend discount model in terms of earnings and retention ratio is

$$\text{Price} \quad P_0 = \frac{D_1}{(r-g)} = \frac{E_1 \times (1-b)}{r-g}$$

$$\text{or} \quad \text{P/E Multiple} \quad \frac{P_0}{E_1} = \frac{(1-b)}{r-g}$$

Retention Ratio, b	80.00%
Required Return, r	12.00%
Growth Rate, g	10.00%
P/E ratio based on expected earnings, E_1	10.00
P/E ratio based on current earnings, E_0	11.00

Market is discounting the current and future earnings of the firms at 10 and 11 times respectively.

(b)

Current Earnings, E_0	₹10.00
Growth Rate, g	10.00%
Required Return, r	12.00%
Expected Earnings, E_1	₹11.00
Retention Ratio, b	80.00%
Price = 10 × (1 + 0.1) × (1 – 0.8) / (0.12 – 0.1)	= ₹110.00

8. Applying P/E Multiple

Theta Ltd is a privately held company that has been doing wonderfully well. It has bagged prestigious contracts for supply of electrical transformers from several electricity boards in India. The current level of profitability of Theta Ltd is ₹12 per share. In order to execute the orders of the electricity boards, it needs to mobilize capital from the capital markets by issuing fresh shares. The merchant bankers appointed for the purpose of mobilising fresh capital have gathered information about the P/E ratios of major companies in order to price the issue of shares.

The P/E multiples of 4 major firms (based on the latest prices and expected future earnings) in the same line of business of electrical goods, as below:

	Firm A	Firm B	Firm C	Firm D
P/E multiple	10.2	12.4	13.5	18.6

The management of the company expects that on the enhanced capital of the firm and upon successful execution on orders on hand the expected earnings level would rise from current level of ₹12 per share to ₹14 per share, which is not disputed.

The Chairman of Theta Ltd thought that his firm is in no way inferior the market leader Firm D and therefore must command the same valuation from the market. On the other hand, CFO of the firm thought that the firm being relatively unknown to the potential investors it would be able to attract valuation no greater than that of Firm A.

The merchant banker caught in the dilemma of pricing the issue tried to resolve by proposing that the price of the issue be done on the basis of average of the valuation for the industry and regarded the four firms as adequate representative sample.

Find out at what price the public offer of Theta Ltd be made according to the (a) Chairman, (b) CFO, and (c) Merchant bankers?

Solution

	Firm A	Firm B	Firm C	Firm D	Average
P/E multiple	10.2	12.4	13.5	18.6	13.675
Expected Earnings, E_1					₹14.00

Price of the issue according to

	P/E Multiple	Future earnings	Price of the issue
The Chairman	18.600	₹14.00	₹260.40
The CFO	10.200	₹14.00	₹142.80
The Merchant bankers	13.675	₹14.00	₹191.45

EXERCISES

Concept Review Questions

1. Why do you think that the valuation of equity shares is more difficult than the valuation of bonds?
2. Describe some of the features of equity shares and their impact on valuation.
3. What do you understand by intrinsic value? How is it related to or different from market value?
4. What is dividend discount model? Describe with its assumptions.
5. How does dividend discount model incorporates the growth of the company in the valuation of its shares?
6. What do you understand by P/E ratio? Explain valuation using P/E ratio with a suitable example.
7. What are different measures of relative valuation and why are they used alongside P/E ratio?
8. Share prices respond to new information. What are the different levels of information?
9. Distinguish between different forms of market efficiency.
10. What implications efficient market hypothesis has on fundamental valuation and technical analysis?
11. What implications efficient market hypothesis has on portfolio management and for portfolio managers?

Critical Thinking Questions

1. The expected dividend on Infosys is ₹12 per share that is currently selling at ₹2,000. The dividend is expected to grow at 20% per annum. An analyst has forecast a price of ₹2,300 after one year for its share. Do you agree with her forecast?
2. If a firm grows, its P/E multiple will always rise. Comment.
3. On the basis of past price data if a financial analyst is able to outperform the market returns, what conclusions can you draw regarding market efficiency?

Practical Assignments

1. Analyse the dividend of Hindustan Lever Ltd for the last 10 years. Project the growth in dividend and then apply dividend discount model with constant growth to project its price for the next year.
2. You are valuing an information technology firm whose market value is not known. However, you have reasonable estimate of its earnings, sales, and capital employed. The firm is planning to come out with a public issue. How would you arrive at the price of the share?

Numerical Problems

1. Price, Growth, and Return

Superior Logistics Ltd had given a dividend of ₹4.00. According to the analysts in the logistic industry the growth rate of dividend is expected to be 8% for times to come. If the market expectation of return is 14% what should be the price of the stock of Superior Logistics? Also project the price of the stock after one year and verify whether the shareholder gets return of 14%.

2. Historical Growth and Price

First Chemicals Ltd has been consistently performing well over last 8 years. The dividend has grown from ₹1.00 per share to ₹10 per share over last 8 years. The growth is likely to be maintained in future too. The investors expect a return of 20%. What is the current market price of the share of First Chemicals?

3. Revised Growth and Price

First Chemicals Ltd has just announced successful development of a new chemical that is expected to propel the growth to 18%. Dividend too would grow proportionately. If investor expectations remain unchanged what would be the new price of the share of First Chemicals?

4. Implied Market Expectation of Return

Shares of Reliance Computers are currently trading at ₹50. The firm had given a dividend of ₹2.50 per share last year. The growth rate of dividend has been 10% in the past, which is likely to remain same. What is the expectation of return on the stock of Reliance Computers?

5. Growth and Expected Return

Stock of Modern Technologies is trading at a price of ₹32.10. It has just given a dividend of ₹2.40 per share. The expected return on the stock of Modern Technologies consistent with the risk of the business it is in is placed at 15%. What is the expected price of the stock of Modern Technologies three years from now? If an investor buys the stock now and sells after three years what return would she obtain? Confirm the calculations.

6. Multiple Growth Rate and Value

A-One Computers has declared a dividend of ₹2 per share. Due to its innovative products, it is likely to register a growth in dividends at 15% for the next four years. Thereafter the growth would coincide with that of industry at 6%. The investors require a return of 16% on the stocks of A-One Computers. What should be the price of the stock of A-One Computers?

7. Future Dividend and Growth

Intel Semiconductors has been growing at the rate of 8% annually. It recently declared a dividend of ₹4.00 per share. In order to develop a new chip it announced that henceforth no dividend would be paid for next two years. The dividend in third year is expected to be ₹5.00 and would grow at 10% per annum instead of current growth of 8%. The required rate of return by investors is 14%. What is the impact on price of the share of Intel Semiconductors?

8. Earnings and P/E Multiple

Apex Motors has earnings of ₹4 per share. These earnings have been growing at 8% for the past several years and the trend is expected to continue. The firm has been funding its requirements by retaining 40% of earnings. What is the price of the share and the P/E multiple?

9. Growth and P/E Multiple

ABC Corporation is earning ₹4 per share currently. These earnings are growing at the rate of 3% annually. The required rate of return is estimated at 10%. Out of the earnings the firm pays 60% as dividend. Due to closure of one of the competing firm the estimates of growth are revised to 6%. What would be the impact on the stock price and the P/E multiple?

CASE STUDY

Euro Ceramics Ltd

Euro Ceramics Ltd came out with a public issue of 56.215 lakh shares at an indicative price of ₹165 per share with book building and provided the basis of indicative price on the relative valuation based on three parameters of P/E ratio, return on net worth, and book value.

The data for preceding three years and weighted average is given here:

Financial Year	2003-04	2004-05	2005-06	Weighted
Weightage	1	2	3	
EPS (₹/Share)	0.70	11.76	17.81	12.94
RONW (%)	7.11	27.67	33.70	27.26
NAV (₹/Share)				52.58
Post-issue NAV				42.31

The post-issue number of shares of the firm would stand at 171 lakh. The net worth would stand increased by ₹8615 lakh if the price of the share is assumed at ₹165.

The industry scenario with respect to P/E ratio, return on net worth, and book values is presented below:

Company	EPS (₹)	P/E Ratio	RONW (%)	Book Value (₹)
Bell Ceramics	0.4	—	2.0	21.4
Cera Sanityware	10.9	8.9	23.1	52.5
Hind Sanityware	4.4	22.3	21.3	33.1
Kajaria Ceramics	3.7	15.5	22.2	18.4
Murudeshwar Ceramics	13.9	5.8	12.4	123.7
Nitco Tiles	8.9	20.7	11.7	115.8
Regency Ceramics	—	9.8	0.1	48.7
SPL	3.8	14.6	5.4	73.2

Based on industry data the company justified the price of ₹ 165 per share as follows:

Industry P/E ratio (for Ceramic—Tiles/Sanitaryware)

Highest	22.30
Lowest	5.80
Average	15.00

Based on the price of ₹165 and current earnings of ₹17.81, the P/E ratio of the firm works out to 9.26.

Discuss

1. Do you think that the price is justified?
2. The firm has current EPS of ₹17.81. What amount of earnings the firm must have to maintain the current EPS level on the enhanced number of shares?

In the CD

Appendix A-7 Measurement of Market Efficiency

Finding Value of a Share with PE Multiple

Finding Value of a Share using DDM

CHAPTER 8 Portfolio Theory

LEARNING OBJECTIVES

After going through this chapter, you will be able to:

- understand the concept of a portfolio, and its return and risk
- learn about feasible portfolios, and the difference between efficient and inefficient portfolios
- measure the relationship of returns of two securities
- understand covariance and coefficient of correlation, and their relationship
- understand the concept of an efficient frontier
- learn how to compute portfolio variance and standard deviation
- examine how the utility of money is related to returns and risks
- understand the concept of capital allocation line (CAL)
- learn to find an efficient frontier using Markowitz Model of portfolio design
- analyse the implications of portfolio theory for portfolio managers
- design an optimum portfolio using Sharpe's Single Index Model
- understand the concept of diversification and the issues to be considered while diversifying
- learn how risk can be segregated into unique risk and market risk
- examine superfluous diversification
- determine an optimum portfolio

TENNIS STOCK AND CRICKET PORTFOLIO

In the hot summer afternoon of June, Ek and Anek, both bosom friends and enthusiastic knowledgeable wagers, sat watching news on the television and sipping beer in a local bar. Announcing the Indian cricket team, the BCCI spokesperson informed, 'We have an extremely balanced side with some very adventurous and some not so adventurous players. We expect to win the next series with this team.' The next news item was on Wimbledon. The seeding is declared. Federer is expected to lift the title and is the top-seeded player in the tournament.

Ek, as his name would imply, always believed in betting on individual performances, told Anek, 'Federer would certainly win the championship. He is unbeatable and his track record is too good. I will put my money on him.'

Anek, differing with the philosophy of Ek reacted, 'But the odds would be too low. I suspect you get only ₹1.20 for a bet on him. I would rather bet on the Indian team winning the test series in England. I think I will get ₹1.60 if India wins.'

Ek suggested, 'Well if you want more return, why don't you bet on Sania Mirza winning the women's Wimbledon title.'

Anek, refusing to accept the suggestion, explained his thinking 'Agreed that the return will be very good if I bet on Sania Mirza, but it is highly risky because chances of her winning are extremely remote. I would rather bet on the performance of the Indian cricket team. Not that I love cricket more than tennis, but putting money on cricket is not as risky as betting on individual performance. It is better to bet on the team performance rather than individual performance.'

Anek further explained, 'Whether or not Tendulkar would hit a century is a poorer bet than a bet on the Indian team's win. It is a risky bet because your fortunes depend upon the performance of single individual. If he fails, you are doomed.'

With a strange look on his face, Ek asked, 'How is the bet on Indian team different? A bet is a bet.'

Anek was quick to respond, 'There are many reasons. If you bet on the Indian team, it is less of a risk because performance is not dependent on a single individual. It is a collective effort. If batsmen fail, bowlers could do well; and if bowlers fail, batsmen have a chance of correcting the damage.'

Looking at the confused expression on the face of Ek, Anek extended the argument, 'We have many bowlers. If Zaheer doesn't strike, Kumble would. Similarly, if Tendulkar fails, we have Dravid to consolidate the innings.'

Not convinced, Ek said, 'I don't agree. Our batsmen have perennial weakness of facing fast seam bowling, especially under overcast conditions. That is a great risk.'

Anek defended, 'But, we too have bowlers who can exploit overcast conditions and cause problems for English batsmen.'

Countered Ek, 'Our bowlers are not as adept as English bowlers are, and with the current lack of form of our batsmen, it is too risky to bet on the Indian team's win.'

Anek changed the line of argument now, 'We have to carry this risk. We possibly cannot do anything about it. But, even here, some have greater chance of resisting the conditions and perform. They are not equally susceptible. That is a risk common to all our batsmen. I possibly cannot do anything about it. And that is the reason the odds are likely to be 1.60.'

Ek kept quiet for a while, brooding on the argument. Breaking the silence, Anek said in a lighter vein, 'This is why I never put my eggs in one basket by betting only on Tendulkar, nor do I gift a basket containing only eggs, because if the person doesn't like eggs, she would not like your gift and you too.'

Ek, looking at the watch changed the subject, 'Oh that reminds me! I have to buy a gift for my girlfriend for her birthday. I think I would apply your principle here at least. I would buy a hamper of assorted sweets now. At least a few of them would certainly be relished. I can't afford to displease her.'

Anek concluded, 'Always remember that cricket is a game that is akin to a portfolio while tennis is not. Recall what we studied in finance together few years back about portfolio theory.'

They finished their last sip of beer, and Ek rushed to the market to buy a gift for his girlfriend.

INTRODUCTION

In the last few chapters, we explained the concepts of risk, returns, and valuation of individual shares. The investment decision does not stop at the identification of individual shares and the understanding of risk and returns associated with it. In fact, it is the beginning of the broader exercise to form a portfolio consisting of many classes of securities and many securities in each class. The study of a single financial asset is not as important as the study of a portfolio because most investors make investments in several securities and hold a portfolio of many financial assets.

A portfolio consists of diverse types of assets. Besides investing directly in financial assets and markets, most people save in various other assets such as insurance policies, provident funds, fixed deposits, etc. Different types of investments appeal to different sets of people and meet their financial and/or other objectives. Investors construct these portfolios to offset the effect of the return of one asset on another. For example, an insurance policy against car theft protects the loss in value of the asset, i.e., the car. The car and the theft insurance policy form a portfolio whose returns and risk compliment each other to provide a stabilizing effect. Insurance policies, in general, are hedges against event risks. They attempt to protect the loss in value of the asset against a particular type of event.

A portfolio consists of several securities and its study is more important than the study of individual asset, as most investors hold portfolios.

When combined to form a portfolio, financial assets too tend to offer similar characteristics; though the effect of hedging may not be as evident or visible as in case of insurance policies. For example, consider an investor having shares of a firm manufacturing air conditioners and a firm engaged in manufacturing synthetic apparel. The business of air conditioning is supposed to do well if the weather turns hot and humid. The firm manufacturing synthetic apparel will do well in pleasant weather, instead of hot and humid conditions. Such a combination of shares in a portfolio protects the returns against unpredictable weather conditions. The concept of hedging gets built automatically when a large number of securities form the portfolio.

Portfolios perform the important function of providing hedge against adverse environmental conditions.

PORTFOLIO RETURN

We all are familiar with averages and weighted averages. If we invest in two securities, A and B, then the expected returns would be the average of the expected returns on Security A and Security B. Let us assume that the expected return on Security A is 10% and the return on Security B is 20%. If we make equal investments in each of them, the expected return of the portfolio would be 15%. As we increase the proportion of investment in Security B, our return would increase.

When portfolio consists of several securities the return on the portfolio is determined by the weighted average of the returns of individual securities constituting the portfolio. This is represented in Equation 8-1.

$$R_p = w_1R_1 + w_2R_2 + w_3R_3 \ldots = \sum_{1}^{n} w_i R_i \quad (8\text{-}1)$$

where w_i is the weight of the security i in the portfolio, and R_i is the expected return on security i.

When returns are uncertain, we deal with the concept of expected returns. The expected return on any security is given by the probability of weighed average of its returns over all scenarios. If there is a possibility of three scenarios—good monsoon, normal monsoon, and poor monsoon with equal chances and the share is expected to provide returns of 24%, 20% and 15% respectively, the expected return of this share is the weighted average of three scenarios, which is 21% $\left[\frac{1}{3}(24+20+15)\right]$.

Expected return of the portfolio is the weighted average of the expected returns of the individual securities constituting it.

Example 8-1 Expected Return and Portfolio's Expected Return

Shares of five firms denoted as 1 to 5 are projected to have returns under three different scenarios as given below:

	Good Economy	*Average Economy*	*Poor Economy*
Probability	25%	50%	25%
		Returns (%) for	
Share 1	20	18	15
Share 2	30	24	20
Share 3	25	12	–6
Share 4	12	24	30
Share 5	40	30	20

Find the expected return on each share. Also, find the return on the portfolio constituted of these five shares in the ratio of 1:2:3:4:5 for share 1, 2, 3, 4, and 5 respectively.

Solution

The expected return for each share is calculated by using the probability-weighted average returns under three different scenarios:

Expected return for share 1 (R_1) = $20 \times 0.25 + 18 \times 0.50 + 15 \times 0.25$ = 17.75%

Expected return for share 2 (R_2) = $30 \times 0.25 + 24 \times 0.50 + 20 \times 0.25$ = 24.50%

Expected return for share 3 (R_3) = $25 \times 0.25 + 12 \times 0.50 - 6 \times 0.25$ = 10.75%

Expected return for share 4 (R_4) = $12 \times 0.25 + 24 \times 0.50 + 30 \times 0.25$ = 22.50%

Expected return for share 5 (R_5) = $40 \times 0.25 + 30 \times 0.50 + 20 \times 0.25$ = 30.00%

The expected return of the portfolio is the weighted average of the returns of the shares, which is given by:

$$R_P = \frac{1}{15}\times 17.75 + \frac{2}{15}\times 24.50 + \frac{3}{15}\times 10.75 + \frac{4}{15}\times 22.50 + \frac{5}{15}\times 30.00 = 22.60\%$$

Example 8-2 Portfolio's Expected Return

Shares of the five firms denoted as 1 to 5 are projected to have returns of 15%, 20%, 12%, 25%, and 30% respectively. Based on this information, answer the following questions:

(a) If the portfolio consists of all the five shares in equal proportions, what is the expected return?

(b) What is the return of the portfolio if 40% of the funds are put in the security of Firm 5 yielding a return of 30% and the remainder is divided equally in the remaining four securities?

Solution

Using Equation 8-1, the expected return will be:

(a) Expected return $R_p = \frac{1}{5}(15 + 20 + 12 + 25 + 30) = \frac{102}{5} = 20.4\%$

(b) 40% invested in Security 5, then each of the other security will have 15% of investment. Then

Expected return $R_p = (0.15 \times 15 + 0.15 \times 20 + 0.15 \times 12 + 0.15 \times 25 + 0.40 \times 30) = 22.8\%$

PORTFOLIO RISK

The risk of a portfolio is measured by the variance of its return. The variance of the portfolio is calculated in the same manner as that of a single asset. The variance of the portfolio σ_p^2 is defined as sum of the squared deviations from the expected value multiplied by the probability of occurrence. If R_p is the return of the portfolio with the expected value of $\bar{R}_p$, the variance of the portfolio is given in Equation 8-2.

$$\text{Var}, \sigma_p^2 = \sum_{1}^{n} p_i (R_p - \bar{R}_p)^2 \quad (8\text{-}2)$$

Example 8-3 Portfolio Return and Risk

Assume a portfolio of the Shares 1, 2, 3, 4, and 5 in the ratio of 1:2:3:4:5 as in Example 8-1. What returns are expected from the portfolio under good, average, and poor economic conditions? What is the portfolio risk?

Solution

The portfolio consisting of Shares 1, 2, 3, 4, and 5 in the proportion of 1:2:3:4:5 would provide returns of 26.87%, 23.20%, and 17.13% under good, average, and poor economic conditions. With probabilities of 25%, 50%, and 25% the portfolio is expected to provide a return of 22.60% as shown below:

		Economy		
Share	***Proportion***	***Good***	***Average***	***Poor***
1	6.67%	1.33	1.20	1.00
2	13.33%	4.00	3.20	2.67
3	20.00%	5.00	2.40	–1.20
4	26.67%	3.20	6.40	8.00
5	33.33%	13.33	10.00	6.67
	100.00%	26.87	23.20	17.13
Probability		25%	50%	25%
		6.72	11.60	4.28
Expected return				**22.60%**

The risk of the portfolio is assessed through its variance or standard deviation. Both these parameters are computed below:

State of economy	*Good*	*Average*	*Poor*	*Exp. Ret. (%)*
Probability (p)	25%	50%	25%	
Return (R in %)	26.87	23.20	17.13	*22.60*
Deviations	4.27	0.60	–5.47	
(Deviation)^2	18.20	0.36	29.88	
$p \times$ (Deviation)^2	4.55	0.18	7.47	
Variance			**12.20**	
Standard Deviation (%)			**3.49**	

Let us consider an example to understand the importance of hedging and diversification in reducing the portfolio risk. We shall confine ourselves to two-securities and then generalize the findings. Consider two firms—Boom Ltd and Toon Ltd. They offer different returns under different economic conditions because they are in different business sectors. Boom Ltd is expected to do better when the economic environment is good, while Toon Ltd does better when economic conditions are rather poor. Assuming three possible economic environments, the returns of Boom Ltd and Toon Ltd are as given below. The probabilities of economic scenarios of good, average, and poor are 30%, 50%, and 20% respectively.

	Good	*Average*	*Poor*
Probability	30%	50%	20%
	Returns (%)		
Boom Ltd	20.00	15.00	10.00
Toon Ltd	12.00	15.00	18.00

Their expected return and risks, assessed by variance or standard deviation, are computed as shown below:

Conditions	*Good*	*Average*	*Poor*	
Probability (p)	30%	50%	20%	
Boom Ltd				**Expected Return**
Return	20.00	15.00	10.00	15.50%
Deviation	4.50	–0.50	–5.50	
$p \times \text{Deviation}^2$	6.08	0.13	6.05	
Variance				**12.25**
Standard Deviation (%)				**3.50%**
Toon Ltd				**Expected Return**
Return	12.00	15.00	18.00	14.70%
Deviation	–2.70	0.30	3.30	
$p \times \text{Deviation}^2$	2.19	0.05	2.18	
Variance				**4.41**
Standard Deviation (%)				**2.10%**

The risk associated, as measured with standard deviation of returns, with Boom Ltd is 3.50% and that of Toon Ltd is 2.10%.

What happens to the returns and risks of the portfolio consisting of Boom Ltd and Toon Ltd? The expected return of the portfolio would be given by the weighted average of the expected returns of the two firms. Unfortunately (or fortunately) the same thing does not hold true about risk. When a portfolio is formed using Boom Ltd and Toon Ltd, the variations of returns of each impact the returns of the portfolio, but not in the same manner.

Portfolio risk reduces because returns of the securities in the portfolio behave differently to a given change.

Another important aspect that needs to be considered is how the returns of the two firms constituting the portfolio co-vary with respect to one another. The variations per se of the individual securities become less important in a portfolio as compared to the nature of interactions of these securities with each other.

COVARIANCE

Covariance is a measure of how returns co-vary with each other. *Variance* refers to the variations in returns of the security with itself, as we multiply the deviations from the mean value with itself. *Covariance* of a portfolio consisting of two securities is determined by how the deviation in return from its mean is related to deviation in return from the mean of another security. If A and E denote the returns, $\bar{A}$ and $\bar{E}$ denote the respective expected values of returns of these two securities. The covariance of two must be measured by the product of deviations of the two securities from their respective means, i.e.,

Portfolio variance is determined by covariance of the securities

$(A - \bar{A}) \times (E - \bar{E})$.

Covariance of Security 1 and Security 2, whose returns are denoted as R_1 and R_2, is given by Equation 8-3.

$$\text{Cov}(R_1, R_2) = \sum_{1}^{n} p_i (R_1 - \bar{R}_1)(R_2 - \bar{R}_2) \tag{8-3}$$

Covariance of the two securities indicates the direction and extent of linkage of behaviour of variations of returns of two securities. Covariance, if positive, implies that the deviations of returns from the expected value of the two securities are in same direction. A negative covariance implies that the deviations are in opposite directions. The extent of relationship is reflected in the magnitude of the covariance.

A positive covariance means that the direction of change in the returns of the two securities is same, while a negative covariance implies the changes are in opposite directions.

In our example of Boom Ltd and Toon Ltd, the returns move in different directions under good, average, and poor economic scenarios. The expected returns of the two firms are 15.50% and 14.70% respectively.

Notice that when the economic scenario is good, the returns of Boom Ltd show a positive deviation of 4.50% from its expected value, while the returns of Toon Ltd have a negative deviation of 2.70% from its expected value. Similarly when economic scenario turns poor, the deviations from the respective expected returns are –5.50% and +3.30% for Boom Ltd and Toon Ltd respectively. We compute the covariance of Boom Ltd and Toon Ltd by using Equation 8-3.

	Economic Scenario			
Conditions	*Good*	*Average*	*Poor*	
Returns (%)				*Expected Return*
Boom Ltd	20.00	15.00	10.00	15.50
Toon Ltd	12.00	15.00	18.00	14.70
Covariance				
Probability (p)	30%	50%	20%	
Deviation—Boom Ltd	4.50	–0.50	–5.50	
Deviation—Toon Ltd	–2.70	0.30	3.30	
p × Product of deviations	–3.65	–0.08	–3.63	
Covariance				*–7.35*
Coefficient of correlation				*–1.00*

$$\text{Cov (Boom, Toon)} = 0.30(20.00 - 15.50) \times (12.00 - 14.70)$$
$$+ 0.50(15.00 - 15.50) \times (15.00 - 14.70)$$
$$+ 0.25(10.00 - 15.50) \times (18.00 - 14.70)$$
$$= -7.35$$

When the two shares react in opposite directions they partially or fully cancel out the change in returns of each other, making the overall returns of the portfolio more stable.

A negative covariance of 7.35 between Boom Ltd and Toon Ltd indicates that the returns of the two change in opposite directions when the economic scenario changes. Therefore, the returns of the portfolio of Boom Ltd and Toon Ltd would be more stable than if the investment was solely in either Boom Ltd or Toon Ltd.

Coefficient of Correlation

While covariance measures the relationship of two securities in absolute terms, the strength of the relationship between the two securities is measured from an easier statistic known as the *coefficient of correlation*. Covariance is a measure of variation of two securities simultaneously, while standard deviation of each security is a measure of the variation of individual security. If covariance is normalized with the individual standard deviations we get a relative measure of the relationship of the two securities.

Coefficient of correlation is a relative measure of the relationship of returns of the two securities. Larger the coefficient greater is the correlation between the two.

Coefficient of correlation, denoted as ρ (rho) is calculated by dividing the covariance by the product of the standard deviations as represented in Equation 8-4.

$$\text{Coefficient of Correlation, } \rho = \frac{Cov\,(R_1, R_2)}{\sigma_1\,\sigma_2} \qquad (8\text{-}4)$$

Coefficient of correlation can have values ranging from −1.00 to +1.00. A negative sign indicates an inverse relationship between two securities. If the coefficient of correlation is negative, the behaviour of returns of the two securities is opposite. If returns of one increase, the returns of the other decrease. The magnitude of coefficient of correlation indicates the strength of the relationship. The values of coefficient of correlation of +1.00 and −1.00 denote perfect positive and perfect negative correlation respectively.

Positive correlation signifies same behaviour and negative correlation implies opposite behaviour of returns of two securities.

Let us find the coefficient of correlation for Boom Ltd and Toon Ltd using Equation 8-4.

$$\text{Coefficient of Correlation, } \rho = \frac{\text{Cov}(R_1, R_2)}{\sigma_1 \sigma_2}$$
$$= \frac{-7.35}{3.50 \times 2.10} = -1.00$$

From the coefficient of correlation of −1.00, we infer that the returns of Boom Ltd and Toon Ltd are perfectly negatively correlated. We shall demonstrate later that it is a desirable characteristic, which does not seem to exist. More likely than not, financial assets are found to have a positive correlation with one another in the real world. A pictorial view of positive and negative correlation is shown in Figures 8-1(a) and (b) respectively.

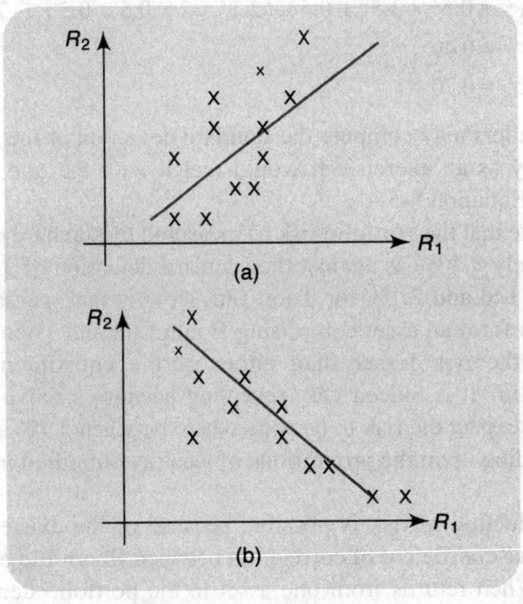

Figure 8-1 (a) Positive correlation (b) Negative correlation

TWO-ASSET PORTFOLIO

As stated earlier, the variance of a portfolio is not as much a function of individual variances of the assets constituting the portfolio as that of the covariances among these securities. The simplest of all portfolios is the combination of only two assets.

Besides selection of assets in a portfolio, another parameter that needs to be decided is the proportion of money to be allocated for each asset. When two assets with variances of σ_1^2 and σ_2^2 are combined to form a portfolio, the variance of the portfolio is given by Equation 8-5[1]:

Variance of the portfolio,

$$\sigma_p^2 = w_1^2\sigma_1^2 + w_2^2\sigma_2^2 + 2w_1w_2\,\text{Cov}(R_1, R_2) \qquad (8\text{-}5)$$

where w_1 and w_2 are the proportions of wealth in asset 1 and 2 respectively, and

$$w_1 + w_2 = 1$$

[1]This expression can be derived as follows:

$$R_p = w_1R_1 + w_2R_2 \text{ and } \bar{R}_p = w_1\bar{R}_1 + w_2\bar{R}_2$$
$$\text{Var}\,(R_p) = (R_p - \bar{R}_p)^2 = [(w_1R_1 + w_2R_2) - (w_1\bar{R}_1 + w_2\bar{R}_2)]^2$$
$$= [w_1(R_1 - \bar{R}_1) + w_2(R_2 - \bar{R}_2)]^2$$
$$= [w_1^2(R_1 - \bar{R}_1)^2 + w_2^2(R_2 - \bar{R}_2)^2 + 2w_1w_2(R_1 - \bar{R}_1)(R_2 - \bar{R}_2)]$$
$$= w_1^2\sigma_1^2 + w_2^2\sigma_2^2 + 2w_1w_2\text{Cov}(R_1, R_2)$$

Variance of the portfolio with equal investment in Boom Ltd and Toon Ltd as per Equation 8-5 is 0.49, equivalent to a standard deviation of 0.70%.

Variance of the portfolio

$$\sigma_p^2 = 0.5^2 \times 3.5^2 + 0.5^2 \times 2.1^2 + 2 \times 0.5 \times 0.5 \times (-7.35)$$
$$= 0.49$$

or $\sigma_p = 0.70$

Readers may compute the standard deviation of the portfolio directly as an exercise. It would match with the one obtained using Equation 8-5.

Note that the portfolio risk as measured by standard deviation is merely 0.70% as against the standard deviation of 3.50% for Boom Ltd and 2.1% for Toon Ltd. How is that we have been able to form an asset comprising Boom Ltd. and Toon Ltd that gives the risk lesser than either of the constituent of the portfolio? It is indeed very revealing because a naïve investor would expect the risk to be somewhere between 2.1% and 3.5% depending upon the proportions of wealth committed in each of them.

Reduction in risk is possible because of the existence of a negative coefficient of correlation between Boom Ltd and Toon Ltd. When returns from one asset in the portfolio decline, the returns from second increase, and while returns from the second show a decline the first asset compensates the loss. This renders stability to the returns of the portfolio, making if safer than either of the asset comprising it.

Risk Return Profile of Two-asset Portfolio

We now evaluate the changes that can take place in the risk and return of a portfolio of two assets merely by changing the proportion of investment in each of the asset. Recall that the portfolio return and risk are given by Equations 8-1 and 8-5 respectively reproduced below:

$$\text{Portfolio Return, } R_p = w_1R_1 + w_2R_2 \quad (8\text{-}6a)$$

$$\text{Protfolio Risk, } \sigma_p^2 = w_1^2\sigma_1^2 + w_2^2\sigma_2^2 + w_1w_2\text{Cov}(R_1, R_2) \quad (8\text{-}6b)$$

where $\text{Cov}(R_1, R_2) = \rho\sigma_1\sigma_2$ and $w_1 + w_2 = 1$

Let us consider a portfolio of Security 1 and Security 2 with expected returns of R_1 and R_2 and standard deviation of σ_1 and σ_2 respectively. We shall examine the two special cases of relationship between the two firms, i.e., where perfect positive or perfect negative correlation between the two securities exists. These are of special significance to us in portfolio theory. Consider a portfolio consisting of two securities with Firm 1 and Firm 2 having the following characteristics:

	Firm 1	Firm 2
Return	15%	30%
Standard Deviation	10%	20%

With perfect positive correlation ($\rho = +1$)

When there is a perfect positive correlation among the securities of Firm 1 and Firm 2, the portfolio return and risk are given by:

$$\text{Portfolio Return, } R_p = w_1R_1 + w_2R_2 \quad (8\text{-}7a)$$

$$\text{Portfolio Risk, } \sigma_p^2 = w_1^2\sigma_1^2 + w_2^2\sigma_2^2 + 2w_1w_2\rho\sigma_1\sigma_2$$

with ρ = 1

$$\sigma_p^2 = w_1^2\sigma_1^2 + w_2^2\sigma_2^2 + 2w_1w_2\sigma_1\sigma_2$$
$$= (w_1\sigma_1 + w_2\sigma_2)^2$$

$$\text{or} \quad \sigma_p = w_1\sigma_1 + w_2\sigma_2 \quad (8\text{-}7b)$$

Note that the standard deviation of the portfolio is also the weighted average of the standard deviations of the individual securities constituting the portfolio, as is the case with portfolio return.

When 100% of the money is invested in Firm 1, the return and standard deviation of the portfolio would be equal to those of Firm 1, i.e., a portfolio return of 15% and standard deviation of 10%. As we change the composition of the portfolio by replacing Firm 1 by Firm 2 in the portfolio (remember to retain the original size of the portfolio) the portfolio return and risk move towards those of Firm 2.

Depending upon the proportion of money in Firm 1 and Firm 2, the return and standard deviation of the portfolio are given by Equations 8-7(a) and 8-7(b) respectively. Any combination of return and risk that satisfies Equations 8-7(a) and 8-7(b) is possible.

Specific combinations of return and risk of the portfolio are shown in Table 8-1(a). The return and risk are depicted graphically in Figure 8-2 by bold dotted line with $\rho = +1$.

When 100% of the money is invested in Firm 2, the portfolio acquires the complete characteristics of Firm 2 with return and standard deviation of 30% and 20% respectively.

Table 8-1(a) Portfolio return and risk with correlation coefficient = 1

All figures in %

w_1	100	80	60	40	20	0
w_2	0	20	40	60	80	100
R_p	15	18	21	24	27	30
σ_p	10	12	14	16	18	20

With perfect negative correlation ($\rho = -1$)

When there is a perfect negative correlation among the securities of Firm 1 and Firm 2, the portfolio return and risk are given by:

$$\text{Portfolio Return, } R_p = w_1R_1 + w_2R_2 \quad (8\text{-}8a)$$

$$\text{Portfolio Risk, } \sigma_p^2 = w_1^2\sigma_1^2 + w_2^2\sigma_2^2 + 2w_1w_2\rho\sigma_1\sigma_2$$

With ρ = –1

$$\sigma_p^2 = w_1^2\sigma_1^2 + w_2^2\sigma_2^2 - 2w_1w_2\sigma_1\sigma_2$$
$$= (w_1\sigma_1 - w_2\sigma_2)^2$$

$$\text{or} \quad \sigma_p = (w_1\sigma_1 - w_2\sigma_2) \quad (8\text{-}8b)$$

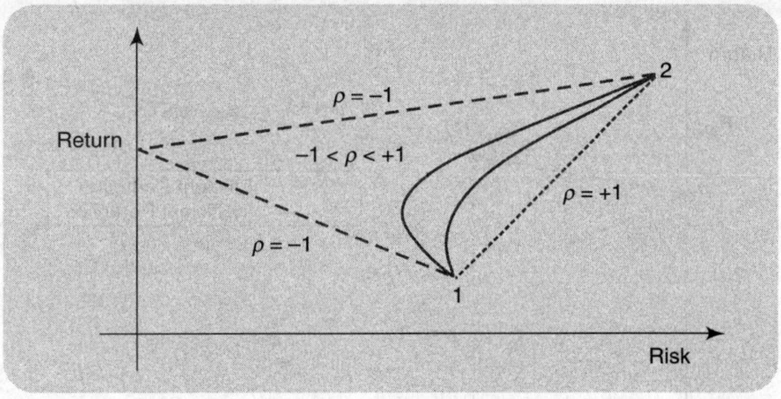

Figure 8-2 Portfolio risk and return

Table 8-1(b) Portfolio return and risk with correlation coefficient = –1

All figures in %

w_1	100	80	60	40	20	0
w_2	0	20	40	60	80	100
R_p	15	18	21	24	27	30
σ_p	10	4	2	8	14	20

Note that while return of the portfolio remains equal to the weighted average of the returns of the individual securities constituting the portfolio, the risk of the portfolio throws up some interesting possibilities.

When 100% of the money of invested in Firm 1 the return and standard deviation of the portfolio would be equal to that of the firm, i.e., a portfolio return of 15% and standard deviation of 10%. As we change the composition of the portfolio by replacing Firm 1 by Firm 2 and maintaining the same size of the portfolio, the portfolio return and risk move towards those of Firm 2. Perfect negative correlation between two securities results in an initial increase in returns (as returns of Firm 2 are higher than that of firm 1), the risk declines due to the offsetting effect of the two securities.

Depending upon the proportion of money in Firm 1 and Firm 2, the return and standard deviation of the portfolio are given by Equations 8-8(a) and 8-8(b). Any combination of return and risk that satisfies these two equations is possible. With different proportions in Firm 1 and Firm 2 different profiles of the return and risk of the portfolio are shown in Table 8-1(b).

The combinations of risk and returns of the portfolio are depicted in Figure 8-2. Small dotted line represents combination when $\rho = 1$. Big dotted line represents combinations when $\rho = -1$. Bold curved lines are combinations when $-1 < \rho < +1$.

Notice in cases of perfect positive and negative correlation, the locus of risk is substantially different. In the instant case of perfect negative correlation we observe that the risk declines when proportion of Firm 2 increases in the portfolio. Since the return of Firm 2 is higher than that of Firm 1, we also see an increase in the return of the portfolio as larger portion of money earns greater returns.

When two securities have coefficient of correlation of –1.00, it is possible to have a zero risk portfolio with positive return by simply adjusting the proportions of investment.

However, the risk cannot fall below zero. As proportions of Firm 2 increase, there comes a point where the offsetting of risk is complete. From there onwards both returns and risk start following the profile of Firm 2.

Perfect negative correlation presents an interesting portfolio. This portfolio is with zero risk and yet has some return that is in excess of the returns of Firm 1. This may be found by equating the portfolio risk given by Equation 8-8(b) to zero.

$$\sigma_p = (w_1\sigma_1 - w_2\sigma_2) = 0 \quad \text{gives} \quad \frac{w_1}{w_2} = \frac{\sigma_2}{\sigma_1}$$

$$\text{or } w_1 = \frac{\sigma_2}{\sigma_1 + \sigma_2} \text{ and } w_2 = \frac{\sigma_1}{\sigma_1 + \sigma_2} \tag{8-9}$$

We may find one such combination of Firm 1 and Firm 2 using Equation 8-9. The portfolio that gives zero risk would have the following values of w_1 and w_2.

$$w_1 = \frac{\sigma_1}{\sigma_1 + \sigma_2} = \frac{20}{10 + 20} = \frac{2}{3}$$

$$\text{and} \quad w_2 = \frac{\sigma_1}{\sigma_1 + \sigma_2} = \frac{10}{10 + 20} = \frac{1}{3}$$

With two third investments in Firm 1 and the remaining one third in Firm 2, we can achieve a zero portfolio risk with 20% portfolio return.

$$\text{Portfolio Return, } R_p = w_1R_1 + w_2R_2$$

$$= \left(\frac{2}{3} \times 15\right) + \left(\frac{1}{3} \times 30\right) = 20\%$$

Efficient Portfolios and Efficient Frontier

Another interesting feature of the portfolio theory can be observed with the coefficient of correlation at –1.00. One can observe the two segments of risk–return profile when the proportions of amount in the portfolio move from Firm 1 to Firm 2. The portfolio characteristics follow a path from A to B (increasing returns but falling risk) and then from B to C (increasing returns and increasing risk) as shown in Figure 8-3 reproducing the portion of Figure 8-2 corresponding to perfect negative correlation.

An efficient portfolio offers higher return for the same risk or lower risk for same return.

The segment AB represents a set of portfolios for which we have another portfolio on segment BC, which has higher return for the same risk. Portfolio (σ_p, R_{p1}) on the segment AB is inefficient as compared to Portfolio (σ_p, R_{p2}) on the segment BC because $R_{p2} > R_{p1}$ for the same risk, σ_p. An investor willing the carry

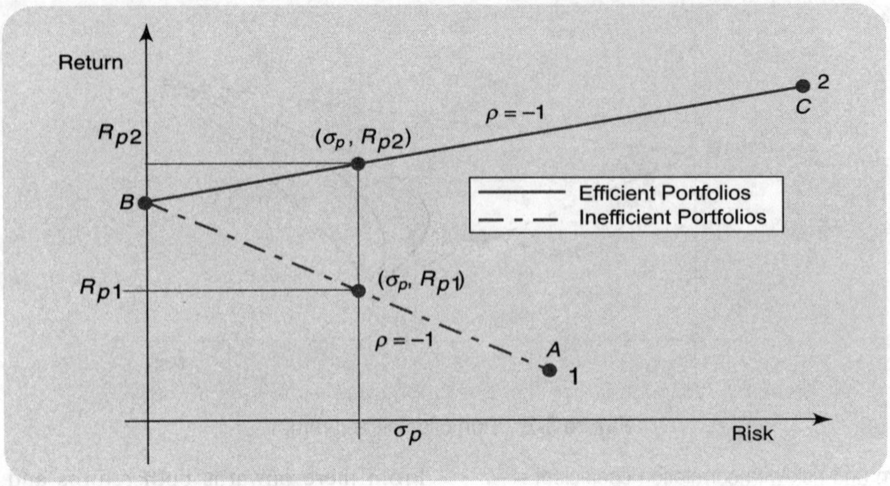

Figure 8-3 Efficient and inefficient portfolios

a risk of σ_p can obtain a portfolio on segment BC that offers a greater return than the one on segment AB.

A portfolio is termed as inefficient when there exists another portfolio with—(1) same risk but higher return; or (2) same return but lower risk. By the same token we may also define an efficient portfolio as one for which there is no portfolio that offers—(1) greater return for the same risk; or (2) lower risk for the same return.

Clearly, any portfolio on segment AB is dominated by some corresponding portfolio on segment BC. The portfolios on segment BC are efficient portfolios while those on AB are inefficient ones. The locus of efficient set of portfolios is known as an *efficient frontier*.

In the real world it is rather difficult to find assets with even a small negative correlation. It is impossible to identify assets that have perfect negative correlation. Most financial assets have positive correlation or at best can be said to have no correlation (coefficient of correlation very close to zero). Under such conditions the possible portfolios would lie on the curved path as in Figure 8-2 relating to coefficient of correlation between 0 and < 1.00, rather than on straight lines corresponding to coefficients of correlation of +1.00 or –1.00.

The determination of an efficient frontier is depicted in Figure 8-4. Curve 1-2 represents portfolios formed by using different proportions of Security 1 and Security 2, with the given coefficient of cor-relation. Portfolio A and Portfolio D are two such portfolios. Similarly, Curve 3-4 represents portfolios consisting of different proportions of Security 3 and Security 4. These securities have different associated risks and returns and have some correlation. Portfolio B and Portfolio C are two such portfolios that use different proportions of Security 3 and Security 4.

Efficient frontier is the locus of efficient portfolios.

A look at Figure 8-4 would reveal that Portfolio A is superior to Portfolio B as it offers greater return for the same amount of risk. Similarly, Portfolio C is more efficient that Portfolio D as it offers the same return with a lower risk. Applying the same logic we find the portfolios on dark portion of the curve outperform the rest. The dark portion of the curve in Figure 8-4 is the efficient frontier.

Feasible Portfolios and Efficient Frontier

When only two risky assets are combined to form a portfolio, the possible combinations on the return–risk space are represented by a curve/line as can be seen in Figures 8-2 to 8-4. When more than two assets are combined in the portfolio, the combinations of portfolios that are feasible by changing proportions of money occupy an area on the return—risk space as shown by shaded area rather than a line.

Feasible portfolios are a set of portfolios formed by a combination of securities that can be obtained by adjusting the proportions of the amount invested in each security.

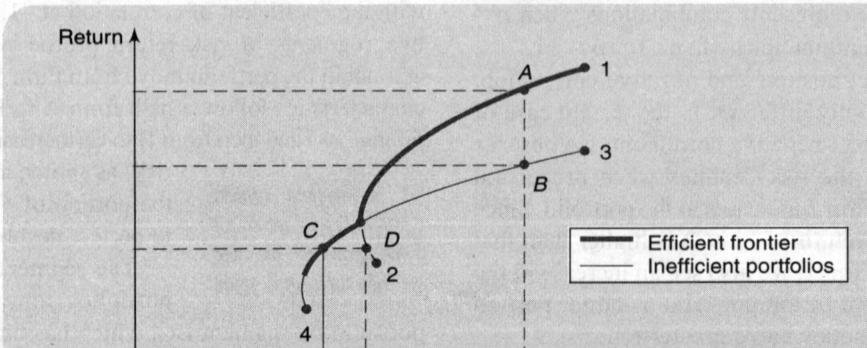

Figure 8-4 The efficient frontier

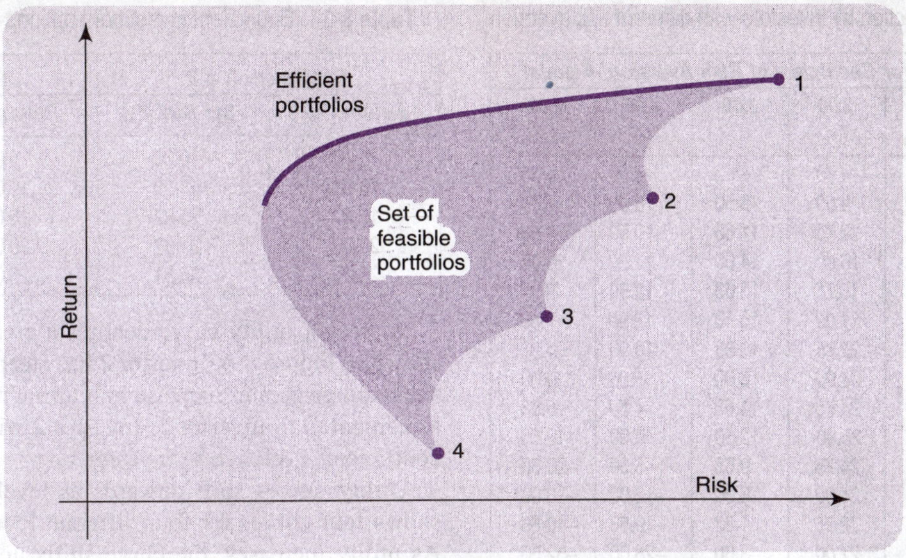

Figure 8-5 Feasible portfolios and efficient frontier

Figure 8-5 shows the space for feasible portfolios and efficient frontier for four securities having different return and risk profile. The area bounded by the curve represents the set of feasible portfolios meaning that any combination of return and risk that lies in the area can be attained by having securities 1 to 4 in some proportion. The dark line represents the efficient frontier implying the superiority of the portfolios falling on it in terms of either more return for given risk or less risk for a given return.

RISK AVERSION AND UTILITY INDIFFERENCE CURVES

It is often seen that the investors value different investment opportunities with a trade-off between risk and return. It is not unusual to find investors say 'I want a 6% return on my bank deposits (assumed to be risk free). However, if I invest in the stock market the return must be 15%'. In terms of investment options, the investment in a risk-free asset with 6% return and that in the stock market (assumed to have 20% risk) with a return of 15% appear to be equivalent. The investor is equating 9% extra return in the stock market with the 20% extra risk being taken.

Investors, in fact, do not have such simplistic substitution of risk with return or vice versa. Further, each investor has a different appetite for risk. Some investors perceive stock market investments to be too risky and yet some investors never wish to keep their money in safe bank deposits. Different investors classify risk by different amounts of return and vice versa. Assuming that risk and returns are the only two considerations in the choice of investments, we further assume that investors can assign a utility score for competing investments. Although there can be many scoring systems that are devised, there is one very commonly used utility function given by Equation 8-10.

Most investors are risk-averse because utility of money decreases with the increased risk for most of them.

$$U = R - 0.005A\sigma^2 \qquad (8\text{-}10)$$

The utility value is represented by U, A is an index that measures an individual investor's risk aversion, and R and σ are the expected return and standard deviation of the investment respectively. The factor of 0.005 is a scaling factor that allows the use of per cent in the values of R and σ instead of decimal.

According to Equation 8-10, the utility of an investment increases with increasing return and decreases with increasing risk. Utility curves will be positively sloped if investors want more return for increased risk. The penalty for reduction in utility from increasing risk is dependent on factor A, named as *coefficient of risk aversion* that is specific to an individual. Higher the value of A, the more risk averse the person is. The value of A can be assigned through some appropriate questionnaires.

Individuals with different coefficient of risk aversion A would choose different investments depending upon which investment maximizes utility. For a given return and risk profile, one can calculate the utility for different investment options. An investor would choose the investment that maximizes the utility of money.

Table 8-2 highlights the contrast in choosing investments by different investors. An investor more averse to risk (with $A = 5$) chooses an investment with 20% return and 20% risk, while an investor who is less averse to risk ($A = 1$) would maximize his/her utility with an investment that yields 100% return and carries an equal risk.

Table 8-2 also provides an insight into the investment selection by investors with different risk appetites. Observe that for an investor with a coefficient of risk aversion at 2 we have several invest-ments that yield equal utility. An investment with 5% return and 5% risk provides the same utility of 4.75 as an investment with 95% return and 95% risk. Similarly, an investor with $A = 5$ treats an investment with 10% return and 10% risk equal to the investment providing 30% return and 30% risk with the utility fixed at 7.50.

Individual investors are characterized by different degrees of risk aversion.

Table 8-2 Investment selection by investors with different risk aversion

Investment Options		Utility for Coefficient of Risk Aversion, A equal				
Return (%)	Std Dev (%)	1.00	2.00	3.00	4.00	5.00
5.00	5.00	4.88	*4.75*	4.63	*4.50*	*4.38*
10.00	10.00	9.50	*9.00*	8.50	*8.00*	*7.50*
15.00	15.00	13.88	*12.75*	11.63	10.50	*9.38*
20.00	**20.00**	18.00	*16.00*	14.00	*12.00*	**10.00**
25.00	**25.00**	21.88	*18.75*	15.63	**12.50**	*9.38*
30.00	30.00	25.50	*21.00*	16.50	*12.00*	*7.50*
35.00	**35.00**	28.88	*22.75*	**16.63**	10.50	*4.38*
40.00	40.00	32.00	*24.00*	16.00	*8.00*	0.00
45.00	45.00	34.88	*24.75*	14.63	*4.50*	–5.63
50.00	**50.00**	37.50	**25.00**	12.50	0.00	–12.50
55.00	55.00	39.88	*24.75*	9.63	–5.50	–20.63
60.00	60.00	42.00	*24.00*	6.00	–12.00	–30.00
65.00	65.00	43.88	*22.75*	1.63	–19.50	–40.63
70.00	70.00	45.50	*21.00*	–3.50	–28.00	–52.50
75.00	75.00	46.88	*18.75*	–9.38	–37.50	–65.63
80.00	80.00	48.00	*16.00*	–16.00	–48.00	–80.00
85.00	85.00	48.88	*12.75*	–23.38	–59.50	–95.63
90.00	90.00	*49.50*	*9.00*	–31.50	–72.00	–112.50
95.00	95.00	49.88	*4.75*	–40.38	–85.50	–130.63
100.00	**100.00**	**50.00**	0.00	–50.00	–100.00	–150.00
110.00	110.00	*49.50*	–11.00	–71.50	–132.00	–192.50
Maximum Utility		50.00	25.00	16.63	12.50	10.00

Investments with maximum utility are in **bold** and those with identical utility are in *italics*.

The investments that provide identical utility value to the investor are also referred as *iso-utility curve*. We can construct the utility indifference curve for an investor with a given value of A. Table 8-3 lists the various combinations of investments that have a utility value of 5.00 for two investors with risk aversion coefficient of 3 and 5 respectively. Returns of 5% with no risk is considered equivalent to a return of 20% with 31.62% of risk for an investor having a coefficient of risk aversion at 3. Similarly, for an investor with coefficient of risk aversion at 5, the investments with return of 10% and 14.14% risk are equivalent to investments with 15% return and 20% risk. Note that for same return of 15% one investor (A = 5) equates risk of 20% while the other (A = 3) takes around 26%.

There are many combinations of return and risk that offer same utility of money.

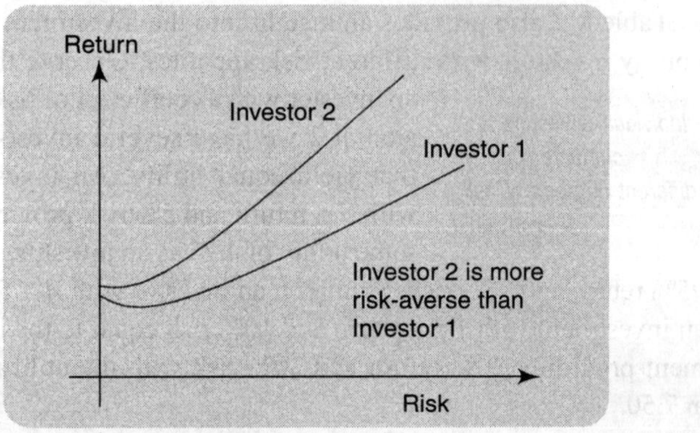

Figure 8-6 Risk aversion and utility

Table 8-3 Equivalent investment options for constant utility U = 5

Coefficient A = 3		Coefficient A = 5	
Return (%)	Std Dev (%)	Return (%)	Std Dev (%)
5.00	0.00	5.00	0.00
10.00	18.26	10.00	14.14
15.00	25.82	15.00	20.00
20.00	31.62	20.00	24.49
25.00	36.51	25.00	28.28

A steeper utility curve denotes a greater aversion to risk as shown in Figure 8-6. Investor 2 has steeper utility implying that she requires greater increase in return with same increase in risk as compared to Investor 1. Investor 2 will have higher value of coefficient A relative to Investor 1.

Utility curves shift upwards as level increases. Figure 8-7 shows four curves for four different levels of utility of money. As utility increases, the curve shifts upwards as may be seen from the Figure 8-7 where $U_4 > U_3 > U_2 > U_1$. Each curve represents the same level of utility of money for different combinations of risk and return of investments to which the investor is indifferent. Two indifference curves corresponding to two different utility levels never intersect for the same investor.

OPTIMUM PORTFOLIO

With known efficient frontier, i.e., the locus of portfolios with maximum return for given risk or least risk for given return, and the indifference curves of the investor, the problem of optimization is concerned with determining the portfolio that satisfies following conditions—(1) it lies on the efficient frontier; and (2) it maximizes the utility for the investor.

Finding a portfolio on the efficient frontier ensures that for given return there is no portfolio with lesser risk or for given risk there is no portfolio with a higher return. Maximization of utility can be achieved through tangency of the utility curves with the efficient frontier.

The portfolio on the point of tangency of the utility curve and the efficient frontier represents the optimum portfolio since no other point on the risk and return space provides greater utility. This point is depicted as Point O at the intersection of efficient frontier and utility curve with U = 3 in Figure 8-8. The intersection of

Optimum portfolio maximizes the utility of money and lies on the efficient frontier.

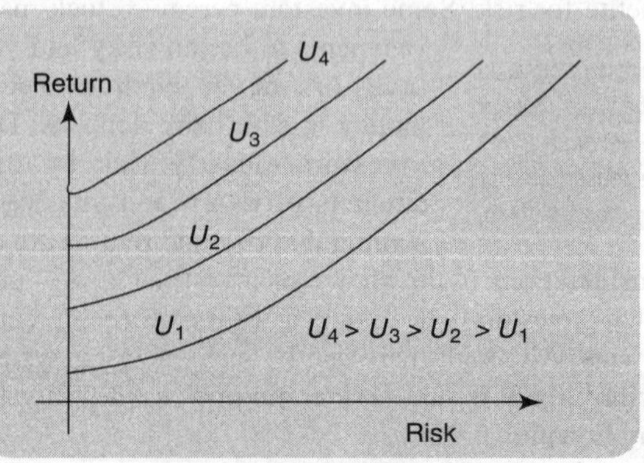

Figure 8-7 Utility indifference curves

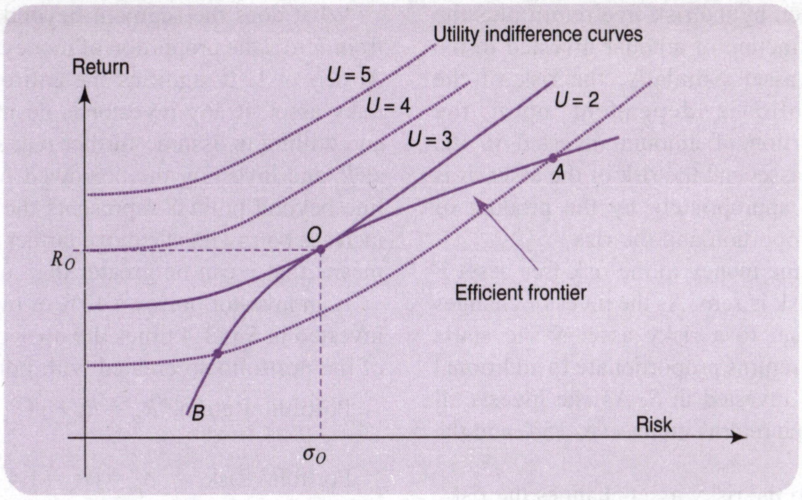

Figure 8-8 Finding optimum portfolio with risky assets

utility curve and the efficient frontier at two points, as is the case with utility curve with $U = 2$, also represents feasible combination of portfolio but its selection is sub-optimal. While Portfolio A provides higher return than the optimum Portfolio O, it also entails greater risk. The risk and return of Portfolio A when mapped on the utility curve represents a lower utility level of $U = 2$. Similarly, Portfolio B has a lower risk than O but its lower return again makes the utility level lower at $U = 2$.

The utility level increases as we move upwards across the efficient frontier. We continue this till we move to a level where the utility curve becomes tangent to the efficient frontier. Moving further upwards increases utility but no portfolio is available to satisfy the higher level of utility. Utility curve beyond the efficient frontier represents non-feasible alternatives as efficient frontier and utility curve do not intersect. This is evidenced from the utility indifference curves at $U = 4$ and $U = 5$ in Figure 8-8.

CAPITAL ALLOCATION LINE

The markets comprise huge number of securities with varying characteristics. It is difficult to pick some securities out of thousands to form a portfolio with the desired parameters. Rather than viewing these securities as independent assets, investors normally classify them into various asset classes. Similar kinds of assets are grouped together. The grouping of assets into various classes helps in profiling the needs of investors and designing of an appropriate portfolio for them. For the sake of convenience, it is easier for people to classify various securities into three distinct classes—safe assets, assets with minimal risk, and risky assets.

Safe assets It comprises government securities such as T-Bills, treasury bonds, and other government securities normally termed as risk-free assets.

Assets with minimal risk Assets in this category include bonds of various types that offer nominal risk and very stable returns.

Risky assets This class of assets includes stocks of various firms. Stocks are regarded as the most risky financial assets.

Normally, the process of portfolio design begins from the basic question of allocation of capital into assets of various risk classes. Most portfolio managers and investors are concerned with allocation of funds in various broad assets. The choice of securities within each asset class is decided once the capital allocation is made.

This process of portfolio optimization is known as the *top-down approach*, where the investor considers asset allocation as the most important part of portfolio construction. The task of identifying the specific securities to be included in each asset class is left to people lower in the organizational hierarchy. The top management of investment companies or of mutual funds is often more concerned with the basic question of how much allocation of capital can be made in various asset classes. Allocation of capital is considered very important because of the belief that portfolio risk can be easily contained and/or controlled by allocation of funds from risky assets to risk-free assets and vice versa. The belief is not wrong as we can see from the discussion that follows.

Top-down approach of portfolio construction starts from selection of class of assets before identifying the securities in each class of asset.

Let us consider the available investment opportunities if the investment spectrum consists only of two classes of assets. We name these assets as risk-free asset, F and risky asset, primarily representing a portfolio of securities, S.

Let us assume that Portfolio F, constituted of risk-free securities, yields a return of 5%. Being risk-free, the portfolio has a zero standard deviation of return. On the other hand, we have a portfolio that is denoted as the risky asset, S having an expected return of R_s of 15% and risk measured by its standard deviation σ_s at 20%. The fraction of money invested in risky Portfolio S is y and the remaining amount $(1 - y)$ is invested in the risk-free Portfolio F. The return and risk of the combined portfolio of risk-free assets and risky assets, is found by using Equations 8-6(a) and 8-6(b).

Portfolio Return, $R_p = y\,R_s + (1 - y)R_f = R_f + y(R_s - R_f)$

Portfolio Risk

$$(\sigma_p)^2 = y^2\sigma_s^2 + (1 - y)^2\sigma_f^2 + 2y(1 - y)\,\text{Cov}(R_f, R_s) = y^2\sigma_s^2$$

$$[\because \text{Cov}(R_f, R_s) = 0 \text{ and } \sigma_f = 0]$$

or $\qquad \sigma_p = y\sigma_s$

The portfolio return is given by the risk-free return plus the excess return earned on the fraction of amount invested in the risky asset. Similarly, the risk of the portfolio is dependent upon the proportion of amount invested in the risky asset and the risk of the asset. It is given appropriately by the product of the proportion and the risk.

> CAL is the locus of portfolios constructed by adjusting the proportions of wealth in risk-free asset and risky asset.

When investor invests all the money in the risk-free asset F ($y = 0$), the return is 5% and risk is zero. As the investor changes position from a risk-free asset to a risky asset S she starts assuming risk and increasing returns proportionate to additional return and the amount being invested in S. As she invests all the money in the risky asset the returns increase to 15% and the risk to 20%.

The allocation of money to the risky asset changes the risk–return profile of the portfolio so constituted. This profile is represented as the *capital allocation line* (CAL) in Figure 8-9. With increasing proportion in the risky asset y, a profile of the risk–return that falls on the segment FS in the Figure 8-9 is obtainable. With increasing y, both return and risk increase at a rate determined by the slope of the line FS, which is CAL. This slope of CAL is dependent the excess return and the additional risk attached with S. The slope of the CAL is given by:

$$\text{Slope of the CAL} = \frac{\text{Excess Return}}{\text{Additional Risk}}$$

$$= \frac{R_s - R_f}{\sigma_s} = \frac{15-5}{20} = 0.50$$

A steeper CAL leads to a more rewarding allocation of funds to the risky asset S. This implies that the investor gets an increased return for the same increase in risk. The slope of CAL is also referred as *reward-to-variability ratio* as it equates reward with the risk. The slope of CAL of 0.5 simply means that the 1% increase in risk results in 0.5% increase in return.

With intercept and slope of the line known, we can represent CAL as:

$$\text{CAL; } R_p = R_f + \text{Slope} \times \sigma_p = R_f + \frac{R_s - R_f}{\sigma_s} \times \sigma_p$$

$$\text{or} \quad R_p = R_f + \frac{\sigma_p}{\sigma_s}(R_s - R_f) \qquad (8\text{-}11)$$

What does the segment beyond FS represent? As we move from F to S the proportion of money in the risky asset y increases. At S, $y = 1$. It signifies the entire investment of funds in the risky asset. If any investor is desirous of increasing the return and willing to assume further risk she may do so by borrowing at R_f and investing the borrowed funds in S. Capital allocation line beyond point S represents the borrowing segment. As we increase borrowing we move farther away from S. This essentially means that y can be greater than one.

If an investor borrows 40% of owned money, the total wealth invested in S is 1.4 times the owned money. The return and risk of the portfolio so created with borrowed funds would be:

$$\text{Portfolio Return, } R_p = R_f + y(R_s - R_f) = 5 + 1.4(15-5) = 19\%$$

$$\text{Portfolio Risk, } \quad \sigma_p = y\sigma_s = 1.4 \times 20 = 28\%$$

We may check if the risk–return combination lies of the CAL or not. The CAL given by Equation 8-11:

$$R_p = R_f + \frac{\sigma_p}{\sigma_s}(R_s - R_f) = 5 + \frac{28}{20}(15-5)$$

$$= 19\% \text{ (Same as calculated above)}$$

Example 8-4 Capital Allocation Line

Mr Xing is considering an investment of ₹4,00,000. He wants to allocate a part of the funds to a portfolio of risk-free securities providing a return of 8%, and the remaining part in a share portfolio, that has an expected return and the standard deviation of 24% each.

(a) What is the capital allocation line faced by Mr Xing?
(b) What does this line mean to him?
(c) If Mr Xing is prepared to assume a maximum risk of 15%, what is the best return he can hope for?
(d) What will be the composition of the funds allocated in different classes of securities by Mr Xing to get a return calculated in (c) above?
(e) In case Mr Xing needs a return of 32%, what minimum risk would he have to assume and how can he achieve the target return of 32%?

Solution

(a) The CAL faced by Mr Xing is:

$$R_p = R_f + \frac{\sigma_p}{\sigma_s}(R_s - R_f) = 8 + \frac{1}{24}(24-8)\sigma_p$$

$$= 8 + \frac{2}{3}\sigma_p$$

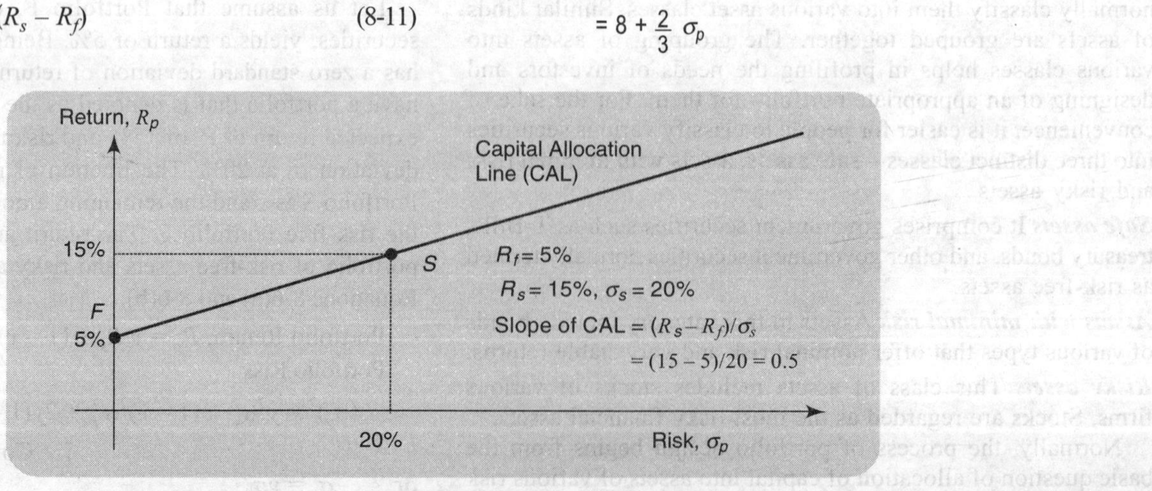

Figure 8-9 Feasible investment set for risky and risk-free assets

(b) The CAL implies that any combination of return and risk that lies on it is achievable by mere allocation of funds in the risky and risk-free assets.

(c) If Mr Xing could take risk no greater than 15% then the maximum return that can be obtained by him is given by CAL as:

$$R_p = 8 + \frac{2}{3}\ \sigma_p = 8 + \frac{2}{3} \times 15 = 18\%$$

(d) The proportion of fund that Mr Xing must allocate to get the return of 18%

Portfolio Return, $R_p = yR_s + (1 - y)R_f = R_f + y(R_s - R_f)$

or $18 = 8 + y \times 16$

or $y = 10/16 = 5/8$

Amount Invested in risky portfolio $= \frac{5}{8} \times 4{,}00{,}000 = 2{,}50{,}000$

Amount Invested in portfolio of risk free securities

= 4,00,000 – 2,50,000

= ₹1,50,000

(e) To get the return in excess of 24% Mr Xing needs to borrow at a risk-free rate. The amount of borrowing is determined by how much extra Mr Xing wants to earn and can be arrived at by using CAL.

Portfolio Return, $R_p = R_f + y(R_s - R_f)$, or $32 = 8 + y \times 16$,

gives $y = \frac{24}{16} = 1.5$

Amount Invested in risky portfolio $= 1.5 \times 4{,}00{,}000$

= ₹6,00,000

Amount to be borrowed at risk-free rate

= 6,00,000 – 4,00,000

= ₹2,00,000

In the discussions above, we stated that returns in excess of what is offered by risky securities can be attained by borrowing at a risk-free rate and then invest the borrowed funds in risky securities. In the real world, lending and borrowing is not done at the same rate. The borrowing rate is invariably higher than the lending rate. In such a case can we continue to assume a CAL as depicted in Figure 8-8? Certainly not, because CAL represents a single slope corresponding to the return on the risk-free asset. In case the lending and borrowing rates differ, CAL would have a kink in the shape at a point where borrowing becomes necessary. Since the borrowing rate is greater than the lending rate, the slope of CAL would decline from the point where borrowing starts, i.e., when more than 100% ($y > 1$) are required to be invested in risky security portfolio, *S*. The CAL would look like as shown in Figure 8-10 with two slopes given by investment rate R_f and borrowing rate R_b.

With different investing and borrowing rates, there would be a kink in the CAL.

Capital allocation line represents the set of feasible alternatives for investment. The risk and return combinations not satisfying CAL are not feasible portfolios

The next issue we attempt to understand is how individuals choose specific portfolios.

CAPITAL ALLOCATION LINE AND UTILITY INDIFFERENCE CURVES

Different investors have different requirements and hence choose different portfolios. All these portfolios necessarily must lie on CAL if investors are assumed to be rational. Also, these portfolios must be optimal for each investor. What is the definition of an optimal portfolio? Should it vary with each individual? These are the few questions we attempt to answer in this section.

Recall that investors view investments as combinations of risk and return. Neither return nor risk is viewed in isolation. A combination of risk and return forms a composite asset and provides some utility. Utility as expressed by Equation 8-10 is reproduced below:

$$U = R_p - 0.005A\sigma_p^2$$

For the risk neutral investor, the value of *A* is equal to zero and the utility is equal to the expected return of the portfolio.

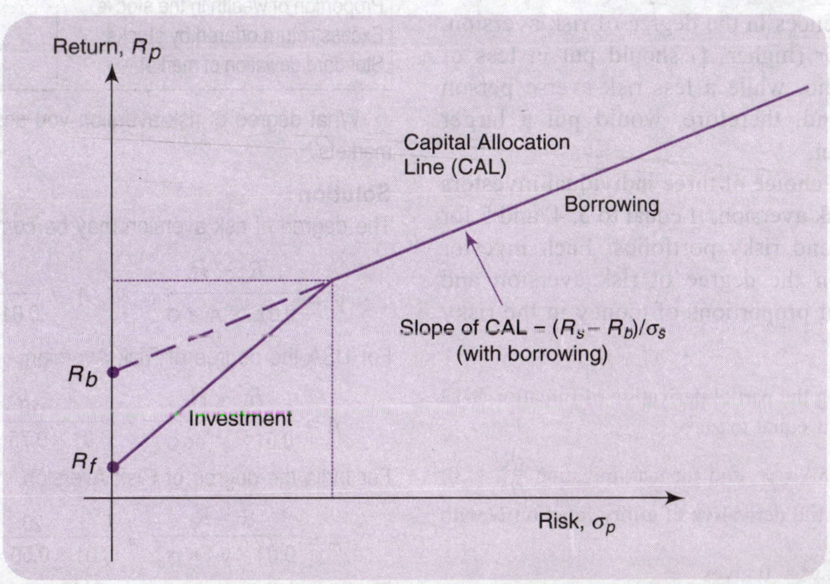

Figure 8-10 CAL for different lending & borrowing rate

Such an investor decides the portfolio only on the basis of the expected return. Increasing degree of risk aversion means an increase in *A*. This leads to a situation where more and more return is sought with increasing risk to have same utility.

With feasible set of investment opportunities as given by CAL and the utility function represented by Equation 8-10, each individual investor must find investment on the CAL that maximizes utility. Thus, maximization of utility is the objective of each rational investor.

Capital allocation line can be obtained by changing the proportion of money, *y* in the risky portfolio. The return and risk of the combination of risky and risk-free asset are given by Equation 8-12.

$$\text{Portfolio Return, } R_p = R_f + y(R_s - R_f)$$
$$\text{Portfolio Risk, } \sigma_p = y\sigma_s \quad (8\text{-}12)$$

Since the only variable in the entire scheme of things is the proportion of investment in the risky asset, *y*, we may express utility as a function of *y* by substituting the values of R_p and σ_p as given by the Equation 8-12. Substituting the values of R_p and σ_p in utility function, we get:

$$U = R_p - 0.005A\sigma_p^2$$
$$U = R_f + y(R_s - R_f) - 0.005Ay^2\sigma_s^2 \quad (8\text{-}13)$$

Utility for investor shall be maximized[2] for specific value of y^* is given by:

$$y^* = \frac{R_s - R_f}{0.01 \times A \times \sigma_s^2} \quad (8\text{-}14)$$

Equation 8-14 states that the proportion of wealth in the risky asset, *y* must be

(a) directly proportional to the excess return the risky portfolio offers over the risk-free portfolio $(R_s - R_f)$.

(b) inversely proportional to the risk associated with the risky portfolio σ_s; and

(c) inversely proportional to the degree of risk aversion *A*.

While excess return and the risk of the portfolio are identical for each investor, the investment strategy would differ for investors because of differences in the degree of risk aversion. A high risk-averse investor (higher *A*) should put in less of money in the risky portfolio, while a less risk-averse person demands greater return and, therefore, would put a larger proportion in the risky asset.

Table 8-4 highlights the choice of three individual investors with different degrees of risk aversion, *A* equal to 3, 4, and 5 for the same set of risk-free and risky portfolios. Each investor maximizes utility based on the degree of risk aversion and accordingly places different proportions of money in the risky asset.

[2]This may be derived by taking the partial derivative of Equation 8-13 with respect to *y* and setting it equal to zero.

$U = R_f + (R_s - R_f)y - 0.005A\sigma_s^2y^2$, and for maximization $\frac{\partial U}{\partial y} = 0$,

Therefore, equating the partial derivative of utility function *U* with respect to *y* to zero

$(R_s + R_f) - 0.010A\sigma_s^2y^* = 0$ gives

$$y^* = \frac{(R_s - R_f)}{0.01A\sigma_s^2}$$

Table 8-4 Utility with investment in risky asset

$R_s - R_f = 15 - 5 = 10\%$			
Standard Deviation $\sigma_s = 20\%$			
y	*Utility at A = 3*	*Utility at A = 4*	*Utility at A = 5*
0.00	5.00	5.00	5.00
0.10	5.94	5.92	5.90
0.20	6.76	6.68	6.60
0.30	7.46	7.28	7.10
0.40	8.04	7.72	7.40
0.50	8.50	8.00	7.50
0.60	8.84	8.12	7.40
0.70	9.06	8.08	7.10
0.80	9.16	7.88	6.60
0.90	9.14	7.52	5.90
1.00	9.00	7.00	5.00
1.10	8.74	6.32	3.90
1.20	8.36	5.48	2.60
1.30	7.86	4.48	1.10
1.40	7.24	3.32	–0.60
1.50	6.50	2.00	–2.50

The maximization of utility as function of proportion of money in the risky asset is shown in Figure 8-10. Both Table 8-4 and Figure 8-11 depict that high risk-averse investors maximize utility with lesser proportion invested in the risky asset. As the degree of risk aversion increases, the proportion in the risky asset decreases.

Example 8-5 Collective Risk Aversion of Investors

Assume that all investors in the market adopt the passive management strategy of investing part in risk-free assets and part in risky assets as represented by the market index. For estimating the risk aversion on collective basis for different markets, assume that a study on India and USA indicates the following:

	USA (%)	*India (%)*
Proportion of wealth in the stocks	75%	50%
Excess return offered by stocks	10%	20%
Standard deviation of market	20%	30%

What degree of risk aversion you associate with the US and Indian markets?

Solution

The degree of risk aversion may be computed from Equation 8-14.

$$y^* = \frac{R_s - R_f}{0.01 \times A \times \sigma_s^2} \quad \text{or} \quad A = \frac{R_s - R_f}{0.01 \times y^* \times \sigma_s^2}$$

For USA the degree of Risk Aversion,

$$A = \frac{R_s - R_f}{0.01 \times y^* \times \sigma_s^2} = \frac{10}{0.01 \times 0.75 \times 20^2} = 10/3 = 3.33$$

For India the degree of Risk Aversion,

$$A = \frac{R_s - R_f}{0.01 \times y^* \times \sigma_s^2} = \frac{20}{0.01 \times 0.50 \times 80^2} = 40/9 = 4.44$$

The calculations suggest that US investors are less risk-averse than Indian investors.

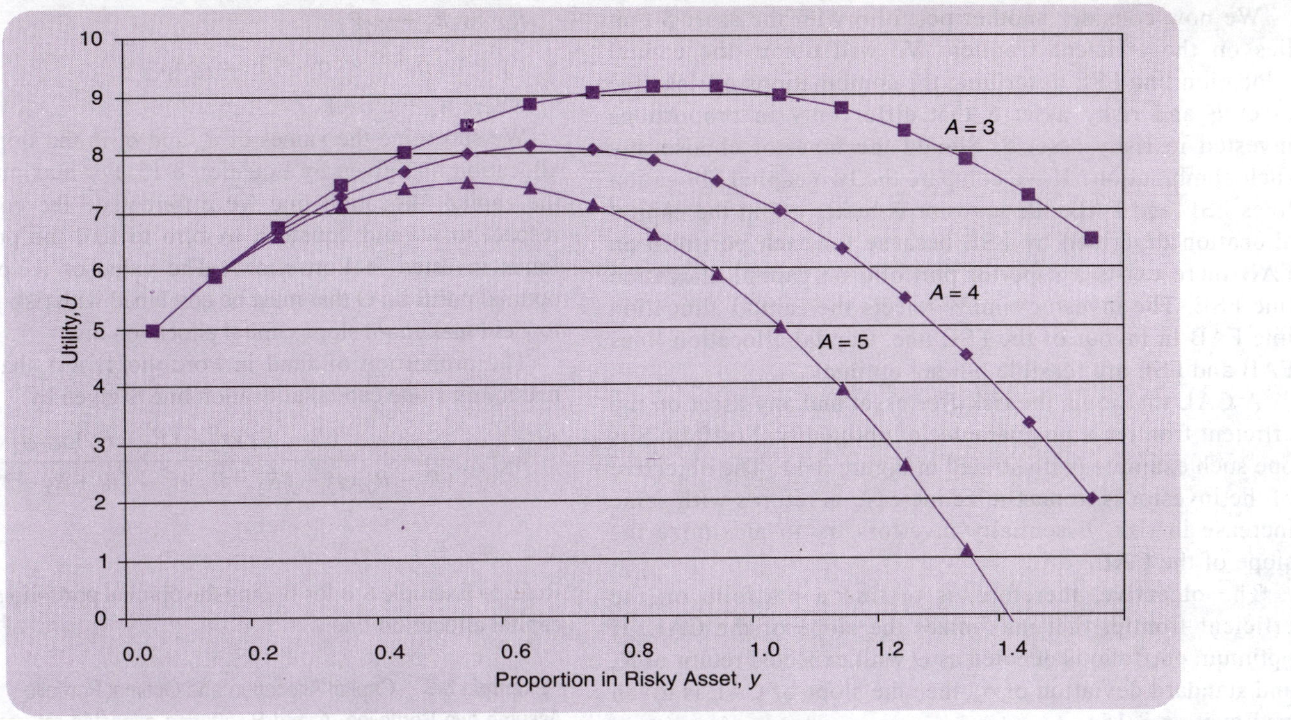

Figure 8-11 Utility U for different investors and y

FINDING OPTIMAL PORTFOLIO

Given a risky asset and a risk-free asset, we now know the locus of the possible portfolios that can be obtained by adjusting the proportion of wealth, y in the risky asset. It is important to know how to choose the risky asset and the reason for maintaining it in the portfolio. We now attempt to answer these two questions in this section.

With the availability of a risk-free asset, the efficient frontier changes to a straight line as it supersedes the efficient frontier of only risky assets.

Consider a set of securities/portfolios in the risk–return space shown as 'X' in Figure 8-12. Any of these assets can be used with the risk-free asset F to form another portfolio that would yield a return and risk combination that lies on the line originating from risk-free asset F and passing through the specific asset. As mentioned earlier, such a line is known as CAL. One such CAL is shown as FAB in Figure 8-12 connecting the risk-free asset F and risky asset A. FAB represents risk and return obtainable with varying proportions in risky asset A.

Is this CAL with asset A the most rewarding for the investors? We can clearly see that it is not, as asset A is not an efficient portfolio. It does not lie on the efficient frontier. There are many assets that are superior to asset A either in terms of better return for the same risk or lesser risk for the same return. Capital allocation line with asset A is, therefore, not optimal.

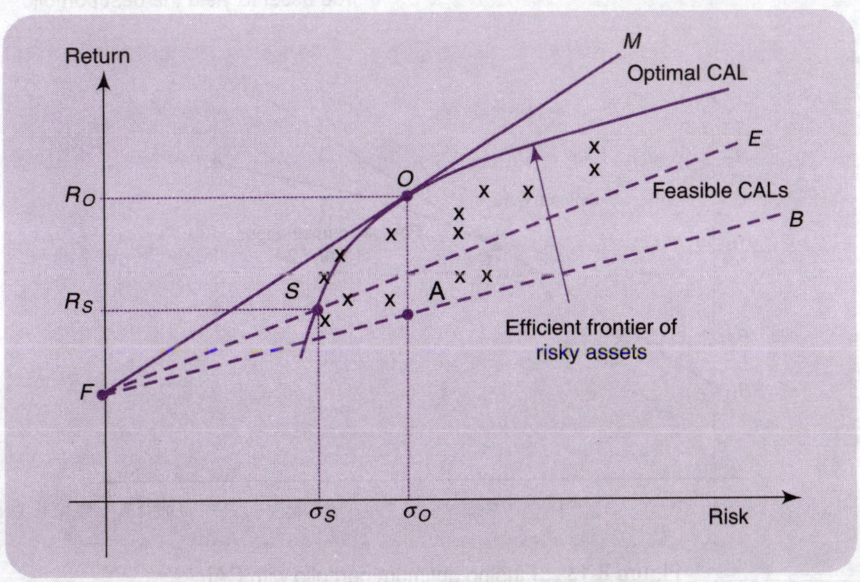

Figure 8-12 Finding optimal CAL

We now consider another portfolio with the asset S that lies on the efficient frontier. We will obtain the capital allocation line FSE describing the combinations of risk-free asset F and risky asset S that differ only in proportions invested in risky asset S. Should the investor choose any such combination? If we compare the two capital allocation lines FSE and FAB, the investor is better off in the capital allocation described by FSE because for each portfolio on FAB there exists a superior portfolio on capital allocation line FSE. The investor simply rejects the capital allocation line FAB in favour of the FSE line. Capital allocation lines FAB and FSE are feasible but not optimal.

A CAL that joins the risk-free asset and any asset on the efficient frontier is no guarantee of optimality. Portfolio S is one such example is illustrated in Figure 8-11. The objective of the investor is to maximize increase in returns with some increase in risk. Essentially investors try to maximize the slope of the CAL.

The objective, therefore, is to find a portfolio on the efficient frontier that maximizes the slope of the CAL. If optimum portfolio is denoted as O with expected return of R_o and standard deviation of σ_o, then the slope of CAL is given by Equation 8-15.

$$\text{Slope of the CAL} = \frac{\text{Excess Return}}{\text{Additional Risk}} = \frac{R_o - R_f}{\sigma_o} \quad (8\text{-}15)$$

Once we have the Portfolio O we can have the CAL that has the maximum slope. This is depicted in Figure 8-13.

We may derive the optimal portfolio and the resultant CAL that yields the maximum slope if the returns and standard deviation of the two portfolios are known. We take two portfolios 1 and 2 with expected returns as R_1 and R_2 and standard deviations of σ_1 and σ_2 respectively. Further, out of the total allocation of fund in the risky asset, w_1 is invested in Security 1 and the remaining $(1 - w_1)$ is in Security 2. This is depicted in Figure 8-13. The portfolio return R_o and standard deviation σ_o can be written as

$$R_o = w_1 R_1 + w_2 R_2$$

$$\sigma_o^2 = w_1^2 \sigma_1^2 + w_2^2 \sigma_2^2 + 2 w_1 w_2 \rho \sigma_1 \sigma_2 \quad (8.16)$$

where $w_1 + w_2 = 1$

We substitute the values of R_o and σ_o in the slope of capital allocation line given by Equation 8-15. For maximum slope of the capital allocation line we differentiate the equation with respect to w_1 and equate it to zero to find the proportion of funds invested in Portfolio 1. The value of w_1 provides the optimal portfolio O that must be combined with risk-free security to yield maximum slope capital allocation line.

The proportion of fund in Portfolio 1, $w_1{}^*$ that yields the maximum slope capital allocation line is given by:

$$w_1{}^* = \frac{(R_1 - R_f)\sigma_2^2 - (R_2 - R_f)\rho\sigma_1\sigma_2}{(R_1 - R_f)\sigma_2^2 - (R_2 - R_f)\sigma_1^2 - (R_1 + R_2 - 2R_f)\rho\sigma_1\sigma_2} \quad (8\text{-}17)$$

and $w_2{}^* = 1 - w_1{}^*$

Refer to Example 8-6 for finding the optimal portfolio and resultant capital allocation line.

Example 8-6 Capital Allocation and Optimal Portfolio

Assume two Portfolios, A and B, offering expected returns of 20% and 25% respectively. The correlation coefficient of the two portfolios is 0.40. The risks of A and B as given by standard deviations are 20% and 30% respectively. The risk-free asset offers a return of 8%. Find the following:

(a) In what ratio would you combine the Portfolios A and B so that you have the best possible capital allocation?
(b) What would be the risk and return of such portfolio?
(c) If combined with the risk-free asset what trade-off of the risk and return would be made?
(d) If capital allocation is done with Portfolio A or Portfolio B, do you expect to achieve the same trade off as with the portfolio obtained in (a)?

Solution

(a) We have to find the optimal Portfolio O that is a combination of Portfolios A and B. The Portfolio O would be combined with the risk-free asset to yield the best portfolio.

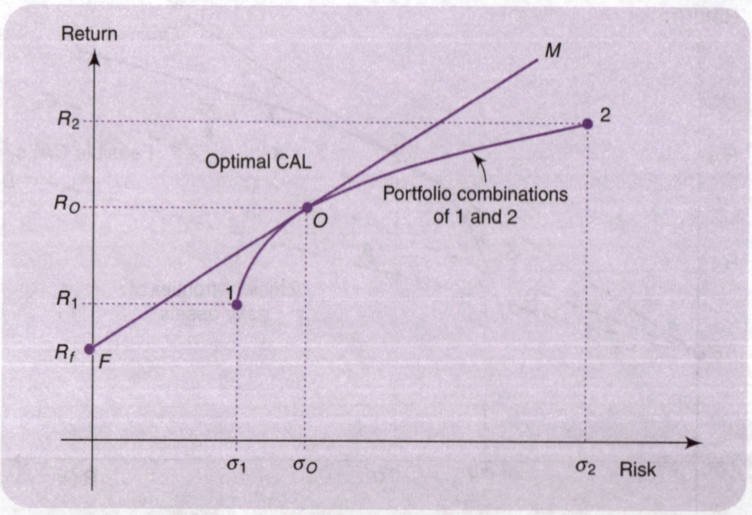

Figure 8-13 Finding optimum portfolio with CAL

Let proportion of money in Portfolio A be w_1 with $(1 - w_1)$ in Portfolio B. By changing w_1 we obtain various portfolios and the w_1^* is the proportion that provides optimal portfolio. The proportion w_1^* is given by Equation 8-17.

$$w_1^* = \frac{(R_1 - R_f)\sigma_2^2 - (R_2 - R_f)\rho\sigma_1\sigma_2}{(R_1 - R_f)\sigma_2^2 + (R_1 - R_f)\sigma_1^2 - (R_1 + R_2 + 2R_f)\rho\sigma_1\sigma_2}$$

$$w_1^* = \frac{(20-8)\times 900 - (25-8)\times 0.4 \times 20 \times 30}{(20-8)\times 900 + (25-8)\times 400 - (20+25-16) \times 0.4 \times 20 \times 30}$$

$$= \frac{10800 - 4080}{10800 + 6800 - 6960} = \frac{6720}{10640} = 0.6316 \text{ or } 63.16\%$$

and $w_2^* = 1 - w_1^* = 1 - 0.6316 = 0.3684$ or 36.84%

The optimal portfolio that would yield a capital allocation line with maximum slope would be obtained if of the total amount allocated to risky portfolio, 63.16% is invested in Portfolio A and remaining 36.4% in Portfolio B.

(b) The return and risk of the optimal portfolio would be:

Optimal Portfolio Return, $R_O = w_1R_1 + w_2R_2$

$$= 0.6316 \times 20 + 0.3684 \times 25$$
$$= 12.63 + 9.21 = 21.84\%$$

Optimal Portfolio Risk, $\sigma_O^2 = w_1^2\sigma_1^2 + w_2^2\sigma_2^2 + 2w_1w_2\rho\sigma_1\sigma_2$

$$= 0.6316^2 \times 20^2 + 0.3684^2 \times 30^2 + 0.6316 \times 0.3684 \times 0.4 \times 20 \times 30$$
$$= 159.57 + 122.15 + 55.84 = 337.57$$

or $\sigma_O = 18.37\%$

(c) The slope of the capital allocation line formed with the optimal portfolio and the risk-free asset is:

$$\text{Slope of the CAL} = \frac{R_O - R_f}{\sigma_O} = \frac{21.84 - 8.00}{18.37} = \frac{13.84}{18.37} = 0.75$$

The slope of 0.75 of the CAL implies that for an increase in risk of 1%, the extra return that can be earned is 0.75%.

(d) If capital allocation is done with Portfolio A and the risk-free asset the benefit in return for same increase in the risk will be lesser as given by reduced slope of such CAL. The extra return for an increase of 1% in risk is 0.60%.

$$\text{Slope of the CAL with Portfolio A} = \frac{R_1 - R_f}{\sigma_1}$$

$$= \frac{20.00 - 8.00}{20.00} = \frac{12}{20} = 0.60$$

Similarly, the CAL using Portfolio B and the risk-free asset would be less than the CAL formed with the optimal portfolio O.

$$\text{Slope of the CAL with Portfolio B} = \frac{R_2 - R_f}{\sigma_2}$$

$$= \frac{25.00 - 8.00}{30.00} = \frac{17}{30} = 0.57$$

The CAL may be super-imposed on the plane of return and standard deviation with the utility curves to find the portfolio the individual investors would choose. The efficient frontier undergoes a substantial change with the presence of a risk-free asset. We stated earlier that the efficient frontier of risky assets is a concave-shaped curved line as shown in Figure 8-8 and its tangential with the utility indifference curve of individual investors would guide the selection of the portfolio.

In the absence of a risk-free asset the investors would be faced with the various securities or portfolio and seek to find the efficient frontier of the risky assets. This efficient frontier is then matched with the utility indifference curves so as to derive maximum utility. With the introduction of risk-free asset the efficient frontier undergoes substantial changes. It is easy to see that all the combinations on the line FOM in Figure 8-13 using Portfolios F and O outperform all portfolios on the efficient frontier that consists of only risky assets. This may be easily seen from Figure 8-14. We may conclude from the above that all investors, rather than combining the risk-free Portfolio F with Portfolio 1 or 2 or any other portfolio, would prefer Portfolio O.

With risk-free assets available all investors can optimize with investment in risk-free asset and the identical risky asset.

A capital allocation line FOM is obtained by using the risk-free asset F. Any combination of risk and return that lies on FOM can be obtained simply by adjusting the proportion of funds in the risky asset O and risk-free asset *F*. At *F* all funds are allocated to F and at O all funds are invested in the Portfolio O. Segment OM would represent borrowing situations implying that stakes in O is increased by borrowing at risk-free rates.

The line FOM is referred to as *capital market line* (CML). All investors, therefore, move up the CML such that utility indifference curve becomes tangential to CML.

Let us consider two different Investors A and B. Investor A is more risk-averse (high coefficient *A*) and has steeper utility indifference curves. Investor B is less risk- averse (low coefficient *A*) and has shallower utility indifference curves. How would the portfolio construction be different for these two Investors A and B?

As stated earlier, individual investors would maximize utility of wealth by choosing the point of tangency with the steepest CAL, different as a complete and ultimate portfolio, that satisfies all constraints to the best as follows:

1. The portfolios lie on the efficient set ensuring maximum return for the same risk or least risk for same return.
2. The steepest CAL ensures that the trade-off of risk and return is optimal. The compensation of return for the same increase in risk is maximum in the case of the steepest CAL.
3. Tangency of utility indifference curve with the CAL ensures that the utility of return and risk is maximized.

Faced with the same set of securities and portfolios along the efficient frontier of the risky assets, both Investors A and B, irrespective of their differences in the attitudes towards risk, would choose the same portfolios of risky asset *O* and risk-free asset F. However, their proportions in the each asset would be different depending upon the degree of risk aversion. With regard to selection of the portfolios, the individual differences do not count. This is amply clear from Figure 8-14, which identifies the optimal portfolio O and is identical for both the investors. Investor A who is more risk averse would end up

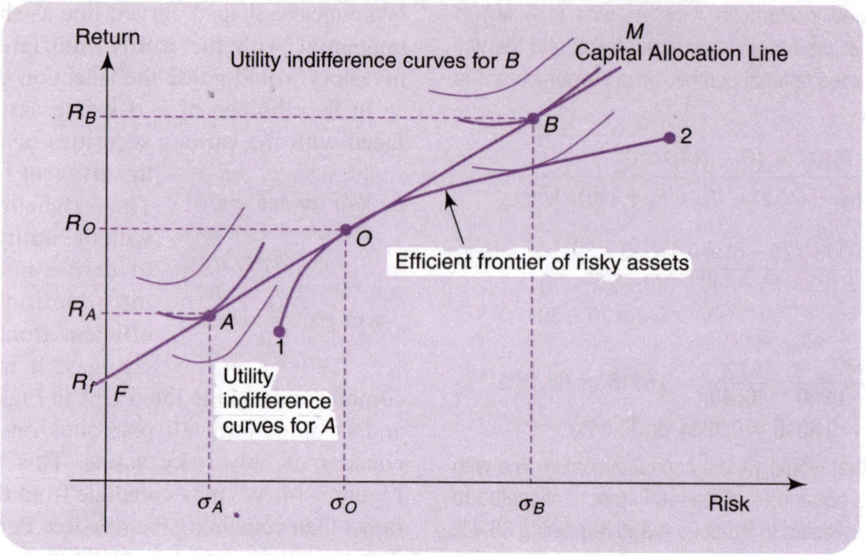

Figure 8-14 Finding optimum portfolio with CAL

investing part of the capital in risk-free asset and part in the risky asset O. In contrast, Investor B is less risk-averse and borrows money at risk-free rate to invest his own as well as the borrowed money in risky asset O to enhance the return. The allocation of funds is governed by Equation 8-14. Investor B assumes greater risk and also has greater level of utility than Investor A. Example 8-7 illustrates the application of the concept.

Separation Theorem

This has important implication for portfolio managers. They can continue to offer the same set of assets to all their clients. Further, they need not conduct separate research for identifying suitable portfolios for each individual client, thereby saving much cost, effort, and time. To accommodate individual preferences of the clients all they need to do is to adjust the proportions of investment in the two assets O and F for each of them. This is known as *separation theorem* since the selection and investment decisions are separated from each other and taken independently.

Example 8-7 Portfolio Allocation

As found in Example 8-6, the optimal Portfolio *O* provides a return of 21.84% with a standard deviation of 18.37%. With risk-free rate of return at 8%, what would be the portfolio of the investors with coefficient of risk aversion of 3 and 5. Also find the investor's return, risk, and the utility for both.

Solution

With the coefficient of risk aversion known the allocation of funds in the risk-free asset and the Portfolio O is given by Equation 8-14.

For an investor whose coefficient of risk aversion is estimated at 3.00, the proportion of funds invested in risky portfolio, y^* is:

$$y^* = \frac{R_O - R_f}{0.01 \times A \times \sigma_o^2} = \frac{21.84 - 8.00}{0.01 \times 3 \times 18.37^2} = \frac{13.84}{10.40} = 1.33$$

The investor would borrow funds equal to 33% of his own and put the entire funds in Portfolio O.

His return, risk, and utility would be:

Return, $R_p = y^* - R_o + (1 - y^*) \times R_f = 1.33 \times 21.84 - 0.33 \times 8 = 26.41\%$

Standard deviation $\sigma_p = y^* \times \sigma_o = 1.33 \times 18.37 = 24.43\%$

Utility, $U = R_p - 0.005A\sigma_p^2 = 26.41 - 0.005 \times 3 \times 24.43^2 = 17.46$

For an investor whose coefficient of risk aversion is estimated at 5.00 the proportion of funds invested in risky portfolio, y^* is:

$$y^* = \frac{R_O - R_f}{0.01 \times A \times \sigma_o^2} = \frac{21.84 \times 8.00}{0.01 \times 5 \times 18.37^2} = \frac{13.84}{16.87} = 0.82$$

The investor would have 82% of the funds allocated to Portfolio O and remaining 18% in a risk-free portfolio.

His return, risk, and utility would be

Return, $R_p = y^* \times R_o + (1 - y^*) \times R_f$
$= 0.82 \times 21.84 + 0.18 \times 8 = 19.35\%$

Standard deviation $\sigma_p = y^* \times \sigma_o = 0.82 \times 18.37 = 15.06\%$

Utility, $U = R_p - 0.005A\sigma_p^2$
$= 19.35 - 0.005 \times 5 \times 15.06^2 = 13.68$

The complete process of portfolio selection is summarized in the following steps:

1. Identify efficient frontier of the risky assets.
2. Establish the optimum risky portfolio using Equation 8-17 that allocates the funds among the risky portfolios in such a manner that provides the largest slope to the CAL.
3. Find out the return and risk of the optimum risky portfolio using Equations 8-6(a) and (b).
4. Allocate funds between optimum risky portfolio and risk-free asset using Equation 8-14 that maximizes utility.
5. Rework out the proportions of funds allocated to risky assets in step (4) in the ratio according to step (2).

An example of the optimization of the portfolio is presented in the Practice Problem 7.

FINDING THE EEFFICENT FRONTIER—MARKOWITZ MODEL

So far we have been working under the assumption that the portfolios available to us were already efficient. The CAL was found using two risky portfolios and the risk-free asset with the assumption that the two risky assets are already well diversified and efficient. The exercise done for finding out the optimum portfolio with two risky portfolios and one risk-free asset would apply equally if we had only two securities instead of efficient portfolios.

In this section we attempt to find the securities that would constitute an efficient portfolio. We generalize the portfolio construction to the case of many risky securities and the risk-free asset. The procedure for portfolio construction in case of securities is identical to the one enumerated earlier. The procedure starts with:

1. Finding of an optimal portfolio of risky asset O by allocating the proportions in two risky assets.
2. Locating the capital allocation with this Portfolio O and the risk-free asset.
3. Finding the ultimate portfolio as combination of risk-free asset and optimal Portfolio O by adjusting the proportion of investment between the two.

We concentrate here on finding the efficient frontier. The investment scenario consists of large number of financial assets/securities that are available for investment. As a starting point we need to have expected return and a measure of risk associated with those returns in respect of all the financial assets that form the whole array of investment. To have such estimates of return and risk it is almost essential that these financial assets are actively traded so as to provide the requisite data. Some people may object to the use of past data since the consideration for portfolio being designed must be based on what is expected to happen and not on what has already happened. Howsoever justified the objection may be, it is generally assumed that past data is good indicator of future as similar events occur in the securities markets. The compulsion to use the past data also results from our inability to find a suitable and better alternative. Projecting returns and standard deviations based on some estimates that necessarily involve subjectivity is equally hazardous.

If assets are actively traded their historical averages and standard deviations would serve as reasonable proxy to expected returns and risks under the presumption of repetitive events, unless the analyst has a reason to differ. In any case there seems no method that can accommodate special events that affect returns.

Besides the estimates of expected returns and the variances (standard deviations), we also need the covariance of each asset with rest of them. In the two-asset case we needed only one such covariance. In an n asset case, we need to have $n \times (n-1)$ covariances. For n financial assets under consideration of a portfolio, we need the following data:

Expected returns for n securities	n
Variance for each of the n securities	n
Covariances for n securities	$n \times (n-1)$

For optimization of the portfolio from among the risky assets we need to apply rules of portfolio selection. Innumerable portfolios can be constructed with the n securities by choosing various securities. Further, the amount of money allocated to each of the asset/security would multiply the options available to the investors. Not all the options are equally desirable. For elimination of huge number of portfolios we assume rational investment behaviour, which implies that:

1. For a given return, the investors opt for least risk, or
2. For a given risk, investors choose maximum return.

The set of portfolios that satisfies any of the above two conditions is called the *efficient frontier*. For design and selection of the ultimate portfolio we need to concentrate only on the portfolios that lie on the efficient frontier. Finding an efficient set of portfolio, therefore, restricts the choices to be evaluated.

Before we proceed to find the efficient frontier, a word about the necessity of having portfolios rather than individual securities is essential. The idea of diversification is age-old. The traditional maxim of *do not put all your eggs in one basket* was given a formal and scientific shape by Harry Markowitz (1952) in his model of portfolio selection. The modern financial theory of portfolio selection postulated diversification of portfolio to reduce risk.

In case of two-asset model we have already observed that the portfolio risk could be lesser than the least of the risk of the two individual assets if held separately. In terms of modern financial theory we can safely state that individual securities are inefficient and unless combined with other securities cannot lead to optimization. Diversification of portfolio by combining securities would lead to—(1) either greater return for the same risk; or (2) lower risk for the same return.

Risk reduction would take place only of the coefficient of correlation is less than the ratio of smaller standard deviation to the larger standard deviation.

In general, risk reduction depends upon the coefficient of correlation between securities. The diversification effect, i.e., reduction in risk is possible when the following relationship[3] holds:

$$\rho < \sigma_1/\sigma_2 \qquad (8\text{-}18)$$

where, σ_1 and σ_2 are the standard deviations of Security 1 and Security 2 respectively and $\sigma_1 < \sigma_2$.

When Equation 8-18 holds it is possible to form a portfolio of two securities that has risk smaller than the any of the securities held singly. This also implies that the risk reduction would not always take place by mere addition of the securities in the portfolio. In this sense one can easily explain that

[3]The relationship may be derived as follows:
Assume that you are invested 100% in the Security 1 that has lower standard deviation, σ_1. The risk of the portfolio is σ_1. Now change the portfolio by divesting small sum, Δ in Security 2 with higher risk, σ_2 as standard deviation. For diversification effect to take place the revised risk of the portfolio should be less than σ_1. Hence

$$(1-\Delta)^2\sigma_1^2 + \Delta^2\sigma_2^2 + 2(1-\Delta)\Delta\rho \cdot \sigma_1\sigma_2 \le \sigma_1^2$$

Expanding and ignoring the Δ^2 terms being small, we get:

$$-2\Delta\sigma_1^2 + 2\Delta\sigma_1\sigma_2 \le 0$$

or $\rho \le \dfrac{\sigma_1}{\sigma_2}$

diversifying the portfolio in stocks belonging to one industry such as pharmaceuticals is not a good idea. The rationale for sector-specific mutual funds cannot be risk reduction, but the belief that the sector identified would offer returns greater than the market.

A number of software programs are available to find the efficient frontier. An efficient frontier can be arrived by either maximizing the returns for a target amount of risk or minimizing the risk for a target amount of return. The target risk or target return is specified by the individual investor.

The return and risk of the portfolio on n assets are dependent upon the following four factors:

1. Returns of individual assets denoted as R_1, R_2, R_3, etc.
2. The risk of each asset measured by variance or standard deviation denoted as σ_1, σ_2, σ_3, etc.
3. The linkage of various assets among themselves specified by coefficients of correlation of each asset with rest of the assets denoted as ρ_{12}, ρ_{13}, ρ_{23}, ρ_{24}, ρ_{34}, ρ_{35}, etc.
4. The proportion of each asset in the portfolio denoted as w_1, w_2, w_3, etc.

With above notations, the mathematical representation of portfolio return and risk is stated at Equations 8-19 and 8-20 respectively,

$$R_p = \sum_{1}^{n} w_i R_i \tag{8-19}$$

$$\sigma_p^2 = \sum_{j=1}^{n} \sum_{i=i}^{n} w_i w_j \mathrm{Cov}(R_i, R_j) \tag{8-20}$$

The optimization programme would have an objective function of either maximization of return as given by Equation 8-19 or minimization of risk as given by Equation 8-20. We may maximize the return as provided by Equation 8-19 by adjusting the weights assigned to each security w_i for a given amount of risk. Alternatively, we may minimize risk given by Equation 8-20 again by adjusting the weights of the security, w_i for given amount of return. Either of the approach would lead to identical results.

The optimization process would be subject to certain constraints. First, the sum of all the weights must be equal to 1. Second, constraint would concern short selling, which refers to the possibility of selling an asset without owning it. Permitting short selling in the formulation of optimization problem implies that the weight of the asset in the portfolio could be negative. Where short selling is prohibited the weight of each asset in the portfolio cannot be negative. The constraints when no short selling is allowed are stated as:

$$\sum_{1}^{n} w_i = 1, \text{ and } w_i \geq 0 \tag{8-21}$$

With the objective function given as Equations 8-19 or 8-20 and the constraints as per Equation 8-21, the efficient frontier can be arrived by using Excel with the tool of *Solver*. One such exercise is given as Appendix A-8 to this chapter in the CD.

With the given expected returns, variance, and the correlation coefficients the efficient frontier would look similar to the one shown in Figure 8-15.

The portfolio that gives the least risk is called the *global minima* and all the portfolios that lie above global minimum risk portfolio are efficient. The portfolios that lie below global minimum risk portfolio are inefficient because there is a portfolio directly above it that offers greater return.

After obtaining the efficient frontier of risky assets we may introduce the risk-free asset. A risk-free asset will further modify the efficient frontier as we draw the CAL with the steepest slope with one risky portfolio O and risk-free asset F. The CAL, representing various combinations of O and F, outperforms the efficient frontier of risky assets. The ultimate portfolio must lie on the CAL maximizing utility as per the procedure already described in preceding section and depicted in Figure 8-14.

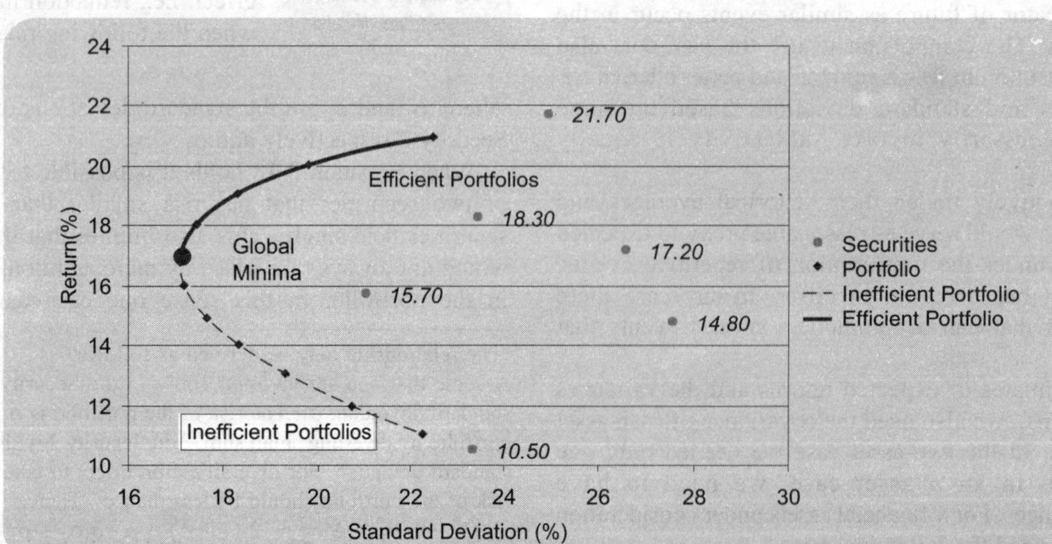

Figure 8-15 Efficient frontier and individual assets

POWER OF DIVERSIFICATION

The benefits of diversification are well understood. The diversification helps in reducing risk. The nature of diversification that helps in reducing risk would be clear in this section.

The general formula for variance of the portfolio of n securities is given by Equation 8-20 reproduced below:

$$\sigma_p^2 = \sum_{j=1}^{n}\sum_{i=1}^{n} w_i w_j \text{Cov}(R_i, R_j)$$

where w_i represents the weight of security i in the portfolio, and $\text{Cov}(R_i, R_j)$ represents covariance of security i with security j.

Without sacrificing objectivity, we make certain simplifying assumptions. For simplicity we assume that—(1) the portfolio of n securities is equally weighted, i.e., $w_i = 1/n$; (2) each of the security has same variance of σ; and (3) each of the correlation coefficient is equal to ρ giving average covariance as AvCov (R_i, R_j). Now segregating the variance term (variance of security i with itself, $\text{Cov}(R_i, R_i) = \sigma_i^2$ from rest of the securities ($i \neq j$) the variance of the portfolio, as given by Equation 8-20 can be re-written as:

$$\sigma_p^2 = \frac{1}{n}\sum_{1}^{n}\frac{1}{n}\sigma_i^2 + \sum_{\substack{j=1 \\ j \neq i}}^{n}\sum_{i=1}^{n}\frac{1}{n^2}\text{Cov}(R_i, R_j)$$

Note that there would be n terms of variances and $n(n-1)$ terms of covariances. The average variance and average covariance are expressed as:

$$\bar{\sigma}^2 = \frac{1}{n}\sum_{1}^{n}\sigma_i^2$$

$$\text{AvCov}, {}_T = \frac{1}{n(n-1)}\sum_{\substack{j=1 \\ j \neq i}}^{n}\sum_{i=1}^{n}\text{Cov}(R_i, R_j)$$

The portfolio variance can be expressed as:

$$\sigma_p^2 = \frac{1}{n}\bar{\sigma}^2 + \frac{n-1}{n}\text{AvCov}(R_i, R_j),{}_T \quad (8\text{-}22)$$

Portfolio risk when securities have no correlation

When average covariance of the securities is zero, we assume that the returns of the securities are not correlated with each other at all. The portfolio return consists entirely of the variances of the securities constituting it. The portfolio risk stands reduced to the firm-specific risk of the securities constituting the portfolio.

$$\sigma_p^2 = \frac{1}{n}\bar{\sigma}^2 \quad \text{or} \quad \sigma_p = \frac{\bar{\sigma}}{\sqrt{n}} \quad (8\text{-}23)$$

The risk of the portfolio would decline with addition of each security and can approach zero. For example, if we have no covariance among the securities in the portfolio and each security has an average standard deviation of 20%, the portfolio of 100 securities would have a standard deviation of only 2% (20/√100). Under the situation of no correlation among the securities the potential for reduction in risk of the portfolio is unlimited and theoretically the risk can be reduced to zero, if short selling is allowed. Practically, the risk can be close to zero if one has a sufficiently large portfolio. Here a large portfolio refers to the number of securities in it rather than its value.

Portfolio risk with positive correlation among securities

When there is a positive correlation among the securities constituting the portfolio, which is the more likely scenario, the resultant variance of the portfolio is dominated by the covariance factor. If we assume for simplicity that all securities have equal standard deviation σ and a common correlation coefficient ρ then the variance between all pairs of securities is $\rho\sigma^2$. The variance of the portfolio is then written as:

Risk of the portfolio is determined by covariance and not as much by the variances of individual securities.

$$\sigma_p^2 = \frac{1}{n}\bar{\sigma}^2 + \frac{n-1}{n}\text{AvCov}(R_i, R_j)$$

$$= \frac{1}{n}\sigma^2 + \frac{n-1}{n}\rho\sigma^2$$

With a higher value of n, the portfolio risk would primarily consist of covariance terms as $1/n$ approaches zero and as $(n-1)/n$ approaches 1, and the portfolio variance would equal $\rho\sigma^2$. Interestingly if the coefficient of correlation is one (there is perfect correlation among the securities in the portfolio), the diversification of portfolio by increasing the number of securities in it is of no value as portfolio risk remains fixed at σ, irrespective of the number of securities.

SIMPLE DIVERSIFICATION

The analysis of diversification has important implications for portfolio construction. While constructing a portfolio the emphasis should be placed on the behaviour of returns of a security with respect to the returns of other securities in the portfolio rather than on the variance or standard deviation of its own returns. This is because in a diversified portfolio the risk is constituted by the covariances of the securities and very little is contributed by the own variance of the individual securities. Diversification helps in eliminating firm-specific risks.

Diversification by adding securities in the portfolio raises many questions. Having recognized that the potential of risk reduction with diversification of the portfolio the issues that remain to be answered are:

1. To what extent can diversification reduce risk?
2. If there is a lower bound to the risk, how big or small should the portfolio size be?
3. How do we include or exclude securities from the portfolio?

The mathematical model of Markowitz quantifies the amount of risk reduction. The behavioural justification for reduction in risk is perceived rather easily. While investing in a single security, the investor carries the return and risk associated with a particular firm. The returns from the security are dependent upon earnings of the firm, which are subject to change due to a host of reasons. The fortunes of the investor fluctuate with those of the firm. With addition of another security, the chances are that when the first firm does poorly, the second firm may perform better, and while second does not do well the first may come out with better than expected performance. Bad performance of one firm may be compensated by good performance of the second firm. As we keep adding securities to the portfolio the chances of achieving compensating effect improve and returns become more and more stable. The issue is whether the poor performance of few of the firms in the portfolio can be fully compensated by improved performance of the returns of the rest of the securities in the portfolio.

To understand whether the compensating effect is partial or full we need to understand the sources of risk in greater detail.

Risk of an asset can be classified into—unique risk emanating from factors affecting individual asset, and the market risk comprising the factors affecting all assets.

As stated above, the performance of the firm is dependent upon several factors. These factors can broadly be classified into two and include:

1. *Factors specific to a firm* Factors such as level of earnings, nature of business, the prospects, quality of management, quality of products, technology adopted, cash flow risks, capital expenditure plans, growth prospects, etc. are unique to the firm and the change in the expected returns due to these factors is referred to as *unique risk*. These factors need to be examined for each firm separately.
2. *Factors common to all firms (market)* These refer to factors such as economic growth, industry growth, government expenditures, levels of taxes, political environment, weather conditions, international issues, budget deficit, balance of payment, threats of war, internal strife, sentiments of the market, etc. These factors are market-wide factors because such factors impact returns of all the firms and the risk emanating from these factors is referred as *market risk*. Here we recognize that the impact on returns of all the firms will be different for any change. The variations in the return would not be same for all securities.

When the securities are added to the portfolio the unique risk of one firm may be offset by the unique risk of another. In the absence of another security in the portfolio, the unique risk is carried by the investor. More the number of securities in the portfolio greater are the chances that the unique risk would be offset. The unique risk is, therefore, also referred to as *diversifiable risk* or *unsystematic risk*.

However, the same cannot be said about market risk. The direction of change in the returns of securities due to market-wide factors is more likely to be same rather than different. By adding more and more securities the market-wide risk cannot be eliminated no matter how large the portfolio becomes. Market risk, is therefore, also known as *non-diversifiable risk* or *systematic risk*.

Unique risk is diversifiable with increasing size of the portfolio but the market risk remains.

The portfolio risk with number of securities in the portfolio is plotted in Figure 8-16. The following observations can be made regarding portfolio risk:

1. As securities are added to the portfolio, its risk diminishes. The risk reduction achieved by the 11th security would be higher than the 51st security in the portfolio.
2. After a certain level, the reduction in risk is nominal no matter how large the portfolio becomes.
3. There is minimum amount of risk below which the portfolio risk cannot be reduced. The risk that remains is the systematic risk. One will have to carry the systematic risk that is inherent in the market irrespective of the size of the portfolio.

Diversification and Portfolio Management

These observations have very important and significant implications for portfolio management. The belief that the increase in the size of the portfolio diminishes the risk factor needs a re-look. No doubt that the risk reduces as size of the portfolio increases but the cost of identifying, research, and monitoring keeps increasing as size increases. Gathering and analysing the information also adds to the effort. Besides, valuable time too is consumed. The question that arises is whether the additional cost, effort, and time spent would yield commensurate benefits. While the costs mount with the addition of each security, the additional amount of benefit in the form of risk reduction diminishes. When portfolio size is small such costs are justified as the benefit of risk reduction seemingly outweighs cost, effort and time.

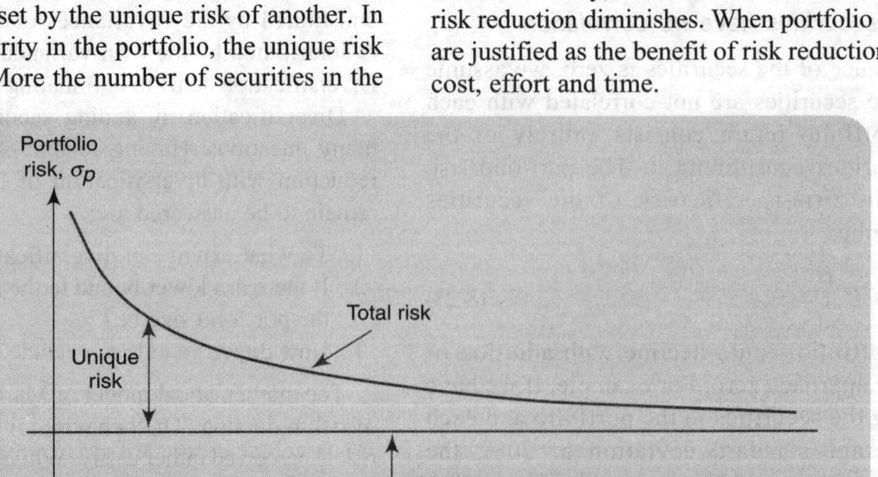

Figure 8-16 Diversification and portfolio risk

However, when the portfolio size has already become large, the cost, effort, and time spent in identifying further securities would not be justified for the amount of risk reduction.

The objective of the portfolio manager must be to achieve desired risk reduction in with as few assets as possible in the portfolio. Observe in Appendix A-8 to the chapter that the global minimum (least risk) portfolio is achieved using only four securities out of total of six under consideration, as shown in the Table 8-5. This helps in bringing down the cost of monitoring of the portfolio. A cursory glance at the various portfolios given in Appendix A-8 reveals that only few financial assets may be enough to meet the desired objectives of return and risk.

Table 8-5 Minimum risk portfolio from six assets

Target Return %	*Minimum Risk*	*Weights of Assets*					
		S	B	C	G	R	F
17.00	9.31	0.004	0.423	—	0.418	—	0.156

Various studies have been conducted to find the right number of securities in the portfolio. It is generally believed that beyond 15–20 securities, no meaningful reduction in risk takes place. A study by Evans and Archer (1968) suggests that unsystematic risk can be reduced by holding as few as 10–15 stocks. The issue of adequacy of the size of the portfolio is rather subjective. To have only the systematic risk present the ideal portfolio would consist of the entire market, i.e., all the assets in the proportions of the market capitalization. This implies having all the securities in the portfolio in the proportion of market capitalization of each security. In case we use an index as a substitute for the market, the portfolio would consist of all securities in the index in the proportion of the market capitalization of each security. In fact, having too many stocks in the portfolio from the same industry may lead to more unsystematic risk because the portfolio is likely to become skewed rather than diversified.

The desire to have more and more securities in the portfolio and making it too large is referred to as *superfluous diversification*. Without meaningful reduction in the risk increasing the size of the portfolio is likely to increase the cost of monitoring and thereby reduce returns. For large investment funds superfluous diversification is rather inevitable as spreading the investment outlay in few securities means large holdings in few firms rather than small holdings in a large number of firms. Besides given the legal constraints of holding stocks in firms beyond a certain level, the buying and selling of huge quantities may mean larger impact costs. However, the important message is that a small investor, who in any case does not have enough funds to own large number of stocks in the portfolio, could be as effective in risk reduction as a large fund would be.

Since market risk cannot be diversified, adding securities in the portfolio beyond a reasonable limit is superfluous.

The strategy is rather apparent with regard to the selection of securities to be included in the portfolio. One must identify securities with low degree of correlation. The ideal situation is to have securities with negative coefficients of correlation. Unfortunately, it is almost impossible to find assets whose returns behave in opposite directions for any change. Therefore, the effort must be to identify assets with as low as possible coefficient of correlation. This can be seen by observing the composition of portfolio of global minimum and their coefficients of correlation (Appendix A-8).

SHARPE'S INDEX MODEL OF OPTIMIZATION

William Sharpe (1964) and other researchers have attempted a simplified model of Markowitz's model of finding an optimum portfolio and achieve similar optimization with substantially reduced data requirements and consequent lesser computations.

The Markowitz model uses correlation of securities with one another and their covariances for determining the portfolio risk and arriving at the optimum combination. The covariance of each asset with another would essentially depend upon the individual characteristics of the assets under consideration. The Sharpe model for optimization of portfolio, instead assumes that two assets influence each other only through broader parameters that can be gauged from the relationship of the each asset with the market factors represented by the index. Therefore, instead of estimating the covariance of each asset with the rest in the portfolio, its variability with the entire group as a whole can be substituted by its relationship with the index. The relationship of the asset with the market can be said to be an aggregate of its covariance with all remaining securities in the portfolio.

Sharpe's single index model substitutes the covariances with one another and instead, uses the covariance of each security with the market.

The relationship of two securities as given by covariance can be represented through market index by following Equation[4] 8-24:

$$\text{Cov}(R_i, R_j) = \beta_i \beta_j \sigma_m^2 \tag{8-24}$$

With this assumption of relationship of returns of each asset being reflected in the aggregate form with that of the market, the data requirement reduces substantially and computation eases significantly. Rather than having correlation of each security with the rest, we now need a parameter that relates its variability with the market. In a spectrum of n securities, the relationship of a security is established through a single collective factor of the market rather than independently with the remaining $(n-1)$

[4]This may be derived as follows:

By definition the covariance between two securities i and j is given by

$$\text{Cov}(R_i, R_j) = \sum (R_i - \bar{R}_i)(R_j - \bar{R}_j)$$

Multiplying and dividing by the market, M variance

$$\text{Cov}(R_i, R_j) = \sum (R_i - \bar{R}_i)(R_j - \bar{R}_j) \frac{(M - \bar{M})(M - \bar{M})}{\sigma_m^2}$$

This simplifies to:

$$\text{Cov}(R_i, R_j) = \frac{\text{Cov}(R_i, M)\,\text{Cov}(R_j, M)}{\sigma_m^2}$$

$$= \beta_i \beta_j \sigma_m^2 \quad \left[\text{Since } \beta_i = \frac{\text{Cov}(R_i, M)}{\sigma_m^2}, \text{ by definition.}\right]$$

securities. Data required under Markowitz's model and Sharpe's model for n securities can be compared as follows:

	Markowitz's model	Sharpe's model
Expected Returns	n	n
Standard Deviations, Risk	n	n
Covariances (correlation coefficients)	$n(n-1)/2$	—
Correlation with market	—	n
Market return and market variance	—	2
Total input data	$n(n+3)/2$	$3n+2$

If we consider a reasonable size of 50 securities, we require 1,325 bits of information under Markowitz's model of optimization while Sharpe's model needs only 152 bits of information. Working with Sharpe's single index model is a trade-off between accuracy and computational ease. The portfolio with the Markowitz model would be an ideal optimization.

Sharpe's single index model relates the expected return of the security R_i to the expected return of the market R_m by following Equation 8-25:

$$R_i = \alpha_i + \beta_i R_m + e_i \tag{8-25}$$

where α_i is the alpha coefficient representing expected return of security i when the market return is zero, β_i is the beta coefficient representing the slope of the line representing sensitivity of the security i with respect to market, and e_i is the error term due to randomness of returns by which it can differ from the forecast return.

The error term is assumed to have the following properties:

- an expected value of zero;
- constant standard deviation; and
- zero coefficient of correlation with the market.

Equation 8-25 states that the returns on the security depend upon its relationship with the market signified by beta.

Equation 8-25 can be obtained through regression, with slope of the line and y intercept providing beta and alpha respectively. The coefficient of determination in the regression equation signifies the percentage of return on the security that can be explained by the variations in the market returns. The variance that can be explained by the index is related to the variations in the market and can, therefore, be regarded as systematic risk. The portion of the risk that cannot be attributed to the variations in the market is, therefore, unsystematic risk related to the specific security.

Sharpe's single index model equates the risk of the security to its two components—systematic risk and unsystematic risk.

Total risk of a financial asset consists of systematic risk and unsystematic risk.

Multi-index model would break-up the risk attributable to as many parameters in the model and an unexplained portion attributable to the security itself. The variance of the returns of the security can be obtained by taking variance of the Equation 8-25 and can be represented as follows:

$$\text{Var}(R_i) = \text{Var}(\alpha_i + \beta_i R_m + e_i)$$

$$\sigma_i^2 = \text{Var}(\alpha_i + \beta_i^2\,\text{Var}(R_m) + \text{Var}(e_i)$$

$$= \beta_1{}^2\sigma_m^2 + \sigma_{ie}^2;\ \text{Var}(\alpha)\text{ being zero}$$

Total Risk = Systematic Risk + Unsystematic Risk

For example, consider a security that has a standard deviation of 15%. The regression of the returns of the security with those of the market reveal a beta of 1.2 as presented in the following equation:

$$R_i = \alpha_i + \beta_i R_m = 1.45 + 1.2R_m$$

$$\sigma_i^2 = \beta_i^2\sigma_m^2 + \sigma_{ie}^2 \tag{8-26}$$

If the standard deviation of the market is 10%, the systematic risk and the unsystematic risk of the security would be:

$$\text{Systematic risk (variance)} = \beta^2\sigma_m^2 = 1.2 \times 1.2 \times 10 \times 10 = 144$$

$$\text{Unsystematic risk} = \text{Total risk} - \text{Systematic risk} = (15 \times 15) - 144 = 81$$

$$\text{The coefficient of determination} = \frac{\text{Risk explained by index}}{\text{Total risk}} = \frac{144}{225} = 0.64 = 64\%$$

Portfolio Beta

If many securities are combined to form a portfolio with w_i as proportion of the investment in security i, the portfolio's return and risk in terms of Sharpe's single index model are represented as:

$$R_p = \sum_1^n w_i \times R_i = \sum_1^n w_i \times (\alpha_i + \beta_i R_m + e_i) \tag{8-27a}$$

$$\text{Portfolio Variance} = \sigma_p^2 = \sigma_m^2 \sum_1^n w_i^2\beta_i^2 + \sum_1^n w_i^2\sigma_{ie}^2 \tag{8-27b}$$

where, w_i, β_i, and e_i represent proportion, beta, and the error portion respectively of security i in the portfolio, and where sum of all investment is one.

Portfolio risk as computed by its variance is equal to the variance of the market multiplied by weighted average of the beta of the portfolio.

Since diversification is expected to eliminate the security specific risk the component the portfolio risk must stand reduced to the systematic risk. This may be represented as follows:

$$\text{Portfolio Variance} = \sigma_p^2 = \sigma_m^2 \sum_1^n w_i^2\beta_i^2$$

Accordingly, the portfolio beta would be weighted average of the betas of the individual securities constituting the portfolio.

$$\beta_p = \sum_1^n w_i\beta_i \tag{8-28}$$

Example 8-8 Sharpe's Model and Diversification

An investor is considering five securities in the portfolio with following expected return, standard deviation, and beta:

Assets	Return %	Standard Deviation %	Beta
Apple	30.00	25.00	1.10
Orange	9.00	12.00	0.40
Mango	15.00	23.00	1.30
Pineapple	22.00	13.00	0.20
Guava	35.00	21.00	1.45
Banana	25.00	20.00	1.20

The market, with index used as a proxy, is expected to have a standard deviation of 13%. The investor has decided to put 10%, 20%, 15%, 15%, 25%, and 15% respectively in Apple, Orange, Mango, Pineapple, Guava, and Banana respectively. Find out the expected return and risk of the portfolio. Of the total risk what risk is attributable to market and what risk is residual in the portfolio?

Solution

The expected return of the portfolio is given by

$$R_p = \sum_{1}^{n} w_i R_i$$

$$= 0.10 \times 30 + 0.20 \times 9 + 0.15 \times 15 + 0.15 \times 22 + 0.25 \times 35 + 0.15 \times 25$$

$$= 22.85\%$$

To determine the portfolio variance we need to find the portfolio beta. The portfolio beta is the weighted average of the betas of the individual securities constituting it.

The portfolio beta is:

$$\beta_p = \sum_{1}^{n} w_i \beta_i$$

$$= 0.10 \times 1.10 + 0.20 \times 0.40 + 0.15 \times 1.30 + 0.15 \times 0.20 + 0.25 \times 1.45 + 0.15 \times 1.20$$

$$= 0.9575$$

With the market variance given, the systematic risk of the portfolio is:

$$\text{Systematic risk} = \beta_p^2 \sigma_m^2$$

$$= 0.9575^2 \times 13^2 = 154.94$$

$$\text{Unsystematic Risk} = \sigma_i^2 = \sum_{1}^{n} w_i^2 \sigma_{ie}^2$$

We need to find the residual risk of each of the security as below:

Assets	Return %	Standard deviation %	Beta	Systematic risk*	Residual variance**
Apple	30.00	25.00	1.10	204.49	420.51
Orange	9.00	12.00	0.40	27.04	116.96
Mango	15.00	23.00	1.30	285.61	243.39
Pineapple	22.00	13.00	0.20	6.76	162.24
Guava	35.00	21.00	1.45	355.32	85.68
Banana	25.00	20.00	1.20	243.36	156.64

*Systematic risk is calculated as $\beta^2 \sigma_m^2$

**Residual variance = Total variance – Systematic risk

$$\text{Unsystematic Risk} = \sigma_i^2 = \sum_{1}^{n} w_i^2 e_i^2$$

$$= 0.10^2 \times 420.51 + 0.20^2 \times 116.96 + 0.15^2 \times 243.39 + 0.15^2 \times 62.24 + 0.25^2 \times 85.68 + 0.15^2 \times 156.64 = 26.89$$

Total risk of the portfolio (variance)

= Systematic risk + Unsystematic risk

= 154.94 + 26.89

= 181.83

Standard deviation of the portfolio = 13.48%

SUMMARY

A portfolio is defined as combination of securities. The return and risk of a portfolio are substantially different than that of a single security.

Portfolio return is given by weighted average of the returns of the individual securities constituting it. The same is not true for portfolio risk, though it is measured in the same way as that of the risk of individual security, i.e., the variance of the portfolio returns. The reason that portfolio risk is not the weighted average of the securities' risk constituting it is that the returns of various securities behave differently for a given change.

The risk of the portfolio is governed by the covariance—the relationship of the change in returns of the two securities. An alternate measure of relationship of returns of two securities is the coefficient of correlation. While covariance is an absolute measure, the coefficient of correlation is a relative measure. The coefficient of correlation can have values between –1.00 to +1.00. A negative coefficient denotes that returns of the two securities behave opposite to one another and the value denotes the strength of the relationship.

Negative values or low value of coefficient of correlation is extremely desirable for an efficient portfolio. With such financial assets, it is possible to have reduced risk of the portfolio. In fact, if two securities have coefficient of correlation of –1.00 it is possible to have a portfolio that has no risk and yet provides positive returns.

It is possible to construct numerous portfolios even with two securities simply by changing the proportions of wealth to be invested in the two. All these portfolios are feasible but not all of them are desirable. A rational investor looks either to maximize returns for a given level of risk or minimize risks for given level of return. The portfolios that satisfy either of the condition are known as efficient portfolios, and locus of such portfolios is known as the efficient frontier.

Most investors are risk averse. They prefer higher returns but lower risks. The utility of the investment is dependent upon the return and risk associated with the portfolio. Investors make investment choices with combinations of returns and risk. Several investments with different return and risk profiles can offer the same level of utility. This fact is an important determinant of portfolio construction. Sharpe has put forward a method of choosing securities for an optimum portfolio. The algorithm of portfolio design is given in Appendix B-8 (provided in the CD).

An optimum portfolio would be one that satisfies two properties—(1) it needs to be an efficient portfolio; and (2) it must maximize the utility.

Existence of a risk-free asset is of tremendous value in portfolio management. If risk-free assets are available, all investors can form different portfolios with some proportion in risk-free assets and some in risky assets. The locus of such portfolios is known as the capital allocation line (CAL). In order to maximize the returns or minimize the risk, investors must choose a CAL that has the maximum slope. Such a CAL becomes an efficient frontier as it outperforms all the portfolios that exist on the efficient frontier of only risky assets. The efficient frontier of only risky asset is a curve while the one with the risk-free asset is a straight line.

A straight-line efficient frontier considerably eases the problems of portfolio design. The optimum portfolio would be one that is tangential to the utility level desired. This has important implication on portfolio management. An optimum portfolio would be a combination of investment in risk-free assets and the remaining in risky assets. The selection of risky assets for all investors is the same. This separates investment decision from financing decision. All investors can be offered the same risky portfolio with amount invested in it varying according to individual preferences. Investors can employ leverage to enhance returns with commensurate rise in the risk.

The selection of optimum portfolio for risky asset can be done on the basis of mathematical model that attempts to minimize risk for a given level of return.

Risk of the portfolio is more of a function of covariance—the relationship of returns of one security with other securities, rather that its own risk, i.e., the variance. Risk reduction through addition of securities in the portfolio is referred to as diversification. For meaningful diversification the selection of securities must be based on the coefficient of correlation. Lower the value of coefficient of correlation; more is its desirability.

Risk of the security is classified into unique risk and market risk. As securities are added in the portfolio, the unique risk gets diversified away. However, the market risk remains and is not diversifiable. Beyond a point, addition of securities does not result in risk reduction and, therefore, further diversification becomes superfluous.

Utilizing the segregation of risk of the security, Sharpe has provided an algorithm for design of an optimum portfolio. Rather than dealing with the covariance, the Sharpe model bases selection of the security on the market risk measured from the beta coefficient. The algorithm starts with selection of a security that offers maximum differential returns per unit of risk, i.e., beta and compares it with the cut-off value. It keeps including the security that has higher excess returns per unit of risk than the cut-off.

Key Terms

Portfolio A combination of two or more securities is referred to as a portfolio.

Portfolio return Portfolio return is the weighted average of returns of the securities constituting it.

Portfolio risk Portfolio risk is the variance of portfolio returns.

Covariance Covariance is the relationship of returns of one security with returns of another.

Coefficient of correlation Coefficient of correlation is another measure of relationship of returns of two securities and is given by covariance divided by the product of variances of the two.

Efficient portfolio An efficient portfolio is one that offers higher returns for a given risk or least risk for a given return.

Efficient frontier Efficient frontier is the locus of efficient portfolios.

Coefficient of risk aversion The measure reflecting the extent of risk aversion an individual has is called coefficient of risk aversion.

Capital allocation line It is the locus of points on the return–risk space that describes the proportions in the risk-free asset and risky asset.

Utility indifference curve It defines the portfolio having different returns and risk, but offering the same utility of money to an investor.

Optimum portfolio Optimum portfolio is one that is efficient and maximizes the utility of money.

Diversification A strategy that demands inclusion of many securities in a portfolio in order to reduce risk is called diversification.

Unique risk The risk of returns that is specific to a security is unique risk. It is a diversifiable risk.

Market risk The change in returns of a security caused by economy and industry-wide factors is market risk. It is a non-diversifiable risk.

Key Formulae

Portfolio return (R_p)

$$w_1R_1 + w_2R_2 + w_3R_3 \ldots = \sum_1^n w_i R_i$$

Portfolio risk

$$\sigma_p^2 = \sum_1^n p_i\,(R_p - \bar{R}_p)^2\,\sigma_p^2$$

$$= \sum_{j=1}^n \sum_{i=1}^n w_i w_j \,\mathrm{Cov}(R_i, R_j)$$

Covariance

$$\sum_1^n p_i\,(R_1 - \bar{R}_1)(R_2 - \bar{R}_2)$$

Coefficient of correlation

$$\rho = \text{Variance} = \sum_1^n p_i \times (X - E(X))^2$$

Variance of the portfolio

$$\sigma_p^2 = w_1^2\sigma_1^2 + w_2^2\sigma_2^2 + 2w_1w_2\mathrm{Cov}(R_1, R_2)$$

Utility $U = R - 0.005A\sigma^2$

Capital allocation line

$$R_p = R_f + \frac{\sigma_p}{\sigma_s}(R_s - R_f)$$

Optimum allocation to risky asset

$$y^* = \frac{R_s - R_f}{0.01 \times A \times \sigma_s^2}$$

Covariance with market Cov $(R_i, R_j) = \beta_i \beta_j \sigma_m{}^2$

Returns with market risk $R_i = a_i + \beta_i R_m + e_i$

Risk of equally weighted portfolio with identical risk and covariance

$$\sigma_p^2 = \frac{1}{n}\bar{\sigma}^2 + \frac{n-1}{n} \text{AvCov}(R_i, R_j),$$

$$= \frac{1}{n}\sigma^2 + \frac{n-1}{n}\rho\sigma^2$$

Security risk and market risk $\sigma_i^2 = \beta_i^2 \sigma_m^2 + \sigma_{ie}^2$

Portfolio risk and market risk

$$\text{Portfolio Variance} = \sigma_p^2 = \sigma_m^2 \sum_1^n f_i^2 \beta_i^2$$

PRACTICE PROBLEMS

1. Expected Return, Variance, and Correlation

Sigma Steel (SS) and Chi Cements (CC) are listed on the stock exchange for the last several years. The stocks behave in tandem depending upon the state of economy but to varying degrees. An analyst has conducted a study to find out how the interrelationship of the returns of the two stock is. He segregated different economic conditions as–Excellent, Good, Normal, and Poor and calculated the returns offered by each firm during such periods. He further estimated that the likelihood of state of the economy for the next 10 years. Summary of his findings is as follows:

Situation	*Probability*	*Past Returns %*	
		SS	*CC*
Excellent	0.15	20.00	15.00
Good	0.15	15.00	12.00
Normal	0.50	12.00	9.00
Poor	0.20	–3.00	–1.00

Find out the following:

(a) The expected return of each of the stock.

(b) Standard deviation of each stock.

(c) Covariance and coefficient of correlation between returns of Sigma Steel (X) and Chi (cements) (Y).

Solution

(a) The expected return on the stock is given by sum of probability × returns under each situation.

$$\text{Expected Return} = \sum_1^n p_i \times r_i$$

$X = SS = 0.15 \times 20 + 0.15 \times 15 + 0.50 \times 12 + 0.20 \times -3$
$= 10.65\ \%$

$Y = CC = 0.15 \times 15 + 0.15 \times 12 + 0.50 \times 9 + 0.20 \times -1$
$= 8.35\ \%$

(b) Standard Deviation, the square root of sum of squared deviations from the expected value, is computed as below

$$\text{Variance} = \sum_1^n p_i \times (X - E(X))^2$$

Prob	*X*	*X – E(X)*	*px(X – E(X))²*	*Y*	*Y – E(Y)*	*pxY – E(Y)²*
15%	20.00	9.35	13.11	15.00	6.65	6.63
15%	15.00	4.35	2.84	12.00	3.65	2.00
50%	12.00	1.35	0.91	9.00	0.65	0.21
20%	–3.00	–13.65	37.26	–1.00	–9.35	17.48
Sum = Variance			54.1275			26.3275
Standard deviation, σ(%)			**7.36**			**5.13**

(c) Covariance and coefficient of correlation reflect the relationship of returns of the two assets and is computed as below:

$$\text{Covariance} = \sum_1^n p_i \times (X - E(X)) \times (Y - E(Y))$$

Prob	*X*	*Y*	*X – E(X)*	*Y – E(Y)*	*p × X – E(X) × Y – E(Y)*
0.15	20.00	15.00	9.35	6.65	9.33
0.15	15.00	12.00	4.35	3.65	2.38
0.50	12.00	9.00	1.35	0.65	0.44
0.20	–3.00	–1.00	–13.65	–9.35	25.53
Covariance					**37.68**

Coefficient of correlation $= \text{Cov}(X,Y)/\sigma_x \times \sigma_y$
$= 37.68 / 7.36 \times 5.13$
$= 0.9980$

2. Historical Data, Return and Risk

You have gathered the stock prices as at the end of each year on March 31 for a firm called All Weather Ltd. For the last six years, the price data is as given below:

Year	*Stock Price (₹)*
2002	130
2003	142
2004	169
2005	154
2006	189
2007	210

Find out the following:

(a) The expected return of the stock.

(b) The risk as measured by variance and standard deviation.

Solution

(a) The expected return on the stock of All Weather Ltd can be found by converting the price data in the % return as shown below:

Year	Price	% Return
2002	130	—
2003	142	9.23
2004	169	19.01
2005	154	–8.88
2006	189	22.73
2007	210	11.11

Expected Return $X = \sum_{1}^{n} \frac{r_i}{n}$

$X = (9.23 + 19.01 - 8.88 + 22.73 + 11.11)/5$

$= 10.64\%$

(b) Standard Deviation is given by:

$$\text{Variance} = \sum_{1}^{n} \frac{1}{n} \times (X - E(X))^2$$

X	X – E(X)	X – E(X)^2
9.23	–1.41	1.99
19.01	8.37	70.10
–8.88	–19.52	380.92
22.73	12.09	146.07
11.11	0.47	0.22
Total		599.30
Variance		119.86
Standard Deviation, (%)		10.95

3. Capital Allocation Line

Following information with respect to two Securites A and B are avaialble:

	Std. Dev. σ (%)	Exp. Return (%)
Security A	40.00%	30.00%
Security B	68.00%	40.00%

Government securities considered to be risk free are providing a return of 6%. Find the following:

(a) Capital Allocation Line (CAL) when risk-free security is combined with Security A

(b) CAL when risk-free security is combined with Security B

(c) What does the CAL tell us?

(d) Draw the CALs in (a) and (b) above

(e) What conclusions can you draw from the two CALs with respect to portfolio considerations of return and risk?

Solution

The financial data of the securities and risk free asset is as below:

	Std. Dev. σ (%)	Exp. Return (%)
Risk-free Security	—	6.00
Security A	40.00	30.00
Security B	68.00	40.00

(a) CAL with risk-free security and Security A

$$\text{Portfolio Return, } R_p = R_f + \frac{R_s - R_f}{\sigma_s} \times \sigma_p$$

$$= 6 + \frac{24}{40} \times \sigma_p = 6 + 0.6 \times \sigma_p$$

CAL implies that for every 1% increase in risk the return would increase by 0.6%

(b) CAL with risk-free security and Security A

$$\text{Portfolio Return, } R_p = R_f + \frac{R_s - R_f}{\sigma_p} \times \sigma_p$$

$$= 6 + \frac{34}{68} \times \sigma_p = 6 + 0.5 \times \sigma_p$$

CAL implies that for every 1% increase in risk the return would increase by 0.5%

(c) CAL provides the locus of risk return that can be achieved with changing proportions of investment in the combination of risk-free security with any other security

(d) CALs with Security A and Security B are depicted in Figure P8-3(d):

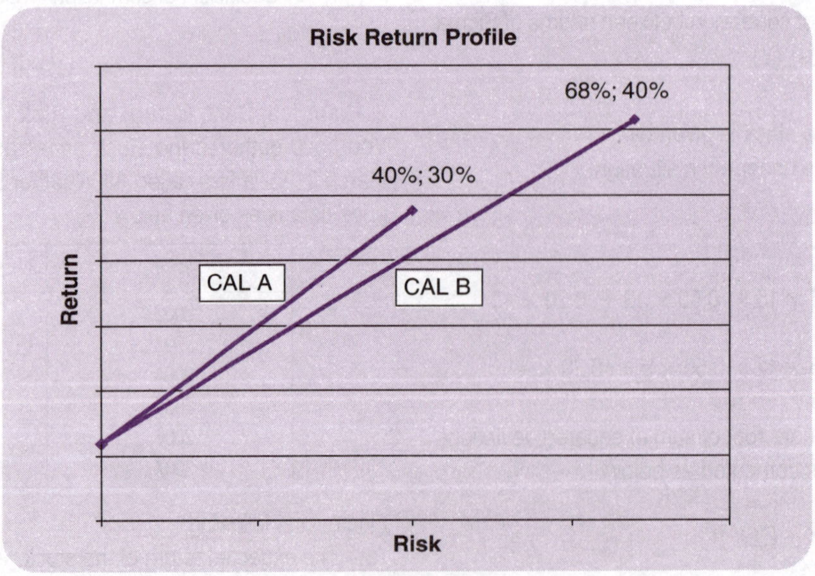

Figure P8-3(d)

(e) Clearly the slope of CAL with Security A is higher.
With the same amount of increase in risk CAL A would provide larger returns than CAL B. CAL A is superior to CAL B.
Therefore combining risk-free security with Security A is more desirable than combining it with Security B.

4. Target Risk and Return

Consider the financial information of risk free security, Security A and Security B in Problem 3 above. An investor is planning to invest his funds in the risk-free security and either of Security A or Security B.
Answer the following:

(a) With the target risk of 20% what maximum returns can he get when investing part of the funds in risk free security and remaining in either Security A or Security B? What would be the composition of these portfolios?
(b) With the target return of 24% what risk he faces when he invests part of the funds in risk free security and remaining in either Security A or Security B? What would be the composition of these portfolios?
(c) Is it possible to obtain a return of 25% with maximum risk of 30% either with Security A or Security B when combined with risk-free security?

Solution

If invesment in risky asset is denoted as *y* then the portfolio return and risk with risk-free security are given by:

Portfolio Return $R_p = y$ ₹+ $(1 - y)\, R_f$
Portfolio risk $\sigma_p = y\, \sigma_s$

The capital allocation line with risk-free security and either of Security A or Security B are:

CAL with Security A: $R_p = 6.0 + 0.6\, \sigma_p$
CAL with Security B: $R_p = 6.0 + 0.5\, \sigma_p$

(a) With targeted portfolio risk of $\sigma_p = 20\%$
Portfolio return with Security A: $R_p = 6.0 + 0.6\, \sigma_p$
$R_p = 6.0 + 0.6 \times 20 = 18\%$

The portfolio would be:
Investment in Security A; $y = \sigma_p / \sigma_s = 20/40 = 0.50$ or 50.00%
Investment in risk-free security = 1 – 0.50 = 0.50 or 50.00%
Portfolio return with Security B: $R_p = 6.0 + 0.5\, \sigma_p$
$R_p = 6.0 + 0.5 \times 20 = 16\%$

The portfolio would be:
Investment in Security B; $y = \sigma_p / \sigma_s = 20/68 = 0.2941$ or 29.41%
Investment in risk-free security = 1 – 0.2941 = 0.7059 or 70.59%

(b) With targeted portfolio return of 24%
Portfolio risk with Security A $24 = 6.0 + 0.6\, \sigma_p$
gives $\sigma_p = 30\%$

The portfolio would be:
Investment in Security A; $y = \sigma_p / \sigma_s = 30/40 = 0.75$ or 75.00%
Investment in risk-free security = 1 – 0.75 = 0.25 or 25.00%
Portfolio risk with Security B $24 = 6.0 + 0.5\, \sigma_p$
gives $\sigma_p = 36\%$

The portfolio would be:
Investment in Security B; $y = \sigma_p / \sigma_s = 36/68 = 0.5294$ or 52.94%
Investment in risk-free security = 1 – 0.5294 = 0.4606 or 47.06%

(c) Targeted risk is no more than 30% with expected return of 25% is not achievable. Portfolio of risk-free security with either Security A and Security B must satisfy the respective CALs. The maximum returns with target risk of 30% as per CALs are:

Security A: $R_p = 6.0 + 0.6 \times 30 = 24\%$
Security B: $R_p = 6.0 + 0.5 \times 30 = 21\%$

5. Two Asset Portfolio

Securities 1 and 2 are providing returns of 25% and 30% respectively. The risks as measured by standard deviations of returns for Security 1 and Security 2 are 20% and 35% respectively.

(a) Determine the profile of return and risk for different portfolios consisting of two shares assuming coefficient of correlation of (i) +1.0 (ii) 0.0 and (iii) –1.00.
(b) Also find the portfolio with least risk for each coefficient of correlation, its return and risk.
(c) Draw the locus of portfolio return and risk for each coefficient of correlation.
(d) What conclusion can you draw from each of the diagram in (c).

Solution

(a) and (b)

	Exp. Return (%)	Std. Dev. (%)
Security 1	25.00	20.00
Security 2	30.00	35.00

Any portfolio consisting of two Securities 1 and 2 would have return and risk as

Portfolio Return, $r_p = X_1 \cdot r_1 + X_2 \cdot r_2$
Portfolio Variance, $\sigma_p^2 = X_1^2 \sigma_1^2 + X_2^2 \sigma_2^2 + 2\rho X_1 X_2 \sigma_1 \sigma_2$

where X_1 and $X_2 = 1 - X_1$ are the proportions of wealth invested in Security 1 and Security 2 respectively.

Assuming different proportions of 0% to 100% in steps of 10% the expected return and standard deviation of portfolio is computed below using the above two equations:

Portfolio		*Return*	*Standard Deviation*		
Proportion (%)		*(%)*	*Coefficient of Correlation, ρ*		
X_1	X_2	r_p	*1.00*	*0.00*	*–1.00*
1.00	0.00	25.00	***0.2000***	0.2000	0.2000
0.90	0.10	25.50	0.2150	0.1834	0.1450
0.80	0.20	26.00	0.2300	***0.1746***	0.0900
0.70	0.30	26.50	0.2450	0.1750	0.0350
0.60	0.40	27.00	0.2600	0.1844	***0.0200***
0.50	0.50	27.50	0.2750	0.2016	0.0750
0.40	0.60	28.00	0.2900	0.2247	0.1300
0.30	0.70	28.50	0.3050	0.2522	0.1850
0.20	0.80	29.00	0.3200	0.2828	0.2400
0.10	0.90	29.50	0.3350	0.3156	0.2950
0.00	1.00	30.00	0.3500	0.3500	0.3500
Least Risk portfolio - Risk, σ_p			**0.2000**	**0.1746**	**0.0200**
Return of least risk portfolio,%			**25.00**	**26.00**	**27.00**
Proportions of investment: X_1			**1.00**	**0.80**	**0.60**
X_2			**0.00**	**0.20**	**0.40**

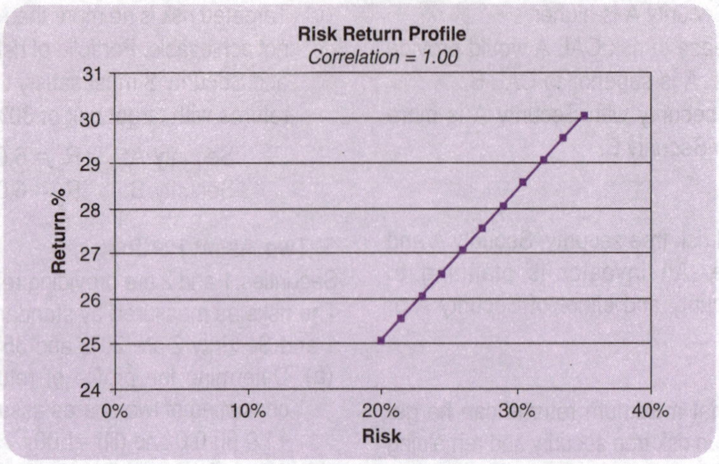

Figure P8-5(a)

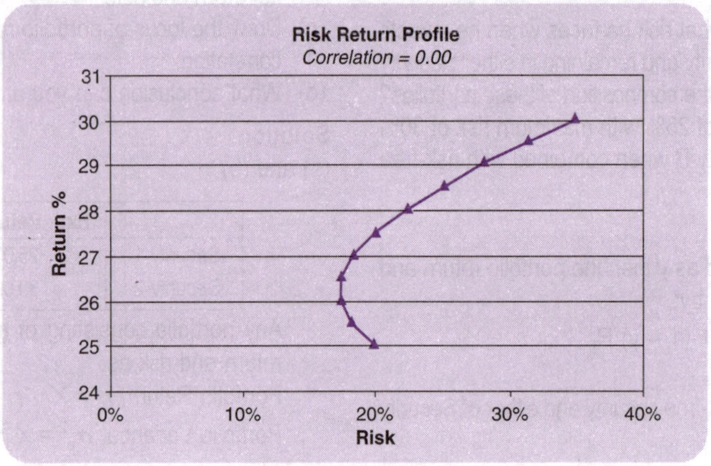

Figure P8-5(b)

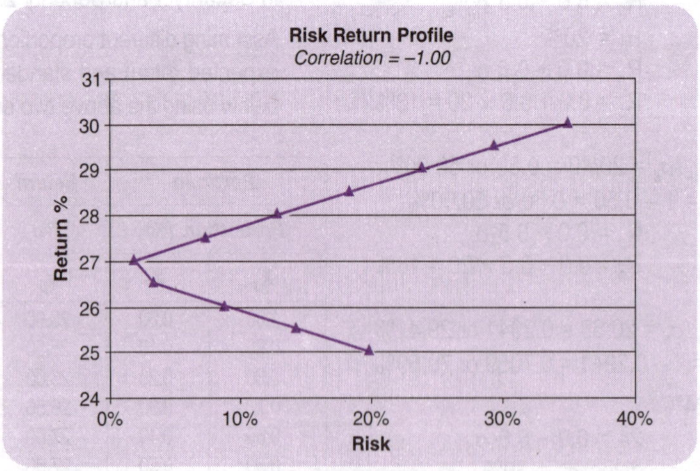

Figure P8-5(c)

(c) The portfolio returns and risk with co-efficient of correlation of 1.00, 0 and –1.00 are shown in Figures P8-5(a), (b) and (c) respectively.

(d) When the coefficient of correlation is 0.00, as the proportion of investment in Security 2 increase the returns would increase with a fall in risk. However with increasing proportions of Security 2 the portfolio would acquire more and more of the characteristics of Security 2 which has higher risk too.

When the coefficient of correlation is 1.00 (Figure P8-5(a)), the returns and risk would move together. The risk would increase as investor desires higher returns.

When there is perfect negative correlation (Figure P8-5(C)) the risk would fall at very high rate with increasing proportions of investment in Security 2 as the returns of both the securities compensate greatly/fully reducing the risk (possibly to zero) yet providing positive and increasing the portfolio returns. As proportion of Security 2 increases, the portfolio starts acquiring the characteristics of Security 2, thereby increasing risk with increasing returns.

6. Diversification Effect

Given the data of Problem 5 regarding Security 1 and Security 2

(a) At what level of coefficient of correlation do you expect the effect of diversification would take place?

(b) Do you think that a portfolio with no risk can be made? If yes, what are the conditions? If no, why not?

Solution

(a) Diversification effect (achieving risk less than the lower of the two securities involved) can be achieved only when the co-efficient of correlation is less than the ratio of risk of the two securities. Coefficient of correlation must be less than 0.20/0.35 = 0.57

(b) Zero risk portfolio is possible only when coefficient of correlation is -1.00 and proportions of investment are inversely proportional to the standard deviations.
Zero risk portfolio would be available when investment in

Security 1, $X_1 = \sigma_2/(\sigma_1+\sigma_2) = 0.35/(0.2 + 0.35) = 0.64$
Security 2, $X_2 = \sigma_1/(\sigma_1+\sigma_2) = 0.2/(0.2 + 0.35) = 0.36$

The zero risk portfolio would not be possible unless both conditions of (i) perfect negative correlation and (ii) proportions of investment are satisfied. It is next to impossible to find securities with perfect negative correlation, while the desired proportions of investment can always be adjusted by the investors.

7. Capital Allocation and Optimal Portfolio*

Assume two portfolios, 1 and 2 offering expected returns of 15% and 20% respectively. The correlation coefficient of the two portfolios is 0.50. The risks of 1 and 2 are given by standard deviations at 10% and 15% respectively. The risk free asset offers a return of 6%. The investor has ₹1,00,000 to invest. She is risk averse with the coefficient determined as 6.00. If you are the portfolio manager and given the task to find the optimum allocation so as the utility is maximized:

(a) How would you allocate her funds in both portfolios and the risk-free asset?

(b) What would be the risk and return of such designed portfolio?

(c) What level of utility would you associate with such allocation?

Solution

We have to find the optimal portfolio O that is a combination of Portfolios 1 and 2. Portfolio O would be combined with the risk-free asset to yield the best portfolio. We first find the proportion in risky Portfolios 1 and 2 of the total allocation to the risky portfolio.*

*The first step involves finding a portfolio that can be combined with the risk-free asset to yield CAL of maximum slope. The portfolio works out the fraction of wealth invested in one asset allocated to the risky assets (as distinct from the total investment in the portfolio, which includes investment in risk-free asset too). With the allocation to one of the asset known we can find the expected return and the risk of the optimum portfolio. All investors have this portfolio in their investment combined with the risk-free asset. The allocation of funds in the risk-free asset and the optimum portfolio would determine the ultimate return and risk the investor assumes depending upon the degree of risk aversion.

Let the proportion of money in Portfolio 1 be w_1 with $(1 - w_1)$ in Portfolio 2. By changing w_1, we obtain various portfolios and the w_1* is the proportion that provides optimal portfolio. The proportion w_1* is given by the following equation:

$$w_1^* = \frac{(R_1 - R_f)\sigma_2^2 - (R_2 - R_f)\rho\sigma_1\sigma_2}{(R_1 - R_f)\sigma_2^2 - (R_2 - R_f)\sigma_1^2 - (R_1 + R_2 - 2R_f)\rho\sigma_1\sigma_2}$$

$$= \frac{(15-6)\times 225 - (20-6)\times 0.5\times 10\times 15}{(15-6)\times 225 + (20-6)\times 100 - (15+10-12)\times 0.5\times 10\times 15}$$

$$= \frac{2025 - 1050}{2025 + 1400 - 1725} = \frac{975}{1700} = 0.5735 \text{ or } 57.35\%$$

and $w_2^* = 1 - w_1^* = 1 - 0.5735 = 0.4265$ or 42.65%

The above allocation would yield a CAL with maximum slope if out of the total amount allocated to risky portfolio, 57.35% is invested in Portfolio 1 and remaining 42.65% in Portfolio 2. Let this be called Portfolio O. The return and risk of the optimal portfolio would be:

Optimal Portfolio Return, $R_o = w_1R_1 + w_2R_2$
$= 0.5735 \times 15 + 0.4265 \times 20$
$= 8.60 + 8.53 = 17.13\%$

Optimal Portfolio Risk, $\sigma_o^2 = w_1^2\sigma_1^2 + w_2^2\sigma_2^2 + 2w_1w_2\rho\sigma_1\sigma_2$
$= 0.5735^2 \times 10^2 + 0.4265^2 \times 15^2$
$+ 0.5735 \times 0.4265 \times 0.5 \times 10 \times 15$
$= 32.89 + 40.93 + 18.34 = 92.16$
or $\sigma_o = 9.60\%$

Now we consider the allocation between Portfolio O and the risk-free asset. The optimum allocation to the Portfolio O, y* that maximizes the utility is:

$$y^* = \frac{R_O - R_f}{0.01\times A\times\sigma_O^2} = \frac{17.13 - 6.00}{0.01\times 6\times 9.60^2} = \frac{11.13}{5.53} = 2.01$$

This implies that the investor must invest twice the amount she has in Portfolio O, and, therefore, must borrow equivalent money. The final allocation would be:

Own funds	₹1,00,000
Borrowed funds	₹1,00,000
Total funds	₹2,00,000

(a) The portfolio:
Funds deployed in Portfolio 1 = 57.35% × 2,00,000 = ₹1,14,700
Funds deployed in the Portfolio 2 = 42.65% × 2,00,000 = ₹85,300
Funds borrowed = 100% × 1,00,000 = ₹1,00,000

(b) Returns = 1,14,700 × 15% + 85,300 × 20% – 1,00,000 × 6% = 0.28265 or 28.265%
Risk of the investor = 2 × 9.60% = 19.20%

(c) The utility is $U = R_p - 0.005A\sigma_p^2 = 28.26 - 0.005 \times 6 \times 19.206^2 = 17.20$

8. Risk in the Diversified Portfolio

Assume that a market called Utopia consists of large number of securities that have identical risk as specified by standard deviation of 30%. These securities too have an identical coefficient of correlation at 0.40. Find out the risk of the portfolio having equal weights with (a) 10 stocks, (b) 25 stocks, and (c) 100 stocks. To what level of minimum risk can the portfolio go with increased diversification?

Solution

(a) The standard deviation of the portfolio of 10 securities is given by:

$$\sigma_p^2 = \frac{1}{n}\sigma^2 + \frac{n-1}{n}\rho\sigma^2 = \frac{30^2}{10} + \frac{9}{10}0.4 \times 30^2 = 30^2 \times 0.46$$

or $\sigma_p = 30 \times 0.68 = 20.34\%$

(b) The standard deviation of the portfolio of 25 securities is given by:

$$\sigma_p^2 = \frac{1}{n}\sigma^2 + \frac{n-1}{n}\rho\sigma^2 = \frac{30^2}{25} + \frac{24}{25}0.4 \times 30^2 = 30^2 \times 0.424$$

or $\sigma_p = 30 \times 0.65 = 19.5\%$

(c) The standard deviation of the portfolio of 100 securities is given by:

$$\sigma_p^2 = \frac{1}{n}\sigma^2 + \frac{n-1}{n}\rho\sigma^2 = \frac{30^2}{100} + \frac{99}{100}0.4 \times 30^2$$

$= 30^2 \times 0.406$

or $\sigma_p = 30 \times 0.64 = 19.2\%$

The minimum risk that can be achieved through diversification is given by:

$\sigma_p^2 = \rho\sigma^2 = 0.4 \times 30^2$ or $\sigma_p = 30\sqrt{0.4} = 18.97\%$

9. Correlation of Stocks through Market Index

It is indeed difficult to examine the behaviour of returns on several stocks with each other. Instead the relationship of returns of various securities can be established through a common portfolio. This common portfolio is often taken as the BSE Sensex.

A study by a mutual fund has revealed following data in respect of three securities:

Security	*σ (%)*	*Correlation with Index, ρ_m*
A	20	0.60
B	18	0.95
C	12	0.75

The standard deviation of market portfolio (BSE Sensex) is observed to be 15%.

(a) What is the sensitivity of returns of each stock with respect to the market?

(b) What are the covariances among the various stocks?

(c) What would be the risk of portfolio consisting of all the three stocks equally?

(d) What is the beta of the portfolio consisting of equal investment in each stock?

(e) What is the total, systematic and unsystematic risk of the portfolio in (d)?

Solution

(a) Sensitivity of each stock with market is given by its beta.

Standard Deviation of Index = 15%

Variance of market Index = 0.0225

Beta of Stocks = $\rho_m\, \sigma / \sigma_m$

<u>Beta</u>

A = 20 × 0.60/15 = 0.80

B = 18 × 0.95/15 = 1.14

C = 12 × 0.75/15 = 0.60

(b) Covariances between any 2 stocks = $\beta_1\beta_2\sigma_m^2$

Covariance matrix

Stock	A	B	C
Beta	*0.80*	*1.14*	*0.60*
A	400.000	205.200	108.000
B	205.200	324.000	153.900
C	108.000	153.900	144.000
Sum of covariances			1802.200
Covariance of equally weighted portfolio			200.244

(c) Total risk of the equally weighted portfolio = variance 200.244

(d) Beta of equally weighted portfolio, $\beta_p = \Sigma\beta_i/N$ 0.847

(e) Systematic Risk, $\beta_p^2\sigma_m^2$ 161.290

Unsystematic Risk = Total Risk – Systematic Risk 38.954

EXERCISES

Concept Review Questions

1. What do you understand by portfolio?
2. Why do you think that the portfolio risk is not the weighted average of the risk of individual securities constituting it?
3. What do you understand by covariance and how is it different from the coefficient of correlation?
4. How do you determine the portfolio risk in case of two assets? Discuss special cases of coefficient of correlation of +1 and –1.
5. Under what conditions is it possible to have a zero-risk portfolio with positive returns?
6. What do you understand by efficient portfolios?
7. What is an efficient frontier?
8. How would you describe risk aversion and ways of measuring it?
9. What do you understand by utility indifference curve? How would they be different for different investors?
10. What is Capital Allocation Line and how does it impact the efficient frontier?
11. Describe features and methodology of Markowitz's Optimization Model of portfolio design.
12. How is the Sharpe Single Index Model different in approach from the Markowitz Model?
13. What is simple diversification and what do you understand by superfluous diversification?

Critical Thinking Questions

1. Security A has expected return of 20% with standard deviation of 25%, while for Security B the expected return is 18% and standard deviation of 30%. A portfolio manager suggested that no one should invest in Security B because its expected return is lower while the risk is higher. Every investor would be better off while investing in Security A. Do you agree with the portfolio manager?

2. Two investors having ₹10 crore each have formed a portfolio selecting stocks at random. One investor has 100 securities while the other has 200 securities. What do you think about the risk profile of the two portfolios? Do you think they would be different? Assign reasons.

Practical Assignments

1. Study the weekly returns of the two stocks for last 25 weeks. Find out the covariance and coefficient of correlation.
2. Identify ten stocks. Find their expected returns and betas. Then devise an optimum portfolio using algorithm of the Sharpe Single Index Model.

Numerical Problems

1. Expected Return, Variance, and Correlation

X and *Y* are two stocks whose returns are governed by the state of the economy. There are five states of economy that can be identified and analysts estimate that the returns of *X* and *Y* under various economic conditions are as follows:

		Returns %	
Economic condition	*Probability*	*Stock X*	*Stock Y*
Boom	0.10	14.00	20.00
Recession	0.20	–5.00	–2.00
Normal	0.40	10.00	9.00
Recovery	0.10	9.00	14.00
Slow	0.20	12.00	18.00

Find the following:

(a) The expected return of each stock.
(b) Standard deviation of each stock.
(c) Covariance and coefficient of correlation between returns of stocks *X* and *Y*.

2. Expected Return, Variance, and Correlation

Two stocks *X* and *Y* have provided returns in the last five years as follows:

Year	*Stock X*	*Stock Y*
2001	8	10
2002	–9	–12
2003	14	18
2004	16	20
2005	20	14

Find the following:

(a) The expected return of each stock.
(b) Standard deviation of each stock
(c) Covariance and coefficient of correlation between returns of Stock X and Stock Y.

3. Two-asset Portfolio

There are two securities under consideration for forming a portfolio—Safety First Ltd and Reasonable Risk Ltd The expected returns are 10% and 20% respectively, and risk as measured by standard deviation is 15% and 30% respectively.

(a) Determine the profile of return and risk for different portfolio consisting of two shares, assuming co-efficient of correlation of (a) +1.0, (b) +0.3, (c) 0.0, and (d) –1.00.
(b) Also find the portfolio with least risk for each coefficient of correlation, and its return and risk.
(c) Under what condition of coefficient of correlation it is advisable to have the portfolio with combination of Safety First and Reasonable Risk?
(d) Is it possible to have a zero-risk portfolio by combining the two stocks? If yes, under what conditions?

4. Relationship of Stock with Index

The returns on Stock A and the market over the last six years are as below:

Year	*Return on stock A (%)*	*Return on market (%)*
2001	34.00	15.00
2002	24.00	30.00
2003	15.00	17.00
2004	9.00	–12.00
2005	–15.00	5.00
2006	21.00	6.00

Find beta and alpha of Stock A using regression methodology.

(a) What is the total risk on Stock A and the market?
(b) What is the covariance of returns of Stock A with the market? Also find the beta using covariance.
(c) How can the risk of Stock A be explained by the market?

5. Designing Portfolio

Given following information about four securities identified by a portfolio manager:

			Coefficient of correlation			
Security	*Return (%)*	*Std dev*	*Acme*	*Booz*	*Candy*	*Dummy*
Acme	18.00	0.20	1.00	0.80	0.75	0.65
Booz	20.00	0.30	0.80	1.00	0.70	0.60
Candy	15.00	0.18	0.75	0.70	1.00	0.90
Dummy	30.00	0.35	0.65	0.60	0.90	1.00

(i) The portfolio manager is targeting a return of around 20% with risk of 20%. Examine the desirability of equally weighted portfolio for meeting the objective.
(ii) If you were to make a portfolio of only two securities which combination would you prefer and why?
(iii) Based on the answer of (ii) find the expected return and risk of the equally weighted portfolio.
(iv) Compare the portfolio performance of (iii) with the portfolio consisting of 40% weight in the security with higher risk.

6. Correlation of Stocks through Market Index

The risk and correlation coefficient with the market of four stocks are as below:

Stock	*Standard Deviation* (σ)	*Correlation with Index* (ρ)
Bunny	25	0.90
	Chummy	20 0.80
	Gummy	18 0.75
Tummy	14	0.65

(i) What is the sensitivity of returns of each stock with respect to the market?
(ii) What are the covariances among the various stocks?
(iii) What is the beta of the portfolio consisting of equal investment in each stock?
(iv) What is the total systematic and unsystematic risk of the portfolio in (iii)?

7. Sharpe's Model of Portfolio Optimization

A portfolio manager has identified six securities for consideration and has gathered following information regarding expected returns, beta, and unsystematic risk:

Security	*Return*	*Beta* (β)	*Unsys. Risk* (σ_i^2)
A	15.00	1.10	50
B	13.50	1.00	25
C	14.00	1.05	20
D	15.50	1.20	25
E	11.00	0.85	40
F	11.50	0.90	16

Further, the expected market return and variance are 15% and 50% respectively. The risk-free rate of return as measured from the return on government securities is 7%.

You are required to form a portfolio using Sharpe's methodology for optimizing the portfolio.

In the CD

Appendix A-8 Optimization of Portfolio using Excel

Appendix B-8 Optimization with Single Index Model–Algorithm and Example

Finding Returns and Risk of Protfolio (Probabilistic Approach)

Finding Returns and Risk of Portfolio (Markowitz/Covariance Approach)

CHAPTER

9

Asset Pricing Models

LEARNING OBJECTIVES

After going through this chapter, you will be able to:

- examine the relationship of expected returns with the risk
- understand the derivation of the capital asset pricing model (CAPM), its assumptions and limitations
- learn about portfolio construction, and assets its return and risk
- learn about single variable and multi-variable models
- understand the concepts related to arbitrage pricing theory (APT)
- examine the similarities and dissimilarities of CAPM and APT

SUBZI MANDI AND ASSET PRICING

Professor Pota, a financial expert attempting to explain the simplicity of finance to his class of MBA students passed a simple comment, 'Shares are like vegetables and the *subzi mandi* (wholesale vegetable market) is like the stock market'.

John, a student, agitatedly asked, 'How can we equate the two? One market caters to the daily needs of all, while the stock market is certainly meant for the more sophisticated, intelligent crowd and is dominated by highly literate people. Theorists in finance and researchers in stock market have earned Nobel prizes'.

Professor Pota responded politely, 'The market behaviour does not change according to who participates in them. Investors in capital markets are like consumers. When it comes to price determination, both literates and the illiterate behave in the same way'.

'What about Nobel prizes? Are they as much worth as potatoes or cabbages?' said John. The Professor, who was not sure about the Nobel Prize, paused for a while and answered, 'If there were a Nobel Prize for research on *subzi mandi* there would have been as many of them as there are for stock market'.

Without waiting for any reaction of the class, Professor Pota continued, 'There is lot of similarity between the two markets, though the variety is far less in *subzi mandi* as compared to the stock market. You see, the *subzi mandi* has a very strong relation to the stock market. Even Miller (1958) of Modigliani–Miller (MM) fame while trying to explain the irrelevance of capital structure drew an analogy from pizzas by explaining that no matter how you cut your pizza, its total size remains the same'.

'You mean the prices of stocks and vegetables are determined by a similar process?' asked another student.

The Professor replied, 'The prices in *subzi mandi* and stock market behave in the same manner. Not only the prices, even the process of price determination is similar. Can you guess how do we forecast the prices of potatoes?'

Taking the initiative, a student, Ganesh, attempted to answer the question posed by the professor, 'The economist uses various econometric models to forecast the prices of potatoes which includes factors such as likely weather conditions, which predominantly includes the amount of rainfall across the nation, acreage under cultivation, yields, besides likely demand for potatoes and may be several other factors.'

Not disputing the answer, Professor Pota reacted, 'It is too complicated. Can we have a simplified model of forecasting prices?'

Not expecting any answers, the professor continued, 'Yes if we take a single factor that affects the prices of all vegetables, it is the weather conditions that are likely in future. The prices of all vegetables are affected by future weather conditions. Some vegetables are more dependent on rainfall while some are not as much dependent. Therefore, the weather can form a single reasonable basis of predicting the prices of potatoes and for that matter, any other vegetable.'

'Why is there so much importance to the weather alone and not any other factors?' asked someone.

Professor Pota was quick to respond, 'Weather is an element that is uncontrollable and common to all. Therefore, it is crucial to price determination. Other factors, such as soil quality, acreage, yield, etc., are controllable to some extent and vary according to the crop you sow. Therefore, including such factors in the determination of the prices though not fallacious but may be redundant. Weather is a common factor that impacts prices of all vegetables the most.'

'It is not yet clear as to why we should ignore other factors while determining the prices of potatoes,' asked another student.

Professor Pota said, 'I will elaborate why other factors are not as important. Determining the price of potatoes based on other factors seems trivial because nobody eats only potatoes in a meal. It is one of the many things that constitute a meal. If potatoes are too expensive, people are likely to substitute it with some other vegetable.'

'But, aren't the prices of all vegetables linked with each other?' queried the same student.

'Yes, to the extent the weather affects them all, they are!' the professor quickly reacted. Almost in the same breath, he added, 'If prices of potatoes are high, the prices of other vegetables too are likely to be high, because if rising prices are due to poor rainfall, it applies to most of the vegetables. So what is relevant is the likely climatic conditions. Rest all can be managed to a fair extent.'

There was total silence almost in disbelief. To be more realistic, the professor added, 'I would attempt to explain that from two perspectives—one of the trader and other of the housewife. Consider the perspective of the trader in vegetables. A trader in the vegetable market is not as much concerned about the prices of potatoes alone. For him, selling potatoes and onions is same. He is concerned with his returns on the basket of vegetables he is selling. Since the prices of all vegetables are dependent on the common factor of weather, the sensitivity of prices to the weather is important.'

'But how is this relevant for the stock market?' asked Ganesh.

Professor Pota said, smiling, 'Good question. Now we come to the point. Like a trader of vegetables, who is concerned about the weather conditions, investors in the stock must be concerned about the impact on the prices of the stocks due to common factor. It is the common factor that the investor cannot do anything about?'

The professor further added, 'This analogy applies to the end-users too. If people cannot afford potatoes, they would afford apples if apples can be substitutes to potatoes. For a housewife, any meal must contain the taste that is obtainable by using various vegetables used in different proportions. The flavours of different vegetables affect each other rather than tastes of individual vegetables. The taste becomes entirely different when a meal is seen as a combination of many vegetables because the flavour of each vegetable gets modified by the presence of other items in the dish.'

Understanding the arguments of the professor, Ganesh summarized, 'Now we understand that if we have to consider the price of potatoes, we must see it in combination with other vegetables and its relationship of taste with them. If that is the case, the factors that are specific to the crop of potato seem irrelevant and, instead, we must concentrate on the weather alone because it is uncontrollable and is the common factor affecting all crops.'

The professor, with a broad smile on his face concluded, 'Exactly this is what capital asset pricing is all about and that's why I said stock market is similar to a *subzi mandi*.'

INTRODUCTION

In the earlier chapter, we examined the role of systematic and unsystematic risk in case of a single security and a well-diversified portfolio. We have so far not considered the determination of returns. Given the same framework as that of portfolio theory, we now examine the capital market theory dealing with the pricing aspects of individual assets in the capital markets. If investors behave rationally as suggested by Markowitz (1952) and capital markets are efficient, the returns offered by individual assets must follow some rule that must fully and truly reflect the investors' choice and state of the capital markets.

We all appreciate the basic idea that the returns must be commensurate with the risk undertaken by the investor. The *capital asset pricing model* (CAPM) is one such model that establishes the formal relationship between risk and return. It seeks a relationship between the risks and returns that must exist in the capital markets at an aggregate level.

The CAPM dominates the modern financial literature the most because of its wide array of applications. Based on the two parameters of return and risk, CAPM helps investors identify assets to invest in. It also clarifies to the investors that which risks get rewarded and which do not. It also helps in knowing what returns to expect and what not to. Besides investing, it has application in the field of corporate finance too. For corporate finance managers, it helps in finding the minimum hurdle rate that project returns must overcome. It helps managers of the firm establish the minimum cost of capital the project must earn to satisfy shareholders who are assumed to hold diversified portfolios and are concerned with only the market risk of the project.

CAPM values the financial asset in terms of the risk associated with it.

Capital asset pricing model was developed by William Sharpe (1964) and John Lintner (1965) who independently, but simultaneously, came out with similar conclusions. The important discovery answered a simple question—what measure of risk is considered appropriate when all investors diversify the Markowitz way?

ASSUMPTIONS OF CAPM

For pricing of financial assets, we need to make certain assumptions. There are several of them. Though they are explained in the discussion of the model it is considered appropriate to list them at one place for easier comprehension of the idea presented by the CAPM. These assumptions are:

assumes CAPM investing, efficient capital markets, absence of taxes, and homogeneous expectations.

1. CAPM assumes that the only two parameters of the asset, the expected return and the risk, form the basis of investment decisions. No other parameter enters the decision-making framework.
2. All investors have homogeneous expectations implying no ambiguity about the measurement of expected return and expected risk, and all investors arrive at the same efficient frontier. Different expectations about the risk and returns would lead to different efficient frontiers for different investors.
3. All investors are rational in their decision-making. Although each investor may exhibit a different appetite for risk, all of them seek lower risk for the same return and higher return for same risk. In addition, investors could differ only in their initial wealth.
4. All investors have identical holding period implying an identical time horizon for considering the investment. What happens after the holding period becomes redundant.
5. The conditions of perfect capital markets prevail such as:
   (a) Free and instantaneous flow of information implying no information gap amongst investors and no cost of information.
   (b) No transaction cost implying that a change in portfolio is possible as many times as one needs to and with no cost.
   (c) No investor is large enough to influence the price.
6. There exist no taxes implying that the tax considerations with regard to sale or purchase of investment and their timings are immaterial.
7. The investor can lend and borrow as much as is required at the same rate, which is referred to as risk-free rate.

THE EFFICIENT FRONTIER

In the previous chapter on portfolio theory, we discussed the concept of efficient frontier. While considering the assets with some expected return and non-zero risk the investors face the *efficient frontier* that provides an option to the investor to choose amongst the portfolios lying on it depending upon the desired degree of risk aversion and the level of utility. All investors attempt to maximize the utility of money that is assumed to grow with the expected return, but place a penalty on the risk associated with the investment. The amount of penalty is dependent on the degree of risk aversion of the investor.

Expanding the scope of investment beyond risky securities the availability of the risk-free asset has significant influence on the efficient frontier. The efficient frontier changes dramatically with the introduction of borrowing and lending at a risk-free rate. Investment in T-Bills or bank deposits is an example of lending at risk-free rates and borrowing at this rate is equivalent to deploying leverage to the investment choices.

Let us assume two stocks, stock A and stock B, with given expected returns and risks. Any investor can form numerous portfolios with the two stocks by changing the proportions of the money in each of them, depending upon the feasible risk–return combination. Few of these portfolios would be efficient and desirable for a rational investor.

In the risk–return space as in Figure 9-1, let us assume that the efficient frontier of risky assets is represented by the curve *ASMB* with two portfolios S and M on it. Both S and M are the portfolios consisting of some proportions of stock A and stock B, which are efficient. With the risk-free asset F, one may draw a *capital allocation line* (CAL) through F and any asset on the efficient frontier S and M included. The investor can choose any portfolio on the efficient frontier and combine it with F. As a result, the investor can obtain any combination of return and risk on the CAL joining the risk-free asset, F and the chosen portfolio lying on the efficient frontier of risky assets. When all the investment is placed in F the investor would earn a return equal to the risk-free rate, while having 100% placed in the chosen portfolio would provide return and risk associated with the same portfolio. By shifting the proportion from risk-free asset to risky asset some combinations of risk and return are obtainable. For example, the investor can obtain the risk–return combination on line FS by adjusting the proportion of money in the risk-free asset F and portfolio S.

If f is the amount allocated to risky asset S, then the portfolio return R_p and risk σ_p are represented by following Equations 9-1 and 9-2.

In case of a risk-free asset the efficient frontier is a straight line providing a linear relationship of return with risk.

$$R_p = (1 - f)R_f + fR_s \quad (9\text{-}1)$$

$$\sigma_p = f\sigma_s \quad (9\text{-}2)$$

where R_s and σ_s are the returns and risk of Portfolio S, R_f is the risk-free rate, and variance of risk-free asset and its covariance with S is zero.

Notice that the portfolios along the line FS is superior to any combination of risky assets alone on the curved segment AS. All combinations of portfolios along the line FS are feasible and dominate portfolios on segment FS in terms of higher return for the same risk. Hence, the *curved* efficient frontier changes to a *straight line.*

Can we further improve upon the straight-line efficient frontier FS? A look at Figure 9-1 would suggest that it is certainly possible simply by changing the choice of the risky portfolio while maintaining the risk-free asset, F in the portfolio. By opting

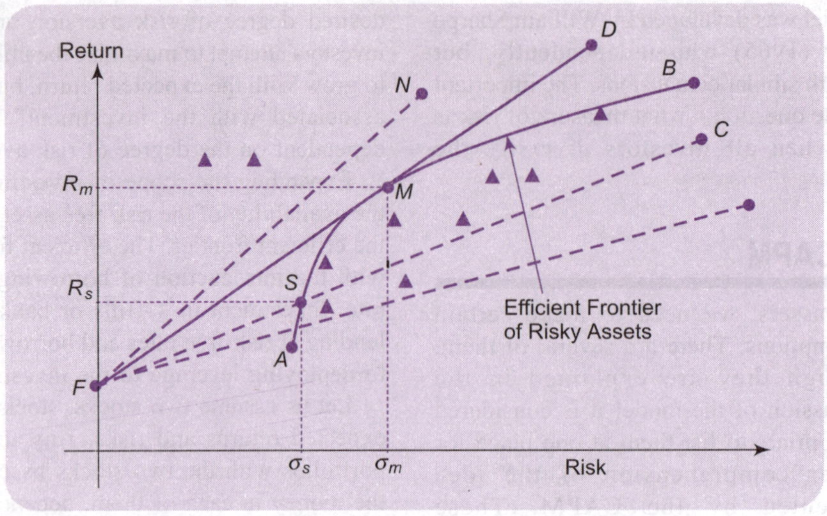

Figure 9-1 Changing efficient frontier with risk-free asset

for Portfolio M instead of S, all portfolios lying on the line segment FS become inferior to those lying on line segment FM. M is the tangential point with F beyond which no portfolio is available. The portfolios represented by line segment FN are not feasible.

Lending and Borrowing

The line segment FM, therefore, becomes the new efficient frontier. With the entire investment made in portfolio M (f =1) the investors can expect a return of R_m with the risk σ_m. Does this mean that investors who want a return greater than R_m would have no option but to limit their expectations to what is offered by Portfolio M? Certainly not, while the returns on the segment FM are possible with shifting investment from M to F, the returns beyond M are possible by borrowing at a risk-free rate and invest those borrowing in the Portfolio M. Mathematically, this means that the proportion of investment, f, in risky portfolio can exceed the value of 1.00. With borrowing at a risk-free rate, the efficient frontier extends beyond the segment FM.

> With borrowing available at risk-free rate, it is possible to obtain returns in excess of returns of the risky assets, assuming commensurate risk.

For example, consider that Portfolio M has expected return of 20% with standard deviation of 25% and the risk-free rate pegged at 5%. With 100% investment in Portfolio M, the investor expects a return of 20% and assumes a risk of 25%. If an investor seeks a lower level of risk, the proportion in the risky asset can be reduced accordingly. The return too would fall proportionately. To have a portfolio risk of 20% the investor can put 80% of the investment in risky portfolio M and remaining 20% in risk-free asset. Then the returns would be limited to 17% as shown below.

$$R_p = (1 - f)R_f + fR_s = 0.2 \times 5\% + 0.8 \times 20\% = 17\%$$
$$\sigma_p = f\sigma_s = 0.80 \times 25\% = 20\%$$

Now let us consider that the investor requires a 35% return. All that the investor has to do is to borrow at a rate of 5% in such a manner that portfolio return is 35%. We may solve Equation 9-1 to obtain the amount of investment required in the Portfolio M. To have a 35% return the investor must borrow an amount equal to her own investment and put the entire sum (her own and borrowed) in the Portfolio M. An increased return implies increased risk. The risk of the portfolio borrowing an equivalent amount and putting 200% in Portfolio M would have the risk twice as much as that of Portfolio M with 100% investment.

$$R_p = (1 - f)R_f + fR_s$$
$$35\% = (1 - f) \times 5\% + f \times 20\%$$
$$f = 2.00$$

And, risk of the portfolio:

$$\sigma_p = f\sigma_s$$
$$= 2.00 \times 25\%$$
$$= 50\%$$

The existence of Portfolio M and the risk-free asset has a very significant and important implication in portfolio management. The straight line joining the risk-free asset and portfolio M is the efficient frontier. All rational investors must choose portfolios that lie on the straight line FMD in Figure 9-2. Any combination of risk and return that lies on the line FMD is achieved merely by adjusting the proportion of investment in the two assets, i.e., the risk-free asset, F and the portfolio, M. Therefore, all investors must necessarily choose both the portfolios.

Investment choices are made with two decisions that seem interrelated. These two decisions are—(1) which securities to invest in; and (2) how much to invest in each security. The first decision, i.e., portfolio selection is an investment decision already made for all investors. All investors must hold the two assets, F and M. All they have to take is the second decision, i.e., the financing decision. How much to lend or borrow is governed by the desired return or the risk. From the above analysis, it is clear that investment decision and financing decision can be taken independent of each other. This is referred to as the *separation theorem*.

Market Portfolio

From the above discussion it is evident that if all investors have homogeneous expectations, identical holding periods, and only

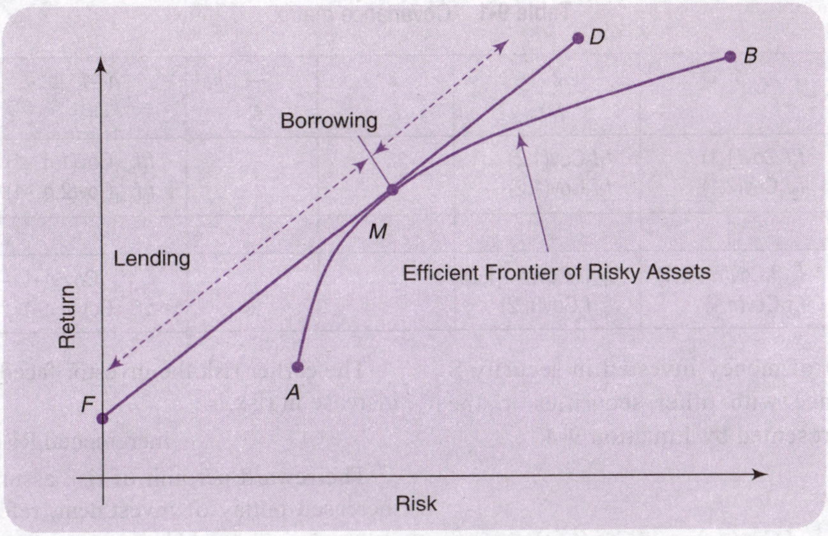

Figure 9-2 Lending and borrowing at risk-free rate

Market portfolio consists of all securities in proportion of their market capitalization.

market assets to invest in, then all of them would choose the same risky portfolio, M. The Portfolio M remains common to all investors irrespective of their attitudes towards risk. What could be this common portfolio? This risky portfolio, M is nothing but a market portfolio. It consists of all securities that are traded in proportion of their market capitalization. This portfolio shall be on an efficient frontier and will also be on maximum slope line from F.

The implication of the common portfolio, M, to be a market portfolio for portfolio management is of great value. It suggests that the holding market portfolio is as efficient as any other carefully designed portfolio. Being efficient, the market portfolio would lead to an inference that a passive strategy to invest in market portfolio is efficient. Therefore, investment in the index as a proxy for market portfolio would be an efficient strategy.

Risk Premium on Market Portfolio

The next question that needs to be answered is that what extra returns over and above the risk-free rate must be provided by the market portfolio? The excess return over the risk-free rate is referred to as the *risk premium*. We need to incorporate the utility function that recognizes that investors are risk averse and maximizes the utility of money. We know that all investors have utility function U as:

Market-risk premium is proportional to the variance of the market portfolio.

$$U = R_p - 0.005\,A\sigma_p^2$$

where $R_p = fR_m + (1-f)R_f$ and $\sigma_p = f\sigma_m$, and R_m and σ_m represent the return and risk, respectively associated with the market portfolio.

For maximizing utility, we use $dU/df = 0$. It would give the optimum proportion of investment in the risky portfolio, M as illustrated in Equation 9-3, which is analogous to Equation 8-14.

$$f = \frac{R_m - R_f}{0.01A\sigma_m^2} \tag{9-3}$$

Again, if all the investors face the same straight-line efficient frontier and the entire adjustment would be on amount of borrowing and lending, then in aggregate, borrowing and lending should cancel out each other. Some investors, desirous of a higher return, would borrow while some others would be willing to lend. On an aggregate basis the borrowing and lending being equal would cancel out each other. This implies that 100% would be invested in market portfolio on an aggregate basis. Therefore, $f = 1$ at an aggregate level and for market as a whole the risk premium,

$$R_m - R_f = 0.01A\sigma_m^2$$

or Market Risk Premium $\propto \sigma_m^2$

Therefore, the market-risk premium must be proportional to the risk contained in the market portfolio.

PORTFOLIO RISK OF AN ASSET

We know that portfolio risk is given by sum of all the covariance of all the securities in the portfolio. It is also known that the contribution of Security S to the portfolio risk is dominated by its covariance with other securities in the portfolio, and not as much by its own variance. Further, portfolio risk is also dependent upon the proportions of investment in the respective securities. The total risk of the portfolio consisting of n securities is the covariance matrix, shown in Table 9-1 which is dependent upon the fractions of investment placed in each security, f_n, besides the covariance of the two securities, Cov (n, m).

The contribution of risk of an individual security to the portfolio risk, is the product of its proportion and its covariance with the rest of the securities.

If each investor has the market portfolio then the contribution of one security, S to the portfolio risk is

Table 9-1 Covariance matrix

Security proportion		1	2 f_1	3 f_2	— f_3	n −1 —	n f_{n-1} f_n
f_1 f_2	1 2	f_1f_1Cov(1,1) f_2f_1Cov(2,1)	f_1f_2Cov(1,2) f_2f_2Cov(1,2)	…	…	f_1f_{n-1}Cov(1,n −1) f_2f_{n-1}Cov(2,n −1)	f_1f_nCov(1,n) f_2f_nCov(2,n)
f_{n-1} f_n	n −1 n	$f_{n-1}f_1$Cov(n −1,1) f_nf_1Cov(n,1)	$f_{n-1}f_2$Cov(n −1,2) $f_{n-}f_2$Cov(n,2)	…	…	$f_{n-1}f_{n-1}$Cov(n−1,n−1) f_nf_{n-1}Cov(n,n−1)	$f_{n-1}f_n$Cov(n−1,n) f_nCov(n,n)

proportional to the amount of money invested in security S and its weighted covariance with other securities in the portfolio. This may be represented by Equation 9-4.

$$f_s\{f_1\text{Cov}(s,1)+f_2\text{Cov}(s,2)\ \ldots\ +f_s\text{Cov}(s,s)\ \ldots +f_n\text{Cov}(s,n)\} = f_s\ \text{Cov}\ (s,m) \qquad (9\text{-}4)$$

If the portfolio consists of all the securities in the market, the contribution of S to the portfolio risk is measured by its covariance with all of the securities, i.e., the market. The component of its own variance $f_s\text{Cov}(s,s)$ will have negligible impact on the overall portfolio risk.

PRICING A FINANCIAL ASSET—THE CAPM

Now we turn our attention to the pricing of a security in an efficient market. Let us continue to assume that the investors are holding the risk-free security and the risky security, the market portfolio, M in their portfolios. Suppose after some research we are able to identify some security, S, that seems to offer better returns than the risky security, M, already in the portfolio. It has an expected return of ₹and standard deviation of σ_s.

Prompted by better returns, the investor would be tempted to borrow some money to invest in a new and attractive opportunity. Let us compare the strategies of the two investors A and B who borrow fractional and equal amount, Δ and put in either the market portfolio M or the new security, S. Strategies of investor A and B denoted as Strategy A and Strategy B are:

Strategy A: Borrow Δ and invest in market portfolio M
Strategy B: Borrow Δ and invest in Security S

Strategy A: Borrow Δ and invest in market portfolio

The investor opting for incremental borrowing invested in the market portfolio would face some extra returns and risk due to changes in the portfolio.

Increase in return for the investor would be:

$$= \Delta(R_m - R_f)$$

The new risk of the portfolio too would change, and would be equal to the proportional amount multiplied by risk of the risky asset. Therefore,

$$\text{New risk, the variance} = (1+\Delta)^2\sigma_m^2 \cong (1+2\Delta)\ \sigma_m^2$$

Ignoring the term Δ^2 as Δ is too small.

The earlier risk the investor faced was σ_m and, therefore, the increase in risk is

$$\text{Incremental Risk} \cong 2\Delta\sigma_m^2$$

The reward per unit of risk assumed by the investor due to increased outlay of investment, referred to as the incremental risk premium, would be:

$$\text{Incremental Risk Premium} \cong \frac{\Delta(R_m - R_f)}{2\Delta\sigma_m^2}$$

Strategy B: Borrow D and invest in Security S

Just like Investor A, Investor B, opting for incremental borrowing invested in the newly found security S, would also face some extra returns and risk due to change in the portfolio.

Increase in return for the investor would be:

$$\text{Increase in Return} = \Delta(R_s - R_f)$$

Likewise, the risk of the portfolio too would change. The new risk would be:

$$= \sigma_m^2 + \Delta^2\sigma_s^2 + 2\Delta\text{Cov}(s,\ m)$$

Again ignoring the term Δ^2 as it is too small to be considered, the increase in risk is represented as:

$$\cong 2\Delta\text{Cov}(s,m)$$

And the incremental risk premium is represented as:

$$\cong \frac{\Delta(R_s - R_f)}{2\Delta\ \text{Cov}(s,\ m)}$$

If the strategy of any of the two offers greater incremental risk premium than the other the investors would opt for that. If strategy B is more rewarding than the strategy A the investors would rush for buying security S either by borrowing more and more or by divesting the market portfolio. This would drive up the price of security S bringing down its returns. This process would continue till the incremental risk premium of the two strategies becomes equal. In an efficient market this would happen more quickly than one would imagine.

Beta, a measure of systematic risk, is defined as ratio of covariance of the asset with the market to the variance of the market.

Therefore, for equilibrium in the prices the incremental risk premium under strategy A and strategy B must be identical. We equate the two to get what is known as CAPM.

Incremental risk premium under A
= Incremental risk premium under B

$$\frac{\Delta(R_s - R_f)}{2\Delta\ \text{Cov}(s,\ m)} = \frac{\Delta(R_m - R_f)}{2\Delta\sigma_m^2}$$

or

$$R_s = R_f + \frac{\text{Cov}(s, m)}{\sigma_m^2}(R_m - R_f)$$

$$= R_f + \beta(R_m - R_f) \quad (9\text{-}5)$$

$$\left[\text{since } \beta = \frac{\text{Cov}(s, m)}{\sigma_m^2}, \text{ by definition.}\right]$$

In a nutshell, we have derived CAPM by the following steps:

1. With the introduction of risk-free security, the curved efficient frontier of risky assets changes to a straight line.
2. All investors choose their portfolios on the new straight-line efficient frontier combining lending or borrowing with the Portfolio M depending upon the risk–return profiles desired.
3. Since all investors have to choose the same portfolio M, it has to be an efficient portfolio. Further, this cannot be anything different than the market portfolio.
4. The risk premium of the market portfolio is proportional to the risk of the market portfolio on an aggregate basis.
5. The inclusion of any security in the market portfolio would add to the risk of the portfolio depending upon its covariance with the market with its own risk becoming relatively insignificant.
6. Upon identification of any attractive opportunity the investors would engage in the arbitrage so as to equalize the incremental risk premium.

Interpreting CAPM

Capital asset pricing model as given by Equation 9-5 implies that the security returns would be equal to the reward for waiting and the risk assumed. The risk assumed by the investor is given by β of the security and must be proportional.

Return on the asset is total of reward for waiting and reward for the risk assumed.

Returns of the security,

$$R_s = \text{Reward for waiting} + \text{Reward for risk}$$

$$= R_f + \beta \times (R_m - R_f)$$

The reward for waiting represents an investment return that is independent of risk. The investor needs to be rewarded for saving and deferring the current consumption for a later date. It is dependent on time and governed by current interest rates prevailing in the market, which in turn are dependent upon several complex economic factors. The other part of the return is dependent upon the risk associated with the investment chosen. The greater the risk assumed, the higher is the expectation of reward. It coincides with and reinforces the general belief that rewards must be commensurate with the risk assumed. All we need is an appropriate measure of risk.

In common parlance risk is a subjective measure. An investment that is considered risky by one investor may be considered as safe by another. Under the Markowitz model of diversification, we attempted to quantify risk by standard deviation of returns. This was a constant figure that left its judgement to the individual investor. The quantification was attempted to reduce the personal bias in interpreting a particular outcome as risky or otherwise.

In CAPM, we bifurcate this risk into two elements—*systematic risk* and *unsystematic risk*. Capital asset pricing model does not concern itself with unsystematic risk assuming efficient markets and adequate diversification on the part of all the investors. It only addresses systematic risk, which becomes relevant for determination of pricing of the financial asset.

Benchmark Values

A benchmark value needs to be developed for measuring risk. A scale for measurement of risk is required. The following are considered reasonable approximations for the values of the risk-free rate and the measurement of β.

1. T-Bills (government securities) are assumed to have zero risk ($\beta = 0$), a risk premium of 0, and a return of R_f. This is regarded as reasonable estimate of the risk-free rate. The yields on the T-bills would, therefore, replace the risk-free rate.
2. The market portfolio is assumed to have $\beta = 1$ and risk premium of $(R_m - R_f)$ is taken as reward for taking the market risk. An index serves the purpose as a reasonable substitute to the market.

The risk of all the securities is measured in terms of their relationship with the chosen market index. If the relationship of the security with the market indicates greater sensitivity, the value of β would be greater than 1. If it is less sensitive than the market, the value of beta would be less than one. For securities that exhibit the same risk in returns and move in exact tandem with the market the value of β would be 1.00.

Returns on T-Bills serves as a good proxy for risk-free rate of return and beta of market portfolio can be taken a 1.00.

The expected risk premium $(R_s - R_f)$ of any security S varies directly with its beta, i.e.,

$$R_s - R_f = \beta \times (R_m - R_f) \quad (9\text{-}5)$$

IMPLICATIONS OF CAPM

Capital asset pricing model has several notable and radical implications for the selection, management, and performance measurement of portfolios.

Portfolio Design

The first implication relates to the consideration of risk in a selection of securities while designing a portfolio. Should we be concerned with the total risk of the firm while considering it for inclusion in the portfolio? According to CAPM, the systematic risk is considered relevant while the unsystematic risk may be ignored. We know that there is little significance to the risk of the individual security as securities are added to a portfolio. Instead, only market risk determines how the inclusion of a security affects portfolio risk. According to CAPM:

- Market risk accounts for most of the risk in a well-diversified portfolio.
- Beta of a security is measure of its sensitivity to market movements.
- Investors must be concerned with the risk that cannot be diversified away.

The second important implication of CAPM relates to *optimality of passive investment* selection strategy. By owning the market portfolio, investors can generate competitive return without taking the trouble of identifying specific securities. The passive selection strategy, therefore, becomes efficient. If all investors follow the passive investment strategy several things would happen. First, the trading in the markets would dry up, impacting the liquidity adversely that becomes contrary to the existence of efficient markets and fair pricing. Second, no investor would research the future potential of firms that would influence the composition of the market portfolio, which is a dynamic phenomenon.

Investing in market portfolio is efficient.

For convenience, we only use an index as a market portfolio and if all investors become passive, the dynamic nature of the market is threatened again, working against the tenets of efficient markets. Capital asset pricing model suggests that the passive management of portfolio is a low-risk and low-cost alternative to active portfolio management. It is concerned about the expected returns and not the risk.

Portfolio Revision

By relying on CAPM for portfolio balancing, portfolio managers can adhere to a strategy of adjusting beta according to the market sentiments. In a rising market the portfolio manager can shift the portfolio in favour of stocks with high beta while in falling markets the orientation may change to having low beta stocks. By doing so the portfolio is expected to outperform the market by registering a larger than market return in bullish conditions and incurring a lesser loss than the market in bearish conditions.

The success of such a simple strategy would, again, defy the efficient market hypothesis. Here, the assumption would be that though CAPM holds, efficient markets do not exist.

Under CAPM, an individual whose portfolio differs from the market is playing a zero sum game. The player has additional risk and no additional return. This logic leads to passive management of stocks, i.e., buying and holding the market portfolio. The ability to decompose return and risk into market and residual components depends upon our ability to forecast beta. Capital asset pricing model claims that the expected residual on every stock is zero. It provides gloomy news for active portfolio managers since the returns on the stock cannot exceed what is prescribed under CAPM and beta of the stock.

Active portfolio management can succeed only when its forecasts are superior to CAPM-based consensus forecast. The ray of hope for the active portfolio management lies in the fact that the assumptions made by CAPM may not hold in practice. Market players have different information and different expectations. Capital asset pricing model helps active portfolio managers to focus on the residual returns that have consensus expectations of zero. The CAPM forecast of expected returns is dependent upon the forecast of beta.

Active portfolio management makes sense only when one's estimate is superior to that of the market.

Rationale for Reward

The other important implication of CAPM with regard to portfolio management concerns the expectations of reward on the portfolio. In an efficient market, all investors are assumed to be knowledgeable and, therefore, are familiar with the virtues of diversification. Most investors possess many securities rather than having investing in a single financial asset. According to CAPM, investors must expect the markets to provide returns commensurate with the risk undertaken. As unsystematic risk can be diversified away, the only relevant risk is systematic risk; the risk emanating from economy-wide factors affecting all stocks. The market would not provide returns for the unsystematic risk, and it would be wrong on the part of investors to expect returns for the unsystematic risk.

Market does not provide returns for the unsystematic risk, as it can be diversified away in a portfolio. While devising a portfolio, the only risk that must be considered is the systematic risk.

According to CAPM, investors are compensated for taking the necessary risk and not for taking unnecessary or avoidable risk. Market risk is inescapable. Residual risk is self-imposed and is avoidable.

Example 9-1 CAPM and Risk

A mutual fund already holds a well-diversified portfolio and is considering inclusion of the following stocks in the portfolio with an additional investment:

Stock	*Beta*	*Proportion (%)*
Meetha Sugar Ltd	1.15	20
Rum Whisky Gin Ltd	0.85	30
Changing Switchgear Ltd	1.20	20
Fast Motors Ltd	0.75	30

(a) What is the risk associated with portfolio of the newly identified securities?

(b) If risk-free rate is 5% and the risk premium on the market is 10%, what return should the mutual fund expect on the new investment?

Solution

Since the fund is already well diversified, the risk of the new securities in the portfolio would only be the systematic risk of each security. This is given by the portfolio's beta, which is the weighted average of the individual securities constituting it.

(a) The beta of the portfolio of new securities is:

Stock	*Beta (β)*	*Proportion (%)*	*Weighted average*
Meetha Sugar Ltd	1.15	20	0.230
Rum Whisky Gin Ltd	0.85	30	0.255
Changing Switchgear Ltd	1.20	20	0.240
Fast Motors Ltd	0.75	30	0.225
Beta of the new security			**0.950**

(b) In terms of CAPM, the expected return on the portfolio should be

$R_p = R_f + \beta \times (R_m - R_f) = 5 + 0.95 \times 10 = 14.5\%$

MEASURING BETA

Beta is the way of separating risk and return into two parts—the market component and the residual component. The yardstick for assessing what returns a security would provide depends upon the asset's market risk. Therefore, market risk of the asset needs to be assessed.

Table 9-2 Monthly returns on security and market

Month	*Returns on Security (%)*	*Return on Market (%)*
January	6.06	7.89
February	–2.86	1.51
March	–8.18	0.23
April	–7.36	–0.29
May	7.76	5.58
June	0.52	1.73
July	–1.74	–0.21
August	–3.00	–0.36
September	–0.56	–3.58
October	–0.37	4.62
November	6.93	6.85
December	3.08	4.55

The connection between security and market is normally established through the prices of the asset in the past. A normal way to assess the relationship of the asset with the market is to perform a regression analysis of the returns of the market taken as an independent variable and security returns as a dependent variable. This may be performed on Excel for which an exercise in the case of Hindustan Unilever Ltd and Nifty is presented in Appendix A-9 to the chapter. An index is deemed a fair representation of the market.

However, a broad idea of the regression is presented here. The past returns of the identified security on y-axis are plotted against the returns on the market on x-axis, with an index used as a substitute. Weekly closing prices can be used for the last one to two years as a reasonable size. From such a scatter diagram, we attempt to establish a simple linear relationship such that, if used for forecast provides the best estimate of security returns with the given expected market behaviour. Such a linear relationship can be represented through Equation 9-6.

$$y = \alpha + \beta x + e \tag{9-6}$$

where y represents the return on security, x is return on index, and α and β are the parameters of regression representing the y-intercept and the slope of the regression line.

Beta of a security (β) can be found by the regression of the past return of the security and market index used as proxy to the market portfolio.

Table 9-2 presents a small sample data on the returns of a security and the index for the preceding 12 months. Figure 9-3 shows the scatter diagram for such data. Regression is performed on the sample data of 12 observations using Excel charts. The result of regression presents the following relationship:

$$y = \alpha + \beta x = 2.2667 + 1.1318x$$

The regression equation shows a value of alpha, α of –2.2667 (the security provides a return of –2.27% when there is no movement in the market, $x = 0$), and β value of 1.13 reflecting the sensitivity of stock returns as 1.13 time the market returns. This implies that a 1% change in market is likely to show up with 1.13% change in the security.

One can directly get the values of regression coefficients using Excel. Feed the data of returns of security and market in the Excel sheet and then use *Tools – Data Analysis – Regression* to get the output. Insert the range of cells containing the data in the dialogue box. This is shown in Figure 9-4. Excel provides a direct output as shown in Figure 9-5. The regression data used in the discussion is highlighted.

The regression equation can be used for the forecast of expected returns on the security. Assuming that the returns on the market

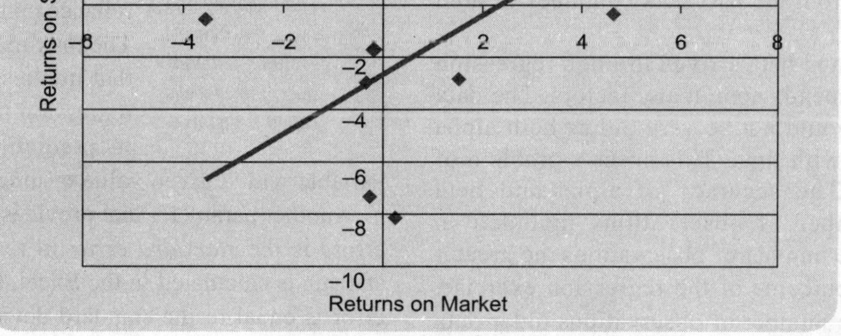

Figure 9-3 Regression

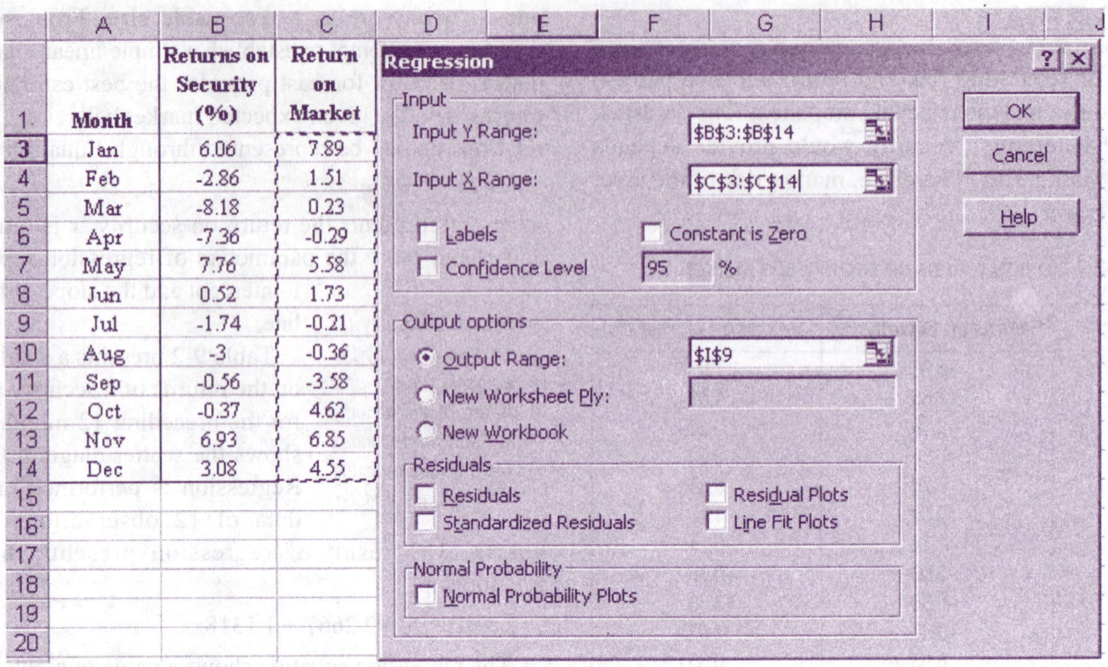

Figure 9-4 Using excel to perform regression

	D	E	F	G
1	**SUMMARY OUTPUT**			
3	*Regression Statistics*			
4	Multiple R	0.758042837		
5	**R Square**	**0.574628943**		
6	Adjusted R Square	0.532091837		
7	Standard Error	3.551110116		
8	Observations	12		
9				
10				
11		***Coefficients***	***Standard Error***	*t Stat*
12	Intercept	**-2.66669239**	1.259575444	-2.1171359
13	X Variable 1	**1.13184813**	0.307948702	3.675443744

Figure 9-5 Regression output in EXCEL

are expected to be 12%, then as per the regression equation the predicted return on the security would be 11.31% as follows:

$y = -2.2667 + 1.1318 \times 12$

$= 11.31\%$

The prediction is naturally based on the assumption that the relationship derived from the past data continues to hold for the future.

The validity of alpha and beta arrived through regression for use in the forecast depends upon many factors. The data used in the regression should not be very old as both alpha and beta tend to change with time. This poses a problem of insufficiency of data. The accuracy of alpha and beta depends upon the number of observations included in regression. The larger the number of observations the greater is the reliability of the outcome of the regression exercise. However, to increase the number of observations older data has to be included. One has to strike a balance between the age and quantity of data for regression. This essentially becomes a managerial compromise.

The reliability and accuracy of the forecast of returns depends upon the statistic called R-squared.

The accuracy of beta is given by the coefficient of determination known as *R-squared* in regression. The higher the value of *R*-squared, the greater is the reliance on the estimate of beta provided. The maximum value of *R*-squared is one that implies that all the points lie on the regression line and no error would result in predicting the value of dependent variable with a given value of independent variable.

Another parameter that provides the idea about the estimation errors is the *standard error* in regression. The standard error statistic is calculated in the Excel. Mathematically, the standard error is equal to the standard deviation divided by square root of number of observations.

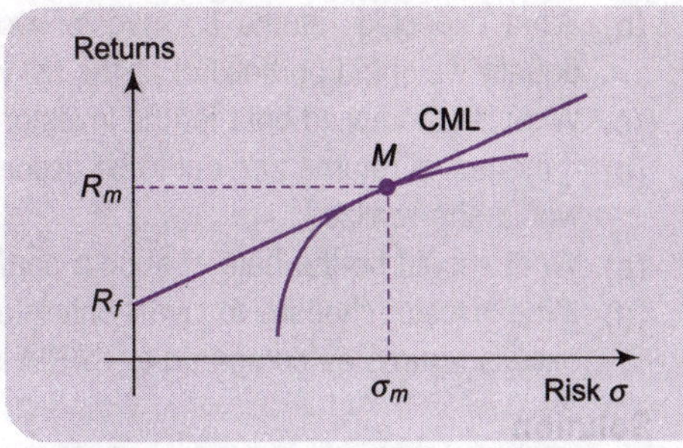

Figure 9-6(a) Capital market line returns

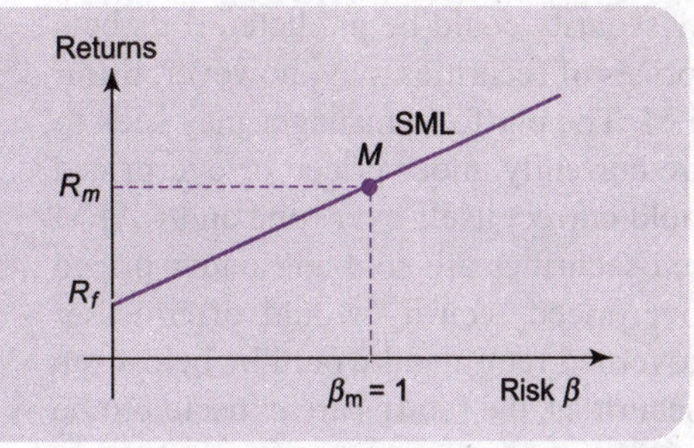

Figure 9-6(b) Security market line returns

$$\text{Standard Error} = \frac{\sigma}{\sqrt{n}} \qquad (9\text{-}7)$$

Based on the assumption that the distribution of estimated statistic is normal, the standard error implies that there are 68% chances of the estimated statistic to lie within one standard error of the mean, and about 95% within two standard errors. In a sample of betas for different shares calculated with the same index and during the same time period, it implies that there is 95% chance that the true beta would lie within ± 2 standard errors of the estimated beta through regression.

There are a few difficulties in the measurement of beta. The returns of the security that need to be regressed have to be adjusted for a dividend or any other corporate action such as issue of bonus shares, rights shares, and stock splits. Another problem that arises is the lack of trading or no trading at all on certain days. It poses difficulty of correlation since the share price remains unchanged while the market moves. This makes returns insensitive to market and provides a lower estimate of beta for the share. Lastly, the decision regarding the length of time to be used for regression is a tricky one. For accuracy one needs a larger number of observations. At the same time, as older data enters the analysis; lesser is the reliance that can be placed on it. The validity of beta for future use depends upon the age of the data used. If observations are recent the likelihood of beta being valid is large. Most betas are arrived at using monthly observations and 60 observations are regarded as appropriate.

CAPITAL MARKET LINE AND SECURITY MARKET LINE

The *capital market line* (CML) joins the risk-free rate with the market portfolio located on the efficient frontier. It is the CAL along which the investors can allocate funds between two securities—the *market portfolio* and the *risk-free asset*. It is a relationship of the returns and the risk measured by standard deviation of the portfolios. This is shown as Figure 9-6(a).

Security market line (SML) is the relationship of expected return and beta of the security as stipulated by CAPM. The market portfolio by definition has a beta of one, while the risk-free asset has beta of zero. The SML depicts, as shown in Figure 9-6(b), the relationship of the expected returns of the security and its risk as measured by beta.

The difference of CML and SML is significant even though Figures 9-6(a) and 9-6(b) look identical. Capital market line is actually a locus of portfolios that is composed of a risky portfolio, M, and a risk-free asset. Along the CML, the proportion in the risky and risk-free assets would differ. The measure of risk in CML is standard deviation. The SML, on the other hand, represents a relationship between expected return to beta. It substitutes the total risk (σ) with the systematic risk (β) on the horizontal axis. Here, the measure of risk is beta assuming the security forms the part of a diversified portfolio.

If the market values the securities as per CAPM they all would lie exactly on the SML. Also, if the market follows the

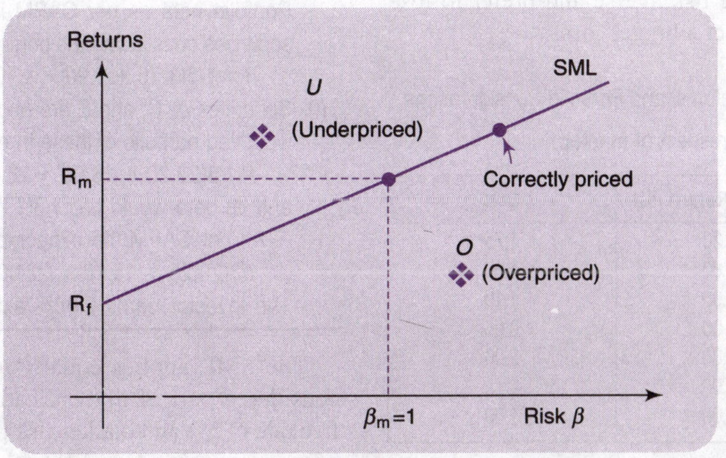

Figure 9-7 Security market line returns

CAPM the returns of any security could be predicted if its beta is known. In reality, the prices of securities may, however, differ from the theoretical CAPM. The portfolio manager may seek to identify securities that are currently under priced or overpriced and hope that market would correct itself over time and CAPM would prevail. Overpriced securities are sold and under priced ones are bought. The overpriced security would offer lesser return than the CAPM-governed return and would be below the SML. For under priced securities, the returns are expected to be higher and, therefore, would occupy a position above SML, as shown in Figure 9-7.

Consider Security O in Figure 9-7. It is overpriced as it offers lesser return than what SML prescribes. An investor can find another security exactly above it that lies on the SML and has the same beta. A zero demand for Security O would cause a drop in price so that the return offered becomes consistent with SML. Similarly, Security U is under priced as it offers greater return than what is prescribed by SML. Another security lying on the SML exactly below Security U offers the same risk β. Those wanting the same risk would seek to buy Security U. The buying pressure on U would cause the prices of the Security U to move up, thereby, reducing its return so as to become consistent with SML.

Capital Market Line relates returns of the security to the total risk while Security Market Line is a relationship of returns with the systematic risk.

What interpretation can be given to a security with a negative beta? In definition of beta it is clear that negative beta means negative covariance of security returns with market returns. It does indicate that the expected returns of the security behave opposite to that of market movement and such a security according to Markowitz's model is a highly desirable asset because of its extraordinary power to reduce risk when included in the portfolio.

However, in reality no one expects a negative return either on the market or on the security. If so, no one would ever make an investment. Yet security with negative expected return exists in the world of insurance. Everybody is happier to lose the insurance premium of the asset, such as a house or car, insured against theft rather than make a claim. The explanation lies in the utility of money. We all are risk averse and prefer to lose smaller sums of money to protect a bigger loss.

Example 9-2 CAPM, Expected Returns, and Portfolio Considerations

Following information is available in respect of market:

Security	Expected Return (%)	Beta
A	22.20	1.75
B	15.80	1.90
C	18.00	1.10
D	9.00	0.95
E	25.80	2.00
T-bills	8.00	—
SENSEX	15.00	1.00

Find out:

(a) Which of the securities are underpriced or overpriced?

(b) What expected returns an investor would have if she forms an equally weighted portfolio of all the risky securities (from *A* to *E*)?

(c) What is the implied beta for the investor on such a portfolio?

(d) If the actual returns turn out to be according to CAPM what returns would she realize?

(e) What should be the beta of such a portfolio where CAPM holds?

(f) If the investor chooses to invest only in undervalued securities what excess returns as compared to CAPM is she expected to realize?

Solution

(a) The expected return of each security needs to be compared with the returns according to CAPM. From the data, it is evident that the risk-free rate, R_f is 8% and the risk premium ($R_m - R_f$) is 7%. As per CAPM, the return of the each security is computed using the following equation:

Expected CAPM Return = $R_f + \beta(R_m - R_f)$

If the expected return is greater than what is prescribed by CAPM, the security is underpriced; if equal, fairly priced; and if less, then overpriced.

Security	Expected Return (%)	Beta	CAPM Return	Remark
A	22.20	1.75	20.25	Underpriced
B	15.80	1.90	21.30	Overpriced
C	18.00	1.10	15.70	Underpriced
D	9.00	0.95	14.65	Overpriced
E	25.80	2.00	22.00	Underpriced

(b) The expected return of equally weighted portfolio

= 1/5(22.20 + 15.80 + 18.00 + 9.00 + 25.80) = 18.16%

(c) The implied beta of the portfolio based on estimated returns is given by following equation:

$R_p = R_f + \beta(R_m - R_f)$

$18.16 = 8 + \beta \times 7$ gives $\beta = 1.45$

(d) As per CAPM: The expected return of equally weighted portfolio

= 1/5(20.25 + 21.30 + 15.70 + 14.65 + 22.00) = 18.78%

(e) The beta of the portfolio based on estimated returns is given by following equation:

$R_p = R_f + \beta(R_m - R_f)$;

$18.78 = 8 + \beta \times 7$ gives $\beta = 1.54$

Portfolio beta as per CAPM is weighted average of betas of the securities constituting the portfolio.

$\beta = 1/5(1.75 + 1.90 + 1.10 + 0.95 + 2.00) = 1.54$

(f) Securities A, C, and E are under priced. The return on the equally-weighted portfolio of these three securities is:

= 1/3(22.20 + 18.00 + 25.80) = 22.00%;

and its beta would be: 1/3(1.75+1.10+2.00) = 1.62

As per CAPM the expected return would be:

1/3(20.25 + 15.70 + 22.00) = 19.32%

The investor earns 2.68% extra returns.

The SML applies equally to portfolios as long as they are considered part of diversification. For example, consider risk-free rate of 5% and market-risk premium of 10%. Then the returns of two securities A and B with beta coefficients of 1.5 and 1.2 respectively will be:

Security A: $R_a = 5\% + 1.5 \times 10\% = 20\%$
Security B: $R_b = 5\% + 1.2 \times 10\% = 17\%$

If we form a portfolio, C, consisting equally of A and B the expected return of C would be:

$$R_c = 0.50 \times R_a + 0.50 \times R_b = 0.50 \times 20\% + 0.50 \times 17\%$$
$$= 18.5\%$$

The beta of the portfolio C would be weighted average of betas of A and B. The beta of portfolio C is:

$$\beta_c = 0.5 \times \beta_a + 0.5 \times \beta_b = 0.5 \times 1.5 + 0.5 \times 1.2 = 1.35$$

We confirm the CAPM return of portfolio C with beta of 1.35. As per CAPM,

$$R_c = R_f + \beta_c \times (R_m - R_f) = 5 + 1.35 \times 10 = 18.5\%$$

Example 9-3 CAPM Returns and Risk

The current price of Stock A is ₹50. It is expected to be ₹40 next year if the economy is in recession. Under normal conditions, the expected price is ₹55 whereas if the economy expands the price would go to ₹60. The probabilities of recession and expansion are 10% each while there is 80% chance for normal conditions to prevail. Stock A does not pay any dividend. Another Stock, B, has an expected return of 9%, a standard deviation of 12%, and the coefficient of correlation with market as 0.2 and with Stock A as 0.6. The standard deviation of the market is 10%. Assuming that CAPM holds, answer the following:

1. Your preference between two stocks for inclusion in the portfolio, if you already hold a well-diversified portfolio and are risk averse.
2. Find out for a portfolio consisting 60% of A and 40% of B—(a) expected return; (b) standard deviation; (c) beta; (d) systematic; and (e) unsystematic risk.

Solution

1. The expected return and standard deviation of stock A are found as below:

Condition	Probability (p)	Price	Return (%)	Deviation^2	p × Deviation^2
Recession	0.10	40	–20	784	78.4
Normal	0.80	55	+ 10	4	3.2
Expansion	0.10	60	+ 20	144	14.4
Variance					**96.0**

Expected Return = 0.1 × –20% + 0.8 × 10% + 0.1 × 20% = 8%
Standard Deviation = 9.80%
Beta of stock A = Cov (A, M) = $\rho_A \, \sigma_A / \sigma_M = 0.8 \times 9.8/10 = 0.784$
Beta of stock B = Cov (B, M) = $\rho_B \, \sigma_B / \sigma_M = 0.2 \times 1.2/10 = 0.240$

The decision to choose the stock for inclusion in the portfolio is based on the incremental risk premium with β being the measure of risk in the already diversified portfolio.

The incremental risk premium for stock A = 8%/0.784 = 10.20%
The incremental risk premium for stock B = 9%/0.24 = 37.5%

The investor must choose stock B offering a greater incremental risk premium.

2. For portfolio consisting of 60% of A and 40% of B;

Expected Return = 0.6 × 8% + 0.4 × 9% = 8.4%
Variance = $(0.6 \times 9.8)^2 + (0.4 \times 12)^2 + 2 \times 0.6 \times 12 \times 9.8 \times 0.6 \times 0.4$
= 34.57 + 23.04 + 33.87 = 91.48

Standard Deviation = 9.56%
Beta of the portfolio = 0.6 × 0.784 + 0.4 × 0.24 = 0.47 + 0.096
= 0.566
Systematic Risk (Variance) = $(\beta\sigma_m)^2 = 32.04$
Unsystematic Risk (Variance) = Total Variance –Systematic Risk
= 91.48 – 32.04 = 59.44

LIMITATIONS OF CAPM

The limitations of CAPM lie in the assumptions made by the model. Some of its assumptions seem unrealistic. Many attempts have been made to test the validity of CAPM by relaxing some of the assumptions. It has been found that CAPM is a very robust model capable of incorporating the required changes. It continues to hold under differing circumstances and helps us to understand asset pricing in the real world. Although, CAPM is not the only way to forecast consensus expected returns, it is arguably the best. The model has withstood many rigorous tests since its inception. This section discusses the likely behaviour of CAPM if some of the assumptions are relaxed.

Limitations of CAPM are embedded in its assumptions but CAPM is fairly robust to accommodate the relaxation of these assumptions.

Single period model

The CAPM is developed as a single period model where the returns and risk for one investment horizon corresponds to the planning period of the investor. While one investor plans investment for one year, another may take a long-term view of five years. If the planning periods for different investors were different, the CMLs and SMLs faced by each investor would be somewhat different. Similarly, if the expectations of investors were different the diversity of expectations would lead to somewhat different SMLs. These SMLs would be a band of lines where the conflicts of opinions and planning periods would persist as shown in Figure 9-8. However, it would not change the principle of asset pricing and linearity.

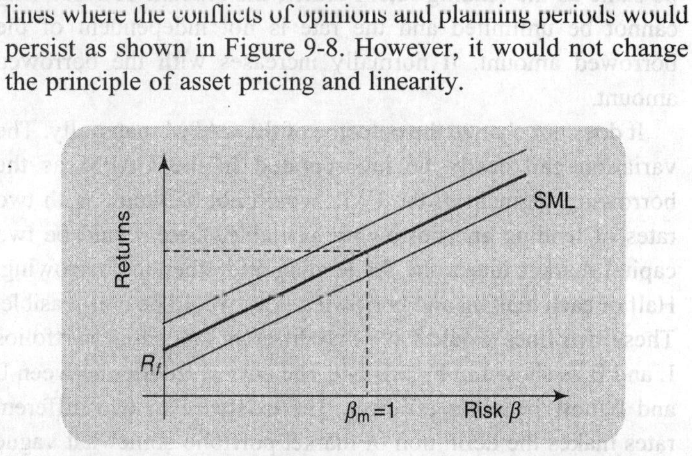

Figure 9-8 Security market line and investment horizons

In one of the studies by Eugene Fama (1970) it has been shown that CAPM can be extended to multi-periods. The assumptions made in the study are that the investors' preferences over successive periods are unchanged. The risk-free rate of returns

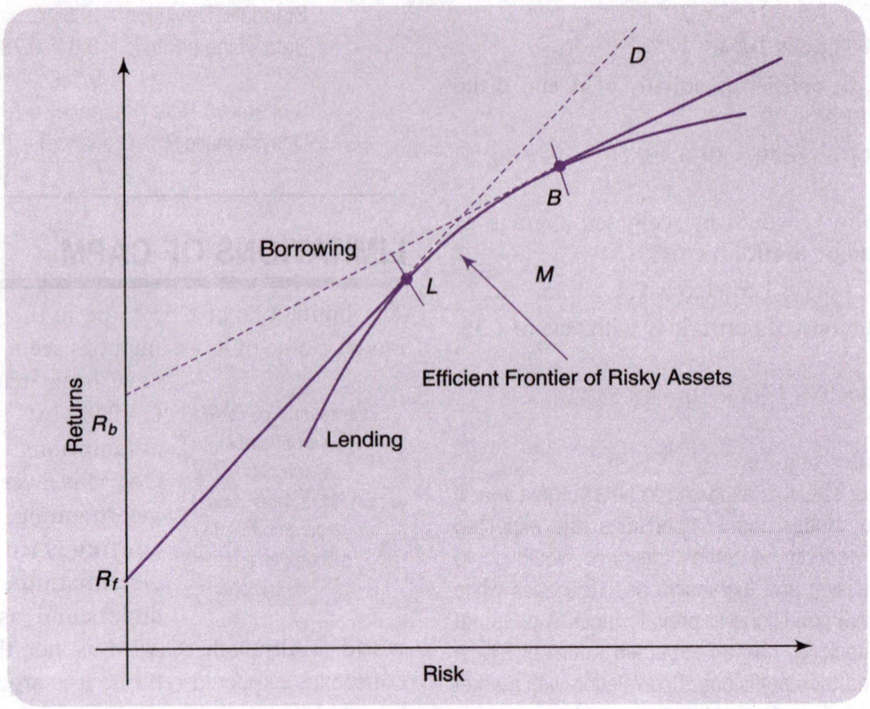

Figure 9-9 Lending and borrowing at different rates

and the probability distribution of security returns do not change unpredictably over time. However, we all know that risk-free rates and security returns do change over time.

Different lending and borrowing rates

Another assumption that is objected to is with respect to unlimited lending and borrowing at the same risk-free rate. The assumption is unrealistic because in the real world, borrowing is done at a higher rate than the lending rate due to the default premium. To cover the risk of default, the borrowing rate cannot be same as the lending rate. Further, the amount of borrowing cannot be unlimited and the rate is not independent of the borrowed amount. It normally increases with the borrowed amount.

It does not change the outcome of the CAPM materially. The variation can easily be incorporated in the CAPM as the borrowing segment of the CML would not be valid. With two rates of lending and borrowing available, there would be two capital market lines; one for lending and other for borrowing. Half of each lending and borrowing lines would be non-feasible. These two lines would have two different tangential portfolios L and B as shown in Figure 9-9. The curved frontier between L and B now becomes efficient. The existence of two different rates makes the definition of market portfolio somewhat vague as all investors do not hold the same market portfolio. If we have many borrowing rates there would be as many tangential portfolios along which different investors could the allocate proportions of investment in the market portfolio and risk-free assets.

Ignores Transaction Cost

Capital asset pricing model ignores transaction costs and limits the constant reshuffling of the portfolio. The expected returns would decline to the extent of transaction cost, which acts as a deterrent to modify portfolios. However, the objection does not take away the central theme of CAPM that returns are governed by systematic risk. The CML rather than a fine line would get transformed to a thick band with thickness representing the transaction costs. Hence, the definition of optimal portfolio would be hazy as shown in Figure 9-10. The process of arbitrage would be somewhat restricted as investors would not revise portfolios unless likely gains exceed the transaction costs. The SML too would be a band rather than a fine line with process of arbitrage stopping somewhat earlier. The securities may remain somewhat under priced or over priced not lying exactly on the theoretical SML, but in its close vicinity.

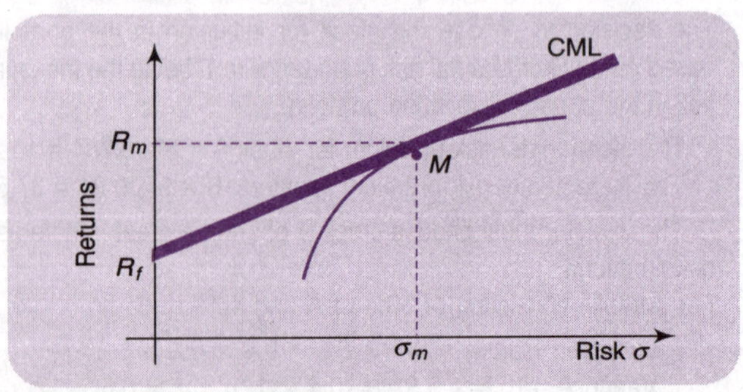

Figure 9-10 Capital market line with transaction cost

Benchmark Errors

In the development of CAPM, we have assumed a market portfolio of all risky assets that helps establish the CAL. In an ideal situation the market portfolio consisting of risky assets would only be efficient. This ideal market portfolio would include all assets such as real estate, metals, derivatives, bonds, bank FDRs, foreign stocks, currencies, etc. Some of these assets are not traded or are so thinly traded that the price information cannot be relied upon. In practice, we choose a proxy such as Nifty or BSE Sensex as market portfolio because of the convenience of price information at all points of time. This proxy excludes non-traded assets as well as thinly-traded assets. Since the benchmarked portfolio (the proxy market portfolio) would not be the most efficient, the CML as well as SML based on the proxy would have a smaller slope than the one obtained from true market portfolio, as shown in Figure 9-11.

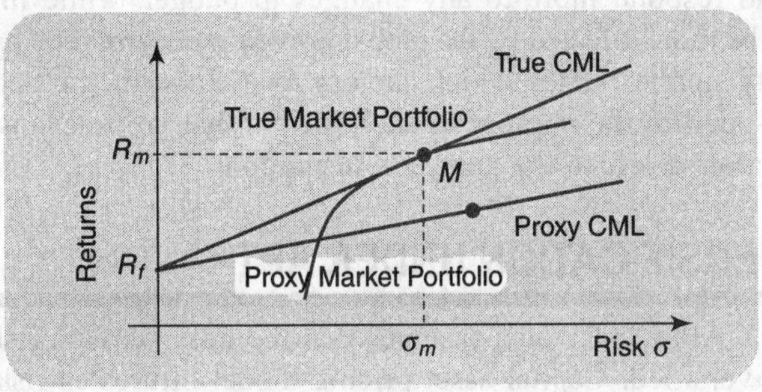

Figure 9-11 CAPM—Benchmark errors

An incorrect derivation of SML leads to two kinds of errors—(1) the estimation of beta of the security is wrong; and (2) the SML so obtained is not accurate distorting the evaluation of performance of the portfolios.

Another benchmark error results from difference in identification of risk-free asset. Since there is no such thing as risk-free in the world, the proxy used for the risk-free asset (such as yields on the T-Bills) would be higher than the true risk-free asset causing a further dip in the slope of the CML, as shown in Figure 9-12. The benchmark used for risk-free rate and the market portfolio would indeed make a difference to the analysis and performance measurement.

By definition, beta is the ratio of covariance of security with the market portfolio to the variance of the market portfolio. As the truer market portfolio would include non-traded assets and global assets, the covariance of the security is expected to decline when estimated with the proxy localized stock index. Further, the variance of index based on global assets is likely to be lower than the localized index. Although it would be difficult to predict the deviation of estimated beta from the true beta, the general belief is that the covariance effect would be larger than the variance and, hence, the estimated beta would be lower than the true beta.

Lack of clarity on risk-free asset and market portfolio leads to errors in estimating the expected returns based on CAPM.

The errors in benchmarking is likely to lead to overestimation of performance of the investment managers because the SML used for evaluation of portfolio performance is not as efficient as the true SML based on true risk-free asset and true market portfolio.

Do the benchmarking problems invalidate the CAPM? Benchmarking only highlights the problem of measurement but really do not invalidate the CAPM as a normative model. It only emphasizes the need for using a wider and more diversified index while testing the model, assessing the sensitivity and systematic risk and evaluating the portfolio performance. It also allows one to adjust to the likely discrepancies that may creep in estimation of beta and eventual asset pricing and performance evaluation.

Empirical research suggests that CAPM is a robust and durable tool for making investment decisions. The limitations of the CAPM do not make it invalid. The limitations only highlight the precautions one must take while applying CAPM to the portfolios, measuring cost of capital, doing portfolio appraisal, and forecasting expected returns.

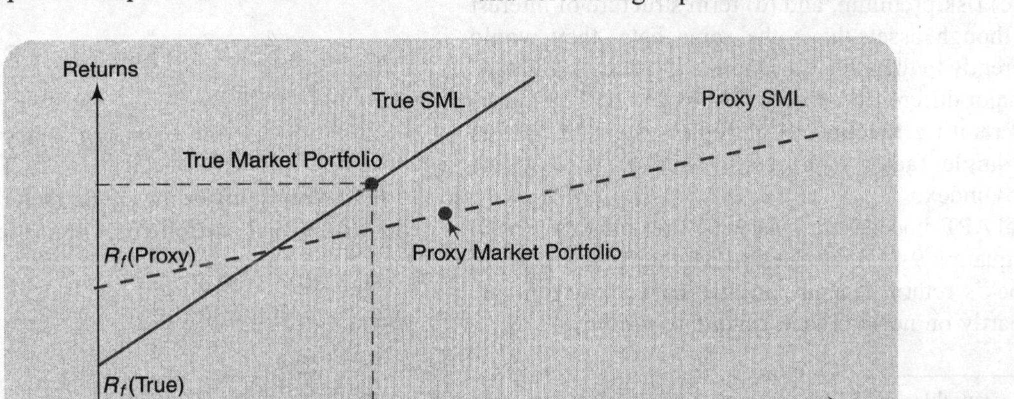

Figure 9-12 True and derived SMLs; benchmark errors returns

ARBITRAGE PRICING THEORY

INTRODUCTION

The various tests conducted on the validity of CAPM have raised some questions and emphasized the need to consider some additional variables in the systematic risk related to the market portfolio while explaining and estimating the returns of a particular security. The CAPM links the return of the security to a single factor, i.e., the market portfolio, which to some analysts appears too simplistic and possibly unrealistic. This led to the further search for finding some alternative asset pricing models to include some more parameters for inclusion in systematic risk.

While consolidating all the environmental risk in a single measure, i.e., market and capturing the sensitivity of returns in the beta we assumed that all securities respond to changes in the macroeconomic environment in a similar fashion. The differences in the returns were adequately captured in the value of beta. To address this issue we focus our attention of the regression statistic called R-squared. Reverting to the example on regression we found the value of R-squared as 57.46% implying, thereby, that about 42% of times the returns are not explained by a single index. This emphasizes the need to have multi-factor model to explain the price behaviour of a security. A better assessment of asset pricing can be had if multiple macroeconomic factors are incorporated in the model.

Multivariate models of determining expected returns disagree with CAPM in assuming the consolidation of systematic risk to a single factor called market risk.

Arbitrage pricing theory (APT) recognizes that returns of the security respond differently to different economic factors and have varying sensitivities to such economic factors. Further, the response of different individual securities is different for the same economic factor. The correlation between securities results when the securities respond to the same economic factor or factors in varying degrees.

Arbitrage pricing theory assumes that the returns of each security depends upon its sensitivities to the unanticipated changes in four economic factors[1], i.e., (a) inflation, (b) industrial production, (c) risk premium, and (d) term structure of interest rates. Even though assets have the same beta, they would respond differently to these basic economic (systematic) factors. This is one major difference between CAPM and APT. It makes the expected return a function of multiple systematic factors rather than single factor captured by market as a whole represented by index.

The general APT model as formulated by Roll and Ross (1980) is given as Equation 9-8. Like the CAPM, the APT also states that each stock's return depends linearly on macro-economic factors and partly on noise (events unique to the firm)

APT Expected Returns for a security R

$$= \lambda_0 + \beta_1\lambda_1 + \beta_2\lambda_2 + \beta_3\lambda_3 + \beta_4\lambda_4 + \text{Noise } (e) \qquad (9\text{-}8)$$

where β_1, β_2, etc., are the sensitivities of the returns with respect to factor 1, 2,..., etc. These can be taken as beta factors in the CAPM parlance. λ_1, λ_2, etc., are the risk premiums of the factor 1, 2, ..., etc, and λ_0 is the expected return with zero systematic risk, i.e., the risk-free rate of return. The noise is the unsystematic risk not related to any of the chosen factors. The return attributable to the firm's specific factors is referred to as noise and is denoted by e.

APT assumes that different securities respond differently to different macroeconomic factors.

Factors that are relevant for a particular security in determining the expected returns can be different for different securities. For example, spending on infrastructure in the Union Budget may have an impact on Tata Steel and the company would respond more to any changes in budget, while Infosys may be more affected by the global growth rate. Arbitrage pricing theory neither states which factors to include in the analysis nor specifies the number of such factors that are relevant. The selection is left to the analyst's discretion.

DIVERSIFICATION UNDER APT

Like CAPM, APT also assumes that the unsystematic risk can be diversified. Capital asset pricing model bifurcates risk into systematic (related to the market) and unsystematic (not explained by the market). As the portfolio becomes larger the unsystematic risk reduces and finally vanishes or becomes trivial to the analysis. Under APT, noise refers to returns that are not explained by the factors chosen in the model. Like CAPM, where the unsystematic risk, termed as noise, can be diversified when the portfolio becomes large enough, under APT too the noise can be diversified.

APT supports the basic idea of CAPM that unique risk is diversifiable.

The portfolio returns under APT with 4 factors, 1, 2, 3 and 4, is represented in Equation 9-9.

$$R_p = \lambda_0 + \sum_1^n w_i\beta_{i1}\lambda_1 + \sum_1^n w_i\ {}_{i2}\lambda_2 + \sum_1^n w_i\beta_{i3}\lambda_3$$

$$+ \sum_1^n w_i\beta_{i4}\lambda_4 + \sum_1^n w_i e_i \qquad (9\text{-}9)$$

In contracts, under the single factor model, the variance of a well-diversified portfolio of n securities is given by:

$$\sigma_p^2 = \beta_p^2\sigma_1^2 + \sigma_{pe}^2$$

where

$$\beta_p = \sum_1^n w_i\beta_i$$

σ_1^2 = Variance of the systematic factor, and

σ_{pe}^2 = Variance of the unsystematic factor

[1]These are the variables listed by Richard Roll and Stephen Ross. Analysts may differ over the set of sensitive factors affecting returns of the securities. Further, these factors need not be uniform for all securities and one may choose different set of factors for different securities.

Since we assume that the unsystematic risks of various securities are unrelated with each other, the unsystematic risk of the portfolio consisting of n securities would be the weighted sum of the unsystematic risk of the individual securities, when the coefficient of correlation of securities with one another is zero. The aggregate unsystematic risk of an equally weighted portfolio, consisting of n securities is $1/n$ of the average unsystematic risk of the individual securities comprising the portfolio as shown here:

$$\sigma_{pe}^2 = \sum_1^n \frac{1}{n^2}\sigma_{ie}^2 = \frac{1}{n}\sum_1^n \frac{1}{n}\sigma_{ie}^2 = \frac{1}{n}[\sigma_{ie(avg)}]^2$$

As n increases, the unsystematic risk of the portfolio becomes smaller and can be ignored.

ASSUMPTIONS OF CAPM AND APT

Capital asset pricing model is a single factor model. Is the systematic risk the only consideration in selection and buying of securities? Is this systematic risk limited only to market portfolio? Is it possible to construct a perfect market portfolio? These are some of the issues that are challenging to theorists.

Capital asset pricing model makes few assumptions that are not required by APT. These are listed as follows:

1. The assumption of market portfolio consisting of all assets in the proportion of market value is a requisite. Further, the market portfolio is also mean variance efficient. On the contrary, APT does not require construction of market portfolio to determine asset pricing. Instead, it requires identification of factors that impact the price and measure sensitivities of returns (the beta factors) with respect to each identified factor. The condition of mean variance efficiency is irrelevant for APT.
2. Another assumption that is dispensed within APT is the consideration of investors' utility function, which places a penalty for the risk. This utility function is assumed to be a quadratic function in CAPM. Arbitrage pricing theory merely assumes that investors prefer more wealth to less wealth. This makes the process of arbitrage as a deciding factor in determining asset pricing.
3. The assumption that security returns have normal distribution is also not required by APT.
4. The assumptions related to risk-free lending and borrowing rates are also dispensed with in APT.

The assumptions that are common to both APT and CAPM are as follows:

(a) Investors prefer more wealth to less wealth.
(b) Investors are risk averse.
(c) All investors have homogeneous expectations
(d) Conditions of perfect capital market exists.

The additional assumption made by APT is that the short selling is allowed that permits set up of arbitrage opportunity.

HOW APT FUNCTIONS

The expected risk premium on a stock must depend upon its sensitivity to several macroeconomic factors. The basic premise of arbitrage pricing theory is that if two portfolios are constructed and have dependence only on one factor, then the process of arbitrage will derive the price of the portfolios to converge, with respect to that factor.

The equilibrium of the market under APT takes place through arbitrage to remove mispricing, if any.

The process of arbitrage will apply to pricing of well-diversified portfolios. However, it must equally apply to pricing of the individual security, if it is assumed that security forms the part of the portfolio. Therefore, each security must offer a return commensurate with its contribution to the risk of a well-diversified portfolio, which would emanate from only systematic factors.

Although arbitrage pricing model is a multi-factor model, we illustrate the process of price discovery and adjustment assuming single factor APT, for the sake of simplicity and convenience. Two-factor APT is discussed in Example 9-5. We explain single factor APT here. Let us assume that returns of the security with single factor APT is governed by Equation 9-10:

$$\text{APT Returns } R = \lambda_0 + \beta_1\,\lambda_1 \qquad (9\text{-}10)$$

where λ_0 is the return on the asset with no systematic risk, λ_1 is the risk premium associated with risk factor 1(say unanticipated changes in the GDP growth), and β_1 represents the responsiveness of the financial asset to the risk factor 1.

If the single factor considered is the unanticipated changes in the GDP growth and assuming the values of the λ_0, λ_1 are 2% and 10% respectively, then APT implies that with no unanticipated change in the GDP growth the returns on the security would be 2%. Further, assume if the GDP growth changes by 1% (becomes 6% instead of forecast 5%) then the risk premium is 10%.

Now assume three securities A, B, and C with beta coefficients of 1.3, 1.8, and 2.0 respectively. The expected annual returns for three securities as per APT Equation 9-10 are:

APT returns for security A: $R_A = \lambda_0 + \beta_A\lambda_1 = 2 + 1.3 \times 10 = 15\%$

APT returns for security B: $R_B = \lambda_0 + \beta_B\lambda_1 = 2 + 1.8 \times 10 = 20\%$

APT returns for security C: $R_C = \lambda_0 + \beta_C\lambda_1 = 2 + 2.0 \times 10 = 22\%$

Assuming that the current market prices of the securities A, B, and C are ₹200, ₹50, and ₹100 respectively, one can work out the expected prices of each security after one year under APT. This is shown in Table 9-3. Now, further assume that we know by other sources of information that the prices estimated a year later for the three securities A, B, and C are ₹230, ₹65, and ₹125 respectively.

Table 9-3 Arbitrage pricing model—data for financial assets

Security	Beta	APT Return	Current Market Price (₹)	Expected APT price (₹)	Estimated Price (₹)	Remarks
A	1.3	15%	200	230	220	Overpriced
B	1.8	20%	50	60	65	Underpriced
C	2.0	22%	100	122	125	Underpriced

Now let us compare the APT prices with the estimated prices and draw conclusion whether the current value of the securities is correctly reflected in the market. In this case there is a clear case of mispricing where Security A is overpriced and securities B and C are underpriced. Under APT any mispricing is corrected through the process of arbitrage. This is under the assumption that any overpricing and/or underpricing that exists today would be corrected by the end of investment horizon.

We may define arbitrage as risk-less profit without an investment. The arbitrage can be set up as follows:

1. *Make no net investment initially* We constitute a portfolio with no investment by short selling the overpriced security and generating the cash, and use the funds so generated to buy the underpriced security such that the total investment is zero. Mathematically, if the weight assigned to n^{th} security is w_n then:

$$\sum w_n = 0$$

2. *Carry no systematic risk for the portfolio* The weights assigned in the portfolio must be so designed that the risk of the portfolio becomes zero. This is possible because the beta of the security sold short would be an opposite sign to the security bought. Again, mathematically we have:

$$\sum w_n \beta_n = 0$$

where β_n is beta of the Security n.

3. *Yet make profit at the end of investment horizon* Having made no investment and facing no risk the profit can be derived by buying the security sold short and selling the security bought at the end of investment horizon. The reversal of the investment position in each security would result in profit on the aggregate portfolio if the securities that were mispriced at the start become correctly priced at the end of the investment horizon.

Effectiveness of APT is dependent upon ability to set up arbitrage with no investment and a zero-risk portfolio.

To understand the process let us apply it to the data presented in Table 9-3. We notice that Security A is overpriced and, hence, we sell one share short and generate ₹200. To make no initial investment, we may use these proceeds to have long positions in underpriced securities B and C. One possible way of attaining such zero investment position is to buy two shares of Security B and one share of security A. Having done so the systematic risk of such a portfolio would be:

Beta of the long position $= (½ \times \beta_B) + (½ \times \beta_c)$

$= (½ \times 1.8) + (½ \times 2.0) = +1.9$

Beta of the short position $= -\beta_A = -1.3$

Beta of the portfolio; $\beta_P = w_A\beta_A + w_B\beta_B + w_C\beta_C = +0.6$

In such a portfolio, while we make no investment, we do face some systematic risk. Hence, this position cannot be taken as arbitrage as one may result in a loss at the end of investment horizon.

In order to have the no systematic risk of the portfolio, we may adjust the proportion of the funds in securities A and B so that beta of the short position is equal to beta of the long position. With ₹200 available from the short sale of Security A, the allocation to Security B and Security C can be done to achieve zero systematic risk as follows:

$$w_A\beta_A + w_B\beta_B + w_C\beta_C$$

where $w_B + w_C = 200$ and $w_A = -200$

$$\frac{w_B}{200} \times 1.8 + \frac{200 - w_B}{200} \times 2.0 = 1.3$$

gives $w_B = 700$ and $w_C = 200 - w_B = -500$

Note that Security C is sold short despite it being underpriced. Normally, investors would buy the same, if the decision were guided by CAPM. The arbitrageur would sell it short so as to obtain a no investment and no risk position. The initial position of the arbitrageur is depicted in Table 9-4. Note that such a set up results in no initial outlay and zero risk.

Table 9-4 Initial position of the arbitrageur

Security	Current Price (₹)	Shares bought (+)/sold (–)	Initial Cash Flow (₹)	Beta
A	200	–1.00	+ 200	–200 × 1.3 = –260
B	50	+14.00	–700	+ 700 × 1.8 = 1,260
C	100	–5.00	+ 500	–500 × 2.0 = –1,000
Net Initial position			0	0

Let us now consider the squaring up of the portfolio at the end of investment horizon taken as one year. As more and more investors set up such portfolios the price adjustment process would begin. Underpriced securities start gaining while securities sold short exhibit price decline. The market, assumed to be efficient, would correct itself over time and provide no arbitrage opportunity. This would result in eliminating any mispricing. The returns on individual securities at the end of the investment horizon, under equilibrium would be determined by the APT Equation 9-10. The resultant position of the arbitrageur would be a profit of ₹65 without investment and without risk, as computed in Table 9-5.

Table 9-5 Final position of the arbitrageur

Security	Shares bought (+)/sold (–)	Price Bought (₹)	Price Sold (₹)	Profit/Loss (₹)
A	–1.00	220	200	(200 –220) × 1= –20
B	+14.00	50	65	(65 – 50) × 14 = 210
C	–5.00	125	100	(100 – 125) × 5 = –125
Profit on the investment (₹)				65

The arbitrage profit in an efficient market would not be permitted. The very process of arbitrage will make the market efficient. The prices would be set right instantly. No arbitrage opportunity can persist for long and investors are quick enough to spot such opportunities that set the market right. The prices would correct in a manner so as not to allow any arbitrage.

Example 9-4 Arbitrage Pricing (Single Factor)

Assume that single-factor APT model applies. The single factor on which the returns depend is unanticipated changes in the GDP. Further, assume that there are two portfolios M and N that satisfy the APT pricing model with returns of 12% and 15% respectively. The betas of M and N with respect to the unanticipated changes in GDP are 1.20 and 1.80, respectively.

(a) What is the arbitrage pricing equation?

(b) Assume there is a Portfolio Q having sensitivity of 1.6 but providing a return of 15%. What strategy would you adopt to make profit with certainty?

Solution

(a) APT Returns for Portfolio M = 12% = $\lambda_0 + 1.2\lambda_1$

APT Returns for Portfolio N = 15% = $\lambda_0 + 1.8\lambda_1$

Subtracting the second equation from first gives λ_1 = 5%

Substituting λ_1 in any of the equation we find λ_0 = 6%

The two equations give λ_0 = 6% and λ_1 = 5%

The risk-free return is 6% and the risk premium for the unanticipated changes in GDP is 5%. The APT equation giving expected return of any security is:

Return on the security R = $\lambda_0 + \beta\lambda_1 = 6 + 5\beta$

(b) Portfolio Q provides a return of 15% with the beta factor of 1.6. The true return according to APT shall be:

$R = 6 + 5 \times 1.6 = 14\%$

Since the Portfolio Q offers a greater return than the theoretical return it would be bought. To set up arbitrage, we need to satisfy two conditions

1. The net investment needs to be zero.
2. The risk of long position is to be offset by the risk of the short position.

A net zero investment is obtained by selling short the portfolios M and N to generate funds for buying the Portfolio Q. The ratio in which the portfolio is short sold is found by equating the betas of the long and short position. If *f* is the proportion of Portfolio M, then

Beta of short position = $f \times 1.2 + (1 - f) \times 1.8$

Beta of long position = 1.5

Equating the two for zero-risk portfolio; f = 1/3 and $1 - f$ = 2/3

We set up the portfolio as below which has no investment and no risk:

Action	Investment	Beta
Bought Portfolio Q	–100	+1.6
Sold Portfolio M	+33 1/3	$-1/3 \times 1.2 = -0.4$
Sold Portfolio N	+66 2/3	$-2/3 \times 1.8 = -1.2$

End of the period profit on the portfolio is as follows:

Profit realized on Portfolio Q = 1 of 15% = 15%

Loss realized on Portfolio M = 1/3 of 12% = 4%

Loss realized on Portfolio N = 2/3 of 15% = 10%

The profit of the arbitrage strategy = 1%

Example 9-5 Arbitrage Pricing (Multiple Factors)

Assume that two factors are considered in the APT model and the following model works:

Expected Returns, $R = \lambda_0 + \beta_1\lambda_1 + \beta_2\lambda_2$

Assume a risk-free rate of 6% and the risk premiums for Factor 1 and Factor 2 as 4% and 5% respectively. Three portfolios with following characteristics are in equilibrium with respect to the two macroeconomic variables:

Portfolio	Beta (Factor 1)	Beta (Factor 2)
A	0.5	1.2
B	1.5	1.0
C	2.5	0.6

(a) Find out the expected returns of the three portfolios A, B, and C. There exists a Portfolio D with betas of 0.6 and 0.8 with respect to Factor 1 and Factor 2 respectively but provides a return of 10%.

(b) How will you take advantage of mispricing of Portfolio D?

(c) What profit can you generate?

Solution

(a) APT returns for Portfolio A = $\lambda_0 + \beta_1\lambda_1 + \beta_2\lambda_2$
$= 6 + 0.5 \times 4 + 1.2 \times 5 = 14\%$

APT returns for Portfolio B = $\lambda_0 + \beta_1\lambda_1 + \beta_2\lambda_2$
$= 6 + 1.5 \times 4 + 1.0 \times 5 = 17\%$

APT returns for Portfolio C = $\lambda_0 + \beta_1\lambda_1 + \beta_2\lambda_2$
$= 6 + 2.5 \times 4 + 0.6 \times 5 = 19\%$

(b) To eliminate mispricing of Portfolio D, we would take opposite positions in Portfolio D on one side and the combinations of Portfolios A, B, and C on the other side. The investment proportions in Portfolios A, B, and C denoted by F_A, F_B, and F_C respectively would be determined such that the betas with respect to Factor 1 and Factor 2 are equal and opposite. This provides the following equations:

Set investment equal to zero:

$F_A + F_B + F_C = 1.0$ (1)

Sets beta for Factor 1 equal to zero:

$0.5F_A + 1.5F_B + 2.5F_C = 0.6$ (2)

Sets beta for Factor 2 equal to zero:

$1.2F_A + 1.0F_B + 0.6F_C = 0.8$ (3)

Multiplying (2) by 2 and subtracting it from (1), we get:

$F_B = 0.1 - 2.0F_C$

Inserting the value of F_B in equation (1) we get

$F_A + 0.1 - 2\,F_C + F_C = 1.0$, gives $F_A = 0.9 + F_C$

Inserting the values of F_A and F_B in Equation (3) we get an equation in terms of F_C alone. Solving we get:

$F_C = 1.9$

$F_B = 0.1 - 2F_C = -3.7$

$F_A = 0.9 + F_C = 2.8$

(c) Portfolio D provides 10% returns while the APT returns are:

$\lambda_0 + \beta_1\lambda_1 + \beta_2\lambda_2 = 6 + 0.6 \times 4 + 0.8 \times 5 = 12.4\%$

Portfolio D, therefore, is overpriced and needs to be sold. The arbitrage portfolio is constituted by short selling the Portfolio D and investing the same amount in the Portfolios A, B, and C in the proportion indicated above. The negative proportion for Portfolio B implies that it too would be short sold. Such a portfolio would have no investment and zero betas with respect to Factor 1 and Factor 2 as shown in the following table.

Arbitrage Portfolio	Investment (Cash flow)	Portfolio Beta for Factor 1 (β_{1P})	Portfolio Beta for Factor 2 (β_{2P})
Position in Portfolio D not in APT equilibrium	+1.0	−0.6	−0.8
Opposite position in Portfolios in APT equilibrium	—	$\beta_{1A}F_A + \beta_{1B}F_B + \beta_{1C}F_C$	$B_{2A}F_A + \beta_{2B}F_B + \beta_{2C}F_C$
Portfolio A	−2.8	+ 0.5 × 2.8	+ 1.2 × 2.8
Portfolio B	+3.7	−1.5 × 3.7	−1.0 × 3.7
Portfolio C	−1.9	+ 1.9 × 2.9	+ 0.6 × 2.9
	−1.0	**+ 0.6**	**+ 0.8**

(d) The end position in the Portfolio D would be a loss of 10% and the cumulative positions in Portfolios A, B, and C would end up with the gain of 12.4% being in equilibrium. The resultant arbitrage profit would be 2.4%. This can be confirmed as follows:

Returns on Portfolio D: −1.0 × 10% = −10.0%
Returns on Portfolio A: 2.8 × 14% = 39.2%
Returns on Portfolio B: −3.7 × 17% = − 62.9%
Returns on Portfolio C: 1.9 × 19% = 36.1%
Total = 2.4%

CAPM AND APT

The CAPM implies that investors hold mean variance efficient portfolios. When the equilibrium is violated the investors shift the portfolios. The small changes of portfolio by large number of investors would create large volumes, which restores the equilibrium. In contrast, under APT if an arbitrage opportunity exists few investors would take very large positions (as it requires no initial outlay) that generates the volumes instantly and push the prices in the right direction. Since it takes fewer investors to correct the market by the arbitrage process under APT, the correction is expected to be much faster than the process of adjustments in the portfolios under CAPM. Hence, under APT it is not necessary that all investors need to be vigilant all the time since only few arbitrageurs capable of identifying the profit-making opportunities would serve the purpose. The assumption that all investors are equally well-informed is not as critical to asset pricing under APT as it is with CAPM.

APT is a flexible model that leaves the determination of factors sensitive to pricing to the individual's judgement.

The CAPM bases the return-determination process on the market portfolio, which is difficult to construct. We use a proxy of market index. In contrast, APT requires construction of a well-diversified portfolio, which is certainly possible and achievable. The need for a market portfolio is dispensed with.

Additionally, the CAPM assumes that probability distribution of security prices remains constant over time and, therefore, past returns provide a valid estimate of the future returns. Arbitrage pricing theory concentrates on the no arbitrage argument and does not require any assumption of normal distribution of returns nor its constancy over time.

Arbitrage pricing theory and CAPM, though contrasted, are not necessarily at loggerheads. They both have a central theme that security prices respond to broad economic factors and have different sensitivities.

Arbitrage pricing theory recognizes the dependence of security pricing on multiple factors. Capital asset pricing model assumes a central role for market portfolio as a benchmark. While APT does not depend exclusively on it, market portfolio returns can be one but not necessarily the only factor. Arbitrage pricing theory views risk more generally than just the relationship of the security with the market.

Limitations of APT

The sensitivities of returns, the beta factors (in CAPM parlance) are difficult to determine due to inadequacy of data with respect to each economic variable. The idea of APT seems appealing but its implementation faces roadblocks. Capital asset pricing model still remains a favourite with analysts due to easier comprehension and availability of pure observations that helps establish a reliable beta factor for asset pricing.

Arbitrage pricing theory does leave the question of determination of factors open-ended, while the CAPM assumes consolidation of all macro factors into a single factor, i.e., return on market portfolio.

Capital asset pricing model postulates a definite single factor of market portfolio as a determinant of return, which makes application and measurement easy, while APT leaves the choice open-ended for the number of factors as well as the choice. This leads to controversies and conflicts among theorists that has prevented the model from becoming popular.

Since the identification of factors determining the price of the security is open-ended in APT, the unanimity on the expected returns on a security is hard to come by.

The validity of CAPM rests on its assumptions, some of which can be challenged. At the same time these assumptions have been relaxed to examine the adaptability of the CAPM. The ability of CAPM to cope with assumptions has been good and, therefore, it helps develop a consensus estimate of return among analysts. The APT, due of open-ended questions of which factors and how many factors to consider leads to subjective interpretations of returns. The efforts for reconciliation among the analysts are likely to be futile due to the divergence of factors to be included in the model and measurement of the sensitivity of returns to the each of the factor. One of the by-products of CAPM is a procedure for determining the consensus on expected return, which is valuable because it is a standard for comparison.

Despite the fact that some of the assumptions can be challenged, research has shown that even in the real world the departure from the expected pricing as per CAPM is not material or significant.

The flexibility of APT makes it inappropriate as a model of consensus expected returns, but it can be an appropriate model for a manager's expected returns. Arbitrage pricing theory says that stock returns can be forecast but how to do so is not clear. The theory by nature is arbitrary.

SUMMARY

Understanding of risk and its resultant impact on the returns of the security is an extremely important but tricky issue. The risk profile of the security, when viewed as single asset and when viewed as part of the portfolio are different. The expected return as the function of risk, therefore, needs closer examination. Capital asset pricing model (CAPM) attempts to establish a relationship between the expected return as and the risk of the security under the assumptions of—(1) security forms the part of the portfolio and not held as a single asset; (2) rational investing and homogeneous expectations; (3) no taxes; and (4) perfect market conditions. Even though some of the assumptions are unrealistic, the basic idea presented by CAPM remains unchallenged.

The risk of the security is constituted of unsystematic risk and systematic risk. Since unsystematic risk is diversifiable in case of a portfolio and all investors are assumed to hold portfolios rather than a single asset, systematic risk is considered as the only relevant risk. The returns would be governed by a systematic risk of the asset. This systematic risk is measured with reference to market portfolio and its measure is referred to as beta, which reflects the sensitivity of returns to the changes in the market returns.

On an aggregate basis, for the entire investing population, the risk premium would be proportional to the variance of the market. The contribution of the individual security to the portfolio risk is the product of the proportion of investment and its covariance with the market portfolio. This covariance with the market portfolio is beta of the security.

Capital asset pricing model relates the expected return of the security to the sum total of reward for waiting, the risk-free rate of return and premium for risk, and the product of beta and excess returns market offers over and above the risk-free rate.

The CAPM is widely used in portfolio design and management. While considering the security for inclusion in the portfolio, only systematic risk needs to be considered. It also suggests that investing in market portfolio is efficient.

The vital and sole determinant of the risk the beta of the security may be measured through regression of the past returns of the security and market returns. One may take returns on the T-Bills as risk-free rate and assume market index with beta of 1.00. The security market line provides an effective basis for investment strategy by selling the overpriced stock and buying the underpriced stock.

Capital asset pricing model is a single factor model that attempts to capture systematic risk through a single parameter. Multivariate models assume that the securities do not have the same response to the changes in the macroeconomic factors and, therefore, returns need to be measured across different macroeconomic variables. Like the CAPM, the multivariate models also subscribe to the view that risks unique to the firm are diversifiable.

Arbitrage pricing theory (APT) is one such multivariate model that attempts to explain asset pricing on the basis of arbitrage. The process is to identify the overpriced and underpriced securities across a chosen macroeconomic variable, set up a zero investment portfolio with zero risk, and then unwind the position at the end of investment horizon under the assumption that mispricing vanishes by then. The limitation of APT would arise with respect to non-unanimity of asset pricing amongst analysts.

KEY TERMS

Market portfolio A portfolio consisting of all securities in the proportion of market capitalization is referred to as market portfolio

Market-risk premium The excess return offered on the market portfolio over the risk-free rate.

Portfolio risk of an asset The change in the risk of the portfolio upon inclusion or exclusion of an asset to/from the portfolio

Beta A measure of systematic risk of the returns of the security is called beta.

Regression A method of finding relationship between two variables based on past data is regression.

R-squared It is the percentage of observations that can be completely explained by the regression equation.

Capital Market Line The relationship of the expected returns of the security with the total risk is capital market line.

Security Market Line The relationship of the expected returns of the security with the systematic risk is security market line.

KEY FORMULAE

Risk of an asset in a portfolio

$$f_s\{f_1\text{Cov}(s, 1) + f_2\text{Cov}(s, 2) \ldots + f_s\text{Cov}(s, s) \ldots + f_n\text{Cov}(s, n)\} = f_s \text{ Cov }(s, m)$$

Capital asset pricing model

$$R_s = R_f + \frac{\text{Cov}(s, m)}{\sigma_m^2}(R_m - R_f) = R_f + \beta(R_m - R_f)$$

Alternatively,

R_s = Reward for waiting + Reward for risk

$= R_f + \beta\,(R_m - R_f)$

Beta of Security $\beta = \dfrac{\text{Cov}(s,m)}{\sigma_m^2}$

Regression Equation $y = \alpha + \beta x + e$

Arbitrage Pricing Model

Returns = $\lambda_0 + \beta_1\lambda_1 + \beta_2\lambda_2 + \beta_3\lambda_3 + \beta_4\lambda_4$ + Noise (e)

Portfolio Returns under APT

$$R_p = \lambda_0 + \sum_1^n w_i\beta_{i1}\lambda_1 + \sum_1^n w_i\beta_{i2}\lambda_2 + \sum_1^n w_i\beta_{i3}\lambda_3 + \sum_1^n w_i\beta_{i4}\lambda_4 + \sum_1^n w_i e_i$$

PRACTICE PROBLEMS

1. Capital Market Line

In a developed stock market like USA the prices and hence the returns on the shares are expected to follow the Capital Asset Pricing Model. Two shares namely IBM and Coca Cola provide returns as per CAPM are found to have beta of 1.15 and 1.50 respectively.

(a) Find the market return and risk-free rate for the US financial markets.

(b) Depict the Capital Market Line (CML) and show where the market return and risk free rate lie.

Solution

(a)

Company	Beta	Expected Return (%)
IBM	0.85	15%
Coca Cola	1.25	21%

As per CAPM the expected return on security is:

$R_s = R_f + \beta \times (R_m - R_f)$

For IBM: Return = $0.15 = R_f + 0.85 \times (R_m - R_f)$

For Coca Cola: Return = $0.21 = R_f + 1.25 \times (R_m - R_f)$

Solving the two equations, we get:

Risk Premium; $R_m - R_f$ = 15.00%

Risk-free rate, R_f = 2.25%

Therefore R_m = 17.25%

(b) Capital Market Line (CML) is shown in Figure P9-1(b) by extending the SML derived from the returns of two shares.

On the CML the market return and risk-free rate corresponding to beta values of 1.00 and 0.00 respectively are also marked.

2. CAPM and Returns

Given that the SML derived in Problem 1 holds, find out the expected returns of following shares with their beta co-efficients given:

Share	Beta
US Steel	2.00
AT & T	1.25
Microsoft	1.30
Citibank	0.95
Boeing	0.80

Solution

The SML as arrived in Figure P9-1(b)

Risk Premium; $R_m - R_f$ = 15.00%

Risk-free rate, R_f = 2.25%

Therefore R_m = 17.25%

Hence return on securities as per CAPM would be

$R_s = 2.25 + \beta \times 15$

Returns for US Steel : $2.25 + 15.00 \times 2.00 = 32.25\%$

AT & T : $2.25 + 15.00 \times 1.25 = 21.00\%$

Microsoft : $2.25 + 15.00 \times 1.30 = 21.75\%$

Citibank : $2.25 + 15.00 \times 0.95 = 16.50\%$

Boeing : $2.25 + 15.00 \times 0.80 = 14.25\%$

3. CAPM and Risk

In the capital markets of USA the risk-free rate of returns is 2.25% and the market risk premium is 15%, as derived in Figure P9-1(b). Assuming that the capital asset pricing model holds what beta co-efficient you associate with five companies with following expected returns:

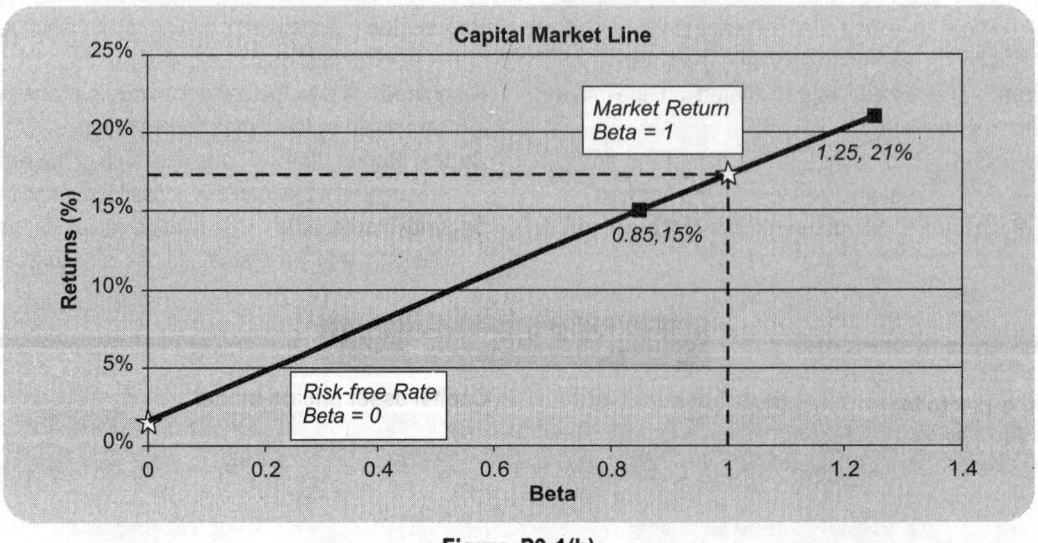

Figure P9-1(b)

Company	Expected Returns (%)
Walmart	15.00
Exxon	18.00
3 M Corp	20.00
Pepsi	35.00
PNC Bank	25.00

Solution

The CAPM with risk-free rate of 2.25% and market risk premium of 15% is as below:

Risk free rate = 2.25%

Market risk premium = 15.00%

The CAPM returns are: ₹= 2.25 + $\beta \times 15$

The beta coefficient is given by = $(R_s - R_f)/(R_m - R_f)$

Company	Expected Beta coefficient
Walmart	(15.00 – 2.25)/15.00 = 0.85
Exxon	(18.00 – 2.25)/15.00 = 1.05
3 M Corp	(20.00 – 2.25)/15.00 = 1.18
Pepsi	(35.00 – 2.25)/15.00 = 2.18
PNC Bank	(25.00 – 2.25)/15.00 = 1.52

4. Portfolio Beta and Return

The return on T-bills considered as closest substitute for the risk free rate of return is 6%. The expected return on the market index, NIFTY is estimated to be 14%. A portfolio manager has short-listed following securities for inclusion in the portfolio;

Stock	Beta
Sleepwell Ltd	0.85
Eatwell Ltd	1.15
Livewell Ltd	1.25
Funwell Ltd	1.65
Stylewell Ltd	0.95
Lookwell Ltd	1.45

What is the expected return of each of the stock as per CAPM?

If an investor wants to constitute a portfolio by following proportions.

Sleepwell Ltd	15%	Funwell Ltd	30%
Eatwell Ltd	20%	Stylewell Ltd	5%
Livewell Ltd	10%	Lookwell Ltd	20%

What would be the returns on the portfolio?

Also find its beta and the expected return using CAPM and the beta so arrived.

Solution

In competitive capital market the returns on the stocks must be governed by CAPM.

Risk free rate of return, r_f = 6.00%

Market Return, r_m = 15.00%

Return on the asset as per CAPM, $r_i = r_f + \beta \times (r_m - r_f)$

Stock	Beta	CAPM Returns
Sleepwell Ltd	0.85	0.06 + 0.85 × (0.15 – 0.06) = 13.65%
Eatwell Ltd	1.15	0.06 + 1.15 × (0.15 – 0.06) = 16.35%
Livewell Ltd	1.25	0.06 + 1.25 × (0.15 – 0.06) = 17.25%
Funwell Ltd	1.65	0.06 + 1.65 × (0.15 – 0.06) = 20.85%
Stylewell Ltd	0.95	0.06 + 0.95 × (0.15 – 0.06) = 14.55%
Lookwell Ltd	1.45	0.06 + 1.45 × (0.15 – 0.06) = 19.05%

Portfolio Beta is given by the weighted average of the beta of the stocks consisting the portfolio.

$$\beta_p = \sum_{i}^{n} w_i \beta_i$$

Portfolio return would then be $r_p = r_f + \beta_p \times (r_m - r_f)$

Also $$r_p = \sum_{i}^{n} w_i r_i$$

Stock	Expected Return	Beta	Weight	Weighted beta	Weighted Return
Sleepwell Ltd	13.65%	0.85	0.15	0.128	2.05%
Eatwell Ltd	16.35%	1.15	0.20	0.230	3.27%
Livewell Ltd	17.25%	1.25	0.10	0.125	1.73%
Funwell Ltd	20.85%	1.65	0.30	0.495	6.26%
Stylewell Ltd	14.55%	0.95	0.05	0.048	0.73%
Lookwell Ltd	19.05%	1.45	0.20	0.290	3.81%
Portfolio				**1.315**	**17.84%**

The beta of the portfolio is 1.315

As per CAPM the returns would be

= 0.06 + 1.315 × (0.15 – 0.06) = 17.84%

The return of the portfolio with weighted average of returns are also same.

5. Underpriced and Overpriced Stocks

A mutual fund is having substantial redemptions falling due in a years time and therefore has an investment horizon of one year. It is on the look out for attractive investment in the equity market. The fund believes that returns are guided by CAPM and therefore beta is the most important parameter. They constituted two groups to undertake independent and simultaneous studies with Group 1 to make estimates of returns based on fundamentals and other factors and Group 2 to make estimates of beta in respect of chosen 12 shares. Both the groups came out with the following findings:

Stock	Expected Return (%) As per Group 1	Beta As per Group 2
A	13.35	0.65
B	15.00	1.12
C	12.60	1.31
D	16.60	1.68
E	21.50	1.11
F	25.50	1.38
G	32.50	1.19
H	26.60	1.41
I	12.80	0.80
J	13.10	0.76
K	6.85	0.65
T-bills	6.65	
Index	16.95	

(a) Find the SML equation.

(b) Identify the overpriced, rightly priced and underpriced securities assuming betas arrived by Group 2 are correct, and depict them graphically.

(c) If the fund buys all the stocks from *A* to *K* in equal proportions what would be the returns according to Group 1 and Group 2?

Solution

As per the data

$R_f = 6.65 \quad R_m = 16.95$

(a) Security returns if guided by CAPM would be

$R_s = 6.65 + \beta \times (16.95 - 6.65)$

(b) The identification of securities whether they are overpriced or underpirced the expected returns are compared with the CAPM returns. If CAPM based returns are more that the expected returns the security is overpriced else it is underpriced.

The expected returns with those of CAPM based returns are compared below:

Security	Return % As per Group 1	Beta	CAPM Returns, % As per Group 2	Pricing
A	13.35	0.65	13.35	Rightly Priced
B	15.00	1.12	18.19	Overpriced
C	12.60	1.31	20.14	Overpriced
D	15.36	1.68	23.95	Overpriced
E	21.50	1.11	18.08	Underpriced
F	25.50	1.38	20.86	Underpriced
G	32.50	1.19	18.91	Underpriced
H	26.60	1.41	21.17	Underpriced
I	10.00	0.80	14.89	Overpriced
J	19.00	0.76	14.48	Underpriced
K	6.85	0.65	13.35	Overpriced
T-bills	6.65	—		
Index	16.95	–1.00		

Securities *A* to *K* are depicted in Figure P9-5(b) indicating the position with respect to CAPM based pricing.

(c) If the fund buys all the shares in equal proportion the returns of the portfolio as per the estimates of Group 1 would be weighted average of returns of the securities consisting the portfolio, i.e.:

$$r_p = \sum_i^n w_i r_i$$

Return of the portfolio consisting of all 11 stocks (equally weighted stocks *A* to *K*) = 18.02

If the fund buys all the shares in equal proportion the returns of the portfolio as per the estimates of Group 2 would be dependent upon the beta of the portfolio, which is weighted average of betas of the securities consisting the portfolio, i.e.:

Beta of the portfolio consisting of all 11 stocks (equally weighted stocks *A* to *K*) = 1.10

Return of the portfolio consisting of all 11 stocks (equally weighted Stocks *A* to *K*) would be based on CAPM, i.e.,

$$r_p = r_f + \beta_p \times (r_m - r_f) = 17.94$$

6. Portfolio Returns

Refer to the data of Problem 5 in respect of securities *A* to *K*.

Find out the expected returns as per Group 1 and Group 2 if you constitute the equally weighted portfolio of:

(a) underpriced stocks only,

(b) overpriced stocks only.

Solution

The returns of the portfolio can be found (a) according to Group 1 directly by taking the average of the returns of selected stocks, and (b) according to Group 2 by first computing the beta of the portfolio and then applying the CAPM.

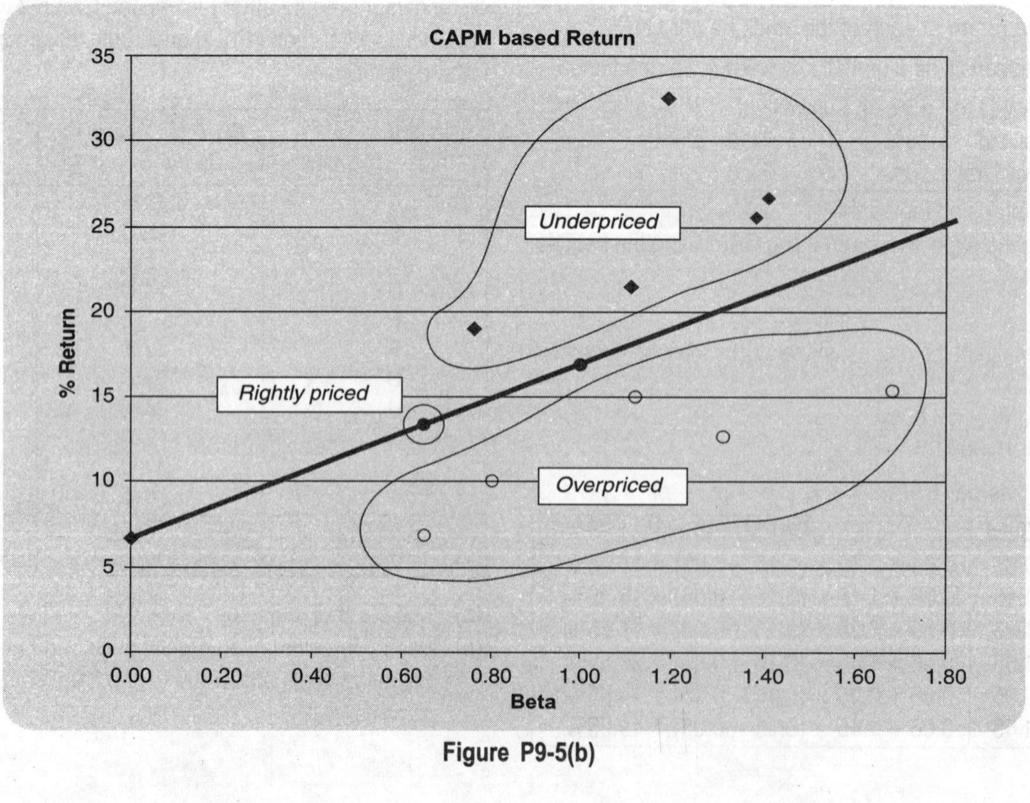

Figure P9-5(b)

(a) Portfolio of equally weighted underpriced stocks

Underpriced Stock	*Returns as per Group 1*	*Beta as per Group 2*	*Expected returns as per Group 2*
E	21.50	1.11	18.08
F	25.50	1.38	20.86
G	32.50	1.19	18.91
H	26.60	1.41	21.17
I	19.00	0.76	14.48
	25.02	1.17	18.70

(b) Portfolio of equally weighted overpriced stocks

Overpriced Stock	*Returns as per Group 1*	*Beta as per Group 2*	*Expected returns as per Group 2*
B	15.00	1.12	18.19
C	12.60	1.31	20.14
D	15.36	1.68	23.95
I	10.00	0.80	14.89
K	6.85	0.65	13.35
	11.96	1.11	18.10

7. Beta through Regression

Over the last 14 years, the returns on the Stock A and market are observed to be as below:

Year	*Return on Stock, A*	*Return on market*
1	34.00%	15.00%
2	24.00%	30.00%
3	18.00%	17.00%
4	20.00%	18.00%
5	24.00%	19.00%
6	−12.00%	−10.00%
7	−15.00%	4.00%
8	21.00%	23.00%
9	15.00%	11.00%
10	19.00%	12.00%
11	15.00%	13.00%
12	9.00%	−12.00%
13	−15.00%	5.00%
14	21.00%	6.00%

(a) Using regression methodology, find beta and alpha of Stock A.

(b) What is the relationship of the returns on the stock and market?

(c) What is the expected return of the stock if the market is expected to provide return of 15% and risk free rate happens to be 6%?

Solution

(a) Calculating Beta and Alpha

Year	$Y = R_i$	$X = R_m$	$X * Y$	$X^2 = R_m^2$
1	34.00%	15.00%	0.051	0.0225
2	24.00%	30.00%	0.072	0.0900
3	18.00%	17.00%	0.0306	0.0289
4	20.00%	18.00%	0.036	0.0324
5	24.00%	19.00%	0.0456	0.0361
6	−12.00%	−10.00%	0.012	0.0100
7	−15.00%	4.00%	−0.006	0.0016
8	21.00%	23.00%	0.0483	0.0529
9	15.00%	11.00%	0.0165	0.0121
10	19.00%	12.00%	0.0228	0.0144
11	15.00%	13.00%	0.0195	0.0169
12	9.00%	−12.00%	−0.0108	0.0144
13	−15.00%	5.00%	−0.0075	0.0025
14	21.00%	6.00%	0.0126	0.0036
Sum	178.00%	151.00%	0.3426	0.3383
Nos. of Observations			14	
Average Return	12.71%	10.79%		

$$\beta = \frac{n\Sigma XY - \Sigma X \ \Sigma Y}{n\Sigma X^2 - [\Sigma X]^2} = \frac{14 \times 3426 - 151 \times 178}{14 \times 3383 - 151^2} = 0.8585$$

$$\alpha = \overline{Y} - \beta\overline{X} = 12.71 - 0.8585 \times 10.79 = 0.0345$$

(b) The relationship between the returns on the stock and the market is depicted in Figure P9-7(b).

(c) The beta of the stock as arrived from the regression is = 0.8585

Risk-free rate, R_f = 6% Market return, R_m = 15%

The expected return on the stock is given by CAPM is

$$R_s = R_f + \beta \times (R_m - R_f)$$
$$= 6.00 + 0.8585 \times (15.00 - 6.00)$$
$$= 13.73\%$$

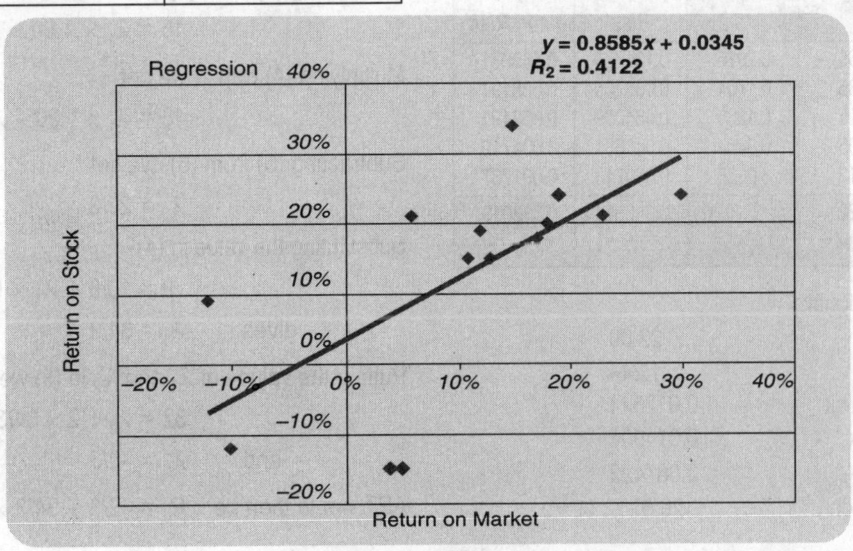

Figure P9-7(b)

8. CAPM and Portfolio

Given the following information for 5 shortlisted securities and the returns of T-bills and market index.

Security	Exp Return %	β	σ %
A	25.00	1.65	54
B	27.00	1.35	42
C	24.00	1.15	35
D	18.00	0.95	22
E	16.00	1.12	25
Index	15.00	1.00	22
T-bill	5.50	0.00	0

(i) For equally weighted portfolio of five securities, find the following:
(a) Return (b) Beta
(c) Systematic risk (d) Unsystematic risk (e) Total risk

(ii) What would happen to the risk and return if the investor borrows 50% and invest in the same portfolio?

Solution

(i) (a) Return on equally weighted portfolio:

$$R_p = \Sigma X_i \times R_i$$

$$R_p = (25 + 27 + 24 + 18 + 16)/5 = 22.00\%$$

(b) Beta of the portfolio is also weighted average of Betas of the individual securities consisting it.

$$\beta_p = (1.65 + 1.35 + 1.15 + 0.95 + 1.12)/5 = 1.244$$

(c), (d) and (e)

Portfolio Risk, $\sigma_p^2 = [\Sigma x_i \times \beta_i]^2 \sigma_m^2 + [\Sigma x_i^2 \times \sigma_{ie}^2]$

Systematic Risk = $[\Sigma x_i \times \beta_i]^2 \sigma_m^2$

Portfolio Beta. $\beta_p = 1.244$

Systematic Risk = 0.074901

For unsystematic risk, following calculations are done:

Market Risk, $\sigma_m^2 = 0.04840$

Security	σ (%)	β	Total Risk	Systematic Risk	Unsystematic Risk
A	0.54	1.65	0.2916	0.131769	0.159831
B	0.42	1.35	0.1764	0.088209	0.088191
C	0.35	1.15	0.1225	0.064009	0.058491
D	0.22	0.95	0.0484	0.043681	0.004719
E	0.25	1.12	0.0625	0.060713	0.001787
Total Average		6.22 1.244		0.388381	0.313019

Portfolio of equal weights:

Return, (%)	22.00
Beta	1.244
Unsystematic Risk	0.012521
Systematic Risk	0.074901
Total Risk	0.087422
Standard deviation	29.57%

(ii) When borrowing is 50%, assumed at risk free rate of 5.5%

Portfolio Return, % = 1.5 × 22 – 0.5 × 5.5 = 30.25%

Portfolio Risk, Standard Deviation, %

= 1.5 × 29.57% = 44.35%

9. Arbitrage Pricing Model

A group of analysts believes that the returns of the portfolios are governed by two vital factors—1. the rate of economic growth and 2. the sensitivity of stock to the developments in the financial markets. The sensitivities of returns with respect to these two factors are denoted by β_1 and beta β_2 respectively.

Further these analysts believe that returns on three carefully crafted Portfolios A, B and C must be predominantly governed by these two factors alone leaving remaining to some company/portfolio specific factors. Assume that these three Portfolios A, B, and C are found to have following beta co-efficients:

Portfolio	Expected Return, %	β_1	β_2
A	16.00	1.00	0.80
B	25.00	1.50	1.30
C	32.00	2.00	1.50

Find out the APT equation governing the returns on the portfolios.

Solution

Arbitrage Pricing Theory for two factors is

$$R_p = \lambda_0 + \lambda_1\beta_1 + \lambda_2\beta_2$$

Putting the given values in the APT to solve for three unknown variables:

For Portfolio A; $16 = \lambda_0 + \lambda_1 \times 1.00 + \lambda_2 \times 0.80$ (1)

For Portfolio B; $25 = \lambda_0 + \lambda_1 \times 1.50 + \lambda_2 \times 1.30$ (2)

For Portfolio C; $32 = \lambda_0 + \lambda_1 \times 2.00 + \lambda_2 \times 1.50$ (3)

Subtracting (1) from (2)

$$9 = \lambda_1 \times 0.50 - \lambda_2 \times 0.50 \quad (4)$$

Subtracting (1) from (3)

$$16 = \lambda_1 \times 1.00 + \lambda_2 \times 0.70 \quad (5)$$

Multiplying (4) with 2, we get

$$18 = \lambda_1 \times 1.00 - \lambda_2 \times 1.00 \quad (6)$$

Subtracting (5) from (6), we get

$$\lambda_2 = 20/3$$

Substituting the value in (4)

$$9 = 10/3 + \lambda_1 \times 0.50$$

gives $\lambda_1 = 34/3$

Putting the values of λ_1 and λ_2 in (3) we get

$$32 = \lambda_0 + 2 \times 34/3 + 1.50 \times 20/3$$

and $\lambda_0 = -2/3$

APT would then be $R_p = -2/3 + 34/3 \times \beta_1 + 20/3 \times \beta_2$

EXERCISES

Concept Review Questions

1. What does CAPM suggest about the pricing of financial assets?
2. List the assumptions made by CAPM and their implications if they are not actually true.
3. How do you define a market portfolio? Why do you think it is optimal to hold a risk-free asset and a market portfolio?
4. How do you distinguish between unsystematic and systematic risk? How would you measure systematic risk?
5. In what way does inclusion of a security in a diversified portfolio affects its risk?
6. According to CAPM, only systematic risk is relevant. Do you agree with the statement?
7. How would you assess the basic inputs required to estimate the expected return of a security?
8. How do multi-factor models differ from single factor model such as CAPM?
9. Describe arbitrage pricing theory (APT) with its assumptions.
10. What are the similarities and dissimilarities of CAPM and APT?

Critical Thinking Questions

1. Beta of a security is found to be –1.50. With a risk-free rate of 5% and risk premium at 10%, the expected return from the security is –10%. Do you think that there would be any demand for such financial security in the market?
2. In the universe of financial assets, the maximum returns offered by Security A is 35% with the risk of 50%. You as an investor need a larger return of 70%. Can your expectations be met realistically? If so, how?
3. A model that makes fewer assumptions is likely to succeed in the real world. Therefore, APT is a superior model than CAPM in describing the returns of a financial asset. Comment.

Practical Assignment

1. Select a share on the National Stock Exchange belonging to the Nifty 50 index. Calculate its beta from regression using Nifty 50 as market portfolio and 52 weekly-closing prices for a calendar year. Use T-bills yield as proxy to the risk-free rate. Using the beta of the stock found using data of same calender year, estimate the returns of the stock based on the returns on the Nifty 50 for each of the 52 weeks for the next calendar year and assuming CAPM holds. Compare the estimated returns with the actual returns of the stock. Do you find CAPM holding?

Numerical Problems

1. Security Market Line

Draw SML for risk-free rate of return of 8% and market return of 15%.

2. SML with Correctly Priced Securities

The return and beta of two securities are given here:

	ABC Ltd	XYZ Ltd
Beta	0.5	1.5
Return (%)	10	18

(a) Assuming that the returns of securities follow the CAPM, what is the SML?

(b) Also find risk-free return, risk premium and market return.

3. Expected Return as per CAPM

The return on T-bills considered as closest substitute for the risk free rate of return is 6%. The expected return on the market index, NIFTY is estimated to be 14%. A portfolio manager has short-listed following securities for inclusion in the portfolio for:

Stock	Beta
Tasty Chocolate Ltd	0.80
Strong Steel Ltd	1.10
Robust Cement Ltd	1.20
Intricate Technical Ltd	1.50
Home Construction Ltd	0.90
Lovely Lights Ltd	1.30

What is the expected return of each of the stock?

4. Beta by Regression

The stocks of Wonderland Ltd have shown following returns as compared to the market index in the last 8 years:

Year	Return on Stock (%)	Return on market (%)
1999	44	15
2000	37	36
2001	32	25
2002	9	–12
2003	–10	–5
2004	12	15
2005	55	24
2006	–12	18

Find out the following:

(i) Beta of Wonderland

(ii) Alpha of Wonderland

(iii) Variance and standard deviations of market and Wonderland

(iv) Covariance of Wonderland with the market

(v) The amount of risk of Wonderland explained by market and not explained by market.

5. Underpriced and Overpriced Stocks

Following data is available in respect of ten prominent stocks (A to J) of National Stock Exchange, and the risk free rate and return on index of NIFTY for the last year:

(i) Find the SML equation.

(ii) Identify the overpriced, rightly priced and underpriced securities.

(iii) If you constitute a portfolio of underpriced securities with equal weights what would be its beta?

(iv) What excess return do you expect to earn on the portfolio in (iii)?

Stock	Expected Return (%)	Beta
A	12.00	0.95
B	10.00	0.85
C	17.60	1.60
D	22.00	1.25
E	23.00	1.35
F	30.00	1.15
G	26.00	1.90
H	9.00	0.80
I	13.10	0.85
J	6.00	0.70
T-bills (364 days)	8.00	0.00
Index	14.00	1.00

6. CAPM and Portfolio

The following information are given for 6 shortlisted securities and the returns of T-bills and market index.

Security	Exp Return (%)	Beta	σ, %
A	30.00	1.60	50
B	28.00	1.30	35
C	25.00	1.10	40
D	20.00	0.95	24
E	18.00	1.05	28
F	8.00	0.70	18
Index	12.00	1.00	20
T-bill	8.00	0.00	0

(i) For equally weighted portfolio of the 6 securities, find the following:
(a) Return (b) Beta
(c) Systematic risk (d) Unsystematic risk (e) Total risk

(ii) What would happen to the risk and return if the investor borrows 45% and invest in the same portfolio?

7. Single Factor APT

Assume that one factor Arbitrage Pricing Model applies. Following two portfolios are in equilibrium:

Portfolio	Expected Return, %	Beta
P	18.00	1.50
Q	8.00	0.50

Find out the APT equation governing the returns on the portfolios.

8. Applying APT and Arbitrage Profit

Assume that the APT derived in the previous problem holds. If there existed a portfolio R with a beta of 1.6 and an expected return of 20%, what strategy would you adopt to make profit?

9. Two-factor APT

Assume that Arbitrage Pricing Model applies. Following three portfolios are in equilibrium:

Portfolio	Expected Return, %	$Beta_1$	$Beta_2$
A	17.00	0.90	0.80
B	20.00	1.50	0.50
C	22.00	1.30	1.10

Find out the APT equation governing the returns on the portfolios.

10. Applying Two-factor APT and Arbitrage Profit

Assume that the APT derived in the previous problem holds. If there existed a Portfolio D with β_1 of 1.22, β_2 of 0.74 and expected return of 23%, what strategy would you adopt to make profit?

If Portfolio D offered a return of 18%, would your strategy change?

In the CD

Appendix A-9 Finding Beta through Regression

Finding Beta through Regression

Finding Expected Returns as per CAPM and Deciding Investment Strategy

CHAPTER 10

Valuation and Corporate Governance

LEARNING OBJECTIVES

After going through this chapter, the readers would understand:

- the importance of valuation of the firms
- different methods of valuation
- the difference between valuing equity and valuing a firm
- how to apply discounted cash flow approach to valuation of the firm using fundamental determinants
- use of comparables approach to determine value of the firm
- what is meant by value-based management
- different measures and determinants of value
- strategies of creating value
- what is meant by Economic Value Added and Market Value Added
- what is corporate governance
- the regulatory framework for corporate governance

MULYAWAN AND FILM DISTRIBUTION

Mulyawan, the owner of 40-year-old Filmistan Distributors, was negotiating to buy the film distribution rights of an untitled film. His son, a 20-year-old MBA student, developed a keen interest in the mechanism of buying the distribution rights.

Son: How do you value the distribution rights for a movie?

Mulyawan: The value of the film is dependent upon the cash generation capacity of the movie. Performance at the box office is a function of many factors.

Son: But, why are you negotiating even before the film is not titled?

Mulyawan: The value needs to be assigned well before the movie is released. In fact, the complex process starts possibly at the same time when the idea of making a movie is conceived. We consider many things like the cast, director, banner of the film, recent past performance at the box office of the cast, the story line, target audience, etc. If we have a cast like Amitabh Bachchan and Rani Mukherjee, and a director like Ram Gopal Varma, the valuation of the film improves drastically because of their past success at the box office.

The deal revolves around the cash generation ability of the film. It is the cash flows that are material to the determination of the value that I quote for the film distribution. Of course, I must include expectations of my return on investment while valuing a movie.

Son: What are the things that would be considered in the cash flows?

Mulyawan: First we make an estimate of the gate money, which in turn, depends upon the number of theatres and the cities where it is planned for release. This fixes the number of prints to be made. Each print costs about ₹1,00,000. If we plan to release at 3,000 theatres, we need about ₹30 crore for the prints alone.

Son: Oh! That is a great amount of money. I never thought it could cost so much.

Mulyawan: Yes, that is why we normally ask for the bid from the theatre owners to maximize our cash flows. Not only this, most of these prints become rather useless after the initial four to six weeks of engagement period.

Son: What is engagement period?

Mulyawan: For a new release, the revenue in the initial phases is very high. This usually lasts for the initial four to six weeks when the box office is very heavy. Movie buffs want to watch the movie just when it is released. We estimate the number of weeks for the initial run, called the engagement period. We enter into a lease agreement or a profit sharing agreement with each theatre owner for the engagement period.

Son: What happens thereafter?

Mulyawan: From the perspective of cash flows, a film has two distinct phases. Cash flows during the engagement period are very high. After some time, the movie is withdrawn from majority of the theatres because some other movie is in the pipeline. It is the time for review. Unless the demand is really high, the prints are phased out. If it is a great success at the box office, we revise the terms with theatre owners. The number of prints required reduces drastically and so does the ticket collection. In most cases, the movie runs only in a few theatres, sometimes as low as 10-20% of the initial launch, where the gate money is far less. This needs to be considered separately till the movie dies down completely.

Son: So it is like terminal value. But is ticket sale the only source of revenue?

Mulyawan: No, we have some other sources of revenue like release of the movie on CDs, DVDs, etc. They augment the cash flows for the distributor. Finally, it is the net cash flow to me that matters. If it matches my expectation, I buy the rights. It looks simple, but you need a lot of skills, experience, and knowledge to do that.

INTRODUCTION

Valuation of assets is an extremely fundamental and important concept. We need and use valuation in almost all activities of life. In terms of finance, the valuation of assets is a prerequisite to make any decision. Managers need to value the assets of the enterprise for a variety of purposes. These include decisions about capital investment, takeovers, and mergers. All these decisions are strategic in nature. As individual investors, while transacting in securities we need to value the firms and assess the value at which to buy and sell securities.

Valuation is bread and butter for all those engaged in financial analysis—brokers, investment bankers, corporate finance managers, etc. It serves as a useful input for decision-making by top management. As the economy becomes liberalized and globalized, the need for valuing assets for strategic growth is assuming greater significance. With deregulation most business houses are relying more on inorganic growth with mergers and acquisitions becoming almost a necessity for survival. Increased availability of finance, evolution of new technology, ever-changing consumer preferences, etc., have caused most business enterprises to think of newer alternatives and business propositions.

Valuation of firms has assumed tremendous significance due to increased globalization and liberalization. It is also an intricate process to understand what drives and creates value.

When we speak of value it implies the fair value. The definition of fair value of an asset is a matter of judgement for individuals concerned with it. Generally, the going market price is regarded as a fair estimate of value as it the price where both buyer and seller converge. However, very often large gaps in the valuation are witnessed, especially in the deals of mergers and acquisitions. When it comes to the matter of control of the enterprises, there is a drastic change in the value. Valuations are often seen to jump by a phenomenal 50–100% almost overnight from the going price in mergers and acquisition deals. Under such situations, the market value cannot be regarded as fair value.

Value-based management has assumed great significance in today's competitive environment. Besides competition, the other factors that have key influence on the need to value the firms are the globalization, mergers and acquisitions, and technological development. The speed at which the environment is changing has compelled the continuous review of the fundamental values of the firm. The multitude of factors that govern the valuation has made the process of corporate valuation complex and diverse. The uncertainty and ignorance add to the confusion. Both uncertainty and ignorance emanate from the dynamic environment, rapid economic development, and technological advancements that are inevitable.

FACTORS AFFECTING VALUATION

Valuation of firm as a composite asset is a complex process where almost all factors that impact the functioning of the firm need to be viewed comprehensively. Use of the rule of thumb is very common in valuation. Normally, analysts attempt to determine the value drivers—the factors that seem critical to value. For example, valuation of telecom service providers is often stated in terms of number of subscribers. The larger the customer base the greater is the value. The number of subscribers is taken as a value driver. On the contrary, the value of a cement manufacturer would be driven by the installed capacity of the tonnes per annum (TPA). Likewise, software firms could be valued on the basis of the number of people it employs. Working with identification of critical factor and assigning value per unit to such a factor is an analysis often criticized for lack of depth. However, such practices cannot be discarded altogether since such rules of thumbs are developed with much experience, time, and unanimity of vast numbers of analysts. We can neither dump or overlook such practices nor accept them as substitute to a more pragmatic and analytical approach.

Availability and credibility of information The accuracy of the valuation is a function of availability of information and its

Besides fundamental factors affecting value there are external factors such as information, demand and supply, efficiency of capital markets, legal environment, and desire for control etc. also impact the value.

credibility. As more and more information becomes available and the uncertainty surrounding the information reduces, the process of valuation becomes easier. The dissimilarity of information and its interpretation results in different valuations by different people for the same asset at the same point of time. Different individuals work with different levels of information and interpret it differently. Further, as the information flows incessantly the valuation keeps changing with time.

State of demand and supply Valuation is also dependent on factors that are directly not considered part of the asset. For example, we all recognize that the value of the firm must be driven by the cash flows of the firm. However, the demand and supply situation at any particular point of time makes the prices of securities move drastically even though the basic determinants of the value do not change by the same proportion. A sudden spurt in demand and investor fancy for a particular financial security has driven the valuation beyond comprehension in a short span of time and lacks justification on fundamental factors.

The classic case of demand and supply playing crucial role in determination of the value comes from automobiles. Till about 15 years back, one could sell a five-year used car for a value greater than the original purchase price because its supply was not adequate. Today, even the one-day old car sells at discount to the purchase value because supply outstrips demand. Similar has been the case of white goods.

Market efficiency The accuracy of valuation is also dependent upon the conditions of the market. The more competitive the markets are the more accurate and fair are they in their valuation. The degree of competitiveness of the market can be gauged from the number of buyers and sellers, availability, and speed of dissemination of information, etc.

The economic conditions of the country and world also affect the valuation process. Developed nations not only have more economic power but also have high literacy and awareness levels. All these factors make the markets more competitive, learned, and matured; features that are essential for fair valuation.

Legal environment Valuation also gets affected by the legal environment the particular market is in. The real estate market may be regulated by several rules and regulations on buyers and sellers, which inhibits the process of fair determination of value. Relatively speaking, the stock markets where securities are traded rather freely with minimal rules and regulations governing the trading process, the valuation is deemed more fair than the valuation of real estate.

Control of Management The value changes drastically when the issue of management control of the firm becomes an issue. Hostile takeover attempts change the valuation in a very short span of time due to competitive bidding. The takeover of Corus by Tata Steel is a case in point. In the opinions of majority of analysts most such attempts are overvalued but in the opinions of acquirers such valuations are fair and realistic. The extra value is often attributed to the price of control of the management.

METHODS OF VALUATION

In this section, we take a look at various approaches used to the valuation of firms. While valuing assets or business we must consider the following—(1) the assets that are being valued; (2) the objective of the valuation; (3) for whom the valuation is being done; and (4) the time frame under consideration.

ADJUSTED BALANCE SHEET APPROACH

The value of the firm can be assessed by examining the balance sheet. All firms prepare account statements at periodic intervals that include a profit and loss account, a balance sheet, and a cash flow statement. More importantly, they are publicly available and, hence, the valuation does not require extra effort to gather information.

Different stakeholders have different focus and, therefore, see the firm in different ways. For example lenders and financial institutions are concerned about the security and safety of the funds lent besides recovery of principal and interest. They, therefore, concentrate more on the value of the assets in place and the income generation. Likewise, creditors for raw material supplies have a short-term focus for the ability of the firm to pay the dues on time. They are, therefore, more concerned with the liquidity position of the firm. Shareholders are concerned with the residual income, dividend, and the market value of the shares owned by them.

Valuation of firm may be based on the reported financial statements suitably adjusted for market values of assets and liabilities.

As deliberated earlier, the fundamental purpose of finance is to maximize the value of the firm from the viewpoint of shareholders. With shareholders being owners of the residual it is best to value the excess of assets over liabilities to find the remainder that belongs to the shareholders. Valuation of residual directly is a difficult process as claimants other than shareholders have definite and measurable claims on the assets.

The shareholders' claim can be used to find if the equity is traded. The adjusted balance sheet approach can be used for valuation by taking the position of assets and liabilities as per the books of account and replace these values by any of the following:

(a) **Market value**: represents the resale price the asset would fetch if sold now. It is assumed here that the assets are in working conditions and are marketable.

(b) **Replacement value:** represents the value of the new asset on the assumption that the existing assets are replaced.

(c) **Liquidation value:** represents the value the asset would fetch under the assumption that the firm is no more a 'going concern'.

The substitution of book values with any of the above is based on the premise that the book values do not reflect the true values of the assets and liabilities. The selection would depend upon the purpose of the valuation. Book values of the assets are mentioned at a historical cost with the preset policies on deprecation, and are not valid in most of the circumstances. The stated face value of the current assets is normally close to the market value. Likewise, liabilities are reflected at face value.

The difference in true values and book values arises due to inflation, and/or technological advancements making assets obsolete. Further, the book values also ignore the value addition due to intangibles like patents and brands. These are not reflected in the financial statements.

The choice with regard to which substitute to use depends upon the circumstances. For example, under takeover cases the assets of the firms are usually valued at replacement cost as if the new capacity was being built, suitably adjusted for the age of the machines. Under liquidation the value of the same asset would decline drastically because of distress sale. The firm is liquidated due to the claims of the pressing creditors is a fact that becomes known to the market. The same asset would fetch a higher value if the sale were made under normal course of business. Which of the value is a fair estimate is anybody's guess. The context becomes important while stating the values of the assets and liabilities.

Following are some of the values used more often for different assets and liabilities that appear on the balance sheet:

Cash It is the easiest asset to value. It is the common denominator that is used to buy any asset or liquidate a liability. The value remains same irrespective of the circumstances, purpose of value, and who the valuer is.

Debtors The balance sheet states the value that is recoverable from the customers over a period of time. The realisable value would be somewhat lower than what is stated on the balance sheet as every business has some bad debts and quality disputes. The amount realisable must be adjusted for the provision for bad debt. Further, the provision for bad debt must also be adjusted against the aging schedule.

Stocks Due to the fact that among the current assets, the farthest from cash is the stock, it demands precaution.

Raw materials and finished goods These should invariably be valued at cost only. It is presumed that market value is close to the cost and that there exists a larger market for raw materials. For consumer products and consumer durables the prices are easily available. For industrial products and/or intermediate products the valuation is rather difficult as compared to products where prices are directly obtainable from the market. Intermediate products are valued greatly by those who need it and are worth nothing for those not capable of using the product directly.

Work-in-process stock It is very difficult to assess as it needs to undergo some value addition. On the other hand, they may not fetch even as mush as raw material contained in the inventory. Even though some value is already added it is not of much significance from the viewpoint of realization. The approach to value work-in-process can be dual. The valuation may be based either on—(1) cost of raw material plus the value addition, or (2) selling price less value to be added.

Other current assets and liabilities These normally include items such as loans and advances, prepaid expenses, security deposits, etc. Such assets normally are stated at face value. Liabilities, whether short-term or long-term are usually neither inflated nor deflated than the stated values on the financial statements.

Investments Investments, if quoted, are the easiest to value as market values are available. However, firms do make investments otherwise in related and group companies that may not be quoted. Such investments are extremely difficult to assess as the cost itself may not reflect the true value of investment.

Fixed assets These include land, building, plant, and machinery, etc. All the fixed assets must be valued depending upon the purpose of valuation. The value of fixed assets changes drastically from replacement value to the distressed sale value. The value of other assets does not change as much due to purpose. Also they are difficult to acquire or uproot. Difficulty of rebuilding fresh fixed asset is the cause of creation of value that is not in line with the historical cost.

A major drawback with the adjusted balance sheet approach is the value of assets not stated in the financial statement. The value of intangible assets like brand, human resources, intellectual capital, etc., is not reflected in the balance sheet. In a world increasingly becoming dominated by the services sector, the intangible assets are overshadowing the tangible assets.

MARKET VALUE APPROACH

The adjusted balance sheet approach is based on the premise that the excess of value of assets over the liabilities belongs to the shareholders. Hence, except for the equity and reserves, all other assets and liabilities are valued by substitution of relevant market values. Wherever the values of equity and debt are available through the market, they should invariably be used since markets, assumed to be efficient and thus fair are the best indicator of true values. There can be no substitutes to the market values obtained directly. The strength of the logic of the market can be realized from the simple fact that shareholders would not accept a lower value than the price of the share in the market even if the most knowledgeable and intelligent sources using alternative methods, arrive at a value of equity that is lower than market price.

> *Market value approach to value a firm is simplest of all and can be found by using the market value of equity and debt of the firm at any point of time.*

Besides equity the debt of the firms are also traded. In such a case, the market value of the debt usually is different than what is mentioned in the financial statements. This happens because the interest rate structure undergoes a change and it is not necessary that circumstances at the time of issue remain same as at the time of valuation. Market values constantly adjust to the changing interest rate scenario.

Value of the firm can be stated as:

Market Value of Equity + Market Value of Debt

i.e., Nos. of shares × Market Price/share + Nos. of debentures × Market Price/Debenture

VALUATION BY DISCOUNTED CASH FLOW

The discounted cash flow (DCF) approach is based on the valuation of the income generation capacity of the assets. Income approach values the assets and/or businesses in term of capacity to generate benefits. These benefits are measured as cash flows at different points of time. In valuing the asset the cash flows generated over the remaining useful life of the asset are relevant. The cash flows are projected on the basis of some assumptions. The time period for which the cash flows are required normally coincides with the remaining life of the asset.

The DCF approach to valuation is being used increasingly by analysts due to several reasons. Increased level of disclosures and transparency, desire for visibility on part of firms, market efficiency, and competitiveness has made it possible to accurately forecast the parameters needed for the valuation of firms. Coupled with these factors the increased desire of investors to unearth undervalued and overvalued assets in the financial market has placed more emphasis on the determination of the intrinsic value of the firm. The DCF approach is one way of establishing the intrinsic value of the assets.

Discounted cash flow valuation is most commonly used tool to value the firm using cash flows and cost of capital as basic inputs for valuation.

In the DCF approach the value of the firm is given by following Equation 10-1, which is no different than DDM or a capital budgeting proposal:

Value of the firm,

$$V = \sum_{n=1}^{\infty} \frac{\text{Cash Flow for period, } n;\ CF_n}{(1 + \text{Discount Rate})^n} \qquad (10\text{-}1)$$

Value of the Firm Vs Value of Equity

While referring to the value we may mean either the value of the firm or value of its equity. The value of the firm is the value to all the stakeholders in the firm. The two kinds of stakeholders who provide capital and expect a return are debt suppliers and equity suppliers. Hence, the value of the firm is the sum of the value of equity holders and the value of debt. Since the value of debt does not change much, the value of the firm and value of the equity become synonymous and differ only by a constant sum. The decisions based on the value of equity should, therefore, be applicable to the firm.

However, there could be some measurement issues. Using the DCF approach, the valuation is done by discounting the cash flows with the appropriate discount rate. The cash flows in the numerator and the discount rate in the denominator have to be consistent with each other. If the entire firm is being valued the cash flow to equity holders as well as debt holders or the preference shareholders have to be considered in the numerator. The relevant discount rate in that case would be the weighted average cost of capital (WACC). If the firm is valued for equity holders only then the cash flows in the numerator must be those accruing to the shareholders. Correspondingly, the discount rate used must be cost of equity.

The value of the firm is equal to the sum of value of its equity and debt.

Whether we value the firm or the equity, both must lead to the same conclusion and the ultimate value. The DCF valuations for equity and firm are given by Equations 10-2 and 10-3 respectively.

$$\text{Value of Equity} = \sum_{1}^{\infty} \frac{\text{Cash Flow to Equity Holders; } CFE_n}{(1 + r_e)^n} \qquad (10\text{-}2)$$

$$\text{Value of Firm} = \sum_{1}^{\infty} \frac{\text{Cash Flow to Firm; } CFF_n}{(1 + r)^n} \qquad (10\text{-}3)$$

where r_e is the cost of equity and r is weighted average cost of capital.

The value of the levered firm is the sum of value of equity and value of other suppliers of capital. For a firm financed only by equity and debt only the value is given by:

Value of the firm = Value of equity + Value of debt

We now demonstrate that the value of the firm would be identical, irrespective of the procedure adopted, highlighting the difference in the numbers used in each of the approach.

Assume that a firm has cash flow before interest and taxes of ₹1,000. For convenience, the cash flow is assumed to be perennial with a growth rate of zero. Assumptions are made only to simplify the computation without taking away the argument. Further, assume that the tax rate is 35% and the cost of equity for the firm financed entirely by equity, r_0 is 18%. The value of the all equity firm is found by discounting the cash flows net of taxes by the capitalization rate, r_0. The formulation for constant and perennial cash flows simplifies to:

$$\text{Value of All Equity Firm} = \frac{\text{Annual Cash Flow to Equity Holders}}{r_0}$$

The relevant annual cash flows and value for the firm are:

Earning Before Interest and Taxes	₹1,000.00
Interest	—
Earning Before Taxes	₹1,000.00
Taxes @ 35%	₹350.00
Cash flow after Taxes	₹650.00

The value of the firm is computed at ₹3,611.11 as below:

$$\text{Value of All Equity Firm, } V_U = \frac{\text{Cash Flow to Equity Holders; } CFE_n}{r_0}$$

$$= \frac{650.00}{0.18} = ₹3{,}611.11$$

One way of arriving at value of the levered firms is to use the MM's proposition that extra value of levered firm is equal to the tax shield provided by debt.

Now let us introduce debt. From MM propositions (explained in chapter 16) we know that the value of levered firm increases by the amount of tax shield the debt generates. For perennial debt the amount of tax shield is tax rate, T multiplied by the amount of debt, D.

Value of the levered firm,

V_L = Value of the unlevered firm, V_U + Value of the tax shield, $T \times D$

$= V_U + TD$

The firm decides to have the debt ratio of 25% with the cost of debt at 9%. We may now find the value of the levered firm as well as value of the debt and the interest outgo on the same.

$V_L = V_U + TD$

$= 3{,}611.11 + 0.35 \times 0.25 \times V_L \Rightarrow V_L = ₹3957.38$

Value of debt $= 0.25 \times V_L = 0.25 \times 3{,}957.38 = ₹989.35$

Interest cost $= 9\% \times 989.35 = ₹89.04$

The other impact of debt is on the cost of equity as the firm now becomes more risky. The cost of equity, r_e in the levered firm is given by:

$$r_e = r_0 + \frac{D}{E}(1 - T)(r_0 - r_d)$$

For the given data the cost of equity becomes 19.95% as shown below:

$$r_e = r_0 + \frac{D}{E}(1 - T)(r_0 - r_d) = 18\% + \frac{1}{3} \times 0.65 \times 9\% = 19.95\%$$

The value of equity is found by discounting the cash flow to equity holders with the cost of equity in the levered firm:

Cash flow Before Interest and Taxes	₹1,000.00
Interest	₹89.04
Cash flow Before Taxes	₹910.96
Taxes @ 35%	₹318.84
Cash flow to Equity holders	₹592.12

$$\text{Value of Equity} = \frac{\text{Cash Flow to Equity Holders, CFE}_n}{r_e}$$

$$= \frac{592.12}{0.1995} = ₹2{,}968.04$$

Value of the firm using value of equity as base is ₹3,957.39.

Value of the Firm = Value of Equity + Value of Debt

$= 2{,}968.04 + 989.35 = ₹3{,}957.39$

Now we value the firm directly by discounting the cash flows to all suppliers of capital with the WACC of the firm. The cash flows are as follows:

Cash flow to equity holders	₹592.12
Cash flow to debt holders net of tax	₹57.88
Total cash flow	₹650.00

WACC in the levered firm:

$$r = \frac{E}{E + D} r_e + \frac{D}{E + D}(1 - T) r_d$$

$$= \frac{3}{4} \times 19.95 + \frac{1}{4} \times 0.65 \times 9\% = 16.425\%$$

The value of the firm:

$$\text{Value of the firm} = \frac{\text{Cash Flow to Equity and Debt Holders}}{\text{WACC, } r}$$

$$= \frac{650.00}{0.16425} = ₹3{,}957.39$$

DCF Valuation with Growth

While valuing a firm, we are attempting to evaluate not only all the capital budgeting decisions already conceived but also those not conceived as yet and for all projects that the firm would undertake in all times to come. One is sure that some of the projects that are being valued have not even been conceived. We enter the unchartered domain with no expertise.

We overcome the problem of projecting and valuing the cash flows for infinite period by making some simplifying but reasonable and realistic assumptions. We all appreciate that all firms are born with some new idea that is expected to have an extraordinary growth in the initial stages. The objective of high growth, therefore, is primary. As competition intensifies the contemplated growth cannot be achieved. Therefore, firms cannot grow indefinitely at a high rate for all times to come. As firms grow, achieving high growth rates consistently becomes impossible. This extraordinary growth for limited time period can be forecast based on product characteristics, state of economy, level of competition, affordability of products, and multitude of other factors.

Stable growth rate When the product achieves maturity and as the firm becomes larger, the growth must stabilize to some realistic level at some point of time. The most acceptable estimate of the stable growth must coincide with the growth rate of the economy. As the firms become larger the growth cannot exceed that of the growth of the economy as the firm becomes synchronized with the economy. A firm cannot outpace the economy for long periods of time. For global firms the realistic stable growth rate would be identical to the global growth rate since they operate globally. Over the long run the two growth rates must coincide if the firm has to remain competitive. However, a firm can have a lower rate of growth than the economy.

The stable growth rate also implies that it is the same for all parameters that are considered as the drivers of value of the firm such as revenue, cash flows, earnings and dividends. In the long run, the growth rates of all value drivers must coincide. For example, the growth rate of earnings and dividends may not coincide because of the adjustment of the payout ratio. Similarly, the growth rate of revenue and earnings depends upon the profit margin, which is high in the initial stages but has to stabilize in the long run.

This rather convenient but realistic assumption resolves the problem of forecasting the cash flows for an indefinite period of time. One needs to make an estimate of growth or cash flows for a reasonable and foreseeable period of time called 'explicit forecast period' and, thereafter, a lower value of growth can be assumed that can be consistently achieved. This is called 'stable growth rate period' extending for an indefinite future. The value of the stable growth rate period is computed as an infinite annuity.

Under DCF valuation the determinants of value are the cash flows and the cost of capital.

Under a constant rate of growth the value of the firm can be computed using Gordon's dividend discount model (DDM).

Though the model looks simple, it encompasses all domains of corporate finance and, virtually, considers all the strategic decisions that an organization takes. The three values needed in valuation through the DCF approach are the—(1) discount rate; (2) growth rate; and (3) cash flows for each period.

Each of the values, in turn, is governed by a set of decisions and the market forces. The discount rate used for computing the present value is a function of the cost of capital of the firm. For valuing equity the appropriate discount rate is cost of equity. In either case, the discount rate becomes a function of financing decision and investment decision. They determine the risk characteristics of the cash flows of the firm, reflected in its beta. Beta determines the cost of equity capital using capital asset pricing model. Other inputs of risk free rate and risk premium required are market determined. This is depicted in Figure 10-1.

The growth rate of the firm's cash flow available to the firm/shareholders is a function of its investment decision, financing decision and the dividend decision. All the three decisions are interlinked and one influences the other two. Investment decision pertains to the selection of assets and projects and the return on them decides the cash flows. Financing decision addresses the question of proportion of debt to be used in financing the activities and deployment of leverage to enhance return on equity. It also decides the risk of the cash flows due to fixed charges of interest. The dividend policy directly influences the cash flows available to the shareholders. It also impacts the financing decision as to the degree of retention would change the debt equity ratio. A simple diagram in Figure 10-2 depicts the determinants of the growth rate of the firm.

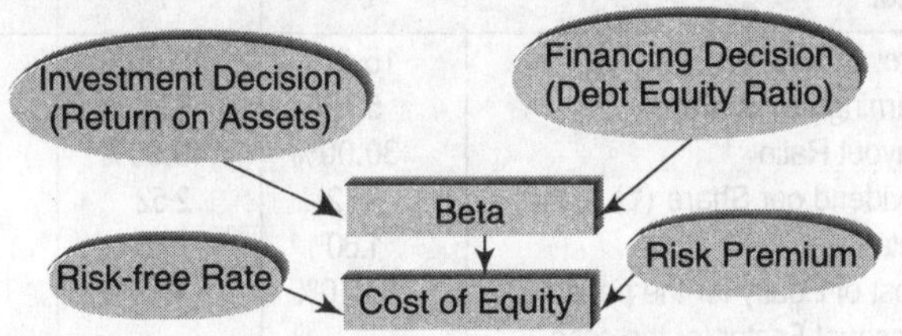

Figure 10-1 Determinants of discount rate

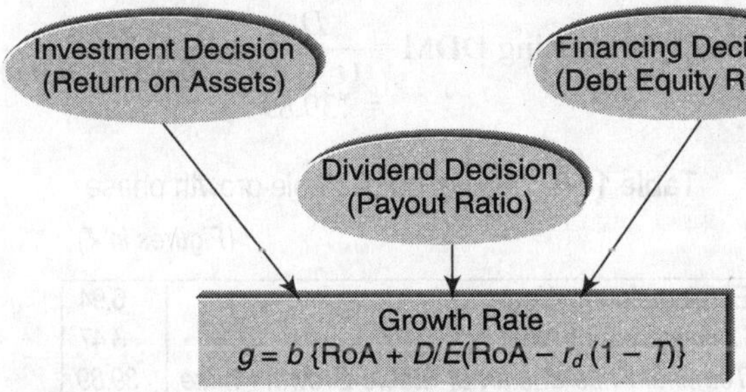

Figure 10-2 Determinants of growth rate

The cash flow generated by the firm is the function of investment policy, and return on assets. These cash flows would grow and would be modulated through the interaction of three policies of investment, financing, and dividend. The value of the firm then can be computed using the growth and the discount rate found earlier. This is depicted in Figure 10-3.

Cash flows of the firm are dependent upon its (1) investment policy (2) financing policy and (3) dividend policy.

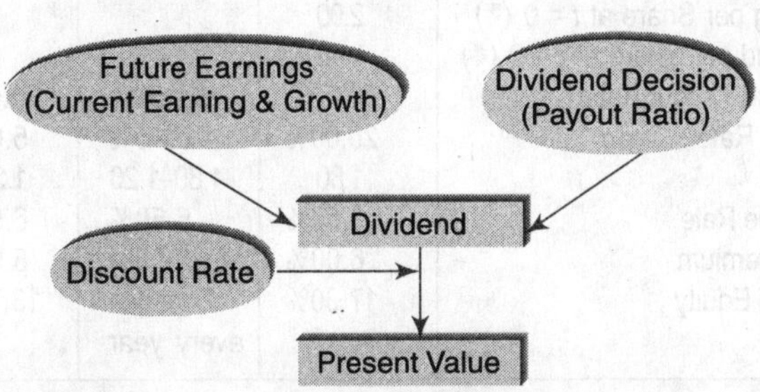

Figure 10-3 Determinants of cash flow to shareholders

Equity Valuation based on Fundamentals

We attempt the valuation of the equity of the firm using dividend discount model. Consider a firm, VarGrow that has developed a new product—alloy wheels for automobiles. The product is acknowledged as being good in quality by the automobile manufacturers, who form the major market. The product is expected to provide a 20% annual growth to the firm for the next five years. To fund the growth, the firm would maintain a rather low dividend payout of only 20% for this period. The expected cash flow being risky in the growth period the beta of the firm is expected to be at 1.80. With risk free rate at 6.50% and market risk premium at 6% the cost of equity of VarGrow is 17.30% using CAPM.

Cost of equity is determined using CAPM and is a function of risk free rate, market risk premium and beta of the firm.

As the competition intensifies the growth would start impinging from fifth year onwards VarGrow would see a transition from high growth period to stable growth period. The transition is expected to last for three years. During the transition the changes would take place in the dividend policy, lowering of beta due to steadiness of the cash flows, and growth rate. The dividend would increase linearly from 20% to 50% while growth rate too would fall linearly to 5% over a period of three years. The cash flow would become rather steady and would cause the beta of VarGrow to fall from 1.80 to 1.20 linearly over three years. Thereafter, the dividend policy, growth rate, and cost of equity are expected to remain constant. The data with the above assumptions is contained in Table 10-1.

We may now attempt the valuation of VarGrow in three parts—(1) the valuation for high growth phase; (2) valuation for transition period; and (3) valuation for stable growth phase using dividend discount model, by projecting dividend in each year and discounting it with the cost of equity relevant for the period.

We first value the growth phase lasting for five years. With current earnings per share of ₹2.00, the projected EPS and DPS for nth year in the growth phase (years 1 – 5) would be:

Table 10-1 Fundamental parameters of 'VarGrow'

	High Growth Phase	Transition Period Phase	Stable Growth Phase
Length (years)	5.00	3.00	Indefinite
Earning per Share at $t = 0$ (₹)	2.00		
Dividend per Share at $t = 0$ (₹)	0.40		
Dividend Payout Ratio	20.00%	30–50%	50.00%
Growth Rate	20.00%	20–5%	5.00%
Beta	1.80	1.80–1.20	1.20
Risk-free Rate	6.50%	6.50%	6.50%
Risk Premium	6.00%	6.00%	6.00%
Cost of Equity	17.30%	Changes every year	13.70%

For Year 3: $EPS_n = EPS_0 \times (1+g)^n$

$$EPS_3 = 2.00 \times (1+0.20)^3 = ₹3.46$$

$$DPS_n = \text{Payout Ratio} \times EPS_n$$

$$DPS_3 = 0.20 \times 3.46 = ₹0.69$$

where g is the annual growth rate in the growth phase.

The cost of equity as determined by CAPM is 17.30% and is constant for the entire growth phase. The dividends are discounted at 17.30% and the cumulative value adds up to ₹2.14, as shown in Table 10-2.

Table 10-2 Valuation for high growth phase

(Figures in ₹)

Year	1	2	3	4	5
Earning per Share	2.40	2.88	3.46	4.15	4.98
Dividend per Share	0.48	0.58	0.69	0.83	1.00
PV of dividend at 17.30%	0.41	0.42	0.43	0.44	0.45
Value of Equity for the High Growth Phase					2.14

The transition phase would last from Year 6–8. All the fundamental parameters of growth, payout ratio, cost of equity changes from year to year impacting on the EPS, dividend, and discount rate, respectively. The computation for EPS for year six to eight is shown below:

$$\text{For Year 6}: EPS_6 = EPS_5 \times (1+g) = 4.98 \times (1+0.15) = ₹5.72$$

$$\text{For Year 7}: EPS_7 = EPS_6 \times (1+g) = 5.72 \times (1+0.10) = ₹6.30$$

$$\text{For Year 8}: EPS_8 = EPS_7 \times (1+g) = 6.30 \times (1+0.05) = ₹6.61$$

Similarly, the dividend for each year can be worked out using the payout ratio of each year, which rises by 10% each year. The cost of equity too undergoes a change every year as beta of the firm changes. The dividend for each year is discounted back to the Year 6 at the cost of equity each year. These would further be discounted back to Year 0 using the relevant discounting factor. The discount factor for Year 6 is 1/(1+0.161), 16.10% being the cost of equity for the sixth year. The discount factors for Year 7 and Year 8 are found by using the cost of equity applicable for each intervening period as follows:

$$\text{Discount Factor for Year 7} = \frac{1}{1+0.1610} \times \frac{1}{1+0.1490} = 0.7496$$

Discount Factor for Year 8

$$= \frac{1}{1+0.1610} \times \frac{1}{1+0.1490} \times \frac{1}{1+0.1370} = 0.6593$$

The value of the dividend for the transition period at its beginning is shown is Table 10-3. The table also shows the present value the dividends of transition phase, at the beginning of the growth phase using the cost of equity of the growth phase as the discount rate.

Table 10-3 Valuation for transition phase

Year	6	7	8
Growth Rate	15.0%	10.00%	5.00%
Earning per Share (₹)	5.72	6.30	6.61
Payout Ratio	30.00%	40.00%	50.00%
Dividend per Share (₹)	1.72	2.52	3.31
Beta	1.60	1.40	1.20
Cost of Equity for the period	16.10%	14.90%	13.70%
Discount Factor for the cash flow of the year	0.8613	0.7496	0.6593
Discounted Value of dividend for the year at beginning of transition phase (₹)	1.48	1.89	2.18
Value of Dividend of Transition Phase at its beginning (₹)			5.55
Value of Dividend of Transition Phase at beginning of Growth Phase (₹)			2.50

Lastly, we value the dividends for the stable growth phase using constant growth dividend discount model. The earning per share for the 9th year is:

For Year 9 $\quad EPS_9 = 6.61 \times (1+0.05) = ₹6.94$

$DPS_n = \text{Payout Ratio} \times EPS_n$

For Year 9 $\quad DPS_9 = 0.50 \times 6.94 = ₹3.47$

The terminal value, also called as continuing value of the VarGrow, shown in Table 10-4 at the beginning of the stable growth phase is:

$$\text{Terminal Value using DDM} = \frac{D_9}{(r-g)} = \frac{3.47}{(0.137-0.05)} = ₹39.89$$

Table 10-4 Valuation of stable growth phase

(Figures in ₹)

Earnings for 9th Year	6.94
Dividend for 9th Year	3.47
Terminal Price at start of Stable Growth Phase	*39.89*

Multi-stage growth model can be applied to determine the value of the firm for varying growth rate over the life of the firm.

The continuing value of the firm is required to be discounted back to Year 0. Since during the transition phase the cost of equity is different in each year the discounting would not be uniform. The continuing value is discounted back at the beginning of transition phase (Year 6) and then to the beginning of growth phase (Year 0) as shown in Table 10-5.

Table 10-5 Present value of the terminal price of VarGrow

Year	6	7	8
Cost of Equity	16.10%	14.90%	13.70%
Discounted Value of Terminal Price at beginning of the year discounted at cost of equity applicable for the period (₹)	26.30	30.53	35.08
Discounted Value of Terminal Price at beginning of the Transition Period (₹)		26.30	
PV of Terminal Price – Today (Discounted at cost of equity of Growth Phase) (₹)		11.84	

The total value of equity of VarGrow is ₹

		₹
1.	Present Value of Growth Phase	2.14
2.	Present Value of Transition Phase	2.50
3.	Present Value of Stable Growth Phase	11.84
	Total Value per Share of VarGrow (1 + 2 + 3)	**₹16.48**

Example 10-1 Value of Equity using Two-Stage DDM

Kitchen Corporation has launched a series of kitchenware that is expected to provide a growth of 20% for the next four years. The current earnings and dividend are ₹5 and ₹1.50 per share, respectively. The dividend pay out would be maintained for the next four years. Currently, T-bills provide yield of 6.50% and market risk premium is 7%. The beta is 1.40. The market conditions are expected to remain unchanged. After 4 years of growth, the firm is likely to have a modest 6% growth, dividend payout of 70% and beta of 1.10. What is the expected price of the share (a) today and (b) at the end of the growth phase?

Solution

(a) The fundamental determinants of the value of equity for the growth and stable phase are as given below:

	High Growth	*Stable Growth*
Length of High Growth Phase (yrs)	4.00	
Earning per Share at $t = 0$ (₹)	5.00	
Dividend per Share at $t = 0$ (₹)	1.50	
Dividend Payout Ratio	30.00%	70.00%
Growth Rate	20.00%	6.00%
Beta	1.40	1.10
Risk-free Rate	6.50%	6.50%
Risk Premium	7.00%	7.00%

The cost of equity of Kitchen Corporation is

During High Growth Phase = 6.50% + 1.40 × 7.00% = 16.30%

During Stable Growth Phase = 6.50% + 1.10 × 7.00% = 14.20%

The earnings dividend and present value at 16.30% for the growth period of next 4 years are:

Value of Equity for the Growth Phase				*Figures in ₹*
Year	1	2	3	4
Earning per Share	6.00	7.20	8.64	10.37
Dividend per Share	1.80	2.16	2.59	3.11
PV of dividend discounted at 16.30%	1.55	1.60	1.65	1.70
Value of Equity for the growth phase				**6.49**

The stable growth from 5th year onwards is valued using DDM as follows:

Value of Stable Growth Phase	*Figures in ₹*
Earnings for 5th year	10.99
Dividend for 5th year	7.69
Terminal Price with r = 14.20% and g = 6%	93.82
PV of Terminal Price at 16.30%	51.28

The price of equity of the firm today is ₹57.77; the sum of the present values of dividend for the high growth period and stable growth period.

Value of Equity of the firm = 6.49 + 51.28 57.77

(b) The value of the equity at the end of high growth period would be equal to the terminal value of the dividends in the stable growth period. Therefore the expected share price at the end of high growth period is ₹93.82.

FREE CASH FLOW APPROACH TO EQUITY AND FIRM VALUATION

The dividend discount model assumes that all the cash flows generated by the firm are either used for growth or are distributed as dividend. The dividend shall be reflected as cash flow to the equity shareholders while the retained portion of the earnings would find its way in providing growth to the dividend in future. The assumption that earnings are either distributed or used for growth is plausible. However, in practice since dividends tend to be sticky (dividend remains constant and the payout ratio changes from period to period) the entire cash available may not be distributed in fixed ratio as dividend.

Further, some highly profitable firms may choose to retain cash to fund growth through acquisitions providing sudden and big leaps in revenue and earnings rather than have conventional steady growth through capacity expansion. In such cases the firm may keep cash for substantial periods of time and deploy them in safe financial securities that in all probability provide returns lesser than expected by equity holders.

Under circumstances where entire available cash is not distributed as dividend, it may not be appropriate to use dividend discount model for valuation of equity. An alternative and a better way of valuation is to evaluate the free cash flows available to equity holders and value them at market determined cost of equity.

Free cash flows to equity (FCFE)

Free cash flow to equity (FCFE) is the distributable cash (not necessarily actually distributed as dividend) that can be arrived by subtracting the funds required for the firm's growth from the available earnings for the shareholders. The funds required for the growth of the firm are in the form of capital expenditure and increase in the working capital. The portion of the net capital expenditure and increase in working capital to be funded from the equity is dependent upon the capital structure of the firm. Assuming a constant debt ratio the funds earmarked for growth from the equity holders are:

Free cash flow approach values the cash flows available to investors after providing for capital expenditure and increase in working capital, deemed essential for growth.

(Capital Expenditure – Depreciation) × (1 – debt ratio)
+ Increase in Working Capital × (1 – debt ratio)

Constant debt ratio implies that the repayment of debt is made out of new issues of debt. Therefore, free cash flow to equity (FCFE) is:

FCFE = Earnings for the shareholders
– (Capital Expenditure – Depreciation) × (1 – debt ratio)
– Increase in Working Capital (1 – debt ratio)

Free cash flows to firm (FCFF)

The amount of free cash flow available to a firm can be found in two alternate ways. Free cash flow to the firm is the sum of payments for the all the suppliers of capital. From the retained earnings we make funds available for growth (Net capital expenditure and increase in working capital), which is not the free cash flow to the firm from the viewpoint of suppliers of capital. The balance may be considered as free cash flow. This would be reflected in the investment made by the firm in financial assets. Debt holders receive interest (net of tax) and principal. Any fresh issue of either debt or equity is deducted for the purpose of free cash flow to the firm. The free cash flow to the firm is:

Under free cash flows approach the firm may be valued separately for debt holders and equity holders. If valued separately the cash flows of each supplier of capital are discounted at the respective cost of capital

FCFF = Earnings for the shareholders + Redemption of capital
– Issue of fresh Capital
+ Interest × (1 – tax rate) + Principal repayments
– New debt issued + Increase in Investment
– After tax income on investment

Alternatively;

FCFF = Operational EBIT (1 – tax rate)
– (Capital Expenditure – Depreciation)
– Increase in Working Capital
+ Post-tax Non-operational Income

For illustration purpose consider the Income Statements and Balance Sheets of CC Corporation as shown in Table 10-6 and Table 10-7, respectively.

Table 10-6 Income statement of CC corporation

(*₹ in lakh*)

	Year I	*Year II*	*Year III*
Sales	400.00	500.00	600.00
Interest Income	—	10.00	15.00
Non Operating Income	15.00	25.00	35.00
Total Income	**415.00**	**535.00**	**650.00**
Expenses other than interest	320.00	410.00	495.00
Interest Expense	20.00	30.00	40.00
Total Cost	**340.00**	**440.00**	**535.00**
PBT	**75.00**	**95.00**	**115.00**
Tax	22.00	30.00	35.00
PAT	53.00	65.00	80.00
Dividend	30.00	40.00	50.00
Retained Earnings	**23.00**	**25.00**	**30.00**

Table 10-7 Balance sheet of CC corporation

(*₹ in lakh*)

	Year I	*Year II*	*Year III*
Equity	200.00	200.00	200.00
Reserves	40.00	65.00	95.00
Debt	200.00	300.00	400.00
Total	**440.00**	**565.00**	**695.00**
Fixed Assets	300.00	330.00	365.00
Investments	—	75.00	150.00
Net Current Assets	140.00	160.00	180.00
Total	**440.00**	**565.00**	**695.00**

The free cash flow to the firm can be worked out. For facilitating projection of cash flow for future it becomes imperative to segregate the income from operations from the total income that may contain non-operational revenues. Similarly, the taxes on operational income and non-operational income are treated separately since tax laws may treat such income independent of each other.

The calculation of earnings before interest and taxes (EBIT) from operations and tax thereon with the assumption of 30% tax rate for Year II and Year III are:

(*₹ in lakh*)

	Year II	*Year III*
Profit Before Tax	95.00	115.00
Add: Net Interest	20.00	25.00
Less: Non-operating Income	25.00	35.00
EBIT from Operations	**90.00**	**105.00**
Taxes on Operational Income		
Provision for Tax	30.00	35.00
+ Tax Shield on Interest @ 30%	9.00	12.00
– Tax on Interest Income @ 30%	3.00	4.50
– Tax on Other Income @ 30%	7.50	10.50
Tax on Operational EBIT	**28.50**	**32.00**
Operational EBIT (Net of Taxes)	**61.50**	**73.00**

The earnings can be used either for growth or are available as free cash flow. Hence, commitments for growth have to be subtracted. Added to this is the post tax non-operational income to provide the free cash flows to the firm for Year II and Year III as shown in the following table.

(₹ lakh)

	Year II	Year III
Operational EBIT Net of Taxes	61.50	73.00
Less:		
Net Capital Investment	30.00	35.00
Increase in WC	20.00	20.00
Add:		
Post-tax Non-operational Income	17.50	24.50
Free Cash Flow to the Firm	**29.00**	**42.50**

Alternatively, the cash flow to the firm can be obtained by adding the payments made to suppliers of capital directly, and the unused portion of the retained earnings that could be distributed but were not and are actually deployed in financial assets to generate some income. The collections made from the suppliers of capital must be subtracted. The free cash flow to the firm for the Year II and Year III are worked out that match with the EBIT approach explained above:

(₹ lakh)

	Year II	Year III
To Equity holders		
Cash Dividend	40.00	50.00
Redemption of capital	—	—
Less: Fresh Issue of capital	—	—
Sub-total A	40.00	50.00
To Debt holders		
Post-tax Interest Expense	21.00	28.00
Repayment of loan	—	—
Less: Issue of fresh debt	100.00	100.00
Sub-total B	(79.00)	(72.00)
To suppliers of capital (*A* + *B*)	(39.00)	(22.00)
Increase in Investment	75.00	75.00
Post-tax income on Investment	7.00	10.50
Net Increase in Investment	68.00	64.50
Free Cash Flow to the Firm	**29.00**	**42.50**

TWO STAGE DCF VALUATION

As stated earlier, the firms begin with projects that yield high growth in the initial periods. As time passes, the growth tapers off to a realistic level. Though the growth rate varies across the high-growth phase, analysts tend to assume a high but constant growth rate for the entire initial phase, rather than adjusting the growth rate in each period of the phase. This is done as a matter of convenience but ideally during this period the cash flow forecast must be made for each year to arrive at the valuation.

Once the high growth rate period is over, the period of sustained stable growth rate begins. The stable growth rate period can be valued easily with the dividend growth model. This is termed as 'terminal value' or 'continuing value' of the firm. This terminal value can be discounted back to the present value at the beginning of the growth phase.

Normally firms exhibit high growth for a limited period only and thereafter settle for normal growth. Each stage must be valued separately.

The valuation model that splits the cash flow in two distinct phases identifiable with two distinct growth rates is termed as the two-stage growth model. The model uses the same principle and method of valuation but the cash flows and growth parameters are different in two phases of 'high growth' and 'stable growth'. The combined value of both the periods is the value of the firm. This is depicted in Figure 10-4 and shown in Example 10-1.

The steps in valuation under the two-stage growth model are simple and are as follows:

1. Project the length of the high growth period, n.
2. Estimate the growth rate during high growth period, g_h.
3. Project the current year cash flow and for each of the n periods of the high growth phase based on the growth rate, g_h.
4. Find out the right rate of discount rate for the cash flows, using CAPM, leverage assumed.
5. Find out the present value of the cash flows for the high growth phase.
6. Estimate the growth rate of the stable growth period, g_s.
7. The ending cash flow of the high growth phase becomes the base for beginning cash flow for the stable growth phase.
8. Find out the terminal value of the stable growth period using constant growth dividend model.
9. Discount the terminal value to the present value.
10. Add the present values of the terminal value of the stable growth period and the cash flows of the high growth period to arrive at the value of the firm.

The process of valuation under two-stage growth model under FCFF is best comprehended by Example 10-2.

Example 10-2 FCFF Valuation–Two Stage

Amusement Parks Limited owns an entertainment park and contemplating an expansion by adding few more rides in the park. Their current balance sheet on book values and market values is given:

Balance Sheet (₹ crore)	Book Value	Market Value
Fixed Assets	110.00	149.17
Net Current Assets	7.50	7.50
Total	**117.50**	**156.67**
Equity Capital	94.00	133.17
Debt	23.50	23.50
Total	**117.50**	**156.67**

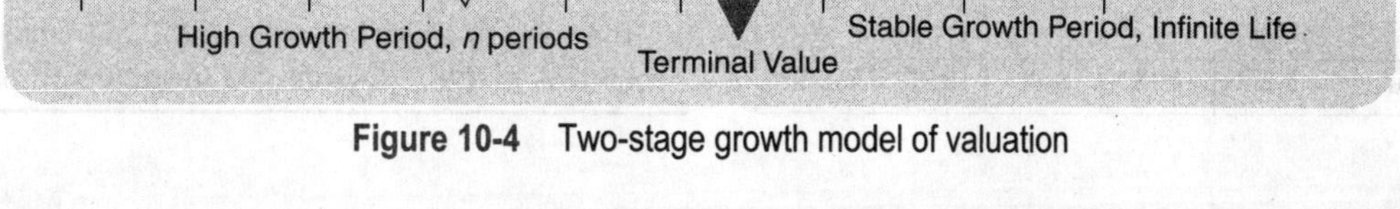

Figure 10-4 Two-stage growth model of valuation

Based on market weights the firm has a debt ratio of 15% and beta of its equity is 1.20. The risk free rate is 6% while market risk premium is 8%. Corporate tax applicable is 35% and post-tax cost of its debt is 9%. The depreciation charged by the firm is 5.5% of the net fixed assets. The capital expenditure plan aggregating ₹135 crore spanning next 4 years is as below:

Year	1	2	3	4
Addition during the year (₹ crore)	20.00	30.00	35.00	50.00

Besides capital expenditure the firm would have nominal working capital at 5% of the total revenue.

The park earns its revenues from entry fee, tickets for rides, rentals from the few kiosks in the park, and the catering. The growth rates and the first year projections net of entertainment tax are projected as below:

Assumptions	*Growth % for next 4 years*	*First Year Projection (₹ in crore)*
Revenue		
Gate Money	10%	5.00
Fee from the Rides	30%	60.00
Rentals from kiosk owners	2%	3.00
Food (% of fee from ride)	65%	39.00
Cash Expenses	60%*	
(of revenue and to decline by 2% every year till the 4th year)		

After four years the free cash flow to the firm are expected to grow at 6% annually forever. Find out the value of the firm and its equity.

Solution

Based on the assumptions given the revenue of Amusement Parks Limited for next 4 years is projected below:

Projection of Revenue (₹ crore)	*Growth*	1	2	3	4
Gate Money	10%	5.00	5.50	6.05	6.66
Fee from the Rides	30%	60.00	78.00	101.40	131.82
Rentals from kiosk owners	2%	3.00	3.06	3.12	3.18
Food	65%	39.00	50.70	65.91	85.68
Total Revenue		**107.00**	**137.26**	**176.48**	**227.34**

The investment in working capital is worked out at 5% of revenue for each of the year:

Working Capital Projection (₹ crore)	*Growth*	1	2	3	4
Initial Working Capital	7.50				
Working Capital for the year	5%	5.35	6.86	8.82	11.37
Increase/(decrease) in WC		**(2.15)**	**1.51**	**1.96**	**2.54**

The computation of depreciation for four years at 5.50% is:

Calculation of Depreciation (₹ crore)		1	2	3	4
Net Block—Opening		110.00	122.85	144.44	169.57
Addition during the year		20.00	30.00	35.00	50.00
Net Block-Closing	125.00	130.00	152.85	179.44	219.57
Depreciation for the year	**5.50%**	**7.15**	**8.41**	**9.87**	**12.08**

Based on the revenue, capital expenditure, increase in working capital and depreciation the free cash flows to the firm for period of growth are worked out below:

FCFF Projection (₹ crore)	1	2	3	4
Revenue	107.00	137.26	176.48	227.34
Cash Expenses	64.20	79.61	98.83	122.76
EBIDT	42.80	57.65	77.65	104.58
Depreciation	7.15	8.41	9.87	12.08
EBIT	35.65	49.24	67.78	92.50
Tax @ 35%	12.48	17.23	23.72	32.38
Adjusted EBIT (EBIT-Tax)	23.17	32.01	44.06	60.13
Gross Cash Flow				
Adj EBIT+ Dep (A)	**30.32**	**40.41**	**53.93**	**72.20**
Less:				
Capital Expenditure	20.00	30.00	35.00	50.00
Change in working capital	(2.15)	1.51	1.96	2.54
Total (B)	17.85	31.51	36.96	52.54
Free Cash Flow (A–B)	**12.47**	**8.90**	**16.97**	**19.66**
Present Value at 14.61%	**10.88**	**6.78**	**11.27**	**11.39**
Value of Growth Period			**40.32**	

Note: The cash flows are discounted at weighted average cost of capital of 14.61%. The cost of equity r_e of the firm as determined by CAPM is:

$$r_e = r_f + \beta (r_m - r_f) = 6\% + 1.20 \times 8\% = 15.60\%$$

The WACC for the firm is:

$$\text{WACC}, r = \text{Proportion of debt} \times \text{Cost of debt} + \text{Proportion of equity} \times \text{Cost of equity}$$

$$= 0.15 \times 9\% + 0.85 \times 15.60\% = 14.61\%$$

The present value of the cash flow of the growth phase of four years is reckoned at ₹40.32 crore.

The value of the period beyond 4 years at 6% growth is found using dividend growth model. The free cash flow for the fifth year are 1.06 × 19.66 = 20.84 crore. The DDM with r = 14.61% and g = 6% gives the terminal value at end of 4th year at ₹242.03 crore, which when converted to present value at WACC of 14.61% comes to ₹140.27 crore.

Value of Stable Growth Period	**₹ crore**
FCFF for 5th year	20.84
Terminal Value at t = 4 years	242.03
Terminal Value at t = 0	**140.27**

The total value of the firm is ₹180.60 crore; the sum of value of growth phase and the terminal value. Subtracting the market value of debt amounting to ₹23.50 crore, the value of equity works out to ₹157.10 crore.

Value of the Firm	**₹ crore**
Value of Growth Period	40.32
Terminal Value	140.27
Total Value	**180.60**
Value of Debt	23.50
Value of Equity	**157.10**

The value of equity presently at ₹133.17 crore is expected to rise by about 18% to ₹157.10 crore due to expansion plan proposed.

Comparison of valuation of equity and firm

We discussed valuation of equity and valuation of firm. The differences in the parameters that are used in the valuation are tabulated in Table 10-8.

Limitations of DCF Approach

The DCF approach to valuation is the most popular and accepted method. Because DCF links the income generating capacity of the asset to its value the method has its own merit. If the basic inputs required for DCF valuation, i.e., the cash flows, discount rates, and growth rates of the cash flows are available and estimated accurately there seems to be no substitute for the method. The validity of the model lies in the accuracy and reliability of the forecast of the values of the determinants. We face the following limitations:

Firms with no or negative cash flow With the requirements of the basic fundamental factors the DCF valuation is most suited to firms that have positive, stable, and predictable cash flows. Firms with long history, positive earnings, and predictable growth rates are easiest to value using DCF technique. However, in the markets, firms that are running into losses and have no cash flows are also traded. The valuation of such firms poses problems in DCF method. The only possible justification for the positive value of the firms but having negative cash flows today is that the markets expects the firm to generate some positive cash flows in future that are being valued by the markets today. Markets view the firm as a 'going concern' and collectively assign a value to such firms that individual analysts may be unable to comprehend. Negative cash flows are considered by promoters of the firm as a necessary investment to make positive gains in future. Though conceptually explainable the DCF method presents difficulties in measurement of fundamental parameters. Any consensus estimate of the growth rate is difficult to obtain. Nor such parameters are available in the historical data.

DCF valuation is difficult to use for the firms that have negative cash flows.

Heavy dependence on economic conditions The cash flows of most firms are dependent upon the conditions of the economy. Some industries and firm have strong linkages with the economic conditions prevailing while some are not as much affected. Projecting cash flows for firms heavily dependent on the economic conditions is rather difficult. For example, consumer product firms are said to be dependent on the monsoons that control the purchasing power of rural segment.

Similarly, firms having idle or under-utilized assets have spare capacity available and show wide fluctuations in the cash flows from period to period. Projecting cash flows for the firms showing steady cash flows in the past are easier to forecast. In a way DCF makes assumption of optimum utilization of assets implicit. Since DCF assumes that income as reflected by the cash flow generation truly reflects the value of assets, full utilization of assets is implied.

Intangibles and option value A conceptual issue with the DCF method of valuation is that it considers only the cash flows. There are many other assets that render value to the firm but do not contribute to the present cash flows. These assets include patents and copyrights that have the value which provide an opportunity to the firm to encash, or to protect the present cash flows from competition. If there is protection from competition it makes cash flows more certain even though not enhancing. These protections must have an impact on discount rate that is not easy to quantify.

DCF valuation ignores the hidden values of strategy.

Another issue not addressed by the DCF approach is the value of managerial decisions that are always available to the firm, particularly the option to delay or option to abandon the projects. The option to expand is the problem already mentioned in the under utilization of assets, where the firm may create large capacities in anticipation of increased demand at later point of time. Further, each firm has an option to discontinue the projects in the light of additional information that becomes available as time elapses. The DCF approach values the cash flows that are

Table 10-8 Comparison of valuation of equity and firm

	Valuation of the Firm	*Valuation of Equity*
Cash Flow	Cash flow to Equity and Debt Holders	Cash flow to only equity holders
Base Year Earnings	EBIT	EPS
Post-tax Cash Flow	EBIT (1 – Tax Rate)	EPS is already post tax
***Less:* Capital Expenditure**	Planned Capital Expenditure net of depreciation	Planned Capital Expenditure net of depreciation × (1 – debt ratio)
Changes in Working Capital	Proportionate to changes in the sales/production levels	Proportionate to changes in the sales/production levels × (1 – debt ratio)
Growth Rate	Growth rate in EBIT; Determined by retention ratio, b and return on assets, ROA ($b \times$ ROA) Not affected by leverage	Growth rate in EPS; Determined by return on assets, retention ratio, post-tax cost of debt and debt ratio
Discount Rate	WACC	Cost of Equity

projected as per the information available now and as such cannot incorporate the values of such options that become available later. We may resort to option pricing theory to value such alternatives available.

Changes in the fundamental determinants The DCF valuation is dependent upon the earnings level, payout ratio, growth rates, and cost of capital. The assumptions of payout, growth, etc. do not remain constant in each period.

Besides the above mentioned factors the DCF valuation is difficult to apply for situations of acquisitions, restructuring, and take-over where the managerial prudence gains precedence over the cash flow. It is also difficult to implement for firms that are not traded for want of data and estimation of risk that ultimately governs the discount rate.

COMPARABLES APPROACH—RELATIVE VALUATION

The comparable approach is based on familiar argument of arbitrage, which states that similar assets must trade at similar prices. The comparable approach comes in handy when the asset being valued is not traded but one can find an equivalent asset that is traded or whose value is known by some alternative and reliable method. The critical issue in comparable approach is to find the similarities in the asset being compared and asset being valued. The advantage of comparables approach lies in placing the reliance on the market rather than on the expertise of analysts to perform the difficult task of valuation.

Another method of arriving at valuation of the firms is market based on the premise that similar asset must trade at similar prices.

The comparables approach finds its roots in real estate business where the value of an apartment is computed on the basis of the value of the already concluded transactions in the recent past for a similar apartment in the same location. This is referred as direct comparable approach where almost identical assets are available for comparison.

In circumstances where direct comparison is not possible we resort to relative valuation where similar but not identical asset is used to arrive at the valuation. It is extremely difficult to find identical firms in corporate world even in the same line of business. The firms have varying sizes, locations, earning capacities, financial characteristics, capital structures and, therefore are not comparable in the true sense. Adjustments need to be made to make a comparison.

Steps in Relative Valuation

In relative valuation the task is divided in following steps:

1. Identify the comparable firm or firms in the same line of business. These firms must have a value determined by the market and all the parameters along which the valuation is contemplated must be available.
2. Identify the parameters of valuation. The usual parameters along which the valuation is done can be sales, EBITDA, book values etc.
3. Estimate the market value along the parameters to find the multiple assigned by the market.
4. Finally project the value of the parameter for the firm being valued and use the value of the multiple to arrive at the valuation.

As a simple example, consider a closely held engineering company for valuation. This engineering firm may have certain technical capabilities. Assume that a firm ABC Ltd projects an earning of ₹30 crore in the coming year. One way of valuation is to project the cash flows of earnings using certain factor of growth indefinitely into the future. Different valuers would arrive at different estimates of cash flows and, hence, different values depending upon the set of assumptions made by each of them.

Relative valuation is based on identifying a comparable and finding the market based multiple to assess the value of the firm in question.

To resolve the conflicts among the analysts we turn our attention to the market valuation. Assuming that the market is supreme and is a better substitute of all the experts, we find the current earnings of a competitor, which is traded on the market. Suppose another firm, XYZ Ltd in the same line of business has projected a profit of ₹45 crore and its market capitalization stands at ₹900 crore. The P/E multiple of the firm XYZ stands at 20. Without any modification to the P/E multiple the value of ABC is computed at ₹600 crore (20×30). There are two key managerial decisions, which determine the efficacy of the relative valuation—the definition of comparable and the choice of multiple.

Defining a Comparable

The basis of relative valuation is the assumption that another firm exists in the market that is comparable to the firm being valued. The objective of comparison with another firm would be met if one can find an exact match of the firm/asset being valued. In the real estate world, it is easier to find such a match but in the corporate world it is easier said than done.

Generally speaking, analysts resort to environmental scanning and industry analysis to identify the exact comparable firm. This is normally difficult. To overcome the problem, a sample is chosen to even out the differences among various firms. The comparison is then made on the basis of average. As a safe alternative one may include all the firms in the industry and arrive at an average. Then the firm may be rated in terms of average.

Choice of Multiple

The price of the stock is directly observable. Similarly, some of the financial information about the firms too is directly observable. One can use the multiple of price of the stock to any firm specific parameter, financial, or otherwise. For example, telecom and internet firms can be valued in terms of customer base. The choice of multiple for relative valuation rests with analyst who determines the relevance of the multiple. Since telecom and internet firms in the initial stages make losses the use of earning multiple in valuation is neither possible nor advisable.

Some of the commonly used multiples are discussed below:

Earning multiple The value of the asset is most commonly linked to its cash generation capacity. Larger the cash generation greater is the asset value. In terms of the stock the price can be seen as a multiple of the earnings available to the shareholders. The ratio of price of the stock to the earning per share (EPS) is known as price earning multiple or the P/E multiple. The P/E multiple can be trailing or leading. When earnings used are current the P/E multiple is trailing and when the projected earnings are used the P/E multiple is called leading.

Book value multiple Book value multiple is the ratio of the market capitalization to the book value of the equity. Book value represents the amount of capital invested in the business by its owners. This includes the original capital contributed and the profits ploughed back in the business, which otherwise could have been distributed and used by the owners. The book value multiple reflects how many times over the contribution is valued by the market as compared to the actual sums put in by the owners. The earnings as a ratio of the market value of the share is the true measure of return on equity. In the financial statements of the firm the book value of equity is replaced by the market value. An alternate way of representing the same is to measure the ratio of the market value to the replacement cost of the assets. This is referred to as *Tobin's Q*.

Revenue multiple The revenue multiple is the ratio of the market capitalization to the revenues generated by the firm. Although sales of the firm are dependent upon the revenue recognition policies, the sales figure is less susceptible to accounting treatment as compared to earnings and book values. Also, the revenue multiple would be far less than the earnings multiple and, therefore, the magnification of error using revenue multiple is less. As an example, consider earnings as 10% of the revenue, then the revenue multiple would be 1/10th of the earning multiple. If there is a 10% error in projection of earnings the valuation would differ 10 times from that is arrived from revenue multiple.

Sector specific multiple Recognizing that each industrial and economic sector has its own peculiar features in respect of financial parameters, economic efficiencies, and structural features, it is believed that the firm in a particular line of business would exhibit somewhat similar characteristics. Large number of studies is made to understand the typical features of each line of business. Valuation can make use of such information available publicly. The sector specific multiples in respect of earnings, revenue and book values are available.

In relative valuation, the analyst must consider the multiple of an exact comparable. Since it is difficult to find an exact match analysts usually resort to a sample of comparable and use averages. Some may choose industry multiples. It is well-known that the average gets distorted by some extreme values present in the sample. While most firms would conform to the average, there always exist some who exhibit unusually high or low multiple. For example, it is not unusual to find some firms in the market with good market value despite negligible earnings giving extremely high P/E multiple. Such outliers need to be ignored in relative valuation. Another way of incorporating the differences among firms is to make subjective judgments about the choice of multiple and giving appropriate weightage to each multiple being developed in the overall valuation process.

Advantages and Limitations of Relative Valuation

We find that relative valuations based on multiples are—(1) far quicker; (2) need no elaborate assumptions; and (3) market based free from individual biases. Relative valuation is easily accepted by all it does not defy convention. Valuation done by any other method, howsoever superior but that does not conform to the market conditions, usually are not easily defensible. The challenges in determining the intrinsic value are many depending upon the subjective factors considered. As relative valuation makes fewer assumptions, the scope of divergence in the opinions is reduced to that extent.

Another factor in relative valuation that can be deemed as a merit as well as a demerit is the dependence of valuation on the sentiments of the market. Higher valuation would result in booming condition in the market, while a lower figure would be justified if depressing conditions prevail. Intrinsic valuation on the other hand is concerned with only the fundamental determinants of the firm with hardly any consideration to the market conditions. If the market valuation differs with the intrinsic valuation, it is assumed that the market would rectify the difference over time. Depending upon the opinion whether the market conditions should impact the valuation or not, the issue can be considered as advantage or disadvantage of relative valuation.

The other merit of relative valuation lies in its simplicity. There is no explicit need to make unnecessary assumptions that are difficult and subjective. As explained earlier that the multiples, as reflected in the market values do take into account all the assumptions that are vital to valuation. In a way multiple is a consolidated figure that builds in all the features like risk of cash flows, growth rates, quantum of cash flows, dividend policies, capital structure, etc., that are regarded as critical determinants of the value of the firm.

Amongst the limitations of relative valuation, the most important one is the carry forward of the market bias in the determination of multiple and resultant valuation. If the market undervalues or overvalues the comparable, the same would affect the valuation. However, it can be argued that individual biases exist in determining the intrinsic values. Also if the market has a biased valuation of the comparables there would be no cause of worry if the same bias persists in valuing the asset. We may average out these biases by using industry multiple of average of a sample.

The limitations of relative valuation include difficulty in finding an exact comparable and carryover of market distortions.

Further, by using the multiples in the relative valuation we tend to assume that the basic characteristics of the firm, such as risk and growth of earnings are identical for the two firms. In the spectrum of comparables, we find that there are large variations in the multiple. Due to the change of multiple over time depending upon the sentiments of the market and a large number of multiples available in the comparable firms it is often said that the analysts can almost justify any valuation done by them. It offers them a great leeway in the relative valuation. While using cash flow techniques the analyst is required to make all company specific assumptions.

Example 10-3 Relative Valuation

A firm, Unknown Ltd, is manufacturing a wide range of chemicals and intending to come out with an IPO to issue one crore shares. It is projecting an earning of ₹3 per share with the revenue of 65 crore. You have been able to identify four firms in the same line and of approximately the same size. The following information about the firms is available:

	Projected ₹ per share			
	EPS	*Book Value*	*Revenue*	*Current Price (₹)*
Firm 1	4.00	40.00	80.00	100.00
Firm 2	4.50	60.00	85.00	120.00
Firm 3	5.00	80.00	90.00	140.00
Firm 4	6.00	72.00	100.00	158.00

What price the firm can issue its shares? Assume that the market gives twice as much importance to earning per share than either to book value or revenue.

Solution

The multiples based on current market price and projected earning, book value and revenue of the four firms are worked out as below:

	Projected ₹ per share				Multiples (times)		
	EPS	*Book Value*	*Revenue*	*Current Price (₹)*	*Earnings*	*Book Value*	*Revenue*
Firm 1	4.00	40.00	80.00	100.00	25.00	2.50	1.25
Firm 2	4.50	60.00	85.00	120.00	26.67	2.00	1.41
Firm 3	5.00	80.00	90.00	140.00	28.00	1.75	1.56
Firm 4	6.00	72.00	100.00	158.00	26.33	2.19	1.58
Average					**26.50**	**2.11**	**1.45**

Since all the four firms are taken for comparison it is advisable to derive the value of Unknown Ltd on the basis of averages. There are no extraordinary multiples that are not considered as representative of sample.

Since the objective is to find the issue price, which impacts the projected book value of the share the multiple with the book value may be ignored.

Based on the two multiples of earnings and revenue, the expected value of the share is placed as:

Based on earnings multiple = 26.50 × 3 = ₹79.50

Based on earnings multiple = 1.45 × 65 = ₹94.25

Weighted average based on the assumption that market value is governed by twice as much by earning than the revenue is

(2 × 79.50 + 1 × 94.25)/3 = ₹84.42

Relative Valuation and Intrinsic Values

However, it does not mean to suggest that the multiple can be applied blindly to the valuation. It also does not mean to suggest that the relative valuation does not make assumptions about cash flows, risk, and growth. These assumptions are implied in the multiple and the analyst is saved from the task of directly making such assumptions regarding cash flows, their risk and growth. For example, consider the case of earnings multiple. The DCF approach would require projection of cash flows, dividend payout ratios, capitalization rate, and growth rate in dividend. The familiar dividend discount model the value of the firm by following formula:

$$P_0 = \frac{D_1}{r-g} = \frac{D_0\,(1+g)}{r-g} = \frac{E_0 \times \text{Payout Ratio}\,(1+g)}{r-g}$$

$$\text{Or}\ \frac{P_0}{E_0} = \frac{\text{Payout Ratio}\,(1+g)}{r-g}$$

Therefore, the P/E multiple indirectly incorporates the dividend policy (the payout ratio), risk of the cash flows in the discount rate, r and the growth rate of dividend g. The P/E multiple explained above makes the same assumptions as those of dividend discount model.

A similar observation can be made regarding price to sales multiple. Earning of the firm is equal to return on sales. Return on sales is defined as a profit margin multiplied by sales. Substituting them in the dividend discount model we can obtain a relationship of revenue multiple as below:

$$P_0 = \frac{D_1}{r+g} = \frac{D_0(1+g)}{r-g} = \frac{E_0 \times \text{Payout Ratio}\,(1+g)}{r-g}$$

$$= \frac{\text{Profit Margin} \times \text{Sales} \times \text{Payout Ratio}\,(1+g)}{r-g}$$

$$\text{Or}\ \frac{P_0}{\text{Sale Value}} = \frac{\text{Profit Margin} \times \text{Payout Ratio}\,(1+g)}{r\text{-}g}$$

A similar exercise is possible with respect to a multiple based on the book value; the net worth. Continuing with the assumption of dividend discount model of all equity financing the earning per share is replaced by (net worth × return on equity). The relationship of book value multiple is derived below:

$$P_0 = \frac{D_1}{r-g} = \frac{D_0\,(1+g)}{r-g} = \frac{E_0 \times \text{Payout Ratio}\,(1+g)}{r-g}$$

$$= \frac{\text{Book Value} \times \text{ROE}_0 \times \text{Payout Ratio}\,(1+g)}{r-g}$$

$$\text{Or}\ \frac{P_0}{\text{Book Value}} = \frac{\text{ROE}_0 \times \text{Payout Ratio}\,(1+g)}{r-g}$$

A word of caution in linking of fundamental factors to the valuation is in order. It may be fallaciously concluded that the P/E multiple of a firms that has growth rate twice as that of another would have twice the multiple. We assume linearity in relative valuation but it cannot be said to exist between the multiple and the fundamental factors. It cannot be said that a

Relative valuation is often done using a linear relationship. It is more of a convenience rather than fundamentally correct.

firm with twice as much growth rate as average would have twice as great P/E ratio as average. One can visualize from the above equations that the fundamental factors are not related linearly with the multiple.

Example 10-4 Relative Valuation and Fundamentals

A firm has following fundamental characteristics;

Current Earnings per Share:	₹4.00
Current Dividend per Share:	₹3.00
Beta of the Firm:	1.30
Growth in Earnings and Dividend:	8%
Return on Sales:	5%
Return on Equity:	20%

Assuming that the current risk-free rate of return is placed at 6% and the market risk premium at 8%, what P/E multiple do you expect for the firm? Also, find the book value multiple and sales multiple.

Solution

The payout ratio of the firm = 3.00/4.00 = 0.75 (75%)

Cost of Equity using CAPM = $R_f + \beta \times (R_m - R_f) = 6 + 1.30 \times 8 = 16.4\%$

The P/E multiple is worked out as under:

$$\frac{P_0}{E_0} = \frac{\text{Payout Ratio } (1+g)}{r - g} = \frac{0.75 \times 1.08}{0.164 - 0.08} = \frac{0.81}{0.084}$$

$$= 9.64 \text{ (trailing)}$$

$$\text{Leading P/E Multiple} = \frac{P_0}{E_j} = \frac{9.94}{1.08} = 8.93$$

The Book Value Multiple is:

$$\frac{P_0}{\text{Book Value}} = \frac{\text{ROE} \times \text{Payout Ratio } (1+g)}{r - g}$$

$$= \frac{0.20 \times 0.75 \times 1.08}{0.164 - 0.08} = 1.98$$

The revenue multiple is:

$$\frac{P_0}{\text{Sale Value}} = \frac{\text{Profit Margin} \times \text{Payout Ratio } (1+g)}{r - g}$$

$$= \frac{0.05 \times 0.75 \times 1.08}{0.164 - 0.08} = 0.482$$

VALUE-BASED MANAGEMENT

Most of the time of the finance function is devoted to the routine accounting matters of booking expenses, ensuring compliances, invoicing etc. All these activities relate to maintenance, which at best can be regarded as necessities rather than the proactive role of finance function to create a shareholder value. All these activities are transactions oriented occupying much of the time of the finance function. Very little attention and time is devoted to strategic functions such as planning, risk management, competitive evaluations that go a long way in creating value for the enterprise.

Most of us concentrate on the earnings of an enterprise as a measure of its performance. Corporate performance can be measured by many tools and techniques such as Return on Net worth, Return on Equity, Earning Per Share, Dividend per Share, P/E Ratio and Market of Book Value already discussed here and in Chapter 2.

Analysts, managers, investors are alike while comparing performances of various firms or making investment choices. They all are driven by the profit and EPS and other such accounting measures. All these measures though important in evaluation do not tell the complete story of how well the capital employed is being used. A firm making profit is not a sufficient condition to ensure value creation for the shareholders. Unless these profits are adequate to compensate the opportunity cost of capital the firm cannot be said to be the creator of value. If the profits are inadequate to cover the cost of capital the firm will be a destroyer of value rather than creator of value.

Earnings vs Cash Flow

Most analysts and investors view the performance of the company from the balance sheet of the enterprise. The balance sheet displays the book value of the assets. It hardly reflects the efficiency with which these assets have been deployed to create value for the shareholders. However, neither the investors nor the analysts are to be blamed for keeping their focus on earnings, as there exists a strong positive correlation between earnings and cash flows, and, therefore, the value of the firm. However, one has to guard against the possibilities of earnings not properly reflecting the economic value of the enterprise. As long as financial statements and economic performance are in tandem the emphasis on earnings or EPS may not be misplaced.

All valuations have their bases in accounting profit and ignore cost of capital. Value-based management focuses on cash flows and cost of capital.

Thinking beyond the earnings will ensure right conclusions. There are a large number of items that distort the cash flows that are derived from earnings. The items of depreciation, inventory valuation, provisions for bad debts, amortization rates are the few examples that create a mismatch between earnings and cash flows.

VALUE-BASED MANAGEMENT

Value-based management is an approach that ensures that firms are run consistently on values rather than on profit. It includes ways to—(1) create value, i.e., the strategies to increase future value; (2) manage the value, i.e., focus on change; and (3) measure the value.

Creating value is the most important factor in the management of the firms. The goal of the finance function is unambiguously stated as an increase in the shareholders' wealth. The focus on enhancing shareholders' wealth has caused a shift in the management thinking to an extent that all functions of the firm get involved in the process of value creation. It does not remain confined to the finance function. Creation or increase in shareholders' wealth is increasingly being used as parameter to determine executive compensation. It has compelled the executive to focus on value creation for the shareholders broadening the scope of thinking from the narrow boundaries of profit generation. It is an attempt to link the performance of various functions to the value creation.

Under the value-based management the scope of marketing function stretches beyond increasing market share and revenue. Likewise, the production function has to think beyond increasing production and the finance function is required to undertake investment strategies that channel the funds in the right avenues that go to create value. It provides a precise metric value on which the entire organization can be built.

Several value-based management styles have been suggested, each of which identifies key drivers of value and uses a measurement tool based on cash flows and cost of capital.

Almost all measures of value emphasize on the cash flows and imply that the value is created only when firms invest capital in a manner that recovers the cost of capital. Unless the expectations of the investors are met, no value addition takes place. It attempts to establish key drivers of value and draws the management's attention to these drivers in a routine as well as a strategic manner.

A large number of value-based management strategies are available that attempt to synthesize various functions of the firm to the process of value creation. A broader framework of value based management includes value to various other stakeholders besides shareholders. These approaches enable to shift attention from the traditional view of measuring value through earnings and think beyond shareholders. All these strategies almost focus their attention to—(1) economic profits based on *cash flows* and *surplus over cost of capital*; (2) identifying the key drivers of the value; and (3) the use their own methods to measure value.

MEASURES OF VALUE

Some of the measures that are used to compute the value are discussed below.

Cash Value Added (CVA)

Cash value added (CVA) is the excess of cash generated over and above the requirement of cash. It is a cash flow based measure of value that includes only the cash items.

Cash Value Added is given by:

Cash value added (CVA) = operating cash flow (OCF) – operating cash flow demand (OFCD)

The operating cash flow is computed for the essential strategic investment and excludes non-strategic investment. Operating cash flow is computed by adding earnings before interest, taxes, depreciation and amortization (EBITDA) and the increase in working capital, and subtracting it from non-strategic investment.

Operating cash flow (OCF) = EBITDA + Increase in Working Capital – Non-strategic Investment

It is clear that investment in working capital is regarded as essential and strategic.

From OCF is subtracted the operating cash flow demand (OFCD) representing the opportunity cost of capital demanded by the investors for the strategic investment. It measures the requirement of investors not in percentage terms but in actual cash flow terms. The difference of OCF and OFCD is the cash value added.

Not being a market-based determinant it can be computed at strategic business unit level. The emphasis is on cash and not on accounting earnings such as EBIT or net profit of the strategic unit being evaluated.

Cash Flow Return on Investment (CFROI)

Developed by Holt Value Associates, cash flow return on investment (CFROI) is a cash flow based corporate performance measure. Boston Consulting Group (BCG) uses it as performance measure and defines it as ratio of sustainable cash flow in a year to the cash invested on the assets of the firm.

$$\text{Cash Flow Return on Investment (CFROI)} = \frac{\text{Sustainable Cash Flow}}{\text{Cash Invested}}$$

Sustainable cash flow is the cash flow adjusted for economic depreciation. Economic depreciation is the annual amount of charge (or sinking fund) on the cash flows of the firm that is required for replacing the asset after its useful life is over and with discount factor of WACC of the firm. For example, if an asset available with the firm is valued at ₹5,00,000 but after 10 years of its useful life the replacement can be done only at ₹7,00,000 the economic depreciation would be based on replacement cost of ₹7 lakh instead of ₹5 lakh. And if the WACC is 12% the amount each year must be based on such that the present value at 12% for 10 years equals ₹7,00,000.

Relative Value of Growth

The firm's management often faces the dilemma as to how to provide increased value to the shareholders. Two common strategies available to them are—increase the revenue by increased marketing and sale promotion effort, and to increase the productivity by undertaking cost cutting exercises wherever possible. Undoubtedly, both are desirable and increase value to the shareholders. Given the constraint of time with the top management it is hard to imagine if management can focus on both the strategies of value addition simultaneously and with equal vigour.

Relative value of growth (RVG) is one parameter that helps resolve this dilemma.

Nathaniel Mass (2005) defined RVG as:

$$\text{Relative Value of Growth (RVG)} = \frac{\text{Value of 1\% Growth (VG)}}{\text{Value of 1\% improvement in Margin (VM)}}$$

where

$$\text{Value of 1\% Growth (VG)} = \text{Value of the Firm with 1\% Extra Revenue} - \text{Current Value of the Firm}$$

$$= \frac{\text{Current Cash Flow}}{\text{WACC} - (g + 1\%)} - \text{Current Value of the Firm}$$

Value of improvement in Margin by 1% (VM)

$$= \frac{\text{Post-tax Increase in Cash Flow}}{\text{WACC} - g}$$

$$= \frac{\text{Current Cash Flow} \times 1\% \times (1 - T)}{\text{WACC} - g}$$

Relative value of growth compares what is achievable by an increase in revenue as compared to increase in profitability. The higher the value of RVG the more desirable it is. It compares the contribution of increase in revenue to that of strategy of cost cutting. With an RVG greater than one, the increase in the value would be higher if the firm focuses on increased revenue than if the focus is on cost cutting to improve margins. It is a measure of how increased revenue, which implies increased market share, impacts shareholders' value creation. Growth in revenue outweighs cost-cutting measures. If RVG is less than one, cost cutting is more effective in value creation than the increase in revenue. Such a situation would signify the maturity of the market where only way to improve value is cost cutting.

Understanding the RVG would help strike a good balance between marketing and production activities. It is useful for making investment decisions, establishing long term focus and formulation of corporate strategy. The limitation of RVG includes its inability to value intangibles besides being a relative measure ignoring the increase in value in absolute terms.

Economic Margin

Economic margin, as a measure of corporate performance, was developed by Daniel J Obrycki and Rafael Resendes (1996). It focuses on economic profit. The approach makes adjustments for differences in capital structure, age and life of the assets, mix of the assets, and investment needed to generate earnings.

Economic margin framework is not only a performance metric but also encompasses valuation based on four main value drivers—profitability, competition, growth, and cost of capital. It is measured as follows:

$$\text{Economic Margin} = \frac{\text{Operating Cash Flow} - \text{Capital Charge}}{\text{Invested Capital}}$$

Where

Operating Cash flow = Net Income + Depreciation & Amortization + After-tax Interest + R&D Expense ± Non-recurring Expenses/Income

Invested capital = Total Assets + Accumulated Depreciation + Gross Plant Inflation adjustment + Capitalized R&D – Non-debt Current Liabilities

The basic difference and premise of economic margin based valuation is that it emphasizes that firms with high excess returns are expected to attract greater competition leading to a shorter competitive advantage period, thus discarding the perpetual cash flow computed to arrive at the terminal value. It states that competition would compete away excess returns.

It is used for finding competition-adjusted performance. The numerator of economic margin like EVA (discussed later) based on economic profit. Unlike EVA, economic margin adds depreciation to the EBIT. Like CFROI the economic margin based on gross assets and helps avoid growth disincentive and not on net assets. However, unlike CFROI the cash flows are unlevered.

Market Value Added

Market value added (MVA) is the excess of market value of the firm as reflected in share price and the value of debt, over the book value of the capital employed. This book value of the capital employed includes the value of reserves and surplus. Mathematically,

Market Value Added (MVA) = Market Value of the firm – Capital Employed

The market value of the firm reflects the present value of the all projects the firm has undertaken. It is the potential of the firm as viewed by investors who value the past as well as future use of funds by the firm. It represents the excess of what the investors can get over what they have put into business.

> *Market value added is a measurement that finds the excess of market value over the capital employed. It is considered good if positive and increasing period after period.*

For example, Infosys, a pure equity IT firm has the book value of equity of ₹5,271.73 crore as on 31 March 2005 with 27.06 crore shares trading at ₹2,294. The market capitalization of Infosys is ₹62,075 crore as on 31 March 2005. Hence, MVA for the firm is ₹56,803 crore; the extra wealth the shareholders can realize over what they have put in.

The market value of the firm is the sum of the values of equity and debt. When debt is considered rather constant, the maximization of shareholders' wealth becomes consistent with maximization of market value of the firm. However, we cannot ignore the value of debt since we are concerned with the efficiency of the assets that are used and not with how were they created. While concentrating on the market value of the firm rather than the value of equity alone we are attempting to offset the effect of capital structure in measuring the efficiency of the firm in deploying capital.

The MVA is considered a better measure of corporate performance than the market capitalization since a firm can always increase the market capitalization by simply issuing more number of shares. How well this new capital is utilized, remains a question mark. It is the excess of value created by the capital over its cost that is relevant for measure of performance and to make a judgment whether the value is created or destroyed.

The problem with MVA is that it is dependent on the market value determined by the price of the stock, which keep changing due to factors other than fundamentals of the firm. Sentiments regarding state of the economy, demand supply scenario, government's fiscal and monetary policies have considerable impact on the stock prices. The stock prices are not purely a function of the firm's potential, though it is one of the important and crucial determinants of the value of the firm. Other factors affecting the stock price cannot be said to be in control of the firm, and, therefore, the MVA will not be an appropriate measure of value created by the firm for its shareholders.

ECONOMIC VALUE ADDED (EVA)[1]

The issue with traditional and accounting measures of the performance of the firm is that they ignore the cost of the resources deployed. They also fail to recognize the value of other assets like intellectual capital that create value for the firm. Although the MVA recognizes all such hidden values in the market price of the share, it is also subject to vagaries of the market. In other words, market value includes the value of the intellectual capital but is subject to change as market value changes every moment.

Economic Value Added (EVA) perhaps is the most popular value based measurement that enables measurement based on the value addition in excess of investors' expectation of return.

Popularized by Stern Stewart & Co, economic value added (EVA) measures the profit that is earned over and above the cost of capital of the firm. The analysts, firms and investors use it to find the value created by the firm for a given amount of capital employed. As per the definition given by Stern Stewart (1991) the EVA is the residual income from operating profits after the cost of capital has been earned and can be stated in the following formula:

EVA = Return on Total Capital Employed
− Cost of Capital × Total Capital

Simply stated, EVA is net operating profit minus an appropriate charge for the opportunity cost of *all capital* invested in an enterprise. It is the amount by which earnings exceed or fall short of the required minimum rate of return that shareholder and lenders could get by investing in other securities of comparable risk. The capital charge is the most distinctive and important aspect of EVA.

EVA is an internal measure of performance of the firm as against the MVA, which is measured by the market. One clear advantage of EVA is its recognition of efficiency of capital along with profits. Conventional measures of performance of firms do not take into account the cost of capital. The EVA compares the profit with cost of capital.

Under conventional financial performance metrics even if some firms are showing profits they may be actually be destroyers of economic value due to lack of efficient utilization of capital. Peter. F. Drucker[2]the renowned management thinker, says, "Until a business returns a profit that is greater than its cost of capital, it operates at a loss. Never mind that it pays taxes as if it had a genuine profit. The enterprise still returns less to the economy than it devours in resources…Until then it does not create wealth; it destroys it." EVA corrects this anomaly by factoring in the cost of equity in the cost of financing calculations. The underlying idea behind EVA is that if managers employ capital they must pay for it, just as if it were a wage. EVA is the measure of wealth that the business creates/destroys. It is the profit the way shareholders define it. If the shareholders expect, say, a 17% return on their investment, firm will be said to have created value for them only to the extent that their share of after-tax operating profits exceeds 17% of equity capital. Everything before that is just building up to the minium acceptable compensation for investing in a risky enterprise..

EVA, unlike the conventional measures, factors in cost of equity in the cost of financing calculations.

The central idea of EVA is to incorporate the cost of capital both of debt and equity. It holds the firm accountable for earnings as well as cost of capital.

EVA, which is a variant of the residual income concept, is not a new discovery. One of the earliest to mention the residual income concept was Alfred Marshall[3]. Marshall defined economic profit as total net gains less the interest on invested capital at the current rate. Marshall said over 100 years ago:

EVA is a variant of the residual income concept that was given by economists over a century back

"When a man is engaged in business, his profits for the year are the excess of his receipts from his business during the year over his outlay for his business. The difference between the value of the stock of plant, material, etc. at the end and at the beginning of the year is taken as part of his receipts or as part of his outlay, according as there has been an increase or decrease of value. What remains of his profits after deducting interest on his capital at the current rate ... is generally called his earnings of undertaking or management."

Though the EVA is a variant of the Economic Profit concept that was propounded by the economists over a century back, its association with market capitalization is of recent origin. Also the adjustments to the accounting profit to eliminate the potential accounting distortions are unique to EVA.

EVA can be defined from two perspectives—"accounting" perspective and "finance" perspective. From accounting perspective, EVA is defined as the difference between the firm's net operating profit after tax (NOPAT) and its weighted-average rupee cost of capital. Since EVA fully accounts for the firm's overall capital costs it differs from traditional metrics of financial performance such as EBIT (earnings before interest and taxes), EBITDA (EBIT plus depreciation and amortization), Earnings after tax etc. This analytical difference is important to the firm's owners because the EVA metric is net of both the direct cost of debt capital and the indirect cost of equity capital—as reflected in the shareholders' required return on common stock. From the accounting perspective EVA can be mathematically expressed as:

EVA can be defined from two perspectives- accounting and finance.

EVA = NOPAT – CAPITAL COST **(10-4)**

= NOPAT – (WACC × Capital Employed)

= (r × Capital Employed) – (c × Capital Employed)

[1]EVA is registered trademark of Stern Stewart & Co.

[2]Drucker P., "The information Executives truly need", Harvard Business Review, Jan- Feb 1995, pp. 54-62.

[3] Alfred Marshall, Principles of Economics, Book II, Chapter IV, 1st ed., 1890 pp. 25.

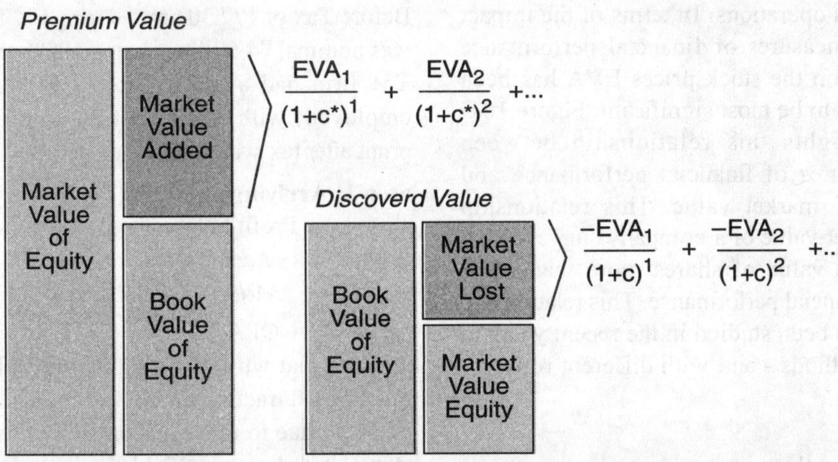

Figure 10-5 Company's market value depends on its future EVA.

Thus,

$$\text{EVA} = (r - c) \times \textbf{Capital Employed}$$

$$\text{EVA}_t = (r - c) \times \textbf{Capital Employed}_{(t-1)} \quad \textbf{(10-5)}$$

Where, WACC = Weighted Average Cost of Capital.
= [Cost of Equity × Proportion of equity in total capital + Cost of debt × Proportion of debt in total capital × (1–tax rate) + Cost of Preference capital × Proportion of Preference Capital in total capital].

From finance perspective, EVA is expressed in terms of its relationship with MVA. Thus MVA is equal to the present value of the firm's expected future EVAs.

MVA = PV of expected future EVA **(10-6)**

The EVA framework has important strategic implications for the company management. Firms having investment opportunities that are likely to yield a return that exceeds the weighted average cost of capital to be employed in such investments would see a positive momentum in the intrinsic value of their shares due a positive EVA outlook. In contrast, firms with returns on invested capital that is expected to fall short of the weighted-average cost of capital should see share price declines as the adverse EVA outlook lowers the intrinsic value of the firm. Thus the EVA framework facilitates the company management to take resources allocation decisions that are compatible with the overall objective of shareholders' wealth maximization.

EVA framework aids in better resource allocation by the firms.

EVA vs MVA

EVA is a period-to-period computation, which can be used to monitor the process of value creation and record historically the growth of the enterprise. The MVA can be interpreted as the present value of all EVAs. The MVA measures the total performance of the firm in economic terms since its inception. It is a cumulative measure while the EVA is a single period measure, usually a year. A firm having a positive EVA is expected to have positive MVA and vice-versa. However, there can be a contradiction in MVA and EVA because the MVA is derived from the share prices, which are forward looking discounting the future potential, while the EVA records performance during a period. We may have negative EVA, yet a positive MVA due to the good potential of the firm.

According to the proponents of EVA other parameters of value like growth, rates of return and dividends do not matter. Growth in EPS will increase MVA only when investments earn more than the cost of capital. Similarly, the rates of return do not matter. What matters is the creation of absolute EVA. Like wise dividend and its growth will be inconsequential as long as the market value falls by the amount of dividend. MVA will be affected only when change in dividend signals some change in fundamental investment policy. The only way for creation of value is undertaking all the projects with positive NPV and rejecting all negative NPV projects – the standard rule of capital budgeting. Once this is done growth in both returns and dividend will take care of themselves automatically. This will lead to maximization of both EVA and MVA.

EVA Vs TRADITIONAL MEASURES OF FINANCIAL PERFORMANCE

Lehn & Makhija[4] in their study point towards the conceptual superiority of EVA over the traditional measures of financial performance. The study suggests that EVA is superior to accounting profits as a measure of value creation because it recognizes the cost of capital and, hence, the riskiness of a

[4]Lehn, K. & Makhija, A. K, "EVA and MVA: As performance measures and signals for strategic change", Strategy and leadership, Vol. 24, May/June, 1996, pp.34-38.

Some studies suggest that EVA influences the market value of stocks more than other conventional measures of financial performance.

firm's operations. In terms of the impact that measures of financial performance have on the stock prices EVA has been found to be most significant. Figure 10-5 highlights this relationship between measures of financial performance and firms' market value. This relationship between EVA and the market value of a company suggests that EVA influences the market value of shares more than other conventional measures of financial performance. This relationship between EVA and MVA has been studied in the recent years in many studies with many methods - and with different results.

Computation of EVA

The computation of EVA is a three-step process.

1. Compute the net operating profit after tax (NOPAT)
2. Find out WACC for the firm, and the capital employed and
3. Find EVA as below:

   EVA = NOPAT – WACC × Capital Employed

Before we illustrate the computation of EVA a short discussion on NOPAT, one of the main constituents of EVA.

NOPAT is arrived at after adjusting the accounting profit to eliminate the potential accounting distortions.

Stewart[5] defines NOPAT as the profits derived from the company's operations after taxes but before financing costs and non cash book keeping entries, except for depreciation, which is reckoned as "a true economic expense." Stewart's definition of NOPAT incorporates regular non operating income. This is a deviation from the traditional concept of operating profit which restricts the operating profit definition to profits from main operations ignoring other income. But in present day business Stewart's definition is more relevant. Stewart identified 164 adjustments to be made to the accounting profit as reported in the Profit and Loss account to eliminate potential distortions in the accounting results based on the Generally Accepted Accounting Principles (GAAP) of a country.

Thus the computation of EVA on one hand removes the distortions in profit that are caused due to discretionary accounting treatment of some transactions like R&D expenditure, inventory valuation etc. This is done by making adjustments to the profits to remove such potentials distortions. Such an adjusted profit that is comparable across firms is termed as NOPAT. On the other hand, the EVA model takes cost of total capital employed, including the cost of equity. These two features that are unique to EVA differentiate it from the conventional measures of performance. Besides, they also make EVA a better and more credible measure of firm's financial performance.

An example will facilitate the understanding of mechanism of calculation of EVA. Consider example of Satyam Computers[6]; an export oriented firm in software. Satyam Computers had Profit Before Tax of ₹77.30 crore during FY 1998-99. The tax obligation was nominal ₹4.50 crore being 100% export unit exempt from tax. The firm had average debt of ₹184.39 crore (58% of capital employed) with an interest outgo of ₹26.43 crore. Net operating profit after tax was derived as below:

Step 1: Arriving at NOPAT

	(₹ crore)
Profit before Tax	77.30
Less: Taxes	4.50
Add: Actual Interest	26.23
NOPAT	99.23

Note that while arriving at NOPAT the tax shield of interest must be subtracted. Since Satyam had no tax (small outgo of tax of ₹4.50 due to other reasons notwithstanding) due to its export status, it had no tax shield available and therefore no adjustment is made.

NOPAT can also be equated as EBIT × (1 – Tax Rate), and EVA can be stated as:

EBIT × (1 – Tax Rate) – Capital Employed × WACC

Step 2: Computing Weighted Average Cost of Capital

Assumed rate of risk free return	12.08%
Expected Risk Premium on Equity (for Software exporters)	10.00%
Beta Variant of Satyam	1.215
Cost of Equity (Using CAPM) = (12.08 + 1.215 × 10)	24.23%
WACC for Satyam = 24.23% × 0.42 + 14.34 × 0.58	18.50%

$$\text{Capital Employed} = \frac{\text{Debt}}{\text{Debt ratio}} = \frac{184.39}{0.58} = ₹317.91 \text{ crore}$$

Equity = Capital employed × Equity ratio
= 317.91 × 0.42 = ₹133.52 crore

Cost of capital (18.50% × 317.91) ₹58.81 crore

Here again note that we have considered cost of debt at 14.34% the actual cost borne by the firm. While computing WACC we must take after tax cost of debt. Since Satyam was tax exempt the pre-tax cost as well as post-tax cost of debt will be same.

Cost of equity has been arrived at by CAPM model with the assumed risk free rate of 12.08% and a risk premium of 10%. The observed beta of Satyam for the period was 1.215.

Step 3: Finding EVA

EVA = NOPAT – Cost of Capital
= 99.23 – 58.81 = ₹40.42 crore

The EVA of ₹40.42 crore implies that during the year 98-99 the firm added economic value of ₹40 crore, i.e., it earned a return of ₹40 crore after providing for the cost of the capital. Thus, the firm was a value creator. Had this figure been negative, the firm would be termed as value destroyer.

Computation of EVA for another firm, Infosys Technologies is shown in Table 10-9 and depicted in Figure 10-6.

[5] Stewart, G. Bennet., "The Quest for Value", Harper Business, 2nd

[6] From Annual Report of Satyam Computers for financial year 1998-99.

[7]As per the Annual Report 2004–05 of Infosys Technologies Ltd

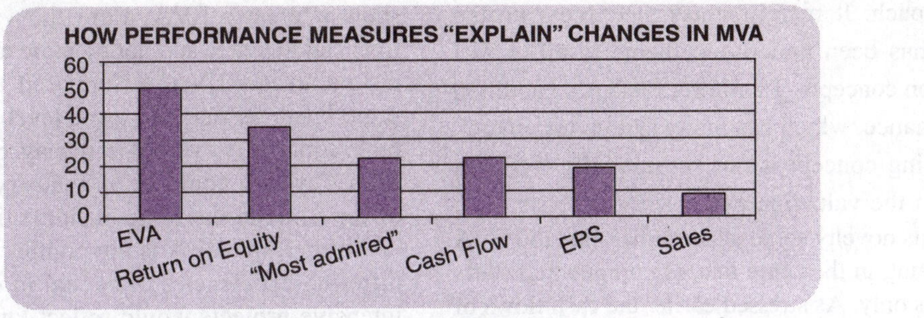

Figure 10-6 EVA vs. traditional measures of performance[8]

Table 10-9 Economic value added—Infosys Technologies

(₹ crore)

	2005	2004	2003	2002	2001
Cost of capital					
Risk-free rate (%)	6.80	5.20	6.00	7.30	10.30
Market premium (%)	7.00	7.00	7.00	7.00	7.00
Beta variant	0.98	1.27	1.57	1.41	1.54
Cost of equity (%)	**13.63**	**14.09**	**16.99**	**17.17**	**21.08**
Debt	—	—	—	—	—
Cost of debt	—	—	—	—	—
WACC (%)	**13.63**	**14.09**	**16.99**	**17.17**	**21.08**
Average capital employed	4,330.95	3,124.82	2,493.40	1,734.97	1,111.47
Economic Value Added					
Operating Profit (excluding extra-ordinary income)	2,048.09	1,357.46	1,079.28	943.39	696.03
Less: Tax	325.58	227.54	201.00	135.43	72.71
Less: Cost of capital	590.31	440.29	423.63	297.89	234.30
Economic Value Added	**1,132.20**	**689.63**	**454.65**	**510.07**	**389.02**

Ways to Improve EVA

There are three variables as shown in Figure 10-6, that determine the EVA:

- Net operating profit after taxes (NOPAT)
- Weighted average cost of capital (WACC)
- Total capital employed

The EVA of the firm will improve with increased earnings for same levels of cost and capital employed. The EVA will also increase if the same level of earning is maintained with reduced cost or lesser capital. The broad strategies for enhancing EVA can be put in following three categories:

- *Process improvements:* It focuses on increasing the efficiency of operations, thereby increasing the spread between the returns on capital employed and cost of capital. This includes better management of net working capital.
- *Exploiting growth potential:* This implies increasing the total capital employed by undertaking all positive NPV projects; since the spread between returns and cost of capital is positive it will enhance EVA.
- *Managing assets and restructuring:* Here the emphasis is on decreasing the exposure from the projects that are not yielding returns in excess of cost of capital.

MVA at any point of time is equal to the discounted present value of all the EVA. If the market and investors can accurately foresee all the potential of the firm, EVA and MVA will be identical.

Drawbacks of EVA

Although EVA represents a novel approach to assess a value the firm creates, many believe that it is no different that the

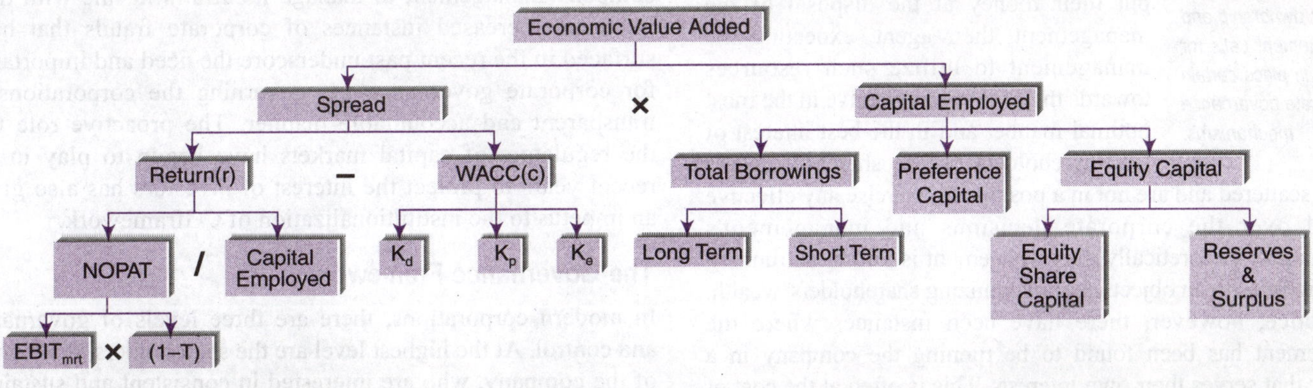

$EBIT_{mrt}$ implies Earnings before interest and taxes net of non recurring transactions k_d, k_p, and k_e imply cost of debt, cost of preference capital, and cost of equity capital respectively. T stands for corporation tax rate.

Figure 10-7 Anatomy of EVA

[8] Ehrbar A. L, "Economic Value Added: The Real Key to Creating Wealth"., New York, John Wiley & Sons Inc.1998, pp 77

residual income approach. It merely states the excess profits over WACC, which has been underlying theme in all capital budgeting and valuation concepts. Therefore, EVA is an addition to the dictionary of finance, which has many synonyms already existing. The underlying concept is not substantially different than the many used in the valuation exercise by analysts.

Not only disputing its novelty some of them may find the EVA approach as self-defeating in the sense that its computation starts from accounting profits only. As stressed earlier the cash flows of the firm are considered to be the main driver of the value of the firm. Due to the distortion, the accounting profits have for the cash flows, adjustments are required to be made for cash flows. Emphasis on NOPAT seems a contradiction to cash flows as basic determinant of value especially in regard to treatment of depreciation. The markets are intelligent enough to arrive at real cash flows from the accounting profit. Markets intuitively account for it through P/E ratios, and do not need another measure of value. The collective judgement of value by the market is deemed superior to the complex computation of EVA.

In any case, the lack of financial disclosures and accounting adjustments of various expense and revenue items that are not consistent and uniform across firms, make the computation of EVA difficult. The accuracy of calculation will always remain a suspect due to inadequate disclosures.

Another problem the EVA faces is with regard to its use as a measure of comparative performance. Different firms have different capital structures and different costs of capital. Two firms in the same line of business with same level of profit will have a different EVA depending upon the cost of capital. The one with lesser cost of capital due to the use of higher debt will show a greater EVA. Here the value is driven by increased financial leverage and not by more efficient utilization of assets—the parameter EVA is supposed to measure. Faced with the same business risk and same level of profit the two firms must rank equal. To overcome it may be suggested to use a single WACC which could be an industry average to assess the EVA of the firms in the same business line.

Further, the EVA is not comparable across industries due to differing efficiencies of capital in different industries. Capital-intensive projects would reflect lower EVA as compared to its true potential, and as compared to firms engaged in projects of small capital such as trading activities and consumer products.

Another major drawback in measuring EVA is in respect of projects that have not matured. All projects have a gestation period over which the full economic potential is realized. In the beginning of the project the cash flows will be less than the true potential, and therefore, the value reflected by the project will be less than its true value. The EVA of the project in the initial years will not provide the measure of the true potential. When calculated as comparative performance the projects that are not fully implemented will understate the EVA as compared to project that have culminated. Here again, we have to rely on the market assessment as true measure of potential of the project and the firm.

EVA as an absolute value may not be of much use. To measure the growth the ratio of EVA with capital employed will be more appropriate. While EVA is not ideal it is definitely a powerful tool to value a firm and when used with discretion and in conjunction with other measures, will provide greater insights to valuation.

CORPORATE GOVERNANCE

Need for Corporate Governance (CG)

Need for CG emerges from the agency conflicts. In company form of business organizations there is a split between ownership and management. Shareholders, the principal, put their money at the disposal of the management, their agent, expecting the management to utilize such resources towards the pre-stated objective in the most optimal manner and in the best interest of the shareholders. These shareholders are widely scattered and are not in a position to exercise any effective control over the corporate decisions and management's performance. Theoretically the management is said to be running the business with an objective of maximizing shareholders' wealth. In practice, however, there have been instances where the management has been found to be running the company in a manner that serves their own interests. This is often at the cost of the interest of the principal, the shareholders. Such a situation is explained as agency conflict i.e. conflict of interests between shareholders and management. Possibility of such an agency conflict in the modern enterprises calls for mechanisms, procedures and structures to be put in place in order to prevent/minimize such conflicts and their consequences.

The split between ownership and management calls for putting in place certain corporate governance mechanisms.

The other stakeholders like lenders, customers, government too, have their stakes locked up in the business and expect the company management to manage its affairs in line with their interests. Increased instances of corporate frauds that have surfaced in the recent past underscore the need and importance for corporate governance i.e. governing the corporations in transparent and accountable manner. The proactive role that the regulators of capital markets have begun to play in the recent years to protect the interest of investors has also given an impetus to the institutionalization of CGframework.

The Governance Framework

In modern corporations, there are three levels of governance and control. At the highest level are the shareholders, the owners of the company, who are interested in consistent and sustained growth of the business. Since shareholders cannot meet frequently, they need to appoint a second level of control, empowered to oversee the managers who run the day-to-day operations of the company. This second level, the Board of

There is a three tier governance structure: Shareholders, Board of Directors, and management.

Directors (referred to as Board at some places) is elected by the shareholders to protect their interests. Board members must always act in the best interest of the stakeholders. The central role of the Board of Directors must therefore be to ensure that the company fulfills its responsibilities to shareholders, the government, the company's business partners, lenders, suppliers, customers, and also to society at large. When in the judgment of the Board the management of the company is not fulfilling these obligations, it is the Board's obligation to intervene and ensure that the interests of shareholders and other stakeholders are served. Boards of Directors and their committees meet throughout the year and provide strategic directions, guidance and oversight to the company management. They are responsible for the selection, evaluation and compensation of management. The third level of governance is done by the company management who are responsible for carrying out the day-to-day operations in the best interest of the shareholders and as per the guidelines laid down by the Board. Company management is headed by the chief executive of the company (President/ CEO). The company management is given reasonable autonomy by the board to carry out their operations effectively.

These three bodies, shareholders, the Board and management, account for the basic structure of a corporation. Besides, there are other supportive structures to ensure that the operations of the firm are run in efficient manner and in the best interest of the shareholders. Most prominent in this regard is the accounting and audit structure. The purpose of the accounting and audit structure is to ensure that the financial performance of the company is measured and reported in a transparent and fair manner as per the laws.

Board of Directors ensures that the management works in the best interest of stakeholders, while management works under strategic direction of the Board.

For a good governance of corporations it is essential that both the basic and support structures work efficiently. This requires activism on part of the shareholders to ensure that there is a competent board in place to guide, supervise, and control the company management to work in the best interest of the stakeholders. But due to the atomistic nature of shareholders they are not in a position to exercise effective control over the board in the general meetings. The Board, too, due to its composition is often found to be lacking in the intent and competence to give the necessary guidance and oversight to the company management. This leaves the stakeholders at the mercy of the company management who have often been found to be working towards their own agenda under the guise of shareholders' wealth maximization. Such a scenario underscores the need to put in place structures and processes that increase the accountability of the company management to the Board and that of Board to the shareholders and finally the accountability of the company as a whole to the various stakeholders and the society. At a macro level the CG framework is more of a regulatory nature focusing upon regulatory and listing requirements with an underlying objective of promoting transparent and efficient markets.

Lack of effective control of the shareholders over the Board and that of Board over the management underscores the need for corporate governance initiatives.

Meaning and definition of Corporate Governance

Corporate governance is the set of customs, processes, regulations, and institutions that aim at administering the affairs on an enterprise in a transparent and responsible manner, in the best interests of its varied stakeholders.

In a *narrow* sense[9], corporate governance involves a set of relationships amongst the company's management, and the various stakeholders like shareholders, auditors etc. These relationships determine the rules, processes, and structures for setting the objectives of the company and defining the means for attaining such objectives. Besides they also lay down the performance expectations and monitoring mechanisms there for. Thus, the key aspects of good corporate governance include transparency of corporate structures and operations; the accountability of managers and the boards to shareholders; and corporate responsibility towards stakeholders.

Corporate governance refers to a set of rules, processes, and structures to ensure that the company is run in a transparent and accountable manner.

In a *broader* sense[10], however, good corporate governance ensures that the companies are run in transparent manner. In this sense corporate governance enhances overall market confidence and thereby efficient allocation of capital. It is important to note that in both the narrow as well as in the broad definitions, the concepts of disclosure and transparency occupy centre-stage. In the first instance, they create trust at the firm level among the suppliers of finance. In the second instance, they create overall confidence at the aggregate economy level. In both cases, they result in efficient allocation of capital.

The thrust of Corporate Governance is to protect the interest of stakeholders in a company and enforce the accountability of the management to the board and that of board to the stakeholders through better disclosure, compliance, and institutionalized checks and balances. At a broader and macro level, Corporate Governance aims at regulating, monitoring, and disciplining the businesses in the best interests of the investors and society. This is to promote market integrity and transparency that facilitate efficient allocation of resources in the economy.

[9] Corporate Governance in India: Theory and practice, National Foundation for Corporate Governance, discussion paper, September 2004, pp.2.

[10] ibid

Principles of Corporate Governance

The theory of corporate governance emphasizes upon carrying out the business function in a responsible, accountable, and transparent manner taking care of the interest of the stakeholders in the business. Business should be run as if it is a trust and the board and management should behave as the trustees of the resources at their disposal. The commonly accepted principles of Corporate Governance are:

Transparency

Corporate Governance should aim at promoting transparency at different levels. At the level of company there should be transparency, to the extent it is practically possible, in the conduct of the company management and the board. At the macro level there should be transparency in reporting by the companies to the stakeholders and to the regulator. Since transparency and disclosure go hand in hand the CG framework should ensure that timely and accurate disclosure is made on all material matters regarding the corporation, including the financial situation, performance, ownership, and governance of the company.

Accountability

The corporate governance framework should ensure the accountability of both, the company to its stakeholders and board and management of the company to its shareholders. This calls for effective monitoring of the company by the regulator and that of management by the board, and the board's accountability to the company and the shareholders.

Protection of Shareholders' rights

Shareholders should have the right to participate in key corporate decisions, such as the nomination and election of board members. To exercise this right it is important that they get timely information regarding the venue and dates of board meetings and should get an opportunity to put items on the agenda of the board meetings, propose resolutions, and ask questions to the board. There should be equitable treatment of all the shareholders including the minority shareholders. Besides, the shareholders should have the right to vote, in person or in absentia. Also, there should be a proper grievance redressal mechanism. The CG framework should facilitate the shareholders to exercise their rights.

Involvement of stakeholders

The corporate governance framework should recognize the rights of stakeholders and provide for active co-operation between corporations and stakeholders in the process of wealth creation. The accessibility of relevant, sufficient and reliable information to the stakeholders assumes significance in this regard. The stakeholders should be given sufficient opportunity to participate in the governance process and also to express their opinion and concerns.

Regulatory framework for corporate governance

Better corporate governance adds considerable value to the operational performance of firms by improving the strategic thinking at the top by inducting independent directors who bring a wealth of experience, and a host of new ideas. Besides it also improves the integrity of the financial reports by institutionalizing the mechanisms and structures that reinforce, along with transparency, the accountability of the management in reporting the businesses performance to the various stakeholders. Further it also creates the checks and balances within the system to protect the interests of the stakeholders.

> *The regulatory framework focuses upon composition and conduct of board, and its committees; reporting and disclosure guidelines; grievance redressal mechanism; norms on certification and compliance.*

Sarbanes-Oxley Act (2002)

The United States federal law that was enacted on July 30, 2002 as a reaction to a number of major corporate and accounting scandals in the country involving the likes of Enron, WorldCom, etc.

Also known as the *'Public Company Accounting Reform and Investor Protection Act'* and *'Corporate and Auditing Accountability and Responsibility Act,'* the law focuses upon the regulation of financial practice and corporate governance of public companies.

Named after Senator Paul Sarbanes and Representative Michael Oxley, who were its main architects, it set new or enhanced standards for all U.S. public company boards, management and public accounting firms. it also set a number of deadlines for compliance.

Contains 11 titles, or sections ranging from independent oversight of public accounting firms to corporate responsibility. From enhanced financial disclosures to corporate fraud accountability.

There are several laws in place in India to ensure that the affairs of public companies are managed in the best interest of the stakeholders. Though the framework laid down by the Indian Companies Act, 1956, Securities contract (regulation) act, 1956 etc. drive the Indian companies to govern their affairs in a transparent and responsible manner, the provisions of Clause 49 of the listing arrangement under the SEBI act, 1992 specially focus on the issue of CG and provides a detailed framework for the same.

Clause 49 lays down the mechanisms, structures, and processes to ensure CG in the listed Indian firms. All the listed Indian companies having a paid up share capital of ₹.3 crores and above or net worth of ₹.25 crores or more are required to comply with Clause 49 of the listing arrangement. The clause provides a detailed regulatory framework regarding the board of directors, audit committees, disclosures, certification and compliance etc. What follows is the detailed description of such structures, mechanisms, or processes that have been either mandated or recommended by the clause 49.

Clause 49 of the listing arrangement

The clause that lays down the framework for the effective corporate governance of the listed Indian companies. The focus of the clause is to enhance accountability of the public firms to their stakeholders and to improve transparency through better disclosure. The salient features of the clause are:

- It applies to listed Indian companies with a paid up capital of at least ₹.3 crores or the net worth of at least ₹.25 crores
- Lays down the norms for the composition of the board of directors; non-executive directors on board to be at least 50%
- Mandatory disclosures by the directors to the company
- Code of conduct for the board members and for the senior management
- Skill enhancement of the board members through training interventions
- Specification of the minimum number of board meetings per year
- Audit committee to oversee the financial reporting process making it more transparent and credible
- Strengthening of the mechanism of whistle blower
- Better and detailed disclosures by the firms
- Certification by the CEO/ CFO of the company
- Grievance redressal mechanism for the shareholders.

Composition of Board of Directors, regulation of their conduct and operation

The Board of directors of the company should have an optimum combination of executive and non-executive directors with not less than fifty percent of the board of directors comprising of non-executive directors. Where the Chairman of the Board is a non-executive director, at least one-third of the Board should comprise of independent directors. A director shall not be a member in more than 10 committees or act as Chairman of more than five committees across all companies in which he is a director. Furthermore it is a mandatory annual requirement for every director to inform the company about the committee positions he occupies in other companies and notify changes as and when they take place. All fees/compensation, if any paid to non-executive directors, including independent directors, shall be fixed by the Board and shall require previous approval of shareholders in general meeting. The Board shall lay down a code of conduct for all Board members and senior management of the company. The code of conduct should be posted on the website of the company and all Board members and senior management personnel should affirm compliance with the code on an annual basis. The Annual Report of the company shall contain a declaration to this effect signed by the CEO. The board shall meet at least four times a year, with a maximum time gap of three months between any two meetings.

Composition, rights and duties of Audit Committee

With the objective of overseeing the company's financial reporting process and the disclosure of its financial information and to ensure that the financial statement is correct, sufficient and credible, a qualified and independent audit committee should be set up by every listed company to which clause 49 applies. All members of audit committee should be financially literate and at least one member shall have accounting or related financial management expertise. The committee shall have minimum three directors as members and two-thirds of the members of audit committee shall be independent directors. The Chairman of the Audit Committee shall be an independent director. The audit committee should meet at least four times in a year and not more than four months shall elapse between two meetings. Besides the monitoring of the firm's financial reporting process the audit committee also needs to carry out the following responsibilities:

- Recommending to the Board, regarding the appointment/ re-appointment/ replacement/ removal of the statutory auditor and the fixation of audit fees.
- Approval of payment to statutory auditors for any other services rendered by the statutory auditors.
- Reviewing, with the management, the annual financial statements and the quarterly financial statements before submission to the board for approval.
- Reviewing the Management discussion and analysis of financial condition and results of operations.
- Reviewing the Statement of significant related party transactions.
- Reviewing, with the management, performance of statutory and internal auditors and the adequacy of the internal control systems.
- Discussion with internal auditors any significant findings and follow up there on.
- Discussion with statutory auditors before the audit commences, about the nature and scope of audit as well as post-audit discussion to ascertain any area of concern.
- To review the functioning of the Whistle Blower mechanism, in case it is in place.
- Carrying out any other function as is mentioned in the terms of reference of the Audit Committee.

To carry out its responsibilities the audit committee is empowered to secure attendance of outsiders with relevant expertise, if it considers necessary; seek information from any employee; investigate any activity within its terms of reference; obtain outside legal or other professional advice.

Mandatory financial and non financial disclosures

The clause, with the objective of ensuring adequate and proper reporting makes the following disclosures mandatory for the companies that fall within its purview:

- A summary statement of transactions with related parties in the ordinary course of business should be placed periodically before the audit committee.
- Details of material individual transactions with related parties and others should be placed before the audit committee, together with management's justification for the same.
- Wherever in the preparation of financial statements, a treatment different from that prescribed in an Accounting Standard has been followed, the fact shall be disclosed in the financial statements, together with the management's explanation for such a deviation.
- The company shall lay down procedures to inform Board members about the risk assessment and minimization procedures. These procedures shall be periodically reviewed to ensure that executive management controls risk through means of a properly defined framework.
- When money is raised through an issue (public issues, rights issues, preferential issues etc.), the category wise uses / applications of funds should be disclosed to the

Audit Committee on a quarterly basis. Also, a statement of funds utilized for purposes other than those stated in the offer document should be placed before the audit committee on an annual basis.

- All pecuniary relationship or transactions of the non-executive directors vis-à-vis the company shall be disclosed in the Annual Report.
- All elements of remuneration package of individual directors should be disclosed by the companies in the corporate governance section of the Annual Report
- As part of the directors' report or as an addition thereto, a Management Discussion and Analysis report should form part of the Annual Report to the shareholders. This Management Discussion & Analysis should, inter alia include the industry structure and developments, perceived opportunities and threats, management's outlook, segment-wise or product-wise performance risks and concerns.
- The shareholders of the company should be provided with the Information regarding the credentials of the director in case of the appointment of a new director or re-appointment of a director.
- Quarterly results and presentations made by the company to analysts should be put on company's web-site, or shall be sent in such a form so as to enable the stock exchange on which the company is listed to put it on its own web-site.

Mechanism for redressal of Investors' grievance

A board committee under the chairmanship of a non-executive director shall be formed to specifically look into the redressal of shareholder and investors complaints like transfer of shares, non-receipt of balance sheet, non-receipt of declared dividends etc.

Certification by the key company officials

The CEO and the CFO, or any other person heading the finance function, shall certify to the Board that:

- They have reviewed financial statements for the year and that to the best of their knowledge and belief these statements do not contain any materially untrue statement or omit any material fact. These statements together present a true and fair view of the company's affairs and are in compliance with existing accounting standards, applicable laws and regulations.
- There are, to the best of their knowledge and belief, no transactions entered into by the company during the year which are fraudulent, illegal or violative of the company's code of conduct.
- They accept responsibility for establishing and maintaining internal controls and have evaluated the effectiveness of the internal control systems of the company.
- They have indicated to the auditors and the Audit committee regarding any significant changes in internal, accounting policies, any instances of significant fraud during the year.

Report on Corporate Governance

There shall be a separate section, containing the prescribed items, on Corporate Governance in the Annual Reports of company, with a detailed compliance report on Corporate Governance. Non-compliance of any mandatory requirement of this clause with reasons thereof and the extent to which the non-mandatory requirements have been adopted should be specifically highlighted. A quarterly compliance report signed either by the Compliance Officer or the Chief Executive Officer of the company should be submitted to the stock exchanges within 15 days from the close of quarter.

Certificate of Compliance

The company shall obtain a certificate from either the auditors or practicing company secretaries regarding compliance of conditions of CGas stipulated in this clause and annex the certificate with the directors' report, which is sent annually to all the shareholders of the company. The same certificate shall also be sent to the Stock Exchanges along with the annual report filed by the company.

Besides the aforesaid mandatory requirements there are certain non-mandatory requirements under clause 49. Some of these non-mandatory requirements are:

Setting up of remuneration committee

The board may set up a remuneration committee, with independent director as its chairman, to determine on their behalf and on behalf of the shareholders the company's policy on specific remuneration packages for executive directors including pension rights and any compensation payment.

Training of Board Members

To enable the board members to discharge their responsibilities effectively a company may train its board members in the business model of the company as well as the risk profile of the business parameters of the company. Besides they may also be made aware of their responsibilities as directors, and the best ways to discharge them.

Mechanism for evaluating non-executive Board Members

The performance evaluation of non-executive directors could be done by a peer group comprising the entire Board, excluding the director being evaluated.

Establishing and strengthening the mechanism of Whistle Blower

The company may establish a mechanism for employees to report to the management concerns about unethical behaviour, actual or suspected fraud or violation of the company's code of conduct or ethics policy. Such a mechanism could also provide for adequate safeguards against victimization of employees who avail of the mechanism and also provide for direct access to the Chairman of the Audit committee in exceptional cases. Once established, the existence of the mechanism may be appropriately communicated within the organization.

SUMMARY

The valuation of firms has become an extremely important activity of finance function in recent times. With increased globalization and liberalization the market environment is becoming less and less regulated, making market valuation as the order of the day. As competitions grow, firms look for expanding product lines and widening customer base shifting focus to inorganic growth.

Valuation of assets has become more and more market oriented. Besides fundamental factors affecting valuation, the market based factors such as conditions of demand and supply, the flow of information, and the level of market efficiency plays an important role in value determination. The issue of change in management control changes the valuation drastically.

One method of valuation is based on the published financial statements. Published statements provide only the book value of assets and liabilities and ignore the organization capital. These values may be far away from the market reality. The values of assets and liabilities as reflected in the balance sheet, therefore, are modified to indicate the market value. Where equity and debt both are traded the valuation is easy and the value of the firm is given by sum of market value of equity and debt.

Most valuation is based on the DCF approach capturing the future cash flows and discounting them at the cost of capital. The basic determinants of the future cash flow are dependent upon the investment needs, financing arrangements, and dividend policy. The determinants of cost of capital are risk free rate, the market risk premium, and the beta of the firm, besides the debt equity ratio and cost of debt.

Growth is a vital determinant of value. Since firms exhibit varying levels of growth in their life span normally multi-stage growth model are employed for valuation where cash flows for each phase of growth corresponding to different growth rates are valued. Under the DCF valuation, either the cash flow to the firm or cash flow to the equity can be valued using appropriate discount rates. DCF valuations, however, ignore the strategic values of enterprises available in the options to the management.

Another popular method of valuation of the firms is based on the premise that similar assets must command similar prices. This approach is called relative valuation. Normally, a key determinant of the value is identified and the multiple with market price is found for a comparable asset that is traded in the market. Using the same multiple for the known asset the valuation of the target firm is done by projecting the value of the key variable. Several modifications in the relative valuation are possible with regard to selection of determinants of value, and adjustments in the multiple. Relative valuation being market-based, carries the market distortions and biases in the valuation of the subject firm. There would be no error as long as distortions continue.

Of late, the focus has been shifting from pure valuation of the firm to the value creation. Value-based management emphasizes the creation of shareholders' or stakeholders' value. The traditional process of valuation ignores aspirations of the shareholders. Value creation is positive only when the firm meets the expectations of the stakeholders besides the operating cost. Most measures of value are cash flow based and incorporate capital cost.

One of the most popular measure of value is economic value added (EVA). The earnings of the firm is adjusted for operating income after taxes called NOPAT, from which the capital cost is subtracted to arrive at the economic value added. The major advantage of EVA is its ability to determine the contribution each strategic business unit makes to the overall value of the firm. Though the EVA calculations take care of market based expectations of the shareholders, it begins with the accounting profits. It is regarded as major drawback of EVA.

KEY TERMS

Adjusted balance sheet approach A method of valuation based on financial statements after making suitable adjustments to the value of assets and liabilities is called adjusted balance sheet approach.

Market value approach A method of valuation of the firm based on market value of equity and debts issued by the firm is called market value approach.

Free cash flow approach A valuation method of discounting the free cash flows of the firm with an appropriate discount rate is called free cash flow approach.

Free cash flow to firm (FCFF) Free cash flows available to all suppliers of capital to the firm after meeting business needs are called FCFF.

Free cash flow to equity (FCFE) Free cash flows available to suppliers of equity capital to the firm after meeting business needs are called FCFE.

Earnings multiple The ratio of market price to the earnings per share is called earnings multiple.

Book value multiple The ratio of market price to the book value per share is called book value multiple.

Revenue multiple The ratio of market value to the revenue is called revenue multiple.

KEY FORMULAE

Value of the Firm

$$V = \sum_{n=1}^{\infty} \frac{\text{Cash Flow for period } n;\ CF_n}{(1+\text{Discount Rate})^n}$$

Value of Equity $= \sum_{1}^{\infty} \frac{\text{Cash Flow of Equity Holders; } CFE_n}{(1+r_e)^n}$

Value of Levered Firm $V_L = V_U + TD$

Book Value Multiple $= \frac{ROE \times \text{Payout Ratio } (1+g)}{r-g}$

Cash Value Added

= Operating Cash Flow – OperatingCash Flow Demand

CFROI $= \frac{\text{Sustainable Cash Flow}}{\text{Cash Invested}}$

Relative Value of Growth

$$\frac{\text{Value of 1\% Growth (VG)}}{\text{Value of 1\% improvement in Margin (VM)}}$$

where

$$VG = \frac{\text{Current Cash Flow}}{WACC - (g + 1\%)} - \text{Current Value of the Firm}$$

$$VM = \frac{\text{Current Cash Flow} \times 1\% \times (1-T)}{WACC - g}$$

Economic Margin $= \frac{\text{Operating Cash Flow} - \text{Capital Charge}}{\text{Invested Capital}}$

Market Value Added

Market Value of the firm – Capital Employed

Economic Value Added

= NOPAT – WACC × Capital Employed

or EBIT × (1 – Tax Rate) – Capital Employed × WACC

PRACTICE PROBLEMS

1. Valuing a Firm with Zero Growth

Deeptam Ventures Ltd has entered the phase of maturity in its life cycle and its cash flows (before interest and taxes) are expected to remain constant at the current level of ₹550.25 lakh. Presently it is an all equity financed firm.

The cost of equity for Divyajyoti Enterprises, which resembles Deeptam in terms of its risk-return characteristics, is 15.75%. You are expected to find out the value of Deeptam Ventures. The tax rate applicable to Deeptam is 38.5%.

What will be the impact on firm's cost of equity, WACC and its valuation if the firm decides to alter its capital structure to have a 25% debt ratio. The cost of debt for firms with the risk profile similar to Deeptam Ventures is 10.25%.

Solution

(a) Value of the firm

= Value to equity holders + Value to debt holders

Since it is an unlevered firm, its valuation model will be:

Value of All Equity Firm V_u

$$= \frac{\text{Cash Flow to Equity Holders; } CFE_n}{r_0}$$

The cash flows for Deeptam Ventures are estimated as follows:

	(₹ in lakh)
Cash flow before interest and taxes	550.25
Interest	0
Cash flow before taxes	550.25
Taxes @ 38.5%	211.85
Cash flow after taxes	338.40

Cost of Equity for Deeptam Ventures (r_0) = 0.1575 (or 15.75%). The value of the firm is computed at ₹2148.60 lakh as below:

$$V_U = \frac{\text{Cash Flow to Equity Holders; } CFE_n}{r_0}$$

$$= \frac{338.40}{0.1575} = ₹2148.60 \text{ lakh}$$

Value of Deeptam ventures (unlevered), V_u = ₹2148.60 lakh

The value of levered firm increases by the amount of tax shield generated by debt. The amount of tax shield that is available on debt depends on the tax rate, T and the amount of debt, D. The value of levered firm therefore is:

Value of the levered firm, V_L =

Value of Unlevered firm (V_u) + Value of Tax Shield

$$V_L = V_u + T \times D$$
$$= ₹2148.60 \text{ lakh} + 0.385 \times 0.25 \times V_L$$
$$= ₹2377.42 \text{ lakh}$$

$$\text{Value of debt} = 0.25 \times V_L$$
$$= 0.25 \times 2377.42 = ₹594.36 \text{ lakh}$$

$$\text{Interest cost} = 10.25\% \times 594.36$$
$$= ₹60.92 \text{ lakh}$$

If Deeptam introduces debt in its capital structure, its cost of equity is likely to go up as its financial risk goes up.

The cost of equity in the levered firm is given by:

$$r_e = r_0 + \frac{D}{E}(1-T)(r_0 - r_d)$$

$$= 0.1575 + \frac{1}{3} \times (1 - 0.385) \times (0.1575 - 0.1025)$$

$$= 0.16878 \text{ (or } 16.88\%)$$

Value of equity is found by discounting the cash flow to equity holders with the cost of equity in the levered firm:

	₹ in lakh
Cash flow before interest and taxes	550.25
Interest	60.92
Cash flow before taxes	489.33
Taxes @ 38.5%	188.39
Cash flow to equity holders	300.94

$$\text{Value of Equity} = \frac{\text{Cash Flow to Equity Holders; } CFE_n}{r_e}$$

$$= \frac{300.94}{0.1688} = ₹1782.80 \text{ lakh}$$

Value of the Firm = Value of Debt + Value of Equity
= ₹594.36 lakh + ₹1782.80 lakh
= ₹2377 (Approx.)

Now we value the firm directly by discounting the cash flows to all suppliers of capital with the WACC of the firm. The cash flows are as follows:

	₹ in lakh
Cash flow to equity holders (₹ in lakh)	300.94
Cash flow to debt holders net of tax (₹ in lakh)	37.47
Total cash flow (₹ in lakh)	338.40

$$\text{WACC of the levered Firm (r)} = \frac{E}{E+D} r_e + \frac{D}{E+D} (1-T)\, r_d$$

$$r = \frac{3}{4} \times 0.1688 + \frac{1}{4} (0.615) \times 0.1025$$

$$= 0.1423 \text{ (or } 14.23\%)$$

$$\textit{Value of the firm} = \frac{\text{Cash Flow to Equity and Debt holders}}{\text{WACC}}$$

$$= \frac{338.40}{0.1423} = ₹2377 \text{ lakh (Approx.)}$$

2. Value of Equity using Two-Stage DDM

To give a boost to its sales that have plateued in the recent years, Metro Ltd has widened its product range by adding three new brands. Such a measure is likely to give a boost to its growth rate for the next seven years to a level of 30%. Thereafter (i.e., beginning from the eighth year) the growth rate is likely to taper off and settle at 8%. The current earnings per share of the firm is ₹5.25 and the company is currently following a policy of 40% payout. The firm is likely to maintain its payout for the next seven years, after which it is likely to go up to 70%. Current beta of Metro Ltd is 1.35, which is likely to come down to a level of 1.10 from eighth year onwards. The current yield on T-bills is 5.50% while the average market risk premium is 7.85%.

Calculate the expected current value of shares of Metro Ltd. Also calculate the expected share price at the end of seventh year. You can assume that the market conditions are likely to remain unchanged during the period.

Solution

The fundamental determinants of the value of equity for the growth and stable phase are as given below:

	High Growth (years 0–7)	***Stable Growth (year 8 onwards)***
Length of High Growth Phase (years)	7	—
Earning Per Share at Year 0	5.25	—
Dividend Payout Ratio	0.40	0.70
Dividend Per Share at Year 0	2.10	
Growth Rate	0.3 (or 30%)	0.08 (or 8%)
Beta	1.35	1.10
Risk-free Rate (in %)	5.50	5.50
Risk Premium (in %)	7.85	7.85

The cost of equity of Metro Ltd is computed as follows:

During High Growth Phase = $r_f + \beta\,(r_m - r_f)$
= 5.50% + 1.35 × 7.85% = 16.10%

During Stable Growth Phase = $r_f + \beta\,(r_m - r_f)$
= 5.50% + 1.10 × 7.85% = 14.14%

The earnings dividend and present value at 16.10% for the growth period of next 7 years are:

Value of Equity for the High growth phase (Year 1–7)

Year	**1**	**2**	**3**	**4**	**5**	**6**	**7**
Earning Per Share (₹)	6.83	8.87	11.53	14.99	19.49	25.34	32.94
Dividend Per Share (₹)	2.73	3.55	4.61	6.00	7.80	10.14	13.18
PV of dividend discounted at 16.10%	2.35	2.63	2.95	3.30	3.70	4.14	4.63
Value of Equity for the high growth phase →							**₹23.70**

The stable growth from 8th year onwards is valued using DDM as follows:

Value of Stable Growth Phase

Earnings for 8th Year (₹) = (Earnings in Year 7) × (1 + 0.08)	35.58
Dividend for 8th Year = (Earnings for 8th year) × (payout)	24.90
Terminal Price with *r* = 14.14% and *g* = 8%	405.62
PV of Terminal Price at 16.10%	142.66

The value of equity of the firm today is the sum of the present values of dividend for the high growth period and stable growth period.

Value of Equity of the firm = ₹23.70 + ₹142.66 = ₹166.36

Expected share price at the end of the 7th year = ₹406.42

3. FCFE Valuation

Converters Ltd is a manufacturer of CNG kits for cars. In view of growing petrol prices the demand for the CNG kits is likely to take the growth in firm's sales to a two digit level. The firm is expected to witness a high growth rate of 25% for the next seven years. At the end of this high growth phase other competitors are likely to enter in this segment and as the result firm will witness a transition from a high growth period to a more stable growth phase. This transition period is likely to last for three years from Year 8 to Year 10. During this transition period the growth rate will fall linearly and settle down at 10% at the end of transition period. The current earnings per share for the firm are ₹3.50.

To fund the maximum of its growing financing needs internally, Converters Ltd will follow the policy of ploughing back 75% of its earnings during the high growth phase. These retained earnings are expected to go down linearly during the three year transition period to a 30% level. The beta of the firm is expected to be maintained at 1.75 level during the high growth period, after which it is likely to fall linearly from 1.75 to 1.15 levels during the three years of transition period. This decline is expected in beta on account of reduced volatility in its cash flows starting from the transition period. The present risk free rate is 5.75% while the historic market risk premium has been 8.5%. You are required to value Converters Ltd using the Free Cash Flow to Equity (FCFE) approach.

Solution

Phase-wise summary of fundamentals for Converters Ltd

	High growth phase (Year 1–7)	*Transition phase (Year 8–10)*	*Stable growth phase (Year 10 onwards)*
Duration of High Growth Phase (yrs)	7	3	Indefinite
Earning Per Share (EPS) at t = 0 (₹)	3.50	—	—
Dividend Payout Ratio	0.25	0.70	0.70
Dividend Per Share (DPS) at t = 0 (₹)	0.875	—	—
Growth Rate (g)	0.25	0.10	0.10
Beta	1.75	Variable	1.15
Risk Free Rate (%)	5.75	5.75	5.75
Risk Premium (%)	8.50	8.50	8.50
Cost of Equity $[r_f + \beta\,(r_m - r_f)]$	20.63	Variable	15.53%

Valuation of Converters Ltd will be done, using the Dividend Discount Model, in three parts – (1) the valuation for high growth phase, (2) valuation for transition period, and (3) valuation for stable growth phase.

To begin with, we will find out the value for the high-growth phase:

For valuation purpose, we need to compute the dividend for the high growth phase using the present EPS and the projected growth rate for the high growth phase. This can be done as follows:

$$EPS_n = EPS_0\,(1 + g)^n$$
$$DPS_n = \text{Payout ratio} \times EPS_n$$

The cost of equity as determined by CAPM is 20.63% as shown in the summary above. This remains constant for the entire growth phase. The projected DPS for the high-growth phase will be discounted using this cost of equity to arrive at the present value of projected dividends during this phase. The summation of PV of dividends will be the value of equity for the high growth phase (Refer Table P10-3(a)).

Table 10-3(a) Valuation for High Growth Phase

(Figures in ₹)

Year	***1***	***2***	***3***	***4***	***5***	***6***	***7***
Earning Per Share	4.38	5.47	6.84	8.54	10.68	13.35	16.69
Dividend Per Share	1.09	1.37	1.71	2.14	2.67	3.34	4.17
PV of dividend (discounted at 20.63%)	0.907	0.940	0.974	1.009	1.045	1.083	1.123
Value of Equity for the High Growth Phase							**7.08**

Valuation of equity during the transition phase (Refer Table P10-3(b)) requires estimation of growth rate, cost of equity individually for each of the three years as they change every year. Since the growth rate falls linearly during these three years of transition, growth rates will be 20%, 15%, and 10% for year 8, 9, and 10 respectively. Similarly the cost of equity (i.e. the discounting factor) also needs to be estimated individually for each of the three years as beta declines linearly during the period.

Lastly, we value the dividends for the stable growth phase using constant growth dividend discount model (Refer Table P10-3(c)). The earning per share for the 11th year is:

$$EPS_{11} = EPS_{10} \times (1 + g)$$
$$= ₹25.33 \times (1 + 0.10) = ₹27.87$$
$$DPS_{11} = \text{Payout ratio} \times EPS_{11} = ₹19.51$$

The terminal value for Converters Ltd at the beginning of the stable growth phase is:

$$\text{Terminal Value using DDM} = \frac{D_{11}}{(r-g)} = \frac{19.51}{(0.1553 - 0.10)} = ₹352.76$$

Table 10-3(b) Valuation for Transition Phase

Year	***8***	***9***	***10***
Growth Rate	20%	15%	10%
Earning Per Share (₹)	20.03	23.03	25.33
Payout Ratio (%)	0.40	0.55	0.7
Dividend Per Share (₹)	8.01	12.67	17.73
Beta	1.55	1.35	1.15
Cost of Equity for the period $[r_f + \beta\,(r_m - r_f)]$ (%)	18.93	17.23	15.53
Discount Factor for the cash flow of the year	0.8408	0.7172	0.6208
Discounted Value of dividend for the year at beginning of transition phase	6.74	9.09	11.01
Value of Dividend of Transition Phase at its beginning (₹)			**26.83**
Value of Dividend of Transition Phase at beginning of Growth Phase (₹)			**7.22**

Table 10-3(c) Present Value for the Terminal Price of Converter Ltd

(Figures in ₹)

Year	*8*	*9*	*10*
Cost of Equity (%)	18.93	17.23	15.53
Discounted Value of Terminal Price at beginning of the year discounted at cost of equity applicable for the period	219.00	260.46	305.34
Discounted Value of Terminal Price at beginning of the Transition Period	—	219.00	
PV of Terminal Price—Today (Discounted at cost of equity of Growth Phase)	—	58.92	

This value is discounted at different rates for years 8, 9, and 10. The PV comes to ₹219.00 in year 8.

The continuing value of the firm is required to be discounted back to Year 0. Since during the transition phase the cost of equity is different in each year the discounting would not be uniform. The continuing value is discounted back at the beginning of transition phase (year 8) and then to the beginning of growth phase (year 0) as follows:

The total value of equity of Converter Ltd is	(₹)
1. Present Value of High Growth Phase	7.08
2. Present Value of Transition Phase	7.22
3. Present Value of Stable Growth Phase	58.92
Total Value per Share of Converter Ltd (1 + 2 + 3)	**73.22**

4. FCFF Valuation

Mico Steels is contemplating the acquisition of Triveni Ores. Iron ore being an important raw material input in steel production, such an acquisition is likely to assure the supply of iron ore by taking care of 65% of iron ore needs of Mico Steels. Triveni Ltd is likely to grow at a rapid pace during the first eight years after acquisition. Thereafter the growth rate will taper off and settle down at negligible level. Triveni Ltd is an unlevered firm with 25.75 crores outstanding equity shares and beta of 1.65. The projected earnings of Triveni Ores for the next eight years are given in Table P10-4(a).

Acquisition of Triveni Ores Ltd will enhance the debt raising capacity of Mico Ltd, which will be able to raise debt up to 25% of its value. The cost of debt for Triveni Ltd will be 9.75 %, the risk frees rate is 5.75% and the historical risk premium is 10.25%. The corporate tax rate is 38.5%. Find out the value of Triveni Ores Ltd.

Solution

Valuation of Triveni Ores Ltd requires estimation of its free cash flows (FCFs) and weighted average cost of capital (WACC). From the earnings projections we can arrive at the cash flows. The FCFs have been estimated in Table P10-4(b).

Table P10-4(a) Earnings Projections for Triveni Ores for the next 8 years

(Figures in ₹ crores unless stated otherwise)

	1	*2*	*3*	*4*	*5*	*6*	*7*	*8*
Profit before depreciation interest and tax (PBDIT)	204.25	238.97	279.60	327.13	382.74	397.86	368.02	322.02
Depreciation	71.49	89.62	106.25	147.21	95.69	208.88	193.21	169.06
Profit before interest and tax (PBIT)	132.76	149.36	173.35	179.92	287.06	188.98	174.81	152.96
Profit after tax (PAT)	81.65	91.86	106.61	110.65	176.54	116.23	107.51	94.07
No. of shares outstanding (in crores)	25.75	25.75	25.75	25.75	25.75	25.75	25.75	25.75
Earnings per share (EPS) (in ₹)	3.17	3.57	4.14	4.30	6.86	4.51	4.18	3.65
Capital expenditure	100.08	124.27	178.94	212.64	202.85	139.25	165.61	144.91
Change in Net Working Capital (ΔNWC)	30.64	35.85	41.94	49.07	57.41	59.68	55.20	48.30

Table P10-4(b) Projection of Free Cash Flows

(Figures in ₹ crores unless stated otherwise)

	1	*2*	*3*	*4*	*5*	*6*	*7*	*8*
PBDIT	204.25	238.97	279.60	327.13	382.74	397.86	368.02	322.02
Less: Depreciation	71.49	89.62	106.25	147.21	95.69	208.88	193.21	169.06
PBIT	132.76	149.36	173.35	179.92	287.06	188.98	174.81	152.96
Tax	51.11	57.50	66.74	69.27	110.52	72.76	67.30	58.89
PAT	81.65	91.86	106.61	110.65	176.54	116.23	107.51	94.07
Add: Depreciation	71.49	89.62	106.25	147.21	95.69	208.88	193.21	169.06
Less: Change in NWC	30.64	35.85	41.94	49.07	57.41	59.68	55.20	48.30
Less: Capital expenditure	100.08	124.27	178.94	212.64	202.85	139.25	165.61	144.91
Free Cash Flows (FCF)	22.42	21.36	–8.02	–3.84	11.96	126.17	79.91	69.92
Terminal Value								**307.74**
Net Cash Flows (NCFs)	22.42	21.36	–8.02	–3.84	11.96	126.17	79.91	377.66
PV factor at 22.72%	0.81	0.66	0.54	0.44	0.36	0.29	0.24	0.19
Present Value of NCFs	18.27	14.18	–4.34	–1.69	4.30	36.94	19.06	73.41

Let us now estimate the cost of equity and WACC for Triveni Ores Ltd. The beta of 1.65 for Triveni ores is an unlevered beta. Since after acquisition of Triveni Ores Ltd, Mico Ltd can raise debt up to 25% of its value, we need to find out levered beta using the unlevered beta.

$$\text{Levered equity beta} = \frac{\text{Unlevered beta}}{\text{Proportion of equity}}$$

$$= \frac{1.65}{0.75} = 2.2$$

Cost of equity for Triveni Ltd (using CAPM model)

$$= [r_f + \beta\,(r_m - r_f)]$$
$$= 5.75\% + (10.25) \times 2.2$$
$$= 28.3\%$$

$$\text{WACC for Triveni Ltd} = 28.3 \times 0.75 + 9.75 \times (1 - 0.385) \times 0.25$$
$$= 22.72\%$$

$$\text{Terminal value} = \frac{FCF_8}{WACC}$$

$$= \frac{69.92}{22.72} = ₹307.74 \text{ crore}$$

$$\text{Value of Triveni Ores Ltd} = \sum_{i=1}^{8} PV \text{ of NCFs}$$
$$= ₹160.12 \text{ crore}$$

5. Relative Valuation

Sanchar Ltd that was set up 10 years back is engaged in telecom business. After years of its successful market presence, the firm wants to up-scale its operations. To meet the financing requirements for its expansion plan, it is contemplating an IPO. The firm is planning to issue 1.5 crore equity shares. The projected earnings per share (EPS) for the firm is ₹3.25 while the projected revenue is ₹90.25 crore.

The price, earnings, book value, and revenue data of four firms–Alpha, Beta, Gamma, and Zeta Ltd–that are similar to Sanchar Ltd in all respects are given below.

	Projected EPS, Book Value, and Revenue (₹ per share)			Current market price (₹ per share)
	EPS	Book Value	Revenue	
Alpha Ltd	5.00	50	90	125
Beta Ltd	3.50	70	84	140
Gamma Ltd	4.50	65	78	165
Zeta Ltd	2.50	80	100	175

The firm is consulting its lead manager regarding the most suitable issue price for the IPO. What is your opinion to the firm regarding the issue price? It has been seen that market gives thrice as much importance to earning per share than either to book value or revenue.

Solution

Since the four firms are similar to Sanchar Ltd, the projected issue price should be based on the average price of the four firms.

The multiples based on current market price and projected earning, book value and revenue for the four similar firms are computed as follows:

	Projected EPS, Book Value, and Revenue (₹ per share)			Current market price per share (₹)	Multiples (times)		
	EPS	Book Value	Revenue		Earnings	Book Value	Revenue
Alpha Ltd	5.00	50	90	125	25.00	2.50	1.39
Beta Ltd	3.50	70	84	140	40.00	2.00	1.67
Gamma Ltd	4.50	65	78	165	36.67	2.54	2.12
Zeta Ltd	2.50	80	100	175	70.00	2.19	1.75
				Average	42.92	2.31	1.73

Since the objective is to find the issue price, which impacts the projected book value of the share, book value multiple may be ignored to avoid circular reference.

Projected EPS for Sanchar Ltd is given as 3.25 while the projected revenue (on a per share basis) can be computed as:

$$\frac{\text{Total projected revenue}}{\text{Projected no. of shares}} = \frac{90.25 \text{ crores}}{1.5 \text{ crores}} = ₹60.17$$

Based on the two multiples of earnings and revenue, the expected value of the share is computed as:

Based on earnings multiple = 42.92 × 3.25 = ₹139.48

Based on revenue multiple = 1.73 × 60.17= ₹104.10

Weighted average based on the assumption that market value is governed by thrice as much by earning than the revenue is: (3 × 139.48 + 1 × 104.10)/4 = ₹130.63

6. Computation of EVA

Compute EVA of Symphony Instruments Ltd from the financials given below:

	(₹ in crore)
Total Assets	500.00
Debt-equity ratio	0.25
Beta	1.19
Sales	1050.00
Cost of goods sold	288.75
Gross Profit	761.25
Administrative, Selling and Distribution overheads	325.00
Profit before interest and tax (PBIT)	436.25
Interest (@ 12% p.a)	12.00
Profit before tax (PBT)	424.25
Taxes (@ 38.5%)	163.34
Profit after tax (PAT)	260.91

The firm finances the asset base with 20% debt. The risk-free rate for the second period can be taken as 5.75% while the risk premium has been estimated as 10.35%. The beta for the firm is 1.19.

Solution

The computation of EVA is a three-step process.

Step 1: Arriving at NOPAT	(₹ *crore*)
Profit before Tax	424.25
Less: Taxes	–163.34
Add: Actual Interest (Post tax)	7.38
NOPAT	268.29

Alternatively, NOPAT can be calculated as:

$$\text{NOPAT} = \text{EBIT} \times (1 - T)$$
$$= 436.25 \times (1 - 0.385)$$
$$= ₹268.29 \text{ crores}$$

Step 2: Computing Weighted Average Cost of Capital (WACC)

WACC computation requires computation of cost of equity and cost of debt.

Cost of equity computation

Assumed rate of risk free return (%) = 0.0575 or (5.75%)

Expected Risk Premium on Equity (%) = 0.1035 or (10.35%)

Beta for Symphony Ltd = 1.19

Cost of equity for Symphony Ltd (using the CAPM model)

As per CAPM model $r_e = r_f + \beta \times (r_m - r_f)$

Cost of Equity r_e (%) = 5.75 + (1.19 × 10.35)

= 0.1807 or 18.07%

Cost of debt computation

Cost of debt before tax = 0.12 or (12%)

Cost of debt after tax = cost of debt before tax × (1 − *T*)

= 0.12 × (1 − 0.385) = 0.0738 (or 7.38%)

Computation of WACC

WACC (%) = (cost of debt × weight of debt)

+ (Cost of equity × weight of equity)

= (0.0738 × 0.2) + (0.1807 × 0.8)

= 0.1593 (or 15.93%)

Cost of capital for Symphony Ltd = (Capital employed × WACC)

= (₹500 crores × 0.1593)

= ₹79.65

Step 3: Finding EVA

EVA (₹ in crores) = NOPAT − Cost of capital

= 268.29 − 79.65

= ₹188.65 crore

Alternatively, EVA *can be stated as:*

EVA = Capital employed × (Return on capital employed − WACC)

$$= \left[\text{Capital employed} \times \left(\frac{\text{NOPAT}}{\text{Capital employed}}\right) - \text{WACC}\right]$$

$$\text{EVA} = 500 \times \left[\left(\frac{268.29}{500}\right) - 15.93\%\right]$$

= 500 × (53.66% − 15.93%)

= ₹188.65 crore

EXERCISES

Concept Review Questions

1. What is meant by valuation of the firm and why is it important?
2. What factors, besides fundamental to the firm, affect its valuation?
3. Describe the adjusted balance sheet approach to valuation. What are the limitations of such a valuation?
4. What is the difference between free cash flow to firm and free cash flow to equity?
5. What are the key fundamental factors or the key determinants affecting valuation of the firm?
6. Why is multi-stage DCF valuation is considered a necessity?
7. What are the merits and demerits of relative valuation?
8. How is value-based management different from DCF valuation?
9. Describe different measures of value.
10. What do you understand by Relative Value of Growth (RVG)?
11. How do you think EVA is different from MVA?
12. Explain the concept of EVA and the method of determining it with the help of an example.

Critical Thinking Questions

1. DCF valuation is a fruitless exercise for valuing the equity of a firm that is traded in the market. It is merely an attempt to justify if the market value is correct. If the market value is diverging from the DCF valuation more reliance must be placed on the market value. Do you agree with the opinion?
2. Value-based management really does not add anything new to the DCF valuation based on free cash flow to firm or equity. Do you agree?
3. If EVA is positive, MVA too has to be positive for any period. Comment.

Practical Assignments

1. Obtain last three years' balance sheet of any firm that has debt and equity. Find out the free cash flow to the firm and free cash flow to equity for the last three years.
2. In Assignment 1, determine if there is any growth in the cash flows to the firm and to the equity holders. Find beta of the firm and compute cost of equity and WACC to finally find the value of the firm.

Numerical Problems

1. Valuing a firm

(a) Find out the value of Zeta Ltd based on the following financial information.

1. The cash flow of Zeta Ltd (before interest and taxes) is at ₹1,50,000. The firm's cash flows are expected to remain constant.
2. The cost of equity for the firm resembling Zeta Ltd, in terms of its business and financial risk, is 16.5%
3. The tax rate applicable to the firm is 38.5%

(b) If the cost of debt to Zeta Ltd is estimated at 9.75% and the firm decides to alter its capital structure and have 20% debt in its capital structure, what will be the impact on firm's cost of equity, WACC and its valuation?

2. Value of Equity using Two-Stage DDM

Illuminated Enterprises, which has been in the business of manufacturing electrical lights, has launched a range of neon lights to give a boost to its growth rate. Such a measure is likely to give a growth rate for the next five years to a level of 25%.

Beginning from the sixth year, the growth rate of the firm is likely to come down and settle at 7%. The current earnings and dividend per share for the firm are ₹4 and ₹2, respectively. The firm is likely to maintain the current level of dividend payout for the next five years, after which the payout ratio is likely to go up to the level of 75%.

Currently T-bills provide yield of 5.75% and market risk premium is 8%. The beta for Illuminated Enterprises is 1.25. Beta value from fifth year onwards is likely to be at 1.15. Assuming that the market conditions remain unchanged, calculate the following for Illuminated Enterprises:

(a) Expected share price today, and
(b) Expected share price at the end of the growth phase

3. FCFF Valuation

Elements Ltd is one of the largest construction companies. The company has reported an EBITDA of ₹1450 crore during the year 2006-07. The interest expense for the firm was ₹160 crore while the depreciation was ₹350 crore in the year 2007. The total capital expenditure for the firm in the year 2007 was ₹300 crore while the working capital investment required to carry out the firm's operations was 8% of the revenues. The total revenues of the firm were ₹14,500 crore for the year ending 31 March 2007. The present risk free rate is 5.5% while market risk premium is 9.5%.

The corporate tax rate applicable to the company is 38.5% while the post tax cost of debt for the company is 9.5%. The beta of the firm is 1.20. The total outstanding debt for the firm was ₹3,120 crore (book value of debt). The market value of which stood at ₹3,250 crore. The current debt–equity ratio for the firm is 1:1.5 which is likely to come down to 1:2.

The firm expects a 15% growth in its revenues, earnings, depreciation, and capital expenditure in the next five years, after which the growth rate is expected to stabilize at 5%. (Capital spending is likely to offset the depreciation in the period of steady growth).

Based on the above information, you are required to determine the following:

(a) Estimated value of the firm
(b) Estimated value of equity capital, using FCFE valuation.

4. Relative Valuation

A firm, Unknown Ltd, is manufacturing a wide range of chemicals and intending to come out with an IPO to issue one crore shares. It is projecting an earning of ₹3 per share with the revenue of ₹65 crore. You have been able to identify four firms in the same line and, approximately, of the same size.

The following information is available with respect to these firms:

	Projected ₹ per share			***Current Price (₹)***
	EPS	***Book Value***	***Revenue***	
Firm 1	6.0	30	100	200
Firm 2	5.0	60	125	240
Firm 3	5.5	100	110	280
Firm 4	6.0	80	130	316

At what price can the firm issue its shares? Assume that the market gives thrice as much importance to earning per share than either to book value or revenue.

5. Computation of EVA

Given below is the extract of financial information of Bygone Ltd

	(₹ in crore)
Sales	300.00
Cost of goods sold	82.50
Gross Profit	217.50
Administrative, Selling and Distribution overheads	150.00
PBIT	67.50
Interest	9.00
PBT	58.50
Taxes (@ 38.5%)	22.52
PAT	35.98

The total assets of the firm are ₹150 crore. The shareholders equity has been used to finance 80% of the total assets of the firm. Assuming that the cost of equity for Bygone Ltd is 16.3% and cost of debt, which constitutes 20% of the assets financing, is 12% before tax compute the economic value added (EVA) for the firm.

CASE STUDY

Amara Raja Batteries*

Amara Raja Batteries (ARB) has been one of the dominant suppliers of automotive and industrial batteries in India. The company owns the brand name 'Amaron' which is the second largest aftermarket brand in the country today. Amaron is distributed through a pan India sales and service network comprising of 130 franchisees, over 95 PitStops, and 10,000 plus active retailers.

Amara Raja has ongoing OE agreements with Ashok Leyland, Eicher Motors, Fiat, General Motors, Hindustan Motors, Honda, Hyundai Motors, Mahindra & Mahindra, Maruti, Swaraj Mazda, and Tata Motors. The company is an exclusive supplier to Daimler Chrysler and Ford and to select platforms such as Honda Accord, Chevrolet Optra, Tavera, and Maruti Swift. Amara Raja exports its automotive batteries to various countries including Japan, Singapore, China, and Australia.

Amara Raja is a leading player in Industrial VRLA batteries. The company had pioneered VRLA technology in India in the early nineties and is supplier to telecom companies including BSNL, VSNL, MTNL, Bharti, Idea, and Hutch.

*Financial information for the case study has been taken from www.Indiaearnings.com, accessed on 10 July 2007.

The company is listed on the Mumbai Stock Exchange and The National Stock Exchange and is actively traded. Assume that the beta of the firm is 1.15. The risk free rate as estimated on the T-bills yield is around 6.5% and the market risk premium is estimated at 12%.

Their operating results for the last five years is given in Table A.

Table A Profit and Loss Account

(₹ crore)

Particulars	Mar '02	Mar '03	Mar '04	Mar '05	Mar '06
Net Sales	163.85	172.47	175.87	235.76	391.69
Other Income	5.99	2.98	4.16	6.42	7.35
Stock Adjustments	7.23	0.93	1.11	7.10	4.16
Total Income	**177.07**	**176.38**	**181.14**	**249.28**	**403.20**
Total Expenses	143.23	152.58	167.51	221.94	349.84
PBDIT	**33.84**	**23.80**	**13.63**	**27.34**	**53.36**
Interest	0.67	0.38	0.18	0.14	1.34
Depreciation	8.41	11.70	12.31	13.63	14.70
Profit Before Tax	24.76	11.72	1.14	13.57	37.32
Tax	6.54	4.32	0.25	4.88	13.48
Net Profit	**18.22**	**7.40**	**1.39**	**8.69**	**23.84**
Equity Dividend	3.99	1.71	1.71	2.28	2.85
Corporate Dividend Tax	—	0.21	0.22	0.32	4.00
Retained Earnings	**14.23**	**5.48**	**0.54**	**6.09**	**16.99**
Per share data (annualized)					
Shares in issue (lakh)	113.90	113.90	113.90	113.90	113.90
Earning per Share(₹)	16.00	6.50	1.22	7.63	20.93
Equity Dividend (%)	35.00	15.00	15.00	20.00	25.00

The financial position for the last five years is shown in Table B:

Table B Balance Sheet

(₹ crore)

	Mar '02	Mar '03	Mar '04	Mar '05	Mar'06
Equity Share Capital	11.39	11.39	11.39	11.39	11.39
Reserves	158.27	163.75	163.21	169.30	189.90
Net worth	**169.66**	**175.14**	**174.60**	**180.69**	**201.29**
Secured Loans	5.62	1.07	4.49	7.36	16.23
Unsecured Loans	7.74	8.67	10.39	15.94	21.64
Total Debt	**13.36**	**9.74**	**14.88**	**23.30**	**37.87**
Total Liabilities	**183.02**	**184.88**	**189.48**	**203.99**	**239.16**
Gross Block	141.06	151.37	158.35	167.23	190.71
Less: Accum. Depreciation	35.87	46.89	59.16	72.37	86.36
Net Block	**105.19**	**104.48**	**99.19**	**94.86**	**104.35**
Capital Work in Progress	**4.28**	**4.23**	**0.95**	**1.29**	**4.82**
Investments	**13.03**	**13.16**	**20.88**	**23.56**	**32.01**
Current Assets	120.37	122.72	119.84	162.67	230.58*
Total CL and Provisions	70.75	69.93	51.38	78.39	132.60
Net Current Assets	**49.62**	**52.79**	**68.46**	**84.28**	**97.98**
Miscellaneous Expenses	**10.90**	**10.22**	—	—	—
Total Assets	**183.02**	**184.88**	**189.48**	**203.99**	**239.16**

* includes a cash balance of ₹20.52 crore

For the financial year ending 31 March 2007, the company reported the gross income of ₹ 605.57 crore with the PBDIT of ₹91.29 crore. The depreciation and interest amount to ₹17.00 crore and ₹3.09 crore, respectively. After providing for tax of ₹25.15 crore the PAT of the company stood at ₹47.04 crore giving an EPS of ₹41.30. It recommended a dividend of ₹3.50 per share on the capital of ₹11.39 crore. With reserves amounting to ₹232.28 crore, the book value of the share increased to about ₹214.

A few critical financial parameters are listed in Table C:

Table C Critical Financial Parameters

	Mar '02	Mar '03	Mar '04	Mar '05	Mar '06
Adjusted Net Profit Margin (%)	9.66	3.72	0.70	3.24	5.35
Profit Before Interest and Tax Margin (%)	13.49	6.09	0.66	5.11	8.67
Return on Capital Employed (%)	14.41	6.98	0.73	6.97	17.45
Return on Net Worth (%)	10.80	4.29	0.79	4.89	12.48
Current Ratio	1.95	1.65	1.91	2.00	1.68
Debt Equity Ratio	0.10	0.07	0.07	0.11	0.16

The company has been on a steady growth path of growth. 'Overall, we are looking at a Capex for this year and some of them would be residual Capex for the previous year as well. We are looking at a Capex of close to ₹90–95 crore and over and above this, we also have ₹88 crore coming in,' said its CEO. He further added, 'We have announced in our release that we expect the expansion to be completed by Q2 of next fiscal, i.e., by September 2007.'

On 26 June 2007, the stock traded at ₹453 and as per the estimates of HDFC Securities it currently trades at 8.5 × and 7.3 × their FY08E and FY09 EPS estimates of ₹53.3 and ₹62.6. According to them, the revenue growth was mainly driven by a robust demand for industrial and automotive batteries. They expected the operating performance of the company to be under pressure with lead prices touching new highs. With two-wheeler batteries and increasing exposure in the industrial battery segment a growth of 35% growth in product volumes with an average realization growth in line with lead prices.

Discuss

1. Estimate the free cash flow to equity for the year ended March 2006.
2. Based on the performance of the firm for March 2007 find the free cash flows to equity.
3. Assuming that the growth in the cash flows to equity as provided in the year 2007 continues for next five years find the free cash flows to equity for next five years.
4. Assume a growth of 5% after five years find the current value of the equity using DCF method.
5. Does your value of equity agree with the relative valuation of HDFC?

In the CD

EVA Calculator

PART THREE

INVESTMENT DECISION

CHAPTER

11

Capital Budgeting-I

LEARNING OBJECTIVES

After going thorough this chapter, you will be able to:

- explain capital budgeting and the different types of capital budgeting proposals
- understand the various techniques of evaluation of investment proposal
- learn about accounting rate of return (ARR) method, payback period method, NPV method, and IRR method
- compute payback period and discounted payback period
- compare the NPV method and IRR method
- examine the relevant cash flows for investment projects
- project cash flows for replacement projects
- match cash flows with the discount rate
- learn how to treat inflation in capital budgeting

SHALINI, LCD TV, AND CAPITAL BUDGETING

Shalini, who works in a renowned multinational company, has just been informed by the Managing Director of her company that she is being transferred to the planning department. 'It is a very key position because we are now embarking upon a major expansion plan. I have complete faith in your abilities and your new role would be to help me take decisions on expansion,' said her MD.

Shalini, though happy, was a bit perplexed. She confided in her husband, Chander, 'How would I meet the expectations of my MD. You have done an MBA in finance. Tell me how to appraise complicated projects. I don't even know how to assess whether to buy a big screen LCD TV for the house or not.'

Chander said, 'That is not exactly a capital budgeting situation that we face in the work environment. But still I would attempt to explain. First, we need to estimate the exact initial cost.'

Shalini responded, 'As a dealer informed, all I know is that dealer quoted ₹1.17 lakh after our last negotiations.'

Chander elaborated, 'That is the cost of the TV only. Have you added the cost of installation, which would be around ₹4,000? A few accessories and cables would cost another ₹2,000. That would make the cost ₹1.23 lakh. Besides, I think we need to consider another thing. The dealer is also prepared to take our old spare music system for ₹3,000 against the payment.'

Shalini enquired, 'What the old music system has to do with the TV?'

Chander clarified, 'It does, because that would reduce our initial cash outlay. So the initial cost of the TV would be ₹1.20 lakh.'

Nodding her head, Shalini clarifying her doubt asked, 'You mean, we need to consider all such small things.'

Chander emphasized, 'Yes, sometimes these small things become big and effect a decision.'

Shalini questioned, 'We have already laid the cable in the house when we bought it. What about its cost?'

With a look of an expert on his face, 'That is a sunk cost. It does not impact our decision to buy an LCD TV. Hence, we ignore it.'

Shalini was getting impressed and more inquisitive. She said, 'What next?'

'Next, we have to project the differential cash flows for the life of the project and compare them to the initial capital outlay. In our case, it is 42' LCD TV,' replied Chander.

Shalini was again bemused at the term and questioned, 'What do you mean by differential cash flow?'

'In simple terms, it is the cash flow between having the TV and not having it. For example, if we have the TV, we would possibly go for a movie only on two out of the four weekends in a month. If each weekend movie costs us around ₹1,000, we would save around ₹2,000 in a month.' said Chander in a professor-like manner.

Asked Shalini, 'What about the other programmes that we shall be watching now?'

Chander, after a little thought answered, 'That is the side-effect that we must include. In our case, it is difficult to put a value to such additional entertainment we would have. Even if we value soaps and serials at paltry ₹10–11 per hour, with three hours of watching every day, it means around ₹1,000 in a month.'

Shalini had another question, 'What about the cost of electricity and the charges to the cable*walla* as security deposit and monthly rentals?'

Chander responded, 'Both of them are costs. It would cost us ₹500 every month for the electricity and cable connection. This would reduce our benefit to ₹2,500 per month. But the security deposit is a one time payment. This must be added to the capital cost and assumed available and released once we do not have the TV.'

'OK. So you are valuing the benefit at ₹2,500 per month or ₹30,000 per annum. That sounds good. For a cost of ₹1,20,000 per annum our return is good 25%.' said Shalini.

'Yes you are right,' said Chander, adding, 'but that is not the way projects are evaluated. There are several other things that need to be examined.'

'Like what?' asked Shalini.

Chander said, 'You see, technology in entertainment is changing very fast. You are assuming that the new LCD TV would last forever and no new superior product would come. In this case, we need to consider the payback period which is four years. Are you sure you would not demand a new TV for the next four years? If you don't, our TV shall remain state-of-the-art and we go ahead buying it.'

Shalini was quick to conclude, 'So we are buying the TV next Sunday.'

Looking at the anxiety on Shalini's face, Chander strongly stated, 'No. Not yet. I was just discussing about how to appraise the proposal and not buying a TV. Your lesson is still incomplete. You had learnt something about the cost of funds. We have not yet accounted for that. The sum of ₹1,20,000 you put in now would have earned you something. We are going to fund this by selling some shares on which we have been earning around 20% return. We have to forego this if we buy a TV.'

Shalini emphatically added, 'But our return is 25% as I just said and you nodded.'

Chander clarified quickly, 'Yes that is true if we ignore the time factor. The benefit of ₹30,000 we have in the first year is not same as the benefit we have in the third year. So we need to value these benefits in terms of time and the opportunity lost to make money otherwise. Even the first year benefit in terms of today's cost is equal to 30,000/1.2 = ₹25,000. Assuming we have this TV for five years and the benefit for each year is ₹30,000 we shall discount at 20% per annum. Further, we would assume that at the end of ten years the TV shall be obsolete and the *kabariwala* (junk collector) would give us no more than ₹5,000 for it.'

'This is getting complicated. Simply tell me are we buying the TV or not,' said Shalini, a little annoyed.

Chander grabbed his book on financial management. Referring to the tables in the end, he summarized, 'I need to calculate if the *value of benefit exceeds the capital cost in today's terms*. If it does, we buy it, else we forget about it. My calculator tells me that the present value of Re 1 every year for next 10 years at 20% discounting is ₹4.1925. Hence, the present value of the benefits is around ₹1,26,000 plus the present value of ₹5,000 the *kabariwala* (junk collector) would give us then and the security deposit that would be refunded. Clearly, since the present value of *benefits exceeds the cost*, we buy the TV.'

Glad at the outcome, Shalini smiled and said, 'So we buy the TV. You are a good husband. I think I shall be taking lot of your help regularly in the coming months.'

'Don't worry, as long as you pay me for my time and knowledge, it is ok,' said Chander joking.

'But that would be added to the cost that can make the TV unviable. I'd rather not pay you anything,' said Shalini laughing.

INTRODUCTION

Capital budgeting decision is perhaps the single most important corporate decision that consumes a major part of the management's time and money. Capital budgeting deals with the question of what assets should a firm acquire. It refers to the desirability of acceptance or rejection of a project based on systematic evaluation of project parameters that are translated in financial terms and weighed against a decision making rule. It is a strategic decision, which determines the growth and survival of a firm in this competitive world. The lack of capital budgeting proposals in any enterprise is a signal that the firm is languishing over a period of time. The firms' management must always be on the look out for fresh business opportunities and its evaluation as to how these opportunities fit into the overall scheme of business.

Capital budgeting decisions relate to acquisition of asset and generally have long-term strategic implications for the firm.

Since the business opportunities available in the environment are always huge as compared to the resources, financial or otherwise, available with the firm, capital budgeting decisions becomes fairly intricate as it impacts other areas of corporate finance like capital structure, dividends and cost of capital. Capital budgeting decision is often referred to as an investment decision of the firm where the allocation of capital among the different projects is decided.

FEATURES OF CAPITAL BUDGETING DECISION

Since the capital budgeting decisions concern the acquisition of asset, they should encompass broader strategic aspects like launching of new products, renovations of existing plants, replacement of machines, buying a technology, initiating R & D programmes, etc. A run-of-the-mill evaluation of capital budgeting proposals is least desired. It is an intricate decision posing several issues that are difficult to resolve. Most capital budgeting decisions are characterized by the following features:

Capital budgeting decisions generally involve large outlays, are difficult to reverse, risky propositions offering no scope of adjustment based on learning.

Non-reversible The strategic decisions are often irreversible; implying that the utmost caution must be exercised while making a decision. Though there are possibilities of abandoning a decision if wrongly made, the cost of such abandonment will be huge. Consider a situation where a firm has acquired a plant only to learn subsequently that the wrong acquisition was made. In case it wants to reverse this decision the cost of doing so would be enormous in most cases.

Large initial outlays followed by small periodic inflows In a typical capital budgeting exercise, the initial outflow of capital is rather large, making it mandatory for the firm to evaluate the financing options, unlike many routine decisions where the capital outlay is not huge. This initial one-time cash outflow is normally followed by regular cash inflows over extended periods spanning the life of the project.

Information gap and inexperience Capital budgeting decisions are either completely or somewhat new to the managers and the management of the firm. Although in some cases, the managers may be experienced about the project being evaluated, the gaps in the knowledge about technology, markets, and processes may impede decision making. Further, more often than not, the managers do not have sufficient and reliable data on which to base judgments and make well-informed decisions. This forces the managers to rely on their intuition, skills, and past experiences on similar projects and situations.

Strategic and risky nature Capital budgeting decisions are long lasting and have long-term implications on the value of the firm. The analytical framework for making such decisions, therefore, includes broader objectives, which may extend well beyond the foreseeable future. To that extent, the uncertainties with the data used in the framework for decision making increase as we go farther into the future, making them highly risky.

Inflexibility Since the decisions are one time, they offer little scope for adjustment for learning with the experience. Unlike working capital decisions, which are repetitive in nature and offer scope of correction based on learning, the capital budgeting decisions have little scope of adjustment with learning. More often than not, one has to live with the decision taken once. Therefore, the evaluation of all courses of action must be reviewed and decided in the beginning itself.

Strategic nature and uncertainties with the capital budgeting proposals call for tremendous amount of planning, care, and systematic evaluation. It becomes a time consuming process since knowledge gaps are to be filled.

A firm undertakes a wide variety of projects over time to ensure its survival and growth. Firms are constantly on the look out for new opportunities for sustained growth. The process of capital budgeting decisions involves the following steps:

1. Identifying investment opportunities
2. Short-listing of identified opportunities that match certain prerequisites
3. Collecting of relevant data of revenue, costs, cash flows, etc.
4. Selecting proper evaluation criteria
5. Make a decision of acceptance or rejection based on the evaluation criteria

TYPES OF PROJECTS

From the perspective of evaluation, these projects may be classified in different ways that have impact on the process of capital budgeting, such as, selection of evaluation criteria, efforts required for gathering information, desired level of accuracy of data, and the urgency of making decisions. Some of the classifications are illustrated in this section.

Small vs large projects

The projects can be classified in terms of their size. Firms normally have to spend considerable energy, cost, efforts, and time in searching, collecting, and evaluating the information. Reliability and accuracy of the data, and selection of appropriate criteria are other issues that must be determined. The time, efforts and cost spent on the exercise of capital budgeting must be justified by the benefits of such exercise. Small projects may not warrant as careful examination as large projects.

New vs expansion projects

Firms normally start with small projects and then go on to expand the capacities gradually over a period of time. The expansion is a result of increased demand for the product. Once the desired level of capacity is achieved firms start thinking in terms of diversifying in related new products or venture out in new unrelated fields. A firm producing paper products may first expand its capacity, then look for opportunities for forward or backward integration, and ultimately may undertake altogether new ventures like buying a ship or entering a telecom business.

In terms of the capital budgeting exercise, the evaluation of an expansion project and a new project is significantly different. The ease and speed with which a firm can collect reliable and accurate information for expansion project is not the same for new projects. It takes much longer and costs more to gather relevant information for new projects. Also the level of confidence in the relevant information for a new project is also lesser. Further, new projects warrant attention at higher managerial levels.

Independent and mutually exclusive projects

Another way the projects can be classified is on the basis of the way they interact among themselves. The projects that do not have any dependence on other projects are called independent projects. Mutually exclusive projects have 'either-or' situation. Acceptance of one project implies the rejection of another. The example of mutually exclusive projects often refers to the selection of one of the many technologies that are available to manufacture a product. As is evident, the evaluation of mutually exclusive projects require deeper thought as only one of many projects can be chosen and rest have to be rejected, while independent projects offer greater flexibility because they can be accepted now or later.

TECHNIQUES OF EVALUATION OF CAPITAL BUDGETING DECISIONS

There are many techniques available to evaluate capital expenditure proposals. All these techniques may not be useful in evaluation of all kinds of projects. One has to choose an appropriate criterion for acceptance or rejection. The selection may be basedon the simplicity of criteria, data requirement, criticality of decision and effectiveness.

The methods of financial evaluation of the projects are categorized into discounted cash flow (DCF) techniques and Non-DCF techniques. DCF techniques value the projects with time value of money.

The techniques of evaluation of capital budgeting can broadly be categorized as—(1) discounted cash flow (DCF) based techniques; or (2) non-DCF based techniques. Discounted cash flow based techniques evaluate the proposals on the basis of cash flows in different periods, timings of such cash flows, and the risk perceived with cash flows. Non-DCF based techniques may not consider all above aspects. We first discuss non-DCF based techniques of—(1) accounting rate of return; and (2) pay back period.

ACCOUNTING RATE OF RETURN

One of the natural ways of deciding whether or not a venture should be undertaken is based on the profit the project would generate. These levels of profit need to be compared with the initial cost of the project. If the levels of profit are deemed to be enough and meet the expectations of the investors, the project is accepted else it is abandoned.

Accounting Rate of Return is defined as average profit as % of average investment over the life of the project.

The accounting rate of return (ARR) is defined as average rate of return over the initial investment as given by Equation 11-1.

$$\text{ARR} = \frac{\text{Average profit}}{\text{Average investment}} \qquad (11\text{-}1)$$

Let us consider an example of computing ARR. All of us are familiar with the accounting statements prepared by any firm. They indicate the income and the expenses that are incurred. The bottom line of such statements is the profit made by the firm. As an illustration let us consider a rather simple situation of a firm MobTel that wants to install a MagicMachine costing ₹10 crore which is capable of producing 10,000 mobile telephone handsets every month. MobTel has entered into a five-year agreement with a marketing firm that has undertaken to lift 80,000 handsets in the first year with 20% increase for next two years for a fixed price of ₹3,000 per handset. MobTel has also concluded a similar agreement with the component supplier who has agreed to supply all the components at a fixed price of ₹2,300 per handset. The MagicMachine is depreciated over its life of five years on a straight-line basis. MobTel attracts income tax at 40%.

Based on the above information, the accountant of MobTel has prepared a statement of income as given in Table 11-1.

Table 11-1 Income statement of MobTel

	1st Year	*2nd Year*	*3rd Year*	*4th Year*	*5th Year*
Nos. of Handsets sold	80,000	96,000	1,15,200	1,15,200	1,15,200
		(₹ in lakh)			
Revenue	2400	2880	3456	3456	3456
Raw Material Cost	1840	2208	2650	2650	2650
Other Expenses	200	250	300	300	300
Depreciation	200	200	200	200	200
Total Cost	2240	2658	3150	3150	3150
Earnings Before Taxes	160	222	306	306	306
Taxes @ 40%	64	89	122	122	122
Net Income	**96**	**133**	**184**	**184**	**184**

Since the net income is varying in each of the year the returns on investment for each year will be different. To make judgment on the basis of the income of any single year will be erroneous. In order to have an overall view of the earnings it will be prudent to average out the income. The average of the income over the life of the magic machine is:

(96 + 133 + 184 + 184 + 184)/5 = ₹156.20 lakh

The initial investment of ₹1,000 lakh was charged uniformly to expense by way of depreciation over the life of the MagicMachine of 5 years. Therefore the average investment was ₹1,000/2 = ₹500 lakh. Using Equation 11-1 we find the ARR as 31.24%

$$\text{ARR} = \frac{\text{Average profit}}{\text{Average investment}} = \frac{156.20}{500} = 31.24\%$$

The Decision-making Criteria

Simply calculating the ARR is not of much help. It is merely a number, which reflects the worthiness of the project in absolute terms. To enable the firm make a conscious decision whether to accept or reject a proposal, it needs to be compared with some acceptance/rejection criteria. The management must, beforehand, set a target rate of return for acceptance of the project. If the ARR exceeds the target rate of return, the firm accepts the proposal, else it is rejected. For example, if the required rate of return for MobTel is 35% they would reject the proposal. On the other hand, if the required rate of return is 25% the management would accept the proposal.

Merits and Demerits

The method of calculation is simple. More often than not, the accounting information is easily available and easy to interpret. One does not require the deep understanding of financial accounting concepts. It is easily comprehendible to all persons with or without an education in finance. However, for capital budgeting decisions the use of accounting information is rather naïve. One must guard against the fallacies of accounting. However, the disadvantages include (1) subjectivity in approach, (2) ignoring the time value of money, (3) ignoring the cash flows and (4) some ambiguity about the definition.

PAYBACK PERIOD METHOD

Another method by which firms make decision is by figuring out when it will get its initial investment back. The rule operates on the basis of projected cash flows expected from a project. The cash inflows from the project are compared with the initial outflow of cash and determine the time (typically, in number of years) it takes to recover the initial cash outflow.

Payback period of the project is the time required to recover the investment. When done on discounted cash flow basis it is called discounted payback period.

As a simple example, to understand the application of payback method, let us consider the cash flows of a project as given in Table 11-2. Of the initial investment of ₹10 lakh, the project provides cash inflows of ₹3 lakh, 5 lakh, 4 lakh and 5 lakh from Year 1 to Year 4, respectively. Now we calculate the time within which one gets back the initial investment. It returns ₹8 lakh in the first two years. During the third year the cash inflow is ₹4 lakh. It can be assumed that remaining ₹2 lakh of the investment will be recovered in six months. By simple extrapolation we can say that the initial investment of ₹10 lakh will be recovered in two-and-a half years. Alternatively stated, the payback period for the project is two-and-a-half years.

Table 11-2 Cash flows of a project

	(Figures in ₹)
Initial cash outflow	10,00,000
Cash inflows	
1st Year	3,00,000
2nd Year	5,00,000
3rd Year	4,00,000
4th Year	5,00,000

Decision-making Criteria

To make a decision for acceptance or rejection of the project this payback period is compared with the predetermined time frame for the project and following rule applied:

If the payback period is < *n*; a predetermined cut-off time period; **Accept the project**

If the payback period is > *n*; a predetermined cut-off time period; **Reject the project**

In the above case, if the decision making criteria is set as a cut-off payback period of three years, the project will be accepted. On the other hand, if the management has prescribed two years as an outer limit for the acceptance of investment opportunities, the project will be rejected as the payback period exceeds two years. The application of the payback rule is fairly simple and straightforward. Accept the projects that have payback period less than the predetermined time limit, else reject.

Merits

The merit of the payback method of evaluating the capital budgeting projects is the simplicity of the rule. As firms take a large number of decisions they need simple but effective rules that eliminate detailed analysis and yet reduce the chances of making a wrong decision. From the management's perspective, the payback rule effectively addresses some of the concerns as highlighted below:

The desire for liquidity and frequent rotation of funds

All firms normally face a shortage of capital as they have more business opportunities than the resources at hand permit. Therefore, the management is always anxious to have pay back as early as possible. Thus, a rule that incorporates the factor of the availability of funds is welcome. The payback rule lays emphasis on liquidity coupled with profitability.

If the payback period is less than the predetermined cut-off, the project is accepted, else rejected. It is one way of resolving risks and emphasizing on liquidity.

Greater efficiency of capital Related to the point mentioned above is the aspect of utilization of capital. The sooner the cash is available, the sooner it is deployed in the investment opportunities, the better shall be the efficiency of capital. It is the endeavour of management to keep the financial resources utilized for most time. The sooner a project pays back, the lesser will be the waiting time for other projects. The timely availability of funds is paramount to the success of the firm.

Reducing risk associated with time Uncertainties of the cash flows increase with time. The more distant cash flows are considered riskier than the near future cash flows. Hence, the projects that have lesser payback period are deemed safer than the projects with longer payback periods. Prescribing a cut-off payback period, in a way, reflects the management's appetite for risk. The measurement of risk is a complex process and payback period attempts to express risk in rather simple form.

In view of the above, the pay back rule is very effective for small projects. However, for the larger projects, the payback rule may be adopted as an additional tool of decision making while the basic framework for evaluation of projects should be more elaborate.

Demerits

The disadvantages of the payback rule are similar to that of the ARR rule. They are:

Arbitrary selection of cut-off The benchmark for acceptance of the project, i.e., the cut-off value of payback period is chosen rather arbitrarily. It is determined subjectively based on the perspective of the management of the firm. Here again, the managerial discretion is not supported by objective data. The arbitrarily chosen cut-off payback period may reject some of the projects that may ultimately result in the enhancement of shareholders' wealth. The focus of the method is on liquidity rather than profitability.

Ignores time value of money The payback rule, like the ARR, ignores the time value of money. It assigns equal importance to all the cash flows that take place prior to payback period. For example, it will treat the following two projects equally desirable:

(Figures in ₹)

	Year 0	Year 1	Year 2	Year 3
Project A	–10,00,000	5,00,000	5,00,000	5,00,000
Project B	–10,00,000	8,00,000	2,00,000	8,00,000

Both the projects A and B payback in two years and are ranked equally. However, Project B gives a larger cash flow in the first year and should be more preferable. This drawback can easily be removed by calculating a discounted payback period where we assign the time value to the cash flows. Assuming a discount rate of 10% the cash flows of Project A and B are as shown in Table 11-3.

Ignores cash flows beyond the payback period The third drawback the payback rule has is that it altogether ignores the cash flows after the payback period. In the above example, there is no importance attached to the cash flow of ₹5 lakh and ₹8 lakh in the third year for projects A and B respectively. Consideration of the post payback period cash flows may alter the preferences of the projects given by the payback rule. Hence, the payback rule by ignoring the cash flows that are generated in the later years may give rise to a conflict between the long-term and short-term objectives of the firm. The focus of payback period method is on short-term objectives of the firm.

Inability to handle multiple cash outflows Finally, the use of the payback rule fails to provide a clear decision in projects involving multiple cash outflows. The rule will not be able to handle the situations where cash outflows take place in subsequent periods.

Despite its disadvantages the payback period remains a popular evaluation criterion because of its applicability in certain situations. For industries, such as electronics and software, which are too dynamic with a high rate of obsolescence, the desirability of early recovery of initial investment is extremely vital and important and may precede any other criteria. Here, it may be fair to treat cash flows beyond payback period as a bonus. This may be a simple and effective way of treating the uncertainty without adopting complicated models of risk analysis.

Example 11-1 Payback Period and Discounted Payback Period

Project M is under consideration for selection. Its initial cash outlay is ₹1,800 and life of five years. The cost of capital of the firm is 12%.

(Figures in ₹)

	Years					
Project	**0**	**1**	**2**	**3**	**4**	**5**
Project M – Cash Flows	–1,800.00	600.00	300.00	1,000.00	800.00	1,100.00

(a) What is the payback period of the project?
(b) If the cut off payback period is three years should the project be accepted?
(c) What is the cut off period on DCF basis?
(d) If cut off payback period remains same at three years even on discounted basis should the firm accept the proposal?

Solution

(a) The cash flows indicate that the capital investment of ₹1,800 can be recovered in slightly less than three years with cash inflows of ₹1,900. By extrapolation we may compute the exact payback period.

Recovery up to Year 2 = 900
Balance to be recovered = 1,800 – 900 = 900

Table 11-3 Illustration: Discounted payback period

(Figures in ₹)	Year 0	Year 1	Year 2	Year 3
Project A: cash flows	–10,00,000	5,00,000/1.1	$5,00,000/1.1^2$	$5,00,000/1.1^3$
Present values		= 4,54,545	= 4,13,223	= 3,75,657
Amount realized after two years			8,67,768	
Amount unrealized after two years			1,32,232	
Time needed in 3rd year to realize the balance				1,32,232/3,75,657 = 0.35 years
Discounted Payback Period for Project A				**2.35 Years**
Project B: cash flows	–10,00,000	8,00,000/1.1	$2,00,000/1.1^2$	$8,00,000/1.1^3$
Present values		= 7,27,273	= 1,65,289	= 6,01,052
Amount realized after two years			8,92,562	
Amount unrealized after two years			1,07,438	
Time needed in 3rd year to realize the balance				1,07,438/6,01,052 = 0.18 years
Discounted Payback Period for Project B				**2.18 years**

The approximate time required to recover the balance assuming uniform cash inflow during the years:

$$= \frac{313.35}{508.41} \times 12 = 10.8 \text{ months}$$

Therefore, the payback period is two years and 10.8 months.

(b) With cut off payback period of 3.0 years the project may be accepted.

(c) Using 12% cost of capital the DCF and its cumulative values are computed below:

(Figures in ₹)

Project	0	1	2	3	4	5
Project M –						
Cash Flow	–1,800.00	600.00	300.00	1,000.00	800.00	1,100.00
Present Value	–1,800.00	535.71	239.16	711.78	508.41	624.17
Cumulative PV		535.71	774.87	1,486.65	1,995.07	2,619.24

Based on DCF, the recovery is made after the third year but before the fourth year. The exact calculation is given below:

Recovery up to Year 3 = ₹1486.65

Balance to be recovered = 1,800 – 1486.65 = ₹313.35

Approximate time required to recover the balance assuming uniform cash inflow during the years:

$$= \frac{313.35}{508.41} \times 12 = 7.40 \text{ months}$$

Therefore, the payback period on DCF basis is three years and 7.40 months.

(d) Since the discounted payback period exceeds the cut off of three years the project must be rejected.

NET PRESENT VALUE METHOD

The net present value (NPV) rule attempts to overcome the limitations of the methods of accounting rate of return and payback. It considers all cash flows over the life of the project as well as assigns time value to each of the cash flows. All the cash flows are discounted to the present value and then compared with the initial outlay, which gives the NPV of the project. The framework of NPV not only provides the rule for acceptance of project but also quantifies the value that will be added or destroyed by acceptance of the project.

Net Present Value (NPV) method evaluates a project after due consideration to the time value of money with cash flows discounted at a rate consistent with the risks of the cash flows.

Mathematically, the NPV of the project is given by Equation 11–2.

$$\text{Net Present Value, NPV} = \sum_{1}^{n} \frac{CF_t}{(1+r)^t} - CF_0 \qquad (11\text{-}2)$$

where CF_t = Cash flow for period t (most often period is equal to year)

t = Period t

n = Life of the project in number of periods

r = Discount Rate

The Decision Rule

The decision making rule is consistent with the objective of the firm which is established as maximization of shareholders' wealth. By accepting the project, the additional wealth created for the shareholders is equal to the NPV of the project. Projects with positive NPV create value for the shareholders.

The decision making rule for the acceptance/rejection of the projects is as below:

ACCEPT	if	$NPV > 0$
REJECT	if	$NPV < 0$

NPV is the value created by the acceptance of the project. It reflects the increase in the market value of the firm.

In the extremely unlikely situation of NPV = 0, the acceptance or rejection of the project neither adds nor destroys the wealth of the shareholders. In such a situation the project is more likely to be rejected as implementing the project is not worth the efforts by the management.

The Procedure

Most investment opportunities typically involve a single outflow at the time of making an investment, CF_0 which is followed by cash inflows for several years till the life of the project. The entire process for calculating the NPV for a typical project can be summarized in the following steps:

1. Estimate the initial cost/investment to implement the project, CF_0.
2. Estimate the net cash flows of the project for each period over its life, CF_t.
3. Discount the each of the estimated cash flows at an appropriate rate to arrive at present value of the cash flows, and add them up.
4. Subtract the initial investment from the present value arrived in Step 3 to get the NPV of the project.
5. Accept the project if NPV is greater than zero, else reject it.

Each of the steps mentioned above need to be discussed in greater detail specifically with respect to projecting the cash inflows and choosing the appropriate discount rate. Both the issues are fairly complex and challenging.

As a simple illustration to highlight the mechanics of the NPV rule for capital budgeting decision, consider Project A and Project B with the cash flows as given in Table 11-4. How these cash flows are arrived at and what all are included or excluded in the cash flows are not discussed here. These cash flows are presumed as given and are to be discounted at 10% assumed to be the cost of capital. At the present moment it is not our concern how 10% discount rate is chosen.

As may be observed from Table 11-4 both Project A and Project B have identical outlays of ₹10 lakh. Project A provides an NPV of ₹2,43,425 while Project B provides an NPV of ₹4,93,614. Clearly, Project B is superior to Project A, providing a greater value addition to the firm.

Net present value with the given discount rate can easily be computed with Excel or any other worksheet programme. Excel provides direct computation of NPV. Feed the data in successive columns, choose *Insert* and *Function* from the menu. Select the *NPV function* and a dialog box appears. Feed the discount rate and the range of cell containing the inflows as shown in Table 11-5. Note that the NPV function in Excel assumes successive cash flow spaced over successive periods and all

Table 11-4 Illustration: Net present value: Discount rate 10%

(*Figures in* ₹)

	Year 0	*Year 1*	*Year 2*	*Year 3*
Project A				
Cash Flow	–10,00,000	5,00,000	5,00,000	5,00,000
Present values of cash inflows	–10,00,000	5,00,000/1.1 = 4,54,545	$5{,}00{,}000/1.1^2$ = 4,13,223	$5{,}00{,}000/1.1^3$ = 3,75,657
Net Present Value		**12,43,425 – 10,00,000 = 2,43,425**		
Project B				
Cash Flow	–10,00,000	8,00,000	2,00,000	8,00,000
Present values	–10,00,000	8,00,000/1.1 = 7,27,273	$2{,}00{,}000/1.1^2$ = 1,65,289	$8{,}00{,}000/1.1^3$ = 6,01,052
Net Present Value		**14,93,614 – 10,00,000 = 4,93,614**		

Table 11-5 Computing NPV through EXCEL

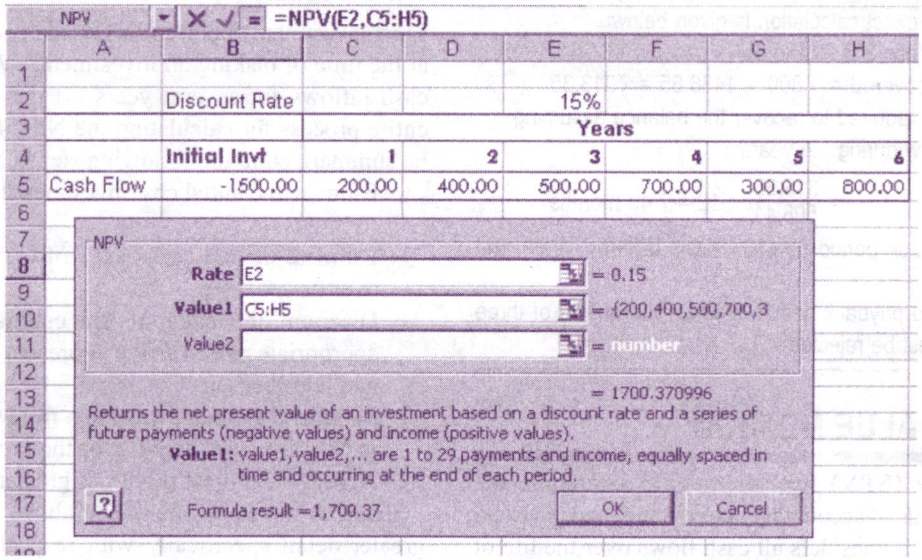

the cash flows are assumed to occur at the end of the period. The first term is discounted by a factor of $(1 + r)$. Therefore, we have to exclude initial investment from the range of cells containing the cash flows. We subtract initial investment later from the result to arrive at NPV of the project (Note in the diagram the *formula result* at 1,700.37. The NPV would be 1,700.37 – 1,500.00 = 200.37).

Additive Property of NPV

The NPV of the firm is the sum of net present values of the individual projects of the firm. Mathematically,

$$\text{NPV}(A + B) = \text{NPV}(A) + \text{NPV}(B) \qquad (11\text{-}3)$$

This is feasible because we are adding the values of the cash flows of the project that correspond to the same time period and are discounting at the same rate. This implies that the cash flows of all the projects can be treated as a composite project and evaluated. In the above example, if we assume both Project A and Project B combine to form a single project, the NPV of the project would be no different than the sum of the individual NPVs of Project A and Project B. This is checked in Table 11-6.

The additive property of NPV helps in isolating the impact that each project makes on the value of the firm.

Table 11-6 Combined net present value

(*Figures in* ₹)

	1st Year	*2nd Year*	*3rd Year*	*4th year*
Project A Cash Flow	–10,00,000	5,00,000	5,00,000	5,00,000
Project B Cash Flow	–10,00,000	8,00,000	2,00,000	8,00,000
TOTAL CASH FLOW	–20,00,000	13,00,000	7,00,000	13,00,000
Present Values at 10%	–20,00,000	13,00,000/1.1 = 11,81,818	$7{,}00{,}000/1.1^2$ = 5,78,512	$13{,}00{,}000/1.1^3$ = 9,76,709
Net Present Value	**27,37,039 – 20,00,000 = 7,37,039**			

This property of NPV is a major advantage of the method as it helps us identify the components of the firm's value. One can find out the impact of the acceptance of the project on the market value of the firm. It is important to mention here that the market value of the firm increases by the amount of NPV of the project that is accepted, the aspect we explain now.

What NPV Tells Us

What do the net present values of ₹2.43 lakh for Project A and ₹4.94 lakh for Project B represent? They simply tell us that after meeting the obligations of the suppliers of capital (including those of shareholders) for the project, as reflected and incorporated in the discount rate, the remaining NPV is the value available today. Who is the claimant of this value if the claims of the suppliers of capital have been satisfied? The answer is, clearly, the shareholders. Shareholders being the owners of the residual have a claim over NPV of the project.

Assume a single shareholder, X for Project A. The implementation of Project A would make X richer by ₹2.43 lakh; the NPV of the project. If X wants to exit and another person, Y becomes interested in the project then exchange of the ownership from X to Y would take place at NPV as X would accept no less and Y would pay no more than ₹2.43 lakh. Therefore, we may say NPV becomes market value of the project if the asset were to trade in the stock exchange. What if some market value already exists prior to acceptance of Project A? The current market value would represent NPV of the existing projects. With the acceptance of the Project A the market value of the firm enhances by ₹2.43 lakh.

INTERNAL RATE OF RETURN METHOD

Internal rate of return (IRR) is akin to the NPV rule. It is a representation of a project in a single parameter that provides a decision making rule for acceptance or rejection of a project. The mechanics of the IRR are similar to the NPV rule. We proceed in the same manner as in NPV by first estimating the cash flows of the project. Once the initial and future cash flows are known we attempt to answer the question that what maximum rate of return these cash flows support. We do not discount these cash flows with the cost of capital but instead discount with the rate that the cash flows support.

To take a rather simple example, consider a project that costs ₹200 and for the next two years provides cash inflows of ₹110 and ₹121, respectively. If the cost of capital is 8%, then under NPV rule using Equation 11-2 we would have calculated the NPV of ₹5.59 as follows:

Net Present Value, NPV

$$= \frac{110}{1.08} + \frac{121}{1.08^2} - 200$$

$$= 101.85 + 103.74 - 100 = ₹5.59$$

Under the IRR rule, we attempt to find the rate of return that is offered by the given cash flows. Since this rate of return is internal to the cash flows we name this exercise as internal rate of return. Mathematically, we find the IRR r by solving the following Equation 11-4:

$$\sum_{1}^{n} \frac{CF_t}{(1+r)^t} = CF_0 \qquad (11\text{-}4)$$

Using Equation 11-4 the formulation of the IRR cash flows is:

$$\frac{110}{1+r} + \frac{121}{(1+r)^2} = 200$$

In the above formulation, we find the discount rate that equates the present values of cash inflows to that of the outflows. Alternatively, we may say that the internal rate of return of the project is that rate which makes the net present value of cash flows zero, as expressed by Equation 11-5.

Internal Rate of Return (IRR) of the project is that rate of return at which the net present value is zero. It is the maximum discount rate that the cash flows of the project can support.

Net Present Value,

$$\text{NPV} = \sum_{1}^{n} \frac{CF_t}{(1+r)^t} - CF_0 = 0 \qquad (11\text{-}5)$$

Normally, it is difficult to solve such equations manually especially when the cash flows extend for several periods. Also it is a time consuming exercise, if done manually. However, with the help of computers this can be solved rather easily and quickly using EXCEL or any other worksheet programme. IRR is a standard mathematical function on all worksheet programmes.

The cash flow data can be fed in a column for different years denoting cash outflow with negative sign and inflows with a positive sign. In the last row formula for IRR may be given specifying the range of cells containing the cash flow information. The syntax is '= *irr*(range of cell)'. This is shown in Table 11-6 in cell B10. The NPV of the cash flow too can be calculated using Excel at any discount rate. This too is shown in Column C of the Excel worksheet in Table 11-7 with a discount rate of 10% fed in Cell C1.

Table 11-7 Calculating IRR on EXCEL

	A	B	C	D
1		Discount Rate	10%	
2	Year	Cash Flow	Present Value at Discount Rate	Present Value At IRR
3	Formula for Row 0	→	B4/(1+$C$1)^A4	B5/(1+$B$10)^A5
4	0	-100.00	-100.00	-100.00
5	1	50.00	45.45	40.98
6	2	30.00	24.79	20.16
7	3	40.00	30.05	22.03
8	4	25.00	17.08	11.28
9	5	15.00	9.31	5.55
10	IRR = irr(b4:b9)	22%		
11	Net Present Value = SUM(C4:C9)		26.69	0.00

In the above example, a simple trial and error method will quickly tell that the value of *r* should be 10%. At this rate the value of cash inflows becomes equal to the value of cash outflows. Or the total value of cash flows becomes zero. The interpretation of *r* can be either of the following:

1. The stream of cash flows by itself generates a return of 10%, i.e., the IRR of the project is 10%.
2. If cash flows are discounted at IRR (10% in this case) the NPV of the project will be zero.

Note that IRR is that rate of discounting which makes the NPV of the project equal to zero. This is cross checked in the Excel worksheet in Column D of Table 11-6 by computing the NPV at discount rate equal to IRR, which is shown in cell D11.

The Decision Rule

The IRR tells us what rate of return is generated by the project cash flows. It will be profitable to invest in the project if this return exceeds the cost of capital. If IRR is greater than cost of capital the firm will be able to generate some positive return after meeting the cost of capital raised from all suppliers of capital. On the other hand if the IRR is less than the cost of capital it would imply that the cash flows will not be enough to meet the expectations of the suppliers of capital. In such a case, it will not be desirable to pursue the project. The decision rule can simply be put as follows:

ACCEPT	if	IRR > Cost of Capital
REJECT	if	IRR < Cost of Capital

NPV AND IRR—A COMPARISON

The mechanics and the concept behind the rules of NPV and IRR are similar. Under the NPV rule, we discount the cash flows at a given rate, which is normally the cost of capital, and arrive at NPV. Under the IRR method, we find a discount rate that makes NPV zero and compare this rate with the cost of capital. The data requirements under both the methods are identical. However, for calculating the IRR one does not need the cost of capital but for NPV we need it. For making the decision under both the methods, cost of capital would be required.

The relationship in the two approaches can be illustrated with a numerical example. Consider a project with initial outlay of ₹100 and cash inflows as shown in Table 11-8.

Table 11-8 Cash flows and NPV at different discount rates

(Figures in ₹)

Year	*0*	*1*	*2*	*3*	*4*	*5*	*NPV*
Cash Flow	**(100.00)**	**50.00**	**60.00**	**30.00**	**20.00**	**10.00**	
Present Values at							
0%	(100.00)	50.00	60.00	30.00	20.00	10.00	70.00
5%	(100.00)	47.62	54.42	25.92	16.45	7.84	52.25
10%	(100.00)	45.45	49.59	22.54	13.66	6.21	37.45
15%	(100.00)	43.48	45.37	19.73	11.44	4.97	24.98
20%	(100.00)	41.67	41.67	17.36	9.65	4.02	14.36
25%	(100.00)	40.00	38.40	15.36	8.19	3.28	5.23
28.23%	(100.00)	38.99	36.49	14.23	7.40	2.88	(0.01)
30%	(100.00)	38.46	35.50	13.65	7.00	2.69	(2.68)
35%	(100.00)	37.04	32.92	12.19	6.02	2.23	(9.60)
40%	(100.00)	35.71	30.61	10.93	5.21	1.86	(15.68)

The project has initial cost of ₹100 with an estimated life of five years. For the next five years, it yields cash inflows of ₹50, ₹60, ₹30, ₹20, and ₹10, respectively. Using progressively increasing discount rates we calculate the NPV of the project using Equation 11-2. Notice that as the discount rate increases, the NPV falls. With the discount rate of zero, the net present value of cash flows is simply an arithmetical summation of cash flows at ₹70. At a 10% discount rate the NPV falls to ₹37.45. As we gradually increase the discount rate to 25%, the NPV falls to ₹5.23 and finally turns negative. At a discount rate of 40%, the NPV becomes –₹15.68. Values of NPV at different discount rates are computed in Table 11-8 and are plotted in Figure 11-1.

As can be observed from the Figure 11-1 and Table 11-8, NPV becomes zero at discount rate of 28.23%. Hence, the IRR of the project is 28.23%.

Besides finding IRR with the graphical depiction of the NPVs with the discount rate, Figure 11-1 can also be used to determine the sensitivity of the cash flows with the change in discount rate. The greater the slope higher is the sensitivity of the cash

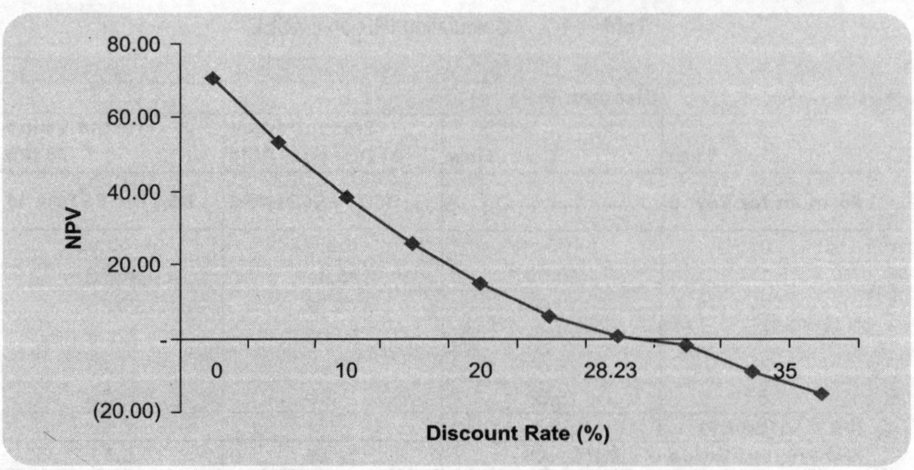

Figure 11-1 Net present value and discount rate

Under most circumstances, the priorities of the projects as given by NPV rule and IRR rule are identical.

flows with the discount rate and the riskier is the project.

Does the IRR method and NPV method provide the same answer about the project's desirability? In almost all cases, the decision to accept or reject the project either by using NPV or IRR will be identical. In the present case, both the rules will provide an identical decision no matter whether we look at the positive NPV or compare the IRR with the cost of capital.

CONFLICT BETWEEN IRR AND NPV

As stated, both the IRR and the NPV rule provide the same answer. However, there could be situations where they may give contradictory results. These situations may arise—(1) if the project has multiple cash outflows instead of a single outflow; and (2) when there are mutually exclusive projects under consideration, (3) when projects have unequal lives or scale of investment and (4) when projects are borrowing and not lending. We discuss each of them here.

Multiple IRRs—Non-conventional Cash Flows

Conventional projects have single cash outflow followed by several cash inflows over the life of the project. However, there can be some projects that may have more than one net cash outflows in different periods. Such instances may include projects where a large working capital is infused in subsequent periods, or a major refurbishing of the plant takes place later, or a large expenditure on advertisement/marketing of products is proposed in later periods. Such kinds of projects may pose a problem in decision making while using the IRR technique.

As an illustration, consider an example where the initial cash outflow is ₹504, which provides a cash flow of ₹2,862 in Year 1. It also needs an out flow of ₹6,070 in Year 2 followed by an inflow of ₹5,700 in Year 3. This may happen due to large modernisation plan needing huge cash outflow in Year 2. Again in Year 4 there is a cash outflow of ₹2,000 that may occur due to tax liability arising in the subsequent year after the useful life of the project is over in Year 3.

The IRR of these cash flows will be calculated using Equation 11-5 as below:

$$504 = \frac{2,862}{1+r} - \frac{6,070}{(1+r)^2} + \frac{5,700}{(1+r)^3} - \frac{2,000}{(1+r)^4}$$

The problem with the above equation is that there are more than one value of r that will satisfy the equation[1] and one wonders which of the IRR should be used in making a capital budgeting decision.

One way of finding out the IRRs is to mathematically solve the given equation. An alternate way is to find out rates at which NPVs become zero. Such an exercise is presented in Table 11-9. Note that the NPV becomes zero at values about 25%, 33%, 42%, and 66% as can be visualized from the Figure 11-2.

Table 11-9 Example Multiple IRRs

(Figure in ₹)

	Year					
Cash Flow	**0** ***–504.00***	**1** ***2862.00***	**2** ***–6070.00***	**3** ***5700.00***	**4** ***–2000.00***	**NPV**
Discount Rate	***Present Values***					
10%	–504.00	2601.82	–5016.53	4282.49	–1366.03	–2.24
15%	–504.00	2488.70	–4589.79	3747.84	–1143.51	–0.76
20%	–504.00	2385.00	–4215.28	3298.61	–964.51	–0.17
25%	–504.00	2289.60	–3884.80	2918.40	–819.20	0.00
30%	–504.00	2201.54	–3591.72	2594.45	–700.26	0.01
35%	–504.00	2120.00	–3330.59	2316.72	–602.14	–0.01
40%	–504.00	2044.29	–3096.94	2077.26	–520.62	–0.01
45%	–504.00	1973.79	–2887.04	1869.70	–452.44	0.01
50%	–504.00	1908.00	–2697.78	1688.89	–395.06	0.05
55%	–504.00	1846.45	–2526.53	1530.66	–346.50	0.08
60%	–504.00	1788.75	–2371.09	1391.60	–305.18	0.08
65%	–504.00	1734.55	–2229.57	1268.89	–269.83	0.03
70%	–504.00	1683.53	–2100.35	1160.19	–239.46	–0.09
75%	–504.00	1635.43	–1982.04	1063.56	–213.24	–0.30
80%	–504.00	1590.00	–1873.46	977.37	–190.52	–0.61
85%	–504.00	1547.03	–1773.56	900.24	–170.74	–1.03
90%	–504.00	1506.32	–1681.44	831.02	–153.47	–1.57

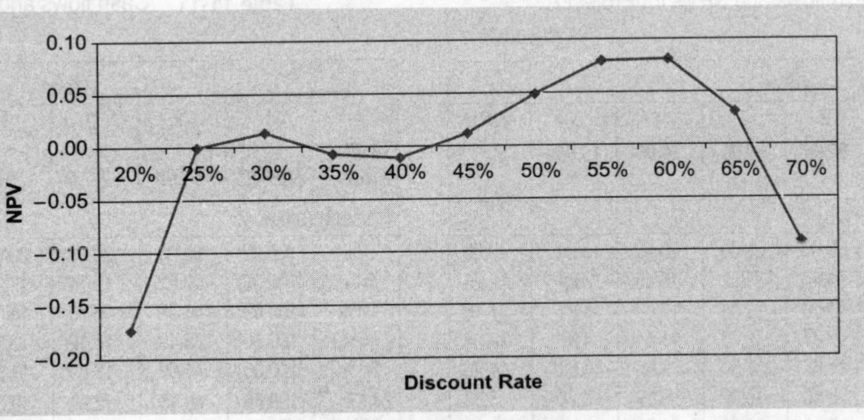

Figure 11-2 NPV and IRR

[1]As per Descartes's Rule of Sign, the maximum number of IRRs is equal to number of times the sign of cash flows changes from positive to negative or negative to positive. Hence, there will be maximum 4 IRRs in the above cash flows.

Observe that the NPV, which is negative at values less than 25%, becomes positive in the range from 25% to 33%, and turns negative, thereafter till 42.5%. The NPV is again positive from 42.5% to 66%.

There are four internal rates of return—25%, 33%, 42.5%, and 66% where the NPV becomes zero. Which of these IRR must be compared with the cost of capital for accepting or rejecting the project is not clear. According to the IRR rule, the project is acceptable if the cost of capital is between 25% and 32%. Further, it is also acceptable if the cost of capital is between 42.5% and 66%. Such ambiguous recommendations defy managerial prudence. Clearly applying the IRR rule for capital budgeting decisions breaks down completely in case of non-conventional cash flows.

Under cases of non-conventional cash flows and mutually exclusive projects, there is a possibility of the conflict in decision-making rules of NPV and IRR.

The solution to the dilemma lies in applying the NPV rule. As a bottom line, IRR rule can only be applied for conventional cash flows.

Mutually Exclusive Projects

Mutually exclusive projects, as defined earlier, imply acceptance of one single project over many. For example, a firm owning a piece of land can either build a warehouse and earn rental income or establish a theatre to run movies and do profitable business. Building a warehouse will rule out business proposition of theatre and vice versa. In such situations, the firm has to choose between the two projects. It cannot have both. Such situations, referred to as mutually exclusive projects, are many in the business world. Choosing one of the multiple technologies available to manufacture a product, or adopting a particular marketing strategy out of many options available are common examples.

In situations of mutually exclusive projects the manager is faced with a decision to choose one. Which of the decision making rule out of IRR and NPV should he use needs to be determined? Will both the decision rules of IRR and NPV lead to identical choice?

We attempt to answer this question through a numerical example. Let us consider two mutually exclusive projects, Project A and Project B. The cash flows of Project A and Project B are given in Tables 11-10 and 11-11, respectively.

As a first exercise, we calculate the NPV of both the projects at different rates of discount ranging from 5% to 40%. The NPVs are shown in Table 11-10 for Project A and in Table 11-11 for Project B. Note that with increased discount rate the NPV falls. The discount rate at which the NPV becomes zero is the IRR of the project. For Project A, the IRR is 28.3%; while for Project B, it is 24.57%.

There is a negative relationship between discount rate and NPV. NPV of some projects decline more rapidly than of others.

According to the rule of IRR, the project with higher IRR would be preferred compared to the project with a lower IRR. Using the IRR rule, we prefer Project A with IRR of 28.3%. Being mutually exclusive we have to accept either A or B. Hence, we choose Project A.

Does the NPV rule give the identical choice? Not necessarily. It depends upon the rate of discount. If the chosen discount rate is 10% we find that Project A has an NPV of ₹37.45 and Project B has an NPV of ₹41.59. As per the NPV rule Project B should be preferred over Project A, which is not consistent with the choice as per the IRR rule. On the other hand if the chosen discount rate happens to be 20% we find that Project A has a higher NPV at ₹14.36 than the Project B with NPV of ₹10.53. Therefore, at a discount rate of 20% Project A is preferred over Project B.

A graphical view of the NPVs of the two projects is given in Figure 11-3, which provides greater clarity of the behaviour of NPV and IRR. While the NPV is dependent upon the discount rate chosen, the IRR isn't. Therefore, while the IRR rule will always provide the same order of choice in selection of projects, the ranking by the NPV rule may change with the chosen discount rate. However, this need not lead to the conclusion that the IRR is a superior method than NPV, being always consistent. In fact, it is the opposite that is true.

Table 11-10 Cash flows and NPVs for Project A

(Figure in ₹)

	Year						
	0	**1**	**2**	**3**	**4**	**5**	**NPV**
Cash Flow	**(100.00)**	**50.00**	**60.00**	**30.00**	**20.00**	**10.00**	
Present Values at							
0%	(100.00)	50.00	60.00	30.00	20.00	10.00	70.00
5%	(100.00)	47.62	54.42	25.92	16.45	7.84	52.25
10%	(100.00)	45.45	49.59	22.54	13.66	6.21	37.45
15%	(100.00)	43.48	45.37	19.73	11.44	4.97	24.98
20%	(100.00)	41.67	41.67	17.36	9.65	4.02	14.36
25%	(100.00)	40.00	38.40	15.36	8.19	3.28	5.23
28.23%	**(100.00)**	**38.99**	**36.49**	**14.23**	**7.40**	**2.88**	**(0.01)**
30%	(100.00)	38.46	35.50	13.65	7.00	2.69	(2.68)
35%	(100.00)	37.04	32.92	12.19	6.02	2.23	(9.60)
40%	(100.00)	35.71	30.61	10.93	5.21	1.86	(15.68)

Table 11-11 Cash flows and NPVs for Project B

(Figure in ₹)

	Year						
	0	**1**	**2**	**3**	**4**	**5**	**NPV**
Cash Flow	**(100.00)**	**50.00**	**20.00**	**20.00**	**40.00**	**60.00**	
Present Values at							
0%	(100.00)	50.00	20.00	20.00	40.00	60.00	90.00
5%	(100.00)	47.62	18.14	17.28	32.91	47.01	62.96
10%	(100.00)	45.45	16.53	15.03	27.32	37.2	41.59
15%	(100.00)	43.48	15.12	13.15	22.87	29.83	24.45
20%	(100.00)	41.67	13.89	11.57	19.29	24.11	10.53
24.57%	**(100.00)**	**40.14**	**12.89**	**10.35**	**16.61**	**20.00**	**(0.01)**
25%	(100.00)	40.00	12.80	10.24	16.38	19.66	(0.92)
30%	(100.00)	38.46	11.83	9.10	14.01	16.16	(10.44)
35%	(100.00)	37.04	10.97	8.13	12.04	13.38	(18.44)
40%	(100.00)	35.71	10.20	7.29	10.41	11.16	(25.22)

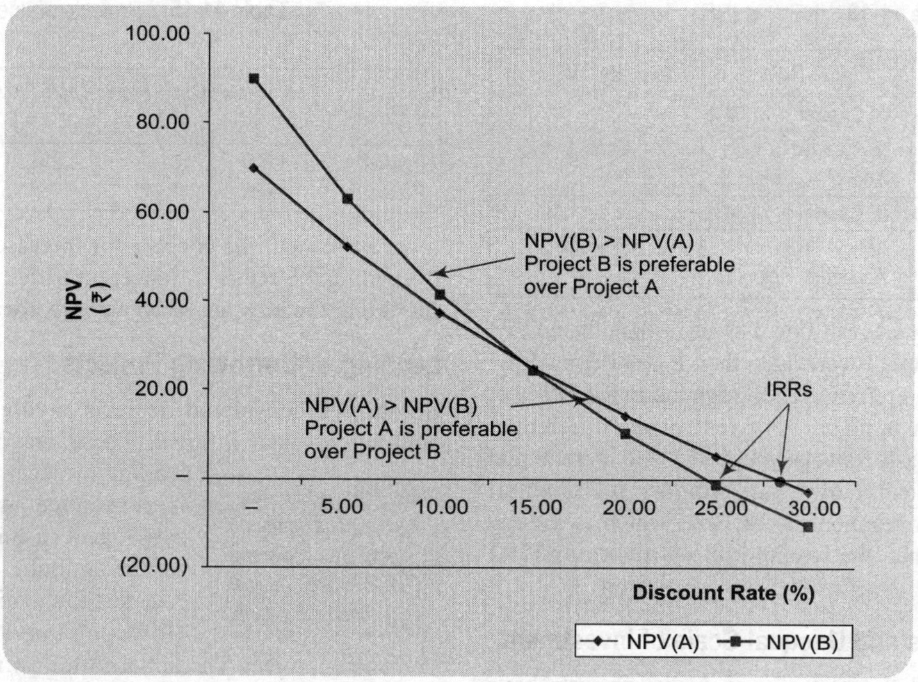

Figure 11-3 NPV of Project A and B

The objective of the firm is to create value for the shareholders. The larger the value creation, the happier is the shareholder. It is the NPV that talks about the absolute value creation. The IRR tells value creation in relative terms only. Project A is more attractive than Project B as it offers relatively higher returns. How much higher is not revealed by IRR. However, we must prefer a project that adds higher value in absolute terms. Shareholders have a big appetite and therefore, they prefer a larger piece of cake, even though a smaller cake may be relatively more attractive to look at.

Point of indifference Since the rate of decrease of the NPV with discount rate is not the same for both the projects, they need to intersect at some point. It is often of interest to know the discount rate at which the NPVs of the two mutually exclusive projects shall be equal. At the discount rate at which the NPVs are equal we are indifferent to the selection of either of the projects. Knowing the point of indifference is more of academic interest rather than of practical significance except for the situations where managers may not have an exact idea of the cost of capital.

Due to varying sensitivities to the discount rate, NPVs of the two projects would intersect at some point. The point of indifference is that discount rate at which the NPV_S of two projects are equal.

One way of knowing the point of indifference is to calculate the NPVs of the projects at different discount rates and keep comparing them till they match. An alternative and simpler method is to find out the IRR for the differential cash flow. This is illustrated for the Project A and Project B in the Table 11-12.

The point of indifference by definition is where the two NPVs are equal, or

$$NPV_A = NPV_B$$

Or $NPV_A - NPV_B = 0 = NPV_B - NPV_A$

This implies that the IRR of the differential cash flow will be one at which the NPV of the first project will be equal to NPV of the second project. In the Table 11-12 we find that the IRR of the difference of cash flows of Project A and Project B is 14.34%. As a cross check NPVs for both the projects is calculated, they are found to be equal at discount rate of 14.34%.

What is meant by the IRR of the differential cash flow? It helps us in reconciling the conflict in the acceptance of two mutually exclusive projects. It becomes a benchmark for making further judgement. If the cost of capital is greater than the IRR of the differential cash flow no conflict is seen between the two methods. However, if the cost of capital is less than IRR of the differential cash flow, NPV and IRR methods would give contradictory results. This is tabulated in Table 11-13.

Table 11-12 Calculating the point of indifference: differential cash flows

(Figure in ₹)

Year	0	1	2	3	4	5	
Cash flow Project A	(100.00)	50.00	60.00	30.00	20.00	10.00	
Cash flow Project B	(100.00)	50.00	20.00	20.00	40.00	60.00	
Cash flow (differential) Project B – Project A	—	—	(40.00)	(10.00)	20.00	50.00	IRR = 14.34%
Present Value			Discount Rate = IRR = 14.34%				**NPV**
Project A	(100.00)	43.73	45.89	20.07	11.70	5.12	**26.51**
Project B	(100.00)	43.73	15.30	13.38	23.40	30.70	**26.51**

Table 11-13 NPV vs IRR

NPV Rule	IRR Rule	Result
If Cost of Capital < 14.34%		
$NPV_B > NPV_A$ Accept B; Reject A	$IRR_A > IRR_B$ Accept A; Reject B	Conflict
If Cost of Capital > 14.34%		
$NPV_A > NPV_B$ Accept A; Reject B	$IRR_A > IRR_B$ Accept A; Reject B	No conflict

The IRR of the incremental cash flow is greater than the cost of capital. If the cost of capital were 12% then Project B must be preferred even though the IRR of Project A is higher. The IRR of the differential cash flows suggests that the incremental cash flows can support incremental investment at 14.34%, which is greater than the required rate of return of 12%; the cost of capital.

IRR of the differential cash flow gives the discount rate at which the NPVs of the two projects are equal.

Unequal Project Lives and Unequal Scale of Investment

It is not necessary that the mutually exclusive projects have identical initial investment or identical project lives. Under such circumstances it is possible to have contradiction in the two rules of NPV and IRR. Here again, the use of NPV rather than IRR is preferred because of our overwhelming preference of increased wealth rather than better rate of return. For some, the argument of preference of greater wealth over a greater rate of return is difficult to comprehend. Consider a simple situation of two mutually exclusive projects A and B of initial investment of ₹1,000 and ₹1,200, respectively. Each project lasts only for one year giving cash inflows of ₹1,200 and ₹1,428, respectively as shown in Table 11-14.

Table 11-14 Projects of unequal investment

(Figures in ₹)

	Cash Flow at t = 0	Cash Flow at t = 1	NPV at 10%	IRR
Project A	–1,000	1,200	90.91	20%
Project B	–1,200	1,428	98.18	19%

The IRR for Project A is 20% and for Project B is 19%. However, the NPVs of Project A and Project B are ₹90.91 and ₹98.18, respectively. The IRR favours Project A while NPV favours Project B. Which project should one prefer? Clearly, Project B. Simply because the end wealth is greater with Project B, as compared to Project A. If one had ₹1,200 in the beginning the end wealth would be ₹1,400 (₹1,200 from Project A plus 200 that is not utilized) with Project A. With Project B, it stands at ₹1,428. This is reflected in higher NPV of the Project B.

Similar would be the outcome with projects of unequal lives. Again consider two projects A and B with initial outlays of ₹1,000. The cash inflow for project A lasting for two years and Project B lasting for one year are given in the Table 11-15. Here again IRR favours Project B having higher IRR while NPV favours Project A with higher NPV. The choice is in favour of Project A giving greater wealth.

Table 11-15 Projects of unequal lives

(Figures in ₹)

	Cash Flow at t = 0	Cash Flow at t = 1	Cash Flow at t = 2	NPV at 5%	IRR
Project A	–1,000	—	1,210	97.50	10%
Project B	–1,000	1,140	—	85.71	14%

In a nutshell, the concern for increased wealth is paramount overriding the returns. Hence, priorities recommended by NPV providing the increase in wealth are always followed.

Lending or Borrowing Projects

So far we considered projects involving initial outlay and subsequent cash inflows. These are investment projects or lending projects. Here the initial outlay is considered as if it is lent and the subsequent cash inflow is the repayment of the amount lent. However, if we reverse the situation the direction of cash flows changes and it becomes a borrowing project. The initial cash flow is positive as if we have borrowed and subsequent cash flows are repayments of the borrowed amount and are cash outflows. What happens to the IRR and NPV in such a case? Consider following two projects with the life of one year and identical cash flows but with reversal of signs:

IRR distinguish between investing and borrowing projects, which one evaluated against opposite criteria.

(Figures in ₹)

	Cash Flow at t = 0	Cash Flow at t = 1	IRR	NPV at 10%
Lending	–100	+120	20%	+9.09
Borrowing	+100	–120	20%	–9.09

According to IRR method, both are acceptable projects because an IRR of 20% for both the cases is in excess of discount rate of 10%. However, the NPV rule clearly spell out that while first project adds value of ₹9.09, the second project loses a value of ₹9.09. This happens because the situations are different in the two cases. In the first case, we are lending ₹100 and demanding back ₹120, which is in excess of our required rate of return of 10%. We create value by doing so. In the second case we are borrowing ₹100 and have to pay back ₹120, while we can deploy the borrowed funds only at 10%. Here we lose value.

The outcome was obvious in this case. However, if we consider the situations as the one given below or for extended time horizon the result may not be apparent. Note that the lending proposal has an IRR of 25% and borrowing proposal has IRR of 40%.

(Figures in ₹)

	Cash Flow at t = 0	Cash Flow at t = 1	IRR	NPV at 10%
Lending	–200	+250	25%	+ 27.27
Borrowing	+300	–420	40%	–81.82

Here, we would give priority to the borrowing project that has higher IRR at 40% than the lending project at 25%. However, borrowing project with a higher IRR suggests higher loss.

Unfortunately, the IRR does not tell us whether it is a lending or borrowing project. The higher the IRR in a borrowing proposal, the greater is the value lost.

Finally, one disadvantage that lies with the IRR is the preoccupation of managers to deal in % terms. Although it is not a demerit of the technique of IRR, it is more to do with the way we ascertain desirability of projects while scanning the environment. Most people compare relative profitability from the rate of return that is offered by different projects. Typically, IRR would be high for short-lived, early cash flow projects that necessarily may not be high NPV projects. We may end up making a wrong choice even though intentions were not so while evaluating the projects based on IRR.

ADVANTAGES OF NPV METHOD

As stated earlier, for most cases of independent projects and no capital constraint NPV and IRR methods give identical results for capital budgeting decisions. However, to avoid any misleading interpretations analysts recommend applying the NPV rule rather than IRR rule for following reasons:

Simplicity NPV is relatively easy to calculate as compared to IRR. The IRR method involves tedious calculations. This advantage of the NPV rule may not seem to be very significant with financial calculators and computers available now.

Reinvestment rate While computing the NPV, the discount rate used is the cost of capital. It implies that the interim cash flows are getting reinvested at the cost of capital. In case of the IRR the discount rate is derived so as to make the NPV equal to zero. The implied assumption of this computation is that the interim cash flows are being reinvested at IRR itself. For example, if the IRR of a stream of cash flow is 20% and the cost of capital is 15%, then while finding NPV all the interim cash flows are assumed to be reinvested at 15%. Under the IRR method, the same cash flows have an assumed reinvestment rate of 20%. Since for the projects that are being accepted the IRR will be higher than the cost of capital, the reinvestment rate in NPV method is on the more conservative side. The NPV method is, therefore, preferable because of the conservative reinvestment rate.

The implied assumption of IRR method is that interim cash flows are reinvested at IRR itself. NPV method assumes reinvestment at discount rate. This assumption of IRR is challenged as it defies conservatism.

Flexibility in choosing the discount rate The calculation of NPV requires the use of a discount rate to the future cash flows, which extends for several periods. This discount rate is normally cost of capital and is currently known. However, it may not be valid in the future and instead, one would like to discount the cash flows of different periods with the respective cost of capital applicable for that period to find out the true NPV rather than use a common rate of discount for all the cash flows, which is the case with IRR method. IRR does not allow the use of different discount rate if the need be so.

Non-conventional cash flows and mutually exclusive projects In cases of non-conventional cash flows and mutually exclusive projects, as discussed in the preceding section IRR rule either cannot be applied or may come in conflict with the NPV rule.

Measuring wealth creation Managers and shareholders alike are normally interested in knowing how much richer they would be if the project is accepted. NPV directly tells how much accretion of the shareholders' wealth will take place upon the acceptance of the project, while the IRR fails to provide that answer as it merely compares IRR with the cost of capital.

Ranking of the project in capital rationing situation Capital is scarce and projects are abundant. Firms normally have several projects for which enough funds are not available. In such situations, the firm needs to know the priority amongst the identified projects, and, therefore, may have to rank them in order of preference. Here again, the NPV must prove to be a more suitable technique since the project that generates greater wealth should be preferred over projects that have higher returns.

Due to numerous advantages and an unambiguous acceptance and rejection criterion, NPV rule is considered superior to the IRR rule.

ADVANTAGES OF IRR METHOD

Whether the NPV method is superior to the IRR method is a matter of discussion. Despite its inability to handle all situations, the evaluation criteria of IRR remains a popular method of appraisal of projects because of the following possible reasons.

Easier comprehension Although it is complex to compute, IRR is easier to comprehend for interpretation. An IRR of, say, 18% would clearly communicate that if the cost of the capital is 10% it is safe to accept the project. Managers and analysts alike prefer to talk in relative terms and specifying % is a more common expression.

No discount rate needed Another advantage, though seemingly trivial, with IRR is the fact that one can compute IRR simply from the cash flows without knowing the discount rate. Though for a complete decision, the cost of capital is required but for comparisons of various independent and conventional projects knowledge of cost of capital is not important. All one needs to know are the IRRs of different projects being compared.

Despite conflicts and drawbacks, IRR remains a popular method because of its ability to compare projects without the consideration of discount rate.

Priority for early cash flows The IRR for the project giving early cash flows would be higher but the same is not true for the NPV method. Since the IRR favours projects with early cash inflows, firms may prefer IRR method as earlier cash inflows mean easier funding for other projects that are on the anvil. Also, earlier cash inflows translates into lesser risk because nearer cashflows are more certain than distant cash inflows.

Example 11-2 NPV and IRR Methods

A firm is considering two mutually exclusive projects, Project R and Project S. Each having a life of five years. The cash flows for five years for both the projects are given below:

Project	Years 0	1	2	3	4	5
Project R- Cash Flow	–2,000.00	600.00	300.00	1,000.00	800.00	1,100.00
Project S- Cash Flow	–1800.00	800.00	700.00	400.00	600.00	700.00

(a) Find out NPV of each project assuming cost of capital at 15%.

(b) Find out IRR of each project.

(c) Which of the project would you choose and why?

(d) If the cost of capital changes to 18%, compute the NPVs of the projects. Does IRR change? Would your decision change? Why or why not?

(e) Find the point of indifference. What does it communicate?

Solution

(a) & (b) The computations of NPV and IRR for Project R and Project S are shown below with cost of capital at 15%.

Project	Years 0	1	2	3	4	5
Project R	–2,000.00	600.00	300.00	1,000.00	800.00	1,100.00
P. V.	–2,000.00	521.74	226.84	657.52	457.40	546.89
NPV = 410.40						IRR = 22.25%
Project S	–1,800.00	800.00	700.00	400.00	600.00	700.00
P. V.	–1,800.00	695.65	529.30	263.01	343.05	348.02
NPV = 379.03						IRR = 24.08%
Present value discount rate is 15%						

(c) According to the IRR rule, we must choose Project S having greater IRR at 24.08%. As per the NPV rule, the selection must be made for Project R with higher NPV of ₹410.40. There is a conflict in these mutually exclusive projects. We would choose Project R because it results in a greater increase in wealth than Project S.

(d) The NPVs of the project at cost of capital of 18% is shown below:

NPVs at discount rate of 18%						
Project	Years 0	1	2	3	4	5
Project R	–2,000.00	600.00	300.00	1,000.00	800.00	1,100.00
P. V.	–2,000.00	508.47	215.46	608.63	412.63	480.82
NPV = 226.01						
Project S	–1,800.00	800.00	700.00	400.00	600.00	700.00
P. V.	–1,800.00	677.97	502.73	243.45	309.47	305.98
NPV = 239.60						

As can be seen in the table, with the discount rate changing, NPV also changes.

However, the IRR does not change for any project.

Now since Project S has higher NPV the choice would be in favour of selecting Project S and rejecting Project R.

(e) The point of indifference is computed by calculating the IRR of the diff erential cash flow. The differential cash flow gives and IRR of 17.04%.

Differential Cash Flow	Years 0	1	2	3	4	5
Project R	–2,000	600	300	1,000	800	1,100
Project S	–1,800	800	700	400	600	700
Differential Cash Flow	–200	–200	–400	600	200	400
IRR = 17.04%						

The NPVs of the Project R and Project S would be equal at cost of capital of 17.04%. This also tells us that for the cost of capital in excess of 17.04% the selection criteria with IRR is consistent with the NPV. For the cost of capital less than 17.04%, there would be a conflict in the selection by the IRR method and the NPV method.

MODIFIED IRR (MIRR)

The source of conflict between IRR and the NPV method of appraising the project is the assumption of reinvestment rate of the cash flows implied in the DCF techniques.

Modified IRR method is an attempt to reconcile with NPV method by overcoming the objection of reinvestment rate.

To overcome the drawback of the IRR method and to make it consistent with the NPV rule, a modified method is developed known as modified IRR. The method works as follows:

1. Find out the terminal values of all the cash flows assuming the reinvestment rate at cost of capital.
2. The total of terminal value is treated as single cash inflow at the end of the project.
3. With only two cash flows (initial investment and terminal value at the end of the project) recompute the IRR. This new IRR is the modified IRR (MIRR).

As an example, consider a project with cash flows as given in Column 2 of Table 11-16. It has an initial cash outflow of ₹10,000. The cash inflows from Year 1 to Year 5 yield an IRR of 17.18%. With the cost of capital at 12%, the project is acceptable as IRR is in excess of cost of capital.

Under the modified IRR method, these cash inflows of each year are converted to Year 5 by compounding them at a reinvestment rate equal to the cost of capital. Here, it is taken as 12%. The terminal values of all the cash inflows add to ₹20,232. This terminal value is now assumed to be single cash inflow in Year 5 as shown in the last column of Table 11-16. With only two cash flows, i.e., the initial outlay in Year 0 and terminal value in Year 5 this is equivalent to the cash flows of the project. The IRR is recomputed. The modified IRR works out to 15.14%, $[10{,}000(1 + r)^5 = 20{,}232]$ which is lower than the

Table 11-16 Modified IRR computation

(Figures in ₹)

Year	Project's Cash Flow	Terminal Value of Cash Flow at 12%	Modified Cash Flow
0	–10,000		–10,000
1	2,000	3,147	—
2	3,000	4,215	—
3	3,500	4,390	—
4	4,000	4,480	—
5	4,000	4,000	20,232
	17.18% ↑ IRR	20,232 ↑ Terminal Value	15.14% ↑ Modified IRR

original IRR. The modified IRR or MIRR will underestimate the true rate of return of the project if the cost of the capital is less than the IRR, which is likely to be the case. The reduced MIRR moderates the bias of pure IRR towards early cash flow.

Modified IRR can now be said to reflect the true profitability of the project having assumed reinvestment at cost of capital. As we increase the reinvestment rate, MIRR converges with the original IRR. The least value of Modified IRR results when the reinvestment rate is zero. MIRR has following advantages:

1. It is consistent with NPV method.
2. It eliminates the problem of multiple IRRs if it exists by taking a single inflow at beginning and single cash outflow at the end of the project.
3. It assumes a more realistic reinvestment rate consistent with conservative policy followed by most finance professionals.

PROJECTING CASH FLOWS

Hitherto, while analysing the different methods of project appraisal we had been assuming that the cash flows of the project are known and given. Irrespective of which method of evaluation is adopted for capital budgeting exercise, the projection of cash flow or profitability is a prerequisite. Possibly, the projection of future cash flow is a more challenging part of the capital budgeting exercise than the selection of technique of evaluation. As long as the firms use DCF technique, the requirement of cash flow cannot be dispensed with.

The projection of cash flows for the project is a more cumbersome exercise and perhaps demands greater managerial application for several reasons. The projection of cash flows by managers is influenced by the individual's frame of mind of being pessimistic or optimistic, risk perception of future, tendency of managers to find short-cuts to the problem, etc. Very little can be done to overcome the influence of these behavioural factors.

Projection of cash flows of the project is done under three broad heads of initial cash outlay, regular cash flows and terminal year cash flows.

Besides these behavioural factors that may distort the projection another reason to have incorrect cash flows is the inability of managers to discern what needs to be included and what needs to be excluded in the cash flows. These are discussed below so as to minimize the errors in forecast of cash flows.

The cash flows are generally categorized into following three categories:

Initial investment The projection of initial cash flow includes the initial outlay. It is rather certain and includes the cost of equipment, working capital, etc.

Cash flow for the life Cash flow for the life of the project more often than not are recurring every year. Though there is no such compulsion to have an annual cash flow, we project cash flows on an annual basis presumably because of the convenient practice of preparing annual performances, reviewing them and to even out the seasonality.

Terminal cash flow At the end of the useful life, the project is deemed closed even though actually it may not happen. Projecting the cash flow in the end is another exercise requiring a distinct set of information and managerial discretion.

PRINCIPLES OF CASH FLOW PROJECTION

Irrespective of the category of the cash flow there are certain well-established principles that need to be observed for the capital budgeting exercise. They are discussed below:

Include only the Relevant and Incremental Cash Flows

The foremost principle of projecting cash flows is to include only those items of cash flow that have an impact on the firm as a whole. Acceptance or rejection of projects impacts the cash flows of the firm on a net basis. The rational approach to evaluate the desirability of the project has to be viewed from the perspective of differential cash flows due to the project. Hence, we need to project cash flows of the firm with and without the project to arrive at the differential or incremental cash flows of the project.

For a new firm such an exercise is extremely simple because all the cash flows in the absence of the project are zero and all the cash flows of the projects are the incremental as well as aggregate for the firm. However, for an existing firm, evaluation of projects like capacity expansion, product development, replacement of capital items, etc., poses problems in the projection of differential or incremental cash flows. One has to take care in identifying the relevant items of revenue and expense while estimating the incremental cash flows. The concept of incremental cash flows is central to the capital budgeting process.

Only differential or incremental cash flows are of importance in capital budgeting decisions.

Initial Outlay Some of the issues that often escape the attention of those projecting initial outlays are highlighted here. We begin with a highly simplified situation and then keep incorporating the impact of each of issues as we discuss them. Remember that it is an illustrative attempt, which by no means can be termed as exhaustive.

Foremost Brewers produces bottled beer branded as 'Pipers'. The production process involves two major steps – fermentation of the feedstock and bottling of the produce. Besides these there are various utilities like boiler plant, generator set, carbonization plant, effluent treatment plant, etc., which help in the process. Consistent with the current market trends and recognizing the consumer preferences Foremost Brewers have to install a canning line to produce canned beer. The canning line costs ₹10 crore and additional fermentation tanks will need ₹3 crore. The firm will use the utilities of effluent treatment plant, carbonization, generators, etc., which already exist. A simplified schematic diagram is shown in Figure 11-4.

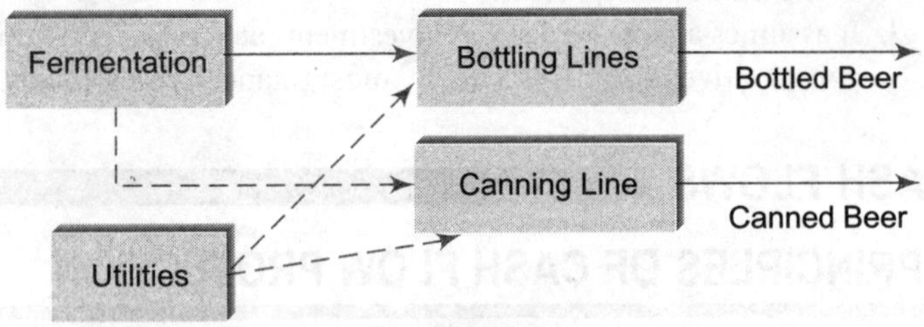

Figure 11-4 Canning line for Foremost Brewers

The cost of the project is estimated as below:

Cost of the project (Initial outlay):	***₹ lakh***
Canning Line	1000
Additional Fermentation Tanks	300
Preliminary Expenses	50
Total	**1350**

This initial cash outlay concerns only the new capital investment that is required. But it is not all that must be considered. There are a few more items that need to be considered in the initial cost. These are—(1) increased requirement of the working capital; (2) the utilization of existing facilities; and (3) some assets becoming obsolete and non-usable. We incorporate each of them progressively and modify the cash flow statement.

Based on the past experience the management and certain assumptions following estimates of cash flows of the new canning line are prepared as shown in Table 11-17.

Note that the projection of operational cash flows and initial cost of the project is a first step only that has included only the cash flows pertaining to the new canning line and suffers from many deficiencies.

Include Side Effects

More often than not managers tend to forget the impact the acceptance of the project is going to make on the existing operations of the firm. In most cases, the inclusion of the project in the business activities of the firm has an impact on the existing operations, because firms normally diversify gradually into related activities. A toilet soap manufacturer may keep adding different brands from time to time with each new product influencing the sales of the existing products. This impact may be synergistic as the overall sales of the firm may be greater than the sum of the sales of individual brands. However, the impact may be negative too as it may result in a decline in sales and profit of existing products and, therefore, result in decline in existing cash flows.

In our situation, the introduction of canned beer may cause a decline in sales of bottled beer as they seem to be substitute product. The question that needs an answer is whether the decline in sales of bottled beer is caused by the firm's own introduction of canned product or it could happen otherwise too. Foremost Brewers may find that decline in sales of bottled beer is inevitable as its competitors would introduce canned beer anyway. In such a situation, loss of sales of existing product would result whether or not Foremost Brewers themselves introduce canned beer or not. Therefore, the incremental cash

Table 11-17 Cash flow projection—Operational—Foremost Brewers (*₹ lakh*)

	Year 0	***Year 1***	***Year 2***	***Year 3***	***Year 4***	***Year 5***
Initial Outlay	–1350					
Revenue		1500	1800	2400	3000	3000
Raw Material		–600	–720	–960	–1200	–1200
Overheads		–500	–600	–700	–1000	–1000
Depreciation*		–240	–240	–240	–240	–240
PBIT		160	240	500	560	560
Add: Depreciation		240	240	240	240	240
Cash flow (Assuming no interest and taxes)		400	480	740	800	800

*Calculated as below: (₹ lakh)

Cost of assets	:	1300
Salvage value	:	100
Useful life of the project	:	5 years
Depreciation	:	(1300 –100)/5 = 240

Major assumptions of operational cash flow:

1. Canning Line has life of five years.
2. It will be depreciated on SLM basis with salvage value of the plant at ₹ 100 lakh.
3. The capacity revenue is ₹ 30 crore with utilization at 50%, 60%, and 80% in Year 1, 2, 3 respectively before full utilization in Year 4 and 5.
4. Raw material consumption is reckoned at 40% of revenue.

flows would exclude the impact of the erosion of sales of existing products.

However, if we assume that the introduction of canned beer will cause some of the existing customers to switch to canned beer from bottled product, we need to incorporate its impact on the incremental cash flows of the canned beer project. Assume that the management has decided to launch the canned beer by the same brand name as that of bottled beer and, therefore, some decline in the sales[2] of bottled beer would take place due to its own action. Further, assume that about 10% of current sales of ₹10 crore will be lost due to the introduction of canned beer. For convenience assume that the profit before interest and taxes of its existing operations would be affected adversely by 5% of the lost sales. In such a scenario, the cash flow projection will be modified as shown in Table 11-18:

Table 11-18 Operational cash flow projection with side effects

(₹ lakh)

	Year 0	Year 1	Year 2	Year 3	Year 4	Year 5
Initial Outlay	–1350					
Revenue		1500	1800	2400	3000	3000
Raw Material		–600	–720	–960	–1200	–1200
Overheads		–500	–600	–700	–1000	–1000
Depreciation		–240	–240	–240	–240	–240
Side effect of loss of PBIT due to lost sales		**–50**	**–50**	**–50**	**–50**	**–50**
PBIT		110	190	450	510	510
Add: Depreciation		240	240	240	240	240
Cash flow		**350**	**430**	**690**	**750**	**750**

Ignore Sunk Cost

The sunk cost is the cost that has been incurred and does not have bearing on the decision making for the capital budgeting process. We need to exclude such a cost from the decision-making process as it is neither relevant nor incremental cash flow. For example consider that the preliminary expenses include the cost of ₹25 lakh incurred by Foremost Brewers for the market survey to examine the desirability of introducing the canned beer. This cost had to be incurred irrespective of whether the firm launches the new product or not. This cost becomes irrelevant to the decision of launching the new product of canned beer, and therefore, must be excluded from the initial cost.

Is it appropriate to exclude this cost? Many managers may feel that excluding the sunk cost would lead to the underestimation of the cost of the project. They could be right, as this cost needs to be recovered from the revenue. However, we have to guard against its relevance to decision making. Suppose after including the cost of survey of ₹25 lakh the NPV of the project works out to – ₹20 lakh (implying that NPV is ₹5 lakh if we exclude the market survey cost). Shall we reject the project? The answer is no because by rejecting the project we lose the opportunity to recover part of the sunk cost as without it the NPV will be –₹25 lakh.

Ignoring the sunk cost the initial outlay is modified as below:

Cost of the project and Sunk Cost	*₹ lakh*
Canning Line	1000
Addl. Fermentation Tanks	300
Preliminary Expenses	50
Less: Market survey cost considered sunk	**–25**
Total	**1325**

Include Opportunity Costs

The exercise of projecting cash flows starts from the items of expenditure and revenues that are visible and impact the cash flows directly. However, there can be certain cost/benefits that may not be visible. We need to include them into our analysis even though the cash flows actually do not occur. The rationale for including these notional cash flows is to account for the value of opportunity foregone.

New projects use the facilities that already exist and do not entail any cash outflow. In case of Foremost Brewers the new canning line will be housed in the surplus land and building already existing with the firm. This land was acquired long time ago. Shall we include the cost of the land in the new project? Or shall we charge rentals for the space utilized for new canning line in the operational cash flow? On the first sight one may decide to ignore it since no cash flow takes place. However, it will be fallacious to do so because by using the land for the project the firm is foregoing an opportunity for its alternative use. The firm could generate some revenue from the land and building, which is termed as opportunity cost. Secondly, by ignoring the opportunity cost we shall be overestimating the cash inflows of the project as we count the facilities coming as free.

Similarly, Foremost Brewers plans to use certain other equipment for the new canning line. If they did not exist the firm would have to provide for the same. The new canning line would cause additional usage of the facilities like DG Set, boiler, etc., which would call for early replacement besides additional recurring cost on maintenance. These costs must be included to reflect the true cash flow for the new project.

To decide whether or not these notional costs should be included in the projection of cash flows the appropriate question to ask is whether the existing resource being used has some alternative use. The rule is simple. If the resource has an alternative use, the opportunity cost must be included in the cash flow projection; otherwise, it should be ignored.

Related to the usage of the existing facilities is the issue of allocation of overhead cost to the project. Normally the costs of common facilities and other overhead cost which are not attributable to a specific project directly are allocated to different projects on some rational basis depending upon management's

[2]The positive synergistic impact on the sales is not ruled out. Depending upon the situation there could be an increase of sales of the existing product.

perception. This allocation of overheads may change the profit and cash flow situation drastically. The principle of incremental cost and not the basis of the allocation of cost should be kept in mind. For example, in case of Foremost Brewers the cost incurred on the DG Set may increase from ₹500 to ₹600 per day due to the additional canning line. The management may also decide to allocate cost in the equal proportion to the existing bottling plant and new canning line. Such an allocation may be appropriate for assessing profitability. However, for the purpose of evaluation of the capital investment proposal only the incremental cost must be attributed to the proposed project that is being examined.

Incorporating opportunity cost for Foremost Brewers

Assume that the land and building had a total cost of ₹150 lakh acquired and building constructed thereon a few years back. Now the canning line will use one-third of the land. Having accepted that the resource of land does not come free of cost for the project, it would be appropriate to charge ₹50 lakh (one-third of ₹150 lakh) on the canning line. Such allocation is appropriate because we need to include the opportunity cost. One may argue that being a sunk cost it must be excluded. However, at the same time we need to recognize the value of the land in the cash flow for making the right decision because of the foregone opportunity. The unutilized space could be rented out if the canning line was not installed.

Table 11-19 Cash flow projects—Including opportunity costs

(₹ lakh)

	Year 0	Year 1	Year 2	Year 3	Year 4	Year 5
Initial Outlay	–1350					
Revenue		1500	1800	2400	3000	3000
Raw Material		–600	–720	–960	–1200	–1200
Overheads		–500	–600	–700	–1000	–1000
Depreciation		–240	–240	–240	–240	–240
Side effect of loss of PBIT due to lost sales		–50	–50	–50	–50	–50
Opportunity cost of rent foregone for the surplus premises		**–12**	**–12**	**–12**	**–12**	**–12**
PBIT		98	178	438	498	498
Add: Depreciation		240	240	240	240	240
Cash flow (Assuming no interest and taxes)		338	418	678	738	738

The cost of land and building is sunk but it has an alternate use and, therefore, the premises can't be assumed to be free of cost. Assuming that Foremost Brewers could get ₹12 lakh per annum by renting out the unused premises[3] the cash flow for the new canning line is altered as shown in Table 11-19.

Incorporate Working Capital

Capital budgeting decisions invariably involve investment in capital assets, which are easy to visualize. Investment in capital assets also demands infusion of some working capital in the form of cash, investment in inventories, and account receivable. Part of this working capital is financed through the credit provided by the suppliers of raw material. The remaining amount, referred to as the net working capital, has to be funded by the firm.

Further, as the project grows with time, the requirements of working capital also grow. As sales increase more and more funds get locked up in receivable, inventories, etc. This increase in working capital in each period is the cash outflow that must be incorporated in the incremental cash flow projections. The increase in net working capital is defined as:

Increase or decrease in net working capital must be incorporated while projecting the cash flows of the project.

Increase in current assets – Increase in current liabilities

When the project has completed its useful life, the working capital is presumed as released. At the end of the project, the release of working capital is equivalent to an inflow. Some of us may believe that since the initial infusion of working capital at the start of the project and its subsequent release at the end of the project offset each other, it is immaterial to include working capital in the capital budgeting decisions. Such a belief is erroneous because we need to provide value for the use of funds during the life of the project as also the time value of money.

The changes in the working capital in the life of the project should be incorporated in the following manner:

1. Project the net working capital requirement in the initial year. In most cases it will be cash outflow.
2. Project the changes in net working capital in each period. An increase means cash outflow while a decrease implies cash inflow for the period.
3. At the end of the useful life of the project, treat the entire working capital as released. It will be cash inflow in most cases.

Providing for net working capital for Foremost Brewers In the case of Foremost Brewers, we assume that the net working capital requirements are 10% of the projected sales for the period[4]. Hence, the working capital cash flows for the life of the projects are as follows:

---

[3]Similar treatment may be given for the other common facilities used by the new project.

[4]Simplified only for illustrative purposes, there are more sophisticated methods to project the net working capital requirements that can be used in the cash flow projections.

Cash Flow Projection for Net Working Capital						₹ lakh
	Year 0	Year 1	Year 2	Year 3	Year 4	Year 5
Initial Outlay	–1350					
Revenue		1500	1800	2400	3000	3000
Net working capital (NWC)		150	180	240	300	300
	150	150	180	240	300	300
Increase (+)/ decrease (–) in NWC	150	30	60	60	—	–300

Separate Financing Cash Flows

The initial cost of the project may be financed in many ways by using combination of debt, equity, or hybrid financing instruments. Depending upon the method of financing the cash flows will be shared amongst the capital suppliers. Should we adjust these cash outflows for interest, principal repayments, and dividends?

The principle of capital budgeting requires that the cash flows that need to be examined are those generated by the asset. While making the capital budgeting decisions we are concerned with the ability of the assets to generate cash benefits and not how these benefits will be shared. Acquisition of asset is an investment decision and how it is funded is a financing decision. It is a different stream of cash flow that must be separated from the stream of cash flows of the investment decision.

Having recognized that the streams of cash flows from investing activity and financing activity are separate, the next question that arises is how to establish a relationship between the two. The objective of the exercise of capital budgeting is to compare the adequacy of cash flows of the project to meet the requirements or expectations of capital suppliers. Whether or not the expectations of capital suppliers are met by the project is examined by the discount rate we choose to arrive at the net present value of the cash flows of the project.

Cash flows that have origins in financing of the project are not included in the cash flows of the project but instead are taken care of in the discount rate.

We segregate the investment and financing by using them separately in numerator and denominator. The numerator consists of the cash flows from investing activities, i.e., the cash flows generated by the assets. The denominator is the discount rate that incorporates the aspirations of the capital suppliers, i.e., the cash flows arising from the financing arrangement. Including the cash flows of the financing activity in the numerator would be erroneous and mean double counting of financing cost. Therefore, we ignore the cost of interest if any while projecting the cash flows of the project.

This is also referred to as *interest exclusion principle.*

Only after-tax Cash Flows are Relevant

As stated earlier, the projects are examined against the expectations of capital suppliers. However, before the claims of the capital suppliers every project must pay the taxes. The prior claim of taxes by the government implies that only the post tax cash flows are relevant from the perspective of the suppliers of capital.

The principle of incremental cash flows also demands that the relevant consideration for applicability of tax is the aggregate income of the firm and not that of the project. Generally, taxes are applicable for the firm as a whole and not on the specific projects, although there are project or location specific tax benefits. Project specific benefits must be accounted for in the project only while estimating incremental cash flow. Where the project is profitable but the firm is not, taxes will not be payable and no cash outflow on account of taxes should be taken into consideration.

Only post-tax cash flows must be considered because taxes are payable before any payment can be made to the suppliers of capital.

The priority of tax claim over the suppliers of capital demands some extra caution in dealing with certain items of expenditure that have features of tax savings. The two most frequently occurring items of such expenses that need attention are depreciation and interest. Both these items have implications on cash flow projections because they are tax deductible. A firm saves tax on these items. We discuss them below:

Interest As stated earlier, the interest cost on the debt must be excluded from the cash flows of the assets as the outflow on the interest is treated as the financing cost and its impact is considered in the discount rate. However, the interest is a tax-deductible expense and influences the tax bill. Yet to arrive at the cash flow to all investors we exclude interest on debt and apply the tax rate to the PBIT. Alternatively, if we calculate the operational cash flows from post-tax profit we add term Interest × (1 –Tax Rate) to arrive at cash flows of the project. Both the methods give identical figures as can be seen from the following:

Operational Cash Flow

$$= \text{Profit Before Interest and Tax (PBIT)} \times (1 - \text{Tax Rate}, T)$$
$$= \text{Profit Before Tax} \times (1 - T) + \text{Interest} \times (1 - T)$$
$$= \text{Profit After Tax} + \text{Interest} \times (1 - T) \quad (11\text{-}6)$$

Depreciation Depreciation on assets is a permissible expense that is allowed to recognize that an asset needs replacement once its useful life is over, consistent with the going concern concept. From the point of view of cash flow, depreciation is a non-cash expense. Yet it appears in the projection of cash flows because it influences the tax amount. Additional complexities arise due to different treatments and methods adopted in calculating the profit for the purpose of financial performance and taxes. Two most prominent methods of charging depreciation[5] are—(1) straight line method (SLM); and (2) written

[5]There are many more methods of charging depreciation. Only two methods are described here for the purpose of highlighting the issues in the projection of cash flows.

down value (WDV). Income Tax Act in India permits the use of WDV method for tax calculation.

Straight line method (SLM) SLM charges depreciation at a constant amount in each year depending upon the life and the salvage value of the asset. If an asset costs ₹100 lakh with a life of ten years at the end of which it is presumed to have a salvage value of ₹10 lakh, the straight-line method of depreciation will charge depreciation at the rate of ₹9 lakh per annum as calculated below:

Depreciation as per SLM
= (Original cost – Salvage Value)/Life of the asset
= (100 – 10)/10 = ₹9 lakh per annum.

The amount of depreciation is uniform for all years.

Written down value method (WDV) The WDV method prescribes a constant rate in terms of % rather than fixed and uniform amount of depreciation for each year. The % of depreciation for the year is applied on the residual value at the end of previous year. Assuming a rate of 20% and the asset value of ₹100 lakh the depreciation for each year will be as follows:

(₹ lakh)

	Year 1	Year 2	Year 3	Year 4	Year 5
A. Value of the asset	100.00	80.00	64.00	51.20	40.96
B. Depreciation @ 20% of A	20.00	16.00	12.80	10.24	8.19
C. Written Down Value	80.00	64.00	51.20	40.96	32.77

Note that in the WDV method—(1) the rate of depreciation is uniform, and not the amount; (2) the value of the asset will never become zero and will be depreciated indefinitely into future unlike in SLM; and (3) the amount of depreciation will be the highest in the first year and will decline gradually as time passes.

For an asset value of Re 1 and the rate of depreciation of d% the depreciation for a period n and the book value after period n are given by:

Depreciation for period $n = d(1 - d)^{n-1}$

Book Value after Period $n = (1 - d)^n$ (11-7)

Including depreciation and tax effects on the cash flows of Foremost Brewers

The physical value of the assets = ₹1,300 lakh
Assumed rate of depreciation as per tax laws = 30%
The depreciation based on WDV method on assumed life of five years:

Depreciation on Written Down Value Method-Foremost Brewers *(₹ lakh)*

	Year 1	Year 2	Year 3	Year 4	Year 5
A. Value of the asset	1300	910	637	446	312
B. Depreciation @ 30% of A	390	273	191	134	94
C. Written Down Value (A – B)	910	637	446	312	218

The cash flow after including the tax:

Depreciation, Taxes and Cash Flow Projection-Foremost Brewers *(₹ lakh)*

	Year 1	Year 2	Year 3	Year 4	Year 5
A. PBIT	160	240	500	560	560
B. Add: Depreciation SLM	240	240	240	240	240
C. Less: Depreciation WDV Method	390	273	191	134	94
D. PBIT for tax purpose (A + B – C)	10	207	549	666	706
E. Tax @ 40% of (D)	4	83	220	266	282
F. Profit After Taxes (PAT) (A – E)	156	157	280	294	278
G. Add: Depreciation (B)	240	240	240	240	240
H. Cash flow (F + G)	396	397	520	534	518

Note: No depreciation can be charged on—(1) preliminary expenses; and (2) net working capital.

Tax shield approach to account for depreciation Since depreciation is not a cash expense but affects the tax amount, sometimes it becomes easier to estimate the cash flows on the basis of tax shield the depreciation provides. This is done by projecting the profit without depreciation (or any other cash items), computing the tax, thereon, and then adding back the tax saved due to depreciation. This is checked as given below.

For Foremost Brewers, the cash flow for the first year is projected below:

		₹ lakh
Profit before Depreciation, Interest and Tax (PBDIT)		400
Less: Tax @ 40%	160	
Add: Tax shield of depreciation (40% of 390)	156	
Cash Flow		396

Tax shield on depreciation in any year is given by:

Tax rate × Amount of depreciation for the year

Example 11-3 Estimating Initial Outlay

Reliance Computer has to replace its old server with the latest version that is costing ₹40 lakh. The new server will have to be imported and its transportation and installation will cost ₹5 lakh. Since the firm is located in an export free trade zone, it qualifies for tax benefits of 20% of the capital investment made in any year. Besides, the firm is also eligible for capital subsidy of 10%. The firm has to dispose its old server at an expected price of ₹5 lakh only against its book value of ₹15 lakh. The firm is profitable and pays income tax at 20%. Find out the initial outlay of the project.

Solution

The initial cash flow is computed as below:

		₹ lakh
Capital Cost of new server		40.00
Add: Incidental cost for installation, transportation, etc.	5.00	
Increase in net working capital	—	
		5.00
Less: Savings of tax on initial investment	8.00	
Capital subsidy available	4.00	
Price realized on the disposal of the existing asset	5.00	

Tax saved on the sale of existing asset			
Price realized	5.00		
Book Value	15.00		
Gain/(loss) on sale of asset	(10.00)		
Tax saved on sale of asset		2.00	
			19.00
Net Initial Cost			26.00

Cash Flow—Terminal Year

All the principles stated above apply to the cash flow of any year. It applies to the terminal year too. The terminal year, however, is characterized by some special cash flows other than operational. We need to address the questions of (a) disposal of asset, (b) net working capital, and (c) effects of taxes thereon. Mostly at the end of the useful life of the project the assets are deemed to be surplus and available for sale. The firm will also be responsible for any tax advantage/disadvantage that may result upon disposal of assets. At the end of the project, the net working capital is also released and is available for alternate use and, therefore, it must be added to the cash flows in the terminal year.

The issue of the release of working capital is rather simple to handle. The initial working capital and subsequent increases in the operations would stand released when the project is considered to be over. The net working capital would simply be added to the operational cash flows in the terminal year. It has no tax implication.

However, the aspect of disposal of assets is not as easy. It has tax implications. Further complexities are added due to the complicated tax treatment of sale of capital assets. Depending upon the tax laws there could be tax savings or tax incidence on disposal of fixed asset. The realized value upon the disposal must be adjusted for taxes.

Terminal year cash flows therefore would be:

Operational cash flow
+ Release of net working capital
+ Salvage value of the asset realized
± Tax saved/paid

Note that the tax laws in India are different. These are mentioned below:

- Only WDV method is allowed for computation of depreciation for tax purposes
- Assets are categorized in the block of assets for different rates of depreciation
- When new assets are bought the purchase price is added to the block of asset
- When assets are sold, the value of the block of asset is reduced by the salvage value

The cash flow implication of the tax is that instead of taxing the gain/loss on sale of fixed asset at the time of the sale, the written down value of the block of asset is reduced by the amount of the salvage value realized. Therefore, the firm does not get depreciation for subsequent periods on the asset sold to the extent of differential of book value and salvage value. We adjust for this loss or gain in the following manner:

If salvage value > book value Tax loss results by the amount equal to the present value of tax shield on the differential of salvage value and book value. This is subtracted from the salvage value for the purpose of determination of cash flow from the sale of asset.

Cash flow from the sale of asset:
= Salvage value – PV of tax shield on (salvage value – book value)

If salvage value < book value Tax benefit accrues by the amount equal to the present value of tax shield on the differential of book value and salvage value. This is added to the salvage value for the purpose of determination of cash flow from the sale of asset.

Cash flow from sale of asset:
= Salvage value + PV of tax shield on (book value – salvage value)

By adjusting the book value of the block of the asset the tax benefit is deferred (assuming salvage value to be less than book value) with progressive reduction in the benefit each year. Depreciation, under the written down value method is a perpetuity and the present value of the depreciation tax shield is given by Equation 11-8.

PV of Depreciation Tax Shield

$$= \frac{T \times d}{r + d}\ (\text{BV} - \text{SV}) \qquad (11\text{-}8)$$

where T = Tax rate,
d = Depreciation rate,
r = Cost of capital (discount rate),
and BV and SV are the book value and salvage value of the asset sold respectively.

Initial cost and terminal year cash flows for Foremost Brewers Assume that Foremost Brewers had two bottling lines used for packaging beer in 750 ml bottles and 375 ml bottles. The installation of new canning line will make bottling line for small bottles redundant. The value of this bottling line in the books was ₹30 lakh but it could be sold for ₹40 lakh. Similarly, after five years the canning line may be sold for ₹20 lakh against its book value of ₹70 lakh. If Foremost Brewers pay 30% tax, the cash flow in the initial year and the non-operational cash flow for the terminal year would be:

The initial cash flow		*₹ lakh*
Capital cost of the new canning line and fermentation tanks		1300
Other cash expenses (excluding sunk cost of market survey)		25
Less: Sale proceed of one bottling line		–40
Tax on sale of small bottling line		
Sale value	40	
Book value	30	
Profit on sale	10	
Tax on sale of asset (30% of capital gain)		3
Additional working capital in the first year		150
Total Cash Outflow in the 1st Year		**1438**

Table 11-20 Cash Flow Projection—Foremost Brewers *(₹ lakh)*

	Year 0	*Year 1*	*Year 2*	*Year 3*	*Year 4*	*Year 5*
Initial Outlay	–1300					
Revenue		1500	1800	2400	3000	3000
Raw Material		–600	–720	–960	–1200	–1200
Overheads		–500	–600	–700	–1000	–1000
Depreciation – SLM		–240	–240	–240	–240	–240
PBIT		160	240	500	560	560
Add: Depreciation		240	240	240	240	240
Cash flow before taxes		400	480	740	800	800
Side effect of loss of PBIT due to lost sales		**–50**	**–50**	**–50**	**–50**	**–50**
Market survey cost regarded as sunk	**25**					
Opportunity cost of rent foregone		**–12**	**–12**	**–12**	**–12**	**–12**
Increase in net working capital	**–150**	**–30**	**–60**	**–60**	**—**	
Tax -as computed		**–4**	**–83**	**–220**	**–266**	**–282**
Sale proceeds of asset sold – net of taxes	**37**					
Sale proceeds of Canning Line + tax saved						**35**
Release of net working capital						**300**
Project's cash flow	**–1438**	**304**	**275**	**398**	**472**	**791**

Terminal Year (non-operational cash flow)		**₹ lakh**
Sale proceeds of canning line		20
Tax on canning line sold		
Sale value	20	
Book value	70	
Profit/(loss) on sale	(50)	
Tax saved		15
Release of net working capital		300
Total Non-operational Cash Flow in the Terminal Year		**335**

Another situation that needs to be considered is when the project is expected to last indefinitely into the future. Here we can't assume that the assets will be disposed, salvage value realized and working capital released. Instead, we have to assume the project continues well beyond foreseeable future. As we go farther into the future, the value of the distant cash flows reduces For practical purposes, we can assume the project to last indefinitely and value it accordingly. Fortunately, we do have the method to take care of such situation by the following formulation:

$$\text{Value of the Cash Flow at the end of period } n;\ PV_n = \frac{CF_{n+1}}{r-g}$$

where CF_{n+1} = Cash flow for the $(n + 1)$th period
r = discount rate; and g = growth rate of the cash flow

We may assume that the project to continue indefinitely yet make cash flow projection for a specified period beyond which assume the cash flows to remain constant or grow marginally. These cash flows can be translated to the present value at the end of initial evaluation period, and included in the overall cash flow of the project.

In case of Foremost Brewers, if we assume that the project will last indefinitely and the cash flow of ₹518 lakh at the end of 5th year will grow at 3% per annum, the value of cash flows at the end of 5th year at discount rate of 15% will be:

Value of the Cash Flow at the end of period n;

$$PV_n = \frac{CF_{n+1}}{r-g} = \frac{518}{0.15-0.03} = ₹4446 \text{ lakh}$$

This will be the terminal year cash flow for the project and may be substituted for the salvage value of the project.

Based of the discussion of various aspects of capital budgeting, the projection of cash flow for Foremost Brewers are presented in Table 11-20 highlighting each change emanating from the principles of capital budgeting. To the cash flows obtained in the last row of Table 11-20, one may choose to apply the IRR method or the NPV method for evaluation of the project for its acceptance or rejection.

CASH FLOWS FOR REPLACEMENT PROJECT

More often than not, firms are faced with the decision to replace an old machine or technology. These projects normally involve a decision to dispose off the old machine and replace it by some new machine that may be more efficient. Similarly, the adoption of new technology attempts to substitute an old product with newer ones with enhanced features or reduced cost. Benefits may accrue on account of the increased price, larger production, or reduced costs.

> *Because of the principle of incremental cash flows the evaluation of replacement project concentrates on the savings made.*

For some, cash flow projections for such projects are rather difficult because we have to apply the principle of incremental cash flow. This demands two projections of cash flows one with the old machine and the other with the new machine. The differential of the two cash flows forms the basis of decision making. An easier approach is to concentrate only on those cash flow items that are likely to change with the decision to replace rather than compiling the two entire sets of cash flows for the new and old machines. Then cash flow projection over the useful life of the project becomes rather easy and repetitive in nature. Depending upon the assumptions of revenues and costs they can be projected with ease. We emphasize only on the factors causing—(1) increase in revenue; and (2) decrease in costs.

Due to the requirement of having incremental post-tax cash flows, few issues pertaining to the initial year and terminal year, need special attention. For the projection of initial cash flow, we consider the cost of new machine and deduct the post-tax cash flow of the existing machine that would be sold. Any increase in working capital requirement must be added to the initial cost.

For cash flow of terminal year the differential of salvage values of the news machine and the old machine are relevant because of our need for incremental cash flow. This necessitates the projection of the salvage value of the old machine at the time of termination of the project with the new machine. One wonders why this is required. We need to remember that the capital budgeting exercise is making a comparison of the situation with and without the old machine. If we do not have the new machine the old machine would continue and all benefits and costs of the old machine remain. While we get the salvage value of the new machine we also lose the salvage value of the old machine.

For illustration of cash flow projection of a replacement machine, refer to Example 11-4.

Example 11-4 Replacement of a Machine

Bharat Auto Industries (BAI) manufactures auto components on lathe machine which has a book value of ₹2 lakh. This machine being depreciated at 20% has another five years of its useful life remaining but can be sold for ₹50,000 today. BAI is contemplating to replace this machine with a new one which delivers more output and is cost efficient too. The cost of the machine is ₹8 lakh with a life of five years and the depreciation of 20%. BAI estimates that with the new machine, it will be able to make extra sales of ₹1 lakh and save cost by ₹1.50 lakh for the next five years. With the increased sales of the requirement of working capital would also change and BAI would need ₹30,000 as shown below:

Increase in debtors	:	₹30,000
Increase in inventories	:	₹20,000
Less: Increase in creditors	:	₹20,000

At the end of five years the benefits of increased revenue and decreased cost will aggregate to ₹75,000 p.a. for indefinite time. BAI has WACC of 15% and pays taxes at 30%. Find if BAI should replace the old machine?

Solution

(Figures in ₹('000s)

Initial cost of the project		
Purchase price of the new machine		800
Less: Cash realized by disposing old machine		–50
Tax saved on disposal of machine:		
Book Value of the old machine	200	
Value realized on sale	50	
Loss on sale of machine	150	
Tax saved @ 30%		–45
Increase in working capital		30
Cash outflow towards new machine		735
Operational cash flow for the initial evaluation period for next five years		
Increased revenue	100	
Savings in cost	150	
Increase in profit	250	
Post-tax increase in profit		175
Depreciation on new machine	200	
Depreciation on old machine	40	
Increased depreciation	160	
Benefit of tax on increased depreciation		36
Incremental cash flow for next 5 years		211

Present Value of incremental cash flow at 15%, 5 years

$= 3.3521 \times 211 = 707.30$

Present value of cash flow of terminal year

Increase benefit of cash flow for indefinite period	75
Post-tax benefit = $75 \times (1 - 0.3) = 75 \times 0.7$	52.5

Value of benefit at the end of fifth year = Cash flow/capitalisation rate $= 75 \times 0.7/0.15 = 350$

Present value of the terminal year benefit $= 350/1.15^5 = 0.4971 \times 350 = 174.01$

NPV = PV of operational cash flows + PV of terminal year cash flow – Initial cost

$= 707.30 + 174.01 - 735.00 = 146.31$

Since NPV of the new machine is positive at ₹1.46 lakh, BAI must replace the machine.

MATCHING CASH FLOWS AND DISCOUNT RATE

Another important consideration while using the DCF techniques is the matching of numbers in the numerator and denominator. In the numerator we have cash flows and in the denominator discount rate is used. There has to be consistency in the use of cash flows and the discount rate.

The capital budgeting decision is usually viewed from perspectives of:

(a) All suppliers of capital, i.e., equity and debt capital; or
(b) Only suppliers of equity capital

While calculating NPV the cash flows must be discounted at rate consistent with the risk of cash flows that are being examined.

The cost of capital that is used as discount rate will depend upon from whose perspective the capital investment proposal is being examined. The cash flows that are discounted will have to be consistent with the stakeholders being considered. If all the stakeholders are considered then relevant discount rate will be Weighted Average Cost of Capital (WACC) unless the risk profile of the new project demands modification of the discount rate. The cash flows being discounted must be those belonging to all stakeholders.

If the analysis is being done from the perspective of equity shareholders then the relevant cash flows will be those belonging to shareholders alone and the relevant discount rate will be the cost of equity. Again the discount rate would be modified if the risk profile of the cash flows of the new project is substantially different than the risk of cash flow changes of the existing operations. The approach that uses cash flows to the equity holders and cost of equity as discount rate, is known as the *equity residual approach*.

Both WACC and equity residual methods would lead to identical decisions regarding the acceptance or rejection of the project if the numbers used are consistent with each other. The method to arrive at the cash flows to all suppliers of capital or suppliers of equity capital is summarized below:

Method	*Appropriate Cash Flows*	*Discount Rate*
WACC Method	**Cash flow to all investors** PBIT (1 – Tax Rate) + Depreciation + Non-cash Expense – Capital Expenditure – Increase in Working Capital	WACC
Equity Residual Method	**Cash flow to equity investors** PAT + Depreciation + Non-cash Expense – Capital Expenditure – Repayment of debt – Increase in Working Capital	Cost of Equity

A numerical example highlighting the approaches and their consistency of results is presented as Example 11-5.

Example 11-5 Matching Cash Flows and Discount Rate

ABC Limited is evaluating a project costing ₹800 lakh which is expected to give Profit Before Interest and Tax (PBIT) of ₹200 lakh per annum forever. Assume no depreciation or any other non-cash expense. The firm faces a tax rate of 40%.

(a) Using Weighted Average Cost of Capital (WACC) of 12%, find the NPV of the project

(b) Assuming that the project is funded through perpetual debt of ₹400 lakh (50% of original cost) at 10%, recompute the NPV of the project using cost of equity as discount rate.

Solution

(a) Using WACC Approach

	₹ lakh
Profit Before Interest and Tax	200
Taxes @ 40%	80
Profit After Tax (Cash flow available to all suppliers of capital)	120

Using the WACC of 12% as discount rate for the cash flows available to all capital suppliers, we find the NPV of the project as ₹200 lakh.

Net Present Value = Present Values of Inflows – Initial Cost

= 120/0.12 – 800 = 1000 – 800 = ₹200 lakh

(b) Using Equity Residual Approach

This method is also referred to as the 'flow-to-equity' approach. Assuming that 50% of the initial cost of ₹800 lakh is funded through a perennial debt at 10%, the market value of the equity will enhance by the NPV of ₹200 lakh.Hence, the debt–equity ratio is 40:60.

Value of the firm V = Value of Debt D + Value of Equity E

= 400 + 400 + Addition of NPV

= 400 + 400 + 200 = ₹1,000 lakh

We now find the cost of equity r_e for a levered firm with cost of debt r_d and tax rate of T as below (Remember that WACC uses market values of debt and equity):

$$\text{WACC} = r_e \times \frac{E}{V} + r_d\,(1 - T) \times \frac{D}{V}$$

$$12 = r_e \times 0.6 + 10 \times 0.6 \times 0.4$$

$$r_e = \frac{12 - 2.4}{0.6} = 16\%$$

The cash flow available to equity shareholders is:

	₹ lakh
Profit Before Interest and Tax (PBIT)	200
Interest on Debt (10% of 400)	40
Profit Before Tax	160
Taxes @ 40%	64
Profit After Tax (Cash flow to equity shareholders)	96

Net Present Value = Cash flow to equity shareholders/Cost of equity – Equity capital

96/0.16 – 400 = 600 – 400 = 200 (Same as obtained with WACC approach)

INFLATION AND CAPITAL BUDGETING

Inflation is an all pervasive phenomenon. How does inflation affect the capital budgeting process? Certainly, we cannot ignore this reality of inflation. There are two parameters entering the process of capital budgeting – the cash flows over the life of the project and the discount rate. They need to be consistent. The problem of consistency of the cash flow and discount rate may arise from inflation.

The principle of consistency in capital budgeting demands that nominal cash flows are discounted at nominal discount rate while real cash flows are discounted at real discount rate.

While projecting cash flows for the project, we make an implied assumption of constant prices of all items of revenue and costs, i.e., all cash flows are projected in terms of today's value of the rupee. The same value is used for all subsequent periods. Though the revenue and cost may be assumed to increase by the same factor of inflation in the subsequent periods the cash flows may be said to be unaffected. Similarly, while discounting these cash flows we also use a discount rate derived from the borrowing cost and cost of equity capital that are published, and exist today. These available figures for discount rate are nominal. However, inadvertently we have got cash flows in real terms while assuming constant prices of Period '0' for all subsequent periods. Would it be right to discount the real cash flows with the nominal cost of capital? Certainly not, instead we have to be consistent with the figures in the numerator and denominator, i.e., with the cash flows and discount rate in the DCF exercise.

The relationship between real rates and nominal rates is given by the Fisher Effect.

(1 + Nominal Rate) = (1 + Real Rate) × (1 + Inflation Rate)

Or, $(1 + r) = (1 + a) \times (1 + I)$

where a = real rate and I = inflation rate

The rule of capital budgeting for deciding the acceptance or rejection of the project would demand consistency in the numbers used in the numerator and denominator. The principle of consistency is violated by using constant prices in projecting cash flows and nominal rates while discounting them. The principle of consistency demands the use of real discount rate with real cash flows and use of nominal discount rate with nominal cash flows. The outcome remains unaffected as long as we follow this principle.

The NPV of the project can be expressed as:

$$\sum_{1}^{n} \frac{NCF_t}{(1+r)^t} - CF_0$$

where NCF_t is nominal cash flow for period t and r is nominal discount rate.

Using the Fisher effect, the NPV with real cash flows and real rate of return is restated as below demonstrating that NPV would not change if nominal figures are replaced by real figures.

$$\text{Net Present Value, NPV} = \sum_{1}^{n} \frac{NCF_t}{(1+r)^t} - CF_0$$

With inflation rate I and real rate a,

$$NPV = \sum_{1}^{n} \frac{CF_t(1+I)^t}{(1+a)^t\,(1+I)^t} - CF_0$$

$$= \sum_{1}^{n} \frac{CF_t(1+I)^t}{(1+a)^t\,(1+I)^t} - CF_0$$

We can use an example to demonstrate that both approaches yield identical results.

Assume a project costing ₹1,000 with a life of two years and the cash flows of ₹600 and ₹700 in Year 1 and Year 2 respectively. Using a discount rate of 10% we get the net present value of ₹123.96 as below:

PV of Cash Flow of Year 1 = 600/1.1 = ₹545.45

PV of cash Flow of Year 2 = $700/1.1^2$ = ₹578.51

Initial Investment = ₹1,000.00

Net Present Value = ₹123.96

Now assume that the inflation rate is 5%. Hence, the real rate must be

(1 + Real Rate) = (1+ Nominal Rate)/(1+Inflation Rate)

= 1.10/1.05 = 1.0476

Or, Real rate = 4.76%

Using real rate we shall get the same NPV if cash flows are translated in real terms:

Year	Nominal Cash flow	Real cash flow	Discounted value
1	600	600/1.05 = 571.43	545.46
2	700	$700/1.05^2$ = 634.92	578.52
Less Initial Investment			–1,000.00
Net Present Value			**123.98**

(The difference is due to round off)

There is only one possible way that we may defend the convention of using the cash flows at constant prices and discount them with the nominal figures available today is to assume that the cost of capital too would show an increase according to the inflation in the subsequent period. In effect, we are saying that the discount rate being used is not nominal but real.

CAUTIONS IN CAPITAL BUDGETING AND CASH FLOW PROJECTION

Capital budgeting exercise and its methods of evaluation assumes a definite life of the project. The acceptance or rejection of each of project is deemed to have no bearing on the subsequent courses of action that a firm may have. It is rarely the case. Invariably, what a firm does in the past either opens up further avenues of investment or constrains the future courses of action. Different projects executed at different points of time during the life of the firm cannot be treated as isolated decisions. New projects were, possibly, the consequences of the old history. In the capital budgeting exercise, we have not accounted for such opportunities that could be made available.

For example, the decision to open up a new style restaurant in an upwardly mobile neighbourhood may be rejected because of the negative NPV of the project. In a routine capital budgeting exercise we would not consider that opening of such restaurant today might also open up avenues to launch few more restaurants later on. The initial decision has a built-in option to abandon or expand depending upon the outcome of the experiment, the value of which was not considered in the capital budgeting exercise. The capital budgeting exercise considers the cash flows of the project without considering the value of the future courses of action that may be available.

Another problem that plagues the capital budgeting decision has its roots in the human behaviour. While projecting the cash flows or choosing the discount rate, we are only dealing with estimates prepared by managers. These estimates carry the biases of the managers concerned. They may overestimate or underestimate the cash flows depending upon what the manager desires. In a way, it is a manifestation of the problem of agency where the managers may not act necessarily in the interest of shareholders. In their own interests, managers may make an otherwise unacceptable project look highly desirable by overstating the cash inflows, underestimating the cash outflows and assuming a lower than real discount rate. Later on, upon the failure of project managers would easily pass on the blame on the circumstances that estimates did not prove correct.

SUMMARY

Capital budgeting decisions are very vital and crucial to the survival and growth of the enterprise. These decisions relating to the acceptance or rejection of the projects have long-term implications and are strategic in nature.

Features of capital budgeting proposals include—(1) their non-reversibility; (2) information gaps; (3) inherent risks in the projects; (4) inflexibilities; and (5) the inability to incorporate changes depending upon the experiences gathered later.

The capital budgeting proposal may be classified in a number of ways depending upon the nature, initial outlays, etc. Mutually exclusive projects are those where acceptance of one precludes acceptance of another. Such projects have to be examined very carefully because the acceptance of one project implies an opportunity foregone to accept possibly a more profitable project.

There are various tools to examine the acceptability of the projects. There can be segregated into DCF-based techniques and non-DCF based techniques. Non-DCF techniques include methods of accounting rate of return (ARR) and payback period. These methods do not place any importance to the fact that when the profit or cash flows are generated. They all are treated with the same value irrespective of their timings of occurrence. The ARR is the percentage return of average profit over average investment. This is compared with expectations of return to make a decision to accept or reject a proposal. The payback period is concerned about the time period it would take to recover the original investment. Again this is compared with the cut-off payback period serving as a benchmark for acceptance of a project. Besides, not attaching the time value of money to the cash flows of the project the payback method suffers the drawback of ignoring the cash flows after the payback period.

The DCF techniques include net present value (NPV) and internal rate of return (IRR) methods. The NPV is the present value of the cash inflows discounted at cost of capital or some other discount rate less initial investment. If the NPV of the project is positive it is accepted else we reject it. The NPV states the contribution a project makes to the value of the firm. Acceptance of project increases the value of the firm by the amount of its NPV.

The internal rate of return (IRR) method is also based on DCF. IRR is that rate of return, which makes the net present value of the project as zero. As the discount rate increases the NPV of the project falls and ultimately turns negative. The IRR is the maximum discount rate that is supported by the cash flows of the project. If the cost of capital is less than the IRR, we accept the project otherwise it is not worth considering.

Generally speaking, the decision rules of acceptance of the project under NPV method and IRR method are consistent with each other and give identical outcomes. However, there are some deficiencies in the IRR method that may cause it to differ from the NPV method. The circumstances that may lead to contradictions in the NPV and the IRR method are non-conventional cash flows of the project and mutually exclusive projects. The source of contradiction is attributed to implicit assumptions about the reinvestment rate of the interim cash flows of the project.

Modified IRR (MIRR) is one way of overcoming the objection of reinvestment rate, where the interim cash flows are assumed reinvested at discount rate for a terminal value and the IRR recomputed.

Due to its unambiguous results, the ability to handle all situations and measure the contribution of the project to the value of the firm NPV techniques is considered a superior tool of evaluation of capital budgeting proposals.

While projecting the cash flows of the project it is usually convenient to split them into three—(1) initial cash outlay; (2) regular cash flows over the life; and (3) cash flows for the terminal year. All the cash flows are made on an incremental basis. This implies the inclusion of cash flows due to the side effects of the project and opportunity costs. Similarly, the sunk costs that have no bearing on the decision must be excluded. Since the capital budgeting decisions are made from the perspective of the suppliers of capital and taxes have precedence over the claims of capital suppliers the cash flows need to be projected on a post-tax basis. Also, capital budgeting is an assessment of the cash generation ability of the assets being examined the cash flows accruing to the financiers like interest and dividend must be separated from those attributable to the capital asset. These are dealt with in the discount rate.

Replacement projects assume special significance for projection of cash flows due to incremental principle. Initial cash flows must be modulated for the salvage value of the asset being replaced. The operational cash flows must consider only those items that are expected to change with the introduction of new asset. The tax shield on the depreciation must be calculated on the basis of depreciation differential of new and old asset. Similarly, at the end of the project the differential of the salvage value net of taxes must be accounted for.

In any capital budgeting exercise, care must be taken to match the cash flows with the appropriate discount rate. The discount rate must reflect the risks inherent in the cash flows. The cash flows may be viewed either from the perspective of shareholders alone or with the debt suppliers too. The discount rate for evaluation must be consistent with the cash flows.

The treatment of inflation in capital budgeting exercise is often flawed. The practice of assuming constant prices while projecting cash flows is generally followed. This means the cash flows are real in nature. At the same time, it has been a practice to use the discount rate through the cost of capital route from the published available information implies that the discount rate is nominal. We essentially have to discount real cash flows with real cost of capital and nominal cash flows with nominal cost of capital.

KEY TERMS

Independent project Projects, which are not related to each other and acceptance on one does not have any bearing on the acceptance of another are independent projects.

Mutually exclusive projects Projects where the acceptance of one precludes acceptance of another are mutually exclusive projects.

Accounting Rate of Return (ARR) It is the average profit as percentage of average investment over the life of the project.

Payback period Payback period is the amount of time required to recover the original investment back.

Discounted payback period It is the amount of time required to recover the original investment back when cash flows are discounted.

Present value Present value refers to the value of the cash flow at time $t = 0$ when discounted with a discount rate.

Net Present Value (NPV) NPV is the present value of cash inflows less present value of the cash outflows.

Internal Rate of Return (IRR) IRR is the discount rate that makes the net present value equal to zero.

Point of indifference Point of indifference is the IRR of the differential cash flows of two projects. At this discount rate the NPVs of the two projects are equal.

Reinvestment rate The rate at which the interim cash flows are reinvested is called reinvestment rate.

Modified IRR (MIRR) MIRR is the method where reinvestment is assumed at cost of capital for the interim cash flows and the IRR is recalculated with such modified cash flows.

Sunk costs Sunk costs are those items of cash flows that have occurred in the past and do not have an impact on the current decision-making.

Opportunity cost The cost that is related to the alternative opportunity foregone is called opportunity cost.

Depreciation tax shield The amount of tax saved on the depreciation is referred as depreciation tax sheild.

SLM method The SLM method of charging depreciation is at a constant percentage of the original cost of the equipment in each year.

Written Down Value (WDV) method Method of charging depreciation on the asset based on fixed percentage of the book value of the asset is called WDV method.

Book value The value of the asset at which the asset is carried in the financial statement is called book value.

Salvage value Salvage value is the expected realizable value at the time of disposal of the asset.

KEY FORMULAE

Accounting Rate of Return $= \dfrac{\text{Average Profit}}{\text{Average Investment}}$

Net Present Value

$$NPV = \sum_{1}^{n} \frac{CF_t}{(1+r)^t} - CF_0$$

Tax Shield on Depreciation = Tax rate × Depreciation

Internal Rate of Return (IRR)

$$\text{Net Present Value, NPV} = \sum_{1}^{n} \frac{CF_t}{(1+r)^t} - CF_0 = 0$$

Depreciation based on the WDV Method

For period $n = d(1-d)^{n-1}$

Book Value based on the WDV Method

Book Value after Period $n = (1-d)^n$

PRACTICE PROBLEMS

1. Payback Period

PayEarly Ltd is planning a major investment to expand its current manufacturing of digital clocks with initial cash outlay of ₹350 lakh. The finance department has projected a following cash flows over the next 7 years considered to be life of the project:

Year	0	1	2	3	4	5	6	7
Cash flows (₹ lakh)	–350	100	150	400	450	300	250	50

What is the payback period of the project?

What is the discounted payback period assuming that discounting is done at 15%?

Solution

Cumulative cash flow, discounted and non-discounted are calculated as shown in the following table:

(₹ lakh)

	Payback period		Discounted payback period at 15%	
Year	Cash flows	Cumulative Cash flows	Cash flows	Cumulative Cash flows
0	–350.00	–350.00	350.00	–350.00
1	100.00	250.00	86.96	–263.04
2	150.00	–100.00	113.42	–149.62
3	400.00	300.00	263.01	113.38
4	450.00	750.00	257.29	370.67
5	300.00	1050.00	149.15	519.83
6	250.00	1300.00	108.08	627.91
7	50.00	1350.00	18.80	646.71

The cumulative cash flow turns from negative to positive in Year 3.

Assuming even cash flow over the year, the cumulative cash flow of – ₹100 lakh would become zero in 3 months of Year 2.

The payback period is 2 years 3 months.

For the discounted payback period the cash flows are discounted at given rate of 15%.

Here also the cumulative cash flow is – ₹150 lakh at the end of two years.

This deficit can be made good in 150/263 years equivalent to 6.84 months.

The discounted payback period is 2 years 6.84 months.

2. Calculating NPV

Light Rollers Ltd (LRL) is considering a project to produce rubber rollers with an initial investment of ₹400 lakh. The project would last for 8 years after which 10% of the initial investment may be realised. LRL has a policy of charging depreciation on SLM basis.

After taking costing of the product a profit before tax of ₹52 lakh is expected for next 8 years. Though the normal rates of tax is 40% LRL would pay only 28% taxes due to tax incentives available. Assume that no tax is payable on the salvage value realized.

If the cost of capital of LRL is 12% what is the NPV of the project and what shall be the decision with respect to its acceptance.

Would your decision change if suddenly the tax benefit is withdrawn and LRL is subjected to normal rate of tax of 40%.

Solution

	₹ lakh	
Cost of the machine	400.00	
Salvage value	40.00	Life = 8 years
Annual depreciation	45.00	

Computation of cash flow and NPV *(₹ lakh)*

	(with 28% tax)	(with 40% tax)
Profit before taxes	52.00	52.00
Taxes @ 28%	14.56	20.80
Profit after tax	37.44	31.20
Add: Depreciation	45.00	45.00
Cash flow after taxes	82.44	76.20
Present value of operational cash flows	**409.53**	**378.53**
Salvage value realised at 10th year	40.00	40.00
Present value of the salvage value	16.16	16.16
Total present value of cash inflows	**425.69**	**394.69**
Less: Initial cost 400.00	400.00	400.00
NPV	**25.69**	**5.31**

Calculation PV factors
Period of annuity = 8 years Required rate of return = 12% Present value of annuity for 8 years at 12.00% = PVIFA (12.00%, 8) = 4.9676
Period of annuity = 8 years Required rate of return = 12% Present value of Re 1 after 8 years at 12.00% = PVIF (12.00%, 8) = 0.4039

As is evident from the calculation of NPV with tax rates of 28% and 40%, the project has positive NPV of ₹25.69 lakh while it is negative at ₹5.31 lakh when the tax rate rises to 40%.

The project is viable as long as tax rate does not go to 40%.

3. Calculating IRR

For the data given in the previous problem find the IRR of the project with a) tax rate of 28% and b) tax rate of 40%.

On the basis of IRR what would be your recommendation?

Solution

The cash flows for the project with two different tax rates are shown below with the salvage value cash flows added to the 8th year cash flow:

	Cash flows (₹ lakh)	
Year	Tax rate 28%	Tax rate 40%
0	–400.00	–400.00
1	82.44	76.20
2	82.44	76.20
3	82.44	76.20
4	82.44	76.20
5	82.44	76.20
6	82.44	76.20
7	82.44	76.20
8	122.44	116.20
IRR	**13.74%**	**11.63%**

IRR of the cash flows has been found using EXCEL

For decision making under the IRR rule we compare the IRR with the cost of capital, 12% in this case. If IRR is greater than the cost of capital we accept the project else we reject it.

With tax rate of 28% the IRR is higher than the cost of capital and therefore is acceptable. With tax rate of 40% the cash flows of the project support the return of 11.63% as against the required return of 12% and is therefore unacceptable.

4. Mutually Exclusive Proposals

Bharat Limited is considering to replace an existing machine for which two suppliers have quoted. Supplier A has proposed a machine costing ₹180 lakh that uses the existing boiler while Supplier B has quoted for the machine for ₹110 lakh but that requires modification in the existing energy supply system costing ₹30 lakh. The machines have a life of 10 years and can be sold for 5% and 10% of the original cost respectively for Suppliers A and B. The additional working capital requirement expressed as % of revenue are 20% and 25% respectively because of larger requirement of fuel for the machine from Supplier B. The details are condensed below:

(₹ in lakh)

	Supplier A	Supplier B
Price of machine	180	135
Annual Cash flows		
Revenue	200	205
Operating cost	150	155
Working capital (% of revenue)	20%	25%
Salvage value % of cost	20%	5%

The firm charges depreciation on SLM basis with zero book value and has a tax rate of 35% for all kinds of income. The cost of capital for the firm is 12%.

Which of the suppliers Bharat Limited prefer:

(a) as per NPV rule

(b) as per IRR rule

Solution

(a) We shall compare the present value of cost of both the alternatives to arrive at the decision to buy from Supplier A or B.

(*₹ in lakh*)

		Supplier A	Supplier B
Initial investment		180.00	135.00
Additional investment		—	30.00
Working capital		40.00	51.25
Initial cash outflow of the project		**220.00**	**216.25**
Annual Cash flows:			
Annual Revenue		200.00	205.00
Annual Operating Costs		150.00	155.00
PBDIT		50.00	50.00
Depreciation		18.00	16.50
PBIT = PBT		32.00	33.50
Taxes 35%		11.20	11.73
PAT		20.80	21.78
Annual Cash flow		**38.80**	**38.28**
PV-Annual regular cash flows (PVA factor = 5.6502)		**219.23**	**216.26**
Terminal Year's cash flows			
Salvage value			
Value realised		36.00	6.75
Book value		—	—
Capital gain		36.00	6.75
Value realised net of tax		23.40	4.39
Release of working capital		40.00	51.25
Terminal year cash inflow		**63.40**	**55.64**
Present value	PV factor = 0.3220	**20.41**	**17.91**
PV of regular cash flows and terminal year		**239.64**	**234.18**
Less: Initial Investment		**220.00**	**216.25**
Net Present value		**19.64**	**17.93**

Calculation of depreciation		
Cost of the machine	180.00	135.00
Additional investment	—	30.00
Life	10.00	10.00
Depreciation SLM	18.00	16.50

Calculation of PV factors	
Period of annuity = 10.00 years	Required rate of return = 12%
Present value of annuity for 10 years at 12% = PVIFA (12% , 10) = 5.6502	
Period of annuity = 10.00 years	Required rate of return = 12%
Present value of Re 1 after 10 years at 12% = PVIF (12% , 10) = 0.3220	

Since the net present value of machine from Supplier A is marginally higher than that of Supplier B, the firm must choose machine from Supplier A.

(b) The cash flows of the machines from Supplier A and Supplier B are as follows:

(*₹ lakh*)

Year	Supplier A: Initial and regular	Supplier A: Terminal year	Supplier A: Total	Supplier B: Initial and regular	Supplier B: Terminal year	Supplier B: Total
0	–220.00		–220.00	–216.25		–216.25
1	38.80		38.80	38.28		38.28
2	38.80		38.80	38.28		38.28
3	38.80		38.80	38.28		38.28
4	38.80		38.80	38.28		38.28
5	38.80		38.80	38.28		38.28
6	38.80		38.80	38.28		38.28
7	38.80		38.80	38.28		38.28
8	38.80		38.80	38.28		38.28
9	38.80		38.80	38.28		38.28
10	38.80	63.40	102.20	38.28	55.64	93.91
	IRR* =		**13.95%**			**13.83%**

*IRR is found using *IRR function* in EXCEL.

The IRR of machines from both the suppliers is greater than the required rate of return of 12%. However since IRR of the machine from Supplier A is higher at 13.95% as compared to 13.83% for the machine from Supplier B the rule favours Supplier A.

5. NPV, IRR, and MIRR

A firm in the business of manufacture of automobile components is considering two mutually exclusive technologies for manufacture of a hydraulic brakes. These two technologies are designated as Option A and Option B with project costs of ₹. 1600 lakh and ₹1850 lakh. Depending upon various features of the product obtainable from the two technologies the firm has developed a forecast of cash flows for 5 years i.e. the life of each project. These cash flows are as below:

(*₹ lakh*)

Year	Option A	Option B
1	350.00	675.00
2	475.00	575.00
3	625.00	725.00
4	575.00	350.00
5	350.00	400.00

Option A is a familiar technology and therefore the firm feels that the current cost of capital of 13% is the appropriate discount rate. However, Option B is considered riskier than the Option A and therefore firm would like to use a discount rate of 15%, some what higher than the current cost of capital.

Find out the following:

(a) NPVs of the Options A and B

(b) IRR of the Options A and B

(c) Which option would you consider with NPV rule and IRR rule

(d) Firm believes that under most probable circumstances it would be able to re-invest the internally generated cash flows of the project at 14%. What would be your decision if that be the case?

Solution

(a) and (b) NPVs and IRRs of the Option A and Option B are calculated as below

	Option A	Option B
Discount rate	13%	15%
Initial cash out flow	1,600.00	1,850.00

Year	*Option A* Cash flow	Present value	*Option B* Cash flow	Present Value
0	–1,600.00	–1,600.00	–1,850.00	–1,850.00
1	350.00	309.73	675.00	586.96
2	475.00	371.99	575.00	434.78
3	625.00	433.16	725.00	476.70
4	575.00	352.66	350.00	200.11
5	350.00	189.97	400.00	198.87
IRR	**14.42%**		**16.19%**	
NPV		**57.51**		**47.42**

(c) Based on the appropriate discount rates for Option A and Option B, the NPVs and IRRs are as below (with favoured options highlighted):

	Option A	Option B
Discount Rate	13.00%	14.00%
NPV (₹ lakh)	**57.51**	47.42
IRR	14.42%	**16.00%**

Based on IRR rule, Option B is preferable having larger IRR. *(IRR is not concerned about the cost of capital while ranking projects)*

Based on NPV rule, Option A is preferred as it has larger NPV than that of Option B, when NPVs are calculated at the appropriate discount rates.

(d) As the firm believes that the re-investment of interim cash flows can be done at 14% only irrespective of the option chosen we need to re-evaluate the cash flows under Options A and Option B with 14% rate of re-investment. We determine the terminal value of cash flows of the two options and find modified IRR.

Re-investment rate = 14.00%

Year	*Option A* Cash flow	Terminal value of inflows	*Option B*	Terminal value of inflows
0	–1,600.00		–1,850.00	
1	350.00	591.14	675.00	1,140.05
2	475.00	703.73	575.00	851.89
3	625.00	812.25	725.00	942.21
4	575.00	655.50	350.00	399.00
5	350.00	350.00	400.00	400.00
Terminal value of cash inflows at 14%		**3,112.62**		**3,733.15**

Option A MIRR, r = $1600 \times (1 + r)^5 = 3112.62$ gives $r = 14\%$

Option B MIRR, r = $1850 \times (1 + r)^5 = 3733.15$ gives $r = 15\%$

Since under the reasonable assumption of re-investment at 14% the modified IRR is greater for Option B the firm should go for Option B.

6. Evaluating Investment Alternatives

A small courier company is in need of a small vehicle to make deliveries. It is intending to choose between two options. One option is to buy a new three wheeler that would cost ₹75,000 and serve for 8 years.

The other alternative is to buy a second-hand vehicle for ₹45,000 now that could serve the firm for 4 years. Thereafter the firm can buy another second-hand vehicle for ₹40,000 that lasts for another 4 years.

The firm can realize the WDV of the vehicles whenever they are discarded. The firm pays 30% tax and is allowed to claim depreciation on vehicles of 25% on WDV basis.

If the cost of capital for the firm is 12% which of the option the firm should adopt?

Solution

Cost of capital	12%
Tax rate	30%
Depreciation	25%

Apart from the capital cost of the vehicles the depreciation tax shield would cause the difference in the cash flows of two options. The depreciation based on 25% WDV is as below:

Depreciation schedule for two alternatives

Year	*New Vehicle* Value	Dep.	*Used Vehicles* Value	Dep.	Value	Dep.
1	75,000.00	18,750.00	45,000.00	11,250.00		
2	56,250.00	14,062.50	33,750.00	8,437.50		
3	42,187.50	10,546.88	25,312.50	6,328.13		
4	31,640.63	7,910.16	18,984.38	4,746.09		
5	23,730.47	5,932.62			40,000.00	
6	17,797.85	4,449.46			30,000.00	7,500.00
7	13,348.39	3,337.10			22,500.00	5,625.00
8	10,011.29	2,502.82			16,875.00	4,218.75
WDV	*7,508.47*		*14,238.28*		*12,656.25*	

The differential cash flows of the two option would consist of (i) the capital cost of the vehicles (ii) the tax shield on the depreciation and (iii) the salvage values realised each time the vehicle is discarded.

We compare these cash flows and find the NPVs of the cost, and choose that has least NPV of costs.

New Vehicle

Year	Capital Cost	Tax Shield – Dep.	Salvage value realized	Total cash outflow	PV of cash outflows
0	75,000.00			75,000.00	75,000.00
1		5,625.00		(5,625.00)	(5,022.32)
2		4,218.75		(4,218.75)	(3,363.16)
3		3,164.06		(3,164.06)	(2,252.12)
4		2,373.05		(2,373.05)	(1,508.11)
5		1,779.79		(1,779.79)	(1,009.90)
6		1,334.84		(1,334.84)	(676.27)
7		1,001.13		(1,001.13)	(452.86)
8		750.85	7,508.47	(8,259.32)	(3,335.80)
Present value of cost					**57,379.46**

Old Vehicles

Year	Capital Cost	Tax Shield – Dep	Salvage value realized	Total cash outflow	PV of cash outflows
0	45,000.00			45,000.00	45,000.00
1		3,375.00		(3,375.00)	(3,013.39)
2		2,531.25		(2,531.25)	(2,017.90)
3		1,898.44		(1,898.44)	(1,351.27)
4	40,000.00	1,423.83	14,238.28	24,337.89	15,467.17
5		3,000.00		(3,000.00)	(1,702.28)
6		2,250.00		(2,250.00)	(1,139.92)
7		1,687.50		(1,687.50)	(763.34)
8		1,265.63	12,656.25	(13,921.88)	(5,622.81)
Present value of cost					**44,856.26**

Since the present value of cost under the option of buying second-hand vehicles is lower, the firm must adopt the strategy of buying the second-hand vehicles.

7. Conflicts between NPV and IRR

Blue Diamonds Limited is a marketing organization that is considering launch of product with two different strategies; Strategy A and Strategy B. It has to choose either of A or B. Both the strategies have initial outlay of ₹20 crore but have different streams of inflows.

Over a period of 5 years, the cash flows of the strategies are as below.

Year	Cash flows in ₹ lakh	
	Project A	**Project B**
0	–2000	–2000
1	500	1000
2	850	875
3	550	500
4	650	140
5	400	200

(i) Find out the NPVs of both the strategies at discount rates between 9% and 19% at intervals of 2%.
(ii) Plot the NPVs of the strategies with different discount rates.
(iii) Find out the internal rate of returns (IRRs) for both the strategies.
(iv) Which of the strategy is preferable based on rule of IRR?
(v) Which of the two strategies is preferable if the cost of capital is (a) 11%, (b) 14%.
(vi) At what rate of discount, the two strategies would be equally preferable? And what does this discount rate mean?

Solution

(i) The net present values of the Strategies A and B with the given cash flows at 9%, 11%, 13%, 15%, 17%, and 19% are as computed Table P11-7(i).

Table P11-7(i) Net Present Value *(All figures in ₹)*

Year	Cash flow	Discount Rates 9%	11%	13%	15%	17%	19%
Strategy A							
0	–2,000.00	–2,000.00	–2,000.00	–2,000.00	–2,000.00	–2,000.00	–2,000.00
1	500.00	458.72	450.45	442.48	434.78	427.35	420.17
2	850.00	715.43	689.88	665.67	642.72	620.94	600.24
3	550.00	424.70	402.16	381.18	361.63	343.40	326.38
4	650.00	460.48	428.18	398.66	371.64	346.87	324.13
5	400.00	259.97	237.38	217.10	198.87	182.44	167.62
	NPV – A	**319.29**	**208.04**	**105.09**	**9.65**	**– 78.99**	**–161.46**
Strategy B							
0	–2,000.00	–2,000.00	–2,000.00	–2,000.00	–2,000.00	–2,000.00	–2,000.00
1	1,000.00	917.43	900.90	884.96	809.57	854.70	840.34
2	875.00	736.47	710.17	685.25	661.63	639.20	617.89
3	500.00	386.09	365.60	346.53	328.76	312.19	296.71
4	140.00	99.18	92.22	85.86	80.05	74.71	69.81
5	200.00	129.99	118.69	108.55	99.44	91.22	83.81
	NPV – B	**269.16**	**187.58**	**111.15**	**39.43**	**–27.98**	**–91.44**

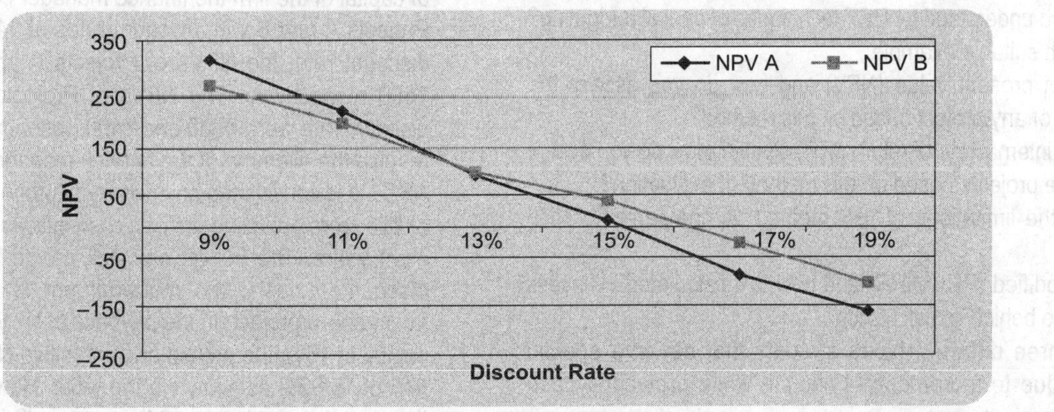

Figure P11-7(ii) NPV Profile

(ii) The profile of net present values of Project A and Project B are plotted in Figure P11-7(ii).

(iii) The internal rate of returns for Project A and Project B are computed below.

(₹ in lakh)

Year	Cash Flows	
	Strategy A	Strategy B
0	–2000	–2000
1	500	1000
2	850	875
3	550	500
4	650	140
5	400	200
IRR of the projects	15.21%	16.15%

(iv) Based on the IRR rule for capital budgeting, Strategy B is preferable as it has higher IRR.

(v-a) If the cost of capital is 11%, the NPVs of the projects are

Strategy A ₹208.04 lakh
Strategy B ₹187.58 lakh

Based on NPV rule, the Strategy A is preferable since it has higher NPV at 11%.

(v-b) If the cost of capital is 14%, the NPVs of the projects are

(₹ in lakh)

Year	Strategy A		Strategy B	
	Cash flow	NPV	Cash flow	NPV
0	–2,000.00	–2,000.00	–2,000.00	-2,000.00
1	500.00	438.60	1,000.00	877.19
2	850.00	654.05	875.00	673.28
3	550.00	371.23	500.00	337.49
4	650.00	384.85	140.00	82.89
5	400.00	207.75	200.00	103.87
NPV		56.48		74.73

Based on NPV rule the Strategy B is preferable since it has higher NPV at 14%

(vi) The point of indifference can be computed by finding IRR of the differential cash flow.

Year	Cash Flows		
	Strategy A	Strategy B	Differential
0	–2000	–2000	0
1	500	1000	–500
2	850	875	–25
3	550	500	50
4	650	140	510
5	400	200	200
IRR of differential cash flow			12.52%

At the discount rate of 12.52%, the NPVs of both the strategies would be equal. When the discount rate is less than 12.52%, the NPV of Strategy A would be higher and it would be the preferable project as compared to Strategy B. However the situation would reverse when the discount rate exceeds 12.52% and then. Strategy B becomes preferable.

EXERCISES

Concept Review Questions

1. What do you understand by capital budgeting? How do you classify different kinds of projects?
2. Why do you think the capital budgeting decisions are vital for any firm?
3. What is a payback period? How do you appraise projects on the basis of payback period and what are the limitations?
4. Payback period and discounted payback period handle the risk associated with the projects in their own way. Comment.
5. What do you understand by DCF techniques of capital budgeting? Explain with suitable example.
6. What is net present value (NPV) and how do you assess the desirability of any project based on this method?
7. What does internal rate of return (IRR) signify? How do you accept or reject the projects based on this method of evaluation?
8. What are the limitations of IRR method as compared to NPV method?
9. What is modified IRR (MIRR) and how is it calculated? Discuss the rationale behind its calculation.
10. Discuss three different types of costs that deserve special attention due to incremental principle while projecting cash flows of a project.
11. While projecting cash flows of the project provide reasons for—(i) excluding interest on the debt; (ii) inclusion of salvage value as cash inflow; and (iii) deducting taxes.
12. How would you treat inflation while evaluating a capital budgeting proposal?

Critical Thinking Questions

1. A firm is considering two mutually exclusive Projects A and B with IRR of 20% and 25%, respectively. Uncertain about the cost of capital of the firm the finance manager computed NPVs of the Projects A and B with discount rates of 14% and 18%. At 14% discount rate, the NPVs of Projects A and B were ₹400 and ₹500 respectively. The NPVs of Projects A and B with 18% discount rate were ₹500 and ₹400, respectively. How would you resolve the dilemma of the finance manager?
2. ABC Ltd is considering an investment proposal requiring an outlay of ₹20 crore providing uniform cash inflows of ₹50 lakh over next eight years. The cut-off payback period is three years. On a discounted basis, the management is inclined to consider favourably a project on the payback of six years. With the cost of capital at 15%, the project has a positive NPV of ₹2.43 lakh and IRR of 18.62% as shown in the table. How would you convince the management to accept the proposal?

			All cash flows in '000s
Year	*Cash Flow*	*PV at 15%*	*Cumulative PV*
0	–2000.00	–2000.00	
1	500.00	434.78	434.78
2	500.00	378.07	812.85
3	500.00	328.76	1141.61
4	500.00	285.88	1427.49
5	500.00	248.59	1676.08
6	500.00	216.16	1892.24
7	500.00	187.97	2080.21
8	500.00	163.45	2243.66
IRR		**18.62%**	
NPV		**243.66**	

3. XYZ Ltd, facing acute shortage of electricity is planning to buy a generator. State the various costs that you would consider in projections of the cash flows and why?
4. An executive committee of the firm in packaging industry already having four colour printing machine is considering the installation of an eight-colour printing machine that would enable them capture additional business and double the turnover. While projecting the cash flows of the machine, the accountants allocated the overheads of finance, HR, purchase, sales, maintenance departments equally on both four- and eight-colour machine on the premise that 50% of the cost must be borne by the new machine constituting 50% of the turnover. As a member of the executive committee, would you accept such a cash flow? Why and why not?
5. A financial analyst regularly involved with the appraisal of the new projects commented: 'We project the revenues and cost as they are prevailing today and project them for the life of the project and use the discount rate derived from the market conditions. Since the revenue and cost offset each other, we do not need to account for inflation in the capital budgeting proposals.' Do you agree with the statement? Give reasons.

Practical Assignments

1. Select a growing company and find out the increase in the capital expenditure from its financial statements for any two consecutive years. Further, take financial statements of next two years and find the increase in cash flows and average it out. Assuming that the increase in cash flow is due to addition in the fixed assets and would continue for the next ten years find out the internal rate of return.
2. In Assignment 1, compute the NPV assuming that the cost of capital is 12%.

Numerical Problems

1. Calculating NPV

Machining Products Limited (MPL) is planning to purchase a CNC Lathe costing ₹220 lakh. It has an estimated life of ten years with salvage value of ₹20 lakh. Over a period of ten years MPL expects a profit before tax of ₹30 lakh every year. It pays a tax of 35% and charges depreciation on SLM basis. Find out whether MPL should buy CNC machine if the cost of capital for them is 10%. Ignore changes in working capital.

2. NPV, IRR, and MIRR

A firm is considering the purchase of 100 sewing machines. Each machine costs ₹18,000 and would yield a cash flow of ₹5,300 for the next five years. If the cost of capital for the firm is 14% find the following:

(i) NPV of the project
(ii) IRR of the project
(iii) Modified IRR of the project

3. Cash flows, NPV, IRR, and Payback Period

Super Dairy Limited (SDL) is planning to buy dairy equipment worth ₹300 lakh. The Milk Board provides 10% subsidy on the capital cost. It can process milk to produce cheese with the capacity of 1,800 tons per annum. The selling price of cheese is taken as ₹50 per kg. The management expects the life of the plant at eight years and the depreciation policy is SLM. However, the plant can be sold at ₹50 lakh at the end of its useful life. The plant is expected to be utilized as below:

Years	*1*	*2*	*3*	*4 to 8*
Cap. utilization	60%	70%	80%	90%

The variable cost constituting primarily of milk is placed at 40% while the fixed expenses are ₹300 lakh per annum. The firm pays 35% tax. The additional working capital required is ₹100 lakh.

Find the following:

(a) Cash flows of the project from Year 0 to Year 8
(b) NPV of the project
(c) IRR of the project
(d) Payback period
(e) Should the project be accepted based on NPV and IRR?

4. NPV and Lease

Ramesh purchased a premium car on a lease of ₹20,000 per month for six years. He continued to pay the instalments for one year after which he faced financial difficulties. He approached the leasing company to revise the terms of lease as he was unable to pay instalments for next one year. He, however, wanted to keep the total repayment period same as before.

The leasing company agreed to waive the next 12 instalments by increasing the amount to ₹27,500 per month for the remaining period. If the opportunity cost of capital for Ramesh is 12%, should he accept the revised payment terms from the leasing company?

Also, find to what revised lease rents Ramesh could accept to remain indifferent.

5. NPV and Managerial Decision

A project is costing ₹120 crore. The life of the project is eight years. The annual cost including depreciation is ₹50 crore. If the required rate of return is 15%, find out what minimum revenue the project must generate to make it viable. Assume depreciation at SLM and tax rate of 40%.

6. Replacing Machine: Net Present Value

Lotus Corporation is contemplating replacing its existing milling machine with an improved version that would increase the production from 12,000 components per month to 18,000. Due to its improved design, the new component would also fetch a better price of ₹90 as against existing price of ₹85 per piece.

The new machine costs ₹12 lakh with an additional amount on installation and training of ₹1.50 lakh to be spent. If purchased, the existing milling machine would be sold for ₹3.5 lakh that has a book value of ₹4 lakh. The remaining life of the existing machine is five years and the firm follows a policy of SLM for depreciation of fixed assets. The life of the new machine too is 5 years.

Installing the new machine would entail some extra recurring cost. The operator's salary would be increased from ₹50,000 to ₹70,000 per month. However, it would save the cost on maintenance and power. While the production would increase by 50%, the rise in maintenance cost would be 20% from existing ₹10,000 per month. Similarly, the power consumption would increase by 25% only from existing ₹6,000 per month. There would be no change in any other cost. Any increase in working capital may be ignored.

Assuming 40% taxes and cost of capital at 10%, examine whether Lotus Corporation should buy the new milling machine or not.

7. Disposal of Machine

Metal Craft Limited has a machine that is not considered up to the mark. The component produced on it can be contracted to a third party. If done so, the increase in cost of purchase net of the in-house manufacturing expenses would be ₹40,000 per annum. The machine can be sold for ₹80,000 while its book value is ₹1,10,000 with five remaining years of life. The depreciation policy of the firm is SLM while the tax rate is 35%. Examine if the machine should be sold or not. The cost of capital is 15%.

8. Make or Buy Decision

Hindustan Rubber Limited (HRL) has been procuring a rubber hose pipe from one of its vendor at a price of ₹125. Due to the increasing requirements of the component it is contemplating production of the same component in-house. The requirements of HRL for the next five years are as follows:

Year	1	2	3	4	5
Quantity required (Nos.)	60,000	67,500	75,000	82,500	90,000

The plant to manufacture the hose pipe costs ₹200 lakh. It is estimated to have a life of five years and a salvage value of ₹20 lakh. The plant can be depreciated at 25% on WDV basis as admissible for tax purposes.

The in-house production of the hose pipe can be done at a significantly less cost of ₹20 per piece as a variable cost, while the fixed cash expenses would amount to ₹15 lakh.

The other major change in the operations would come from the area of working capital management. HRL is currently keeping a stock of 1.6 months of requirement. If produced in-house, the overall stocking would increase to three months at the cost of production. The firm would also enjoy credit on the raw material of 0.5 months.

Examine whether HRL should go for in-house production of rubber hose pipe if tax rate is 40% and cost of capital is 10%.

9. Mutually Exclusive Proposals

Bharat Airlines Limited is considering the purchase of an aircraft. It has two alternatives—a Boeing or an Airbus. The initial investment, annual operational costs, and the salvage value at the end of 20 years are given below:

₹ in lakh	*Boeing*	*Airbus*
Initial investment	700	920
Annual Operating Costs		
Operational cost	150	100
Maintenance cost	140	120
Other costs	60	50
Salvage value	35	92

The firm pays 40% tax and charges depreciation on SLM basis. The life of aircraft is 20 years. Which aircraft should Bharat Airlines buy if the cost of its capital is 12%?

10. NPV vs IRR

A firm has two mutually exclusive proposals, A and B, under consideration requiring an initial outlay of ₹1,000 each. Both the projects have a life of seven years with the following cash flows:

		Cash flows in ₹
Year	*Project A*	*Project B*
0	–1000	–1000
1	50	500
2	100	350
3	250	250
4	300	60
5	400	100
6	450	100
7	500	150

(i) Find out the NPVs of both the projects at discount rates between 8% and 20% at intervals of 2%.

(ii) Plot the NPVs of the project with different discount rates.

(iii) Find out the internal rate of returns (IRRs) for both the projects.

(iv) Which of the project is preferable based on rule of IRR?

(v) Which of the two projects is preferable if the cost of capital is (a) 12%, (b) 15%.

(vi) At what rate of discount, both the projects would be equally preferable? And what does this discount rate mean?

CASE STUDY

GUPTA BRICKS—Bull's Trench Kiln and Vertical Shaft Brick Kiln

Mr Gupta owned the traditional family business of producing brick in a small town in Madhya Pradesh. His firm, Gupta Bricks, was doing good business off late and was operating at almost the full capacity.

The capacity of brick production was mainly limited by Bull's Trench Kiln (BTK); the most commonly used technology for firing the bricks. He had two Bull's Trench Kilns with an average capacity of 30,000 bricks per day. Operating on an average of 250 days in a year his annual production was about 75 lakh bricks per BTK.

Currently, the construction industry was passing through a boom. He wondered as to how to capitalize on the boom in the construction industry that has been facing a tremendous demand. The real estate prices were spiralling upwards. Besides new construction the demand for bricks was augmented due to rebuilding too. Built-up residences were being demolished and rebuilt by the affluent people who wanted to modernize construction for stylish living.

The last two years had witnessed increased prices and almost full capacity utilization. His income statement for the last two years is presented in Table A:

Table A Gupta Bricks—Income Statement for the last two years

Year	Year 1		Year 2	
Production and Sales '000 Nos.	14,000		15,000	
Income Statement				
(₹ in '000s)	Total	Per '000 bricks	Total	Per '000 bricks
Revenue	**14,000**	1.00	**16,500**	**1.10**
Raw Material	4,289	0.31	5,043	0.34
Expenses				
Labour	3,055	0.22	3,369	0.22
Fuel	2,948	0.21	3,255	0.22
Overheads	1,030	0.07	1,120	0.07
Total	**11,322**	**0.81**	**12,787**	**0.85**
Cash Profit	**2,678**	**0.19**	**3,713**	**0.25**
Depreciation	100	0.01	100	0.01
Book Profit	**2,578**	**0.18**	**3,613**	**0.24**
Taxes	928	0.07	1,301	0.09
Profit After Tax	1,650	0.12	2,312	0.15

Manufacturing of Bricks

The process of making brick consists of the following steps:

- Gathering, crushing, grinding, screening of clays and shale
- Mixing the raw materials; making the brick; and setting, and drying, and finally
- Firing in the kilns

The crusher breaks up the large chunks of clay or shale and passes it to conveyors heading for the grinders. The grinders pulverize the material to a fine consistency. The pulverized material passes over a vibrating screen in which the fine material passes through to the next step and the coarse material is returned to the grinder for re-grinding.

Once screened, the material is sent to the pug mill where it will be tempered to make a homogeneous plastic mass ready for shaping in the required brick form. The pug mill consists of a chamber that houses one or two revolving shafts with blades rigidly attached, which thoroughly mix the material. Water is added to provide the proper plasticity and materials, such as manganese, are added to change the body colour. The next step is to make the material into the shape of the brick. They can be handmade, or extruded.

The final process is firing into the kiln. Most manufacturers use BTK for the purpose. The bricks remain inside the kiln for 20 to 30 days.

The Plan

Gupta Bricks has been using BTK for ages and is contemplating shifting to different technology that has been implemented not long ago. The desire to change the technology was prompted by concerns for the pollution, which the government was enforcing. However, the motivation to change to a newer technology called, Vertical Shift Brick Kiln (VSBK) emanated from its potential to make financial savings besides complying with the forthcoming and much anticipated legislation on pollution. Fortunately, Mr Gupta had enough resources to change over to VSBK technology.

The VSBK technology has been tried and tested successfully by several organizations, though it was not gaining as much acceptance among the brick kiln owners as was thought of. Mr Gupta was always looking for some modernization and improvements. Thus far, his innovations were primarily focussed on the marketing because he always believed in maintaining continuous touch with major contractors in the area and emphasized timely delivery of bricks at the sites. This was for the first time that he was seriously considering the migration to newer technology of VSBK, though he too was not in favour of abandoning the BTK technology. He had two BTKs with each having a capacity of 75 lakh brick per annum based on 250 days of working. BTKs could not function in rainy days.

His initial thought was to add another BTK. However, he was constrained by the paucity of the land required to make his proposal come good. As an alternative he could consider installation of three 2-shaft kilns with each kiln produces about 10,000 bricks per day (having a size of 230mm × 110mm × 70mm) and abandoning one BTK. The VSBK kiln with two shafts could be set up in 2000 sq.m. of land, and four shafts in 4000 sq.m, excluding the brick-moulding area. With an initial investment of approximately ₹25 lakh Mr Gupta intended replacing the existing BTK with three VSBKs of two shafts.

A 2-shaft kiln produces about 8,000 bricks per day (having a size of 230mm × 110mm × 70mm). Operation is round-the-clock and annual production of up to 30 lakh bricks per annum could be achieved. Because the new kilns could be operated throughout the year unlike

BTKs even during the monsoon Mr Gupta estimated that he could produce for 350 days in a year, and increase his production. With the installation of three VSBKs, Mr Gupta could not only match the production of one of the existing BTK but exceed it by good 10–15% if the demand situation required so.

Each of the VSBK was estimated to cost around ₹10 lakh inclusive of the ramp and the elevated platform.

Advantages of VSBK

The VSBK technology was environment friendly. Performance of the VSBK kiln was better than other existing kilns for firing bricks. It is a better kiln in terms of the health and safety of the workers too. Besides polluting less, the VSBK had several economic advantages.

It also gives unmatched flexibility of operation, good product quality, and substantial saving in energy costs. One could plan a precise production schedule and produce exact quantity of bricks that is required. Once operational, loading and unloading is carried out simultaneously. In general, one batch of bricks is loaded (and one unloaded) every one-and-a-half to two hours. The bricks remain inside the kiln for approximately 24 to 30 hours instead of the 20 to 30 days required with a BTK. This reduces the working capital substantially. In the estimates of Mr Gupta the reduction in working capital was offset by his desire to keep extra inventory.

The other advantage of the VSBK was the improved quality if one follows good firing practices. In fact, the products are superior to those of produced by BTKs and possibly could fetch about 3% higher prices because VSBK – fired bricks show a fine, deep red colour and have a good, metallic ring depending upon the soil composition and particle size distribution.

Besides increased production, somewhat increased prices the major advantage of VSBK was the saving potential in the fuel cost. The external coal consumption can be reduced drastically. In some cases, with the plastic soil and medium calorific value (2,300 kcal/kg) internal fuel, e.g., sponge iron waste, good quality fired bricks have been produced at even 10 kg of external coal per 1,000 bricks compared to normal 180 kg per 1,000 bricks in traditional kilns. Fuel costs alone are expected to be about 20% lower than those associated with the operation of conventional kilns.

Mr Gupta was concerned about the newer skills required to operate the VSBKs, which needed specially trained firemen and fire-masters. The technology provider will provide on-the-job training for firemen. This will normally take 3 to 4 weeks once the new kiln has been commissioned. The supplier of VSBKs had agreed to locate the suitable personnel in the area and train them. However, Mr Gupta estimated that his wage bill would go up by about 10% for one of the BTKs.

A VSBK can be used for many years if good firing and maintenance practices are observed. The expected service life of a VSBK is between 10 to 15 years.

The maintenance costs are bound to increase by ₹60,000 per annum because once a year, before the start of the firing process the refractory brick wall lining of shaft needs filling of joints with refractory mortar and occasional replacement of a few of refractory bricks.

Considering the number of advantages, Mr Gupta was favourably inclined to replace one of his BTKs with the new VSBKs. Being a renowned person in his town he wanted to set up an example to his competitors and remain ahead of them in all respects.

Mr Gupta was of traditional views and did not believe in any debt. He could feel happy if his investment had the payback of less than five years. This amounted to about 20% return on investment. His expectations were well met by this criteria of RoI because he thought his cost of capital was only 14%.

Discuss

Discuss whether or not Mr Gupta should replace one of his BTKs with three 2-shafts VSBKs.

In the CD

Finding NPV of Cash Flows

Finding IRR of Cash Flows

CHAPTER

12 Capital Budgeting-II

LEARNING OBJECTIVES

The chapter is aimed to explain the following:

- how to extend the principles of capital budgeting to more complicated but closer to real-life situations of:
  - selecting among the mutually exclusive projects with different useful lives
  - selecting from the different machines while replacing the existing asset
  - making decision under the constraint of funds
- what is Profitability Index (PI) method
- how to take care of risks in capital budgeting through
  - sensitivity analysis
  - scenario analysis, and
  - simulation
- what are sequential decisions, and how decision trees can be used to analyse the decision process involving several small decisions as part of a bigger decision
- conventional methods of handling risk by: (1) breakeven analysis, and (2) payback period
- what is risk-adjusted discount rate, and how can it be used for handling risk in investment proposals
- what is meant by certainty equivalent, and how to use the approach to incorporate risk in capital budgeting

SHALINI, LCD TV, AND RISKS IN CAPITAL BUDGETING

Having bought the 42" LCD TV a few days later, Shalini came running to Chander and expressed, 'You told me a few things about evaluation of capital budgeting proposals a few days back. In my office today, I examined the purchase of a grinding machine. But my MD asked me several questions, and I could not answer those questions.'

Chander: 'What were they?'

Shalini: 'He asked me, "You have examined the cash flows of the grinding machine. It is showing a marginal positive NPV of ₹2.30 lakh with the capital cost of 50 lakh." Even though the project is positive NPV, he found it too risky and therefore would not accept it. I argued a great deal with him, but he said you have to consider the risks in the project. I do not understand what is risk analysis and why should he reject a positive NPV project.'

Chander: 'You see, when we project the cash flows of any project, we make several assumptions. The acceptance or rejection of a project is dependent upon the NPV based on those assumptions. The risk lies in the validity of the assumptions we make. How well these assumptions would come true in real life in future is a big question. By risk analysis, all he means is what-if analysis.'

Shalini: 'How do you examine the validity of assumptions? These are made by marketing and production departments. We simply translate these assumptions into financial figures.'

Chander: 'Yes, you are right. Still, we may do some value addition. For example, we estimated the annual benefit of our LCD TV at ₹30,000 per annum. It was based on the assumption of saving on the movie outing twice a month at ₹1,000 for every outing. What happens if this is not true, and instead, we end up saving only ₹900 per outing? There is a fair chance of that.'

Shalini: 'How do we account for this?'

Chander: 'Simple. We recalculate the NPV using ₹900 as the saving per outing. The change in NPV with respect to change in any of the assumption is called sensitivity analysis, i.e., how vulnerable is the project to the changing conditions. Likewise, what would happen if the dealer does not give us ₹3,000 for the old spare music system we have. Again, our project cost would increase, reducing the NPV.'

Shalini: 'What if the *cablewalla* also increases his rate?'

Chander: 'Yes, that too is possible. We can examine one assumption at a time. When we do this, it is called sensitivity analysis.'

Shalini: 'What happens if all these things happen together?'

Chander: 'In fact, that is more likely to happen in a business situation. All the variables that have been assumed tend to move together. We call them scenarios. Each scenario consists of the values of the variables that determine the NPV. We calculate the NPV under all scenarios, assign probability to each scenario, and find the expected NPV, which works as a guide to decision-making.'

Shalini: 'But such scenarios would be few and not consider all possibilities. Would it give a fair view?'

Chander: 'Yes, you are right. At best, people can handle 4–5 scenarios. In fact, none of which may actually take place!'

Shalini: 'Then, what do we do?'

Chander: 'That is easy to understand but hard to implement. We resort to mathematics. Since all the possible situations cannot be handled and since all the events are beyond our control, we perform hundreds of calculations for different situations by simulating, and calculate the NPV of the project.'

Shalini: 'That is a long and tedious process.'

Chander: 'Yes. Therefore, we need computers to perform this kind of analysis. We identify each critical variable and assign random numbers to each variable. Then, we pick them randomly from the computer and find the values of respective variables corresponding to those numbers. For each set of random numbers, we calculate the NPV from the formula already fed in the computer.'

Shalini: 'Again, we would get hundreds of NPVs. Which one of them is correct?'

Chander: 'Again, we work on the expected value and find the average of all the iterations to make a decision.'

Shalini: 'All this seems fairly complicated. Do we need to take so much of pain for the exercise?'

Chander: 'Yes. It depends upon the risk involved and the size of the project. If the project size is too large, it is worth the pain and the wait.'

Shalini: 'Isn't there a simpler way?'

Chander: 'Yes. The most popular way is to incorporate the risk of the project in the discount rate. Higher the risk, higher should be the discount rate. Remember, we used the discount rate of 20%, which we earn on the stock market, while trying to evaluate the decision to buy the LCD TV. I think that was too high. The cash flows that we used were not as risky as the stock market returns. A more appropriate discount rate for our LCD TV could be 9%, i.e., slightly higher than the returns we get on the fixed deposits with bank because our cash flows were rather certain.'

Shalini: 'That means the LCD TV had the higher NPV. Now, I think, I can afford to pay you for the lessons that you have given me.'

INTRODUCTION

Capital budgeting decisions in the real world are complex. They are not as simple as the capital budgeting exercises discussed in the previous chapter, where we examined the different evaluation techniques for capital budgeting and the principles to be followed for projecting the cash flows of the project. All these techniques and principles continue to remain the same and are valid, irrespective of simplicity or complexity of capital budgeting proposals.

Business situations involve capital budgeting decisions that are complex in nature. However, principles of capital budgeting continue to be applied to these situations.

We shall now examine some complex investment projects because they are closer to real life situations. While the earlier chapter provided the necessary conceptual background, here we shall deal with some specific applications. This would be followed by discussion on the how to incorporate risks in the capital budgeting proposals. These common situations are considering proposals of—(1) different lives; (2) different scales; (3) replacement of existing assets with new ones; and (4) under constraint of funds. (Capital rationing)

PROJECTS WITH UNEQUAL LIVES

More often than not, firms are required to choose between two or more alternative technologies to manufacture the same product. In the earlier chapter, we discussed the project of a canning line for Foremost Brewers. They may be facing a decision of choosing between two alternative models from two different suppliers. For example, one supplier may have cheaper equipment with an estimated

It would be wrong to compare the NPVs of two projects having different economic lives and selecting the one with higher NPV.

life of five years, while another model from another supplier may be expensive but is expected to have a longer life of ten years. Here, the selection of one model/supplier from the two short-listed is a situation that is analogous to mutually exclusive projects. But these have different useful lives.

These technologies not only have different initial outlays but also have different cash flows and different lives. Under these circumstances, making a choice between two technologies is difficult because the evaluation cannot be compared purely on the basis of NPV or IRR for the reason that they have different lives. The benefits and costs are essentially not comparable in the true sense. Here, two issues must be emphasized. Firstly, we must reiterate here that normally we are looking at most cost effective options in such evaluations. Therefore, the perspective is to select a technology that has the least NPV of costs, and not the maximization of NPV. Secondly, consistent with the going-concern concept we assume that the technology is required indefinitely irrespective of which one is chosen and, therefore, would need to be replaced at the end of useful life.

Assume that a firm is engaged in the business of producing moulded products. The firm keeps replacing the existing equipment periodically whenever the existing machines wear out or a new technology develops. Assume that the time has come to replace an existing machine with a newer version. It is considering two suppliers that manufacture the same machine. Supplier A has offered a machine that costs ₹40 lakh, has an annual running cost of ₹12 lakh. This machine has a useful life of six years. Another Supplier B has offered a machine that costs ₹30 lakh with annual running cost of ₹14 lakh but with useful life of four years. For simplicity assume no taxes and no depreciation benefits. (They need to be considered in practice). How do we decide which one to choose?

Conventional evaluation would require the computation of NPV of costs at a specific discount rate, comparing them, and making a selection in favour of the one with lower NPV of costs[1]. Assuming the cost of capital at 15% we find the NPV of the costs of the two machines as follows:

Supplier A

$$\text{Net Present Value } (A) = \left[40 + \frac{12}{1.15} + \frac{12}{1.15^2} + \frac{12}{1.15^3} + \frac{12}{1.15^4} + \frac{12}{1.15^5} + \frac{12}{1.15^6}\right]$$

$$= \{40 + 12 \times (0.869 + 0.756 + 0.657 + 0.572 + 0.497 + 0.432)\}$$

$$= 40 + 12 \times 3.784 = 40.000 + 45.396$$

$$= ₹85.396 \text{ lakh}$$

Supplier B

Net Present Value (B)

$$= \left[30 + \frac{14}{1.15} + \frac{14}{1.15^2} + \frac{14}{1.15^3} + \frac{14}{1.15^4}\right]$$

$$= \{30 + 14 \times (0.869 + 0.756 + 0.657 + 0.572)\}$$

$$= 30 + 14 \times 2.854 = 30.00 + 39.956 = ₹69.956 \text{ lakh}$$

Note that the NPV calculated above is for the cash outflows and not inflows. Common sense tells us that we must choose the supplier with least cost in terms of their net present values. A direct comparison of NPV favours Supplier B who has a lower NPV of cost at ₹69.956 lakh as compared to the Supplier A with NPV of costs at ₹85.396 lakh. However, these costs ignore the important factor of time for which they are to be incurred. In case of Supplier A, the cost of ₹85.396 lakh will provide service for six years while for Supplier B, the relevant period is four years having a cost of ₹69.956 lakh. Would it be a right decision? Perhaps not. We have ignored the issue of replacement of machines when they wear out. The machine from Supplier B needs to be replaced earlier after four years as against machine from Supplier A whose machine lasts for six years.

The correct approach would be to compare the machines for equal lengths of time. One approach towards a solution to the problem is to extend the cash flows for subsequent periods so as to make the lives of the two proposals equal. This would be achieved when both machines get replaced at the same point of time. This common period is 12 years in this case, where two alternatives become equivalent with the following options:

> *One way of evaluating projects with different lives is to extend the cash flows of each till the lives of the projects become identical and then compare their NPVs.*

- Buy from Supplier A now and replace at the end of six years, or
- Buy from Supplier B now, and replace at the end of four years and at the end of eight years

Both the options will now provide service for 12 years and we compare the NPV over 12 years. We actually do not need to buy multiple times but repeat the cash flow hypothetically to make a fair comparison of the two alternatives. After making the lives equal compute the NPVs of both the options and the one that gives least NPV of cost is chosen. The NPVs of the two options with reiteration of cash flows up to 12 years are worked out in Table 12-1.

From Supplier A, the net present value of the cost is ₹85.40 lakh. For the second purchase in the sixth year, the NPV will be same. This NPV at 6th year need to be converted to today's NPV. This works out to ₹36.89 lakh. The total NPV of the costs if two machines are purchased (one now and the other six years later) is ₹122.29 lakh. Similarly, for Supplier B, the purchases are made now, four years later and eight years later each with the NPV of costs of ₹69.95 lakh at the beginning of each purchase. Translating these NPVs to today's value provides the total NPV of cost at ₹132.85 lakh.

Now the comparison seems fair because both the machines are compared over equal length of time. The NPV of the machine from Supplier A is ₹122.29 lakh is lower than that of the NPV of the machine from Supplier B at ₹132.85 lakh. Now we should favour Supplier A.

[1]If we need to be consistent with the principle of maximizing the NPV we need to use negative sign for the cash flows being costs.

Table 12-1 Matching cash flows for same useful life

YEAR — Figures in ₹ lakh

0	1	2	3	4	5	6	7	8	9	10	11	12
Supplier A												
Cash outflows												
40	12	12	12	12	12	12	**1st Machine**					
					2nd Machine	40	12	12	12	12	12	12
												Present Value
85.40 ←												NPV 1st Machine
36.89 ←			$85.40/1.15^6$ ←			85.40 ←						NPV 2nd Machne
122.29 ←												**TOTAL NPV**
Supplier B												
30	14	14	14	14	**1st Machine**							
			2nd Machine	30	14	14	14	14				
							3rd Machine	30	14	14	14	14
												Present values
69.95 ←												NPV 1st Machine
40.01 ←		$69.95/1.15^4$ ←		69.95								NPV 2nd Machine
22.89 ←				$69.95/1.15^8$ ←				69.95				NPV 3rd Machine
132.85 ←												**TOTAL NPV**

An Alternative Approach—Equivalent Annual Value (EAV) Method

The projections of cash flows to match lives of the projects and recomputing of the NPVs of the two mutually exclusive projects would become very unwieldy if the lives of equipment are large. For example, if two machines have useful lives of 15 and 20 years, respectively one would have to reiterate cash flows for 60 years.

We need to adopt a simpler approach. One way of comparing the two machines is to compare their costs on an annual basis rather than on common life basis. To arrive at an annual cost we need to work out the value of uniform annual cash flows over the life of the machine that equates with the NPV calculated. This is referred to as the equivalent annual value (EAV).

EAV is computed by dividing NPV with the annuity factor at the given discount rate for the periods equal to the life of the project.

We need to find the cash flow, which if paid annually over the life of the machine, will provide an NPV equal to ₹85.396 lakh for Supplier A and ₹69.956 lakh for Supplier B. To do this, we take help from tables of annuity factor[2]. The annuity factor at 15% for period of 6 years is 3.784 while for four years it is 2.854.

Therefore, the EAV for:

Supplier A: ₹85.396/3.784 = ₹22.567 lakh

Supplier B: ₹69.956/2.854 = ₹24.511 lakh

Mathematically, EAV is given by Equation 12-1.

Equivalent Annual Value (EAV)

$$= \frac{\text{Net Present Value}}{\text{Annuity Factor for } n \text{ years at discount rate of } t} \qquad (12\text{-}1)$$

[2]The annuity factor at discount rate of r (denoted as decimal) and for n period is given by $\dfrac{1-\dfrac{1}{(1+r)^n}}{r}$

What do these figures mean? For the machine from Supplier A, it implies that ₹22.567 lakh if paid each year for six years will result in NPV of ₹85.396 lakh. Therefore, the NPV of costs of ₹85.396 lakh is equivalent to an annual cost of ₹22.567 lakh for six years at 15%. Similarly, in case of machine from Supplier B if ₹24.511 lakh is paid each year for four years it would result in an NPV of ₹69.956 lakh. The EAV is ₹24.511 lakh. Clearly, in terms of annualized cost, the machine from Supplier A is preferred. EAV places the total cost on an annual basis.

Alternatively, the EAVs of the NPV may be compared to make selection in favour of one.

The EAVs of the two machines may be compared and the one with lower value may be chosen. If EAV happens to be cash inflow or revenues then the project with higher EAV would be chosen.

Example 12-1 Equivalent Annual Value (EAV) of BW Forgings

BW Forgings is considering replacement of a grinding machine. There are two alternatives: Machine M and Machine N under consideration with useful lives of three and four years, respectively. The costs are given as below:

	Cash Costs (₹)					
	0	1	2	3	4	Total Cost
Machine M	1,500.00	500.00	600.00	700.00	—	3,300.00
Machine N	2,000.00	300.00	400.00	500.00	600.00	3,800.00

The cost of capital for BW Forgings is 15%. Which machine should they choose? Ignore salvage values and depreciation tax shields.

Solution
The present values of costs with discount rate of 15% for Machine M and Machine N are computed below:

	Cash Costs (₹)					
	0	1	2	3	4	Total Cost
Cash Flows						
Machine M	1,500.00	500.00	600.00	700.00		3,300.00
Machine N	2,000.00	300.00	400.00	500.00	600.00	3,800.00
Present Values at 15%						
Machine M	1,500.00	434.78	453.69	460.26	—	2,848.73
Machine N	2,000.00	260.87	302.46	328.76	343.05	3,235.14

Since the present value of the cost of Machine M is lesser than Machine N, one is inclined to select Machine M. However, accounting for the life of the machine and its replacement at the end of its life, the correct decision making criteria would be equivalent annual cost. This is computed below:

Equivalent Annual Value

	NPV (₹)	Life (yrs)	PV-Annuity	EAV
Machine M	2,848.73	3.00	2.2832	1,247.69
Machine N	3,235.14	4.00	2.8550	1,133.15

Since EAV of the Machine N is smaller, we choose Machine N.

REPLACEMENT DECISION

Another special case that deserves attention in capital budgeting is the determination of policy for the replacement of assets at periodic intervals. Here we are talking of the replacement decision in a different context. The replacement decision just considered in the previous section related to the circumstances where the existing equipment had already outlived its utility and had to be replaced. The choice was selecting between the two new machines.

The context here, in the replacement decision, is different. We are attempting to formulate a policy as to when to replace the existing machines, irrespective of whether they still have some utility left or not. If the existing machine has become obsolete the decision to replace was forced on the firm. It was not a replacement decision, but a selection of one from many possible replacement alternatives. If a firm continues to persist with the policy not to replace till the life of the existing machine is over it may be supporting an uneconomical situation. The replacement of existing machine raises the question of time of replacement that is most economical to the firm.

As a typical case, consider a firm engaged in the transport business owning a fleet of trucks. It may have a policy to replace a vehicle only when it breaks down and is beyond repairs. Such a policy may prove costly in the long run. Supporting high running cost of old vehicles to save high capital cost of new vehicle may look attractive and hence, the decision to postpone the replacement continues till one is forced. However, as a prudent policy the firm needs to decide how often or after how much time a truck needs to be replaced, taking into consideration the various determinants of cost and revenue. As the vehicles become older, the fuel efficiency falls, maintenance costs increase, besides, vehicles becoming prone to frequent accidents and break-downs increasing idle time and reducing utilization, etc. On the other hand, replacing old trucks with new ones entails capital expenditure. With the conflict of cash flows in two situations, the firm needs to find an optimum balance in recurring and capital costs. Here, the relevant policy decision concerns replacement at appropriate time.

Replacement decision refers to the determination of optimum replacement policy as to how often the firm must replace existing assets.

The above situation is a case of project with unequal lives in capital budgeting and the answer can be attempted with either the EAV approach or the reiterative procedure.

Consider a firm, First Forwarder, which owns a fleet of trucks for its business. The firm needs to replace its old trucks with new ones on a regular basis. At present, a new truck costing ₹10 lakh, has a maximum life of five years, after which it necessarily must be replaced. The firm has an option to replace them earlier if it makes economic sense. The current cost of capital for the firm is 12%. The firm has gathered data on the cash flows for each year of operation for the entire life of four years. The resale value of the truck is ₹6.50 lakh, 6.00 lakh, 3.00 lakh, and 1.50 lakh if sold at the end of first, second, third, and fourth year, respectively. For simplicity, assume no taxes and depreciation benefits. The data is presented in Table 12-2.

Table 12-2 Cash flow data for Truck

	Cash flows for the year (₹ in '000s)				
	0	1	2	3	4
Initial cost	–1,000				
Revenue		1,000	1,000	800	700
Operating costs		–500	–550	–600	–650
Salvage value if sold at the end of year		650	500	300	150

We need to analyse what replacement policy the firm needs to adopt. The management has ruled out replacement after one year as it is too cumbersome. The choices available to the management are:

- Replace every four years
- Replace every three years
- Replace every two years

These options are mutually exclusive as we have to choose only one of the alternatives. Also, these alternatives have different useful lives of two, three, and four years. A comparison of NPV for all the options will lead to an erroneous conclusion. The options available with the firm can be analysed on the basis of EAV method or by matching the lives of the options.

In order to match the lives of different options we need to extend the period of analysis to 12 years. If the firm chooses to replace the trucks every four years the firm will be actually replacing three times. Similarly, by replacing the trucks every three and two years the firm ends up replacing them four and six times, respectively over a period of 12 years. The NPV over 12 years under each option can be worked out and the option that gives the highest NPV will determine the optimum replacement policy. Readers may do this as an exercise.

Instead, we adopt a more convenient method of computing the EAVs of the cash flows under each alternative under review. Under the EAV method, the NPVs calculated for each option are converted to equivalent annual value using the annuity factor at 12% for the relevant period. This is presented in Table 12-3.

As can be seen from Table 12-3, the equivalent annualized value under three different options are:

Replacement every four years : ₹45.45 lakh
Replacement every three years : ₹67.04 lakh
Replacement every two years : ₹120.56 lakh

What do these equivalent annual values convey? For the replacement policy of every two years, the cash flows of the vehicles are equivalent of receiving ₹120.56 lakh every year. Similarly, the cash flows under the three-year and four-year replacement are equivalent to ₹67.04 lakh and ₹45.45 lakh every year. Hence, these values become directly comparable. Being the present values of cash inflows, the option with the maximum EAV is chosen. Since replacement after every two years provides the highest NPV, it is the optimum replacement policy.

Replacement policy too may be framed on the basis of EAVs.

Table 12-3 Analysing Replacement Policy (*₹ in '000s*)

Year	0	1	2	3	4	TOTAL
PV factor at 12%		0.8928	0.7972	0.7118	0.6355	
Replacement every four years						
Operating CF	−1000	500	450	200	150	
Salvage Value					150	
Total CF	−1000	500	450	200	300	
Present Values	−1000	446.40	358.74	142.36	190.65	138.15
Annuity Factor at 12% for 4 years						3.0373
Equivalent Annual Value						45.48
Replacement every three years						
Operating CF	−1000	500	450	200		
Salvage Value				300		
Total CF	−1000	500	450	500		
Present Values	−1000	446.40	358.74	355.90		161.04
Annuity Factor at 12% for 4 years						2.4018
Equivalent Annual Value						67.04
Replacement every two years						
Operating CF	−1000	500	450			
Salvage Value			500			
Total CF	−1000	500	950			
Present Values	−1000	446.40	757.34			203.74
Annuity Factor at 12% for 4 years						1.6900
Equivalent Annual Value						120.56

FINDING A COMPETITIVE PRICE

A common business situation is to submit bids for the tender where the lowest bid is awarded the contract. The competitive bidding forces different bidders to quote a lowest price with the motivation that substantial capacities can be booked for long periods of time. Sometimes, this becomes extremely competitive. The price quoted is often so non-remunerative that losers of the tender feel elated while the winner carries on with the loss making proposition.

To guard against such situations, the technique of NPV may be fruitfully deployed.

Assume that a firm MeshWire Ltd has been asked to quote a price for the supply of 5 lakh pieces of wire mesh over a period

Table 12-4 Cash Flows and Present Values for WireMesh Ltd

Year	0	1	2	3
Price (₹)		5.50	5.50	5.50
Quantity (Nos. in thousands)		100.00	150.00	250.00
				(*₹ in '000s*)
Sales		550.00	825.00	1,375.00
Variable Cost @ 60%		330.00	495.00	825.00
Fixed Cost		100.00	110.00	120.00
Cash flow from Operations		120.00	220.00	430.00
Tax @ 34%		40.80	74.80	146.20
Post-tax Cash Flow		79.20	145.20	283.80
Depreciation		50.00	50.00	50.00
Tax Shield of Depreciation		17.00	17.00	17.00
Operating Cash Flows		96.20	162.20	300.80
Initial and Terminal Cash flows	−600.00			300.00
PV Factor at 10%		0.9091	0.8264	0.7513
Present Values of Cash Flow	−600.00	87.45	134.05	226.00
PV of Terminal Year Cash Flows				225.39
Total PV of cash flows	−600.00	87.45	134.05	451.39
Net Present Value				72.89

of three years with 1.00 lakh, 1.50 lakh, and 2.50 lakh pieces for the next three years, respectively. The managers at MeshWire have estimated that special wire mesh requires an additional investment and working capital of ₹5.00 lakh and 1.00 lakh, respectively. At the end of three years, the additional equipment can realize ₹2.00 lakh net of taxes and the working capital would be released.

The regular selling price of the WireMesh is ₹6,000 but anticipating strong competition and prestige attached with the order the managers at the firm have proposed a price of Rs 5,500 and prepared estimates of cash flows as given in Table 12-4. Assuming 60% variable cost, depreciation of 10% on straight-line basis with a tax rate of 34%, cost of capital of 10%, present value is arrived at.

Based on the above assumptions and the cash flows as per Table 12-4 the net present value of the proposal comes to about ₹73,000. The managing director of the firm believes that price of ₹5,500 is too high and the firm would lose to competitors. He wants to know the minimum price that can be quoted.

We may use Excel to arrive at the minimum price. We go to Excel and choose *Tools–Goal Seek*. A dialogue box appears where we fill the target value of NPV in Cell F56 as zero by changing the price in given Cell D40 as shown in Figure 12-1.

Though apparently a marketing decision we may apply principles of capital budgeting to find a competitive price.

Once we click OK, the result is displayed in the cell, as shown in Figure 12-2. We get the result as ₹4,810 as a minimum selling price with NPV equal to zero, implying that at this price the order neither adds or destroys the value of the firm. Any price less than ₹4,810 would make the proposal a negative NPV project.

The exercise may be repeated for a target profit. Figure 12-3 shows that for a target value addition of ₹5,000 the firm must charge a minimum price of ₹5,280.

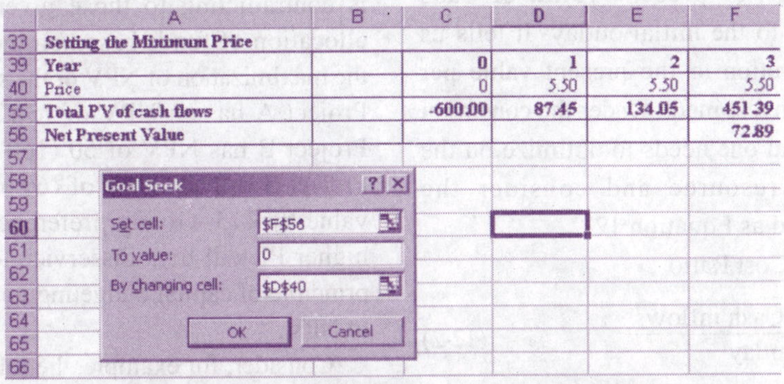

Figure 12-1 Using EXCEL—GOAL SEEK function

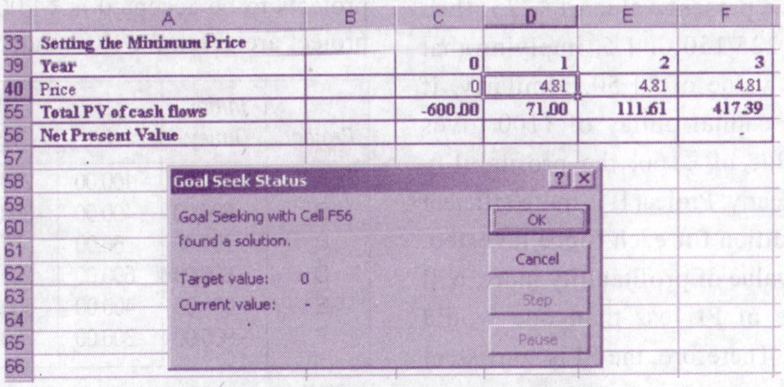

Figure 12-2 Using EXCEL—GOAL SEEK function

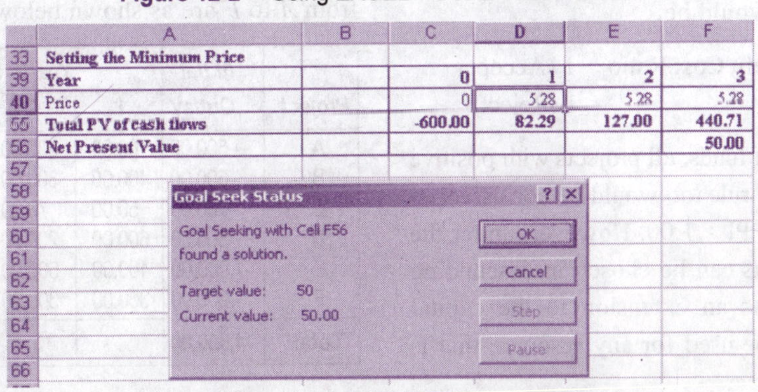

Figure 12-3 Using EXCEL—GOAL SEEK function

CAPITAL RATIONING

Capital rationing refers to the situation where a firm has more positive NPV projects than it can fund from its own or borrowed resources. Under these circumstances the managers have to decide which of the projects should be undertaken. Though ideally a firm would like to execute all the positive NPV projects, it will have to leave some for the want of funds. How does one decide which projects to execute and which to omit?

Profitability Index (PI) Method

Besides NPV and IRR, another DCF-based technique that incorporates the constraint of funds is Benefit Cost Ratio or Profitability Index method. The Profitability Index (PI) is one parameter that indicates the utility of capital.

Profitability index refers to the productivity of capital in terms of addition to present value per unit of capital outlay.

Profitability index (PI) is defined as the ratio of present value of cash inflows to the initial outlay. It tells us the accretion to the present value per unit of invest-ment. Under the constraint of capital one needs to optimize on the scarce resource and consider the efficiency of capital. It is defined as Equation 12-2.

Profitability Index or Benefit Cost Ratio

$$= \frac{\text{Present Value of Cash inflows}}{\text{Initial Outlay}} \quad (12\text{-}2)$$

For example, if Project A with capital outlay of ₹150 provides cash inflows that have present value of ₹225, then the profitability index will be 225/150 or 1.5, implying that each rupee invested creates a value of ₹1.50. Similarly, if another Project B with initial capital outlay of ₹100 gives cash inflows with present value of ₹160, the profitability index will be 160/100 or 1.60. Clearly, Project B is more efficient as it provides greater value addition for each rupee invested. For positive NPV projects the value of profitability index will be greater than one. A value of PI less than one would indicate a loss of present value. Therefore, the PI is consistent with the NPV method of evaluation of investment projects. The decision making criteria would be:

If Profitability Index/ Benefit Cost Ratio > 1 (Accept)
< 1 (Reject)

When there is no constraint of funds, all projects with positive NPV would be accepted. The PI rule too would be consistent as we accept all projects that have PI > 1.00. However, under the constraint of capital, the projects can be chosen in descending order of Profitability Index. As an extension to the capital constraint, the PI method can be used for any resource that is under constraint. For example, if managerial expertize is a constraining factor one may find the NPV added per unit of managerial time. Or, if electric power is a constraint, one can work out NPV added per unit of power. Then according to the PI choose projects for implementation.

Under situations of scarcity of capital the projects may be executed in descending order of Profitability Index.

Profitability Index and NPV

The objective under capital rationing is to put the capital to its best use. Allocation of resources based on PI may sound appropriate and provide a ranking similar to that of NPV. Since PI gives the value addition per unit of capital invested, we should be maximizing the NPV if projects are selected on the basis of ranking given by PI. However, at times it may give ranking that is contradicting to those given by NPV. In such a case the allocation of funds based on the PI may not necessarily lead to the maximization of NPV or the shareholders' wealth. For example, Project A has an NPV of 75 (225 – 150) and PI of 1.5, while Project B has NPV of 60 (160 – 100) and PI of 1.6. Choosing Project B will add NPV of ₹60 only, while Project A will enhance value by ₹75. Giving preference to Project B on the basis of a higher PI will be a disservice to the shareholders. The guiding principle of capital budgeting unambiguously is the maximization of NPV.

Consider, for example, the following six projects that are being evaluated by a firm. The aggregate initial outlay required for all projects to be accepted is ₹4,000 lakh. The cash flows of each project are given for five years.

Project	Initial Outlay	Year's Cash Flow (₹ lakh) 1	2	3	4	5
A	–500.00	100.00	200.00	350.00	140.00	500.00
B	–600.00	400.00	300.00	180.00	300.00	200.00
C	–200.00	50.00	70.00	90.00	120.00	200.00
D	–800.00	600.00	200.00	300.00	150.00	600.00
E	–1,000.00	400.00	500.00	600.00	300.00	600.00
F	–900.00	300.00	300.00	300.00	400.00	180.00

With cost of capital of 12% the NPVs of the various projects from *A* to *F* are as shown below:

Project	Initial Outlay	Year's Cash Flow (₹ lakh) 1	2	3	4	5	NPV at 12%
A	–500.00	100.00	200.00	350.00	140.00	500.00	370.53
B	–600.00	400.00	300.00	180.00	300.00	200.00	428.56
C	–200.00	50.00	70.00	90.00	120.00	200.00	154.25
D	–800.00	600.00	200.00	300.00	150.00	600.00	544.47
E	–1,000.00	400.00	500.00	600.00	300.00	600.00	713.92
F	–900.00	300.00	300.00	300.00	400.00	180.00	176.89
Total	**4,000.00**						**2,388.63**

If the firm had ₹4,000 lakh to invest, it would face no problem in executing all the projects and it would cause an increase in the value of the firm by ₹2,388 lakh.

Generally, the rankings given by NPV and PI are consistent, but in case of divergence, the principle of maximization of NPV prevails and guides the selection.

Now consider that the firm faces a capital constraint of ₹2,500 lakh. It may choose projects according to descending order of NPV or PI. The ranking of projects as per NPV and PI criterion are shown in the following table:

Project	*Initial Outlay*	*NPV at 12%*	*Rank NPV*	*PI*	*Rank PI*
A	–500.00	370.53	4	1.74	2
B	–600.00	428.56	3	1.71	3
C	–200.00	154.25	6	1.77	1
D	–800.00	544.47	2	1.68	5
E	–1,000.00	713.92	1	1.71	4
F	–900.00	176.89	5	1.20	6

Seeking to maximize the NPV per unit of capital invested, it uses PI ranking as a method of choosing the projects. Starting with highest PI, the firm chooses Projects C, B, A, E in that order exhausting ₹2,300 lakh which leaves ₹200 from the budget inadequate to execute any further projects. The NPV of the firm would increase by ₹1,667.29 lakh with the acceptance of the projects based on PI. However, if it makes the choice with NPV rank it accepts Projects E, D, and B exhausting ₹2,400 lakh of the budget and adding ₹1,686.95 lakh to the value. The results of the two approaches are tabulated below:

Criteria	*Projects Chosen*	*Capital Cost*	*Increase in NPV*
As per PI	C, A, B, and E	2,300 lakh	1,667.27 lakh
As per NPV	E, D, and B	2,400 lakh	1,686.95 lakh

We find that the NPV rule gives better results. This is due to the indivisibility of the projects. The selection of projects on the basis of PI may prelude the acceptance of two smaller projects due to selection of project with higher outlay. Two smaller projects may provide a greater increase in the aggregate NPV than the single large project.

However, if the projects are divisible, i.e., when they can be implemented partially, the rule of PI seems to work fine as may be seen from the data below:

Criteria	*Projects Chosen*	*Capital Cost*	*Increase in NPV*
As per PI	C, A, B, E and 1/4th of D	2,500 lakh	1,803.39 lakh
As per NPV	E, D, B and 1/5th of A	2,500 lakh	1,761.06 lakh

Divisibility of the projects implies full utilization of capital budget and there are no additional constraints on the acceptance of projects. In such a situation, the Profitability Index Method would provide optimum results. For mutually exclusive projects or indivisible projects we shall continue to use NPV rule.

Example 12-2 Capital Rationing

Consider five projects A, B, C, D, and E. All projects are independent and have a useful life of three years with following cash flows:

PROJECT	*CASH FLOWS (₹)*				
	A	*B*	*C*	*D*	*E*
Year					
0	–500	–700	–800	–300	–400
1	300	400	300	150	200
2	400	400	500	100	200
3	50	200	400	250	250

Find:

(a) IRR of each project and rank them in order of preference

Table E12-2 Ranking as per NPV, IRR, and PI

(Figures in ₹)

PROJECT	*Cash Flows*				
	A	*B*	*C*	*D*	*E*
Year 0	–500	–700	–800	–300	–400
Year 1	300	400	300	150	200
Year 2	400	400	500	100	200
Year 3	50	200	400	250	250
IRR	28.4%	22.7%	22.2%	27.5%	27.6%
Ranking as per IRR	1	4	5	3	2
PV of cash in flows at 10%	640.87	844.48	986.48	406.84	534.94
Profitability Index (PI)	1.28	1.21	1.23	1.36	1.34
Ranking as per PI	3	5	4	1	2
NPV at 10%	140.87	144.48	186.48	106.84	134.94
Ranking as per NPV	3	2	1	5	4

(b) NPV of each project assuming cost of capital at 10% and rank them in order of preference
(c) Profitability Index of each project and rank them in order of preference
(d) The capital budget is ₹2,000. Which of the projects will be chosen if projects are (i) indivisible and (ii) divisible (can be implemented in part with proportionate NPV)
(e) What happens if the capital budget is reduced to ₹1,500?

Solution

(a), (b), and (c)

The NPV, IRR, and Profitability Index (PI) are computed in Table E12-2. The priorities of the projects are decided in the descending order of NPV. The rankings as per NPV, IRR and PI are displayed in Figure E12-2

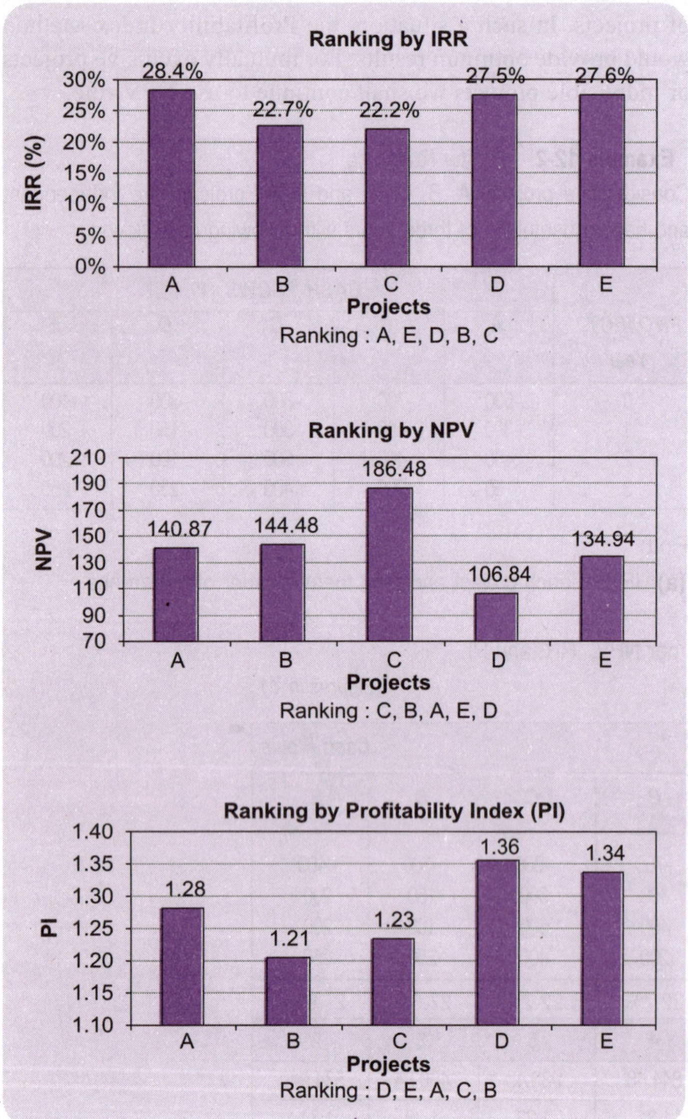

Figure E12-2 Raning as per NPV, IRR, and PI

(d) and (e)

Based on the ranking projected by each method, projects are selected and a cumulative addition to the NPV is found. The method that gives maximum NPV is chosen. This is illustrated in the table below:

Project Selected	Initial Outlay	Cumulative Outlay	Budget = 2000 Indivisible	Budget = 2000 Divisible	Budget = 1,500 Indivisible	Budget = 1,500 Divisible
NPV Rule						
C	800		186	186	186	186
B	700	1500	145	145	145	145
A	500	2000	141	141	—	—
Total NPV			**472**	**472**	**331**	**331**
IRR Rule						
A	500		141	141	141	141
E	400	900	135	135	135	135
D	300	1200	107	107	107	107
B	700	1900	145	145	—	62
C	800		—	23		
Total NPV			**528**	**551**	**383**	**445**
PI Rule						
D	300		107	107	107	107
E	400	700	135	135	135	135
A	500	1200	141	141	141	141
C	800	2000	186	186	—	70
Total NPV			**569**	**569**	**383**	**453**

When projects are indivisible Based on the three methods of selection of projects, i.e., NPV, IRR, and PI the highest NPV results from choosing projects D, E, A, and C giving total increase in NPV of 569 with capital budget of ₹2,000 using the PI method.

With capital budget of ₹1,500 both IRR and PI give identical selection of projects though with different priorities. Projects D, E, and A are selected to induce an increase in the NPV of ₹383.

When projects are divisible Again, based on the three methods of selection of projects, i.e., NPV, IRR, and PI the highest NPV results from choosing projects D, E, A, and C giving a total increase in the NPV of ₹569 with capital budget of ₹2,000. When projects are divisible, the NPV and PI method do not cause any change in the NPV as the total budget is exhausted in the selected projects. However, with the IRR method, a surplus of ₹100 is left after full adoption of projects A, E, D, and B which permits one-eighth of the Project C providing one-eighth of its NPV of ₹23. Despite this, the selection based on the PI method provides a greater NPV and the choice reflected by PI method is adopted.

With a capital budget of ₹1,500, projects C and B exhaust the budget under the NPV method. Both the IRR and PI permit the selection of part projects. Under the IRR method, three-seventh of the Project B is accepted, providing a proportionate NPV of ₹62. Under the PI method three-eighth of Project C can be implemented with proportionate NPV of ₹70. Comparing the NPV under different selection criteria, the choice given by PI method is optimum with NPV of ₹453 with projects D, E, A, and three-eighth of C.

RISKS IN CAPITAL BUDGETING

The cash flows of the project are subject to variations as they are estimated on the basis of certain assumptions that may or may not remain valid in real life situations. Any kind of projection has risks inherent in them. If they were certain they wouldn't be called projections. These uncertainties about the cash flows render risk to the capital investment proposals with regard to their acceptance.

These risks of cash flows can be viewed from the following perspectives:

- How do uncertain cash flows of the project impact the return of the project itself (referred to as project risk or standalone risk)?
- How does the return of the firm, consisting of several projects, get affected (referred to as corporate risk)?
- How does the return to shareholders, assumed to be holding diversified portfolio, get affected; (referred to as market risk)?

The essence of portfolio theory states that it is only the market risk that is relevant on the assumption that investors hold diversified portfolios. Accordingly, consideration of market risk alone will suffice for the maximization of the shareholders' wealth. However, in practice it may not be true because: (i) there exist many investors who are not diversified enough so as to ignore other risks, (ii) besides shareholders there are many other stakeholders in the firm like employees, suppliers, customers, lenders, etc., who are concerned about the project and corporate risks. The actions of non-diversified investors and other stakeholders are not guided by the portfolio theory.

It is important to assess the risks of the project on standalone basis as it contributes to the risk of total cash flows of the firm.

Further, in practice even the well diversified investors like institutional investors, mutual funds, and pension funds do not ignore corporate and project risk as they dwell greatly on the prospects of the firm and tend to project specific aspects while choosing securities for investment. Despite the fact that project specific details constitute unsystematic risk, a large diversified investor in his/her own wisdom emphasizes upon the corporate risk and project risk in the selection of portfolios. It is indeed hard to comprehend the market risk without the understanding of corporate and project risks.

SENSITIVITY ANALYSIS

The risk for the capital budgeting projects emanates from the variability of its cash flow. Cash flows are projected on the basis of few critical assumptions. Normally, such assumptions relate to key variables such as the level of output, selling price of the product, cost structure, administrative, and other overheads, etc. Any change in these key determinants will cause a change in cash flows and the NPV of the project.

One way of handling the risk in the cash flow is to measure the sensitivity of each assumption to the cash flows and the resultant NPV, thus computed. The idea behind the sensitivity analysis is to gauge the change in NPV for a given change in any one of the key factors. For example, one may like to know whether a decline in the selling price by 10%, which managers may see as distinct possibility, can be sustained by the project. Sensitivity analysis helps managers identify which of the assumption is the most critical for the project. It not only helps them making an initial decision of acceptance/rejection of project but also lets them focus their attention on the key variables, in order of their criticality to the project's viability, in an ever-changing environment.

Sensitivity analysis measures the change in NPV of the project with respect to change in one of the independent variables impacting the NPV.

Let us consider an example. Sensor Corporation is considering a project costing ₹8,000 with a useful life of ten years to manufacture and market special sensors. It makes certain assumptions for projecting the operational cash flows. It expects to sell 3,000 units per annum at a selling price of ₹3.20 with variable cost of ₹1.80 per unit. The fixed costs, which include selling expenses are expected to be ₹1,200. Depreciation charge is ₹1,200. With no interest and after paying taxes of 40% it expects cash in flow of ₹2,280 for the next ten years.

The NPV of the project at 15% discount rate is a handsome ₹3,443.

However, the managers of Sensor feel that the selling price is rather arbitrarily assumed at a higher level that may not be sustainable. The reasons for the apprehension of selling price not being realistic may be many. They may foresee competition, lack of demand, or could it be pure overestimation. Concerned about the assumptions about the selling price, they may like to assess how the project behaves. They would like to analyse the project with the change in selling price. The fall in selling price is expected anywhere between 5% and 20%.

To assess the impact of selling price we decrease the selling price sequentially by 5% to 20% and recalculate the NPV. The exercise is presented in Table 12-5.

The sensitivity of the project with respect to the selling price can be defined as % change in NPV from the normal case for a given change in the key variable determining the NPV of the

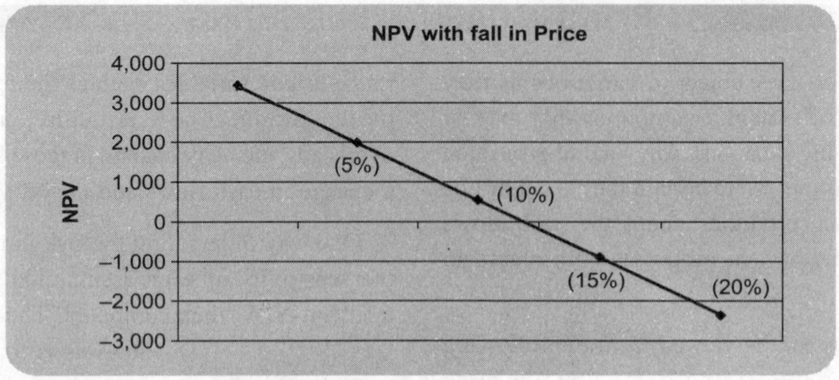

Figure 12-4 Sensitivity analysis

project[3]. We observe that the NPV of the project falls by ₹1,446 (3443 – 1997) with a 5% drop in selling price. This is equivalent to 8.40% drop in NPV with 1% drop in selling price.

The sensitivity analysis can also estimate the level of decline in price the project can sustain. Note that the NPV becomes negative when the selling price drops by 11.90%. If the selling price drops below ₹2.64 the project turns unviable with negative NPV. Managers can take a view on the possibility of such a fall in price actually taking place. The sensitivity of the NPV of the project is presented in Figure 12-4. The higher the slope of the NPV the greater is the sensitivity of the project with respect to the independent variable.

Sensitivity analysis helps in determining the extent to which the project is sensitive to exogenous variables.

Sensitivity analysis can be done for any variable considered of critical importance in the decision making exercise. The sensitivities of the NPV of the Sensor Corporation for increase in initial cost, cost of capital, variable cost, and fixed expenses are given in Table 12-6. Note that only one variable is allowed to vary while all other determinants of NPV are held constant. Sensitivity analysis reflects upon the following:

1. How sensitive the NPV of the project is to a particular variable,
2. Which of the variable is comparatively more critical than others for the viability of the project to enable managers to determine the priorities of monitoring the variables, and
3. To what extent the adversity in a variable is permissible to keep the project alive, and examine whether or not such adversity can actually happen.

From a cursory glance at Table 12-6, we can conclude that the project of Sensor Corporation is the most sensitive to an increase in variable cost (besides the selling price) and, therefore, managers must focus their attention to control the variable cost. One possible way of keeping the variable cost under control is to enter into a long-term contract with raw material suppliers to safeguard the interests of the firm and shareholders by not letting the NPV of the project slip into negative territory. Likewise on the marketing front, Sensor Corporation can explore the possibility of entering into similar long-term fixed price contracts with potential customers even at a price somewhat lower than the projected price of ₹3 per unit. Therefore, the sensitivity analysis helps in controlling the risk of the project in the capital budgeting decision.

Table 12-5 Sensitivity analysis: sensor corporation

Initial Investment (₹)	8,000	8,000	8,000	8,000	8,000
Life of the project (Years)	10	10	10	10	10
Discount Rate	15%	15%	15%	15%	15%
Operating Level (Nos.)	3,000	3,000	3,000	3,000	3,000
Selling Price falls by		**5%**	**10%**	**15%**	**20%**
Selling Price (₹)	**3.20**	**3.04**	**2.88**	**2.72**	**2.56**
					(Figure in ₹)
Revenue	9,600	9,120	8,640	8,160	7,680
Variable Cost	5,400	5,400	5,400	5,400	5,400
Contribution	4,200	3,720	3,240	2,760	2,280
Fixed Costs	1,200	1,200	1,200	1,200	1,200
Depreciation	1,200	1,200	1,200	1,200	1,200
PBIT	1,800	1,320	840	360	(120)
Interest	—	—	—	—	—
PBT	1,800	1,320	840	360	(120)
Tax @ 40%	720	528	336	144	(48)
PAT	1,080	792	504	216	(72)
Cash Flow from Operations	**2,280**	**1,992**	**1,704**	**1,416**	**1,128**
PV of Cash in flows	11,443	9,997	8,552	7,107	5,661
Net Present Value at 15%	**3,443**	**1,997**	**552**	**(893)**	**(2,339)**
Sensitivity					
Fall in NPV for 1% fall in selling price				−289	
% fall in NPV for 1% fall in selling price				−8.40%	

Despite its usefulness in determining the more crucial factors on which NPV is dependent, sensitivity analysis suffers from the disadvantage of not being able to incorporate the likelihood of the variable taking the assumed figure. The selection and the quantum of change in the independent variable are purely discretionary and subjective to the manager conducting the sensitivity analysis. This makes the outcome of the sensitivity analysis subjective. Further, the interrelationship of variables is not considered since only one variable is examined at a time.

[3]**The analysis may also be conducted for the change in IRR but changes in NPV are more practical and communicative.**

Table 12-6 Sensitivity analysis: Sensor Corporation

(Figures in ₹)

	Normal	Initial cost increases by 10%	Cost of capital increases by 10%	Variable cost increases by 10%	Fixed Cost increases by 10%
Initial Investment (₹)	8,000	8,800	8,000	8,000	8,000
Life of the project (Yrs)	10	10	10	10	10
Discount Rate	15%	15%	16.5%	15%	15%
Operating Level (Nos.)	3,000	3,000	3,000	3,000	3,000
Selling Price (₹)	3.20	3.20	3.20	3.20	3.20
Revenue	9,600	9,600	9,600	9,600	9,600
Variable Cost	5,400	5,400	5,400	5,940	5,400
Contribution	4,200	4,200	4,200	3,660	4,200
Fixed Costs	1,200	1,200	1,200	1,200	1,320
Depreciation	1,200	1,320	1,200	1,200	1,200
PBIT	1,800	1,680	1,800	1,260	1,680
Interest	—	—	—	—	—
PBT	1,800	1,680	1,800	1,260	1,680
Tax	720	672	720	504	672
PAT	1,080	1,008	1,080	756	1,008
Cash Flow from Operations	**2,280**	**2,328**	**2,280**	**1,956**	**2,208**
Net Present Value	**3,443**	**2,884**	**2,818**	**1,817**	**3,081**
	Sensitivity				
Change in NPV for 1% change in the variable		(56)	(63)	(163)	(36)
% change in NPV for 1% change in the variable		−1.62%	−1.82%	−4.72%	−1.05%

SCENARIO ANALYSIS

While sensitivity analysis is the most widely used tool of assessing the risk of the project, the managers are often interested in knowing how the project would behave if several variables change at the same time. The scenario analysis is a tool that overcomes the limitation of the sensitivity analysis as the variables are strongly correlated with each other, i.e., a change in one is often linked with the change in another variable, it is necessary to analyse the impact of changes in several parameters, simultaneously. For example, if the market is good the firm may be able to charge higher price and yet sell more quantity. On the contrary, if the product has a bad price in the market then its quantity sold would be lower than expected. Though in the projections of cash flows, the price and quantity sold may form two independent assumptions but they may be closely related in reality so as to overly underestimate or overestimate the cash flows.

> *Scenario analysis measures the change in NPV of the project under different scenarios changing several variables at a time because of interrelationship of variables among themselves.*

Due to a strong correlation among the variables determining the cash flows, managers must first visualize a broad scenario with its likelihood, then assign a value to all the variables under each scenario, and finally, compute the NPV under each scenario. The expected value of the NPV is the measure of the potential of the project. The risk of the project can be assessed through its standard deviation or the coefficient of variation (Expected NPV/Standard deviation).

As an example, consider five different scenarios for Sensor Corporation, denoted as excellent, good, normal, bad, and worst. Under each of the five scenarios with changes in the four variables of demand, selling price, variable cost and overheads from the projections made earlier in the 'Normal' column of Table 12-7 are presented below:

Table 12-7 Scenario description: Sensor Corporation

	Excellent	Good	Normal	Bad	Worst
Demand Level (Nos.)	+10%	+5%	**3,000**	−5%	−10%
Selling Price (₹/unit)	+ 5%	Same	**3.20**	−5%	−10%
Variable Cost (₹)	+10%	Same	**5,400**	Same	+10%
Overheads	+ 5%	−5%	**1,200**	+10%	+20%

Under each scenario, the NPV[4] is calculated in Table 12-8. With the estimated probabilities to each scenario the expected NPV of the project is ₹1,978 as against NPV of ₹3,443 under 'normal' scenario. Due to the interplay and compounding of variables the effects on NPV become skewed and the risk cannot be measured from the change in NPV per unit of change in the independent variable, as was measured under sensitivity analysis.

Table 12-8 Scenario analysis: Sensor Corporation

(Figures in ₹unless specified)

Initial Investment	8,000	8,000	8,000	8,000	8,000
Life of the project (Years)	10	10	10	10	10
Discount Rate	15%	15%	15%	15%	15%
SCENARIO	**Excellent**	**Good**	**Normal**	**Bad**	**Worst**
Operating Level (Nos.)	3,300	3,150	3,000	2,850	2,700
Selling Price	3.36	3.00	3.20	3.04	2.88
Revenue	11,088	9,450	9,600	8,664	7,776
Variable Cost	5,940	5,400	5,400	5,400	5,940
Contribution	5,148	4,050	4,200	3,264	1,836
Fixed Costs	1,260	1,140	1,200	1,320	1,440
Depreciation	1,200	1,200	1,200	1,200	1,200
PBIT	2,688	1,710	1,800	744	(804)
Interest	—	—	—	—	—
PBT	2,688	1,710	1,800	744	(804)
Tax @ 40%	1,075	684	720	298	(322)
PAT	1,613	1,026	1,080	446	(482)
Cash Flow from Operations	**2,813**	**2,226**	**2,280**	**1,646**	**718**
Present Value of Cash in flows	14,117	11,172	11,443	8,263	3,601
Net Present Value	**6,117**	**3,172**	**3,443**	**263**	**(4,399)**
Probability (%)	**15%**	**20%**	**30%**	**20%**	**15%**
Expected NPV			**1,978**		
Standard Deviation of NPV					**1,607**
Coefficient of Variation					**0.81**

[4]What applies to sensitivity analysis also applies to scenario analysis. We may examine the change in IRR with each scenario as measure of risk but we continue with NPV due to its established superiority over IRR as method of evaluation of capital budgeting proposals.

To have a more clear view of risk, we may compute the expected NPVs by assigning probabilities to different scenarios. The expected NPV, given by Equation 12-3, of Sensor Corporation is:

$$\text{Expected NPV} = \sum_{1}^{n} p_i \times \text{NPV}_i \tag{12-3}$$

$$= (0.15 \times 6{,}117) + (0.20 \times 3{,}172) + (0.30 \times 3{,}443) + (0.20 \times 263) - (0.15 \times 4{,}399)$$

$$= ₹1{,}978$$

For measurement of aggregate risk in the project we may compute the variance or standard deviation or coefficient of variation. These are computed below using Equation 12-4:

$$\text{Variance} = \sum_{1}^{5} p_i \times (X_i - \overline{X})^2 \tag{12-4}$$

where X_i = NPV of the scenario i, $\overline{X}$ = Expected NPV,

p_i = Probability of scenario i

Therefore, the variance of sensor corporation is:

$$= 0.15 \times (6{,}117 - 1{,}978)^2 + 0.20 \times (3{,}172 - 1{,}978)^2 + 0.30 \times (3{,}443 - 1{,}978)^2 + 0.20 \times (263 - 1{,}978)^2 + 0.15 \times (-4{,}399 - 1{,}978)^2$$

$$= 25{,}81{,}445$$

And, the standard deviation = $\sqrt{2581445} = 1607$

For finding the relative risk of the project coefficient of variation may be used. As an absolute measure of risk, variance or standard deviations are adequate measures. When the projects have different sizes, different expected NPV and different standard deviations they need to be compared for relative risk. The coefficient of variation provides a partial answer to this problem. The coefficient of variation for Sensor Corporation is 0.81 stating the change in expected NPV per unit change in risk, is computed below using Equation 12-5:

$$\text{Coefficient of Variation} = \frac{\text{Expected NPV}}{\text{Standard Deviation of NPV}}$$

$$= \frac{1978}{1607} = 0.81 \tag{12-5}$$

The major limitation of scenario analysis is its inability to consider sufficiently large number of scenarios to reasonably assess true expected value of NPV and its variability.

SIMULATION ANALYSIS

Known as the Monte Carlo simulation, this technique tries to overcome the objection with scenario analysis. The Monte Carlo simulation is mathematically complex and can't be considered as a suitable technique if computers are not available. Monte Carlo simulation synthesizes a sufficiently large number of combinations of variables of a project with respective NPVs, with a large number of possible NPVs becoming statistically more reliable to assess expected value and risk of the project.

Monte Carlo simulation is done with following steps:

1. Identify the exogenous variables that determine the cash flows of the project and its NPV. We also need to determine how each variable is related to NPV. These variables are normally demand, selling price, variable cost, etc. of the project and are beyond the control of the management.
2. Specify the probability distribution for each of the exogenous variable.
3. Allocate the random numbers to all the possible values of each variable.
4. Pick random numbers for each variable, and for corresponding values compute the NPV of the project. This is iteration 1.
5. Perform sufficiently large iterations by repeating steps 1 to 4 and get all the NPVs.
6. Find the mean and standard deviation of the NPVs to make assessment of risk of the project.

For Sensor Corporation, we consider three variables of demand, selling price, and variable cost. For convenience and illustration purpose, we have assumed a discrete distribution for all three variables. In actual practice, infinite values of demand, price, and variable cost are possible. Depending upon the probability of occurrence, we assign random numbers to each value. This is done in Table 12-9. Allocation of a range of random numbers to the different values is proportional to the probability.

Simulation is an exercise that generates large number of NPVs their expected value and standard deviation.

Now, we pick a set of random numbers, one for each variable and find the corresponding values of the variables. For these values based on the random numbers picked we compute the NPV.

Table 12-9 Simulation: Sensor Corporation

Demand Level			Selling Price			Variable Cost		
Value	*Probability*	*Random Number*	*Value*	*Probability*	*Random Number*	*Value*	*Probability*	*Random Number*
2,600	0.10	00–09	2.75	0.20	00–19	1.70	0.20	00–19
2,700	0.20	10–29	2.85	0.25	20–44	1.80	0.60	20–79
3,000	0.30	30–59	3.00	0.35	45–79	1.90	0.20	80–99
3,100	0.10	60–69	3.15	0.10	80–89			
3,200	0.20	70–89	3.30	0.10	90–99			
3,500	0.10	90–99						

Table 12-10 illustrates the random numbers picked that determine the values of the variables for the iteration of NPV calculation. For example, as the first draw of number, we get 18, 81, and 62, respectively for the demand level, selling price, and variable cost, respectively. These random numbers correspond to the demand level of 2,700, selling price of ₹3.15, and variable cost of ₹1.80. For these independent variables, we compute the cash flows and NPV of the project.

Table 12-10 Simulation: Sensor Corporation

	Iteration 1		Iteration 2		Iteration 3	
	Random Number	Value	Random Number	Value	Random Number	Value
Demand Level (Nos.)	18	2,700	51	3,000	76	3,200
Selling Price (₹/unit)	81	3.15	13	2.75	46	3.00
Variable Cost (₹/unit)	62	1.80	93	1.90	11	1.70

For the three iterations as given in Table 12-10, the computations of NPV are done in Table 12-11. Depending upon the accuracy of results desired we determine the number of iterations to be performed. The larger the iteration, the closer would it be to reality.

Table 12-11 Simulation: Sensor Corporation

	Iteration 1	Iteration 2	Iteration 3
Initial Investment (₹)	8,000	8,000	8,000
Life of the project (Years)	10	10	10
Discount Rate	15%	15%	15%
Demand Level (Nos.)	2,700	3,000	3,200
Selling Price	3.15	2.75	3.00
			Figure in ₹
Revenue	8,505	8,250	9,600
Variable Cost	4,860	5,700	5,440
Contribution	3,645	2,550	4,160
Fixed Costs	1,200	1,200	1,200
Depreciation	1,200	1,200	1,200
PBIT	1,245	150	1,760
Interest	—	—	—
PBT	1,245	150	1,760
Tax @ 40%	498	60	704
PAT	747	90	1,056
Cash Flow from Operations	**1,947**	**1,290**	**2,256**
Net Present Value at 15% for 10 years	**1,772**	**(1,526)**	**3,322**

When sufficiently large iterations are performed we can get the distribution of the variables to check if the random numbers selected in the iterations generate the probability distribution that matches the assumed distribution. For example, if 1,000 iterations are performed, the distribution of demand must match what is reflected in column two of Table 12-9.

The mean and standard deviation of NPVs of the simulated iterations will truly represent the worth and the risk of the project.

The simulation of NPVs and the measurement of expected values and the risks are closest to real-life situations as it recognizes the existence of infinite numerous values and combinations of variables. Besides the statistical accuracy, the basic difference in simulation and scenario analysis is in its assumptions of relationship of variables. The scenario analysis assumes strong correlation among the exogenous variables while simulation treats these variables as independent of each other. The sensitivity analysis considers only one variable at a time and, therefore, the interrelationship amongst variables is not recognized. The limitations of sensitivity analysis and scenario analysis are best overcome in simulation.

However, simulation has its own shortcomings. The data requirement is huge and cumbersome. The probability distributions of the variables identified are difficult to ascertain. Further, each variable is treated as independent of others, whereas, in reality they are interrelated. Also, the value of even a single variable is dependent upon its own values in the past. For example, if the selling price is increased from ₹3.00 to ₹3.15, there is no possibility of it becoming ₹5 in the next period. Such a situation is ignored by simulation since every iteration is independent of the previous one. Simulation hopes to remove such deficiency by increasing the number of iterations, which adds to the cost and time. Lastly, simulation may measure the risk but it does not convey the desirability of acceptance or rejection of the project and for which we need to adopt some other method, unless we decide to use the expected NPV of the simulation as decision making tool.

DECISION TREE ANALYSIS

Decision tree analysis is a tool to arrive at sequential decisions. Sequential decisions are those that involve a series of decisions depending upon the happenings in the past and the earlier decisions taken. The technique helps in systematic representation of a complex situation by breaking it down into a series of small decisions over time. With many variables clouding the thought process it is advised to view one variable/time period at a time and analyse the impact. The utility of decision tree emanates from the fact that business decisions are not isolated but form a sequence of small decisions.

Decision tree analysis deriving its name from the graphical depiction of a problem handles the risks associated with the situations by assigning the probabilities to each of the branches. The decision tree analysis presents the risk element associated with the decisions and calls it a chance event. For example, all cash flow projections are based on the various demand scenarios. Each of the demand scenarios may be represented as a branch and assigned a probability. The expected value of the cash flow at any point with probability of p_i and cash flows at CF_i then may be represented as Equation 12-6.

$$\text{Expected Value of the Cash flows} = \sum_{1}^{n} p_i \times CF_i \qquad (12\text{-}6)$$

The decision tree is constructed with—(1) decision points, representing the various courses of managerial actions available at a given point of time, and followed by (2) the chance events

A decision tree is a powerful tool of analysing sequential decisions. It breaks up complex decision into smaller decisions and calculates the NPV backwards to arrive at most pragmatic decision based on maximisation of NPV.

that follow each action that impacts the future courses of actions and is again followed by decision points. This chain of decision points and chance events continues till all decisions are exhausted. Each chance event is assigned a probability and for each decision point, the cash flows are determined. These probabilities and cash flows are analysed from the end to arrive at judicious decision at time $t = 0$. The appearance of decision tree would be as depicted in Figure 12-5.

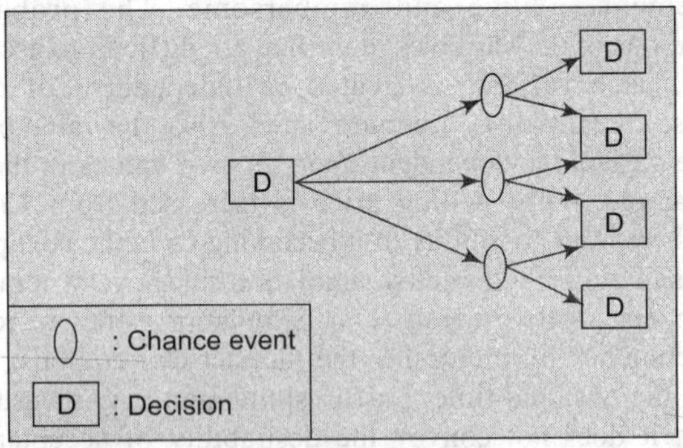

Figure 12-5 Pictorial View—Decision Tree

An example will help understand the whole process of decision tree analysis. A common business situation that can be analysed is the decision choice a firm makes to start with a pilot plant and expand or not to expand later on depending upon the demand scenario faced in the initial stages. We take a similar situation for our analysis.

Consider a firm planning to buy a palletization plant for which it has two options—buy a one big machine right away or start with a smaller machine and add second machine after a year. The dilemma is on account of the uncertainty about the demand and not to invest heavily so as to avoid an unfavourable condition of lack of demand, subsequently. The firm expects to be better informed a year later and feels that the uncertainties about the demand profile may be somewhat resolved by then.

The first decision faced by the firm is whether or not to install a large machine or a small machine. Subsequent decisions would depend upon the demand situation during the first year of operation. There is 60% probability that the demand would be high for the forthcoming year. If it were so, the expected cash generation with a large capacity machine would be ₹200, while with a smaller machine, it would be ₹100. There is only one other possibility, and that is of low demand, probability of which is 40%. However, if the demand were low the cash generation would be ₹100 and ₹70 with large and small machine, respectively.

The demand situation from Year II onwards is dependent upon the state of demand in the first year. It is assumed that demand situation from Year II onwards would continue for substantial time in future. If the demand were high during the first year, then for the subsequent years the probability of demand remaining high is 50%. However, if the demand were low in the first year the chances that the demand would be high, subsequently, is only 40%. The firm may have various options

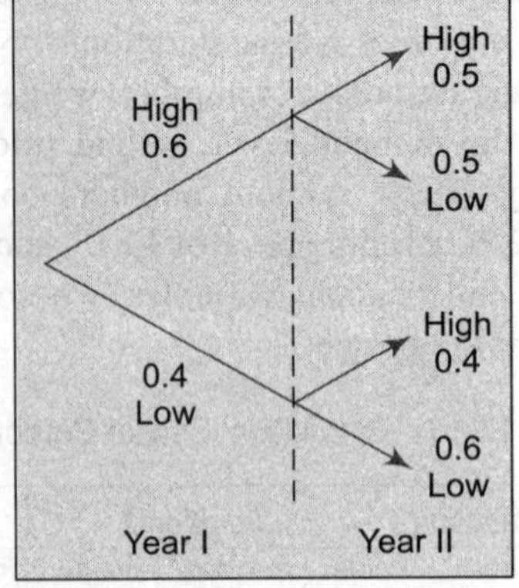

Figure 12-6 Demand Scenario for Palletization

available at the end of Year I. The demand scenario is depicted in Figure 12-6.

If the firm decides to have the large capacity machine, the cash flows of the project for Year II are expected to be ₹300 with annual growth of 8%. However, if the demand were low, the cash flow for Year II would stand reduced to ₹150 and the growth rate to mere 3%. There is no further decision to be made at the end of Year I if the firm goes with the large machine now.

There are many possibilities at the end of Year I, if the firm goes with the small machine now. It may buy another small machine, or buy a large machine, or abandon the machine(s) bought. Buying a large machine is ruled out with one small machine already in place since the demand is not expected to be large enough to book a huge capacity on one small and one big machine. The firm may decide to go in for another small machine. Irrespective of the demand situation in Year I, the firm has two options after first year—(1) buy another small capacity machine, or (2) to continue with the first machine only. However, at the end of Year II it has two options again—(1) to continue with the machine or machines as the case may be; or (2) abandon all the machines and exit from the project. Salvage values would be ₹100 and ₹200 for the first and second machine respectively. The expected return is 18%.

Various options of the firm under different conditions are summarized in Table 12-12.

Table 12-12 Data for Decision Tree

Year I Scenario			*Year II onwards*			*Growth*
Demand	*Prob.*	*Cash Flow Year I (₹)*	*Demand*	*Prob.*	*Cash Flow Year II (₹)*	*Rate (%)*
Big Palletization Plant						
High	0.6	200	High	0.5	300	8 %
			Low	0.5	150	3 %
Low	0.4	100	High	0.4	300	8 %
			Low	0.6	150	3 %
Small Palletization Plant						
High	0.6	100	High	0.5	150/Machine	8 %
			Low	0.5	50/Machine	3 %
Low	0.4	70	High	0.4	150/Machine	8 %
			Low	0.6	50/Machine	3 %

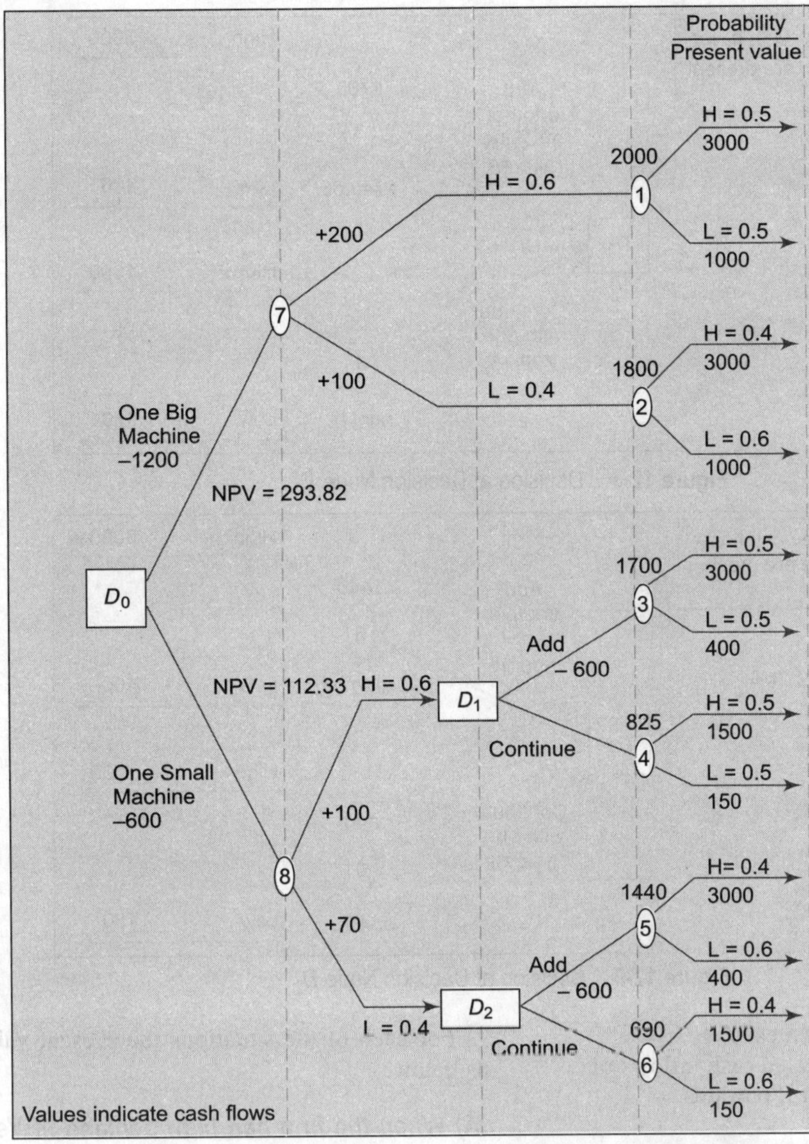

Figure 12-7 Decision Tree for Palletization Plant

The decision tree with decision and chance events is depicted in Figure 12-7.

We now begin our analysis from the end of tree by computing the cash flows for each branch, finding the expected cash flows, calculate the net present values and choosing the higher of the NPVs at each decision point. This continues till the present stage of the decision tree, i.e. D_0.

When the Firm Chooses to go for a Large Machine Now

When the demand was high in Year I

The expected cash flow of the firm at the end of Year I would depend upon the probability distribution of demand and the cash flows. If the demand were high for Year II onwards the present value of the cash flows would be ₹3,000 as calculated below:

$$\text{Present value at Year I} = \frac{CF_2}{r-g} = \frac{300}{0.18-0.08} = ₹3{,}000$$

If the demand were low for Year II onwards the present value of the cash flows would be ₹1,000 as calculated below:

$$\text{Present value at Year I} = \frac{CF_2}{r-g} = \frac{150}{0.18-0.03} = ₹1{,}000$$

The expected value of the cash flow at Node 1 would be

$0.5 \times 3{,}000 + 0.5 \times 1{,}000 = ₹2{,}000$

Total expected cash flow at the end of Year I at Node 7
= Cash flow of Year I + Expected cash inflows Year II onwards
= $200 + 2{,}000 = ₹2{,}200$

And the present value is = $2{,}200/1.18 = ₹1{,}864.40$

When the demand was low in Year I

We calculate the expected cash flow in the same manner as before and the expected value of the cash flow at Node 2 would be:

$0.4 \times 3{,}000 + 0.6 \times 1{,}000 = ₹1{,}800$

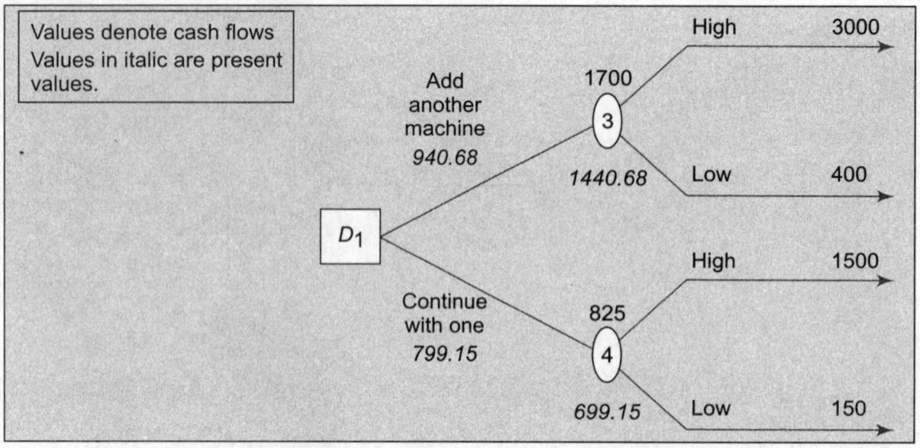

Figure 12-8 Decision at Decision Node D_1

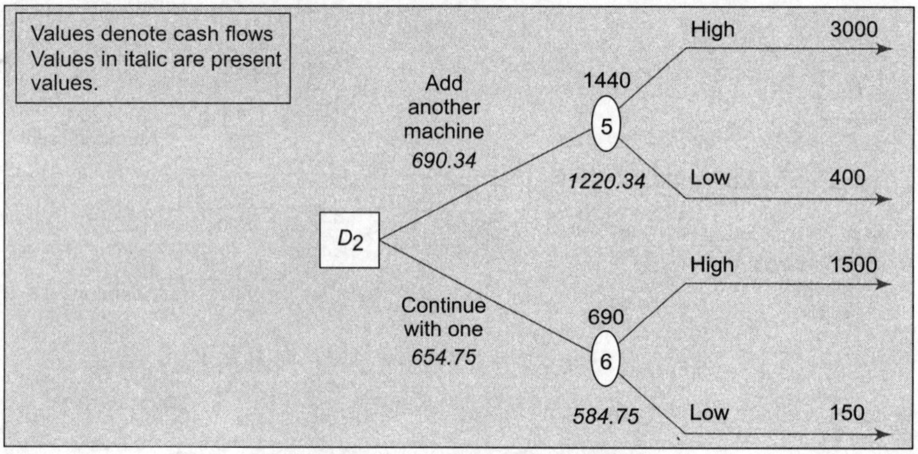

Figure 12-9 Decision at Decision Node D_2

Total expected cash flow at the end of Year I
= Cash flow of Year I + Expected cash inflows of Year II onwards
= 100 + 1,800 = ₹1,900

And the present value would be 1,900/1.18 = ₹1,610.17

With all the expected values of cash flows known we may compute the expected discounted cash flow at Year 0. It would be:

Expected PV of Cash Flows at $t = 0$

$$= \frac{0.6 \times 1,864.40 \times 0.4 \times 1,610.17}{1.18} = ₹1,493.82$$

And, NPV = 1,493.82 – 1,200 = ₹ 293.82

When the Firm Chooses to go for a Small Machine Now

Initially, when a firm chose a large machine it faced no further or sequential decision. However, in case of the installation of a small machine at $t = 0$, the firm faces the decision at another time or a sequential decision at $t = 1$; whether to continue with the same machine or install another. Buying of large machine at $t = 1$ is ruled out. It has following four situations:

	Demand in First Year	*Decision*
A	High	(i) Buy another machine
	High	(ii) Continue with the old machine
B	Low	(i) Buy another machine
	Low	(ii) Continue with the old machine

For each of the situations the present values are calculated as below:

(A) When the firm had high demand in Year I

There are two possible situations—(1) installation of another small machine; and (2) continuing with the first machine only. Both the situations are analysed.

(i) When the firm had installed another small machine in Year I With another machine installed at the end of Year I, the firm faces a chance event of high or low demand in Year II. If the demand were high, the firm gets the value of ₹3,000 as before at a growth rate of 8%. However, if it faced low demand its cash flows constitute of ₹100 from operations and ₹300 from the salvage values of the two machines being abandoned. The expected cash flow at Node 3 would be:

Expected cash flow from operations in Year II:
= 0.5 × 3,000 + 0.5 × 400 = ₹1,700

Present value of cash flows in Year I at 18%
= 1700/1.18 = ₹ 1,440.68

And the net present value at Decision Point 1 at the end of Year I:

= PV of cash flows of Year II + cash flow of Year I – cost of one small machine
= 1440.68 + 100 – 600 = ₹940.68

(ii) When the firm continued with only one small machine in Year II When another machine was not installed, the cash flows faced by the firm would be the expected value of cash flows with high and low demand.

With high demand in Year II and onwards:

$$\text{Present value at Year I} = \frac{CF_2}{r-g} = \frac{150}{0.18-0.08} = ₹1{,}500$$

With low demand in Year II and onwards:

Expected cash flow = Cash flow of one small machine in Year II + Salvage Value
= 50 + 100 = 150

Therefore, the expected cash flow at Node 4 for Year II = 0.5 × 1500 + 0.5 × 150 = ₹825

The cash flows and present values at decision point D_2 are shown in Figure 12-8.

Present value at Year I at Decision Point D_1 = 825/1.18 = ₹699.15

Net Present value at decision point 1 at the end of Year I
= PV of cash flows of Year II + cash flow of Year I
= 699.15 + 100 = ₹799.15

The cash flows and present values at decision point D_1 are shown in Figure 12-8.

Net present value at decision point D_1 With the two branches of with another machine and with single machine representing two mutually exclusive projects the decision would be to choose the option that has a higher NPV. Hence, the decision is in favour of installing another machine if the demand faced in Year I was high since the present value of the cash flows with another machine bought is higher than without another machine. At D_1 the present value is ₹940.68.

(B) When the firm had low demand in Year I

Again there are two possible situations—(1) installation of another small machine; and (2) continuation with the first machine only. Both the situations are analysed below.

(i) When the firm had installed another small machine in Year I With another machine installed at the end of Year I, the firm faces a chance of facing high or low demand in Year II. If the demand were high, the firm gets the value of ₹3,000 as before at growth rate of 8%. However, if it faced low demand its cash flows constitute of ₹100 from operations and ₹300 from the salvage values of the two machines being abandoned. The expected cash flow would be:

Expected cash flow from operations at Node 5 in Year II
= 0.4 × 3,000 + 0.6 × 400 = ₹1,440

Present value of cash flows in Year I at 18% = 1440/1.18 = ₹ 1,220.34

And the net present value at decision point 1 at the end of Year I
= PV of cash flows of Year II + cash flow of Year I
– cost of one small machine
= 1220.34 + 70 – 600 = ₹690.34

(ii) When the firm continued with only one small machine in Year II When another machine was not installed the cash flows faced by the firm would be the expected value of cash flows with high and low demand.

With high demand in Year II and onwards:

$$\text{Present value at Year I} = \frac{CF_2}{r-g} = \frac{150}{0.18-0.08} = ₹1{,}500$$

With low demand in Year II and onwards:

Expected cash flow = Cash flow of one small machine in Year II + Salvage value
= 50 + 100 = 150

Therefore the expected cash flow at Node 6 for Year II = 0.4 × 1500 + 0.6 × 150 = ₹690

Present value at Year I at decision point D_2 = 690/1.18 = ₹584.75

Net present value at decision point 1 at the end of Year I
= PV of cash flows of Year II + cash flow of Year I
= 584.75 + 70 = ₹654.75

Net present value at decision point D_2 Here again, we would choose the option with a higher NPV. Hence, the decision is again in favour of installing another machine since the present value of the cash flows with another machine bought is higher at ₹690.34 than without another machine at ₹654.75. At D_2 the present value is ₹690.34. The cash flows and present values at decision point D_2 are shown in Figure 12-9.

The expected cash flow at decision point D_0 with the branch from small machine is:

Probability of high demand × Present value at D_1
+ Probability of low demand × Present value at D_2
= 0.6 × 940.68 + 0.4 × 690.34 = 564.41 + 276.14
= ₹840.55

And the present value would be 840.55/1.18 = ₹712.33

The net present value would be:
= ₹712.33 – 600
= ₹112.33

With large machine providing expected NPV of ₹293.82 and the strategy of installing small machine results in NPV of ₹112.13 the decision is clearly in favour of going for the large machine straight away.

The decision tree is a powerful tool that represents a concept in a simplified manner. It eases comprehension of a complex problem. It helps in eliminating undesirable propositions and arriving at the most profitable option based on a pragmatic evaluation. The necessity of the calculation of the cash flows has merits as well as demerits. While it increases the computational requirements manifold even for some *prima facie* unwarranted option, it also forces the managers to question the validity of each decision that is of essence to any evaluation process. The decision tree would become more and more unwieldy as decision points and chance events increase.

CONVENTIONAL WAYS OF HANDLING RISKS

The tools of incorporating risks in the evaluation of capital budgeting process are varied. Some of these tools have been discussed in the previous paragraphs/sections. These tools are specific to the determination of risks of the cash flows and handle specific nature of risk in their own ways. A sensitivity analysis focused on critical variables and recomputation of NPVs with specific changes to be evaluated against the NPV under normal and assumed conditions. Scenario analysis achieved the same comparison based on simultaneous and multiple changes due to interrelationship of variables that exists in the real world. Simulation, again, focused on the key determinants of the value of the project and analysing a larger set of scenarios based on the likely probability distribution of each variable. The decision tree recognized the situation of sequential decisions existing in the business scenarios. All these techniques were complicated, statistical, and sophisticated.

There are few simpler techniques of assessing risk associated with capital budgeting proposals that are considered equally effective and easy to comprehend. These techniques are based on existing or projected cash flows or they incorporate the risk in the capital budgeting process itself rather than addressing the issue separately. These techniques are as follows:

1. Breakeven Analysis
2. Payback Period
3. Risk-adjusted discount rate method
4. Certainty equivalent method

Breakeven Analysis

Breakeven analysis has been discussed in detail in Chapter 3. It focuses on the determination of minimum volume/revenue that would result in the recovery of all expenses. The concern of the management is not to make the loss. As long as profit results the variations in the profit is considered a non-issue. The techniques based on standard deviation disregard this approach and consider any deviation from the expected level as risky. Under breakeven analysis, managers make an assessment regarding the possibility of not achieving the breakeven level of sales. The farther is the expected level of operation from the breakeven level, the safer is the project. This is referred to as the margin of safety. This is a rather simplistic view of risk but in certain cases it serves the objective of risk assessment. Breakeven analysis, requires a minimum amount of data as no further inputs are required besides those already prepared for the evaluation of the project, and risk may be assessed based on the evaluation.

Breakeven point can provide an insight into the risk of project. Lower the breakeven point safer is the project.

For example, the breakeven point for a project may be at 50% of capacity utilization, while another comparable project may have capacity utilization at 65%. Given all other factors remaining the same for both the projects, the first project with lower breakeven point at 50% capacity utilization would be regarded as less risky. This is a relative measure of risk. BEP may also be used as an absolute measure. For example, if the first project is expected to operate at 70% capacity utilization and the pessimistic scenario is assumed at minimum of 60% capacity utilization, the project may be considered as safe because it still leaves a 10% margin of safety.

Payback period in itself is a capital budgeting techniques based on risk considerations. Lower the payback safer is the project.

Payback Period

The evaluation of investment proposals by the payback method is discussed in the previous chapter. As one would realize, the payback period method accounts for risk associated with the project in the decision rule itself. When a cut-off payback period is decided as a benchmark for acceptance or rejection, the underlying thought is the risk associated with the cash flows of the project. The recovery of principal, i.e., the initial investment is paramount for the firm. The earlier the investment is recovered, the safer the project is deemed. The time elapsed between the investment and its recovery is considered proportional to the risk.

Normally, firms decide on a cut-off on the payback period for some of the projects. It may appropriately shorten or lengthen the cut-off for specific projects, taking in to account its risk rather subjectively.

A major debatable issue with the payback period as a tool for associating risk is its concern solely with time. Cash flows are risky because of the assumptions of projection of cash flows are not likely to fall in place. Implicit in the method is that assumptions would remain valid in near term and would fall apart only in the later stages of the project. Though this seems to be a reasonable thought, it may not be true. All the uncertainties with the cash flows cannot be attributed to time. Firms would do well to concentrate on making the assumption closer to reality.

Risk-Adjusted Discount Rate (RADR)

Another commonly and possibly the most acceptable and logical method is the adjustment of risk in the discount rate.

Central to the idea of risk-adjusted discount rate is the generally accepted view that more risk is acceptable if the returns are good and less risky ventures become acceptable even if they offer rather paltry returns. To take an example from capital markets, assume that two shares A and B are trading at identical price ₹100. Share A is expected to grow to ₹120 and Share B to ₹150 in a year from now. An investor is willing to buy only one share at ₹100 (It can be capital rationing situation or mutually exclusive investment Share A and Share B from the same industry). The required return by the investor is 15% but he is less sure of Share B touching a value of ₹150. The investor is not willing to invest in Share B unless it offers a return of 20% to commensurate with the risk of price in a year from now. Therefore, he chooses to discount the cash flow of Share A at 15% and Share B at 20% and then compare the NPV to make a decision in favour of Share B with an NPV of ₹125 against an NPV of ₹104 for Share A.

Recognizing that the cash flow projections are only estimates and the actual flows would vary, an appropriate adjustment for the risk has to be incorporated in the capital investment decisions. In fact, it will be only be by coincidence that the estimates of cash flows will actually fructify in future. One way of adjusting for the risk is to discount more risky cash flows with a higher rate and less risky projects with lesser rate. It is based on the premise that more risky projects need to offer higher returns before they are accepted. Therefore, the hurdle rate must be higher for such projects. If the project clears a higher hurdle rate it is worth considering.

Risk-adjusted discount rate method uses a higher discount rate for more risky cash flows and lesser discount rate for less risky cash flows.

More often than not, the hurdle rate is the weighted average cost of capital, WACC. A word of caution is in order here regarding the use of WACC as discount rate. While using WACC as a discount rate we have assumed that the project has the same risk as that of the firm as a whole. We have also recognized that opportunity cost of capital r_0 for all equity financing incorporates only the business risk of the project. We modified this to get cost of equity r_e for increased leverage to account for the other risk called financial risk. Finally, we obtained the weighted average cost of capital by including the cost of debt and used it as discount rate. One would assume that the cost of the equity modulated for the financial risk and business risk would cover all the risks of the project. Indeed it is so, provided the cash flows of the project are only as risky the existing cash flows of the firm. However, if the cash flows of the project are not consistent with the risk of the firm the use of WACC as discount rate is inappropriate.

While, WACC is already a risk-adjusted discount rate for the projects that are in the same line of business as existing, it cannot be used as universal discount rate for all projects of the firm. For other projects, an alternative way for adjusting for the risk of the project is to derive the discount rate on the basis of capital asset pricing model (CAPM) by adjusting the cost of equity (refer pure-play approach in Chapter 9) and arrive at appropriate discount rate. The appropriate discount rate may be represented as:

Risk-adjusted discount rate
= Risk-free rate + Premium for the risk

Here, the premium for the risk would be consistent with the risk of the cash flows being evaluated. Using a higher discount rate would decrease the present value of the cash flow and, therefore, the riskier cash flows would be valued lesser than the safer ones. Such an adjustment should automatically accept or reject an investment proposal incorporating its risk profile. For example, consider the following cash flows of a short-lived project of three years for a firm:

		(₹)
Year 0	:	–10,000
Year I	:	3,000
Year II	:	4,000
Year III	:	6,000

With the above cash flows the NPV of the investment proposal at a discount rate of 10% is:

$$\text{NPV at } 10\% = \frac{3{,}000}{1.10} + \frac{4{,}000}{1.10^2} + \frac{6{,}000}{1.10^3} - 10{,}000 = ₹540.95$$

At 10% discount rate, the project is acceptable with a positive NPV.

However, the firm feels that a return of 10% is not an appropriate for the quality of cash flows the project represents. According to the firm, the appropriate return for such cash flows is 15% and not 10%. If we discount the cash flows at 15% the NPV is:

$$\text{NPV at } 15\% = \frac{3{,}000}{1.15} + \frac{4{,}000}{1.15^2} + \frac{6{,}000}{1.15^3} - 10{,}000 = -₹421.63$$

Clearly, the project is not acceptable since it does not meet the expectations of a return of 15% for such a quality of cash in flows. A project that is acceptable at 10% becomes unacceptable at 15% only on the premise that the quality of the cash flow deserves a return of 15% and not 10%. Depending upon the background and the expertise of the firm, the cash flows would represent different kinds of risks. Different firms would view the same cash flows differently from the perspective of risk. Therefore, a project can never be unacceptable by all or none. There would always be someone who finds the project favourable.

What applies to NPV method would also apply to the IRR method. We may use the IRR of the project against a higher cut-off hurdle rate for riskier projects.

A ratio of coefficient of variation of the project to that of the firm will provide an idea about the relative risk of the project. For example, if the WACC of the firm is 15% and the risk-free rate is 8% it can be said that the risk premium for the firm is 7%. If this firm is considering a project that is deemed 20% more risky, the risk premium of the project will be 1.2 × 7 = 8.4%. Add to this the risk-free rate of 8%, the relevant discount rate works out to 16.4%. If the project has positive NPV at discount rate of 16.4% it is accepted or else rejected.

Risk adjustment through beta Despite the simplicity of the argument for using risk-adjusted discount rate, it suffers from few limitations. The first limitation is operational in nature, which casts problems in making a reasonable assessment of premium to be added on account of risk. This is usually incorporated through beta. The use of beta as measure of risk has some implied assumptions that may not hold true. One has to guard against the following:

- When there exists no firm with adequate historical published data for the prices of securities, making computation of beta, a measure of market risk, difficult
- When unsystematic risk is large compared to systematic risk
- When a firm consists of large number of small projects in the same line cannot be considered to be diversified enough so as to treat entire risk consisting of only the systematic risk
- When capital markets are imperfect

Beta as a measure of risk and determinant of the premium for risk can at best be used for projects of similar nature. Since beta cannot incorporate the entire risk of the cash flows of the project, managers may have to use another premium determined on subjective basis. The subjectivity of managers in assessing the relative risk of the project will make a selection of discount rate controversial.

Compounding risk with time Another more plausible objection related to the use of risk-adjusted discount rate lies in treatment of cash flows of different periods. By using a higher discount rate for a risky project, the distant cash flows are being penalized more than the nearer cash flows. To illustrate, consider the cash flow of a project for Year 1 and Year 2 of ₹100 each with a risk-adjusted discount rate of 25%. The present value of these cash flows would be:

$100/1.25 + 100/1.25^2 = 80 + 64 = 144$

Here the cash flow for Year 2 is discounted at 25% for two years by a factor of $1/1.25^2 = 0.64$ as compared to the cash flow of Year 1 with a discount factor of 0.80, while in reality the cash flows of Year 1 and Year 2 may be equally risky. In this case, we unnecessarily penalized the distant cash flow while computing the present value. This compounding of risk, depending upon the time, the cash flow that occurs is a distortion of the true representation of risk even though one may justify that later cash flows inherently carry a greater risk than the earlier ones. In fact, in certain situations it may be exactly the opposite. The cash flows in the formative years of the project may be more risky in nature. But once they fructify, the management becomes more certain of the future cash flows.

Cash flow and discount rate Lastly, an objection that is more basic in nature. By using a risk-adjusted discount rate, we essentially are transferring the risk of cash flows, a figure used in the numerator, to the discount rate, a figure used in the denominator. Though there has to be consistency in both the figures, the question as to what extent the deficiency of one is compensated by adjustment to another is debatable.

Certainty Equivalent Approach

The certainty equivalent approach is based on the premise that if the cash flows are deemed risky, we must modify them so that the correct decision is taken. In the risk-adjusted discount rate method we attempted to modify the discount rate to handle the risk of the cash flows. This had two demerits; (i) we were compounding the risk of the cash flows with time and (ii) resolving the issue of risk of cash flows not by cash flows but with discount rate. As a judicious method, the evaluation of the investment proposal must separate discounting for risk and time. Adding a risk premium to the discount rate is like mixing oil with water. A project value has a distinct risk profile and a definite time value. Under the risk-adjusted discount rate method, we mixed the time value and compensation for risk.

Certainty equivalent approach computes the NPV of the project by converting the risky cash flows into equivalent risk-free cash flows and the discount them with risk free-rate.

Instead of adjusting the discount rate, the certainty equivalent approach attempts to correct the cash flows for risk and use an appropriate discount rate. It is a two-step process of segregating the risk element and time element of the cash flows:

- First convert the uncertain cash flows to certain cash flow to reflect the risk element of the project, and then
- Use the risk-free rate as discount rate for certain cash flows to provide for time value of money.

Mathematically, it can be represented as:

$$\text{Net Present Value, NPV} = \sum_{1}^{n} \alpha_t \frac{CF_t}{(1+r_f)^t} - CF_0$$

where α_t = certainty equivalent factor for period t ranging between 0 and 1

r_f = risk-free rate

The decision rule will be:

Accept the project if its certainty equivalent NPV is positive else reject it.

The certainty equivalent factor is used to convert uncertain cash flows into certain cash flows. Note that initial cash flow is not modified being a certain cash flow. By the use of risk-free rate as a discount rate, we are attaching the time value and avoiding the mistake of compounding the distant cash flows with unrealistically low discount factor that possibly it does not deserve.

Certainty equivalent and probability distribution The conversion of uncertain cash flows to certain cash flow is possible in a number of ways. If the probability distribution of the cash flow is known, we may adjust the uncertain cash flows by subtracting certain number of standard deviations from the expected value. Assuming that the cash flows have normal distribution with a known mean and standard deviation, and the estimated cash flow is the expected value of the probability distribution, one can find the certainty equivalent of the cash flows using normal distribution tables. If the cash flow has a normal distribution with an expected value of ₹100 and standard deviation of ₹15, the certainty equivalent will be:

$\bar{E} - 3\sigma = 100 - 3 \times 15 = 55$

This implies that the expected cash flow of ₹100 is equivalent to ₹55 with 99.87% certainty.

As an example of application of certainty equivalent approach, consider a project with an initial investment of ₹180 with a life expectancy of three years and uniform expected cash in flows of ₹100 in each of the three years. Using WACC at 20% as discount rate, the NPV of the project is:

$100/1.20 + 100/1.20^2 + 100/1.20^3 - 180 =$ ₹30.65

The expected cash flows are assumed normally distributed with standard deviation of ₹10 the certainty equivalent cash flows are ₹70 each year. Assuming a risk free rate of 10% the NPV of the project under certainty equivalent approach will be:

$70/1.10 + 70/1.10^2 + 70/1.10^3 - 180 = -$ ₹5.92

Thus, in the WACC method, the project is acceptable while with the certainty equivalent approach, the venture is too risky to be undertaken. According to the certainty equivalent approach, uncertain cash flows of ₹100 discounted at 20% must be equivalent to certain cash flows of ₹70 discounted at 10%. If the NPVs are different, it implies that the risk assessment of the project is wrong.

Certainty co-efficient An alternate way of approaching the certainty equivalent approach for those not statistically minded is to assign the uncertainty factor subjectively. Each year's cash flow is assigned a risk factor ranging between 0 and 1, rather subjectively. For example, a certainty coefficient factor value of 0.8 for a cash flow would suggest that the projected cash flow of ₹100 would for sure result in a cash flow of ₹80. One may assign a uniform value for all the cash flows for the entire life of the project or may use a progressively decreasing value of certainty equivalent factor as cash flows become more and more distant. This approach may be used when the validity of the assumption of normal distribution is doubtful, a subjective assessment of certainty can be used.

Assume in the earlier example that the managers are certain that cash flows for the three years would, for sure, be realized to the extent of 90%, 80%, and 70%, respectively, the NPV of the project would be:

$$0.9 \times 100/1.10 + 0.8 \times 100/1.10^2 + 0.7 \times 100/1.10^3 - 180 = -₹20.52$$

Certainty equivalent and RADR As a comparison between the risk-adjusted discount rate method and certainty equivalent approach, consider a situation when the two approaches give identical result. For this to happen the discounted values of the cash flows for every period must be equal. Therefore,

$$\alpha_t \cdot \frac{\text{CF}_t}{(1+r_f)^t} = \frac{\text{CF}_t}{(1+r)^t}$$

Or $$\alpha_t = \frac{(1+r_f)^t}{(1+r)^t}$$

Also $$\alpha_{t+1} = \frac{(1+r_f)^{t+1}}{(1+r)^{t+1}}$$

If both the approaches have to give identical results then the certainty equivalent coefficient must decline by a factor of $\frac{(1+r_f)}{(1+r)}$ for each period. For example, if the risk free-rate is 10% and the risk-adjusted discount rate is 20% we advertently or inadvertently assign the certainty equivalent coefficients for successive periods by a factor of 1.10/1.20 = 0.9167. If so, the results from the two approaches would be identical.

The risk-adjusted discount rate assigns the risk factor in the denominator, while the certainty equivalent approach adjusts uncertain cash flows in the numerator for valuation under the DCF technique.

The element of subjectivity is confined to a single parameter of assigning risk premium in risk-adjusted discount rate. Thereafter, everything falls in place if the selection of premium for risk is correct. However, if there is an error it keeps getting compounded. This is unlikely to happen in the certainty equivalent approach. Managers may find the use of risk adjusted discount factor an operationally easier approach. Certainty equivalent approach is more subjective as it requires attaching certainty factor to each year cash flows.

RISK ANALYSIS METHODS: A FINAL WORD

Providing for uncertainty or risk in capital budgeting exercise is a matter of debate. One has a wide variety of tools available for handling risk; from simple breakeven analysis to simulation and other complicated statistics based methods. Depending upon the amount of initial outlay, the criticality of the cash flows to the overall cash flows and other factors the analysis of risk and tools of handling the same may be decided.

Each method has its own merits and demerits and utility of the stakeholders in the project. For example, it would purely be impractical and fruitless to run a simulation exercise for a paltry investment or while attempting to decide upon a replacement policy. One may do it for academic purposes, but it does not make sense on business considerations. An appropriate method applicable to a situation must be chosen.

No method can be said to be superior or inferior to another in all circumstances. For example, financial institutions or lenders to the project rely heavily on sensitivity analysis while providing financial assistance for the project in order to keep an eye on the variables that are crucial to the positive net present value of the project. They also focus on breakeven point to assure themselves of the recovery of principal and interest. They would find simulation or scenario analyses to be too cumbersome and not serving their purpose as they monitor progress of the project on the basis of a select few crucial variables. On the other hand, managers of the firm may be more concerned about the scenario analysis rather than sensitivity analysis.

Also, the risk-adjusted discount rate method might seem more relevant for a management seeking a higher return and not minding extra risk for increased return while lenders may prefer certainty equivalent approach over risk adjusted discount rate because of their greater concern for safety rather than increased return.

SUMMARY

Capital budgeting decisions are not simple in real life situations. Most capital budgeting decisions revolve around consideration of mutually exclusive projects, which may be categorized as:

1. Mutually exclusive projects with the projects having unequal lives
2. Deciding on how often the asset must be replaced
3. Submitting competitive price without incurring losses
4. Making decision under constraint of capital

Projects with unequal lives are often related to the replacement of old technology with new one from alternative sources of supply that last for different periods of time apart from being different in cash flow characteristics. One way of handling such decisions is to extend the cash flows of each technology for a number of periods till the lives of the two competing equipment match. This is rather tedious. An alternative approach is to compare the cost of each technology based on annual costs. For this purpose, we make use of annuity tables and translate the present values of cost for equivalent annualized value (EAV). The option with lower EAV of costs is chosen.

The second important type of decision relates to a policy formulation with regard to how often the old equipment needs to be replaced.

Some firms continue with the existing asset till they last. The decision to replace is not made by them but is forced on them by the asset when it breaks down completely and goes beyond repairs. Such a philosophy is not a prudent one as firms keep incurring unduly large costs without realizing that by early replacement the scope of saving costs exists. Determination of such policy is also based on the principles of mutually exclusive option lasting for different times. The policy of how often the replacement is made is again based on equivalent annualized value of the cash flows. The policy that gives the largest equivalent annualized value is adopted.

The third situation that is often faced by business enterprises is to find a minimum price that must be quoted for long contracts for high volumes. Though this appears to be a marketing problem it can be resolved utilizing the principles of capital budgeting.

Lastly, but perhaps most importantly, a firm faces a situation of limited funds and finds themselves to accept all positive NPV projects. Such a situation is referred to as capital rationing. Here, the firm has to make the best use of the capital and changes its focus to addition of present values of inflows per unit of initial investment. This is akin to marginal efficiency of capital. The method to be adopted under the conditions of capital rationing is the profitability index (PI). The PI is the present values of inflow per unit of capital outlay. Projects with higher PI are preferred over those with lower PI.

The capital budgeting exercise is based on the future cash flows that are estimated. The decision assumes that these projected cash flows are certain and, hence, the decision made is correct. This can hardly be true. We need to recognize the fact that the projected cash flows used are liable to change and the decision of capital budgeting must incorporate the risk emanating from the changes in the cash flows.

The sensitivity analysis refers to finding out the critical variables in the assumptions of cash flow and then finding out the changes in the NPV of the project with a given change in each of the variables. More often than not the critical determinants of the cash flows are taken as selling price and proportions of variable cost. Only one variable is assumed to change at a time.

Scenario analysis is similar to sensitivity analysis in approach. However, here we recognize that business scenarios change simultaneously because of the interrelationship among the variables. Each scenario is analysed for changes in the NPV and assessed for the risk the project has. Here, the risk assessment cannot be done on a single variable basis. It has to be on aggregate basis and for all scenarios the expected NPV, its variance and standard deviation need to be arrived at.

Simulation overcomes the problem of scenario analysis since the sufficient number of scenarios may not be conceived and decisions based on statistical parameters may not be dependable. With the availability of fast computing devices it is possible to generate large number of scenarios and find out the NPVs under each so as to make statistical data dependable and relevant for decision making.

The decision tree analysis handles the issues of risk in a different manner. It recognizes that business decisions are taken in sequential manner where the past governs the future courses of actions. It is a systematic depiction of all the alternatives available. The computation is based on NPVs of each of the option in a roll back manner. The decision at any point is based on the NPV and branches with lower NPVs are dropped. As we proceed from backwards, the size of the decision tree truncates with clear decision made at each decision point till we reach the first decision point. All decisions are made on a pragmatic basis of maximizing the NPV.

Conventional tools of assessing risk include computation of breakeven point and finding the payback period. The lower the breakeven point, the safer is the project. Similarly, the faster the project pays back the original investment, the better it is. Two other techniques that build in the risk in the decision making process itself are: (i) risk-adjusted discount rate and (ii) certainty equivalent approach.

The method of risk-adjusted discount rate is based on the premise that uncertain cash flows need to offer a greater return to become attractive enough for acceptance. Therefore, the cash flows that are more risky must be assessed against a greater hurdle rate. This can easily be achieved by increasing the discount rate by adding a suitable premium commensurate with the risk of the cash flows being evaluated. The discount rate must be consistent with the quality of cash flows. Though fundamentally sound and appealing and convenient to use, it suffers from the limitation of compounding the risk with time. If all cash flows are discounted at higher rate, the distant cash flows erode in value extremely fast as compared to near cash flows. It may be true that distant cash flows are more risky and must be valued less but compounding decrease in value seems unwarranted.

Certainty equivalent approach emphasizes on replacing the risky cash flows of the project with equivalent certain cash flows and then discounting them at a risk free rate. The approach handles the risk in the cash flow separately and then matches it with an appropriate discount rate. It eliminates the compounding of risk with time.

No single method can be said to be superior to the rest. The usefulness and applicability of a particular method to handle or assess the risk of the project is dependent upon the objective of the evaluator, criticality of the risk to the overall risk of the portfolio, magnitude of risk, and the stakeholder assessing the risk.

KEY TERMS

Equivalent Annualized Value is an annual and equal cash flow spread over life of the project that gives the present value same as that of project when discounted at same rate.

Capital Rationing refers to a situation where the firm faces projects requiring higher outlay than the resources available with the firm.

Profitability Index is defined as present value of cash inflows per unit of initial capital outlay.

Sensitivity of the project is the % change in net present value of the project with a given change in one of the independent variable.

Scenario Analysis is the study of changes in the net present value of the project with different scenarios encompassing different values of the variables.

Simulation Analysis is also a study of changes in the net present value of the project with respect to number of variables values of which are picked from the random numbers generated.

Decision Tree is a graphical depiction of various options available followed by chance events that may happen.

Risk-adjusted Discount Rate is arrived by adding a suitable risk premium, based on the risk of the cash flows being examined, to the risk-free rate.

Certainty Equivalent refers to the amount of certain cash flows that is considered equivalent to the uncertain cash flows.

KEY FORMULAE

Equivalent Annual Value (EAV)

$$= \frac{\text{Net Present Value}}{\text{Annuity Factor for } n \text{ years at discount rate of } r}$$

Profitability index or Benefit Cost Ratio

$$= \frac{\text{Present Value of Cash inflows}}{\text{Initial Outlay}}$$

PRACTICE PROBLEMS

1. Matching Lives for NPV

WallConstructions Ltd are considering purchase of a special purpose fabrication machine for making concrete walls. Two machines are being offered by a supplier that differ in their useful lives. Model A can work well for two years while the Model B is more rugged and lasts for three years.

The supplier has priced the two models very smartly so that both the models sell well. Model A with 2 year useful life was priced at ₹50 lakh while Model B with three years life was quoted at ₹85 lakh. The marketing department of the supplier organisation convinced the management of WallConstructions Ltd that buying either of the model would be equally profitable to them.

After study of the various aspects associated with the fabrication, the management came out with the following projections of the cash inflows from the two models:

₹ lakh	Cash Flows			Capital Cost
Year	1	2	3	
Model A	35.0	25.0		50
Model B	45.0	35.0	25.0	85

If the cost of capital for WallConstructions Ltd is 11% which of the two models should they procure?

Solution

Since the two models have different useful lives their NPVs are not comparable directly. To make assessment, we assume that each machine would be replicated at the end of useful life with same cash flows till the period where the lives become equal. This happens at the end of six years.

(₹ Lakh)

Model A	Cash flows				
Year	1st m/c	2nd m/c	3rd m/c	Total CF	PV at 11%
0	−50.00			−50.00	−50.00
1	35.00			35.00	31.53
2	25.00	−50.00		−25.00	−20.29
3	0.00	35.00		35.00	25.59
4		25.00	−50.00	−25.00	−16.47
5			35.00	35.00	20.77
6			25.00	25.00	13.37
Net present value					4.50

Model B	Cash flows				(₹ Lakh)
Year	1st m/c	2nd m/c	3rd m/c	Total CF	PV
0	−85.00			−85.00	−85.00
1	45.00			45.00	40.54
2	35.00			35.00	28.41
3	25.00	−85.00		−60.00	−43.87
4		45.00		45.00	29.64
5		35.00		35.00	20.77
6		25.00		25.00	13.37
Net present value					3.86

Since Model A has marginally higher net present value WallConstructions Ltd should buy Model A.

2. Probabilistic Approach to NPV

Certainty Enterprises are considering two projects A and B with initial outlays of ₹50 lakh and ₹60 lakh. The inflows of the projects are sensitive to the economic conditions that are expected to prevail over 10 years; the life of each of the project. The cash flows for the 4 different economic conditions of Excellent, Good, Average and Poor with their respective probabilities are as below

(₹ Lakh)

	Probability	Cash flows	
		A	B
Initial cost	Certain	−50.00	−60.00
Excellent	0.30	15.00	18.00
Good	0.20	12.00	14.00
Average	0.30	10.00	12.00
Poor	0.20	8.00	7.00

(a) What is the net present value of the projects under the different economic conditions?

(b) What NPV you expect for each of the project?

(c) What are the risk associated with each of the projects in terms of standard deviation and co-efficient of variation?

(d) Which of the two projects would you choose?

Solution

(a) Calculation of NPV under various scenarios

Project A				₹ *lakh*
Scenario	*Annual Cash flow*	*Present value*	*Initial cost*	*NPV*
Excellent	15.00	75.28	50.00	25.28
Good	12.00	60.23	50.00	10.23
Average	10.00	50.19	50.00	0.19
Poor	8.00	40.15	50.00	–9.85

Project B				₹ *lakh*
Scenario	*Annual Cash flow*	*Present value*	*Initial cost*	*NPV*
Excellent	18.00	90.34	60.00	30.34
Good	14.00	70.26	60.00	10.26
Average	12.00	60.23	60.00	0.23
Poor	7.00	35.13	60.00	–24.87

(b) and (c) Calculation of expected NPVs, Variance, Standard Deviation and Co-efficient of variation

Project A				
Scenario	*Prob, p*	*NPV*	*p × NPV*	*Dev²*
Excellent	0.30	25.28	7.58	0.01
Good	0.20	10.23	2.05	6.43
Average	0.30	0.19	0.06	17.60
Poor	0.20	–9.85	–1.97	18.76
Expected value of NPV				**7.72**
Variance				**42.80**
Standard deviation				**6.54**
Coefficient of variation				**0.85**
Profitability Index				**1.15**

Project B				
Scenario	*Prob, p*	*NPV*	*p × NPV*	*Dev²*
Excellent	0.30	30.34	9.10	0.58
Good	0.20	10.26	2.05	6.41
Average	0.30	0.23	0.07	17.55
Poor	0.20	–24.87	–4.97	32.21
Expected Value of NPV				**6.25**
Variance				**56.74**
Standard Deviation				**7.53**
Coefficient of variation				**1.21**
Profitability Index				**1.10**

Co-efficient of variation = Standard deviation/Expected NPV

(d) The summary of the two projects is given below:

	Project A	Project B
Expected NPV	7.72	6.25
Variance	42.80	56.74
Standard deviation	6.54	7.53
Co-efficient of variation	0.85	1.21

Since the expected NPV for Project A is higher it would be preferred over Project B. Risk parameters too are in favour of Project A as reflected in the lesser standard deviation and co-efficient of variation.

Calculation of PV factors	
Period of annuity = 10.00 years	Required rate of return = 15%
Present value of annuity for 10 years at 15.00%	
= PVIFA (15.00%, 10) = 5.0188	

3. Risk Management with NPV

In Problem 2, for the projects A and B find out the probabilities that the

(a) NPV would be negative

(b) NPV would be more than ₹10 lakh

Solution

	Project A	Project B
Expected NPV	7.72	6.25
Standard deviation	6.54	7.53

$$z \text{ = value} = \frac{x - \overline{X}}{\sigma}, \text{ where } \overline{X} \text{ is the expected NPV}$$

Probability of expected NPV

		Project A	Project B
(a) less than zero	z	(1.1794)	(0.8294)
Prob < z		11.91%	20.34%
(b) NPV > ₹10 lakh	z	0.3491	0.4981
Prob < z		36.35%	30.92%

4. Decision Tree

ABC Computers Ltd (ACL) is facing an option to develop 2 models; Model A and Model B of personal computer. Both the models are expected to be hot sellers for next two years. The capital expenditure involved in the development of Model A is ₹225 crore while Model B costs ₹250 crore. Because of familiarity of the existing users, Model A that is an improved version of existing one, offers a certain cash flow of ₹140 crore and ₹180 crore for next two years.

However in respect of Model B having capital expenditure of ₹250 crore, ACL is not very sure of the cash inflows. It expects a cash inflow of ₹150 crore in the first year with 70% possibility. Under exceptional circumstances the product may do better to yield a cash inflow of ₹180 crore.

The cash inflows in the second year are dependent upon what happens in the first year. If the firm faces a normal cash inflow of ₹150 crore in the first year the chances are that it would repeat with probability of 30%, improve to ₹180 crore with 40% chance and do exceptionally well with cash inflow of ₹220 having 30% probability.

If the firm faces better prospects in the first year, the chances are that it would have second year cash inflows of ₹220 crore, ₹230 crore and ₹250 crore with probabilities of 50%, 30% and 20% respectively.

Examine both the models and recommend to ACL which of the two models they must go ahead. Assume cost of capital of 12%

Solution

Cost of capital for ACL = 12%

MODEL A

For Model A the net present value is worked out as below:

₹ crore	*Cash inflow*	*Present value*
First year	140.00	125.00
Second year	180.00	143.49
Present values of cash inflows		**268.49**
Less: Initial investment		225.00
Net present value		**43.49**

MODEL B

The cash flows along with respective probabilities are as given below:

Year 1		*Year 2*	
Probability	*Cash flow*	*Probability*	*Cash flow*
		0.3	150
0.7	150	0.4	180
		0.3	220
		0.5	220
0.3	180	0.3	230
		0.2	250

Since the cash flows second year are sequentially dependent upon the cash flows of the first year we examine the evaluation of the Model B with a decision tree.

The decision tree is as follows:

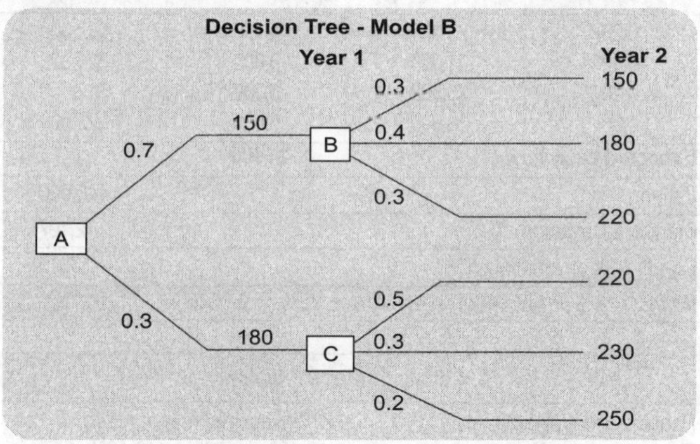

We examine the Model B by finding the expected present values working backwards with the decision tree. We first calculate the expected present values at Nodes B and C and then at Node A using the probabilities given.

Discount rate = cost of capital = 12%

(₹ crore)

Present value of Year 2 cash flows at the end of Year 1

Expected cash flow at 'B' = 0.3 × 150 + 0.4 × 180 + 0.3 × 220 = 183.00

Present value of expected cash flow at 'B' = 183/(1 + 0.12) = 163.39

Expected cash flow at 'C' = 0.5 × 220 + 0.3 × 230 + 0.2 × 250 = 229.00

Present value of expected cash flow at 'C' = 229 / (1 + 0.12) = 204.46

Present value of Year 1 cash flows at Year 0

Value of the cash flow at	*Node B*	*Node C*
Cash flow of Year 1	150.00	180.00
PV of cash flow of Year 2	163.39	204.46
Total Cash flow at Year 1	313.39	384.46

Expected cash flow at 'A' = 313.39 × 0.7 + 384.46 × 0.3 = 334.71

Present value of expected cash flow at 'A' (Year 0) = 334.71/(1 + 0.12) = 298.85

Less: Capital expenditure 250.00

Expected NPV of the project 48.85

Since expected NPV for Model B is higher, the firm must develop Model B.

5. Sensitivity of NPV

Delicate Foods Limited are in the business of powdered milk and associated products. They have been witnessing a lot of volatility in the revenue of the firm due to varying demand conditions and would like to understand in greater detail the impact on the profitability of the project. They projected the profitability and cash flows for varying level of revenue for the range between ₹150 lakh to ₹450 lakh as follows:

(₹ *lakh*)

Revenue	*150*	*210*	*270*	*330*	*390*	*450*
Variable cost	100	140	180	220	260	300
Contribution	50	70	90	110	130	150
Fixed cost	20	25	30	35	40	45
Depreciation	25	25	25	25	25	25
Profit Before Tax	5	20	35	50	65	80
Tax @ 40%	2	8	14	20	26	32
Profit After Tax	3	12	21	30	39	48
Cash Accruals	28	37	46	55	64	73

Assuming a life of 10 years with repetitive cash flows and 15% cost of capital answer the following:

(a) NPVs at different levels of revenue.
(b) Plot the NPVs as function of revenue.
(c) The relationship between the NPV and the revenue
(d) Using the result of c) above find the
 (i) NPV at revenue of ₹175 lakh
 (ii) NPV at revenue of ₹300 lakh
 (iii) Revenue at which NPV is zero.

Solution

(a) The NPVs at different levels of revenue with 15% discount rate are calculated as below

(₹ *lakh*)

Revenue	*150.00*	*210.00*	*270.00*	*330.00*	*390.00*	*450.00*
Cash flow	28.00	37.00	46.00	55.00	64.00	73.00
PV	140.53	185.69	230.86	276.03	321.20	366.37
Investment	175.00	175.00	175.00	175.00	175.00	175.00
NPV	– 34.47	10.69	55.86	101.03	146.20	191.37

Calculation of PV factors	
Period of annuity = 10.00 years	Required rate of return = 15%
Present value of annuity for 10 years at 15.00% = PVIFA (15.00%, 10) = 5.0188	

(b) The sensitivity of NPV with respect to revenue is shown below:

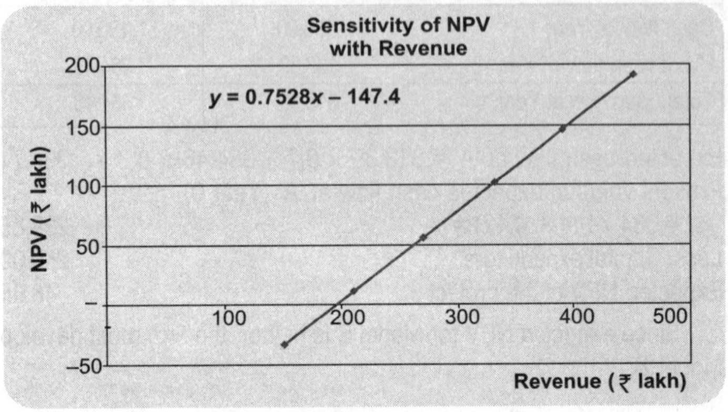

(c) The relationship of NPV with revenue is governed by following equation:

$Y = 0.7528\ x - 147.4$ where Y is NPV and x is revenue.

This implies that if revenue increases by ₹10 lakh the NPV would increase by ₹7.528 lakh.

(d) (i) If revenue is ₹175 lakh the NPV would be

$Y = 0.7528\ x\ 175 - 147.80 = -$ ₹16.06 lakh

(ii) If revenue is ₹300 lakh the NPV would be

$Y = 0.7528\ x\ 300 - 147.80 =$ ₹78.04 lakh

(iii) For NPV = 0 we must have

$0 = 0.7528\ x - 147.80$

Revenue $x = 147.80/0.7528 =$ ₹196.33 lakh

6. Risk Adjusted Discount Rate

Risk Governors Ltd is considering two mutually exclusive proposals both having an initial outlay of ₹90,000. The proposals denoted as A and B have uncertain cash inflows depending upon the market conditions. There are four possible market scenarios having probabilities of 20%, 40%, 20% and 20%. The cash inflows of A and B under four possible market conditions are forecast as below: Is

			Cash flows in ₹
Market Scenario	***Probability***	***Cash flow A***	***Cash flow B***
I	0.20	20,000	22,000
II	0.40	25,000	24,000
III	0.20	28,000	26,500
IV	0.20	30,000	28,000

The firm recognises the fact that project appraisal must take into account the riskiness of the cash flows. To objectively decide upon the appropriate discount rate the management of Risk Governors Ltd have devised a formula for arriving at Risk Adjusted Discount Rate (RADR) based on co-efficient of variation (CV) as follows:

RADR = 8% + CV × 25%

Assuming that each proposal lasts for 5 years and RADR is used to evaluate the proposals which one would you prefer and why?

Solution

We work out the expected value of the cash flows, its standard deviation and co-efficient of variation. Based on the coefficient of variation we determine the appropriate discount rate for finding the NPV of the proposals.

Proposal A			
Prob., p	***Cash flow (₹)***	***p × Cash flow***	***p × Dev²***
0.20	20,000	4,000	6,272,000
0.40	25,000	10,000	144,000
0.20	28,000	5,600	1,152,000
0.20	30,000	6,000	3,872,000
Expected cash flow (₹)			**25,600**
Variance			11,440,000
Standard Deviation, %			3,382
Co-efficient of variation, CV			0.1321
RADR = 8% + CV × 25% =	8% + 25% × 0.1321 =		11.30%

Calculation of PV factor	
Period of annuity 5.00 years	Required rate of return 11.30%
Present value of annuity for 5 years at 11.30% = PVIFA (11.30%, 5) = 3.6679	

PV of the expected cash inflows (₹) – Proposal A 93,898

Proposal B			
Prob., p	***Cash flow (₹)***	***p × Cash flow***	***p × Dev²***
0.20	22,000	4,400	1,682,000
0.40	24,000	9,600	324,000
0.20	26,500	5,300	512,000
0.20	28,000	5,600	1,922,000
Expected cash flow (₹)		**24,900**	
Variance			4,440,000
Standard Deviation, %			2,107
Co-efficient of variation, CV			0.0846
RADR = 8% + CV × 25% =	8% + 25% × 0.0846 =		10.12%

Calculation of PV factor	
Period of annuity 5.00 years	Required rate of return 10.12%
Present value of annuity for 5 years at 10.12% = PVIFA (10.12%, 5) = 3.7796	

PV of the expected cash inflows (₹) – Proposal B 94,113

	Proposal A	***Proposal B***
Expected value of cash flow (₹)	25,600	24,900
Standard deviation (₹)	3,382	2,107
Co-efficient of variation	0.1321	0.0846
Risk Adjusted Discount Rate, RADR	11.30%	10.12%
NPV at RADR (₹)	3,898	4,113

Expected value of the cash flows for Proposal A is less and therefore if discounted at the same rate as that of Proposal A, it would have lower NPV than the Proposal A.

However, taking into account the risks of the cash flows we find that the NPV of the cash flows of Proposal B is higher.

Therefore Proposal B must be preferred over Proposal A.

7. Capital Rationing

The management of Capital Choosers Ltd has 5 Projects A, B C, D and E on hand. The initial outlays, annual cash flows and life of the projects is as under:

	Project A	Project B	Project C	Project D	Project E
Initial outlay, ₹ lakh	100.00	150.00	175.00	180.00	135.00
Expected annual cash inflow, ₹. Lakh	22.00	34.00	49.00	43.00	37.00
Life of the project, Years	10.00	9.00	6.00	8.00	7.00

(a) Find NPV and Profitability Index of each project assuming the cost of capital at 15%.
(b) Rank the projects in order of preference based on PI criteria
(c) Rank the projects in order of preference based on NPV criteria
(d) If firm faces the capital constraint of ₹500 lakh and projects can be implemented in parts what amount of wealth can be created when projects are chosen on the basis of (i) PI criteria, (ii) NPV criteria?

Solution

(a) The NPV and Profitability Index for each project are computed at 15% cost of capital:

	Project A	Project B	Project C	Project D	Project E
Annual cash inflow, ₹ Lakh	22.00	34.00	49.00	43.00	37.00
Life of the project, Years	10.00	9.00	6.00	8.00	7.00
PV of cash inflows, ₹ lakh	110.41	162.23	185.44	192.95	153.94
Initial outlay, ₹ lakh	100.00	150.00	175.00	180.00	135.00
NPV, ₹ lakh	10.41	12.23	10.44	12.95	18.94
Profitability Index, PI	1.1041	1.0816	1.0597	1.0720	1.1403

Years	6	7	8	9	10
Present value of annuity for years at 15%	3.7845	4.1604	4.4873	4.7716	5.0188

(b) The ranking of the projects based on the Profitability Index is as below:

Rank	Project	PI	Outlay	Cum Outlay
1	E	1.1403	135.00	135.00
2	A	1.1041	100.00	235.00
3	B	1.0816	150.00	385.00
4	D	1.0720	180.00	565.00
5	C	1.0597	175.00	740.00

(c) The ranking of the projects based on the NPV is as below:

Rank	Project	NPV	Outlay	Cum Outlay
1	E	18.94	135.00	135.00
2	D	12.95	180.00	315.00
3	B	12.23	150.00	465.00
4	C	10.44	175.00	640.00
5	A	10.41	100.00	740.00

(d) (i), (ii) If firm faces capital constraint of ₹500 lakh and chooses projects based on the PIs till the budget is exhausted the preference would be Projects E, A and B in full and remaining funds in D to the extent of availability of funds.

If firm selects based on the NPVs the preference would be Projects E, D and B in full and remaining funds in C to the extent of availability of funds.

The addition of wealth based on criterion would be as below:

Based on PI			Based on NPV		
Project	Outlay	NPV	Project	Outlay	NPV
E	135.00	18.94	E	135.00	18.94
A	100.00	10.41	D	180.00	12.95
B	150.00	12.23	B	150.00	12.23
D	115.00	8.28	C	35.00	2.09
Increase in NPV		49.86	Increase in NPV		46.21

EXERCISES

Concept Review Questions

1. Why is it wrong to compare the NPVs of two mutually exclusive projects with different lives? What is the way to overcome the deficiency of such an approach?
2. What do you understand by equivalent annualized value (EAV)? Explain its meaning and way of computing by taking a suitable example.
3. Why is it necessary to make a well defined replacement policy?
4. How are sensitivity analysis and scenario analysis different?
5. What are the limitations of simulation?
6. In what way does the decision tree analysis handle the risk of the projects?
7. What is risk-adjusted discount rate? What are its advantages and limitations?
8. How does certainty equivalent approach overcome the limitations of risk-adjusted discount rate method of handling the risk of the project?

Critical Thinking Questions

1. Explaining the replacement policy the Managing Director of AB Ltd stated 'It is a waste of money to replace the asset before its useful life is over, not because you are losing the remaining value of the asset but also incurring avoidable cost on the new asset'. Do you agree with the statement? Give reasons for your answer.
2. The Managing Director of AB Ltd also stated 'When it comes to choosing between two technologies, it is always advisable to choose the more expensive and longer lasting technology as compared to the cheaper equipment with lesser useful life because expensive

technology is always priced so as to outperform the economic benefits of the cheaper machine. As such there is no need to evaluate the two competing technologies.' Comment on the statement made by the managing director.

3. Capital rationing is a hypothetical situation for a good successful firm because it would always find sufficient funds from the equity or debt markets so as to accept all profitable ventures that are on hand. Do you agree?
4. A manager in a bank appraising a project found from sensitivity analysis, that a project is too risky with respect to the selling price assumed. To this the Director of the firm stated that he believed in scenario analysis to make a judgment about the risk of the project and asked the manager of the bank to consider scenarios rather than sensitivity. Was the director right in his suggestion?

Practical Assignments

1. Identify a project and its profitability and assumptions (the best source would be a prospectus of an IPO). Examine the assumptions of the cash flow and identify the critical variables that are likely to impact the cash flows. Find out the NPV of the project and conduct a sensitivity analysis with respect to at least three variables.
2. In Assignment 1, do a scenario analysis also for at least four different scenarios assuming different values for at least three variables.

Numerical Problems

1. Unequal Lives

Zeta Products are considering installation of a grinding machine. It has two suppliers of machine in mind. Machine A has a life of three years and it costs ₹10 lakh. Machine B has a life of 4 years and it cost ₹14 lakh.

The estimated post-tax cash inflows of the two machines are as below:

(₹ *lakh*)

Year	1	2	3	4
Machine A	4.0	4.5	5.0	–
Machine B	4.5	4.8	5.1	5.6

If the cost of capital for Zeta Corporation is 10%, which of the two machines should they procure?

2. Probability Approach to NPV

National Paper Mills is considering expansion into manufacture of glazed paper or craft paper. Though both the projects can be undertaken, due to capital constraints, only one of them can be implemented now. The glazed paper project involves an outlay of ₹25 crore, while the craft paper project can be implemented with ₹20 crore. The markets are uncertain and the estimates of NPV for both the projects with corresponding probabilities are as below:

(₹ *lakh*)

Glazed Paper		*Craft Paper*	
Probability	*NPV*	*Probability*	*NPV*
0.20	400.00	0.10	250.00
0.30	650.00	0.40	500.00
0.30	850.00	0.30	750.00
0.20	155.00	0.20	250.00

(i) What is the expected NPV of each project?
(ii) What is the risk of each project, as measured from standard deviation and coefficient of variation?
(iii) What is the profitability index of each project?
(iv) What conclusion would you draw based on expected NPV, its standard deviation, and coefficient of variation?
(v) If the firm faces a constraint of capital, which project should be undertaken?

3. Decision Tree

Child Entertainment Ltd (CEL) is in the business of developing fancy toys that last normally no more than 2–3 years. They have come out with another fancy toy that is expected to last for two years. The capital investment is ₹275 lakh.

During the first year, CEL expects the post-tax cash flows of ₹150 lakh with a probability of 60% or ₹180 lakh with a probability of 40% depending upon the demand for the new toy.

During the second year, the probabilities of demand being low, medium, and high are 40%, 40%, and 20%, respectively. If initial demand during the first year is high, then the second year cash flows are expected to be ₹200 lakh, ₹240 lakh, and ₹290 lakh, respectively.

However, if initial demand during the first year is low, then the second year cash flows are expected to be ₹160 lakh, ₹200 lakh, and ₹250 lakh, respectively.

For the kind of business CEL is into, the appropriate discount rate for investment is 15%. Advise whether CEL should go ahead with the investment.

4. Scenario Analysis

A firm is considering a capital investment of ₹40 lakh for a project that has a life of 5 years. The cash flows are dependent upon the general economic conditions. The project team has considered 4 different scenarios of poor, average, good, and excellent with respective probabilities of 20%, 30%, 30%, and 20%, respectively. The cash flows fro three years under 4 different scenarios are given below:

(₹ *lakh*)

Scenario	Prob.	Year 1	Year 2	Year 3
Poor	0.20	12.00	15.00	18.00
Average	0.30	15.00	19.00	24.00
Good	0.30	20.00	25.00	35.00
Excellent	0.20	27.00	35.00	44.00

Assuming cost of capital at 12%, find out the following:

(i) The NPV of the project under different scenarios of poor, average, good, and excellent.
(ii) The expected NPV of the project.

(iii) Risk as assessed from standard deviation and coefficient of variation.

(iv) Find out the probabilities of NPV being (a) negative (b) 80%, (c) 90%, (d) 100%, (e) 110%, and (f) 120% of the expected NPV.

(v) The management does not accept any proposal that has more than 20% chance of providing negative NPV. Under such condition, what is your recommendation regarding acceptance of the project?

5. Sensitivity Analysis

Sensitive Controls Limited have a project on hand costing ₹20 crore with a life of 10 years. The expected revenue is ₹21 crore per annum with a variable cost estimated at 50%. The fixed cost is ₹2 crore, while depreciation is on the basis of SLM. The tax rate is 40%, and the cost of capital for the firm is 14%.

The management of the Sensitive Controls Limited is apprehensive of the cash flow estimates. The apprehension emanates from uncertainty of revenue and the proportion of the variable cost. Due to inherent risk in the projections, the management also believes that the suppliers of capital for the project may not be very comfortable with the returns equal to the current cost of capital.

Find out the following:

(i) The estimated annual cash flows of the project.

(ii) Assuming uniform cash flows of the project for its entire life and current cost of capital as appropriate discount rate, find the NPV of the project.

(iii) Find out the NPV of the project assuming the revenues can change from 70% to 130% of the expected revenue, and plot the NPV with respect to the level of revenue. Find out from the plot the approximate minimum revenue that the project must generate so as to keep the NPV positive.

(iv) Find out the NPV of the project assuming that the variable cost can change from 35% to 65% of the expected revenue, and plot the NPV with respect to the variable cost as proportion of expected revenue. What is the maximum proportion of variable cost the project can afford?

(v) Find out the NPV of the project for a cost of capital ranging between 11% and 17%, and plot the NPV with respect to cost of capital. What is the maximum cost of capital that would keep the project acceptable?

6. Risk-adjusted Discount Rate

A firm has several projects on hand. These projects have varying size, annual cash flows, lives, and risks as given below:

	Project A	Project B	Project C	Project D	Project E
Initial outlay (₹ lakh)	100	120	135	165	200
Expected annual CF (₹ lakh)	30	45	55	70	90
Life of the project (Yrs)	5	5	6	6	4
Coefficient of variation of CF	0.40	0.60	0.80	1.20	0.60
Beta of the project	1.30	1.20	0.95	1.40	1.60

(CF = Cash Flow)

(i) Find out the order of preference of different projects based on discount rate arrived at using CAPM model assuming risk-free rate at 8% and market return at 14%.

(ii) Rank the projects based on cost of capital and coefficient of variation as the benchmark assigning a premium of 15% for the coefficient of variation over a constant rate of 10%.

(iii) Rank the projects based on management's view of the cost of capital for different projects as follows:

Project	Project A	Project B	Project C	Project D	Project E
Management's discount rate	12.00%	13.00%	15.00%	18.00%	20.00%

7. Capital Rationing

Refer to the projects in Problem 6. If the firm faces a capital constraint of ₹500 lakh, which of the project would be accepted under (a) NPV criterion, (b) PI criterion.

What would be the addition to the NPV in each case? Use cost of capital as per CAPM for calculating NPVs. Assume that the projects can be implemented in parts.

8. Certainty Equivalent

Riskless Enterprises is a steadily growing company that follows a rather conservative approach to its capital expenditure plans due to the inherent risks involved.

The firm normally does not take capital expenditures that last more than 5 years and follows a policy of converting the risky cash flows to their certainty equivalents by assigning certainty equivalent factors of 0.9, 0.8, 0.7, 0.6, and 0.5 for the cash flows of Year 1 to Year 5, respectively.

The post-tax cash flows of two such mutually exclusive projects, A and B, are given below:

Estimated cash flows

Year	Project A	Project B
0	–250	–250
1	60	100
2	70	120
3	80	100
4	120	20
5	120	40

The cost of capital for the firm is 15%, while the risk-free return is 6%.

(i) Which project should be undertaken based on NPV rule?

(ii) Which project must be undertaken if certainty equivalent approach is followed?

(iii) What is the IRR of each project based on risky and certain cash flows?

(iv) Based on IRR rule, which project must be undertaken?

(v) Which project would you recommend if (a) shareholders are dominant, (b) debt holders are dominant?

CASE STUDY

GUPTA BRICKS—The Risks in Vertical Shaft Brick Kiln

Mr Gupta's son, Ramesh, who was studying finance in London, was in India when he was considering the installation of VSBKs in place of one of the BTKs (for details refer to the case study of Chapter 11). Ramesh was very enthusiastic about finance and found an opportunity to apply his concepts of capital budgeting to his father's business proposal.

Ramesh conducted an exhaustive analysis of the whole situation and came out with the differential cash flows making following assumptions:

- There would be an increase of 10% in production and sales due round-the-clock functioning of VSBKs.
- Due to improved product quality there would be an increase of 3% in the price of the bricks produced by the VSBK as compared to those produced in BTK.
- Due to an increase in quality and the process of firing savings in raw material would also be to possible the extent of 2%.
- There would be additional maintenance cost of ₹60,000 per annum.
- The wage bill would mount by 10% due to specialized fire master required
- The fuel cost would be saved at least to the extent of 20%.

Besides these, he also considered the net impact of depreciation tax shields that would be available on VSBK but lost on the existing BTK.

Based on these assumptions, he arrived at following cash flow and the NPV of the VSBK as given in Table A.

Ramesh found that the project had the positive net present value and was trying to convince his father that he must go in for new technology because it met all his requirements. The project had positive NPV of ₹4.15 lakh with the payback period of less than five years and offered a 20% Return on Investment.

Mr Gupta, on the other hand, was somewhat reluctant to accept Ramesh's arguments. He perceived that the project was too risky and thought that it could become a negative NPV project if any of the savings in the cost or increase in revenue did not materialize. Being a new technology and not as tested as BTK, he was not sure whether implementing VSBK would increase the production by 10%.

Though he was not as much concerned about the increased price he considered two factors – increase in production and savings in fuel cost as the most important and critical. He wanted Ramesh to tell him what would be the impact on the project's viability

Table A Evaluating VSBK

Replacement of BTK with VSBK					*₹'000s*
A. Cost of equipment				**3,200**	
Life (years)			10		
Depreciation on VSBK			320		
Depreciation on BTK lost			50		
Increase in depreciation			270		
Net Tax Saved on Depreciation			**97**		
B. Tax Saved on BTK removed					
(1) Current value			500		
(2) Disposal realized			50		
(3) Loss on BTK			450		
(4) Tax saved			162		
Net Initial Cost A – B(2) – B(4)				**2,988**	
Incremental Cash Flows				**₹'000s (unless specified)**	
	Existing Per BTK	Inc./Dec. (%)	Value.	Pro-posed	Net impact
Increase in Revenue					
Volume sold (000s)	7,500	10%	750	8,250	
Price (₹/Brick)	1.10	3 %	0.03	1.13	
Revenue ('000s)	8,250			9,347	1,097
Decrease in cost					
Per '000s	0.34	–2%	–0.01	0.33	
RMC	2,522			2,718	–197
Increase in maintenance	0			60	–60
Increase in Labour Cost					
(Per unit)	0.22				
Total labour cost ('000s)	1,685	10%	168	1,853	–168
Fuel Per '000s	0.22	–20%	–0.04	0.17	
Total Fuel ('000s)	1,628			1,432	195
Annual Incremental Cash Flow				867	
Post-tax Value of Incremental Cash Flow				555	
Tax Saved on Extra Depreciation				97	
Annual Incremental Cash Flow				652	
PV Annuity Factor 14% 10 years				5.2160	
Present Value					**3,403**
Present Value of Terminal Cash Flow					**0**
Present Value of Inflows					**3,403**
Initial Cost					2,988
Net Present Value					**415**
Pay back period (years)					**4.91**
ROI					**20%**
Profitability Index					**1.06**

1. If the savings in fuel cost were only 15%, instead of 20% and
2. If the increase in production materialized only to the extent of 5% rather than 10%.

Mr Gupta with his vast experience had a belief in the Murphy's law that if anything can go wrong, it will. He thought of the worst case scenario wherein about 5% increase in production, with no increase in price and 15% savings in the fuel cost, all of them happening simultaneously.

On the other hand, young Ramesh thought that he had already considered a rather conservative scenario. His discussion with the supplier revealed that there existed a possibility of achieving an increase of 20% in production and potential for saving in fuel cost up to 40% rather than 20% considered by him. The supplier of the machine wanted the evaluation to be done with a 20% increase in production, 2% increase in price, and a minimum of 30% saving in the fuel cost. For the supplier, it was the most likely and realistic scenario.

Confused with the opposing opinions of his father and that of the supplier, Ramesh was wondering how to proceed next. Ramesh thought that the projections prepared by him were the most likely scenario and had 50% chances of coming true. That was the reason he prepared his analysis. He gave a 20% probability that what his father stated could be true. He also thought that the scenario described by the supplier too had a chance of 30% to be true.

Discuss

How would you want Ramesh to proceed further?

In the CD

Finding Sensitivity of NPV with Discount Rate

CHAPTER

13 Cost of Capital

LEARNING OBJECTIVES

The chapter is aimed to explain the following:

- what is opportunity cost of capital
- what is weighted average cost of capital (WACC)
- how to calculate cost of debt, the difference between redeemable and perpetual debt, and their costs
- what are the implications of tax on the cost of debt
- how to incorporate the flotation cost and issues at premium or discount
- what kinds of debts to include in the cost of capital
- what is preferred capital and its cost
- describing the features of equity capital, and the difficulties faced while measuring its cost
- how to calculate the cost of equity capital by using: (1) dividend capitalization method, (2) earnings-based approach, and (3) CAPM-based approach
- what are the differences in internal and external equity and their implications on cost
- various ways to assign weights to the different components of cost
- what is marginal cost of capital, its relationship with weighted average cost of capital and determination of optimal capital budget
- how to incorporate risk of the project on the cost of capital
- the application of pure play technique

IT'S ALL ABOUT THE RIGHT BLEND

Kuldeep Tours and Travels is in the business of running taxis on hire. The business was set up three years back by Kuldeep's father, a retired mechanical engineer. The business has a fleet of ten Tata Indica cars. Currently, all the taxis of the firm are running on diesel. The firm prefers taxis that run on diesel due to the low costs of running them. These days, Kuldeep, who has a sound grounding in finance, is looking after the day-to-day operations of the business. His father's concerns are limited to strategic issues only. Kuldeep wants to adopt an aggressive business policy with an all out focus on profit maximization.

In view of increased demand for taxis, the firm has decided to add 20 more vehicles over the next one year to its existing fleet of taxis. Kuldeep and his father sit across the table to discuss the issue.

Kuldeep: I propose to buy only CNG-run cars, because driving on gas reduces running costs considerably. The cost of driving on natural gas is 20–40% lower than diesel. On an average, the cost of running on CNG comes out to ₹1.30 per kilometer, while that on diesel, the cost is around ₹2.20 per kilometer. If we buy CNG fitted cars, the ratio of CNG-run and diesel-run cars would be 2:1. A high proportion of CNG-run cars in the fleet will bring down the running costs. It is just like increasing the proportion of low cost debt in the financing mix so as to bring down the overall cost of capital.

Father: Son, the analogy of debt is fine, but why do you forget that like debt, the CNG option has its own risks. Have you thought about the availability of CNG? It is not an option for long distance travel due to the shortage of CNG stations in interior areas. Also, the one time storage capacity of CNG is limited. Do not forget that there is a limit to which we can utilize the boot space for fitting additional CNG cylinders.

The boot space belongs to the customers who hire the taxis. Not to mention the maintenance cost issue, CNG causes dryness in the engine as a result of which, the fixed and regular servicing cost of the CNG-run vehicles comes to be higher than that for the diesel vehicles. CNG tends to have lower octane levels and continues to contain impurities that hinder continuous combustion in the engine chamber. Running the car on gas for an extended period may also lead to engine damage. The risk of a breakdown in the absence of maintenance is higher for such vehicles. So, as an entrepreneur, you must not only be looking at the cost savings but also the associated risks. There is a limit to which you can use the lower cost option without adding to your risk.

Kuldeep: Does it imply that we have to forgo the low cost option of CNG-run taxis and opt for 100% diesel vehicles? Doing so would mean forgoing the probable savings on account of low running costs. Would it not compromise with our profits?

Father: No, I never said that. The idea here is to take the benefit of both CNG- and diesel-run vehicles. Since your total running cost is the weighted average of the cost of running both CNG-run vehicles and diesel-run vehicles, you should try to bring down the running costs by maximizing the usage of the CNG-run vehicles but also manage the risks associated with them. For running within the city limits, you should try to maximize the usage of CNG-run taxis, but for long distance service, diesel-run taxis would be a better idea. By having a mix of both CNG and diesel taxis in your new fleet, you will be able to capture the savings from CNG-run taxis, yet contain the related risks.

INTRODUCTION

Globalization has brought a number of choices to our doorstep. As consumers we often have to compare objects ranging from shoes to televisions while making a purchase. Just like HR managers are required to make performance assessment of staff at regular intervals and marketing managers are required to achieve sales beyond predetermined targets, the finance managers are required to evaluate the opportunities that come across regularly over a period of time. The question that arises in the minds of the finance manager is whether or not to make use of the opportunities offered by the technological advancements, market development, or economic development of the society. Today, the economy continuously offers business opportunities that need to be examined and evaluated by business enterprises.

Cost of capital is an essential input for several corporate finance decisions as it serves as a benchmark.

In any kind of a situation, one needs a standard against which the comparison or assessment is made. In the context of the financial management and for the purpose of evaluation of business opportunities, the returns of the business opportunities need to be compared with a benchmark. If returns exceed this benchmark we give a favourable thought to the business opportunity, else we reject the same. This benchmark against which the benefits of the business opportunities are compared is called discount or the hurdle rate. In most cases, this hurdle rate happens to be the 'cost of capital'.

OPPORTUNITY COST OF CAPITAL

While evaluating an investment option, a question that is foremost in the mind of the investor is what are the alternative ways of using the fund? Can he compensate it if the investment under consideration is taken up. In our individual capacity we always make an investment based on higher returns that are offered by different instruments belonging to the same risk class. This benchmark becomes the hurdle rate for selecting the investment. As a simple definition, opportunity cost refers to the returns foregone on the next best available option.

Applying the definition of opportunity cost of capital in case of business situations is not as simple as for individual investing. The case of individual investing was simple because there was only one investor and only one type of capital. If we extend the concept of opportunity cost of capital to multiple investors some difficulties would arise in arriving at the hurdle rate. Suppose, we now want to analyse the situation when the investment is pooled by several investors who may have different expectations of returns, what happens to the opportunity cost and the hurdle rate? Should it change according to each investor's expectations? If we do so, some would reject the investment while the rest will accept. Essentially, the expectations of investors must converge. The opportunity cost remains the same and so does the hurdle rate because this is what the market can afford. Hence, one parameter in determining the hurdle rate is the market determined opportunity cost of capital.

Market-oriented opportunity cost forms the basis of determination of cost of capital.

Besides market-oriented returns, the hurdle rate must also account for the risk associated with the investment. The opportunity cost must compare the investment of the same risk class. We cannot use the opportunity cost of a bank fixed deposit, an extremely safe option, while evaluating the investment in stock market; an inherently risky investment.

Further numerous investors who contribute to the capital of the firms also raise loans. The existence of loans affects the hurdle rate in at least two ways. One, the loans bring down the cost of funds for the firm as the interest cost is tax deductible and two, they modify the expectations of the equity investors because the claim of the debt holders is prior to their claims. Also claims of debt holders are fixed irrespective of profit or loss the investment makes. The prior and fixed nature of claims of the debt holders increases the risk for the equity holders. Therefore, the hurdle rate becomes dependent upon proportion of debt besides its cost.

With the different types of sources of funding at varying expectations of return, should the evaluation of investment proposals be done against the specific sources of funding the investment? It would be fallacious to do so. For example, consider a project offering a return of 10%. The expectations of debt holders are 6%, while the equity investor expects a return of 12%. If we weigh the proposal from the perspective of the debt holders, we accept the project as it satisfies the claims of debt holders. However, if evaluated from the perspective of equity holders we would reject the project because it falls short of their expectations. This would result in contradictions and suggest that the firm keeps borrowing limitlessly. Therefore, a composite benchmark needs to be developed that takes care of aspirations of all kinds of investors because of their interrelationship. The firm deals with them in totality and not individually. Since all projects must be evaluated against the same benchmark, the aggregation of claims of debt and equity holders becomes a prerequisite for the appropriate discount rate. Therefore, it must consider the following:

Incorporate business risk The benchmark must incorporate the risk of the project. The higher the risk of the project, higher must be the discount rate. The riskiness of the project is manifested in the variability of the cash flows. More often than not, managers tend to offset the risk of cash flows by raising the qualifying bar, i.e., to revise upwards the discount rate while appropriate way would be risk-adjusted discount rate approach.

Cost of capital must incorporate the business risk and the financial risk.

Incorporate financial risk The variability of the cash flows pertains to the business risk where the market environment and other related factors cause uncertainty in cash flows. The other factor affecting the discount rate is capital structure. The expectations of the returns for the capital providers changes with changing capital structure. The risk faced by equity capital suppliers increases as firm borrows more and more. This is called financial risk. The discount rate must appropriately reflect the element of financial risk the equity capital suppliers are exposed to.

WEIGHTED AVERAGE COST OF CAPITAL (WACC)—PREVIEW

The discount rate to be used for the cash flows must be chosen in a manner that reflects the aspirations of all categories of capital suppliers. The two broad kinds of suppliers of capital to a firm are (i) those who lend funds and expect a fixed return irrespective of success or failure of project, and (ii) those who are willing to merge their fortunes with the performance of the project, expecting high returns, if profits permit and sacrifice returns if the project does not succeed.

The weighted average cost of capital (WACC) is one number that will take into account the expectations of all suppliers of capital. This may be used as a hurdle rate that must be overcome if the project is to be accepted. Crossing of this hurdle rate will imply that all capital suppliers are satisfied with the benefits of the project.

Weighted Average Cost of Capital, WACC is single composite number that reflects the claims of all suppliers of capital on an aggregate basis.

In order to develop a single number, we need to consider the cost of suppliers of all kinds of capital, individually. Depending upon the proportions of each kind of capital, a weighted average may be found. Mathematically, this can be represented as

$$\text{WACC} = w_e \times r_e + w_p \times r_p + w_d \times r_d \qquad (13\text{-}1)$$

Where

w_e = Proportions of equity
r_e = Cost of equity
w_p = Proportion of preference capital
r_p = Cost of preference capital
w_d = Proportion of debt
r_d = Cost of debt

While we introduced debt and equity as sources of capital in the preceding section, no mention of preference capital was made. We shall discuss the same when we discuss its cost. We now examine the cost of individual components of the capital.

COST OF DEBT

The cost of borrowed funds is the easiest to determine. The people who lend to the firm at fixed rates are debenture holders, banks, financial institutions, subscribers to commercial paper, etc. The main characteristic of these kinds of suppliers of capital is that they need a fixed return on the capital provided.

The cost of debt is normally the coupon rate that is payable by the firm to the holders of the debt instruments. If a firm raises funds from public through an issue of debenture at 12% at par (issue price equal to face value on which interest is payable) the cost of debt would be 12% at the time of issue of debenture. However, if the debenture were traded in the market, its price would reflect the true and latest trends of the expectations of the interest rates in the market. Market price in excess of issue price would imply decline in the interest rate while market price of the instrument lesser than the issue price would indicate rise in the interest rate since the time of the issue. Using 12% as the cost of debt will be erroneous if the market price of the debenture is different from the issue price/face value.

Cost of Redeemable Debt

Normally, debt is issued with certain terms of repayment. The principal is payable either as bullet payment upon the completion of period of borrowing or is payable in instalments over periodic intervals. Equation 13-2 accurately and appropriately determines the cost of debt denoted by r_d that pays a fixed sum in each period and is repayable at the end of the debt tenure.

Cost of redeemable debt is determined by equating the cash flows of the instrument to its market price.

$$P_0 = \sum_{t=1}^{N} \frac{C_t}{(1+r_d)^t} + \frac{R}{(1+r_d)^N} \qquad (13\text{-}2)$$

Where P_0 = Current market price of the debenture
C_t = Coupon payments (interest) at time period t
N = Number of periods left for maturity of the debenture
R = Redemption value of the debenture
r_d = Cost of debenture

Solution for the Equation 13-2 is obtained by the process of trial and error to match the price of the debt with those of the present value of the cash out flows of coupon payments and the repayment of principal at an assumed rate. With the usage of computers one can very quickly find the value of discount rate by using *IRR function* in the EXCEL.

Cost of Perpetual Debt

In case of perpetual debt the cost of debt is easiest to determine as Equation 13-2 simplifies to:

$$P_0 = \frac{C_t}{r_d} \quad \text{or} \quad r_d = \frac{C_t}{P_0} \qquad (13\text{-}3)$$

Cost of perpetual debt is simply coupon rate divided by the current market price.

Therefore, the cost of perpetual debt, r_d is equal to the coupon payments divided by price of debenture as stated in Equation 13-3.

One may wonder about the applicability of cost of perpetual debt since most of the debt/loans are given for fixed duration of time. Equation 13-3 becomes applicable in the circumstances where firms work for a specific target of debt–equity ratio where the ratio of debt is kept constant by reissuing the debt once the old debt is redeemed. Therefore, the debt becomes perpetual as one lender replaces another.

Post-tax Cost of Debt

On the face of it, the coupon rate of bonds/debenture or the interest rate specified on any other kind of debt instrument is the cost of the debt that a firm takes. However, from the perspective of the shareholders of the firm the interest that is paid out to the lenders is not borne entirely by the shareholders. A big part of this cost is borne by government as payment of interest is recognized as an expense and the firm saves the tax on such outgo of interest.

Effective cost of debt is less to the extent of tax saved on the interest payments.

The effect on the earnings that are available to shareholders would not reduce by the amount of interest, but by a smaller amount; the difference being the amount of tax. If a firm pays 40% tax and has an interest outgo of ₹100, the effective outgo on interest payment would only be ₹60 since the firm will now have to pay ₹40 less of tax. The funds available to the shareholders would, therefore, reduce by ₹60 and not by the amount of interest, i.e.,₹100.

Since we analyse situations from the perspective of the shareholders being the owners of post-tax residual income only, the effective cost of debt would, therefore, be as per Equation 13-4.

$$\text{Post-tax cost of debt} = r_d(1 - T) \qquad (13\text{-}4)$$

Where T = Corporate tax rate

Example 13-1 Cost of Redeemable Debt

A firm wants to raise debt by issue of a short-term bond with a face value of ₹100 with a coupon rate of 11%, payable annually redeemable at a premium of 5% at the end of three years. The firm will have to incur flotation cost of 5%. Find the cost of debt with tax rate of 40%.

Solution

Using Equation 13-2 we can find out the cost of bonds as follows:

$$P_0 = \sum_{t=1}^{N} \frac{C_t}{(1+r_d)^t} + \frac{R}{(1+r_d)^N}$$

$$95 = \frac{11\times 0.6}{1+r_d} + \frac{11\times 0.6}{(1+r_d)^2} + \frac{11\times 0.6}{(1+r_d)^3} + \frac{105}{(1+r_d)^3}$$

Solving the above equation we get post-tax cost of debt r_d = 10.12%

Note that (i) interest payments are tax deductible while the repayment is not, and hence, factor of $(1 - T)$ is not required in the numerator of the last term relating to the redemption amount, and ii) the funds realized are net of flotation cost.

Historical yields and current yields One issue that needs to be addressed is which yields must be used in determining the cost of debt. Firms keep issuing debts at different points of time that are traded in the markets. Further, these debts may either be on floating rate basis or fixed rate basis. The coupon rate in case of fixed rate bonds are decided on the basis of capital markets conditions prevailing at the time of issue. For example, a firm may have issued bonds three years back at 10% coupon because it was consistent with the conditions prevailing then. The rates have fallen to 8% in the current scenario and if asked to issue bonds today the coupon rate must be 8%. What is the appropriate cost of debt: 8% or 10%? The answer is unambiguous: 8%, which is the current yield in the market. The coupon rates for the issues made in the past have no relevance. In fact, the price of the bond issued three years ago would have already risen to provide a yield of 8%.

What if the firm is visiting the capital markets for the first time? The answer lies in using the yields for a comparable bond in the market. This would determine the cost of debt for a new firm.

Treating flotation cost and issue at discount/premium For mobilizing funds from the capital markets the firms are required to incur costs such as expenses for due-diligence, road shows, advertising, printing of application forms, brokerage, underwriting, etc., to induce and educate potential investors. All these costs are incurred at the initial stage. Such costs associated with the mobilization of capital are referred to as flotation costs, and are normally expressed as % of the value of funds being mobilized because major proportion of such costs like brokerage, underwriting, etc., are specified and payable on the price of the issue.

To mobilize debt one has to incur floatation cost which increase the cost of debt.

Naturally, such costs of flotation would increase the cost of debt so raised. It is because the firm pays interest on the face value of the debt but realizes money lesser than the face value to the extent of flotation cost.

Also, in order to be consistent with conditions prevailing in the capital market the debt may be issued at premium or at discount to the face value of the bonds. Further, the redemption of the bond may be at a premium or discount to the face value, depending upon the market conditions and as an inducement for investors to subscribe to the issue.

These market-oriented factors impact the overall cost of the debt since each of them has cash flow implications. Flotation costs would increase the cost of debt while premium over face value would reduce it. Similarly, a premium on redemption would increase the cost of debt. The best way to find the cost of debt is to modify the cash flows in Equation 13-2 and solve it in the usual fashion either by trial and error or by using EXCEL with *IRR function*. However, an approximate idea of the cost of the debt can be had from Equation 13-5.

$$r_d = \frac{C(1-T) + (f \pm d/p \pm p_m/d_m)/N}{(P_0 + R)/2} \quad (13\text{-}5)$$

where f represents flotation cost, d and p are the discount/premium over face value and p_m/d_m is premium/discount on the redemption, and N is the tenure of the instrument.

Example 13-2 Cost of Debt with Flotation

A firm wants to issue debenture with following features:

Face value (Rs)	100.00	Tenure (Years)	5
Premium on issue	5%	Premium on redemption	10%
Coupon rate	12%	Flotation cost	3%
Tax rate	40%		

Find the cost of debt for the firm. Assume annual payment of coupon.

Solution

The cash flow of the debenture are:	Cash Flow (₹)
Amount realized on issue (97% of ₹105)	101.85
Coupon payment 1	7.20
Coupon payment 2	7.20
Coupon payment 3	7.20
Coupon payment 4	7.20
Coupon payment 5 and Redemption	117.20
IRR—Cost of Debt	8.42%

The problem can be solved with approximate value of cost of debt using Equation 13-5

(a) Coupon payment net of taxes = 7.20%
(b) Cost of flotation, premium on redemption less premium on issue = 8%
(c) Apportionment over the tenure of debenture = 8/5 = 1.60%
(d) Average of issue price and redemption price = (105 + 110)/2 = 107.50

Approx. cost = (a + c)/d = (7.20 + 1.60) × 100/107.50 = 8.19%

Which Debt to Consider?

A firm raises debt capital from a variety of sources, for a variety of purposes and in a variety of forms. Besides mobilizing capital from capital market through issue of debentures, firms also raise long-term borrowings from financial institutions and short-term borrowings from commercial banks for working capital. They also use other means of raising short-term capital through inter-corporate loans, issue of commercial paper, bill discounting, etc. The other prominent and widely used source of debt capital is the supplier of raw materials, who provides credit for the supplies he makes.

The question of which sources of capital must be considered while estimating the cost of debt depends upon the perspective of the exercise. More often than not the situations are analysed from the perspective of the long-term stakeholders in the firm. By that definition only suppliers of equity capital and long-term loans must be considered. The following must be kept in mind while deciding about the cost of total debt that must be considered:

While computing the cost of debt the claims of the suppliers of long-term debt are only considered.

- Though commercial banks provide short-term capital for working capital, for most firms it is rather a permanent feature of capital structure. In fact, with the growth of the firm the bank credit keeps mounting. On the contrary, financial institutions make an exit after providing project finance for specified time. Ironically, the providers of short-term capital may have much longer interest in the firm than the providers of, supposedly, long-term capital. Therefore, it will be erroneous to ignore the cost of funds raised for working capital from banks while calculating the overall cost of capital of the firm.
- Similarly, suppliers of raw material provide credit on the supplies made by them on a perpetual basis. This credit obviously does not come free of cost. Suppliers normally raise the prices proportionately with the credit periods. However, this cost is not explicitly stated, It is implied in the prices of the supplies made by them. From the viewpoint of cost of funds the implied cost can be ignored as the impact of raised prices is taken into account in the cost of materials, and the cash flow that is to be discounted is reduced by the same extent of increased prices.

COST OF PREFERENCE CAPITAL

The preference capital raised by the firm is more in the nature of debt rather than equity capital from the point of view of cost.

Preference shareholders are promised a fixed amount of dividend, with the stipulations that unless the commitment to preference shareholders is met, no dividend to equity shareholders can be paid.

Just like debenture holders and loan providers have prior claims on the cash flows of the firm, the preference shareholders also enjoy the same rights. However, there is a difference in the treatment of the dividend payable to the preference shareholders from the interest payable to loan providers. While interest is a tax deductible expense, dividend is not. Therefore, the cost of the preference capital is higher compared to debt for the same amount of interest or dividend promised. To keep same cash flow to equity capital suppliers, a firm will have to earn higher if it has to pay same rate of dividend on preference capital as the interest rate on the debt.

Preference capital is in between pure debt and equity that explicitly states a fixed dividend that has claim prior to that of equity holders. Unlike interest on debt, dividend is not tax deductible.

Simply stated, the cost of preference capital is the amount of dividend payable. If the preference capital is traded or redeemable after a specified time, the cost of preference capital can be found from the following Equation 13-6, similar to the one used for finding cost of debenture:

$$P_0 = \sum_{t=1}^{N} \frac{D_t}{(1+r_p)^t} + \frac{R}{(1+r_p)^N} \qquad (13\text{-}6)$$

Where P_0 = Current market price of preference share
D_t = Dividend payments during time period t
N = Number of periods left for maturity of the preference share
R = Redemption value of the preference share
r_p = Cost of preference share capital

Also, since the dividend to preference shareholders is payable only out of income arrived at after tax, there is no difference in the pre-tax or post-tax cost of preference capital. They are identical unlike the cost of debt where the pre-tax and post-tax cost differs by the amount of tax saved.

Cost of preference capital is determined by equating the cash flows of the instruments to its market price. There is no adjustment of tax.

Example 13-3 Cost of Preference Share

A firm has issued preference shares of the face value of ₹100 with the promised dividend of ₹12.00 per annum after incurring a flotation cost of 2%.

(a) What is the cost of preference share to the firm? Assume that the firm will continue to have the same level of preference capital for times to come.

(b) After a year the preference share marketed at ₹100 face value is trading in the market at a price of ₹90. Do you think the cost of preference share has changed? If yes, by how much?

Solution

(a) The cost of preference share = $D/(P - f)$
= 12/(100 – 2) = 12/98 = 12.24%

(b) The cost of preference shares will change in accordance with the market price. If the market price goes up, the cost of preference share will fall and vice-versa. The cost of the instrument has to be seen from the perspective of price at which the instruments can be issued at present. Current market price is one ready indicator of the funds the firm can fetch.

Assuming fresh flotation cost of 2% and the same rate of dividend the cost of preference capital would become 12/90 × (1 – 0.02) = 13.61%

COST OF EQUITY

The cost of equity is most difficult to find since equity shareholders are owners of residual profits. There is no legal commitment made to pay equity shareholders. The entire residual that is left after meeting all commitments including those of suppliers, workers, government besides other suppliers of capital, belong to the equity shareholders. It is extremely difficult to know what residual will be available to the equity shareholders.

Further, it is also equally difficult to arrive at the expected return that will satisfy the equity shareholders. This stems from the fact that there are no directly observable phenomena that can reflect accurately the expectations of the equity shareholders. There is no explicitly stated cost of equity. There are as many expectations as there are investors who provide capital to various firms. The divergence of the expectations does not disturb us while computing the cost of equity in terms of its opportunity cost. The market price of the share serves as an ideal substitute as it reflects the collective expectations of all shareholders.

Equity capital is normally classified in two ways; (i) the profits that are not distributed but used by the firm in funding the growth, called retained earnings and referred as *internal equity* and (ii) equity capital raised afresh to fund the projects and growth, called *external equity*.

In terms of their costs there are a few differences between the two, but the approaches for determination of cost essentially remain same. There are basically two approaches to arrive at cost of equity capital, namely dividend capitalization approach and capital asset pricing model (CAPM) approach. Both of them are driven by market conditions and measure the cost of equity in an indirect manner.

Before we proceed to describe the two approaches we must be aware that sometimes it is argued that since there is no explicit cost stated and there is no contractual obligation to pay a return, the cost of internally generated funds is zero. This argument does not hold due to opportunity costs that need to be considered for the funds retained by the firm. If not retained, the funds would be distributed to the shareholders. They would earn some return on the same. Therefore, there is an opportunity as well as expectation of a return. This must constitute the basis of cost and merely because shareholders do not explicitly demand a return the cost of the funds provided by them cannot be treated as zero.

Cost of equity capital is most difficult to ascertain due to absence of any legal obligation to pay any explicitly stated cost. However, it does not mean that the cost of equity is zero.

Dividend Capitalization Approach

Shareholders provide the capital to firms to earn income, which comes from two sources. One is a recurring income in the form of dividend an investor receives by holding to the share. This is known as dividend yield. The other is appreciation in the price expected over a period of time. This appreciation in price is naturally governed by the expected growth in the income and, therefore, the dividend.

Dividend capitalization approach determines the cost of equity by equating the stream of expected dividend to its market price.

If the equity shares are traded in the market at a price of P_0 and if it is expected that the firm will pay a dividend of D_1 in the next year, it may be reasonable to assume that one is willing to buy the stock at P_0 to earn the dividend of D_1. This would imply that the return expected is the dividend yield given by $r_e = D_1/P_0$.

This can be derived by making extremely simplistic assumption that the current price of the equity share is nothing but the discounted cash flow of the dividend expected from the share. Mathematically, this is put as:

$$P_0 = \frac{D_1}{(1+r_e)} + \frac{D_2}{(1+r_e)^2} + \frac{D_3}{(1+r_e)^3} + \frac{D_4}{(1+r_e)^4}$$

If dividend is constant, i.e., $D_1 = D_2 = \ldots = D$

$$\text{Then } P_0 = \frac{D}{r_e}; \text{ or } r_e = \frac{D}{P_0} = \text{Dividend Yield} \qquad (13\text{-}7)$$

Normally for traded equity shares the dividend yields are very low, in the order of 2-4% for good companies. A look at the data of stock prices and dividend paid by the firm will confirm that statement. Since equity shareholders do have the option of investing in much safer securities (say government T-Bills or dated securities) and they offer much better returns than the dividend yields it shall be naïve to presume that the cost of equity is equal to the dividend yield.

A variant on the dividend capitalization model is often used where more realistically it is recognized that the dividends from period to period are not constant but grow. The price of the stock takes into account the growth prospects of the firm. If we attach a constant growth of '*g*' in dividend from one period to another in the above model the cost of equity capital can be arrived at as below:

$$P_0 = \frac{D_1}{(1+r_e)} + \frac{D_1(1+g)}{(1+r_e)^2} + \frac{D_1(1+g)^2}{(1+r_e)^3} + \frac{D_1(1+g)^3}{(1+r_e)^4}$$

$$\text{then } P_0 = \frac{D_1}{r_e - g}; \text{ or } r_e = \frac{D_1}{P_0} + g \qquad (13\text{-}8)$$

This can give a far more realistic estimate of the cost of equity capital than with the assumption of constant dividend. If we continue to assume as before, that the dividend expected in the next period would be 4% of the current price but the market believes that the dividend will grow at a constant rate of say 10% the cost of equity becomes 14%.

Example 13-4 Cost of Equity Capital using Dividend Discount Model

Raj Plastic has been in operation for the last 15 years and its shares in the stock market are currently trading at ₹120. The most recent dividend by the firm was ₹10 per share. Historically, the dividend of Raj Plastics has been growing at 10% but a majority of financial analysts are of the opinion that firm would grow at 12% per annum and so would be the dividend. Find out the cost of equity from the perspective of (a) management of Raj Plastics and (b) financial analysts.

Solution

(a) The cost of equity r_e is given by (as per management):

$$r_e = \frac{D_1}{P_0} + g = \frac{D_0(1+g)}{P_0} + g = \frac{10 \times 1.10}{120} + 0.10$$
$$= 0.1917 = 19.17\%$$

(b) The cost of equity r_e is given by (as per financial analysts):

$$r_e = \frac{D_1}{P_0} + g = \frac{D_0(1+g)}{P_0} + g = \frac{10 \times 1.12}{120} + 0.12$$
$$= 0.2133 = 21.33\%$$

One of the major limitations of the dividend capitalization model includes that it cannot be applied to firms that do not pay dividend at all or the pay out is not proportional to the growth in earnings. The dividend growth model also assumes that dividends will grow at a constant rate of *g* indefinitely into the future. This is clearly impossible. However, the limitation can be overcome by using multi-period growth models by assuming high growth initially and a relatively smaller growth in the later periods in the Equation 13-8.

The other limitation of the model is that it is extremely sensitive to the growth estimate. Since the dividend yield is very low, the growth estimates dominates the cost of equity. These growth estimates may vary from analyst to analyst and there can never be a consensus among them (if it was so, there isn't any need for so many of them to exist). It would be best to average these estimates of growth to eliminate individual biases.

Earnings-based approach to cost of equity Some managers tend to replace the dividend yield and growth with the earning yield to arrive at the cost of equity capital. Without getting into the dividend policy of the firm it is rightly assumed that the entire earnings belong to the shareholders, and sooner or later they shall be distributed to them. It is assumed that part of the earnings is distributed as dividend while the remaining is retained to fund the growth of the firm. By retaining the earnings the firm is only delaying the dividend but promising to compensate the delay by offering greater returns to the shareholders in future. Finally, the dividend payout will be 100% of earnings.

Therefore, it is reasonable to assume that the expected future cash earning of the firm will drive the stock price. The cost of equity would therefore be:

Cost of equity; r_e = Cash Earning Yield

$$= \frac{\text{Cash EPS for next period}}{\text{Current Market Price}}$$

$$= \frac{\text{Cash EPS}_1}{P_0} \qquad (13\text{-}9)$$

It is observed that even the earning yields (as replacement of dividend yield) of majority of the firms are abysmally low to justify those to be the cost of equity capital. Earnings yield as cost of capital, therefore, may not meet the test of reality. This is because of the reason that firms drive growth by retaining the earnings and deploy them to yield better returns than those expected by the equity holders. Earnings based measure of cost of equity can be used only when the firms keep investing the retained earnings at the same rate as that of expectations of the shareholders.

This may be examined by seeing the Equation 13-8 in a slightly different perspective. The earnings of the firms are either distributed as dividend or retained. If the amount retained as constant % of earnings is b (hence, the pay out ratio is '$1 - b$') then the amount of dividend in period one would be $E_1 \times (1 - b)$. Further, if the retained earnings provide a return of k the growth of earnings would be $b \times k$. Putting these values in Equation 13-8 we get:

$$P_0 = \frac{D_1}{r_e - g} = \frac{E_1 \times (1-b)}{r_e - b \times k}$$

And when $r_e = k$; $P_0 = \dfrac{E_1}{r_e}$ or $r_e = \dfrac{E_1}{P_0}$

Therefore, under the special case when the firm uses the earnings at the same rate as expected by shareholders, earnings based approach to measure the cost of equity holds.

The other limitation with the dividend capitalisation model is that it does not consider the risk of the project as determinant of the discount rate. The element of variability of the project cash flows is not recognized explicitly. The risk of the project is manifest in the estimates of growth, which more often than not, are determined subjectively rather than objectively.

Example 13-5 Estimating the Growth in Dividend g

Ruchi Auto, a manufacturer of auto components, is planning to raise a capital of ₹100 crore. The current price of the share in the market is ₹230 and the firm has paid a dividend of ₹20 per share. The track record of the growth in dividend and earnings has been encouraging as Ruchi Auto has doubled dividend in the last five years. The dividend pay out per share for the last five years has been as follows:

Year	2005	2004	2003	2002	2001
Dividend (₹/Share)	20.00	17.50	15.00	12.50	10.00

(a) What is the cost of equity for Ruchi Auto?

(b) Would the cost of equity change if the Ruchi Auto has to incur a flotation cost of 3%?

Solution

(a) Applying the dividend capitalization model to arrive at the cost of equity, we need to estimate the growth in dividend of Ruchi Auto. Since the track record of the firm is given we can estimate the compound annual growth of dividend.

$(1 + g)^4 = 20/10 = 2$ gives $g = 0.1892$ of 18.92%

Using Equation 13-8, the cost of equity r_e is given by:

$$r_e = \frac{D_1}{P_0} + g = \frac{D_0(1+g)}{P_0} + g = \frac{20 \times 1.1892}{230} + 0.1892$$
$$= 0.2926 = 29.26\%$$

(b) With a flotation cost of 3%, the cost of equity increases as the price realized will be less by 3% of ₹230. Incorporating the flotation cost in Equation 13-8 we get cost of equity

$$r_e = \frac{D_1}{P_0(1-f)} + g = \frac{D_0(1+g)}{P_0(1-f)} + g = \frac{20 \times 1.1892}{230 \times 0.97} + 0.1892$$
$$= 0.2958 = 29.58\%$$

CAPM-based Approach

One way to consider the risk is to adjust the discount rate which is determined based on the perceived risk of the project.

CAPM-based cost of equity accounts for the risk of the cash flows that the dividend capitalization approach ignores.

The rationale for making the desired rate of return stems from the fact that one needs to offer higher returns to the investors if they are asked to invest in the risky venture. Therefore, there is a need to incorporate the risk of the project explicitly in the cost of capital.

The capital asset pricing model provides for the direct adjustment of the risk in the expected returns. A highly simplistic mathematical presentation would state that expected returns from a project are directly proportional to the risk of the project. The higher the risk, the higher is the expectation of the returns and vice versa. Recognizing the linear relationship of expected return and risk, we need to quantify risk and develop a measure.

Determinants of cost of equity under CAPM include three parameters; the risk free rate, the market return and β, as measure of risk.

We define this risk as Beta (β) and assign specific meaning to the values of 0 and 1. The value of zero is assigned to β for ventures that have no risk at all. The value of 1 is assigned as a standard for the project that offers risk equivalent to that of the market governed by general economic conditions. Since investors have a choice to invest in the market and the risk of returns provided by the market is presumed to be standard it is assigned a value of 1. The projects having greater risk than the market will have a β of greater than 1, while those with lesser risk than the market will have a β of less than 1.

The next question that needs to be answered is what returns are expected from a project that is presumed to have no risk at all. Strictly speaking there is no venture that is entirely free of risk. However, investment in government securities can be considered to be virtually risk free. Therefore, risk-free returns can be assumed to be the returns offered by government securities like *T*-bills and bonds.

Conforming to the above characteristics following equation will correctly define the expected cost of equity r_e for a risky venture:

$$r_e = r_f + \beta \times (r_m - r_f) \qquad (13\text{-}10)$$

where; r_f = Expected return on risk free securities,
r_m = Expected return on the market, and
β = Expected risk of the project.

Now we need to find out the appropriate values to find the expected cost of equity. While the values of r_f and r_m are available for immediate past, the future values cannot be forecast. Since economic conditions change only gradually over time, it will be reasonable to assume that trends depicted in the recent past would continue to be reflected in not-so-distant future.

The problem of measurement of the risk of the project β is rather complex. It is not a directly observable phenomenon. It has to be derived from relevant observable parameters. β is the relationship of the returns of the firm with the returns of the market in the same period. One way to find out this relationship is through regression of past data of returns of the firm with the returns of market. Returns of the security with that of market in the recent past are observed and compared. The linear relationship between the cost of equity and the risk as measured from β is depicted in Figure 13-1. The cost of equity would rise proportionately with the risk of the project by the amount of differential of the market return r_m and risk free rate r_f.

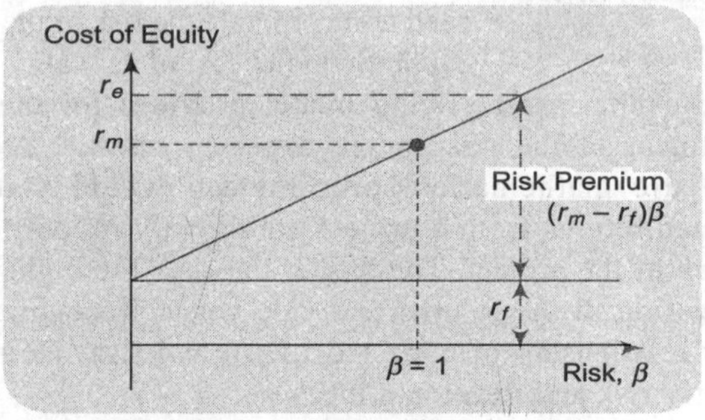

Figure 13-1 Cost of equity—CAPM based

Once the information on risk-free returns, returns on the market, and β are available, the cost of equity can be calculated by Equation 13-10. For risk-free returns of 5%, market returns of 14% and with security β of 0.8 the cost of equity for the firm is 12.2% as shown below:

$$r_e = r_f + \beta \times (r_m - r_f) = 5 + 0.8 \times (14 - 5) = 12.2\%$$

Dividend Capitalization vs CAPM-based Approaches

As one would observe the computation of cost of equity capital through CAPM-based approach has the advantage of (i) incorporating the risk of the project, and (ii) elimination of need to know the policies on dividend. This makes CAPM-based measurement of cost of equity preferable over the dividend capitalization based approach. The dividend capitalization approach does not consider the risk of the project. Further, the assumptions of dividend capitalization approach includes constant pay out ratio, which makes its application difficult for firms with volatile dividend record or no dividend record. The CAPM-based approach does not require any such assumption regarding dividend and instead derives cost of equity on the market-based information.

CAPM based determination of cost of equity is regarded as superior as it relies on the market based information and incorporates risk.

The disadvantages would emanate from the assumption that past is appropriate guide to the risk of the project as β is based on past data. If β does not remain constant the cost of equity may not be true. However, changes in β with time are expected to be less volatile than the changes in dividend pay out. In most cases the assumptions that past β would remain valid for near future is more likely to hold. The limitation of past being sufficient indicator of future also exists with dividend discount models where dividends in the past are considered to be an indicator of future dividends.

Realizing the different sources of deriving the cost of equity in the two models discussed above it is more likely that both models will give different values of cost of equity. Both the models stand on sound financial logic that is difficult to dislodge. Using the two approaches, one is likely to find two different estimates of cost of equity. Only by coincidence they may give identical figures. Since both the models have some limitations and stand on sound financial logic it would be better to calculate the cost of equity by both the methods and average them out, as a managerial decision, though a theorist may continue to argue for superiority of one method over the other.

Example 13-6 Cost of Equity using CAPM

Beta Corporation is a listed at stock exchange and the current price of its share is ₹200. The earnings and dividend had been growing at 10% and the last dividend was ₹12. Through regression analysis, the beta of the firm is estimated at 1.20. The expected market return is 16% while the returns in the government securities are prevailing at 6%. Find out the cost of equity for Beta Corporation using DDM and CAPM. Why do you think that there is difference in the two figures?

Solution

As per DDM the cost of equity:

$$r_e = \frac{D_1}{P_0} + g = \frac{D_0(1+g)}{P_0} + g = \frac{12 \times 1.10}{200} + 0.10 = 0.1660 = 16.60\%$$

As per CAPM the cost of equity is:

$$r_e = r_f + \beta \times (r_m - r_f) = 6 + 1.2 \times (16 - 6) = 18.00\%$$

The difference in the cost of equity is due to the fact that DDM projects the cost of equity on the basis of growth estimates of the firm, while CAPM assumes the return on equity of a stock when it is part of a well diversified portfolio and markets become the sole determinant of the return on a particular security. CAPM estimates the return on the basis of systematic risk while DDM considers the factors affecting growth of specific firm.

Cost of equity for non-traded firms

Both the dividend capitalization approach and CAPM-based approach to determine cost of equity are based on the firm's market information and apply to firms that are traded in the market. How do we compute cost of equity for privately held firms? There are many possible ways of getting this answer. One may use comparative pricing and use the data of a firm that is listed and traded and is engaged in the same activity. The cost of equity for the firm in the same line can serve as a useful guide and starting point. Of course, adjustments based on the size of the firm, capital structure, etc., would need to be made. Another possible way is to use the CAPM-based approach of risk premium. Rather than obtaining the risk premium based on market return and β of the firm a subjective assessment about the risk premium desired by the promoters can be added to the risk free rate to arrive at cost of equity.

Cost of External Equity

The cost of equity as derived from dividend capitalization approach applies to the internally generated funds. This was under the assumption that the growth of dividend is funded by retained earnings. At times the firms are also required to issue fresh capital. This is called external equity as opposed to the internal equity, i.e., retained earnings.

Cost of external equity is more than the cost of retained earnings due to (i) floatation costs, (ii) under utilization of capital raised, and (iii) the under pricing of newly issued stocks.

Would the cost of equity by issuing fresh stock be identical to that of retained earnings? Theoretically, they must be identical. Funding growth through fresh issue of capital and distributing entire earnings do not make any difference to the outcome or change the aspirations of investor. They must be indifferent to such swapping of funds. The firm distributes to the shareholders what it owes to them and collects back to implement new projects.

However, practical considerations demand some changes. There are following three major differences in the real world that have cost implications.

1. Existence of flotation cost
2. Under utilization of external equity
3. Under pricing of fresh capital

First, the issuance of fresh equity involves some flotation cost. These costs include fees to merchant bankers, underwriting commission, administrative cost, etc. Sometimes these costs related to flotation are as high as 10% depending upon the amount mobilized. Flotation costs come down as the issue size increases. A small modification to the Equation 13-8 would handle the issue of flotation cost. If flotation costs, f, are expressed as % of price, the market price of equity would be as per Equation 13-11. We have used it in Example 13-5.

$$r_e \text{ for external equity} = \frac{\text{Cost of internal equity}}{(1-f)}$$

$$= \frac{1}{(1-f)}\frac{D_1}{P_0} + g \qquad (13\text{-}11)$$

As per Equation 13-11 the cost of equity for fresh issue of capital will be adjusted for the factor of flotation cost. If the cost of flotation is 5% of the issue price and cost of internal equity determined either through dividend discount model or CAPM-based approach is 16% then the cost of fresh equity shall be 16.84% (16/0.95).

Second, fresh issues of capital are made in 'chunks' where the entire funds mobilized are not used instantaneously. Large projects do have considerable gestation period and unless the project is executed fully, the use of funds will be partial only. This time lag between the mobilization of funds and its use has a cost. The funds are idle for some time and firms normally deploy these funds in short-term risk free securities to earn some income. Such a situation is less likely with the retained funds since surpluses are generated periodically and deployed accordingly. For most growing firms, retained funds can be assumed used instantaneously.

Commercial consideration demands that the fresh equity issue be made at a price lower than the current market price. If offered at the market price, investors may not subscribe because prospective investors can obtain the same from the open market. They have no incentive to buy from the firm. Further, a fresh issue of shares would increase supply and cause the price to fall. Another reason for under pricing of the new issue is the common belief amongst investors that firms issue new shares only when the markets are booming and stocks are priced higher, i.e., valued more than their intrinsic worth. Even though fairly priced, the market belief would cause under pricing of new issue. The under pricing would make external equity more expensive than the retained earnings. The cost of fresh equity may be computed by Equation 13-12 as follows:

$$r_e \text{ for external equity} = \frac{1}{(1-f)}\frac{D_1}{P_0'} + g \qquad (13\text{-}12)$$

where P_0' is the issue price.

ASSIGNING WEIGHTS

Having studied the cost of capital from different sources, the next question to be answered is the proportion of capital from each of the source. The firm's cost of capital that must be used as discount rate is the weighted average of each of the sources used as given by Equation 13-1. There are three ways the proportion of capital from each source can be determined. These are

Computation of WACC requires proportions of capital from each source besides cost of each source. The proportions may be based on (1) marginal, (2) book value, or (3) market value.

1. Marginal proportions
2. Book value proportions
3. Market value proportions

Marginal Proportions

Using marginal proportions means using the proportions of each source that have been used to raise the incremental capital. Proportions based on actual amounts raised from each source to fund the new project are used to determine the WACC.

Some managers believe that the cost of specific sources of funding the project is relevant for capital budgeting decision. The rationale forwarded for the use of the weights based on specific sources of capital is that if the project is able to generate adequate cash flows to meet the obligations undertaken to execute the same, the project must be accepted. However, this notion is extremely misplaced. Proportions of specific sources of funding to arrive at cost of capital are irrelevant and distort the capital budgeting process.

As an example, consider that a firm is evaluating a project costing ₹10 crore with an internal rate of return at 8%. It decides to raise the entire capital from loans costing 8%.

If the tax rate is 35%, then the post-tax cost of raising capital is:

$r_d \times (1 - t) = 8 \times 0.65 = 5.2\%$

Using 100% weight for debt the cost of capital would then be 5.2%. Accordingly, if the cash flows are discounted at 5.2% it would result in positive NPV and the project is accepted. The project would add to the value of shareholders by the amount of NPV. Ignoring such a project would mean a lost opportunity to add to the shareholders' wealth.

However, there is a serious fallacy in the argument advocating the use of proportions based on sources of incremental funding. Further, looking into the future, the firm decides to implement another project of ₹10 crore again with an IRR of 10%; higher than the one executed earlier. Having exhausted its debt capacity earlier, it is required to mobilize equity of ₹10 crore. If the cost of new equity is 12% then it becomes the discount rate using marginal proportions. This project now results in a negative NPV and, hence, would be rejected. Both the decisions are incorrect. If only we had changed the order of financing, i.e., raising equity first and then debt the decisions would be reversed. What was accepted would now stand rejected, and what is rejected would stand accepted.

The situation just described does not take into account either the past record or the future requirements. In the example most of us would agree that the firm decided to have 100% debt funding only because the capital structure permitted such debt. Possibly, the firm was already having high proportion of equity and had the borrowing capacity available then. Incremental funding at such a low cost of 5.2% was possible due to the past earnings of the firm. More and more projects would find acceptance at such low cost of capital being used as discount rate, which would be a wrong decision. Similarly, the firm had to resort to equity funding later because it had exhausted the debt capacity and rejected a more profitable project. If the firm had considered both past and future, it would have possibly avoided the mistake.

Hence, the past and current capital structure cannot be ignored while considering cost of capital. Today's incremental cost of capital, in fact, gets benefits of yesterday and affects the tomorrow's cost of capital.

Therefore, while deciding about the cost of capital and hence the discount rate for the capital budgeting decision we need to consider the target capital structure of the firm. It is a different matter that at any point of time the actual capital structure may not conform to the target capital structure. It is possible for a firm to have a target debt–equity ratio of 1:2 while current debt–equity ratio might be 1:3 permitting to raise debt to achieve the target capital structure. Since firms do not always raise funds in the same ratio as that of target capital structure because of practical considerations of flotation costs, amounts to be raised, etc., the specific sources of funding a particular project becomes irrelevant in determining the cost of capital.

Since cost of each source of capital rises with the quantum raised use of marginal weights based on target capital structure is recommended while computing WACC.

Therefore, the appropriate weight to be used in determination of WACC is the weight of target capital structure.

Despite the fact that firm may not be able to raise incremental capital in the same proportions as the current capital structure, one would still use existing proportions in the cost of capital as it dwells in the past and also considers future requirements. In a nutshell, historical as well as future considerations must determine today's actions.

Use of weights of actual sources of funding is inappropriate and leads to errors, and instead weights based on target capital structure must be used.

Using the cost of specific sources used to finance a project is fallacious for many reasons. Firstly, suppliers of specific capital consider *interalia* the existing as well as final capital structure while deciding upon the quantum of capital and its cost. Due consideration is given to the historical capital structure and industry norms. Secondly, capital is fungible. A company may undertake numerous projects and it may be difficult to assign a specific source of capital to any project. The firm as a single entity uses all sources of capital for all its activities. Finally, firms normally strive to raise funds in such a manner so as not to distort its existing capital structure in the long run, minor short term deviation notwithstanding. They continue to strive towards a target capital structure, although it is achieved over a very long period of time.

Book Value Vs Market Value Proportions

Having accepted that the proportions that must be used in determination of WACC are the proportions of target capital structure a question as to how these weights must be valued arises. There are two ways the target capital structure may be looked at; (i) on the basis of book values and (ii) on the basis of market values.

Assume that a firm has total funds of ₹100 crore in the form of equity and debt and they are reflected in the books as follows:

Nature of Funding	*Amount (₹ crore)*	*Proportion*	*Post-tax Cost*
Equity including reserves	75.00	75%	20%
Debt	25.00	25%	8 %
Total	100.00	100%	

Assuming the cost of equity at 20% and post-tax cost of debt at 8% the WACC based on the book value weights would be:

WACC (Book value) $= 0.75 \times 20\% + 0.25 \times 8\% = 17.00\%$

The liabilities of a firm are represented in the financial statements at book value, i.e., the costs at which they were actually raised in the past and they are used in determining the proportion in the computation of WACC.

If equity and debt were traded in the market, the market values of each will be different than what is reflected in the financial statements. Assume that both equity and debt are listed on stock exchange. The value of equity shares and debt in the market are ₹180 crore and ₹20 crore, respectively at current market price. Based on market value, the proportion of each in the capital structure would be as shown below:

Nature of Funding	Market Value (₹ crore)	Proportion	Post-tax Cost
Equity	180.00	90%	20%
Debt	20.00	10%	8%
Total	200.00	100%	

Using same cost of equity and debt as before, the WACC based on the market value weights would then be:

WACC (Market value) = 0.90 × 20% + 0.10 × 8% = 18.80%

What are the proportions of debt and equity in the capital structure? Is it 1:3 based on book value proportions or is it 1:10 based on market value proportions. From the viewpoint of mobilization of fresh capital, it is argued that if the new capital is to be raised, it would be done at prevailing market rates and not at what the books tell. The current cost of each source of capital is determined by the current market price and not what has been recorded. Therefore, the use of proportions based on market values is more appropriate than using proportions based on book values.

However, there are many merits in using the book value weights. The merits of using book value proportions are—(1) its simplicity, and ready availability leading to operational ease; (2) book values are free from vagaries of market, which cause values to change on a day-to-day basis; (3) book value information published in public documents is not subjective; and (4) most financial analysis by banks and financial institutions is based on book values.

Use of weights based on book value though convenient and practical but lacks conviction. Therefore, the use of weights based on market values, being true reflectors of investors' expectations, is the most appropriate.

Due to dynamic conditions of the market, it will be hard to find consistency and unanimity in the proportions if they are based on market values. Use of book value proportions will not be controversial with respect to its mathematical accuracy. It is widely accepted that the use of proportions based on market value is most appropriate while computing the cost of capital of the firm. The market values are true indicators of expectations of the investors, and the firm is supposed to fulfil these expectations if it plans to raise new funds from them. From this viewpoint, using market value proportions scores over book value proportions and is a good reason that overwhelms all advantage of using book value weights. Despite the convenience in using the book values one must use the market value weights in the target capital structure, which ultimately determines WACC and the appropriate discount rate for capital budgeting decisions.

Example 13-7 Weighted Average Cost of Capital

Flag Products Limited (FPL) has been maintaining a capital structure based on market value proportions of 25:15:60 for debt, preference, and equity capital which it believes is optimal. The 10% debt of FPL is selling at 20% discount to the face value and the 12% preference share is selling at par. FPL growing at 15% per annum had paid the dividend of ₹4 per share in the previous year, and its share of face value of ₹10 is trading at ₹60. Flag Products Limited has a reserve of ₹25 per share. The corporate tax payable by the firm is 40%. What is the WACC for FPL based on book value and market value weights?

Solution

Post Tax Cost of Debt; $r_d = \dfrac{10(1-0.4)}{0.80} = 7.50\%$

Cost of Preference Capital; $r_p = \dfrac{D_p}{P_0} = \dfrac{12}{100} = 0.12 = 12.00\%$

Cost of Equity; $r_e = \dfrac{D_1}{P_0} + g = \dfrac{D_0(1+g)}{P_0} + g = \dfrac{4 \times 1.15}{60} + 0.15$

$= 0.2267 = 22.67\%$

Book value proportions can be arrived as under;

Debt selling at 20% discount to face value:

Book value = Market value/0.80 = 25/0.8 = 31.25

Preference capital selling at par:

Book value = Market value = 15

Equity capital:

Book value = capital + reserves = 10 + 25 = 35

Computation of WACC

Source	Cost (%)	Market Value Weights			Book Value Weights		
		Market value	Weight	Weighted cost %	Book value	Weight	Weighted cost %
Debt	7.50	25	0.25	1.875	31.25	0.385	2.888
Preference Capital	12.00	15	0.15	1.800	15.00	0.185	2.220
Equity Capital	22.67	60	0.60	13.602	35.00	0.430	9.748
WACC %				17.277			14.856

* With the face value of ₹10 the firm has reserves of ₹25 giving a book value of ₹35 against market price of ₹60

MARGINAL COST OF CAPITAL

WACC as discount rate for appraisal of project makes a significant assumption that the acceptance or rejection of the project does not impact the capital structure of the firm. Whenever the project size is comparable to the existing operations it is hard to imagine that the capital structure would remain unaltered. When the new funding requirements are significant, with respect to existing resources, the firm would see a rise in the WACC even if the capital structure remains unaltered. For example, debts are provided by the lenders at an increasing rate with the volume of debt. This tends to push up the WACC.

In such cases, considering the present WACC as the discount rate for project for making decision could be erroneous. The relevant cost of capital for discounting the cash flows would be the incremental cost of capital, i.e., the marginal cost of capital. Let us consider an example of a firm that has the existing capital structure of equity and debt in the ratio of 2:1. The cost of equity and post-tax cost of debt are 25% and 10%, respectively, therefore, the WACC is 20%.

This firm is considering a project costing ₹200 lakh that is financed equally with equity and debt of ₹100 lakh each. The new debt is being raised at 12% and it is assumed that with the acceptance of the project the cost of equity would increase to 26% from 25%. The new capital structure with market proportions are given in the table below:

Source	Before Project		After Project	
	Cost %	Market Value ₹(lakh)	Cost %	Market Value ₹(lakh)
Equity	25.0	800	26	900
Debt	10.0	400	10	400
New Debt	—	—	12	100
Cost of Capital (WACC)	20.00%		20.43%	

The new capital structure gives WACC at 20.43% as follows:

$$\text{WACC} = \frac{9}{14} \times 26\% + \frac{4}{14} \times 10\% + \frac{1}{14} \times 12\% = 20.43\%$$

As one would imagine that the marginal cost of capital is the weighted average of the cost of newly raised capital. The cost of new equity and debt are 26% and 12%, respectively. As the project is funded equally with equity and debt, the cost of capital and, therefore, the discount rate to be used should only be 19%. Wrong. Such an approach ignores the impact of new funding on the existing capital structure of the firm. With new funds added to finance the new project the capital structure has changed.

Marginal cost of capital is the cost of incremental finances required for the project and is an appropriate discount rate.

The correct approach would be to calculate the change in the overall cost as a consequence of raising additional funds, providing for the change in the capital structure of the firm. The incremental cost of raising additional funds of ₹200 lakh is ₹46 lakh comprising cost of equity of ₹34 lakh ($26 \times 900 - 25 \times 800$) and cost of new debt of ₹12 lakh. Therefore, the cost of new funds is 23%. This is the marginal cost of capital, taking into account the changes in capital structure.

Even when the capital structure is constant the marginal cost of capital changes because of the increasing costs of its components. As the amount of funding increases, the costs rise. For example, consider a firm having a target capital structure of equity at 60% and debt at 40%. The cost of each component is dependent upon the quantum of funds raised from each source. Let us assume the following costs at different levels:

Cost of funds from various sources:

Equity		Debt	
Up to ₹60 crore	20%	Up to ₹20 crore	10%
Between ₹60–75 crore	22%	Between ₹20–30 crore	11%
More than ₹75 crore	24%	More than ₹30 crore	12%

The cost of incremental funds would increase with increasing amounts of finance. Also, the WACC too would be dependent upon the aggregate level of financing and show an increasing trend.

We first find out at what aggregate level the costs would change. If debt has to be 40% then the first change in cost would take place at ₹50 crore because a debt of ₹20 crore can support only as much with the given capital structure. At this level we exhaust the capacity at 10% debt and have to get debt at 11%. Similarly, another change would take place at the aggregate level of finance of ₹75 crore because we exhaust the debt availability at 11% too. Thereafter, the debt would be available at 12%. This is found as follows:

Maximum permissible capital outlay with 10% cost of debt

$$= \frac{\text{Maximum debt up to 10\%}}{\text{Proportion of debt}} = \frac{₹20 \text{ crore}}{0.40}$$

= ₹50 crores

Maximum permissible capital outlay with 11% cost of debt

$$= \frac{\text{Maximum debt up to 11\%}}{\text{Proportion of debt}} = \frac{₹30 \text{ crore}}{0.40}$$

= ₹75 crores

The WACC for financing up to ₹50 crore would be:

$$\text{WACC} = 0.6 \times 20\% + 0.4 \times 10\% = 16\%$$

Marginal cost of raising fund (provided that the aggregate requirement is within ₹50 crore) is also same as WACC. However, when funds requirement exceed ₹50 crore the incremental funds can be arranged at 16.4%.

Cost of incremental funds (marginal cost of capital, MCC)

$$= 0.6 \times 20\% + 0.4 \times 11\% = 16.4\%$$

Marginal cost of capital remains the same till we reach another break point. However, WACC would be dependent upon aggregate funds raised. For aggregate funds of ₹60 crore, the equity and debt in the ratio of 60:40 would be ₹36 crore and ₹24 crore, respectively. While all equity is available at 20%, debt in excess of ₹20 crore is obtained at 11%. Therefore, WACC would be:

$$\text{WACC} = \frac{1}{60}(36 \times 20\% + 20 \times 10\% + 4 \times 11\%) = 16.07\%$$

Since there are changes in the cost of equity, the cost on incremental funds and WACC would change when the equity at lower cost is exhausted. We may find such break point in the same fashion as we did for debt. These break points are:

Maximum permissible capital outlay with 20% cost of equity

$$= \frac{\text{Maximum equity up to 20\%}}{\text{Proportion of equity}} = \frac{₹60 \text{ crore}}{0.60}$$

= ₹100 crore

Maximum permissible capital outlay with 22% cost of equity

$$= \frac{\text{Maximum equity up to 22\%}}{\text{Proportion of equity}} = \frac{₹75 \text{ crore}}{0.60}$$

= ₹125 crore

Table 13-1 and Table 13-2 give the MCC and WACC at various levels of funding.

Table 13-1 Cost of Incremental Funds (Marginal Cost of Capital)

	Breaking Value				
Up to ₹ crore	***50***	***75***	***100***	***125***	***> 125***
Equity	30.00	45.00	60.00	75.00	75.60
Debt	20.00	30.00	40.00	50.00	50.40
Cost of Equity	20%	20%	20%	22%	24%
Cost of Debt	10%	11%	12%	12%	12%
MCC (%)	**16.00**	**16.40**	**16.80**	**18.00**	**19.20**

One may note that at each breaking point the cost of incremental funds increases and becomes constant at 19.2% for funding above ₹125 crore. Marginal cost of capital rises in steps and remains constant till the next breaking point. However, the same is not the case with WACC. It rises every time with each additional funding. However, it would never exceed 19.2% the maximum marginal cost of capital because part of funds would be available at cheaper rates. At a level of ₹150 crore the WACC come at 17.07% as may be seen from Table 13-2.

Table 13-2 WACC at Different Levels of Funding (*₹ crore*)

Total Funds	**50**	**60**	**75**	**90**	**100**	**115**	**125**	**150**
Equity at 60%	30	36	45	54	60	69	75	90
at 20%	30	36	45	54	60	60	60	60
at 22%	—	—	—	—	—	9	15	15
at 24%	—	—	—	—	—	—	—	15
Debt at 40%	20	24	30	36	40	46	50	60
at 10%	20	20	20	20	20	20	20	20
at 11%	—	4	10	10	10	10	10	10
at 12%	—	—	—	6	10	16	20	30
WACC (%)	**16.00**	**16.07**	**16.13**	**16.24**	**16.30**	**16.52**	**16.64**	**17.07**

A graphical view of MCC and WACC is presented in Figure 13-2.

Optimal Capital Budget

The capital budgeting exercise is the computation of the NPV of the project at a discount rate. If the NPV is positive, we accept the project. Alternatively, the internal rate of return of the project must exceed the discount rate. The question that arises is which of the two: WACC or MCC is an appropriate rate to compare with the IRR of the project.

When marginal cost of capital equals marginal revenue, it is an optimal capital budget.

It must be emphasized here that it is the marginal cost of capital that governs the value addition to the firm and not WACC. Incremental benefits must exceed incremental cost if the value is to be added. As WACC represents the cost of the funds being raised at different points of time and it would not be fair to value a project against this cost. WACC would trail MCC. If the MCC is rising WACC will never exceed it. At best it can be equal to MCC. Under such a case if projects are valued against WACC, some projects having an IRR greater than WACC but less than MCC would be accepted. The cost incurred to execute such projects would be larger than the benefits and hence they would be destroying value because we count the benefit of earlier projects to the new projects.

The argument favouring the use of marginal cost of capital as discount rate, rests on the familiar principle of economics providing the rule for optimality. With increased usage of resources the marginal revenue decreases and marginal cost increases. The optimization of resource is obtained at a point where marginal revenue equals the marginal cost.

As an illustration, consider the following projects, A to H with capital outlays and in descending order of the internal rate of return.

Projects	***A***	***B***	***C***	***D***	***E***	***F***	***G***	***H***
Outlay (₹)	30	20	25	25	15	10	25	30
Cumulative Outlay (₹)	30	50	75	100	115	125	150	180
IRR	25%	23%	21%	20%	19%	18%	17%	16%

These internal rates of return should be plotted against the increasing budget, called investment schedule. On the same plot the MCC too is plotted. The intersection of MCC with the investment schedule provides the optimal point up to which the firm must invest. This is plotted in Figure 13-3. It may be noted that projects F and G stand rejected despite their IRRs being greater than WACC.

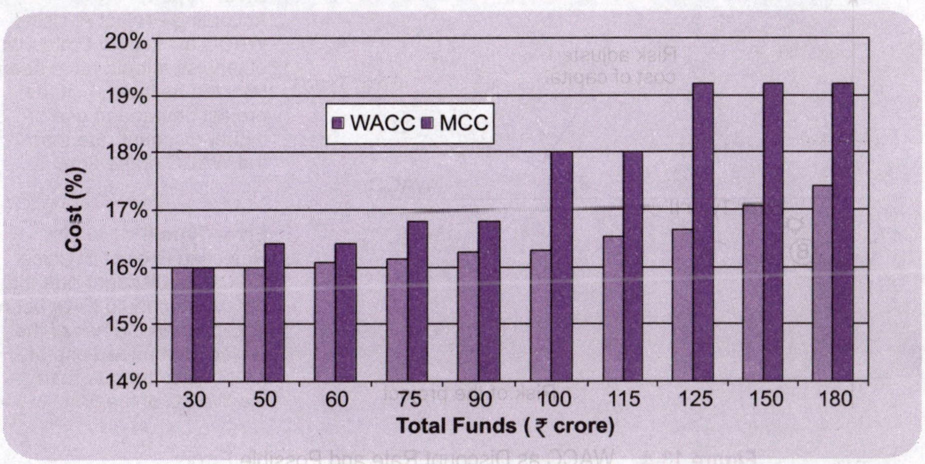

Figure 13-2 WACC & MCC

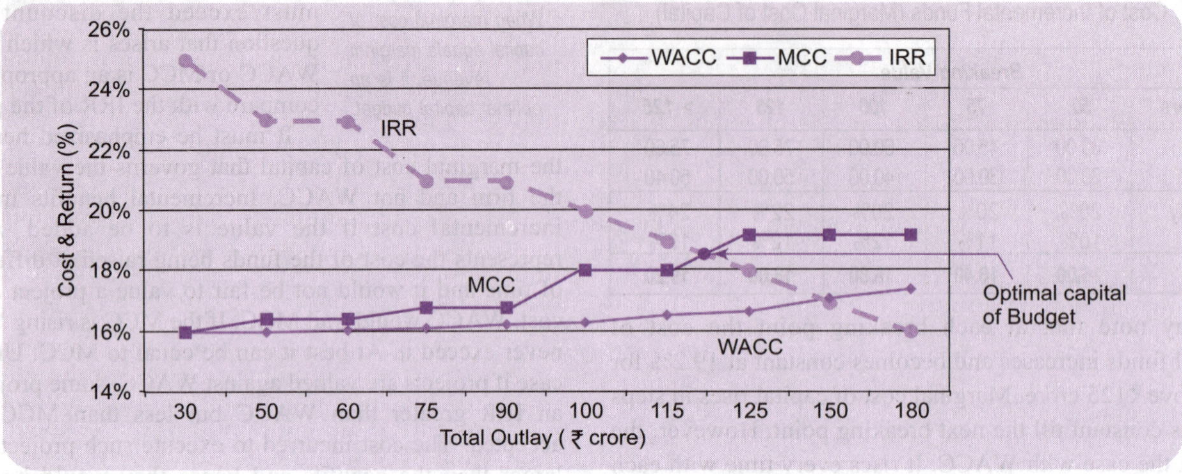

Figure 13-3 Optimal Capital Budget

WACC AS DISCOUNT RATE AND RISK

In most cases the marginal cost of capital is the same as weighted average cost of capital, WACC and therefore, we continue to use WACC as discount rate as WACC. Further, we assume that the capital structure is constant and WACC is based on target capital structure. Another implied assumption while using WACC as discount rate for capital budgeting is that the projects being evaluated bear the same risk as the overall risk of the firm.

In most cases, these assumptions hold since most projects are relatively small in size and pertain to the activities similar to the main business of the firm. Projects relating to capacity enhancement, product improvement, cost reduction, replacement of machines developing by-products, etc., fall in the category of investment where the use of WACC is befitting.

However, the use of WACC as discount rate for all projects is fraught with risk. While it can serve as guiding tool WACC is not the universal discount rate. It is well established that the discount rate to be used for arriving at the present values must be based on the risk of the project irrespective of cost of funds that are used to finance the project. Using existing WACC as discount rate may not be consistent with the risks of the cash flows.

When using WACC as discount rate care must be taken to adjust it for the risk of the project that may not the same risk as that of the existing line of business.

Blind use of WACC may lead to two kinds of errors. Suppose WACC for firm is 12% and it is considering a low risk project that demands a discount rate of 8%. This conventional project has a positive NPV at 8% but it becomes a negative NPV at 12%. If evaluated with WACC as a discount rate, the project would be erroneously rejected. Same is the case when there is some unconventional project that demands a discount rate of 15% and it is a negative NPV project. However, if this project has a positive NPV at 12% it would be accepted. Again wrongfully. Managers have to guard against such errors. Blind use of WACC as discount rate for all projects is not recommended. This is presented in Figure 13-4.

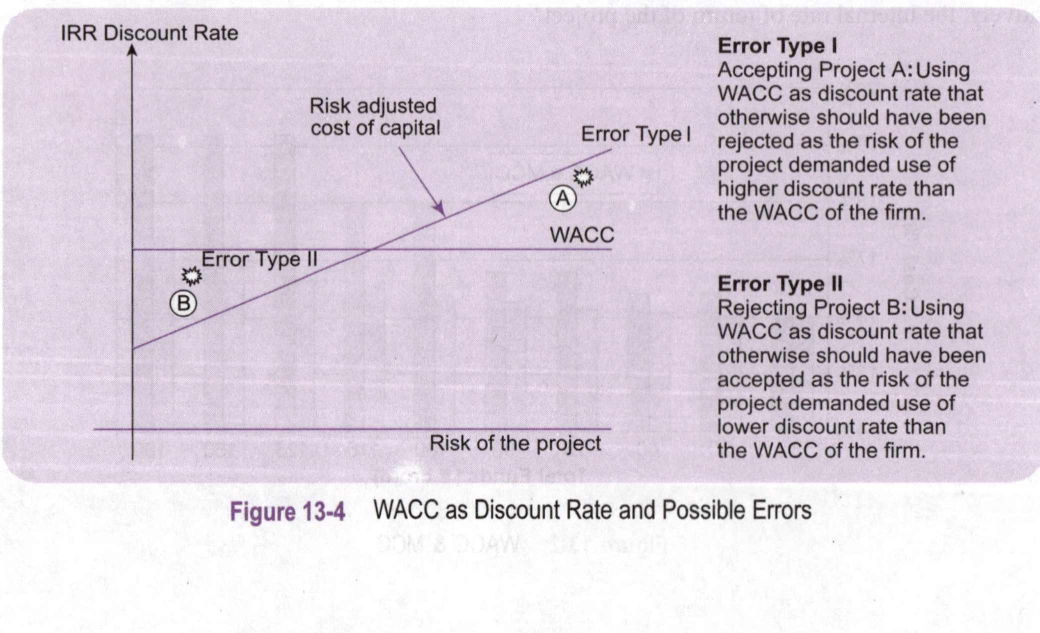

Figure 13-4 WACC as Discount Rate and Possible Errors

Example 13-8 Capital Structure, Capital Budgeting, and Cost of Capital

Simple Enterprises has clearly stated corporate philosophy for their capital structure and dividend payout. They believe in financing all capital expenditures by maintaining a debt and equity proportions of 40:60 based on market values. Similarly, they have a clearly stated dividend payout policy of 50% of earnings on cash basis. Last year they declared a dividend of ₹2, which has been growing at 10%. Simple Enterprises expects to maintain the same growth in future. They have a plan to invest ₹1,000 lakh. After payment of corporate tax of 40% the expected cash flow for the year is estimated at ₹300 lakh. Simple Enterprises can mobilize debt at 12% with a flotation cost of 3% while fresh equity can be mobilized with a flotation cost of 5%. The current market price of the share is ₹50. Find out the WACC to be used by Simple Enterprises for evaluating the investment opportunity.

Solution

The financing for the project of ₹1,000 lakh with the desired capital structure and existing dividend payout is as below:

	₹ lakh
Funds required	1,000
Debt Finance (40%)	400
Equity (60%)	600
Internal Accruals available:	
Post-tax Cash flow generated	300
Less: Dividend payout (50%)	150
Internal Accruals	150
Fresh Equity to be mobilized	450

$$\text{Post-tax Cost of Debt; } r_d = \frac{C(1-T)}{(1-f)} = \frac{12(1-0.4)}{(1-0.03)} = 7.42\%$$

$$\text{Cost of Internal Accruals} = \frac{D_1}{P_0} + g = \frac{D_0(1+g)}{P_0} + g$$

$$= \frac{2\times 1.10}{50} + 0.10 = 0.144 = 14.40\%$$

$$\text{Cost of External Equity} = \frac{D_1}{P_0(1-f)} + g = \frac{D_0(1+g)}{P_0(1-f)} + g$$

$$= \frac{2\times 1.10}{50\times 0.95} + 0.10 = 0.1463 = 14.63\%$$

Computation of WACC

Source	Value ₹(lakh)	Weight	Cost (%)	Weighted Cost (%)
Debt	400	0.40	7.42	2.97
Internal Accruals	150	0.15	14.40	2.16
External Equity	450	0.45	14.63	6.58
Weighted Average Cost of Capital (WACC) %				**11.71**

PURE PLAY APPROACH: UNLEVERING AND RELEVERING OF BETA

There are situations where a firm may decide to undertake a project that is unrelated to its present business activity. For example, a petrochemical company may decide to enter the telecom business or an IT company may want to open a bank. Under such situations the business environment to be faced by the firm for the proposed activity will be substantially different than its existing business environment. The question is whether the use of existing WACC of the firm is appropriate as a discount rate for evaluation of the new project. The cases of unrelated diversification are plenty in the corporate world.

The use of current WACC as discount rate is inappropriate because the business risk of the new venture is substantially different than the existing business. The providers of capital, especially equity require adequate compensation according to the risk they undertake. The discount rate must necessarily recognize the risk. Another situation discouraging the use of WACC pertains to a business conglomerate having various divisions with diversified activities. Under such circumstance a WACC based on business risk of different business activities is recommended rather than the use of the firm's WACC.

Pure play approach is one way of adjusting the risk of the project in the discount rate, by identifying a firm doing business in the same line as that of the proposed project.

The most widely used method for projects of varying risk profiles is the pure play approach. As stated earlier, the risk adjusted cost of equity capital as per the CAPM-based approach is determined by β of the firm. However, we have to use β that is relevant for the new proposed activity. We need to construct this β artificially because beta of the firm is not valid.

Assume that a firm, PetChem Industries Limited (PIL), having substantial interest in petrochemicals is planning a foray into telecommunications infrastructure and services by introducing mobile telephones. What β must be used for evaluation of this project? Beta of PIL is obviously not appropriate because the new activity has no common business risk with the existing operations. Further, the cost of equity is a function of financial leverage. With increased leverage, the risk to shareholders too increases, in justification of greater returns.

Appropriate beta must consider (i) the business risk of the proposed venture and (ii) the financial risk emanating from the proposed financial leverage. We describe below the method to construct a suitable β.

Step I: Identify a pure-play firm engaged in same/similar activity Firstly, PIL needs to identify a publicly traded firm purely engaged in telecom business. A reasonable similarity would also serve the purpose as long as it is safe to assume that the business risk of the new venture is identical to the pure-play firm. The higher the number of pure-play firms, the better it is. It will provide a more accurate estimate and remove the structural bias that will continue to exist if we use a single firm. Let us assume that Indian Telecom Limited (ITL) is one such pure-play firm.

Step II: Find β of the pure-play firm The next step is to know the β of ITL. Since ITL is publicly traded firm the β of ITL is publicly available. Alternatively, it can be obtained directly by performing a regression analysis on the price data of ITL and market index say NIFTY. Assume that β of ITL is 1.2.

Step III: Unlever the observed β β obtained in step II is applicable to the equity shareholders of ITL. The observed β of ITL not only reflects the business risk of ITL but also considers the financial risk faced by its equity shareholders. We need to adjust the observed β for the capital structure of ITL. The observed β needs to be converted into a β that relates to shareholders of ITL as if its operations were financed wholly by equity, i.e., unlevering of observed β. This can be done by following relationship between unlevered beta and levered beta as given by Equation 13-13.

$$\beta_u = \beta_d \frac{D}{D+E} + \beta_L \frac{E}{D+E} \quad (13\text{-}13)$$

Where

β_u = Beta of the unlevered firm
β_d = Beta of debt
β_L = Beta of equity for levered firm; the observed beta
D = Market Value of Debt
E = Market Value of Equity

The equation above makes use of additive property of β which means that β of assets is simply the weighted average of the individual sources comprising the asset, i.e., the beta of the asset created with some equity and some debt will be equal to weighted average of betas of the equity and debt. This weighted average is computed using market value proportions.

The Equation 13-13 needs to be modified for the tax shield the firm enjoys with debt. Since interest is tax deductible, the value of debt D needs to be replaced by $D \times (1 - T)$; the post-tax value of debt. In most cases, the beta of debt β_d can be assumed to be very low as the value of debt does not change much with change in the equity market conditions. Assuming β_d is equal to zero and adjusting for tax shield of the debt in Equation 13-13 we get a relationship between levered and unlevered beta as Equation 13-14.

$$\beta_u = \beta_d \frac{D(1-T)}{D(1-T)+E} + \beta_L \frac{E}{D(1-T)+E} \quad (13\text{-}14)$$

with $\beta_d = 0$

$$\beta_u = \beta_L \frac{E}{D \times (1-T) + E} \quad (13\text{-}15)$$

$$= \frac{\beta_L}{\{1 + (1-T) \times D/E\}}$$

Assume that the observed beta of ITL is 1.2. Besides reflecting the business risk of the telecommunication business, the observed beta of ITL also represents the financial risk of ITL. Therefore, the observed beta is levered beta. And this has to be unlevered, i.e., converted into β of equity as if ITL was all equity financed.

While using beta of the pure-play firm, it must be unlevered for the financial leverage to reflect only the business risk and then relevered for the proposed capital structure of the project.

If the debt equity ratio based on market values of ITL is 1:5 and its marginal tax rate is 30% the beta of ITL, as if it were all equity financed, will be 1.0526.

$$\beta_u = \beta_L \frac{E}{D \times (1-T) + E}$$

$$= \frac{\beta_L}{\{1 + (1-T) \times D/E\}} = \frac{1.20}{1 + 0.7 \times 1/5} = 1.0526$$

Step IV: Relevering Beta The beta arrived at in step III represents the sensitivity of ITL stock as if it were wholly financed by equity. Unlevering of beta implies segregation of the two components of the risk, i.e., the business risk and the financial risk that are present in observed beta. Unlevered beta represents only the business risk.

This now needs to be relevered with the proposed financing pattern of the project. This can be done again using the Equation 13-14 incorporating debt–equity ratio (D^*/E^*) and tax rate (T^*) of the proposed project.

$$\beta_L^* = \beta_u\{1 + (1 - T^*) \times D^*/E^*\}$$

If PIL proposes to finance the telecom project with a debt–equity ratio of 2:5 and has a tax rate of 35% the beta of the project using Equation 13-14 works out to 1.3262.

$$\beta_L^* = \beta_u\{1 + (1 - T^*) \times D^*/E^*\} = 1.0526(1 + 0.65 \times 2/5)$$
$$= 1.3262$$

This is the appropriate beta that must be used for computing the cost of equity of the telecom project of PIL.

Step V: Calculating cost of equity of the project After incorporating the business risk of the project and the leverage of the proposed venture in its beta, the cost of equity may be calculated using the CAPM reproduced here:

$$r_e = r_f + \beta \times (r_m - r_f)$$

For the telecom project of PIL using the risk-free return r_f of 6% and market return of r_m of 16% the cost of equity is 19.262%.

$$r_e = r_f + \beta \times (r_m - r_f) = 6 + 1.3262 \times (16 - 6) = 19.262\%$$

Step VI: Finding the discount rate The WACC of the telecom project of PIL that is to be used as discount rate is found by using the following equation:

$$\text{WACC} = w_e \times r_e + w_d \times r_d$$

The cost of equity is arrived at by using CAPM. Assuming the pre-tax cost of debt to be issued by PIL is 8%, the WACC for telecom project of PIL with debt at 40% of equity (debt–equity ratio at 2:5) would be:

$$5/7 \times 19.26\% + 2/7 \times 8\% \times (1 - 35\%) = 15.244\%$$

The pure-play approach as described above assumes that the telecom project of PIL will be able to raise debt at 8% and equity at 19.262%. In fact, both these figures will use the legacy of PIL as one entity. The debt capacity as depicted in the debt equity ratio of 2:5 for the project may be possible only because the firm's capital structure permitted such a financing pattern. The fact that other activities influence the project's financing pattern is ignored in the pure-play approach. Despite the limitation of pure-play technique, its use should not be discouraged. Using the firm's WACC as a matter of convenience would be more inappropriate.

In case pure-play is not available There are instances where pure-play firm is not available or its published data may not be too reliable. These situations may arise when a firm ventures into relatively newer markets/products or is a pioneer in the industry, or authentic dependable information is not available. Under these circumstances, the firm may choose to rely on its own data to that of others. However, the basic idea of pure-play approach, i.e., to construct the β consistent with risk of the cash flows is retained. The only exception is that the benchmarkfor constructing the β becomes firm's own β rather than the pure-play firm's β.

The steps involved here would be:

1. Have the β of firm as benchmark
2. Remove the effects of financial leverage
3. Adjust for operating leverage for revenue volatility
4. Adjust for operating leverage again for cost structure
5. Relever the β for financial leverage using the proposed capital structure with marginal weights, and finally
6. Use CAPM to arrive at the cost of equity and debt to be and find marginal WACC to be used as discount rate.

Let us take the case of PIL as taken earlier and assume no data is available for ITL. Even if it is available it is not considered matured enough to adequately depict the business characteristics. Instead, PIL considers its own information more reliable.

Another way to adjust the risk of an unrelated diversification project based on the beta of the firm itself is to adjust it for revenue volatility and cost structure apart from unlevering and relevering.

Assume its equity β and debt β are 1.10 and 0.20, respectively, which are fairly steady. This becomes the bench-mark now and the starting point to artificially construct β for telecom project. We decide to unlever this β of the financial leverage of PIL whose debt equity ratio is 3:10. We find the value of unlevered β of PIL using Equation 13-14:

$$\beta_u = \beta_d \frac{D(1-T)}{D(1-T)+E} + \beta_L \frac{E}{D(1-T)+E}$$

$$= 0.2 \times \frac{3 \times 0.65}{3 \times 0.65 + 10} + 1.1 \times \frac{10}{3 \times 0.65 + 10} = 0.95$$

This implies the β of PIL would be 0.95 if it were wholly financed by equity.

Now we estimate the revenue volatility of the telecom project in relative terms with respect to the economic activity. Assuming that the telecom revenues are 20% more volatile than the revenue of existing business, the revenue adjusted β for telecom project will be:

$$\text{Revenue adjusted } \beta = \beta_u \times \text{Relative Revenue Volatility}$$
$$= 0.95 \times 1.2 = 1.14$$

The other component of operating leverage is the cost structure. The returns for equity shareholders vary more if the proportion of fixed cost to total cost is higher just as was with the case with financial leverage. Hence, for a relatively higher proportion of fixed cost β should be higher and for lower proportion of fixed cost β would be lower. Assuming that the telecom business has only 15% fixed cost component while at present PIL's fixed cost component is 28%, then the adjustment for operational difference can be done as on similar lines as for revenue volatility as follows:

$$\text{Project's unlevered } \beta = \text{Rev. Adj. } \beta \left[\frac{1+\text{project's fixed cost}}{1+\text{firm's fixed cost}}\right]$$

$$= 1.14 \times \frac{1.15}{1.28} = 1.02$$

Now we have unlevered β of the project that has taken into account the revenue volatility, and cost structure differences. This adjusted beta needs to be modified for the financial leverage of the project. Assuming the project's debt–equity ratio of 2:5 the relevered β of the project can be found taking marginal tax rate of 35% and debt beta of 0.2 as before using the Equation 13-14.

$$\beta_u = \beta_d \frac{D(1-T)}{D(1-T)+E} + \beta_L \frac{E}{D(1-T)+E}$$

$$1.02 = 0.2 \frac{2 \times 0.65}{2 \times 0.65 + 5} + \beta_L \frac{5}{2 \times 0.65 + 5}$$

gives $\beta_L = 1.23$

This is the β of the equity of the project with the capital structure as above. Now we can find cost of equity using CAPM, cost of debt and finally the WACC to be used as discount rate for evaluation of the project as below:

Cost of Equity $r_e = r_f + \beta_L(r_m - r_f) = 6 + 1.23(16 - 6) = 18.3\%$

Cost of Debt $r_d = r_f + \beta_D(r_m - r_f) = 6 + 0.2(16 - 6) = 8\%$

WACC $r = r_e \times w_e + r_d \times w_d(1 - T) = 18.3 \times 5/7 + 8 \times 2/7 \times 0.65 = 14.56\%$

FACTORS AFFECTING COST OF CAPITAL

The foregoing discussion on the cost of capital would reveal that there are a host of factors that impact the cost of capital of the firm. The cost of different components of the capital is market determined. These are general factors and influence the cost of all firms. The prevailing yields in the debt markets would alter the expectations of debt suppliers. Because of the tax deductibility of the interest, the cost of debt is also influenced by the tax rate. The higher the tax rate, the greater is the tax shield on the debt and lesser is the cost of debt. Similarly, the returns in the stock market govern the expectations of equity suppliers. General economic conditions play a dominant role in the determining the market returns. Since all these factors keep changing with time the cost of capital cannot be said to be static in nature. It has to be constantly reviewed since not only the cost of individual components would change with time but also the weights of each components being market determined too would change.

Besides market-oriented factors that affect the cost of capital, in general for all the firms there are some critical firm specific factors that influence the cost of capital of the firm. Investment policy, dividend policy, and capital structure decisions are closely linked and each of them affects the cost of capital.

From the perspective of cost of capital, it is assumed that WACC would fairly represent the cost of capital. This applies only if the new investments are having similar risk profile as that of the current activity of the firm. In most cases it remains true as firms usually undertake projects in the same line of business. If there is unrelated diversification, care needs to be taken to adjust the cost of capital for risk.

Similarly, dividend policy and the capital structure are very closely inter-linked. We have worked out the cost of capital under implied assumptions of—(1) the firm follows dividend policy of constant pay-out; and (2) a target capital structure using market valued weights. In case of change in any of these, the WACC would undergo a change. Managers have to safeguard against such possible changes while evaluating projects that may necessitate changes in composition of cost of capital for use as discount rate.

SUMMARY

The cost of capital is an extremely important input requirement for capital budgeting decision. Without knowing the cost of capital, no firm can evaluate the desirability of the implementation of new projects. Cost of capital serves as a benchmark for evaluation.

The basic determinant of the cost of capital is the expectations of the suppliers of capital that are dependent upon the returns that could be available to them by investing in the alternatives. The returns provided by the next best alternative investment is called the opportunity cost of capital.

The weighted average cost of capital (WACC) is a composite figure reflecting the cost of each component of cost of capital multiplied by the weight of each component.

The cost of debt and the cost of preferred debt are easy to calculate because the cost of such means of financing is explicitly stated in the instruments. Preferred capital is like debt because of its prior claim on cash flows over shareholders. The cash flows of the instruments govern their costs. In case of debt, the effective cost of the debt reduces due to the tax saved on the interest payable on debt instruments. However, no such adjustment of the tax is required for preference capital. Flotation expenses increase the cost whenever fresh debt or capital is raised.

The cost of equity capital is the most difficult to determine because there is no legal binding to pay any compensation and no explicit mention of charges to be paid on such capital. The cost of equity capital is determined either by the dividend capitalization approach or the CAPM-based approach. The price to be used in any of the model is the market determined. β is the primary determinant of risk governs the cost of equity.

After the cost of each of the components is determined, they need to be multiplied by the respective proportions to arrive at WACC. The weights based on the target capital structure are most appropriate though the current capital structure may not conform. These weights can either be based on book values or the market values. Though book value weights are easy and more practical, the use of market value based weights is technically superior.

Further, since the cost of each component of capital does not remain constant as the quantum of funding increases, the incremental cost of raising funds is most appropriate as discount rate. The cost of incremental funding is referred to as the marginal cost of capital. In practice, this must be used in determination of the optimal capital budget.

The discount rate for appraisal of the projects must be appropriate to the risk of the project. In most cases, WACC adequately represents the risk since most projects selected by the firms belong to the line of activity. However, where the proposed project has substantially different risk profile, a risk-adjusted WACC must be used as discount rate for the cash flow. The most popular method by which such risks are incorporated is called a pure-play technique. The pure-play approach is based on the identification of a firm that most resembles the risk profile of the new project. The data of the comparable firm is first adjusted for its leverage to find an all equity beta, called unlevering and then re-adjusted for the proposed capital structure of the project, called relevering. The value of β so arrived is used in calculating the WACC.

KEY TERMS

Opportunity cost The returns foregone in the next best investment option is called opportunity cost.

Weighted average cost of capital WACC is the composite cost of capital with cost of each component of capital multiplied by its proportion in the capital structure.

Preference capital Preference capital is the capital where the fixed amount of dividend is paid with prior claim to that of shareholders. No dividend to equity shareholders can be paid unless claims of preference shareholders are satisfied.

Internal equity Internal equity refers to the retained earnings that are not distributed to the shareholders and are deployed in the business for its needs.

External equity External equity refers to the issue of fresh capital by the firm.

Flotation cost Flotation costs are the expenses incurred in mobilizing any kind of capital from the market.

Dividend capitalization model The dividend capitalization model states that the present value of dividend would be equal to the price of the share.

P/E ratio The price of the share divided by the earnings per share is called P/E ratio that is often used as a benchmark for valuation.

Marginal proportions The proportions of different sources of capital in raising the incremental finances are marginal proportions.

Book value weights The proportions of different sources of cost of capital based on the value as recorded in the books of the firm are book value weights.

Market value weights The proportions of different sources of cost of capital based on their market value are market value weights.

Marginal cost of capital The cost of raising incremental cost is called marginal cost of capital.

Unlevering β Elimination of financial leverage from observed β is called unlevering of beta.

Relevering β Incorporating the financial leverage to the unlevered β is called relevering of beta.

KEY FORMULAE

WACC $= w_e \times r_e + w_p \times r_p + w_d \times r_d$

Cost of perennial debt $r_d = \dfrac{C_t}{P_0}$

Cost of redeemable debt $P_0 = \sum_{t=1}^{N} \dfrac{C_t}{(1+r_d)^t} + \dfrac{R}{(1+r_d)^N}$

Post-tax cost of debt $= r_d(1 - T)$

Cost of preference capital $P_0 = \sum_{t=1}^{N} \dfrac{D_t}{(1+r_p)^t} + \dfrac{R}{(1+r_p)^N}$

Cost of equity as per DDM $r_e = \dfrac{D_1}{P_0} + g$

Cost of equity as per CAPM $r_e = r_f + \beta \times (r_m - r_f)$

Cost of equity after flotation cost

$$r_e = \frac{\text{Cost of internal equity}}{(1-f)}$$

$$= \frac{1}{(1-f)}\frac{D_1}{P_0} + g$$

Relationship between levered and unlevered β

$$\beta_u = \beta_L \frac{E}{D \times (1-T) + E} = \frac{\beta_L}{\{1 \times (1-T) \times D/E\}}$$

Beta adjustment for different cost structure

Project's unlevered β

$$= \text{Revenue Adjusted } \beta \left[\frac{1 + \text{project's fixed cost}}{1 + \text{firm's fixed cost}}\right]$$

Beta adjustment for revenue volatility

Revenue adjusted $\beta = \beta_u \times$ Relative Revenue Volatility

PRACTICE PROBLEMS

1. Cost of Debt and Preference Capital

Udhaar Enterprises Limited has borrowed from the market by issue of debentures with the coupon rate of 10.50%. It is a profitable enterprise paying 36% tax.

(a) What is the cost of debt if it sells (i) at par (ii) at 5% premium (iii) at 5% discount to the face value?

(b) If instead of debt, the firm had issued a preference share with the promised dividend of 10.5%, what would be the cost of preference share when it sells (i) at par (ii) at 5% premium (iii) at 5% discount to the face value?

(c) Why do you think that there is a difference in the cost of debt and preference capital despite identical features and cash flows?

Solution

(a) **Cost of debt:**

Coupon rate = 10.50% Face value = ₹100.00
Coupon Payment = ₹10.50 Tax = 36.00%
Current market price = ₹100.00

(i) Cost of perpetual debt = Coupon × (1 – T)/Market price
= 10.5 × (1 – 0.36)/100 = 6.72%

(ii) Market price at 5% premium to the face value = ₹.105.00
Cost of debt = 10.5 × (1 – 0.36)/105 = 6.40%

(iii) Market price at 5% discount to the face value = ₹.95.00
Cost of debt = 10.5 × (1 – 0.36)/95 = 7.07%

(b) **Cost of preference capital:**

Dividend rate = 10.50% Face value = ₹100.00
Dividend = ₹10.50
Current market price = ₹100.00

Cost of perpetual preferential capital = Dividend/Market price

(i) Cost = 10.5/100 = 10.50%

(ii) Market price = ₹.105.00
Cost = 10.5/105 = 10.00%

(iii) Market price = ₹95.00
Cost = 10.5/95 = 11.05%

(c) Difference in the cost of debt and cost of preference capital is due to tax treatment of dividend and interest. Interest on debenture is tax deductible while dividend is not and is paid out of post-tax profit.

2. Cost of Redeemable Debt and Preference Capital

Combined Metals Limited are planning a simultaneous issue of debenture and preference share. The features of the debenture and preference shares are as below:

	Debenture	Preference Share
Face value	₹100.00	₹100.00
Issue price	₹90.00	₹110.00
Coupon/Dividend	8.00%	12.00%
Term	10 yrs	10 yrs
Redemption price	₹110.00	₹100.00
Flotation cost	1.00%	2.00%

(a) Assuming a tax rate of 40%, find the cost of debenture and preference shares.

(b) What difference does it make to the shareholder if the capital is raised by issuing debenture or preference shares? Which is advantageous?

(c) If the impact on shareholders wealth is not equal by issue of instruments, why should Combined Metals Limited issue the disadvantageous instrument?

Solution

(a) The cost of debenture and preference share can be found by the returns that the cash flows of each instrument can afford. These are found as below:

Cash flows of the simultaneous issue — *Figures in ₹*

Year	Debentures Inflow	Debentures Outflow	Debentures Total	Preference Shares Inflow	Preference Shares Outflow	Preference Shares Total
0	90.00	0.90	89.10	110.00	2.20	107.80
1		4.80	–4.80		12.00	–12.00
2		4.80	–4.80		12.00	–12.00
3		4.80	–4.80		12.00	–12.00
4		4.80	–4.80		12.00	–12.00
5		4.80	–4.80		12.00	–12.00
6		4.80	–4.80		12.00	–12.00
7		4.80	–4.80		12.00	–12.00
8		4.80	–4.80		12.00	–12.00
9		4.80	–4.80		12.00	–12.00
10		114.80	–114.80		112.00	–112.00
Cost of debt = 7.08%				**Cost of preference capital =10.69%**		

Notes: *Cost is found by IRR of the cash flows.*
Inflows of instruments are equal to issue prices.
Outflows consists of flotation cost, interest/dividend, and redemption price.

(b) We can examine the impact of fund raising with different instruments by the changes that would be made to the shareholders income

The numbers of instruments that would be required to be issued to raise ₹100 are:

Nos. of debenture = 100/Issue price × (1–flotation cost)
= 100/90 × 0.99 = 1.1223

Nos. of pref. shares = 100/Issue price × (1–flotation cost)
= 100/110 × 0.98 = 0.9276

Assuming EBIT level of ₹100 and raising of ₹100 the impact on shareholders earnings would be:

	Debenture	*Preference Share*
Nos of instruments for raising ₹100	1.1223	0.9276
EBIT	100.00	100.00
Interest	8.98	—
PBT	91.02	100.00
Tax	36.41	40.00
PAT	54.61	60.00
Preference dividend	—	11.13
Income for shareholder	**54.61**	**48.87**

(c) By issue of preference shares the shareholders would be poorer by ₹5.74 for every ₹100 raised.

Issue of preference share is disadvantageous to the shareholders. The company may still like to issue the preference share because of non-binding obligation of dividend as against binding obligation of interest on debenture. Also it helps maintain the capital structure towards equity.

3. Cost of Debt and Coupon

Wiser Corporation is planning to raise debt from the market by issuing bonds for five years. Consistent with the reputation of the firm, the management wants to issue the bond at 10% premium to the face value. However it would be redeemed at par. Wiser Corporation needs to decide on the coupon rate of the bond in such a manner that the cost of debt does not exceed 2% over the current yield on 5-year government paper.

Assume that the coupons are payable annually on par value of ₹100. The current yield on 5-year government paper is 6%.

Solution

Current YTM	6.00%
Premium over YTM	2.00%
Cost of debt	8.00%

The relationship of coupon and issue price is stated as:
Issue price = Coupon × Annuity factor at YTM
+ Redemption price x Discount factor at YTM

Issue price = ₹110.00 Redemption value = ₹100.00

If coupon rate is c, then

$$c \times 3.9927 + 100 \times 0.6806 = 110$$

gives c = 10.50%

Calculation of PV factors	
Period of annuity = 5.00 years	Required rate of return = 8%
Present value of annuity for 5 years at 8.00% = PVIFA (8.00%, 5) =	3.9927
Period 5.00 = years	Required rate of return = 8%
Present value of Re 1 after 5 years at 8.00% = PVIF (8.00%, 5) =	0.6806

4. Cost of Debt and Market Price

Find the cost of debt when debenture issued at par is selling at a price of (a) ₹95 and (b) ₹105.

The details of the debenture are as below:

Coupon Rate	12%	Periodicity	Annual
Face Value	₹100.00	Redemption value	₹100.00
Coupon payment	₹12.00	Time to maturity	5 years
		Tax rate	35%

Solution

(a) Market price ₹95.00

Cash flows of the Debenture						Figures in ₹
Year	**0**	**1**	**2**	**3**	**4**	**5**
Market price	95.00					
Interest (Net of tax)		–7.80	–7.80	–7.80	–7.80	–7.80
Redemption						–100.00
Cash Flow	95.00	–7.80	–7.80	–7.80	–7.80	–107.80
Cost of debt = IRR of the cash flows of debenture = 9.09%						

(b) Market price ₹105.00

Cash flows of the Debenture						Figures in ₹
Year	**0**	**1**	**2**	**3**	**4**	**5**
Market price	105.00					
Interest(Net of tax)		–7.80	–7.80	–7.80	–7.80	–7.80
Redemption						–100.00
Cash Flow	105.00	–7.80	–7.80	–7.80	–7.80	–107.80
Cost of debt = IRR of the cash flows of debenture = 6.59%						

5. Cost of Equity using DDM

The shares of Indian Handicrafts Ltd is quoted on the stock exchange. The company paid a dividend of ₹8.50 last year. The market is expecting that the amount of dividend this year would be ₹9.50. If the market price of share of Indian Handicraft Ltd is ₹200, what is the cost of equity?

What would happen to cost of equity if the market revises expectations of dividend from ₹9.50 to (a) ₹9.60, (b) ₹9.70?

Solution

Last dividend ₹8.50 Expected Dividend ₹9.50

Current market price ₹200.00

The growth rate can be determined by the dividend amount

$D_1 = D_0 \times (1 + g)$

or $9.50 = 8.50\,(1 + g)$

gives $g = 9.50/8.50 - 1 = 0.1176$ or 11.76%

Cost of equity, $r_e = D_1/P_0 + g$

$= 9.5/200 + 0.1176 = 16.51\%$

Revised expectation of dividend	**₹9.60**	**₹9.70**
Revised growth rate	12.94%	14.12%
Expected market price = $D_1/(r_e - g)$	₹268.64	₹404.66
Cost of equity, E_1/P_0	16.51%	16.51%

The cost of equity would remain same because it is determined by earning potential and not how these earnings are distributed.

6. Cost of Equity Capital with CAPM

Beta Enterprises has been doing well on the Indian stock markets for past several years. Various analysts are trying to study the returns of Beta Enterprises with a broad based index in the market. According to them, the returns on the shares of Beta Limited change by a factor of 1.25 times as that of index.

If expectation of returns on the market is 14% while the returns on the government securities is 6.10%, what returns do you expect for Beta Enterprises?

Solution

Given

Risk-free rate of return, $r_f = 6.10\%$

Market Returns, $r_m = 14.00\%$

Beta of the stock, $\beta = 1.25$

Risk Premium, $r_m - r_f = 7.90\%$

Cost of equity as per CAPM, $r_e = r_f + \beta\,(r_m - r_f)$

$= 6.10 + 1.25(1400 - 6.10)$

$= 15.98\%$

7. WACC—Book Value, Market Value

Mentor Technologies Ltd is planning to raise capital from market by way of debt as well as equity.

Merchant bankers to the issue of debt and equity capital have advised as follows: The firm can issue a 12% debenture with face value of ₹1,000 redeemable at par after 8 years. Coupon shall be payable annually. The current yield in the market would not fetch them a price of more than ₹980 per debenture. The issue expenses would be 1.5% of the money mobilized.

For the equity issue the merchant bankers have advised that the company would have to offer a discount of 5% on the current market price of ₹120 per share. The company can go ahead with the plan of dividend of ₹6 as against ₹5 paid last year. The flotation cost would be 2% of the issue proceeds.

Following is the composition of the liabilities of the Mentor Technologies based on books of accounts and market values (all the securities of the firm are traded in the capital markets).

₹ crore	Book Value	Market Value
Equity	100	820
Reserves	400	
Debt	200	180
Total	**700**	**1000**

Assuming that the firm pays tax of 36%, answer the following:

(a) What is the cost of debenture after discount to face value and flotation costs?

(b) What is the cost of equity after allowing for discount to the current market price and the flotation costs?

(c) What would be the weighted average cost of capital based on (i) book value weights and (ii) market value weights?

Solution

(a) **Cost of debenture (debt)**

Face Value: ₹1000.00		Coupon:	12.00% on face value
Issue Price: ₹980.00		Flotation Cost:	1.50% of issue price
Redemption: ₹1000.00		Tax rate:	36.00%

All figures in ₹

Year	Issue Redemption	Flotation cost	Coupon Payment	Total cash flow
0	980.00	−14.70		965.30
1			−76.80	−76.80
2			−76.80	−76.80
3			−76.80	−76.80
4			−76.80	−76.80
5			−76.80	−76.80
6			−76.80	−76.80
7			−76.80	−76.80
8	−1000.00		−76.80	−1076.80
Cost of debt = IRR of cash flow = 8.29%				

(b) **Cost of equity**

Current market price	₹120.00
Discount for new issue	5.00%
Issue price	₹114.00
Flotation cost	2.00% of issue price
Last year's dividend	₹5.00
Expected dividend	₹6.00

Cost of equity can be worked out as under:

Cost of equity, $r_e = D_1/P_0 \times (1 - f) + g$

$D_1 = D_0 \times (1 + g)$

$6 = 5 \times (1 + g)$

$g = 6/5 - 1 = 1.2 - 1 = 0.2 = 20.00\%$

Cost of equity, $r_e = 6/114(1 - 0.02) + 0.2 = 25.37\%$

(c) (i) **WACC with book value weights**

	Book Value			
	₹ crore	Weight	Cost	Weighted cost
Equity	100	71.43%	25.37%	18.12%
Reserves	400			
Debt	200	28.57%	8.29%	2.37%
Total value	700			
WACC with book value weights				20.49%

(c) (ii) **WACC with market value weights**

	Market Value			
	₹ crore	Weight	Cost	Weighted cost
Equity	820	82.00%	25.37%	20.80%
Reserves				
Debt	180	18.00%	8.29%	1.49%
Total value	1000			
WACC with market value weights				22.30%

EXERCISES

Concept Review Questions

1. What is cost of capital and weighted average cost of capital?
2. What is the significance of weighted average cost of capital?
3. Why the cost of debt is adjusted for taxes while the cost of preference is not?
4. Despite no legal binding to pay dividend the cost of equity is not zero but is highest. Explain.
5. Compare dividend capitalization and capital asset pricing model approach to the determination of cost of equity.
6. Why do you think the CAPM-based approach is superior to dividend capitalization approach to determine the cost of equity?
7. What is the difference between internal equity and external equity and why should external equity cost more than the internal equity?
8. What is marginal cost of capital? How is it different from WACC? Can WACC ever exceed marginal cost of capital?
9. What are the advantages of using book value weights while computing WACC?
10. Why should one use market value weights in computation of WACC?
11. Between marginal cost of capital and WACC which one is a better discount rate and why?
12. What do you understand by unlevering and relevering of β, and why should it be done?

Critical Thinking Questions

1. If the cost of debt is far less than the cost of equity why do firms not finance entire funding requirement by way of debt?
2. A firm had issued three bonds at different points of time with total values of ₹5 crore, ₹10 crore, and ₹10 crore with different coupon rates of 8%, 10%, and 12%, respectively. It calculated the average cost of debt as 10.40% (shown below) and used it in the computation of WACC.

$$\frac{5}{25}\times 8\%+\frac{10}{25}\times 10\%+\frac{10}{25}\times 12\%=10.40\%$$

Was the firm right in using such a method?
3. A firm called PREFEQ explicitly stated that its target debt–equity ratio is 1:4. As of today, its debt–equity ratio stood at 1:3 with the costs of debt and equity at 8% and 20% respectively. It had new project costing ₹10 crore with an IRR of 18%. Striving to achieve its target capital structure it decided to finance the entire project by equity at the marginal cost of 20% and used it as discount rate only to reject the new project. Was PREFEQ right in its decision?
4. While using CAPM approach to find the cost of equity one is required to use a risk-free rate. There are two options of short-term T-bills or long-term dated securities the yield on which may be used as a reasonable substitute. Which of the two yields: on the T-bills or on the long-term dated securities is a better substitute.

Practical Assignments

1. Take the balance sheet of a large company like Reliance Industries Limited and calculate its weighted average cost of capital using book value weights and market value weights.

2. Analyse three public issues of equity of less than ₹100 crore, from ₹100 to 500 crore, and more than ₹500 crore and identify the expenses of flotations and their costs for each of them.

Numerical Problems

1. Cost of Perpetual Debt

Permanent Debt Limited keeps a fixed amount of debt in its books. It pays a coupon of 15%. Its debt sells at par in the market. What is the cost of debt if the firm pays 35% tax?

What is the cost of debt if it sells (a) at 5% premium, (b) at 5% discount to the face value?

2. Cost of Redeemable Debt

Dhatu Nigam Limited has decided to issue debentures with the face value of ₹100 and a coupon of 12% payable annually. The tenure of the debentures is 8 years when it would be redeemed at a premium of 5% to the face value. The flotation cost is placed at 5% of the issue price. The firm pays 40% tax. What is the cost of debt if the firm is able to market its debenture (a) at par, (b) at a price of ₹110, and (c) at a price of ₹90?

3. Cost of Perpetual Preference Capital

ABC Limited has issued 14% preference shares of ₹100 each. The current price of the preference shares is ₹100. What is the cost of preference capital for ABC Limited?

What would be the cost of preference capital if the price of preference shares is changed to (a) ₹90, and (b) ₹120?

4. Cost of Redeemable Preference Capital

ABC Limited has issued 12% preference shares redeemable at the end of 7 years at a premium of 10% with the face value of ₹100 but issued at ₹105 with a flotation cost of 5%. What is the cost of preference capital issued by ABC Limited?

5. Cost of Debt, Different Repayment Schedules

A debenture of ₹100 is issued with 5 years to maturity that carries an annual coupon of 15%. The debenture is issued at ₹100 only. The firm pays tax of 35%.

Find the cost of debt under the following conditions:

(i) When repayment is made at the end of 5th year.
(ii) When repayment is made in equal instalments of ₹20 each at the end of each year.
(iii) When repayment is made in equated annual instalments.

6. Cost of Debt with Flotation

Find the cost of debt for all the three options of repayment in Problem 5 with a flotation cost of 5%.

7. Cost of Debt and Market Price

Find the cost of debt when a new debenture is issued at a price of (a) ₹90, and (b) ₹110.

The details of the debenture are as below:

Coupon rate:	*15%*	*Periodicity:*	*Annual*
Face value:	₹100.00	Redemption value:	₹100.00
Coupon payment:	₹15.00	Time to maturity:	5 years
		Tax rate:	35%

8. Cost of Equity and Dividend

The current market price of shares of Syntex Garments is ₹300 with expected earnings level of ₹30. Find out the cost of equity when the proposed dividend per share is:

(i) ₹12, (ii) ₹15 and (iii) ₹18

What conclusion do you draw from the results of (i), (ii), and (iii)?

9. Cost of Equity: DDM

ABC Ltd has expected earnings at ₹30 per share of which it expects to distribute ₹15 as dividend. The market price of its share is ₹300.

Find the following:

(i) Current cost of equity.
(ii) Cost of new equity if the firm issues fresh shares at current market price but with a flotation cost of 5%.
(iii) Cost of existing equity if a dividend tax of 15% is imposed on the distributed earnings when (a) current level of dividend amount is maintained, (b) when dividend to the shareholders is reduced by the extent of dividend tax.
(iv) Cost of equity with dividend tax and flotation cost.

10. Cost of Equity Capital with CAPM

Apex Retails Limited has its shares quoted in the market for last several years. Its beta is estimated to be 1.20. The yield on T-bills is 5% and the market return is expected to be 15%. Find the cost of equity for Apex Retail Limited.

11. Cost of Equity, Capital Appreciation, and Dividend Yield

Metal Forge Limited has been growing at 20%. It had paid a dividend of ₹4.00 per share last year. The expected return by the investors of Metal Forge Limited is 14%.

The current growth is expected to last for another 5 years, and thereafter, it would be normal growth of the industry at 8%. Find out the following:

(i) The current price of the share.
(ii) The price of the share after 1, 2, 3, 4, and 5 years.
(iii) The capital appreciation and the dividend yield for each of the 5 years.
(iv) Confirm that the cost of equity remains at 14% for each of the year.

12. Determining Optimal Capital Structure

The financial analyst of a large corporation has prepared the following profile of cost of debt and equity for different levels of debt on the basis of his survey for his organization.

Debt (%)	*Cost of debt (%)*	*Cost of equity (%)*
0.00%		14.00%
10.00%	10.00%	15.00%
20.00%	11.50%	15.00%
40.00%	12.00%	15.50%
50.00%	12.50%	16.00%
60.00%	14.00%	18.00%
70.00%	15.00%	20.00%

Assuming that the survey has given reliable results, find out what is the optimal debt ratio for the firm, and what would be the cost of capital for the optimal? Also, plot the cost of capital for different levels of debt.

13. WACC—Book Value, Market Value and Specific Sources

Anand Industries has three sources of capital–equity shares, preference shares, and straight debt, costing 18%, 15%, and 7%, respectively.

The proportions of different kinds of capital as reflected in the balance sheet and as per the market values are as under:

Capital	Proportions	
	Book value	Market value
Equity	50%	70%
Preference	20%	15%
Debt	30%	15%

Find out the WACC based on (a) book values (b) market values.

Anand Industries wishes to raise the capital for an expansion programme with equity, preference shares, and debt at 15%, 35%, and 50%. What would be the cost of capital for the expansion programme?

14. Cost of Capital—Book Value Weights and Market Value Weights

Megha Steel Limited has capital employed of ₹100 crore whose market value is ₹150 crore as shown in the following table:

₹ crore	Book values	Market values
Equity Shares	30	130
Retained Earnings	45	
Preference Shares	7	6
Debentures	18	14
Total	**100**	**150**

The firm paid dividend of ₹20 last year, which has been growing at 8%. It also pays income tax at 35%. Following further information is available in respect of various sources of capital:

Equity shares: Fresh shares can be issued at a price of ₹220 with a flotation cost of 4%.

Debentures: Fresh debentures can be issued with following features:

Coupon Rate	12%	Periodicity	Annual
Face Value	₹100.00	Redemption value	₹100.00
Coupon Payment	₹12.00	Time to maturity	15 years
Issue Price	₹95.00	Flotation cost	1.50%

Preference shares: New preference shares can be issued as follows:

Dividend	15%	Flotation Cost	2.00%
Face Value	₹100.00	Issue Price	₹110.00

Find the cost of specific sources of capital. Find WACC based on (a) book values, and (b) market values.

CASE STUDY

Acme Consultancy Ltd

Acme Consultancy Ltd (Acme) is one of the world's leading information technology companies. Through its network delivery model, and innovative networking, it facilitates the global organizations to address their business challenges effectively. The motto of the organization is to continuously innovate and transform themselves to stay ahead of competition. Acme helps enterprises stay agile and respond better to changing market conditions by optimizing business processes, making their IT infrastructure resilient, and ensuring faster business results.

Acme continues to invest in new technologies, processes, and people, helping its customers to succeed. It works with businesses across industries to help them manage their operations in a better and efficient manner. The list of businesses facilitated by Acme consulting is long and wide and it ranges from banking to accounting, from security to manufacturing to logistics to name a few. Rightly, it calls itself as a business solution provider.

In the recent months, the company's stock price has been depressed, and management is concerned about re-examining the financial structure. The management is also concerned with the financing of forthcoming acquisitions: should Acme continue to take advantage of its strong cash flow, or should it begin to use debt financing? If it does raise additional debt, the proceeds will be used for a stock buyback. You have been asked to evaluate whether the company has an appropriate amount of debt.

In March 2007, the following information about Acme's current position was collected:

Summarized Income Statement	Mar 07 (₹ in crore)	Mar 06 (₹ in crore)	Mar 05 (₹ in crore)
Total Income	**15,155.86**	**11,303.41**	**8,146.33**
Expenditure	10,638.34	7,967.19	5,890.53
Profit before Interest, Depreciation, and Tax	**4,517.52**	**3,336.22**	**2,255.80**
Interest & Financial Charges	3.43	4.49	10.40
Depreciation	343.41	257.38	133.22
Profit Before Tax	**4,170.68**	**3,074.35**	**2,112.18**
Tax	413.39	357.48	280.76
Profit After Tax	**3,757.29**	**2,716.87**	**1,831.42**
Equity Dividend	1,125.39	660.56	552.13
Equity Dividend (%)	1,300.00	1,350.00	1,150.00
Earning per Share (₹)	36.66	53.63	36.60
Book Value	82.35	114.64	69.17

Current share price is ₹1,200 and the number of shares outstanding is 5,703,576. The beta of the stock based on the BSE index is 1.3. The total outstanding debt amounts to ₹50.74 crore with AAA rating for company's debt.

Market rate on bonds with rating AAA comes to 5.65% while the prevailing rate on 10-year Government bond is 4.80%. The company's marginal tax rate is 36.75%. The pre-tax profit for year 2008 is estimated to be ₹4,980.37 crore.

Summarized Balance Sheet	Mar-07 ₹ (in crore)	Mar-06 ₹ (in crore)	Mar-05 ₹ (in crore)
Sources of Funds			
Share Capital	97.86	48.93	48.01
Reserves and Surplus	7,961.13	5,560.40	3,273.04
Total Shareholders' Funds	**8,058.99**	**5,609.33**	**3,321.05**
Total Debt	**50.74**	**35.5**	**120.74**
Total Liabilities	**8,109.73**	**5,644.83**	**3,441.79**
Application of Funds			
Net Block	1,460.61	1,169.78	908.16
Capital Work in Progress	757.85	280	120.28
Investments	3,252.04	1,963.52	1,404.42
Current Assets, Loans, and Advances			
Inventories	12.06	22.94	
Sundry Debtors	2,799.80	2,325.83	1,468.05
Cash and Bank Balance	557.14	171.17	120.74
Loans and Advances	1,932.13	1,497.51	731.15
Less: Current Liablities and Provisions			
Current Liabilities	1,756.85	1,245.38	783.43
Provisions	905.05	540.54	527.58
Net Current Assets	**2,639.23**	**2,231.53**	**1,008.93**
Total Assets	**8,109.73**	**5,644.83**	**3,441.79**

Based on the company's business, its interest coverage and other factors, the following table displays what an increase in long term debt would do to the company's ratings and its cost of borrowing as well as key ratios:

Additional debt (in crore)	New Rating	Interest rate	Interest expense	Interest coverage ratio	Debt/ capitalization
0	AAA	6.76%	3.43	1216	0.63%
250	AAA	6.95%	20.80	189	3.71%
500	A+	7.35%	40.18	9114	6.79%
750	A–	8.15%	64.56	5586	9.87%
1000	BB–	9.45%	98.00	3966	12.96%

Corporate bond spreads: Basis points over treasury curve

Rating	1 yr	2 yr	3 yr	5 yr	7 yr	10 yr	30 yr	Typical Interest Coverage Ratios
AAA	40	45	50	60	74	85	96	>8.50
BBB+	105	115	128	145	165	186	208	2.50-3.00
B+	375	400	425	500	550	610	765	1.75-2.00
CCC	600	650	800	900	1025	1150	1300	0.80-1.25

The share price behaviour of Acme's shares was as follows:

Year	Price			
	Open (₹)	High (₹)	Low (₹)	Close (₹)
2004	538.00	669.00	479.28	667.75
2005	674.90	875.43	545.50	851.23
2006	853.50	1,225.00	727.50	1,218.60
2007	1,250.00	1,399.00	1,050.00	1,129.60
January	1,250.00	1,399.00	1,200.00	1,278.60
February	1,300.00	1,350.00	1,170.00	1,188.45
March	1,200.00	1,320.00	1,129.85	1,231.20
April	1,223.00	1,330.00	1,171.10	1,265.70
May	1,275.00	1,299.50	1,205.00	1,208.60
June	1,220.00	1,244.00	1,118.20	1,149.25
July	1,152.00	1,200.00	1,100.70	1,158.45
August	1,145.00	1,188.40	1,050.00	1,129.60

The industry debt–equity ratios for the past five years were as follows:

Years	Debt to equity
March 2003	0.06
March 2004	0.09
March 2005	0.08
March 2006	0.08
March 2007	0.10

Discuss

1. Should Acme take on additional debt? If so, why, and how much?
2. What is the weighted average cost of capital before and after the additional debt?
3. How much does Acme's value increase as a result of the lower cost of capital? What will be the estimated price per share after the company takes on new debt?

Note:

Assume that the additional value comes from the savings from a lower cost of capital each year, and that the savings will continue indefinitely.

In the CD

Finding WACC

CHAPTER

14 Real Options

LEARNING OBJECTIVES

The chapter is aimed at

- explaining what is meant by real option
- highlighting the difference between financial options and real options
- describing three important real options faced in corporate world:
  - option to delay
  - option to expand
  - option to abandon
- describing valuation of real options by discounted cash flow (DCF) method
- highlighting the limitations of DCF valuation in its application to real options
- applying binomial model with (a) equivalent portfolio approach and (b) risk neutral approach to the real options
- application of Black–Scholes model in valuing real options
- attempting a reconciliation of the values of the real option obtained by different methods

THE REAL VALUE OF REAL ESTATE!

Prithvi and Rooma, very accommodating couple for the last 20 years, walked into their rented home after visiting various sites for their new dream house that both of them wanted to own. After a long day on the roads in dusty hot summer, and sipping their cup of tea in the evening, they started discussing the merits and demerits of the various houses and the plots they had seen and evaluated over the past several months.

Rooma: We have been to so many properties in the last several weeks. We have yet to decide whether we want a ready-built flat or a vacant piece of land. I can shortlist only two properties that seem appropriate. First, the ready-built two-story condo in plush Model Town and second, the land of 250 square yards adjoining it.

Prithvi: Which one do you like?

Rooma: I would prefer the ready-built house.

Prithvi: Why?

Rooma: Simply because of financial reasons. The ready-built house costs us less. My back-of-the-envelope calculations indicate a saving of ₹25 lakh. The built house costs ₹75 lakh. And if we build a similar house on the adjoining plot, it would cost us ₹50 lakh. Add the price of the land of ₹50 lakh and the total would come to ₹100 lakh. This is a good ₹25 lakh more than the ready-built house, which has everything that we want.

Prithvi: But I prefer to buy the plot of land adjoining the flat we saw.

Rooma: We can have the same accommodation at ₹25 lakh cheaper. I do not find any justification for paying ₹25 lakh extra. What are your reasons?

Prithvi: Well, buying a piece of land gives us several advantages. I call them options.

Rooma: What options are you talking about? We only have option to buy the plot or the ready-built house.

Prithvi: No. I am talking of different kind of options we have with the plot.

Rooma: What are they?

Prithvi: In fact, there are many, but I can easily count four of them.

Rooma: What are they?

Prithvi: First, we have the option to delay. We have time to start construction any time within two years of possession. That way, we can phase out our investment and cash outflows. That gives us a lot of convenience of planning.

Rooma: But then, we lose the benefit of living in our own house and continue to pay the rent for the house. I do not value this option very much.

Prithvi: OK, but there is some value. And, I think it is of greater value than the rent saved. Of course, some of the value is lost by the extra rent that we pay during this period.

Rooma: What else?

Prithvi: Second, we have the flexibility to adjust the construction of the house in terms of sizes of bedrooms, number of toilets, etc. I am fond of some open space in the house. In the ready-built house, there is no open space. We can have this flexibility of designing the house exactly to our taste and style.

Rooma: Yes, that looks like some advantage. Even I found that the kitchen in the house to be somewhat small. I would like to have a bigger kitchen which can accommodate all modern gadgets.

Prithvi: Not only we have the flexibility of design but also have the flexibility to control the quality of building material, wood, fittings, etc., that we wish to use.

Rooma: Yes, I agree. But, what else? You were talking of four advantages.

Prithvi: Also we have the option to expand. In the already-built house, the builder has not left even an inch of space, and there is no scope of expanding the living space. We can expand the house to include more bedrooms on the third floor as and when we need it. I expect my parents to move with us once my father retires. So we have to provide enough space for them. Also, our son would get married in a few years. He too would need some space exclusive to him. How do we create it in the ready-built house? I do not know.

Rooma: Yes, that is right. But, we already have enough bedrooms in the ready-built house and capacity to accommodate more family members.

Prithvi: Well, another important option is to sell or abandon the idea. We can sell the plot any time till we start the construction. This is valuable for a period of two years at least.

Rooma: This is no great deal. We can sell the house too as we sell the plot.

Prithvi: There can be many more options. If you think you may identify some more advantages, but I can easily identify these four. Since you have these options attached with the plot that are not there with the already-built house, the plot naturally costs more.

Rooma: Yes, I agree, but the big question is how much more. And, how do you assess what extra value you should pay for these options and flexibilities?

Prithvi: Yes, we can sell the house too. But, there are always more buyers for a plot than for an already-built house. Therefore, you get a better price for the plot. To that extent, the plot becomes more valuable than the ready-built house.

Prithvi: Attaching a value to these options is really difficult. You see one of the factors would be the price you pay, the current market value, the time up to which the plot retains its character of a plot and does not become a house, the likelihood of appreciation in the value of the land, the interest rate prevailing. But to quantify this value is indeed a difficult task

Rooma: Why?

Prithvi: Simply because these options are not traded in the market place. It is difficult. If people start talking in terms of value, which they do by way of closed-door negotiations, it would become feasible to assess the real value of real estate options. Only a few sellers and buyers exist. They do not disclose every thing. Even if they disclose some detailas, there is no guarantee of truth. All these make determination of fair value indeed difficult. We may value them on the basis of similar assets on which more information is available and that is more authentic too.

Rooma: This realization is enough for me. You value these options the way you like.

Prithvi: Yes, I believe a plot is worth more than the area it comprises because of the choices or options it offers.

Unable to comprehend fully what Prithvi was talking and under pressure of time to prepare for dinner, Rooma excused herself to proceed to the kitchen.

INTRODUCTION

Strategic decisions are not as straightforward as routine capital budgeting problems. Firms and managers usually have an option to invest in real assets. Standard capital budgeting problem is solved by the discounting of cash flows at an appropriate discount rate to arrive at an NPV. If this happens to be positive we go ahead with the project, else we reject it. Traditional capital budgeting problems assume no action once the project is accepted or rejected on the basis of discounted cash flows. The implied assumption is that nothing can be altered once the decision is taken.

In real life situations, the problems are not as clearly defined as is assumed in capital budgeting exercises. There remain

Routine capital budgeting exercise of discounting the cash flows to find NPV is flawed because values so arrived ignore the managerial actions that are available later.

substantial ambiguities about the timing of investment, gaining or losing the competitive advantage as time elapses, the strategic position of the firm in the competitive world. Such strategic decisions often relate to expenditure of research and development where the outcome of the efforts as well as cash flows is totally unknown. In fact, the firm has an option of whether to invest or not, and if yes when to escalate the capital investment. If the initial outcome is not on expected lines, the firm has to decide whether or not to abandon the effort.

Standard techniques to evaluate capital budgeting decisions consider only the current information. It assumes that all managerial actions are absent once the cash flow estimates are prepared. In practice, this is not the case. Capital budgeting decisions are not passive and static. Instead they are subject to managerial actions with several options as time progresses. For example, after having implemented a project, managers have the option of reducing capacity utilization or undertake intensive advertising campaign if volumes are not picking up. On the other hand, if the product finds more than expected acceptance the managers have options to increase production, raise prices, develop more product variants, etc. The list of future course of actions available is endless. In fact, each capital budgeting decision is a complex set of options.

Sometimes these options embedded in the capital budgeting proposals are quite explicit. For example, the firms always have the right to exit anytime after the project is undertaken, though this possibility is not considered while projecting the cash flows. Capital budgeting decisions are also strategic in nature, the value of which is ignored in discounted cash flow (DCF) techniques. For example, an R&D effort to develop a new product would most likely be a negative NPV project and, hence, would most likely be rejected if standard procedure of evaluation is adopted. First, a firm has to make efforts to develop a product, and test the market before it can decide to set up a full plant, which is a standard capital budgeting problem. The decisions to establish developmental facilities and to test market the product are strategic decisions a firm has to take.

In the standard capital budgeting exercise the value of these managerial actions is ignored. Techniques based on the DCF approach assume that once the action has been taken the possibility of changes in cash flows due to managerial action does not exist. This holds good for financial assets like stocks and bonds where once purchased, the investor does not have any control over the cash flows attributable to the financial asset. In case of real assets there is some leeway always available to influence the cash flows of the project, sometimes substantially at other times marginally.

All capital budgeting proposals have some options available in them. The options available on real assets are called real options as distinct from financial options.

KINDS OF REAL OPTIONS

Three basic real options are – option to delay, option to expand and option to abandon, besides options that allow managerial flexibility for adjusting prices, volumes, shutting and re-opening, etc.

As distinct from financial options, the options on real assets are referred to as real options. Firms and managers usually have three different kinds of options on the projects and are referred as follows:

- Option to delay the project,
- Option to expand the project, or
- Option to abandon the project.

Option to Delay

Also referred to as option to wait, the option to delay a project refers to the decision of timing the commencement of the project. Managers have several choices as to the right time to start a project. The conflict arises while considering the pros and cons of being an early bird. Starting early may be beneficial on one hand while on the other hand it may also mean greater risk. Firms may face a choice of starting now or a year later. They are mutually exclusive projects. Delaying a project may mean leaving the field open to competitors and foregoing the advantage of early bird and capitalizing on the market share acquired in the nascent stage. The option to delay is a valuable one where there exists some kind of exclusivity about the venture or where the entry barriers are substantial. It is a meaningless option if competitors can start the same project.

In the strategic sense, no project is acceptable merely because it has positive net present value now. It is possible to have a greater net present value if the project is delayed. This may happen due to greater certainty of cash flows, reduction in discount rate, expanding markets due to increased awareness, etc., all or which go to increase the net present value. Similarly, no project can be permanently rejected merely because it has a negative net present value now. It may turn positive later due to greater demand, higher prices, lack of competition, reduced capital cost, etc.

Option to Expand

The option to expand is practised by firms exploring new markets and new products. Capacity expansion to meet increased demand also provides an option to expand the size of the project. This is also referred to as growth option. Firms also have options to start a pilot project and depending upon its outcome, may decide to go for full-fledged investment later. Normally, the data available for starting a pilot project is uncertain and inadequate. The pilot project may be having a negative NPV, and, therefore, may be rejected. But it provides a competitive edge to the firm and the possibility of expansion at a later stage. Starting the pilot may be well worth the effort.

Similarly, increasing price or increasing production adds value to the project as cash flows improve and so does the NPV. While projecting the cash flows, we assume constant prices and expected volumes and, therefore, underestimate the value of the project by not considering the value of the option to expand, the biases of managers notwithstanding. Most capital budgeting exercises are done on steady assumptions.

Option to Abandon

The option to abandon is the option to discontinue operations before the project completes its useful life. Normally, the cash flows are projected for the entire useful life of the project and rarely do we account for the possibility of the firm making an early exit. Having undertaken a project on its promising future, the expected cash flows of the project may not materialize. Under such situations, the firm always has an option available to abandon the project and realise salvage value, as doing so may be more beneficial than continuing the business.

Similarly, scaling down the operating level or suspending operations temporarily are the options available that reduce the cash flows and the NPV. By ignoring the value of such an option we are overstating the cash flows and the NPV of the project in a standard capital budgeting exercise.

These embedded options in the strategic capital investment add value to the project. This value must be considered while evaluating the capital budgeting decision. The value of these options sometimes makes a negative NPV of the project worthy of favourable consideration. The strategic value of these options is significant and should not be ignored as they create further opportunities for the firm that can be exploited later. The firms that recognize such values tend to outperform the competition.

The options available add value to the projects that is not captured in standard capital budgeting exercise.

The identification of options and valuing them is tricky proposition since the business scenario is complex. Several options may be built into a single business scenario. For example, assume that an infrastructure development firm is considering the construction of a road to connect two towns that reduces the distance and time of travel. However, the level of traffic between the towns is low and the toll charges have a ceiling prescribed by the government. These factors make the investment as a negative NPV project. However, this project may have multiple options embedded in it, simultaneously. The construction project may have an option to grow (expand from a single to a double lane), or an option to abandon (handover the project to government at a predetermined price after some years), or an option to delay (deferring the project till more traffic is generated or toll ceiling gets revised upwards). All of these flexibilities will add value to the project. More importantly, if valued it can convert a negative NPV project into a positive one.

While spotting options is difficult and requires substantial managerial foresight, valuing these options is equally tricky and requires deeper mathematical skills. Most options are valued on the basis of the tools developed for valuation of financial assets, which are traded and where data required for valuation is available rather easily. Besides inadequacy of data for valuation of real options, the ambiguity in description of opportunities through real options also poses considerable problems. Valuing real options by the tools developed for valuing options on financial assets is the popular alternative available currently, though other tools like decision trees are also available.

Real options are strategic in nature and are difficult to value in a well-defined mathematical model or framework.

In this chapter, we shall be valuing these options on real assets by drawing an analogy from financial assets.

DIFFERENCES IN FINANCIAL AND REAL OPTIONS[1]

Before we attempt valuation of real options on the basis of financial options, let us consider the distinguishing features that will help explain the distortions in valuation of real options.

Real assets are not traded Principles used in option pricing theory assume a set up of equivalent portfolios. The call option can be replicated by owning the underlying the asset by borrowing at a risk-free rate. This replication has the same pay off as that of call option and, hence, the two must trade at the same price to prevent arbitrage. This implies that both the call option as well as replicated portfolio are widely traded assets. Such an assumption, in case, of real assets is far from reality, as the underlying assets, which are the cash flows of the project itself do not have many buyers and sellers, and as such are not tradable. Valuing real options, as if they are financial options demands conclusions with care.

Real options can be valued on the basis of models for options on financial assets. However real options are significantly different and make the applicability of valuation models doubtful.

Variance of real options is difficult to estimate Another difficulty with real option is the estimate of its variance. It is extremely difficult to obtain variance of the projects though techniques such as simulation, scenario analysis, etc., exist. In case of financial assets, it is far easier to obtain the estimate of variance because the price data is available. The option pricing for financial assets assumes that this variance remains constant over the period of option. Since financial assets are short-term, the assumption seems valid. For real options this assumption cannot hold as most real options are long-term in nature. Even if variance of the project may be obtainable it cannot be regarded as constant over the life of the option.

Exercise of real options is time consuming Exercise of real options is a time consuming process unlike financial options where the exercise takes place rather instantaneously. Exercise of call option on a stock can be done the moment the stock price exceeds exercise price and whenever the investor desires. In contrast, exercise of real options such as setting up additional capacity will require substantial time. This gestation period means

[1]*Source*: Damodaran, Aswath, *Corporate Finance: Theory and Practice*, John Wiley & Sons Inc.

a substantial delay from the time the decision to exercise was made to the time the exercise is actually implemented. The benefits of exercise of the option accrue much later than the decision to exercise was made. Effectively it means that the option period is lesser than what appears to be.

Terms of exercise of real options are not clearly defined Further, the terms of exercise of financial options are well defined. In case of real options this right to exercise is ambiguous. Also, the actual exercise of the real option is also doubtful and deferred due to human behaviour. Exercise of financial options requires only economic and financial considerations while the exercise of real options involves subjectivity and managerial prudence. The data required to value real options and the considerations to exercise the same are not as well defined as that of options on financial assets.

VALUING REAL OPTIONS

Although valuing real options is complex, here we attempt to value some simple looking real options to provide insights to the valuation process. We have attempted to value each of the three kinds of real options described above by three different methods using—(1) DCF approach; (2) binomial model; and (3) Black–Scholes formula. It is pertinent to mention here that one would not get identical results with all the three possible approaches for various reasons, some of which are discussed here.

OPTION TO DELAY—TIMING DECISION

Some high technology firms engaged in developmental work often face a situation regarding the timing of the investment. When a product is in the preliminary stage the doubts over its commercial viability or success are rather high. Under such situations a firm may prefer to wait since uncertainty reduces as time elapses. Making an investment earlier than warranted exposes the firm to greater risk, which can be reduced significantly if the firm waits a while to have clarity over the future scenario.

Option to delay is the flexibility available to the management to time the implementation of the project.

The apprehensions of the firm to invest now, as compared to later may emanate from any reason. Normally, the demand situation is fluid for new products or the products are in the infancy stage and still require some refinements. An unrefined product may not receive a great response from the customers and may kill the future market. The firm may have to make an extra effort to launch a more refined product later. At the same time, if not launched now, the firm may be apprehensive of losing business to competition, which may take greater initiative and show more entrepreneurship. The firm may not want to lose the advantages normally associated with an early bird. Under such circumstances, the option to delay the investment is ruled out since the firm's competitors would introduce the product anyhow.

However, in some circumstances where the firm has exclusivity by way of a right or a patent the option to delay the implementation or timing of the investment is somewhat a matter of choice.

Value Option to Delay with DCF Method

One way to value an option to wait is standard DCF analysis. In the nascent stage cash flows are uncertain. In terms of financial management this uncertainty and ambiguity is reflected in the negative NPV at present, calling for its rejection but strategically the managers are not inclined to do so. The dilemma arises due to negative NPV of the project. The DCF technique gives the decision criteria as now or never. If the NPV is negative we do not consider the project. But future potential may be large enough to more than offset the negative NPV of the project if undertaken now. Under these situations another alternative emerges, i.e., to wait until the uncertainty about the project reduces to an acceptable level. In terms of DCF valuation we expect the NPV of the project to improve and turn positive either due to improved cash flows or reduction in discount rate.

Merely because NPV of a project is positive it is not necessary that the project must be implemented now. By deferring the project one may attain higher NPV.

The rule The standard technique of capital budgeting to evaluate the timing decision is to find out NPVs of the different timing options and choose the one that has the maximum NPV.

Let us consider a simple example to illustrate the decision making process.

Assume that a software firm, SoftBank has developed a new banking product and is uncertain about its demand potential. SoftBank expects the product to have a life of four years and its launch will cost ₹100 lakh today. SoftBank knows that there is no competitor emerging in the product developed. If the firm faces a good demand for its product the annual cash in flows are expected to be ₹50 lakh. However, if the demand is not good the annual cash flows will reduce to ₹30 lakh. The managers at SoftBank estimate equal likelihood of the 'good' and 'not so good' demand scenario. The expected annual cash flow would be ₹40 lakh ($0.50 \times 50 + 0.50 \times 30$). With a 12% discount rate considered appropriate for the risk of the cash flows the expected NPV of the project if launched now is ₹21.49 lakh:

$$\text{NPV} = \frac{40}{1.12} + \frac{40}{1.12^2} + \frac{40}{1.12^3} + \frac{40}{1.12^4} - 100 = ₹21.49$$

With a positive NPV, the project must be implemented now. However, some managers of SoftBank feel that it is worthwhile to wait for another year for the launch of the product, as the preferences of the customers will be better known and there is no sign of competition emerging at least till the next year. The cost of launching the product a year later is no different than what it is now. The decision to implement a year later will depend upon the demand scenario prevailing then. If the demand remains

Table 14-1 The option to delay for Softbank

(₹ lakh)

	Year 0	1	2	3	4	NPV	Prob p	p × NPV
OPTION I: Launch now								
GOOD								
Cash flow	(100.00)	50.00	50.00	50.00	50.00			
PV	(100.00)	44.64	39.86	35.59	31.78	51.87	0.50	25.93
NOT GOOD								
Cash flow	(100.00)	30.00	30.00	30.00	30.00			
PV	(100.00)	26.79	23.92	21.35	19.07	(8.88)	0.50	(4.44)
						Expected NPV		**21.49**
OPTION II : Launch a year later								
GOOD								
Cash flow	(100.00)	50.00	50.00	50.00	50.00			
PV at Year '0'	(89.29)	39.86	35.59	31.78	28.37	46.31	0.50	23.16
NOT GOOD								
Cash flow	—	—	—	—	—			
PV	—	—	—	—	—	—	0.50	—
						Expected NPV		**23.16**
						Discount rate used is 12%		

good SoftBank must go ahead with the launch else, it must drop altogether (this would be an option to abandon).

The above situation can be considered as following two mutually exclusive options and the decision will be based on the rule of higher NPV.

Option I : Launch now
Option II : Launch a year later

As a first step, we compute the NPV of the project for immediate launch. If we considered the NPV of Option I, being positive we would have gone ahead with immediate implementation foregoing the Option II. We cannot let Option II lapse unless immediate launch proves a better choice. To choose between the two we need to compare NPVs of both the options. The expected NPVs of Option I and Option II are computed in Table 14-1.

Option to delay a project (a) helps in reducing the uncertainties of the cash flows and (b) provides for learning. Therefore it adds value to the project.

The expected NPV of Option I is ₹21.49 lakh and that of Option II is ₹23.16 lakh. Since the expected NPV of Option II is greater, the product must be launched a year later. The value of the option to wait for one year, therefore, is the difference of the two NPVs, i.e., ₹1.67 lakh. We have assumed the following here:

1. The firm implements the project if the demand scenario is 'good' in Year 1.
2. Firm abandons the project if the demand scenario is 'not so good' in Year 1.
3. The initial outlay and the cash flows from for next four years remain same.
4. The discount rate too remains same at 12%.

While first two assumptions seem valid, the last two may be challenged. The annual cash flows for the life of the project may turn out to be more or less than ₹50 lakh. If competition catches up, the likely cash flows may reduce and in case the demand proves better than expected they may increase.

The NPV of the option to wait is higher by ₹1.67 lakh being the difference of NPVs of Option II and Option I. Note that all variables of the DCF technique are the same under both the options. In fact, the NPV of Option II will be somewhat different because of two reasons. First, the initial investment of ₹100 lakh in year one is certain and therefore, discounting it at the current cost of capital is not justified. This investment must be discounted at a much lower rate than the WACC. Some recommend the use of risk-free rate. This will increase the value of the initial investment and decrease the NPV of the delay option. Second, the use of the same WACC under both the options is also fallacious because of increased certainty of the cash flow in option to delay. Under Option II we do not make an investment if low demand is experienced in year one. Therefore, the discount rate under Option II should be lower than the one used in Option I, not because the rates have fallen or changed but because there is less uncertainty under Option II than under Option I. This will increase the NPV of the delay option.

Higher NPV of the project when delayed indicates that the option to wait is valuable.

Likewise, if there are other options of different timing of investments are available the same may be analysed utilising the DCF technique and comparing expected NPVs to choose the option with largest NPV.

Value Option to Delay with Binomial Model[2]

Since there are only two possible situations, the timing option for SoftBank is tailor made to the binary model of option pricing. The situation for the SoftBank is displayed in Figure 14-1. The present value, in case the demand is high, is ₹151.87 lakh being the present value of the annual cash flows of ₹50 lakh discounted at WACC of 12%. Similarly, the present value of the cash inflows, in case the demand is not so good is, ₹91.92 lakh with an annual cash flows of ₹30 lakh.

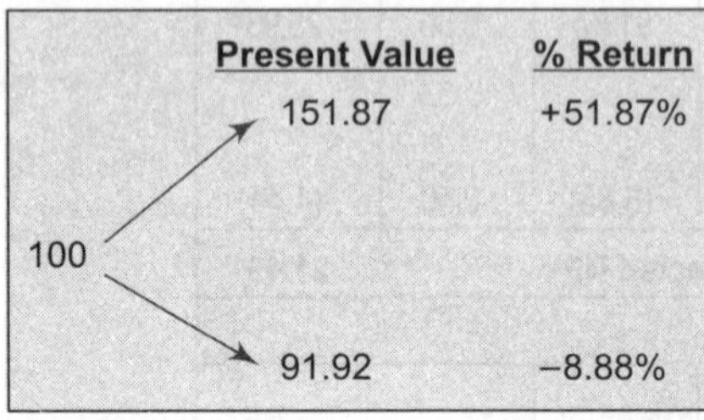

Figure 14-1 *Option to wait; binary option pricing*

The firm has the option to delay by one year implying, thereby, that it implements the project with exercise price of ₹100 lakh. In case the demand is good the firm implements the project and the pay off is ₹51.87 lakh. In case the demand is not so good, the firm does not implement. The pay off of the call option in that case is nil.

Binomial method of valuation of financial option can be applied to value the real options too.

We adopt the risk neutral method to value the call option. Assuming that the probability of high demand is p, then under the risk neutral valuation the pay off of the two branches must yield return equal to risk-free rate taken as 9%. Then:

$$p \times 51.87\% + (1 - p) \times (-8.88\%) = 9\%$$

$$p = 29.43\%$$

With a probability of 29.43%, the value of the call is computed at ₹15.26 lakh.

$$\text{Value of the call} = 0.2943 \times 51.87 + 0.7551 \times 0$$
$$= ₹15.26 \text{ lakh}$$

The option pricing through binomial model suggests that the option to wait is worth ₹15.26 lakh as against the NPV of the project at ₹21.49 lakh, if implemented today. Therefore, SoftBank must implement the project now. It is not worth waiting for another year.

Discounted cash flow and binomial option valuation Here we face a contradiction in the outcomes by DCF valuation and the binomial model. Which of them is correct? It is hard to disbelieve the DCF approach because it has been used so successfully in financial framework. However, we must point out the deficiencies of the DCF analysis when the situation involves options. In the DCF approach, we made two vital assumptions—first was regarding the probability of the demand being good at 50% and second was regarding the discount rate of 12%. The probability assigned to the demand being good was subjective and each individual would assign different values depending upon his perception. The NPV, therefore, would be different for different persons. On the contrary, option valuation by binomial method is independent of the individual's expectations and perceptions. It is more objectively defined.

Second, we assumed a discount rate of 12% for all situations. While valuing an option there are contingent situations, which change the risk of the cash flows. Here, the option to wait includes a decision not to implement the project if in the first year the demand faced is not so good. The risk faced in such a situation would be zero. There cannot be a single discount rate that captures all the situations and corresponding risks. We necessarily have to use different rates of discounting the cash flows for different situations. The validity of using single discount rate is questionable. Valuation of option however, is independent of the individual's preferences for probabilities and the discount rate.

Due to the presence of option the risk profile of the cash flows changes in each scenario and therefore standard DCF analysis is not suitable because no single rate of discount can capture all the risks of the cash flows.

Under the risk neutral assumption in binomial option pricing, we neither need the probabilities of the different demand scenarios nor do we need a discount rate. With the binary model, taking into account the contingent situations, the use of DCF method is inappropriate. However, which of the two methods gives an accurate result remains a moot point.

Option valuation is dependent upon current price of the underlying asset. Current price is assumed to contain the probability estimates. Risk neutral method implies probability of facing upside demand of 50 lakh per annum of 29.43% as against the assumed figures of 50% in the DCF method. The other determinant of the option price is the risk. The risk is supposed to be contained in the estimates of the volatility. This also means that the implied volatility in the binary model[3] is 41.78% as against 28.00% in the DCF method, calculated later in the chapter.

Value Option to Delay with Black–Scholes Model

The binomial model takes care of two possible future values of the underlying asset. We can use Black–Scholes option pricing model (BSM) to value the option to wait, which provides further insight to analysis, as it allows all possible values and continuous compounding. The BSM developed for pricing financial options can be used to value real options too though with certain limitations as stated in the earlier part of this chapter.

Note that the option to wait resembles a call option on a stock (option to buy at predetermined price within specified time), and we can use BSM to value the option to wait. To value this call option we require the following five inputs:

1. Exercise Price E
2. Expiration Time t
3. Risk-free rate r_f
4. Spot Price of the underlying asset S
5. Variance of return σ^2

---

[2]For description of binomial method of option pricing refer to the appendix to the chapter in the CD

[3]The volatility implied in the binary option pricing is given by $(1 + u) = e^{\sigma\sqrt{t}}$

Here, the first three inputs are straightforward and do not require much explanation. The exercise price E is ₹100 lakh, the value of initial investment. The time to expiry t of this option is one year. And the risk-free rate r_f can be obtained from the yield on the government securities. Let us assume this at 6%.

The underlying asset on the option is the cash flow of the delayed project. The expected present value of the cash inflows only of the project (not the expected NPV which is the intrinsic value of the option) will be equivalent to the spot price, S. The spot price of the underlying asset values can be arrived as below:

Present Value of inflows; the spot price (₹ lakh)

	Year					PV	Prob	p
	1	2	3	4	5		p	× PV
Cash flow	—	50.00	50.00	50.00	50.00			
PV	—	39.86	35.59	31.78	28.37	135.60	0.50	67.80
Cash flow	—	30.00	30.00	30.00	30.00			
PV	—	23.92	21.35	19.07	17.02	81.36	0.50	40.68
Present Value at t = 0, S								**108.48**

The last input required is the variance of returns. We need to compute the variance of the expected returns on the option to delay at the time when the option expires, i.e., after one year. The value of the underlying asset at the expiration is as below:

Present Value of inflows at expiry of the option (₹ lakh)

	Year				PV	Prob	p ×
	1	2	3	4		p	PV
Cash flow	50.00	50.00	50.00	50.00			
PV	44.64	39.86	35.59	31.78	151.87	0.50	75.93
Cash flow	30.00	30.00	30.00	30.00			
PV	26.79	23.92	21.35	19.07	91.12	0.50	45.56
Present Value at t = 1							**121.49**

Note that the expected value of the asset at the time of expiration is 12% higher than the values at the beginning of the option period as the cash flows are discounted at WACC of 12%.

Calculating Variance of Option

	Expected Price at t = 1 (₹ lakh)	Spot Price (₹ lakh)	% Return	Prob.	p × Return	p × dev²
Good	151.87	108.48	40%	0.50	0.20	0.0392
Not Good	91.12	108.48	−16%	0.50	(0.08)	0.0392
Expected Return					**12%**	
Variance						**0.0784**
Standard Deviation						**28.00%**

One standard model of valuing options is Black–Scholes option pricing formula developed for valuing options on financial assets.

The variance of the call option is 0.0784, which is equivalent to the standard deviation of 0.28 (28.00%). Now all the inputs for valuing the options are available for using Black–Scholes Model applicable for valuing financial options. The Black–Scholes Option Pricing model for valuing call options is reproduced below as Equation 14-1:

$$c = \mathrm{S}N(d_1) - Xe^{-rt}N(d_2)$$

$$\text{where} \quad d_1 = \frac{\ln(S/X) + (r + \sigma^2/2)t}{\sigma\sqrt{t}}; \text{ and} \qquad (14\text{-}1)$$

$$d_2 = \frac{\ln(S/X) + (r - \sigma^2/2)t}{\sigma\sqrt{t}} \quad \text{or} \quad d_2 = d_1 - \sigma\sqrt{t}$$

The values of the input are:

Spot Price, S	₹108.48 lakh
Exercise Price, X	₹100.00 lakh
Time to expiry, t	1 year
Interest Rate, r_f	6%
Standard Deviation, σ	28%

Inserting these values in Equation 14-1 we find the value of the call option to be ₹19.83 lakh. Therefore, the value of the option to delay by one year is ₹19.83 lakh, as per option pricing model.

It may be observed that the NPV of the option is lower than the NPV of the project if implemented today (₹21.49 lakh). Option pricing method recommends implementation now. The NPV of the delayed project is computed as ₹23.16 lakh as per DCF method and it recommends delaying implementation by a year. How do we reconcile the contradiction?

The answer possibly lies in the assumptions of option pricing not holding good. The standard deviation of the project is computed with the limited number of scenarios and, hence, may not be reflecting the variability truly. Options derive their values from the volatility. The larger the variance, the greater is the value of the option. The implied volatility of the cash flow appears to be higher than what is assumed in the option pricing model. However, our failure to accurately project the variance of the cash flows in the real world situations should not be treated as a deterrent to the use of the model. Instead, we must strive for a better estimate of volatility.

OPTION TO EXPAND

Option to expand concerns the ability of the firms to improve cash flows subsequently.

Many strategic situations demand initial investment in the initial stages despite its negative NPV because it provides the firm with an opportunity to make further investment, which is profitable enough to compensate for the loss incurred in the first investment. Firms cannot let go the initial investment opportunity simply because they lose more profitable business that arises subsequently as consequence to the initial investment. We shall examine how to value such opportunity to expand the business that is basically embedded in the first investment.

Consider a firm, GrowMotors, which is developing an electric car that requires no fuel and works on batteries and solar energy. The initial cost of the project of developing the pilot model is estimated at ₹200 crore. The product is new and offers considerable advantages over usual petrol driven cars. However, the selling price is relatively high and the new car suffers from a drawback of low speed. Since the product is high priced and cannot run beyond the speed of 50 kmph, the consumer response regarding its acceptability is doubtful. Based on the estimates for the next three years, the cash flows are projected evenly at ₹75 crore, annually (assumed for simplicity). The project has a negative NPV of ₹13.49 crore as can be seen from the Table 14-2, and, therefore, not worthy of consideration. The discount rate used is 10% being the risk adjusted WACC considered appropriate for the risky venture of electric car.

Table 14-2 GrowMotors—launch of electric car (Phase I)

Discount Rate 10% (₹ crore)

	Year			
	0	*1*	*2*	*3*
Cash flow	(200.00)	75.00	75.00	75.00
Present Value	(200.00)	68.18	61.98	56.35
Net Present Value	(13.49)			

However, this project has an option to grow embedded in it. GrowMotors is engaged in continuous and sustained developmental work and is confident of coming out with an improved model. It expects to remove the deficiencies of the car in the next three years. Let this be called Phase II, that would commence in the third year. It will cost another ₹600 crore to launch the improved model in terms of the present value at Year 3. This is clearly a call option with an exercise price of ₹600 crore that is available only when the Phase I is implemented and arises only when the present investment of ₹200 crore is made now. Depending upon the experiences gained in the period of initial launch, the decision to introduce the Phase II will be made. However, at present the management expects any of the following two scenarios:

1. 60% probability of facing a good demand with cash flow of present value of ₹1,000 crore providing NPV of ₹400 crore in Year 3, or
2. 40% probability of facing a poor demand with cash flow of present value of ₹300 crore providing NPV of ₹–300 crore in Year 3.

This is depicted in Figure 14-2.

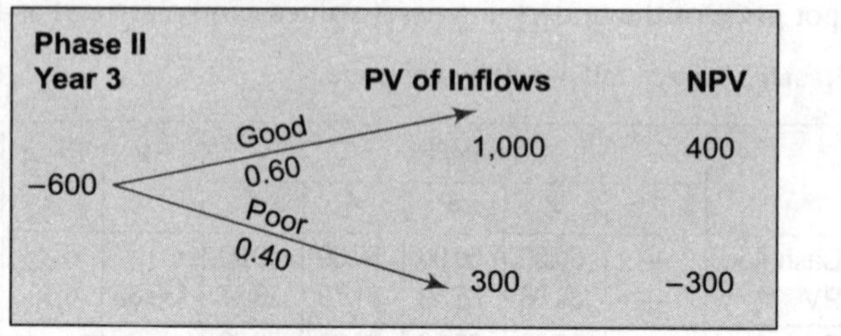

Figure 14-2 Option to expand—GrowMotors

Conventionally evaluated, the expected NPV at year three of the commercial model is:

$$0.60 \times 400 + 0.40 \times (-300) = ₹120 \text{ crore}$$

Value option to expand with DCF method

The launch of the commercial model in Phase II as a standalone project is positive NPV as of today. Note that the Phase II has considerable uncertainty. However, this is a contingent project, which cannot be pursued without Phase I. At the end of Year 3 the option to expand will be exercised depending upon the demand scenario. If the demand is poor the investment (exercise of option) will not be made, and if the demand happens to be

Table 14-3 GrowMotors—Launch of electric car (Phase I and Phase II)

			Discount Rate	10%	
Present Value with High Demand			**Expand**		
			Year		
Cash flow (₹ crore)	*0*	*1*	*2*	*3*	*PV at T = 0*
Phase I					
Investment	-200.00				-200.00
Inflows		75.00	75.00	75.00	186.51
Phase II					
Investment	—	—	—	-600.00	518.30*
Inflows	—	—	—	1000.00	751.31
Net Present Value with High Demand					219.53
Present Value with Low Demand			**Do not expand**		
Phase I					
Investment	-200.00				-200.00
Inflows		75.00	75.00	75.00	186.51
Phase II					
Investment	—	—	—	—	—
Inflows	—	—	—	—	—
Net Present Value with Low Demand					-13.49

*Being certain discounted at 5%

good the investment will be made. In such a case, the NPV of the project to expand would be (Refer Figure 14-2):

$0.60 \times 400 + 0.40 \times 0 =$ ₹240 crore.

Therefore, the NPV of the electric car project with the option to launch Phase II will be positive ₹126.32 crore as shown in Table 14-3 and Figure 14-3.

(₹ crore)

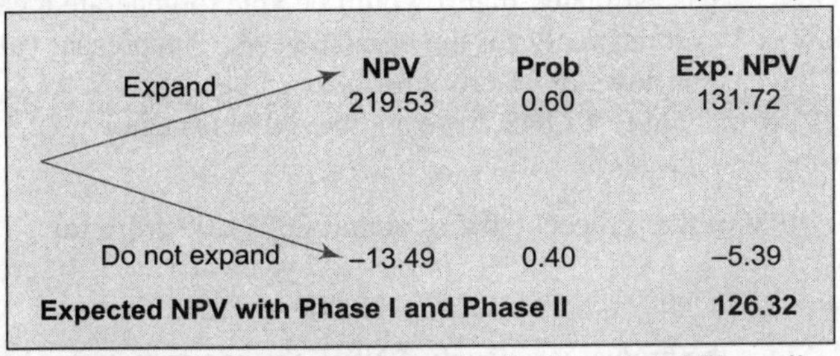

Figure 14-3 NPV GrowMotors—with Phase I and Phase II

Notice that under the DCF approach we have used the risk-free rate of 5% for discounting the initial investment of ₹600 crore because of its certainty. Rest of the figures, carrying operational risk, are discounted at WACC of 10%. If we go by the standard capital budgeting process, the pilot Phase I as a standalone project, we would end up rejecting it. However, with the option to expand, the project becomes viable.

In the appraisal of the Phase I, we did not consider the value of the option to expand. We need to value the same. This option to expand is a call option with exercise price of ₹600 crore with time to expiry as three years.

Value Option to Expand with Binomial Model

We shall consider the value of this option to expand using binomial method since as there are only two outcomes of demand scenario possible. The payoff of the call option at expiry is as below:

(Figures in ₹crore)

Demand Scenario	*Good*	*Poor*
Value of the underlying asset	1,000	300
Exercise Price	600	600
Payoff from the call option	400	0

This time we value the call option with equivalent portfolio approach, as against the risk neutral method used in the earlier section for valuing the option to wait. The equivalent portfolio can be constructed with owning some fraction of the asset, (known as delta of option) and borrowing so as to give the same payoff as that of the call option. The delta of the call option is given by:

Delta = Spread of payoff of call/Spread of values of underlying asset

$= (400 - 0)/(1{,}000 - 300) = 400/700 = 4/7$

Therefore, we shall buy 4/7 fraction of the underlying asset and borrow in a manner that makes the payoff equivalent to the payoff of the call option. The amount of borrowing that will equate the cash flow of the call option to expand will be ₹171.43 crore on expiration date, being the difference of value of asset and pay off of call (4/7th value of asset – Payoff of call option: 571.43 – 171.43, or 171.43 – 0). The value of the portfolio of 4/7th of the asset and borrowing on the expiry of the option period of three years is identical to that of the call option and is as depicted below:

(Figures in ₹ crore)

Demand Scenario	*Good*	*Poor*
Value of the asset on expiry	1,000.00	300.00
Value of 4/7th underlying asset	571.43	171.43
Repayment of loan and interest	171.43	171.43
Payoff from the portfolio	**400.00**	**0.00**

Since the portfolio and call option are equivalent at maturity, they must command the same price today. Hence, we need to find the value of the asset and the loan today. Here the underlying asset is the present values of the cash flows from the asset. The expected value of the asset at Year 3 is:

(₹ crore)

Demand Scenario	*PV of Cash flows*	*Probability*	*p × Cash flow*
Good	1000	0.60	600
Poor	300	0.40	120
Expected Value			**720**

The current value of the underlying asset can be computed by discounting the Year 3 value at WACC of 10%. The current value of underlying asset is $720/1.10^3 =$ ₹540.95 crore and the value of 4/7th is ₹309.11 crore. The borrowing will be done at a risk-free rate of 5% and the present value of borrowing is $171.43/1.05^3 =$ ₹148.09 crore. We arrive at the value of the call by setting it equal to the current value of the equivalent portfolio. Therefore, the value of the call is:

= Value of 4/7 share –Present Value of borrowing

$= 309.11 - 171.43/1.05^3$

$= 309.11 - 148.09 =$ ₹161.02 crore

Value of the Phase I of electric car project

= NPV of the Phase I + Value of the embedded call option

$= -13.49 + 161.02 =$ ₹147.53 crore

Value Option to Expand with Black–Scholes Model

Value of the call as per Black–Scholes Model is given by Equation 14-1.

Amongst the five inputs required to find the value of the call, we already have four; the exercise price X as ₹600 crore, risk-free rate r_f as 5%, time to expiry t of three years and spot price of the underlying asset S as ₹540.95 crore (PV of expected values, $720/1.10^3$). The remaining input of standard deviation of the underlying asset σ is calculated in Table 14-4.

Table 14-4 Calculation of standard deviation of returns

Expected value of asset at t = 0, S	*Value of the asset at t = 3*	*Return Relative*	*Annual returns (%)*	*Prob.*	*Expected Value*	*Variance*
540.95	1000	1.85	22.73	0.60	13.64	158.01
	300	0.55	–17.84	0.40	–7.14	237.02
Expected Return (%)					6.50	
Variance						395.03
Standard Deviation (%)						19.88

With all the inputs known for GrowMotors' option to expand can be valued using the Black–Scholes model

Values for Black–Scholes Model—GrowMotors

Exercise Price, X	₹600.00 crore
Spot Price, S	₹540.95 crore
Standard deviation, σ	19.88%
Annual Interest, r_f	5.00%
Time for Expiration, t	3.00 years

Inserting the values of input in the Black–Scholes model, we get the value of the call as:

$$c = N(d_1) \times S - N(d_2) \times \text{PV of } X$$
$$= 0.6205 \times 540.95 - 0.4851 \times 516.42 = ₹85.16 \text{ crore}$$

The value of the call option is ₹85.16 crore.

Note that delta of the option under binomial method and under Black–Scholes model is 0.5714 and 0.6205, respectively which is one source of variation in the value of the call. The other sources of variation in the value of the call by binomial method and Black–Scholes method are rooted in the calculation of volatility made in both the models.

OPTION TO ABANDON

All projects are subject to constant review by the managers of the firm taking into consideration the latest happenings and their future potential. One of the possible scenarios relates to the discontinuation of the project where the managers face adverse conditions that no more generate the expected cash flows. In such conditions, managers may estimate that the project will be better off if assets are disposed of rather than put to continued use. Withdrawal from the existing project may also be triggered by another more profitable opportunity that may arise with the passage of time.

Option to abandon relates to the situation where the firm can take a decision to exit the activity to reduce or avoid cash losses.

Such a right to abandon or make an exit is valuable as it may release financial resources for exploring new and more profitable business avenues, or simply help contain future losses that may result due to continuation of the project. Such an option is analogous to a put option where the holder has an option to sell at a predetermined price within a predetermined time period.

Consider an example, Ganga Toll Bridge Company (GANGA) that is contemplating to participate in a tender to build a bridge across a river. The tender stipulates the maximum toll fee that can be charged. The terms and conditions of the tender specify that the bridge must be made toll free after 25 years. The cost of building the bridge is ₹10 crore.

Based on the present level of traffic and its future estimates, GANGA has estimated that it would be able to generate a cash flow of ₹1 crore evenly for the next 25 years. The present value of the cash inflows of ₹1 crore for next 25 years at a WACC of 12% works out to ₹7.843 crore and the NPV is negative ₹2.157 crore.

$$\text{NPV of the project} = \text{PV of annuity of ₹1.00 crore for 25 years at 12\%} - 10 \text{ crore}$$
$$= 7.843 - 10.000 = -₹2.157 \text{ crore}$$

Since the project is a negative NPV, the company is not keen on pursuing the project.

The company has also expressed its apprehensions to the local government that based on the present and future levels of traffic building a bridge is not a viable proposition. In response, the local government disclosed following further information:

1. The local government is also planning to develop an amusement park and a township on the other side of the river, which is likely to enhance the traffic on the bridge. The estimated time to complete the development is five years.
2. In view of its developmental objective the local government has also offered to buy back the bridge at the end of five years at ₹6 crore from the toll bridge company if it finds the bridge non-remunerative at that time.

In the light of new information made available GANGA has been asked to reconsider their stand.

The additional information now available has changed the features of the project. First, it is now a project with a put option (option to sell) at the end of five years with GANGA realizing ₹6 crore. Second, the likely scenario of traffic would change with the amusement park and the new township after five years. The company estimates that the government's plan has 60% chances of succeeding, in which case the increased traffic would result in the cash flows of ₹2.50 crore, annually for the next 20 years. If the plan does not succeed, the traffic would provide a cash flow of ₹0.50 crore annually for the next 20 years in which case GANGA may abandon the project and handover to government at ₹6 crore.

Value Option to Abandon with DCF Method

Under the revised scenario GANGA faces the following situation:

1. It implements the project now and expects cash flows of ₹1 crore for the next five years when it is time to take another decision.

   At the end of five years GANGA faces two possible scenarios of traffic:
2. If the traffic volume is high it gives an annual cash flow of ₹2.50 crore for 20 years, which if valued at 12% has a present value of ₹18.674 crore, then the company continues with the project.

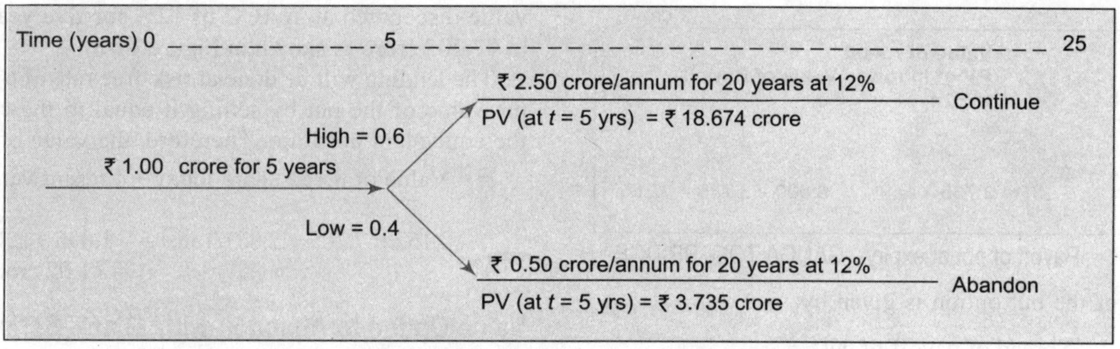

Figure 14-4 Option to abandon—GANGA

3. If traffic volume is low it gives annual cash flow of ₹0.50 crore for 20 years which if valued at 12% has present value of ₹3.735 crore, GANGA abandons the project and realizes ₹6.00 crore from the government because the asset is worth less than put option.

The new scenario is presented in Figure 14-4.

DCF Valuation without the put option Without the additional new information the NPV of the project was negative at ₹2.157 crore. With the traffic scenario changing from the sixth year onwards we revalue the project assuming (a) annual cash flows of ₹1 crore for first five years, and (b) the expected value of two possible traffic scenarios of high and low with the probability of 0.6 and 0.4, respectively for the next 20 years. All the cash flows are discounted at 12% considered appropriate for the risk associated with the project. The expected value of the cash flows at $t = 5$ years is ₹12.698 crore.

Expected value of cash flows ($t = 5$ years)
$= 18.674 \times 0.6 + 3.735 \times 0.4 =$ ₹12.698 crore.

When further discounted at 12% for five years it gives a present value of ₹7.205 crore at $t = 0$.

We add the present value of the cash flows of ₹1 crore for five years to provide a net present value of ₹0.81 crore. This makes the project marginally acceptable even without the exercise of the put option. This is depicted in Figure 14-5.

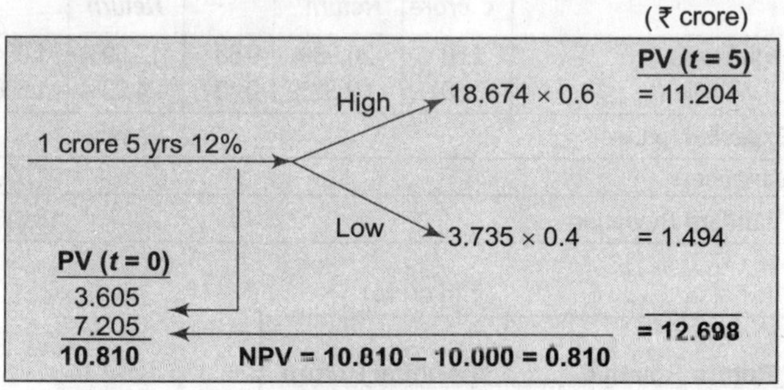

Figure 14-5 Expected Value & NPV without Put Option

DCF valuation with option of abandonment The offer of local government is a put option for the company with an exercise price of ₹6 crore with time of expiry as five years. GANGA at the end of five years can exercise the option depending upon the situation at that time. This changes the cash flows for the Low traffic scenario from ₹3.735 crore to ₹6 crore because the company exercises the option to abandon the project. This would enhance the value of the project. Here again, we have discounted all the cash flows at WACC of 12%. This may be challenged because cash flows with low traffic are certain, while the cash flows with high demand carry the usual business risk. If the cash flow of the low traffic demand is discounted at risk-free rate of 6% the net present value of the project increases to ₹1.755 crore.

The value of the project with put option is shown in Figure 14-6. Clearly the put option adds value to the capital budgeting exercise.

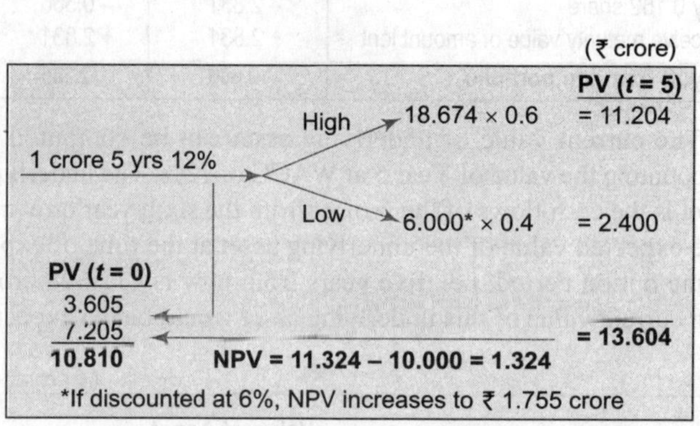

Figure 14-6 Expected Value & NPV with Put Option

Value Option to Abandon with Binomial Model

Since GANGA faces only two possible traffic situations we may use binomial method to value the put option. The underlying asset is the present value of the cash flows of the bridge that are likely from sixth year onwards. Note that the cash flows of the first five years do not form the part of the underlying asset.

Major advantage of using the option pricing models for valuing real options is that one does not need to know either the expected value or the discount rate.

For the two branches the value of the asset at the expiry of option period of five years is known and given in Figure 14-4. Using the same values for high and low traffic scenarios the put option would be worthless if the high demand is faced while the value would be ₹2.265 crore (6.000 – 3.735) in case the company faces low traffic. The payoff of put option is shown in Figure 14-7.

To set up an equivalent portfolio we first find delta of the option. One part of the equivalent portfolio would be short selling of the underlying asset equal to delta of the option. The other part would be lending an amount such that its maturity value is equal to sum of value of delta shares and value of put.

(₹ crore)

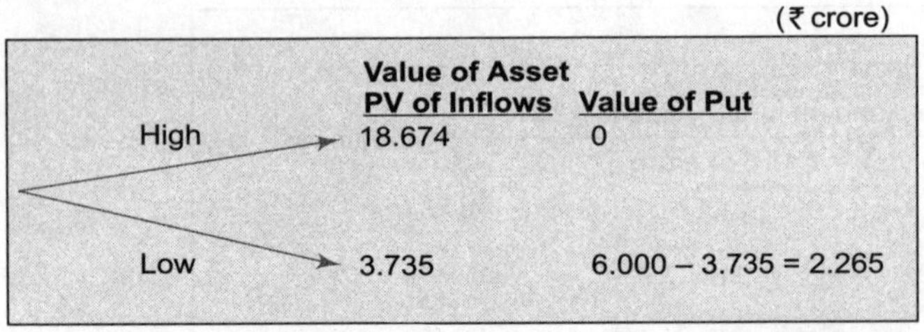

Figure 14-7 Payoff of put at expiry—GANGA TOLL BRIDGE

The delta of the put option is given by:

$$\text{Delta} = \frac{\text{Spread of payoff of put}}{\text{Spread of values of underlying asset}}$$

$$= \frac{2.265 - 0}{18.674 - 3.735} = \frac{2.265}{14.939} = 0.152$$

Therefore, we short sell 0.152 of the underlying asset. The payoff of the portfolio at expiry of option period at $t = 5$ years would be as follows:

Cash flows (₹ crore)

Traffic Scenario	*High*	*Low*
Value of the underlying asset	18.674	3.735
Buy 0.152 share	– 2.831	– 0.566
Receive maturity value of amount lent	+ 2.831	+ 2.831
Payoff from the portfolio	**0.000**	**2.265**

The current value of underlying asset can be computed by discounting the value of Year 5 at WACC of 12%. The underlying asset is the cash flows of the project from the sixth year onwards. The expected value of the underlying asset at the time of expiry of the option period, i.e., five years from now is ₹12.698 crore. The current value of this underlying asset would be the expected value discounted at WACC of 12% for five years. This comes to ₹7.205 crore as shown in Figure 14-8.

(₹ crore)

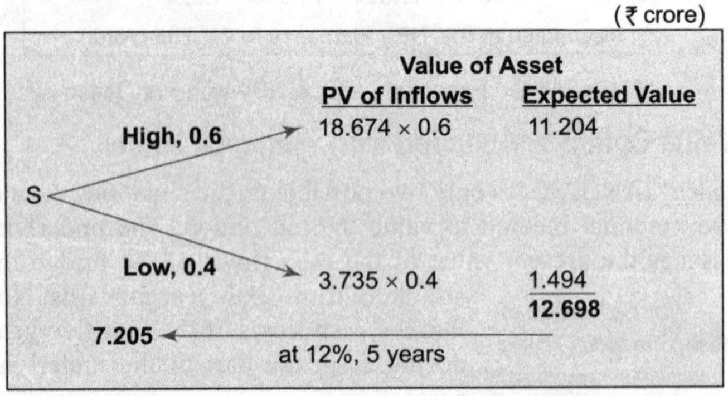

Figure 14-8 Value of underlying asset—GANGA

The lending will be done at risk-free rate of 6%. We arrive at the value of the put by setting it equal to the current value of the equivalent portfolio. Therefore, the value of the put is:

= – Value of 0.152 share today + Present value of amount lent

$$= -0.152 \times 7.205 + 2.831/1.06^5 = -1.095 + 2.115$$
$$= ₹1.02 \text{ crore}$$

Value Option to Abandon with Black–Scholes Model

Value of the put as per Black–Scholes Model is given by:

$$p = -[1 - N(d_1)] \times S + [1 - N(d_2)] \times \text{PV of } X$$

where $d_1 = \{\ln (S/X) + (r_f + \sigma^2/2) \times t)\}/\sigma\sqrt{t}$, and

$$d_2 = d_1 - \sigma\sqrt{t}$$

$N(d_1)$, $N(d_2)$ = Area under the cumulative normal distribution at d_1 and d_2, respectively

Alternatively, the value of put can also be obtained using put call parity that links the prices of call and put options .

Amongst the five inputs required to find the value of the put, we already have four; the exercise price X as ₹6.00 crore, risk-free rate r_f as 6%, time to expiry t of five years and spot price of the underlying asset S as ₹7.205 crore. The remaining input of standard deviation of the underlying asset σ is can be found from the variability of the returns on the underlying asset. The return when the traffic scenario is high is 159.5%, which is equal to the annualized return of 20.98%. Similarly, the annualized return with low traffic scenario is –12.33%. The scenario of expected returns on annualized basis is depicted in Figure 14-9.

The calculation of standard deviation of the annualised returns on the underlying asset is shown in Table 14-5. It is 16.31%.

Table 14-5 Standard deviation of returns on underlying asset

	Annual Cash Flow ₹ crore	*Annual Return*	*Prob.*	*Expected Return*	*Variance*
High Traffic	2.50	20.98%	0.60	12.59%	1.0643
Low Traffic	0.50	– 12.32%	0.40	– 4.93%	1.5965
Expected return				7.66%	
Variance					0.0266
Standard Deviation					16.31%

(₹ in crore)

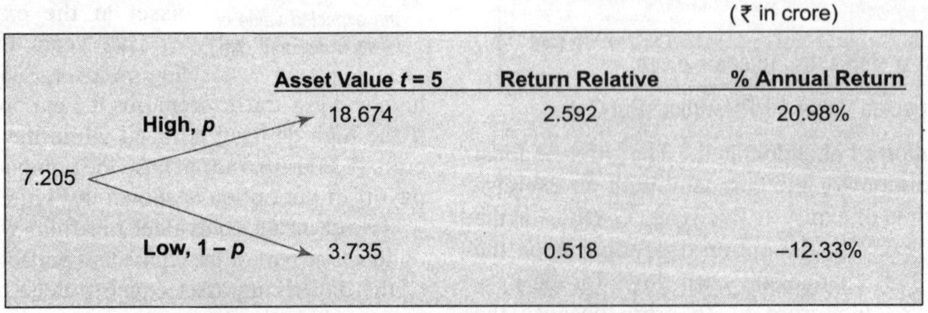

Figure 14-9 % Return for Black–Scholes valuation of put option—GANGA

Now we may compute the value of put option using Black Scholes model.

With these inputs we find:

$d_1 = -1.5067$ and $N(-d_1) = 0.0659$
$d_2 = -01.1420$ and $N(-d_2) = 0.1267$

Inserting the values of input in the Black–Scholes Model, we get the value of the put as:

$P' = ₹0.089$ crore

The option to sell back the bridge to government is valuable which can be seen from visualising what happens after the fifth year. The put option works as insurance for GANGA in the event the demand keeps low due to non-development of amusement park and the new township. The company can also use this valuation to negotiate the buyback price upwards of ₹6 crore to accept the project.

The difference in the valuation of put with binomial model and Black–Scholes formula is due to the difference in the volatility. In the Black–Scholes model the annual volatility is taken as 16.31%. For a five year period, this volatility is equivalent to $\sigma\sqrt{t} = 16.31\sqrt{5} = 36.49\%$. As against this the volatility in the binomial method for a five year period is 101.60% as shown in Table 14-6.

Table 14-6 Standard deviation of returns on underlying asset

	Annual Cash Flow ₹crore	*5 Year Return*	*Prob*	*Expected Return*	*Variance*
High Traffic	2.50	159.20%	0.60	95.52%	41.2942
Low Traffic	0.50	–48.20%	0.40	–19.28%	61.9413
Expected return				76.24%	
Variance					1.0324
Standard Deviation					101.60%

This is equivalent to annual standard deviation of $\sigma/\sqrt{t} = 101.66/\sqrt{5} = 45.43\%$. Using the value of σ as 45.43 we get the put value of ₹1.108 crore.

Despite the advantages of the real option approach over other tools of managing and incorporating risk in the capital budgeting process, it remains a tool that is scantily used. The real problem is the identification of complex options available in capital budgeting exercise. Rarely are the situations as simple as the ones explained above. Several options run on all projects simultaneously. For example, a launch of the project may be deferred, expanded later after execution or abandoned if the initial experience is not on expected lines. To value all kinds of options that run concurrently would indeed be a difficult task.

SUMMARY

Capital budgeting decisions are seldom routine. They are strategic in nature where the management has the flexibility to make decisions subsequent to implementation of project. These decisions have the implication on the cash flows of the project. These cash flows once projected are assumed constant over the life of the project. The decision is made on the basis of these static cash flows. The standard capital budgeting exercise ignores the strategic value of the decision.

The flexibility of the management and their ability to change the cash flows of the project subsequently, is referred to as an option on real asset. One is too familiar with the options on the financial asset. Options on real asset are normally of three types – option to delay, option to expand, and option to abandon.

Option to delay refers to the decision of timing of implementation of the project, while the option to expand is the flexibility to increase production, increase price or add product lines to enhance the cash flows of the project later depending upon the experiences gained in the initial phases. It is like a call option that has the exercise price equal to the cost of additional investment required at a later date. The option to abandon refers to the flexibility of the management to exit the project having implemented it realizing the salvage value. It is equivalent to a put option that is exercised when the cash flows of the project fail to meet the expectations, with the exercise price equal to the salvage value.

Standard capital budgeting analysis on the DCF basis treats the situation as now or never. The project is implemented only if the NPV of the project is positive. The real options approach suggests that there exists a possibility of increasing the value by deferring the implementation. It is like a call option because there is no compulsion of implementing the project late. The option to delay can be valued in many ways. The DCF approach is to compare the NPVs of different options by changing the timing of implementation. Since the option to implement now or later, are two mutually exclusive projects we choose the timing of implementation that provides the largest NPV.

Many real options situations are apt for valuation by binomial method. The advantages of binomial method over the decision tree using DCF are the elimination of requirement of knowing (a) the probabilities of the various scenarios and (b) the discount rate. The current price of the asset and its volatility are assumed to contain the expected value. The estimates of probabilities for likely future price are extremely subjective. The process of valuation of option by the binomial method is independent of individual's risk preferences. While this remains true for financial assets, which are traded the same may not be applied to real assets because they are not traded. This makes the price of options independent of individual's choice. It is a risk neutral valuation.

The valuation of real options on the basis of model developed for options on financial assets suffers from limitations of (a) non-tradability of real options, (b) exercise not being instantaneous, (c) problems of estimating the volatility of the cash flows, and (d) inability to clearly define the option.

KEY TERMS

Real Option Real options are options on the real assets as distinct from financial assets.

Option to Delay Option to delay is the decision resting with the management to decide when to implement a project. It is also referred as option to wait or timing decision.

Option to Expand Option to expand refers to the flexibility to start a project at lower scale and then expand as time progresses and uncertainties resolved.

Option to Abandon Option to abandon is a decision to exit the project and realize the salvage value in case the cash flows happen to be lesser than expected. It is equivalent to a put option.

Binomial Method A method to arrive at the value of an option assuming only two possible future courses to action or values of the asset is referred as binomial method.

Equivalent Portfolio Approach Equivalent portfolio approach for valuing an asset assumes that equivalent portfolios must command the same price at all times else they give rise to arbitrage opportunities.

Risk Neutral Valuation Risk neutral valuation of an asset is based on the premise that markets value the assets so as to provide risk-free return. The current price of the asset incorporates the future estimates of the price.

Delta of an Option Delta of an option is the ratio of spread of payoff of the option to the spread of the price of the asset. It is helpful in constructing equivalent portfolio.

KEY FORMULAE

Black–Scholes Formula for valuing Call Option

$$c = N(d_1) \times S - N(d_2) \times \text{PV of } X$$

where $d_1 = \{\ln (S/X) + (r_f + \sigma^2/2) \times t)\} / \sigma\sqrt{t}$

$d_2 = d_1 - \sigma\sqrt{t}$

$N(d_1)$, $N(d_2)$ = Area under the cumulative normal distribution at d_1 and d_2 respectively

Black–Scholes Formula for valuing Put Option

$$p = N(-d_2) \times \text{PV of } X - N(-d_1) \times S$$

$$\textbf{Delta of Call Option} = \frac{\text{Spread of payoff of call}}{\text{Spread of values of underlying asset}}$$

EXERCISES

Concept Review Questions

1. What are real options? How do they add value to capital budgeting proposals?
2. What are the different kinds of real options? Define.
3. What are the differences in real options and financial options?
4. Why do you think that DCF analysis is not an appropriate tool for evaluating capital budgeting proposals involving real options?
5. What is the relevance of equivalent portfolio approach to option valuation?
6. Describe the risk neutral approach to value an option.
7. In terms of options terminology, what is the difference between option to grow and option to abandon?

Critical Thinking Questions

1. In terms of Black–Scholes model of valuation of call and put option for options to wait, to expand and to abandon describe:
   (a) What would be the underlying asset?
   (b) What would be the exercise price?
   (c) How would you find out volatility?
2. What would happen to the option valuation if the risk-free rate changes from 6% to 10% in the example of GANGA under the option to abandon?
3. Identify which real option exist in following scenarios:
   (a) A firm holding a patent for a product is ready to launch it since the project has a positive NPV of ₹100 lakh evaluated at a WACC of 15%. However, it believes that the awareness about the product would increase over the next two years and since there is no threat from competition, the cash flows of the project would improve.
   (b) A firm is considering two alternative technologies to produce switchgears. One technology involves the production on a custom designed assembly line that is not resalable and the other is on a readily available standard machine that can be resold in the future at a substantially good price.

Practical Assignment

1. You have been short listed as a prospective vendor to supply die cast components for a new automobile model being developed by a large auto manufacturer. The initial cost of the project is ₹5 crore while the off take promised by the auto major is good enough to provide a cash flow for next three years that has an NPV of ₹4 crore only. However, depending upon the success of the new model that can be known only after two years, the off take of die cast components is likely to increase significantly. The chances are 70%. These raised volumes would generate cash flows of ₹1 crore annually for the next 25 years. No additional investment is required.
   (a) Would you accept the project?
   (b) Is there any real option available in the situation? If yes, then describe it.
   (c) What is the exercise price?
   (d) How would you value the option, if such an option exists?

Numerical Problems

1. Option to Delay

Fair Amusements Ltd is planning to open an amusement park that would cost ₹100 crore. It is expected to generate ₹15.60 crore as free cash flows for the next 20 years. The cost of capital of the firm is 13%.

The local government is planning to provide free transport facility to the amusement park by the next year. The probability of its happening is 60%. In such a case the cash flows to the amusement park would jump to ₹18 crore. If such a facility is not provided the annual cash flows would decline to ₹12 crore.

Examine whether the firm must go ahead with the project right now or should it defer the implementation by one year. Assume that the cost of the project remains same at ₹100 crore even if it is deferred.

2. Option to Delay: Applying BSM

Find the value of the option in Problem 1 as per Black–Scholes option pricing model. Assume standard deviation of returns at 20%.

3. Option to Abandon

Ace Technologies Ltd is considering a buy out of a firm, Speciality Software, for a price of ₹400 crore. It is expected to provide annual cash flow of ₹50 crore for next 20 years. The cost of capital of Ace Technologies is 12%. Should it go ahead with the acquisition?
The estimate of the annual cash inflow has been prepared on the basis of 50% chance of getting cash flow of ₹75 crore and 50% chance of having only ₹25 crore as annual cash inflow. This is due to the fact that efforts on the product improvement may succeed or may not succeed.

Meanwhile, the original promoters of Speciality Software have offered to buy back the firm for ₹350 crore two years later but they would have to pay ₹425 crore now instead of ₹400 crore. Should you go ahead with such proposition?

4. Option to Abandon: Applying BSM

Find the value of the option in the Problem 3 as per Black–Scholes option pricing model. Assume standard deviation of returns at 40%.

5. Option to Expand

The Ministry of Tourism in India is planning to develop an island as recreation and leisure resort for which it is in the process of granting exclusive rights to an airline for transporting tourists to and fro from the mainland. The initial cost of the aircraft is placed at ₹100 crore. How well the tourist spot would be accepted by travellers is extremely uncertain rendering volatility to the cash flows.

Though the cash flows of the airline would vary from year to year according to tourist interest, it is estimated that on an average the cash flows can be considered as annuities for 30 years as follows:

Probability	*Annual Cash inflows*
0.2	₹5.00 crore
0.3	₹10.00 crore
0.3	₹15.00 crore
0.2	₹20.00 crore

Considering the uncertainty of the cash flows, the expected rate of return is 15%.

Given the above scenario should the airline undertake the project?

The tender conditions allow that once the airline is awarded the contract it would have exclusive right to expand. This option is available for next 5 years. If the option is exercised, the cost of additional aircraft is placed at ₹110 crore.

Would the decision of airline change with the exclusive rights it would obtain by participating in the initial tender?

CASE STUDY

Sewa Steel Limited—The Metallurgy of Real Option

Sewa Steel Limited (SSL), a large producer of steel, having integrated the steel plant with Blast Furnace and Basic Oxygen Furnace, was on expansion path for enhancing the capacity of molten steel. For its planned increase in the capacity of steel-making, it faced substantially enhanced requirement of metallurgical coke. Consistent with its policy of backward integration, SSL was considering setting up a separate unit for producing metallurgical coke through one of its wholly-owned subsidiaries. The subsidiary, responsible for its own profitability was required to establish the viability of the project. The project team constituted for the evaluation of the project had compiled the following data for the new facility:

- **Initial cash outlay** Capital cost of the project was estimated at ₹1,200 crore which included the cost of land, building, plant, and machinery. In view of the assured market and prompt payments, the working capital requirements were nominal and ignored.
- **Cost of capital** The project was to be funded with 1/3rd of debt and 2/3rd of equity. The weighted average cost of capital of the project was assessed at 12% with the mix of debt and equity and was considered an appropriate rate of discounting the cash flows.
- **First year cash flow** The project was sensitive to the capacity utilization levels. The project team took a lot of effort to accurately project the cash flows of the first year because that formed the basis of cash flows for all subsequent years. It was estimated at ₹80 crore.
- **Life of the Project** The life of the project was reckoned at 20 years. After 20 years, the project was assumed to provide cash flows with marginal growth of 1%. For convenience, it was assumed to last forever.
- **Growth of cash flows** With the study of the requirements of the parent unit for metallurgical coke, the growth in the output and the cash flows was reckoned as follows:

	Year 1–5	*Year 6–10*	*Year 11–20*	*Year 20 onwards*
Growth rate of cash flows (%)	10%	7%	3%	1%

Based on these broad assumptions, the project assessment team projected the following cash flows for the project and applied the discounted cash flow approach to evaluate the desirability of the implementation project as given below:

Present Value					(₹ *in crore)*
Year	*Cash Flow*	*Present Value*	*Year*	*Cash Flow*	*Present Value*
1	80.00	71.43	11	169.21	48.64
2	88.00	70.15	12	174.28	44.73
3	96.80	68.90	13	179.51	41.14
4	106.48	67.67	14	184.90	37.83
5	117.13	66.46	15	190.44	34.79
6	125.33	63.49	16	196.16	32.00
7	134.10	60.66	17	202.04	29.43
8	143.49	57.95	18	208.10	27.06
9	153.53	55.36	19	214.35	24.89
10	164.28	52.89	20	220.78	22.89

The present value of the cash inflows over the next 20 years aggregated ₹978.38 crore. The terminal value of the project at the end of 20 years was ₹2,027.13 crore, which in terms of present value worked out to ₹210.15 crore. Therefore, the aggregate present value of the cash inflows worked out to ₹1,188.53 crore. With the initial cost standing at ₹1200 crore, the project had a marginally negative NPV of ₹11.47 crore.

The project team was not convinced of the viability of the project. After several rounds of discussions among themselves, finally, they decided to present the findings to the Managing Director (MD). Presented with the analysis, the MD was of the view that though the project team had taken all precautions in estimating the cost of the project, the cost of capital, and the cash flows; the application of the discounted cash flow technique was faulty. According to him, while DCF captured all the explicit factors of the cost and growth, it has ignored some strategic issues. Among the strategic aspects, the MD listed quite a few of them as follows:

- Ability to expand at a later stage
- Adjust the prices and the profit margin
- Control the level of production
- Delay the implementation

Among several strategic decisions listed above, the MD was particularly interested in the option to delay the implementation of the metallurgical coke project. The primary reason for such an option to be valuable was the volatility in the prices of coke. It was considered to be too high. The current prices that formed the basis of the projection were subdued. Another factor that caused the possibility of deferring the implementation of the project was the fact that no threat from any competitors existed due to very high capital outlay of the project and the control over the supply chain Sewa Steel enjoyed.

The project team started reworking over the value of the project trying to incorporate the option value emanating from the delay of the project. They considered that the project could be delayed by three years before any threat of competition could emerge. The cash flows of the project deferred by three years were taken as the asset. However, there would be loss of cash flow for three years. The yield on the three year government notes was at 7%. The MD had mentioned that it is the volatility in the coke prices that makes him think of deferring the project. His estimate of volatility in prices of coke was 40%.

Discuss

Re-evaluate the project's viability with the option to delay by three years.

In the CD

Appendix A-14 Binomial Option Pricing Model

CHAPTER 15 Mergers and Acquisitions

LEARNING OBJECTIVES

After reading this chapter, you will be able to:

- understand the meaning and definition of merger
- explain the difference between mergers, acquisitions, and takeovers
- learn about the synergies that emerge from the M&A for the combining firms
- examine various types of mergers and the rationale behind them
- apply cost–benefit analysis in an M&A deal
- understand the valuation framework for M&A
- learn important terms and concepts that are used in M&A literature
- analyse M&A in the Indian business environment

UNITED WE STAND

Shantilal & Sons was a family-owned business running a chain of 12 big-scale departmental stores in Mumbai. Till five years back, the business was being managed by Mr Shantilal, a veteran in the business who started with a small grocery shop 35 years back and over the years, his hard work, strong business acumen, staunch belief in quality, and focus on customer delight resulted in a turnover of ₹15 crore. Five years back, there was a division in the family, and each son got four departmental stores as the part of settlement. Mr Shantilal decided to retire from the business and keep himself engaged in managing the activities of the charitable trust that was set up in the name of his late father.

During the past five years, the entire landscape of the retail sector in India has been transformed. The entry of the big corporate giants such as Reliance, Marks & Spencer, Bharti, etc., has revolutionized the sector. The scale of business has been redefined, along with the quality of services and management. Post the division of the business, Mr Shantilal's three sons are struggling in view of the massive changes that the sector has been a witness to. Their margins have been shrinking and market base has been cut down drastically.

Realizing the problem faced by his sons, Mr Shantilal decided to intervene by calling his three sons to their ancestral home, a common bond between them, to discuss the issue. The father broke the ice thus:

'Have the three of you not heard the story of an old man who called his four sons and asked them to tie up the sticks in a bundle and then break the bundle? None of them could break it, but when the sticks were untied and the sons were asked to break them one by one, they could easily do so. The moral of the story is very simple but carries a deep meaning for life. Today, when the business world is moving towards consolidation, our business has got disintegrated. Combination gives you a bigger customer base, greater access to capital on better terms, better bargaining power, economies of scale, avoiding of overlaps, duplications and wastes, better quality of delivery. Besides, it also reduces the risk of hostile takeovers. In this era of cut-throat competition and hostile environment in the sector when we need to combine our physical, financial, and knowledge resources, we are competing against each other and giving undue advantage to our competitors.

The basic dictum is: when in crisis, hang around. Let me caution you, went on Mr Shantilal, 'as they say, "a stitch in time saves nine". If you do not realize the need of the hour, then you are running against the risk of being eaten up by the sharks.'

INTRODUCTION

Business newspapers and journals often report the news of mergers and acquisitions (M&A) happening in some or other part of the world. It has emerged during the past decade, as one of the most dominant activities in the field of corporate finance and strategy.

The contextual factors of business have undergone a sea change in view of the following two developments world over:

- The emergence of buyers' driven market that is putting pressures on the bottom-line of the companies, particularly in the wake of the increased competition.
- The increased competition caused, *inter alia*, by deregulation and liberalization especially in the developing economies of Asia, Latin America, and, Eastern Europe.

Due to the aforesaid developments, companies are finding it difficult to retain their market share. The problem before the firms world over is two-fold: enhancing or at least retaining their volumes and maintaining, if not increasing, their margins. The problem gets further compounded by the increasing assertiveness on part of the shareholders who expect increasing returns on equity, eroding margins and shrinking market share notwithstanding. Firms in response to the challenge of enhancing shareholder's value amidst downward pressure on their margins and volumes are adopting strategies of diversification, corporate restructuring and consolidation, etc.

Mergers and acquisitions have emerged as one of the most potent tools of corporate consolidation and restructuring. Using the M&A option, firms are combining with one or more firms in related/unrelated lines of business. Such combinations are benefiting the combining firms either by bringing down their operating costs or by increasing their market base or product line. Sometimes such combinations benefit by increasing the bargaining power of the combined entity while in some other cases they may facilitate in risk mitigation through diversification. For the firms that have entered moderate growth phase, M&A offers a mechanism to bolster their top and bottom line. M&A is also looked at as a long-term investing decision from the view of acquiring/merged firm as it provides such firms with productive investment avenue(s) to park their surpluses enhancing their expected future income. It is for this reason that the evaluation of merger is done like a capital budgeting decision.

MEANING AND DEFINITION OF MERGER

Every business is guided by the goal of wealth maximization. The wealth can be maximized by either internal or external growth. Internal growth can be achieved through either product extension or capacity expansion. External growth can be achieved, *inter-alia*, by mergers and acquisitions of existing business firm (s). Such a route to growth is termed as inorganic growth and is often seen as a faster way for firm(s) to grow.

Merger refers to a fusion of two or more firms with a view to bring in certain operational efficiencies. The assets and liabilities of the merging companies get transferred to the merged entity.

According to the Oxford Dictionary, the term 'merger'[1] means 'combining of two things, especially companies, to one'. In the business parlance, the term merger refers to a fusion between two or more enterprises, which results in the emergence of a single enterprise. Such a fusion involves the transfer of assets and liabilities of the merging companies to the merged (combined) company. The shareholders of the merging company/ companies normally become the shareholders in the merged company and all firms, except one, lose their identity.

Such a combination involves the integration of operations of merging organizations with a view to improving the operational efficiency of merging entities. In a merger the existing company or companies may decide to form a new company through the transfer of all their property to a new entity. In the second case, where a new entity is formed, the other companies lose their existence. It is this new corporation, thus, formed by absorbing the other companies that remains in existence post merger. The companies that transfer their assets to the other company are termed as transferor or merging companies and the company to which such assets are transferred is known as transferee or the merged company.

In India the word amalgamation is used for merger in legal parlance.

The Indian Companies Act, 1956 and the Indian Income Tax Act, 1961 use the term 'amalgamation' instead of merger. According to Section 2 (IB) of the Income Tax act, 'amalgamation, in relation to companies, means the merger of one or more companies with another company or the merger of two or more companies to form one company (the company or companies which so merge being referred to as the amalgamating company or companies and the company with which they merge or which is formed as a result of the merger, as the amalgamated company). Such a merger, according to the act, should be done in such a manner that all the assets and liabilities of the amalgamating company or companies immediately before the amalgamation becomes the assets and liabilities of the amalgamated company by virtue of the amalgamation. Also, the shareholders holding not less than nine-tenths in value of the shares in the amalgamating company or companies become shareholders of the amalgamated company by virtue of the amalgamation.

Merger or amalgamation (henceforth, in the chapter and elsewhere in the book the two terms will be used synonymously) can take either the form of absorption or consolidation. Combining two or more companies into an 'existing company' is referred to as merger through absorption[2] (i.e., $A + B + C = A$, or B, or C). All companies, except one, lose their identity in such a merger. For example, the absorption of Tata Fertilisers

[1] *The Concise Oxford English Dictionary*, 10th ed. (Revised), p. 892 Oxford University Press, New Delhi, 2002.

[2] http://india.gov.in/business/growing_business/mergers_acq.php, accessed on 10 March 2008

Mergers can take the form of either absorption or consolidation.

Ltd (TFL) by Tata Chemicals Ltd (TCL); TCL, an acquiring company (buyer), survived after merger while TFL, an acquired company (seller), ceased to exist. TFL transferred its assets, liabilities, and shares to TCL. Merger through consolidation[3] is a combination of two or more companies into a 'new company' (i.e., $A + B + C = D$). In this form of merger, all companies are legally dissolved and a new entity is created. Here, the acquired company (or companies as the case may be) transfers its assets, liabilities, and shares to the acquiring company for cash or exchange of shares. For example, the merger of Hindustan Computers Ltd, Hindustan Instruments Ltd, Indian Software Company Ltd, and Indian Reprographics Ltd into an entirely new company called HCL Ltd.

M&A can be looked at as strategic corporate restructuring decision or as an investment decision.

M&A deals can be viewed from three different perspectives: as corporate restructuring decision, as a strategic decision, and as an investment (or capital budgeting decision). Corporate restructuring involves changes in ownership structure/business mix/asset mix with a view to enhancing the shareholders' wealth. M&A are often viewed as corporate restructuring decisions as they affect the ownership structure and, thereby, the control pattern of the merging companies. They also alter, normally, the financial structure of the merged firm. M&A decisions may involve diversification, forward, backward integration, product or market extension, etc. All such decisions have a long-term impact on the companies involved. The implications of such decisions are in terms of increased efficiency, reduction in cost or competition, increasing the revenue, etc. It is due to these long-term implications for the companies involved, that the M&A deals are viewed as strategic decisions. M&A are also viewed as capital budgeting decisions as they entail huge capital outlays that the acquiring/merged company has to pay as purchase consideration for the M&A deal. Also, like investment decisions such decisions significantly influence the future cash flows of the merged firm and have the element of irreversibility.

Mergers, Acquisitions, and Takeovers

Mergers, acquisitions, and takeovers are commonly used interchangeably. But in reality, they have slightly different meanings. While a merger refers to the combining the businesses of two or more firms in a manner that all but one firms lose their identity. As discussed earlier, it may take the form of absorption or consolidation. An acquisition may be defined as an act of acquiring effective control by one company over assets or management of another company without any physical combination of their businesses. In an acquisition two or more companies may remain independent, separate legal entities, but there may be a change in control of the companies. The deal between Tata and Corus is an example of acquisition as Tata acquired Corus by increasing its shareholding in the European Steel giant and the acquired company still maintains its separate legal status and independent existence. Through huge financial investment in Corus, Tata Steel is having a significant say in its major policy decisions. Generally the terms acquisition and takeover are used synonymously as in both the cases the acquiring (taking over) firm can have control over the acquired (target) firm without having a full legal control. Even a minority ownership (of less than 50%) is sufficient in certain situations to control the affairs of another firm. There is no need to combine the operations of the two firms physically to acquire (or take over) and both the firms, acquired and acquiring retain their separate identity. However, sometimes a distinction is made between acquisition and takeover.

While merger refers to physical combination of the operations acquisition aims at acquiring effective control over the assets and management without any physical combination.

An acquisition can either be friendly or unfriendly. If the acquisition is agreeable to the target firm it is a friendly acquisition. A forced or unfriendly acquisition is termed as takeover as in such a case the management of 'target' company would oppose a move of being taken over. When the managements of acquiring and target companies mutually and willingly agree for the takeover, it is called acquisition. Thus, when one business acquires another on friendly terms, it is termed as an *acquisition* but when it is against the wishes of the target firm, i.e., when it is unfriendly it is termed as a *takeover*. The Mittal–Arcelor deal was a takeover as initially the management of Arcelor was against Mittal's proposal. Notwithstanding this distinction between acquisition and takeover, technically there is no difference, as stated earlier, between a merger and an acquisition.

SYNERGIES FROM M&A

M&A bring in certain operating and financial synergies that are mainly economies of scale in operations and financing.

The basic reason behind M&A is that it creates a synergy for the companies involved in the process, i.e., a combined firm is more valuable than the sum of the individual combining firms. This synergy emerges as a merger enables the combined firm to carry out its operations in a more efficient and profitable manner than it were done by the combining firms individually. For example, if one company has an outstanding product line but weak distribution channel, while the other company has a problem with its product line but has great distribution channel, then potentially, the two companies could create a synergy with a merger as both will be able to combine their respective strengths. In certain cases, synergy comes in the form of staff reduction brought about by the reduction in or elimination of overlapping functions. For example, if before merger both the companies had their individual R&D departments, after the merger only one R&D department would be needed. Although the size of such a department would become bigger, duplication would be eliminated, particularly in the areas of overlap. There are two different types of

[3]ibid

synergies— operational and financial— that accrue to the firms on account of M&A.

Operating Synergy

M&A increases the scale of operations of the combined firm and, thus, enables them to exploit the benefit of economies of scale that the individual combining firms were unable to get pre-merger. Such economies accrue due to the combining of the physical, financial, and human resources. The productivity of such resources increases as they are spread over larger number of units of output in the combined firm. Such an optimal utilization of resources brings down the cost per unit of output. Operating economies also accrue in specific management functions such as production, R&D, marketing, or finance. Such economies may be achieved through a merger between firms, which have competencies in different areas. For instance, when a firm, whose core competence is R&D, merges with another having a strong marketing strategy, the two businesses would complement each other. The acquisition of Betapharm by Dr. Reddy's is an example of such a combination. Dr. Reddy's has R&D and manufacturing as its core competence. It acquired Betapharm that has a wide distribution network in Europe. Other economies in operations emerge on account of increased capacity of the combined firm to exploit the resources and harness the potential of the combining firms that could not be done by them due to the limitations of their scale and managerial capabilities. This happens as the firms with more efficient management are able to identify firms that are good potential but are operating at lower efficiency. They merge/acquire such firms as they have the managerial ability to improve the latter's performance. Besides, a vertical integration, i.e., combining of firms at different stages of the industry value chain also creates operational synergies by cutting down the costs of communication and bargaining.

The increased scale of operations of the combined firm brings in operational economies through better resource utilisation, and benefits from each other's core competencies.

Financial Synergy

M&A combine the financial resources of the combining firms, increasing their capacity to further mobilize financial resources at a lower cost. The enlarged equity base of the combined firm increases the capacity of the combined firm to raise further debt, which is a cheaper source of financing. Also, with the increased asset base of the combined firm its credit worthiness increases and as the result it is in a position to raise more resources than what the combining firms could have been able to do individually, and that too at a lower cost. There have been cases where post merger, due to its sheer size, the combined firm has been able to raise funds internationally at much lesser cost as compared to domestic finances.

The large capital base of the combined firm enables it to attract easy and convenient financing.

ADVANTAGES OF M&As

Mergers and acquisitions bring significant benefits to the combining companies. By affecting both the top line and the bottom line, M&As, eventually, create value for the shareholders. It is not that every single M&A necessarily creates the value for the shareholders, but most of them surely do and that is the reason why the firms world over have taken recourse to this option of inorganic growth. The major advantages of the M&A for the companies involved in the deal are:

By enhancing the growth rate, and cutting down the competition the M&A deals boost the top-line as well as bottom-line of the combining firms, besides mitigating the business risk through diversification.

Drives growth Resources put a constraint on the rate of growth that the firms can achieve internally through the expansion of its capacity or extension of its product line. M&A overcomes these constraints by combining the resources of the merging companies together. Also growth gets accelerated at a very fast rate through M&A as it not only combines the market share of the merging companies (in case of horizontal mergers) it also combines their core competencies (in case of vertical mergers). For example, the combination of a pharmaceutical manufacturing company and an R&D company brings together their core strength that may accelerate the rate of growth for both of them. Similarly, a company may lack technical and (or) marketing skills or distribution network for entering into new products/markets. Such a company can acquire existing company/companies with requisite infrastructure and skills and grow quickly.

Enhances profitability Combining two different companies bring together certain operational economies, thus, enhancing their profitability. Duplication of overlapping functions like distribution, R&D, etc., can be avoided by the combined firm, which may bring down the cost of operations for the combined firm. Besides it also brings in certain economies of scale to the combined firm. On account of up-scaling of its operations the combined firms may be able to spread their fixed costs over larger number of units and, thus, bring down per unit cost of production. Also, certain other benefits of scale in terms of better bargaining power and discounts accrue to the merged unit. All these boost the profitability of the combined entity.

Mitigates risk Merging of two companies belonging to unrelated industries (conglomerate merger) cuts down the element of cyclicality, if any, in their business. Such a combination of unrelated (diversified) business that have negatively correlated income stream protects the existing business of the acquiring/merged firm. Besides the combination of management and other resources it increases the resilience of the firm to withstand and overcome the crisis situations.

Cuts down the competition Merging with (or acquiring) the competitors not only increases the market share of the combined firm, it also reduces the competition significantly. This reduction in competition is direct in case of horizontal merger and indirect in case of vertical mergers as the benefits of upstream/downstream integration in vertical mergers put the combined firm to a significant cost advantage over its competitors and, hence, erodes the competition significantly.

Reduces tax liability Merging with firms having accumulated losses and unabsorbed depreciation in their financial statements allows the merged firm to set-off this unabsorbed depreciation and accumulated losses against the post-merger profits of the merged firm. The provisions under Section 72A and 72AA of the Indian Income Tax Act, 1961 allow this facility to set-off and carry forward the losses against the profits of the merged entity. Such a set-off brings down the taxable income and the associated tax outflows for the merged firm.

TYPES OF MERGERS AND THEIR RATIONALE

Depending upon the similarities of product line or the stage of operations of the merging firms, mergers can be categorized into—horizontal, vertical, or conglomerate

Mergers may be effected to increase profits and reduce losses through the reduction of competition, diversification of production, bringing in operational economies, or through revival or rejuvenation of failing businesses by the infusion of new management and personnel. The underlying rationale or motivation behind the M&A depends primarily upon the type of merger. Let us understand the different types of mergers and the rationale behind them.

Mergers appear in three forms, horizontal, vertical, and conglomerate, based on the competitive relationships between the merging parties. A *horizontal merger* brings together related businesses; a *vertical merger* integrates businesses that are similar but operate at different stages of value chain. Such businesses share a supplier–customer relationship with the other units involved in the merger. A conglomerate merger involves combining unrelated businesses.

Horizontal Merger

Combining of firms dealing in similar products/ services is known as horizontal merger.

In a horizontal merger, both the merging firm and the merged firm produce and sell identical or similar products in the same geographic area. So if the parties involved in a merger are in direct competition with each other, it is termed as horizontal merger. For example, the acquisition of Parle products by Coke or the merger of Brooke Bond India with Lipton India to form Brooke Bond Lipton India Ltd are some examples of horizontal combination. Such a merger reduces the number of firms competing in the relevant market and, eventually, results in market concentration. Since horizontal mergers have the affect of bringing down the competition and increasing the concentration in the industry such mergers are actively on the scanner of the regulators. The purpose of horizontal merger is elimination or reduction in competition; putting an end to price cutting; and bringing in economies of scale in production, research and development, marketing or other functions.

Vertical Merger

Combination of firms operating at different stages of value chain within the industry is vertical merger.

A combination of two or more firms that fall in the same industry but operate at different stages of production–distribution chain is termed as vertical merger. Such a merger involves combining with either a customer or a supplier. For example, a merger of cotton spinning unit with a cotton weaving unit is a vertical merger as the two units are in the same industry but at the different stages of value chain. Vertical merger may take the form of forward or backward merger (alternatively known as forward or backward integration). When a company combines with the supplier of material, it is called backward merger and when it combines with the customer, it is known as forward merger. The backward and forward mergers are alternatively referred to as upstream mergers and downstream mergers, respectively. The joining of a pharmaceutical company with a drugstore chain is an example of downstream merger while the merger of an oil distribution company with an oil refining company is an example of upstream merger. Consumers can benefit from the increased efficiencies in the form of lower prices and/or better service resulting from supply chain integration caused by the M&A.

A vertical merger is an important instrument available for the firms who want to move up or down the value chain. The purpose of such a merger may range from lowering the costs of inputs and distribution overheads to assured supplies of inputs or posing entry barriers for the potential competitors. The acquisition of German drug major Betapharm by Dr. Reddy's Laboratories Ltd is an example of vertical integration as the acquisition is expected to give Dr. Reddy's (a drug manufacturing company) access to the supply chain of Betapharm into Germany and the rest of the Europe. Vertical mergers also affect the competitive situation in the industry as combining firms are in a position to collectively affect the prices of the end products by forming cartels. But unlike horizontal mergers, they do not affect the competition directly and, hence, are not watched as scrupulously as horizontal mergers by regulators.

Conglomerate Merger

Mergers of unrelated businesses are termed as conglomerate mergers. Such mergers involve firms that are neither competitors nor the part of the same supply chain, i.e., if the merging units do not relate either horizontally or vertically the combination is known as conglomerate merger. It is a type of combination in which firm(s) established in one industry combine with other

Combination of unrelated businesses is termed as conglomerate merger.

firm(s) in unrelated industry. It generally involves diversification of business activities and therefore is considered to pose no threat to competition. Such a merger results in the broadening of the business portfolio of merged company. Mitigation of risk is the basic motivation behind such mergers as they involve businesses that are diverse and, hence, have unrelated income streams. It results in the reduction of total risks through substantial reduction of cyclicality of operations. The merger of Alstom Transport and Alstom System with Alstom Power India Ltd is an example of conglomerate merger.

Such a merger may either aim at market expansion or product extension. When the merger involves two or more companies that sell the same products in different markets it aims at market expansion. The aim of the merger is product extension when two or more firms selling different but related product(s) in a common market. Such a merger allows the new, larger company to pool their products and sell them with greater success to the already common market that the two separate companies shared.

Conglomerate mergers may either be aimed at market expansion or product extension.

M&A: COSTS BENEFIT ANALYSIS

As discussed earlier, M&A deals create synergy for both the merging and the merged firms. This can be represented symbolically as:

M&A should be evaluated like a capital budgeting decision. The NPV should form the basis for M&A decisions.

$$V(AB) > V(A) + V(B)$$

where

$V(A)$ = Value of A Ltd

$V(B)$ = Value of B Ltd

$V(AB)$ = Value of the merged company

M&A is an investment decision for the merged/acquiring company as it requires huge capital outlay for the purchase of the assets of the merging company/companies. Post-merger prospective cash inflows also get a boost on account of such a decision. For the merging/acquired companies it is a disinvestment decision as it leads to release of funds tied up in the balance sheet of such companies. Irrespective of whether it is looked at from the investment perspective or from the disinvestment perspective it creates value for both the merged and the merging firms. Merger is successful if it creates a positive NPV for all the firms that are involved. And it is this positive NPV that is one of the key reasons for the firms to enter into M&A deals.

COMPUTATION OF COSTS AND BENEFITS TO THE FIRMS INVOLVED IN M&A

As discussed earlier, M&A create positive NPV to all the firms involved. Computation of NPV is based on a cost–benefit analysis which requires computation of the difference between the present value of the combined or merged entity (PV_{AB}) and the sum of the present value of firms taken separately. For a typical merger (through absorption) involving two firms the benefit to the merged firm can be calculated as:

$$\text{Benefit} = (PV_{AB}) - (PV_A + PV_B)^*$$

where AB = Combined firm

A = Acquiring/merged firm

B = Acquired/target firm

Computation of cost of merger depends on whether the purchase consideration for merger is paid for in cash by the merged company or by the issue of shares. If the purchase consideration is paid in cash by the merged entity to the merging/acquired entity (Firm B in our case), the cost of the merger from the point of view of Firm A (acquiring company) can be calculated as:

NPV is the difference between the present value of the combined (merged) firm and the sum of the present values of individual merging firms.

$$\text{Cost} = \text{Cash purchase consideration} - PV_B$$

$$\text{Thus, NPV for } A = \text{Benefit} - \text{Cost}$$

$$= [PV_{AB} - (PV_A + PV_B)] - (\text{Cash purchase consideration} - PV_B)$$

The net present value of the merger from the point of view of Firm B (merging firm) is the same as the cost of the merger for A. Hence,

$$\text{NPV to B} = \text{Cash purchase consideration} - PV_B$$

Normally, the purchase consideration is paid by issuing shares in the merged company to the shareholders of the merging company. If so, the NPV computation requires an estimation of the proportion of shareholding of the shares in the merged company by the shareholders of merging company. This can be explained with the help of Example 15-1.

Example 15-1 Cost-benefit Analysis of Merger

Firm Alpha plans to acquire Firm Beta. Following are the pre-merger vital statistics of the two firms:

	Alpha (A)	Beta (B)
Market price per share (₹)	50	20
Book value per share (₹)	34	16
Number of outstanding shares	4,50,000	2,25,000
Market value of the firm (₹)	2,25,00,000	45,00,000

Firm Alpha offers to the shareholders of Firm Beta one share in exchange for every two shares held by them in Beta Ltd. The merger is expected to bring gains, which have a PV of ₹50 lakh. Should Alpha Ltd acquire Beta Ltd?

Solution

The cost to the acquiring/merged company can be computed as follows:

$$\text{Cost} = \alpha PV_{AB} - PV_B$$

Where α represents the fraction of the shares in the combined entity received by shareholders of Beta.

The share of B in the combined entity denoted by α is computed as follows:

$$\alpha = 112500\ (450000 + 112500) = 0.2$$

*The symbol AB that has been used for the combined firm does not denote a new firm formed on account of merger but it is to denote the synergistic impact of merger in the value of merged firm. Although in the situation Firm A has acquired Firm B.

If we assume that the market value of the combined entity will be equal to the sum of present value of the separate entities and the benefit accruing to the combined firm on account of merger, then,

$PV_{AB} = PV_A + PV_B +$ Benefit on account of merger
$= 225 + 45 + 50 = ₹320$ lakh

Cost $= PV_{AB} - PV_B = 0.2 \times 320 - 45 = ₹19$ lakh

Thus,

NPV to A = Benefit – Cost
$50 - 19 = ₹31$ lakh

NPV to B = Cost to A = ₹19 lakh

Thus, in this case both Alpha and Beta are net gainers from the merger as both get a positive NPV.

MERGER AS A CAPITAL BUDGETING DECISION: A VALUATION FRAMEWORK

Having seen the cost–benefit analysis of merger, let us discuss the valuation framework for M&A.

When a firm plans to acquire another firm, it should consider the acquisition as a capital budgeting decision. Hence, such a proposal must be evaluated as a capital budgeting decision from the viewpoint of acquiring/merged firm. This requires determining the cash flows over the estimated finite time horizon during which incremental benefits of merger will accrue, determining the cost of capital, and, finding out the present value of incremental cash flows using the discount rate. The steps involved in the determination of NPV of M&A deal are as follows:

Step 1 Determination of the time period for the evaluation of the deal. The time period depends upon the period for which the benefits of merger are expected to be available to the combined firm.

Step 2 Determine the (without merger) after-tax cash flows of the acquiring firm over the evaluation period.

Step 3 Determine the discount rate.

Step 4 Determine the PV of the cash flows (arrived at Step 2) of the acquiring firm without merger using the discount rate computed at Step 3.

Step 5 Determine the post-merger cash flows (after-tax) of the combined firm (CF). The cash flows consist of the cash flows of both merging firms and the merged firm and reflect the benefits of synergy that accrue to the firms on account of merger.

Step 6 Determine the PV of cash flows of the combined firm using the discount rate computed at Step 3.

Step 7 Determine the ownership position of the shareholders of acquiring firm in the merged (combined) firm. The ownership position (OP) can be computed using the following model:

$$OP = \frac{N_x}{[N_x + ER(N_y)]}$$

where

N_x = number of outstanding equity shares of Firm X (the merged/acquiring firm) before the merger.

N_y = number of outstanding equity shares of Firm Y (the merging/acquired firm) before the merger.

ER = exchange ratio representing the number of shares of Firm X exchanged for every share of Firm Y.

The denominator in the above model denotes the total number of outstanding shares post-merger in the combined firm. The numerator denotes the number of shares of the acquiring firm. Hence, the model denotes the fraction of shares that the shareholders of acquiring firm hold in the combined firm.

Step 8 Calculate NPV of the merger proposal from the point of view of X (acquiring firm) as follows:

$$NPV(X) = OP[PV(CF)] - PV(X)$$

Where

$NPV(X)$ = NPV of the merger proposal from the point of view of shareholders of X, the acquiring firm

OP = ownership position of the shareholder of Firm X in the combined firm (CF)

$PV(CF)$ = PV of the cash flows of the combined firm .

$PV(X)$ = PV of the cash flows of Firm X, without the merger.

Example 15-2 Computation of NPV of Acquisition for the Acquiring Firm

X Ltd is a firm which in order to increase its market share is considering the proposal to acquire Y Ltd, which is considered as a very promising prospect due to its excellent R&D team. If X Ltd acquires Y Ltd, it will be a backward integration for X Ltd, a manufacturer, with R&D firm and is likely to drive significantly the growth rate of X Ltd that has been presently languishing at 11–12%. If the acquisition takes place the cash flows are projected to grow @ 25% per annum post-acquisition for the next five years, after which, cash flows of the combined firm are expected to grow at a rate of 9% per annum, which is the expected growth rate of economy. The projected post-tax cash flows for X Ltd for the next five years (without acquisition) are as follows:

Year	1	2	3	4	5
CF (X) (₹ in lakh)	500.00	557.50	621.61	693.10	772.80

If the acquisition takes place the expected cash flows (after tax) of the combined firm (X′)* are projected as:

Year	1	2	3	4	5
CF (X′) (₹ in lakh)	637.00	796.25	995.31	1244.14	1555.18

The required rate of return for the firms that have risk–return characteristics similar to X Ltd is 14%. The number of equity shares outstanding in X Ltd are 2,00,000 while those in Y Ltd are 1,00,000. If the acquisition takes place, the exchange ratio is likely to be 0.5 in the combined firm for the shareholders of Y Ltd. What is the expected NPV for X Ltd from acquisition?

Solution

Step 1 Since the benefit of acquisition will be availed over an infinite period of time, the period of evaluation has been divided into two phases; abnormal growth phase (year one through five) and the normal growth phase (year five onwards).

*X′ denotes combined firm

Step 2 Projected after-tax cash flows of the acquiring Firm X have already been given in the problem.
Step 3 The discount rate has been stated as 14%.
Step 4 The present value of cash flows of the acquiring firm (without acquisition) has been estimated as follows:

$$PV(X) = \frac{500.00}{(1.14)^1} + \frac{557.50}{(1.14)^2} + \frac{621.61}{(1.14)^3} + \frac{693.10}{(1.14)^4} + \frac{772.80}{(1.14)^5} + \frac{772.80(1.09)}{0.14 - 0.09}$$

$$= 2098.89 + 16847.13$$

$$= ₹18946.02 \text{ lakh}$$

Step 5 The post-merger projected cash flows of the combined firm (X') have already been estimated and given in the problem above
Step 6 The present value of the cash flows of combined firm can be estimated as follows:

$$PV(X') = \frac{637.00}{(1.14)^1} + \frac{796.25}{(1.14)^2} + \frac{995.31}{(1.14)^3} + \frac{1244.14}{(1.14)^4} + \frac{1558.18}{(1.14)^5} + \frac{1555.18(1.09)}{(0.14 - 0.09)}$$

$$= 3387.609 + 33902.832$$

$$= ₹37290.44 \text{ lakh}$$

Step 7 Ownership position for the shareholders of X Ltd in the combined firm can be estimated as follows:

$$OP = \frac{2,00,000}{[2,00,000 + 0.5\,(1,00,000)]} = 0.8$$

Step 8 NPV of the merger proposal from the point of view of X can be computed as follows:

$$NPV\ (X) = (37290.44 \times 0.8) - 18946.02$$

$$= ₹10886.34 \text{ lakh}$$

Thus, the acquisition is likely to create value of ₹10886.34 lakh for the acquiring firm.

Calculation of Exchange Ratio from the Perspective of the Acquired and the Acquiring Firm

Exchange ratio (ER) is the number of shares that the shareholders of acquired (merged) firm receive in the combined firm to the number of shares that they held in the merging (acquired) firm.

Whenever a firm acquires another firm, the compensation to the shareholders of the acquired firm is usually paid in the form of shares of the acquiring firm. In other words, shares of acquiring firm will be given in exchange for shares of acquired firm. This ratio is termed as 'exchange ratio' or 'swap ratio'. Exchange ratio (ER) may be defined as the number of shares of the acquiring company that a shareholder will receive for one share of the acquired company. An ER of 0.6 implies that shareholders of acquired firm will receive 60 shares in the combined firm for every 100 shares held in the acquired firm.

Exchange ratio (ER) is an important factor in an M&A deal.

Exchange ratio is a very important factor in M&A deal. The acquiring firm will want to keep this ratio as low as possible, while the acquired firm will want it to be as high as possible. In any case, both firms would ensure that post merger, their equivalent price per share will at least equal their pre-merger price per share. Larson–Gonedes (LG) model (1969)[4] of exchange ratio determination and shareholders' expectation can be used for determining the exchange rates for the two firms (i.e. maximum and minimum exchange rates). The actual exchange will lie somewhere in between the two exchange rates. The model was revisited and simplified by Conn and Nieisen[5]. Let us understand the LG model for exchange rate determination:

The symbols used in this model are:

ER = Exchange ratio
P = Price per share
EPS = Earning per share
PE = Price earning multiple
E = Earnings
S = Number of outstanding equity shares
AER = Actual exchange ratio

In addition, the acquiring, acquired, and combined firms will be referred to by subscripts A, B, and AB, respectively.

Firm A would ensure that the wealth of its shareholders is preserved post-merger. This implies that the price per share of the combined firm is at least equal to the price per share of Firm A before merger:

$$P_{AB} = P_A$$

Let us consider, for the sake of simplicity, that $P_{AB} = P_A$

As known, $\frac{P}{E} \times EPS$ = Market price per share

Price earnings ratio of the combined firm × Earnings per share of the combined firm gives the Market price per share of the combined firm.

$$P_{AB} = PE_{AB} \times EPS_{AB}$$

Since P_{AB} has been assumed to be equal to P_A we get our first equation as:

$$P_{AB} = PE_{AB} \times EPS_{AB} = P_A \tag{15-1}$$

Earnings per share of the combined firm can be expressed as:

$$EPS_{AB} = \frac{E_A + E_B}{[S_A + S_B(ER_A)]} \tag{15-2}$$

ER_A = number of shares of Firm A given in lieu of one share of Firm B.

By substituting the formula of EPS_{AB} (given in Equation 15-2) in Equation 15-1 we get:

$$P_{AB} = \frac{PE_{AB}(E_A + E_B)}{[S_A + S_B(ER_A)]}$$

From the above equation, we may solve for the value of ER_A to arrive at the maximum exchange ratio acceptable to the shareholders of Firm A as follows:

[4]Larson, Kermit D. and Nicholas J. Gonedes, 'Business Combination: An exchange ratio determination model', *The Accounting Review*, October, pp. 720–728.
[5]Conn, Robert L. and James F. Nieisen, 1977, 'An Empirical Test of the Larson-Gonedes Exchange Ratio Determination Model', *The Journal of Finance*, vol. 32, no. 3, June, pp. 749–759.

$$ER_A = \left(\frac{S_A}{S_B}\right) + \left[\frac{E_A + E_B}{P_A S_A} PE_{AB}\right]$$

Similarly, the minimum exchange ratio acceptable to the Firm B(ER_B) can be computed as follows:

The basic condition is that the price that the shareholders of Firm B would be expecting in the combined firm should be at least equal to the price of shares of Firm B. Thus:

$$P_{AB}\,(ER_B \geq P_B) \qquad (15\text{-}3)$$

Assuming again, for the sake of simplicity, that $P_{AB} = P_B$ and substituting P_{AB} from Equation 15-1 in Equation 15-3 we get:

$$PE_{AB} \times EPS_{AB} \times ER_B = P_B$$

Substituting the value of EPS_{AB} from Equation 15-2 in the above equation, and solving the equation for ER_B we get:

$$ER_B = \frac{P_B S_A}{[(PE_{AB})(E_A + E_B) - P_B S_B]}$$

The above model can be used to find out the exchange ratio (maximum and minimum) for the combining firms at the different levels of their P/E fractions. Let us see the computation of exchange ratio for the combining firms with the help of the following example:

Example 15-3 Determination of Exchange Ratio (*ER*) using the LG Model

Two companies *A* & *B* decide to merge. The relevant financials of the two firms are as follows:

	Firm A	*Firm B*
Total earnings, *E* (₹ lakh)	210	60
No. of shares outstanding, *S* (in lakh)	20.5	8
Earnings per share, EPS (₹)	10.24	7.50
Price earnings ratio, *P/E* (times)	10	7
Market price per share, *P* (₹)	40	14

Determine the exchange ratio for Firm A and Firm B using LG model.

Solution

As per LG model, the exchange ratio for the two firms will be determined as follow:

$$ER_A = \left(\frac{S_A}{S_B}\right) + \left[\frac{(E_A + E_B)}{P_A S_A} PE_{AB}\right]$$

$$ER_A = \left(\frac{20.5}{8}\right) + \left[\frac{(210 + 60)}{40 \times 20.5} PE_{AB}\right]$$

Using the above equation, the ER_A can be computed for the various levels P/E fraction of the combined firm (AB). The calculations are given in Table A:

Similarly, the *ER* can be computed for Firm B using the following model:

$$ER_B = \frac{P_B S_A}{[(PE_{AB})(E_A + E_B) - P_B S_B]}$$

$$= \frac{14 \times 20.5}{[(PE_{AB})(210 + 60) - 14 \times 8]}$$

Using the above equation, the ER_B can be computed for the various levels *P/E* fraction of combined firm (*AB*). The calculations are given in Table B.

Thus, *ER* would be settled somewhere in between the minimum and maximum exchange ratios that have been determined for different levels of expected *PE* multiples of the combined firm. During the negotiations for the *M&A* deal the combined (acquiring) company would like to keep the *ER* as low as possible while the merging (acquired) firm would want it to be as high as possible. As the result, the *AER* will lie somewhere between Max. *ER* and Min. *ER*.

This relationship between the *ER* and *PE* fraction of combined firm has been expressed in the Figure 15-1. As it can be seen in the figure for every level of *PE* of the combined firm (PE_{AB}) there is a unique exchange rate for both the firms *A* and *B*). The shareholders of both the firms will benefit from the merger if the *AER* lies in quadrant I. If *ER* lies in quadrant II the shareholders of acquiring firm suffer from unanticipated losses, if it lies in quadrant IV the shareholders of acquired firm will suffer from unanticipated losses, and if *ER* lies in quadrant III, then merger will lead to erosion of wealth for both the firms.

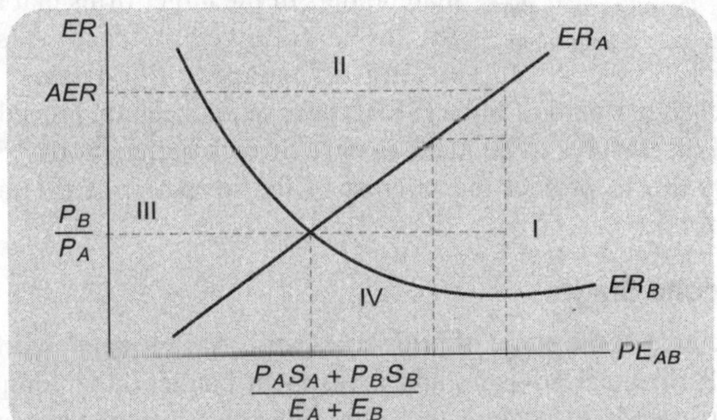

Figure 15-1 Determination of Exchange Ratio

There are other more practical approaches for determining the exchange ratio for merger. The practical bases for determining the exchange ratio are:

- Earnings per share (EPS)
- Market value per share
- Book value per share

Table A

PE_{AB}	1	2	3	4	5	6	7	8	9	10	11	12	13	14	15
Max ER_A	2.23	1.90	1.57	1.25	0.92	0.59	0.26	0.07	0.40	0.73	1.06	1.39	1.72	2.05	2.38

Table B

PE_{AB}	1	2	3	4	5	6	7	8	9	10	11	12	13	14	15
Min. ER_B	1.82	0.67	0.41	0.30	0.23	0.19	0.16	0.14	0.12	0.11	0.10	0.09	0.08	0.08	0.07

In the above mentioned three approaches the basis of determining the ER gets changed. Like if EPS is taken as the basis of determining the ER then ER will be determined based on the EPS of the merged (acquiring) and merging (acquired) firms. Supposing the EPS of the acquired firm is ₹2, while that of acquiring firm is ₹4 then the ER will be determined as 0.5, i.e., for every two shares in the acquired firm the shareholders of the acquired firm will get one share in the combined firm.

M&A DEAL

The M&A deal in most of the cases is a long drawn process that starts with the identification of the target company by the acquiring firm. The deal can be divided into three stages as illustrated in this section.

First Stage

A process of M&A typically begins with a tender offer, which is an intention by the acquiring company to purchase some or all of the shares of a target company. The offer typically contains a price that is usually at a premium to the market price. In this process, the acquiring company discreetly buys up shares in the target company, or builds a position. However, there are certain regulatory procedures to protect the interest of the shareholders of the target firms that have got to be followed in case of such buying of shares. Securities and Exchange Board of India (SEBI) laws require certain procedures and disclosures to be made in case of such acquisitions.[6] Such laws are to protect the interest of the investors of the target firm.

The M&A deal takes place in a phased manner. After identifying a target firm the acquiring firm makes a tender offer, discovers the acquisition price, and finally makes the proposal to the target firm.

Second Stage

The next is the stage of price discovery. At this stage, working with financial advisors and investment bankers, the company that intends to acquire the other company formulates a price that it is willing to pay to its target firm. After discovering the price, the acquiring firms(s) make a public announcement in the newspapers primarily disclosing its intention to acquire shares of the target company from existing shareholders by means of an open offer. The disclosures in the announcement include the offer price, number of shares to be acquired from the public, identity of acquirer, purpose of acquisition, future plans of acquirer, if any, regarding the target company, change in control over the target company, if any, the procedure to be followed by acquirer in accepting the shares tendered by the shareholders and the period within which all the formalities pertaining to the offer would be completed. The acquirer is required to make such a public announcement through the merchant banker (MB) within four working days of the entering into an agreement to acquire shares or deciding to acquire shares/ voting rights of target company. The objective of such an announcement is to ensure that the shareholders of the target firm get timely information of an exit opportunity available to them through ensuing open offer. The price, so discovered, is then publicized to the press along with a deadline by which the target company must either accept or reject the proposal. The period of time between the public announcement of a merger/acquisition and the actual close of the deal is usually associated with a process known as *due diligence*. During this period, the acquiring organization carefully analyses available data from the target organization, to determine whether its financial condition is as it has been advertised.

Third Stage

The target company responds to the proposal made by the acquiring firm. The various options available for the target firm are to accept the offer as it is, to reject the proposal outright, or to negotiate the terms of the deal so as to arrive at the best terms. There are several issues of concern to the target firm that need to be ironed out at this stage of the deal. They range from the purchase consideration offered to the target firm by the acquiring firm to the softer issues like extent of absorption of the workforce of the target firm by the acquiring firm. In case of retrenchments, the compensation packages to be offered, etc. This stage is the most crucial from the management perspective. Once the terms of the deal are finalized, the deal requires the approval of the shareholders of the target firm who may either accept or reject the deal.

ACCOUNTING FOR M&A

As discussed earlier in the chapter, a merger leads to a physical combination of the operations of the combining firms while in case of an acquisition or a takeover, the combining firms retain their separate legal status. An acquisition is essentially a strategic financial investment whereby the acquiring firm, through its financial investment in the target firm, acquires the control of the latter. The accounting treatment of an acquisition should recognize the value of the purchased financial stake in the target firm as an investment. If the acquisition is financed by issuing shares of the acquiring firm to the shareholders of the acquired (target) firm, the impact of acquisition will be on the share capital as the acquired firm's share capital would increase by the amount of the acquisition price that has been paid through the issue of shares. There will be a corresponding increase in the investments on the asset side of the acquiring firm. If the acquisition is made by paying cash then the cash account on the asset side would be reduced by the amount of acquisition price paid for in cash, while the investments will increase by a corresponding value. In case the acquisition price is higher than the fair value of the investment then the excess will be recorded as goodwill on the assets side of the balance sheet.

Merger (or amalgamation) can take the form of either consolidation or absorption. In case of a merger by consolidation,

[6]For details of such guidelines refer to the SEBI, 'Substantial acquisition of shares and takeover regulation', *Takeover Code*, 20 February 1997.

the assets and liabilities of the combining firms are transferred to the new entity formed as the result of merger. The pooling of interest method of accounting is followed to account for such a merger. Under this method, the assets, liabilities, and reserves of the transferor company are recorded by the transferee company at their existing carrying amounts as shown in Table 15-1.

Table 15-1 Balance sheet of merging and merged firm(s)

(₹ in crore)

	Firm A (Merging firm)	*Firm B (Merging firm)*	*Firm C (Merged firm)*
Assets:			
Net Block	64	77	141
Current Assets	24	36	60
Total	88	113	201
Liabilities			
Share Capital	40	50	90
Reserves and Surplus	10	20	30
Long-term loans	15	15	30
Current liabilities	23	28	51
Total	88	113	201

In case the merger is by absorption, the pre-merger assets and liabilities of the merging firms become the assets and liabilities of the firm that absorbs other firm(s) and all merging companies, except for one, lose their identity. The purchase method of accounting is used to account for such a merger that takes the form of absorption. Under this method, the pre-merger assets and the liabilities of the merging firm(s) are stated in the books of the merged firm either at their existing carrying value or at an amount that adjusts for the purchase price that is paid to the target firm. If the acquisition price is higher than the fair market value of the assets and liabilities of the target firm, the difference is shown as the goodwill in the books of merged firm. Conversely, it is shown as capital reserve in the books of the merged firm. This can be seen in Table 15-2. Firm A absorbs Firm B at a value of ₹80 crore and assumes all its assets and liabilities.

Table 15-2 Balance Sheet of merging and merged firm(s)

(₹ in crore)

	Firm A (Merging firm)	*Firm B (Merging firm)*	*Firm C (Merged firm)*
Assets:			
Net Block	64	77	146
Current Assets	24	36	59
Goodwill	—	—	6
Total	88	113	211
Liabilities			
Share Capital	40	50	90
Reserves and Surplus	10	20	40
Long-term loans	15	15	30
Current liabilities	23	28	51
Total	88	113	211

The fair value of the assets and the liabilities of Firm B are estimated as follows:

Net fixed assets: ₹82 crore (146 Cr – 64 Cr)

Current assets: ₹35 crore (59 Cr – 24 Cr)

Long-term debt and current liabilities are taken at book value. Value of Goodwill in the deal has been estimated as follows:

	(₹ in crore)	*(₹ in crore)*
Payment made to B Ltd		80
Fair value of fixed assets of B Ltd	82	
Fair value of current assets of B Ltd	35	
Fair value of total assets of B Ltd transferred to A Ltd	117	
Less: Fair value of long-term loans of B Ltd	15	
Less: Fair value of current liabilities of B Ltd	28	
Fair value of total liabilities of B Ltd transferred to A Ltd	43	
Fair value of net assets of B Ltd (117 – 43)		74
Value of goodwill		6

M&A TERMINOLOGY

In this section, we discuss the various terms and concepts that come up in the context of merger and which one must be familiar with. The terms that we now proceed to discuss and explain may not follow any sequence and may also not be interconnected but they surely are a part of the M&A literature.

Due Diligence

It has multiple meanings based upon the context in which it is used. Generically, it refers to the care that a reasonable person should take before entering into an agreement or a transaction with another party. It is done through a process of investigation or audit of a potential transaction or deal so as to find out all relevant facts pertaining to the ensuing transaction. There are various types of due diligence such as technological due diligence, environmental due diligence, organizational due diligence, financial due diligence, etc.

Due diligence in context of M&A refers to an investigation and analysis of the price of the deal and the associated risks.

In context of M&A it refers to assessing the price and identifying the financial risks involved in an M&A deal. The decisions to merge/acquire/takeover are based on the due diligence report. Critical issues addressed by such an analysis from the perspective of the acquiring/merged firm may include: value of target firm(s); synergies from the deal; estimated value creation for the acquiring/merged firm from the deal, etc. A similar due diligence could be performed by the seller on the buyer with a view to judge the purchasing power of the buyer.

Leveraged Buyout

A leveraged buyout (LBO) is a term used in context of M&A financing. When a controlling interest in a company's equity is acquired principally through borrowed funds, it is called a leveraged buyout. It is a financing strategy of an M&A deal wherein a significant amount of debt capital is used to meet the

Acquisition of controlling interest in a target firm principally through debt is termed as LBO.

cost of acquisition. The Tata–Corus deal is an example of LBO. Often, the assets of the company being acquired, in addition to the assets of the acquiring company, are used as collateral for the debt raised for financing M&A deals. The purpose of leveraged buyouts is to allow companies to make large acquisitions without having to commit a lot of capital. In a typical LBO deal, the debt component can go up to 90% of the total capitalization of the target/acquired firm. Besides the benefit of low financing cost and tax shield associated with debt LBO also aims at disciplining the management of the acquiring firm(s) by forcing them to cut down the wasteful expenditure in wake of heavy debt servicing burden.

Management Buy Outs

When the managers and/or executives of the company buy or acquire controlling interest in the company from the existing shareholders, it is termed as management buy out (MBO). Along with M&As, MBOs have assumed an important role in corporate restructuring. The goal of an MBO may be to increase the management's stake in the company. In most cases, the MBO is followed by companies going private with management buying out all the outstanding shares with the financial support of venture capitalists. This happens as the management feels that it has the expertise to grow the business better if it controls the ownership of the business. An example of MBO is Tata Infomedia, which the management bought out with the support of ICICI Venture. One main criticism of MBOs is that they create incentive for managers to deliberately not manage the firms' operations efficiently. By their doing so, they would be able to bring down the stock prices and purchase shares at depressed prices. Post MBO they may gain significantly due to the stock prices rising on account of efficient management of the firm.

MBO refers to the acquisition of controlling interest in a firm by its management.

Poison Pill

A strategy used by management of a target company to discourage a hostile takeover. In such a strategy, the target company attempts to make its stock less attractive to the acquirer by increasing the cost of takeover. Such a strategy may take the form of issuing rights by the target company to its existing shareholders to acquire a large number of new securities, usually common stock or preferred stock. These new rights usually allow holders (other than an acquirer) to convert the right into a large number of common shares if anyone acquires more than a set amount of the target's stock (typically 10–20%). This immediately dilutes the percentage of the target owned by the acquirer, and makes it more expensive to acquire control of the target. There are two types of poison pills—flip-in and flip-over. A flip-in poison pill allows existing shareholders (except the acquirer) to buy more shares at a discount. By purchasing more shares cheaply, investors get instant profits and, more importantly, the additional number of shares dilutes the shares held by the competitors. The flip-over strategy allows stockholders to buy the acquirer's shares at a discounted price after the merger.

Poison pill is a strategy used by the target firm to prevent its hostile takeover making the own stock less attractive for the acquirer.

M&A IN INDIA

The news of Indian companies acquiring a US or European firm that may have been surprising most of us a few years back has become common place today. A growing number of Indian companies have been on a buying spree in Europe, Asia Pacific, and other parts of the world in the quest to become players in the global market. These big ticket acquisitions by Indian companies globally are the signs that Indian companies are prepared to take over. The inbound mergers, acquisitions, and takeovers of Indian firms by the global players have been outperformed by the outbound mergers in the recent years as indicated in the Tables 15-3 and 15-4.

Outbound M&A by Indian firms have outperformed the inbound mergers by their global counterparts.

Table 15-3 M&A activity in India in 2006[7]

Nature of mergers	*Percentage*
Outbound mergers	62%
Inbound mergers	26%
Domestic mergers	12%

Note: The above percentages are based on the deals valuing more than US$ 20 million.

Table 15-4 Inbound Vs Outbound M&A: deal value[8]

(In US$ million)

	Inbound deals	*Outbound deals*
2001	1634	40
2002	3204	792
2003	1581	599
2004	1409	901
2005	3549	3569
2006	3898	6361

Note: The above deal values are based take into account deals valuing more that US$ 20 million.

Based on the figures given in Tables 15-1 and 15-2, it can be easily inferred that cross-border mergers involving Indian firms are gaining significance compared to domestic M&A. In cross-border M&A deals that have taken place, outbound M&As have outperformed the inbound M&A activity. The outbound M&A has really picked up since 2005 and was significantly higher than inbound M&A activity in 2006 in terms of both, the

[7] *Source:* Country perspectives: Mergers and acquisition activity in India, Rohit Kapur, KPMG India Presentation to CII, 30 January 2007.

[8] ibid

Significant growth witnessed by services sector companies, strategic shift by Indian firms to move up the value chain and the huge surpluses on account of booming domestic economy have been the major drivers of outbound M&A activities by Indian firms.

number and the value of deals. In fact, 2006 will be a remembered as a landmark year in India's corporate history as a year when Indian companies covered a lot of new ground by acquiring a number of strategically significant companies all across the globe. This comprised 62% of the total mergers and acquisitions (M&A) activity in India in 2006. The most important feature of these M&As was that over 95% of acquisitions were made with cash payments. This reflects the buying power of Indian firms.

The following factors have been responsible for this significant growth in the outbound mergers, acquisitions and takeovers by Indian firms:

1. The outsourcing phenomenon, especially in IT industry has helped Indian companies by exposing Indian managers to western business culture and practices preparing them to handle operations in such destinations. Indian IT companies like Wipro and Infosys have witnessed exponential growth in their profits that has generated huge surpluses over the years. These surpluses are being utilized for such acquisitions with a view to increasing their market through such geographical expansion and also to protecting their businesses models against US business cycles by diversifying into markets other than US.
2. Outbound mergers are also giving opportunities to Indian companies to go up in the value chain. If on one hand the big MNCs are shifting their low value activities to low cost manufacturing and service destinations like China and India, Indian firms through these outbound mergers, acquisitions, and takeovers are targeting the end of the value chain to boost their margins. The Tata–Corus deal is an example of this strategic shift of Indian firms.
3. A booming domestic economy has increased the surpluses that the Indian companies, across the board, are carrying on their balance sheets. This coupled with the availability of easy international financing is facilitating the Indian firms to lever their existing surpluses and invest them in acquiring global firms. This is not only bringing them the economies of scale but also bringing down their cost of production and delivery by integrating their supply chains.

On account of the aforesaid factors, Indian companies have already made 382 deals worth ₹1,047 billion ($26 billion) in the first half of 2007, a substantial rise of 126% in deal value over the same period last year. Some of the top outbound M&A deals involving Indian firms are shown in Table 15-5.

Table 15-5 Some of the major global M&A deals involving Indian firms in 2006-07

S No.	*Acquirer*	*Target Company (Country)*	*Industry*	*Deal (approximate value) ($ million)*	*Major Synergies from the deal for the acquirer*
1	Tata Steel	Corus Group plc (UK)	Steel	12,000	Access to high-end European market. A combination of low cost of production in India and high-end market in Europe will boost the margins significantly.
2	Hindalco	Novelis (Canada)	Steel	6000	To establish a global integrated low-cost aluminium production facilities combined with high-end aluminium rolled product capabilities. The complementary expertise of both the companies is likely to create and provide a strong platform for sustainable growth and ongoing success.
3	Videocon	Daewoo Electronics Corp. (Korea)	Electronics	730	Give access to 25 manufacturing facilities in South Korea, the US, and the UK, and will give Videocon a global presence.
4.	Dr. Reddy's Labs	Betapharm (Germany)	Pharmaceutical	597	Will give Dr. Reddy's access to the German and European markets and also the wide distribution network of Betapharm.
5	Suzlon Energy	Hansen Group (Belgium)	Energy	565	Geographical diversification and vertical integration in the sector will also give suzlon access to R&D facilities in Europe along with the presence that it already has in low cost manufacturing destinations like India and China.
6	HPCL	Kenya Petroleum Refinery Ltd (Kenya)	Oil and Gas	500	Give HPCL opportunities in the upstream and increase its supply source. Unleash its capacities.
7	Ranbaxy Labs	Terapia SA (Romania)	Pharmaceutical	324	To increase its product portfolio by adding 157 products of Terapia and to increase its presence in Europe.
8	Tata Steel	Natsteel (Singapore)	Steel	293	Give Tata Steel access to the key Asia-Pacific markets of Nat steel in China, Thailand, Vietnam, Philippines, Australia, and Malaysia.
9	Videocon	Thomson SA (France)	Electronics	290	Videocon will own Thomson's three manufacturing facilities in Poland, Mexico, and China. Also allows Videocon to take over the R&D facilities at various places in Europe and China and access to a large resource of the patents and IPRS relating to technologies in colour picture tube segment.
10	VSNL	Teleglobe (Canada)	Telecom	239	Expand VSNL's ownership interests in undersea cable networks and provide it with more than 200 direct and bilateral agreements with leading voice carriers.

As can be seen in Table 15-5, the outbound M&A by Indian firms is distributed across the sectors and is not merely concentrated to few sectors such as IT as it was in the initial years. The sectors attracting outbound mergers, acquisitions and, takeovers by Indian firms are varied and include metals, pharmaceuticals, industrial goods, automotive components, beverages, telecommunications, Information technology, and banking, with pharmaceuticals, IT, and metals being the prominent ones. In 2006, the largest proportion of outbound deals occurred in Europe (50% of deal value), followed by North America (24% of deal value).

The outbound M&A deals by Indian firms are widely distributed across the sectors with IT, pharmaceutical, automobile telecommunications, metals, banking and financial services being the prominent ones.

REGULATORY FRAMEWORK OF M&A IN INDIA

Mergers and acquisition deals, particularly the horizontal M&As, may affect the competitive situation in the industry. Since M&As (particularly horizontal M&As) have the potential to cut down the competition significantly, they are on the active scanner of Competition Commission of India (CCI). Mergers and acquisitions also affect the shareholders of the combining firms. This brings the M&A under the SEBI's purview. Due to the restructuring of the firms and its tax impact, the Companies Act and the Income Tax Act regulations also come into the picture in an M&A deal. Due to this multi-pronged impact of M&A deals, a comprehensive legal framework has evolved in India to regulate such deals. This regulation is mainly from the viewpoint of the impact of the deal on the—competitive position in the industry, shareholders, tax aspects, etc. The M&A activities in the Indian market are regulated by the provisions contained in the following:

1. Indian Companies Act, 1956
2. Competition Act, 2002
3. Income Tax Act, 1961
4. The Securities Exchange Board of India (Substantial Acquisition of Shares and Takeovers) Regulations, 1997
5. Listing agreement of stock exchanges
6. Takeover code of SEBI

SUMMARY

M&A has emerged as a potent tool for corporate consolidation and restructuring that is being used by the firms world over with a view to either reduce costs or to increase revenues through market expansion or product extension. It also facilitates in risk mitigation by combining with firms in unrelated businesses. In case of firms that have entered the maturity phase, M&A propels their growth.

Merger denotes fusion of two or more corporations with a view to improving operational efficiency of merging entities. Mergers may be done with an existing company or companies may decide to merge to form a new company. Merger can take either the form of absorption or consolidation. M&A deals can be viewed from three different perspectives: as corporate restructuring decision, as a strategic decision, and as an investment decision.

While merger refers to the combining of two or more firms wherein the businesses of the merging firms is combined and all but one of the combining firms lose their existence an acquisition refers to an act of acquiring effective control by one company over assets or management of another company without any physical combination of companies. Technically, *acquisition* and *takeover* are two different terms having the same meaning; yet sometimes, the term *takeover* is used to denote an unfriendly acquisition that is forced upon the target firm against the wishes of its management. In India, amalgamation is the legal term used for merger.

M&A bring in certain operating and financial synergies for the combining firms on account of economies of scale. M&A are advantageous for the combining firms as they boost both the top-line and the bottom-line of the combining firms by enhancing the growth rate and cutting down the competition. Besides they also mitigate the business risk through diversification.

There are three types of mergers; horizontal, vertical, and conglomerate. While horizontal merger involves combining of firms dealing in similar products/ services vertical merger is the combination of firms operating at different stages of value chain within the industry. Combination of unrelated businesses is termed as conglomerate merger.

Since M&A entail huge capital outlay, have long-term implications for cash flows of the acquired/merged firms they are evaluated like a capital budgeting decisions. The NPV forms the basis for M&A decisions. The NPV in M&A is the difference between the present value of the combined (merged) firm and the sum of the present values of individual merging firms. The determination of exchange ratio is one of the important aspects of an M&A deal. Exchange ratio (ER) is the ratio of number of shares that the shareholders of acquired (merged) firm receive in the combined firm in exchange for the number of shares held by them in the merging (acquired) firm. The M&A deal takes place in a phased manner. After identifying a target firm the acquiring firm makes a tender offer, discovers the acquisition price, and finally makes the proposal to the target firm.

In line with the global trends, Indian business environment has also witnessed growing number and value of M&A deals. One major shift that has been noticed of late is that the number and value of outbound M&A deals by Indian firms has outpaced the number of the inbound deals. Besides the M&A deals today are happening in varied sectors unlike a few selected sectors in past.

KEY TERMS

Synergy The idea that the value and performance of two companies combined will be greater than the sum of the separate individual parts. Symbolically it is represented as:

Value (AB) > Value (A) + Value (B)

Economies of scale The increase in production efficiency on account of increase in the activity level. Such economies occur as with the increase in the activity level the fixed costs get spread over larger volumes and as the result the average cost per unit gets lowered. In an M&A deal, the combined firm gets the benefit of the economies of scale as the scale of operations of the combined firm goes up.

Swap ratio The literal meaning of the term swap is exchange. In M&A parlance, it is used for exchange of shares in a combined firm against the shares in the combining firms. It is the ratio in which the shareholders of the combining firms are allotted shares in the combined/merged firm. Alternatively, it is referred to as exchange ratio. A swap ratio of 1:2 or 1 for 2 means that the shareholders of combining firm(s) will get one share in the combined firm for every two shares held in the combining firm(s)

Target firm A firm that is being targeted by another firm for the takeover. A firm becomes target due to its perpetually weak financial performance causing the shareholders to sell their shares. This pushes down the share prices and makes the firm a good prospect (target) for acquiring firms.

Cross border M&A An M&A transaction involving companies that are located or regulated in different countries. Such deals often involve more than two countries, for example, a US private equity firm sells investment in German manufacturing firm to Indian buyer.

Inbound M&A An M&A deal in which a target Indian firm is acquired by/merged with an overseas firm.

Outbound M&A M&A deals in which an overseas target firm is acquired by/merged with an Indian firm.

PRACTICE PROBLEMS

1. Computation of Costs and Benefits of Merger

Alpha Ltd is planning to merge with Beta Ltd. The key value metrics of the two firms are given below:

	Alpha Ltd	*Beta Ltd*
Market price per share (₹)	445	272
Book value per share	174	87
Number of Shares outstanding	25,00,000	10,50,000
Market value of the firm (₹)	1,11,25,00,000	28,56,00,000

The synergistic impact of merger is likely to benefit both the firms. The total gains of ₹875 lakh are likely to accrue, in PV terms, to the firms. The purchase consideration is proposed to be paid by Alpha Ltd to Beta Ltd by issuing shares in Alpha Ltd to the shareholders of Beta Ltd. One share in Alpha Ltd for every 1.5 shares in Beta Ltd is proposed to be offered. How is the proposed merger going to benefit the two firms?

Compute the NPV of the deal for the two companies involved in the merger.

Solution

The cost in this case is defined as:

$$\text{Cost} = \alpha \, PV_{\text{Alpha + Beta}} - PV_{\text{Beta}}$$

Where α represents the fraction of the combined entity received by the shareholders of Beta Ltd. Since the swap ratio is 1 for 1.5, the total shares of Alpha to be issued to the shareholders of Beta Ltd would be:

$$\frac{10{,}50{,}000}{1.5} = 7{,}00{,}000$$

In the above example, the share of Beta in the combined entity is:

$$\alpha = 7{,}00{,}000/(25{,}00{,}000 + 70{,}00{,}000)$$
$$= 0.21875$$

Let's assume that the market value of the combined entity will be equal to the sum of present value of the separate entities and the benefit of merger. Then,

$$PV_{\text{Alpha + Beta}} = PV_{\text{Alpha}} + PV_{\text{Beta}} + \text{PV of Benefit}_{\text{Alpha + Beta}}$$
$$= 1{,}11{,}25{,}00{,}000 + 28{,}56{,}00{,}000 + 8{,}75{,}00{,}000$$
$$= ₹1{,}48{,}56{,}00{,}000$$
$$\text{Cost} = \alpha \, PV_{\text{Alpha + Beta}} - PV_{\text{Beta}}$$
$$= 0.21875 \times 1{,}48{,}56{,}00{,}000 - 28{,}56{,}00{,}000$$
$$= ₹3{,}93{,}75{,}000$$

Thus,

NPV to Alpha = Benefit – Cost

8,75,00,000 – 3,93,75,000 = 4,81,25,000

NPV to Beta = Cost to Alpha = 3,93,75,000

2. Mergers and Acquisition as a Capital Budgeting Decision

Emphasis Ltd has prepared a strategic roadmap for the next 10 years to boost its growth. The strategic plan has proposed inorganic growth as the main growth driver. To give effect to its strategic plan, the firm has identified Metamorphosis Ltd as a target firm for horizontal merger. Such a merger would increase the market share of Emphasis Ltd from 32% at present to 54%.

The cash flows of Emphasis Ltd are expected to grow at 27.5% for the next 10 years on account of merger. This is significantly above the current growth rate of 9.5%. The growth rate after 10 years is likely to normalize and come down to the 12% level. In case Emphasis Ltd does not merge with Metamorphosis Ltd, its growth rate beyond year 10 is expected to come down to 6.5%. The projected post-tax cash flow for Emphasis Ltd at the end of first year is ₹1000 lakh in absence of merger. However if Emphasis Ltd combines with Metamorphosis Ltd, the cash flow at the end of first year is projected to be ₹1785 lakh. The required rate of return for the firms that have risk-return characteristics similar to Emphasis Ltd is 14.5%.

The number of equity shares outstanding in Emphasis Ltd are 4,50,000 while those in Y Ltd are 2,00,000. If the acquisition takes place, the exchange ratio is likely to be 0.5 in the combined firm for the shareholders of Y Ltd.

Do you approve of the merger? Your advice should be based on the NPV to the acquiring firm (Emphasis Ltd).

Solution

The decision to acquire Metamorphosis depends on the value that is likely to be created (NPV) on account of such an acquisition. This can be calculated by finding the difference between PV of Cash Flows of the Combined Firm and the PV of Cash Flows of Emphasis Ltd without acquisition.

For the purpose of Cash Flow estimation of Emphasis Ltd (without acquisition), growth rate can be split into: g_1 and g_2. With g_1 representing growth rate for year 1–10 and g_2 representing growth rate from year 10 onwards.

Since the benefit of acquisition will be availed over infinite period of time. The period of evaluation has been divided into two phases; abnormal growth phase (Year 1 through 10) and the normal growth phase (Year 10 onwards). The growth rate for Combined Firm during the abnormal growth phase (Year 1–10) can be termed as g_a. While for period thereafter (i.e. beyond year 10, which is expected to be normal growth period) can be termed as g_n. Now let us estimate Cash Flows for NPV computation.

After-tax cash flows of the acquiring firm Emphasis Ltd (without acquisition) for the abnormal growth phase are estimated as follows:

Cash Flow for Year n = Cash Flow Year 1 $(1 + g)^n$

Computation of Present Value of Cash flows (Year 1–10) without merger for Emphasis Ltd.

Year	CF (Emphasis) (₹ In lakh)	PV Factor @ 14.5%	Present Value (₹ in lakh)
1	1000.00	0.8734	873.36
2	1095.00	0.7628	835.22
3	1199.03	0.6662	798.75
4	1312.93	0.5818	763.87
5	1437.66	0.5081	730.51
6	1574.24	0.4438	698.61
7	1723.79	0.3876	668.11
8	1887.55	0.3385	638.93
9	2066.87	0.2956	611.03
10	2263.22	0.2582	584.35
		Sum of PV →	7202.76

Terminal value of Emphasis Ltd (without acquisition) can be computed as follows:

$$\frac{\text{Cash Flow of Year 10 } (1+g_2)}{r-g_2}$$

$$\frac{2263.22\,(1+0.065)}{0.145-0.065} = ₹30,129,14 \text{ lakh}$$

PV of cash flow for Emphasis Ltd for normal growth period (Year 10 onwards)

$$= \frac{\text{Terminal Value}}{(1+r)^n}$$

$$= \frac{30,129,14}{(1+0.145)^{10}} = ₹7779.14 \text{ lakh}$$

PV of Emphasis Ltd (without merger) will be:

PV of abnormal growth phase + PV of normal growth period

= 7202.76 + 7779.14

= ₹14,981.90 lakh

The post-merger cash flows for the normal growth period (year 10 onwards) of the combined firm are estimated as follows:

Cash flow for year n = –Cash flow for Year 1 $(1 + g_a)^n$

Computation of Present Value of Cash flows (abnormal growth period) for Emphasis Ltd (post-merger):

Year	CF (Emphasis) (₹ in lakh)	PV Factor @ 14.5%	Present Value (₹ in lakh)
1	1785.00	0.8734	1558.95
2	2275.88	0.7628	1735.95
3	2901.74	0.6662	1933.05
4	3699.72	0.5818	2152.52
5	4717.14	0.5081	2396.91
6	6014.36	0.4438	2669.05
7	7668.30	0.3876	2972.08
8	9777.09	0.3385	3309.52
9	12465.79	0.2956	3685.28
10	15893.88	0.2582	4103.69
		Sum of PV →	26517.00

Terminal value of Emphasis Ltd post merger can be computed as follows:

$$\frac{\text{Cash Flow for Year 10 } (1+g_n)}{r-g_n}$$

$$= \frac{15893.88\,(1+0.12)}{0.145-0.12} = ₹7,12,045.75 \text{ lakh}$$

PV of cash flow for combined firm for normal growth period (Year 10 onwards)

$$= \frac{\text{Terminal Value}}{(1+r)^n}$$

$$= \frac{7,12,045.75}{(1+0.145)^{10}} = ₹1,83,845.5 \text{ lakh}$$

So PV of combined firm will be:

PV of abnormal growth phase + PV of normal growth period

= 26,517.00 + 1,83,845.50

= ₹2,10,362.51 lakh

Ownership position (OP) for the shareholders of Emphasis Ltd in the combined firm can be estimated as follows:

$$\text{OP} = \frac{4,50,000}{4,50,000 + 0.5(2,00,000)} = 0.81818$$

NPV of the merger proposal from the point of view of the combined firm can be computed as follows:

NPV (combined firm) = (2,10,362.51 × 0.818) – 14,981.90
= ₹1,57,094.63 lakh

Thus, the merger is likely to create value for the acquiring firm (Emphasis Ltd) by ₹1,57,094.63 lakh. Hence acquisition is approved.

3. Determination of Exchange Ratio (ER) using LG Model

Two companies, Inquest Ltd and Impress Ltd, have decided to merge. The relevant financials of the two firms are as follows:

	Inquest Ltd	**Impress Ltd**
Total earnings, *E* (in ₹lakh)	450	125
No. of shares outstanding, *S* (in lakh)	25	10
Earnings per share, EPS (₹)	18.00	12.5
Price earnings ratio, P/E (Times)	10	7
Market price per share, *P* (₹)	150	65

Using the LG model, determine the exchange ratio for the merger.

Solution

$$ER_{\text{Inquest}} = \left(\frac{S_{\text{Inquest}}}{S_{\text{Impress}}}\right)\left[\frac{E_{\text{Inquest}} + E_{\text{Impress}}}{P_{\text{Impress}} \times S_{\text{Inquest}}} PE_{\text{combined firm}}\right]$$

$$= \left(\frac{25}{10}\right) + \left[\left(\frac{450 + 125}{150 \times 25}\right) PE_{\text{Combined firm}}\right]$$

Using the above equation, the ER $_{\text{Inquest Ltd}}$ can be computed for the various levels.

P/E fraction of combined firm. The calculations are given in the following table:

$PE_{\text{Combined firm}}$	Max. $ER_{\text{Inquest Ltd}}$	$PE_{\text{Combined firm}}$	Max. $ER_{\text{Inquest Ltd}}$
1	–2.65	9	–1.12
2	–2.81	10	–0.97
3	–2.96	11	–0.81
4	–3.11	12	–0.66
5	–3.27	13	–0.51
6	–1.58	14	–0.35
7	–1.43	15	–0.20
8	–1.27		

Similarly, the ER can be computed for the firm Impress Ltd using the following model:

$$ER_{\text{Impress}} = \frac{P_{\text{Impress}} \times S_{\text{Impresst}}}{[(PE_{\text{Combined firm}})(E_{\text{Impresst}} + E_{\text{Impress}}) - P_{\text{Impress}} \times S_{\text{Impress}}]}$$

$$ER_{\text{Impress}} = \frac{65 \times 25}{[(PE_{AB}) \times (450 + 125) - 65 \times 10]}$$

Using the above equation the ER_B can be computed for the various levels P/E fraction of combined firm (AB). The calculations are given in the following table:

$PE_{\text{Combined firm}}$	Min. ER_{Impress}	$PE_{\text{Combined firm}}$	Min. ER_{Impress}
1	–21.67	9	0.36
2	3.25	10	0.32
3	1.51	11	0.29
4	0.98	12	0.26
5	0.73	13	0.24
6	0.58	14	0.22
7	0.48	15	0.20
8	0.41		

Thus, ER would be settled somewhere in between the minimum and maximum exchange ratios that have been determined for different levels of expected PE multiples of the combined firm. During the negotiations for the M&A deal, the combined (acquiring) company would like to keep the ER as low as possible, while the merging (acquired) firm would want it to be as high as possible. As a result, the AER will lie somewhere between Max. ER and Min. ER. At P/E of 15 there is a trade off between maximum and minimum exchange ratio. However, the actual exchange ratio will depend upon the negotiations between the two firms.

4. Exchange Ratio to Earn a Fixed EPS Post-Merger

Management of Amtech Ltd is under immense pressure to boost its sagging earnings. The firm has been advised by its consultants "Matrix Solutions" to follow the route of inorganic growth as an immediate solution to its problem. In the medium term as the market picks up the earnings position is likely to improve on its own. The current profit after tax (PAT) for Amtech Ltd is ₹125 lakh and the EPS is ₹3.125. Current market value per share for Amtech Ltd stands at ₹57.25.

Matrix Ltd, as a part of their consulting package, has identified Susceptible Ltd as the suitable target firm. The current PAT of Susceptible Ltd is ₹75 lakh. Its EPS is ₹7.5 and the market price of its shares is ₹87.5.

If Amtech wants its EPS to go up to the level of ₹5.75, what exchange ratio should it offer to the shareholders of Susceptible Ltd?

Solution

The following financial information is available for the two firms:

	Amtech Ltd	**Susceptible Ltd**
PAT (₹ in lakh)	125.000	75.000
EPS	3.125	7.500
Market Value per share (₹)	57.250	87.500
No. of Shares outstanding (lakh)	40.000	10.000
PAT of combined firm (₹ in lakh)	200.000	

Since the EPS post merger is expected to be ₹5.75, the exchange ratio can be computed as follows:

$$\frac{\text{Combined PAT}}{\text{No. of shares in combined firm}} = ₹5.75$$

$$\frac{125 + 75}{40 + x} = ₹5.75$$

x = 5.22 lakh

Thus, exchange ratio = 5.22/10 = 0.522

EXERCISES

Concept Review Questions

1. What do you understand by merger? What are the advantages of mergers?
2. Distinguish between mergers, acquisitions, and takeovers?
3. What are the various types of mergers and what is the rationale behind them?
4. How is the cost–benefit analysis done in an M&A deal?
5. Discuss the different stages involved in an M&A deal.

Critical Thinking Questions

1. What are the factors that have led to an increase in the M&A activity worldwide?
2. M&A decisions are viewed as corporate restructuring decision, strategic decision, and investment decision? Elaborate.
3. NPV forms the basis of evaluation of the M&A deal. If the NPV from the M&A deal is positive for the firms involved, M&A is likely to be a value creator. Discuss in the light of the basic valuation model for M&A.
4. The direction, scale, and sectors of M&A deals involving Indian firms have undergone significant change over the years. Analyse the statement and discuss the key reasons responsible for the increasing scale of M&A activities involving Indian firms.

Practical Assignment

Pick up any latest M&A deal. Generate the details of the deal and then study the deal in the light of the following:

- Nature of the deal: merger, acquisition, or takeover. If it is a merger, what type of merger is it?
- Synergies likely to emerge to the combining and combined firm(s) from the deal
- The valuation for the merger
- The basis of exchange rate determination

Numerical Problems

1. Computation of Costs and Benefits of Merger

Given below are the financials of A Ltd and B Ltd before the merger takes place. B Ltd is likely to merge with A Ltd.

	A Ltd	B Ltd
Market price per share (₹)	100	50
Book value per share	45	24
Number of Shares outstanding	5,00,000	3,00,000
Market value of the firm (₹)	5,00,00,000	1,50,00,000

One share in A Ltd is offered to the shareholders of B Ltd for every 2 share held in B Ltd. The merger is expected to bring gains, which have a PV of ₹ 125 lakh.

Compute the NPV of the deal for the two companies involved in the merger.

2. M&A as a Capital Budgeting Decision

Fema and Fench (F&F) is considering the proposal to acquire Belco Ltd. Such an acquisition is likely to increase the market share of F&F from 23% at present to 45%. Cash flows for the combined firm are projected to grow at 27.5% post acquisition for the first 5 years. The projected rate of growth in cash flows is likely to come down and stabilize at 10% post fifth year.

The projected post-tax cash flows for F&F for the next 5 years (without acquisition) are as follows:

Year	1	2	3	4	5
Cash Flow for F&F (₹ in lakh)	450	510.75	579.70	657.96	746.79

If the acquisition takes place, the expected cash flows (after tax) of the combined firm (CF) are projected as:

Year	1	2	3	4	5
Cash Flow for CF (₹ in lakh)	575.00	733.13	934.73	1191.79	1519.53

The required rate of return for the firms that have risk-return characteristics similar to *X* Ltd is 13.75%. F&F has 20 lakh shares outstanding while Belco Ltd has 15 lakh outstanding shares. The swap ratio will be 3 shares in the combined firm for every 4 shares held by the shareholders of Belco Ltd in the firm. Should Fema and Fench go ahead with the acquisition of Belco? Evaluate in the light of value likely to be created/eroded for F&F.

3. Determination of Exchange Ratio (ER) using the LG Model

Two companies (A&B) decide to merge. The relevant financials of the two firms are as follows:

	Firm A	Firm B
Total earnings, *E* (in lakh)	400	150
No. of shares outstanding, *S* (in lakh)	20	10
Earnings per Share, EPS (₹)	20	15
Price Earnings ratio, PE (Times)	12	8
Market Price per share, *P* (₹)	40	14

Based on the above information you are required to determine the maximum and the minimum exchange rate for the merger.

4. Exchange Ratio to Earn a Fixed EPS Post-merger

Alpha Ltd wants to boost its EPS quickly and has been advised by its consultants "Value creators" to adopt the inorganic route for the purpose.

The company, on the advice of its consultants, is planning for acquiring Beta Ltd. The acquisition of Beta Ltd is likely to create a synergy of 10% post acquisition. Alpha Ltd wants to peg its EPS at ₹8 level post merger. Following are the EPS, market value and number of shares for Beta Ltd:

	Alpha Ltd	Beta Ltd
EPS (₹)	5	5
Market Value per share (₹)	60	50
Number of shares	12,00,000	10,00,000

Determine the exchange ratio that will result in the EPS of ₹ 8 post acquisition.

CASE STUDY

Hindalco's acquisition of Indal*

Background of Indal

Kolkata-based Indal was incorporated in 1938. The company is the third largest producer of aluminium in India, after Hindalco Industries and National Aluminium Co. The company has vertically integrated the aluminium operations from bauxite mining, alumina refining, power generation, and aluminium smelting, to semi-fabricated products of sheet, foil, and extrusions, as well as aluminium scrap recycling. The company was promoted by Alcan Aluminium of Canada. The equity shares of Indal are listed on the Mumbai, Calcutta, and National Stock Exchanges. Its GDRs are listed on the Luxembourg Stock Exchange. The company came under the fold of the Aditya Birla group in March 2000. The group, via Hindalco Industries—the largest manufacturer of primary aluminium, acquired a 74.5% stake in Indal for ₹1,008 crore. The addition of Indal consolidated the Aditya Birla group's numero uno position in the Indian aluminium industry.

Background of Hindalco

Hindalco Industries is India's largest aluminium manufacturing company. Like Indal, it is a vertically integrated aluminium producer—from bauxite mining, alumina relining, power generation, and aluminium smelting, to downstream aluminium products. The group currently holds a 74.5% stake in Indal. On 21 July 2002, the board of Hindalco Industries approved the acquisition of the balance 25.5% stake in Indal. The consolidation of stake in Indal appears to be part of the Aditya Birla group's restructuring initiative to emerge as a global player in the non-ferrous metals market.

Scenario

Aluminum industry, which is highly capital intensive and scale sensitive, depends on two major variable cost components viz. alumina and power. Bauxite from which alumina is obtained, being a bulk commodity, has forced companies to be concentrated near bauxite deposits. Given the higher price realization of 25–50% between primary metals and downstream products over the past couple of years the focus of aluminium industry has been shifting from primary metal to a wider basket of value-added downstream products, such as rolled products, extrusions and foils.

The major companies in the Indian aluminium industry are Hindalco, NALCO, BALCO and Indal with Hindalco having the largest manufacturing capacity in the industry. The Indian aluminium industry, in line with the global trends in the global aluminium industry that underwent a major consolidation last year with giants teaming up with each other, took a step in the same direction. The public sector National Aluminium Company (NALCO) is planning a ₹2,000 crore expansion to increase its primary metal capacity from 2.3 lakh tonnes to 3.45 lakh tonnes with an addition of 120 MW captive power to take it to 840 MW.

At the international level, the process of consolidation that has ushered is likely to gather further momentum in the years to come. Given the relatively optimistic demand outlook and examining the production forecast of all aluminium majors, the industry is staring at a supply deficit of 1.74 lakh tonne of primary metal in 2004-05. From the feasibility studies conducted by several consultants, it is clear that the setting up of greenfield capacities in India may not create adequate shareholder value to justify the investments and risks involved.

The Financials

	Target: Indian Aluminium Co.			*Acquirer: Hindalco Industries*		
	Mar '00	*Mar '01*	*Mar '02*	*Mar '00*	*Mar '01*	*Mar '02*
Total Income	1203.9	1425.7	1575.5	2448.4	2718.0	2873.1
Total Expenses	1010.1	1169.4	1322.8	1392.0	1531.1	1667.5
Non-recurring Exp.	3.1	10.2	15.0	22.8	0.3	2.9
PBDIT	193.8	256.3	252.7	1056.3	1186.9	1205.6
Depreciation	56.5	63.0	62.2	135.7	143.1	154.5
Interest	37.3	40.8	38.0	59.7	63.6	46.2
PBT	100.0	152.5	152.6	860.9	980.2	1005.0
Tax Prov.	16.1	36.5	35.5	248.5	302.1	319.0
PAT	83.9	116.0	117.1	612.4	678.1	686.0
Net worth	772.0	856.7	800.1	3799.2	4378.8	4581.6
Capital	71.1	71.1	71.1	74.5	74.5	74.5
Reserved	700.9	785.5	729.0	3724.8	4304.4	4507.1
Borrowings	409.4	400.7	430.9	575.2	714.5	957.7
GFA	1190.6	1224.5	1307.6	3910.9	4349.8	5180.0
NFA	768.6	752.5	779.1	1996.4	2147.7	2691.1
Investments	85.0	202.7	265.6	1132.9	1917.5	1985.3
Net Curr.assets	307.5	292.8	183.2	1240.6	1023.8	858.8
Expenses (nwo)	15.4	9.3	3.1	—	—	—
Total Assets	1181.4	1257.3	1231.0	4374.4	5093.3	5539.3
Dividend (%)	50.0	40.0	40.0	80.0	120.0	135.0
RCNW (%)	8.2	14.9	12.2	17.9	16.2	13.9
ROCE (%)	10.6	17.9	15.4	22.8	21.8	18.7
Debt/Equity (times)	0.5	0.5	0.5	0.2	0.2	0.2
EPS(₹)	11.80	16.31	16.46	82.23	91.06	92.12
BVS(₹)	108.56	120.46	112.52	510.15	588.03	615.26

The Aditya Birla Group plans to consolidate its holding in Indian Aluminium Co., a company it gained control of in March 2000. Subsequently, on 25 July 2002, Hindalco Industries made an open offer to acquire the remaining stake in India at ₹120 per share, aggregating ₹218.19 crore. On the successful completion of the offer, Indal will become the wholly owned subsidiary of Hindalco Industries. On public holding falling below 10%, a final open offer at ₹120 per share will be made by Hindalco Industries. Following the completion of this final offer, the shares of Indal will be removed from the list of the bourses.

---

*Sources:

1. Mergers and acquisitions database of CMIE.
2. 'Building muscle to bid for Nalco', *The Hindu*, 29 July 2002.
3. 'Consolidation in aluminium', *The Hindu*, 02 April 2000.

The M&A Deal	
Target Company	Indian Aluminium Co.
Ownership-Target Company	Aditya Birla Group
Activity	Aluminium
Ownership-Acquirer Company	Aditya Birla Group
Lead Manager	DSP Merrill Lynch
Registrar	MCS
Stock Exchange Listed On	BSE, CSE, LXSE, NSE
Announcement Date	26 July 2002
Opening Date	14 October 2002
Ruling Price (BSE) ₹)	117.05
Total Amount (₹ crore)	218.19
Offer Amount (₹ crore)	218.19
Offer Price (₹)	120.00
Latest Price (BSE) (₹)	17.20 (30 Sept. 2002)
EPS (₹)	15.81
Offer P/E	7.59
BVS (₹)	112.52
Offer P/BV	1.07

Merger with Hindalco Industries would create a powerhouse with revenues of nearly ₹6,000 crore and PBIT of over ₹1,500 crore (based on 31st March 2002 results).

(As on 31 March 2002)

(₹ in crore)

	Turnover	PBIT	Net Worth
Hindalco Industries	2331.4	988.6	4581.6
Indian Aluminium Co.	1386.4	179.2	800.1
Indo Gulf Corpn.	2238.4*	419.5*	1547.0
Total	5966.2	1687.3	6928.7

Note: *Minus the Fertilizers Business.

Post-merger Scenario

Hindalco will benefit significantly from the merger because its growth has been affected due to the non-availability of additional metal volumes. Its brownfield expansion will give additional volumes in the next 2-3 years. Hindalco will be able to save time on setting up a new greenfield venture to expand capacity. Besides, it will have access to value added products, a wider geographical area and a wider customer base. The foils and sheets business of Indal will go a long way in adding value to Hindalco's portfolio. In terms of margins, Hindalco was better off because of its complete integration with access to captive power and primary metal. The deal has also boosted Hindalco's export prospects. Indal had made inroads into the export markets for alumina and semi-fabricated products. It recently modernized its rolled products facility to bring it on a par with international standards. Hindalco has a surplus metal capacity but insufficient alumina and downstream capacity. Indal is metal-strapped although it has large alumina and downstream capacity. Indal has been resorting to duty-free imports to convert into downstream products. Up to 40% of its requirement of primary metal is outsourced which leads to higher costs for Indal.

Post-expansion, the combine will have a total alumina capacity of nearly 13 lakh tonnes. Hindalco's cost of power at 55 paise per kWh for its captive power is among the lowest, while Indal was sourcing power from the grid at ₹4.56 per kWh against 75 paise per kWh for captive power. Post-merger, Hindalco would leverage on the collective competitive strength of Hindalco and Indal through a slew of activities ranging from homogenizing systems and processes, integrating logistics, cost optimization and product rationalization and marketing/manufacturing strategies. And the dividends from these activities have begun to be reflected in the financial performance of Indal in the first nine months of 2000-01. In this period, Indal recorded a decent 16.7% rise in turnover to ₹941.36 crore and 55% jump in post-tax earnings to ₹84.78 crore.

The Indal scrip experienced an uptrend from 5 July 2002. On that day, it surged 4.9% in intra-day trading to close at ₹96.10 per share. The scrip was previously trading between ₹89 and 91. Subsequent trading days saw the scrip cross the ₹100 mark. A considerable appreciation in the scrip was also witnessed on 18 July 2002. On that day, the scrip surged 8.7% in intra-day trading to close at ₹114.05. This was the day of media reports of the proposed deal. From then on, the scrip traded above ₹110 per share. The open offer announcement by the Birla group caused the Indal scrip to trade over ₹115 per share.

INDAL vis-à-vis COSPI*

	Return (%)	Excess Returns (%)
Yearly Returns		
2000	195.50	121.76
2001	–39.00	5.20
2002	–4.09	–14.15
Cumulative Returns		
April 1999 to March 2002	72.87	66.17
Monthly Returns		
April. 2002	8.45	6.46
May 2002	–0.45	3.62
June 2002	0.56	–4.33
July 2002	30.35	39.32
August 2002	0.94	–2.82
September 2002	–0.46	5.88
Cumulative Returns		
April 2002–September 2002	42.19	51.39

*COSPI is the index developed by the Centre for Monitoring Indian Economy (CMIE). It constitutes of all the listed Indian firms with trading on at least 75% of the days. The index conveys broad market.

Hindalco (Yearly share prices pre- and post-acquisition)

Date	Open (₹)	High (₹)	Low (₹)	Close (₹)*	Spread (₹) H – L	Spread (₹) C – O
Year 2000	779.00	806.00	619.90	725.95	186.10	–53.05
Year 2001	785.25	964.95	496.10	639.80	468.85	–145.45
Year 2002	634.00	864.35	469.35	586.35	395.00	–47.65
Year 2003	580.10	1,430.00	530.15	1,408.30	899.85	828.20
Year 2004	1,424.70	1,503.00	725.00	1,426.80	778.00	2.10
Year 2005	1,439.90	1,487.00	112.60	143.40	1,374.40	–1,296.50
Year 2006	148.00	251.40	139.00	174.10	112.40	26.10
Year 2007	175.40	191.90	125.25	154.35	66.65	–21.05

Hindalco (Monthly pre- and post-acquisition Share Prices in 2002)

Date	*Open (₹)*	*High (₹)*	*Low (₹)*	*Close (₹)*	**Spread (₹)*	
					H – L	*C – O*
January 2002	634.00	730.00	622.30	719.60	107.70	85.60
February 2002	720.10	864.35	712.50	773.90	151.85	53.80
March 2002	770.75	798.95	725 25	770.05	73.70	–0.70
April 2002	775.00	778.00	700.00	728.30	78.00	–46.70
May 2002	729.95	759.90	690.00	696.20	69.90	–33.75
June 2002	705.00	727.10	677.00	710.55	50.10	5.55
July 2002	718.00	718.00	611.00	627.60	107.00	–90.40
August 2002	616.05	634.00	530.30	594.05	103.70	–22.00
September 2002	610.00	610.00	520.00	522.60	90.00	–87.40
October 2002	522.00	532.00	469.35	495.55	62.65	–26.45
November 2002	495.00	550.00	489.00	540.30	61.00	45.30
December 2002	550.00	595.00	535.00	586.35	60.00	36.35

BSE SENSEX in year 2002

	High	*Low*	*Average*	*Closing (Month End)*
January	3437.78	3246.15	3353.31	3311.03
February	3712.74	3311.73	3528.58	3562.31
March	3690.27	3459.08	3580.73	3469.35
April	3512.55	3301.21	3435.13	3338.16
May	3462.01	3114.05	3302.91	3125.73
June	3362.42	3161.09	3257.03	3244.7
July	3358.58	2987.65	3214.87	2987.65
August	3181.23	2950.09	3053.16	3181.23
September	3187.26	2991.36	3085.53	2991.36
October	3009.76	2834.41	2949.76	2949.32
November	3228.82	2948.04	3058.19	3228.82
December	3398	3207.36	3315.84	3377.28

Discuss

1. What kind of integration is it—vertical or horizontal?
2. What is the rationale of acquisition from Hindalco's perspective? Justify in the light of major synergies expected to be available to Hindalco from the merger.
3. How is the deal expected to benefit Indal?
4. What is the minimum exchange ratio based on the LG model?

In the CD

Finding NPV from Merger

PART FOUR

FINANCING AND DIVIDEND DECISIONS

CHAPTER

16 Capital Structure–Theory

LEARNING OBJECTIVES

This chapter aims at explaining:

- capital structure
- different theories of capital structure
  - net income approach
  - net operating income approach
  - traditional theory
- Miller and Modigliani's propositions of irrelevance of capital structure for the value of a firm
- home-made leverage
- the effect of taxes on the value of a firm and its capital structure
- the advantage of debt when personal taxes exist
- the cost of financial distress
- the conflict of debt holders and shareholders and agency cost of debt
- trade-off theory
- agency cost of equity
- Donaldson's pecking order theory for raising capital
- signalling and asymmetric information hypothesis
- free cash flow hypothesis

GOODWILL GARAGE–GOOD WITH DEBT

Swami Shankar, a happy-go-lucky man was living a comfortable life with his wife and two children studying in college. Shankar managed Goodwill Garage, the automobile workshop that he had inherited from his father, reasonably well and was hoping that his young son would continue the tradition.

The other day, three customers were ready to take delivery of their vehicles repaired and serviced by Dhani Mahajan, his very competent and sincere lieutenant.

The Mercedes owner said that he would pay only after 15 days of checking if the vehicle runs fine. Swami Shankar agreed. The owner of the BMW said, 'The defect repaired this time was not done in the earlier service. You should not demand payment.' Swami Shankar let him go too. The Volkswagen's customer wanted a discount of 25% being a regular customer. Swami Shankar agreed with a smile on his face.

Dhani Mahajan watched with anxiety wondering how Swami Shankar survives. This was no different than what Dhani Mahajan saw practically the every second day. He hesitantly asked, 'Why do you keep losing every day? You know all these guys are making excuses not to make payment.' Swami Shankar replied without much thought, 'You need to do this for continuing business. This is the way I have survived for so long. So did my father. You should not bother about it. *Yeh to mere baap ka maal hai* (this is my father's property).

Few years passed. One fine morning Dhani Mahajan resigned. 'Why are you doing so?' asked Swami Shankar. 'I have got a million from my uncle who left me this fortune. I need not work any more. I will lend and earn interest and live peacefully hereafter,' replied Dhani Mahajan gleefully. 'You shouldn't stop working,' quipped Swami Shankar. Immediately, sensing a good opportunity to grow, he asked, 'Why don't you lend to me. I will add a few more facilities and increase business. I can now take 150 vehicles every day and don't have to turn away customers.'

Dhani Mahajan paused for a while and agreed to lend at 12% and asked hesitantly, 'But what about the security for the money that I will lend you?'

Swami Shankar paused for a while and said, 'You continue to work and see what is happening. You have been here for years. You know I have not run away with anybody's money. You see it every now and then that others take me for a ride and have taken away my money. You trust me for the security of your money.'

A contract was drawn up and both Swami Shankar and Dhani Mahajan were happy until one evening when the same story repeated. This time Dhani Mahajan intervened. 'You cannot lose money from customers by offering free service, extended warranties, and ad-hoc discounts,' claimed Dhani Mahajan.

Swami Shankar was surprised at Dhani Mahajan's reaction. He immediately asked, 'You never behaved earlier in this fashion. What is the matter with you?'

'I have to protect my interest. If you continue doing so, you would not be in a position to pay my interest. I need it because I have to share it with my cousins.' replied Dhani Mahajan.

Swami Shankar returned home irritated and worried about what Dhani Mahajan said. With visible signs of worry on his face, his wife asked, 'You look disturbed. What is the problem?'

Swami Shankar said, 'Dhani Mahajan has started interfering too much in my work since the time he has lent money to me. No doubt he talks sense, but I do not like his questioning one bit. After all, I am the owner of the garage.' Swami Shankar explained in detail to his wife how Dhani Mahajan objected to his granting credit, executing extended warranties, and allowing rebates.

His wife trying to justify the actions of Dhani Mahajan said, 'Dhani Mahajan has been talking in your interest only, though he should only be concerned about recovery of his interest and principal.'

Swami Shankar replied, 'Exactly. Then why should he interfere so much in the management.'

His wife again justified, 'After all, he allowed you to grow. If he did not lend money to you, someone else would have opened another garage and taken away your business. You did not have enough money otherwise to add newer and extra facilities. He has given you an opportunity to expand your business and we have started having some more comfort in life. In fact, you owe him a lot apart from the money he lent.'

'But I still think that I should not have borrowed,' Swami Shankar said.

Attempting to remove the notion from Swami Shankar's mind, 'You should not think this way. Though your business has increased only 150%, now you bring double the money you used to bring earlier. You have added value to the business and yourself. As an owner, you get more than what you used to get earlier. Dhani Mahajan gets only the fixed amount of interest from you.'

Brooding over his wife's words, Swami Shankar retired to his bed after dinner.

INTRODUCTION

Capital structure decision is perhaps the key strategic decision that has occupied much of the time and attention of academicians and managers alike. Important as it is for the survival and growth of the firms it also remains one of the most controversial subjects in the world of finance. Capital structure decision refers to the proportion of debt and equity and finding out whether there is a capital structure that can be said to be optimum for the shareholders of the firm.

Capital structure decision is one of the key decisions that focuses on finding the capital structure with the single objective of maximization of value of the firm.

The issue revolves around the question of an optimal capital structure, if there is any. Put simply, it means that can the value of the firm be enhanced by changing the mix of debt and equity? We know there are primarily two sources of funds, i.e., debt and equity. The question of capital structure deals with whether a firm must borrow and if yes, to what extent so as to increase the value of the firm. Unfortunately, there is no definite answer available. There are conflicting theories about the existence of optimum capital structure.

COMMON ASSUMPTIONS FOR ANALYSIS

Before we analyse different theories pertaining to capital structure, here are few statements, which always must be kept in mind. These are important assumptions for analysing any proposition concerning the evaluation of capital structure.

Capital structure decision assumes (i) replacement of one form of capital with another, (ii) firm value is consistent with shareholders wealth, and (iii) would be optimum when cost of capital is minimized.

- *To analyse the effects of capital structure, one form of capital needs to be replaced with another* While analysing the capital structure, we shall always assume that the investment decision of the firm remains same. We consider replacement of one form of capital with another keeping the total value of assets constant. The addition of debt or equity would result in the augmenting of assets, which shall ultimately result in the increase of earnings before interest and taxes (EBIT).
- *Maximization of value of the firm is consistent with maximization of shareholders' wealth* The framework for determination of capital structure would assume that optimal capital structure would be one that maximizes the value of

the firm. The value of the firm is the sum total of market values of its debt and equity. Our attempt is to find the structure of debt and equity that maximizes the value of firm based on the market values. This is consistent with the objective of the finance function, which, in no uncertain terms, acts in the interest of shareholders of the firm, and all decisions are made to maximize the shareholders' wealth. As the market value of debt remains almost constant, maximization of value of the firm would automatically imply maximization of shareholders' wealth.

- *Optimal capital structure is one that minimizes WACC* Determination of the value of the firm is done by the net present value of the projects arrived at by discounting the cash flows at a specific rate. The value of the firm can be increased if lower discount rate is used. In most cases, the discount rate used is weighted average cost of capital (WACC). Lower the WACC, and, hence, the discount rate, the higher will be the NPV of the project and the value of the firm. Therefore, maximization of firm's value will take place at the point where the capital structure minimizes the WACC.

  The emphasis on the minimization of WACC rather than the maximization of the value of the firm is due to the difficulties one faces with the measurement of impact of managerial decisions on the values of the firm, given by market prices of its stock and debt securities. It is difficult to estimate how the market values will change with the changing capital structure. However, it is far easier to see how the cost of capital would change with the changing mix of debt and equity in financing of an enterprise. Hence, the capitalization rates assume significance in determining the optimal capital structure.
- *Constancy of earning levels* While analysing the changes in the capital structure, it is essential to assume that the earnings of the firm remain constant and they are distributed to the stakeholders. If the earnings change, the value of the firm too would change. The retention of earnings implies that the firm is planning to fund its growth through internal accruals and we assume no growth of earnings.

As a measure of capital structure, we shall use the debt–equity ratio, the ratio of market value of debt (D) to the market value of equity (E). Although there could be several other measures available, but the most commonly accepted numbers are debt–equity ratio at market rates, the value of debt to the value of equity, or alternatively the debt ratio, the proportion of debt to total value.

Target capital structure When faced with the question of optimal capital structure, do we necessarily keep the same structure all the time if at all we are able to find one? At least this is what we target at. Whether or not the firms achieve it is a separate question. The target capital structure is the one that the management thinks is the most suited to the firm in the business environment it is operating.

Target capital structure is the debt–equity ratio deemed most appropriate by the management for the business it is in.

We assume that each firm works towards achieving the target capital structure. If it has a lower proportion of debt it raises the debt to finance the investment opportunities. And if the debt is too large, the firm raises equity capital. Firms may not be maintaining the target capital structure all the time and we assume that deviations are not too great. In any case, with changing market values exact adherence to the target capital structure is not possible when it is defined in terms of market values.

Target capital structure is determined by taking several factors into account. These factors range from pure financial issues like taxes and interest to practical issues like market practices, lenders' perspectives, and industry norms. We shall revert to them in the next chapter. With the target capital structure in mind, we now consider the various approaches to the capital structure.

NET INCOME APPROACH

The net income approach for capital structure focuses on the cash flows to the respective suppliers of capital and their capitalization rates. As we all know, debt suppliers get an interest on the amount of debt provided by them. Once the interest is paid, the remainder is available to the shareholders. The net income approach assumes that the cost of debt as well as equity remains constant irrespective of level of debt.

If we assume perennial debt, constant earnings and 100% pay out as a dividend, cost of debt r_d, the cost of equity r_e and the WACC, r are given by Equations 16-1 to 16-3.

$$\text{Cost of Debt; } r_d = \frac{\text{Interest}}{\text{Market value of debt}} = \frac{I}{D} \quad (16\text{-}1)$$

$$\text{Cost of Equity; } r_e = \frac{\text{Earnings for equity shareholders}}{\text{Market value of equity}} = \frac{\text{EBIT} - I}{E} \quad (16\text{-}2)$$

$$\text{WACC; } r = \frac{\text{Earnings to all capital suppliers}}{\text{Market value of the firm}} = \frac{\text{EBIT}}{D+E} \quad (16\text{-}3)$$

The assumption that both the cost of debt and the cost of equity remain constant irrespective of the capital structure implies that the suppliers of debt and equity capital are not concerned with the level of debt the firm has. Instead, they are concerned only with their desired returns, respectively.

Net Income approach assumes that capitalization of the firm is based on the net income derived by each supplier of capital discounted at fixed rates irrespective of levels of debt.

We also assume that the cost of debt is less than the cost of equity and the return on assets is always greater than the cost of debt; else, the firm will have no incentive to borrow.

Let us consider some numbers to illustrate the net income approach. Assume a firm is considering implementation of a project costing ₹10 crore. The assets are expected to yield an EBIT of ₹5 crore each year. The firm is considering three scenarios of capital structure with debt–equity ratios calculated at values of 1:9 (Scenario A), 1:1 (Scenario B), and 9:1 (Scenario C). The outcomes of three scenarios are presented in Table 16-1.

Table 16-1 Net Income Approach

(₹ *in lakh*)

	Scenario A	*Scenario B*	*Scenario C*
Project Cost	1,000.00	1,000.00	1,000.00
Sources of Finance			
Equity (Book Value)	900.00	500.00	100.00
Debt (Book Value)	100.00	500.00	900.00
Capitalization Rate			
Equity, r_e	20%	10%	20%$_e$
Debt, r_d	10%	20%	10%
EBIT	500.00	500.00	500.00
Interest (I)	10.00	50.00	90.00
EBT	490.00	450.00	410.00
Taxes	Assumed no taxes		
Earnings available to shareholders (EAT)	490.00	450.00	410.00
Market value of debt (I/r_d)	100.00	500.00	900.00
Market value of firm (EBIT – I – Taxes)/r_e	2,450.00	2,250.00	2,050.00
Total Value of the firm	2,550.00	2,750.00	2,950.00
Overall Capitalization rate (r)	19.61%	18.18%	16.95%

It is assumed here that the suppliers of debt and equity are indifferent to the level of debt raised by the firm and demand uniform returns of 10% and 20%, respectively. Further, we have assumed no taxes. With debt–equity ratio of 1:9 the market values of debt, equity, WACC, and total value of the firm are computed as per Equations 16-1, 16-2, and 16-3.

Market Value of Debt:

$$D = \frac{\text{Interest}}{r_d} = \frac{10}{0.10} = ₹100 \text{ lakh}$$

Market Value of Equity:

$$E = \frac{\text{Earnings for equity shareholders}}{r_e}$$

$$= \frac{490}{0.20} = ₹2{,}450 \text{ lakh}$$

WACC:

$$r = \frac{\text{Earnigs to all capital suppliers}}{\text{Market value of the firm}}$$

$$= \frac{\text{EBIT}}{D+E} = \frac{500}{100+2450} = 19.61\%$$

Total value of the firm = Value of debt + Value of equity
= 100 + 2,450 = ₹2,550 lakh.

Similarly, we may compute the values of debt, equity, and WACC for the other two scenarios of capital structure with 50% debt and with 90% debt.

A graphical view of rates of return with different levels of debt is presented in Figure 16-1. Due to the fact that rates of return on debt and equity are constant and cost of debt is lower than the cost of equity, the overall cost of funds will fall down with increasing debt. With pure equity the cost of capital will be equal to cost of equity and with pure debt it will be equal to the cost of debt.

The total value of the firm is the sum total of value of equity and value of debt. The value of debt is given by the income earned by debt holders divided by capitalization rate. As the amount of debt increases, the value of debt also increases from ₹100 lakh to ₹500 lakh to ₹900 lakh under Scenarios A, B, and C, respectively.

Net Income approach states that capitalization rates are constant and increasing debt would reduce overall capitalization rate (WACC) and increase the value of the firm.

Similarly, the value of equity is given by earnings available to equity holders divided by capitalization rate of equity holders. With an equity capitalization rate of 20%, the value of equity is ₹2,550, ₹2,750, and ₹2,950, respectively under Scenarios A, B, and C.

Since the capitalization rate of debt is lower than that of equity, the overall capitalization rate of firm would keep declining, and total value of the firm would keep increasing with increasing debt ratio. According to the net income approach, the optimal capital structure is 100% debt as can be seen from the Figure 16-1.

Optimal capital structure under net income approach is 100% debt.

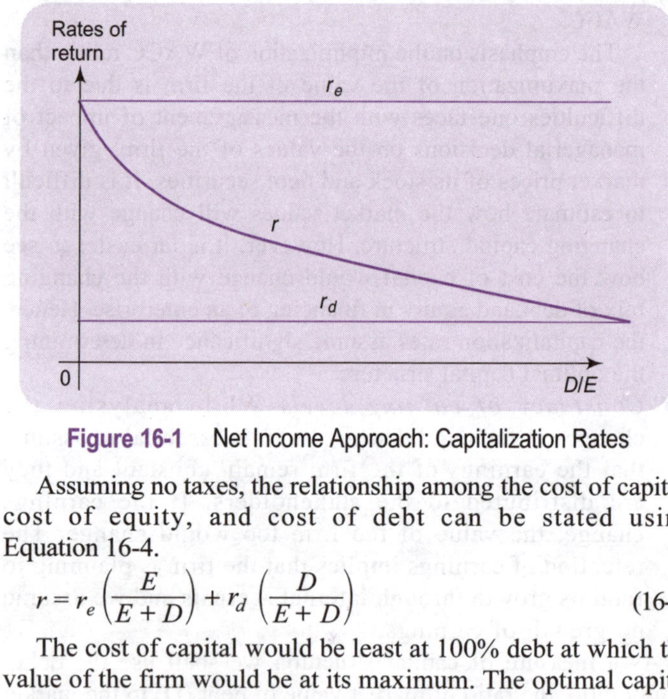

Figure 16-1 Net Income Approach: Capitalization Rates

Assuming no taxes, the relationship among the cost of capital, cost of equity, and cost of debt can be stated using Equation 16-4.

$$r = r_e\left(\frac{E}{E+D}\right) + r_d\left(\frac{D}{E+D}\right) \qquad (16\text{-}4)$$

The cost of capital would be least at 100% debt at which the value of the firm would be at its maximum. The optimal capital structure would, therefore, be 100% debt.

NET OPERATING INCOME APPROACH

Unlike the net income approach, this approach assumes that the cost of capital remains constant regardless of the level of debt. As cheaper debt replaces equity, the shareholders recognize the increased level of risk and hence, revise their expectations of return. The market capitalization rate adjusts exactly to offset the advantage of cheaper debt. As such overall capitalization rate remains constant.

The basic premise of net operating income approach is that the net operating income of the assets is constant. It cannot change simply because the sources of finance to acquire these assets have changed. Capital structure should have no impact on the earning capacity of the asset. Varying proportions of debt and equity cannot add to the productivity of the assets. Since the earning potential is mainly governed by the business risk the overall value of the firm remains constant irrespective of what the mix of equity and debt is used to acquire those assets. Changing capital structure will merely allocate the proportions of cash flows between suppliers of debt and equity capital.

Earning capacity remains the same, no matter how and to whom it is distributed The earning power is subject to the cost structure and the business environment both of which are not dependent upon the sources of funds. Therefore, as a starting point for any analysis we use earnings before interest and taxes (EBIT).

Net operating income approach assumes that value of the firm remains constant because overall capitalization rate remains constant.

The numerical example of the net income approach is reproduced in Table 16-2 with modified assumptions. Note that the overall value of the firm remains constant at ₹2,500 lakh for different capital structures determined on the basis of EBIT level of ₹500 lakh and overall capitalization rate of 20%.

$$\text{Market value of the firm} = \frac{\text{Earnings to all capital suppliers}}{r}$$

$$= \frac{500}{0.2} = ₹2{,}500 \text{ lakh}$$

For debt level of 10% the value of debt is found by using alternate form of Equation 16-1.

$$\text{Market value of debt} = \frac{\text{Interest}}{r_d} = \frac{10}{0.10} = ₹100 \text{ lakh}$$

The market value of equity is the difference between total value and the value of debt, i.e., 2,500 – 100 = ₹2,400 lakh. Likewise, we may find the market value of equity for the other two scenarios of capital structures as done in Table 16-2.

Table 16-2 Net Operating Income Approach

(*₹ in lakh*)

	Scenario A	*Scenario B*	*Scenario C*
Project Cost	1,000.00	1,000.00	1,000.00
Sources of Finance			
Equity (Book value)	900.00	500.00	100.00
Debt (Book value)	100.00	500.00	900.00
Capitalization Rate			
Debt, r_d	10%	10%	10%
Overall, r	20%	20%	20%
EBIT	500.00	500.00	500.00
Interest (I)	10.00	50.00	90.00
EBT	490.00	450.00	410.00
Taxes	Assumed no taxes		
Earnings available to shareholders (EAT)	490.00	450.00	410.00
Market value of debt (I/r_d)	100.00	500.00	900.00
Market value of firm (EBIT/r)	2,500.00	2,500.00	2,500.00
Value of equity (E)	2,400.00	2,000.00	1,600.00
Equity capitalization rate (EAT/E)	20.42%	22.50%	25.63%

With an overall capitalization rate and cost of debt (r_d) constant, the cost of equity would rise as the ratio of debt increases. If we denote the capitalization rate for an all-equity financed firm as r_0, then at any level of debt the WACC, r too must equal r_0. Therefore, we may write:

$$r_0 = r_e\left(\frac{E}{E+D}\right) + r_d\left(\frac{D}{E+D}\right) \qquad (16\text{-}5)$$

Cost of equity Equation 16-5 can be rewritten to express the cost of equity as function of debt–equity ratio as Equation 16-6.

$$r_e = r_0 + (r_0 - r_d)D/E \qquad (16\text{-}6)$$

Under net operating income approach the cost of equity rises so as to compensate the reduced cost of debt keeping the overall capitalization rate constant.

Equation 16-6 can be interpreted in a logical manner. With 100% equity funding ($D/E = 0$) the overall cost of capital will be equal to the opportunity cost of equity, r_0 the cost for all equity financed firm. With increasing debt, the excess of r_0 and cost of debt will add to the cost of equity in the ratio of market values of debt and equity. In the above example, the cost of equity under pure equity capital structure r_0 is 20%. The cost of equity under three scenarios is:

Scenario A : $r_e = 20 + (20 - 10) \times 100/2400 = 20.42\%$
Scenario B : $r_e = 20 + (20 - 10) \times 500/2000 = 22.50\%$
Scenario C : $r_e = 20 + (20 - 10) \times 900/1600 = 25.63\%$

This matches with the computation shown in Table 16-2.

The graphical view of net operating income approach is presented in Figure 16-2.

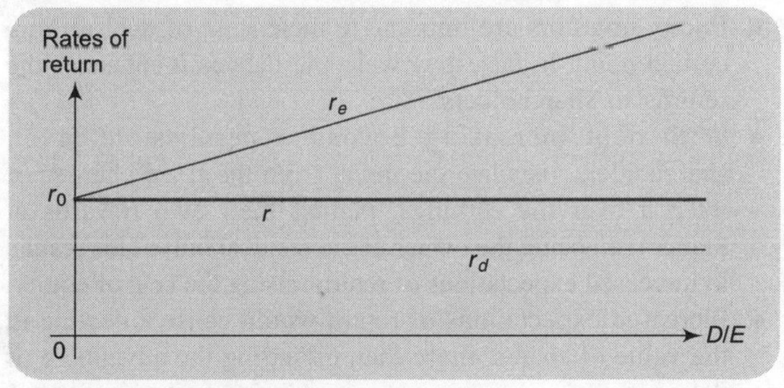

Figure 16-2 Net operating income approach: Capitalization rates

The major implication of net operating income approach is that all capital structures are optimal. Alternatively stated, none of the capital structure is optimal. We cannot change the overall cost of capital of the firm merely by changing the mix of debt and equity. The value of the firm is always constant, dependent upon the business risk of the firm and independent of level of debt. Increased debt merely changes the expectations of equity shareholders because their earnings are under threat. To continue to be shareholders, they seek higher rates of return.

Under net operating income approach no capital structure is optimal, alternatively all capital structures are optimal.

TRADITIONAL APPROACH

The net income approach and net operating income approach take extreme positions. There is no conflict about the assumption of constancy of cost of debt. However, the net income approach assumes constancy of cost of equity capital causing change in the overall capitalization rate while the net operating income approach presumes constancy of overall capitalization rate causing a change in the cost of equity.

Traditional approach recognises the advantage of debt only up to certain level. Any increase in debt beyond a point causes cost of equity to rise.

Traditional approach recognizes assumptions of both the approaches not wholly but in parts only. Rather than assuming constancy of cost of equity or the overall capitalization rate, it assumes as follows:

About the cost of debt

- The cost of debt remains constant over fairly extended levels of debt because its suppliers feel fairly secured about the returns expected by them.
- Exceeding a certain point of leverage, debt suppliers perceive increased risk of non-recovery of interest and/or principal. To dissuade firms from borrowing at dangerously high levels the lenders first increase the cost of funds and then impose more and more stringent conditions on the management restricting their operational freedom. Instead, they participate actively in the management of firm. From financial viewpoint these are equivalent to raising cost of debt.

About the cost of equity

- Equity investors are immune to increasing of debt up to a certain point. In fact, they welcome debt as it enhances the returns to shareholders.
- With debt increasing beyond a permissible level, shareholders visualise the threat from the fixed charges of interest over the earnings, putting their own rewards at higher risk, being the owner of the residual only. This results in increased expectations of return raising the cost of equity.
- Increased expectations of return would cause a decline in the value of shares, more than offsetting the advantage of debt.

Implications

The implications of the assumptions about the cost of debt and cost of equity for the overall capitalization rate are:

- Initially the cost of capital for the firm will fall as cheaper debt replaces expensive equity.
- Even though the cost of equity rises with increased debt, the advantages of debt would outweigh the increased cost of equity.
- Beyond a certain level of debt, the cost of equity starts rising disproportionately, which more than offsets the advantage of debt, raising the overall cost of capital for the firm.
- Since the cost of capital falls initially and then starts rising, there exists a point where the cost of capital would be least. At its lowest point, the cost of capital would maximize the value of the firm and, hence, is the optimal capital structure.
- At this point, the marginal cost of equity will be equal to marginal cost of debt.

Though it may be extremely difficult to arrive at the exact point at which WACC is at the lowest, the arguments presented under traditional view on capital structure seem to be very appealing. The value of the firm under three different scenarios *A*, *B* and *C* are worked out in Table 16-3. The cost of debt is assumed at 10%, 11%, and 12% while the cost of equity is taken at 20%, 20% and 30% in the three scenarios respectively. The value of the firm increases and then declines. The WACC declines first and then increases. This happens due to increased cost of equity in Scenario C.

According to traditional approach, with increasing level of debt the overall cost of capital falls initially because debt is cheaper than equity later it rises because equit;' holders expect greater returns due to increasing perceived risk from the debt holders.

The capitalization rates under traditional approach are depicted in Figure 16-3 where point 'C' represents optimal capital structure; i.e., the debt–equity ratio that minimises the WACC and, hence, maximizes the value of the firm.

Table 16-3 Traditional approach

(₹ in lakh)

	Scenario A	Scenario B	Scenario C
Project Cost	1,000.00	1,000.00	1,000.00
Sources of Finance			
Equity (Book value)	900.00	500.00	100.00
Debt (Book value)	100.00	500.00	900.00
Capitalization Rate			
Debt	10%	11%	12%
Equity	20%	20%	30%
EBIT	500.00	500.00	500.00
Interest (I)	10.00	55.00	108.00
EBT	490.00	445.00	392.00
Taxes	Assumed no taxes		
Earnings available to shareholders	490.00	445.00	392.00
Market value of debt (I/r_d)	100.00	500.00	900.00
Market value of equity (EAT/r_e)	2,450.00	2,225.00	1,307.00
Value of the firm, *V*	2,550.00	2,725.00	2,207.00
Capitalization rate, WACC (EBIT/V)	19.61%	18.35%	22.65%

The traditional view of the capital structure rests on the premise that shareholders would not seek higher returns if the debt remains within some limits, and would need larger returns if the debt increases. The perceived risk of the equity investors is immaterial up to a certain point but jumps substantially thereafter. Unfortunately there is no evidence to prove this and it remains a conjecture only.

We shall revert back to the traditional viewpoint with a trade-off theory that provides similar conclusions with explanations of tax advantage and cost of financial distress.

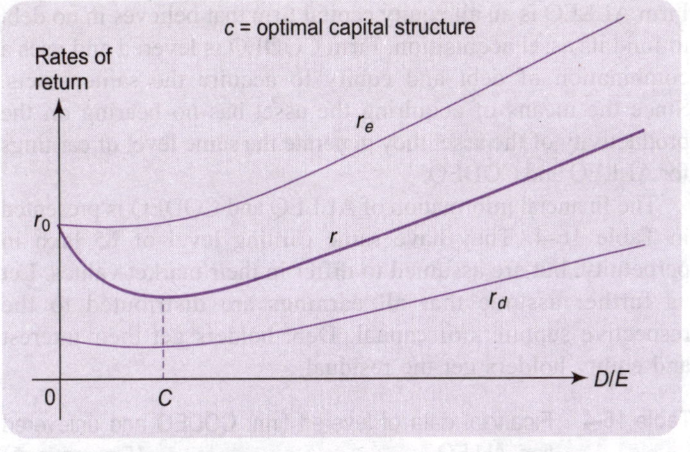

Figure 16-3 Traditional approach capitalization rates

MODIGLIANI AND MILLER (MM) THEORY—WITHOUT TAXES

Franco Modigliani and Merton Miller (MM for short) made a classic contribution to explain the capital structure. Their theory of capital structure substantiates the view of *net operating income approach* and provides behavioural explanation of the theory that capital structure is immaterial to the value of the firm.

The question is what combination of the debt and equity would maximize the value of the firm. MM provides the answer through three propositions; first considered without the corporate taxes and later with existence of taxes. We first consider MM propositions without taxes.

Proposition I (No Taxes)

The market value of the firm is independent of its capital structure and is given by capitalizing its expected return at a rate appropriate to its class.

The total value of the firm remains same as determined by its assets no matter how they are acquired. It is only the nature of claims on the earnings that changes with changing debt ratio, the capital structure. Just as the size of bread does not change, no matter how many slices it is cut into and who shares those slices, the value of the firm remains constant no matter how the earnings are shared between debt holders and equity holders.

> MM's Proposition I without taxes implies that capital structure is irrelevant. The value of levered firm and unlevered firm would be equal.

Denoting a firm financed entirely by equity as 'unlevered' firm and the firm using some debt as 'levered' firm, and the market values of unlevered and levered firms as V_U and V_L respectively, then according to MM's Proposition I we have:

$$V_U = V_L \quad (16\text{-}7)$$

i.e., the value of levered firm will be same as that of the unlevered firm.

Proposition II (No Taxes)

Proposition II specifies the expected return on equity as the leverage increases, in overall terms. The capitalization rate and the capital structure is stated as below:

The expected yield on the equity capital is equal to the pure equity return plus a premium for the financial risk, which is equal to the spread between pure equity return and cost of debt in the proportion of debt–equity ratio.

This can be explained in terms of the firm's overall cost of capital, which is defined as weighted average of the expected returns to the total market value of all the securities issued by the firm. In their view, the average cost of capital of any firm is completely independent of its capital structure. This capitalization rate will be equal to the expected returns from the assets as if they were financed entirely from equity. Let us call this pure equity return as r_0.

> MM's Proposition II without taxes states that with increasing leverage the cost of equity rises exactly to offset the advantage of reduced cost of debt to keep the value of the firm constant.

Even though the total value remains constant, the debt–equity ratio causes important changes in the values of debt and equity. The cost of equity in the levered firm r_e will rise as the leverage increases, thereby, changing the value of equity. The cost of equity in a levered firm will be as given by the net operating income approach. It is given by Equation 16-6 reproduced here:

$$r_e = r_0 + (r_0 - r_d)D/E$$

Hence, the cost of equity r_e depends upon the required rate of return on the assets r_0, the required rate of return by the debt holders r_d, and the debt–equity ratio D/E. The cost of equity is a linear function of debt–equity ratio with the slope given by difference of the asset capitalization rate and the cost of debt as depicted in Figure 16-4.

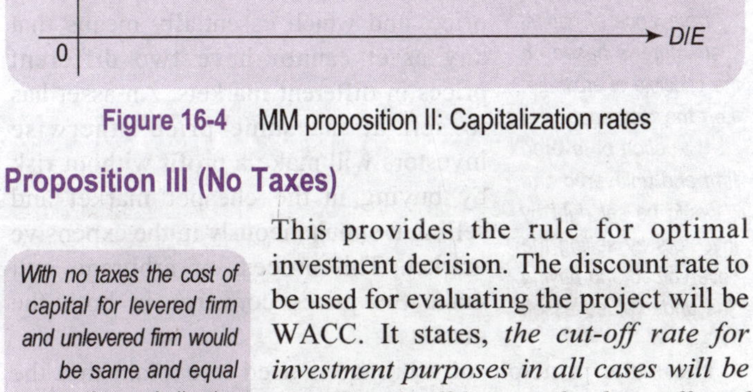

Figure 16-4 MM proposition II: Capitalization rates

Proposition III (No Taxes)

This provides the rule for optimal investment decision. The discount rate to be used for evaluating the project will be WACC. It states, *the cut-off rate for investment purposes in all cases will be WACC and will be completely unaffected by the type of security issued to finance the investment.*

> With no taxes the cost of capital for levered firm and unlevered firm would be same and equal to the capitalization rate of the all equity financed firm.

WACC of the unlevered will be given by r_0. WACC for the levered firm would also be r_0 as can be seen below:

$$\text{WACC for levered firm} = r_e \frac{E}{E+D} + r_d \frac{D}{E+D} \qquad (16\text{-}8)$$

Using Proposition II, i.e., $r_e = r_0 + (r_0 - r_d)D/E$, we get
WACC for levered firm = WACC unlevered firm = r_0

Example 16-1 The Cost of Equity and WACC

Assuming a world of no taxes, the WACC of a firm is 15% with the capital structure of debt to equity ratio of 1:3. The cost of borrowing is 9%. Find the cost of equity of the firm. What will be its WACC if the firm mobilizes further debt so as to have the debt equity ratio of 1:1? Will the cost of equity remain same as before?

Solution

The cost of equity can be arrived at from Equation 16-6:

$$r_e = r_0 + (r_0 - r_d)D/E$$
$$= 15 + (15 - 9) \times 1/3 = 17\%$$

The WACC will remain same for the firm as per the MM propositions with the change in the debt equity structure. However, the cost of equity will change with the new debt–equity ratio of 1:1. The new cost of equity will be 21% again using Equation 16-6:

$$= 15 + (15 - 9) \times 1 = 21\%$$

We may verify that the WACC of the firm remains same irrespective of level of debt using Equation 16-8.

$$r = r_e\left(\frac{E}{E+D}\right) + r_d\left(\frac{D}{E+D}\right)$$
$$= (21 \times 0.5) + (9 \times 0.5)$$
$$= 10.5 + 4.5 = 15\% \text{ (Same as before)}$$

The Arbitrage Argument—Behavioural Process of Investors

The Proposition I of MM is no different from the net operating income approach. The assumption that the overall capitalization rate remains constant due to exact offsetting effect of the cost of equity with increased leverage of net operating income approach is proved by MM.

MM provides an economic justification for constancy of value of the firm with changing leverage. This justification comes from the process of arbitrage. Arbitrage is the process that establishes the law of one price, and which essentially means that any asset cannot have two different prices in different markets. An asset has to sell at the same price otherwise investors will make a profit without risk by buying in the cheaper market and selling it simultaneously in the expensive market. This process of arbitrage will make the prices converge in both the markets.

MM Propositions of irrelevance of capital structure is based on the principle of arbitrage, i.e., the discrepancy in valuation of levered firm and unlevered firm would be set right by investors by selling the overvalued and buying the undervalued asset.

The same principle of arbitrage is used to explain that the market value of the firm will be the same regardless of its capital structure. Let us assume two firms; namely ALLEQ and CODEQ. They are identical in every respect, except their capital structures. Firm ALLEQ is an all equity capital firm that believes in no debt to fund its asset acquisition. Firm CODEQ is levered and uses a combination of debt and equity to acquire the same assets. Since the means of acquiring the asset has no bearing on the productivity of the asset they generate the same level of earnings for ALLEQ and CODEQ.

The financial information of ALLEQ and CODEQ is presented in Table 16-4. They have same earning level of ₹5 lakh in perpetuity, but are assumed to differ in their market values. Let us further assume that all earnings are distributed to the respective suppliers of capital. Debt holders get their interest and equity holders get the residual.

Table 16-4 Financial data of levered firm, CODEQ and unlevered firm, ALLEQ (*Figures in ₹*)

	ALLEQ	*CODEQ*
EBIT	5,00,000	5,00,000
Interest @ 10%	—	1,00,000
EBT	5,00,000	4,00,000
Taxes (Assumed no taxes)	—	—
EAT	5,00,000	4,00,000
Market value of debt	—	10,00,000
Market value of equity, Capitalization rate 20%	25,00,000	20,00,000
Value of the firm	25,00,000	30,00,000

The market value of the firms would be the total value of debt and equity of each of the firm. The value of ALLEQ comprising only equity would be would be ₹25,00,000.

Market value of the equity of ALLEQ

$$= \frac{\text{Earnings to equity suppliers}}{r}$$

$$= \frac{\text{Dividend}}{r} = \frac{5,00,000}{0.20} = ₹25,00,000$$

The value of CODEQ would be the sum of the value of its debt and value of its equity. With capitalization rates remaining same the total value of CODEQ is ₹30,00,000 with debt– equity ratio of 1:2 as computed below:

Market value of equity of CODEQ

$$= \frac{\text{Earnings to equity suppliers}}{r}$$

$$= \frac{\text{Dividend}}{r} = \frac{4,00,000}{0.20} = ₹20,00,000$$

Market value of debt of CODEQ

$$= \frac{\text{Interest}}{r_d} = \frac{1,00,000}{0.10} = ₹10,00,000$$

Notice that the value of CODEQ is higher than ALLEQ. This causes the process of arbitrage to begin. Since CODEQ is expensive and ALLEQ is cheaper, it makes sense for the investors of CODEQ to divest from it and invest the proceeds in ALLEQ. Keeping their exposure same, it provides them the opportunity to make some profit, as presented below:

1. An investor who excels in the art of arbitrage, named ARBIT owns 10% of CODEQ. Realizing that ALLEQ is going cheap,

he decides to sell his holding in CODEQ. He realizes ₹2,00,000 (10% of the market value he holds).

2. Since ARBIT was holding 10% of CODEQ it can be assumed that he is comfortable with the debt level CODEQ had. In order to keep his risk profile identical to that of CODEQ, he borrows an amount equal to 10% of debt of CODEQ. The cost of his borrowing is assumed to be identical to that of CODEQ i.e. 10%. He borrows ₹1,00,000 (10% of the value of debt of CODEQ).
3. ARBIT would like to keep his position same as before and therefore acquires 10% of ALLEQ by investing ₹2,50,000 (10% of market value of ALLEQ).

By following the three above mentioned steps ARBIT acquires an equivalent portfolio as he had as an investor in CODEQ. Table 16-5 gives the cash flow position and returns of ARBIT before and after investing in ALLEQ:

Table 16-5 Cash flow and returns for investor swapping position

	Swapping position – Cash flow	
Initial cash flow		
Selling 10% of CODEQ		+2,00,000
Borrowing		+1,00,000
Investing 10% in ALLEQ		–2,50,000
Surplus (Deficit) cash		+50,000
	If invest in CODEQ	*If invest in ALLEQ*
Returns		
10% of shareholders' fund	40,000	50,000
Less: Borrowing cost	—	10,000
Net Income	40,000	40,000

One may wonder that in order to be indifferent to the investment in either of the firms ARBIT needs to borrow only ₹50,000 and not ₹1,00,000 to acquire 10% stake of ALLEQ. However, that would not have kept the financial leverage of ARBIT and CODEQ identical. ARBIT must have same leverage of 1:2 as that of CODEQ to make the comparison fair.

Notice that the returns of ARBIT are identical whether he invests in CODEQ or ALLEQ. But he has surplus cash of ₹50,000 now, which can provide some positive returns. If he invests the same at the rate of his borrowing at 10% he will get ₹5,000 extra. Alternatively, he may invest this surplus money where an opportunity exists while keeping his return and risk profile same as before and as if he continued to stay invested in CODEQ.

Since ALLEQ is undervalued and CODEQ is overvalued more and more investors would adopt the same strategy as that of ARBIT resulting in selling pressure in CODEQ and buying pressure in ALLEQ. This will bring down the value of CODEQ and increase the value of ALLEQ. We only need to guess for how long this process would continue. This process will continue till the values of ALLEQ (the unlevered firm) and CODEQ (the levered firm) become equal.

What if unlevered firm is valued more than levered firm?

We considered the levered firm, CODEQ was valued more than the unlevered firm, ALLEQ. If the unlevered firm (ALLEQ) is valued higher than the levered firm (CODEQ), the reverse process would apply. The investors of ALLEQ can sell their investment and acquire same proportion of debt and equity of CODEQ. This will provide them with the same returns for a lower investment. The surplus funds can be invested elsewhere to yield some additional returns.

Thus, the levered firm cannot be valued higher than unlevered, nor can the levered firm have value higher than unlevered firm. Both the firms essentially must have the same value. If not, the process of arbitrage would make it so. Differing capital structure cannot cause the overall value of the firm to change. Stated otherwise, the value of the firm will remain same regardless of its capital structure, i.e., $V_U = V_L$.

MM Proposition II and Proposition III

Having established that the value of levered firm and unlevered firm cannot differ, the question arises about the level of adjustment required in capitalization rates to establish the equality of value. Since the earnings level and total value remain unchanged with increased borrowing the equity holders must revise their expectation. With no debt financing the expectations of equity holders, r_0, would be the governing factor for determination of the firm value.

$$V_U = V_L \quad \text{or} \quad \frac{\text{EBIT(unlevered)}}{r_0} = \frac{\text{EBIT(levered)}}{r}$$

Since EBIT (unlevered) and EBIT (levered) are same, the WACC of levered firm would be same as the capitalization rate of unlevered firm, i.e.,

$$r = r_0 = \frac{E}{E+D}r_e + \frac{D}{E+D}r_d$$

This may be reorganized as follows:

$$r_e = r_0 + (r_0 - r_d)D/E$$

Assumptions and Limitations of MM's Theory of Irrelevance

While stating and explaining the MM's position regarding capital structure, a number of assumptions were made. These assumptions are also the limitations of MM's propositions and are narrated below:

Identical expectations of earnings For the arbitrage process to begin, investors need to estimate the earning potentials of various firms in the same risk class and the opinions of all investors must be identical. If it is not so, the arbitrage process will be distorted and hampered due to differing opinions of investors. In practice the expectations of investors differ, who in general are naïve. Even the intelligent and literate analysts who all have undergone similar education and training in the discipline of finance do not converge to a single figure of expected earnings for a firm. Else there wouldn't be so many research firms and advisers existing.

All earnings are distributed While comparing the returns of ARBIT as an investor of either ALLEQ or CODEQ we had assumed that all the earnings of the firms are distributed. Retention by either of the firms would alter the growth, return and valuation process of the firms. They have to be identical for both the firms for comparison to be meaningful, even though MM have also advocated the irrelevance of dividend.

No transaction cost It was also assumed that while the changing positions from one firm to another to execute the arbitrage no costs were incurred in either buying or selling. The presence of transaction cost will reduce the returns of the investors and, hence, discourage arbitrage and frequent changes of portfolios. However, the presence of transaction costs changes the MM's proposition only marginally, as arbitrage would not be executed if it doesn't result in benefit in excess of transaction cost. Arbitrage would continue till such time it more than compensates the cost of transactions.

Critical assumptions made by MM in their argument of irrelevance of capital structure are perfect capital markets, absence of taxes and ability and willingness of individual investors to create homemade leverage.

Free and instantaneous flow of information Not only do investors have homogeneous expectations of earnings of the firms, the exchange of information among them is assumed to be instantaneous and free of cost. Again if it costs something to obtain the information the values of the firm can differ to the extent of cost involved in the gathering of information. Also if the flow of information is not instantaneous, the correction in the values of the firm will also not be so. Distortions in values can continue to exist for sometime and would be transitory in nature. However, in the real world information flows are continuous. By the time one piece of information reaches all investors, there will be a host of other information that would not have spread among investors. Hence, the values may differ permanently due to incessant flow of information albeit difference may be marginal, as vital and crucial information regarding valuation travel very fast in today's world.

Absence of taxes So far we have assumed total absence of taxes, corporate as well as personal. The MM proposition with the presence of corporate taxes will be discussed in subsequent section. The presence of personal taxes will, once again, reduce the returns of investors, which is a deterrent to frequent buying and selling of securities.

Replication of leverage in personal capacity, the home-made leverage MM's argument of arbitrage rests on the fact that investors are able to replicate the debt–equity structure of the corporate in their personal capacity. This is regarded as the most critical assumption of MM theory of capital structure. This borrowing in the personal capacity by investors, referred to as homemade leverage, is assumed a perfect substitute for corporate leverage. This may not be possible due to a variety of reasons. Some of them are:

MM Propositions assume that investors have the capability to replicate the leverage of the firm in their personal capacities at the same cost.

1. The terms and conditions of the lenders are substantially different for lending to individuals and to firms regarding security, documentations, debt–equity ratios, and the interest rates. Even small size corporations enjoy a better credit rating than the high net worth individuals and, hence, can borrow at lesser rates than individuals.
2. Normally corporate borrowers have limited liabilities whereas with individuals there is an unlimited liability with the risk of attachment of their personal assets in case of default. This very fact may dissuade individual investors to borrow in their personal capacities particularly when firms they invest in can borrow more conveniently.
3. Additionally, arbitrage with homemade leverage assumes that initial position of the investors is free from borrowing. It is quite possible that the investor's initial investment itself may have been set up with leverage. In such a case there will be dual leverage; one directly in the personal capacity and other indirectly through investment in the levered firm. This will destroy the argument of equivalence.

One would realize that the assumptions for the capital structure theory of MM are difficult and seem impractical. They relate to perfect markets in terms of expectations, information, and indifference to leverage in personal capacity and in corporate world. The limitations of MM's proposition can best be summarized in the words of Ezra Solomon: 'A perfect capital market should be defined as in which MM theory holds'.

MM'S APPROACH WITH CORPORATE TAXES

Proposition I (Under Taxes)

MMs have considered the implication of corporate taxes on the capital structure. Continuing with the same example of ALLEQ and CODEQ, but with the presence of corporate taxes we reproduce the data in the Table 16-6 assuming 40% corporate tax.

Table 16-6 Financial data of levered and unlevered firms under taxes

(Figures in ₹)

	ALLEQ	CODEQ
EBIT	5,00,000	5,00,000
Interest @ 10%	—	1,00,000
EBT	5,00,000	4,00,000
Taxes @ 40%	2,00,000	1,60,000
EAT	3,00,000	2,40,000
Earnings available to suppliers of debt and equity	3,00,000	3,40,000

It may be noticed that earnings available to suppliers of capital are not identical for levered and unlevered firms, as was the case with no taxes. When corporate taxes are applicable the earnings available to stakeholders of levered firm are higher.

It is no coincidence that the extra amount happens to be the amount of taxes saved. While ALLEQ pays ₹2,00,000 as taxes CODEQ pays only ₹1,60,000, as the expense of interest is tax deductible. This is known as the *tax shield of debt*. The cost of debt, therefore, is not the interest rate charged (10%) but is

> MM Proposition I under taxes states that value of the levered firm would be greater than the value of unlevered firm by the amount of present value of tax shield of debt.

lesser by the amount of taxes saved thereon. With a tax rate T of 40% the effective cost of debt reduces to only 6%, or $r_d \times (1 - T)$.

Since the levered firm offers more cash flow to suppliers of capital, the value of the levered firm will be greater than that of the unlevered firm. This extra amount must equal the amount of tax saved in each period. In other terms, for the purpose of valuation, the excess value will be equal to the present value of the tax saved.

In case of perpetual debt the value of levered firm will exceed by an amount equal to tax rate × amount of debt; being the present value of the tax shield. If the tax is saved every year ($r_d \times T \times D$) then the present value of the amount of tax saved will be given by Equation 16-9.

$$\text{PV of tax shield} = \frac{r_d \times D \times T}{(1+r_d)} + \frac{r_d \times D \times T}{(1+r_d)^2} + \frac{r_d \times D \times T}{(1+r_d)^3} + \frac{r_d \times D \times T}{(1+r_d)^4} \ldots$$

$$= \sum_{n=1}^{\infty} \frac{r_d \times D \times T}{(1+r_d)^n} = \frac{r_d \times D \times T}{r_d}$$

$$= D \times T = \text{Tax rate} \times \text{Debt} \qquad (16\text{-}9)$$

The tax savings on the interest paid on the debt being certain must be discounted at the cost of debt only. These cash flows are unlike operational cash flows, which are discounted at WACC or any such other discount rate consistent with the risk of cash flows.

The value of ALLEQ, the unlevered firm with assumed capitalization rate of 20% works out to ₹15,00,000. Mathematically, the value of unlevered firm is given by Equation 16-10:

$$V_U = \frac{\text{EBIT}\,(1-T)}{r_0} \qquad (16\text{-}10)$$

where EBIT represents earnings of the asset.

With no debt, the net earnings available to the shareholders would be EBIT$(1 - T)$. If the earnings were perennial the value of the firm would be given by the earnings divided by the capitalization rate r_0.

As compared to this, CODEQ, the levered firm is financed by way of debt of ₹10,00,000 and remaining ₹5,00,000 by equity. The impact of such debt financing on the valuation as is stated as:

$$V_L = V_U + \text{Value of Tax Shield}$$

$$= \frac{\text{EBIT} \times (1-T)}{r_0} + \frac{T \times D \times r_d}{r_d}$$

$$= \frac{\text{EBIT}\,(1-T)}{r_0} + T \times D$$

where T and D are the corporate tax rate and the amount of debt, respectively. Remember that earnings EBIT and debt D are constant and perennial.

Proposition I of MM with taxes can be restated as:

The value of the levered firm will be higher than the unlevered firm by the amount of tax shield on debt enjoyed by the levered firm.

Mathematically, it is stated as Equation 16-11.

$$V_L = V_U + T \times D \qquad (16\text{-}11)$$

MM Proposition II (Under Taxes)

> MM Proposition II under taxes recognises that with increasing debt the cost of equity would rise though at a lesser rate than what it would in the absence of taxes.

The cost of equity for the levered firm undergoes a change with the amount of debt. With no taxes the cost of equity with increasing leverage goes up and offsets the advantage of cheaper debt replacing expensive equity, so as to keep the value of the firm constant. With corporate taxes, the debt becomes more valuable due to a tax shield provided by interest paid on the debt. This tax shield benefits the equity holders, and hence, the cost of equity would not rise as much had there been no taxes.

Cost of equity for a levered firm, r_e[1] is given by Equation 16-12 as below:

$$r_e = r_0 + \frac{D}{E}(1-T)(r_0 - r_d) \qquad (16\text{-}12)$$

Note that the expression is similar to the one obtained with no taxes, with an extra term of $(1 - T)$ present. The cost of equity in a levered firm would rise by the differential of all equity cost (r_0) and cost of debt (r_d), but the proportion of increase would be $(1 - T)$ times the debt equity ratio.

The proposition II of Miller and Modigliani can be stated that with increased debt the cost of equity would rise because equity holders would like to be compensated for the additional risk they assume because of the likely threat to their cash flows. Debt holders having a prior and fixed claim on the cash flows leave lesser for equity holders at increased risk. The cost of equity when the firm has no debt accounts for only the business risk. With debt financing we add risk due to capital structure, called financial risk, to the business risk. Alternatively, we may state:

Cost of equity
= reward for business risk + reward for financial risk.

---

[1]If value of equity in levered firm is E and value of its debt is D then the cash flow to the stake holders in the firm are:

= Cash flow to equity holder + Cash flow to debt holders

$= E \times r_e + D \times r_d$

Also $V_L = V_U + T \times D$, and $V_L = E + D$ gives $V_U = E + D(1 - T)$

In terms of MM Proposition I, the value of levered firm is $V_L = V_U + T \times D$.

In terms as cash flows to stake holders we may have it as

Cash flow to capital suppliers

$= V_U \times r_0 + T \times D \times r_d = \{E + D\,(1 - T)\}\, r_0 + T\,D\,r_d$

Finally, equating the two cash flows;

$E \times r_e + D \times r_d = \{E + D\,(1 - T)\}\, r_0 + T\,D\,r_d,$

Gives

$$r_e = r_0 + \frac{D}{E}(1-T)(r_0 - r_d)$$

The values of the firms ALLEQ and CODEQ with corporate taxes and cost of equity are worked out below:

Value of unlevered firm, $V_U = \dfrac{\text{EBIT} \times (1-T)}{r_0}$

Value of ALLEQ, $V_U = \dfrac{5{,}00{,}000 \times (1-0.4)}{0.2}$

$= ₹15{,}000{,}000$

Value of levered firm $V_L = V_U + PV_{TS}$

Assuming perpetual debt

Present value of tax shield $PV_{TS} = D \times T$

$= 10{,}00{,}000 \times 0.4 = ₹4{,}00{,}000$

Value of CODEQ; $V_L = 15{,}00{,}000 + 4{,}00{,}000 = 19{,}00{,}000$

Value of equity of CODEQ; $E = V_L - D$

$= 19{,}00{,}000 - 10{,}00{,}000 = ₹9{,}00{,}000$

Equity capitalization rate for CODEQ;

$$r_e = r_0 - (r_0 - r_d)\frac{D}{D+E}$$

$$r_e = 20\% + (20\% - 10\%)\frac{\text{Cash flow to share holders}}{r_e} = 26.67\%$$

This may be checked with the cash flow approach to valuation. The value of CODEQ would be the value of cash flows of shareholders and debt holders discounted at the respective rates. The value of the firm based on cash flow would be:

Value of the firm = PV of the cash flows to shareholders and debt holders

$$= \frac{\text{Cash flow to debt holders}}{r_d} + \frac{\text{Cash flow to debt holders}}{r_d}$$

$$= \frac{2{,}40{,}000}{0.2667} + \frac{1{,}00{,}000}{0.10}$$

$$= 9{,}00{,}000 + 10{,}00{,}000 = ₹19{,}00{,}000$$

MM Proposition III (Under Taxes)

We have noticed that the market value of levered firm is more as compared to unlevered firm. The increased value of levered firm accrues to equity shareholders and, hence, the cost of equity does not rise as much as it would for unlevered firm. The third question is that of cost of capital of the levered firm. The weighted average cost of capital (WACC) declines for the levered firm despite increased capitalization rate of equity capital. The WACC for CODEQ, the levered firm will be:

MM Proposition III under taxes recognizes that with increasing debt the cost of capital too would rise though at a lesser rate than what it would in the absence of taxes.

$$\text{WACC}_L = r_e\frac{E}{D+E} + r_d(1-T)\frac{D}{D+E}$$

$$= 26.67\frac{9}{19} + 10(1-0.4)\frac{10}{19} = 15.79\%$$

The expression again is similar to the one obtained under no taxes with the exception of term $(1-T)$ appearing. This represents the fact that the cost of debt r_d with no taxes stands reduced to $r_d(1-T)$ when taxes become applicable.

Example 16-2 **Valuation and Cost of Capital for Levered and Unlevered firms under MM**

A firm is financed entirely by equity capital with expected rate of return of 15%. It has EBIT of ₹450 lakh. The corporate tax stands at 33.33%. As a financing option and considering the capital structure the firm is expecting to borrow ₹900 lakh at an attractive rate of 8% and retire equity by an equivalent amount. Find out the following:

(a) The market value of the firm when it is financed entirely by equity.
(b) The market value of the firm after it borrows from the market.
(c) What benefits do the equity shareholders draw from this borrowing?
(d) What is the cost of equity capital after borrowing?
(e) What is the cost of capital for the firm after borrowing?
(f) Find market value of equity using answer to (d).

Assume perpetual income and debt.

Solution

(a) When the firm is financed entirely by equity:

$$\text{Market value of the firm} = \frac{\text{Earnings for shareholders}}{\text{Capitalization rate}}$$

$$= \frac{\text{EBIT} \times (1-T)}{r} = \frac{450 \times (1-1/3)}{0.15}$$

$$= ₹2{,}000 \text{ lakh}$$

(b) When the firm replaces equity with debt worth ₹900 lakh, the value of the firm increases by the amount of tax shield enjoyed on the interest paid on debt. For perennial debt the value of the tax shield is given by

Present value of tax shield = Tax rate × Debt amount
= (1/3) × 900 = ₹300 lakh

The total value of the firm would increase by ₹300 lakh from the earlier position of all equity financing. Hence, the value of the firm after availing debt would be:

Value of levered firm
= Value of unlevered firm + Amount of tax shield
= 2,000 + 300 = ₹2,300 lakh

(c) Value of equity = Value of the firm – Value of debt
= 2,300 – 900 = ₹1400 lakh

The equity shareholders of the firm gain by the amount of tax shield. The value of equity should have reduced to ₹1,100 lakh from ₹2,000 lakh after borrowing of ₹900 lakh. Instead, the value of remaining equity increases by ₹300 lakh; the amount of tax shield. The benefit of tax shield accrues to the equity shareholders.

(d) The revised cost of equity after raising debt is:

$$r_e = r_0 + (r_0 - r_d)\frac{D \times (1-T)}{E}$$

$$= 15 + (15 - 8)\frac{900\,(1-1/3)}{1400} = 18\%$$

(e) The cost of capital for the firm after debt:

$$\text{WACC} = r_e\left(\frac{E}{E+D}\right) + r_d \times (1-T)\frac{D}{D+E}$$

$$= 18\left(\frac{1400}{2300}\right) + 8 \times (1 - 1/3)\frac{900}{2300} = 13.04\%$$

(f) Using cost of equity arrived at in (d) we may find the value of equity in the levered firm from:

$$\text{Value of equity} = \frac{(\text{EBIT} - r_d \times D)(1-T)}{r_e}$$

$$= \frac{(450 - 0.08 \times 900)(1 - 1/3)}{0.18}$$

$$= ₹1{,}400 \text{ lakh}$$

Conclusions of MM's Irrelevance of Capital Structure

The implications of Modigliani and Miller's approach with taxes can be summarized as below:

Value of the firm The value of the levered firm will be higher than the unlevered firm by the present value of the amount of taxes saved.

Cost of equity capital The cost of equity capital will rise with increasing leverage, like in case of a world without taxes. However, the premium, related to the financial risk with taxes present, will be smaller by the factor of tax rate.

Cost of capital Due to reduced premium for financial risk and constancy of cost of debt, the weighted average cost of capital WACC for the levered firm will decline with increasing leverage.

Optimal capital structure Due to continuous reduction in the cost of capital with increasing leverage it will be beneficial for the firm to keep borrowing and increase value. Hence, the optimal capital structure; the one that maximizes the value of the firm or minimises the cost of capital, will be 100% debt. The minimum cost of capital will be equal to the post tax cost of debt.

In the presence of corporate tax, the optimal capital structure would be 100% debt according to MM propositions.

The implication of MM on the value of the firm and the cost of financing in the world with taxes are depicted in Figure 16-5 (a) and (b), respectively. The value of the firm rises by the amount of tax shield, which is directly proportional to the amount of debt taken. Similarly, the cost of equity too rises with the increasing debt.

At this point, a caveat is in order. How and when does debt replaces equity needs to be understood clearly. The process of replacing equity with debt or vice versa is governed by the way stock markets function. Typical sequence of events in the stock market would be (i) announcement of issue of debt, (ii) followed by mobilisation of debt, and (iii) lastly actual retirement of equity.

Efficient markets respond to the news rather than the actual happening. The benefits of debt are captured in the market price of the share just on the announcement. Therefore, the market price jumps to reflect the value of the tax shield even before the debt is actually raised and equity replaced. Hence, debt retires equity at the revised price and not at the price prevailing prior to the change in the capital structure is made. An example, would make the process of change in the capital structure clear and holding the validity of the valuation of the firms under MM propositions.

Example 16-3 Changing Capital Structure

In the preceding example for valuation and cost of capital for the levered and unlevered firms assume that the unlevered firm had 10 lakh shares outstanding prior to the issue of debt. With the issuance of the debt how many shares will be purchased and what shall be the market price of the shares?

Solution

Value of the unlevered firm = ₹2,000 lakh
Nos. of shares outstanding = 10 lakh
Market price before the issue of debt = ₹200 per share.

When the issue of debt is announced, the market value of the firm rises by the amount of tax shield and the entire benefit of the tax shield accrues to the shareholders. Hence, the market value of the shares would rise by ₹300 lakh (by the amount of tax shield). The new price of the share would therefore be:

₹2300 lakh/10 lakh = ₹230 per share

The number of shares that will be retired by raising debt
= 900/230 = 3.913 lakh

Nos. of shares outstanding = 10 – 3.913 = 6.087 lakh
Market value of remaining shares = 6.087 × 230 = ₹1,400 lakh

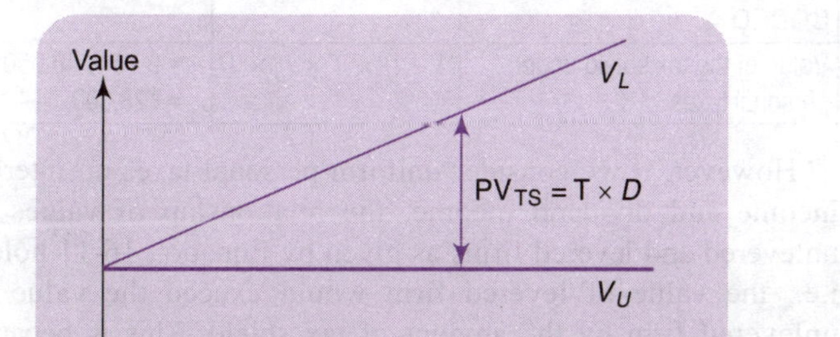

Figure 16-5 (a) MM proposition (with taxes): Value of the firm

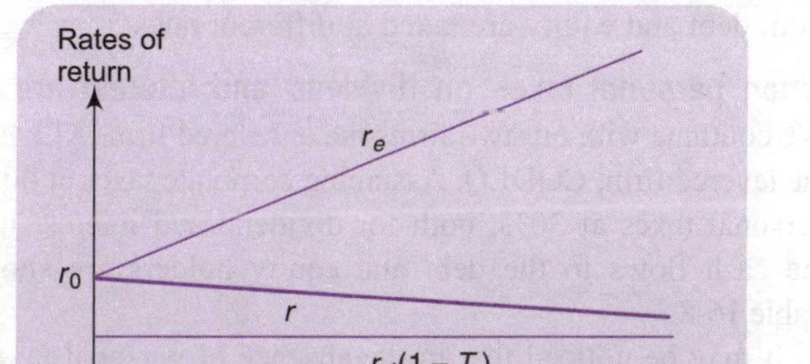

Figure 16-5 (b) MM proposition (with taxes): Capitalization rates

Table 16-7 MMs Propositions—with and without corporate taxes

	Without Taxes	With Taxes
Proposition I Value of the firm	$V_L = V_U$ $V_L = E + D$	$V_L = V_U + PV_{TS}$ $V_U = \text{EBIT}(1 - T)/r_0$
Proposition II Cost of equity	$r_e = r_0 + (r_0 - r_d)\frac{D}{E}$	$r_e = r_0 + (r_0 - r_d)\frac{D(1-T)}{E}$
Proposition III Cost of capital	$\text{WACC}_U = \text{WACC}_L = r_0$ $\text{WACC};\ r = r_e\frac{D}{E+D} + r_d\frac{D}{E+D}$	$\text{WACC}_L = \text{WACC}_U\left(1 - \frac{PV_{TS}}{D+E}\right)$ $\text{WACC}_L;\ r = r_e\frac{E}{E+D} + r_d\frac{D(1-T)}{E+D}$

Where PV_{TS} = Present value of tax shield; For perennial debt it is $T \times D$

The implications of Miller and Modigliani with and without taxes are summarized in Table 16-7.

CAPITAL STRUCTURE WITH PERSONAL TAXES

So far we ignored personal taxes. Investors are required to pay taxes on the incomes derived from subscribing to financial instruments. In most countries, including India, the tax rates differ with nature of income. The income from equity investments and income from debt instruments are taxed at different rates.

In India, while the dividend income on shares is tax exempt in the hands of individuals, firms are required to pay a dividend distribution tax on the amount distributed as dividend. If the entire earnings are retained, no such tax is payable. The current rate of dividend distribution tax is 15%. The interest income is taxed in the hands of the investors. However, firms save tax on the interest. The tax payable by an individual on interest is based on the level of his income and varies from nil to 30%.

What is the impact of personal taxes on the value of the firm and the returns of the investors? Naturally, the returns would fall by the amount of taxes paid on the respective incomes earned by the debt holders and shareholders. What happens to the value of the firm with the personal taxes introduced? We shall examine it under two cases—(i) where the income from debt and equity are taxed at the same rates, and (ii) where the income from debt and equity are taxed at different rates.

When personal taxes on dividend and interest are equal

We continue with our two firms the unlevered firm, ALLEQ and the levered firm, CODEQ. Assuming corporate taxes at 40% and personal taxes at 30%, both for dividend and interest income the cash flows to the debt and equity holders are shown in Table 16-8.

It may be noticed that in the absence of personal taxes, the combined income derived by the equity as well as debt suppliers is higher by ₹40,000 (3,40,000 - 3,00,000) for levered firm compared to unlevered firm. This is equal to the tax shield provided by debt, i.e., 40% of interest amount of ₹1,00,000. When personal taxes are charged from the personal income of investors, the returns of the investors would fall by the tax amount. Since the investors of CODEQ have a higher income they would pay greater amount of tax than the investors of all equity firm ALLEQ. Therefore, the value of tax shield enjoyed by CODEQ would stand reduced by the amount of additional personal taxes paid by investors, denoted as t in CODEQ.

With personal taxes, the value of the tax shield declines by the amount of personal taxes.

Table 16-8 Cash flow to debt and equity holders—levered and unlevered firms with corporate and personal taxes

(Figures in ₹)

	ALLEQ	CODEQ
EBIT	5,00,000	5,00,000
Interest @ 10%		1,00,000
EBT	5,00,000	4,00,000
Taxes @ 40%	2,00,000	1,60,000
EAT	3,00,000	2,40,000
Personal tax on equity income @ 30%	90,000	72,000
Personal tax of interest income @ 30%	—	30,000
Earnings available to suppliers of debt and equity, after tax	2,10,000	2,38,000

Tax advantage of levered firm, CODEQ with corporate taxes but without personal taxes	$T \times r_d \times D$	$= 0.40 \times 1,00,000$ = ₹40,000
Additional personal taxes paid by investors of levered firm CODEQ	$t \times T \times r_d \times D$	$= 0.30 \times 40,000$ = ₹12,000
Value of the tax shield under personal taxes	$(1 - t) \times T \times r_d \times D$	$= 0.70 \times 40,000$ = ₹28,000

However, if we consider uniform personal taxes on interest income and dividend income, the relationship of values of unlevered and levered firms as given by Equation 16-11 holds, i.e., the value of levered firm would exceed the value of unlevered firm by the amount of tax shield. This is because cash flows of shareholders of unlevered firm would now be discounted at $r_0 \times (1 - t)$ instead of r_0. Similarly, income of levered firm too would get discounted at lesser rate by a factor of $(1 - t)$; i.e., equity income at $r_e \times (1 - t)$ and debt income at

$r_d \times (1 - t)$ instead of r_e and r_d, respectively. Further, the tax shield too would be discounted at $r_d \times (1 - t)$. For perpetual tax shield the present value of the tax shield remains same at ₹4,00,000.

$$\text{Present value of the tax shield} = \frac{(1-t)\times T \times r_d \times D}{(1-t)\times r_d}$$
$$= T \times D = 0.40 \times 10{,}00{,}000$$
$$= ₹4{,}00{,}000$$

This may be looked at another way in relative terms. Assuming that a firm has ₹1.00 to distribute either as an interest to debt holders or as a dividend income to the equity holders. Debt holders pay tax on the interest income at t_d and shareholders pay taxes on dividend at t_e. But prior to this, the firm has to pay corporate taxes of T, in case it wants to pay earnings as dividend rather than interest. Post tax cash flows to the stakeholders in case of distribution of EBIT of Re 1.00 as interest or as dividend are depicted in Figure 16-6[2].

Differential personal tax rates on interest and dividend and capital gains makes debt beneficial for the firm as long as $(1 - t_d) > (1 - T)(1 - t_e)$.

With different corporate and personal taxes the objective of the firm must be to choose a capital structure that maximises the cash flow to its capital suppliers. In case it has zero debt, the cash flow to equity holders would be $(1 - T)(1 - t_e)$.

In case the firm has only debt the cash flow to the stakeholders would be: $(1 - t_d)$

It would be advantageous to have debt as long as additional cash flow to debt holders exceeds the cash flow to equity holders:, i.e.,

$$(1 - t_d) > (1 - T)(1 - t_e) \quad (16\text{-}13)$$

Alternatively, the tax advantage can be stated as:

$$\text{Net tax advantage of debt} = (1 - t_d) - (1 - T)(1 - t_e)$$

As long as the net tax advantage of debt is positive the firm must continue to borrow. When tax rates on interest income and dividend income is same (when $t_d = t_e = t$) the net tax advantage reduces to $(1 - t) \times T$ as was done for CODEQ in Table 16-8. Further, the presence of corporate taxes and the taxes on equity income favour debt while an increase in tax on the interest income would reduce the attractiveness of debt.

When tax rates on dividend and interest are different In practice, the personal tax rates for dividend and interest are different. Shareholders in most cases pay less taxes because tax rates on dividend are lesser as compared to the interest income

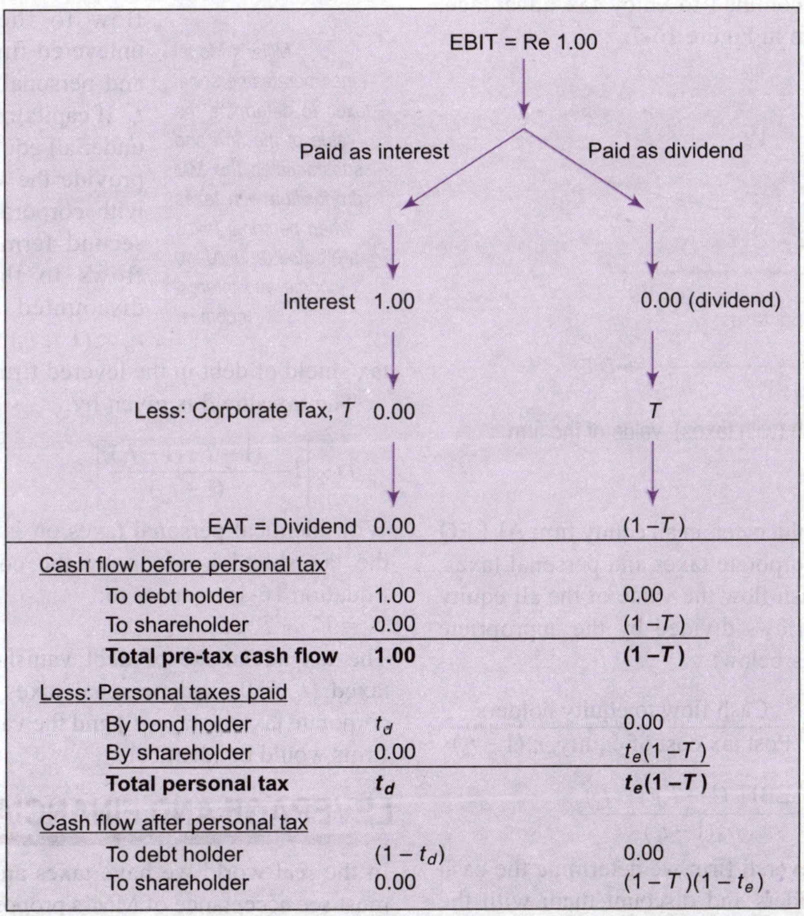

Figure 16-6 The impact of tax on cash flows to debt holder and equity holder

[2]*Source*: *The Principles of Corporate Finance* by Brealey & Myers, 6th ed., 2000, Tata McGraw Hill.

In such situations, we expect the capital structure to favour equity rather than debt, as equity shareholders pay lesser tax than debt holders. For ALLEQ and CODEQ we present the data with personal income tax on dividend and interest income at 15% and 30%, respectively in Table 16-9.

Table 16-9 Financial data of levered and unlevered firms under corporate and different personal taxes

(₹)

	ALLEQ	CODEQ
EBIT	5,00,000	5,00,000
Interest @ 10%		1,00,000
EBT	5,00,000	4,00,000
Taxes @ 40%	2,00,000	1,60,000
EAT	3,00,000	2,40,000
Personal tax on equity income @ 15%	45,000	36,000
Personal tax of interest income @ 30%	—	30,000
Earnings available to suppliers of debt and equity	2,55,000	2,74,000

As personal taxes increase the value of the tax shield comes down. However, levered firm remains more valuable than the unlevered firm. Some of the tax advantage of levered firm gets offset by personal taxes. As long as personal taxes are not 100% the levered firm will continue to enjoy tax advantage, howsoever marginal, as shown in Figure 16-7.

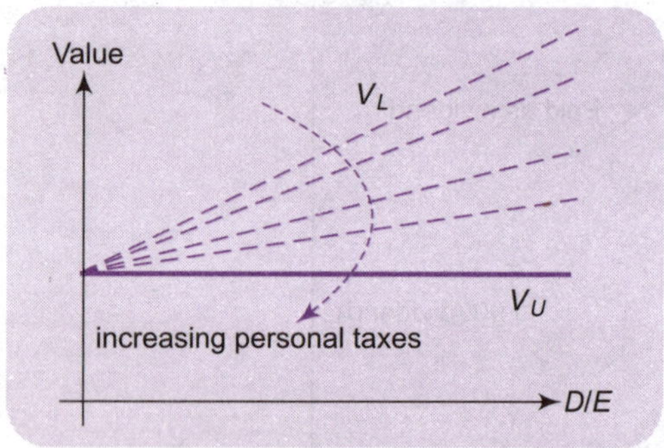

Figure 16-7 MM position (with taxes): value of the firm

Miller's Model

The cash flows to the equity holders for an all equity firm ALLEQ would be EBIT reduced by corporate taxes and personal taxes, t_e. Therefore, for perennial cash flow the value of the all equity firm would be annual cash flows divided by the appropriate discount rate. This is given as below:

$$\text{Value of All Equity Firm} = \frac{\text{Cash flow to equity holders}}{\text{Post tax cost of equity, } r_0(1-t_e)}$$

$$= \frac{\text{EBIT }(1-T)(1-t_e)}{r_0(1-t_e)}$$

To find out the value of levered firm we determine the cash flows to equity and debt holders and discount them with the appropriate discount rates. To the equity holders the cash flow available after corporate tax is $(\text{EBIT} - r_dD) \times (1-T)$. After personal taxes the cash flow reduces to $(\text{EBIT} - r_dD) \times (1-T) \times (1-t_e)$.

Similarly, the cash flow to debt suppliers after personal tax of t_d is $r_dD \times (1-t_d)$. The sum of cash flows to the suppliers of capital would form the basis of the value of the firm. This may be represented as under:

Post tax income of investors

$$= (\text{EBIT} - r_dD)(1-T)(1-t_e) + r_dD\,(1-r_d)$$

$$= \text{EBIT}(1-T)(1-t_e) - r_d\,D(1-T)(1-t_e) + r_dD(1-t_d)$$

$$= \text{EBIT}(1-T)(1-t_e) + r_dD(1-t_d)\left[1-\frac{(1-T)(1-t_e)}{(1-t_d)}\right]$$

Value of the levered firm; V_L

= Present value of the cash flows to be discounted at appropriate rates

$$= \frac{\text{EBIT}(1-T)(1-t_e)}{\text{Cost of equity in all equity firm}}$$

$$+ \frac{r_dD(1-t_d)}{\text{Cost of debt}}\left[1-\frac{(1-T)(1-t_e)}{(1-t_e)}\right]$$

$$= V_U + D\left\{\left[1-\frac{(1-T)\,(1-t_e)}{(1-t_d)}\right]\right\} \quad (16\text{-}14)$$

The first term of Equation 16-14, i.e., EBIT × (1 – T) × (1 – t_e) in post tax cash flow to the investors represents the cash flow to the equity investors in an unlevered firm with corporate taxes at T and personal taxes on equity income as t_e. If capitalized at post tax cost of equity under all equity funding, $r_0(1-t_e)$ it will provide the value of the unlevered firm with corporate and personal taxes. The second term represents post tax cash flows to the debt investors and if discounted at post tax cost of debt $r_d \times (1-t_d)$ would provide the value of tax shield of debt in the levered firm.

Miller's Model incorporates personal taxes to determine the value of the firm and substantiates the MM proposition with taxes when personal taxes are equal on dividend income and interest incomes.

The tax shield is given by:

$$D \times \left[1-\frac{(1-T)\,(1-t_s)}{(1-t_d)}\right]$$

With identical personal taxes on interest and dividend ($t_e = t_d$) the tax shield is given by the corporate tax rate only, and Equation 16-14 reduces to:

$$= V_U + T \times D$$

The tax advantage of debt vanishes if equity income is not taxed ($t_e = 0$) and personal taxes on interest income equals corporate tax rate ($t_d = T$) and the value of levered and unlevered firms would be identical.

LEVERAGE AND FINANCIAL DISTRESS

In the real world we have taxes and, therefore, in practice we must see acceptance of MM's propositions, which suggest 100% leverage to maximize shareholders value and minimize the cost of capital. One may argue that at 100% debt there shall be no shareholders left and the cherished objective of finance manager of maximization of shareholders' wealth vanishes. However, it does not take away the argument in favour of increasing debt till the last shareholder exists. If that is true, we as shareholders must favour high debt firms compared to low debt firms. Contrary to the theoretical positions we find the practice to be exactly opposite. Most successful firms have no or very little debt. Also most of the firms that have failed had inordinately high amount of debt. The high amount of debt possibly has been the single largest reason for corporate failures and bankruptcies.

Apparently, capital structure matters for reasons other than taxes. Managers as well as shareholders are literate enough to recognize the advantage of tax as highlighted by MM and to challenge MM's propositions if they do not agree. There are issues that seem to dominate the tax advantage else managers' and shareholders' preference for equity cannot be explained. Behaviour is independent and can neither justify nor defy theories. In fact, theories have to be found to explain behaviour.

Cost of Financial Distress

One of the factors that seem to negate the tax advantage is the financial distress the firm undergoes when it assumes debt. Financial distress is described as the difficulty a firm may face in meeting its commitments, which also includes interest to be paid to the lenders of the funds. It may range from minor liquidity crisis to total insolvency. Overcoming temporary liquidity crisis is the starting point for borrowing in most firms. It is the compulsion of meeting day-to-day needs that leads to borrowing rather than to borrow deliberately to avail the tax advantage and increase the value of the firm.

When financial distress becomes severe and firm actually makes a default in the commitments the costs associated with debt increase significantly. However, at low levels of leverage these costs may not be felt by the firm as the probability of defaulting as well as the cost of financial distress are low. Financial distress is dependent upon many factors such as cost structure of products, levels of competition, technological innovations, stability of demand, etc.

It is extremely difficult to estimate the cost of financial distress. There is no substitute for managerial wisdom and shareholders' intelligence. Financial distress cost can be divided in two categories, (i) direct costs such as cost of litigation and administration, loss due to distress sale, reduction in value of assets due to non-use, etc, and (ii) indirect costs such as management time in warding off the creditors, managing by crisis rather than planning, faulty decision making in choosing right business opportunities, etc.

Each time the firm raises debt, it increases the fixed commitment, which increases the chance of getting less for equity shareholders. As a firm goes for higher debt the lenders raise the interest rate too. Further, it is seen as constraining the freedom of shareholders. Lenders, in order to protect their own interest, put several covenants that come in the way of making free and fair decisions from the viewpoint of shareholders. The interest of the lenders is often conflicting with those of shareholders. Consent to the covenants put by lenders, is not seen favourably by shareholders and markets. The value of the firm may not rise despite the availability of the tax shield of debt.

The direct costs of financial distress are quite nominal, compared to the value of the firm. They are fairly low and do not justify the low levels of debt most successful firms have. It is the indirect costs emanating from the perception of dangers that high levels of debt may cause which seems to affect the capital structure in favour of equity. In the opinion of the market, if the borrowing does not come in the way of the interest of shareholders, only then would the market value rise. Further, any kind of borrowing may not be viewed very kindly by shareholders, especially those of the successful firms, because they themselves may be very keen to fund the capital requirements either by way of foregoing dividends or by way of subscribing to the fresh capital. Since the firm is successful, any intervention by lenders is regarded as an infringement on the rights of shareholders notwithstanding the tax advantage of debt.

With increasing debt, the cost of financial distress rises and offsets the tax advantage. As long as the cost of financial distress is lower than the tax advantage the value of the firm will rise with increasing leverage. As leverage keeps increasing the perceived costs of financial distress offset the benefits of tax savings. Any increase in the probability of financial distress raises the cost of capital.

Costs of financial distress tend to decrease the value of the firm offsetting the advantage of tax shield of debt.

Agency Cost of Debt

In a levered firm we may have conflict of interest between shareholders and debt holders. The conflict of interest under normal circumstances is not very perceptible, but becomes exaggerated under conditions of high debt with mounting costs of financial distress. These conflicts are easy to visualise when firms are on the verge of bankruptcy.

One feature of debt is that it claims a fixed amount of principal and interest irrespective of business conditions. The bondholders are indifferent to the risk of business. The business risks are borne by equity holders only being claimant of residual. However, under conditions of likely bankruptcy bondholders also become prone to some risk, though not as much as equity holders. The return to the bondholders is guided by the actions of the shareholders being decision makers and managers of the firm.

As an example, consider a firm facing bankruptcy. So far it has not defaulted on the obligations of debt but may do so if similar conditions continue for some more time. The current values of its debt and equity are nominal. It faces a choice of two mutually exclusive projects—a rather conservative project, SAFE and a make-or-break project, RISKY. Both the projects are of same size and assume that the funds can be made available for initial investment. With bad and good scenarios equally likely the SAFE project yields an increase in the value of ₹1,600 and ₹3,200 respectively, while for RISKY project the pay-offs are ₹500 and ₹4,000, respectively.

The expected value of SAFE project is ₹2,400 and for RISKY project is ₹2,250. The fixed claim of debt holders for this inordinately high debt firm is ₹1,000. For the SAFE project, the risk is lower and the expected value is higher than the RISKY project, and principle of capital budgeting demands that SAFE project be implemented. The data is displayed in Table 16-10.

Table 16-10 Agency cost of debt

Condition	Prob	SAFE			RISKY		
		Value	Bond	Equity	Value	Bond	Equity
Bad	0.5	1,600	1,000	600	500	500	—
Good	0.5	3,200	1,000	2,200	4000	1,000	3,000
Expected Value—Total		2,400			2,250		
Expected Value—Equity		1,400			1,500		

Under normal circumstances, the entire increase in value would accrue to the equity shareholders. However, since the firm is facing bankruptcy and is on the verge of defaulting the payment obligations to the bondholders, the perspective of the managers working for the shareholders changes dramatically. Instead of focussing on the increase in the expected value of the project his attention turns on the increase in the value to the shareholders. Observe that an increase in the value of equity is greater if RISKY project is accepted and good conditions prevail. If conditions are bad the shareholders are indifferent to both SAFE and RISKY project. It does not take long for one to realise that the gain of shareholders is at the expense of bondholders. Hence, with bankruptcy imminent, the firm is more likely to accept the RISKY project though the prudence demands otherwise. It is like gambling with borrowed money which if succeeds can do lot of good and if it fails the lender loses because the gambler (read shareholder) doesn't have anything to lose further.

Inordinate amount of debt acts against the principles of capital budgeting and encourages managers to take undue risk to increase the welfare of shareholders at the expense of debt holders.

Besides taking risks, the firms facing bankruptcy are hesitant to bring in any fresh equity if they have any worthwhile projects to undertake. In the earlier example, we assumed the funds were available to choose either SAFE or RISKY project. The question of who funds the initial cost was not addressed. Since the firm is already on the verge of bankruptcy the chances are that shareholders would be required to fund the projects by their own funds. Even if the firm selects SAFE project and is required to bring in fresh equity of ₹2,000 the shareholders would be hesitant to fund, because any increase in value will first accrue to the bondholders.

Extending the argument further, shareholders may also attempt to take as much advantage as they can before the actual bankruptcy occurs. Since the control of the firm rests with equity holders they may take decisions to benefit themselves such as announcing extraordinary dividend (if any cash is left with the firm). They may decide to generate cash by selling some unencumbered assets, which at present seem useless but may have potential to generate cash flows.

Who Bears Agency Costs

Thus, firms facing bankruptcy are likely to exhibit actions or behaviour that defy pragmatism. Strategies such as (i) favouring extremely risky projects even when safer projects even with higher NPV are available, (ii) reluctance to bring in any fresh equity if situations so demand, and (iii) draining cash and other productive resources of the firm, do have costs as they are detrimental to the firm. The discussion the preceding paragraphs may cause one to feel that it is the bondholders who bear this cost. The firm faces bankruptcy due to its reduced ability to service the debt. It must be kept in mind that shareholders cannot gain unless the obligations to service the debt are fulfilled. Any correct decision not taken simply because it will first benefit the debt holders, is wrong. The costs of myopic and erroneous decision making are ultimately and unarguably borne by shareholders themselves.

Agency cost of debt relate to the conflict of interest between debt holders and shareholders. Though it appears that debt holders bear this cost the fact remains that agency cost are borne by shareholders themselves.

Bondholders or lenders, sensing that behaviours of firms facing bankruptcy are likely to damage them, take some protective measures. First they raise the interest rates to compensate for the high risk they are exposed to in the vulnerable firms. Besides the lenders may impose certain restrictions like (i) restricting declaration of dividend before fulfilling obligations of debt, (ii) prior approval for any major expansion projects, (iii) restricting the sale of assets, (iv) seek additional protection in the form of collateral security besides primary security, (v) restriction on raising any further loans, (vi) periodic monitoring, (vii) nominating directors on the boards of the firms to check actions of shareholders, and (viii) building convertibility clauses in the loan agreements whereby loans may be converted to equity in situations leading to bankruptcy, etc. All such actions reduce the cost of loan funds and are attempts to keep the conflict between bondholders and shareholders within manageable limits. Acceptance of protective covenants of the lenders by the firms implies reduced cost of debt due to (i) additional protection the creditors have and (ii) shareholders forego some freedom of actions.

TRADE-OFF THEORY OF CAPITAL STRUCTURE

With the introduction of cost of financial distress and cost of agency with increasing debt the tax advantage of debt reduces. This gives rise to a trade-off between the advantage and disadvantage of debt.

Because the cost of the financial distress and cost of agency cannot be computed as clearly as the tax advantage of debt we may not be able to determine the exact optimal capital structure. It is the perceived balance between the advantage of debt and the costs of financial distress and agency that will, rather subjectively, determine the level of debt a firm can afford. This leads to a point of optimal capital structure where the marginal cost of financial distress becomes equal to the additional tax

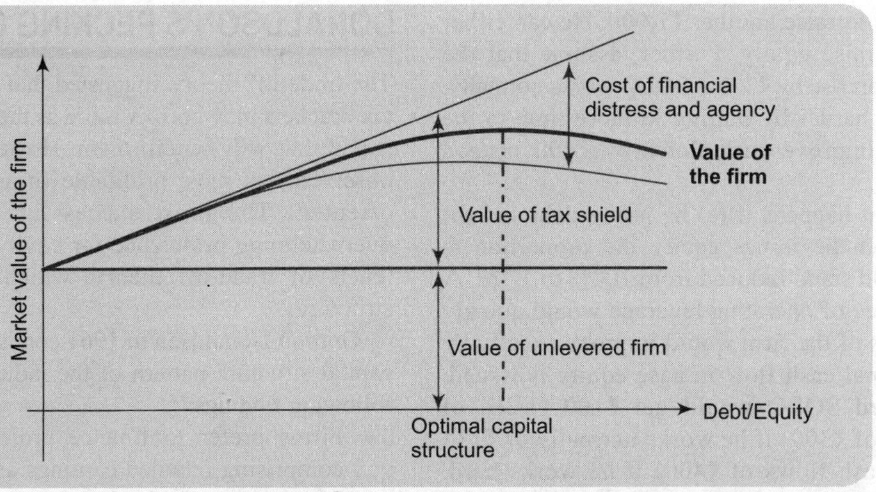

Figure 16-8 Trade-off theory: Cost of financial distress and tax shield

Trade-off theory suggests that there exists an optimal capital structure when the tax advantage is offset completely by cost of financial distress and agency cost of debt.

advantage any further borrowing will bring. This is known as trade-off theory and suggests that there exists an optimal capital structure for each firm, which is the fine balance between the advantage of debt in the form of tax shield and disadvantage of debt perceived in the form of costs of financial distress and cost of agency. This basic idea behind trade-off is depicted in Figure 16-8.

Trade-off theory would state the value of levered firm as:

Value of levered firm = Value of unlevered firm
+ PV of tax shield
– PV of costs of financial distress

Few of the important implications of trade-off theory can be summarized as under:

Firstly, the firms that face high business risk can afford little debt as compared to firms in less risky business environment. An increase of debt for a firm already in high business risk class would see a rise in agency cost and the cost of financial distress more rapidly than the firms in low business risk class.

Secondly, firms already paying more taxes stand to gain more by raising debt as the tax shield of debt would be greater as compared to the firm paying lesser rate of tax. Hence, profitable firms in high tax brackets should raise more debt as the larger cost of financial distress and agency would be needed to offset the tax shield.

Thirdly, the costs of financial distress and agency would be lower in the firms having tangible assets as compared to firms whose value is predominantly governed by their intangible assets. Knowledge-driven firms, such as those in the software sector or internet business, derive their values from the intellectual base they possess. Such firms rely heavily on people and their knowledge. The value of the firm becomes volatile as people move. Any act that restricts freedom, as would happen through the covenants of lenders, would be disliked and could be a sufficient reason to switch jobs, especially for senior managers seriously impacting the value of the firm. On the contrary, the firms with tangible assets of land, building, and machineries, etc., such as steel makers and cement producers may provide a lot of comfort to lenders and shareholders alike, as such firms are less dependent upon knowledge of people. Neither shareholders nor lenders may actually feel threatened with increasing levels of debt till it assumes significantly high proportion. Such feeling of security emanates from recourse to the assets being available.

Uniformity in business risk and similarities of nature of assets in particular industrial and business sectors are primarily responsible for establishing norms for debt–equity ratio. One often witnesses similar debt–equity ratios for the firms in particular business, which represents the collective wisdom of managers in those sectors. Only under extreme circumstances firms and lenders, primarily financial institutions, deviate from the established norms of debt–equity ratio. Such established capital structure is a fine balance between two conflicting issues of benefits of debt on one hand and cost of financial distress and agency on the other.

Agency Cost of Equity

Both the amount of tax shield and the cost of financial distress rise as the amount of debt increases. Conversely, reduced debt would reduce the benefit of tax shield as well as decrease the cost of financial distress. Reduced debt provides another advantage in the form of reduction in the cost referred as agency cost of equity.

Agency cost of equity refers to the tendency of shareholders to increase debt and not equity so as to gain maximum advantage with least work.

The agency cost of equity results from the changing degree of involvement the owners have in the survival and growth of the firm with changing debt–equity ratio. It is a well-known fact that we take better care of our own house than we do for a rented one. This is a common behaviour, which is also exhibited in the corporate world. Let us again assume some numbers to demonstrate this rather common behaviour that one does harder work when the degree of ownership increases. This has strong implication for capital structure as it favours debt as against equity.

Assume that a firm has worth of ₹500 and is 100% owned by its proprietor, SOLO. As some excellent business opportunity is available SOLO needs to raise another ₹1,000. He can either issue debt at 15% or raise equity. Further, assume that the cash flows of the firm can rise by ₹300 if SOLO works normally. However, if he works harder by putting in more time to the project the firm can improve cash flows by ₹400 instead of ₹300.

Let us examine what happens if (a) he issues debt and (b) he issues equity. When he issues equity the proportionate holding of SOLO would stand reduced from 100% to 1/3rd. A discussion on the degree of operating leverage would quickly reveal that his earnings of the firm would improve exactly by the amount of additional cash flow in case equity is issued. When equity is issued SOLO would get ₹100 (1/3rd of additional cash flows of ₹300) if he works normally or ₹133 (1/3rd of additional cash flows of ₹400) if he works hard. This is presented in Table 16-11.

Table 16-11 Agency cost of equity: shirking work (₹)

	Soft Paddle			Hard Grind		
	Addl. Cash flow	Interest	Cash for SOLO	Addl. Cash flow	Interest	Cash for SOLO
Debt	300	150	150	400	150	250
Equity (1/3rd ownership)	300	—	100	400	—	133

However, if debt is issued, SOLO remains the 100% owner of the firm. His gain would be ₹150 (₹300 – interest; 15% of ₹1,000) if he works normally, and ₹250 (₹400 – interest) if he works hard. We may conclude the following:

(a) When debt is issued the rise in earnings is greater,
(b) When debt is issued the rise in earnings is steeper as more effort is put than in case of issue of fresh equity, and
(c) Since proportionate ownership reduces issue of fresh equity would cause SOLO not to work harder.

In the above example, if SOLO issues debt and works normally he can earn more than what he would earn had he issued fresh equity and works harder. Therefore, SOLO would favour issuance of debt.

Extending the conclusions of SOLO, we may infer that managers who are the owners would shirk from work if fresh equity is issued. In fact, any dilution in ownership causes them to behave more like hired employees. Therefore, managers would strive for additional perquisites as means of increasing their own welfare and economic being. The cost associated with shirking of work and craving for perquisites is referred to as cost of agency for equity. This favours debt and savings in the agency cost of equity can be viewed as another benefit of debt apart from the tax shield. Such an analysis would be valid if the issuance of equity causes a substantial change in ownership of managers; fractional changes may not make the agency cost of equity material to the capital structure.

The trade-off model can now be viewed as a fine balance of (i) tax advantage of debt, (ii) savings of agency cost of equity on one side and (iii) cost of financial distress and (iv) agency cost of debt on the other side.

DONALDSON'S PECKING ORDER THEORY

The trade-off theory suggested that the profitable firms in high tax brackets may borrow more as they have larger amount of tax shield that will benefit them. However, in actual practice it is observed that most profitable firms are predominantly equity oriented. The most successful firms have exhibited an overwhelming preference for equity over debt. This defies the tenets of trade-off theory, which suggests a target capital structure.

Gordon Donaldson in 1961 conducted a study to examine the capital structure pattern of the industry and came out with the following findings:

- Firms prefer to finance projects with internal accruals comprising retained earnings and depreciation.
- Firms set a dividend pay out ratios after considering the future investment opportunities such that expected cash flows are sufficient to cover the capital expenditures under normal circumstances.
- Dividends are 'sticky'—the firms are reluctant i) to raise dividend unless very confident of maintaining the enhanced level in future, or ii) to cut dividend unless they have to.
- If the firm has more internal accruals than needed for capital investment, it will invest in marketable securities, retire debt, increase dividends, buy back shares, or resort to acquisitions.
- If the firm has insufficient internal accruals to meet capital expenditures it will draw down on marketable securities, then go for external finance. If it goes for external finance then it will first issue debt, then convertible bonds, and finally the equity stock.

Donaldson's theory suggests that firm:

1. will finance from internal accruals, then
2. raise debt or convertible debt, and finally
3. resort to issue of equity.

With pecking order of financing, it seems that there is no defined target debt–equity ratio that can be arrived through trade-off theory. Pecking order splits the equity into two parts – internally generated funds and fresh issue of equity. While internally generated funds are preferred over debt the same is not true when it comes to mobilizing equity through a fresh issue. Raising debt is preferred over raising fresh equity.

Donaldson study suggests the pecking order of financing specifies that firms (i) will finance from internal accruals, then (ii) raise debt or convertible debt, and finally (iii) resort to issue of equity.

Two kinds of equity sandwiching debt as per the pecking order of financing is inconsistent with the trade-off theory. One plausible explanation may lie in the behaviour of the capital markets as to how it views the mobilization of capital by the firms. The deployment of internally generated funds for projects is viewed rather positively, and as healthy sign by the capital markets. On the other hand, raising equity issue may cause a doubt and some concern in the minds of existing shareholders that the stocks are overpriced and hence firm wants to raise capital by equity route. Also the issuance of equity invites new shareholders to partake the benefits of projects, diluting the relative share of existing shareholders. Since debt does not let the control dilute or curtail benefits of equity the existing shareholders are not averse to funding through debt.

This explains why profitable firms dislike debt even though they have recourse to it. They keep increasing the retained earnings and building a borrowing capacity. Should an opportunity of investment arise and firm finds itself short of internally generated funds it can utilize its borrowing capacity. This also explains why growing firms having more investment opportunities than what can be afforded by internal funds, resort to borrowing first before mobilizing fresh equity. In a nutshell, the firms build their borrowing capacity in good times and use it when the need arises.

Pecking order theory relies on the assumption that mobilisation of fresh capital is not greeted with cheers in the capital markets.

SIGNALLING OR ASYMMETRIC INFORMATION THEORY

The inconsistency of Donaldson's finding and trade-off theory may be resolved by what is referred as signalling or asymmetric information theory of capital structure. Proposed by Stewart Myers, the theory suggests that Donaldson's finding may be explained if asymmetric information and divergent expectations of investors exist.

Contradiction in Donaldson's pecking order and trade-off models can be explained partially on the information asymmetry that exists between shareholders and managers if the firm.

The trade-off theory assumes that there is no information gap and investors have homogeneous expectations and, hence, stocks are priced at their fair or intrinsic values. If this assumption is not true, i.e., different groups of investors have asymmetric information and expectations are not homogeneous, the findings of Donaldson may be explained reasonably. This can best be explained through some numbers.

Assume that a firm has 100 shares outstanding and the current market price is ₹50. The managers of the firm believe that the shares are underpriced and the intrinsic worth of the firm is good enough to command a price of ₹55. Since the managers are better informed than the investors such a possibility is recognized. The information gap between managers and shareholders is not far from reality. Note that this is inconsistent with the assumptions of strong form of efficient market hypothesis.

Further assume that the firm needs capital investment of ₹5,500 with NPV of ₹500. The increased NPV would be reflected in the price of the shares. The firm needs to raise finance either through debt or issuance of fresh equity. With respect to issuance of equity, its managers broadly face two situations; (i) to remove the existing information gap between investors and themselves before making a fresh equity issue or (ii) let the asymmetric information persist.

If the managers make conscious efforts to remove the information asymmetry, then the firm would be able to issue fresh shares at ₹55, else it will have to price them at ₹50. The post issue scenario when the information asymmetry would be resolved is presented in Table 16-12.

A look at Table 16-12 would reveal that the old shareholders would be at loss subsequent to the issue of fresh capital if the there is asymmetric information. More importantly, the new shareholders would be benefited due to undervalued shares. Both old and new shareholders would benefit if the information asymmetry is resolved prior to the fresh issue.

The result would be no different if the market overvalues the stock compared to its intrinsic value. This can be seen from Table 16-13 where the intrinsic worth of the share is placed at ₹45 as against the market price of ₹50.

From Tables 16-12 and 16-13, it can be concluded that if information asymmetry remains the issue of fresh capital is not advisable since existing shareholders would lose. However, if the firm issues debt instead of equity the entire benefit of increased NPV of ₹500 would accrue to existing shareholders, and the question of under or over valuation due to information asymmetry becomes rather redundant. Hence, firms may prefer to issue debt rather than fresh equity if there exists information asymmetry and non-homogeneous expectations.

Table 16-12 Signalling theory: Stocks undervalued due to information asymmetry

	Asymmetric information (Information gap not resolved before the issue)	*Symmetric information (Information gap resolved before the issue)*
Market price (₹)	50	55
Market value of existing shares (₹)	5,000	5,500
Nos. of shares to be issued to raise ₹ 5,500	5500/50 = 110	5500/55 = 100
Value of the firm		
Existing shares	5,500	5,500
New shares	5,500	5,500
Project NPV	500	500
TOTAL	11,500	11,500
Nos. of shares	220	200
New market price (₹)	52.27	57.50
Outcome	Old shareholders lose while new shareholders gain	Both new and old shareholders gain

Table 16-13 Signalling theory: Stocks overvalued due to information asymmetry

	Asymmetric information (Information gap not resolved before the issue)	*Symmetric information (Information gap resolved before the issue)*
Market price (₹)	50	45
Market value of existing shares (₹)	5,000	5,500
Nos. of shares to be issued to raise ₹ 5,500	5500/50 = 110	5500/45 = 122.22
Value of the firm		
Existing shares	4,500	4,500
New shares	5,500	5,500
Project NPV	500	500
TOTAL	10,500	10,500
Nos. of shares	220	222.22
New market price (₹)	47.73	47.25
Outcome	Both old and new shareholders lose	Both new and old shareholders gain

Also, note that the loss of value to existing shareholders due to information asymmetry would not be felt if the projects were high positive NPV projects. If the same project had an NPV of ₹2,000 instead of ₹500 any loss in the value due to information asymmetry would be more than compensated by the increase in value due to higher NPV, and the loss in value would not be apparent.

It can be further argued that in case of over valuation by the market the firm must issue shares and use the funds to retire debt, even if the firm does not have positive NPV project. It would benefit the existing shareholders since new shares issued at higher price than the intrinsic worth would mitigate the losses of existing shareholder as and when the true intrinsic value becomes known to the investors. In the case of overvaluation sooner or later, the stock price would fall from ₹50 to ₹45. However, if the firm issues shares worth ₹5,000 at ₹50 before the information asymmetry is resolved, the new value of the share will be ₹47.50 as shown below:

$$\text{New Price} = \frac{\text{Intrinsic value} + \text{New capital}}{\text{Total number of shares}}$$

$$= \frac{\text{EBIT}\,(1-T)(1-t_e)}{r_0(1-t_e)} = ₹47.50$$

With the existence of information asymmetry the managers would not want to issue fresh capital unless a firm has an extremely profitable opportunity available. If in the opinion of managers the prospects are bleak with markets unaware, the firm may issue fresh capital. Any announcement of the issue of fresh capital, therefore, could serve as a signal to existing shareholders that the picture is not rosy. Existing shareholders may also believe that since fresh capital is being issued the stock is overvalued.

The pecking order of financing by Donaldson can be explained logically in the face of reality that exists in capital markets where a different group of investors, managers of the firm included, have different views on the prospects as well as expectations from the firm. More often than not, shares are undervalued as investors are not as well informed about the prospects of the firm. This doubt keeps the price lower than the intrinsic worth of the firm. Without getting into the controversy of overvaluation or undervaluation, it may be said that the firm would continue to use internal accruals as long as it could, and if further requirement of funds necessitates access to the market, the firm would prefer debt rather than fresh equity.

Firms would do well to retain earnings even if they may not have any immediate use of the funds, and keep building the borrowing capacity should an opportunity arise in future. First, it may use retained earnings, then issue debt and only as a last resort issue equity. Since firms build the reserve borrowing capacity, the debt–equity ratio would be lower than the optimum suggested by trade-off theory.

Free Cash Flow Hypothesis

The free cash flow hypothesis works on the premise that the availability of cash induces irrational behaviour and leads to wasteful activities on part of the managers. This is evidenced in the fact that cash rich firms have often offered higher prices for the acquisitions than their actual worth or the market price, simply because of easy availability of cash with them.

Free cash flow hypothesis states that managers would have tendency to waste if cash available is high. Debt would reduce the availability of free cash flow and therefore check indiscretion.

On the contrary, if the cash flow is constrained, the opportunities for wasteful expenditure reduce. Since the dividend is cash out flow, its payment would reduce the free cash flow with managers. Similarly, a debt would imply cash flow obligations of interest and repayment of principal constraining the availability of free cash flow to the managers. The presence of debt in the capital structure would constrain the opportunity for wasteful expenditures by managers, not merely because of the covenants placed by lenders on the freedom of managers but also because of reduced availability of free cash. A capital structure more in favour of debt would force more careful evaluation and spending by managers, and therefore, the firm will have greater value with debt in its capital structure.

Summary

Capital structure decision relates to finding out an optimum level of debt that a firm must have in order to maximize its value. There are two opposing schools of thoughts regarding optimum capital structure. One school of thought believes that the value of the firm is dependent upon its capital structure and there exists an optimal capital structure. The opposing school of thought argues that capital structure is irrelevant to the value of the firm.

To analyse the impact of capital structure on the value of the firm we make certain simplifying assumptions. These assumptions relate to perfect capital markets, absence of taxes, and constancy of all other parameters like earnings.

The net income approach assumes that the value of the firm is determined by the cash flows to the respective capital suppliers discounted at appropriate capitalization rates. These rates of capitalization are assumed to remain constant at all levels of debt. Since debt is cheaper than equity, the overall capitalization rate (WACC) of the firm would fall as proportion of debt increases. The optimal capital structure would be 100% debt.

The net operating income approach suggests that the value of the firm is determined by the earning capacities of its assets and not how they are acquired. Therefore, the overall capitalization rate remains constant, irrespective of the level of debt. The constancy of the capitalization rate is achieved by an increase in the cost of equity with the increasing level of debt.

The traditional view of capital structure opines that there is an acceptable level of debt up to which shareholders welcome it and do not revise their expectations. This brings down the cost of capital with increasing debt. Beyond a level of debt the expectations of the equity holders increase more than the advantage of reduced cost of debt and the overall capitalization rate starts mounting. Therefore, there exists an optimal capital structure coinciding with the point of least cost of capital.

Modigliani and Miller (MM) agree with the net operating income approach and provide a justification through the process of arbitrage for the irrelevance of capital structure. The value of the levered firm and unlevered firm would be driven equal by the investors by creating homemade leverage in their personal capacities in case the values of the two firms are different. The cost of equity would rise proportionately with the increasing proportion of debt keeping the overall cost of capital constant. To prove their argument of irrelevance of capital structure MM made several assumptions, the most important of them being the absence of taxes.

In the presence of taxes, the MM proposition changes radically. In the world of corporate taxes, the value of the levered firm is proved to be greater than the value of unlevered firm by the amount of tax shield the debt provides. The advantage of tax also causes a smaller increase in the cost of equity in a levered firm as compared to the unlevered firm. While with no taxes the capital structure is irrelevant MM propositions suggest 100% debt as the optimum capital structure when taxes are present.

Miller further incorporates personal taxes in the model. According to the Miller model, the outcome of MM remains the same except for the fact that value of tax shield decreases when investors are taxed in their personal capacities

Despite the substantial advantage of debt due to taxes and optimality of 100% debt as capital structure, most successful corporations are observed to have overwhelming preference for equity. This is attributed to the perceived cost of financial distress that arises only when the firms have debt in their capital structure. Under extremely high level of debt there also exists the agency cost of debt. The cost of financial distress and the agency cost of debt tends to reduce the tax shield of debt. The optimal capital structure is therefore a trade-off between the tax advantage of debt and cost of financial distress and agency cost of debt.

A study by Donaldson revealed that firms follow a pecking order of raising capital. Firms first use internal accruals to fund growth, then raise debt if required, and finally resort to the issue of fresh equity. While firms have a preference for equity financing, when it comes to raising funds from the market, firms exhaust the borrowing capacity first before mobilizing fresh capital. The phenomena can be partly explained by the information asymmetry existing between shareholders and managers. Shareholders generally believe that firms issue capital only when market price exceeds the intrinsic worth of the firm.

The free cash flow hypothesis favours raising debt because the obligations of interest reduces free cash flows available to managers and, therefore, checks managerial indiscretion.

Key Terms

Target capital structure Target capital structure is the debt ratio the firm strives to achieve.

Optimal capital structure An optimal capital structure is that debt – equity ratio that maximises the value of the firm.

MM's Proposition I The market value of the firm is independent of its capital structure and is given by capitalizing its expected return at a rate appropriate to its class.

MM's Proposition II The expected yield on the equity capital is equal to the pure equity return plus a premium for the financial risk, which is equal to spread between pure equity return and cost of debt in the proportion of debt–equity ratio.

MM's Proposition III The cut-off rate for investment purposes will in all cases be WACC and will be completely unaffected by the type of security issued to finance the investment.

Tax shield The present value of the tax saved on the interest on debt is called tax shield.

Net tax advantage of debt The excess of post tax earnings of debt holders over the post-tax earnings of equity holders is the net tax advantage of debt.

Cost of financial distress It refers to the perceived costs due to increased amount /ratio of debt in the firm.

Agency cost of debt The indirect cost of actions of shareholders due to excessive debt resulting from the conflicts of debt holders and shareholders is referred to as agency cost of debt.

Agency cost of equity The indirect cost of actions of managers resulting from the conflicts of interests of managers and shareholders is referred to as agency cost of equity.

Pecking order of financing A hierarchical preference of financing followed by firms in raising funds by the firms is pecking order of financing.

Asymmetric information The gap in the information of managers and various groups of shareholders regarding the performance of the firm that results in mismatch of valuation of firm by different groups is referred as asymmetric information.

Free cash flow hypothesis A hypothesis that states that excess availability of free cash causes financial indiscretion.

KEY FORMULAE

Cost of debt

$$r_d = \frac{\text{Interest}}{\text{Market value of debt}} = \frac{I}{D}$$

Cost of equity

$$r_e = \frac{\text{Earnings for equity shareholders}}{\text{Market value of equity}} = \frac{\text{EBIT} - I}{E}$$

WACC

$$r = \frac{\text{Earnings to all capital suppliers}}{\text{Market value of the firm}} = \frac{\text{EBIT}}{D+E}$$

$$= r_e\left(\frac{E}{E+D}\right) + r_d\left(\frac{D}{E+D}\right)$$

MM's Proposition I

With taxes $V_L = V_U + T \times D$

With no taxes $V_L = V_U$

MM's Proposition II

With taxes $r_e = r_0 + \frac{D}{E}(1 - T)(r_0 - r_d)$

With no taxes $r_e = r_0 + (r_0 - r_d)D/E$

MM's Proposition III

With taxes

$$\text{WACC}_L = \text{WACC}_U\left(1 - \frac{PV_{TS}}{D+E}\right)$$

$$r = r_e\left(\frac{E}{E+D}\right) + r_d\left(\frac{D(1-T)}{E+D}\right)$$

With no taxes

$$\text{WACC}_L = \text{WACC}_U = r_0$$

PV of Tax Shield

$$= \sum_{n=1}^{\infty} \frac{r_d \times D \times T}{(1-r_d)^n} = \frac{r_d \times D \times T}{r_d}$$

$$= D \times T = \text{Tax Rate} \times \text{Debt}$$

Value of unlevered firm with taxes

$$V_U = \frac{\text{EBIT}(1-T)}{r_0}$$

Net tax advantage of debt $= (1 - t_d) - (1 - T)(1 - t_e)$

Value of unlevered firm with corporate and personal taxes

$$\frac{\text{Cash flow to equity holders}}{\text{Post-tax cost of equity, } r_0(1-t_e)} = \frac{\text{EBIT}(1-T)(1-t_e)}{r_0(1-t_e)}$$

Value of levered firm with corporate and personal taxes

$$V_U + D\left[1 - \frac{(1-T)(1-t_e)}{(1-t_d)}\right]$$

PRACTICE PROBLEMS

1. Determining Capital Structure

Clay Products Limited is an all equity firm with the market value of its equity at ₹20 crore. Its current cost of equity capital is 15%. The management is planning a capital expenditure of ₹15 crore that would increase the earning levels by 1.5 times.

For the first time in the history of the enterprise, the management is motivated by enthusiastic bankers to avail debt and have been offered very attractive and competitive interest rate slabs as follows:

PLAN	*I*	*II*	*III*	*IV*	*V*
Amount of debt (₹ crore)	3.00	6.00	9.00	12.00	15.00
Cost of debt (%)	8.00%	8.50%	9.50%	10.00%	11.00%

The finance manager of the firm believes that the cost of equity, which is currently at 15% would increase with the increasing amount of debt. His estimate of the cost of equity is as follows:

PLAN	*I*	*II*	*III*	*IV*	*V*
Cost of equity (%)	15.50%	15.50%	16.00%	18.00%	21.00%

Examine how much amount of debt Clay Products should have. Assume tax rate at 36%.

Solution

We shall examine the value of the firm at various levels of debt with enhanced earnings. The level of debt that gives the maximum value to the firm, i.e., value of debt plus value of equity would be chosen.

Current market value of equity = ₹20.00 crore

Current cost of equity = 15%

Current level of EAT to shareholders

= Market value × Cost of equity

= 20 × 0.15 = ₹3.00 crore

Tax rate = 36%

Current Level of earnings, EBIT = 3/(1 – 0.36) = ₹4.688 crore

New level of EBIT/old level = 1.5

New level of EBIT = 1.5 × 4.688 = ₹7.03 crore

We compute the value of the firm under different capital structures, and the costs of debt and equity are as follows:

(₹ crore)

PLAN	No debt	I	II	III	IV	V
Debt level		3.00	6.00	9.00	12.00	15.00
Cost of debt		8.00%	8.50%	9.50%	10.00%	11.00%
EBIT	7.03	7.03	7.03	7.03	7.03	7.03
Interest	0.00	0.24	0.50	0.78	1.08	1.41
EBT	7.03	6.79	6.54	6.25	5.95	5.62
Taxes	2.53	2.44	2.35	2.25	2.14	2.02
EAT	4.50	4.35	4.18	4.00	3.81	3.60
Cost of equity, r_e	15.00%	15.50%	15.50%	16.00%	18.00%	21.00%
Value of equity, E	30.00	28.04	26.99	25.01	21.16	17.13
Value of debt, D	0	3.00	6.00	9.00	12.00	15.00
Total value, V, $(E + D)$	30.00	31.04	32.99	34.01	33.16	32.13
WACC, EBIT/V	23.44%	22.65%	21.31%	20.68%	21.20%	21.88%

The desirable capital structure would be one that gives the least weighted average cost of capital and greatest value of the firm consistent with the objective of maximization of value.

Plan III with debt of ₹9 crore is preferable as it gives the maximum value to the firm at ₹34.01 crore and least weighted average cost of capital (WACC) at 20.68%.

2. Replacing Equity with Debt – With and Without Taxes

Daily Needs Limited, which is in the business of packaged foods has been an all equity financed firm. Its current level of earnings are ₹28 crore. The shareholders expect a 14% return from the firm and the shares of the company is accordingly priced in the market. It has been offered a debt of ₹50 crore at 6% by the financial institutions. Daily Needs Limited, not in need of finances, have been advised to retire equity to the extent of availability of debt in order to increase the value of the firm.

(i) Find out the total value of the firm, value of equity, cost of equity, and WACC if there are no taxes. Can debt help?

(ii) Calculate the same parameters with a tax rate of 30%.

Solution

(i) **With no taxes**

EBIT	₹28.00 Crore
Amount of debt	₹50.00 Crore
Cost of equity, r_e	14.00%
Cost of debt, r_d	6.00%

The total value of the firm is given by

= 28/0.14 = ₹200.00 crore

With debt, the value of the firm does not change as long as the asset base remains constant and debt only substitutes the equity.

The value of equity would therefore be

= Total value – Debt value

= 200 – 50 = ₹150.00 crore

If debt is assumed, the cost of equity increases proportionately as given below:

$$r_e = r_0 + (r_0 - r_d)D/E$$

$$= 0.14 + (0.14 - 0.06)50/150 = 16.67\%$$

Since cost of equity increases proportionately, the cost of capital too remains same.

$$\text{WACC} = r_e \times E/V + r_d\,(1 - T) \times D/V$$

$$= 16.67 \times \frac{150}{200} + 6 \times \frac{50}{200} = 14\%$$

Debt does not increase the value of the firm. Debt merely allocates the value among the shareholders and debt holders.

(ii) **With taxes**

With taxes, the value of levered firm increases by the amount of tax shield.

Tax rate = 30%

Value of tax shield = $T \times D$ = 0.3 × 50 = ₹15.00 crore

or $V_L = V_u + T \times D$ = 200 + 15 = ₹215.00 crore

Value of equity, E = Total value (V_L) – Value of debt (D)

Value of debt, D = ₹50.00 crore

Therefore, value of equity, E = ₹165.00 crore

If debt is assumed the cost of equity increases proportionately but not as much as it would under no taxes, as given below:

$$r_e = r_0 + (r_0 - r_d)(1 - T)\,D/E$$

$$= 0.14 + (0.14 - 0.06)\,(0.7)50/165 = 15.70\%$$

The cost of capital would be given by:

$$\text{WACC} = r_o \times E/V + r_d\,(1 - T) \times D/V$$

$$= 15.70 \times \frac{165}{215} + 0.7 \times \frac{50}{165} = 13.02\%$$

Debt increases the value of the firm by the amount of tax shield available.

3. Net Income vs Net Operating Income Approach (With Taxes)

Master Equity Limited (MEL) and Master Debt Limited (MDL) are two firms in the same line of business and also have almost the same size. They differ only in the way they are financed. MDL has a debt of ₹400 crore while MEL is free from debt.The cost of debt is 15%.

Find out the value of firms assuming tax of 35%, EBIT level of ₹275 crore, and cost of equity as 20% under net income approach.

Also find the value of the MDL, the levered firm under the net operating income approach.

What is the cost of equity and WACC of firms under NI and NOI approaches?

Solution

NI Approach

The values of the two firms under the net income approach and their respective cost of capital (WACC) are worked out as follows:

₹ crore	Master Equity	Master Debt
Level of debt	0	400
Cost of debt, %	—	15.00%
EBIT	275.00	275.00
Interest	—	60.00
EBT	275.00	215.00
Taxes 35%	96.25	75.25
EAT	178.75	139.75
Cost of equity, r_e	20.00%	20.00%
Value of equity, *E*	893.75	698.75
Value of debt, *D*	—	400.00
Total value, *V*, *E* + *D*	893.75	1098.75
WACC, EBIT(1 – *T*)/*V*	20.00%	16.27%

NOI Approach

₹ crore	Master Equity	Master Debt
Level of Debt	0	400
Cost of debt, %	—	15.00%
EBIT	275.00	275.00
Interest	0.00	60.00
EBT	275.00	215.00
Taxes 35%	96.25	75.25
EAT	178.75	139.75
Opportunity cost (%)	20%	20%
Value of firm	893.75	1033.75
Value of debt, *D*	—	400.00
Value of equity, *E*	893.75	633.75
Cost of equity	20%	22%
Cost of debt	—	10%
WACC, EBIT(1 – T)/V	20.00%	17.29%

Value of levered firm,

$$V_L = V_u + \text{Value of tax shield}$$
$$= V_u + T \times D$$

Value of levered firm ₹ *crore*

Value of unlevered firm, V_U = Value of MEL =

= EBIT × (1 – *T*)/r_e = 275 × (1 – 0.35)/0.2 = 893.75

Value of Tax Shield, *T* × *D* = 0.35 × 400 = 140.00

Value of levered firm, V_L = 1033.75

Value of equity, *E* = Total Value, (V_L) – Value of Debt (*D*)

Value of debt, *D* 400.00

Therefore, value of equity, *E* 633.75

Cost of equity, r_e is given by

$$r_e = r_0 + (r_0 - r_d)(1 - T)\ D/E$$
$$= 0.2 + (0.2 - 0.15)\ (0.65)400/633.75 = 22.05\%$$
$$\text{WACC} = r_e \times E/V + r_d\ (1 - \text{T}) \times D/V = 17.29\%$$

Alternatively, WACC = EBIT (1 – *T*)/*V* = 17.29%

4. Net Income and Net Operating Income Approach

Two firms, X and Y, are implementing the same project with debts of ₹500 lakh and ₹700 lakh respectively. The cost of debt for X and Y are 12% and 15% respectively. The expected level of earning before interest and taxes are ₹300 lakh annually.

(a) If both the firms are subject to 35% tax, find the level of earnings for the shareholders of each firm.

(b) If costs of equity for Firm X and Firm Y are taken as 22% and 24% respectively, find out the value of equity, value of the firm, and the overall cost of capital for both the firms.

(c) A consultant argued that cost of equity cannot be fixed or assumed in view of debt. Instead if the project was to be financed entirely by equity, the cash flows of the firm justify a return of 20%. The value of the firm is driven by the earning potential of asset and not the way they are acquired. Assuming the contention of consultant is right, find value and cost of equity, and the total cost of capital for Firm X and Firm Y.

Solution

(a)

₹ lakh	Firm X	Firm Y
Level of debt, *D*	500.00	700.00
Cost of debt, r_d, (%)	12.00%	15.00%
Tax rate, *T*	35.00%	35.00%
Income Levels		
EBIT	300.00	300.00
Interest	60.00	105.00
EBT	240.00	195.00
Taxes	84.00	68.25
EAT for equity holders	156.00	126.75

(b) With cost of equity assumed the values can be found using net income approach as follows:

$$\text{Value of equity} = \frac{\text{Cash flow to equity}}{\text{Cost of equity}}$$

$$\text{WACC} = \frac{\text{Cash flow to debt and equity holders}}{\text{Total value of the firm}}$$

(₹ *lakh*)

Net Income Approach	Firm X	Firm Y
Cost of equity, r_e	22.00%	24.00%
Cash flow to equity holders	156.00	126.75
Value of equity, *E*	709.09	528.13
Value of debt, *D*	500.00	700.00
Value of firm, *V* = *E* + *D*	1,209.09	1,228.13
WACC for the firm	16.13%	15.88%

(c) The contention of the consultant is to adopt NOI approach for valuation and cost of capital.

Under NOI approach, we first find the value of each firm as if it were free of debt. This value is given by:

$$\frac{\text{EBIT} \times (1 - T)}{r_0}$$

We add the value of tax shield on the debt to arrive at the total value of the firm.

From total value of the firm, we subtract the value of debt to arrive at the value of equity.

The cost of equity is calculated by dividing the earnings of the shareholders by the value of equity.

WACC of the firms would remain same at the opportunity cost of capital.

(₹ *lakh*)

Net Operating Income Approach	*Firm X*	*Firm Y*
EBIT	300.00	300.00
Tax rate	35.00%	35.00%
Opportunity cost, r_0	20.00%	20.00%
Value of all equity firm, EBIT $(1 - T)/r_0$	975.00	975.00
Value of tax shield on debt, $T \times D$	175.00	245.00
Value of the firm, V	1150.00	1220.00
Value of debt, D	500.00	700.00
Value of equity, $E = V - D$	650.00	520.00
Cost of equity, r_e	24.00%	24.38%
Cost of debt	12.00%	15.00%
WACC, EBIT$(1 - T)/V$	16.96%	15.98%

Alternatively the cost of equity and WACC may be found directly as below:

$$\text{Cost of equity} = r_e = r_0 + (r_0 - r_d)(1 - T)\ D/E$$

$$\text{Firm X} = 0.2 + \left(0.08 \times 0.65 \times \frac{500}{650}\right) = 24.00\%$$

$$\text{Firm Y} = 0.2 + \left(0.05 \times 0.65 \times \frac{700}{520}\right) = 24.38\%$$

$$\text{WACC} = r_e \times E/V + r_d\,(1 - T) \times D/V$$

$$\text{Firm X} = 0.24 \times \frac{650}{1150} + 0.12 \times 0.65 \times \frac{500}{1150} = 16.96\%$$

$$\text{Firm Y} = 0.2438 \times \frac{520}{1220} + 0.15 \times 0.65 \times \frac{700}{1220} = 15.98\%$$

5. Capitalization, Debt, and Value

A study by a research firm has revealed that the expected returns from operation in the liquor industry is 20%. As liquor industry is not entitled to raise debt, this may be regarded as opportunity cost of capital.

For a sample project, the research firm has projected the following:

(₹ *crore*)

EBIT	25.00
Interest	—
EBT	25.00
Taxes 40%	10.00
Earnings for shareholders	15.00
Capitalisation rate	20.00%
Market value	75.00

With a changing environment, debt is now available for liquor industry.

Promoters of Firm X are ready to accept the recommendations of the research firm. However, they feel that, the cost of equity of 20% is high and would justify a debt level of ₹60 crore. Without the debt, the cost of equity should be 18%.

However promoters of Firm Y hold the opposite view and feel that the capitalization rate must be 22% without debt and 24% with debt of ₹50 crore.

What values the promoters of Firm X and Firm Y would assign if they can arrange loans at 12% and 14% respectively. Assume a tax rate of 40%.

Also comment upon the sources of difference in valuation.

Solution

The values by the promoters of Firm X and Firm Y under conditions of no debt and with debt are worked out as follows:

(₹ *crore*)

	Firm X		*Firm Y*	
	w/o debt	*w/ debt*	*w/o debt*	*w/ debt*
Level of debt, D	—	60.00	—	50.00
Cost of debt, r_d, (%)	12.00%	12.00%	14.00%	14.00%
EBIT	25.00	25.00	25.00	25.00
Interest	—	7.20	—	7.00
EBT	25.00	17.80	25.00	18.00
Taxes	10.00	7.12	10.00	7.20
EAT	15.00	10.68	15.00	10.80
Cost of equity, r_e	18.00%	20.00%	22.00%	24.00%
Value of equity, E	83.33	53.40	68.18	45.00
Value of debt, D	—	60.00	—	50.00
Value of the firm, $V = E + D$	**83.33**	**113.40**	**68.18**	**95.00**

The difference in values is attributable to two factors: (i) the advantage of tax shield when debt is taken and (ii) due to change in the capitalization rate. The difference in the values can be reconciled as follows:

(₹ *crore*)

	Firm X		*Firm Y*	
	w/o debt	*w/ debt*	*w/o debt*	*w/ debt*
Value of the firm, $V = E + D$	83.33	113.40	68.18	95.00
Value as per research firm	75.00	75.00	75.00	75.00
Difference in value	**8.33**	**38.40**	**–6.82**	**20.00**
Value of tax shield, $T \times D$	—	24.00	—	20.00
Change in value of the firm due to change in the cost of equity	8.33	14.40	–6.82	—

6. MM's Arbitrage and Capital Structure

Let there exist two firms X and Y, identical in all respects except their capital structure. While X has no borrowing, Y has a debt of ₹100 crore at 12%. The EBIT for both the firms is ₹40 crore. Market values of equity shares of X and Y are ₹280 crore and ₹250 crore respectively. The debt of Y trades at par. Both firms pay 30% tax.

If market value of X is correctly determined, what should be the value of Y?

If an investor is holding 5% stake in Y, what action can you recommend to him to increase his welfare?

Solution

The data of the two firms is presented here:

(₹ crore)

	X, All Equity Firm	Y, the levered firm
Level of debt,	0	100
Cost of debt, %	0.00%	12.00%
EBIT	40.00	40.00
Interest	0.00	12.00
EBT	40.00	28.00
Taxes 30%	12.00	8.40
EAT	28.00	19.60
Value of equity, *E*	280.00	250.00
Value of debt, *D*	0.00	100.00
Total value, *V*, *E* + *D*	280.00	350.00

If valuation of X is presumed correct, then the value of Y must be greater by the amount of tax shield it enjoys on the debt it carries.

(₹ crore)

Value of X	280.00
Value of tax shield, $T \times D$	30.00
Theoretical value of *Y*	310.00
Actual value of *Y*	350.00

Therefore, *Y* is **overvalued.**

Strategy: Buy the undervalued and sell the overvalued.

Therefore, investors of Y must sell their holding and buy X.

Investor in Y would act as follows:

1. Sell holding in Y and realize cash
2. Borrow an amount so as to keep the level of debt same as Firm Y, in the personal capacity
3. From the sum available, buy X to the extent possible

By doing so, the income accruing to the investor would be larger. The working is as follows:

Investor holding in Y	5.00%
Sell holding in Y and realize	₹12.50 crore
Raise debt as per the debt of Y	₹ 5.00 crore
Total funds available	₹17.50 crore

% holding that can be bought in X = 17.5/280 = 6.25%

The comparison of income is as below:

(₹ crore)

	Continue with Y	When switched to X
Share of profit from X	—	1.75
Share of profit from Y	0.98	
Less; Cost of borrowing, 12%	—	-0.60
Net Income	**0.98**	**1.15**

EXERCISES

Concept Review Questions

1. Differentiate between net income and net operating income approaches for determining the value of the firm with the changes in the capital structure.
2. How does the traditional view of the capital structure differ from net income approach and net operating income approach?
3. What does MM's Proposition I state about the value of the firm in the (a) absence of taxes and (b) in the presence of taxes? What different implications it has for the optimal capital structure?
4. What do you understand by (a) arbitrage and (b) homemade leverage? Explain their relevance in establishing the theory of irrelevance of capital structure?
5. How do cost of equity and WACC change with increasing levels of debt assuming that MM's propositions hold?
6. What is tax shield and how does it change the value of the levered firm as compared to the unlevered firm?
7. Describe Miller's model with corporate and personal taxes. Is Miller's model consistent with MM's model of capital structure and value of the firm with (a) no taxes (b) with corporate tax but no personal tax, and (c) with corporate and personal tax but no difference in rates of personal taxes on different types of incomes?
8. What are the implications of trade-off model on the value of the firm?
9. Differentiate between agency cost of debt and agency cost of equity.
10. What does Donaldson's pecking order of financing suggest and how can this be explained under signalling theory?
11. What is free cash flow hypothesis and what implication does it have on the capital structure of the firms?

Critical Thinking Questions

1. According to the theory of irrelevance of capital structure, it is the earning power of the asset that determines the value of the firm and not how the acquisition of asset has been financed. The presence of taxes does not change the earning capacity of the assets of the firm. If that is the case, why should the theory of irrelevance change?
2. Net operating income (NOI) approach and MM's propositions conclude that capital structure is irrelevant to the value of the firm. Is there any difference between the two approaches?
3. 'All successful firms have equity as predominant source of capital and their market values are always higher than the firms using debt in the same line of business. Since the debt has a cost and equity has no cost the increased amount equity would bring down the cost of capital and therefore maximize the value of the firm.' Do you agree with the statement?
4. Free cash flow hypothesis is an alternative version of agency cost of equity. Do you agree with the statement?

Practical Assignment

1. From the financial statements of six top IT firms and six top firms in the FMCG sector, find out the level of debt in comparison with the market value of equities of these firms. You would most likely find out rather negligible level of debt for these firms. Despite obvious tax advantage of debt that enhances the value of the firm, debate the possible reasons these firms may have in not opting for debt.

Numerical Problems

1. Determining Capital Structure

Radiant Technology has a project costing ₹15 crore for making high-end microchips on hand. It shall provide the earning level of ₹4 crore annually. With a view to decide the desired capital structure the firm compiled following data with respect to cost of debt and cost of equity for debt levels of 20% to 70% of the cost of the project, that is reproduced below:

PLAN	I	II	III	IV	V	VI
Debt ratio	20%	30%	40%	50%	60%	70%
Amount of debt (₹ lakh)	300	450	600	750	900	1050
Cost of Debt (%)	8.00%	8.00%	8.00%	9.50%	10.00%	10.50%
Cost of Equity (%)	15.50%	15.50%	16.00%	18.00%	21.00%	25.00%

Examine which of the capital structure is best for Radiant Technology.

2. Capital Structure and Cost of Equity—With and Without Taxes

ABC Ltd is an all equity firm having a constant earnings of ₹24 crore and cost of equity at 12%. It is offered a debt of ₹ 100 crore at 8%.

(i) Find out the total value of the firm, value of equity, cost of equity and WACC if there are no taxes. Can debt help?

(ii) Find out the total value of the firm, value of equity, cost of equity and WACC if there are taxes of 40%. Can debt help?

3. Replacing Debt with Equity

Mangal Dass Enterprises is in the business of manufacture and export of garments. Currently in its capital structure it has a debt of ₹15 crores with cost of 10%. The cost of equity is reckoned at 15%. It has earnings level of ₹3.75 crores and does not pay any taxes being tax-exempt unit.

The Managing Director of the firm believes that the level of debt is too high and would like to repay the debt by issuing additional shares to the extent of ₹5 crore. According to him, the reduced level of leverage would reduce the cost of capital because of two reasons—cost of debt falling from existing 10% to 9%, and cost of equity falling from 15% to 14%.

Evaluate the option of the Managing Director to replace debt with equity. Also find the WACC and value of the firm in both the situations.

4. Replacing Equity with Debt

Consider the data of Mangal Dass Enterprises in the Problem 3. The Vice President (Finance) of the firm was of the opinion that reducing debt was not an appropriate decision. Instead he was of the view that debt must be increased to retire equity. The revised cost of debt would be marginally higher at 10.50% and the desired return by the shareholders would jump to 16% from existing 15%.

Would you be in favour of retiring equity with debt? Again find the value of the firm and WACC under revised conditions as per Vice President (Finance).

5. Cost of Equity and Capital Structure

Again refer to the data of Mangal Dass Enterprises in Problems 3 and 4. Both Managing Director and Vice President (Finance) made an estimate of the cost of equity under changing capital structure that substantiated their viewpoint.

Do you think that their estimates of cost of equity were correct? What do you think the correct cost of equity is under both the propositions? Assume that the firm is correctly valued today.

6. Net Income vs Net Operating Income Approach, with Taxes

Assume that there exist two firms, X and Y identical in all respects except for their capital structure. X has no debt while Y carries a debt of ₹10 crore at pre-tax cost of 10%.

Find out the value of firms X and Y assuming tax of 36% and EBIT level of ₹400 lakh and cost of equity as 15% under net income (NI) approach.

Also find the value of the levered firm Y under Net Operating Income (NOI) Approach.

What is the cost of equity and WACC of Firms X and Y under NI and NOI approaches?

7. Arbitrage, Capital Structure and Value – No Taxes

There exist two identical firms X and Y with X having no debt. However, Y has a debt of ₹100 lakh at 8%. The earning level of the two firms is same at ₹50 lakh per annum with no growth. The value of the equity for X in the market is ₹400 lakh and for Y is ₹325 lakh and debt valued at par. Assume that X is correctly priced in the market.

Demonstrate that how an investor in Y holding 10% equity of Y can benefit from the valuation by the market.

What would be the ultimate impact of the actions of the investor upon the valuation of the firm?

8. Arbitrage, Capital Structure and Value—With Taxes

Let there exist two firms X and Y identical in all respects except their capital structure. While X has no borrowing Y has a debt of ₹600 lakh at 10%. The EBIT for both the firms is ₹300 lakh. Market values of equity shares of X and Y are ₹13 crore and ₹9 crore, respectively. The debt of Y trades at par.

If market value of X is correctly determined, what should be the value of Y?

What should the investors do to achieve balance in the valuation?

CASE STUDY

Space Technologies Limited—Adding Value

Space Technologies Limited (STL) has been one of the market leaders in the field of software development. For a decade or so, it consistently outpaced its rivals in the industry and displayed phenomenal growth. Their growth in income levels, EBIT, and EPS has been of the order of 25–30% on a compounded basis for the last four years. It consistently followed the policy of dividend pay out of 20% of earnings. The performance of the company is depicted in Table A.

Table A Financial Performance—Space Technologies Limited

(₹ crore)

Year	*2004*	*2005*	*2006*	*2007*	*CAGR (%)*
Income	4,761	6,860	9,028	13,149	27.61%
EBITDA	1,584	2,325	2,989	4,225	26.55%
Depreciation and Amortisation	231	268	409	469	
EBIT	1,353	2,057	2,580	3,756	
Interest	—	—	—		
EBT	1,353	2,057	2,580	3,756	27.77%
Tax	227	325	303	352	
EAT	1,126	1,732	2,277	3,404	30.41%
Dividend—Regular	196	310	412	649	
Dividend—Special	668		830		

Its performance at the stock exchanges too was impressive enough. Looking at the continuous growth of the STL, the market had discounted their earnings with a multiple of 30 consistently year after year. The management of STL was able to build the confidence of the market, not only through the consistent growth but also due to complete transparency to the shareholders in terms of disclosure of information far beyond what is prescribed under the law. These voluntary disclosures had made the STL as one of the darling shares in the stock market.

Due to increased earnings, the compounded average growth rate for the shareholders was of the order of 30% ignoring the dividend yield. The market capitalization of the firm had increased almost three times from ₹34,000 crore to ₹101,000 crore in just last four years. The earnings and the PE multiple and the market capitalization are shown in Table B.

Due to excellent financial performance and the margins in the business, the firm never felt it necessary to resort to borrowing as may be inferred from the balance sheet of STL in Table C. In fact, they had so much of cash that they could float a bank of their own. Besides being heavily oriented towards equity financing, the firm also successfully evaded any thoughts of unrelated diversification, which has been the desire of many cash rich firms all over the world. They remained focused on their core business of software development.

Table B Share performance—Space Technologies Limited

Year	*2004*	*2005*	*2006*	*2007*
Nos. of Shares (Crore)	53.12	53.91	54.93	56.43
Per Share Data (₹/Share)				
EPS	21.20	32.13	41.45	60.32
DPS—Regular	3.69	5.757.50	11.50	
DPS – Special	12.50	—	15.00	—
PE Multiple (times)	30.22	32.59	33.62	29.76
Stock Price	640.62	1,046.98	1,393.56	1,795.05
Market Capitalization (₹ Crore)	**34,028**	**56,446**	**76,553**	**101,303**

Table C Balance sheet—Space Technologies Limited

(Figures in ₹)

Year	*2006*	*2007*
Net worth	6,897	11,162
Debt	—	—
Total	**6,897**	**11,162**
Fixed Assets	2,133	3,107
Investment	876	839
Deferred Tax Asset	56	79
Current Assets	6,049	8,961
Less: Current Liabilities	2,217	1,824
Net Current Assets	3,832	7,137
TOTAL	**6,897**	**11,162**

Three top executives of the company, Mr Mathur, Mr Singh, and Mr Nair, all of whom had their basic qualification as MBA in Finance, were talking with lot of pride about the financial performance and continued growth and the success of the management to build the investors' confidence in creating value for the shareholders. Consistent with the management's philosophy they did not want to leave anything that could add to the value to the shareholder with each of them holding substantial employee stock options. While the performance of the stock and reward to shareholders, with respect to dividend pay out and capital appreciation, were more that exemplary there was only one single thought that was crossing their minds. Inordinately high and ever increasing amount of *cash and cash equivalent* available were suggesting that there was not enough or desired level of utilisation of the resources.

Year	*2006*	*2007*
Cash and Cash Equivalent (₹ crore)	4,463	5,650
Cash and Cash Equivalent to Total Asset (%)	64.71%	50.62%

The cash, which predominantly included bank deposits and investment in the liquid mutual funds were standing at more that 50% of the total assets. The amount of cash and cash equivalent was ₹5,650 crore as at the end of financial year 2007.

Mr Mathur initiated a debate and said, 'It is a poor reflection on management's ability to deploy resources in the optimum manner. Having such a huge amount of cash is certainly against the principles of value creation. It means we cannot find enough business and growth opportunities to use the resources available at hand. Usually firms face an opposite situation of resource crunch. They are always short of resources.'

Mr Singh reacted, 'I cannot but agree with you. I think we must find a better use of the cash than investing in low yield safe financial instruments. Our growth has been extraordinary. So far we have been dependent upon the organic growth. Acquisition of some business makes sense. It gives us the ready business and uses the idle resources that we have.'

Mr Nair had reservation about what Mr Singh said. He spoke, 'I do not agree with the philosophy of acquisition. Whether negotiated or hostile, my experience is that the take-overs have always been expensive. Just recently Tatas acquired Corus. They started acquisition of Corus Steel at 455 p and ended up paying 608 p in the deal, a good 35% up from the initial valuation. There is never a fair price in acquisition.'

Mr Mathur supporting the views of Mr Singh said, 'Even if we pay something more than what the firm may deserve, it is still better than the keeping the resource idle. We would add greater value to the shareholders than what we are adding now.'

Mr Nair emphasized, 'Having resources does not mean we waste it. To my mind keeping it for better use and waiting for the right opportunity is a better solution.'

Mr Mathur came out with another suggestion. He said, 'Then let us return this cash back to the shareholders. We are unnecessarily following the policy of distribution of only 20% of earnings, whereas we may distribute more. Let shareholders find a better use of the cash in their individual capacities.'

Mr Nair again disagreed and said, 'I think that would be a disservice to the shareholders. No one has complained why are we keeping so much cash with us. In fact our shareholders are more than happy with us. You can see it in the appreciation of our share price. In any case, the dividend does not constitute much of the return to the shareholders. We should rather continue with the 20% payout policy and distribute dividend on special occasions rather that regularly. Regular high dividend is misconstrued and raises unnecessary hopes.'

Mr Mathur reacted, 'In the last four years we have paid out ₹1,500 crore as special dividend and yet we have loads of cash with us.'

Mr Nair suggested, 'We may invest in the stock market. That would give better yield than what we get in investing in fixed deposits with the bank and in liquid mutual funds.

Mr Mathur agreed but said with some reservations, 'Yes certainly we may do it. But no company does that unless it is an investment company for several reasons, the most important being the risk of losing money. Shareholders would not approve of such a plan.'

Mr Singh said, 'I have an idea to use the cash. Why don't we use part of the cash and part of borrowing to buyback the shares. It would help add value in many ways – the number of shares would decrease for the same earning level, the EPS would improve as long as our interest cost remains within acceptable limits.'

All of them agreed to the proposal promising to return the next day with their proposed plan.

Mr Mathur, Mr Singh, and Mr Nair submitted their plans named Plan A, B, and C as shown in Tables D, E, and F, respectively.

All the plans had common assumptions of (a) a growth of 40% in EBIT over current levels, (b) availability of debt at 10% pre-tax cost, (c) repurchase of shares at the current market price, and d) corporate tax rate of 20%. The plans differed with each other as follows:

- **Plan A** assumed that the initial ₹3,000 crore required to fund the buyback would come from the available cash balance of ₹5,650 crore. Balance need of funds would be raised by debt.
- **Plan B** assumed that the initial funds to the extent of ₹2,500 crore would come from debt (approximately 25% of the current net worth) while for the remaining cash available would be utilized.
- **Plan C** fixed the buyback level at ₹6,000 crore to be funded equally by debt and the available cash balance.

Table D Using cash for value—Plan A

(₹ crore)

Fixed Cash					
(% of Shares Bought Back)	*0%*	*3%*	*4%*	*5%*	*6%*
Funds Required	—	3,039.09	4,052.12	5,065.15	6,078.18
Cash	—	3,000.00	3,000.00	3,000.00	3,000.00
Loan		39.09	1,052.12	2,065.15	3,078.18
Interest at 10%		3.91	105.21	206.52	307.82
Projected EBIT	5,258.40	5,258.40	5,258.40	5,258.40	5,258.40
Interest	—	3.91	105.21	206.52	307.82
EBT	5,258.40	5,254.49	5,153.19	5,051.88	4,950.58
Taxes at 20%	1,051.68	1,050.90	1,030.64	1,010.38	990.12
EAT	4,206.72	4,203.59	4,122.55	4,041.51	3,960.47
Nos. of Shares Bought	—	1.69	2.19	2.71	3.22
Outstanding Shares	56.43	54.74	54.25	53.72	53.21
EPS (₹/Share)	74.54	76.79	76.00	75.23	74.43
PE Multiple (Times)	30.00	30.00	30.00	30.00	30.00
Stock Price (₹)	2,236.24	2,303.69	2,279.96	2,256.88	2,232.87
Market Capitalization (₹ crore)	**126,202**	**126,108**	**123,677**	**121,245**	**118,814**

Table E Using cash for value—Plan B

(₹ *crore*)

Fixed Borrowing					
(% of Shares Bought Back)	***0%***	***3%***	***4%***	***5%***	***6%***
Funds Required	—	3,039.09	4,052.12	5,065.15	6,078.18
Cash	—	539.09	1,552.12	2,565.15	3,578.18
Loan	—	2,500.00	2,500.00	2,500.00	2,500.00
Interest at 10%		250.00	250.00	250.00	250.00
Projected EBIT	5,258.40	5,258.40	5,258.40	5,258.40	5,258.40
Interest	—	250.00	250.00	250.00	250.00
EBT	5,258.40	5,008.40	5,008.40	5,008.40	5,008.40
Taxes at 20%	1,051.68	1,001.68	1,001.68	1,001.68	1,001.68
EAT	4,206.72	4,006.72	4,006.72	4,006.72	4,006.72
Nos. of Shares					
Bought	—	1.69	2.19	2.71	3.22
Outstanding Shares	56.43	54.74	54.25	53.72	53.21
EPS (₹ /Share)	74.54	73.19	73.86	74.58	75.30
PE Multiple (Times)	30.00	30.00	30.00	30.00	30.00
Stock Price (₹)	2,236.24	2,195.79	2,215.90	2,237.45	2,258.94
Market Capitalization (₹ crore)	**126,202**	**120,202**	**120,202**	**120,202**	**120,202**

Table F Using Cash For Value—Plan C

Fixed Total Amount	***Crore***
Cash	3,000
Borrowing	3,000
Total Funds for Buyback	**6,000**
Nos. of Shares	
% of Market Capitalization	5.92%
Shares Bought	3.34
Remaining Shares	53.09
Projected EBIT	5,258.40
Interest at 10%	300.00
EBT	4,958.40
Taxes at 20%	991.68
EAT	3,966.72
Nos. of Shares Bought	3.34
Outstanding Shares	53.09
EPS (₹ /Share)	74.71
PE Multiple (Times)	30.00
Stock Price (₹)	2,241.41
Market Capitalization (₹ crore)	**119,002**

Discuss

Discuss Plans A, B, and C with their pros and cons.

CHAPTER

17 Designing Capital Structure

LEARNING OBJECTIVES

This chapter is aimed at providing insights into

- the meaning of leverage
- operating leverage and its impact on earnings
- financial leverage and capital structure
- EBIT–EPS analysis for evaluation of various financing plans
- what is meant by Degree of Operating Leverage, Degree of Financial Leverage, and Degree of Total Leverage
- cash flow approach to determine capital structure
- various factors to be considered in defining the target capital structure

GOODWILL GARAGE—GOOD WITH DEBT (PART II)

The next day Swami Shankar decided to go straight to his chartered accountant, Gyan Dinkar, rather than to his workshop. He wanted to confirm whether his wife's statements the previous evening were correct. He was not convinced by his wife's utterances. Swami Shankar explained his problem to Gyan Dinkar. Their conversation went like this.

Swami: I was wondering whether I did right by borrowing money. My wife tells me that since the time I borrowed I have started giving her more money at home. I normally do not keep any record of how much I have earned. I simply conduct my business in the manner that I like. I am too engrossed in it. You keep a record of my earnings. Tell me if I have increased my earnings and if yes, how?

Gyan: Your wife is both right and wrong. Yes, you have increased your earnings since the time you borrowed. To my mind, you have done the right thing by borrowing money.

Swami: How?

Gyan: Borrowing affects your earnings and welfare in two ways. First, it allows you to grow. Your wife realizes this more than you do. It allows you to expand. Naturally, if the business grows, your earnings also grow. Another reason that this debt became favourable to you was because it cost you less.

Swami: How? Don't I pay interest on my borrowing?

Gyan: Yes, you do. But what you get is more than what your lender gets. But first, let me tell you how borrowing helps. Your increased earnings may be split in two components: the first, increased business and the second, reduced costs of debt that allow you greater return on your own capital.

Swami: I don't understand what you say.

Gyan: Normally people think that borrowing helps only because it augments resources. No doubt it does. But that is not the only impact of borrowing. To realize what debt does to business is to replace the equity with debt, assuming that your income level remains the same. I will give a small example to make you understand what I have said.

Swami: Ok. Go ahead.

Gyan: Suppose you had invested ₹1000 in a business that provides you a 10% return on investment. That means you earn ₹100 every year. Is that right?

Swami: Ok.

Gyan: Now you pay tax, of say 30%, on ₹100. That means you take ₹70 home. Your return on investment is 7%. As the entire investment was your own, your return on equity too would be 7%.

Swami: Please continue.

Gyan: Now assume a different scenario. You continue to have the same business, but borrow ₹500 and withdraw an equivalent amount of your own money, keeping total investment constant. Now the business is funded by ₹500 of your own and ₹500 of debt at, say, 6%. Would it change the earning power?

Swami: No.

Gyan: Exactly. You would continue to earn the same return on investment no matter where the investment comes from. So you still get ₹100 as income. Is that right?

Swami: Yes.

Gyan: Now there is a catch. One benefit given by the government is that the interest you pay is tax deductible.

Swami: What do you mean by tax deductible?

Gyan: You earn ₹100 after incurring all business expenses. So the interest that you pay on the debt is also regarded as a business expense, just like the salaries you pay to your employees. Now you pay ₹30, i.e., 6% of ₹500. Your earnings remain constant at ₹100, but now you pay lesser tax. For tax purposes, your income now would be ₹70 and not ₹100. With a 30% tax rate, you would now pay ₹21 as against ₹30 that you would pay if you don't borrow. The tax saved flows to you.

Swami: Ok.

Gyan: Your net earning after tax would be ₹49. But because your investment is reduced to ₹500, your return would be 9.8%, as against the 7% you would earn if you used only your own finances.

Swami: Oh! That is good. That means I must keep borrowing.

Gyan: Yes, you are right, but only as long as business does well. Just as your earnings are subject to change, so is your return on investment subject to change as the business scenario changes. The change in return on your investment is larger if you have more debt. If you do better than expected, you earn a larger amount; if you do worse than expected, you lose a larger amount.

Swami: So how do you decide how much to borrow?

Gyan: That is a very difficult question to answer. In fact, there seems to be no simple formula for making such a decision. People generally work with conventions and experiences. Although you can make an assessment of the risks in your business, it is difficult to determine the optimum level of debt.

INTRODUCTION

We discussed various theories of the capital structure of a firm with the focus on the value of the firm, with tax advantage, cost of financial distress, and agency cost playing major roles in determination of the capital structure. Here we concentrate on some operational issues that provide a window to evaluate different kinds of financing plans and their impact on the returns and risks to shareholders.

A firm deploys resources to generate revenues. The difference between revenue and the cost of utilization of resources provides income. Claims on these revenues are of two types. One type of charge is a fixed charge, which needs to be incurred irrespective of the level of production, revenues, or cash flows. It is not dependent upon the revenue generation capacity. The other charge is not fixed, and varies according to the levels of production and sales. The residual that is left after all the commitments are met is issued as equity claim.

There are two kinds of charge on the cash flows of the firm: fixed and variable. Furthermore, the fixed charge is also of two types: one resulting from the cost structure and the other from the financing structure.

There are two kinds of fixed charges on cash flows. One of them emanates from the cost structure of the products the firm sells, while the other comes from the financing structure the firm uses in the acquisition of the assets. Both of these fixed charges have a significant bearing on the earnings of the shareholders of the firm. The impact of these fixed charges on the earnings of the owners of the firm is referred to as *leverage*. Just as the lever is used to magnify the use of force, firms use these fixed charges to magnify the earnings of their owners. Hence, we use the term leverage for our study of fixed charges.

Cost structure Normally, there are two types of cost: *fixed* and *variable*. Examples of fixed cost would be salaries to personnel, administrative overhead expenses, and depreciation. These are costs that have to be incurred regardless of the level of sales. Examples of variable cost would be the cost of raw materials, packing expenses, taxes and duties, incentives, and commission. The incidence of these costs is dependent upon the level of sales. These costs vary directly with the level of sales.

Apart from purely variable and fixed costs, there are some costs that are semi-variable in nature. Such costs include electricity expenses, traveling, etc., which are partly fixed and partly vary with the level of sales. However, for the purpose of our study of leverage, we can assume only two kinds of costs: fixed and variable. Strictly speaking, no cost can be called either fixed or variable in the true sense. Here, we are concerned with the predominant cost behaviour, which may be either fixed or variable.

Financing structure The other fixed charge arises from the financing structure the firm uses to fund its operations. Earnings derived from use of assets have to be shared among the suppliers of capital. Assets can be created by—borrowing; raising capital from investors who are content with a fixed amount of income; taking the assets on hire or lease; or raising capital from investors who are willing to take home the remainder after satisfying everybody else's claim. The financing structure of the firm used for creation of assets can again be categorized into two classifications. The first kind involves fixed charges on earnings, regardless of the level of earnings, such as interest on borrowing, dividend on preference capital, lease rentals, etc. The other kind of financing comes from equity shareholders who share the remaining earnings, if any, left after satisfying the fixed claims.

OPERATING LEVERAGE

A lever is used to magnify the effect of force applied at one point to another point. Leverage is referred to as use of a lever. In the financial world, *leverage* can be defined as the influence of fixed expenses over the operating cash flows or earnings. Fixed expenses can be used as a lever to magnify the operating cash flows and earnings.

Operating leverage can be defined as change in earning before interest and taxes (EBIT) due to change in sales. If all the costs of the product are variable, the expected percentage change in the income before taxes will be equal to the percentage change in sales. To examine this, let us consider two firms, A and B, with varying composition of fixed and variable costs. Assume that Firm A procures electric bulb assemblies at ₹80 a piece and sells them at a price 25% higher than the purchase price. It has no other cost of any kind. The income of the firm shall be ₹20 from a sale of ₹100. This profit of 20% of sales will remain constant, i.e., if the firm doubles its sales, the income will also double. The percentage change in earnings will be equivalent to the percentage change in sales. In other words, a 1% change in sales will result in a 1% change in earnings.

Operating leverage is the study of the impact of fixed cost on the earnings of the firm.

Now, consider Firm B, identical to Firm A in all respects except the cost structure. It has also got the same sales and earnings as Firm A, but is able to get the electric bulb assembly at 70% of the sale price, i.e., ₹70 per piece, because it has hired sales professionals at fixed salaries to promote sales and attend to customer complaints. Assume that Firms A and B both have sales of ₹100, with identical profits of ₹20, as shown in Table 17-1.

Let us consider the impact of changes in sales on earnings. If the revenue of Firm A doubles, the profit would double, too. However, for Firm B, the change in earnings would be more than double. In fact, it has gone up by 150% against a 100% rise in sales, as can be seen from Table 17-1.

Table 17-1 Operating leverage: Effect of change of sales on earnings

(Figures in ₹)

	Firm A		Firm B	
	Present	**Future**	**Present**	**Future**
Sales	100	200	100	200
Variable cost	80	160	70	140
Fixed cost	—	—	10	10
Earnings before interest and taxes (EBIT)	20	40	20	50
% change in sales	100%		100%	
% change in EBIT	100%		150%	

It can be seen that the change in earnings of firm B is greater than the change in earnings of Firm A. Why has the change in earnings been more than proportionate in the case of Firm B? It is because Firm B has been able to use its sales professionals to achieve higher sales at a relatively lesser cost, i.e., ₹70 rather than ₹80 per bulb assembly, when compared with the operations of Firm A. In fact, Firm B hired sales professionals on fixed salaries precisely for that reason. Firm B has been able to use this fixed cost to its advantage.

The simple example of Firm A and Firm B highlighted how the fixed cost can be used to advantage. Similar situations often exist in the complex corporate environment. Normally, whenever a firm considers a project it has to choose between alternative methods of producing the same product. These alternative methods normally have different cost structures.

To illustrate the concept of operating leverage, let us consider a firm, String Shoes, who has two possible routes to manufacture shoes. Method A uses highly automated machinery, having a high rate of depreciation, a high maintenance cost, and larger infrastructure requirements; hence, Method A has a high proportion of fixed cost. Under Method B, the firm can produce the same shoes by using contract labour, and hence, incur more variable cost. For the purpose of simplicity, let us assume that (*a*) there is no quality and price differentiation in the products derived from Method A and Method B; (*b*) both the methods require the same amount of capital—Method A involves higher capital expenditure while Method B requires higher working capital—and (*c*) the entire funding is done through equity. In essence we are assuming that all parameters are identical except for the cost structure of the product, so that we can examine the impact of changing business conditions on the earnings of the firm.

The relevant data for Method A and Method B are presented in Exhibit 17-1. The price of the product is assumed at ₹600. Variable costs under Method A and Method B are ₹300 and ₹200 per unit, while fixed costs are ₹100 lakh and ₹200 lakh respectively. The entire cost of the project, ₹1,500 lakh, is funded through equity, and hence, the Return on Investment (RoI) is equal to the Return on Equity (ROE). Under normal conditions, String Shoes expects, to earn a post-tax return of 8% with expected sales of 1.00 lakh pairs of shoes at an average price of ₹600 per pair. Profits under Method A and Method B are identical, as shown in the following table:

₹ lakh	Method A	Method B
Sales	600	600
Variable cost	300	200
Fixed cost	100	200
EBIT	200	200

The presence of fixed cost magnifies the earnings o f the firm. Earnings are better under favourable business conditions and poorer if conditions are unfavourable, when compared to firms with smaller or nil fixed cost.

Both the methods of production are at par for the expected level of operations. However, String Shoes faces a business risk emanating from various factors affecting sales volume. Although any one of the outcomes is possible, we restrict our analysis to seven different scenarios: Terrible, Very Bad, Bad, Average, Good, Very Good and Excellent. The earning levels of two extreme scenarios of 'Terrible' and 'Excellent' are shown in Table 17-2.

Table 17-2 Impact on EBIT due to changing cost structure

(*₹ in lakh*)

	Method A			Method B		
	Terrible	Average	Excellent	Terrible	Average	Excellent
Sales	120	600	1080	120	600	1080
Variable cost	60	300	540	40	200	360
Fixed cost	100	100	100	200	200	200
EBIT	–40	200	440	–120	200	520
% Change	–120%		120%	–160%		160%

We observe that in both the good and the bad scenarios, the change in EBIT is larger for the method that has a larger element of fixed cost.

Degree of Operating Leverage

The ability of the firm to leverage the fixed cost to achieve more than proportionate change in earnings is referred to as operating leverage. It is measured numerically by the *degree of operating leverage* (DOL), which is defined in Equation 17-1.

$$\text{DOL} = \frac{\Delta\text{EBIT}/\text{EBIT}}{\Delta\text{sales}/\text{sales}} = \frac{\%\text{ change in EBIT}}{\%\text{ change in sales}}$$

$$= \frac{\text{sales} - \text{variable cost}}{\text{sales} - \text{variable cost} - \text{fixed cost}}$$

$$= \frac{Q(P-V)}{Q(P-V)-F} \qquad (17\text{-}1)$$

As we can see from Equation 17-1, a larger fixed cost would result in a larger DOL. Under Method A, the DOL is 1.5, as the change in EBIT is 1.50% for a 1.00% change in sales in either direction. For Method B, the DOL is 2.0, which means that a 1% change in sales will cause the EBIT to change by 2.0%.

Degree of Operating Leverage (DOL) is a relationship between the percentage change in EBIT with 1% change in sales. The minimum value of DOL is 1.00.

The relationship between EBIT and ROE is direct. EBIT and the ROE are computed under each scenario in Exhibit 17-1. It can be observed that under Method B, which has a greater proportion of fixed cost, ROE is more sensitive to changes in the level of sales as compared to Method A. This may be seen in Exhibit 17-1.

To the extent the firm can control its operating leverage, the risk of variability of EBIT, and hence the ROE, with the variability of sales can be contained. Under a given situation in the business environment, the firm with a lesser fixed cost will be less vulnerable. The lower the operating leverage, the more stable would the income be. Once a technology is chosen, the operating leverage becomes largely fixed. However, the firm to some extent can control operating leverage by making relevant decisions while considering issues such as the sub-contracting of activities like payroll, maintenance contracts, job work, etc.

The expected value and standard deviation of the ROE is computed in Exhibit 17-1. This has been done for discrete observations. In real life, any sales scenario is possible. The figure in Exhibit 17-1 depicts the expected value and its variability if we assume a continuous distribution of sales, rather than the discrete changes considered in the example of String Shoes. The choice of operating leverage to the extent available to the management is governed *inter alia* by the confidence the management has on the expected level of operations in terms of utilization of assets and the affordability of the changes in the operating income.

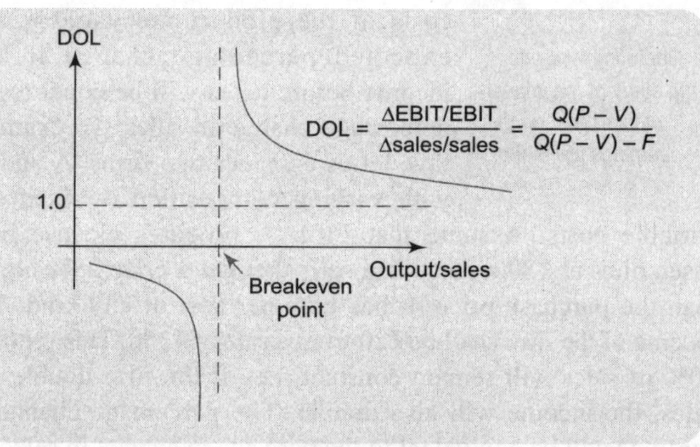

Figure 17-1 Degree of operating leverage

The behaviour of DOL is presented in Figure 17-1. The following observations can be made about DOL:

- DOL always has a value in excess of 1.0. The value '1' signifies that the entire cost is variable and any change in sales will result in an equivalent change in earnings.
- The value of DOL is unique at each level of operation.
- DOL is undefined at breakeven point.
- Negative values of DOL signify that the firm is operating below breakeven point. They do not signify the inverse relationship.
- While operating above the breakeven point, the value of DOL declines and approaches 1 as the firm moves away from breakeven point. This is because the fixed cost per unit decreases as the number of units increase.

Exhibit 17-1 Impact of operating leverage

	Method A	Method B
Selling price (₹/unit)	600	600
Variable cost (₹/unit)	300	200
Fixed cost (₹thousands)	10,000	20,000
Tax rate (%)	40%	40%
Investment (₹thousands)	150,000	150,000

				Method A ₹thousands				Method B ₹thousands			
Scenario	Prob	Sales (Nos.) ('000s)	Revenue ('000s)	Fixed Cost	Variable Cost	PAT	ROE	Fixed Cost	Variable Cost	PAT	ROE
Terrible	5%	20.0	12,000	10,000	6,000	–2,400	–1.60%	20,000	4,000	–7,200	–4.80%
Very bad	8%	50.0	30,000	10,000	15,000	3,000	2.00%	20,000	10,000	0	0.00%
Bad	12%	85.0	51,000	10,000	25,500	9,300	6.20%	20,000	17,000	8,400	5.60%
Average	50%	100.0	60,000	10,000	30,000	12,000	8.00%	20,000	20,000	12,000	8.00%
Good	12%	125.0	75,000	10,000	37,500	16,500	11.00%	20,000	25,000	18,000	12.00%
Very good	8%	150.0	90,000	10,000	45,000	21,000	14.00%	20,000	30,000	24,000	16.00%
Excellent	5%	180.0	108,000	10,000	54,000	26,400	17.60%	20,000	36,000	31,200	20.80%
Expected value of ROE						8.14%				8.19%	
Standard deviation of ROE						4.05%				5.40%	

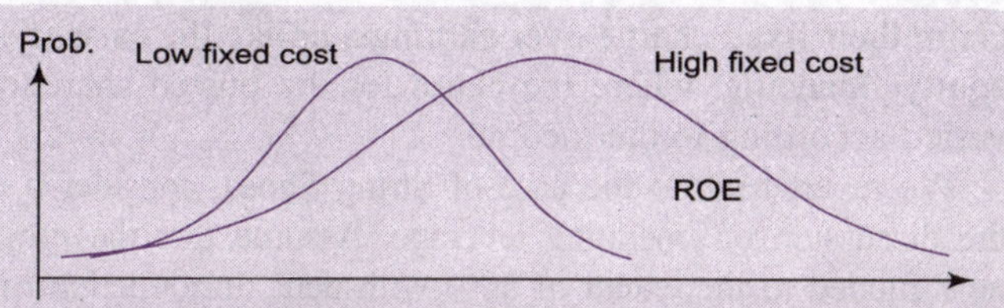

A low fixed cost implies a lower operating leverage, lower profits and less variability in profits and ROE, as reflected in lower standard deviation (Method A).

A high fixed cost will cause larger variations in profits and ROE with changes in sales, and the distribution of profit will be spread over a larger range, as indicated in the higher standard deviation (Method B).

Degree of operating leverage can be thought of as one of the measures of the business risk the firm faces. It measures the sensitivity of earnings to changes in sales. The environment in which the firm operates governs its sales. Factors that constitute the business environment include industry prospects, governmental controls, level of competition, technology, etc., and each firm operates within the limitations imposed by its environment. The business environment determines business risks. Factors affecting demand, supply, price, substitutes, competition, and elasticity of demand and supply etc cause the operating profit of the firm to change.

The larger the Degree of Operating Leverage, the larger is the change in earnings. This makes earnings riskier too. It is a measure of business risk.

Different firms see different levels of operating profit and its variability, given the same environment on which they can hardly exercise any influence. The variability of earnings with changes in any of the above factors would in turn be determined by the extent to which the cost structure is fixed. The firm with a higher proportion of fixed cost would see a relatively large change in its earnings, as compared to the firm with a lower proportion of fixed cost. The cost structure in terms of fixed and variable is a function of factors like industry, technology, and level of automation. Businesses such as steel, cement, and airlines need heavy investments and thus have high fixed cost proportions; therefore, they see wilder fluctuation in income, as compared to businesses such as retailing, textile which have a greater proportion of variable cost. Operating leverage, therefore, is a parameter that is predominantly not in the control of management, but awareness of its implications in management is handy.

The best way that management can hope to deploy the concept of operating leverage is in the selection of product technology. Different technologies to manufacture the same product have different cost structures. Managers can focus their attention on the cost structure associated with each technology and choose the one that suits their requirements for desired level of EBIT and acceptable levels of its variability. Once the choice is made, the managers can do little subsequently. Hence, operating leverage becomes a strategic issue rather than a tactical one.

Although there is very little managers can do to alter the DOL, a good knowledge of operating leverage is certainly desirable for examining the impact of changes in EBIT with changes in level of sales, to assess risk and plan better. Managers can make a fair estimate of the likelihood of reaching certain levels of sales that are consistent with the risk profiles assumed.

Example 17-1 Understanding DOL

Rank Chemicals is operating at a sales level of ₹400 lakh. Rank Chemicals has a variable cost of ₹250 lakh (62.5%) and fixed expenses of ₹100 lakh. What changes in profit do you expect if the sales (a) rise by 5% and (b) decline by 5%?

Solution

The DOL of the firm is

$$= \frac{\text{Sales} - \text{variable cost}}{\text{Sales} - \text{variable cost} - \text{fixed cost}}$$

$$= \frac{400 - 250}{400 - 250 - 100} = 3.00$$

This implies that a 1% change in sales would result in a 3% change in earnings. Hence, a 5% decline in sales would cause income to fall by 15% and likewise, a 5% rise in sales would result in a 15% increase in income. This may be verified from the following brief projections:

All figures in ₹ lakh

	Current level	5% increase	5% decrease
Sales	400.00	420.00	380.00
Variable cost (62.5%)	250.00	262.50	237.50
Fixed cost	100.00	100.00	100.00
Profit	50.00	57.50	42.50
% change		+15%	–15%

FINANCIAL LEVERAGE

The other kind of fixed commitment made by the firm is interest to be paid on funds borrowed. Besides debt, there could be other commitments of similar nature to pay fixed charges for funds deployed to acquire and operate assets. These include preference capital, on which a fixed rate of dividend is paid, and leased assets, for which fixed rentals are paid. Residual earnings are used to service the shareholders. The pie that is available to the shareholders is measured in terms of Earnings Per Share (EPS), which is derived by dividing Earning Before Taxes (EBT) or Earnings After Taxes (EAT) by the number of shares, respectively for pre-tax and post tax EPS. It can also be measured by ROE, which is EBT or EAT divided by value of equity. Here, we are not concerned about taxes, which are deemed as fixed and beyond the control of firm. An analysis based on pre-tax or post-tax earnings would lead us to similar conclusions.

Financial leverage refers to the use of debt financing and the resultant sensitivity of the earnings available to shareholders (EPS) by the substitution of their capital with fixed charge finance. If the firm has no fixed financial charges, then any change in the levels of EBIT will be transferred to shareholders as it is. The change in the shareholders' wealth would be identical to that of the change in EBIT. In such a case, all the business risk is borne by the shareholders.

Financial leverage is the study of the impact of fixed cost of interest on earnings for shareholders.

However, if some of the equity capital is substituted by fixed charge capital, changes in EPS will be larger as compared to all equity financing option. Replacing equity with debt leaves the risk with the remaining equity shareholders. Debt compounds the business risk for the remaining shareholders. A simple discussion will illustrate this point. There is a certain amount of business risk a firm faces. Assume there are 100 equal shareholders contributing ₹10 each in a firm having an expected income of ₹100, providing an expected income of Re 1 to each of them. If the income rises to ₹200, each shareholder would get ₹2, and if income falls to ₹50, each shareholder would be left with Re 0.50 only. All the 100 shareholders bear the business risk in equal proportion.

Now assume that 50 shareholders are replaced by raising a debt of ₹500, leaving only 50 shareholders. The debt, costing 5%, has a fixed charge of ₹25. With EBIT likely to fluctuate between the same range of ₹50 and ₹200, the earnings for the shareholders would now range between ₹25 and ₹175. For the shareholders continuing in the business the income would now be between Re 0.50 and ₹3.50. Hence, the remaining shareholders are exposed to more risk. Thus, use of debt compounds the business risk to the remaining equity shareholders. The debt providers who replaced the 50 equity holders do not bear the business risk. This happened because the debt providers will claim their fixed charge over earnings, unlike the case of 100% equity financing, where the claim for the ousted shareholders varied according to the income.

We revert back to the case of String Shoes, considered under the discussion on operating leverage. Assume that the project is now funded to the extent of 50% with debt. Introduction of debt will cause the earning to the shareholders and its variability to change. The firm has two options to fund the total requirement of ₹1,500 lakh. It can obtain the entire funds through equity, under Plan A, or avail debt at 10% to replace half of the equity, under Plan B. We again present the changes in the EPS for the two plans under the scenarios 'Terrible' and 'Excellent' in Table 17-3.

Table 17-3 Impact on EPS due to changing financial structure

(₹ in lakh)

	Plan A			Plan B		
	Terrible	Average	Excellent	Terrible	Average	Excellent
EBIT	–40	200	440	–40	200	440
Interest	—	—	—	75	75	75
EBT	–40	200	440	–115	125	365
Taxes 40%	–16*	80	176	–46*	50	146
PAT	–24	120	264	–69	75	219
# of shares	150	150	150	75	75	75
EPS (₹)	–0.16	0.80	1.76	–0.92	1.00	2.92
% Change	–120%		120%	–160%		160%

*Assumed that the tax would be payable when the firm performs better in future

We observe that under financing Plan B, the change in the EPS is larger than that under Plan A, which involves no fixed charge. A look at Exhibit 17-2 would reveal that the variability of the EPS under Plan B is larger than under Plan A.

Exhibit 17-2 Effects of financial leverage

Selling price	(₹/unit)	600
Variable cost	(₹/unit)	300
Fixed cost	(₹ thousand)	10,000
Tax rate	(%)	40%
Investment	(₹ thousand)	150,000

Financing Plan	*Plan A*	*Plan B*
Debt	—	75,000
Equity	150,000	75,000
No. of shares	15,000	7,500

All figures in thousands unless otherwise mentioned

					PLAN A				PLAN B			
Scenario	*Prob.*	*Sales (Nos.)*	*Revenue*	*EBIT*	*Interest*	*EBT*	*PAT*	*EPS (₹)*	*Interest*	*EBT*	*PAT*	*EPS (₹)*
Terrible	5%	20	12,000	–4,000	—	–4,000	–2,400	–0.16	7,500	–11,500	–6,900	–0.92
Very bad	8%	50	30,000	5,000	—	5,000	3,000	0.20	7,500	–2,500	–1,500	–0.20
Bad	12%	85	51,000	15,500	—	15,500	9,300	0.62	7,500	8,000	4,800	0.64
Average	50%	100	60,000	20,000	—	20,000	12,000	0.80	7,500	12,500	7,500	1.00
Good	12%	125	75,000	27,500	—	27,500	16,500	1.10	7,500	20,000	12,000	1.60
Very good	8%	150	90,000	35,000	—	35,000	21,000	1.40	7,500	27,500	16,500	2.20
Excellent	5%	180	108,000	44,000	—	44,000	26,400	1.76	7,500	36,500	21,900	2.92
					Expected value			**0.81**				**1.03**
					Standard deviation			**40.53%**				**81.05%**

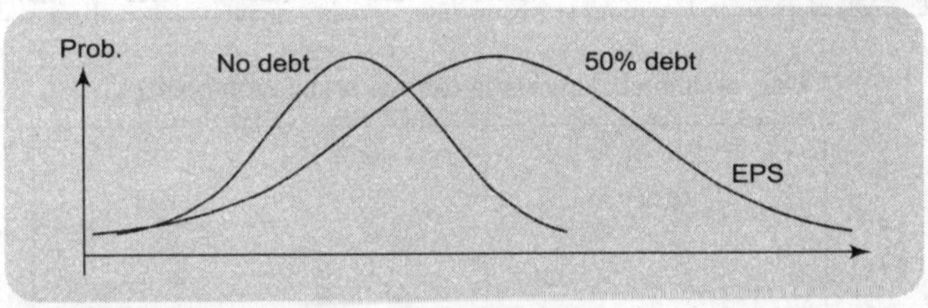

No debt implies lower financial leverage, lower profits and less variability in EPS and RoE, as reflected in the lower standard deviation. (Plan A)

High debt will cause larger variations in profits, EPS and ROE, with changes in sales. The distribution of profit/EPS/ROE will be spread over a larger range, as indicated in the higher standard deviation. (Plan B)

Degree of Financial Leverage (DFL)

Just as a fixed cost leverages the EBIT for changes in sales, as studied under the section on operating leverage, the presence of a fixed charge in the financing of the firm leverages the EPS for a given change in EBIT. This is called financial leverage. Use of debt causes fixed charges on the capital by way of interest, and since this fixed capital replaces more expensive equity, the remaining equity earns a greater return.

Degree of Financial Leverage (DFL) is the percentage change in the Earnings per Share with 1% change in the EBIT level. The minimum value of DFL is 1.00.

Degree of financial leverage (DFL) is defined as given below.

$$\text{DLF} = \frac{\Delta\text{EPS}/\text{EPS}}{\Delta\text{EBIT}/\text{EBIT}} = \frac{\%\text{ change in EPS}}{\%\text{ change in EBIT}}$$

$$= \frac{\text{EBIT}}{\text{EBIT} - I - D_p/(1-T)} \qquad (17\text{-}2)$$

where I = interest on debt and all fixed financing charges which are tax deductible, and

D_P = fixed dividend on preference capital and all other fixed financing charges which are not tax deductible.

Financial leverage analyses, with given levels of EBIT, what changes will accrue to shareholders if the financing pattern is changed. With all equity financing the DFL is equal to 1. This is the minimum value of DFL. As more debt replaces equity, DFL increases beyond 1. When DFL has a value greater than 1, it implies that with increase in debt (i) the returns to shareholders will increase, and (ii) the sensitivity of the ROE too will increase.

Financial leverage under Plan A for Shoe String, as measured by DFL, is 1 (which is the least value for a 100% equity financed firm), implying that any change in EBIT would cause a similar change in EPS. Under Plan B the DFL is 1.60 (EBIT/(EBIT–I) = 200/125), signifying that a 1% change in EBIT would result in a 1.6% change in EPS.

The characteristics of DFL are similar to those of DOL, as can be seen in Figure 17-2, and the observations are also similar. These are stated below:

- DFL always has a value in excess of 1.0. The value of 1 signifies that entire funding is done through equity. The firm has no interest burden.
- A DFL value less than 1 is possible when the firm is unable to generate any income. The firm cannot meet its fixed operational cost and EBIT is negative.
- The value of DFL is unique at each level of operation.

Exhibit 17-3 Behaviour of DOL and DFL

All figures in thousands unless otherwise mentioned

Sales	0	100	200	300	399	400	401	500	600	700	800	900	1,000	1,500	2,000
Variable cost	0	50	100	150	200	200	201	250	300	350	400	450	500	750	1,000
Fixed cost	200	200	200	200	200	200	200	200	200	200	200	200	200	201	202
EBIT	–200	–150	–100	–50	–1	0	1	50	100	150	200	250	300	549	798
DOL	**0.00**	**–0.33**	**–1.00**	**–3.00**	**–399.00**	**∞**	**401.00**	**5.00**	**3.00**	**2.33**	**2.00**	**1.80**	**1.67**	**1.37**	**1.25**

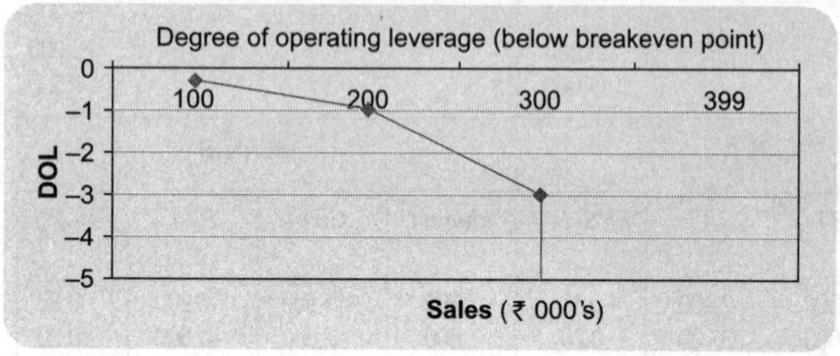

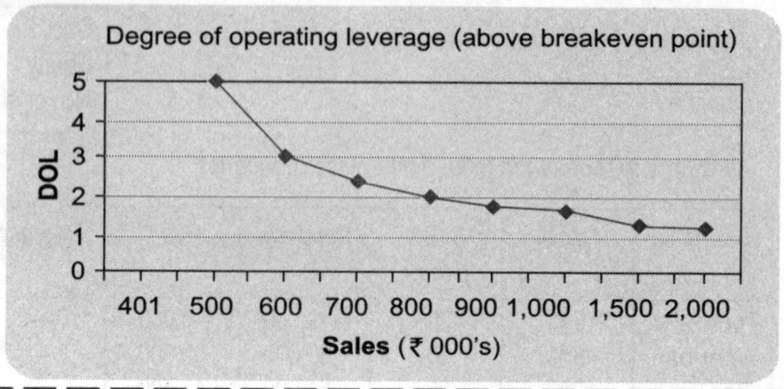

Sales	0	100	200	300	400	499	500	501	600	700	800	900	1,000	1,500	2,000
Variable cost	0	50	100	150	200	250	250	251	300	350	400	450	500	750	1,000
Fixed cost	200	200	200	200	200	200	200	200	200	200	200	200	200	201	202
EBIT	–200	–150	–100	–50	0	50	50	51	100	150	200	250	300	549	798
Interest	50	50	50	50	50	50	50	50	50	50	50	50	50	50	50
EBT	–250	–200	–150	–100	–50	–1	0	1	50	100	150	200	250	499	748
DFL	**0.80**	**0.75**	**0.67**	**0.50**	**0.00**	**–99.00**	**∞**	**101.00**	**2.00**	**1.50**	**1.33**	**1.25**	**1.20**	**1.10**	**1.07**

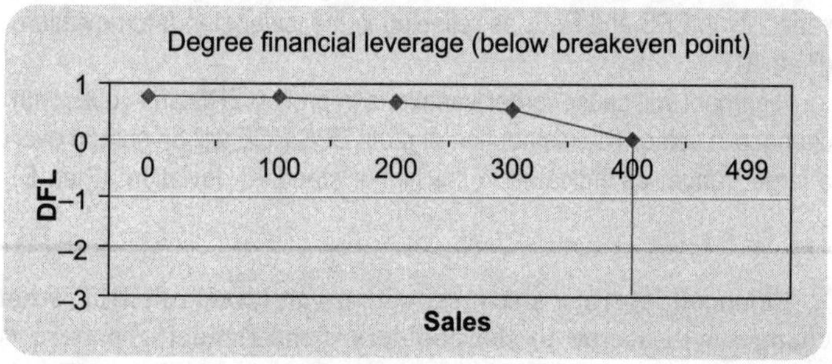

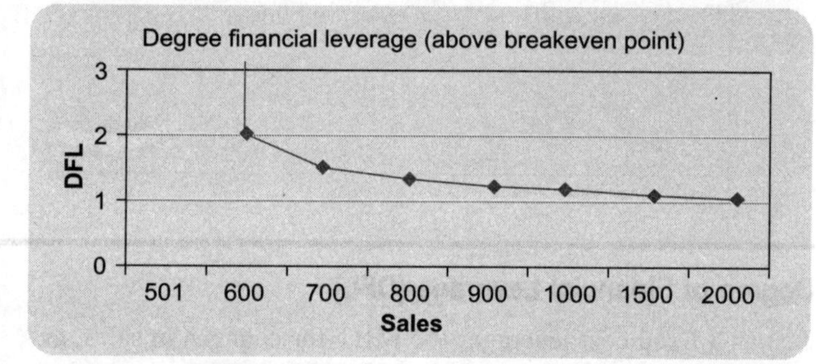

- At breakeven point the DFL is undefined. By breakeven point here, we mean a financial breakeven point, defined as the level of EBIT that is just enough to meet the financial fixed cost (interest).
- Negative values of DFL signify that the earnings of the firm are not enough to cover interest costs, and there is a loss for the equity shareholders. On the whole, the firm is operating below breakeven point. A negative sign does not signify an inverse relationship.
- While operating above the breakeven point, the value of DFL declines and approaches 1, as the firm moves away from the breakeven point.

As DOL measures the business risk of the firm, DFL reflects upon the financial risk of the firm, i.e., the sensitivity of shareholders' returns to financing mixes of debt and equity in creating assets.

Unlike operating leverage, the choice of financial leverage is not imposed on the firm by its external environment. Instead, it largely depends upon the management philosophy of funding growth either by equity or by debt. The environment places a restriction on the maximum borrowing that a firm can enjoy, as for most industries the upper limits to debt are specified in terms of debt–equity ratios conventionally followed by financial institutions and markets. Therefore, financial leverage is largely a choice that rests with management, and depends on the growth

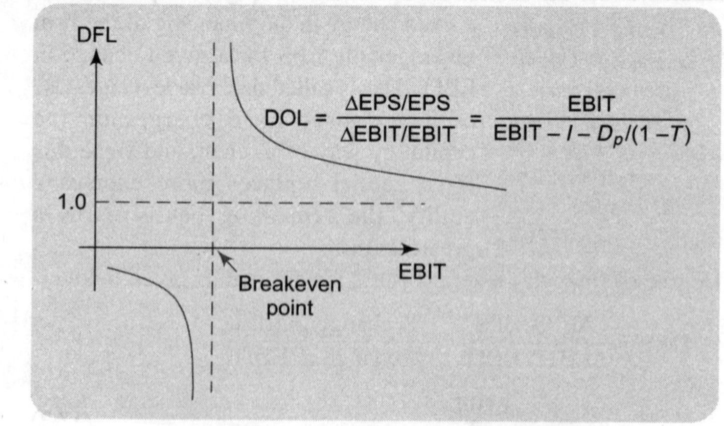

Figure 17-2 Degree of financial leverage

opportunities available. As stated earlier, financial leverage compounds business risks. In a given scenario involving business risk and operating leverage, a firm's management can take a conscious decision to the extent it can afford the financial leverage, depending upon the risk perception and the risk-bearing capacity.

Deployment of leverage has both good and bad effects. Leverage enhances earnings for shareholders, but it also increases their risks. Leverage becomes a choice between reward and risk. A desire for increased reward is necessarily associated with increased risk.

The larger the value of DFL, the greater is the change in earnings for the shareholders, and hence, the greater is the risk. DFL is a measure of financial risk.

The behaviour of DOL is presented in Exhibit 17-3 for different levels of operations, assuming 50% variable cost and fixed cost at 50. Similarly, a plot of DFL too is made for different levels of EBIT with interest cost of 50.

Example 17-2 Understanding DFL

Ruchi Corporation is considering a project costing ₹800 lakh. The project offers expected earnings of ₹100 lakh under normal conditions. These earnings can change by ±50% under conditions of expansion and recession. Ruchi Corporation has two alternate financing plans: raise 100% equity financing through issue of 10 lakh shares of value ₹80 each, or avail of a loan of ₹400 lakh—equivalent to 50% of the project cost—at interest of 12.50%, while issuing 5 lakh shares at ₹80 each.

(a) What is the DFL for Ruchi Corporation under 100% equity financing arrangement, and under a 50% debt arrangement?
(b) What interpretations do you assign to the values of DFL?
(c) Project expected earnings to shareholders under expansion and recession.

Solution

(a) Calculation of DFL

(Figures in lakh)

	100% equity	50% equity
EBIT (₹)	100.00	100.00
Interest, *I*	—	50.00
EBT	100.00	50.00
Nos. of shares	10.00	5.00
EPS (₹Per share)	10.00	12.00
DFL = EBIT/(EBIT–*I*)	1.00	2.00

(b) With 100% equity financing, DFL is 1 indicating equivalent changes in EPS with EBIT. A 50% rise or fall in sales will lead to a 50% rise or fall in EPS. Hence, expected EPS would be ₹15 and ₹5 under conditions of expansion and recession respectively.

Financing with 50% debt would have a larger DFL, computed at 2. The change in EPS is expected to be twice as much as that of sales. A 50% rise or fall in sales will cause a 100% rise or fall in EPS.

(c) Expected earnings

₹ in lakh	*100% equity*		*50% equity*	
	Expansion	Recession	Expansion	Recession
EBIT	150.00	50.00	150.00	50.00
Interest, *I*	—	—	50.00	50.00
EBT	150.00	50.00	100.00	—
No. of shares	10.00		5.00	
EPS (₹)	15.00	5.00	20.00	0.00

EBIT–EPS ANALYSIS

To understand the implications of debt financing on returns to shareholders, we compare the earnings available to the shareholders (EPS) with various financing alternatives. The comparison of the financing alternatives must be made at the expected value of EBIT.

To study the impact of the level of debt on returns to shareholders, let us examine a project. AutoComp Ltd plans to manufacture and supply OEM automobile components to a major automobile manufacturer. The cost of the project is estimated to be ₹10 crore and the automobile manufacturer has agreed to pricing patterns that would yield 15% return on assets. With corporate tax at 40%, the post-tax return would be a mere 9%. If the entire project were funded by way of equity, the ROE would be 9%, too. Promoters feel that this return is too meagre. What can be done to provide a greater ROE?

EBIT-EPS analysis is a powerful analytical tool that helps in evaluation of different financing patterns and in establishing a target capital structure.

Our discussion about financial leverage suggests that to enhance the ROE, we may resort to debt. The cheaper debt would substitute for equity and provide a greater return on the remaining equity. We examine the various financing plans, with debt ranging from 10% to 90%, in Table 17-4. Keeping the expected level of EBIT constant at 15%, we observe that the ROE can be enhanced from a poor 9% with all equity financing to an attractive 36% if we resort to 90% debt under Plan E.

Table 17-4 Evaluating different plans

(₹ *lakh*)

	Financing Plans					
₹ Lakh	*All Equity*	*A*	*B*	*C*	*D*	*E*
Debt ratio	0 %	10%	30%	50%	70%	90%
Cost of the project	1000	1000	1000	1000	1000	1000
Equity	1000	900	700	500	300	100
Debt	0	100	300	500	700	900
Cost of debt	10%	10%	10%	10%	10%	10%
Return on assets	15%	15%	15%	15%	15%	15%
EBIT	150	150	150	150	150	150
Interest	0	10	30	50	70	90
EBT	150	140	120	100	80	60
Tax 40%	60	56	48	40	32	24
PAT	90	84	72	60	48	36
No. of shares (lakh)	100	90	70	50	30	10
EPS (₹ /share)	0.90	0.93	1.03	1.20	1.60	3.60
ROE	9.0%	9.3%	10.3%	12.0%	16.0%	36.0%

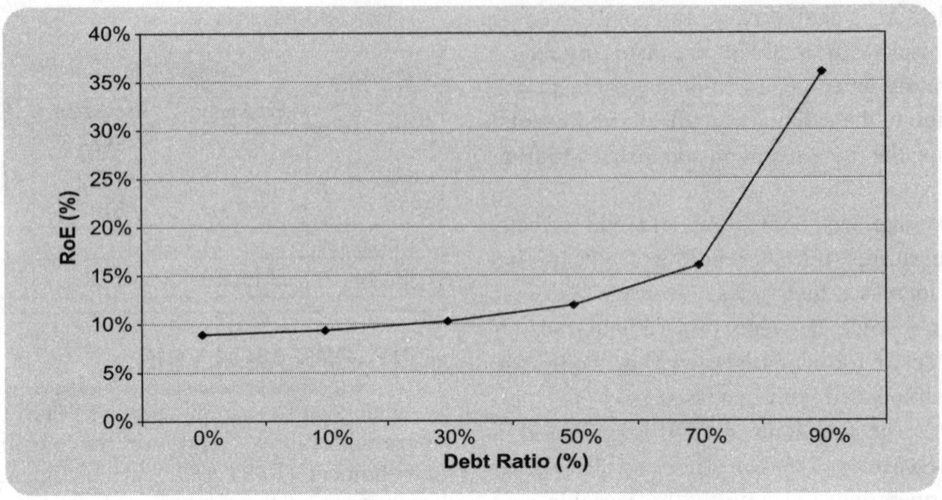

Figure 17-3 Return on Equity (as function of debt ratio)

We observe that ROE increases as the debt ratio increases. Mathematically, ROE is expressed as the percentage post-tax earning after paying interest on debt, as stated in Equation 17-3.

$$\text{ROE} = \frac{(\text{EBIT} - I)(1 - T)}{E} \quad (17\text{-}3)$$

As leverage increase the change in EPS and Return on Equity is steeper and steeper. Therefore increased amount of debt makes returns to shareholders higher and riskier.

At 60% debt level for AutoComp's project, we can expect ROE to be somewhere in between 12% and 16%. We can find ROE to be 13.5%

$$\text{ROE} = \frac{(\text{EBIT} - I)(1 - T)}{E}$$

$$= \frac{(150 - 60) \times 0.6}{400} = 13.5\%$$

The plot showing ROE as a function of debt ratio is shown in Figure 17-3.

It may be observed from Figure 17-3 that the rise in ROE is slower at lower levels of debt, but is steeper at higher levels of debt. Depending upon the level of ROE desired, one may fix the target capital structure. For example, if the promoters of AutoComp desire an ROE of 13.5%, they could opt for debt of 60% of their requirement, as computed above. The relationship of ROE and return on assets can also be expressed as given in Equation 17-4.

With EBIT – EPS analysis the capital structure can be planned with desired return on equity or EPS and risk appetite.

$$\text{ROE} = \frac{(\text{EBIT} - I)(1 - T)}{E}$$

$$= \left[\frac{r_a(E + D) - r_d \times D}{E}\right] \times (1 - T)$$

$$= \left[r_a + (r_a - r_d)\frac{D}{E}\right] \times (1 - T) \quad (17\text{-}4)$$

Equation 17-4 may again be used to determine the target capital structure. For example, if a 15% ROE is desired in the AutoComp project, we arrive at the debt–equity ratio of 2:1 that yields 15% ROE.

$$\text{ROE} = \left[r_a + (r_a - r_d)\frac{D}{E}\right] \times (1 - T)$$

$$15\% = \left[15 + (15 - 10)\frac{D}{E}\right] \times 0.6$$

$$\frac{D}{E} = 2$$

Desirability of Financial Leverage

But is the desired ROE the sole criterion for determining the target capital structure? The latter half of Figure 17-3 suggests that very high ROEs are achievable with high debt ratios. But is such high financial leverage desirable?

We started our analysis with a rather assured level of EBIT and kept ROE expectations within acceptable levels while choosing the capital structure. What happens if the desired level of EBIT is not achieved? ROE would be under threat of falling short of expectations. Let us examine how the business risk changes ROE.

Assume that AutoComp has opted for a debt ratio of 50% (debt–equity ratio of 1:1) that provides a return of 12% under normal conditions. To examine the impact of changes in the business environment, let us consider different capital structures. There may be numerous financing options available to AutoComp, but for ease of explanation, let us consider only two such options as follows:

Option I: Achieve 100% equity financing through issue of 10 lakh equity shares priced at ₹10 each, denoted as 'All Equity' in Table 17-4.

Option II: Achieve a debt–equity ratio of 1:1 by arranging a debt of ₹5 crore at a cost of 10%, and raising the balance of ₹5 crore by issuing 5 lakh shares priced at ₹10 each, denoted as 'Plan C' in Table 17-4.

Let us consider EPS under the two options with five different possible scenarios: 'Bad', 'Fair', 'Normal', 'Good', and 'Excellent'. Under normal circumstances, AutoComp expects a return of 15% on assets. However, if the business scenario is gloomy, the return can fall to as low as 5%. On the other extreme, if the business circumstances turn out to be extraordinary, the firm can expect excellent returns of 25%. The anticipated performance of AutoComp under 5 different business scenarios and two financing options, 100% equity financing and 50% debt, is presented in Table 17-5.

Return on Assets given by EBIT varies from ₹ 50 lakh, under the most pessimistic scenario 'Bad', to ₹ 250 lakh, under the most optimistic scenario 'Excellent'. Under the all-equity financing and the 50% debt financing options, the impact on the returns to shareholders, gauged either by EPS or ROE, would change by different amounts and proportions because the DFL is different.

Table 17-5 Evaluating financing plan with changing business risk

₹ lakh	Business Scenario: Bad	Fair	Normal	Good	Excellent
Investment			1000		
Return on Assets	**5%**	**10%**	**15%**	**20%**	**25%**
Option I: All Equity Financing					
EBIT	50	100	150	200	250
Interest	0	0	0	0	0
EBT	50	100	150	200	250
Tax 40%	20	40	60	80	100
PAT	30	60	90	120	150
No. of shares	100	100	100	100	100
EPS (₹/share)	**0.30**	**0.60**	**0.90**	**1.20**	**1.50**
ROE	**3.0%**	**6.0%**	**9.0%**	**12.0%**	**15.0%**
Option II: 50% Equity & 50% Debt Financing					
EBIT	50	100	150	200	250
Interest	50	50	50	50	50
EBT	0	50	100	150	200
Tax 40%	0	20	40	60	80
PAT	0	30	60	90	120
No. of shares	50	50	50	50	50
EPS (₹/share)	**—**	**0.60**	**1.20**	**1.80**	**2.40**
ROE	**0.0%**	**6.0%**	**12.0%**	**18.0%**	**24.0%**

Looking at Table 17-5, the following observations can be made:

- When the business scenario is better than expected, EPS is greater if the firm employs leverage as compared to all-equity financing, as can be seen under the 'Normal', 'Good' and 'Excellent' scenarios.
- The rise of EPS in a levered firm is steeper when compared to an all-equity financed firm.
- When the business scenario is not as good as expected, EPS in an all-equity firm will be greater than in a firm with debt financing, as reflected under the 'Bad' business scenario.
- When the going is not good, the shareholders of a levered firm face a steeper decline in EPS when compared to the shareholders of a firm with all-equity financing.

The general effect of leverage on shareholders earnings can be summarized in other words as follows.

- Substitution of equity with debt enhances earnings for equity shareholders, as cheaper debt replaces more expensive equity.

  Although EPS for shareholders increases, the variability of EPS too increases. In effect, this means that the shareholders are exposed to greater risk as more and more debt substitutes for equity.

The impact on EPS of changing levels of EBIT can be gauged directly by DFL. For the two financing options, DFL is 1.00 and 1.50, as shown below:

Degree of financial leverage (DFL)

$$\text{for 100\% equity financing} = \frac{\text{EBIT}}{\text{EBIT} - I - D_p/(1-T)}$$

$$= \frac{150}{150-0} = 1.00$$

$$\text{for 50\% equity financing} = \frac{\text{EBIT}}{\text{EBIT} - I - D_p(1-T)}$$

$$= \frac{150}{150-50} = 1.50$$

DFL implies that under 100% equity-financing, EPS would change by the same percentage as EBIT would. If EBIT changes by 33.33% from ₹150 to ₹200, EPS would also change by one-third. EPS therefore rises to ₹1.60 from ₹1.20. Similarly, under the 50% debt plan, the change in EPS would be 1.5 × 33.33% = 50%. EPS rises from ₹1.20 to ₹1.80.

Increases in debt make EPS more volatile.

A graphical view of the effect of leverage on EPS under the two financing options is presented in Figure 17-4.

As can be seen from Figure 17-4, beyond a certain level of EBIT, the use of debt is advantageous, as it provides higher EPS to the remaining shareholders, when compared to the firm that uses lesser debt. However, if the level of EBIT is not sufficiently large, then it is beneficial to have less debt. The financing option with a lower amount of debt provides higher earnings per share. The relationship of EBIT to EPS would become steeper as the debt ratio increases.

Point of Indifference

With changing levels of EBIT, as governed by the business risk of the firm, the preferred financing option changes from no leverage or low leverage to high leverage. As this transition is made, there would be a point of indifference of the level of earning, at which the two financing options provide the same amount of EPS for shareholders. It can easily be derived from the following equation:

$$\frac{(\text{EBIT}^* - I_1)(1-T)}{n_1} = \frac{(\text{EBIT}^* - I_2)(1-T)}{n_2} \tag{17-5}$$

where EBIT* = level of EBIT for point of indifference

T = tax rate

I_1 and I_2 = interest payments under financing options 1 and 2, respectively

n_1 and n_2 = numbers of shares under financing options 1 and 2, respectively

Increased borrowing provides a steeper relationship between EBIT and EPS, with advantage and disadvantage of debt depending upon the level of earning. The greater the earning, the larger is the advantage and the lesser the earning, the larger is the disadvantage.

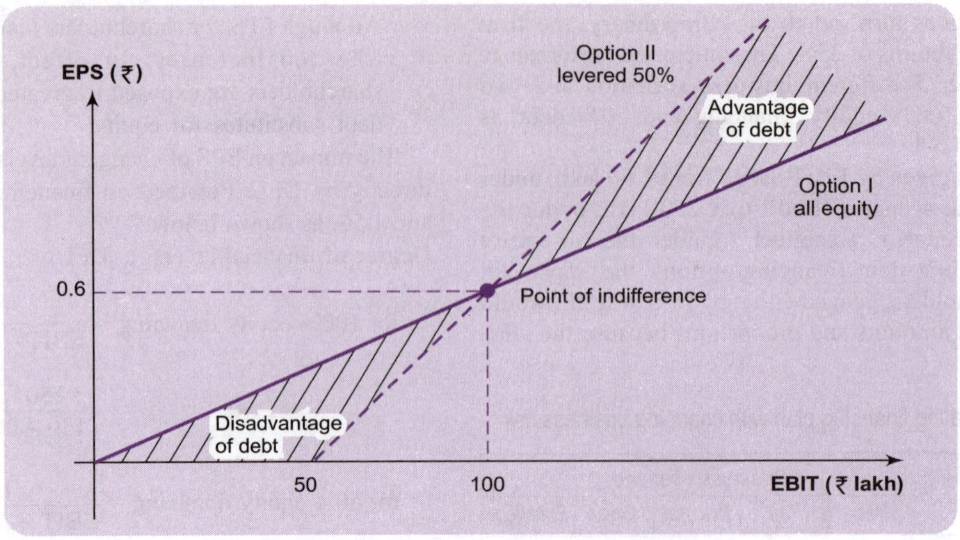

Figure 17-4 Effect of leverage on EPS

For the two financing options, 100% equity and 50% debt, the point of indifference is at EBIT of ₹100 lakh.

$$\frac{(\text{EBIT}^* - I_1)(1-T)}{n_1} = \frac{(\text{EBIT}^* - I_2)(1-T)}{n_2}$$

$$\frac{(\text{EBIT}^* - 0) \times 0.6}{100} = \frac{(\text{EBIT}^* - 50) \times 0.6}{50}$$

$$\text{EBIT}^* = 100$$

The EPS under both the financing options at EBIT of ₹100 lakh is Re 0.60.

The point of indifference of EBIT for the two financing options provides an important decision-making parameter while comparing the financing options. It is a guiding tool for managers to compare any two financing options and make a choice between the two. If the level of EBIT for the point of indifference is relatively low and managers are fairly confident of achieving that level, then the firm may decide to use an increased level of leverage to maximize EPS, which in turn maximizes shareholders' wealth. However, if EBIT at the point of indifference appears to be higher than the expected level, it is advisable to decide the financing structure more in favour of equity. In a way, the point of indifference provides an insight to the level of risk the firm faces with respect to the level of EBIT.

ROI–ROE ANALYSIS

The EBIT–EPS analysis is done with absolute numbers available, where total earning potential is measured by EBIT and the return to shareholders is measured in terms of EPS. Often, the comparison is more convenient in percentage terms. If EBIT is replaced by ROI and EPS is replaced by ROE, and both are expressed in percentage terms, we obtain a relationship between ROI and ROE similar to that between EBIT and EPS. Even the observations made for the EBIT–EPS analysis would remain the same, and can be summarized as follows:

- As long as ROI is greater than the cost of debt, the excess of ROI over the cost of debt contributes to enhancement of the ROE. Therefore it is more beneficial to choose a capital structure favouring leverage. The ROE in this case will be given by Equation 17-4.

$$\text{ROE} = \{\text{ROI} + (\text{ROI} - r_d)\, D/E\} \times (1 - T) \qquad (17\text{-}4)$$

- When ROI is not enough to meet the cost of debt, it is advantageous to have the capital structure oriented towards equity.
- The point where ROI is equal to the cost of debt will be the point of indifference from the viewpoint of the capital structure.

Example 17-3 Comparing Financing Plans

A firm is considering implementation of a project costing ₹10 crore. The current market price of its share is ₹50. It has got the following three financing plans available:

Plan A: Issue 20 lakh shares to raise the entire financing of ₹10 crore.

Plan B: Issue 10 lakh shares to raise ₹5 crore and arrange a debt at 10% for the remaining ₹5 crore.

Plan C: Issue 10 lakh shares to raise ₹5 crore as equity, issue preferential shares at 8% for ₹3 crore, and arrange a debt at 10% for the remaining ₹2 crore.

The firm expects a return on assets of 20% (projected EBIT of ₹2 crore). It attracts tax at the rate of 30% on its profits.

Submit the following:

(a) Your calculation of EPS under all the three financing plans
(b) Your calculation of DFL at EBIT level of ₹2 crore under all the three financing plans
(c) Your interpretation of the DFL
(d) The financing plan you would opt for if you were very confident of achieving the EBIT level of ₹2 crore
(e) Your calculation of the ROI under all the financing options
(f) Your expectation of changes in the EPS for the three financing plans if EBIT increases by 12%
(g) Your thoughts on how ROE will change with equity being substituted by debt or preferential share capital
(h) The capital structure you would propose if equity investors desire a return of 25% and no preferential share capital is to be raised

Solution

(a) and (b) Calculation of EPS and DFL: EBIT–EPS Analysis

Assuming a 20% return on assets, EBIT of the firm is ₹200 lakh

(₹ lakh)

	Plan A	*Plan B*	*Plan C*
EBIT	200	200	200
Interest	—	50	20
EBT	200	150	180
Tax @ 30%	60	45	54
EAT	140	105	126
Preference dividend	—	—	24
Equity shareholders' fund	140	105	102
No. of equity shares	20	10	10
EPS (₹/share)	700	10.50	10 20
Degree of financial leverage	$\frac{EBIT}{EBIT - I - D_p/(1-T)}$		
	1.00	1.33	1.37

(c) When the entire financing is by way of equity, 1% change in the EBIT level will lead to an equivalent change in the EPS; the return to equity shareholders. When the capital structure is leveraged, the return to equity shareholders will rise or fall at a higher proportion than the change in the level of EBIT. The magnification of return to equity shareholders is dependent upon (i) the quantum of debt substituting equity, and (ii) the excess of return on assets over the cost of debt. This can be seen in financing Plans B and C, for which DFL is greater than 1. EPS will rise by 1.33% and 1.37% for an increase of 1% in EBIT, for financing Plans B and C respectively.

(d) With reasonable certainty of the projected EPS of ₹2 crore, and with a view to maximize shareholders' wealth, the option that gives the highest EPS, i.e., financing Plan C, is most preferred.

(e) ROE is computed as follows:

	Plan A	*Plan B*	*Plan C*
Earning for the equity shareholders (₹) lakh	140	105	102
Market value of equity (₹) lakh	1000	500	500
ROE (%)	14.0%	21.0%	20.4%

This can also be found by dividing EPS by the current market price of the equity share, i.e., ₹50.

(f) The change in EPS and the new level of EPS will be

	Plan A	*Plan B*	*Plan C*
For a 12% change in EBIT the EPS will change by	1.00 × 12%	1.33 × 12%	1.37 × 12%
% change in EPS	12.0%	16.0%	16.4%
New EPS (₹per share)	7.84	12.18	11.87

(g) The relationship of ROE to the changing capital structure can be derived as given below:

$$\text{ROE} = \frac{EAT}{E} = \frac{(EBIT - I)(1-T) - D}{E}$$

$$= \frac{\{(E + D + P) \times r_a - r_d \times D\}(1-T) - r_p \times P}{E}$$

$$\text{ROE} = r_a(1 - T) + (r_a - r_d)(1 - T)\, D/E + \{r_a(1 - T) - r_p\}\, P/E$$

where E, D, and P are the market values of equity, debt, and preferential share capital respectively, r_a, r_d, and r_p are the rate of return on capital employed, rate of interest on debt, and rate of dividend on preferential shares, respectively.

Interpretation The interpretation of the above equation is fairly straight forward. If a firm is all-equity financed without any debt or preferential share capital, the ROE is the same as the after-tax return on assets, and is equal to $r_a(1 - T)$. If debt is introduced, the ROE will be enhanced by the excess of return over the cost of debt, multiplied by the debt–equity ratio. Similarly, when preferential capital is introduced, the return gets enhanced by the excess of all equity returns $[r_a(1 - T)]$ over the cost of preferential share capital r_p, multiplied by the ratio of preferential share capital to equity capital.

(h) If the desired ROE is 25%, we substitute the target ROE of 25% in the equation

$$\text{ROE} = r_a(1 - T) + (r_a - r_d)(1 - T)\, D/E$$
$$25\% = 20\%\,(1 - 0.3) + (20\% - 10\%)\, D/E$$

gives $D/E = 1.1$, implying debt of ₹5.24 crore and equity of balance ₹4.76 crore

Limitations of EBIT-EPS Analysis

The limitations of the EBIT–EPS analysis (ROI–ROE analysis) are as follows:

EBIT-EPS, though a powerful tool, suffers from limitations because it ignores (a) growth potential, (b) the risk of EBIT, and (c) the time value of money.

1. The major limitation of the EBIT–EPS analysis arises from its focus on EPS as the primary determinant of the value of the firm. It has been argued that apart from EPS, there are other important factors that create value to the firm. These factors include the growth rate, another primary determinant of value of the firm. The EBIT–EPS analysis helps in analysing the financing options and choosing the best option among them for target capital structure at a particular point of time. It ignores the long-term perspective.
2. The second important element is the risk associated with EBIT. An evaluation of the financing plan would cover the financial risk associated with the capital structure; the EBIT–EPS analysis treats EBIT as a given figure oblivious of the business risk. This objection seems rather trivial because we have recognized that risk can be segregated into two types: business risk and financial risk. Since EBIT does not change with financing structure the risk of EBIT is otherwise. The risk in EBIT can be incorporated by taking different scenarios and assigning the probabilities to each of them.
3. The EBIT–EPS analysis ignores the time value of money, a perennial obsession with all practitioners and academicians of finance.

Combined/Total Leverage

We analysed the impact of two separate kinds of fixed cost on earnings that would ultimately affect equity shareholders. These two fixed costs were (i) the fixed cost in the cost structure and the (ii) fixed cost in the financing structure. The presence of both these costs enhanced returns to shareholders. At the same time, these costs also increased the variability of these returns. In our endeavour to increase returns to equity shareholders, we made the investment of equity riskier.

These risks are known as business risk and financial risk, and are measured respectively by DOL and DFL. The aggregate risk of the firm is the combination of the two and can be defined as total leverage as percentage change in EPS due to 1% change in the sales. The total risk can be expressed as a product of the two risks, and is called Degree of Total Leverage (DTL). DTL can be expressed as:

Degree of Total Leverage (DTL) is the study of impact of changing level of sales on the EPS. It is the product of DOL and DFL. It is measure of combined risk.

$$\text{DTL} = \frac{\%\text{ change in EPS}}{\%\text{ change in sales}}$$

$$= \frac{\%\text{ change in EPS}}{\%\text{ change in EBIT}} \times \frac{\%\text{ change in EBIT}}{\%\text{ change in sales}}$$

$$= \text{DFL} \times \text{DOL}$$

$$\text{DTL} = \frac{\text{sales} - \text{variable cost}}{\text{EBIT}} \times \frac{\text{EBIT}}{\text{EBIT} - \text{interest}}$$

$$= \frac{\text{contribution}}{\text{EBIT} - \text{interest}} \qquad (17\text{-}5)$$

DTL helps in striking a balance between operating leverage and financial leverage. A firm normally assumes a particular pre-defined level of risk in its business. If the same firm decides to undertake riskier projects, the risk of the firm as a single entity will increase due to an increase in DOL. In order to keep total risk at the same level, the firm can tilt its financial leverage more in favour of equity when financing a new venture. Refer to Example 17-4.

Example 17-4 Designing Capital Structure

Safety Business Ltd has Project I running with an EBIT level of 10% of sales. Its variable cost is 60% of sales and it has interest cost of 20% of EBIT. They are considering an expansion programme equivalent to the current business level, with two mutually exclusive projects designated Project II and Project III, with the following characteristics:

	Project II	*Project III*
Variable cost (% of sales)	50	30
EBIT (expressed as % of sales)	10	10

The management of Safety Business Ltd feels that the current level of risk it has taken is adequate and it cannot accept any further risk with the addition of a new project.

Discuss how Safety Business Ltd can contain its risk at the present level. Which of the two projects, II and III, is more acceptable?

Solution

Both Project II and Project III have higher operating risks than Project I, as the proportions of fixed costs are higher than in Project I. In other words, DOL of the firm will be higher than the current DOL of Project I. Acceptance of either of the projects would alter the operating leverage. However, the total risk of the firm, as measured by DTL, may be controlled partially by adjusting the DFL. The increase in operating leverage can be partially offset by designing the capital structure in such a manner that it reduces DFL.

Any increase in risk from the present level is unacceptable, and, therefore, the firm will have to adjust DFL to examine if the desired level of risk is achievable. The total risk of the firm, i.e., DTL, is a product of DOL and DFL. The DOL of Project I is 4 (Contribution/EBIT = 40/10), as can be seen from table below. The DFL of Project I is 1.25 (10/8). Therefore, DTL of the firm is 5 (4 × 1.25), implying a 5% change in shareholders' earnings with a 1% change in sales (Note that the presence of taxes does not make any difference to the analysis).

A summary of Project I and Project II is given below.

	Project I	*Project II*	*Project I & II*
Sales	100	100	200
Variable cost	60	50	110
Contribution	40	50	90
Fixed cost	30	40	90
EBIT	10	10	20
Interest	2	?	?
EBT	8	?	?

Project II

If Project II is accepted, the firm will have income as stated in column 3 of the preceding table. DOL of the firm would become 4.5 (90/20). To keep the overall risk constant, DTL must remain at 5. This gives the new DFL:

new DFL = 5.00/4.50 = 1.11

With EBIT fixed at 20, the total interest outgo is governed by

20/(20 – interest) = 1.11

This gives a total interest of 2, which is the current level. The firm can afford no more debt. Hence, the project must be funded entirely by equity to keep aggregate risk same.

Projects III

A similar analysis with Project III would reveal that the new operating leverage is 5.5 (110 ÷ 20).

The total risk of Safety Business Ltd cannot go below 5.5 because the minimum value of DFL can be only 1. Hence, the firm must choose Project II instead of Project III to maintain the maximum acceptable risk level.

The combined position of Safety Business Ltd with Project III is presented below:

	Project I	*Project III*	*Project I & III*
Sales	100	100	200
Variable cost	60	30	110
Contribution	40	70	90
Fixed cost	30	60	90
EBIT	10	10	20

RATIOS AND INDUSTRY NORMS FOR CAPITAL STRUCTURE

The EBIT–EPS analysis or the ROI–ROE analysis incorporates the expectations of shareholders and the business environment.

By way of DOL, industry chara[...] to the extent they impact the ea[...] the shareholders, are incorporated[...] coupled with DFL, defines the magn[...] of earnings and ROE. It also incl[...] what appetite for risk the sharehold[...] have with respect to a particular project.

The capital structure must conform to the various norms prevailing in the industry and financial markets.

Financial markets that are fairly developed, however, work on well-established financing norms. These norms keep evolving with time and form the basis of lending to the firms. These norms place a constraint on the financing structure of the projects. The focus of EBIT–EPS is more oriented towards the shareholders' perspective. Lenders normally focus on the ability of the firm to service debt in terms of interest and principal obligations under normal and distress circumstances. The safety of a loan is normally assessed by financial institutions on the basis of the coverage of interest provided by earnings and cash flows.

Interest Coverage Ratio

Industry norms for the capital structure inter alia include (a) interest cover, (b) debt service coverage ratio, and (c) debt–equity ratio. These norms normally place a higher limit on the amount of debt.

One prominent ratio that is considered while providing debt is the *interest coverage ratio*. It is defined as:

$$\text{Interest coverage ratio} = \frac{\text{EBIT}}{\text{Interest}}$$

Under a 'normal' scenario, the interest cover for AutoComp is 3.00, as shown below, implying that earnings levels are three times the interest obligations.

	Bad	Fair	Normal	Good	Excellent
EBIT	50	100	150	200	250
Interest	50	50	50	50	50
Interest cover	1.00	2.00	**3.00**	4.00	5.00

If the interest cover is within acceptable norms, the loan is assumed to be safe.

The interest cover provides an impression about the safety of the interest portion of debt only. It is a relevant figure for determining capital structure because we assume continuing debt.

Cash Coverage Ratio

However, another practical consideration from the viewpoint of financial institutions is the recovery of the principal amount. The maximum tenure of a loan is generally fixed by the charters of the financial institutions. They do not assume perennial loans. To assess the chances of recovery of principal amount, the ability of the firm to provide sufficient cover is judged by the cash coverage ratio, which is defined as given below:

Cash flow coverage

$$= \frac{\text{EBIT} + \text{depreciation} + \text{non-cost expense}}{\text{Interest} + \dfrac{\text{loan instalment}}{(1-T)}}$$

Note that the cash cover adjusts the loan principal repayment by a factor of $1/(1-T)$ because repayment is done on a post-

L[...]	
Re[...]	
Inter[...]	
Tax ra[...]	
Pre Tax[...]	
Debt Serv[...]	**0.89**

On aggrega[...]mount to ₹150 lakh over the entir[...]ars, and the post-tax value of the principa[...] ÷ 0.6 = ₹833 lakh. The cash coverage ratio is [...]which is not adequate to cover the loan repayment.

$$\text{Cash flow coverage} = \frac{175 \times 5}{150 + \dfrac{150}{0.6}} = 0.89$$

A cash coverage ratio of less than 1.00 clearly is not permissible. Assuming that the financial institutions grant loans for a maximum repayment period of five years and with a minimum cash cover ratio of 1.75, we find that the maximum loan is ₹254 lakh with 10% interest and 40% tax rate. This can be done by using *Goal Seek* in *Tools* in Excel, as shown in Figure 17-5. This freezes the capital structure of AutoComp at about 25% debt ratio.

Debt Equity Ratio

The third important parameter that both financial institutions and industry follow in providing debt is the norms on the debt–equity ratio prevailing in the industry. These norms develop over a period of time and are time tested. Generally speaking, the institutions follow these norms; in cases of deviation, the reasons need to be explained. Assuming that in the auto component industry the debt–equity norm is 1:2, the debt capacity can be fixed at one-third of the cost of the project, subject to the cash flow and adequate debt service.

The cash flow approach to the determination of capital structure focuses on liquidity, solvency, and safety.

The focus of financing based on ratios and cash flows places emphasis on liquidity and safety of operations. The perspective of this analysis is more towards the debt side, rather than towards shareholders' welfare. This perspective is often misconstrued as conflicting with the interests of shareholders, but this is not so in fact. Although shareholders would crave greater returns by taking up as much debt as possible, the debt providers would permit such borrowings only within manageable and acceptable

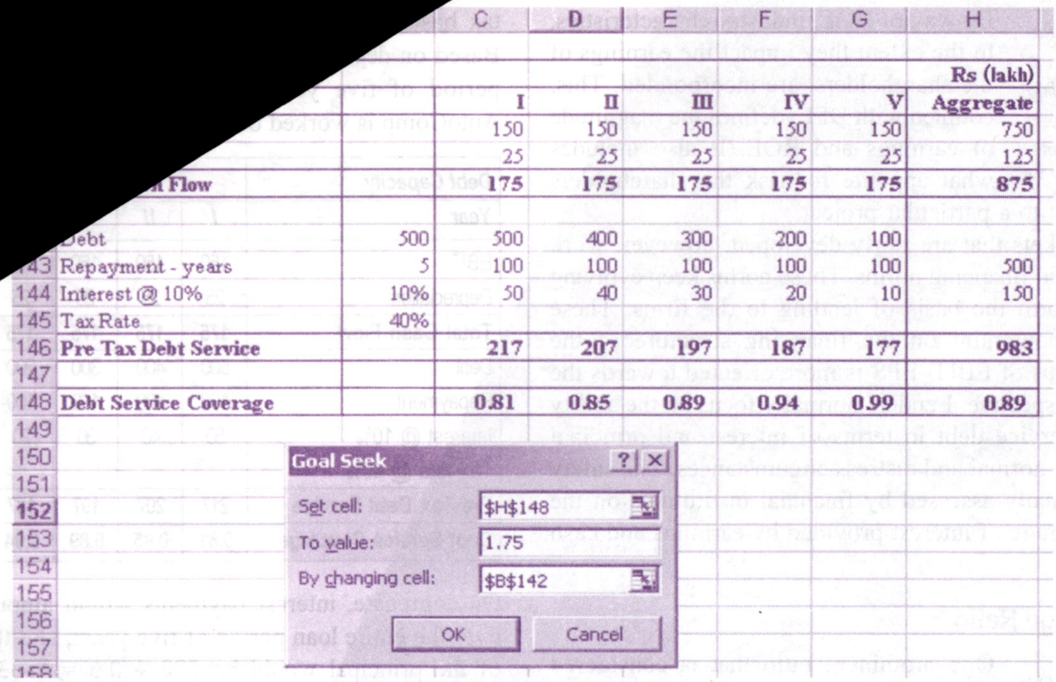

		C	D	E	F	G	H
							Rs (lakh)
		I	II	III	IV	V	Aggregate
		150	150	150	150	150	750
		25	25	25	25	25	125
	...n Flow	**175**	**175**	**175**	**175**	**175**	**875**
	...ebt	500	500	400	300	200	100
...43	Repayment - years	5	100	100	100	100	100	500
144	Interest @ 10%	10%	50	40	30	20	10	150
145	Tax Rate	40%						
146	**Pre Tax Debt Service**		**217**	**207**	**197**	**187**	**177**	**983**
147								
148	**Debt Service Coverage**		**0.81**	**0.85**	**0.89**	**0.94**	**0.99**	**0.89**

Figure 17-5 Fixing the maximum debt

limits, which ultimately is in the interest of the shareholders. Containing debt within acceptable norms would contain the risk that is ultimately borne solely by the shareholders.

DEFINING TARGET/OPTIMAL CAPITAL STRUCTURE

Arriving at the optimal target capital structure, as defined by the firms, is a complex decision that involves several strategic as well as operational choices. We discuss some of the issues that must be kept in mind, with the caution that such a discussion can never be exhaustive because in practice most capital structure decisions are situational.

Profitability

The EBIT–EPS analysis focuses upon the capital structure that maximizes EPS. Does that mean that the optimal capital structure is one that maximizes earnings to the shareholders? The answer is a difficult one to give. Most of us relate share prices to the earnings of the firm. The theory of corporate finance for capital structure echoes the same view. However, to be unambiguous, we define the optimal capital structure as the one that maximizes the value of the firm. If it coincides with the maximization of EPS, we treat that capital structure as optimal. But for several fundamental reasons such as growth prospects, interest rates, and risk perception and fictional reasons like expectations, demand and supply conditions in the financial markets, and vagaries of the market, the total focus on current EPS may be misleading. Although current EPS is an important factor affecting the value of the firm, it is not the only determinant of stock price. Hence, the focus instead must be on the value of the firm, rather than on EPS alone.

Market and operational risks

The use of debt surely enhances dividends and hence earnings to shareholders. The dividend capitalization model of corporate valuation would, therefore, rightly predict an increase in share price with increased EPS and dividend. However, the use of debt will also add to the risk of earnings. This increased risk would depress the share price. Therefore, leverage would act as a moderating and compensating tool for the valuation of the firm. The question of what degree of increase in EPS would offset increase in risk is difficult to address in an unambiguous manner.

The value of the firm is the sum of the values of its debt and equity. If the firm is financed entirely by equity, the value of the firm will be equal to that of equity. Changes in capital structure can be achieved if debt replaces some of the equity. This would cause the value of equity to change. If a firm raises 50% debt to retire 50% equity, the remaining equity would trade at a new price, which, depending upon how the debt is perceived, can be lower than, equal to, or higher than the price prevailing before the debt. If the debt is viewed positively, as a lever to increase earnings, share prices would rise. If viewed as an encumbrance to the earnings of shareholders, share value will decline. Whatever be the case, because the value of debt essentially remains constant, the value of the firm will depend upon what happens to the value of the equity. Therefore, a value maximization proposition gets translated into maximization of value to equity shareholders.

Liquidity and norms

The other important consideration in defining the target capital structure is governed by the environment in financial markets, particularly environment relating to institutional finance. The amount and/or proportion of debt is governed by its availability. Availability of loan cannot be taken for granted if the amount or proportion of loan does not conform to the norms of debt–equity ratio, debt service, etc. For the most part, such norms set a limit on the amount of borrowing. Even if an EBIT–EPS analysis may suggest higher leverage for increasing EPS, loans to the required extent may not be available. Therefore, while deciding the target capital structure, a study of financing norms is essential. One can have debts lower than prescribed but deviations on the higher side are often not permissible, except when financial restructuring is considered.

Although an EBIT–EPS analysis may focus on reduced costs and the tax advantage of debt, and financing norms may place an upper limit on borrowing capacity, the target capital structure is not purely governed by analytical considerations. There are several other issues that merit consideration in defining the target capital structure but possibly lack an analytical framework.

Financial flexibility and investment policy

Financial flexibility is one such issue for which an analytical framework is difficult to develop. Normally, investment opportunities generated from the environment are random. Therefore, the investment policy of the firm is rather hazy. Firms normally do not know what investments opportunities would be forthcoming. These uncertainties may relate to sudden technological development or acquisitions, or may result from the legal and social environment. To be well prepared to make use of any investment opportunities that arise, a firm may want to build up its borrowing capacity and as such, may refrain from making full use of its debt capacity at any point of time. An assurance that funds would be available when needed allows the management to concentrate on business and proactive environmental scanning. Valuing this assurance is extremely difficult because devising an analytical framework for it seems impossible. At this point, we recognize the fact that mobilizing debt is quicker and easier than mobilizing fresh equity. Therefore, keeping a borrowing capacity available all the time allows for considerable managerial flexibility, which is critical if no suitable investment opportunity is allowed to lapse.

Management and control

Another critical and vital issue is management control of the firm. There could be some strategic considerations of prevention of hostile take-over bids and tactical considerations of management of the enterprise on routine matters. Although not directly related to the firm's debt–equity mix, it is more concerned with the shareholding pattern of the firm. The legal environment in India prescribes two important shareholding proportions: 51% and 26%.

Apart from EBIT-EPS analysis and cash flow approach the other considerations in designing of capital structure include financial flexibility, control and quality of assets.

Control of the firm cannot be challenged if promoters hold a minimum of 51%, and any special resolution requires 75% voting in favour for acceptance. Any special resolution can be blocked by a 26% vote against. Considerations of control constrain the mobilization of fresh equity capital, because any increase in capital by way of a fresh issue would reduce existing promoters' holdings, and also add new shareholders. Even if the issue of fresh capital does not cross the critical thresholds of 51% and 26%, management becomes answerable to new shareholders, much to the discomfort of the present management or promoters. Keeping in mind the primary consideration of growth of the firm, many professionally managed firms have overlooked these thresholds of 51% and 26%, and are enjoying management control with much lesser shareholding.

Quality of asset and security

The nature and quality of the asset base also impact the capital structure. If the assets are tangible and form a good security, mobilizing debt is rather easy, and perhaps more economical when compared with a firm that derives its value from intangibles. Therefore, firms functioning in conventional areas such as steel, cement, etc., with large investments in plant and machinery, have rather easy access to loans, and can have capital structures oriented towards debt. Investments in real estate and plant and machinery are regarded as better collaterals for loans. In contrast, industries such as software development, information technology, etc., who derive their worth on the basis of human capital, have capital structures heavily oriented towards equity, as getting debt is rather difficult because of lack of confidence in the security of their assets.

CORPORATE DEBT RESTRUCTURING

Notwithstanding their best efforts and intentions, sometimes firms find themselves in financial distress due to both controllable and non-controllable factors. For the revival of such firms as well as for the safety of the money lent by creditors (including banks and financial institutions), timely support through restructuring, in genuine cases, is called for.

Corporate Debt Restructuring (CDR) refers to the reorganization of a firm's outstanding financial obligations that has the impact of reducing the debt burden of the firms in question. It is done with an objective of either decreasing the interest rate on debt obligations or increasing the time period available to pay back such obligations. Sometimes, such restructuring may also be done to replace debt obligations towards creditors with their stake in the equity capital of the firm. Whatever may be the mode of CDR, it results in reducing the debt obligations of the firms and hence, enhances their capacity to repay such obligations.

The need for a corporate debt restructuring often arises when a company is going through financial hardship and is having difficulty in meeting its obligations. In such a situation, CDR is one of the options available before such distressed firms to preclude their bankruptcy. Such firms may renegotiate their obligations with the creditors so as to bring down their debt burdens. It also saves the creditors from the hassle of going through the procedure of filing for bankruptcy that may not often recover their stake, locked up in such distressed firms, in full. From the creditors' perspective, CDR is a proactive step to prevent incipient delinquency in corporate accounts. Therefore, this system resolves the financial difficulties of the corporate sector and enables entities to become viable. Other available options to restructuring may include re-financing or filing for bankruptcy. In practice, restructuring brings to the table the interests of the company along with those of the creditors. This is what differentiates CDR from other creditor friendly approaches.

In India, CDR has gained currency in context of the rising non-performing assets (NPAs) of the banking sector. Factors such as demand contraction in export markets, increase in raw material prices (even as prices of finished goods remained inelastic), delays in project implementation, and foreign exchange derivative contracts backfiring due to adverse exchange rate movements have reduced the ability of most of the effected Indian firms to service their debt obligations, efficiently and timely. This caused the threat of rising NPAs, from industrial credits, of the banking sector and has reinforced the need for CDR. Though cyclical industries such as airlines have been in the forefront of CDR, the option has also been equally used by industries such as textiles, steel, and retail.

There are arrays of options available to help firms in distress. Depending upon what is most suited in a given situation, the debt would be restructured. Lenders would consider increasing the repayment period and convert a part of debt into convertible instruments as a part of the restructuring process under CDR. In an extreme situation, there may be a change in the management where it is found that the present set of people are not able to make a turnaround. In certain cases, the CDR package may focus upon the waiver of part of interest, concessions in payment, or converting the un-serviced portions of interests into term loans. Some CDR packages may aim at re-phasing of recovery schedules, reduction in margins, or reassessment of credit facilities including working capital. There could be instances where debt restructuring is done to reduce equity capital or to convert debentures into equity with a view to provide relief on the compulsory payment of interest on the debentures.

Countries like the UK, Thailand, Korea, Malaysia, etc. have successfully incorporated an institutional mechanism for restructuring of corporate debt. Based on their experience and to fulfill the requirement of having a similar mechanism in India, a Corporate Debt Restructuring System was evolved and detailed guidelines were issued by the Reserve Bank of India in 2001 for implementation by financial institutions and banks. CDR allows financially troubled companies with multiple lenders and loans of more than ₹20 crore to restructure those loans. CDR is a non-statutory voluntary mechanism applicable only to standard and substandard assets of banks and financial institutions with high priority given to potentially viable cases. Thus, the main concern of CDR is to revive those units that have a potential to grow.

SUMMARY

Fixed charges in the earnings statement of the firm can be used to magnify income. This is referred to as leverage. These fixed changers on the cash flow of the firm are of two types: one emanating from the cost structure and the other from the financing structure.

The manufacturing of a product generally has two types of costs: fixed and variable. The higher the proportion of fixed costs, the greater is the variability of the earnings. A firm having a larger proportion of fixed costs would show improved earnings when business conditions are good, but would exhibit poorer performances when conditions are bad; the opposite is true of a firm having a lower proportion of fixed costs. This is known as operating leverage. The degree of operating leverage (DOL) is the sensitivity of earnings to changes in sales. It is a measure of the business risk the firm carries, and is measured by the percentage change in earnings arising from a 1% change in sales.

Like fixed costs in the cost structure, firms also have fixed costs in the financing structure. These fixed charges in the financing structure arise from the use of debt. The use of more debt means a higher fixed cost by way of interest on loans. With more loans, equity is correspondingly reduced, and so is the number of shares. As interest costs increase, the sensitivity of the shareholders' return, measured as EPS or ROE, increases. A firm that uses more debt can enhance shareholder earnings in good times, but make them poorer in bad times, as compared to a firm with a lesser amount of debt. A change in shareholder earnings arising from a change in EBIT is called degree of financial leverage (DFL), which specifies the percentage change in EPS with a 1% change in EBIT. It is a measure of the financial risk that emanates from the changing capital structure of the firm.

EBIT–EPS is an analytical tool that helps in analysing the different financing plans a firm may have, to determine what is best for shareholders in terms of EPS. A graphical representation of the EBIT–EPS analysis clearly depicts the relationship of EPS with changing levels of EBIT. The slope of the line would reflect the sensitivity of EPS. The line for financing plans that use larger amounts of debt would be steeper, indicating a greater rise or fall than a corresponding change in EBIT. With prior determination of the desired level of returns to shareholders and the most likely

EBIT level, a firm may decide upon the most favourable financing plan.

The risk of returns to shareholders can be measured by the degree of total leverage, which is the product of DOL and DFL. It reflects change in EPS based on change in sales. It is a composite measure of risk, and combines business risk and financial risk.

While EBIT–EPS helps in determining a financing plan, the choice may be constrained by the prevailing norms of capital structure in the industry. The norms are often specified in terms of debt–equity ratio, debt service coverage ratio, and interest cover. These norms incorporate the opinions of the lenders on the financing structure of the firm, and could supersede the choice of the shareholders that was determined by the EBIT–EPS analysis.

The final choice of capital structure must strike a fine balance between shareholders' opinions and lenders' viewpoints. The other determinants of the target or optimal capital structure include the aspects of financial flexibility, level of control desired, and the quality of asset base the firm has.

Corporate debt restructuring is done with an objective of either decreasing the interest rate on debt obligations or increasing the time period available to pay back such obligations.

KEY TERMS

Operating leverage The impact of changing fixed cost on the operating profits of the firm is called operating leverage.

Degree of operating leverage The percentage change in operating income due to a 1% change in sales is the degree of operating leverage. It is a measure of business risk and the sensitivity of earnings to sales.

Financial leverage Financial leverage refers to the relationship between debt and earning per share.

Degree of financial leverage The degree of financial leverage is the percentage change in earning per share with a 1% change in earnings before interest and taxes.

EBIT–EPS analysis EBIT–EPS is graphical or tabular presentation of various financing plans to evaluate the impact of various levels of debt on EPS.

Degree of total leverage The degree of total leverage is the percentage change in EPS based on a 1% change in sales.

KEY FORMULAE

Degree of Operating Leverage (DOL)

$$= \frac{\Delta EBIT/EBIT}{\Delta sales/sales} = \frac{\%\text{ change in EBIT}}{\%\text{ change in Sales}}$$

$$= \frac{\text{sales} - \text{variable cost}}{\text{sales} - \text{variable cost} - \text{fixed cost}} = \frac{Q(P-V)}{Q(P-V)-F}$$

Degree of Financial Leverage (DFL)

$$= \frac{\Delta EPS/EPS}{\Delta EBIT/EBIT} = \frac{\%\text{ change in EPS}}{\%\text{ change in EBIT}}$$

$$= \frac{EBIT}{EBIT - I - D_p/(1-T)}$$

Return On Equity (ROE)

$$= \frac{(EBIT - I)(1-T)}{E}$$

$$= \left[r_a + (r_a - r_d)\frac{D}{E}\right] \times (1-T)$$

$$= \{ROI + (ROI - r_d)\ D \div E\} \times (1-T)$$

Point of Indifference

$$\frac{(EBIT^* - I_1)(1-T)}{n_1} = \frac{(EBIT^* - I_2)(1-T)}{n_2}$$

Degree of Total Leverage (DTL)

$$\frac{\%\text{ change in EPS}}{\%\text{ change in sales}}$$

$$= \frac{\%\text{ change in EPS}}{\%\text{ change in EBIT}} \times \frac{\%\text{ change in EBIT}}{\%\text{ change in sales}} = DFL \times DOL$$

$$= \frac{\text{sales} - \text{variable cost}}{EBIT} \times \frac{EBIT}{EBIT - \text{interest}} = \frac{\text{contribution}}{EBIT - \text{interest}}$$

Interest Coverage Ratio $= \dfrac{EBIT}{\text{interest}}$

Debt Service Coverage Ratio

$$= \frac{EBIT + \text{depreciation} + \text{non-cash expense}}{\text{interest} + \dfrac{\text{loan instalment}}{(1-T)}}$$

PRACTICE PROBLEMS

1. Operating Leverage

Alternatives Fuels Limited (AFL) have three ways of producing solar energy that have different composition of cost but identical levels of profit.

These alternatives denoted as A, B, and C have variable costs of 70%, 60%, and 50% respectively. The fixed cost for alternatives A, B, and C are ₹10 lakh, ₹20 lakh, and ₹30 lakh respectively for targeted level of sales of ₹100 lakh.

(a) Find out the degree of operating leverage under the three different cost structures and predict the changes in the level of profitability.

(b) Confirm your prediction with the change in level of sales by 20% in either direction.

(c) What alternative would you recommend for AFL if:
   (i) chances of achieving sales 20% higher than expected are very high?
   (ii) chances of achieving sales 20% lower than expected are very high?

Solution

(a) The decision to choose the cost structure must be based on the change of EBIT with changing level of sales, i.e. the degree of operating leverage (DOL)

The DOL for three different alternatives of cost structure is as follows.

(₹ *lakh*)

Cost Structure	A	B	C
Sales	100.00	100.00	100.00
Less: Variable Cost	70.00	60.00	50.00
Contribution	30.00	40.00	50.00
Less: Fixed Cost	10.00	20.00	30.00
Operating Profit, EBIT	20.00	20.00	20.00
DOL = Contribution/EBIT	1.50	2.00	2.50

Predicted change in EBIT based on DOL

	A	B	C
% increase in EBIT with 20% increase in sales	30%	40%	50%
% increase in EBIT with 20% increase in sales	–30%	–40%	–50%

(b) The verification of the predicted change is as follows:

₹ *lakh*

	A	B	C
For increase in sales by 20%			
Sales	120.00	120.00	120.00
Less: Variable Cost	84.00	72.00	60.00
Contribution	36.00	48.00	60.00
Less: Fixed Cost	10.00	20.00	30.00
Operating Profit, EBIT	26.00	28.00	30.00
% increase in EBIT	30%	40%	50%
For decrease in sales by 20%			
Sales	80.00	80.00	80.00
Less: Variable Cost	56.00	48.00	40.00
Contribution	24.00	32.00	40.00
Less: Fixed Cost	10.00	20.00	30.00
Operating Profit, EBIT	14.00	12.00	10.00
% increase in EBIT	–30%	–40%	–50%

(c) If chances of achieving sales 20% higher than expected are high, AFL must opt for cost Structure C; while if the chances of achieving sales 20% lower than expected are high, the firm would be better off with cost Structure A.

2. Degree of Financial Leverage

Assume that Alternatives Fuels Limited have decided the Cost Structure B. They have three alternatives of financing the project designated as Plan I, II, and III corresponding to debt levels of ₹50 lakh, 60 lakh, and 70 lakh at a cost of 12%, respectively.

Find out the degree of financial leverage (DFL) for each of the financing plan. Also find out the degree of total leverage (DTL) for each financing plan. What do DFL and DTL mean in each case?

Solution

With the selection of Cost Structure B, the degree of financial leverage is computed below for each of the Financing Plan I, II, and III.

(₹ *lakh*)

Financing Plan	*I*	*II*	*III*
Debt	50.00	60.00	70.00
Cost of debt	12%	12%	12%
Cost Structure B			
EBIT	20.00	20.00	20.00
Less: Interest	6.00	7.20	8.40
EBT	14.00	12.80	11.60
DFL = EBIT/EBT	1.43	1.56	1.72
DOL for cost structure B	2.00	2.00	2.00
DTL = DTL × DFL	2.86	3.13	3.45

DFL means the % change in the earnings of equity holders with 1% change in level of EBIT. It states the impact of capital structure on the earnings of the shareholders. For Financing Plans I, II, and III, the values are 1.43, 1.56, and 1.72 respectively.

DTL means the % change in the earnings of equity holders with 1% change in level of sales. It takes into account the cost structure and financing structure while evaluating the impact of change in sales on the shareholders' earnings. For Cost Structure B and Financing Plans I, II, and III, the values are 2.86, 3.13, and 3.45 respectively.

3. Degree of Total Leverage

Find out the DFL as well as the DTL for Cost Structure A and C in Problem 1 and for the financing Plans I, II and III in Problem 2.

As the conservative management is more concerned about the decrease in sales, what cost structure and financing structure would you prefer?

Also find out the desired cost structure and financing structure for the management that is very optimistic about increased sales volume.

Solution

Under Financing Plans I, II, and III the degree of financial leverage are found as below. DTL is computed by multiplying the DFL with the DOL of the respective cost structure.

(₹ lakh)

Financing Plan	I	II	III
Debt	50.00	60.00	70.00
Cost of debt	12%	12%	12%
Cost structure A			
EBIT	20.00	20.00	20.00
Interest	6.00	7.20	8.40
EBT	14.00	12.80	11.60
DFL = EBIT/EBT	1.43	1.56	1.72
DOL	1.50	1.50	1.50
DTL	2.14	2.34	2.59
Cost structure C			
EBIT	20.00	20.00	20.00
Interest	6.00	7.20	8.40
EBT	14.00	12.80	11.60
DFL = EBIT/EBT	1.43	1.56	1.72
DOL	2.50	2.50	2.50
DTL	3.57	3.91	4.31

Degree of Total Leverage

Cost Structure / *Financing Structure*	A	B	C
I	2.14	2.86	3.57
II	2.34	3.13	3.91
III	2.59	3.45	4.31

The preferred combination for conservative shareholders is the one that has the least degree of total leverage, i.e., Cost Structure A and Financing Plan I having DTL of 2.14 implying that 1% increase or decrease in sales would cause increase or decrease of 2.14% in the earnings of the shareholders.

The preferred combination for risk taking shareholders is the one that has the largest degree of total leverage, i.e., Cost Structure C and Financing Plan III having DTL of 4.31 implying that 1% increase in sales would cause an increase of 4.31% in the earnings of the shareholders.

4. Capital Structure and Value

Combinations Ltd is a renowned company in the business of manufacture of chemicals. Its current level of operations are as follows:

(₹ crore)

Current EBIT	12.00
Interest	3.60 (Debt of ₹30 crore at 12%)
EBT	8.40
Taxes @ 30%	2.52
PBT	5.88
Nos. of shares	2.50 crore
EPS	₹2.35 per share
Current market price	₹51.00 per share
PE multiple	21.68

Current capital structure at market values:

	₹ crore
Debt	30.00
Equity	127.50

The firm is considering an expansion plan worth ₹150 crore. Debt for amount of ₹50 crore to ₹100 crore is available at increasing cost from 12% to 13.5%. Similarly the new shares can be issued at progressively decreasing price with increasing debt. The firm has shortlisted the following six options with different amounts of debt and equity.

₹ crore	*Financing Plan* A	B	C	D	E	F
Additional equity	100.00	90.00	80.00	70.00	60.00	50.00
Additional debt	50.00	60.00	70.00	80.00	90.00	100.00
Additional shares	2.00	1.80	2.00	1.75	2.40	2.00
Additional interest	6.00	7.50	8.75	10.40	11.70	13.50
Price of share (₹)	50.00	50.00	40.00	40.00	25.00	25.00
PE multiple	20.00	22.00	25.00	20.00	12.00	7.00
Cost of debt	12.00%	12.50%	12.50%	13.00%	13.00%	13.50%

The expansion programme would result in an increase in EBIT of ₹12 crore. For different financing plans, find out the following:

(a) Revised level of earnings available to the shareholders
(b) Revised market price and EPS
(c) Value of debt, equity, and the firm
(d) Debt equity ratio and debt ratio after the expansion
(e) Plot the values of debt, equity, and firm after expansion
(f) The desired financing option

Solution

(a) Additional amount of interest and additional number of shares are as shown below for different financing plans:

Figures in crore	*Financing Plans* A	B	C	D	E	F
Additional equity	100.00	90.00	80.00	70.00	60.00	50.00
Additional debt	50.00	60.00	70.00	80.00	90.00	100.00
PE multiple (times)	20.00	22.00	25.00	20.00	15.00	10.00
Price of share	50.00	50.00	40.00	40.00	25.00	25.00
Additional shares	2.00	1.80	2.00	1.75	2.40	2.00
Cost of debt	12.00%	12.50%	12.50%	13.00%	13.00%	13.50%
Additional interest	6.00	7.50	8.75	10.40	11.70	13.50

The values of debt, equity, and the firm are worked out for different financing plans after the expansion assuming an increase in the EBIT level by ₹15 crore.

Figures in crore	*Financing Plans* A	B	C	D	E	F
Increase in EBIT	15					
EBIT	27.00	27.00	27.00	27.00	27.00	27.00
Interest	9.60	11.10	12.35	14.00	15.30	17.10
EBT	17.40	15.90	14.65	13.00	11.70	9.90
Tax	5.22	4.77	4.40	3.90	3.51	2.97
EAT	12.18	11.13	10.26	9.10	8.19	6.93

(b) Total number of shares, new EPS and the market price of the share would be as below:

	A	B	C	D	E	F
Nos. of shares, crore	4.50	4.30	4.50	4.25	4.90	4.50
EPS, ₹per share	2.71	2.59	2.28	2.14	1.67	1.54
PE multiple	20.00	22.00	25.00	20.00	15.00	10.00
Market Price, ₹	54.13	56.94	56.97	42.82	25.07	15.40

(c) The value of equity, debt, and the firm under different financing plans would be as shown below:

(₹ *crore*)

₹ *crore*	A	B	C	D	E	F
Value of equity	243.60	244.86	256.38	182.00	122.85	69.30
Value of debt	80.00	90.00	100.00	110.00	120.00	130.00
Value of the firm	323.60	334.86	356.38	292.00	242.85	199.30

(d) Debt-equity ratio and debt ratio under different financing plans would be:

	A	B	C	D	E	F
Debt-equity ratio	0.32	0.36	0.39	0.60	0.97	1.88
Debt Ratio	0.24	0.27	0.28	0.37	0.49	0.65

(e) The values of debt, equity, and the firm for increasing level of debt is as shown below:

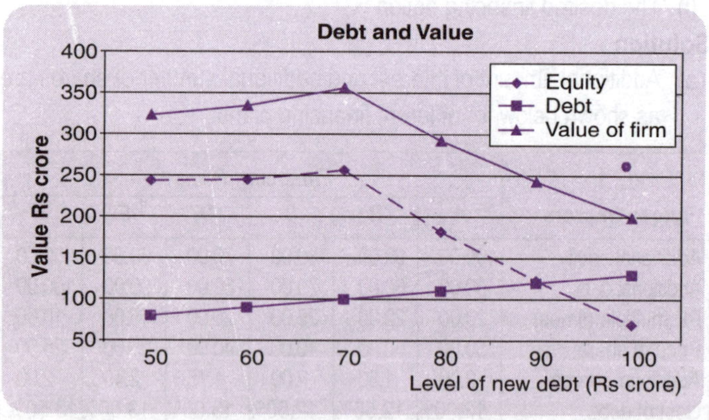

(f) It is clear from the market values in tables and the graph that Financing Plan C is the best as it maximizes the value of the firm as well as that of the equity. The firm must opt for Financing Plan C.

5. EBIT-EPS Analysis

New Ventures Limited is planning a plantation project costing ₹300 crore. It is considering two financing alternatives. Under the first alternative, it can issue shares for ₹50 worth ₹200 crore and raise the remaining ₹100 crore at 12%. Under the second alternative, it can issue shares worth ₹150 crore again at a price of ₹50 per share and raise the remaining ₹150 crore by loan at 14%. The firm pays 30% tax.

The returns from the project are extremely volatile and can be anywhere between 10% to 20% as return on the assets. This is one of the reasons that the management wants to issue lesser number of shares till the revenues stabilize.

(a) Find out the EPS under both the financing plans with return on asset varying from 10% to 20% in steps of 2.5%.

(b) Depict the relationship of EPS with EBIT under both the financing plans.

(c) What would be your recommendations if you are confident that the firm would achieve a return on asset of (i) 12.5% and (ii) 17.5%?

(d) At what level of EBIT, the two financing alternatives are indifferent to EPS?

Solution

(a) The parameters of two financing alternatives are summarized below:

₹ *crore*	*Debt*	*Equity*	*Total*	*Cost of debt*	*Nos. of shares (crore)*
Financing Plan I	100	200	300	12.00%	4.00
Financing Plan II	150	150	300	14.00%	3.00

Under Financing Plan I, the EPS at different level of EBIT is as follows:

(₹ *crore*)

ROA, %	*10.00%*	*12.50%*	*15.00%*	*17.50%*	*20.00%*
EBIT	30.00	37.50	45.00	52.50	60.00
Interest	12.00	12.00	12.00	12.00	12.00
EBT	18.00	25.50	33.00	40.50	48.00
Taxes	5.40	7.65	9.90	12.15	14.40
EAT	12.60	17.85	23.10	28.35	33.60
Nos. of shares. (crore)	4.00	4.00	4.00	4.00	4.00
EPS, (₹ per share)	3.15	4.46	5.78	7.09	8.40

Under Financing Plan II, the EPS at different level of EBIT is as follows:

₹ *crore*

EBIT	30.00	37.50	45.00	52.50	60.00
Interest	21.00	21.00	21.00	21.00	21.00
EBT	9.00	16.50	24.00	31.50	39.00
Taxes	2.70	4.95	7.20	9.45	11.70
EAT	6.30	11.55	16.80	22.05	27.30
Nos. of shares. (crore)	3.00	3.00	3.00	3.00	3.00
EPS, (₹/share)	2.10	3.85	5.60	7.35	9.10

(b) The relationship of EPS with EBIT under the two financing plans is depicted below:

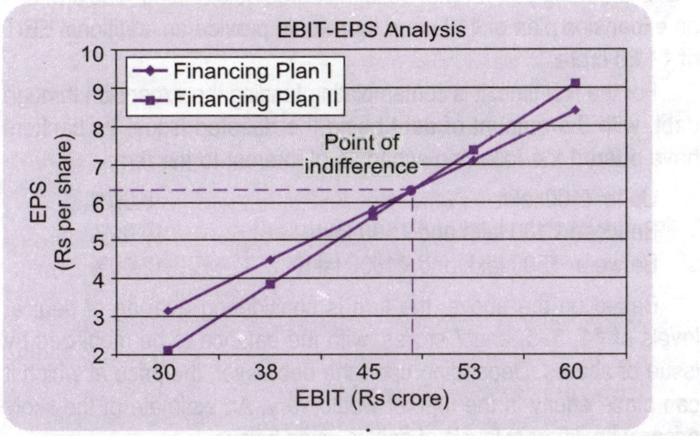

(c) The EPS for the two financing plans for ROA of 12.5% and 17.5% are:

	ROA	
EPS (₹/share)	***12.50%***	***17.50%***
Financing Plan I	4.46	7.09
Financing Plan II	3.85	7.35

For ROA of 12.5%, the EPS is higher for Financing Plan I, and hence is preferred over Financing Plan II. With ROA rising to 17.5%, Financing Plan II gives higher EPS to the shareholders and would be preferred.

(d) The EBIT level at which the two financing plans would be indifferent to the shareholder is given by:

$$\frac{(\text{EBIT}^* - I_1)(1-T)}{n_1} = \frac{(\text{EBIT}^* - I_2)(1-T)}{n_2}$$

$$\Rightarrow \quad (n_2 - n_1)\,\text{EBIT}^* = I_1 \times n_2 - I_2 \times n_1$$

$$\Rightarrow \quad (4-3) \times \text{EBIT}^* = 21 \times 4 - 12 \times 3$$

$$\text{EBIT}^* = ₹48.00 \text{ crore}$$

EXERCISES

Concept Review Questions

1. What do you understand by business risk? How can this be measured?
2. What is the degree of operating leverage and how can it be used for determining the capital structure?
3. What is meant by financial leverage? What is the measure of financial risk of the firm?
4. In what way can the degree of operating leverage and the degree of financial leverage be used to find an optimal capital structure?
5. List the various properties of the degree of operating leverage and the degree of financial leverage.
6. With the help of a graph, explain the relationship between EBIT and EPS with changing financing plans?
7. What does the point of indifference on the EBIT–EPS analysis signify? What happens when the EBIT level is (a) below and (b) above the point of indifference?
8. What are the parameters considered by financial institutions while evaluating a proposal for a loan from a firm?
9. What different factors would you consider while devising a target capital structure for (a) a cement plant, (b) a software development firm, (c) a call centre, and (d) a toll bridge company?

Critical Thinking Questions

1. A financial analyst opined that a firm must never borrow because borrowing can never be beneficial to shareholders. Fixed charges of interest would deplete the cash flows to shareholders, and thus, they would always be poorer, when compared to the shareholders of an unlevered firm, by the amount of interest paid. Do you agree with the statement?
2. According to the EBIT–EPS analysis, any project can be made attractive enough for shareholders because ROE can be improved drastically by increasing the debt ratio as per the following equation:

$$= r_a + (r_a - r_d)\frac{D}{E} \times (1-T)$$

Therefore, the firm must avail of as much debt as possible, leaving the choice of capital structure to the suppliers of debt. Do you find the statement and the conclusion valid?

3. An appraisal of a firm's proposal by a financial institution found that cash flows of the firm were not adequate for serving the 50% debt applied for by the firm, and instead offered a loan to the extent of 30%. At this level, ROE stood at 15%—the minimum shareholders expect. The firm clarified that with a reduced debt amount, ROE would fall and, therefore, the financial institution must sanction 50% debt. As a manager in the financial institution, what would be your response?

Practical Assignments

1. Pick up five top firms in the steel industry and find out their debt–equity ratio for the last 5 years. Do you find some similarities in the capital structures of these firms? On the basis of the data, develop a norm for a new firm for its capital structure.
2. Find out the following ratios for the five firms mentioned in Assignment 1.
   (a) Interest cover
   (b) Debt service coverage ratio
   (c) Debt–equity ratio

Numerical Problems

1. Operating Leverage

Beta Limited and Theta Limited operate in the same line of business of manufacture of rubber components. However, their cost structures and financing structures differ substantially. An analysis of their financial performance has revealed the following data:

₹ (lakh)	Beta Ltd	Theta Ltd
Sales	750	1100
Variable cost	300	500
Fixed cost	250	200
Operating profit, EBIT	200	400
Interest	75	80
Profit before tax	125	320

(i) Find out DOL and DFL for both.
(ii) What is your interpretation of DOL and DFL?

2. Applying Leverages
The following information is extracted from the financial statements of Rana Auto Components Ltd

	₹ lakh
Fixed cost	500
EBIT	1000
Profit before tax, PBT	800

Find out the change in PBT caused by a 3% change in sales.

3. Choosing Alternative Technologies and Operating Leverage
Sheetal Auto Components is considering the manufacture of sheet metal components with a capacity of 1200 lakh units. The project cost is estimated to be ₹100 crore.

There are three technologies, A, B, and C, available to them from three different plant manufacturers that offer similar quality, but different degrees of automation. While the overall cost of manufacture remains the same for all the technologies, the composition of costs differs, and is as follows:

Technology	A	B	C
Variable cost (₹/pc)	10	9	8
Fixed cost (₹ lakh)	1000	2000	3000

The selling price estimated by the management is ₹15 per piece, while projecting a sales of 10 crore pieces annually.

As the project is new, management also believes that sales may decline by as much as 50%.

Do you think that selection of the right technology would have a role to play in mitigating the risk of declining sales? What would you do in the circumstances?

4. Capital Structure and DFL
With the EBIT level of ₹40 crore, Sheetal Auto Components has a choice of three alternative capital structures. The project cost of ₹100 crore can be funded by debts of 25%, 40%, and 60% at costs of 10%, 11%, and 12%, respectively.

Find out DFL for the three alternative capital structures. Use the data of Problem 3.

5. EBIT–EPS Analysis and maximization of Stock Price
Rotomac Corporation is an all-equity firm with current EPS of ₹3.25. Its share is trading at ₹42, with 50 lakh shares outstanding. The firm has an expansion plan of ₹12 crore that would provide an additional EBIT of ₹1.80 crore.

For the first time, it is contemplating funding the expansion through debt, with the amount of debt being the debated issue. Its bankers have offered the following schedule of interest to the firm:

Up to ₹100 lakh	8.00%
Between ₹100 lakh and ₹500 lakh	10.00%
Between ₹500 lakh and ₹1000 lakh	12.00%

Based on the above, the firm is considering availing of debt at levels of ₹1, 3, 5, and 7 crores, with the balance to be mobilized by issue of shares. Depending upon the debt level, the price at which it can place equity in the market would vary. An estimate of the likely prices with different levels of debt is given below:

Level of debt (₹ lakh)	100	300	500	700
Price of new shares (₹)	42	42	38	36

The level of debt affects the stock valuation, and it is expected that for four different levels of debt the PE multiple would be 14 for a debt of up to ₹3 crore and would decline to 13 and 12 respectively for debts of ₹5 crore and ₹7 crore.

Consistent with the objective of maximizing the price of the share, which of the financing options would you prefer? Assume tax rate of 36%.

6. Indifferent Level of EBIT
ABC Ltd needs ₹500 lakh for an expansion plan that is expected to yield 15% return on assets. At present, its return on asset is 12%, and the firm is all-equity funded. For the proposed expansion, it has alternatives of funding the entire expenditure either through debt or equity. The following information is available:

Nos. of shares already existing	20 lakh
Price at which the shares can be issued (₹)	50
Existing interest (₹)	30 lakh
Interest rate on debt	10%
Tax rate	40%

Find out the new EPS with equity and debt financing. Also find at what level of earnings the firm is indifferent to mode of financing.

7. EBIT–EPS Analysis and Capital Structure
Modi Networks Limited is a major player in the computer hardware components industry. Some select financial data of the firm are presented below:

Capital Structure	₹ crore	Profit & Loss	₹ crore
		Sales	200
		Cost	170
Equity 6 crore	60	EBIT	30
Reserves	60	Interest	4
Debentures 10%	40	PBT	26
Total	160	Taxes 30%	7.80
		PAT	18.20

The stock of the firm is currently traded at PE ratio of 15.

The firm is considering an expansion plan costing ₹80 crore, with an EBIT of 14%. EBIT would decline due to the reduction of the sales prices of products, in order to increase sales volume.

Management has two financing plans in mind—raise the required fund by issue of debentures at 12%, or raise equity at a discount of about ₹5 on the current price.

(i) With the expansion, sales would rise to a minimum of ₹250 crore and a maximum of ₹350 crore. Examine EPS of the firm at sales levels of ₹250 crore, ₹300 crore, and ₹350 crore under the two alternatives for funding the expansion: debt and equity. Also draw a graph of EBIT and EPS.

(ii) What would the recommended mode of financing be if management believes that sales of (a) ₹325 crore and (b) ₹225 crore can be achieved?

(iii) What is the level of EBIT at which the firm is indifferent to mode of financing?

(iv) Find the value of the shares at three different levels of sales, assuming PE ratio of 12 when financed through debt and 16 when financed through equity.

CASE STUDY

Premier Casting Limited—Who Casts the Benefit?

Premier Casting Limited (PCL) had been doing excellent business for the last four years. It share value had increased four times in four years, from ₹25 to ₹100, providing returns much beyond the expectations of shareholders and management. The earnings level had jumped by about 25%. The shareholders had seen about 100% rise over the last year due to enhanced earning and re-rating of the company on the market. The price of the share was hovering around ₹100 in early March 2006 when the market was expecting an earning level of ₹23 crore and an EPS of ₹8.32. The performance of the firm for the last year and the current year, on the verge of completion, is presented in Table A.

Table A Select financial data-Premier Casting Limited

(₹ lakh)

	March 2005	*March 2006 Estimated*
EBIT	1,850	2,300
Interest	1,000	1,000
EBT	850	1,300
Taxes	306	468
EAT	544	832
Nos. of Shares (lakh)	100.00	100.00
EPS (₹/share)	5.44	8.32
PE Multiple	10.00	12.10
Price (₹/share)	54.40	100.67
Value of Equity (₹ lakh)	5,440	10,067

Buoyed by the excellent returns, the promoters of the firm assumed an aggressive stand, and were on a shopping spree for enhancing business. They were then operating at about 80% capacity utilization, and had an order book that would require production in excess of 100% capacity. They seemed to have no choice but to go for inorganic growth. Ravi Prakash (RP), the Managing Director, and his younger sibling Kavi Prakash (KP), the Dy. Managing Director, who held about 40% of the equity, were negotiating with the neighbouring First Casting Limited (FCL), a closely held company that was almost three-fourth of the size of PCL. The promoters of FCL were demanding ₹100 crore. Both the brothers thought it to be an excellent bargain, and were very keen to acquire the firm in view of promising business opportunities and the scope for enhancing their capacity, something that was needed to fulfil the orders expected in the near future.

The need for acquisition was well established, but the question of funding it was a lingering issue. The firm had always believed in the philosophy of maintaining a reasonable level of debt and equity while funding growth and business operations. KP always believed in an equal proportion of equity and debt. According to him, there could not be a finer or better balance between the two sources of funding. Their philosophy had been to pay earnings in dividend after retaining the funds required for growth, based on a debt–equity ratio of 1:1. There were no administrative or fundamental hurdles from the banks and financial institutions providing the loans. The plan was to retain only half as much money as required for growth and distribute the remaining as dividend, and thus, PCL had no ready cash available that could be used for acquisition. The elder brother was indifferent to financing questions, as he concentrated more on technical, marketing, and operational aspects.

Faced with an inadequate cash balance, mobilizing funds to the extent of ₹100 crore for the acquisition posed a major challenge. They passed on the task of finding the requisite funds, and more importantly the policy for funding, to their long-time associate and trusted Vice President Finance, Kevin Xavier (KX).

After considerable discussion regarding the expected level of earning after the acquisition of FCL, the management was convinced that EBIT would jump to about ₹35 crore from the current level of ₹23 crore. After lot of thought and lengthy deliberations with bankers, KX had three possible alternatives before him for funding the acquisition. These were:

All equity option One option was to fund the entire ₹100 crores by way of equity. This was possible by placing the shares privately with the institutional investors for the required ₹100 crore. Considering the market capitalization of ₹100 crore for the existing equity, it was indeed a difficult task. However, discussions with some private investors who looked for promising returns and not for management control had assured him that the placing of equity of an amount equivalent to the current market capitalization was possible provided the shares were offered at a discount of a minimum of 5% on the current market price. About 105 lakh additional shares would be needed, at ₹95 per share.

Debt and equity in equal proportions Another alternative was to continue with the existing funding philosophy of PCL: equal amounts of equity and debt. Assuming the same market conditions, KX believed that private investors would have no problems in subscribing ₹50 crore at ₹95 per share. Apart from issuing about 63 lakh additional shares, KX had to mobilize an equivalent amount by way of loans. Given PCL's excellent track record with lenders and its promising future, the existing lenders would gladly provide the required ₹50 crore.

All debt option Although this option was not initially in the scheme, KX thought of it when his talks with the banks revealed that they were not averse to accepting a debt–equity ratio of 2:1. As such, the entire funds could be made available by the existing lenders, or syndicated by them. KX was more than pleased to hear such commendations from his lenders.

KX presented an analysis of the three alternatives, as shown in Table B.

Table B Comparison of financing schemes

(*₹ lakh*)

Projected	*All equity*	*Equal*	*All Debt*
Funds required	10,000	10,000	10,000
Fresh equity	10,000	5,000	—
No. of fresh shares (lakh)	105.26	52.63	—
Debt issued	—	5,000	10,000
Interest rate	10%	10%	10%
Additional interest cost	—	500	1,000
EBIT	3,500	3,500	3,500
Interest	1,000	1,500	2,000
EBT	2,500	2,000	1,500
Taxes	900	720	540
EAT	1,600	1,280	960
No. of shares (lakh)	205.26	152.63	100.00
EPS (₹/share)	7.79	8.39	9.60
Expected PE multiple	15.00	12.00	9.00
Expected price (₹/share)	116.92	100.63	86.40
Value of equity (₹lakh)	24,000	15,360	8,640

Although both the brothers agreed with the projections of KX, they had differing opinions about the method of funding the acquisition. RP and KP had a look at all the alternatives. The option of mobilizing equity by privately placing shares worth ₹100 crore would mean a considerable dilution in the management stake. RP was much inclined to go by the all-equity route. He agreed with the expected PE multiple of 15 and thought that it only could be higher. With an expected price of ₹117, he thought 17% returns was good enough, despite the fact that he had witnessed a 100% growth in the stock price over the last year.

However, KP differed from his elder brother. He appreciated the virtues of equity financing over debt, but was not particularly comfortable with the reduced proportion of their equity holding if they chose the all-equity route. Any issue of fresh capital to new shareholders meant a dilution in management control. He said that their combined holding would fall to 20% from the existing 40%. Given the promising future and returns, he did not discount the possibility of hostile takeover attempts. According to him, defending a mere 20% stake could be a serious problem; most probably they would not be successful in doing so. According to him, going for equity and debt in equal proportions would be the ideal solution. 'While it captures the virtue of equity, it is also consistent with the current financing policy of the company. Even though it also meant dilution in the controlling stake the resultant holding of about 26% was reasonable, and could be defended. We could bring it back to 40% with some efforts of either buy back or open market purchase from their personal wealth,' said KP. Furthermore, KP was also concerned about the level of EPS, as it would decline from the current level of ₹ 8.32 to the projected level of ₹7.39 under the all-equity route. KP continued, 'The price appreciation is coming because of our assumption of improving PE ratio, otherwise all-equity means earning less than what we earn now. This is not what we are working for.'

Unfortunately, KX did not agree with either of the brothers. His opinion was to go in for 100% debt, as it meant retaining the same controlling equity stake of 40% in the company. Besides, EPS would show a considerable increase from the existing ₹8.32 to ₹9.60. Even though the debt–equity ratio of 2:1 would not be seen favourably by the market, KX was of the opinion that the situation was only short-term in nature. The loan would stand liquidated over a period of time and, therefore, they should have no problem in coming back to the desired long-term debt–equity level of 1:1, a practice followed traditionally.

RP could not resist from pointing out that taking debt was too risky, and was not equitable to the shareholders. 'In any case, a major part of the additional earnings of ₹12 crore is taken away by lenders. At 10% cost of debt, we straight away pay ₹10 crore. What is left for the shareholders who take all the pains of managing the business?' said RP.

'You can't prevent it happening. If we go the equity route, new shareholders would take away most of the money. In fact we get less than what we are getting now,' retorted KP.

Listening to the brothers, KX was in a dilemma, and did not know how to react.

Discuss:

1. Discuss the advantages and disadvantages of each of the financing schemes.
2. Draw an EBIT–EPS chart of the three financing alternatives.
3. Find out the points of indifference of the financing alternatives.
4. What implications does the point of indifference have for managerial decision making?

CHAPTER 18

Leasing and Hire Purchase

LEARNING OBJECTIVES

This chapter is aimed at providing the readers with

- understanding of what is a lease
- familiarization with terminology of lease transactions and with various kinds of leases
- knowledge of how to evaluate a lease proposal with net advantage of lease method and equivalent loan method
- knowledge of what are the relevant cash flows of lease
- knowledge of what adds value to the lease transaction
- good and bad reasons for a lease
- description of accounting for lease
- description of hire purchase and how is it different from a lease

DO YOUR BEST AND LEASE THE REST

SITCO Tiles Ltd (STL) is in the business of manufacturing ceramic tiles of different sizes and specifications. The company's fully automated integrated ceramic tile manufacturing facility is close to Gailpur, Rajasthan. The plant has been built in technical collaboration with the world leaders 'Sacmi Impianti' of Italy. The company falls in the mid-size segment and has its customer base spread mainly over Northern India, particularly Delhi, Haryana, Punjab, and Uttar Pradesh. The state-of-the-art manufacturing facility had enabled the company to complete its production schedule on time, but over the years, the company has been facing outbound logistics problems.

Till last year, the company had its own fleet of 20 delivery trucks (5 Tata model SFC 407 trucks and 15 full size Tata model 1210 trucks). The average life of the delivery trucks was around 5.5 years and maintenance expenditure on the trucks was increasing due to the aging fleet. At any time, if 2 or 3 delivery trucks were down or under maintenance, which is quite normal given the average life of the fleet, it meant that 10–15% of the delivery schedule of the company would get disrupted. The problem could be aggravated in times of peak demand.

The Managing Director of STL was struggling to dispose of the aging fleet of vehicles, and was intending to replace them with new vehicles. The Vice President Finance advised him that getting funds for the new vehicles from banks would be a difficult task. He was also of the opinion that the replacement of vehicles would solve the problem only temporarily. As the fleet became older, the same problem would resurface.

The Vice President Finance suggested leasing of vehicles instead. Although the company would forego the advantage of depreciation and related tax benefits, at the same time it would be entitled to charge the lease rentals as a tax-deductible expense. The problems of maintenance of fleet and also of scrapping of the trucks at the end of their useful lives would also be taken care of.

In the previous year the company, after much discussions and deliberations, entered into a leasing contract with one of the leading transport service providers 'Transco'. Since then, both the customers and the drivers of the delivery trucks have been happy. Now maintenance of the trucks is not the responsibility of the company, because the company has entered into a maintenance lease contract with Transco. As per the lease contract, Transco will recall its trucks after two years of service and will replace them with new trucks. This has improved the fuel efficiency of the fleet, as the trucks are newer, better equipped, and serviced regularly. The moment any truck goes for regular servicing or maintenance, it is replaced by Transco and as the result, the delivery schedule is strictly adhered to.

Retention of the drivers had been one of the major challenges for STL. The reduction in the average life of the fleet has reduced the turnover of the drivers, as the drivers are now happy driving these new trucks. STL is availing the benefits of owning the trucks without having to bear the associated risks and maintenance responsibilities. The lease agreement has also given STL the flexibility in planning its fleet make-up, as under the 'special clause' of the contract, STL can review its fleet make-up at any time, in the light of its business requirements, and ask Transco to alter its fleet composition as per its needs. Most importantly, STL is now able to focus on its core competence—manufacturing of ceramic tiles.

INTRODUCTION

Leasing and hire purchase are well-accepted means of acquiring specific assets that can be used by corporations without incurring a huge capital outgo, while reaping the benefits that an owner of the asset would derive. There are situations where a corporation may want to acquire an asset to exploit an opportunity but faces capital constraints. It may be apprehensive of issuing fresh equity, for capital markets may not be conducive for this purpose. Furthermore, the cost of the asset either is not large enough to warrant incurring rather high floatation costs, or the asset has a life that is not long enough to service the fresh equity perennially. For similar reasons the firm may not want to raise debt capital either. It may not be in a position to obtain further debt, or it may be too expensive.

Leasing is an asset-based financing mechanism.

Under such circumstances, leasing offers a convenient alternative source of acquiring assets that can be put to productive use by payment of rentals akin to the instalments on loans. Leasing is an asset-based finance option where an asset is given on rent by the owner to the user. By exploiting the asset, the user generates enough revenues to pay predetermined sums to the owner at periodic intervals. These periodic payments are referred to as lease rentals. Raising equity or debt involves managing the liability side of the balance sheet. In contrast, leasing or hire purchase is asset-based finance and concentrates on the asset side of the balance sheet.

LEASE

A lease is a contract in which the owner of the asset, called *lessor*, allows the use of the asset to another party, called *lessee*, for a specified period of time, referred to as the *lease period*, in exchange for periodic payments, called *lease rentals*. Most of us have entered into lease agreements of some sort at some time or the other. The hiring of a taxi for a day is the simplest example of leasing in our day-to-day life. Similarly an apartment on rent is an example of a lease where the tenant pays rent to live in the apartment owned by the landlord, for a fixed period of time as agreed upon. A typical lease is depicted in Figure 18-1.

Leasing separates ownership and usage. One who uses the asset is called lessee and the one who owns the asset is called a lessor.

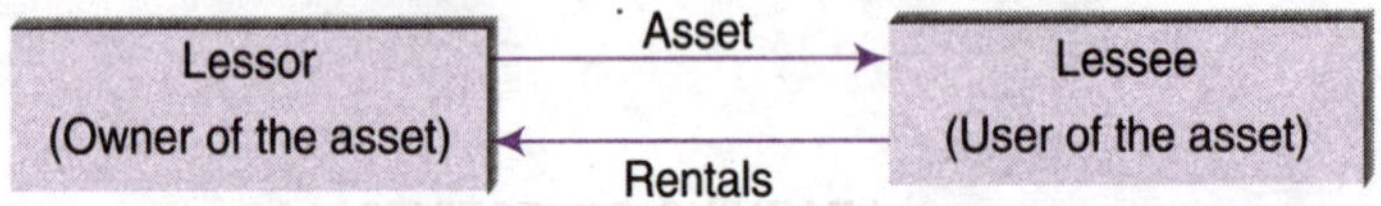

Figure 18-1 Lease arrangement

The lessor owns the asset but does not use it, while the lessee uses the asset but does not own it. Normally assets are owned by the firms because they have to put them to use for making economic gains. Under a lease, assets are not owned by the firms. Leasing provides the unique advantage of separating ownership and usage. Leasing enables (i) possession of the asset to the party interested in deriving benefits by exploiting the asset, and (ii) ownership to another party interested in deriving the benefits that are attached with ownership. Depreciation is one expense that can be claimed by the owner only and becomes important because it is a non-cash expense that is tax deductible. This reduces the burden for the owner of the asset.

FEATURES AND TYPES OF LEASES

Leases can be classified broadly in two categories—*financial lease and operating lease*. Although the economic rationale for both financial and operating leases remains the same, they are different administratively. Used as one of the means of financing the equipment, the lease agreement normally provides for an operator to accompany the equipment. The lessor does so because he/she is responsible for the running and maintenance of the equipment, or the lessee may not have the necessary skills to operate the equipment. Such lease is known as an operating lease. Hiring a taxi with its driver would be an example of an operating lease. Lease contracts not providing for an operator are termed financial leases. Fine-tuning of various clauses in the lease contracts over time has now made it increasingly difficult to differentiate between financial and operating leases.

Financial lease is a financing mode while an operating lease includes other benefits for the lessee.

Amortization of lease Amortization of lease refers to the issue of whether the full cost of the asset and profit thereon is recovered in a single lease agreement. If the entire cost and profit are recovered through lease rentals, the lease is classified as fully amortized.

When the lease rents cover the capital cost and profit, the lease is said to be fully amortized.

Operating leases are very popular in the airline industry, where aircraft are often taken on lease by an airline, and upon completion of the lease period, the manufacturer/lessor may offer the lease to another airline. The economic life of the asset exceeds the lease period, and several leases can be completed before the asset becomes obsolete. Since the period of lease is less than the economic life of the asset, the lease rentals do not cover the entire cost and profit for the lessor. Operating leases do not fully amortize the cost of the asset in a single lease contract. In contrast, a financial lease is purely an alternative means of financing the asset required by the lessee. In most cases of financial lease, the asset is purchased on the request of the lessee, who may have inadequate funds for acquisition of the asset. Given that the asset is acquired for almost exclusive use of the lessee, the lessor amortizes the asset fully by recovering the entire cost and profit thereon through lease rentals over the lease period.

While operating leases may be executed for reasons other than finance, financial leases are used purely as a financing mechanism. The reasons for having operating leases may include non-familiarity of operation of the asset by the lessee, avoidance of risk of obsolescence, and uncertainty or unwillingness to have the asset for long time. The costs of maintenance, insurance, etc., are borne by the lessor in case of operating leases, while it is the lessee who bears such costs under financial leases.

Primary and secondary lease period In case of a financial lease, the option to cancel the lease lies with the lessee while the lessor makes the investment. In order to prevent any loss that the lessor might incur because of cancellation of lease, the lease agreement is split into two distinct periods. The first period, referred to as primary lease period, prohibits cancellation of lease by the lessee, and during this period, the higher lease rentals are fixed such that the entire investment in the asset and some profit thereon for the lessor are recovered. Subsequently, the lessee can continue to permit the use of the asset for another period, called secondary lease period, with the option of cancellation given to the lessee. The lease rentals are substantially less during secondary lease period.

Risk and rewards of ownership Substance rather than the form of the lease contract must decide if the lease is financial or operating. One important test of ownership lies in assessing who bears the risk and earns the reward from the asset. In case of an operating lease, the risk and reward associated with ownership are not transferred to the lessee, and remain with the lessor, while a financial lease transfers substantial risks and rewards to the lessee from the lessor. One indication of who bears the risk and reward, though not conclusive, would be the party that bears the cost of maintenance and insurance of the asset. If the risks of loss due to impairment, theft, malfunctioning, etc. are borne by the lessee, the virtual ownership lies with the lessee. Hence, such a lease would be classified as a financial lease.

Table 18-1 provides a comparison between operating and financial lease.

Sale and Lease-back

An innovation over the financial lease is a sale and lease-back transaction. The financial lease is viewed as an alternative means of financing of an asset. The sale and lease-back transaction goes one step further, where a firm owning and using the asset sells it to another party (the lessor) and then leases it back. The sale transaction is entered into with the sole objective of generating funds for the firm. The second leg of the transaction is to keep possession of the asset and continue its use, as was the case prior to the sale. Effectively, the transaction enables raising a loan and repaying it in instalments. The sale consideration is the amount of the loan and lease rentals are the instalments. A sale and lease-back transaction is depicted in Figure 18-2 below:

Sale and leaseback is a unique mechanism of raising finance while continuing to utilize the asset.

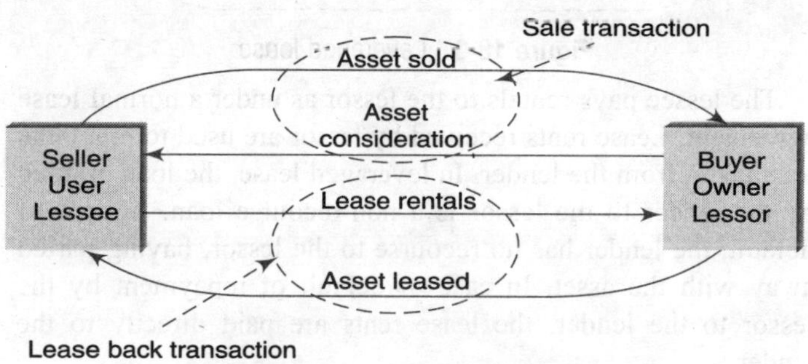

Figure 18-2 Sale and lease-back

A sale and lease-back transaction may work out to be a cheaper option than borrowing an equivalent amount of money

Table 18-1 Comparison of operating and financial lease

Feature	*Operating Lease*	*Financial Lease*
• Amortization	• Not fully amortized	• Fully amortized
• Maintenance	• By lessor	• By lessee
• Insurance	• By lessor	• By lessee
• Cancellation	• Rests with lessee only	• Generally non-cancellable
• Renewal	• Lessor reserves the right to offer lease to another party	• Lessee usually has a right to renew
• Period of lease	• Normally less than the economic life of the asset	• Normally equal to the economic life of the asset
• Disposal at the end to economic life	• Lessor repossesses the asset	• Lessee normally buys the asset
• Risk and reward	• Remains largely with the lessor	• Transferred substantially to the lessee

by pledging the asset in question. In the sale and lease- back transaction, the lessor can claim depreciation because the ownership of the asset is transferred. However, at the same time the seller foregoes an equal amount of depreciation. If the value of the depreciation tax shield is less to the seller of the asset than it is for the buyer, sale and lease-back becomes a cheaper alternative to borrowing.

Another reason why the sale and lease-back transaction may be a better economic substitute to a loan lies in the strength of the security. In the sale transaction, the lessor becomes the owner, while in the lending transaction, the user remains the owner of the asset and pledges it to the lender to secure funds. Legal ownership of the asset is considered a better security than a pledge of the same asset against a loan.

Leveraged Lease

In a leveraged lease, there are three parties involved. As the name suggests, a leveraged lease implies acquisition of an asset by borrowing. Beside the lessor and the lessee, there exists a lender who finances the acquisition of the asset for the lessor, who in turn leases it out to the lessee. A schematic diagram of a leveraged lease is presented in Figure 18-3.

A leveraged lease involves raising a loan for the acquisition of an asset and then leasing the same to the lessee.

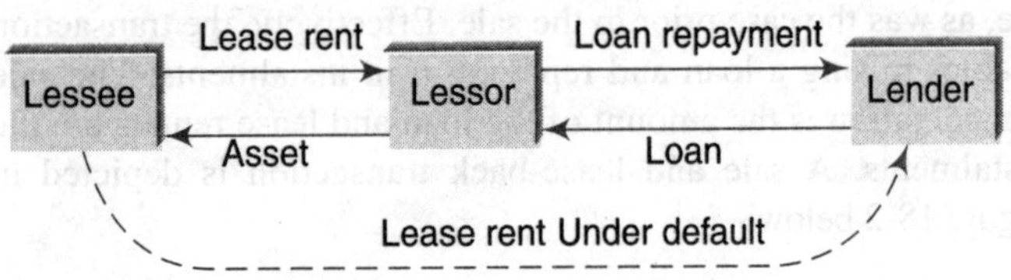

Figure 18-3 Leveraged lease

The lessee pays rentals to the lessor as under a normal lease agreement. Lease rents received by lessor are used to repay the loan taken from the lender. In leveraged lease, the loan granted by the lender to the lessor is a non-recourse loan. In case of default, the lender has no recourse to the lessor, having parted away with the asset. In case of default of repayment by the lessor to the lender, the lease rents are paid directly to the lender.

LEASE vs BUY DECISION

All leases, especially financial leases, are substitutes for outright purchase of the asset. As a capital budgeting decision the lease option seems irrelevant. If a project or acquisition is acceptable with our standard NPV analysis, it need not be evaluated again if the option is to lease the asset. A lease decision has to be viewed as an alternative mode of financing, and does not impact the decision to acquire an asset per se. Leasing as a mode of finance cannot make an unacceptable project acceptable, or vice versa, except in rare circumstances where projects have extremely marginal positive or negative NPVs. A marginally negative NPV project may become a marginal positive NPV project if leasing is a cheaper alternative to borrowing.

Leasing is a financing decision and not an investment decision.

Having made the decision to acquire the asset, the question of whether to buy the asset or lease it arises. The analytical tool used for evaluation of the lease proposal as against buying is to compare the net present value of the cost of lease option with that of the buy option. Naturally, if the NPV of the cost of lease option is smaller than the NPV of the cost of buying option, one prefers to lease.

Cash Flows of Lease

For evaluation of lease or buy proposal, one does not need to concentrate on the income side of the cash flows, since the acquisition of asset either by leasing or buying does not impact the revenue generation capacity of the asset in question. A comparison of the cost of lease and the cost of buy should provide sufficient data to make a financial decision.

Differential cash flows of the lease form the basis of evaluation of a lease proposal. These differential cash flows relate to avoiding capital cost, paying lease rents net of taxes, and foregoing the depreciation tax shield.

To evaluate a leasing proposal, we examine the differential cash flows that are associated with leasing, i.e., the cash flows that exist with one option but are absent from the other option. Although there could be various types of cash flows specified in a lease agreement, there are three very prominent, distinct, and basic cash flows, which are common in each lease agreement. These are:

1. *Capital cost of the asset:* Initial investment is absent in the lease option, but cash outflow must occur in the purchase option for possessing the asset.
2. *Payment of lease rents:* Periodic payments of lease rents are made in the lease option but are absent in the purchase option. Lease rents paid by the lessee are a deductible expense for tax purposes. The effective cash outflow of lease rents will be net of tax.
3. *Depreciation tax shield:* Although depreciation is not a cash flow, the tax shield offered by it is equivalent to cash. The tax shield of depreciation is available in the purchase option but is absent in the lease option.

Besides the three cash flow items, there could be several others items of cash flows depending upon the lease agreement, characteristics of the asset, cost savings, etc. In the buy option, the salvage value will be realized by the owner but would not be available to the lessee. Similarly, certain front-end payments like lease management fee are often payable at the beginning of the lease. Further lease agreements would specify who would bear asset-related expenses like repairs, insurance, annual maintenance contracts, etc. If these expenses are different for the lease and buy options, they have to be considered in the financial analysis of the lease.

Expenses or cash flows common to both the options need not be considered while evaluating a lease proposal. Expenses such as electricity, operator's salary, rent for housing the asset, etc., have to be incurred by the user, irrespective of whether the asset is leased or bought. Similarly, revenues generated by the asset, cost savings affected when the asset replaces an old one, extra production due to improved quality of the asset, etc., are items that do not change with the manner in which the asset is acquired. Such cash flows of either income or cost become irrelevant to the analysis of lease proposals.

As an example, consider a proposal to lease a new car that is replacing an old one. The new car offers many savings over the old car, such as those stated below:

1. The new car uses diesel as fuel instead of expensive petrol, and has a fuel efficiency of 15 km/litre as against 10 km/litre for the old vehicle. Use of cheaper fuel and better fuel efficiency would result in savings of ₹20,000 per annum.
2. The new car, being more expensive, would attract higher insurance premiums of ₹5,000 per annum.
3. The new car would need little repair and maintenance, and result in savings of ₹30,000 per annum.
4. The new car would provide service for an additional 4 years, as compared to the old vehicle.

Do we consider all the savings and additional benefits that the new car offers over the old one while evaluating the proposal to lease or buy? Certainly not! All the cash flows that result from the replacement of the old vehicle with the new one are relevant for the capital budgeting exercise where the decision to replace the old asset is evaluated. Having made the decision to replace the car, the next stage of evaluation is how to acquire the asset, i.e. through lease or outright purchase. For evaluating lease proposals, most such cash flows become irrelevant.

EVALUATING FINANCIAL LEASE

Based on the cash flows of the lease and buy options, there exist two methods to evaluate a lease vs buy decision. These methods provide the same result. They are—(1) net advantage of leasing method; and (2) equivalent loan method.

There are two methods to evaluate a lease – Net Advantage of Lease Method and Equivalent Loan Method.

Let us consider an example to understand the process of evaluation of lease. Assume that Rama Taxi Company is planning to introduce a fleet of new cars. It has the option of leasing or buying the cars. Each new car costs ₹10 lakh and has been offered on lease by a financing firm on a lease rent of ₹3.00 lakh for a period of 5 years. Being a financial lease, the lessee is responsible for all repairs, maintenance, and insurance. If leased, the firm cannot claim depreciation, of 20% on SLM basis, on the car. The firm pays tax at 40% and foregoes the benefit of tax shield on depreciation if the car is leased. For simplicity, we assume no salvage value of the car after useful life of 5 years.

Net Advantage of Leasing Method

Net advantage of leasing (NAL) method concentrates on the incremental advantage of leasing the asset over buying it. This advantage is expressed in terms of differential cash flows of lease over buying, which are as below:

Rama Taxi Company, by opting to lease each car, would

1. Avoid the capital expenditure of ₹10.00 lakh
2. Forego the depreciation tax shield of 40% on ₹2.00 lakh for 5 years
3. Incur cash out flow equal to the lease rentals of ₹3.00 lakh for 5 years
4. Save tax on the lease rents at 40% of ₹3.00 lakh for 5 years.

Table 18-2 shows the cash flows relevant for analysis of lease proposal, with negative signs (–) indicating cash outflow.

Apart from avoidance of capital cost, foregoing the depreciation tax shield, and after-tax outflow of lease rents, another aspect of the saving of opportunity cost of capital requires some elaboration. One may argue that by leasing, the firm saves the opportunity cost of capital resulting from avoidance of capital cost equal to the value of the asset to be leased. As in cases of capital budgeting, this aspect would be considered in the discount rate used in arriving at the present value of the cash flow.

Decision Rule

Under the NAL method, the present value of the differential cash flows of lease and buy options is computed. If it is greater than 0 we lease, otherwise we buy.

The last row of Table 18-2 provides the differential cash flows for the lease period, referred to as net advantage of leasing over buying. To make a decision in favour of or against leasing, we calculate the net present value of the differential cash flows, i.e., NAL and adopt the following rule:

If NPV of NAL > 0; Lease the asset
If NPV of NAL < 0; Buy the asset

Table 18-2 Cash flows; lease vs buy

(₹ '000s)

Year	*0*	*1*	*2*	*3*	*4*	*5*
If leased:						
Pay Lease Rent		-300.00	-300.00	-300.00	-300.00	-300.00
Less: Tax Saved on Lease Rents (40%)		120.00	120.00	120.00	120.00	120.00
Post tax cash flow of lease		–180.00	–180.00	–180.00	–180.00	–180.00
If Bought:						
Initial Cost	-1,000.00					
Depreciation		200.00	200.00	200.00	200.00	200.00
Tax Saved on Depreciation (40%)		80.00	80.00	80.00	80.00	80.00
Post-tax Cash Flows of Buying	–1,000.00	80.00	80.00	80.00	80.00	80.00
Cash Flow (Lease – Buy)	1,000.00	–260.00	–260.00	–260.00	–260.00	–260.00

A positive NPV would indicate that leasing is cheaper than buying and negative value signifies advantage of buying over leasing.

Deciding the discount rate The rate at which one must discount the cash flows must be consistent with the risk associated with them. Alternatively it could be the opportunity cost of capital. While making a comparison with the buying option, one would argue that the appropriate rate of discount should be the WACC of the firm computed on the basis of target capital structure using market weights for equity and debt. However this argument does not reflect the factual position with respect to the cash flows that are being evaluated. It would have been appropriate to use WACC as discount rate if the cash flows being discounted were carrying the same risk as that of the operational cash flows of the firm. This is not the case with the cash flows of the net advantage of leasing, as shown in Table 18-2.

We take an alternative view of the leasing transaction. As mentioned earlier, leasing is regarded as a substitute for borrowing. Lease rents can be deemed as payment of interest and the principal of the loan equivalent to the capital cost of the asset. Furthermore, these payments are certain and are not dependent upon environmental factors that normally affect the operational cash flows of revenue and cost. Apparently, lease rents do not carry the same risk as operational cash flows and hence cannot be discounted with WACC.

The factors that determine the cash flows of NAL are the rates of depreciation and tax. Any change in rates of depreciation or tax would render variability to the cash flows of leasing. If rates of depreciation and the corporate tax are assumed to be fixed, the tax shields of lease rents and depreciation are also certain and free from risk. The little risk that the cash flows are subjected to emanates from the assumption that the firm will generate enough income to pay taxes. Another element of risk may come from the possibility of change in the tax rate in future.

Differential cash flows of the lease being certain the relevant discount rate is the post tax cost of debt and not WACC, as is common with capital budgeting exercise.

In view of the facts that (a) lease rents are more like debt service payment, and (b) cash flows of lease are not subject to the same risk as operational cash flows, the appropriate rate of discounting the cash flows of leasing is the post-tax cost of debt. In case one wants to provide for (i) the continued ability of the firm to generate taxable income in future to avail tax deductibility of lease rents and depreciation, and (ii) possibility of change in the rates of depreciation for tax purposes and corporate tax rate, one may add a small premium to the post-tax cost of debt to have an extremely appropriate discount rate, truly reflecting the nature and risk of the cash flows of lease.

In view of the facts that depreciation rates and corporate tax rates seldom change, and when they do, the changes are small, we follow the practice of using post-tax cost of debt as discount rate. A remark about use of post-tax cost of debt rather than pre-tax cost is in order here. Recall that while computing the cost of capital we used post-tax cost of debt and ignored the interest tax shield from the cash flows. Continuing with the same practice, we do not include the interest cost and use post-tax cost of debt for discounting the cash flow. Post-tax cost of debt captures the tax shield of the interest and justifies the exclusion of interest tax shield from the cash flows of lease. For elaboration refer to Example 18-3.

Reverting to Rama Taxi Company, we have net advantage of leasing cash flows as given by the last row of Table 18-2, reproduced as Table 18-3. Assuming that the post-tax cost of debt of Rama Taxi Company is 10%, we find the present values of the cash flows. If Net Advantage of Leasing in present value terms is positive we go for lease, otherwise we buy. The present value of NAL at 10% comes to + ₹14,400, indicating that Rama Taxi Company must lease the car.

Table 18-3 Cash flows; lease vs buy

(₹ '000s)

Year	*0*	*1*	*2*	*3*	*4*	*5*
Cash Flow (Lease – Buy)	1,000.00	–260.00	–260.00	–260.00	–260.00	–260.00
Present Value at 10%	1,000.00	–236.36	–214.88	–195.34	–177.58	–161.44
Net Advantage of Leasing (Discount at 10%)						**14.40**

Example 18-1 Net Advantage of Leasing

XYZ Corporation is planning to procure a server for IT applications costing ₹45 lakh. Due to fast changing developments in the field of information technology and to avoid the risk of obsolescence, the firm is considering leasing the server for a period of 3 years at a rental of ₹18 lakh per annum payable in arrears. There is no salvage value for the server after 3 years. Alternatively, the firm can buy the server by borrowing at 12%. The firm pays tax at 40%. The depreciation rate that can be claimed by the firm is 33.33%.

(a) Find whether it is beneficial for XYZ Corporation to lease the server or buy it.

(b) If the salvage value is reckoned to be ₹3 lakh at the end of 3 years, does your decision change?

Solution

(a) Following data about the equipment is available.

	(₹ lakh)		(%)
Cost of Equipment	45.00	Cost of Debt (Pre-tax)	12.00%
Lease Rentals	18.00	Cost of Debt (Post-tax)	7.20%
Salvage Value	0.00	Rate of Depreciation	33.33%
Life (Years)	3.00	Tax Rate	40.00%

Cash flows of lease are as follows:

(*₹ in lakh*)

Year	*Present Value*	*0*	*1*	*2*	*3*
A. Lease Option					
Lease Rentals			−18.00	−18.00	−18.00
Tax Saved on Lease Rents			7.20	7.20	7.20
Cash Flow – Lease		0.00	−10.80	−10.80	−10.80
A. Present Value (Lease)	−28.24	0.00	−10.07	−9.40	−8.77
B. Buy Option					
Initial Cost		−45.00			
Depreciation			15.00	15.00	15.00
Tax Saved on Depreciation			6.00	6.00	6.00
Cash flow		−45.00	6.00	6.00	6.00
B. Present Value (Buy)	−29.31	−45.00	5.60	5.22	4.87
Net Advantage of Leasing NAL	(*A* – *B*)	45.00	−16.80	−16.80	−16.80
Present Value of NAL	1.07	45.00	−15.67	−14.62	−13.64

NAL is > 0 and hence we must go for lease. Since net present value of the costs of lease option is less by ₹1.07 lakh, it costs less to lease the server, and hence, XYZ Corporation must go for lease.

(b) If there is salvage value at the end of three years the buy option may become more valuable to the extent of increased cash flow due to salvage value realized. However, the firm will have to pay taxes if there is profit on sale of asset. In case there is a capital loss it would result in saving of tax on the operational income. The cash flows for buy option are shown below with depreciation charged to the lessor to the extent of salvage value at ₹14 lakh each year and salvage value realized.

(*₹ lakh*)

Year	*Present value*	*0*	*1*	*2*	*3*
Initial Cost		−45.00			
Depreciation			14.00	14.00	14.00
Tax Saved on Depreciation			5.60	5.60	5.60
Salvage Value Realized					3.00
Tax Saved on Salvage					0.00
Cash flow		−45.00	5.60	5.60	8.60
Present Value (Buy)	−27.92	−45.00	5.22	4.87	6.98
Net Advantage of Leasing NAL (*A* – *B*)		45.00	−16.40	−16.40	−19.40
Present Value of NAL	−0.32	45.00	−15.30	−14.27	−15.75

CAUTION: Realization of salvage value is an operational cash flow and must be discounted at WACC of the firm and not at cost of debt. In the absence of WACC the cash flow pertaining to the salvage value is also discounted at post-tax cost of debt.

The present value of buy decision is lesser than that of lease option. In case the salvage value is realizable, the decision to buy rather than lease is more economical (by an amount of ₹0.32 lakh).

Practical Considerations in Cash Flows of Lease

The practical situations in leasing are somewhat different than assumed in the analysis. Some of these differences are stated below.

1. *Lease rents in arrears or advance:* Normally lease rentals are payable in advance and not in arrears as was assumed in the analysis. Caution must be taken in reflecting the cash flows in appropriate periods and discounting them. However, tax relief is based on accrual basis and hence the lease payment made in advance would be eligible for tax deductibility in the next period and not in the same period as that of payment. Refer to Example 18-4.

While computing cash flows of lease one must consider the terms and conditions of the lease agreement, which specifies the relevant cash flows.

2. *Different methods and rates of depreciation:* Similarly, the rates and methods of depreciation for tax purposes and for reporting purposes are often different. One should use the method and rates applicable for tax purposes to evaluate lease proposals. Refer to Example 18-2.
3. *Front-end fee:* Leasing firms also charge some management fee, which must be included in the cash flow net of taxes in the same year.
4. *Salvage value:* When an asset is bought, the owner recovers some amount of the asset by selling it after the useful life is over. In practice, the asset may continue with the user. However for evaluation purposes all capital budgeting proposals are analysed for the period extending up to the useful life of the project only. Thereafter it is deemed abandoned, and all salvage values are assumed to be realized. The net advantage of leasing would reduce by the present value of the salvage realized. Further salvage value would result in savings or liability for taxes, depending upon the book value then. The net present value of NAL must be adjusted for salvage value net of taxes. Remember to use appropriate discount rate (mostly WACC of the lessee firm) while discounting the salvage value, as it is an estimate and is subject to the usual risk, equal to that of operational cash flows of the firm.

Example 18-2 Leasing with WDV Depreciation

A firm is has to install a generator set costing ₹1500 lakh. A leasing firm has offered it on lease, for a period of its useful life, for five years on a lease rent of ₹450 lakh per annum. Alternatively, the firm can buy the generator by borrowing at 20%, claim depreciation of 25% on Written Down Value basis, and realize its salvage value of ₹100 lakh. All other costs remain identical whether the firm leases or buys the generator. Find if the firm should lease the generator.

Solution

The data required for analysis of decision is presented below:

	₹ lakh		(%)		₹ lakh		%
Cost of Equipment	1500.00	Tax Rate	35.00	Lease Rentals p.a.	450.00	Cost of Debt (Pre-tax)	20.00
				Salvage Value	100.00	Cost of Debt (Post-tax)	13.00
				Life (Years)	5.00	Depreciation WDV	25.00

Year	*PV*	*0*	*1*	*2*	*3*	*4*	*5*
Lease Option							₹ lakh
Lease Rentals			–450.00	–450.00	–450.00	–450.00	–450.00
Tax Saved on Lease Rents			157.50	157.50	157.50	157.50	157.50
Cash Flow – Lease			–292.50	–292.50	–292.50	–292.50	–292.50
Present Value (Lease)	–1028.79		–258.85	–229.07	–202.72	–179.40	–158.76
Buy Option							
Initial Cost Saved		–1500.00					
Tax Saved on Depreciation*			131.25	98.44	73.83	55.37	41.53
Salvage Value**							100.00
Tax Saved on Salvage							89.58
Cash Flow – Buy		–1500.00	131.25	98.44	73.83	55.37	231.11
PV of Cash Flow – Buy	–1096.19	–1500.00	116.15	77.09	51.17	33.96	125.44
Net Advantage of Lease		1500.00	–423.75	–390.94	–366.33	–347.87	–523.61
PV (NAL)	67.40	1500.00	–375.00	–306.16	–253.88	–213.36	–284.20
*Tax Saved on Depreciation							
Book Value in Beginning			1500.00	1125.00	843.75	632.81	474.61
WDV Depreciation 25%			375.00	281.25	210.94	158.20	118.65
Book Value in end			1125.00	843.75	632.81	474.61	355.96
Tax Saved on Depreciation			131.25	98.44	73.83	55.37	41.53
**Salvage Value@							100.00
Tax on Salvage Value							
Book Value							355.96
Profit							–255.96
Tax Saved							89.58

@Here again the cash flow pertaining to the realization of salvage value is discounted at post-tax cost of debt. In practice the discount rate must be WACC of the firm.

The lease option has lesser cost by ₹67.40 lakh in present value terms and hence the generator must be leased.

Example 18-3 Leasing and Borrowing

In Example 18-2, the firm actually borrows at 20% per annum for 5 years with repayment of loan in equated annual instalment payable at the end of the year. How would you evaluate the decision to lease or borrow?

Solution

Using the same parameters of cost of borrowing, tax rate, and life of the machine we can compute the cash flow that will consist of (a) the payment of instalments, (b) savings of tax on depreciation, (c) savings of tax on the interest portion of the instalment, (d) the cash flow for the salvage value, and (e) the tax advantage/disadvantage over the salvage value.

Year		*1*	*2*	*3*	*4*	*5*
(a) Instalment Paid		–501.57	–501.57	–501.57	–501.57	–501.57
Tax Saved on Interest						
Outstanding - Beginning		1500.00	1298.43	1056.55	766.29	417.97
EMI in Arrears		501.57	501.57	501.57	501.57	501.57
Interest on Loan		300.00	259.69	211.31	153.26	83.59
Principal Repaid		201.57	241.88	290.26	348.31	417.97
(b) Tax Saved on Interest		105.00	90.89	73.96	53.64	29.26
(c) Tax Saved on Depreciation		131.25	98.44	73.83	55.37	41.53
(d) Salvage Value						100.00
(e) Tax on Salvage Value						89.58
Book Value	355.96					
Profit/Loss	–255.96					
Cash Flow - Borrow (a to e)		–265.32	–312.24	–353.78	–392.56	–241.20
Present Value	–1096.19	–234.80	–244.53	–245.19	–240.76	–130.91

We find that the present value of the loan instalment with tax shield on interest considered is identical to the one calculated under buy option in Example 18-2.

Example 18-4 Lease Rents Payable in Advance

Ankit Software Limited has to install 100 computer terminals for their call centre business. Each terminal costs ₹1.20 lakh. Because of fast changing technology, the firm will have to replace the terminals in 3 years with advanced versions by selling each terminal for a paltry ₹20,000. The firm can depreciate the computers' at 40% on WDV basis, and borrow at 12%. The firm pays tax at 40%. The weighted average cost of capital for Ankit Software is 10%.

A leasing company has offered these computers on 3 years' lease at an annual rent of ₹50,000 per terminal per annum payable in advance. Lease rents include expenditure on repair and maintenance, which otherwise would be 2%, 5%, and 8% respectively. Evaluate the proposal of the leasing company for Ankit Software, and advise for or against the leasing option.

Solution

	₹ lakh		%
Cost of Equipment	120.00	Tax Rate	40.00
Lease Rentals in Advance	50.00	Cost of Debt (Pre-tax)	12.00
Salvage Value	20.00	Cost of Debt (Post-tax)	7.20
Life (Years)	3.00	Cost of Capital	10.00
		Rate of Depreciation	40.00

(*₹ in '000s*)

Year	***Present value***	***0***	***1***	***2***	***3***
Lease Option					
Lease Rentals		–50.00	–50.00	–50.00	
Tax Saved on Lease Rents			20.00	20.00	20.00
Cash Flow – Lease		–50.00	–30.00	–30.00	20.00
Present Value (Lease)	–87.86	–50.00	–27.99	–26.11	16.23
Buy Option					
Initial Cost		–120.00			
Depreciation					
Opening Value of the Asset			120.00	72.00	43.20
Depreciation WDV			48.00	28.80	17.28
Closing Value			72.00	43.20	25.92
Tax Saved on Depreciation			19.20	11.52	6.91
Cash Flow – Buy - Certain		–120.00	19.20	11.52	6.91
(a) Present Value at Post-tax Cost of Debt		–120.00	17.91	10.02	5.61
Operational Cash Flows					
Salvage Value Realized					20.00
Book value ₹25.39 lakh					
Tax Saved on Salvage					2.37
Expenses on Repairs			2.40	6.00	9.60
Cash flow – Buy – Operational		0.00	–2.40	–6.00	12.77
(b) Present Value (Buy) at WACC		0.00	–2.18	–4.96	9.59
TOTAL PV – Buy (a + b)	–84.00	–120.00	15.73	5.07	15.20
Present value of NAL	–3.85	70.00	–43.71	–31.17	1.03

Since the present value of NAL is negative, the firm must borrow.

Evaluating Operating Lease

The evaluation of an operating lease is no different than that of a financial lease. Recall that the major difference between the financial lease and the operating lease that has cash flow implication is the answer to the question of who bears certain operating expenses related to the asset. For example, the lease agreement may contain a clause that the maintenance of the asset would be undertaken by the lessor. Instead, if the asset is bought, the expense on maintenance would be incurred by the lessee, and hence must be incorporated in the differential cash flows of leasing.

Evaluation of an operating lease is no different than financial lease except that there could me more items of cash flows in an operating lease.

After including such cash flows pertaining to the acquisition of asset in the framework of the lease or buy decision, care must be taken in choosing the right discount rate for arriving at the present value of such cash flows. These cash flows cannot be discounted at post-tax cost of debt as the expenses for maintenance are estimates only and face the same amount of risk as the other operational cash flows. Example 18-5 will illustrate the point better.

Example 18-5 Evaluation of Operating Lease

Innovative Bridges Limited (IBL) is planning to buy a specialized crane for use in various projects. The manufacturer of the crane has offered it on lease for a period of 4 years at a lease rent of ₹20 lakh per annum payable in advance. The lease rent includes cost of operator, maintenance, and insurance. Alternatively IBL can buy the crane outright at ₹50 lakh, but will have to bear the cost of operator, estimated at ₹5 lakh per annum with an annual increase of 10%, and maintenance cost, estimated at ₹6 lakh for the first year, with 20% annual increase. If the crane is bought outright the manufacturer has indicated willingness to take back the crane for furbishing at ₹15 lakh. Cranes are grouped under items eligible for 35% depreciation on WDV basis. IBL can arrange a loan at 10%, while WACC is placed at 12%. IBL pays tax of 40%. Find whether the firm should lease the crane or buy it.

Solution

The data given is tabulated as follows:

	₹ *lakh*		%
Cost of Equipment	50.00	Tax Rate	40.00
Lease Rentals	20.00	Cost of Debt (Pre-tax)	10.00
Salvage Value	15.00	Cost of Debt (Post-tax)	6.00
Life (Years)	4.00	WACC (Post Tax)	12.00
		Depreciation WDV	35.00%

Cash Flows of Leasing (₹ *in lakh*)

Year	*NPV*	*0*	*1*	*2*	*3*	*4*
A. Lease Option						
Lease Rentals		–20.00	–20.00	–20.00	–20.00	
Tax Saved on Lease Rents			8.00	8.00	8.00	8.00
Cash Flow – Lease		–20.00	–12.00	–12.00	–12.00	8.00
Present Value (Lease)	**–45.74**	**–20.00**	**–11.32**	**–10.68**	**–10.08**	**6.34**
B. Buy Option						
(i) Capital Cost & Depreciation Tax Shield						
Initial Cost		–50.00				
Depreciation[1]			17.50	11.38	7.39	4.81
Tax Saved on Depreciation[1]		7.00	4.55	2.96	1.92	
Cash Flow - B (i)		**–50.00**	**7.00**	**4.55**	**2.96**	**1.92**
Present Value B (i)	**–35.34**	**–50.00**	**6.60**	**4.05**	**2.48**	**1.52**
Discounted at post tax cost of debt						
(ii) Operational Savings						
Operator's Salary			–5.00	–5.00	–5.00	–5.00
Maintenance Cost			–4.00	–4.80	–5.76	–6.91
Total Operational cost			–9.00	–9.80	–10.76	–11.91
Tax Saved			3.60	3.92	4.30	4.76
Operating Cost (Net of tax)			–5.40	–5.88	–6.46	–7.15
(iii) Salvage Value[2]						
Cash Flow (Net of Tax)						12.57
Total B (ii) and B (iii)			–5.40	–5.88	–6.46	5.42
B. Present Value	**–10.66**		**–4.82**	**–4.69**	**–4.60**	**3.45**
Discounted at Post-tax WACC						
Net Advantage of Leasing						
A – B (i) (ii) & (iii)	**0.26**	**30.00**	**–13.10**	**–10.04**	**–7.96**	**1.37**
[1]Depreciation						
Book Value – Beginning			50.00	32.50	21.13	13.73
Depreciation 35% WDV			**17.50**	**11.38**	**7.39**	**4.81**
Book Value – End			32.50	21.13	13.73	8.93
[2] Salvage Value Net of Tax						
Salvage Value Realized						15.00
Book Value at the end						8.93
Capital Gain/(Loss)						6.07
Tax Paid (–)/Saved						–2.43
Cash Flow (Net of Tax)						**12.57**

The present value of NAL is marginally positive and hence IBL should go for leasing of the crane.

The net advantage of leasing can be stated mathematically as below:

Net Advantage of Leasing Method

$$PV(NAL) = \sum_{1}^{n} \frac{L_t(1-T)+d_tT}{\{1+r_d(1-T)\}^t} + \sum_{1}^{n} \frac{E_t(1-T)}{(1+r)^t} - \frac{S_n}{(1+r)^n} \quad (18\text{-}1)$$

where

C_0 = Capital cost of the asset
L_t = Lease rent for period t
d_t = Depreciation for period t
T = Tax rate
r_d = Cost of debt for lessee firm
E_t = Extra expense for period t, if bought
S_n = Post tax salvage value realized
r = Post-tax WACC of the lessee firm
n = Period of lease

Equivalent Loan Method

Equivalent loan method of evaluation of leases works on the premise that the cash flows of lease represent the additional cash available to the firm that does not go for lease, as compared to the firm opting to go for lease. Reverting to the last row of Table 18-2 of Rama Taxi Company (reproduced below) as Table 18-4 we may state that the firm that does not opt for leasing would have additional cash of ₹2,60,000 available every year.

Equivalent loan method is based on the premise that cash flows of the lease provide additional borrowing capacity that enables service of debt.

Table 18-4 Cash flows; lease vs buy (Rama Taxi Company)

(₹ '000s)

Year	1	2	3	4	5
Cash Flow (Lease – Buy)	–260.00	–260.00	–260.00	–260.00	–260.00

These additional cash flows available to the firm that does not lease can support an additional loan. Alternatively stated, this firm (exactly the same as Rama Taxi Company, except that it does not lease) can have additional borrowing capacity as compared to Rama Taxi Company, to the extent that can be serviced by the additional cash flows of Table 18-4. This additional borrowing may be used to acquire the asset, whereas Rama Taxi Company procured its asset on lease. The decision is now clear. If this additional borrowing is in excess of the cost of asset the firm must go in for buying, otherwise it must lease.

If cash flows of the lease are adequate to service a loan that exceeds the capital cost of the asset it is advantageous to buy the asset rather than lease it.

The equivalent loan that can be serviced by the cash flows of lease can be found by discounting them at post-tax cost of debt. The rule for decision-making would then be

If Equivalent Loan > Cost of Asset; Buy the asset
< Cost of Asset; Lease the asset

With annual cash flow of ₹2,60,000 for 5 years, tax at 35% and interest cost at 15%, the firm can service a debt of ₹9,91,930, as shown in Table 18-5.

Table 18-5 Computing equivalent loan

(₹ '000s)

Year	1	2	3	4	5
Cash Flow	260.00	260.00	260.00	260.00	260.00
Present Value at 9.75%	236.90	215.86	196.68	179.21	163.29
Equivalent Loan					**991.93**

We observe that additional cash flows can service a debt of only approx. ₹9.92 lakh while the capital cost of the asset is ₹10.00 lakh. Since the amount of loan that can be serviced is less than the capital cost of the asset, taking a loan would be disadvantageous and the leasing option is preferred to the buying one.

We may verify that the amount of loan of ₹9.92 lakh can be serviced fully by the additional cash flows of ₹2.60 lakh annually for 5 years. Table 18-6 provides the verification that the cash flows of lease can serve the exact loan amount, as calculated in Table 18-5.

Comparing NAL and Equivalent Loan Method Net advantage of leasing method and equivalent loan methods would lead to identical conclusions. We may confirm this in the case of Rama Taxi Company. We had concluded earlier that with 10% post-tax cost of debt, the net advantage of leasing was to the extent of ₹14,400. To validate the same figure by equivalent loan

Table 18-6 Checking equivalent loan calculation

Year	1	2	3	4	5
(a) Loan Amount at Beginning	991.93	828.65	649.44	452.76	236.90
(b) Interest at 15%	148.79	124.30	97.42	67.91	35.54
(c) Tax Saved on Interest @ 35%	52.08	43.50	34.10	23.77	12.44
(d) Interest Post-tax (b – c)	96.71	80.79	63.32	44.14	23.10
(e) Amount Paid	260.00	260.00	260.00	260.00	260.00
(f) Principal Repaid (e – d)	163.29	179.21	196.68	215.86	236.90
Loan Amount at end (a – f)	828.65	649.44	452.76	236.90	0.00

Table 18-7 Comparing equivalent loan and NAL methods

(₹ '000s)

Year	0	1	2	3	4	5
Net Advantage of Leasing Method						
Cash Flow (Lease – Buy)	1000.00	–260.00	–260.00	–260.00	–260.00	–260.00
Present Value at 10%	1000.00	–236.36	–214.88	–195.34	–177.58	–161.44
Net Advantage of Leasing						**14.40**
Equivalent Loan Method						
Addl. Cash Flow		260.00	260.00	260.00	260.00	260.00
Present Value at 10%		236.36	214.88	195.34	177.58	161.44
Equivalent Loan that can be taken						**985.60**
Capital Cost of the Asset						**1000.00**
Shortfall Suggesting that Leasing is Beneficial by the Amount						**14.40**

method, we calculate the amount of loan that can be serviced by the cash flows of ₹2,60,000 with the post-tax cost of debt of 10%. This is computed in Table 18-7 as ₹9,85,600, as against the requirement cost of asset of ₹10,00,000. The loan amount is short by ₹14,400. Therefore we may state that leasing the asset rather than borrowing is advantageous to the extent of ₹14,400, the same result as computed by the NAL method.

Mathematically the equivalent loan can be expressed as given in Equation 18-2.

Equivalent Loan Method

Equivalent Loan

$$= \sum_{1}^{n} \frac{L_t(1-T)+d_tT}{\{1+r_d(1-T)\}^t} + \sum_{1}^{n} \frac{E_t(1-T)}{(1+r)^t} - \frac{S_n}{(1+r)^n} \quad (18\text{-}2)$$

where

L_t = Lease rent for period t — d_t = Depreciation for period t

T = Tax rate — r_d = Cost of debt for lessee firm

E_t = Extra expense for period t, if bought — S_n = Post-tax salvage value realized

r = Post-tax WACC of the lessee firm — n = Period of lease

WHERE FROM THE VALUE COMES

We considered the lease transaction from the lessee's viewpoint. What about the lessor? The cash flows that are considered for the lessee are also the cash flows for the lessor, though with opposite signs. The lessee saves the capital cost of the asset but the lessor incurs it. The lessee foregoes depreciation tax shield, the lessor avails of it. The lessse pays lease rents, the lessor receives them. Therefore the cash flows for the lessor must be exactly opposite to those of the lessee, as indicated in Table 18-8 for the lease proposal of Rama Taxi Company.

Table 18-8 Cash Flows - Lessor and Lessee

(₹ '000s)

Cash Flow—Lessee (Lease – Buy)	1000.00	–260.00	–260.00	–260.00	–260.00	–260.00
Cash Flow—Lessor (Lease – Buy)	–1000.00	260.00	260.00	260.00	260.00	260.00

Given that this is the case, the net present value of the combined cash flows of the lessee and lessor would be zero. What is gained by the lessee is exactly the same amount as lost by the lessor, and vice versa. Therefore, the value of the lease is zero. This raises an interesting issue. If the lessee accepts the lease proposal, the lessor must reject it, and if the terms are favourable to the lessor, the lease becomes unacceptable to the lessee. Apparently there cannot be a meeting ground mutually beneficial for both lessor and lessee, because neither is interested in losing money.

How do we create value in a lease transaction? There could be many sources that can explain why leasing takes place, despite the fact that the combined value of lease of lessor and lessee is zero. Hitherto we assumed that the same set of assumptions apply to lessor and lessee. However, in real life situations there are some factors that cause differences between lessor and lessee, and these factors can create value in a lease transaction. These are mentioned below.

Broadly speaking leasing adds no value since the advantage for the lessee is equally a disadvantage for the lessor. Only market imperfections can provide the value to the lease.

Difference in the rates of tax for lessor and lessee Due to various kinds of tax exemptions and benefits available, the lessor firm and lessee firm may face different rates of tax. The difference in taxes would create value in the lease transaction.

Difference in the ability of the lessor and lessee to avail of depreciation tax shield Depreciation has been used as a tax planning tool and some firms pay greater emphasis to depreciation than others, creating a difference in the value attached to the depreciation tax shield. Firms making a loss are relatively less concerned with depreciation, because even though the carry forward is allowed, availing of the tax shield in future remains a question mark. If the lessor can avail of greater depreciation, the lease becomes attractive.

Difference in the ability to save operational cost of the lessor and lessee Operating leases include the cost of some services provided by the lessor, which otherwise the lessee would obtain on his own. Due to specialized nature, the manufacturer lessor may provide these services more effectively and economically. Lessee may have to incur greater costs and this would make lease work for both lessor and lessee.

Difference in cost of capital We assumed that the rates of discounting the cash flows, i.e., the cost of debt, and WACC are identical for lessor and lessee. If they are different then the value of lease may be different for lessor and lessee.

COMPUTATION OF MAXIMUM AND MINIMUM LEASE RENT

As stated earlier, the cash flows of lessor and lessee would be exactly equal and opposite. Both the parties to the lease contract would like to maximize the net advantage of leasing. From the lessee's viewpoint the net advantage of leasing decreases with the increase in lease rent. The lease rent that makes the net advantage of leasing zero is the maximum that is acceptable by lessee. The same lease rent would be the minimum acceptable to the lessor. Mathematically, it is stated as shown in Equation 18–3.

Maximum lease rent acceptable to lessee = Minimum lease rent acceptable to lessor (Net Advantage of Leasing = 0) given by

$$0 = C_0 - \sum_{1}^{n} \frac{L_t(1-T)+d_tT}{\{1+r_d(1-T)\}^t} + \sum_{1}^{n} \frac{E_t(1-T)}{(1+r)^t} - \frac{S_n}{(1+r)^n} \quad (18\text{-}3)$$

where C_0 is the cost of asset

Maximum Acceptable Lease Rent for Lessee

As explained, there could be many factors that can create value in a lease transaction, i.e. both lessor and lessee derive positive net advantage from leasing. One of the common situations that can create value is the inability of the lessee to avail the depreciation tax shield, as it does not make profit and pay taxes. In such a case the cash flows of lease would constitute only the lease rentals, L_t. If Rama Taxi Company did not pay taxes the cash flows of lease would be as given in Table 18-9.

Table 18-9 Cash Flows; Lease vs Buy (Rama Taxi Company)

(₹ '000s)

Year	0	1	2	3	4	5
Cash Flow (Lease – Buy)	1000	$-L_t$	$-L_t$	$-L_t$	$-L_t$	$-L_t$

Note that the cash flows are before tax. Recall that we had assumed the post-tax cost of debt of Rama Taxi Company at 10% with 40% tax rate. Therefore the pre-tax cost of debt would be 16.67% (10%/0.6), which is the correct discount rate. The value of the lease would therefore be:

$$NAL = 1000 - L_t \times A^5_{16.67\%}$$

Maximum acceptable lease rent fro the lessee and the minimum acceptable rent for the lessor may be different and provide the ground for negotiation of the actual lease rents.

where $A^5_{16.67\%}$ is annuity of 5 years at 16.67%.

For the maximum lease rent the Net Advantage of Leasing must be zero, or

$$NAL = 0 = 1000 - 3.2238\ L_{t(Max)}$$

Gives $L_{t(Max)}$= 310.19 or ₹3,10,119 per annum.

Any lease rent less than ₹3.1019 lakh would give positive net present value and should be acceptable to the lessee.

Minimum Acceptable Lease rent for Lessor

To find what minimum lease rent would be acceptable to the lessor we examine the cash flow of the lessor. In the case of Rama Taxi Company, assume lease payments of L_t The cash flow for the lessor, assuming availability of depreciation tax shield and 40% tax on the lease rents received, is given in Table 18-10.

The minimum lease rent that would be acceptable to lessor can be found by equating the NPV of the cash flows of the lease to zero.

$$NAL = 0 = -1000 + 0.6\,L_t \times A^5_{10\%} + 80 \times A^5_{10\%}$$

where $A^5_{10\%}$ is annuity of 5 years at 10.00% and is equal to 3.7908. This gives

$$L_{t\,(Min)} = 306.327 \text{ or ₹3,06,327 per annum.}$$

The lower and upper boundaries to lease rent provide the scope for negotiation of lease rent in between where the NPV of the lease would be positive for both lessor and lessee. In the case of Rama Taxi Company, the lease rents in the range of ₹3.06 lakh and ₹3.09 lakh would please both lessor and lessee.

Example 18-6 Determining the Lease Rent

As a manager in a leasing firm you are required to quote for the lease rents for equipment costing ₹15 lakh. The life of the asset is 4 years, after which you may realize the salvage value of ₹5 lakh. You can claim depreciation at 35% on WDV basis. Your firm pays 35% tax on operational income and 10% on capital gains. The cost of debt is 12% while WACC is 10%. What minimum lease rent would be acceptable to you?

If a firm that does not pay tax, nor can avail of depreciation benefits, wants to lease the equipment, what maximum lease rent could you quote that would be accepted.

Find out the value of the lease for lessor and lessee if a lease rent of ₹3,75,000 has been fixed.

Table 18-10 Cash Flows for Lessor (₹ '000s)

Year	0	1	2	3	4	5
Receive lease rent		L_t	L_t	L_t	L_t	L_t
Less: Tax paid on lease rents (40%)		$0.4L_t$	$0.4L_t$	$0.4L_t$	$0.4L_t$	$0.4L_t$
Post-tax lease rent		$0.6L_t$	$0.6L_t$	$0.6L_t$	$0.6L_t$	$0.6L_t$
Initial cost	–1000					
Depreciation		200	200	200	200	200
Tax saved on depreciation (40%)		80	80	80	80	80
Post-tax Cash Flows of Lessor	**–1000**	**80 + 0.6L_t**	**80 + 0.6L_t**	**80 + 0.6L_t**	**80 + 0.6L_t**	**80 + 0.6L_t**

Solution

Lease Rent Calculation for Lessor

Cost of Equipment	₹15.00 lakh	Life (Years)	4	Lease Rentals in Arrears		Cost of Debt (Pre-tax)	12.00%
Rate of Depreciation	35.00%	Salvage Value	₹5.00 lakh	Tax Rate	35.00%	Cost of Debt (Post-tax)	7.80%
				Capital Gains Tax	10.00%	Cost of Capital	10.00%

(₹ *in '000s*)

Year		*0*	*1*	*2*	*3*	*4*
Initial Cost		–1500.00				
Depreciation						
Opening Value of the Asset			1500.00	975.00	633.75	411.94
Depreciation WDV			525.00	341.25	221.81	144.18
Closing Value			975.00	633.75	411.94	267.76
Tax Saved on Depreciation			183.75	119.44	77.63	50.46
Cash Flow – Buy – Certain		–1500.00	183.75	119.44	77.63	50.46
Present Value at Post-tax Cost of Debt		–1500.00	170.45	102.78	61.97	37.37
Salvage Value						
Salvage Value Realized	500.00					
Book Value	267.76					
Capital Gains/Loss	232.24					
Tax Saved/Paid						–23.22
Net Salvage Value Realized						476.78
Present Value (Salvage) at WACC						325.64
Determining Breakeven Lease Rents For Lessor (Minimum)						
Capital Cost of the Asset						1500.00
Less: Present Value of the Salvage					325.64	
Less: Present Value of Depreciation Tax Shield					372.57	
Value to be Realized by Lease Rents						801.78
Annuity Factor at		7.80% for 4 years				3.3269
Minimum Post-tax Lease Rents Per Annum						241.00
Minimum Pre-tax Lease Rents Required Per Annum						370.77
Determining Breakeven Lease Rents for Lessee (Maximum)						
Capital Cost of the Asset						1500.00
Less: Present Value of the Salvage*					325.64	
Less: Present Value of Depreciation Tax Shield					0.00	
Value to be Realized by Lease Rents						1174.36
Annuity Factor at		12.00% for 4 years				3.0373
Maximum Acceptable Post-tax Lease Rents Per Annum						386.64
Maximum Acceptable Pre-tax Lease Rents Per Annum						386.64
*Even if lessee firm pays no taxes it would still pay tax on the salvage value Arising out of capital gains						
With lease rents of ₹3,75,000 per annum fixed, the value of the lease for both lessor and lessee would be positive and can be calculated as follows:						
Value of Lease For Lessor						
Capital Cost of the Asset						1500.00
Less: Present Value of the Salvage					325.64	
Less: Present Value of Depreciation Tax Shield					372.57	
Value to be Realized by Lease Rents						801.78
Annuity Factor at		7.80% for 4 years				3.3269
Lease Rent Received		Pre-tax = 375				Post Tax = 243.75
Value of the Lease Rents Realized						810.94
Value of the Lease for the Lessor						9.16
Value of Lease For Lessee						
Capital Cost of the Asset						1500.00
Less: Present Value of the Salvage					325.64	
Less: Present Value of Depreciation Tax Shield					0.00	
Value to be Paid by Lease Rents						1174.36
Annuity Factor at		12.00% for 4 years				3.0373
Lease Rent Paid		Pre-tax = 375				Post-tax = 375.00
Value of the Lease Rents Realized						1139.01
Value of the Lease for the Lessor						35.35

REASONS FOR LEASE

There are several reasons given by people in favour of leasing rather than borrowing. Some of these reasons are flimsy and lack conviction, but some of them are valid. We examine these reasons in two categories—wrong reasons and valid reasons.

Wrong Reasons for Leasing

100% financing Proponents of leasing forward a reason that leasing provides 100% financing of the capital goods, while the lenders normally insist on some margins against their finance. Leasing does not involve any payment towards the capital cost of the asset. The argument does not carry much weight since by borrowing cash equivalent to capital, cost of the asset increases and lease payments are analogous to the repayment of the borrowed capital and interest thereon.

Off-balance sheet financing There is a perception that the capital structure of the firm remains at what it was prior to the leasing, because leased assets as well as the obligations to pay future lease rents do not appear on the balance sheet. On the other hand, if the asset is procured through borrowing, the loan as well as the asset appear on the balance sheet. The capital structure measured in terms of debt–equity ratio gets affected. This belief is apparently wrong, since all those providing debt are more concerned about the repayment capacity rather than debt–equity ratio. As such leasing cannot increase the debt capacity of the firm. To a certain extent, it may help in overcoming the debt equity norms prevailing in the industry. This too is not of much help since the value of the lease assets and corresponding liability on account of lease rents are required to be disclosed separately. A lease therefore does not result in any tangible benefit of retaining the debt capacity.

Availability of 100% finance, off balance sheet financing and protection of financial ratios are some of the invalid reasons for entering in to lease agreement.

Improved financial performance Most financial analysts measure the performance of the firm through a variety of ratios. These ratios, such as asset turnover, return on investment, etc., are normally taken from the balance sheet. Since lease finance is regarded as an off balance sheet item, the ratios so calculated will wrongly depict an improved performance in better utilization of assets and capital employed. However, for intelligent investors and analysts it shall be meaningless, and they would neither work too hard nor take too long to make a fair assessment of the performance, taking into consideration the leased assets and corresponding liabilities.

Valid Reasons for Leasing

Tax advantage Amongst the right reasons for a lease to exist, the most important one is the tax advantage. It makes sense for a firm paying low tax to undertake leasing, as tax shield available on the interest rate on borrowing as well as on depreciation will have lower value than if the firm were in a high tax bracket. The leasing firm in a high tax bracket would derive greater advantage of tax shield of depreciation and interest, and, therefore, would be able to lower the lease rent. In such a situation, both lessee and lessor would have positive net present value as both have them view the deal with respect to the different tax rates faced by each.

Shifting risks Another real reason that can cause lessee to undertake the lease rather than the borrow option is the shifting of certain kinds of risks to the lessor. These risks include the risk of technological obsolescence of the capital asset. Fast changing technology in many fields prompts firms to enter into short-term cancellable leases so as to allow them to replace the leased assets, if need arises, more conveniently. The manufacturer-lessor can absorb the changes in technology rather easily, as compared to the user-lessee, because of its ability to refurbish, modernize, or re-make the old asset.

Valid reasons for lease include tax advantage, avoidance of obsolescence risk, convenience etc.

Economy Cost savings due to the specialized knowledge of the manufacturer-lessor could be another reason to prefer lease. The lessee would like to concentrate on its core competencies, rather than on running and maintaining assets requiring special skills. For example, banks would do well to lease ATMs, as the skills for running and maintaining them are not available in the banks. And even if such skills could be hired, it would likely cost the banks more than what it would to the leasing or manufacturer firms, for whom this would be core business. As another example, consider servers and computers. People with goods skills in running and maintaining them would like to work for a firm in the information technology line, rather than with the users of such assets. Besides being economical, such leasing or manufacturer firms would have more specialized knowledge in running and maintaining such machines.

Transaction cost, speed, and convenience Better convenience and faster speed of the lease transaction, as compared to the borrowing transaction, also contribute towards the popularity of lease. Borrowing generally involves greater scrutiny by the lenders and elaborate documentation, which not only take a longer time in processing, but also increase the transaction cost indirectly in the form of managerial attention and follow up required for arranging loans. Lease transactions are not subject to as intensive and extensive scrutiny as loan transactions, saving valuable time and effort. Besides, lease transactions, unlike loan transactions, are not subject to rather stringent and restrictive covenants, which limit managerial freedom. Leasing avoids rather unnecessary conditions which are normal with loans.

Administrative ease Certain firms also believe that leasing transactions also save time and effort in the lessee's organization. Normally capital expenditure in most firms requires justifications and approvals from higher levels. This is not the case with revenue expenditure, which is dealt with in a routine manner and at lower levels. Lease rents, being a revenue item, do not need elaborate justification, as in the case of capital expenditure. Therefore, leasing, as compared to buying, saves time and effort of the managers in the lessee's organization.

Lesser risk for lessor Ownership of an asset is better security than its pledge. Under the lease transaction, the ownership rests with the lessor, making repossession of the asset easier in case of default in lease rent payments. In the case of loan transactions, the repossession of assets is more difficult and time-consuming for the lender if the borrower defaults in payment. The superior nature of security should make the lease a cheaper transaction, as the lessor carries a lower risk than the lender.

Example 18-7 Leasing: A Comprehensive View

ABC Ltd needs a special purpose small motor designed by Moto Corporation. This motor, costing ₹15,000, is available only on lease by Moto Corporation for a period of 5 years at rent of ₹2,100 payable in arrears. This motor provides a saving of electricity of ₹6,000 per annum. After 5 years the value of the motor is zero. ABC Ltd pays tax at 35% and can avail a loan at 10% from a bank.

An employee of ABC Ltd has developed the same motor that can provide savings of electricity of ₹9,000 per annum.

1. Find if ABC Ltd should lease the motor or buy it from the employee if he agrees to give it for ₹15,000.
2. If the employee is not willing to supply the motor at ₹15,000 what maximum price can ABC Ltd offer?
3. Realizing the saving potential the bank wants to negotiate the interest rate on the loan. What maximum rate of interest should ABC Ltd be willing to pay to the bank?
4. In view of the offer by the employee ABC Ltd finds that the lease rents of Moto Corporation are exorbitant. What maximum lease rent can ABC Ltd pay so as to prefer a lease rather than purchase from the employee?

Solution

The data available is summarized as below

Cost of Equipment	15,000	Life (Years)	5
Rate of Depreciation	SLM	Salvage Value	0
Lease Rentals	2,100	Cost of Debt (Pretax)	10%
Tax Rate	35%	Cost of Debt (Post-Tax)	6.50%

Year	*Present Value*	*0*	*1*	*2*	*3*	*4*	*5*
A. Lease Option							
Lease Rentals			–2,100	–2,100	–2,100	–2,100	–2,100
Reduction in Electricity Cost			6,000	6,000	6,000	6,000	6,000
Tax Saved on Lease Rents			735	735	735	735	735
Tax Paid on Electricity Savings			–2,100	–2,100	–2,100	–2,100	–2,100
Cash Flow – Lease			2,535	2,535	2,535	2,535	2,535
Present Value (Lease)	10,535		2,380	2,235	2,099	1,971	1,850
B. Buy Option							
Initial Cost		–15,000					
Depreciation			3,000	3,000	3,000	3,000	3,000
Tax Saved on Depreciation			1,050	1,050	1,050	1,050	1,050
Reduction in Electricity Cost			9,000	9,000	9,000	9,000	9,000
Tax Paid on Savings in Electricity			–3,150	–3,150	–3,150	–3,150	–3,150
Cash flow		–15,000	6,900	6,900	6,900	6,900	6,900
Present Value (Buy)	13,674	–15,000	6,479	6,083	5,712	5,364	5,036
Net Advantage of Leasing (A – B)	10,535	15,000	–4,365	–4,365	–4,365	–4,365	–4,365
Present Value of NAL	–3,140	15,000	–4,099	–3,848	–3,614	–3,393	–3,186
Maximum Capital Cost the Firm can Pay							
Equivalent Loan Method							
Additional Cash Flow Available			4,365	4,365	4,365	4,365	4,365
PV of Additional Cash Flow			4,099	3,848	3,614	3,393	3,186
Loan Amount that can be Serviced		18,140					
The maximum price that can be offered is ₹ 18,140.							
Maximum Rate of Loan the firm can pay							
Internal Rate of Return							
Cash Flow of Lease		–15,000	4,365	4,365	4,365	4,365	4,365
Internal Rate of Return							**13.96%**
The maximum rate that can be paid by the firm to the bank for borrowing and not lease							
Lease Rents that make Leasing more Attractive							
Depreciation Tax Shield			1,050	1,050	1,050	1,050	1,050
Savings in Electricity Net of Tax			1,950	1,950	1,950	1,950	1,950
Total			3,000	3,000	3,000	3,000	3,000
Present Value	12,467		2,817	2,645	2,484	2,332	2,190
Capital Cost of the Asset							15,000
Less: Present value of Depreciation Tax Shield & Savings							12,467
Value to be realized by Lease Rents							2,533
Annuity Factor at	6.50% for 5 years					4.1557	
Maximum acceptable post tax lease rents per annum							610
Maximum acceptable pre tax lease rents per annum							938
If the lease rents are less than ₹ 937 the lease option becomes more attractive.							

ACCOUNTING FOR LEASES

The framework presented for leases and its evaluation differs significantly from the accounting aspects of leases. The differences need to be highlighted. From accounting viewpoint globally and locally in India, assets under financial leases are treated just as any other asset owned by the lessee. International Accounting Standard IAS–17, as well as Indian Accounting Standard AS–19, deals with the treatment to be given in the books of accounts for lease assets. Select features are discussed below.

Accounting standards, both international and Indian, lay emphasis on the substance of the lease rather than its form. They distinguish between the financial lease and operating lease on the basis of who bears the risk and earns reward of the lease contract. A lease is classified as financial lease if the risks and rewards incidental to ownership are transferred from lessor to the lessee, even though the legal title may or may not be ultimately transferred at the end of the lease period. There are many situations which would indicate who is *de facto* owner of the asset. Some of the tests of real and not legal ownership are:

- Whether the rents are fixed in a manner such that the lessor recovers the cost of the asset and earns some profit.
- Whether the period of lease covers the major part of the useful/economic life of the asset.
- Whether the lessee bears the loss due to idle capacity and risk of technological obsolescence of the asset.
- Whether the lease is non-cancellable over useful/economic life of the asset, or if cancellable, the lessee pays additional money.
- Whether the lessee becomes the owner of the asset at the end of the lease period, or has the option to buy it at a substantially lower price than the estimated market price, or can continue with the lease at a substantially lower rent than the market rate.
- Whether the asset can be used by any party other than the lessee.

If the answer to any of the above is in the affirmative, the lease will be classified as financial lease, according to global or Indian accounting standards, as the substance of the contract implies that leasing has been used only as a financing mode. Accounting standards do not explicitly discuss operating lease. Any lease that is not a financial lease is called an operating lease.

Once the nature of lease is determined as financial, the accounting standard specifies that leased assets be recognized in the balance sheet as a separate group of assets. An equivalent amount is recorded as lease payable on the liability side of the balance sheet. The value of the asset and matching liability must be recorded at the lower of (a) cash price determined on the basis of arm's length, and (b) present value of the minimum lease rents discounted at the rate of return implied in the lease contract.

Consider an example. Assume that a knitting machine costs ₹20,000, which has a life of 4 years with residual value of ₹2,000. The machine is offered on lease of ₹6,500 per annum. The value at which the machine will be recorded in the books of the lessee would be the lower of ₹20,000 and the present value of lease rents. The rate implied in the lease contract would take into account the residual value, assuming that at the end of the lease period the lessee would own the asset by paying the residual value. We assume that this residual value is a reasonable and fair estimate of the value that can be realized at the end of the lease period. The implied rate of return can be determined by computing the IRR of the cash flows of the leased asset and the lease rentals. This is done as follows:

IRR of the cash flows of lease rentals and capital cost represent the implied cost of leasing

Computing implied rate of interest

(₹ '000s)

Year	0	1	2	3	4	IRR
Cash Flow assuming purchase after lease period	–20.00	6.50	6.50	6.50	8.50	
Implied Rate of Interest in the Lease						**14.29%**

The value of the asset can be arrived at with the minimum lease rents, which exclude payment of residual value, i.e., ₹6,500, discounted at the implied rate of return of 14.29%. Payment of residual value is not optional, and hence cannot form part of minimum lease payments.

Value of the asset in the books of lessee (₹ '000s)

(a) Fair Value of the Asset 20.00
(b) PV of Minimum Lease Rents at IRR 18.83

Year	1	2	3	4
Lease Rent	6.50	6.50	6.50	6.50
Present Value at IRR	5.69	4.98	4.35	3.81

Value of the Asset and Liability in the books—Minimum of (a) and (b) 18.83

The lease shall be recorded in the balance sheet as

Lease Payable	18.83	Leased Assets	18.83

For subsequent years the value of leased assets and lease payable would decline. Lease payments are deemed to constitute a finance charge and repayment of principal. Therefore each lease rent needs to be segregated in to two components—finance charges and repayment of lease liability. The rate of interest used for determination of finance charges would be the implied rate found earlier and equal the IRR of lease transaction. The balance amount of the lease rent would go to reduce the lease liability. After recording the initial value of the asset lease liability at the beginning of the lease, the liability would reduce with each lease rent paid.

Value of the leased asset and its corresponding liability has to be disclosed separately in the balance sheet, with the amount being equal to present value of lease rents payable discounted at implied cost of leasing.

Allocation of interest from lease rents

(₹ '000s)

Year	1	2	3	4
Lease Payable—Beginning	18.83	15.02	10.66	5.69
Interest at IRR	2.69	2.15	1.52	0.81
Lease Rent	6.50	6.50	6.50	6.50
Principal Repaid	3.81	4.35	4.98	5.69
Lease Liability—End	15.02	10.66	5.69	0.00

Since lease rentals are deemed as repayment of loan, the lessee would charge depreciation on the asset like any other asset, as well as finance charges in the profit and loss account. The value of the asset would decline by the amount of depreciation each year, as shown below:

Depreciation and value of leased asset

(₹ '000s)

Year	1	2	3	4
Leased Asset Gross Value	18.83	18.83	18.83	18.83
Depreciation for the Period	4.71	4.71	4.71	4.71
Accumulated Depreciation	4.71	9.41	14.12	18.83
Leased Assets—Net Value	14.12	9.41	4.71	0.00

The expensed items of depreciation and finance charges as well as the position of asset and liability would be as follows:

Accounting for lease related items

(₹ '000s)

Year	1	2	3	4
Balance Sheet at the end of the Period				
Asset—Leased Asset (Net)	14.12	9.41	4.71	0.00
Liability—Lease Payable	15.02	10.66	5.69	0.00
P & L Account for the Period				
Finance Charges	2.69	2.15	1.52	0.81
Depreciation	4.71	4.71	4.71	4.71

It can be easily observed that the treatment in the books of accounts of the lessee's firm is at divergence with the analytical framework presented earlier. Accounting convention treats assets under financial lease as if the assets were owned by the lessee.

However, the position assumed under the Income Tax Rules is quite contrary. It is specifically mentioned as per the Indian Income Tax Act that the lessor being the owner is entitled to claim depreciation, and the lessee being the user is entitled to expense out the entire lease rents, not with standing what is stated in the accounting standards.

HIRE PURCHASE

Another popular means of acquiring an asset is hire purchase. The hirer (the one who takes the asset on hire) pays a fixed instalment periodically over the hire purchase period, just as the lessee pays lease rents in a lease transaction. The similarity between hire purchase and lease possibly ends here. In the treatment of taxes, ownership, and cash flows, the hire purchase transaction becomes different from a lease transaction. Hire purchase transactions are extremely popular in the automobile industry. Normally, some part of the equipment cost has to be paid in advance by the hirer while the finance company contributes the major portion. Alternatively, some deposit is to be placed with the finance company, which may be refunded or adjusted against the last few instalments.

In a hire purchase transaction, the asset is procured by the finance company which lets it out for use by the hirer for a specified period, and lets the purchase take place at the end of the hire period, subject to full and timely payment of all the instalments. The asset is purchased in the name of the hirer to enable him to claim depreciation. The hirer becomes the complete and legal owner of the asset only upon payment of the final instalment. Each instalment is treated as hire charges, to facilitate recovery of asset in case of defaults.

Each instalment of hire purchase is like repayment of a loan along with interest. The amount of each instalment is bifurcated into principal and interest. The hirer can claim only the interest portion as expense and not the principal. In contrast, under a leasing transaction the entire lease rent is claimed as deductible expense. The tax shield available to the hirer is only partial, while to the lessee it is on the full amount. A comparison of lease and hire purchase is presented in Table 18-11.

Instalments of hire purchase transactions are normally fixed on the basis of flat rate of interest. For example, if the rate of interest is 5% per annum and the hire purchase is for 10 years the interest charged for the transaction would be 50% (5% p.a. × 10 years). If the cost of the asset is ₹10,000 then the annual instalment would be ₹1,500 (₹15,000/10). The allocation of interest for each payment required for claiming expense deduction by the hirer can be done by two methods – IRR method or Sum of the Years Digit (SYD) method. Both IRR and SYD functions are available in EXCEL.

The method to be followed for calculation of interest based on IRR is to find the internal rate of return of the cash flows with cost of the asset as cash inflow in period '0' and hire

Table 18-11 Comparison of lease and hire purchase

	Lease	*Hire purchase*
Ownership	With lessor	Remains with hirer and transferred upon payment of final instalment
Ownership at end	Lessee has no right to own the leased asset	Hirer has right to own upon payment of final instalment
Depreciation	Claimed by lessor	Claimed by hirer
Tax deductibility	To the lessee for the entire amount of lease rent	Instalment is split in principal and interest; tax deductibility only on the interest portion of the instalment
Extent of finance	Entire capital cost is borne by lessor	Some portion of the capital cost is contributed by hirer
Claim on salvage value	With the lessor	With hirer

Hire purchase is different than a financial lease because the hirer in contrast to lessee is regarded as owner of the asset and is entitled to depreciation benefits. Each instalment consists of interest and repayment of principal and interest tax shield is available to the hirer.

purchase instalments as cash outflows in each year. IRR would be the rate of interest, and the amount of interest is obtained by the principal amount outstanding at the beginning of the period. Interest is charged on the reducing balance.

The calculation of interest based on SYD method would be to allocate the total amount of interest in the ratio of time remaining for hire purchase instalment. For a principal amount of ₹10,000 and a flat interest rate of 5% per annum for a period of 10 years, the total amount of interest is ₹5,000 and the annual instalment amount is ₹1,500. The total amount of interest is divided into 55 parts (sum of the years from 1 to 10). For the first year, the interest is assumed to be 10 times that of the final year. The interest for all the years can be calculated as:

$$\text{Interest for the first year} = \frac{10}{55} \times 1500 = ₹272.73$$

$$\text{for the second year} = \frac{9}{55} \times 1500 = ₹245.45$$

$$\text{for the third year} = \frac{8}{55} \times 1500 = ₹218.18$$

and so on.

The balance amount out of the instalment is repayment of principal.

Table 18-12 shows the allocation of interest for different periods out of the instalments in hire purchase contracts based on IRR and SYD methods.

Lease Vs Hire Purchase

Comparison between the cash flows of lease and hire purchase would form the basis in choosing the appropriate alternative. The cash flows net of tax T would be as follows:

Cash Flows under Lease

Cash out flow for lease rents = $-L_t \times (1-T)$

where L_t is lease rent for period t

Cash Flows under Hire Purchase

Cash out flow of principal = $-P_t$

where P_t is the principal in instalment for period t.

Cash out flow of interest (net of tax) = $-I_t \times (1-T)$

where I_t is the interest component in the instalment for period t.

Cash inflow of depreciation tax shield = $d_t \times T$

where d_t is depreciation for period t.

Cash in flow of salvage value net of tax the end of period = S_n

To find which of the options must be preferred, discount the cash flows of lease and hire purchase at post-tax cost of debt with the exception of salvage value to be discounted WACC, being cash flow of uncertain nature. The lower of the two discounted cash flows would be the preferred alternative. An example follows.

Example 18-8 Choosing between Lease and Hire Purchase

Assume that equipment costing ₹15,000 is offered on lease as well as hire purchase by a finance firm. The period of the contract is 5 years and salvage value is zero.

The equipment is charged for depreciation on a straight line basis. If leased, the rent would be ₹3,750, while the instalment under hire purchase arrangement is ₹3,600. The cost of debt is 10% while the rate of tax is 35%. Suggest which mode of financing should be adopted.

Table 18-12 Hire purchase—Allocation of interest (IRR method and SYD method)

Principal Amount	₹1000
Nos. of Instalments	8
Flat Rate of Interest	4% p.a.
Amount of Interest	₹320
Amount of Instalment	₹165

Year		1	2	3	4	5	6	7	8	IRR
IRR of the Cash Flow	–1000.00	165.00	165.00	165.00	165.00	165.00	165.00	165.00	165.00	6.62%
Interest Allocation based on IRR Method										
Principal—Opening		1000.00	901.18	795.83	683.50	563.74	436.05	299.91	154.76	
Interest		66.18	59.64	52.67	45.24	37.31	28.86	19.85	10.24	
Instalment		165.00	165.00	165.00	165.00	165.00	165.00	165.00	165.00	
Principal Repaid		98.82	105.36	112.33	119.76	127.69	136.14	145.15	154.76	
Principal—Closing		901.18	795.83	683.50	563.74	436.05	299.91	154.76	0.00	
Interest allocation based on Sum of The Years Method										
Principal—Opening		1000.00	906.11	803.33	691.67	571.11	441.67	303.33	156.11	
Interest		71.11	62.22	53.33	44.44	35.56	26.67	17.78	8.89	
Principal Repaid		93.89	102.78	111.67	120.56	129.44	138.33	147.22	156.11	
Principal—Closing		906.11	803.33	691.67	571.11	441.67	303.33	156.11	0.00	

Solution

Cost of Equipment	₹15,000	Life (Years)	5	Lease Rentals	₹3,750	Cost of Debt (Pre-tax)	10%
Rate of Depreciation	SLM	Salvage Value	0	Tax Rate	35%	Cost of Debt (Post-tax)	6.50%

Year	*0*	*1*	*2*	*3*	*4*	*5*
A. Lease Option						
Lease Rentals		–3,750	–3,750	–3,750	–3,750	–3,750
Tax Saved on Lease Rents		1,313	1,313	1,313	1,313	1,313
Cash Flow – Lease		–2,438	–2,438	–2,438	–2,438	–2,438
Present Value (Lease)	–10,129	–2,289	–2,149	–2,018	–1,895	–1,779
B. Hire Purchase Option						
Depreciation		3,000	3,000	3,000	3,000	3,000
Tax Saved on Depreciation		1,050	1,050	1,050	1,050	1,050
Amount of Interest Paid[1]		–1,000	–800	–600	–400	–200
Tax Saved on Interest		350	280	210	140	70
Prepayment of Principal		–2,600	–2,800	–3,000	–3,200	–3,400
Cash Flow – Hire Purchase		–2,200	–2,270	–2,340	–2,410	–2,480
Present Value (Hire Purchase)	–9,688	–2,066	–2,001	–1,937	–1,873	–1,810

[1]Hire Purchase – Allocation of Interest

Principal Amount	₹15,000		
Nos. of Instalments	5	Amount of Interest	₹3,000
Flat Rate of Interest	4% p.a.	Amount of Instalment	₹3,600

Year	*1*	*2*	*3*	*4*	*5*
Interest Allocation based on Sum of The Years					
Principal—Opening	15,000	12,400	9,600	6,600	3,400
Interest	1,000	800	600	400	200
Principal Repaid	2,600	2,800	3,000	3,200	3,400
Principal—Closing	12,400	9,600	6,600	3,400	0

SUMMARY

Leasing is a very popular means of asset-based financing. Leasing is a unique method of separating the ownership and the utilization of the asset. It is an alternative to borrowing that the firm resorts to while procuring the asset for its economic exploitation.

The two parties to a lease agreement are called the lessee—the one who uses the asset but does not own it—and the lessor—the one who owns the asset but does not use it. The lessee pays lease rentals to the lessor over the lease period as consideration for using the asset. Such agreements are generally entered into to acquire special kinds of assets, where the firms need to use them but do not want to carry the risks associated with ownership, like risk of obsolescence. The lessor is entitled to claim depreciation on the asset leased while the lessee enjoys the tax shield on the lease rents.

Leases are basically of two types—operating lease and financial lease. A financial lease is merely a financing mechanism where the lessee becomes the owner at the end of the lease period. An operating lease is much beyond mere financing, and the ownership usually does not pass on to the lessee at the end of the lease period. There are other kinds of lease agreements that include "sale and lease-back" and "leveraged lease".

Contrary to general belief, leasing is not an investment decision but a mere financing decision. It is a method of acquiring an asset, which alternatively could be procured through borrowing. The decision whether to lease or to borrow can be made on the basis of the differential cash flows of the lease. The cash flows of the lease primarily constitute three factors—(i) the avoidance of capital cost of the asset, (ii) payment of lease rentals net of tax, and (iii) foregoing of the depreciation tax shield.

The two methods that can be used for evaluation of the lease are net advantage of lease method (NAL) and equivalent loan method. The differential cash flows of lease represent the net advantage of lease. When discounted at post-tax cost of debt, the present value of net advantage of lease is arrived at. If this is positive we go for lease, otherwise it is advisable to buy the asset outright. The post-tax cost of debt is the appropriate discount rate for evaluation of differential cash flows because it is certain.

The equivalent loan method of evaluation of lease proposal finds out what level of loan the differential cash flows of lease can service. If the differential cash flows of lease can service a loan that exceeds the capital cost of the asset, it is more economical to buy the asset, otherwise leasing the asset is preferable. Both NAL and Equivalent Loan methods give identical decisions because the cash flow and discount rate used are identical.

Broadly speaking, the net advantage of lease for the lessee is net disadvantage to the lessor. Cash flows of lease cannot offer advantages to both lessee and lessor unless there are differences in the benefits of lessee and lessor. These differences can render the net advantage of leasing positive both for lessee and lessor. To know this we need to compute the maximum lease rent that is acceptable to the lessee and the minimum lease rent acceptable to the lessor. The actual lease rent can be negotiated in between the two.

Since leasing provides 100% finance as against loans that demand some margin from the borrower, it is often thought to be an advantage offered by the leasing option. Other reasons often cited in favour of lease are its nature of off-balance sheet financing and protection of financial position. However these reasons are only flimsy. The good reasons to go for lease are tax advantages and avoidance of risk associated with ownership, like obsolescence and convenience.

Accounting for leases is extremely typical. The leased assets are required to be disclosed separately with an equivalent liability. The amounts are the present value of the lease rent payable in the future. Accounting standards treat the leased asset in the same way as an owned asset.

Hire purchase is also one of the ways an asset can be acquired. It differs from lease in the sense that under hire purchase the user of the asset is also the owner of the asset, and is entitled to claim depreciation and its associated tax shield.

KEY TERMS

Lease Lease is an asset-based financing mechanism that enables use of the asset without owning it on payment of lease rents.

Lessee The one who uses the asset and pays the lease rents to the owner is called lessee.

Lessor The owner of the asset who leases it to the lessee against the consideration of receiving lease rents is called lessor.

Financial lease A lease that serves only as substitute to the acquisition by borrowing is a financial lease.

Operating lease A lease that provides additional benefits besides financing of the asset is called an operating lease.

Amortization The recovery of capital cost and return through lease rentals is called amortization. If full recovery is made, the lease is fully amortized.

Sale and lease-back The arrangement of first selling the asset already owned to raise funds and then obtaining it back on lease from the buyer/lessor is a sale and lease back transaction.

Leveraged lease The acquisition of an asset by the lessor through borrowing and then leasing the asset to the lessee is leveraged lease.

Net advantage of lease The difference of the cash flows of lease over cash flows of buying is referred to as net advantage of lease.

Equivalent loan The additional amount of loan that can be serviced by the additional cash flows of lease is called equivalent loan.

Maximum lease rent Maximum lease rent is the amount of lease rent that makes net advantage of lease zero for the lessee.

Minimum lease rent Minimum lease rent is the amount of lease rent that makes net advantage of lease zero for the lessor.

Cost of leasing The internal rate of return of the cash flows of the lease is implied cost of leasing.

Hire purchase Hire purchase is another mode of asset-based financing where the hirer pays the rents but is entitled to the benefits of ownership.

KEY FORMULAE

Net advantage of leasing

$$C_0 = \sum_{1}^{n} \frac{L_t(1-T)+d_tT}{\{1+r_d(1-T)\}^t} + \sum_{1}^{n} \frac{E_t(1-T)}{(1+r)^t} - \frac{S_n}{(1+r)^n}$$

Equivalent loan

$$\sum_{1}^{n} \frac{L_t(1-T)+d_tT}{\{1+r_d(1-T)\}^t} + \sum_{1}^{n} \frac{E_t(1-T)}{(1+r)^t} - \frac{S_n}{(1+r)^n}$$

PRACTICE PROBLEMS

1. Fixing Lease Rentals

Sun Tourist is planning to take on lease a fleet of 15 cars with each car costing ₹9 lakh. The cars have a useful life of 5 years after which the value would be ₹2 lakh, at which the firm would buy back the car from the leasing company. The leasing company requires a return of 15%. Find out the lease rents under the following schemes of installments:

(a) Equated lease rentals payable in arrears
(b) Equated lease rentals payable in advance
(c) Stepped up lease rentals to increase by 20% annually and payable in arrears
(d) Stepped down lease rentals to decrease by 20% annually and payable in arrears
(e) First four installments of ₹2,00,000 each in arrears and remaining in the 5th year.
(f) Equated three instalment deferred by two years.

Solution

Following data is available:

Cost of fleet of cars	₹9,00,000
Life	5 years
Residual Value	₹2,00,000
Required rate of return	15%

(a) *Equated annual lease rentals in arrears*

The residual value of the asset

= ₹2,00,000

Present value factor for 5 years at 15.00%
= PVIF (15.00%, 5) = 0.4972
Present value of the residual = ₹99,435
Amount to be recovered by way of lease rentals = ₹8,00,565
Present value of annuity for 5 years at 15.00%
= PVIFA (15.00%, 5) = 3.3522
Annual lease rentals = Cost/PVIFA(15.00%,5)
= 8,00,565/3.3522 = ₹2,38,821

(b) *Equated annual lease rentals in advance*
Annual lease rentals in advance would be equal to the discounted lease rents in arrears at 15%.
Therefore, lease rentals in advance would be = ₹2,07,670

(c) Stepped up lease payments with 20% increase each year
Let the first year lease rental be x

Required return	15%
Annual increase	20%

Then the present value of lease payments, that must be equated with the amount to be recovered, would be:
$= x \times \text{PVIF}(15\%,1) + 1.20x \times \text{PVIF}(15\%,2) + 1.20^2x \times \text{PVIF}(15\%,3) + 1.20^3x \times \text{PVIF}(15\%,4) + 1.20^4x \times \text{PVIF}(15\%,5)$
This may be solved for value of x, as under:

Year	PV factor	Rent	Rent x PV factor	Lease rents
1	0.8696	1.0000	0.8696	₹1,68,799
2	0.7561	1.2000	0.9074	₹2,02,559
3	0.6575	1.4400	0.9468	₹2,43,071
4	0.5718	1.7280	0.9880	₹2,91,685
5	0.4972	2.0736	1.0309	₹3,50,023
Sum			4.7427	
Amount to be recovered by lease rent			₹8,00,565	
First year lease rental				₹1,68,799

(d) *Stepped down lease payments with 20% decrease each year*
Let the first year lease rental be x

Required return	15%
Annual increase	–20%

Then the present value of lease payments, that must be equated with the amount to be recovered, would be:
$= x \times \text{PVIF}(15\%,1) + 0.80x \times \text{PVIF}(15\%,2) + 0.80^2x \times \text{PVIF}(15\%,3) + 0.80^3x \times \text{PVIF}(15\%,4) + 0.80^4x \times \text{PVIF}(15\%,5)$
This may be solved for value of x, as under:

Year	PV factor	Rent	Rent x PV factor	Lease rents
1	0.8696	1.0000	0.8696	₹3,34,730
2	0.7561	0.8000	0.6049	₹2,67,784
3	0.6575	0.6400	0.4208	₹2,14,227
4	0.5718	0.5120	0.2927	₹1,71,382
5	0.4972	0.4096	0.2036	₹1,37,105
Sum			2.3917	
Amount to be recovered by lease rent			₹8,00,565	
First year lease rental				₹3,34,730

(e) *Fixed payments each year except the last year*
Amount of lease rent every year = ₹2,00,000
Nos of years for fixed lease rents = 4 years
PV of fixed lease rentals = PVIFA(15.00%,4) = 2.8550
PV of lease rentals of first four years= 2.8550 × 200000
= ₹5,70,996
Remaining amount to be recovered = ₹2,29,569
PV factor of final lease rental of amount of x
= PVIF (15.00%,5) = 0.4972
Amount of final lease rental
= Amount to be recovered – PV of fixed lease rents/PVIF(15%,5) = ₹4,61,745

(f) *Deferred lease rental*
Moratorium period = 2 years
Nos of instalments from Year 3 onwards = 3
Present value of annuity for 3 years at 15.00%
= PVIFA (15.00%, 3) = 2.2832
Amount of three instalments = amount financed/PVIFA(15%,3)
= ₹3,50,629
Future value factor for deferment of two years = 1.3225
Amount of instalment = ₹4,63,707

2. Comparing Lease Plans

Sun Control Systems needs to install solar panels costing ₹12 lakh. It has useful life of 8 years and have zero residual value. A leasing company has offered various lease plans for a period of 8 years, as below:

(a) Equated lease rentals of ₹2,12,000 payable in arrears.
(b) Equated lease rentals of ₹1,95,000 payable in advance.
(c) Stepped up lease rentals plan with first year payment of ₹1,55,000 with an increase of 10% every year and payable in arrears.
(d) Stepped down lease rentals plan with first year payment of ₹2,85,000 with a decrease of 10% every year and payable in arrears.
(e) First seven instalment of ₹1,50,000 each in arrears and ₹8,40,000 in the 8th year.

You are required to recommend the best lease plan for Sun Control Systems.

Solution

Various lease plans may be compared with the cost each of the lease plan has.

The cost of the lease may be found by calculating the IRR of the cash flows of the lease. The lease plan that has least IRR is the one with least cost.

The IRR of different lease plans is computed as follows:

(₹ '000s)

Year	Equal rentals in arrears	Equal rentals in advance	Stepped up with increase of 10%	Stepped down with decrease of 10%	Fixed amount with final balloon
0	–1200.00	–1005.00	–1200.00	–1200.00	–1200.00
1	212.00	195.00	155.00	285.00	150.00
2	212.00	195.00	170.50	256.50	150.00
3	212.00	195.00	187.55	230.85	150.00
4	212.00	195.00	206.31	207.77	150.00
5	212.00	195.00	226.94	186.99	150.00
6	212.00	195.00	249.63	168.29	150.00
7	212.00	195.00	274.59	151.46	150.00
8	212.00	0.00	302.05	136.31	840.00
IRR*	**8.40%**	**8.30%**	**8.49%**	**8.38%**	**8.59%**

** IRR is computed using EXCEL.*

Tax implications not considered being common to all plans.

Based on the IRR of each plan we find that the Plan (b) "Equated rentals payable in advance" is the best, as it has the least cost for Sun Control Systems.

3. Determining Lease Rents

Worthwhile Leasing Limited needs to quote for leasing of machines on per-thousand basis. The lease period is 5 years and the residual value at the end of 5 years would be 3%.

If the leasing firm requires a return of 22% after considering the depreciation tax shield, what rate should it quote for semi-annual installments payable in arrears and in advance?

Solution

Amount to be funded	₹1,000
Period of lease	5 years
Required return, *r*	22.00%
Residual value, *R*	₹30
Semi-annual periods, *n*	10
Semi-annual returns	11.00%

Present value of annuity for 10 semi-annual periods at 11.00%

= PVIFA (11.00%, 10)

= 5.8892

Present value factor for 10 periods at 11.00%

= PVIF (11.00%, 10) = 0.3522

Let semi-annual lease rents payable in arrears = x

Then the lease rents and residual values must satisfy the following:

$x \times$ PVIFA(r%, n periods) + R $\times$ PVIF(r%, n) = Lease amount

$x \times 5.8892 + 30 \times 0.3522 = 1000$

Solving for x we get, x = ₹168.0074

The instalments payable in advance would be less by the 11%.

The amount of installment payable in advance would be

= ₹151.3580

4. Net Advantage of Lease

ABC Ltd is considering to buy a milling machine costing ₹9,50,000 which has a useful life of 5 years after which ABC Ltd can post tax realize ₹75,000. If ABC Ltd buys the machine, it can claim a depreciation of 25% on WDV basis. It will have to incur additional operational cost of ₹60,000 per annum.

Alternatively, the firm can go for lease of 5 years for which it would have to pay lease rents in arrears of ₹3,30,000.

Assuming the cost of debt at 12%, WACC at 12% and tax rate at 35%, find the following:

(a) Whether the firm should go for lease or buy the machine?

(b) What is the maximum lease rent that the firm can pay?

Solution

Following data is available:

	(₹ '000s)		(%)
Cost	950	Cost of debt	12.00%
Lease rent	330	Tax rate	35.00%
Additional operating cost	60	Post-tax cost of debt	7.80%
Post-tax salvage value	75	Depreciation WDV	25.00%
Period (years)	5	Post-tax WACC	12.00%

(a) Cash flows and their present value for lease alternative as against buying are as below:

(₹ '000s)

Year	0	1	2	3	4	5
Purchase cost avoided	950.00					
Depreciation tax shield lost		–83.13	–62.34	–46.76	–35.07	–26.30
Post-tax lease rents		–214.50	–214.50	–214.50	–214.50	–214.50
Net advantage of lease (NAL)	950.00	–297.63	–276.84	–261.26	–249.57	–240.80
Present value at post-tax cost of debt	950.00	–276.09	–238.23	–208.55	–184.81	–165.41
Present value of Net Advantage of Lease						–123.09
Add: PV of operating cost						140.59
Less: PV of salvage value						–42.56
PV of NAL with operating cost and salvage values considered						–25.06

Notes

Year	1	2	3	4	5
Depreciation					
Opening value	950.00	712.50	534.38	400.78	300.59
Depreciation (25%)	237.50	178.13	133.59	100.20	75.15
Closing value	712.50	534.38	400.78	300.59	225.44
Tax shield on depreciation	**83.13**	**62.34**	**46.76**	**35.07**	**26.30**
Operating cost					
Additional operating cost	60.00	60.00	60.00	60.00	60.00
Post-tax operating cost	39.00	39.00	39.00	39.00	39.00
PV at WACC	*34.82*	*31.09*	*27.76*	*24.79*	*22.13*
Cumulative PV at WACC					**140.59**
Salvage value					
Post-tax salvage value					75.00
Present value of salvage at WACC					**42.56**

Since the Net Advantage of Leasing is negative, the firm must buy the machine rather than go for the lease at ₹3,30,000 per annum.

(b) The leasing alternative is expensive by about ₹25,000 in present value terms.

To eliminate this disadvantage, the lease rents must reduce such that the present value of these lease rents is less by ₹25,000.

This may be done as follows:

Years = 5

Interest rate = 7.80%

Present value of annuity for 5 years at 7.80%

= PVIFA (7.80%, 5) = 4.0138

Net disadvantage of leasing with lease rent of ₹3,30,000

= ₹25,000

The lease rent therefore must decrease by = ₹6,228

Maximum lease rent that the firm can pay = 3,30,000 – 6,228

= ₹3,23,772

5. Lease vs Borrow

Super Analytic Limited (SAL) needs to have a special computer system for a project costing ₹12 crore. The project is likely to run for 5 years after which the computer system is worthless. A leasing firm has offered the lease for a period of 5 years with lease rents of ₹3.50 crore annually payable in arrears.

On the other hand, SAL can borrow from its existing bankers at 12% with equal installments spread over the life of the project of 5 years.

SAL pays taxes at 40% and charges depreciation at 25% on written down value basis.

Find out which of the alternative of leasing and borrowing is more attractive for SAL.

Solution

We have the following data available:

Cost (₹ lakh)	1200	Cost of debt	12.00%
Lease Rents (₹ lakh)	350	Tax Rate	40.00%
		Post-tax cost	7.20%
Life (years)	5	Depreciation, WDV	25.00%

Loan alternative

When the firm decides to avail the loan, it pays the installments of loan over the life of the asset, the period of lease.

The amount of equated installment is worked out on the basis of period of loan and the interest rate applicable for the loan.

Nos. of years = 5

Loan taken= ₹1,200 lakh

Interest rate= 11%

Present value of annuity for 5 years at 11.00%

= PVIFA (11.00%, 5) = 3.6959

Amount of installment = loan amount/PVIFA(r,n)

= ₹324.68 lakh

This loan installment consists of interest and repayment of principal. The firm would be entitled to deduction of interest for tax purposes.

The amount of loan for repayment of principal and interest with the tax savings is worked out as follows:

(₹ *lakh*)

Year	**1**	**2**	**3**	**4**	**5**
Loan outstanding -opening	1,200.00	1,007.32	793.44	556.03	292.51
Amount of interest	132.00	110.80	87.28	61.16	32.18
Amount of repayment	192.68	213.88	237.41	263.52	292.51
Loan outstanding - end	1,007.32	793.44	556.03	292.51	0.00
Tax saved on interest	**52.80**	**44.32**	**34.91**	**24.47**	**12.87**

Besides savings of tax on interest, the firm would also be entitled to the tax saving on the depreciation. Though depreciation is not cash saving, the tax saved thereon is cash flow saved. Depreciation tax shield is worked out as follows:

(₹ *lakh*)

Year	**1**	**2**	**3**	**4**	**5**
Value of Asset–opening	1,200.00	900.00	675.00	506.25	379.69
Depreciation	300.00	225.00	168.75	126.56	94.92
Value of Asset - closing	900.00	675.00	506.25	379.69	284.77
Tax saved on depreciation	**120.00**	**90.00**	**67.50**	**50.63**	**37.97**

Cash flows of the loan, net of tax shields on interest and depreciation for the period of borrowing are as follows:

(₹ *lakh*)

Year	***1***	***2***	***3***	***4***	***5***
Cash flows of loan					
Loan installment	324.68	324.68	324.68	324.68	324.68
Tax saved on interest	–52.80	–44.32	–34.91	–24.47	–12.87
Tax saved on depreciation	–120.00	–90.00	–67.50	–50.63	–37.97
Net cash flow of borrowing	151.88	190.36	222.27	249.59	273.85
PV of cash flows at post tax cost of borrowing	141.68	165.65	180.43	189.00	193.43
Total cost of borrowing					**870.19**

Lease alternative

For the cost of the lease, we have no tax shield available for either interest or depreciation.

However the lease rentals are deductible as expense for tax purpose. Therefore, tax would be saved on the amount of lease rentals paid. Cash flows of the lease option are as follows:

(₹ *lakh*)

Year	**1**	**2**	**3**	**4**	**5**
Cash flows of lease					
Lease rent	350.00	350.00	350.00	350.00	350.00
Tax saved	140.00	140.00	140.00	140.00	140.00
Net lease payment	210.00	210.00	210.00	210.00	210.00
Present value	195.90	182.74	170.46	159.02	148.34
Total cost of leasing					**856.45**

Since the cost of borrowing is more, SAL must opt leasing of the computer system.

EXERCISES

Concept Review Questions

1. What do you understand by a lease? Explain its various terms.
2. What is a sale and lease-back transaction? How does this method help the lessee?
3. What are the cash flows of lease? Why do you feel that the differential cash flows of lease and buy option are appropriate methods of evaluation of lease proposal?
4. What do you understand by net advantage of lease? What are the rules for an appropriate decision?
5. Why is the post-tax cost of debt the appropriate rate of discounting the cash flows of lease, rather than the WACC of the firm?
6. How is hire purchase transaction different from a lease transaction?

Critical Thinking Questions

1. Both the lessor and leasse pay the same amount of taxes and are entitled to the same amount of depreciation. Yet there can be common grounds for entering into a lease transaction. What can such considerations be?
2. Can the two methods of evaluation of financial lease, i.e., net advantage of lease and equivalent loan, give contradicting results? Why or why not?
3. A manager of the firm asserts that when he leases an asset he avoids borrowing, and it helps in keeping the debt–equity ratio of the firm within acceptable limits. Therefore, he opts for leasing wherever possible, since it is a tangible advantage to avoid debt and yet reap the benefits of using the asset. Do you agree with his viewpoint?

Practical Assignments

1. Visit any car financing company and examine how they fix the lease rental for the various brands, sizes, and tenure of lease of the cars. Do you find any variations in return in financing of small, medium, and large cars? Also find if there is any difference in returns between 3-year and 7-year leases? If you notice any variations in return, find out the reasons.
2. Repeat Assignment 1 for housing loans of 10-year, 15-year and 20-year tenures. Calculate IRRs of lease payments.

Numerical Problems

1. Fixing Lease Rentals under Different Plans

A firm is planning to take on lease a DG set costing ₹5 lakh having useful life of 5 years after which its value would be nil. The firm has different lease structures in mind. The leasing company requires a return of 20%. Find out the lease rents under the following patterns:

(i) Equated lease rentals payable in arrears
(ii) Equated lease rentals payable in advance
(iii) Lease rentals to increase by 20% annually and payable in arrears
(iv) First four instalments of ₹1,00,000 each in arrears and remaining in the fifth year.

2. Lease vs Borrow

In order to have an uninterrupted supply of electricity, ABC Limited needs to install a DG set costing ₹10 lakh. It has a useful life of 5 years and the salvage value can be taken as nil. The firm has two options to acquire the DG set: to lease it for a payment of ₹2,75,000 annually in arrears, or obtain a loan at 12% interest, repayable in 5 equal instalments.

If the firm can charge depreciation on straight line method and has a tax rate of 36%, which of the alternatives must the firm pursue?

3. NAL Method

Evaluate Problem 2 by using Net Advantage of Leasing method. Do the cash flows of lease and buy change under this method? Furthermore, would your conclusion change?

4. Equivalent Loan Method

Evaluate Problem 2 and decide the lease vs borrow issue by the equivalent loan method. State at what capital cost of equipment the buying option would be more economical.

5. Lease vs Borrow—Depreciation Methods and Patterns of Loans

Solid Builders Ltd are planning to procure a mobile mixing machine that costs ₹12 lakh. It has an expected life of 8 years with no salvage value at the end. A leasing company has offered a lease for the machine at rents of ₹2.60 lakh annually payable in arrears. The company also has the option of getting a term loan at 13% for 8 years. The firm pays income tax at 40%. Evaluate the desirability of lease with following conditions:

(i) With depreciation on SLM basis and equated annual repayment of loans
(ii) With depreciation on WDV basis and repayment of loan in 8 annual instalments of ₹1.50 lakh along with interest.

6. NAL Method

A DG set costing ₹40 lakh with useful life of 4 years and residual value of ₹10 lakh is taken on lease of ₹9 lakh per annum, payable in arrears.

The DG set could be procured at 16% loan. In such a case the depreciation would be charged on SLM basis. The firm has a tax rate of 50%. Find if DG set should be leased.

7. Leveraged Lease

Dynamic Enterprises Ltd has given on lease a plant worth ₹400 million. As it had only 20% of the amount on hand, it borrowed the remaining 80% at 20% interest.

The period of loan and the lease is 8 years. If Dynamic Enterprises requires a pre-tax return of 25%, what minimum lease rentals must it fix?

CASE STUDY

Oriental Trading Company*

Background

Oriental Trading Company Ltd (OTC) is in the business of trading in fun products ranging from toys to party products, from crafts and hobbies to holiday products. The company has witnessed an average annual growth rate of 20% during the last 5 years and is expected to sustain this rate of growth at least in the coming 3–5 years due to the potentially untapped market, particularly in tier 2 cities in India, and also a huge export potential for its products.

The company has its corporate office in Andheri, Mumbai. The corporate office has a floor area of 20,000 square feet and is equipped with offices for the Chairman, the Managing Director, the three VPs, a conference room, a reception area, recreation room, an open space with partition for staff, a computer server room, and a kitchen area. The office houses a staff of 200 personnel and the current occupancy rate for the company is 70%. The available office space is estimated to be sufficient for the company's requirement for the next 5 years, with minor modifications.

The leasing option was seen as the most practical and affordable option 3 years back, and hence the company entered into a lease contract for 3 years. The lease contract will be due for renewal on 31st March this year (6 months from now). Real estate prices have really skyrocketed in recent months. Also, with vacancies declining, particularly in the key business locations, the lessors are trying to encash on the opportunity.

In view of this, the current lease contract can be renewed only with a 20% hike in the starting lease rentals, and also with a clause allowing 10% annual hike. The financials of the company are as follows:

Financials

Oriental Trading Company Ltd
Balance Sheet as on 31 March 2006

(₹ *in lakh*)

Assets	*Amount*	*Liabilities*	*Amount*
Fixed Assets (including office equipment and fittings)	150	Share capital	2919
		Reserves and Surplus	1354
		Long term loans	—
Cash and Cash Equivalents	3579	Accounts payable	132
Short-term Investments	178	Accruals	14
Accounts Receivables	373		
Inventories	139		
Total	4419	Total	4419

*Ideated and adapted from Real Estate and Capital Structure Decisions—Lease-Versus-Buy analysis, Frederik Pretorius, Centre for Asian Business Cases, University of Hong Kong, 10th February 2003, Ref. No. 03/158C.
Source: http://www.realestatemumbai.com/
http://www.indiainfoline.com/

Income Statement for Oriental Trading Company Ltd
for the year ended 31 March 2006 (₹ *in lakh*)

Net Sales	2037.43
Operating costs	826.14
Depreciation	27.35
Rent	475
Operating income	708.95
Other income	113.95
Earnings before interest and tax (EBIT)	822.90
Interest	12.00
Less: Earnings before tax	810.90
Tax	298.00
Earnings after tax	512.89
Dividends	205.16
Retained earnings	307.74

Notes:
1. The operating costs are exclusive of depreciation
2. The rent payments include, in addition to the rent paid for the 2 warehouses of the company, the lease rental payment for the corporate office premises at the rate of ₹150 per square foot.
3. Other income comprises of interest income and income from investments. The share of the 2 heads of income being 35% and 65% respectively.
4. The corporate tax rate for resident Indian companies is 35%. An additional surcharge of 5% is also levied. The effective tax rate for the company for the previous year has been 22%.
5. The total number of shares outstanding at the end of the year is 20,00,000.

In terms of location, the choice before the company is restricted to South Mumbai, which area offers the best strategic advantages for the company's business. The company has to weigh the respective cost benefits of the leasing strategy and the buying strategy in order to be able to take a final decision.

Leasing Option

The leasing option gives a lot of flexibility to the company, as the company can lease according to its changing business requirements in terms of size and location. At times of slump in the real estate market, benefits can be availed by the company as it can strike a favourable deal. It also helps the company to utilize its resources for its core business initiatives, instead of tying them up in real estate. Besides, it enables the lessee to charge the lease rentals paid to revenues and further, to transfer maintenance responsibility to the lessor. The prevalent lease rentals for similar kinds of office space in different locations of South Mumbai are as follows:

Lease rentals for different locations in South Mumbai

(₹ /sq.ft.)

₹/sq.ft./month	*Worli*	*Lower Parel*	*Bandra Kurla*	*Andheri Kurla*	*Malad*	*Powai*
Avg. Base Rent	185	125	180	75	43	68
Gross Rent	207	133	202	80	46	72
Average Efficiency (%)	75%	70%	70%	70%	82%	80%
Net Effective Occupancy Cost	276	190	289	114	56	90

Buying Option

The benefit of buying office space is that the company is able to capture the rising real estate value on its balance sheet. Several companies have in the recent past realized heavy capital gains on the sale of office spaces that they owned. They then leveraged the sale price that they realized by taking mortgage loans and acquiring much bigger office space.

Owning office space has proved to be a beneficial proposition for such companies. But the flip side of ownership is that these companies could not avail of the benefit in times of slump in the real estate market. With interest rates hardening, these companies have ended up paying heavy amounts of interest, that eroded their profits, on mortgage loans.

Purchase of property allows for double deductibility: for depreciation and for the interest paid on the mortgage loan. However it increases the firm's debt–equity ratio, which may erode the firm's future debt-raising potential. If the company decides to buy its own office space, then it will have to do so at prevailing costs, which are as follows:

Cost of acquisition of office space in South Mumbai

Location	*Cost per square feet (₹)*
Worli	11000–21000
Parel	6500–14000
Bandra Kurla	11000–28000
Andheri Kurla	6500–8500
Malad	5000–7000
Powai	4500–6500

Decision Problem

There are 3 options before the company: first, to continue at its current official location with the 20% initial hike, and 10% annual hike thereafter, in the lease rentals; second, to shift to another leased office space at some suitable location in South Mumbai; and third, to buy its own office premises.

As per standard practice in the real estate market, for commercial leases a 3-year lease contract is standard. If the company decides to buy the required office space, it will have to make a 40% down payment and finance the balance with a floating rate mortgage loan at an interest rate of 11.25% per annum. If it decides to go along with the renewal of the current lease contract, it will have to accommodate the 20% hike in the lease rentals that will erode its bottom line. Shifting to other leased premises may take care of this significant hike in the lease rentals, but this may be a temporary relief only.

The crucial issue facing the firm is: should it go in for leasing of office space or buy its own office space? The basic concern before the company in taking a decision is the probable impact of the decision on the balance sheet, its profits, and the dividend payout, besides its debt–equity ratio.

Interest Rates Prevailing

Savings Bank	*Call Money*	*Term Loans*	*Best Rate*
3.5%	5.25%–6.25%	7.05%–8.30%	8.5%–9.85%

In the CD

Finding EMI and its Segregation in Interest and Repayment of Principal

(i) Payment in Advance
(ii) Payment in Arrears

CHAPTER

19 Dividend Decision

LEARNING OBJECTIVES

After going through this chapter, the readers would know

- what is dividend
- relevance of dividend for the value of the firm
- about the conflicts of the relevance and the irrelevance theory, especially the Gordon's model and Miller and Modigliani theory of irrelevance
- what is home-made dividend and its mechanism in making dividend irrelevant
- valuation of the firm with dividend capitalization model
- limitations of model of irrelevance
- factors in the real world that influence the policies on dividend
- about passive residual dividend policy and the different features that a dividend policy must have
- what is signalling and clientele effect
- what are the alternative forms of dividend, e.g. (i) bonus shares, (ii) split shares, and (iii) share buyback
- the advantages and disadvantages of share buyback in comparison to cash dividend payment

SMRIDHI AND SIDHANT–DIVIDEND FOR PIZZAS

Smridhi and Sidhant Mehra, both retired professionals in finance, had invested a major part of their savings in the stock market. The academic parity of both the husband and the wife as professional bankers, and an abundance of time at the disposal of both of them often led to healthy debates on matters of finance.

Smridhi received the mail and was very excited and enthusiastic, because experience told her, based on the appearance of the envelopes, that they contained advices of dividend and/or corporate actions. She was delighted to see the ECS advice of dividend from Hindustan Lever Ltd, confirming dividend at ₹6 per share, as against ₹5 paid the previous year. The second envelope contained a bumper news (in fact, she already knew about both these developments through the newspapers) from ITC Ltd: her two shares had been made equal to 30 shares through a 1:2 bonus, followed by a simultaneous 1:10 split.

Sidhant: What is there to be so pleased about?

Smridhi: Well, I am happy because I am richer this year. I have more money to spend. I am ordering pizza for lunch this afternoon.

Sidhant: I find nothing great about it. The company has given you what already belonged to you. If it had not given it to you this year, it would have given it next year. There is nothing to be happy about in realizing the ownership of something that you already own.

Smridhi: I do not agree. All right, the dividend money belonged to me. But the fact that they have enhanced the amount provides good signals for the future.

Sidhant: A judgement of how rich or poor you are, is made on the basis of the amount of money you earn and not by how much you spend or save.

Smridhi: Yes, the income level determines wealth. But people assess your wealth by the money you spend. People think that the more you spend, the richer you are. It is a perception of people that, more often than not, proves correct. Income is not disclosed publicly, but what you spend is in the knowledge of everybody. Your spending sends signals to all those watching you. Everybody assumes that you spend in proportion with your earning, though there may be some aberrations.

Sidhant: You must concentrate on what the company earns and not what it distributes.

Smridhi: No doubt, earnings are important, but dividends too are important because dividends reflect earning levels. The part that is given to you is certain, while the earnings remain with the company. How well they would use it is always a moot point.

Sidhant: I am sure firms can invest better than you because of the collective expertise and the knowledge they possess.

Smridhi: Not necessarily. If that were so, so many companies would not be winding up. Firms commit bigger mistakes than individuals do.

Sidhant: Then, you must apply your mind in choosing better companies to invest in.

Smridhi: Yes, I do that. But it does not dilute the importance of dividend. Dividend is important because it satisfies the current needs of consumption.

Sidhant: Well, you can always buy and sell shares in the market according to your consumption needs.

Smridhi: That is impractical. If I were investing in bank deposits only, you would then suggest, by the same logic, that I keep all the money in fixed deposits and nothing in liquid form, either in current accounts or savings accounts. Shall we keep making and breaking fixed deposits as per our daily needs?

Sidhant: That certainly is inconvenient.

Smridhi: Precisely for the same reasons of convenience, dividends are welcome. That is why current income becomes important. And to that extent, increased dividends provide additional current income.

The pizza they had ordered was delivered at their home by then.

Sidhant: This reminds me of Miller and Modigliani. Pizza has the same value, no matter whether it is a single piece, or cut in four or eight pieces.

Smridhi: No. There is a difference. We cut it into pieces for the convenience of eating. Besides, a pizza cut into many pieces can fetch a better value than the whole single piece.

Sidhant: Why?

Smridhi: If the pizza was split into eight pieces, you could possibly sell them to eight different customers. There would be eight customers now, and you would have a higher number of people craving for it. For all you know, each piece could be sold at more than one-eighth of the value of the whole pizza. Therefore, as a pizza seller, you may benefit more by selling eight one-eighth pieces, rather than a single whole.

Sidhant: Well, you have given me some practical insights to why firms issue bonus shares or split the shares. But I still believe that the income of the firm is the only factor in the potential of returns from investing.

INTRODUCTION

The part of earning that is distributed is called dividend. The optimum dividend policy would be one that maximizes the value of the firm.

A firm earns for its shareholders. Income remaining after meeting all other obligations of the firm belongs to the shareholders. Shareholders left with this residual income face another vital question as to what must be done with the income earned. Basically, they face one question that throws open three choices. The single question that needs to be answered is: what fraction of earnings must be distributed, and what fraction must be retained? The first choice is to retain 100% of the earnings in the business and deploy these funds to implement projects that will enhance future income. The second choice facing the firm is to distribute 100% of the earnings among the shareholders themselves, and let individual shareholders decide for themselves what to do with the income so distributed. The third choice is to retain a part of the earnings and distribute the remainder to the shareholders. Naturally, this choice will raise another question: what fraction of earnings is to be retained, and what fraction is to be distributed?

The question of the ratio of retained to distributed earnings is referred to as *dividend decision* or *policy*. The guiding philosophy of the dividend decision is naturally to adopt a policy that maximizes the shareholders' wealth. Therefore, from the viewpoint of financial management, the objective is to find out the dividend policy that will maximize or enhance the value of the firm.

There are two divergent schools of thoughts on dividend policy. One school of thought believes that the dividend policy matters in determining the value of the firm, while the other school of thought advocates that the dividend decision is irrelevant to the determination of the value of the firm. We shall have a look at both the philosophies.

RELEVANCE OF DIVIDEND

The school of thought that considers the value of the firm to be dependant on the dividend policy includes two models: Walter's Model and Gordon's Model. Both the models are similar, and make similar assumptions with similar conclusions.

There are two schools of thought regarding dividend policy. One set of people believes that dividend policy affects the value of the firm, while the other regards dividend policy as irrelevant.

These models of valuation of the firm link the dividend policy to investment opportunities available. These models support the view that dividend policy is material to the value of the firm, and is dependent upon the kind of investment opportunities that are available to the firm, in comparison with the expectations of shareholders.

Assuming sufficient business opportunities are available to the firm, then the dividend policy affecting the firm's value will depend upon the returns that are being offered by these opportunities, compared to the expectations of shareholders. If these business opportunities offer higher returns than the expectations of shareholders, then a dividend policy oriented towards retention of earnings for exploiting new business opportunities will be more rewarding to shareholders than a policy that favours distributing the earnings and forgoing any profitable business opportunities. In such situations, the dividend policy favouring retention of earnings should lead to a larger increase in the value of the firm than the dividend policy favouring distribution of earnings.

On the contrary, if available business opportunities provide a return that is less than the expected return to the shareholders, then retention of earnings to finance the new business opportunities will diminish the value of the firm rather than adding to it. In such a situation, distributing earnings to shareholders, rather than retaining them in the business, will be advisable. A dividend policy favouring greater payout will add more value to the firm.

WALTER'S MODEL

Walter developed one of the earliest models linking the value of the firm to its dividend policy. The value of the firm as per Walter's Model is given in Equation 19-1.

$$P_0 = \frac{D}{r} + \frac{k(E-D)/r}{r} \tag{19-1}$$

where P_0 = current price,
D = dividend,
E = earnings
r = expected returns by shareholders, and
k = reinvestment rate of the firm

Walter's Model considers the value of the firm to be the sum of two components; (i) an infinite stream of dividend, D and (ii) an infinite stream of retained earning, $E - D$ reinvested at a constant rate k, which are generated each year for an infinite length of time.

Equation 19-1 may be derived as follows:

Walter's Model links the value of the firm to the earning level, dividend level, reinvestment rate, and shareholders' expectations.

Present value of constant dividend n perpetuity

$$= \frac{D}{1+r} + \frac{D}{(1+r)^2} + \frac{D}{(1+r)^3} + \frac{D}{(1+r)^4} + \dots$$

$$= \frac{D}{r}$$

Present value of first retained earnings reinvested at k

$$= \frac{(E-D)k}{(1+r)^2} + \frac{(E-D)k^2}{(1+r)^3} + \frac{(E-D)k^3}{(1+r)^4} + \dots$$

$$= \frac{(E-D)k}{r(1+r)}$$

Present value of second retained earnings reinvested at k

$$= \frac{(E-D)k}{(1+r)^3} + \frac{(E-D)k^2}{(1+r)^4} + \frac{(E-D)k^3}{(1+r)^5} + \dots$$

$$= \frac{(E-D)k}{r(1+r)^2}$$

Present value of third retained earnings reinvested at k

$$= \frac{(E-D)k}{(1+r)^2} + \frac{(E-D)k^2}{(1+r)^3} + \frac{(E-D)k^3}{(1+r)^4} + \dots$$

$$= \frac{(E-D)k}{r(1+r)^3}$$

When all the retained earnings are added for an infinite period, they would add up to $\frac{k(E-D)/r}{r}$. Adding this to the dividend stream, we get Equation 19-1.

Equation 19-1 can alternatively be viewed as returns to shareholders, consisting of the sum of (i) dividend yield and (ii) the capital appreciation in price, as given in Equation 19-2.

$$r = \frac{D}{P_0} + \frac{\Delta P}{P_0} \tag{19-2}$$

Capital appreciation is provided by the retained earnings as amount retained with the ratio of reinvestment rate and shareholders' expectations.

$$\Delta P = \frac{k}{r}(E-D)$$

and the value of the firm is

$$P_0 = \frac{D + \frac{k}{r}(E-D)}{r}$$

Assumptions and Limitations

In the above analysis, we have made following assumptions, which are also the limitations of the model:

1. Funding of new projects is done solely from earnings. Issuing fresh equity or raising debt to fund the growth is not considered. In reality, this is rarely the case, as most firm resort to outside financing at some point of time. However, this assumption is necessary to highlight the impact of the dividend policy on the value of the firm. Based on this assumption alone the conclusions made will be unaffected even if some amount of external funding, either through equity or through borrowing, is used to fund the growth.
2. Growth opportunities do not alter the risk profile of the firm as a whole, and therefore, the market capitalization rate remains constant. This assumption too holds in the normal course, as most firms engage in diversification projects in fields that are related. Furthermore, each of the diversification projects is comparatively small, relative to the size of the firm. Under such circumstances, the risk profile undergoes a change that is gradual; therefore, the conclusions made will be true for the reasonably foreseeable future. However, such conclusions may not hold true from a long-term viewpoint, as the risk profile may change substantially over longer periods; they may also not hold true if the firm undertakes a diversification plan that is unrelated, or is too big compared to the current level of operations.
3. The firm is a going concern and the pricing model assumes perpetual earnings. This assumption too seems reasonable; the effects of distant cash flows on the price of shares in the valuation model are minimal, as they are discounted. A change in the cash flow for the next year has a far greater impact on prices than the cash flow of tenth year.
4. Lastly, there is an implied assumption that the reinvestment rate *k* remains constant. Normally, all available projects do not have the same rate of return. Different projects have different rates of return, and the firm chooses projects in descending order—first accepting the project with the highest rate of return—and keeps choosing projects till funds are available, or any other constraint is faced. However, as long as the assumptions of comparative values of reinvestment rate and market capitalization rate hold good, the conclusions made about the impact on prices would remain valid.

Walter's model assumes inter-dependence of the investment and dividend decisions.

According to Walter's Model, the capital budgeting decision and dividend decision are interrelated. The capital budgeting policy determines the value of the firm, as the assets created provide

Table 19-1 Impact of dividend policy on price–Walter's Model

Growing Firm	*Declining Firm*	*Normal Firm*
Reinvestment Rate (k > r)	*Reinvestment Rate (k < r)*	*Reinvestment Rate (k = r)*
	Current Dividend Payout 50%	
$E = ₹\ 20$ $D = ₹\ 10$ $k = 20\%$ $r = 16\%$	$E = ₹\ 20$ $D - ₹\ 10$ $k = 12\%$ $r = 16\%$	$E = ₹\ 20$ $D - ₹\ 10$ $k = 16\%$ $r = 16\%$
	Current Market Price, P_0	
$P_0 = \frac{D + \frac{k}{r}(E-D)}{r}$ $= \frac{10 + \frac{0.20}{0.16}(20-10)}{0.16} = 140.63$	$P_0 = \frac{D + \frac{k}{r}(E-D)}{r}$ $= \frac{10 + \frac{0.12}{0.16}(20-10)}{0.16} = 109.37$	$P_0 = \frac{D + \frac{k}{r}(E-D)}{r}$ $= \frac{10 + \frac{0.16}{0.16}(20-10)}{0.16} = 125.00$
	Expected Price – Increased dividend pay out to 75%, i.e. ₹ 15 per share	
$P_0 = \frac{15 + \frac{0.20}{0.16}(20-15)}{0.16} = 132.81$	$P_0 = \frac{15 + \frac{0.12}{0.16}(20-15)}{0.16} = 117.19$	$P_0 = \frac{15 + \frac{0.16}{0.16}(20-15)}{0.16} = 125.00$
	Expected Price – Decreased dividend pay out to 25%, i.e. ₹ 5 per share	
$P_0 = \frac{15 + \frac{0.20}{0.16}(20-5)}{0.16} = 148.48$	$P_0 = \frac{5 + \frac{0.12}{0.16}(20-5)}{0.16} = 101.62$	$P_0 = \frac{5 + \frac{0.16}{0.16}(20-5)}{0.16} = 125.00$
	Impact of the dividend policy on the price	
If dividend payout increases, the price decreases.	If dividend payout increases, the price increases.	Price remains the same irrespective of dividend payout.

value to the firm. The dividend policy becomes a key determinant of the value of the firm because it will materially affect the capital budgeting process.

As per Equation 19-1, the value is a function of expected dividend, capitalization rate, reinvestment rate, and the amount reinvested, all of which lead to capital appreciation in future. The impact of the dividend policy of a firm on its value can be seen in Table 19-1.

We have taken three firms with identical levels of current earnings, and the same dividend policy, with a payout ratio at 50%. These three firms are different only in terms of their future prospects; this explains the different current prices of their shares. One of the firms, classified as a *growth firm*, offers a reinvestment rate in excess of the return desired by the market. The second firm is a *declining firm* that does not have more profitable business opportunities. The third firm, classified as a *normal firm*, has just enough projects to meet the market expectations of return. For all the three firms, price is calculated with increased and decreased dividend payout in Table 19-1.

Conclusions of Walter's Model

As is evident from Table 19-1, the key determinant of the dividend policy and value of the firm is the reinvestment rate of retained earnings. The following observations can be made

(a) For a *growing firm*, the market value will (i) increase if dividend payout ratio is decreased and (ii) decrease if dividend pay out is increased. This is because shareholders on their own cannot earn more on the distributed earnings than the firm would with the money retained. Therefore, a 0% payout would maximize the share price of the firm.

(b) For a *declining firm*, the opposite will happen. Here, the shareholders can earn more on distributed earnings than the firm can provide from retained earnings. A dividend policy of 100% payout will maximize the value of the firm.

(c) However, for a *normal firm*, investors are indifferent to the dividend policy because retained earnings will yield the same return as distributed earnings. Therefore, the share price for such a firm remains constant, and the dividend policy becomes irrelevant.

The optimum dividend policy is determined by reinvestment rate, k. If k exceeds shareholders' expectations r, then the optimum dividend policy is 100% retention; if k < r, then the optimum is 100% payout, and when k = r the dividend policy is immaterial.

GORDON'S MODEL

It starts with a valuation model similar to that of Walter's Model. The value of the firm, as per the constant growth dividend capitalization model, is the discounted value of the dividend in perpetuity. Dividend is not constant, because the portion of earnings that is retained is reinvested in the growth of the firm,

Table 19-2 Impact of dividend policy on price (Gordon's Model)

Growing Firm	*Declining Firm*	*Normal Firm*
Reinvestment Rate k > r	*Reinvestment Rate k < r*	*Reinvestment Rate k = r*
	Current Dividend pay out 50%	
E_1 = ₹ 20 D_1 = ₹ 10 k = 20% r = 16%	E_1 = ₹ 20 D_1 = ₹ 10 k = 12% r = 16%	E_1 = ₹ 20 D_1 = ₹ 10 k = 16% r = 16%
	Current Market Price P_0	
$P_0 = \frac{E_1 \times (1-b)}{r-bk} = \frac{10}{0.16-0.10}$ = ₹ 166.67	$P_0 = \frac{E_1 \times (1-b)}{r-bk} = \frac{10}{0.16-0.06}$ = ₹ 100.00	$P_0 = \frac{E_1 \times (1-b)}{r-bk} = \frac{10}{0.16-0.08}$ = ₹ 125.00
	Expected Price – Increased dividend pay out to 75% i.e. ₹ 15 per share	
$P_0 = \frac{15}{0.16-0.05}$ = ₹ 136.36	$P_0 = \frac{15}{0.16-0.03}$ = ₹ 115.38	$P_0 = \frac{15}{0.16-0.04}$ = ₹ 125.00
	Expected Price – Decreased dividend pay out to 25%, i.e., ₹ 5 per share	
$P_0 = \frac{5}{0.16-0.15}$ = ₹ 500.00	$P_0 = \frac{5}{0.16-0.09}$ = ₹ 71.43	$P_0 = \frac{5}{0.16-0.12}$ = ₹ 125.00
	Impact of the dividend policy on the price	
If dividend pay out increases, the price decreases.	If dividend pay out increases, the price increases.	Price remains the same irrespective of dividend pay out.

Another model that supports the relevance of dividend policy is Gordon's Model. Its assumptions and conclusions are similar to Walter's Model.

and hence, results in the growth of dividend period after period. If earnings and dividend for the next period 1 are E_1 and D_1 respectively, and the growth in dividend each year is g, then the value of the firm is given by Equation 19-3, as derived in Chapter 7.

$$P_0 = \frac{D_1}{r - g} \tag{19-3}$$

We modify Equation 19-3 to incorporate the dividend policy of the firm. If the earnings level for the next period is E_1, and if b is the retention ratio, the amount of dividend is $E_1(1 - b)$. The reinvested funds are $E_1 \times b$, and if they are reinvested at k, the growth in absolute terms will be $E_1 \times b \times k$. The relative growth, g, will be $b \times k$. Incorporating the above changes, the valuation of the firm can be given by Equation 19-4.

$$P_0 = \frac{E_1 \times (1 - b)}{r - bk} \tag{19-4}$$

Therefore, the dividend policy as reflected in the retention ratio of b is one of the important determinants of the valuation of the firm. This formulation is similar to Walter's Model, and has a similar set of assumptions. The impact of changes in the retention ratio on the value of the firm is presented in Table 19-2.

The crux of Gordon's Model lies in the relationship between dividend and growth and the balancing of the two. An increase in dividend, taken in isolation, would lead to an increase in price as the value of the numerator in Equation 19-3 increases. But as we increase the dividend, the lesser amount is retained, and hence, a lesser growth g is expected. A reduction in growth would push the price of the share downwards. There would be two opposite forces operating on the value of the firm.

Like Walter's Model, the value of the firm under Gordon's Model is also dependent upon the reinvestment rate and shareholders' expectations.

The data in Table 19-2 reveal that the value of the firm must (i) rise with increasing retention, if the firm's reinvestment rate exceeds shareholders' expectations (and *vice versa*), (ii) fall with increasing retention, if the reinvestment rate is lower than the expectations of shareholders (and *vice versa*), and (iii) remain the same if the reinvestment rate equals shareholders' expectations.

The impact of changes in the dividend policy on the value of the firm is evident from the data in Table 19-2. When the firm matches investors' expectations ($k = r$), the price of the share becomes independent of the dividend policy. The value of the firm under such circumstances purely becomes a function of the earning power of the assets, E_1, and the shareholders' expectations, r, as shown in Equation 19-5.

$$\text{When } k = r; \quad P_0 = \frac{E_1 \times (1 - b)}{r - bk} = \frac{E_1}{r} \tag{19-5}$$

When the firm is unable to match the expectations of the shareholders ($k < r$), retention is not favourable, because investors can generate more than the firm can. The optimum dividend policy will then be a 100% payout, i.e. $b = 0$. Again, the value of the firm would be the same, as given by Equation 19-5.

When $k < r$, then optimum value would be at $b = 0$;

$$P_0 = \frac{E_1 \times (1 - b)}{r - bk} = \frac{E_1}{r}$$

The earning power of the firm is less than shareholders' expectations ($k < r$), and so, the value of the firm would naturally be less to that extent.

The problem with Gordon's Model arises when k exceeds r. When a firm can exceed the expectations of investors, the optimum dividend payout would be 0%, i.e. $b = 1.00$. This makes the price of the share indeterminable, going by Equation 19-5. An additional assumption in Gordon's Model would then be that ($b \times k < r$) or ($b < r \div k$). This seems reasonable because the growth rate of dividend g cannot exceed the market capitalization rate r. This is realistic, as it is difficult to imagine a situation where the firm can offer a growth of, say, 20% in dividend and the investors seem pleased with a return less than 20%. If a firm can offer 20% growth, the investors must immediately revise their expectations to beyond 20%, and therefore, r would be greater than $b \times k$.

Walter's Model vs Gordon's Model

The assumptions of both Walter's Model and Gordon's Model are the same. The conclusions too are identical. Yet for the same set of parameters, the two models arrive at different values. With earnings and dividend at ₹20 and ₹10 respectively, a reinvestment rate of 20%, and shareholders' expectations at 16%, the value of the firm as per Walter's Model is ₹140.63.

Walter's Model keeps the dividend amount constant in each period, while Gordon's Model assumes growing dividend in each period.

$$P_0 = \frac{D + \frac{k}{r}(E - D)}{r}$$

$$= \frac{10 + \frac{0.20}{0.16}(20 - 10)}{0.16}$$

$$= ₹140.63$$

For the same parameters, the value of the firm as per Gordon's Model is ₹166.67.

$$P_0 = \frac{E_1 \times (1 - b)}{r - bk} = \frac{20(1 - 0.5)}{0.16 - 0.5 \times 0.20} = ₹166.67$$

The difference in value is due to the assumption of growth. Walter's Model assumes constant earnings and dividend for each period, while Gordon's Model assumes a growth in dividend as well as in earnings for each period. Dividend payout is constant, but the dividends are not constant in Gordon's Model.

Example 19-1 Value with Walter's Model and Gordon's Model

Assume that a firm has current earnings of ₹10 per share. It can use these earnings in projects that provide a return of 15%. The expected return to shareholders is 20%. What is the value of the firm under (a) Walter's Model and (b) Gordon's Model, if it retains (i) 40%, (ii) 50%, and (iii) 60% of the earnings?

Solution

(a) As per Walter's Model, the market price of the share is

With 40% payout,

$$P_0 = \frac{D + \frac{k}{r}(E-D)}{r} + \frac{4 + \frac{0.15}{0.20}(10-4)}{0.20}$$

$$= ₹40.50$$

With 50% payout,

$$P_0 = \frac{5 + \frac{0.15}{0.20}(10-5)}{0.20} = ₹43.75$$

With 60% payout,

$$P_0 = \frac{6 + \frac{0.15}{0.20}(10-6)}{0.20} = ₹45.00$$

(b) As per Gordon's Model the price of the share would be:

With 40% payout,

$$P_0 = \frac{E_1 \times (1-b)}{r - bk}$$

$$= \frac{10\,(1-0.6)}{0.20 - 0.6 \times 0.15} = ₹36.36$$

With 50% payout,

$$P_0 = \frac{10(1-0.5)}{0.20 - 0.5 \times 0.15} = ₹40.00$$

With 60% payout,

$$P_0 = \frac{10(1-0.4)}{0.20 - 0.4 \times 0.15} = ₹42.86$$

Bird-in-the-Hand Theory

Data in the last column of Table 19-2 and in Equation 19-5 relating to the event when $k = r$ suggest that the value of the firm is independent of its dividend policy. However, the argument of Gordon, which says that the return expected by shareholders is not completely independent of dividend payout, is stretched further. The argument is referred to as the *bird-in-the-hand argument*, based on the famous proverb, 'a bird in the hand is better than two in the bush.'

The bird-in-the-hand argument suggests that increased dividend means increased certainty of cash flows. This helps in reducing the discount rate, and so, the value of the firm must increase with increased dividend.

Returns to shareholders consist of dividend yield and capital gains, as can be seen from Equation 19-4, reproduced below in an alternate form as Equation 19-6:

$$r = \frac{D_1}{P_0} + g \qquad (19\text{-}6)$$

Here, the first term is the dividend yield and the second term is the capital gain. It is argued that the dividend yield component is more certain than the capital gain component. Therefore, it would be logical that the more certain component, dividend, must be discounted at a lower rate than the more uncertain component, capital gains.

Therefore, if the earning level remains the same, the expected market capitalization rate must change with a change in the dividend policy. The higher the dividend, the lower the discount rate must be. If current dividend is withheld with a promise to make it available later, the discount factor must increase, due to uncertainty of the promise. Therefore, the price must fall if dividend payout is reduced. Conversely, when a greater proportion of earning is distributed, the certainty of returns is greater, reducing the discount rate and leading to an increase in the share price.

Assuming that the discount rate is a function of the dividend, refer to the data presented in Table 19-3. Assuming an earning of ₹25 per share and a constant reinvestment rate of 20% on the retained funds, the impact of changing dividend payout on share price is examined under Gordon's Model.

Here it is assumed that the capitalization rate in the market is a function of the dividend payout. The larger the payout, the smaller is the capitalization rate. Initially, it is assumed that return expected by investors is 20%, with a low payout ratio of 20%. As the payout increases from 20% to 80% (from ₹5 to ₹20 per share) the expected return falls gradually from 20% to 14%. The price is calculated using the formula for dividend capitalization model under constant rate of growth. We observe that price increases from ₹125 to ₹200 per share. Appreciation of price is due to recognition of the fact that investors put a greater value on current income, as compared with the promise of future income.

According to Myron Gordon and John Lintner, too, it is the market capitalization rate that undergoes change with any change in the dividend policy. According to them, investors are averse to risk. They give more value to returns that are certain. The value of returns that are uncertain is less. Even though in theory

Table 19-3 Dividend policy and price—bird-in-the-hand argument (Gordon Model)

Capitalization rate r (%)	20%	18%	16%	14%
Earning (₹/share)	25	25	25	25
Reinvestment rate k (%)	20%	20%	20%	20%
Dividend payout (₹)	5	10	15	20
Retention ratio b (%)	80%	60%	40%	20%
Price of the share $P_0 = \frac{D_1}{r-g}$	$P_0 = \frac{5}{0.20-0.16}$ = ₹ 125.00	$P_0 = \frac{10}{0.18-0.12}$ = ₹ 166.67	$P_0 = \frac{15}{0.16-0.08}$ = ₹ 187.50	$P_0 = \frac{20}{0.14-0.04}$ = ₹ 200.00

all earnings belong to shareholders, the dividend policy decides the timing of the distribution of these earnings. Retained earnings will be made available to shareholders at a later point of time, hopefully with growth. Investors consider the portions that are distributed less risky, and attach greater value to them. The growth component is more risky. After all it is just a promise, and not all promises are fulfilled. Some promises never fructify. Hence, retained earnings are valued less than distributed earnings.

IRRELEVANCE OF DIVIDEND

MM THEORY OF IRRELEVANCE

Miller and Modigliani (MM), the proponents of irrelevance of dividend to value of the firm, disagreed with Gordon's Model about the change of discount rate with change in the dividend policy. Instead, they argued that the market capitalization rate, r, is governed by earning power and the risks associated with it. For shareholders wealth, it is immaterial how these earnings are distributed or retained. Shareholders' wealth is governed by the firm's investment policy. As long as investment policy is held constant, the basic earning power of the assets and the risks to the cash flows remain the same. Therefore, the value of the firm must also remain the same, irrespective of dividend policy.

The MM argument of irrelevance of dividend rests on the assumption that it is the earnings and the investment policy that determine the value of the firm, not the manner of distribution of earnings.

The argument does not imply that dividends are irrelevant. It means that while dividend may be relevant to shareholders' wealth, the dividend policy is not. All cash flows belong to the shareholders, and the dividend policy is merely a question of timing of the distribution of these cash flows to shareholders. For any increase in the current dividend, shareholders must give up an equal amount from future dividends in present value terms, as the cash balance of the firm would stand depleted by an amount equivalent to the dividend. Any increase in the current level of dividend will cause an equal decline in the value of the stock.

Looking from the viewpoint of current and future dividends, it is again a question of sacrificing the present for a better future, or having a better present by sacrificing the future. Mere switching of the timing of the cash flow does not alter the size of the cash flow, which remains the key determinant of the value of the firm, in contrast to the timing of its distribution. Increased dividends today are compensated by reduced dividends tomorrow, and *vice versa*. Any cut in dividend would be followed by an equal gain in future dividends, and any increase in current dividend would result in an equal decrease in future dividends, in present value terms.

Increased dividends today are compensated by reduced dividends tomorrow, and vice versa.

The substance of the argument of irrelevance lies in the constancy of capital structure and investment policy. Now let us examine the impact of change in the dividend policy on the price of shares, keeping the investment policy and capital structure constant. Assume that the current price of the share is P_0 and the return desired by shareholders is *r*.

Assume that the firm wants to increase the amount of dividend to D_1 from the earnings per share (EPS) of E_1. Keeping the investment same as before at *I*, any increase in dividend will leave a shortfall in investment. To fill the gap, the firm will have to issue fresh shares, which can be sold at an ex-dividend (refer to Exhibit 19-1) price P_1,

Exhibit 19-1 Important dates for dividend

Declaration date: Dividends are declared in a meeting of the Board of Directors that needs to be notified to stock exchanges at least seven days in advance. The date on which the directors of the company declare dividend is called the *dividend declaration date*.

Record date: The *record date* is the date on which all those shareholders whose names are on the books of the firm are paid dividend. It is announced on the date of declaration of dividend. This date needs to follow notice of duration of a minimum of 15 days to stock exchanges. The company closes its stock transfer book on this date.

Ex-dividend date: The *ex-dividend date* is the date on which prices on stock exchanges are adjusted for the amount of dividend. All buyers prior to this date get the dividend. This is normally a day before the record date, to enable the company to update its stock transfer book.

Payment date: The *payment date* is the date of actual payment of the dividend. The payment date has to be within 30 days of the declaration date.

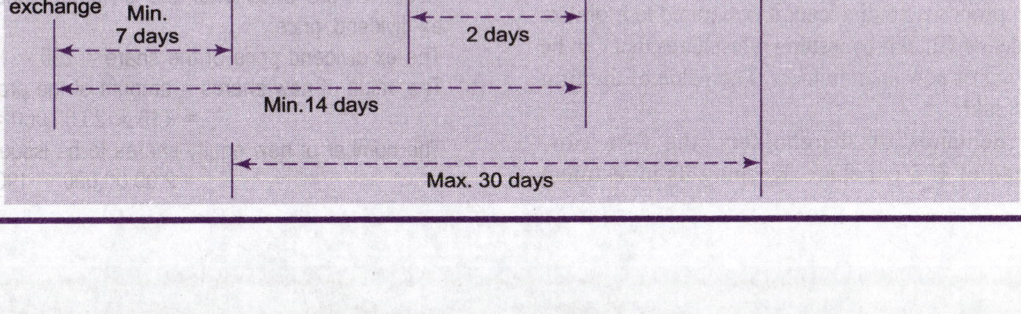

To retain investment, the firm would have to issue a larger number of new shares when it increases dividend. The value of the firm would remain the same, with the transfer of wealth from old to new shareholders.

otherwise the value of the firm would be lost if the desired investment is sacrificed. The shortfall could also have been met by raising debts, if the capital structure is immaterial (remember that the capital structure too is immaterial, as per MM). However, keeping the capital structure same as before, any increase in dividend will have to be substituted for by issue of fresh capital, and not debt.

Considering a holding period of one year, we know that the current market price of shares is the sum of the present value of the expected dividend and the expected price at the end of the next period. Mathematically,

$$P_0 = \frac{1}{1+r}(D_1 + P_1) \qquad (19\text{-}7)$$

and, the market value of the firm having n number of shares outstanding is:

$$nP_0 = \frac{1}{1+r}(nD_1 + nP_1) \qquad (19\text{-}8)$$

where P_0 = current market price of the share
D_1 = expected dividend in the next period
P_1 = expected market price in period 1 (ex-dividend price)
n = number of shares outstanding
r = equity capitalization rate

To compensate for the dividend, the firm has to issue new shares. If Δn is the additional number of shares, then fresh equity would be raised at P_1, the ex-dividend price. To meet the shortfall in the desired investment, a number of additional shares are issued.

$$\Delta n \times P_1 = I - (nE_1 - nD_1) = I - nE_1 + nD_1 \qquad (19\text{-}9)$$

Equation 19-8 can be rewritten as:

$$nP_0 = \frac{1}{1+r}(nD_1 + nP_1 + \Delta nP_1 - \Delta nP_1)$$

$$= \frac{1}{1+r}\{nD_1 + nP_1 + \Delta nP_1 - (I - nE_1 + nD_1)\}$$

$$= \frac{1}{1+r}\{(n+\Delta n)P_1 - I + nE_1\} \qquad (19\text{-}10)$$

Equation 19-10, for current value of the share, is independent of dividend and instead, is a function of investment I, earnings E_1, and discount rate r. The incremental dividend is replaced by new equity, raised by issuing Δn shares.

Consider a firm having 1,000 shares outstanding, with a current market value of ₹500 per share. The firm has announced an investment of ₹6 lakh and expected earnings of ₹4 lakh. Based on the announcements, the returns expected are 20%, and hence, the expected price is ₹1.2 × 500 = ₹600, with value of the firm standing at ₹6 lakh. If the firm proposes no dividend, it is required to mobilize the required remainder of ₹2 lakh by issuing new shares that can be sold at ₹600 to existing or new shareholders. The value of the firm would increase to ₹8 lakh.

In response to demands of shareholders, the firm now announces a dividend of ₹25 per share. Keeping its investment policy unchanged, the firm now has to mobilize another ₹25,000.

With a dividend of ₹25 announced, the share price would be ₹575. New shareholders would pay no more and no less than the value they get.

$$P_0 = \frac{1}{1+r}(D_1 + P_1)$$

or ex-dividend price,

$$P_1 = (1+r)P_0 - D_1$$
$$= 600 - 25$$
$$= ₹575$$

The number of new shares required to be issued is 391.40.

$$\text{No. of new shares to be issued} = \frac{\text{Funds required}}{\text{Ex-dividend price}}$$

$$= \frac{6,00,000 - 4,00,000 + 25,000}{575} = 391.40$$

These shares would aggregate to ₹2.25 lakh, of which ₹25,000 could be distributed as dividend to shareholders and ₹2,00,000 used as net capital expenditure. The value for shareholders would remain the same as before. Shareholders would get ₹25,000 as dividend, with an offsetting loss in the market value of share of (600 – 575) × 1000 = ₹25,000. If there were no dividend paid, the old shareholders would have had ₹6,00,000 as market value of the shares. Likewise, any amount of dividend would result in an equivalent amount of capital loss, as shown in Table 19-4.

The total value would increase by ₹2,00,000, due to net investment. The issue of fresh capital means there is transfer of value from old shareholders to new shareholders, keeping the aggregate value the same, as depicted in Figure 19-1. The issue of fresh shares amounts to taking money from one set of investors and passing it on to another. This act should not change the value of the firm.

Example 19-2 Dividend policy

MM Corp's share is trading at ₹200, with 20,00,000 shares outstanding. It has a current income of ₹4 crore, providing EPS of ₹20. Its earnings are earmarked for capital investment. MM Corp announces a dividend of ₹10 per share, leaving only ₹2 crore for capital expenditure. MM Corp decides to raise the shortfall of ₹2 crore by issuing fresh shares. Find the following.

(a) At what price can new shares be issued?
(b) How many shares should be issued?
(c) What is the value of the firm after the issue of new shares?
(d) How does the new value of MM Corp compare with its value before the dividend announcement?

Solution

(a) If the firm pays a dividend of ₹10 per share, it has to raise an equivalent amount through new shares. The new shares could be issued at the price after the dividend announcement, i.e., the ex-dividend price.
The ex-dividend price of the share = 200 – 10 = ₹190
(b) The value of new shares = amount of the proposed dividend
= ₹10 × 20,00,000 = ₹200 lakh
The number of new equity shares to be issued
= 2,00,00,000 ÷ 190 = 1,05,263

Table 19-4 Irrelevance of dividend (*all figures in ₹ unless specified otherwise*)

		With Dividend			
Dividend per share	***No Dividend***	***25***	***30***	***35***	***40***
Existing shares (Nos.)	1,000	1,000	1,000	1,000	1,000
Current price (₹)	500	500	500	500	500
Returns required (%)	20%	20%	20%	20%	20%
Projected price (ex-dividend)	600	575	570	565	560
Investment required	600,000	600,000	600,000	600,000	600,000
Earnings available	400,000	400,000	400,000	400,000	400,000
Dividend	—	25,000	30,000	35,000	40,000
New capital required	200,000	225,000	230,000	235,000	240,000
No. of new shares issued	333.33	391.30	403.51	415.93	428.57
Total market value (₹)	**800,000**	**800,000**	**800,000**	**800,000**	**800,000**
		Total market value allocated			
Old shareholders					
Market value	600,000	575,000	570,000	565,000	560,000
Add: dividend received	—	25,000	30,000	35,000	40,000
Total	**600,000**	**600,000**	**600,000**	**600,000**	**600,000**
New shareholders					
Market value	200,000	225,000	230,000	235,000	240,000
Less: dividend not received	—	25,000	30,000	35,000	40,000
Total	**200,000**	**200,000**	**200,000**	**200,000**	**200,000**

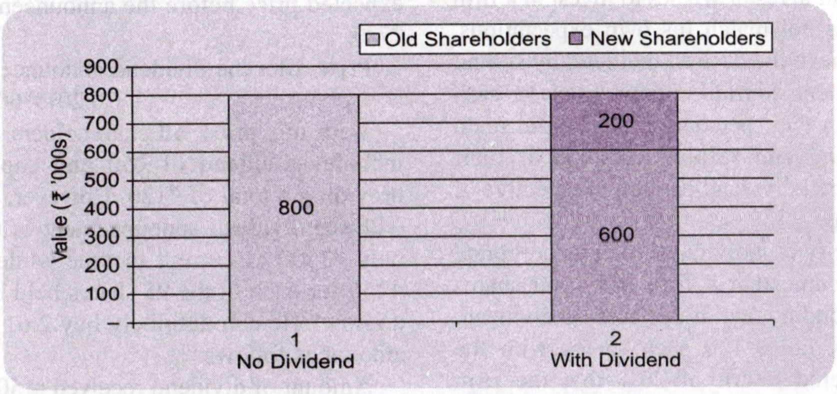

Figure 19-1 Value of the firm

(c) The total number of shares after the new issue
= 20,00,000 + 1,05,263 = 21,05,263.
The total value of MM Corp after the new issue
= number of shares × price
= 21,05,263 × 190 = ₹40 crore.

(d) The value of MM Corp before the new issue
= number of shares × price
= 20,00,000 × 200 = ₹40 crore

The value of the firm remains the same, and is independent of the dividend policy.

The irrelevance of dividend is depicted in Figure 19-2, which highlights the fact that constant earnings and constant investments determine the value of the firm. Dividend out of earnings is like a flexible pipe, where the outflow of dividend to shareholders is ploughed back as fresh capital by the same or new shareholders. Dividend is compensated by issue of fresh capital, keeping investment constant. A larger payout of dividend implies mobilization of equivalent extra fresh capital to keep the investment intact. As long as earning potential and investment policy are constant, the value of the firm does not change.

HOME-MADE DIVIDEND

The irrelevancy of dividend can also be demonstrated by the ability of investors to make their own dividend policy in their individual capacities, in case the firm's dividend policy does not suit them. This is important because divergence among different investors with respect to dividend cannot be denied. On an aggregate basis, one cannot assume that dividends are preferred or hated. Some investors may prefer dividend, whereas others may like retention. The flexibility of the individual investor is an important dimension in arguments on the irrelevancy of dividend. We examine the issue of individual investors, with

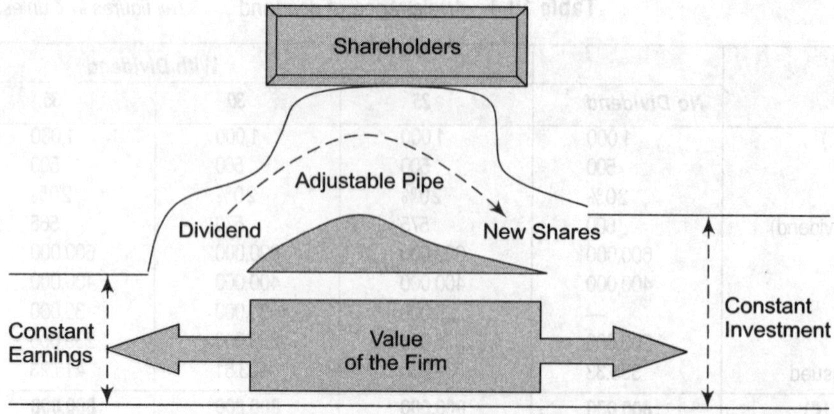

Figure 19-2 Dividend irrelevance: earnings and investment determine value

regard to dividend policy suiting their own personal requirements. MM have demonstrated that an individual investor has the capacity to have the desired dividend, irrespective of the dividend policy of the firm.

In the first place, investors have the choice of investing in firms whose dividend policy matches their own requirements. In a perfectly competitive capital market, there would be firms available which meet shareholders' requirements in terms of dividend policies.

Even if for some reason an investor wishes to invest in a firm whose dividend policy does not match his own expectations, the investor can simply achieve the desired dividend by selling or buying shares, to supplement shortfall or convert excess cash into investment. Investors in their personal capacity can undo corporate actions by buying and selling fractions of their holdings to achieve the desired dividend payout, irrespective of the firm's dividend decision.

Let us examine the capacity of individuals to undo corporate dividend policy. Let us assume that a firm has 1000 shares outstanding, and it declares no dividend. Mr X holds 100 such shares with the expected return of 20% that the firm provides by way of capital appreciation in stocks, although there is no dividend. The current price in period 0—the buying price for Mr X—is ₹500. This price is expected to move up to ₹600 by the end of the period. The expected wealth of Mr X by the end of the period is ₹60,000 (100 shares at ₹600 each). However, for his own reasons, Mr X desires a dividend of ₹3,000 which the firm does not provide because it declares no dividend. What can Mr X do to satisfy his need for current income?

Home-made dividend enables individual investors to make their own dividend policy by buying and selling shares to achieve current income. They can undo corporate action in their individual capacities.

Mr X can definitely sell some shares to have his current income. He needs to sell five shares at ₹600 each to get the desired cash flow of ₹3,000. His returns at the end of period would then be:

Cash realized by selling five shares = 5 × 600 = ₹3,000
Value of the remaining 95 shares = 95 × 600 = ₹57,000
Total wealth = ₹60,000
Investment made = 500 × 100 = ₹50,000

$$\text{Returns obtained} = \frac{10{,}000}{50{,}000} \times 100 = 20\%$$

Therefore, Mr X's position is the same as that of other investors who desire no current income. He neither gains nor loses any returns, as compared to other investors in the firm, and continues to get a return of 20%, like the others.

Now assume that in period '1' the firm changes its dividend policy and decides to give a dividend of ₹50 per share. Assuming that the stock continues to provide the same return of 20%, the expected price before the announcement of dividend would be ₹720.

Price after the dividend announcement
= (1 + 0.20) × 600 – 50 = ₹670

With this price, all shareholders earn a return of 20% that includes dividend of ₹50 and capital appreciation of ₹70, providing a total of ₹120. However, Mr X again is dissatisfied with the dividend announcement of the firm because he needs only ₹3000 as current income while he would receive ₹4750 (₹50 for each of the 95 shares held by him now). What can he do now? He can definitely buy 2.6119 shares with the surplus amount as follows:

Amount of dividend received = 50 × 95 = ₹4,750
Current income desired = ₹3,000
Surplus available that can be invested = ₹1,750
Stock price = ₹670
No. of additional shares bought = 1750/670 = 2.6119

What about his return? Does it stay at 20% like it would have for his fellow investors in the firm? Let us see his wealth at the end of period '1'.

Total number of shares at the end of period '1' = 97.6119
Market value of shares = 97.6119 × 670 = ₹65,400
Dividend retained = ₹3,000
Total wealth at the end of period '1' = ₹68,400

Thus, his ending wealth is ₹68,400. What returns has he been provided with?

Value of investment at the beginning = 95 shares × ₹600
= ₹57,000
Percentage return in period '1' = (68,400 – 57,000)/57,000
= 20%

Thus, irrespective of the dividend policy of the firm, Mr X can have the same returns and yet fulfil his desire to have current income. He can construct his own dividend policy. Like Mr X, every other investor would enjoy the same freedom of adjusting holdings by buying and selling of shares. Keeping the aggregate returns same as offered by the firm, the mix of current income and capital appreciation is entirely in the hands of the individual investor. He does not need to depend on the firm to provide a mix of current income and capital appreciation. In any case, the firm's dividend policy can provide only one single mix of current income and capital appreciation that would match the needs of some investors, while leaving the others to find their own ways. They would have to resort to home-made dividend to meet their individual needs.

It is evident from the feasibility of home-made dividend that the dividend policy is irrelevant even at the level of the individual shareholder. Thus, the value of the firm becomes independent of the dividend policy. The value of the firm is determined by its capacity to provide returns, which is primarily determined by its investment policy.

Under perfect market conditions, the theory of irrelevance holds ground. But several real world factors make the dividend policy relevant. Prominent among these factors is the presence of taxes and frictions in the markets.

From the foregoing discussions, the following conclusions can be made.

1. The firm can remain unaffected by its dividend policy, by funding through issue of new equity.
2. Shareholders too can remain indifferent to the firm's dividend policy; because of home-made dividend, they can implement their own.
3. Hence, dividend policy is irrelevant to the valuation of the firm. This is not meant to suggest that dividends as such are irrelevant. One must remember that it is only the allocation of distribution of cash between now and later, which is irrelevant.

Gordon's Model vs Irrelevance

Gordon's Model emphasizes dividends. Valuation, as given by Equation 19-3, is reproduced below

$$P_0 = \frac{D_1}{r-g}$$

The value of a firm paying a dividend of ₹20 per share with a growth rate of 5% and a capitalization rate of 15% is ₹200. The firm decides to increase dividend by ₹20, to make it ₹40 per share. Would the price double if somehow the growth is maintained? If the shortfall due to extra dividend is recouped by issue of new equity, the growth would be maintained. Does the equation hold?

The answer to this question is that the share price does not double, and yet Equation 19-3 holds. The firm issues new equity, equivalent to ₹20 per share, to fund the extra dividend. These new equity shareholders will have a claim on the future cash flows meant for providing for the growth of the firm. The new equity raised is 10% of the value of the share price, and therefore, 10% of the next period's cash flow would get diverted from existing shareholders to new shareholders. The shortfall of 10% would again be met from issuing equity. In other words, the growth rate of dividend for existing shareholders falls by an equivalent amount of 10%. The effective growth rate becomes –5% (5% – 10%). Thus, the share price remains the same, as shown below.

The theory of irrelevance of dividend does not imply that dividends per se are irrelevant, but only states that the dividend policy is irrelevant for determination of the value of the firm.

Old price prior to increase in dividend

$$P_0 = \frac{D_1}{r-g} = \frac{20}{0.15-0.05} = ₹200$$

New price after increase in dividend

$$P_0 = \frac{D_1}{r-g} = \frac{40}{0.15-(0.05-0.10)} = ₹200$$

By allowing the issue of new equity, the existing shareholders have allowed new subscribers a claim on future earnings, which originally belonged to the existing shareholders. The effective growth rate for existing shareholders falls, because overall cash available remains the same. In effect, existing shareholders had a trade off between current dividend and growth rate.

The major difference between relevance and irrelevance comes from the interplay of the dividend and investment policies. Gordon's Model assumes a decline in growth with increase in dividend, making dividend and investment interrelated decisions. MM prove the irrelevance of dividend with an independent investment policy, where any extra dividend is replenished by new shares to keep investment constant.

The irrelevance of dividend and capitalization models are often presumed to be contradictory. This is a misconception. These models are not at loggerheads. It must be clarified that the irrelevance of dividend model does not state that the value of the firm is not equal to the discounted value of the stream of dividend. It remains so. What the theory of irrelevance states is that the value of the firm can not be altered by changing the amount of dividend, because it is a mere reallocation of cash flow from one period to another such that the total value remains the same.

Bird-in-the-Hand vs Irrelevance

A comparison between the bird-in-the-hand argument and the irrelevance argument is also desired. The major difference between the two approaches lies in the assumptions about the constancy of the capitalization rate, i.e., the expectations of shareholders. Gordon argues that because dividend is more certain, an increase in it would cause the discount rate to fall. As the discount rate decreases, the price, which is inversely related to the discount rate, must increase. Miller and Modigliani assume that the amount of dividend distributed provides no cause for revision of the discount rate, which is primarily determined by the uncertainty of cash flows. It remains the same, and hence, the value stays the same.

The bird-in-the-hand argument assumes a decline in discount rate, and therefore, an increase in the value of the firm with increasing dividend. The theory of irrelevance assumes that both the discount rate and the value remain constant with dividend payout.

According to Gordon, investors have a greater preference for cash dividends than for retained earnings, due to the certainty of cash flow. Therefore, firms that pay larger dividends are valued more, as compared with firms paying lesser or no dividends, all other things remaining the same. Dividends become preferable because they resolve uncertainty. One fallacy pointed out in the argument is that comparison of the price change with dividend must be made at the same point in time, i.e. now and not later. The fact remains that the price falls by the amount of dividend on the ex-dividend date. Another counter to the 'bird-in-the-hand' argument can come from home-made dividend. Investors who wish to have certain cash flows can resort to buying and selling of shares as per their needs, while keeping the returns the same.

The positions of Gordon and MM are depicted in Figures 19-3 (a) and (b).

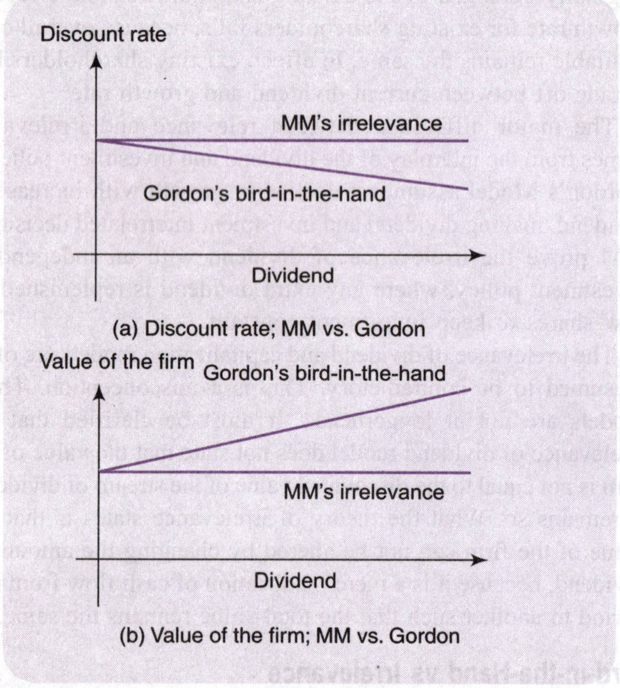

Figure 19-3

ASSUMPTIONS OF THE THEORY OF IRRELEVANCE OF DIVIDEND

In the above analysis, a number of assumptions were made which, for the sake of convenience, need to be listed. They are:

Constancy of investment policy The investment policy is the key determinant of the value of the firm. The investment policy is set beforehand and the dividend policy is not allowed to influence the investment policy. It is the investment policy that determines the levels of cash flows as well as the business risk, both of which are determinants of the value of the firm.

Investor's indifference to dividend income and capital gains Any change in dividend is replaced by new equity. The new issue can be made at a price that exactly offsets the extra dividend gained by shareholders in the current period. It is assumed that investors are indifferent to dividend income and capital gain or loss. It is immaterial that extra dividend now is offset by loss in price, or that reduced dividend is offset by gain in price.

No uniform taxes For investors to be indifferent to capital gains and dividend income as stated above, it is necessary that neither dividend nor capital gains are taxed at all; if they are taxed, then the treatment should be tax neutral.

Absence of flotation costs When new equity replaces extra dividend, it also implies that this can be done at no additional cost, i.e., there are no flotation costs. The extra dividend is raised through new equity, without the loss of value and without incurring any cost.

Uniform/homogeneous expectations Investors and firms face homogeneity in the expectations of future cash flows. The growth contemplated in dividend will actually fructify, and even if it does not, all of the investors will at least believe so. That would eliminate speculation about the future price of the share.

Perfect capital markets In creating the home-made dividend policy of the firm it was assumed that investors can buy and sell shares to adopt their own dividend policy, independent to the policy of the firm. This effectively implies that

(i) there were no transaction (brokerage) costs involved,
(ii) the shares were infinitesimally divisible and could be sold and bought,
(iii) the buying and selling actions of investors do not influence the price,
(iv) all investors are equally well informed, with no cost of information, and
(v) all investors interpret the information in a homogeneous way.

LIMITATIONS OF THE THEORY OF IRRELEVANCE OF DIVIDEND

The argument of irrelevance of dividend under conditions of perfect market is well established. However, in the real world several assumptions of irrelevance are challenged by arguments that propagate the idea that value is dependent upon the dividend policy. These are discussed below.

Investment policy The key assumption in the theory of irrelevance is the independence of the investment and dividend policies. In practice, this assumption does not seem to hold because most companies do not seem to invest more than what they have. These firms depend on internal generation of funds. Capital rationing is self-imposed. Therefore, their investment policy is not independent of earning capacity. These firms are found to distribute dividend too. Therefore, their investment and dividend policies are linked, and are not independent of each other.

Existence of taxes In our discussion on the proposition related to irrelevance of dividend, we assumed the total absence of taxes. In a real world situation, income for investors is taxed. What is more important is that taxes depend upon the nature of income. Dividend and capital gains are treated differently, attracting different rates of tax. Normally, capital gains are taxed

Preferential tax treatment of capital gains favours retention of earnings for increasing the value of the firm.

lower than dividend. In India, however, dividend is not taxed in the hands of investors. Firms are required to pay a dividend distribution tax of 15% while distributing dividend. Capital gains are exempt from tax if the gains result after a holding period of more than 12 months. The reduced tax for capital gains favours retention of earnings.

Let us consider two firms with the same level of earnings of ₹100; one pays no dividend, while the other pays all its earnings in dividend. Given the dividend distribution tax of 15%, the shareholders would get a total of ₹85, in the case of the firm paying dividend. The firm that does not pay dividend will show an increase equivalent to the earnings in its assets value. There would be a capital gain of ₹100, and with tax rate of 10%, the net increase in wealth of the shareholders of the firm paying no dividend would be ₹90, ₹5 higher than shareholders of the firm paying dividend. This is shown in Table 19-5.

Table 19-5 Impact of tax on shareholders' wealth (₹)

	Firm with No Dividend	Firm with Dividend
A. Earnings available	100	100
B. Dividend proposed	Nil	100
C. Dividend distribution tax (15%)	—	15
D. Post-tax cash flow to shareholders		85
E. Rise in the value of the firm	100	
F. Capital gains	100	—
G. Tax on capital gains (10%)	10	—
H. Post-tax capital gains	90	—
I. Post-tax cash flow to shareholders (*D* + *H*)	90	85

It is clear from the data in Table 19-5 that if the capital gains tax is lower than the dividend, it must favour retention. The value of the firms paying less dividend or no dividend would be higher than the value of firms paying higher dividend.

Another issue related to the taxes on dividend and capital gains, which is difficult to evaluate financially, is the applicability of tax only on realization. Dividend tax is paid when dividend is given, but capital gains tax is deferred till the gain is actually realized. Till such time the capital gain remains unrealized, no tax is payable. The deferment of capital gains tax also favours retention.

Transaction cost The theory of irrelevance of dividend assumed substitution of shareholding with level of current income. The shift from wealth of shareholding to current income and *vice versa* was assumed at no cost. Changes in the composition of wealth from portfolio to cash and back would necessitate buying and selling of shares frequently. Investors would have to incur cost of brokerage while transacting in shares. For dividend payments, there are no transaction costs. Hence, replacement of cash with shareholding would be more expensive. If transaction costs were 1%, and to have a current income adjustment of ₹100 would leave investors poorer by 1% each time the adjustment was made. Therefore, the presence of the transaction cost favours dividend. Added to this would be the cost of inconvenience in keeping a record of the buying and selling transactions.

Flotation cost The irrelevance of dividend theory assumed replacement of dividend by fresh capital through issue of fresh shares. Apart from being a time-consuming process, the issuance of capital has direct costs that are avoidable and unnecessary. To save Flotation cost, firms would favour retention, and shareholders must agree with this.

Underpricing The issue of fresh capital cannot take place at current market prices. There is a tendency to price the new issue below the current market price. Prospective investors need to be enticed to subscribe to the issue. They would not find investment attractive enough if the issue price is set equal to the market price. Also, due to volatility in share prices, the firm cannot charge the market price while issuing securities. Even if the firm exercises the option of calling for bids instead of announcing the price, it is likely that the prices bid by investors would be lower than the market price. Invariably, firms have to underprice shares while making a fresh issue.

The presence of transaction costs makes dividends more valuable, while floatation cost, the phenomenon of underpricing, and legal hassles favour retention of earnings.

This implies issuing larger number of shares than warranted, which has crucial implications in terms of servicing of equity for all times to come, and in terms of dilution of control. The phenomenon of underpricing raises cost of capital; it also reduces NPV of the projects, and hence, the value of the firm. Therefore, it is advisable to retain earnings, rather than distribute them first and then replenish them by issue of fresh shares.

Legal considerations The legal environment for issue of shares is more cumbersome than it may initially seem to be. Compliance with the laws of the land and the prerequisites for a public issue of shares are onerous and present roadblocks; they also take up precious time of the management, which may beneficially be utilized for business development and growth, adding value to the firm. Several laws come into force when it comes to mobilization of fresh capital. The presence of these laws favours retention of earnings.

DIVIDEND POLICY

PASSIVE RESIDUAL DIVIDEND POLICY

As an outcome of limitations present in the real world, most factors favour retention of earnings rather than cash dividend. The tax advantage from capital gains is substantial, and favours retention. Other factors include the presence of floatation costs, the phenomenon of underpricing and legal hassles that are also in favour of retention of earnings, rather than its distribution. The presence of transaction costs is the only factor that favours cash dividend payment.

Due to factors overwhelmingly supporting retention, firms ought to follow the following dividend policy:

1. Identify all possible positive NPV projects.
2. Retain the required cash to accept all such projects, so as to increase the value of the firm.
3. Maximize returns to shareholders through increase in the price of shares.
4. Distribute the remaining cash balance only when all positive NPV projects are funded.
5. Raise fresh capital only when internally generated earnings are not enough to accept all the positive NPV projects.

Such a policy of dividend is referred to as *passive residual dividend policy*. This policy dictates returning only excess cash. Following such a policy must lead to optimal results.

The passive residual dividend policy would imply fluctuating dividend from period to period, because the flow of earnings and the availability of positive NPV projects can hardly be said to be steady. Both earnings and available opportunities are volatile by nature. Therefore, following a passive residual dividend policy essentially implies volatile dividends over time.

However, the empirical evidence is contrary. Several studies have revealed that dividends are sticky and follow a smoother pattern than earnings, a phenomenon that is substantiated by general observation. Firms generally do not raise dividend unless they are absolutely sure of sustaining the trend in future. Similarly, they do not reduce dividend unless they feel that the drop in earnings is due to bad economic conditions, or to other reasons that are likely to prevail for an extended time. Therefore dividends are likely to be more stable than earnings.

The passive residual dividend policy suggests acceptance of all positive NPV projects and distribution of only leftover earnings as dividend.

Information Content of Dividend (Signalling Theory)

The failure of firms to follow the passive residual dividend policy forces us to examine dividend in greater detail, and to look for some explanations to justify the stickiness of dividend beyond returns and value of the firm.

Many people argue that the dividend policy of the firm does not merely provide a cash flow back to shareholders, but also communicates a lot about the prospects of the firm. It is well accepted that share prices move constantly as new information flows in. Investors continuously strive for newer information, and the value of the firm keeps changing. Much of the information available publicly to investors pertains to the past, but stock prices are mainly driven by the prospects of the firm. The markets are always a step ahead. They work on future expectations rather than on the present or the past. Financial markets always discount not only all past information, but also future prospects.

The signalling hypothesis emphasizes that dividends convey plenty of information that is tangible, besides providing returns. Therefore, change in dividend policy is important for revaluation of the firm.

The level of dividend is an important indicator of the earning prospect of the firm. Managers are often reluctant to alter the level of dividend with the level of earnings because this communicates a lot about their earning prospects. Managers tend to raise dividend only when they are confident of maintaining increased levels of earnings in the foreseeable future. Similarly, a decline in dividend is announced only when the prospects of the firm seem to be bleak. Dividend is neither decreased nor increased with minor changes in earning levels. The attempt is to maintain an absolute level of dividend till such time a major change in earnings is anticipated that can support the new level of dividend.

Therefore, an announcement about increased dividend provides a signal to investors that management is confident that earnings levels will remain adequate in the future too, such that the enhanced level of dividend can be sustained. Likewise, an announcement confirming decreased dividend conveys management's projection of a poor business scenario in the future.

This signalling via dividend assumes that other information available to investors, such as directors' reports, financial statements, financial analyst recommendations, press releases, etc, is not as convincing in judging future prospects as a simple announcement of dividend. Furthermore, the management of the firm more often than not underplays negative factors and overemphasizes positive factors. Financial analysts, being conservative in approach, generally overstate negative factors and underplay positive factors. There may also be conflicting opinions of analysts and experts that may leave the investor confused, rather than resolve his dilemma. This happens because talk is free, and opinions that are proven wrong can be excused conveniently with the *ifs and buts* used in opinions expressed earlier. Unlike reports, dividend costs money, and therefore, the credibility of dividend is more than information available otherwise. Dividend trends can convey a lot more information than tonnes of paper and volumes of publicity, because the proof of the cake lies in its eating.

Signalling, Gordon and MM The signalling hypothesis loses its significance and base for argument if the firm follows an erratic dividend policy. If dividends change from period to period the signals cannot be credible. It is only when a stable dividend policy is pursued by the firm that the information content is maximum. By and large, most firms follow a stable dividend policy, and so the signalling hypothesis becomes significant. The fact that an increase in dividend brings cheer to financial markets and a decrease often causes a price decline provides credibility to the signalling hypothesis. The information content of dividend is unambiguous, whereas all other sources of information cannot be relied on as much, because of very speculative nature of the markets, which thrive on conflicts of opinions.

The information content of dividend tends to reduce uncertainties surrounding the functioning of the firm. However, it differs from Gordon's bird-in-the-hand approach, which associates reduction in uncertainty to reduction in discount rate.

Dividends reduce the perceived risk and the cost of getting information.

Supporters of the MM theory of irrelevance support the information content of dividend, but argue that investors respond as much also to changes in dividend as reflectors of changes in earnings. Investors' response to changed dividend is due to revised expectations of the earnings level. Therefore, the value of the firm does not change due to changes in dividend, but due to changes in earning expectations, the basic element that drives the value of the firm, as per the theory of irrelevance.

Despite the ability of individual investors to undo the corporate dividend policy through home-made dividend, investors tend to prefer dividends over capital gains for behavioural reasons.

Investors' Preference for Current Income

The theory of irrelevance of dividend assumes that investors are indifferent to capital gains and dividend. They were assumed to be the perfect substitutes in the absence of taxes and/or uniform treatment of tax. Investors could also create home-made dividend policy by selling shares to meet shortfalls in dividend, and buying shares if in receipt of excess dividend.

As far as the taxation issue is concerned, the distribution of dividend is not favoured in the current system of taxation. At present, dividends in India are subject to the dividend distribution tax, though not in the hands of investors, while capital gains, if long-term (holding period greater than 12 months), are exempt from tax. This was discussed earlier in Table 19-5.

Differential tax treatment apart, the question is whether the investor is indifferent to dividend and capital gains. A study by Hersh Shefrin and Meir Statman reveals that investors prefer dividend over capital gains, even though capital gains are more tax efficient. For behavioural reasons, investors tend to value dividend more than capital gains. One plausible explanation could be that while dividend is treated as a regular income that helps meet regular needs for funds, liquidating shares to compensate for shortfalls in dividend is regarded as an erosion of wealth. Many investors consider securities to be assets of a capital nature. For such investors, current expenditure should be met with current income, and only for funding expenditure of a capital nature should one think of liquidating capital assets.

Shefrin and Statman offer the behavioural aspects of investors as bases to defend their preference for dividend over capital gains, through arguments that talk of (i) *lack of self-control* and (ii) *aversion to regret*.

Lack of self-control It refers to those behavioural aspects of people which make them adopt rules which are devised to check unwanted tendencies. Such rules are plentiful. The success of anti-smoking clinics, alcohol and drug de-addiction centres, and health clinics proves that people resort to damage control knowing fully that in the first place, simple control over wrong habits would have been more cost effective. Similarly, in the financial domain, people have a tendency to meet regular expenditure through regular income and resort to liquidation of capital assets only in extreme situations. In the absence of taxes and transaction costs, such a policy has no merit, and yet, this is the behaviour most common to investors.

Aversion to regret It refers to the avoidance of perceived loss in value that could arise from exercising one's alternative choices of actions. To pay for a seven course dinner at a five star hotel, one can either use dividend received from the firm or can sell part of one's shareholding. If income from dividend and capital gains were the same, it would make no difference from which source the dinner is paid for. Besides the rules of self-control that human beings have for themselves, people are also averse to situations which may lead to regret. Most people will pay their dinner bill from the dividend and avoid selling shares for reasons of aversion of regret, though either source of payment will leave them equally poorer. If the bill is paid by selling shares, and subsequently share prices rose, most people would experience greater regret having taken such an action. Such regret is likely to be less if the dinner bill is paid out of dividend received.

The behavioural pattern of investors suggests that people lacking self-control and having greater aversion to regret prefer dividends to capital gains.

Clientele Effect

As stated earlier, investors may prefer dividend for reasons of their own, despite the fact that capital gains are more tax efficient than dividend. For example, retired people could form one group that may need money on a regular basis and look forward to dividend. They may not want to create home-made dividend by buying or selling the contents of their portfolio of stocks. On the contrary, young people who are earning well do not depend on dividend as a source of income may instead believe in increasing their wealth by investing more. Similarly, some institutional investors would like to meet their administrative overheads with a regular flow of dividend income. They may be prohibited from selling stock for legal reasons too. Therefore, investors can be grouped according to their preference for dividend or capital gains, and may be referred to as *clienteles*.

Investors can be grouped as clienteles according to their preference for dividend or capital gains. A change in the dividend policy would cause the clienteles to shift their investment.

The clientele effect refers to investors' selection of firms that match their preference for dividend. Markets constitute of large bases of investors, and these bases can be grouped according to their preference or otherwise for dividend. Some may like more dividend, while some other may prefer capital gains; yet another group may like to have both. Investors who favour dividend may choose high-dividend-paying companies for their portfolios, while the group that does not need dividend would pick stocks that offer more capital appreciation. Individuals' preferences for dividend mean that they would invest in firms with matching dividend policies. Firms get the investors they deserve and investors get the firms they choose.

With the needs of firms and investors matched, it is not advisable to change the dividend policy because this would provoke investors to switch. Switching would entail transaction costs and payment of capital gains tax. If a changed dividend policy causes larger numbers of investors to buy, prices would increase; if there are more investors selling, prices would fall. Therefore, firms should not change their dividend policy.

However, this argument does not seem to be very convincing. Although there is no denying the existence of clienteles, the question of whether the firm should influence its dividend decision on these clienteles is a moot one. The argument that firms should not change their dividend policies for the sake of retaining the same clientele is a debatable one. As investors can choose firms they like, so too can firms find new clientele with a change in their dividend policies. From the viewpoint of the firm, one clientele is as good as another.

RESIDUAL DIVIDEND POLICY – REVISITED

The preceding discussions suggest that firms, while deciding on their dividend policies, must give consideration to a multitude of real-world factors that may have an impact on the valuation of the firm. The overall guiding principle, of course, remains the maximization of the value of the firm. Some of these factors that have been discussed are: (i) available investment opportunities, (ii) risk profile of the firm, (iii) level of earnings and its sustainability, (iv) dilution of control, (v) floatation costs, (vi) target capital structure, (vii) tax structure, (viii) investors' preferences, and (ix) existence of clienteles.

The residual dividend policy implies distribution of the left-over cash flows. A firm determines its target payout ratio on the basis of the following factors, which are mentioned in the order of their importance.

Available investment opportunities Recognizing the fact that value enhancement can be achieved only by accepting all positive NPV projects, the acceptance of all available business opportunities is paramount. The process of value creation by exploitation of available investment opportunities cannot be subordinated to any other process. Irrespective of the relevance of the dividend policy to value creation, one cannot contest the overwhelming influence the investment policy has on the value of the firm. Therefore, the investment policy must get precedence over the dividend policy.

Key considerations in passive residual dividend policy are: (i) identification of investment opportunities, (ii) fixing the target capital structure to find residual and then, (iii) smoothing them to preserve the information content, investors' preferences, and clienteles.

The residual policy would imply no distribution of dividend as long as positive NPV projects are available. Only after meeting requirements of funds for new projects would the remainder be distributed as dividend.

Target capital structure In meeting investment needs, it is not suggested that the entire capital for new projects should come from retained earnings. All future projects can be funded with a combination of equity and debt. Each firm must, therefore, have a target capital structure, which should guide the funding pattern. The question of whether the firm must pay dividend and raise debt, in accordance to the target capital structure, to fund future projects is difficult to answer. It would be sub-optimal for a firm to move to an all-equity capital structure because this would forgo the value provided by the tax shield that debt provides. At the same time, paying dividend cannot be regarded as harmful for the process of value creation. Hence, it may be prudent to raise debt within the bounds of the target capital structure and not withhold dividend. However, paying dividend and issuing equivalent fresh capital is imprudent due to (i) floatation cost and (ii) underpricing, which eats away some value.

Based on the above, the amount of dividend as residual can be worked out as below:

Dividend = Net income – capital outlay for new projects
– debt to be raised as per target capital structure

Pure vs Smoothed Residual Dividend Policy

Paying dividend strictly as per the above equation is referred to as *pure residual dividend policy*. It is likely to result in dividends that fluctuate from period to period, because earnings as well as investment opportunities cannot be forecast with much accuracy, especially for growing firms. Paying dividend as a residual of earnings and investment is against the tenets of value creation and would make returns on equity volatile. Apart from adding to the variability of returns, the pure residual dividend payout has the following disadvantages:

1. It takes away the argument of the information content of dividends, because persistent variability in dividend provides ambiguous signals to investors. At best, it can lead to confusion in the minds of investors.
2. If the dividend is being paid to satisfy the preference of investors for current income over capital gains, the pure residual dividend policy does not seem to be consistent with the idea of clientele effect. If investors require current income to meet current expenditure, they do so for known and certain liabilities. In such a situation, varying dividend would imply buying or selling shares to match current requirements for funds. Clientele effect too is based on the fact of fixed dividend rather than varying dividend. Varying dividend is also against the premise of clientele effect.

To overcome the shortcomings of the pure residual dividend policy, the firm can adopt a policy of dividend distribution that reduces the element of uncertainty, provides useful signals, and does not disturb clienteles. Continuing to follow the residual policy, the amount of dividend needs to be smoothed over time. The firm may decide the level of initial dividend and then raise it gradually, even if this leaves the firm with some extra liquidity. This extra liquidity provides a cushion to maintain fixed dividend payouts in case there are temporary aberrations in projected cash flows and growth plans.

Besides providing such a cushion, the *smoothed residual dividend policy* remains consistent with the arguments of (i) the *information content* of dividends; as the changes in dividend will signal whether the growth plans are as scheduled and are on course, (ii) *investors' preference for current income*, to render stability to current income to meet current liabilities, and

(iii) *clientele effect:* to retain same investors who need not switch to another firm to match their needs, saving them transaction costs.

Most firms tend to follow the stable dividend policy with slow and steady growth to indicate steady cash flows. The general principle is to increase or decrease dividend only if it becomes necessary. Drastic changes in dividend are generally avoided and serve no useful purpose.

FACTORS AFFECTING DIVIDEND POLICY

The preceding discussions would reveal that in perfect market conditions, the dividend policy is irrelevant but in a real world situation, there are several factors that impact the dividend policy and valuation. A firm has to consider many factors while setting a dividend policy in practice. The objective remains the undisputed maximization of shareholders' wealth.

Amongst the factors that favour high dividend payout are (1) low outlay required on available investment opportunities, (2) the desire of investors for current income, (3) the resolution of uncertainty, (4) the presence of transaction costs, and (5) the presence of agency cost—a high dividend payment tends to reduce agency costs, etc.

Among the factors that favour low payout are (1) larger outlays needed by investment opportunities, (2) preferential treatment of capital gains as compared to dividends, (3) the presence of floatation costs, (4) the phenomenon of underpricing, and (5) constraining legal and administrative factors that have to be addressed when issuing new shares, etc.

Besides the factors that govern the level of dividend, there are a few important considerations that are more concerned with the stability of dividend rather than its level. Access to debt markets in days of poor earnings helps keeping the dividend stable. Most institutional investors demand a regular and constant flow of dividend. Once a level is decided, it is maintained till the need to change arises. When changing the level of dividend, the firm needs to consider (1) what signal the change in dividend provides to the shareholders, (2) what reaction the change would have on the firm's clientele, and (3) the question of whether the change would cause shifting of clientele and impact the complexion of shareholding patterns. Another important consideration is the sustainability of the changed dividend.

Firms decide their dividend policies based on several practical considerations, as stated above. You may refer to Box 19-1.

Box 19-1 **IT majors sit on a growing cash mountain***

Riding high on the booming economy and growing outsourcing opportunities, the top five Indian information technology players—Tata Consultancy Services, Infosys Technologies, Wipro, Satyam, and HCL Technologies—have piled up net cash in excess of ₹20,000 crore.

The net cash figure jumped 31% to ₹21,148.42 crore in 2006-07 from ₹16,151.36 crore in the previous year. Analysts estimate the figure will increase by 60% in the current financial year.

The logic lies in the revenue and net profit numbers of these companies. For instance, the total turnover of the five companies for 2006-07 stood at ₹57,397 crore—a jump of nearly 40% over the last fiscal number of ₹41,033 crore. If these companies continue growing at this pace, their total income should surpass $20 billion by 2009 even after factoring in rupee appreciation and wage inflation, say analysts. The aggregate net profit of these companies increased by around 56% to ₹13,135 crore in the 2007 financial year. After accounting for analysts' estimates of the net profit and likely dividend to be given to shareholders in the 2008 financial year, these five firms are expected to have ₹33,743 crore net cash—a 59.5% jump over the previous year's figures.

So what are they doing with the money? Almost all of them said the best thing to do with their cash mountains was to turn them over to shareholders. The five companies paid ₹3,391.50 crore as dividend to shareholders in 2006-07, against ₹3,341 crore in the previous year (which included a special dividend from Infosys).

They also plan to use the cash for capital expenditure requirements (which are not much, as these are service firms), acquisition, and hedging against adversities. 'As with any IT firm we use cash to pay dividend, for capital expenditure and expansion, to fund existing business and develop sale and marketing presence, for potential acquisition and to hedge against adversities like 9/11 kind of a situation', said an HCL Technologies spokesperson.

Cashing In	₹ Crore				
	2003–04	2004–05	2005–06	2006–07	2007–08*
TCS	631.96	1062.16	2058.48	3076.00	6987.53
Infosys	2798.51	2917.00	4372.00	6157.00	10181.20
Wipro	2243.47	2799.67	4060.23	5564.00	8174.36
Satyam	2469.79	3177.68	4092.25	4139.42	5565.53
HCL Tech	1600.37	1391.59	1568.36	2212.00	2835.00
Total	9744.10	11348.10	16151.32	21148.42	33743.62

A TCS spokesperson said the company uses cash for capital expenditure rewarding shareholders with dividend, and funding inorganic growth.

IT firms generally dole out anywhere between 10% and 20% of their cash reserves as dividend.

Wipro, on the other hand, has been using cash to acquire companies, and plans to buy companies (each deal worth $100 million) in the pharmaceutical and aviation sectors. The company, which is sitting on ₹5,564 crore in cash, says it prefers the cash acquisition route to equity.

Infosys Technologies is sitting on the largest pile of cash (₹6167 crore). V. Balakrishnan, CFO of Infosys Technologies, said, 'The robust financial model followed at Infosys allows the company to balance profitability as well as invest in growth and maintain the liquidity position of the company'. Infosys is making substantial investments in scaling up.

**By Leslie D'Monte and B. G. Shirsat, reproduced from Business Standard, 27 April 2007*

ALTERNATIVE FORMS OF DIVIDEND

Firms normally reward shareholders with regular cash dividends. We have seen that firms follow a stable dividend policy and refrain from increasing dividend, even when earnings continue to grow. These earnings get accumulated over a period of time, enhancing the shareholders' wealth and causing share prices to rise consistently.

Besides cash payment, firms also have alternative methods to provide rewards to shareholders that directly or indirectly are in the interest of shareholders. These special types of dividend avoid any possibilities of miscommunication arising from the increased dividend, because such actions are taken as one-off measures.

Besides cash dividends, firms can also reward shareholders with non-cash tools such as bonus shares and split shares. The rationale for such measures is to bring the price to a more trading friendly zone and increase investors' participation.

There are ways other than regular or periodic cash dividend to reward shareholders. Three other ways of rewarding shareholders are very popular. They are as follows:

1. Bonus shares
2. Stock splits, and
3. Share buyback

The first two are non-cash forms of rewarding shareholders, whereas buyback of shares comes in the cash form. We discuss all of them in the same order.

BONUS SHARES

Issue of bonus shares is a way of capitalizing reserves into shares. It only changes the form and not the content or wealth of shareholders.

Adhering to a stable dividend policy despite continuous excess earnings implies an accumulation of reserves Shareholders are owners of the capital subscribed and residual profit that is retained in the business. These retained profits appear as 'Reserves and Surplus'. The sum of the capital subscribed and the reserves is referred to as *shareholders' fund*. These retained profits keep enhancing the value of the reserves and surplus, period after period. This increase in book value is reflected in share prices. The book value of a share is defined as the shareholders' fund divided by the number of shares, i.e., how much a share is worth in the books of account of the firm.

When the proportion of reserves and surplus becomes relatively high in relation to subscribed capital, firms normally issue bonus shares, to get back to an appropriate proportion of subscribed capital to reserves and surplus. The issue of bonus shares is a mere reorganization of shareholders' funds, keeping the overall value same as before.

As an example, consider the following structure of shareholders' funds of a firm A.

	₹ lakh
Paid-up share capital	500
Reserves and surplus	4500
Total Shareholders' Fund	**5000**

The firm finds that the book value of the share, at 10 times the face value, is too high. This would cause the price of the shares also to be extremely high. To reduce the book value and the share price, the firm may issue bonus shares in the ratio of 2:1 (2 additional shares for every one held). The new structure of shareholders' fund now becomes

(After Bonus Issue)	₹ lakh
Paid-up share capital	1500
Reserves and surplus	3500
Total Shareholders' Fund	**5000**

The funds from reserves and surplus are transferred to paid-up capital. Shareholders get additional shares without paying cash. Firm A has transferred a sum of ₹10 crore from reserves and surplus to paid-up capital.

Bonus share issues bring about in the following results.

1. The number of shares increases by the ratio of bonus shares. In the present case, the number of shares becomes three fold.
2. The proportionate holding of each investor remains the same, because all investors get bonus shares in proportion to their existing holding in the firm. Thus, neither is control impacted nor is the ownership or shareholding pattern affected.
3. The book value of the shares falls proportionately. If the face value of the share is ₹10, then the book value of the share prior to bonus issue by Firm A is ₹100. The new book value after issue of bonus shares is around ₹33.33 ($5000/1500 \times 10$).
4. It is a mere restructuring of the shareholders' fund. The earning level of the firm remains the same. However, EPS falls because the number of shares has increased. In this case, EPS will fall to one-third of the earlier level, as the number of shares has tripled.
5. In accordance with the fall in book value and EPS, the key value driver, the market value, also falls proportionately, conserving the total wealth of the shareholders. The share price will fall to one-third as the number of shares triples.

The issue of bonus share, being a mere restructuring of shareholders' fund, should not create any value for the firm. Yet most respectable firms have a history of issuing bonus shares for a variety of reasons. Some of these reasons are given below.

1. Firms that are candidates for issue of bonus shares usually witness a price level that is rather high for small investors. Given an investment choice between one share of ₹20,000 and 1000 shares of ₹20, most investors would opt for the latter, despite risk being at the same level for both investments. It is believed that the issue of bonus shares brings the price of shares down to a more acceptable trading range, inviting greater participation by investors.
2. With an increased number of shares and reduced prices, liquidity in the market increases. This is supposed to benefit small investors. Firms also believe that the investor base would expand, too.

3. The issue of bonus shares is regarded as a very strong signal that all is well with the firm and that management is confident of improving EPS and book value of the shares in future.
4. Last, but not the least, despite the same level of earnings with the issue of bonus shares, investors do not expect dividends to fall proportionately. Instead, expectations are that dividends would fall less than proportionately, providing greater cash flow to the investors

The issue of bonus shares by firms seems to be an outcome of management's reluctance to increase dividend drastically, which results in accumulation of earnings over a period of time. Saddled with huge reserves, the firm announces issue of bonus shares and yet does not raise dividend per share (DPS). These huge reserves reach the hands of the investors soon, as the firm maintains the same DPS. Issue of bonus shares can, therefore, be treated as advance notice of arrival of increased cash.

STOCK SPLITS

The stock split too is a reward to shareholders that works in the same way as bonus shares. Under stock split, the firm provides additional shares to investors. Splitting of shares is done by simply increasing the number of shares without capitalizing the reserves, unlike issue of bonus shares, as highlighted in Table 19-6.

Table 19-6 Comparison of bonus and splitting

(₹ *lakh*)

	Prior to bonus/split	*Remarks*
Paid-up share capital		
Comprising 50 lakh shares of ₹10 each	500	
Reserves and surplus	4500	
Total	**5000**	
After issue of bonus shares 3:1		
Paid-up share capital		
Comprising 200 lakh shares of ₹10 each	2000	Number of shares increased
Reserves and surplus	3000	through capitalization of reserves.
Total	**5000**	
After splitting shares in ratio of 4:1		
Paid-up share capital		
Comprising 200 lakh shares of ₹2.50 each	500	Number of shares increased by changing the face value of the
Reserves and surplus	4500	shares and keeping the value of reserves same.
Total	**5000**	

Stock splits are identical to bonus share issues in respect of the effects on valuation, liquidity, price, book value, and EPS. The only difference between the two lies in the books of accounts. In the case of bonus share issue 'reserves and surplus' is capitalized and transferred to paid-up capital, while in the case of split 'reserves and surplus' as well as 'capital' remain unaffected. The number of shares simply gets multiplied.

The impact of stock split is same as that of bonus share issue. It is merely a different tool of communication. Book value of shares would change in both the cases, though by different amounts. In the case of split, the change in book value is due to the increased number of shares, while in the case of bonus share issue, the impact on book value is two fold. Reserves come down and the number of shares increases.

Bonus shares and stock splits increase the number of shares, yet keep the same share-holding pattern. They increase proportionately the number of shares and liquidity, but keep the total wealth of the shareholders the same.

For long-term investors, split and bonus shares are extremely advantageous. In India, tax laws treat the cost of acquisition for bonus and split shares as zero. The ex-bonus or ex-split price can be taken in entirety as capital gains. Although dividends too are tax-free in the hands of investors, firms can save dividend distribution tax (currently at 15%).

SHARE BUYBACK

Following a stable dividend policy, firms normally do not increase dividend payout, despite increased earnings, for the sake of reducing chances of misinterpretation of the information content of dividend, and also as in pursuit of a policy to retain a good proportion for future requirements, should good opportunities come by. Firms may be uncertain of future capital expenditure requirements with several projects under study. These may relate to acquisitions that require huge outlays. When flush with sufficient funds, with no relevant growth opportunities in sight, firms may decide to return the excess cash back to shareholders.

Here, the firm faces two choices for returning the excess cash—either give bumper dividend or buy back shares. An increasingly popular method of rewarding shareholders in a form other than regular cash is the share buyback. Under share buyback, the firm buys its own shares from whoever wants to sell his holding at a specified price during a specified period. Till 1998, share buyback was not allowed in India. After it was allowed, several firms in India have offered share buyback. The features of current regulations are given in Box 19-2.

Share buyback is a substitute for dividend payment when it is large. It provides an option to shareholders to continue or exit their investment in any desired ratio.

In theory, it is really immaterial whether the firm pays its shareholders a higher amount of dividend or offers them share buyback to the extent of the proposed dividend. However, real world conditions render many advantages to a share buyback as compared to a one-time huge dividend. There are two key parameters to be decided in a share buyback—the number of shares to be bought back and the price at which to buy them.

The mechanism of share buyback works like this. As an example, imagine a firm has 150 lakh shares outstanding at present, selling for ₹550 each. The firm has been paying a modest dividend of ₹10 per share, providing a meagre dividend yield of less than 2%. Over a period of time, it has accumulated substantial cash of about ₹100 crore, deployed at present in extremely safe government securities.

Box 19-2 Current regulations of share buyback in India

Share buyback can be done in two ways:

1. **Through tender offer**, where the firm announces a buyback programme to all its shareholders to buy a specified number of shares at a predetermined price. The offer remains open for a short period, usually 15 – 30 days.
2. **Through open market purchases in the stock exchanges**, where the firm announces a maximum price and buys shares up to the prescribed limit, set in money terms, from the stock market. This option is kept open for a long time, usually a year, and enables procurement at market-oriented prices. This also keeps the price of the share stable for a longer time.

The buyback programme has to be devised within the following framework:

- The amount of share buyback cannot exceed 25% of the paid-up share capital and free reserves.
- Post buyback, the debt-equity ratio should not exceed 2:1.
- Shares bought back cannot be re-issued.
- Firms are not allowed to issue fresh shares till six months of the conclusion of a buyback programme.

The management of the firm believes that about ₹30 crore would be adequate to meet its expansion plans for the foreseeable future. If retained, the excess cash would remain deployed in low-yield but safe government securities, doing shareholders no good. Management would like to return this cash to shareholders.

One option available to the firm is to give a dividend of ₹47 per share. Shareholders could use this cash in any manner they like. From the firm's point of view, such a step may not be advisable because it has the potential to create a false impression about the earnings of the firm. The other alternative is to make an offer to repurchase shares from shareholders. The working of buyback could be as under:

No. of shares outstanding
= 150 lakh

Current market price per share
= ₹550

Amount of surplus cash available for distribution
= ₹7,000 lakh

Equivalent dividend per share
= 7,000/150 = ₹46.67

Premium considered appropriate for buyback
= 20%

Price of buyback = 1.20 × 550 = ₹660

No. of shares that can be bought back

$$= \frac{7,000}{660} = 10.60 \text{ lakh}$$

No. of outstanding shares post buyback
= 150 – 10.60
= 139.40 lakh

In practice, it has been observed that with buyback announcements the share price normally increases, causing an increase in wealth for those shareholders who choose to remain invested with the firm.

Assuming that the resources used for buyback do not impinge upon the growth prospects of the firm, and that the same earnings are maintained, EPS post buyback increases with the reduced number of shares. Even if the firm maintains the same capitalization in terms of the PE ratio, the price is likely to show an increase. This may be seen from the data presented in Table 19-7.

Table 19-7 Impact of share buyback on the price of the share

Current EPS of the share	₹5.00
No. of shares outstanding	10,00,000
Current market price	₹45.00
Price–earning PE ratio	45 ÷ 5 = 9.00
No. of shares to be bought back	1,00,000
EPS after share buyback (Total earnings/shares outstanding after buyback)	5 × 10,00,000 ÷ 9,00,000 = 50/9
Expected market price of the share after share buyback	PE ratio × new EPS = 9 × 50/9 = ₹50

Advantages of Share Buyback

There are several advantages that share buybacks seem to offer:

Indicative of worth of the firm The impetus to the practice of share buyback is often attributed to the need for a firm's management to somehow tell investors that the market is undervaluing the firm. Through buyback programmes, the firm can infuse confidence in investors when the market is bearish. The buyback price offered by the firm works as a floor, and a premium is offered for buying back, so that investors know the minimum worth of their shares in the opinion of the management. This forces revaluation of the share by the market. The premium offered by the firm over and above the prevailing market price sends very strong signals about the future prospects of the firm.

Besides communicating the worth of the shares in the opinion of management, a buyback would create an upward pressure on the price due to reduced supply of shares after the buyback. It may be noted that shares bought back cannot be re-issued, and firms are not allowed to have any fresh public issue until a certain time period elapses after the completion of the buyback programme.

Reduce information asymmetry It is argued that investors, analysts, and managers of the firm have different opinions on valuation because of gaps in the information each one of them possesses. Managers of the firm are supposed to be better informed, whereas the general investors are least informed. This is referred to as *information asymmetry*. The buyback price announced by the management will help bridge the information gap and bring about convergence of the different perspectives of the various investor groups on the value of the firm.

A share buyback has advantages of (a) communicating the worth of the firm (b) increasing promoters' shareholding, (c) providing protection against hostile takeover,and (d) altering shareholding pattern and capital structure.

Control shareholding pattern and threat of takeover Buyback of shares results in increasing the proportion of shareholding of the promoters and their associates. This is due to the fact that the promoter group is not allowed to participate in the buyback programme, for obvious reasons of possible misuse and unjust enrichment. The increased

Box 19-3 Deemed dividend—capital reduction vs buyback*

Colgate-Palmolive India Limited recently announced a *deemed dividend* at ₹9 per share, apart from a special 70th anniversary dividend of ₹2 per share. The deemed dividend is proposed through a return of ₹122.40 crore (excluding dividend distribution tax) to shareholders. The amount would not be liable to tax in the hands of shareholders, clarified the company.

The announcement said that the reduction in capital which is in excess of the company's operational needs is proposed under Section 100 of the Indian Companies Act, 1956, and would be achieved by reduction in the face value of existing shares from ₹10 to Re 1 per share. The proposal of reduction of capital is subject to the approval of shareholders and confirmation by the Bombay High Court. The number of shares issued, paid-up, and outstanding and the shareholding pattern would remain unchanged.

Return of capital to shareholders should not have any tax implication either for the company or for the shareholders, who are receiving a part of their investment. Section 2(22)(d) of the Income Tax Act, 1961 treats this distribution by the company to its shareholders as deemed dividend.

According to one opinion the reduction in share capital amounts to extinguishment of rights of capital gains, and the assessees (shareholders in this case) are liable to pay capital gains tax as a result of reduction in the face value of shares of the company.

The amount distributed by the company on reduction of share capital has two components—distribution attributable to accumulated profits of the company and distribution attributable to capital. Distribution to the extent of accumulated profit is, therefore, to be treated as deemed dividend. Distribution over and above the accumulated profit, after reducing the cost of shares, is to be treated as capital gains.

For Colgate-Palmolive India Limited, the distribution of ₹9 per share upon reduction of capital would, therefore, be treated as deemed dividend (as accumulated profits are available to that extent) and would be tax exempt in the hands of the shareholders, under section 10(34) of the Income Tax Act. However, the company would be liable to pay dividend distribution tax of 16.995% on the amount distributed.

**Based on an article by D Murali, Business Line, 10 May 2007*

shareholding of the promoters is indicative of their sustained interest and involvement, and of the good long-term prospects of the firm. The remaining shareholders have increased faith in the firm once the buyback programme is over. Value would increase because involvement becomes long-term, and the supply of shares would drop. Furthermore, due to the increased price, the reduced supply of shares in the market, and increased promoters' holdings, the threat of hostile takeover is automatically reduced. It provides a cover to the existing management, who otherwise would need to infuse their own capital if they wanted to increase their shareholding.

Controlling the capital structure With the reduced number of shares after the buyback, the debt–equity ratio in terms of book values would increase. Debt may be used to buy back equity shares and so, this route can be used to control or modify the capital structure of the firm. This advantage is apparently trivial, because it has been observed that more often than not firms that have large reserves and are almost 100% equity financed usually offer buybacks. Such firms remain debt-free even after the buyback.

A choice to shareholders A share buyback is open to those who are willing to sell, and there is no compulsion for shareholders to participate in it. Those who want to stay invested in the firm can do so. Those who want a cash dividend need not create their own home-made dividend. The firm creates it for them. Those who do not want to sell and who believe in capital gains being more tax efficient can remain invested. Furthermore, each investor has the flexibility of working out the exact number of shares to sell, depending upon his need for current cash flow. If dividend were distributed instead, all shareholders would be forced to receive fixed amounts of cash, irrespective of their preferences in terms of current income or capital appreciation. Distribution of dividend implies less capital gains, something that does not suit all shareholders.

Preserving information content of dividend A share buyback permits a stable dividend policy to be pursued. On the other hand, if a large dividend were to be distributed, the firm would have to make extra efforts to communicate that this is a one-off event and should not be construed as increased ability of the firm to generate increased earnings. It allows the preservation of the signalling value of dividend.

Disadvantages of Buyback

However, there can be some disadvantages to share buybacks, which include the following.

It cannot be recurring Cash dividends are 'sticky' (they are maintained at a given level, or exhibit steady growth unless the situation changes drastically), and therefore, shareholders may prefer dividends, which are more predictable in comparison with share buybacks, which are one-time opportunities and are not regular features.

Excessive pricing To induce shareholders to exercise the option of buyback, firms necessarily have to offer a price that is more than the current market price. This may lead to overpricing, and paying prices that are more than warranted may benefit those exiting at the cost of those choosing to remain invested. One can judge this by observing the price of the share immediately after the conclusion of a buyback programme. If it is less than the offered price, one may conclude that the buyback was at a price higher than warranted. It may be considered by some of the shareholders as a waste of money which could have been saved if the same amount were distributed as dividend; this could have created more value.

Method of Buyback

Share buyback can be done either through *tender offers* or through *open offers*. Under tender offers, the firm can buy directly from shareholders a specified number of shares at a predetermined price over a specified period of time. Alternatively, under open offers, the firm can buy, from secondary markets, a specified number of shares at varying prices subject to a maximum price, within a specified time period, which usually lasts much longer. As compared to a tender offer, an open offer is a superior and more efficient way of share buyback because (a) it staggers the cash flow, (b) keeps prices steady for a longer time, and (c) the firm pays a market-determined price for repurchase, rather than an announced price which is likely to be in excess of the market price and intrinsic worth.

SUMMARY

Dividends are periodic payments by a firm to its shareholders as reward for their investment. 'Dividend policy' refers to the decision on how much of earnings or what proportion of earnings must be distributed so as to enhance the value of the firm.

Whether or not the dividend decision can contribute to the value of the firm is a debatable issue. There is one school of thought that believes that the dividend policy impacts the value of the firms, while another school of thought believes in the opposite philosophy of irrelevance of dividend policy in determination of the value of the firm.

Major proponents who believe in the relevance of dividend are Walter and Gordon, who have developed similar models for valuation of the firm based on dividend. They believe that investment policy and dividend policy are interrelated and not independent of each other. Depending upon the returns of the investment opportunities available to the firm, the value of the firm can increase or decrease with its dividend policy. If the firm is able to exceed the expectations of its shareholders, the optimum dividend policy would be 100% retention. If firm is not able to deploy the earnings at the expected rate, the optimum dividend policy would be 100% payout. Only when the ability of the firm exactly matches the shareholders' expectations will the dividend policy have no impact on the value of the firm.

On the contrary, the other school of thought, led by MM, believes that under perfect market conditions, the dividend policy is irrelevant to the value of the firm. According to them, the key determinants of the value of the firm are the level of earnings and the investment policy. As long as investment policy is held constant, there is no reason for the value of the firm to change. Dividends cannot alter the complexion of investment because firms can always replenish the cash outflow on account of dividend through issue of fresh capital. There would only be a transfer of value from old shareholders to new shareholders, with total value remaining the same

Furthermore, if the dividend policy of the firm does not suit individual investors, they can resort to buying and selling of their shares to earn the desired level of current income and yet keep their total wealth constant. This is referred to as home-made dividend, which can undo the corporate dividend policy at the individual investor's level.

Extending Gordon's argument further, dividends are thought to resolve uncertainties in cash flow. Dividends are certain and nearer, and so, the increased amount must lower the discount rate and raise the firm's value. This is called the bird-in-the-hand argument. According to MM, the increased dividend does not alter the riskiness of the earnings. If earnings remain the same, the discount rate must remain unchanged.

However, in the real world there are several factors that influence the dividend policy. Factors such as taxation favour retention because capital gains are taxed at a lower rate than dividend income. Similarly, the existence of floatation cost, inability of the firm to issue fresh shares at prices lower that current market value, floatation costs, and legal framework also favour as much retention as possible.

The factors that favour high payout of earnings as dividend include transaction costs, investors' preference for current income, and their reluctance to sell capital assets. Recognizing these conflicting factors, it is opined that a passive residual dividend policy must be optimal. It recognizes the value of investment opportunities and the increased cost of replacing internal equity with external equity. Only the remainder from the investment can be paid as dividend. This calls for a fluctuating dividend payout, while it is desirable to have a stable dividend for other reasons.

Factors that emphasize the stability of dividend are the signalling power of dividend, the need of investors to have current income, and the existence of clienteles. Besides providing returns to shareholders, any change in dividend communicates the ability of the firm to maintain a revised dividend policy. A change in the dividend policy also causes shifting of investor groups, called clienteles, and creates avoidable activity in the stock markets.

Bonus shares and stock splits are the rewards that are non-cash in nature. The rationale behind bonus shares and stock splits is bringing share prices to a more acceptable trading range, to increase investors' interest, liquidity and broaden the shareholder base. They also communicate the increased ability of the firm to service a larger number of shares in future.

Share buyback is another unique method, with many more advantages, of returning excess cash to shareholders. It gives two choices to shareholders: remain invested, or sell the shares back to the firm. It also communicates to shareholders the perception of management that the firm is undervalued. Share buyback can influence the shareholding pattern, increase promoters' holdings and alter capital structure. The disadvantage of share buyback is the possibility of excess price being paid to those exiting shareholders who opt for buyback.

KEY TERMS

Relevance of dividend The value of the firm is determined *inter alia* by the dividend on shares.

Irrelevance of dividend The dividend policy is irrelevant for determination of the value of the firm.

Bird-in-the-hand argument Dividend being more certain, part of the return can be discounted at a lower rate, causing the value of the firm to increase as dividends increase is referred as bird-in-the-hard argument.

Home-made dividend The ability of individual investors to adjust their current income by buying and selling shares without affecting their return is referred to as home-made dividend.

Underpricing The inability of the firm to issue fresh shares at a price lower than the current current market price is referred to as underpricing.

Passive residual dividend policy The practice of fixing dividend as a residual of earnings only after meeting investment needs and utilizing all internal equity, without mobilizing external equity is referred as passive residual dividend policy.

Signalling theory The opinion that a change in dividends is an important and tangible piece of information about the future prospects of the earnings of the firm is referred as signalling theory.

Clientele effect Investors can be segregated into groups, called clienteles, according to their preference for current income and capital gains. Clienteles choose to invest in firms which have dividend policies that match the clienteles' needs for current income.

Bonus shares The shares issued by capitalization of reserves into capital of the firm, proportionately increasing the number of shares while keeping the value of the portfolio the same are bonus shares.

Stock split The shares issued by a firm splitting a share into more than one, without capitalization of reserves is called share split. Shareholders' wealth remains the same, due to a proportionate decrease in price.

Share buyback A tool to return excess cash to shareholders in lieu of dividend, giving them the options of either remaining invested or converting their holdings into cash.

KEY FORMULAE

Walter's Model of valuation $P_0 = \dfrac{D}{r} + \dfrac{k(E-D)/r}{r}$

Gordon's Model of valuation $P_0 = \dfrac{D_1}{r-g}$

or $P_0 = \dfrac{E_1 \times (1-b)}{r-bk}$

Market capitalization rate $r = \dfrac{D_1}{P_0} + g$

Shareholders' return $r = \dfrac{D}{P_0} + \dfrac{\Delta P}{P_0}$

Value of new shares to be issued under irrelevance argument

$\Delta n \times P_1 = I - (nE_1 - nD_1) = I - nE_1 + nD_1$

PRACTICE PROBLEMS

1. Walter's Model and Payout

Flat Even Ltd (FEL) has an earning level of ₹5 crore. If invested back in the business, it can earn ₹1.5 crore additional. The investors in FEL have expectations of 35%. Find the following as per Walter's Model:

(a) The value of FEL if it follows payout of (i) 0%, (ii) 30%, and (iii) 60%

(b) The optimum payout ratio

(c) The maximum value the share of FEL can command

Solution

(a) The company has a potential to offer returns of 30% (1.50/5.00)

Therefore, k = 30.00%

Available earnings, E = ₹5.00 crore

Return required, r = 35.00%

The value as per Walters Model is:

$$P_0 = \frac{D + \frac{k}{r}(E-D)}{r}$$

(i) With 0% payout we have D = ₹0.00 crore

$$P_0 = \frac{0 + \frac{0.30}{0.35}(5.00-0)}{0.35} = ₹12.24 \text{ crore}$$

(ii) With 30% payout D = ₹1.50 crore

$$P_0 = \frac{1.50 + \frac{0.30}{0.35}(5.00-1.50)}{0.35} = ₹12.86 \text{ crore}$$

(iii) With 60% payout D = ₹3.00 crore

$$P_0 = \frac{3.00 + \frac{0.30}{0.35}(5.00-3.00)}{0.35} = ₹13.47 \text{ crore}$$

(b) Since the firm is able to deploy the funds at 30% only as against the expectations of the investors of 35%, the optimum payout would be 100%.

(c) At 100% payout, the value of the firm would be:

$$P_0 = \frac{D + \frac{k}{r}(E-D)}{r}$$

with $E = D$; $P_0 = \dfrac{D}{r}$

Here $E = D$ (for 100% payout) and the maximum value of FEL is:

P_0 = D/r = 5.00/0.35 = ₹14.29 crore

2. Gordon's Model: Reinvestment and Share Value

Paradigm Garments Ltd has been doing reasonably well in the market through its off-beat, fashion garments. The current operations yield 20% return and is matched by shareholders' expectations. With current level of earnings at ₹10 per share, the market price of the share is ₹50.

The management, desirous of growth, is facing three alternatives: (i) To enter conventional garments line that provides a return of 15% but expands the market, (ii) Expand the current operations in other geographies that would yield same 20%, and (iii) Enter another niche of high end apparel that has low volumes but provides handsome 25% return.

As a matter of philosophy, the management funds all its operations through plough back of the earnings. Since the three operations are scalable, the management again faces three alternatives of retaining 50%, 60%, or 70% of the earnings.

What happens to the share price if the firm (a) enters conventional garments line, (b) expands current operations, and (c) ventures into high end apparel niche? Provide an explanation to the change in the share price.

Solution

As per Gordon's Model, the value of share is given by:

$$P_0 = \frac{D_1}{r-g} = \frac{E_1(1-b)}{r-bk}$$

Expected earnings level, E_1 = ₹10.00

Expected return, r = 20%

(a) If the firm enters the conventional garments line, the value of the share with re-investment rate of 15% with different levels of retention is worked out as follows:

Reinvestment rate, k = 15%	
Retention, b	**Price**
50%	$\frac{10\times(1-0.5)}{0.2-0.5\times0.15}$ = ₹40.00
60%	$\frac{10\times(1-0.6)}{0.2-0.6\times0.15}$ = ₹36.36
70%	$\frac{10\times(1-0.7)}{0.2-0.7\times0.15}$ = ₹31.58

With reinvestment rate k less than the expected rate of return by the investors, an increased retention (decreased payout) would result in fall in the share price because the firm is not able to meet the investors' expectations.

(b) If the firm opts for expansion of the current line, the re-investment rate of the retained surplus would be 20% and the value of the share would be as follows:

Reinvestment rate, k = 20%	
Retention, b	**Price**
50%	$\frac{10\times(1-0.5)}{0.2-0.5\times0.2}$ = ₹50.00
60%	$\frac{10\times(1-0.6)}{0.2-0.6\times0.2}$ = ₹50.00
70%	$\frac{10\times(1-0.7)}{0.2-0.7\times0.2}$ = ₹50.00

With reinvestment rate k equal to the expected rate of return by the investors, an retention/payout would have no impact on the share price because the firm is able to meet exactly the investors' expectations. As such dividend policy seems irrelevant to the value of the firm.

(c) With entry into the high-end apparel, the retained funds would provide a return of 25% and the share price would be:

Reinvestment rate, k = 25%	
Retention, b	**Price**
50%	$\frac{10\times(1-0.5)}{0.2-0.5\times0.25}$ = ₹66.67
60%	$\frac{10\times(1-0.6)}{0.2-0.6\times0.25}$ = ₹80.00
70%	$\frac{10\times(1-0.7)}{0.2-0.7\times0.25}$ = ₹120.00

With reinvestment rate k more than the expected rate of return by the investors, an increased retention (decreased payout) would result in rise in the share price because the firm is able to exceed the investors' expectations.

3. Dividend Policy and Expected Return

Glad Corporation follows a current dividend policy of distributing 40% of its earnings. The shares of the company trade at ₹200. The management is of the opinion that an increase in the dividend payout from current 40% to either 50% or 60% would increase the value of the firm and provide better returns to the investors.

Assuming that the firm continues to remain in the same business and an expected earnings of ₹40 per share in the coming year, examine the shareholders' return if Glad Corporation changes its payout to (a) 50% and (b) 60%.

What conclusion do you draw from the results?

Solution

Expected Earnings per Share, E_1 = ₹40.00

Expected Dividend per Share, D_1 = ₹16.00

Current Market Price, P_0 = ₹200.00

Retained Earnings = ₹24.00

Returns to the shareholder comprise of the dividend yield and the growth in price. Growth in the price is dependent upon the retained earnings, hence the payout policy.

Growth, $g = \dfrac{\text{Retained earnings}}{\text{Price}} = \dfrac{24}{200} = 12.0\%$

Current returns to the shareholders, r_e

$= E_1/P_0 = D_1/P_0 + (E_1 - D_1)/P_0$

$= D_1/P_0 + g$

$= 16/200 + 0.12$

$= 0.08 + 0.12 = 20.00\%$

(a) When dividend is 50% = ₹20.00

Retained earnings = ₹20.00

Growth, g = Retained earnings/Price = 20/200 = 10.00%

Returns to the shareholders, r_e

$= D_1/P_0 + g$

$= 20/200 + 0.1$

$= 0.10 + 0.1 = 20.00\%$

(b) When dividend is 60% = ₹24.00

Retained earnings = ₹16.00

Growth, g = Retained earnings/Price = 16/200 = 8.00%

Returns to the shareholders, r_e

$= D_1/P_0 + g$

$= 24/200 + 0.08$

$= 0.12 + 0.08 = 20.00\%$

The shareholders' return remains same irrespective of the dividend policy. The amount of present dividend lost is gained exactly by the growth rate and vice versa.

4. Gordon's Model: PE Multiple and Dividend Policy

Vedic Nourishers Ltd is in the business of producing energy drinks in different flavours. Due to good opportunity of investments yielding a 25% return, they have been retaining 60% of their earnings while distributing the rest.

(a) If investors expect a return of 20% and the firm expects earnings of ₹10 per share find out the (i) PE multiple of the firm and the (ii) current market price.

(b) The management of the firm believes that the market perception of the firm can be improved, but it does not have projects that can yield better than 25% return. What changes in the policy can you suggest if the firm needs to improve its PE multiple to (i) 10, (ii) 12, and (iii) 20.

(c) Find out the expected price of the share of Vedic Nourishers Ltd after one year assuming that the target PE multiples are achieved.

Solution

(a) The current scenario of the expectation, dividend policy reinvestment is as below:

Retention,	b =	60%
Distribution,	$(1 - b)$ =	40%
Expected return,	r =	20%
Investment rate,	k =	25%

The PE multiple as per Gordon's model is:

$$P_0 = \frac{E_1(1-b)}{r - bk}$$

or $$\frac{P_0}{E_1} = \frac{(1-b)}{r - bk}$$

(i) The current PE multiple $= \dfrac{(1-b)}{r-bk}$

$$= \frac{0.4}{(0.2 - 0.6 \times 0.25)} = 8.00$$

Expected earnings, E_1 = ₹10.00

(ii) Current Price, P_0 = ₹80.00

(b) With the same parameters of reinvestment rate and expectations of investors, the perception of the company may be changed by changing the PE multiple. The PE multiple as a function of dividend policy is expressed as:

$$\text{PE Ratio } X = \frac{1-b}{0.20 - 0.25b}$$

For different target PE multiples, the dividend policy as reflected in the retention ratio b is worked out as follows:

Target PE multiple =	**10**	**12**	**20**
r =	20%	20%	20%
k =	25%	25%	25%
gives $(1 - b)$=	$2 - 2.5b$	$2.4 - 3b$	$4 - 5b$
Solving for b, we get:			
b =	66.67%	70.00%	75.00%
(c) Growth, $g = b \times k$	16.67%	17.50%	18.75%
Revised dividend	₹3.33	₹3.00	₹2.50
New price	₹100.00	₹120.00	₹200.00
Price next year, P_1	₹116.67	₹141.00	₹237.50

5. Multiple Growth Rates and Fair Value

Gandhi Software Limited is in the business of software development and occupies a prominent position in the industry. For the last 5 years, the industry has been growing at a compounded annual growth rate of 25% which is far in excess of the economic growth in the country. The last dividend by the firm was ₹20 per share.

Being a leader in the software industry, Gandhi Software Limited has always exceeded the growth rate of the industry. According to some analysts, reflecting the mood of some optimistic investors, the expected growth rate of the firm would be 20% higher than the industry. Another group believes that the firm would grow at a rate equal to the industry growth rate of 25%.

Differing with the two groups, there is another group of analysts which has projected the growth of Gandhi Software Limited as well as the overall growth rate of the industry to be around 15% only; somewhat higher than the expected national economic growth.

(a) What is the appropriate share price of Gandhi Software Limited according to the three groups of analysts? Assume that all groups are unanimous in their opinion about the expected return of 35%.

(b) If the current market price of the share is ₹320, what is the implied growth rate in the current market price?

(c) With the actual market price at ₹320, which group of investors buys and which investor group sells the shares of the firm?

(d) What are the factors that influence the future market price?

Solution

(a) Three group of investors designated as Group A, B, and C have varying estimates of growth of the firm, while they are unanimous about the remaining determinants of the fair value of the firm. According to each of them, the value of the firm determined through Gordon's model is:

	Group A	Group B	Group C
Current dividend, D_0	₹20.00	₹20.00	₹20.00
Growth in dividend, g	30.00%	25.00%	15.00%
Expected dividend, D_1	₹26.00	₹25.00	₹23.00

Required return, r = 35.00%

The value of the share is given by:

$$P_0 = \frac{D_0(1+g)}{r-g}$$

Value of the common stock:

Group A: $\frac{20(1+0.30)}{0.35-0.30} = ₹520$

Group B: $\frac{20(1+0.25)}{0.35-0.25} = ₹250$

Group C: $\frac{20(1+0.15)}{0.35-0.15} = ₹115$

(b) The actual market price of the share = ₹320

The expected return from the investment = 35.00%

Growth rate implied by the market price may be found using DDM as follows:

$$\text{Value of stock, } P_0 = \frac{D_0(1+g)}{r-g}$$

$$320 = \frac{20\times(1+g)}{0.35-g}$$

$$g = 0.2706 \text{ or } 27.06\%$$

(c) Given the price of the share at ₹320, Group A would be buying the share as the intrinsic value of the share is more than the current market price. Group B and Group C would sell the shares because according to them, the intrinsic worth of the share is less than the current price. In future, the share must find its intrinsic worth.

(d) The future price of the share would be determined by the group of investors that dominates the process of buying and selling. The process of continuous buying and selling would continue till all investor groups converge on their estimates of future growth rate.

6. Dividend and Value

The management of Confusion Ltd are in a dilemma regarding the declaration of their first ever dividend. The shareholders have been witnessing a 25% growth in the share price period after period, and as a result, today the market price is ₹400. The management is contemplating a dividend of ₹50 per share for the coming year. What would be the price of the share of Confusion Ltd if:

(a) dividend is actually declared and

(b) dividend is not declared

Solution

(a) If dividend is declared then the price would be given by

$$P_0 = \frac{1}{1+r}(D_1 + P_1)$$

$$400 = \frac{1}{1+0.25}(50 + P_1)$$

Solving for P_1, we get:

P_1 = ₹450

(b) If dividend is not declared, then the price would be:

$$P_0 = \frac{1}{1+r}(D_1 + P_1)$$

$$400 = \frac{1}{1+0.25}(0 + P_1)$$

Solving for P_1, we get:

P_1 = ₹500

The gain of dividend is compensated by the loss in price, keeping the returns same. If dividend is declared, the price of the share would fall by the amount of dividend.

7. Irrelevance of Dividend

Expanding Corporation is providing 25% returns to its shareholders. The current market price of its share is ₹80 with 1.25 crore shares outstanding.

The firm is expected to earn ₹4 crore in the year, while its investment requirements of the period is ₹6 crore. It has been distributing dividend at 75% of the earnings.

In view of its expansion requirement, it is exploring the proposition of skipping the dividend altogether for the year while mobilizing the remaining funds by issue of fresh shares.

Examine the value of the firm when the firm (a) continues with the current dividend policy of 75% payout and (b) decides to skip the dividend for the year.

Solution

The current position of the firm is as below:

Expected return,	r = 25%
Current market price,	P_0 = ₹80.00
No. of shares,	n = 1.25 crore
Investment required,	I = ₹6.00 crore
Earnings available,	E_1 = ₹4.00 crore
Planned dividend,	D_1 = ₹3.00 crore

(a) **Price when dividend is declared**

Dividend per share = ₹2.40

The relationship of returns and the share price is:

$$P_0 = \frac{1}{1+r}(D_1 + P_1)$$

$$P_1 = (1 + r) \times P_0 - D_1$$

The firm can issue shares at the price expected to prevail at the end of Period 1. As per the value of the share, the expected market price and the number of new shares required to be issued are computed as below:

Expected market price,

$P_1 = (1 + 0.25) \times 80 - 2.4 = ₹97.60$

Capital to be mobilized

$= I - (E_1 - D_1) = 6 - (4 - 3) = ₹5.00$ crore

Number of new shares to be issued,

$\Delta n = 5/97.60 = 0.05123$ crore

Total number of shares after the issue,

$n + \Delta n = 1.25 + 0.05123 = 1.30123$ crore

The current market capitalization is ₹100 crore. (1.25 crore shares @ ₹80)

Market value of shares after the issue for existing shareholders,

$P_1 \times n = ₹122.00$ crore

Dividend received by existing shareholders,

$n \times D_1 = ₹3.00$ crore

Total cash flow for existing shareholders at the end of Period 1 $= ₹125.00$ crore

Present value for existing shareholders = ₹100.00 crore

Market value of shares after the issue,

$P_1 \times (n + \Delta n) = ₹127.00$ crore

Value for the new shareholders, $P_1 \times \Delta n = ₹5.00$ crore

Value for the existing shareholders = ₹122.00 crore

(b) **Value when dividend is not declared**

Expected market price, $P_1 = (1 + 0.25) \times 80 - 0 = ₹100.00$

Capital to be mobilized $= I - (E_1 - D_1)$
$= 6 - (4 - 0) = ₹2.00$ crore

Number of new shares to be issued, $\Delta n = 0.02$ crore

Total number of shares, $n + \Delta n = 1.27$ crore

Market value of shares after the issue for existing shareholders,

$P_1 \times n = ₹125.00$ crore

Dividend received by existing shareholders,

$n \times D_1 = ₹0.00$ crore

Total cash flow for existing shareholders at the end of Period 1 $= ₹125.00$ crore

Present value for existing shareholders = ₹100.00 crore

Market value of shares after the issue, $P_1 \times (n + \Delta n)$ $= ₹127.00$ crore

Value for the new shareholders,

$P_1 \times \Delta n = ₹2.00$ crore

Value for the existing shareholders = ₹125.00 crore

The value for existing shareholders remains same at ₹125 crore in terms of market price and dividend.

EXERCISES

Concept Review Questions

1. What is dividend?
2. Explain Walter's Model of valuation of the firm based on dividend.
3. How does Gordon's Model differ from Walter's Model in valuation of the firm based on dividend?
4. What are the differences in the assumptions made by the theory of relevance and the theory of irrelevance of dividend?
5. What do you understand by bird-in-the-hand theory? Would you agree with the argument made in the theory? Why or why not?
6. What do you understand by passive residual dividend policy? If it is optimal, why do firms not follow it in practice?
7. What are the practical considerations that make a dividend policy relevant?
8. Despite the tax advantage of capital gains, investors prefer dividend income. What could the possible reasons be for this preference for dividend?
9. What are the implications of the signalling theory on the dividend policy of the firm?
10. What do you understand by clientele effect?
11. What are the advantages offered to firms following such methods of non-cash dividend as issue of bonus shares or stock split?
12. How do bonus shares and stock splits affect stock prices?
13. What is share buyback? What are its advantages?
14. Explain the circumstances under which share buyback, rather than cash dividend, is a preferred mode of rewarding shareholders?

Critical Thinking Questions

1. A model of regression for determination of the price of a certain stock, P_0, as a function of dividend and retained earnings is developed with the following formulation:

$$P_0 = a + b_1 \times D + b_2 \times (E - D) + e$$

where a, b_1 and b_2 are the regression coefficient, and e is the error term. D represents dividend and $(E - D)$ represents retained earnings. What do you think the values of b_1 and b_2 would be if (a) dividends are relevant, and (b) dividends are irrelevant?

2. A firm that strongly believed in the residual dividend policy had investment opportunities worth ₹100 lakh. Its earnings for the current period were also ₹100 lakh. The target capital structure of the firm involved a debt–equity ratio of 1:1.

   Following its policy, the firm decided to fund the investment opportunities with ₹50 lakh debt and ₹50 lakh from earnings. The remaining ₹50 lakh from earnings was distributed as dividend.

   Do you think the firm was right in raising debt? What could be the implications on the value of the firm if it had decided to fund the investment entirely with earnings?

3. Given a choice between bonus shares of 1:1 or a stock split of 1:1, which mode of non-cash dividend would you prefer?

Practical Assignment

1. Evaluate one of the recent buyback issues of any firm and find out the following:
   (a) How the price of the share buyback was worked out;
   (b) How much funds were reserved for buyback programme;
   (c) How this amount was worked out;
   (d) What impact it has on the growth prospects of the firm;
   (e) How the debt–equity ratio is affected;
   (f) How the buyback is going to affect EPS.

Numerical Problems

1. Walter's Model and Payout

ABC Ltd has been earning ₹10 per share. The firm is in a business where it can use internally generated funds at 12.5% return. If the return expected by investors in the firm is 15%, find the following:

(i) The value of the share of ABC Ltd if it follows a payout of (a) 0%, (b) 25%, and (c) 50%

(ii) The optimum payout ratio

(iii) The maximum value the share of ABC Ltd can command

2. Dividend Policy and Value

Multiactivity Ltd has a series of projects that can generate returns of 10%, 12%, and 14%. At present, it has earnings of ₹12 per share, of which 25% is the minimum dividend payout that has to be maintained due to investors' preference for current income.

The Managing Director of the firm is considering three alternative dividend policies of 25%, 50%, and 75% payout.

(i) What is the likely impact on the value of the share of the dividend policy under different reinvestment rates?

(ii) What conclusions can you draw?

3. Gordon's Model

Meta Films Ltd has a projected earnings level of ₹15. It has a payout policy of 25%, while retaining 75%. It is able to reinvest the funds at 20%. The expectations of return by the shareholders of Meta Films are 16%.

(i) What is the value of the Meta Films share in the market?

(ii) What would be the price of Meta Films stock be after one year?

(iii) Verify whether the investors get their desired return of 16%.

4. Walter's Model vs. Gordon's Model

What would be the price of the stock of Meta Films in Problem 3 if Walter's Model is applied?

(i) Do you find the price the same under Walter's Model?

(ii) Explain the difference in the prices obtained by the two models.

5. Irrelevance of Dividend

The current market price of the shares of Zenith Corporation is ₹200. It has projected a dividend of ₹10 per share in the coming year. The market expects a return of 20%.

What would the price of the share of Zenith Corporation be if (a) dividend is actually declared, and (b) it is not declared?

6. Multiple Dividend Growth Rates and Value

Macy Garments Ltd is in the business of fashion designing, and has low volumes. It is expected to grow at the rate of 50% over the next two years. However, it would not be possible to have this level of growth beyond two years, when it is expected to grow at 30% for another three years. The growth rate thereafter is expected to be around 10%.

What is the value of its share at the end of each of the five years if the cost of capital is 15%?

7. Changing Dividend Policy and Value

Radiant Corporation, a market leader dealing in refrigeration products, has been paying dividend consistently over the last several years. The growth rate of dividend on an average has been 12%. The capitalization rate of Radiant Corporation is 16%.

Consistent with its developmental philosophy, Radiant Corporation acquired a technology for a new refrigerant that called for a huge investment, but offered a potential of growth of 14% in earnings and in dividend as well.

Radiant had always believed in financing projects through internal accruals, and never faced any problems in funding growth opportunities as well as in maintaining dividend. It was for the first time that the management of Radiant faced a situation where it had to compromise dividend for the sake of implementing a new project, although with the objective of better growth.

Radiant's management decided to skip dividend for the next three years. However, as a measure of good corporate governance and to reassure investors, it announced that dividend would recommence four years later at ₹12 only, and would offer a better growth rate of 14% instead of 12%.

What do you think would the impact on the market price of shares of Radiant Corporation of the announcement of a new project and the resultant postponement of dividend?

8. Investment and Dividend as Residual

Flat Products Ltd has been following a policy of 100% payout, as it did not have any expansion plans. All its ongoing earnings are distributed as dividend. Its present levels of earnings are ₹16.00 crore while the shares outstanding are ₹500 lakh, providing an EPS of ₹3.20, which is distributed as dividend.

It has just identified an opportunity that requires an investment of ₹10 crore, which would take one year to implement. Thereafter, the project provides an income of ₹5 crore annually. Consistent with its past practice of no debt, Flat Products has decided to fund the expansion from internal resources by reducing dividend.

If the market capitalization is 10%, find out the price of the share of Flat Products today and the impact of the investment decision on this price. Explain any increase or decrease in the price of the share consequent upon acceptance of investment.

9. External Funding, Dividend and Value

Examine the relevant data of Flat Products Limited in Problem 8 when funding is achieved by borrowing at 6%. State the impact on Flat Products' share price. Assume no taxes.

CASE STUDY

ICI India Limited – Buyback of Shares*

ICI India Ltd (ICI) manufactures and markets paints, specialty chemicals, adhesives, fragrances, starch, and flavours. ICI was formed in 1954 for the manufacture of explosives, and later diversified into several businesses such as fertilizers, catalysts, rubber chemicals, water treatment chemicals, pharmaceuticals, etc. After several rounds of business restructuring, it is focussed at present on paints, specialty chemicals, etc.

Since inception, it has been consistently rewarding shareholders. Select financial data of ICI is presented in Table A:

* Extracted from Public Announcement of Buyback of Shares dated 21 September 2006, by ICI India Limited.

Table A Select financial data: ICI India Limited–Buyback

(₹ *crore*)

As on 31 March	*2005-06*	*2004-05*	*2003-04*
Operating income	876.24	754.34	685.12
Other income	31.59	28.07	22.87
Total income	907.83	782.41	707.99
EBITDA	121.94	93.00	83.13
PAT	50.15	47.18	109.09*
Dividend incl. tax	27.96	25.76	57.64
Paid-up capital	40.87	40.87	40.87
Must be presented as below:			
Reserves excl. capital and revaluation reserves	510.46	488.33	479.28
Debt	—	16.00	20.00
EPS (₹/share)	12.27	11.54	26.69
Book value (₹/share)	128.44	123.01	120.17
Debt–equity ratio	—	0.03	0.04
Return on net worth	9.76%	9.49%	23.44%

* including exceptional income of ₹54.27 crore

With the objective of returning cash to its shareholders, ICI announced a programme to buy back shares at the meeting of its Board of Directors on 26 July 2006, with the following features:

1. The buyback to be effected with open market purchases through stock exchanges, without any negotiated deals, and offloading of promoters' shares at the price prevailing in the market, but not exceeding ₹350.00 per share, commencing on the 29th of September 2006 for a period of about one year.
2. The maximum amount of buyback would not exceed ₹131.23 crore, representing 25% of the capital and free reserves of ₹524.93 crore as on 31 March 2006, as stipulated under the law.
3. The buyback would be funded through the surplus cash available with the firm, without resorting to any borrowing.
4. The promoters of ICI, i.e., the Imperial Chemical Company plc, which holds 2,07,76,213 shares equivalent to 50.83% of the share capital, shall not tender any of its shares in the buyback, and hence, management control would continue to rest with Imperial Chemical Company plc.
5. Shares bought back would be cancelled and would not be re-issued till six months of completion of buyback programme have elapsed, as required under the law.
6. The debt–equity ratio post buyback would remain well within the stipulated norms of maximum of 2:1.

The rationale for buyback of shares included (a) returning cash to shareholders and optimizing returns to them, (b) enhancing shareholder value, and (c) improving EPS without impairing growth prospects.

Under the takeover guidelines, the promoters would be required to make an open offer for an additional 20% of the shares in case their holding exceeded 55% in the course of the buyback programme. ICI's management, therefore, decided to limit the buyback programme to the number of shares that would confine the promoters' holding to less than 55%.

The management of ICI offered a buyback price at a premium of about 20% over the closing prices of the share on the date of announcement of the buyback. The closing prices of ICI shares on the day of notice to stock exchanges of the proposed buyback, i.e., 17 July 2006, and on the day after the resolution indicating the buyback price of ₹350 per share was passed, i.e., 26 July 2006, were as shown in the following table.

Closing Price	*17 July 2006*	*26 July 2006*
BSE (₹ per share)	301.90	294.35
NSE (₹ per share)	303.00	295.00

The stock prices for the 6 months preceding the announcement of buyback and the previous three calendar years at the Bombay Stock Exchange (BSE) are given in Table B:

Table B Stock Market Data ICI Limited—Buyback

(₹ *per share*)

Price in BSE	*High*	*Low*	*Average*
Calendar year 2003	203.50	103.90	140.51
Calendar year 2004	237.40	157.25	185.83
Calendar year 2005	351.90	212.60	278.41
March 2006	410.60	377.05	394.28
April 2006	402.55	350.35	375.43
May 2006	374.95	319.80	354.80
June 2006	355.35	252.65	288.72
July 2006	308.25	280.00	292.99
August 2006	313.05	294.00	303.69
September 2006 (till 19 Sept)	351.05	308.80	328.71

The prices of ICI shares at the NSE were similar to those of the BSE.

Discuss

1. What is the advantage of a share buyback? Compare the two scenarios if ICI paid ₹131.23 crore as dividend, instead of using this amount for buyback.
2. What would the impact on other income of ICI be when the buyback is complete?
3. What changes in the shareholding pattern did you perceive consequent to the buyback programme?
4. What is the maximum number of shares ICI can repurchase without (a) exceeding the limit of the pre-set amount and (b) without invoking the takeover guidelines?
5. Post buyback, what impact do you see on the stock price, assuming the same PE ratio is maintained?

In the CD

Finding Value of the Firm as per Walter's Model and Gordon's Model

CHAPTER

20 Sources of Finance

LEARNING OBJECTIVES

After reading this chapter, you should be able to understand:

- the role played by financial markets in converting savings into productive investments
- the different segments of financial markets
- the financial products available and the services offered by financial markets
- domestic capital market and its constituents
- primary vs secondary markets
- Initial Public Offering (IPO) as a source of long-term financing
- conventional sources of long-term financing like term loans and project financing
- venture capital funding and its utility for financing the newer and riskier projects
- investment banking as the process of financial intermediation
- services provided by investment bankers
- sources of short-term financing like working capital loans, lines of credit, commercial papers, factoring, and forfaiting

FOOD FOR THOUGHT

Khazanchi and Udyami are childhood friends. Despite having their early education together, both had chosen different careers. Khazanchi had become a proficient investment banker, while Udyami was head of software development with one of the major IT companies. This evening, as part of their family get-together, Mr and Mrs Khazanchi had invited Mr and Mrs Udyami for a dinner at Regency, a five star hotel.

"What is the occasion?" asked Udyami.

"I just concluded a big assignment today with a major IT company for an issue of ADR," replied Khazanchi.

Udyami rather inquisitively asked, "All these years, I never asked you what is your job all about? You neither invest nor are you a banker, and yet you call yourself an investment banker!"

Looking at the bearer who had just come to handover the menu cards, Khazanchi said, "My position is just like this bearer. He advises us what is available in the restaurant, asks about our preference, and suggests suitable dishes according to our specifications and taste. He himself does not eat those recipes. I do the same. I tell my clients what is on offer in the menu of financial products markets and what meets their tastes. Like this bearer who does not bother about his own taste, I too have to be concerned with what my clients want. In fact, I go a step further. If need be, Istructure customized products to suit the needs of my clients. Just like the chef prepares dishes as per specifications and tastes of guests that may otherwise not be there in the standard menu.

Not very satisfied with the explanation, Udyami said, "A gentleman had come to see me this morning. He called himself a venture capitalist. He too was sounding like you."

Khazanchi replied, "Venture capitalist is someone who provides you a start after which he vanishes from the scene, normally, only to return to reap the benefits. He works like an appetizer leaving the main course to your choice but would come to share the desserts."

Mrs Khazanchi, who found some similarity with venture capitalists reacted, "He is just like me who likes to have some soups and then straight have a dessert leaving the main course for you people."

Mrs Udyami not be left out of discussions said, "I am more interested in the main course and prefer not to gobble up the starters."

Khanzanchi explained, "That is very much like a project financier or a banker who does not participate at the start-up stage but rather joins for the main course when the starters are over."

Taking the discussion further, Udyami said, "My management is planning a major expansion and is mulling over the plan for additional capitalization. What we are debating over is whether we should go for IPO or should place debt privately."

With an air of a Prefessor, Khazanchi said "Public issue or an IPO is like a full five course meal. Unlike bankers, capital markets are always hungry and connoisseurs. Capital markets relish everything from appetizers to desserts. Shareholders are interested in all. They start with appetizers, have a drink or two, participate in the main course, and also enjoy the desserts and may be coffee thereafter."

Udyami asked, "What is the ADR business that you said you have accomplished today?"

With a smile on his face Khazanchi said, "All these Thai, Continental, and Chinese dishes that you see on the menu card are like ADRs and GDRs. Although these foreign dishes are served as the main course, they are cooked in Indian style with Indian condiments and flavours added."

Bearer who was overhearing all the conversation while waiting for the order said, "I never imagined that finance can be so literally food for thought. Sir! Can we now have some thought for food."

Thereafter, they all ordered their food to the bearer.

INTRODUCTION

Once the vexatious issue of debt-equity mix is resolved, the next problem that the finance manager has to grapple with is to choose the most suitable source(s) of debt/equity financing. If, in a given situation, debt emerges as the preferred source of financing, the next important issue is what form should the debt take? Should the firm go for borrowings externally, or should it raise the term-loans privately, or go ahead with public issue of debentures? Should the firm prefer direct financing or should it go ahead with the indirect financing format like leasing? Similarly, in situations where equity emerges as the preferred mode of financing, the issue before the firm is: how should equity be raised—internationally or domestically? In certain situations, the conventional sources of equity financing may not be available due to high riskiness caused by the newness of business model/ product/technology, etc. In such a situation, venture capital financing may be the most appropriate source of financing. Similarly, several sources of financing have emerged to finance the firms' working capital requirements. Besides the conventional sources of short-term financing like lines of credit offered by banks, several new sources of financing like *commercial papers*, *factoring*, etc., have emerged as preferred sources of financing.

To be able to pick up the most appropriate financing alternative, the finance manager must be aware of the different financing options that are available to meet the long-term and short-term financing needs of firms along with the terms and conditions of their availability. Most of the firms, instead of directly getting involved in the fund-raising process, outsource the function of raising capital to financial intermediaries called *investment bankers* who provide a basket of pre- and post-capital issue services. It is essential for the finance managers to understand the services offered by these financial intermediaries.

Besides discussing the role played by financial markets in channelizing savings towards productive channels, this chapter aims at discussing the different financing options available to Indian firms (the financing options for individuals is beyond the scope of this chapter) to meet their long-term and short-term financing requirements along with the terms and conditions of their availability. This chapter also discusses the various services provided by financial intermediaries that facilitate the process of raising finances. In addition to the various financing options detailed in this chapter, there are certain other financing options available to Indian firms that have been suitably dealt with in the book in appropriate context. To have a complete understanding of the financing options, this chapter should be supplemented with the financing options detailed in Chapter 6 (Valuation of Bonds), Chapter 7 (Valuation of Shares), and Chapter 18 (Leasing and Hire Purchase).

The short-term financing options discussed under the heading 'Money Market' in this chapter should go on to supplement the discussion on 'Working Capital Management' in Part V of this book (Chapters 21–24) as the said options are availed for working capital financing.

ROLE OF FINANCIAL MARKETS

Financial markets act as a conduit through which the funds are channelized from the units whose current income exceeds their current consumption needs (referred to as surplus units) to the units whose investment needs exceed their present and past savings (referred to as deficit units). Such firms are dependent on outside sources to finance their present and future investment needs. This process is depicted in Figure 20-1.

Financial markets channelize the resources from the surplus units to the deficit units.

By affecting such a transfer, the financial markets enable the surplus units to park their funds fruitfully. In absence of such a transfer, such funds would be lying idle. The deficit units get benefited as they get the necessary funds to meet their investment requirements. The economy as a whole gets benefited, as in case of a well-functioning and efficient financial market, the funds would automatically be driven to the most productive avenues of investments. However to the extent the capital markets lack efficiency, there is a risk of funds being frittered away which may make the investors and the economy worse

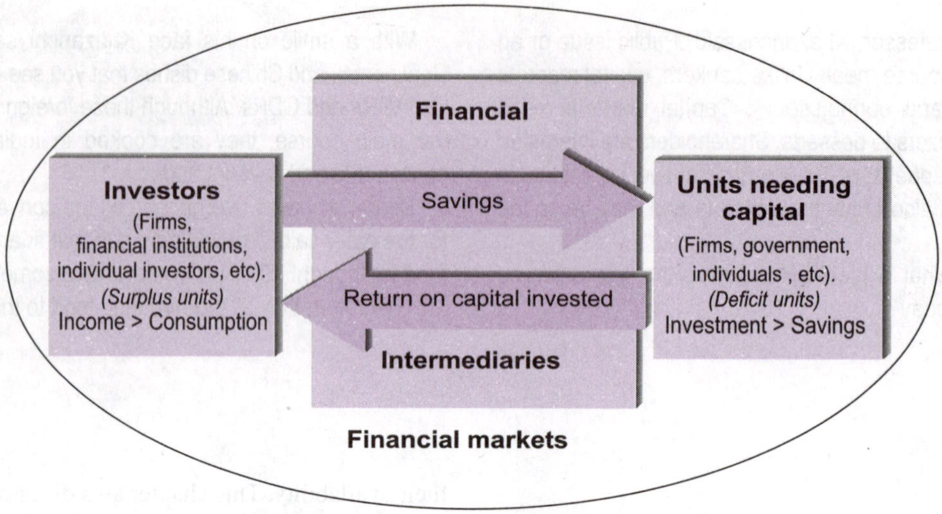

Figure 20-1 Role played by financial markets

off. Financial intermediaries play a very important role in this process of funds transfer. They intermediate in the process of funds transfer by various pre- and post-capital issue services to the firms raising capital.

Since this chapter focuses on the liabilities side of the balance sheet, we will discuss the subject from the perspective of the firms that raise funds and not from the perspective of investors or financial intermediaries. Hence, the subsequent sections give an overview of the financing options and services available to the firms that want to raise funds.

Financial intermediaries facilitate the process of funds transfer.

FINANCIAL MARKETS: SEGMENTS, PRODUCTS, AND SERVICES

Instead of looking at the financial markets as a physical entity, one must look at it as an assemblage of different players, such as investors, units raising capital, financial intermediaries, regulators, etc., and the various financing instruments and services. Financial markets, as shown in Figure 20-2, can broadly be segmented into *capital market* and *money market*. Such segmentation is based on the duration of financing and the purpose for which finance is raised.

Financial markets consist of players, instruments, and services. They can broadly be categorized into money market and capital market.

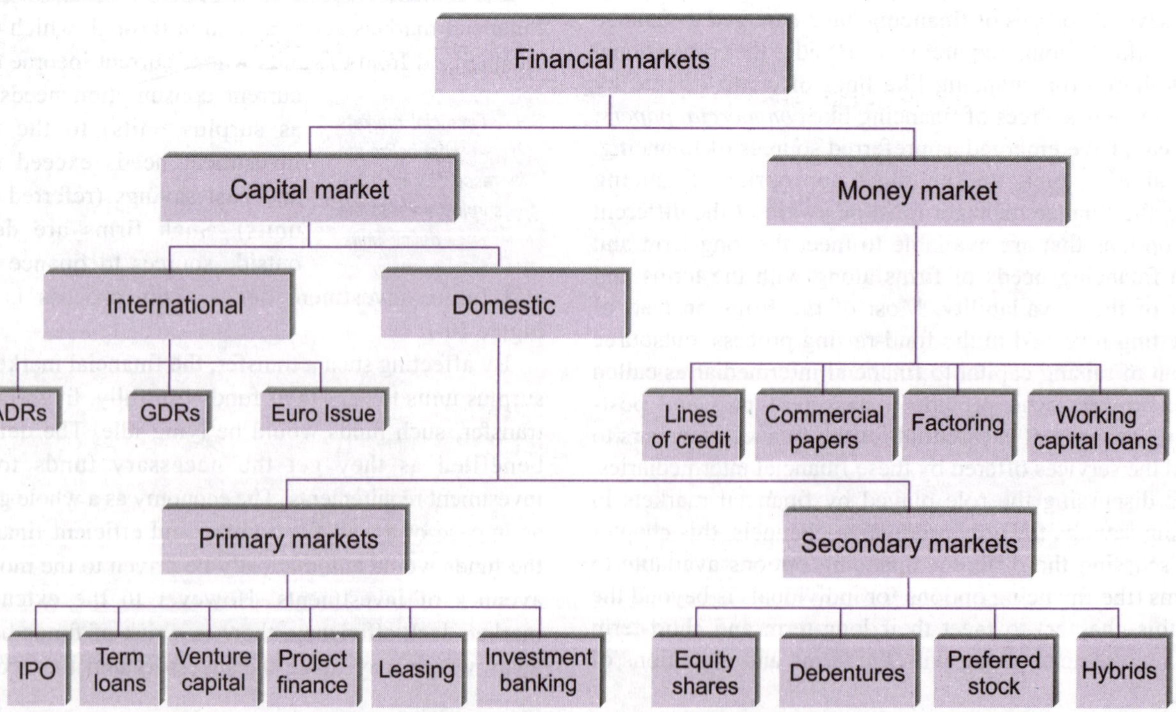

Figure 20-2 Financial markets: Segments and Financing options

LONG-TERM SOURCES OF FINANCE—EQUITY

The *concept of going concern* warrants availability of finance on a continuing basis. Any claim on capital that is redeemable is a sufficient cause for discontinuity of operations. Therefore availability of long term capital to the firm has to be viewed differently than short term capital. In this section, we discuss the two forms that long-term capital can take—*equity* and *debt*.

Equity Capital

Share capital, referred as *equity*, is one such source and instrument to provide capital on a continuing basis. A firm needing funds mobilizes the required amount of equity capital from public at large by inviting subscriptions based on projected financial performance of the project. Financial markets classify the equity broadly on the basis of—(a) geographical domain such as domestic and international capital markets and/or (b) nature of offering, i.e., Initial Public Offer (IPO) (also called as *primary markets*) or Follow-on Public Offer (FPO) (also referred to as *secondary markets*).

The classification of equity capital based on geographical domain is due to the substantially varying regulatory environments prevailing in different nations with respect to reporting, governance and disclosure requirements on part of the issuing firm. Further, the business ethics, practices, culture and norms too vary significantly from country to country, thereby making the process of mobilization of equity different in each country or region. Some of these factors also influence the valuation of equity as the levels of awareness of investors about equity investment and associated risk perceptions are different.

The distinguishing features of the equity capital include: (a) management control and voting rights, (b) ownership of residual profits that are not subject to any minimum, (c) no legal binding to distribute the residual, and (d) its perennial nature absolving the issuer to redeem the liability. These characteristics make equity the backbone of funding of the firm. The investors having no recourse to the issuing firm seek exit in the secondary markets where those willing to invest and those willing to exit the firm exchange the ownership. The continuity of funds to the issuing firm is maintained as one investor gets replaced by another. This can be accomplished by making the instrument of equity transferable and tradable in the secondary markets. The value at which the investors exchange the equity becomes a function of corporate performance, awareness levels of investors, future outlook, corporate governance, efficiency of capital markets, etc.

Capital market is the market for long-term financing. The financing options available in the capital markets are to meet the firms' financing needs that exceed the period of one year. The investors in capital markets include individual investors, firms, and financial institutions. These investors have surplus that they want to invest productively for long-term.

Capital markets can be categorized as domestic and international. Although there are other constituents of capital markets, such as commodities markets, derivatives markets, etc., they are beyond the coverage of this chapter as the instruments traded in these markets such as options, futures, swaps, etc., relate to the asset side of the balance sheet and are used as risk management tools. Since the chapter focuses on the liabilities side of the balance sheet, it talks only about those options that relate to long-term and short-term financing.

DOMESTIC CAPITAL MARKETS

The capital market is the market for firms, individuals, and government to raise long-term funds through the issue of equity and debt instruments. It includes the stock market and the bond market. Capital market in India is regulated by the apex regulatory bodies like Securities and Exchange Board of India (SEBI) and Ministry of Finance. The Indian capital market, like elsewhere, constitutes of *primary market* and *secondary market* of equity and debt instruments.

> *Capital market is the market for long-term financing. Funds can be raised using the debt or the equity option.*

Primary market is the market for new issues of securities (both equity and debt), as distinguished from the *secondary market*, where previously issued securities are bought and sold. The proceeds from the issues of securities in the primary markets go to the firms issuing them. Unlike the secondary markets, the primary markets should not be looked at as a physical entity or a geographical location but rather should connote a composition of players, instruments, and regulators who are involved in the process of new issue of long-term debt or equity.

> *Primary market is the new issue market. Issues made in the primary market subsequently get traded in the secondary market.*

Secondary market is the market where securities are traded after they are initially offered in the primary market. Stock exchanges are known as secondary markets. Secondary markets provide exit routes to the investors in the primary markets.

Although the two are different, they are inexorably linked as the sentiments in one affects the performance of the other. Primary and secondary markets can be better understood by drawing an analogy from the new car market and the market for used cars. The manufacturer/seller of new car goes to the new car market to generate revenues. He generates the revenues and vanishes from the scene. Once the consumer buys a new car, he has to go to the used car market to sell the same. The sales in the used car market do not add on to the revenues of the manufacturer/seller. However, the presence of a vibrant used car market provides the exit option for the buyers of new cars, and thus lends vibrancy to the latter. Similarly, there are primary and secondary markets for equity and debt securities. The firms planning to raise capital go to the primary market or the new issues market. The investors who invest in the primary market, in case they want to disinvest, should go to the secondary markets. The secondary market purchases and sales do not affect the capitalization of the firm, but the ease of exit in the secondary market increases the confidence of investors in the primary market providing liquidity and premium to the scrips.

IPOs, term loans, venture capital financing, project financing, and leasing are the prominent sources of raising funds from the primary markets. Investment bankers assume special significance as they facilitate the process of raising funds from the primary markets by providing various pre-issue and post-issue management services to the firms planning to raise capital from the primary markets. We now proceed to discuss these services. Leasing will not be taken up in this chapter as leasing as a financial service has been dealt with at length in Chapter 18. The secondary market instruments, mentioned in Figure 20-2, have been discussed elaborately in Chapters 6 and 7.

Initial Public Offerings (IPOs)

Initial public offering, or simply 'public offering', is the first sale of stock to the public by a firm (company) that is entitled to issuing shares to public at large. It does not mean that the firm in question is raising capital for the first time. What it essentially means is that hitherto the firm was financed through promoters' contribution, privately placed debt, or equity capital. Now since the firm is able to meet the listing requirements and expects to command the confidence among the investors by virtue of its track record of performance, it feels it is the right time to go public to meet its requirement for additional financing. Every firm makes only one IPO over its lifetime. All public issues of equity made after the IPO are termed as follow-on public offer. Investment bankers or merchant bankers assume significant roles in the IPO process. In an IPO, the issuer may obtain the assistance of an underwriting firm, which helps it determine what type of security to issue (common or preferred), the best offering price, and the time to bring it to market.

IPO is the first sale of stock by a firm (company) to the public. All public issues of equity made after the IPO are termed as follow-on public offer.

IPOs generally involve one or more investment banks as *underwriters*. A large IPO usually involves a 'syndicate' of investment banks led by a major investment bank. The investment bank that leads the syndicate in the IPO is called the *lead manager*. The lead manager enters into a contract with the firm issuing its IPO. The lead manager also enters into contracts with other investment banks involved in the issue management. Such a contract clearly defines the roles and responsibilities of the investment banks, particularly the proportion of the issue underwritten by each one of them. Besides other responsibilities like road shows, book building, decision on the bankers and brokers to the issue, the investment banks may be required to underwrite the issue that they are managing. Underwriting is a financial service (as a part of issue management) whereby the issue manager (referred to as *underwriter* in this role) guarantees against any under-subscription of public issue. To the extent the issue remains undersubscribed, the underwriter purchases them and becomes the shareholder of the firm by virtue of such a holding. The underwriting of the issue by the issue managers (investment banks) not only guarantees 100% subscription to the public issue, it also links the fortune of the issues managers with that of the issuing firm. The underwriter charges an underwriting commission for providing such a service. This commission is dependent on the prospects of the issue being fully subscribed.

The investment bankers also advise the issuing firms on pricing the public issue. This role of investment bankers assumes significance after emergence of free pricing regime as a consequence of abolition of the office of Controller of Capital Issue (CCI) in 1992. In such a scenario, it becomes important that the issue is appropriately priced (neither overpriced nor underpriced). The norm of compulsory underwriting of the public issue by the underwriters puts a check on the underwriters from overpricing the public issue as any under-subscription on account of an ambitious offer price has eventually got to be purchased by the investment bankers themselves.

Investment bankers advise the issuing firm on the pricing of the IPO. The price is discovered following the process of 'book building'.

Book Building

The pricing of the public issue is done following the process of *book building*. Book building is basically a capital issuance process used in IPO which aids price and demand discovery. It is a process used for marketing a public offer of equity shares of a company. The process of book building involves nomination of the lead merchant banker as a *book runner* by the issuing firm. The issuer also specifies the number of securities to be issued and the price band for orders. Investors place their orders. This process is called *bidding* and is similar to open auction. These orders are input into the *electronic book* which remains open for a minimum of 5 days. Bids cannot be entered at less than the floor price. Bids can be revised by the bidder before the issue closes. After the book building period is over, the book runner evaluates the bids on the basis of the evaluation criteria which may include the following:

- Price aggression
- Investor quality
- Earliness of bids, etc.

The book runner and the company conclude the final price at which it is willing to issue the stock and allocation of securities. The size of the issue gets frozen based on the price per share discovered through the book building process. Allocation of securities is made to the successful bidders. The process of book building gets regulated by SEBI laws in India.

Investment Banking

Investment bankers provide a wide array of pre- and post-capital issue services to the firms that want to raise capital either through public issue or private placement. They are termed as financial intermediaries, as they are an important link between the investors and issuers of the capital. It is due to this intermediation and facilitation in the funds transfer that the investment bankers are often referred to as *merchant bankers*. Merchant banking, as a commercial activity, took shape in India through the management of Public Issues of capital and Loan Syndication. It originated in 1969 with the setting up of the Merchant Banking Division by ANZ Grindlays Bank. The main service offered at that time to the corporate enterprises by the merchant banks included the management of public issues and some aspects of financial consultancy. The early and mid-seventies witnessed a boom in the growth of merchant banking organizations in the country with various commercial banks, financial institutions, and broker's firms entering into the field of merchant banking.

Investment bankers provide the issuing firms with a wide array of pre- and post-capital issue services.

A merchant banker, as defined by SEBI, is a person who is engaged in the business of issue management either by making arrangements regarding selling, buying, or subscribing to securities as manager, consultant, advisor, or rendering corporate advisory service in relation to such issue management.

The services provided by investment bankers to the firms issuing capital range from preparation of offer documents, legal compliances, issue price discovery, underwriting of public issue to post-issue monitoring. Besides most of the investment banks also offer strategic advisory services for mergers, acquisitions, divestiture, or any other from of financial restructuring. A couple of these services that relate to issue management have already been discussed in the preceding section on IPO.

The process of follow-on offer remains essentially the same as that of IPOs. An added advantage of follow-on offer is the availability of the firm's track record to the investors overcoming several issues of valuation. It also facilitates easy decision-making for prospective investors as the historical price data is available to them.

Offer for Sale

Offer for sale, unlike IPO or FPO, is not the new issue of capital. The existing promoters or investors of the firm holding substantial capital offer their holding to the public for subscription. Offer for sale can be motivated by any one or more of the following objectives:

a) willingness of the existing shareholders to make an exit from the firm,
b) to meet the listing requirement in order to have minimum number/proportion of share capital to be available in the market for trading, and
c) to have better visibility for the firm by increasing the distribution of capital to the public.

Offer for sale has widely been used by venture capitalists and private equity investors to find an exit route for the investments made by them in young companies. When these young companies get matured and reach a stage to command a fair price in the eyes of the general public, they mobilize the capital from them.

The divestment programme of the government of India too has been as offer for sale where the government holding in the public sector enterprises has been offloaded to general investors in the secondary markets. Note that offer for sale is not a fresh issue of capital but is an attempt to use the secondary market for diffusing the concentrated shareholding.

Rights Issue

Another popular way of mobilizing fresh capital from investors is to offer the subscription of shares to existing shareholders. Such an issue is called a *rights issue*. For example if a firm needs another 10% of its already issued capital, then it can approach the existing investors to provide funds equal to 10% of their existing subscription. The firm that is already listed has a wide base of investors who also serve as trusted and willing providers of fresh capital when needed. Further, the rights issue does not disturb the shareholding pattern as the proportionate holding of pre- and post-rights issue remains unaffected. Rationally speaking, offering the shares to all implies dilution of control and proportionate holding of the existing shareholders. This can be done only with the approval of existing owners. An offer of rights provides an opportunity to the existing shareholders to meet additional requirement of capital in the proportion of their holding. Only upon the inability of existing shareholders to provide fresh capital should the firm resort to other investors.

The floatation costs under the rights issue are substantially less as compared to an IPO/FPO, as the requirements of due-diligence, brokerage, collection of subscriptions, publicity, underwriting, etc., stand diluted. Issuance of capital on rights basis has a greater chance of success as compared to an IPO/FPO.

AMERICAN AND GLOBAL DEPOSITORY RECEIPTS

The ushering of the era of liberalization and globalization has increased the interaction between world economies. With the global integration of capital markets and with the deregulation, the definition of capital market has widened in scope to include international capital markets as well. Today, Indian firms have easier access to international capital markets than what it was in the past. This has enabled them to access the cheaper sources of financing available internationally. Indian firms have raised resources from international capital markets through the issue of American Depository Receipts (ADRs) and Global Depository Receipts (GDRs).

Global Depository Receipts

GDRs are the receipts issued by the depository (usually a large international bank) against the shares issued by an Indian firm (or any other foreign firm) and that are deposited with the depository. They can be used to tap multiple capital markets with a single instrument. GDRs have found favour with Indian firms. They are essentially equity instruments that are freely transferable outside India. The dividend in respect of the shares represented by the GDR is paid in Indian rupees only. They are listed and traded on a foreign stock exchange. Trading takes place between professional market makers on an *OTC* (over-the-counter) basis. The shares correspond to the GDR in a fixed ratio. The holders of GDRs can, at any time, convert them into underlying shares by surrendering them to the depository. Prior to conversion, the GDRs do not carry any voting rights; and once the conversion takes place, the underlying shares are listed and traded on the domestic exchange. Most of the Indian companies have their GDR issues listed on the Luxembourg Stock Exchange and the London Stock Exchange.

> GDRs are the receipts issued by a depository against the shares of a firm. These receipts are freely tradable in markets abroad.

GDRs facilitate trade of shares, and are commonly used to invest in companies from developing or emerging markets. The prices of GDRs are often close to values of related shares, but they are traded and settled independently of the underlying share. Several international banks, such as JPMorgan Chase, Citigroup, Deutsche Bank, Bank of New York, issue GDRs.

American Depository Receipts

ADRs, similar to GDRs, are negotiable instruments, denominated in US dollars, and issued by the US Depository Bank. An Indian firm (or any other non-US firm) that seeks to list in the US, deposits its shares with a US bank. The bank acting as a depository bundles the specified number of shares of the issuing company as a depository receipt (ADR) and issues them to the investors in US. The ADRs thus issued represent the ownership of deposited shares. There is no legal or technical difference between an ADR and a GDR except for the fact that ADRs are specific to US markets. As they are listed on the New York Stock Exchange (NYSE) and the NASDAQ (National Association of Securities Dealers Automated Association), ADR issues offer access to the US institutional and retail markets, while GDR issues offer access only to the US institutional market. ADR listing requires comprehensive disclosures and greater transparency as compared to a GDR listing.

> Depository receipts issued against the shares that are tradable in USA are called American Depository Receipts.

GDRs can be converted into ADRs by surrendering the existing GDRs and depositing the underlying equity shares with the ADR depository in exchange for ADRs. The company has to comply with the Securities and Exchange Commission (SEC) requirements to materialize this exchange offer. However, the company does not get any funds by this conversion. The trend is towards the conversion of GDRs into ADRs, as ADRs are more liquid and cover a wider market. Besides these, many European investors have been disappointed by the poor performance of Indian GDRs in traditional industries and are unwilling to provide more capital.

VENTURE CAPITAL AND PRIVATE EQUITY

It is often said that those with brilliant business ideas do not have capital and those having capital do not have business ideas to implement. Entrepreneurs often develop products and ideas for which they require substantial capital during the formative stages of their companies' or the products' life cycles. On the other hand, there are a number of resourceful people who like to assume risk through deployment of capital owned. Venture capital and private equity funds are the mediums that make these two sets of people meet and complement each other's requirements.

Many young entrepreneurs commence their activities only to realize later that the financial resources at their hands are inadequate. Most new business ideas get evaporated in the nascent stages and are not explored fully to examine whether they had the potential to become big. As new business ideas have large gestation periods in terms of product design, product development, its execution, and acceptance, there would be prolonged periods of cash outflows without any certainty of cash inflows in future. Only those people with deep pockets can have the capability to touch the crescendo and make the business self-sustaining thereafter.

Venture capital is a broad subcategory of private equity that refers to equity investments made, typically in less mature companies, for the launch, early development, or expansion of a business. Venture investment is most often found in the application of new technology, new marketing concepts, and new products. There is more in common in venture capital and private equity than the differences. The discussions in this section would apply to both venture capital and private equity.

Origins of venture capital or private equity are attributed to Georges Doriat, father of venture capital who in 1946 founded

American Research and Development Corporation (ARDC) raising capital from institutional investors to encourage private investment for the businesses of the soldiers returning from World War II. Amongst the few beneficiaries of venture capital are firms like Digital Equipment Corporation, the producers of PDP series of computers, and Fairchild Semiconductor credited with the first commercial exploitation of integrated circuits. Initial success of the venture capitalists providing returns as high as 100% p.a. possibly led to a rapid development of the niche and made it more organized.

It is indeed hard to define venture capital but as such the concept is ancient. What distinguishes the industry in the modern days is that it has now become more organized. People with similar outlook on risk of business pool in financial resources and create a venture capital fund aimed at identifying and funding the enterprises that deserve capital infusion with return potentials high enough to meet the risk-return expectations.

Venture Capital Needs

In most cases, technical entrepreneurs also do not have an option to access the capital markets on their own due to lack of credibility and the fragile nature of the business idea being implemented. If at all they attempt to access the capital markets on their own, they may face several limitations. First there may not be enough takers for the idea for the promoters because of its newness. Secondly they do not have an adequate track record or the required credibility to generate confidence in the market. Finally on pure financial grounds, access to capital market does not make sense because a larger number of shares may have to be issued even if the markets accepted the idea, which the promoters may not favour because they would have to service the large equity so issued perennially.

Similarly the debt markets too would be out of bounds because providers of debt are always reluctant to provide capital to risky ventures. Lenders are too conscious of risk. Debt is normally associated with conventional ventures and financial institutions are guided by stringent capital structure (debt equity, and coverage ratios) norms as well as security norms, primary or collateral, which young entrepreneurs and new projects are unable to meet.

New entrepreneur and ideas are constrained to mobilize capital by equity or debt presenting an opportunity for those willing to assume risk and expect commensurate rewards.

The situation just described is ripe for those who are willing to explore new avenues by putting their capital at risk but lack domain knowledge and necessary technical or managerial skills. These people may become providers of capital to those starved of it. Such financing is motivated by high anticipated returns consciously recognizing the high levels of risks associated in relatively unknown and unexplored ventures as well as the promoters. This capital for untested ideas and promoters is called *venture capital* or *private equity*. Venture capital does not come cheap for the entrepreneurs. For them venture capital is a forced choice despite its high cost of such funding.

In a way, it may be said that venture capitalists attempt to turn the philosophy of capital and debt markets upside down. Equity capital and debt capital are difficult to mobilize for the firms when they actually need it because of the high levels of risk associated. Also when the businesses have matured and offer rather steady and certain cash flows, both capital and debt markets are too eager to offer resources. In a nutshell, the capital is not available when needed and is available when not needed. Venture capitalists tend to do exactly the reverse. They offer capital when needed in the risky environment and exit through the capital markets when the cash flows of the venture are ascertained and assured. Thus venture capital and capital markets complement the needs rather than competing with each other.

Venture capital and private equity complement the capital and debt markets rather than compete with them.

Another possible reason for growth of venture capital and private equity is the increased burden of compliance in the capital markets. If one goes public, the regulations are too vast and numerous placing extraordinary burden both in terms of compliances and disclosure requirements. New entrepreneurs neither have the time nor the inclinations to comply with regulatory requirements because of their preoccupation with the success of the idea they are nurturing. In their enthusiasm to see their project succeed, they are ready to have expensive venture capital to pay high returns rather than get bogged down with compliances.

Advantages of Venture Capital

Besides complementing the capital and debt markets, the venture capital also complements the needs of the firm. Unlike debt providers who are concerned with the fixed return and constrain the freedom of the management, venture capitalists become a part of the firm and are ready to sink or swim with the firm. Venture capital has a number of advantages over other forms of finance, such as:

- It injects long-term equity finance which provides a strong capital base for future growth.
- The venture capitalist acts as a business partner, sharing risks and rewards as well as the management. Capital markets as providers of equity are neither willing to assume risks beyond certain limits nor participate in the management.
- Venture capitalists are rewarded by business success and the capital gain.
- Venture capitalists add strategic value to the firm and provide assistance based on their past experience with other such ventures funded by them in the past.
- Venture capitalists have wide networking in many areas that can be exploited by the firm as it adds value to the firm. This is especially handy when additional rounds of financing are required.

- Venture capitalists may be capable and willing to provide additional funding as it protects their own interest besides that of the firm. They become a part and parcel of the firm and its promoters once they get involved in the first round of financing.

Today the venture capital is mobilized from high net worth individuals and various types of funds that create a venture fund. The scope of the fund is normally defined very broadly to enable them invest in vast range of businesses but mostly venture funds invest in relatively new products, technologies, and newer markets. The venture fund is usually managed by professional managers, for a fee, who constantly scout for business opportunities and undertake the due-diligence.

The presence of these professional mangers with the required domain knowledge complements the needs of providers and seekers of capital better. These managers are equipped with good analytical abilities and comprehend the needs better. These managers discharge an important function of bridging the gap of domain knowledge on part of providers of funds and financial acumen on part of fund seekers. Normally a major part of their fee comes from capital gains from the invested capital. At times these managers also happen to be small contributors in the venture fund.

FEATURES OF VENTURE CAPITAL FINANCING

There are several features that distinguish venture financing from other modes of financing. While conventional modes of financing include equity and capital, the distinctions are more to do with the philosophy of venture financing in terms of quantum, timing, selection, and manner of financing. Some of these features are discussed below.

High Risk and High Returns

Venture capital as another source of finance is different from other modes of financing. We all know that debt providers have focus on low/nominal risk and need bare minimum compensation by keeping the return expectations low. Similarly providers of equity capital are willing to assume business risk of the firm and ready to align their fortune with that of the firm. The venture capitalist moves a step forward in the risk-return space. Providers of equity capital do assume risk but are averse to extreme situations. Typically, investors in equity/capital markets are more risk averse than venture capitalists. It is indeed difficult to draw a line between different levels of risk. However, the difference between venture capitalists and those investing public through capital markets essentially lies in the levels of risk assumed by them. Desire for increased benefits is justified because of the uncertainty of cash flows as well as the lack of security.

Venture capital is characterized by high risk and high returns with large shareholding.

Large Shareholding

Large proportions of capital: Unlike investors through capital markets who hold small holdings, venture capitalists hold a sufficiently large proportion of shareholding. Such large proportion of holding enables them to participate in management decisions, if they choose so. In most cases, venture capitalists do add strategic value to the firm in any of the areas of technology transfer, product development, market development, human resource, etc. The funding by venture capital though has monetary value but is denominated in equivalent percentage holding of the equity capital.

Strict Due-diligence

Firms financed by venture capitalists are neither listed nor known. The critical performance measures remain confined to select few who have nurtured the idea. The financial performance measures and requirements are too hazy, and in most cases, the entrepreneurs remain ignorant about such measures. Venture capitalists undertake the due-diligence with great earnest and the appraisal is minute. The idea behind strict due-diligence is to make proper assessment of risk and place appropriate checks and balances. Strict due-diligence should not be construed as non-willingness to assume risk; instead it should be taken as an attempt to gauge the risk properly. In contrast due-diligence by merchant bankers prior to the issuance in the capital markets or by financial institutions for debt financing is mainly procedural, and compliance oriented and is done in a well-structured format. Due-diligence for venture funding, though strict, has no such boundaries as each project is different and may require different focus. Due-diligence by venture fund would also include subjective assessment and may dilute or enhance the legal documentation.

Funding in Tranches

In most venture capital endeavours, funding is completed in tranches rather than in a single shot. It serves many purposes. Funding in tranches places cash in the hands of the management according to their needs. It is commonly believed that availability of excess cash causes indiscretion. Another purpose of funding in tranches is that control can be exercised more frequently where suitable directions may be provided by the fund. Yet another objective of funding in tranches is to value the venture on each tranche. Again the monetary value of the funding would be denominated in percent shareholding. Therefore even if the monetary value of the two tranches may be equal, the latter tranche would transform in lesser number of shares than the first tranche, if the valuation of the firm has improved in the interim. This motivates the management or promoters to add as much and as fast value as possible.

To protect their interest venture capitals conduct strict due-diligence, provide fund in tranches and participate in management.

Sometimes different tranches in the venture capital financing are given different names. The initial investment by venture fund is referred as *seed money* or *start-up capital*. In this early stage, the sums are small. The promoters in this stage also contribute whatsoever little they have. The idea of the venture is at a very nascent stage. Depending upon the progress over a period of time, the funding can be done in several rounds. With progressive development of the idea, the clarity improves and valuations become more and more firm. When the idea is fully developed, the commercial exploitation would demand its full-blown execution. At this stage of the development, funds are mainly required for expansion. Finally at the pre-exit stage, the venture capitalist provides funds as bridge finance awaiting funds from new investors participating in the IPO. Under progressive funding, the successive amounts of money are converted into percent of shareholding or number of shares. As successive valuations increase with time, each tranche is converted into lesser number of shares.

Participation in Management

Another distinguishing feature of venture funding is the role played by the fund in management of enterprises. Though participation in management of the firm is done with the explicit motive of protecting the interests of the venture fund, the implicit objective is to see that the process of value creation remains intact. To ensure a steady rise in value of the firm, venture fund plays a constructive role by providing inputs in technical, development, production, human resource, and marketing functions of an enterprise. Venture fund provides strategic inputs to the firm being financed.

Exit Orientation

One of the most important features of venture funding is akin to perspective of a lender. Just as a lender sanctions loans for a definite period of time, the focus of the venture capitalist too is for a specific duration. Such focus resembles more with lenders than the equity investor though venture capitalists fund by way of equity and by way of high cost debt. The difference lies in the way the returns are obtained. The returns of venture capitalists are derived from exiting the business rather than by continuing in business. Therefore the mechanism of exit assumes great significance for the venture capitalist.

Venture capitalists focus on capital gains and hence are concerned with the timing and mode of disinvestment.

PROCESS OF APPRAISAL FOR VENTURE FUNDING

The process of funding by venture capitalists/fund essentially involves the same phases as would be for any financing of equity or debt but with a shift in emphasis and philosophy of funding. The orientation of venture capitalists is different than the debt providers or equity providers at mature stage.

The process of venture funding involves: (a) identification of new ventures, (b) screening of available opportunities, (c) conducting due diligence on selected ventures, (d) structuring the funding, (e) valuation at different times, and (f) determining exit options.

Identification of Potential New Ventures

Once the fund has been set up and the corpus generated or assured, the venture fund managers look for suitable business opportunities in terms of the projects that are likely to meet the target rate of return. Since the ventures are at a nascent stage and are not known to the public at large, the task of finding a suitable project is indeed a difficult one. Fund managers continuously scan the environment and remain in touch with a few promoters. Word of mouth is the most cost-effective way of identifying suitable projects. Seldom do the venture funds advertise the availability of resources. Another important and potential source of finding suitable projects is conferences and seminars where the focus is on technology and product development.

Screening of Available Opportunities

Once a reasonable list of possible ventures is available, the venture fund has to decide prima-facie some limited ideas that need to be nurtured. The initial screening is done with respect to suitability of the ventures with the objectives of the fund. Despite limited marketing effort to create awareness and availability of funds, the venture funds usually have more demand for funds than they can meet with the corpus. Screening of the projects may use the principle of diversification. Venture funds can achieve limited diversification by (a) identifying number of projects from diverse industries, (b) at different levels of execution, (c) not belonging to same set of promoters.

In the initial appraisal process, the venture capitalist meets with the entrepreneur and the key members of the management team to review the business plan and understand the concept. It is an important time for the promoters to demonstrate their understanding of their business and ability to achieve the strategies outlined in the plan. The venture capitalist will look carefully at the functional skills and backgrounds. Based on the initial evaluation, a preliminary set of terms and conditions is outlined, normally referred as *term sheet* or *memorandum of understanding* (MoU).

Conducting Due-diligence

Once a few projects are shortlisted that meet the broad objectives of the fund, the process of due-diligence commences. Due-diligence is an exercise to assess the potential risks associated and the likelihood of overcoming the risk factors associated. Fund managers get into the minute details of the projects as well as make technical assessments about the capability of the management team, its

The appraisal by venture capitalists is same as done by any supplier of capital except that the focus is on greater risk and commensurate returns.

integrity, and credibility of the claims made. It is indeed an assessment of the capability of the management team to overcome the likely threats.

Due-diligence involves in-depth study of alternative technologies and potential markets for the product. Here a venture fund manager may face some limitations in understanding of the idea, technology and markets. It is common for the fund managers to seek assistance from experts with specific domain knowledge.

It is often seen that research-oriented technical people, typically the seekers of venture fund, lack commercial acumen. The success of venture fund ultimately depends upon the commercial exploitation of the idea rather than mere development of the product, technology or markets. The venture capitalist studies the industry carefully to obtain information about competitors, examines entry barriers, reviews potential for commercial exploitation, draws product life cycles, etc. The due-diligence may continue with reports from other consultants. Hence, venture fund managers have the onerous task of identifying technically sound entrepreneurs who have strong commercial orientation too.

Usually due-diligence starts with a close scrutiny of business plan prepared by entrepreneurs, the timeline suggested, and the various milestones that can be observed and monitored. The venture fund, while committing funds, have to make assessment of several risks they are exposed. First they are required to gauge the successful development of the product. Then comes the assessment of the risks associated with the acceptance of the product by the market. Commercial exploitation of the product may involve another set of risks as mass production machines and trained manpower may not be available. Finally the venture capitalist faces the risk regarding the integrity of promoters with regard to their honest intentions, efforts, and transparency.

Structure of Funding

Structuring of the venture funding may be seen from two diverse angles – mode and frequency of disbursal, and control of enterprise. As discussed earlier, venture funding is normally done in several tranches as it has many advantages. The most common form of venture funding is by participation in the equity of the firm. Though other forms of funding like *preference capital* or *debt funding* is not ruled out, such funding would essentially be conflicting with the concept of venture capital. Therefore the amount of capital contributed is translated in number of shares and percent of holding. Usually venture funds allow majority holding with the promoters, though they themselves may hold substantial share capital.

The second aspect of fund structuring is to determine the approach to the management of the firm. There are two possible ways – *hands-off* and *hands-on*. Hands-on approach involves active participation of the venture fund in the management of enterprise, while hands-off approach would keep away from day-to-day functioning of the firm. Hands-on approach may not be desirable by the promoters as it may be construed as an unnecessary intervention detrimental to the objective of value creation. However, monitoring by way of participation at the board level, access to critical information and periodic reviews of achievements are almost invariably present in all venture funding endeavours.

The structure would also involve certain protective covenants regarding the constitution of board, and representation of venture fund in the board, some kind of veto powers, prior approval to undertake certain activities, etc. Such protective measures are adopted to protect the interest of the venture fund and take effective steps to correct and guide the future course of action, so that the valuation is not eroded and the risks remain within manageable bounds. As an extreme measure, the venture funding may reserve a right to change the management despite minority holding.

These covenants are often seen as deterrents and threats by the management but form rather an essential part of venture funding. However, such protective covenants and clauses by the venture capitalist are aimed at enhancing or maximising the shareholders' wealth; an undisputed objective of the firm. These are in the interest of promoters too as they hold the majority stake and therefore the interventions by venture capitalists must be seen by the promoters in the right earnest as value enhancers rather than undue interference.

Determining Exit Options

The final phase of the appraisal process is the parting of the venture capitalist from the enterprise. In case of debt financing, the returns are periodical and the tenure is decided in advance. In case of equity participation, the time involvement is indefinite. Secondary markets provide the exit route to the investor by replacing one investor with another. Since venture firms are not traded, the venture capitalist has to find an appropriate way to exit the venture, though *secondaries* exist in the private equity domain. These alternatives are discussed separately. It would suffice to say that exit options form a part of the appraisal process and is an important consideration in venture funding that must be addressed at the initial stages itself, rather than deferred for a later time. Of the various exit alternatives, the venture capitalist keeps multiple options open while initiating the venture capital financing as a measure of abundant caution. These alternatives include clauses such as *drag along* (forcing promoters to sell off if a suitable buyer is found) and *tag along* (sell off with promoters if they want to exit at an attractive valuation).

EXIT OPTIONS

One of the most distinguishing features of the venture capitalist is recognition of the fact that venture capitalist/fund does not stay with the firm forever. At some point of time, the venture capitalist would like to divest from the firm after fulfilling the

Venture capitalists have three exit routes available – buyback of shareholding by the promoters, selling the stake to another strategic investor, and divesting through an offer for sale in the capital market at the time of IPO.

target return. The returns sought by the venture capitalists are in the form of capital gains. They do not look forward to dividends from the shares as a regular income. It would not be incorrect to say that venture capitalists may prevent any dividend distribution in recognition of the facts that (a) retention of funds in high growth business is desirable, (b) distribution of dividend would decrease valuation, and (c) if the need for funds arises subsequently, then the dividends received may have to be funded again.

For the exit purpose, the venture capitalist has to decide on the tentative time of disinvestment and the prospective valuation of the firm at the time of tentative exit. The usual time frame of the venture capitalist is around 5–7 years. At the end of this period, the fund looks for an exit to recycle. Venture fund is essentially in the business of high returns and high risk. When the firm is fully developed, the prospective returns from the venture are not likely to remain attractive for the venture capitalist though they may be good enough for another class of investors ready to sacrifice their returns for assuming lesser risk.

The exercise of valuation needs to be done in the early stages of financing. Both timing and valuation become important in realising the target return. The investment is made in terms of holding of shares. The desired return, r for the investment, I for n periods must be related to the value at the end V_n as follows:

$$I \times (1+r)^n = V_n = \begin{pmatrix} \text{Proportionate} \\ \text{shareholding} \end{pmatrix} \times \begin{pmatrix} \text{Value of} \\ \text{the firm} \end{pmatrix}$$

The exit routes available are:

1. buyback of shareholding of venture capitalist by the promoters,
2. selling of the stake to another strategic investor who takes the venture forward, and
3. off-loading of the shares through an offer for sale in the capital market at the time of IPO.

Buyback by Promoters

At the end of a certain time or achievement of certain milestones, the venture fund may offer an option to the promoters to buy the shares back. Such an option seems relatively non-feasible. Assuming that the promoters of the firm are starved of capital, it is difficult to imagine that they would become resourceful enough to buy out the venture fund. The only possible motive for the buyback by promoters of the shares held by the venture fund is to retain or increase the proportionate shareholding in the venture. For funding the buyback, the promoters may resort to borrowing as it becomes a feasible option at this relatively matured stage of the firm. In the agreement with the venture fund, the promoters usually have the 'right of first refusal' at a given price.

Sell to Another Strategic Investor

The next option available to make an exit is to scout for another strategic investor. At this stage, since the venture is fairly developed, high net worth individuals as well as financial institutions would be more willing to participate in the venture by way of equity or debt. A strategic investor could mobilise funds on his own or borrow as borrowing avenues open. Normally demand for high returns by the venture capitalist forces the strategic investors to borrow. If most of the financing is obtained by borrowing, the acquisition is termed as *leverage buyout* (LBO). LBOs certainly exceed the debt equity norms prevailing in the industry. Such borrowing would have substantial impact on the capital structure of the firm, which in turn affects valuation. Borrowing beyond the conventional norms by the strategic investors is because they are rather liberal in valuation.

An IPO in Capital Markets

The last option available to the venture capitalist is by public float. When the cash flows of the firm become steady and the product is accepted in the market, further needs of funding may be met by capital markets by issuing additional shares. Along with additional new shares, the holding by venture capitalist too may be placed as 'offer for sale'. Issuance of shares through capital market is cumbersome, time-consuming, and subject to scrutiny by several agencies controlling the capital markets like SEBI, Registrar of Companies, etc.

As compared to the option of exit through capital markets, the option of seeking another strategic investor is relatively easy and fast. Further, the valuations can be better understood by strategic investors than naïve investors and therefore IPO may have to be conservatively priced. Pricing in private placement with strategic investors may be far more attractive from the viewpoint of the venture capitalist.

VALUATION OF THE FIRM

The primary concern of the venture fund is to make an exit at an appropriate time when the value of the firm is adequate to provide desired returns. Since participation of the venture fund is in terms of equity, the returns depend upon the final value of the firm at the tentative time of exit. The value of the venture fund would be in proportion of the shareholding. For example, if the value of the firm at the time of exit is ₹100 crore and the venture fund holds 20% equity it would get ₹20 crore. If the fund provided were ₹3 crore five years back, then the return derived by the venture fund would be governed by

$$3 \times (1+r)^5 = 20$$

The valuation of the firm at the time of exit faces several limitations. The method of relative or comparative valuation is apparently ruled out because there would not be a similar firm listed on the market and its valuation known. The other plausible approach is to project the cash flows of the firm and value them, which too is difficult in view of the great uncertainty attached with the venture. The assumptions of profitability, growth, commercial success, etc. are likely to change as time elapses.

Yet another issue is that the proportionate holding would also change because venture funding is done in tranches. If subsequent tranches are provided by the same venture fund, the proportionate holding would increase; but if done by another venture fund or a new investor, the proportionate holding of the existing investor stand diluted.

In light of the absence of sound and time-tested methods, the valuation of the firm becomes extremely tricky and subjective. It may be appreciated that valuation cannot be done without inputs from the promoters of the venture. Such valuation would lack the confidence and may lead to conflicts. It may not be agreed by the incumbents; the promoters, who may like to overvalue in order to prevent dilution. On the contrary, the venture fund may prefer to undervalue the venture in order to increase their proportionate holding and to provide cushion of the desired return. Entrepreneurs always have an optimistic viewpoint, while funding partners always prefer conservative estimates recognising the fact that all assumptions do not hold good. Therefore valuation requires much thought from the experts in the field needing innovative ideas as (a) all conventional ways of valuation are not suited, (b) valuation is subjective, and (c) there exists conflicting interests of seemingly collaborative partners.

Valuation of a newborn firm at maturity of the investment is perhaps the most challenging task for venture capitalists.

PRIVATE EQUITY

It is indeed very difficult to distinguish between private equity and venture capital except that the stage of product lifecycle is different in both the cases. *Investopedia* defines private equity as equity capital that is not quoted on a public exchange. According to this definition, all venture funding would be private equity but all private equity is not venture capital. Private equity consists of investors and funds that make investments directly into private companies or conduct buyouts of public companies that result in a delisting of public equity. Private equity is placed in more matured companies than venture capital. It more often than not takes the shape of financing for expansion rather than development of a business idea.

Unlike stocks, mutual funds, and bonds, private equity funds usually invest in more illiquid assets. By purchasing companies, firms gain access to those companies' assets and revenue sources, which can lead to very high returns on investments.

Private equity and venture capital have more in common than their differences. Both are characterised by high expectations of returns sought by private investors willing to assume greater risk than the normal investors in the equity market. Individuals with common risk-return profiles combine and pool resources to create a fund that seeks businesses with potential to offer greater-than-normal returns. Such funds are rather illiquid in the beginning, and the investors are willing to wait for an appropriate time to make an exit when the return expectations are likely to be met.

There are more similarities in venture capital and private equity rather than dissimilarities.

Box 20-1 Facebook Private Shares Soar

Facebook is being valued at more than $ 33 billion as investors try to secure a stake in the social networking site in anticipation of its flotation in US stock markets. The latest data shows that shares in *Facebook* are changing hands for up to $ 76, more than double their value at the start of this year. While *Facebook* is still privately held, the shareholders are able to sell the company's stock through 'secondary market' trading. By buying these shares at these prices, some investors are calculating that *Facebook* is worth more than eBay or Dell, or nearly twice as much as Yahoo!

Secondary market trading can inflate the value of a private company, as relative scarcity of its shares may encourage a buyer to overpay. But with founder Mark Zuckerberg thought to be planning to float *Facebook* in the next couple of years, there is already strong interest in what would be tech sector's biggest IPO since Google went public six years ago.

Facebook is expected to earn about $1.3 billion of advertising revenue, a figure that is tipped to rise sharply to $1.8 billion in 2011. *Facebook* attracted its 500 millionth user last month. It is also benefitting from the smartphone boom across the world.

Source: The Hindustan Times; HT Business 27 August 2010

Why Private Equity

Private equity is more amenable to situations where the time of funding is of essence. In areas where technological obsolescence is fast, firms do not have enough time to mobilise funds. Firms have to rely either on the capital markets or debt financing to capitalise on the opportunity. Capital and debt markets consume time, which is vital in making assessment for funding. Moreover accessing capital and/or debt markets would demand many disclosures amounting to leaking of the idea in the larger public domain that the promoters may not favour. In view of speedy access and confidentiality, firms may prefer private equity. Private equity by way of its speedy action provides the firm the advantages of early movers.

Another advantage of private equity is the avoidance of the regulatory environment that is imposed on capital and debt markets. These markets are subject to several regulations and constraints that inhibit speedier actions. The accountability of these markets does not justify the risk levels associated with the financing of relatively new firms, new products, and acquisitions at more-than-fair price.

Another situation that provides an impetus to private equity is in the area of mergers and acquisitions. The hectic fast-paced activities in the acquisition of firms demands prior arrangement of funds required for the bidding process. In the absence of private capital, the area of mergers and acquisitions would be confined to rich and wealthy. Access to private capital would add participants in the market and make it more competitive. Capital markets and debt markets suffer from their own inertia and are not amenable to speedy actions; a prerequisite of takeover bids.

Private equity investors often resort to heavy borrowings. As stated earlier, such acquisitions are called leveraged buyouts (LBOs). It serves two purposes – bring down the quantum of own funds and magnify the returns on the funds provided. The debt used in buyouts has a relatively fixed cost that is less than the return on assets of the firm being acquired. The fund's return on equity becomes higher than if it hadn't borrowed money. However debt makes the return on equity riskier too. In making these leveraged buyouts, if the acquired company's return on assets falls below the cost of debt, then the private equity fund's return becomes negative too. Leveraged buyouts intend to service debt from continuing cash flows of the firm acquired or by making an exit at a substantial profit. If so, the new shareholders in effect pay for the debt.

Among the most common investment strategies in private equity include leveraged buyouts, distressed investments, and mezzanine capital. *Mezzanine capital* refers to subordinated debt or preferred equity securities that often represents junior portion of debt but senior to common equity. This form of financing is often used by private equity investors to reduce the amount of equity capital required to finance a leveraged buyout or a major expansion. Mezzanine capital allows firms to borrow additional capital beyond the levels that traditional lenders are willing to provide through bank loans. In compensation for the increased risk, mezzanine debt holders require a higher return for their investment than secured or other more senior lenders.

Growth capital refers to equity investments, most often minority investments, in relatively mature companies that are looking for capital to expand or restructure operations, enter new markets, or finance a major acquisition without a change of control of the business. Companies seeking growth capital are likely to be those who can generate positive cash flows, but it is not enough for major expansion that can transform the firm from nascent stage to growth. Since risks of financing for this transition phase reduce substantially, the return expectations would be toned down too. As compared to venture financing, the growth capital must cost less. The present incumbents would like a debt funding for such expansion but possibly the cash flows and the stage of firm is not yet right for debt providers. In these circumstances, the promoters are ready to dilute the holding and share the returns with the providers of private equity.

The differences between private equity and venture capital are condensed in Table 20-1. All these differences are discussed in the discussions above and do not require any further elaboration.

Table 20-1 Difference Between Venture Capital and Private Equity

	Private Equity	*Venture Capital*
Investment target	Mature stage of business	Early and nascent stages of business
Nature of target	Matured and established industries	Relatively untested products, technologies, ideas, and markets
Proportion of debt	A combination of equity and debt is more likely structure	Mostly no debt is available. Venture funding is mostly pure equity
Time horizon	3–5 years	3–10 years
Risk profile	Only business risks assumed as the venture is matured	Both project and business risks
Management participation	Mostly hands-off	Mostly hands-on

LONG TERM SOURCES OF FINANCE — DEBT

Most firms also have debt. Unlike equity which is always long-term in nature, debt can be either long-term or short-term. Long-term debt has implications on capital structure as the firm decides to have a target proportion of debt because (a) debt reduces the overall cost of capital and (b) provides enhanced return to the shareholders. Short-term debt is resorted to overcome the temporary illiquidity. We now focus on long-term sources and instruments of debt.

DEBENTURES/BONDS

The major instrument to raise debt is a debenture/bond where a firm directly invites subscription from public on the pre-decided terms and conditions contained in the indenture. These terms and conditions including the features and types of the bonds are described in Chapter 6. Innovations in the products are aplenty.

Debentures are normally secured by way of charge of the lenders on the assets created out of debt so raised. Another feature of corporate debentures that is almost essential is the rating. Since debentures constitute a firm and fixed commitment of cash flow by way of interest and principal on due dates, it is essential to establish the adequacy of cash flows of the firm to service the obligations. It is presumed that investors of debentures neither have access to such financial data nor have the capacity to analyse the same. Realising the limitations of general investors, it has been made mandatory for the issuing firm to have the debentures rated by some credible agencies,

Box 20-2 Tata Steel Issues Perpetual Bonds

Tata Steel, the world's seventh-largest steel maker has made the debt market and probably the equity investors sit up with a very interesting perpetual bond product. Tata Steel has boasted about raising ₹1,500 crore through these high-yield perpetual bonds.

Perpetual bonds means the issue has no maturity period, and only the company has the option to buy-back the bonds at any time it chooses. Tata Steel has listed this bond in the wholesale debt market and expects it to fetch an interest of 11.8% per annum.

In an interview with CNBC-TV18's Latha Venkatesh, Koushik Chatterjee, Group CFO of Tata Steel, said that the company wanted to come up with a product which captures the essence of equity at a lower cost than equity cost and gives a higher yield to the investors. 'We started working on a product which meets the legal requirement, the regulatory framework and the accounting disclosure issues and this is what we have arrived at,' he said.

According to him, this product will fetch benefits to investors from the insurance companies and pension funds, who have long-term asset liability requirements to match. He also said that perpetual bond issue helps funding sources and this bond is lesser expensive compared to equity.

'Appetite for this bond should be high. It is an important product for companies with value-accretive investments,' added Chatterjee.

Talking about the tenure of the product, he said that technically it has a tenure of 10 years but it doesn't create obligation on the issuer to repay the distribution cost.

JP Morgan Securities India and ICICI_Bank were the arrangers for the issue.

Source: www.moneycontrol.com accessed on 25 March 2011

called *rating agencies*. The rating by the competent rating agency is expected to aid the investors in taking a well-informed decision to invest. Rating agencies and their symbols are discussed in Chapter 6.

Market for debenture can be broadly classified into two – the general public (or retail debt) and the institutional investors. The legal environment is controlled by SEBI by placing conditions of listing and trading. The interest of the retail investors is guarded by a trust that oversees the timely payment and status of the security of the funds. However, major subscribers of the debentures are financial institutions and banks. The debentures may be privately placed by the firm to select institutional investors.

Being cheaper source of funds, debentures reduce the cost of capital and enhance income to the equity shareholders. While resources are augmented, the control of the firm remains with the existing shareholders without any dilution. The major disadvantage of debentures is increased riskiness of the returns to the shareholders due to fixed and prior payment of interest on debt irrespective of cash flows of the firm. Due to increased risk, the equity holders raise their expectations of returns increasing the cost of equity. Hence a balance between the lesser cost of debt and increased expectations of return by the shareholders need to be found.

Term Loans

Term loans are the basic vanilla commercial loans. They are the conventional source of financing that are available to Indian firms. They are so called due to their being available for a fixed term, at the end of which they need to be repaid. They typically carry fixed interest rates, monthly or quarterly repayment schedules, and include a predetermined maturity date. Such loans can be classified into *intermediate-term loans* and *long-term loans*.

Term loans are the basic vanilla commercial loans that carry a fixed rate of interest and maturity period.

Intermediate-term loans are available usually for a period of up to three years, and are generally repaid in monthly installments. Long-term loans commonly have a maturity period of 3–10 years. Some of them may go up to 20 years. Long-term loans are collateralized by a business's assets and typically require quarterly or monthly payments derived from profits or cash flow. These loans may carry certain restrictive covenants that may pose restrictions on the firm in raising additional loans, or in declaring the dividends, or may sometime require that a certain amount of profit be set aside to repay the loan. The rate of interest on the term loans depends on the prime lending rates of the banks and also the creditworthiness of the borrowers.

Traditionally, Development Financial Institutions (DFIs), like IFCI, IDBI, etc., have been extending term loans to Indian industry. But with the ushering in of the era of universal banking and the changing role of the DFIs and most of them being converted into banks through the process of reverse merger, the Indian banks have started extending the term loan assistance to the firms. Term loans are today finding less favour with Indian firms as that are costly compared to newly emerged sources of intermediate and long-term financing like *external commercial borrowings*. Also because of the emergence of another source of financing as leasing that gives a lot of flexibility to the buyers and can be customized to their specific needs. Moreover, the development of equity market in the country has facilitated the raising of funds through equity and now, unlike in the 1970s when the Indian firms had to rely forcefully on the term loans as their main source of financing, an average Indian firm has easy access to equity financing. As the result, today such term loans are the appropriate sources of financing for small firms as well as those firms that do not have access to other cheaper and flexible sources of financing.

The most critical part of term loans is the project appraisal with regard to the technical feasibility and financial viability. Since the major chunk of debt is provided by a single or a few institutions, they have to take utmost care in advancing a term loan to a firm. Project appraisal is a very comprehensive exercise. Technical feasibility of the project is concerned with the ability of the management to achieve the development of products, their capacity, product mix, markets for finished goods and raw materials, etc. Financial viability of the project is concerned with the ability of the firm to make timely payment of interest and recovery of principal amount of loan. The critical parameters of financial appraisal are as follows.

a) Breakeven analysis for assessing the likelihood of achieving it, computing margin of safety for the risk measurement, likely time frame to achieve breakeven for determining the moratorium period for the loan.
b) Complete analysis of the projected cash flow statements and other financial statements over the likely tenure of the loan to adjudge the ability of the project to make timely repayment as computed from debt service coverage ratios to provide the comprehensive view of the riskiness of the project.
c) Compare and analyse the capital structure with respect to the norms prevailing in the industry.

Since most financial institutions have considerable exposure by way of term loans, they impose some restrictive covenants on the management of the firm. These often relate to expansion plans, payment of dividend, further borrowing, representation on the board of directors, etc. Most term loans are also secured by way of charge over the assets of the firm.

Project Finance

Project finance is a method of financing very large capital-intensive projects, with long gestation periods, where the lenders rely on the assets created for the project as security and the cash flow generated by the project as the source of funds for repayment of their dues. It is often more complicated and more expensive than alternative financing methods. It is commonly used in infrastructure projects, such as mining, transportation, telecommunication, and public utility industries. Such financing is typically secured by all of the project assets, including the revenue-producing contracts. Project lenders are given a lien on all these assets, and the lenders can assume control of a project if the firm has difficulties complying with the loan terms.

Project finance is the financing option available to large capital-intensive projects that require huge capital and involve high risks.

Generally, a Special Purpose Entity (SPE) or Special Purpose Vehicle (SPV) is created for each project, thereby shielding other assets owned by a project sponsor from the detrimental effects of a project failure. As a special purpose entity, the project company has no assets other than the project. Capital contribution commitments by the owners of the project company are sometimes necessary to ensure that the project is financially sound.

Risk identification and allocation is a key component of project finance. A project may be subject to a number of technical, environmental, economic, and political risks. To cope with these risks, it is usually preferable to distribute the risk by involving multiple parties in the financing. Usually, a project financing scheme involves a number of equity investors, known as *sponsors*, as well as a syndicate of banks which provide loans to the operation. The loans are most commonly non-recourse loans, which are secured by the project itself and paid entirely from its cash flow. A riskier or more expensive project may require limited recourse financing secured by a surety from sponsors. A complex project finance scheme may incorporate corporate finance, securitization, options, insurance provisions, or other measures to mitigate the risk. Project finance shares many characteristics with maritime finance and aircraft finance.

Characteristics of project financing

The lenders to the project look primarily at the earnings of the project as the source from which loan repayments will be made. Their credit assessment is based on the project, not on the creditworthiness of the borrowing entity.

The key features of project financing that funds lent are:

- Secured by project assets
- Follow complex financing structures
- Different formats such as BOT, BLT, and PPP format of financing

The security taken by the lenders is largely confined to the project assets created by funds lent. As such, project financing is often referred to as *limited recourse financing* because lenders are given recourse against project assets only.

Most project finance structures are complex. The risks in the project are spread among various parties; each risk is usually assumed by the party which can most efficiently and cost-effectively control or handle it.

Project financing can take different formats, such as Build-Operate-Transfer (BOT), Public Private Partnership (PPP), Build-Lease-Transfer (BLT), etc.

Build-Operate-Transfer (BOT) is a form of project financing, wherein a private entity receives a franchise to finance, design, construct, operate and maintain a facility for a specified period, after which the ownership is transferred back to the funding entity. The period is often as long as 20–30 years. During the time that the project proponent operates the facility, it is allowed to charge the facility users with appropriate tolls, fees, rentals, and charges stated in their contract to enable the project proponent to recover its investment, and operating and maintenance expenses in the project. Several toll bridges and express ways in India have been financed using the BOT model.

Built-Lease-Transfer (BLT) Under the BLT arrangement, the control of the project is transferred from the project owners to the lessee. Although the legal ownership remains with the owners, the project is leased to the lessee for operational purpose for the specified period after which it gets transferred back.

Public Private Partnership (PPP) A project financing format in which a venture is funded and operated through a partnership of government and one or more private sector companies is called Public Private Partnership. These schemes are sometimes referred to as PPP or P3. In some types of PPP, the government uses tax revenue to provide capital for investment, with operations run jointly with the private sector or under contract (see contracting out). In other types (notably the Private Finance Initiative), capital investment is made by the private sector on the strength of a contract with the government to provide agreed services. Government contributions to a PPP may also be in kind (notably the transfer of existing assets).

Typically, a private sector consortium forms *special purpose vehicle* (SPV) to build and maintain the asset. It is the SPV that signs the contract with the government and the subcontractors to build the facility and then maintain it. A typical PPP example would be a hospital building financed and constructed by a private developer and then leased to the hospital authority. The private developer then acts as landlord, providing housekeeping and other non-medical services to the hospitals.

External Commercial Borrowings (ECBs)

ECBs are the foreign currency denominated loans raised by Indian firms.

The Indian companies are free to raise ECBs from any internationally recognized source, such as banks, export credit agencies, suppliers of equipment, foreign collaborators, foreign equity holders, and international capital markets. ECBs supplement domestically available resources for expansion of existing capacity as well as for fresh investment. Indian companies have preferred this route to raise funds because the cost of borrowing is low in the international markets. Indian corporates are allowed to raise foreign loans for financing infrastructure projects. ECBs need sound risk management — both interest rate and forex risk. Any default has wider repercussions in terms of increasing the risk premium for the subsequent borrowers from India.

Foreign Currency Convertible Bonds (FCCBs)

FCCBs are foreign currency denominated bonds issued by Indian companies. They carry a fixed coupon rate and are convertible into a fixed number of ordinary shares at a preferred price. Such bonds are listed and traded abroad and subscribed to by non-residents.

FCCBs are bonds issued by Indian companies that are listed and traded abroad and subscribed to by a non-resident in foreign currency. Such bonds carry a fixed coupon rate and are convertible into a fixed number of ordinary shares, either in whole or in parts, at a preferred price. Till conversion, the company has to pay interest in dollars, and if the conversion option is not exercised, the redemption is also made in dollars. These are hybrid securities and give the benefit of both equity and debt. They are less dilutive than equity and are cheaper than debt. In case of FCCBs, equity dilution is not immediate and happens gradually as the bonds get converted into underlying local shares in a phased manner.

The interest rate is low, but the exchange risk is more in FCCBs, as the interest is payable in foreign currency. Hence, only those companies with low debt-equity ratios and large forex earnings potential opt for FCCBs. The minimum maturity period for FCCBs is five years, but there is no restriction on the time period for converting the FCCBs into shares.

The interest rate in FCCBs is much lower than bond issuances or loan syndications. The equity component in a FCCB is an attractive feature for investors. Higher the premium for conversion of equity, higher will be the yield on the FCCB.

SHORT-TERM SOURCES OF FINANCE

Money market consists of players and instruments related to working capital financing.

Short-term financing primarily relate to arranging finance to overcome the temporary liquidity problems. It is generally obtained against the security of short-term assets such as inventories, receivables, etc. Working capital financing is normally classified as short term. Money market is the market tapped by the firms to meet their working capital financing needs. The instruments traded in the money market have a maturity of up to one year. Traditionally, in India, the commercial banks have been the key players in the money market, as they were the main source of working capital financing. Efficient money markets facilitate the easy availability of short-term financing to the firms. Since the money market operations have a direct impact on the liquidity position, and thereby the level of inflation; the Reserve Bank of India is the apex regulator of money market operations. Over the years, the Indian money market has grown and the number of financing options available to Indian firms has multiplied. Besides the conventional sources of short-term financing like lines of credit, short-term loans, bill discounting, etc., several other fund-based and fee-based financing options, such as Commercial Papers and Factoring have evolved over the years that provide Indian firms an easy access to short term financing. Let us look at some of the prominent financing options that are available to Indian firms to meet their current financing requirements.

LINES OF CREDIT

A line of credit (LOC) is a credit facility that allows a borrower to take advances, during a defined period, up to the preset *line limit* or *credit limit* and repay the advances along with the interest at his discretion. Unlike the term loans where the amount of loan and the maturity period is fixed, LOC gives a lot of flexibility to the borrower in terms of the amount borrowed and the repayment schedule. An operating line of credit is an important component of a company's finances and many businesses could not survive without this basic banking product. A line of credit may also be used to support an import/export letter of credit that is often used in international transactions.

Line of credit is the source of meeting the working capital requirements of businesses. These are extended by firms' banks with a preset credit limit. The interest that the firms pay is on the amount of credit availed and not on the entire credit limit approved.

For businesses, an operating line of credit is used to provide liquidity during the operating cycle of the business. Such lines of credit are extended by the firms' banks. The benefit of LOC as a means of working capital financing is that—although the firms are allowed to avail the credit facility up to their respective line limit, the interest that the firms have to pay is only on the credit availed and not on the entire LOC. Thus, it is governed by the "pay as per usage principle".

The banks keep on monitoring the line usage according to inherent risk. The level of control is determined by the perceived credit risk and the line limit. For smaller lines to companies with good credit, there may be no active controls on line of credit usage; that is, the customer can take advances and repay the same at will. Typically, line usage is only analysed annually, or at renewal. If the line does not properly revolve during the year, the line of credit would generally be converted to a fully amortizing term loan and the line of credit is closed out.

For larger lines of credit and for companies deemed to have a higher credit risk, the line may be more closely monitored. For a fully controlled line, a borrower would be required to submit a daily accounting of accounts receivable and accounts payable along with a borrowing base certification calculating how much is available on the line and how much of an advance is needed that day.

COMMERCIAL PAPER (CP)

Commercial paper (CP) is an unsecured money market instrument issued in the form of a promissory note by highly rated corporate borrowers to meet their working capital requirements. It has a fixed maturity period. This option of financing has been made available to Indian firms since 1990 with a view to enable highly rated corporate borrowers to diversify their sources of short-term borrowings and to provide an additional instrument to investors. Commercial paper can essentially be compared as an alternative to lines of credit with a bank. Once a business becomes large enough and maintains a high enough credit rating, then using commercial paper is always cheaper than using a bank line of credit. There are four basic kinds of commercial paper: *promissory notes*, *drafts*, *cheques*, and *certificates of deposit*. Corporates, primary dealers (PDs), satellite dealers (SDs), and the financial institutions (FIs) have been permitted to raise short-term resources through CPs as per the limit fixed by the Reserve Bank of India.

Commercial Paper is an unsecured money market instrument with a fixed maturity period issued by highly rated corporate borrowers to meet their working capital. They have maturity period varying from 7 days to 1 year.

Initially, only top-rated corporates with tangible net worth of not less than ₹10 crore were allowed to issue CP with maturity between 3–6 months from the date of issue. Further, issuance of the CP had to be carved out of the working capital (fund based) limit, and it was also stipulated that CP could be issued in multiples of ₹25 lakh and the amount to be invested by a single investor should not be less than ₹1 crore. But these guidelines have been relaxed over the years. The present guidelines for issuing CPs are follows:

1. ***Eligibility for the issue*** A corporate would be eligible to issue CPs provided: (a) the tangible net worth of the company, as per the latest audited balance sheet, is not less than ₹4 crore; (b) the company has been sanctioned a working capital limit by bank(s) or all-India financial institution(s); and (c) the borrowal account of the company is classified as a standard asset by the financing bank(s) or institution(s).
2. ***Rating requirement*** All eligible participants shall obtain the credit rating for issuance of CP from either the Credit Rating Information Services of India Ltd (CRISIL) or the Investment Information and Credit Rating Agency of India Ltd (ICRA) or the Credit Analysis and Research Ltd (CARE) or the FITCH Ratings India Pvt Ltd or other such credit rating agencies as may be specified by the Reserve Bank of India from time to time, for the purpose. The minimum credit rating shall be P-2 of CRISIL or such equivalent rating by other agencies.

3. ***Maturity*** CP can be issued for maturities between a minimum of 7 days and a maximum of up to one year from the date of issue. The maturity date of the CP should not go beyond the date up to which the credit rating of the issuer is valid.
4. ***Denominations*** CP can be issued in denominations of ₹5 lakh or multiples thereof. Amount invested by a single investor should not be less than ₹5 lakh (face value).
5. ***Limits and the amount of issue of CP*** CP can be issued as a *standalone* product. The aggregate amount of CP from an issuer shall be within the limit as approved by its board of directors or the quantum indicated by the credit rating agency for the specified rating, whichever is lower. Banks and FIs will, however, have the flexibility to fix working capital limits duly taking into account the resource pattern of companies' financing including CPs. A financial institution can issue CPs within the overall umbrella limit fixed by the RBI.
6. ***Mode of issuance*** CP can be issued either in the form of a promissory note or in a dematerialized form through any of the depositories approved by and registered with SEBI. CP will be issued at a discount to the face value as may be determined by the issuer. No issuer shall have the issue of CP underwritten or co-accepted.
7. ***Issue expenses*** The issuing firm has to bear *stamp duty, rating fee, and issuing and paying agent fee.* Such charges are subject to change from time to time.

Procedure for Issuance

Every issuer must appoint an Issuing and Paying Agent (IPA) for issuance of CP. The issuer should disclose to the potential investors its financial position as per the standard market practice. After the exchange of deal confirmation between the investor and the issuer, the issuing company shall issue physical certificates to the investor or arrange for crediting the CP to the investor's account with a depository. Investors shall be given a copy of IPA certificate to the effect that the issuer has a valid agreement with the IPA and the required documents are in order.

Companies Issuing Commercial Papers in India

The factor that has hampered the growth of CP market in India has been the stringent requirements in terms of net worth and credit rating. The result of such guidelines has been that the option of CP financing has been available to only a select few. However, with the increasing scale of operations of Indian firms, more and more firms are using it as a preferred source of meeting their working capital financing requirements. Some of the prominent Indian firms issuing CPs include Infosys Technologies Ltd, Godrej and Boyce Manufacturing Ltd, Tata Motors, Tata Power, Ranbaxy Laboratories, DLF, etc.

FACTORING

Factoring is a continuing financial arrangement between the client (a firm) and the factor (financial institution), whereby the factor purchases the accounts receivables or book debts of the client either with or without the credit risks associated. It is a collection and finance service that aims at improving the client's cash flow by turning its accounts receivables into cash. Such an arrangement provides the factor with an opportunity to park their funds and unties the funds of the client blocked in the receivables. Factoring receivables is an ideal financial solution for new and emerging firms that may not have an easy access to the conventional sources of short-term financing, as they may not have strong financials. Since creditworthiness for the purpose of factoring is evaluated based on the financial strength of the customer (debtor), such firms can leverage on the financial strength of their customers.

Factoring refers to sale of accounts receivables by the client (a firm) to the factor (a bank). Such a transaction unlocks firms' cash that gets tied up in receivables. Factoring can be with recourse or without rocourse. Risk in factoring without recourse is higher for the factor.

Besides purchasing the accounts receivables; the factor, as per the factoring arrangement, may provide the following services to the client:

- Credit management
- Debt collection services
- Sales ledger administration
- Credit policy formulation
- Risk coverage (in case of factoring without recourse)

A full-fledged factoring arrangement does away with the need of having an in-house credit department for the client.

Factoring is a fund-based financial product. The process of factoring is depicted in Figure 20-3. In factoring, a financial institution (factor) buys the accounts receivable of a company (client) and pays up to 80–90% of the amount immediately on agreement. Factoring company pays the remaining amount (balance 10–20%) after deducting the operating and financing costs to the client when the customer pays the debt. Collection of debt from the customer is done either by the factor or the

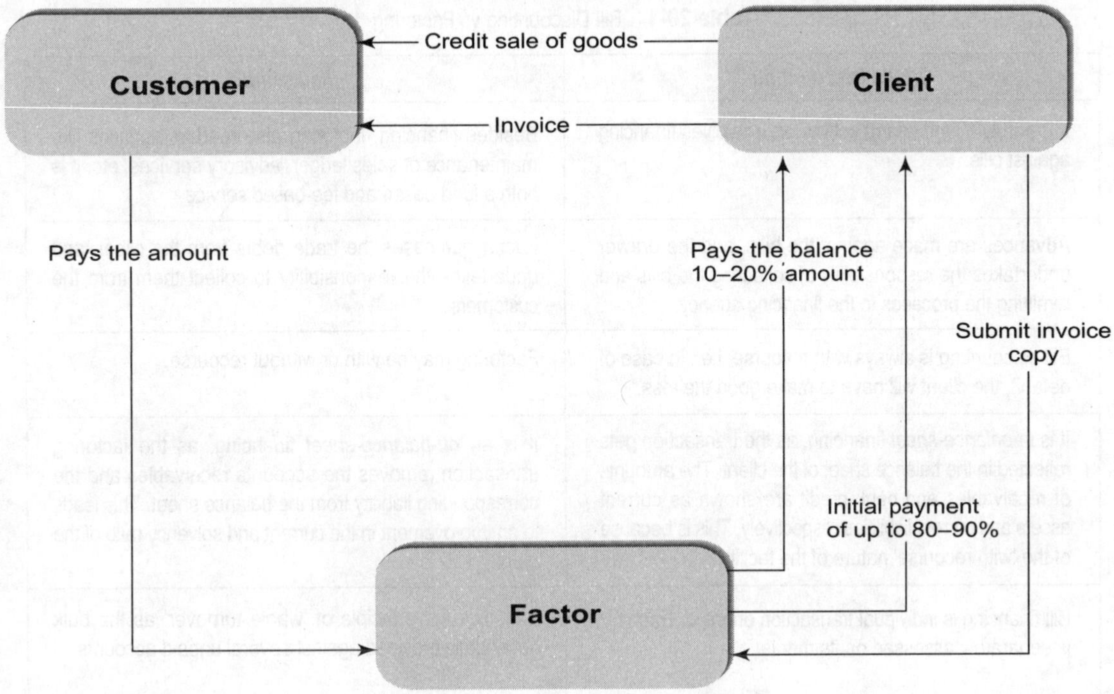

Figure 20-3 Factoring process

client depending upon the type of factoring. Credit rating is not mandatory for factoring. But the factoring companies usually carry out credit risk analysis before entering into the agreement.

Factoring is a means for financing working capital requirements of the firms. It improves the cash flow position by unlocking the funds blocked in the receivables. To the extent it improves the cash flows by untying the cash flows tied up in receivables, it cuts down the firms' dependence on the external sources of financing. By offloading the sales accounting and administration, the management has more time for planning, running, and improving the business, and exploiting the opportunities. The reduction in overheads brought about by the factor's administration of the sales ledger and the improved cash flows because of the quicker payments by the customers result in interest savings and contribute towards cost savings. However, factoring could prove to be costlier to in-house management of receivables, especially for large firms which have access to similar sources of funds as the factors themselves and which on account of their size have well-organized credit and receivable management. Factoring is perceived as an expensive form of financing and also as the finance of the last resort.

In addition to the funds provided, the factor offers certain other services, such as collection of receivables, sales ledger administration, etc., to the client.

Although factoring is categorized as a fund-based financial product, it has features of fee-based service also. Factoring service provided by the factor to the client has two components—financing of the receivables, which is a fund-based activity; and receivables collection, and sales ledger administration services, etc., which are fee-based activities. The cost of factoring constitutes of finance cost (for the advance given by the factor to the client) and operating cost (for the services provided by the factor like collection, sales ledger administration, etc.). Factoring cost vary according to the transaction size, financial strength of the customer, etc. The cost of factoring varies from 1.5% to 3% per month depending upon the financial strength of the client's customer. Usually, the period for factoring is 90 to 150 days. Some factoring companies allow even more than 150 days.

Types of Factoring

Factoring can be *with recourse* or *without recourse*. In case of with-recourse factoring, the risk of non-payment by the customer is borne by the client and not the factor. If the customers don't pay the amount on maturity, the factor will recover the amount

Table 20-1 Bill Discounting vs Factoring

Bills Discounting	*Factoring*
It is purely a fund-based activity, as it involves financing against bills.	Besides financing, factoring also renders services like maintenance of sales ledger, advisory services, etc. It is both a fund-based and fee-based service.
Advances are made against the bills, and the drawer undertakes the responsibility of collecting the bills and remitting the proceeds to the financing agency.	Factor purchases the trade debts from the client, and undertakes the responsibility to collect them from the customers.
Bill discounting is always with recourse, i.e., in case of default, the client will have to make good the loss.	Factoring may be with or without recourse.
It is *in-balance-sheet* financing, as the transaction gets reflected in the balance sheet of the client. The amounts of receivables and bank credit are shown as current assets and current liabilities respectively. This is because of the 'with recourse' nature of the facility.	It is an *off-balance-sheet* financing, as the factoring transaction removes the accounts receivables and the corresponding liability from the balance sheet. This leads to an improvement in the current and solvency ratio of the client.
Bill financing is individual transaction oriented. Each bill is separately assessed on its merits.	It follows the principle of 'whole turnover' as the bulk advance is provided against several unpaid accounts.

from the client. This is the most common type of factoring. Recourse factoring is offered at a lower interest rate since the risk borne by the factor is low.

In non-recourse factoring, the factor undertakes to collect the debts from the customer. Balance amount is paid to the client at the end of the credit period or when the customer pays the factor, whichever comes first. The advantage of non-recourse factoring is that the risk of the debt going bad is passed on by the client to the factor, and the client is protected from the bad debt losses. On the due date, if the debt turns sticky or bad, the factor has no recourse to the client and has to bear the loss arising out of bad debts. Since the factor bears the risk of bad debts, the cost of factoring without recourse is higher than the cost of with-recourse factoring.

Reverse Factoring

Factoring of payables is called *reverse factoring*. The buyer of goods/services is extended a credit period by the seller under the terms of sale. But to avail this credit period, the buyer has to forgo certain benefits like credit discount that can be availed only on making the payment within the stipulated period. The factor provides factoring service to the buyer by factoring the payables. The factor charges interest on the amount of payables factored depending upon the period involved and recovers the money from the client (buyer in this case) on the due date. This benefits the buyer by way of enjoying discounts from the seller and at the same time, enjoying his credit period. Reverse factoring is an unsecured fund-based service as the factor does not seek any charge on stocks.

Factoring vs Bill Discounting

In addition to the rendering of factoring services, banks and financial institutions also provide bills discounting facilities to provide finance to the client. Often, due to the similarities between factoring and bill discounting, the factoring is vaguely referred to as bill discounting, although there are significant differences between the two. The comparison of factoring and bill discounting is depicted in Table 20-1.

Forfaiting

What factoring is to a domestic credit sale transaction, forfaiting is to an international transaction.

The word *forfaiting* is derived from the French term *a forfait* which means *relinquishing a right.* In context of financial services, it refers to the exporter relinquishing his right to a receivable due at a future date in exchange for an immediate cash payment, at an agreed discount. Thus forfaiting is the discounting of international trade receivables on a without-recourse basis. What factoring is to a domestic transaction, forfaiting is to an international transaction.

The process of forfaiting involves purchasing of an exporter's receivables (the amount importers owe to the exporter) by the forfaiter at a discount. The forfaiter pays cash to the exporter, and the importer is obliged to pay its debt to the forfaiter. By purchasing these receivables—which are usually guaranteed by the importer's bank—the forfaiter not only unlocks the cash tied up in the receivables of the exporter, but also insures himself against the default risk of the importer. While giving the exporter a cash payment, forfaiting allows the importer to buy goods for which it cannot immediately pay in full. The receivables, becoming a form of debt instrument that can be sold on the secondary market, are represented by bills of exchange or promissory notes, which are unconditional and easily transferred debt instruments.

SUMMARY

Having resolved the issue of debt-equity mix, the next issue that the finance manager is faced with is to choose the most suitable source(s) of financing. To be able to pick up the most appropriate financing alternative, the finance manager must be aware of the different financing options that are available in financial markets to meet the long-term and short-term financing needs of firms along with the terms and conditions of their availability.

Financial markets act as a conduit through which the funds are channelized from the surplus units to the deficit units. Financial markets consist of players, financing instruments and services, and can broadly be segmented into *capital market* and *money market*. Capital market is the market for long-term financing, while money market provides financing to meet the working capital needs of the firms.

Capital market constitutes of *primary market* and *secondary market* of equity and debt instruments. *Primary market* is the market for new issues of securities. Previously issued securities are bought and sold in the secondary market. Initial Public Offerings (IPOs), term loans, venture capital financing, project financing, and leasing are the prominent sources of raising funds from the primary markets.

IPO is the first sale of stock to the public by a firm. Term loans are the basic vanilla commercial loans. They are available at a fixed rate of interest for a fixed term, at the end of which, they need to be repaid. *Project finance* is a method of financing very large capital-intensive projects, with long gestation periods. Venture capital is a type of private equity capital available to businesses that have to face high levels of risk due to the newness of their product/technology/idea/business model.

An *investment banker* provides a wide array of pre- and post-capital issue services to the firms that want to raise capital either through public issue or private placement.

Equity shares, preference shares, debentures, and hybrid securities are the commonly traded instruments in the secondary market. All the instruments that are traded in secondary markets are issued in primary markets. Thus, the secondary market provides an exit route to the investors in the primary markets. Investment bankers, by providing pre- and post-issue management, play a very active role in financing.

Increased interactions between world economies has improved the access of Indian firms to the international capital through the issue of Global Depository Receipts (GDRs), American Depository Receipts (ADRs), Foreign Currency Convertible Bonds (FCCB), and External Commercial borrowings (ECB).

Money market is the market that the firms tap to meet their working capital financing needs. The instruments traded in the money market have a maturity of up to one year. Traditionally, In India, the commercial banks have been the key players in the money market, as they were the main source of working capital financing. Besides the conventional sources of short-term financing like lines of credit, short-term loans, bill discounting, etc.; several other fund-based and fee-based financing options, such as *commercial papers* and *factoring* have evolved over the years that provide the Indian firms an easy access to short-term financing. Equity and debt are two forms of long-term sources of capital. Venture capital is a broad subcategory of private equity that refers to equity investments made, typically in less mature companies.

KEY TERMS

Primary market The market for new issues of securities (both equity and debt). It includes the players, instruments, and the regulators that are involved in the process of new issue of long-term debt or equity.

Secondary market The market where securities are traded after they are initially offered in the primary market. They provide exit routes to the investors in the primary markets. Stock exchanges are also known as secondary markets.

Investment banking Investment bankers are financial intermediaries. They provide a wide array of pre- and post-capital issue services to the firms that want to raise capital either through public issue or private placement. They are an important link between the investors and issuers of the capital.

Term loans Loans that carry fixed interest rates and a predetermined maturity date. They are one of the most common sources of conventional financing.

Venture capital Private equity capital available to businesses that face high degrees of risk due to newness of their product/technology/idea/business model. It is alternatively referred to as idea financing.

Global Depository Receipts (GDRs) Receipts issued by the depository (usually a large international bank) against the shares issued by an Indian firm (or any other foreign firm) and that are deposited with the depository. They are essentially equity instruments that are freely transferable outside India. They are listed and traded on a foreign stock exchange.

American Depository Receipts (ADR) Like the GDRs, they are also negotiable instruments, denominated in US dollars that are issued by the US Depository Bank. Any non-US firm that seeks to list in the US, deposits its shares with a US bank. These shares are bundled as a depository receipt (ADR) by the US bank that issues them to the investors in US.

Lines of credit A credit facility that allows a borrower to take advances, during a defined period, up to the preset limit and repay the advances at the borrower's discretion. It gives a lot of flexibility, unlike term loans, to the borrower in terms of the amount borrowed and the repayment schedule.

Commercial Paper (CP) An unsecured money market instrument issued in the form of a promissory note by highly rated corporate borrowers to meet their working capital requirements.

Factoring A continuing financial arrangement between the client (a firm) and the factor (financial institution), whereby the factor purchases the accounts receivables or book debts of the client, either with or without the credit risks associated.

EXERCISES

Concept Review Questions

1. Define financial markets and discuss its various segments in detail.
2. While capital markets deal in long-term sources, money markets provide working capital financing to firms. Elaborate.
3. Define term loans. What kind of firms prefer such loans?
4. What is factoring? How is it different from bill discounting? What are the different services offered by the factor to their clients?
5. Describe the instruments that are available to Indian firms to raise capital from the international capital markets.
6. What are commercial papers? Discuss the guidelines for the issue of CPs.

Critical Thinking Questions

1. 'Financial markets improve the productivity of the economy by channelizing the savings towards the most productive avenues.' Discuss.
2. 'Sentiments in secondary markets affect the primary markets as well.' Examine the statement.
3. 'The option of issuing commercial papers as a means of working capital financing is available only to a select few firms.' Examine the statement.
4. 'A full-fledged factoring is a replacement of an in-house credit department.' Analyse.
5. 'A venture capitalist funds those businesses which others do not dare to.' Analyse.

Practical Assignments

1. Visit the RBI website and read the latest ECB guidelines.
2. Visit the website of Bombay Stock Exchange (www.bseindia.com) and study eligibility criteria for listing of companies on the Exchange.

3. Select an IPO that has been made in the recent past, and trace the entire event chronologically so as to understand the process of IPO.
4. Next time when you visit the bank with which you have an account, find the corporate financing products offered by the bank and the terms and conditions on which they are offered.
5. Prepare a list of leading investment banks of the country, visit their websites, and find out the services offered by them.
6. Visit the RBI website and read the guidelines for the issue of ADRs and GDRs by Indian companies.
7. Explain the role played by investment bankers in IPOs.

PART

FIVE

WORKING CAPITAL MANAGEMENT

CHAPTER 21

Working Capital Management—An Introduction

LEARNING OBJECTIVES

After reading this chapter, you will be able to understand:

- the need for and the importance of investing in current assets
- the concept of operating cycle and its relevance in the management of working capital
- techniques to reduce the operating cycle
- principles underlying the management of current assets
- how to estimate working capital requirements

BE EFFICIENT TO LOOK HEALTHY

Mescos Limited (Mescos) has received an order to export 1.20 lakh pair of footwear to Germany. The delivery schedule is very stringent: delivery has to be completed within two months in a phased manner. This is the first time that Mescos has grabbed such a big order to export directly.

The company has of late modernized and expanded its manufacturing unit, doubling its manufacturing and storage capacities, of which only 55% is being used currently. There will be no capacity constraint, as the order can be met by increasing one production shift. At present, there are only two shifts in operation.

Having completed the entire feasibility study and planning, the company approaches its bank, 'The Dependable Bank', with an application for raising its working capital limit by ₹1.20 crore. Two days after submitting its application for additional working capital financing, the company, to its dismay, gets back its loan application with the following comments from the credit appraisal team of the bank:

- The firm seems to be steadfast in focusing upon capacity expansion, particularly in view of an increased market for formal and lifestyle footwear. The efficiency of the firm has declined over the period, as reflected in the pile up of inventory in the balance sheets of the company.
- There is a noticeable slackness in the collection of receivables by the company. This is evident in the reduced receivables turnover ratio from 10 to 8 and the increased percentage of bad debts of the firm from 1.50 to 2.15 during the past one year. Concern over these two issues has already been voiced by the bank to the company in a previous meeting with the Chief Financial Officer of the company.
- The increasing exposure of the firm to debt has brought its interest coverage and debt service coverage ratios to precarious levels.

Upon receipt of the communication by the bank pointing the deficiencies in the working capital management the Managing Director of Mescos called for an emergency meeting with the Chief Financial Officer to understand the complexities. His enthusiasm of the big order stood somewhat diluted.

INTRODUCTION

Traditionally, *working capital* has been defined as the firm's investment in current assets. Working capital decisions are of tremendous importance for any firm, as they affect the business's liquidity position. The principles underlying the management of working capital are both similar and dissimilar to those discussed in chapters 11, 12, and 13, on the management of long-term assets. Like long-term investment decisions, working capital decisions require an evaluation of the benefits and costs associated with each component of current assets. Like long-term investment decisions, cash flows play an important role in working capital decisions as well. The primary difference between long-term decisions and working capital decisions relates to the time horizon of the decision-making. While long-term financial decisions have cash flow implications for a period that may extend up to 20 years, or even more, short-term financial decisions, i.e., working capital decisions typically affect the cash flows of the firm for a shorter time frame, extending up to a maximum of one year, normally. Unlike the case of long-term investment decisions, this makes the concepts of risk and time value of money less pertinent to working capital decision-making, as the value of money and the risk profile do not undergo any consequential change within a short time frame. Instead, the concept of operating cycle and its management assumes significance in the context of working capital management (WCM). Firms have a greater degree of flexibility in working capital decisions, compared to long-term financial decisions, because working capital directly corresponds to sales.

Chapters 21 to 24 look at various issues governing WCM. This chapter is introductory in nature, and looks at the principles underlying effective management and control of working capital. Chapters 22 to 24 discuss issues that are specific to the management of individual components of working capital—*inventory*, *receivables*, and *cash*.

MEANING OF WORKING CAPITAL

The concept of working capital is, perhaps, one of the most misunderstood issues in the literature of finance. The reason is that it is subject to multiple connotations. From the accountants' perspective it refers to the current assets–current liabilities differential; from the finance managers' angle it implies the total investment made in current assets; from the production managers' view it refers to the total funds that a firm needs to carry out its day-to-day operations. For definitional purposes, this book adopts, for obvious reasons, the finance managers' view of working capital. For the sake of simplicity, we postpone issues of similarity or otherwise of the three perspectives to later paragraphs.

Working capital refers to the investment made by firms in current assets. It is the measure of firms' liquidity position.

Working capital, alternatively referred to as current or circulating capital, is the investment made by firms in their current assets. Current assets comprise all assets such as cash, marketable securities, accounts receivables, and inventories that the firm expects to convert into cash within the year. It is these current assets that determine the liquidity position of the business. The higher the investment in current assets, the better is the health of the firm from the liquidity perspective. Before we get to the issue of profitability–liquidity tangle, let us understand the concepts of gross and net working capital.

Gross working capital (GWC) is the broader concept of working capital, as it talks about the total investment made by a firm in current assets. It is referred to as the managers' concept of working capital, as it denotes the liquidity position of the firm. Other factors remaining the same, the higher the GWC of a firm, the better its liquidity position. However, the increased holding of current assets, i.e., the GWC, by a firm increases its cost of carrying these assets and thus adversely affects its profitability. Furthermore, an increased GWC increases the risk of obsolescence of inventory in industries in which obsolescence rates are high. Besides, it also causes a slowdown in the turnover of current assets.

Gross working capital refers to the total investment in the current assets while net working capital is the difference between current assets and current liabilities.

Net working capital (NWC) refers to the difference between current assets and current liabilities (CA – CL). This differential denotes that part of current assets which is financed by long-term sources of financing. It is referred to as the accountant's definition of working capital. An increasing NWC indicates an improving liquidity position of the firm, as it reflects an increasing usage of long-term financing sources to partly finance short-term assets. The availability and cost of short-term funds are subject to market vagaries; thus, to the extent a firm uses long-term funds to finance investments in current assets, it precludes the possibility of non-availability of short-term funds for financing these assets. This improves the firm's liquidity position. However, increased usage of long-term sources of financing increases the firm's cost of financing, as long-term funds are normally costlier than short-term financing.

Although there are two different approaches to defining working capital, both concepts (GWC and NWC) are equally important in the management of working capital, as both are related. One is a measure of the level of current assets while the other measures the extent to which long-term sources of financing have been used to finance current assets.

SCOPE OF WORKING CAPITAL MANAGEMENT

Working capital management relates to the current assets (CA) and current liabilities (CL) components of the balance sheet, as indicated in Figure 21-1. All these components form part of the operating cycle. The scope of WCM is very wide. Working capital decisions affect the firm's profits through their impact on sales, operating costs, and interest expense. They affect the firm's risk through their impact on the variability of the firm's cash flows, the probability of not receiving the cash flow, and the ability to generate cash in a crisis. The working capital policy touches upon almost every functional area of the business's operation. Working capital management affects and gets affected by the different operational decisions in a firm. For example, the production department's decision to

The working capital policy touches upon almost every functional area of business's operation.

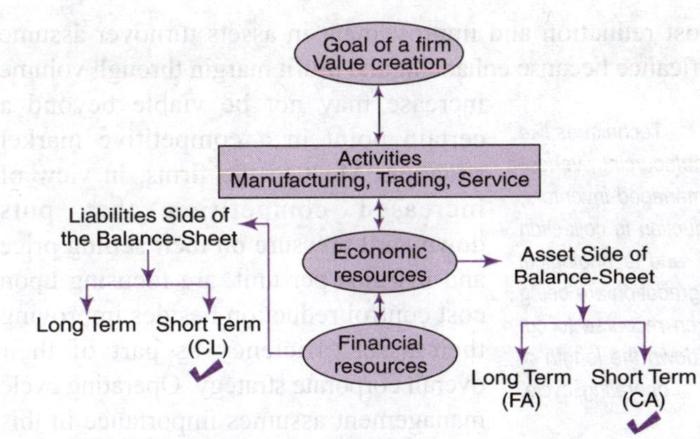

Figure 21-1 Scope of working capital management

increase the level of raw material inventory so as to meet production schedules shall increase the total working capital requirement of the firm. Similarly, if the marketing department, in order to boost up its sales liberalizes its credit policy and offers a longer credit period to the customers, the level of debtors in the firm's books would increase, causing an increase in the total working capital requirements.

WORKING CAPITAL NEEDS OF DIFFERENT TYPES OF BUSINESS

The amount of working capital requirement depends, inter alia, upon the nature of business.

The quantum of working capital requirements is closely related to the nature of business of the firm, which in turn, is related to the operating cycle. For example, in a bakery unit, the requirement may be very low, as the operating cycle may hardly be for one or two days. Similarly, in case of an electric supply company, or a transport company, or a company that is still in a sellers' market, working capital requirements may be much less. This is due to the shorter operating cycle, which is due to the fact that sales for such businesses is mainly on cash basis. As the result, the time lag between credit sales and collection of accounts receivables is cut down. As against this, a company manufacturing heavy machine tools or turbines will naturally be having a much longer operating cycle, as it would be selling mostly on credit, and consequently would require a much higher level of working capital. Also for such businesses, the value of raw material inventory, finished goods inventory, and credit sales is high due to the costly nature of products they deal in.

Seasonal industries, such as those manufacturing woolen clothes and blankets, geysers, etc., may require a much higher level of working capital in peak seasons and a much lower requirement during slack seasons. Table 21-1 demonstrates this relationship between current assets (working capital) and total assets for different industrial sectors. As can be seen in the table, the highest level of working capital/current assets is maintained by trading firms. This is because investment in the inventory of finished goods is the single most significant investment for such firms.

Table 21-1 Current assets to total assets ratio for different industries

Industries	*Current assets to total assets (%)*
Trading	75–77
Medicines	65–70
Machinery	60–68
Engineering	60–65
Sugar	59–65
Rubber	50–55
Aluminium	45–50
Paper	40–45
Cement	32–35
Electricity Gen. and Supply	25–30
Shipping	15–18

OPERATING CYCLE AND ITS RELEVANCE FOR WORKING CAPITAL MANAGEMENT

The total duration taken by a firm to complete one chain of operations that begins with the procurement of inputs and ends with the realization of credit sales is known as operating cycle.

The operating cycle, as shown in Figure 21-2, is the total duration taken to complete one cycle of operation, i.e., the time it takes to turn the investment of cash (for the purchase of raw materials and finished goods) back into cash (through collection of accounts receivables). For manufacturing firms, it typically consists of three activities: procurement of inputs, transfor-mation of inputs into outputs, and distribution (selling) of output. The total time involved in operating cycle can be broken up into the following three constituents:

- *Inventory conversion period (ICP)* The total time involved from the procurement of inputs till the conversion of inputs into outputs is called inventory conversion period. It consists of three successive stages—raw material conversion period, work-in-progress conversion period, and finished goods conversion period.
- *Receivables conversion period (RCP)* Time lag in converting credit sales into cash is called receivable conversion period. It depends on the credit period offered to customers and collection efforts of the firm. It is alternatively referred to as Accounts Receivable conversion period, Debtors conversion period, or Book Debts conversion period.

Inventory conversion period, receivables conversion period and payables deferral period are the three constituents of the operating cycle.

- *Payables deferral period (PDP)* The period for which the firm can defer its payments is referred to as payables deferred period. The longer the period, the lesser would be the firm's need to seek working capital financing from external sources.

The operating cycle, can be subdivided into the *gross operating cycle* and the *net operating cycle*. The *gross operating cycle* (GOC) refers to the total time involved from the procurement of inputs to the realization of cash on account of sales. It can be represented as an equation as follows:

$$GOC = ICP + RCP \qquad (21\text{-}1)$$

The *net operating cycle* (NOC) implies the net time for which the working capital needs to be arranged. It ignores the period for which the firm is able to defer payables (PDP). The firm does not need financing for the period it defers its payables, as it is getting financed indirectly by those deferrals. The longer this period, the lesser is the firm's reliance on direct sources of working capital financing. NOC can mathematically be represented as:

$$NOC = GOC - PDP \qquad (21\text{-}2)$$

The operating cycle in part determines how long it takes for a firm to generate cash from its current assets and, therefore, the risk and costs of its investments in current assets, or working capital. The length of the operating cycle depends on the technology adopted. Adopting an improved production technology normally causes a reduction in the conversion time. Similarly, an improved supply chain reduces the lead and delivery time. The firm's credit policies also affect its operating cycle. Normally, a relaxation in the credit policy elongates the operating cycle.

Gross operating cycle (GOC) and net operating cycle (NOC) are the two measures of the operation cycle. NOC is alternatively referred to as cash cycle.

Another concept closely related to operating cycle is the *cash conversion cycle.* Normally, the term operating cycle is used to refer to the GOC, while the term cash conversion cycle or the cash cycle means the NOC. It is the period for which the firm is required to arrange for finance for its working capital needs.

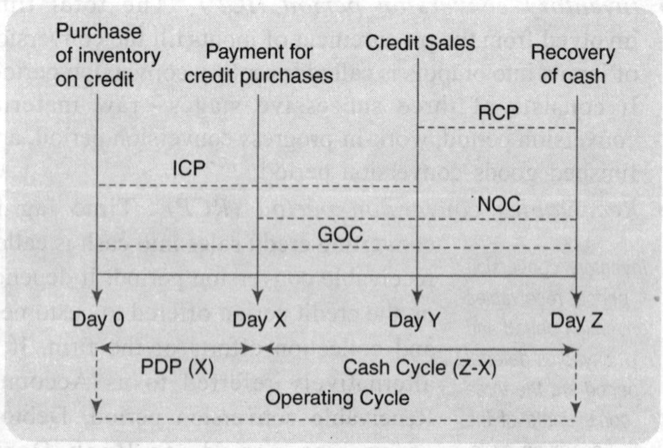

Figure 21-2 Operating cycle vs cash cycle

Techniques Adopted by Firms to Cut Down their Operating Cycle

Returns, such as return on investment (ROI), return on equity (ROE), profit margin, etc., depend on two basic factors:

1. Profit margin and
2. Asset efficiency (turnover)

Cost reduction and improvement in assets turnover assume significance because enhancing the profit margin through volume increase may not be viable beyond a certain point in a competitive market situation. Most of the firms, in view of increased competition that puts downward pressure on their selling price and margins per unit, are focusing upon cost control/reduction besides improving their asset efficiency as part of their overall corporate strategy. Operating cycle management assumes importance in this context. Firms across the board are trying to cut down their operating cycle so that they can reduce the blockage of funds in their value chain. The blocked funds thus freed can be redirected either towards more yielding investments or to pay back the firms' existing liabilities which realigns their debt–equity ratios and reduces future interest burdens. Sometimes outsourcing is taken recourse to cut down the operating cycle. This also brings down the cost of operations, as the firms need not to focus upon all activities down the value chain, but only on those activities in which they have core competency, and outsource the other activities/ processes at lesser cost to firms that have core competence in such processes.

Techniques like outsourcing, vendor managed inventory, reduction in collection float, and technological upgradation are being taken recourse to cut down the length of operating cycle.

The prominent techniques that the firms are taking recourse for cutting down their operating cycle are:

- Outsourcing of various processes (such as production, distribution, collection, etc.)
- Setting up vendor-managed inventories
- Reducing the collection float by using banks with accelerated clearing capabilities
- Bringing about technology upgradation to achieve reductions in the conversion period for in-house operations

All these techniques are dealt with elaborately in Chapters 22 to 24, on WCM in suitable contexts.

The Relationship of Working Capital Management to Business Solvency

The level and the quality of current assets (working capital) held by a firm have a direct impact on its liquidity (or short-term solvency) position. As is known, current assets have the basic feature of transformation. One form of current asset converts itself into the other form until cash is realized eventually at the end of the operating cycle of the business. It is this cash, which is used by the business to repay its current obligations, or to pay for procurement of the inputs needed in its operations. Without cash, or at least access to it, bankruptcy becomes a grim possibility. Thus the liquidity position of the business depends on the level of current assets it holds. The higher the level of current assets, the higher would be the capacity to transform these current assets and generate cash. Consequently, the liquidity position of the business denoted by the current ratio (ratio of current assets to current liabilities) shall also be high. Although the extra investment

The level and quality of current assets held by the firm determine its solvency.

in current assets affects the profitability position adversely, from the viewpoint of the liquidity position of the business, it is justified.

Apart from the level of current assets, the quality of current assets is an equally important aspect that affects the liquidity position of the business. The higher the investment in the more liquid current assets such as cash and receivables, the better is the liquidity position of the business. From the viewpoint of liquidity, the business should always prefer cutting down its investment in less liquid assets such as inventory, as these assets generally take longer to convert into cash. Such a policy improves the quick ratio (ratio of current assets less inventories to current liabilities) of the business.

WORKING CAPITAL MANAGEMENT

Working capital management refers to the management of short-term assets (the current assets). It involves planning and controlling the level and mix of a firm's current assets as well as the pattern of their financing. It is alternatively referred to as current assets management. Specifically, WCM requires the finance manager to decide on the two issues:

Working capital management is alternatively referred to as current assets management as it relates to the management of level and financing of firms' current assets.

- What should be the optimal level of current assets held by the firm?
- How should these current assets be financed?

Thus, WCM is essentially concerned with managing the liquidity position of the business, and entails two related problems—managing the firm's investment in current assets, and managing the firm's use of current liabilities.

This chapter provides the basic principles underlying the analysis of both the aforesaid problems. The enunciated principles are then applied in subsequent chapters.

Managing Current Assets

Current assets can be defined as assets that can be converted to cash within the operating cycle or within one year. They are also referred to as short-term assets. There are two main characteristics of current assets:

1. They have a short life span that usually extends to an operating cycle or to a period not exceeding 12 months.
2. Any one form of current asset gets transformed into other forms of current assets (and ultimately into cash) rapidly.

Cash, accounts receivable, inventory, marketable securities, and prepaid expenses are some of the prominent examples of current assets that appear on the Balance Sheets of various firms. The importance of current assets lies in the fact that they fund the ongoing, day-to-day operations of firms. These assets determine the liquidity position of the firms. A high level of current assets denotes a high liquidity position, and vice versa. It is for this reason that lenders, particularly short–term lenders, expect the firm to have a high level of current assets.

Current assets that are also referred to as short term assets fund the day-to-day operations of firms. They are important as they determine the liquidity position of the firm.

Firms acquire fixed assets because of the future cash flows those assets are expected to generate. Likewise, firms invest in current assets because of the expected benefits derived from such assets. In this chapter, our interest in the firm's short-term investment (current assets) decisions relates to their effect on the firm's liquidity position.

As a means of increasing its liquidity, the firm may choose to invest additional funds in current assets, particularly cash and/or marketable securities. Such an action involves a tradeoff, however, since these assets earn little or no return. The firm thus finds that it can reduce its risk of illiquidity only by reducing its overall return on invested funds, and vice versa. The optimal level of current assets is decided in the light of the tradeoff between the cost of liquidity and the cost of illiquidity. It is at this tradeoff point that the total cost is lowest. The larger the investment in current assets, the higher is the liquidity position of the firm; the more, however, is the opportunity cost (cost of liquidity) of funds blocked in the current assets, as indicated in Figure 21-3. The profitability–liquidity tangle needs to be resolved in deciding the issue of the optimal level of current assets. A higher investment in current assets increases the liquidity position of the business, but brings down profitability due to the higher blockage of funds in idle current assets that give an abysmally low return, if any.

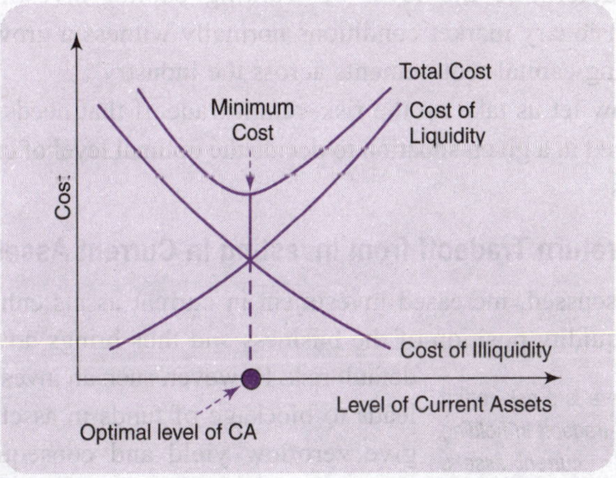

Figure 21-3 Optimal level of investment in current assets

Carrying out of operations in an efficient manner, without blocking extra funds in current assets, is the guiding criterion in deciding the level of current assets.

Nature and type of business; length of operating cycle; seasonality of operations; degree of uncertainty; and prevailing and emerging market conditions are the factors that determine the level of investment in current assets.

The level of a firm's investment in current assets depends on:

Type of business The type of business the firm is in and the related industry characteristics and practices affect the level of current asset investments. The retailing business entails a large portion of investments in current assets, as compared to manufacturing businesses, which may be more capital-intensive.

The length of operating cycle The longer the operating cycle, the longer will be the blockage in its various stages, and hence, the more will be the investment in working capital.

Uncertainty in operating cycle Degree of uncertainty associated with supplies, availability of short-term credit at a short notice, etc affect the working capital decisions. Assured supplies reduce the uncertainty and thus do away with the need to block additional funds in current assets as a cushion to tide over supply constraints. Similarly, an easy access to short-term credit on convenient terms does away with the need for forcefully raising funds for a longer duration than required and unnecessarily blocking them in current assets to justify their utilization.

Seasonality Seasonality of operations and the production policy of the firm has an impact on firm's working capital needs. A firm manufacturing and selling seasonal products such as air conditioners, sugar, etc., will witness large variations in its working capital requirements. There will be a surge in working capital investments during the peak season and a decline during the lean season. Similarly, firms with seasonal production policy will have a higher investment in working capital during the peak season, as compared to those following a steady production policy.

Market conditions Prevailing and emerging market conditions also determine the level of working capital investments. Expansionary market conditions normally witness a growth in working capital requirements across the industry.

Now let us take up the risk–return tradeoff that needs to be resolved in a given situation to decide the optimal level of current assets.

Risk-return Tradeoff from Investing in Current Assets

As discussed, increased investment in current assets enhances the liquidity position of the business and thus brings down its default risk. However, such an investment leads to blockage of funds in assets that give zero/low yield and consequently affects the returns adversely. Thus, determining the optimal level of investment in current assets is essentially deciding about this risk-return tradeoff. Let us understand this risk-return tradeoff involved in managing the firm's liquidity, with the help of an example.

There is a risk–return tradeoff in holding current assets. Increased investment in current assets increases liquidity (thus decreasing the risk) but reduces profitability (return).

Firms A and B are identical in every respect but one: Firm B has invested ₹150,000 in marketable securities, which has been financed with 'common equity'. That is, the firm raised additional capital of ₹150,000 through sale of its common stock and invested this additional capital in marketable securities to strengthen its liquidity position. The balance sheets and net incomes of the two firms are as follows:

Balance Sheet	*Firm A*	*Firm B*
Cash	20,000	20,000
Marketable securities		150,000
Accounts receivable	220,000	220,000
Inventories	425,000	425,000
Current assets	665,000	815,000
Net fixed assets	1,250,000	1,250,000
Total	**1,915,000**	**2,065,000**
Current liabilities	300,000	300,000
Long-term debt	380,000	380,000
Common equity	1,235,000	1,385,000
Total	**1,915,000**	**2,065,000**

Net income and ratios

	Firm A	*Firm B*
Net income	210,650	216,050
Current ratio (current assets/current liabilities)	2.22 times	2.72 times
Net working capital (current assets – current liabilities)	365,000	515,000
Return on total assets (Net income/total assets)	11.00%	10.46%

Note that Firm A has a current ratio of 2.22 (reflecting NWC of ₹365,000) and earns 11% return on its total assets. Firm B, with its investment in marketable securities, has a current ratio of 2.72 and has a NWC of ₹515,000. The marketable securities earn a return of only 6% before taxes (3.6% after taxes with a 40% tax rate), and therefore, Firm B earns only 10.46% on its total investment. Thus, investing in current assets, particularly in marketable securities, does have a favourable effect on the firm's liquidity, but also has an unfavourable effect on the firm's rate of return earned on invested funds. The risk–return tradeoff involved in holding current assets (marketable securities in case of Firm B) is one of added liquidity versus reduced profitability. During the year Firm B held ₹150,000 in marketable securities with a 6% or ₹9000 return for the year. After paying taxes at a rate of 40%, the firm earned ₹5400 on this investment.

Having discussed the issue of the optimal level of current assets, now let us take up the second issue in the management of working capital: financing of current assets, i.e., the management of current liabilities.

Managing Current Liabilities

The other important issue in the management of working capital relates to the financing of current assets, i.e., deciding about the mix of current versus long-term debt. Here too, a risk–return tradeoff needs to be resolved by the firm. Other things remaining the same, the more the use of short-term debt or current liabilities in the financing mix, the less the liquidity of the firm. But that is only one side of the coin (i.e., the risk perspective), as short-term sources of financing (i.e., current liabilities) render certain benefits too. Current liabilities are, normally, not only less costly than long-term financing, they also provide the firm with a more flexible means of financing current assets.

Increased usage of short-term sources of financing (i.e., current liabilities) increases profitability but reduces liquidity.

Before we take the risk–return tradeoff any further, let us discuss the advantages and disadvantages of using current liabilities as the source of financing.

Advantages of Current Liabilities

The advantages of using current liabilities to fund the level of current assets are (i) flexibility and (ii) interest cost.

Flexibility Current liabilities offer the firm a flexible source of financing. They can be used to match the timing of a firm's needs for short-term financing. For example, if a firm needs funds for a three-month period each year to finance a seasonal expansion in inventories, then a three-month loan can provide substantial cost savings over a long-term loan (even if the interest rate on short-term financing should be higher). This results from the fact that the use of long-term debt in this situation involves borrowing for the entire year rather than for the three-month period for which the funds are needed; this increases the interest cost the firm has to bear. This brings us to the second advantage, generally associated with the use of short-term financing.

Current liabilities provide cheaper and flexible financing options. However there are availability and cost related uncertainties with the current liabilities.

Interest Cost In general, interest rates on short-term debt are lower than on long-term debt for a given borrower. This relationship is usually referred to as the term structure of interest rates. For a given firm, the term structure might appear as follows:

Loan Maturity	Interest Rate*
Up to 3 months	11.75%
3–6 months	12.00%
6–9 months	12.75%
9 months–1 year	13.50%
1–3 years	14.25%
3–5 years	15.75%
5–10 years	16.00%

Note that this term structure reflects the rates of interest applicable to a given borrower at a particular point in time; thus, it would not describe the rates of interest available to another borrower or even those applicable to the same borrower at a different point in time.

Disadvantages of Current Liabilities

The use of current liabilities or short-term debt as opposed to long-term debt subjects the firm to a greater risk of illiquidity. That is, short-term debt, due to its very nature must be repaid or rolled over more often, and so it enhances the possibility that the firm's financial condition might deteriorate to a point where the needed funds might not be available.

A second disadvantage of short-term debt is the uncertainty of interest costs from year to year. For example, where a firm borrows during a six-month period each year to finance a seasonal expansion in current assets, it might incur a different rate of interest each year. This rate reflects the current rate of interest at the time of the loan, as well as the lender's perception of the firm's riskiness. If long-term debt were used, then the interest cost would be known for the entire period of the loan agreement.

*The interest rates are determined based on the prime lending rates (PLR). Normally the banks add a spread to their PLR to estimate the lending rates. The figures given in the table are the average figures. The rate of interest chargeable in a given situation depends upon the creditworthiness of the borrower.

Risk-return Tradeoff from Using Current Liabilities

Let us understand the risk-return tradeoff from using current liabilities with the help of an example.

Two firms, A and B, are identical in all respects other than the mix of their short-term and long-term financing. Their comparative financial statements are as follows:

Balance Sheet as on 31 December

	Firm A	Firm B
Current assets	6,00,000	6,00,000
Net Fixed assets	14,00,000	14,00,000
Total	**20,00,000**	**20,00,000**
Accounts payable	2,00,000	2,00,000
Notes payable	—	4,00,000
Current liabilities	2,00,000	6,00,000
Long-term debt	4,00,000	—
Common equity	14,00,000	14,00,000
Total	**20,00,000**	**20,00,000**

Net Income and Ratios

	Firm A	Firm B
Net operating income	4,40,000	4,40,000
Less: Interest expenses	44,000	9,000
Earnings before taxes	3,96,000	4,31,000
Less: Taxes (40%)	1,58,400	1,72,400
Net income	2,37,600	2,58,600
Current ratio	3	1
Net working capital	4,00,000	0
Return on Total Assets	11.59%	12.61%

As can be seen from the balance sheets above, all the assets and liabilities for the two firms are the same, other than the notes payable and long-term debt. Both firms had the same seasonal needs for financing throughout the past year. During the four-month period beginning with August and extending through November, both firms needed ₹2,00,000 to support a seasonal build up in inventories. In addition, the firms required ₹4,00,000 to finance a seasonal expansion in accounts receivable in the month of December. Firm A financed its seasonal financing requirements using ₹4,00,000 in long-term debt, carrying an annual interest rate of 11%. Firm B, on the other hand, satisfied its seasonal financing needs using short-term borrowing, on which it paid interest at 9% per annum.

Firm A, having financed its seasonal requirements through long-term sources, will have to pay interest for the entire year (including the off-season period when the funds are not needed). The interest expense for firm A has been 11% × ₹4,00,000 = ₹44,000.

Firm B borrowed only for the period it needed the funds (₹2,00,000 for four months and ₹4,00,000 for one month) at a lower rate of interest (compared to the rate of interest on long-term borrowings), and, therefore, its interest expense for the year was only ₹9,000. Firm B's interest expense for the year has been computed as:

$$₹4,00,000 \times 0.09 \times \frac{1}{12} + ₹2,00,000 \times 0.09 \times \frac{4}{12}$$

$$= ₹3,000 + ₹6,000 = ₹9,000$$

The end result of the two firms' financing policies gets reflected in their current ratio, NWC, and return on total assets. Firm A, using long-term rather than short-term debt, has a current ratio of 3 and NWC of ₹4,00,000, whereas firm B's current ratio is only one, which represents zero NWC. However, owing to its lower interest liability on account of short-term financing, the return on total assets of Firm B is 12.61%, which is higher than the 11.59% return for Firm A.

Thus, reliance on long-term sources of financing reduces the risk of liquidity, but because long-term sources are costlier than short-term sources of financing, and also because, interest on long-term sources may have to be paid for periods during which funds are lying idle, usage of long-term sources of financing brings down the return on investment. Once again we see that the risk-return tradeoff involves an increased risk of illiquidity versus increased profitability.

WORKING CAPITAL FINANCING POLICIES

The financing of working capital is very crucial to management of working capital as it makes a significant impact on the firm's profitability and liquidity position. Theoretically, there can be three possible approaches to working capital financing: matching, conservative, and aggressive. The mix of short-term and long-term sources of working capital financing varies in each approach, and consequently, the impact of each of the three approaches on the profitability and liquidity position of the business also varies.

The working capital financing policy may have a significant impact on the profitability–liquidity position of the firm. Theoretically, the policies of working capital financing can be categorized as: matching; conservative; and aggressive.

Matching Approach

This is the conventional approach to financing. As per this approach, the duration of requirement of funds should be matched with the duration of the sources of financing, as can be seen in Figure 21-4. That is, while the fixed assets and the permanent (core) current assets must be financed by long-term sources of finance, the temporary current assets alone should be financed by short-term sources of funds. This approach follows the middle path of working capital financing.

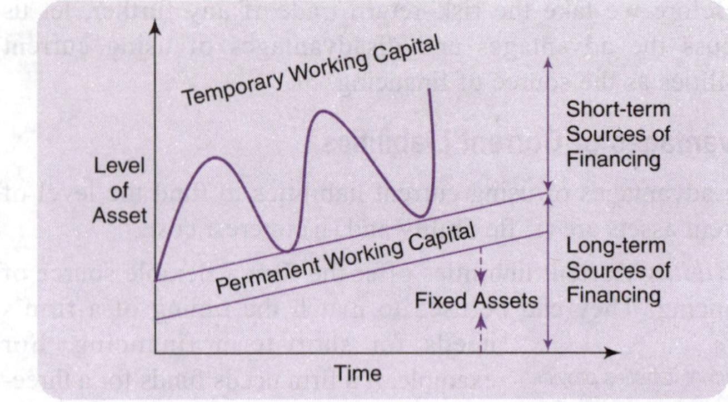

Figure 21-4 Matching approach to working capital financing

Conservative Approach

This approach favours maximum reliance on long-term sources of financing. A firm following this approach would finance not only its fixed assets and its permanent working capital from long-term sources, but would also partly finance its temporary (seasonal) working capital requirements from long-term sources as can be seen in Figure 21-5. The conservative approach is termed as a low profitability and high liquidity approach to working capital financing because more reliance on long-term funds impacts returns adversely, although it strengthens the liquidity position of the business. In Figure 21-5, *a* and *b* denote the part of seasonal working capital needs that is financed from short-term sources of financing, and *x* and *y* denote disinvestment of, and investments in, respectively, of marketable securities.

While matching approach refers to using short-term financing sources to finance seasonal financing needs and long-term sources for permanent requirements, conservative and aggressive approaches favour relying more on the long-term and short-term sources of financing respectively.

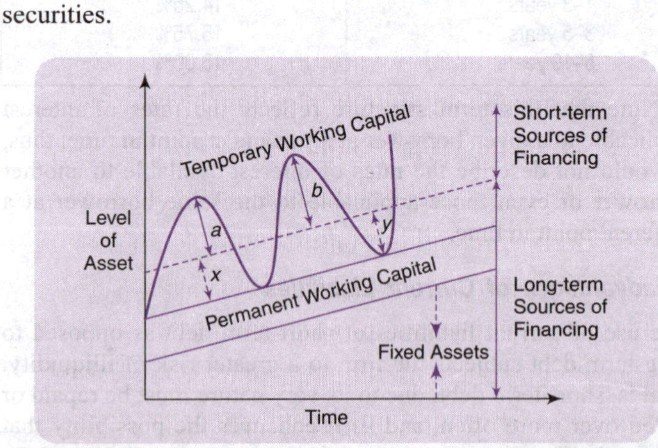

Figure 21-5 Conservative approach to working capital financing

Aggressive Approach

Aggressive approach to working capital financing favours maximum reliance on short-term sources for working capital financing. The working capital financing policy of a firm is said to be aggressive if it finances a part of its permanent working capital requirements from short-term sources. This is a high profitability and low liquidity approach to working capital financing (see Figure 21-6).

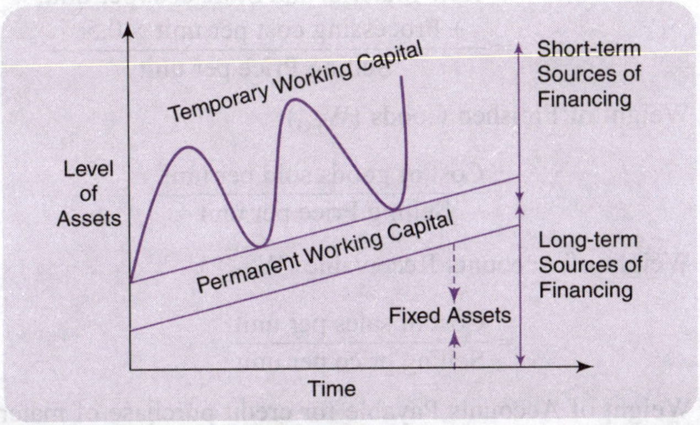

Figure 21-6 Aggressive approach to working captial financing

Although the terminology matching, conservative, and aggressive may not be standard and universally applicable, the idea behind classifying the working capital financing policy of firms under these three broad categories is to make working capital financing policies across firms and over time comparable for the purposes of analysis and decision making. A firm may be more aggressive in its working capital financing vis-à-vis other firms in the sector, or compared with its own financing policy in the past.

WORKING CAPITAL POLICY

As discussed, overall working capital policy depends on two factors; the level of current assets (that we refer to as current assets policy) and the financing of current assets (that can be alternatively referred to as working capital financing policy or level of current liabilities). Whether the working capital policy of the firm is aggressive or conservative in relation to its policy in the past or vis-à-vis its competitors depends upon its current assets policy and its current assets financing policy, as shown in Figure 21-7. Depending upon the level of current assets and their financing, working capital policy of firms can be categorized into one of the four quadrants.

Depending upon the current assets policy and the current assets financing policy a firm's working capital policy can be categorized as conservative, aggressive or moderate.

As can be seen in the figure, if the firm on one hand maintains low level of current assets while on the other it depends more on short-term sources of financing its overall working capital policy is termed as aggressive. Firms that maintain a higher level of current assets and also rely heavily on long-term sources for financing their current assets fall in Quadrant I and their working capital policy is termed as conservative. Other firms would fall in either Quadrant II or III and are said to have a moderate working capital policy.

As firms evolve and as the competition intensifies, the firms become more cost conscious and start focusing on better resource utilization, they move towards Quadrant IV and their working capital policy normally becomes more aggressive. Moreover, with the growing size of firms and long years of performance their credibility increases. Also, they establish good relations with suppliers and bankers. This cuts down the uncertainty with respect to supply of inputs and short-term sources of financing and as a result it does away with the need to carry extra level of current assets.

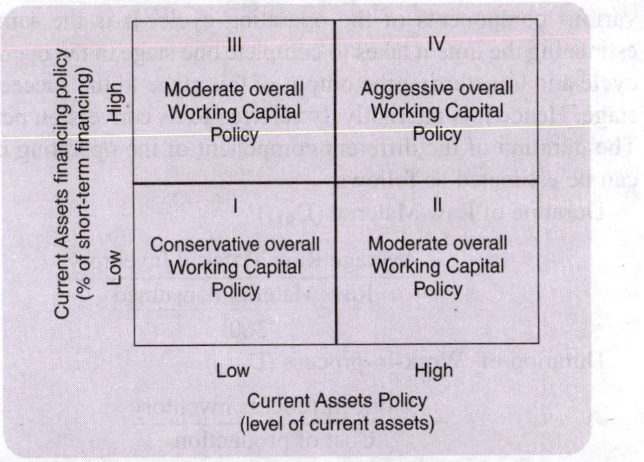

Figure 21-7 Overall working capital policy

ESTIMATION OF WORKING CAPITAL REQUIREMENTS

Accurate estimation of working capital requirements is of tremendous importance, as the funding of working capital requirements depends upon this estimate. Estimation is essentially a projection that depends on both past data and the projected level of activity for which the working capital is required. It requires information from varied sources. The production department provides inputs on the rate of material consumption and labour usage and on production overheads based on past performance. The stores section provides data on average inventory held by the firm in the past, while the marketing department provides sales projections for the period for which working capital is to be estimated. The personnel department submits information about the salary bill and other manpower-related costs, and the accounts department provides an estimate of the various overheads likely to be incurred for the period.

Estimation of working capital requirements is based on past data and future projections. It requires estimation of the duration and weights of different components of the operating cycle.

Working capital essentially refers to funds that need to be blocked in the various stages of the firm's value chain (i.e., the different components of current assets), to carry out the desired level of activity in a smooth and efficient manner. Its estimation requires the estimation of funds to be blocked in the different components of current assets and the duration of their blockage. The operating cycle and its components (ICP, RCP, and PDP) that have been discussed earlier in the chapter form the basis of such estimation.

Estimation of working capital can be stated as a four step process:

Step 1: Determining the *duration* of blockage of funds. This gives the time period for which the money will be tied up in the various components of the operating cycle. It is the same as estimating the time it takes to complete one stage in the operating cycle and transferring the output of this stage to the succeeding stage. Hence it is alternatively referred to as conversion period. The duration of the different component of the operating cycle can be estimated as follows:

Duration of Raw Material (D_{RM})

$$= \frac{\text{Average Raw Material Inventory}}{\frac{\text{Raw Material consumed}}{360^{1}}}$$

Duration of Work-in-process (D_{WIP})

$$= \frac{\text{Work-in-process inventory}}{\frac{\text{Cost of production}}{360}}$$

Duration of Finished goods (D_{FG})

$$= \frac{\text{Finished goods inventory}}{\frac{\text{Cost of goods sold}}{360}}$$

Duration of Accounts Receivable (D_{AR})

$$= \frac{\text{Average Debtors}}{\frac{\text{Credit sales}}{360}}$$

Duration of Accounts Payable (D_{AP})

$$= \frac{\text{Average Creditors}}{\frac{\text{Credit Purchase}}{360}}$$

The raw material inventory has been divided by the raw material consumed, given in the extract of P&L account, to get the D_{RM}. The work-in-process inventory and finished goods inventory have been divided by the sum of raw material, wages and overheads to arrive at the D_{WIP} and D_{FG} respectively. D_{RM}, D_{WIP}, and D_{AR} denote the total time period it takes to convert the raw material inventory, the work-in-process inventory, and the receivables (or debtors) into their next stages, and eventually into realization of cash. The longer the duration, the more the blockage of funds in the three components of inventory, and the more the blockage, the more the requirement for working capital. If the estimation is to be done on a weekly or monthly basis, the denominator should be divided by 52 or 12 respectively.

Step 2: Estimation of *weights* of the different components of operating cycle in the total funds to be blocked in working capital. The weights can be computed as follows:

Weight of Raw Material (W_{RM})

$$= \frac{\text{Raw Material and Stores cost per unit}}{\text{Selling Price per unit}}$$

Weight of work-in-process (W_{WIP})

$$= \frac{\text{Raw Material and Store cost per unit} + \text{Processing cost per unit} \times 0.5}{\text{Selling Price per unit}}$$

Weight of Finished Goods (W_{FG})

$$= \frac{\text{Cost of goods sold per unit}}{\text{Selling Price per unit}}$$

Weight of Accounts Receivable (W_{AR})

$$= \frac{\text{Cost of sales per unit}}{\text{Selling price per unit}}$$

Weight of Accounts Payable for credit purchase of material (W_{AP})

$$= \frac{\text{Raw Materials and Stores cost per unit}^{3}}{\text{Selling Price per unit}}$$

Step 3: Determination of weighted operating cycle (WOC). WOC can be computed as follows:

$$WOC = D_{RM} \times W_{RM} + D_{WIP} \times W_{WIP} + D_{FG} \times W_{FG} + D_{AR} \times W_{AR} - D_{AP} \times W_{AP}$$

Step 4: Computation of working capital requirements is as follows:

$$\text{Working Capital Requirement} = \text{Sales per day} \times WOC + \text{Cash Balance Required}$$

Example 21-1 illustrates the process of estimation of working capital

Example 21-1 Estimates of Working Capital

Estimate the working capital requirements for Amkit India Ltd for an estimated sales level of 15000 units per month. The company has a policy of maintaining cash balance that is sufficient enough to meet its cost of production for three days. Following are the financials of the company:

Balance Sheet of Amkit India Ltd

Liabilities	*(₹ in '000)*	*Assets*	*(₹ in '000)*
Share Capital	3000	Fixed Assets	2200
Reserves	2000	Raw materials	800
Sundry Creditors	400	Work-in-progress	200
		Finished goods	1000
		Sundry debtors	1000
		Cash	200
	5400		5400

[1]No. of days in a year has been taken as 360 in the denominator. This is for the ease of computation and also due to the assumption that there are atleast 5 days in a year when there is no business activity. However, readers may take 365 days in the denominator instead of 360.

[2]Multiplying the processing cost by 0.5 is a standard practice to indicate that the WIP is 50% complete as regards processing.

[3]This is only for the deferrals of payment to the suppliers. Credit purchases are the most prominent deferrals (i.e., spontaneous sources of financing). If there is any other deferral its weight can be computed similarly.

Extract from a Monthly Income Statement of Amkit India Ltd

	(In ₹)
Raw material	400,000
Wages	100,000
Overheads	300,000
Profits	200,000
	1,000,000

Cost Structure of Amkit India Ltd

Components	*Cost and price per unit (In ₹)*
Raw Material	20
Labour	5
Overheads	15
Profit	10
Selling price	50

Solution

Step 1: Determining the *duration* of blockage of funds can be done as follows:

	(in lakh)	*(in months)*
D_{RM}	8/4	2.00
D_{WIP}	2/8	0.25
D_{FG}	10/8	1.25
D_{AR}	10/10	1.00
D_{AP}	4/4	1.00

Step 2: Estimation of weights of the different components of operating cycle can be done as follows:

Cost Structure of Amkit India Ltd

	Cost per unit (in ₹)	*Weight of components*
Raw material	20	0.4
Labour	5	0.1
Overheads	15	0.3
Profit	10	0.2
Total	50	1.0

Steps 3 and 4 have been clubbed together in the following table:

Computation of Working Capital Requirements

(*₹ in lakh*)

	RM	*WIP*	*FG*	*Debtors*	*Total*
RM	6.00	0.75	3.75	3.00	13.5
Direct Labour	—	0.19	0.94	0.75	1.88
Overheads	—	0.56	2.81	2.25	5.62
Profit	—	—	—	1.50	1.50
Total	6.00	1.50	7.50	7.50	22.50
Less: Sundry Creditors					3.00
					19.50
Add: Cash Balance					0.60
Working Capital Requirements for Amkit India Ltd				20.10	

Explanation of computed values given in the table:

1. Value of raw material that is blocked in raw material inventory has been computed in the table as follows:
   No. of units for which material is needed = 15,000 for a month
   Cost of raw material (per unit) = ₹20
   For one month, the value of raw material needed
   = 15,000 units × ₹20 per unit
   = ₹3,00,000
   But duration of raw materials (D_{RM}) is 2 months. This implies that the firm, on an average, procures raw material sufficient for 2 months. Hence, investment in raw material becomes 3,00,000 × 2 = ₹6,00,000.
2. Value of raw material blocked at the stage of work-in-process has been computed as follows:
   15,000 units × ₹20 per unit = ₹3,00,000 per month
   Since the duration of blockage at the stage of WIP is 1/4th of a month, the total blockage of raw material at this stage would be ₹3,00,000 × 0.25 = ₹75,000
3. Value of raw material blocked at the stage of finished goods has been computed as follows:
   15,000 × 20 × 1.25 (i.e., D_{FG}) = ₹3.75 lakh per month
4. Value of raw material blocked at the stage of Debtors (or Accounts Receivables) has been computed as follows:
   15,000 × 20 × 1.00 (i.e., D_{AR}) = ₹3.00 lakh
5. Value of direct labour blocked at the stage of WIP has been computed as follows:
   15,000 × 5 × 0.25 = ₹18,750 (approximated to ₹0.19 lakh in the table).
   Similarly, direct labour cost blocked at the finished goods and receivables stages have been computed as ₹0.94 lakh and ₹ 0.75 lakh respectively, applying the duration of 1.25 months and 1.00 month respectively.
6. Overheads blocked at the stage of WIP has been computed as follows:
   15,000 × 15 × 0.25 = ₹56,250 (approximated as ₹0.56 lakh in the table).
   Similarly, the value of overheads blocked at the stage of finished goods and receivables have been computed as ₹2.81 lakh and ₹2.75 lakh respectively, applying the duration of 1.25 months and 1.00 month respectively.
7. Value of sundry creditors (or Accounts Payables) has been estimated assuming that the creditors constitute suppliers of raw materials and the firm has fully availed the credit facility offered by its suppliers, i.e., 100% purchases have been made on credit basis. The value of funds provided by sundry creditors as an indirect financing has been computed as follows:
   Units purchased × Value of raw material per unit × D_{AP}
   = 15,000 × 20 × 1
   = ₹3,00,000
8. Cash balance has been computed as:
   Total production in month = 15,000 units
   Cost of production = ₹40 per unit

So, total cost of production for 30 days = 15,000 × 40 = 6,00,000

Cost of production for 3 days = ₹60,000.

Since the firm has a policy of maintaining cash, sufficient to meet its cost of production for three days, its cash balance will be ₹60,000.

The table can be read both horizontally and vertically. The columns indicate the value of funds required to be blocked in different components of cost in order to achieve the target sales level of 15,000 units. Rows indicate the value of each component blocked in different stages of value chain.

For instance, the raw material that the firm needs to procure to achieve the targeted sales of 15,000 units is of ₹6 lakh value; but since the production process is ongoing, at a given point, the total amount of funds blocked in raw materials across the value chain is ₹13.5 lakh, which is much higher.

WORKING CAPITAL FINANCING BY BANKS

Apart from financing for investing in fixed assets, business also require funds on a continual basis for carrying on their day-to-day operations. Such operating cash outflows include payment for purchase of raw material, manufacturing expenses, administration, selling and distribution expenses etc. While part of the raw material may be purchased on credit, the business would still need to pay for other expenses. The time lag between sales its cash realised requires the business arrange for funds to meet its day-to-day operations. Such funds are termed as working capital and assume tremendous significance for the efficient and uninterrupted conduct of business operations. This section focuses upon the working capital financing by the banks in response to the working capital loan application by firms. There are other sources of working capital financing like lines of credit, commercial papers, factoring etc. that have been discussed in Chapter 20 on Sources of Finance.

Banks have been providing the working capital finance to meet the short-term financing needs of industry. To ensure the smooth flow of credit from the banks to the industry, RBI has constituted various committees like Daheja committee;Tandon committee; Chore committee; Marathe committee etc. to review the prevailing norms pertaining to the flow of credit from the banking sector to the industry from time to time. Tandon committee set up by RBI assumes significance in context of banks' financing of working capital requirements of firms. Banks follow the norms proposed by the committee regarding the assessment of Working Capital Gap and the determination of Maximum Permissible Bank Finance.

Tandon Study Group

Tandon study group was constituted by RBI in July 1974 to frame guidelines for rational allocation and optimal use of bank credit. The committee was set up in the background of growing demand for the bank credit by the different sectors of the economy. It was felt that cheap credit available from the banks was being used for building up disproportionate stocks of materials so as to realize trading profits by the manufacturing firms that they were not made for. The prevalent cash credit system was being put to misuse by the firms as they were indulging into double financing. The practice under the cash credit system was to lend to the extent of 75% of the value of inventory and receivables, the remaining 25% being the margin. This value of inventory included purchases of material on credit. Thus, this amounted to double financing-from creditors as well as banks. Also, bank lending under the system was focused on the security in form of inventory and receivables and had no relationship with the operations of the borrower. As the result those borrowers who had large inventory built- ups were entitled to higher financing than the borrowers who had low inventory and receivables blockages due to better inventory handling and efficient collecting systems.

The Terms of Reference (TOR) of the Group were:

- To suggest guidelines for commercial bank to follow-up and supervise credit from the point of view of ensuring proper end-use of funds.
- To make suggestions for prescribing inventory norms for different industries both in the private and public sectors and indicate the broad criteria for deviating from these norms.
- To make recommendations for obtaining periodical forecasts from borrowers of (a) business/production plans, (b) credit needs
- To suggest criteria regarding satisfactory capital structure and sound financial basis in relation to borrowings.
- To make recommendations as to whether the existing pattern of financing working capital requirements by cash credit/overdraft system etc. requires to be modified. If so, to suggest suitable modifications.
- To make recommendations on any other related matter as the Group may consider germane to the subject of enquiry of any other allied matter which may be specifically referred to it by the Reserve Bank of India.

Observations and Recommendations

The Study Group submitted its report to the RBI in 1975. The main recommendations can be broadly be classified under two heads- recommendations on banks' lending norms and those related to inventory and receivables norms.

Lending norms

The Group identified working capital gap viz., the borrower's requirements of finance to carry current assets (based on norms) other than those financed out of his other current liabilities, could be bridged partly from his owned funds and long term borrowings and partly by bank borrowings. It suggested that the maximum permissible level of bank borrowings could be worked out in three ways:

First method Under the first method, the difference between the acceptable level of current assets and the anticipated quantum of other current liabilities (i.e. other than bank finance, viz. largely comprising sundry creditors) will be calculated, and this will be termed as the "Working Capital Gap" (WCG). And, the Net Working Capital (NWC), [or the margin, or the Owner's Equity (OE)], should be minimum 25% of the working capital gap. Thus, under the first method, the banker will finance maximum up to 75% of the working capital gap.

Second method Under the second method, the Net Working Capital (NWC) should be minimum 25% of the total value of the acceptable level of current assets. The remaining 75% will first have to be financed by the other current liabilities (mainly Sundry Creditors) and the banker may finance the balance amount of the working capital requirements.

Third method The third method is quite similar to the second method, except that the composition of the acceptable current assets is a slightly changed. That, is, under this method, the acceptable current assets would mean the total current assets (as commonly understood by us) less the value of the Core Assets. And, the Core Assets, according to the Tandon Committee, constitute "the absolute minimum level of the raw material, goods in process, finished goods and stores, which are in the pipe line, so to speak, to ensure a continuity of production". The entire Core Assets, however, are to be financed out of the Owner's Equity (OE) only.

The three alternatives may be illustrated by taking the following example of a borrowers' financial position, projected at the end of the next year:

Balance Sheet

Current Liabilities		***Current Assets[4]***	
Creditors for purchase	100	Raw materials	200
Other current liabilities	50	Stocks-in-process	20
	150	Finished goods	90
Bank borrowings, including bills discounted with bankers	200	Receivables including bills discounted with bankers	50
		Other current assets	10
	350		**370**

The first method would mean the banker financing upto a maximum of 75% of the working capital gap of 220[5], i.e., 165 and the borrower providing at least 55 out of his long-term funds, i.e., owned funds plus long-term borrowings. This method will give a minimum current ratio of 1:1.

The second method would mean the borrower financing a minimum of 25% of total current assets (0.25 × 370=92.5) through long-term funds and the gap, i.e., maximum of 127.5 (277.5–150), will be provided by the bank. This will give a current ratio of at least 1.3:1.

The third method would mean a further reduction in bank borrowing and strengthening of the current ratio. This method will provide the largest multiplier of bank finance.

The Maximum Permissible Bank Finance (MPBF) and the current ratios under the three methods are given in Table 21-2.

Table 21-2 Maximum Permissible Levels of Bank Finance

1st Method		***2nd Method***		***3rd Method***	
Total current assets	370	Total Current assets	370	Total current assets	370
Less: Current Liabilities other than bank borrowings	50	Less: 25% of above from long-term sources	92.5	Less: Core current assets from long-term sources[6]	95
			277.5		**275**
Working capital gap	220	Less: current liabilities other than bank borrowings	150	Real current assets Less: 25% of above from long-term sources	275 69
			127.5		**206**
Less: 25% of above from long-term sources	55	Working capital gap	220	Less: current liabilities other than the bank borrowings	150 56
Maximum bank borrowings permissible	165	Maximum bank borrowings permissible	127.5	Working capital gap Maximum bank borrowings permissible	220 56
Excess borrowings	35	Excess borrowings	72.5	Excess borrowings	144
Current ratio	1.17:1	Current ratio	1.33:1	Current ratio	1.79:1

Inventory and receivable norms

The committee suggested that the borrowers be allowed to retain only the reasonable level of current assets, particularly inventory and receivables. The banker should finance only the normal level of inventory based on the production plan, lead time, economic ordering levels and reasonable factor of safety. These levels of inventory and receivables to be financed should be in tune with the practices of borrower's firm and industry.

Besides its observations on the working capital gap and maximum permissible bank finance the Tandon committee also gave the norms for inventory and receivables in different industries. It also recommended for periodic information and reporting system.

The present practice of the commercial banks is to assess the working capital requirements of the corporate borrower based upon:

(a) Projected values of assets and liabilities of the borrowing firm (Projected Balance Sheet method)

(b) Projected cash flows of the borrowing firm (Cash Budget method)

(c) Projected turnover of the borrowing firm (Turnover method).

---

[4] As per suggested norm or past practice, whichever is lower in relation to projected production for the next year.

[5] Working capital gap = CA –CL. Current assets =370 and Current liabilities, except bank loan = 220. Thus WC gap = 220

[6] It is presumed that the amount of permanent current assets (the minimal amount that remains invested in the current assets all through the year) is 95.

Summary

Traditionally, working capital has been defined as the firm's investment in current assets. Working capital and its management determine the solvency position of the business. Gross working capital refers to the total investment in current assets, while Net Working Capital (NWC) is the difference between current assets and current liabilities. As working capital policy touches upon almost every functional area of business, the scope of Working Capital Management (WCM) is very wide.

The total duration taken by a firm to complete one chain of operations that begins with the procurement of inputs and ends with the realization of credit sales is known as operating cycle. Inventory conversion period (ICP), receivables conversion period (RCP) and the payables deferral period (PDP) are the three constituents of the operating cycle. Gross operating cycle (GOC) and net operating cycle (NOC) are the two measures of the operating cycle. NOC is alternatively referred to as cash cycle. Funds get tied up in the operating cycle, and so firms take recourse to techniques such as outsourcing, vendor-managed inventory, reduction in collection float, and technological upgradation to cut down the length of the operating cycle.

Managing working capital entails considering two related problems: of managing the firm's investment in current assets, and of managing the firm's use of short-term or current liabilities. Thus the two key issues in WCM are:

- What should the optimal level of current assets held by the firm be?
- How should these current assets be financed?

Investing in current assets does have a favourable effect on the firm's liquidity, but it also has an unfavourable effect on the firm's rate of return earned on invested funds. Financing of current assets also involves a risk-return tradeoff. Other things remaining the same, the greater the reliance upon short-term debt or current liabilities in financing current assets, the lower will liquidity be. On the other hand, the use of current liabilities offers some very real advantages to the user in that they can be less costly than long-term financing and they provide the firm with a flexible means of financing its fluctuating needs for assets.

Theoretically, the policies of working capital financing can be categorized as: matching; conservative; and aggressive. While the matching approach uses short-term financing sources to finance seasonal financing needs, and long-term sources for permanent requirements, conservative and aggressive approaches rely more on long-term and short-term sources of financing respectively. Depending upon its current assets policy and the current assets financing policy, a firm's working capital policy can be categorized as conservative, aggressive or moderate.

Estimations of working capital requirements are based on past data and future projections. They require estimations of the duration and weights of different components of operating cycle, The amount of working capital requirement depends, *inter alia*, upon the nature of business. Banks follow the norms proposed by the various committees set up by the RBI for the assessment of working capital gap and the determination of maximum permissible bank finance.

Key Terms

Gross and net working capital A valuation metric that is calculated by deducting current liabilities from current assets ia called Net Working Capital. Alternatively, working capital is also defined as total investment in current assets, i.e., Gross Working Capital.

Current Assets (CA) Short-term assets that are available with the firm for a short duration (operating cycle or the maximum of one year) are called Current Assets. They determine the liquidity position of the business. Cash, inventory (including raw material, work-in-process and finished goods), and receivables are prominent examples of current assets.

Current Liabilities (CL) Usually appearing on a company's balance sheet, current laibilities represent the amount owed for interest, accounts payable, short-term loans, expenses incurred but unpaid, and other debts due within one year.

Liquidity Liquidity refers to the ability to generate cash quickly. The liquidity position depends on the level of current assets held. Generally, the higher the level of current assets, the higher is the liquidity position, as these current assets get transformed, in the normal course of business operations, into cash.

Raw materials conversion period (RMCP) It is the total time required to convert raw material into the next stage, i.e., work-in-process. It is also known as Duration of Raw Material (D_{RM}). It is the measure of a firm's efficiency in handling its raw material inventory.

Work-in-process conversion period (WIPCP) WIPCP is the time taken to transform the work-in-process into finished goods. It is the duration for which the semi-finished inventory remains blocked in the assembly line. It is alternatively referred to as duration work in progress (D_{WIP}) and denotes the efficiency of the production process.

Finished goods conversion period (FGCP) Also known as Duration of Finished Goods (D_{FG}), it refers to the shelf life of the finished goods inventory. It denotes the total time taken by the firm to convert its ready-to-sell stock into sales.

Permanent/Core working capital Permanent Working Capital (PWC) represents the working capital requirements of the company even at the lowest level (bottom) of its sales cycle. It constitutes the permanent (core) current assets that must be held by the firm invariably.

Temporary/Fluctuating working capital Temporary Working Capital (TWC) represents that component of working capital which keeps on changing in accordance with seasonal demands, or even some market factors affecting demand. It is alternatively referred to as fluctuating working capital.

Supply chain A network of organizations, people, activities, information, and resources involved in moving a product or service from supplier to customer.

KEY FORMULAE

Duration of raw materials (D_{RM})

$$D_{RM} = \frac{\text{Average Raw Material Inventory}}{\text{Raw Material Consumed/360}}$$

Duration of work-in-process (D_{WIP})

$$D_{WIP} = \frac{\text{Work-in-process inventory}}{\text{Cost of production/360}}$$

Duration of finished goods (D_{FG})

$$D_{FG} = \frac{\text{Finished goods inventory}}{\text{Cost of goods sold/360}}$$

Duration of Accounts Receivable (D_{AR})

$$D_{AR} = \frac{\text{Average Debtors}}{\text{Credit sales/360}}$$

Duration of Accounts Payable (D_{AP})

$$D_{AP} = \frac{\text{Average Creditors}}{\text{Credit Purchases/360}}$$

Weight of raw material (W_{RM})

$$W_{RM} = \frac{\text{Raw Material and Stores cost per unit}}{\text{Selling Price per unit}}$$

Weight of work-in-process (W_{WIP})

$$W_{WIP} = \frac{\text{Raw Material and Store cost per unit} + \text{Processing cost per unit} \times 0.5}{\text{Selling Price per unit}}$$

Weight of finished goods (W_{FG})

$$D_{FG} = \frac{\text{Cost of goods sold per unit}}{\text{Selling Price per unit}}$$

Weight of accounts receivable (W_{AR})

$$W_{AR} = \frac{\text{Cost of Sales per unit}}{\text{Selling Price per unit}}$$

Weight of accounts payable (W_{AP})

$$W_{AP} = \frac{\text{Raw Materials and Stores cost per unit}}{\text{Selling Price per unit}}$$

Weighted Operating Cycle (WOC)

$$= D_{RM} \times W_{RM} + D_{WIP} \times W_{WIP} + D_{FG} \times W_{FG} + D_{AR} \times W_{AR} - D_{AP} \times W_{AP}$$

Working capital requirement

$$= \text{Sales per day} \times \text{WOC} + \text{Cash Balance Required}$$

PRACTICE PROBLEMS

1. Impact of Current Assets on Risk-return

Two firms (X Ltd and Y Ltd) are similar in all respects except for their investment in current assets and the pattern of their financing. The assets and liabilities of the two firms on 31 March stood as shown in the following table.

The profit after tax (PAT) for the two firms stood at ₹25 lakh and 25.528 lakh respectively. The marketable securities fetch a return of 8% for Y Ltd. The tax rate applicable to both the firms is 34%.

Analyse the impact of differential current assets level and their pattern of financing on their profitability-liquidity position. Also, discuss the implications of your analysis for the current assets management.

(₹ *in lakh*)

	X Ltd	*Y Ltd*
Cash	40	40
Marketable securities	—	10
Accounts receivable	20	20
Inventories	45	45
Current assets	105	115
Net fixed assets	150	150
Total	**255**	**265**
Current liabilities	45	45
Long-term debt	42	42
Common equity	168	178
Total	**255**	**265**

Solution

Computation of key measures of liquidity and profitability

	X Ltd	Y Ltd
Net income	25.00	25.53
Current ratio (CA/CL)	2.33	2.56
Net working capital (CA – CL)	60.00	70.00
Return on total assets	9.80%	9.63%

Note that Firm X has a current ratio of 2.33 and earns 9.80% return on its total assets. Firm Y, with its investment in marketable securities, has a current ratio of 2.56, which is higher than the current ratio of X Ltd. Since the marketable securities earn a return of only 8% before taxes (5.28 % after taxes), Firm Y earns only 9.63 % on its total investment.

Thus, investing in current assets, particularly in marketable securities, does have a favourable effect on firm's liquidity. But, it adversely affects its profitability due to low (or zero) yield on such assets. During the year, Firm B held ₹10 lakh in marketable securities, with 8% return or ₹80,000 for the year. After paying taxes at a rate of 34%, the firm earned ₹52,800 as return on this investment.

2. Impact of Current Assets Financing on Risk-return

Two firms (Hit Ltd and Fit Ltd) are similar in all respects except for the pattern of financing their current assets. The assets and liabilities of the two firms stood as follows:

(*₹ In lakh*)

	Hit Ltd	Fit Ltd
Current assets	400	400
Net Fixed assets	800	800
Total	1200	1200
Accounts payable	80	80
Notes payable	—	150
Current liabilities	80	80
Long-term debt	150	—
Common equity	970	970
Total	1200	1200

The earnings before interest and tax (EBIT) for the two firms stood at ₹200 lakhs. In view of the sudden spurt in seasonal demand for their products, both Hit Ltd and Fit Ltd have made additional investments in inventory to the tune of ₹150 lakh. Hit Ltd has financed this investment by raising a long-term debt from market. The debt carries an interest rate of 11.5% p.a. Fit Ltd has financed the seasonal built up in its inventory by notes payable in three months and carrying an interest rate of 7.5% p.a. The tax rate applicable to the two firms is 34%.

Analyse the impact of the differential current asset financing of the two firms on their profitability-liquidity position. Also, discuss the implications of the two financing patterns from the working capital perspective.

Solution

Net Income and ratios

	Hit Ltd.	Fit Ltd.
EBIT (₹ in lakh)	200.00	200.00
Less: Interest expenses (₹ in lakh)	17.25	2.81
Earnings before taxes (₹ in lakh)	182.75	197.19
Less: Taxes (@34%) (₹ in lakh)	62.14	67.04
Profit after tax (PAT) (₹ in lakh)	120.62	130.14
Current ratio (CA/CL)	5.00	1.74
Net working capital (₹ in lakh) (CA – CL)	320.00	170.00
Return on Total Assets (PAT/Total Assets)	10.05%	10.85%

As can be seen from the balance sheets, all the assets and liabilities for the two firms are same other than the notes payable and long-term debt. Both firms had the same seasonal needs for financing a seasonal build up in inventories. Hit Ltd financed its seasonal financing requirements by raising ₹150 lakh in long-term debt that carry an annual interest rate of 11.5%. Fit Ltd, on the other hand, satisfied its seasonal financing needs using short-term borrowing on which it paid interest @ 7.5% p.a.

Since Hit Ltd has financed its seasonal requirements through long-term sources it will have to pay the interest for the entire year (including the off season period for which the funds are not needed). The interest expenses for Hit Ltd. has been 11.5% × ₹150 lakh = ₹17.25 lakh.

Fit Ltd borrowed only for the period it needed the funds (i.e., for three months) and did so at a lower rate of interest (compared to interest on long-term borrowings), its interest expense for the year was only ₹2.81 lakh. Interest expense for Fit Ltd for the year has been computed as:

$$150 \text{ lakh} \times 7.5\% \times \frac{3}{12} = ₹2.81 \text{ lakh}$$

Hit Ltd, using long-term rather than short-term debt, has a current ratio of 5 and net working capital of ₹320 lakh as compared to current ratio of 1.74 and NWC of 170 lakh for Fit Ltd. This is due to the presence of additional current liabilities (i.e., Notes Payable) in the financial structure of Fit Ltd. However, owing to its lower interest on account of short-term financing, the return on total assets for Fit Ltd is 10.85%, which is higher than the 10.05% return for Hit Ltd.

3. Computation of Operating Cycle

Following information has been extracted from the financial statements of a manufacturing firm:

(*Figures in ₹ crore unless stated otherwise*)

Average credit period allowed by suppliers (in days)	60
Average debtors outstanding	6
Raw material consumed	60
Cost of production	145
Cost of goods sold	157.5
Sales	200
Inventory of raw material	5.75
Work-in-progress	6.75
Finished goods	4.80

Compute the operating cycle for the firm assuming that the information given above is for a full one year period.

Solution

The duration (or length) of an operating cycle depends on the duration of its components. To compute the operating cycle, we first need to compute the duration of its various components.

$$\text{(a)}\ D_{RM} = \frac{\text{Average Raw Material Inventory}}{\text{Raw material consumed}} \times 360$$

$$= \frac{5.75}{60} \times 360 = 34.5 \text{ days}$$

$$\text{(b)}\ D_{WIP} = \frac{\text{Average WIP Inventory}}{\text{Cost of Production}} \times 360$$

$$= \frac{6.75}{145} \times 360 = 16.76 \text{ days}$$

$$\text{(c)}\ D_{FG} = \frac{\text{Average finished goods inventoery}}{\text{Cost of goods sold}} \times 360$$

$$= \frac{4.80}{157.5} \times 360 = 10.97 \text{ days}$$

$$\text{(d)}\ D_{AR} = \frac{\text{Average Debtors}}{\text{Credit Sales}} \times 360$$

$$= \frac{6}{200} \times 360 = 108 \text{ days}$$

(It has been assumed that credit period offered to the customers was fully availed and hence the entire sales have been taken as credit sales for D_{AR} computation.)

Gross Operating Cycle (GOC) = $D_{RM} + D_{WIP} + D_{FG} + D_{AR}$
= 34.50 + 16.76 +10.97 + 108.00
= 170.23 days

This implies that it takes approximately 170 days for the raw material to convert into cash eventually. As can be seen, the operating cycle is long in this case mainly due to low turnover of receivables.

Net Operating Cycle (NOC) = GOC – DAP
= 170.23 – 60.00
= 110.23 days ≃ 110 days

The credit period offered by the firm to its customers is higher than the credit period offered by the suppliers to the firm. Hence, the firm needs to finance its working capital needs for 110 days. For the remaining 60 days, it is being financed indirectly by its suppliers. To reduce its dependence on external financing for meeting its working capital requirements, the firm should reduce this gap between the duration of credit offered and the duration of credit availed.

4. Estimation of Working Capital Requirements

Prepare a working capital forecast from the following information:

(a) Production level during the previous year was 10 lakh units. During the current year, the firm is likely to maintain its level of production at the previous year's level.

(b) The expected ratio of costs to selling price for the firm are as follows:

Raw materials	: 40%
Direct wages	: 20%
Overheads	: 20%

(c) The past data of the firm tells that raw material normally remains in stores for a period of 3 months before production. Every unit of production remains in process for 2 months and is assumed to be constituting of 100% of raw materials, wages, and overheads.

(d) Finished goods remain in the warehouse of the firm for 3 months.

(e) Credit allowed by creditors is 4 months from the date of delivery of raw materials and credit given to customers is 3 months from the date of dispatch.

(f) The firm on an average maintains a cash balance of ₹1,50,000. Wages and other expenses are paid by the firm with a lag of 15 days.

(g) The selling price of the firm's products is ₹10 per unit.

(h) The firm also maintains a contingency provision of 10% in addition to the regular cash balance.

Solution

Total sales = 10,00,000 × 10 = 1,00,00,000

Statement of Working Capital Requirement

	(in ₹)	*(in ₹)*
Debtors (100,00,000 × 0.80 × 3/12)	20,00,000	
Finished Goods (100,00,000 × 0.80 × 3/12)	20,00,000	
Work-in-progress (100,00,000 × 0.80 × 2/12)	13,33,333	
Raw Materials (100,00,000 × 0.40 × 3/12)	10,00,000	
Total Current Assets		**63,33,333**
Creditors (100,00,000 × 0.40 × 4/12)	13,33,333	
Wages (100,00,000 × 0.20 × 1/24)	83,333	
Expenses (100,00,000 × 0.20 × 1/24)	83,333	
Total Current Liabilities		**15,00,000**
Net Working Capital (NWC) = CA – CL		**48,33,333**
Add 10% for contingencies		4,83,333
		53,16,667
Cash		1,50,000
Working Capital Requirement		**54,66,667**

EXERCISES

Concept Review Questions

1. Define and contrast the terms working capital and net working capital.
2. What advantage and disadvantage are generally associated with the use of short-term debt? Discuss.
3. Discuss the following concepts and their relevance for working capital management.
   (a) Permanent working capital
   (b) Temporary working capital
   (c) Spontaneous sources of financing
   (d) Current liabilities
4. How do Indian banks arrive at the maximum permissible finance for working capital requirements?

Critical Thinking Questions

1. 'Firms are making efforts to cut down the operating cycle chain because a significant amount of funds gets tied up in it.' Discuss in context of Indian firms.
2. 'Working capital management is all about managing the level and financing of current assets.' Comment.
3. 'The use of current liabilities as opposed to long-term debt subjects the firm to a greater risk of illiquidity.' Examine.

Practical Assignment

1. Study the working capital management of manufacturing firm(s) of choice over the period and compare it with its own performance in the earlier period(s) and vis-à-vis its competitors with respect to the following parameters of working capital performance:
   (a) Its gross and net operating cycles. Has the firm been able to cut down its GOC and NOC? If so, try and find out the reasons for this.
   (b) Its inventory and receivables conversion periods and its payables deferral period. Are the inventory and receivables turnover showing an improving trend? If so, find out the techniques that the company has adopted to achieve this.
   (c) Total funds blocked in the current assets components of the balance sheet. Is it going up in relation to sales? If so, what are the reasons and implications for this?
   (d) The mix of short-term and long-term financing used by the firm. Has this mix undergone a change over the period? If so, is it good or bad for the firm?

Numerical Problems

1. Impact of Current Assets on Risk-return

Two firms (Alpha Ltd and Beta Ltd) are similar in all respects except for their level and mix of current assets. The assets and liabilities of the two firms stood as follows:

(₹ in lakh)

	Alpha Ltd	*Beta Ltd*
Cash	400	400
Marketable Securities	—	100
Accounts receivable	200	200
Inventories	415	415
Current assets	1,015	1,115
Net fixed assets	1,480	1,480
Total	**2,495**	**2,595**
Current liabilities	415	415
Long-term debt	415	415
Common equity	1,665	1,765
Total	**2,495**	**2,595**

The profit after tax for the two firms stood at ₹250.00 lakh and 255.28 lakh respectively.

Marketable securities fetch a return of 8% for Beta Ltd. The tax rate applicable to both the firms is 34%. Analyse the impact of the difference in the level and mix of current assets of the two firms on their profitability liquidity position. Also discuss the implications of your analysis for current assets management.

2. Impact of Current Assets Financing on Risk-return

Two firms (Zeta Ltd and Gamma Ltd) are similar in all respects except for the pattern of their current assets financing. The assets and liabilities of the two firms stood as follows:

	Zeta Ltd (₹ in lakh)	*Gamma Ltd (₹ in lakh)*
Current assets	815	815
Net Fixed assets	1,650	1,650
Total	**2,465**	**2,465**
Accounts payable	175	175
Notes payable	—	375
Current liabilities	175	550
Long-term debt	375	
Common equity	1,915	1,915
Total	**2,465**	**2,465**

The tax rate applicable to the two firms is 34%. Earnings before interest and tax (EBIT) of both the firms stood at ₹408 lakh. In view of the sudden spurt in seasonal demand for their products, both Zeta Ltd and Gamma Ltd have made additional investments in inventory to the tune of ₹375 lakh. Zeta Ltd has financed this investment by raising a long-term debt from the market. The debt carries an interest rate of 12% per annum. Gamma Ltd has financed the seasonal built up in its inventory by notes payable carrying an interest rate of 8% per annum with a maturity period of three months. Analyse the impact of the differential current asset financing policy of the two firms on their profitability–liquidity position. Also discuss the implications of the two financing patterns from the working capital perspective.

3. Computation of Operating Cycle

The following information has been extracted from the financial statements of Makers and Shapers

	As on 31 March 2006 (₹ in lakh)	As on 31 March 2007 (₹ in lakh)
Raw Materials & Stores	560	520
Work-in- process	280	250
Finished goods	250	230
Accounts receivable	456	435
Trade creditors	265	270

The following costs were incurred by the firm during the year 2006-07:

	(₹ in lakh)
Purchase of Raw materials and stores	750
Manufacturing overheads	650
Excise duty	235
Depreciation	126
Selling and Administration overheads	896
Revenue	3400

You are required to compute the operating cycle for Makers and Shapers.

4. Estimation of Working Capital Requirements

Flamingo Enterprise is operating at 50% capacity. The annual output of the firm at the current capacity level is 300,000 units. The increasing market size and demand for its products have made the company's management increase its capacity level to 80% in the financial year 2007-08.

The cost structure for Flamingo Ltd is as follows:

	(₹ per unit)
Materials and Stores	8
Wages	4
Variable overheads	4
Selling price	20

The current assets and current liabilities of Flamingo Ltd stood as follows on 31 March 2007.

	(units)	(₹)
Materials and stores	80,000	640,000
Work in process	40,000	480,000
Finished goods	50,000	800,000
Accounts receivables	—	780,000
Accounts payable	—	400,000
Wages payable	—	320,000
Other expenses payable	—	120,000

The total fixed overheads for the firm at its current capacity level amount to ₹3.5 lakh.

Since the firm has surplus capacity available, increasing the production level in the next financial year will not add much to the fixed overheads. They will go up marginally by 10%. Ascertain the additional working capital requirements for Flamingo Ltd making the following assumptions:

1. The prices of material are likely to remain unchanged in the coming year. Even the wage rate is likely to remain unchanged.
2. Work-in-process is 50% complete as regards wages and variable overheads
3. The time lags in the payments made to/by the firm are likely to remain unchanged in the coming financial year.

CASE STUDY

Maruti Udyog Limited (MUL)-I*

Background

Maruti Udyog Ltd, (MUL) incorporated in 1981, is a private foreign company primarily engaged in the manufacture of passenger cars. It was formed by a joint venture between the Government of India and Suzuki Motor Company of Japan. The Government of India owns about 10% of the company, while Suzuki Motor Corporation and the Indian public own 54.21% and 3% respectively.

MUL's plants are located in Gurgaon and Manesar, and its product range includes ten basic models with over 50 variants; of these, the company manufactures nine models locally and one is imported from Suzuki. The company's models include the Maruti 800, the Omni, the premium small car Zen, the Alto, the Wagon R, the Gypsy, the Esteem, the luxury car Baleno, the MPV Versa, and the luxury SUV Grand Vitara XL7, targeting all segments of customers. Through its subsidiaries, the company also provides allied services, such as sale and purchase of pre-owned cars, lease and fleet management service for corporate clients, insurance, and finance services.

Financials

The financials of the company are given in Tables A, B, and C.

*This case study has been developed based on the information collected from the annual reports, management discussions and analyses and other information available at the company's official website, besides the various secondary sources of information, including reports, news items, etc. Some of the views expressed in the case study may not be in conformity with the official viewpoint. The purpose of the case study is to enable the reader to see the application of the specific concepts discussed in this chapter and not to comment on the performance of the company.

Table A Summarized Profit and Loss Account (₹ crore)

	Mar 2002	Mar 2003	Mar 2004	Mar 2005	Mar 2006	Mar 2007
Income						
Sales	9251.2	9222.1	11157.2	13506.5	15147.4	17494.2
Other income	126.9	156.4	198.9	214.0	250.9	338.7
Change in stocks	141.9	−102.0	3.2	141.7	236.0	−243.1
Non-recurring income	44.6	89.8	133.0	130.6	54.7	84.8
Expenditure						
Raw materials, stores, etc.	5896.8	5665.5	7050.5	8685.2	9431.9	10863.0
Wages and salaries	228.9	213.6	201.1	196.0	228.7	288.4
Energy (power & fuel)	49.4	78.1	95.8	58.1	79.4	133.6
Indirect taxes (excise, etc.)	2014.0	1810.8	1943.8	2413.2	2737.5	2510.1
Advertising and marketing expenses	323.3	403.7	287.2	223.9	249.1	362.3
Distribution expenses	158.8	204.1	118.8	113.3	106.9	137.6
Others	326.3	283.6	371.4	408.9	752.3	804.7
Less: expenses capitalized	—	—	12.8	22.4	6.7	14.3
Non-recurring expenses	39.9	62.6	104.6	50.4	22.0	12.9
Profits/losses						
PBDIT	527.2	644.3	1331.9	1866.2	2087.9	2576.3
Financial charges (incl. lease rent)	66.0	52.7	43.4	36.0	20.4	37.6
PBDT	461.2	591.6	1288.5	1830.2	2067.5	2538.7
Depreciation	342.9	322.1	494.9	456.8	285.4	271.4
PBT	118.3	269.5	793.6	1373.4	1782.1	2267.3
Tax provision	13.8	123.1	251.5	519.8	593.0	705.3
PAT	104.5	146.4	542.1	853.6	1189.1	1562.0
Appropriation of profits						
Dividends	39.7	48.2	48.9	66.0	115.3	151.9
Retained earnings	64.8	98.2	493.2	787.6	1073.8	1410.1

Table B Assets of MUL (₹ crore)

	Mar 2002	Mar 2003	Mar 2004	Mar 2005	Mar 2006	Mar 2007
Gross fixed assets	4457.1	4523.1	4641.6	5095.2	5046.6	6385.7
Land and building	252.1	250.5	269.2	432.2	460.9	608.7
Plant and machinery	4083.5	4214.9	4244.5	4563.1	4431.4	5467.6
Other fixed assets	49.1	48.4	53.0	57.8	62.3	70.5
Capital WIP	72.4	9.3	74.9	42.1	92.0	238.9
Less: cumulative depreciation	1954.6	2258.1	2735.9	3179.4	3259.4	3487.1
Net fixed assets	2502.5	2265.0	1905.7	1915.8	1787.2	2898.6
Investments	96.8	103.2	1677.3	1516.6	2051.2	3409.2
In group/associate cos.	0.1	0.1	85.3	90.6	136.3	153.9
In mutual funds	—	—	1586.8	1436.5	1925.4	3265.7
Other investments	96.7	103.1	5.2	−10.5	−10.5	−10.4
Marketable investment	14.5	14.5	1597.9	1447.6	1936.5	3276.8
In group / associate cos.	0.0	0.0	11.1	11.1	11.1	11.1
Quoted investment	14.5	14.5	11.1	11.1	11.1	11.1
Market value of quoted investment	42.8	50.8	150.9	200.1	289.8	270.4
Deferred tax assets	0.0	231.7	125.5	125.4	121.1	110.1
Inventories	681.1	487.0	439.8	666.6	881.2	713.2
Raw materials and stores	437.0	338.1	249.6	390.5	302.3	375.8
Raw materials	371.5	264.2	228.1	309.9	282.7	348.0
Stores and spares	65.5	73.9	21.5	80.6	19.6	27.8
Finished and semi-finished goods	244.1	148.9	190.2	276.1	578.9	337.4
Finished goods	219.2	128.4	172.4	226.2	554.1	306.5
Semi-finished goods	24.9	20.5	17.8	49.9	24.8	30.9
Receivables	1347.6	1306.4	1338.9	1276.0	1458.1	1709.9
Sundry debtors	839.3	671.1	689.4	599.5	646.1	747.4

(*Contd*)

(*Contd*)

Debtors exceeding six months	71.3	76.7	73.6	45.4	47.4	101.7
Accrued income	17.6	20.0	11.0	19.7	25.9	24.1
Advances/loans to corporate bodies	3.3	43.0	68.2	56.8	174.8	46.5
Group/associate cos.	3.3	43.0	68.2	56.8	174.8	46.5
Other cos.	—	—	—	—	—	—
Deposits with govt./agencies	264.7	409.6	351.7	406.8	446.6	654.6
Advance payment of tax	—	—	—	—	—	—
Other receivables	222.7	162.7	218.6	193.2	164.7	237.3
Cash and bank balance	71.9	989.4	240.2	1029.4	1401.6	1422.8
Cash in hand	43.8	17.4	25.5	61.9	46.2	94.6
Bank balance	28.1	972.0	214.7	967.5	1355.4	1328.2
Intangible / DRE not written off	119.2	88.7	16.3	0.0	0.0	0.0
Total assets	4819.1	5471.4	5743.7	6529.8	7700.4	10263.8

Table C Liabilities of MUL (₹ *crore*)

	Mar 2002	*Mar 2003*	*Mar 2004*	*Mar 2005*	*Mar 2006*	*Mar 2007*
Net worth	2707.3	3098.0	3591.2	4378.8	5452.6	6853.9
Authorized capital	135.0	155.0	155.0	155.0	155.0	372.0
Issued equity capital	132.3	144.5	144.5	144.5	144.5	144.5
Paid-up equity capital	132.3	144.5	144.5	144.5	144.5	144.5
Preference capital	—	—	—	—	—	—
Reserves and surplus	2575.0	2953.5	3446.7	4234.3	5308.1	6709.4
Free reserves	2555.9	2916.8	3394.0	4164.1	5292.3	6699.4
Share premium reserves	37.3	424.1	424.1	424.1	424.1	424.1
Other free reserves	2518.6	2492.7	2969.9	3740.0	4868.2	6275.3
Specific reserves	19.1	36.7	52.7	70.2	15.8	10.0
Borrowings	748.2	641.7	427.2	406.1	166.3	723.6
Bank borrowings (short-term)	448.2	341.7	127.2	106.1	96.3	116.1
Debentures/bonds	300.0	300.0	300.0	300.0	70.0	40.0
Foreign borrowings	—	—	—	—	—	567.3
Borrowings from corporate bodies	—	—	—	—	—	0.2
Secured borrowings	395.1	300.0	311.9	307.6	166.3	156.3
Unsecured borrowings	353.1	341.7	115.3	98.5	—	567.3
Current portion of long term debt	—	—	—	30.0	30.0	40.1
Total foreign currency borrowings	146.4	142.7	—	—	—	—
Deferred tax liabilities	—	438.8	308.8	235.4	199.0	277.6
Current liabilities and provisions	1363.6	1292.9	1416.5	1509.5	1882.5	2408.7
Current liabilities	1065.3	950.2	1096.1	1120.3	1411.2	1918.2
Sundry creditors	477.5	321.1	405.0	463.7	555.1	909.6
Interest accrued/due	43.5	42.6	41.1	20.3	14.7	24.3
Other current liabilities	544.3	586.5	650.0	636.3	841.4	984.3
Provisions	298.3	342.7	320.4	389.2	471.3	490.5
Tax provision	10.2	33.0	56.8	87.6	108.4	115.5
Dividend provision	39.7	42.7	43.3	57.8	101.1	130.0
Dividend tax provision	0.0	5.5	5.6	8.1	14.2	21.9
Other provisions	248.4	261.5	214.7	235.7	247.6	223.1
Total liabilities	4819.1	5471.4	5743.7	6529.8	7700.4	10263.8

Management opinion

The management of MUL is satisfied with the overall financial performance of the company, particularly the efficient management of its working capital. The following achievements have been cited by management in support of the efficient management and control of working capital:

- The operation cycle duration (both GOC and NOC) has been brought down by the firm through efficient handling of its inventory and receivables, and also by optimizing the spontaneous sources of financing
- By adopting the innovative techniques of inventory control and management such as usage of bar codes, delivery instruction

system, vendor managed inventory, and localization of input sourcing, the company has been able to successfully implement JIT inventory management. This has significantly reduced the amount of funds tied up in the inventory. The inventory turnover ratio has gone up over the years while there has been a significant decline in the stock accumulation rate and the ratio of inventory vis-à-vis gross and NWC. This efficient handling of inventory has brought in significant savings in the opportunity cost for the firm without having any adverse impact on the sales.

- Due to its significant brand pull and the 'reliability factor' associated with the Maruti brand, the company has been able to gradually tighten the terms of credit to its suppliers while continuing to enjoy longer periods of credit from its creditors. The debtor turnover ratio has gone up significantly, causing a reduction in the debtor conversion period by almost 50% over the past six years. A combination of tight inventory control and stringent credit policy along with increased duration of the deferrals has brought down the NWC cycle for the firm over the years.

All in all, the liquidity position of the firm has improved over the past five to six years due to the increased efficiency in its operations.

Discuss

Are you convinced with the claim made by the management regarding the working capital performance of MUL? Back your arguments on every claim by the management with suitable facts, figures, and analyses.

CHAPTER

22

Inventory Management

LEARNING OBJECTIVES

After going through this chapter, you should be able to understand:

- the meaning of inventory
- the motives behind holding inventory
- basic issues in inventory management and the underlying principles that guide management of inventory
- how to determine the optimal level of inventory under the conditions of certainty using the EOQ model
- assumptions and limitations of the basic EOQ model
- adjustments to the basic EOQ model to incorporate variations and uncertainty
- what are reorder point and safety stock and how to determine them
- how to decide whether the inventory policy should be altered or not
- techniques for monitoring and controlling inventory

IT'S A TIGHTROPE WALK

Samthar Petrol Filling Station was set up seven years back by Mr Rajat Bansal, an industrialist, on the Delhi–Kolkata Highway (NH-2). For these seven years, this was the only filling station over a stretch of about 50–60 kms on either side of Mathura. The station was set up on a large area of 30,000 sq ft and has four underground storage tanks.

Over the past two years, petrol filling stations have mushroomed because of increasing traffic volumes. The 145-km stretch between Delhi and Mathura today has eight new petrol stations, while the 54-km Mathura–Agra stretch has six. This increase in number of petrol filling stations has not only changed the virtual monopoly that was enjoyed by Samthar, but has also brought down its revenues drastically to a level of concern. On a recent visit to the petrol station, Mr Bansal asked the Manager of his Samthar Project about possible ways to overcome the problem of declining revenues. The following discussion took place between them:

Mr Bansal: Mr Manager! How can we address the problem of declining revenues from our Samthar Project?

Manager: Sir, given the increased competition that we have to cope with, the problem of declining revenues can be handled by better capacity utilization. The unutilized space that we have can be hired out for setting up a small shopping arena that may house a restaurant and some rest rooms for travellers, apart from the shops. All these will be value-added services that we can offer and will attract more customers, besides increasing our revenues. Also, we can increase the utilization of our petrol/diesel storage capacity, as only 55–60% of our total storage capacity is being used now.

Mr Bansal: As far as your proposal for setting up a shopping facility is concerned, I recommend you work out a detailed business model. The proposal seems to be interesting. But why do you think that we need to increase our existing level of stock?

Manager: Sir, the idea here is to economize on the procurement costs. With bigger one-time purchases, we will be able to reduce the frequency of purchase and bring down the fixed component of procurement costs. Besides, it will also enable us to spread the costs of procurement over larger volumes and as a result bring down the procurement costs per unit. Moreover, it will give us a better bargaining power vis-a vis our suppliers that may lead to better economy in terms of better discount, etc.

Mr Bansal: But, what about the cost that we will have to bear on the additional level of inventory that you propose to hold? Additional stock will lead to more blockage of funds, which have opportunity costs. Besides, expenses on insurance will also go up on account of this additional inventory. The decision to raise the inventory level is not that easy, as you have to trade-off the benefits of the additional inventory with the costs that will have to be incurred on holding that additional inventory. It is like a tightrope walk, which needs a lot of balance. I suggest that in addition to the details that I have asked you to work out, kindly also work out the cost benefits of this additional inventory proposal.

INTRODUCTION

Inventory management is about determining and maintaining an optimal level of inventory, i.e., a level that is neither inadequate nor excessive.

Inventory management involves the control of assets being produced/procured to be sold in the normal course of the firm's operations. The general categories of inventory include raw materials inventory, work-in-process (WIP) inventory, and finished goods inventory. The three categories of inventory taken together constitute the biggest component of current assets. The management of inventory assumes significance in the light of the magnitude of funds blocked in them. A comfortable cushion of inventory enables the firm to absorb both supply and demand shocks. However, possessing a high level of inventory for long periods of time is likely to affect the bottom-line adversely due to increased inventory storage, obsolescence, and spoilage costs. Conversely, an inventory level that is too low is not good either, because the business runs the risk of losing out on potential sales and potential market share as well. Thus the thrust of inventory management is to arrive at the optimal level of inventory.

MEANING OF INVENTORY

For a typical manufacturing firm inventory comprises of raw material, work-in-process and finished goods. For a trading business it refers to the finished goods stock held for sale.

Inventory represents value locked up at both ends of the production system. For a typical manufacturing firm, this blockage is in the form of raw material at one end of the production system, WIP (or semi-finished) goods within it, and completely finished goods at the other end. For a trading/merchandising firm such as Big Bazaar, inventory refers to the stock of finished goods for sale, while in the case of a manufacturing business, the definition of inventory includes raw material, WIP (or semi-finished) goods, and finished goods. Thus, the definition of inventory is specific to the nature of business. Although spares and stores are also shown as a part of inventory for financial reporting purpose, they are excluded from the definition of inventory in the chapter because they are procured to facilitate production/operations and not for sale.

MOTIVES FOR HOLDING INVENTORY

There are three specific motives for holding inventory:

Transactionary motive The basic purpose of holding inventory is to carry out production/procurement and/or selling transactions in an uninterrupted manner.

Precautionary motive Since uncertainty and associated risks are inevitable, the business must always plan for them. There might be uncertainty associated with the supply of basic inputs or with the demand for outputs. An adequate raw material inventory level tides over temporary supply side constraints and reduces input availability risks. Similarly, sufficient inventory of WIP and finished goods enables the firm to overcome uncertainties related to the production line and the demand side respectively. This is termed the 'precautionary motive of holding inventory'.

Speculative motive In addition to transactionary and precautionary motives, firms might also be holding inventory in anticipation of gain from expected rises in future prices of raw material or finished goods. This is referred to as 'speculative motive'. For example, if an oil refinery with the objective of gaining from an anticipated hike in international oil prices increases its crude oil reserves, it is said to be doing so with a speculative motive.

PURPOSE OF INVENTORY

Inventory decouples the different stages of the production–distribution function and insulates succeeding stages of operation from the bottlenecks in the preceding stages. It also provides certain economies.

Imperfections in the market cause both demand and supply side uncertainties. If the productive-distributive systems were perfectly integrated backward to the input sources and forward to an efficient market, and the plant operations ran smoothly and flexibly in response to the demand and supply, then perhaps, there would not have been any necessity to hold inventories at the different stages of the production–distribution line of the enterprise.'[1] However, to the extent this is not feasible, there is always the possibility of demand and supply shocks.

[1] Bhattacharya, H., *Working Capital Management: Strategies and Techniques*, Prentice Hall of India, New Delhi, 2002, p. 142.

Inventory becomes a necessity for absorbing such demand and supply shocks that occur on account of market imperfections.

Another rationale for holding inventories is that in a sequential productive-distributive system, they enable the decoupling of the operations of the firm—that is making each function of the business independent of other functions so that delays or shutdowns at some stage in production distribution function no longer affect production and delivery schedules. To better illustrate the decoupling function that inventories perform, we will look at several general types of inventories.

Raw Materials Inventory

Raw material inventory consists of basic materials used as inputs in the firm's production operations. For a steel manufacturing firm, iron ore is the main raw material; for a construction company, cement, iron, bricks, etc., are the basic raw materials. All manufacturing firms maintain a raw materials inventory, regardless of the specific form of the inventory. Its purpose is to decouple the production function from the purchasing function—that is, to make these two functions independent of each other, so that delays in shipment of raw materials do not cause production delays. In the event of a delay in shipment, the firm can meet its need for raw materials by dipping into its existing raw material inventory.

> Holding of raw material inventory decouples production function from purchase function.

Another reason for maintaining raw material inventories is that firms find it economical to buy raw materials in large quantities. This gives the firm flexibility in purchasing. Sometimes, firms maintain large raw material inventories in anticipation of a price increase by suppliers, materials shortage, a labour transporters' strike affecting the supplies, and other similar factors. For manufacturing firms, which have production/manufacturing as a core business activity, the raw material inventory assumes special significance for the reason that it reduces supply side uncertainties. It is thus no wonder that for such firms, raw material constituted 46.75% of the total inventory investments in the year 2005-06 as can be seen in Table 22-1.

Work-in-process Inventory

Work-in-process inventory consists of partially finished goods requiring additional work before they become finished goods. The more complex and lengthy the production process, the larger will be the investment in WIP inventory. The purpose of WIP inventory is to decouple the various operations in the production process so that machine failures and work stoppages at any stage of operation do not affect the subsequent stages. Assume, for example, that there are ten different production operations in a sequential production system, each one involving the piece of work produced in the previous operation. If the machine performing the first production operation breaks down, a firm with no WIP inventory will have to shut down all ten production operations. Yet, if a firm has WIP inventory, the remaining nine operations can be continued with, as the firm holds in its inventory goods that have passed processing at the first stage. Thus, until such time as the first stage operations get restored, production can continue by drawing on inputs from the WIP inventory for the second stage operation, rather than directly from the output of the first operation. Thus the WIP inventory breaks the sequential dependence of operations and related interruptions. Although irrespective of their nature, firms maintain WIP inventories, investment by manufacturing firms in this component of inventory is much higher than that of trading firms. In reality, there is hardly any WIP inventory for trading firms. Again, this difference is due to the nature of their respective operations (Refer to Tables 22-1 and 22-2).

> WIP inventory decouples different operations in production process.

Finished Goods Inventory

The finished goods inventory consists of unsold goods on which production processes have been completed. The purpose of a finished goods inventory is to decouple production and sales functions, so that sales remain unhindered by stoppages/slowdown in the production process. Firms holding such an inventory can absorb temporary bottlenecks in the production process, meet delivery schedules, and service customers' demands despite the lag in the production schedules. For example, there was a strike in the production facility of Hero Motorcycle & Scooter India (IIMSI) in April 2006 that lasted for a month. If HMSI did not carry an inventory of motorcycles and scooters, sales would have virtually ceased during the strike period. Sufficient finished goods inventories carried by dealers ensured that the strike did not have an impact on sales. A finished goods inventory allows a firm, flexibility in its production scheduling.

> Holding of finished goods inventory decouples production and sales fucntions.

Table 22-1 Inventory as a percentage of total assets and current assets for manufacturing Indian firms*

	1999–2000	*2000–01*	*2001–02*	*2002–03*	*2003–04*	*2004–05*	*2005–06*
Sales / Inventory (times)	5.77	6.65	7.00	6.82	7.30	7.15	7.05
Inventory Holding Period (days)	63.24	54.90	52.13	53.51	50.02	51.05	51.75
Inventory / Current Assets (%)	37.25	37.30	35.92	36.38	35.02	34.49	34.82
Inventory / Total Assets (%)	16.04	15.83	14.53	15.57	15.39	16.44	16.83
Raw Materials / Total Inventory (%)	42.12	40.35	41.53	41.17	43.30	46.67	46.75
Work-in-Process / Total Inventory (%)	14.32	14.26	13.82	13.19	13.15	14.64	13.84
Finished Goods / Total Inventory (%)	42.13	43.98	43.34	44.38	42.30	37.85	38.62

Source: Prowess database of Centre for Monitoring of Indian Economy, India
*Based on a sample of 5060 Indian manufacturing firms.

Table 22-2 Inventory as a percentage of total assets and current assets for trading Indian firms*

	1999-2000	*2000-01*	*2001-02*	*2002-03*	*2003-04*	*2004-05*	*2005-06*
Sales/Inventory (times)	4.05	3.24	3.48	14.33	8.61	15.10	18.80
Inventory Holding Period (days)	90.03	112.74	104.93	25.47	42.37	24.17	19.41
Inventory / Current Assets (%)	48.85	55.99	51.41	20.00	25.48	16.26	15.26
Inventory / Total Assets (%)	34.49	41.27	39.28	12.61	20.30	12.51	10.65
Raw Materials / Total Inventory (%)	4.27	2.67	2.96	16.12	6.71	16.24	17.06
Work-in-Process / Total Inventory (%)	0.80	1.03	0.50	4.07	0.71	1.57	2.14
Finished Goods / Total Inventory (%)	92.22	94.98	94.86	75.32	91.59	81.23	79.53

Source: Prowess database of Centre for Monitoring of Indian Economy, India
*Based on the sample of 756 Indian trading firms.

Another reason for maintaining such inventories is that, in general, it is cheaper to produce in large quantities and at a steady rate over time. A refrigerator manufacturer may find that by manufacturing refrigerators throughout the year, profits are increased. The inventory of refrigerators would build up during the winter. As the refrigerators are sold in the spring, summer, and fall, the inventory would be depleted. The economies would come from better utilization of plant capacity and a stable labour force. Although the finished goods component of inventory is maintained by all firms, blockage in this component is maximum for trading firms. Despite the year-on-year reduction in the finished goods inventory of the trading firms over the past several years, it constituted 79.53% of the total inventory for the year 2005-06 (refer Table 22-2). It is due to the nature of their business. Since trading firms have sales as their core business operation, such a high percentage of investment in the finished goods component of inventory enables them not only to delink their delivery schedule from their production schedule, but also to tap any sudden opportunity for sales.

INVENTORY MANAGEMENT

Inventory management involves an interface between all the departments along the productive distributive channel of the firm. Such departments are the direct stakeholders, and have their own interests in inventory management. The purchase department, in order to benefit from the economies of scale, indulges in bulk buying, which may cause an overstocking of raw material. The production department's focus is on output maximization through improved operational efficiency, for which unhindered production is a prerequisite. Therefore, the production department would always want sufficient inventory of WIP so that interruption at some stage in the production line does not affect its output, i.e., finished goods. Similarly, the marketing department, with its objective to maximize sales, would focus on maximizing investment in the finished goods inventory, as it enables the firm to exploit any sudden spurt in demand.

Inventory management involves reconciling the interests of the different departments involved in the production distribution function.

These individual goals of the different departments may lead to sub-optimization of organizational resources. The role of the finance department, therefore, assumes significance. The finance department, not being a direct stakeholder in the purchase-production–distribution process, can decide about the optimal level of inventory investments in a dispassionate manner. It not only reconciles the varied and often conflicting goals of the purchase, production, and marketing departments with regard to inventory investments, it also looks at inventory management from the broader perspective of shareholders' wealth maximization.

Proper inventory management requires a total systemic view that integrates both the suppliers and the customers into the business. It is no wonder that many times the dividing line between inventory management and supply chain management gets blurred. Instead of taking a functional view of inventory and looking at it in isolation, inventory management should be seen as a subset of overall corporate strategy. Inventory management is intricately linked to overall business strategy, and so reflects the prevailing strategy in a firm. For example, if a firm adopts a cost-cutting strategy, its inventory investment also comes down. Similarly, the inventory level normally goes up with expansionary business strategy.

The issue of optimal investment in inventory is decided in the light of incremental gains from inventory investments and the incremental costs of holding inventory

The underlying principles that govern inventory management are discussed in this section.

Efficient operation of purchase-production-distribution function Firms should maintain inventories at levels that are adequate for ensuring uninterrupted operations. Inventory holding decouples the different stages of operations and therefore, the higher the investment in the inventory, the stronger the possibility of the firm being able to absorb supply and demand shocks caused by uncertain market conditions. However, an increased inventory level also slows down inventory turnover, besides increasing the risk of obsolescence, particularly in businesses with a high rate of change in technology.

Inventory management is guided by the principles of efficient business operation and cost minimization.

Cost minimization principle Although high levels of inventory investments facilitate uninterrupted operations, the inventory level must be adequate and not excessive, as the funds tied up in the inventory come at a cost. These funds can be put to alternative uses. Further, to the extent the firm is able to cut down its inventory holding, it would be saving related carrying costs. Firms have become conscious about cost minimization through inventory reduction because every penny saved contributes to shareholder wealth. Firms are discovering innovative techniques such as vendor-based inventory management, improvements in the supply chain, outsourcing, etc., to minimize their inventory holding. These techniques enable them to minimize the costs of holding inventory without affecting their smooth operations.

Actually, the decision-making process with respect to investment in inventory involves a trade-off between risk and return. Although reduced investment in inventory saves money, there is always a risk that if the level of inventory is too low, the various functions of business may not be effectively decoupled and delays in production and customer delivery may result in loss of sales for the firm. As the size of the inventory increases, storage and handling costs in addition to the required return on capital invested in inventory will rise. Therefore, as the firm increases its level of inventory, the risk of running out of inventory is lessened, but cost of holding inventory (which is also referred to as carrying cost) increases. Thus, deciding the optimal level of inventory investment assumes significance, and is the thrust of inventory management. Reorder point and inventory control are the other two points given attention in inventory management. Issues of critical importance in inventory management can be summarized as:

Determining optimal level of inventory and reorder point, and monitoring and control of inventory are the critical issues in inventory management.

- What should be the optimal level of investment in the inventory?
- When should orders be placed for the replenishment of inventory to ensure that the firm does not run out of stock?
- Should the firm change its current inventory policy?
- Monitoring and control of inventory

The chapter takes up these four issues in inventory management in detail.

Importance of Inventory Management

Inventories form a link between production and sale. Maintaining inventory is important for the firm because it allows the firm to service customer needs adequately. Maintaining inventory also requires investment of capital. Excess investment in inventories adversely affects the firm's measures of financial performance and efficiency. For example, excess inventory lowers the return on total assets and inventory turnover ratio. Proper management of inventory is an important managerial task. Since production shutdowns result in increased costs, and since delays in delivery can cause loss of customers, the management and control of inventory is an important duty of the finance manager.

Due to the sheer size of funds blocked in inventory, its management assumes significance.

Inventory represents the second largest investment in the assets of manufacturing companies, next only to plant and machinery. As can be seen in Table 22-1 inventory constituted around 34.82% of the current assets and 16.83% of the total assets held by Indian manufacturing firms in the year 2005-06. For trading firms, the figures stood at 15.26% and 10.65% respectively for the same year (Refer Table 22-2). Given this substantial investment in inventory, the importance of inventory management can hardly be overemphasized. Inventory management also assumes significance from the revenue perspective because the turnover of inventory is one of the primary sources of revenue generation and subsequent earnings for the companies' shareholders and owners. It is for this reason that inventory turnover is taken as a key indicator of operating efficiency. A higher turnover indicates improved efficiency and increased profitability.

Over the past two decades, inventory management has been the major focus of corporations worldwide. Inventories have attracted maximum attention in cost-cutting efforts due to the sheer size of funds that are tied up in them. The *lean-thinking* revolution in technology (both production and information technology) has enabled firms to cut down their inventory holding through speedier conversions and better supply chains. As is evident from Tables 22-1 and 22-2, the inventory holding period for trading firms has come down drastically from 90 days in 1999-2000 to almost 20 days in 2005-06. Even for manufacturing firms, it has been reduced from 63 days to 52 days approximately. Inventory turnover during the stated period has increased from 4 times to almost 19 times for trading firms and from 5.77 to 7.05 times for manufacturing firms. These facts signify the importance that inventory management has assumed in the overall corporate strategy of cost control besides indicating this scope of improving overall productivity through efficient inventory management and control. The emergence of techniques such as outsourcing also points to the increased importance that inventory management has assumed.

DECIDING OPTIMAL LEVEL OF INVENTORY

Proper inventory management requires achievement of a balance between inventory carrying costs and ability to adequately meet demand. Extreme levels of inventory—too high or too low—are not desirable. High levels of inventory enhance the firm's capability to meet demand, but also result in high carrying costs. Too little inventory, although resulting in lower carrying costs, increases the opportunity cost of being out of stock and increases customer dissatisfaction. In this section we define costs associated with carrying inventory and then look at a model for managing inventory.

Optimal level of inventory involves a tradeoff between carrying costs and ordering costs. At this point the total cost is minimum.

Carrying cost It is the cost of maintaining inventory in a company's warehouse. It is alternatively referred to as holding cost and has two parts:

(a) the cost associated with physically carrying inventories, such as warehouse rent, insurance of inventory, and the cost of handling, inspection and supervision of inventory, etc., that is spent on storing inventory. It also includes costs of obsolescence, shrinkage or theft, and cost of physical damage of inventory;

(b) financial cost of funds tied up in the inventory, which is generally the opportunity cost of alternative investments. This cost has a positive correlation with the level of inventory, and hence is assumed to be a variable cost in inventory management. Total carrying costs increase as inventory increases.

Ordering cost Costs that are incurred at the time an order is placed are called ordering cost. These costs are periodic and normally remain constant regardless of the size of the order. They are also referred to as reorder costs or set-up costs. All costs associated with writing and placing an order, such as cost of processing orders, cost of follow up with the vendors, cost of receiving new shipment, cost incurred on handling the accounts payable invoice, etc., are the main constituents of ordering costs. These costs do not vary with the size of the order but with the number of orders. Total order costs decrease as the number of units ordered each time increases. This happens because with more units being ordered each time, the number of orders placed decreases.

Stock-out cost The third type of inventory cost is the cost of being out of stock. Such a cost is borne by firms due to shortage in the finished goods inventory. It is alternately called backorder cost. It includes discrete costs such as lost profit due to loss of present sales, cost of replacing a specific piece of inventory, and certain intangible costs such as loss of goodwill of the firm due to poor customer service, that affects the future revenues and profits of the firm. Such costs vary inversely with the inventory level. The impact of stock-out costs depends upon whether the customer shifts to competitors in the event of non-availability. If so, stock-out costs are high. Firms typically control shortage costs by maintaining an adequate level of 'safety stocks'.

These costs are important in determining the level of inventory. The relationship between stock-out costs and carrying costs of inventory determines whether a firm should over- or under-produce. If the carrying cost of inventory is less than stock-out costs (which is true in most cases), the firm should over-produce and keep an inventory.

Optimal Inventory Dilemma

Consider two firms A and B. Both buy the same raw material and sell a similar finished product. Firm A buys very small quantities of raw material and maintains a small finished goods inventory. Firm B buys very large quantities of raw material and consequently, has a large inventory. Managers for both firms claim that their inventory management system is better. Are they both right? Perhaps, but it is more likely that both are mismanaging inventory. Firm A is successful in keeping inventory carrying costs down, but probably it is paying higher reorder costs. The reverse would be true for Firm B. The total number of orders Firm B places over a specified time period would be small and its total reorder costs would be low because it buys in large quantities. However, its inventory carrying costs would be high. A more reasonable approach would be to balance carrying and ordering costs. Probably the answer lies in determining the appropriate number of units that should be ordered, i.e., the Economic Order Quantity (EOQ). Thus, judging the inventory held by both A and B against the EOQ shall tell which of the two is managing its inventories better.

ECONOMIC ORDER QUANTITY MODEL

As discussed in the previous sections, the basic issue in inventory management is to arrive at the optimal level of inventory, i.e., a level that enables unhindered production–distribution functions without excessively tying funds in inventory. This, therefore involves a tradeoff between profitability and liquidity. The quantity of inventory to be ordered and the timing of order are the underlying issues that need to be resolved to arrive at the optimal level of inventory.

How much to order and when to order are the two basic issues that the theory on inventory addresses.

The two questions that the inventory theory tries to address are:

1. How much should be ordered?
2. When should it be ordered?

The first question, how much, arises due to the presence of ordering costs and other issues which depend on the frequency of ordering. The smaller the order size, the more the frequency of ordering and consequently, the more the ordering costs. The second question, when to order, arises due to supply side uncertainties. Let us take up these two issues one by one.

Economic Order Quantity

Inventory models deal with the question of how much to order by defining an EOQ. The EOQ involves a tradeoff between ordering costs (or setup costs) and carrying costs. A larger order quantity reduces order frequency, and, therefore, total ordering costs, but increases the average inventory level, and, therefore, carrying costs. The optimal order quantity, i.e., the EOQ is given by Equation 22-1

Economic Order Quantity (EOQ) refers to the lot size of inventory that is most economical to procure and hold.

$$\text{EOQ}(Q) = \sqrt{\frac{2 \times D \times O}{C}} \qquad (22\text{-}1)$$

where D is the demand in units, O is the ordering cost per order, and C is the carrying cost per unit per period.

The EOQ(Q) is the point at which both ordering costs and carrying costs are equal. This is the point of tradeoff between carrying and ordering costs, as at this point the total cost of inventory shall be lowest. Hence, this is the most economical quantity that can be ordered by the firm. Combining the carrying and ordering costs shows that total inventory costs decrease up to a point with the increase in inventory. Beyond this point—labeled EOQ in Figure 22-1—total inventory costs increase with increasing inventory. Any inventory in excess of this optimal quantity (EOQ) erodes the profits of the firm.

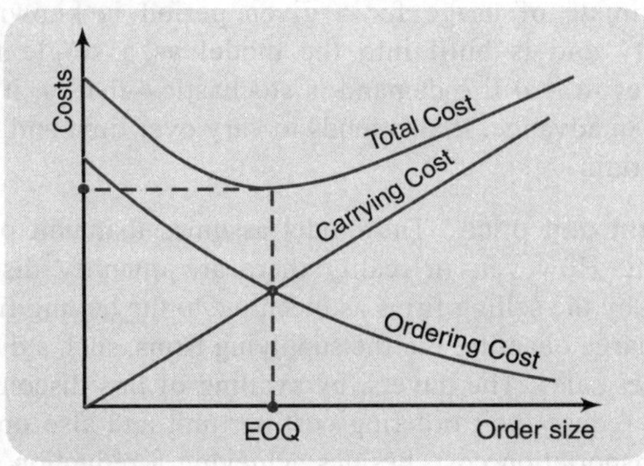

Figure 22-1 Inventory costs and EOQ

Example 22-1 Computation of Optimal Inventory Level Using EOQ Model and Iterative Process

A unit manufacturing plastic containers consumes 1350 units of molded plastic uniformly through the month. The current cost of acquisition is ₹20 per unit and the carrying cost for the firm, 30% on average based on recent data available, is not likely to change in the coming months. The firm has to bear a cost of ₹2400 every time it places an order. Compute the optimal inventory level for the year ahead using EOQ model.

Solution

Annual demand = D = 1350 × 12 = 16,200

$$\text{EOQ } (Q) = \sqrt{\frac{2 \times D \times O}{C}}$$

$$Q = \sqrt{\frac{2 \times 16{,}200 \times 2{,}400}{6}} = 3600 \text{ units}$$

Thus, the firm will be able to minimize its total cost if it places orders for 3,600 units (the EOQ).

The result given by the EOQ model can be cross-checked using the tedious iterative process for determining optimal inventory level.

Iterative process

Quantity per order	*No. of orders*	*Average inventory*	*Ordering costs*	*Carrying cost (Col. 4 × 20 × 0.30)*	*Total cost (Col.4 + Col. 5)*
(1)	*(2)*	*(3)*	*(4)*	*(5)*	*(6)*
16,200	1	8,100	2,400	48,600	51,000
8,100	2	4,050	4,800	24,300	29,100
4,050	4	2,025	9,600	12,150	21,750
3,600	**4.5**	**1,800**	**10,800**	**10,800**	**21,600**
2,025	8	1,012.5	19,200	6,075	25,275
1,620	10	810	24,000	4,860	28,860
810	20	405	48,000	2,430	50,430

It is evident from the table in Example 22-1 that total cost is higher at any order quantity other than 3600. Thus, the result from this circuitous iterative process matches with that achieved using the EOQ model.

Assuming that the usage rate is uniform, the ordering and usage process is shown in Figure 22-2. At time t_0, 3600 units are received and consumed over the period $t_0 - t_1$. At t_1, another 3600 units are ordered, we can see that the average inventory level is 1,800, so that total carrying cost for the year is 1,800 × 20 × 0.30 = ₹10,800. We must place a total of 4.5 orders per year (16,200/3,600), so the total ordering costs also are ₹10,800 per year. The sum of ordering and carrying costs is ₹21,600 per year. With a little arithmetic, we can verify that total costs are higher at any order quantity other than 3600.

The basic EOQ model can be re-arranged to arrive at the following: (a) Nos. of orders described as N, (b) optimal number of supply days per order described as S, and (c) optimal amount per order described as A. These variants of EOQ model given in Equations 22-2 to 22-4 aid in proper inventory planning and management. These are illustrated with the data used in Example 22-1.

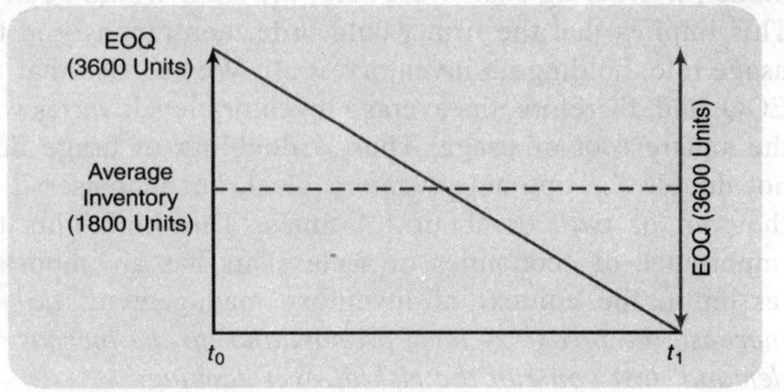

Figure 22-2 The ordering and consumption of optimal inventory

*Optimal number of orders (N)**

$$N = \sqrt{\frac{D \times C}{2 \times O}} \qquad (22\text{-}2)$$

$$= \sqrt{\frac{16{,}200 \times 6}{2 \times 2{,}400}} = 4.5$$

*Optimal number of supply days per order (S)**

$$S = \sqrt{\frac{2 \times (365)^2 \times O}{D \times C}} \qquad (22\text{-}3)$$

$$= \sqrt{\frac{2 \times 1{,}33{,}225 \times 2{,}400}{16200 \times 6}}$$

= 81.11 days**, this denotes the number of days for which EOQ supplies would suffice.

*The derivation of these variants of EOQ model is provided in Appendix A-22 given in the CD.

**If we presume that there are 360 days in a year, instead of 365 days built into the model above, S becomes 80 days. Not only does 360 days seem to be realistic, it also gives a convenient result, normally a whole number. We leave the issue of whether it should be 365 or 360 days to the discretion of the readers. However, we prefer 360 over 365 days, leaving 5 days per year as days off.

Optimum amount per order (A)*

$$A = \sqrt{\frac{2D \times P \times O}{I}} \quad (22\text{-}4)$$

$$= \sqrt{\frac{2 \times 16{,}200 \times 20 \times 2{,}400}{0.30}} = 72{,}000$$

(*P* denotes the purchase price per unit.)

The EOQ formula is widely used in inventory control to determine optimal order quantities. To use the EOQ formula in quantitative applications, the cost of financing must be included as a component of carrying cost, which is often approximated using the interest cost of debt. Arriving at a more realistic estimate of cost of financing requires estimation of the risk-adjusted rate of return.

In addition to its usefulness in quantitative applications, the EOQ model yields several useful qualitative insights from the managerial perspective. As can be inferred from the model, if ordering costs were zero, the EOQ would be zero. This implies that the firm would order continuously at the usage rate, holding no inventory at all. We see also that the EOQ, and, therefore, the average inventory level, varies with the square root of usage. Thus, a doubling of usage does not double the optimal inventory level, but increases it by the root of two, or about 1.4 times. This highlights the importance of economies of scale. This has an important lesson in the context of inventory management: *do not increase the inventory level proportional to the increase in demand, lest you run the risk of overstocking.*

Assumptions of EOQ Model

The major weakness of the EOQ model is its restrictive assumptions. Certain assumptions such as constant demand do not hold well in reality. At the outset, before we proceed further to discuss the assumptions of the model, we strongly advocate the utility of the model, as it tends to yield quite good results, notwithstanding the assumptions and their limitations. The structure of the EOQ model is such that it is highly insensitive to variation or errors in prediction of demand/usage. In a real life situation, even if there are some variations due to uncertain/incorrect estimates, their effect gets blunted to a large extent due to the square root function. In situations where the assumptions of the model do not hold valid, the model can be suitably modified to accommodate the situation[2].

The EOQ model is based on the assumptions of certainty as regards demand, costs, price, and delivery time.

As discussed, the assumptions of the EOQ model are the cause of limited applicability of the model in its original form. Let us now briefly discuss the assumptions of the EOQ model and delve further to find out how they limit its applicability.

Constant or uniform demand The EOQ model assumes that demand is constant and known. Due to this assumption, the estimate of usage for a given period is known with certainty and is built into the model as a single figure. However in real life demand is stochastic—that is, it is not known in advance. It also tends to vary over time and hence, is uncertain.

Constant unit price The model assumes that unit price is constant. However, in reality there are quantity discounts offered by the selling firms as incentive to the buying firms to buy in large quantity. For the supplying firms, such a discount promotes sales. The buyers, by availing of this discount, are able to reduce their ordering cost per unit and also optimize the transportation cost, besides achieving a reduction due to bulk buying in their stock-out costs. The buyer, of course, has to tradeoff these savings with the incremental costs on the funds blocked in the inventory. Due to the quantity discount, there are multiple selling prices for the same item. Hence, in reality the unit price may vary from customer to customer, and there may be no single constant unit price, unlike the assumption in the model.

Constant carrying costs The basic EOQ model assumes that inventory carrying cost is a fixed percentage of the average value of inventory. However, in reality the unit carrying cost may vary substantially as the size of the inventory rises, either decreasing because of economies of scale of storage efficiency, or increasing as storage space runs out and new warehouses have to be rented.

Constant ordering costs As per the model, the cost of every order remains uniformly the same, irrespective of the order size.

Instantaneous delivery The basic EOQ model discussed above assumes that delivery is instantaneous when an order is placed, as there is no time lag between the placing of order and receipt of the supplies. This indicates a zero lead time situation. The model also assumes that there are no stock-out costs, as the lead time is zero and the stock-out cost depends on the lead time.

These assumptions also point out the limitations of the basic EOQ model. An understanding of the assumptions and consequent limitations of the EOQ model provides the finance manager with a strong base for making inventory decisions. The EOQ model presented here, despite the assumptions involved, is a useful managerial device for gaining a perspective on inventory management.

We have discussed the assumptions and the limitations of the model and can now move on to discussing briefly ways to modify the basic model to accommodate certain variations and uncertainties that exist in real life, but have not been accounted for in the basic model. In the process, we shift from the basic EOQ model to the modified one.

The basic EOQ model can be modified to arrive at the modified EOQ model so as to overcome limitations arising from restrictive assumptions and accommodate and incorporate

---

[2]For detailed discussion on how adjustments to EOQ models can be made to accommodate demand and cost variations, refer to Bhattacharya, H., *Working Capital Management: Strategies and Techniques*, Prentice Hall of India, New Delhi, 2002, pp 166-167.

*The derivation of this variant of EOQ model is in the appendix given in the CD.

The restrictive assumptions of EOQ model can be relaxed and model be modified to account for demand, price, cost, and delivery time related uncertainties.

certain real life situations. Example 22-2 illustrates one such modification that can be made to the basic EOQ model.

Modified EOQ Model

The basic EOQ model can be modified and adjusted for the conditions of varying demand and unit price. Adjustment can also be made to incorporate inflation in EOQ computation.

Adjustment for demand variation The EOQ model assumes that demand is constant and known. The inventory pattern under such an assumption of certainty is shown in Figure 22-3. In real life, demand is stochastic—that is, it not known in advance. It also tends to vary over time and hence, is uncertain. An inability to meet such unanticipated demand results in lost sales, which carries an opportunity cost. This first assumption of constant demand in the basic model can be relaxed and the model be suitably adjusted to accommodate the uncertain demand. An intuitive way to handle unanticipated demand is to carry safety stock or inventory over and above the quantity determined by using the basic EOQ model. The EOQ model can be modified to accommodate this stochastic and varying demand through the inclusion of safety stock. It is suggested that in such situations, firms should move from constant inventory pattern (shown in Figure 22-3) to inventory pattern for the varying demand (shown in Figure 22-4). As shown in Figure 22-4, the firm may decide to maintain y units in safety stock to accommodate variations and uncertainties in demand. Its average inventory in such a case would be $y + \frac{Q}{2}$ units. Due to unexpected demand, if the inventory level goes below the EOQ (Q), the firm will have a cushion available in the form of safety stock that can be used to meet the increased demand. The firm will place an order for $y + \frac{Q}{2}$ units of inventory at the reorder point (denoted as a in Figure 22-4), so that by the time it reaches the zero inventory position (denoted by b in the Figure), the inventory gets replenished, given the lead time (L). This provision of safety stock also takes care of situations where actual lead time exceeds projected lead time, as the firm would be having a sufficient cushion in the form of safety stock, and can dip into this safety stock to meet its inventory requirements.

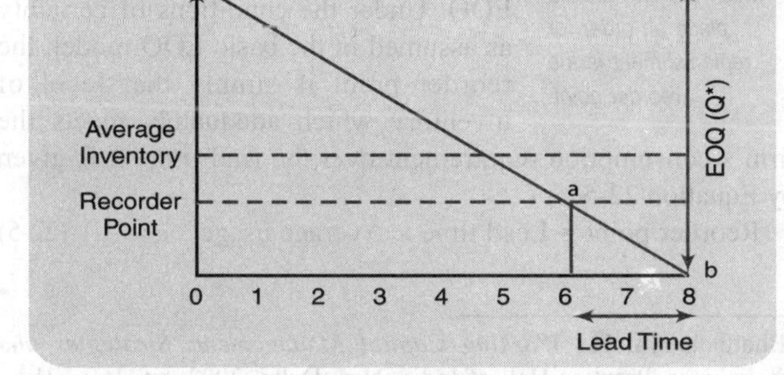

Figure 22-3 Inventory Pattern: Constant demand

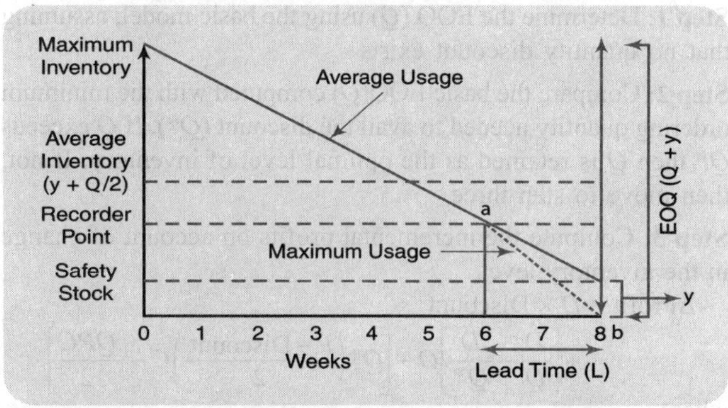

Figure 22-4 Inventory Pattern: Varying demand

How does one determine the optimal level of safety stock to maintain? A balance has to be struck between carrying cost of safety stock and the inventory shortage costs. Safety stock levels are dependent on lead time to delivery, the probability distribution of the demand for the item, and customer service level policies. In general, a rule of thumb that gives approximately correct answers is

$$y = 1.85 \times \sqrt{L \times D}$$

where y = safety stock in units; L = average lead time to delivery as a fraction of the time period; D = demand per time period.

In the earlier example of the unit manufacturing plastic containers, the safety stock, assuming that the average lead time was 2 weeks, would be

$$y = 1.85 \times \sqrt{\frac{2}{52} \times 16200} = 46.179 = 46 \text{ units}$$

There are other complex ways to accommodate the stochastic nature of demand in the EOQ model, dealt with in detail in the course on Production and Operations Management.

Adjustment for variable unit price The second assumption of constant unit price can similarly be relaxed to incorporate the quantity discount that is normally available on bulk buying. Quantity discount varies directly with the order size and hence makes the assumption of constant per unit price redundant. The basic EOQ model can be modified to relax the condition of constant per unit price and incorporate the quantity discount. To avail the benefit of quantity discount, firms are encouraged to do bulk buying. While on the one hand this brings down the ordering costs due to the quantity discount, on the other hand it increases the cost of holding inventory.

The issue before the firm is whether to avail the discount. If the discount is availed, and the minimum order size to avail the discount (hereafter referred to as Q^*) exceeds the EOQ (Q), the firm will have to increase the optimal level of inventory. The inventory held by the firm would normally be settled at a level higher than that determined using the basic EOQ model. The optimal level of inventory in case of quantity discount has to be determined. This can be done by considering the impact of change in inventory level on the firm's profit. A four-step process can be followed to resolve the problem:

Step 1: Determine the EOQ (Q) using the basic model, assuming that no quantity discount exists

Step 2: Compare the basic EOQ(Q) computed with the minimum ordering quantity needed to avail the discount (Q^*). If Q exceeds Q^* then Q is retained as the optimal level of inventory. If not, then move to step three

Step 3: Compute the incremental profits on account of change in the inventory level

$$\Delta \text{Profit} = D \times \text{Discount} + \left[\frac{D}{Q} - \frac{D}{Q^*}\right]O - \left[Q^*\left(\frac{P - \text{Discount}}{2}\right)C - \frac{QPC}{2}\right]$$

where

ΔProfit = change in profit deriving from change in inventory level

D = demand

Q = EOQ

Q^* = minimum ordering quantity needed to avail the discount

O = ordering cost

P = purchase per unit price

C = carrying cost

The first term on the right-hand side of the above model ($D \times$ Discount) denotes the savings on account of quantity discount. The second term $\left[\frac{D}{Q} - \frac{D}{Q^*}\right]O$ is the saving in ordering cost because of reduced frequency of ordering, which in turn is due to bulk buying triggered by the quantity discount. The third term in the model $\left[Q^*\left(\frac{P - \text{Discount}}{2}\right)C - \frac{QPC}{2}\right]$ is the increase in the inventory carrying cost caused by increased inventory holding to avail the quantity discount. With these components the model compares the benefit in terms of quantity discount and ordering costs with the additional carrying cost, the resultant being the incremental profit.

Step 4: If the incremental profit obtained at step 3 is positive Q^* becomes the optimal level of inventory, if not, Q, i.e., EOQ, is retained as the optimal inventory level.

Example 22-2 Incorporating Quantity Discount in the Basic EOQ Model

In Example 22-1, assume that the supplier offers a quantity discount of ₹2 per unit, provided the order size exceeds 5000 units. What will be the optimal level of inventory?

Solution

Step 1: Determining the EOQ (Q) using the basic model, assuming that no quantity discount exists

$$\text{EOQ (Q)} = \sqrt{\frac{2 \times D \times O}{C}}$$

$$(Q) = \sqrt{\frac{2 \times 16200 \times 2400}{6}}$$

$$Q = 3600 \text{ units}$$

Step 2: Compare the basic EOQ (Q) computed at step 1 with the minimum ordering quantity needed to avail the discount (Q*). Since Q* (5000 units) exceeds Q (3600 units) the impact on profit of change in the level of inventory has to be determined

Step 3: Computation of incremental profits caused by change in the inventory level

$$\Delta\text{Profit} = 16{,}200 \times 2 + \left[\frac{16{,}200}{3{,}600} - \frac{16{,}200}{5{,}000}\right]2{,}400 - \left[5{,}000\left(\frac{20-2}{2}\right)0.30 - \frac{3600 \times 20 \times 0.30}{2}\right]$$

$$= ₹3901.26$$

Step 4: Since the incremental profit is positive, Q* (5000 units) is the optimal level of inventory

Adjustment for inflation In this era of universal inflation, a constant price assumption in the EOQ model is unrealistic. Hence, the model needs to be adjusted for inflation that causes the price per unit to increase with time. Such a rise in prices supports increased inventory levels of both raw material and finished goods. The increased level of raw material inventory in times of rising prices brings about savings in the cost of input, while the increased levels of WIP and finished goods inventories bring additional profits in the form of higher prices for the output. To account for inflation, the rate of inflation can be deducted from the annual carrying cost (C-i). The rationale behind such a treatment is that the rise in inventory value in the wake of inflation offsets to a certain extent the carrying cost associated with the increased inventory holding.

Similarly, other limitations caused by the restrictive assumptions can be overcome by making suitable adjustments/ modifications[3] to the basic EOQ model.

DECIDING WHEN TO ORDER

Having discussed the first issue of how much to order, i.e., determining the EOQ, we now move on to the second issue of when to order, i.e., ascertaining the reorder or the order point.

Reorder Point

The reorder point refers to that level of inventory at which the firm should place an order for the replenishment of inventory, to ensure that replenishment takes place before the remaining inventory reaches zero level. It depends on the lead time, average usage, and the EOQ. Under the conditions of certainty as assumed in the basic EOQ model, the reorder point is simply that level of inventory which adequately meets the firm's consumption requirement over the lead time. It is given by Equation 22-5.

The level of inventory at which the firm should place an order for replenishment is the reorder point.

Reorder point = Lead time × Average usage (22-5)

[3]Bhattacharya, H., *Working Capital Management: Strategies and Techniques*, Prentice Hall of India, New Delhi, 2002, pp. 169-171.

Example 22-3 Determining the Reorder Point

Assuming the lead time to be 15 days in Example 22-1, find out the reorder point.

Solution

Let us recall some variables from Example 22-1.

EOQ (Q) = 3600 units

Monthly consumption, D = 1350 units

Optimal number of supply days per order, S = 80

Based on the above information, let us determine the reorder point and understand its relevance in inventory management.

$$\text{Average usage} = \frac{1350}{30} = 45 \text{ units per day}$$

$$\text{Reorder point} = \text{Lead time} \times \text{Average usage}$$

$$= 15 \times 45 = 675 \text{ units}$$

If there is no lead time, i.e., if the delivery is instantaneous, as assumed in the basic EOQ model, the new order will be placed on the 80th day, as soon as the inventory level reaches zero level. But as the lead time is 15 days, the order will be placed on the 65th day (80 – 15).

At this point, the firm is left with the unconsumed portion of EOQ, i.e., 675 units [3600 – (65 days × 45 units per day)] in the inventory as computed earlier. Going by the average rate of consumption of 45 units per day, these 675 units will last for 15 days. Thus on the 80th day, by the time the firm reaches zero inventory level, the replenishments will have taken place.

Safety Stocks

The reorder point has been determined under the assumption of certainty. This model assumes that usage and lead time are certain, and can be predicted accurately. However, it may not be so in reality. In practice, uncertainty is likely to exist with respect to delivery times, production rates, and sales rates. Strikes occur, suppliers fail to deliver, and unexpected surges in demand appear. When delivery is delayed or usage increases unexpectedly, a stock-out is likely to occur. To reduce the likelihood of stock-outs, firms hold safety stocks, additional inventory over and above that prescribed by the EOQ formula. This has been denoted by y in Figure 22-4.

Safety sock is an additional level of inventory intended to enable the firm to continue to meet demand in case sales levels turn out to be higher than predicted and in case there are unexpected delays in either receiving raw materials or in producing goods.

Suppose the plastic containers manufacturing firm as in Example 22-1 to 22-3, actual usage is 50 units per day, and the firm, based on the reorder point model that assumes certainty, orders for replenishment on the 65th day. The firm will then be out of stock from the 72nd day through the 80th day (the date of replenishment). Similarly, if the actual lead time exceeds the projected lead time by 5 days, then from the 80th day till the 85th day, the firm will be out of stock. Thus, if the actual usage increases or the delivery of inventory is delayed, the firm can face the potentially costly problem of stock-out. Safety stock assumes significance in this context of uncertainty.

If we incorporate uncertainty in the reorder point model discussed before, the model becomes more robust. The modified reorder point model becomes:

Reorder point = Lead time × Average usage + Safety stock

Safety stock provides cushion against demand and supply side uncertainties. Determining the optimal level of funds to be blocked in safety stock assumes importance, since the holding of safety stock is imminent. What the level of safety stock should be, is a very pertinent question that needs to be addressed. Finding the optimal level of safety stock involves a tradeoff between stock-out costs and carrying costs. When a stock-out occurs, several kinds of costs may be incurred, including some out-of-pocket and some opportunity costs. A stock-out in raw material may cause production delays or stoppages and higher costs of scheduling and set-up. In continuous–process industries such as paper or synthetic fibres where the relationship between on-time delivery and inventory level is not linear, a production stoppage would cause a loss of sales or, at a minimum, inconvenience to customers.

The cost of stock-out includes lost contribution as well as damage to the firm's reputation. Calculating stock-out costs is a difficult problem, and one that requires a situation specific solution. In each situation, it is necessary to identify out-of-pocket and opportunity costs incurred because of the stock-out.

The optimal size of the safety stock depends on stock-out costs, carrying costs, and the probability that stock-outs will occur. The optimal level thus varies directly with:

1. Stock-out costs either in lost contribution or production inefficiency,
2. Uncertainty of rate of usage and sales.
3. Uncertainty of delivery times.

Although there are complex probabilistic quantitative models for determining safety stock, it can intuitively be determined by projecting the maximum possible usage. If both lead time and usage rate are uncertain in a given situation, then the optimal level of safety stock can be determined as follows:

Safety stock = Maximum possible usage – Normal usage
= (Maximum possible daily usage
× Maximum possible lead time)
Less: (Avg. daily usage × Avg. lead time)

In Example 22-3, based on past data provided by the production department, the company feels that daily usage varies between 20 and 70 units. The purchase department quotes a maximum lead time of 30 days, which was due to a strike by the transport operators. The safety stock can be computed as follows:

Safety stock = (Maximum possible daily usage
× Maximum possible lead time)
Less: (Avg. daily usage × Avg. lead time)
= (70 units × 30 days) – (45 × 15)
= 1425 units

Thus reorder point for the plastic containers manufacturing company on account of usage and supply time variations becomes

Reorder point = 675 + 1425
= 2100 units

The intuitive model for estimating the safety stock is a fast and convenient approach, as it does not take into account the probability of the usage rate being above normal, and also the probability of actual lead time varying from normal lead time. This may cause a conservative estimate of safety stock, leading to overstocking. Probabilistic models can be used instead to get better results.

It is important to note that having safety stock does not eliminate the possibility of a stock-out. The safety stock is intended to give a known probability of a stock-out such that the expected cost of a stock-out (cost times probability) is balanced against the inventory carrying cost. The quantitative models show us the important effect of uncertainty—the greater the uncertainty, the higher the optimal level of inventory.

ANALYSIS OF INVESTMENT IN INVENTORY

Having discussed the issues of optimal investment in inventory and the point of reorder, we now move on to the next issue in inventory management—should additional investments be made in the inventory? Any decision to invest further funds assumes significance because huge funds are tied up in inventory. A decision to increase the level of inventory involves an evaluation of profitability on the additional investment in inventory. To resolve the issue, we adopt the incremental analysis.

The decision to increase the level of inventory depends on its impact on the wealth of the shareholders. Incremental analysis is used to evaluate such decisions.

Inventories represent another important use of a firm's funds and are, therefore, an important concern of the finance manager. At any point in time, a firm has a given investment in inventory. As in the case of accounts receivable, we will view a decision to expand inventories as an investment decision. It is the responsibility of the finance manager to see to it that inventories are set at the level that maximizes the value of the firm. The inventory policy will maximize the value at a point where incremental returns from investment in the inventory equal incremental cost of funds used to finance the investment in inventory.

Such an incremental analysis can be described as a four-step process:

Step 1: Estimation of incremental profit on account of alteration in the level of inventory. It can be estimated as follows:

$$\Delta OP = \Delta Cont - \Delta Cost$$

where ΔOP = change in operating profit caused by alteration in inventory

$\Delta Cont$ = change in contribution caused by alteration in inventory

$\Delta Cost$ = change in cost caused by alteration in inventory

Step 2: Estimation of incremental investment in inventory. Incremental investment in inventory includes incremental working capital also, as more working capital is required to handle the increased level of operations.

$$\Delta Invest = \Delta Inv + \Delta NWC$$

where $\Delta Invest$ = change in the total investment caused by change in the level of inventory

ΔInv = change in inventory investment

ΔNWC = change in working capital investment due to alteration in inventory

Step 3: Estimation of rate of return on the incremental inventory $E(r)$

If the rate of return on incremental investment in inventory exceeds the required rate of return the additional investment adds value to the shareholders.

$$E(r) = \frac{\Delta OP}{\Delta Invest}$$

Step 4: Compare $E(r)$ with required rate of return (r). If $E(r) > r$ then incremental investment in inventory creates value for the shareholders, otherwise it does not.

As with receivables, the marginal return on investment in inventory declines as inventory is increased, and the optimum lies at the point at which marginal return $E(r)$ equals the rate required by suppliers of funds.

To illustrate the calculation of expected return on investment in inventory, consider the case of Asia Motors.

Asia Motors Ltd is a manufacturer of bearings used in two-wheelers. The company follows a policy of mass production. The production schedule is jointly planned by the sales and production departments. Asia Motors' sales totaled ₹7.8 crore in 2005. In the past, inventories had been tightly controlled and were dictated to a large extent by production requirements. Inventory turnover in 2005 was 6.3 times, a figure considered quite good by industry standards. However, Asia Motors management had become increasingly concerned over sales lost due to stock-outs of finished goods inventories. At the end of the year 2005, total inventory value was ₹8,00,000, of which ₹2,00,000 was in finished goods.

Anticipating the problem of stock-outs, management initiated a study to determine whether finished goods inventories should be increased. From historical records of orders received and despatched, management estimated that, at the present inventory level, lost sales due to stock-outs were running at an annual rate of ₹6,25,000. Lost contribution amounted to about ₹2,50,000 because variable costs totalled about 60 per cent of sales.

The magnitude of the lost contribution figure convinced management that further study was necessary. Lost sales were estimated at four alternative levels of finished goods inventories, each of which represented an incremental increase over current levels. The results are listed in Table 22-3. The analysis showed that if the finished goods inventory was increased from the current level of ₹2,00,000 to ₹2,78,000, lost sales would decline from ₹6,25,000 to ₹4,75,000 and an additional contribution of ₹60,000 (last column in the table) would be realized. Similarly, the additional contribution at inventory levels B, C, and D was also determined.

Table 22-3 Asia Motors Ltd: Lost Sales

(₹ in thousand)

Policy	Inventory level[a]	Lost sales	Lost contribution[b]	Incremental contribution
Current	200	625	250	—
A	278	475	190	60
B	414	303	121	69
C	620	153	61	60
D	868	63	25	36

[a]Finished goods inventory only.
[b]variable costs equal 60% of sales.

Carrying costs amounted to 5% of the value of the inventory. This figure excluded financing costs. Incremental operating profit was estimated as shown in Table 22-4. By moving to level A, carrying costs would increase by ₹4,000. Subtracting this figure from the incremental contribution of ₹60,000 gives a pretax increase in operating profit of ₹56,000.

Table 22-4 Asia Motors Ltd: Incremental Operating Profit

(₹ in thousand)

Policy	Inventory level	Carrying cost[a]	Incremental carrying cost	Incremental contribution[b]	Incremental operating profit	
					Before tax	After tax[c]
Current	200	10	—	—	—	—
A	278	14	4	60	56	28
B	414	21	7	69	62	31
C	620	31	10	60	50	25
D	868	43	12	36	24	12

[a] 5% of inventory level.
[b] From Table 22-3.
[c] Taxes at 50%.

From the data in Tables 22-3 and 22-4, expected return on investment was calculated as in Table 22-5.

Table 22-5 Asia Motors Ltd: Expected Return on Investment in Additional Inventory

Policy	Inventory level (in thousands of rupees)	Inventory investment[a] (in thousands of rupees)	Inventory operating profit after tax[b] (in thousands of rupees)	Inventory E(R) on investment after tax (%)
Current	200	—	—	—
A	278	78	28	35.9
B	414	136	31	22.8
C	620	206	25	12.1
D	868	248	12	4.8

[a] out-of-pocket outlay.
[b] from Table 22-4.

To move from the current policy to level A, Asia Motors must invest an additional ₹78,000 in the finished goods inventory.

We have identified the costs that vary and those that remain fixed as sales expand due to recovery of lost sales. The validity of the analysis depends on our ability to correctly identify fixed and variable costs in the range of sales in question.

We see in Table 22-5 that the incremental or marginal return $E(r)$ declines. As finished goods inventories are increased, each successive increment recaptures less lost sales and, therefore, less lost contribution. At levels A and B, $E(r)$ appears to be quite attractive. Policy D, returning only 4.8% after taxes, does not seem attractive. Which policy should Asia Motors adopt? The answer depends on the target or required rate of return on investment in inventories.

An important feature of the analysis above is that it examines the incremental return on successive increments of inventory. To move from the current policy to level D would require a total investment of ₹6,68,000. This investment would generate additional operating profit of ₹9600, an $E(r)$ of 14.4%. However, the $E(r)$ on the last increment, from level C to level D, is only 4.8%. By looking at several increments, we can better determine the point at which marginal $E(r)$ falls below the required rate within increments; the figures in Table 22-5 represent averages. The marginal $E(r)$ on the last rupee of investment in increment B is quite a bit lower than the average $E(r)$ of 22.8% on increment B as a whole.

INVENTORY MONITORING AND CONTROL

In this section of the chapter we take up an issue of immense importance—monitoring and control of inventory. The issue assumes importance due to the fact that funds that are blocked in the production–distribution system incur costs. To the extent that a firm is able to untie the funds that are blocked in inventory, it can divert them to alternate uses and thereby create value for shareholders. It is no wonder that inventory control has emerged as one of the prominent issues in cost management and control.

On the one hand, we have a simple *two-bin system* of inventory control that is suited for small firms. Under this system, the company maintains two bins. Once the inventory contained in the first bin gets exhausted, stock is reordered while the inventory in the second bill becomes available for consumption/sale. On the other hand, we have a comprehensive *material requirement planning* (MRP) system that classifies the items of inventory between independent (end product, e.g., car) and dependent items (subordinate items needed to produce the end product, e.g., metal sheets of given specifications to mould them into the body of car). Such a classification enables firms to focus on proper monitoring and control of dependent items and thus meet the production and delivery schedules of the independent items.

Computerization and networking of all the activities in the production–distribution channel has facilitated the process of regular tracking of inventory. This has helped firms to move

Box 22-1 **Managing retail inventory**

Every product that one purchases at a retail store has a barcode tag. This small tag is of immense utility. At the time of final billing at the cash counters, the information contained in these barcode tags (which includes manufacturing batch number, date of procurement, etc.,) is transferred to computer terminals through scanners. The moment this information is fed into the computer terminal at the payment counter, the inventory of that particular item gets reduced by the number of units of the item sold. This latest status of inventory is available with all the departments in the production–distribution channel, since all terminals are on the network. This information helps the purchase department in placing timely orders for inventory replenishment. It also helps the marketing team in analysing shifts in the patterns of customer demand, if any, in terms of the size, brand, and other parameters of the products, and altering the product mix accordingly.

If the firm is sharing this information selectively with its suppliers, as Wal-Mart does in certain cases, it will also help the suppliers to plan their production and delivery. The most interesting feature of this entire technology is that the flow of information across the supply chain is parallel and not sequential. This saves a lot of time and recurring costs that would be spent on generating and disseminating such an information, besides enabling effective monitoring and control of inventory.

from a periodic to a perpetual inventory management system and has streamlined the process of inventory management and control. Firms are using customized software to track their entire value chain right from the stage of placing of orders with suppliers, to the final sale point. This serves a dual purpose: first, it enables an almost effortless tracking of inventory and second, by generating an itemized ageing schedule, or the turnover of the different items in the inventory, it helps the firm in understanding customer preferences vis-à-vis the different items and brands in the inventory. The second feature is more suited for the retail format of business. Inventory monitoring and control at a typical retail store has been illustrated in Box 22-1.

Although the terms 'monitoring' and 'control' may be used synonymously, there is a thin difference between the two. Monitoring focuses on optimization of available inventory resources through a proper tracking of the entire value chain, whereas the thrust of inventory control is on minimization of the total cost of inventory that includes carrying, ordering, and stock-out costs. A proper monitoring system is a pre-requisite for effective control. Notwithstanding this difference between monitoring and control of inventory, in practice there may be a lot of overlap when it comes to monitoring and control techniques. Due to this lack of a neat distinction, we club them together for further discussion.

Techniques of Inventory Control

Several techniques used in inventory monitoring and control have evolved over the years that are used by firms worldover. Some of the widely used techniques are discussed below.

Ratio analysis

We can monitor inventory by looking at financial ratios in much the same way as we can monitor receivables. We reproduce here for the convenience of readers the inventory-related ratios that have been elaborately discussed in Chapter 2, Historical and Comparative analysis.

$$\text{Inventory Turnover Ratio} = \frac{\text{Cost of Goods Sold (COGS)}}{\text{Average Inventory}}$$

$$\text{Inventory Holding Period} = \frac{\text{Average Inventory}}{\text{COGS}} \times 360^*$$

Raw Material Inventory Turnover Ratio

$$= \frac{\text{Raw Material Consumption}}{\text{Average Raw Material Inventory}}$$

Raw Material Inventory Holding Period

$$= \frac{\text{Average Raw Material Inventory}}{\text{Raw Material Consumption}} \times 360^*$$

Work-in-Process (WIP) Turnover Ratio

$$= \frac{\text{Cost of Production}}{\text{Average WIP Inventory}}$$

WIP Inventory Holding Period

$$= \frac{\text{Average WIP Inventory}}{\text{Cost of Production}} \times 360^*$$

Finished Goods (FG) Turnover Ratio

$$= \frac{\text{Cost of Sales}}{\text{Average FG Inventory}}$$

FG Inventory Holding Period

$$= \frac{\text{Average FG Inventory}}{\text{Cost of Sales}} \times 360^*$$

The Inventory Holding Period (IHP) is the ratio of the rupee value of inventory to the cost of goods sold per day. It suggests the number of days' worth of sales on hand, which is why it is alternately referred to as analysis of ageing of inventory. Combined with the demand projections, this ratio helps in scheduling production and procurements. For example, automobile manufacturers keep a close watch on the holding period of car lots. If it is more than average, they tend to offer rebates and financing incentives. If it is less, they may step up production. Another way to monitor inventory is the inventory turnover ratio (ITR). It expresses the relationship between goods sold to the goods that were in the inventory. The inventory turnover ratio indicates, on average, how many times inventory flows through—from raw materials to goods sold— during the period. If the turnover is above the average, this may suggest a possible stock-out. A lower than usual ITR

Comparison of inventory turnover and holding period with their respective averages facilitate in inventory monitoring and control.

*360 here denotes the days of consumption, production and sales in (a year) in RM holding period, WIP holding period, and FG holding period respectively. It is for computational case that 360 has been used instead of 365. However, the readers can take 365 instead.

may be due to either slowdown in production (resulting in relatively more WIP) or sluggish sales, which may perhaps need a boost through sales incentives or discounted prices. These ratios, however, need to be interpreted carefully. Is a higher turnover good or bad? It could be either. A high turnover may mean that the firm is using its investment in inventory efficiently. But it might mean that the firm is risking a shortage of inventory. Not keeping enough on hand (relative to what is sold) incurs the risk of lost sales and customer goodwill.

ABC Analysis

In cases where the inventory consists of multiple items, the same degree of control may not be desirable for all the items in the inventory. Some items in the inventory may score high in terms of volume, but less in terms of their value, while others may be high value items of lesser volumes. This second category of items assumes importance in monitoring and control of inventory, as it constitutes the bulk of the inventory value.

ABC analysis is a selective approach to inventory control and is used in firms that have multiple items in inventory. Based on Pareto's 80–20 principle, it advocates a greater emphasis on controlling those inventory items that account for the bulk of the usage value. For this purpose, all items in the inventory are classified into one of three categories—A, B, or C. Category A represents the most important items; it generally consists of 15–25% of the volume of inventory and on an average, accounts for around 60–75% of the value of inventory. This category is most important from the viewpoint of inventory control, as value blocked in this category is highest. Category B, representing around 20–30% in both volume and value, is of moderate importance from the inventory control perspective. Category C is the least important for monitoring and control of inventory, as its contribution in value terms is least (10–15% of the inventory), although these items are large in terms of volume (40–60% of the total volume of inventory). Due to such a categorization, the ABC classification is also referred to as the VED (Vital, Essential, and Desirable) classification. V represents category A items that are vital for inventory control, E stands for category B items that are essential, and D, being the same as category C, represents items that are least important for inventory control, and are hence termed desirable.

In ABC analysis, inventory is categorized according to relative importance for the purpose of monitoring and control.

Categorization of items under the three categories can be described as a four-step process.

Step 1: Rank all the items of inventory in descending order, on the basis of their usage value, and number them serially from 1 through *n*.

Step 2: Record the total of annual usage values of all the items and express this as a percentage of the value of total usage. Also find out the cumulative percentage of the total usage

Step 3: Classify the inventory items, looking at the cumulative percentage of the total usage and the percentage of items, into categories A, B, and C

For illustration, consider the following information of Silicon Ltd.

Items No.	Annual usage (units)	Unit price (₹)
1	24,000	2.14
2	15,000	18.00
3	11,000	54.00
4	11,000	52.00
5	12,000	58.00
6	22,000	1.69
7	18,000	13.00
8	16,000	12.00
9	18,000	1.08
10	20,000	1.10

The items in the inventory of Silicon Ltd can be classified using the ABC classification as follows:

Step 1:

Items No.	Units	Unit Price (₹)	Total Usage (₹)	Rank
5	12,000	58.00	696,000	1
3	11,000	54.00	594,000	2
4	11,000	52.00	572,000	3
2	15,000	18.00	270,000	4
7	16,000	13.00	208,000	6
8	18,000	12.00	216,000	5
1	24,000	2.14	51,360	7
6	22,000	1.69	37,180	8
10	20,000	1.08	21,600	9
9	18,000	1.10	19,800	10

Step 2:

Rank	Items No.	Total usage (₹)	Total usage (in percentage)	Cumulative percentage of total usage
1	5	696,000	25.91	25.91
2	3	594,000	22.12	48.03
3	4	572,000	21.30	69.32
4	2	270,000	10.05	79.38
6	7	208,000	7.74	87.12
5	8	216,000	8.04	95.16
7	1	51,360	1.91	97.07
8	6	37,180	1.38	98.46
9	10	21,600	0.80	99.26
10	9	19,800	0.74	100.00
		2,685,940	100.00	

Step 3:

Category	Item Nos.	No. of items	Percentage of total items	Cumulative percentage of annual usage	Net (%)
A	5,3, and 4	3	20.36	69.32	69.32
B	2,7, and 8	3	29.34	95.16	25.84
C	1,6,9, and 10	4	50.3	100.00	4.84

The final classification that emerges from this three-step process is given in Table 22-6 and its graphic description in Figure 22-5.

Table 22-6 ABC classification of inventory

Units	*Percentage of total*	*Category*	*Cumulative percentage*	*Unit Price (₹)*	*Total cost (TC) (₹)*	*Percentage of TC*	*Cumulative TC*
12,000	7.19			58.00	6,96,000	25.91	
11,000	6.59	A	20.36	54.00	5,94,000	22.12	69.32
11,000	6.59			52.00	5,72,000	21.30	95.16
15,000	8.98	B	49.70	18.00	2,70,000	10.05	
18,000	10.78			13.00	2,16,000	8.04	
16,000	9.58			12.00	2,08,000	7.74	
24,000	14.37	C	100.00	2.14	51,360	1.91	100.00
22,000	13.17			1.69	37,180	1.38	
20,000	11.98			1.10	21,600	0.80	
18,000	10.78			1.08	19,800	0.74	
1,67,000	**100.00**				**26,85,940**	**100.00**	

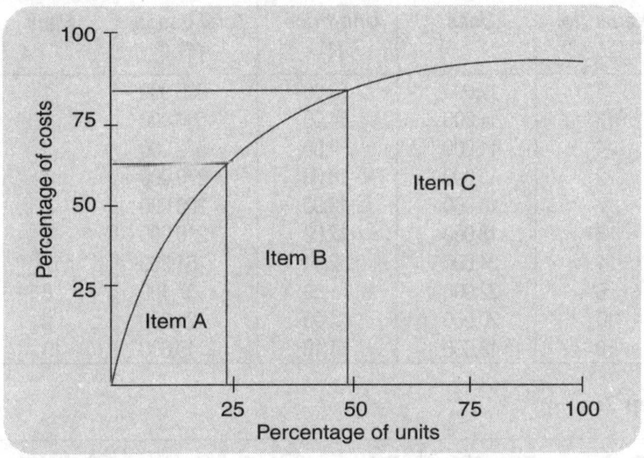

Figure 22-5 ABC classification of inventory

Vendor Managed Inventory (VMI)

VMI is an arrangement between the buyer and the supplier of a product whereby the buyer passes onto supplier selected information regarding the level of inventory in the buyer's stock of the products supplied by the supplier and the supplier takes full responsibility for maintaining an agreed inventory of his supplies in buyer's stock. A third party logistics provider is involved to make sure that the buyer has the required level of inventory by adjusting the demand and supply gaps. For example, the responsibility of monitoring the inventory level of Gillette products in Wal-Mart stores is that of Gillette, not of Wal-Mart. Gillette continuously tracks the inventory position of its products in Wal-Mart stores and replenishes them on time.

> *The responsibility to monitor and replenish the inventory is that of the vendor and not of the buyer in the VMI.*

The concept of shared risk is the most prominent feature of VMI. Often, if the inventory does not sell, the vendor (supplier) will repurchase the product from the buyer (retailer). In other cases, the product may be in the possession of the retailer but is not owned by the retailer until the sale takes place, meaning that the retailer simply has to store the product without blocking his own funds in the inventory. For the assistance provided by the vendor in setting the product, he gets a predetermined commission or profit.

VMI helps foster a closer understanding between the supplier and the manufacturer by using Electronic Data Interchange formats. Use of statistical models for forecasting the level of inventory in the entire supply chain also assume significance in VMI.

VMI benefits the vendors by providing them with the information regarding the inventory position of the retailer, which enables them to provide need-based supplies to the retailer and also to plan their own inventory position accordingly. It helps retailers by reducing the risk of stock-outs, besides cutting down the cost of holding, monitoring, and controlling inventory. And finally, the customer benefits from the knowledge that the store staff has regarding the inventory position and make-up at the vendor's (manufacturer's) end due to close contact with the vendor. The knowledge of product lines offered by different vendors help the customers to choose from the competing products.

Techniques of Inventory Reduction

In some cases, inventory is so bloated that a high proportion of it may become obsolete before it is sold. Worse, too much inventory is a certain indicator of more serious and costly business process and systems problems that can be rooted very deeply across the organization. Firms cutting across sectors have realized the importance of inventory reduction, the benefit it offers in terms of cost minimization, waste reduction and operational efficiency. It is no wonder that there has been a consistent decrease in inventory holding by Indian firms, both manufacturing and non-manufacturing, as is evident from the figures shown in Tables 22-1 and 22-2. Let us discuss some of the prominent techniques of inventory reduction that the firms are taking recourse to.

Just-In-Time (JIT)

It is a Japanese concept of an inventory management that was developed by Taiichi Ohno, a chief engineer at Toyota Motor Company in Japan. The underlying philosophy of JIT is to reduce

The JIT ensures the supply of inventory just at the time they are needed. Thus it does away with the need of holding excess inventory.

the level of inventory to zero so that the firm is able to cut down its carrying cost. Contrary to traditional thinking, JIT considers cost of funds tied up in inventory as a waste, as it does not add any value to the firm. Although a minimal level of inventory is necessary, as the firm may not be able to function without it, the focus of JIT is on shedding the excess inventory: the safety stock that does not contribute to the production process.

In short, the JIT inventory system is all about having 'the right material, at the right time, at the right place, and in the exact amount'. It should not be seen as a mere procedure, it is an organization process that focuses upon total quality management and elimination of waste. Inventory reduction and cost minimization are just two aspects of this philosophy that have much bigger ramifications for the organization and that cut across the entire supply chain. It requires commitment from all the levels in the organization and also from the suppliers.

JIT can be successful only if suppliers are able to adhere to their delivery schedules and ensure that the supplies reach the production facility/selling point just in time. The interlinkage between the various players in the supply chain is expressed in Figure 22-6.

Some Indian firms have adopted JIT successfully and others are in different stages of implementation of JIT. Maruti Udyog Ltd (MUL) and Hero Honda Motors Ltd are some examples of firms that are using JIT successfully. Firms such as MUL have set up ancillary units adjacent to their production units to ensure an assured supply. These ancillary units provide the key inputs that are required in the production process. The company does not carry any surplus inventory in its stock, since the supplying units are located at the doorsteps of MUL and supplies are assured.

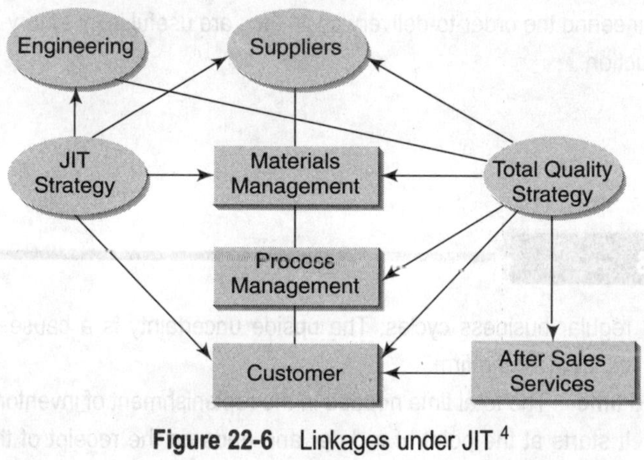

Figure 22-6 Linkages under JIT [4]

[4]Bhattacharya, H., *Working Capital Management: Strategies and Techniques*, Prentice Hall of India, New Delhi, 2002, p. 244.

Outsourcing

Outsourcing has assumed importance since the 1990s. It refers to the delegation of non-core operations from internal production to an external entity specializing in the management of that operation. It has emerged at a rapid scale in view of cost-consciousness of firms. Outsourcing enables firms to cut down their costs as the supplier, due to the benefits of economies of scale, is able to produce and supply at a cost that is lower than the in-house production cost. The time and resources thus saved through outsourcing can be directed at the core business operations. Of course, quality control assumes importance in this regard, and the buyers do ensure a strict quality check. The cost consideration becomes all the more important when the products are being sourced from low-cost destinations, particularly from across the border, as translation costs also get built into the total cost to the buyer. It is no wonder that most manufacturers in developed countries are outsourcing lower end manufacturing facilities to the developing countries. Another benefit of outsourcing is that to the extent the manufacturing process is outsourced the inventory from the buyer's stock gets transferred to the supplier's stock. This not only saves carrying costs, it also increases the buyer's turnover. Unilever India Ltd and Bata are the two prominent examples of outsourcing, as they have gradually shifted from manufacturing in-house to outsourcing the products. This has enabled these firms to move up in the value chain, from production to distribution.

Improving supply chain management

By streamlining the entire supply chain, a company can reduce inventory, improve time to market, compress cycle times, free up more cash, decrease costs and improve profitability.

Firms world over are trying to speed up the order-to-delivery cycle and improve the entire supply chain which helps them to reduce all forms of inventory. Networking between manufacturers, suppliers, and customers is bringing about such an improvement in supply chain. This provides a 'window' on manufacturers operations.

Through this window, suppliers (for example) can find out when the customer will run out of the item they supply and automatically restock it. This streamlining of the supply chain enables manufacturers to reduce inventory buffers, decrease cycle time, and achieve significant cost reductions. Many manufacturers are working closely, like partners, with their suppliers and their customers. This is helping them not only in reducing their inventory levels but also in cost reduction, better demand estimation, and improved delivery schedules.

Re-engineering

To reduce their inventory buffer through better inventory control and reduced lead time firms world over are rejigging their business processes. Such a processes re-engineering is not only helping them to shorten their order-to-delivery cycle but is also raising the standards of their customer services.

Developing flexible manufacturing

When a manufacturer is rigidly set up for long production runs, there is a tendency to maintain higher than necessary production levels even in the face of reduced demand. The 'inflexible' manufacturer maintains high production to absorb overhead. This may make some bad numbers look good, but the costs and inefficiencies are not eliminated; they are buried in inventory. To minimize inventory and improve customer responsiveness, more and more manufacturers today are building flexibility into their operations—flexibility in how they operate in order to quickly respond to changing customer demand.

SUMMARY

Inventories represent the value that is blocked at both the ends of the production system. For a typical manufacturing firm, they consist of raw material, work-in-process, and finished goods. They serve as buffers to decouple the purchasing, production, and sales activities of the firm, so that all do not have to proceed at the same rate and unexpected events are not disruptive. Such buffers are necessary because of transaction costs and uncertainty. As inventories are expanded, some costs rise and others decline. The costs that rise with inventory are termed carrying costs. They include storage costs, servicing costs, and risk of loss in value. Total ordering costs of inventory decline with the increasing level of inventory.

The inventory theory provides a framework for analysing inventory costs. The economic order quantity (EOQ) model deals with the tradeoff between carrying costs and ordering costs. Minimizing the sum of all inventory costs leads to the point of maximum operating profit. As in the case of accounts receivable, the optimal inventory policy must consider not operating profit alone, but also return on investment. The expected return on incremental investment in inventory can be calculated by identifying the various elements of cost associated with different inventory levels, calculating incremental operating profit, and dividing by the required incremental investment.

The EOQ model is a certainty-based model, which is the cause of its limitations. However, the model can be modified and suitably adjusted to incorporate uncertainties of price, cost, demand and supply.

The objective of both credit policy and inventory policy is to maximize the value of the firm. In both cases, the policy that accomplishes this objective lies at the point where marginal expected operating return falls below the return necessary to compensate suppliers of funds.

Management of inventory assumes importance due to the fact that funds that are blocked in the production–distribution system incur costs. To the extent that a firm is able to untie the funds that are blocked in inventory it can create value for shareholders. It is in this context that inventory control has emerged as one of the prominent issues in cost management and control. Techniques like ratio analysis, ABC analysis, and vendor managed inventory are taken recourse to monitoring and controlling the investment in inventory. While techniques like JIT, outsourcing, improved supply chain, improved production scheduling and re-engineering the order-to-delivery cycle etc., are useful in inventory reduction.

KEY TERMS

Supply side uncertainties Uncertainties associated with the availability of inputs (raw material) needed by the firm. This may be on account of shortage of inputs, a sudden hike in the price of the inputs, increase in the supply time, etc.

Demand side uncertainties Uncertainties associated with the demand for the output of the firm. This may be on account of regular business cycles. The upside uncertainty is a cause of concern for the firm.

Lead time The total time needed in the replenishment of inventory. It starts at the point of reorder and ends on the receipt of the supplies.

KEY FORMULAE

Economic order quantity

$$\text{EOQ } (Q) = \sqrt{\frac{2 \times D \times O}{C}}$$

Optimal number of orders $N = \sqrt{\dfrac{D \times C}{2 \times O}}$

Optimal number of supply days per order

$$S = \sqrt{\frac{2 \times (365)^2 \times O}{D \times C}}$$

Optimum amount per order $A = \sqrt{\dfrac{2 \times D \times P \times O}{I}}$

Incremental profits on account of change in the inventory level

$\Delta\text{Profit} = D \times \text{Discount}$

$$+ \left[\frac{D}{Q} - \frac{D}{Q^*}\right] O - \left[Q^* \left(\frac{P - \text{Discount}}{2}\right) C - \frac{Q \times P \times C}{2}\right]$$

Re-order point = Lead time × Average usage + Safety Stock

Safety stock = Maximum possible usage – Normal usage
= (Maximum possible daily usage × Maximum possible lead time)
Less: (Avg. daily usage × Avg. lead time)

Incremental profit on account of alternation in inventory

$\Delta\text{OP} = \Delta\text{Cont.} - \Delta\text{Cost}$

Estimation of incremental investment in inventory

$\Delta\text{Invest} = \Delta\text{Inv.} + \Delta\text{NWC}$

Estimation of rate of return on the incremental inventory

$$E(r) = \frac{\Delta\text{OP}}{\Delta\text{Invest}}$$

Inventory turnover ratio $= \dfrac{\text{Cost of goods sold}}{\text{Average inventory}}$

Inventory holding period $= \dfrac{\text{Average inventory}}{\text{Cost of goods sold}} \times 360^*$

Raw material turnover ratio

$$\frac{\text{Raw material consumption}}{\text{Average raw material inventory}}$$

Raw material holding period

$$\frac{\text{Average raw material inventory}}{\text{Raw material consumption}} \times 360^*$$

WIP turnover ratio $= \dfrac{\text{Cost of production}}{\text{Average WIP inventory}}$

WIP holding period $= \dfrac{\text{Average WIP inventory}}{\text{Cost of production}} \times 360^*$

Finished goods turnover ratio

$$= \frac{\text{Cost of sales}}{\text{Average finished goods inventory}}$$

Finished goods holding period

$$= \frac{\text{Average finished goods inventory}}{\text{Cost of sales}} \times 360^*$$

(*It can also be taken as 365)

PRACTICE PROBLEMS

1. Determining the Economic Order Quantity

A unit manufacturing electronic meters consumes 20,000 units of moulded steel boxes every month. The material is consumed at an uniform rate during the month. The cost of acquiring the inputs is ₹100 per month for the firm and the carrying cost for the firm is 27.5% on an average. The acquisition cost is likely to remain constant in the near future. The cost of placing an order is ₹50,000 per order. Compute the optimal inventory for the year ahead using EOQ model.

Solution

Annual demand $D = 20{,}000 \times 12 = 2{,}40{,}000$
Ordering cost O = ₹50,000
Carrying cost C = ₹27.5 (27.5% of acquisition cost of ₹100)

$$\text{EOQ}(Q) = \sqrt{\frac{2 \times D \times O}{C}}$$

$$= \sqrt{\frac{2 \times 2{,}40{,}000 \times 50{,}000}{27.5}} = 29{,}542 \text{ units}$$

2. Incorporating Quantity Discount in the Basic EOQ Model

Spring Enterprises require 30,000 units of inputs annually to sustain its production at the current level. The carrying cost is ₹32 per unit while the ordering cost is ₹5,000 per order. The cost per unit of input is also ₹32.

Determine the EOQ for Spring Enterprises. What would be the firm's policy of inventory acquisition if the firm's suppliers offer quantity discount as follows:

Order Size (Units)	Discount (%)
1000–3999	0.00
4000–7999	1.00
8000–11999	1.25
12000–15999	2.00
16000 and above	3.00

Solution

Demand D = 30,000 units
Ordering cost O = ₹5,000
Carrying cost C = ₹32

$$\text{EOQ}(Q) = \sqrt{\frac{2 \times D \times O}{C}}$$

$$= \sqrt{\frac{2 \times 30{,}000 \times 5{,}000}{32}} = 3062 \text{ units}$$

Since Q is 3062 units, the number of orders per year

$$= \frac{D}{Q} = 9.80 \text{ (or 10 orders)}$$

Now let us evaluate discount and total cost for different order sizes (Refer Table P22-2).

Thus with quantity discounts in the offing, the firm should place ten orders of 3000 units each as this minimizes the total cost for the firm. As can be seen from the computation above, the total cost keeps on declining consistently as the number of orders increases and becomes minimum at 10 orders. It again starts increasing from this point as the order size is increased.

3. EOQ with Quantity Discount

Alpha Ltd consumes 25,000 units of input per year to maintain its production at the current level. The cost of its input is ₹125 per unit. The cost of placing an order for Alpha Ltd is ₹4,000 per order while the carrying cost of inventory for the firm is 12.5% per annum.

The purchase manager with a view to maximize the inventory of inputs that would reduce the frequency of purchases has been advocating for bulk purchases. The reason being stated by the purchase manager is the discount of 2.5% on bulk purchases that the firm would be able to get from its suppliers in case the firm orders for entire 25,000 units of inputs required at one go.

Are you convinced with the argument of purchase manager?

Solution

To evaluate the proposal, we need to first find out the EOQ. Then total cost of EOQ should be compared with the total cost of bulk purchases to decide which option is better.

Demand D = 25,000 units

Ordering cost O = ₹4,000

Carrying cost C = ₹15.625

$$\text{EOQ}(Q) = \sqrt{\frac{2 \times D \times O}{C}}$$

$$= \sqrt{\frac{2 \times 25{,}000 \times 4{,}000}{15.625}} = 3578 \text{ units}$$

Since Q is 3578 units, the number of orders per year

$$= \frac{D}{Q} = 6.9877 \text{ (or 7 orders)}$$

Comparison of bulk purchases option and EOQ purchases

	Bulk Purchases	***EOQ Purchases***
Order size (in units)	25,000	3,578
No. of orders placed	1	7
Ordering cost (per order) (in ₹)	4,000	4,000
Ordering cost (total) (in ₹)	4,000	28,000
Carrying cost (per unit) (in ₹)	15.625	15.625
Average inventory (Size of order/2)	12,500	1,789
Total carrying cost (₹)	1,95,312	27,953
Discount on bulk purchases	–78125	—
Total cost (in ₹)	1,21,187	55,953

Since the total cost in EOQ purchases is lesser than the total cost of bulk purchases, the argument given by the purchase manager does not hold good. It is better if the firm goes for the purchases of EOQ.

4. ABC Classification of Inventory

Classify the following items using the ABC method of inventory classification.

Item No.	***Annual usage (Units)***	***Unit Price (₹)***
1	1,20,000	120.00
2	1,10,000	100.00
3	1,00,000	90.00
4	1,13,000	32.00
5	1,50,000	22.00
6	1,80,000	10.00
7	2,40,000	5.00
8	2,20,000	4.00
9	1,60,000	2.00
10	2,05,000	1.00

Table P22-2 Discount and total cost for different order sizes

(All figures are in ₹ unless stated otherwise)

No. of orders	***1***	***2***	***3***	***4***	***5***	***6***	***7***	***8***	***9***	***10***	***11***
Size of order (in units)	30000	15000	10000	7500	6000	5000	4286	3750	3333	3000	2727
Average inventory (in units)	15000	7500	5000	3750	3000	2500	2143	1875	1667	1500	1364
Value of order	960000	480000	320000	240000	192000	160000	137143	120000	106667	96000	87273
Carrying cost	480000	240000	160000	120000	96000	80000	68571	60000	53333	48000	43636
Ordering cost	5000	10000	15000	20000	25000	30000	35000	40000	45000	50000	55000
Total cost	485000	250000	175000	140000	121000	110000	103571	100000	98333	98000	98636
Less: Discount	28800	9600	4000	2400	1920	1600	1371	0	0	0	0
Net Cost after discount	456200	240400	171000	137600	119080	108400	102200	100000	98333	**98000**	98636

*Figures in the table have been rounded off.

Solution

Categorization of items under A, B, and C categories is a three step process.

Step 1 Ranking of all the items in the inventory in descending order based on their total cost (or usage value) and raking them serially from 1 to 10

Item No.	Annual usage (Units)	Unit Price (₹)	Total cost (TC) (₹)	Rank	Percentage in total items
8	1,20,000	120	1,44,00,000	1	7.51
10	1,10,000	100	1,10,00,000	2	6.88
3	1,00,000	90	90,00,000	3	6.26
4	1,13,000	32	36,16,000	4	7.07
2	1,50,000	22	33,00,000	5	9.39
6	1,80,000	10	18,00,000	6	11.26
7	2,40,000	5	12,00,000	7	15.02
1	2,20,000	4	8,80,000	8	13.77
9	1,60,000	2	3,20,000	9	10.01
5	2,05,000	1	2,05,000	10	12.83
Total	**15,98,000**		**4,57,21,000**		**100.00**

Step 2 Calculating the percentage contribution of items to the total cost (or usage) and also calculating the cumulative percentage of items (rank-wise)

Rank	Item No.	Total cost (TC) (₹)	Total cost (in percentage)	Cumulative Percentage of TC
1	8	1,44,00,000	31.50	31.50
2	10	1,10,000,00	24.06	55.55
3	3	90,00,000	19.68	75.24
4	4	36,16,000	7.91	83.15
5	2	33,00,000	7.22	90.37
6	6	18,00,000	3.94	94.30
7	7	12,00,000	2.62	96.93
8	1	8,80,000	1.92	98.85
9	9	3,20,000	0.70	99.55
10	5	2,05,000	0.45	100.00
		4,57,21,000.00	**100.00**	

Step 3 Classification of items based on the cumulative percentages and their percentage in total inventory (quantity) into A, B, and C categories

Category	Item Nos.	No. of Items	Percentage of Total Items	Cumulative Percentage of annual usage	Net (%)
A	8,10, and 3	3	20.65	75.24	75.24
B	4,2, and 6	3	27.72	94.30	19.06
C	7,1,9, and 5	4	51.63	100.00	5.70

EXERCISES

Concept Review Questions

1. Why do firms invest in inventory? What are the benefits from the investment in inventory? What are the costs of investing in inventory?
2. Distinguish between the economic order quantity and the just-in-time inventory models of inventory management.
3. What are carrying costs and ordering costs and how are they important in inventory management?
4. What is the reorder point and how is it relevant to inventory management? What is the role of safety stock in the determination of reorder point?

Critical Thinking Questions

1. Where inventory occupies a prominent position in business operations, it will usually play a key role in deciding the success of the venture. Comment.
2. Compare and contrast the motives for holding cash and inventory. What are the similarities and differences in these motives?
3. 'Inventory provides cushion against demand side and supply side uncertainties.' Comment.
4. 'The inventory policy of a firm is intricately linked with the overall corporate strategy.' Discuss.
5. 'Although the proportion of the different components of inventories is industry-specific, its importance is universal.' Elaborate.
6. 'Alteration in the level of inventory is justified only if the expected rate of return on incremental investments in inventory exceeds the cost of funds blocked in them.' Examine.

Practical Assignments

1. Select a manufacturing company of your choice and study the inventory holding pattern of the company, using the inventory turnover ratio (or the inventory holding period). Based on these measures, compare the inventory management trend with other companies in the industry.

   If the inventory turnover of the firm has improved, find out the measures taken by the firm that have facilitated the improvement in the inventory management. Are these measures similar to those adopted by MUL in the case study?
2. Select a manufacturing sector of your choice. Based on the sample of the prominent firms falling in the sector do the value chain mapping of the sector so as to find out whether the sector has moved up the value chain during the past 5–7 years or not.

   (Hint: one of the possible ways could be studying the inventory level and composition over the period and also vis-à-vis the competitors). If there has been upscaling, find out the ways the firm has been able to move downstream.

Numerical Problems

1. Determining the EOQ

A unit manufacturing bangle containers consumes 17,500 units of plastic fibres every month. The material is consumed uniformly throughout the month. Based on the data available, the current per unit cost of acquisition is ₹55 and the carrying cost for the firm is 35% on an average, and the figures are not likely to change in the coming months. The firm has to bear a cost of ₹36,000 every time it places an order. Compute the optimal inventory for the year ahead using the EOQ model.

2. Incorporating quantity discount in the basic EOQ model
Alpha Ltd consumes 30,000 units of raw materials annually at the current level of its production. Raw material is currently priced at ₹65 per unit. The cost of ordering raw materials is ₹2,500 per order and the carrying cost for Alpha Ltd is 25% of the average value of inventory. With the market facing a recessionary condition, the suppliers of Alpha Ltd have liberalized their credit policy and are offering a discount of 3% on the purchases of raw materials provided the purchases exceed 1200 units.

In the light of the above situation, answer the following questions:
(a) The EOQ of Alpha Ltd without the discount
(b) Do you recommend Alpha Ltd to avail the discount offered by their suppliers?
(c) If Alpha Ltd decides to avail the quantity discount, what will be its EOQ?

3. EOQ with quantity discount
Season enterprises require1,20,000 units of a certain item annually. The cost per unit is ₹6. The carrying cost is ₹10 per unit, while the ordering cost is ₹500 per order. Determine the EOQ for Season enterprises.

What would be the firm's policy of inventory acquisition if the firm's suppliers offer quantity discount as follows:

Quantity ordered (units)	***Discount (%)***
4500–5999	3
6000 and above	4

4. Determining the reorder point
Using the figures given in Problem 22-1, find out the reorder point assuming the lead time for the bangle manufacturing unit is 11 days.

5. ABC classification of inventory
Classify the following items using the ABC method of inventory classification:

Item Serial No.	***Annual Usage(units)***	***Price per unit(in ₹)***
1	12,000	0.5
2	2,000	100
3	4,000	80
4	7,000	1.5
5	200	1.2
6	1200	0.8
7	600	50
8	1200	0.4
9	300	0.6
10	70	500

CASE STUDY

Maruti Udyog Limited (MUL)-II*

Inventory Management at MUL

With raw material consumption cost (including the cost of raw material stores and spares) as a percentage of net sales ranging from 75–83%, the management of inventory for the firm has always assumed importance from the viewpoint of operational efficiency, and also the bottom line of the firm. Around 70% of the firm's components are outsourced. Inventory management, therefore, plays a key role in the company's operations. The average inventory turnover ratio of the company has increased from 11.9 in 2005–06 to 13.9 in 2006–07. In the light of the significant importance of inventory, the firm has been paying special attention to its inventory management. The inventory management performance at MUL for six consecutive financial years is given in Table A.

Table A Inventory management performance at MUL

	2001-02	*2002-03*	*2003-04*	*2004-05*	*2005-06*	*2006-07*
Net Sales (₹ crore)	70677.00	71265.00	93456.00	109108.00	120034.00	145922.00
Average Stock of raw materials (₹ crore)	477.00	317.85	246.15	269.00	296.30	315.35
Average Stock of stores and spares (₹ crore)	123.10	69.70	47.70	51.05	50.10	23.70
Average Stock of semi-finished goods (₹ crore)	28.80	22.70	19.15	33.85	37.35	27.85
Average Stock of finished goods (₹ crore)	144.40	173.80	150.40	199.30	390.15	430.30
Average days of raw materials stock	38.52	25.45	16.10	14.04	14.14	12.00
Average days of finished goods stock	7.38	8.76	6.38	7.37	13.34	12.29
Average days of semi-finished goods stock	1.56	1.28	0.85	1.29	1.29	0.85

Source: Prowess database of Centre for Monitoring of Indian Economy, India.

* The case study has been developed based on the information collected from the Annual Reports, management discussions and analyses and other information available at the company's official website, and also various secondary sources of information, including reports, news items, etc. Some of the views expressed in the case study may not be in conformity with the official viewpoint. The purpose of the case study is to enable the reader to understand the application of the specific concepts discussed in this chapter, and not to comment on the performance of the company.

Initiatives in inventory management

MUL's manufacturing is undertaken using the just-in-time (JIT) inventory management. The application of JIT has been facilitated by the following initiatives taken by the company in the recent past.

Use of Bar Codes

The company's production in Gurgaon introduced barcode technology, which has reduced their inventory cost. The barcode is used at various levels for automatic data identification purposes. All documents such as purchase orders, delivery chalans, etc., are barcoded at the time of delivery by various vendors. These barcodes are scanned at various levels, such as the main security gate, and even at internal departments for data entry applications. This reduces processing time and increases the accuracy of data entry and speed of operation. Besides, it also saves investment in raw material by doing away with the need for raw material storage, as trucks from different vendors go straight into the production centre, and the raw material is used at the time of requirement.

Delivery Instruction System

The company has streamlined the sourcing and stocking of materials and components through its 'delivery instruction system'. Web initiatives helped Maruti to bring down procurement time and costs. The implementation of the 'Delivery Instruction System', one of the best practices Maruti had picked up from Suzuki, was aimed at streamlining the scheduling and handling of materials and components. Every 15 days, this system provided vendors with details of Maruti's component requirements, including the product specifications, across the different variants of the various models. Maruti connected to its vendors through an Internet-based information network, which maintained online information regarding order status and delivery instructions. The system has helped in reducing both inventory levels and lead times required for the supply of various components and sub-assemblies, and enabled vendors to plan and dispatch their products more efficiently. Extensive e-buying in consumables and services cut procurement costs.

Kanban Production System

e-Nagare, an electronic communication system, is used to implement the 'Kanban Production System', an important concept of JIT that helps to facilitate the pull production concept. This system is implemented at the suppliers' end as well. By logging on the system, the suppliers get to know the amount of different parts to be supplied and the due dates. Then, depending on the lead time, they start to manufacture the product. Changes to the requirements are made as fresh forecasted data is available. Forecasting is done 15 days in advance for domestic suppliers. For international suppliers, where the lead time is of the order of two to three months, forecasting is done five months in advance. Thereafter, a rolling plan is followed, where the requirements in the database are updated, according to the vehicles actually manufactured, to plan for vehicles to be manufactured.

The e-Nagare system is linked to the material requirement planning (MRP) module implemented in the company. The module uses master production schedule (MPS), bill of material (BOM), and item master file. The MPS specifies what items to produce, when to produce them, and in what quantities to produce them. Bill of material specifies all the parts, and their quantities, that are used to manufacture a product. Item master file specifies the inventory of different items on hand. Earlier, the material was first transferred to the stores and then issued by the materials manager to the assembly line. Using this issuance system, the inventory records were maintained. But now, using the MRP module, the inventory is maintained by subtracting from the inventory on hand the amount of material used. The amount of material used is calculated by multiplying the number of cars made with the material required to make one car (using BOM).

Vendor Management

Since its inception, Maruti has helped establish an organized automobile component industry in India through its vendor development program. Maruti reduced the number of vendors from 370 in 2000 to 299 in 2003 and has plans to reduce the number further to 100. Seventy per cent of MUL's suppliers are situated within a 100 km radius. They account for more than 80% of MUL's raw material requirement. This has enabled vendors to eliminate packaging—and thereby save on costs of packaging—and to supply components directly to the assembly line. The company has also been benefited from its location in one of the prominent automobile clusters of the country—the NCR. Most of the suppliers have set up their manufacturing units either in Gurgaon or in the adjoining areas of Manesar, Sonepat, and Dharuhera. This has enabled MUL to cut down its raw material inventory significantly. Some of the prominent suppliers of the company that have set up their manufacturing facilities close to the MUL premises are: Bharat Seats Ltd, Jai Bharat Maruti Udyog Ltd, Caparo Maruti Ltd, Suzuki Metal India Ltd, Krishna Maruti Ltd, Lica Auto Industries, Minda Group, Lifelong, etc.

Instead of assembling components from many small suppliers, Maruti started buying from big, tier-I suppliers, who assembled supplies from others. This resulted in better coordination, smaller inventories, and consequently, lower costs. That makes for operational efficiencies and also gives the vendors better economies of scale. 'By lowering the time and cost involved in dealing with more vendors, it has increased its supply chain efficiencies. While measures such as commonalized procurement and other manufacturing synergies have paid off with MUL's tier-I suppliers, the model will now be replicated with the tier-2 vendors. Most of its vendors have developed flexible manufacturing systems, which enable them to align their production to Maruti's changing requirements. Going forward, we plan to have technically and financially capable set of vendors who can match up to MUL's standards,' says a Maruti executive. Maruti executives say they have streamlined the system to an extraordinary extent through a combination of controlling workshop costs, lean management systems, and improved delivery schedules. For instance, the man-hours spent per car have been reduced by nearly 54% in the last three years.

A large number of its vendors depend on Maruti's purchases for a substantial majority of their turnover. The company has a policy of having two sources for one component. This ensures the timely availability of supplies to MUL and economies of scale to the vendors. To facilitate just-in-time production, Maruti encouraged vendors who were located in far-away places to build a warehouse near Gurgaon, where its manufacturing facility was located. Maruti promised to compensate them for expenses incurred in maintaining the warehouses. The role of the vendors has gradually evolved from tactical to strategic, where the vendors work in close coordination with Maruti to meet its long-term goals in terms of component development, quality, delivery, and cost control. The company maintains long-term relationships with the suppliers. When the company plans to launch a new model, and some parts are required which are not available in India, it tries to develop the product with existing suppliers by getting into R&D with them. If this is not possible, it looks for other suppliers who have the capability to develop the new product.

In line with Japanese tradition, Maruti supported its vendors in various ways. It helped them in setting up plants, automating the process, and finally, in value engineering. Maruti sometimes reduced the cost of capital for its vendors by taking advantage of its superior credit rating and borrowing on their behalf. It also started working with some of its major vendors to implement the Maruti Production System (on the lines of the Suzuki Production System) that focused on eliminating wasteful activities in the manufacturing process. The company set cost reduction targets for vendors and promised to share the benefits with the vendors.

Reduction of Vendor Costs

Maruti has begun working with some of its major vendors to implement the MPS, which focuses on the elimination of wasteful activities in their manufacturing processes. This helps reduce their costs of production, and also reduces the costs of components. In addition, it plans to begin to integrate its vendors into the worldwide purchase system or WWP, whereby a vendor may become the sole supplier for a Suzuki product in several countries including India. This would generate economies of scale for the vendor, and also result in reduction of Maruti's costs. Through value analysis, or VA, it aims to minimize the cost of manufacturing a component without changing its functional utility. Through value engineering, or VE, it aims to minimize costs at the stage of design of the component, before commencement of production. It has the support of 250 engineers trained in VA and VE to help it conceive and implement its VA/VE activities.

Finding the capacity utilization of the trucks entering its factory at 60 per cent levels, the company introduced the 'milk run system'. Under this system, MUL decided to pool material from different vendors, so that a truck's carrying capacity is fully utilized.

Localization

MUL strives to increase the proportion of locally sourced components and raw materials in its products, a concept known as *localization*. It has increased the levels of localization in its existing models and new models over time by working closely with its vendors in India to develop their capacity to manufacture and supply components that match its quality and technical requirements at costs lower than the cost of imported components. The minimum localization maintained is 70% and the maximum is 96%. It is MUL's strategy to introduce new models with a minimum of 75% localization level, and increase the same to at least 90% within three years of introduction of the model.

The principal raw materials for the company are steel, non-ferrous metals, rubber, and engineering plastics. In order to mitigate the price-related risk caused by exchange rate volatility, and also to bring down the cost of inputs, MUL has gradually reduced its dependence on imported steel. About 2–3 years back, the proportion of domestic to imported steel was 20:80. As of date, this proportion has become 50:50. This proportion is expected to increase in the future in favour of domestic steel. (Refer Table B)

This is required to achieve high levels of localization that help to keep the cost of the vehicle down. The company has been streamlining its supplier base. In the last 1.5 years, the company has reduced the number of suppliers from 400 to 214.

Table B Sourcing of Raw Materials (Indigenous vs Imported)

(*₹ crore*)

	Mar 2003	Mar 2004	Mar 2005	Mar 2006	Mar 2007
Raw materials consumed	5267.7	6634.9	8141.9	8877.9	10137.4
Indigenous	3895.7	5281.1	6538.4	7211.9	8857.1
Imported	1372.0	1353.8	1603.5	1666.0	1280.3
Stores and spares consumed	14.5	16.5	15	16.7	36.6
Indigenous	9.4	9.7	10.4	10.9	23.3
Imported	5.1	6.8	4.7	5.8	13.3

Discuss

1. Are you satisfied with the claim of the management regarding the improvement in the management of inventory by MUL? If so, on what basis
2. What steps has MUL taken in the recent past to improve its inventory management?
3. What techniques has the company taken recourse to in order to cut down its ordering costs and carrying costs?
4. How has MUL successfully implemented the JIT?

In the CD

Appendix A-22 Derivation of EOQ Model

CHAPTER

23 Receivables Management

LEARNING OBJECTIVES

After going through this chapter, you should be able to understand:

- the significance of accounts receivable management in the overall financial management of firms
- credit policy and its constituents—credit terms, credit standards, and collection efforts
- the impact of change in the components of credit policy on the other financial variables and consequently on the firm's overall financial performance
- the practical techniques which firms can take recourse to strike optimal credit terms and ensure that sales are made to creditworthy customers
- the procedures that firms follow to expedite collection on receivables

CHANGE ONLY FOR THE BETTER

Pure Sure is a brand of mineral water packaged and distributed by Neer Udyog. The product is sold in containers of three different sizes (1 litre, 5 litres, and 20 litres). Neer Udyog had been enjoying a virtual monopoly in the packaged drinking water industry till about five or six years back. The market share of the firm in this segment till three years back was 35–37%.

Over the years, competition in the segment has intensified, as shown by the emergence of one Indian brand that overtook Neer Udyog as the market leader five years back, achieving a market share of 52–55%. The remaining market share in this segment was fragmented among small, unorganized players who had little or no brand appeal, and who were targeting the local populace only. Neer Udyog has been selling its product by offering a credit period of 1 month to its distributors.

Over the past two years, the packaged water segment has witnessed increased competition due to the entry of some big international aerated drink brands. A year back, Neer Udyog reviewed its pricing strategy and decided to re-segment its product after a downward revision of the selling prices (by ₹2, ₹3, and ₹5 for its 1 litre, 5 litre, and 20 litre containers respectively). In order to take a step further to overcome competition, the firm is considering changing its terms of sales by changing its credit period from one month to two months and introducing a cash discount of 1%.

The Vice President (Marketing) and Vice President (Finance) of Neer Udyog hold contradictory positions on the issue. The marketing department, focused on expanding sales volumes, is pushing hard for the alteration in the firm's credit policy, as it feels that such a change will boost its volumes by giving it an edge over its competitors. The firm, according to the marketing department, will be able to lever its brand value with such an alteration in its credit policy. The finance department, with its focus on value creation, is interested in the costs and benefits of the change in the credit policy. The VP (Finance), knowing fully well what implications a change in the credit policy may have on the overall financial health of the firm, has asked his team to work out the increase in sales (both in volume and value terms) that is expected as a result of the change in credit policy.

On account of the credit policy changes and the opportunity cost of the additional funds that would get tied up in the receivables due to the liberalization of credit policy, the VP (Finance) also wanted to know:

- The extent of increase in the inventory on account of the increased level of production and supplies.
- The extent of increment in receivables.
- The financial implications of the cash discount, increase on the bad-debts portfolio and the collection costs that will have to be incurred because of the proposed change in the firm's credit policy.

The VP (Finance) is aware that it is the cost–benefit analyses of the present and the proposed policy that will enable the firm to take a decision on whether the existing credit policy needs to be liberalized. Any move to change the credit policy would be acceptable only if it creates more value for the shareholders than the existing policy.

INTRODUCTION

In the previous two chapters we developed a general overview of working capital management and took an in-depth look at the management of inventory. The current chapter focuses upon the management of another significant component of working capital: accounts receivable. The management of accounts receivable assumes significance due to the amount of funds blocked in them. It is due to their size that the receivables affect both the top line and the bottom line. Since accounts receivable—or simply receivables—are a function of the firm's credit policy, the terms 'accounts receivable management' and 'credit policy management' shall be used interchangeably in the chapter and elsewhere in the book. As will be seen later in the chapter, loosening of the credit policy or the receivables policy normally boosts sales and hence, pushes the top line upwards. However, this additional volume of credit sales generally comes along with increased collection costs and bad-debt losses.

The major issue for the firm therefore is whether an alteration in its receivables (credit) policy is beneficial. The relationships between the credit policy variables and their impact on the wealth of the shareholders in case of any policy change are issues of prominence in receivables/credit management. Another related issue is the management of collections.

MEANING AND IMPORTANCE OF ACCOUNTS RECEIVABLE

The total monetary value of unpaid customer invoices is termed *accounts receivable*. They represent the accounts (customers) to whom value has been transferred in the form of sale of goods or services, and who are yet to pay for such value transfers. Since a corresponding value transfer is a legal obligation for the customer (purchaser), it is shown as a current liability in the books of the purchaser and as a current asset in the books of the seller. These receivables normally come in the form of operating lines of credit and are usually due within a relatively short period of time, ranging from a few days to a year. Most companies extend this indirect credit facility by selling on credit basis (of course, with attached conditions known as credit terms, to be discussed later in the chapter) to their regular customers to save them from the inconvenience of arranging funds to make a cash down payment for each transaction. For regular customers, it is like a revolving credit facility.

Accounts receivable or simply receivables represent the value of unpaid customers' invoices. Their management and control assume importance as they constitute a sizeable portion of a firm's assets.

Management and control of accounts receivable assume significance for the reason that they account for a large portion of the firm's assets. As can be seen in the figures from a sample of Indian manufacturing firms in Table 23-1(a) providing sector-wise proportions of account receivable, that receivables constitute around 22% of assets of manufacturing firms. Thus, because of their sheer magnitude, any change in the firms' credit policies can affect the levels of accounts receivables, and thereby the firms' profitability. For example, an increase in accounts receivable—that is, additional extension of trade credit—not only results in higher sales, but also requires additional financing to support the increased investment in accounts receivable. The costs of credit investigation and collection efforts and the chances of bad debts also increase.

All firms by their very nature are involved in selling either goods or services. Some of these sales will be for cash, but a large proportion will involve the extension of credit. Whenever a sale is made on credit, it increases the size of the firm's accounts receivable. Thus, the importance of accounts receivable management depends upon the degree to which the firm sells on credit. Table 23-1(a) lists, for selected sectors, the percentage of total assets made up by accounts receivable.

Table 23-1(a) Sector-wise accounts receivable as a percentage of total assets

Sectors	*Receivables / Total Assets*	*Receivables / Current Assets*
Manufacturing Firms*	22.22	45.97
Automobile Sector	26.77	42.47
Capital Goods Sector	47.12	58.45
Consumer Durables	27.05	33.02
FMCG	17.52	34.16
Healthcare	28.05	52.17

Source: Prowess database of Centre for Monitoring of Indian Economy, India
*Based on a sample of 5,060 listed Indian manufacturing firms

In Table 23-1(a), we can see that accounts receivable typically comprise slightly over 22% of the assets of the manufacturing sector. This percentage varies from industry to industry, and may go up to as high as 45–50% in the case of the capital goods industry. Although accounts receivable as a percentage of current assets and total assets have come down over the years, as can be seen in Table 23-1(b) the percentage of funds tied up in them is still substantial, and requires regular and effective monitoring and control. In effect,

Table 23-1(b) Time-wise analysis of receivables as a percentage of assets

Year	1997	1998	1999	2000	2001	2002	2003	2004	2005	2006
Receivables / total assets	27.32	24.73	24.21	24.72	25.26	23.41	23.93	23.35	23.63	22.22
Receivables / current assets	58.90	58.16	59.13	57.41	59.51	57.85	55.89	53.16	49.57	45.97
Current assets / sales	58.35	57.90	54.26	52.51	44.75	44.58	44.91	43.61	44.93	45.35

Source: Prowess database of Centre for Monitoring of Indian Economy, India

when we discuss management of accounts receivable, we are emphasizing the management of around one-quarter of the firm's assets. Moreover, since cash flows from a sale cannot be invested until the account is collected, control of receivables assumes additional significance. Efficiency of collection of receivables impacts both profitability and liquidity of the firm.

The level of sales is one of the key determinants of the size of the investment in accounts receivable. Typically, the more the growth in regular/seasonal sales, the higher will be the investment in accounts receivable.

Another important factor that determines the level of investment in accounts receivables, as can be seen in Table 23-1(a), is the nature of business. The blend of credit and cash sales depends on the nature of business operations. For a typical retail store, sales are largely on cash basis and hence, the receivables component may be very low, as compared to a business dealing with capital goods, where sales may primarily be on credit basis. Last and most important, the level of investment in accounts receivable depends on the credit policy of the firm, i.e., the terms of sale (or credit terms), the credit standards, and the collection efforts. Let us now look at the variables that get influenced by the credit policy. This will be followed by a discussion on the components of credit policy.

IMPACT OF CREDIT POLICY

Credit policy and any change therein are expected to have a direct impact on sales, level of investment, particularly in working capital components, bad-debt losses, and collection costs. Any proposed alteration in the credit policy should be evaluated in the light of its impact on these variables. Some of these variables have positive impact while others have negative implication for the firm. This section studies the relationship that exists between credit policy and these variables.

Credit policy influences the sales, investment levels, bad debts losses, and collection costs.

Sales Sales are normally expected to increase with the stretching of credit period. The demand for a firm's product is greatly influenced by the ease with which the products can be purchased on credit. Sales will be at their lowest level if they are strictly for cash. Those who want to buy on credit will patronize other manufacturers who extend credit. Sales will be at their maximum level when the firm does not screen buyers for creditworthiness. Rather, credit is extended to all who want to buy the firm's products. It is within these two extremes–of all credit and no credit–that the credit policies of firms normally fall.

Investment Levels Liberalization of credit policy normally leads to increase in sales. To service this additional demand, firms may have to increase their productive capacity, which requires additional investments. Also, the increased sales cause an increased blockage of funds in currents assets, particularly in inventory and receivables.

Bad-Debt Losses Bad-debt refers to the default a customer can make in paying for the goods purchased on credit. Not only the profit on sale is forgone but the firm also loses the cost that it incurred in producing those goods. Without credit sales, the firm will not incur any bad-debt losses. Relaxation of credit standards may result in credit sales to those customers who may later turn out to be not creditworthy. This results in an increase in bad-debt losses.

Collection Costs As credit terms are liberalized, the firm's volume of accounts receivable increases. This leads to an increase not only in the costs related to invoicing and bookkeeping of these increased receivables, but also in the costs of collection on these increased receivables as the collection staff has to do more follow-up for longer periods and for larger number of customers.

COMPONENTS OF CREDIT POLICY

Credit policy, or accounts receivables policy, has three main constituents: (i) credit terms, (ii) credit standards, and (iii) collection efforts.

There are three constituents of credit policy: credit terms; credit standards; and collection efforts.

Credit Terms

Credit terms refer to the terms and conditions under which credit sales are made to customers. Specifically, there are three decision points pertaining to credit terms: (i) the duration of credit allowed to the customers, called the net date; (ii) the discount allowed, if any, for cash payment; (iii) the period within which payment should be made to avail of discount for early payment. These terms are generally stated in the form "*a*/*b* net *c*", indicating that the customer will get *a* per cent discount if the payment is paid within *b* days; otherwise, the account must be settled within *c* days. For example, credit terms of 1.5/15 net 30 indicate that a

Credit terms refer to the terms of credit sales to current and prospective customers. They include credit period, rate and period of cash discount.

1.5% discount will be available to customers on the total payment due from them if the payment is made by them within 15 days; otherwise they have to settle their accounts within 30 days.

What if the customer decides to forgo the discount and not pay until the final payment date? If such a decision is made, the customer has the use of the money for the time period between the discount date and the final payment date, i.e., between the 15th and the 30th day in our example. However, failure to take the discount represents a cost to the customer. For instance, if the terms are 1.5/15 net 30, the cost associated with such a policy is approximately 36%. To be exact the analysed opportunity cost of passing up this 1.5% discount in order to withhold payment for an additional 15 days is 36.55%[†]. This is determined by Equation 23-1 as follows:

Opportunity cost of forgoing the discount

$$= \frac{a}{1-a} \times \frac{360}{c-b} \quad (23\text{-}1)$$

Substituting values from the example, we get:

$$\frac{0.015}{1-0.015} \times \frac{360}{30-15} = 36.55\%$$

These credit terms vary from industry to industry. Except for firms that are the market leaders, and those having a significant brand pull, other firms are typically credit policy takers and not givers. Similarly, new entrants in already established industry segments are normally credit policy takers.

A change in credit policy affects sales and consequently profits. Proposed change in credit policy should be analysed in the light of its impact on other financial variables.

As discussed previously, liberalization of credit policy normally increases sales and consequently, profits. However, it also increases investment levels, bad-debt losses, and collection costs, and thereby, causes an adverse impact on profits. An appropriate credit policy balances profits from increased sales due to more liberal credit terms with increased costs due to increased investments, bad-debt losses, and collection costs. The ideal credit policy allows for the liberalization of credit terms to the point where the marginal revenue from a new category of credit accounts is exactly equal to the marginal costs of selling and servicing such accounts.

While designing a new credit policy or altering an existing one, firms have to take into account the impact of the proposed credit policy on each of the financial variables, and on the overall financial health of the firm. Before we move on to an analysis of credit policy and its impact on the firm's financial health, it is mandatory to understand the nuts and bolts of the credit policy, and their impact on each of the firm's financial performance variables. As discussed before, there are three variables of credit policy: *credit period, discount rate*, and *discount period*.

Credit period Credit terms are specified on the invoices sent out by firms. A typical credit term may state: "*a*/*b* net *c*". As discussed earlier in the chapter, the first number *a* is *the discount rate* and indicates that a *a*% discount may be granted if the invoice is paid within the number of days specified by the second term, i.e., *b* days. The second term *b* is the *discount period* and indicates the number of days during which the credit discount is valid. The last number *c* indicates the credit period. *The credit period* specifies the number of days that a firm can take to pay the invoice without being considered to be delinquent. With terms of *a*/*b* net *c* the credit period is *c* days, and the full amount of the invoice is due within *c* days.

One way to liberalize credit terms is to increase the credit period. Conversely, credit terms can be tightened by shortening the credit period. In either case, the decision to change the credit period depends on assessment of the impact of the proposed change on the other financial variables like sales, collection costs, bad-debts, etc. Let us consider an example to highlight the changes in profitability due to change in credit terms.

Example 23-1 Evaluating the Change in Credit Period

Suyog Corporation is currently selling on credit terms of 1.5/15, net 30. Its annual gross sales are ₹500 crore currently and all its sales are on credit basis. Fifty per cent of its clients avail the 1.5% discount and make payment on the fifteenth day, while the others avail of the full credit period of 30 days.

The company's management is considering two alternative credit plans:

Plan A: to change the credit terms to 1.5/15 net 45;

Plan B: to shift to credit terms of 1.5/15 net 60.

Plan A is expected to increase sales by 10% from current levels, whereas Plan B is likely to boost sales by 15%. Suyog's margins on sales before credit-related costs and taxes are 20%. Investments in accounts receivable carry a 12% before-tax cost. Suyog's management feels that lengthening of the credit period may make the idea of availing the full credit period more lucrative for customers, and as a result, increase the base of customers availing of the full credit period.

However, they feel that with the present plans, there will be no change in the rupee volume of sales on which the discount is taken. That is, all incremental sales will be paid for after the 15-day discount period. In addition, management feels that 1% of all incremental sales under Plan A and 2% under Plan B will prove to be uncollectible. No additional credit costs will be involved in clerical or administrative functions. Which of the plan should be accepted by Suyog?

Solution

In order to arrive at a decision regarding the change in credit policy, the firm's management has to study the impact of the changed credit period on the other financial variables and consequently on the overall profits.

The variables to be considered in deciding between the present credit terms and Plan A or B are: (i) profits on increased sales; (ii) increase in accounts receivable; (iii) increase in the cost of financing the additional receivables, and (iv) increase in bad-debt losses. Thus an incremental analysis of change in credit terms is needed.

The effects of the three credit terms on these variables are summarized in Table 23-2. Under Plan A, sales increase by 10% or ₹50 crore (0.10 × ₹500 crore). Sales are expected to increase by ₹75 crore under Plan B. Marginal profits before taxes and credit-related expenses are ₹10 crore (0.2% × ₹50 crore) for Plan A and ₹15 crore for Plan B.

[†]We have used 360 days in a year for computational ease. Readers may like to use 365 days instead.

Extension of credit period may prompt buyers who are not availing of the discount, and making their payments on the 30th day, to avail of the extended credit period. Incremental investment in receivables is estimated by calculating total receivables first. Under the present credit terms, 50% of sales are paid up in 15 days, and the other 50% in 30 days. The average sale is outstanding for 22.5 days [0.5(15) + 0.5(30)]. Daily sales are ₹1.389 crore (₹500 crore /360 days). Total accounts receivable equals ₹31.25 crore[1] [22.5 days × ₹1.389 crore].

Table 23-2 Analysis of Credit Terms: Suyog Corporation.[§]

(*₹ in crore*)

	Present	*Plan A*	*Plan B*
Current sales	500.00		
Increase in sales (%)	—	10.00	15.00
Increase in sales, ΔS	—	50.00	75.00
Margin on sales (%)	20.00	20.00	20.00
Marginal profits ΔP	—	10.00	15.00
Average sales outstanding (Days)	22.50	31.37	40.44
Daily sales	1.389	1.53	1.60
Total receivables	31.25	47.92	64.59
Increase in receivables	—	16.67	33.34
Incremental cost of receivables	—	2.00	4.00
Increase in bad-debt losses	—	0.50	1.50
Increase in costs due to change in credit terms	—	2.50	5.50
Increase in profits—	7.50	9.50	

Under Plan A, total sales amount to ₹550 crore (₹500 crore + 50 crore). The rupee amount subject to payment by the 15th day remains at ₹250 crore or 45.45% (₹250 crore/ ₹550 crore). The other 54.55% of clients now take 45 days to pay. The average sale will be outstanding for 31.37 days [0.4545 × (15 days) + 0.5455 × (45 days)]. Daily sales amount to ₹1.53 crore (₹550 crore/360 days). Total receivables are ₹47.92 crore (₹1.53 crore × 31.37 days).

Under Plan B total sales are ₹575 crore. The percentage of discount takers is 43.47% (₹250 crore / ₹575 crore). The average sales is outstanding for 40.44 days [0.4347 (15 days) + 0.5653 (60 days)]. Daily sales are ₹1.60 crore (₹575/360) and receivables are ₹64.59 crore (₹1.60 crore × 40.44 days).

Increase in receivable would reflect in the increase of working capital outlay. Incremental receivables are 16.67 crore (₹47.92 crore – ₹31.25 crore) for Plan A and ₹33.34 crore (₹64.59 crore – ₹31.25 crore) for Plan B. The before-tax cost of financing these receivables is 12%. Therefore, the increase in investment costs for Plan A is ₹2 crore (₹16.67 crore × 0.12) and is ₹4 crore (₹33.34 crore × 0.12) for Plan B.

Besides there would be change in the losses due to bad debts. The incremental bad-debt losses would be ₹0.5 crore (0.01 × 50 crore) for Plan A and ₹1.5 crore (0.02 × ₹75 crore) for Plan B.

The total incremental cost of credit policy change is ₹2.5 crore for Plan A and ₹5.5 crore for Plan B. The incremental profits after adjusting for credit costs are ₹7.5 crore for Plan A and ₹9.5 crore for Plan B. Both plans are superior to the present plan. However, Plan B gives higher profits, compared to Plan A.

Discount rate The discount is offered to customers as an inducement to pay promptly. The choice before customers is whether to avail of the discount and make the payment before the net date, or forgo the discount and pay on the net date and hence avail of the full credit period. In case the customer does not avail of the discount, he gets financed for the additional period but he has to bear the opportunity cost in terms of the discount forgone. The opportunity cost of not availing the discount is given by:

$$\frac{360 \text{ days} \times \text{credit discount}}{\text{credit period} - \text{discount period}}$$

For terms of 1.5/10 net 30, the opportunity cost of not taking the discount is 27% [(360 days × 1.5%)/(30 – 10)]. Obviously, this opportunity cost has to be high enough to motivate a financially strong credit buyer to take the discount. For example, terms of 1/10 net 70 imply an opportunity cost of 6%. At this cost, firms will prefer to use trade credit rather than borrow from banks, and the credit discount is no longer a viable credit policy instrument.

Although changing the credit discount has some influence on demand, its most visible impact is on reducing the average collection period and the level of accounts receivable. Let us understand the feasibility of change in the discount rate offered by the seller with the help of an example.

Example 23-2 Evaluating the Change in Discount Rate

Assume that Suyog Corporation, having its present credit terms as "1.5/15 net 30", is considering altering its credit terms in view of increased competition, to "2.0/15 net 30" under Plan C or "2.5/15 net 30" under Plan D. Either of the new plans would not affect the sales volume. However, under Plan C, 70% of the credit buyers would take the credit discount and, under Plan D, 90% would take the discount.

Should Suyog switch to either Plan C or D?

Solution

The analysis here would be similar to the one done for the credit period. Gross sales volume remains unchanged at ₹500 crore for both plans, C and D. 50% of the buyers avail the discount under the present policy (this amounts to ₹250 crore), while 70% (amounting to ₹350 crore) and 90% (amounting to ₹450 crore) would avail the credit facility under Plan C and Plan D respectively, as indicated in Table 23-3. The credit discount for the present plan is ₹3.75 crore (1.5% × ₹250 crore). For Plan C, it is ₹7 crore (2% × ₹350 crore), and ₹11.25 crore (2.5% × 450) for Plan D. The incremental cost of going to a more liberal credit discount under Plan C is ₹3.25 crore, and ₹7.50 crore for Plan D.

The increase in credit costs due to a larger credit discount reduces the level of investments in accounts receivable. Total receivables under the present plan were calculated to be ₹31.25 in Table 23-2.

Under Plan C, the average collection period is 19.5 days [0.7 (15 days) + 0.3 (30 days)].

Since daily sales are ₹1.389 crore, total receivables are ₹27.08 crore (19.5 days × ₹1.389 crore).

[1] Sales are reasonably assumed to be equally distributed among buyers. Also, it is assumed that the daily sales volume is constant.

[§] The calculations have been rounded off to two decimal places.

Under Plan D, the average collection period is 16.5 days [(0.9 × 15 days) + (0.1 × 30 days)]. The total receivables under Plan D are ₹22.92 crore (16.5 × 1.389).

Under Plan C, receivables decrease by ₹4.17 crore (₹31.25 crore – ₹27.08 crore).

The decrease in investments under Plan D is ₹8.33 crore (₹31.25 crore – ₹22.92 crore).

Table 23-3 Analysis of credit terms: Changing credit discounts for the Suyog Corporation

(Figures in ₹ crore unless specified otherwise)

	Present	Plan C	Plan D
Gross sales volume	500.00	500.00	500.00
Average daily sales	1.389	1.389	1.389
Average sales outstanding (In days)	22.50	19.50	16.50
Sales with discounts (%)	50	70	90
Sales with discounts	250	350	450
Credit discounts (%)	1.5	2.0	2.5
Credit discounts	3.75	7.00	11.25
Increase in discounts	0	3.25	7.50
Total receivables	31.25	27.08	22.92
Decrease in receivables	0	4.17	8.33
Decrease in investment costs	0	0.50	1.00
Increase in profits	0	–2.75	-6.50

The cost of investments in receivables is 12%. Cost savings on account of reduction in receivables is ₹0.50 crore for Plan C and ₹1 crore for Plan D. Cost savings less increase in discount costs gives increase in profits before taxes. As shown in Table 23-3, neither Plan C nor Plan D results in increasing profits over the present levels. Consequently, Suyog should not implement any of the plans under consideration.

Discount period The analysis of changing discount periods is very similar to the analysis of changing credit discounts. As the discount period is increased, the opportunity cost of not taking a discount increases. Therefore, it becomes more attractive for a credit buyer to take the discount. However, as the discount period is extended, existing discount takers take advantage of the liberalized credit terms and delay their payments until the end of the new discount period. Whether extending the discount period is desirable depends on whether total receivables increase or decrease. Let us understand this by extending the example of Suyog Corporation.

Example 23-3 Evaluating the Change in Discount Period

Suyog is considering changing its credit terms to "1.5/18 net 30" or "1.5/20 net 30" under Plans E and F, respectively. The percentage of sales subject to the discount would be 60% and 80% under Plan E and Plan F, respectively. Should Suyog Corporation switch to either Plan E or Plan F? Gross sales would not be affected by these alternative plans.

Solution

Table 23-4 Analysis of Credit Terms: Changing Discount periods for Suyog Corporation

(Figures in ₹ crore unless specified otherwise)

	Present	Plan E	Plan F
Gross sales volume	500.00	500.00	500.00
Average daily sales	1.389	1.389	1.389
Average sales outstanding (in days)	22.50	22.80	22.00
Sales with discounts (%)	50.00	60.00	80.00
Sales with discounts	250.00	300.00	400.00
Credit discounts	3.75	4.50	6.00
Increase in discounts	—	0.75	2.25
Total receivables	31.25	31.67	30.56
Decrease in receivables	—	0.42	0.69
Decrease in investment costs	—	0.05	0.08
Increase in profits—	–0.08	–2.17	

Sales subject to discounts would be ₹250, 300, and 400 crore for the present credit terms, Plan E and Plan F, respectively. Credit discount at 1.5% would be ₹3.75 crore for the present plan, and ₹4.50 crore and 6.00 crore for Plans E and F, respectively. The increase in discounts for Plan E as can be seen in Table 23-4 is ₹0.75 crore for Plan E and ₹2.25 crore for Plan F.

The total receivables under Plan *E* would be [0.6 (18 days) + 0.4 (30 days)] × 1.389 crore = ₹31.67 crore.

The same entry would be [0.8 (20 days) + 0.2 (30 days)] × ₹1.389 = 30.56 crore for Plan F.

A decrease in investment costs due to a decrease in receivables is ₹0.42 crore for Plan E and ₹0.69 crore for Plan F.

Taking into consideration the increased discounts being given, we find that neither of the two new plans is acceptable.

Simultaneous Changes in Credit Terms

Having discussed the impact of change in the credit terms individually, we now move on to understand the collective impact of the changes in the credit terms. Most firms, from a practical standpoint, will consider changes in all credit terms simultaneously. The expected collective impact of these changes in the individual credit terms is determined using a cost–benefit analysis. Extending the credit period influences sales most strongly, whereas changing the other two credit terms has a strong impact on the level of receivables outstanding. A firm considering to change all credit terms needs to carefully examine the potential impact of the changes on incremental profits. Let us examine the impact of a simultaneous change in credit period, discount rate, and discount period by extending further the example of Suyog Ltd .

Example 23-4 Evaluating a Simultaneous Change in Credit Terms

Suyog Ltd is contemplating recasting its credit policy by changing from terms of "1.5/15 net 30" to either "2/20 net 45" under Plan G or "2.50/20 net 60" under Plan H. Under Plan G, sales are expected to increase by

5%, whereas with Plan H sales would have the potential of increasing by 10%. Marginal returns before credit-adjusted costs and taxes would be 20% of sales.

Under Plan G, 55% of sales would involve the discount, while under Plan H, 60% avail discount. Those who take the discount would pay at the end of the discount period and others would, in general, pay by the end of the credit period. Bad-debt losses would increase by 1% of incremental sales for Plan G and 2% of incremental sales for Plan H. Collection costs would increase by ₹10,00,000 and ₹30,00,000 under Plans G and H, respectively.

Which one of the two credit terms does appear to be better for Suyog Ltd?

Solution

Under Plan G, sales and marginal profits would increase by ₹25 crore and ₹5 crore, respectively. Under Plan H, sales would increase by ₹50 crore and profits by ₹10 crore. These marginal profits are before credit adjusted costs and need to be adjusted for changes in the investment levels in receivables and in discount taken.

Given credit terms of "2/20 net 45" with 55% sales subject to availing discount, the average collection period for Plan G is 0.55 (15 days) + 0.45 (45 days) = 31.25 days.

Daily sales are ₹525/360, i.e., ₹1.389 crore. Therefore, total receivables for Plan G would be 31.25 days × ₹1.389 crore = ₹43.40 crore.

Similarly, total receivables for Plan H would be [0.60 (20 days) + 0.4 (60 days)] = 36 days × 1.389 crore = ₹50.01 crore

From total receivables, we can calculate incremental receivables and the cost of increased investments in receivables, as shown in Table 23-5.

Table 23-5 Analysis of Credit Terms: Changing Credit Terms for Suyog Corporation

(Figures in ₹ crore unless specified otherwise)

	Present	Plan G	Plan H
Increase in sales (%)	—	5	10
Increase in sales	—	25	50
Margin on sales (%)	20	20	20
Marginal profits	—	5	10
Average collection period	22.5	35.25	36
Daily sales	1.389	1.389	1.389
Total receivable	31.25	43.407	50.01
Increase in receivable	—	12.157	18.76
Increase in investment costs		1.459	2.251
Increase in bad-debt losses	—	0.25	1.00
Sales with discount	250	275.03	300.06
Credit discounts (%)	1.5	2.00	2.50
Credit discounts	3.75	5.50	7.50
Increase in discounts	—	1.75	3.75
Increase in collection costs	—	0.10	0.30
Increase in credit costs	—	3.559	7.303
Increase in profit	—	1.441	2.697

Bad-debt losses for Plan G would be ₹25 crore × 0.01, or ₹0.25 crore, and for Plan H, ₹1 crore. The cost of giving discounts and increased collection costs are shown in Table 23-5. Given the total credit-related cost increases of ₹3.559 crore for Plan G, its profitability before taxes is ₹1.441 crore (₹5 crore – ₹3.559 crore). Similarly, Plan H would increase pretax profits by ₹2.697 crore. Of these two, Plan H is the better one.

Credit Standards

Applying credit standards to judge worthiness of customers is an important credit policy variable. It determines the amount of funds blocked in receivables.

A second decision variable in credit policy is to judge the creditworthiness of the customers, i.e., determining whether the customers who request credit sales qualify for trade credit. This assumes importance as the credit standards followed by the firm go on to determine not only the amount of funds tied up in the receivables, but also the quality of the receivables and hence, the liquidity of the firm. Relaxation in credit standards give a boost to the firm's sales, as it increases its catchment area by bringing those customers into its fold who could not qualify for trade credit previously under the more stringent credit policy. Whether this enhances the firm's overall profits or not depends on the cost of this credit offered.

There are several costs associated with extending credit to customers with low credit standing. First, as the probability of customer default increases with the extension of credit to customers with low credit rating it becomes more important to identify which of the possible new customers would be a poor risk. Thus, more time is spent investigating the customers with poor credit standing, and the costs of credit investigation increase. Default costs also vary directly with the quality of the customer. If the customer's credit rating is lower, chances that the account will not be paid on time increase. In the extreme case, payment does not occur at all, and the account must be written of. Thus, taking on lower-quality customers results in increases in default costs. Collection costs also increase as the quality of the acceptable customer is lowered. The increase in delinquent accounts will force the firm to spend more time and money in collecting them. In a nut shell, decline in customer quality results in increased costs of credit investigation, collection, and default.

In determining whether or not credit should be granted to an individual customer, we are primarily interested in the customer's liquidity position. Thus, liquidity ratios, other obligations, and the overall profitability of the firm become the focal point in this analysis. Credit-rating services provide information on the financial status, operations, and payment history for most firms. Other possible sources of information would include credit bureaus, trade associations, chambers of commerce, competitors, bank references, public financial statements, and, of course, the firm's past relationships with the customer. Once information regarding the creditworthiness of current and prospective customers is generated from these cost-effective and reliable sources, the next thing is to determine the credit risk in individual accounts using the credit standards for the firm. It is this comparison between the credit risk of individual customers and the acceptable level of credit risk as per the firm's credit standards that lead to a decision regarding the extension of trade credit.

One way to evaluate credit risks of customers is through the use of *credit scoring*. Credit scoring involves the numerical evaluation of each applicant, in which an applicant receives a score based upon his or her answers to a simple set of questions. This score is then evaluated relative to a predetermined standard; its level relative to the standard determines whether or not credit should be extended. The major advantage of credit scoring is that it is inexpensive, easy to perform, and reduces subjective evaluation.

Techniques used for constructing credit-scoring indexes range from the naïve, simple approach of adding up default rates associated with the answers given to each question, to sophisticated evaluations using *Multiple Discriminant Analysis* (MDA). Table 23-6 shows a credit 'scorecard' used by a large automobile dealer. The weights or scores attached to each answer are based upon the autodealer's past experience with credit sales. For example, the scorecard indicates that individuals with no telephone in their home have a much higher probability of default than those with a telephone.

Another model that could be used for credit scoring has been provided by Edward Altman, who used multiple discriminant analysis (MDA) to identify businesses that might go bankrupt. MDA is a statistical technique for calculating the appropriate importance to be given to each question used in evaluating the applicant. In this landmark study, for the period of 1946 to 1965 Altman used financial ratios to predict which firms would go bankrupt.

Table 23-6 Credit Scorecard

Living quarters						Score
Own home no mortgage 6	Own home mortgage 3	Rent a house 2	Live with someone 1	Rent a apartment 0	Rent a room 0	
Bank accounts						
None 0	1 4	More than one 6				
Other Loans (annual liability)						
None 6	up to Rs 10,000 4	1,00,001-2,00,000 2	Above 2,00,000 0			
Years at present address						
Under ½ 0	½-2 1	3-7 3	8 or more 4			
Size of family (including customer)						
1 2	2 4	3-6 3	7 or more 0			
Annual household income						
Under Rs 200,000 0	Rs 2,00,001–400,000 1	Rs 400,001–8,00000 2	Rs 8,00,001 20,00,000 6	More than 20,00,000 8		
Length of present employment						
Under ½ year 0	½-2 1	3-7 years 2	8 years or more 4			
Percentage of selling price on credit						
Under 50 5	50-69 3	70-84 1	85-99 0			
Interview discretionary points (+ 5 to –5)						
If a previous customer, were payments received promptly?						Yes/No*
Are you willing to take responsibility for authorizing loan?						Yes/No
Total						

Credit scorecard		
Customer's Name		
Street address		
City, state, pin code		
Home/office telephone		
Credit scorer		
Credit scorecard evaluation		
Rupee amount: ₹ 0 - ₹ 3,00,000		
0-18 Reject	19-21 Refer to main credit	22 or more Accept
Rupee amount: ₹ 3,00,001-₹ 6,00,000		
0-21 Reject	22-24 Refer to main credit	25 Accept
Rupee amount: More than ₹ 600,000		
0-23 Reject	26-27 Refer to main credit	27 or more Accept

*Refer to main credit if answer to either question is No.

Using multiple discriminant analysis, Altman came up with the following index:

$$z = 3.3\left(\frac{\text{Credit}}{\text{Total Assets}}\right) + 1.0\left(\frac{\text{Sales}}{\text{Total Assets}}\right) + 0.6\left(\frac{\text{Market value of equity}}{\text{Book value of debt}}\right) + 1.4\left(\frac{\text{Retained earning}}{\text{Total assets}}\right) + 1.2\left(\frac{\text{Working capital}}{\text{Total assets}}\right)$$

Altman found that of the firms that went bankrupt over this time period, 94% had Z scores of less than 2.7 one year prior to bankruptcy and only 6% had scores above 2.7%. On the other hand, of those firms that did not go bankrupt, only 3% has Z scores below 2.7 and 97% had scores above 2.7. Such a model can be used with suitable modification to suit the nature of business/industry to judge creditworthiness of customers.

Again, the advantages of credit-scoring techniques are their low cost and ease of implementation. The credit scorer needs little or no training, and with simple calculations, can easily spot those credit risks that need more in the way of screening before credit should be extended to them.

A firm reviewing a request for credit needs to judge the credit applicant's willingness and ability to pay. If either of these two factors is missing, the firm would increase its chances of suffering losses on credit extended to the applicant. Willingness to pay is judged by the applicant's past repayment behaviour. Its ability to pay is judged by the strength of its financial statements in relation to the amount of credit desired, using credit scoring models or discriminant analysis.

Determining the Credit Limit

Once the firm decides to grant credit to a customer, the next important issue facing the firm is that of establishing the credit limit i.e. deciding as to what level of credit should be extended to customers. Heuristic or statistical procedures could be utilized for the purpose.

Heuristic approach

The heuristic approach is based on intuitive judgments or simple common sense backed by long experience and grounding in the business. There are eight factors that need to be considered in the decision to establish a credit limit and grant credit. The credit limit is the maximum amount of credit purchases allowed to the credit applicant at any one time and is stated as a percentage of tangible net worth. The lower limit is minus 15% and is tantamount to denying new credit to the applicant. The upper limit is 80% and is equivalent to the sum of the maximum percentage points on the eight credit granting factors. Let us discuss the eight-factors that are taken into consideration while deciding the credit limit.

Credit requirements The first factor is the applicant's credit requirements (C). This factor is a measure of the applicant's dependency on the creditor. If the applicant plans to buy less than 25% of his requirements from the creditor, he gets 0% toward his credit line. If he plans to buy between 25% and 50%, he gets a 5% allowance. If he plans to buy over 50%, he gets a 10% allowance (see Table 23-7).

Pay habit The second factor is pay habits (P), and is a measure of the willingness and ability to pay. Payments during the discount period gets a rating of 10%. Payments during the credit period are rated as 5%. Habitually late payments rate minus 5%.

Years in business The third factor is years in business (Y), and is a measure of the ability of the firm to pay. Being in business less than 3 years has no effect on increasing the limits. If Y is between 3 and 10 years, the limit is increased by 5%. If the firm has been in existence for more than 10 years, it rates 10%.

Table 23-7 Heuristic Approach to Establishing the Credit Limit

Contributing factor	Rating	Contribution to Credit Limit : Per cent of Net Worth
Applicant credit requirements (C)	$C < 25\%$	0
	$25\% < C < 50\%$	5
	$C > 50\%$	10
Pay habits (P)	Takes discount	10
	Pays on time	5
	Pays late	–5
Years in business (Y)	$Y < 3$ years	0
	$3 < Y < 10$	5
	$Y > 10$	10
Profit margin (M)	$M < 5\%$	0
	$5\% < M < 14\%$	5
	$M > 14\%$	10
Current ratio (R)	$R > 2.2{:}1$	10
	$1.5 < R < 2.2$	5
	$R < 1.5$	0
Total debt to assets (T)	$T < 30\%$	10
	$50\% > T > 30\%$	5
	$T > 50\%$	–5
Inventory turnover (I)	$I > 10$	10
	$5 < I < 10$	5
	$I < 5$	0
Qualitative (Q)	Q = high	10
	Q = average	5
	Q = low	–5

Profit margin The fourth measure is the profit margin (M). If margins are less than 5%, 0% is contributed to the credit limit. If it is more than 5% but less than 14% it gets a 5% rating. Margins in excess of 14% contribute 10% to the credit limit.

Current ratio The fifth measure is the current ratio (R). A current ratio of over 2.2 to 1 is considered to be a good indication of ability to pay and helps contribute 10% toward the credit limit. A current ratio of less than 1.5:1 is considered to be relatively weak and does not help increase the credit limit. While a current ratio that is less than 2.2 contributes 5% towards credit limit.

Total debt to asset ratio The sixth measure is the ratio of total debt to total assets (T), and represents the ability to pay. If T is less than 30%, the applicant is seen to be conservatively leveraged, and 10% is added to the credit limit. On the other hand, a T of over 50% implies increased financial riskiness and rates a minus 5% towards the credit limit.

Inventory turnover The seventh factor is the inventory turnover (I). A higher inventory turnover implies high efficiency; I can help contribute anywhere from 0% to 10% toward the credit limit, as shown in Table 23-6.

Qualitative factor The last factor is a qualitative factor (Q), and lets the credit manager use discretion in subjective evaluation of the credit applicant's willingness and ability to pay.

It should be kept in mind that the factors mentioned here and their contribution to the credit limit is based on a particular firm's actual experience. The factors and their contributions to the credit limit may vary according to accounts payable, and the economic environment would also be considered in developing a heuristic credit evaluation decision model.

As an example we can apply the heuristic model presented here to evaluate Sponge Metal. Assume that Sponge is requesting a credit line to purchase its raw materials requirements. What is the maximum credit line to establish for Sponge? The contributions of the various factors to the credit limit are shown in Table 23-8. The existing credit line for Sponge Ltd is ₹7,50,000. The tangible net worth of the firm is ₹42,96,100. The last factor, Q, is rated average because of Sponge's dependence on only 12 customers.

Table 23-8 Application of the Credit Limit Model for Sponge Metal Products

Factor	*Sponge's Rating*	*Contribution to Credit Limit (%)*
1. Sponge's requirement (C)	$C < 25\%$	0
2. Pay habits (P)	Takes discount	10
3. Years in business (Y)	$Y > 10$	10
4. Profit margins (M)	$M = 4.6\% < 5\%$	0
5. Current ratio (R)	$R = 2.89 > 2.22$	10
6. Total debt to total assets (T)	$T = 0.28 < 0.3$	10
7. Inventory turnover (I)	$I = 12 > 10$	10
8. Quantitative (Q)	Average	5
Total Contribution		**55**

As can be seen in Table 23-4, total contribution of the eight factors to the credit limit is 55% of tangible net worth, or ₹42,96,100 × 0.55, i.e., ₹23,62,900. The value of existing credit lines for Sponge Metals is ₹7,50,000. Sponge can be extended additional credit up to ₹23,62,900 – ₹7,50,000 = ₹16,12,900.

Statistical approach

In quantitative approaches to credit analysis, the firm relies on financial information as well as on the payment records of firms that were granted credit in the past. Past customers can be readily classified into good risk and bad risk categories. The financial information on customers is used in conjunction with a statistical procedure called *multiple discriminant analysis* to develop a statistical credit scoring model.

Discriminant analysis, first of all, provides an indication of those measures which are most important in distinguishing between good risk and bad risk customers. That is, the firm may start out by using 30 ratios and variables in its analysis. Discriminant analysis might indicate that only five of these ratios and variables are important in characterizing good risk and bad risk customers. Second, discriminant analysis will develop weights for each ratio or variable to form a discriminant function that may look like:

Discriminant score = 3.5 (current ratio) + 1.7 (profit margins)
+ 7.1 (debt to assets) + 0.3 (inventory turnover)
+ 1.9 (quick ratio)

The weightage for each of the factors (represented by 3.5, 1.7, 7.1, 0.3, and 1.9 in above equation) are developed by discriminant analysis. Current ratio, profit margins, and so forth, are discriminant variables identified as important by the model. The sum of the products of the weights and the variables is the discriminant score. The analysis selects weights such that discrimination between good risk and bad risk accounts is maximized. A perfect set of weights would create a discriminant score such that all bad risk firms would have scores on one side of the discriminant score. Once the discriminant credit scoring model has been developed, it can be applied to credit applicants. The weights can be used to calculate a score for the credit applicant. The credit applicant's score can be compared with the discriminant score to see whether the applicant falls in the good risk or bad risk category. If the applicant falls in the good risk category, a similar type of procedure as described in heuristic approach can be used to establish a credit limit for the applicant.

Collection Policy

Once credit has been extended to a customer, it is very important to regularly monitor the credit. This is essential not only for quick recovery on maturity, it can also indicate, in a timely manner, accounts likely to become delinquent. Using tools like financial analysis, ageing schedule, etc., firms can monitor their receivables and ensure their quick collection.

The key to maintaining control over the collection of accounts receivable is that the probability of default increases with the age of the account. Thus, control of accounts receivable focuses on the control and elimination of past-due receivables. One common way of evaluating the current situation is *ratio analysis*. By examining the average collection period, the ratio of receivables to assets, the ratio of credit sales to receivables (called the accounts receivable turnover ratio), and the amount of bad debts relative to sales over time, the finance manager can determine if receivables are drifting out of control. In addition, an ageing of accounts receivable provides a break-up both in rupee and in percentage terms of the proportion of receivables that are past due. Comparing the current ageing of receivables with past data offers further insight into the degree of control that is being maintained over receivables. An example of an *ageing account* or schedule appears in Table 23-9.

As can be seen from Table 23-9 such a schedule tells at a glance, what value and percentage of firm's receivables are collected within 30 days, 60 days, and so on. A comparison of the current ageing schedule with that of the past tells how good the company has performed in monitoring and controlling the receivables.

Table 23-9 Ageing Account

Age of Accounts receivable (days)	*Rupee Value (in lakh)*	*Percent of total*
0–30	2340	39%
31–60	1500	25%
61–90	1020	17%
91–120	720	12%
Over 120	420	7%
Total	**6000**	**100%**

When an account becomes delinquent, a firm can resort to a series of actions to try to collect on the account. These actions include writing a letter, calling on the phone, calling in person, using a collection agency, and legal action. The particular collection procedures followed have a direct impact on bad-debt losses and the average collection period. The firm has an obvious interest in reducing both bad-debt losses and the average collection period, which lower total receivables and investment in receivables. In general, the more the firm spends on collection, the lower its delinquency costs (bad-debt losses) and the cost of maintaining excess receivables. However, the marginal productivity of collection expenditures declines as the firm spends more on collections.

Another important issue in credit monitoring is access to information regarding the creditworthiness and financial performance of the buyer. Apart from published financial information, this can be obtained from credit bureaus that have started rendering their services in India, and also from banks. Companies all over the world are normally outsourcing this collection function. This not only saves cost, but also enables them to focus on their core competency.

The discussion on collection policy has assumed that sales are independent of collection policy. Most firms recognize that instituting a very aggressive collection policy may be very irritating for some customers who are slow in paying. An aggressive collection policy may therefore adversely affect sales. A second result of an aggressive collection policy may be to force more customers to take the discounts. These two factors need to be recognized before a firm implements a collection policy that equates marginal collection expenditures with marginal reductions in delinquency costs.

SUMMARY

Much of our concern with accounts receivable is derived from the fact that they make up around 25% of a typical manufacturing firm's assets. Thus, because of their sheer magnitude, any change in their levels affects profitability. In effect, when we discuss management of accounts receivable, we are discussing the management of one-quarter of the firm's assets. Management of accounts receivable focuses on credit policy and collection procedures.

Credit policy directly influences sales, investment levels, bad-debt losses, and collection costs. The demand for a firm's products is greatly influenced by the ease with which the products can be purchased on credit. As credit terms are made more liberal, the firm's investments in cash, accounts receivable, inventories, and, sometimes even physical investments increase in a complementary fashion. The decision to change the existing credit policy is taken based on the incremental analysis of the change in credit terms. An appropriate credit policy balances profits from increased sales due to more liberal credit terms with increased costs due to increased investments, bad-debt losses, and collection costs. The ideal credit policy allows for the liberalization of credit terms to the point where the marginal revenues from a new category of credit accounts is exactly equal to the marginal costs of selling and servicing such accounts. One way to liberalize credit terms is to increase the credit period. Conversely, credit terms can be tightened by shortening the credit period. Credit policy can also be altered by changing credit standards, i.e., by selling to customers with higher or lower risk profiles. Models and techniques like heuristic approach, credit scoring, etc., are put into practice for evaluating the creditworthiness of customers.

Active collection efforts are needed by firms to collect the accounts as and when they get due. By examining the average collection period, the ratio of receivables to assets, the ratio of credit sales to receivables (called the accounts receivable turnover ratio), and the amount of bad debts relative to sales over time, the finance manager can determine whether or not receivables are drifting out of control. In addition, an ageing of accounts receivable provides a break-up both in rupee and in percentage terms of the proportion of receivables that are past due. Comparing the current ageing of receivables with past data offers further insight into the degree of control that is being maintained over receivables.

Once the delinquent accounts have been identified, an effort should be made to collect them. A variety of collection procedures can be utilized by the firm in its efforts to collect on delinquent accounts. The initial efforts should be very low key and should become stricter as per the response from debtors. Legal action is taken as the last resort in realizing the amounts due.

KEY TERMS

Credit policy Credit policy refers to the terms and conditions of credit sales by firms. It constitutes three components—credit terms, credit standards, and collection efforts.

Credit terms Terms of extending trade credit to buyers (customers) are called credit terms. They include credit period, period of discount, and the rate of discount offered.

Credit standards Credit standards refer to the yardsticks applied to judge the creditworthiness of buyer (or borrower). Also referred to as the criteria that should be fulfilled by the buyer/ borrower in order to be eligible for credit.

Accounts receivable Account receivable denotes those accounts from which money is to be received for goods or services that have been rendered to them, but which they have not yet paid for.

KEY FORMULAE

Opportunity Cost of Foregoing Discount = $\frac{a}{1-a} \times \frac{360}{c-b}$

PRACTICE PROBLEMS

1. Changing the Credit Period

The management of Sapient Ltd, in view of increased competition from overseas owing to reduction in excise duty, is facing an intense competition in the sector. To give a boost to its sliding sales, the management is contemplating an increase in the credit period offered to its customers. At present the company offers 30 days of credit period to its suppliers and it proposes to increase it to 60 days, expecting its sales level to go up from ₹550 lakh at present to ₹623.75 lakh on account of changed credit policy.

Since the company has sufficient surplus production and distribution capacity available, such an increase in sales can be accommodated without any corresponding increase in the overheads.

However, such a relaxation in credit policy is likely to increase bad debt losses from 1.5% of sales at present to 2.75%. The variable cost-to-sales ratio for the firm is 0.60 and is likely to be maintained in near future also. The receivables turnover ratio for the firm is 13, which is likely to go down to 8 under the proposed policy.

The opportunity cost of capital for Sapient Ltd is 12.5%. Do you recommend lengthening of credit period by the firm?

Solution

Current Sales (₹ in lakh)	550.00
Sales under proposed credit policy (₹ in lakh)	623.75
Incremental sales under proposed credit policy (₹ in lakh)	73.75
Variable cost ratio (Variable cost / Sales)	0.60
Contribution ratio (Contribution / Sales)	0.40
Profits on incremental sales (Incremental sales × contribution ratio) (₹ in lakh)	29.50
Receivables turnover ratio (Present policy)	13
Receivables turnover ratio (Proposed policy)	8
Opportunity cost of capital for the firm	0.125 (or 12.5%)

Comparison of present and proposed credit policy

(*₹ in lakh*)

	Present	*Proposed*
Average daily sales (Sales/360)	1.528	1.733
Receivables (Sales / Receivables turnover)	42.31	77.97
Cost of receivables	5.29	9.75
Incremental cost of receivables	—	4.46
Bad debt losses	8.25	17.15
Incremental bad debt losses		8.90
Incremental profit		16.14

Since the change in credit policy is expected to create value of ₹16.14 lakh, the proposed lengthening of credit period is recommended for Sapient Ltd.

2. Choosing between Alternate Credit Policies

Pai Vista, a manufacturer of DVDs, presently follows a policy of "all cash and no credit." With the increased competition from Chinese manufacturers, the company's sales have been witnessing a consistent decline. The finance manager of the firm is evaluating two credit policies, which he thinks would be able to give a boost to the firm's sales. The two options are as follows:

	Credit Policy A	*Credit Policy B*
Collection period (in months)	1	2
Increase in sales (in %)	10%	15%
Bad debt losses (in %)	15%	2%

The current sales of the firm are ₹125 lakhs and the total costs are ₹75 lakh. Which of the two policy should the finance manager of the firm prefer in case the firm wants to maintain its current level of profitability? Assume that the firm's required return on investment in its receivables is 12.5%.

Solution

(*₹ in lakh unless stated otherwise*)

Present sales (₹ in lakh)	125
Total cost (₹ in lakh)	75
Present profits (₹ in lakh)	50
Present profitability (in %)	0.4 or 40%
Required rate of return in receivables	0.125 or 12.50%

Receivables turnover ratio for the two policies can be computed as follows:

Receivables turnover ratio (RTR)

$$= \frac{\text{No. of months or days in a year}}{\text{Credit period}}$$

For Policy A,

$$\text{RTR} = \frac{12 \text{ months}}{1 \text{ month}} = 12$$

For Policy B,

$$\text{RTR} = \frac{12 \text{ months}}{2 \text{ months}} = 6$$

Comparison of two policies

(₹ *in lakh*)

	Credit Policy A	*Credit Policy B*
Additional sales	12.50	18.75
Profitability on additional sales	5.00	7.50
Additional bad debts losses	0.1875	0.375
Additional receivables	1.0417	3.1250
Investment in additional receivables	0.6250	1.8750
Cost of additional investments	0.0781	0.2344
Additional cost	0.2656	0.6094
Incremental profitability	4.7344	6.8906

Since Policy B (extending 2 months of credit period to the customers) is likely to yield more profits than Policy A, Policy B should be chosen by Pai Vista Ltd.

3. Introduction of Discount in the Credit Policy

Saanidhya Enterprises in the recent years has witnessed an average growth rate of 20% in its top-line. The company recorded a sale of ₹452 lakh in the current year. Although the profitability performance of the firm has exceeded the expectations in the recent years, the firm has been facing liquidity crunch with the receivables turnover slowing down.

The firm, as per its present credit policy, is giving a credit period of one month to its customers. The company does not offer any cash discount. In order to improve its liquidity position, the company management is considering liberalizing its credit terms by introducing a 3% cash discount if the payment is made within 10 days. Such a measure is expected to induce the debtors to pay their dues before the current maturity period of 30 days, although it would not affect the firm's sales.

Based on a survey done by an external agency on behalf of the firm, it is estimated that 70% of the customers would avail the discount facility and make the payment within 10 days. This would bring down the average collection period to 10 days.

Should Saanidhya Enterprises introduce cash discount? The company's required rate of return on its receivables is 14.5%.

Solution

The decision to introduce cash discount should be taken based on the cost-benefit analysis. If the firm benefits in net terms on account of introduction of discount, the scheme must be implemented.

Facts of the problem

Present Sales (₹ in lakh)	452
Collection period without cash discount (in days)	30
Collection period with cash discount (in days)	10
Likely reduction in collection period (in days)	20
Firm's Required rate of return	14.5%
Percentage of accounts availing cash discount	70%
Cash discount (%)	3.0%

Cost-benefit analysis of introduction of cash discount

(₹ *In lakh*)

Accounts Receivables (without cash discount) $= \text{Sales} \times \dfrac{\text{Collection Period}}{360}$	37.67
Accounts Receivables (with cash discount) $= \text{Sales} \times \dfrac{\text{Collection Period}}{360}$	12.56
Reduction in accounts receivables on account of cash discount = (₹37.67 lakh – ₹12.56 lakh)	25.11
Savings due to reduced blockage of funds in accounts receivables = (25.11 x 14.5%)	3.64
Loss on account of cash discount (assuming it is availed by all 70% accounts) = (Present Sales x 70% x 3%)	9.49
Net gain on account of proposed cash discount	–5.85

Since the cost of cash discount outweighs their savings, the introduction of cash discount is not advisable.

4. Analysing Credit Policy Change

The current sales of Sigma Designs is ₹1050 lakh. The variable cost of the firm is 75% of the sales. The company with a view to expand its sales is reviewing its present credit policy, which is net 45 days. The present credit period offered by the firm to its customers is fully availed. The average collection period of the firm is 50 days.

The company management is considering changing the credit terms from net 45 to 3/10 net 60. Due to this proposed change in credit policy, the firm's sales are expected to go up by 15%. Although bad debts losses on existing sales will remain unchanged, the same for the additional sales are expected to go up by 2%. The current bad debts of the firm are 1.5% of sales. The average collection period for the new policy is expected to be 35 days. It is expected that 60% of the firm's customers will to avail the cash discount and pay on the 10th day.

Analyse the impact of the change in credit policy on the firm's profits assuming a 18% required rate of return. You can ignore taxes in your computations.

Solution

Current Sales, S (₹ in lakh)	1050
Variable cost ratio, V	75%
Bad debts ratio, b_n (on incremental sales)	1.5%
Proportion of customers likely to avail the cash discount, P_n	60%
Discount rate, d_n	3 %
Required rate of return	18%
Expected growth in sales due to change in credit policy	15%
Average collection period (under current policy) in days	50
Average collection period (under proposed policy) in days	35
Incremental Sales (ΔS)	157.5

$$\Delta P = \Delta S(1 - V) + K\Delta R - b_n\,\Delta S - \Delta DIS$$

where ΔP = Incremental profit

ΔS = Incremental sales

$\Delta S\,(1 - V)$ = Incremental contribution

$K\Delta R$ = Opportunity cost of incremental investment in receivables

ΔDIS = Incremental discount

As per the above model, the incremental profit
= (Profits on incremental sales)
– (Opportunity cost of incremental receivables
+ Incremental bad debts
+ Discount availed by customers)

$\Delta S(1 - V) = 39.375$

$$K\,\Delta R = K[(ACP_o - ACP_n)\frac{S}{360} - V\frac{\Delta S}{360}ACP_n$$

$= 5.81$

where ACP_o = Average collection period under current credit policy
ACP_n = Average collection period under new credit policy
$b_n\,\Delta S = 2.36$
$\Delta DIS = P_n(S + \Delta S)d_n = 21.74$

Therefore, ΔP = ₹21.09 lakh

Thus, change in credit terms is likely to increase the firm's profits, hence introduction of cash discount is acceptable.

5. Multi-period Analysis of Changing the Credit Policy

The current sales of Alpha Ltd are ₹312 lakh. The sales projections of the firm put its next year's sales at ₹328 lakh. The company management is considering lengthening its terms of sale to give a boost to its top-line. Such a measure is likely to slow down its receivables turnover. As a result, the blockage of funds in receivables will increase because the receivables conversion period is likely to increase from 30 days to 45 days. However, the projected sales of ₹355 lakh in the first year is what the management is aiming to achieve by this change in credit policy.

The rate of growth in top-line for the proposed policy is expected to be 10% compared to 9% under the present policy. Variable cost-to-gross sales ratio for the firm is 0.75 and is likely to be maintained in the near future as well. The appropriate risk-adjusted discount rate for the cash flows is 15%. Expected life of the product being sold by the company is 5 years.

The production equipment currently in place will have to be replaced at the end of fourth year to increase the production capacity. The expected cost of replacement would be ₹210 lakh. The equipment can be scrapped at a value of ₹175 lakh at the end of the project.

If the firm implements the proposed credit policy, the CAPEX for increasing capacity additional capacity will be made at the end of the second year for ₹275 lakh and will have a salvage value of ₹100 lakh.

The firm's policies are such that the inventory turnover is 25 times a year with this ratio based on gross sales. Under the present policy, the total bad debts is 1.5% of sales. Under the proposed policy, this is likely to increase to a level of 2% of the sales. Collection costs for the firm is not likely to change if the new policy is adopted. The firm does not offer a cash discount.

The firm is in 38.5% tax brackets and depreciates its assets from their initial value to their expected salvage value by the straight line method. It is anticipated that the inventory and the receivables shall fetch their book value.

Should the firm make proposed changes in its terms of sales?

Solution

Present Policy

Facts of the problem	
Last year's gross sales (₹ in lakh)	312
First year's gross sales (₹ in lakh)	328
Growth rate	9%
Receivables turnover (in days)	30
Bad debt expenses (as % of sales)	1.5%
Discount rate	15%
Inventory turnover (times)	25
Variable cost ratio	0.75
Tax rate	38.5%

₹ lakh	*Year*					
	0	*1*	*2*	*3*	*4*	*5*
Gross sales	312.00	328.00	357.52	389.70	424.77	463.00
Sales net of bad debts	307.32	323.08	352.16	383.85	418.40	456.05
Receipts						
Accounts receivables balance	25.61	26.92	29.35	31.99	34.87	38.00
Cash receipt from sales	281.71	321.77	349.73	381.21	415.52	452.92
Payments						
Inventory balance	12.48	13.12	14.30	15.59	16.99	18.52
Increase in the inventory		0.64	1.18	1.29	1.40	1.53
Cost of goods produced for sale		246.00	268.14	292.27	318.58	347.25
Total cost of goods produced for sale		246.64	269.32	293.56	319.98	348.78
Capital expenditure		—	—	—	210.00	—
Salvage value of new equipment						175.00
Income Tax Calculations						
Sales net of bad debts		323.08	352.16	383.85	418.40	456.05
Cost of goods produced for sale		246.00	268.14	292.27	318.58	347.25
Depreciation		—	—	—	—	35.00
Earnings Before Tax		77.08	84.02	91.58	99.82	73.80
Taxes (@38.5%)		29.68	32.35	35.26	38.43	28.41
Earnings After Tax		47.40	51.67	56.32	61.39	45.39

Computation of NPV

(₹ lakh)

Cash receipt from sales	—	321.77	349.73	381.21	415.52	452.92
Total cost of goods produced for sale	—	246.64	269.32	293.56	319.98	348.78
Capital expenditure	—	—	—	—	210.00	—
Salvage value of new equipment	—	—	—	—	—	175.00
Recovery of receivables	—	—	—	—	—	38.00

(Contd)

(*Contd*)

Recovery on inventory	—	—	—	—	—	18.52
Taxes paid	—	29.68	32.35	35.26	38.43	28.41
Net Cash Flow	—	45.451	48.067	52.393	−152.892	307.247
Total NPV	—	—	—	—	—	**175.66**

Propsosed Policy

Facts of the problem	
Last year's gross sales (₹ in lakh)	312
First year's gross sales (₹ In lakh)	355
Growth rate (in %)	9 %
Receivables turnover (in days)	45
Bad debts expenses	2 %
Discount rate	15 %
Inventory turnover (times)	25
Variable cost ratio	0.75
Tax rate	38.5%

(₹ lakh)

	Years					
	0	**1**	**2**	**3**	**4**	**5**
Gross sales	312.00	355.00	386.95	421.78	459.74	501.11
Sales net of bad debts	305.76	347.90	379.21	413.34	450.54	491.09
Receipts						
Accounts receivables balance	38.22	43.49	47.40	51.67	56.32	61.39
Cash receipt from sales	342.63	375.30	409.07	445.89	486.02	
Payments						
Inventory balance	12.48	14.20	15.48	16.87	18.39	20.04
Increase in the inventory	—	1.72	1.28	1.39	1.52	1.66
Cost of goods produced for sale		266.25	290.21	316.33	344.80	375.83

(*Contd*)

(*Contd*)

Total cost of goods produced for sale		267.97	291.49	317.72	346.32	377.49
Capital Expenditure		—	275.00	—	—	—
Salvage value of new equipment		—	—	—	—	100.00
Income Tax Calculations						
Sales net of bad debts		347.90	379.21	413.34	450.54	491.09
Cost of goods produced for sale		266.25	290.21	316.33	344.80	375.83
Depreciation		—	—	58.33	58.33	58.33
Earnings Before Tax		81.65	89.00	38.68	47.41	56.92
Taxes (@ 38.5%)		31.44	34.26	14.89	18.25	21.92
Earnings After Tax		50.21	54.73	23.79	29.15	35.01

Computation of NPV

(₹ lakh)

Cash receipt from sales	342.63	375.30	409.07	445.89	486.02
Total cost of goods produced for sale	267.97	291.49	317.72	346.32	377.49
Capital expenditure	—	275.00	—	—	—
Salvage value of new equipment	—	—	—	—	100.00
Recovery of receivables	—	—	—	—	61.39
Recovery on inventory	—	—	—	—	20.04
Taxes paid	31.44	34.26	14.89	18.25	21.92
Net Cash Flow	43.23	-225.46	76.46	81.32	268.05
Total NPV	—	—	—	—	**97.15**

Since the NPV from the present credit policy is higher than the NPV from the proposed credit policy, any change in credit policy is likely to erode value. Hence, it is suggested that the firm retains its present credit policy.

EXERCISES

Concept Review Questions

1. What is meant by management of accounts receivable and why does it assume importance?
2. How does credit policy influence the following?
   (a) Sales
   (b) Investment in receivables
   (c) Bad-debt losses
   (d) Collection costs
3. What are the components of credit terms? Explain each component briefly.
4. How can discriminant analysis be utilized in evaluating an applicant's creditworthiness?
5. How is the firm's credit policy linked to the management of its accounts receivable?
6. How does changing credit period affect sales and credit-related costs? Explain.
7. What is meant by collection policy? How is the conceptual foundation of collection policy similar to or different from credit policy framework? Explain briefly.

Critical Thinking Question

1. Evaluate the following statement: "A credit department that never has a delinquent account is an asset to the firm."

Practical Assignment

1. Study the management of accounts receivables of firm(s) of choice over the period and compare it with its own performance in the earlier period(s) and vis-à-vis its competitors against the following parameters:
   (a) Its receivables conversion period. Has the firm been able to expedite its collection process?
   (b) The incidence of bad-debts and the collection costs. Has it been going up or coming down? How have they been behaving vis-à-vis the sales?
   (c) Has the firm been able to enhance its sales without blocking additional funds in its receivables? If so, find out the techniques deployed by the firm for achieving the same.
   (d) Has the firm become more/less efficient with regards to its receivables management?

Numerical Problems

1. Changing the Credit Period

Transient Ltd is currently operating at a 65% capacity utilization level, with its sales pegged at ₹950 lakh. As per its current credit policy, the firm is offering a credit period of 20 days. The average collection period for Transient Ltd is 30 days. In view of increased competition that has started to erode its bottom line recently, the firm's management has been contemplating relaxing its credit terms. As per management's projections, such liberalization of firm's credit policy is likely to boost its sales by 30%. However, since the proposed change is likely to increase the average credit period for the firm by 30 days, one section of the company's management is opposed to any change in the credit policy and is advocating a status quo. The variable costs for the firm are 75% of the sales. Are you in favour of the change proposed in the firm's credit policy? Assume the opportunity cost of capital for Transient Ltd is 12%.

2. Choosing Credit Policies

Networking Ltd, the leader in networking business in the country, has been enjoying its status of market leader, and in a virtual monopolistic situation, has been selling on 100% cash basis. The emerging competition in the sector from new players has forced the firm to revisit its terms of sales, it is now evaluating two alternate credit policy options. The two options are:

On Incremental Sales	*Credit Policy A*	*Credit Policy B*
Collection period (in months)	1.0	2.5
Increase in sales (in %)	15.0	17.0
Bad-debt losses (in %)	1.5	3.0

The current sales of the firm are ₹400 lakh and total costs are ₹312 lakh. Which of the two policies should be chosen by Networking Ltd? Assume that the firm's required return on investment in its receivables is 14%.

3. Evaluating Discount in the Credit Policy

Green & Clean has been performing well on the profitability front with its sales growing at an average of 15–20% over the past four years. However, the firm has been facing liquidity problems in the recent past. In order to improve its liquidity position, the firm's management is considering liberalizing its credit terms by introducing a cash discount. Such a measure is expected to induce debtors to pay their dues before the current maturity period of 30 days and, therefore, is likely to bring down its average collection period by 15 days. In net terms, the funds tied up in receivables are likely to come down due to the introduction of cash discount. Should Green & Clean introduce cash discount?

The current sales of the firm are ₹655 lakh. The company is planning a cash discount policy of 3/10, net 30. Based on the market research done by the company, it is expected that 80% of the accounts are likely to avail of the cash discount facility. The company's required rate of return on its receivables is 18%.

4. Analysing Credit Policy Change

The present terms of sales for Chougule Trading Company are net 30 days. All the sales of the company are on credit basis and the average collection period is 32 days. The current sales of the company are 50 lakh units at an average selling price of ₹ 250 per unit. The variable cost-to-sales ratio for the firm is 65%, while the bad-debts-to-sales ratio is 2.5%. In order to expand sales, the company management is considering changing its credit terms from net 30 to 3/10, net 30. Due to this proposed change in credit policy, the firm's sales are expected to go up by 18%. Although bad-debt losses on existing sales will remain unchanged, they are expected to go up by 2% on the additional sales. The average collection period for the new policy is expected to be 29 days. 40% of the firm's customers are expected to avail of the cash discount and pay on the tenth day.

Analyse the impact of the change in credit policy on the firm's profits, assuming a 20% required rate of return. Ignore taxes.

5. Multi-period Analysis and Credit Policy

The current sales of ABC Ltd are ₹285.46 lakh and it is expected to be ₹310.00 lakh next year.

Sales are expected to grow at 7.5% per annum. The company is considering its terms of sale. The change in the credit policy is likely to increase the accounts receivable turnover period from 45 days to 60 days.

Under the proposed terms, the next year's sales are expected to increase to ₹342 lakh, although the growth in sales is likely to remain the same as under the present policy. Variable costs of production are 70% of gross sales, and the appropriate risk-adjusted discount rate for the cash flows is 13.5%. Expected life of the product being sold by the company is 5 years. The production equipment currently in place has a maximum capacity to produce enough output for a maximum of ₹360 lakh in sales.

Under the present policy, the firm will have to purchase additional production capacity at the end of the fourth year at a cost of ₹ 150 lakh. This capacity will be scrapped at the end of the life of the product at the salvage value of ₹79 lakh. If the firm implements the proposed policy, the capital expenditure for the additional capacity will be made at the end of the second year for ₹188 lakh, and will have a salvage value of ₹ 84 lakh at the end of the product's life.

The firm's policies are such that the inventory turnover is 20 times a year with this ratio, based on gross sales. Under the present policy, bad-debts total 2% of sales; under the proposed policy this is likely to increase to a level of 2.5% of sales. Collection costs for the firm are not likely to change if the new policy is adopted. The firm does not offer a cash discount.

The firm is in the 38.5% tax bracket and depreciates its assets from their initial value to their expected salvage value by the straight line method. It is anticipated that the inventory and the receivables shall fetch their book value.

Should the firm make proposed changes in its terms of sales?

CASE STUDY

Neer Udyog Limited

Background

Neer Udyog Limited was set up as a private limited company 15 years back. The promoters of the company were Shri Ambalal Sarabhai and Shri Suresh Mehta. The company has been a pioneer in the bottled water segment. The promoters of the company could foresee the potential in the packaged water market in the years to come, and became the first ones to launch the product fifteen years ago. The prophecy of the promoters has been proven right and the packaged water market has reached a value in excess of ₹1,000 crore.

Over almost twelve years, Neer Udyog maintained its position as the market leader in the bottled water industry, but now the scenario in the industry has undergone a transformation, and the market today is glutted with players and brands. Innumerable brands in the bottled water market are posing stiff competition, and the category is now growing faster than the retail segment, attracting a number of major players including multinationals like Coke and Pepsi, and above all, the most trusted Indian brand, 'Bisleri'. All these big brands have the advantage of their huge distribution networks, which were built up over the years for their aerated soft drinks and are now being used by them for their bulk water products also. Along with these big players, regional players compete side by side, enjoying local clout.

All in all, the segment is a witness to intense competition, and the firms are devising strategies like consolidation, cost control, etc., to stay afloat. The market share of Neer Udyog has gradually eroded over the past 5–6 years, and the major challenge before the firm in the short run is to maintain its market share. In the medium/long term the firm wishes to regain its position of market leader.

Product

Till a few years back, mineral water used to be an elitist indulgence or something to do with health. Now it is being looked at as a safe drinking water option. Over the years, the product has undergone a major transformation, and the segment has been redefined as bulk water market, which includes water delivered at homes and offices and dispensed from coolers, as well as the gallon- or larger-sized bottled water containers sold from retail stores. Neer Udyog Ltd has been selling its product in three sizes: 1, 5, and 20 litres. With the intensification of competition, there has been a downward pressure on selling prices in the packaged water market.

Financials

Summarized Balance Sheet as on 31 March

(₹ *in lakh*)

	2004	2005	2006
Assets			
Gross Fixed Assets	125.00	138.00	153.00
Less: Accumulated Depreciation	27.50	29.39	31.37
Net Fixed Assets	97.50	108.61	121.64
Inventory	25.00	27.60	30.60
Accounts Receivables	6.25	6.90	7.65
Cash	0.85	0.90	1.10
Marketable Securities	4.25	4.50	5.50
Current Aassets	36.35	39.90	44.85
Total Assets	**133.85**	**148.51**	**166.49**
Liabilities			
Long-term Debt	23.00	21.00	21.00
Share Capital	67.35	60.01	59.44
Reserves and Surplus	15.00	17.50	21.00
Creditors	11.00	12.50	14.35
Short-term Borrowings	13.00	32.30	44.60
Other Payables	4.50	5.20	6.20
	133.85	**148.51**	**166.49**

Summarized Profit and Loss Account for the year ending on 31 March

(₹ *in lakh*)

	2004	2005	2006
Gross Sales	264.75	293.87	311.50
Net Sales	256.81	285.06	302.16
Less: Cost of Goods Sold	154.08	171.03	181.30
Gross Profit	102.72	114.02	120.86
Less: Administrative Expenses	15.00	16.50	17.63
Selling and Distribution expenses	6.00	7.20	7.86
Bad debts	0.11	0.12	0.12
Collection expenses	1.54	1.71	1.81
Interest	2.76	2.52	2.52
Profit before Taxes	77.32	85.97	90.92
Less: Taxes	30.93	34.39	36.37
Profit after Taxes	46.39	51.58	54.55

Actual and Projected Monthly Sales

(₹ *in lakh*)

	Actual Sales 2005-06	***Projected Sales 2006-07***
April	25.45	26.72
May	27.25	28.61
June	30.45	31.97
July	32.60	34.23
August	32.70	34.34
September	33.50	35.18
October	27.25	28.61
November	22.40	23.52
December	17.30	18.17
January	17.50	18.38
February	20.45	21.47
March	24.65	25.88
Total	311.50	327.08

Credit Policy

The firm had earlier been following a policy of cash sales, but with increasing competition over the years, it has liberalized its credit policy. The current credit policy of the firm is to offer a credit period of one month to its distributors, but the firm does not offer any cash discount.

The marketing department of the firm has been pushing hard to liberalize its credit policy, as it feels that such a strategy will give a boost to the firm's top line. The marketing department projections suggest that if the firm liberalizes its credit policy to "1/10 net 60", it will be able to achieve a sales growth of 15% in the coming financial year, as compared to the projected 5% that it is expected to achieve with its existing credit policy.

The low level of bad debts and collection costs of the firm are being stated as the reasons in support of the liberalization of the credit policy. However the VP (Finance) is not convinced by the logic given by the marketing department.

Discuss

1. Should Neer Udyog go ahead with lengthening of its credit terms?

CHAPTER 24

Cash Management

LEARNING OBJECTIVES

After going through this chapter, you should be able to understand the following:

- why do firms hold cash
- the cash flow process and its relevance for the financial health of the firm
- principles underlying the management of cash
- how do firms maximize the availabilty of cash
- working capital cycle and its relationship with financing requirements
- impact of collection float on firms' profits
- how do firms minimize the collection float
- disbursement management
- how to control disbursements to maximize the availability of cash
- forecasting cash position for better cash management
- determination of optimal working capital balance
- choosing the right mix of cash and marketable securities

REGULATE THE FLOW TO PREVENT CONGESTION

"Managing the liquid resources of firms like ours is a tough choice," said Mr Gupta, the chief of treasury operations of Apex Ltd, at an induction and orientation programme for management trainees in the firm's finance department.

Looking at the perplexed faces of his audience, Mr Gupta sensed the need to elaborate the significance of cash management.

"Extra cash improves liquidity, but cuts profitability, and so, one has to strike a balance all the time. There is always a profitability–liquidity tangle to be resolved. Unlike other areas of financial decision-making, cash management cannot be compartmentalized into short-term and long-term. Cash has no colour or creed, and the job of the treasury manager is to ensure that adequate cash is available for both long-term and short-term commitments.

He further added; today's treasurers need rapid and reliable information so that risk and exposure can be accurately monitored for improved decision-making. Efficient cash management processes are needed to execute payment, collect receivables, and manage liquidity. Good cash management is simple. It involves:

1. Knowing when, where, and how your cash needs will occur;
2. Knowing the best sources for meeting additional cash needs;
3. Being prepared to meet these needs when they occur, by keeping good relationships with bankers and other creditors.

The starting point for good cash flow management is developing a cash flow projection. Smart business owners know how to develop both short-term (weekly, monthly) cash flow projections to help them manage daily cash, and long-term (annual, 3–5 year) cash flow projections to help them develop the necessary capital strategy to meet their business needs. They also prepare and use historical cash flow statements to understand how they used money in the past.

I wish you all the very best at this juncture of your career and suggest that you remember all your life the five basic tenets of cash management:

1. Bill promptly,
2. Follow up aggressively,
3. Pay slowly,
4. Project accurately, and
5. Invest discretely."

INTRODUCTION

Cash is the last link of working capital. Management of cash assumes significance as the level of cash, like any other current asset affects liquidity and profitability position. Cash here refers to ready money, available in the bank or with the business. It includes cash in hand, demand deposits with banks, and the cash invested in marketable securities. Since cash is the most liquid current asset; the higher the cash in hand and bank balance, the stronger is the liquidity position and the creditworthiness of the firm, other factors remaining the same. But this liquidity comes at a cost. Cash, though most liquid, is the least productive of current assets. The funds tied up in cash in hand and in current accounts of banks give a yield of zero. The determination of optimal cash balance assumes importance, as it affects the profitability–liquidity position of the firm.

Maximizing cash availability while simultaneously minimizing idle cash is the thrust of cash management. Although the twin objectives—cash availability maximization and idle cash minimization—are seemingly contradictory, they are important from the profitability–liquidity standpoint. Apart from explaining the underlying principles of cash management, this chapter focuses on ways to achieve the aforesaid of cash management. The three techniques highlighted in the chapter to achieve the objective of maintaining an optimal case balance are:

1. Managing collections and disbursements,
2. Reliable forecasting and reporting systems,
3. Maximizing interest income by selecting the optimal mix of cash (held for transaction requirements) and marketable securities.

MOTIVES FOR HOLDING CASH

In his treatise on economics, Keynes[1] has suggested that money demanded by firms can be kept as income deposits, business deposits, or savings deposits. Although all money that is held by firms may not be segregated into these three compartments, and may broadly be held primarily for business and secondarily for other purposes, the three basic motives for holding cash are: *transaction motive, precautionary motive,* and *speculative motive.*

Cash is held by firms with three motives: transaction, precautionary, and speculative.

Transaction motive There is normally a time lag between the incurring of costs (inputs and overheads) and the receipts of corresponding sales proceeds. All businesses need cash to finance their operations during this time lag, and this creates the motive of financing called *transaction motive.*

Holding of cash facilitates the firms' operations by paying for the cost incurred and repaying the liabilities due.

Transaction requirements also include cash balances used to meet irregular outflows, as well as the planned acquisition of fixed assets and inventories. The level of such cash balances depends primarily on the length of the firm's operating cycle, which in turn depends upon the industry characteristics of the firm. If the cash inflows and outflows have an element of certainty, such as those for utility firms, which enjoy quasi-monopolies and assured revenues, the need to hold cash balances for transaction purposes is less, as compared to businesses such as retail chains, where cash flows have high variability. Normally, firms hold most of their cash requirements for transaction purposes either as cash in hand or as cash at bank.

Precautionary motive Firms need to maintain a cash balance to be able to satisfy possible, but as yet indefinite, needs such as providing for contingencies requiring sudden expenditure, and for unforeseen opportunities of advantageous purchases. Cash balance held to cater to such needs is known as precautionary balance. Precautionary balances are a buffer stock of liquid assets. The firm's need for a precautionary cash balance depends, inter-alia, upon the predictability of its cash flows. For example, airlines businesses face a high degree of cash flow uncertainty due to several factors, such as rising fuel costs, strikes by operating personnel, etc. As a result, even minimum cash balances maintained by airline companies are normally high. It also depends upon access to external funds at short notice, which in turn depends on the credit standing of the firm in the market. The higher the creditworthiness of the firm, the more is the ability to raise cash at short notice, and hence, the lesser would be the cash balance held for precautionary purpose.

Lack of perfect synchronization between inflows and outflows necessitates that businesses keep some buffer cash to tide over crisis situations.

As the precautionary balance is akin to the buffer stock of cash that may or may not be required, it is advisable for firms to invest their precautionary balance in marketable securities, instead of letting it lie idle as cash in hand, so that the balance gives them some minimum yield. In case of need, this balance can be used by disinvesting the marketable securities.

Speculative motive Cash is held for speculative purposes in order to take advantage of anticipated profit-making situations. Petroleum marketing companies, for example, may be holding cash to temporarily increase their inventory in view of anticipated increases in petroleum prices, as this would enable them to gain from these increases. Generally, the speculative motive is the least important component of a firm's preference for liquidity. The transaction and precautionary motives account for most of the reasons why a company holds cash balances. Although the possibility of firms holding cash for speculative purposes can not be denied, the literature does not reckon the speculative motive as a genuine motive for holding cash, as it goes against the spirit of the terms of contract that exists between the firm and its

Cash may be held by some businesses to make some speculative earnings, although for a non-speculative business, holding of cash with a speculative profit motive is not a genuine motive.

[1] John Maynard Keynes, *The General Theory of Employment, Interest and Money*, Harcourt, Brace, New York, 1936, p. 170

investors. Nonetheless, if the firm holds cash for speculative purposes, it should always remain invested in marketable securities till such time as the opportunity for gain arises.

The strength of all these three types of motive will partly depends on the costs and the reliability of sources of temporary (or short term) financing, in particular an overdraft facility or its equivalent. Obviously, there is no necessity to hold idle cash to bridge over intervals if it can be obtained without difficulty at moments when it is actually required. This strength will also depend on what we may term the relative cost of holding cash. If the cash can only be retained by forgoing the purchase of a profitable asset, this increases the cost, and thus weakens the motive towards holding a given amount of cash. If deposit interest is earned, or if bank charges are avoided by holding cash, this decreases the cost and strengthens the motive. It is possible, however, that this is likely to be a minor factor except where large changes in the cost of holding cash are in question.

CASH FLOW PROCESS AND ITS RELEVANCE

The flow of cash into and out of the business over a period of time is referred to as cash flow. Cash inflow can be in the form of cash received from customers, lenders, and investors. Cash outflow can arise as a result of payments made to employees, suppliers, and creditors. The net cash flow position of the business is either positive or negative. When cash inflow exceeds outflow, it results in positive cash flows. Such a cash flow position is beneficial to the business. However, surplus cash lying with the business entails opportunity cost. When cash outflow exceeds inflow, the net cash flow for the firm is termed negative. A negative cash flow position is a point of concern for the firm because if such a position lasts, it may jeopardize the sustainability of the business. Firms have to identify the reasons for such a negative cash flow position and take the necessary corrective measures. Figure 24-1 depicts the process of resources generation and disposition in a typical manufacturing firm. As can be seen in the figure, cash flows occur on account of both regular operating transactions and episodic non-operating transactions. Cash flows that typically occur in businesses can be classified into three heads: *operating cash flow, investing cash flow,* and *financing cash flow*.

Cash flows in and out of the business on account of operating, investing, and financing activities. The operating cash flows are of utmost importance from the working capital perspective.

Operating cash flows Operating cash flows, often referred to as working capital or regular cash flows, are generated from the firm's mainline operations. It is the cash generated from the sale of a product or service of a particular business. The examples of operating cash outflows are payments for inputs and overheads, while the inflows primarily consist of cash sales and collections from receivables. As these cash flows determine the sustainability of the firm's operations, they need to be monitored carefully.

Investing cash flow Investing cash flow is generated internally from non-operating activities such as acquisition of fixed assets, purchase of financial investments, disposal of used assets, etc. Such cash flows are important, as they affect the productive capacity of the business. To maintain the productivity of the firm, regular investing cash outflows need to be incurred.

Financing cash flow It is the cash flow to and from external sources, such as lenders, investors, and shareholders. Raising a new loan, the repayment of a loan, the issuance of stock, and the payment of dividend are some of the activities that would be included in this section of the cash flow statement.

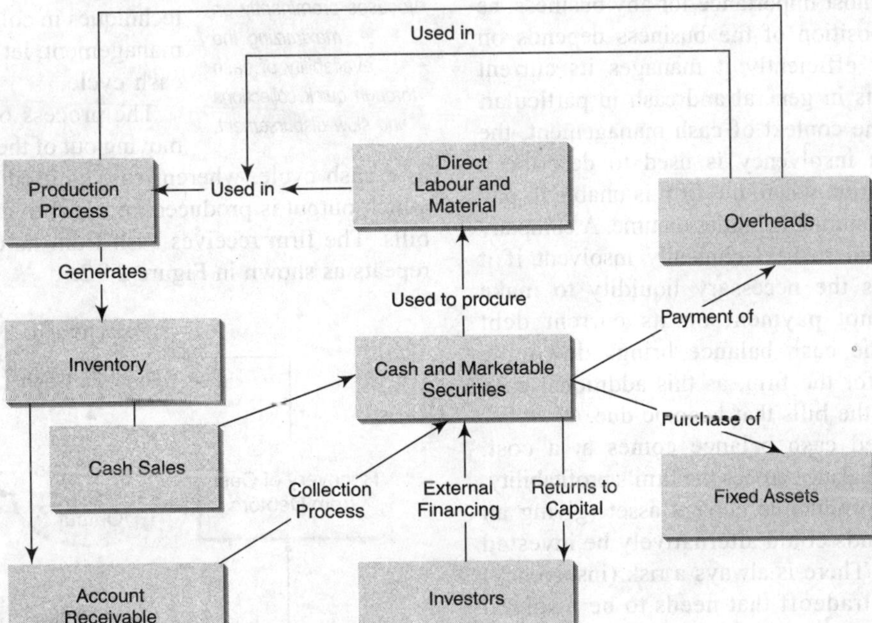

Figure 24-1 Resource flow in a manufacturing firm

It is essential for firms to generate a net cash flow surplus from mainline operations, as this not only determines the liquidity health of the firms, but can also be used for capital servicing and for financing the future expansion needs of the firms. The sustainability of the firm's operations and its credibility in the capital market depends upon how efficiently it manages this net operating cash flow surplus, and how well it synchronizes its inflow and outflows to ensure that the cash balance is neither excessive nor inadequate.

The cash flow surplus from operating activities determines liquidity health and sustainability of operations. This surplus also contributes towards capital servicing and future financing needs. Hence, its management assumes significance for the business.

Potentially profitable companies can fail because of poor cash management, while apparently non-profitable companies can be kept alive by efficient cash management techniques. Cash is the lifeblood of a business. Of course, profitability and other financial issues are all important; but when it comes down to the one financial matter that must always be rigorously managed, cash tops the list. The importance of cash and its proper management stems from the fact that there is a lack of a perfect synchronization of inflows and outflows. No matter how accurately the cash flow projections are made, there is always the possibility of lead and lag between the inflows and the outflows. In cases where the inflows precede the outflows, the issue of productively parking the cash for the period it is lying as surplus with the business is of importance to the firms. But when the outflows precede the operating inflows, the business has to have a sufficient cash buffer to ensure that it is able to meet outflow requirements on account of purchase of inputs, payment for overheads, or meeting other obligations.

PRINCIPLES OF CASH MANAGEMENT

Cash management is of utmost importance for any business, as the short-term solvency position of the business depends on how efficiently it manages its current assets in general and cash in particular. In the context of cash management, the term insolvency is used to describe a situation where the firm is unable to pay its maturing liabilities on time. A company is said to be technically insolvent if it lacks the necessary liquidity to make prompt payment on its current debt obligations. Increasing the cash balance brings down the probability of insolvency for the firm, as this additional cash provides a cushion to pay the bills that become due.

The key objective of cash management is to ensure that sufficient cash is available to finance day to day operations, while at the same time idle funds are minimized.

However, this increased cash balance comes at a cost. Increase in the level of cash balance erodes the firm's profitability, because cash is the least productive current asset (giving an explicit yield of zero). Funds could alternatively be invested in more productive assets. There is always a risk (insolvency) and return (profitability) tradeoff that needs to be resolved in the management of cash. The finance manager must strike an acceptable balance between holding too much cash and too little cash. A large cash balance minimizes the chances of insolvency, but penalizes the company's profitability. A small cash component frees excess balances for investment in both marketable securities and longer-lived assets; this enhances company profitability, and thereby, the value of the firm's common shares, but increases the chances of running out of cash. This risk-return tradeoff can be reduced to two prime objectives for the firm's cash management system:

1. Holding enough cash balance to carry out the operating needs of the business
2. Minimizing funds tied up in the idle cash balance.

To achieve these twin objectives, the firms need to focus on the three important aspects of cash management (also referred to as key decision areas in cash management) listed below.

The three focal issues in cash management are: collection and disbursement management; reliable cash forecasting system; determining the optimal mix of cash in hand and cash invested productively in marketable securities.

- Managing collections and disbursements
- Reliable cash forecasting and reporting system
- Maximizing the interest income by selecting the optimal mix of cash (held for transaction requirements) and marketable securities.

The reminder of this chapter dwells on these three decision issues.

COLLECTIONS AND DISBURSEMENTS MANAGEMENT

One of the main focuses of cash management is to maximize the availability of cash, which can be achieved by managing collections and disbursements, i.e., expediting collections and slowing down disbursements. Before we take up the underlying issues and techniques in collection and disbursement management, let us understand the firm's cash cycle.

Cash management focuses prominently on maximizing the availability of cash through quick collections and slow disbursement.

The process of cash flowing into and moving out of the business may be viewed as a cash cycle, wherein cash is used to procure inputs, from which output is produced and sold to customers, who pay their bills. The firm receives cash from its customers and the cycle repeats as shown in Figure 24-2.

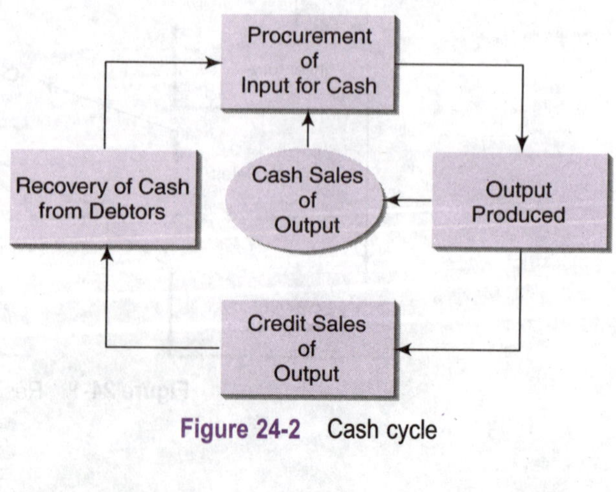

Figure 24-2 Cash cycle

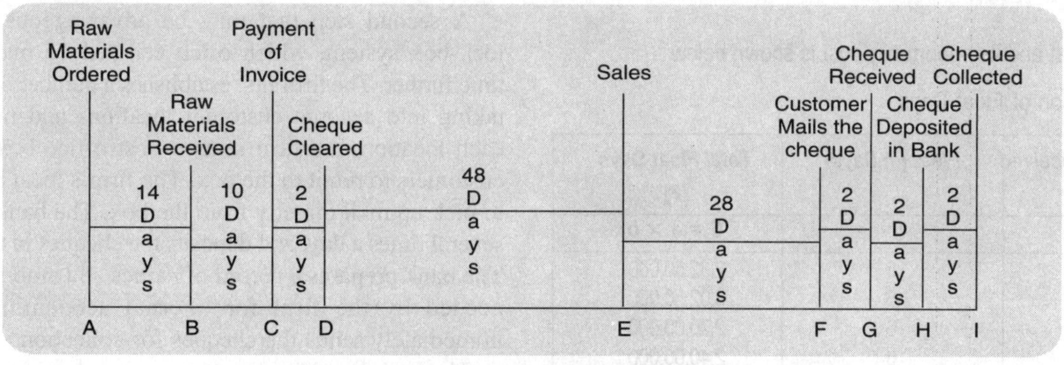

Figure 24-3 Working capital cycle of a typical manufacturing firm

Collection management assumes significance particularly for firms that follow a policy of liberal credit terms and standards, as the extent of funds blocked in receivables is high. The higher the extent of blockage, the more is the firm's financing requirement. To the extent a firm is able to bring down this blockage in receivables, its working financing requirements come down. To understand this blockage phenomenon and its impact on the firm's bottom line, let us revisit the concept of working capital cycle (or operating cycle) that has been discussed at length in Chapter 21. The working capital cycle is shown in Figure 24-3 from the perspective of blockage of funds.

In Figure 24-3, firm XYZ orders for raw material at point A and receives it 14 days later at point B. Terms of 2/10, net 30 are offered by suppliers, so the firm pays the invoice 10 days later at Point C. However, it takes two days for the cheque to clear, and the firm's bank account is not charged until point D (though taken as two days, firm's account is actually debited on the next day of presentation in the bank). Suppose the firm turns over its inventory six times in the year. The product is sold 60 days after the raw material is received and the customer is billed. The collection period is 30 days, 28 for the customer to pay and 2 for the cheque to arrive by mail (at point G). XYZ processes the payment and deposit it two days later, at point H. Another two days elapse while XYZ's bank collects the funds from the customer's bank.

The financing requirements of working capital depend upon the working capital cycle.

The firm's total financing requirement is affected by the total time lag from point B to point I. The firm can control some, but not all, of the factors that determine the various lags. Some of the lags affect the cash balance, while others affect other components of working capital, such as accounts receivable and inventory. In addressing ourselves to cash management, we are concerned with time periods BCD and FGHI. Time period AB is beyond the firm's control and does not directly affect its financial statements, although it may affect production schedules. Time period BE is determined by the firm's production process and inventory policy, and affects the total investment in inventory. Time period EF is determined by the firm's credit terms and the payment policies of its customers, and affects the total investment in accounts receivable. The larger the delay in collection (F to I), the more is the requirement for funds to maintain continuity in operations. Firms aim at cutting down this time lag between points F and I. The delay in collection is termed as *collection float*.

Collection Float and its Impact on Profitability

Collection float refers to the total time lag from the point the customer mails the payment (cheque/draft—point F in Figure 24-3) till the funds actually become available to the firm (point I in the figure). This time lag is on account of mail time delay, time taken by the firms to process the cheques/drafts received from customers before sending them to their bank, and the time taken by the bank to clear the cheque/draft and credit the value to the firm's account, making the funds actually available for use by the firm. Thus, collection float is the sum of mail float, processing float, and availability float. It assumes significance for the firm, as cutting down of the float expedites the availability of funds to the firm, and to that extent, it reduces dependence on external sources of finance for operational needs. Furthermore, the funds tied up in the working capital chain (between point F and I in Figure 24-3) entail an opportunity cost. The higher this blockage, the more will be the opportunity cost for the firm. Example 24-1 explains the concept of collection float.

Collection float is the time gap between customers making the payments and those becoming actually available to the firm.

Collection float has an inverse relationship with profits. Firms try to minimize the collection float to enhance their profits.

Example 24-1 Impact of Collection Float

Asbestos Ltd is likely to receive the following four payments in the coming week:

Payments to be received (Amt. in ₹)	*Day of the week*
77,50,000	Monday
60,50,000	Tuesday
45,00,000	Thursday
40,00,000	Saturday

As per past trends, the delays involved in Float are normally as follows:

Payments received on	*Float*
Monday	1 mail + 2 processing and availability = 3 days
Tuesday	1 + 1 + 3 = 5
Thursday	1 + 2 + 3 = 6
Saturday	1 + 2 + 3 = 6

Show the impact of the collection float on the firm, assuming the opportunity cost of capital to be 10%.

Solution

Computation of float and its opportunity cost is shown below

Step 1: Computation of Float Days

Payments to be received (Amt. in ₹)	*Float (in Days)*	*Total Float Days (₹)*
(a)	*(b)*	C = a × b
77,50,000	3	2,32,50,000
60,50,000	5	3,02,50,000
45,00,000	6	2,70,00,000
40,00,000	6	2,40,00,000
		10,45,00,000

Step 2: Computation of Daily Float

Average Daily Float (Total float days ÷ number of days) = 104,500,000 ÷ 7	14,928,571

Step 3: Computation of Opportunity Cost of Average Daily Float

= (1,49,28,571.43 ÷ 0.10) ÷ (365 ÷ 100)

= 4,090.02

This daily opportunity cost, when converted into annual opportunity cost of the funds blocked due to collection float, becomes 4090.02 × 365, or 1,492,897. This clearly highlights the magnitude of the impact of collection float.

Having discussed the importance of expediting collections by reducing the collection float, we now turn to the techniques available for the same.

Taking the Entry Points Closer to the Customers and Improving the Internal Processing

To the extent a firm is able to reduce the lag between the time the customer mails the cheque and the time the funds get collected, that is, from points F to I in Figure 24-3, the collection float is minimized and cash availability is expedited. Of the six days lag in Figure 24-3, two days are due to mail time, two days are due to processing time within XYZ, and two days are due to collection time within the bank. We will have more to say later about collection within the banking system. Let us now focus on the four days lag from points F to H.

Firms should take the entry points closer to the customers. This cuts down the mail float and expedites the availability of funds.

Small firms that operate in limited geographical areas often can do little to reduce mail time. However, improvements often can be made in processing time within the firm. Suppose XYZ has credit sales of ₹5 crore per year. With approximately 250 working days per year, XYZ's collections average ₹2,00,000 per working day. If XYZ could reduce its collection period by a single day (taking XYZ's borrowing cost as 9%), a saving of about ₹18,000 per year would be realized (2,00,000 × 9%). These potential saving could be compared to the cost of faster processing to determine whether the change in processing should be made. We can conclude that internal processing should be speeded up to the point at which the cost of further improvement exceeds the savings achieved.

A second step that may be advantageous is to establish a lock-box system, which often can reduce mail and processing time further. The firm first establishes a number of collection points, taking into account customer locations and mail schedules. At each location, the firm rents a post office box and instructs its customers to remit to the box. The firm's local bank is authorized to pick up mail directly from the box. The bank does so, perhaps several times a day, and deposits the cheques in the firm's account. The bank prepares a record of names and amounts and other data needed by the firm for internal accounting purposes, and immediately sends the cheques for collection.

The lock-box system results in two benefits to the firm: first, the bank performs the clerical tasks of handling the remittances prior to deposit, services which the bank may be able to perform at lower cost. Second, and often more important, the process of collection through the banking system begins immediately upon receipt of the remittance and does not have to wait until the firm completes its processing for internal accounting purposes. In terms of the activities in Figure 24-3, the activity represented by HI now takes place simultaneously with GH. The firm processes remittances for internal accounting purposes using data supplied by the bank and can schedule this processing at any time, without delaying collection. By using a lock-box system, as much as four days in mailing and processing time can be reduced for XYZ. Most utility companies who have to collect small sums of monies from huge number of customers have adopted lock-box system in some form or the other.

Setting up of lock-boxes brings down the mail and internal processing floats.

Banks charge for their services in connection with a lock-box plan, by way of either fees or compensating account balance requirements. Whether the savings will outweigh the costs for a particular company depends mainly on the geographical dispersion of customers, the amount of the average remittance, and the firm's financing cost.

We see that a major advantage of speeding up collections is freeing of blocked cash, and thereby, reduction in the firm's total financing requirements. There are other advantages as well. By transferring clerical functions to the bank, the firm may reduce its costs, improve internal control, and reduce the possibility of fraud. By getting cheque to banks on which they are written sooner, the incidence of cheques getting dishonoured for insufficient funds may also be reduced.

Reducing collection time in the banking system

We have made several references to the time required to collect a cheque through the banking system (HI in Figure 24-3), but we have made no proposals to shorten it. Let us look at the process of cutting down collection time in the banking system. Suppose a customer in New Delhi purchases electronics equipment from a firm in Mumbai, and remits a cheque drawn on a New Delhi bank. The seller deposits the cheque in a bank in Mumbai, but the funds are not available for use until the cheque has been presented physically to the New Delhi bank, a process that depends on mail service between the two cities and may take several days. A very extensive clearing network has been established in India that involves the commercial banks and the Reserve Bank of India. In the majority of cases, clearing times has been reduced to two days or less, using the facilities of direct inter-bank clearing.

With the advent of technology and computerization in banking systems the delays in collection have been minimized. Electronic clearing system (ECS) and real time gross settlement (RTGS) (described in Box 24-1 and Box 24-2, respectively) have been introduced that have major implications in cash management. They have not only reduced the collection time in the banking system but have also gone a long way in facilitating the receivables management.

Box 24-1 **Electronic Clearing Service (ECS)***

ECS is a mode of electronic funds transfer from one bank account to another bank account using the services of a Clearing House. This is normally for bulk transfers from one account to many accounts or vice-versa. This can be used both for making payments like distribution of dividend, interest, salary, pension, etc., by institutions or for collection of amounts for purposes such as payments to utility companies like telephone, electricity, or charges such as house tax, water tax, etc., or for loan installments of financial institutions/banks or regular investments of persons.

ECS (Credit) transaction can be initiated by any institution who have to make bulk or repetitive payments to a number of beneficiaries. The clearing house would debit the account of the ECS user through the account on the appointed day and credit the accounts of the recipient banks, for affording onward credit to the accounts of the ultimate beneficiaries. Beneficiaries have many benefits like avoiding frequent visits to bank for depositing the physical paper instruments, preventing loss of instrument and fraudulent encashment, and prompt realization of proceeds after receipt of paper instrument. The payee saves on administrative machinery for printing, dispatch and reconciliation, avoids loss of instruments in transit and chances of frauds. Similary banks avoid handling papers.

ECS (Debit) transaction allows the users to recover an amount at a prescribed frequency by raising a debit. The ECS user has to collect ECS mandate for raising such debits. These mandates have to be endorsed by the bank branch maintaining the account. Banks will treat the electronic instructions received through the clearing system on par with the physical cheques.

To the corporates bodies, the system ensures trouble-free collection eliminating the need to go to the collection centres/banks, saves on administrative machinery for collecting the cheques, monitoring their realization and reconciliation resulting in better cash management. It also avoids chances of frauds due to fraudulent access to the paper instruments and encashment. It also enables realization of the payments on a single date instead of fractured receipt of payments.

**Adapted from the website of Reserve Bank of India, http://www.rbi.org.in/ 23 March 2008*

Box 24-2 **RTGS System**

"RTGS" stands for Real Time Gross Settlement. RTGS system is a funds transfer mechanism where transfer of money takes place from one bank to another on a "real time" and on "gross" basis. This is the fastest possible money transfer system through the banking channel. Settlement in "real time" means payment transaction is not subjected to any waiting period. The transactions are settled as soon as they are processed. "Gross settlement" means the transaction is settled on one-to-one basis without bunching with any other transaction. Considering that money transfer takes place in the books of the Reserve Bank of India, the payment is taken as final and irrevocable.

Electronic fund transfer system (EFT) or national electronics funds transfer system (NEFT) are electronic fund transfer modes that operate on a deferred net settlement (DNS) basis which settles transactions in batches. In DNS, the settlement takes place at a particular point of time. All transactions are held up till that time. For example, NEFT settlement takes place 6 times a day during the weekdays and 3 times during Saturdays. Any transaction initiated after a designated settlement time would have to wait till the next designated settlement time. Contrary to this, in RTGS, transactions are processed continuously throughout the RTGS business hours.

The RTGS system is primarily for large value transactions. The minimum amount to be remitted through RTGS is ₹1 lakh. There is no upper ceiling for RTGS transactions. No minimum or maximum stipulation has been fixed for EFT and NEFT transactions.

Under normal circumstances, the beneficiary branches are expected to receive the funds in real time as soon as funds are transferred by the remitting bank. The beneficiary bank has to credit the beneficiary's account within two hours of receiving the funds transfer message. If the money cannot be credited for any reason, the receiving bank would have to return the money to the remitting bank within 2 hours.

The RTGS service window for customer's transactions is available from 9.00 hours to 15.00 hours on weekdays and from 9.00 hours to 12.00 noon on Saturdays. However, the timings between these hours would vary depending on the customer timings the branches have.

As on 31 January 2007, more than 26,000 bank branches are RTGS enabled.

On a typical day, RTGS handles about 14,000 transactions a day for an approximate value of ₹1,50,000 crore.

Source: www.rbi.org.in as on 23 March 2008

In this regard, it needs to be mentioned that a firm can negotiate with its bank and ensure that the bank makes funds available to it, albeit conditionally, to the extent of the value of cheques it deposited for clearing. Firms should be careful in selecting banks to deal with, and should go with the banks that provide them with accelerated clearing facilities, as this would cut down the time lag between the firms depositing payments in the banking system, and the funds actually becoming available to the firms. Services such as factoring (discussed in Chapter 20), offered by banks, release the funds tied up.

Concentrating Banking

By taking the entry points closer to the customers using tools such as lock-boxes, etc., firms are able to ensure that funds enter the system soon. By improving the efficiency of processing of payments at the firm level, and collection at the bank level, the collected funds can become usable funds. However, the actual usage depends on how quickly the funds that lie scattered are concentrated into a central pool.

The funds collected should be pooled into the centralized account quickly to make them usable.

Many firms need only a single bank account. Larger firms that operate over wide geographical areas usually need more than one, sometimes dozens. Where many accounts are needed, concentration accounts can be used to minimize the total requirement for working balances. Suppose a company has a number of branch offices, each with a local bank account. Branches collect accounts receivable and make deposits in their local accounts. Each day, funds above a certain predetermined minimum level are transferred to a central concentration account, usually at the firm's headquarters.

The funds transferred to the concentration account are available for disbursements and for other purposes. As we will see later, the more variable a firm's cash flows, the higher the requirement for working cash balances.

By pooling its funds for disbursement in a single account, the aggregate requirement for working balances is lower than it would be if balances were maintained at each branch office. Concentration, in short, permits the firm to 'store' its cash more efficiently.

Controlling Disbursements

Just as speeding collections quickly turns accounts receivable into cash, and thereby reduces the firm's financing requirements, slowing disbursements also does the same. In an earlier chapter, we discussed trade credit as a source of funds. We concluded that the proper policy was to pay within the terms agreed upon, taking cash discounts when offered. We also concluded that there is no point in paying sooner than agreed. By waiting as long as possible, the firm maximises the extent to which accounts payable are used as a source of funds, a source which requires no interest payment.

Firms should try to delay disbursements up to the point it does not adversely affect relationships with suppliers.

Firms with expense-generating activities over a wide area often find it advantageous to make disbursements from a single central account. In that way, schedules can be tightly controlled and disbursements can be made on exactly the right days. An alternate arrangement is to disburse from decentralized locations, but to wire transfer funds for this purpose, the exact amount needed in each local account for all disbursements scheduled on a given day needs to be ascertained accurately.

Some firms find it advantageous to exploit the 'cheque book float', which is the time between the writing of a cheque and its presentation for collection, represented by CD in Figure 24-3. If this lag can be exploited, it offsets at least partially the lag in the other direction in collecting cheques from customer (HI). Normally, a firm's balance on the bank's books is higher than in its own cheque book because of lag CD. Knowing this, a firm may be able to reduce its working cash requirements. Banks understand cheque book float also, and can be expected to set compensating balances and fees based on balances on their books. If a firm exploits cheque book float too far, it increases the likelihood of cheques being dishonoured because of insufficient funds, and the resultant displeasure of both bank and payee.

CASH FORECASTING

Besides efficient management of their collections and disbursements, firms need to develop a reliable system of cash forecasting and reporting. A reliable forecasting system enables the firms to identify the periods of cash leads and lags in advance, and thus facilitate investment planning for periods of projected surplus and resource planning for periods of projected deficits. As can be seen in Example 24-2, ABC Ltd, through cash forecasting, has been able to identify July, August, and October as the months with cash deficit. Such identification will enable the firm to raise the required funds in a timely and efficient manner. Similarly the firm has also identified September, November, and December as months with cash surplus, for which productive investment opportunities can be identified. Such a cash projection will facilitate the firm in investing surplus funds expected to be available in these months. This would help maximize interest income by making timely short-term investments and minimizing idle funds.

A reliable system of cash forecasting helps in identifying the amounts of cash surpluses and deficits along with the periods in which they fall. This facilitates proper resource planning.

An accurate forecasting system forms the bedrock of effective cash management, as cash forecasting involves projections of all possible cash flows expected during the forecast periods. Cash forecasting is a comprehensive exercise that requires information about the different items of probable cash flows (inflows and outflows). Cash forecasting is an integrated exercise that requires information from different sources/departments. The starting point of cash forecasting is the sales projections that form the basis of forecasting the other components of cash inflows and outflows. In the light of these projected sales, the other departments like production, marketing, and personnel prepare their respective budgets, which are eventually integrated into the overall cash forecast for the firm.

The time horizon for forecasting may range from one day to one year, depending upon the requirements. Both short-duration and long-duration forecasts should correspond with each other. The process of moving from forecasts of shorter duration to those of longer duration is known as *scheduling*, while the process of moving from long-duration forecasts to short-duration forecasts is known as *distribution*.

Example 24-2 Cash Forecasting

ABC Ltd wants to forecast its cash requirements for the period July to December 2007, based on the following information.

- Historically, 12% of the firm's sales has been on cash basis. Of credit sales, 55% is realized in the next month, and 32% is realized in the second month from sales.
- Sales for the months of May and June were ₹ 700 lakh and 755 lakh respectively. The sales department has submitted the following forecasts for sales in the coming months:

Months	*Sales Forecasts (₹ in lakh)*
July	850
Aug	856
Sept	876
Oct	805
Nov	750
Dec	678

- The projected expense details given by the production deparment are as follows:
- Direct material is 38% of sales.
- Direct labour is 34% of sales for July, August and September, but is expected to rise to 35% for the period thereafter. As per past trends, direct labour is generally paid for in the month it is incurred.
- The suppliers grant the terms of sales of net 60 days, which are fully utilised.
- Fixed monthly expenses such as rent, etc., are estimated to be ₹124.5 lakh. Tax payment, due to be paid in the months of July and October, is estimated to be ₹46 lakh. Repayment of long-term debt is due in the month of October to the tune of ₹105 lakh.
- The capital planners' conference that met in December 2006 had estimated the amount of progress payments, due in August, October, and December on the firm's new construction, at ₹110 lakh. Interest on inter-corporate lending by the firm is likely to be received in the month of October. The total loans given by the firm amount to ₹200 lakh at 10.5% interest per annum, and the interest is received on a quarterly basis.
- The firm wishes to maintain a cash balance at the level of 5% of monthly sales. Surplus cash, if any, is invested by the firm in marketable securities.

Prepare a cash forecast on monthly basis

Solution

Monthly cash forcast (July to December, 2007) for ABC Ltd

	May	*June*	*July*	*Aug.*	*Sep.*	*Oct.*	*Nov.*	*Dec.*
Sales	700.00	755.00	850.00	856.00	876.00	805.00	750.00	678.00
Cash Receipt Forecasts:								
Cash sales			102.00	102.72	105.12	96.60	90.00	81.36
Collections one month prior			415.25	467.50	470.80	481.80	442.75	412.50
Collections 2 months prior			224.00	241.60	272.00	273.92	280.32	257.60
Total Receipts		**741.25**	**811.82**	**847.92**	**852.32**	**813.07**	**751.46**	
Cash Disbursement Forecasts:								
Direct material payments		323.00	325.28	332.88	305.90	285.00	257.64	
Direct labour payments		289.00	291.04	297.84	281.75	262.50	237.30	
Monthly fixed expenses		124.50	124.50	124.50	124.50	124.50	124.50	
Tax payments			46.00			46.00		
New construction				110.00		110.00		110.00
Repayment of loan						105.00		
Total Disbursements			**782.50**	**850.82**	**755.22**	**973.15**	**672.00**	**729.44**
Net cash flow			**–41.25**	**-39.00**	**92.70**	**–120.83**	**–141.07**	**–22.02**
Beginning cash			37.75	42.50	42.80	43.80	40.25	37.50
TOTAL CASH			**–3.50**	**3.50**	**135.50**	**–77.03**	**181.32**	**59.52**
Desired cash			**42.50**	**42.80**	**43.80**	**40.25**	**37.50**	**33.90**
Borrowings		**–46.00**	**–39.30**		**–117.28**			
Investment in marketable Securities					**91.70**		**143.82**	**25.62**

CASH VS MARKETABLE SECURITIES

Given that the firm has been able to maximize the availability of cash through quick collections and delayed disbursements, and that the amounts and periods of deficit/surplus have been identified, the next important issue facing the firm is to decide the mix of cash and marketable securities. For the purpose of discussion, in this section we will make a slight departure from the definition of cash given in the introduction to the chapter. Here, cash includes cash in hand and cash held in form of other demand deposits with banks (together referred to as working balance in this section), but excludes marketable securities. This is because unlike marketable securities, the other two items give a yield of zero. Thus, the higher the cash held by the firm, the better is its liquidity position. However, this increased cash adversely affects its profitability position, as the funds tied up in cash have their opportunity costs. The profitability position of the firm improves if it converts cash into marketable securities, which give returns to the firm. Thus, the decision on how much of surplus should be retained in cash and how much should be invested in marketable securities has implications for the profitability–liquidity position of the firm.

Determining the optimal cash balance assumes significance as cash is the most liquid but least productive current asset.

The key issue relating to cash is to determine how much cash a firm should maintain as a working balance. Let us clarify here that what we refer to as cash in hand actually refers to the cash balance that the firm is maintaining in its current account; this is because the cash balance in current accounts, like cash in hand, does not give any return to the firm. We will address this question here, and in the next section discuss the investment of amounts above the working balance.

The key issue is to determine the mix of cash held as working balance and cash invested in marketable securities.

The working balance is maintained for transaction purposes. If the firm maintains too small a working balance, it may run out of cash. It then must liquidate marketable securities, if available, or borrow from outside. Both the options entail costs that are known as transaction costs.

Too high a working balance maintained by the firm may help in reducing the cash crunch, and hence the liquidity problem, but in maintaining such a balance the firm forgoes the opportunity to earn interest on marketable securities. This interest forgone is referred to as the opportunity cost of the funds tied up in the working balance. Thus, the entire issue boils down to determining the optimal level of working balance, i.e., the balance that is neither excessive nor inadequate. Finding such an optimal balance involves a tradeoff of transaction costs against opportunity costs. By keeping a low working balance, a firm would be able to reduce its opportunity costs, but it may have to incur more transaction costs, because of the high number of transactions involving: (1) disinvestment of marketable securities to generate required working balances as and when needed and (2) investments of surplus cash in marketable securities at times when cash available exceeds the working balance requirements. The situation will be reversed with firms that maintain a very high working balance. Thus, transaction costs fall as the working balance level rises. Opportunity costs, on the other hand, rise as the level of working balances rises. Management should try to find the point where the sum of the two costs is at a minimum. However, locating the optimal point and maintaining the working balance at that level consistently may not always be practical or feasible, as this optimal balance keeps on fluctuating depending upon demand and supply constraints, transaction costs, opportunity costs, prospects and costs of external financing, etc. Yet, it serves as the referral point for firms to monitor their working balance and take the necessary actions. There are several models that can be used to determine the optimal level of working balance.

A high level of working balance reduces the transaction costs but increases the opportunity cost.

The issue of optimal level of working balance is resolved in the light of tradeoff of opportunity costs and transaction costs.

Models to Determine the Optimal Working Balance

The models to determine the optimal working balance of a firm can be classified into two categories—certainty-based models and uncertainty-based models. Certainty-based models follow the EOQ approach of inventory management and apply it to determining the optimal level of working balance. Uncertainty-based models, which seem to be more realistic due to their assumption of uncertain cash flows, follow the stochastic modelling. Their models follow the control limits approach. The Baumol's model discussed in this section follows the certainty approach while the Miller–Orr model subscribes to the uncertainty assumption. Although there are other models, such as Beranek[2] and Stone[3], this section discusses only the Baumol and Miller–Orr models in detail, as the other models are extensions of the two basic models (the Beranek model extends the Baumol model by focusing upon cases with lumpy outflows and steady inflows, while the Stone model extends the Miller–Orr model by adding two sets of outer and inner control limits).

Baumol's Model[4]

It uses the EOQ method of inventory control to determine the optimal level of working balance under conditions of certainty. Like the EOQ model, the objective function of the Baumol model is of cost minimization, i.e., minimizing opportunity costs and transaction costs.

Baumol's model with its assumptions of certainty proposes the optimal level as a point where the total of opportunity costs and transaction costs is minimized.

---

[2] Beranek, William, *Analysis for Financial Decisions*, (Homewood, Ill: Richard D. Irwin, 1963)

[3] Stone, Bernell, 'The Use of Forecasts and Smoothing in Control-Limit Models for Cash Management,' *Financial Management*, Spring 1972, pp. 72-84.

[4] Baumol, William, 'The Transactions Demand for Cash: An Inventory Theoretic Approach,' *Quarterly Journal of Economics*, November 1952, pp. 545-56.

The firm attempts to minimize the sum of holding costs (opportunity costs) and conversion costs (transaction costs). Let us look at the assumptions of the model before we discuss the model in detail. The model is based on the following assumptions:

1. The cash requirements of a firm can be forecasted with certainty.
2. The firm's cash payments occur at a steady rate over the period.
3. The opportunity cost of holding cash is known, and remains constant over time.
4. The transaction cost remains constant through out the period.

Assume that the firm starts with an opening cash balance of C as shown in Figure 24-4, and the total fund requirement of the firm during the period is T. With steady cash outflows, this cash balance C gets used up over the period, till it reaches a level of zero at time t_1. At this point, the firm will disinvest its marketable securities to the tune of ₹ C, so as to restore its cash position. This can be seen in Figure 24-4. The average cash balance of the firm is $C/2$ because the model assumes a steady reduction in its cash balance. Assuming the opportunity cost of funds to be K, the opportunity cost of working funds would be K(C/2). This is the cost that the firm will have to forgo due to blockage of funds in the working balance. It goes up with increase in the average working balance with the total funds requirement for the firm during the period as T, and the cash balance during the period as C, the number of transactions during the period will be T/C. Assuming the fixed cost per transaction to be b, the total transaction cost will be $\left[b \times \frac{T}{C}\right]$. The total cost (opportunity cost and transaction cost) will be:

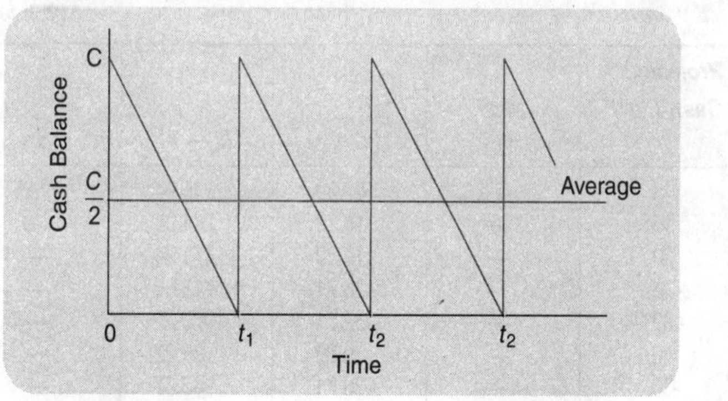

Figure 24-4 Baumol's model of working balance

$$\text{Total cost} = b \times \left(\frac{T}{C}\right) + K \times \left(\frac{C}{2}\right) \qquad (24\text{-}1)$$

The objective function is to minimize the total cost. This will be done at the point where the opportunity cost is equal to the transaction cost.

$$K \times \left(\frac{C}{2}\right) = b \times \left(\frac{T}{C}\right)$$

Or $KC^2 = 2bT$

Or $C^2 = 2bT$

Or $C = \sqrt{2bT/K}$ (24-2)

This point of optimal level of working balance can be graphically represented, as in Figure 24-5. Equation 24-2 signifies that the optimal working balance, C (or cash balance), depends upon the square root of the rupee volume of transaction. This varies directly with fixed transaction costs, b, and inversely with opportunity cost, K. The equation denotes that at times when a higher return can be earned by investing in marketable securities, firms would prefer a lesser working balance. However, increased transaction costs may force the firms to hold a higher working balance.

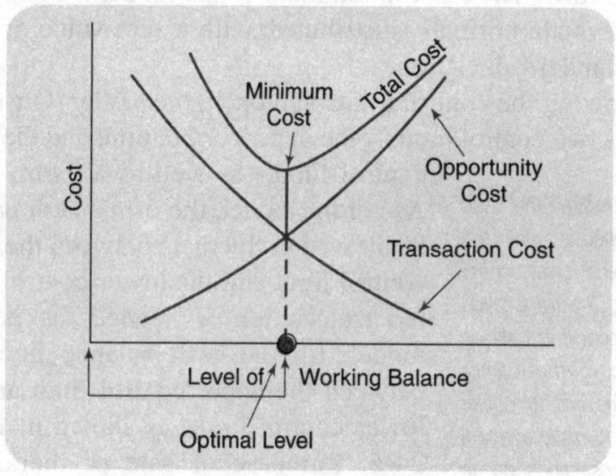

Figure 24-5 Optimal level of working balance

The Baumol's model can be better understood with the help of an example.

Example 24-3 Baumol's Model of Optimal Cash Balance

A firm has estimated that total disbursements during the coming year will be ₹720 lakh. The outflows will be incurred steadily over the period. The firm has been parking its surplus cash in a portfolio of securities, with an average yield of 12% per annum. The cost per transaction (disinvestment or investment) for the firm has been ₹1000. Find the optimal working balance.

Solution

The optimal working balance as per Baumol's model is:

$$C = \sqrt{\frac{2bT}{K}}$$

$$= \sqrt{\frac{2 \times 1000 \times 720}{0.12}} = ₹10{,}95{,}445$$

The number of transaction during the year will be:

$$\frac{7{,}20{,}00{,}000}{10{,}95{,}445} = 65 \text{ transactions}$$

The Baumol's model is similar to the EOQ model of inventory management, and its limitations are also similar to those of the EOQ model. The model may not be useful in uncertain conditions, where the cash outflows are not steady.

Miller–Orr Model[5]

The EOQ model may not work under conditions of uncertainty, as cash balances may be volatile and not steady. For conditions

[5]Miller, Merton H. and Daniel. Orr, 'A Model of the Demand for Money by Firms,' *Quarterly Journal of Economics,* August 1966, pp. 413-35.

The Miller–Orr model adopts the stochastic approach to decisions regarding the optimal working balance.

of uncertainty, stochastic models may be more suitable. The Miller–Orr model overcomes the limitations of the Baumol model by incorporating the uncertainty in determining the optimal level of working balance. The model assumes that most firms do not use their cash flows uniformly, and also cannot predict their daily cash inflows and outflows. The model incorporates this uncertainty by allowing for daily variation in the cash flow. The assumption made in the model is that the net cash flows are normally distributed, with a zero value of mean and a standard deviation.

Following the control limits approach, the Miller–Orr model provides two control limits—the upper control limit and the lower control limit—as well as a return point. As per the model, the firm's cash balance is allowed to fluctuate between the upper control limit and the lower control limit. No transaction is needed, as per the model, till the cash balance fluctuates between the upper control limit and the lower control limit, as shown in Figure 24-6. Purchase or sale of marketable securities takes place only when one of these limits is reached. As can be seen in the figure, when the firm's cash flow touches the lower limit on day t_2, it enters into a disinvestment transaction and sells marketable securities to the tune of (R-L). Such a transaction brings the cash balance of the firm back to the normal level, i.e., the return point. Similarly, when the firm's cash balance touches the upper limit on day t_5, the firm undertakes investment transactions and buys marketable securities to the tune of (H-R). Such investment transactions bring the firm back to a normal level of cash balance, i.e., the return point. For the rest of the days in the figure, no investment or disinvestment transaction gets triggered, as the firm's working balance is within the upper and the lower control limits.

Till the time the cash balance is within the upper and lower control limits, no transaction takes place. It is only on breach of these limits that the investment or disinvestment transactions occur.

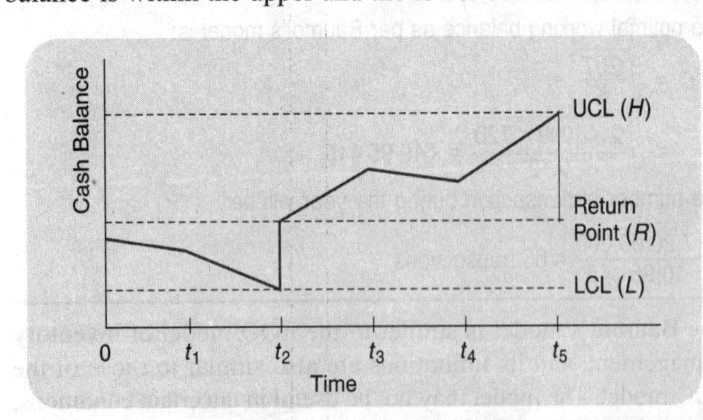

Figure 24-6 Miller–Orr model

The lower limit is set by the firm based on its desired minimum 'safety stock' of cash in hand. It depends on the past levels of cash held by the firm, and also on the volume of business expected in the period for which the working balance is being estimated. Once the firm has decided its lower control limit, it has to determine its upper control limit and the return point. The optimal values of the upper control limit (*H*) and the return point (*R*) depend upon the fixed transaction cost (*b*), opportunity cost (*K*), and the variance of the firm's cash flows (s^2). The variance of cash flows can be estimated based on the past cash flow behaviour of the firm. As per the model, the value of return point is estimated as follows:

$$R \text{ (Return Point)} = L + \sqrt[3]{\frac{3bs^2}{4K}} \quad (24\text{-}3)$$

The upper control limit is defined as follows:

$$H \text{ (Upper Control Limit)} = 3 \times \sqrt[3]{\frac{3bs^2}{4K}} + L \quad (24\text{-}4)$$

Example 24-4 provides an illustration of Miller–Orr Model.

Example 24-4 Optimal Cash Balance Using Miller–Orr Model

Projected cash flows of Zeta Ltd for the coming week are as follows:

Day	*1*	*2*	*3*	*4*	*5*	*6*	*7*
Projected Cash Flow (₹ in lakh)	48	15	20	–26	–32	10	–30

The firm incurs a fixed cost of ₹2,000 per transaction every time it invests or disinvests. The average return that the firm earned during the previous year by investing its surplus in marketable securities was 12%. The company's management always keeps a minimum cash balance of ₹25,000. Based on the above information, find the the return point and the upper control limit using the Miller–Orr model.

Solution

The working of Miller–Orr Model is shown below:

Calculation of variance of projected cash flows

(*₹ in lakh*)

Projected Cash Flow x_i	*Mean* ($\bar{x}$)	$(x_i - \bar{x})$	$(x_i - \bar{x})^2$	(S^2)
48	—	47.29	2235.94	—
15	—	14.29	204.08	—
20	—	19.29	371.94	—
–26	—	–26.71	713.65	—
–32	—	–32.71	1070.22	—
10	—	9.29	86.22	—
–30	—	–30.71	943.37	—
	$= \Sigma x_i/n$ = 0.7143	$\Sigma = 0$	$\Sigma = 5625.43$	$\Sigma(x_i - \bar{x})^2/n$ = 5625.43/7 = 804

Minimum cash balance (*L*) = ₹ 25,000

Transaction cost (*b*) = ₹2,000

Opportunity cost (*K*) = 0.12

$$\text{Return point } (R) = L + \sqrt[3]{\frac{3bs^2}{4K}}$$

Therefore, $R = 0.25 + \sqrt[3]{\frac{3 \times 0.02 \times 804}{4 \times 0.12/365}}$

= 0.25 + 33.27 = ₹33.52 lakh

$H = 3R + L = 3 \times 33.52 + 0.25$ = ₹100.68 lakh

Investing the surplus cash

Having determined the optimal working balance, the next issue in cash management is to productively invest the surplus cash in marketable securities. This would maximize the firm's interest income by minimizing idle resources. A firm might invest excess cash in many types of interest-bearing assets. To choose among the alternatives, we must establish criteria based on our reasons for investing excess cash in the first place.

The final issue in cash management is of parking the surplus cash in securities that are highly liquid.

We are investing either temporary transaction balances or precautionary balances, or both. When we need the cash, we want to be able to obtain it quickly. Given these objectives, we can rule out equity shares and other investments with returns that are not contractual and with prices that often vary widely. Debt securities, with a contractual obligation to pay, are our best candidates.

In selecting among debt securities, there are three principal characteristics we should examine: *default risk, maturity, and marketability*. The primary purpose of parking the surplus funds is to have a liquidity cushion, and therefore, the surplus funds should be invested in those instruments that are highly liquid or marketable. Securities that have a low level of default risk and have shorter maturity periods are the ones that are normally said to be marketable. Such securities may not be carrying a high yield as the risk element and the maturity period is short.

SUMMARY

The term cash in this chapter refers to total liquid assets, made up of working cash balance plus interest-bearing securities and deposits. Firms hold cash (liquid assets) for two reasons: to facilitate their day-to-day transactions (transactionary motive) and to overcome crisis situations (precautionary balance). The overall problem of cash management comprises of four issues: (1) collecting and disbursing funds efficiently; (2) developing a reliable system of cash forecasting to identify the leads and lags in cash flows; (3) determining the appropriate working cash balance and (4) investing the remaining excess cash.

The objective of cash management is to maximize the availability of cash and also, to maximize interest income. The two may seem to be contradictory. In order to maximize the availability of cash, firms should follow the policy of quick collections and slow disbursements. Also, they should concentrate the collected funds in a central pool quickly to make the collected funds usable.

A reliable system of cash forecasting is a *sine qua non* of an effective cash management system. Cash forecasting is an integrated exercise requiring inputs from different sources and departments. The duration of forecast may be as short as one day and as long as one year. Forecasting enables the firms to identify the periods of cash surplus/deficit and do their resource planning accordingly.

The next issue after maximizing cash availability is minimizing idle funds. This requires determination of the optimal level of working balance, using either the heuristic or the model-based approach. The focus here is to minimize blockage of funds in the working balance and to invest surplus funds in marketable securities. The issue is resolved in the light of the transaction costs of investments/disinvestments and the cost of opportunity forgone by having a high level of working balance.

KEY TERMS

Cash In general, cash refers to the ready cash available with firms. It is also termed cash-in-hand. The definition of cash includes cash in hand, cash in the firm's bank accounts, and also cash invested in marketable securities.

Collection float Collection float is the total time gap between the times of payments dispatched by the customers and the times funds actually become available for usage.

Disbursement float Disbursement float is the total lag between the time the firm mails payment to its suppliers and the time the firm's account is actually debited.

Marketable securities Marketable securities are securities that are capable of being liquidated easily.

PRACTICE PROBLEMS

1. Collection Float on Revenues or Profits

Sumangalam Ltd is likely to receive the following six payments in the coming week:

Day of the week	*Payments to be received (₹)*
Monday	1,20,00,000
Tuesday	1,15,00,000
Wednesday	10,00,000
Thursday	8,55,00,000
Friday	12,50,00,000
Saturday	6,50,0000

As per the past trend, normally the delays involved in Float are as follows:

Payments received on	*Float*
Monday	1 mail + 2 Processing and Availability =3 days
Tuesday	1+1+1=3
Wednesday	1+1+1=3
Thursday	1+1+1=3
Friday	1+1+3=5
Saturday	1+2+2=5

You are expected to analyse the impact of collection float on the firm's costs/ revenues/ profits. Assume that the required rate of return for the firm is 12%.

Solution

Step 1: Computation of Float Days

Payments to be received (Amt. ₹)	*Float (in Days)*	*Total Float Days (₹)*
120,00,000	3	360,00,000
115,00,000	3	345,00,000
10,00,000	3	30,00,000
855,00,000	3	25,65,00,000
125,00,0000	5	62,50,00,000
65,00,000	5	32,50,000
	Total	95,15,00,000

Step 2: Computation of Daily Float

$$\text{Average Daily Float} = \frac{\text{Total Float Day}}{7}$$

$$= \frac{95,15,00,000}{7} = ₹46,42,857.14$$

Step 3: Computation of Opportunity Cost of Average Daily Float

$$= \frac{\text{Average Daily Float} \times 12}{100}$$

$$= \frac{46,42,857.14 \times 12}{100} = ₹5,57,142.86$$

$$\text{Daily opportunity cost of float} = \frac{5,57,142.86}{365} = ₹1526.42$$

2. Cash Forecasting

Sugandh Co. is in the business of manufacturing and selling perfumes. The sales forecast for the firm of the months January–March 2007 is as follows:

Months	*Sales (₹ in lakh)*
January	215
February	225
March	257

The actual sales of the last two months of the previous calendar year have been ₹187 lakh and ₹199 lakh respectively. The past records of sales indicate that on an average the firm has been selling 25% on cash basis. Out of the credit sales made by the firm, 65% is realized in the month following the sales while 34% is realized in the second month. The firm had made inter-corporate lending of ₹550 lakh that fetch an interest of 11% per annum. The interest is received half yearly (in March and September). The non-operating cash outflows expected in the month of February are projected as ₹32.5 lakh.

A capital expenditure is due towards the replacement of assets in the month of January. The amount for the same has been estimated at ₹105 lakh. The production department has given the following details regarding the cost of production:

- Direct material has been estimated at 51.5% of the sales.
- Labour and other overheads have been projected at 21.75% of the sales.
- The expenses are paid for in the month incurred.
- Company's cash balance on 31 December 2006 was ₹1,25,000.
- The company wants to maintain a cash balance that is sufficient to meet 6% of its expected monthly cash outflows at all times during the period January–March.

You are required to forecast the cash position of the firm on a monthly basis.

Solution

Facts of the Problem (*₹ in lakh*)

	Nov.	*Dec.*	*Jan.*	*Feb.*	*Mar.*
Monthly sales	187	199	215	225	257
Interest	—	—	—	—	30.25
Non operating cash flows	—	—	—	32.50	—
Capital expenditure	—	—	105	—	—
Cash sales				25%	
Collections in first month				48.75%	
Collections in second month				25.5%	
Direct materials (as % of sales)				51.5%	
Labour and other overheads (as % of sales)				21.75%	
Desired cash balance				6 %	

Cash Forecast (*₹ in lakh*)

	Months				
	Nov.	*Dec.*	*Jan.*	*Feb.*	*Mar.*
Sales	**187**	**199**	**215**	**225**	**257**
Cash Receipt Forecasts					
Cash Sales			53.75	56.25	64.25
Collections one prior month			97.01	104.81	109.69
Collections 2nd prior month			47.69	50.75	54.83
Interest					30.25
Total Receipts			198.45	211.81	259.01
Cash Disbursements Forecasts					
Direct Material Payments			110.73	115.88	132.36
Labour and overhead Payments			46.76	48.94	55.90
Non-operating outflows				32.50	
Capital expenditure			105.00		
Total Disbursements			262.49	197.31	188.25
Net Cash Flow			–64.04	14.50	70.76
Beginning Cash			1.25	–15.75	–11.24
Total Cash			–62.79	–30.24	82.60
Desired Cash			15.75	11.84	11.30
Surplus/ Borrowings			–78.54	–18.41	71.30

3. Cash Forecasting

Supreme Ltd consults you to forecast their daily cash requirements for the month of January 2007 based on the following information:

The past data reveals that the firm's cash sales have been 30% on an average. 50% of the sales are realized in the next month while 19% are realized in the second month. Sales for the previous two months (November and December) were ₹175 lakh and ₹176.5 lakh respectively. The sales department has submitted the following forecasts for the sales in the coming months:

Month	January	February	March	April	May	June
Sales Forecast (₹ in lakh)	178	178.5	177	195	215	256

The projected expenses details given by the production department. are as follows:

Direct Material: 42% of sales

Direct Labour: 25% of sales for January, February, and March but is expected to rise to a level of 26.5% for the period thereafter.

As per the past trend, the direct labour is generally paid for in the month it is incurred.

The suppliers grant the terms of sales of net 60 days, which are fully utilized. Monthly fixed expenses like rent etc., are estimated to be ₹45 lakh. Capital expenditure worth ₹215 lakh is due in June. The company has a policy of maintaining a cash balance at a level of 5% monthly sales. Surplus cash, if any is invested in marketable securities.

Prepare monthly cash forecast for Supreme Ltd for the months January through June indicating the cash defecit/cash surplus months.

Solution

Cash Forecast for Supreme Ltd for January–March 2007

	Months					
	January	February	March	April	May	June
Sales	178	178.5	177	195	215	256
Cash Receipt Forecasts						
Cash sales	53.40	53.55	53.10	58.50	64.50	25.60
Collections one prior month	88.25	89.00	89.25	88.50	97.50	129.00
Collections 2nd prior month	33.25	33.53	33.82	33.91	33.63	56.55
Total Receipts	174.90	176.08	176.17	180.91	195.63	211.20
Cash Disbursements						
Direct Material Payments	73.50	74.13	74.76	74.97	74.34	81.90
Direct Labour Payments	44.50	44.63	44.25	51.68	56.98	67.84
Monthly fixed expenses	45.00	45.00	45.00	45.00	45.00	45.00
Capital Expenditure						215.00
Total Disburse-ments	163.00	163.75	164.01	171.64	176.31	409.74
Net Cash Flow	11.90	12.33	12.16	9.27	19.31	–198.60
Beginning Cash	8.82	8.90	8.925	8.85	9.75	10.75
Total Cash	20.72	21.23	21.08	18.12	29.06	–187.84
Desired Cash	8.90	8.92	8.85	9.75	10.75	12.80
Investment in marketable securities	11.82	12.30	12.23	8.37	18.31	—
Borrowings	—	—	—	—	—	–200.64

EXERCISES

Concept Review Questions

1. What are the principal motives for holding cash and liquid assets?
2. What is the focus of cash management?
3. Suppose a firm's cash inflows and outflows are variable but completely predictable. How are the concepts of inventory theory applicable to such a problem?
4. Suppose a firm's cash inflows and outflows are completely random. What approach might a firm use to set its minimum working balance?
5. What is cash forecasting and how does it help in better cash management?

Critical Thinking Questions

1. From the standpoint of cash management, on what parts of the cash cycle should attention be focused?
2. 'The efficiency of cash management depends on how efficiently the firm manages its inventory and receivables.' Comment.
3. 'Cash balance should be neither inadequate nor excessive, as both these conditions are adverse.' Discuss.
4. What are the techniques that can be taken recourse to, cut down the cash cycle?
5. 'Disbursements should be delayed to the extent that it does not jeopardize relationships with suppliers.' Elaborate.

Practical Assignment

1. Study the different services offered by Indian banks to cut down the mail, processing, and availability floats.

Numerical Problems

1. Impact of Collection Float on Revenues/Profits

Numero Uno Ltd Is likely to receive the following four payments in the coming week

Payments to be received (Amount ₹)	*Day of the week*
1,05,40,000	Monday
82,28,000	Tuesday
61,20,000	Thursday
54,40,000	Saturday

As per the past trend, normally the delays involved in Float are as follows:

Payments received on	*Float*
Monday	1 mail + 2 Processing and Availability = 3 days
Tuesday	1+1+2 = 4
Thursday	1+2+3 = 5
Saturday	1+2+3 = 4

You are expected to analyse the impact of firm's collection float on its costs/revenues/profits. Assume that the required rate of return for the firm is 10%.

2. Cash Forecasting

Safe Pouch is in the business of manufacturing the Plastic pouches that increase the shelf life of vegetables and fruits by preserving their freshness. The sales forecast for the firm for the months April through September 2007 is as follows:

Months	*Sales (₹ in lakh)*
April	136.00
May	145.00
June	147.00
July	127.50
August	125.00
September	120.00

The actual sales of the last two months of the previous financial year have been ₹110 lakh and ₹123 lakh, respectively. The past records of sales indicate that on an average the firm has been selling 30% on cash basis. Out of the credit sales made by the firm 60% is realised in the month following the sales while 38.5% is realised in the second month.

The firm expects to receive ₹5.5 lakh as interest on the different loans given by the firm. This is due in the month of June. A dividend receipt is also due in the month of June to the extent of ₹5 lakh. The non operating cash outflows expected in the month of August are projected as ₹17 lakh. A capital expenditure is due towards the replacement of assets in the month of September. The amount for the same has been estimated at ₹65 lakh. The production department has given the following details regarding the cost of production:

Direct material has been estimated at 48% of the sales. Labour and other overheads have been projected at 29% of the sales.

The expenses are paid for in the month incurred. The beginning cash balance with the firm was ₹85.000 on 1st April.

The company wants to maintain a cash balance that is sufficient to meet 6% of its expected monthly cash outflows at all times during the period April-September.

You are required to forecast the cash position of the firm on a monthly basis.

3. Cash Forecasting: Comprehensive Illustration

Mirage Ltd consults you to forecast their cash requirements for the period July–Dec 2005 based on the following information:

The past record of firm's sales and its collections tell that on an average its sales have been 20% on cash basis. 50% of the sales are realized in the next month while 28.5% are realised in the second month following sales.

Sales for the previous two months (May and June) were ₹119 lakh and ₹124 lakh, respectively. The sales department has submitted the following forecasts for the sales in the coming months:

Months	*Sales Forecasts (₹ in lakh)*
July	127.72
Aug	134.11
Sept	138.13
Oct	140.89
Nov	142.30
Dec	142.73

The firm has made some investments and its average monthly return on those investments is estimated at ₹11.45 lakh during the next six months. The projected expenses details given by the production department are as follows:

Direct Material — 38% of sales

Direct Labour — 29% of sales for July, August and September but is expected to rise to a level of 32% thereafter. As per the past, trend the direct labour is generally paid for in the month it is incurred.

The suppliers grant the terms of sales of net 60 days, which are fully utilised. Monthly fixed expenses like rent etc. are estimated to be ₹21.5 lakh. Tax payment due to be paid in the months of July and October is estimated to be ₹18 lakh. No repayments on firm's outstanding debt are due during the next 6 months. The capital Planners conference that met in December 2006 had estimated the amount of progress payments on firm's new construction at ₹65 lakh which is due in August and December. The company's has a cash balance of ₹1,25,000 on 1 July 2007. Mirage ltd. has a policy of maintaining a cash balance at the level of 5% of monthly sales.

Surplus cash, if any, is invested in marketable securities. Prepare cash forecast for Mirage Ltd for the months July through December clearly indicating the surplus/deficit months, cash balance/ marketable securities investments.

Distribute the forecast for the month of July into daily cash forecast using the following information:

Ignoring holidays there are 21 working days working days in the month of July, 5 in each of the first 4 weeks and one in the final week. The firm has found from the research on prior patterns that for the months with the structure of July, 35% of cash receipts occur in the first week of the month, 24% in the second week, 20% in the third week, 17% in the fourth week and the remaining 4% in the last week.

For the months similar to July, in a given week 30% is received on Monday, 25% on Tuesday, 20% on Wednesday, 10% on Thursday, and remaining 15% on the last working day of the week i.e. Friday. Payment for materials and wages and fixed expenses are made on the last day of the month.

4. Cash vs Marketable Securities—Baumol's Model

Firm ABC follows a made to order production system. As per its policy it receives a monthly advance from its distributors before its starts processing their orders. The firm follows a uniform monthly production policy. For the upcoming month, the firm expects to receive ₹2,50,00,000 from its suppliers as an advance. Such advance money will be consumed by the firm during the month in its production and marketing functions. By investing in money market instrument it can earn 0.65% per month. Transaction costs are estimated at ₹2,500 per (investment/ disinvestment) transaction. What is the firm's best investment strategy for the firm to convert its surplus cash into marketable securities and how much will that earn? Analyse using the Baumol's model.

5. Cash vs Marketable Securities—Miller–Orr Model

Firm ABC can earn 0.025% per day in investments. Based on historic data, the firm has estimated the standard deviation of its daily cash flows at ₹35,000. The transaction cost for investments/ disinvestments for the firm are ₹750 per transaction. The firm wishes to maintain a minimum cash balance of ₹1,50,000 at all times. Assuming that the firm's starting balance is ₹1,50,000 and the following cash flows occur during the next five days.

Day	*Net Cash Flow*
1	–85,000
2	125,000
3	–70,000
4	45,000
5	105,000

Show the investments and disinvestments that the firm will make during the next five days using the Miller–Orr model.

In the CD

Optimal Cash Balance—Baumol's Model

Optimal Cash Balance—Miller-Orr Model

PART

SIX

INTERNATIONAL FINANCIAL MANAGEMENT

CHAPTER 25 Foreign Exchange: Rates and Markets

LEARNING OBJECTIVES

The chapter is aimed at

- providing understanding of foreign exchange markets and rates
- familiarizing readers with the different systems of exchange rates
- explaining various terms used in foreign exchange markets
- providing a basic understanding on the mechanism of forward contracts and swap deals
- deriving forward rates from swap points
- deriving merchant rates
- explaining arbitrage as the key process in the determination of stable exchange rates
- explaining and deriving the ground rules of quoting foreign exchange rates that permit no arbitrage

FOREIGN EXCHANGE: AN EXCHANGE THAT NEVER SLEEPS

Mr Harkirat Singh is the Spot Forex Dealers Association's top euro dealer based in New York. Just yesterday morning, he traded about US$ 500 million in euro, darting in and out of the market 50 times. As the US dollar inched up, he bought. As it retreated, he sold.

Currency traders like Mr Singh are riding high these days. As politicians dicker over what to do about the US dollar after last month's stock-market crash, traders at the world's top 30 to 50 banks hold day-to-day control of the currency markets.

The first two hours of the day are consumed by a blizzard of trades with European banks. Computerized dealing systems let traders do business with London, Frankfurt, or Zurich at the push of a button, without even a phone call. Typically, Spot Dealers Association will buy 'five dollars'—trader jargon for US$ 5 million—then resell it at a razor-thin profit margin seconds later.

In a flurry of four transactions, Spot Dealers Association dumps the US$ 10 million it just bought, and sells another US$ 8 million as well. It gets rates ranging from 1.9321 to 1.9441 for each sterling pound.

At about 01:00 p.m., the euro traders encounter their one difficult stretch of the day. They have sold US dollars, expecting further drops. But the US dollar is inching up. Mr Hanslal Mehta, another senior dealer, slams his phone down, snarling: "It's up, it's up, it's going up."

Rather than fight the momentary trend, the traders begin buying US dollars. "The dollar is going uptown," Mr Mehta declares. He holds his new positive position on the US dollar for only a brief spell, but profits from it as well. All morning calls from incoming banks and customers light up dealers' phone boards, which hold 120 direct phone lines.

The trading frenzy continues until about noon New York time, when the European trading day ends. Only then can traders at Spot Forex, New York, relax. "It's like a ball and chain," complains James Young, senior sterling trader. "I can't go out to lunch."

INTRODUCTION

Globalization of business is the theme of almost all firms in the world. As world economies are growing and becoming more and more open because of relaxation of regulations concerning international trade, the firms are doing businesses in various currencies and markets. International markets present several financial challenges in terms of additional understanding required, due to the extra dimension of choosing the currency for finance and trade. As the world economy becomes more and more integrated, a finance manager is required to make additional decisions with respect to strategic issues such as currency of borrowing, impact on capital structure, and tactical issues such as currency of invoicing.

Besides the selection of currency for finance and trade, another important dimension that figures prominently on the agenda of finance managers is the exposure to additional risk emanating from dealing in currencies other than the domestic currency, and the need to devise methods to mitigate this risk. Apart from the broadening of the conceptual scope for understanding of interest rate structures in various countries and financial assets denominated in foreign currency, the finance manager has the onerous task of gathering, assimilating, and analysing the vast pool of information that is generated all over the world. In this way, an international firm, referred to as a *multinational corporation* (MNC), becomes different from a purely domestic firm, which essentially deals in a single currency.

One may argue that concepts of corporate finance essentially must remain the same irrespective of the currency being evaluated. All the three major decisions a firm makes—the investment decision, the financing decision and the dividend decision—should be independent of the currency of the funds being considered in each of these decisions. The argument is valid, but the presence of multiple currencies makes each of these decisions more complicated, as the number of choices available increases significantly. Numerically, it is a simple calculation involving exchange rates to convert one currency into another, but the decision-making framework changes drastically with regard to international business, as managerial inputs are different, and significantly larger.

With the choice of several currencies, the evaluation of all decisions of finance is not as simple as it is in the case of a single currency.

Cross-border evaluation of financial decisions becomes further complex due to the varying legal environments and substantially different accounting practices and conventions, business practices, and expectations of investors, customers, and suppliers prevailing in various economies. Furthermore, markets for financial assets in different economies do not have the same level of efficiency and besides, financial instruments available in different markets vary, and understanding of each such financial instrument is critical to decision-making. All these factors make decision-making in the international environment extremely complex as compared with a single economy.

An additional dimension to transactions denominated in currencies other than domestic is the exposure to the risk of changes in currency conversion rates. All transactions denominated in foreign currencies face exchange rate risks, because the foreign exchange rates change much in the same way as stock prices change in the stock markets. Multinational corporations deal in various currencies, and have assets and liabilities denominated in several currencies. They need to bring all these transactions, assets, and liabilities down to a single currency—the domestic currency of the country where MNC is based.

FOREIGN EXCHANGE MARKETS

Foreign exchange markets, mainly consisting of banks globally, are *Over–The-Counter* (OTC) markets, where individuals and corporate traders place their requirements for either buying or selling specific currencies to various participants. There is no organized exchange where foreign exchange could be traded, unlike stock exchanges where customers can place their orders for buying and/or selling of stocks in the physical or electronic markets. The OTC nature of foreign currency markets places an additional burden on corporate finance managers to explore various avenues and possibilities, which apart from consuming time, requires deeper understanding and negotiating skills.

Another feature of foreign exchange markets is that they are operative all the time. Foreign exchange transactions are primarily conducted during banking hours. Some centres are always open, as banks across the globe constitute the market. The major centres of trading in foreign exchange are Tokyo, Sydney, Hong Kong, Singapore, London, Frankfurt, Zurich, and New York. Foreign exchange rates fluctuate all the time, and are always available in some part of the world.

The communication medium of trading is *SWIFT*, an acronym for Society for Worldwide Inter-bank Financial Transactions, a Belgian non-profit cooperative society connecting all major banks and centres with one another.

People from various cultures and nationalities conduct the trade, and thus, there is a need for clarity of communication. The International Standards Organization (ISO) has developed a unique three-letter code for each of the world's currencies. The Indian rupee is always denoted as INR while transacting business in international markets, even though we may use the term ₹ when dealing locally. Similarly the US dollar is denoted as USD, while in the USA, the symbol $ would suffice.

Foreign exchange markets can be bifurcated into two distinct layers. Certain transactions are conducted within and amongst banks, while other transactions take place between banks and their customers. Transactions conducted by and within banks are called *inter-bank transactions*, while those conducted by banks with their customers are known as *merchant transactions*. Inter-bank transactions constitute around 80 to 90% of the total volume of trading in foreign exchange.

There exist two distinct markets called inter-bank market and merchant market in the foreign exchange trade.

FOREIGN EXCHANGE TRANSACTIONS

Various kinds of rates and transactions are made in the foreign exchange market. A basic understanding of these rates and transactions is essential.

Spot vs Forward vs Swaps

Transactions in foreign exchange can either be spot or forward, depending upon the time of settlement. When currency buy or sell transactions are conducted, the actual exchange of cash (debit or credit to accounts) in the two currencies takes place later, and is referred to as settlement. Traders in foreign exchange can choose to enter into transactions and settle them at different dates. Naturally exchange rates, which are agreed upon mutually, would differ depending on the time of settlement. If the transactions are to be settled immediately, then they are termed spot transactions, and the exchange rates applicable for such transactions are known as spot rates. In trades involving foreign exchange, spot transactions are to be settled within two business days of the transaction, to allow for clearance and confirmation on the communication network. The settlement date is also referred to as value date.

Spot transactions in foreign exchange markets are settled in two business days.

It is also possible to have the value date on the same day or on the next day after the date of transaction, depending upon the transacting parties. Both the legs of the transactions are settled on the same day, the value date. For example, if Citibank has bought €10,000 from Barclays Bank at US$ 1.20 per €, Citibank would receive euros on the same day as Barclays Bank receives US dollars. Any mismatch of timing of delivery would result in credit risk.

Forward transactions Transactions in foreign currency can also be made for settlement at a later date. Such transactions, where the rates are fixed straightaway, but the exchange of currencies is set for a later date, are known as forward contracts. For example, a 1-month forward contract for buying of US dollars by an Indian importer at ₹45.00 implies that physical exchange of US dollars and rupees would take place one month after the date of transaction, at the rate of ₹45 per US$, which has been decided right now. It does not matter what exchange rate actually prevails on the day of settlement.

Banks usually quote rates for delivery in whole months, and standard contracts for 1, 2, 3, 6, and 9 months are generally available. However, banks can also quote rates for forward periods that are not exact multiples of a month. Traders can book contracts for any number of days forward. Such contracts are called *broken date or odd date contracts.*

Forward contracts are settled at a later date, but at rates negotiated in advance. These rates are usually available in advance for whole number of months.

The value date for forward contracts is determined by adding the agreed number of calendar months to the value date that would have corresponded to a spot transaction done on the same date. For example, a two-month forward transaction done on 20 March would become due for settlement on 22 June (settlement day for spot transaction on 20 March plus two calendar months).

Swap transactions A *swap transaction* is a combination of spot and forward transactions and consists of both. The spot and forward legs of the swap are opposite and equal in value. For example, bank A may buy US$ 10,000 spot from another bank B and simultaneously enter into a one-month forward contract to sell US$ 10,000 to bank B. The rates for buying spot and selling forward would be different, but are known beforehand. With both buying and selling prices known, the bank is not exposed to any risk of fluctuating exchange rates. The purchase of foreign currency today and sale at a later date, or the sale today and purchase later, is a composite contract in the swap deal. However, the same position is obtainable with two independent but opposite and equal contracts—one spot and the other forward. An independent forward contract is called *outright forward contract.* Two independent contracts—one spot and one outright forward—are more expensive than the composite swap contract.

A swap is a composite contract consisting of two legs with the second leg being opposite and equal to the first leg, but settled on the expiry of first leg.

Composite swap contracts are of great utility to banks, as they avoid assuming risk and the problem of finding an exactly matching counter-party. Swaps can do this by having offsetting positions in a single contract. Banks usually trade on behalf of their customers who are exporters and importers. The deals of a bank with its customers are on outright basis. Assume that a bank buys US$ 10,000 one-month forward at ₹46 per US$ on outright basis from an exporter. The contract means that after one month, the exporter would deliver US$ 10,000 to the bank and receive ₹4,60,000 from it. After paying ₹4,60,000 to the exporter, the bank would end up with US$ 10,000. The rupee amount payable by the bank is certain, but it does not know at what rate it would be able to sell US$ 10,000 after a month. Depending upon the rate prevalent then, the bank may realize more than, less than, or just ₹4,60,000. Thus, by buying US dollars from an exporter, the risk of exchange rate fluctuations passes from the exporter to the bank. The bank must find a buyer (a customer who is an importer) who needs exactly the same amount at exactly the same time. Although not impossible, this is indeed a difficult proposition.

No bank would assume such a position, since it is not a bank's business to take risks on behalf of its customers. Hence, in turn it would book a contract with another bank to buy US$ 10,000 one-month forward. Such a step would mean that the bank, after receiving US$ 10,000 from its customer, would sell this amount to another bank at a rate known in advance. However, the second bank would then face the same exchange risk as the first bank, which could be eliminated by the second bank by selling forward to a third bank. Thus, the foreign exchange risk could be passed on from one to another bank till a bank is found that is prepared to carry the risk of foreign exchange rate fluctuations or whose currency is US dollars.

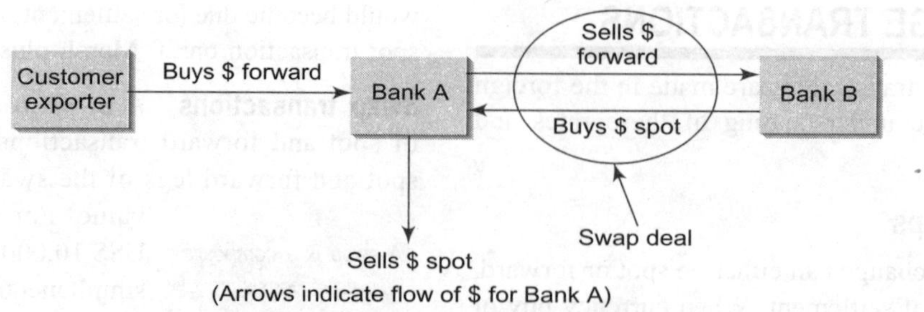

Figure 25-1 Swap transaction for bank A

Alternatively, to put an end to the transfer of risk from one party to another, a more convenient way is to have a swap deal. When buying dollars forward, the second bank would sell an equal quantity on spot basis to the first bank. The US dollars so received can be sold in the market at prevailing spot prices. By doing so, the timings of the cash flows in foreign currency are matched with spot buying and selling and forward buying and selling. Furthermore, all exchange rate risk is eliminated, with no exposure to foreign currency. Figure 25-1 depicts the flow of foreign currency (US dollars) for Bank A under a swap deal. Note that cash flows on spot basis as well as forward basis in foreign currency are matched with all the rates known at present, eliminating the uncertainty of foreign exchange markets.

Most inter-bank deals are swap deals, which help eliminate exchange rate risk

FOREIGN EXCHANGE RATES

Trading in foreign exchange, unlike trading in shares and other financial assets, is not done in any organized exchange. For exchange-traded assets, only a single price is available. The buyer and seller both pay brokerage. With brokerage of 1% and the price of a share at ₹200, the buyer would pay ₹202 and the seller would receive ₹198, with ₹4, the total transaction cost for the buyer and the seller, being the income of the brokers.

Bid Rate vs Ask Rate

Foreign exchange markets are OTC markets, with various banks serving as dealers in foreign exchange. Two rates for foreign exchange are quoted by banks—one for buying and the other for selling foreign currency. The two rates are called *bid rate* and *ask rate* respectively, and are defined below.

Bid rate: It is the rate at which a bank buys foreign currency.

Ask rate: It is the rate at which a bank sells foreign currency.

Banks make profits in foreign exchange transactions by buying currencies at lower rates and selling them at higher rates. Therefore, the ask rate is always higher than the bid rate. The convention is to specify the bid rate first when quoting rates. The difference between the ask rate and the bid rate is the profit for the bank in doing a round transaction, and is known as *spread*. Percentage spread is defined as below:

Foreign exchange rates are always a two-way quote, one for buying foreign currency—the bid rate, and other for selling—the ask rate.

$$\% \text{ spread} = \frac{\text{ask rate} - \text{bid rate}}{\text{mid rate}} \times 100 \qquad (25\text{-}1)$$

Where mid rate is the average of bid and ask rates.

Example 25-1 Bid Rate, Ask Rate, and Spread

A bank quotes the following rates for US dollars.

₹ per US$: 45.00 45.50

What amount would you (a) get if you sell US$ 1,000 (b) pay to buy US$ 1,000? Find the profit for the bank, if it bought and sold US$ 1,000. What is the spread for the bank?

Solution

When a customer sells foreign currency, the bid rate becomes applicable. The customer would get ₹45.00 × 1,000, i.e., ₹45,000, while selling US$ 1,000.

When a customer buys foreign currency, the ask rate becomes applicable. The customer would have to pay ₹45.50 × 1,000, i.e., ₹45,500, while buying US$ 1,000.

The profit for the bank is ₹500 (45,500 – 45,000).

The spread for the bank

$$\% \text{ spread} = \frac{\text{ask rate} - \text{bid rate}}{\text{mid rate}} \times 100$$

$$= \frac{45.50 - 45.00}{45.25} \times 100 = 1.10\%$$

Direct Rate vs Indirect Rate

The price of a commodity or any other product is specified in terms of monetary units, for example, ₹10 per kg. In a non-conventional or rather odd way, the price of monetary unit in terms of commodity may also be specified, for example, ₹10 per kg may also be expressed as 0.10 kg per rupee. Foreign currency quotations, however, may be specified either way, because both the parameters are monetary. The price quotation for US dollars may be mentioned either as number of rupees per US dollar or number of US dollars per rupee. A foreign exchange rate is the price of one currency in terms of another.

Almost all nations follow the convention of quoting foreign exchange rates in the direct way, i.e., the number of units of domestic currency per unit of foreign currency.

Direct rate Expressing the price of a foreign currency in terms of the local currency is called the *direct rate*. Direct rate refers to the number of units of home currency per unit of foreign currency. For example, ₹43.50 per US$ in India would be a direct rate in India; US$ 1.022 per € is a direct rate in the USA. Effective August 1993, all quotations in India have been direct.

Indirect rate Expressing the price of the local currency in terms of a foreign currency is called the *indirect rate*. Indirect rate refers to the number of units of foreign currency per unit of home currency. For example, US$ 0.025 per rupee in India would be an indirect rate in India; € 1.02 per US$ is an indirect rate in the US.

Note that in the context of two countries, what is direct rate in one country becomes indirect rate for the other country. In India, ₹50 per US$ is a direct rate, while it is an indirect rate for the US. Similarly, US$ 0.02 per rupee is a direct quote in the USA, while it is indirect in India.

Most countries follow the convention of direct rates. However, England follows indirect rates where all quotations are expressed as number of units of foreign currency per pound.

For reasons of convenience, a few currencies, such as the Indonesian rupiah and the Japanese yen are quoted per 100 units.

Cross Rates

The trading of local currency in a country is confined to a few selected foreign currencies. For example, in India the rupee could be well traded against the US dollar, the euro, the sterling pound, etc., and hence, direct rates are readily available. However, trade in Saudi riyals or Mexican pesos may not be as frequent, while volumes may be too small. Getting direct quotes for currencies of such low-volume trade is rather difficult. However, these currencies would be active against more recognized and acceptable international currencies, such as the US dollar and the euro.

When no explicit exchange rate is available for two currencies it can be synthesised by using a common currency that is actively traded against both of them.

Rather than attempting to find the direct rate for the Indian rupee against the Saudi riyal, an alternate way is to synthesize the rate through use of a common currency against which both the currencies are actively traded. If both the Indian rupee and the Saudi riyal are actively traded against the US dollar then the two rates can be used to derive the rate for Indian rupee vis-à-vis Saudi riyal by multiplying the rates of the Indian rupee per US dollar and the Saudi riyal per US dollar, being a vehicle currency.

Exchange rate, Indian rupees to Saudi riyal

$$= \frac{₹}{\text{US\$}} \times \frac{\text{US\$}}{\text{Saudi riyal}}$$

$$= \frac{₹}{\text{US\$}} \div \frac{\text{Saudi riyal}}{\text{US\$}}$$

When using cross-rates for synthesizing rates, two cautions are in order—(1) use the same set of rates, i.e., bid rates are multiplied to get bid rates and ask rates must be multiplied to get ask rates; and (2) use correct expression of rate, i.e., the correct numerator and denominator of the quotation. Using cross-rates would normally involve inversion of at least one of the rates. For example, the Saudi riyal per US dollar rate would be available, while we may need to use the US dollar per Saudi riyal rate. We all know that the reciprocal of the given rate involves transforming the numerator and denominator.

The system of two-way quotes in foreign exchange markets presents an issue while inverting rates. When inverting rates from one currency to another, the reciprocal of the bid rate becomes the ask rate, and the reciprocal of the ask rate becomes the bid rate. For example the exchange rate for euro in terms of US $ dollars may be expressed as:

Exchange rate, US$ per €	1.2000	1.2500

This may be converted into an expression that gives number of euros per US$ by inverting the ask rate to get bid and inverting the bid rate to get ask as follows:

Exchange rate, US$ per €	1.2000	1.2500
Exchange rate, euro per US$	0.8000	0.8333
	(1 ÷ 1.2500)	(1 ÷ 1.2000)

The use of cross-rates reduces the number of quotations drastically. If every currency is to be expressed with respect to every other currency, the number of quotations for n convertible currencies are $n(n-1)/2$, while with cross-rates only $(n-1)$ quotations would be required, as all currency rates can be expressed in terms of a single identified currency, termed *vehicle currency*. Using the vehicle currency, the rest of the rates may be computed.

Example 25-2 Cross Rates

The following rates are available in Indian foreign exchange markets:

₹ per US$	44.75	45.50
₹ per €	57.50	58.25

A bank wants to quote a rate for a customer who wants to trade euros for US dollars. How can the rates be quoted (expressed as amount of US dollar per euro)?

Solution

Using the Indian rupee as the vehicle currency, the rates of the euro in terms of the US dollar can be synthesized as follows:

$$\text{Number of US\$ per euro} = \frac{₹}{\text{euro}} \times \frac{\text{US\$}}{₹}$$

We first need to express the rates with common denominator. While rate of euro is expressed in the format desired, the rate of US dollar is to be inverted (to be expressed as amount of US dollar per Rupee), as required in the cross-rates. This is done as follows:

Exchange rate, ₹ per US$	44.75	45.50
Exchange rate, US$ per ₹	0.0220	0.0223
	(1 ÷ 45.50)	(1 ÷ 44.75)

Now the bid and ask rates are computed by direct multiplication of respective rates.

$$(\text{Amount of US\$ per euro})_{Bid} = \left(\frac{₹}{€}\right)_{Bid} \times \left(\frac{\text{US\$}}{₹}\right)_{Bid}$$
$$= 57.50 \times 0.0220 = 1.2638$$

$$(\text{Amount of US\$ per euro})_{Ask} = \left(\frac{₹}{€}\right)_{Ask} \times \left(\frac{\text{US\$}}{₹}\right)_{Ask}$$
$$= 58.25 \times 0.0223 = 1.3017$$

Spot Rate vs Forward Rate

As stated earlier, settlement in transactions in foreign exchange may be done at a later date. Forward transactions are those contracts where the rate of exchange has been fixed on the date of contract, but the settlement (the actual exchange of currencies) takes place at a later date, as specified in the contract. Like stock prices, spot rates change with time because various economic and political forces impact the exchange rates on a continuous basis. The exchange rate, therefore, has to be dependent upon the time of delivery of the currencies. The spot rate and the forward rate, therefore, have to be different. What is valid today may not be valid tomorrow, though the spot rate and the forward rate could be the same by way of mere chance. Essentially, the exchange rate would depend upon the timing of the settlement of the transaction.

What should the forward rate be? Is there a relationship between spot rate and forward rate? These are some questions that dwell on the minds of many. They will be addressed later. However, we would like to dispel a common notion that the forward rate necessarily has to be higher than the spot rate. This notion is rather misplaced. Some of us tend to believe that if the US dollar is available today at ₹45, the 6-month forward rate necessarily must be more than ₹45. The logic advanced is that by deferring cash flow till the date of settlement, one would earn or save some interest in the interim. According to this logic, if the interest rate is 10% per annum in India, the 6-month forward contract should be at least 5% higher than the spot rate, as one can earn this interest in the next six months. It is true that interest would be earned or saved over the forward contract period, but we overlook the fact that the same also applies to the counter-party for the other currency; the US dollar in this case. The person required to deliver rupees earns interest in rupees, and at the same time the counter–party, required to deliver US dollars against rupees, also earns or saves interest in US dollar till the date of delivery. Therefore, both the parties earn or save interest as cash flows are deferred.

It is not necessary that forward rates have to be higher than the spot rates on account of deferred settlement. It depends upon the relative interest rates in the two currencies.

Since interest is earned or saved by both the parties for the forward contract period, the forward rate becomes dependent on the interest rates applicable for the two currencies in question. We shall revert to the exact relationship later. At this juncture, it must be recognized that foreign exchange rates for forward contracts, though related to the spot rate, can be higher than, lower than, or equal to spot rates.

FORWARD PREMIUM/DISCOUNT

In the system of direct rates that expresses the price of a foreign currency in terms of domestic currency, if forward rates are higher than spot rates, this means that the foreign currency will be more expensive in the future than it is at present, and thus, it is said to be at *premium*. Similarly, if forward rates are lower than spot rates, this implies that the foreign currency will be cheaper in future than it is at present, and so, it is said to be at *discount*.

When forward rates are higher than spot rates, the foreign currency is said to be at premium and when lower than spot it is at discount.

How expensive or cheap is a foreign currency, is stated conventionally on an annual basis. Therefore, the premium or discount of a foreign currency is normally calculated on an annual basis, depending upon the available forward rate and spot rate. Forward rates are available for varying contract periods. One can get foreign exchange rates for any forward period on demand, as one is working in an OTC market, but it is more common to find forward rates available at monthly intervals. The annual premium or discount on a foreign currency can be computed by using the forward rate as follows:

Annualized forward permium/discount(%)

$$= \frac{\text{forward rate}_{\text{mid}} - \text{spot rate}_{\text{mid}}}{\text{spot rate}_{\text{mid}}} \times \frac{12}{\text{forward period (in months)}} \times 100 \quad (25\text{-}2)$$

Forward rates for many periods are available, raising a dilemma as to which of the forward periods is most appropriate for calculating annualized premium or discount. Purely on the consideration that trading thins down as forward period extends in time, it is most appropriate to estimate annualized premium or discount on a foreign currency on the basis of an 1-month forward rate, rather than the forward rate of any other contract period, presuming that contracts with near maturity are traded more and have adequate liquidity that is essential to fair pricing.

Foreign exchange rates are quoted in pairs (bid and ask rates), and the premium or discount is calculated using the average of the two, called *mid rate*. Another important feature of forward rates is the spread in forward contracts. Banks and dealers are exposed to greater risk while dealing with forward contracts because forward rates are only estimates. Given the increased degree of risk, banks would expect a greater reward, which is derived from spread (the difference between the ask and bid rates). Therefore, spread in forward quotations is larger than spread in spot rates. By the same logic, the spread increases in proportion to the maturity of forward contracts, i.e., the spread in a 6-month forward contract would be higher than the spread in a 1-month forward contract.

Example 25-3 Forward Premium/Discount

Consider the following rates of foreign exchange for euro.

Spot (₹ per €)	57.90	58.10
1-month Forward (₹ per €)	57.50	57.80

(a) Find whether the euro is at premium or discount.
(b) Calculate the annualized premium or discount for euro.
(c) What interpretation do you give to this figure?
(d) What do you think would be the average (mid) rate for 3-m, 6-m and 12-m forward contracts, assuming spreads of Re 0.50, Re 0.80 and Re 1.00 respectively?

Solution

(a) The foreign currency concerned, euro, is at discount to the rupee because the one-month forward rates are lower than the spot rates.
(b) The amount of discount is:

Annualized forward permium/discount (%)

$$= \frac{\text{forward rate}_{\text{mid}} - \text{spot rate}_{\text{mid}}}{\text{spot rate}_{\text{mid}}} \times \frac{12}{\text{Forward period (in months)}} \times 100$$

$$= \frac{57.65 - 58.00}{58.00} \times 12 \times 100$$

$$= -7.24\%$$

(c) Euro is likely to depreciate at the rate of 7.24% per annum.

(d) Assuming that the premium/discount calculated using the 1-month forward rate is a fair representative of forward rates for the whole year, the likely forward rates for 3 months, 6 months, and 12 months are given below.

3-m forward rate (mid) = 58.00 × [1 – (0.0724/4)
= ₹56.95 per €

6-m forward rate (mid) = 58.00 × [1 – (0.0724/2)
= ₹55.90 per €

12-m forward rate (mid) = 58.00 × (1 – 0.0724)
= ₹53.80 per €

Assuming even distribution of spread for the bid and ask rates, the forward rates are:

3-m forward rate (₹ per €)	:	56.75	57.25
6-m forward rate (₹ per €)	:	55.50	56.30
12-m forward rate (₹ per €)	:	53.30	54.30

OUTRIGHT FORWARD VS SWAP

We described a swap transaction as either of the following:

buy foreign currency spot and sell forward; or
sell foreign currency spot and buy forward.

A swap is a composite deal that has two equal legs; one spot and another forward that is equal and opposite to spot[1]. The exposure to foreign currency is nullified at the end of the swap period. Both legs being equal and opposite, the net flow of foreign exchange is zero. A swap contract merely changes the timings of the cash inflow and the outflow of foreign currency.

Swap deals are quoted in a different fashion. Two rates are required for a swap deal, one for the spot leg and another for the forward leg. Spot rates are readily available, but the rates for the forward leg are not explicit, and instead, are quoted through the swap points. Spot rates alongside swap points are used to arrive at the rates applicable for the forward leg. This can best be explained with an example. Assume that a dealer wants to buy euro now and sell euro one month later. This is a swap transaction where the spot leg is a buy and the forward leg is a sell for the dealer. Let's further assume that a bank quotes the rates given below.

Spot (₹ per €)	58.5800 – 58.6000
Swap points[2] 1 m	500/700

The dealer can achieve the outcome by entering into two independent contracts: buy euro spot and sell the same quantity 1-month forward. The rates for the 1-month forward deal are arrived at from the swap points using the following rules.

Forward rates are arrived by adding or subtracting the swap points to the spot rates. When order of swap point is low/high the points are added and when high/low they are subtracted from spot rate.

When swap points are Low/High: The foreign currency is at premium and the rate for the forward deal is arrived at by adding the swap points to the spot rates. *When swap points are High/Low*: The foreign currency is at discount and the rate for the forward deal is arrived at by subtracting the swap points from the spot rates.

Using the above rule, the rate for the forward contract is arrived at as given below.

Spot (₹ per €)	58.5800 – 58.6000
Swap points 1 m	500/700
1-month forward rate	58.6300 – 58.6700

(Swap points being low/high are added to the spot rates)

The dealer can buy euro spot at 58.6000 (the ask rate for spot deal) and sell euro 1-m forward on outright basis at 58.6300 (the bid rate for the forward deal).

Instead of booking two independent contracts, the dealer can book a composite swap contract. Here the spot transaction would be executed at the same rate (the ask rate as the dealer buys and the bank sells euro) at ₹58.6000 per euro. However, the rate for the forward leg would differ and is reached in the following fashion.

1. The rate for the spot leg becomes the reference rate to which relevant swap points are either added to or subtracted from.
2. If swap points are low/high they would be added to the spot rate, and if high/low they would be subtracted from the spot rate.
3. If forward leg is 'buy' for the bank, the bid points are relevant, and if it is 'sell', then ask points are relevant.

Here the reference rate is 58.6000 and the forward leg is 'sell' for dealer and 'buy' for the bank; therefore, bid points become relevant. Furthermore, as swap points are low/high, they would be added to the reference rate for the forward leg. The forward rate would, therefore, be 58.6000 + 0.0500, i.e. 58.6500, yielding a profit of Re 0.0500 per euro for the dealer. Note that the profit for the dealer was lower at Re 0.0300 per euro if he had booked two independent spot buy and 1-m outright forward sell contracts.

A swap deal is always cheaper than the equivalent two independent forward contracts.

A composite contract of swap is always cheaper than the combination of two independent contracts of a spot deal followed by an outright forward contract. This comparison is shown in Table 25-1.

Table 25-1 Swap and outright forward

₹ per Euro

	Swap	Outright Forward
(a) Buy now and sell later:		
Spot 'buy'	58.6000	58.6000
Forward 'sell'	58.6500	58.6300
Profit	0.0500	0.0300
(b) Sell now and buy later:		
Spot 'sell'	58.5800	58.5800
Forward 'buy'	58.6500	58.6700
Loss (–)	**– 0.0700**	**– 0.0900**

[1]It is not necessary to have first leg as spot under the swap. One can buy (sell) 1-month forward and sell (buy) an equal amount 2-month forward. Such a swap is called a forward-forward swap.

[2]In inter-bank quotations, the rates are quoted up to four decimal places. The first two decimal places are called Basis Points, abbreviated to 'bp' and the last two decimal places are referred to as Points-in-Points, abbreviated to PIPs. Swap points are quoted in PIPs.

Swap points directly give the profit or loss under a swap deal with lower points representing profit and higher the loss.

Also note that swap points directly indicate profit or loss margins, obviating the need for computation and facilitating quick decisions. Here, ₹0.0500 per € is the profit if we buy first and sell later, and ₹0.0700 per € is the loss if we sell first and buy later.

Example 25-4 Swap vs outright forward

The following rates are available in the foreign exchange market.

Spot (₹ per €)	58.5800 – 58.6000
Swap points 1-m	700/500

Find out the profit or loss of a dealer for the swap deal and spot and outright forward deal if (a) he buys euro spot and sells one month later, (b) he sells euro spot and buys one month later.

Solution

Swap points are high/low, and so the euro is at discount to rupee. The outright forward rates are arrived at by subtracting the points from the spot rates.

1-m forward rate 58.5100–58.5500

(a) *Buying euro spot and selling forward*

With two independent contracts of spot buy and forward sell

The dealer	buys spot at	58.6000
	sells forward at	58.5100
Loss		0.0900

With the swap deal

The dealer	buys spot at	58.6000
	sells forward at	58.5300

(Reference rate is 58.6000, bank buys in the forward leg and hence, bid points are relevant, which are subtracted)

Loss	0.0700

(b) *Selling euro spot and buying forward*

With two independent contracts of spot buy and forward sell

The dealer	sells spot at	58.5800
	buys forward at	58.5500
Profit		0.0300

With the swap deal

The dealer	sells spot at	58.5800
	buys forward at	58.5300

(Reference rate is 58.5800, bank sells in the forward leg and hence, ask points are relevant, which are subtracted)

Profit	0.0500

INTER-BANK RATE AND MERCHANT RATE

Banks conduct foreign exchange transactions with their customers at different rates, called merchant rates.

Trading in foreign exchange can be classified into two groups—(1) amongst banks themselves; and (2) between banks and their customers. Banks are required to cater to the needs of their customers who are importers and exporters. Importers need to buy foreign currency from the banks for payments to be made to suppliers. Similarly, exporters need to sell foreign currency received from customers against the supplies made by them. Besides, there could be other business transactions that may require buying and selling of foreign currency by customers of banks. To meet these demands, banks quote foreign exchange rates to their customers.

The rates quoted by the bank to its customers are known as *merchant rates*, and they apply to transactions between the bank and its customers. When one bank quotes to another bank, the rates are called *inter-bank rates*, which apply when banks trade among themselves.

Both bid and ask rates are quoted by banks while dealing within themselves; the rates quoted by banks to their customers are also in pairs. The two rates are known as *telegraphic transfer (TT) buying rate*—the rate at which the bank buys foreign currency from it customers, and *TT selling rate*—the rate at which the bank sells foreign currency to its customers. TT buying and TT selling rates apply when banks perform the function of a moneychanger only.

Apart from dealing purely in different currencies on behalf of customers and exchanging money, banks are also expected to provide many other services that relate to foreign exchange transactions. For example, banks are also required to handle export documents of the consignments exported by their customers, apart from buying foreign currency from such customers. Similarly, a bank also advances money against bills to its customers before it realizes money from the counter-party. Where banks discharge additional functions, such as handling documents or paying customers in advance before actually getting reimbursement, they are entitled to additional remuneration. This remuneration is built into the foreign exchange rates, and is called the *bill rate*. For buying, the rate is called the *bill buying rate*, and for selling, the rate is known as *bill selling rate*.

Besides exchanging currency banks are expected to render other services too, for which separate rates called bill buying and bill selling are quoted

Deriving Merchant Rates

Merchant rates are derived from the inter-bank rates. When dealing with customers, banks normally cover themselves in the inter-bank market. The rates that are prevalent in the inter-bank market, therefore, become the starting point for the rate that is quoted to customers. Banks would like to earn a spread on the transactions conducted for their customers. This spread is referred to as *exchange margin*[3].

Inter-bank rates form the basis of arriving at merchant rates.

TT buying rate The TT buying rate applies when the bank buys foreign currency. The TT buying rate is computed by subtracting the exchange margin from a base rate, which would be the bid rate in the inter-bank market. The exchange margin represents the profit that could be earned by the bank. The bank would buy foreign exchange from customers at lower rates than it would get selling foreign currency to another bank in the inter-bank market. TT buying rate is given by:

[3]Exchange margin are prescribed by FEDAI (Refer Box 25-1). Banks may charge lesser margin than what is prescribed by FEDAI.

Base Rate (bid in the inter-bank market) – Exchange Margin

Assuming that for US dollar in the inter-bank market, the bid rate is ₹45.4550 and an exchange margin of 0.125% is appropriate, the TT buying rate would be

$$\text{TT Buying Rate} = 45.4550 - 0.125\% \times 45.4550$$
$$= 45.4550 - 0.0568 = 45.3982$$

(rounded off to ₹45.40 per US$)

TT selling rate As the bank buys foreign currency at a lower rate than the prevalent inter-bank bid rate to earn profit, it also needs to sell foreign exchange to customers at a higher rate than the rate at which it can buy from the inter-bank market, i.e. the inter-bank ask rate. The bank buys required foreign exchange from the inter-bank market for sale to its customers. The TT selling rate is thus computed by adding the exchange margin to the inter-bank ask rate.

TT Selling Rate = Base Rate (Ask in the Inter-bank market) + Exchange Margin

Assuming that for US dollars in the inter-bank market, the ask rate is ₹45.4650 and an exchange margin of 0.125% is appropriate, the TT selling rate would be

$$\text{TT Selling Rate} = 45.4650 + 0.125\% \times 45.4650$$
$$= 45.4650 + 0.0568$$
$$= 45.5218$$

(rounded[4] off to ₹45.52 per US$)

Bill buying rate The bill buying rate is applicable where—(1) the bank handles documents for exports; and (2) the bank pays its exporter-customer before it realizes payment from the importer. Bill buying is equivalent to a forward transaction in foreign currency, because the bank parts with funds before it gets reimbursed by the importer. The forward period is dependent upon—(1) the time taken to have the documents reach the importer, called the *transit period*[5]; and (2) the credit period granted by the exporter to the importer, called the *usance period*. The total of the transit period and the usance period would elapse between the time the bank makes payment to its exporter-customer and the time it receives payment from the importer.

Documents of export normally include a bill of exchange, besides the invoice, the packing list, the bill of lading, etc. These documents are delivered to the importer through the bank. The payment by the importer to the exporter is made according to the tenure mentioned on the bill of exchange. If no credit period is allowed by the exporter, the payment is due immediately. Such a bill of exchange is called a *sight* or *demand bill of exchange*. The bill of exchange permitting usance period, i.e., payment at a later date, is called *usance bill*.

For bill buying rates, the bank would add a margin for the forward period, besides the exchange margin. The forward margin is dependent upon the swap points. If the currency is at discount, the forward rate would be lower than the spot, and if the currency is at premium, the forward rate would be higher than the spot.

As we know, forward rates are determined by adding/subtracting the swap points, which are specified for monthly intervals. The forward period, consisting of the transit period and the usance period, may not add up to whole months, and hence, the bank would round off the forward period. The direction the round off would take place depends upon whether the currency is at premium or at discount. The governing rule is that the bank would like to pay as little as possible, to increase its own margin. If the currency is at discount, it becomes cheaper as time elapses. Therefore, banks round off the forward period to the nearest month on the higher side (buying as late as possible) if the currency is at discount. Similarly, if the currency is at premium, it becomes dearer as time elapses, and the bank would round off to the nearest month on the lower side (the earliest opportunity to buy).

Box 25-1 Foreign Exchange Dealer's Association of India

The Foreign Exchange Dealer's Association of India (FEDAI) was set up in 1958 as an association of banks dealing in foreign exchange in India (typically called Authorized Dealers or ADs) as a self-regulatory body. It is incorporated under Section 25 of The Companies Act, 1956. Its major activities include framing of rules governing the conduct of inter-bank foreign exchange business among banks vis-à-vis public and liaison with RBI for reforms and development of forex market. At present, some of its functions cover the following:

- Guidelines and rules for forex business
- Training of bank personnel in the areas of foreign exchange business
- Accreditation of forex brokers
- Advising/assisting member banks in settling issues/matters in their dealings
- Represent member banks on government/Reserve Bank of India/other bodies.
- Announcement of daily and periodical rates to member banks

Given the continuing integration of the global financial markets and the increased pace of deregulation, the role of self-regulatory organizations such as FEDAI has also been transformed. In such an environment, FEDAI plays a catalytic role for the smooth functioning of the markets through closer co-ordination with the RBI, other organizations such as FIMMDA, the Forex Association of India and various market participants. FEDAI also maximizes the benefits derived from synergies of member banks through innovation in areas such as new customized products, benchmarking against international standards on accounting, market practices, risk management systems, etc.

Source: www.fedai.org

[4]Merchant rates are rounded to two decimal place and inter-bank rates are specified up to four decimal places, with the last two digits being multiples of 25. Rules for rounding off are prescribed by FEDAI.

[5]Transit periods too are prescribed for different countries by FEDAI.

When foreign currency is at discount

Bill buying rate = Inter-bank bid rate – Discount for transit plus usance period* – Exchange margin

(*transit plus usance period rounded to higher month)

When foreign currency is at premium

Bill buying rate = Inter-bank bid rate + Premium for transit plus usance period@ – exchange margin

(@transit plus usance period rounded to lower month)

In addition to the adjustment of forward period in the foreign exchange rate, the bank is also entitled to charge interest for the funds provided for the transit period and usance period. The bill buying rate merely accounts for changes in the foreign exchange, and is a forward rate, while interest is the cost of funds charged if the bank provides advance funds to the exporter client.

As an example, consider the inter-bank bid rate for US dollar at ₹45.4550. An exporter wants the bank to buy a bill drawn on an importer in the USA, with usance period of three months. The transit period is 20 days. The US dollar is at premium and the swap points are as follows:

3-months	300/400
4-months	400/550

The forward period is 3 months 20 days. The swap points indicate that the US dollar is at premium. The bank would round off the forward period to three months and use 3-month swap points. With an exchange margin of 0.15%, the merchant rate for the exporter would be:

	₹ per US$
Inter-bank spot bid rate (the base rate)	45.4550
Add: Forward premium for 3 m	0.0300
	45.4850
Less: Exchange Margin (0.15%)	0.0682
	45.4167
	(rounded off to ₹45.42)

Now consider the same example, but with the following swap points indicating US dollar at discount:

3-months	400/300
4-months	500/650

The forward period is 3 months 20 days. Here, the bank would round off the forward period to four months and use four-month swap points. With an exchange margin of 0.15%, the merchant rate for the exporter would be:

	₹ to US$
Inter-bank spot bid rate (the base rate)	45.4550
Less: Forward discount for 4 m	0.0500
	45.4050
Less: Exchange Margin (0.15%)	0.0681
	45.3369
	(rounded off to ₹45.34)

Bill Selling Rate The bill selling rate becomes applicable when the bank makes payment on behalf of its importer-client for the bill of exchange drawn on him. For handling documents, another exchange margin is loaded on the TT selling rate.

Bill Selling Rate = TT Selling Rate + Exchange Margin

Note that the bill selling rate has two exchange margins loaded, one for the foreign exchange transaction already built into the TT selling rate, and the other for handling the documents.

Forward Transactions for Merchants

The four rates mentioned above apply to spot transactions. Customers of the banks may also demand foreign exchange rates in advance and may like to enter into forward transactions. For arriving at forward rates, the bank uses the same principle as described with the bill buying rate; i.e., buy as late as possible when the currency is at discount and as early as possible when it is at premium. The reverse applies while selling, i.e., sell as early as possible when the currency is at discount and as late as possible when it is at premium. In forward transaction, besides the transit and usance periods, the forward period is also to be considered while rounding off to lower/higher months. Forward buying and selling rates are computed as follows:

When foreign currency is at discount

Forward Buying Rate = Spot ask rate – Discount for transit, usance and forward period rounded to higher month – Exchange margin

Forward Selling Rate = Spot ask rate – Discount for forward period rounded to lower month + Exchange margin

When foreign currency is at premium

Forward Buying Rate = Spot bid rate + Premium for transit, usance and forward period rounded to lower month – Exchange margin

Forward Selling Rate = Spot ask rate + Premium for forward period rounded to higher month + Exchange margin

Example 25-5 Merchant Rates

The following information is given: (₹ to US$)

Spot		45.6000/6500		
Swap	1-m	3500/3000	2-m	5500/5000
	3-m	8500/8000	4-m	1.1500/1.1000
	5-m	1.3500/1.3000	6-m	1.5500/1.5000

With a transit period of 20 days, an exchange margin of 0.15%, and a bill selling exchange margin of 0.20%, calculate the following:

(a) ready bill buying rate
(b) 2-m forward rate for demand bill
(c) 2-m forward rate for 60-day usance bill
(d) 3-m forward TT selling rate
(e) 3-m forward bill selling rate

Solution

(a) *Ready bill buying rate*

Forward + Usance + Transit = 0 + 0 + 20d = 20d
(rounded off to higher to 1-m) (US$ at discount)

Spot Buying Rate	45.6000
Less: Forward Discount 1-m	–0.3500
	45.2500
Less: Exchange Margin 0.15%	–0.0679
Merchant Rate	**45.1821**
	(rounded off to 45.18)

(b) *Two-month forward ready buying rate:*

The period involved is 20-d + 0 + 2-m = 2-m 20-d (rounded off to 3 m)

Spot Buying Rate	45.6000
Less: Forward Discount 3m	−0.8500
	44.7500
Less: Exchange Margin 0.15%	−0.0671
Merchant Rate	44.6829
	(rounded off to 44.68)

(c) Two-month forward 60-day usance bill buying rate

Forward Period = Forward + Usance + Transit = 2-m + 2-m + 20-d = 4-m 20-d

Spot Buying Rate	45.6000
Less: Forward Discount 5m	−1.3500
	44.2500
Less: Exchange Margin 0.15%	−0.0664
Merchant Rate	44.1836
	(rounded off to 44.18)

(d) and (e) Three-month forward TT and bill selling buying rates

Spot Selling Rate	45.6500
Less: Forward Discount 3m	−0.8000
	44.8500
Add: Exchange Margin 0.15%	+0.0673
Merchant TT Selling Rate	**44.9173**
	(rounded off to 44.92)
Add: Bill Exchange 0.20%	+0.0898
Merchant Bill Selling Rate	**45.0071**
	(rounded off to 45.01)

Option Forwards

Under forward contracts, parties are committed to settle their individual obligations on the due date. A forward contract is a firm contract that has to be settled on the specific date. Banks are in a better position to meet these commitments exactly on the specific date, but it is a rather difficult proposition for the merchants dealing in exports and imports. For example, an exporter expecting a payment in one month's time from his customer may decide to sell the foreign currency 1-month forward to the bank. Although a commitment has been made to sell the foreign currency to the bank, the exporter may not realize his payment as expected. In such a case, the exporter would default, as he is not ready with the foreign currency to be delivered to the bank on the scheduled date. A similar case may happen with an importer who may not like to buy the foreign currency on the date fixed in a forward contract booked by him.

Some flexibility in the timing of the maturity of the forward contract is desired by merchants, as they can predict their cash flows only on an approximate basis. When the exact timing of the cash inflow/outflow is uncertain, then forward contracts can be booked for delivery within a given period, called *option period*, rather than on a specific date. For example, an exporter expecting payment any time between two to three months would like to have flexibility whereby he can deliver the foreign exchange between two and three months of booking a forward contract. Such a contract is called *option forward contract*, and is depicted in Figure 25-2.

Option forward contracts are not fixed date contracts, but instead provide flexibility to settle within a period, called the option period.

Under an option forward contract, the merchant, having booked the forward contract at $t = 0$, has an option period for delivery between two dates; the earliest date and the latest date, rather than a fixed date.

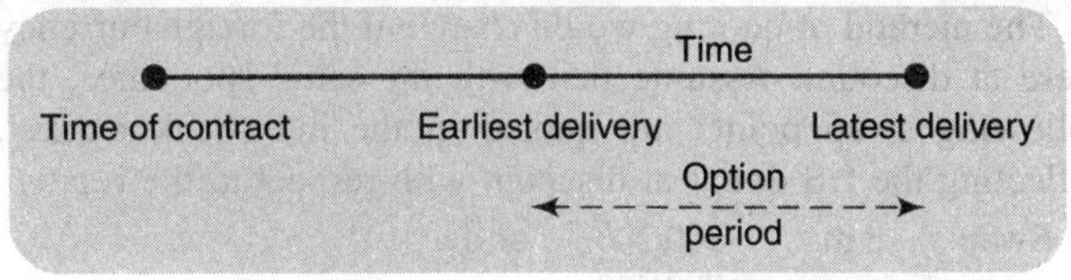

Figure 25-2 Option forward contract

Rates offered by banks in option forward contracts are based on the principle of least risk and maximum gain. The assumption is that the customer would exercise the delivery option that is most advantageous to him, putting the bank at an equal disadvantage. To offset the risk of unfavourable rates, the bank adopts an approach that minimizes the perceived advantage to the customer. Here the bank can choose to quote rates based on earliest or latest delivery depending upon whether—(1) the bank is buying or selling; and (2) whether the currency being transacted is at premium or discount. The advantage to the bank can be maximized if banks adopt the following strategies for quoting option forward rates.

	Buy	**Sell**
Premium	Earliest	Latest
Discount	Latest	Earliest

Rates based on the above strategies would no doubt be expensive for the customer. But the customer must be prepared to pay a price for exercising the option and, therefore, must not feel aggrieved.

As an example, consider the following scenario in the foreign exchange market:

Rupee to US$	Spot	:	45.3500 – 45.6550
Swap	3 m	:	250/300
	6 m	:	500/650

The swap points indicate that the US dollar is at premium with respect to the rupee. The rates for outright forward contract are obtained by adding the swap points to the spot rates. Accordingly, 3-m forward and 6-m forward rates are:

3-m forward	:	45.3750 – 45.6850
6-m forward	:	45.4000 – 45.7200

If a customer needs rates for the option period from that day to the next three months, the bank would quote the most favourable combination from the spot rates and 3-month outright forward rates. The foreign currency, US dollar, being at premium, the bank would prefer to buy at the earliest (the least rate) and sell at the latest (the highest rate) over the option period. The option forward rates for the option period from zero to three months are given below.

Option Forward Rates:

(Option Period 0 to 3m) : 45.3500 – 45.6850

Similarly, for option period between three and six months, the bank would quote

Option Forward Rates:

(Option Period 3 m to 6 m): 45.3750 – 45.7200

The method of quoting would change if the foreign currency were at discount. Assume that with the same spot rates, the following swap points are quoted in the inter-bank market, reflecting the US dollar at discount with respect to the rupee.

Swap	3 m:	300/200	and
	6 m:	700/450	

Outright forward rates are now obtained by subtracting the swap points from the spot rates. Accordingly, the rates are:

3-m forward	:	45.3200 – 45.6350
6-m forward	:	45.2800 – 45.6100

Using the same principle of least advantage to the customer, the option forward rates for option period from 0 to 3 months and 3 to 6 months would be:

Option Forward Rates

(option period 0 to 3 m): 45.3200 – 45.6550

(option period 3 to 6 m): 45.2800 – 45.6350

Example 25-6 Option Forward

On 31 December, an importer asked a bank to quote rates for sale to him of: (a) euro for delivery on 28 February, and (b) US dollar for a delivery any time in April. The following rates are available.

		₹ per US$ (Mumbai)	Euro per US$ (Singapore)
Spot		44.3700 – 44.3800	1.1000 – 1.1050
Swap	1-m	300/400	50/70
	2-m	1100/1250	100/130
	3-m	1900/2200	145/185
	4-m	2600/2950	190/240
	5-m	3500/3900	250/300

The bank needs an exchange margin of 5p.

Solution

Swap points reflect that the US dollar is at forward premium against the rupee as well as the euro. For outright forward rates, swap points will be added to the spot rate.

(a) *Euro for fixed delivery*

Customer buys euro, sells US dollars;

Bank sells euro, buys US dollar.

Customer buys US dollars, sells rupees;

Bank sells US dollar, buys rupees.

Spot Selling Rate for $	44.3800
Add: Premium (2 m)	+ 0.1250
Add: Exchange margin	+ 0.0500
$ Selling Rate (₹/$)	44.5550
Spot Buying Rate for €	1.1000
Add: Premium (2 m)	+ 0.0100
	1.1100

Merchant rate (₹ to €) = 44.5550 ÷ 1.1100

= 40.1396 (rounded off to ₹40.14 per €)

(b) *The US dollar for option delivery in April*

The US dollar is at premium, and hence, bank prefers latest delivery (30 April, i.e., 4 m premium)

Spot Selling Rate	44.3800
Add: Premium (4 m)	+ 0.2950
Add: Exchange margin	+ 0.0500
Merchant rate (₹ to US$)	= 44.7250

(rounded off to ₹44.73 per US$)

Option Forward vs Swap

It can be seen that option forwards are an expensive proposition to merchants, as they pay a higher price for the entire option period. As the option period lengthens, the cost in the form of unfavourable rates would increase. For example, an option forward contract for selling foreign currency that is at a premium would provide the least rate, forgoing the additional value that would have been obtained if the sale were deferred.

By curtailing the option period, merchants can save cost. The way to curtail the option period is to first enter into a swap deal, and when the timing of cash flows becomes more certain, enter into an option forward contract. A swap deal is a cheaper alternative. A swap deal alters the timing of the cash flow and saves cost.

For example, on 1 August, an importer books forward to buy US dollars for settling an expected payable three months later (due on 1 November). On 20 October, he learns that shipment is delayed by 15 days. On 30 October, he does a 15–day swap for spot sale and forward purchase of US dollars.

Such a swap deal would be cheaper than the option forward contract, if booked on 1 August. The importer defers the cash flow; delivers US dollars from the forward deal in the spot leg of the swap. The option forward contract would offer an absolutely firm rate, while for swap, uncertainty about swap points remains till 30 October.

Swap vs Roll-over Forward

Forward contracts are suitable for covering foreign exchange risks for short periods. For deferred payments or receipts extending beyond 6 or 12 months, forward contracts are not suitable instruments. Forward contracts may not be allowed, or available, beyond a specific maturity (six months in India), or if available, may be expensive. In order to cover risk in the long term, roll-over forward contracts are generally used. For example, for a loan repayable over five years, the borrower may book forward a buy contract for six months and then keep rolling over every six months till the end of the five–year period. Such rolling over of the forward contract every six months would be very expensive. Therefore, roll over forwards are not suitable to cover long-term exposures. Swaps enable roll over of the obligations in a cheaper way, and provide certainty of value of long-term exposures.

As an example, consider a term loan of US$ 10 million, repayable in 10 six-monthly instalments of US$ 1 million each. This can be covered through a swap as follows:

- Book forward contract of US$ 10 million for about six months
- After six months, take US$ 1 million for the 1st instalment and do a six-month swap of US$ 9 million spot sale and forward purchase
- Repeat swap every six months with reduced value.

FOREIGN EXCHANGE RATES AND ARBITRAGE

Having discussed the various rates, the question of whether the various dealers in foreign exchange would quote the same rate for a currency remains. More broadly, the question is how the process of quoting rates is determined. At a macro level, there is a large number of economic factors that impact the prices of various currencies almost continuously. Attempting to understand the factors that determine foreign exchange rates is a subject matter of economics. At micro level, or at the level of day-to-day operations, we are more concerned about how the rates from different sources are reached. We shall explore this process in this section.

The question of the determination of rates is analogous to stock market quotations. Unconcerned about the fair value of a financial asset like stocks or bonds, we all appreciate that an asset cannot have two prices. Having two prices provides an opportunity to investors to make an immediate profit without making an investment or assuming risk. Shares of Reliance Industries Limited in various stock exchanges in India at any one point of time necessarily have to be identical. If this is not so, one can buy shares in a market where prices are low, and simultaneously sell in a market where prices are high, pocketing the difference of prices in the two markets as profit that is earned without making any investment and without taking any risk. For example, if the share is trading at ₹1250 at NSE and at ₹1275 at BSE, one can buy at NSE and sell at BSE simultaneously, earning a profit of ₹25 less transaction costs per share. This kind of profit is called *arbitrage profit*.

Arbitrage is a process that makes prices converge in different market. It is not concerned with whether the prices are fair or not.

Here the focus is on differences of price, rather than the absolute price or the question of which of the prices is correct. The process of arbitrage would make the prices converge and eliminate such profits very quickly. The visibility of arbitrage opportunity is extremely high in cases where trading in financial assets takes place at exchanges where the prices are displayed all the time. The same process of arbitrage makes the prices of foreign exchange converge to identical rates by different traders and/or banks.

However, arbitrage opportunities in foreign exchange markets are not as visible as they are in the case of stocks and bonds. There are two primary reasons: first, the foreign exchange markets are OTC markets, where the rates are not displayed for viewing, and hence, fewer investors are aware of the rates and of discrepancies, if any, and second, foreign exchange quotations are two-way quotes, with one price for buying and another for selling. Identification of arbitrage opportunities in foreign exchange markets is relatively difficult. Apart from these factors, foreign exchange market may place restrictions on trading and prohibit taking of speculative positions, unlike stock markets, where such restrictions are mostly absent.

We shall examine and derive some rules for foreign exchange markets that may help traders to save some cost, if possible. Let us consider a simple example where two banks, Bank A and Bank B (assuming both are American banks and follow the convention of direct rates) have offered the following rates.

Rate, US$ per €	*Bid*	*Ask*
Bank A	1.3160	1.3260
Bank B	1.3280	1.3380

As we know, foreign exchange rates are quoted in pairs: the bid rate for buying, the ask rate for selling. The above rates are for buying and selling of euro in the USA. Normally, inter-bank markets specify rates up to four decimal places. Also remember that the bid rate is always lower, and precedes the ask rate.

The rates of Bank A mean that it would buy euro at US$ 1.3160 and sell euro at US$ 1.3260. This means that customers can sell one euro and get US$ 1.3160 (the bid rate), and if they wish to buy one euro, they will have to pay US$ 1.3260 (the ask rate). Similarly, from Bank B, customers can sell one euro for US$ 1.3280 and pay US$ 1.3380 to get one euro. A customer sells foreign currency at the bid rate and buys foreign currency at the ask rate.

To derive profit, one needs to 'sell high and buy low'. In foreign exchange markets, if the ask rate of one is higher than the bid rate of another, this would offer an arbitrage opportunity, and the difference between ask of one and bid of another can be earned as profit. The conditions for arbitrage are exhibited in Figure 25-3, and can be simply expressed as:

For arbitrage: $Bid_2 > Ask_1$

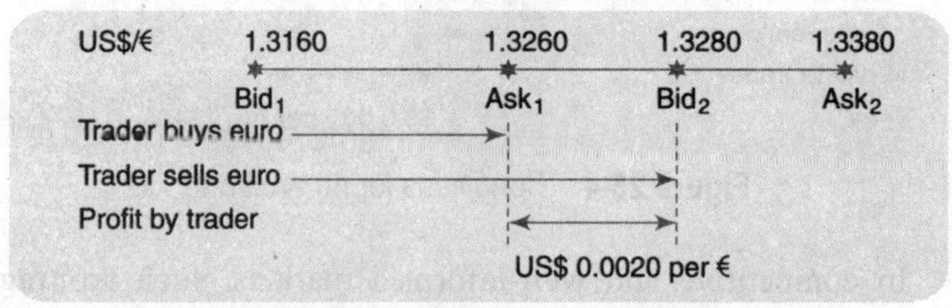

Figure 25-3 Condition for arbitrage

With the given rates, speculators would buy euros from Bank A by paying the ask rate of US$ 1.3260 and sell the same amount of euros to Bank B to receive the bid rate of US$ 1.3280, making a profit of US$ 0.0020 per euro without making any investment or carrying any risk.

Obviously, the rates that offer arbitrage opportunities cannot exist for long in the market. Arbitrage opportunities vanish very quickly. Traders make merry in such conditions, but banks would soon go bankrupt. Foreign exchange rates are not traded, and thus, Bank A and Bank B are not aware that the mismatch exists. However, market forces will communicate a lot to both the banks, automatically forcing both Bank A and Bank B to adjust the rates.

Banks do business by buying and selling foreign currency; under ideal conditions, they would have no net position in any currency. Here, both the banks expect to sell the same amount of euro as they buy, so as to avoid any exposure or build-up of foreign currency either in substantial amounts or for long periods. Bank A would face great demand for euro, indicating that it can raise the ask rate. Continuing with the same rate would also result in depletion of its stock of euro. Similarly, Bank B would face a situation where it would be buying a lot of euro US$ 1.3280. This indicates that it can revise its quote downwards and also prevent unnecessary build-up of euro. Arbitrageurs would stimulate upward revision of the ask rate of Bank A and downward revision of the bid rate of Bank B. If the quotes of Bank *A* and Bank B overlap (the ask rate of one is greater than the bid rate of the other), the arbitrage opportunity would vanish. Traders would not be able to generate profit by buying from one and selling to the other if the banks revise the rates, as shown below.

For arbitrage-free foreign exchange rates the bid price of one trader must be less than the ask price of another, with both the quotes expressed in similar fashion.

Rate, US$ per €	*Bid*	*Ask*
Bank A	1.3160	1.3275
Bank B	1.3270	1.3380

The condition where no arbitrage opportunity can exist is depicted in Figure 25-4, where the rates of the two banks overlap. This may also be stated as:

$$\textbf{For no arbitrage:} \quad \text{Bid}_2 < \text{Ask}_1$$

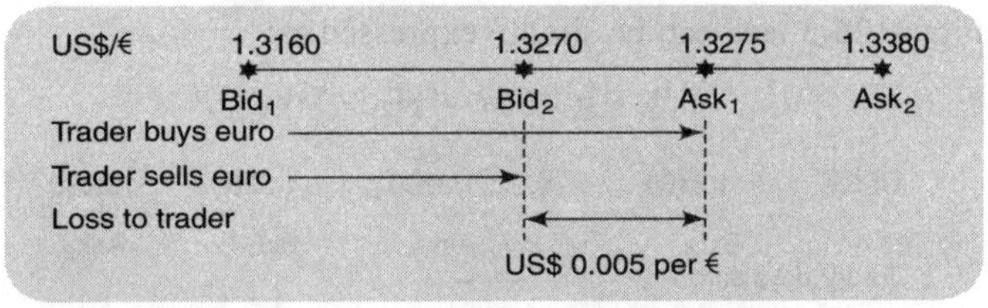

Figure 25-4 Conditions for no arbitrage

In competitive and well-informed markets, such arbitrage opportunities do not exist at all, and if they do, then they vanish as quickly as they are spotted.

Arbitrage in Two Markets

We considered the existence of arbitrage in one country, where the rates available and quoted had the same format. Although the principle of arbitrage essentially remains the same if the arbitrage is to be found in two different countries, spotting of such opportunity is slightly difficult and not apparent, because quotations are not made in the same format. For example, consider a US bank and a German bank, located in different countries, which follow a system of direct rates and offer the following rates.

	Bid	*Ask*
US Bank *(US$ per €)*	1.3160	1.3260
German Bank *(€ per US$)*	0.7475	0.7525

Here, the arbitrage opportunity, though it exists, is not directly visible from the quotes. To facilitate identification of whether quotes are overlapping, one needs to have the rates in the same format. Either of the rates has to be inverted. We invert the rates of the German bank from rate for euro per US dollar to rate for US dollar per euro, as available in the quotes of the American bank. Remember that while inverting rates, the ask rate is used to obtain the bid rate, and vice versa. This is shown below.

While inverting rates ask rate is inverted to get bid rates and vice versa.

German Bank *(rate, € per US$)* (direct quote)	0.7475	0.7525
(Rate, US$ per €) (Indirect quote)	1.3289 *(1/0.7525)*	1.3378 *(1/0.7475)*

Now the arbitrage opportunity is evident, as the ask rate of the American bank is lower than the bid rate of the German bank. Traders can buy euro in USA and sell it in Germany to get a profit of US$ 0.0029 per €

Note that the arbitrage exists only in one direction. The reverse arbitrage i.e. buying euro in Germany and selling them in USA would result in loss. You may verify that loss in this case would be US$ 0.0218 for each €.

Arbitrage using only two currencies is very conveniently visible. But in reality, with several currencies involved, spotting such instances is difficult. One has to trade in many currencies before profits can be derived. One would have to use cross-rates and vehicle currency to identify arbitrage opportunities.

SUMMARY

With increased globalization and gradual removal of regulatory controls for businesses across borders, understanding foreign exchange rates and their market has become as necessary as the understanding of domestic markets. For large firms dealing on a global basis, an insight into the mechanism of how foreign exchange markets operate is vital. The risk profile in international business alters substantially, as the accounting conventions and the legal environments are different for the two contracting parties.

Foreign exchange markets, unlike stock markets, are over-the-counter (OTC) markets, where currency rates are negotiated between two parties without anything being disclosed to others. They operate all the time. There are two distinct markets in foreign exchange: the one within banks, called inter-bank markets, and the other for transactions of traders with banks. The foreign exchange market is dominated by transactions amongst banks.

In foreign exchange markets, the banks serve as brokers, but unlike stock market brokers, earn their profit through buying at lower rates, called bid rates, and selling at higher rates, called ask rates. Foreign currency can be bought or sold for future delivery with rates determined today. Such contracts, where the physical exchange of currencies takes place at a later date, are called forward contracts, and the rates are called forward rates. Forward contracts have a firm date and firm value for settlement. They are excellent instruments that provide perfect hedge. Forward rates are generally available for whole numbers of months, though it is possible to obtain contracts of delivery at any point of time.

A combination of a spot transaction followed by an equal and opposite forward transaction is called a swap. A swap deal nullifies the outstanding foreign exchange position when the forward leg is completed. This can also be achieved by a spot transaction followed by an equal and opposite forward transaction, making two independent contracts. A swap deal is always cheaper than two independent contracts of spot and forward, and is a more efficient tool for covering foreign exchange risk.

The rates that banks charge among themselves, called inter-bank rates, are different from the rates charged to customers, called merchant rates. Merchant rates provide exchange commissions and handling charges for the banks, and are derived from inter-bank rates. These commissions and charges are governed by FEDAI. Merchant transactions are of two kinds: one involves the exchange of currencies and the other involves dealing with documents. There are four kinds of merchant rates applicable: TT buying, TT selling, bill buying, and bill selling.

When firms cover foreign exchange risk through a forward contract, the exact delivery date is fixed. However, commercial transactions on credit may not adhere to the exact payment schedule. In circumstances where no exact date of settlement can be forecast, and only an approximate idea of realization or payment can be made, option forward contracts are available that permit delivery of foreign currency within a time period, rather than on a specific date.

The basic principle that determines the quotations of foreign exchange at different places at the same point of time is the process of arbitrage. Any discrepancies in the rates at different places or of different banks are exploited by traders to make profits without having to make any investment or assume any risk. Arbitrage forces the convergence of exchange rates all over the world. An exchange rate is the price of one currency in terms of another, and cannot be different in different markets.

KEY TERMS

Bid rate The bid rate is the rate at which a bank buys foreign currency. Traders sell foreign currency at this rate.

Ask rate The ask rate is the rate at which a bank sells foreign currency. Traders buy foreign currency at this rate.

Forward contract A forward contract fixes the delivery date, in the future, of a specified amount of currency for which the exchange rates are decided at the time of entering contract.

Value date The value date is the date of settlement of foreign exchange transactions, when the two currencies contracted for are paid into the respective accounts of the contracting parties.

Spot transactions Spot transactions in foreign currency markets are those transactions where the exchange rate is fixed on the date of contract for settlement within two business days.

Swap A swap is a composite contract consisting of a spot transaction followed by an equal and opposite forward transaction.

Swap points Swap points indicate the profit or loss that would be incurred in doing a swap transaction.

Direct rate Under the direct rate system, foreign exchange rates are quoted in terms of number of units of the home currency per unit of the foreign currency. For example, ₹45 per US$ or ₹59.00 per € would be direct rates in India.

Indirect rates Under the indirect rate system, foreign exchange rates are quoted in terms of number of unit of foreign currency per unit of home currency. For example US$ 0.02 per rupee or € 0.155 per rupee would be indirect rates in India.

Cross rate When rates for a currency are not available directly, one can synthesize the rates using a common intermediate currency. For example, the exchange rate for Indian rupee to peso can be arrived at by using the rupee to US dollar rate and then the US dollar to peso rate.

Inter-bank rate Inter-bank rates are the rates that apply to transactions amongst banks.

Merchant rate Merchant rates are those rates that banks quote to their customers.

Arbitrage Arbitrage is a strategy that results into profit without (a) making own investment and (b) taking risk.

KEY FORMULAE

Spread $\%\text{ spread} = \dfrac{\text{ask rate} - \text{bid rate}}{\text{mid rate}} \times 100$

Forward premium/discount

Annualized forward permium/discount (%)

$$= \frac{\text{forward rate}_{mid} \times \text{spot rate}_{mid}}{\text{spot rate}_{mid}} \times \frac{12}{\text{forward period (in months)}} \times 100$$

PRACTICE PROBLEMS

Given the following exchange rate scenario as on 21 April 2008:
(Use the following rates for Problems 1 to 6)

₹ per unit of FC	*Bid*	*Ask*
US $	39.85	39.87
Euro	63.07	63.10
British Pound	79.70	79.72
Japanese Yen (for 100 Yens)	38.40	38.43
Swiss Franc, CHF	39.17	39.20
Singapore Dollar, SG $	29.45	29.47
Chinese Yuan	5.69	5.70
Korean Won	4.02	4.03
African Rand	5.13	5.15
Australian Dollar, Aus $	37.38	37.40
Swedish Kroner	6.71	6.75
Danish Kroner	8.45	8.48
Canadian Dollar, Can $	36.69	36.73
Thai Baht	126.47	126.49

1. Exchange Rate for Exporters

How much money would be realized by Indian exporters for

(a) US $ 1,000
(b) Chinese Yuan 20,000
(c) Singapore $ 25,000
(d) Japanese Yen 10,00,000

Solution

For exporters selling foreign currency, the bid rate is applicable.

	Currency	FC Amount	Bid Rate	Equivalent ₹
(a)	US $	1,000	39.85	39,850
(b)	Chinese Yuan	20,000	5.69	1,13,800
(c)	Singapore $	25,000	29.45	7,36,250
(d)	Japanese Yen	10,00,000	38.40 (per 100)	3,84,000

2. Exchange Rate for Importers

How much money would be payable for

(a) Euro 10,000 (b) GBP 20,000
(c) Australian $ 20,000 (d) Thai Baht 10,00,000

Solution

For importers buying foreign currency, the ask rate is applicable.

	Currency	FC Amount	Ask Rate	Equivalent ₹
(a)	Euro	10,000	63.10	6,31,000
(b)	GBP	20,000	79.72	15,94,400
(c)	Australian $	20,000	37.40	7,48,000
(d)	Thai Baht	10,00,000	126.49	12,64,900

3. Exchange Rate for Travel Abroad

You are proceeding on a world tour and need the following currencies:

(a) Canadian $ 10,000
(b) African Rand 20,000
(c) Swedish Kroner 15,000
(d) Korean Won 25,000

How much money in Indian rupee you must have?

Solution

For travellers buying foreign currency, the ask rate is applicable.

	Currency	FC Amount	Ask Rate	Equivalent ₹
(a)	Can $	10,000	36.73	3,67,300
(b)	African Rand	20,000	5.15	1,03,000
(c)	Swedish Kroner	15,000	6.75	1,01,250
(d)	Korean Won	25,000	4.03	1,00,750
			Total money required	6,72,300

4. Bid Ask Spread

You had ₹1,00,000 with you while travelling to USA. You had them converted into US $. However, your decision to travel changed and instead you were required to curtail your journey up to London only. The US $ you had now are required to be converted in British pounds. How many British pound would you have now? What is the loss?

Solution

Amount available = ₹1,00,000

While buying US $ worth ₹10,000 the bank would apply ask rate.

Nos. of US $ obtained were = 1,00,000/39.87 = 2,508.15

Due to the change of travel plan, now you are required to sell US $ to get rupees and then buy GBP. US dollar would be sold at bid rate.

Rupees obtained by selling US $ = 2508.15 x 39.85 = 99,949.84

British pound that can be made available would be

= 99,949.84/79.72 = 1,253.76

The loss incurred would be equal to the bid ask spread in US $ rates. The loss is = ₹50.16

5. Indirect Rates

In India, the foreign currency rates quoted are direct (Nos. of rupees per unit of foreign currency). If the same rates are to be quoted in a foreign country, what bid and ask rates would be offered for the following currencies:

(a) Korean Won (b) African Rand
(c) Swedish Kroner (d) Danish Kroner

Your answer must be up to 4 decimal places.

Solution

The rates quoted for these currencies in India are

	Bid	*Ask*
Korean Won	4.02	4.03
African Rand	5.13	5.15
Swedish Kroner	6.71	6.75
Danish Kroner	8.45	8.48

Number of rupees per unit of foreign currency

While converting the rates in the indirect format, we need to invert the bid rate to get the ask rate and vice versa. For example, we get rates of Korean Won as follows:

$$\text{Bid}_{(\text{Won}/₹)} = \frac{1}{\text{Ask}\ (₹/\text{Won})} \text{ and } \text{Ask}_{(\text{Won}/₹)} = \frac{1}{\text{Bid}_{(₹/\text{Won})}}$$

$$\text{Bid}_{(\text{Won}/₹)} = \frac{1}{4.03} = 0.2481 \text{ and } \text{Ask}_{(\text{Won}/₹)} = \frac{1}{4.02} = 0.2488$$

The rates for Indian rupees in the respective countries would be quoted as below:

	Bid	Ask
Korean Won	0.2481	0.2488
African Rand	0.1942	0.1949
Swedish Kroner	0.1481	0.1490
Danish Kroner	0.1179	0.1183
Number of foreign currency per Indian rupee		

6. Using Cross Rates

Using Indian Rupee as vehicle currency, work out the bid and ask rates for

(a) Euro/ US $
(b) CHF/Singapore $
(c) GBP/Swedish Kroner

Solution

While working out the cross rate using a common currency, we apply the chain rule.

For working out the rates of euro/US $ we use following equations:

$$\text{Bid}_{(\text{Euro/US\$})} = \text{Bid}_{(₹/\text{US\$})} \times \text{Bid}_{(\text{Euro}/₹)}$$

$$= \frac{\text{Bid}_{(₹/\text{US\$})}}{\text{Ask}_{(₹/\text{Euro})}}$$

$$\text{Ask}_{(\text{Euro/US\$})} = \text{Ask}_{(₹/\text{US\$})} \times \text{Ask}_{(\text{Euro}/₹)}$$

$$= \frac{\text{Ask}_{(₹/\text{US\$})}}{\text{Bid}_{(₹/\text{Euro})}}$$

Using the above equations, we get

(a) Euro/US $
Bid = 39.85/63.10 = 0.6315
Ask = 39.87/63.07 = 0.6322

(b) CHF/SG $
Bid = 29.45/39.20 = .7513
Ask = 29.47/39.17 = 0.7524

(c) GBP/Swedish Kroner
Bid = 79.70/6.75 = 11.8074
Ask = 79.72/6.71 = 11.8808

7. Forward Premium/Discount

In the foreign exchange market, one of the dealers in foreign exchange has quoted following spot and 6-m forward rates in respect of four currencies - US Dollar, Euro, Swiss Francs, and British Pound:

	₹ per unit of foreign currency			
Currency	**Spot**		**6-m Forward**	
US $	40.12	40.16	39.32	39.38
Euro	63.06	63.10	65.08	65.14
CHF	37.86	37.90	37.54	37.60
GBP	79.70	79.74	80.20	80.26

(a) Find the annualized premium/discount for each currency with respect to rupee.
(b) Based on answer in a) what forward rate do you expect for 12-m forward for each currency?

Solution

Premium or discount of the currency is computed on the basis of the average of bid and ask rates. If the forward rate is higher than the spot, the currency is said to be at premium with respect to the local currency. If the forward rate is less than the spot, the foreign currency is at discount.

Mid rates (average of bid and ask rates) for the forward and spot market are as follows:

Currency	Spot			6-m Forward		
	Bid	Ask	Mid	Bid	Ask	Mid
US $	40.12	40.16	40.14	39.32	39.38	39.35
Euro	63.06	63.10	63.08	65.08	65.14	65.11
CHF	37.86	37.90	37.88	37.54	37.60	37.57
GBP	79.70	79.74	79.72	80.20	80.26	80.23

(a) Annualized premium/discount for each currency is computed below:

Annualized forward premium (+)/discount (–)

$$= \frac{F-S}{S} \times \frac{12}{\text{months}} \times 100$$

$$\text{USD} = \frac{39.35-40.14}{40.14} \times \frac{12}{6} \times 100 = -3.9362\% \approx -3.94\%$$

$$\text{Euro} = \frac{65.11-63.08}{63.08} \times \frac{12}{6} \times 100 = 6.4363\% \approx -6.44\%$$

$$\text{CHF} = \frac{37.57-37.88}{37.88} \times \frac{12}{6} \times 100 = -1.6367\% \approx -1.64\%$$

$$\text{GBP} = \frac{80.23-79.72}{79.72} \times \frac{12}{6} \times 100 = 1.2795\% \approx -1.28\%$$

(b)

Currency	Spot (mid)	Premium/ Discount	12-m Forward (mid)
US $	40.1400	-3.9362	38.56
Euro	63.0800	6.4363	67.14
CHF	37.8800	-1.6367	37.26
GBP	79.7200	1.2795	80.74

8. Swap and Outright Forward

Following rates are quoted in respect of US $ for Indian rupee.

Spot (₹/$)	40.25	40.50
6-m swap	50/75	

(a) Find out the profit/loss for a trader who wants to sell dollar now and buy 6 months later on (i) outright basis and (ii) swap basis.
(b) Find out the profit/loss for a trader who wants to buy dollar now and sell 6 months later on (i) outright basis and (ii) swap basis.

Solution

Outright forward rate may be computed by adding the swap points to the spot rate as the swap points are Low/High.

Spot (₹/$)	40.25	40.50
Swap points	50	75
Outright forward (₹/$)	40.75	41.25

For buying dollar spot and selling later, if done on outright basis, the rates applicable for spot buy and forward sell would be market determined with both the transactions as independent of each other.

In the swap deal, it would be a composite deal where rate for the forward leg is determined based on the swap points applicable for the second leg.

(₹/$)	Outright basis	Swap basis
(a) Spot buy—sell later		
Spot buy	40.50	40.50
Forward Sell	40.75	41.00
Profit/loss	0.25	0.50
(b) Spot sell—buy later		
Spot sell	40.25	40.25
Forward buy	41.25	41.00
Profit/loss	–1.00	–0.75

9. Merchant Rates

Following exchange rates are quoted in the inter-bank market:

Spot (₹ per euro)	64.0000	64.3000
1-m swap	3000	2000
2-m swap	5500	4000
3-m swap	8000	5500

On the basis of the given data, you are required to calculate the following:

(a) TT buying rate

(b) TT selling rate

(c) Bill buying rate for 1-month usance and 10 days as transit period. Assume that the bank charges 0.125% for bill handling.

Solution

Based on the rates, the forward rates are worked out by subtracting the swap points from spot (being high/low)

Outright forward rate	₹/€	
1-m	63.7000	64.1000
2-m	63.4500	63.9000
2-m	63.2000	63.7500

The forward rates indicate that euro is at discount with respect to rupee.

TT rates are arrived on the basis of spot rate in the inter-bank market by adding/deducting the exchange margin for the bank. For TT buying rate, exchange commission is deducted; while for selling rate, it is added.

	₹/€
(a) Interbank bid rate-Spot	64.00
less: Exchange margin	0.15
TT buying rate	63.85
(b) Interbank ask rate-Spot	64.30
add: Exchange margin	0.15
TT selling rate	64.45

(c) For the 1-m usance bill, the period for the forward transaction would be calculated. It shall then be rounded off to whole number of months. If foreign currency is at premium, the rounding off is in lower number; and if at discount, then to higher number of months.

Forward period = Transit period + Usance period = 10 days + 1 month = 2 months (rounded higher, euro being at discount)

	₹/€
Inter-bank bid rate Spot	64.0000
less: 2 month swap points	0.5500
Inter-bank 2-m forward rate	63.4500
Bank's margin	0.0793
Bill buying rate	63.3707 (rounded off to 63.37)

10. Arbitrage in Foreign Exchange Markets

Following rates in the foreign exchange markets of different countries are being quoted at the same point of time:

(Assuming all countries follow the convention of quoting direct rates)

New York (Nos. of US $)		
Euro	1.5912	1.5935
Pound	1.9817	1.9842
London (Nos. of Pound)		
US $	0.5016	0.5025
Euro	0.8025	0.8050
Paris (Nos. of Euro)		
US $	0.6284	0.6300
Pound	1.2454	1.2475

Do you think that there exists an arbitrage in the foreign exchange market? If the scope for arbitrage exists, how can it be exploited?

Solution

To examine arbitrage, we have to compare the ask rate (the rate at which bank sells and customers buy) at one place with the bid rate (the rate at which bank buys and customers sell) at another place.

If the ask rate at one place is less than the bid rate at another place, then we can profit by buying at the first place and selling at the second place.

To facilitate the comparison of ask and bid rates we need to convert the rates of different places in the same format.

		US $ per Euro
New York	1.5912	1.5935
Paris	1.5873	1.5913

Ask rate is higher than the bid rate, and therefore there exists no arbitrage opportunity. We shall incur a loss of $ 0.0062 for every euro bought in New York and sold in Paris, as is demonstrated here:

Buy € in	New York at	1.5935
Sell € in	Paris at	1.5873
Profit/Loss		–$0.0062

		US $ per £
New York	1.9817	1.9842
London	1.9900	1.9936

Ask rate is lower in New York than the bid rate in London, and therefore there exists arbitrage opportunity. We shall make arbitrage profit by buying pound in New York and sell in London. A profit of $ 0.0058 would result for every pound bought in New York and sold in London, as is demonstrated here:

Buy £ in	New York at	1.9842
Sell £ in	London at	1.9900
Profit/Loss		$0.0058

		€ per £
Paris	1.2454	1.2475
London	1.2422	1.2461

Ask rate is higher than the bid rate and therefore there exists no arbitrage opportunity. We shall incur a loss of Euro 0.0052 for every Pound bought in Paris and sold in London, as is demonstrated below:

Buy £ in	Paris at	1.2475
Sell £ in	London at	1.2422
Profit/Loss		– € 0.0053

EXERCISES

Concept Review Questions

1. As there is no commission/brokerage payable in foreign exchange trades, how do banks derive their profits while dealing in foreign currency with their customers?
2. How do banks arrive at foreign exchange rates for their customers?
3. What is the difference between spot and forward transactions in foreign exchange markets?
4. How do you define a swap transaction? Why do banks undertake swap rather than entering two separate transactions on spot and outright forward bases?
5. There is no rate available for Saudi riyal against rupee in India. However, both Indian rupee and Saudi riyal are actively traded against the US dollar. What method would you adopt to quote a rate for Saudi riyal in terms of Indian rupee?
6. An exporter has granted credit to his European customer for 30 days for €10,000. Looking at the track record, it is found that the customer normally pays in 45 days. Should the exporter book a forward sell contract of €10,000 for 30 days or 45 days? Is there any other alternative available to him?
7. The following rates are available in the foreign exchange markets in New York and London:

In New York (US$ per £)	1.6500	1.6580
In London (£ per US$)	0.6000	0.6100

How do you think you can take advantage of these rates? If asked to correct the rates, which of the rates would you modify and by how much? Give reasons for your decision.

Critical Thinking Questions

1. Foreign exchange markets, being Over-the-Counter with rates available worldwide, are more efficient than organized markets like stock markets. Do you agree with the statement? Give reasons.
2. Given forward rates for periods of 1, 2, 3, 6, and 9 months, which of the rate would you use to arrive at annualized forward premium/discount and why? Would the annualized premium/discount be the same using any forward rate? Provide reasons for your answer.
3. One analyst obsessed with the time value of money stated that forward rates must always be higher than spot rates because under forward contracts, actual exchange of cash takes place later. Do you agree with the statement?
4. An exporter has hired you as a consultant. He also offers very high credit periods of four to six months to his customers, and to cover risks, books option forward contracts with option periods of four to six months. What better and more economical alternatives can you suggest?
5. It is observed that at exchange counters, the rates for exchanging cash and traveller cheques are different. Customers normally get higher rates for traveller cheques. What reasons can you ascribe to this variation?

Practical Assignments

1. Choose a currency and 10 different banks on a given day. Get exchange rates for the currency from the 10 banks. Ascertain the reasons for variations in their rates. Compare their rates to identify if any arbitrage opportunity exists.
2. Find out the spot rates and 1-month forward rates for the last 12 months for US$ from the same source and on the same date of each month. Find out the annualized premium or discount and construct a graph. Attempt to find out the reasons for changes in the forward premium or discount over the preceding 12 months.
3. Find out the bid and ask rates for each of the last 30 days for the US dollar and the sterling pound against the Indian rupee. From these rates, synthesize the US dollar to sterling pound rate expressed as number of US dollars per sterling pound, then compare these rates on the same date with those prevailing in London. What differences do you find in the spread of direct rates in London and those synthesized by you?

Numerical Problems

1. Identifying Applicable Exchange Rate

Given the following exchange rate scenario:

Per US $	*Bid*	*Ask*
Euro	0.7275	0.7325
Pound	0.4930	0.4970
Yen	118.0000	121.0000
CHF	1.1950	1.2000
SG $	5.4200	5.4300
HK $	7.8150	7.8250
Aus $	1.5100	1.5250
NZ $	1.1700	1.1800
Can $	1.3200	1.3300
Rupee	40.5000	40.9000

Answer the following questions using the above data:

(i) How much money would be realized by
  (a) Indian exporter for US$ 1,000
  (b) Swiss exporter for US$ 500
  (c) Hong Kong exporter for US$ 1,500
  (d) Japanese exporter for US$ 2,000

(ii) How much money would be payable by
  (a) English importer for US$ 5,000
  (b) Singapore importer for US$ 2,500
  (c) Australian importer for US$ 3,500
  (d) Canadian importer for US$ 10,000

(iii) How many US $ would be received by
  (a) An Indian for ₹5,000
  (b) A New Zealander for NZ $ 500
  (c) A Japanese for Yen 1,00,000
  (d) A Canadian for Can $ 4,000

(iv) How many US $ would be payable for buying
  (a) Indian ₹10,000
  (b) Swiss Franc 1,00,000
  (c) € 3,000
  (d) HK $ 10,000

2. Using Cross Rates
Using the data given in Problem 1, work out the bid and ask rates for
  (a) HK$ per €
  (b) Japanese yen per CHF
  (c) Indian rupee per pound
  (d) Can $ per Aus $

3. Vehicle Currency
India follows a system of direct quotes in foreign exchange markets. All the currencies are quoted in terms of the number of local currency units, i.e., rupees per unit of foreign currency. Following rates exist:

Currency	Bid rate	Ask rate
US $	40.50	41.00
Euro	55.60	56.80
Pound	82.10	82.50
Yen per ₹100	34.05	35.25
CHF	33.60	34.00
SG $	26.75	27.45
HK $	5.20	5.40
Can $	38.40	39.00

An Englishman is travelling from New Delhi to Tokyo. He has £ 10,000 with him. He has to convert these pounds into Japanese yen at Delhi. How many yen would he get?

4. Buying and Selling Currencies
An exporter has received €10,000 and at the same time has to remit CHF 15,000. How much Indian rupee would be payable or receivable after the completion of the transactions? Use the exchange rates given in Problem 3.

5. Cross Rates
Using the exchange rate of Problem 3, work out the bid and ask rates using rupee as the vehicle currency for
  (a) HK$ per €
  (b) Japanese yen per CHF

6. Finding Arbitrage
We arrived at following cross rates using US $ and Indian rupee as vehicle currency respectively in Problem 2 and Problem 5.

HK $ per €		Japanese yen per CHF	
With rupee as vehicle		With rupee as vehicle	
10.2963	10.9231	100.1471	104.9107
With US $ as vehicle		With US $ as vehicle	
10.6689	10.7560	98.3333	101.2552

Is there any arbitrage opportunity?

7. Competition for Profitable Use
Assume that foreign exchange in India is freely available. A broker in foreign exchange dealing in US$ and euro has offered following quote for US$ and euro:

Spot Exchange Rate (US$ per €)   1.3500   1.3600

A customer tenders €1,000 for conversion into US$ to the broker. The broker is required to cover the transactions in the interbank market for all the dealings with individuals. Four banks, A, B, C, D have offered following rates for € and US $ in terms of Indian rupee.

	₹/€		₹/US $	
	Bid	Ask	Bid	Ask
Bank A	55.6500	55.8500	41.1000	41.2500
Bank B	55.6000	55.9000	41.1500	41.3000
Bank C	55.5500	55.7500	41.0500	41.1550
Bank D	55.6800	55.9000	41.0000	41.2000

Find what rate of exchange would be applicable to the customer?
How would you execute the cover operations?
Find if you can make some money in the cover operations with the bank when allowed to deal with (i) multiple banks and (ii) a single bank.

8. Competition for Profitable Use
Examine all the questions of Problem 7 if another customer tenders US$ 1,000 for conversion into euro.

9. Applying Cross Rates
A customer requested the bank to remit CHF 250,000 to Zurich under an LC for import of diamonds on 27 October. The bank could effect the remittance only on 3 November. The rates on two dates were as follows:

		Oct 27		Nov 3	
Bombay	₹ /$	44.050	44.550	44.000	44.450
London	$/pound	2.1500	2.1560	2.1570	2.1630
	CHF/pound	2.9575	2.9590	2.9380	2.9390

If bank wants to charge exchange margin of 0.125% how much amount the customer stand to lose or gain?

10. Option Forwards
An exporter from Germany is required to execute an order worth US$ 2 million. The payment terms are immediate upon execution. He is expecting to execute the order anytime between 2 and 3 months. Since US$ is expected to depreciate with respect to euro, he would like to cover the risk of exchange rate through a forward contract. What rates bank would quote to the customer under following two scenarios:

	Scenario A		Scenario B	
Spot Euro/$	1.5280	1.5285	1.5280	1.5285
2-m Swap	35	40	30	25
3-m Swap	55	65	45	35

11. Speculation in the Foreign Exchange Markets
With respect to rupee - US $ exchange rate following scenario exists today:

Spot (₹/$)	40.60	40.80
6-m Swap	50	80

A company has also prepared a forecast for the expected spot rate six months later. The forecast is summarized as follows:

Probability	0.20	0.30	0.30	0.20
Bid Rate	40.50	40.70	40.90	41.00
Ask Rate	40.75	40.95	41.20	41.35

The company believes that its forecast is fairly reliable and would like to put it to a profitable use if there exists and opportunity to do so. Being an exporter and importer it has the option of booking forward contracts for buying or selling the foreign currency. It is thinking of booking a forward contract now and cancel it by entering into an opposite contract upon maturity of the forward contract. Do you think that such an opportunity exists? If so what strategy would you adopt and how much profit can be generated on a forward contract of US$ 100,000?

CASE STUDY

Diamond Edge Inc: Assessment of Potential Arbitrage Opportunities*

To overcome saturated demand conditions in the domestic market, Diamond Edge Inc, a US manufacturer of roller blades, has chosen Thailand as its primary export target for 'Turbo', Diamond Edge's primary product. The company's primary customer in Thailand, Entertainment Products, has committed itself to the purchase of 180,000 Turbo units annually for the next three years at a fixed price of Thailand Baht (THB) 4,594 per pair. Diamond Edge also imports from Thai suppliers some of the rubber and plastic components needed to manufacture Turbo because of quality and cost considerations.

In recent times, Thailand has experienced weak economic growth and excess supply of Baht for sale over the demand for Baht in the foreign exchange market. This has put downward pressure on the Baht's value. The withdrawal of funds from Thailand has aggravated the situation further and caused a continued decline in the Baht's value. Diamond Edge has net cash flows in Baht resulting from its exports to the country, and deterioration in the Baht's value would affect the company negatively.

Ben Johnson, Diamond Edge's CFO, would like to ensure that the spot and forward rates the company is quoted by its bank are reasonable. If the exchange rate quotes are reasonable, then arbitrage would not be possible. However, if the quotations are not appropriate, arbitrage may be possible. Under these conditions, Ben Johnson would like Diamond Edge to use some form of arbitrage to take advantage of possible mispricing in the foreign exchange market. Although Diamond Edge is not an arbitrageur, Ben Johnson believes that arbitrage opportunities could offset the negative impact resulting from the Baht's depreciation, which would otherwise seriously affect Diamond's profit margins.

Ben Johnson has identified three arbitrage opportunities as profitable, and would like to know which one of these is the most profitable. Thus, Ben Johnson has consulted you, Diamond Edge's financial analyst, asking you to prepare an analysis of the arbitrage opportunities he has identified. This would allow the CFO to assess the profitability of these arbitrage opportunities very quickly.

1. The first arbitrage opportunity identified by Ben Johnson relates to locational arbitrage. He has received spot rate quotations from two banks in Thailand: Minzue Bank and Sobat Bank, both located in Bangkok. The bid and ask prices of Baht for each bank are displayed in the following table.

	Minzue Bank	*Sobat Bank*
Bid	US$0.0224	US$0.0228
Ask	US$0.0227	US$0.0229

Determine whether the foreign exchange quotations are appropriate. If they are not appropriate, determine the profit the company could generate by withdrawing US$ 100,000 from its checking account and engaging in arbitrage before the rates are adjusted.

2. Apart from the bid and ask quotes for the Thai Baht provided in the previous question, Minzue Bank has provided the following quotations for the US$ and the Japanese Yen.

	Quoted Bid Price	*Quoted Ask Price*
Value of a Japanese Yen in US dollars	US$ 0.00857	US$ 0.00868
Value of a Thai Baht in Japanese Yen	JY 3.47	JY 3.49

Determine whether the cross exchange rate between the Thai Baht and Japanese Yen is appropriate. If it is not appropriate, determine the profit you could generate for Diamond Edge by withdrawing US$ 100,000 from Diamond Edge's checking account and engaging in triangular arbitrage before the rates are adjusted.

3. Ben Johnson has obtained several forward contract quotations for the Thai Baht to determine whether covered interest arbitrage may be possible. He was quoted a forward rate of US$ 0.0295 per Thai Baht for a 90-day forward contract. The current spot rate is US$ 0.0297. Ninety-day interest rates available to Diamond Edge in the United States are 2.25%, while 90-day interest rates in Thailand are 3.95% (these rates are not annualized). Ben Johnson is aware that covered interest arbitrage, unlike locational and triangular arbitrage, requires an investment of funds. Thus, he would like to be able to estimate the US dollar profit resulting from arbitrage over and above the US dollar amount available on a 90-day US deposit.

*Adapted from Madura, Jeff 2001, *International Financial Management*, 6th edition, Thomson Asia Pte Ltd, Singapore, pp 27, 28, 83, 84 and 115.

Determine whether the forward rate is priced appropriately. If it is not priced appropriately, determine the profit you could generate for Diamond Edge by withdrawing US$100,000 from the company's checking account and engaging in covered interest arbitrage. Measure the profit as the excess amount over what you could generate by investing in the US money market.

4. Why are arbitrage opportunities likely to disappear soon after they have been discovered? To illustrate your answer, assume that covered interest arbitrage involving the immediate purchase and forward sale of Baht is possible. Discuss how the Baht's spot and forward rates would adjust until covered interest arbitrage is no longer possible. What is the resulting equilibrium state called?

In the CD

Finding % Bid-Ask Spread in the Spot Rates, and % Annualized Premium/Discount in the Forward Rates

CHAPTER 26 Determining Foreign Exchange Rates

LEARNING OBJECTIVES

The chapter is focused on

- explaining how exchange rates would be determined on the basic principle of economics of matching demand and supply
- how various economic and monetary policies impact exchange rates
- developing an appreciation that the principles of economics would be far more applicable for currency prices than for commodities
- explaining the concept of appreciation and depreciation of currency and its measurement
- developing familiarity with various parity conditions that should govern exchange rates and changes in them
- explaining the Fisher Effect and the International Fisher Effect and achieving familiarity with the process of international investing
- explaining interest rate parity to link forward rates with spot rates
- deriving arbitrage-free forward rates based on interest rate parity
- understanding limitations in forecasting of exchange rates

DEMYSTIFYING THE MAZE

Sipping cups of tea in the Tea House, Ramesh, with Suresh, was engrossed in reading the newspaper. Suresh said, 'I was just reading in the newspaper that the government is considering full convertibility of Indian rupee on capital account in the next one year. You are working in a bank. What does it really mean?

Ramesh responded, 'In the simplest of terms, it implies that the government would no more be bothered about what currency you keep your money in, where you invest, and how and when you convert your money from one currency to another.'

Suresh inferred, 'Oh, that will be good. I can now invest in stock markets worldwide, and not be confined to looking at returns on the stock markets in India alone. If the stock markets in Indonesia or China offer returns of 30%, as compared with returns on NSE at 20%, I would rather invest in Indonesia.'

Broodingly, Ramesh said, 'Well, you can do that. But things are not as simple as that. Agreed that your returns elsewhere could be higher, but now we have the added dimension of what would happen to the exchange rates of Indonesian rupiah to Indian rupee.'

With a strange look on his face, Suresh questioned, 'But why should that bother us? Don't we know it now?'

Explained Ramesh, 'Well, we know it now, but we do not know it for the future.'

Quizzed Suresh, 'But, can we forecast it?'

Replied Ramesh, 'Yes, we can. But it is not a simple exercise, because the exchange rates move much in the same way as the stock prices. You know how difficult it is to forecast stock prices.'

Suresh again asked, 'Why do I need to forecast the exchange rates to know the returns on the stock market? In any case, I do not think that the returns would change drastically.'

Emphasized Ramesh, 'No, they are dependent upon the exchange rates, and therefore, I do need to forecast the exchange rates.'

Not convinced, Suresh asked, 'Tell me how.'

Ramesh explained, 'Because there is a gap between the times when I invest and when I disinvest. My returns would not be purely determined by the returns on the stock exchanges of the respective countries. Assume that returns in the Indian stock market are expected to be 20%, while those in the USA are 10%. Naturally, that would cause people in the USA to get motivated to invest in India. So, the first thing that they have to do is to convert their dollars into Indian rupees.'

Agreed Suresh, 'Yes, that is true.'

Ramesh elaborated, 'Suppose that someone has US$ 10,000 to invest. If the exchange rate is ₹40 per dollar, he gets ₹4,00,000. After a year, this ₹4,00,000 becomes ₹4,80,000, assuming that the expectations about returns on the Indian stock market come true. That is a cool 20% gain. But there lies the catch.'

Suresh nodded, and Ramesh continued, 'Now the investor has to convert these Indian rupees back into dollars.'

Casually, Suresh remarked, 'Yes, he would get ₹4,80,000 divided by 40, which is US$ 12,000.'

Ramesh again emphasized, 'No, the amount of dollars the investor gets is dependent upon the exchange rate when he exits the Indian stock market. Now, if the rupee has depreciated by 20% to, say, ₹48 per dollar, he would get lesser dollars. In fact, he would get back only US$ 10,000. So, his return is nil. Had he invested in the US stock market, he would have been better off, and got US$ 11,000 for the original investment of US$ 10,000.'

Suresh nodded his head, and rather surprisingly questioned, 'Oh, I see. But, what if the Indian rupee appreciated?'

Quickly, Ramesh responded, 'The investor would be too happy. If the Indian rupee appreciated by 20% to, say, ₹32 per dollar, his ₹4,80,000 would become US$ 15,000. His return would then be 50% in dollar terms.'

Suresh concluded as if he fully understood the subject of appreciation and depreciation of the rupee, 'If only the exchange rates remained constant, then it makes sense to invest at a place where returns are higher.'

Ramesh concurred with Suresh: 'Exactly, you have got the point. That means one has to forecast the exchange rate.'

Becoming more interested, Suresh asked a quick question, 'How do we forecast it?'

Although he did not know much, Ramesh attempted to answer, 'Difficult question to answer. In fact, one of the factors would be the returns in the different markets. If we expect the rupee to appreciate, then return on dollars invested in India is 50%, which is much above the 10% return offered by the US stock market. The exchange rate would tend to negate this if the markets in various countries are to remain in balance and coherent with each other.'

Curious, Suresh again asked, 'What other considerations must be there while forecasting the exchange rate?'

Ramesh paused for a while, recollected his thoughts, and responded, 'There can be numerous ways by which we may forecast exchange rates. Each of the ways would focus on some parameter of the economy. Depending upon the time horizon of the forecast, the method may change.'

Suresh continued to ask, 'What economic parameters are important?'

Ramesh tried to explain, 'The basis to any forecasting method would be the arbitrage. We saw arbitrage in the example of the stock market returns. Markets will not let that happen. If returns in the Indian market are 50% and returns in the USA are 10%, then the exchange rate must adjust in such a manner that the returns equalize across the two countries, and for that matter, across the world.'

Suresh concluded, 'You mean if in India there is 20% return and in the USA the return is 10%, the extra 10% return in India would get wiped out by the depreciation of the rupee?'

Agreeing with Suresh, Ramesh reinforced, 'Yes, ideally that must happen. In the short term, when the capital moves almost instantly, the money would always chase higher returns. Therefore, the exchange rate has to adjust very fast to offset any additional returns one country may offer over another. The exchange rate must appreciate or depreciate by an amount proportional to the differential in returns.'

Curious to know more, Suresh again asked, 'Well, is this the only way to forecast?'

Ramesh confidently added, 'Certainly not. In the long term, every commodity is subject to arbitrage. As the prices in the stock market move, so do the prices of any commodity. The broad indicator of these prices is inflation in the country. The process of arbitrage would apply equally to wheat or rice. In value terms, they must cost the same across all nations, else people would begin trading in wheat and rice too, by buying them in countries where they are cheap and selling where they are expensive.'

Surprised, Suresh again asked, 'Are people really doing this?'

Emphasizing the point, Ramesh said, 'Yes, if it saves money, people would certainly do it. For example, you may buy a bottle of Pepsi in India for ₹10 and sell it for 50 cents in the USA. At ₹40 a dollar you get ₹20 and make a profit of ₹10. Of course, it is subject to many limitations, such as utility, styling, cost of transportation, etc.'

With some understanding, Suresh concluded, 'So, not only must the returns of the stock markets be equal, but the price of commodities across the world must be such that they cost the same.'

Reaffirming the thought, Ramesh stated, 'Yes, the only mechanism that can help achieve this is the change in the exchange rates. Changes in prices are not under our control. Prices are subject to inflation, which depends on so many factors. Because foreign exchange markets can respond quickly, the adjustments must be reflected in the exchange rates.'

Suresh, wanting to conclude, said, 'So, a study of inflation would throw some light on the future exchange rates.'

Agreeing, Ramesh too said, 'Yes, we may use this model to forecast.'

In a hurry to leave, Suresh said, 'Well, things don't seem to be as simple as I thought. I think now I have to study more of economics than finance to understand the behaviour of exchange rates.'

Concurring with the views, Ramesh too expressed his dilemma. 'Yes, I too would have to update my knowledge of banking, because now in our bank, we may have to offer deposits in many currencies, rather than the rupee alone.'

INTRODUCTION

An exchange rate is defined as the number of units of the home currency to be paid, or received, in exchange for one unit of a foreign currency, e.g., ₹47 per US dollar. Using the direct rate convention, it is the price of foreign currency in terms of local currency. There are various ways the prices of foreign currencies can be determined. At one end of the spectrum, the prices could be fixed, and at another extreme, they may be allowed to vary according to pure market forces.

Under the regulated regime in vogue for a long time, and till as recently as 1974 when the Bretton Woods System of exchange rate determination came to an end, exchange rates were determined by the respective governments with varying degrees of control. While some nations had absolutely fixed exchange rates specified by their respective governments, some nations intervened in the foreign exchange markets heavily, so as to keep exchange rate movement within a narrow and a desirable band. In such a system, not much was affecting the exchange rates except the national economic policies and the willingness of various nations to let the rates change only to an extent they desired. The business community too did not have to bother much about likely changes in exchange rates, as movements were narrow and predictable, and did not warrant much concern in the context of managing foreign exchange exposures.

Under the flexible exchange rate system, the determination of exchange rates is a complex economic phenomenon incorporating domestic and global economic factors.

With the advent of the flexible exchange rate system, where the governments exercised little or no control over exchange rates, the question of determination of exchange rates became extremely complex. Under the flexible exchange rate system, market forces govern the exchange rate, just as the price of any other commodity is determined by forces of demand and supply under a free economy. Like the prices of most commodities, products, etc. are determined by factors governing demand and supply, exchange rates, the prices of foreign currencies too are determined by factors affecting demand and supply under the flexible exchange rate system. The flexible exchange rate system places an increased burden on managers to develop an ability to forecast the direction and quantum of change in various currencies where their firms have exposure, and also to devise various ways and means of managing the risk arising out of volatility in the exchange rates.

However, there remains one key difference in the way prices of commodities or products are determined, as compared with prices of foreign exchange. The prices of commodities and other products are predominantly determined by domestic economic factors, and not as much by global economic factors, but the prices of currencies are greatly influenced by world economy factors, because foreign exchange is almost exclusively used for international trade. For example, the exchange rate of the US dollar in India would change not only because of changes in the interest rate structure in India, but also because of developments in interest rates in the USA, and for that matter, in any part of the world. Understanding of the factors that impact foreign exchange rates needs global perspective, rather than the narrower knowledge limited to a single economy.

DETERMINATION OF FOREIGN EXCHANGE RATES

The basic economic theory of price determination states that demand and supply are the key determinants of the equilibrium price of a product. All those factors that affect the demand and/or supply of a product determine its price. It is the matching of the demand and supply that governs equilibrium price. We present here a very brief discussion on the determination of exchange rates based on the fundamentals of economics, with the objective of providing a bird's eye view of how various economic factors cause changes in exchange rates. It is vital for managers to understand the direction of changes in exchange rates arising from macroeconomic policy changes, to enable them to take appropriate precautions and limit exposures, and determine the desirability of managing such exposures.

It is extremely essential to understand the link between likely direction and quantum of change in the exchange rate with changes in the macroeconomic factors.

We all know, from the basic theory of economics, that the demand schedule is negatively sloped and the supply schedule is positively sloped. The sensitivities and the extent of changes of demand and supply are dependent upon the *inter alia* features of the product and general economic conditions.

Distinguishing Features of Exchange Rate Markets

Like with any other commodity, all of us would agree that the interaction of demand and supply schedules must determine the prices of foreign exchange. It is important to appreciate key differences between the commodity and foreign exchange markets that have significant impact on the schedules of demand and supply. Some of the basic differences in the commodity and foreign exchange markets relating to their structural features are discussed below.

Unlike commodities, demand and supply of foreign currency are characterized by many unique features that let factors of demand and supply operate more efficiently than in the market for commodities.

Universal and uniform utility, and unlimited appetite

Money has power to satisfy many needs, irrespective of its colour and denomination. As against this, every product primarily has the capacity to fulfil a single need. Wheat, rice, etc., satisfy hunger, clothes provide protection to the body, and automobiles fulfill transportation needs, but money is a commodity that has the capacity to satisfy multiple needs. In fact, all material, if not spiritual, needs are fulfilled by money. It can buy almost anything, being a universal denominator, and the sensitivity of foreign exchange rates should be far greater when compared with that of any other commodity/product. Furthermore, there can be distortions in demand for a product in terms of its utility to different consumers. There is no such differentiation of utility in respect of currencies.

Constraints of supply Most products face some limitations in terms of the quantity of supplies in a given economy or geography. The supply of money does not face any capacity constraint or production lead time. Currency can be printed almost instantaneously to increase supply. Supply can be withdrawn quickly through open market operations. The process of adjustment of supply is smooth and quick, unlike with commodities and other products. Therefore, adjustment to the equilibrium price is expected to be far quicker.

Absence of transportation cost Due to the distances involved, the prices of a commodity or a product in two distant geographical markets can differ substantially. Furthermore, these differences are sustainable, and the two markets can still remain in equilibrium. This is possible due to transportation cost. Transportation costs are absent in the case of transactions of foreign exchange. Foreign exchange contracts can be bought and sold with extremely nominal transaction cost (analogous to transportation costs), minimizing the price differentials in different geographical and national markets.

Other factors Furthermore, there are other facilitating factors too. The *non-perishable* nature of foreign currency, absence of storage costs, and independence from seasons and weather conditions also help remove discrepancies in prices in different markets. The perishable nature of commodities and various products distorts the supply and demand preferences of suppliers and consumers respectively. In addition, *hoarding* of commodities and products entails costs, and sometimes may be regarded as unethical, too. There is no such cost or stigma attached to accumulation of wealth. Both the factors, the non-perishable nature and lack of storage costs, help in truer determination of competitive price.

In what is stated above, it may be seen that the condition for free and fair markets, i.e., the basic prerequisite of determination of fair price as an interaction of the demand and supply schedules, is far more easily satisfied in the foreign exchange market than in any commodity or product market.

However, disregarding the constraints, we examine the direction of change in foreign exchange rates due to changes in the broad economic variables affecting demand and supply. Managers in the commercial world are not as concerned with the determination of the absolute level of exchange rates as they are with the direction of change of exchange rates. Therefore, more than the consideration of how a given exchange rate was arrived at, the more important question is, how would the rates respond to changes in the economic policies.

Factors Affecting Demand and Supply

For simplicity, but without losing the substance of the argument, let us assume that there are only two nations, India and the USA, with the rupee and the dollar as their respective currencies. In such an extremely simplified position, we shall examine the factors that affect the exchange rates. As is known, the price of the dollar in terms of the rupee is governed by all the factors affecting the demand and supply of the dollar in India. The economic model depicted in Figure 26-1 looks familiar and simple.

> *Like any other commodity, the price of foreign currency would be determined by the intersection of the demand and supply schedules of the foreign currency.*

Here, the intersection of the demand and supply schedules, where demand and supply are equal, determines the exchange rate of the dollar.

Demand for foreign currency is broadly determined by importers wanting to import goods and services. Therefore, all those economic policies that affect the propensity to buy imported goods and services must have an impact on foreign exchange rates. Restrictions on imports through law, or discouraging imports by imposing and increasing custom duties, must lead to reduced demand for foreign currency, i.e., the dollar, in India, leading to reductions in its price. This is called *depreciation* of the dollar, the foreign currency, or *appreciation* of the rupee, the local currency.

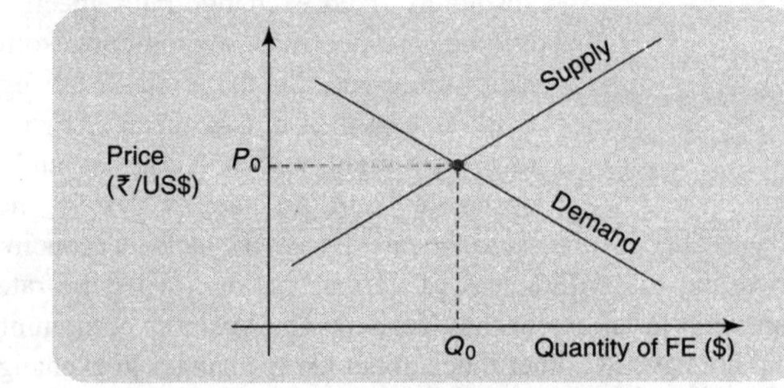

Figure 26-1 Price of foreign exchange

Like demand for the dollar comes from importers, supply of the dollar is made by exporters who sell Indian goods to America. Any policy changes directed towards increasing exports, such as subsidies and tax holidays, would help generate more foreign exchange, bringing down the price of the dollar. Likewise, any policy change resulting in reduction or withdrawal of incentive would make Indian goods more expensive in the USA, reducing the demand for Indian goods and thus, the supply of the dollar. Apart from Indian policies regarding exports, American policies governing imports would also dictate the ultimate supply position of foreign currency, and hence, the exchange rates.

Appreciation of foreign currency Any increase in demand for foreign currency would shift the demand schedule upwards from D to D', as shown in Figure 26-2. If supply remains unchanged at S, the intersection with the supply schedule would be at A, reflecting the exchange rate change from P_0 to P_1 with $P_1 > P_0$. The equilibrium quantity of demand and supply would be at Q_1, instead of Q_0. This indicates appreciation of the dollar and depreciation of the rupee.

Similarly, any decrease in supply would cause appreciation of foreign currency. A decrease in supply of the dollar shifts the supply schedule upwards from S to S' in Figure 26-2, intersecting with the unchanged demand schedule at B, which corresponds to the exchange rate level of P_1. The equilibrium quantity of demand and supply is at Q', which is lower than the original quantity demanded, Q_0.

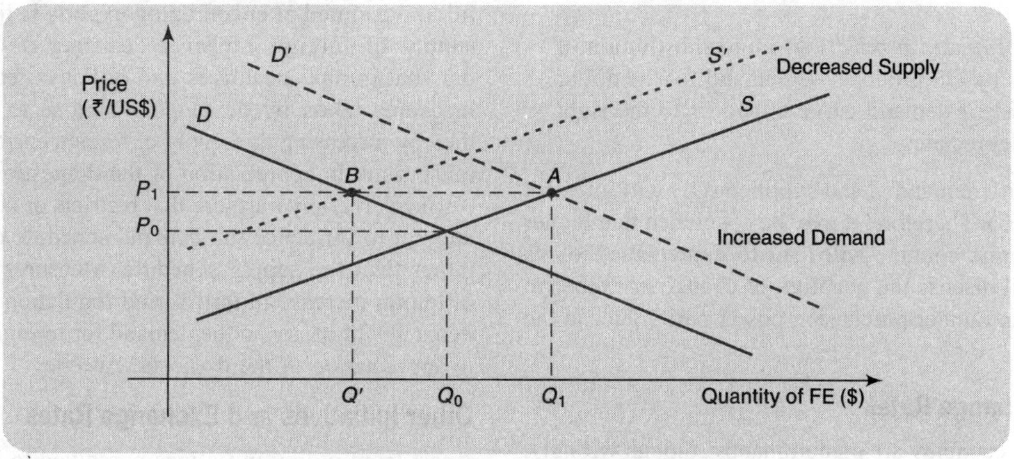

Figure 26-2 Appreciation of foreign exchange

Any increase in demand or decrease in supply causes appreciation (increase in the value) of the foreign currency. Appreciation means more units of local currency are required to buy the same amount of foreign currency.

> *An increase in the price of a foreign currency is called appreciation. It means more units of domestic currency are required for the same amount of foreign currency.*

Depreciation of foreign currency Similarly, any decrease in demand for foreign currency would shift the demand schedule downwards from *D* to *D′* (as depicted in Figure 26-3), intersecting with the unchanged supply schedule *S* at a level *A* lower than the original intersection level *O*, indicating depreciation of foreign currency (lesser number of units of local currency are required to buy the same amount of foreign currency). In the same way, any increase in supply of foreign currency causes depreciation, as the unchanged demand schedule *D* and the new supply schedule *S′* intersect at point *B*, lower than the earlier intersection point *O*. The depreciation of foreign currency is shown in Figure 26-3.

Besides exports and imports, another source of supply and demand for the currencies is derived from the desire to invest in one another's capital and money markets. If returns in the capital markets of one country are greater, this would attract increased inflow of the other country's currency. The consequent increase in the supply of that currency leads to its depreciation. If the return on investment in the capital markets of the USA is more attractive than the return on investment at home, there would be greater demand for the dollar, causing its appreciation.

> *Exports, foreign direct investment, and portfolio investments are major sources of supply of foreign exchange. Imports, foreign outward investment, and withdrawal of portfolio investment constitute demand for foreign currency.*

To understand how the demand and supply schedules change and impact the exchange rates in an economy, let us review some of the economic and monetary factors, both on a macro as well as a micro basis.

Inflation and Exchange Rates

Inflation rates are specific to each nation's economy, and seldom do people realize their implications on exchange rates. The most common cause of inflation is increased money supply in the country, relative to the supply of goods and services. The demand and supply schedules of the foreign currency get impacted in the following manner.

Supply side

Rupee supply increases in India → inflation in India → price of Indian goods will rise relative to American goods → Americans will buy less Indian goods → decrease in the supply of the dollar → shift of supply curve upwards to the left (*S′*) → rupee depreciates.

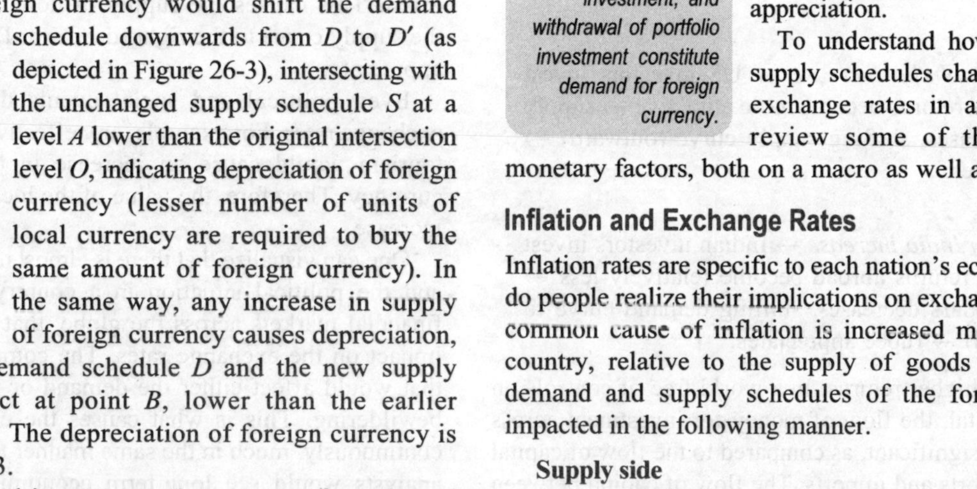

Figure 26-3 Depreciation of foreign exchange

Demand side

Higher prices of Indian products → more substitution of Indian products by US products → demand for the dollar will rise → shift of demand curve outwards to the right (D') → rupee depreciates.

The new quantity demanded and supplied (Q_1) will intersect at a higher level (P_1). Therefore, it may be concluded that higher inflation in the home country will lead to depreciation of its currency. We shall discuss the quantum of change in exchange rates due to inflation under purchasing power parity later in the chapter.

Interest and Exchange Rates

Interest rates in an economy are predominantly, though wrongly, regarded to be a purely domestic phenomenon with little bearing on exchange rates. However, most developing nations follow the policy of raising investment-specific interest rates in an attempt to attract foreign investment, while keeping domestic investment rates untouched. In conditions of free movement of capital across borders, any change in interest rates would affect the demand and supply schedules of foreign exchange in the following manner.

Supply side

Interest rates in India increase → US investors invest more in India as returns become more attractive → supply of dollars increases, shifting supply curve (outward) → rupee appreciates.

Demand side

Interest rates in India increase → Indian investors invest less abroad, as returns abroad become relatively less → demand for dollars decreases, shifting demand curve to the left (inward) → rupee appreciates.

Money chases higher returns. In a world free of controls on movement of capital, the flow of money for investment across borders would be significant, as compared to the flow of capital on account of exports and imports. The flow of capital between nations for investment purposes mainly guided by relative returns is called *portfolio investment*, and appears under the capital account in the balance of payment of nations.

Merchandise exports and imports form a part of the current account in the balance of payments. Depending upon the nature of control on flow of money exercised in an economy, the factors affecting exchange rate determination would change. In nations with fully convertible currencies that permit unchecked portfolio investments in money markets, the flow of foreign exchange inwards or outwards would be influenced more by the interest rate differentials in the money markets of various countries, even though factors fundamental to an economy can never be ignored.

Policy Initiatives and Exchange Rates

Inflation and interest rates in an economy are broader economic phenomena, but there are other policy initiatives of a fiscal or monetary nature that influence exchange rates. Any policy initiative aimed at encouraging exports is likely to increase the supply of foreign exchange, causing its depreciation. Duty drawbacks, tax incentives and holidays, etc., are some of the measures taken by developing nations to encourage exports, thereby increasing the supply of foreign currency. Such measures must result in appreciation of the domestic currency.

Similarly, any measure that restricts or controls imports is an attempt to influence the demand schedule of foreign exchange rather than the supply schedule. Measures such as imposition of quota, increase in tariffs, and regulation of imports of some items would constrain the demand for foreign currency, resulting in appreciation of the domestic currency.

Other Initiatives and Exchange Rates

Apart from policy initiatives perceived to be influencing only the domestic economic scenario, there are a few direct measures that governments take to encourage foreign investment. For example, a developing country like India opens up its economy for foreign investment by raising the sectorial foreign investment limits. This would result in appreciation of domestic currency. If India offers incentives for investment in any industrial sector, it would encourage more US companies to build plants in India. This causes the supply of dollars to increase, shifting the supply curve to the right (downward) and making the rupee appreciate.

Even political and social events do impact the foreign exchange rates. For example, any effective measures to promote tourism would cause an increase in the supply of foreign currency. Therefore, the value of the local currency would also increase.

One can visualize that there is almost no event in the economy and the political situation in a country and worldwide, and financial markets across the globe, that would fail to have an impact on the exchange rates. The complexities of the factors that would affect either the demand or the supply or both are bewildering. This is what causes the exchange rate to move continuously, much in the same manner that stocks move. Some analysts would see long-term economic policies as a major determinant of the strength of the currency. They would concentrate on balance of payment deficit or surplus, its trend, likely patterns of exports and imports of goods and services, while other analysts would pay more attention to monetary policies for determining the capital flows in and out of the country.

CALCULATING APPRECIATION AND DEPRECIATION

Most managers and analysts are more concerned about the appreciation and depreciation of currencies, rather than spot rates, while making business decisions. To them, a conversion rate of ₹45 per US dollar is less important than the question of how this value is going to change over time. The changes in value of the currency are normally specified in terms of percentage changes from a base period. A currency is said to be appreciating if its value increases with time, and depreciating if it declines with time. The amount of depreciation or appreciation under the system of direct rates is given in Equation 26-1.

Amount of appreciation (–)/depreciation (+) of local currency

$$= \frac{S_1 - S_0}{S_0} \qquad (26\text{-}1)$$

Where S_1 and S_0 are spot rates at time 0 and 1 respectively. If the current rate of the British pound is ₹80.00, and the expected rate in the next period is ₹85.00, then the rupee is said to be depreciating with respect to the pound. The amount of depreciation is calculated as:

Amount of appreciation (–)/depreciation (+) of local currency

$$= \frac{S_1 - S_0}{S_0} = \frac{85.00 - 80.00}{80.00} = 0.0625 = 6.25\%$$

In terms of amounts, most of us believe that depreciation of one currency must exactly correspond to appreciation of the second currency. However, this is not so mathematically. If the same rates are expressed from the viewpoint of the pound, the appreciation of the pound would be given by Equation 26-2.

Mathematically, the amount of appreciation of one currency is not the same as the amount of depreciation of the other currency, though colloquially they are treated as equal.

Amount of appreciation (–)/depreciation (+) of foreign currency

$$= \frac{1/S_1 - 1/S_0}{1/S_0} = \frac{S_0 - S_1}{S_1} \qquad (26\text{-}2)$$

Using the same figures as before, the appreciation of the pound against the rupee is calculated as

Amount of appreciation (–)/depreciation (+) of foreign currency

$$= \frac{S_0 - S_1}{S_1} = \frac{80.00 - 85.00}{85.00} = 0.0588 \equiv 5.88\%$$

Thus we see that a 6.25% depreciation of the rupee has corresponded to a 5.88% appreciation of the pound. The discrepancy is because different base rates have been used for the two currencies, and hence, appreciation of one currency should not be treated as an exactly equal depreciation of the second currency.

PURCHASING POWER PARITY (PPP)

Our study of the determination of foreign exchange rates based on fundamental economic factors already provided us with an introduction to inflation rates as one of the key determinants of exchange rates and movements. Here, we elaborate further, to formulate a quantitative relationship between the spot rates of two currencies and the inflation rates in the respective countries. This would provide an insight into the magnitude of likely changes in the exchange rates based on inflation rates prevailing in the two countries.

Purchasing power parity is based on the law of one price, which applies to any product irrespective of its geographical location and the currency in which it is bought or sold. A single price of the product must prevail no matter where it is sold or in which currency the price is denominated. Currency is merely a medium to buy goods. Issuance of currencies by a government grants purchasing power to the holders of the currency, to buy any product they desire. These products are bought or sold to satisfy certain needs. The level of satisfaction in meeting these needs, as measured from the financial values paid, must be equal across borders.

The relationship of exchange rates with inflation rates, first propounded by the Swedish economist Gustav Cassel, is referred to as *purchasing power parity* (PPP). The focus of PPP is on the process of arbitrage that must make prices equal across nations. For simplicity again, assume there are only two nations, India and the USA, whose currencies are the rupee and the dollar respectively, and one single commodity called gold. Assume further that the following prices of gold prevail in India and the USA on a given date:

In India	per 10 gms	₹10,000
In the USA	per oz (assume 28 gms/oz)	US$ 650

According to PPP, the per gram value of gold must remain the same, irrespective of the currency in which it is priced. Hence,

Value per gm of gold in India = Value per gm of gold in USA

The gold prices, therefore, would determine the spot prices of the two currencies.

$$\frac{₹10{,}000}{10} = \frac{\text{US\$ } 650}{28} \text{ gives ₹43.08 per \$}$$

The foundation of PPP lies in the process of arbitrage that would remove deviations, if any, in the foreign exchange rates if they were not in conformity with PPP. Arbitrageurs will act in the following way if there is a disparity between the PPP-prescribed values and actual currency exchange rates determining the relative value of the currencies. Consider two different scenarios where the exchange rates are different from what is prescribed by PPP.

Actual exchange rate in India, say ₹40, is less than the PPP rate (₹43.08) If the actual exchange rate is less than ₹43.08 per dollar, then the Indian rupee is overvalued and the US dollar is undervalued in terms of gold. The arbitrageurs would buy gold in the currency that is undervalued and sell in the currency that is overvalued. The arbitrageurs can realize profits as follows:

Buy 1 gm gold in the USA ⇒ pay $ 23.21 ⇒ ship gold to India ⇒ sell gold in India ⇒ realize ₹1,000 for 1 gm gold ⇒ convert ₹ to $ at exchange rate of ₹40 ⇒ get $ 25 ⇒ make profit of $ 1.79.

Actual exchange rate in India, say ₹45, is more than the PPP rate (₹43.08) If the actual exchange rate in more than ₹43.08 per dollar, then the Indian rupee is undervalued and the US dollar is overvalued in terms of gold. The arbitrageurs would buy gold in the currency that is undervalued, i.e., in India, and sell in the currency that is overvalued, i.e., in the USA. The arbitrageurs can realize profits as follows:

Purchasing Power Parity says that the spot exchange rate must be in the ratio of prices of a common basket of goods in two currencies.

Buy 1 gm gold in India ⇒ pay ₹1,000 ⇒ ship gold to the USA ⇒ sell gold in the USA ⇒ realize $ 23.21 for 1 gm gold ⇒ convert $ to ₹ at exchange rate of ₹45 ⇒ get ₹1,044.45 ⇒ make profit of ₹44.45.

Hence, we see that the process of arbitrage will set right any deviation in the exchange rate that is not in conformity with the PPP. The process of arbitrage will drive the exchange rate, so as to render equal purchasing power to each currency.

The illustration of arbitrage of gold can be extended to any commodity. If that is the case, then one may state that on an aggregate basis, general price levels in the two economies would determine the exchange rates. The price levels in general terms can be measured by referring to the price indices of different countries. Accordingly, as per PPP, the spot exchange rate must be equal to the ratio of prices of common baskets of goods, as given by Equation 26-3.

$$\text{Spot Exchange Rate (₹/\$)} = \frac{\text{Price of basket of goods in India in ₹.}}{\text{Price of same basket of goods in USA in \$}} \qquad (26\text{-}3)$$

For example, if a particular basket of goods costs ₹4,500 in India, and the same basket of goods is available for US$ 100 in the USA, then the exchange rate should be ₹45 per US$, according to PPP. As such, PPP provides a relationship between goods markets and currency markets.

Limitations of PPP

Does PPP hold? To examine the validity of PPP, we need to compare the actual exchange rate with the PPP rate. In most cases, it has been found that the actual prices differ from those determined by PPP. One study by *The Economist* rated prices in different countries for Big Mac, the McDonald hamburger that is served in more than a 100 nations with exactly the same recipe and taste. It was found that the prices of Big Mac do not conform to PPP. In 1999, most currencies were either undervalued or overvalued when compared with PPP, and the deviations were as large as 40–60% in some cases[1]. As per PPP, the value of Big Mac should be equal across nations, and the ratio of the price in local currency and in US dollars must determine the exchange rate.

The validity of PPP is in doubt for a variety of reasons.

The failure of the actual exchange rate to conform to PPP may have many causes, some of which are examined here.

Transportation cost For execution of arbitrage, it is necessary to transport the goods from one location to another, which will add to the cost. Unless the arbitrage profits exceed the transportation cost, there would be no incentive to undertake the process. To the extent of transportation cost the price differential would exist even under PPP.

Trade barriers The essence of PPP rests on the arbitrage process. If the process of arbitrage is hampered for any reasons, price convergence would not occur and PPP is not likely to hold. The assumption of free trade is crucial. Most nations have trade restrictions in the form of tariffs, quotas, permissions, and other regulations that distort the prices and the process of arbitrage. These barriers to trade let the price disparities prevail.

Product differentiation The value of a product is contained not just in the physical or physiological need that it satisfies; it encompasses many other intangible factors. The value of the product is a composite representing several needs, basic or contrived. Price disparities for the same product in the same nation are glaring. For example, a cup of tea expected to satisfy the same need of providing refreshment may cost as low as ₹2 and as high as ₹500 in India, depending upon the location, source, styling, etc. In the international scenario, such product and price differentiations are likely to be increasing rather than decreasing. Although Big Mac is served with a uniform taste across various countries, in environments and styles that are as uniform as possible, it is priced differently, depending upon the location.

Non-traded goods and services Even if goods arbitrage is allowed to take place freely, the validity of PPP remains in doubt. As world economies grow and advance, the proportion of services as compared to goods in GNPs is rising. Due to this increased proportion of services, disparities in exchange rates are not only likely to persist, but may widen too, because the services are non-traded goods. The process of arbitrage is rather difficult to execute for services. At best, PPP can apply to traded goods. For non-traded goods, arbitrage cannot set right the disparities in prices and exchange rates. For example, land on Marine Drive in Mumbai cannot be shifted to Manhattan in New York, and vice versa, and therefore, prices of land in India and in the USA are not subject to PPP. Such prices become trivial for determination of exchange rates according to PPP. Aberrations may be partially overcome by comparing the prices of traded goods only.

Definition of the basket of goods and services For verification or empirical testing of PPP, it is essential to constitute a basket of goods that represent same value and utility. It is indeed extremely difficult to create a basket that has the same utility across the globe. The commodities included in the basket and the weight given to each of them represent the relative importance of each commodity, which is a function of intangible factors such as culture, tradition, and history. For example, weight of wheat in a price index in India would differ substantially from a similar index in any of the nations in the West. Commodities such as wheat, vegetables, etc., do not provide the same utility to Europeans as they do to Indians because of the availability of substitutes that change the relative proportions of each commodity.

Goods prices change slowly Differences in speeds of change make up another reason why PPP may not hold, and may pose problems in empirical testing. The process of

[1]For deviations of actual exchange rate with the PPP implied rate, refer to Exhibit on page 122 of *Multinational Financial Management* by Alan Shapiro (7th Edition, John Wiley & Sons).

adjustment of changes in price levels is slower than the process of adjustment of changes in exchange rates. Therefore, PPP could stand violated in the short term. One opinion is that PPP ultimately would hold, but with a time lag. The changes in the nominal exchange rates would take cognizance of the changing level of prices much in advance.

RELATIVE FORM OF PPP

Recognition of the fact that PPP is found not to hold does not imply that its study has no utility in determination and forecast of exchange rates. The PPP described above is called its *absolute version*, which states that the spot exchange rate must represent the ratio of the price levels of common basket of goods. The relative version of PPP concentrates not on absolute exchange rates, but instead on the magnitude and direction of changes in the exchange rates over a period of time. It establishes the relationship between the inflation rates and changes in the spot exchange rates.

We make an important observation relating to the fact that PPP does not hold. The observation is that the reasons responsible for deviation of exchange rates from PPP appear to be of a permanent, persisting nature. If the same distortions are likely to persist from one period to another, any changes in the exchange rates in the same intervening period can still be linked to the changes in price levels.

For example, assume that in the beginning of the year 2005 the price of a basket of goods in India is ₹4,500, while the same basket was priced at US$ 100 in the USA, providing an exchange rate of ₹45 per dollar if the PPP were to hold. However, the actual exchange rate is ₹50 per dollar, signifying undervaluation of the rupee. The variance may be attributable to any of the factors, discussed above, that cause the PPP not to hold. Irrespective of what causes the deviation, our further forecast of future spot rates a year later should hold as long as same reasons persist till the next year. For example, if the distortion in price is attributable to differences in taste, the same reason would continue to be valid even the next year.

Relative purchasing power parity is concerned with the changes in exchange rates.

We apply the same concept of absolute PPP; the ratio of prices of the common basket of goods dictating the spot prices, to the changes in the spot rates. As per PPP, in a given Period 1, the spot exchange rate S_1 is a ratio of prices P_1^d in Period 1 in India (the home country) and P_1^f in the USA (the foreign country), as shown in Equation 26-4.

Spot exchange rate (₹ per $)

$$S_1 = \frac{\text{Price of basket of goods in India in ₹.}}{\text{Price of same basket of goods in the USA in \$}} = \frac{P_1^d}{P_1^f}$$

$$= \frac{4,500}{100} = ₹45 \text{ per \$} \qquad (26\text{-}4)$$

Now assume that annual inflation rate in India is I_d and in the USA is I_f. After a year, the prices of the same basket of goods would stand increased by the amount of inflation in each country. Paying little attention to the distortions in the actual exchange rates in Period 1, we move to the second year; Period 2, again applying the absolute PPP for the spot exchange rates in Period 2, S_2. The price levels in Period 2 in India and the USA are now P_2^d and P_2^p respectively, which differ from the prices of Period 1 by the amount of inflation during the period. As per PPP, the spot rate in Period 2 would be as per Equation 26-5.

The relative PPP is more likely to hold, and can be fruitfully used by managers for forecast of exchange rate behaviour.

Spot exchange rate (₹ per $)

$$S_2 = \frac{\text{Price of basket of goods in India}}{\text{Price of same basket of goods in the USA}}$$

$$= \frac{P_2^d}{P_2^f} = \frac{P_1^d(1+I_d)}{P_1^f(1+I_f)} \qquad (26\text{-}5)$$

Assuming that the same factors continue to operate on the prices of goods in the two periods, the relationship between exchange rates of Period 1 and Period 2 can be stated as

Spot exchange rate (₹ per $)

$$S_2 = \frac{P_2^d}{P_2^f} = \frac{P_1^d(1+I_d)}{P_1^f(1+I_f)} = S_1\frac{(1+I_d)}{(1+I_f)} \qquad (26\text{-}6)$$

Re-arranging Equation 26-6, we get Equation 26-7, which shows a relationship between the changes in spot exchange rates:

$$S_2 = S_1\frac{(1+I_d)}{(1+I_f)}$$

$$\text{or} \quad \frac{S_2}{S_1} = \frac{(1+I_d)}{(1+I_f)}$$

$$\text{or} \quad \frac{S_2 - S_1}{S_1} = \frac{(I_d - I_f)}{(I + I_f)} \qquad (26\text{-}7)$$

For a relatively small inflation rate in a foreign country, Equation 26-8 can be approximated as

$$\frac{S_2 - S_1}{S_1} = \frac{\Delta S}{S_1} \approx (I_d - I_f) \qquad (26\text{-}8)$$

This is referred to as *relative purchasing power parity*, which states that changes in nominal exchange rates would be approximately equal to differences in the inflation rates of the two countries. Equation 26-8 applies to a single period of one year where annual inflation rates are specified. For an *n*-period case (each period of one year) relative PPP can be stated as given in Equation 26-9,

Relative PPP states that change in spot rates would be approximately equal to differential of inflation rates in two countries; the currency with higher inflation rate depreciates as much.

$$S_n = S_1\frac{(1+I_d)^n}{(1+I_f)^n} \qquad (26\text{-}9)$$

where S_n is the nominal exchange rate at Period n.

The outcome of relative PPP as given by Equation 26-8 or Equation 26-9 is an important one for corporate managers. Most managers are rather unconcerned about why differences in exchange rates exist with those of PPP (it may be an important issue for economists). It is taken as a hard fact with which each one of us has to live. As long as reasons for deviations continue to hold, changes in the exchange rates would be governed by changes in the price levels. Corporate managers are more concerned about the directions in which, and the amounts by which, exchange rates are likely to move. The answers to these questions are provided by relative PPP to a reasonably accurate extent.

Relative PPP connects domestic economic factors to foreign exchange markets. Foreign exchange markets cannot remain aloof from important domestic economic happenings, a broad indicator of which is the inflation rate in the economy. The inflation rate can be regarded as the single most important measurement of the state of the economy. Higher rates of inflation reflect faster erosion of value of the currency relative to any other currency that exhibits lower rates of inflation. This must necessarily be reflected in the exchange rates by depreciation of the currency facing higher inflation.

Example 26-1 Forecasting Exchange Rate

The current exchange rate for the Australian dollar with the US dollar is A$ 1.80 per US$. The Consumer Price Index (CPI) in the USA is 100, while the same goods as in the baskets of the USA are priced at 200 in Australia. The rates of inflation in the USA and Australia are 2% and 5% respectively. What exchange rate do you anticipate (number. of Australian dollars per US dollar) (a) after six months, (b) after one year, and (c) after two years?

Solution

As per the PPP, the exchange rate should have been in the ratio of the price of the common basket of goods, i.e., A$ 2.00 per US$. However, assuming that the discrepancy would continue for the next two years, exchange rate forecasts using the current spot rates and the inflation rates can be made. Inflation in Australia is higher than the USA by 3%, and therefore, we must see a depreciation of the Australian dollar by 3% per annum.

Using Equation 26-9 we may forecast the currency exchange rate as follows

(a) $S_{1/2} = S_0 \dfrac{(1+I_d)^{1/2}}{(1+I_f)^{1/2}} = 1.80 \dfrac{(1+0.05)^{1/2}}{(1+0.02)^{1/2}}$ = A$1.8263 per US$

(b) $S_1 = S_0 \dfrac{(1+I_d)^1}{(1+I_f)^1} = 1.80 \dfrac{(1+0.05)^1}{(1+0.02)^1}$ = A$1.8529 per US$

(c) $S_2 = S_0 \dfrac{(1+I_d)^2}{(1+I_f)^2} = 1.80 \dfrac{(1+0.05)^2}{(1+0.02)^2}$ = A$1.9074 per US$

Nominal and Real Exchange Rates

Very often we hear terms such as *real exchange rates* and *nominal exchange rates*. Nominal exchange rates do not account for inflation, while real rates would. The relationship between real and spot rates is given as Equation 26-10.

$$R_1 = S_i\left(\frac{\text{Relative price level in foreign country in Period 1}}{\text{Relative price level in home country in Period 1}}\right) \tag{26-10}$$

where *R* and *S* represent the direct real and nominal exchange rates (number of units of home currency per unit of foreign currency) in Period 1, respectively.

Real rates are computed on the basis of change in the purchasing power of the currencies. If nominal rates change so as to completely offset the impact of changes on the purchasing powers of the currencies, real rates remain unchanged from one period to another. It is implied that PPP holds when real rates remain the same.

Depreciation or appreciation of a currency in nominal terms does not reflect true changes in the competitive position of a firm. To assess the change in the competitive position, changes in the exchange rates on a real basis are important. To illustrate the concept, let us consider an example of an Indian exporter who makes a supply to a German customer worth euro 100. With cost at ₹4,000 and revenue of ₹6,000 at the current exchange rate of ₹60 per euro, the current profit is ₹2,000.

If the changes in the nominal exchange rates are in accordance with PPP, the real exchange rates do not change from one period to another.

Assume that India and Germany face inflation of 20% and 10% respectively. In the next period after one year, the Indian exporter can increase the price by 10% to euro 110, consistent with the German inflation rate, without attracting the wrath of the customer, as prices of all other products would have risen by 10% in Germany. The German customer, therefore, should not object, and should let the price rise by 10%. At the same time, the exporter faces a cost of ₹4800, increased by 20% in accordance with the inflation rate in India.

Now let us consider different scenarios of the exchange rate market. If exchange rates in nominal terms move according to inflation, we must not see any change in the competitive position of the Indian exporter. If the change in exchange rate is according to PPP, the new exchange rate must be ₹65.45 per euro, as computed below:

$$S_1 = S_0 \frac{(1+I_d)^1}{(1+I_f)^1} = 60.00 \frac{(1+0.2)^1}{(1+0.1)^1} = ₹65.45 \text{ per } €$$

With product price at € 110, realization would be ₹65.45 × 110 = ₹7,200; with cost at ₹4,800, profit stands at ₹2400 in Year 1. This profit is equivalent to ₹2,000 in terms of prices of Year 0.

If exchange rate changes cancel out the price level changes in the accordance with inflation, the competitive position of the firms stands unchanged; if not, it would favour either the exporter or the importer.

If the rupee depreciates excessively, the benefit of extra depreciation must pass on to the exporter. However, if the depreciation is lesser than warranted by PPP, it implies appreciation of rupee in real terms. This must lead to deterioration of the competitive position of the exporter. A look at Table 26-1 would confirm this view.

Table 26-1 Competitive position with changes in nominal exchange rate

(Figures in ₹)

	Year 0	Year 1		
		Rupee depreciates excessively	Rupee depreciates normally as per PPP	Rupee does not depreciate as much
Nominal exchange rate (₹ per €)	*60.00*	*70.00*	*65.45*	*62.00*
Sales: € 100 in Period 0 and € 110 in Period 1	6,000	7,700	7,200	6,820
Cost	4,000	4,800	4,800	4,800
Profit	2,000	2,900	2,400	2,020
Profit in terms of Period 0 prices		**2,417**	**2,000**	**1,683**
Competitive position		**improves**	**remains same**	**deteriorates**
Real exchange rate (₹ per €)		**64.17**	**60.00**	**56.83**

Example 26-2 Forecasting Exchange Rate

Assume that the exchange rate in 1980 was ₹25.00 per £ and in 2005, the rate was quoted as ₹64.00 per £. However, price levels too changed in both the countries between 1980 and 2005. The price index in India in 2005 stood at four times that of 1980. Prices in Britain doubled during the same period.

(a) What is the depreciation of the rupee over the last 25 years (the period 1980 to 2005)?

(b) How much is the real depreciation?

Solution

(a) In nominal terms, the depreciation of the rupee was to the extent of 156%, as reflected in the ratio of spot rates for the intervening period of 25 years.

$$\frac{S_2}{S_1} - 1 = \frac{64}{25} - 1 = 1.56 = 156\%$$

Changes in the nominal exchange rate do not truly indicate changes in the competitive position. The changes in the real exchange rates would reflect the true changes in the relative competitive position. Assuming that the price base in India and Britain in 1980 was consistent with the exchange rate prevailing then, the current exchange rate of 2005 has to be adjusted for inflation in the two countries.

(b) The real exchange rate and depreciation in real terms are given by

$$\text{Real exchange } R_2 = S_2 \frac{\text{Relative price level in Britain}}{\text{Relative price level in India}} = 64\left(\frac{2.00}{4.00}\right)$$
$$= ₹32 \text{ per £}$$

$$\text{Real depreciation} = \frac{R_2}{R_1} - 1 = \frac{32}{25} - 1 = 0.28 = 28\%$$

FISHER EFFECT

Fisher Effect describes relationships between interest rates and inflation rates. Earning interest on investments is the reward for waiting and for deferment of consumption needs. The value of this reward gets eroded due to the presence of inflation in the economy. There would be no incentive to invest if the return offered by the investment does not cover increased costs over the period of investment. For example, if the return offered on an investment is 6% per annum and the inflation is 10%, investors would not be interested in investing because what is available today for ₹100 would cost ₹110 a year later, while the investment would provide only ₹106. Such an investment would make the investor poorer rather than richer.

Investors are interested in real increase in wealth and not in nominal increase.

While evaluating an investment opportunity, therefore, the investor concentrates not on the nominal returns offered, but on the increase in real wealth. The welfare of the investor is appropriately gauged by the real returns, net of inflation. On a regular basis, all returns are specified in nominal terms, and thus, they must be adjusted for inflation. Nominal returns must be bifurcated into two components: one for inflation and the other for the real return. This relationship (Equation 26-11) is formally termed the *Fisher Effect*.

$$(1 + r) = (1 + a)(1 + I) \qquad (26\text{-}11)$$

where r = nominal return, a = real return, and I = inflation,

If the inflation rate is 5% and the nominal investment rate is 8%, the real rate of return would be

$$(1 + a) = \frac{(1 + r)}{(1 + I)} = \frac{1.08}{1.05} = 1.0286;$$

or real rate of return, $a = 2.86\%$

Equation 26-11 is often approximated and simplified (by ignoring the product term, $a \times I$, which is too small), to give Equation 26-12.

$$r = a + I$$

$$\text{or} \qquad a = r - I \qquad (26\text{-}12)$$

The implication of the Fisher Effect on the international flow of capital is that just like individual investors focus on real returns, international investors too would consider the inflation rates in the country/currency of investment before making investment choices. Capital would not flow in merely because a country offers higher nominal returns, unless the real returns offered abroad are higher than the real returns in the local markets. For example, if Mexico offered 12% returns against 6% available in the USA, that would not be enough motivation for US investors to invest in Mexico, unless in real terms they feel richer by doing so. They would net out the returns after inflation.

According to the Fisher Effect, the real returns across nations/currencies must be equal. In case of differences in the real returns, capital will flow out from the country offering lesser returns to the one where returns are higher. Increased inflow of

The Fisher Effect states that real returns across borders must be equal. Capital flows across borders would make real returns equal in two countries.

capital would cause returns to fall in the country, which initially offered higher returns, till such time the returns become equal across both nations.

Mathematically, the Fisher equation is represented for two countries (currencies) 1 and 2, whose nominal returns, real returns, and inflation rates are denoted as *r*, *a*, and *I*, with suffixes 1 and 2 respectively, as shown below in Equation 26-13.

$$(1 + r_1) = (1 + a_1)(1 + I_1);$$
$$(1 + r_2) = (1 + a_2)(1 + I_2)$$

Equating real returns of the two countries $a_1 = a_2$ gives

$$\frac{(1+r_1)}{(1+I_1)} = \frac{(1+r_2)}{(1+I_2)} \qquad (26\text{-}13)$$

In the approximate form, the Fisher condition states that the differential of the nominal returns and the inflation rates must be equal for two nations, as derived below in Equation 26-14.

$$a_1 \approx r_1 - I_1; \quad \text{and} \quad a_2 \approx r_2 - I_2$$

and $a_1 = a_2$ gives

$$r_1 - I_1 \approx r_2 - I_2 \qquad (26\text{-}14)$$

Implications The implication of the Fisher effect is that even if a country offers lower nominal returns, capital can still flow into the country if it has extremely low rates of inflation. For example, if the USA offered 8% nominal returns and Mexico offered 15% nominal returns, the common belief would be that capital will flow from the USA to Mexico. In general, this may be true if inflations rates in both countries are comparable. However, if the inflation rates in the USA and Mexico were 3% and 12% respectively, the direction of flow of capital would reverse, because the real rate of return in the USA would be 5% against 3% in Mexico, causing flow of capital from Mexico to the USA and not vice versa.

Raising interest rates is no guarantee of inflow of capital, unless inflation is contained and real returns increase.

Another implication of the Fisher effect is that nominal interest rates in countries with higher inflation rates would be higher. As inflation increases, interest rates too must increase to offset the increased cost, and to provide incentive to invest.

Constraints The basic requirement for the Fisher condition to hold is the free flow of capital without restrictions. However, most developing countries do allow free inflow but have some controls that restrict outflow prohibiting transfer of financial gains back to the investing nation. These controls and restrictions on outflow of capital are more in the nature of political risk. To the extent this political risk is higher in some nations, the Fisher condition would stand distorted. Investors would demand additional premium for the political risk assumed while investing abroad. For example, a foreign country may offer real returns of 10%, while domestic investment fetches only 5% on real basis. Apparently, there is arbitrage of 5% available, yet the capital may not flow out because the risk premium to cover the additional political risk in investing abroad is in excess of 5%.

International investing is governed by increase in the real wealth, and not nominal wealth.

The validity of the Fisher condition is also a function of how integrated and homogeneous the world capital markets are. Do countries freely allow issuance and redemption of capital and other financial instruments denominated in currencies other than their own? If yes, we call capital markets *integrated* and *homogeneous*. As world capital markets become increasingly efficient and integrated and economies open up, reduction in political risk lets the process of arbitrage operate. Firms would issue capital and financial instruments in countries and currencies where the cost is least. Under such a scenario, the difference between interest rates and inflation rates of nations must converge.

Another fact that may impede the applicability of the Fisher condition is the additional currency risk implied in international investments. Investments abroad require conversion of local currency into foreign currency at the beginning and then re-conversion back to local currency at the maturity of the investment. The second conversion has to be done at the exchange rates prevailing, causing uncertainty of returns. If currency risks are deemed to be high in international transactions, investors may prefer to invest only locally. This would slightly distort the Fisher condition, due to the additional risk premium demanded by investors to cover currency rate fluctuations.

Besides increase in real wealth, other factors that affect international investments are political risk, volatility in exchange rates, and taxes.

Taxation is another vexed issue in international investing. The real return that must be considered in international investing is net of taxes. In domestic investments, the taxation aspect is often ignored in comparing various investments, as the tax rate remains constant. However, for international investments, evaluation is based on post-tax returns, as tax rates across nations differ substantially.

Finally, a question that often arises is: which of the many differentials that may exist in countries with many interest rates and a single inflation rate is appropriate for comparison? The answer is not easy to find, though it may be said that the nominal returns for various financial assets are commensurate with the risk associated with those assets. When comparing real returns across borders, assets of the same financial class must be considered. However, since risk is relative rather than absolute comparison of risks and identification of assets with identical risk profiles internationally may indeed be a difficult task.

INTERNATIONAL FISHER EFFECT

We stated above that international investments involve currency exchange twice, i.e., at the time of making investment in a foreign currency and at the time of exit, when the foreign currency is converted back to local currency. The second conversion entails risk.

Let us examine the process in more detail. Assume that in the home country the nominal return offered is r_h and the current foreign exchange rate is S_0 in direct terms (number of units of home currency per unit of foreign currency). Nominal return in foreign currency is r_f. Assume that a firm wants to invest abroad for a period of one year.

The maturity value of the investment in terms of foreign currency would then be:

$$\frac{1}{S_0} \times (1 + r_f)$$

This amount needs to be converted back to the firm's local currency. Assume that the expected exchange rate after one year is $\hat{S}_1$. Therefore, the expected maturity value in terms of local currency after one year is:

$$\frac{1}{S_0} \times (1 + r_f) \times \hat{S}_1$$

The maturity value of the domestic investment made would be $(1 + r_h)$. As long as expected realization from foreign investment exceeds that from domestic investment, capital would flow out. Stated another way, the returns at home and abroad would represent expectations of the future spot exchange rate, $\hat{S}_1$. Mathematically, this is represented as:

$$\frac{1}{S_0} \times (1 + r_f) \times \hat{S}_1 = (1 + r_h) \qquad (26\text{-}15)$$

Equation 26-15 can further be stated as:

$$\frac{\hat{S}_1}{S_0} = \frac{(1 + r_h)}{(1 + r_f)} \qquad (26\text{-}16)$$

$$\text{or} \quad \frac{\hat{S}_1 - S_0}{S_0} = \frac{(r_h - r_f)}{(1 + r_f)} \qquad (26\text{-}17)$$

$$\approx (r_h - r_f), \text{ if } r_f \text{ is low.}$$

Equations 26-16 and 26-17 are referred to as the *International Fisher Effect*, which implies that countries/currencies with higher nominal interest rates are expected to depreciate. Conversely, countries with lower interest rates would see their currencies appreciating. Higher nominal gains from investment in currencies with high interest rates arc partly offset by likely depreciation of the currency. Under perfect capital market conditions, the depreciation of the currency would completely offset the additional gain, making the net gain equal to the one obtained by investing in currencies with lower nominal interest rates.

For an n-period case, the International Fisher Effect can be represented as shown in Equation 26-18.

$$\frac{\hat{S}_n}{S_0} = \frac{(1 + r_h)^n}{(1 + r_f)^n} \qquad (26\text{-}18)$$

Results of International Fisher effect are no different from those arising from combinations of the Fisher effect and relative PPP.

A higher inflation rate implies that nominal interest rates must be high too.

Recall that relative PPP states that the expected change in spot rates would be equal to the inflation rate differentials, while the Fisher effect equates real returns across borders. Substituting Equation 26-11 in Equation 26-16, we get what is stated in the relative PPP Equation 26-8, as demonstrated below:

$$\frac{\hat{S}_1}{S_0} = \frac{(1 + r_h)}{(1 + r_f)} = \frac{(1 + a_h)(1 + I_h)}{(1 + a_f)(1 + I_f)}$$

with $a_h = a_f$ as per Fisher effect

$$\frac{\hat{S}_1}{S_0} = \frac{(1 + I_h)}{(1 + I_f)}$$

$$\text{or} \quad \frac{\hat{S}_1 - S_0}{S_0} = \frac{(I_h - I_f)}{(1 + I_f)}$$

$$\approx (I_h - I_f), \text{ if } I_f \text{ is low.}$$

As long as nominal interest rates move in tandem with inflation rates, the predicted changes in the spot exchange rates of two currencies, whether done through interest rate differential or inflation rate differential, would lead to identical results. Countries that have high inflation would find their currencies depreciating. Due to higher inflation, these countries would also have to offer high interest rates. Therefore, viewed either from the viewpoint of inflation or from the viewpoint of nominal interest rates, the forecasts must be identical.

The pegging of exchange rates to a currency is an attempt not to let the International Fisher condition prevail. Pegging of exchange rates and maintaining a high rate of interest attract foreign capital, as interest arbitrage becomes available to foreign investors. Erosion in gains due to depreciation of currency is checked by fixing the exchange rates. Only if they were allowed to move would arbitrage vanish.

Example 26-3 International Investing and International Fisher Effect

Assume that bank deposits in Mexico offer a return of 12% in Mexican pesos, while deposits in India offer 6% in Indian rupees. The current exchange rate is ₹4.00 per peso. Assuming free flow of capital between India and Mexico,

(a) What returns can be expected for an Indian investor investing in Mexico?

(b) Would the returns be the same if both India and Mexico pegged their respective currency to the US dollar?

Solution

(a) Assume that the Indian investor wants to invest ₹10,000

equivalent pesos at current exchange rate = 10,000 ÷ 4.00

= peso 2,500

Maturity value of Mexican investment after a year

= 2,500 × (1 + 0.12) = peso 2,800

To realize returns in domestic currency, the investor is required to convert Mexican pesos back to Indian rupees at the spot rate expected to prevail a year later. As per the International Fisher Effect, the expected rate of exchange after one year is

$$\frac{\hat{S}_1}{S_0} = \frac{(1 + r_h)}{(1 + r_f)}$$

$$\hat{S}_1 = S_0 \frac{(1 + r_h)}{(1 + r_f)} = 4.00 \frac{(1 + 0.06)}{(1 + 0.12)} = ₹3.7857 \text{ per peso}$$

The expected realization of Mexican pesos in Indian rupees is 2800 × 3.7857 = ₹10,600, providing a return of 6%, i.e., equal to what the investor could have got by investing at home. The extra return in the foreign market was offset by the depreciation of the foreign currency.

(b) If both Indian rupee and Mexican peso were pegged to the dollar, the exchange rate would not be allowed to adjust as per International Fisher Effect. The returns from investing in Mexican peso would be translated into the same amount in Indian rupees. The maturity value of the invested pesos would then be 2,800 × 4.00 = ₹11,200; a return of 12% in rupee terms.

INTEREST RATE PARITY

The International Fisher condition for investment relates changes in expected future spot rates to interest rate differentials. We stated earlier that a forward contract for buying and selling foreign currency can be booked to eliminate risks of uncertain future spot rates. The forward rates are determined by what is known as *interest rate parity* (IRP). Here again, we use the all-important and potent process of arbitrage to find an equilibrium condition between money markets of two currencies and foreign exchange markets providing spot as well as forward rates for currency exchange.

Let us consider a case with no transaction cost in either the money markets or the foreign exchange markets. Assume that the current spot exchange rate for US dollars in India is ₹44.00 per dollar. Further, assume that the money market in India offers 15% return, while that of the USA gives 5% return per annum. Both the interest rates are taken to be valid for identical risk free markets in India and the USA. However, we do not know the forward rates in the currency markets in India.

When Forward Rate is too Low

Without a clue to how forward market rates are determined, let us make a wild guess and offer a rate of ₹45 per dollar for a six-month forward contract. If so, an arbitrageur would work as follows:

Today: at $t = 0$ the arbitrageur will take the following four actions simultaneously

1. borrow US$ 1 at 5% for 6 months (maturity amount = US$1.025)
2. convert dollars into rupees in the foreign exchange market at a spot rate of ₹44 per US$
3. invest the rupees obtained for 6 months in Indian money markets, and,
4. buy dollars 6-m forward for the amount to be paid at maturity of the borrowing, US$ 1.025, at a 6-m forward rate of ₹45.00 per US$.

By taking the above actions, the arbitrageur is investing no money of his own, and also taking no risk, as all the cash flows are known with certainty. Note that maturities of borrowing, investing, and the forward contract coincide.

After 6 months At the maturity of borrowing, investment, and the forward contract, there would accrue certain cash flows. At $t = 6$ months, the arbitrageur has an asset through investment in rupees and has a coinciding liability, to pay back the borrowed amount. The value of the asset is ₹47.30 and the value of the liability is US$ 1.025, which is covered by the forward contract at ₹45.00, and thus, has a value of ₹46.125.

As the amount payable is less than the amount receivable, there would result a profit that is gained without any investment or risk. The amount of profit shall be ₹1.175 for every dollar borrowed, as shown in Figure 26-4.

Clearly, the forward rate of ₹45.00 is unsustainable, and arbitrageurs demanding too many dollar forwards will drive the prices of 6-m forward contracts up.

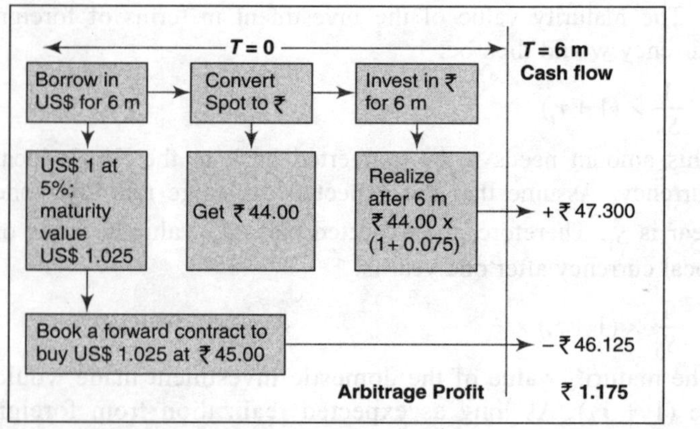

Figure 26-4 Arbitrage in money markets and foreign exchange markets

When Forward Rate is too High

Increased demand for buy of the dollar in the forward market would cause an upward revision in the price of the forward contract. Without knowing how much increase is enough, let us again estimate that the price of the six-month forward contract of ₹48.00 is appropriate.

Here again at $t = 0$, the arbitrageur would act to make some risk-free profit by taking the following four actions simultaneously.

1. borrow ₹44 at 15% for 6 months (maturity amount = ₹47.30)
2. convert rupees into dollars in the foreign exchange market at a spot rate of ₹44 per US$
3. invest the dollars so obtained for 6 months in US money markets, and,
4. buy rupee (or sell dollars) 6-m forward for the amount to be paid at maturity of the borrowing, ₹47.30, at a 6-m forward rate of ₹48.00 per US$.

Again, there was no risk and no investment, with the maturities of borrowing, investing, and the forward contract coinciding.

After 6 months At the maturity of borrowing, investment, and the forward contract there would accrue certain cash flows. At $t = 6$ months, the arbitrageur has an asset through investment in dollars, and has a coinciding liability, to pay back the borrowed amount, The value of the asset is US$ 1.025, and the value of the liability is ₹47.30, which is covered by the forward contract at ₹48.00, and thus, has a value of US$ 0.9854.

As the amount payable is less than the amount receivable, there would result a profit that is gained without any investment or risk. The amount of profit shall be US$ 0.0396 for every ₹44 borrowed, as shown in Figure 26-5.

The position can be viewed in terms of the rupee too. The Indian investor, rather than buying rupees forward, may like to sell the maturity value of the dollars invested in the US markets. Keeping the final position in rupees would result in a profit of ₹1.90, as shown below.

Sell forward US$ 1.025 obtained post investment	₹49.20
Liquidate the rupee liability	–₹47.30
Get profit (for every ₹44 borrowed, or every dollar invested)	₹1.90

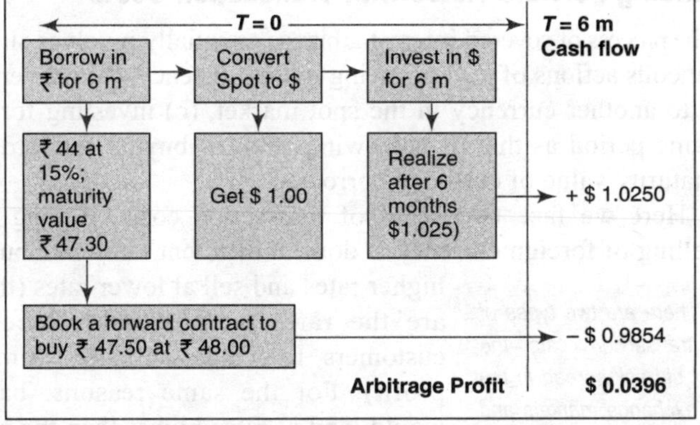

Figure 26-5 Arbitrage in money markets and foreign exchange markets

Thus we see that if the forward rate were either too low or too high, the arbitrageurs would make a profit by taking positions in the money market: borrowing one currency, converting spot, and investing in another. The only way to eliminate arbitrage profit is to adjust the forward rate, because neither the spot rates nor the money market rates in the two currencies can be influenced. In the first case of borrowing dollars (foreign currency), the forward rate must be adjusted upwards just enough to eliminate the profit of ₹1.175. Similarly, in the second case of borrowing in rupee (the domestic currency), the forward rate must be revised downwards just enough to eliminate the profit of ₹1.90. Any excess revision in either direction would make arbitrage possible one way or the other. We need to find a state of equilibrium.

Before we work out an exact solution, we would like to put in a word about arbitrage. Some of us may wonder: why should one engage in borrowing of a currency and incurring interest costs if he has his own money? No doubt, one can definitely invest one's own money, but such a step would not classify as arbitrage. Earning profit on one's own money is construed as a reward for investment, i.e., as return on capital invested. Furthermore, by borrowing, we are supplementing resources, and the profit on our own capital is multiplied with certainty, since we earn risk-free profit. Arbitrage would be defined as making profit (a) without one's own investment and (b) with no risk. Note that when we borrowed dollars or rupees and executed the arbitrage, neither was any investment of our own made, nor was any risk assumed because all the cash flows were determined at the start of the process itself.

Forward markets in exchange rates provide rates free of risk. They are determined such that no arbitrage is possible.

To obtain a solution to find an arbitrage-free forward rate, let us work with symbols. Let the spot exchange rate be S_0 and the forward rate be F_1 for one period case. The interest rates in the domestic and foreign money markets are r_h and r_f respectively.

By borrowing one unit of the foreign currency and converting it at the spot rate, we get S_0 of the domestic currency. Investing in domestic currency, we create an asset that matures to a value of $S_0 \times (1 + r_h)$. At the same time, we create a liability of $(1 + r_f)$ by borrowing in foreign currency, which matures into an equivalent liability of $(1 + r_f) \times F_1$ in domestic currency, using the forward market. If the value of the asset exceeds the value of the liability of borrowing, arbitrage profit would result. For no arbitrage to take place, the asset value must be less than the liability value. Hence, we get inequality in Equation 26-19.

$$S_0(1 + r_h) \leq F_1(1 + r_f) \qquad (26\text{-}19)$$

$$F_1 \geq S_0 \frac{(1 + r_h)}{(1 + r_f)}$$

Similarly, by borrowing one unit of the domestic currency and converting it at the spot rate, we get $1/S_0$ of the foreign currency. By investing in foreign currency, we create an asset that matures to a value of $(1/S_0) \times (1 + r_f)$. At the same time, we create a liability of $(1 + r_h)$, which matures into an equivalent liability of $(1 + r_h)/F_1$ in foreign currency using the forward market. Again, we should not let the value of the asset exceed the value of liability, to prevent arbitrage. Hence we get another inequality, in Equation 26-20.

$$\frac{(1 + r_f)}{S_0} \leq \frac{(1 + r_h)}{F_1} \qquad (26\text{-}20)$$

$$F_1 \leq S_0 \frac{(1 + r_h)}{(1 + r_f)}$$

Both the conditions specified by Equation 26-19 and Equation 26-20 can be satisfied if and only if

$$F_1 = S_0 \frac{(1 + r_h)}{(1 + r_f)} \qquad (26\text{-}21)$$

Equation 26-21 is referred to as *interest rate parity* (IRP), that establishes the relationship of the forward rate with the spot rates through the money markets of the two currencies. Violation of the IRP would make borrowing in one currency and investing in another profitable. Therefore, money markets and foreign exchange markets have to operate in tandem to eliminate any arbitrage profits. Forward rates, being facilitators of currency risk management, have to align with the broader economic fundamentals governing money market conditions in the two economies. Any increase in the domestic interest rate compared with foreign interest rates would see increasing forward rate and vice versa.

Interest rate parity links forward rates to interest rates. The currency providing higher rates of interest would be at discount of approximately equal to interest rate differential.

Forward rates are commonly specified as premium of discount over spot rates. Premium implies that the foreign currency is more expensive in future than in spot. Similarly, discount means that foreign currency is cheaper in future than in the spot market. The forward rate/premium is expected to increase with increase in domestic interest rates, or with fall in the foreign interest rates. The premium should fall with a decrease in domestic interest rates and a rise in foreign interest rates. The ratio of forward to spot rate can be expressed as

$$\frac{F_1}{S_0} = \frac{(1 + r_h)}{(1 + r_f)} \qquad (26\text{-}22)$$

Re-arranging Equation 26-22, we get forward premium/discount over spot rates as Equation 26-23.

Forward premium (+)/discount (–)

$$= \frac{F_1 - S_0}{S_0} = \frac{(r_h - r_f)}{(1 + r_f)}$$
$$\approx (r_h - r_f), \text{ if } r_f \text{ is low} \qquad (26\text{-}23)$$

Equation 26-23 in the approximate form means that the forward premium would be approximately equal to the interest rate differential. The currency with higher rates of interest would be at discount, and the currency with lower interest rates would be at premium to the spot rates.

The generalized form of interest rate parity for an n-period case can be stated as Equation 26-24.

$$F_n = S_0 \frac{(1 + r_h)^n}{(1 + r_f)^n} \qquad (26\text{-}24)$$

Forecasting and IRP

IRP has important forecasting implications. Forward rates are assumed to be the unbiased predictor of future spot rates. In the short term, IRP may be used for forecast of future spot rates, even if IRP does not hold in the true sense, i.e. the forward premium or discount may not represent interest rate differentials exactly. Yet it may be used for forecasting changes in spot rates in the short run. What was stated for purchasing power parity can also be said for IRP. If the causes of distortion of rates were to continue from one period to another, the changes in premium or discount could be forecast based on the changes of interest rates in the intervening period.

In the above analysis, we made the following important assumptions:

1. Free flow of capital across borders
2. Freedom of investors to borrow and invest in any currency desired
3. The rates of interest in two countries are risk free and are of comparable financial assets
4. Any political risk taken by investors for investing and/or borrowing abroad is ignored
5. Absence of transaction costs

With the exception of transaction costs, all other factors causing mismatch in the forward and spot rates must be minimized. All nations, including developed ones, do place some restrictions on the flow of capital in and out of the country. Are competitive and politically independent exchange rates and financial instruments available? The nearest instruments that satisfy the conditions for IRP to hold are present in the euro-markets[2]. Therefore, in order to test the validity of IRP, the rates prevailing in the euro-markets are often considered most appropriate because these markets offer very competitive rates and are free from exchange control mechanisms, as also from political interference.

[2] Euromarkets are markets for deposit and lending of money outside the home country. For example, US dollars deposited or lent in London would be called eurodollars. Likewise, the Yen transacted outside Japan would be referred to as euro-yen.

Finding Forward Rates with Transaction Costs

The process of covered interest arbitrage essentially involves simultaneous actions of (a) borrowing in one currency, (b) converting it to another currency in the spot market, (c) investing for the same period as that of borrowing, and (d) buying forward the maturity value of currency borrowed.

Here we face two types of transaction costs. Buying and selling of foreign currency is done at different rates. We buy at higher rates and sell at lower rates (these are the rates banks would force on customers, to enable the banks to make profit). For the same reasons, banks would lend at rates higher than the rates paid for accepting deposit. For conversion of one currency into another, we face transaction costs in the form of bid-ask spread. In addition, while lending and borrowing, we face transaction costs in the form of investments at lower rate and borrowings at higher rate.

There are two types of transaction costs—the bid ask spread in the exchange markets and the difference in investing and borrowing rates, that provide flexibility in forward rates.

With transaction costs in the foreign exchange markets and the money markets, greater scope is available in quoting forward rates in a manner that does not allow arbitrage. Let us work with a numerical example to illustrate the process of quoting a set of valid forward rates.

Assume that the following rates are quoted in the currency and money markets:

Spot rate (US$ per €)		1.3000	1.3100
Interest rates	US$	5.50%	5.75%
	€	4.00%	4.25%

To arrive at valid twelve-month forward rates that do not permit arbitrage, we follow the same process of borrowing and investing in different currencies and using spot and forward markets for currencies. Assume that the twelve-month forward bid and ask rates are F_b and F_a respectively.

(a) Borrow euro and invest in US We borrow € 1 at the euro borrowing rate (4.25%) for a year, convert it to dollars at the spot bid rate ($ per € 1.3000), invest the dollars at 5.50%, and book a forward contract at forward ask rate, F_a, to buy maturity amount of euro borrowed. This is shown in Figure 26-6.

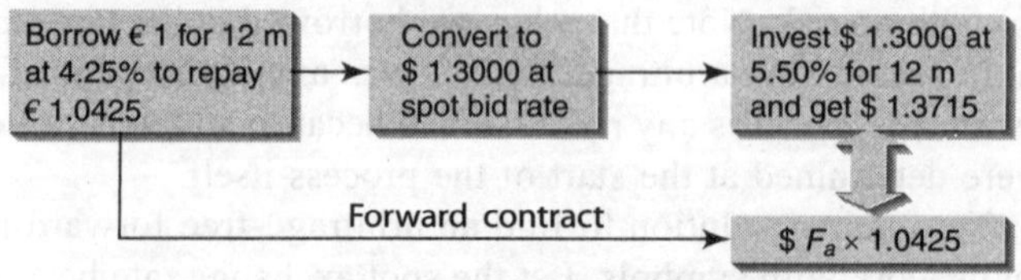

Figure 26-6 Finding arbitrage-free forward ask rate

For arbitrage-free forward rates, the amount payable under forward contract must be more than the amount realizable through investment in US dollars. This gives the following condition for no arbitrage:

$$F_a \times 1.0425 \geq 1.055 \times 1.3000$$

$$F_a \geq \frac{1.3715}{1.0426} \geq (\$/€)\ 1.3156$$

(b) Borrow dollar and invest in Europe To find the forward bid rate, we now borrow US$ 1 at the dollar borrowing rate (5.75%) for a year, convert it to euro at the spot ask rate (US$ to euro 1.3100), invest euro at 4.00% and book a forward contract at forward bid rate F_b to buy the maturity amount of dollars borrowed. This is shown in Figure 26-7.

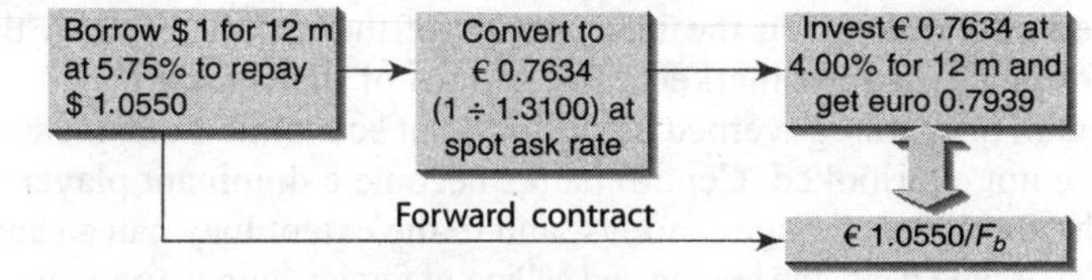

Figure 26-7 Finding arbitrage-free forward bid rate

For an arbitrage-free forward rate, the amount payable under the forward contract must be more than the amount realizable through investment in euro. This gives the following condition.

$$\frac{1.0575}{F_b} \geq \frac{1.04}{1.3100}$$

or $$F_b \leq \frac{1.0575}{0.7939} \leq (\$/€)\ 1.3320$$

With the twelve-month forward bid rate ($ to euro) less than 1.3320, and the ask rate higher than 1.3156, we may quote any number of forward rates that would satisfy the no-arbitrage condition. However, there are additional conditions that also need to be considered for arriving at valid rates. These are listed below:

1. The ask rate must be higher than the bid rate.
2. The bid-ask spread in forward rates must be more than the bid-ask spread in the spot market to compensate traders for taking greater risks in the forward transactions.
3. The forward premium/discount must reflect approximately the differential of interest rates in the two currencies, to be consistent with IRP.

The following would be some examples of forward rates that satisfy the condition of no arbitrage, but yet are not valid rates.

Forward bid rate must be less than 1.3320	Forward ask rate must be greater than 1.3156	Fallacy
1.3310	1.3175	Ask rate is less than the bid rate
1.3100	1.3160	The forward bid-ask spread is less than the spot bid-ask spread
1.3100	1.3250	IRP is not satisfied

However, twelve-month forward rates of 1.3150–1.3300 would be one valid quotation that satisfies all the conditions.

Example 26-4 Determining Valid Forward Rates

The foreign exchange markets in India for US dollars exhibit the following scenario:

Spot (₹ per $) 44.00 44.25

Interest rates in India are 10.00%–10.50%, while those in the USA are 8.00%–8.50%. What are the valid forward rates that must prevail in the market?

Solution

Borrowing US dollars, converting spot, and investing in India, while simultaneously covering the borrowing in US dollars would give the following boundary conditions:

$$F_a \times 1.0850 \geq 44.00 \times 1.10$$

$$F_a \geq \frac{48.40}{1.085} \geq (₹/\$)\ 44.61$$

Similarly, borrowing in rupees, converting them into dollar spot and investing the dollars in the USA while simultaneously covering the rupee borrowing in the forward market gives us the following boundary conditions for the forward bid rate:

$$\frac{1.105}{F_b} \geq \frac{1.08}{44.25}$$

$$F_b \leq \frac{1.105 \times 44.25}{1.08} \leq (₹/\$)\ 45.27$$

From the IRP we know that the dollar must be at premium of around 2% (the differential of the interest rates). The mid rate in the spot market is ₹44.125 per $. With 2% premium, the twelve-month forward rate must be approximately 2% higher, say about ₹45.00.

We also know that the bid ask spread in the spot market is 25 bp. If a bid ask spread of 40 bp is regarded as adequate in the twelve-month forward contract, the bid and ask rates of ₹44.80 and ₹45.20 respectively seem to be valid rates.

FORECASTING EXCHANGE RATES

Interrelationship of International Parity Conditions

We discussed various theories of determination of exchange rates based on inflation rates (PPP), interest rates (International Fisher Effect), and forward rates (IRP). In ideal circumstances, they must essentially lead to the same result, although they take different routes to forecasting of future spot exchange rates. A corporate finance manager has to find a balance in using any of the theories and get into the validity of the assumptions made in each of them. The interrelationship among the various theories of exchange rate determination or forecasting of the changes in the exchange rates is presented in Figure 26-8[3].

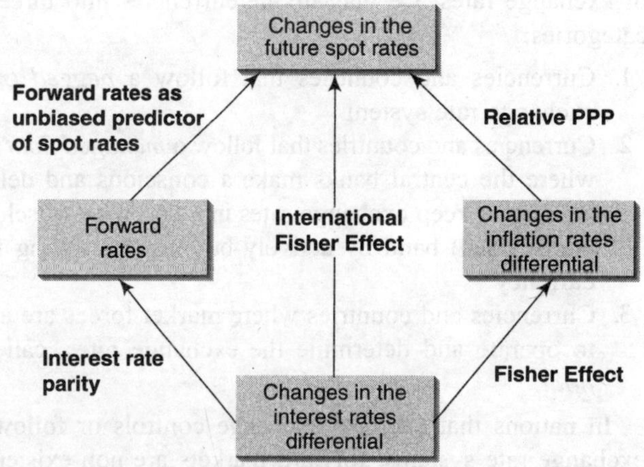

Figure 26-8 Interrelationship of parity conditions for forecasting

[3]Adapted from *Multinational Financial Management* by Alan Shapiro 7th Edition, John Wiley & Sons, Inc.

exchange rates

While PPP relates the changes in the exchange rates to the inflation rates differential, the International Fisher Effect attributes changes to the differential of nominal interest rates. However, the Fisher Effect relates the changes in the nominal interest rates to inflation rates, and if inflation and nominal interest rates move in tandem, then the outcome of PPP would be identical to that of the International Fisher Effect. The differential of interest rates is also linked with the forward premium/discount through IRP. Forward rates can be thought of as unbiased predictors of future spot rates, as the forward premium/discount is the best estimate with currently available information of the direction and magnitude of changes in the spot rates.

Any of the international parity relations may be used for forecasting exchange rates. Under balanced markets, all would provide the same result. They are not conflicting, but are complimentary to each other.

Besides macroeconomic factors, other factors too influence the exchange rates. For example, political uncertainty is a big consideration in decisions to invest abroad, directly or indirectly. Politically unstable countries do not attract much investment in any form. Similarly, factors such as xenophobia may deter investment from abroad. Thus, political and social factors also guide the flow of capital. In our analysis, we have totally ignored the element of risk associated with international investing. Even if borders were open for free flow of capital, foreigners may not be motivated enough to execute arbitrage opportunities available because of political risk perceived in such endeavours.

Any method may be applied to forecast exchange rate, depending upon the validity of the assumptions of each.

Exchange Rate Systems and Forecasting

However, one must realize that the one basic and necessary condition for validity of each of the theories is the feasibility of international arbitrage and its efficient execution. Concentrating on only on economic factors, and from the viewpoint of forecast of exchange rates, we may divide currencies into three broad categories:

1. Currencies and countries that follow a *pegged* or fixed exchange rate system
2. Currencies and countries that follow a *managed float* system where the central banks make a conscious and deliberate attempt to keep exchange rates in a specified (disclosed or undisclosed) band by actively buying and selling foreign currency
3. Currencies and countries where market forces are allowed to operate and determine the exchange rates, called *free float*.

In nations that exercise exchange controls or follow fixed exchange rate systems, forward markets are non-existent. The international environment is closed to the economy for the purpose of exchange rates. They are determined officially. In such circumstances, there prevails an unofficial exchange rate, which alone can be an indicator of the quantum of devaluation or revaluation of the currency. It is well recognized that it is only a matter of time before the currency would see either a devaluation or a revaluation, depending upon when the political leaders would ultimately recognize economic fundamentals. The quantum of change in the value of the currency is dependent upon how long political will persists and overlooks pressure from economic fundamentals.

Under the system of managed float, the focus of the exchange rates forecast is on the intervention of the central bank in the foreign exchange markets. The actions of the central banks are again primarily governed by politics, but economic fundamentals are not overlooked. Central banks become a dominant player in the foreign exchange markets, and to the extent they can sustain the desired band, the buying and selling of foreign currency continues. The currency finds a new level when such interventions are stopped. A policy of interventions embodies the economic philosophy of the government. When interventions continue, it is not hard to know what band of exchange rates the central bank is aiming for. The frequency and extent of interventions reflect the severity of the pressure on the exchange rates. Along with information on interventions, the prediction of changes in the philosophy is extremely crucial to the forecast of exchange rates in such situations.

Under conditions of free float, where exchange rates are governed by market forces, each of the parity conditions would have a role to play in the forecasting of rates. Each of the theories would become more and more accurate and applicable. However, when free market forces are allowed to operate and govern exchange rates, it is not an easy task to forecast currency values because of the huge number of factors influencing the exchange rates simultaneously. It would be fallacious to project or forecast future exchange rates based on a single parameter such as differentials of inflation rates or interest rates. There are several methods to forecast rates and the choice of the best method rests with the analyst.

Market-based forecast One way of estimating future exchange rates is to rely entirely on forward rates. This method is commonly known as *market based forecast*. An analyst treats forward premium/discount as an unbiased predictor of future spot rates. If this is not true then the speculators will take positions to profit such situation. For example, if the twelve-month forward rate for euro is ₹62.00, and speculators believe that 12 months later the spot rate would be ₹60.00, they would sell euro twelve-month forward. If the estimates of speculators come correct, then upon maturity of the forward contracts they would buy euro spot at ₹60.00 and realize ₹62.00 under the forward contracts, resulting in a speculative profit of ₹2.00. As more and more speculators sell euro forward, there would be a downward pressure on the forward rate or premium, till it matches with the expectations for future spot rates. Similarly, if the forward rate happens to be ₹58.00 against expectations of ₹60.00, most speculators would buy euro forward and sell spot on maturity. This would cause upward pressure on the forward rate.

For a large number of participants in the market with diverging opinions about future spot rates, forward rates would be driven closer to the expected future spot rates. Forward rates would keep changing to accommodate the changing expectations of future spot rates. Thus, forward premium/discount could be used as an unbiased predictor of future spot rates.

Regression Based Approach to Forecasting Exchange Rates

Exchange rates respond to a host of factors. Macroeconomic variables of a fiscal or monetary nature are responsible for causing movements in exchange rates. Besides, political factors too influence exchange rates. Under models based on regression, we may consider only the deterministic variables, and must exclude extraordinary events such as changes in the political environment. Normally, analysts consider macroeconomic variables such as interest rate differentials, inflation rate differentials, growth rate differentials, money growth differentials, etc. If these macroeconomic variables are denoted as $f_1, f_2,$ etc., then a three-variable regression model for changes in the exchange rate ΔS would look like Equation 26-25.

Exchange rates respond to a host of factors, and therefore, a regression-based approach may be used to determine sensitivity with respect to each independent variable.

$$\Delta S = a_0 + a_1 \times f_1 + a_2 \times f_2 + a_3 \times f_3 + e \quad (26\text{-}25)$$

where f_1, f_2, f_3 are the independent variables influencing changes in the spot rates, and a_1, a_2, a_3 are the regression coefficients representing the sensitivity of exchange rate changes with respect to variables f_1, f_2, and f_3, respectively. a_0 is the constant and e represents the error term in the regression, the spot rate changes not explained by any of the macroeconomic variables used in the model.

For example, the factors f_1, f_2 and f_3, may represent inflation rate differential, interest rate differential, and income growth rate differential respectively. Using past data for these variables and the changes in the spot rate, a regression equation that provides the values of regression coefficients may be developed. The regression model may provide an output similar to that of Equation 26-26.

$$\Delta S = 0.02 + 0.4 \times f_1 + 0.5 \times f_2 + 1.1 \times f_3 \quad (26\text{-}26)$$

Here, the values of coefficients of a_1, a_2 and a_3 are 0.4, 0.5, and 1.1 respectively, denoting that spot rates would change by 0.4%, 0.5%, and 1.1% respectively with a 1% change in inflation rate differential, interest rate differential, and income growth rate differential.

Having obtained the value of the regression coefficients, one may forecast the changes in the exchange rates based on the anticipated values of independent variables considered in the model. For example, in the above equation if an analyst forecasts 5.1% inflation rate differential, 3.4% interest rate differential, and 1.2% income growth rate differential, her forecast for changes in the spot rate would be 5.08%, as shown below.

$$\begin{aligned}\Delta S &= 0.02 + 0.4 \times 5.1\% + 0.5 \times 3.4\% + 1.1 \times 1.2\% \\ &= 0.02 + 2.04 + 1.70 + 1.32 \\ &= 5.08\%\end{aligned}$$

Forecasting exchange rates based on the regression of selected macroeconomic variables poses several problems. First, the identification of the relevant variables poses a major challenge to analysts predicting the exchange rates. Second, a limitation faced in development of such models is the determination of whether a variable is leading or lagging the changes in the exchange rates. For example, if exchange rates move on expectations of increased economic growth, then the present exchange rates have already discounted the anticipated economic growth. Finally, the confidence level of forecasts based on regression depends upon the accuracy of coefficients. A sufficiently large sample of past data is required to find regression coefficients, which may be a constraining factor in the use of regression-based forecasting.

SUMMARY

Just like the price of a commodity is derived from factors affecting demand and supply of that commodity, a currency rate, which is the price of one currency in terms of another, is also governed by factors affecting demand and supply of foreign currency. Exporters constitute the supply of foreign currency while importers demand it. A balance of demand and supply would determine exchange rates, which are supposed to be stable. However, some countries do not let factors affecting supply and demand operate freely, and instead fix exchange rates by law. In such cases, the economics of demand and supply are overcome over a shorter period of time. Changes in exchange rates can be sudden and substantial under such systems, when economic forces accumulate over time and force these changes.

In countries where no regulations to check exchange rates exist and free market conditions prevail, the foreign exchange markets are likely to follow the principles of economics speedily and rigorously, due to several foreign exchange features. Features that lead to lesser friction and faster adjustment in demand and supply schedules are comparatively unlimited supply of money, absence of storage cost, absence of transportation cost, independence of weather conditions, and the non-perishable nature of money. Like prices of any commodity adjust to changes in economic fundamentals, currencies too respond to such changes. Any factor leading to increased demand or reduced supply of a foreign exchange would cause its appreciation. Similarly factors that lead to increased supply or reduced demand would cause depreciation of a foreign currency.

A large number of factors cause changes in exchange rates. The macroeconomic factors of inflation and interest rates are predominant determinants. Movement in exchange rates is caused not only by what is happening in the domestic environment, but also by happenings around the world. Exchange rates would move even when economic conditions in a country remain unchanged.

Changes in exchange rates are governed more by the differentials of inflation and interest rates than their absolute values in one country. In forecasting exchange rates, an analyst has to identify the relevant factors that cause changes. The selection of factors for forecasting is dependent upon the forecasting horizon. For horizons up to one year, the interest rates differential is a major consideration, while in forecasting for periods beyond one year, the inflation rates differential becomes a guiding tool.

Appreciation of one currency implies depreciation of another. Mathematically, the quantum of appreciation of one currency is not exactly equal to the quantum of depreciation of another.

Purchasing power parity, using the law of one price, states that spot exchange rates are a ratio of the prices of a common basket of goods in the two countries. Several studies reveal that PPP does not hold because of factors such as trade barriers, transportation cost, product differentiation, style, tastes, culture, etc. Even though PPP does not hold true, it can be used as a potent tool for forecasting changes in the spot rates if used in its relative version. Relative PPP asserts that the currency that faces higher inflation would depreciate by an amount approximately equal to the differential of the inflation rates. Countries with higher inflation face depreciation of their currencies, while currencies of countries with lower inflation appreciate.

The exchange rates that are available are nominal, i.e., they do not account for inflation. Exchange rates net of inflation are called real rates. According to PPP, changes in the nominal exchange rates leave the real rates unchanged. The competitive position of firms remains unchanged as long as real rates do not change.

The Fisher Effect, which deals with international investments, states that the real rate of returns across nations must be the same. This links inflation rate and interest rates. Nations with high inflation would necessarily have to offer higher nominal rates. Further, the differential of interest rate and inflation rate of one country would be equal to the difference between interest rate and inflation rate of the second country.

The International Fisher Effect is concerned with determination of changes in spot rates with the changes in differential of interest rates of two countries. It also states that exchange rates would move in such a manner that the extra returns available in foreign currency would be eroded by its depreciation, thus making foreign returns equal to domestic returns.

Interest rate parity establishes the premium or discount of foreign currency to the differential of the interest rates in two currencies. Currencies offering higher interest rates would be at discount to those currencies that have lower interest rates. Again, the principle used is the covered interest arbitrage, where borrowing is made in one currency and invested in another, while simultaneously a forward contract is booked to cover the borrowing. Forward premium/discount can further be used as a forecasting tool, assuming the forward premium/discount to be an unbiased predictor of future spot rates.

Forecasting future spot rates based on a single factor could be misleading because foreign exchange rates respond to many factors. A regression based approach is suggested to incorporate all the factors that affect exchange rates, thus removing any possible aberrations that may arise from predictions based on a single factor.

KEY TERMS

Appreciation When the value of one currency rises over time with respect to another, it is said to be appreciating. The percentage rise in value is the amount of appreciation.

Depreciation When the value of one currency falls over time with respect to another, it is said to be depreciating. The percentage fall in value is the amount of depreciation.

Purchasing power parity The spot rate at any time must be in the ratio of the prices of a common basket of goods in two given currencies.

Relative purchasing power parity The change in spot rates would be approximately equal to the differential of the inflation rates in two countries, The currency of a country with lower inflation would appreciate, whereas the currency of a country with higher inflation would depreciate.

Real exchange rate Nominal exchange rate adjusted for rate of inflation is real exchange rate.

Nominal exchange rate Exchange rates commonly available: published in newspapers, quoted by banks, traders, etc., are nominal exchange rates.

Fisher Effect Real rates of returns across borders in different currencies must be equal. Real returns are approximately equal to nominal returns less inflation.

International Fisher Effect Changes in spot rates are governed by the nominal interest rates in the two currencies.

Forward premium The percentage amount by which the forward rate is higher than the spot rate (under the direct rate system) is forward premium.

Forward discount The percentage amount by which the forward rate is lower than the spot rate (under the direct rate system) is forward discount.

Interest rate parity Forward premium or discount would be approximately equal to the differential of interest rates in two currencies. The currency with higher interest rate is at discount and the currency with lower interest rate is at premium.

Regression based forecasting Finding a relationship of exchange rate change with respect to independent variables, mostly macroeconomic in nature, to forecast is called regression based forecasting.

KEY FORMULAE

Purchasing power parity

$$\text{Spot Exchange Rate (₹/\$)} = \frac{\text{Price of basket of goods in India in ₹}}{\text{Price of same basket of goods in USA in \$}}$$

Relative purchasing power parity

$$S_n = S_1 \frac{(1+I_d)^n}{(1+I_f)^n}$$

Appreciation or depreciation

$$\frac{\text{Amount of appreciation (–)}}{\text{Depreciation (+) of local currency}} = \frac{S_1 - S_0}{S_0}$$

Real exchange rate

$$R_1 = S_1 \left(\frac{\text{Relative Price Level in Foreign Country in Period 1}}{\text{Relative Price Level in Home Country in Period 1}} \right)$$

Relationship of real and nominal returns

$(1 + r) = (1 + a)(1 + I)$

Fisher Effect $r_1 - I_1 \approx I_2 - I_2$

International Fisher Effect

$$\frac{\hat{S}_1 - S_0}{S_0} = \frac{(r_h - r_f)}{(1 + r_f)} \approx (r_h - r_f), \text{ if } r_f \text{ is low}$$

$$\frac{\hat{S}_n}{S_0} = \frac{(1 + r_h)^n}{(1 + r_f)^n}$$

Interest rate parity

$$F_1 = S_0 \frac{(1 + r_h)}{(1 + r_f)}; \quad F_n = S_0 \frac{(1 + r_h)^n}{(1 + r_f)^n}$$

Regression model of forecasting changes in spot rates

$$\Delta S = a_0 + a_1 \times f_1 + a_2 \times f_2 + a_3 \times f_3 + e$$

PRACTICE PROBLEMS

1. PPP—Nominal and Real Rates

A year back, the exchange rate was ₹40 per $. As compared to the last year, rupee has appreciated by 10%. The inflation rate in India was 5% while it was 10% in USA.

(a) What is the nominal exchange rate today?

(b) If PPP were to hold, what should have the exchange rate?

(c) Has rupee appreciated or depreciated with respect to dollar in real terms and by how much?

Solution

(a) Exchange rate a year ago (₹/$) = 40.00

Appreciation of rupee = 10%

The current exchange rate is

$= S_0 \times (1 \pm \text{Depreciation/appreciation})$

$= 40 \times (1 - 10\%) =$ ₹= 36.00/$

(b) Inflation in India = 5%

Inflation in USA = 10%

Appreciation as per PPP should have been equal to the differential of the inflation rate of USA and India, i.e., 5%.

As per PPP, the exchange rate should have been $40 \times (1 - 0.5) = 40 \times 0.95 =$ ₹. 38.00/$

(c) In real terms, the value of rupee has increased by 5%.

If the nominal rate had been ₹38.00, the value of rupee in real terms would remain unchanged.

2. Future Spot Rate and Forward Rate

(a) The current scenario in the money markets provide returns of 12% and 8% in Germany and USA respectively. If the inflation rate in USA is 6%, how much would be the inflation in Germany if parity conditions hold?

(b) If the current exchange rate in USA is US $ 1.60 per €, what exchange rate do you expect after one year?

(c) Again assuming the current exchange rate at 1.60, what rates would be quoted in the forward market in USA for € for 12-m period?

Solution

(a) Inflation rate in USA, I_u	6.00%
Interest rate in USA, r_u	8.00%
Interest rate in Germany, r_g	12.00%
Inflation rate in Germany = I_g	

If the real rates of return in USA and Germany are denoted by a_u and a_g respectively, then according to Fisher condition

$$a_u = a_g$$

The relationship of inflation rate, interest rate, and real rate is given by:

$$(1 + r_u) = (1 + a_u) \times (1 + I_u)$$

$$(1 + r_g) = (1 + a_g) \times (1 + I_g)$$

Equating the real returns, we get:

$$\frac{1 + r_u}{1 + I_u} = \frac{1 + r_g}{1 + I_g}$$

$$1 + I_g = \frac{1 + I_u}{1 + r_u} \times 1 + r_g$$

$$= \frac{1.06}{1.08} \times 1.12 = 1.0993$$

Inflation rate in Germany, I_g = 9.93%

(b) Current exchange rate in USA (US $/€) = 1.60

Expected spot rate after one year would be an, appreciation of $ approximately by 9.93%, i.e., the differential of inflation rates in two countries.

$$\frac{S_1}{S_0} = \frac{1 + I_u}{1 + I_g}$$

$$S_1 = \frac{1 + I_u}{1 + I_g} \times S_0$$

$$= \frac{1.06}{1.0993} \times 1.6 = 1.5428$$

(c) Forward rate is governed by interest rates

$$\frac{F_1}{S_0} = \frac{1 + r_u}{1 + r_g}$$

$$F_1 = \frac{1 + r_u}{1 + r_g} \times S_0$$

$$= \frac{1.08}{1.12} \times 1.60 = 1.5428$$

3. Investing Abroad

An Indian firm wants to invest in USA. The current exchange rate in India is ₹38.00 per US $ while the 12-m forward rate is ₹39.00 per $. They have ₹10 lakh to invest for one year.

Investing in India would provide a return of 9% while the targets for the firm is to earn at least 12% return. It decides to explore the USA markets for different investment opportunities which range from 6% to 18% depending upon the risk return profile of the various classes of investment.

If the firm is not willing to take any risk in the foreign exchange markets, find out in what class of investment the firm must invest in USA so that it gives a return of 12% in rupee terms.

Solution

Current spot rate = ₹38.00 per $
12-m Forward rate = ₹39.00 per $
Amount invested = ₹10,00,000
Return desired = 12.00%
Maturity value desired in Indian rupee = ₹11,20,000
Converted to US $ today at spot rate, we get = $ 26,315.79
Invested at x
Maturity value in $ = 26315.79 × (1 + x)
Conversion to ₹ after one year at 12-m forward rate
= 26315.79 × (1 + x) × F

Therefore (1 + x) = 11,20,000/(26,315.79 × 39.00) = 1.0913
Investment return required in USA = 9.13%

4. Speculation in the Forward Market

Currently the exchange rate for US dollar is ₹40.9500 in the inter-bank market. Based on the interest rates of 10.5% in USA and 7.00% in India, the dollar is at annualized discount of 3.50% in the forward markets.

A foreign exchange dealer (bank) is expecting that the interest rates in India would rise by 1.50% in one month's time.

Assuming that the forecast about the change in the interest rate scenario is correct, what action do you propose for the bank to make gains from such a forecast? Also calculate the expected gains from the suggested action.

Solution

Current spot rate = ₹40.95 per $

	Current interest rate	Expected interest rate
US $	10.50%	10.50%
₹	7.00%	8.50%
Differential	3.50%	2.00%

The strategy of the speculation would be to take actions based on the forecast of interest rates.

Based on the interest rate differential, US dollar is at 3.50% discount to the Indian rupee currently.

Since interest rates in India are expected to rise after one month, the discount on dollar would reduce. Therefore, dollar would become expensive after one month.

The strategy would therefore be to buy dollar today and sell later.

Hence, the dealer would buy dollar 6-m forward, and after 1 month would sell dollar 5-m forward so as to gain from the differential.

Also, to have risk-free position, the dealer would sell dollar 1-m forward now and after a month would buy it spot.

The actions now and one month later are:

Today	*1 month later*
Buy dollar 6-m forward	Sell dollar 5-m forward
Sell dollar 1-m forward	Buy dollar spot

Based on the current exchange rate and interest rate scenario, following are the swap points and forward rates:

	Swap points	*Forward (₹/$)*
1-m	0.1194	40.8306
6-m	0.7166	40.2334

After 1 month, the spot rate would be equal to the 1-m forward rate.

Therefore, expected spot rate after 1 month = ₹40.8306 per $
Swap points after rise would be = 2.00%

The forward rate scenario then would be

	Swap points	*Forward (₹/$)*
5-m	0.3403	40.4903

The expected cash flows of the actions today and 1 month later would be:

₹/$

	1-m later	6-m later
Today		
Buy US $ 6-m forward at		–40.2334
Sell US $ 1-m forward at	40.8306	
There is no cash flow today.		
1 month later		
Buy US $ spot	–40.8306	
Sell US $ 5-m forward at		40.4903
Net cash flows	**0.0000**	**0.2569**

The profit expected from the strategy would be ₹0.2569 for every dollar transacted.

5. Speculation in the Forward Market

Refer to the data in Problem 4. Assume that the current situation remains same. However another banker forecasts that interest rates in USA are going to increase by 1% while rates in India would decline by the same amount one month later. How would the banker benefit from such forecast?

Solution

Current spot rate = ₹40.95 per $

	Current interest rate	Expected interest rate
US $	10.50%	11.50%
₹	7.00%	6.00%
Differential	3.50%	5.50%

Based on the interest rate differential, US dollar is at 3.50% discount to the Indian rupee currently.

Since interest rates are expected to fall in India and rise in USA after one month, the discount on dollar would increase. Therefore, dollar would become cheaper after one month than what it is now.

The strategy would therefore be opposite, i.e., to sell dollar today and buy later.

Hence, the dealer would sell dollar 6-m forward, and after 1 month buy dollar 5-m forward so as to gain from the differential.

Again, to have risk-free position, the dealer would buy dollar 1-m forward now and after a month would sell it spot.

The actions now and one month later are:

Today	*1 month later*
Sell dollar 6-m forward	Buy dollar 5-m forward
Buy dollar 1-m forward	Sell dollar spot

Based on the current exchange rate and interest rate scenario, following are the swap, points and the forward rates:

	Swap points	*Forward (₹/$)*
1-m	0.1194	40.8306
6-m	0.7166	40.2334

After 1 month, the spot rate would be equal to the 1-m forward rate. Therefore, expected spot rate after 1 month = ₹40.8306 per $

Swap points after rise would be = 5.50%

The forward rate scenario then would be:

	Swap points	*Forward (₹/$)*
5-m	0.9357	39.8949

The expected cash flows of the actions today and 1 month later would be:

₹/$

	1-m later	*6-m later*
Today		
Sell US $ 6-m forward at		40.2334
Buy US $ 1-m forward at	–40.8306	
There is no cash flow today.		
1 month later		
Sell US $ spot	40.8306	
Buy US $ 5-m forward at		–39.8949
Net cash flows	**0.0000**	**0.3385**

The profit expected from the strategy would be ₹0.3385 for every dollar transacted.

6. Arbitrage in Foreign Exchange and Money Market

In New York, British pound (£) is trading at 2.1150 while the 12-m forward rate is 2.2150. The interest rates prevailing in USA and England are 8% and 4% respectively. Do you think that money markets and foreign exchange markets are in tandem with each other? If they are not, how would one exploit the situation?

Solution

	Exchange Rate ($/£)	*Interest Rate*
Spot rate	2.1150	£ 4.00%
12-month Forward	2.2150	$ 8.00%

Interest rate differential = 4.00%

Interest rate differential suggests that pound must be at about 4% annualized premium.

Annualized discount for dollar in the foreign exchange markets = 4.73%

There exists an arbitrage by borrowing in USA and investing in England. By doing so, the investor stands to lose 4% in the money markets if the exchange rates remain static. However, since the forward discount on dollar is 4.73% the investor would gain the discount. The net arbitrage gain would be about 0.73%. We may see this by borrowing $ 100.

The investor would take the following simultaneous actions today:

Borrow $ ⇒ convert spot to £ ⇒ Invest £ ⇒ Buy $ forward

$1 ⇒ £ 1/2.1150 ⇒ £ 1/2.1150 × 1.04 ⇒ $ 1.08

After 12 months, the matured amount of loan would be paid from the matured value of rupee investment.

Amount of $ borrowed	$ 100.00
Maturity value of $ after 12 months	$ 108.00
Pound equivalent at spot rate	£ 47.2813
Maturity amount of pound after 12 months	£ 49.1726
Book forward contract for buying $ at	$ 2.2150 per £
At the end of 12 months	
Maturity value of £ invested after 12 months	£ 49.1726
Amount to be paid for $108 at forward rate	£ 48.7585
Profit to be made	£ 0.4141

7. Arbitrage Free Forward Rates

Following exchange rates and interest rates are prevailing with respect to US$:

Spot Exchange Rate (₹/US$)		42.5000	42.7500
6-m Interest Rate	₹	8.00%	8.50%
	US$	4.00%	4.50%

You are required to arrive at 6-m forward rates that offer no arbitrage opportunity.

Solution

Spot Exchange Rate (₹/$)		42.5000	42.7500
6-m Interest Rate	₹	8.00%	8.50%
	US $	4.00%	4.50%

For no arbitrage condition, we borrow in one currency, convert spot into another currency, invest and book a forward contract to buy back the borrowed currency, such that at maturity the invested amount does not exceed the liability of the borrowed amount.

Actions now:

Borrow US $ 1 → Convert Spot to ₹ at bid rate → Invest ₹ for 6-m → Sell 6-m forward the maturity amount of ₹ to get US $ at forward ask rate

Six months later:

Get US$ by the forward contract to liquidate the liability and see if we can make profit.

Amount borrowed @	1.50%	$ 1.00
₹ in the spot market at	42.5000	₹42.5000
Invested at the rate of	8.00%	
Maturity value of ₹ invested		₹44.2000
Forward ask rate,		F_a
US$ available after 6 m		$44.2000/F_a$
US$ liability – payable		$ 1.0225

For no arbitrage, US $ available must be less than the liability.

or $44.2000/F_a \leq 1.0225$

or $F_a \geq$ ₹43.2274 per $

For getting the forward bid rate, we reverse the borrowing and investing actions.

Borrow ₹1 → Convert Spot to \$ at ask rate → Invest \$ for 6-m → Sell 6-m forward the maturity amount of \$ to get ₹ at forward bid rate

Instead of borrowing US dollar, we now borrow Indian rupee, convert it to dollar and invest. We sell the matured investment in dollars forward to get Indian rupee.

Amount borrowed @	8.50%	₹1.0000
US \$ at spot ask rate of	42.7500	\$ 0.0234
Invested at the rate of	4.00%	
Maturity value of US \$ invested		\$ 0.0239
Forward bid rate,		F_b
₹ available after 6 m		$0.0239 \times F_b$
₹ liability		₹1.0425

For no arbitrage, ₹ available must be less than the liability.

or $0.0239 \times F_b \leq 1.0425$

or $F_b \leq$ ₹43.6930 per \$

The process gives the upper bound for the bid rate and lower bound for the ask rate. Any rate satisfying the conditions can be set.

EXERCISES

Concept Review Questions

1. List out ten macroeconomic factors that impact exchange rates. Also state in which directions exchange rates would move if they change.
2. What are the distinguishing features of foreign exchange markets as compared to commodities markets for determination of price as an intersection of demand and supply schedules?
3. What is purchasing power parity? Explain.
4. What are the reasons that purchasing power parity does not hold? Do you think that it will ever hold?
5. What is relative purchasing power parity? Despite the fact that it is derived from PPP in its absolute form, which does not hold, can it be fruitfully used for managerial decisions? If so, how?
6. What are nominal and real returns? Also, describe what are nominal and real exchange rates?
7. What is Fisher Effect? What implications does it have for international investing?
8. Highlight the difference between Fisher Effect and International Fisher Effect.
9. Describe how you would apply interest rate parity to determine forward rates.
10. Other than the presence of transaction cost in international investing and exchange of foreign currencies, what other factors would you consider in quoting valid forward rates?
11. How are different parity conditions linked with each other? Can you think of situations where they provide a different forecast of exchange rates?
12. What are the limitations faced in the regression model for forecasting of exchange rates?

Critical Thinking Questions

1. The Reserve Bank of India, in order to control liquidity, keeps changing the Statutory Liquidity Ratio (the proportion of money to be invested in government securities) and Cash Reserve Ratio (the proportion of cash to be retained by banks). What impact do such changes have on exchange rates?
2. Issue of T-bills by the government would lead to appreciation of the rupee with respect to all other currencies. Do you agree with the statement?
3. How are exchange rates expected to behave with (a) increase in the bank rates (b) deficit financing of fiscal budget?

Practical Assignments

1. Find out T-bill yields in India and the USA. Also find out the forward rates of the US dollar from any bank for one month, three months, and six months. Compute the divergence of forward rates from interest rate parity. Assign reasons for such divergence.
2. Repeat the exercise for the USA and Britain and compare the 1-m, 3-m, and 6-m forward rates of the US dollar and the sterling pound. Compute the divergence with interest rate parity and assign reasons for the same. Do you find the divergence of the same order as in Assignment 1?

Numerical Problems

1. Purchasing Power Parity—Absolute and Relative

The prices of seven commodities in India and Germany in their respective currencies, rupees and euro, as well as the actual average exchange rates are given below for two successive years.

	Weight in Index		Prices			
			2004		2005	
	Germany	India	Germany	India	Germany	India
			euro	₹	euro	₹
Wheat	0.20	0.30	0.20	25.00	0.26	35.00
Mutton	0.30	0.20	1.05	100.00	1.25	125.00
Cabbage	0.10	0.20	0.40	20.00	0.45	22.00
Shirt	0.05	0.05	4.50	450.00	5.00	470.00
Tutor	0.15	0.05	3.00	150.00	3.30	160.00
100 bricks	0.10	0.05	3.50	250.00	3.75	300.00
Petrol	0.10	0.15	0.60	45.00	0.62	48.00
Total	1.00	1.00				
Actual Exchange Rate (₹ per euro)				58.25		60.60

(a) Verify whether the PPP in its absolute form holds.

(b) Verify whether the PPP in its relative form holds.

2. Forecasting Exchange Rate using PPP

Inflation rate in India is currently at 5%, while in Pakistan, it is at 15%. What behaviour do you expect from the exchange rates for Indian rupee (INR) to Pakistani rupee (PKR)? If the current exchange rate is PKR 1.25 per INR 1.00, what rate do you expect after (a) one year (b) 2 years and (c) 6 months?

3. Arbitrage in Foreign Exchange and Money Markets

In the spot market, the rupee is trading at ₹42.00 per dollar and the 6-m forward rate is ₹42.80. In the money market, the yields of comparable T-bills in India and the USA are 12% and 8% respectively. Given the conditions in the foreign exchange markets and money markets, do you think there arbitrage opportunities exist? If yes, how would you execute the arbitrage?

4. Arbitrage in Foreign Exchange and Money Markets

In the Problem 3, do you think arbitrage opportunities would still exist if the forward rate was modified to ₹43.50?

5. Covered Interest Arbitrage

Based on the following information, find out if any arbitrage opportunities exist.

Spot ($/£)	2.1850	2.1950	Interest rate, $	6.50%	6.75%
3-m swap	300	200	Interest rate, £	5.00%	5.25%

If there was an arbitrage opportunity, how would the rates be modified?

6. Arbitrage Free Forward Rates

The following exchange rates and interest rates prevail with respect to the euro and US dollar markets:

Spot exchange rate (US$/€)		1.44	1.45
6 m interest rate	€	4.00%	4.50%
	US$	8.00%	8.50%

You are required to arrive at 6-month forward rates that offer no arbitrage opportunity.

7. Choosing Investment Location

A treasurer has surplus funds of 1 million pounds with an option to invest in either Germany or England.

Exchange rates prevailing are:

			Interest rate		
Spot (€/£)	1.5000	1.5100	England	£	10.00%
12-m swap	550	500	Germany	€	6.00%

Where should he invest his surplus funds? The withholding tax in Germany is 10%. Assume England does not provide tax credit for investment income in Germany. Would your decision change if England provided tax credit?

Assume no tax on capital gains on account of conversion of currency.

8. Forward Hedge and Money Market Hedge

An Indian exporter is expecting to receive US$ 10,000 after three months. Worried about the depreciation of the dollar against the Indian rupee, he needs to hedge his receivables. Given the following data, what alternatives are available to the exporter?

Exchange Rate			Interest Rate		
(₹$)	40.60	40.80	₹	13.00%	13.50%
3-m swap	40	60	$	5.75%	6.00%

9. Choosing Currency to Borrow

An Indian treasurer needs to borrow for six months. He could borrow at 11% in Indian rupees. His banker has also given him an option to borrow in any currency desired by him, provided he covers the borrowing by carrying no foreign exchange risk. The following rates for spot, 6-m forward and interest are prevailing:

Currency	Spot	6-m forward	Interest rate (%)
Euro	57.50	57.70	4.00%
US$	41.45	41.50	5.00%
British pound	83.60	83.80	6.00%
Swiss Franc	32.15	32.50	2.00%
Can $	38.65	39.00	8.00%
Aus $	32.25	32.75	10.00%
HK $	6.25	6.20	12.00%

Find in which currency should the treasurer borrow.

10. Speculation and Borrowing

A company has been offered borrowing rates for different currencies for its requirement of funds as shown below. At the same time, the consultant of the firm has projected exchange rates that are expected to prevail after 6 months, given in Column 4. In what currency should the company borrow (a) if it does not want to carry any risk of foreign exchange rate fluctuations, and (b) if it is willing to assume the risk, provided the cost of borrowing falls down?

Currency	Spot	3-m forward	Expected spot rate	Interest rate (%)
Euro	57.60	57.70	57.30	4.00%
US$	41.60	41.50	41.65	5.00%
British pound	84.15	83.80	83.65	6.00%
Swiss franc	32.15	32.50	32.85	2.00%

CASE STUDY

PANTALOON EXPORTS LIMITED–TAKING SHIRT OFF FOR EXCHANGE RATE

Pantaloon Exports Limited (PEL) is a firm engaged in the production of a variety of garments. It supplies predominantly to the USA and European markets, but does not cater to domestic markets. A tender for the supply of regular shirts was floated by a global player, T-Mart. The Request for Proposal (RFP) specified requirements for 250,000 pieces of high quality corduroy shirts. PEL was very happy to be among the short-listed suppliers. After a successful evaluation by the technical team of T-Mart, they were asked to submit a financial bid.

Through some investigations in the market, they came to know that three more Indian firms had been short-listed and had been asked to submit financial bids. The RFP had clearly stated that the tender was open only for Indian firms; for suppliers from other nations, separate RFPs were floated.

Mr Mohan Dass, the Managing Director (MD), Mr Ved Prakash Marwah, the Vice President (Marketing) (VPM), and Mr David Fraser, the Director Finance (DF), constituted the team that assumed the responsibility for preparing the financial bid. The supply for 250,000 shirts was phased over 10 months at equally spaced monthly intervals commencing two months from now. Thus, in the coming 12 months the entire supply would be completed. The RFP was silent on payment terms. Naturally, this was one of the considerations for T-Mart. It would favour the firm that offered longer credit periods. The order was prestigious for PEL, as it could provide the company with an opportunity to get a foothold in the large retail chain of T-Mart. It simply did not want to lose the order.

Cost estimates revealed that the cost per piece would average ₹200, and the total cost would be ₹50 million. PEL was entitled to an export benefit of 7% on the sale value. The MD and the VPM were inclined to quote the actual cost as the sale price because that would give them a profit of 7% by way of the export incentive from the government. The DF agreed to this proposition. With this unanimous view on the sale value in rupee terms, the two questions that evoked animated debate were (i) how much credit to offer and (ii) at what exchange rate to convert the rupee value into US dollars.

Both the issues were linked to exchange rates. For the last four years, the rupee had shown a steady trend, with little orientation towards depreciation. According to the MD and the VPM, extending credit would be beneficial as the rupee was expected to depreciate, though marginally. Thus far, the rupee had been depreciating, and extending credit to T-Mart was not a problem at all. In fact, extended credit periods would be in our interest, said the MD. The DF, however, did not agree. The DF had been more vigilant about the exchange rate movements. He did not believe that the past depreciation would continue, or that a steady rate would hold. Recent trends showed some appreciation of the Indian rupee. Since net profit margin was limited to about 7%, the DF was worried about the erosion of profit due to appreciation of the rupee. He presented data on exchange rate behaviour in the recent past, as given in Table A.

Table A Exchange rate—recent past—₹ to $

	Spot Rate	*12-m Forward Premium (%)*
90 days prior	41.38	3.90
75 days prior	41.30	3.72
60 days prior	41.27	3.62
45 days prior	41.05	3.26
30 days prior	40.78	2.98
15 days prior	40.62	2.24
Current rate	40.50	2.50

Looking at the data relating to recent foreign exchange movement, he opined, 'I am not in favour of extending any credit. The more credit we give, the more we lose on the exchange rate, apart from incurring the local cost of interest on the funds and constraining our liquidity, too.' The MD proposed to use the six-month forward rate to convert his bid into dollars and book 10 forward contracts for the expected realization of each consignment. According to the VPM, it was too risky to book forward contracts. The VPM said, 'In case we fail to win the bid, we face a liability that is easily avoidable. At this stage it is unwarranted. It would take about one more month to know if we win the bid.' He suggested using a fourteen-month forward rate to convert the bid into dollars.

The DF suggested that if the forward rate was used, PEL would underbid. He opined that since the forward premiums were continuously declining, they would not be appropriate. 'Instead, we must use spot rates likely to prevail after six to eight months. In the last 90 days, the rupee has appreciated by more than 2%. If the rupee continues the recent trend, we will wipe away all the profit we intend to make. Therefore, we must use future spot rates for bidding, while we can book forward contracts once we are successful,' he said. Asked the MD, 'Forward rates are the best indicators of future spot rates. What other method do we have to forecast spot rates better than the forward markets?'

The DF replied, 'We can do it on the basis of the inflation rates differential in India and the USA. At present, inflation in India is of the order of 4% and in the USA, it is 3%. But it is likely to drop to 3% in India. That would suggest no change in the value of the dollar. The other way is to use the six-month interest rates. The data on my hand reveals that six-month yields in India and the USA are 5.9% and 5.6% respectively.'

'But all this data, though helpful, does not justify the current premium on the dollar,' said the MD.

'I agree. I think the market is moving on some very short-term indicators such as FII inflow in the stock markets, and of course, our mounting oil imports. Recently, I read about a model, developed by some foreign exchange expert, which seems to have withstood empirical testing for past changes in exchange rates. It relates exchange rate movement to import of oil and inflows of FIIs, the two most sensitive factors determining exchange rate changes.'

The DF stood up and wrote on the board the following model:

$$\Delta F = 0.02 \times \Delta O - 0.10 \times \Delta I$$

where ΔF = percentage change in the US dollar exchange rate,

ΔO = the import of oil in India for the period in billion dollars,

and ΔI = FII inflows in India for the period in billion dollars.

Continued the DF, 'According to the model, if changes in oil imports match the changes in FII inflows every month, the rupee would appreciate by 0.08% or at 0.96% per annum. In fact, I expect FII inflows to be about twice as much as the increase in oil imports in the coming six months. That would mean an appreciation of the rupee by about 2%.'

In the CD

Finding Expected Spot Rates as per PPP, and Forward Rates as per IRP

CHAPTER 27

Managing Foreign Exchange Exposure

LEARNING OBJECTIVES

After reading this chapter, you will understand:

- how the changing exchange rate impact the financial and competitive positions of the firms.
- what are the different kinds of risk faced by the firms due to changing foreign exchange rates
- meaning of different kinds of exposures and their distinguishing features
- what is meant by
  - transaction exposure
  - economic exposure
  - translation exposure
- measurement of each of the exposure
- hedging transaction exposure by
  - forward hedge
  - money market hedge
- management of economic exposure
  - strategically
  - financially
- methods of translation of financial statements
  - current/Non-current method
  - monetary/Non-monetary method
  - temporal method
  - all current method
- management of translation exposure through
  - balance sheet
  - derivatives

INSECURITY IN SECURITY DEPOSIT

Technology Export Limited (TEL) was a firm developing specialized software for its foreign clients. The firm was managed by Mr Narayan who was a very well-qualified computer engineer having obtained his master's degree from Stanford University, USA. He was in the process of negotiating a contract with a London-based firm that wanted him to develop a scheduling software for the underground railway system. The project involved posting of 5 engineers at least for a period of 6 months in London.

Looking at the fact that TEL was a new entrant, the customer insisted for a security deposit of £100,000. With a strong likelihood of getting some further business and continued post-development support, he thought favourably to concede the requirement of the customer. In case the business does not move in the expected direction, he would call back the funds. He was fortunate to have the required funds of £100,000. He decided to consult Mr Berry, the partner of Berry and Associates, his chartered accountant.

Berry: Though I appreciate your line of thought and agree with it, but I see a problem here.

Narayan: What is the problem?

Berry: There are two in fact—(1) appreciating rupee with respect to British pound, and (2) our fast-approaching closing of the accounts. I am worried about the impact of this transaction on your balance sheet and profitability.

Narayan: What the foreign transactions has to do with our profitability? It is not an expense. If at all it must have an impact on the profits of the firm, it should be positive and not negative.

Berry: Assume that you have given the security deposit of £100,000 to the customer. Now you have to show this asset in your balance sheet, like you show the values of all other assets held in India. The exchange rate at present is ₹80 per pound, so the value of the security deposit would be equal to ₹80 lakh in the balance sheet.

Narayan: That is ok.

Berry: But I expect the rupee to appreciate by at least 10% before the next 31 March. Indian economy is doing well. Inflation is under control and within well-accepted limits. Interest rates are low too. There is nothing that can stop rupee to appreciate by about 10%.

Narayan: What is bad about it? It should be good for us too if it is good for the nation.

Berry: Yes, but it would have a significant effect on our performance.

Narayan: Why and how?

Berry: You see, today, we have assets worth ₹80 lakh. On 31 March, assume that pound depreciates by 10%, then the value of our asset would fall down by 10% and we have to show the value of the security deposit at ₹72 lakh instead of ₹80 lakh.

Narayan: So what?

Berry: Since our value of asset has declined, it would have an impact on the profits. The profit would decline by ₹8 lakh, i.e., the difference in the value of asset today and the value that prevails on 31 March.

Narayan: But this is purely notional. In fact, we still have the deposit of £100,000.

Berry: Yes, you are right. But this is the way the translation is done. We have to recognize the depreciation in the value of the asset.

Narayan: When we do not have actual loss, why should that be reported at all? What if pound appreciates later on?

Berry: The principles of accounting require that the value of asset and liabilities must reflect the current price. It assumes the reality of what would have happened if you were to liquidate the assets and the liabilities in foreign currencies. If the pound were to appreciate later, we would record a profit.

Narayan: It is funny.

Berry: Yes, it is. But the principle has a meaning. Suppose you were to liquidate the asset, what value in Indian rupee would you realize. Assuming you call back the deposit on 31 March, you would realize only ₹72 lakh instead of ₹80 lakh you originally sent while making the deposit. Therefore, we would have incurred a loss of ₹8 lakh and that is what is reflected in the financial statements.

Narayan: Our bottom line is already very thin. We cannot afford to do that. What is the remedy?

Berry: One remedy that I can think of is that you take a loan in British pounds.

Narayan: How does that help?

Berry: You see, the value of asset has decreased causing the loss. Likewise, the value of liability too would decrease if you had taken a loan. There would be a gain to the same extent. The impact of values of asset and liability due to exchange rate changes is opposite on the profit and loss account. That way, the net impact on the profit would be confined to the difference of the value in the asset and liability. If you take loan in pounds, of say £90,000, then the loss would be confined to the value of £10,000 only, instead of £100,000.

Narayan: So, the actual loss has no meaning.

Berry: No, it has got more meaning. In fact, it is the cash loss when you actually undertake the transaction of converting one currency to another. The loss on the balance sheet on the closing of account is merely a loss in the books. It is called translation loss. But it is the cash loss that everybody is more worried about.

Considering the advice of Mr Berry, Narayan started thinking in terms of raising a loan in British pounds rather than remit money for the security deposit from India.

INTRODUCTION

All firms, domestic or multinational, are affected by changes in the foreign exchange rates. Multinational Corporations (MNCs) are affected more while pure domestic firms are affected less. Amongst the pure domestic firms, those heavily dependent upon imports and exports are affected more; while those with no import content and/or no exports may have rather insignificant effect due to changes in the exchange rates.

To realize how serious and large the impact of changes in the foreign exchange rates can be, consider a simple situation of a merchant exporter having sent goods on credit of 90 days for US $100. The exporter supplied the goods on the presumption that he would realize ₹4,500 as the prevalent exchange rate of ₹45.00 per dollar is expected to remain unchanged. The merchant exporter operated on the margin of 4% with his

Fluctuating exchange rates are a cause of concern to all exporting and importing firms due to its direct impact on the bottom line.

total cost inclusive of interest for the credit period of 3 months reckoned at ₹4,320. However, when he realized the money after 3 months, the exchange rate stood at ₹43.50; a fall of about 3.33% and net realization came to ₹4,350. Thus his expected profit of ₹180 reduced to a paltry ₹30; a fall of more than 83%. The sensitivity of profit to the exchange rate changes is tremendously high as we see that a rather small decline of about 3.33% resulted in a loss of profit of more than 83%. The exporter faced the risk of depreciation of the foreign currency. Likewise importer liable to make payments at future dates would fear appreciation of foreign currency but would be delighted to see depreciation as it reduces the liabilities to pay in domestic currency.

There are many kinds of exposures a firm faces due to unanticipated changes in the foreign exchange rates. Exposure is defined as changes in the value of assets, liabilities, income or expenses denominated in foreign currency and resulting from fluctuations in the exchange rates of these currencies. Without worrying about what causes the foreign exchange rates to change, we are more concerned about the kinds of exposures a firm may have and possible remedies to reduce or eliminate such exposures.

The risks from fluctuating foreign exchange rates called exposures are classified into three categories; Transaction Exposure, Translation Exposure, and Economic Exposure.

We classify the foreign currency exposure into the following three types:

1. Transaction exposure
2. Economic exposure
3. Translation exposure

We will now discuss each of these exposures separately.

TRANSACTION EXPOSURE

The example cited above highlighted the transaction exposure faced by the firm. Transaction exposure arises out of contracts denominated in the foreign currency that are already entered but are not settled as yet. Hence it is often called as contractual exposure. The exposure is over once the contract is settled.

Typical examples of transaction exposure include transactions denominated in foreign currency of (a) export made on credit (b) imports made on credit, (c) borrowings made and instalments payable, and (d) lending done and instalments receivable.

A distinguishing and most important feature of transaction exposure is that the value of cash flow changes as the foreign exchange rates change. For example, if an Indian company borrows US $1 million repayable in 10 quarterly instalments, it faces transaction exposure each quarter when it pays the instalment. The amount paid in local currency at each repayment would be different from what is expected.

MEASUREMENT OF TRANSACTION EXPOSURE

The measurement of transaction exposure is extremely simple. It is simply the value of the contracts denominated in the foreign currency that is not settled yet. For example, if an exporter has US $1,000 as receivable after one month, his exposure is simply US $1,000. The measurement of risk arising out of this contract of invoicing US $1,000 would essentially depend upon the volatility of the exchange rate over a period of 30 days. The period of exposure would be 30 days. When the money is realized, the transaction exposure vanishes. Volatility can be measured by the standard deviation of exchange rates. Alternatively, one can project the worst case and best case exchange rates scenarios to gauge the risk exposure.

Transaction exposure defined as the risk for changes in the exchange rates for the contracts that are entered but not yet settled.

Importers and exporters face threat from movement of exchange rate in different directions. What is good for importer is bad for exporter and vice-versa.There is an important issue to note regarding measurement of exposure or risk. While measuring risk, only the unanticipated fluctuations in the foreign exchange are relevant. The anticipated changes in the exchange rates are already built into the transactions that are being entered in foreign currency. The exporters would usually provide for likely depreciation in foreign currency for the duration of booking the sales and actual realization of money. Likewise importers would provide for likely appreciation in foreign currency when they actually pay for the liability being booked today.

Transaction exposure has impact on the cash flows in near future and concerns only the unanticipated changes in the currency exchange rates.

IMPORTANCE OF TRANSACTION EXPOSURE

As stated earlier, the exposure can be classified into three types, i.e., Translation, Transaction, and Economic. While as a manager, one is required to manage all the three for effective control of risk, the management of transaction exposure is considered most vital amongst the three exposures. The reasons are not far to seek. The importance of managing transaction exposure can be argued as follows:

Due to its impact on the immediate cash flows, transaction exposure is considered most important of the three exposures.

Impact on cash flow Transaction exposure has immediate impact on the cash flow, which may be adversely affected. Besides posing problems in day-to-day cash management, any impact on cash flows also has long-term implications on the valuation of the firm.

In contrast, translation exposure is only notional and remains so till profits are repatriated, assets disposed off, or liabilities liquidated, which gives rise to transaction exposure.

Further, economic exposure impacts all the firms in some degree or the other. The competitive position of the firm changes as the foreign exchange rates change. This remains valid for all the firms in the same business, and therefore the impact of economic exposure may not be as high as one may estimate.

Style of managing exposures Management of foreign exchange may be tactical or strategic in nature. Since implications of transaction exposure are essentially short-term, the tools and instruments available for managing transactions exposure are mostly tactical. Other exposure possibly can be managed more effectively by strategic interventions.

Interrelationship of exposures Lastly and most importantly, management of translation and economic exposures gives rise to transaction exposure. It is a moot point that whether the exposures that otherwise do not impact cash flows in the immediate future should be converted in the exposure bearing risk for cash flows in the immediate future.

IRRELEVANCE OF EXCHANGE RATE RISK MANAGEMENT[1]

There are several arguments made for not managing the transaction exposure. All the arguments seem somewhat valid under perfect market conditions.

There have been substantial arguments for not managing the transaction exposure. Since management of transaction exposure entails cost and places burden on the profitability of the firm, some analysts are strongly in favour of avoiding such costs associated with hedging the exposures.

PPP Argument

The first argument for irrelevance of the management of foreign exchange exposure emanates from the purchasing power parity (PPP) argument. As per PPP, change in exchange rates is matched by equivalent price movements. What is lost due to the adverse movement in the exchange rates affecting the firms dependent on the imports and exports will be compensated by the changes in cost of firms that are not dependent upon exports and imports. For example, consider the exporters who denominate their receivables in foreign currency. Any depreciation of foreign currency would adversely affect the cash inflows of the exporters. This depreciation of foreign currency is due to reduced inflation, which would cause a decline in the local prices too. Hence, a similar risk of reduced cash inflow is faced by the firms catering only to domestic markets. This places exporting firms and non-exporting firms at an equal disadvantage and makes management of foreign exchange exposure rather irrelevant.

The counter-argument in favour of managing the foreign currency exposure lies in the validity of PPP. If PPP holds, the argument for not managing the exposure seems to hold. But is PPP valid in reality? Since one is not sure about the validity of PPP, it is argued that firms that consciously attempt to manage the risk of foreign currency are viewed more favourably by managers, lenders, and shareholders.

Home-made hedging The second argument for discouraging the conscious efforts on the part of firms to manage the currency risk results from the famous and familiar arguments given by Miller and Modigliani in respect of irrelevance of capital structure and dividend policy. Miller and Modigliani have proved that under perfect market conditions, desired leverage or dividend is achieved by investors in their personal capacities, by personal borrowing.

Extending the same argument to currency exposure, it can be stated that investors in firms recognize that their interests could be adversely affected by the currency exposure faced by the firms. Therefore, they can take appropriate steps in their personal capacities to hedge against such risks. The argument is that the firms need not bother unnecessarily over the issues that can be managed by the investors themselves.

The counter-argument favouring management of currency exposure by firms is that firms can achieve a hedge more effectively and efficiently than any of the individual investors. Further, management by individuals assumes adequate knowledge and familiarity of the financial instruments and mechanisms of hedging—a remote possibility indeed.

Diversification Another argument for irrelevance of management of currency exposure comes from the *portfolio theory*. According to the portfolio theory, individuals can diversify specific risks away by holding portfolios rather than individual security. If investors hold well-diversified portfolios, it is assumed that foreign exchange risk would be diversified away since the risks for importers and exporters offset each other.

Without taking away the merit in the argument of diversification, one may find it difficult to implement in practice. Most diversifications are confined to single economy, and it is difficult to find investors who are globally diversified. Further, even in a single economy, it is difficult to find importing and exporting firms in a manner that evens out the risk from exchange rate fluctuations because most nations do not exhibit balanced trade.

RELEVANCE OF EXCHANGE RATE RISK MANAGEMENT

The arguments in favour of managing the currency risk include that the value of the firms is dependent upon the stability of revenue/cash flows. By covering the risk of currency rate fluctuations, the firms are attempting to make the cash flows stable. This endeavour, therefore, must stand good for the investors in the firm. It is likely to result in better valuation of the firms. The firms that do not manage exchange rate risk face rather volatile cash flows, which cannot be a positive factor for valuation of the firm. Not only shareholders but lenders too

[1]This section is based on discussions by Jeff Madura; *International Financial Management*.

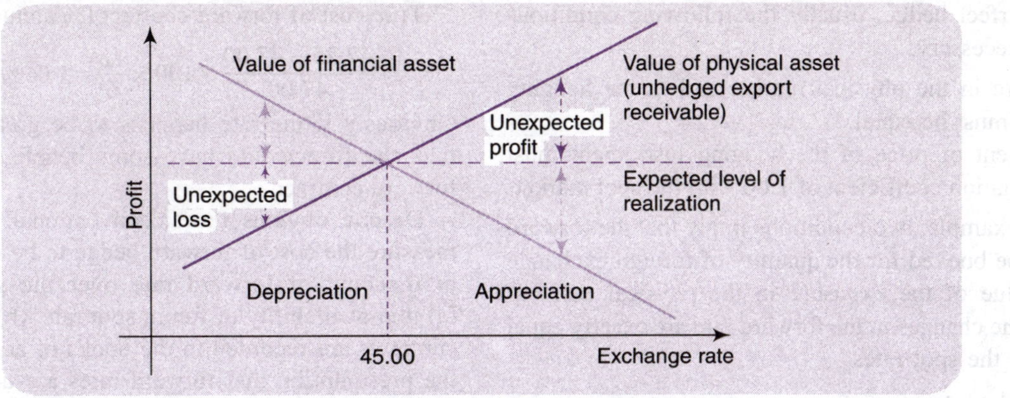

Figure 27-1 Perfect hedging

view the firms that manage risk more positively and lend cheaper, causing cost of capital to be lower, benefiting all stakeholders in the firm.

The arguments for irrelevance of managing foreign exchange risk assume efficient markets. The assumption needs to be tested; and as long as the markets remain inefficient, the need for hedging remains. In fact, the availability and use of hedging instruments would make markets more efficient rather than their absence.

CONCEPT OF HEDGING

Having established the need for managing transaction exposure one needs to understand the concept of hedging. The risk faced by the transactions denominated in the foreign currency emanates from likely adverse movement of exchange rates. Exporters fear depreciation of foreign currency for the receivables, while importers are concerned about appreciation of the foreign currency for the payables. Their concern is uncertainty or deviations of the planned cash inflow or outflow when the receivable or payable matures.

Hedging is a concept that renders stability to the cash flows. Some of us may have a belief that hedging improves profit by improving the cash flows. It is an extremely misplaced notion. Hedging in fact has a cost, and hence profits could be lower compared to the firm that does no hedging. A firm that does not hedge assumes risk of adverse movement of exchange rates. If exchange rates move favourably, the firm gains unexpected profits. The firms that hedge their foreign currency exposures assume no risk of incurring unexpected loses, but at the same time also forego the potential for making unexpected profits.

Hedging against the adverse movement of foreign exchange rates is done by taking a position in a financial asset that is equivalent and opposite to the exposure in the physical asset. The unexpected losses due to adverse movement in the position of physical asset are covered by equivalent unexpected profits in the position taken in the financial asset chosen for hedging. Similarly if profit is made in the physical asset, the hedging instrument would incur equivalent loss to keep the position unchanged. An example would facilitate better understanding.

Forward hedge Consider an exporter has an exposure in foreign currency having sent goods worth US $1,000 on credit. The expected realization is at ₹45 per $. If dollar appreciates to, say ₹46, he would have an unexpected profit of ₹1,000; while if it depreciates to say ₹43.50, the unexpected loss is ₹1,500. Now let us suppose that the exporter uses forward contract as hedging mechanism. He sells the receivable forward at a rate of ₹45. Having sold the receivable forward at ₹45.00, a notional profit or loss would result depending upon the rate prevailing at the time of maturity of the forward contract when the forward sell contract is deemed extinguished by notional purchase of the equivalent quantity of foreign exchange.

The graphical position of portfolio comprising the asset and the hedging instrument (a forward contract) is depicted in Figure 27-1. Notice that the net realization is pegged at ₹45 per $; the contemplated figure irrespective of what happens to the exchange rate at the time of realization. Table 27-1 shows that the profit or loss from the contemplated realization is completely offset by the equivalent loss or profit on the position taken in the hedging instrument; the forward contract. Such a situation where the hedging instrument completely offsets the gain or loss is referred as *perfect hedging*. Forward contract is one such instrument that results in a perfect hedge.

Table 27-1 Perfect hedging

	Amount in US $	Exposure at current rate of ₹ 45/$	$ appreciates to ₹ 46	$ depreciates to ₹ 43.50
Position in the financial Asset	1,000	+45,000	+1,000	–1,500
Position in the Forward Contract	1,000	–45,000	–1,000	+1,500
Net Position		0	0	0

To have a perfect hedge, usually the following conditions are considered necessary:

1. The exposure in the physical market and in the hedging instruments must be equal.
2. The movement of price of the hedging instrument must have a correlation coefficient of 1.00 with the spot market.

In the above example, two conditions imply that the forward contract would be booked for the quantity of foreign exchange equal to the value of the exposure in the physical asset of receivable, and the changes in the forward rate are exactly equal to the change in the spot rates.

Cost of forward hedge As stated earlier, hedging through forward contract provides stability to the cash flows rather than increasing them. By hedging through forward contract, the firm foregoes the benefits that may accrue due to favourable movement of exchange rates while protecting against the losses due to unfavourable movements. This is an implicit cost of forward contract.

The cost of forward hedge is gauged by forward premium or discount over the spot rates.

The explicit cost of the forward contract is often taken as the premium or the discount the forward rate has over the spot rate. The annualized % premium or discount of forward rate is determined as follows:

Cost of forward contract

= Premium(+)/discount(–)% annualized on forward contract

$$= \frac{F_1 - S_0}{S_0} \times 100 \times \frac{12}{\text{forward contract period in months}}$$

where F_1 denotes the forward rate for period '1', S_0 is the current spot rate.

If the 6-m forward rate and spot rate are ₹47.25 per \$ and ₹45.00 per \$ the cost of forward hedge would be 10%; equal to the forward premium as shown below:

Cost of forward contract

= Premium(+)/discount(–)% annualized on forward contract

$$= \frac{47.25 - 45.00}{45.00} \times 100 \times \frac{12}{6} = 10\%$$

Is it the true cost of hedging? The answer is no, because the effectiveness of the forward hedge must be judged not from the current spot rate but from the actual spot rate at the time when the forward contract matures. Effectively it means that the cost of the forward contract must be gauged from what the firm would end up paying/receiving if it had not hedged.

Assuming the spot rate at the time of maturity of the forward contract is S_1, the true cost of forward hedge is given by:

True cost of forward contract (% annualized)

$$= \frac{F_1 - S_1}{S_0} \times 100 \times \frac{12}{\text{forward contract period in months}}$$

If after 6 months the spot rate turns out to be ₹47.00, then the true cost of forward hedge would merely be 1.06% as computed here:

True cost of forward contract (% annualized)

$$= \frac{47.25 - 47.00}{47.00} \times 100 \times \frac{12}{6} = 1.06\%$$

Obviously if the rate happens to be greater than the forward rate, the firm would have some benefit from booking of the forward contract.

Despite obvious flaws, conventionally people continue to measure the cost of forward hedge to be equal to the premium or discount of forward rate over the spot rate because of (a) non-availability of future spot rate, (b) the way the forward contracts are recorded in the books of accounts, and (c) under the presumption that forward rates are unbiased predictors of future spot rate.

TOOLS FOR MANAGING TRANSACTION EXPOSURE

Hedging through various financial instruments available is referred to as *tactical hedging*. It deals with the specific transactions, the resulting exposures from these transactions, and the ways to manage it. Various financial instruments are available to cover the exchange rate risk.

Since hedging has a cost associated with it, most firms do not hedge all exposures and all transactions. To save cost, most firms resort to selective hedging, i.e., hedge only those transactions that are deemed risky to the cash flows. The rules for selective hedging are simple. The question of whether to hedge or keep the position exposed depends upon the perception and likely movement of the exchange rates over the period of exposure.

Given a unidirectional trend in the exchange rate movement, as has been the case with India till recent past, the need for hedging had been rather low. Hedging makes more sense when there is an even chance of movement of exchange rate in either direction. The predictability of the direction of movement is crucial to the decision to hedge. For example if dollar were appreciating all the time in the past, the exporter does not face the risk of receiving lesser than the spot rate. If the plan is based on spot rate, the exporter may not feel the need to hedge the receivable. On the contrary, if the exchange rates were fluctuating either way, then the risk of realizing lesser than the spot rate becomes a distinct possibility and may prompt the exporter to hedge.

Since hedging has a cost it is appropriate for firms to manage transaction on selective basis rather than covering all transactions.

Another situation that warrants hedging is the disagreement of the firm with the market about the forecast of foreign exchange rates at the time of maturity. Consider, for example, an exporter expecting a receivable in 90 days. A 90-day forward contract at ₹46 per \$ is offered and the exporter believes that the spot rate after 90 days would be less than ₹46; the forward contract rate. Sensing an opportunity to get extra money, the exporter may decide to book the forward contract. Though the exporter has an underlying trade transaction to support the forward contract, essentially the decision to book the forward contract is partly motivated by speculation. Similarly, few traders may underbook or overbook a hedging position as compared to the exposure in the physical asset/liability. They too can be motivated by the desire to speculate.

In general, the principle of selective hedging for forward contract would be as follows:

For Accounts Receivable:

Depreciating local currency (Appreciating foreign currency) **(Do not Hedge)**

Appreciating local currency (Depreciating foreign currency) **(Sell Forward)**

For Accounts Payable:

Depreciating local currency (Appreciating foreign currency) **(Buy Forward)**

Appreciating local currency (Depreciating foreign currency) **(Do not Hedge)**

Forward Hedge

Hedging receivable through forward contract The mechanism of hedging through forward contract can be explained through a simple example. Consider a firm expecting a receivable denominated as US $10,000 to mature after 6 months. The current spot rate is ₹45 per $. Assume that 6-m forward contract is available at ₹43.00 per $. The forward rate suggests depreciating $ and appreciating rupee. The firm faces two choices;

Option 1: To sell the receivable forward and assure itself of firm realization at ₹43 per $; or

Option 2: Leave the exposure unhedged and convert the receivable in local currency at whatever spot rate prevailing at maturity. It may decide to do so if it believes that the spot rate would be higher than the forward rate of ₹43.

Under Option 1, the firm would be insulated from the vagaries of foreign exchange market. It would end up realizing the same amount for the receivable irrespective of the spot rates prevailing then. Under Option 2, where the position is exposed, the firm stands to gain as much as it stands to lose. This is depicted in Table 27-2 under different scenarios of spot rate at the time of realization of receivables (assumed to coincide with maturity of forward contract). Note that when hedged through forward contract, the firm would be:

(i) better off if the spot rate turns out to be lower than the forward rate,

(ii) indifferent if the spot rate is equal to the forward rate, and

(iii) worse off if the spot rate is higher than the forward rate.

Hedging payable through forward contract The mechanism of hedging payable through forward contract is same as that of receivable. Consider the same firm now with a payable denominated as US $10,000 to mature after 6 months. Assume the same current spot rate of ₹45 per $ but now the 6-m forward contract is ₹47.00 per $. The forward rate suggests appreciating $ and depreciating rupee. The firm again faces two choices;

Option 1: To buy a forward contract at ₹47.00 and assure itself of a fixed liability at ₹47 per $; or

Option 2: Leave the exposure unhedged and buy $ spot at whatever rate prevailing at the time when payable becomes due. It may decide to do so if it believes that the spot rate would be lower than the forward rate of ₹47.

The position of importer is depicted in Table 27-3 under different scenarios of spot rate at the time of maturity of liability (assumed to coincide with maturity of forward contract). Note that when hedged through forward contract, the firm would be:

Table 27-2 Hedging receivable with forward contract

Spot rate at the time of realization and maturity of forward contract	*Option 1: Firms sells forward at ₹ 43.00 (Amount realized)*	*Option 2: Firm does not sell forward (Amount realized)*
42.22	₹ 43,000	₹ 42,220
43.00	₹ 43,000	₹ 43,000
44.10	₹ 43,000	₹ 44,100
Outcome	**Amount of realization is certain and independent of spot rate**	**Cash inflow varies depending upon the spot rate and firm makes unexpected gains or losses.**

Table 27-3 Hedging payable with forward contract

Spot rate at the time of realization and maturity of forward contract	*Option 1: Firms buys forward at ₹ 47.00 (Amount paid)*	*Option 2: Firms deos not buy forward (Amount paid)*
46.25	₹ 47,000	₹ 46,250
47.00	₹ 47,000	₹ 47,000
48.40	₹ 47,000	₹ 48,400
Outcome	**Amount of realization is certain and independent of spot rate**	**Cash inflow varies depending upon the spot rate and firm makes unexpected gains or losses**

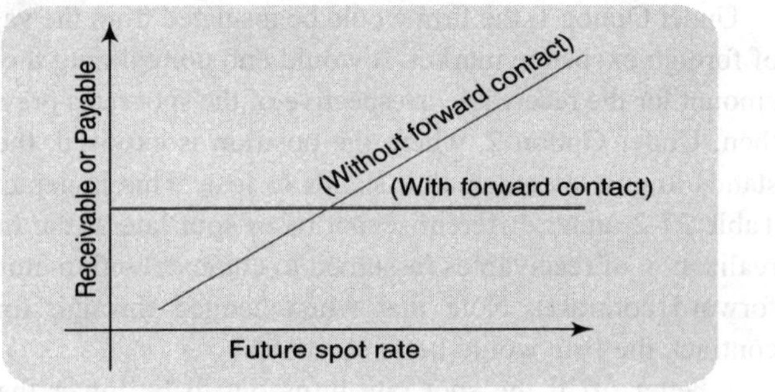

Figure 27-2 Forward hedge

(iv) worse off if the spot rate turns out to be lower than the forward rate,
(v) indifferent if the spot rate is equal to the forward rate, and
(vi) better off if the spot rate is higher than the forward rate.

A graphical view of the forward hedge as compared to the unhedged position can be had from Figure 27-2, which shows constancy of value of receivable or payable when forward contract is booked, and linear variation in the value with respect to the future spot exchange rate.

Forward contract fixes the value of asset or liability at the time of booking the contract in domestic currency.

Under both the transactions of receivable and payable, apart from two choices of booking and not booking a forward contract, the firm also faced a decision with respect to the value of the forward contract. The value of forward contract may differ from the value of the financial transaction. In such a situation, hedging is coupled with the speculative motive where the firms takes a view on the future spot rate and compares with the forward rate prevailing.

Money market hedge

An alternative mechanism for covering foreign exchange exposure of either receivable or payable is available that does not use forward market at all. Firms can make an assessment about the money markets prevailing in two currencies involved and take a decision to borrow in one currency, and invest in another by converting spot. Of course, we assume that borrowing and investing in the currencies are readily available options in the two countries. As would be seen, such a mechanism would enable lock-in a firm rate for receivable or payable. We illustrate this with an example each on receivable and payable.

Money market hedge uses the spot market and the money markets of two currencies to synthesize a forward rate.

Money market hedge for receivable Assume a firm has €1,000 receivable after 6 months. The spot rate is ₹58 per €. Also assume that the firm is free to borrow and invest in rupees as well as euro. The interest rates are 10% and 6% for euro and rupee respectively. The interest rate structure indicates depreciating euro and appreciating rupee.

Money market hedge for receivable requires borrowing in foreign currency, converting spot and investing in local currency.

To set up a money market hedge, the firm must do the following 3 steps today:

1. *Borrow foreign currency* Borrow euro at 10% so that the maturity value of the borrowing after 6 months is €1,000. The amount borrowed is €1,000/1.05 = 952.38. By doing so, the assets and liabilities stand matched at the date of maturity of receivable and loan, and the liability becomes self-liquidating.
2. *Convert borrowing in local currency* Convert in rupees spot to realize ₹58.00 × 952.38 = ₹55,238.09.
3. *Invest in local market* Invest for 6 months at 8% to have the maturity value = ₹55,238.09 × 1.04 = ₹57,447.62

After 6 months, the loans raised in euro would be liquidated by the receivable as both mature at the same time, and the matured value of invested rupees is deemed as realization of receivable. To arrive at the effective rate of realization, the matured value of the invested rupee is divided by the amount of receivable. Therefore, the effective rate of realization works out to ₹57.4776 per €.

The operations with money markets of the two currencies and the spot market of foreign currency provide all the cash flows with certainty at the time of exposure and therefore work as a hedge. Note that money market hedge does not use the forward market for assured cash flows, but in a way synthesizes a rate that otherwise could be considered equivalent to the forward rate. Reverting to interest rate parity, it can be stated that the interest rate structure indicates depreciating euro and appreciating rupee. It is presumed that the forward markets would reflect the same exchange rate as synthesized using money markets and spot markets.

The steps of money market hedge for receivable are depicted in Figure 27-3.

Money market hedge for payable To understand the mechanism of money market hedge for payable let us consider the firm now has a 6 month payable of €10,000. Assuming the spot rate same as before at ₹58 per €. However now we consider interest rates in rupee at 10% and that of euro at 8%. The interest rate structure in the two currency suggests appreciation of euro and hence the desire for the firm to hedge.

Money market hedge for payables requires borrowing in local currency, converting spot and investing in foreign currency.

To set up a money market hedge for the payable the firm must do the similar steps as for money market hedge for receivable, with currency of borrowing and investing becoming different. The chronological steps would be:

1. *Borrow local currency* Borrow rupees at 8% such that after conversion to foreign currency and investing the same for the period of payable the amount matches the value of payable.
2. *Convert borrowing in foreign currency* Convert the borrowed rupees to euros in the spot market at the prevailing rate.
3. *Invest in foreign currency market* Invest euros for 6 months at prevailing interest rate to have the maturity value that matches with the value of the payable.

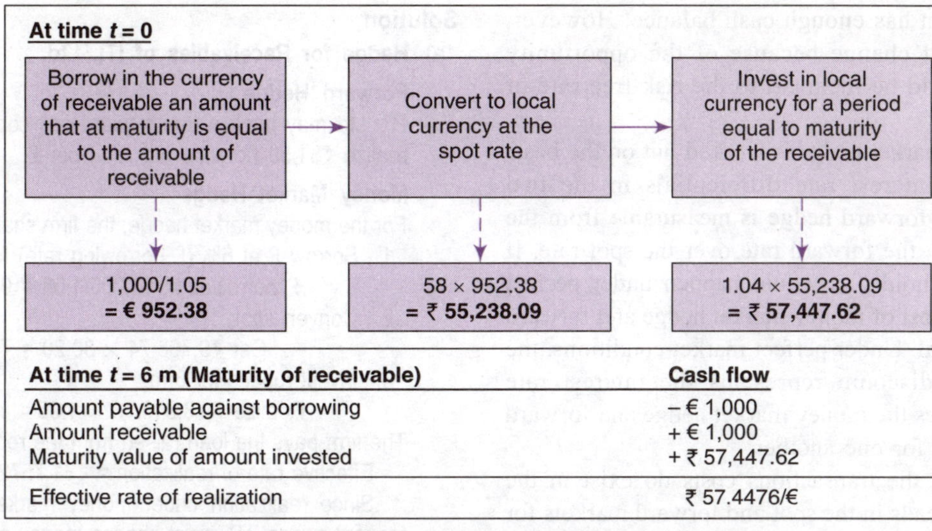

Figure 27-3 Mechanism of money market hedge—receivable

However the calculation of the amount to be borrowed would be opposite to the chronology of the steps. We calculate the amount as follows:

Amount of payable required after 6 months	€10,000.00
Amount of euro required today if invested at 8% euro; 10,000/1.04	€9,615.38
Amount of rupee required to be borrowed today at spot rate; 58.00 × 9615.38	₹5,57,692.31
Maturity amount of the rupee borrowed; ₹1.05 × 5,57,692.31	₹5,85,576.92

After 6 months the loans raised in rupee would service the payable. To arrive at the effective rate for the payable the cash flows of rupee and euro must be valued at the same point of time to account for the time value of money. The effective exchange rate paid is:

₹5,85,576.92/€10,000 = ₹58.5576/€

Again note that while setting up the money market hedge all the determinants of the cash flows i.e., amount of payable, period of investing, amount to be borrowed are known with certainty. Again the money market hedge does not use the forward market for assured cash flows but in a way synthesizes a rate that otherwise could be considered equivalent to the forward rate. The steps of money market hedge for payable are depicted in Figure 27-4.

Comparing Money Market Hedge and Forward Hedge

We have seen both in the money market hedge for receivable and payable, the firm can use the money markets in two currencies and the spot markets to crystallize the exchange rate at the time of creation of exposure. Alternatively, the firm could use the forward market to achieve the same objective of removing uncertainty of the cash flow at the time of maturity of receivable or payable.

It would be interesting to note the differences in the ways the forward and money market hedge work. Money market hedge essentially is a loan contract. We borrow in one currency and invest in another. The borrowing can be substituted by the

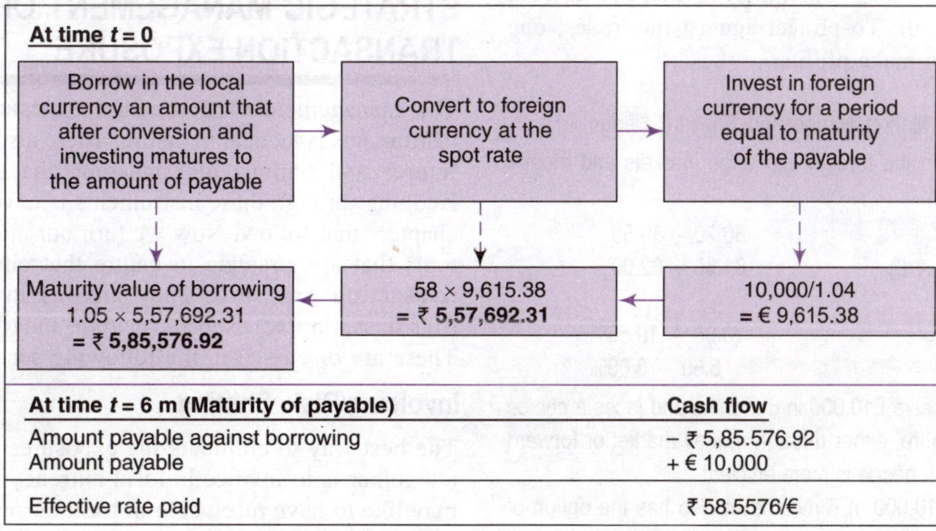

Figure 27-4 Mechanism of money market hedge—payable

owned funds if the firm has enough cash balance. However, the logic still does not change because of the opportunity cost of own funds would be identical to the risk free rate of borrowing.

The cost of money market hedge is worked out on the basis of spot rate and the interest rate differentials in the two currencies. The cost of forward hedge is measurable from the premium or discount on the forward rate over the spot rate. If the interest rate parity holds, as would happen under perfect market conditions, the cost of money market hedge and forward hedge would be identical. Under perfect market conditions, the forward premium or discount represents the interest rate differential, which makes the money market hedge and forward hedge exact substitutes for one another.

However, in reality, the transactions costs do exist in the form of bid and ask spreads in the spot and forward markets for foreign exchange, and different rates for borrowing and lending in the money markets of the two currencies. This generally makes one of the hedges more efficient than the other. Therefore, managers of the firm have two options to choose from and are required to evaluate both forward hedge and money market hedge. The one that provides better cash flows is preferred. Example 27-1 compares the two.

Due to presence of the transaction costs either of the forward hedge or money market hedge would be more economical.

Since money market is a home-made forward rate, it may be compared with the relevant forward rate for making a decision in favour of one of the hedges. The rule for selection of hedge is simple and stated below:

For receivable: Choose the hedge that gives higher rate

For payable: Choose the hedge that gives lower rate

While the effectiveness of the two hedges can be compared with respect to cost of each, the comparison of hedged position with the unhedged position cannot be made till the period of exposure ends and the spot rate at maturity of payable/receivable becomes known. Unhedged position carries risk to the extent of volatility in the exchange rates, both money market and forward hedge entail no risk at all. To protect against the losses, one foregoes the potential to make profits.

Example 27-1 Money Market Hedge and Forward Hedge

Following scenario exists in the foreign exchange markets and money markets in India and Britain:

Spot Rate (₹/£)	:	80.20 – 80.50
6-m Forward Rate (₹/£)	:	81.50 – 82.00
Interest Rates		
₹	:	10.00 – 10.50%
£	:	5.50 – 6.00%

(a) ITL Ltd expects to receive £10,000 in 6 months and faces a choice of covering the exposure, either through money market or forward market. Find out which hedge is more efficient.

(b) IPL Ltd has to pay £10,000 in 6 months. It also has the option of covering the exposure, either through money market or forward market. Find out which hedge is more efficient.

Solution

(a) **Hedge for Receivables of ITL Ltd**

Forward Hedge

ITL Ltd may book a 6-m forward sell contract for receivable and realize ₹81.50 (forward bid rate) per £.

Money Market Hedge

For the money market hedge, the firm shall take following steps:

1. Borrow £ at 6% (£ borrowing rate) for 6 m:
   £ borrowed = 10,000/1.03 = 9,708.74
2. Convert spot:
   Get ₹9,708.74 × 80.20 = 7,78,640.78
3. Invest rupees for 6 m:
   Realize 7,78,640.78 × 1.05 = 8,17,572.81

The firm pays the loan raised from the receivable.

Effective rate of realization = ₹81.7572 (higher than forward)

Since realization under money market hedge is higher than forward hedge, ITL must choose money market hedge.

(b) **Hedge for Payables of IPL Ltd**

Forward Hedge

IPL Ltd may book a 6-m forward buy contract for payable and undertake to pay ₹82.00 per £ (forward ask rate).

Money Market Hedge

For the money market hedge, the firm shall take following steps:

1. Borrow ₹ at 10.50% (the borrowing rate for rupee).
2. Convert spot to £ at spot ask rate.
3. Invest £ at 5.50% (£ investing rate) for 6 m.

Investment required today	= £10,000/1.0275 = £9,732.36
Equivalent rupees needed today	= 80.50 × 9,732.36
	= ₹7,83,454.99
Value of rupee borrowed after 6 months	= 1.0525 × 7,83,454.99
	= ₹8,24,586.37
Effective rate of payment	= ₹82.4586 (higher than forward)

Since payment under money market hedge is higher than forward hedge, IPL must choose forward hedge.

STRATEGIC MANAGEMENT OF TRANSACTION EXPOSURE

The management of transaction exposure with the financial instruments is tactical in nature. There also exist other tools like futures and options for managing the transaction exposure. Hedging through these instruments is covered in the respective chapters that follow. Now we turn our attention to some of the tools that are strategic in nature that eliminate or reduce the transaction exposure. They are (a) invoicing/risk shifting (b) risk sharing, (c) exposure netting, and (d) leading and lagging. These are discussed in the following section.

Invoicing/Risk Shifting

The best way to eliminate the exposures from the transactions altogether is to invoice in local currency. An exporter in India may like to have receivable in local currency and eliminate the necessity of shopping for instruments of hedging the foreign currency risk. In such a case, the cash flows on the firm would become immune to the exchange rate fluctuations as both cost and revenue are denominated in local currency. Exports would be just like the domestic sale. Similarly, an importing firm may ask its suppliers to invoice in importer's home currency ensuring a bottom line independent of foreign exchange rate fluctuations.

Invoicing in local currency protects one party but exposes the counter-party to the equivalent risk. For example, an Indian car producer importing engines may negotiate a contract with a German supplier on deferred payment basis in Indian rupee rather than euro. By such a contract, the Indian car manufacturer completely avoids the risk from the foreign exchange markets as all its procurement is now in Indian currency. However, the German supplier receiving payment in Indian rupee has to convert into euro. It has to undergo all that which the Indian firm would have if the invoicing were in euro. In effect, the risk shifts from one party to another. If the supplies are denominated in euro, the risk is borne by Indian firm and otherwise by German supplier when denominated in rupee.

The best way to eliminate the transaction exposure is to make and accept invoices only in local currency. The risk passes to the counter-party to the transaction.

Is such a strategy advisable or does it result in savings of cost of hedging? Though it may appear as if the hedging cost is avoided; but in reality the answer is no unfortunately, if the markets are competitive. Assuming that neither the importer nor the exporter has an upper hand in dealing with each other and both are knowledgeable enough about the vagaries of foreign exchange market, it is immaterial who bears the risk of foreign exchange exposure. Just as we know that asking for credit from the supplier translates into increased price or foregoing the cash discount; similarly in foreign exchange transactions, the party assuming the foreign currency risk incorporates the risk in the increased price. Increased price is compensation for the risk assumed which otherwise could be assumed by the counter-party, who foregoes the advantage of reduced price.

However, in practice, the two contracting parties are never on equal footing. The needs and the positions of two parties are always different making negotiations of price and terms of the contract favouring the stronger party.

Spot vs Forward Rate Irrespective of who dominates the negotiation of price and other terms of the contract, a caution is in order. The conversion of one currency into another is not a simple case of multiplication of the current exchange rate. It is fraught with risk. We illustrate this with an example.

Assume that an Indian supplier, as matter of policy, denominates its exports in Indian currency only and avoids any risk of foreign exchange fluctuations. It is negotiating a high value order for supplies on 6 months credit to a buyer in Singapore. The price agreed is ₹1,000 per piece. Upon insistence by the buyer in Singapore, the Indian firm agrees to invoice the goods in Singapore dollar (SG $). In complete ignorance of how the financial markets operate, oblivious of the anticipated depreciation of SG $, and in the enthusiasm of procuring an all important order; the marketing manager converts the quotation from Indian rupee price of ₹ 1,000 to SG $40 using the current spot rate of ₹25 per SG $. By doing so, the firm has inadvertently assumed the risk of foreign exchange. As anticipated, the SG $ depreciates to ₹23 in 6 months; the time of realization of sale. It finds itself receiving ₹920 instead of ₹1,000; ₹80 short of what it would have realized if only the goods were invoiced in accordance with the existing policy.

While negotiating credit terms, it must be borne in mind to use the forward rate and not the spot rate as basis of negotiation of price.

Using spot rate to convert the currency of invoicing is a common mistake made in negotiations of the price. Foreign exchange rates fluctuate with time. If one is unmindful of the mismatch of timing of exchange rate and cash flow, it results in transaction exposure. In the instant case the marketing manager must use forward rate while converting the quotation from one currency to another.

In financial terms, it amounts to booking of the forward contract at the time of invoicing protecting the cash flow in local currency as indicated in Table 27-5. If the forward rate is used for converting the price into another currency, the price quoted would be SG $43.48; and if the forward actually turns out to be the spot rate at the time of maturity of the receivable, the sum realized would be ₹1,000.

Risk Sharing

In contrast to invoicing in one currency where the entire risk of foreign exchange exposure shifts from one party to another, an alternate and more acceptable way is to have some price adjustment clause in the contract where the risk of exchange rate fluctuations of each party is specified and shared.

For example, in the example of the previous section, the Indian exporter having agreed to invoice in Singapore dollar carried the entire risk of exchange rate. If it appreciated, the exporter benefited to the extent of appreciation, and lost if it depreciated. For assuming this risk, the exporter was entitled to have a mark-up on the price to compensate for the additional risk. The increase in price would be detrimental to the

Risk sharing is attained through a price adjustment clause that places neither party at extreme disadvantage.

Table 27-5 Risk shifting

	Price (₹)	Conversion Rate (₹/SG $)	Equivalent Price (SG $)	Spot rate at the time of realization	Sum Realized (₹) (₹/SG $)	Variance (₹)
Using Spot rate	1,000.00	25.00	40.00	23.00	920.00	–80.00
Using Forward rate	1,000.00	23.00	43.48	23.00	1,000.00	NIL

buyer importer. Assuming that both the importer and exporter are knowledgeable about the risk being assumed by each party, the situation warrants a fair deal sharing risk rather than a lopsided contract imposing the entire risk on the single party. If such a contract can be devised where position of each party with respect to risk of exchange rate is explicitly stated, then both parties would have no reason to feel aggrieved.

Risk sharing in contrast to risk shifting is recognition of the fact that none of the contracting parties are burdened with the adverse cash flows. One such example of risk sharing is presented below in the context of Indian exporter quoting for the Singapore buyer via a price adjustment clause as shown in Table 27-6 (a).

The price adjustment clause with respect to exchange rate recognizes that:

(a) The risk must be borne by the exporter for the exchange rate within a reasonable range (say from ₹24.50 to ₹25.50).
(b) If Singapore dollar appreciates beyond acceptable limit, the exporter who would lose otherwise should be allowed a 50% compensation by adjusting the price upwards to the extent of amount of decrease from the lower exchange rate.
(c) If Singapore dollar depreciates beyond acceptable limit to the benefit of the exporter, a partial amount must be passed on to the buyer by adjusting the price downwards to the extent of amount of increase from the higher exchange rate.

For each situation, the cash flow for Indian exporter is shown in Table 27-6(b).

Risk sharing by incorporating a price adjustment clause divides the risk between two contracting parties as is shown in Figure 27-5, where within a limited range of exchange rate movement, the risk is borne by the exporter; and outside the acceptable band, the risk is partly borne by the exporter and partly by the importer as indicated with dotted lines of reduced slope when the exchange rate is beyond acceptable limits. Without the price adjustment, the value of the receivables varies linearly with the exchange rate as shown with the dark line in Figure 27-5.

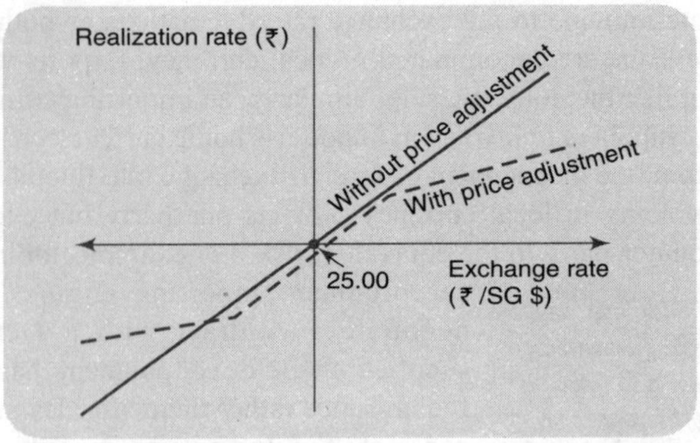

Figure 27.5 Risk sharing for exporter

Range forward Independent of negotiations between the two contracting parties regarding risk sharing, a somewhat similar outcome can be achieved through financial markets. An instrument called *range forward* is available where the buyer of the contract can contain extreme losses by assuming part of the risk of fluctuations of foreign exchange rates.

Range forward is a financial instrument that accomplishes the same objective as that of price adjustment clause as risk-sharing mechanism.

Under forward contract, an exporter would freeze the realization rate independent of the spot rate prevailing at the time of maturity of receivable. The same principle holds good for an importer who freezes the value of the liability. In a contract of range forward, the value of asset or liability is not completely independent of the spot rate on the maturity of the contract. For some acceptable rage of foreign exchange rate, the importer/exporter assumes risk and books the receivable or payable at the actual rate prevailing at the time of maturity. For wilder movement he protects.

In the context of the example of Indian exporter, a range forward could work as shown in Table 27-7.

Table 27-6(a) Risk sharing through price adjustment

Event	*Exchange Rate*	*Adjusted Price*
SG $ appreciates beyond acceptable limit	Less than ₹ 24.50/SG $	SG $ 40.00 + ½(24.50 – S_1)
SG $ remains within the acceptable limits	Between ₹ 24.50 to ₹ 25.50/SG $	SG $ 40.00
SG $ depreciates beyond the acceptable limits	More than ₹ 25.50/SG $	SG $ 40.00 – ½(S_1 – 25.50)

Table 27-6(b) Risk sharing through price adjustment

Event	*Exchange Rate (₹/SG $)*	*Adjusted Price (SG $)*	*Amount Realized (₹)*	*Amount w/o Price adjustment*
SG $ appreciates beyond acceptable limit	23.50	40.00 + ½(24.50 – S_1) = 40.50	951.75	940.00
SG $ remains within the acceptable limits	25.00	40.00	1,000.00	1,000.00
SG $ depreciates beyond the acceptable limits	26.50	40.00 – ½(S_1 – 25.50) = 39.50	1,046.75	1060.00

Table 27-7 Range forward

Event	*Exchange rate*	*Value of receivable*
SG $ appreciates beyond acceptable limit	Less than ₹24.50/SG $	₹24.50/SG $
SG $ remains within the acceptable limits	Between ₹24.50 to ₹25.50/SG $	Actual Rate
SG $ depreciates beyond the acceptable limits	More than ₹25.50/SG $	₹25.50/SG $

The exporter is prepared to bear some risk when the exchange rate remains, say within a range of ₹24.50 to ₹25.50 per SG $. When SG $ depreciates below ₹24.50, the exporter realizes ₹24.50; and when it appreciates above ₹ 25.50, he realizes no more than ₹25.50 for his receivable. The value of receivables change linearly with exchange rate within a limited range. It has a floor (the minimum that would be realized) and a cap (the maximum rate that would be realized) as shown in Figure 27-6. Such an instrument is known as *range forward.*

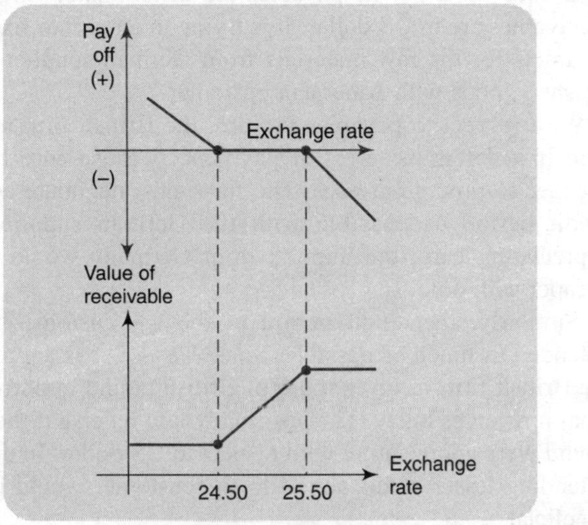

Figure 27-6 Range forward

As we know, forward contract has a cost. Also the buyer of forward contract foregoes the potential of making profit in order to protect the losses. The range forward would be more economical as compared to a forward contract because the buyer of the range forward contract assumes some risk in an acceptable range.

Natural Hedge and Exposure Netting

When a firm has simultaneous and equivalent positions in the receivable and payable, the currency rate movements do not impact the aggregate cash flows of the firm. Assume a rather unlikely situation of a firm that has a receivable and a payable of the same amount of €10,000, both maturing exactly on the same dates. Does the firm face a currency exposure or risk of the exchange rate movement? Clearly the answer is no as what is adverse for receivable becomes favourable for payable and *vice versa*. The loss and gain compensate each other. Such a situation where asset and liabilities match in terms of amount of exposure and timing of maturities is referred as *natural hedge.* Receivable protects payable and payable protects receivable. Under such cases, no instrument is required for hedging the exposures.

Receivable and payable in same currency provide a natural hedge due to offsetting effect, and hence may be netted.

Complete natural hedge is rather rare in any firm. Except for very large multinational firms having worldwide operations and dealings in many currencies, most firms either remain largely exporter or importer, but not both. Even if the firm happens to be an exporter as well as an importer, the natural hedge is difficult to achieve. Either the amounts or the maturities of receivable and payable differ.

Even when timing, amount, and currencies of exposure differ, the principle of netting can still be used beneficially. Though there would not be complete offsetting, but partial benefits can be materialized, either by reduction of amount or reduction of duration of exposure. Consider a situation of same timing and same currency but different amounts. For example, if a firm has 90-day receivable of US $10,000 and a 90-day payable of US $5,000, we may say that natural hedge is available for US $5,000 only (lower than the amount of exposure). It would be wrong to assume an exposure of US $15,000 and wastefully book two different contracts for covering a risk of US $10,000 receivable and US $5,000 payable, because the impact on cash flows is not in the same direction for receivable and payable. The firm can save a substantial cost by covering only the remaining US $5,000 receivable for exchange rate risk and yet achieve the objective of hedging.

Similarly, netting can be done for different timings of receivable and payable. Assume a firm has 90-day receivable and 45-day payable of US $10,000 each and books separate forward contracts for both. The cost of hedging is proportional to the period of exposure. The firm incurs hedging cost for a period of 135 days for an exposure of US $20,000. Alternatively, the firm can take a view that increased liability of payable up to 45 days would be matched notionally by increased value of receivable though not realized and hence is not considered a risk. The exposure carried by the firm is for the later 45 days of receivable and should be hedged. This way, the firm incurs cost only for 45 days for US $10,000. The effectiveness of such netting on time basis is dependent upon the volatility in the foreign currency market. However, it provides the benefit of availability of information at the end of first 45-day period, which should be more certain than what is available 90 days before.

The third situation arises when the currency of exposures are different. Can we use netting in such cases? The answer is in the affirmative if there exists a relationship in the exchange rates of two currencies. For example, a firm in India may have a receivable of US $10,000 and a payable of €8,000. At current exchange rate of US $1.25 per euro, the exposures are equivalent and opposite. If both the exposures are treated differently, which shall be the case when the firm is unmindful of the relationship of the two currencies, the firm may book two separate forward contracts for US $10,000 receivable and €8,000 payable. This may represent an avoidable cost. The firm needs to adopt a portfolio approach to the exposures in various currencies where not only the movements in rates of individual currencies are relevant, but the inter-relationships of various currencies also assume significance. A study of the inter-relationship would result in saving of costs of hedging. If movement of US dollar and euro with respect to rupee have perfect and positive correlation, then the exposure in euro is no different than that of US dollar and vice versa. A 5% change in US dollar receivable also implies a 5% change in euro payable. The exposures in US dollar and euro provide a natural hedge. The net exposure would be limited to the extent the movement in US dollar and euro differ and do not offset each other.

Note that in case of negative correlation of exchange rate movements of the two currencies, the receivables alone or payables alone in two currencies provide the natural hedge. We do not need receivable and payable to offset each other.

To implement exposure netting, centralization is almost a necessity, the need for which can immediately be perceived and requires no explanation.

Cross hedge The concept of *cross hedging* is related with the similarity and dissimilarity of the currencies. Firms may have exposures in currencies where instruments of hedging may not be available. Consider an exposure of a Korean firm having an exposure in Mexican Peso. Ideally, it would like to cover its exposure in Mexican Peso through an instrument specified in terms of Korean Won and Mexican Peso. Assume that the chosen instrument is a forward contract and no such contracts are offered in the financial markets of Korea. However, contracts in US dollar are available. Another fact known to the Korean firm is the strong positive correlation of Mexican Peso with US dollar. Laws permitting the Korean firm can book a forward contract in US dollar and cover its exposure in Mexican Peso. Any depreciation or appreciation of Mexican Peso with Korean Won would be reflected in US dollar; a strongly correlated currency with Mexican Peso. This hedge may not be a perfect hedge because the % change in exchange rates of US $ and Mexican Peso with respect to Korean Won may not be equal.

A cross hedge can be implemented in the currency on which no contract is available through a closely linked currency that offers forward contracts. This is known as cross hedge.

For estimating the effectiveness of cross hedge, one needs to establish the relationship and find a degree of correlation using past data. Greater the value of R^2 (explains the fraction of variation explainable) in the regression, better is the cross hedge. To make the hedge more effective in case of lower degree of correlation, the size of forward contract may be altered (overbook or underbook as the case may be) to offset the losses in the currency of exposure.

Leading and Lagging

Leading and lagging is another managerial strategy that hedges exposures with a policy statement. It manages receivables and payables at macro level rather than attempting to hedge individual transactions. Leading and lagging as a strategy relates to the credit period to be extended to the customers and credit period to be availed from creditors while taking into account the likely movement of exchange rates.

Leading and lagging receivables and payables relate to advancing and deferring of the cash flow depending upon the likely movement of exchange rates.

Consider an example where a British firm believes that British pound would strengthen against euro and weaken against US dollar. Assume that the firm procures from Germany and supplies its product to USA. Its payables are denominated in euro and receivables are in US dollar. It is trying to enter into fixed price contracts for the raw materials from German supplier and for finished goods with American customer.

With respect to payables in euro, the British firm stands to gain if it defers its terms of payment, because euro becomes cheaper as time progresses. The firm must negotiate as long a credit period as possible with the German supplier. With depreciating euro, the imports from Germany would become cheaper with time.

Similarly, the credit period to the US customer may be extended as much as possible. Since US dollar is appreciating, the British firm receives more of British pound tomorrow than what it receives today. The position would reverse if the British pound were appreciating with respect to US dollar. In that case, extending lesser credit period to the customer would be more beneficial.

Advancing the cash flow is called *leading* and deferring the cash flow is referred as *lagging*. The rules for leading and lagging the receivables and payables are based on principle of: (a) receive as much as possible and (b) pay as low as possible. These are summarized below:

If the foreign currency is appreciating:

Lead the payable
Lag the receivable

If the foreign currency is depreciating:

Lag the payable
Lead the receivable

ECONOMIC EXPOSURE

Economic exposure is concerned with impact of changes in exchange rates on the cash flows of the firm on an aggregate basis rather than for individual transactions. Multinational corporations and firms whose inputs and/or outputs are largely denominated in foreign currency are more susceptible to the exchange rate movements as compared to the firms dealing purely in the domestic markets. For example, most firms in India in the area of information technology and software development

The impact of changes in the aggregate cash flows due to change in the exchange rate is referred as economic exposure.

are export oriented, and cash flows and profits are critically dependent on the exchange rates. Similarly, firms in petroleum sector depend too much on imports of oil, again denominated mostly in US dollar. The cash flows in such firms are heavily dependent on the exchange rate, and hence the value of the firm.

The value of the firms—as reflected in its stock price—takes into account the changes in the competitive position of the firm. All firms face competition from within the country and from outside world. For example, compare an automobile manufacturer who produces cars with all domestic resources, with the firm who imports entirely. Due to depreciation of foreign currency, the cars supplied by importers would become cheaper adversely affecting the cash flows in terms of revenue as well as profits of the local firm. As a result, the value of the firm would decline affecting its shareholders. The loss in value has resulted despite the firm not having undertaken any transaction denominated in foreign currency, yet it results in change in its competitive position. Therefore, even in the absence of transaction exposure, the stakeholders of the firm—particularly the shareholders—are not insulated from the happenings in the foreign currency markets. This change in competitive position of the firm due to exchange rate changes is referred as economic exposure.

With the appreciation of local currency, the firm faces increased competition from foreign products because imports become cheaper. Both local sales and export sales, if any, of the local firms are expected to decline. Similarly, inputs of the local firm too would have more competitive import substitutes. If markets for imported inputs are also competitive, the local firm may see a decline in the cost of inputs. The net impact of appreciation of local currency would depend on the level of competitiveness in the markets for finished goods and raw materials. Therefore, the exposure of the firm with respect to foreign currency rates is dependent upon several vastly different factors such as market structures, competitiveness of import substitutes, elasticity of demand, etc.

Similar observations can be made with respect to depreciation of local currency, which makes exports more competitive and imports expensive. Depreciation of local currency would cause foreign competition to reduce. It is likely to result in increased cash inflows, both from local as well as export sales. Cash outflows for procurement of inputs too would increase as domestic prices of the inputs can be raised as prices of imported substitutes rise. Again, the net impact on cash flows becomes specific to the characteristics of the firm, markets, and price elasticities of the products demanded and supplied.

With increased globalization of trade and economics, it is hard to imagine that competitive position of the firms, domestic or multinational corporations, would remain unaffected due to changes in the foreign exchange rates. The changes in values of the foreign currencies reflect the economic happenings around the world as well as the expectations of the economic performance across the globe. The foreign exchange markets behave exactly like stock markets where information keeps flowing on a continuous basis and prices keep on adjusting based on the new information. Though the changes may appear to be random, but they are driven by a complex structure of economies and their dependence on vastly different factors. Therefore, economic exposure is faced by all the firms on a continuous basis, unlike transaction exposure or translation exposure, which occur only when firms undertake transactions denominated in foreign exchange.

MEASURING ECONOMIC EXPOSURE

We defined economic exposure as the impact of the changes in the exchange rates on the competitive position of the firm. The primary determinants of the strength of the firm are its cash flows and its net income. If they undergo a change for any reason, the competitive position of the firm changes.

Scenario Analysis

To measure economic exposure of the firm, we may use the changes in the cash flows of the firm with a likely scenario of exchange rates. A sample of such calculation is presented in Table 27-8. For the purpose of illustration, consider a firm that generates revenue with domestic and export sales and also procures inputs from domestic and foreign markets. For simplicity, consider an exposure of exports and imports in a single currency of US dollar only. The projected cash profit of

Table 27-8 Measuring economic exposure

	Domestic Sale (₹)	*Export Sale ($)*	*Equivalent ₹*	*Total*
Panel 1: Present Forecast at Exchange Rate of ₹45/$				
Sales	2100	20	900	3000
Variable Cost	800	30	1350	2150
Overheads	300	—	—	300
Cash Profit				550
Panel 2: Rupee appreciates to ₹42/$ causing decline in domestic and export sales as well as cost of inputs				
Sales	2000	19	798	2798
Variable Cost	800	28	1176	1976
Overheads	300	—	—	300
Cash Profit				522
Panel 3: Rupee depreciates to ₹47/$ causing decline in domestic and export sales as well as cost of inputs				
Sales	2100	22	1034	3234
Variable Cost	850	32	1504	2354
Overheads	300	—	—	300
Cash Profit				580

₹550 is expected with the current exchange rate of ₹45 per $ as shown in the first panel of Table 27-8. The impact on the cash flow is analysed under two different exchange rate scenarios of rupee appreciating to ₹42 per $ and rupee depreciating to ₹47 per $ depicted respectively in Panels 2 and 3 of Table 27-8. Both the cases have some impact on domestic sales and purchases too due to changing competitive position in the foreign markets of inputs and outputs.

A glance at Table 27-8 would reveal that an appreciation of domestic currency of rupee by about 6.67% would make cash flow of the firm fall by 28 (550 – 522); a decline of 5.09%. Similarly, a depreciation of the rupee by 4.44% would cause the cash flows of the firm to jump from estimated ₹550 to ₹ 580; a rise of 5.45%. We may conclude that cash flows of the firm are more sensitive and have favourable impact due to depreciation of local currency. The firm has to guard against the unfavourable impact that results from appreciation of local currency.

Market value of the firm—A Proxy to Cash Flow

A scenario analysis establishing the changes in the cash flow position of the firm arising due to changes in the exchange rates presupposes an understanding of the business intricacies of the markets for the finished product and raw material markets the firm deals with. Besides, knowledge of and access to the firm's internal policies are also required to evaluate different scenarios. The task of assessing the economic exposure becomes simpler if a proxy for the cash flows may be used. For traded firms, the suitable proxy is the stock price, assuming that stock price is nothing but the present value of net future cash flows. The stock price changes with changing economic conditions, and therefore must respond to the happenings in the foreign exchange markets. Besides, stock price also truly reflects the change in the competitive position of the firm.

It is extremely difficult to measure economic exposure for those who are outsiders to the firm, even though they are most concerned about the firm's competitive position.

A regression of the past data of stock price with different exchange rates would help establish a relationship and dependence of the firm on the exchange rates. This historical analysis can be used to find the likely stock price with the anticipated rate in future.

The advantage of using the stock price as a measure of economic exposure of the firm is that such analysis may be carried out without the in-depth (a) understanding of currency markets, (b) economic conditions, and (c) access to the information specific to the firm. Measurement of economic exposure with the changes in the stock price also serves another useful purpose, which is possibly difficult to account for in the scenario or sensitivity analysis. An exposure is defined as the changes in the competitive position due to unanticipated changes in the exchange rates. Since stock prices already discount anticipated events, including the expected changes in the exchange rates, the measurement based on changes in the stock price would only account for the new information that has not been discounted in the existing price.

Important differences between economic exposure with the transaction and translation exposure are highlighted in Table 27-14 at the end of the chapter.

Only Real Rates Matter

'What kinds of changes in the exchange rates matter and alter the competitive position of the firm' is a key question. Changes in nominal exchange rate are immaterial for economic exposure, unless they signify the change in the real exchange rates. Economic exposure is concerned with the changes in the competitive position of local firms with respect to foreign firms assuming that local firms would be subjected to similar impact. If the changes in the nominal exchange rates are consistent with the changes in the inflation rates—as would happen if PPP holds—the competitive position of local firm with respect to foreign firm remains unchanged. What is lost by the increase in the nominal exchange rates is compensated by the increased inflation rate. Change in real exchange rate only causes economic exposure.

Fundamental factors affecting real rates are significant while measuring economic exposure. Changes In nominal rates are immaterial.

For illustration purpose, consider a small example. Assume that there are two suppliers of shirts—one manufacturing locally and the other importing entirely from Britain. The cost of manufacture of a shirt for a domestic producer is ₹1,200, while an imported shirt costs £ 20. With the current exchange rate at ₹60 per £, the cost of imported shirt is exactly equal to ₹1,200 keeping the competitive position of domestic producer and imported supplier at par with one another.

Now assume that the inflation rates in India and Britain are 20% and 10% respectively. According to PPP, the new nominal exchange rate after one year should be ₹65.45 ($60 \times 1.2/1.1$). This would imply that the real exchange rates have not changed. Under the circumstances where the real exchange rates remain unchanged, it can be demonstrated that the competitive positions of domestic producer and importer remains unaffected. While local manufacturer faces increased cost due to inflation in India, the imported supplier faces impact on two counts: (i) inflation in Britain and (ii) increased exchange rate. The combined impact of inflation and exchange rate changes on the importer is exactly equal to increased inflation faced by the domestic producer.

However, the relative competitive position would be affected if the change in nominal exchange rates is not consistent with PPP, causing depreciation or appreciation of the currency in real terms. As per PPP, the depreciation of rupee should be equal to the differential of inflation rates in the two countries, i.e., 10%. Assume that the actual depreciation of rupee is more than 10%, say the exchange rate is now ₹70 rather than ₹64.45. In such a case, the importer would face an additional cost in the form of extra depreciation of rupee making his products more expensive relative to the domestic producer.

Table 27-9 Change in real rates only have economic exposure

	Cost today	*Cost a year later*	
		Real Rates Constant	*Real Rates Change*
Exchange Rate	₹60/£	₹65.45/£	₹70.00/£
Local manufacturer	₹1,200	₹1,440 (increased by 20% due to inflation)	₹1,440 (increased by 20% due to inflation)
Importer Equivalent ₹	£20 ₹1,200 (@ ₹60/£)	£22 ₹1,440 (@ ₹65.45/£) Increased by 10% due to inflation and remaining 10% due to change in nominal exchange rate	£22 ₹1,540 (@ ₹70.00/£) Increased by 10% due to inflation and remaining due to change in nominal exchange rate
Impact	Competitive position is identical costs being same	Relative position remains same if changes in nominal exchange rates are consistent with PPP i.e., real rates do not change.	Relative position of local manufacturer improves as rupee as depreciated more making product of importer relatively more expensive as compared to the domestic producer.

The effect of exchange rate changes on the competitive position is presented in Table 27-9. It must also be noted that the competitive positions change due to large number of facto ₹, and changes in exchange rates is only one of them. Thus, firms face economic exposures otherwise too, but that is not the issue being discussed here.

Fixed Rates—No Solution

Connected with the issue of changes in real exchange rate is the notion that firms would not face any economic exposure if a country followed fixed exchange rates. The notion gains ground, though wrongly, on the premise that since exchange rates do not change, the risk associated with changing exchange rate too vanishes automatically. It is extremely inappropriate to assume so. The fact remains that when exchange rates are fixed, the risk associated with transactions denominated in foreign exchange is eliminated, i.e., transaction exposure does not exist. However, economic exposure continues because fixing nominal exchange rates does not imply that real rates are also fixed.

The argument that no economic exposure is present where exchange rates are fixed is a myth. In fact, fixed exchange rates essentially mean that real exchange rates are certain to change.

As explained earlier, the economic exposure results not from the changes in the nominal exchange rates but due to the changes in the real exchange rates. By fixing the exchange rate, by law, we are defying the law of one price, i.e., not letting the PPP prevail. Exchange rate can be regulated through exchange control laws but inflation cannot be. The inflation rates of the two countries, in all probability, would differ. By fixing the exchange rate in nominal terms, there is no appreciation or depreciation of currency in nominal terms. The fact is that by fixing the exchange rate in nominal terms, the currency would appreciate or depreciate in real terms by the differential of inflation rates in real terms, not reflected in exchange rate quotations.

Again, consider a small example to understand the economic exposure despite fixed exchange rate. China has pegged its currency, Yuan with US$. Consider a Chinese shoe exporter invoicing in US$ to its customers. The price is US $10 and the fixed exchange rate is Yuan 8 per US $. Thus, the exporter is assured of revenue of Yuan 80. The exporter incurs its entire cost in Chinese Yuan placed at Yuan 60 per a pair of shoes providing a profit of Yuan 20. What would happen to his position after one year? Does he face economic exposure? Let us examine his position assuming an inflation rate of 10% in China and no inflation in USA (assumed only for simplicity). Though the revenue of the Chinese shoemaker remains fixed at Yuan 80, his cost rises by 10% due to inflation from Yuan 60 to Yuan 66. This would deplete the profit of the firm by Yuan 6 (from Yuan 20 to Yuan 14), as depicted in Table 27-10.

Fixed exchange rates may not change the competitive position of domestic firms with one another but it alters the relative position globally.

Table 27-10 Economic exposure with fixed exchange rate

	Now	*A Year Later*
Selling Price $10	Yuan 80	Yuan 80
Cost in Yuan	60	66
Profit	20	14
Profit declines by 30%. Though nominal rate remains constant, in real terms, Yuan has devalued by 10% (the amount of differential of inflation rates of China and USA).		

Economic exposure results due to changes in the real exchange rates. When nominal rates move as per PPP, there is no change in the real exchange rates. When nominal rates defy PPP, as would be the case when exchange rates are fixed, economic exposure is inevitable.

MANAGING ECONOMIC EXPOSURE

Management of economic exposure is complex because the sources of changes in the operating cash flows causing the firm's competitive position to change are too many. Operating cash flows change not only due to changes in the real exchange rates but also due to all macro-economic and behavioural factors. The responses of customers, competitors, suppliers, lenders, investors, etc., to a given change in the price level are difficult to predict since economic rationale does not prevail all the time. The behaviour of people to a change in the economic, political, and social environments is too complex to be formulated into a mathematical model capable of analysing the impact of a change.

Therefore, management of economic exposure becomes more of strategic nature concerned with stabilizing the future cash flows over a long period of time, unlike management of translation and transaction exposures that focus on the stable cash flows in the immediate future.

To Manage or Not to Manage

A few managers and experts often argue that there is no need to manage the economic exposure as long as the transaction exposure is managed well. Since individual transactions cause variations of cash flows, collectively they represent the economic exposure. The argument is valid only partially. Transaction exposure and translation exposure are the subsets of economic exposure. Economic exposure is much broader than transaction exposure and translation exposure. Sales and purchases in foreign currencies can be hedged through a variety of financial instruments available. Similarly, balance sheet exposure of the assets and liabilities denominated in foreign currency too can be managed, though they do not affect cash flows unless liquidated. However, changes in the cash flows due to consumer behaviour, competitor's reaction, etc., to exchange rate changes forming part of economic exposure are not hedged. Economic exposure is a superset that encompasses transaction and translation exposures and therefore needs to be managed besides hedging transactions and translations.

According to one argument: Since cash flows are affected by transaction exposure, a firm that manages transaction exposure well need not be concerned about managing economic exposure

Strategic Management of Economic Exposure

As stated earlier, the management of economic exposure is strategic in nature and hence cannot be confined to finance function alone. The management of economic exposure is not exclusive to finance function. All other functions like marketing, production, purchase, etc., and the respective strategies are equally responsible and concerned about the management of economic exposure.

One strategic way of managing economic exposure is to spread the manufacturing locations of various plants. Most MNCs manage economic exposure by locating the manufacturing plants in many countries rather than export from a single location. Besides expanding the marketing base by increased geographical coverage, such spreading of plant locations reduces volatility of the aggregate cash flows of the firm due to exchange rate changes since products are invoiced in local currencies rather than foreign currencies.

Diversifying the markets, though primarily done to increase the sales and the profits, also renders stability to operating cash flows. While launching products in new geographical territories, pricing strategies in the new markets are some of the marketing-based interventions seldom thought as risk-reduction strategies. Indeed, they do reduce economic exposure and some of them are executed to respond to the competitors' moves. It can be classified as one of the strategies to manage economic exposure, though to most managers, stability of cash flows is only secondary to increased cash flows.

Strategic management of economic exposure involves all the functions of a business; production, marketing, procurement, etc. besides finance function.

Product differentiation as a management strategy is a concept favourite of marketing function with several motives in mind. Besides differentiating the products from those of the competitors', it is expected to take care of the changing consumer preferences. It is also done to broaden the market base by capturing as many segments as possible. Little does marketing function realize that they serve an extremely useful finance function of providing stability to the cash flows by product differentiation because competitive position of the firm is more stable when a firm has many differentiated products to offer to its customers.

Purchase-based activities that lead to reduced economic exposure are: (i) vendor development, (ii) cultivating domestic vendors to reduce dependence upon foreign vendors, and (iii) entering into fixed price long-term contracts for supplies. All these activities are aimed at reducing the uncertainty of cash outflows.

Though cash flows of most firms are primarily dependent upon the operating activities of sales and purchases, the role of finance is often overlooked in managing the economic exposure. Financing structure too can expose firms to wider fluctuations in operating cash flows than what is normally expected. From financing viewpoint, the management of economic exposure is to follow a golden rule to borrow in the currency in which the cash flows of the firm are generated. By borrowing in a currency other than that of cash flow generation, the interest and repayment of principal become dependent upon the exchange rates giving rise to transaction exposure. These payments of interest and principal would increase if the currency of borrowing appreciates.

Tactical Management of Economic Exposure

Tactical management of economic exposure concerns itself with its management over a short term; may be up to one year. According to an argument, it is not required to manage the economic exposure because economic exposure is a superset of transaction exposure, and it shall stand automatically managed if transaction exposure is managed well. It is not a completely valid argument since economic exposure concerns with changes in the cash flow of the firm with changing exchange rates. Further, for economic exposure changes in the real exchange rate matter. The management of transaction exposure deals with the threats arising out of changes in the nominal exchange rates.

In a nutshell, it may be reiterated that economic exposure is a superset and not a subset of transaction exposure. A comparison of transaction exposure and economic exposure is presented in Table 27-11.

Financial hedge

Covering economic exposure purely by financial instruments has a specific advantage of tactical management. Hedging strategies related to marketing and production are extremely strategic and take a long time to implement. Further, reversal of such strategic intervention is rather impossible. Financial hedge is easy to implement and is reversible if things do not work out the way they were aimed at. Forwards, futures, and options provide easy solutions to cover economic exposure.

Financial hedge to manage economic exposure means taking speculative position in the foreign exchange markets and giving rise to transaction exposure.

Hedging through financial derivatives has some drawbacks as well. This strategy involves taking a speculative position on the movement of exchange rates. It converts economic exposure to transaction exposure having cash flow implications in immediate future. The desirability of such financial intervention to manage the economic exposure therefore becomes specific to corporate philosophy.

Table 27-11 Transaction exposure and economic exposure

Transaction exposure	*Economic exposure*
• Contract specific • Relates to transaction cost • Concerned with changes in the nominal exchange rates • Managed tactically • Short term in nature	• Economy specific • Relates to opportunity cost • Concerned with changes in the real exchange rates • Managed strategically • Long term in nature

Financial hedge to cover the economic exposure can be done by booking a forward contract such that loss in the cash flows are compensated by gains in the forward contract and vice versa, so as to have stable cash flows. The desirability of booking a forward contract is questionable. It amounts to taking a speculative position on the movement of exchange rate causing transaction exposure having cash flow implications. Economic exposure gets converted into the transaction exposure if we manage by forward contract or any other similar derivative instrument.

TRANSLATION EXPOSURE

Translation exposure, also called accounting exposure or balance sheet exposure, results from the translation of assets and liabilities and items of profit and loss account from one currency to another. The values of these items would differ from time to time depending upon the rates of foreign exchange prevailing at the time of translation of financial statements from one currency to another.

Translation exposure arises due to conversion of financial statements denominated in foreign currency into domestic/ another currency.

Multinational corporations usually have many subsidiaries in various countries and the financial statements of each of the subsidiaries are denominated in the local currency where the subsidiary is located. MNCs while evaluating overall performance and in order to comply with the laws of the land, which generally demand presentation of financial statements in domestic currency for the worldwide operations, are required to convert financial statements of all its subsidiaries located in various countries to the local currency before they can be consolidated with the financial statements of the parent. The changing rates of foreign exchange change the values of the assets and liabilities as well as profits.

As an example, assume that an Indian company's subsidiary in Germany has placed a deposit of € 100 with a German bank. At the time of placing this deposit, the exchange rate was, say ₹55 per €; and therefore in the books of Indian firm, the value of deposit was reflected as ₹5,500. Assuming that the German subsidiary continues to keep this deposit for another year and euro appreciates to ₹60 after one year, the value of the deposit in the books of Indian parent would now be shown as ₹6,000. The difference of ₹500 would be shown as 'reserves arising out of translation' in the liability side.

Note that though there is no change in the value of the deposit in terms of euro, the value in rupee stands increased merely due to depreciation of rupee in the intervening period of one year increasing the value of deposit into local currency while consolidating the accounts. However, the change in the value is only notional and not real as long as the deposit remains in Germany. The impact of change would become real when the deposit is withdrawn and euro is converted back into rupee.

As long as assets, liabilities, and profits of the subsidiary are not converted or remitted back to the parent, the exposure resulting from translation remains only notional. Cash flows to the parent are not affected in the immediate future. However, at some point, it makes the difference when assets, liabilities, and profits are actually converted.

Translation exposure is notional in nature without any cash flow implications. It arises only while consolidating the accounts.

The impact of translation is indirect. Profits in the books would be inflated if the local currency has depreciated and vice versa. For example, a profit of US $100 would be reflected in the consolidated accounts of the Indian parent company as ₹4,500 if the exchange rate was ₹45, and ₹5,000 if the exchange rate was ₹50 per US $. We all know that accounting earnings drive the prices of the stocks. Therefore, there could be an impact on share price due to translation. However, this is debatable under conditions of efficient markets where such notional gains or losses would be ignored while valuing the firm.

Apart from the impact on valuation of the firm, another effect of translation could be changes in the interpretation based on financial analysis where ratios relating to the liquidity, capital structure, profitability, etc., dictate judgement. Depending upon the direction of movement of foreign exchange rates, there could be favourable or unfavourable impact on the debt-equity ratio, current ratio, etc. which are very crucial in forming opinions. Again, it may be argued that intelligent and aware analysts would discount such notional impact resulting form the changing values of assets and liabilities due to translation. Since translation does not impact cash flows, such notional changes need to be ignored for valuation or judgement of the strengths and weaknesses of the firm.

TRANSLATION METHODS

Foreign exchange rates fluctuate all the time like the prices of any other commodity or financial asset. Do we need to translate the financial statements all the time because the exchange rates keep on changing? Fortunately, the answer is no. Translation of balance sheet and profit and loss account is mandated only when the accounts of the parent owning the subsidiaries are published. The financial statements of the subsidiaries are required to be consolidated then. In most cases, this is required to be done on annual basis on the day of closing of books of accounts of the parent, when the parent prepares its financial statements.

Translation exposure relates to the assets and liabilities that are regarded as exposed to currency rates and emanates only from items that are translated at the closing rates. The translation exposure is thus the difference between the exposed assets and exposed liabilities because exposures in assets and liabilities move in the opposite direction.

Many exchange rates are available for translation of subsidiaries' accounts for consolidation purposes. Also different rates may be used for different items of assets, liabilities, revenue, and cost. Therefore, different methods can be used for translating the accounts of the subsidiaries. Broadly speaking, there exist four methods; with variations in each of them being used in different countries. We shall discuss them now.

Four prominent methods of translation are: current/non-current, monetary/non-monetary, temporal, and all current.

Current/Non-current Method

Under *Current/Non-current method,* the items are segregated with respect to their maturities. Current assets and current liabilities that are short-term in nature, i.e., convertible into cash within a year, are translated at current rates, i.e., closing rate as on the date of conversion to reflect the true nature value of the asset and liability. As the time progresses, the values of current assets and liabilities keep changing. All items of non-current nature, whether assets or liabilities, including equity capital are translated at historical rates, i.e., the exchange rate that prevailed at the time when the assets were acquired or liabilities created. It essentially means that the fixed assets and long-term liabilities are not subject to change with changes in the exchange rates, while the value of current assets and current liabilities do change with time.

Items of profit and loss account are translated using average rates for the period under consideration, except those related to non-current assets and liabilities where historical rate would be used. One such item is depreciation that relates to the fixed asset and is translated at historical rate; the rate applicable to the fixed assets.

Monetary/Non-monetary Method

Under this method assets and liabilities are classified either as monetary or non-monetary rather than based on maturities. Monetary items are those that represent a claim, receivable or payable, for a fixed sum of foreign currency. Non-monetary items are physical assets and liabilities.

For monetary items, current rate is used while non-monetary items, including equity capital, are translated at historical rates. With respect to Current/Non-current method, the difference arises in respect of few items. For example, inventories of stocks, though current asset are non-monetary in nature and represent physical asset. They would be translated at historical rates in Monetary/Non-Monetary method. Under Current/Non-current method, the same would be translated at closing rate being a current asset.

Similarly, long-term debts would be translated at closing rate under this method while historical rate would be used in the Current/Non-current method. The idea behind the method is that it is the monetary assets and liabilities only that carry the risk of changes in the values with changing exchange rates and therefore must be translated at rates as recent as possible. Non-monetary assets and liabilities are assumed to maintain the same values as real rates do not change if assumptions of PPP hold.

Items of revenue and cost use average rate prevailed during the period except those related to non-monetary assets and liabilities. The rates used here would be same as those used for relevant non-monetary assets or liabilities. Depreciation related to fixed assets is converted at the same rate as that of fixed asset. Similarly, cost of goods sold pertaining to the inventory is also translated at the rate used for inventory.

Temporal Method

Temporal method is a variant of Monetary/Non-monetary method. The underlying principle in the temporal method is to use the same type of exchange rate for translation that are used for carrying an item in the balance sheet. Items are neither classified as current/non-current nor as monetary/non-monetary. If the market value is used in balance sheet, the translation would take place at current rate, and if assets and liabilities are carried at original cost, they would be translated at respective historical rates. This usually leads to a difference in the translation of inventories. Since they are carried to the balance sheet at market rates, the translation is done at current rate, unlike monetary/non-monetary method where they shall be converted at historical rate being a non-monetary item.

All Current Method

Simplest of all methods is *all current method* where only closing rates are used for all items. However, equity is translated at historical rates. Items of profit and loss are translated at average rates during the period.

A summary of rates to be used for translation of various assets and liabilities under different methods is presented in Table 27-12.

Table 27-12 Comparison of translation methods

Item	*Current/ Non-current*	*Monetary/ Non-monetary*	*Temporal*	*All Current*
Cash	C	C	C	C
Debtors	C	C	C	C
Creditors	C	C	C	C
Inventory*	C	H	C	C
Fixed Assets	H	H	H	C
Term Liabilities	H	C	C	C
Equity	H	H	H	H

* Assumed at market rates, C = Current Rates, H = Historical Rates

Translating the accounts of the subsidiaries with non-uniform rates for all the items would result in a translation gain or loss. The translation exposure is computed on the items that are exposed to exchange rate changes. Following rules would apply for translation exposure:

Translation Exposure	**Translation Gain/Loss**
When local currency depreciates	
exposed assets > exposed liabilities	Gain
< exposed liabilities	Loss
When local currency appreciates	
exposed assets > exposed liabilities	Loss
< exposed liabilities	Gain

MEASURING TRANSLATION EXPOSURE

To understand the impact of translation on the balance sheet, consider a small example. Assume that there is a Swiss subsidiary of an Indian firm keeping its accounts in Swiss Francs (CHF). Assume the balance sheet totals CHF 100 and the rate was ₹30 per CHF. The balance sheet in CHF and Indian rupees is shown in Table 27-13. Now assume that Indian rupee has depreciated to ₹40 per CHF and no change in the balance sheet has taken place in the interim period of one year. The same balance sheet would be translated in Indian rupees after one year with different items translated either at historical rate (₹30 per CHF) or at current rate (₹40 per CHF) under different methods.

Translation exposure is measured by the difference of asset and liabilities that are translated at current rates.

The translation is shown in Table 27-13 under three different methods; Current/Non-current, Monetary/Non-monetary, and All Current. The items are classified based on the principles of each method. The translation exposure is computed on the items that are exposed and translated at current rate. The exposure is computed as net of exposed asset over exposed liabilities multiplied by the difference in the exchange rates. This is shown separately in the translated balance sheet of the Indian parent.

Example 27-2 Translation Methods and Measurement of Translation Exposure

Assume an American firm has a subsidiary in Germany having the following assets and liabilities denominated in euros:

Table 27-13 Impact of translation under different translation methods

	Now		***Translation in Indian rupees after a year with Indian rupee depreciating by 33.33% to ₹40.00 per CHF***					
	1 CHF = ₹ 30.00		***Current/Non-current***		***Monetary/Non-monetary***		***Current***	
Balance Sheet	***CHF***	***Indian ₹***	***Nature***	***Value***	***Nature***	***Value***	***Nature***	***Value***
Fixed Assets	35	1,050	NC	1,050	NM	1,050	C	1,400
Stocks	30	900	C	1,200	NM	900	C	1,200
Debtors	25	750	C	1,000	M	1,000	C	1,000
Cash	10	300	C	400	M	400	C	400
TOTAL	**100**	**3,000**		**3,650**		**3,350**		**4,000**
Net worth	40	1,200	NC	1,200	NM	1,200	NC	1,200
Term Liabilities	30	900	NC	900	M	1,200	C	1,200
Trade Creditors	30	900	C	1,200	M	1,200	C	1,200
Translation Gain/(loss)	—	—		350		–250		400
TOTAL	**100**	**3,000**		**3,650**		**3,350**		**4,000**
Translation Exposure (Assets – Liabilities)								
Assets translated at current rates				65		35		100
Liabilities translated at current rates				30		60		60
In CHF				**35**		**–25**		**40**
In Indian rupees				**1,050**		**–750**		**1,200**
Translation Gain/Loss				**350**		**–250**		**400**

NC = Non-current *NM = Non-monetary* *C = Current* *M = Monetary*

Balance Sheet (*Euros in thousands*)

Assets		*Liabilities*	
Fixed Assets	12.00	Net worth	12.00
Stocks	5.00	Term Liabilities	5.00
Debtors	4.00	Trade Creditors	6.00
Cash	2.00		
	23.00		**23.00**

The current rate of exchange is 1 euro = US $1.20. The US parent is required to consolidate its subsidiary's accounts with it.

1. Find out the exposure of the US parent if it follows (a) Current/Non-current method and (b) Monetary/Non-monetary method.
2. What would be the translation gain/loss if US $ appreciates to 1.12 per euro? Draw the accounts of the subsidiary in US $ after its appreciation under both the methods.

Solution

The balance sheet in euro and US $ is shown in columns 2 and 3 respectively of the following table.

	Now		*Translation in US $ after its appreciation to $1.12/euro*	
	1 euro = US $1.20		*Current/ Non-current*	*Monetary/ Non-monetary*
Balance Sheet	**euro**	**US $**	**US $**	**US $**
Fixed Assets	12.00	14.40	14.40	14.40
Stocks	5.00	6.00	5.60	6.00
Debtors	4.00	4.80	4.48	4.48
Cash	2.00	2.40	2.24	2.24
TOTAL	**23.00**	**27.60**	**26.72**	**27.12**
Net worth	12.00	14.40	14.40	14.40
Term Liabilities	5.00	6.00	6.00	5.60
Trade Creditors	6.00	7.20	6.72	6.72
Translation Gain/(loss)	—	—	**–0.40**	**0.40**
TOTAL	**23.00**	**27.60**	**26.72**	**27.12**
Assets translated at current rates			11.00	6.00
Liabilities translated at current rates			6.00	11.00
Translation Exposure (Assets – Liabilities)				
In euro			**5.00**	**–5.00**
In US $			**6.00**	**–6.00**
Translation Gain/Loss			**–0.40**	**0.40**

The US firm faces an exposure of US $6,000 (€ 5,000) under both the methods. However due to differences in the classification of various items under current/non-current method, the net assets have exposure; while under monetary and non-monetary method, the exposure is – US $6,000 with liabilities exceeding assets.

The balance sheet of the subsidiary under the two methods is shown in Columns 4 and 5 of the above table. The translation gain/loss is as follows:

Under Current/Non-current Method; Loss = 5.00 (1.20 – 1.12)
= –0.40

Under Monetary/Non-monetary Method; Gain = –5.00 (1.20 – 1.12)
= 0.40

MANAGING TRANSLATION EXPOSURE

Management of translation exposure can be done in several ways. They are classified as: balance sheet hedge and derivatives hedge.

Balance Sheet Hedge

Translation exposure is often managed by making efforts to make equal the assets and liabilities translated at current rate.

Balance sheet hedge uses the principle of netting out those assets and liabilities which are exposed to exchange rate fluctuations. Translation exposure is defined as net of assets and liabilities that are converted at current rates of exchange. In case the parent has several subsidiaries, then the cumulative position of all subsidiaries must be considered hoping that exposed assets of one would cancel out against the exposed liabilities of another.

On a standalone basis of a single subsidiary, the attempt is to match the exposed assets and exposed liabilities by undertaking some transaction to offset the exposure. Consider the case of a German subsidiary of a US parent as in Example 27-2 with the following balance sheet drawn in euros.

Balance Sheet (*Euros in thousands*)

Assets		*Liabilities*	
Fixed Assets	12.00	Net worth	12.00
Stocks	5.00	Term Liabilities	5.00
Debtors	4.00	Trade Creditors	6.00
Cash	2.00		
	23.00		**23.00**

Applying the monetary/non-monetary method of translation, the US parent faces net liability translation exposure of €5,000 (liabilities less assets translated at current rates). To eliminate the translation exposure, the US parent can do any of the following:

1. Liquidate the entire stocks of €5,000 immediately to get cash: Stocks being non-monetary and cash being monetary would equate assets with liabilities exposed to currency fluctuations.
2. Convert $6,000 (5,000 × 1.20) from parent and remit €5,000 to German subsidiary: This too would make translation exposure zero.
3. Pay off liabilities, either term or current by €5,000 by borrowing dollar and immediately converting to euros to remove the imbalance in the exposed assets and liabilities.

The major limitation with the balance sheet hedge to cover the translation exposure is that the actions required may not be feasible for reasons of law or otherwise.

Derivatives Hedge

Managing translation exposure through derivatives creates speculative position and gives rise to transaction exposure.

In the above example, the US parent faces a net liability exposure of €5,000. This would cause a translation loss if euro appreciated and result in a gain if euro depreciated. The translation loss can be offset by entering into a forward contract in a manner that would result in equivalent profit.

Assume that euro is likely to appreciate to \$1.30 per € from its current rate of \$1.20 per € by the next date of balance sheet. The expected translation loss would be:

Net Liability Exposure: €5,000

Translation Loss: [5,000 × (1.30 – 1.20)] = US \$ 500

Assume that the 12-m forward rate for euro is at \$1.25 and the expected spot rate after 12 months is \$1.30. If the US parent buys euro 12-m forward and then sells spot later, the expected profit would be US \$0.05 per € if the same spot rate prevails as was indicated by the forward rate. The calculation is shown below:

At the date of next balance sheet (12 months later)	**(per euro)**
Cash outflow for delivery against forward contract	US \$1.25
Cash inflow for spot sale of euro	US \$1.30
Profit on the forward position	US \$0.05

To cover a translation loss of US \$500, the US firm needs to buy 12-m forward contract for €10,000. The size of the forward buy contract can be arrived at from the following formula:

Size of the Forward Contract

$$= \frac{\text{Potential Loss upon Translation (in local currency)}}{\text{Forward rate} - \text{Expected future spot rate}}$$

Net liability exposure usually necessitates buying the foreign currency forward and net asset exposure involves selling foreign currency forward.

As may be easily seen from the above, the effectiveness of the forward hedge to cover the translation loss would essentially depend upon the accuracy of the forecast of foreign exchange rate with respect to the actual rate. If future spot rate turns out to be exactly equal to the forecast rate, the hedge would be perfect.

Though the translation exposure can be managed through a forward contract, it is not advisable to do so because entering into a forward contract creates transaction exposure. Since translation exposure is limited to books, the merit of covering the same through a mechanism that has cash flow implications is questionable. Besides, forward hedge has its cost that is incurred to negate a notional loss and not an actual loss. Thus, managing translation exposure may seem irrelevant.

Example 27-3 Managing Translation Exposure Through Derivatives

A subsidiary of Indian firm is expected to earn \$10,000 in profit net of taxes for the coming year. Current exchange rate is ₹45. By the next year, the dollar is expected to depreciate to ₹40. However, the 12-m forward rate is ₹42 per \$. The Indian firm does not repatriate the profit.

(a) What is the translation loss expected?

(b) How can this be covered by forward market?

(c) Do you recommend such an action?

Solution

(a) With the profit of \$10,000 expected next year, the Indian firm would face net asset exposure for translation of US \$10,000, as cash/bank balance would increase by the amount of profit. With the expected future spot rate to decline by ₹5, the Indian firm faces a translation loss of ₹50,000.

(b) There is a net asset exposure for the Indian firm that would necessitate selling of the foreign currency forward. The loss can be covered in the forward market by selling dollar 12-m forward at ₹ 42 and then buying the same in the spot market later. Assuming the future spot rate is ₹40 as expected, the forward contract would result in profit as follows:

Rupee cash flow for selling US \$ under forward contract	+42.00
Rupee cash flow for buying US \$ spot	–40.00
Net Profit per \$ of forward contract	2.00

Therefore, the size of forward contract in US \$ = 50,000/2 = US \$25,000

(c) Such an action is not recommended since Indian firm does not repatriate the profit. Booking of forward contract causes unnecessary transaction exposure and avoidable cost. The gains of the forward contract have cash flow implications, which are being adjusted against unrealized losses.

We discussed three different kinds of exposures faced by the firms with respect to changes in the foreign exchange rates. A comprehensive though not exhaustive comparison of the three exposures is presented in Table 27-14.

Table 27-14 Comparison of different kinds of foreign exchange exposures

	Transaction Exposure	*Economic Exposure*	*Translation Exposure*
Definition	Changes in the amount of future cash flows, for contracts entered in foreign currency but not settled.	Changes in the amount of future cash flows determined by future competitive position.	Changes in the income statement, and values of assets and liabilities; Denominated in Foreign currecny.
Real or Notional	Real	Real	Notional
Retrospective or Prospective	Retrospective and prospective as well; Contracts **entered:** past but **not settled:** prospective	Retrospective	Retrospective in nature; deals with activities happened in the past
Currency	Concerns only foreign currency	Concerns both local and foreign currency	Concerns only foreign currency
Management	Tactical	Strategic Tactical management causes transaction exposure	Tactical; creates transaction exposure

Needless to mention that it is the transaction exposure that is central and receives most attention of the finance discipline. All innovations in the financial markets and instruments are focussed and aimed at managing transaction exposure only. Even though the aggregate cash flows arising out of the fluctuating exchange rate may not be significant, the impact on the bottom line is significant with seemingly minor change in the exchange rates. This demands ensuring definite cash flows for profit planning and growth. Economic exposure is more strategic in nature while translation exposure is notional. If the changes in the exchange rates are within a reasonable range, both economic exposure and translation exposure do not seem to be greatly damaging.

SUMMARY

All businesses are affected by changing foreign exchange rates. The various risk faced by the firms due to changing values of the currencies, termed as foreign exchange exposures, are classified into three categories: the translation exposure, the transaction exposure, and the economic exposure. Some firms are affected more and some less, depending upon the amount of transactions denominated in foreign exchange and the level of foreign competition faced.

Transaction exposures arise from the transactions denominated in foreign exchange, which have not been settled as yet. Translation exposure results from the conversion of financial statements of a subsidiary that maintains its accounts in foreign currency into local currency using the exchange rates at different times. Economic exposure is concerned with the change in the competitive position of the firm due to varying exchange rates.

The management of transaction exposure is regarded vital since such exposure has cash flow implications in immediate future. However, several arguments made against the effective management do not find favour of financial community. The need for management of transaction exposure need not be overemphasized.

Transaction exposure can be managed either strategically or tactically. Tactical or financial management of the transaction exposure requires setting up a position in the financial instrument such that the anticipated losses on the physical transactions of sale, purchase, loan, etc., are compensated by an equal profit in the financial instrument used. Such a strategy is called hedging. A position, which exactly and completely offsets the gains/losses in the physical transaction is called perfect hedging. Hedging, often confused with maximization of profit, is a strategy that renders stability to the cash flow. Hedging comes with a cost.

Since hedging has a cost, most organizations resort to hedging on a selective basis, i.e., hedge only when adverse movement is anticipated in exchange rates. Most simple and effective hedge is provided by a forward contract. A forward contract involves selling or buying of the foreign currency in advance for delivery at a later date. Forward contract provides a perfect hedge as it freezes the cash flow at the time of booking of the contract. An alternate way to synthesize the forward rate is to execute a money market hedge. Money market hedge does not use forward market; instead, it utilizes spot market and the money markets in the two currencies. Due to the presence of transaction cost, a finance manager always faces a choice of hedging either through the forward market or the money market, one of which would be more cost efficient.

Strategic management of transaction exposure include risk shifting or risk sharing where invoicing in foreign currency is avoided. It also focuses on the sharing of risk of exchange rate by both contracting parties by incorporating price adjustment clause. Exposure netting suggests setting off the exposures of payables with receivables and also combining the exposure in similar currencies. Leading and lagging the payables and receivables controls or minimizes the risk of foreign exchange by negotiating a favourable credit period for receivables and payables.

Economic exposure evaluates the changes in the cash flow with fluctuations of exchange rates to assess the changes in the competitive position of the firm. Value of stocks can be used as a reasonable substitute to the cash flow obviating the need for making a large number of assumptions required for projecting the cash flows. Economic exposure is mostly managed strategically on a long-term basis though tactical management through the financial instruments is also possible. Management of economic exposure through financial instruments creates transaction exposure, questioning the desirability of such management.

Translation exposure arises due to the necessity of periodic consolidation of accounts of subsidiaries. Also known as accounting exposure, it results due to the changing rate of foreign exchange from period to period. Various translation methods are used for conversion of accounts from one currency to another using different rates for different assets, liabilities, and revenue items. This gives rise to imbalance in the balance sheet with the difference being reflected as "reserves out of translation".

Management of translation exposure is done by making equal the items of asset and liabilities translated at current rates. This process is referred to as balance sheet hedge. Alternatively, financial management of exposure may be done by taking a position in financial derivative instruments. The desirability of such strategy is again in doubt as it amounts to taking a speculative position on exchange rate and transforming a notional exposure to cash flow exposure.

KEY TERMS

Transaction exposure Transaction exposure arises due to contracts entered in foreign currency that are yet to be settled. Uncertainty with respect to the value of the contract in local currency persists till they are settled.

Economic exposure Economic exposure refers to the changes in the competitive position of a firm due to changes in exchange rates. It is measured in terms of changes in the cash flows of the firm with changes in the exchange rates.

Translation exposure Translation exposure arises from translation of accounts from one currency to another using different rates for different items of assets, liabilities and revenue items, and at different points of time.

Hedging Hedging refers to a strategy that attempts to cover the risk of changing value of asset/liability with adverse movement of exchange rates.

Perfect hedge Perfect hedge is the one where anticipated losses are fully and exactly compensated by the gains in the hedging instrument.

Forward hedge When hedging instrument used is a forward contract, it is called a forward hedge. It is a perfect hedge.

Cost of forward hedge Cost of forward hedge is given by the premium/discount on the forward rates compared to the spot rates, on an annualized basis.

Selective hedging Movement of exchange rate can be favourable or unfavourable. Selective hedging refers to hedging of only those transactions that are affected adversely due to anticipated movement of exchange rates.

Money market hedge A substitute for forward hedge where the forward rate is synthesized by borrowing in one currency and investing in another currency using spot market for conversion.

Risk shifting Risk shifting is invoicing in domestic currency, passing the risk of exchange rates entirely onto the counter-party, or any such arrangement where two contracting parties share the exchange rate risk.

Range forward Range forward is a financial instrument that does not cover the risk within a specified range of exchange rates. Beyond this range, the value of the asset/liability is frozen.

Exposure netting Exposure netting refers to the setting off of the exposures of assets and liabilities against one another in single currency or in the currency that is expected to behave similarly.

Cross hedge Cross hedge refers to covering of the risk through positions in the currency which is either positively or negatively correlated to the currency of exposure for which no financial contracts are available.

Leading and lagging Leading and lagging is a strategy related to adjustment of credit period given or taken in respect of receivables and payables depending upon the likely direction of movement of exchange rates.

Current/Non-current method A method of translation where assets and liabilities are categorized based on their maturities to determine which of the exchange rates would be used for conversion of one currency to another.

Monetary/Non-monetary method A method of translation where assets and liabilities are categorized based on their nature of monetary or non-monetary to determine which of the exchange rates would be used for conversion of one currency to another.

Temporal method A variant of Monetary/Non-monetary method for translation of financial statements.

All current method A translation method where only current rates are used for translation for all items in the financial statements except equity, which is carried at historical rate.

Translation reserve Translation reserve is the amount of difference of assets and liabilities resulting from using different rates for different items in the financial statement.

Balance sheet hedge Balance sheet hedge is a method to eliminate the translation exposure by making the amount of assets and liabilities that are translated at current rates equal.

PRACTICE PROBLEMS

1. Forward Hedge vs Money Market Hedge for Receivable

A Japanese auto dealer has supplied cars in Germany for which the payment of € 6.15 million is due after 6 months from now. Following exchange rate scenario is prevailing in the markets in Tokyo:

Spot Exchange rate (J ¥/€)	160	175
6-m Swap points (J ¥/€)	5	4

The dealer is inclined to book a forward contract to sell euro as yen is showing a rising trend. The banker of the dealer has suggested that it would be better to have euros now than later by borrowing the same. The interest rate applicable for the euro loan would be 5%.

Examine the desirability of the proposal of the banker. The interest rates prevailing in the yen market are 2%.

Solution

The banker has suggested money market hedge against the forward hedge.

The dealer has two alternatives of either booking a forward contract or implement a money market hedge as suggested by the banker.

The interest rates prevailing are:

For J¥: 2.00% *For € : 5%:*

If the dealer books a forward contract:

Spot Exchange rate (J ¥/€)	160	175
6-m Swap points (J ¥/€)	5	4
Outright forward rate (J ¥/€)	155	171

The exporter can sell his receivable at outright forward bid rate of J ¥155/€

The amount realizable in €	6.15 million

The amount realizable in ¥ under forward contract

= 953.25 million

If dealer borrows € now and converts them spot to ¥:

The dealer can execute the money market hedge by taking following actions:

1. Borrowing the foreign currency in such a manner that its maturity value is liquidated by the receivable.
2. Convert the borrowing at the spot exchange rate into local currency at spot bid rate.
3. For comparison with the forward hedge, this amount is presumed to be invested at the domestic interest rate.
4. The borrowed foreign currency is liquidated when the receivable is realized.

Euro to be borrowed for 6 months at 5% = €6.00 million which matures to €6.15 million and liquidated by the receivable.

Equivalent J ¥ converted at spot bid rate = 6 × 160

= J¥ 960.00 million

Maturity amount after investing for 6 months at 2%

= J¥ 969.60 million

Money market hedge gives higher amount than the forward hedge.

The dealer therefore must follow the advise of the banker and borrow euro to have yen now.

2. Pay Now or Later

An Indian importer is negotiating payment terms for acquiring a machine costing €25,000 that is payable after 3 months. The exchange rate market is quoting following rates:

Spot exchange rate (₹/€)	59.80	60.10
3 m Swap points	120	160

(a) If the cost of borrowing for the importer is 12.00% per annum, should the importer pay now or after 3 months?

(b) Would your decision change if the supplier offers a cash discount of (i) 1%, (ii) 2%?

Solution

(a) Swap points are Low/High. They suggest depreciation of Indian rupee. If he decides to pay later, he would end up paying higher sum. The increased amount of funds have to be compared with his cost of borrowing to arrive at the decision to pay now or later.

Spot exchange rate (₹/€)	59.80	60.10
3-m Swap points	120	160
3-m Outright forward rate (₹/€)	61.00	61.70

If the importer decides to avail the credit period:

Amount payable (€)	25,000
Rate under forward contract (₹/€)	61.70

The Indian firm by booking the forward contract would pay

= 25000 × 61.70 = ₹15,42,500

If the firm decides to pay now, its cash outflow would be:

= 25,000 × 60.10 = ₹15,02,500

Cost of borrowing = 15%

Interest payable for three months = 1,502,500 × 0.15 × 3/12

= ₹56,344

Effective amount payable

= Payment on spot basis + interest thereon

= 15,02,500 + 56,344 = ₹15,58,844

Since the amount payable by deferring the payment by booking a forward contract is less, the firm must avail the credit period rather than resort to borrowing from the bank.

(b) *If the vendor for the machine offers a discount of 1%*

(i) Amount payable in the spot = 24,750 × 60.10 = ₹14,87,475

Cost of borrowing = 15%

Interest payable for three months = 1,487,475 × 0.15 × 3/12

= ₹55,780

Effective amount payable

= Payment on spot basis + interest thereon

= 1,487,475 + 55,780 = ₹15,43,255

Cash discount of 1% is not enough. Continuing to avail the credit of 3 months would remain beneficial as it would cost less.

(ii) *If the vendor for the machine offers a discount of 2%*

Amount payable in the spot = 24,500 × 60.10 = ₹14,72,450

Cost of borrowing = 15%

Interest payable for three months

= 14,72,450 × 0.15 × 3/12

= ₹55,217

Effective amount payable

= Payment on spot basis + interest thereon

= 14,72,450 + 55,217 = ₹15,27,667

Cash discount of 2% is good enough to overcome the benefit of availing the credit period. The effective amount payable by availing the 2% cash discount is better than availing the credit period. The firm must accept 2% cash discount.

3. Discounts and Exchange Rates

Credit Corporation has supplied a lot of shoes to one of its regular overseas customers who would pay in US dollars after 6 months.

Having exhausted the borrowed funds from the bank, it needs to replenish funds. One way of replenishing the funds is to offer a discount for early payment. The cost of borrowing is 12%.

In the foreign exchange market, the spot and forward market are as follows:

Spot (₹/$)	40.55	41.05
6-m swap	150	200

In view of the premium on US dollar, the Managing Director is of the opinion that no request for an early payment should be made as he would realize a greater amount if payment remains deferred. Two other members of the committee are in favour of giving a discount of 1% and 2% respectively.

As the Chief Financial Officer you are required to evaluate such discount and also advise what maximum discount could be offered to the customer without compromising the profitability?

Solution

Spot (₹/$)	40.55	41.05
6-m swap	150	200

Based on the above rates, the 6-m forward rates are as follows:

6-m forward rate (₹/$)	42.05	43.05

If no discount is offered, the firm would realize forward bid rate if it books a forward contract.

Receive after 6 months ₹42.0500

If discounts are offered, the firm would realize the spot rate which is lower than the forward rate but would save interest on the borrowed funds.

Rate of interest payable = 12%

If offered a discount of 1%

	₹
Amount realized now = (1 – 0.01) × 40.55 =	40.1445
Add: Amount of interest saved for 6 months @ 12.00%	2.4087
Effective exchange rate realized	*42.5532*

Rate realized after 1% discount is higher than if realized after 6 months under forward contract. Therefore, 1% discount can be offered.

If offered a discount of 2%

	₹
Amount realized now = (1 – 0.02) × 40.55 =	39.7390
Add: Amount of interest saved for 6 months @ 12.00%	2.3843
Effective exchange rate realized	*42.1233*

Rate realized after 2% discount is also higher than if realized after 6 months under forward contract. Therefore, 2% discount can also be offered.

The maximum discount that can be offered should be such that the realization after considering the savings of interest must equal the rate that would be realized under forward contract, if no discount is offered. Let that amount be *a*.

Amount realized net of discount = *a*

Then, $(a \times \text{spot rate}) + \frac{\text{interest rate}}{2} \times a \times \text{spot rate}$

= 6-m forward rate

$\Rightarrow (a \times 40.55) + (0.06 \times a \times 40.55) = 42.05$

$\Rightarrow$ Amount of realization, $a = 97.83\%$

Therefore, maximum discount that can be offered, $(1 - a) = 2.17\%$

4. Forward Hedge vs Money Market Hedge for Payable

Indian Steel Limited has imported some consumables worth £10,000 from England for which the payment is due in 3 months' time. The foreign exchange rates are as follows:

Spot exchange rate (₹/£)	84.55	84.85
3-m Swap points	40	80

In the money market, the yields on three month T-bills are as follows:

India : 8.00% England : 4.00%

Examine whether Indian Steel Limited must execute the forward hedge or money market hedge to eliminate the exchange rate risk it is exposed to.

Solution

Spot exchange rate (₹/£)	84.55	84.85
3-m Swap points	40	80
3-m Outright Forward rate (₹/£)	84.95	85.65

The firm can buy the required £ at forward ask rate as hedge against rising £.

Amount of £ to be paid	= £10,000
Forward exchange rate	= ₹85.65 per £
Amount payable after 3 months	= ₹8,56,500

Alternatively, Indian Steel Limited can resort to the following actions:

1. Borrow local currency
2. Convert local currency into £ at the spot ask rate.
3. Invest the £ obtained for the period so as to mature on the scheduled date of payment.
4. Upon maturity of investment in £, pay for the liability.

The amount of borrowing in the local currency is worked backwards as follows:

Amount payable after 3 months	= £10,000
£ required today for investment at 4.00%	= £ 9,901
Amount required now at ask rate of ₹84.85	= ₹8,40,099
Add: Interest on borrowing for 3 months @ 8.00%	= ₹16,802
Effective amount payable	= ₹8,56,901

Since amount payable under money market hedge after providing for interest is more than the forward contract, the importer must execute forward hedge.

EXERCISES

Concept Review Questions

1. What are the different kinds of exposures that a business enterprise have to face with regard to foreign currency exchange rates?
2. What is transaction exposure and why do you think it is most important?
3. What is drawback of measuring cost of forward hedge with forward premium/discount?
4. What are the different methods of translation? Discuss each of them.
5. How would you measure economic exposure? Elaborate your answer.
6. Compare forward hedge and money market hedge for receivables.
7. Highlight the difference in the steps one takes while hedging receivables and payables through money market hedge.
8. How do you measure translation exposure?

Critical Thinking Questions

1. Money market hedge provides a synthetic forward rate. Synthetic forward rates are always higher than market forward rates. Therefore, one should never implement money market hedge. Do you agree with the statements? Justify your answer.
2. Two manufacturers of plastic products source their raw material from vendors located abroad. One manufacturer has one supplier

of materials with fixed price contracts, while the other sources the same material on periodic basis from multiple suppliers. Who is facing greater economic exposure?

3. A firm in India has floated a subsidiary in London with equity capital of £1,00,000. With the contribution of equity, it purchased a flat in London. For the whole year, the firm did not conduct any other transaction. Does the Indian firm face a translation exposure while consolidating the account after a year?

Practical Assignments

1. Identify 10 major firms that have substantial imports and exports, and study their profit and loss account for the last five years. Under the head of other income, look for the gains on fluctuations of foreign exchange (in case of loss, look at the appropriate expense head). The figures are sometimes revealed in the cash flow statement too. Compare the figure with the profit/loss for the year and determine how sensitive the profits are to the fluctuations in the foreign exchange rates.
2. Observe 3-m forward rate continuously for 6 months at periodic intervals (say 15 days) and project the likely rate for the 3-m forward rates for the next 6 months.

Numerical Problems

1. Forward Hedge for Receivable

An Indian firm has receivable of US $10,000 due six months from now. The spot and forward rates are as follows:

Spot exchange rate (₹/$)	41.60	41.70
6-m Swap	40	65

The exporter does not want to have any uncertainty about the amount to be realized.

(a) What should he do?

(b) How much amount can he realise for his receivable?

2. Forward Hedge for Payable

An Indian importer has payable under a letter of credit of € 15,000 due 3 months from now. The exchange rate scenario is as below

Spot exchange rate (₹/€)	55.50	56.00
3-m Swap points	75	60

The importer is expecting an appreciation of euro by about 3% in next three months.

(a) Is his expectation consistent with the market scenario?

(b) What action is appropriate for the importer?

(c) What would be his liability in Indian rupee?

3. Forward Hedge vs Money Market Hedge for Receivable

A trader in Singapore is expecting an inward remittance of Aus. $1 million in 6 months' time.

The exchange rates and interest rate scenario are as follows:

Spot Exchange rate (SG $/Aus $)	0.8010	0.8100
6-m Swap points	100	200
Interest rate	SG $ 8.00%	Aus $ 6%

The trader has two alternatives of either booking a forward contract or implement a money market hedge. Evaluate what course of action he must pursue.

4. Forward Hedge vs Money Market Hedge for Payable

An importer in Hong Kong has a payable of euro 20,000 under a letter of credit. The due date is three months ahead. The foreign exchange rates are as follows:

Spot exchange rate (HK $/€)	10.65	10.75
3-m Swap points	25	30

In the money market the yields on three month T-bills are

Hong Kong	15.00%	Germany	5.00%

Examine whether the importer must execute the forward hedge or money market hedge.

5. Risk-Free Investment Abroad

A bank has surplus funds of ₹10 crore for a temporary period of 6 months as it is finding lack of credit worthy borrowers. Its cost of funds in rupees is 8%. It faces an opportunity to lend funds in USA in US $ at 6%. The spot rate is ₹40.30 while 6-m forward rate is ₹40.90. What additional risk the bank faces while lending abroad. What can be done to overcome the risk? Should it invest abroad in US $?

6. Translation Exposure

A subsidiary of an US company in Great Britain has following balance sheet that needs to be translated in US $ as at the closing on 31 December. The subsidiary was floated a year back when the exchange rate was $2.10 per £. On 31 December the exchange rate moved to $ 2.30 per £ due to depreciation of US dollar. Translate the financial statement of the British subsidiary in US dollar using: (a) All Current method, (b) Monetary/Non-monetary method, and (c) Current/Non-current method. Compute the amount of translation reserve and translation exposure under each method.

Balance sheet of subsidiary in £ ('000s)

Liabilities		*Assets*	
Capital	800	Fixed Assets	600
Debt	160	Current assets	
Current Liabilities	200	Inventory	260
		Receivable	180
		Cash	120
TOTAL	1160	TOTAL	1160

CASE STUDY

ABC LTD—TRANSLATION AND TRANSACTION EXPOSURE

ABC Ltd has been one of the major players in the country in its field of chemicals. It produced and supplied speciality chemicals and adhesives and was presently operating at about full capacity with an annual turnover in excess of ₹1,000 crore The industry had been growing at about 25% per annum while the growth of ABC Ltd was constrained due to the capacity it had. The limitation of growth is evidenced in its income statement presented in Table A.

Table A Income statement

₹ crore

	Mar-06	*Mar-05*	*Mar-04*
Income	**1,130**	**940**	**650**
Material	630	512	340
Wages	66	58	52
Overheads	254	218	140
Total	950	788	532
PBDIT	**180**	**152**	**118**
Interest	5	5	4
Depreciation	65	55	46
Profit before tax	**110**	**92**	**68**
Tax	31	31	23
Profit after tax	**79**	**61**	**45**
Dividend	24	12	—
Retained earnings	**55**	**49**	**45**

It had drawn an ambitious plan to expand its business with almost an equal size to that of existing business and asset level. It wanted to become a global player in its field. It planned to increase its turnover twofold in next 3 years. The asset base consisted of about ₹350 crore of fixed assets at market values. It needed another ₹350 crore to execute the plans over the next 2–3 years.

The firm had believed in the philosophy of funding the growth and expansion of the assets through retained earnings. Unfortunately, the firm did not have enough resources to execute its plans. As a first choice, it considered the mobilization of funds through fresh equity issue. Around November 2006, the CFO of ABC Ltd, Mr Kulkarni held discussions with several experts of capital markets. The share was moving around in the range of ₹100 to ₹125. Consultations with merchant bankers revealed that ABC Ltd could issue fresh capital at no more than ₹150 per share arrived on the basis of PE multiple and Book Value multiple. The EPS of the firm was ₹15.50 and PE multiple of 10 was considered appropriate. Similarly, the book value of the share was around ₹93, which too projected a price of ₹150 based on book value multiple of around 1.5. These valuations were optimistic considering the current market price. According to Mr Kulkarni's opinion, such valuations were not attractive enough.

The balance sheet of ABC Ltd for the last three years is given in Table B.

Table B Balance sheet

₹ crore

	Mar-06	*Mar-05*	*Mar-04*
Capital	51	51	51
Reserves	425	370	321
Shareholders' Fund	**476**	**421**	**372**
Loans	45	45	30
Deferred Tax liability	10	8	6
Total	**531**	**474**	**408**
Fixed Assets	341	302	247
Investment	32	32	32
Net Current Assets	158	140	129
Total	**531**	**474**	**408**

Mr Kulkarni thought that the situation was ripe for using the debt capacity built over the years. He was keen to raise the required sum of ₹350 crore by debt based on the debt-equity ratio of around 1:1. The little debt the firm had was for financing of working capital. Since the focus was on achieving growth through exports, he turned his attention to international capital markets for mobilizing required resources for expansion. The amount needed for the implementation of the expansion plan was around ₹350 crore. The other factor that motivated the consideration of debt in foreign currency was lower interest rates prevailing abroad. In view of favourable investment climate in India and lower interest rates prevailing in the US dollar, Mr Kulkarni along with all other members decided to raise funds in US dollar.

The decision to raise funds in foreign currency warranted consideration of additional risk factor of fluctuations of foreign exchange. While interest rates were attractive in US dollar at around 4%, the depreciation of rupee could offset the advantage of low interest. Mr Kulkarni reviewed the exchange rates for the last five years as presented in Table C. Further, he looked more closely on the exchange rates of US dollar for the 12–14 months as presented in Table D and depicted in Figure 1.

Table C Exchange rates*

₹/US $

Period	*High*	*Low*	*Closing*
Year 2002	49.06	47.96	48.03
Year 2003	48.02	45.27	45.61
Year 2004	46.46	43.39	43.58
Year 2005	46.33	43.30	45.07

Table D Exchange rate* *₹/US $*

Period	*High*	*Low*	*Closing*
Jan-06	45.05	44.07	44.07
Feb-06	44.56	44.15	44.44
Mar-06	44.69	44.32	44.01
Apr-06	45.30	44.61	44.97
May-06	46.43	44.86	46.43
Jun-06	46.40	45.82	46.08
Jul-06	46.95	45.98	46.51
Aug-06	46.72	46.43	46.55
Sep-06	46.53	45.86	45.96
Oct-06	45.84	45.02	45.02
Nov-06	45.34	44.45	44.76
Dec-06	44.83	44.23	44.23
Jan-07	44.61	44.17	44.17
Feb-07	44.31	44.06	44.31

*RBI Reference Rate

The long-term trend for the rupee in the exchange market was rather steady. If at all, there was an indication it pointed towards small appreciation of rupee. Mr Kulkarni was rather assured that his interest cost would remain at around 4% only; same as prevailing in the US dollar debt market. If any depreciation took place, it would add to the interest cost in rupee terms, while appreciation would reduce the cost.

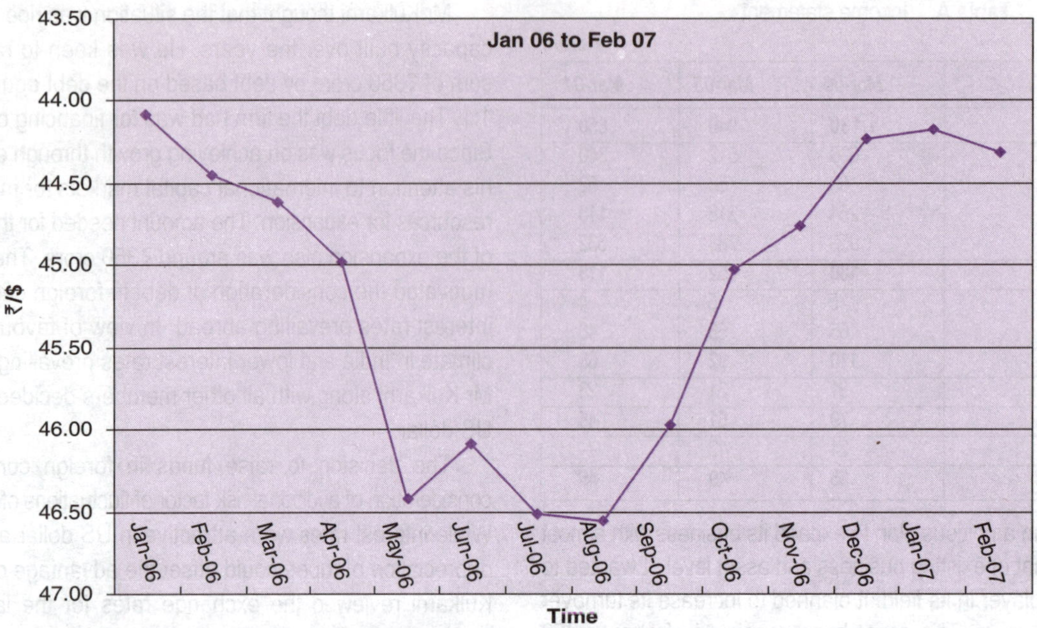

Figure 1 Exchange rates

Reassuring himself, Mr Kulkarni decided to come out with the foreign currency borrowing. However, top management's philosophy of relying on equity made Mr Kulkarni to offer the borrowing with right to conversion into equity. Apart from meeting the requirements of the top management, Mr Kulkarni was also induced from the fact that valuation of the firm by foreign investors would be higher, and it shall fetch better price for equity than what could be possible in the domestic equity markets.

The news of expansion plan and decision to borrow to fund the expansion were seen as a positive signal in the market, and then the stock price started showing appreciation expecting a substantial rise in the EPS. From a range of around ₹120 to ₹150, the stock price jumped to ₹237 in February 2007. The stock price for the period of last two years for calendar years 2005 and 2006 is shown in Table E and is depicted in Figure 2.

Table E Stock price

₹/Share

Month	*Closing Price*	*Month*	*Closing Price*
Jan-05	86	Jan-06	172
Feb-05	85	Feb-06	152
Mar-05	81	Mar-06	124
Apr-05	80	Apr-06	126
May-05	83	May-06	119
Jun-05	99	Jun-06	100
Jul-05	107	Jul-06	95
Aug-05	152	Aug-06	119
Sep-05	163	Sep-06	127
Oct-05	149	Oct-06	133
Nov-05	167	Nov-06	114
Dec-05	182	Dec-06	196

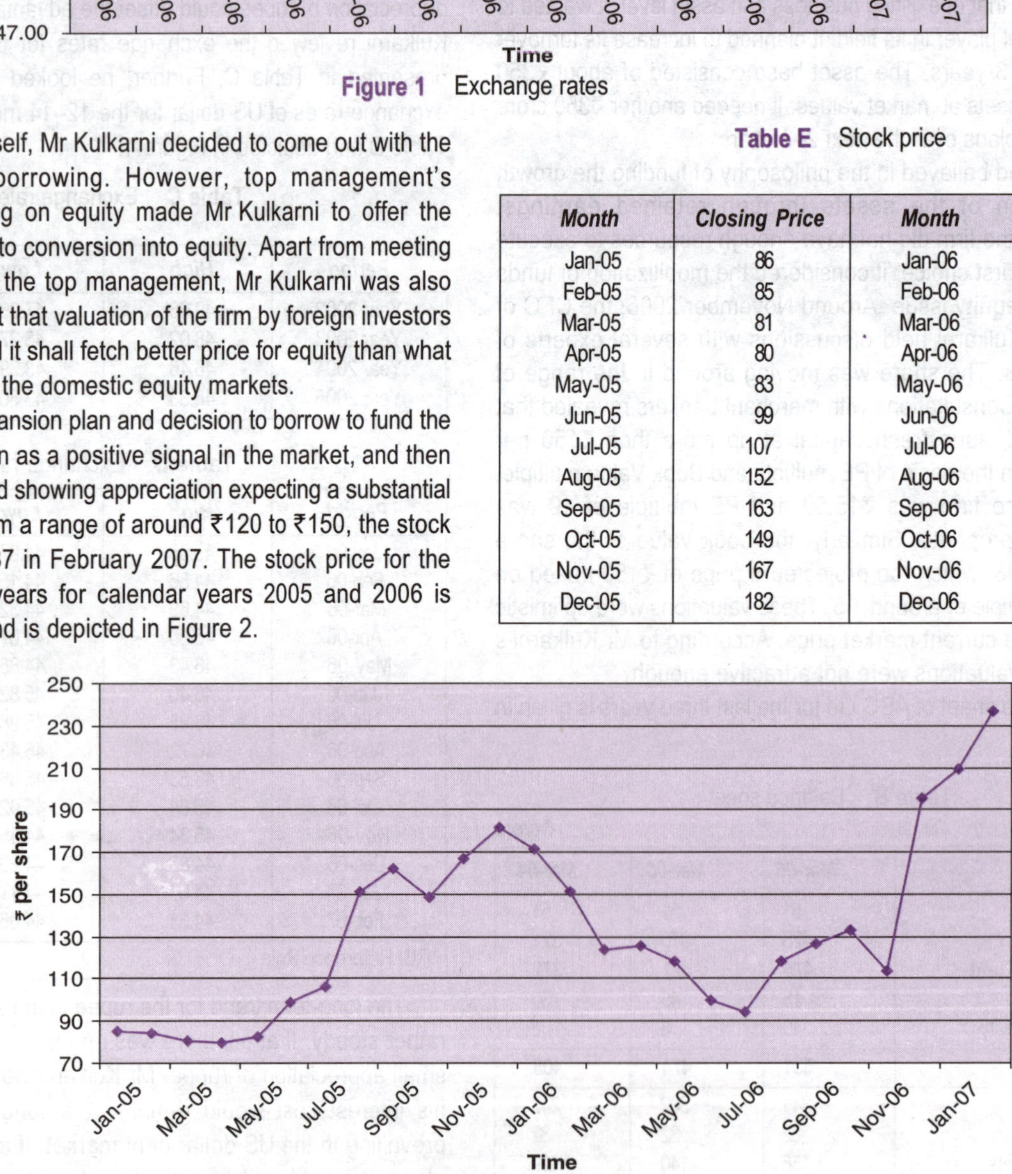

Figure 2 Stock price movement

Table F Stock price—last 6 months

Sep-06	127.00
Oct-06	133.00
Nov-06	114.00
Dec-06	196.00
Jan-07	210.00
Feb-07	237.00
3-m Average	**214.33**
6-m Average	**169.50**

Based on all the considerations of utilizing the debt capacity and attraction of better valuation by foreign investors, ABC Ltd decided to come out with the issue of Foreign Currency Convertible Bonds (FCCB) of US $80 million expected to yield about ₹354 crore required for the expansion of capacity. Floatation costs were estimated at about US $1 million. This was an added advantage of the debt issue because the estimated cost of floatation was of the order of 3–5% for an equity issue.

Accordingly an attractive and investor-friendly instrument was offered in the global markets. The features of the bond were as follows:

Objective :	Expansion, doubling of the capacity.
Nature :	FCCBs would not be secured and therefore would be treated as unsecured loan in the balance sheet.
Face value :	US $1,000
Interest :	Payable at 4% annually in arrears
Maturity :	5 years maturing on March 2012
Listing :	Singapore and London Stock Exchanges
Conversion :	Each bond shall be convertible into Equity shares of the company at the option of the holder any time before maturity at a fixed price of ₹200 and fixed foreign exchange rate of ₹44.50 per $, being the rate prevailing on the date of offering.

The conversion price of ₹200 was arrived on the basis of average of closing prices of the share for the last 3 months and 6 months as tabulated in Table F.

On 15 March 2007, the firm received the proposed money through the FCCBs, and it was deposited in the bank net of flotation costs. The transaction was recorded in the books as follows:

In crore

	US $	₹		US $	₹
FCCB Liability	8.00	356.00	Bank Deposit	7.90	351.55
Issue Expenses against reserves	–0.10	–4.45			

Following events occurred between 15 March and 30 March.

1. Immediately upon subscription, some of the bondholders decided to convert their holding into equity shares at ₹200 as the share price had already moved beyond ₹230. The aggregate value of the bonds so converted into equity till 31 March 2007 was US $10 million.
2. Out of the 79 million held in the banks in London
   (a) Mr Kulkarni repatriated US $10 million on 22 March when the exchange rate was ₹43.66
   (b) Mr Kulkarni also decided to pay US $20 million directly to the supplier of capital goods who had already supplied some of the machinery required for expansion. This was done on 28 March when the exchange rate was ₹43.47.

Discuss

On 31 March 2007, the exchange rate had moved to ₹43.59. As on 31 March 2007, Mr Kulkarni was required to prepare his balance sheet at the closing rates. Find out the following:

1. The loss incurred by ABC Ltd upon conversion into equity.
2. How would you translate the conversion of FCCB liability into equity capital and what treatment would be accorded to the loss incurred on conversion to equity?
3. What is the loss of the cash flow upon: (a) remittance of money into India and (b) payment to capital goods supplier directly in the foreign exchange?
4. How much would be the loss or profit upon translation of foreign currency asset of bank deposit and liability of FCCB on 31 March 2007?

PART SEVEN

DERIVATIVES AND RISK MANAGEMENT

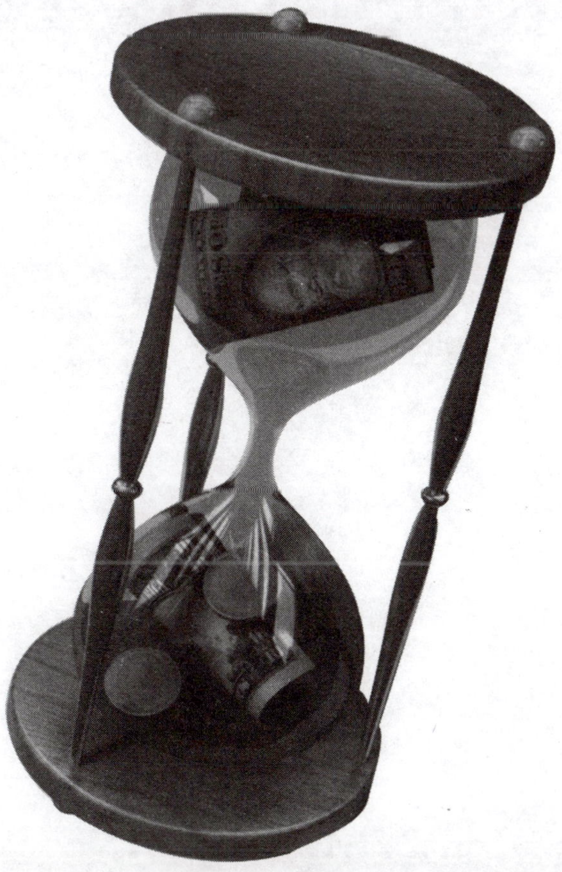

CHAPTER

28 Risk Management, Forwards & Futures

LEARNING OBJECTIVES

This chapter is aimed at providing information on

- different kinds of risks
- non-financial way of managing business risks
- derivatives and their functions
- forward contract, its features, and uses as a hedging tool
- forward contract and using it as speculative tool and for arbitrage
- futures contract and its different kinds
- differences in forward and futures contracts
- how forward contracts and futures contracts are priced
- differences between commodity futures and financial futures
- uses of commodity futures for hedging, speculation and as spread strategies
- currency futures, their pricing and hedging applications
- stock index futures, their pricing, and applications of hedging, speculation and arbitrage

FUTURES LOOK GOOD FOR SURAKSHIT—DRIVING RISK TO SAFETY

Mr Surakshit Gupta was wondering how not to lose the opportunity of making some money. He was an avid investor, completely obsessed with equity research. An extremely confident person about his research, he always sounded very convincing in his words and logic. Mr Gupta always believed in fundamentals and followed principles while investing on cash basis. Any kind of leverage or borrowing was simply unacceptable.

He had spotted some undervalued shares. Not only were these identified shares expected to perform exceedingly well, he was also optimistic about the general outlook. His present portfolio mostly consisting blue chip stocks had outperformed the market. He did not want to liquidate any of the stocks in his portfolio to take a position in the newly identified shares. He was wondering by the time he gets money from his insurance policy, maturing in next two months, it would be too late to invest because the prices would have gone up by then. Understanding his dilemma that if he invested after three months, a major part of the gain would be wiped out, his broker friend, Mr Prayogik, suggested a way out.

Prayogik: Why don't you divest a part of the existing portfolio and invest in these newly identified securities?

Surakshit: I don't want to touch my existing portfolio. That has outperformed the market in the past and would continue to do so. Though the prospect of return on the existing portfolio are not likely to be as good as on the new securities I have identified, that is not a good enough reason for me to divest the existing holding. I would persist with the existing securities simply because it carries little risk.

Prayogik: Well, if you wish to continue to hold the existing portfolio and do not have money now and also don't want to lose the opportunity to make gains, then the way out is to buy futures of the stocks identified.

Surakshit: You know I am not a speculator. Futures are too risky. I always invest cash. In any case, how does it help?

Prayogik: No, you have a misconception. You buy futures today. All you need to pay is a small sum as margin money to take some position. That covers your potential losses. In any case, futures contracts are settled on a daily basis where you get the profit or pay the losses. You have to discipline yourself to the maximum loss that you can take and unwind your position then. So, it is not risky if you follow discipline.

Surakshit: That is very difficult.

Prayogik: Well, if you are confident of your forecast, you buy the futures today and sell after three months when you have enough cash to take physical position. That way, you can protect the losses and your effective cost of purchase would be the price prevailing today.

Surakshit: What about the shares on which there is no futures contract?

Prayogik: Even then, the futures are very good instrument. In such a case, if not the entire but at least a part of the gain can be pocketed by taking a position in the index futures. You know that returns are partly due to good market sentiments and partly due to fundamentals of the firm. The part of the returns attributable to the market can be captured by taking position in the stock index futures.

Surakshit: You seem to favour derivatives a lot.

Prayogik: Yes. I find many more advantages with them. The most significant advantage is for people like me who do not understand the intricacies of finance, or do not have enough time and analytical skill or desire to make effort for equity research like you. Simply taking a position on the index futures gives you market returns with least of capital. You need not bother about identifying the stock. If you feel good about the future, simply buy index futures and you would get market returns. There in no need for equity research as long as you are happy with the market returns.

Surakshit: What other benefit do you have with futures?

Prayogik: It is a very safe instrument for hedging.

Surakshit: How?

Prayogik: I have many clients like you who want to stick to their portfolios and not churn every now and then because frequent adjusting involves transaction costs. More importantly, the reason why you are changing your portfolio may not come out to be true. So you lose unnecessarily. Futures are good for such people.

Surakshit: What else?

Prayogik: You can beat the market with futures by adjusting the beta of the portfolio. You see when sentiments are up, everybody wants beta of the portfolio to be greater and greater. If beta is greater than 1, you beat the market. You simply buy the futures rather than identifying high beta securities. Similarly, when the market sentiments are down, you wish to reduce the beta of your portfolio to have losses lower than the market. You simply sell futures. That way, the need for changing the portfolio every now and then is eliminated.

Surakshit: Oh, that is good. Now I understand how you make more money than I do, despite spending so much of my time on the research. I never touched derivative because I regarded them to be too dangerous.

Prayogik: Remember, it is the greed that makes derivatives explosive. For need-based use, derivatives are very safe.

INTRODUCTION—RISK MANAGEMENT

Risk is inherent in all the activities we do in our day-to-day life, and all of us remain concerned about it. We all would like to eliminate it altogether. In most cases, complete elimination of risk is not possible, but certain steps can be taken to mitigate the risk. In our personal life, when we buy an insurance policy against theft in the house or for a vehicle, we are attempting to minimize the potential loss we may incur if some unfortunate event takes place.

Each one of us in everyday life faces variety of risks and also manages them with appropriate tools and strategies.

The risk is normally gauged from: (i) the probability of an adverse event happening and (ii) the expected magnitude of loss in case such an event occurs. The preparedness and the measures to mitigate risk are determined by the combined impact of the probability and magnitude of loss. If there is a high probability of small losses (stock prices, commodity prices) or small probability of large losses (earthquakes, tsunami, etc.), the magnitude of risk may be same but the strategies of risk management may differ. In business enterprises, the management of risk is mainly confined to situations of high probability of small losses. The management of the other kind of risk of small probability of large losses are more strategic in nature such as capital budgeting decisions. We now turn our focus on the management of the risks that emanate from conduct of normal operations of the business.

Managing Risk

There are various ways different people manage different kinds of risks. Insurance policy is a classic example of managing risk with which we all are familiar.

One possible way to avoid the risk is **not to undertake an activity** at all. There are people who abstain from air travel because they see too great a risk with that mode of transport. Likewise, certain people do not invest in equity market due to the risk associated with stock market and prefer to invest in safer avenues. While certain activities can be avoided purely on the ground of high risk and one can still live without it, not investing in the equity market for instance, it may not be possible to abstain from mandatory activities. One has to find better avenues to manage risk rather than avoidance of the activity altogether.

Another way of managing risk is to **diffuse the risk** across the sources of risk. Many call centres prefer to have multi-location operations to protect themselves against natural disasters. Similarly, investors prefer to have investment in many alternatives to protect themselves against fall in expected return from a single investment, as risk of failure of many investments simultaneously is far less than the risk of failing of a single investment. Likewise, firms do not have a single supplier or a single customer to manage business. They prefer to have many suppliers/customers, as it is not possible that all the suppliers would fail to deliver and all the customers would be weaned away by competitors at the same point of time.

Lastly, one can manage the risk by **transferring** it to another party who is willing to assume risk. Insurance company does not do anything to contain the risk *per se*, but assumes risk on your behalf. It is the business of the insurance company to assume risk for an income. Similarly, there are people who are willing to assume risks of other kind for a consideration. Risk as such does not and cannot vanish but gets transferred from one who wants to avoid it to the one who is willing to accept the risk upon exchange of consideration.

There exist a wide array of financial instruments and financial markets that enable business enterprises to contain risks inherent in their day-to-day operations. Non-financial risks, such as financial loss due to a certain key employee leaving an organization, failure of R&D department to develop a product, breakdown of production machine, losses due to vagaries of nature, etc., are not in the scope of discussions.

Types of Business Risks

Leaving aside the risks of the nature described earlier, we concentrate here on the day-to-day risks that have large probabilities of small losses. Some of the risks that a business enterprise faces and for which suitable financial instruments and deep markets exist, are described briefly here.

Business risks are characterized by small losses but with high probability and concerns about changes in prices, exchange rates, and interest rates.

Price risk All markets, be it of commodity, stocks, or materials, are dynamic. The forces of demand and supply vary continuously. The prices are never stable, though they strive for equilibrium. This change in price causes the profit of a business enterprise change, which is a cause of anxiety for managers of the firm. The investors also face the same situation when they invest in financial securities, the prices of which vary causing uncertainty of returns.

Exchange rate risk Exchange rate risk emanates from the transactions pertaining to foreign currency where a firm faces uncertainty regarding the exchange rate at which the foreign currency will be converted in the domestic currency or vice versa. As an example, consider a firm that sells goods on credit and realizes its sales proceeds in foreign currency. Even though the price in foreign currency is frozen, the firm faces an uncertainty regarding the amount that will be realized in domestic currency depending upon the rate prevailing at the time of realization of sales. Similarly, an importer having to pay in foreign currency at a later date would be uncertain about the actual amount to be paid in domestic currency.

Interest rate risk Like the changes in the prices and the exchange rates, the interest rates too keep changing depending upon various macro-economic factors, both national and international. All firms needing capital resort to borrowing, while those with surplus funds invest. Both the borrowers and investors face the risk of changes in the interest rates subsequent to the transaction.

DERIVATIVES

The three kinds of risk described in the preceding section can be managed through products that are classified as derivatives. Derivatives are agreements that derive their values on the basis of some asset, called an underlying asset. An example will illustrate the meaning of a derivative product.

Derivatives are product that derive their value from some other asset called underlying asset

Consider that an Indian exporter is expecting to realize $1,000 in six months' time from now. He had priced his product with a profit of ₹2,000 based on the current market price of ₹45 per $. The actual money that will be realized by him in Indian rupees will depend upon the exchange rate prevailing six months later. This rate is not known today. The exporter expects ₹45,000 but may end up getting ₹44,000 if the exchange rate is ₹44 six months later. On the other hand, he may realize ₹46,000 if the exchange rate goes up to ₹46/$. If the rate happens to be ₹44, his profit will stand reduced to half by ₹1,000. Though he can't do much to control the prices of dollar in the currency market and hence his profit, he can definitely take some measures to reduce the uncertainty of the exchange rate and consequential profit.

One of the ways that he can choose to reduce the uncertainty is to sell dollar to a party who needs them six months later and negotiate the exchange rate today. By doing so, he will be assuring himself of definite profit. Such a contract will be called a forward contract where the actual exchange of currency will take place later but at a price that is determined today. Of course, the price at which this forward contract will be negotiated will be dependent upon the current price of dollar, which is known as the spot price. Since the price of the forward contract is determined or in other words derived from the spot market of the foreign currency market, such a contract is classified as derivative. The spot price of foreign exchange, on the basis of which forward contract price will be negotiated, is called the underlying asset.

Similarly, a forward contract can be negotiated for any commodity, subject to legal constraints and feasibility. For example, a farmer growing wheat can sell his crop before harvesting at a price negotiated today. The physical delivery of crop and exchange of cash will take place on the due date of the contract but at a price that is determined today. By selling the crop in advance at a known price will help the farmer to concentrate on his work rather than to worry about the price that will prevail when he harvests the crop. Here, the underlying asset will be the crop of wheat, whose current prices will govern the price of the forward contract.

For the sake of definition of a derivative, we may state that a derivative is a contract whose price is derived from the price of the underlying asset and which remains distinctly different from and independent of the underlying asset for all remaining features.

Derivative Products

Forwards are the oldest form of a derivative contract. Several financial innovations have taken place, especially in 1970s and thereafter, and a host of derivative products have come into existence since then. Innovations continue unabated making products more and more complex. The growth, both in terms of new innovations and the volumes of trading in derivatives, has been enormous. The innovations in the derivatives markets have made financial instruments so complex that understanding them requires special aptitude and knowledge.

The prolific growth in the derivatives trading has also occurred due to the vast number of business applications, the investors and academicians have devised. These applications cover a wide array of situations, ranging from speculation to hedging to profiting from mispricing. Due to the wide variety of applications, the interest of investors is continuously increasing.

Participants in Derivative Markets

The participants in the derivative markets can be broadly classified in three different categories depending upon their motives. These are:

1. Hedgers
2. Speculators
3. Arbitrageurs

Hedgers are those who enter into a derivative contract with the objective of covering risk. A farmer growing wheat faces uncertainty about the price of his product at the time of the harvest. Similarly, a flour mill needing wheat also faces uncertainty of price of input. Both the farmer and the flour mill can enter into a forward contract, where the farmer agrees to sell his product when harvested at a predetermined price to the flour mill. Such a contract will eliminate risk of price for both the parties. The contract was entered into with the objective of hedging against the price risk. Such participants in the derivatives markets are called hedgers.

There are three kinds of participants in derivatives market with different motives: hedging, speculation, and arbitrage.

Speculators are those who enter into a derivative contract to make profit by assuming risk. If only hedgers were to operate in the derivative markets, the number of participants in the market will be extremely limited. A farmer would find it difficult to locate a flour mill with perfectly matched and complimentary requirements in terms of quantity, quality, and timing of delivery of the asset (wheat in this case). If middlemen are permitted to operate, the hedgers need not look for exact match; instead they can deal with the middlemen who would buy the product from the farmer in advance with anticipation of higher price in future at the time of harvest. Such middlemen will be speculating on the future price and bid a current price in a manner that results in gain for him. By entering into a contract on the derivatives, the speculators are assuming risk of price in future.

The third category of participants is an **arbitrageur**. While hedgers and speculators want to eliminate and assume risk respectively, the arbitrageurs take a risk-less position and yet earn profits. They are constantly monitoring the prices of different assets and identify opportunities to make profit that emanate from mispricing of products. The most common example of arbitrage is the price difference that may be prevailing in different stock markets. For example, if the share price of Hindustan Lever is ₹175 in NSE and ₹177 in BSE, the arbitrageur will buy at NSE and sell at BSE simultaneously and pocket the difference of ₹2 per share. An arbitrageur takes risk-neutral position and makes profits because markets are imperfect. Naturally such imperfections cannot exist for long. These imperfections are extremely short-lived. The arbitrageurs cashes upon these short-lived opportunities. Such actions restore the balance in prices and remove distortions in the pricing of assets.

Each type of participant is equally essential for proper and efficient functioning of the market. None of them can be termed as desirable or undesirable.

Functions of Derivative Markets

The derivatives were invented to fulfil the need of hedging against the price risk. Besides, hedging derivatives perform three other important functions.

Price discovery First the derivatives and its market increase the competitiveness of the market as it encourages more number of participants with varying objectives of hedging, speculation, and arbitraging. With broadening of the

Derivatives perform important function of efficient price discovery, transfer of risk, and leveraging.

market, the changes in the price of the product are watched by those who trade on the slightest of reasons. Even a minor variation in price prompts action on the part of speculators. Active participation by large number of buyers and sellers ensures fair price. The derivative markets therefore facilitate price discovery of assets due to increased participants, increased volumes, and increased sensitivity of participants to react to smallest of price changes.

Facilitate transfer of risk Hedgers amongst themselves could eliminate risk if two parties face risk from opposite movement of price. The wheat farmer needing to sell his product faced a risk from the fall in price while the flour mill needing to buy wheat was worried about the rise in price. Since the risk was emanating from opposing directions, the convergence of the two was possible. If both farmer and flourmill wanted to hedge against price rise, the two would not have met. When speculators enter the market, they discharge an important function and help transfer of risk from those wanting to eliminate to those wanting to assume risk.

Leveraging Taking position in derivatives involves only fractional outlay of capital when compared with the position in the underlying asset in the spot market. Assume a speculator is convinced that price of wheat will be ₹16 per kg in six months and a farmer agrees to sell at ₹15.50 per kg. To take advantage, the speculator will have to pay the full price of ₹15.50 per kg now and realize ₹16.00 six months later. Instead, if a mechanism is available by which he can absolve himself of making the full payment, he will be too glad to enter into a contract. Derivatives as products and their markets provide such exit routes by letting him enter into a contract and then permitting him to neutralize the position by booking an opposite contract at a later date. This magnifies the profit manifold with same resource base. This also helps build volumes of trade, further helping the price discovery process.

Classification of Derivatives

Derivative instruments are broadly classified into four categories. They are: forwards, futures, options, and swaps.

There is a wide menu of instruments available as derivatives. Each of the instruments is different in some respect or the other—conceptually, operationally, or in its uses. The derivative products that are continuously evolving can broadly be categorized as below:

Forwards: *Forwards* are those contracts where the buyer and seller agree to exchange the asset and its price at a predetermined price on an agreed date.

Futures: *Futures* are similar to forward contracts in terms of its pricing and concept, but are operationally different from forwards in terms of other features. The features of futures contracts are standardized in terms of quantity, delivery dates, delivery venues, quality of the product, etc., unlike forward contracts. These features will be discussed later.

Options: *Options* are contracts for delivery in future like forwards and futures except that one of two parties involved holds an option whether to enforce the contract or not, while the other party is obligated to perform at the option of the first party.

Swaps: *Swaps* are agreements between two parties to exchange a set of cash flows according to a predetermined method.

Another source of variety of derivatives emanates from the vast range of underlying assets. One can have derivative contract on any asset, financial or otherwise. These assets can be physical or hypothetical. It is the compulsion of delivery of the underlying assets that makes the price of derivatives linked to the spot price of the asset. However, in some cases, the underlying asset can be hypothetical such as index futures where the delivery of the underlying asset is not possible, yet one can trade in them for beneficial outcome.

Derivatives can be classified on the basis of pay offs, underlying asset, trading

Based on the underlying asset, the derivatives can be classified as:

- Commodities: The commodities on which derivatives contracts exist are:
  - Agricultural products, such as rice, wheat, cotton, oils, soya, tea, coffee, rubber, etc.
  - Metals, such as copper, tin, gold, silver, etc.
- Currencies, such as US $, Canadian $, Singapore $, Euro, Yen, Mexican Peso, etc.
- Interest rates
- Equity shares
- Stock indices

Derivatives can further be grouped according to the markets they are dealt in. The derivatives can be of two types, namely:

(a) Over-the-counter (OTC) products, or
(b) Exchange traded products.

When two mutually consenting parties enter into a contract with matching needs that are known to each other, such contracts are called over-the-counter (OTC) products. These contracts are specific to the parties involved and are not traded in the market. These contracts are customized to the requirements of counter parties and are normally settled by delivery of underlying asset, though there is a possibility of exiting the obligations by entering into a subsequent contract opposite to the first one.

Other kind of derivatives, namely the exchange traded products, are traded on the organized exchanges where the buyer and seller need not know each other, the exchange being the counter-party for both buyer and seller. They are standard products whose specifications are designed by the exchange authorities taking into consideration the characteristics of the underlying assets.

FORWARD CONTRACTS

Forward contracts are all-pervasive. Knowingly or unknowingly, we all enter into a forward contract. In most cases, we all acquire assets and pay the consideration for the same simultaneously. All transactions of cash are made on the spot. However, in some cases, we book a purchase in advance and execute the

Forward contract is an agreement between two contracting parties to buy/sell an asset on a given date and at a predetermined price.

delivery and its consideration at a later point of time. Booking a movie ticket on phone is one such example. It is a sort of forward contract because we buy the ticket and pay its price only after reaching the cinema hall. Similarly, most automobiles are booked in advance and the price is paid only upon the physical delivery of the vehicle. This too is an example of a forward contract where asset and cash is exchanged at a later date.

Features of Forward Contract

Following are the features of a forward contract:

- Like any contract, a forward contract also involves minimum of two parties, a buyer and a seller of asset. It is an OTC product where all relevant aspects of asset, quantity, price, and delivery date are fixed on one-to-one basis customized to the needs of the parties involved.
- The price at which the exchange of asset will be done is negotiated in advance. By doing so, both buyer and seller attempt to avoid the price risk by locking in a price today.
- On due date of the contract, seller makes the delivery and buyer pays the price. There is a mutual obligation between the buyer and the seller to perform according to the requirement. The seller is committed to make delivery on due date, and the buyer is obligated to pay the consideration.
- The buyer and seller of the contract assume risk, referred as counter-party risk on each other. The seller may fail to deliver the asset and/or the buyer may fail to make the payment on the agreed date. While entering the forward contract, both the contracting parties are aware of the possible default by the other party and take adequate precaution to prevent such default on either side.
- Once a forward contract is booked, both parties are obligated to perform. The cancellation can only be done through mutual consent of both the parties any time prior to the maturity of the contract.
- No exchange of money is done at the time of entering the forward contract, though any of the party can insist on initial deposit adjustable against price and delivery to mitigate counter-party risk.

Forward contracts in India are available in major foreign currencies through various banks authorized to deal in foreign currencies. Importers who need foreign currencies and exporters who realize their sales in foreign currency deal with the banks to buy and sell the foreign currencies respectively. The spot and forward rates are available on demand and are also published as indicative rates only. One cannot force a contract on the published rates. Banks normally quote rates of foreign currencies for spot sale and purchase as well as on forward basis for standard tenures of 1 month, 3 months, and 6 months.

Table 28-1 gives the spot and forward rates of foreign currencies as on 16 September, 2005 as quoted by State Bank of India. How these rates are arrived at is beyond the domain of this chapter. Here, we present the meaning of these quotations. Spot rate is the rate at which transaction will be done for settlement to take place now (in fact, within two business days as per the convention in the foreign exchange markets). For example, consider spot rates of Pound Sterling. The bank will buy Pound Sterling from exporters at ₹79.34, whereas sell the same to importers at ₹79.61. The exchange of Pound Sterling and Indian rupee will be done on the spot, i.e., within two business days.

Table 28-1 Spot and forward foreign exchange rates as on 16 September 2005

As quoted by State Bank of India								
Import				*Currency*	*Export*			
6m	*3m*	*1m*	*Spot*		*Spot*	*1m*	*3m*	*6m*
44.13	44.06	44.02	43.97	US $	43.83	43.83	43.85	43.92
54.57	54.22	54.01	53.87	Euro	53.69	53.63	53.73	53.98
79.71	76.56	79.65	79.61	Pound Sterling	79.34	79.28	79.27	79.32
35.41	35.07	34.85	34.72	Swiss Franc	34.61	34.56	34.66	34.90
7.32	7.27	7.24	7.22	Danish Kroner	7.20	7.19	7.21	7.24
33.68	33.74	33.83	33.81	Australian $	33.69	33.80	33.76	33.72
37.46	37.31	37.21	37.14	Canadian $	37.01	36.95	37.00	37.12
								₹ per unit of foreign currency

Source: Business Line, 17 September 2005

If importers and exporters want to buy or sell the foreign currency for future settlement, they may do so by booking a forward contract with the bank. For example, if an exporter expects to realize Swiss Franc 6-m later, he can sell the same to the bank today by booking a 6-m forward sell contract at ₹34.90 per Swiss Franc. The physical exchange of currencies will take place 6-m later at a price of ₹34.90 fixed today. At the end of six months, the exporter will deliver to the bank Swiss Francs and the bank will pay ₹34.90 for each Swiss Franc.

Hedging Through Forward Contracts

Forward contract can be used to remove the uncertainty of the price in future by buying and selling them now.

Exporters who expect to realize the sales in foreign currency face the risk of falling price of foreign currency. They need protection in the loss of the value of the asset; the account receivable. If the foreign currency appreciates, the value of the asset would rise and exporters would welcome such a change. It is the unfavourable movement (depreciating foreign currency in this case) that is a cause of concern. This concern may be mitigated by selling the anticipated receipts in foreign currency by entering a forward contract with the bank wherein the exporter promises to deliver the foreign currency in exchange of receipt of the domestic currency at a rate fixed now.

Currency forward is an agreement to give or take delivery of foreign currency in exchange of domestic currency at a future-specified date and at an exchange rate determined today.

Similarly, importers who have to make a definite payment in foreign currency at a future date are apprehensive of its rising price. They see an increase in the value of payable which must be confined to an acceptable level. The apprehension about the rising prices of the foreign currency can be removed by freezing the exchange rate now by entering into a forward contract to buy the foreign currency where the importer would obtain the requisite foreign currency in exchange of delivery of domestic currency with a rate known now.

Based on the data in Table 28-1, we present below two examples demonstrating how hedging can be done for receivables and payables.

Example 28-1 Hedging by Exporter

An exporter, EXPressive Ltd, has sold merchandise worth £1,00,000 to a customer in England. EXPressive expects to receive the money in three months from now. The spot price of Pound is ₹79.34. The exporter is expecting depreciation of pound during the next three months and expects the price to be at ₹79.00 then. What can EXPressive do to protect itself from depreciating pound? For all data, refer to Table 28-1.

Solution

The 3-m forward rate available from the bank is ₹79.27. EXPressive can sell a 6-m forward contract for £ 1,00,000 to the bank. After three months, the settlement will be done as follows:

EXPressive will deliver to the bank	:	£ 1,00,000
Bank will pay to EXPressive	:	₹79,27,000

By booking the forward contract, EXPressive has mitigated the anticipated losses. If forward contract was not booked, EXPressive would have sold its Pound Sterling at the spot price prevailing then. If the rate had fallen to ₹79.00 as anticipated, they would have realized only ₹79,00,000. Through forward sale of Pound Sterling, they benefited by ₹27,000. On the other hand, if Pound Sterling appreciated to ₹79.50, the collection would be ₹79,50,000, i.e., ₹23,000 more than what is being realized from the forward contract.

Example 28-2 Hedging by Importer

An importer, IMPressive Ltd, has purchased a machine from a supplier in Germany for € 10,000 for which the payment is due in six months. The current price of Euro is ₹53.84. The importer is expecting Euro to appreciate to a level of ₹55.00 in six months' time and is worried about rising value of Euro. What can be done to safeguard importer's interest?

Solution

The importer is expecting cash outflow of ₹5,50,000 if his anticipation about value of Euro proves correct. To safeguard its position IMPressive may buy € 10,000 6-m forward from the bank, which quotes a rate of ₹54.57 (refer Table 28-1). At the time of making the payment in Euro after 6 months:

Bank will provide IMPressive	:	€ 10,000
IMPressive will pay to the bank	:	₹5,45,700

By booking of a forward buy contract IMPressive has ensured that it does not end up paying more than ₹54.57 per €. Whether or not the importer benefited economically from such a deal will be known only at the expiry of forward contract, i.e. by the spot rate at the time of settlement of the forward contract. If Euro appreciated to a level more than ₹54.57, then IMPressive benefits from the forward contract. On the other hand, if the price of Euro remained below ₹54.57, IMPressive would be better off without a forward contract.

One common misconception about hedging is that it improves the profitability and it can compensate the losses anticipated. It needs to be clarified that forward hedge cannot provide the desired price. In fact, the spot price (S_0) of the asset is market determined and no one can alter it. Forward contracts ensure a price for the hedger irrespective of the future spot price of the currency, S_1. The forward price (F_1) too cannot be changed.

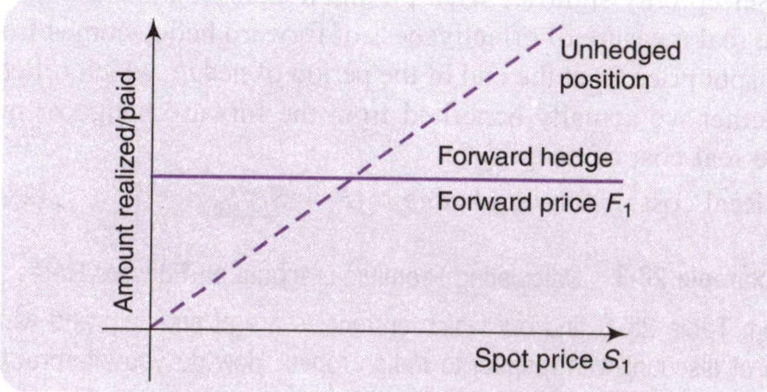

Figure 28-1 Pay off of a forward hedge

When an exporter books a forward contract, he realizes the forward price F_1 that is fixed in advance for his receivables irrespective of the price prevailing at the time of realization. When he is unhedged, the amount realized will depend upon the spot price S_1 prevailing at the time of receiving the foreign currency as shown in Figure 28-1. Similar would be the case in respect of an importer buying the forward contract for foreign currency.

Also note that—by hedging through the forward contract, the risk was transferred from the customers to the bank. While customers were assured of the definite price, the bank assumed the risk of price change in the foreign exchange. One may argue why the banks should bear the risk of fluctuations in the price, banks being more conservative in approach than businessmen. The answer is simple enough. Banks have many options. Firstly, banks usually cover themselves up for the risk by entering into another contract of opposite nature with another party. Secondly, banks can resort to netting of exposures. Having bought \$10,000 and sold \$8,000 for delivery on the same future date, the bank needs to cover itself only for the net exposure of \$2,000, rather than sell \$10,000 and buy \$8,000 separately to nullify its position. Netting of exposure will cost much less.

Cost of forward hedge Since exporter and importer have assured themselves of a fixed price removing uncertainties, the assurance cannot come free of cost. We need to know what costs are borne by hedgers.

Traditionally, the cost of forward hedge is measured in terms of premium or discount over the spot price. If forward price is higher than the spot price, the currency is said to be at premium. When forward price is less than the spot price, the foreign currency is said to be at discount. The cost of forward hedge is measured as % premium or discount over the current spot price as below:

$$\text{Cost of hedging} = \text{Premium or Discount } (+/-) = (F_1 - S_0)/S_0 \quad (28\text{-}1)$$

When foreign currency is more expensive in future than in spot, i.e., $F_1 > S_0$, it is said to be at premium; and when cheaper than spot, i.e., $F_1 < S_0$, it is at discount.

In fact, the efficacy of the forward hedge can be measured only after the forward contract period is over. The real cost or benefit of the forward hedge must be measured, not when it was set-up but when it ended. The cost of forward hedge at the time of set-up only signifies what premium or discount is available. The real measure of effectiveness of forward hedge comes from the spot price S_1 at the end of the period of hedge, which reflects whether we actually benefited from the forward hedge or not. The real cost of hedging is:

$$\text{Real cost of forward hedge} = (F_1 - S_1)/S_0 \qquad (28\text{-}2)$$

Example 28-3 Calculating Premium/Discount on Forward Rates

From Table 28-1, find out which currencies are at premium and which are at discount with respect to Indian rupee. How do you interpret the premium or discount?

Solution

The premium or discount on the currencies can be found by using Equation 28-1. Normally, the premium and discount are expressed in annualized % terms. The premium/discount in annualized % is given by:

Annualized premium (+)/discount(–)

$$= \frac{\text{forward rate} - \text{spot rate}}{\text{spot rate}} \times \frac{12}{\text{period of forward in months}} \times 100$$

The annualized premium/discount is computed for all the currencies below with negative sign denoting discount.

Annualized Premium/Discount for exporters

Currency	*Spot Rate ₹/Unit of FC*	*3 m Forward ₹/Unit of FC*	*Annualized Premium/ Discount (%)*
US $	43.83	43.85	0.18%
€	53.69	53.73	0.30%
Pound Sterling	79.34	79.27	–0.35%
Swiss Franc	34.61	34.66	0.58%
Danish Kroner	7.20	7.21	0.56%
Australian $	33.69	33.76	0.83%
Canadian $	37.01	37.00	–0.11%

If the currency is at premium, it implies that the foreign currency will appreciate in future. A premium of 0.83% for Australian dollar indicates that the value of Australian dollar will increase by 0.83%, and it is expected that the spot price of Australian dollar one year later will be ₹33.97 (33.69 × 1.0083). Similarly, a discount indicates decreasing value of the foreign currency. British pound is expected to decline by 0.35% by next year and the spot price then should be around ₹79.06 (79.34 × 0.9965).

Speculation with Forward Contracts

In Examples 28-1 and 28-2, the exporter and importer covered the risks on assets owned. The exporter was holing foreign currency receivable, and the importer was holding a fixed amount of domestic currency for the foreign currency denominated payable. Hence, they booked the forward contracts with the purpose of hedging their receivables and payables respectively and had all the intentions of honouring their commitments.

In contrast to actions of EXPressive and IMPressive, consider a financial firm, BETTERS Ltd, who are neither users nor suppliers of foreign exchange. They research on the foreign exchange movements and forecast rates. Whenever they find forward rates attractive, they trade on them with the sole objective of making a profit.

Forward contracts can also be used for speculation in the currency exchange rate markets by holding a view contrary to the market and taking a position.

As per Table 28-1, the spot price of US dollar is ₹43.83 and 6-m forward price is ₹43.92 at an annualized premium of mere 0.41%. BETTERS feel that the US dollar is undervalued and should command a better premium than what is indicated by the forward rate. Therefore, BETTERS buy US dollars 6-m forward at ₹43.92. They keep a continuous watch on the exchange rate movement specifically on US dollar. They are convinced that in six months' time, the US dollar will command a better price. They can do either of the following:

1. Whenever forward rate of US dollar crosses the price of ₹43.92, they can neutralize their position by booking a sell contract such that the maturity of the new sell contract coincides with the maturity of the original buy contract. Suppose three months later, the 3-m forward contract is available at ₹44.00. BETTERS can book a 3-m forward contract to sell US dollar at ₹44.00 and earn a profit of ₹0.08 for each dollar. Note that the delivery dates of both the first and second contracts coincide, although it is not at all necessary to match maturity dates to take speculative position.
2. Alternatively, they can wait till the contract matures when BETTERS were required to take the delivery of dollar by paying an equivalent at ₹43.92, the contracted rate. Rather than taking delivery, BETTERS sell the dollar at spot price, booking either profit or loss depending upon the spot price prevailing then.

The actions of BETTERS Ltd are termed as speculative since they held the contrary view to what the markets indicated and were prepared to assume a position on their own regarding the future movement of the prices of US dollar. In fact, they were not attempting to cover any risk as they did not have either the foreign currency or needed it in future, but instead were taking risk by opening the first forward contract in the hope to neutralize the exposure subsequently. In case the likely movement was not in their favour, they would lose some value.

Arbitrage with Forward Contract

As defined earlier, the process of arbitrage requires set-up of a riskless position, in contrast to speculative actions which set-up an initial position and wait for an opportune time to square up the initial position. It is not possible to find an opportunity to make arbitrage profit from the same source, as the rates offered by the same bank will

Different currency exchange rates by different banks for a currency may provide opportunities for arbitrage.

be offered in such a manner that they result into profit for the bank and hence loss for the customers. However, it is possible to find another bank that offers rates such that a smart and aware investor can buy from one source at cheaper rates and sell to another at higher rates simultaneously.

From Table 28-1, we note that State Bank of India offers following rates for Swiss Franc:

Exchange rates of State Bank of India

Import				*Currency*	*Export*			
6m	*3m*	*1m*	*Spot*		*Spot*	*1m*	*3m*	*6m*
35.41	35.07	34.85	34.72	Swiss Franc	34.61	34.56	34.66	34.90

Hypothetically, let us assume that Citibank offers the following exchange rates at the same time for Swiss Franc:

Exchange rates of Citibank

Import				*Currency*	*Export*			
6m	*3m*	*1m*	*Spot*		*Spot*	*1m*	*3m*	*6m*
34.41	34.07	33.85	33.72	Swiss Franc	33.61	33.56	33.66	33.90

An arbitrageur spots an opportunity to make profit from the rates available from State Bank of India and Citibank. The arbitrageur can sell Swiss Franc 6-m forward at ₹34.90 to State Bank of India, and simultaneously buy Swiss Franc 6-m forward from Citibank at ₹34.41.

Note that by buying from one and selling to another, the arbitrageur has assured himself of a profit of ₹0.49 for each Swiss Franc transacted, without involving any capital or entering into any obligation that cannot be fulfilled. His position stands nullified as he buys the Swiss Francs from Citibank and sells simultaneously the same amount to State Bank of India.

FUTURES

We discussed the mechanism of forward contract as a tool of risk management, speculation, and possible arbitrage in the preceding section. We now discuss the futures contracts that are like forwards in their applications but differ substantially in operations.

Futures are relatively new derivatives. The value of derivative fluctuates with the value of the underlying asset. The underlying asset can be a commodity, metal, stock, currency, bond, index, T-bills, a reference interest rate or any other real or hypothetical asset.

Why Futures

Futures contracts came into existence to overcome some of the problems that exist with the forward contract. In a forward contract, there is a very strong inclination for at least one party to default in fulfilling its commitment towards the other party to the contract depending upon the price scenario of the underlying asset. Post contract, the scenario will favour only one of the parties to the contract.

One way of eliminating the counter-party risk is to involve another party to the transaction. The forward contract is executed on a one-to-one basis and the two parties assume the counter-party risk. It can be easily visualized that one default will lead to chain reaction and the whole market may collapse with one default triggering another.

Risk of default would seriously limit the volumes of trade in the forward markets.

The issue of counter-party risk can be solved if the transaction is done on an exchange that serves as counter-party to both buyer and seller. Rather than conducting business on one-to-one basis, they do business on the exchange. Both buyer and seller become liable to the exchange which in turn meets commitments to both. In case of default by one party, the exchange meets the commitment from alternate sources. To protect itself, the exchange can develop suitable risk containment measures. With the exchange serving as guarantor, both buyer and seller of the contract are assured of performance as depicted in Figure 28-2. This also eliminates the need to know each other and establish credibility before undertaking a forward deal.

The role of the guarantor, to ensure a default-free performance, can be performed by an organized body, i.e., an exchange. Rather than settling the transaction on the due date, both the buyer and seller can make their promises good to an exchange obviating the need of the buyer and seller to know each other. This is depicted in Figure 28-2.

However, if the trades have to take place on an exchange, the product cannot be tailor-made to the specific needs of the two parties and instead would have to be standardized. Exchange cannot commit itself to the quantity, quality, and timing of the asset as per the specific requirements of individual buyers and sellers. If the exchange has to serve as counter-party, it has to deal in standardized products in terms of quantity, quality, and timing of the assets it is dealing in.

Futures are like standardized forward contracts that are exchange traded. The standardization is in terms of size, delivery, and price.

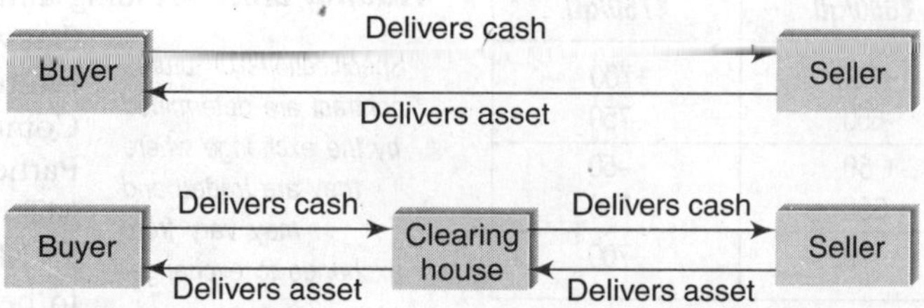

Figure 28-2 Role of clearing house

For example, an exporter selling $10,254 forward for delivery on 26 December and another selling $11,999 for delivery on 29 December will be difficult to comply with by the exchange. Instead, it will be easier for the exchange to deal in a standard contract, of say $10,000, for one particular date of delivery in the month of December. Instead, individual buyers and sellers would have to adjust their own requirement and decide the best possible course of action by choosing from the menu of standard products available in an exchange.

Futures may be defined as a standardized forward contract that is traded on an exchange where a seller agrees to deliver the specified quantity of an asset of defined quality on a predetermined date at a price fixed in advance with the buyer.

How a Future Contract Works

Let us contrast forward and future contract with an example. Assume a farmer who is producing wheat is expecting to harvest his crop that is estimated to be around 50 quintals. To remove uncertainty of price, he could sell this crop forward to a grain trader at a price of say ₹700 per quintal. Irrespective of the price of wheat in April, the farmer would realize ₹700 from the grain trader per quintal.

Unlike forwards, futures contracts de-link the delivery and price and yet provide more efficient and effective way of hedging.

Necessary prerequisite for the forward deal was locating a suitable grain dealer willing to accept delivery of wheat in April. If a futures contract existed on the exchange with wheat as underlying asset, rather than hedging through a forward contract, the farmer could opt to do the following:

1. Sell 5 futures contracts (assuming standard futures contract size of 10 quintals) on the exchange now,
2. Subsequently, the farmer buys back 5 futures contracts in April or any time prior to April, and
3. Sell wheat in the grain market at whatever price prevailing in April.

Assume that the futures contract for delivery in April is trading at ₹700 (in fact, this price may be immaterial). A necessary condition for futures is—on the day of delivery, the prices in the spot market and futures market must converge to prevent arbitrage. Hence, futures will be selling close to spot price on the day of the delivery in April. Let us examine the position of the farmer if he operates in the futures market, assuming two possible price scenarios of increased price at ₹750 and decreased price at ₹650.

(₹/quintal)

	Cash flow	
Spot Price in April	**₹650/qtl**	**₹750/qtl**
Selling 5 wheat futures contracts	+700	+700
Buying 5 wheat futures contracts	–650	–750
Gain/loss on futures trading	+ 50	–50
Price realized by the farmer	+ 650	+750
Net price realized for wheat	700	700

Note that by operating in the futures market and the physical market simultaneously, the farmer assures himself of the same price as under the forward contract. However, the mechanism is different. In case of forward contract, the farmer operates in the physical market alone. In case of hedging through futures, the farmer operates in two independent markets; the physical market where the commodity is traded and the financial market where the futures contract is traded. Both the markets are closely linked for the purpose of price determination as law of one price operates. The loss or gain in futures market is compensated by the gain or loss in the physical market ensuring a fixed price for his produce.

Besides avoiding the counter-party risk, the big advantage of futures contract is the flexibility to make an exit at whatever time prior to April. The farmer can choose to buy back his futures contract any time prior to April. He also gets the flexibility to sell his produce to anyone who offers the best price for his wheat in the physical market. In case of forward deal, the farmer was tied to the single party with whom he had entered the contract for delivery and exchange of agreed price. Here, delivery is de-linked. Delivery is made in the physical market at whatever price but financial market compensates for the gain or loss in the expected price.

Major advantages of the futures as against the forward contract are: (i) the elimination of counter-party risk, (ii) flexibility of exiting anytime, and (iii) de-linking of delivery.

Features of Futures Contract

As we know, the futures contract is a standardized product traded on the exchange. Each exchange lays down specifications of the contract in great detail for complete and unambiguous understanding of the product being dealt, lest it leads to conflicts. Explained below are a few of the terms.

Contract month Contract month refers to the month in which the delivery will be made. The exchange specifies the time when the contracts for delivery in a particular month will come into force and when it will close for trading. For example, the Rice contracts will open for trading 4 months prior to the delivery month. The opening date and last date of trading will be specified by the exchange. Unlike forwards where the delivery is as per the contract between the two parties, in a futures contract, the delivery date is fixed by the exchange.

This has important implications in terms of the period for which hedging can be done or speculative position can be taken. For example, in case of rice, there will be four contracts corresponding to the next four months available for trading at any point of time.

Trading unit Trading unit refers to the standard contract size that will be traded on the exchange. Each futures contract for rice on MCX (Multi Commodity Exchange) is for 10 MT. Participants can trade in multiples of 10 MT. This implies that in order to hedge 15 MT, either one or two contracts have to be traded.

Specifications of futures contract are determined by the exchange where they are traded and may vary from exchange to exchange.

Price quotation Quotation is the basis of price. The price quoted for the product is generally the way prices are quoted in the physical market. For example, the price quotation for futures contract on rice is ₹ per quintal. Hence, the quotation or ₹ 550 would mean ₹550 per quintal and the contract size is ₹55,000 (Value of 10 MT). Similarly, for contract in gold, the price quoted is for 10 grams while the contract size is 1 kg.

Tick size Tick size is the minimum change that will be recognized in the price quotation. For rice contract, it is Re 1. Hence a price quotation of ₹551.50 is not possible. The tick size for the contract, the minimum amount by which the value of contract changes, will be ₹100 (Re 1 per quintal over 10 MT).

Open interest The number of contracts outstanding at any point of time is called as open interest. When a new contract is introduced, the investors start taking a view on the market of the underlying asset and take an exposure on the futures contract. Under normal circumstances, initially the open interest rises with time as more and more investors start evincing interest in the new contract and either buy or sell a contract depending upon their individual opinion. But as the maturity of contract approaches, the investors tend to reduce their exposure and unwind the initial position. Hence, open interest starts declining as maturity approaches.

Open interest is the number of futures contract outstanding. It reduces to zero upon maturity of the contract.

Ultimately on the expiry of contract, all positions would be squared up. The positions that are left exposed by the investors are compulsorily settled by the exchange assuming that no delivery is sought. The positions are settled by exchanging the difference of closing price and the price of initial contract.

Differences Between Forward and Futures Contracts

As can be seen from the discussions above, the principle and purpose of the forward contract and a futures contract are same. However, there are key differences that need to be understood.

To cover the default risk, futures require initial margin and are marked to market on daily basis.

Besides the standardization and exchange-traded products, the futures have two substantial differences from forward contracts as follows:

1. Initial and Variation Margin, and
2. Marking to the market.

Margin requirements The exchange serves as counter-party to both buyers and sellers of futures contract. Delivery of the underlying asset and the cash flow are the two essential ingredients of the futures contract. Despite the fact that most contracts are neutralized prior to the delivery, the link of delivery and resultant cash flow cannot be broken. The exchange works to eliminate the counter-party risk, and therefore it has to assure itself of the financial standing of the participating member. It further needs to curb the tendency of overtrading by the members.

To assure itself of financial credibility of the participants, the exchange prescribes the margin to be deposited with it. The margin is some percentage of the contract value and is prescribed by the exchange depending upon the volatility in price of the underlying asset.

The initial margin is intended to cover the loss that the trader can incur. On account of the losses when this margin falls below a certain specified level, the exchange may become uncomfortable and insecure because any further decline in price will wipe out the entire margin. The exchange therefore prescribes a minimum level below which the margin should not fall. If it does, the exchange asks the trader to replenish the margin to restore the original level. This is referred as *variation margin.*

Marking to the market One unique feature with the futures contract is the practice of settling the difference of price on daily basis. This daily settlement is referred to as *marking-to-the-market*.

At the end of each day, the profit or loss on the position is calculated and the loss, if any, is made good to the exchange by the investor. Likewise, any profit at the end of each day is credited to the account of the investor. Profit or loss is settled at the end of each day as if the investor was closing out the position. This way, the position is marked daily to the end-of-the-day price, though the net impact remains same. Table 28-2 illustrates the mechanism of marking to the market.

The final profit/loss will be given by the difference of selling and buying prices, as would be the case with a forward contract.

The differences in the forward and futures contract are tabulated in Table 28-3.

Cost of Carry Model: Pricing Forward/Futures Contract

We now attempt to understand how the price of a forward/futures contract is decided. The pricing of forward and futures contracts uses the same principle, since economically it is the same contract that specifies the price today for future delivery of the asset.

As a most simple case, let us consider an asset that provides no income to the owner of the asset. Let the asset be 100 gms of

Table 28-2 Marking to the market

Day	*Price (₹)*	*Cash Flow (₹)*	*Remarks*
Day 1	410	None	A long position opened for one contract (400 shares) valued at ₹ 1,64,000
Close Day 1	420	(420 – 410) × 400 = + 4,000	Investor receives ₹ 4,000
Close Day 2	400	(400 – 420) × 400 = –8,000	Investor pays ₹ 8,000
Close Day 3	390	(390 – 400) × 400 = –4,000	Investor pays ₹ 4,000
Exit Day 4	440	(440 – 390) × 400 = +20,000	Position closed out with contract value of ₹ 1,76,000. Investor gets ₹ 20,000
Net Profit		(440 – 410) × 400 = 12,000	

Table 28-3 Comparison between forward and futures contracts

Features	Futures	Forwards
Location	Exchange	Over-the-counter
Counter-party	Unknown to each other, Exchange serves as counter party	Counter-parties are known to each other
Counter-party risk	Minimal	Exists
Initial cash flow	Initial and Variation margins required	None
Explicit cost	Brokerage required to be paid	No intermediary and no cost
Settlement	Implicitly daily by marking-to-market	No marking-to-market
Final settlement	By delivery or cash settled	By delivery
Exit prior to maturity	Possible by entering an opposite contract to square up the position	Generally not possible,
Quantity specification	Fixed standard size/lot	Any quantity
Time of delivery	On fixed dates	Any time mutually decided by the parties concerned
Cost of hedging	Very nominal	High
Period of hedging	Contracts available for limited period	Unlimited

Futures' price is based on spot price and the cost of carry for the period less benefits of ownership.

gold. Let the current price of gold, S_0, be ₹7,000 per 10 gms. The owner of the asset sells the asset 12-m forward at price F_1. Once the contract period is over, the ownership will get transferred to the buyer upon payment of the contracted price F_1. Purely from financial perspective, the buyer of the contract has owned the asset on deferred payment basis, while the seller of the asset will receive payment only after the end of contract period though he has sold the asset now.

The new buyer has saved the cost of interest. Since there is a certainty of delivery and cash payment, we can safely assume that he saved the interest cost r applicable for risk-free investment. Let us assume $r = 10\%$. If the contracted price was F_1, he needs to have $F_1/(1 + r)$ today so as to mature to F_1 at the expiry of the contract period. Hence, the current price of the asset S_0 must be less than $F_1/(1 + r)$, else he would not enter into a forward contract. Mathematically,

$$S_0 < F_1/(1+r), \text{ or } F_1 > S_0 \times (1+r) \quad (28\text{-}3)$$

From the viewpoint of current owner of gold, if he had sold the asset on the spot at current price and invested at risk-free rate, his wealth would have grown to a minimum of $S_0 \times (1 + r)$. Therefore, the forward contract price F_1 must exceed $S_0 \times (1 + r)$ to motivate him to enter a forward deal. Mathematically,

$$F_1 > S_0 \times (1+r) \quad (28\text{-}4)$$

The only way the two inequalities of 28-3 and 28-4 can be satisfied is by equating the two. The forward deal will take place when the buyer and seller of asset feel indifferent to a price. Therefore, the forward contract will take place if and only if:

$$F_1 = S_0 \times (1+r) \quad (28\text{-}5)$$

Here, we have assumed annual compounding of interest. If the compounding period is made infinitesimally small, then Equation 28-5 is represented as below:

$$F_1 = S_0 \times e^{rt} \quad (28\text{-}6)$$

Equations 28-5 and 28-6 are also referred as *cost of carry model;* this implies that futures' price would be equal to spot price plus cost of carry for the futures' period.

It can be shown that the price of futures other than as given by Equations 28-5 and 28-6 will give rise to arbitrage opportunity.

Convergence of futures price and spot price

As per the cost of carry model discussed above, the difference in the futures price and the spot price called basis represents the cost of carry for the remaining period for the expiry of the contract. Accordingly, the futures contract with longer maturity will be priced higher than the contract with shorter maturity. As maturity nears, the difference between the futures price and spot price shrinks, and on the day of maturity, the two prices must necessarily be identical, as shown in Figure 28-3.

The difference of futures price and spot price is called basis. As time progresses, basis declines and becomes zero on the day of maturity, i.e. spot and futures price converge.

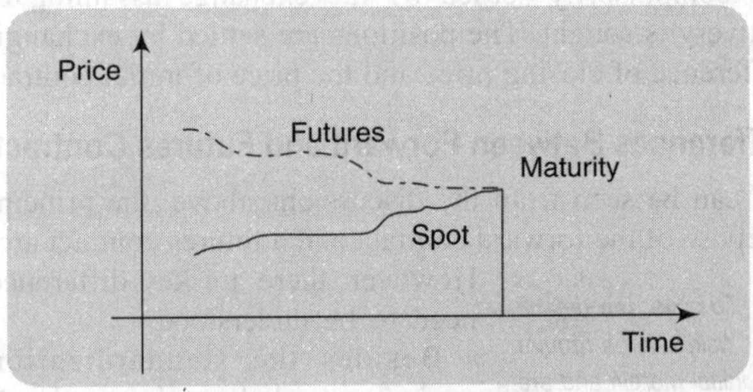

Figure 28-3 Convergence of price

Convergence of prices of underlying and the futures contract happens due to compulsion of delivery, at the option of buyer or seller attached with the futures contract. Note that delivery is not obligatory in the futures contract, and one nullifies the open position by entering into a contract opposite to that of the original contract, and exchanging the price difference. This is the most common way all investors square up their positions in the futures contracts. Even though settlement of futures contract is rarely done through delivery, yet the futures price can be no different than the one prevailing in the physical market. The mere possibility of either buyer or seller forcing the delivery is a sufficient reason for the prices in the physical and the financial markets to converge. If provision of delivery is withdrawn, futures will reduce to a pure speculative instrument and the very purpose for which they were invented will be lost. On the date of the delivery, the prices in the physical and financial markets must essentially converge; and if they do not, then arbitrage will drive them to common value.

Relationship between futures and forward price

In efficient and perfect markets, the forward price and futures price must be identical. However, from cash flow point of view, there are two major differences between forward and futures contract. Forward contracts are not subject to: (a) *Initial margin requirement*, and (b) *Marking to the market.* The cash flows from forward contract and the futures may be different, though the net position at the end may be the same. Both forward and futures prices should yield the same profit in the end except for the interest on interim payments. A gain of ₹100 in forward market may mean a gain of ₹300 on day 1 and a loss of ₹200 on day 2 in the futures market.

The relationship of spot prices with the interest rate determines the difference in pricing of futures and forwards. If there exists no correlation between the spot price and the interest rate, the cash inflows and outflows arising out of the process of marking to the market would tend to cancel out each other. In such a case, there is no reason to believe that futures and forward prices should be different.

When spot prices are positively correlated with interest rates, long position in futures will be better than in the forward, as it will provide the interim cash inflows which may be invested. Hence, futures price will exceed the forward price. With negative correlation of spot prices and interest rates, the forward prices will be higher than the futures prices.

The table below illustrates the relationship between the prices of futures and forward with respect to the behaviour of interest rates.

Correlation of Spot and Interest	*Relationship of Futures and Forward Price*
Positive Correlation	Futures Price > Forward Price
Negative Correlation	Futures Price < Forward Price
No Correlation	Futures Price = Forward Price

Types of Futures

Futures can be classified on the basis of underlying asset. As stated earlier, there can be a host of assets on which a futures contract can be created. It is a matter of standardization of the contract. Broadly, futures are categorized into two: (i) Commodity futures, and (ii) Financial futures.

Futures are broadly of two types; the commodity futures and financial futures depending upon the underlying asset.

Commodity futures are those where the underlying asset is a commodity. Contracts are available in India on agricultural commodities, such as Wheat, Rice, Soya, Coffee, Sugar, Tea, Jeera, Pepper, Edible oils, Cotton, Coconut, etc. Contracts on metals like Gold and Silver are also available. Futures contracts on oil also fall under commodity futures.

Financial futures are those where underlying asset is a financial product. They can further be categorized into four:

(i) **Currency futures** are those where the underlying assets are currencies. Futures contracts on various currencies are available in major centres like Chicago, London, Singapore, etc.

(ii) **Stocks futures** are those where the underlying assets are stocks. Stock futures were introduced in 1882 by Kansas City Board of Trade. Stock futures were introduced in India on 12 June 2000 for Indices and on 9 November 2001 on select individual securities at NSE.

(iii) **Interest rate futures** are those where underlying assets are interest rates. In India, interest rate futures were launched on 24 June 2003 at NSE.

(iv) **Index futures** are those where the underlying assets are stock indices, like BSE Sensex, or NIFTY.

Another classification can be based on the nature of the underlying assets from the perspective of being deliverable or non-deliverable. Certain futures contracts are made on hypothetical assets, which do not exist in the physical form. Futures contracts on indices and freight are non-deliverable.

Hedging Strategy Using Futures

Hedging strategy with futures revolves around compensating anticipated losses in the spot market with the equivalent gains in the futures market. This is done by taking a position on the futures market that is opposite of the position in the spot market.

Long and short positions

When a party holds the underlying asset, it is said to be *long on the underlying*. For example, a jeweller holding gold or silver is long on the underlying asset. Similarly, when a party requires the underlying asset, it is said to be *short on the underlying*. For example, a tea exporter who is in need of tea stock to execute the pending orders is short on tea, the underlying commodity/asset.

In the futures market, if one buys a contract, he is said to be *long*; and the one who sells the contract is said to be *short*. To execute a hedge, the following steps are taken:

1. One who is long on the asset goes short on the futures and the one who is short on underlying goes long in the futures.
2. At an appropriate time, one can neutralize the position in the futures market, i.e., go long on futures if one was originally short and go short on futures if one was originally long, and receive/pay the difference of prices.
3. Sell or buy the underlying asset in the physical market at the prevailing price.

Refer to Example 28-4 which illustrates the hedging strategy.

Perfect vs imperfect hedge

Hedging with futures involves taking futures position opposite to that of the physical asset hoping to compensate for the likely losses in the physical market with the gain in futures.

In Example 28-4, the hedging strategy of the sugar mill resulted in exact offsetting of gains and losses in the futures and the physical market. However, the profit or loss would be completely offset or not is dependent upon many factors. If the loss in the physical market is fully offset by the gains in the futures market and

Example 28-4 Hedging for Sugar Mill

A sugar mill in Uttar Pradesh is expected to produce 100 MT of sugar in the month of April. The current price today (in the month of February) is ₹22 per kg. April futures contract in sugar due on 20 April is trading at ₹25 per kg.

The sugar mill apprehends that a lesser price than ₹25 per kg will prevail in April due to the excessive supply expected at that time. How can the sugar mill hedge its position against the anticipated decline in sugar prices in April?

Solution

To execute the hedging strategy, the sugar mill has to take opposite position in the futures market. The sugar mill is long on the asset in April. Therefore, it needs to sell the futures contract today. The number of contracts that needs to be sold is dependent upon the exposure in the physical asset and the value that one needs to cover. Assuming that 100% cover of the position in the asset is desired, we can find the number of contracts to be sold.

$$\text{Number of contracts to be sold} = \frac{\text{Quantity to be hedged}}{\text{Quantity in each futures contract}}$$

$$= \frac{100\text{ MT}}{10\text{ MT}} = 10$$

The sugar mill would go short on futures in February. Prior to April before the future contract expires, the sugar mill buys the future contract to nullify its position in the futures market. The underlying asset, sugar, is sold in the spot market. The price realized by the sugar mill in two different scenarios of decline or rise in sugar prices, using the principle of convergence of price on the due date of the contract, is worked out as shown below:

When the price falls to ₹22 per kg.	Cash flow
In the futures market	(₹ per kg.)
Sold futures contract in February	+ 25.00
Bought futures contract in April	–22.00
Gain in the futures market	**+ 3.00**
Price realized in the spot market	+22.00
Effective price realized	₹25.00

Here the loss of ₹3 (₹25 – ₹22) in the spot market is made up by the equal gain in the futures market.

When the price rises to ₹26 per kg.	
In the futures market	
Sold futures contract in February	+ 25.00
Bought futures contract in April	–26.00
Loss in the futures market	**–1.00**
Price realized in the spot market	+26.00
Effective price realized	₹25.00

Here the gain of Re 1 (₹26 – ₹25) in the spot market is offset by the equal loss in the futures market.

Due to the fact that prices of sugar in the spot market and futures market must converge, a fixed price of ₹25 per kg is realized by the sugar mill. The loss or gain in the spot market is fully compensated by gain/loss in the futures market.

vice versa, then such a hedge is known as perfect hedge as depicted in Figure 28-4. Since the positions in the physical and financial markets are opposite, the loss or gain in two positions too would be opposite. For perfect hedge, i.e. for exact offset, the following conditions have to be met: (a) the underlying and futures must be of the same asset, (b) the quantity of the underlying and the futures must match, (c) the time of maturity of the futures contract and the period of hedging must coincide, and most importantly, (d) the principle of convergence of futures and spot prices must hold.

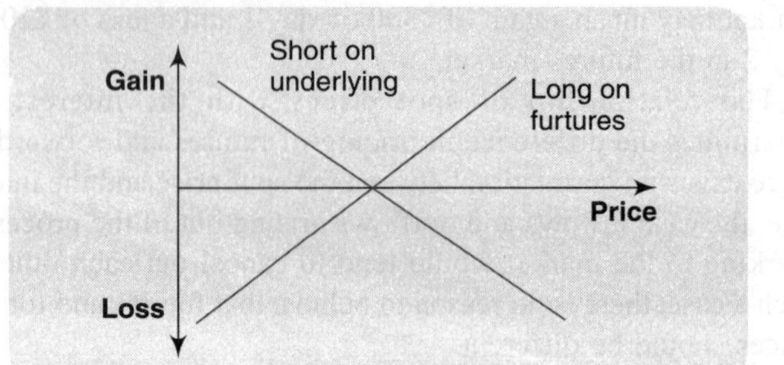

Figure 28-4 Perfect hedge

While executing hedging through futures, certain limitations are faced which makes the hedge imperfect. Realization of exact price, which one desires, is difficult to achieve because of the following reasons:

Mismatch of asset and quality It is not necessary that the futures contract on same asset, on which price risk is to be covered, is available. For example, a sugarcane grower cannot cover a price risk of his produce if the futures contract on sugarcane is not available. It does not mean to suggest that no hedging is possible under the situation of non-availability of the futures contract on the commodity. One has to find a commodity that is available through futures, and has a positive correlation with the prices of the commodity to be hedged. The effectiveness of the hedge will depend upon the degree of correlation in prices of the commodity and the futures contract. If correlation between the two commodities is perfect, then the hedge could be implemented.

As regards to sugarcane grower, the hedge is possible through the futures contract available on sugar, as prices of sugarcane and sugar go hand-in-hand. A hedge executed through a futures contract on an asset that is different than the underlying asset is referred as **cross-hedge**.

The mismatch in assets also covers the differences in quality of commodities. Different qualities of sugar are sold on different prices, and futures contracts on all qualities may not be available. However, as long as there is a correlation of prices, an effective hedge can be set up.

Mismatch of quantities Another reason that leads to deviations from a perfect hedge is the inability to cover the exact quantity of the asset to be hedged. As is known, futures contracts are standardized in terms of quantity. For example, one standard contract of sugar futures is of 10 MT. Quantity that is not a multiple of 10 MT cannot be hedged exactly. If the sugar mill wanted to hedge 95 MT, it had a choice of booking either 9 or 10 contracts for hedging. It would either be under-hedged or over-hedged.

Mismatch of period of hedging Since the futures contracts are also standardized with respect to the delivery dates, the exact matching of period to hedge cannot be achieved except by coincidence. For example, if the sugar mill wanted to hedge against the price risk till 30 April, it could not do so because the April contract expires on 20 April. The sugar mill may have the choice to book a futures contract for April or May, which may expire on 25 May, or take position on April futures contract. If it books April contract, the position remains exposed for the period between 20th and 30th April. By booking the May contract, the period of exposure in the assets is covered; but while exiting the May contract, the convergence of prices in the physical and financial markets would not happen leaving losses and gains unequal in the two markets. Also, beyond the date of liquidation of asset on 30 April and continuing to keep the position in futures open amounts to speculation.

Hedging price risk with futures is not perfect. Price risk gets replaced by a much smaller risk called the basis risk.

CURRENCY FUTURES

Currency futures serve the same purpose as currency forward contracts do. Currency forwards and futures are used by importers/exporter to cover the exchange rate risks in respect of their receivables/payables. Forward contracts by far are extremely popular because they are available with all commercial banks. All importers and exporters necessarily deal with banks for their day-to-day requirements, and find it operationally convenient to hedge through forwards.

Currency futures are the derivatives based on the exchange rate and are used for hedging against fluctuation in the exchange rate.

In India, trading in futures on currencies began in August 2008. Overseas, especially in USA, the use of futures contracts is widespread. As already stated, the cost of hedging through futures, being exchange-traded, is expected to be much smaller than the forward contracts. However, forward contracts offer perfect hedge as the exchange rate realized or paid is known with certainty at the time of booking contracts. The limitations of futures that make its hedge imperfect, i.e. mismatches of quality and quantity and timing of the hedge, do not occur in forward contracts being over-the-counter product matching specific needs of the exporters and importers.

Currency futures are contracts in foreign currency with exchange rate of the currency as the underlying asset. In 1972, International Monetary Market introduced currency futures at Chicago Mercantile Exchange. Standard contracts in various currencies are available at Chicago Mercantile Exchange.

Currency futures at CME are traded in standard lots of different currencies quoted in terms of number of US dollar per unit of other currency, with

- Tick size of $ 0.01
- Delivery standardized in March, June, September, and December
- **Standard Lots** of Australian $: 10,000; Canadian $: 100,000; Sterling Pounds: 62,500; Yen: 12,500,000; CHF: 125,000, Euro: 125,000

Pricing Currency Futures

Pricing of foreign currency futures will depend upon interest rates of the currencies involved in the contract. The concepts of interest rate parity and covered interest arbitrage are central to the determination of forward rates of the various currencies. Under free trade policies and free flow of capital across international borders, the interest rates in the two currencies must determine the exchange rates.

As a standard concept of economics, the price of any commodity is determined by the factors that affect the demand and supply of the commodity. Foreign currency is no different. The demand for foreign currency emanates from importers, and supply predominantly constitutes of exporters who enter transactions of goods and services abroad in currencies other than the domestic currency. Apart from the usual risks of trade, the importers and exporters face additional risk of exchange rates of currencies. Importers and exporters have a genuine need to hedge the transactions entered in foreign currency by them.

Besides hedgers, there are speculators and arbitrageurs operating in the foreign exchange markets subject to exchange control regulations in place in an economy. World over, the speculators and arbitrageurs constitute a majority of transactions. In fact, actual transactions that are being hedged form a miniscule volume of 3–4% in the foreign exchange markets. Irrespective of speculation or hedging, the pricing of the forward contracts is based on the condition that satisfies no-arbitrage condition.

Price of currency futures depends upon the spot price and the interest rate differential in two currencies.

To examine how the arbitrage works to determine the forward exchange rate, let us consider an example. Assume that a trader has ₹10 lakh today available for one year. He has a choice of either (a) to invest in rupees or (b) convert these rupees into US dollar at today's rate, invest the US dollar and reconvert the matured US dollar back into rupees one year later. In an efficient market, the two strategies of investment must yield the same reward. Also, the outcome of both the strategies must be certain. Therefore, we assume that the investment must be made in the risk-free securities in either market.

If the spot price of US $ is ₹50.00 and risk-free interest rates in rupees and US dollar are 5% and 3%, then the two strategies will give the following wealth:

(a) Invest ₹10,00,000 at 5% for a year and get ₹10,50,000
(b) Convert rupees in US $ at the spot rate of US $ 1 = ₹50.00 to get US $ 20,000 which are invested at 3% to yield US $ 20,600 after 1 year at maturity.

Both the investment strategies are depicted in Figure 28-5. For either strategy, the investor must be indifferent in terms of value in both the markets, i.e. Indian and US financial markets. If this has to happen, then the spot exchange rate one year later must be such that US $ 20,600 are equal to ₹10,50,000. This implies an exchange rate of ₹50.97 per US $. In symbolic terms, if the spot rates today and one year later are S_0 and S_1 and the

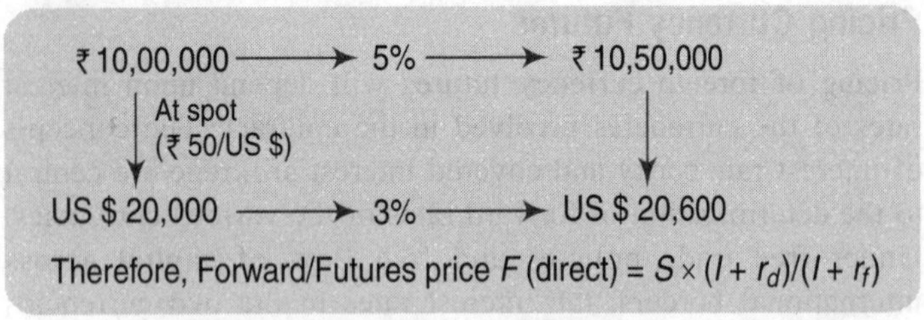

Figure 28-5 Determination of forward exchange rate

domestic and foreign interest rates are r_d and r_f respectively, then the relationship of the two spot rates is given by Equation 28-7 as follows:

$$S_1 = S_0 \times \frac{(1+r_d)}{(1+r_f)} \quad (28\text{-}7)$$

In the above argument, we ignored the aspect of risk. There are two sources of risk, i.e., the rates of interest for making investment and the exchange rates one year later. To be on equal levels of risk, we assumed investment at risk-free rates in both rupee and dollar markets. However, the second source of risk remains. While converting the matured amount into rupee, the investor is not aware of the future spot rate S_1. If the investor knew exactly what rate he would get after a year for the US $ invested today, then the risk of exchange rate fluctuation would also be eliminated. This uncertainty can be easily eliminated if the investor sells US dollar forward. Under conditions of certainty, the amount realized under two investment strategies will be:

(a) Investment of S_0 in rupee = $S_0 \times (1 + r_d)$

(b) Investment in US dollar

- Matured amount = $(1 + r_f)$
- Rupee realized by selling dollar forward at forward rate of $F_1 = (1+ r_f)/F_1$

For no arbitrage:

$$S_0 \times (1 + r_d) = (1 + r_f)/F_1$$

or

$$F_1 = S_0 \times \frac{(1+r_d)}{(1+r_f)} \quad (28\text{-}8)$$

With continuous compounding, the above Equation 28-8 gets modified to:

$$F_1 = S_0 \times e^{(r_d - r_f)t} \quad (28\text{-}9)$$

Reconciliation of interest rate parity and cost of carry models for determining the forward / futures price The price of futures/forward arrived through interest rate parity and the no-arbitrage argument in fact is same as the cost of carry model. Under the cost of carry model, futures price and the spot price are related by the cost of carry for the period of contract. In case of currency, this happens to be risk-free rate of interest. The future value of an asset is given by $S_0 e^{r_d t}$. If exchanged, the asset would have earned the risk-free rate of interest in the foreign currency. Therefore, the effective cost of carry is the differential of interest rates of two currencies. If r_d is less than r_f, it becomes a case of negative cost of carry as the dividend on the asset is larger than the cost of carrying in local currency.

Forward contracts help achieve a perfect hedge by assuring an exchange rate that can be ascertained today. An exporter expecting to receive his collection in foreign currency can sell the receivables forward. Likewise, an importer having a foreign currency payable can know his exact outflow in domestic currency if he buys the foreign currency forward.

Use of forward contracts fixes the future cash inflows/outflows in domestic currency as demonstrated in Example 28-5. This implies no foreign exchange risk.

Example 28-5 Converting Foreign Exchange Liability into Local Currency using Forwards

Consider an importer negotiating the purchase of a machine worth US $ 1,00,000. The machinery supplier is prepared to offer deferred payment facility at 5% interest with repayment spread over 5 annual equal instalments. The importer is apprehensive of appreciation of US dollar. A bank is prepared to offer forward contracts for US dollar at ₹51.00, 52.10, 53.40, 54.60, 55.90 per $ for 1, 2, 3, 4, and 5 years respectively. Find out how the importer can cover the foreign exchange risk. Also, find the rupee equivalent interest rate once he eliminates the exchange risk.

Solution

The importer can book forward contracts for repayments and interests due at the end of each year. His cash flow will be as follows:

Cash flows for the importer

Principal ($)	*Interest ($)*	*Principal +Interest ($)*	*Exchange Rate (₹/$)*	*Equivalent ₹*
–100,000	0	–100,000	50.00	–5,000,000
20,000	5,000	25,000	51.00	1,275,000
20,000	4,000	24,000	52.10	1,250,400
20,000	3,000	23,000	53.40	1,228,200
20,000	2,000	22,000	54.60	1,201,200
20,000	1,000	21,000	55.90	1,173,900

Effective Interest rate in Indian rupees
= IRR of the cash flows **7.30%**

The effective cost of funds (inclusive of the forward premium paid) comes to 7.30%.

Futures contracts in various currencies perform the same function as that of currency forwards. As stated earlier, futures contracts are standardized in terms of size (the quantity of currency) and delivery dates so that they become tradable on the exchange. The large number of buyers and sellers ensures liquidity and fair price. Though the pricing mechanism of forwards and futures remains same in theory, futures are more competitively priced simply because they are tradable and generate a lot more volume than the forward contracts.

In case of forward, the party assuming risk of exchange rate fluctuations builds his reward for the risk in the rates quoted for forward contracts. In foreign exchange markets, two rates are quoted: one for buying the foreign currency known as *bid rate* and the other for selling foreign currency known as *ask rate*, the difference being the reward for the party offering the forward contract. For futures contracts, there exists only one price at which sale or purchase is made. Being exchange traded, all transactions of buy and sell are subject to brokerage as in the stock market. The amount of brokerage is expected to be lower than bid-ask spread.

Hedging Through Currency Futures

Hedging currency exchange rate fluctuations with currency futures is no different than hedging price risk through commodity futures. We use the same principle of taking position in the futures market opposite to that of in the physical market. Subsequently, we enter into another futures contract offsetting the initial contract. As in case of commodities, we strive to nullify the gain/loss in physical market by loss/gain in the futures market so as to achieve a target price with as much certainty as possible. One must be reminded that the target price should not be construed as profitable price. A target price in case of forward contract is fixed and is governed by the forward rates available. One cannot have desired exchange rates that are out of line of market conditions. The ultimate price realized in the hedge through futures is dependent upon the prices of futures at the time of cancelling the contracts and ultimate price prevailing in the spot market.

A few examples will illustrate the mechanics of hedging through futures for importer and exporter, known as *long hedge* and *short hedge*, respectively.

Hedging for importer

Hedges that involve taking a long position on futures contract is known as *long hedge*. It is appropriate when one has to purchase a certain asset in future and needs to lock-in the price.

In June 2003, an Indian importer buys a machine at US $ 50,000. Payment is due after 6 months in December. The spot exchange rate is ₹45.5625 while December futures is trading at ₹46.6500 indicating an appreciation of dollar by about 2.4% in 6 months. The importer feels that the dollar will appreciate much more. What shall he do? Assume futures contract in rupee are available for ₹25 lakh.

> *An importer is short on foreign currency. To hedge against appreciating foreign currency, he goes long on the futures contract.*

Hedging strategy As hedging strategy, the importer buys the futures contract now and sells close to the delivery date before December. Though he knows the exact amount of dollar to be covered, the importer has to determine the size of the contract that he has to buy. At current spot rate, the exposure in terms of rupee is US $ 50,000 × 45 = ₹22,50,000.

With one contract in rupee at ₹25,00,000, the number of contracts that the importer must buy is 1.

$$\text{Nos. of contracts bought} = \frac{\text{Exposure amount}}{\text{Value of one contract}}$$
$$= 1.11 \qquad \text{(Rounded to 1)}$$

Having bought rupee futures, the importer would cancel the position in the futures by selling the rupee futures at a date close to the actual date of payment in December. Let us examine the two different scenarios of exchange rates at the time when the payment becomes due in December.

When US$ appreciates to ₹47.5600 and futures sells for ₹47.5700

The importer exits the futures contract at ₹47.57 and buys the foreign currency in the spot market at the prevailing spot rate.

Importer buys $ 50,000 at spot rate:	
Cost = 50,000 × 47.5600	= ₹23,78,000
Sells the futures contract booked earlier:	
Nos. of dollar bought = 25,00,000/46.65	= $ 53,590.57
Nos. of dollar sold = 25,00,000/47.57	= $ 52,554.13
Net gain on futures	= $ 1,036.44
Equivalent rupees = $ 1,036.44 × 47.56	= ₹49,293
Net rupees paid	= ₹23,28,707

Effective Exchange Rate = ₹46.5741 per $

As against spot price of ₹47.56, the importer ends up buying dollar at ₹46.5741.

US$ depreciates to ₹44.5625 and futures sells for ₹44.5700

Importer buys $ 50,000: Cost = 50,000 × 44.5625	= ₹22,28,125
Sells the futures contract booked earlier:	
Nos. of dollar bought = 25,00,000/46.65	= $ 53,590.57
Nos. of dollar sold = 25,00,000/44.57	= $ 56,091.54
Net loss on futures	= $ 2,500.97
Equivalent rupees = $ 2,500.97 × 44.5625	= ₹1,11,449
Net rupees paid	= ₹23,39,574

Effective Exchange Rate = ₹46.7915 per $

As against spot price of ₹44.5625, the importer ends up buying dollar at ₹46.7915.

It may be observed that if US $ appreciates to ₹47.56 the effective cost to the importer remains close to the opening futures price. Similarly, when the US $ depreciated, the effective price paid by the importer was again close to the opening futures price.

Hedging for exporter

Exporters are long on the asset and to cover the risk through the futures, they have to take an opposite position in the futures, i.e. go short on the futures. This strategy is appropriate when one has to sell foreign currency in future and needs to lock-in the price.

> *An exporter is long on foreign currency. To hedge against depreciating foreign currency, he goes short on the futures contract.*

For example, consider a British exporter expecting to receive $ 5 million in 6 months' time in coming June. He is expecting dollar to depreciate and pound to appreciate as is reflected in the spot and futures rates given below:

Spot: $1.5530/£, and June Futures: $1.5600/£

Hedging Strategy Hedging strategy would involve selling the futures now and covering later. The exporter is facing a loss in the receivable and he is long on US dollar in the physical market, and therefore he must go short in the futures market, i.e., buy pound/sell dollar. Again, determining the number of contracts to be traded are:

Standard contract in British pound is £ 62,500.

Nos. of contract to be purchased

= $ 5 million/1.5530/62,500 = 51.51

Nos. of contracts purchased = 52 (Rounded off)

Say, in June, prior to the settlement date, the following rates were prevailing:

Spot : $1.6250/£, and June Futures: $ 1.6275/£

The exporter squares up and sells the futures contract.

Gain on futures market:

$(1.6275 - 1.5600) \times 52 \times 62{,}500 = \$\ 219{,}375$

This is equivalent to £135,000. (Using spot price of $1.6250/£)

Loss on the receivable

$= (1/1.5530 - 1/1.6250) \times 5$ million $=$ £142,652

Net loss = £142,652 – £135,000 = £7,652

If the exporter had not hedged, he would have received £30,72,196 (50,00,000/1.6275). With hedging, he receives £135,000 extra from futures contract, making realization rate at $1.5590/£.

STOCK INDEX FUTURES

All of us have heard about terms like SENSEX and NIFTY. They are indices devised by respective stock exchanges to measure the day-to-day activity of the movement of prices of stocks.

There is a huge number of shares listed on the stock exchanges and changes in price of each of the stock will indicate state of the market. It would indeed be a difficult task. In order to make qualitative and quantitative judgement of the happenings in the market, one has to develop a representative sample just as we develop a basket of goods that are included in the consumer price index to measure inflation. Since indices are developed to include all sectors of economy and all prominent stocks in each sector, the changes in the value of index are regarded as indicator of market risk.

Stock index futures can be defined as a commitment to buy or sell a portfolio of stocks comprising the index. As the price of stocks change, the value of index changes. Since stock index is a hypothetical product and does not have a physical form, it is a non-deliverable asset. Unlike commodities and currency futures where delivery can be enforced, stock index cannot be delivered. In theory, the index may be deliverable, and the delivery will consist of shares in the stock index in their relative proportion. However, for all practical purposes, we can deem the stock index to be non-deliverable.

Stock index futures is a derivative with stock index as the underlying asset.

Since delivery of index is impractical, the contracts in stock index futures are necessarily cash settled. Cash settlement implies the exchange of difference in the prices upon cancellation of the original contract. Stock exchanges deem all outstanding open positions as squared up at the price of the day of closing of futures contract.

Stock index futures were introduced in India in mid 2000 after some legal hurdles were overcome. The act governing the securities, i.e. Securities Contracts Regulation Act (SCRA) had prohibited dealing in futures and options. With the passing of Derivative Bill by the Parliament, the stock index trading began on BSE on 9 June, 2000, and at NSE on 12 June 2000 with trading on SENSEX and NIFTY respectively. Though several other indices and futures on them have come into existence since then, the futures on BSE SENSEX, NSE NIFTY-50 are two of the most popular index futures.

Stock exchanges define the characteristics of the futures contract, such as the underlying index, market lot, and the maturity date of the contract. The futures contracts are available for trading from introduction to the expiry date. The stock exchange acts as *market maker* by offering two-way quotes. The stock exchange also acts as a *clearing house* and each member signs a separate agreement. Though the regulations permit futures contracts up to 12 months, the exchanges in India have introduced three contracts for next three months. In the month of January, the three contracts would be referred as Jan, Feb, and Mar contracts. The day of settlement has been fixed as last Thursday of each month. Next month contract would be introduced on the last Friday of the month.

Specifications of Stock Index Futures

Contract size Minimum contract value is fixed in a manner so as to be close to ₹2 lakh at the time of introduction. Minimum lot for BSE SENSEX was fixed at 50, while for NIFTY, it was 200.

Contract value Each point is considered to be equivalent to 1 rupee. If the BSE SENSEX is at 4,500, then the contract value will be $50 \times 4{,}500 =$ ₹2.25 lakh.

Tick size Indicates the minimum change and is fixed at 0.05 points for BSE SENSEX and NIFTY. Hence, the minimum change in value of NIFTY contract will be $200 \times 0.05 =$ ₹10

Margins Initial margin and mark-to-market (MTM) margins are to be compulsorily deposited with broker.

Initial Margin: To cover the largest potential loss in a day.

MTM Margin: Daily settlement.

Time of expiry/delivery Life is 3 months, 3 series will be open at all times (1 month, 2 months, and 3 months contracts).

Maturity/expiry On last Thursday of each month. New series comes into existence on the next Friday.

Settlement Always cash settled as stock indices cannot be delivered. Contracts can be closed at any time. Open positions are automatically closed on the last day of trading at a price determined by spot cash value of the index.

Besides index futures, we have futures contracts on individual stocks in India. Futures contracts on very active stocks (currently around 80) exist on the Indian stock market. Stock futures are financial contracts where the underlying asset is specific stock.

Unlike stock index futures, the delivery of stock futures is possible because the stock in question can be delivered. However, for the sake of uniformity, the stock futures are cash settled only at present, and there is no requirement of delivery. The final settlement is done at the closing price on the last day of the contract.

World over, the futures contracts on index are preferred, as they are used as hedging mechanism. Futures on individual stocks do not exist. Futures on individual stocks exist only in very few countries. USA too has only stock index futures. The futures on individual stocks do not exist for following reasons:

1. Institutional investors and large equity holders use futures for portfolio hedging, for which stock indices are more suitable.
2. Price volatility in individual stocks is much higher than the index comprising them.
3. Risk of clearing and requirements of margining are very high.
4. Stock indices are more difficult to manipulate compared to individual stocks.

Pricing Stock and Stock Index Futures

The pricing of futures on stock of index follows the cost of carry model. The cost of carry is rather easy to determine in case of financial assets. In case of financial futures, the cost of carry is the interest costs incurred, if a similar position is taken in cash market and carried to maturity of the futures contract less any income typically dividends resulting in this period.

Futures price = Spot price + Cost of carry r – Benefits of ownership d

$$F = S\left(1+\frac{r}{m}\right)^{mn}$$

where, r = rate of interest (annual)
m = No. of compounding periods in a year
n = period of futures in years

$$F = S\ e^{(r-d)t}$$

where, t = period of futures in years

Theoretical value or the fair value of the index future is dependent upon the cost of carry and the benefits of dividend accruing during the period. The cost of carry model is based on the arbitrage argument. An example would illustrate the application of cost of carry model of pricing index futures.

Consider the present value of NIFTY index is 3150. The 3-m interest rate is 12% per annum while the dividend yield on the index is estimated to be 6%. Based on the data given as above, the fair value of the index future with 90 days remaining for maturity is calculated as below:

Fair value of the index future

= Current value of index + Cost of carry for 90 days – Dividend for 90 days

$= 3150 + 3150 \times 12\% \times 90/365 - 3150 \times 6\% \times 90/365$

$= 3150 + 40.60 - 20.30 = 3170.30$

Stock index is a non-deliverable asset, yet we can use the cost of carry model for pricing it.

If the futures contract sells for anything different than the fair price, it offers arbitrage opportunity. Consider the futures contract on index is selling for 3180. Clearly, the index futures are overpriced. An investor can take simultaneous steps of: (a) sell the futures, (b) buy the underlying assets (this may be done through basket buying/program trading) at the current value of index of 3150 by (c) borrowing the amount at 12%. By doing so, the investor is assured of the profit upon closing out the position close to the maturity of the futures contract irrespective of the value of the index then. Because of convergence, the index and the futures contract would be at the same price at the closing date. The investor would (a) buy back the futures, (b) sell the underlying stocks, and (c) pay the borrowing along with interest. Table 28-4 gives the profit for the investor at two different closing levels of index of 3000 and 3300. In both the cases, the profit is ₹9.70; the difference of actual price and fair price.

Table 28-4 Fair pricing of future and arbitrage
(Cash flow in ₹) except future prices

Index closing value	*3000.00*	*3300.00*
Initial Position		
Sell Futures	3180.00	3180.00
Borrow funds	3150.00	3150.00
Buy underlying stocks	–3150.00	–3150.00
Closing Position		
Buy Futures	3000.00	3300.00
Profit/loss on futures	**+180.00**	**–120.00**
Sell underlying stocks	+3000.00	+3300.00
Interest payment	–40.60	–40.60
Dividend received	+20.30	+20.30
Pay borrowings & interest	–3190.60	–31290.60
Net cash flow on borrowing & underlying stocks	**–170.30**	**+129.70**
Profit of portfolio of future and underlying stocks	**9.70**	**9.70**

Example 28-6 Fair Value of the Index Future and Adjustment of Dividend

(a) NIFTY index consists of 50 stocks. Its current value is 2,450. If risk-free rate of interest is 6%, find the true value of 1, 2, and 3 months (assume 30, 61, and 92 days away) futures contracts.

(b) The share of State Bank of India (SBI) has a weight of 7% in the index and is being traded at a price of ₹850. SBI has announced a dividend of ₹25 per share that will be paid 45 days from now. What will be the impact of this dividend on the prices of the futures?

Solution

(a) The value of futures will exceed the spot price by the cost of carry amount for the period of maturity of futures as calculated below:

Cost of Carry Model

Risk-free rate of interest	6 %	6 %	6 %
Spot value of index	2450	2450	2450
Days to maturity	30	61	92
Fair Value of Futures	1 month	2 months	3 months
$F = S_0 \times e^{rt/365}$	2,462.11	2,474.69	2,487.33

(b) Dividend is like negative cost. It implies reduction of cost of carry. Adjustment of dividend that is payable after some time can be made either to the spot value or the terminal value.

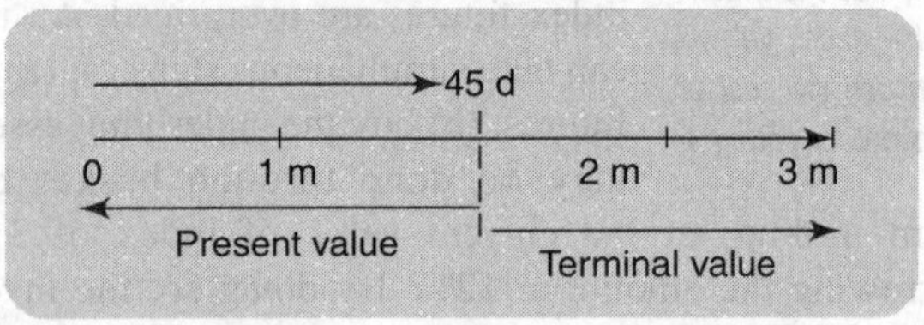

The dividend is payable after 45 days. 1-m futures contract expires before dividend, and hence its price remains unaffected. On the other hand, 2-m and 3-m futures contracts will change in value with the dividend payment. The amount of dividend in the index futures can be worked out as below:

Adjustment of Dividend

Proportion of SBI share	7%
Value of share in the index	171.50
Share price of SBI share (₹)	850.00
Nos. of shares in the index	0.2017
Dividend per share (₹)	25.00
Amount of dividend (₹)	5.04
Dividend receivable after t_d days	45
PV of Dividend (₹) $D_0 = D_1 \times e^{-rt_d/365}$	5.01

Spot value of index must be reduced by ₹5.01 for 2-m and 3-m futures contracts. Again, applying cost of carry, we get the prices as:

	2m	3m
Price of Index Futures $F = (S_0 - D_0) \times e^{rt/365}$	2,469.63	2,482.25

Alternatively, the terminal value of dividend can be subtracted from the price of the futures.

	1m	2m	3m
Terminal Value of Dividend	–	5.06	5.08
Price of Futures (*F* – Terminal Value of Dividend)	2,462.11	2,469.63	2,482.25

Apart from the theoretical value, the actual value may vary depending on demand and supply of the underlying at present and expectations about the future. Under normal market conditions, futures contracts are priced above the spot price. It is possible for the futures price to be below the spot price. Such a situation is known as *backwardation*. The fair value as per the cost of carry model gives the value of the futures under ideal conditions. But in reality, the actual price may deviate from the fair value. If this be the case, the divergence from fair value represents an opportunity for arbitrage.

Example 28-7 Pricing, Profiting, and Mark to Market

The following data is available as on 27 December 1999.

BSE SENSEX	4,500
1-m futures maturing Jan 27	4,568
Value of SENSEX futures	₹2,28,400
Initial margin 5%	₹11,420

(a) Find the fair value of the futures contract assuming an interest rate of 12% p.a.

(b) Is there an opportunity to profit from the above calculation? If yes, how?

(c) How does mark to market margin affect the profit?

(d) How does initial margin affect the profit?

(e) What are the other costs in transactions of futures?

Solution

(a) Fair/True value of the futures contract
= Current price of underlying + Cost of carry
= 4,500 + 45 = 4,545 (assuming a financing cost of 12% p.a)

(b) Yes, there is an opportunity to make profit since the actual price is different than the fair value. Here, the actual price is 4,568. Clearly, the futures is overpriced. One must sell futures in the hope that it will approach fair value; and when that happens, the investor must buy futures contract to make a profit.

(c) Mark-to-market margins:
Next day, 1 January 2000, the BSE closes at 4,535;
Pay mark-to-market margin (loss)
= 50 × (4,568 – 4,535) = ₹1,650
January 2, 2000 Index closes at 4,590;
Get mark-to-market margin (gain)
= 50 × (4,590 – 4,535) = ₹2,750
This continues till one closes out the contract. The mark-to-market margin does not affect the profit. It remains same. In fact, the profit is the sum of all mark-to-market cash flows.

(d) The initial margin is only a security provided by the client through the clearing member to the exchange. It can be withdrawn in full after the position is closed. Therefore, it does not affect the above calculation of profit or loss.

(e) There would be a funding cost or transaction cost in providing the security. This cost must be added to the total transaction costs to arrive at the true picture. Other items in transaction costs would include brokerage, stamp duty, etc.

Uses of Stock Index Futures

Index futures can be used in many ways. The applications of futures are normally categorized in following three ways:

(a) Hedge against risk
(b) Speculation
(c) Arbitrage

We consider them in order.

Hedging through stock index futures

The investors who are long on the portfolio or the stock usually fear decline in the value of the assets in case the market falls. They need to protect the value of their portfolio. They can do so by going short on the index futures. Similarly, there are investors who are short on the underlying (they have planned to buy stocks in future expecting to receive funds) fear a rise in price. They can go long on the index futures.

Stock index futures can be used for hedging a portfolio by going short on futures.

For example, consider a very large mutual fund which is fearing a fall in the value of the portfolio in near future. The period of uncertainty is expected to be temporary and the fund has a long-term conviction on its portfolio. With owning the portfolio and expecting the market to go down, it has the following two options:

Do nothing Having faith on the long-term fundamentals, the mutual fund may decide to remain invested and do nothing against the temporary fall expected in the value. In such a case, the fund faces a risk of temporary fall becoming permanent, and lose the value forever. The fund carries the risk of fall in the market.

Alternatively, the fund can sell the portfolio now and buy it back later when the prices have fallen. Such a strategy suffers from the following drawbacks:

(i) *Transactions cost* First selling and then buying back the portfolio would result in higher transaction costs.

(ii) *Impact cost* If it is a large fund, its action of selling may trigger others to sell and prices may fall due to panic selling, bringing the prices further down. Similarly, while repurchasing the stock, the prices may go up. Besides the transactions cost, the mere action of first selling and then buying the stock may cause the prices to change unfavourably bringing down the returns. The effect on price due to actions of selling and buying and vice versa is known as *impact cost*. This does not consider the transactions costs of brokerage, taxes, etc.

(iii) *Market may not fall actually* In such a case, the fund will unnecessarily incur the transactions cost and impact cost.

Hedge with index futures Availability of index futures presents an extremely preferred option that does not suffer the limitations of cost and yet provides protection of value. The fund is long on asset; and in order to protect the value, one must go short on futures. The fund must sell futures now and buy later, keeping the portfolio intact. Such a strategy will save the transaction costs as well as impact cost. How do firms hedge against the fall in the value of the portfolio is shown in Example 28-8.

Example 28-8 Hedging against Adverse Price Movement

Consider a mutual fund having a huge portfolio of ₹100 crore. Today is 2 February, and the expectation of general budget on coming 28 February is not very promising. The current value of BSE SENSEX is 6,500. February and March futures maturing on 25 February and 25 March consisting of 50 SENSEX are selling at 6,525 and 6,600 respectively. How can the fund insulate against the uncertainty of budget?

Solution

Hedging strategy

The fund is long on asset and must go short on futures. It must sell futures contracts of March as uncertainty of budget lasts till 28 February and cannot be covered by selling February contracts expiring prior. To cover fully, the fund must sell March futures contracts.

Nos. of contracts to be traded:

Value of one BSE SENSEX contract $= 50 \times 6600 =$ ₹3.30 lakh

Value of the portfolio to be hedged = ₹10000 lakh

Nos. of contracts to be sold = 10,000/3.30 $\cong$ 3,030 contracts (assuming that fund is diversified enough and a change of 1% in market causes equivalent change portfolio value)

The fund buys back the index at an appropriate time after 28 February.

If the market goes down by 5% as anticipated

The value of portfolio stands reduced by ₹5 crore (₹100 crore to ₹95 crore). The March futures falls from 6,600 to 6,260 when the fund squares up its position.

Gain on futures = $(6{,}600 - 6{,}260) \times 50 \times 3{,}030 \cong$ ₹515.10 lakh

Therefore, the fund more or less compensates itself for the loss incurred on the portfolio value. Remember that futures cannot provide permanent protection; and if the market sentiments become bearish, the fund will have to resort to other methods, including rolling over of the hedge. A longer period of uncertainty can be covered by closing out the position in March futures and opening a new position by going short on, say, June futures.

If the market goes up by 5% against expectations

The value of portfolio stands increased by ₹5 crore (₹100 crore to ₹105 crore). The price of March futures rises from 6,600 to 6,900 when the fund squares up its position.

Loss on futures = $(6{,}600 - 6{,}900) \times 50 \times 3{,}030 \cong$ ₹454.50 lakh

Therefore, an increase in portfolio value is offset more or less by the loss incurred on the futures contracts, keeping the value of portfolio almost constant. Note that hedging through futures does not mean protecting against loss while preserving gain. It only ensures a constant value of the portfolio.

Long hedge can be used to protect against the rising market. An investor awaiting funds cannot take position in the cash market till funds are received. If the investor is expecting a rise in the market, he can protect his buying price of the portfolio by:

1. going long on futures now,
2. cancelling out his position by selling the futures contract later,
3. investing in the cash market.

The examples of such situation include an investor willing to invest proceeds of the real estate that is already sold but consideration of money has not been yet realized. He is as much concerned with the rise in the equity values as is an investor holding securities concerned with the fall in prices. Situations like where a new fund receives subscription over a period of time and is yet to construct a portfolio are also included such as:

(a) The fund is awaiting outcome of its equity research efforts to exactly identify suitable securities for investment, and/or

(b) The fund does not want to enter the market in a big way to save itself of large impact cost, and instead builds its portfolio gradually by investing in futures and closing out gradually to buy securities of equivalent amount.

Futures also provide protection against the market risk (systematic risk) of a stock as demonstrated in Example 28-9.

Example 28-9 Protection against Market Risk

An investor buys the stocks of Hindustan Lever Ltd (HLL) worth ₹20 lakh due to its very strong fundamentals. However, the market in general is considered to remain weak for about the next three months. The beta of HLL is 1.2 and the current value of NIFTY is 2250 and 3-m futures is selling at 2310. Answer the following:

1. How can the investor hedge himself against the expected fall in the market?
2. Analyse his position (a) if the market falls by 10% in 3 months and HLL drops to ₹178 from ₹200 (b) if the market registers a rise of 6% and HLL rises to ₹215 from ₹200.
3. Given the standard deviations of the market as 12% and HLL as 18%, what is the risk of unhedged and hedged portfolio?

Solution

1. One option for the investor was to wait for three months and then buy. He runs the risk of rise in prices of the share of HLL after 3 months. With stock index futures available, he does not need to defer the purchase and take the risk of rise in prices. A better strategy would be to buy the share now; and to protect against the risk of falling market, take a short position in 3-m futures. Since beta of HLL is 1.2 (implies a fall of 1% in market will result in 1.2% decline in stock value), the futures position must be 1.2 times the position in physical market. Therefore, the investor takes the following steps:
   - Buys stock worth ₹20 lakh due to strong fundamentals, and
   - Sells 3-m futures worth ₹24 lakh (1.2 × 20 lakh) to insulate against market risk.

   Nos. of shares of HLL = 20,00,000 / 200 = 10,000

   $$\text{Nos. of futures contract sold} = \frac{\text{Value to be hedged}}{\text{Value of 1 futures contract}} = \frac{24{,}00{,}000}{200 \times 2310} \approx 5.19 \text{ (Rounded, 5 contracts)}$$

2. (a) Market falls by 10% to 2025 from 2250 and HLL falls to ₹178:

   Selling price of futures = 2310
   Purchase price of futures = 2025
   Gain in futures market = 285
   Gain in position of futures = 5 × 200 × 285
   = ₹2,85,000
   Loss on HLL 10,000 shares = (200 − 178) × 10,000
   = ₹2,20,000
   Net Gain = ₹65,000

   If the investor was unhedged, his loss would be ₹2,20,000

   (b) Market rises by 6% to 2385 from 2250 and HLL rises to ₹215:

   Selling price of futures = 2310
   Purchase price of futures = 2385
   Loss in futures market = 75
   Loss in position of futures = 5 x 200 x 75 = ₹75,000
   Gain on HLL 10,000 shares = (215 −200) × 10,000
   = ₹1,50,000
   Net gain = ₹75,000

   If the investor was unhedged his gain would be ₹1,50,000

3. If the investor remained unhedged, he would carry the entire risk of HLL of 18%. With hedged position in futures, the amount of variance reduction is:

   $$\beta^2 \sigma_m^2 = (1.2)^2 \times (12)^2 = 207.36 \text{ or standard deviation} = 14.4\%$$

   $$\text{Residual variance} = (18)^2 - \beta^2 \sigma_m^2 = (18)^2 - (1.2)^2 \times (12)^2 = 116.64 \text{ or } 10.8\%$$

   Hedged portfolio will reduce the risk of the asset from 18% to 10.8%.

Speculation with stock Index futures

Hitherto, we looked at the risk reduction features of the stock index futures. It will not be wrong to say that derivatives markets were designed for the purpose of hedging against the risk. Ironically, the same derivative markets can serve the opposite purpose and may be used to create or magnify risk. The risk is increased when a participant in the market does not have any position in the underlying cash/physical asset. The risk due to absence of position in the physical market is compounded by the fact that a much lower financial outlay is required in the derivatives markets.

Futures provide the opportunity to take a view on the market. It is a leveraging mechanism that enables increased returns. As a simple strategy of benefiting from the expected move in the market, one can buy or sell futures rather than take a position in the cash market involving a large cash outlay. The leveraging strategies are listed below.

- If markets are expected to go up:
  Buy futures now and sell later.
- If markets are expected to go down:
  Sell futures now and buy later.

The use of futures involves outlay in the form of initial margins only. If the margin requirement is 10%, the investor can take position 10 times larger than the position in the cash market. Accordingly the returns, positive or negative, will be magnified 10 times.

Stock index futures are used for taking speculative positions and make way for magnified returns with equally magnified risk.

Assume that an investor has ₹10 lakh to invest. He is currently bullish about the market. The current level of SENSEX is 6,500 and 3-m futures contract of 50 SENSEX is trading at 6,650. The margin requirement is 20%. The investor has the option to buy a balanced portfolio from a mutual fund. However, he is highly optimistic about the rise of the market and expects a minimum level of SENSEX at 10% higher in 3 months' time. How can he benefit from his optimistic forecast?

As an alternative, the investor can buy the balanced portfolio in the cash market. If market goes up by 10%, his profit will be 10% of the investment in the cash market, i.e., ₹1,00,000. In case the market falls by 5%, his loss will be ₹50,000.

Alternatively, if the investor is extremely confident of his forecast, he can take a larger risky position in futures by buying 15 contracts on index futures leaving him a cash balance of ₹2,500, which is ignored.

Value of 3-m futures = 50 × 6,650 = 3,32,500

Margin required per contract @20% = ₹66,500

$$\text{Nos. of contracts that can be bought} = \frac{₹10,00,000}{₹66,500} = 15$$

The investor subsequently sells these contracts at a higher price.

If the market goes up by 10%

The selling price of the contract = 7,150

Purchase price = 6,650

Profit = 500

Total profit = 15 × 50 × 500 = ₹3,75,000

If the market falls by 5%

The selling price of the contract = 6,175

Purchase price = 6,650

Loss = 475

Total loss = 15 × 50 × 475 = ₹3,56,250

Hence with futures, the gains and losses as well would be magnified as compared to the position in cash. While the gain on the investment can be as high as 237.50% with only 10% rise in the market, the loss would be equally high at more than 35% with 5% fall in the market.

Futures can also be used in falling market. An investor can benefit from a predicted fall in the price of stock by selling futures. As the price of the future falls in line with the underlying stock, the investor will make a greater positive return.

Arbitrage with stock Index futures

We explained the arbitrage with futures when the price of the futures is away from the fair value. This may be used as a tool of *yield enhancement* on the portfolio. The use of futures as a tool of yield enhancement is illustrated in Example 28-10.

A portfolio consisting of stock index futures and T-bills produces same returns as stock portfolio replicating the index, if there is no mispricing of futures. If the theoretical price and actual price differ sufficiently, then arbitrage opportunities arise that result in increased yield. One can adopt the following strategies in case there is mispricing of futures.

> *When there is mispricing of futures, it is an excellent tool of enhancing yields on the portfolio.*

If Actual Price < Theoretical Price : Buy Futures

If Actual Price > Theoretical Price : Sell Futures

Example 28-10 Arbitrage with Futures; Yield Enhancement

An investor is considering an investment in market portfolio to capitalize on the probable increase in the value of securities and earn the dividend yield. He has ₹10 lakh to invest. BSE Sensex is trading at 6,650 while 2-m futures contract with 60 days to maturity is selling for 6,670.

Assuming risk-free rate of interest of 8% and a dividend yield of 4%, find the fair value of 2-m future contract. Also analyse the investment strategies of: investing in Sensex (Strategy I) and investing in T-bills and futures (Strategy II).

Compare the positions of Strategy I and II with (a) 10% increase, (b) 10% decrease, and (c) no change in Sensex after 2 months.

Solution

The fair value of 2-m futures contract on Sensex:

$$F = S_0 \times e^{\frac{(r-d)t}{365}} = 6{,}693.87$$

The actual price of futures is 6,670 which is lower than the fair value. Hence, futures are underpriced.

Rather than buying the portfolio in the physical market, the investor can replicate the portfolio by buying futures contract and invest in T Bills. The strategy will have the same risk as that of the portfolio in the physical market. A comparison of payoff under the two strategies is presented below:

Strategy I : Invest in the portfolio of index

Amount invested in securities	1,000,000

Strategy II : Invest in T Bills and go long on futures

Amount invested in T Bills	1,000,000

Nos. of futures bought

Current value of 2-m futures	6,670
Nos. of indices in a futures contract	50
Value of one futures contract	₹333,500
Nos. of contracts bought (rounded off)	3.00

The payoff of the strategies are analysed for three different scenarios of 10% increase, no change, and a 10% decrease in the market from the current level of 6,650:

(₹)

	Increase by 10%	*No change*	*Decrease by 10%*
Strategy I			
Have a portfolio of ₹10 lakh			
Value of the portfolio	1,100,000	1,000,000	900,000
Dividend yield 4% of 10,00,000 for 2 months	6,667	6,667	6,667
Total value of investment	**1,106,667**	**1,006,667**	**906,667**
Strategy II			
Investment in T Bills and buy 3 futures			
Value of T Bills	1,000,000	1,000,000	1,000,000
Interest on T-bills	13,333	13,333	13,333
Position on Futures			
Selling price of futures	7,315	6,650	5,985
Purchase price of futures	6,670	6,670	6,670
Profit/loss on index points	645	–20	–685
Profit/loss on futures	96,750	–3,000	–102,750
Total value of investment	**1,110,083**	**1,010,333**	**910,583**

As can be noticed, Strategy II is always superior to the Strategy I; and hence in case of mispricing of futures, the yields can be improved by investing in futures and T-bills.

When futures are overpriced, a reverse strategy can be used as follows:

- Sell futures
- Borrow at risk-free rate
- Invest in the cash market buying the securities consisting index.

Refer to Example 28-11 for better understanding.

Example 28-11 Arbitrage when Futures Overpriced

Current value of NIFTY is 1990 with a dividend yield of 4%. 3-m futures contract is selling at 2030 and the risk-free interest rate is 10%. Half of the stocks in index will pay dividend in next three months.

(i) Spell out a strategy that yields risk-less profit.

(ii) Evaluate gains if the index after 3 months is at: (a) 1,900 and (b) 2,080.

Solution

(i) The fair value of 3-m index futures

= Spot Value + Cost of Carry – Dividend

$= 1990 + 1990 \times 0.10/4 - 1990 \times 0.04 /2$

$= 1990 + 49.75 - 39.80 = 1999.95$

≈ 2000

The futures at 2030 are overpriced. The strategy that would yield profit will be as follows:

- Sell futures, borrow funds at 10%, and invest in index securities.
- After an appropriate time: buy back futures, sell the securities, and refund the loan with interest.

(ii) The pay off under two scenarios will be as given below:

	Index at 1900	*Index at 2080*
Position in futures		
Selling Price	2030.00	2030.00
Buying Price	1900.00	2080.00
Gain/loss	130.00	–50.00
Position on Index		
Buying Price	1990.00	1990.00
Selling Price	1900.00	2080.00
Gain/loss	–90.00	90.00
Dividend Received	39.80	39.80
Interest paid	–49.75	–49.75
Profit	**30.05**	**30.05**

SUMMARY

Risk is all-pervasive in our day-to-day life. All of us keep taking steps to avoid or minimize the risk that each one of us faces. From business perspective, risk can be categorized in two ways; those with high losses but low probability, and those with small losses but high probability. The ways to handle these two kinds of risk are different. Most business risks come under the second category.

There are three ways to manage a risk: (i) not to undertake any risky activity, (ii) to transfer the risk from one to another, and (iii) diversification and taking positions in various instruments devised specifically to manage risk. Normally, business enterprises face risks emanating from changes in the price, exchange rates, and interest rates. Derivatives on each of them are the instruments of managing such risks.

Derivatives are defined as products whose price is derived from some other asset, called underlying asset. There are derivatives on commodities, exchange rate, stocks, indices, and interest rates. The participants in derivatives markets are classified into three categories with three different motives. *Hedgers* are those who take positions in the derivatives market to cover the risk that they are exposed to in their business transactions. On the other hand, *speculators* are those whose business is to take risk. They take positions in the derivative markets with the motive of making profit on the transactions. They have no risk to cover. *Arbitrageurs* are the most conservative lot who intend to earn profit without taking any risk whatsoever. They perform an important function of restoring the balance in the prices in case they begin to differ in different markets or from the theoretical position. All kinds of participant are equally important for efficient functioning of the market.

Derivative markets discharge three important functions: (a) efficient price discovery, (b) facilitating transfer of risk from those who want to avoid to those who want to assume risk, and (c) leveraging the returns on equity.

The four broad classes of derivative are: (1) forwards, (2) futures, (3) options, and (4) swaps, though there are many variants available. Derivative can be classified on the basis of risk profile, underlying assets and the kinds of markets.

Forward contracts are the widely known and the oldest form of derivatives. It is an agreement to buy/sell an asset at a specified date with a price determined today. They are over-the-counter product as the terms and conditions of the contract are decided mutually by the two parties concerned. The price is decided today but physical exchange of asset and cash takes place subsequently. In India, forward contract is the most popular instrument of covering fluctuations in the currency rates. Exporters, expecting to realize the foreign exchange for the sales made on credit, sell the foreign currency to banks at a rate negotiated today. Likewise importers, getting supplies on credit, can buy the foreign currency forward.

Cost of the forward hedge is normally ascertained by the premium or discount of the forward rate over the spot rates, though the true cost of hedging can only be known only at the end of hedge period.

Forward contracts on foreign currency are also used for taking a speculative position on the currency rates.

Futures is another instrument that provides cost-effective and efficient means of hedging the exposures in prices. A futures contract is a standardized forward contract that is traded on the exchange eliminating the counter-party risk that is always present in the forward contract. Besides, futures contract de-links the delivery of the asset by making it feasible for hedger to take position in the futures exchange independently of the physical market. Futures contract can have underlying assets of: (1) commodities, (2) currencies, (3) stocks and stock indices, and (4) interest rates. Specifications of the futures contract are finalized by the exchange where the futures are traded.

Though the pricing of forward and futures is based on the common principle of cost of carry, the two may differ slightly due to additional cash flows of initial margin and marking-to-the-market attached with the futures contract that are absent in the forward contract. Further, the cost of carry model and the no-arbitrage argument may not be fully applicable for the commodity futures due to convenience yield and inability of going short on the commodity.

The difference of futures price and spot price is called *basis*. As maturity of futures contract approaches, the basis reduces and becomes zero on the day of maturity of futures contract. Despite de-linking of the financial and physical markets, the principle of convergence of the prices in the two markets makes the hedge possible. Principle of hedging with futures involves taking opposite positions in the physical and financial markets. If one is long on the asset, he goes short on the futures; and if one is short on the asset, he goes long on futures. The hedge is completed on the maturity of futures contract or by its cancellation if one desires so. The exit possibility at any time during the tenure of the futures contract is another important benefit of futures over forwards, which provides this flexibility only upon the acceptance by the counter-party to the forward transaction.

The hedge through the futures market cannot be perfect except by coincidence due to presence of basis risk. However, price risk which is much larger gets replaced by basis risk which is much smaller under a futures hedge. Futures can also be used for speculation purposes using spread differential with respect to various commodities, various markets, and various times to maturity.

Currency futures have exchange rates as the underlying asset. They can be used for hedging against the fluctuating exchange rates in respect of foreign currency receivables and payable. The principle of taking opposite position in the financial market to that of physical market remains same in hedging. With a view contrary to the market rates, currency futures can also be used for speculative gains.

Stock and stock index futures have stock/indices as the underlying asset. The uses of stock index futures range from hedging positions in stock to speculation to yield enhancement. Despite a non-deliverable underlying asset, the pricing of stock index futures is governed by cost of carry model. The principle of convergence of price applies too.

Key Terms

Price risk The uncertainty about the price of any product is referred as price risk.

Exchange rate risk Receipts and payments denominated in foreign currency are subject to prevailing exchange rates that keep changing, rendering cash flows uncertain.

Interest rate risk The impact on cash flow due to changes in the interest rates is referred as interest rate risk.

Derivatives Derivatives are instruments that derive their value from the prices of some other asset, called underlying asset.

Hedgers Hedgers are those who attempt to reduce the risk on the asset and liabilities they already have.

Speculators Speculators are those who take a different view on the price than what is reflected in the prices of derivatives and take independent position to gain from the movement of price as expected by them.

Arbitrageurs Arbitrageurs look for mispricing in different products and/or markets and take risk-less position to profit from the price differentials.

Forward contract Forward contract is an agreement to buy or sell a product at a specified future date and at a predetermined price.

Futures Futures is a forward contract that is standardized in terms of quantity, quality, and delivery date and are traded on the exchanges.

Tick size Tick size is the minimum change in the price quotation that would be reflected in the futures price.

Open interest Open interest is the number of futures contracts outstanding at any point of time.

Marking-to-the-market Marking-to-the-market is the process that deems closing of outstanding positions in the futures at the closing/clearing rate of the day and exchange of price difference of loss or profit, as the case may be.

Basis The difference of futures price and spot price is called as basis.

Convergence The phenomenon of reduction of difference between the futures price and the spot price with time is known as convergence. On the date of maturity, the spot and futures price must converge.

Cash settlement The practice of exchanging the price difference while extinguishing the position in the futures contracts, rather than by delivery, is called cash settlement.

Key Formulae

Fair value of forward/futures contract

Without continuous compounding

$$F_1 = S_0 \times (1 + r)$$

With continuous compounding

$$F_1 = S_0 \times e^{rt}$$

Price of the forward/futures contract on currencies

Without continuous compounding

$$F_1 = S_0 \times \frac{(1 + r_d)}{(1 + r_f)}$$

With continuous compounding

$$F_1 = S_0 \times e^{(r_d - r_f)t}$$

Price of the forward/futures contract on stock index

Without continuous compounding

$$F_1 = S_0 \times (1 + r)$$

With continuous compounding

$$F_1 = S_0 \times e^{(r - y)t}$$

PRACTICE PROBLEMS

1. Pricing a Forward Contract

A share is currently trading at ₹125. It is expected to give a dividend of ₹10 per share after 4 months. Assume that the risk-free rate of return is 10% per annum.

What would be the approximate value of the forward contract (assuming annual compounding) on the share for delivery after (i) 3 months, (ii) 6 months, and (iii) 12 months?

What would be the value of the forward contract with continuous compounding?

Solution

The price of the forward contract is given by cost of carry model. The forward price would be higher than the spot price by the amount of cost of carry for the period of the forward contract. However, the benefits accruing to the holder of the underlying asset would not be available to the holder of the forward contract, and therefore the value of the forward contract must be adjusted accordingly.

Price of the forward contract

= Spot price – PV of the benefits accruing during the period
+ Cost of carry for the forward period

Mathematically, $F = (S_0 - D) \times (1 + r)$

where D is PV of benefits during the period.

Given:

Current stock price, S_0	₹125.00
Risk free interest rate, r	10.00% p.a.
Dividend, D	₹10.00 after 4 months

(a) (i) For forward period of 3 months, there would be no dividend as it is paid after 4 months.

Present value of benefit, D = ₹0.00

Maturity of the forward, t = 3 months = 0.25 years

Therefore, 3-m forward contract price, F_3 = (125 – 0) x (1 + 0.1 x 3/12) = ₹128.13

(ii) & (iii) For forward periods of 6 and 12 months, there would be dividend of ₹10 in between 4 months from today.

Present value of benefit, $D = 10/(1 + 0.1 \times 4/12)$ = ₹9.90

Forward period = 6 months = 0.5 years

$F_6 = (125.00 - 9.90) \times (1 + 0.1 \times 6/12)$ = ₹120.86

Forward period = 12 months = 1 year

$F_{12} = (125.00 - 9.90) \times (1 + 0.1 \times 12/12)$ = ₹126.61

(b) With continuous compounding the price of the forward contract would be given by:

$$F = (S_0 - D) \times e^{rt}$$

PV of dividend $D = D_t \times e^{rt} = 10.00 \times e^{0.10 \times 4/12}$ = ₹9.67

$F_3 = (125.00 - 0.00) \times e^{0.10 \times 0.25}$ = ₹128.16

$F_6 = (125.00 - 9.67) \times e^{0.10 \times 0.5}$ = ₹121.24

$F_{12} = (125.00 - 9.67) \times e^{0.10 \times 1}$ = ₹127.46

2. Pricing a Futures Contract on Index

On the National Stock Exchange, the current value of index, NIFTY is 5,000.

If the dividend yield on the index is 3% and risk-free rate is 10%, find out the value of futures contracts on NIFTY for (a) 3 months, (b) 6 months, and (c) 12 months.

Ignore marking-to-the-market and initial margin on the futures contracts.

Solution

Given:

Current value of NIFTY, S_0	5,000.00
Risk-free interest rate, r	10.00% p.a.
Dividend yield on the index, y	3.00% p.a.

With continuous yield and compounding, the price of the futures contract is given by:

$$F = S_0 \times e^{(r-y) \times t} = 5{,}000 \times e^{0.07 \times t}$$

Price of futures contract for

(a) 3 months $F_3 = 5{,}000 \times e^{0.07 \times 0.25}$ = 5,088.27

(b) 6 months $F_6 = 5{,}000 \times e^{0.07 \times 0.5}$ = 5,178.10

(c) 12 months $F_{12} = 5{,}000 \times e^{0.07 \times 1}$ = 5,362.54

3. Hedging with Commodity Futures

Bharat Oil Corporation (BOC) imports crude oil for its requirements on a regular basis. Its requirements are estimated at 100 tonnes per month.

Of late, there has been a surge in the prices of oil. The current price (month of June) of crude oil is ₹5,500 per barrel. The firm expects the price to rise in coming months to ₹5,800 by August. It wants to hedge against the rising prices for its requirements of the month of August.

Multi Commodity Exchange (MCX) in India offers a futures contract in crude oil. The contract size is 100 barrels and August contract is currently traded at ₹5,668 per barrel.

(a) How can BOC hedge its exposure against the rising price of crude oil?

(b) If BOC hedges its exposure at MCX, how many contracts it must book?

(c) Analyse the position of BOC if in the month of August (i) the spot price is ₹5,750 and futures price is ₹5,788, (ii) the spot price is ₹5,417 and futures price is ₹5,455.

(d) What would be the price paid if the positions in the physical market and futures market were matched?

Ignore marking-to-the-market and initial margin on futures contracts.

Solution 1 tonne = 7.33 barrels

(a) Hedging strategy would be to take position in the futures market opposite to that of in the physical market.

BOC is short on crude oil and therefore they must go long on the futures of crude oil.

Following would be the hedging strategy:

June	:	Buy futures contract
August	:	Purchase crude oil at the price prevailing then in the spot market, and sell the futures contracts.

(b) Quantity to be imported/hedged = 100 tonnes or 733 barrels
Contract size = 100 barrels
Nos of contracts bought = 733/100 ≃ 8 (rounded off)

(c) In August, the firm would buy its requirements of crude oil in the market and unwind its position in the futures market by selling the contracts bought in June. By doing so, the gains/loss in the physical market would be offset significantly.

August futures on crude oil = ₹5,668 per barrel

(i) *When the price of crude oil rises:*

Spot crude oil price = ₹5,750 Futures price = ₹5,788

Purchase price in the spot for = 733 × 5750 = ₹42,14,750

Cash flow on futures position

Buying price	5668
Selling price	5788
Profit	120

Realizations from futures market

= 8 × 100 × 120 = –₹96,000

Net amount paid ₹41,18,750

Effective price per barrel = 41,18,750/733 = ₹5,619

(ii) *When the price of crude oil falls:*

Spot crude oil price = ₹5,417

Futures price = ₹5,455

Purchase price in the spot for = 733 × 5417 = ₹39,70,661

Cash flow on futures position

Buying price	5668
Selling price	5455
Profit	–213

Realisations from futures market = 8 × 100 × –213

= ₹1,70,400

Net amount paid ₹41,41,061

Effective price per barrel = 41,41,061/733 = ₹5,649

(d) If positions in the physical market and futures market were matched then

The effective price would be $S_1 - (F_1 - F_0)$

When price rose the effective price paid is

= 5750 – (5788 – 5668) = ₹5,630 per barrel

When price fell the effective price paid is

= 5417 – (5455 – 5668) = ₹5,630 per barrel

4. Hedging with Currency Futures

Assume it is June 30. An American importer has to make a payment of € 240,000 in September. Since euro has been appreciating in the past and the trend is expected to continue, the importer wants to hedge the exposure in euro.

One of the instruments available to him is the futures contract in euro at Chicago Mercantile Exchange. The contract size is € 125,000 and the next contract has expiry in September. The current spot price and September futures price are \$1.5550 per € and \$1.5700 per Euro, respectively.

(a) Explain how would the import hedge his exposure in euro.
(b) How many futures contracts should he trade?
(c) What would be his position in September when he actually pays the liability and squares up his exposure in futures if (i) the spot price and futures price of euro are \$1.5600 and \$1.5625 respectively, (ii) the spot price and futures price of euro are \$1.5950 and \$1.5975 respectively?
(d) What would be the price paid if the positions in the physical market and futures market were matched?

Ignore marking-to-the-market and initial margin on the futures contracts.

Solution

(a) Hedging strategy would be to take position in the futures market opposite to that of in the physical market.

Importer is short on euro and therefore he would go long on the futures of euro.

Following would be the hedging strategy:

June : Buy euro Sept. futures contract now

Sept : Purchase € 240,000 at the price prevailing then in the spot market, and Sell the futures contracts.

(b) Amount to be hedged = € 240,000

Contract size = € 125,000

Nos of contracts bought = 240000/125000 = 2 (rounded off)

Sept futures contract of euro = \$1.5700 per €

(c) In September the importer would buy its required Euros at the spot price prevailing then in the market and sell the contracts bought in June. By doing so the gains/loss in the physical market would be offset significantly.

(i) *When Euro appreciates little to \$1.5600:*

Spot price of euro = \$1.5600 Futures price = \$1.5625 per €

Purchase price in the spot for euros

= 240,000 × 1.5600 = \$ 374,400

Cash flow on futures position

Buying price	1.5700
Selling price	1.5625
Profit	–0.0075

Realizations from futures market

= 2 × 125,000 × –0.0075 = \$1,875

Net amount paid for € 240,000 = \$ 376,275

Effective exchange rate paid

= 376,275/240,000 = \$1.5678 per €

(ii) *When Euro appreciates substantially to \$1.5950:*

Spot price of euro = \$1.5950

Futures price = \$1.5975 per €

Purchase price in the spot for euros

= 240,000 × 1.5950 = \$382,800

Cash flow on futures position

Buying price	= 1.5700
Selling price	= 1.5975
Profit	= 0.0275

Realizations from futures market

= 2 × 125,000 × 0.0275 = –\$6,875

Net amount paid for € 240,000 = \$375,925

Effective exchange rate paid

= 375,925/240,000 = \$1.5664 per €

(d) If positions in the physical market and futures market were matched, then

The effective exchange rate would be = $S_1 - (F_1 - F_0)$

When price rose, the effective exchange rate paid is

= 1.5600 – (1.5625 – 1.5700) = \$1.5675

When price fell, the effective exchange rate paid is

= 1.5950 – (1.5975 – 1.5700) = \$1.5675

5. Hedging Long Position with Stock Futures

Safety Mutual Fund is holding a portfolio of ₹50 crore. Due to anticipated rise in the stock markets, they had an aggressive portfolio with a beta of 1.40. However, due to sudden political developments, the markets are not expected to have the rising trend. This political uncertainty is expected to be resolved in one month's time. The mutual fund is convinced of the fundamentals of the securities in the portfolio.

One possible way of overcoming the decline in the value of the portfolio is to sell now and buy after one month. However, this is ruled out in view of the transaction costs involved. Safety Mutual Fund is therefore considering to cover the risk through the futures market.

Current value of index in the Bombay Stock Exchange, is 17,550 while the 1-m futures contract is traded at 17,730.

(a) With 1 point of Sensex at Re 1.00 and contract size of 50 indices, find out how Safety Mutual Fund can protect against the expected fall in the stock market in next one month.

(b) Evaluate the position of the portfolio if Sensex falls to (i) 17,000 and (ii) 16,000 after 1 month.

(c) What conclusion do you draw from the results of (b)?

(d) What would be the position of the portfolio if market instead of falling actually rose to 18,000?

(e) What conclusion do you draw from the results of (d)?

Ignore marking-to-the-market and initial margin on the futures contracts.

Solution

(a) Current value of BSE Sensex = 17,550

Price of 1-m futures on BSE Sensex = 17,730

Current value of the portfolio = ₹50.00 crore

Beta of the portfolio = 1.40

Safety Mutual Fund is long on the asset. They can protect the decline in the value of the asset by going short on the futures. Therefore, they must sell futures contract now equivalent to the exposure. The value that needs to be covered in the futures market is dependent upon the beta of the portfolio.

Value to be covered = Beta × Value of the portfolio

= 1.4 × 50 = ₹70.00 crore

Current value of 1 futures contract = 17,550

Nos. of Sensex in 1 futures contract = 50

Value of 1 futures contract = ₹8.775 lakh

Nos. of futures contracts to be sold

= 7000/8.775 = *797.72 contracts*

= 798.00 contracts (rounded off)

At the end of one month, the mutual fund would buy the futures. The price of futures would then be equal to the spot value of the Sensex.

(b) (i) *Sensex moves to 17,000*

New value of Sensex = 17,000

% change in the Sensex = –3.13%

% change in the value of the portfolio

= 1.4 × –3.13% = –4.39%

New value of the portfolio = ₹47.81 crore

Gain in the futures market

Value of futures sold

= 798 × 17,730 × 50 = ₹70.74 crore

Value of futures bought

= 798 × 17,000 × 50 = ₹67.83 crore

Profit/Loss in the futures market = ₹2.91 crore

Value of the portfolio (at the end of hedge period) = ₹50.72 crore

(ii) *Sensex moves to 16,000*

New value of Sensex = 16000

% change in the Sensex = –8.83%

% change in the value of the portfolio

= 1.4 × –8.83% = –12.36%

New value of the portfolio = ₹43.82 crore

Gain in the futures market

Value of futures sold

= 798 × 17,730 × 50 = ₹70.74 crore

Value of futures bought

= 798 × 16,000 × 50 = ₹63.84 crore

Profit/Loss in the futures market = ₹6.90 crore

Value of the portfolio (at the end of hedge period) = ₹50.72 crore

(c) The conclusion that can be drawn from the value of the portfolio with the fall in the Sensex is that the portfolio is protected for any level of fall in the market. The value is ₹50.72 crore.

Had the position in the futures market been identical to that of the exposure, the portfolio would have the value of ₹50 crore. The minor variation is due to slightly larger exposure in the futures market.

(d) *Sensex moves to 18,500*

New value of Sensex = 18,500

% change in the Sensex = 5.41%

% change in the value of the portfolio

= 1.4 × 5.41% = 7.58%

New value of the portfolio = ₹53.79 crore

Gain in the futures market

Value of futures sold = 798 × 17,730 × 50 = ₹70.74 crore

Value of futures bought = 798 × 18,500 × 50 = ₹73.82 crore

Profit/Loss in the futures market = –₹3.07 crore

Value of the portfolio (at the end of hedge period) = ₹50.72 crore

(e) The value of the portfolio remains same even if the Sensex rises instead of falling. By taking the position in futures, Safety Mutual

Fund has forgone the opportunity to increase the value of the portfolio to ₹53.79 crore if the Sensex rises to 18,500.

6. Hedging Short Position with Stock Futures

Dynamic Mutual Fund is expecting an inflow of ₹75 crore from which they would constitute a portfolio with a beta of 1.50. They anticipate a rise in the stock markets in the coming month and are wondering that after a month, the prices of the shares would rise. They wished that they had the funds now to invest.

Dynamic Mutual Fund is considering to cover the risk of rising market through the futures.

Current value of index in the Bombay Stock Exchange, is 17,550 while the 1-m futures is traded at 17,730.

(a) With 1 point of Sensex at Re 1.00 and contract size of 50 indices, find out how Dynamic Mutual Fund can protect against the expected rise in the stock market in next one month.

(b) Find out how much fund would be required by Dynamic Mutual Fund to acquire the contemplated portfolio after a month if Sensex rises to (i) 18,700, and (ii) 19,700.

(c) What conclusion do you draw from the results of (b)?

(d) What would be the position of the Dynamic Mutual Fund if the market instead of rising actually fell to 16,500?

(e) What conclusion do you draw from the results of (d)?

Ignore marking-to-the-market and initial margin on the futures contracts.

Solution

(a) Current value of BSE Sensex = 17,550
Price of 1-m futures on BSE Sensex = 17,730
Current value of the portfolio = ₹75.00 crore
Beta of the portfolio = 1.50

Dynamic Mutual Fund is short on the asset. They can protect against the rise in the market and keep the investment value close to ₹75 crore by going long on the futures. Therefore, they must buy futures contract now equivalent to the short position. The value that needs to be covered in the futures market would dependent upon the beta of the portfolio.

Value to be covered = Beta × Value of the portfolio
= 1.5 × 75 = ₹112.50 crore
Current value of 1 futures contract = 17,550
Nos. of Sensex in 1 futures contract = 50
Value of 1 futures contract = ₹8.775 lakh
Nos. of futures contracts to be bought
= 11250/8.775 = 1,282.05 contracts
rounded to 1,282 contracts

At the end of one month, the mutual fund would sell the futures. The price of futures would then be equal to the spot value of the Sensex.

(b) (i) *Sensex moves to 18,700*
New value of Sensex = 18,700
% change in the Sensex = 6.55%
Expected % change in the value of the portfolio
= 1.5 × 6.55% = 9.83%
Investment required to acquire the portfolio
= ₹82.37 crore

Gain in the futures market
Value of futures bought
= 1282 × 17,730 × 50 = ₹113.65 crore
Value of futures sold
= 1282 × 18,700 × 50 = ₹119.87 crore
Less: Profit/Loss in the futures market = ₹6.22 crore
Net funds required to acquire the portfolio
= ₹76.15 crore

(ii) *Sensex moves to 19,700*
New value of Sensex = 19,700
% change in the Sensex = 12.25%
Expected % change in the value of the portfolio
= 1.5 × 12.25% = 18.38%
Investment required to acquire the portfolio
= ₹88.78 crore

Gain in the futures market
Value of futures bought
= 1282 × 17,730 × 50 = ₹113.65 crore
Value of futures sold
= 1282 × 19,700 × 50 = ₹126.28 crore
Profit/Loss in the futures market = ₹12.63 crore
Net funds required to acquire the portfolio
= ₹76.15 crore

(c) The conclusion that can be drawn is that irrespective of the rise in the Sensex, the investment required is ₹76.15 crore. Had the position in the futures market been identical to that of the exposure, the portfolio would involve net investment of ₹75 crore. The minor variation is due to slightly larger exposure in the futures market.

(d) *Sensex moves to 16,500*
New value of Sensex = 16,500
% change in the Sensex = –5.98%
% change in the value of the portfolio
= 1.5 × –5.98% = –8.97%
Investment required to acquire the portfolio = ₹68.27 crore
Gain in the futures market
Value of futures bought
= 1282 × 17,730 × 50 = ₹113.65 crore
Value of futures sold
= 1282 × 16,500 × 50 = ₹105.77 crore
Profit/Loss in the futures market = –₹7.88 crore
Net funds required to acquire the portfolio = ₹76.15 crore

(e) The investment required to acquire the contemplated portfolio remains same even if the Sensex falls instead of rising. By taking the position in futures, Dynamic Mutual Fund has forgone the opportunity to benefit from the fall in the market. If they do not take position in futures, the acquisition would cost ₹68.27 crore if market fell to a level of 16,500.

EXERCISES

Concept Review Questions

1. What do you understand by risk? What are the different kinds of risk faced by the business enterprises?
2. What is the difference between forward and futures contracts?
3. Futures is a standardized forward contract. Comment
4. Hedging with futures is never perfect except by coincidence. Justify the statement.
5. What do you understand by marking-to-the-market? Explain its purpose with suitable example.
6. How do you measure the cost of forward hedge?
7. What is basis and basis convergence?
8. Compare price risk with basis risk. What are the sources of basis risk?
9. Futures could be used for hedging as well as for speculation. If one is holding a futures contract, how would you find out whether the position taken in futures is hedging or speculation?

Critical Thinking Questions

1. A gold trader has observed that gold prices and stock prices move in opposite directions. He is holding some stock of gold and expecting a decline in the prices. Applying the principle of hedging of taking opposite positions, he shorts the stock index futures. Is he hedging or is it an inadvertent speculation?
2. In the year 2006, wheat farmers were able to realize about ₹100 per quintal above the procurement price of the Government. In early 2007, Government of India, in the wake of short supply of wheat and rising prices, imported about 30 lakh tons of wheat at a much higher price than the prevailing domestic price. Under immense pressure from certain political parties to contain inflation, the Government banned futures trading in wheat and paddy. What do you think is the fall out of this strategy?
3. One financial expert opined that "Futures contract is nothing but a forward contract rolled over on daily basis." Do you subscribe to the same opinion? Justify your answer.
4. According to a political philosophy, "Futures and other derivatives are tools of speculation and fuel inflation." What argument can you forward to negate such philosophy?

Practical Assignments

1. Observe the actual value of the index and the price of 1-m index future on NIFTY at NSE. For next 20 successive days till maturity of the futures contract, observe the index value and the price of the same contract. Find out the basis for each day and plot it. Calculate the implied cost of carry, and observe if the price of the contract and value of the index converge or not. If not, assign a reason after further investigation.
2. Identify a futures contract on the same commodity that is traded on at least two multiple exchanges. Compare the contract specifications of the two with respect to product quality, delivery centres, and timing of the delivery. Then, compare the prices of the contract at two exchanges. Do you find the prices as same? If they are different, assign reasons for the same.

Numerical Problems

1. Pricing a Forward Contract

A share is trading at ₹250. What would be the value of the forward contract on the share for delivery after 6 months? Assume the risk-free rate of return is 6% per annum.

2. Price of Forward and Dividend

If the stock in Problem1 is expected to pay a dividend of ₹2.50 per share exactly 3 months from now, what impact do you see on the forward price?

3. Pricing a Forward Contract

The NIFTY Stock Index is at 4,120. What would be the value of the 3-m futures on NIFTY. Assume that the risk-free rate of return is 6% per annum and the yield on NIFTY stocks is 4%. One futures contract on NIFTY is for 200 indices.

4. Speculation with Index Futures

The current value of NIFTY is 4050. Index futures on NIFTY consist of 200 with a value of Re 1 per point. The 3-m futures on NIFTY is currently selling at 4100. Historically, the dividend yield on NIFTY stocks is 3%. The yield on T-bills for 90-day maturity is 7.5%. Find out the following:

(a) The fair price of NIFTY future.
(b) Assuming that the market would correct to the fair price, what actions can you take to make profit?
(c) If the market does not correct till the maturity of the futures contract, could you still make profit without taking any risk?
(d) Would the profit accrue irrespective of the position of market at maturity?

Assume that after three months, the spot market (a) rises to 4200, (b) declines to 3800.

5. Hedging a Receivable

Today is 15 March. A French firm has exported goods to USA worth US $ 1.5 million. The firm expects the payment to arrive by 15 June. The spot exchange rate in Paris is US $ 1.2550 per € and 3-m forward rate is 1.2840. In the futures market, June futures maturing on 24 June are quoted at 1.2710. Answer the following:

(a) What do the forward and future rates indicate for exchange rate of dollar?
(b) How would the French exporter hedge his receivable in the futures market?
(c) The spot rate and futures rate on 15 June are 1.2450 and 1.2475 respectively. When the exporter realizes his bills, what gain/loss would he make in the futures hedge? Also, work out the effective exchange rate the exporter gets when he hedges in the futures market.
(d) Compare the futures hedge with the forward hedge.

Assume size of the futures contract on euro as 1,25,000.

6. Hedging Receivable

Examine the position of the French exporter in Problem 5 if the rates on 15 June are as below:

Spot 1.2700 June Futures 1.2725

(a) Would he end up paying more in this case?
(b) What conclusion could you draw for the hedging strategy?

7. Hedging a Payable

Today is 15 March. A British firm has received documents under letter of credit for a payable of US $ 3 million in three months' time due on 15 June. The spot exchange rate in London is US $ 1.6050 per £ and 3-m forward rate is 1.5900. In the futures market, June futures maturing on 24 June are quoted at 1.5940. Answer the following:

(a) What do the forward and future rates indicate for exchange rate of dollar?
(b) How would the British importer hedge his payable in the futures market?
(c) The spot rate and futures rate on 15 June are 1.6450 and 1.6475 respectively. When the importer pays his liability, what gain/loss would he make in the futures hedge? Also, work out the effective exchange rate the importer pays when he hedges in the futures market.
(d) Compare the futures hedge with the forward hedge.

Assume size of the futures contract is £ 62,500.

8. Hedging a Receivable

Examine the position of the British exporter in Problem 7 if on 15 June the rates are as below:

Spot ($/£) 1.5800 June Futures ($/£) 1.5825

(a) Would he end up paying more in this case?
(b) What conclusion could you draw for the hedging strategy?

CASE STUDY

BOMBAY SUGAR MILLS—BITTER SUGAR AND SWEET FUTURES

Bombay Sugar Mills (BSM), one of the largest sugar producers in the country, came out with its disappointing performance for the quarter that ended in June 2007. It showed a loss of ₹47.31 crore, as against a profit of ₹65.43 crore in the corresponding period last year. In an interview with a news channel, its Managing Director attributed the poor results to sharp drop in the sugar prices and very high procurement cost for the basic inputs. The performance was declining quarter after quarter as the procurement cost kept increasing and realization kept falling. This is shown in the Table A.

Table A Quarterly Performance of Bombay Sugar Mills

₹ crore

Quarter ending	*Jun-07*	*Mar-07*	*Dec-06*	*Sep-06*	*Jun-06*
Net Sales	365.26	396.90	337.11	388.22	392.96
Other Income	2.17	2.22	1.66	2.04	0.70
Total Income	367.43	399.12	338.77	390.26	393.66
Expenditure	–382.09	–341.00	–285.60	–329.21	–286.67
Operating Profit	–14.66	58.12	53.17	61.05	106.99
Interest	–20.72	–15.01	–5.52	–7.00	–9.57
Gross Profit	–35.38	43.11	47.65	54.05	97.42
Depreciation	–20.52	–19.41	–17.06	–14.38	–13.77
Profit before Tax	–55.90	23.70	30.59	39.67	83.65
Tax	8.59	–3.73	–11.41	–7.46	–18.22
Profit after Tax	–47.31	19.97	19.18	32.21	65.43
Net Profit	–47.31	19.97	19.18	32.21	65.43

A greater sign of worry was that the trend was expected to continue for the next three quarters.

The primary reason for the dismal show is largely attributed to the structure of the industry in the country. Sugar industry in India is heavily controlled by the Government in many ways. There are three kinds of stakeholders in the industry. At one end, there are farmers who grow and supply the sugarcane, and at the other end are the consumers of sugar, with the mills falling in between and converting the sugarcane into sugar.

The two ends of the spectrum, i.e., the producers and the consumers, are protected leaving the manufacturers in the lurch. While sugarcane farmers are protected through an assurance of a minimum price they get for their produce, the consumers are protected by control of free-sale sugar quota and public distribution system. These protections are often at the expense of sugar mills.

The most important tool by which the Government influences the industry is the fixing of the Statutory Minimum Price (SMP) that sugar mills are supposed to pay to the farmers for sugarcane. These are fixed by Central Government. Besides SMP, every state also announces another price called State Advised Price (SAP), which is set on the basis of SMP and is much higher. Most sugar mills, depending upon the state they are located in, end up paying a much higher price for the sugarcane than the SMP announced. SMP serves only as a benchmark and is not the price that is actually paid. The data for the past 10–15 years reveal an increasing pattern of SMP as given in Figure 1. While in 1992–93, the SMP was ₹31 per quintal, it rose ₹79.50 in 2005–06. However, the actual price paid is around 50–60% higher than the SMP in any year.

While the SMP is fixed on the basis of expected sucrose recovery from the sugarcane, the efficiency of the sugar mills has to be shared with the farmers. There is very little incentive for productivity on part of the management. In case the recovery improves, the SMP is jacked up accordingly. For example, for 2005–06 the SMP was ₹79.50 per quintal on basis of recovery of 9%; and for every increase in recovery by 0.1%, the SMP rises by ₹0.88.

The ever-increasing prices of sugarcane ensured that there is sufficient production of sugarcane because growing sugarcane remains more attractive to farmers as compared to other crops. With abundant supply of sugarcane always available in each season, the prices of sugar mostly remain low as all mills operate on near capacity. Though

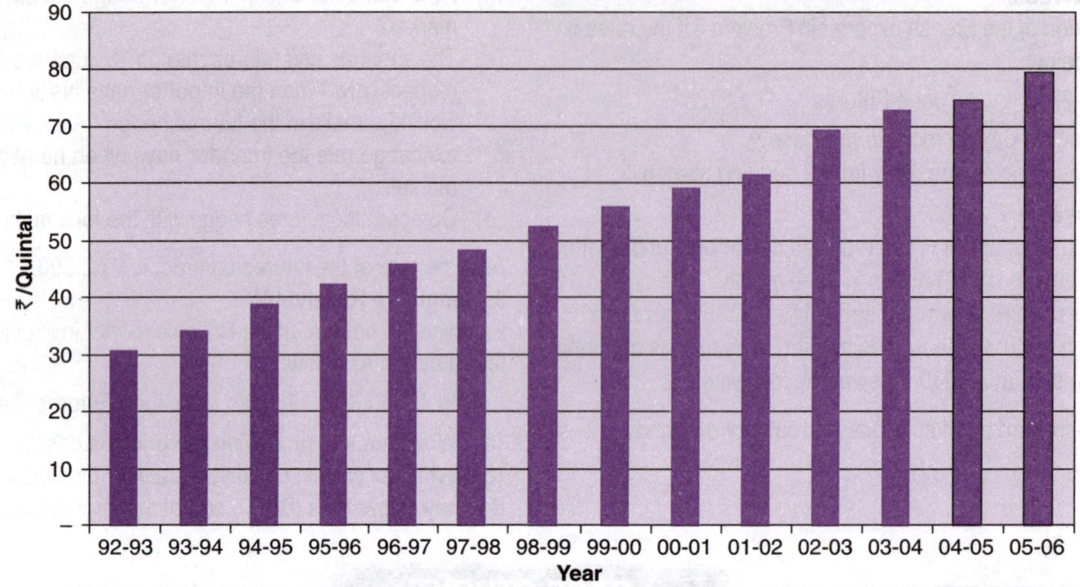

Figure 1 Statutory minimum price–Sugarcane

there is realization that the high levels of SMP and SAP may cause imbalance in crops, the political compulsions keep SMP higher and higher each season. Besides producing sugarcane, the area under the cultivation is also increasing because land not that suitable for the crop is also cultivated with sugarcane resulting in a fall of yield per acre. This too has impacted the recovery of sugar for the sugar mills. Content of sucrose has remained constant at about 10% as against 12% in other countries, despite several efforts to improve the sucrose content.

On the end-product side, the Government specifies a % of the total production as levy sugar at notified price to be distributed to poor through Public Distribution System. The levy to free sale ratio has reduced from 40:60 to 15:85 over the years. Levy prices are about 20% below the cost of production.

Though there is no price control in free-sale sugar, the supplies are regulated through the mechanism of monthly release quota. Producers are not allowed to sell the quantities of sugar in the manner they desire. Therefore, prices are not determined by free competition. Instead, they become a function of releases of free-sale sugar quantity by the Government. Instead, monthly quotas are released for each mill by the Government.

These constraints and limitations are very well known to all and sundry. Yet, the Managing Director, who believed in teamwork and active participation constituted a team comprising senior managers of all departments – Marketing, Finance, and Production to know what different remedies they may have to come out of the difficult situation the firm is in. He requested them to think off beat and come out with some solution that offered the firm some insulation from the vagaries of the market, or rather its dependence on Government actions. The concern of the Managing Director was to make the performance steady.

Hedging Alternatives

The three members of the team met after a couple of days to suggest the following:

The Vice President Finance, Mr Chattri, had learnt about the financial markets well. He informed that he would like to be a very active participant in the derivatives market of futures to make the bottom line steady. He wanted to deal in futures in sugar and *gur*, which could protect the price in the short-term for the next six months. Other members of the team were not as aware and asked Mr Chattri to elaborate on the scheme.

Mr Chattri narrated the scheme like this:

"There are contracts available for different periods in the market for which physical settlement was not required. We can estimate the prices of sugar and *gur*. This estimate would be based on anticipated release order from the Government in near future. Greater the amount to be released, lower would be the price in that month and vice versa.

Under the given scenario for the sugar industry, we can fruitfully employ trading in futures, if not to enhance the profit, then to stabilise it. That way, we shall be able to service not only the farmers but also the shareholders better". He stated the following:

"Futures contract in sugar (quoted in ₹/quintal) comes into force 6 months prior. For example, January 2008 contract becomes available in July 2007. There are two contracts generally available, S-30 and M-30, for small and medium grain of sugar respectively. Each contract is for 10 Tons. Exposures per client is limited to 10,000 tonnes. Margin requirements are about 3%.

We may ensure a price for ourselves by undertaking the following actions:

1. Forecast the release of quotas by the Government on an aggregate basis.
2. On the basis of the quota, project the expected price.
3. Compare the forecast price with the price of the futures contract for the month.
4. If the futures price is higher than the forecast price, sell futures contract and square up anytime before delivery. By doing so, we would realize the price at which we sold the futures contract.

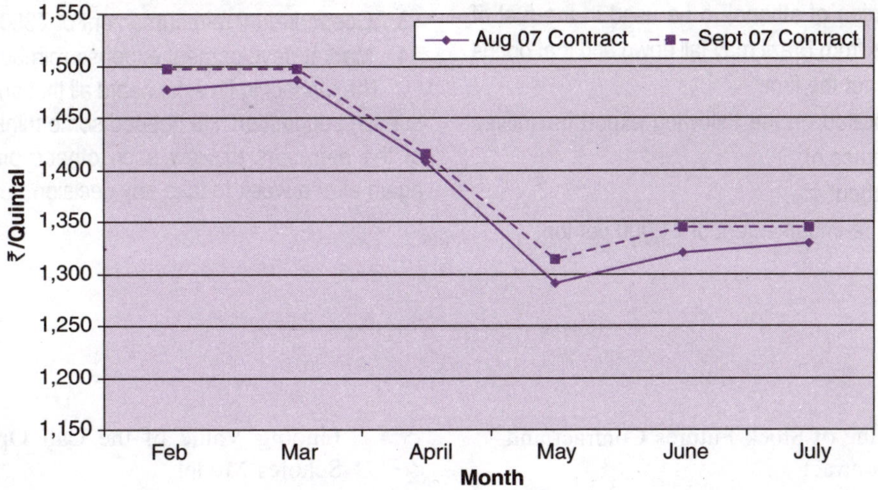

Figure 2 Futures contract prices

5. If futures price is lower than the forecast price, do not take any steps. By doing so, we would be able to ensure the price level much in advance and plan better for procurement."

To reinforce his viewpoint, he presented data on how the futures price of the Sugar contract had moved in the last six months as given in Table B and graphically depicted in Figure 2. He elaborated that had they known that the prices would fall in August, he would sell the August futures contract in February at ₹1,477 and bought back at ₹1,330 in July, thus making a gain of ₹147 per quintal. That would have made his realization at ₹1,477 per quintal.

Table B Price of sugar contract at NCDEX

(*₹/Quintal*)

In the Month of	*Contract*					
	Aug-07	*Sep-07*	*Oct-07*	*Nov-07*	*Dec-07*	*Jan-08*
Feb	1,477	1,498	—	—	—	—
March	1,487	1,497	—	—	—	—
April	1,408	1,416	1,417	—	—	—
May	1,292	1,315	1,312	1,300	—	—
June	1,321	1,345	1,349	1,350	1,352	—
July	1,330	1,345	1,353	1,335	1,324	1,329
Prices are from NCDEX and are taken in mid month						

Vice President Production, Mr Utpadak suggested that the release order and the market prices of the Government were not under the firm's control. Likewise, there was little that the firm can do about the SMP or SAP, despite the fact that the firm enjoys excellent relations with the political forces present and to be. For providing the hedge against the fluctuating levels of profit, he suggested to increase the capacities somehow from power generation and distillery, which could be done by appropriately increasing the crushing capacity. With increased crushing capacity, not only per unit cost of production would fall, but quantities and proportions of saleable by-product of co-generation and distillery too would increase. The increasing proportion of the by-product in the overall revenue would reduce dependence of profit on the prices of sugar and sugarcane.

Vice President Marketing, Mr Vyapari, agreed with Mr Utpadak that there is little that the firm can do under the circumstance either to influence the procurement market and industry structure. He said, "The firm must look beyond Indian borders. There is little sugar exported from India, despite the fact that it is the second largest producer in the world after Brazil." According to him, the prices prevailing in the world were far higher and India was among the countries where the prices ruled the least. He presented the data given in Table C.

Table C Domestic sugar prices across world

(*cents/lbs*)

Country	*Price*	*Country*	*Price*	*Country*	*Price*
Japan	74	UK	45	Argentina	35
France	63	USA	42	India	17
Australia	58	South Africa	41	Brazil	12

Source: www.illovosugar.com

USA was the best target market. He opined that as a result of the ongoing global sugar production deficit, together with significant long-term structural changes within the world sugar market, the sugar price whilst still volatile, increased significantly from US 8.0 cents/lb in April 2005 to US19.7 cents/lb In February 2006.

He shared the good news that yesterday the Government has freed export of sugar from any kind of permission. He said, "We soon should be among the first few to board the bus. So, I think, this is just a bureaucratic hurdle or the bottleneck that has been removed by the Government that you don't need to go and have the permission from them for export. Further, the major player in the world sugar market 'Brazil' that initiates the leads in the international sugar prices has already announced that due to growing requirement of ethanol, it would increase the proportion of ethanol to be used in the fuel of gasoline. Therefore, exports from Brazil may fall down and that opens up a window of opportunity for the firm."

Mr Vyapari also elaborated on the following export incentives available that can be made use of:

1. DEPB entitlement of about 4%.
2. Internal transportation re-imbursement of ₹1,000 per ton.
3. Ocean freight reimbursement of ₹350 per ton.
4. Market development expense reimbursement of ₹500 per ton.

The Managing Director heard all that and thought there are merits in each suggestion. He needed some thinking and also asked each of the members to view each other's proposals and come back again after a week to take any decision.

In the CD

Finding Fair Value of Stock Futures Contract and Index Futures Contract

Finding Value of the Call Option using Black–Scholes Model

CHAPTER 29 Options

LEARNING OBJECTIVES

This chapter is aimed at providing the following:

- basic concept of options
- terminology used in describing options
- introduction to call and put options, their payoffs
- understanding of intrinsic value and time value of an option
- valuation of option by the Black–Scholes model
- determinants of option price and its application
- relationship between call and put prices—put call parity
- concept of implied volatility
- hedging strategies using options

THE TRICKY TENDER

Mr S.K. Jindal (SKJ), the Managing Director of Hindustan Constructions Ltd (HCL) was engrossed with his Marketing Manager, Mr V. K. Maheshwari (VKM) and Finance Manager, Mr Rajat Mehta (RM), trying to give final touches to the bid for a large construction contract in Dubai. The bid is estimated in the vicinity of ₹225 crore and SKJ had proposed to bid US $ 50 million computed at the then prevailing exchange rate of ₹45 per US $.

Developments in the foreign exchange markets over the last month were not too encouraging for HCL. In fact, in today's meeting, all the three wore an extremely worried look. All of them were seeing the risk of losing the bid because the tender price had to be jacked up. Of late, the exchange rate had moved from ₹45 to ₹42.50 with rupee showing remarkable appreciation of more than 5.5% in a short span of time of a little over one month.

SKJ: That rupee appreciation is really very steep. What it effectively meant is that our bid amount would rise from earlier $ 50 million to $ 52.95 million. That is an increase in our bid by 5.88%. In fact, seeing the competition, I was thinking of revising the bid downwards to about $ 48 million.

VKM: I am apprehensive that, at this price, we may not be successful in getting the award.

SKJ: That is right. But I am further worried that even if we get the award at $ 52.94 million, what happens if the rupee continues to appreciate at this rate. By the time we get mobilization advance, another month will be gone. Newspapers are flooded with articles suggesting that Rupee may appreciate to ₹40 per US $ by then.

VKM: Is there no mechanism by which we can freeze the price of the Dollar that we would realize in the four equal instalments spread over the next 12 months? I am worried that by the time we get the tender awarded to us and get the first instalment, half of our profit would be eaten away by the Rupee appreciation.

SKJ: What can we do?

VKM: We may book a forward contract as we do for our regular collections in the foreign exchange. At least, we would know what price we are getting. We would not have any shocks.

RM, who until now was a mute spectator to the conversation of the Managing Director and the Marketing Manager, intervened.

RM: No. We may still have some shocks. Do not forget the fact that forward contract is a two-way contract. We have to execute our part. If we sell US $ 10 million 3-m forward, what happens if we do not get the contract and the mobilization advance? We would still have to deliver $ 10 million, which we would not have if we fail the bid. I don't recommend such a risky approach until we are sure that we have won the bid and got the mobilization advance.

SKJ: Once we get the contract, we are assured of getting dollars. Can we book the forward contract then for the remaining three instalments?

VKM: Oh, I realize that forward is a risky business in the present scenario. I always thought forward was a very safe mechanism.

RM: Yes it is, as far as the price is concerned. But it does not give you choice to execute or not to execute the contract. You stand committed to do your part, and so does the other party. To answer Mr SKJ's question, we may book the forward contract once we succeed in the tender.

SKJ: Then, what do we do now?

RM: We may buy a put option.

VKM: What is that?

RM: Under a put option, we have a right to sell but have no such obligation to do so. In the forward, we are obligated to deliver the foreign exchange on the due date.

SKJ: What does that mean?

RM: It means that if for any reasons I do not want to sell the foreign exchange, I may choose to do so. That means if I fail the bid, I do not sell the foreign exchange; and if I succeed, I would sell the foreign exchange at the rate that we agree today.

SKJ: What about the other party?

RM: He would have to perform his part if I want.

SKJ: That is funny. Why should he give you this right and bind himself unnecessarily?

RM: Because he would be compensated to do that as I would have to pay him something upfront, called premium.

SKJ: That means my cost would increase.

RM: Yes. No right without any obligation can come to you free of cost. Since we know the cost, we may add it to all our cost.

SKJ: But on what basis, the cost of the put option is determined?

RM: The most important factor in determining the cost are naturally the current price of dollar, and the exchange rate at which you want a right to sell. Besides that, if you want to have the right for more time, naturally the cost increases. Further, since it involves cash flow at a later date, the interest rate too becomes a factor. The most important aspect that I can think of is the likelihood of exchange rate crossing the value you desire to protect. Greater the chances of price crossing the cut off, called the strike price, greater is the premium. That means greater the risk, larger is the premium.

SKJ: I understand how we get protection, but what I cannot figure out is how the person giving us this right makes money?

RM: He pockets the premium and hopes that within the specified time, you do not exercise the option. Like, if we buy a put option at ₹43 per \$, we exercise it only when the rupee appreciates beyond ₹43, say to ₹42/\$. He only hopes that the exchange rate for rupee remains above ₹43.

SKJ: This is a very useful tool that does not have equal obligations from the two parties. It seems unfair. Usually, all contracts are fair for both the parties.

RM: This contract too is a fair contract, because we pay the fee front-end. Yes, after we pay the fee and enter the contract, the payoff of the two parties become different and opposite. What I lose is his gain, and what I gain is his loss. On the whole, it results in no gain and no loss, like any other equitable contract and therefore, it is a fair contract.

All three concurred that under the circumstances, they must book a put option. SKJ asked RM to urgently find the price of the put option for a strike price of ₹42.

INTRODUCTION

An option is a unique instrument that confers a right, but no obligation to buy or sell another asset, called the underlying asset. Like forwards and futures, it is a derivative instrument. For example, an option on the share of a firm, say ITC Ltd, would confer a right to the holder to either buy or sell a share of ITC. Naturally, this right would be available at a price, which is in turn derived from the price of the share of ITC. Hence, an option on ITC would be priced according to the price of ITC share prevailing in the market. Of course, this right can be made available at a specific predetermined price and remains valid for a certain period of time rather than extending indefinitely in time.

Options are unique instruments that confer right but create no obligation to perform.

The unique feature of the option is that while it confers the right to buy or sell the underlying asset, the holder is not obligated to perform. The holder, at his option, can force the counter-party to honour the commitment made. Obligations of the holder would arise only then. Therefore, an option may be defined as a contract that gives the owner the right but no obligation to buy or sell at predetermined price within a given time frame. It is the absence of obligation to perform for one of the parties that makes the option contract a substantially different derivative product from forwards and futures, where there is equal obligation on both the parties to a contract.

TERMINLOGY OF OPTIONS

Before we discuss how an option contract works, it would be handy to familiarize with the basic terms that are often used in describing options. These basic terms are described below:

Call option An option to BUY the underlying asset at a predetermined price within a specified interval of time is called a CALL option.

Put option An option to SELL the underlying asset at a predetermined price within a specified interval of time is called PUT option.

Buyer or holder The person who obtains the right to buy or sell but no obligation to perform is called the owner/holder of the option. One who buys an option has to pay a premium to have that right.

Writer or seller One who confers the right to the holder is called seller/writer of an option. To confer this right, the writer charges a premium.

Premium While conferring a right to the holder, who is under no obligation to perform, the writer is entitled to charge a fee upfront. This upfront amount is called the premium. This is paid by the holder to the writer and is also called the price of the option.

Strike price The predetermined price at the time of buying/writing of an option at which it can be exercised is called the strike price or exercise price.

Expiry date/Maturity date The right to exercise the option is valid for a limited time. The latest time when the option can be exercised is called the time to maturity. It is also referred as expiry date.

European/American option The options that can be exercised at any time before maturity are called American options. Options that can be exercised only upon maturity are called European options.

CALL OPTION

A small example from stock markets would help clarify all the terms of the options. Assume that the share of ITC is currently trading at ₹180. An investor, John, believes that the share price is going to rise at least to ₹220 in the immediate future of next three months. John does not have adequate funds to buy the share now, but he is expecting to receive a substantial amount of money in the next three months. He cannot afford to miss an opportunity to own this share. Waiting for three months implies not only a greater outlay at a later point of time, it also means foregoing of substantial potential gains. Another investor, Mohammad, holds contrary views and believes that optimism of John is exaggerated. He is willing to sell the share.

A call option is a right but no obligation to buy an asset at predetermined price within the specified time.

What can John do under these circumstances where he cannot buy the shares on outright basis now? Amongst the many alternatives that may be available to John is included an instrument called a call option. He can instead buy a call option from Mohammad stating that John has a right to buy a share of ITC from Mohammad at a price of ₹190 at any time during the next three months. This would be a call option (the option to buy). John is the holder of the option, while Mohammad is writer/seller of the option. In case John decides to buy the share (exercise the option), he would pay ₹190, the strike/exercise price. The period up to which John can exercise this option is three months. Note that John has the option, which he may not exercise, but Mohammad has no such choice, and he stands committed to deliver the share at ₹190 from John, irrespective of the price of ITC share at that time. Naturally, Mohammad would not provide such a right for free as he is obligated to perform at the option of another. Therefore, Mohammad would charge some fee, called option premium, to grant this right to John. This premium is determined *interalia* by the price of the underlying asset, the ITC share. We shall discuss later how this premium is decided.

We now discuss the circumstances when John would exercise his option. He would use this opportunity only when the actual price of the ITC share has gone beyond ₹190 (the exercise price). Imagine it has moved to ₹200. By exercising the option, he stands to gain immediately ₹10 as he gets one share from Mohammad by paying ₹190 and sells immediately in the market at ₹200. Logically, John would not exercise the option if the price remains below ₹190, because he can buy the share from the market at a cheaper rate. But, John loses the premium paid. If price remains below ₹190, Mohammad would not be asked to deliver and the upfront premium would be his profit.

We may generalize the outcome of a call option in the following manner:

'As long as the price of the underlying asset S remains below the strike price, X the buyer of the call option will not exercise it; and the loss of the buyer would be limited to the premium paid on the call option c.' Therefore,

When $S < X$	Buyer lets the call expire	loss = premium, c
When $S = X$	Buyer lets the call expire	loss = premium, c
When $S > X$	Buyer exercises the call	gain = $S - X - c$

Mathematically, the value of the call is given by Equation 29-1.

$$\text{Value of the call option} = \text{Max}\,(0, S - X) - c \qquad (29\text{-}1)$$

A graphical depiction of the payoff of the holder and writer of the call option is easier to comprehend and is presented in Figure 29-1(a) and (b), respectively.

PUT OPTION

Put option is similar to call option except the fact that it is an option to sell. Again, we take a small example from stock markets to clarify how put option works. Assume that the share of ITC is currently trading at ₹180. An investor, John, in possession of the share (it is not necessary to have the

A put option is a right but no obligation to sell an asset at a predetermined price within the specified time.

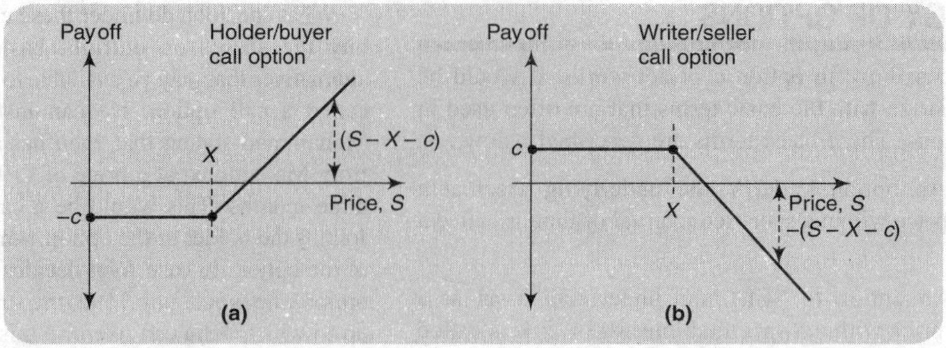

Figure 29-1(a) and (b) Graphical view; payoff of call option for buyer and seller

Unlike forwards and futures, options have an unsymmetrical nonlinear payoff, because they do not create an obligation.

share to enter into an options contract) believes that the share is likely to fall to ₹150 in the immediate future of next three months. John is not sure of the fall but would like to exit from his investment at ₹175. He is seeking protection against the heavy fall in the price. Another investor, Mohammad, holding contrary views believes that pessimism of John is exaggerated. He is willing to buy the share at ₹175, since he feels that ₹175 is the lowest the share will fall.

John believes ITC is a good long-term buy, but he is unsure when the scrip would show potential. He does not want to exit unnecessarily. Under these circumstances, John can buy a put option (the right to sell) from Mohammad stating that he has a right to sell a share of ITC to Mohammad at a price of ₹175 at any time during the next three months. In case John decides to sell the share (exercise the option), he would receive ₹ 175, the strike/exercise price in next three months. John has the option, which he may not exercise, but Mohammad has no such choice and he stands committed to pay the agreed price and claim the share. As in case of the call option, Mohammad would not grant such a right for free and charge some fee, called option premium. This premium is determined *inter alia* by the price of the underlying asset, the ITC share.

John would exercise his option only when it is profitable to do so. The option would become profitable when the actual price of the ITC share goes below ₹175 (the exercise price). Imagine that it has moved to ₹160. By exercising the option, John stands to gain immediately ₹15 by placing the share to Mohammad and realize ₹175 from him, and using the proceeds to acquire a share of ITC from the market at ₹160. This keeps his earlier position intact and yet gives ₹15 as profit. Logically, John would not exercise the option if the price remains above ₹175. However, under all circumstances, he loses the premium paid.

We may generalize the outcome of a put option in the following manner:

'As long as the price of the security remains below the strike price, the buyer of the option will exercise it, because he stands to gain; otherwise his loss would be limited to the premium paid on the put option p.' Therefore,

When $S < X$	Buyer exercises the option	gain $= X - S - p$
When $S = X$	Buyer exercises the option	loss = premium, p
When $S > X$	Buyer lets the contract expire	loss = premium, p

Mathematically, the value of the put is given by Equation 29-2.

$$\text{Value of the put option} = \text{Max}\ (0, X - S) - p \qquad (29\text{-}2)$$

The graphical view of the payoff for put option holder and writer is shown in Figure 29-2 (a) and (b) respectively

All options are a zero-sum game; what is gained by the holder of an option is exactly the same amount that is lost by the writer and vice versa. Table 29-1 (a) shows the payoff of the holder and the writer of the call option at an exercise price of ₹190 and the asset prices ranging from ₹125 to ₹225. The payoff is governed by the actions of the option buyer. If the price of the asset increases beyond the exercise price, the call option holder would buy the asset at the exercise price and sell the same asset in the market and have profit. The call option writer would have to obtain the asset from the market and realize only the exercise price. Market price being higher, he would incur a loss. If price remains below the exercise price, the holder does not exercise the option.

Options are zero-sum game; the gain of holder is the loss of writer and vice-versa.

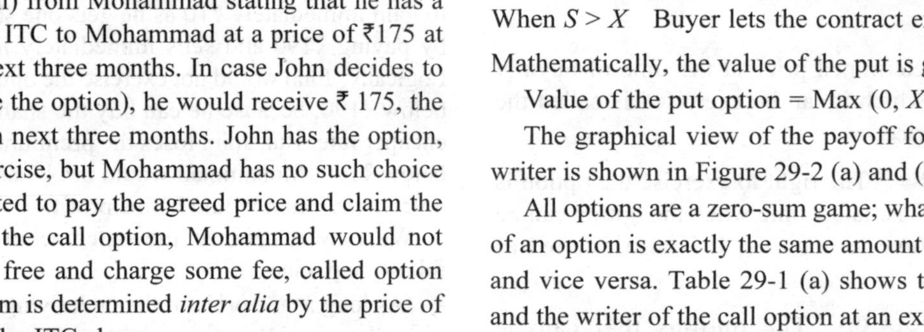

Figure 29-2(a) and (b) Graphical view; payoff of put option for buyer and seller

Table 29-1 (a) Payoff of call option X = 190

Price of the asset	Payoff — Call Holder			Payoff — Call Writer		
	Buy from writer	Sell in the market	Profit/Loss	Sell to holder	Buy from market	Profit (+) /Loss (–)
125 150 175	Holder does not exercise the call option; Loses premium paid at the time of buying the call option.			Obligation of writer does not arise; Gains premium received at the time of writing the call option.		
200	190	200	10	190	200	–10
225	190	225	35	190	225	–35

Table 29-1(b) shows the payoff of the put option for the holder and the writer. Here, the option becomes profitable if the price remains below the exercise price; and therefore, the holder exercises his option. Here, he would sell at the exercise price and buy back the asset from the market. The writer would have to buy from the holder and sell in the market.

Table 29-1(b) Payoff of put option X = 160

Price of the asset	Payoff — Put Holder			Payoff — Put Writer		
	Sell to writer	Buy from the market	Profit/Loss	Pay to holder	Sell in the market	Profit (+)/ Loss (–)
125	160	125	35	160	125	–35
150	160	150	10	160	150	–10
175 200 225	Holder does not exercise the put option; Loses premium paid at the time of buying the put option.			Obligation of writer does not arise; Gains premium received at the time of writing the put option.		

Over-the-Counter (OTC) vs Exchange Traded

Options can also be categorized as OTC or exchange-traded, depending upon where and how it is constructed. Options may be like forward contracts, which are specific to the two contracting parties, or they can be like futures, which may be bought and sold on the specific exchanges. In the exchange-traded options, the contracts need to be standardized. The standardization of option contract would be in terms of the following:

- **Quantity of underlying asset** Only a specific quantity of the underlying asset could be traded on the exchange, and it needs to be predetermined.
- **Strike prices** Only specific strike prices can be handled in a standardized product traded on the exchanges. OTC products can have any strike price as agreed by the two contracting parties.
- **Expiration dates** Like strike price, the expiration dates too must be known before trading can take place in options at the exchanges.
- **Nature of exercise of option** For exchange-traded options, it must be known whether the options are American or European in nature.
- **The ways of settlement** Normally, exchange-traded options are cash settled. Cash settlement refers to the exchange of difference of prices at the time of entering and closing the position in the contracts rather than settling by exercising the option. Cash settlement is done by facilitating the cancellation of the contract by entering into an equal and opposite contract to the original one.

In-the-Money (ITM), At-the-Money (ATM), and Out-of-the-Money (OTM) Options

Depending upon the payoff of the options, they are often referred as either In-the-Money (ITM), At-the-Money (ATM), or Out-of-the-Money (OTM). At any time, ITM options are those which if exercised would result in positive cash flow to the holder. Similarly, OTM options would result in cash outflow if exercised and ATM would have no cash flows.

A call option becomes profitable when the price of the underlying asset exceeds the exercise price. Similarly, a put option is worth exercising when the price of the asset is less than the exercise price. The call option is called ITM when the asset price exceeds exercise price. A put option would be in-the-money as long as the asset price is lower than the exercise price. When the asset price equals the exercise price, it is called the ATM option. It applies to both call and put options. Similarly, when asset price is lower than exercise price for call option, it is out-of-the-money; while put option would be out-of-the-money when asset price exceeds exercise price. We can also refer to the price of the underlying asset as the spot price.

OPTION PRICING

To obtain a right without the obligation, the option holder has to pay a premium to the one conferring the right at a price called option price.

The valuation of the option, i.e., the premium payable by the holder is dependent upon several factors. The two most important factors to determine the price would be: (a) the extent to which the option is in-the-money, and (b) the chances that before expiry, the option will become deeper in-the-money or will turn into in-the-money if it is out-of-the-money. Therefore, the price of an option has two components called *intrinsic value* and *time value*.

Intrinsic value The value attached to the option if it is exercised now is called the *intrinsic value of the option*. The difference between spot price and exercise price will determine this value. For call option, the intrinsic value is $\text{Max}\{(S - X), 0\}$; and for put option, the intrinsic value is $\text{Max}\{(X - S), 0\}$. The value of an option can never fall below its intrinsic value.

The option premium consists of two components: the intrinsic value and the time value.

Time value The value attached to the chances that the strike price will be pierced in times to come, before expiry of the option contract is called the *time value of an option*. Time value of an option can be derived from the observed actual price and the intrinsic value. It is given by the difference of actual price and the intrinsic value. It will be paid by the buyer for the probability that the option will turn in-the-money before expiration. Time value cannot be negative. At best, it can have zero value. Time value may be written as given in Equation 29-3.

Time value of an option

= Actual Price (or Observed Price) – Intrinsic Value (29-3)

Time value of the option is greatest for ATM options. The entire premium paid for ATM options is attributable to the time value as the intrinsic value of the option is zero. As the spot price moves away from the exercise price, the time value starts falling. For deep out-of-the-money options, the time value approaches zero. Also for deep in-the-money options, the time value approaches zero and most of the premium paid is attributable to the intrinsic value of the option.

Boundary Conditions for Call Option Pricing

A call option is a right to buy the asset at the exercise price. Therefore the maximum value of the call option c cannot exceed the price of the asset itself, as no one would pay more money to buy an option than what is required to buy the asset itself. Therefore,

Maximum value of the call option cannot exceed the value of the asset itself on which the option is bought.

Maximum price of the call option,

$$c_{max} = S \quad \text{or} \quad c \leq S \tag{29-4}$$

Similarly, the minimum price that a call option would sell for is the intrinsic value of the option adjusted for the present value of exercise price. The minimum bound for the call option price is:

$$c_{min} = S - Xe^{-rt} \quad \text{or} \quad c \geq S - Xe^{-rt} \tag{29-5}$$

where Xe^{-rt} represents the present value of the exercise price.

A call option with an exercise price of ₹80 and having a spot value of the asset at ₹ 100 must sell for more than ₹20 (Spot Value – Exercise Price). Any price less than the intrinsic value presents an arbitrage opportunity. Consider the following strategy if the call option sells for ₹10.

"Buy a call for ₹10, short a stock for ₹100, and generate a cash flow of ₹ 90." At expiry, following would be the payoff:

	Value of stock	*Value of call*	*Total*
If S < 80	–S	—	–S
If S > 80	–S	S – 80	–80

The cash outflow at maturity is always less than ₹80 irrespective of the price of the asset as against ₹90 already generated earlier.

Therefore, the option value will always exceed its intrinsic value, i.e., the difference between the spot price and the present value of the exercise price. In case of an American option, the boundary conditions for price of the call will apply. The condition for maximum price needs no elaboration. For the minimum value, the call holder will pay X at the time of exercise of the option, and the condition will hold since $S - Xe^{-rt}$ will always be higher than $S - X$. Further, it can be proved that it is sub-optimal to exercise an American option before maturity for non-dividend paying stock.

The composition of the price of call option is shown in Figure 29-3.

As an example, a call on the stock of WIPRO with an exercise price of ₹1,500 and a spot price of ₹1,450 may be selling at ₹75. It is easy to see that the intrinsic value of the call is ₹ 50; and the balance ₹25 which is the time value is attributed to the fact that the price of WIPRO can go beyond ₹1500 before the option expires.

Boundary Conditions for Put Option Prices

A put option is a right to sell the underlying asset at an exercise price X. Irrespective of the price of asset, the put option cannot sell for more than the exercise price. The maximum price for put option is, therefore, the exercise price X. For European option, the put price p has to be less than the present value of X, i.e.

Maximum value of a put option cannot exceed the exercise price.

$$p_{max} = Xe^{-rt} \quad \text{or} \quad p \leq Xe^{-rt} \tag{29-6}$$

The minimum price that a put option would sell for is its intrinsic value, i.e.

PV of X – Spot price

or $$p_{min} = Xe^{-rt} - S \quad \text{or} \quad p \geq Xe^{-rt} - S \tag{29-7}$$

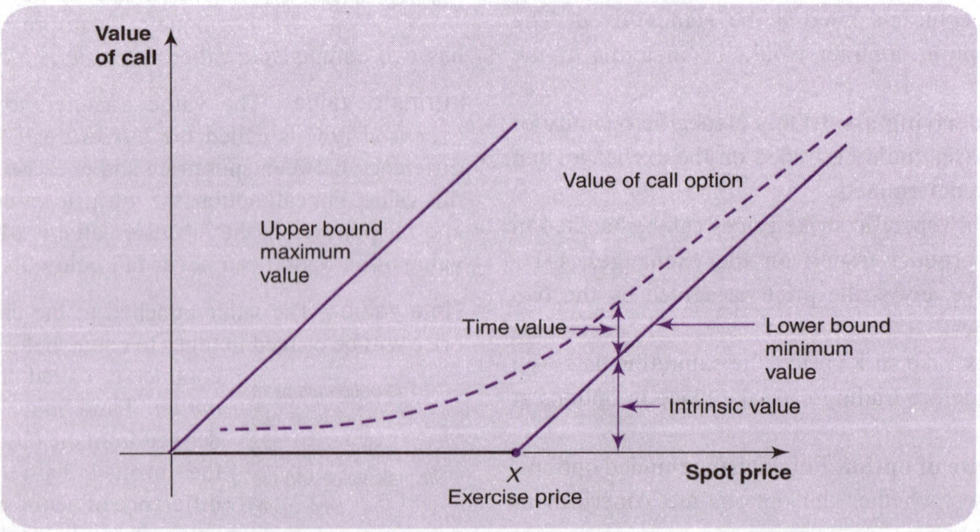

Figure 29-3 Value of call option

Violation of this condition presents arbitrage opportunity. For example, if an asset sells for ₹100, then the 6-m put option for exercise price of ₹120 must be priced more than ₹13.21 $\left(\text{i.e., } \frac{120}{1.06} - 100\right)$ assuming 1% per month as risk-free return without continuous discounting.

To illustrate the arbitrage, consider the following portfolio if the put price is ₹10, i.e., lesser than the lower bound of the put price.

A put option at ₹10, a stock at ₹100 and funded by borrowing of ₹110 for 6 months at 12% with an obligation to pay back ₹110 × 1.06 = ₹116.60. After 6 months, the payoff of the portfolio is as under:

	Value of stock	*Value of put*	*Total*
If $S < 120$	S	$120 - S$	120
If $S > 120$	S	—	S

With an obligation to pay only ₹116.60, the arbitrageur always ends up with a profit, as the value of the portfolio is always greater than ₹120.

With regard to the early exercise, what can be stated for call option does not hold good for put option. For American put, early exercise of the option may be preferred for an ITM option, as the investor realizes a larger amount of $(X - S)$ as against $(Xe^{-rt} - S)$. Consider an example of an Investor A with a 6-m put option at $X = 100$ and a share as against Investor B holding cash of ₹94.34 (PV of exercise price at 1% risk-free rate, 100/1.06). At any point of time before maturity, Investor A is at least worth ₹100 $(X - S + S)$ as he exercises his put option and sells stock as can be seen from the following:

	Value of stock	*Value of putl*	*Total*
If $S < 100$	S	$100 - S$	100
If $S > 100$	S	—	S

As against this, Investor B attains ₹100 only after 6 months. Though the put option held with the long position in stock provides an insurance against the falling price of the stock, early exercise of put option may be desirable to realize the exercise price and forego the insurance if the prices are falling.

Since an American put option may be beneficially exercised prior to maturity, the value of American put option shall be more than the value of a corresponding European put. The intrinsic value for deep in-the-money American put is $(X - S)$ representing the minimum bound. The European put option may sometimes be valued lesser than the intrinsic value to the extent of the differential of the present value of X and S. The differential will be maximum when the price of the underlying asset is zero.

A comparative of values of American and European puts is presented in Figure 29-4.

Example 29-1 Option Prices and Payoffs

A 2-m call option on Infosys with a strike price of ₹2,100 is selling for ₹140 when the share is trading at ₹2,200. Find out the following:

(a) What is the intrinsic worth of the call option?
(b) Why should one buy the call for a price in excess of the intrinsic worth?
(c) What are the circumstances under which the option holder would exercise his call?
(d) At what price of the asset the call option holder would break-even?
(e) If the price of Infosys becomes ₹2,150 (lower than the break even price), should the option holder exercise the call option?
(f) What is the payoff of the holder and the writer if the price of Infosys share is: (i) ₹2,000, (ii) ₹2,250, and (iii) ₹2,500 on the date of expiry of the option?

Solution

(a) The intrinsic worth of the option is $(S - X) = 2{,}200 - 2{,}100 =$ ₹100
(b) The price of the option is ₹140, i.e., ₹40 more than the intrinsic worth. This is the time value of the option and is paid because there are chances that in the next two months, the price of Infosys may rise further and the holder stands to gain more than ₹100.
(c) The option holder would exercise his call if the price of the asset S surpasses the exercise price X, i.e., when $(S > 2{,}100)$.
(d) Call option holder would break even when payoff of the call $(S - X - c) = 0$, which happens at $S =$ ₹2,240.

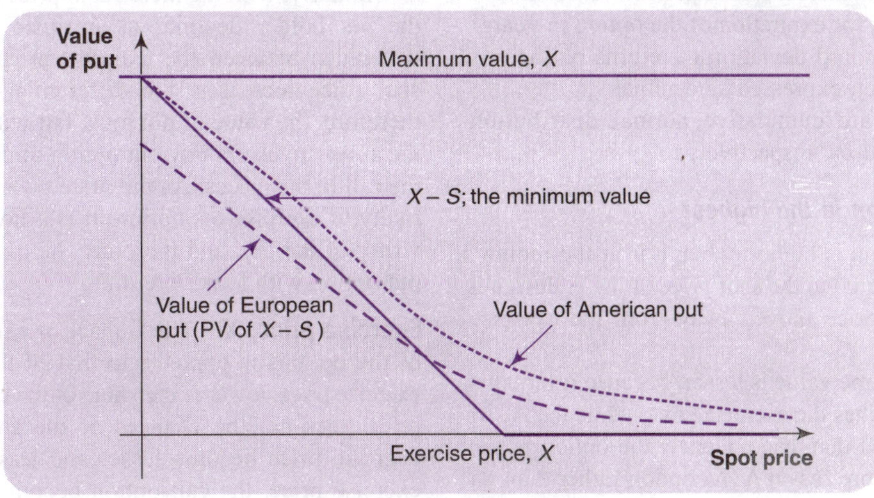

Figure 29-4 Value of the put option

(e) If the price of the asset is above the exercise price, the call option must be exercised irrespective of whether it breaks even or not. The premium paid is a sunk cost. If the price of the stock is ₹2,150, the option holder stands to gain ₹50 upon exercise of the option, which would partly refund the premium paid and contain the losses to ₹90. If he does not, the loss would be ₹140.

(f) The payoff of the call holder and the writer at various prices is:

	Call Option Holder Max (S – X – c, –c)	Call Option Writer –Max (S – X – c, –c)
S = 2,000	–140	+ 140
S = 2,250	+ 10	–10
S = 2,500	+260	–260

BLACK–SCHOLES OPTION PRICING MODEL

While pricing options, the intrinsic value is always apparent, but estimating the time value of the option poses problem. The time value of the option reflects the possibility of it becoming ITM before maturity date, as well as the extent to which it can be ITM.

The basic valuation model, which was developed by Myron Scholes and Fisher Black in 1973 using complex mathematics, is the single most important development in the theories of finance. The work, which fetched Nobel Prize to its inventors, is now called Black–Scholes Model (BSM) of option pricing and forms the backbone of modern option pricing theory.

Black–Scholes Model of option price for European Call on non-dividend paying stock is given by Equation 29-8.

$$c = SN(d_1) - Xe^{-rt}N(d_2) \quad (29\text{-}8)$$

where $d_1 = \dfrac{\ln(S/X) + (r + \sigma^2/2)t}{\sigma\sqrt{t}}$; and

$$d_2 = \frac{\ln(S/X) + (r - \sigma^2/2)t}{\sigma\sqrt{t}} \quad \text{or} \quad d_2 = d_1 - \sigma\sqrt{t}$$

where c = call premium;

S = spot price of the underlying assest

X = exercise price;

r = annual risk-free interest rate expressed as decimal

t = time remaining for expiration of the option in years

σ = annualized standard deviation of returns on the underlying asset, expressed as decimal

$N(d_1)$ and $N(d_2)$ are cumulative normal distribution functions at d_1 and d_2, respectively

Time value of ATM option is the highest

The time value of an option is highest when it is at-the-money, i.e., the exercise price is equal to the spot price of the underlying asset. It declines as the price moves away from the exercise price in either direction.

For OTM option, the time value is lesser, because it remains worthless till the price reaches the exercise price, while the ATM option has already reached that stage. Hence, the option buyer will be prepared to pay more for an ATM option rather than an OTM option. Similarly, in case of ITM option, though the threshold for making profit has already been achieved, there is a likelihood with the passage of time that erosion in the profit will take place with a decrease in the intrinsic value. An ATM option not having any intrinsic value does not face the situation of erosion in intrinsic value.

The entire premium of the ATM option consists of time value. This is true for OTM option too, but it is behind ATM option in the race to become ITM. Therefore, it has lesser time value. The ITM option, though ahead of the ATM option, has the drawback of losing the intrinsic value. Hence, an ITM option has less time value than an ATM option.

Factors affecting the option price

As per BSM, there are six factors that affect the price of the call option. Five of them are present in the Black–Scholes formula. These are: (i) spot price of the underlying asset *S*, (ii) the exercise price *X*, (iii) the volatility of the prices of the underlying asset σ, (iv) the risk-free rate of return *r*, and (v) the time left for expiration of the option *t*. The last factor that affects the option price is the dividend yield which does not figure in the Black–Scholes formula derived for non-dividend paying stock. The impact of each of these factors on the premium of the option is discussed below.

There are five determinants of the option: (i) price of the non-dividend paying asset; (ii) price of the asset, (iii) the exercise price, (iv) the interest rate, and (v) the volatility and time left to expiration.

Price of the underlying asset, *S* As the price of the asset increases, the value of the call also increases. The value of the call is driven by the differential of *S* and *X*. Higher the asset price, higher the differential, and hence higher the value of the call. Most investors buy a call option to benefit from the price rise, and therefore must pay a higher premium if the asset price increases. If the call is OTM and the spot price increases, the chances of its touching the strike price also increases. If the call is already ITM, its intrinsic value increases even further with the increase in spot price. A call option becomes more expensive, as the writer of the call assumes greater risk with rising spot price.

Similarly, with the increase in price of the asset, the payoff of the put holder declines as intrinsic value of the put is the difference between the exercise price and the spot price. As spot price increases, the differential ($X - S$) decreases, and therefore, the value of put must fall with increase in the price of the asset. Investors buy put option to protect themselves against the fall in the prices. As the price goes up, the put holder is less likely to exercise his option. It is a favourable situation for the writer of the put, and therefore, he can be induced to write the put option with lesser premium.

Exercise price, *X* The impact of exercise price on the value of the options is opposite to that of the spot price. Higher the exercise price, lower is the value of the call option. As the exercise price goes up, the chances of the share price exceeding the exercise price become lesser and lesser. With increase in the exercise price, the call option becomes more and more OTM. The value of the call is driven by the differential of the spot price and the exercise price. With the increase in the exercise price, the value of the call falls.

As the value of the call decreases with an increase in the exercise price, the value of the put increases, because exercising the put option by the holder becomes more and more profitable. Accordingly, the value of put option must increase with any increase in the exercise price.

Time left for expiration, *t* Intuition would tell us that the chances of achieving the desired outcome improve if there is more time available in hand. This general statement must also hold true for options. Farther the expiration date, more valuable is the option, because the chances of approaching the strike price become higher. Conversely, if the time available is less, then the option is less valuable. Irrespective of whether it is an option to buy (call) or an option to sell (put), the chances of an option turning in-the-money increase with increased availability of option period.

Therefore, a call or a put of 3 months must cost more than the call/put option having its expiry in 1 month. As the time to maturity approaches, the value of call as well as that of put decreases.

Variability of the price (risk) of the stock, σ It is easy to notice the impact of the three variable of option price, i.e., spot price, exercise price, and time left for expiration. On the other hand, how volatility of the underlying asset affects option premium is not as apparent. Volatility refers to the standard deviation of the return of the asset. Larger the standard deviation, larger is the volatility. In terms of shape of the normal distribution curve, it will become flatter and wider as the standard deviation increases. The expected profit from the option, either a call or a put, would increase with the increase in the standard deviation. As the risk involved is more, the price of the asset varies in a wider range. Hence, it has a greater chance of becoming ITM. It will not be wrong to say that it is the volatility of the price of the asset that imparts value to an option. Call and put options become more valuable as the volatility of the underlying asset increases.

Interest rate, *r* Interest rates also affect the option premium. Again, like volatility, the affect is not as apparent as it was with other determinants of option premium. To understand the impact of interest rate on the option premium, one has to look into the timing of the cash flows that are attached with owning or writing an option. Assuming the intentions of exercising the option at expiry or prior, we can assume that the cash flows for the underlying transaction is deferred in the options contract.

In case of a call option, the holder has a liability to pay the exercise price to own the asset at the time of exercise to the call writer. The buyer essentially has deferred the cash flow for owning the asset, and therefore he can earn an interest on the money equal to the exercise price over the option period. Payment is made only when the call is exercised. It is a liability that arises only upon exercise. If the interest rate increases, the earnings for the holder of the option would be more, and hence he would be willing to pay an additional premium. The other way of ascertaining the direction of change in value of the call option is to view the call premium dependent upon the difference of the spot price and the present value of the exercise price, i.e.,

$$c \geq S - \text{PV of } X \quad \text{or} \quad S - Xe^{-rt}$$

With the increase in the interest rate, the present value of X decreases, thereby making the call more expensive.

Similarly, holding a put is a deferred potential asset that results into inflow of the money only at the time of exercise. The holder of the put foregoes interest for the option period. This sacrifice of income would be more if the interest rates increase. To compensate for the loss of interest, the holder will be willing to pay a lesser premium if the interest rates are higher. With the increased rate of interest, the present value of the potential asset is less. Therefore, the value of put is less when interest rate is high. Alternatively, with increased interest rates, the difference of present value of exercise price and spot price decreases as can be seen from the value of the put:

$$p \geq Xe^{-rt} - S$$

Black Scholes Model of option pricing can be modified to account for the dividend during the option period.

Dividends The factor of dividend does not appear in the Black–Scholes formula. It is derived for the non-dividend paying stock. Robert Merton developed an extension of BSM to account for the dividend, which is given by Equation 29-9 as follows:

$$c = Se^{-dt}N(d_1^*) - Xe^{-rt}N(d_2^*) \tag{29-9}$$

where $d_1^* = \dfrac{\ln(S/X) + (r - d + \sigma^2/2)t}{\sigma\sqrt{t}}$

and $d_2^* = \dfrac{\ln(S/X) + (r - d - \sigma^2/2)t}{\sigma\sqrt{t}}$ or $d_2^* = d_1^* - \sigma\sqrt{t}$

There are two adjustments—one for the dividend and another for the interest rate. The adjustment for dividend is made in the present value of the spot price, which is discounted at the dividend yield rate, and the rate of interest is reduced by the amount of the dividend yield.

Dividend on the assets is a benefit of ownership that does not accrue to the option holder. The holder of the call option becomes its owner only upon its exercise. The benefit of dividend keeps accruing only to the owner of the asset. The price of the asset falls by the amount of dividend once it is paid. As the dividend does not accrue to the call holder and the price of the asset falls, the premium of the call decreases.

Just as the value of the call decreases with increased dividend, the value of the put increases as the holder of the put option retains the ownership of the asset till its exercise and all benefits keep accruing to the holder of the put option.

Following is the summary of the impact of various factors that determine the option price:

VARIABLE (increasing)	*CALL*	*PUT*
Share Price	↑	↓
Strike Price	↓	↑
Time for Expiration	↑	↑
Volatility	↑	↑
Risk-free Rate	↑	↓
Dividends	↓	↑

Applying Black–Scholes Model

The application of Black–Scholes Model is rather easy. One simply has to plug in the values of the variables to get the call premium. An example follows.

Example 29-2 Application of Black–Scholes Model: Call Premium

Given the following information about a share:

Current market price	:	₹50
Annual Volatility	:	30%
Risk-free interest rate	:	10%

Find out the value of 3-m call option with exercise prices of (a) ₹40, (b) ₹50, and (c) ₹60. What are the intrinsic value and the time value of the calls in each case?

Solution

As per the Black–Scholes Model, the value of the call is given by:

$$c = SN(d_1) - Xe^{-rt}\,N(d_2)$$

where $d_1 = \dfrac{\ln(S/X) + (r + \sigma^2/2)t}{\sigma\sqrt{t}}$

and $d_2 = \dfrac{\ln(S/X) + (r - \sigma^2/2)t}{\sigma\sqrt{t}}$ or $d_2 = d_1 - \sigma\sqrt{t}$

(a) For exercise price of ₹40

First, we find the values of d_1 and d_2. All values used are annual and in decimal form. We have $S = 50$, $X = 40$, $r = 0.10$, $t = 0.25$, and $\sigma = 0.30$. These are plugged in the formula.

$$d_1 = \frac{\ln(50/40) + (0.10 + 0.30 \times 0.30/2) \times 0.25}{0.30 \times \sqrt{0.25}} = 1.7293$$

$$d_2 = d_1 - 0.30 \times \sqrt{0.25} = 1.7293 - 0.15 = 1.1593$$

From Normal distribution tables or using Excel function NORMSDIST(d), we find out the area under the Normal distribution for values less than d_1 and d_2.

We have:

$$N(d_1) = 0.9581 \quad\text{and}\quad N(d_2) = 0.9429$$

Inserting the values in the equation in the call premium c:

$$c = S\,N(d_1) - Xe^{-rt}\,N(d_2)$$
$$= 50 \times 0.9581 - 40\,e^{-0.1 \times 0.25} \times 0.9429$$
$$= 47.9050 - 39.0124 \times 0.9429 = ₹11.12$$

The intrinsic value of the call is ₹10 (= 50 – 40) and the remaining value of ₹1.12 represents the time value.

(b) For exercise price of ₹50

We have:

$$d_1 = \frac{\ln(50/50) + (0.10 + 0.30 \times 0.30/2) \times 0.25}{0.30 \times \sqrt{0.25}} = 0.2417$$

$$d_2 = d_1 - 0.30 \times \sqrt{0.25} = 0.2417 - 0.15 = 0.0917$$

$$N(d_1) = 0.5955 \quad\text{and}\quad N(d_2) = 0.5365$$

Inserting the values in the equation in the call premium c:

$$c = S\,N(d_1) - Xe^{-rt}\,N(d_2)$$
$$= 50 \times 0.5955 - 50\,e^{-0.1 \times 0.25} \times 0.5365$$
$$= 29.7750 - 48.7655 \times 0.5365 = ₹3.61$$

The call is ATM with zero intrinsic value, and the entire call premium of ₹ 3.61 belongs to the time value.

(c) For exercise price of ₹60, we get:

$d_1 = 0.9738$, $d_2 = 1.1238$, $N(d_1) = 0.1651$, and $N(d_2) = 0.1305$

and Call premium, c = ₹0.62

Here the call is out-of-money and the entire premium represents the time value; the value attached with the likelihood of call becoming in-the-money before expiry.

The time value is maximum for at-the-money call.

Assumptions of Black–Scholes Model

The following assumptions are made while deriving the option price using the Black–Scholes Model.

Prices are log-normally distributed The BSM assumes the behaviour of the spot price of the underlying asset to be random, which implies that the price is log-normally distributed. Log-normal distribution is similar to the normal distribution with a difference that the random variable can take any positive or negative value under normal distribution, while it is restricted to positive values under lognormal distribution. The other property of log-normal distribution is that the natural log of the variable is normally distributed.

No dividend till the expiration date of the call option Black–Scholes Model assumes that no dividend is paid during the tenure of the option. In practice, the firms declare dividend from time to time, and in an efficient market, the price falls by the amount of dividend when it is disbursed. One way of overcoming this problem is to reduce the present value of the dividend from the spot price of the asset using continuous compounding rates.

It applies to European options The BSM applies to European options, which can be exercised only upon maturity. American options can be exercised at any point of time till the maturity date. One would imagine that the American option being exercisable at any time should be more valuable than the European option. However, it is always more prudent to sell the call option rather than exercise it. We know that the option has intrinsic value as well as time value. When one exercises an American call option well before its maturity, he realizes only the intrinsic value and foregoes the time value. The call will always be selling for more than its intrinsic value. Hence, it is better to sell than to exercise the call option. Since it is always more prudent to sell the call rather than to exercise it, the BSM can be applied to American options too without much problem.

Other assumptions of BSM include: (a) markets are efficient, (b) there exist no transaction cost, and (c) risk-free interest rates remain constant over the option period.

Interpreting Black–Scholes Model

The log-normal distribution of price implies that the natural log is normally distributed, i.e., ln (*S*) is normally distributed. The mean and standard deviation of the natural log of the variable, i.e., ln (*S*), are given by:

$$\text{Mean} = \ln(S) + (\mu - \sigma^2/2)t \quad (29\text{-}10)$$

$$\text{Standard deviation} = \sigma\sqrt{t} \quad (29\text{-}11)$$

where S is the current price, μ is the expected return per annum, and σ is the annual volatility of the price. μ is the annualized expected return in a short period of time.

Let us interpret the BSM for each of the term that is included in the formula for determining the call price c.

$$c = SN(d_1) - Xe^{-rt}N(d_2)$$

where $d_1 = \dfrac{\ln(S/X) + (r + \sigma^2/2)t}{\sigma\sqrt{t}}$

and $d_2 = \dfrac{\ln(S/X) + (r - \sigma^2/2)t}{\sigma\sqrt{t}}$ or $d_2 = d_1 - \sigma\sqrt{t}$

The first term $SN(d_1)$ can be said to be the cash inflow, and the second term of $Xe^{-rt}N(d_2)$ can be said to be potential cash outflow of the exercise price.

The term $N(d_1)$ refers to the delta of the option which represents the fraction of the stock bought for each call written in the hedged portfolio. Since the first term is the value of the fraction of stock owned, it is equivalent to an asset.

The expression Xe^{-rt} reflects the present value of the exercise price discounted on the continuous basis. $N(d_2)$ can be interpreted as the probability of the call becoming ITM. And if it does become ITM, it entails a cash outflow of X, the present value of which is Xe^{-rt}. Therefore, it is a potential liability.

The call price is the surplus of the asset owned, less the likely liability for the call written. Hence, the difference of the value of the stock position taken per call and the present value of the expected liability represents the call value at any point of time.

Put pricing using BSM The BSM model can also be applied to the pricing of a put option. The put price as per the BSM is given by:

$$p = Xe^{-rt}N(-d_2) - SN(-d_1) \quad (29\text{-}12)$$

where $d_1 = \dfrac{\ln(S/X) + (r + \sigma^2/2)t}{\sigma\sqrt{t}}$

and $d_2 = \dfrac{\ln(S/X) + (r - \sigma^2/2)t}{\sigma\sqrt{t}}$ or $d_2 = d_1 - \sigma\sqrt{t}$

p = put premium; S = spot price of the underlying asset

Equation 29-12 is similar to that of the call price with changed signs of X and S; and d_1 and d_2 being replaced by $-d_1$ and $-d_2$ respectively, we can directly apply the Black–Scholes Model for determination of put prices.

Example 29-3 Application of Black–Scholes Model: Put Premium

Given the following information about a share:

Current market price	:	₹50
Annual Volatility	:	30%
Risk-free interest rate	:	10%

Find out the value of 3-m put option with exercise prices of: (a) ₹40, (b) ₹50, and (c) ₹60.

What are the intrinsic and time values of these options?

Solution

As per the Black–Scholes Model, the value of the put is given by:

$$p = Xe^{-rt}N(-d_2) - SN(-d_1)$$

where $d_1 = \dfrac{\ln(S/X) + (r + \sigma^2/2)t}{\sigma\sqrt{t}}$

and $d_2 = \dfrac{\ln(S/X) + (r - \sigma^2/2)t}{\sigma\sqrt{t}}$ or $d_2 = d_1 - \sigma\sqrt{t}$

(a) For exercise price of ₹40

First, we find the values of d_1 and d_2. We have:

$S = 50$, $X = 40$, $r = 0.10$, $t = 0.25$, and $\sigma = 0.30$

These values are plugged in the formula.

$$d_1 = \frac{\ln(50/40) + (0.10 + 0.30 \times 0.30/2) \times 0.25}{0.30 \times \sqrt{0.25}}$$

$$= 1.7293$$

$$d_2 = d_1 - 0.30 \times \sqrt{0.25} = 1.7293 - 0.15 = 1.1593$$

From Normal distribution tables or using Excel function NORMSDIST(d), we find out the area under the Normal distribution for the values less than $-d_1$ and $-d_2$.

We have:

$$N(-d_1) = 0.0419 \text{ and } N(-d_2) = 0.0571$$

Inserting the values in the equation in the put premium p

$$p = Xe^{-rt}N(-d_2) - S\,N(-d_1) = 40\,e^{-0.1 \times 0.25} \times 0.0571 - 50 \times 0.0419$$

$$= 2.2267 - 2.0950 = \text{Re } 0.13$$

The intrinsic value of the put is zero, and the entire value of ₹0.13 represents the time value, the value attached with the chances that the put would turn ITM before expiry.

(b) For exercise price of ₹50

We have:

$$d_1 = \frac{\ln(50/50) + (0.10 + 0.30 \times 0.30/2) \times 0.25}{0.30 \times \sqrt{0.25}} = 0.2417$$

$$d_2 = d_1 - 0.30 \times \sqrt{0.25} - 0.2417 - 0.15 = 0.0917$$

and $N(-d_1) = 0.4045$ and $N(-d_2) = 0.4635$

Inserting the values in the equation in the put premium p:

$$p = Xe^{-rt}N(-d_2) - N(-d_1) = 50\,e^{-0.1 \times 0.25} \times 0.4635 - 50 \times 0.4045$$

$$= 22.6028 - 20.2250 = ₹2.38$$

The put is ATM with zero intrinsic value and the entire premium of ₹2.38 belongs to the time value.

(c) For exercise price of ₹60, we have

$d_1 = 0.9738$, $d_2 = 1.1238$,

$N(-d_1) = 0.8349$, and $N(-d_2) = 0.8695$

and Put premium p = ₹9.14

Here, the put is ITM with an intrinsic value of ₹10. The present value of exercise price is ₹58.52, and the minimum value of an European put option would be ₹8.52. The remaining premium of Re 0.62 represents the time value, the value attached with the likelihood of put remaining ITM before expiry.

Notice that: (a) Put can sell for less than its intrinsic value, and
(b) The time value is maximum for ATM option.

RELATIONSHIP OF CALL AND PUT PRICES—PUT CALL PARITY

There exists a relationship between the prices of call and put options, known as the *put call parity*, which is derived on the principle of no arbitrage. For this, we examine a special combination that is of significance. The combination is that of stock, a call option, a put option, and the debt/bond. Let us consider an example where an investor creates a portfolio of the following securities:

For same underlying asset, same exercise price, and same time to expiry, call price would exceed put price by the amount of the differential of spot price and the present value of the exercise price.

1. Goes long on a share
2. Writes a call for $X = 100$ maturing at time t and commanding a premium of c.
3. Buys a put for $X = 100$ also maturing at time t and selling at a premium of p.

After having formed the portfolio, let us examine the position of this portfolio under various prices of the underlying asset at the time of expiration. Table 29-2 depicts the position of the portfolio for a price range of ₹0 to ₹200.

Table 29-2 Value of the portfolio of stock, short call, and long put at expiration

(Figures in ₹)

Stock Price	0	50	75	100	125	150	200
Long Stock	0	50	75	100	125	150	200
Short Call at $X = 100$	—	—	—	—	–25	–50	–100
Long Put at $X = 100$	100	50	25	—	—	—	—
Total Value of the Portfolio	100	100	100	100	100	100	100

From the last row of Table 29-2, it is evident that the value of the portfolio remains constant at the exercise price $X = 100$, irrespective of the price of the underlying asset. When price falls below ₹100, the put becomes valuable and protects the loss on the asset. When price goes beyond ₹100, the call holder exercises the option and the asset in hand gets delivered in exchange for the exercise price of ₹100, foregoing any gain from the rise in price.

A payoff of the individual securities and the combined payoff of the portfolio is depicted in Figure 29-5.

With no uncertainty in the value of the portfolio at expiration, we can state the following:

1. An investor can borrow an amount equivalent to the present value of exercise price to create the portfolio. Since the value of the portfolio is certain at the expiration date, the lenders would lend money at risk-free rate. The portfolio can be funded by borrowing an amount equal to the present value of the maturity amount of X, the exercise price.
2. This portfolio can be said to be equivalent to a bond which matures to the value equal to that of the exercise price, and whose maturity coincides with the expiry of options.

Since the maturity value of the portfolio and the bond are equal at maturity, the law of one price demands that the initial cost of the portfolio must be equal to the present value of the bond.

> Initial cost of the portfolio of long stock, short call and long put
> = Amount that can be borrowed at risk-free rate
> = Present value of the bond maturing to the exercise price

If S_0 is the current price of the share, c is the call premium, and p is the put premium, then:

$$S_0 - c + p = \text{PV of } X = X/(1 + r)$$
$$= Xe^{-rt} \text{ (for continuous compounding)} \quad (29\text{-}13)$$

Equation 29-13 is known as *put call parity*, establishing a relationship between the call and put prices. An alternative form of the put call parity is that the difference of the call and put

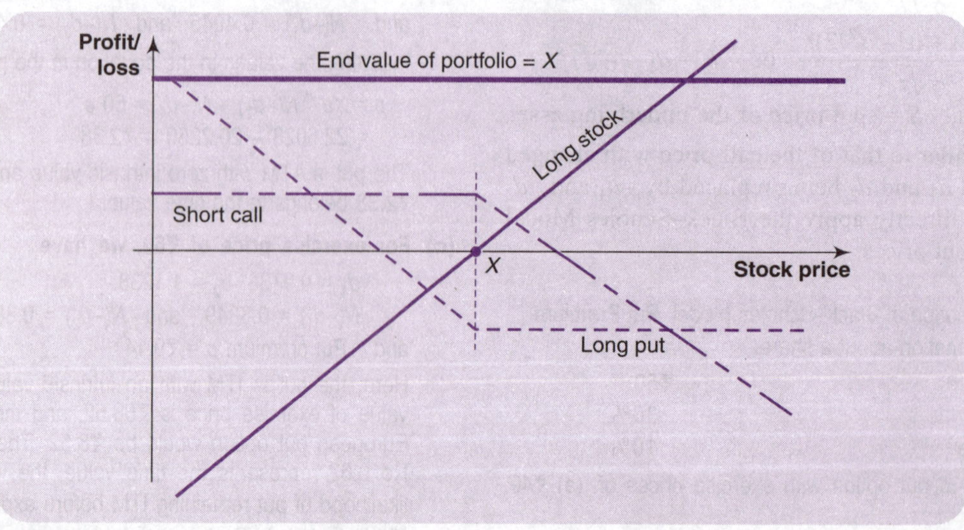

Figure 29-5 Put call parity; a risk-less portfolio

prices must be equal to the difference of spot price and present value of the exercise price. Rearranging Equation 29-13 gives a more familiar form of put call parity.

$$c - p = S_0 - X e^{-rt} \quad (29\text{-}14)$$

This also implies that the call price for ATM options must always be higher than the put price for the same underlying asset, same exercise price and same expiration.

Applying Put Call Parity

If put call parity is not true, the situation will offer arbitrage opportunities. An example will highlight the arbitrage available.

Assume the current stock price is ₹100. A call with exercise price of ₹100 with two months to maturity is selling at ₹12. The risk-free rate is 1% per month, and therefore a bond maturing after two months is selling for 100/1.02 = ₹98.04. We examine this situation for put with the exercise price of ₹100 and two months to maturity with put prices of: (a) ₹6 and (b) ₹11.

If the put price is comparatively lower at ₹6, the investor can do as follows:

If the Put Price is ₹6			*Figures in ₹*
At t = 0		*At t = 2 months*	
Action	*Cash flow*	*Action*	*Cash flow*
Buy the portfolio Buy stock –100 Write call +12 Buy put –6	–94.00	Sell the portfolio	+100.00
Short sell the bond	+98.04	Buy the bond and deliver	–100.00
Net Cash flow	**+4.04**		**0.00**

Since, at maturity, the value of the portfolio is risk-less, an investor buys the portfolio at ₹94 and short sells the bond to realize ₹98.04 having a net cash inflow of ₹4.04 now. After two months, the investor can sell the portfolio at ₹100, buy the bond, and meet the short sale commitment. Alternatively, he could borrow ₹98.04 at 1% per month now and after 2 months, pay the maturity value of the loan of ₹100 by liquidating the portfolio. Hence, the initial cash flow of ₹4.04 is the profit from the risk-less position.

In case the put price is higher at ₹11, the investor can take a reverse position, i.e., sell the portfolio and buy the bond, and yet profit from arbitrage as may be seen from the following:

If the Put Price is ₹11			*Figures in ₹*
At t = 0		*At t = 2 months*	
Action	*Cash flow*	*Action*	*Cash flow*
Sell the portfolio Sell stock +100 Buy call –12 Write put + 11	99.00	Buy the portfolio	–100.00
Buy the bond	+ 98.04	Sell the bond	+100.00
Net Cash flow	**+ 0.96**		**0.00**

Here again, the maturity value of ₹100 is fixed. The investor can sell the bond and utilize the proceeds to buy the portfolio back, resulting in no cash flow. However, he generates a profit of Re 0.96 at the time of setting up the risk-less position. As an alternative to the bond, the investor could lend ₹98.04 at risk-free rate.

The put price that will eliminate the arbitrage profit is arrived by using Equation 29-14. Accordingly, the equilibrium put price will be:

$$p = c - S_0 + \text{PV of } X$$
$$= 12 - 100 + 98.04 = ₹10.04$$

In the first case, the put price of ₹6 was too low, and therefore the investor bought the put; while in the second case, the put was overpriced at ₹11 inducing the investor to write the put.

Implications of Put Call Parity

Rearranging the equation, we can state the call price as:

$$c = S_0 - X e^{-rt} + p$$

Call price = Intrinsic value + Time value

The intrinsic value of the call being the difference between the spot price and the present value of the exercise price, we may say that the put price reflects the time value of the call. Since a put cannot sell for less than zero, a call will always have some time value. For an OTM put, the put premium reflects the time value of call as well as the put.

Put call parity also establishes a link between capital markets, derivative markets, and debt markets. While we all know that the derivatives are driven by capital markets dealing in the underlying assets of shares, the link between the derivatives markets and debt markets was not very apparent. Through put call parity, we now know that the returns on the bonds also affect the prices of derivatives. Therefore, in an efficient economy, all three markets must be in balance.

The other implication of put call parity relates to the synthetic creation of an asset. Put call parity relates the prices of call, put, stock, and bonds. A bond can be replicated using stock, call, and put. Likewise, the payoff of stock can be obtained using bonds, call, and put. In fact, amongst the four assets of call, put, bond, and stock, the profile of one asset can be replicated using the other three. Rearranging Equation 29-15 will provide the combination for synthesizing the asset. A synthetic put can be obtained by buying a bond, buying a call, and short selling a stock. Synthetic creations can help establish a position in an asset at lower cost in the event of a temporary imbalance in the capital markets, the derivative markets, and the debt markets.

Put Call Parity for American Options Put call parity for European options can help establish a relationship for American puts and calls. The put prices for European option are given by rearranging Equation 29-14.

$$p = c - S_0 + Xe^{-rt}$$

Since it is not beneficial to exercise call before expiration, the values of American and European calls are equal for non-dividend paying stocks. However, the same cannot be said for American put, which commands a higher price than the European put. If prices of American call and put options are denoted as C and P respectively, we may say that:

$$C = c \quad \text{and} \quad P > p$$

The put call parity relationship for American options can be stated as below:

$$c - S_0 + Xe^{-rt} \quad (29\text{-}15)$$

Implied Volatility

The volatility used in the Black–Scholes model is an unobservable statistic. Using historical volatility in the Black–Scholes formula for arriving at option prices may not match with the market prices prevailing for calls and puts. The reason for divergence between the theoretical price as per Black–Scholes model and the actual market price may lie in the different estimates of volatility used by the market that does not conform to the historical volatility.

The fact that options are traded, the price of an option implies a volatility in the prices of the underlying asset, which may be different from the measured volatility based on historical data.

To illustrate implied volatility, we may use BSM to calculate the price of a call option at ₹29.36 with $S = 500$, $X = 500$, $t = 0.25$ years, and $r = 10\%$ using $\sigma = 23\%$ as measured by the historical data. The actual market price happens to be ₹35. How do we explain this divergence in the price? The only plausible explanation can lie in the different estimates of volatility used by the market and the Black–Scholes model, as there exists no ambiguity about the other four variables, S, X, t, and r that affect the call price.

While the BSM used the historical volatility in its calculation of the call premium, the market is more concerned with the future volatility of return. As long as the historical volatility truly represents the future volatility, the actual prices would be identical to the theoretical price. Since the market price represents the collective wisdom of investors, we have to accept it as true even though it does not agree with the theory. All theories must explain practice, else it becomes redundant. Assuming that the market price of the call is correct and also assuming the BSM as valid, the call price must reflect a volatility that is implied in the Black–Scholes formula. Hence, given the four parameters, S, E, t, and r, and the market-determined call price, we can solve for σ in the BSM. This volatility derived from the BSM is implied in the call premium prevailing in the market and makes the equation of option price hold.

Estimating implied volatility Since call premium is an increasing function of volatility and the market price of the call, which is at ₹35, is greater than the figure arrived at using the BSM. we can say that the implied volatility is greater than 23%. We have to find the value of σ in the BSM that matches the call premium of the market. Unfortunately, there is no direct way to solve for σ using the market-determined call prices. The only option we seem to have is to use a trial and error method to arrive at σ that satisfies the BSM and the market price. Hence, we start increasing the value of σ and solve for the call premium. As a first attempt, we increase the value of σ from 23% to 30% and calculate the call premium. We get a value of ₹36.12. Since this is greater than the market price, we may try a reduced number of 28% as the next approximation. This time, the call premium comes to ₹34.21. Now, we are fairly close to the market price. As another attempt, we assume a value of 29% and get a call premium of ₹35.11. Using linear extrapolation of the two figures of ₹34.21 and ₹35.11 for volatilities of 28% and 29% (Re 0.90 per 1%), we conclude that the implied volatility in the call price of ₹35 is around 28.88%.

Does implied volatility mean that the historical volatility is of no significance? Certainly not. Historical volatility provides insight into what has been the general level of risk with the stock prices. On the other hand, implied volatility is something that is assigned by the market for future. Though the future is not necessarily dependent upon the past, it is not independent of it either. One must find an explanation for divergence in the estimates of volatility. Historical volatility will provide a base for further study of causes of divergence.

HEDGING STRATEGIES WITH OPTIONS

Hedging may be defined as those actions that protect against the adverse happening of events. Options can precisely perform that role. In our day-to-day life, we act in a manner that resembles options, yet we do not realize having used them.

For example, each one of us obtains an insurance of some form or the other. For example, consider a car insurance against theft or a house insurance against fire each year. We pay insurance premium to protect against the loss of asset due to theft or fire. Insurance firms charge premium and hope that the fire or theft does not take place. If it does, you recover the loss from the insurance firm. If the fire or theft does not take place, the insurance firm feels good. In any case, the premium paid to the insurance firm is foregone. It is the price of buying peace of mind. By taking an insurance policy, we have hedged against the loss in the value of the asset owned. In options terminology, buying an insurance policy is nothing but the equivalent of holding a put option that protects against the loss in the value of the asset owned. The insurance firm has in fact written a put. You exercise your option if the fire takes place, and the insurance firm is obligated to compensate the loss.

As another example, consider buying a property/real estate. While buying a property, we normally enter into an 'agreement to sell' which states the firm price of the property and provides for a token payment by the prospective buyer to the prospective seller at the time of the agreement with the balance amount to be paid within an agreed time period. Before the expiry of the agreement to sell, the prospective owner has the right to pay the balance and take delivery of the property in question. If the prospective buyer does not exercise the option within the stipulated time, the prospective seller is absolved of the obligation to deliver the property. This agreement to sell closely resembles a call option, which is exercised if the price goes up and is not exercised when the price falls down. The prospective buyer would exercise the option if the price of the property has gone up. Instead, if the price has fallen, the buyer would not seek delivery of the property and let the agreement to sell expire. In either case, the front-end payment made is forfeited, and belongs to the seller. Such an agreement to sell provides protection to the buyer and is a hedge against the rise in price of the property.

Depending upon the situation, people need protection against the change in price. Sometimes, fall in value is damaging as was in the case of the insurance policy, where one already owned an asset—called long on asset in financial terminology—and needed protection against the fall. At other times, the rise in value is adverse as was the case in buying of property, where one did own an asset—called short on asset in financial terminology—and needed protection against the rise in prices. Both the situations emphasize the need for hedging.

Option is an excellent instrument to hedge, because it protects against the adverse movement in prices and at the same time, retains the upside potential to gain from a position in the asset.

Hedging

Examples from financial market are most apt to explain and comprehend the concept of hedging. When an investor takes a position in the stock, he faces the risk of losses when the prices move opposite to the anticipated direction. If one has purchased a stock, he expects to gain from the rise in price. If the price falls instead, he incurs a loss. Similarly, an investor who has taken a short position in stock expects to gain from the fall in the price. Instead, if the price rises, the investor faces a loss. Combining the position in the stock with those of the options protects one from the losses from the adverse movement in price without affecting the returns from the favourable movement of price. The returns from the favourable side are reduced marginally to the extent of the premium paid to buy the option.

Hedging long position in stock/asset—the protective put

An investor takes a long position in a stock in the hope of a rise in price. A long position in stock carries a risk if the price falls. If the purchase price of the asset was S_0 and the current price is S, the loss or profit is given by $S - S_0$. If $S < S_0$, the investor suffers a loss.

If the investor buys a put giving him the right to sell at exercise price along with the stock to form a portfolio – called long on asset with a put - the loss in the long position in stock can be covered by exercise of the put in the event of a fall in price. This is called a *protective put*. The payoff of the protective put is shown in Figure 29-6, which emerges from the payoff of the long position in stock and the put option.

A long position in assets deteriorates with a fall in price. Buying a put option is a way to get protection from the expected loss. In case the prices move up, the long position continues to gain from such movement.

Note that the loss in case of fall in price is contained to the premium paid for the put. In case of rise in price, the profit from the stock stands reduced by the amount of premium paid on the put. In a long position on the asset, the profit will be $S - S_0$; while with the put, the profit will be $S - S_0 - p$, where p is the put premium, when $S > S_0$.

An example of a protective put with IPCL stock as the underlying asset is shown in Exhibit 29-1.

Exhibit 29-1 explains the hedging strategy, contains a table for payoff and depicts the graphical view of the combined position

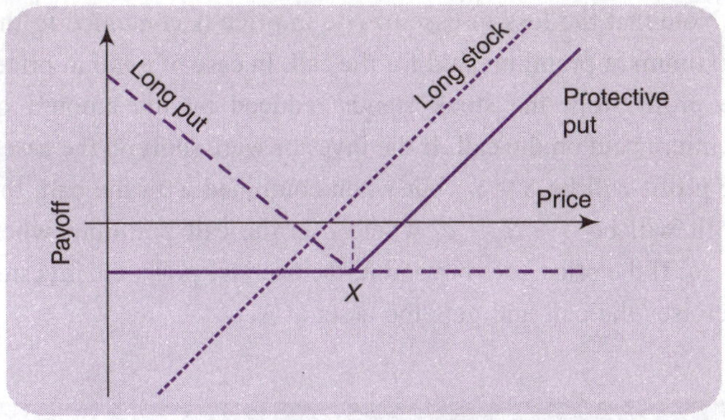

Figure 29-6 Protective put

of long on asset with put option. If the investor does not buy the put— remains unhedged—his profit and loss could be very large. Buying a put restricts the losses to ₹8 and yet retains the profit potential, except for the premium paid on the put as may be seen from the figure in Exhibit 29-1.

Hedging short position in stock/asset—short on asset and long on call

Now consider an opposite position with no asset in possession. Many of you would wonder what protection one needs on an asset that is not owned. Of course, one has nothing to lose because one does not own. Yet, protection is required if one is intending to own the asset in near future. In future, if the price falls, it would be favourable; but if it rises, then owning the asset would become more expensive, which is precisely why protection is required. We call this position as *short on asset.*

An investor is assumed short in a stock expecting a fall in price. He carries a risk with rising price. If the current price of the asset is S_0 and the expected price is S, the loss or profit is given by $S - S_0$. If $S < S_0$, the investor gains, else he suffers a loss. To get protection from the losses that may result from the rise in price, the investor buys a call option on the stock. In the event of a rise in price, the investor can exercise the call owned and compensate for the losses incurred on the short position in stock. The payoff of the combined position of short stock and long call is shown in Figure 29-7.

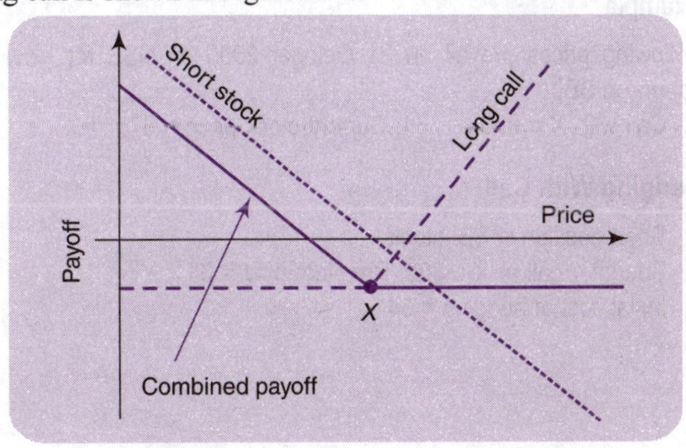

Figure 29-7 Long on stock and long on call

Note that the loss in case of rise in price is contained to the maximum of premium paid for the call. In case of a fall in price, the profit from the stock stands reduced by the amount of premium paid on the call. If the investor were short on the asset, the profit will be $S - S_0$; but when combined with the call, the profit will be $S - S_0 - c$, where c is the call premium when $S < S_0$. If the price goes beyond X, the exercise price, the investor exercises the call and gets the asset at X.

An example of hedging a short position on a stock of State Bank of India (SBI) is shown in Exhibit 29-2 with a strike price of ₹880 and a call premium of ₹34. With the call option, the investor is assured of getting the stock of SBI at no more than ₹880. If the price remains below ₹880, he does not need to exercise the call; instead, he gets his desired stock at a lower price in the market.

Exhibit 29-1 Protective Put

Strategy

- Long position on stock
- To hedge against fall in price: buy a put on the same asset for the period of hedge

Example

The following prices prevail on 21 October 2005 on NSE in November 2005 option on IPCL:

Put with X = 220 p = 8; Current stock price = 220

Protective Put

Long position in IPCL stock

Bought 1 Put at X = 220; Premium paid = 8

Initial cost of protective put = 8

Table for payoff for protective put

When Spot Price S	Long Stock	Long Put X = 220	Initial Cost	Total
S < 220	S – 220	220 – S	–8	–8
S > 220	S – 220	—	–8	S – 228

Graphical View: Protective Put Payoff

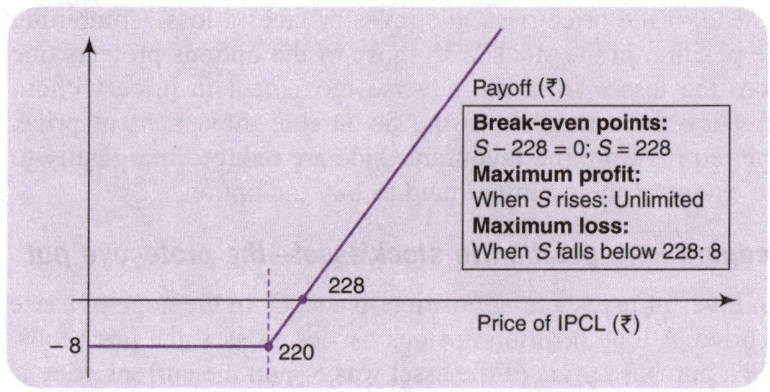

Exhibit 29-2 Hedging Short Position in Stock

Strategy

- Short position on stock
- To hedge against rise in price: Buy a call on the same asset for the period of hedge.

Example

Following prices prevail on 21 October 2005 on NSE for Nov. 05 option on SBI:

Call with X = 880 c = 34; Current stock price = 875

Hedging With Call

Short position in SBI stock

Bought 1 call at X = 880; Premium paid = 34

Initial cost of hedging = 34

Table for Payoff of Short on Asset and Long on call

When Spot Price S	Short Stock	Long Call X = 880	Initial Cost	Total
S < 880	880 – S	—	–34	846 – S
S > 880	880 – S	S – 880	–34	–34

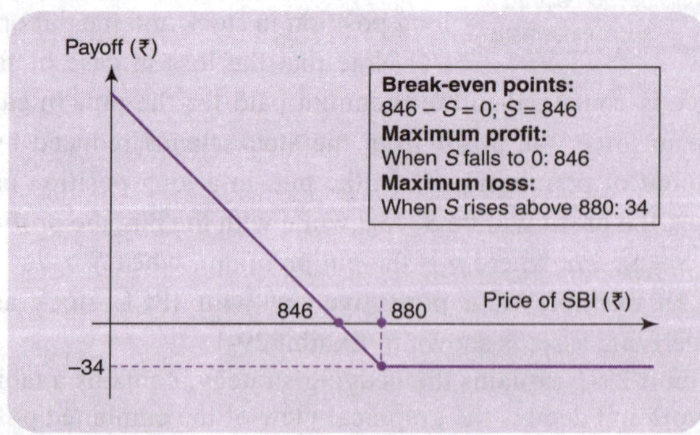

SUMMARY

Options are derivatives that provide a right without an obligation. This unique feature, of a right without an obligation, makes options different from other derivatives like forwards and futures. This feature also makes the payoff of the options non-symmetrical with uneven gains or losses from equal upside and downside movement of prices.

The basic options are of two kinds; a call option and a put option. A call option is an option to buy an underlying asset at a predetermined price in a specified time. A put option is an option to sell with the same features as that of a call. The person who obtains the right but no obligation is called as the holder/buyer of the option, while the one who confers the right and is obligated to perform is the writer/seller of an option. For conferring this right without creating an obligation on the holder, the writer charges a front-end premium. This premium motivates one to write the option. The option to buy or sell at a predetermined price, called exercise/strike price, lasts for a definite time, which is called the expiration date, after which it automatically expires.

Option holders exercise the options depending upon the price of the underlying asset. A call option is exercised if the price of the asset is higher than the exercise price, because only then it results in profit. Similarly, a put option is exercised when the price of the asset is less than the exercise price. Options can be entered between two parties with conditions determined by the concerned parties, or they can be exchange-traded in the standardized form.

Options exercisable at any time before maturity are American options and those exercisable only on maturity date are called European options. Options which when exercised result in cash inflow for the holder are called in-the-money (ITM), those which result in no cash flow are called at-the-money (ATM), and those which result in cash outflow are called out-of-the-money (OTM).

The option premium payable by the option holder to the option writer depends upon five factors: (i) the spot price of the underlying asset, (ii) the exercise price, (iii) the risk-free interest rate, (iv) volatility in the price of the asset, and (v) the time left for expiration. The premium consists of two parts—the intrinsic vale and the time value. For a call option, intrinsic value is the difference between the spot price and the strike price of a call; for a put option, it is the difference between the strike price and the spot price of a put. Intrinsic value cannot be negative. The excess of market price over intrinsic value is the time value, which is always positive, but diminishes as maturity approaches and becomes zero on maturity.

A European call is no different from an American call in terms of its pricing, because it is more beneficial to sell a call rather than exercise it before maturity. The same cannot be said about the European and American puts. An American put is more valuable than a European put, because early exercise of the put may result in greater cash inflow and more time value of money.

The Black–Scholes Model of valuation of options is a landmark in finance literature. It values the option on a non-dividend paying stock on the basis of five factors: (i) spot price of the underlying asset, (ii) the exercise price, (iii) volatility of the price, (iv) the risk-free interest rate, and (v) the time left for expiration. With greater volatility, the option price increases both for call and put options. The values of call and put options decrease as time elapses. For the rest of the determinants of price, call and put prices behave in an opposite manner.

Except for volatility, the other four determinants of option price are known. With call prices also observable, they imply volatility in the prices of the underlying asset, which can be treated as collective assessment of the market to the risk in the asset prices. Implied volatility by option price may not be same as the volatility measured from the past prices of the underlying asset.

Put call parity establishes the relationship between the call and the put prices. The basis to arrive at the relationship is to set up portfolios providing identical payoffs.

Options can be used as tools for hedging as well as creating portfolios with desired risks and return characteristics. A put option provides protection against the fall in price, while a call option protects one from the losses due to the rise in prices.

KEY TERMS

Option A right without any obligation to buy or sell an asset at a predetermined price within a specified time.

Call option An option to buy an asset is a call option.

Put option An option to sell an asset is a put option.

Holder/Buyer One who obtains the right to buy or sell is called the holder or buyer of an option.

Writer/Seller One who confers the right to buy or sell is called the writer or seller of an option.

American options Options exercisable at any time before expiry are called American options.

European options Options exercisable only at the time of expiry are called European options.

Exercise/Strike price The price at which the asset is bought or sold is called the exercise price.

Intrinsic value Cash flow to the holder that results from exercising an option is the intrinsic value. It cannot be negative.

Time value That part of option price assigned for the chances that the option would turn in-the-money before expiry.

Implied volatility The volatility implied in the call prices as per Black–Scholes Model of option price determination.

KEY FORMULAE

Value of the call option = Max (0, $S - X$) $- c$

Value of the put option = Max (0, $X - S$) $- p$

Black–Scholes Model for value of call $c = SN(d_1) - Xe^{-rt}N(d_2)$

where $d_1 = \dfrac{\ln(S/X) + (r + \sigma^2/2)t}{\sigma\sqrt{t}}$; and

$d_2 = \dfrac{\ln(S/X) + (r - \sigma^2/2)t}{\sigma\sqrt{t}}$ or $d_2 = d_1 - \sigma\sqrt{t}$

Black–Scholes Model for value of put $p = Xe^{-rt}N(-d_2) - SN(-d_1)$

where $d_1 = \dfrac{\ln(S/X) + (r + \sigma^2/2)t}{\sigma\sqrt{t}}$; and

$d_2 = \dfrac{\ln(S/X) + (r - \sigma^2/2)t}{\sigma\sqrt{t}}$ or $d_2 = d_1 - \sigma\sqrt{t}$

Put Call Parity $c - p = S_0 - Xe^{-rt}$

PRACTICE PROBLEMS

1. Payoff - Call and Put Options

There exists a call option on a stock with the strike price of ₹50 selling at a premium of ₹6 expiring in 2 months from now. A put option with similar features trades at a price of ₹5.

(a) Determine the payoff of the call option with and without premium.
(b) Determine the payoff of the put option with and without premium.
(c) Plot the payoff of the call holder
(d) Plot the payoff of the put holder
(e) Determine the payoff of the call and put option writers with and without premium.
(f) Plot the payoff of the call and put writers with premium.

Solution

(a) and (b) The payoff of the holder of call and put option for stock prices ranging between ₹0 and ₹100 is given in Table P29-1(a):

The payoff of call option holder is:

Max ($-c$, $S - X - c$) where c is call premium.

The payoff of put option holder is:

Max ($-p$, $X - S - p$) where p is put premium.

(c) See Figure P29-1(a)
(d) See Figure P29-1(b)
(e) See Table P29-1(b)
(f) See Figure P29-1(c)

Table P29-1(a) Payoff call and put option holder

Figures in ₹

	Call		Put	
Strike Price	50		50	
Premium	6		5	
Spot Price	**Without premium**	**With premium**	**Without premium**	**With premium**
0	0	–6	50	45
10	0	–6	40	35
20	0	–6	30	25
30	0	–6	20	15
40	0	–6	10	5
50	0	–6	0	–5
60	10	4	0	–5
70	20	14	0	–5
80	30	24	0	–5
90	40	34	0	–5
100	50	44	0	–5

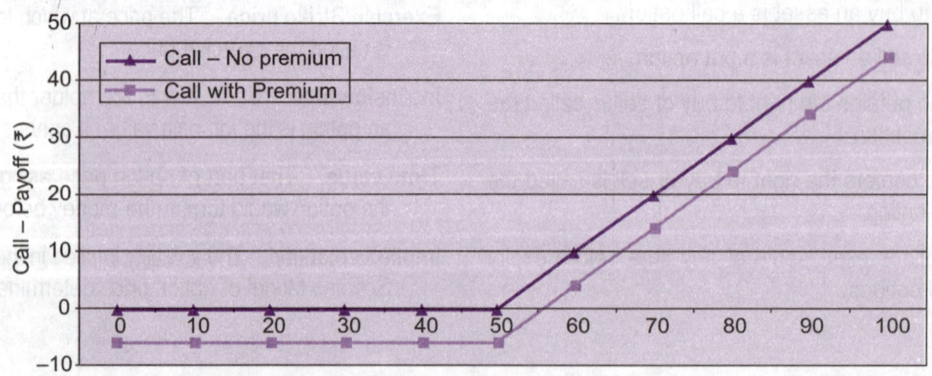

Figure P29-1(a) Call Option – Payoff – Holder

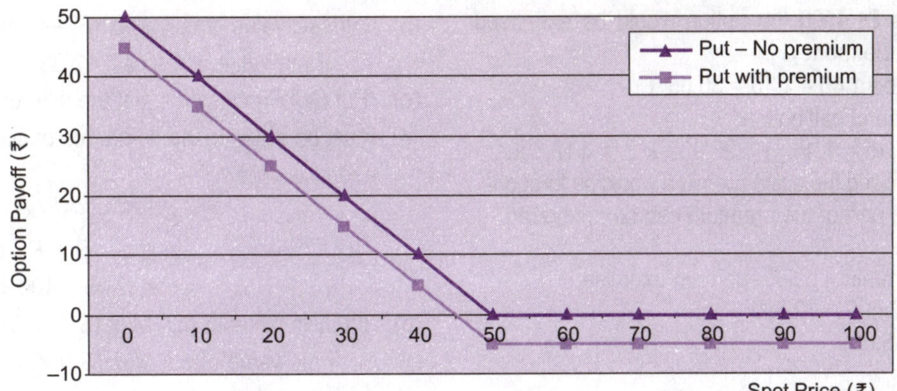

Figure P29-1(b) Put Option – Payoff – Holder

Table P29-1(b) Payoff of call and put option writer

				Figures in ₹
	Call		*Put*	
Strike price	*50*		*50*	
Premium	*6*		*5*	
Spot Price	*Without premium*	*With premium*	*Without premium*	*With premium*
0	0	6	–50	–45
10	0	6	-40	–35
20	0	6	–30	–25
30	0	6	–20	–15
40	0	6	–10	–5
50	0	6	0	5
60	–10	–4	0	5
70	–20	–14	0	5
80	–30	–24	0	5
90	–40	–34	0	5
100	–50	–44	0	5

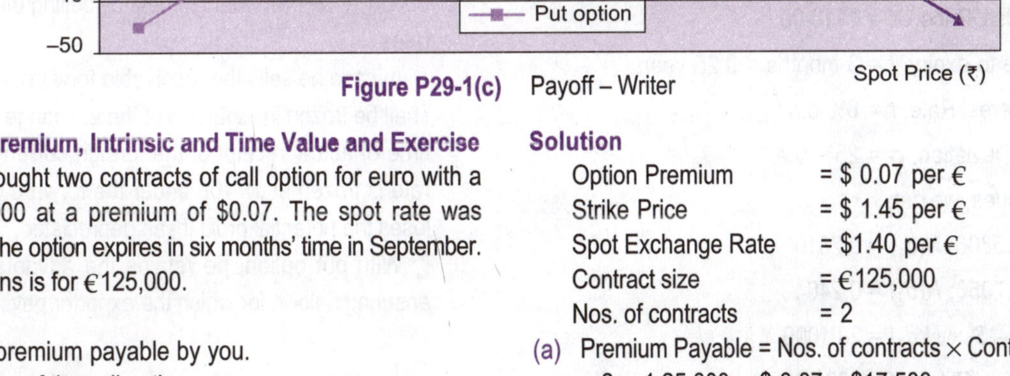

Figure P29-1(c) Payoff – Writer

2. The Call Option–Premium, Intrinsic and Time Value and Exercise

On 12 March, you bought two contracts of call option for euro with a strike price of $1.4000 at a premium of $0.07. The spot rate was $1.4500 per € then. The option expires in six months' time in September. One contract of options is for €125,000.

Find the following:

(a) The amount of premium payable by you.
(b) The intrinsic value of the call option.
(c) Time value of the call option.
(d) If on expiry the spot price is $1.4500 would you exercise the call? If so, what is the amount of profit?

Solution

Option Premium	= $ 0.07 per €
Strike Price	= $ 1.45 per €
Spot Exchange Rate	= $1.40 per €
Contract size	= €125,000
Nos. of contracts	= 2

(a) Premium Payable = Nos. of contracts × Contract Size × Premium
= 2 × 1,25,000 × $ 0.07 = $17,500

(b) Intrinsic value of the Call = max(S – x, 0) = 0

(c) Time value of the option = Price of the option – Intrinsic Value
= 0.07 – 0 = $ 0.07

(d) If the actual price is \$1.4500 the option would be exercised because the call is in the money.

The profit would be 1.45 – 1.40 = \$0.05 €.

The gain on exercise of call option

= (1.45 – 1.40) × 1,25,000 × 2 = \$12,500

If the call is not exercised the entire premium would be foregone. By exercising the call, part of the premium can be recovered. The net loss would be

= premium paid – gain on exercise
= 17,500 – 12,500
= \$ 5,000

3. Option Pricing – Black–Scholes Model

The following data is given:

Current stock price	= ₹100.00
Strike Price	= ₹110.00
Time to expiration	= 3 months
Risk free rate of return	= 6.00%
Variance of return on the stock	= 0.0625

(a) Find out the value of the call option using Black–Scholes Model.
(b) Find out the intrinsic value and the time value of the call option.
(c) Using put call parity, find out the value of the put option with same parameters.
(d) Find out the intrinsic values and time values of the put option.

Solution

(a) The value of the call option for non-dividend paying stock is given by Black–Scholes Model (BSM):

$$c = SN(d_1) - Xe^{-rt}N(d_2)$$

where $$d_1 = \frac{\ln(S/X) + (r + \sigma^2/2)t}{\sigma\sqrt{t}};\ \text{and}$$

$$d_2 = \frac{\ln(S/X) + (r - \sigma^2/2)t}{\sigma\sqrt{t}} \text{ or } d_2 = d_1 - \sigma\sqrt{t}$$

Following values may be inserted in the BSM to find the value of the call.

Spot Price, S = ₹100.00

Exercise Price, X = ₹110.00

Time to expiry, t = 3 months = 0.25 years

Interest Rate, r = 6% p.a.

Standard Deviation, σ = 25% p.a.

Inserting the values, we get:

$d_1 = -0.5800$; $N(d_1) = 0.2810$

$d_2 = -0.7050$; $N(d_2) = 0.2404$

$S \times N(d_1) = 28.1000$

$PV\ of\ X = 108.3623$

$PV(X) \times N(d_2) = 26.0503$

Call Value = $S \times N(d_1) - PV(X) \times N(d_2)$ = ₹2.05

(b) Intrinsic value of call, $Max(S - X, 0)$ = ₹0.00

Time value of the call = 2.05 – 0 = ₹2.05

(c) Put Call Parity states that the difference of the call and put price must be equal to the difference of spot and present value of the exercise price.

$$c - p = S - PV(X)$$
$$p = c - S + PV(X)$$
$$= 2.05 - 100 + 108.36 = ₹10.41$$

(d) Intrinsic value of put, Max $(S - X, 0)$ = ₹10.00

Time value of put Max $(S - X, 0)$ = 10.41 – 10.00 = ₹0.41

4. Hedging Receivable with Put

A Japanese exporter has a 90-day receivable from a customer in USA for US \$ 10 million. The spot rate is J¥ 110 per \$. Yen has shown a rising trend in the recent past and the exporter needs to protect the value of receivable. The 90-day forward rate for US \$ is J¥ 108.

In the options market, banks are willing to offer a put option for strike price of J¥ 105 at a premium of J¥ 2.

(a) How does put option benefit the exporter as compared to the forward contract?
(b) Under what condition the exporter would exercise the put option and when would he break even?
(c) Depict the net realizable value with the put option and compare it with the realization under forward contract.

Solution

(a) With the put option bought, the exporter protects the value of the receivable at the exercise price of the option. In this case, the value of the receivable shall be protected if yen appreciates beyond J¥105.

In case yen appreciates more than the exercise price, the exporter would exercise the put option and sell the receivable at the strike price, i.e., J ¥105.

However, if direction of movement is otherwise, i.e., yen depreciates instead of appreciating, the exporter would let the put option lapse and would benefit by selling the receivable at market rates.

In case he sells the receivable forward, the realization amount shall be frozen irrespective of the exchange rates prevailing at the time of actual receipt of the foreign currency amount. While the rate is frozen at J¥ 108 under the forward contract, the exporter loses the potential profit if yen depreciated.

With put option, he retains the advantage of profiting while ensuring a floor, for which the exporter pays a premium front-end.

	J¥/ \$
Strike price of the put option	105
Premium paid	2
Forward rate	108

Table P29-4 Net realizable value with put option

J ¥/$ Spot rate at maturity	Put Option Revenue	Premium	Net Revenue	Forward
93	105	2	103	108
95	105	2	103	108
97	105	2	103	108
99	105	2	103	108
101	105	2	103	108
103	105	2	103	108
105	105	2	103	108
107	107	2	105	108
109	109	2	107	108
111	111	2	109	108
113	113	2	111	108
115	115	2	113	108
117	117	2	115	108
119	119	2	117	108

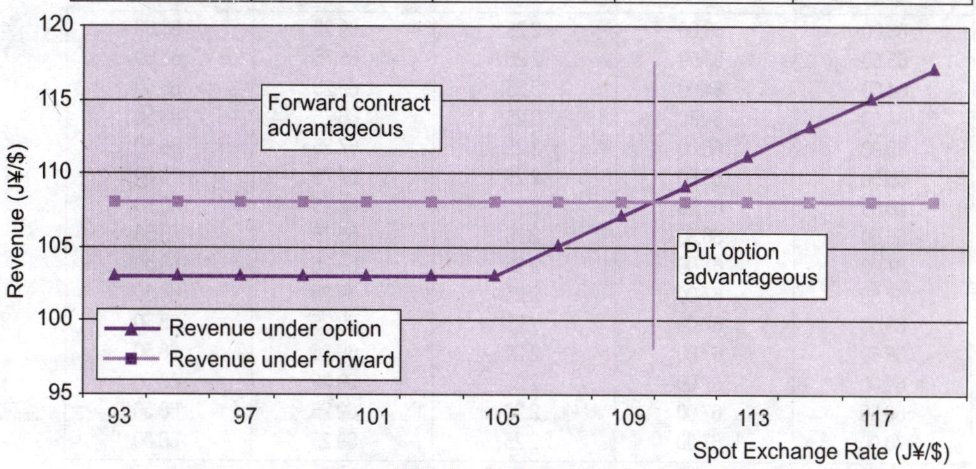

Figure P29-4 Put option vs Forward

(b) The exporter would exercise put option when the spot exchange rate is less than the strike price of J ¥ 105/$

However, he would break even when he also recovers the premium paid. When spot exchange rate is less than J ¥ 103 per $ the firm would break even.

The minimum revenue under option would be J ¥ 103 per $ while under forward contract, it would be fixed at J ¥ 108. If at the end of 90 days, the exchange rate is more than J ¥110 (forward price + the put premium) put option shall be more beneficial.

(c) See Table P29-4 and Figure P29-4.

5. Hedging Payable with Call

An Indian firm has imported goods worth €10,00,000 for which the payment is required to be made 6 months later.

The spot rate is ₹65.20 per € and the forward annualized premium is 10%. Forward contract for 6-month is available for ₹68.50. A call option with strike price of ₹67.00 is available at the premium of ₹3.05.

(a) What would be the cost of payable if the firm books a forward contract to buy euro?

(b) In case the firm goes for call options, what would be the maximum cost for paying €10,00,000?

(c) Comparing the cost of payable in (a) and (b), what could be the rationale for booking an options contract?

(d) Depict the cost of payable assuming the exchange rate at the end of 6 month from ₹63 to ₹70, and indicate when the options hedge would be more beneficial than the forward hedge?

Solution

(a) The forward premium is indicating that the foreign currency is going to appreciate by about 10%. If the firm books the forward contract, it would end up paying @ ₹68.50 irrespective of the actual appreciation of euro. The cost would be ₹6.85 crore.

(b) If the firm goes for call option, it has the right to buy euro at the strike price of ₹67.00. Therefore, its maximum cost would be strike price plus the premium.

	₹/€
Strike price of the call option	67.00
Premium paid	2.25
Forward rate	68.50

Max price = Strike price of the call option + the premium
= 67.00 + 2.25 = ₹69.25

The maximum amount that would be paid under options hedge
= 10 x 69.25 = ₹692.5 lakh or ₹6.925 crore

(c) Though the maximum price payable with the call option is much higher than what would be with the forward contract, it may still make sense to go for hedging with call option.
With the call option, the firm would retain the financial gains that the firm could make if the appreciation of euro is lesser than 10% as indicated by the forward rate.

(d) The cost for payable with options hedge and forward hedge for the exchange rate scenario between ₹63 and ₹70 are as given in Table P29-5. Refer to Figure P29-5.

Options hedge would be beneficial if:

Spot rate + premium of call ≤ Forward rate

or Spot rate ≤ Forward rate – Call premium
≤ 68.50 – 2.25 = ₹66.25

Table P29-5 Cost for payable with options hedge and forward hedge

₹/€ Spot rate at maturity	Call Option			Forward
	Cost	Premium	Total Cost	
63.00	63.00	2.25	65.25	68.50
63.50	63.50	2.25	65.75	68.50
64.00	64.00	2.25	66.25	68.50
64.50	64.50	2.25	66.75	68.50
65.00	65.00	2.25	67.25	68.50
65.50	65.50	2.25	67.75	68.50
66.00	66.00	2.25	68.25	68.50
66.50	66.50	2.25	68.75	68.50
67.00	67.00	2.25	69.25	68.50
67.50	67.00	2.25	69.25	68.50
68.00	67.00	2.25	69.25	68.50
68.50	67.00	2.25	69.25	68.50
69.00	67.00	2.25	69.25	68.50
69.50	67.00	2.25	69.25	68.50
70.00	67.00	2.25	69.25	68.50

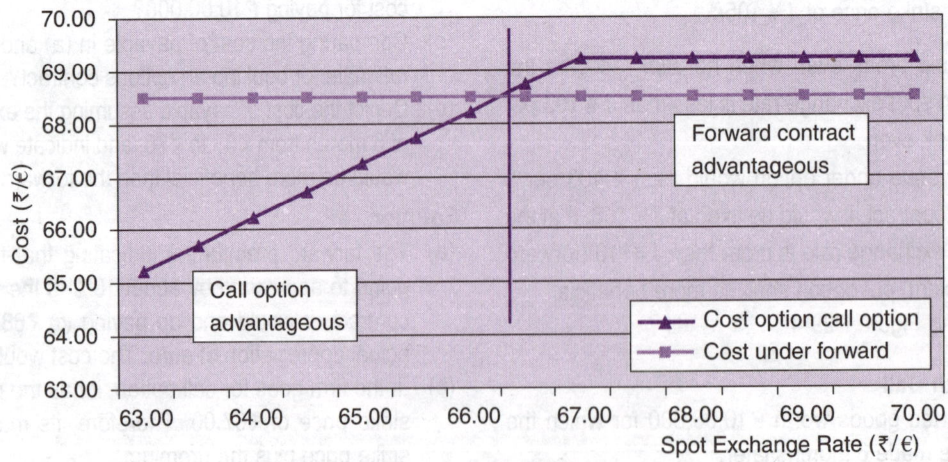

Figure P29-5 Call option vs Forward

EXERCISES

Concept Review Questions

1. What are the features of options that differentiate it from forwards and futures?
2. What do you understand by ITM, ATM, and OTM options?
3. The price of the call option is composed of intrinsic value and time value. What do you understand by these terms? Given the market price, how do we arrive at intrinsic value and time value of a call option?
4. What are the factors that affect the price of the call options? In which direction the call price and the put price are expected to move with: (a) increasing stock price, (b) increasing exercise price, (c) increasing volatility, (d) increasing interest rate, and (e) decreasing time to expiration.
5. What do you understand by 'put call parity'?
6. What is implied volatility and how would you assess it?
7. What are the assumptions that the Black–Scholes model makes to arrive at the price of a call option?
8. In terms of option value, what do you mean by (i) intrinsic value, and (ii) time value?

Critical Thinking Questions

1. American calls are more valuable than European calls, because they offer the flexibility of exercising the option at any time during the tenure of the options. Do you agree? Justify your answer.
2. Why is it considered sub-optimal to exercise the call option before maturity?
3. As hedging instruments, options are always superior to forwards and futures. Do you agree with the statement?
4. You have gone to your broker to conduct options trading at the stock exchange. You place the first order to buy a call option on the shares of Tata Steel with the strike price of ₹500 when the stock is trading at ₹490. Your broker asks you to deposit 10% margin. Would you agree to his demand? Explain. Would your stand change if you were: (a) buying a put option, (b) selling a call option, or (c) selling a put option?

Practical Assignments

1. Observe the actual prices of call option and put option on a stock with identical exercise price and time to expiration over a period of one month. Arrive at the put prices from the call prices using put call parity and compare it with the actual put price. How would you be able to implement arbitrage if there is discrepancy in the actual price and the put price derived from call and put call parity?
2. Observe the actual price of the call for 30 days, and calculate the theoretical price from Black–Scholes model using historical volatility. Do you find any difference in the two prices, and if yes, what are the factors to which you attribute this difference?

Numerical Problems

1. Option Pricing—Black–Scholes Model

Given the following data:

Current stock price	₹83.00
Strike price	₹80.00
Time to expiration	3 months
Risk-free rate of return	8.00%
Variance of return on the stock	0.36

(a) Find out the value of the call option using Black–Scholes Model.
(b) Using put call parity, find out the value of the put option with the same parameters.

2. Investing with Mispriced Options

In Problem 1, find out the following:

(a) Intrinsic value and time value of the call and put options.
(b) If the actual price of the call is: (i) ₹12.50 and (ii) ₹11.00, what investment opportunities exist to make profit?
(c) If the actual price of the put is: (i) ₹8.50 and (ii) ₹7.00, what investment opportunity exist to make profit?

3. Put Option

A share is currently trading at ₹110, while a put option with 2 months to expire with a strike price of 120 is trading at ₹14. Find the following:

(a) The intrinsic value of the put option
(b) Time value of the put option
(c) The price of the call option with same features if the risk-free rate of interest is 12%
(d) If the price fell to ₹80 on expiry of the option, the profit and loss of the holder and the writer of the option

4. Income Generation with Options

An investment fund is holding an index portfolio worth ₹1 crore with a beta equal to that of the index. The following options are available in the market:

Strike Price	*Call option*	*Put option*	*Expiry*
3,700	₹60.00	₹75.00	2 months

The current value of the index, which is 3680, is not likely to change much in the next 2 months or so.

(a) What can the investment fund do to improve upon the yield on the portfolio?
(b) Examine what happens if after 2 months, the index is at (i) 3500, (ii) 3680, and (iii) 3900.

5. The Call Option—Premium, Intrinsic Value, Time Value and Exercise

On 12 March, you bought two contracts of call option for euro with at strike price of $1.4000 at a premium of $0.07. At that time, the spot rate was $1.4500 per €. The option expires in six months' time in October. One contract of options is for € 125,000. Find the following:

(a) The amount of premium payable by you.
(b) The intrinsic value of the call option.
(c) Time value of the call option.
(d) If on expiry, the spot price is $1.4500, would you exercise the call? If so, what would be the amount of profit?

6. Call Option vs Forward

A French firm has bought a call option for US dollar with a strike price of €0.80 per $ at a premium of €0.02 per $. The option expires in 6 months. The prevailing 6-m forward rate is €0.81 per $.

(a) When would the firm exercise the call option?
(b) What is the exchange rate in the spot market at which the firm would break even?
(c) What is the maximum cost the French firm would have under: (i) options and (b) forward contract?
(d) Find out the cost under forward and option for a range of spot price between 0.76 and 0.84, and plot the cost. Also, find under what circumstances, options would be a better alternative than the forward contract.

7. Put Option vs Forward

A French firm has a £ receivable of 1 million. Anticipating a decline in the value of the £, the firm buys a put option with a strike price of €0.62 per £, a premium of €0.02 per £. The option expires in 6 months. The prevailing 6-m forward rate is €0.61 per £.

(a) When would the firm exercise the put option?
(b) What is the exchange rate in the spot market at which the firm would break even?
(c) What is the minimum revenue the French firm would have under: (a) options and (b) forward contract?
(d) Find out the realization under forward and option for a range of spot price between 0.58 and 0.66 and plot the revenue. Also, find under what circumstances, options would be a better alternative than the forward contract.

8. Hedging Foreign Currency Payable with Call Option

A German importer is due to pay US $ 1 million in 2 months' time. The current spot rate is €0.82 per $. The importer fears appreciation in the value of dollar. He is thinking of capping his liability at around €0.84 per $. A call option with 2 months to expiry is available at a cost of €0.005 per $. The contracts in dollar are of the size of $100,000 with a nominal brokerage of €10 per contract.

(a) What can be the strategy that the German importer can adopt to hedge his payable?
(b) Find out the effective cost of the payable for the German importer if the dollar: (i) depreciates to 0.80 and (ii) appreciates to 0.86. Also, mention the maximum price the German importer would lock-in if he buys the call option.

Ignore time value of money.

9. Hedging Foreign Currency Receivable with Put Option

An Indian firm has planned a debt issue of US $ 100 million. The subscription is likely to take 4 months' time when the proceeds of the issue would be remitted back to India. The current exchange rate is ₹44/$. In the recent past, the Indian rupee has appreciated a lot, and the trend is expected to continue. The expectations are that in coming months, the Indian rupee would appreciate to ₹42 per $. An OTC put option for 4 months is available with a strike price of ₹43.50 at a premium of Re 0.55. The firm buys the put.

Find out the effective exchange rate at which the firm would remit the dollar back if the exchange rate after 4 months is: (a) ₹45 per $ and (b) ₹42 per $. Assume cost of funds at risk-free rate of 6%.

In the CD

Finding Value of the Put Option using Black Scholes Model and Checking the Validity of Put Call Parity

CHAPTER

30 Interest Rate and Currency Swaps

LEARNING OBJECTIVES

After going through this chapter, the readers would

- understand the basic concept of swap
- understand why and how swaps evolved
- distinguish between interest rate and currency swaps
- familiarize with the terminology of swap
- know how to hedge interest rate risk and exchange rate risk through swaps
- understand how swaps, besides being a hedging tool, can be effectively used as a tool for reducing financing costs
- know how to value swaps as a pair of bonds and/or a series of forward contracts
- appreciate the roles of intermediary in a swap deal

SWAP ASSETS—NO ONLY THE LIABILITIES

Sthir and Chalit had been friends since their schooldays. Despite their very contrasting poor and rich economic backgrounds, they had maintained their friendship for the last 35 years. Not only the schooling, but also their professional education was at the same institution. After completing education, they were working for the same IT firm in their hometown of Bangalore.

They have identified two adjoining flats where they would like to live in the neighbourhood of each other. The flats are costing ₹40 lakh each. Each of them had ₹20 lakh of their own and needed ₹20 lakh as loan from the bank. Chalit, through his family connection, has been dealing with Asia Bank. They approached the bank for a housing loan.

After meeting the Bank Manager at the Asia Bank, Sthir decided to spend the evening with another common friend, Salaha Kaar, an engineer and an MBA, working as a consultant in the field of finance, to take his advice.

Sthir: Today, we had gone to the bank for getting a housing loan for each one of us. Chalit enquired with the bank manager whether he could sanction a loan of ₹20 lakh for a house costing ₹40 lakh. He was too glad to know this, but asked whether he wanted loan on a fixed rate basis or on a floating rate basis.

Salaha: Ok.

Sthir: We asked what it means. He told that borrowing funds on a fixed rate means that the interest would be fixed right now and would stay the same for the entire tenure of the loan. But under floating rate loan, the interest rate would be determined every six months according to the market rates prevailing then, and the instalment would be fixed accordingly. If the rate were high, the interest too would be high; and if it were low, the interest on the loan too would be low.

Salaha: That is correct.

Sthir: Chalit wanted a floating rate loan because he thought the interest rates are going to fall in future, and therefore he could cut down his interest cost. The branch manager offered loan on the basis of an interest rate based on 6-m MIBOR (Mumbai Inter Bank Offer Rate) + 1% to him.

Salaha: So what happened next?

Sthir: It was surprising to me that he offered loan at 2% above MIBOR. I am wondering why he offered a higher rate to me as compared to Chalit?

Salaha: Simple. As I know, his entire family has been dealing with the bank for long. His family members might have some deposits with the bank. In simple words, the lower interest rate offered to him is because of the fact that he enjoys better credibility with the bank.

Sthir: This is wrong. We draw the same salary and have the same paying capacity. We are buying the house of similar value, of the same size, and in the same locality. Why should this differentiation be there?

Salaha: Sorry. I really cannot answer this question exactly. Nor do I think the branch manager can. Unfortunately, this is the way the market functions. When you buy a SONY TV, you are prepared to pay a higher price despite the fact that some local brand TVs are available at lower prices. This is the credibility gap. You should not feel bad about it.

Sthir: Ok. But, I was more interested in a fixed rate loan because I did not want to worry about the changing interest rate scenario. I just wanted to have peace of mind for 10 years knowing what exact instalment I would have to pay each month. He offered me a loan at 10%. But again, I found that the branch manager was discriminating. Strangely, he offered the same loan, on a fixed interest rate basis, at 8% to Chalit.

Salaha: Do not feel discriminated against. Again, it is the same reason of credibility that he could get the loan on the fixed rate cheaper than what you could get. But, I observe something interesting in the rates you mentioned.

Sthir: What is so interesting?

Salaha: Wait, let me recapture what you said. In a nutshell, there are two conclusions—one, Chalit was able to get loan 1% cheaper on floating rate basis and 2% cheaper on fixed rate basis, and two, you want a loan on fixed rate while Chalit is interested in availing loan on floating rate.

Sthir: Exactly.

Salaha: What if I suggest a scheme where both of you have to pay a lesser cost. You are agreeable to pay 10% fixed, and Chalit is ready for MIBOR plus 1%.

Sthir: Yes.

Salaha: Well, I can reduce the cost for both of you.

Sthir: How?

Salaha: I would ask you to approach the bank to grant you a loan on floating basis at MIBOR + 2% and ask Chalit to avail the loan at 8% fixed.

Sthir: But, this is exactly the opposite of what we want.

Salaha: Wait. I have told you only the first part of the transaction. There is another transaction to follow, which would convert your liability to fixed and Chalit's liability to floating, and more importantly would save money for both of you.

Sthir: What is that second part?

Salaha: After you enter your independent contracts for the housing loan with the bank, you and Chalit must enter into an agreement with each other. In this agreement, Chalit would pay you MIBOR + 2%, and in return, you pay Chalit 9.5% fixed.

Sthir: What happens by doing so?

Salaha: Look at what you pay and receive now. What you pay to the bank, i.e., MIBOR + 2%, you receive the same from Chalit. That gets cancelled. Now, what you pay to Chalit is 9.5%. Therefore, your cost becomes 9.5% and that saves you 0.5%. If you go fixed with the bank, you end up paying the bank 10%.

Sthir: Ok, but what about Chalit?

Salaha: Chalit too would save money. Look at what he pays and receives. He pays the bank 8% and receives from you 9.5%. So, he has an extra 1.5% with him. He also pays you MIBOR + 2%. That means, effectively he pays MIBOR + 0.5%. If he were to borrow from the bank on floating rate, he would pay MIBOR + 1%.

Sthir: That is great. How do you think the bank would allow such a transaction. But, what if the bank comes to know of this?

Salaha: It does not matter. The contract between you and Chalit is separate from your individual contracts with the bank. All the three contracts are independent of each other. The bank need not even know about the arrangement between you two.

Sthir: Tell me, does the bank not know that this could happen?

Salaha: Yes, they do know this. But, unfortunately, they cannot help it. The only way that can be removed is to quote similar rates in the floating and fixed rate basis. This would happen only if there are exactly identical customers. Moreover, when you two have the contract, you take the risk on each other for non-payment. Since both of you have been excellent friends for long, there is no such problem.

Sthir: Oh, that is a wonderful scheme. Let me call Chalit.

Salaha: Yes, you do that, but what about my consultancy charges? Better pay me something.

Both Sthir and Salaha laughed away and digressed their discussions to another matter.

INTRODUCTION

Necessity is the mother of invention. The evolution of *swaps* as a financial instrument is the classical and a rather latest example of the proverb. Financial experts believe that swaps developed out of the constraints and the regulatory controls faced by the large corporations in 1970s. When multinational corporations operating in various countries could not remit funds back and

Swaps as a financial instrument came into existence due to the presence of exchange controls which restricted the movement of capital from one country to another.

forth among their subsidiaries due to exchange controls, they came out with innovations of back-to-back or parallel loans among themselves. Upon removal of restrictions on the capital flows, these loans later developed into a full financial product called swaps.

Parallel loans involve four parties—two multinational corporations and two subsidiaries in two different countries. Imagine, IBM as one USA based company with a subsidiary in London, and British Telecom as another company having operations in New York. The subsidiary of British Telecom needs money in US $, while the subsidiary of IBM in London requires funds in British £. Due to regulatory controls, neither IBM USA nor British Telecom can fund their subsidiaries. To overcome the problem, British Telecom can arrange funds in British £ to fund the requirement of the subsidiary of IBM in London. Similarly, IBM USA may raise funds in US $ to fund the operations of British Telecom in New York. Such an arrangement is called *back-to-back* or *parallel loans*. These amounts would be re-exchanged at maturity at a rate determined in advance. Besides overcoming the regulatory controls, there are other economical advantages that caused the development of swaps as a full blown financial product and which remained popular even after the removal of regulatory controls. By this simple arrangement, each firm gains access to the capital markets in a foreign country and makes use of their comparative advantage of borrowing in different capital markets.

Back-to-back/parallel loans posed several difficulties of finding parties with identical needs in terms of amount of principal, timing and duration of loans, periodicity and nature (fixed or variable) of interest payments, all of which must match to conclude a successful deal. Solutions to these problems were found by intermediary banks, which later became dealers in swaps.

Swaps overcame the operational difficulties faced in parallel loans and developed into an instrument independent of the underlying loan transaction.

Swap and its Terminology

A swap, in its simplest form, may be defined as an exchange of future cash flows between two parties as per agreed contract. The basis of future cash flow can be exchange rate for currency and/or the interest rate.

If the exchange of cash flows is done on the basis of interest rates prevalent at the relevant time, it is known as *interest rate swap*.

Where the exchange of cash flows is in two different currencies on the basis of a predetermined formula of exchange rates, it is known as *currency swap*. More complex swaps involve two currencies with fixed and floating rates of interest in two currencies. Such swaps are called *cocktail swaps*.

First, we concentrate on interest rate swaps.

INTEREST RATE SWAPS

As stated earlier, the basis of exchange of cash flow under interest rate swap is the interest rate. The cash flows from one party to another remain in the same currency.

Interest rate swaps are generally used for creating synthetic, fixed, or floating rate liabilities or assets with a view to hedge against adverse movement of interest rates. Interest rate swaps can be categorized in different ways, as discussed below.

Fixed-to-floating In fixed-to-floating rate swaps, the party pays a fixed rate of interest to the bank or the swap dealer, and in exchange, receives a floating rate interest determined on the basis of a reference/benchmark rate at predetermined intervals of time. Such a swap is used by a firm which has a floating rate liability, and anticipates a rise in the interest rates. Through the swap, the firm will cancel out the receipts and payments of floating rate and have cash outflow based on a fixed rate of interest.

Under Interest Rate Swaps (IRS), the series of cash flows from one party to another is decided on the basis of interest rates.

Floating-to-fixed In this kind of swap, the party pays a floating rate of interest to the bank or the swap dealer, and in exchange, receives a fixed rate interest at predetermined intervals of time. Such a swap is used by a firm which has a fixed rate liability, and anticipates a fall in the interest rates. Through the swap, the firm will cancel out the receipts and payments of fixed rate liability and have cash outflow based on a floating rate of interest.

Basis swap In contrast to the fixed-to-floating or the floating-to-fixed swaps, where one leg is based on a fixed rate of interest, the basis swaps involve both the legs on a floating rate basis. However, the reference rates for determining the two legs of payment are different. Basis swaps are used where the parties in the contract are tied to assets or liabilities based on one reference rate and want to convert the same to another reference rate. For example, if a firm having liabilities based on T Bills rate wants to convert it to MIBOR based rate, then the firm can enter a basis swap where it pays MIBOR based interest to the swap dealer in exchange of receiving interest based on T Bills rate.

Interest rate swaps were first conceived as a tool of hedging against fluctuating interest rates. The most common type of swap is a simple exchange between two parties of interest determined periodically, on the basis of a benchmark on a notional principal amount. It can be elucidated with the help of an example.

IRS has two legs of payment of interest, both of which may be based on different parameters; with one leg fixed and the other floating, or both floating but on different benchmarks.

Let us consider two parties, A and B, who have borrowed from the market on fixed and floating rates respectively. Assume that Party B has borrowed funds by issuing bonds that carry an interest 200 bps above 6-m MIBOR (Mumbai Inter Bank Offer Rate). MIBOR is a reference rate. Hence, Party B pays market-determined rates each time the interest is to be paid. Similarly, assume that Party A has issued bonds that carry 12% interest. For simplicity, further assume that both the parties have same periodicity of interest payments on same amount of borrowings from the market.

Cash Flow for the Swap

	Party A	*Party B*
1. Payment to investors 2. Payment to counter-party 3. Receipt from counter-party	12% MIBOR + 3% 13%	MIBOR + 2% 13% MIBOR + 3%
Effective interest rate (1 + 2 – 3)	**MIBOR + 2%**	**12%**
Impact	**Fixed rate liability (12%) changed to variable rate liability (MIBOR + 2%)**	**Variable rate liability (MIBOR+2%) changed to fixed rate liability (12%)**

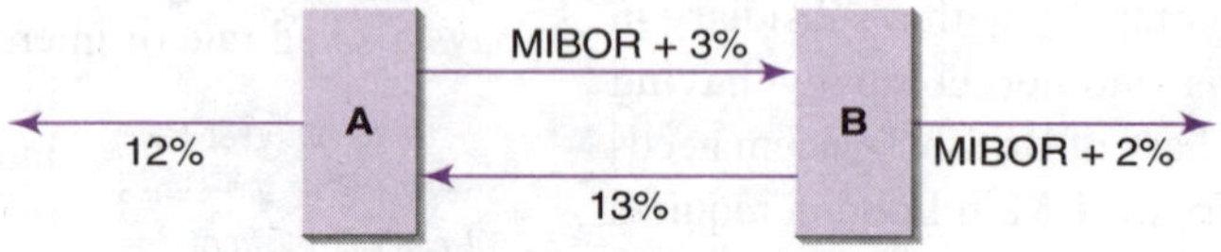

Figure 30-1 Interest rates swap: A schematic view
Changing fixed rate liability into floating and vice versa

Both the parties are currently not satisfied from their existing borrowing terms. They have differing outlook on the future interest rate scenario. Party A feels that interest rates are going to fall, and having borrowed on a fixed rate basis, it would incur higher cost in servicing the debt. Likewise, Party B too feels dissatisfied having borrowed on floating rate basis, but it holds an opposite opinion about future interest rates. Party B believes that the rates will go up, and therefore they would end up paying higher interest in future.

This difference of opinion about future interest rates forms the basis of a swap arrangement between the two. The arrangement would involve Party A to receive a floating rate interest at specified periods on a notional principal amount from Party B, and pay a fixed rate of interest. Similarly, Party B would receive a fixed rate of interest periodically in exchange of payment of a floating rate of interest to Party A. This exchange of interest changes the character of their borrowings from fixed rate to floating rate and vice versa for the two parties in question as depicted in Figure 30-1.

Swaps have the capability to alter the characteristics of an asset or a liability.

Features of Interest Rate Swap

As may be seen from the example mentioned above, a swap has the following features.

Series of cash flows The swap involves a series of payments in exchange of receipts at the same time. The transaction does not end with a single cash flow but has many cash flows.

Notional principal amount It may be noted that no principal amount is exchanged. However, for calculation of the interest amount to be exchanged, a notional amount is used for both the legs. This makes the swap an independent instrument, as the principal is not linked to the periodic interest payments. This feature opens up the avenues for many parties, as those with no requirement of funds but with an opinion on the interest rate movement may participate in a swap deal. This widens the swap market.

Only differential cash flow Is exchanged Further, even full payment of interest is not exchanged. Instead, only the differential amount of interest is exchanged between the parties on a specified date when the floating rate is known. In the above example, the cash flow on the basis of a notional principal of ₹100 lakh to Party A, which pays MIBOR+3% and receives 13% at six monthly intervals are given in Table 30-1. MIBOR is assumed here.

Cash flows under IRS are based on a notional principal and are netted, making them independent of the original loan amount and widening the market by increasing the participants.

Table 30-1 Cash flows for Party A under swap

Notional Principal amount: ₹1,00,00,000				
Time (Months)	***Reference rate MIBOR (% p.a.)***	***Cash outflow (₹)***	***Cash inflow (₹)***	***Net cash flow (₹)***
6	10.0	6,50,000	6,50,000	—
12	9.5	6,25,000	6,50,000	25,000
18	9.0	6,00,000	6,50,000	50,000
24	10.2	6,60,000	6,50,000	–10,000
30	11.0	7,00,000	6,50,000	–50,000
36	11.2	7,10,000	6,50,000	–60,000

Again, this feature makes life easier for the contracting parties as two huge sums of interest are reduced to one small sum widening the scope of market.

As can be seen from the above cash flows that as long as MIBOR remains below 10%, Party A benefits and generates positive cash flows for itself. When MIBOR goes beyond 10%, Party A becomes a loser. Note that only the differential of the cash flow as given in the last column of Table 30-1 is either paid or received by Party A and not the cash inflows and outflows shown in the preceding columns.

RATIONALE FOR SWAP: THE COMPARATIVE ADVANTAGE

The motivations to enter into a swap arrangement can be many. Besides speculative motive of taking a view on the future interest rates as in the above example, the intentions to have swaps can include resolving asset liability mismatch, managing off-balance sheet transactions, hedging against interest rate risk, transforming debt structure, reducing cost of funds, etc.

Theory of comparative advantage has been used to devise swap transaction in a manner that both parties in the swap reduce their costs of funds. Generally, a firm with higher credit rating is able to procure funds at lower rates of interest than a firm with lower credit rating, irrespective of whether the borrowing is on fixed or floating rate basis. The firm with a higher credit rating is said to enjoy the absolute advantage over the firm with a lower credit rating in both fixed rate and floating rate markets. The advantage of higher rated firm over the lower rated firm is called the *credit quality spread.*

Despite the presence of credit quality spread in both fixed rate and floating rate markets, it may be beneficial for the higher rated firm to engage in a swap deal with a lower rated firm due to the likelihood that the spread in both the markets may not be identical. The differential of the absolute advantage measures the comparative advantage, which in turn forms the basis of the swap deal. This comparative advantage is the aggregate benefit that both concerned parties of the swap deal can share in proportion to the bargaining powers of each.

Swaps serve as a tool of reducing the financing cost. This is possible due to the presence of credit quality spread in different kinds of markets.

An example will illustrate the mechanism and rationale of a swap. Assume that a highly rated firm AAA can raise funds in the fixed rate market at 10%, and in the floating rate market, at MIBOR + 1% (or 100 bps; 1% = 100 basis points). The current rate of MIBOR is 8%. Another Firm A, which is rated comparatively lower than AAA, can mobilize its capital at 12% and MIBOR + 2% in the fixed rate and floating rate markets respectively. Clearly, Firm AAA has an advantage over Firm A in both kinds of the markets—fixed and floating—as can be seen below:

	Firm AAA	Firm A	Advantage AAA
Fixed Rate	10%	12%	200 bps
Floating Rate	MIBOR + 100 bps	MIBOR + 200 bps	100 bps

We further assume that Firm AAA is interested in borrowing at a floating rate (at MIBOR + 100 bps), and Firm A wants to borrow in the fixed rate market (at 12%). Notice that for the lower rated firm, the spread in the fixed rate market is greater. Even though Firm AAA has absolute advantage in both fixed rate and floating rate markets, it has greater comparative advantage in the fixed rate market. To put it in another way, Firm A has relative advantage in floating rate market. The comparative advantage of Firm AAA is 100 bps, i.e., the difference of absolute advantage in the fixed and floating rate market. The comparative advantage of 100 bps is available for exploitation by both the firms. Let us assume that they are willing to share this advantage equally. Both the firms can set up the swap as follows:

1. Firm AAA goes to the fixed rate market and borrows at 10% rather than tapping the floating rate market at MIBOR + 100 bps.
2. Firm A mobilizes funds from the floating rate market at MIBOR + 200 bps rather than mobilizing from the fixed rate market at 12%.
3. Having accessed different markets as against their original choice, Firm AAA and Firm A enter into a swap where:
   (a) Firm AAA pays Firm A floating at MIBOR + 200 bps
   (b) Firm A pays Firm AAA fixed at 11.5%

The schematic diagram and cost of funds for both the firms are presented in Figure 30-2. As against a fixed payment of 10% to its original lenders, Firm AAA now pays floating at MIBOR + 200 bps and receives 11.5% fixed. This not only transforms the liability from fixed to floating which is precisely what the firm wanted in the first place, but also reduces the cost by 50 bps to MIBOR + 50 bps as against MIBOR + 100 bps. Similarly, Firm A

Cost of Funds for Firms

	AAA	A
1. Payment to investors 2. Payment to counter-party 3. Receipt from counter-party	10% MIBOR + 2% 11.5%	MIBOR + 2% 11.5% MIBOR + 2%
Cost of borrowing (1 + 2 – 3)	**MIBOR + 50 bps**	**11.5%**
Impact	**Firm can raise funds at MIBOR + 50 bps as against MIBOR + 100 bps without the swap; gaining 50 bps**	**Firm can raise funds at 11.5% as against 12% without the swap; gaining 50 bps**

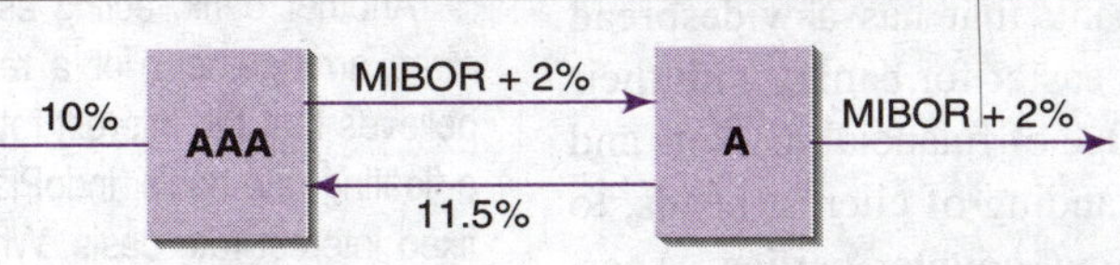

Figure 30-2 Interest rate swap: a schematic view: reducing cost of funds

Cost of Funds for Firms

	AAA	A
1. Payment to investors	10%	MIBOR + 2%
2. Payment to bank	MIBOR + 2.1%	11.6%
3. Receipt from bank	11.5%	MIBOR + 2%
Cost of borrowing (1 + 2 – 3)	**MIBOR + 60 bps**	**11.6%**

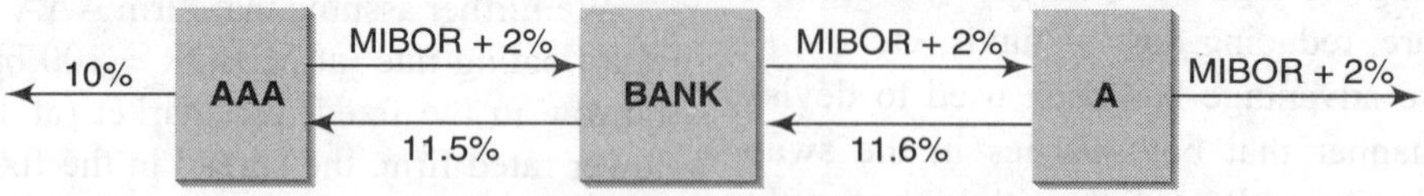

Figure 30-3 Interest rate swap: A schematic view with intermediary

too can transform its liability to fixed rate as desired and also reduce the cost of funds by 50 bps to 11.5% as against 12%.

The exploitation of the comparative advantage by the firms is a clear case of arbitrage on the credit rating. The fixed rate market demanded a greater premium from the lower-rated firm than did the floating rate market, forcing the firm to access the floating rate market. The premium demanded by the higher-rated firm for fixed rate was lower than the market, making the swap deal attractive. The question that arises is how a competitive market can allow this aberration to take place. The answer appears to lie in the information gap between the market as a whole. Since Firm AAA could rely on Firm A more than the market, it could offer a better credit than the market. It is like someone approaching a friend for financial assistance rather than approaching the market. A friend is likely to offer better terms than the market. Will this credit arbitrage continue? Very much yes, as long as the gaps in information and credibility remain.

Role of Intermediary: The Swap Dealer/Bank

The above illustration assumed that the needs of Firm AAA and Firm A are perfectly matching.

Swaps usually face two problems:

1. Finding a counter-party and the default risks associated with it, and
2. Matching of needs in terms of the principal amount of borrowing, its timing, periodicity of payment of interest, and final redemption of the borrowing.

Indeed, it is a difficult task. Swap dealers can help overcome these problems by assuming the following functions:

Facilitating the swap deal The difficulties of finding a matching counter-party can be reduced if an intermediary is involved. The intermediary or the swap dealer is normally a bank that has a widespread network. It is easier for banks, with their deep knowledge of financial markets and exact understanding of clients' needs, to locate matching counter-parties. Apart from finding counter-parties, the banks also have the ability to assume exposures on their own resulting from mismatch of timings, amounts, etc. Of course, for providing a facilitating role, banks need to earn some remuneration. This is achieved by splitting the total advantage. In the above example, the benefits of swap were shared by the concerned parties. With a bank being introduced in the deal to facilitate and mediate the transaction, the total benefit will now be shared among three parties.

Financial intermediaries in the swap deal promote market development by assuming counter-party risks and narrowing down the gaps between the financial needs of the parties concerned.

With the introduction of a bank which needs 20 bps for itself, the benefits to the counter-parties will stand reduced to 40 bps each from 50 bps. The cash flows in such a case will be as given in Figure 30-3.

Assuming counter-party risk Besides taking positions on the swaps, banks also discharge an important function of mitigating the counter-party risk. With the involvement of the bank, neither Firm AAA nor Firm A are concerned with the default that either of the party can make.

Warehousing Of late, banks have started performing the role of market-maker in swaps. One can obtain a quote on demand for a swap; and banks, without waiting for a matching counter-party, are willing to enter swaps on their own. The bank carries the risk of interest rate fluctuations till a matching counter-party is found. This risk is covered through interest rate futures. Hedging through interest rate futures has to be done only for the net exposure in swaps, as banks are likely to have a portfolio of swaps, which can nullify the interest rate risk for a major part of the exposure.

Example 30-1 Interest Rate Swap to Reduce Funding Cost

Two Indian firms, IndoPlas and IndoCar, are contemplating to raise a finance of ₹100 crore each. They have been offered the following loans by a bank.

	Fixed Rate	Floating Rate
IndoPlas	12.00%	MIBOR + 70 bps
IndoCar	11.00%	MIBOR + 30 bps

Another bank, acting as a swap intermediary, is willing to work out a swap arrangement for a remuneration of 5 bps from each firm. IndoCar believes that the interest rate would fall, and hence wants to raise funds in a floating rate basis. IndoPlas feels otherwise, and likes to raise funds on a fixed interest rate basis. What can be the swap arrangement between the two parties? What would be the saving in financing the cost of each firm?

Solution

The absolute advantage for IndoCar is 100 bps in the fixed rate market, while it is 40 bps in the floating rate market. Though IndoCar wants to raise finance at a floating rate, the firm must access the fixed rate market, and then enter into a swap deal with IndoPlas to convert the fixed rate liability into floating rate. The total benefit to be availed is 60 bps; the differential of absolute advantage of IndoCar in the two markets. Of this benefit, 10 bps would go to the bank, while the remaining 50 bps may be shared equally by both the parties. One such structure is presented below.

The aggregate cost of funds for IndoCar would be MIBOR + 5 bps; a saving of 25 bps if it had accessed the floating rate market. Similarly, IndoPlas obtains funds at 11.75% against 12%; an advantage of 25 bps.

Cost of funds for firms

	IndoCar	*IndoPlas*
1. Payment to investors	11%	MIBOR+0.7%
2. Payment to bank	MIBOR+0.05%	11.05%
3. Receipt from bank	11%	MIBOR
Cost of borrowing (1 + 2 – 3)	**MIBOR + 5 bps**	**11.75%**

Interest rate swap: A schematic view with intermediary

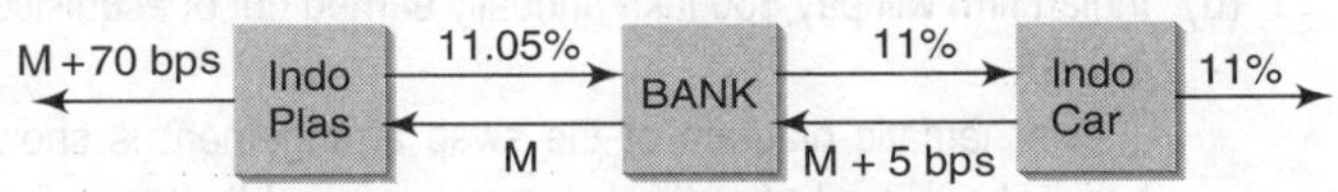

CURRENCY SWAPS

In a currency swap, the exchange of cash flows between counter-parties takes place in two different currencies. Since two currencies are involved, currency swaps become different from interest rate swaps in its uses, functionality, and administration.

Currency swaps, also called financial swaps, have a series of exchanges of cash flows in different currencies decided on the basis of exchange rates.

Currency swaps cover a different kind of risk. It is a way of converting liabilities or assets from one currency to another. While in case of interest rate swaps, assets or liabilities are transformed from fixed interest rate to floating or vice versa, providing a hedge against fluctuating interest rates; currency swaps provide a hedge against exchange rate risks, as it transforms liability/asset from one currency to another.

Let us consider an example to see how multinational firms face currency risks and how can these be overcome through a swap deal.

Assume that an Indian firm needs funds for its US operations. The firm raises funds in Indian rupees and commits to serve the interest obligation and the final repayment in Indian rupees. The funds raised in rupees are converted in US $ to acquire assets in USA. These assets provide income in US $. The Indian firm is facing a risk of appreciation of rupee. If rupee strengthens in the currency markets, the firm receives lesser rupee profit for the fixed return earned in US $. Similarly, an US firm which needs to acquire assets in India and raises funds in dollars faces the same risk. Its earnings will be in Indian rupees, and the liabilities are to be serviced in US $. Like the Indian firm, the US firm too faces a risk of shortfall in US $ if dollar appreciates (or rupee depreciates).

Currency swaps are useful in: (a) hedging the exchange rate risk, (b) transforming asset/liability from one currency to another, and (c) reducing the financing cost for each of the counter-party in the deal.

The vulnerability of Indian firm and the US firm is due to the uncertainty of exchange rate movement, which may take place in either direction. While appreciation of rupee harms the Indian firm, it benefits the US firm. In case rupee depreciates, the US firm is at loss, while the Indian firm gains. The risks for both the firms arise, because it is difficult to predict what direction the exchange rates would take. Even though it is possible to make an estimate of the likely direction of exchange rates based on many theories, we are concerned here with the unexpected and adverse movement of exchange rates.

The element of risk can be removed if the Indian firm and US firm enter into a swap as depicted in Figure 30-4. A look at Figure 30-4 would reveal that the Indian firm has financed its US operations by creating rupee liability. This liability, which is to be serviced by income generations in US $, faces a currency exchange rate risk. Likewise, the US firm having funded Indian operations through US $ would be serviced by rupee income, which needs to be converted to US $ for payment of interest and principal in future whenever they fall due.

Under the swap transaction, the mismatch of cash inflows and cash outflows in different currencies for both the firms can

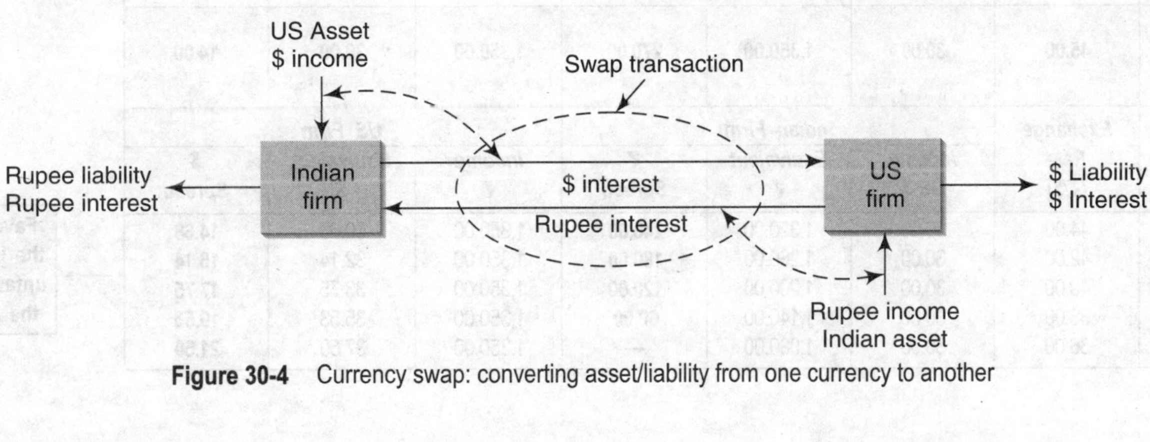

Figure 30-4 Currency swap: converting asset/liability from one currency to another

be eliminated, if the US firm agrees to pay rupee generated out of its Indian operations to the Indian firm in exchange for the Indian firm agreeing to pay dollar generated out of its US operations. Thus, the rupee asset income flows to the Indian firm, facilitating service of rupee liability. In exchange, the US $ asset income flows to the US firm to meet its US $ obligations. Through the swap, both the firms will have assets and liabilities translated in the same currency eliminating the currency risk.

Example 30-2 Swap to Eliminate/Reduce Exchange Rate Risk

Assume that an Indian software firm, Inso Ltd, wants to acquire a US firm with a cost of $ 2.00 crore. For this purpose, it raises the required capital of ₹90 crore (current exchange rate of ₹45/$) at 12%. The US acquisition is expected to yield 15% return. At the same time, a US engineering firm, USENG Inc., is negotiating a joint venture to contribute US $2.00 crore which promises to yield 15% return in India. USENG Inc. raises the required dollar at a cost of 8%. Assume that all the liabilities need annual payments, and conversion of currencies by the Indian and US firms is done annually.

1. Examine the risk faced by Inso Ltd and USENG Inc. if the:
   (a) Rupee appreciates to 44, 42, 40, 38, and 36 per $ over the next five years.
   (b) Rupee depreciates to 46, 48, 50, 52, and 54 per $ over the next five years
2. Show how a swap arrangement between the two can help eliminate the risk of exchange rate fluctuations.

Solution

1. Inso Ltd is targeting an annual profit of ₹270 lakh, as given below:

Income in US $ = 15% of $ 200 lakh	= $ 30 lakh p.a.
Equivalent ₹	= ₹1,350 lakh p.a.
Interest payment = 12% of ₹9,000 lakh	= ₹1,080 lakh p.a.
Anticipated Profit = (1350 – 1,080) lakh	= ₹270 lakh p.a.

If Indian rupee appreciates, the firm will receive lesser annual income than expected, and hence it faces a risk of reduction in profit to the extent of appreciation in rupee, the liability being fixed in rupees.

Similarly, USENG Inc. is targeting an annual profit of $ 14 lakh, as below:

Income in ₹	= 15% of ₹9000 lakh	= ₹1,350 lakh p.a.
Equivalent $		= $30 lakh p.a.
Interest payment	= 8% of $200 lakh	= $16 lakh p.a.
Anticipated Profit	= 30 – 16	= $14 lakh p.a.

If Indian rupee depreciates, the firm will receive lesser annual income than expected, and hence it faces a risk of reduction in profit to the extent of depreciation in rupee, the liability being fixed in dollars.

While appreciation of rupee is good for the US firm and detrimental to the Indian firm, the position reverses if rupee depreciates. The impact on the spreads of both the firms for the exchange rate scenario is presented below:

2. By entering into a swap arrangement both the firms can eliminate the volatility of spread. Under the swap arrangement at current rate of ₹45 per $:
   (a) US firm will pay Indian ₹1350 lakh annually earned out of its joint venture in India.
   (b) Indian firm will pay $30 lakh annually earned out of acquisition in USA.

   A schematic diagram of the swap arrangement is shown here. The spread after the swap arrangement becomes fixed for both the firms irrespective of the exchange rate.

   The US firm will lock in a return of $ 16 lakh, and the Indian firm will assure a profit of ₹270 lakh after the swap arrangement. Without the swap, the income for both the firms in US and India were subject to fluctuations due to currency exchange rate.

All figures in lakh

Year	*Exchange Rate (₹/$)*	*Indian Firm* Income US $	*Indian Firm* Equivalent ₹	*Indian Firm* ₹ Spread	*US Firm* Income ₹	*US Firm* Equivalent $	*US Firm* $ Spread
5	54.00	30.00	1,620.00	**540.00**	1,350.00	25.00	**9.00**
4	52.00	30.00	1,560.00	**480.00**	1,350.00	25.96	**9.96**
3	50.00	30.00	1,500.00	**420.00**	1,350.00	27.00	**11.00**
2	48.00	30.00	1,440.00	**360.00**	1,350.00	28.13	**12.13**
1	46.00	30.00	1,380.00	**300.00**	1,350.00	29.35	**13.35**
Now	**45.00**	**30.00**	**1,350.00**	**270.00**	**1,350.00**	**30.00**	**14.00**

Favourable for the Indian firm and unfavourable for the US firm

Year	*Exchange Rate (₹/$)*	*Indian Firm* Income US $	*Indian Firm* Equivalent ₹	*Indian Firm* ₹ Spread	*US Firm* Income ₹	*US Firm* Equivalent $	*US Firm* $ Spread
1	44.00	30.00	1,320.00	**240.00**	1,350.00	30.68	**14.68**
2	42.00	30.00	1,260.00	**180.00**	1,350.00	32.14	**16.14**
3	40.00	30.00	1,200.00	**120.00**	1,350.00	33.75	**17.75**
4	38.00	30.00	1,140.00	**60.00**	1,350.00	35.53	**19.53**
5	36.00	30.00	1,080.00	—	1,350.00	37.50	**21.50**

Favourable for the US firm and unfavourable for the Indian firm

Cash flows after swap		***Figures in lakh per annum***
	Inso Ltd	***USENG Inc.***
Income earned abroad	+ $ 30	+ ₹ 1350
Paid to counter-party	– $ 30	– ₹ 1350
Received from counter-party	+ ₹ 1350	+ $ 30
Interest obligation	– ₹ 1080	– $ 16
Spread	+ ₹ 270	+ $ 14

Currency swap: Converting asset/liability from one currency to another

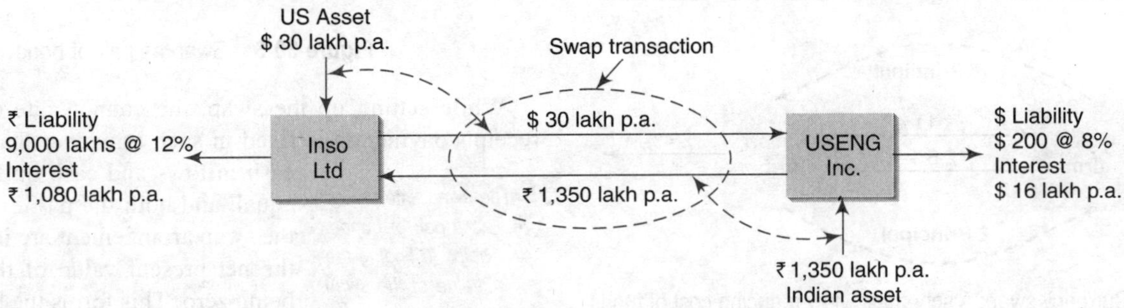

Reducing Cost of Funds Through Currency Swap

Like interest rate swaps, currency swaps can also be used to reduce funding cost for multinational firms which require funds in different currencies. Again, the guiding principle is theory of comparative advantage. In interest rate swap, the comparative advantage emanated from the differential pricing in the floating rate and fixed rate markets. Here, the comparative advantage will result from two distinct and separate markets governed by a different set of rules altogether, and operating in vastly different economic conditions.

Though the exchange rate mechanism provides a link among these markets and economies, the link is a frail one as compared to the strong linkages the capital and debt markets have in a single economy. The quality spread in domestic markets is based on the credit rating of the parties. In the international markets, the credit rating for the same firm may vary substantially across nations, as firms are generally better known in their own country and lesser known in a foreign country. Further, exchange control regulations of the land may discourage the non-residents to borrow by stipulating a higher rates of interest and/or taxes. Therefore, the comparative advantage is likely to be more pronounced in two markets in two different economies, as compared to similar markets of the same economy. As such, the credit quality spread is expected to be larger in different currency markets than the credit quality spread in fixed/floating rate markets.

A greater spread in credit quality increases the comparative advantage. Increased comparative advantage opens up more avenues for currency swaps. However, the size of the market may be limited, as only the multinational firms will be the beneficiaries of currency swap transactions.

As a simple example, consider two multinational firms—one Indian and another British. Both the firms enjoy excellent and equivalent credit rating in their respective countries. However, their funding requirements are confined to their own countries. Now, they need to raise funds across the nations for their ever-increasing needs of expansion, and to capitalize on the interest rate differentials that may exist in various currencies.

Following is the cost of capital for two firms in India and Britain in their respective currencies:

	Indian Market (Rupee)	***British Market (Pound)***
Indian Firm	10%	6%
British Firm	14%	4%
Advantage—British Firm	–4%	2%

Clearly and naturally, the Indian firm enjoys an advantage over the British firm in India, and the British firm commands more credibility in Britain as compared to the Indian firm. Notice that the absolute advantage may not be in favour of the same firm as was the case in the interest rate swap. The comparative advantage here is 6%. If the two firms borrow in the required currency, the total cost of funds will be 20%, i.e., the Indian firm borrows pound at 6% and the British firm borrows rupee at 14%. However, if they borrow as per the comparative advantage theory and exchange each other's commitment, the total cost of funds can be reduced to 14% with the British firm borrowing pound at 4% and the Indian firm borrowing rupee at 10%. Both the firms can benefit by 6% in aggregate if they enter into a swap arrangement wherein:

(a) Indian firm mobilizes funds in rupees in the Indian market at 10%,
(b) They lend the rupee funds to the British firm at 11%,
(c) The British firm raises funds in the British market in pound at 4%,
(d) They lend the same funds to the Indian firm at 5%,
(e) Exchange the interest payment periodically, and
(f) Finally, exchange the principal upon redemption.

The schematic diagram of the swap arrangement and the cost of funds for both the firms is shown in Figure 30-5.

Cost of funds for firms

	Indian Firm	*British Firm*
1. Payment to investors	Rupee 10%	Pound 4%
2. Payment to counter-party	Pound 5%	Rupee 11%
3. Receipt of from counter-party	Rupee 11%	Pound 5%
Cost of borrowing (1 + 2 – 3)	**Pound 4%**	**Rupee 10%**

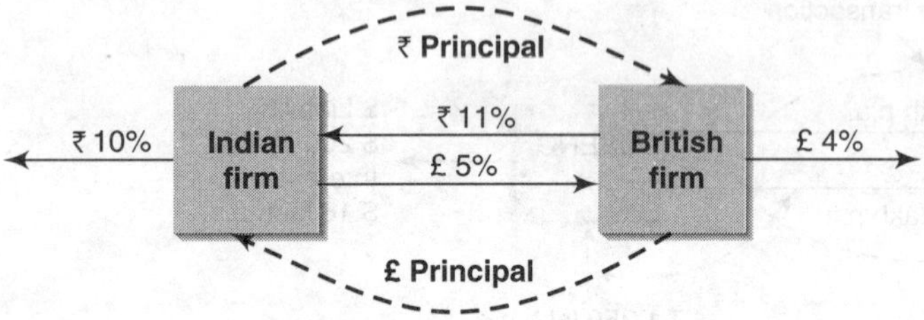

Figure 30-5 Currency swap: A schematic view reducing cost of funds

Through the swap, the Indian firm is now able to obtain pound funds at 4% as against 6% in the absence of swaps; a benefit of 2%. Similarly, the British firm gains access to rupee funds at 10% as against 14%; a benefit of 4%. The aggregate benefit is equal to the comparative advantage of 6%, which may be shared by the two firms depending upon the strengths and negotiating skills of the two firms involved.

It was assumed in the example that the Indian firm and the British firm exchanged the principal amount of borrowing, and as a natural outcome, will have to exchange the repayment at the time of redemption. However, it is not essential to do so, as both the firms can use the spot market for buying and selling the currencies required, independent of each other, both at the time of raising funds and at its redemption.

VALUING AND INTERPRETING SWAP

The value of an interest rate swap is the net difference between the present value of the payments to be received and the present value of the payments to be made. At the inception of the swap, the value of swap is zero to both parties; later, it becomes positive to one and negative to the other, depending on the movement of interest rates.

A swap transaction may be interpreted at least in two ways. It can be thought of as either a pair of bonds or a series of forward agreements. Either of these two interpretations of the swap helps in initial pricing of the swap as well as the value to be attached to it if and when one wants a premature closure.

Interest rate swaps can be seen as a pair of bonds; one as liability with cash outflow of interest and another as an asset with cash inflow of interest.

Swap as pair of bonds

The most common interpretation of interest rate swaps is to consider the inflows and outflows of interest at periodical intervals equivalent to that of the bonds. In an interest rate swap, one leg of transaction is on a fixed rate and the other leg is on the floating rate of interest. The cash flow of the swap is equivalent to receiving an interest on the floating rate bond owned and paying an interest on the fixed rate bond issued. The situation is clearly depicted in Figure 30-6.

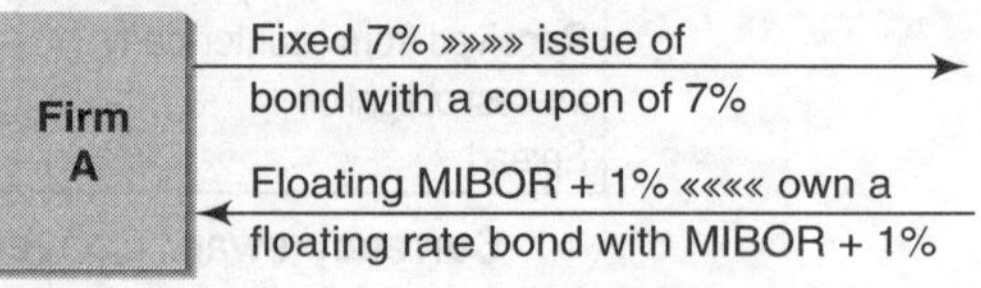

Figure 30-6 Swap as pair of bond

While setting up the swap, the coupon rate (the fixed leg receipts/payments) is fixed in such a manner that the value of cash inflows and cash outflows remains equal, and both the parties concerned in the swap arrangement are in equilibrium; the net present value of the cash flows being zero. This forms the basis of fixing the initial price of the swap determined in terms of fixed rate of interest, payable or receivable upon exchange of a floating benchmark rate.

The swap, interpreted as a pair of bonds, helps in finding the value of the swap subsequent to its initiation. The value of swap is zero when it is set up.

However, the interest rates are dynamic and the value of cash flows as determined at the start of the swap will not remain same as time elapses. The value of the swap will depend upon the behaviour of bond prices with respect to changes in the interest rates. The following rules about bond prices may come in handy while valuing swaps:

1. The value of fixed rate bond will increase with the fall in interest rates and vice versa.
2. The value of floating rate bond remains equal to par value, as the coupon rate is aligned with the market rates on each periodic payment of interest.
3. The value of floating rate bond changes subsequent to payment of each interest. If the interest rate structure has changed, it again gets aligned to the par value on the next payment of interest.

Since the change in value of the floating rate bond will only be nominal and temporary (it changes only during the two interest payments), the value of swap, determined on the basis of difference in the present values of the fixed and floating legs, is predominantly dependent upon the value of fixed rate bond.

At any point of time, the value of the swap will be the differential of present values of the fixed rate bond and the floating rate bond. The value of the bond with fixed rate payments will be equal to the sum of coupon payments and the notional principal amount discounted at an appropriate rate. The discount rate to be used for each coupon payment is known from the term structure of interest rates. The value of the fixed interest payment leg V_c is given by:

$$V_c = \sum_{1}^{n} \frac{C_i}{(1 + r_i)^n} + \frac{P}{(1 + r_n)^n}$$

where C_i = Coupon payment at time i

r_i = Discount rate for period i

n = Number of periods remaining

and P = Notional principal amount

Similarly, we can find the value of the floating rate bond V_f which is equal to present value of the next interest payment and the principal. As we know that the value of the floating rate bond converges to the par value on each payment date, the value of the floating leg can be expressed as:

$$V_f = \frac{F_1}{(1+r_1)} + \frac{P}{(1+r_1)}$$

where F_1 = Next payment of interest

r_1 = discount rate for period 1

and P = Notional principal amount

And, the value of the swap will be equal to the differential of the fixed leg and floating rate cash flows given as below:

Value of swap =

PV of fixed coupon bond – PV of floating rate bond

or $V_s = V_c - V_f$

$$V_s = \sum_{1}^{n} \frac{C_i}{(1+r_i)^n} + \frac{P}{(1+r_n)^n} - \frac{F_1}{(1+r_1)} - \frac{P}{(1+r_1)}$$

This is the value of the swap for a party receiving fixed and paying floating. The value of the swap for the counter-party paying fixed and receiving floating will be exactly opposite.

Let us consider a simple example of valuation of swap, assuming it to be a pair of bonds. Assume that, two years ago, Firm A has entered a 5-year interest rate swap, where it receives fixed 8% and pays MIBOR+1%. For simplicity, we assume annual payments. There are three remaining annual payments. Since the time of the swap, the interest rates have moved upwards causing the value of the swap to change. Note that the value of the swap was zero two years ago when it was set up. The payment of the floating rate, fixed one period in advance, is at the rate of 9.5%. The term structure of interest rates is as given below:

1-year: 10% ; 2-year: 10.5% ; 3-year: 11%

We find the value of the floating rate bond for an assumed principal payment of ₹100 by discounting the interest (₹9.50) and the principal (₹100) at 10%.

Value of the floating rate bond = 109.50 / 1.10 = ₹99.545

The value of fixed rate bond will be:

$$V_c = \frac{8}{(1+0.10)} + \frac{8}{(1+0.105)^2} + \frac{8}{(1+0.11)^3} + \frac{100}{(1+0.11)^3}$$

$$= 7.273 + 6.552 + 5.849 + 73.119$$

$$= ₹92.793$$

The value of swap = PV of inflow – PV of outflow

= 92.793 – 99.545 = – ₹6.752

The present value of inflow of the fixed leg for Firm A is ₹92.793 and that of floating rate outflow is ₹99.545. The swap can be cancelled if Firm A pays ₹6.752 (that will make the PV of the swap zero) now to the counter-party, who paid fixed rate and received floating rate.

Swap as series of forward contracts

In a swap, regular payments of interest are made and received by the counter-parties. Next cash flow of interest can be considered as forward transaction. Similarly, all subsequent cash flows are regarded as future dated delivery commitments. The timings of each cash flow is known in advance, and hence the swap can be regarded as a series of forward contracts maturing on specified dates with the amounts of respective interest payments, as shown in Figure 30-7. Swap is a single contract encompassing several forward contracts.

Interest Rate Swaps may also be viewed as a series of forward contracts, where the floating rate cash flows are equivalent to expected interest rates implied by the term structure of interest rates.

The valuation of swap requires computation of present values of fixed rate leg and the floating rate leg. While the interest payments of fixed rate leg are known for the entire remaining duration of the swap, the cash flows of the floating rate leg is known for only the next period. For all subsequent periods, the cash flows for the floating rate leg will be determined only one period in advance. Hence, all the payments cannot be known today. This poses problem in valuation of swap when we assume it to be a series of forward rate agreements.

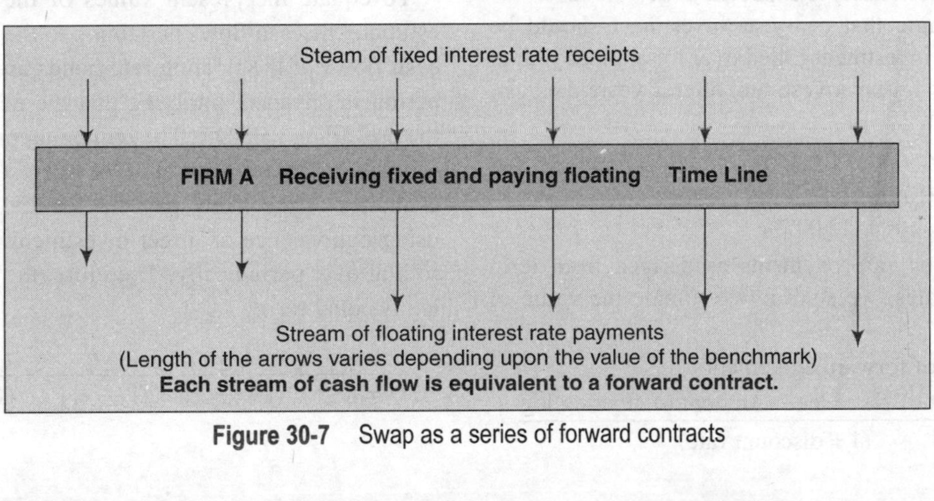

Figure 30-7 Swap as a series of forward contracts

Treating the swaps as a series of the forward rate agreements swap arrangement of the above example can be viewed as follows:

Period t	Year y	Firm receives %	Firm pays %
1	3	8.00	9.50 fixed at $t = 0$
2	4	8.00	Rate to be determined at $t = 1$; $y = 3$, say ${}_1r_2$
3	5	8.00	Rate to be determined at $t = 2$; $y = 4$, say ${}_2r_3$

With the given term structure of interest rates, the floating rate payments are implied. The term structure of the interest rate as used in earlier section is given as below:

One year yield investment starting today; ${}_0r_1 = 10.00\%$

Two year yield investment starting today; ${}_0r_2 = 10.50\%$

Three year yield investment starting today; ${}_0r_3 = 11.00\%$

where ${}_0r_n$ implies the interest rate for the investment period starting at 0 and ending at the nth period.

The forward rates of interests are built in the term structure of interest rates. The implied forward rate can be calculated on the argument of equivalence of investment under the two strategies of: (a) direct investment for planned horizon, and (b) making investment now and rolling it over from period to period to cover the entire planned horizon. For details, refer to Chapter 6 on bonds. From the above data, we may have either direct investment for two years at 10.5%, (i.e., ${}_0r_2$) or invest for one year at 10%, (i.e., at ${}_0r_1$) and then rollover the matured amount for another year at 1-year rate one year from now, (i.e., ${}_1r_2$). Both the strategies must yield the same end value of the investment. Given this condition, we have the following relationship:

$$(1 + {}_0r_1) \times (1 + {}_1r_2) = (1 + {}_0r_2)^2$$

or $$1.10 \times (1 + {}_1r_2) = 1.105^2$$

or $${}_1r_2 = 11.002\%$$

The present term structure of interest rate implies that the market expects 1-year investment yield one year later at 11.002%. The investor can invest for 2-year period at 10.5% and get ₹1.2210. Alternatively, he can invest for one year at 10% and get ₹1.10 after one year. This amount would be reinvested at 11.002% for one more year to give an ultimate wealth of ₹1.2210. Therefore, the second interest payment for the floating rate (to be decided one year from now) is expected to be 11.002%.

Using the same logic that a 3-year investment should be equivalent to a 2-year investment rolled over for another year at the rate prevailing for 1-year investment after 2 years, i.e., ${}_2r_3$, we have:

$$(1 + {}_0r_2)^2 \times (1 + {}_2r_3) = (1 + {}_0r_3)^3$$

or $$1.105^2 \times (1 + {}_2r_3) = 1.11^3$$

or $${}_2r_3 = 12.007\%$$

With estimated floating rate payments as derived from term structure of interest rates, we shall now estimate the value of the swap as:

Net Present Value of forward agreement

$$= \frac{\text{Amount of fixed leg} - \text{Amount of floating leg}}{(1 + \text{discount rate})^n}$$

$$\text{Value of first swap payment} = \frac{(8.00 - 9.50)}{1.10} = -1.364$$

$$\text{Value of second swap payment} = \frac{(8.00 - 11.002)}{1.105^2} = -2.458$$

$$\text{Value of third swap payment} = \frac{(8.00 - 12.007)}{1.11^3} = -2.930$$

The value of swap comes to –₹6.752 as computed with the assumption of swap as a pair of bonds.

Swap Quotes and Initial Pricing

Many banks in the international markets play the role of market-maker for swaps. These banks quote two-way swap rates in terms of fixed rate of interest for receiving and paying floating rates of interest. A bid rate is the fixed rate of interest that the bank will pay to receive floating; and an ask rate or an offer rate is the fixed rate of interest that the bank will receive for paying floating. The average of two rates is known as the *swap rate*. At swap rate, the value of the swap is zero, i.e., the values of fixed and floating rates are equal.

Banks function as market-maker in swaps by offering two-way quotes for paying and receiving a fixed rate against floating interest, offering easy entry and exit.

In order to determine the initial swap rate, we equate the present values of the cash flows of the fixed rate bond and floating rate bond. The cash flows of the fixed rate bond are known for the entire duration of the swap. The cash flows pertaining to the floating rate are not known.

How do we price a swap? We again use the term structure of interest rates to derive the cash flows of the floating rate leg, as they are the best estimates available.

Let us consider an example for quoting a 5-year swap with an annual exchange of cash flows. The pricing will be done in the form of % interest of the fixed leg to be received/paid for paying/receiving a benchmarked floating rate of interest. Internationally, the benchmark is LIBOR (London Inter Bank Offer Rate). However, here we assume exchange of MIBOR for a fixed interest for five years.

To equate the present values of the two legs, we need to estimate the cash flows pertaining to the floating rate bond. The cash flows of the floating rate bonds are decided normally one period in advance; implying that the next payment is equal to the prevailing MIBOR. The remaining payments will have to be estimated. The term structure of interest rates provides the best estimates of the likely pay out for the floating leg payments, using equivalence of direct investment for planned horizon or rolling over periodically. Therefore, the PV of the floating rate leg is equal to:

$$\frac{{}_0r_1}{(1 + {}_0r_1)} + \frac{{}_1r_2}{(1 + {}_0r_2)^2} + \frac{{}_2r_3}{(1 + {}_0r_3)^3} + \frac{{}_3r_4}{(1 + {}_0r_4)^4} + \frac{{}_4r_5}{(1 + {}_0r_5)^5}$$

Assuming a fixed payment of interest of X in the fixed leg, the PV of the fixed rate leg is given by:

$$\frac{X}{(1+{}_0r_1)}+\frac{X}{(1+{}_0r_2)^2}+\frac{X}{(1+{}_0r_3)^3}+\frac{X}{(1+{}_0r_4)^4}+\frac{X}{(1+{}_0r_5)^5}$$

For initial pricing, we have to equate the cash flows of fixed and floating rate and solve for the only unknown X.

With the term structure of interest rates for five years at 6.5%, 7.0%, 7.5%, 8.0%, and 8.5%, we can arrive at the discount factors and floating rate payments as implied forward rates, as shown here:

Year	*Interest Rate*	*Implied Forward Rate given by*	*Implied Forward rate*	*Discount Factor*
1	${}_0r_1$ = 6.5%	$(1+{}_0r_1)\times(1+{}_0r_2) = (1+{}_0r_2)^2$	${}_0r_1$ = 6.500%	0.9390
2	${}_0r_2$= 7.0%	$(1+{}_0r_1)\times(1+{}_1r_2) = (1+{}_0r_2)^2$	${}_1r_2$ = 7.502%	0.8734
3	${}_0r_3$= 7.5%	$(1+{}_0r_2)^2\times(1+{}_2r_3) = (1+{}_0r_3)^3$	${}_2r_3$ = 8.507%	0.8050
4	${}_0r_4$= 8.0%	$(1+{}_0r_3)^3\times(1+{}_3r_4) = (1+{}_0r_4)^4$	${}_3r_4$= 9.514%	0.7350
5	${}_0r_5$= 8.5%	$(1+{}_0r_4)^4\times(1+{}_4r_5) = (1+{}_0r_5)^5$	${}_4r_5$ =10.523%	0.6650

Substituting these values in the two equations, we get:

$$X(0.9390+0.8734+0.8050+0.7350+0.6650)$$
$$=(6.500\times 0.9390)+(7.502\times 0.8734)$$
$$+(8.507\times 0.8050)+(9.514\times 0.7350)$$
$$+(10.523\times 0.6650)$$

or $\quad 4.0174X = 0.3349$

$$X = 0.0834 \text{ or } 8.34\%$$

The swap rate will be 7.57% for paying or receiving MIBOR. To this equilibrium swap rate, the dealer/bank will add its spread to cover its administrative cost as well as the cost of taking counter-party risk. Assume that the bank wants to have 40 bps as bid-ask spread, then the swap quote of the bank would be (7.37% – 7.77%). This means that the bank will pay 7.37% fixed for receiving MIBOR, and receive 7.77% fixed for paying MIBOR. As the tenure of the swap becomes longer, the spread increases.

Example 30-3 Value of a Swap

A firm had entered into a swap arrangement for a notional principal of ₹1 crore with a bank wherein it paid 9% fixed and received MIBOR semi-annually. It has three more years to go and has just exchanged the cash flow. The 6-m MIBOR for the next payment of interest was reset at 8%. Next day, the markets exhibited a fall and the 6-m MIBOR fell to 7%, leading the firm to believe that it is overpaying. It wants to cancel the swap arrangement. How much should the firm ask the bank to pay to cancel the swap deal?

Solution

The value of the swap for the firm is determined on the basis of discounted cash flows. Since the rates have changed, the discount rate used would be 7%; the prevalent market rate. The value of the cash outflows on the fixed basis discounted at 7% is ₹115.63, as shown here:

Present value of cash flow of the fixed leg

Fixed leg payment – Cash outflow	9.00%
Present 12-m MIBOR	7.00%
Next Interest payment on floating rate	8.00%

(₹ *lakh*)

Time months	*Years*	*Cash flow*	*DCF at 7.00%*
—	—	4.50	
6	0.50	4.50	4.42
12	1.00	4.50	4.35
18	1.50	4.50	4.27
24	2.00	4.50	4.20
30	2.50	4.50	4.13
36	3.00	104.50	94.25
Present Value of Fixed Leg			**115.63**

The present value of the inflow at floating rate would be the next interest payment known, decided a period in advance, plus the face value of ₹100 discounted at 7%. This amount works out to ₹100.48.

(₹ *lakh*)

Value of floating leg		
Interest to be received after 6-m		4.00
Principal to be received after 6-m		100.00
		104.00
Present Value at	**7.00%**	**100.48**

The present value of the cash outflow is more by ₹15.15 lakh for a principal of ₹100. The firm may exit the swap by paying ₹15.15 lakhs to the bank.

Pricing Currency Swap

We can price the currency swap on the same lines and principle as that of the interest rate swap, i.e., equating the value of cash inflows with the value of cash outflows. These cash flows are in different currencies and need to be converted to the domestic currency. If the present values of cash flows of domestic currency and foreign currency are V_d and V_f respectively and the spot rate is S, then the value of the swap, which pays domestic and receives foreign currency, is given by the formula:

$$V_s = S \times V_f - V_d$$

The initial pricing of the swap is set such that the present values of foreign and domestic currency cash flows are equal, and the value of swap is zero. The most common currency swaps involve exchange of principal in the beginning, periodic payment of interest on predetermined interest rates at predetermined intervals, and re-exchange of principal at the end of the swap contract. We have to value these cash flows to know the worth of the swap deal, any time subsequent to the contract, as spot rates as well as risk-free rate change.

Any change in the term structure of interest rates in either of the currencies involved or in the exchange rates causes disequilibrium in cash flows, and imparts value to the swap. Paying interest in domestic currency and receiving in foreign currency is like having issued a bond in domestic currency and owning a foreign currency bond. A fall in the domestic interest rate will increase the value of the domestic cash flows, and a fall in the foreign currency interest rate would increase the value of foreign currency cash flows.

How the value of a currency swap is determined can be seen through a simple example. Let us assume that Firm A has entered into a 5-year swap, wherein it receives Indian rupees at 8% and pays US dollars at 4% annually on the exchange of a principal amount of US $ 100 lakh when the exchange rate was ₹45 per $. Assuming a flat term structure of interest, the value of the swap at its initiation is zero, as can be seen from Table 30-2.

Table 30-2 Value of the swap at the beginning

(Figures in lakh)

Year	₹ Interest and principal	US $ Interest and principal	PV Discounted at 8% (₹)	PV Discounted at 4% (US $)
1	360.00	4.00	333.33	3.85
2	360.00	4.00	308.64	3.70
3	360.00	4.00	285.78	3.56
4	360.00	4.00	264.61	3.42
5	360.00	4.00	245.01	3.29
*5	4,500.00	100.00	3,062.62	82.19
			4,500.00	**100.00**
Equivalent Domestic Currency @ ₹45/$				**4,500.00**
Value of Swap				—

*Principal amount

The initial value of the swap is zero, as one would expect, because no deal would take place, if any of the party believes in receiving less and paying more in the given interest rate and exchange rate scenario. Firms receiving and paying ₹/$ must feel equivalence in both the currencies at the current interest rates and exchange rate so as to enter into a swap deal.

Valuation of swap can also be done on the basis of treatment of payments as a series of forward contracts. The forward rates can be worked out from the interest rate structure using interest rate parity. The cash flow of interest of $ 4 lakh in the Years 1–5 and the principal of $ 100 lakh in Year 5 are equivalent to forward contracts of the amounts in each year. Given the interest rates of 8% and 4% for rupee and dollar, the 1-year forward rate using interest rate parity is given by:

$$E_1 = S_0\left(\frac{1+r_d}{1+r_f}\right) = 45\left(\frac{1.08}{1.03}\right) = 45 \times 1.0385 = ₹46.43/\$$$

The valuation of swaps is based on discounted cash flow technique, and the problem arises with projection of the floating leg of cash flow that is unknown

Likewise, one can find out the implied forward rates for all subsequent periods at which the dollar cash flows can be converted into local currency. The differential of equivalent of dollar cash flows and the local currency will be the net cash flow of the firm under the swap. The differential is discounted at the interest rate applicable to rupee.

Table 30-3 *Value of currency swap as series of forward contracts*

(Figures in lakh)

Year	₹ Interest & Principal	$ Interest & Principal	Implied Forward Rate (₹/$)	Equivalent ₹	Value of forward	PV of forward
1	360.00	4.00	46.73	186.92	173.08	160.26
2	360.00	4.00	48.53	194.11	165.89	142.22
3	360.00	4.00	50.39	201.58	158.42	125.76
4	360.00	4.00	52.33	209.33	150.67	110.75
5	360.00	4.00	54.35	217.38	142.62	97.06
*5	4,500.00	100.00	54.35	5,434.56	–934.56	–636.05
Total						**0.00**

*Principal amount

Assuming the swap as a series of forward contracts, the value comes to zero as expected, and is in conformity with the calculation based on the assumption of swap as a pair of bonds, as may be seen from Table 30-3.

The value of the currency swap will change if the interest rates in either currency or the exchange rate changes subsequent to the swap. The swap becomes valuable to one of the parties depending upon the direction of its movement. The change in the exchange rate of the currency will impart a value to the swap, as $S \times V_f = V_d$ will not hold good any more.

Let us calculate the value of swap assuming that the domestic interest rate has gone up from 8% to 10% while the dollar interest rate remains same at 4%. Note that the absolute values of the cash flows pertaining to the interest and principal as fixed at the time of setting up of the swap deal do not change. With the change in the domestic interest rates, the discounted value of the rupee cash flow changes. The calculations are shown in Table 30-4.

Table 30-4 Value of the swap with the change in interest rates

(Figures in lakh)

Year	₹ Interest and principal	US $ Interest and principal	PV ₹ Discounted at 10%	PV US $ Discounted at 4%
1	360.00	4.00	327.27	3.85
2	360.00	4.00	297.52	3.70
3	360.00	4.00	270.47	3.56
4	360.00	4.00	245.88	3.42
5	360.00	4.00	223.53	3.29
*5	5,000.00	100.00	3,104.61	82.19
			4,469.29	100.00
PV in Equivalent Rupees				**5,000.00**
Value of swap				**–530.71**

*Principal amount

As may be seen from Table 30-4, with the rise in interest rates in the rupee, the discounted value of the rupee cash flow falls; and if the firm is paying rupee, the value of the swap becomes ₹531 lakh. For a firm that receives rupee and pays dollar, the value of the swap is positive ₹531 lakh. These values can be used to reverse the positions in the swaps taken earlier.

Readers are advised to check if the value is same when the swap is taken as a series of forward contracts.

Motivations and Contradictions

As stated earlier, there are many motivations for firms to enter into swap contracts. Swaps can serve as hedging instruments for covering exchange rate risk via currency swaps or interest rate risk via interest rate swaps. More complex swaps involving different currencies and fixed and floating interest rates can cover the two risks simultaneously. Another reason, though manifestation of hedging only for entering into swap contracts, is the desire to change the complexion of asset or liability from one currency to another or from fixed interest rates to floating and vice versa. However, the most prominent reason for firms to engage in swaps is their ability to reduce the funding cost by utilizing the difference in credit quality spreads. This feature of the swaps seems to be the overwhelming reason of its popularity. How long can this credit quality arbitrage can be exploited is a moot point.

The advantage and popularity of swaps rests on the validity of the theory of comparative advantage of international trade. The theory of comparative advantage would predict disappearance of swaps as an instrument to reduce financing cost, as with time, the opportunities of credit arbitrage should vanish. However, the increasing volumes of swap transactions defy this logic. As long as imperfections in the capital markets persist, swaps would continue to grow. These imperfections have their roots in controls, incentives, and protection exercised by various governments, making access to capital markets discriminatory. Governments may prohibit non-resident firms to access capital markets or may offer subsidized loans to promote development. Such aberrations based on domicile of the firms are likely to continue and would offer scope for swaps, as a tool of reducing financing cost.

Not only the volumes of swaps are increasing, innovations in swaps too are taking place at a fast pace. *Swaptions*, the options on swaps, are also becoming popular. A call swaption gives one the right to receive a fixed payment of interest, and a put swaption gives the holder a right to pay a fixed rate of interest. In each case, the holder pays a nominal front-end premium to cover the risk of rising or falling interest rate.

Unlike other derivatives like options and futures, swaps are over-the-counter products that take into account the specific needs of counter-parties with financial institutions and banks serving as intermediaries.

SUMMARY

Swaps, as financial instruments, evolved in 1970s due to the exchange controls exercised by several nations impeding the free flow of capital amongst the subsidiaries of multinational corporations located in various countries. These controls on cross border flows of capital forced the MNCs to arrange parallel loans to address the mutual problems of funding the subsidiaries in currencies other than their own. Later, these parallel loans developed into full blown financial products called swaps.

A swap can be defined as an exchange of cash flows based on the terms and conditions as agreed upon by the contracting parties. In case of interest rate swaps, the exchange of cash flow is based on interest rates; while in case of currency swaps, it is based on currency exchange rates. Interest rate swaps involve only exchange of netted cash flow based on a notional principal. In currency swaps, the principal amount is exchanged when the contract is initiated and is re-exchanged upon conclusion of the deal.

Interest rate swaps have two legs. Based on how the interest under the two legs is determined, swaps are classified as fixed-to-floating, floating-to-fixed, or basis swap. In most swaps, one leg involves payment of interest at fixed rate and is constant over the life of the swap, while the interest on the other leg is determined at periodical intervals based on a reference rate. This instrument allows one to change the characteristics of an asset/liability from fixed rate to floating for one party and vice versa for the second party. Depending upon the perception of the behaviour of future interest rate, swaps may be used as a hedge against the movement of interest rates.

However, swaps are used more for taking advantage of the imperfect markets that offers an opportunity for firms to reduce the aggregate financing cost. The rationale behind swaps is rooted in the theory of comparative advantage of international trade. Despite the fact that a firm may enjoy an absolute advantage in all kinds of markets for borrowing funds as compared to another firm, the differential of advantage in different markets would not be identical. There would be comparative advantage in one of the markets that may be exploited by the parties in the swap deal for their mutual benefit. This is done by accessing the markets first for raising money, and then entering into a swap.

Banks and financial institutions act as intermediaries in a swap deal and serve many useful purposes. Besides finding parties with matching financial needs, they serve the useful role of: (a) filling the gap in matching needs temporarily till the exact match is found, (b) assuming counter-party risk, and (c) facilitating an exit from swap deals by offering two-way quotes.

Currency swap involves two currencies and start with the exchange of principal amount of loan, followed by exchange of interest in two currencies for the period of the swap, and finally re-exchange of principal back at the conclusion of a deal. This helps in transforming an asset/liability from one currency to another. Again, currency swaps too serve as a tool of reducing financing cost for both the firms involved in a swap.

Valuation of swap can be viewed at least in two different ways—as a pair of bond or as a series of forward contracts. The initial value of the swap is always zero, as none of the parties pays in excess of receipts while agreeing to a swap deal. However, subsequent to the deal, the interest rates and exchange rates undergo a change, making a swap more valuable for one party. The value of a swap may be determined by using discounted cash flow technique. The problem faced in valuing the swap relates to the projections of the cash flows of the floating leg. In case of interest rate swaps, the term structure of interest rate may be used; while for currency swaps, implied forward rates are used to address the problem of finding the cash flow on the floating leg.

Based on the valuation, banks offer two-way quotes for paying and receiving a fixed rate of interest in exchange of a benchmarked floating rate. They serve as market-makers in swaps, offering much warranted liquidity to firms in entering and exiting a swap deal whenever they feel the need to do so.

Despite increased integration of capital markets worldwide, both volumes and innovations are growing in the swap markets defying the reasoning that the comparative advantage must vanish over a period of time.

KEY TERMS

Parallel loans Parallel loans refer to the mutual arrangement between two MNCs having subsidiaries where each parent firm finances the subsidiary of another located in its country.

Swap Swap is an exchange of cash flows between two parties according to the terms of the contract.

Interest rate swaps Under interest rate swaps, one party pays a fixed rate of interest in exchange of receiving an interest based on a floating rate from the counter-party.

Basis swap In basis swap, both the legs of cash flows of interest are floating but are based on different benchmarks.

Currency swap Under currency swap, the exchange of cash flow is based on exchange rates. The principal amount too is exchanged in the beginning and re-exchanged at the conclusion of the contract.

Value of swap The amount of money that one party must pay to another so that the present value of the cash flow is equated.

KEY FORMULAE

Value of fixed leg of interest rate swap

$$V_c = \sum_{1}^{n} \frac{C_i}{(1+r_i)^n} + \frac{P}{(1+r_n)^n}$$

Value of currency swap

$$V_s = S \times V_f - V_d$$

Value of floating leg of interest rate swap

$$V_f = \frac{F_1}{(1+r_1)} + \frac{P}{(1+r_1)}$$

Value of interest rate swap

$$V_s = V_c - V_f$$

PRACTICE PROBLEMS

1. Protection against Falling Interest Rates

A firm has issued fixed rate bonds to the subscribers. The coupon rate of the bond was 15% which was consistent with the then prevailing market conditions. Since the time of the issue five years back, the interest rates have fallen to about 12%. It is expected that the interest rates would fall further in coming few years as the economy has been doing well in the recent past and the same trend is likely to continue.

The chairman is concerned that the firm is paying inordinately high cost of borrowing funds as the coupon at 15% has been committed. He is thinking of some remedy to contain the cost of funds in coming years.

As a banker, you have offered the firm a swap whereby the bank would pay 12.00% fixed for receiving MIBOR on floating basis. The current MIBOR is 12.25%.

If the firm enters into the swap arrangement, what would be the cost of funds? Draw a schematic diagram reflecting the swap arrangement.

Would it be advisable to go for swap on the rates being offered by the bank?

Solution

The firm is currently paying a cost of 15% fixed irrespective of the current interest rates in the market. By entering into a swap arrangement, the nature of liability of firm would stand transformed from fixed to variable because the fixed outflow of interest would be matched by the fixed inflow from the bank and the firm would be paying the bank on floating basis. This can be seen from the given diagram.

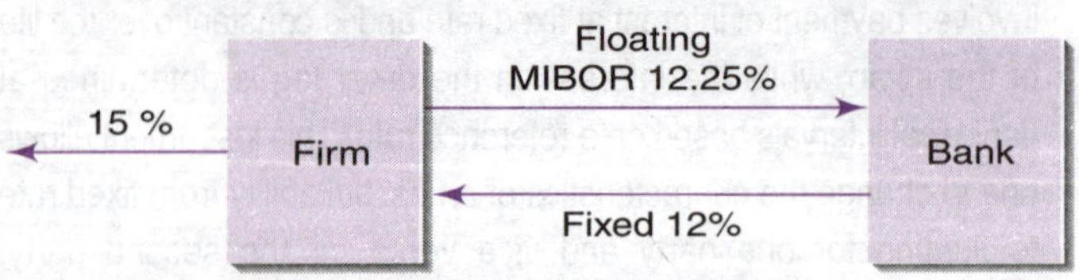

Current cost of funds for the firm is fixed at 15%.
After the swap, the cost of funds for the firm:

Payment to bond holders	15%
Payment to bank	MIBOR
Receipt from bank	–12%
Cost of funds for the firm	MIBOR + 3%

With the current rate of MIBOR at 12.25%, the cost of funds would rise to 15.25%.

The swap would be beneficial for the firm only when the interest rates are likely to come down further.

2. Hedging against Rising Interest Rates

Variable Masters Ltd always believed in following what the markets demanded. The philosophy of the management to follow the market oriented practices were also reflected in the borrowing policies of the firm. The endeavour of the finance department was always to avail the funds at variable rates of interest in order to be consistent with management practices.

Three years back, Variable Masters Ltd had mobilized ₹100 crore from the bank on MIBOR + 50 bps. The tenure of the loan was 7 years. After availing the loan, the interest rates declined initially but of late they have started rising. The buzz in the market is that interest rates would rise in times to come. This has caused worries, as the interest liability of the firm would go up if rates indeed rise.

The Financial Controller of Variable Masters has approached another bank to have a swap arrangement where the firm would pay a fixed rate of interest in exchange of receiving MIBOR based payment from the bank. The bank has agreed to pay MIBOR in exchange of receiving 8% fixed.

If the firm enters into the swap arrangement, what would be the cost of funds? Draw a schematic diagram reflecting the swap arrangement.

Solution

The firm is currently paying a cost of MIBOR + 50 bps. By entering into a swap arrangement, the nature of liability of firm would stand transformed from variable to fixed, as the variable outflow of interest would be matched by the variable inflow from the bank and the firm would be paying the bank on fixed basis. This can be seen from the given diagram.

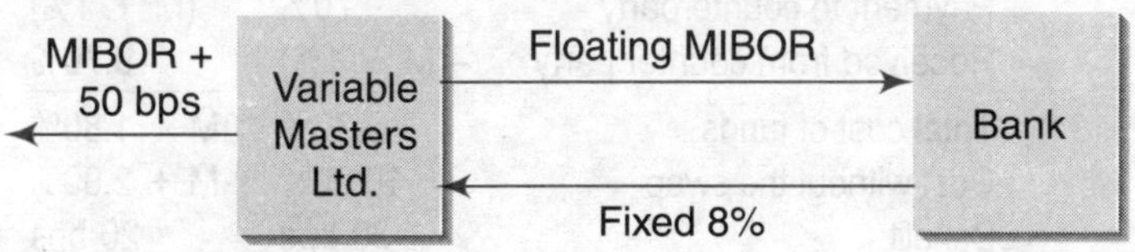

Current cost of borrowing for the firm is MIBOR + 0.50%

After the swap the cost of funds for the firm would be fixed at 8.50%:

Payment to bond holders	MIBOR + 50 bps
Payment to Bank	8%
Receipt from bank	–MIBOR
Cost of funds for the firm	8.50%

3. Currency Swap

Star Trading House (STH) has borrowed a sum of ₹1,000 million in US dollar in the euro markets in London. The equivalent loan amount of US $ 25 million is payable at the end of five years. The current exchange rate is ₹40/$. The interest payable in US dollar is at the rate of 5.00% and is to be paid at the end of each year.

A consultant in foreign exchange who enjoys the confidence of the management of STH has suggested that the cost of funds, though fixed in US dollar at 5%, it is not as cheap it seems from the viewpoint of cost in rupee terms. In fact with appreciation of US dollar, the cost of funds is rather high.

He further suggested that it would be appropriate to convert the liability of US dollar into euro. Even though the prevailing interest rate in euro is higher at 8%, it would be worthwhile to transform the liability given that appreciation of euro would be marginal.

The current exchange rate for US $ is ₹40, while for euro it is ₹61.80. The consultant has prepared the following forecast of the exchange rate for US dollar and euro for the next five years.

(₹ per unit)

Year	*US dollar*	*Euro*
1	41.00	62.00
2	44.00	62.25
3	47.00	62.50
4	49.00	62.75
5	50.00	63.00

HSBC Bank in London is ready to offer a US dollar-euro swap where it would pay 5% US dollar in exchange of receiving 8% euro. Assume that STH enters into the swap arrangement with HSBC Bank.

(a) Draw a schematic diagram indicating the flow of payments for STH and the bank.

(b) What would be the cost of funds for STH If it enters into the swap?

(c) Do you recommend entering into for the arrangement? Why or why not?

Solution

(a) The flow of funds from and to the bank is as shown here.

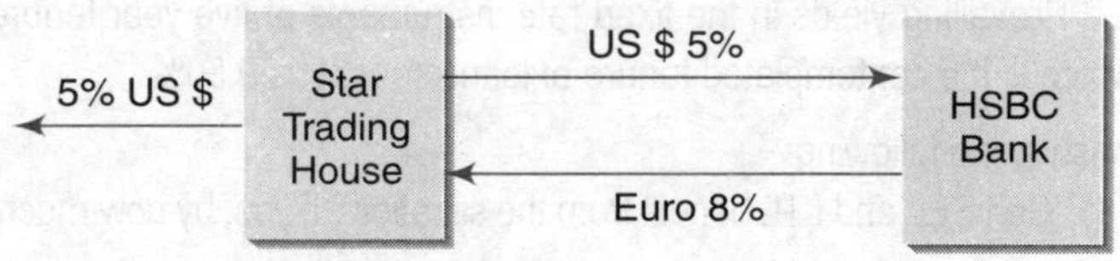

(b) Current cost of borrowing for the firm in US dollar is 5%

After the swap, the cost of funds for the firm would be fixed at 8.00% in euro:

Payment to bond holders	US $ 5%
Payment to bank	Euro 8%
Receipt from bank	–US $ 5%
Cost of funds for the firm	Euro 8%

(c) The rupee cost of funds in US dollar and euro, assuming the forecast of the consultant to be true, is worked out on the basis of the rupee cash flows as under:

	US dollar	Euro
Existing loan amount (₹ million)	1,000	1,000
Current Exchange rate (₹/unit of foreign currency)	40.00	61.80
Interest rate payable in foreign currency	5.00%	8.00%
Equivalent loan in foreign currency (million)	25.00	16.18

Cost of loan if in US dollar				Cost of loan if in Euro			
Year	Interest	Ex rate	₹ cash flow	Year	Interest	Ex rate	₹ cash flow
—	-1,000.00	—	-1,000.00				
1	1.25	41.00	51.25	1	1.29	62.00	80.26
2	1.25	44.00	55.00	2	1.29	62.25	80.58
3	1.25	47.00	58.75	3	1.29	62.50	80.91
4	1.25	49.00	61.25	4	1.29	62.75	81.23
5	26.25	50.00	1,312.50	5	17.48	63.00	1,100.97
IRR of ₹ cash flow			9.83%				8.41%

After the swap, the cost of loan is 8% in euro terms. However incorporating impact of exchange rate, the cost in rupee terms works out to 9.83% if liability remains in US dollar, and 8.41% if the liability is transformed to euro through the swap.

In the present circumstances, Star Trading House must enter into the swap with the bank, as it reduces the cost by 1.42% in rupee terms.

4. Reducing Cost through Swap

Solar Equipment Ltd (SEL) and Lunar Technologies Ltd (LTL) are in the same line of business and compete with each other. They both are in need of funds and are exploring the markets for raising money. The survey in the lending market has offered them the following rates with fixed and floating rate:

	Fixed rate	Floating rate
Solar Equipments Ltd	T + 50 bps	M + 100 bps
Lunar Technologies Ltd	T + 100 bps	M + 200 bps

Fixed rate markets are governed by the returns that are prevailing in the bonds market, while floating rates are based on MIBOR.

Prevailing yields in the fixed rate instruments of five year tenure, which is the contemplated tenure of loans sought, is 9.50%.

Answer the following:

(a) Can SEL and LTL benefit from the situation? If yes, by how much?

(b) What strategies should both the firms follow to avail the benefit?

(c) If SEL desires to share the benefit to the extent of 60% while letting LTL avail remaining 40%, what cost of funds each of the firm would have?

(d) Draw a schematic diagram to explain the strategy that you would implement to derive the benefit.

(e) Compute the cost of funds for STL and LTL after they enter into a swap arrangement.

Solution

(a) From the data of the market, it can be seen that SEL has advantage over LTL in both the markets of fixed rate and floating rate.

In the fixed rate market, SEL can mobilize at 10% while LTL can do it at 10.50%, i.e., 50 bps cheaper than LTL.

In the floating rate market, SEL can mobilize at M + 1% while LTL can do it at M + 2%, i.e., 100 bps cheaper than LTL.

	Fixed rate	Floating rate
Solar Equipments Ltd	10.00%	M + 100 bps
Lunar Technologies Ltd	10.50%	M + 200 bps
Advantage of SEL, bps	50	100

It is the comparative advantage that is crucial to the decision making. The comparative advantage in favour of SEL is the difference of absolute advantage.

The present market scenario offers an advantage of 50 bps in the cost of funds for both the firms on an aggregate basis.

(b) SEL must access floating rate market at M + 100 bps and then enter into a swap with LTL.

Similarly LTL must access the fixed rate market to mobilize capital and then enter into a swap with SEL.

(c) The total benefit available is 50 bps that can be shared by SEL and LTL. Since SEL wants 60% of benefit, the cost of funds would be made lesser by 30 bps for SEL and the same swap would benefit LTL by 20 bps.

(d) SEL and LTL can enter into a swap arrangement after accessing the loan markets at floating rate and fixed rate respectively. Under the swap, SEL would pay 9.70% to LTL in exchange of receiving M + 1.00% as shown in the schematic diagram.

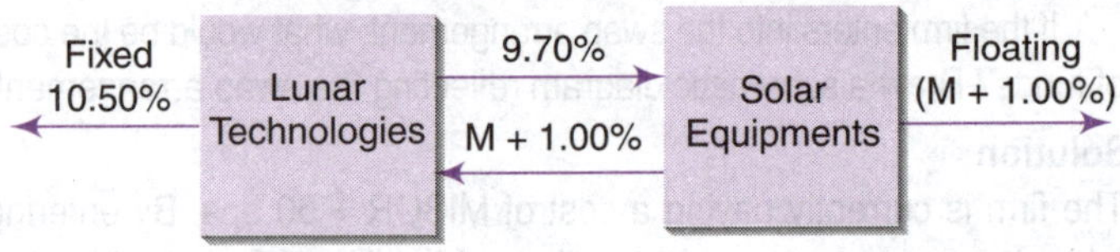

(e) After accessing the markets and entering into the swap arrangement, the cost of funds is worked out as follows:

	SEL	LTL
Payment to market	M + 1%	10.50%
Payment to counterparty	9.70%	(M + 1%)
Received from counter party	–(M + 1%)	–9.70%
Total cost of funds	9.70%	M + 1.80%
Cost without the swap	10.00%	M + 2.00%
Benefit	30 bps	20 bps

5. Reducing Cost of Borrowing through Swap

Eros Plc and Atlas Plc are two competing and growing firms in Britain catering to the European markets for supplies of office needs. Both the firms are expanding rapidly and in order to fund the growth, are exploring for raising debt from the market.

Eros Plc can mobilize funds at 5.40% in the fixed rate market while in the floating rate market it can do so at LIBOR + 50 bps. Atlas Plc can raise funds at 6.3% on fixed rate basis and at LIBOR + 70 bps in the floating rate market.

Eros Plc is wanting to raise money on floating rate basis, as it expects a fall in the interest rate structure. Contrary to Eros Plc, Atlas

Plc is convinced of rise in the interest rates in future, and therefore wants to raise funds on fixed rate basis.

HSBC Bank has advised them to raise money in the markets of opposite choice and then enter into a swap through them by paying 10 bps each.

(a) Show how the swap can benefit both the firms and to what extent?

(b) If the bank is involved as intermediary and wants 10 bps from each of the firm, with Eros Plc wanting 60% of the remaining benefit, what would be the cost of funds for each?

(c) What function would the bank discharge as intermediary?

Solution

(a) The position of the two firms in the two markets is as follows:

	Fixed rate market	Floating Rate market
Eros Plc	5.40%	LIBOR + 50 bps
Atlas Plc	6.30%	LIBOR + 70 bps
Advantage – Eros Plc	90 bps	20 bps

Comparative advantage, i.e., the difference of the two absolute advantages is 70 bps. The comparative advantage can be exploited by the two firms by arranging a swap between them. If the advantage of 70 bps is to be shared equally, the cost of funds for each of them can come down by 35 bps.

(b) With the bank fixing its earnings at 20 bps (10 bps from each of the party), the comparative advantage that can be exploited by Eros Plc and Atlas Plc reduces to 50 bps. As agreed between the two Eros plc would avail the benefit of 30 bps leaving the remaining 20 bps for Atlas Plc.

Following cash flow structure may be formed under the swap:

1. Eros Plc would access the fixed rate market mobilizing funds at 5.40%.

   Under the swap, it would receive fixed 5.40% from the bank and pay floating L + 20 bps to the bank.

2. Atlas Plc would access the floating rate market mobilizing funds at L + 70 bps.

   Under the swap, it would pay fixed 5.50% to the bank and receive floating L + 10 bps from the bank

Swap arrangement is shown in the given diagram.

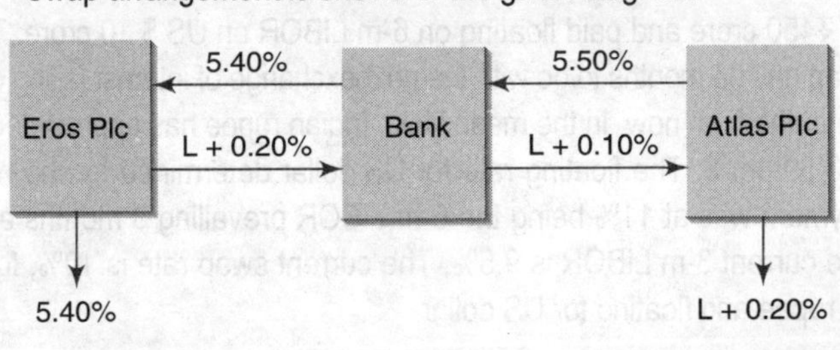

After the swap, the cost of funds for each firm would be as follows:

	Eros Plc	Atlas Plc
Payment to the market	5.40%	L + 70 bps
Payment to bank under swap	L + 20 bps	5.50%
Receipt from bank under swap	–5.40%	–(L + 10 bps)
Cost of funds with swap	L + 20 bps	6.10%
Cost of funds without swap	L + 50 bps	6.30%
Benefit of swap	30 bps	20 bps

(c) The role performed by the bank under the swap would be to assume the counter-party risk. In case Eros Plc and Atlas Plc enter into the swap directly both would assume risk of interest payment on each other.

The environment after the swap would be favourable to one and unfavourable to the another leaving scope of default. With the bank in between, both parties are assured of cash flows at specified intervals.

6. Cancelling a swap

A company has borrowed through a fixed rate instrument of 8%. The swap quote from the bank is 7.80/7.90, i.e., bank pays 7.80 fixed for receiving LIBOR and would receive 7.90% fixed for paying LIBOR. The company enters the swap deal with the bank.

After some time, the swap market changes to 6.40/6.50 and the company again reverses the original swap by entering into 2nd swap opposite to that of the first one.

(a) What does the structure of the first swap achieve?

(b) What is the cost of funds for the firm before and after the swap?

(c) What is the structure of 2nd swap and what does it do?

(d) Find the cost of funds for the company after the second swap?

Solution

(a) The company would undertake the transform the fixed rate liability to floating rate, as it possibly expects a decline in the interest rates. Following would be the structure of the swap with the bank.

(b) Cost of funds after swap = L + 0.2%

(c) The company would enter into a swap opposite to that of the first one. In the first swap, the firm received fixed and paid variable. Now in the second swap, it would pay fixed while receiving LIBOR. This would enable cancelling the floating leg. The company would gain the differential of the fixed legs of first and second swap.

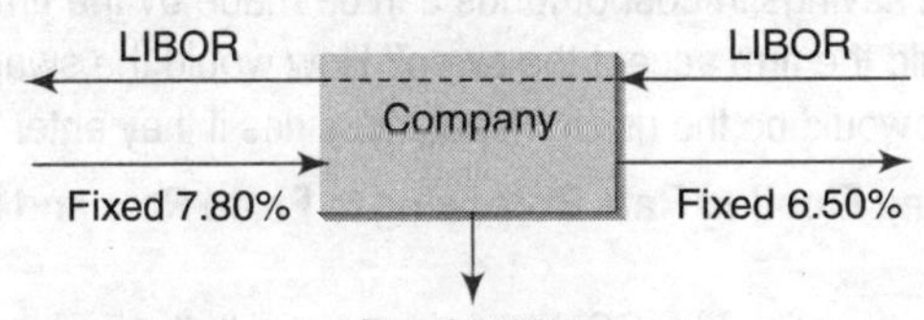

(d)

Pay fixed to borrowers	8.00
Receive fixed from bank (1st swap)	–7.80
Pay fixed to bank (2nd swap)	6.50
Effective cost after 2nd swap	6.70

EXERCISES

1. What are parallel loans and their problems?
2. What is a swap contract? Explain how it can be used as a hedging instrument.
3. How do swaps reduce the cost of financing for both the parties involved in the deal?
4. Swaps are used as a tool for changing the characteristics of an asset or liability. Elaborate.
5. What is the difference between interest rate swap and currency swap, and what are their uses?
6. What do you understand by valuation of swap? What problems are you likely to face, and what are the ways of resolving these problems?
7. What functions do the banks or financial institutions discharge in a swap deal?

Critical Thinking Questions

1. Swaps reduce the cost of financing for both the parties in a swap transaction. If both the firms benefit, who loses?
2. At the time of entering an interest rate swap, the term structure of interest rate was flat, and the first exchange of cash flow was to take place after 6 months. At the time of first exchange, the interest rate declined but the term structure remained flat. In whose favour is the swap tilted now?

Practical Assignment

Visit the website of International Swaps and Derivatives Association (www.isda.org) and familiarize yourself with the standards and terminology used in swap deals.

Numerical Problems

1. Changing Fixed Rate Borrowing to Floating Rate and Reducing Cost

Ispat Industries Ltd had raised funds through the issue of fixed rate 5-year bonds with a fixed interest rate of 12%. The issue was made two years ago. Since then, the interest rates have declined, and the low level of interest rate is likely to continue for some time. At present, the yield on 3-year treasury bonds is 9%. The bankers of Ispat Industries have offered a swap to them at 50 bps over treasuries for MIBOR. The current MIBOR is 8.75%.

(a) What savings in cost of funds can be made by the firm?
(b) Should the firm accept the swap? How would the swap work?
(c) What would be the risk for Ispat Industries if they enter the swap?

2. Changing Floating Rate Borrowing to Fixed Rate and Reducing Cost

Cement Corporation Ltd (CCL) had come out with the Foreign Currency Bonds at a floating rate three years ago. The bonds had the maturity of seven years and carried a floating rate of interest at LIBOR + 2.5%. At the time of the issue, CCL had anticipated a decline in the interest rates. However, in the last three years, the rates have gone up. The trend of interest rates suggests further rise. Barclays Bank in London has offered a swap at 75 bps over 4-year treasury yield for LIBOR. The yield on 4-year treasury is 8.25% and 6-m LIBOR is at 9.5%.

(a) What swap should CCL enter into, and what kind of savings the swap would result in?
(b) If CCL enters the swap, what risks does it carry?

3. Reducing the Cost of Borrowing through Swap

First Chemicals is an AAA rated company engaged in manufacture of chemicals. It needs funds of ₹100 crore that can be raised either at a floating rate of MIBOR + 50 bps or at a fixed rate of 10.40%. At the same time, Royal Oils, an AA rated firm too needs funds of the same magnitude and can raise them at MIBOR + 100 bps with a floating rate borrowing or at 11.50% in the fixed rate market. The tenure of borrowing by both the firms is 7 years.

First Chemicals is inclined to raise funds on a floating rate basis, while Royal Oils is happy raising money on fixed rates.

(a) Show how the swap can benefit both the firms, and what would be the extent of benefit?
(b) If a bank is involved as intermediary and wants 5 bps from each of the firm, how would the cost of funds change?
(c) What function would the bank discharge as intermediary?

4. Value of Swap

Indian Petro Ltd had entered into a swap with a bank under which it was paying 13% fixed for receiving LIBOR. The swap required annual payments of interest. The next cash flow is due 90 days from now for which the LIBOR was set at 11% nine months ago. Since the time of entering the swap arrangement, the structure of interest rate has declined. Currently, the 5-year swap is being quoted at 10% against LIBOR. 3-m LIBOR is 8%. What is the value of the swap?

5. Value of Currency Swap and Cancellation

An Indian firm, Indian Steel, had entered a swap with a bank some time ago, exchanging a rupee loan for US dollar. The exchange rate prevailing at that point of time was ₹45 per US $. The swap was agreed with the bank, wherein Indian Steel received fixed 12% interest on ₹450 crore and paid floating on 6-m LIBOR on US $ 10 crore. The swap has 63 months to go with the next exchange of interest falling due 3 months from now. In the meanwhile, Indian rupee has appreciated to ₹43.50 per $. The floating rate for US dollar determined for the next payment was at 11% being the 6-m LIBOR prevailing 3 months ago. The current 3-m LIBOR is 9.5%. The current swap rate is 10%, fixed for rupee and floating for US dollar.

(a) What is the value of the swap for Indian Steel today?
(b) If the bank wants to cancel the swap today, what amount should Indian Steel demand to agree for cancelling the arrangement?
(c) What would be the value of swap if the exchange rate had remained constant?

CASE STUDY

General Products—The Rosy Swap

Mr Lever, the Managing Director of General Products, was preparing to go out for the party on the eve of the New Year, when his Vice President Finance, Mr Malhotra, presented him with the following projections of the profitability estimates for the year closing in the forthcoming March.

	₹ crore
Sales	51.00
Raw material	35.10
Expenses other than interest	7.00
PBIT	8.90
Interest	6.40
Profit before tax	2.50
Tax 40%	1.00
Profit after tax	1.50
Nos. of shares (crore)	0.50
EPS (₹)	3.00

Mr Lever disappointingly looked at the likely scenario and said that the major cost that deteriorates the earnings for the shareholder is the interest on the debt he carries. To him, the interest cost of about ₹12.80 per share was too high. Thinking that little could be done to avoid debts, he proceeded for the evening celebrations.

Preoccupied with the worrying thoughts of high interest burden, Mr Lever couldn't resist talking about the high proportion of the interest cost to some of his banker friends who were present in the party. Bankers informed him that since the time he raised the debt on fixed rate at 8%, the interest rates have fallen. And he must swap his fixed rate loan for a floating rate loan. According to the bankers, it would give him substantial savings considering the high proportion of debt his firm was saddled with.

Next morning, he discussed the idea of converting the fixed rate liability into a floating rate liability. Mr Lever said, "The current level of debt is ₹80 crore and the current cost is 8%. A small savings of 0.5% on the interest rate means a saving of ₹40 lakh. With a mere 50 lakh shares, the EPS would increase by Re 0.80, and with the PE multiple of 20, the jump in the stock price could be as high as ₹16." He asked his Vice President Finance, Mr Malhotra, to immediately get in touch with the bankers to find out more about the swap transaction that the bankers had casually mentioned to him the previous night.

After a few telephone calls and a couple of hours, Mr Malhotra had the following data before him:

Swap rate Bank pays 7.2% for receiving MIBOR. General Products would receive fixed 7.2% on semi-annual basis matching the interest payment on the debt of ₹80 crore every June and December for three years.

Current MIBOR rate 6.90%

Expected futures contract yields were

6-m :	6.80%	12-m :	6.85%	18-m :	7.25%
24-m :	7.30%	30-m :	7.60%	36-m :	7.70%

The term structure of interest rate for the next three years was as follows:

6 month :	6.45%	1 year :	6.60%
2 years :	6.80%	3 years :	6.90%

The present debt of ₹80 crore had three years to mature.

Analysing the data, Mr Malhotra realized that the current swap quote had the potential of saving the interest cost. His current cost of 8% fixed can become floating at MIBOR + 0.8% if he enters the swap now. With MIBOR currently at 6.9%, the cost of debt in immediate future would be 7.7%; a saving of 0.3%. But, he was not very sure of the future.

Should he enter the swap transaction with the bank? Justify your answer.

PART EIGHT

APPENDICES

APPENDIX A-1

Future Value of Re 1 at r% after n Periods

APPENDIX A-2

Present Value of Re 1 Discounted at r% for n Periods

APPENDIX A-3

Future Value of Amuity of Re 1 at r% for n Periods

APPENDIX A-4

Present Value of Annuity at r% for n Periods

APPENDIX A-5

EMI Payable in Advance at r% for n Years

APPENDIX A-6

EMI Payable in Arrears at r% for n Years

APPENDIX A-7

Area Under the Normal Distribution Curve

1st Part For Positive Values

2nd Part For Negative Values

APPENDIX A-1

Future Value of Re 1 at *r*% after *n* Periods

Period *n* / Interest *r*	1%	2%	3%	4%	5%	6%	7%	8%	9%	10%	11%	12%	13%	14%	15%
1	1.010	1.020	1.030	1.040	1.050	1.060	1.070	1.080	1.090	1.100	1.110	1.120	1.130	1.140	1.150
2	1.020	1.040	1.061	1.082	1.103	1.124	1.145	1.166	1.188	1.210	1.232	1.254	1.277	1.300	1.323
3	1.030	1.061	1.093	1.125	1.158	1.191	1.225	1.260	1.295	1.331	1.368	1.405	1.443	1.482	1.521
4	1.041	1.082	1.126	1.170	1.216	1.262	1.311	1.360	1.412	1.464	1.518	1.574	1.630	1.689	1.749
5	1.051	1.104	1.159	1.217	1.276	1.338	1.403	1.469	1.539	1.611	1.685	1.762	1.842	1.925	2.011
6	1.062	1.126	1.194	1.265	1.340	1.419	1.501	1.587	1.677	1.772	1.870	1.974	2.082	2.195	2.313
7	1.072	1.149	1.230	1.316	1.407	1.504	1.606	1.714	1.828	1.949	2.076	2.211	2.353	2.502	2.660
8	1.083	1.172	1.267	1.369	1.477	1.594	1.718	1.851	1.993	2.144	2.305	2.476	2.658	2.853	3.059
9	1.094	1.195	1.305	1.423	1.551	1.689	1.838	1.999	2.172	2.358	2.558	2.773	3.004	3.252	3.518
10	1.105	1.219	1.344	1.480	1.629	1.791	1.967	2.159	2.367	2.594	2.839	3.106	3.395	3.707	4.046
11	1.116	1.243	1.384	1.539	1.710	1.898	2.105	2.332	2.580	2.853	3.152	3.479	3.836	4.226	4.652
12	1.127	1.268	1.426	1.601	1.796	2.012	2.252	2.518	2.813	3.138	3.498	3.896	4.335	4.818	5.350
13	1.138	1.294	1.469	1.665	1.886	2.133	2.410	2.720	3.066	3.452	3.883	4.363	4.898	5.492	6.153
14	1.149	1.319	1.513	1.732	1.980	2.261	2.579	2.937	3.342	3.797	4.310	4.887	5.535	6.261	7.076
15	1.161	1.346	1.558	1.801	2.079	2.397	2.759	3.172	3.642	4.177	4.785	5.474	6.254	7.138	8.137
16	1.173	1.373	1.605	1.873	2.183	2.540	2.952	3.426	3.970	4.595	5.311	6.130	7.067	8.137	9.358
17	1.184	1.400	1.653	1.948	2.292	2.693	3.159	3.700	4.328	5.054	5.895	6.866	7.986	9.276	10.761
18	1.196	1.428	1.702	2.026	2.407	2.854	3.380	3.996	4.717	5.560	6.544	7.690	9.024	10.575	12.375
19	1.208	1.457	1.754	2.107	2.527	3.026	3.617	4.316	5.142	6.116	7.263	8.613	10.197	12.056	14.232
20	1.220	1.486	1.806	2.191	2.653	3.207	3.870	4.661	5.604	6.727	8.062	9.646	11.523	13.743	16.367
21	1.232	1.516	1.860	2.279	2.786	3.400	4.141	5.034	6.109	7.400	8.949	10.804	13.021	15.668	18.822
22	1.245	1.546	1.916	2.370	2.925	3.604	4.430	5.437	6.659	8.140	9.934	12.100	14.714	17.861	21.645
23	1.257	1.577	1.974	2.465	3.072	3.820	4.741	5.871	7.258	8.954	11.026	13.552	16.627	20.362	24.891
24	1.270	1.608	2.033	2.563	3.225	4.049	5.072	6.341	7.911	9.850	12.239	15.179	18.788	23.212	28.625
25	1.282	1.641	2.094	2.666	3.386	4.292	5.427	6.848	8.623	10.835	13.585	17.000	21.231	26.462	32.919
26	1.295	1.673	2.157	2.772	3.556	4.549	5.807	7.396	9.399	11.918	15.080	19.040	23.991	30.167	37.857
27	1.308	1.707	2.221	2.883	3.733	4.822	6.214	7.988	10.245	13.110	16.739	21.325	27.109	34.390	43.535
28	1.321	1.741	2.288	2.999	3.920	5.112	6.649	8.627	11.167	14.421	18.580	23.884	30.633	39.204	50.066
29	1.335	1.776	2.357	3.119	4.116	5.418	7.114	9.317	12.172	15.863	20.624	26.750	34.616	44.693	57.575
30	1.348	1.811	2.427	3.243	4.322	5.743	7.612	10.063	13.268	17.449	22.892	29.960	39.116	50.950	66.212

(Contd)

(*Contd*) **Appendix A-1**

16%	17%	18%	19%	20%	21%	22%	23%	24%	25%	26%	27%	28%	29%	30%	40%
1.160	1.170	1.180	1.190	1.200	1.210	1.220	1.230	1.240	1.250	1.260	1.270	1.280	1.290	1.300	1.400
1.346	1.369	1.392	1.416	1.440	1.464	1.488	1.513	1.538	1.563	1.588	1.613	1.638	1.664	1.690	1.960
1.561	1.602	1.643	1.685	1.728	1.772	1.816	1.861	1.907	1.953	2.000	2.048	2.097	2.147	2.197	2.744
1.811	1.874	1.939	2.005	2.074	2.144	2.215	2.289	2.364	2.441	2.520	2.601	2.684	2.769	2.856	3.842
2.100	2.192	2.288	2.386	2.488	2.594	2.703	2.815	2.932	3.052	3.176	3.304	3.436	3.572	3.713	5.378
2.436	2.565	2.700	2.840	2.986	3.138	3.297	3.463	3.635	3.815	4.002	4.196	4.398	4.608	4.827	7.530
2.826	3.001	3.185	3.379	3.583	3.797	4.023	4.259	4.508	4.768	5.042	5.329	5.629	5.945	6.275	10.541
3.278	3.511	3.759	4.021	4.300	4.595	4.908	5.239	5.590	5.960	6.353	6.768	7.206	7.669	8.157	14.758
3.803	4.108	4.435	4.785	5.160	5.560	5.987	6.444	6.931	7.451	8.005	8.595	9.223	9.893	10.604	20.661
4.411	4.807	5.234	5.695	6.192	6.727	7.305	7.926	8.594	9.313	10.086	10.915	11.806	12.761	13.786	28.925
5.117	5.624	6.176	6.777	7.430	8.140	8.912	9.749	10.657	11.642	12.708	13.862	15.112	16.462	17.922	40.496
5.936	6.580	7.288	8.064	8.916	9.850	10.872	11.991	13.215	14.552	16.012	17.605	19.343	21.236	23.298	56.694
6.886	7.699	8.599	9.596	10.699	11.918	13.264	14.749	16.386	18.190	20.175	22.359	24.759	27.395	30.288	79.371
7.988	9.007	10.147	11.420	12.839	14.421	16.182	18.141	20.319	22.737	25.421	28.396	31.691	35.339	39.374	111.120
9.266	10.539	11.974	13.590	15.407	17.449	19.742	22.314	25.196	28.422	32.030	36.062	40.565	45.587	51.186	155.568
10.748	12.330	14.129	16.172	18.488	21.114	24.086	27.446	31.243	35.527	40.358	45.799	51.923	58.808	66.542	217.795
12.468	14.426	16.672	19.244	22.186	25.548	29.384	33.759	38.741	44.409	50.851	58.165	66.461	75.862	86.504	304.913
14.463	16.879	19.673	22.901	26.623	30.913	35.849	41.523	48.039	55.511	64.072	73.870	85.071	97.862	112.455	426.879
16.777	19.748	23.214	27.252	31.948	37.404	43.736	51.074	59.568	69.389	80.731	93.815	108.890	126.242	146.192	597.630
19.461	23.106	27.393	32.429	38.338	45.259	53.358	62.821	73.864	86.736	101.721	119.145	139.380	162.852	190.050	836.683
22.574	27.034	32.324	38.591	46.005	54.764	65.096	77.269	91.592	108.420	128.169	151.314	178.406	210.080	247.065	1,171.356
26.186	31.629	38.142	45.923	55.206	66.264	79.418	95.041	113.574	135.525	161.492	192.168	228.360	271.003	321.184	1,639.898
30.376	37.006	45.008	54.649	66.247	80.180	96.889	116.901	140.831	169.407	203.480	244.054	292.300	349.593	417.539	2,295.857
35.236	43.297	53.109	65.032	79.497	97.017	118.205	143.788	174.631	211.758	256.385	309.948	374.144	450.976	542.801	3,214.200
40.874	50.658	62.669	77.388	95.396	117.391	144.210	176.859	216.542	264.698	323.045	393.634	478.905	581.759	705.641	4,499.880
47.414	59.270	73.949	92.092	114.475	142.043	175.936	217.537	268.512	330.872	407.037	499.916	612.998	750.468	917.333	6,299.831
55.000	69.345	87.260	109.589	137.371	171.872	214.642	267.570	332.955	413.590	512.867	634.893	784.638	968.104	1,192.533	8,819.764
63.800	81.134	102.967	130.411	164.845	207.965	261.864	329.112	412.864	516.988	646.212	806.314	1,004.336	1,248.855	1,550.293	12,347.670
74.009	94.927	121.501	155.189	197.814	251.638	319.474	404.807	511.952	646.235	814.228	1,024.019	1,285.550	1,611.022	2,015.381	17,286.737
85.850	111.065	143.371	184.675	237.376	304.482	389.758	497.913	634.820	807.794	1,025.927	1,300.504	1,645.505	2,078.219	2,619.996	24,201.432

APPENDIX A-2

Present Value of Re 1 Discounted at *r*% for *n* Period

$$PV = \frac{1}{(1+r)^n}$$

Period n / Interest r	1%	2%	3%	4%	5%	6%	7%	8%	9%	10%	11%	12%	13%	14%	15%
1	0.9901	0.9804	0.9709	0.9615	0.9524	0.9434	0.9346	0.9259	0.9174	0.9091	0.9009	0.8929	0.8850	0.8772	0.8696
2	0.9803	0.9612	0.9426	0.9246	0.9070	0.8900	0.8734	0.8573	0.8417	0.8264	0.8116	0.7972	0.7831	0.7695	0.7561
3	0.9706	0.9423	0.9151	0.8890	0.8638	0.8396	0.8163	0.7938	0.7722	0.7513	0.7312	0.7118	0.6931	0.6750	0.6575
4	0.9610	0.9238	0.8885	0.8548	0.8227	0.7921	0.7629	0.7350	0.7084	0.6830	0.6587	0.6355	0.6133	0.5921	0.5718
5	0.9515	0.9057	0.8626	0.8219	0.7835	0.7473	0.7130	0.6806	0.6499	0.6209	0.5935	0.5674	0.5428	0.5194	0.4972
6	0.9420	0.8880	0.8375	0.7903	0.7462	0.7050	0.6663	0.6302	0.5963	0.5645	0.5346	0.5066	0.4803	0.4556	0.4323
7	0.9327	0.8706	0.8131	0.7599	0.7107	0.6651	0.6227	0.5835	0.5470	0.5132	0.4817	0.4523	0.4251	0.3996	0.3759
8	0.9235	0.8535	0.7894	0.7307	0.6768	0.6274	0.5820	0.5403	0.5019	0.4665	0.4339	0.4039	0.3762	0.3506	0.3269
9	0.9143	0.8368	0.7664	0.7026	0.6446	0.5919	0.5439	0.5002	0.4604	0.4241	0.3909	0.3606	0.3329	0.3075	0.2843
10	0.9053	0.8203	0.7441	0.6756	0.6139	0.5584	0.5083	0.4632	0.4224	0.3855	0.3522	0.3220	0.2946	0.2697	0.2472
11	0.8963	0.8043	0.7224	0.6496	0.5847	0.5268	0.4751	0.4289	0.3875	0.3505	0.3173	0.2875	0.2607	0.2366	0.2149
12	0.8874	0.7885	0.7014	0.6246	0.5568	0.4970	0.4440	0.3971	0.3555	0.3186	0.2858	0.2567	0.2307	0.2076	0.1869
13	0.8787	0.7730	0.6810	0.6006	0.5303	0.4688	0.4150	0.3677	0.3262	0.2897	0.2575	0.2292	0.2042	0.1821	0.1625
14	0.8700	0.7579	0.6611	0.5775	0.5051	0.4423	0.3878	0.3405	0.2992	0.2633	0.2320	0.2046	0.1807	0.1597	0.1413
15	0.8613	0.7430	0.6419	0.5553	0.4810	0.4173	0.3624	0.3152	0.2745	0.2394	0.2090	0.1827	0.1599	0.1401	0.1229
16	0.8528	0.7284	0.6232	0.5339	0.4581	0.3936	0.3387	0.2919	0.2519	0.2176	0.1883	0.1631	0.1415	0.1229	0.1069
17	0.8444	0.7142	0.6050	0.5134	0.4363	0.3714	0.3166	0.2703	0.2311	0.1978	0.1696	0.1456	0.1252	0.1078	0.0929
18	0.8360	0.7002	0.5874	0.4936	0.4155	0.3503	0.2959	0.2502	0.2120	0.1799	0.1528	0.1300	0.1108	0.0946	0.0808
19	0.8277	0.6864	0.5703	0.4746	0.3957	0.3305	0.2765	0.2317	0.1945	0.1635	0.1377	0.1161	0.0981	0.0829	0.0703
20	0.8195	0.6730	0.5537	0.4564	0.3769	0.3118	0.2584	0.2145	0.1784	0.1486	0.1240	0.1037	0.0868	0.0728	0.0611
21	0.8114	0.6598	0.5375	0.4388	0.3589	0.2942	0.2415	0.1987	0.1637	0.1351	0.1117	0.0926	0.0768	0.0638	0.0531
22	0.8034	0.6468	0.5219	0.4220	0.3418	0.2775	0.2257	0.1839	0.1502	0.1228	0.1007	0.0826	0.0680	0.0560	0.0462
23	0.7954	0.6342	0.5067	0.4057	0.3256	0.2618	0.2109	0.1703	0.1378	0.1117	0.0907	0.0738	0.0601	0.0491	0.0402
24	0.7876	0.6217	0.4919	0.3901	0.3101	0.2470	0.1971	0.1577	0.1264	0.1015	0.0817	0.0659	0.0532	0.0431	0.0349
25	0.7798	0.6095	0.4776	0.3751	0.2953	0.2330	0.1842	0.1460	0.1160	0.0923	0.0736	0.0588	0.0471	0.0378	0.0304
26	0.7720	0.5976	0.4637	0.3607	0.2812	0.2198	0.1722	0.1352	0.1064	0.0839	0.0663	0.0525	0.0417	0.0331	0.0264
27	0.7644	0.5859	0.4502	0.3468	0.2678	0.2074	0.1609	0.1252	0.0976	0.0763	0.0597	0.0469	0.0369	0.0291	0.0230
28	0.7568	0.5744	0.4371	0.3335	0.2551	0.1956	0.1504	0.1159	0.0895	0.0693	0.0538	0.0419	0.0326	0.0255	0.0200
29	0.7493	0.5631	0.4243	0.3207	0.2429	0.1846	0.1406	0.1073	0.0822	0.0630	0.0485	0.0374	0.0289	0.0224	0.0174
30	0.7419	0.5521	0.4120	0.3083	0.2314	0.1741	0.1314	0.0994	0.0754	0.0573	0.0437	0.0334	0.0256	0.0196	0.0151

(*Contd*)

(Contd) **Appendix A-2**

6%	17%	18%	19%	20%	21%	22%	23%	24%	25%	26%	27%	28%	29%	30%	40%
0.8621	0.8547	0.8475	0.8403	0.8333	0.8264	0.8197	0.8130	0.8065	0.8000	0.7937	0.7874	0.7813	0.7752	0.7692	0.7143
0.7432	0.7305	0.7182	0.7062	0.6944	0.6830	0.6719	0.6610	0.6504	0.6400	0.6299	0.6200	0.6104	0.6009	0.5917	0.5102
0.6407	0.6244	0.6086	0.5934	0.5787	0.5645	0.5507	0.5374	0.5245	0.5120	0.4999	0.4882	0.4768	0.4658	0.4552	0.3644
0.5523	0.5337	0.5158	0.4987	0.4823	0.4665	0.4514	0.4369	0.4230	0.4096	0.3968	0.3844	0.3725	0.3611	0.3501	0.2603
0.4761	0.4561	0.4371	0.4190	0.4019	0.3855	0.3700	0.3552	0.3411	0.3277	0.3149	0.3027	0.2910	0.2799	0.2693	0.1859
0.4104	0.3898	0.3704	0.3521	0.3349	0.3186	0.3033	0.2888	0.2751	0.2621	0.2499	0.2383	0.2274	0.2170	0.2072	0.1328
0.3538	0.3332	0.3139	0.2959	0.2791	0.2633	0.2486	0.2348	0.2218	0.2097	0.1983	0.1877	0.1776	0.1682	0.1594	0.0949
0.3050	0.2848	0.2660	0.2487	0.2326	0.2176	0.2038	0.1909	0.1789	0.1678	0.1574	0.1478	0.1388	0.1304	0.1226	0.0678
0.2630	0.2434	0.2255	0.2090	0.1938	0.1799	0.1670	0.1552	0.1443	0.1342	0.1249	0.1164	0.1084	0.1011	0.0943	0.0484
0.2267	0.2080	0.1911	0.1756	0.1615	0.1486	0.1369	0.1262	0.1164	0.1074	0.0992	0.0916	0.0847	0.0784	0.0725	0.0346
0.1954	0.1778	0.1619	0.1476	0.1346	0.1228	0.1122	0.1026	0.0938	0.0859	0.0787	0.0721	0.0662	0.0607	0.0558	0.0247
0.1685	0.1520	0.1372	0.1240	0.1122	0.1015	0.0920	0.0834	0.0757	0.0687	0.0625	0.0568	0.0517	0.0471	0.0429	0.0176
0.1452	0.1299	0.1163	0.1042	0.0935	0.0839	0.0754	0.0678	0.0610	0.0550	0.0496	0.0447	0.0404	0.0365	0.0330	0.0126
0.1252	0.1110	0.0985	0.0876	0.0779	0.0693	0.0618	0.0551	0.0492	0.0440	0.0393	0.0352	0.0316	0.0283	0.0254	0.0090
0.1079	0.0949	0.0835	0.0736	0.0649	0.0573	0.0507	0.0448	0.0397	0.0352	0.0312	0.0277	0.0247	0.0219	0.0195	0.0064
0.0930	0.0811	0.0708	0.0618	0.0541	0.0474	0.0415	0.0364	0.0320	0.0281	0.0248	0.0218	0.0193	0.0170	0.0150	0.0046
0.0802	0.0693	0.0600	0.0520	0.0451	0.0391	0.0340	0.0296	0.0258	0.0225	0.0197	0.0172	0.0150	0.0132	0.0116	0.0033
0.0691	0.0592	0.0508	0.0437	0.0376	0.0323	0.0279	0.0241	0.0208	0.0180	0.0156	0.0135	0.0118	0.0102	0.0089	0.0023
0.0596	0.0506	0.0431	0.0367	0.0313	0.0267	0.0229	0.0196	0.0168	0.0144	0.0124	0.0107	0.0092	0.0079	0.0068	0.0017
0.0514	0.0433	0.0365	0.0308	0.0261	0.0221	0.0187	0.0159	0.0135	0.0115	0.0098	0.0084	0.0072	0.0061	0.0053	0.0012
0.0443	0.0370	0.0309	0.0259	0.0217	0.0183	0.0154	0.0129	0.0109	0.0092	0.0078	0.0066	0.0056	0.0048	0.0040	0.0009
0.0382	0.0316	0.0262	0.0218	0.0181	0.0151	0.0126	0.0105	0.0088	0.0074	0.0062	0.0052	0.0044	0.0037	0.0031	0.0006
0.0329	0.0270	0.0222	0.0183	0.0151	0.0125	0.0103	0.0086	0.0071	0.0059	0.0049	0.0041	0.0034	0.0029	0.0024	0.0004
0.0284	0.0231	0.0188	0.0154	0.0126	0.0103	0.0085	0.0070	0.0057	0.0047	0.0039	0.0032	0.0027	0.0022	0.0018	0.0003
0.0245	0.0197	0.0160	0.0129	0.0105	0.0085	0.0069	0.0057	0.0046	0.0038	0.0031	0.0025	0.0021	0.0017	0.0014	0.0002
0.0211	0.0169	0.0135	0.0109	0.0087	0.0070	0.0057	0.0046	0.0037	0.0030	0.0025	0.0020	0.0016	0.0013	0.0011	0.0002
0.0182	0.0144	0.0115	0.0091	0.0073	0.0058	0.0047	0.0037	0.0030	0.0024	0.0019	0.0016	0.0013	0.0010	0.0008	0.0001
0.0157	0.0123	0.0097	0.0077	0.0061	0.0048	0.0038	0.0030	0.0024	0.0019	0.0015	0.0012	0.0010	0.0008	0.0006	0.0001
0.0135	0.0105	0.0082	0.0064	0.0051	0.0040	0.0031	0.0025	0.0020	0.0015	0.0012	0.0010	0.0008	0.0006	0.0005	0.0001
0.0116	0.0090	0.0070	0.0054	0.0042	0.0033	0.0026	0.0020	0.0016	0.0012	0.0010	0.0008	0.0006	0.0005	0.0004	0.0000

APPENDIX A-3

Future Value of Annuity of Re 1 at r% for n Periods

$$FVA(r, n) = \frac{(1+r)^n - 1}{r}$$

Period n / Interest r	1%	2%	3%	4%	5%	6%	7%	8%	9%	10%	11%	12%	13%	14%	15%
1	1.000	1.000	1.000	1.000	1.000	1.000	1.000	1.000	1.000	1.000	1.000	1.000	1.000	1.000	1.000
2	2.010	2.020	2.030	2.040	2.050	2.060	2.070	2.080	2.090	2.100	2.110	2.120	2.130	2.140	2.150
3	3.030	3.060	3.091	3.122	3.153	3.184	3.215	3.246	3.278	3.310	3.342	3.374	3.407	3.440	3.473
4	4.060	4.122	4.184	4.246	4.310	4.375	4.440	4.506	4.573	4.641	4.710	4.779	4.850	4.921	4.993
5	5.101	5.204	5.309	5.416	5.526	5.637	5.751	5.867	5.985	6.105	6.228	6.353	6.480	6.610	6.742
6	6.152	6.308	6.468	6.633	6.802	6.975	7.153	7.336	7.523	7.716	7.913	8.115	8.323	8.536	8.754
7	7.214	7.434	7.662	7.898	8.142	8.394	8.654	8.923	9.200	9.487	9.783	10.089	10.405	10.730	11.067
8	8.286	8.583	8.892	9.214	9.549	9.897	10.260	10.637	11.028	11.436	11.859	12.300	12.757	13.233	13.727
9	9.369	9.755	10.159	10.583	11.027	11.491	11.978	12.488	13.021	13.579	14.164	14.776	15.416	16.085	16.786
10	10.462	10.950	11.464	12.006	12.578	13.181	13.816	14.487	15.193	15.937	16.722	17.549	18.420	19.337	20.304
11	11.567	12.169	12.808	13.486	14.207	14.972	15.784	16.645	17.560	18.531	19.561	20.655	21.814	23.045	24.349
12	12.683	13.412	14.192	15.026	15.917	16.870	17.888	18.977	20.141	21.384	22.713	24.133	25.650	27.271	29.002
13	13.809	14.680	15.618	16.627	17.713	18.882	20.141	21.495	22.953	24.523	26.212	28.029	29.985	32.089	34.352
14	14.947	15.974	17.086	18.292	19.599	21.015	22.550	24.215	26.019	27.975	30.095	32.393	34.883	37.581	40.505
15	16.097	17.293	18.599	20.024	21.579	23.276	25.129	27.152	29.361	31.772	34.405	37.280	40.417	43.842	47.580
16	17.258	18.639	20.157	21.825	23.657	25.673	27.888	30.324	33.003	35.950	39.190	42.753	46.672	50.980	55.717
17	18.430	20.012	21.762	23.698	25.840	28.213	30.840	33.750	36.974	40.545	44.501	48.884	53.739	59.118	65.075
18	19.615	21.412	23.414	25.645	28.132	30.906	33.999	37.450	41.301	45.599	50.396	55.750	61.725	68.394	75.836
19	20.811	22.841	25.117	27.671	30.539	33.760	37.379	41.446	46.018	51.159	56.939	63.440	70.749	78.969	88.212
20	22.019	24.297	26.870	29.778	33.066	36.786	40.995	45.762	51.160	57.275	64.203	72.052	80.947	91.025	102.444
21	23.239	25.783	28.676	31.969	35.719	39.993	44.865	50.423	56.765	64.002	72.265	81.699	92.470	104.768	118.810
22	24.472	27.299	30.537	34.248	38.505	43.392	49.006	55.457	62.873	71.403	81.214	92.503	105.491	120.436	137.632
23	25.716	28.845	32.453	36.618	41.430	46.996	53.436	60.893	69.532	79.543	91.148	104.603	120.205	138.297	159.276
24	26.973	30.422	34.426	39.083	44.502	50.816	58.177	66.765	76.790	88.497	102.174	118.155	136.831	158.659	184.168
25	28.243	32.030	36.459	41.646	47.727	54.865	63.249	73.106	84.701	98.347	114.413	133.334	155.620	181.871	212.793
26	29.526	33.671	38.553	44.312	51.113	59.156	68.676	79.954	93.324	109.182	127.999	150.334	176.850	208.333	245.712
27	30.821	35.344	40.710	47.084	54.669	63.706	74.484	87.351	102.723	121.100	143.079	169.374	200.841	238.499	283.569
28	32.129	37.051	42.931	49.968	58.403	68.528	80.698	95.339	112.968	134.210	159.817	190.699	227.950	272.889	327.104
29	33.450	38.792	45.219	52.966	62.323	73.640	87.347	103.966	124.135	148.631	178.397	214.583	258.583	312.094	377.170
30	34.785	40.568	47.575	56.085	66.439	79.058	94.461	113.283	136.308	164.494	199.021	241.333	293.199	356.787	434.745

(Contd)

(*Contd*) **Appendix A-3**

16%	17%	18%	19%	20%	21%	22%	23%	24%	25%	26%	27%	28%	29%	30%	40%
1.000	1.000	1.000	1.000	1.000	1.000	1.000	1.000	1.000	1.000	1.000	1.000	1.000	1.000	1.000	1.000
2.160	2.170	2.180	2.190	2.200	2.210	2.220	2.230	2.240	2.250	2.260	2.270	2.280	2.290	2.300	2.400
3.506	3.539	3.572	3.606	3.640	3.674	3.708	3.743	3.778	3.813	3.848	3.883	3.918	3.954	3.990	4.360
5.066	5.141	5.215	5.291	5.368	5.446	5.524	5.604	5.684	5.766	5.848	5.931	6.016	6.101	6.187	7.104
6.877	7.014	7.154	7.297	7.442	7.589	7.740	7.893	8.048	8.207	8.368	8.533	8.700	8.870	9.043	10.946
8.977	9.207	9.442	9.683	9.930	10.183	10.442	10.708	10.980	11.259	11.544	11.837	12.136	12.442	12.756	16.324
11.414	11.772	12.142	12.523	12.916	13.321	13.740	14.171	14.615	15.073	15.546	16.032	16.534	17.051	17.583	23.853
14.240	14.773	15.327	15.902	16.499	17.119	17.762	18.430	19.123	19.842	20.588	21.361	22.163	22.995	23.858	34.395
17.519	18.285	19.086	19.923	20.799	21.714	22.670	23.669	24.712	25.802	26.940	28.129	29.369	30.664	32.015	49.153
21.321	22.393	23.521	24.709	25.959	27.274	28.657	30.113	31.643	33.253	34.945	36.723	38.593	40.556	42.619	69.814
25.733	27.200	28.755	30.404	32.150	34.001	35.962	38.039	40.238	42.566	45.031	47.639	50.398	53.318	56.405	98.739
30.850	32.824	34.931	37.180	39.581	42.142	44.874	47.788	50.895	54.208	57.739	61.501	65.510	69.780	74.327	139.235
36.786	39.404	42.219	45.244	48.497	51.991	55.746	59.779	64.110	68.760	73.751	79.107	84.853	91.016	97.625	195.929
43.672	47.103	50.818	54.841	59.196	63.909	69.010	74.528	80.496	86.949	93.926	101.465	109.612	118.411	127.913	275.300
51.660	56.110	60.965	66.261	72.035	78.330	85.192	92.669	100.815	109.687	119.347	129.861	141.303	153.750	167.286	386.420
60.925	66.649	72.939	79.850	87.442	95.780	104.935	114.983	126.011	138.109	151.377	165.924	181.868	199.337	218.472	541.988
71.673	78.979	87.068	96.022	105.931	116.894	129.020	142.430	157.253	173.636	191.735	211.723	233.791	258.145	285.014	759.784
84.141	93.406	103.740	115.266	128.117	142.441	158.405	176.188	195.994	218.045	242.585	269.888	300.252	334.007	371.518	1,064.697
98.603	110.285	123.414	138.166	154.740	173.354	194.254	217.712	244.033	273.556	306.658	343.758	385.323	431.870	483.973	1,491.576
115.380	130.033	146.628	165.418	186.688	210.758	237.989	268.785	303.601	342.945	387.389	437.573	494.213	558.112	630.165	2,089.206
134.841	153.139	174.021	197.847	225.026	256.018	291.347	331.606	377.465	429.681	489.110	556.717	633.593	720.964	820.215	2,925.889
157.415	180.172	206.345	236.438	271.031	310.781	356.443	408.875	469.056	538.101	617.278	708.031	811.999	931.044	1,067.280	4,097.245
183.601	211.801	244.487	282.362	326.237	377.045	435.861	503.917	582.630	673.626	778.771	900.199	1,040.358	1,202.047	1,388.464	5,737.142
213.978	248.808	289.494	337.010	392.484	457.225	532.750	620.817	723.461	843.033	982.251	1,144.253	1,332.659	1,551.640	1,806.003	8,032.999
249.214	292.105	342.603	402.042	471.981	554.242	650.955	764.605	898.092	1,054.791	1,238.636	1,454.201	1,706.803	2,002.616	2,348.803	11,247.199
290.088	342.763	405.272	479.431	567.377	671.633	795.165	941.465	1,114.634	1,319.489	1,561.682	1,847.836	2,185.708	2,584.374	3,054.444	15,747.079
337.502	402.032	479.221	571.522	681.853	813.676	971.102	1,159.002	1,383.146	1,650.361	1,968.719	2,347.751	2,798.706	3,334.843	3,971.778	22,046.910
392.503	471.378	566.481	681.112	819.223	985.548	1,185.744	1,426.572	1,716.101	2,063.952	2,481.586	2,982.644	3,583.344	4,302.947	5,164.311	30,866.674
456.303	552.512	669.447	811.523	984.068	1,193.513	1,447.608	1,755.683	2,128.965	2,580.939	3,127.798	3,788.958	4,587.680	5,551.802	6,714.604	43,214.343
530.312	647.439	790.948	966.712	1,181.882	1,445.151	1,767.081	2,160.491	2,640.916	3,227.174	3,942.026	4,812.977	5,873.231	7,162.824	8,729.985	60,501.081

APPENDIX A-4

Present Value of Annuity at r% for n Periods

$$PVA(r, n) = \frac{1 - \frac{1}{(1+r)^n}}{r}$$

Period n / Interest r	1%	2%	3%	4%	5%	6%	7%	8%	9%	10%	11%	12%	13%	14%	15%
1	0.9901	0.9804	0.9709	0.9615	0.9524	0.9434	0.9346	0.9259	0.9174	0.9091	0.9009	0.8929	0.8850	0.8772	0.8696
2	1.9704	1.9416	1.9135	1.8861	1.8594	1.8334	1.8080	1.7833	1.7591	1.7355	1.7125	1.6901	1.6681	1.6467	1.6257
3	2.9410	2.8839	2.8286	2.7751	2.7232	2.6730	2.6243	2.5771	2.5313	2.4869	2.4437	2.4018	2.3612	2.3216	2.2832
4	3.9020	3.8077	3.7171	3.6299	3.5460	3.4651	3.3872	3.3121	3.2397	3.1699	3.1024	3.0373	2.9745	2.9137	2.8550
5	4.8534	4.7135	4.5797	4.4518	4.3295	4.2124	4.1002	3.9927	3.8897	3.7908	3.6959	3.6048	3.5172	3.4331	3.3522
6	5.7955	5.6014	5.4172	5.2421	5.0757	4.9173	4.7665	4.6229	4.4859	4.3553	4.2305	4.1114	3.9975	3.8887	3.7845
7	6.7282	6.4720	6.2303	6.0021	5.7864	5.5824	5.3893	5.2064	5.0330	4.8684	4.7122	4.5638	4.4226	4.2883	4.1604
8	7.6517	7.3255	7.0197	6.7327	6.4632	6.2098	5.9713	5.7466	5.5348	5.3349	5.1461	4.9676	4.7988	4.6389	4.4873
9	8.5660	8.1622	7.7861	7.4353	7.1078	6.8017	6.5152	6.2469	5.9952	5.7590	5.5370	5.3282	5.1317	4.9464	4.7716
10	9.4713	8.9826	8.5302	8.1109	7.7217	7.3601	7.0236	6.7101	6.4177	6.1446	5.8892	5.6502	5.4262	5.2161	5.0188
11	10.3676	9.7868	9.2526	8.7605	8.3064	7.8869	7.4987	7.1390	6.8052	6.4951	6.2065	5.9377	5.6869	5.4527	5.2337
12	11.2551	10.5753	9.9540	9.3851	8.8633	8.3838	7.9427	7.5361	7.1607	6.8137	6.4924	6.1944	5.9176	5.6603	5.4206
13	12.1337	11.3484	10.6350	9.9856	9.3936	8.8527	8.3577	7.9038	7.4869	7.1034	6.7499	6.4235	6.1218	5.8424	5.5831
14	13.0037	12.1062	11.2961	10.5631	9.8986	9.2950	8.7455	8.2442	7.7862	7.3667	6.9819	6.6282	6.3025	6.0021	5.7245
15	13.8651	12.8493	11.9379	11.1184	10.3797	9.7122	9.1079	8.5595	8.0607	7.6061	7.1909	6.8109	6.4624	6.1422	5.8474
16	14.7179	13.5777	12.5611	11.6523	10.8378	10.1059	9.4466	8.8514	8.3126	7.8237	7.3792	6.9740	6.6039	6.2651	5.9542
17	15.5623	14.2919	13.1661	12.1657	11.2741	10.4773	9.7632	9.1216	8.5436	8.0216	7.5488	7.1196	6.7291	6.3729	6.0472
18	16.3983	14.9920	13.7535	12.6593	11.6896	10.8276	10.0591	9.3719	8.7556	8.2014	7.7016	7.2497	6.8399	6.4674	6.1280
19	17.2260	15.6785	14.3238	13.1339	12.0853	11.1581	10.3356	9.6036	8.9501	8.3649	7.8393	7.3658	6.9380	6.5504	6.1982
20	18.0456	16.3514	14.8775	13.5903	12.4622	11.4699	10.5940	9.8181	9.1285	8.5136	7.9633	7.4694	7.0248	6.6231	6.2593
21	18.8570	17.0112	15.4150	14.0292	12.8212	11.7641	10.8355	10.0168	9.2922	8.6487	8.0751	7.5620	7.1016	6.6870	6.3125
22	19.6604	17.6580	15.9369	14.4511	13.1630	12.0416	11.0612	10.2007	9.4424	8.7715	8.1757	7.6446	7.1695	6.7429	6.3587
23	20.4558	18.2922	16.4436	14.8568	13.4886	12.3034	11.2722	10.3711	9.5802	8.8832	8.2664	7.7184	7.2297	6.7921	6.3988
24	21.2434	18.9139	16.9355	15.2470	13.7986	12.5504	11.4693	10.5288	9.7066	8.9847	8.3481	7.7843	7.2829	6.8351	6.4338
25	22.0232	19.5235	17.4131	15.6221	14.0939	12.7834	11.6536	10.6748	9.8226	9.0770	8.4217	7.8431	7.3300	6.8729	6.4641
26	22.7952	20.1210	17.8768	15.9828	14.3752	13.0032	11.8258	10.8100	9.9290	9.1609	8.4881	7.8957	7.3717	6.9061	6.4906
27	23.5596	20.7069	18.3270	16.3296	14.6430	13.2105	11.9867	10.9352	10.0266	9.2372	8.5478	7.9426	7.4086	6.9352	6.5135
28	24.3164	21.2813	18.7641	16.6631	14.8981	13.4062	12.1371	11.0511	10.1161	9.3066	8.6016	7.9844	7.4412	6.9607	6.5335
29	25.0658	21.8444	19.1885	16.9837	15.1411	13.5907	12.2777	11.1584	10.1983	9.3696	8.6501	8.0218	7.4701	6.9830	6.5509
30	25.8077	22.3965	19.6004	17.2920	15.3725	13.7648	12.4090	11.2578	10.2737	9.4269	8.6938	8.0552	7.4957	7.0027	6.5660

(Contd)

(*Contd*) **Appendix A-4**

16%	17%	18%	19%	20%	21%	22%	23%	24%	25%	26%	27%	28%	29%	30%	40%
0.8621	0.8547	0.8475	0.8403	0.8333	0.8264	0.8197	0.8130	0.8065	0.8000	0.7937	0.7874	0.7813	0.7752	0.7692	0.714
1.6052	1.5852	1.5656	1.5465	1.5278	1.5095	1.4915	1.4740	1.4568	1.4400	1.4235	1.4074	1.3916	1.3761	1.3609	1.224
2.2459	2.2096	2.1743	2.1399	2.1065	2.0739	2.0422	2.0114	1.9813	1.9520	1.9234	1.8956	1.8684	1.8420	1.8161	1.589
2.7982	2.7432	2.6901	2.6386	2.5887	2.5404	2.4936	2.4483	2.4043	2.3616	2.3202	2.2800	2.2410	2.2031	2.1662	1.849
3.2743	3.1993	3.1272	3.0576	2.9906	2.9260	2.8636	2.8035	2.7454	2.6893	2.6351	2.5827	2.5320	2.4830	2.4356	2.035
3.6847	3.5892	3.4976	3.4098	3.3255	3.2446	3.1669	3.0923	3.0205	2.9514	2.8850	2.8210	2.7594	2.7000	2.6427	2.168
4.0386	3.9224	3.8115	3.7057	3.6046	3.5079	3.4155	3.3270	3.2423	3.1611	3.0833	3.0087	2.9370	2.8682	2.8021	2.263
4.3436	4.2072	4.0776	3.9544	3.8372	3.7256	3.6193	3.5179	3.4212	3.3289	3.2407	3.1564	3.0758	2.9986	2.9247	2.331
4.6065	4.4506	4.3030	4.1633	4.0310	3.9054	3.7863	3.6731	3.5655	3.4631	3.3657	3.2728	3.1842	3.0997	3.0190	2.379
4.8332	4.6586	4.4941	4.3389	4.1925	4.0541	3.9232	3.7993	3.6819	3.5705	3.4648	3.3644	3.2689	3.1781	3.0915	2.414
5.0286	4.8364	4.6560	4.4865	4.3271	4.1769	4.0354	3.9018	3.7757	3.6564	3.5435	3.4365	3.3351	3.2388	3.1473	2.438
5.1971	4.9884	4.7932	4.6105	4.4392	4.2784	4.1274	3.9852	3.8514	3.7251	3.6059	3.4933	3.3868	3.2859	3.1903	2.456
5.3423	5.1183	4.9095	4.7147	4.5327	4.3624	4.2028	4.0530	3.9124	3.7801	3.6555	3.5381	3.4272	3.3224	3.2233	2.469
5.4675	5.2293	5.0081	4.8023	4.6106	4.4317	4.2646	4.1082	3.9616	3.8241	3.6949	3.5733	3.4587	3.3507	3.2487	2.478
5.5755	5.3242	5.0916	4.8759	4.6755	4.4890	4.3152	4.1530	4.0013	3.8593	3.7261	3.6010	3.4834	3.3726	3.2682	2.484
5.6685	5.4053	5.1624	4.9377	4.7296	4.5364	4.3567	4.1894	4.0333	3.8874	3.7509	3.6228	3.5026	3.3896	3.2832	2.489
5.7487	5.4746	5.2223	4.9897	4.7746	4.5755	4.3903	4.2190	4.0591	3.9099	3.7705	3.6400	3.5177	3.4028	3.2948	2.492
5.8178	5.5339	5.2732	5.0333	4.8122	4.6079	4.4187	4.2431	4.0799	3.9279	3.7861	3.6536	3.5294	3.4130	3.3037	2.494
5.8775	5.5845	5.3162	5.0700	4.8435	4.6346	4.4415	4.2627	4.0967	3.9424	3.7985	3.6642	3.5386	3.4210	3.3105	2.496
5.9288	5.6278	5.3527	5.1009	4.8696	4.6567	4.4603	4.2786	4.1103	3.9539	3.8083	3.6726	3.5458	3.4271	3.3158	2.497
5.9731	5.6648	5.3837	5.1268	4.8913	4.6750	4.4756	4.2916	4.1212	3.9631	3.8161	3.6792	3.5514	3.4319	3.3198	2.498
6.0113	5.6964	5.4099	5.1486	4.9094	4.6900	4.4832	4.3021	4.1300	3.9705	3.8223	3.6844	3.5558	3.4356	3.3230	2.498
6.0442	5.7234	5.4321	5.1668	4.9245	4.7025	4.4985	4.3106	4.1371	3.9764	3.8273	3.6885	3.5592	3.4384	3.3254	2.499
6.0726	5.7465	5.4509	5.1822	4.9371	4.7128	4.5070	4.3176	4.1428	3.9811	3.8312	3.6918	3.5619	3.4406	3.3272	2.499
6.0971	5.7662	5.4669	5.1951	4.9476	4.7213	4.5139	4.3232	4.1474	3.9849	3.8342	3.6943	3.5640	3.4423	3.3286	2.499
6.1182	5.7831	5.4804	5.2060	4.9563	4.7284	4.5196	4.3278	4.1511	3.9879	3.8367	3.6963	3.5656	3.4437	3.3297	2.500
6.1364	5.7975	5.4919	5.2151	4.9636	4.7342	4.5243	4.3316	4.1542	3.9903	3.8387	3.6979	3.5669	3.4447	3.3305	2.500
6.1520	5.8099	5.5016	5.2228	4.9697	4.7390	4.5281	4.3346	4.1566	3.9923	3.8402	3.6991	3.5679	3.4455	3.3312	2.500
6.1656	5.8204	5.5098	5.2292	4.9747	4.7430	4.5312	4.3371	4.1585	3.9938	3.8414	3.7001	3.5687	3.4461	3.3317	2.500
6.1772	5.8294	5.5168	5.2347	4.9789	4.7463	4.5338	4.3391	4.1601	3.9950	3.8424	3.7009	3.5693	3.4466	3.3321	2.500

APPENDIX A-5

EMI Payable in Advance at *r*% for *n* Years (Rupees per '000s)

Year	1%	2%	3%	4%	5%	6%	7%	8%	9%	10%	11%	12%	13%	14%	15%
1	83.7156	84.0987	84.4825	84.8670	85.2523	85.6382	86.0249	86.4123	86.8005	87.1893	87.5789	87.9691	88.3600	88.7517	89.1440
2	42.0670	42.4695	42.8740	43.2807	43.6894	44.1001	44.5129	44.9278	45.3447	45.7636	46.1845	46.6074	47.0323	47.4592	47.8880
3	28.1846	28.5949	29.0087	29.4259	29.8465	30.2706	30.6980	31.1288	31.5630	32.0005	32.4413	32.8855	33.3328	33.7835	34.2374
4	21.2438	21.6590	22.0791	22.5040	22.9337	23.3682	23.8074	24.2512	24.6998	25.1530	25.6108	26.0731	26.5400	27.0113	27.4872
5	17.0795	17.4986	17.9239	18.3553	18.7929	19.2366	19.6864	20.1421	20.6038	21.0714	21.5449	22.0242	22.5092	22.9999	23.4962
6	14.3036	14.7259	15.1558	15.5932	16.0381	16.4904	16.9501	17.4171	17.8914	18.3727	18.8612	19.3566	19.8590	20.3681	20.8840
7	12.3210	12.7462	13.1803	13.6234	14.0753	14.5359	15.0051	15.4830	15.9693	16.4640	16.9669	17.4780	17.9970	18.5239	19.0585
8	10.8342	11.2621	11.7003	12.1488	12.6074	13.0760	13.5546	14.0431	14.5411	15.0488	15.5657	16.0919	16.6271	17.1712	17.7239
9	9.6780	10.1084	10.5506	11.0043	11.4695	11.9460	12.4337	12.9325	13.4421	13.9623	14.4930	15.0339	15.5848	16.1453	16.7154
10	8.7531	9.1860	9.6320	10.0909	10.5625	11.0468	11.5435	12.0524	12.5733	13.1059	13.6499	14.2050	14.7711	15.3476	15.9343
11	7.9966	8.4319	8.8816	9.3455	9.8236	10.3155	10.8210	11.3398	11.8718	12.4164	12.9734	13.5425	14.1231	14.7150	15.3177
12	7.3662	7.8038	8.2572	8.7262	9.2105	9.7100	10.2242	10.7528	11.2956	11.8520	12.4217	13.0041	13.5989	14.2055	14.8235
13	6.8329	7.2728	7.7299	8.2038	8.6944	9.2012	9.7240	10.2623	10.8157	11.3836	11.9656	12.5611	13.1694	13.7901	14.4226
14	6.3759	6.8181	7.2788	7.7576	8.2543	8.7685	9.2998	9.8475	10.4113	10.9904	11.5844	12.1924	12.8138	13.4480	14.0942
15	5.9800	6.4244	6.8886	7.3723	7.8751	8.3966	8.9362	9.4932	10.0672	10.6572	11.2627	11.8829	12.5168	13.1638	13.8231
16	5.6336	6.0802	6.5480	7.0365	7.5454	8.0740	8.6218	9.1880	9.7719	10.3726	10.9893	11.6210	12.2670	12.9262	13.5977
17	5.3280	5.7768	6.2481	6.7415	7.2563	7.7920	8.3479	8.9231	9.5167	10.1277	10.7552	11.3982	12.0555	12.7263	13.4094
18	5.0565	5.5075	5.9823	6.4804	7.0012	7.5439	8.1077	8.6917	9.2947	9.9158	10.5538	11.2074	11.8757	12.5573	13.2513
19	4.8136	5.2668	5.7450	6.2479	6.7746	7.3242	7.8959	8.4884	9.1007	9.7315	10.3795	11.0434	11.7220	12.4139	13.1180
20	4.5951	5.0504	5.5321	6.0397	6.5722	7.1287	7.7080	8.3090	8.9303	9.5705	10.2281	10.9018	11.5902	12.2918	13.0053
21	4.3975	4.8549	5.3401	5.8523	6.3906	6.9538	7.5407	8.1499	8.7800	9.4292	10.0962	10.7792	11.4768	12.1875	12.9098
22	4.2179	4.6774	5.1660	5.6829	6.2269	6.7968	7.3911	8.0084	8.6469	9.3049	9.9807	10.6727	11.3790	12.0981	12.8286
23	4.0539	4.5156	5.0076	5.5291	6.0787	6.6552	7.2569	7.8820	8.5287	9.1952	9.8795	10.5799	11.2944	12.0215	12.7595
24	3.9037	4.3675	4.8629	5.3889	5.9442	6.5271	7.1360	7.7687	8.4235	9.0981	9.7905	10.4988	11.2211	11.9556	12.7005
25	3.7656	4.2315	4.7303	5.2608	5.8216	6.4110	7.0268	7.6670	8.3295	9.0119	9.7121	10.4280	11.1575	11.8988	12.6502
26	3.6381	4.1061	4.6083	5.1433	5.7096	6.3052	6.9280	7.5755	8.2454	8.9353	9.6429	10.3659	11.1022	11.8498	12.6071
27	3.5202	3.9903	4.4958	5.0353	5.6070	6.2088	6.8383	7.4928	8.1700	8.3671	9.5817	10.3114	11.0540	11.8076	12.5702
28	3.4107	3.8828	4.3917	4.9357	5.5128	6.1206	6.7567	7.4181	8.1022	8.8062	9.5275	10.2635	11.0120	11.7710	12.5387
29	3.3088	3.7830	4.2952	4.8436	5.4260	6.0398	6.6823	7.3505	8.0413	8.7518	9.4794	10.2214	10.9754	11.7394	12.5116
30	3.2137	3.6900	4.2055	4.7583	5.3459	5.9657	6.6144	7.2891	7.9863	8.7032	9.4367	10.1843	10.9434	11.7121	12.4883

(*Contd*)

(*Contd*) **Appendix A-5**

16%	17%	18%	19%	20%	21%	22%	23%	24%	25%	26%	27%	28%	29%	30%	40%
89.5370	89.9307	90.3251	90.7202	91.1159	91.5123	91.9094	92.3071	92.7055	93.1045	93.5042	93.9045	94.3055	94.7071	95.1094	99.1660
48.3189	48.7516	49.1863	49.6229	50.0614	50.5019	50.9442	51.3884	51.8344	52.2823	52.7320	53.1836	53.6370	54.0921	54.5491	59.2139
34.6944	35.1547	35.6181	36.0847	36.5543	37.0271	37.5029	37.9817	38.4636	38.9484	39.4362	39.9269	40.4204	40.9169	41.4162	46.5582
27.9674	28.4520	28.9409	29.4341	29.9315	30.4331	30.9389	31.4487	31.9626	32.4805	33.0023	33.5279	34.0575	34.5908	35.1278	40.6905
23.9981	24.5054	25.0182	25.5362	26.0596	26.5881	27.1217	27.6603	28.2039	28.7523	29.3055	29.8634	30.4259	30.9929	31.5643	37.5016
21.4064	21.9354	22.4707	23.0124	23.5602	24.1140	24.6738	25.2394	25.8106	26.3874	26.9697	27.5572	28.1500	28.7477	29.3504	35.6182
19.6007	20.1503	20.7072	21.2712	21.8422	22.4199	23.0042	23.5950	24.1920	24.7951	25.4041	26.0188	26.6391	27.2647	27.8956	34.4509
18.2850	18.8544	19.4317	20.0169	20.6097	21.2098	21.8171	22.4313	23.0521	23.6793	24.3128	24.9522	25.5974	26.2481	26.9040	33.7056
17.2947	17.8828	18.4797	19.0849	19.6982	20.3193	20.9479	21.5836	22.2263	22.8756	23.5312	24.1929	24.8603	25.5332	26.2112	33.2207
16.5309	17.1370	17.7522	18.3763	19.0088	19.6493	20.2976	20.9532	21.6158	22.2850	22.9606	23.6420	24.3291	25.0215	25.7188	32.9013
15.9308	16.5538	17.1864	17.8280	18.4784	19.1369	19.8032	20.4769	21.1575	21.8447	22.5379	23.2369	23.9413	24.6506	25.3645	32.6893
15.4522	16.0913	16.7401	17.3982	18.0650	18.7401	19.4228	20.1129	20.8097	21.5127	22.2217	22.9360	23.6553	24.3792	25.1073	32.5477
15.0662	15.7202	16.3842	17.0575	17.7396	18.4297	19.1274	19.8321	20.5433	21.2605	21.9832	22.7108	23.4430	24.1794	24.9194	32.4529
14.7518	15.4199	16.0980	16.7854	17.4813	18.1851	18.8963	19.6141	20.3381	21.0676	21.8022	22.5414	23.2846	24.0314	24.7816	32.3893
14.4938	15.1751	15.8662	16.5665	17.2750	17.9913	18.7145	19.4440	20.1792	20.9195	21.6644	22.4133	23.1659	23.9216	24.6800	32.3465
14.2807	14.9742	15.6774	16.3894	17.1095	17.8369	18.5708	19.3105	20.0556	20.8052	21.5589	22.3163	23.0767	23.8397	24.6050	32.3177
14.1038	14.8086	15.5229	16.2457	16.9761	17.7134	18.4568	19.2056	19.9592	20.7169	21.4781	22.2425	23.0095	23.7786	24.5496	32.2983
13.9564	14.6716	15.3960	16.1285	16.8682	17.6144	18.3662	19.1229	19.8838	20.6484	21.4161	22.1864	22.9588	23.7330	24.5085	32.2852
13.8330	14.5578	15.2914	16.0327	16.7808	17.5348	18.2939	19.0575	19.8248	20.5953	21.3683	22.1436	22.9205	23.6988	24.4781	32.2763
13.7295	14.4631	15.2050	15.9542	16.7098	17.4707	18.2363	19.0058	19.7785	20.5540	21.3316	22.1109	22.8916	23.6732	24.4555	32.2704
13.6424	14.3840	15.1335	15.8898	16.6519	17.4190	18.1902	18.9648	19.7422	20.5218	21.3032	22.0860	22.8697	23.6540	24.4387	32.2664
13.5690	14.3179	15.0743	15.8369	16.6048	17.3772	18.1532	18.9322	19.7136	20.4968	21.2814	22.0669	22.8531	23.6397	24.4263	32.2637
13.5070	14.2626	15.0250	15.7933	16.5664	17.3434	18.1237	18.9064	19.6911	20.4773	21.2645	22.0524	22.8406	23.6289	24.4170	32.2619
13.4545	14.2161	14.9841	15.7574	16.5350	17.3161	18.1000	18.8859	19.6735	20.4621	21.2515	22.0412	22.8311	23.6208	24.4102	32.2606
13.4101	14.1771	14.9500	15.7278	16.5094	17.2940	18.0809	18.8696	19.6595	20.4503	21.2414	22.0327	22.8239	23.6147	24.4050	32.2593
13.3724	14.1444	14.9217	15.7033	16.4884	17.2761	18.0657	18.8567	19.6486	20.4410	21.2336	22.0262	22.8184	23.6101	24.4012	32.2592
13.3405	14.1168	14.8980	15.6831	16.4712	17.2615	18.0534	18.8464	19.6400	20.4338	21.2276	22.0212	22.8143	23.6067	24.3984	32.2588
13.3133	14.0936	14.8783	15.6665	16.4572	17.2497	18.0436	18.8382	19.6332	20.4282	21.2230	22.0174	22.8111	23.6042	24.3963	32.2586
13.2902	14.0741	14.8619	15.6527	16.4457	17.2402	18.0357	18.8317	19.6278	20.4238	21.2194	22.0144	22.8088	23.6022	24.3948	32.2584
13.2706	14.0576	14.8481	15.6413	16.4362	17.2324	18.0293	18.8265	19.6236	20.4204	21.2166	22.0122	22.8070	23.6008	24.3936	32.2583

APPENDIX A-6

EMI Payable in Arrears at r% for n Years (Rupees per '000s)

Principal Amount = 1000

Year	1%	2%	3%	4%	5%	6%	7%	8%	9%	10%	11%	12%	13%	14%	15%
1	83.7854	84.2389	84.6937	85.1499	85.6075	86.0664	86.5267	86.9884	87.4515	87.9159	88.3817	88.8488	89.3173	89.7871	90.2583
2	42.1021	42.5403	42.9812	43.4249	43.8714	44.3206	44.7726	45.2273	45.6847	46.1449	46.6078	47.0735	47.5418	48.0129	48.4866
3	28.2081	28.6426	29.0812	29.5240	29.9709	30.4219	30.8771	31.3364	31.7997	32.2672	32.7387	33.2143	33.6940	34.1776	34.6653
4	21.2615	21.6951	22.1343	22.5791	23.0293	23.4850	23.9462	24.4129	24.8850	25.3626	25.8455	26.3338	26.8275	27.3265	27.8307
5	17.0937	17.5278	17.9687	18.4165	18.8712	19.3328	19.8012	20.2764	20.7584	21.2470	21.7424	22.2444	22.7531	23.2683	23.7899
6	14.3155	14.7504	15.1937	15.6452	16.1049	16.5729	17.0490	17.5332	18.0255	18.5258	19.0341	19.5502	20.0741	20.6057	21.1450
7	12.3312	12.7674	13.2133	13.6688	14.1339	14.6086	15.0927	15.5862	16.0891	16.6012	17.1224	17.6527	18.1920	18.7400	19.2968
8	10.8432	11.2809	11.7296	12.1893	12.6599	13.1414	13.6337	14.1367	14.6502	15.1742	15.7084	16.2528	16.8073	17.3715	17.9454
9	9.6860	10.1253	10.5769	11.0410	11.5173	12.0057	12.5063	13.0187	13.5429	14.0787	14.6259	15.1842	15.7536	16.3337	16.9243
10	8.7604	9.2013	9.6561	10.1245	10.6066	11.1021	11.6108	12.1328	12.6676	13.2151	13.7750	14.3471	14.9311	15.5266	16.1335
11	8.0032	8.4459	8.9038	9.3767	9.8645	10.3670	10.8841	11.4154	11.9608	12.5199	13.0923	13.6779	14.2761	14.8867	15.5091
12	7.3723	7.8168	8.2779	8.7553	9.2489	9.7585	10.2838	10.8245	11.3803	11.9508	12.5356	13.1342	13.7463	14.3713	15.0088
13	6.8386	7.2850	7.7492	8.2312	8.7306	9.2472	9.7807	10.3307	10.8968	11.4785	12.0753	12.6867	13.3121	13.9510	14.6029
14	6.3812	6.8295	7.2970	7.7835	8.2887	8.8124	9.3540	9.9132	10.4894	11.0820	11.6905	12.3143	12.9526	13.6049	14.2704
15	5.9849	6.4351	6.9058	7.3969	7.9079	8.4386	8.9883	9.5565	10.1427	10.7461	11.3660	12.0017	12.6524	13.3174	13.9959
16	5.6383	6.0903	6.5643	7.0600	7.5768	8.1144	8.6721	9.2493	9.8452	10.4590	11.0900	11.7373	12.3999	13.0770	13.7677
17	5.3325	5.7865	6.2637	6.7639	7.2866	7.8310	8.3966	8.9826	9.5880	10.2121	10.8538	11.5122	12.1861	12.8748	13.5770
18	5.0607	5.5167	5.9972	6.5020	7.0303	7.5816	8.1550	8.7496	9.3644	9.9984	10.6505	11.3195	12.0043	12.7038	13.4169
19	4.8176	5.2756	5.7594	6.2687	6.8028	7.3608	7.9419	8.5450	9.1690	9.8126	10.4746	11.1539	11.8490	12.5588	13.2820
20	4.5989	5.0588	5.5460	6.0598	6.5996	7.1643	7.7530	8.3644	8.9973	9.6502	10.3219	11.0109	11.7158	12.4352	13.1679
21	4.4011	4.8630	5.3534	5.8718	6.4172	6.9886	7.5847	8.2043	8.8458	9.5078	10.1887	10.8870	11.6011	12.3297	13.0712
22	4.2214	4.6852	5.1790	5.7018	6.2528	6.8307	7.4342	8.0618	8.7117	9.3825	10.0722	10.7794	11.5023	12.2393	12.9890
23	4.0573	4.5232	5.0202	5.5475	6.1041	6.6885	7.2992	7.9345	8.5927	9.2718	9.9701	10.6856	11.4168	12.1617	12.9190
24	3.9070	4.3748	4.8751	5.4069	5.9690	6.5598	7.1776	7.8205	8.4866	9.1739	9.8803	10.6038	11.3427	12.0950	12.8593
25	3.7687	4.2385	4.7421	5.2784	5.8459	6.4430	7.0678	7.7182	8.3920	9.0870	9.8011	10.5322	11.2784	12.0376	12.8083
26	3.6412	4.1130	4.6198	5.1605	5.7334	6.3368	6.9684	7.6260	8.3072	9.0098	9.7313	10.4695	11.2224	11.9881	12.7647
27	3.5231	3.9969	4.5070	5.0521	5.6304	6.2399	6.8781	7.5428	8.2313	8.9410	9.6695	10.4145	11.1738	11.9453	12.7274
28	3.4135	3.8893	4.4027	4.9521	5.5357	6.1512	6.7961	7.4676	8.1630	8.8796	9.6148	10.3661	11.1313	11.9084	12.6954
29	3.3115	3.7893	4.3059	4.8597	5.4486	6.0700	6.7213	7.3995	8.1016	8.8248	9.5663	10.3236	11.0943	11.8764	12.6680
30	3.2164	3.6962	4.2160	4.7742	5.3682	5.9955	6.6530	7.3376	8.0462	8.7757	9.5232	10.2861	11.0620	11.8487	12.6444

(*Contd*)

(*Contd*) **Appendix A-6**

16%	17%	18%	19%	20%	21%	22%	23%	24%	25%	26%	27%	28%	29%	30%	40%
90.7309	91.2048	91.6800	92.1566	92.6345	93.1138	93.5944	94.0763	94.5596	95.0442	95.5301	96.0174	96.5060	96.9959	97.4871	102.4715
48.9631	49.4423	49.9241	50.4086	50.8958	51.3857	51.8782	52.3733	52.8711	53.3715	53.8746	54.3802	54.8885	55.3994	55.9128	61.1877
35.1570	35.6527	36.1524	36.6560	37.1636	37.6751	38.1905	38.7097	39.2329	39.7598	40.2906	40.8252	41.3636	41.9057	42.4516	48.1102
28.3403	28.8550	29.3750	29.9001	30.4304	30.9657	31.5061	32.0515	32.6018	33.1571	33.7173	34.2823	34.8521	35.4267	36.0060	42.0468
24.3181	24.8526	25.3934	25.9406	26.4939	27.0534	27.6189	28.1905	28.7680	29.3513	29.9405	30.5353	31.1358	31.7419	32.3534	38.7516
21.6918	22.2461	22.8078	23.3767	23.9528	24.5360	25.1261	25.7231	26.3268	26.9372	27.5540	28.1773	28.8068	29.4425	30.0842	36.8055
19.8621	20.4358	21.0178	21.6080	22.2062	22.8122	23.4259	24.0472	24.6758	25.3116	25.9545	26.6042	27.2607	27.9236	28.5930	35.5993
18.5288	19.1215	19.7232	20.3339	20.9532	21.5810	22.2171	22.8612	23.5131	24.1727	24.8396	25.5137	26.1947	26.8824	27.5766	34.8291
17.5253	18.1362	18.7569	19.3871	20.0265	20.6749	21.3319	21.9973	22.6708	23.3522	24.0411	24.7372	25.4404	26.1502	26.8665	34.3280
16.7513	17.3798	18.0185	18.6672	19.3256	19.9932	20.6697	21.3548	22.0481	22.7493	23.4580	24.1740	24.8968	25.6262	26.3618	33.9980
16.1432	16.7883	17.4442	18.1103	18.7863	19.4718	20.1663	20.8694	21.5807	22.2998	23.0262	23.7597	24.4999	25.2463	25.9986	33.7789
15.6583	16.3192	16.9912	17.6736	18.3661	19.0680	19.7789	20.4984	21.2259	21.9609	22.7031	23.4521	24.2073	24.9684	25.7350	33.6327
15.2670	15.9430	16.6300	17.3276	18.0352	18.7522	19.4781	20.2123	20.9542	21.7034	22.4595	23.2218	23.9900	24.7637	25.5424	33.5347
14.9485	15.6384	16.3395	17.0511	17.7727	18.5034	19.2427	19.9901	20.7449	21.5066	22.2746	23.0485	23.8279	24.6122	25.4011	33.4689
14.6870	15.3900	16.1042	16.8288	17.5630	18.3061	19.0576	19.8166	20.5827	21.3553	22.1338	22.9176	23.7064	24.4997	25.2970	33.4247
14.4711	15.1863	15.9126	16.6489	17.3947	18.1490	18.9112	19.6807	20.4567	21.2387	22.0261	22.8184	23.6151	24.4158	25.2202	33.3949
14.2919	15.0184	15.7557	16.5029	17.2590	18.0234	18.7952	19.5737	20.3584	21.1485	21.9435	22.7430	23.5464	24.3533	25.1633	33.3749
14.1425	14.8795	15.6269	16.3838	17.1494	17.9226	18.7029	19.4894	20.2815	21.0786	21.8801	22.6856	23.4945	24.3065	25.1213	33.3613
14.0175	14.7641	15.5208	16.2866	17.0605	17.8417	18.6293	19.4228	20.2213	21.0243	21.8313	22.6418	23.4553	24.2715	25.0900	33.3522
13.9126	14.6680	15.4331	16.2068	16.9882	17.7764	18.5706	19.3700	20.1741	20.9822	21.7938	22.6084	23.4257	24.2453	25.0669	33.3461
13.8243	14.5878	15.3605	16.1414	16.9295	17.7238	18.5236	19.3283	20.1370	20.9494	21.7648	22.5829	23.4033	24.2257	25.0497	33.3419
13.7499	14.5208	15.3004	16.0876	16.8816	17.6813	18.4861	19.2951	20.1079	20.9238	21.7425	22.5634	23.3864	24.2109	25.0369	33.3391
13.6871	14.4646	15.2504	16.0434	16.8425	17.6470	18.4559	19.2688	20.0850	20.9039	21.7252	22.5485	23.3735	24.1999	25.0275	33.3372
13.6339	14.4175	15.2089	16.0069	16.8106	17.6191	18.4318	19.2479	20.0669	20.8884	21.7119	22.5371	23.3638	24.1916	25.0204	33.3360
13.5889	14.3730	15.1743	15.9768	16.7845	17.5966	18.4124	19.2313	20.0527	20.8763	21.7016	22.5284	23.3564	24.1854	25.0152	33.3351
13.5507	14.3447	15.1455	15.9520	16.7632	17.5784	18.3969	19.2181	20.0416	20.8669	21.6937	22.5218	23.3508	24.1807	25.0113	33.3345
13.5183	14.3168	15.1215	15.9315	16.7457	17.5636	18.3844	19.2076	20.0328	20.8595	21.6876	22.5167	23.3466	24.1772	25.0084	33.3341
13.4908	14.2933	15.1015	15.9145	16.7315	17.5516	18.3744	19.1992	20.0258	20.8538	21.6828	22.5128	23.3434	24.1746	25.0062	33.3339
13.4674	14.2734	15.0848	15.9005	16.7198	17.5419	18.3663	19.1926	20.0204	20.8493	21.6792	22.5098	23.3410	24.1726	25.0046	33.3337
13.4476	14.2568	15.0709	15.8889	16.7102	17.5340	18.3598	19.1873	20.0160	20.8458	21.6763	22.5075	23.3391	24.1711	25.0034	33.3336

APPENDIX A-7 (IST PART)

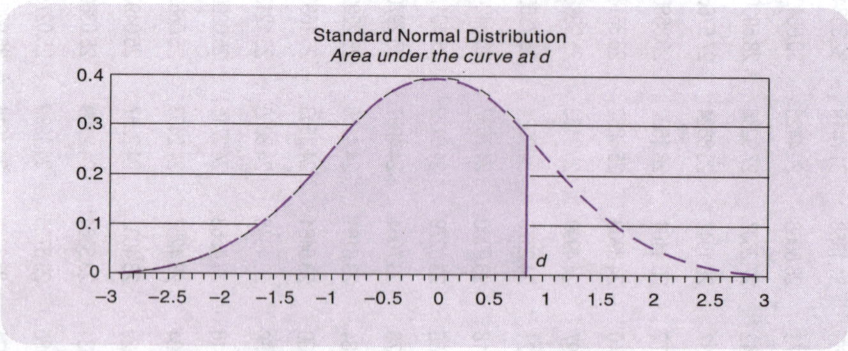

Area Under the Normal Distribution Curve (for positive values)

d	0.00	0.01	0.02	0.03	0.04	0.05	0.06	0.07	0.08	0.09
0.0	0.5000	0.5040	0.5080	0.5120	0.5160	0.5199	0.5239	0.5279	0.5319	0.5359
0.1	0.5398	0.5438	0.5478	0.5517	0.5557	0.5596	0.5636	0.5675	0.5714	0.5753
0.2	0.5793	0.5832	0.5871	0.5910	0.5948	0.5987	0.6026	0.6064	0.6103	0.6141
0.3	0.6179	0.6217	0.6255	0.6293	0.6331	0.6368	0.6406	0.6443	0.6480	0.6517
0.4	0.6554	0.6591	0.6628	0.6664	0.6700	0.6736	0.6772	0.6808	0.6844	0.6879
0.5	0.6915	0.6950	0.6985	0.7019	0.7054	0.7088	0.7123	0.7157	0.7190	0.7224
0.6	0.7257	0.7291	0.7324	0.7357	0.7389	0.7422	0.7454	0.7486	0.7517	0.7549
0.7	0.7580	0.7611	0.7642	0.7673	0.7704	0.7734	0.7764	0.7794	0.7823	0.7852
0.8	0.7881	0.7910	0.7939	0.7967	0.7995	0.8023	0.8051	0.8078	0.8106	0.8133
0.9	0.8159	0.8186	0.8212	0.8238	0.8264	0.8289	0.8315	0.8340	0.8365	0.8389
1.0	0.8413	0.8438	0.8461	0.8485	0.8508	0.8531	0.8554	0.8577	0.8599	0.8621
1.1	0.8643	0.8665	0.8686	0.8708	0.8729	0.8749	0.8770	0.8790	0.8810	0.8830
1.2	0.8849	0.8869	0.8888	0.8907	0.8925	0.8944	0.8962	0.8980	0.8997	0.9015
1.3	0.9032	0.9049	0.9066	0.9082	0.9099	0.9115	0.9131	0.9147	0.9162	0.9177
1.4	0.9192	0.9207	0.9222	0.9236	0.9251	0.9265	0.9279	0.9292	0.9306	0.9319
1.5	0.9332	0.9345	0.9357	0.9370	0.9382	0.9394	0.9406	0.9418	0.9429	0.9441
1.6	0.9452	0.9463	0.9474	0.9484	0.9495	0.9505	0.9515	0.9525	0.9535	0.9545
1.7	0.9554	0.9564	0.9573	0.9582	0.9591	0.9599	0.9608	0.9616	0.9625	0.9633
1.8	0.9641	0.9649	0.9656	0.9664	0.9671	0.9678	0.9686	0.9693	0.9699	0.9706
1.9	0.9713	0.9719	0.9726	0.9732	0.9738	0.9744	0.9750	0.9756	0.9761	0.9767
2.0	0.9772	0.9778	0.9783	0.9788	0.9793	0.9798	0.9803	0.9808	0.9812	0.9817
2.1	0.9821	0.9826	0.9830	0.9834	0.9838	0.9842	0.9846	0.9850	0.9854	0.9857
2.2	0.9861	0.9864	0.9868	0.9871	0.9875	0.9878	0.9881	0.9884	0.9887	0.9890
2.3	0.9893	0.9896	0.9898	0.9901	0.9904	0.9906	0.9909	0.9911	0.9913	0.9916
2.4	0.9918	0.9920	0.9922	0.9925	0.9927	0.9929	0.9931	0.9932	0.9934	0.9936
2.5	0.9938	0.9940	0.9941	0.9943	0.9945	0.9946	0.9948	0.9949	0.9951	0.9952
2.6	0.9953	0.9955	0.9956	0.9957	0.9959	0.9960	0.9961	0.9962	0.9963	0.9964
2.7	0.9965	0.9966	0.9967	0.9968	0.9969	0.9970	0.9971	0.9972	0.9973	0.9974
2.8	0.9974	0.9975	0.9976	0.9977	0.9977	0.9978	0.9979	0.9979	0.9980	0.9981
2.9	0.9981	0.9982	0.9982	0.9983	0.9984	0.9984	0.9985	0.9985	0.9986	0.9986
3.0	0.9987	0.9987	0.9987	0.9988	0.9988	0.9989	0.9989	0.9989	0.9990	0.9990

APPENDIX-7 (2ND PART)

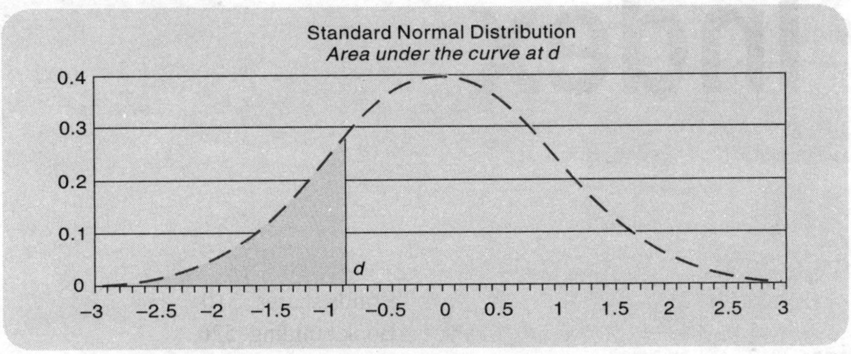

Area Under the Normal Distribution Curve (for negative values)

d	0.00	0.01	0.02	0.03	0.04	0.05	0.06	0.07	0.08	0.09
0.0	0.5000	0.4960	0.4920	0.4880	0.4840	0.4801	0.4761	0.4721	0.4681	0.4641
−0.1	0.4602	0.4562	0.4522	0.4483	0.4443	0.4404	0.4364	0.4325	0.4286	0.4247
−0.2	0.4207	0.4168	0.4129	0.4090	0.4052	0.4013	0.3974	0.3936	0.3897	0.3859
−0.3	0.3821	0.3783	0.3745	0.3707	0.3669	0.3632	0.3594	0.3557	0.3520	0.3483
−0.4	0.3446	0.3409	0.3372	0.3336	0.3300	0.3264	0.3228	0.3192	0.3156	0.3121
−0.5	0.3085	0.3050	0.3015	0.2981	0.2946	0.2912	0.2877	0.2843	0.2810	0.2776
−0.6	0.2743	0.2709	0.2676	0.2643	0.2611	0.2578	0.2546	0.2514	0.2483	0.2451
−0.7	0.2420	0.2389	0.2358	0.2327	0.2296	0.2266	0.2236	0.2206	0.2177	0.2148
−0.8	0.2119	0.2090	0.2061	0.2033	0.2005	0.1977	0.1949	0.1922	0.1894	0.1867
−0.9	0.1841	0.1814	0.1788	0.1762	0.1736	0.1711	0.1685	0.1660	0.1635	0.1611
−1.0	0.1587	0.1562	0.1539	0.1515	0.1492	0.1469	0.1446	0.1423	0.1401	0.1379
−1.1	0.1357	0.1335	0.1314	0.1292	0.1271	0.1251	0.1230	0.1210	0.1190	0.1170
−1.2	0.1151	0.1131	0.1112	0.1093	0.1075	0.1056	0.1038	0.1020	0.1003	0.0985
−1.3	0.0968	0.0951	0.0934	0.0918	0.0901	0.0885	0.0869	0.0853	0.0838	0.0823
−1.4	0.0808	0.0793	0.0778	0.0764	0.0749	0.0735	0.0721	0.0708	0.0694	0.0681
−1.5	0.0668	0.0655	0.0643	0.0630	0.0618	0.0606	0.0594	0.0582	0.0571	0.0559
−1.6	0.0548	0.0537	0.0526	0.0516	0.0505	0.0495	0.0485	0.0475	0.0465	0.0455
−1.7	0.0446	0.0436	0.0427	0.0418	0.0409	0.0401	0.0392	0.0384	0.0375	0.0367
−1.8	0.0359	0.0351	0.0344	0.0336	0.0329	0.0322	0.0314	0.0307	0.0301	0.0294
−1.9	0.0287	0.0281	0.0274	0.0268	0.0262	0.0256	0.0250	0.0244	0.0239	0.0233
−2.0	0.0228	0.0222	0.0217	0.0212	0.0207	0.0202	0.0197	0.0192	0.0188	0.0183
−2.1	0.0179	0.0174	0.0170	0.0166	0.0162	0.0158	0.0154	0.0150	0.0146	0.0143
−2.2	0.0139	0.0136	0.0132	0.0129	0.0125	0.0122	0.0119	0.0116	0.0113	0.0110
−2.3	0.0107	0.0104	0.0102	0.0099	0.0096	0.0094	0.0091	0.0089	0.0087	0.0084
−2.4	0.0082	0.0080	0.0078	0.0075	0.0073	0.0071	0.0069	0.0068	0.0066	0.0064
−2.5	0.0062	0.0060	0.0059	0.0057	0.0055	0.0054	0.0052	0.0051	0.0049	0.0048
−2.6	0.0047	0.0045	0.0044	0.0043	0.0041	0.0040	0.0039	0.0038	0.0037	0.0036
−2.7	0.0035	0.0034	0.0033	0.0032	0.0031	0.0030	0.0029	0.0028	0.0027	0.0026
−2.8	0.0026	0.0025	0.0024	0.0023	0.0023	0.0022	0.0021	0.0021	0.0020	0.0019
−2.9	0.0019	0.0018	0.0018	0.0017	0.0016	0.0016	0.0015	0.0015	0.0014	0.0014
−3.0	0.0013	0.0013	0.0013	0.0012	0.0012	0.0011	0.0011	0.0011	0.0010	0.0010

Index